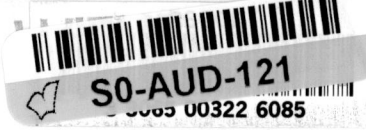

Historical Statistics of the United States

Historical Statistics of the United States

Earliest Times to the Present

MILLENNIAL EDITION

VOLUME TWO

PART B
WORK AND WELFARE

Editors in Chief
Susan B. Carter
Scott Sigmund Gartner
Michael R. Haines
Alan L. Olmstead
Richard Sutch
Gavin Wright

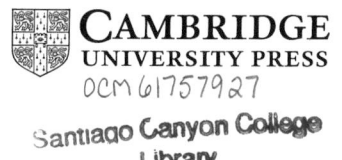

CAMBRIDGE
UNIVERSITY PRESS

CAMBRIDGE UNIVERSITY PRESS
Cambridge, New York, Melbourne, Madrid, Cape Town, Singapore, São Paulo

Cambridge University Press
40 West 20th Street, New York, NY 10011-4211, USA

http://www.cambridge.org
Information on this title: www.cambridge.org/9780521817912

First published 2006

Printed in the United States of America

A catalog record for this publication is available from the British Library.

Library of Congress Cataloging in Publication Data

Historical statistics of the United States : earliest times to the present / Susan B. Carter ... [et al.]. – Millennial ed.
p. cm.
Rev. update of: Historical statistics of the United States, colonial times to 1970. Bicentennial ed. Washington : U.S. Dept. of Commerce, Bureau of the Census, 1975.
Includes bibliographical references and index.
ISBN 0-521-81791-9 (set)
1. United States – Statistics. I. Carter, Susan B. II. Historical statistics of the United States, colonial times to 1970. III. Title.

HA202.H57 2006
317.3 – dc22 2005027089

ISBN-13 978-0-521-81791-2 (set of five volumes hardback)
ISBN-10 0-521-81791-9 (set of five volumes hardback)

ISBN-13 978-0-521-58496-8 (volume 1 hardback)
ISBN-10 0-521-58496-5 (volume 1 hardback)

ISBN-13 978-0-521-58540-8 (volume 2 hardback)
ISBN-10 0-521-58540-6 (volume 2 hardback)

ISBN-13 978-0-521-81790-5 (volume 3 hardback)
ISBN-10 0-521-81790-0 (volume 3 hardback)

ISBN-13 978-0-521-85389-7 (volume 4 hardback)
ISBN-10 0-521-85389-3 (volume 4 hardback)

ISBN-13 978-0-521-85390-3 (volume 5 hardback)
ISBN-10 0-521-85390-7 (volume 5 hardback)

ISBN-13 978-0-511-13297-1 (on-line edition)
ISBN-10 0-511-13297-2 (on-line edition)

SUMMARY CONTENTS

VOLUME 1

Part A. Population

Introduction 1-3
Aa. Population Characteristics 1-17
Ab. Vital Statistics 1-381
Ac. Internal Migration 1-489
Ad. International Migration 1-523
Ae. Family and Household Composition 1-653
Af. Cohorts 1-691
Ag. American Indians 1-715

VOLUME 2

Part B. Work and Welfare

Ba. Labor 2-3
Bb. Slavery 2-369
Bc. Education 2-387
Bd. Health 2-499
Be. Economic Inequality and Poverty 2-621
Bf. Social Insurance and Public Assistance 2-693
Bg. Nonprofit, Voluntary, and Religious Entities 2-837

VOLUME 3

Part C. Economic Structure and Performance

Ca. National Income and Product 3-3
Cb. Business Fluctuations and Cycles 3-71
Cc. Prices 3-147
Cd. Consumer Expenditures 3-225
Ce. Saving, Capital, and Wealth 3-287
Cf. Geography and the Environment 3-333
Cg. Science, Technology, and Productivity 3-415
Ch. Business Organization 3-477
Cj. Financial Markets and Institutions 3-583

VOLUME 4

Part D. Economic Sectors

Introduction 4-3
Da. Agriculture 4-7
Db. Natural Resource Industries 4-275
Dc. Construction, Housing, and Mortgages 4-395
Dd. Manufacturing 4-573
De. Distribution 4-705
Df. Transportation 4-761
Dg. Communications 4-977
Dh. Services and Utilities 4-1061

VOLUME 5

Part E. Governance and International Relations

Ea. Government Finance and Employment 5-3
Eb. Elections and Politics 5-141
Ec. Crime, Law Enforcement, and Justice 5-209
Ed. National Defense, Wars, Armed Forces, and Veterans 5-333
Ee. International Trade and Exchange Rates 5-441
Ef. Outlying Areas 5-587
Eg. Colonial Statistics 5-627
Eh. Confederate States of America 5-773

Appendixes

1. Weights, Measures, and Monetary Values 5-809
2. States and Census Regions 5-815
3. Origin of *Historical Statistics of the United States* 5-819

DETAILED CONTENTS OF VOLUME TWO

Guide to the Millennial Edition Monty Hindman and Richard Sutch 2-xi

PART B. WORK AND WELFARE

Chapter Ba. Labor 2-3

Editor: Susan B. Carter *Associate editors*: Lee A. Craig, Robert A. Margo, Joshua L. Rosenbloom, Matthew Sobek, and William A. Sundstrom

Essays

Labor *Susan B. Carter* 2-3

Labor Force *Susan B. Carter* 2-13

Occupations *Matthew Sobek* 2-35

Wages and Wage Inequality *Robert A. Margo* 2-40

Hours and Working Conditions *William A. Sundstrom* 2-46

Labor Unions *Joshua L. Rosenbloom* 2-54

Household Production *Lee A. Craig* 2-59

Tables

Workforce *Thomas Weiss* 2-63

Employment and Unemployment *Susan B. Carter and Matthew Sobek* 2-77

Employment, by Industry *Susan B. Carter and Matthew Sobek* 2-101

Occupations *Matthew Sobek* 2-133

Wages *Robert A. Margo* 2-254

Hours and Working Conditions *William A. Sundstrom* 2-301

Labor Unions *Joshua L. Rosenbloom* 2-336

Household Production *Lee A. Craig* 2-363

Chapter Bb. Slavery 2-369

Editors: Stanley L. Engerman, Richard Sutch, and Gavin Wright

Essay

Slavery *Stanley L. Engerman, Richard Sutch, and Gavin Wright* 2-369

Tables

Slave Population *Susan B. Carter* 2-375

Slave Prices and Values *Richard Sutch* 2-381

Manumitted and Fugitive Slaves, and Slave Revolts *Susan B. Carter* 2-384

Chapter Bc. Education 2-387

Editor: Claudia Goldin

Essay

Education *Claudia Goldin* 2-387

Tables

Kindergarten, Elementary School, and Secondary School *Claudia Goldin* 2-398

Higher Education *Susan B. Carter and Claudia Goldin* 2-439

Educational Attainment *Claudia Goldin* 2-464

Earnings, by Education *Claudia Goldin* 2-471

Revenues and Expenditures *Claudia Goldin* 2-480

Chapter Bd. Health 2-499

Editor: Richard H. Steckel

Essay

Health, Nutrition, and Physical Well-Being *Richard H. Steckel* 2-499

Tables

Expenditures *Richard H. Steckel* 2-509

Hospitals *Richard H. Steckel* 2-520

Health Care Practitioners *Richard H. Steckel* 2-541

Health Insurance *Richard H. Steckel* 2-550

Incidence of Disease *Richard H. Steckel* 2-564

Nutrition and Health-Related Behaviors *Richard H. Steckel* 2-572

Physical Well-Being *Richard H. Steckel* 2-582

Chapter Be. Economic Inequality and Poverty 2-621

Editors: Peter H. Lindert (Economic Inequality), Linda Barrington and Gordon M. Fisher (Poverty)

Essay

The Distribution of Income and Wealth *Peter H. Lindert* 2-621

Poverty *Linda Barrington and Gordon M. Fisher* 2-625

Tables

Distribution of Income *Peter H. Lindert* 2-652

Distribution of Wealth *Peter H. Lindert* 2-658

Mean and Median Income *Peter H. Lindert* 2-660

Poverty Lines *Linda Barrington and Gordon M. Fisher* 2-663

Characteristics of the Poverty Population *Linda Barrington and Gordon M. Fisher* 2-674

Chapter Bf. Social Insurance and Public Assistance 2-693

Editor: Price V. Fishback *Associate editors*: Joan Underhill Hannon, Melissa A. Thomasson, and Stephen T. Ziliak

Essay

Introduction *Price V. Fishback* 2-693

Public Assistance: Colonial Times to the 1920s *Stephen T. Ziliak with Joan Underhill Hannon* 2-693

Social Welfare: 1929 to the Present *Price V. Fishback and Melissa A. Thomasson* 2-700

Tables

Poor Relief *Joan Underhill Hannon and Stephen T. Ziliak* 2-720

Social Welfare Expenditures *Price V. Fishback and Melissa A. Thomasson* 2-734

Social Welfare Programs *Price V. Fishback and Melissa A. Thomasson* 2-751

Private Welfare *Price V. Fishback and Melissa A. Thomasson* 2-820

Chapter Bg. Nonprofit, Voluntary, and Religious Entities 2-837

Editor: Peter Dobkin Hall

Essay

Nonprofit, Voluntary, and Religious Entities *Peter Dobkin Hall with Colin B. Burke* 2-837

Tables

Nonprofit Institutions *Colin B. Burke* 2-851

Voluntary Associations *Colin B. Burke* 2-885

Religion *Colin B. Burke* 2-900

Philanthropy *Colin B. Burke* 2-923

Index I-1

GUIDE TO THE MILLENNIAL EDITION

Monty Hindman and Richard Sutch

Editions and Copyright

Previous editions. This is the fourth edition of *Historical Statistics of the United States*. The U.S. Bureau of the Census published the prior editions in 1949, 1960, and 1975, the last known as the Bicentennial Edition. Cambridge University Press publishes this, the Millennial Edition, with the permission of the Census Bureau. Some of the data and table documentation presented here are used without explicit quotation, but with permission, from the earlier editions. The Census Bureau takes no responsibility for the design of this edition or the accuracy of its content, which rests solely with the contributors, the editors, and Cambridge University Press.

Electronic edition. This edition of *Historical Statistics of the United States* is available in electronic form from Cambridge University Press. A compact disk containing the Bicentennial Edition of *Historical Statistics of the United States* is also available from the Press.

Copyright. Permission to quote or reprint copyright material should be obtained directly from the copyright owner. Much of the data reproduced in this work were originally published by agencies of the U.S. government and are in the public domain. Generally speaking, original data that have been published elsewhere under copyright protection may be freely used for educational, scholarly, or journalistic purposes (but not commercial purposes) with proper citation to the original source under the fair use provision of U.S. copyright law. Cambridge University Press has made every effort to secure, where necessary, permission to reproduce protected material. In almost every case the permission requested was freely granted. In a few instances, however, the copyright owner requested a specific citation. These citations may be found in the listing of Copyright Citations at the end of Volume 5.

Data Revisions and Updates

Reproduction and revision of data from prior editions. Although this volume provides many data series from prior editions of *Historical Statistics of the United States*, users should be aware that some data from these editions have subsequently been revised. Our contributors sought to present the most recently available data, and thus users probably will wish to use the data presented here rather than that in previous editions. In some cases, data from the earlier editions were judged to be unreliable or obsolete and were not reproduced.

Data updates. The data series in *Historical Statistics of the United States* do not have a uniform end date; instead, each table reports the data available at the time the contributor compiled the data. Many series in these volumes are continued on a regular basis with periodic updates and revisions by the agency, group, or individual responsible for the original data. Figures for many of the current series are presented in the *Statistical Abstract of the United States*, published annually by the U.S. Bureau of the Census. The updating of industrial statistics will be complicated by the switch in 1997 from the Standard Industrial Classification (SIC) system to the North American Industrial Classification System (NAICS); see the Introduction to Part D.

Additional data. In many cases, additional data can be found in the source documents, in references mentioned in the table documentation or chapter essays, and through the Internet sites of the groups or agencies noted in the sources for the data presented here.

Errors. In a work as large as this, errors of both commission and omission are likely to have occurred. Users who discover errors are urged to communicate them to Cambridge University Press, 40 West 20th Street, New York, New York 10011-4211, USA.

Data Selection

General principles. The criteria for the selection of data to be included in this edition varied broadly, depending on the particular subject matter. Generally, summary measures or aggregates at gross levels and immediately below were given highest priority for inclusion. Below such levels, selection was governed by the interplay of the following: the amount of space already devoted to a particular subject; the attempt to achieve a relatively balanced presentation among subject fields; whether other data already covered a particular topic; the quantity and quality of the data available; and the extent to which the data might enhance the value of other material in the book. During the early phases of the project these selection criteria were conveyed to our contributors, upon whose judgment we ultimately relied.

Data reliability. Our contributors have attempted to select data that they consider to be generally reliable and to reproduce faithfully the data reported in their sources. They have also provided citations and technical descriptions to assist users in making independent assessments of both the data's reliability and their suitability for a project at hand.

Original versus derived data. Primary emphasis was placed on the presentation of original, unmodified figures rather than derived data because they offer greater flexibility to users. Derived data – for example, averages, percentages, ratios, and index numbers – were provided if they were the accepted standard for presentation (for example, unemployment rates), if the table contributor judged that the derived data would be particularly helpful, or if the use of derived data saved a significant amount of space.

Topical coverage. Because the last thirty years have witnessed the expansion of data collection into areas that were only inadequately covered, if at all, in the 1970s, this edition has a broader topical scope than its predecessors. A tentative list of topics emerged after extensive discussions between the project's editors in chief and Cambridge University Press. The outline was widely circulated to scholars, reference librarians, and government statistical bureaus. After a revision of that outline, the project recruited contributors, who offered additional suggestions. What emerged from this process was an outline for the project that was both designed by the profession and feasible to accomplish.

Temporal coverage. Contributors were asked to take the data series under their charge as far backward and forward in time as possible. They were also encouraged to include important lapsed series – those that begin and terminate in the past – because such series are sometimes available only in out-of-print documents. Most data series in *Historical Statistics of the United States* provide annual or decennial data spanning at least twenty years, with the main exceptions being for special topics (the colonial period and the Confederate States of America), for newly developed series providing the only data available to represent an important subject field, and for short series that served as important extensions of longer series.

Data frequency. Annual data were given preference for inclusion, but certain series are presented only for years in which a national census was conducted and, in some instances, only for scattered dates, as dictated by data availability. When both annual figures and benchmark data exist, both series are sometimes shown. A major exception was made for Chapter Cb, which presents many of its series on a monthly or quarterly basis. Although this volume mainly provides annual data, underlying data are sometimes available more frequently from the original sources.

Geographical coverage. The data in *Historical Statistics of the United States* generally cover the nation as a whole, defined by the recognized borders of the country for the year in question. As new states were admitted to the Union, the coverage of the typical statistical series in this volume expands to include the new additions, without any special notation in the table documentation. The documentation should be consulted to determine if such changes in the boundaries of the United States are likely to have affected the series. When the year of a state's inclusion in a series differs significantly from its year of statehood, this fact was noted in the documentation whenever possible. Refer to Appendix 2 for the dates of statehood.

Subnational data. Because of limitations of space, data are generally not shown for regions, states, or localities. The underlying sources sometimes provide data in finer geographical detail than shown here. Some tables provide data for U.S. census regions or divisions; see Appendix 2 for more information on such regional classifications.

Outlying areas. In almost all cases, outlying areas are not included in the national totals reported here. Refer to Chapter Ef for additional information on such areas.

Organization of the Volume

Arrangement of the data. In this edition of *Historical Statistics of the United States,* data are arranged by broad subjects in five parts, each published in a separate volume and each volume containing several chapters. The tables in most chapters are further organized into various subsections (see the Detailed Table of Contents in each volume).

Essays. Each chapter is introduced by one or more essays that provide a general guide to the data, the sources, and the historical trends that have been emphasized in the scholarly literature. They contain a list of references that may be consulted by those interested in more detail.

Series identifiers. Each data series is assigned a unique alphanumeric identifier. The two letters in the identifier indicate the chapter in which the series resides. Within a chapter, series are numbered sequentially. Sets of contiguous series are identified by means of a series range (for example, series Da42–47). Source citations and table documentation are linked to the data series by means of such identifiers, which may be preferred over page numbers for use in reference citations.

Table identifiers. An entire table is identified by the range of series that it contains. For example, the first two tables in the chapter on vital statistics contain ten and twenty series, respectively; thus, they are identified as Table Ab1–10 and Table Ab11–30. Similarly, a group of contiguous tables is identified by a series range. Using the same example, these two tables could be referred to jointly as Tables Ab1–30.

Table Documentation

Table contributors. Each table provides the names of the contributors who selected, collected, and described the data. The editorial staff also reviewed the data and table documentation for accuracy, completeness, and clarity of presentation.

Sources. In most cases, full citations are given for data sources; however, when numerous issues of a publication were used, the source citations are usually limited to "annual issues" or similar notations. When data are reproduced from the Bicentennial Edition, the source citation lists the original source rather than the Bicentennial Edition, except under special circumstances.

Unpublished data. Nearly all the data reported here have been previously published or accepted for publication. Rare exceptions for previously unpublished data were allowed if a contributor felt that the data were particularly important and if peer review accepted the data for inclusion.

Integrated Public Use Microdata Series. A number of series reported in this edition are extracted from the Integrated Public Use Microdata Series (IPUMS). The IPUMS is composed of representative samples drawn from the returns of the decennial censuses of the population. All censuses from 1850 to 1990 are included, with the exception of 1930, which is under development, and 1890, the manuscripts for which were destroyed by fire. The IPUMS data and documentation are available over the Internet.*

Internet sources. Some data series in *Historical Statistics of the United States* are based on electronic sources; however, owing to the fleeting nature of specific Internet addresses or Web-based

* Steven Ruggles, Matthew Sobek, et al., *Integrated Public Use Microdata Series: Version 2.0* (Historical Census Projects, University of Minnesota, 1997).

file names, we do not use them when identifying sources. Instead, we use more general phrasing to direct users to the Internet source.

Table documentation. Most tables are accompanied by documentation defining relevant terms and concepts, providing methodological and historical background, noting unusual values or comparability issues, explaining methods used to calculate derived data, and providing references to sources containing more detailed data or more extensive discussion. Unlike prior editions, which consolidated table documentation at the beginning of chapters, this edition locates the documentation with the tables, the intent being to increase its visibility, convenience, and thus use. Many tables are fully self-documenting, without cross references to other parts of this work; however, when cross references to other tables or essays are provided, the user is encouraged to follow those references.

Footnotes. There is no sharp demarcation between the type of information conveyed in the ordinary table documentation and that conveyed in the footnotes. Roughly speaking, footnotes are used for two purposes: to draw attention to issues of particular importance (footnotes as warnings) or to comment on matters related to specific columns, rows, or cells in a table.

Footnote order. Within a table, footnotes are numbered sequentially as follows: first the general footnotes that apply to the entire table; then left-to-right across the table header (the footnotes governing specific series); and finally footnotes attached to the table stub and the data area, proceeding in top-to-bottom, then left-to-right fashion (as used here, the directional terms apply to tables with standard page orientation). A footnote's first appearance within a table determines its position within the sequential numbering.

Total and subtotals. In most cases, a table's header structure will clearly indicate the total–subtotal relationships among the series. The typical practice in this volume is to provide the total series first, followed by its components. Often the sum of the components will equal the total, perhaps with small deviations attributable to rounding or other causes; however, sometimes the breakdowns provided in a table are not exhaustive, and the components will add to an amount less than the total. Users should consult the table documentation and exercise caution in this regard.

Race and ethnicity. Many tables provide disaggregations by race or ethnicity. This volume typically uses the terms "white," "black," "Asian" (or "Asian American"), "Indian" (or "Amerindian" or "Native American"), and "Hispanic." Note that a person identified as Hispanic may be of any race. See the essay on definitions and measurement of race and ethnicity in the Introduction to Part A for a discussion of racial classification and identification as it applies to the collection of historical statistics in the United States.

Dates

Date ranges. Throughout the table documentation and the chapter essays, date ranges are inclusive: for example, 1964–1987 includes both 1964 and 1987.

Year of record. The identification of the year of record – in other words, the precise meaning of the years shown in a table stub – was complicated by the failure of some sources to state whether the data were prepared on a calendar year, fiscal year, or some other basis; by changes in the year of record over time; and, in some instances, by imprecision or silence in the source concerning the beginning or ending date for the year of record. Table contributors attempted to clarify such matters, but ambiguity remains in some tables.

Transition quarters. Sometimes the year of record changes in the middle of a table, and values are provided for the "transition quarter" – the gap between the end of the old year of record and beginning of the new. In such cases, users will see a (TQ) designation in the table stub. Nearly all transition quarters in this volume are associated with the year 1976, when the federal government changed the end of its fiscal year from June 30 to September 30. In rare cases, the (TQ) designation will be for a transition period that is not actually a quarter, but some other fraction of a year.

Units, Measures, and Monetary Values

Units of measure. Series are usually expressed in the units reported in the original source. In some cases, however, units were converted to make two or more data series comparable, or to create a single series when splicing data from multiple sources. The approach taken in these volumes was to restrict the units information to true *measures* and to rely on the table title and layered headers to convey other details about the things being counted or measured. Sometimes series are expressed in units too complex for pithy statement; in these rare cases, a generic unit of measure is given, with further elaboration left to the table documentation.

Billion and trillion. The American and Canadian definitions of billion (10^9) and trillion (10^{12}) are used throughout, not the definitions used in England, Germany, and many other countries.

Index numbers. Some series are expressed in terms of index numbers. In such cases, the base period of the index is provided where the unit of measure would normally be found. For a discussion of index numbers, see the essay on prices and price indexes in Chapter Cc and the essay on national income and product in Chapter Ca.

Weights and measures. Most data series are expressed in American units (the U.S. Customary System) rather than metric units (the International System). For a discussion of these two systems and for conversion information, see Appendix 1.

Monetary values. Unless otherwise noted, monetary values are expressed in current or nominal terms – in other words, the actual historical values (usually U.S. dollars), not adjusted for previous or subsequent changes in prices. This standard was adopted to avoid attaching the word "current" or "nominal" to every reference to a monetary unit. When monetary values have been adjusted in some fashion, this is stated explicitly and the relevant base period is given. For a discussion of monetary values, see Appendix 1 and the essay on prices and price indexes in Chapter Cc.

Data Values

Data precision and significant digits. In making decisions regarding the precision with which data values should be presented, fidelity to sources was our primary consideration. Thus, the underlying data files for *Historical Statistics of the United States* – available in the electronic edition – retain the full precision provided by table contributors, even though this level of detail might be deemed excessive by scientific standards for the reporting of significant digits. In most cases, the detail comes straight from the sources themselves; therefore, exact reproduction provides a valuable check for researchers wanting to trace the provenance of a number or hunt down an anomaly. In other cases, excessive precision comes from spreadsheet calculations made by table contributors (for example, in the computation of derived data). Here, too, we did not impose our judgments concerning the appropriate precision and instead retained the full detail provided by contributors. Users should note that historical sources sometimes change the precision with which they report data over time. Also, some tables contain series reported in the sources at different levels of detail but that, for ease of comparison, are provided here in consistent units. The usual indication of varying precision – whether in a single series or across multiple series within a table – is a run of data values with trailing zeros, either before or after the decimal point. In such cases, users will need to exercise judgment concerning the precision of the data.

Decimal precision for display purposes. While the underlying data files retain all of the detail provided by table contributors, the data displayed in the print edition of *Historical Statistics of the United States* are shown in rounded fashion, typically with no more than three digits following the decimal point. Similarly, tables generated for display purposes by the electronic edition are formatted using the same rounding conventions; however, the underlying files available for downloading provide the values at full precision.

Zero values and (Z). A zero in a data series means exactly that: a reported value of zero. In some cases, an underlying data value may be so small that it rounds to zero when displayed at the level of decimal precision chosen for the series. In such cases, a (Z) marker is used rather than a zero value. Stated more precisely, the (Z) notation indicates a *nonzero value that is not shown or possibly not known*. In the former case – a nonzero value not shown – (Z) means that the value falls below the threshold of our rounding convention: the number rounds to zero, as displayed in this volume (full precision for such values is available through the electronic edition). In the latter case – a nonzero value not known – (Z) means that the original source did not provide a specific value. Owing to these complexities, the meaning of the (Z) marker is specifically documented in every table that uses the device.

Dash as a data value. The "—" marker means that a value is not being reported. There are several possible reasons: the data are not available anywhere; the data were not provided in the source but conceivably could be found with sufficient research; the data were available in the source but the table contributor decided that they should not be reported (for example, unreliable data); or the data might conceivably be reported as a zero, but the table contributor decided for conceptual reasons to represent it as "no value reported" (for example, if a category or program covered by the series did not yet exist). Some sources do not carefully distinguish between zero values and missing data. Table contributors attempted to eliminate such confusion, but in some cases the "—" marker could mean that the value, if shown, would be zero.

Historical Statistics of the United States

Millennial Edition

Volume 2

Part B

Work and Welfare

CHAPTER Ba

Labor

Editor: Susan B. Carter

Associate Editors: Lee A. Craig, Robert A. Margo, Joshua L. Rosenbloom, Matthew Sobek, and William A. Sundstrom

LABOR

Susan B. Carter

> The annual labour of every nation is the fund which originally supplies it with all the necessaries and conveniences of life, . . . [whose quantity] must in every nation be regulated by two different circumstances; first, by the skill, dexterity, and judgment with which its labour is generally applied; and, secondly, by the proportion between the number of those who are employed in useful labour, and that of those who are not so employed. Whatever be the soil, climate, or extent of territory of any particular nation, the abundance or scantiness of its annual supply must, in that particular situation, depend upon those two circumstances. (Smith 1776, p. 1)

Writing in the American Revolutionary War year 1776, Adam Smith identified labor as the key for understanding international differences in the standard of living and quality of life. For earlier thinkers, the "wealth of nations" was their stock of gold and other precious metals. With these they could purchase implements of military power and pay the salary of a standing army. Such resources not only secured the nation's own stock of wealth but could also be used to plunder the wealth of others.

Smith's insight was to recognize that the true "wealth of nations" is the productive capacity of the population. Although he based his analysis on a close reading of the historical development of European nations, perhaps the best illustration of his principles was about to unfold with the development of the American economy.

In this broad sense, then, "labor" is the subject of nearly every chapter of *Historical Statistics of the United States*. It also commands an enormous literature of its own. For recent overviews, written from the point of view of quantitatively oriented economic historians, see David Galenson (1996) for the colonial era, Robert Margo (2000) for the nineteenth century, and Claudia Goldin (2000) for the twentieth century.

The discussion that follows is meant to direct readers to material in other chapters of *Historical Statistics* that are relevant for understanding the development of labor in the American economy. I use the structure outlined by Smith as an organizational device.

Proportion Employed in Useful Labor

For narrative purposes, let us begin with Smith's second "circumstance," the proportion of the population employed in "useful labour." As Smith argues, this proportion is an important determinant of economic well-being. Other things being equal, high employment rates mean high levels of income per capita. Nations in which there are few dependents have higher levels of income per capita than nations that support large numbers of the young, old, or idle. In addition, because labor productivity tends to be higher in the market than in the nonmarket sector, the transfer of labor out of the household and into the market increases total output. This would be true even if official labor force statistics were to include the output of the household sector, which typically they do not. If output in the household sector is ignored, the effect of a shift of labor to the market sector is especially important (see Folbre and Wagman 1993; Wagman and Folbre 1996; and the essay on the labor force in this chapter).

One measure of the proportion of the population employed in "useful labour" is the labor force–to-population ratio. This is not a perfect measure of Smith's concept because it excludes nonmarket

Acknowledgments

Susan B. Carter thanks Richard Sutch, Gavin Wright, and Matthew Sobek for valuable comments on the introductory essay on labor. This work was supported in part by funding from the National Science Foundation, the Center for Social and Economic Policy at the University of California, Riverside, and Stanford University.

Susan B. Carter thanks Richard Sutch, Gavin Wright, Monty Hindman, and Matthew Sobek for valuable comments on the essay on the labor force. She thanks Victoria Nayak and Dustin Chambers for research assistance. The National Science Foundation and the Center for Social and Economic Policy at the University of California, Riverside, provided financial assistance.

Thomas Weiss thanks Matthew Sobek, who provided data from the Integrated Public Use Microdata Series (IPUMS) used in the workforce tables. This work was supported in part by funding from the National Science Foundation.

William A. Sundstrom thanks Susan Carter for her comments and suggestions during the preparation of the essay. He also thanks Scott Blashek, George Carlson, Susan Carter, Monty Hindman, Matt Sobek, and Aklilu Zegeye for their assistance in preparing the tables. This work was made possible in part by funding from the Leavey School of Business at Santa Clara University.

Joshua L. Rosenbloom thanks Barry T. Hirsch and David A. Macpherson for their assistance in the preparation of several of the tables included in the section on unions, and especially for their efforts in compiling (from Current Population Survey tapes) the data on union membership by industry contained in Table Ba4870–4883.

Lee A. Craig thanks Laura Phillips for her assistance in preparing the tables in this chapter. Alastair Hall provided valuable comments on the essay, and Susan B. Carter was especially generous with her comments on and supplemental material for the essay on household production.

labor and includes work that some might not deem "useful." Moreover, it makes no adjustment for changes in hours. For a discussion of change in hours of work per worker over time, see the essay on hours and working conditions in this chapter.[1] The statistical record reveals a high and growing labor force–to-population ratio in America for most of the last two centuries (see, for example, Tables Ba1–78, Ba417–424, and Ba478–486). These estimates put the employment ratio at over 35 percent in 1800; by 2000 it had grown to approximately 51 percent. Both of these levels are high by international standards, especially considering that – except in the case of slaves – relatively few young children were or are engaged in labor in America. The labor force–to-population ratio fell only during the period 1929–1966. The decline was the result of markedly reduced immigration resulting from restrictive legislation, the onset of the Great Depression, and the post–World War II baby boom.

Part of the explanation for the high and growing labor force–to-population ratio that characterized much of American history is demographic. Although American fertility was extremely high during the eighteenth century, it began to fall during the early years of the nineteenth. This more or less continuous fall, interrupted only by the post–World War II baby boom, reduced the dependency ratio; that is, it reduced the fraction of the population that was either too young or too old to work. Measured as the number of persons "young" (0–14 years) and "old" (65 years of age and older), divided by the number of persons in the middle working ages (15–64 years), and multiplied by 100, the U.S. dependency ratio was only 37.1 in 1850 when it is first reliably possible to make this calculation; by 1990 it had fallen to 28.6 (see Chapter Ab on vital statistics). By contrast, at the turn of the twenty-first century many developing countries experience dependency ratios in excess of 75, with some as high as 100 (U.S. Bureau of the Census 2003).

The effects of the early fertility decline were reinforced by a heavy influx of immigrants throughout much of the last two centuries. Immigrants tend to arrive during their young working ages. This means that immigration increases the population in the 15–64 age group relative to those who are young and old (compare Tables Aa185–286 and Ad226–230). Moreover, because a major reason for emigrating in the first place is to obtain employment, immigrants also tend to have high labor-force participation rates relative to the native-born population of the same age and gender (see Table Ad752–759).

The long-term secular increase in women's labor force participation reinforced the positive demographic developments. Women's participation rates are given in Tables Ba40–49, Ba404–416, and Ba535–550. They show a more than threefold increase in the proportion of the prime-age adult female population engaged in the labor force since 1800. Women's labor force participation evolved from a relatively brief interlude between the end of schooling and marriage into a relatively permanent career attachment across the life cycle, including, increasingly, mothers of young children.[2]

The increasing labor force participation of women more than offset three other developments that exerted downward pressure on the economywide labor-force participation rate. These were the reduction in the labor of black workers following emancipation, as their participation rates adjusted to the standards of free rather than slave labor; the reduction in labor force participation among young males as schooling levels advanced; and the marked reduction in the labor force participation of older males as voluntary retirement became the American norm.[3]

"Skill, Dexterity, and Judgment"

Even more important than the labor force–to-population ratio, in Smith's view, was the "skill, dexterity, and judgment" possessed by those who work. To such factors Smith credited the "greatest improvements in the productive powers of Labour." Skill, dexterity, and judgment are developed through three interrelated but distinct processes: division of labor; investments in physical and human capital; and invention, innovation, and diffusion of new technologies and organizational structures.

Division of Labor

The division of labor refers to specialization in production and the exchange of goods and services. Specialization and exchange can take place at a variety of levels. Largely self-sufficient agriculturalists may produce extra farm products for exchange for manufactured items or for services produced on neighboring farms, in a nearby town, or in a distant land. An example is the Samuel Swayne household of Chester County, Pennsylvania, in the latter part of the eighteenth century, which was described by Marc Egnal (1996, pp. 7–8). The Swaynes operated a ninety-one-acre farm they received at their marriage in 1756 and that they supplemented with an additional thirty-five acres purchased sixteen years later. Most of the labor of the Swayne household was reserved for the production of goods and services for its own consumption, but some was directed toward producing goods for exchange. Swayne made saddletrees (leather frames that served as foundations for saddles), and his wife churned butter and made cheese for sale in the local market. They produced wheat, flax, Indian corn, flaxseed, beef, rye, and pork for sale outside the community. The Swaynes used the proceeds from these sales to purchase goods such as books, fabric, sugar, tea, and wine.

Another form of specialization and division of labor involves localities or regions. One well-known example is the "triangular trade" that developed during the eighteenth century, in which New England produced rum for export to Africa, Africa produced slaves for export to the Caribbean area, and the Caribbean exported sugar to New England, where much of it was made into rum (see, for example, Table Eg474–513). Another example is the rapid expansion of regional specialization and interregional trade after 1815, with the "West" (what we would today call the Midwest) specializing in grains, the South in cotton and tobacco, and the Northeast in manufactured products (Atack and Passell 1994, pp. 160–4).

Yet a third form of the division of labor involves the specialization among and within occupations, industries, and firms. One example that will be familiar to many is the evolution of the one-room rural schoolhouse, in which a single teacher taught all grades

[1] Moses Abramovitz and Paul A. David estimate that hours worked per capita rose over the period 1800 to 1890, fell from 1890 through 1966, and then rose over the period 1966 through 1989 (Abramovitz and David 2000, Table 1.3, p. 14).

[2] This important development is discussed more fully in the essay on the labor force in this chapter.

[3] These participation rates are shown in Tables Ba391–403 and Ba519–534 and discussed in greater detail in the essay on the labor force in this chapter.

and subjects, into graded classrooms with specialized teachers for individual grades and subjects. A related development was the creation of separate institutions for the elementary, middle, secondary, and postsecondary educational levels.

The division of labor stimulates labor productivity and wages in a number of ways. By specializing in each area of comparative advantage, labor concentrates in the activity in which its relative productivity is highest. Repetition develops workers' skills, and so they become more proficient. Focus on a single activity eliminates lost time in moving from one to another. Close familiarity with a specific task generates new ideas for enhancing productivity; specialization provides an incentive to invest in skills, tools, machinery, and structures to make the work faster, more accurate, and less physically demanding.

Given its abundant advantages, why don't all societies adopt the division of labor? The answer is contained in Smith's often-quoted remark, "The division of labor is limited by the extent of the market." In other words, in order for specialization to be profitable, one needs trading partners. Had Robinson Crusoe specialized, he would not have survived his stay on his deserted island. Crusoe was isolated from the large populations with their high level of wealth that would have made specialization both possible and attractive. If, instead, Crusoe had washed ashore in the newly formed United States of America in 1776, he would have found an extensive market and one that was uniquely well positioned to grow larger still.

Because of its high fertility, low mortality, and extensive immigration, the United States had a large and growing population. By 1820, the U.S. population was almost half the size of that of the United Kingdom (U.K.); by 1870, the U.S. population had overtaken that of the U.K.; and by the year 2000, the United States was the third most populous country in the world after only China and India (Maddison 1995, p. 106; U.S. Bureau of the Census 2003).

This large and growing population was also becoming wealthier. Robert E. Gallman estimates that the U.S. economy in 1774 was already approximately a third the size of Great Britain's, despite the fact that the U.S. population was proportionately smaller and that the economy had not yet embarked upon the Industrial Revolution. Between 1774 and 1909, the U.S. economy grew about 175-fold, or at an average annual rate of 3.9 percent (see Chapter Ca on national income and product). This compares with an estimated average annual growth rate for the British economy over the same period of about 2.2 percent. Thus, by 1909, the U.S. economy was almost two and a half times the size of Great Britain's (Gallman 2000, pp. 2–5).

Low barriers to trade facilitate interactions among labor market participants, thereby further promoting the division of labor. In this light, the constitutional prohibition on tariffs and other impediments that might restrict interstate commerce was an important stimulus to the division of labor. This stimulus was reinforced by early governmental efforts at the federal, state, and local levels to actively promote internal trade by surveying the land, dredging rivers and streams, building turnpikes and canals, and offering inducements to private companies to undertake transportation improvements. For all these reasons, the United States was in the forefront of a worldwide "transportation revolution" that occurred in the early nineteenth century and that measurably increased the speed and reduced the cost of moving goods and people from place to place (for details see the essay on transportation in Chapter Df and Table Cf83–87).

Overall, then, by virtue of its rapidly growing population and wealth and its falling barriers to internal trade, the U.S. domestic market grew to become the world's largest and wealthiest by the end of the nineteenth century, and it maintained that position throughout the twentieth century. Other countries have taken advantage of the division of labor by responding to international markets, and indeed the United States has pursued this strategy as well. However, because of their common language and culture, nations with large internal markets have a particular advantage in capturing this "Smithian" source of economic growth.

The developing division of labor is perhaps most easily visible in the occupation and industry statistics presented in Tables Ba652–813 and Ba1033–4213 and discussed in the essay on occupations in this chapter. As these statistics refer to the nation as a whole, however, they necessarily omit labor specialization at the regional and local level.

Like most other economies of the time, eighteenth-century America was largely agricultural and, unlike England, had not yet commenced its Industrial Revolution. Nonetheless, as early as 1800, more than a quarter of the labor force was employed outside this primary sector, with the two largest categories of nonagricultural employment at the time being ocean transportation and domestic service (see Table Ba814–830). Over the nineteenth and twentieth centuries, the agricultural share of the labor force declined further as labor moved into more productive occupations. By 1890, the agricultural share of the labor force was less than 50 percent of the total; by 1990, it was just a little more than 1.5 percent (see Table Ba1033–1046). Only during the Great Depression of the 1930s, when agriculture provided employment for those who could not find work in other sectors, did agricultural employment experience a respite from the relentless downward trend in its share of employment.

The occupations that outpaced agriculture were diverse and constantly changing. During the nineteenth century, manufacturing employment grew most spectacularly in both absolute and relative terms. In 1810, manufacturing accounted for only 3.2 percent of the labor force; by 1870, it claimed between 19 and 24 percent of the labor force, and at its peak in 1950, it claimed 34 percent of the total (Tables Ba814–830 and Ba1033–1046).

Clerical, sales, and service occupations outside of domestic work grew rapidly in the late nineteenth and early twentieth centuries. In 1870, the first year in which the census of occupations included the entire labor force, clerical and sales and service occupations (excluding domestic work) accounted for only 3.4 and 1.4 percent of the labor force, respectively. By 1920, their respective shares were 13.1 and 4.4 percent; and by 1990, these had advanced to 25.6 and 12.8 percent (Table Ba1033–1046). These important shifts in the occupational distribution of the labor force were both the source of improvements in income per capita and the cause and consequence of the entry of women into the labor force.[4]

Physical Capital

Output per worker may advance as a result of the development of the division of labor alone. Indeed, Kenneth Sokoloff (1986)

[4] See the essay on occupations in this chapter for more detail on the occupational and industrial distribution and its change over time. See the essay on hours and working conditions in this chapter for the changing character of the size of firms in which workers were employed. The essay on productivity in Chapter Cg describes the pace and pattern of labor productivity change over time, and the essay on wages and wage inequality in this chapter describes the pattern of wages.

ascribes productivity advances in early-nineteenth-century American textile manufacturing almost entirely to this source. At the same time, expansion of the physical capital stock – machinery, factories, livestock, and land – can enhance labor productivity regardless of the division of labor. A farmer with a horse-drawn plow can cultivate more acres in a day than one who pushes the plow by hand.

Given the obvious advantages of employing physical capital in the production process, why don't all societies make use of it? The explanation has to do with relative prices and the legal status of labor. If labor is plentiful, inexpensive, and "free," then it pays to organize production using hand techniques even if machinery is readily available; only if labor is scarce, expensive, and "free" does it pay to invest in machinery. Free labor in this context means that the worker retains legal control over the disposition of his or her own labor and cannot be compelled to complete a labor agreement by threat of punishment. Since the beginning of the nineteenth century – and with the important exception of the American South, which is discussed in detail in the section on slave labor – American labor is and has been scarce, expensive, and free. It is for these reasons that capital-intensive techniques have been and continue to be a prominent feature of the American economy.[5]

The origins of labor scarcity date to the earliest European settlements in North America. The arrival of Europeans decimated the indigenous population through disease and calculated political and military strategies, leaving the continent sparsely populated (see the essay in Chapter Ag on American Indians). European settlers and their offspring then enjoyed a relative abundance of land, game, fish, timber, and minerals. As the objective of the colonists in British North America was settlement, they adopted a legal environment that encouraged small landholdings; democratic institutions that encouraged broad-based input into local, state, and national decision making; and a political system of checks and balances designed to limit the exercise of power by any single group.

As a result of these institutions, independent family-based enterprises became the norm. The easy availability of self- or family employment meant that hired laborers could be had only at high wages. Thus, those who sought to expand output beyond what could be produced by the family looked for strategies that might mitigate the impact of high wages on their profitability. To this end, they actively recruited foreign workers; encouraged immigration; and pioneered ways to substitute capital, raw materials, and land for labor. Robert Gallman (2000) and Moses Abramovitz and Paul David (2000) have made estimates of average annual growth rates of capital relative to the population and to the labor force for specified subperiods during the nineteenth and twentieth centuries. Growth in capital per worker was a particularly important source of economic growth in the nineteenth century. Abramovitz and David (2000, Table 1.6, p. 23) estimate that this so-called capital deepening accounted for almost half (49 percent) of the total growth in output per worker during the period 1800–1855 and 65 percent of a much more rapid rate of output per worker growth during the period 1855–1890.

The high and growing capital-labor ratios were effected through a variety of technological and organizational responses, three of which are particularly worthy of mention. These appeared first in America and were progenitors of developments that would later be emulated worldwide.

The first was the "American System of Manufactures," perhaps best exemplified by rifle production in the Enfield Armory in Connecticut. Prior to the adoption of the American System, rifles were handcrafted to the specifications of individual customers by an artisan who worked with general-purpose tools, such as files, hammers, and tongs. With respect to the American System, a large volume of standardized rifles were manufactured by a large number of highly specialized workers operating highly specialized single-purpose machines and making heavy use of capital and raw materials. Early characterizations of the American System emphasize the importance of interchangeable parts, although more recent research suggests that interchangeable parts were more the exception than the rule before 1870. Before then, quality was not high enough to make such interchangeability a practical reality in most industries (Hounshell 1984). The American System as developed in small-arms production was soon adopted in the production of other manufactured goods. Thus, the modern factory production techniques that today are employed worldwide had their origin in the high-wage environment of nineteenth-century America (see the essay in Chapter Dd on manufacturing).

The second organizational response was the early development of the machine-tool industry, that is, an industry that specialized in the manufacture of machines for use in other industrial processes. The viability of such an industry depended crucially on an extensive domestic market of final manufactured goods and on the capital-intensive nature of a wide range of industrial enterprises throughout the economy. The search for mineral inputs for this industry, such as iron and coal, prompted mineral exploration efforts that had far-reaching consequences for the economy. Thus, the mineral-rich products that fueled America's international ascendancy and, by extension, the mineral discoveries that revolutionized economies around the world also had their origin in the high-wage environment of nineteenth-century America (Rosenberg 1963; also see the essay on natural resources and the environment in Chapter Cf).

The third factor of significance was the early growth of large-scale corporations. These made their appearance in the American railroad and telegraph industries during the mid-nineteenth century. The railroad and telegraph companies expanded rapidly over the nineteenth century in response to an unprecedented increase in the demand for transportation and communication services. This demand for transportation services, in turn, was stimulated by the vast geographic extent of the nation, its large domestic market, and the strong regional variation of its resource base. Technological breakthroughs in the 1820s and 1830s gave an edge to railroads over water and road transportation systems in much of the country, and the railroad industry expanded rapidly. Annual statistics on the miles of railroad track laid between 1830 and 1890 are shown in Table Df874–881. What these statistics do not show is the growing size of the corporations that owned these rail systems. The railroad industry was characterized by returns to scale; that is, large companies were more profitable than small ones. As a consequence, the industry became highly concentrated in the hands of a small number of rail-service providers. The large size of these rail companies presented unprecedented challenges to labor management. As the business historian Alfred D. Chandler Jr. (1977, p. 79) emphasized:

[5] For a fuller discussion of "free" labor, see the section on labor market institutions in this essay.

> They were the first to require a large number of full-time managers to coordinate, control, and evaluate the activities of a number of widely scattered operating units. For this reason, they provided the most relevant administrative models for enterprises in the production and distribution of goods and services when such enterprises began to build, on the basis of the new transportation and communication network, their own geographically extended, multiunit business empires.

Thus, the unprecedented economic and geographic expansion of the American product market laid the basis for the innovation of labor management systems and internal labor markets. This innovation revolutionized labor systems in the United States and throughout the world during the twentieth century (Jacoby 1985). For statistics on manufacturing employees by size of employing unit, see Table Ba4703–4705.

Human Capital

"Human capital" refers to those productive human skills that are developed through investments in education, apprenticeship, and other formal and informal on-the-job training. Human capital can advance productivity directly, as it does when it leads to faster or more accurate completion of some given task. Human capital can also advance productivity indirectly, as it does when it enables workers to identify and seize new opportunities, such as adopting a new type of seed or a different method of cultivation, or to switch to a more advantageous venue, such as abandoning the thin and rocky soils of New England for the fertile lands of the Midwest or quitting agriculture altogether to take up more profitable employment in industry. Human capital also stimulates invention. In the nineteenth century, it was human capital in the form of the work experience of thousands of individual farmers, mechanics, and craftsmen that generated the stream of inventions that transformed American agriculture and industry. In the early twentieth century, the locus of American invention and innovation shifted to industrial research laboratories and research universities. In this case, the connection between human capital in the form of formal schooling and invention is especially clear (see the essay on science and technology in Chapter Cg).

In the American context, formal schooling is the form of human capital that has received the greatest attention. One reason is that from as early as the mid-nineteenth century until recently, America led the world in formal educational attainment. Claudia Goldin describes this American ascendancy in terms of three transformations (see the essay in Chapter Bc on education). The first of these was achieved in about 1850 when the majority of free American youth completed the eighth grade. The second was achieved in about 1940 when the majority of youth completed high school. The third is ongoing at the beginning of the twenty-first century as a growing fraction of youth complete four years of college. Historical statistics on the educational attainment of the population by sex and race since 1940 are shown in Table Bc737–792. Labor-force participation rates by educational attainment are shown in Table Ba507–518.

Not only did America lead the world in terms of educational attainment for much of the nineteenth and twentieth centuries, but the rest of the world also gradually adopted the American educational model – what Goldin terms the "American template." This template reflected the American political philosophy, which she characterizes as "egalitarianism" and which consisted of several elements: "public funding, openness, gender neutrality, local (and also state) control, separation of church and state, and an *academic curriculum*" (Goldin 2001, p. 265; emphasis added). Americans insisted on an academic rather than a vocational curriculum because the academic but not the vocational curriculum provided *general* skills. General skills are those that are useful in a variety of circumstances. General skills "survive transport across firms, industries, occupations, and geography" (Goldin 2001, p. 275). Americans insisted on these general, portable skills because of the dynamism of the American economy; in America, the locus of opportunity shifted rapidly across industries, occupations, technologies, and locales.

If human capital development in the form of formal schooling is so attractive, why didn't all societies embrace it? Part of the answer has to do with demand-side factors. In a stagnant economy experiencing little change in its technology, industrial organization, composition of its output, and the geographic location of its production, there is no payoff to training that goes beyond the acquisition of the current stock of skills; only dynamic economies reward those who can craft solutions to new problems and seize new opportunities. Thus, the principal demand-side factor explaining the growth of formal schooling in America was and is the dynamic economic environment. Some milestones in this dynamic development with special implications for labor include the development of the American System of Manufactures, which reduced the demand for skilled artisans; growth of the machine-tool industry, which stimulated demand for engineering skills; development of large-scale industries, such as the railroad and the telegraph, which stimulated demand for managerial and organizational skills to run them; and the advent of "knowledge-based progress" in the twentieth century.

Some evidence pointing to the power of these demand-side factors are the estimated rates of return to formal schooling. These appear to have been higher than returns to other forms of human capital investment perhaps as early as the 1820s. It also seems probable that rates of return to formal schooling in America were higher than in other parts of the world at that early date. Robert Margo reports that while wages of artisans fell relative to those of unskilled labor during the early period of industrialization, those of educated labor rose.[6] Rates of return to formal education have fallen during only two periods of American history. One was the period of the 1930s, 1940s, and 1950s – the era that Goldin and Margo describe as the "Great Compression," when the Great Depression, then World War II, and finally the rapid expansion of manufacturing in response to a dramatic growth in world demand for American products in the immediate post–World War II period favored less educated workers (Goldin and Margo 1992). The second period of decline in the relative wage advantage of highly educated workers was during the 1970s, when a downturn in the economy coincided with the labor force entry of the large, highly educated "baby boom" generation.[7]

The other reason formal schooling developed as rapidly and extensively as it did in America has to do with supply-side factors.

---

[6] Margo (2000) and the essay on wages and wage inequality in this chapter.

[7] On the business cycle, see the essay on economic fluctuations, recessions, and depressions in Chapter Cb. On the characteristics of the baby boom cohort as compared with those of other cohorts, see the essay in Chapter Af on cohorts. For evidence on relative earnings by skill category over time, see Tables Ba4253–4267 and Ba4381–4395, as well as Figure Ba-K. For income at different times according to years of education, see Tables Bc814–901.

Human capital development requires wealth. There is the cost of instruction itself – the wages of teachers and administrators, the physical plant, and books and supplies. Even more expensive, in general, is the implicit cost of the student's time in school. Those engaged in on-the-job training reduce their production. Those engaged in formal schooling may have to suspend production and forgo the associated income altogether. In order for human capital accumulation to take place, a society or an individual must be wealthy enough to absorb these expenses. We have already documented the high and growing wealth in the American economy.

A related issue is the relationship between adults and youths. Human capital is most beneficial to the individual and to society when it is acquired at young ages. This is because young people have more years in which to reap the benefits in terms of higher productivity and wages. However, young people generally find it difficult or impossible to finance their own human capital investments, because their earning capabilities are typically low and they have not had time to accumulate assets. For these reasons, youths are generally dependent for their human capital development on the decisions and resources of their elders. Not all elders are willing to provide schooling for youths, even if they are able. Schooling expands youths' opportunities; youths may take up these opportunities to distance themselves from their parents. In the past, throughout the world and in many parts of the world even today, parents rely on their grown children to provide economic security for their old age. Where they do so, they are reluctant to educate their children, especially their daughters.

Americans largely abandoned their reliance on grown children for old-age security early in the nineteenth century. After this transition, planned, self-financed retirement became the norm. Once accumulated savings secured old age, children became precious. They were sent to school and little work was expected of them. Daughters as well as sons enjoyed these benefits (Fishlow 1967; Lindert 1978; Kaestle and Vinovskis 1980; Tyack and Hansot 1990; Carter, Ransom, and Sutch 2003). School enrollment rates were high, and boys and girls attended in relatively equal proportions (see Tables Bc258–264 and Bc438–446). An unintended consequence of educating daughters as well as sons was the creation of a large pool of inexpensive female teachers. The schools' willingness to hire female teachers and female teachers' willingness to teach for low wages were important ingredients in facilitating the ongoing expansion of the American educational system (Carter 1986; Perlmann and Margo 2001).

A third supply-side factor was the system of local control. This allowed communities to adjust school structure, curriculum, and financing in response to local conditions. Local control meant that schools reflected local needs and, therefore, garnered public support (see the essay in Chapter Bc on education).

Improvements in Technology and Industrial Organization

Technological improvements permit more output from a given set of inputs. They almost always boost labor productivity. A familiar example is Eli Whitney's cotton gin (1793), which replaced hand methods of removing cotton seeds from the bolls. Contemporary observers testified that the gin would "separate more by one hand in a day than formerly in the space of months" (Green 1956, p. 49). Organizational changes can improve output in the same way. A famous early organizational innovation is the hog-slaughtering "disassembly" lines established first in Cincinnati and then in Chicago in the early 1870s. Live hogs were herded into the upper floor of slaughterhouses and moved by gravity and overhead conveyer devices through a sequence of consecutive steps involving slaughtering, butchering, and dressing. The meat for wholesale and retail distribution emerged at the far end of the slaughterhouse without once retracing its steps (Giedion 1948). Such sequential ordering of production was not possible in early factories that relied on water or steam power for their energy. Instead, the power-intensive elements of production were located near the power source, and other intervening operations performed elsewhere in the building. Because consecutive steps in the production process were performed at different places around the plant, a large number of workers had to be employed in simply moving partially finished goods from one part of the factory to another. The introduction of electrical power into factories in the 1890s and its widespread adoption in the 1920s allowed for the rationalization of the workflow. Because electricity could be distributed as easily to one as to another point in the factory, production was reorganized to manage the flow of production in a logical fashion and to reduce the need to move semifinished products back and forth around the plant. These changes afforded considerable savings in labor, plant size, and working capital (David 1990). To the extent that such technological and organizational changes raise labor productivity, they also prompt a rise in wages.

Scholars have argued that as early as the first half of the nineteenth century, technological innovation in America was faster than elsewhere. In an influential book, H. J. Habakkuk (1962, p. 5) reports commentary by contemporary observers to this effect and asks, "Why should mechanisation, standardization and mass-production have appeared before 1850 and to an extent which surprised reasonably dispassionate English observers?" At the same time, there is abundant evidence that America was a heavy borrower of industrial technologies from other countries. To briefly summarize a large and complicated literature, it seems that in certain industries, such as firearms, steamboats, farm machinery, sewing machines, and other machine tools, the United States was the primary source of new and distinctive technological inventions and innovations. In other industries, especially cotton textiles, most of the technology employed in America was borrowed from abroad (Habakkuk 1962; Rosenberg 1976; Hounshell 1984). The longest-running quantitative measure of this technological activity is the series on patents (series Cg30). By 1810, the United States had surpassed Great Britain in patents per capita (Khan and Sokoloff 2001, p. 239).

The characterization of American industrial and organizational inventions, innovations, and practice over the last 200 years is the subject of a large literature. See the essay on science and technology in Chapter Cg, Engerman and Sokoloff (2000), and Mowery and Rosenberg (2000) for recent surveys. Also see the essay on productivity in Chapter Cg for an assessment of the role of improvements in technology and industrial organization as a source of American productivity growth.

Technological and organizational improvements rarely affect all inputs equally. Those that do are said to be "neutral." Generally speaking, however, changes in technology affect the demand for capital and for labor differently and may have different effects on skilled versus unskilled labor as well. See the essay on wages and wage inequality in this chapter for a discussion of the impact of technological and organizational changes on various types of labor over time.

Laws, Institutions, and the Operation of the American Labor Market

The American labor market operates within a complex, idiosyncratic, and changing set of laws and institutions. These laws and institutions influence a wide range of labor market outcomes. We have already referred to the impact of educational institutions on labor skills, of immigration policy on the size and character of the labor force, and of Indian policy on "land abundance" for European settlers. These are but a few examples.

The basic law of employment specifies the ownership and control over human labor itself. Three major categories of such ownership and control have been practiced historically: slavery and serfdom, "contract labor" such as indentured servitude, and free labor. A slave is the property of a master who exercises complete legal and physical control. Slaves pass their enslaved status on to their offspring. Contract laborers are born free and their children are born free, but when they voluntarily enter into a labor contract, they are bound for the specified period of time to perform their agreed-upon duties or face punishment. Free laborers enter labor relations voluntarily and are free to quit at any time. Unlike contract laborers, they are not bound to remain until the task or term of work is completed. If they do depart before the work is complete, they lose compensation for the uncompleted work, but they do not face punishment.

Orthogonal to these three labor systems are laws controlling married women's right to make contracts and to control their own property, earnings, and activities. Throughout most of the world until the nineteenth century and in some parts of the world even today, a wife was forbidden to "make contracts, buy and sell property, sue or be sued, or draft wills. Her husband owned any wages she earned, and he controlled any property she brought to the marriage. A husband also could control his wife's economic activities outside the home, such as limiting a particular shopkeeper from selling to his wife" (Geddes and Lueck 2002, p. 1079). Other legal restrictions societywide often limited the labor of married women.

At their founding, the American colonies recognized slavery and indentured servitude, but over time abolished both of these forms of coercive labor. The abolition of slavery began in the North in 1777 and was complete in the "Free States" by 1803. Slavery continued in the South, however, until the Civil War, and the Thirteenth Amendment to the Constitution outlawed this practice. Indentured servitude vanished by the 1820s. In 1864, Congress legalized contract labor for immigrants, but in 1885 reversed itself and banned the practice. According to Robert Steinfeld (1991), America was the first nation to embrace the institution of free labor on a wide scale.

American labor institutions originated out of the English labor practice and law at the time of initial colonization during the early seventeenth century. As Steinfeld demonstrates, English law at that time sanctioned both slave and consensual labor contracts. The distinction between the two is that slaves had no say in the disposition of their labor, whereas free persons did. Free persons could sign labor contracts in exchange for wages, training, or transatlantic transportation. He also demonstrates that the consensual labor contracts offered at the time subjected workers to what we would describe today as "unfree labor" (Steinfeld 1991, p. 3). Although workers entered into these labor agreements voluntarily, they faced stiff penalties if they failed to fulfill their promises. Thus, if an individual agreed to work for some specified period of time, produce some product, or provide some service, he or she would not only risk the loss of compensation for failing to deliver but also face fines, imprisonment, whippings, disfigurement, or other punishments. Under such circumstances, hired labor in the seventeenth and eighteenth centuries was closer in nature to indentured servitude than it was to the free labor we know today. Today, employees have the right to quit at any time without fear of coercive retribution.

The motivation for adopting these systems of "unfree" labor was the relative ease of attaining self-employment in the American environment. The abundance of land, game, fish, timber, and minerals and the consequent low price for the right to exploit these resources meant that even those who started with few assets of their own could soon purchase access by accumulating savings over a few years of wage work. Those seeking to expand employment in their enterprise beyond the family labor force found it necessary to resort to some form of unfree labor. This insight is attributable to Evsey Domar (1970), who demonstrated that free land, free laborers, and rent-earning landlords cannot exist simultaneously. In a land-rich environment, property owners can profit from hired labor only by placing restrictions on their laborers' rights.

Indentured Servitude and Other Forms of Contractual Labor

Indentured servitude was the first form of unfree labor to enjoy widespread adoption in the American colonies. According to this system, Europeans voluntarily signed contracts, called "indentures," in which they pledged to work for a specific period of time in return for food, shelter, and clothing and often passage to America, training, and "freedom dues" upon the completion of their service. The length of the required service varied with the reimbursements; those who could afford to pay their own passage could negotiate for a shorter period of service. The length of required service also varied with the characteristics of the servant. Young, healthy men in possession of craft skills were offered shorter periods of service because of their higher productivity than those without such characteristics. The length of service also varied with supply and demand. A decrease in the supply of servants or an increase in demand for labor caused the period of service to fall, effectively raising the price of the servant for the master.

By about 1630, after the initial establishment of the colonies had been completed, indentured servants constituted the majority of new arrivals from Europe. With the end of religious persecutions in Europe, the rise in wages, and the fall in transportation costs, the number of persons willing to enter servitude fell, and colonists were forced to offer shorter terms of service in order to attract them. Increases in the value of colonial export products also led to reductions in the length of service as planters searched for ways to entice more potential workers. These forces eventually drove the price of indentured servants above the price of black slaves imported from Africa or the Caribbean. Colonists who wished to use bound labor relied increasingly on slave labor. By the time of the American Revolution, slaves had largely replaced indentured servants in the South, although they continued as an important source of labor in Pennsylvania and the Chesapeake Bay area. After 1820, the institution of indentured servitude disappeared entirely (Steinfeld 1991; Galenson 1996).

In addition to indentured servants, restrictive contracts formed the basis of the employment relation for apprentices and domestic servants, as well as for laborers. Peter Way (1993) shows that early American canals were built with a labor force that comprised slaves and white laborers who signed contracts committing them to remain with the project until the work was complete. Coercive labor contracts were also ubiquitous in the market for Northern agricultural labor through the first half of the nineteenth century. Although most Northern farms made do with family labor, those that employed hired hands bound them to honor either specific periods of service or the completion of specific tasks (Rothenberg 1992; Steinfeld 1991, Chapter 2).

Slave Labor

Slave labor was a powerful and quantitatively important institution in colonial America. Slavery was legal throughout British North America, and it was practiced in all of the colonies that would ultimately become the United States. In 1770, blacks (almost all of whom are presumed to have been slaves) accounted for an estimated 21.7 percent of the total population. They were heavily concentrated in the South. In Virginia, North Carolina, South Carolina, and Georgia, they accounted for 42.0, 35.3, 60.5, and 45.5 percent of the population, respectively. At the same time, slaves were present in the Northern colonies as well, in particular in Rhode Island, New York, and New Jersey, where they accounted for 6.5, 11.7, and 7.0 percent of the 1770 population, respectively (Table Eg1–59).

In 1800, slaves accounted for over 30 percent of the workforce nationally and slightly over 50 percent of the workforce in the South. Almost all slave labor was engaged in agriculture, especially in the cultivation of tobacco. Enslaved women and children were just as likely as enslaved men to work in the fields. See Tables Ba79–339.

Vermont was the first to abolish slavery in 1777, and by 1804, all of the Northern states had outlawed this practice. Slavery continued to be practiced throughout the South until 1865 at the conclusion of the Civil War and the passage of the Thirteenth Amendment to the Constitution. The essay in Chapter Bb describes the origins of slavery in the American colonies, its development, and subsequent abolition. The essay in Chapter Eg discusses the role of slavery in the colonial economy. The essay in Chapter Eh focuses on the Confederate States of America and the Civil War.

The institution of slave labor produced a distinctive economic dynamic in the South. Gavin Wright (1984, p. 11) argues that the distinctiveness of the Southern labor market even today had its origins in behaviors motivated by slaveholding in the early nineteenth century:

> As compared to the American North, the incentives of slave property tended to disperse population across the land, reduce investments in transportation and in cities, and limit the exploration of southern natural resources. Above all, slave owners had no incentives to open up labor market links with outside areas, and the resulting inelasticity of the labor supply squeezed out labor-intensive manufacturing activity, such as the pre-[Civil]war textile industry which grew during the 1840s but stagnated during the cotton boom of the 1850s.

With the abolition of slavery, Southerners ceased to engage in these distinctive practices. Wright (1984, p. 11) calls particular attention to the "reallocation of land from corn to cotton, new enthusiasm for railroads and local development, and the rise of new manufacturing and mining sectors." He also shows that after the abolition of slavery, the Southern labor market began to function much like the labor market in the rest of the country. Despite the evils of debt peonage, sharecropping, and racism, Southern labor turnover was high, and laborers migrated from lower- to higher-wage areas. At the same time, the absence of formal linkages with the rest of the nation (in the slave era, the South had stronger trade connections with Europe than it did with the Northern states), the absence of appropriate industrial technologies (the American System of Manufactures was not well suited to the low-wage, labor-abundant South), and a reluctance to invest heavily in education for fear of enabling the out-migration of youths kept the Southern labor market separate from that of the rest of the nation. Until World War I, the Southern labor market operated in isolation from that in the rest of the country. Southern migration took place only within the South, despite the availability of higher wages, better working conditions, and more political freedom for blacks in other regions of the country. As the vast majority of blacks lived in the South, an important implication of this Southern labor-market isolation is that it perpetuated the poverty, low educational attainment, and agricultural employment of the black population. In Wright's phrase, blacks were the "poorest group in the country's poorest region."[8] William Collins (1997) demonstrates that this isolation of the Southern labor market was caused by mass European immigration, coupled with racist hiring practices of Northern employers, who favored white immigrants over Southern blacks.

Labor shortages during World War I and the restrictive immigration legislation of the 1920s sparked the "Great Migration," which ended the isolation of the Southern labor market. The Great Migration refers to the wholesale migration of black Southerners to Northeastern and Midwestern cities. It began in the last decade of the nineteenth century, accelerated substantially during World War I and then again during the 1920s, subsided somewhat during the Great Depression of the 1930s, but then accelerated once again during the World War II years. Although Southerners of all races migrated to the North, black Southerners participated to a disproportionate degree.[9] The Great Migration is credited with substantial gains for blacks on a wide range of fronts, including improvements in educational attainment (Table Bc438–446), increased occupational integration (Table Ba4207–4213), and greater equality in black–white earnings (Tables Ba4431–4439 and Ba4512–4520).

Although the exodus of blacks sparked some improvements for the black workers who remained in the South, Gavin Wright (1987) demonstrates that it was not until the enactment of New Deal labor policies during the 1930s that the Southern labor market really began to resemble the labor market in the rest of the nation. The National Recovery Act (NRA) raised the wage in many Southern industries, and Works Progress Administration (WPA) employment opportunities were offered at wages that were much higher than those prevailing in the South. Other influential New Deal policies were those that encouraged unionization and established a relatively high minimum wage.

---

[8] Wright (1987). See also Rosenbloom (2002) on the isolation of the Southern labor market.

[9] See the essay in Chapter Ac on internal migration and Collins (1997).

Free Labor

"Free labor" in this context refers to a labor system in which employees have the right to quit. As Robert Steinfeld (1991) demonstrates, free labor was not an institution that America inherited from the English; it was a unique American development. Although free labor first appeared in America in the early eighteenth century, it was not until the early years of the nineteenth century that it emerged as the dominant mode. Steinfeld attributes the appearance and spread of free labor to two consequences of the American Revolution: a heightened resolve to abolish black slavery and a broad-based demand to extend the suffrage. He argues that following the Revolution, "Americans began to think about indentured servitude quite differently, as a form of involuntary rather than voluntary servitude and as essentially indistinguishable from slavery" (Steinfeld 1991, p. 7). Their post-Revolutionary agitation for broadened suffrage pushed in the same direction: "One of the principal new tests for the suffrage that states began to adopt was the test of legal self-government. Did an individual have the legal right to control and dispose of his or her own person, or did that right lie in another? If individuals enjoyed the legal right to control and dispose of themselves, they would be qualified to exercise the suffrage" (Steinfeld 1991, p. 185). Thus, under this interpretation, suffrage required the abolition of unfree labor. Peter Way (1993) suggests that an economic motive may have played a role as well. Free laborers are cheaper than unfree when the supply of labor is great and where demand fluctuates the way it did in the building of canals in the late eighteenth and early nineteenth centuries. During good times, inexpensive free labor could be recruited in Scotland and Ireland; during bad times, free laborers could be dismissed, sparing the company the cost of their room and board, forcing laborers to finance their own unemployment. By the early nineteenth century, the two labor systems were chattel slavery and free labor, where free laborers not only entered into the employment relation voluntarily but had also secured the right to depart at will.

Free labor became an increasingly important institution in America over the nineteenth century and for most of the twentieth century as well. Although the free share of the Southern labor force remained roughly constant during the nineteenth century up until the abolition of slavery, it rose as a share of the national labor force. This was because of the substantial immigration of free laborers to the North, but not to the South, especially after 1840. Thus, while free workers accounted for 69.5 percent of the labor force in 1800, on the eve of the Civil War in 1860 the free share was 78.3 percent (calculated from Tables Ba1–10 and Ba40–49).

There is an additional sense in which free labor was growing in importance over time, that is, in distinguishing self-employed and unpaid family workers from hired workers. Stanley Lebergott estimates that as late as 1900, hired labor accounted for only a little more than half (55.4 percent) of the labor force (calculated from series Ba470, Ba910, and Ba918). The continuing importance of owner-operated farms and small retail and service establishments limited the extent of hired labor economywide. By 1960, wage and salary workers comprised 84 percent of the labor force according to Lebergott, and 86 percent according to the U.S. Bureau of Labor Statistics (BLS) (series Ba981). In 2000, wage and salary workers were estimated to account for 93 percent of the labor force. The decline in self-employment and rise in (free) wage and salary workers have been a largely uninterrupted development, except for a mild reversal of the trend toward wage and salary work in the late 1970s and early 1980s (series Ba981). One confounding development has been the growing use of S-corporations as a legal form for small individual and family enterprises. To reduce risk and taxation, an increasing number of small enterprises have adopted this legal form. When they do so, the formerly self-employed individual is reclassified as an employee of the new corporation (see Table Ch1–18). The number of S-corporations has risen rapidly over time, especially since the mid-1980s. This trend may be masking a substantial amount of what we would otherwise classify as self-employment.

The Rights of Married Women

American law adopted the English practice of "coverture," which refers to the constricted status of married women under common law. In the oft-quoted words of the prominent English jurist Sir William Blackstone, marriage creates under coverture a "unity of person between the husband and wife; it being held that they are one person in law, so that the very being and existence of the woman is suspended during the coverture, or entirely merged and incorporated in that of the husband" (Blackstone 1756). In other words, under coverture, husbands exercised legal control over their wives' activities and owned their wives' output; the absence of coverture is self-ownership. Coverture has been shown to have limited married women's commercial and patenting activities in nineteenth-century America (Khan 1996). It is also probable that coverture reduced investments in women's education and job-related skills (Schultz 1995).

American laws regarding coverture were written at the state level, and it is therefore possible to observe regional differences in the decline of this institution over time. R. Richard Geddes and Dean Lueck (2002) develop a chronology of women's property rights by state over time and use the data to explore the causes of this important legal change. In their view, the principal causes of the decline in coverture, at least in the American environment, were increases in wealth, the market wage, the rate of return to education, and the complexity of market work. According to available estimates, women's self-ownership became law throughout the country by the late 1890s (Table Ba5091–5095).

Nonetheless, twentieth-century depression and wartime exigencies produced a series of labor laws that severely limited married women's employment opportunities between the 1920s and the 1950s. These were the so-called marriage bars that prohibited employers from hiring married women and required them to fire experienced, formerly single female employees upon their marriage. Claudia Goldin (1991) documents the rise of such practices beginning in the 1920s, just as women were beginning to extend the number of years they devoted to the labor force. The institution of such regulations posed few costs to employers, in Goldin's view, because they were imposed at a time when most married women considered their jobs to be temporary. Nonetheless, these regulations surely must have inhibited investments in human capital by women who would have preferred longer employment careers. Marriage bars were suddenly abandoned in the 1950s under pressure from the markedly growing labor supply of married women.

Labor Market Structure

In addition to the basic law of employment, there are countless other laws, institutions, and practices that affect labor market operation. Stephen Nickell and Richard Layard (1999) classify these under five headings: labor taxation, especially payroll taxes, income taxes, and consumption sales taxes; employment protection legislation regulating hours of work, employee compensation, and job security; trade union activity and minimum wages; support for the unemployed and active labor market policy aimed at reducing unemployment; and education and skill formation. Quantitative evidence on the historical development of these labor market institutions are displayed in various chapters of *Historical Statistics of the United States*. The essay in Chapter Ea on government finance and employment discusses the development of the federal income tax, its level, its incidence, and change over time. The essay on hours and working conditions in this chapter discusses the development of hours of work, worker safety, and job security legislation. The essay on labor unions in this chapter discusses trade unions and their growth and evolution over time. Table Ba4422–4425 displays time series data regarding the federal minimum wage. The essays on public assistance and on social welfare in Chapter Bf describe private and social income support for the unemployed and for those who are out of the labor force. The essay on economic fluctuations, recessions, and depressions in Chapter Cb discusses the evolution of active labor market policy. Educational institutions are described in the essay in Chapter Bc on education, as well as in this essay.

The constellation of institutions that affect labor market operations are sometimes referred to collectively by the term "labor market structure." For some purposes, labor market structure can be usefully viewed as lying along a single dimension. At one end of the spectrum lie "unfettered" labor markets that mimic textbook examples of perfect competition. At the other end are highly "structured" labor markets with substantial legal, political, and social institutions that modify the forces of market competition. A popular way of viewing the development of the American labor market is to see it as moving along this continuum from less to more structure over time. Christopher Tomlins (2000) provides an overview and analysis of the major legal developments. Price Fishback (1998) offers a comprehensive description of the operation of the relatively "unfettered" labor markets at the turn of the twentieth century. He also provides an assessment of their operation and the political economy of the emergence of additional labor market structure over the course of the twentieth century. In Fishback's view, the relatively unfettered labor markets at about 1900 "functioned well enough that workers typically had multiple opportunities and were able to move to take advantage of them to improve their situation" (Fishback 1998, p. 759). At the same time, laborers clearly expressed their dissatisfaction with many of the labor practices of the day, and there were a considerable number of issues that were viewed as problems by both workers and employers. Fishback concludes that many of the Progressive era labor regulations, especially worker compensation laws, unemployment insurance, and minimum wages, were beneficial not only to workers but also to a "significant subset of employers" (Fishback 1998, p. 761). For this reason, they are likely to remain a part of the American landscape, at least until the underlying conditions change.

Labor markets can also be compared according to these structures. An active area of labor market research in the closing years of the twentieth century is the identification of connections between different labor market structures and their associated labor market outcomes.[10]

[10] For overviews, see Blau and Kahn (1999) and Nickell and Layard (1999).

References

Abramovitz, Moses, and Paul A. David. 2000. "American Macroeconomic Growth in the Era of Knowledge-Based Progress: The Long-Run Perspective." In Stanley L. Engerman and Robert E. Gallman, editors. *The Cambridge Economic History of the United States,* volume 3. Cambridge University Press.

Atack, Jeremy, and Peter Passell. 1994. *A New Economic View of American History: From Colonial Times to 1940*. 2d edition. Norton.

Blackstone, Sir William. 1756. *Commentaries on the Law of England, in Four Books*. Clarendon.

Blau, Francine D., and Lawrence M. Kahn. 1999. "Institutions and Laws in Labor Markets." In Orley Ashenfelter and David Card, editors. *Handbook of Labor Economics,* volume 3A, Chapter 25. Elsevier Science.

Carter, Susan B. 1986. "Occupational Segregation, Teachers' Wages and American Economic Growth." *Journal of Economic History* 46 (2): 373–83.

Carter, Susan B., Roger L. Ransom, and Richard Sutch. 2003. "Family Matters: The Life-Cycle Transition and the Unparalleled Antebellum American Fertility Decline." In Timothy W. Guinnane, William A. Sundstrom, and Warren Whatley, editors. *History Matters: Essays on Economic Growth, Technology, and Demographic Change*. Stanford University Press.

Chandler, Alfred D., Jr. 1977. *The Visible Hand: The Managerial Revolution in American Business*. Harvard University Press.

Collins, William. 1997. "When the Tide Turned: Immigration and the Delay of the Great Black Migration." *Journal of Economic History* 57 (3): 607–32.

David, Paul A. 1990. "The Dynamo and the Computer: An Historical Perspective on the Modern Productivity Paradox." *American Economic Review* 80 (2): 355–61.

Domar, Evsey. 1970. "The Cause of Slavery or Serfdom: A Hypothesis." *Journal of Economic History* 30 (1): 18–32.

Egnal, Marc. 1996. *Divergent Paths: How Culture and Institutions Have Shaped North American Growth*. Oxford University Press.

Engerman, Stanley, and Kenneth Sokoloff. 2000. "Technology and Industrialization, 1790–1914." In Stanley L. Engerman and Robert E. Gallman, editors. *The Cambridge Economic History of the United States,* volume 2. Cambridge University Press.

Fishback, Price V. 1998. "Operations of 'Unfettered' Labor Markets: Exit and Voice in American Labor Markets at the Turn of the Century." *Journal of Economic Literature* 36 (2): 722–65.

Fishlow, Albert. 1967. "The American Common School Revival: Fact or Fancy?" In Henry Rosovsky, editor. *Industrialization in Two Systems: Essays in Honor of Alexander Gerschenkron*. Wiley.

Folbre, Nancy, and Barnet Wagman. 1993. "Counting Housework: New Estimates of Real Product in the United States." *Journal of Economic History* 53 (2): 275–88.

Galenson, David W. 1996. "The Settlement and Growth of the Colonies: Population, Labor, and Economic Development." In Stanley L. Engerman and Robert E. Gallman, editors. *The Cambridge Economic History of the United States,* volume 1. Cambridge University Press.

Gallman, Robert E. 2000. "Economic Growth and Structural Change in the Long Nineteenth Century." In Stanley L. Engerman and Robert E. Gallman, editors. *The Cambridge Economic History of the United States,* volume 2. Cambridge University Press.

Geddes, R. Richard, and Dean Lueck. 2002. "The Gains from Self-Ownership and the Expansion of Women's Rights." *American Economic Review* 92 (September): 1079–92.

Giedion, Sigfried. 1948. *Mechanization Takes Command: A Contribution to Anonymous History*. Oxford University Press.

Goldin, Claudia. 1991. "Marriage Bars: Discrimination against Married Women Workers from the 1920s to the 1950s." In Patrice Higonnet, David S. Landes, and Henry Rosovsky, editors. *Favorites of Fortune: Technology, Growth, and Economic Development since the Industrial Revolution*. Harvard University Press.

Goldin, Claudia. 2000. "Labor Markets in the Twentieth Century." In Stanley L. Engerman and Robert E. Gallman, editors. *The Cambridge Economic History of the United States,* volume 3. Cambridge University Press.

Goldin, Claudia. 2001. "The Human-Capital Century and American Leadership: Virtues of the Past." *Journal of Economic History* 61 (2): 263–92.

Goldin, Claudia, and Robert A. Margo. 1992. "Great Compression: The U.S. Wage Structure at Mid-Century." *Quarterly Journal of Economics* 107 (February): 1–34.
Green, Constance McLaughlin. 1956. *Eli Whitney and the Birth of American Technology*. Little, Brown.
Habakkuk, H. J. 1962. *American and British Technology in the Nineteenth Century*. Cambridge University Press.
Hounshell, David A. 1984. *From the American System to Mass Production, 1800–1932: The Development of Manufacturing Technology in the United States*. Johns Hopkins University Press.
Jacoby, Sanford M. 1985. *Employing Bureaucracy: Managers, Unions, and the Transformation of Work in American Industry, 1900–1945*. Columbia University Press.
Kaestle, Carl F., and Maris A. Vinovskis. 1980. *Education and Social Change in Nineteenth-Century Massachusetts*. Cambridge University Press.
Khan, B. Zorina. 1996. "Married Women's Property Laws and Female Commercial Activity: Evidence from United States Patent Records, 1790–1895." *Journal of Economic History* 56 (2): 356–88.
Khan, B. Zorina, and Kenneth L. Sokoloff. 2001. "The Early Development of Intellectual Property Institutions in the United States." *Journal of Economic Perspectives* 15 (3): 233–46.
Lindert, Peter H. 1978. *Fertility and Scarcity in America*. Princeton University Press.
Maddison, Angus. 1995. *Monitoring the World Economy, 1820–1992*. Development Centre of the Organization for Economic Co-operation and Development.
Margo, Robert A. 2000. "The Labor Force in the Nineteenth Century." In Stanley L. Engerman and Robert E. Gallman, editors. *The Cambridge Economic History of the United States,* volume 2. Cambridge University Press.
Mowery, David, and Nathan Rosenberg. 2000. "Twentieth-Century Technological Change." In Stanley L. Engerman and Robert E. Gallman, editors. *The Cambridge Economic History of the United States,* volume 3. Cambridge University Press.
Nickell, Stephen, and Richard Layard. 1999. "Labor Market Institutions and Economic Performance." In Orley Ashenfelter and David Card, editors. *Handbook of Labor Economics,* volume 3C, Chapter 46. Elsevier Science.
Perlmann, Joel, and Robert A. Margo. 2001. *Women's Work? American Schoolteachers 1650–1920*. University of Chicago Press.
Rosenberg, Nathan. 1963. "Technological Change in the Machine Tool Industry, 1840–1910." *Journal of Economic History* 23 (4): 414–43.
Rosenberg, Nathan. 1976. *Perspectives on Technology*. Cambridge University Press.
Rosenbloom, Joshua L. 2002. *Looking for Work, Searching for Workers: American Labor Markets during Industrialization*. Cambridge University Press.
Rothenberg, Winifred B. 1992. "Structural Change in the Farm Labor Force: Contract Labor in Massachusetts Agriculture, 1750–1865." In Claudia Goldin and Hugh Rockoff, editors. *Strategic Factors in Nineteenth Century American Economic History: A Volume to Honor Robert W. Fogel*. University of Chicago Press.
Schultz, T. Paul, editor. 1995. *Investment in Women's Human Capital*. University of Chicago Press.
Smith, Adam. 1776. *An Inquiry into the Nature and Causes of the Wealth of Nations*.
Sokoloff, Kenneth. 1986. "Productivity Growth in Manufacturing during Early Industrialization: Evidence from the American Northeast, 1820–1860." In Stanley L. Engerman and Robert E. Gallman, editors. *Long-Term Factors in American Economic Growth*. National Bureau of Economic Research. Studies in Income and Wealth, volume 51. University of Chicago Press.
Steinfeld, Robert J. 1991. *The Invention of Free Labor: The Employment Relation in English and American Law and Culture, 1350–1870*. University of North Carolina Press.
Tomlins, Christopher L. 2000. "Labor Law." In Stanley L. Engerman and Robert E. Gallman, editors. *The Cambridge Economic History of the United States,* volume 3. Cambridge University Press.
Tyack, David, and Elisabeth Hansot. 1990. *Learning Together: A History of Coeducation in American Public Schools*. Yale University Press.
U.S. Bureau of the Census. 2003. *International Data Base*. Downloaded from the Census Bureau Internet site on June 19, 2003.
Wagman, Barnet, and Nancy Folbre. 1996. "Household Services and Economic Growth in the United States, 1870–1930." *Feminist Economics* 2 (1): 43–66.
Way, Peter. 1993. *Common Labor: Workers and the Digging of North American Canals, 1780–1860*. Johns Hopkins University Press.
Wright, Gavin. 1984. *Old South, New South: Revolutions in the Southern Economy since the Civil War*. Basic Books.
Wright, Gavin. 1987. "Postbellum Southern Labor Markets." In Peter Kilby, editor. *Quantity and Quiddity: Essays in U.S. Economic History*. Wesleyan University Press.

Labor Force

Susan B. Carter

For much of human history, and in much of the world even today, the vast majority of the population work for a living. Except for those too young, too old, or too sick, and except for the "idle classes" – those with power or resources to command food, clothing, and shelter from others – people work, and do so for most of their lives.

In contrast to this common human reference to labor, the term "labor force" has a technical definition that was created and refined during the social, economic, and political crises accompanying the Great Depression of the 1930s. To determine an individual's status according to the labor force concept, people are asked about their activities during a specific reference week and, on the basis of their answers, are classified as either employed, unemployed, or out of the labor force. The labor force, according to this measure, is the sum of the employed and the unemployed.

The employed are defined as those adults who, during the reference week, (1) did any work at all as paid employees, worked in their own business, in their profession, or on their own farm, or who worked fifteen hours or more as unpaid workers in a family-operated enterprise; plus (2) those who did not work but who had jobs or businesses from which they were temporarily absent due to illness, bad weather, vacation, child care problems, labor dispute, parental leave, or other family or personal obligations – whether or not they were paid by their employers for the time off and whether or not they were seeking other jobs.[1] Each employed person is counted only once, even if he or she holds more than one job. Multiple jobholders are counted in the job at which they worked the greatest number of hours during the reference week. Included in the total are employed citizens of foreign countries who are residing in the United States. Excluded are persons whose only activity consists of unpaid work around their own home, such as housework, painting, repairing, and so forth, or volunteer work for religious, charitable, and similar organizations.

The unemployed are those who had no employment during the reference week, but who were available for work and who had made specific efforts, such as contacting employers, to find work during a specified period. Those who are neither employed nor unemployed are classified as "out of the labor force." Additional details for assigning individuals across the categories employed,

[1] "Adults" were defined as persons fourteen years of age and older through 1947 and persons sixteen years of age and older beginning in 1947. There are two values for the labor force in 1947, one for each age grouping. See Table Ba478–486.

unemployed, and out of the labor force are spelled out in the text for Table Ba478–486.

The U.S. Bureau of Labor Statistics (BLS), in collaboration with the Census Bureau, first implemented the labor force concept in 1940. It was devised during the 1930s to assist macroeconomic policymakers who needed an indicator that would tell them whether their interventions into the economy were having the desired effect of lowering unemployment. An earlier definition of unemployment was based on replies to the question, "Do you have an occupation?" and, if not, "Are you willing and able to work?" Analysts found that people in objectively similar situations often answered these questions differently. For this reason, the answers could not be used reliably to compare labor force participation rates across individuals or cities, or to compare changes in such rates over time. The cornerstone of the modern labor force concept is the objectivity of the criteria used to assign individuals across categories: clearly specified activities rather than attitudes, and a clear reference period for which the criteria are applied (Lebergott 1975).

Although the labor force concept is highly precise on the questions "who is in and who is out of the labor force" and "who is employed and who is unemployed," it does not distinguish among many other aspects of labor that are critical to the development of the economy and to the well-being of workers. For example, persons working sixty hours a week, those working one hour a week, and those on vacation are all included "in the labor force" and "employed" and on equal footing in the official framework. Workers with highly developed skills and those supplying purely manual labor are counted equally. Much of the work done by women is not counted at all. For these reasons, most historical or policy questions involving change in the labor force must be studied in conjunction with data on change in hours of work, the skills of the workforce, wages, working conditions, occupations, child care and other family services, and household production.

Despite its limitations, "labor force" has proved to be a highly useful concept for policymakers. Statistics on the unemployment rate and labor force participation are among the most commonly cited indicators of the health of the economy, often making headlines when the latest figures are released. Increases in the unemployment rate and decreases in the labor force participation rate correlate strongly with other measures of economic downturn. Indeed, for some scholars, these labor market indicators are the premier measures of economic fluctuations (see the essay on economic fluctuations, recessions, and depressions in Chapter Cb).

Modern Labor Force Estimates

The three major sources of data on the size and composition of the labor force are the decennial censuses of population, the Current Population Survey (CPS), and the Current Employment Statistics survey (CES). The census and CPS are surveys of households; the CES is a survey of employers.

The census of population made its first inquiries regarding work behavior in 1850, when it asked free males fifteen years of age and older to report their occupation, if any. In 1860, the census extended the inquiry to free women. The year 1870 is the first for which occupation statistics are available for the majority of the black population, as they were enslaved and their occupations not enumerated at the time of the earlier censuses. Not until 1940 did the census shift its questions regarding work behavior to reflect the labor force concept discussed previously.[2]

The effort that would become the CPS was also begun in 1940 when the census initiated a monthly national sample survey of households. For studies of the labor force in the second half of the twentieth century and beyond, the CPS is the most widely used source. These data are also the source for official estimates of unemployment. The CPS provides labor force data at a much higher frequency and with more personal background characteristics than does the census. The major background characteristics are age, sex, marital status, presence of children, race, Hispanic origin, industry, occupation, and unemployment according to reason and duration. Tables Ba478–506 provide an overview of labor force estimates based on the CPS. More than ten other tables provide additional detail. Here, we report annual averages calculated from the monthly figures.

The CES is the third major source of national, historical labor force data. These data are collected by the BLS from the monthly payroll records of a sample of nonfarm business establishments. The firms submit the data voluntarily. In 1999, the Bureau surveyed 400,000 establishments employing about a third of all wage and salary workers. The surveys provide detailed industry data on employment, hours, and earnings of workers on nonfarm payrolls. The CES counts workers each time they appear on a payroll during the reference period. Thus, unlike the CPS, a person with two jobs is counted twice. Tables Ba840–848 and Ba866–879 provide an overview of labor force estimates based on the CES. Many tables in this chapter and in others provide additional industry detail.

Historical Labor Force Estimates

The evident value of the labor force concept for understanding the development of the economy has prompted scholars to devote considerable effort to developing historical labor force and unemployment estimates consistent with the modern definition. The principal starting point for all of these estimates is the census of population.

From 1850, when it first asked about occupation, through 1930, after which it abandoned the approach, census employment figures were based on the "gainful worker" concept. A gainful worker is defined as a person (over a given age) who reports an occupation. Scholars have devoted considerable attention to the comparability of the gainful worker and labor force concepts and have achieved widespread agreement on three points. First, the gainful worker and the labor force concepts probably would have yielded similar statistics for prime-age males had both questions been asked at the same time. Second, the gainful worker and labor force concepts produce different estimates for youthful and older males and for females of all ages. This is because when the census asked about occupation, it did not indicate the period of time for which the question of occupation pertained. This was not a serious problem in the case of prime-age males, because most of them were employed year-round, but many scholars believe that the question elicited inconsistent responses from youthful and older males and from females. Stanley Lebergott (1975, p. 124) considered this a serious problem:

[2] See the Integrated Public Use Microdata Series (IPUMS) Internet site for a convenient listing of the precise questions asked by census enumerators and the portion of the population to which the questions were directed at each census date.

> The question as posed by the enumerator made no reference to time. The response thus varied substantially with the individual. Many persons who were retired or permanently disabled and who had not worked for some time reported their former line of work and were counted as gainful workers. On the other hand, many employed persons did not enter themselves as gainful workers, because they considered themselves as students or housewives and their current employment as only temporary.

Finally, the third point of scholarly consensus is that although the instructions to enumerators regarding the occupation question became more precise (and lengthy) over the years, they were generally consistent from one census to the next, except in the case of the 1910 Census. In that year, the census included special instructions to enumerators that substantially raised the gainful worker rates of children and women – especially black women – relative to reports for the previous and following censuses. For example, the labor force participation rate of black women rises from 43.7 percent in 1900 to 58.1 percent in 1910 and then falls back down to 42.9 percent in 1920, according to the official census definition (series Ba424). The special entreaties to enumerators also reduced the recorded labor force participation rates of older men. The interpretation of the 1910 figures is the subject of a large literature.[3]

Prime-Age Males

Because the gainful worker and labor force concepts produce similar results for prime-age males, the estimation of this segment of the labor force for the period 1850–1930 is a fairly straightforward matter. That said, scholars who developed these estimates have invested tremendous effort to ascertain that the overall estimates and estimates for individual sectors are consistent with other evidence on the development of the economy.[4]

To greatly simplify a complicated procedure, the estimation process for prime-age males for the years 1850–1930 involves taking the gainful worker figures of the censuses, purging them of evident errors, adding in the male slaves who were omitted from the occupational counts of 1850 and 1860, and checking the resulting levels and trends for consistency with other relevant statistical series.

Perhaps the most serious estimation problem for the prime-age male labor force for these years has nothing to do with the overall size of the labor force but is with the distribution of laborers between agriculture and nonagriculture. The problem arises because the census of occupations categorized many agricultural workers as "laborers, not elsewhere classified." The occupation statistics developed by Matthew Sobek and displayed in Tables Ba1033–3687 make an adjustment to "laborers, not elsewhere classified" for the years 1850–1880 by recoding those who resided on a farm as farm laborers. For all other years it reports laborers exactly as the census reported them. For this reason, the Sobek statistics regarding the occupational distribution of the labor force probably understate the share of the labor force in agriculture for the years 1900–1930. The Lebergott and Weiss estimates of the agricultural labor force, shown in Table Ba814–830, incorporate adjustments to the census figures for agricultural laborers.[5]

Estimates of the prime-age male labor force for the period prior to 1850 required even greater efforts. To produce the estimates presented in Table Ba814–830, both Lebergott and Thomas Weiss began with the 1850 and 1860 figures and worked backward in time. They examined the demographic and geographic structure of the population; the fragmentary data from the censuses of manufacturing that were conducted in 1820 and 1840; and a variety of industry-specific data. For example, Lebergott's estimates of employment in teaching are based on contemporary sources, such as statistics of scholars and schools and local studies, that he then projects to the country as a whole. Weiss took a similar approach except that he generated individual estimates for each state. He evaluates fragmentary data on manufacturing employment in light of demographic data such as age, gender, race, and rural residence in order to judge their consistency and coverage and to improve their overall reliability. The art as well as the science of such work lies in getting all of the pieces of the puzzle to fit.

Historical estimates of the prime-age male labor force are presented in several tables. For the decennial census years from 1800 through 1900, Weiss offers estimates of the labor force participation of males sixteen years of age and older, with disaggregations by race, in Tables Ba1–39. For decennial census years from 1860 through 1990, Sobek offers estimates of male labor force participation rates by five-year age groups in Table Ba391–403.

Females

Estimating the labor force participation rates of women prior to 1940 poses its own difficult set of problems and is the subject of another vast literature. A point of agreement is that the early censuses missed a substantial amount of women's market work. Worker surveys undertaken independently of the population census consistently indicate far more female, but not male, employment.

There are several reasons why women's paid employment was undercounted. One is that census enumerators may have forgotten to ask about women's gainful employment. The commentary on occupation statistics in the Censuses of 1870 and 1880 speculated that women and children employed in factories had been "omitted in large numbers." Special instructions to the enumerators of the 1910 Census that were designed to reduce their oversight of women's work resulted in dramatic jumps in the recorded gainful worker rates for women. When these special exhortations were dropped for the 1920 Census, the recorded gainful worker rates for women returned to their former low levels. A second reason is that the women themselves or their husbands may have been reluctant to report women's gainful employment. As Nancy Folbre and Marjorie Abel note, "both the middle-class 'cult of domesticity' and the working-class concept of the 'family wage' dictated that a wife's proper place was in the home." They refer to census commentary on the 1880 occupation returns that mentions specifically the "indisposition of the persons themselves or the heads of families to speak of them [women] as in employment" (Folbre and Abel 1989, p. 551).

Finally, there is evidence that the census itself – at least in 1880 – published female employment totals that were far smaller than the returns collected by enumerators. Comparing the Public Use Microdata Samples (PUMS) of the manuscript census with

[3] See Smuts (1960); Lebergott (1964); Oppenheimer (1970); Conk (1978); Folbre and Abel (1989); Goldin (1990); and Sobek (2001).

[4] Key efforts are Durand (1948); Carson (1949); Long (1958); Lebergott (1964, 1966, 1975, and 1984); and Weiss (1992, 1999).

[5] For a discussion of the methods underlying these estimates, see Lebergott 1964, pp. 156–61, and Weiss 1999.

the published totals for 1880, Susan Carter and Richard Sutch (1996) discovered that the original enumerations exceeded the published totals by 35, 44, and 146 percent, respectively, for girls ages 10–15, women ages 16–59, and women ages 60 years and older. They deduced that a large share of women who were recorded by census enumerators as "housekeepers" (together with a sizable number of women who reported other occupations) were systematically edited out of the gainful worker totals. This was the case despite the fact that the term "housekeeper" was reserved for those who engaged in housekeeping activity for pay, whereas the term "keeping house" was used for those engaged in housekeeping for their own families.

Thus, there is abundant evidence to suggest that published census estimates of female employment in the gainful-worker era are too low. The question is, by how much? Claudia Goldin (1986) undertook a detailed examination of the 1890 Census returns in an effort to quantify the magnitude of the omissions and to develop female labor force estimates for the pre-1940 period that are designed to be consistent with the labor force concept. She argues persuasively that it was not the shift from the gainful worker to the labor force concept per se that is the source of incomparabilities, but the inappropriate omission of female workers in three particular sectors: boardinghouse keepers, family-based agriculture, and manufacturing.

Theoretically, the shift from the "gainful worker" to the "labor force" concept might have reduced female employment totals if, for example, the gainful worker concept captured women whose part-time and intermittent work would be missed by the labor force concept. Because the labor force concept measures only those who are working or searching for work in a given reference week, an individual in the pre–labor force era would have had to be gainfully occupied on average half of the year and, if engaged in unpaid family labor, for more than fourteen hours per week to be included. Because estimates of women's hours and weeks of work in the late nineteenth and early twentieth centuries indicate that those women who were engaged were engaged mostly full time, Goldin concludes that the gainful worker and labor force definitions would have produced similar employment estimates had both been used to collect data during the period when the census collected female gainful worker statistics (1870–1930).

The standard labor force participation rate in 1890 for women 15–64 years of age is 19.0 percent for all women and 4.6 percent for married women (Goldin 1986, p. 559). Had the omitted female boardinghouse keepers, manufacturing workers, and unpaid family farm laborers been included, Goldin (1986, p. 577) estimates that the labor force participation rate for all women would have been somewhere between 24.6 and 25.7 percent, and the rate for married women somewhere between 12.3 and 14.0 percent. Thus, for married women especially, the inclusion of omitted work has a large effect on their estimated labor force participation rate.

Abel and Folbre (1990) used the manuscript census returns for two small Massachusetts communities in 1880 to make their own adjustments to the official gainful worker figures for married women. They added into the gainful worker ranks those married women living in households with boarders who were not boarders themselves and who were not listed with an occupation. They made similar adjustments for females engaged in family businesses and in home- and factory-based manufacturing. Overall, the Abel–Folbre adjustments (Abel and Folbre 1990, p. 174) raise married women's estimated labor force participation rate from 10.1 to 47.3 percent in one community and from 9.9 to 68.2 percent in the other. Clearly, official and adjusted estimates of women's labor force participation imply substantially different views of women's economic role in the economy at the time.

It should be emphasized that the historical estimates of female labor force participation presented here do not incorporate the adjustments suggested by Goldin or by Abel and Folbre. They therefore certainly understate female employment levels both relative to males at the same time and relative to females in the latter part of the twentieth century.

A different question regarding women's work is whether market-based measures, such as labor force and gainful employment, are misleading when a substantial share of the productive energies of many women are devoted to nonmarket activities. For certain questions, such as how output has changed over time, the market measure produces serious distortions. At least since the late nineteenth century when women's labor force participation began to rise over time, the market measure understates total output in the early years and exaggerates the growth of output over time. Goldin (1986) estimates that in 1890, approximately 14 percent of farm housewives' sixty-five-hour workweek was devoted to household production of the clothing, baked goods, and meals that, by 1980, were purchased on the market. Folbre and Wagman (1993) estimate that in 1800, the total output of the economy would have been somewhere between a fifth and a third larger than standard estimates, had the value of household production been included. For a more extended discussion, see the essay on household production in this chapter. For implications for measures of economic growth, see the essay on national income and product in Chapter Ca.

Youth

There is widespread agreement that the censuses also underreported the occupations of youth relative to those of prime-age males. The reasons are similar to the reasons offered for the underenumeration of women's market work. Employed youth typically worked part-time or part-year. Their status was reported by parents who might consider them primarily as students or who may have wished to conceal their gainful activity. Census enumerators may have failed to ask about the employment status of youth.

It is not clear, however, whether youth employment would have been higher if measured according to the labor force concept. The fact that some employed youths were not recorded as gainfully occupied biases the gainful worker measure downward, as compared with the labor force measure of youth employment. However, there may be an upward bias to the gainful worker measure if, for instance, youths recorded with an occupation worked only a small number of hours each day or only part-time during the year. This issue remains unresolved.

The two estimates of youth employment prior to 1940 that we present here are derived from responses to the census of population's gainful worker question. Weiss's estimates for the decennial census years 1800–1900 pertain to youths ages 10–15 and are disaggregated by sex, race, and legal status (Tables Ba1–24 and Ba40–63). His national estimates were built up from state-level estimates. They are based on the assumption that participation rates for free youths in each state were equal to the average youth participation rate for the years 1870–1910 as developed by Alba Edwards (see Edwards 1943, Weiss 1999, p. 30). For slaves, Weiss assumed a labor force participation rate of 90 percent for males and females in all age groups, including youths. His estimates are based on a close reading of the scholarly literature and reflect the views of many quantitatively oriented economic historians (see Weiss 1999 for additional detail). By construction, the Weiss figures show largely unchanging labor force participation rates for white boys and girls over the period, but a marked decline in the participation of black youths following the abolition of slavery.

The youth employment estimates prepared by Sobek for the years 1860–1970 are derived from the Integrated Public Use Microdata Series (IPUMS) and are disaggregated by sex and age for the free population ages 10–15 (Table Ba355–390).[6] Beginning in 1880, they show an almost continuous decline in youth participation rates for both boys and girls and at every age. The exception is the apparent rise in the participation rates of 14- and 15-year-olds between 1940 and 1960.

Both the Weiss and Sobek youth employment estimates differ sharply from the older estimates developed by Alba Edwards of the U.S. Census Bureau, who revised the published occupation figures for youths for the years 1870–1940 in an effort to improve their comparability. Edwards's estimates indicate a substantial *increase* in the labor force participation of youths between 1870 and 1900. Over this period, according to Edwards, the employment incidence of boys grew by more than a third, rising from 19.3 to 26.1 percent, while that of girls increased from 7.0 to 10.2 percent. After 1900, he reports that youth employment rates fell dramatically, so that by 1930, fewer than 5 percent of 10- to 15-year-olds were gainfully occupied.

This view of rising youth employment rates during industrialization was challenged by Carter and Sutch (1996), who discovered that the published census totals for youths in 1880 were only 75 percent of the level originally collected by census enumerators. Because the published statistics for 1880 formed the basis for Edwards's adjustment of the 1890 numbers, and because the 1870 statistics were collected and tabulated using the same protocol as in 1880, the Carter–Sutch finding calls into question the validity of Edwards's series. If the IPUMS figures are accepted and substituted for those from the published volumes, the stylized facts of long-term change in youth employment show a decline, not an increase. The Sobek series, which is calculated directly from the IPUMS, naturally shows this decline. The Weiss series, which is based on the assumption that the true youth employment rate is the average of the published rates for the years 1880–1910, shows no trend. Neither of these scholars embraces the view that youth labor force participation was rising during the period of industrialization.

Older Males

Generating estimates of the older male labor force for the years before 1940 involves all of the problems regarding the labor force estimation of prime-age males plus one more. Because the census question regarding gainful occupation did not indicate a reference time period, the gainful worker figures may overstate the labor force participation of elders. Some older workers reported their former line of work even though they were retired. The question is how many.

Roger Ransom and Richard Sutch (1986) proposed removing from reported gainful employment all workers 60 years of age and older who reported six or more months of unemployment – a group they call the "permanently unemployed." They argue that these older men reporting long-term unemployment were, by the modern definition, really retired. If accepted, their calculations imply high but *falling* rates of male retirement between 1870 and 1900 and a small rise between 1900 and 1930. The retirement rate in this context is the percent of men 60 years of age and older who are not gainfully occupied. Jon Moen, Robert Margo, and Dora Costa argue that all of the older, long-term unemployed are properly included in the labor force (Moen 1987, 1988; Margo 1993b; Costa 1998). Moen and Costa generated male retirement rate estimates that are quite low in the nineteenth century and that begin to rise, but slowly, about 1880.

The dispute has important consequences for a variety of issues in American economic and social history. If the Ransom–Sutch estimates are accepted, then the retirement rate for men ages 60 and older had reached one third as early as 1900. This implies that there was little or no trend in the overall participation rates of the elderly between 1900 and 1930 and that New Deal–era social legislation initiated a trend toward increased retirement. If the Moen and Costa estimates are accepted, then retirement rates would appear to have increased throughout the industrial era, and Social Security emerges as just one of several determinants of the relatively high retirement rates of the post–World War II period. Because they remain controversial, we have not included retirement estimates in this work.

Characteristics of the Labor Force

The term "characteristics of the labor force" refers to demographic factors, such as gender, age, race, ethnicity, nativity, marital status, and presence of children; labor productivity factors, such as job experience, education, and vocational training; full versus part-time status; matters of deployment, such as the occupational, industrial, and geographic distribution of the labor force; and legal and institutional factors, such as slavery, contract labor, trade unions, and the size and organization of employing units.

In an economy as dynamic as that of the United States, the characteristics of the labor force are constantly changing. Table Ba-A, together with five brief snapshots taken at roughly fifty-year intervals beginning in 1800, was constructed to highlight the principal shifts. Many of these labor force characteristics are discussed individually and in detail elsewhere in these volumes.

1800

In 1800, America was a largely agricultural economy; approximately three fourths of the labor force were occupied in this one sector (Table Ba814–830). More than 30 percent of the workforce nationally and slightly more than 50 percent of the workforce in the South were slaves. The majority of these slaves were engaged in the cultivation of tobacco for export and in the cultivation of food for their own consumption. Because enslaved women and children were just as likely as enslaved men to work in the fields, women's and children's share of total employment was also high at this time. Slave labor was concentrated in the South, yet certain Northern states also made heavy use of slave labor in 1800. In New York and New Jersey, slaves accounted for 7.5 and 12.7 percent of the labor force, respectively (see Tables Ba79–339 and the essay in Chapter Bb on slavery).

Among the free agricultural labor force, the vast majority were engaged in family-owned farm operations, and most of the others

[6] See the Guide to the Millennial Edition for information on the IPUMS.

TABLE Ba–A Labor force – selected characteristics expressed as a percentage of the labor force: 1800–2000

Year	Agriculture	Manufacturing	Domestic service	Clerical, sales, and service	Professions	Slave	Nonwhite	Foreign-born	Female
1800	74.4	—	2.4	—	—	30.2	32.6	—	21.4
1860	55.8	13.8	5.4	4.8 [1]	3.0 [1]	21.7	23.6	24.5 [1]	19.6
1910	30.7	20.8	5.5	14.1	4.7	—	13.4	22.0	20.8
1950	12.0	26.4	2.5	27.3	8.9	—	10.0	8.7	27.9
2000	2.4	14.7	0.6	38.0 [2]	15.6	—	16.5	10.3 [2]	46.6

[1] Values for 1870 are presented here because the available data for 1860 exclude slaves.

[2] 1990.

Sources

Agricultural share of the labor force: 1800 and 1860 from Thomas Weiss, series Ba829–830; 1910 and 1950 from Matthew Sobek, series Ba652–653; and 2000 from U.S. Bureau of the Census, *Statistical Abstract of the United States: 2002*, Table 591.

Manufacturing share of the labor force: 1860 from Stanley Lebergott, series Ba814 and Ba821; 1910 and 1950 from Sobek, series Ba652 and Ba657–658; and 2000 from *Statistical Abstract of the United States: 2002*, Table 591.

Domestic service share of the labor force: 1800 and 1860 from Lebergott, series Ba814 and Ba828; 1910 and 1950 from Sobek, series Ba1033 and Ba1042; and 2000 from *Statistical Abstract of the United States: 2001*, Table 593.

Clerical, sales, and other service occupations as a share of the labor force: 1870–1990 from Sobek, series Ba1033, Ba1038–1039, and Ba1043.

Professionals as a share of the labor force: 1870–1950 from Sobek, series Ba1033–1034; and 2000 from *Statistical Abstract of the United States: 2001*, Table 593.

Slave share of the labor force: from Weiss, series Ba1–2, Ba9–10, Ba40–41, and Ba48–49.

Nonwhite share of the labor force: 1800 and 1860 from Weiss, series Ba1–2, Ba5–6, Ba40–41, and Ba44–45; 1910 and 1950 from Sobek, series Ba1033, Ba1089, and Ba1117; and 2000 from *Statistical Abstract of the United States: 2002*, Table 561.

Foreign-born share of the labor force: 1870–1990 from Sobek, series Ba1033 and Ba1145.

Female share of the labor force: 1800 and 1860 from Weiss, series Ba1–2 and Ba40–41; 1910 and 1950 from Sobek, series Ba1033 and Ba1061; and 2000 from *Statistical Abstract of the United States: 2002*, Table 561.

Documentation

Note that "clerical, sales, and service" excludes domestic service.

were slave plantation owners or white overseers on slave plantations. The labor of women and children in the fields was considerably less prevalent among the free when compared with the slave population. This is not to say that free women and children were idle. Rather, the women were engaged in household production primarily intended for the use of their families, while children assisted in farm and household chores and were engaged in various sorts of skill development. Older children were also frequently engaged in land-clearing and other farm-building activities. The labor of independent Northern farmers and their families was supplemented by that of indentured servants and other contract laborers. It is difficult to determine from extant records how prevalent contract labor was for the economy as a whole, although a number of local studies suggest that this form of labor was fairly common, especially in the Middle Atlantic region.[7] Outside of agriculture, the primary occupations in 1800 were connected with ocean-going transportation and domestic service (Table Ba814–830). Many workers engaged in different occupations at different points during the year, working, for example, in agriculture during the spring planting and fall harvest, in fishing during the summer, and in home manufactures during the winter.

1860

Jumping ahead a little more than half a century to 1860 on the eve of the Civil War, the American labor force is familiar in some ways but markedly different in others. Perhaps the most significant change in the labor force over these sixty years was the growing difference between labor force characteristics in the North and South.

In the South, slavery remained a powerful institution. It grew in profitability and expanded geographically in a westward direction. The invention of the cotton gin in 1793 and its rapid diffusion in the years that followed greatly enhanced the value of the short-fiber cotton that was well suited to that region's soil and climate. This technology – in combination with rising world demand for raw cotton stimulated by the Industrial Revolution in textiles manufactures – made cotton "king" and shifted the majority of slave laborers out of tobacco into this newly profitable crop. Cotton cultivation spread steadily westward within the "Cotton Belt," a region that stretched from South Carolina and the Piedmont of Georgia in the East through central Alabama, Mississippi, Louisiana, and southeastern Arkansas. By 1860, it had even made inroads into eastern Texas. The shifting geographic location of the slaves who cultivated this cotton can be seen in Table Bb1–98. The slave share of the Southern labor force remained roughly constant, but this constancy masked strikingly different developments within the region. States of the Cotton South experienced marked growth in the slave share of their labor force, so much so that by 1860, slaves accounted for approximately 70 percent of the labor force in the states of South Carolina, Georgia, and Mississippi, and upward of 60 percent in a number of neighboring states (see Tables Ba79–339). Slaves declined not only as a share of the labor force but even in absolute numbers in the states of Delaware and Maryland (see the essay in Chapter Bb on slavery). Despite the rapid growth of the slave population, slave ownership remained profitable, and the average price of slaves rose through most of this period (see Sutch 1965 and Table Bb209–214).

Except for a brief flurry of manufacturing efforts in the 1840s when world cotton prices temporarily declined, the Southern economy remained firmly agricultural throughout the antebellum era (Bateman and Weiss 1981). Gavin Wright (1986, 1987) explains the South's lack of manufactures and also its lack of towns, schools, and transportation improvements in terms of the economic logic of the institution of slavery. Under slavery, asset holders' wealth takes the form of movable human property instead of immovable land, homes, and factories. Because slaveholders' assets are mobile, they have little incentive to invest in the infrastructure – towns, roads, and schools – which stimulates a rise in the price of these immovable homes, farms, and shops. Because slave assets "crowd out" physical capital in the portfolios of slave owners, investment

[7] See the essay on labor in this chapter and Rothenberg (1992).

in physical capital is reduced and economic development is held back (Ransom and Sutch 1986).

In the North, both slavery and indentured servitude largely vanished from the labor force in the early years of the nineteenth century. Independent self-employed family enterprises and "free" hired labor emerged as the dominant institutions within the labor force. Agriculture had fallen as a share of total employment and its character had changed. Prompted by substantial improvements in internal transportation, Northern agriculture expanded westward to take advantage of more fertile soils and cheaper land. Farms became increasingly specialized, concentrating in the cultivation of grains and cereals in the West and orchard crops, vegetables, and dairy products in the East (Atack and Bateman 1987).

During the first half of the nineteenth century, the Northern labor force also began to move out of agriculture and into manufacturing, construction, trade, transportation, and services. This movement was at first gradual, but after the 1820s, it began to pick up considerable momentum as the gap in productivity between manufacturing and agriculture expanded.[8] Virtually all of the 18 percentage point drop from 74.4 to 55.8 percent in agriculture's share of the total labor force that appears in Weiss's estimates for the period 1800–1860 is due to the decline in the relative importance of agriculture within the Northern states (Table Ba814–830).

To a disproportionate extent, the movement of the labor force out of agriculture involved the incorporation of groups that had not heavily participated before these industrial transformations. One group was composed of young adult females who left their family farm households for wage employment, most famously to work in the cotton textile mills of New England, but also in a variety of other manufacturing industries and in a variety of services (Goldin and Sokoloff 1982). The growing importance of these young women to the labor force, especially of New England in this period, can be gleaned from a study of Tables Ba79–339, from which one can calculate the growing share of free adult women in the labor force. For example, these estimates put the female share of the 1860 labor force ages 16 years and older at 22.4 and 21.2 percent in Rhode Island and Massachusetts, respectively.

Foreign-born workers from Europe constituted the other important addition to the Northern labor force during the first half of the nineteenth century. Significantly, these immigrants did not venture into the slave South but flocked in large numbers to the free labor markets of the North. Immigration from Europe to the North grew gradually over the first part of the nineteenth century and intensified in the 1840s, when Irish seeking to escape their country's disastrous potato famine emigrated to America. Irish emigration to the Northern states continued even after the crisis of the famine had subsided. The Irish were joined by immigrants arriving from England, Scotland, Germany, and other areas of northwestern Europe. These immigrants were attracted by the manufacturing and construction jobs (primarily in the construction of canals and railroads) available in New England and the Middle Atlantic states. (See Table Ad106–120 for annual estimates of flows of European immigrants beginning in 1820 and Table Ad231–245 for immigrant occupation at the time of their arrival in the United States.) Some historians credit the rapid expansion of American industry during this period to this large influx of foreign labor. Without this augmentation to the supply of labor, wages could have risen to the point that further expansion of manufacturing might not have been profitable. Foreign laborers were more likely than their native-born counterparts to take up positions as wage laborers in manufacturing, construction, and transportation. The foreign-born were underrepresented among self-employed farmers and even among farm laborers. Because output per worker was considerably higher outside as compared to within agriculture, the increasing concentration of the labor force in nonagricultural activities was a major source of improvement in output per worker economywide (see the essay on national income and product in Chapter Ca).

The expansion of Northern manufacturing undercut the markets and the income of many American artisanal craftsmen who had previously dominated the production of these goods. In industries such as iron implements, textiles, stonecutting, and woodcutting, to name only a few, the wages of skilled craftsmen fell relative to those of common labor (Table Ba4253–4267). One response of artisanal workers to these developments was to form, for the first time, organized craft labor unions as a way of gaining more control over development within their industries. During economic downturns, labor demonstrations took place in many Northern cities; by 1860, several trades could boast national organizations that represented their interests.[9]

1910

On the eve of World War I, the labor force looked markedly different from what it had been a half-century earlier. Slavery had been abolished by the passage of the Thirteenth Amendment to the Constitution in 1865. Agriculture had shrunk to less than a third of total employment; manufacturing now employed one in five workers. Clerical, sales, and service positions outside of domestic service had grown in relative importance by more than threefold. The foreign-born and women (there is some overlap in these two categories) each accounted for a little more than a fifth of the workforce (see Tables Ba1033–1074 and Ba1131–1158). Large-scale establishments powered by inanimate forces such as water, coal, steam, and the recently introduced electricity were the norm. At the same time, differences between the Northern and the Southern labor markets were as prominent as they had been on the eve of the Civil War.

The most important change in the Southern labor force during the half-century following 1860 was the South's defeat in the Civil War and the subsequent abolition of slavery. Ransom and Sutch emphasize that one immediate effect of the abolition of slavery was that former slaves could decide for themselves about how much labor to supply. In response to this newfound freedom, former slaves radically reduced their labor force participation to fit the norms of other free laborers:

> Emancipation gave the ex-slave the freedom to lighten his burden and, for the first time, reserve a portion of his time for himself. The slave was literally worked to the limit of his economic capacity. Once free, he quite naturally chose to work less, so that he might reserve a portion of each day in which to enjoy the fruits of his labor, fruits that had previously been taken from him by his master. The result was that the amount of labor offered by each freedman and his family was substantially less than when slavery forced every man, woman, and child to work long hours throughout the

[8] Sokoloff (1986) and the essay on national income and product in Chapter Ca.

[9] See the essay on labor unions in this chapter and Wilentz (1984).

> year. Rather than work like slaves, the freedmen chose to offer an amount of labor comparable to the standard for free laborers of the time. (Ransom and Sutch 1977 [2001], p. 44)

The authors estimate that the withdrawal of former slave labor was on the order of 28 to 37 percent of the total black labor force (Ransom and Sutch 1977 [2001], Appendix C). Their estimates include separate calculations for withdrawals from the labor force and also changes in days worked per week and hours worked per day for those who remained engaged. Ransom and Sutch argued that the rate of labor force withdrawal differed across demographic groups. The Weiss calculations presented here reflect this view. For adult males, Ransom and Sutch and Weiss estimate that the decline was relatively modest. By contrast, among adult women and among children of both sexes, the labor force withdrawal was substantial. Weiss estimates that the total black labor force – including those who were formerly free, in addition to those who were formerly enslaved – declined by 12.4 percent for males and 60.0 percent for females between 1860 and 1870. Recall that the labor force records whether a person is in or out; it does not take account of adjustments in days or hours of work by those who continue to participate (series Ba17 and Ba56). As evidence suggests that many ex-slaves who retained their attachment to the labor force nonetheless reduced their days or hours of employment, the Weiss figures underestimate the total work reduction of ex-slaves.

Ransom and Sutch go on to demonstrate that the sizable reduction in black labor in the South had profound implications for many institutions and economic outcomes in the postbellum Southern economy. Rather than working as wage laborers as Southern whites had hoped, the blacks' withdrawal from the labor force enabled them to bargain successfully for the farm tenancy, which gave them considerably greater autonomy. Wright (1986, 1987) demonstrates how the abolition of slavery stimulated other positive developments within the Southern economy. These included increased manufacturing activity and improved movement of Southern laborers from low- to high-wage regions within the South. Nonetheless, even by 1910, the Southern labor market remained isolated from that of the rest of the nation. Southern wages were low and few Southern workers moved from the low-wage South to the high-wage North (see the essay on labor in this chapter for additional details).

In the North, the characteristics of the labor force also changed substantially between 1860 and 1910. Continued improvements in transportation, led by the significant expansion of the railroad network, including the completion of the transcontinental railroad in 1869, further stimulated the westward movement of the labor force and Northern agriculture's continuing specialization in marketable crops. Agricultural productivity nationwide grew substantially between 1870 and 1910, with virtually all productivity improvements occurring in the North (series Da1119). Because of these agricultural productivity gains, agricultural employment *fell* as a share of total employment.

In America, between the Civil War decade and 1910, farmers' and farm laborers' share of the total workforce fell from 46 percent to 31 percent nationwide (Table Ba1033–1046). A disproportionate share of this transition of the labor force out of agriculture occurred within the North.

The largest relative employment gains nationwide occurred among clerical, sales, service, and professional occupations. In 1870, none of these individual sectors employed more than 3 percent of the labor force nationwide; collectively they employed less than 8 percent of the workforce. By 1910, however, these occupations had more than doubled their share, registering 19 percent of the total labor force (Table Ba1033–1046). At the same time, the employment of operatives, generally engaged in semiskilled manufacturing work, rose as well. From a rather substantial 13 percent of the labor force in 1870, operatives came to occupy 16 percent of the national labor force by 1910 (Table Ba1033–1046). Manufacturing operatives were increasingly employed in large manufacturing establishments where they had less say in the organization of their work and the terms of their employment. These shifts in the balance of employer and employee power prompted a whole host of responses, including strikes, formation of labor unions, passage of labor legislation, and the rise of internal labor markets characterized by job ladders, employer-sponsored retirement schemes, and other forms of personnel management (Nelson 1975; Jacoby 1985).

Enabled by another remarkable transportation improvement – the ocean-going steamship – immigrants continued to arrive from Northern and Western Europe in large numbers and were joined at the end of the nineteenth century by immigrants from Southern and Eastern Europe. Early in the period, there had also been a brief influx of immigrants from China and Japan, but these flows were halted by legislation and international agreements that reduced immigration from Asia to a trickle by 1910 (see the essay in Chapter Ad on international migration).

The immigrants tended to locate wherever wages were high and employment was growing most rapidly at the time of their arrival. Immigrants during this period were attracted to the burgeoning manufacturing and construction sectors. While 22 percent of the total 1910 labor force were foreign born, foreign-born workers accounted for 31 percent of all operatives and 41 percent of laborers outside of agriculture (Tables Ba1131–1158). Not only did immigrant laborers facilitate the expansion of these growing sectors over the long run, but they also played an important role in overcoming short-run bottlenecks. Because immigrants timed their arrival (and departure) to coincide with the availability of employment opportunities, their involvement in the American economy allowed for longer economic expansions and shorter contractions than would have been the case had employers been forced to rely on domestic labor supplies alone (Carter and Sutch 1999).

Women's employment had also grown as a share of the labor force over this period as women began to enter new industries and occupations. In 1910, women accounted for 21 percent of the labor force, up from 15 percent in 1870 (Tables Ba1033–1046 and Ba1061–1074). Women's share of professional employment grew from 27 percent to 45 percent over the same period, largely because of their increasing employment in teaching (Perlmann and Margo 2001). Women also made significant advances in clerical, sales, and, to a lesser extent, service work (Rotella 1981). At the same time, women's employment outside the home remained largely restricted to the period of life after the end of schooling and before marriage. Few married women were employed in wage work during the period. Those married women who did engage in employment outside the home were likely to be married to men who were unemployed or disabled or who otherwise faced difficulty in earning an adequate income (Goldin 1990).

A different milestone for the American labor force over the second half of the nineteenth century was the achievement of near-universal literacy by 1910. Among persons 14 years of age and older, the percentage illiterate in 1910 was only 7.7. A disproportionate share of the illiterate population were blacks living in the South who had not yet overcome the educational disadvantages imposed by slavery. Among blacks 14 years of age and older in 1910, 31 percent were illiterate. Among whites, only 5 percent of the native-born but 13 percent of the foreign-born were illiterate (Table Bc793–797). This would be a remarkable achievement for any country at the beginning of the twentieth century, but it was especially notable in America, as such a large proportion of the labor force arrived as young adults, having received their education in countries that were behind in their educational development.

So far we have emphasized long-term trends in the characteristics of the labor force between 1860 and 1910, but an important new development during this period was the appearance of labor market fluctuations that condemned large numbers of wage workers to involuntary unemployment for extended periods of time. The most severe depressions of this period occurred from October 1873 to March 1879; from March 1887 to May 1888; from January 1893 to June 1894; from December 1895 to June 1897; and from May 1907 to June 1908 (see Table Cb5–8 and the essay on economic fluctuations, recessions, and depressions in Chapter Cb). These industrial downturns prompted worker unrest and encouraged the formation of labor unions and legislative initiatives designed to protect industrial workers from some of the consequences of unfettered labor market operation (Keyssar 1986).

1950

By 1950, the United States was clearly the world's largest and most powerful economy, and its labor force looked markedly different from what it had been just forty years earlier. Manufacturing was the country's single largest industrial sector, occupying 26 percent of the labor force. Clerical, sales, service, and professional occupations had grown more rapidly, while agriculture and domestic service work had declined. Foreign-born workers had declined to less than 9 percent of the labor force, their lowest share in more than a century and a half. While women's share of total employment changed only slightly, white women's occupational distribution was substantially altered. White women had largely abandoned domestic service by 1950 and moved into white-collar occupations in the professions, into nondomestic services, and especially into secretarial and clerical work, which by 1950 had become the single largest occupational category for white women workers. Almost a third were engaged in office work at that date (Table Ba1103–1116).

Blacks had moved out of the rural South in large numbers to take up jobs in urban, industrial employment. A high school diploma had become the educational norm. The labor market of 1950 was regulated by a vast array of new laws at the federal, state, and local levels that affected a range of labor market outcomes, including the minimum wage, overtime pay, worker health and safety insurance, and retirement. A few years earlier, Congress had passed the Employment Act of 1946, charging the federal government with responsibility for maintaining maximum employment.

Between 1910 and 1950, the pace of economic growth quickened, partly because of the continued growth in capital per worker and also because of the increasing importance of knowledge-based improvements in technology and industrial organization (see Table Ca-C in Chapter Ca). In the first half of the twentieth century, these latter factors had become the major source of increases in output per capita (Abramovitz and David 2000). The rapid advance in productivity prompted substantial shifts of the labor force across industries and occupations. The manufacturing sector grew. The agricultural sector began to contract beginning in the 1920s, when food prices fell and many farmers' incomes were not sufficient to cover their expenses (series Ba3759, Cc68, and Da1295). Stimulated by technological advances and stimulating their further development was the continuing growth in the educational attainment of the labor force. Whereas the majority of the workforce had completed only primary school at the beginning of the century, by 1950 high school graduation had become the norm.

Punctuating these long-term trends were several unique and turbulent events. The United States was involved in two world wars; it endured a crippling, eleven-year depression; and it closed its doors to mass immigration. The outbreak of the world war in Europe in 1914 had a powerful impact on the American labor force. The arrival of immigrants from Europe slowed considerably, as fewer potential immigrants were allowed to leave their home countries and as transportation across the Atlantic became riskier and more expensive. All the while, demand for American manufactured products soared as warring nations sought armaments, military provisions, and civilian goods that their own factories were unable to adequately supply under wartime conditions. The combination of reduced foreign labor and increased labor demand led to rising wage rates and employment shortages. These conditions inspired Northern industrialists, for the first time on a large scale, to begin recruiting Southern blacks for their Northern industrial positions. These labor recruitment efforts initiated the "Great Migration" of blacks out of the South (Collins 1997). In 1910, only 11 percent of the black population lived outside the South, but by 1950, 32 percent of the black population and a considerably larger percentage of the black labor force did so. For most blacks, the abandonment of the South also meant the abandonment of agriculture for industry. This Great Migration produced large gains for blacks in terms of wages, education, and political expression (Margo 1990). It played an important role in the integration of Southern and Northern labor markets (Wright 1986, 1987; Rosenbloom 2002).

Following World War I, immigration returned to its prewar levels but was soon halted by the severely restrictive regulations embodied in the Quota Acts of the 1920s. The high unemployment associated with the onset of the Great Depression of the 1930s brought the small remaining immigrant flow to a complete halt. In fact, more foreign-born persons left the United States for other countries than arrived here from abroad. There was a limited resumption of immigration during World War II, but the flows remained small. Thus, by 1950, the foreign-born share of the labor force was considerably smaller than it had been for well over a century.

The economic boom of the 1920s witnessed acceleration in the growth of large corporations and the development of elaborate personnel management systems. Corporations expanded their clerical, sales, service, and professional staffs and opened many of these new positions to female workers. The prosperous 1920s, however, were followed by the Great Depression of the 1930s, the most catastrophic of the recurrent industrial depressions that had first appeared in the latter half of the nineteenth century. At its depth in 1932, almost a fourth of the total labor force and a third of the nonagricultural labor force were unemployed (Table Ba470–477). Despite a partial recovery in 1937, the Great Depression lasted fully eleven years, ending only when the government began mobilizing the economy to fight World War II (see the essay on economic fluctuations, recessions, and depressions in Chapter Cb).

During the 1930s, the government expanded both its size and its reach. It enacted a broad range of measures that substantially altered the operation of the labor market and that remained prominent institutional features of the economy at the end of the twentieth century. Federal social security, old-age assistance, and unemployment insurance were all introduced at this time (see the essay on social welfare in Chapter Bf). So were laws that enhanced organized labor's ability to recruit new union members and to pursue its interests vis-à-vis employers. Because these laws were national in scope, they played an important role in standardizing the operation of labor markets in different regions of the country, in particular in bringing conditions in the low-wage South onto a par with those in the rest of the nation. Although scholars differ on the details of whether this New Deal legislation would have been enacted about that time even in the absence of the Great Depression, all agree that the legal and institutional changes of that decade played a powerful role in changing the nature of labor market operation in the years that followed (Bordo, Goldin, and White 1998).

The onset of World War II prompted further changes in the American labor force. Unemployment fell as the government geared up for wartime production and drafted young adult males into military service. By 1945, almost 12 million men and a quarter of a million women were engaged as military personnel on active duty (Table Ed26–47). The number of males engaged in active duty at this time is equivalent to about two thirds of the total male population 15–29 years of age in that year (Table Aa125–144). To accomplish its production goals, the government enticed millions of women – married and single – into the labor force. This wartime work experience permanently changed public perceptions of women's economic roles and is widely believed to have contributed to the marked expansion of women's roles in the years that followed (Goldin 1990).

2000

From an historical perspective, perhaps the single most striking characteristic of the 2000 labor force is the prominent role of women. In 2000, women comprised nearly half of the total labor force, and almost half of these female workers were married. The growth in women's share of the labor force was accomplished through two complementary processes, an increase in women's participation rates and a decline in men's. The share of women 16 years of age and older participating in the labor force grew from 33.9 percent in 1950 to 60.2 percent in 2000 (Table Ba535–550). Overall, men's participation rates fell from 86.4 percent to 74.7 percent, with virtually the entire decline occurring among older men. In 2000, only 67 percent of males 55–64 years of age and 18 percent of those 65 years of age and older were labor force participants. This compares with 87 percent and 46 percent, respectively, in 1950 (Table Ba519–534).

Foreign-born workers were a much more prominent presence in the 2000 labor force than they had been fifty years earlier. Immigrant flows had resumed in the post–World War II era, and they were fed by entrants from different parts of the world. In 1950, the overwhelming majority of the foreign-born workforce was of European origin, whereas by 2000, persons from Asia and Latin America formed the majority. The successive waves of migration from Latin America were so large in the previous fifty years that, in 2000, almost 11 percent of the total labor force was of Hispanic origin (Tables Ba551–570).

The 2000 labor force was highly educated. Thirty percent had a college degree, while fewer than 10 percent had not completed high school (U.S. Census Bureau 2002, Table 564). White-collar work in the professions and in clerical, sales, and service occupations accounted for over half of the total workforce (Table Ba1033–1046); manufacturing had declined to almost half its 1950s level, while agriculture had shrunk to a mere 2 percent of the labor force economywide (Table Ba652–669).

Unions were far less powerful than they had been a half century earlier. Union members accounted for only 13 percent of the workforce in 2000 (series Ba4788 divided by series Ba479). At the same time, unemployment posed less of a threat to workers. Between 1950 and 2000, unemployment averaged 5.7 percent, down from an average of 6.8 percent during the previous fifty-year period. Moreover, prior to 1950, unemployment had reached 22.9 percent in 1932 and exceeded 10 percent for a total of eight years. In the post-1950 period, the highest level of recorded unemployment was 9.7 percent in 1982 (series Ba475 and Ba485).

This new face to the 2000 labor market was the product of a complex set of developments that included both continuity and change compared with the previous period. Among the most important are the continuing growth of labor productivity, rising incomes, and low unemployment; the resumption of large-scale immigration; and the revolution in the social and political roles of minorities and women.

Labor productivity continued to advance, with improvements in the quality of inputs, such as more educated labor and more sophisticated machinery and organization, leading the advance.[10] This labor productivity growth, combined with growth in the labor-to-population and capital-to-labor ratios, produced an overall rate of growth of real gross domestic product per capita of 2.2 percent per annum, a rate that exceeded that for any of the previous periods discussed here (Table Ca-C in Chapter Ca). A 2.2 percent annual growth rate sustained for fifty years translates into a threefold increase in real per capita income.

The growth in both labor productivity and per capita income influenced the deployment of the labor force in a variety of ways. As incomes rose, consumers shifted demand away from standardized products and toward custom-made manufactured goods, imported specialty products, and services, especially health care, transportation, education, and insurance. The rise in demand for these new goods, increasing international specialization and trade, and rapid technological advance prompted shifts in the deployment of the labor force across industries. Manufacturing employment as a share of total employment fell from 26 percent to 15 percent. Within manufacturing, the share of workers employed by the very large firms (those employing 1,000 or more workers) fell as well from 33 percent to only 20 percent of the labor force (series Ba4705). Business services – such as advertising, building services, personnel supply services, and computer and data processing services; educational services; and other professional services such as health, legal, and social services – more than doubled their labor force share since 1950 to reach 5.9, 9.4, and 12.9 percent of the labor force, respectively, by 2000 (Table Ba652–669).

The growing female share of the paid labor force is bound up with these industrial and occupational shifts in a variety of interesting and mutually reinforcing ways. Women's activities figure in the demand side, because it was women's willingness to reallocate their time from unpaid household work to the paid labor force that contributed to the strong and growing effective demand for products such as education, transportation, and insurance, which cannot

[10] Abramovitz and David (2000) and the essay on productivity in Chapter Cg.

be produced in the home. Women's activities figure in the supply side, because their high levels of education and labor market entry have facilitated the rapid growth of employment without a rapid increase in the costs of production.

After World War II, immigration to the United States resumed. With the recovery of the economy, the American labor market was once more attractive to potential immigrants. Furthermore, the United States had created loopholes in the program of strict numerical control of immigration. In acknowledgment of strategic wartime alliances and in an effort to influence the character of postwar international relations, the United States loosened bans on immigration from Asia, created special admission categories to accommodate persons displaced by World War II, and encouraged the immigration of the highly educated. These programs were expanded with the onset of the Cold War that followed (for a list of these programs, see Table Ad-J in Chapter Ad; for numbers admitted by program, see Table Ad989–1004).

Another source of foreign-born labor in this period was migrant labor for agriculture, which was drawn largely from Mexico. Tight labor markets during World War II produced an agricultural laborers program that was continued into the 1950s and early 1960s. During most of the 1950s and early 1960s, the number of workers entering the United States under the auspices of this program was more than double the number of persons admitted as regular immigrants (Table Ad1023–1029). When the United States ended the program unilaterally in 1964, the migrant labor flows continued, but in an undocumented form.

In 1965, the United States repealed the Quota Acts of the 1920s that had starkly restricted immigration from much of the world and substituted the Preference System. The Preference System allowed for higher annual levels of immigration and greatly facilitated the entry of immigrants from Asia (see the essay in Chapter Ad on international migration). Following the mid-1960s, the share of the American labor force born in Asia and Latin America grew rapidly. These foreign-born workers in the late twentieth century were a more diverse group than those a hundred years earlier. Back then, the majority of immigrants came out of agricultural backgrounds and took up places in unskilled occupations in the growing manufacturing sector of the economy. There were few professionals, but also few agricultural workers. At the end of the twentieth century, a much higher share of the foreign-born workforce was employed in professional positions than was true a century earlier. At the same time, it is also true that a disproportionate share of the foreign-born population is employed as agricultural laborers and as manual service workers in the hospitality industry. In 1990, the foreign-born share of the agricultural labor force was more than double its share of the labor force overall (Tables Ad231–255 and Ba1131–1158 and Figure Ba-B).

We postpone the discussion of changes in the labor market roles of minorities and women during the second half of the twentieth century to the next section on labor force participation.

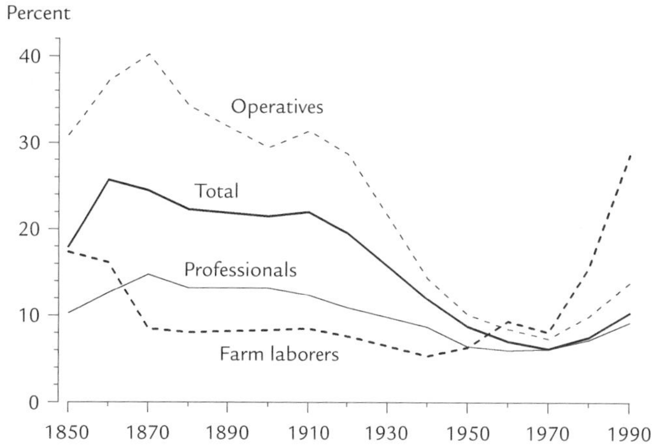

FIGURE Ba-B Foreign-born share of employment, by major occupational group: 1850–1990

Sources

Series Ba1131–1132, Ba1139, Ba1142, Ba1145–1146, Ba1153, and Ba1156.

Labor Force Participation

Although most workers report that their own labor force participation is a necessity rather than a matter of choice, the historical record reveals enormous variation over time in the participation rates of different groups. For example, in the nineteenth century, labor force participation of married women was rare, and that of youth and older men was much more common than today. Thus, a long-term perspective reveals that societywide labor force participation rates are clearly flexible.

Economists explain patterns and trends in labor force participation with reference to an economic model originally developed to explain consumers' choices among commodities (Killingsworth 1983). According to this model, the individual is assumed to select between two goods, one purchased in the market and the other produced at home. Leisure is included among the home-produced goods. Individuals participate in the labor force in order to earn the money they require for the purchase of these market goods. They face a number of constraints in this process: their time is fixed at twenty-four hours per day; their assets and nonmarket income are not boundless; their productivities and returns in the market and nonmarket venues are limited in specific ways; and they have biophysical requirements for sleeping and eating.

This consumer choice model of labor force participation is generally recast from an individual to a family or household perspective to take account of the fact that individuals' decisions are influenced by the wages and the household productivity of other family members. According to this model, family members make their labor supply decisions simultaneously, rather than piecemeal, and so it remains to be explained why families sent older children into the labor force while keeping the wife/mother in household labor in the late nineteenth century but did the opposite in the late twentieth century.

Labor force participation may also be cast in a life-cycle perspective, in which individuals' decisions regarding current activity are made with an eye to the future and are influenced by the value of assets that they have already accumulated. A typical life-cycle employment pattern involves working and saving as a young adult and then reducing the work effort and drawing down savings at older ages (Modigliani 1966).

The economist's labor supply model was developed to explain individual differences in labor force participation at a single point in time. For example, why is one 58-year-old employed in the labor force while a neighbor is retired? Is it differences in earnings opportunities, income of spouses, pensions, health, or something else? Alternatively, one might ask why education is positively correlated with labor force participation. Is it simply that better-educated individuals have access to higher wages, or is there some independent effect of education itself? A primary goal of such investigations is to answer policy-related questions. One might be interested, for example, in predicting the impact of a proposed change in Social Security benefits on the probability of retirement at different ages. Appropriately, for this purpose, such modeling focuses on factors that distinguish among individuals at some single point in time and leaves aside factors that influence all individuals and that change slowly over time.

To explain long-term change in labor force participation, one must bring these "background characteristics" explicitly into the analysis. Economic historians distinguish among two major categories of background characteristics: cohort effects and trends.

Cohorts – or, more specifically, birth cohorts – refer to individuals born about the same time. "Cohort effects" refer to developments that distinguish the life experience of one birth cohort from another. Familiar examples are war, famine, economic depression, political struggles, legislative change, and technological developments, such as the advent of television, the automobile, or airline travel. Such events appear to have a lifelong impact on those coming of age at the time they occur (see the essay in Chapter Af on cohorts). The impact of such events is reinforced by the fact that, for a variety of reasons, individuals' behavior depends to some extent on the behavior of those around them (Schelling 1978). Thus, for example, individuals are more likely to marry at young ages if their peers are doing so.

Many decisions that affect lifetime labor supply behavior are made as young adults. Especially pertinent are decisions regarding education, marriage, family size, and geographic location. For example, a woman who has a large number of children may find that she is unable to respond to an unexpected decline in discrimination or to an increase in wage rates for many years, perhaps ever. Cohort effects can differ markedly from one birth cohort to the next.

Trends also influence long-term change in labor supply. The term "trends" refers to social norms, legal regimes, and institutions that change over time and that affect all individuals in the economy. Such norms, laws, and institutions are typically not part of the economist's model of labor supply precisely because the economist focuses on differences across individuals or cohorts at a single point in time, whereas norms, laws, and institutions are typically the same for everyone. Nonetheless, if the focus is on long-term change, then trends may be quite important. To take one example, discrimination against women in professional employment or social attitudes that stigmatize married women's employment may lead some women to decide against labor market participation altogether. A reduction in such discrimination and stigma may be more important than changes in wages in explaining change in women's labor force participation over time.

Goldin (1983, 1990) parsed the determinants of change in women's labor force participation between 1940 and 1970 into the three categories embraced here: point-in-time effects, such as income and wages that can improve or deteriorate from one year to the next; cohort effects, such as educational attainment, marital status, and fertility, which are generally fixed by age 30 or so; and trends in difficult-to-quantify factors, such as social norms, laws, and institutions. She concludes that each of these categories, on its own, can account for only about a third of the total change in women's labor force participation over time. In other words, it is important to consider all three categories.

Male Labor Force Participation

The long-term pattern of male labor force participation since 1870 is shown in Figure Ba-C and Table Ba417–424. In nineteenth-century America, an estimated 90 percent of adult white males 16 years of age and older, and a slightly higher percentage of nonwhites, were engaged in the labor force. Beginning about 1920, this high rate of labor force participation began to decline so that by 2000, the respective participation rates of whites and nonwhites were only 75 percent and 71 percent (Table Ba551–560).

The entire decline in male labor force participation over the twentieth century occurred at the younger and, especially, the older ages; the participation rates of males 20–44 years of age changed not at all (Figure Ba-D and Table Ba519–534). Young males increasingly delayed their entry into the labor force in order to extend their schooling, while older males began their retirement at increasingly younger ages. Earlier retirement is by far the largest component in the overall decline in the labor force participation of men over time. As Table Ba519–534 indicates, the labor force participation rate of males 55–64 years of age was close to 90 percent between 1947 and 1960. During the 1970s and 1980s, this rate fell substantially but then remained essentially unchanged during the 1990s. In 2000, the labor force participation rate of males 55–64 years is 67.3 percent.

The long-term trend toward more retirees who begin their retirement at increasingly early ages is thought to be a reflection of three principal developments: rising real incomes, the movement out of self-employment, and the rise of institutions such as Social Security and old-age pensions. Rising incomes have allowed individuals to enjoy more of all goods, including more retirement. Self-employment has given way to wage and salary employment in large business enterprises that have been able to offer increasingly attractive rewards to employees (Tables Ba910–983). Nonetheless, the improved earnings in wage and salary work come at the expense of less flexibility regarding the extent, pace, and content of the work. The self-employed worker controls these qualities himself or herself, which means that in self-employment, the worker can accommodate the various personal circumstances that change with

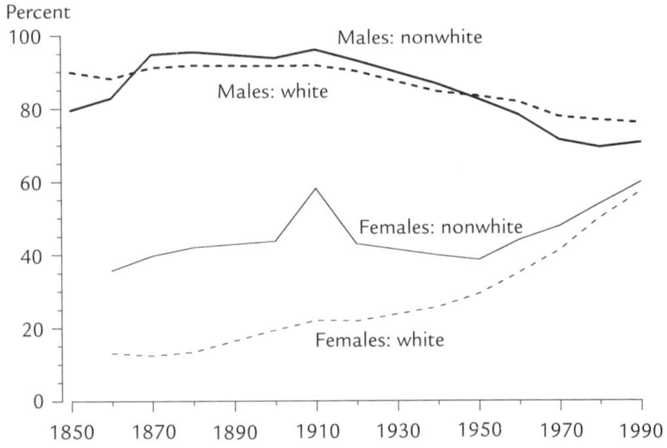

FIGURE Ba-C Labor force participation rate, by sex and race: 1850–1990

Sources

Series Ba419–420 and Ba423–424.

Documentation

These series cover noninstitutionalized civilians age 16 and older.

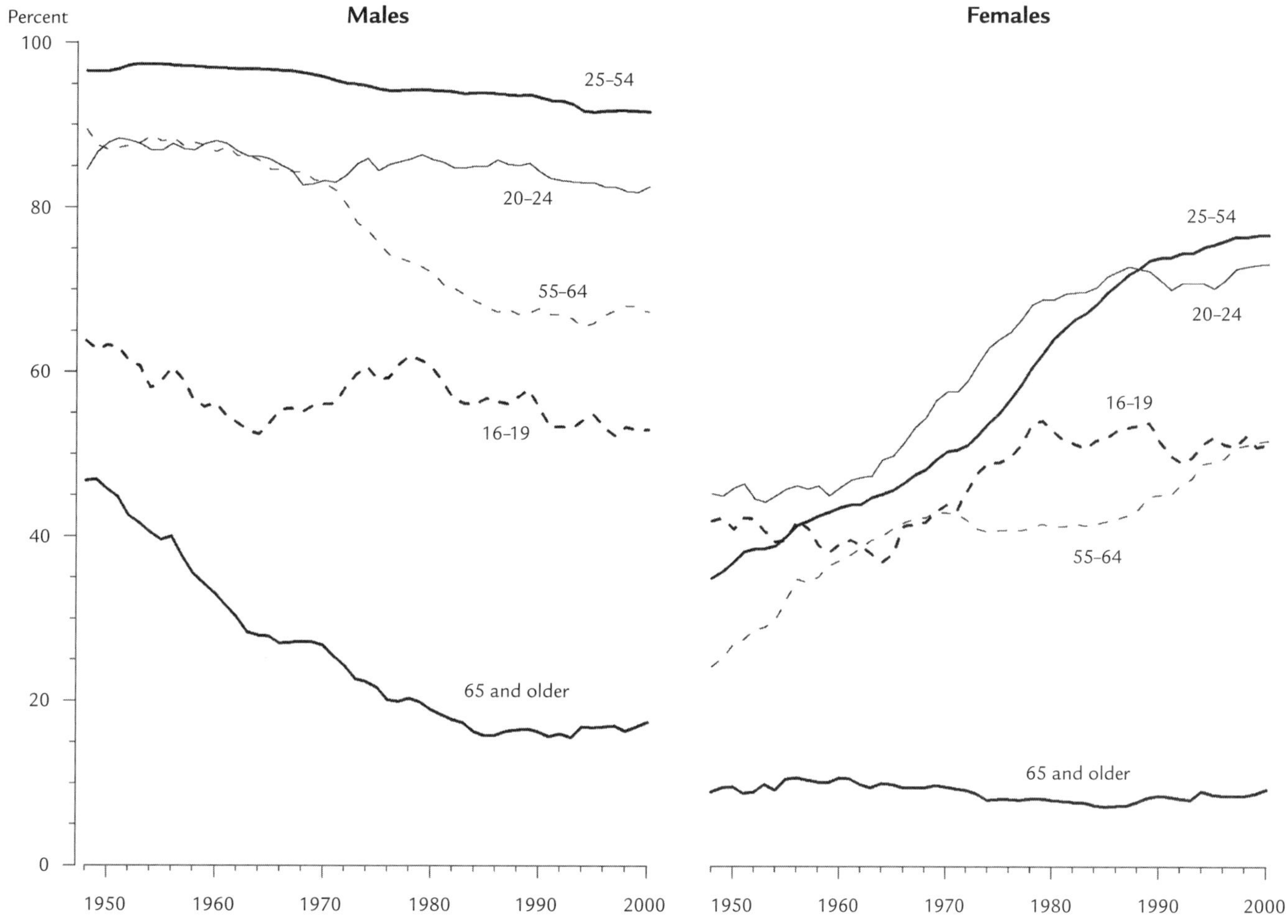

FIGURE Ba-D Labor force participation rate, by sex and age: 1948–2000

Sources

Series Ba528–534 and Ba544–550.

Documentation

The labor force participation rates for the 25–34, 35–44, and 45–54 age groups are fairly similar over time. For display purposes, these groups have been averaged, using weights based on the number of workers in the groups (series Ba522–524 and Ba538–540).

age. Large enterprises tend to adopt elaborate and rather inflexible internal personnel policies that limit workers' ability to make such adjustments. In fact, some employment policies of large firms, pension policies in particular, are specifically designed to encourage workers' early retirement. These firm-based pensions reinforce the effect of Social Security, veterans' benefits, and other public pensions in encouraging older workers to withdraw from the labor force at relatively young ages. A different long-term trend working in the opposite direction is improvements in health. Dora Costa has shown that over the twentieth century, not only has mortality fallen, but the average level of health has also improved (Costa 1998). Because poor health is one reason why workers retire, health improvement, taken by itself, ought to have prompted reductions in retirement over time. This has not happened. Overall, then, rising real incomes, the movement out of self-employment, and the rise of pensions have overwhelmed the effects of long-term improvements in health, leading to substantially lower rates of labor force participation among older males over time.

Labor force participation rates of males, but especially older males, also vary with the business cycle. Downturns in the economy and increases in the unemployment rate are associated with reductions in the labor force participation, whereas periods of economic expansion lead to increases (Coleman and Pencavel 1993; see also Table Ba519–534). It is also the case that older males with the lowest levels of education exhibit the lowest levels of labor force participation and that differences in the participation rates of those with the highest and the lowest levels of educational attainment have grown over time (compare series Ba511 and Ba514). Taken together, these data suggest that for at least some older males, difficulty in obtaining employment may play a role in their decision to leave the labor force. They are also consistent with the view that interesting work conducted in a pleasant environment may be increasingly necessary in order to keep older workers in the labor force.

It is interesting that long-term changes in wage rates appear to have little or no effect on the labor force participation decisions of males. According to the simple model of labor supply described previously, an increase in the market wage has two offsetting effects. On the one hand, an increase in the wage means that a given hour's worth of work generates more income and therefore more command over market-produced goods and services. This produces a positive relationship between the wage and labor force participation. On the other hand, an increase in the wage increases income and therefore offers the possibility of purchasing more of all goods, leisure and early retirement included. This consideration produces a negative relationship between the wage and labor force participation. The first effect has been shown to dominate for males who are already labor market participants; that is, higher wages appear to induce male workers to work longer hours. However, for males both in and out of the labor force, changes in the wage rate do not appear to affect the participation decision one way or the other (Pencavel 1986; Coleman and Pencavel 1993; Blundell and MaCurdy 1999).

Female Labor Force Participation

Figure Ba-C and Table Ba417–424 display official statistics concerning the long-term pattern of female labor force participation. These statistics show a sizable, steady advance for white women since the first census estimates of female employment in 1860. At that time, only 13.1 percent of 16- to 64-year-olds were gainfully occupied, according to the census count. By 1990, the rate was almost 60 percent. The long-term pattern of nonwhite women's labor force participation is complicated by the experience of slavery and then emancipation. An estimated 90 percent of enslaved women were engaged in the labor force. The 1870 Census, the first following emancipation, estimates the labor force participation rate of all nonwhite women at 39.2 percent, a rate higher than that of white women at the time but far below that of women under slavery. Over time, the labor force participation rate of nonwhite women rose so that in 1990, it too stood at almost 60 percent. As described in detail previously, scholars have shown that these official estimates certainly understate the extent of women's paid employment in the nineteenth and early twentieth centuries. However, even after adjusting for these underestimates, the substantial rise in women's labor force participation remains.

In the nineteenth century, many women lived their lives without ever becoming engaged in market work; for most of those who did participate, the experience was a relatively brief life episode (Tables Ba425–469 and Ba571–578). In 1880, the first year for which female labor force participation rates by marital status are available, 33.7 percent of single, 23.5 percent of widowed and divorced, but only 5.7 percent of married women were labor force participants. Over the twentieth century, the participation of women in all marital status categories grew, with the largest gains made by married women who were living with their husbands (the official category is "married, spouse present"). In 1999, 68.7 percent of single, 61.2 percent of married, and 49.1 percent of widowed and divorced women 16 years of age and older were labor force participants (Table Ba571–578).[11] As one can infer from these statistics, by the end of the twentieth century, a large proportion of women were participating in the labor force throughout their adult lives, even while caring for young children. In 1999, fully 59.2 percent of married women with spouse present and with children under the age of 3 were in the labor force (Table Ba579–582).

The process by which the female population transitioned from low to high rates of labor force participation can be summarized in a simple phrase: women's labor force participation has increased across the board. Women's labor force participation increased within every age group. Between 1948, when the modern annual data on women's labor force participation begins, through our last year of data, 1999, women's labor force participation increased in each and every age group (Table Ba535–550 and Figure Ba-D). Only among young adults and only in recent years has there been a trending down of female labor force participation. This is a case in which the labor force participation rates of young women mirror those of young men. Both increasingly postponed labor market entry in order to extend their schooling.

Women's participation at every age has increased with each successive birth cohort. For many years, economists characterized women's labor force participation over the life cycle as a "two-peaked" pattern, that is, heavy participation before marriage, withdrawal from the labor force at the time of marriage or birth of the first child, and then a return to the labor force after the youngest child was in school. This two-peaked pattern is suggested by cross-sectional data displaying the labor force participation rates of women of different ages at some point in time (see Figure Af-A in Chapter Af). However, Goldin (1990) has shown that an entirely different pattern emerges if one rearranges the data in a way that highlights the actual experience of successive cohorts of women as they age. For example, to view the labor market experience of women born in 1920, select the labor force participation rate of 20-year-olds in 1940, 30-year-olds in 1950, and so on. This measure is called a "cohort" measure because it follows the actual experience of a group of women, all of whom were born at the same time. The labor force participation rates of successive cohorts of women born in the twentieth century are shown in Figure Af-B in Chapter Af. In this figure, it is clear that all cohorts of women born in the twentieth century increased their labor force participation as they aged, at least up to age 55. The apparent withdrawal of women from the labor force during the peak child-bearing years that is so striking in cross-sectional data for a single year does not represent the actual experience of any true cohort (see the essay in Chapter Af on cohorts).

Women's labor force participation increased at every level of family income, though much more rapidly in high-income than in low-income households. In the nineteenth century, female labor force participants tended to come from the more economically disadvantaged segments of the population – daughters and wives of men who were sick, injured, unemployed, missing, or dead. Over the twentieth century, the expansion of white-collar professional, managerial, clerical, sales, and service occupations and women's entry into these positions prompted substantial increases in labor force participation among women from middle- and upper-income households. By 1940, 49 percent of college-educated women were in the labor force, as compared with only 22.9 percent of women with less than a high school education. By 1990, the respective percentages were 82.0 and 47.2 (Table Ba507–518). At the same time, the educational attainment of successive cohorts of women rose. In 1940, the percentage of the female population 25 years of age and older who had completed four or more years of college was only 3.8 percent. By 1997, the figure was 21.7 percent (series Bc750). Together, the increase in women's educational attainment and the disproportionately rapid growth in the labor force participation of well-educated women powered the growth in female labor force participation overall.

Although it is clear how women's labor force participation increased, it is considerably less clear exactly *why*. The simple economic model of labor force participation highlights nonwage income, and the market wage has two potentially powerful influences.

[11] The average age of the widowed and divorced women is considerably greater than that of women who are single and married, husband present. This age effect is the primary reason for their low participation rate.

An increase in a woman's nonwage income (typically the income of her spouse) is expected to reduce her labor force participation, and yet, even though the income of married men increased steadily over time for most (but not all) married men (Tables Ba4224–4233, Ba4381–4390, Ba4440–4483, Ba4512–4520, and Be67–84), married women's labor supply has increased, rather than decreased, as the model might lead us to expect.

Of course, women's wages have also increased over time (Tables Ba4224–4233 and Ba4512–4520). As noted earlier, an increase in women's wage produces two offsetting effects. On the one hand, it encourages labor force participation through what is called the "substitution effect." An increase in the wage rate makes it easier to acquire, say, bread by abandoning work in one's own kitchen, working for wages, and then spending the resulting income to purchase bread from a bakery. On the other hand, an increase in the wage will increase potential income, offering the possibility of purchasing more of all goods, leisure (and home cooking) included. Among women, the substitution effect has been found to predominate. That is, rising wages seem to encourage women to enter the labor force. At the same time, the rise in women's labor force participation rates, especially after World War II, far exceed the rise that would be predicted by the rise in wage rates alone (Goldin 1983, 1990; Pencavel 1998). To fully understand this long-term increase, we need to consider cohort effects and trend variables as well.

We have already noted in the descriptive section of this essay that successive cohorts of women have increased their involvement in the paid labor force (Figure Af-B). To some extent, these changes can be attributed to factors such as increased education, postponement of marriage, and reduced fertility – developments that have improved the rewards of women's market work and facilitated their labor force participation. Women's educational attainment has increased steadily over time. In fact, changes in the space of just a generation or two are truly enormous. For example, among women born between 1911 and 1920, 53 percent of whites and 85 percent of nonwhites had not completed high school by the time they reached their twenties; among the next generation, born between 1931 and 1940, the respective percentages were only 34 and 58. Jumping ahead to the cohort born between 1961 and 1970, only 11 percent and 14 percent of white and nonwhite women, respectively, had not completed high school (Table Af295–336). Over the same time period, college graduation became increasingly common. Among women born between 1911 and 1920, only 5 percent of whites and 2 percent of nonwhites had graduated from college, whereas among the cohort born between 1961 and 1970, the respective proportions were 23 percent and 17 percent (Table Af355–390).

Not all changes from one cohort to another facilitated labor force participation, however. White women born between the two world wars were far more likely to marry and have large families than women born into earlier and especially later cohorts. Among the cohort of white women born between 1911 and 1920, 62 percent were married by the time they reached their twenties; jumping ahead to the cohort born between 1931 and 1940 reveals a marriage rate in this age group of 77 percent. These high marriage rates, however, disappeared quickly. Among white women born between 1951 and 1960, only 56 percent were married by their twenties. Fertility followed the same pattern across cohorts, with depressed fertility for women born prior to World War I, elevated fertility for women born between the world wars, and sharply reduced fertility among the cohorts of women born after World War II. The sharply reduced marriage and fertility rates, together with their high levels of education, are an important element of the explanation for the long-term increase in female labor force participation rates, especially for the acceleration after 1970.

The emphasis in the previous paragraph on cohort-by-cohort change in educational attainment, marriage, and fertility decisions on labor force participation does not imply that these prior changes are made independently of labor market developments. On the contrary, these seemingly personal decisions have been shown to respond to a variety of economic forces societywide. For example, in a highly influential book, Richard Easterlin (1980) argues that the high marriage and fertility of cohorts born in the interwar period appear to be a response to high household incomes in the 1950s – incomes that far exceeded the income expectations they had formed as young adults growing up during the Great Depression of the 1930s. Likewise, Easterlin argues that the sharply reduced rates of marriage and fertility displayed by the post–World War II baby boom generation are a response to the disappointing economic conditions when this generation came of age during the 1970s.

"Trends" also play an important role in explaining the secular increase in women's labor force participation over time. In contrast to "point-in-time effects" and cohort effects, trends are evolving influences with largely universal impacts. We highlight here two trends especially evident in the twentieth century that have received considerable attention in the scholarly literature on women's labor force participation. The first is the rise of a consumer culture, coupled with advances in the technology of household production. The second is change in the social norms, laws, and institutions regarding the employment of women outside the home. Although we discuss these trends individually, they are closely intertwined with each other.

Economic historians have traced back many centuries the linkage between the introduction of new market goods and change in basic norms of family life, including norms regarding labor force participation. For example, Jan DeVries (1994) argues that the introduction of new textile, art, and home improvement commodities in eighteenth-century Europe provided a powerful incentive for workers to work longer hours in order to be able to afford these attractive new products.

In American history, the expanding offerings of new consumer goods are also strongly linked to changing patterns of work, especially to changes in women's work. Prior to American industrialization, when consumer goods were largely imported and expensive, families produced most of what they consumed. They raised their own food, processed some for storage, and prepared their daily meals. They built their own homes and produced household goods, such as soap, candles, brooms, toys, furniture, and mattresses. They also produced their own thread, cloth, and apparel. The appearance of inexpensive commercial substitutes for many of these products, along with the advent of American industrialization and improvements in internal transportation, prompted many families to abandon home production and purchase from the market much of what they had formerly produced at home. Household production fell (Tables Ba4999–5081), sales of commercially produced products rose, and many young people, especially women, left home to work in industrial employment. These new industrial workers were drawn disproportionately from large, relatively prosperous rural families that no longer required their assistance with home production. As Thomas Dublin (1994, p. 118) put it, "although economic motives undoubtedly loomed large for these women workers, family economic need was not the principal motivation that led them to enter the mills. Mill employment offered young single women economic and social independence unknown to previous generations of New England women." Although historians offer different views of its relative importance, there is ample evidence that for many of these young women, one of the attractions of earning their own wages was the opportunity to purchase more fashionable dresses and hats for themselves and household furnishings for when they married. Some women worked in order to further their schooling. All of these goods were, at the time, newly available consumer goods. They were attractive in that they enabled these young women to better connect with the larger world beyond their rural origins (Dublin 1981).

The impact of these new goods on married women's work was more complex. On the one hand, the appearance of inexpensive consumer goods allowed married women to forgo many arduous and time-consuming activities such as soap and candle making. The appearance of utilities, such as running water, indoor plumbing, gas, and electricity, eliminated the necessity for other back-breaking tasks, such as hauling water, tending wood or coal furnaces and stoves, and removing the soot that such heating devices produced (also see the essay on utilities in Chapter Dh). At the same time, Ruth Schwartz Cowan (1983) shows that productivity enhancements offered by the commercial substitutes for household production and by the new household technologies shifted, but did not reduce, married women's work in the home. She argues that social standards for cleanliness and for other household services – especially child care and meal preparation, but also standards of leisure for husbands and children – rose faster than household productivity. The result, which she signals in the title of her influential book, *More Work for Mother*, was more time spent in household work for married women and less participation in paid labor.

Joel Mokyr (2000) argues that rising social standards for household cleanliness in the late nineteenth century were due, at least in part, to the scientific discovery of the germ theory of disease. A practical implication of the germ theory is that good hygiene could reduce the incidence of disease and speed the recovery of the ill. In Mokyr's view, the widespread acceptance of the germ theory helped to raise the social valuation of women's traditional household maintenance chores. Cleaning became more than a cosmetic or aesthetic improvement, according to this new view; it was an integral input into the health and well-being of the family. As commercial sources of housecleaning and nursing services were largely unavailable to all but the very wealthy, he argues, families maximized their well-being by deploying mothers' labor in the home.

In the twentieth century, new consumer goods began to have a more direct effect on the allocation of married women's labor. On the one hand, new goods that unambiguously reduce household work, such as prepared foods and meals eaten away from home, became much more popular and readily available. For example, over the twentieth century, but especially since the 1950s, expenditures on food consumed away from home grew substantially. By 2000, such expenditures accounted for almost 40 percent of all expenditures on food (Tables Cd1–77 and Cd153–263). On the other hand, families' consumption bundles shifted to include goods such as automobiles, various types of insurance (old age, health, homeowners, and automobile), and college education. As Clair Brown (1994) notes, an important characteristic of all of these goods is that by their nature, they cannot be produced in the home. For married women to acquire them for their families, they must enter paid employment.

Overall, then, expenditures on kitchen and other household appliances soared, along with expenditures on goods that by their nature must be produced in the market (series Cd180). Over the same period, women's time spent in household work declined, and time spent in market work has grown (Tables Ba4641–4646 and Ba5096–5119).

Changing social norms, laws, and institutions also impact women's labor force participation. The precise impact of such factors is difficult to quantify, of course, but it is clear that they have played an important role in shaping long-term change in women's market work. To describe one example, Joel Perlmann and Robert Margo (2001, Chapter 3) examine differences across recently settled Illinois counties in 1850 in their propensity to employ female teachers. Illinois in this period is an interesting case study because its underlying economic environment was largely homogeneous, but it was settled by migrants from a variety of regions throughout the East that had different but entrenched attitudes regarding women's roles and, in particular, the acceptability of women as teachers. Perlmann and Margo show that most of the variation in women's employment in school teaching across Illinois communities in 1850 is explained by acceptability of women's teaching in migrants' communities of origin. If women taught in the counties from which settlers had come, then women were likely to teach in the new communities established by these pioneers. However, if in the next town over, pioneers arrived from communities in which teaching was men's work, then even in their new Illinois environment, they employed men but not women as teachers.

Given the evident power of such social norms, what, specifically, describes the profound changes in American women's labor force participation rates over time? A partial answer is that, at a fundamental level, there appears to be no necessary connection between the technical characteristics of employment in any particular occupation or industry and the gender composition of employment. In a study that was especially well constructed to standardize for the effects of industry, industrial technology, and norms regarding the length of the workday and worker safety protections, Gary Saxonhouse and Gavin Wright (1984) demonstrate that occupations deemed "men's work" in Japan can be "women's work" in the United States and vice versa. Differences between these social definitions appear to depend entirely on the relative supplies of male and female labor in the two countries at some influential point in time. Occupations designated as men's work in nineteenth-century America (clerical work, for example) are women's work today (Rotella 1981; Davies 1982). The reverse is also true. Occupations, such as assisting with childbirth, evolved over time from women's to men's work (Walsh 1977).

Again, when and under what circumstances do social norms regarding women's and men's work change? The scholarly literature identifies several underlying conditions that appear to extend social definitions of employment to include women and to encourage women's involvement. Foremost among these are temporary shortages of male workers, the appearance of new technologies, and rapid expansion in the demand for workers, including work reorganization. Thus, Perlmann and Margo find that temporary shortages of male teachers during the Civil War prompted school boards in many communities across the country (including recently settled communities in Illinois, which had never before employed women to teach school) to hire women for the first time (Perlmann and Margo 2001). Significantly, the (positive) wartime experience of such communities with their (temporary) wartime female teachers appears to have permanently changed their attitudes regarding the acceptability of women for teaching posts. At the conclusion of the Civil War, and beyond, the female share of the teaching force across communities was above the prewar level, despite the return of male teachers who had been called away for wartime military deployment.

Myra Strober and Carolyn Arnold (1987) tell a similar story regarding the feminization of the bank teller occupation during World War II. The demand for banking services, which continued and expanded during wartime, coupled with markedly reduced supplies of male labor, prompted banks to reorganize financial services delivery in a way that created jobs for women and redirected a greater share of the banking labor force toward service activities. Even with the war's end and the return to the civilian labor force of former male bank employees, the structure of bank occupations retained its heavy reliance on female workers.

There are other stories as well. Elyce Rotella (1981) and Margery Davies (1982) explain women's entry into clerical work in terms of the rapid increase in demand for workers in the occupation; the development of new technologies, especially the typewriter; and the reorganization of work, which removed record keeping as a stepping stone to a managerial position and redefined it as a new, self-contained work category. Mary Roth Walsh (1977) accounts for the narrowing of opportunities for women in health care over the nineteenth century in terms of the development of occupational licensing procedures with legal clauses that directly or indirectly excluded women.

Social norms regarding responsibility for the care of children, the aged, and the infirm are another arena with enormous implications for women's labor force participation. Historically, societies have vested such responsibilities in women. Although some European nations have accepted increasing social responsibility for such matters, especially over the latter half of the twentieth century, the United States has not. Norms regarding women's responsibility for such care have changed far more slowly than norms relating to the style and content of women's paid employment. Thus, employed women, to a far greater extent than employed men, must juggle the demands of career and family. Many women responded by delaying marriage and reducing their fertility in order to pursue careers. Women who are already mothers when they enter employment are often faced with difficult choices as they balance the demands of child care and employment.

Over the long term, legal changes have greatly enlarged the sphere for women's self-determination and participation society-wide. Many of these have had direct effects on women's labor force participation. Before the mid-nineteenth century, for example, control over married women's earnings and assets rested with their husbands. Wives were required to obtain their husbands' permission in order to participate in the labor force, sign contracts with merchants, and engage in many other activities essential to earning an independent livelihood. Table Ba5091–5095 displays the timing of the repeal of such laws on a state-by-state basis, beginning with Maryland in 1842 and concluding with Utah in 1897.

In the latter part of the nineteenth century, following a noticeable increase in women's industrial employment, states began to regulate the hours and working conditions of women and children. Women's night work and hours of employment per working day were restricted in many states, and women were excluded from employment in mining and certain types of manufacturing processes that were deemed to pose a risk to their health or to that of their unborn children. Ronnie Steinberg (1982) has compiled a useful summary of these regulations on a topic-by-topic and state-by-state basis for the period 1900–1970. The overall effect of such legislation is not entirely clear. Women's hours of work fell in response to the passage of restrictive hours legislation, but they fell no faster than men's hours over the same time period. Women's employment in the regulated manufacturing industries did not fall. These findings suggest that this Progressive-era protective legislation for women workers may have improved the ability of male workers who were not directly affected by the legislation to bargain for reduced hours and safer working conditions, so that hours fell and safety improved for both male and female workers (Goldin 1990, Chapter 7). Thus protected by law, more women were able to seek employment without encountering opposition from parents, husbands, and the general community.

In the years that followed, the emphasis of gender-specific employment legislation shifted from special protection for women workers to gender equality in wages and employment. Key legislative developments were the Equal Pay Act of 1963; Title VII of the Civil Rights Act of 1964; Executive Order 11246 (1965) and Executive Order 11375 (1967), or "Affirmative Action"; and Title IX of the Educational Amendments Act of 1972. "Comparable worth" legislation was passed by a number of states beginning in the 1980s but did not achieve national coverage. An Equal Rights Amendment to the Constitution was first introduced in Congress in 1923 and passed by Congress in 1972; however, it was not ratified by the necessary thirty-eight states by the July 1982 deadline (it was ratified by thirty-five states).

It is difficult to specify the precise impact of legislation on women's labor force participation, occupations, wages, and educational attainment over time. The limitations of such a legislative approach are obvious. The Equal Pay Act of 1963 required only equal pay for workers in essentially the same job with the same employer. Because gender-based occupational segregation at the time of the law's passage was extensive (Table Ba4207–4213), the law applied to only a small proportion of the jobs in which women worked. Title VII of the Civil Rights Act of 1964, in prohibiting discrimination in all aspects of employment – hiring, firing, training, promotion, and compensation – was potentially far more powerful. Scholarly studies do find positive impacts of such laws (see Blau and Ferber 1994 for a review of the evidence).

Unemployment

Since the advent of the modern labor force concept in the 1940 Census, the unemployed have been defined as noninstitutionalized civilians 16 years of age and older (14 years and older before 1947) who had no employment during a particular reference week but who were available for work and who made specific efforts to find a job within the previous four weeks. Job-search efforts might include applying to an employer, registering with an employment service, or checking with friends regarding employment opportunities. Persons on layoff from a job and expecting recall are also classified as unemployed according to this definition. The unemployment rate is calculated by dividing the number unemployed by the number in the labor force, where the labor force is the sum of the employed and the unemployed. Annual estimates of the number unemployed and the unemployment rate based on these definitions are shown in Table Ba478–486.

Although our focus here is on unemployment, it is important to note that the downturns in economic activity that produce unemployment also produce a number of other labor market adjustments. During downturns, opportunities for highly paid overtime work are reduced (Table Ba4640). Some workers who prefer full-time schedules may be offered only part-time work (Table Ba4614–4625). Others may be offered night work or other less attractive work schedules (Shiells and Wright 1983). Workers with jobs are more likely to be absent from work due to illness, vacation, and other reasons (Table Ba4649–4655). Occupational injury rates also rise during depressions (Table Ba4750–4767).[12]

Historical Unemployment Estimates

Prior to 1940, the government measured unemployment in a number of different ways. The decennial federal census first inquired about unemployment in 1880 when it asked those who reported an occupation how many months out of the previous twelve they had been unemployed. A similar question was asked in 1900. In 1910, the census asked two unemployment questions, one relating to unemployment at the time of the census and a second regarding weeks of unemployment in the previous year.[13] Additional information on unemployment prior to 1940 may be found in surveys conducted by numerous federal and, especially, state agencies. The most important of the federal unemployment surveys were U.S. Commissioner of Labor (1905), U.S. Immigration Commission (1911), and the special U.S. census of unemployment taken in 1937. For a description of unemployment data collected by state agencies, see Keyssar (1986) and Carter, Ransom, and Sutch (1991). Goldin (2000) displays summary statistics on unemployment gleaned from a number of state surveys conducted in the late nineteenth century. Margo (1993a) makes use of state labor bureau data from the 1930s to study unemployment during the Great Depression.

The first annual estimates of unemployment for the period prior to 1940 that are based on the modern unemployment definition were developed by Stanley Lebergott (1964). Lebergott's work was part of a broad-based effort across the economics profession during the 1950s and 1960s to reconstruct the statistical record regarding the long-term growth of the American economy. The goal was a better understanding of the American growth experience that could inform efforts by less developed countries to improve their own standard of living. Lebergott began with the 1940 labor force and unemployment figures and worked backward in time, proceeding in two steps. He first generated estimates of labor force and unemployment for the decennial census years by taking available census data on unemployment by sex and race and adjusting them to better accord with the labor force concept. He referred to these as "benchmark" estimates. He then generated intercensal unemployment estimates by first estimating an annual series on the labor force between census benchmark dates and then subtracting from it annual estimates of employment. These annual estimates of employment were constructed by a wide variety of methods, depending on available evidence in different sectors of the economy. David Weir (1992) offers a clear and concise description of the details of the Lebergott estimation process.

The upward jump in both the unemployment rate and the inflation rate in the early 1980s prompted the economics profession to shift its focus away from economic growth to economic stabilization. At that time, academic interest in the historical unemployment estimates shifted as well. Data developed for the study of growth began to be used for the study of economic stability in long-term perspective. Viewed in this way, these data presented a puzzle. Prices, employment, and gross national product all appeared to have become increasingly stable over time, yet theory suggests that increasingly stable prices should destabilize the economy. The apparent incongruity between theory and evidence spurred a variety of investigations, including a reexamination of Lebergott's unemployment estimates.

This reexamination was inaugurated by Christina Romer (1986a, 1986b), who argued that the apparent increasing stability of the economy over time is an artifact of the methods used to reconstruct economic statistics for the prewar period. Although these methods might have been acceptable for their original purpose – the calculation of long-term growth rates – Romer argued that they exhibited spurious volatility, making the resulting estimates inappropriate for the study of long-term change in economic stability. To drive home her point, Romer (1986b) used "prewar methods" to transform postwar employment and labor force data. The result was a postwar unemployment series that was nearly as volatile as the pre-1930 series. In a widely cited conclusion, Romer (1986b, pp. 2, 32) stated that the apparent increasing stability of the economy over time was a "figment of the data" and that "economists may have misjudged the effectiveness of stabilization policy and the long-run changes in the economy."[14]

Romer's papers prompted a number of scholars to reconsider Lebergott's original sources and methods. A careful, detailed reexamination of his intercensal interpolation methods led Weir (1992) to argue that Romer's criticisms reflected a misunderstanding of Lebergott's methods. For the most part, Weir validated Lebergott's procedures and findings, while calling attention to a number of issues in need of further work. Weir did, however, take exception to two elements of Lebergott's series. One was the unemployment estimates for the 1890s, which Lebergott developed according to a different methodology from the one that he employed for later years. Adapting the procedures Lebergott developed and refined for the years 1900–1940, Weir produces substantially lower unemployment rate estimates for that decade. The second had to do with the treatment of "emergency workers" during the Great Depression. Beginning in 1929 and continuing through 1943, the federal government created a series of employment programs for otherwise unemployed workers. The major programs were the Works Progress Administration (WPA) and the Civilian Conservation Corps (CCC). Together they employed several million workers during their peak years of operation from 1933 through 1941. The numbers employed in such programs were assembled by Michael Darby

[12] These issues, along with other changes that accompany cyclical fluctuations in the labor market, are discussed in Lilien and Hall (1986).

[13] In 1910, the unemployment question was asked of wage and salary workers only. The self-employed and employers were omitted.

[14] For a discussion of Romer's methodology see Goldin (2000), pp. 589–91.

and are shown in series Ba477. Standard practice for the Bureau of Labor Statistics (BLS) at the time was to count these workers as "unemployed." Its rationale was that these people would have been unemployed had they not been assisted by government relief efforts. Therefore, if the unemployment rate is a measure of the failure of the private sector, government relief workers ought to be excluded from the employment figures. Subsequent long-term employment and unemployment estimates constructed by Lebergott continued this practice (Lebergott 1964, pp. 184–5). Darby, however, was interested not so much in the failure of the private economy as in how many workers were receiving paychecks. From his perspective, it was appropriate to count emergency workers as employed. Weir followed Darby and counted the emergency workers as employed, and this treatment made Weir's unemployment rate estimates for the Great Depression considerably lower than Lebergott's. Thus, whereas Lebergott dates the depth of the Depression in 1933 with an unemployment rate of 25.2 percent, Weir estimated that it reached the bottom in 1932 with an unemployment rate of 22.9 percent (Lebergott, 1964, p. 512, and series Ba475).

To provide a century's worth of conceptually consistent data on the labor force, employment, and unemployment, Weir linked his revisions of the Lebergott series with official federal data collected according to the labor force concept, beginning in 1948 and continuing to 1990. A revised and updated version of these federal data is reported in Table Ba478–486. Minor discrepancies in the years of overlap for Tables Ba470–486 reflect revisions to the data made by the BLS after Weir completed his research. For studies that take a long-term view spanning 1948, the Weir series is preferred. For those taking only a post-1948 perspective, the official series is preferred. The Weir estimates through 1947 and the BLS estimates beginning in 1948 are shown in Figure Ba-E.

The long-term unemployment series continues to attract scholarly revisions. Carter and Sutch (1992) use microlevel surveys of workers and firms to recalculate aggregate unemployment rate estimates for the 1890s. They argue that two sources of unemployment have been neglected in the standard calculations: (1) unemployment created by industrial suspensions of operation, in which the entire firm closed for several days to several months, throwing all employees out of work and (2) unemployment created by the failure of business establishments. Because these processes created a large amount of unemployment in this period, their inclusion in

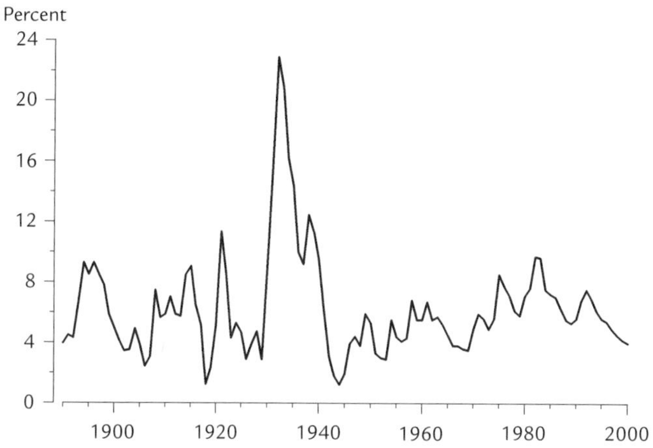

FIGURE Ba-E Unemployment rate: 1890–2000

Sources

Through 1947, series Ba475; thereafter, series Ba485.

the unemployment rate estimates largely offsets the effect of Weir's downward revisions, restoring the depression of the 1890s to its former infamy.

John James and Mark Thomas (2003) make use of the IPUMS sample from the 1910 Census to construct a new unemployment rate estimate for that date. Although unemployment data were collected in that census, it was not published in the regular report of that census. Lebergott based his own estimates for that year on a mimeographed report produced by the Census Bureau in 1948. This report showed the distribution of weeks of unemployment by occupation, but excluded information on the demographic characteristics of workers, such as sex and age. On the basis of the evidence available to him, he estimated the unemployment rate of nonfarm employees at 11.6 percent. When James and Thomas examined the IPUMS sample from the 1910 Census, however, they found substantially lower unemployment rates for nonfarm employees – 5.0 percent for 1909 and 5.3 percent for 1910. They convincingly argue that the lower rates ought to be accepted. Since Weir adopted Lebergott's census benchmark unemployment figures, James and Thomas's results suggest that a downward revision to the Weir unemployment rate series in the years surrounding 1910 is warranted as well.

Long-Term Trends in Unemployment

Unemployment is a modern development. In an economy comprising exclusively independent family-owned and family-operated enterprises, unemployment does not exist. Workers in such an economy may endure economic setbacks because of bad weather, disease, or other natural disasters. Their circumstances may be reduced by war or injurious government policy. Alternatively, they may find that competitors have lured away markets for their tradable commodities or have made such markets less remunerative. Yet none of these economic setbacks represent unemployment. Unemployment is the condition of someone who is willing and able to work but who cannot find employment. For the self-employed, there is always something to do, even in slow times. Unemployment, therefore, presupposes a class of workers who are dependent on wage or salary earnings for their livelihood. Even as late as 1900, only about two thirds of the labor force were wage and salary workers (Tables Ba814–830 and Ba910–921).

The history of American unemployment dates from the appearance of "free labor" in the early nineteenth century. "Free" labor in this context refers to labor's legal right to employment at will, especially the legal right to abandon employment without threat of fines or punishment. Although the embrace of free labor was beneficial for laborers overall, the abandonment of labor contracts in favor of free labor also led to employer-initiated terminations of employment – in other words, unemployment.

Alexander Keyssar (1986) provides a colorful, highly readable, and detailed account of the emergence of unemployment in the Massachusetts economy over the course of the nineteenth and early twentieth centuries. Massachusetts is an interesting microcosm from which to view changes in the larger society, as it was an early industrializer and its public officials kept unusually good statistical records of the consequences.

Although theory predicts that industrialization is a necessary precondition for unemployment, Keyssar shows that it is not a sufficient condition. The reason is that the early production of manufactured products took place within an agricultural setting in which any reduction in industrial employment could be offset by reallocating labor into some alternative sphere. The appearance of modern unemployment, in his story, required the abandonment of agriculture for full-time industrial work. Thus, unemployment is linked to urbanization and to the mass migration of foreign workers, who had no claim to domestic agricultural roots. Because these urban, industrial, and largely foreign-born workers relied wholly on wage labor income for their sustenance and typically had few assets with which to establish a farm or business establishment of their own, these workers were the first Americans to suffer modern unemployment.

Nineteenth-century industrial employment was characterized by frequent interruptions in labor demand. Some of these resulted from seasonal shifts in the supply of raw materials, such as grain, fleece, or fiber. Others resulted from seasonal shifts in demand for industrial products, such as agricultural implements and shoes. Seasonality in both the supply of raw materials and the demand for industrial products remained an important determinant of shifts in the aggregate demand for labor throughout the nineteenth century (Engerman and Goldin 1994).

One response to seasonality as well as to other business disruptions was the suspension of business operations, a widespread practice in the nineteenth century. Firms of that era often closed for a day or two at a time, idling their entire workforce. In normal times, shutdowns were scheduled in advance for vacations and holidays and for routine maintenance and improvements. High or low water, disruptions in the supply of raw materials, and other unforeseen events led to unscheduled closures. Data assembled by Carter and Sutch for the industrial states of Massachusetts, New Jersey, and Pennsylvania for the period 1890–1919 indicate that even in the year of the most continuous operation (1906), firms were closed for an average of one and a half weeks (Carter and Sutch 1992, p. 353). Temporary plant shutdowns were also used to reduce output during economic depressions. In the depression year 1893, for example, average downtime for the industrial establishments in the three states was nearly six weeks. In the modern era, complete plant shutdowns to accommodate disruptions in supplies or reductions in demand are rare (Lilien and Hall 1986, p. 1006; Kniesner and Goldsmith 1987, p. 1244).

Seasonality and industrial suspensions made nineteenth-century unemployment a more democratic and less protracted experience than it is today. In a comparison of the unemployment experience of male nonagricultural workers in 1910 and 1970, Margo (1990) found that the average worker in 1910 was more likely than his grandson in 1970 to become unemployed, but that once unemployed, he was more likely to be quickly reemployed. Margo also found that personal characteristics of workers in 1910 played a small role in determining whether or not a worker would become unemployed.

By the second half of the twentieth century, unemployment became concentrated among minority workers and among those with the fewest job skills (see Figure Ba-F). Over the period since 1954, when the relevant data first become available, nonwhite males have experienced an average unemployment rate that is 5.4 percentage points higher in any given year than that experienced by white males. The additional unemployment rate burden of nonwhite females is 5.2 percentage points (Table Ba583–596). The racial differential in unemployment is especially large during years of high unemployment overall. Thus, in 1983, just a year after the post–World War II unemployment rate peak of 9.7 percent overall, the racial differential in unemployment was 9.7 percent for males and 9.2 percent for females. Put another way, nonwhites

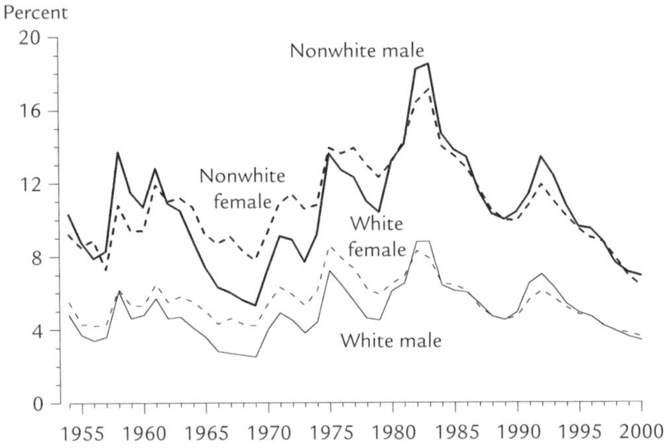

FIGURE Ba-F Unemployment rate, by sex and race: 1954–2000

Sources

Series Ba589–590 and Ba592–593.

experienced unemployment rates that were over twice as high as those of whites during recession years. A comparison of the unemployment rates of males and females of the same race suggests that females' unemployment is more stable across the business cycle than that of males. Economic booms are more effective in reducing male than female unemployment, and economic depressions throw more males than females out of work. This gender difference derives from two sources. One is that men are more likely to be employed in the more cyclically sensitive sectors of the economy, such as construction, transportation, and manufacturing. The other is that men's labor force participation is less sensitive to the business cycle than is women's. This means that in a recession, when men lose their jobs they are likely to remain in the labor force as unemployed persons looking for work. By contrast, when women lose their jobs they are more likely than men to exit the labor force and not be counted as unemployed.

Unemployment duration refers to the length of time a worker who becomes unemployed remains unemployed. Along with the increasingly selective nature of the unemployment experience itself, over the past century the duration of unemployment for those who become unemployed has increased. In the nineteenth century, although workers ran a high risk of unemployment at any particular time, they also stood a good chance of fairly rapid reemployment. In the twentieth century, the average risk of unemployment was lower, but the duration of unemployment was lengthy. For the post–World War II period as a whole, average unemployment duration is 13.0 weeks; for the period since 1975, it is 14.9 weeks (series Ba597). The concentration in the incidence and the lengthening duration of unemployment is attributed to reduced seasonality, growth of firm-specific job skills that give firms the incentive to retain skilled workers during economic downturns, unionization, the development of unemployment insurance, and a shift of employment into relatively stable sectors, such as the professions and services (see Margo 2000, p. 242; Goldin 2000, pp. 591–9).

In addition to factors such as interruptions in the supply of raw materials, seasonal reductions in demand, changes in consumer tastes, or increased market competition that generate unemployment at a particular firm or in a particular industry, macroeconomic factors generate unemployment across many firms and industries simultaneously throughout the economy. A mild rise in overall unemployment is called a contraction or recession; a severe rise is called a depression. Recessions and depressions are called "macroeconomic" phenomena because they are a product of the interconnected nature of developed market economies. For example, when bad weather interrupts production in a manufacturing plant and its workers become unemployed, those workers typically reduce their own purchases. This may lead to reduced product demand and therefore unemployment in sectors not directly affected by the bad weather. The opposite is true as well. Strong demand for labor in one sector leads to increases in worker income that spill over into increased demand for products and therefore labor throughout the economy. A reduction in unemployment to a previous low is called a recovery; a more sustained reduction in unemployment is called an expansion. The combination of economic contraction and expansion is called a business cycle. For a detailed description of these business cycles, along with a discussion of their causes and consequences, see the essay on economic fluctuations, recessions, and depressions in Chapter Cb. Dates for business cycles beginning in 1790 are given in Tables Cb1–8.

The more highly specialized the economy and the more interdependent its economic actors, the more vulnerable it is to business cycles. One measure of this interdependence is the share of wage and salary workers in the total workforce. For 1800, Lebergott estimates that less than 20 percent of the labor force comprised wage and salary workers; by 1900, this figure had risen to approximately 66 percent; by 2000 it was 93 percent (series Ba981). The rise in the wage and salary share of the labor force is associated with a general increase in the amplitude of unemployment peaks during economic crises in the nineteenth century. Thus, Lebergott (1964, p. 187) estimates unemployment at 3–5 percent of the labor force in the crisis of 1819; 6–8 percent in 1838 and again in 1858; 12–14 percent in 1876; and 6–8 percent in 1885. By far, the worst economic crisis of that century occurred in the 1890s. Carter and Sutch (1992, p. 366) estimate an unemployment rate of approximately 12–14 percent in the peak depression year of 1894 and unemployment rates in excess of 10 percent for the seven-year depression episode running from 1893 through 1899.

Not every downturn was worse than the previous one, but many observers detected a trend toward more violent movements of output and employment over time. Following the financial panic of 1907, Congress created the National Monetary Commission with a mandate to explore strategies for stabilizing the economy. Following the commission's recommendations, Congress in 1913 passed the Federal Reserve Act, which provided for the creation of a central bank to conduct monetary policy and to regulate the workings of the private banking sector. The economy experienced sharp but brief recessions in 1914–1915 and again in 1921–1922. Then, beginning in 1930, unemployment began climbing and reached an unprecedented high of 23 percent by 1932. It was not until 1942, when the economy was mobilized to fight World War II, that unemployment returned to the low levels of the 1920s (Table Ba470–477).

The high Great Depression–era levels of unemployment, together with their unprecedented duration, provoked a political crisis within the United States (and also within many other developed industrial economies that were experiencing similar economic circumstances). In the 1932 presidential election, the Republican incumbent, Herbert Hoover, was defeated by Democrat Franklin D. Roosevelt, who campaigned on the promise of an active role for the federal government in ending the crisis. During his first 100 days in office, Roosevelt sent to Congress a record number of bills designed to give immediate relief to the unemployed, raise the wages of those who remained employed, and indirectly promote employment through programs aimed at reversing deflation and enhancing the profitability of private business establishments. Economic historians generally conclude that these programs worked in the right direction, but that Roosevelt's policies, in particular his fiscal policies, were far too limited to have secured the nation's recovery from such a serious economic depression (see Atack and Passell 1994, pp. 633–46, for an excellent discussion of the debate). In particular, this scholarship cautions against the view that Roosevelt was the first Keynesian. The reference here is to the views of John Maynard Keynes (1935), who argued in *The General Theory of Employment, Interest and Money* that governments should offset reductions in private spending during depressions in order to maintain unemployment at low levels. It was not until America's involvement in World War II that Roosevelt authorized a level of deficit spending that was sufficient to reduce unemployment to its pre–Great Depression level. Nonetheless, the Great Depression left an important legacy regarding the responsibility of the federal government for the health of the economy. This is reflected in the passage of the Employment Act of 1946, which charged the federal government with maintaining the economy at full employment. It is also reflected in the fact that voters in the post–World War II era appear to hold the president responsible for the economic health of the country and regularly refuse to reelect presidents who have experienced a rise in unemployment during their term in office.

The overall success of federal government efforts since World War II to maintain unemployment at low levels is the subject of continuing scholarly debate. David Weir (1992) argues that the postwar economy is significantly more stable than the prewar economy, not only overall but also in every major sector. James and Thomas (2003) conclude that pre-1914 labor markets were more volatile than those of the postwar era, even after they reduce the estimated level of unemployment around 1910. Goldin (2000, pp. 589–91) argues that differences among competing estimates of pre- and postwar employment volatility are not yet fully resolved.

References

Abel, Marjorie, and Nancy Folbre. 1990. "A Methodology for Revising Estimates: Female Market Participation in the United States before 1940." *Historical Methods* 23: 167–76.

Abramovitz, Moses, and Paul A. David. 2000. "American Macroeconomic Growth in the Era of Knowledge-Based Progress: The Long-Run Perspective." In Stanley L. Engerman and Robert E. Gallman, editors. *The Cambridge Economic History of the United States,* volume 3. Cambridge University Press.

Atack, Jeremy, and Fred Bateman. 1987. *To Their Own Soil: Agriculture in the Antebellum North.* Iowa State University Press.

Atack, Jeremy, and Peter Passell. 1994. *A New Economic View of American History: From Colonial Times to 1940.* 2d edition. Norton.

Bateman, Fred, and Thomas Weiss. 1981. *A Deplorable Scarcity: The Failure of Industrialization in the Slave Economy.* University of North Carolina Press.

Blau, Francine D., and Marianne Ferber. 1994. *The Economics of Women, Men, and Work.* 2d edition. Prentice Hall.

Blundell, R., and Thomas MaCurdy. 1999. "Labor Supply: A Review of Alternative Approaches." In Orley C. Ashenfelter and David Card, editors. *Handbook of Labor Economics*, volume 3A, Chapter 27. Elsevier.

Bordo, Michael D., Claudia Goldin, and Eugene N. White. 1998. "The Defining Moment Hypothesis: The Editors' Introduction." In Michael D. Bordo, Claudia Goldin, and Eugene N. White, editors. *The Defining Moment: The Great Depression and the American Economy in the Twentieth Century.* University of Chicago Press.

Brown, Clair. 1994. *American Standards of Living, 1918–1988.* Blackwell.

Carson, Daniel. 1949. "Changes in the Industrial Composition of Manpower since the Civil War." In Studies in Income and Wealth, volume 11. National Bureau of Economic Research.

Carter, Susan B., Roger L. Ransom, and Richard Sutch. 1991. "The Historical Labor Statistics Project at the University of California." *Historical Methods* 24 (2): 52–65.

Carter, Susan B., and Richard Sutch. 1992. "The Great Depression of the 1890s: New Suggestive Estimates of the Unemployment Rate." *Research in Economic History* 14: 347–76.

Carter, Susan B., and Richard Sutch. 1996. "Fixing the Facts: Editing of the 1880 U.S. Census of Occupations with Implications for Long-Term Trends and the Sociology of Official Statistics." *Historical Methods* 28 (1): 5–24.

Carter, Susan B., and Richard Sutch. 1999. "Historical Perspectives on the Economic Consequences of Immigration into the United States." In Charles Hirschman, Philip Kasinitz, and Joshua DeWind, editors. *The Handbook of International Migration: The American Experience.* Russell Sage Foundation.

Coleman, Mary T., and John Pencavel. 1993. "Changes in Work Hours of Male Employees, 1940–1988." *Industrial and Labor Relations Review* 46 (2): 262–83.

Collins, William. 1997. "When the Tide Turned: Immigration and the Delay of the Great Black Migration." *Journal of Economic History* 57 (3): 607–32.

Conk, Margo. 1978. *The United States Census and Labor Force Change: A History of Occupation Statistics, 1870–1940.* UMI Research Press.

Costa, Dora L. 1998. *The Evolution of Retirement: An American Economic History, 1880–1990.* University of Chicago Press.

Cowan, Ruth Schwartz. 1983. *More Work for Mother: The Ironies of Household Technology from the Open Hearth to the Microwave.* Basic Books.

Davies, Margery W. 1982. *Woman's Place Is at the Typewriter: Office Work and Office Workers, 1870–1930.* Temple University Press.

DeVries, Jan. 1994. "The Industrial Revolution and the Industrious Revolution." *Journal of Economic History* 54 (2): 249–70.

Dublin, Thomas. 1981. *Farm to Factory: Women's Letters, 1830–1860.* Columbia University Press.

Dublin, Thomas. 1994. *Transforming Women's Work: New England Lives in the Industrial Revolution.* Cornell University Press.

Durand, John D. 1948. *The Labor Force in the United States, 1890–1940.* Social Science Research Council.

Easterlin, Richard A. 1980. *Birth and Fortune: The Impact of Numbers on Personal Welfare.* Basic Books.

Edwards, Alba M. 1943. *Comparative Occupation Statistics for the United States, 1870 to 1940.* U.S. Government Printing Office.

Engerman, Stanley L., and Claudia Goldin. 1994. "Seasonality in Nineteenth-Century Labor Markets." In Thomas Weiss and Donald Schaefer, editors. *American Economic Development in Historical Perspective.* Stanford University Press.

Folbre, Nancy, and Marjorie Abel. 1989. "Women's Work and Women's Households: Gender Bias in the U.S. Census." *Social Research* 56: 545–70.

Folbre, Nancy, and Barnet Wagman. 1993. "Counting Housework: New Estimates of Real Product in the United States." *Journal of Economic History* 53 (2): 275–88.

Goldin, Claudia. 1983. "The Changing Economic Role of Women: A Quantitative Approach." *Journal of Interdisciplinary History* 13 (Spring): 707–33.

Goldin, Claudia. 1986. "The Female Labor Force and American Economic Growth, 1890–1980." In Stanley Engerman and Robert Gallman, editors. *Long-Term Factors in American Economic Growth.* University of Chicago Press.

Goldin, Claudia. 1990. *Understanding the Gender Gap: An Economic History of American Women.* Oxford University Press.

Goldin, Claudia. 2000. "Labor Markets in the Twentieth Century." In Stanley L. Engerman and Robert E. Gallman, editors. *The Cambridge Economic History of the United States,* volume 3. Cambridge University Press.

Goldin, Claudia, and Kenneth Sokoloff. 1982. "The Relative Productivity Hypothesis in American Manufacturing." *Journal of Economic History* 42 (4): 741–74.

Jacoby, Sanford M. 1985. *Employing Bureaucracy: Managers, Unions, and the Transformation of Work in American Industry, 1900–1945.* Columbia University Press.

James, John A., and Mark Thomas. 2003. "A Golden Age? Unemployment and the American Labor Market, 1880–1910." *Journal of Economic History* 63 (4): 959–94.

Keynes, John Maynard. 1935. *The General Theory of Employment, Interest and Money.* Harcourt, Brace.

Keyssar, Alexander. 1986. *Out of Work: The First Century of Unemployment in Massachusetts.* Cambridge University Press.

Killingsworth, Mark R. 1983. *Labor Supply.* Cambridge University Press.

Kniesner, Thomas J., and Arthur H. Goldsmith. 1987. "A Survey of Alternative Models of the Aggregate U.S. Labor Market." *Journal of Economic Literature* 25: 1241–80.

Lebergott, Stanley. 1964. *Manpower in Economic Growth: The American Record since 1800.* McGraw-Hill.

Lebergott, Stanley. 1966. "Labor Force and Employment, 1800–1960." In Dorothy S. Brady, editor. *Output, Employment, and Productivity in the United States after 1800.* Studies in Income and Wealth, volume 30, by the Conference on Research in Income and Wealth. National Bureau of Economic Research.

Lebergott, Stanley. 1975. "Labor." In U.S. Bureau of the Census. *Historical Statistics of the United States, Colonial Times to 1970,* Bicentennial Edition, 2 volumes. U.S. Government Printing Office.

Lebergott, Stanley. 1984. *The Americans: An Economic Record.* Norton.

Lilien, David M., and Robert E. Hall. 1986. "Cyclical Fluctuations in the Labor Market." In Orley Ashenfelter and Robert Layard, editors. *Handbook of Labor Economics,* volume 2. Elsevier Science.

Long, Clarence D. 1958. *The Labor Force under Changing Income and Employment.* Princeton University Press for the National Bureau of Economic Research.

Margo, Robert A. 1990. "The Incidence and Duration of Employment: Some Long-Term Comparisons." *Economics Letters* 32: 217–20.

Margo, Robert A. 1993a. "Employment and Unemployment in the 1930s." *Journal of Economic Perspectives* 7: 41–59.

Margo, Robert A. 1993b. "The Labor Force Participation of Older Americans in 1900: Further Results." *Explorations in Economic History* 30 (October): 409–23.

Margo, Robert A. 2000. "The Labor Force in the Nineteenth Century." In Stanley L. Engerman and Robert E. Gallman, editors. *The Cambridge Economic History of the United States,* volume 2. Cambridge University Press.

Modigliani, Franco. 1966. "The Life Cycle Hypothesis of Saving, the Demand for Wealth and the Supply of Capital." *Social Research* 33 (Summer): 160–217.

Moen, Jon R. 1987. "The Labor of Older Men: A Comment." *Journal of Economic History* 47 (September): 761–7.

Moen, Jon R. 1988. "From Gainful Employment to Labor Force: Definitions and a New Estimate of Work Rates of American Males, 1860 to 1980." *Historical Methods* 21 (4): 149–59.

Mokyr, Joel. 2000. "Why 'More Work for Mother'? Knowledge and Household Behaviour, 1870–1945." *Journal of Economic History* 60 (1): 1–41.

Nelson, Daniel. 1975. *Managers and Workers: Origins of the New Factory System in the United States, 1880–1920.* University of Wisconsin Press.

Oppenheimer, Valarie Kincade. 1970. *The Female Labor Force in the United States: Demographic and Economic Factors Governing Its Growth and Changing Composition.* University of California Press.

Pencavel, John H. 1986. "Labor Supply of Men: A Survey." In Orley Ashenfelter and Richard Layard, editors. *Handbook of Labor Economics,* volume 1. North-Holland.

Pencavel, John. 1998. "The Market Work Behavior and Wages of Women, 1975–94." *Journal of Human Resources* 33 (4): 771–804.

Perlmann, Joel, and Robert A. Margo. 2001. *Women's Work? American Schoolteachers 1650–1920.* University of Chicago Press.

Romer, Christina. 1986a. "New Estimates of Prewar Gross National Product and Unemployment." *Journal of Economic History* 46: 341–52.

Romer, Christina. 1986b. "Spurious Volatility in Historical Unemployment Data." *Journal of Political Economy* 94: 1–37.

Ransom, Roger L., and Richard Sutch. 1977 [2001]. *One Kind of Freedom: The Economic Consequences of Emancipation.* Cambridge University Press.

Ransom, Roger L., and Richard Sutch. 1986. "The Labor of Older Americans: Retirement of Men on and off the Job, 1870–1937." *Journal of Economic History* 46 (March): 1–30.

Rosenbloom, Joshua L. 2002. *Looking for Work, Searching for Workers: American Labor Markets during Industrialization.* Cambridge University Press.

Rothenberg, Winifred B. 1992. "Structural Change in the Farm Labor Force: Contract Labor in Massachusetts Agriculture, 1750–1865." In Claudia

Goldin and Hugh Rockoff, editors. *Strategic Factors in Nineteenth Century American Economic History: A Volume to Honor Robert W. Fogel.* University of Chicago Press.
Rotella, Elyce. 1981. *From Home to Office: U.S. Women at Work, 1870–1930.* UMI Research Press.
Saxonhouse, Gary, and Gavin Wright. 1984. "Two Forms of Cheap Labor in Textile History." In Gary Saxonhouse and Gavin Wright, editors. *Technique, Spirit and Form in the Making of the Modern Economies: Essays in Honor of William N. Parker.* JAI Press.
Schelling, Thomas C. 1978. *Micromotives and Macrobehavior.* Norton.
Shiells, Martha, and Gavin Wright. 1983. "Night Work as a Labor Market Phenomenon: Southern Textiles in the Interwar Period." *Explorations in Economic History* 2 (4): 331–50.
Smuts, Robert W. 1960. "The Female Labor Force: A Case Study in the Interpretation of Historical Statistics." *Journal of the American Statistical Association* 55: 71–9.
Sobek, Matthew. 2001. "New Statistics on the U.S. Labor Force, 1850–1990." *Historical Methods* 34: 71–87.
Sokoloff, Kenneth. 1986. "Productivity Growth in Manufacturing during Early Industrialization: Evidence from the American Northeast, 1820–1860." In Stanley L. Engerman and Robert E. Gallman, editors. *Long-Term Factors in American Economic Growth.* National Bureau of Economic Research Studies in Income and Wealth, volume 51. University of Chicago Press.
Steinberg, Ronnie. 1982. *Wages and Hours: Labor and Reform in Twentieth-Century America.* Rutgers University Press.
Strober, Myra H., and Carolyn L. Arnold. 1987. "The Dynamics of Occupational Segregation among Bank Tellers." In Clair Brown and Joseph A. Pechman, editors. *Gender in the Workplace.* Brookings Institution Press.
Sutch, Richard. 1965. "The Profitability of Ante Bellum Slavery – Revisited." *Southern Economic Journal* 31 (April): 365–77.
U.S. Bureau of the Census. 2002. *Statistical Abstract of the United States: 2002.* 122nd edition. U.S. Government Printing Office.
U.S. Commissioner of Labor. 1905. *Nineteenth Annual Report of the Commissioner of Labor, 1904: Wages and Hours of Labor.* U.S. Government Printing Office.
U.S. Congress. Senate. Committee on Immigration. 1911. *Reports of the Immigration Commission* [a.k.a. the Dillingham Commission]. Committee on Immigration, United States Senate, 61st Congress, 3rd Session. December 5, 1910. 42 volumes. U.S. Government Printing Office.
Walsh, Mary Roth. 1977. *Doctors Wanted: No Women Need Apply: Sexual Barriers in the Medical Profession, 1835–1975.* Yale University Press.
Weir, David R. 1992. "A Century of U.S. Unemployment, 1890–1990: Revised Estimates and Evidence for Stabilization." *Research in Economic History* 14: 301–46.
Weiss, Thomas. 1992. "U.S. Labor Force Estimates and Economic Growth." In Robert E. Gallman and John Joseph Wallis, editors. *American Economic Growth and Standards of Living before the Civil War.* University of Chicago Press.
Weiss, Thomas. 1999. "Estimates of White and Nonwhite Gainful Workers in the United States by Age Group, Race, and Sex: Decennial Census Years, 1800–1900." *Historical Methods* 32 (1): 21–35.
Wilentz, Sean. 1984. *Chants Democratic: New York City and the Rise of the American Working Class, 1788–1850.* Oxford University Press.
Wright, Gavin. 1986. *Old South, New South: Revolutions in the Southern Economy since the Civil War.* Basic Books.
Wright, Gavin. 1987. "Postbellum Southern Labor Markets." In Peter Kilby, editor. *Quantity and Quiddity: Essays in U.S. Economic History.* Wesleyan University Press.

OCCUPATIONS

Matthew Sobek

Occupations are among the most revealing and valuable pieces of socioeconomic information pertaining to individuals that survive in the historical record. Few types of evidence have been put to as much or as varied use by social scientists. At the level of families and individuals, occupations have been used as indicators of social status, class, and income, among other things. Aggregate occupation statistics for localities, population subgroups, and the nation have likewise been heavily utilized as measures of group economic well-being, social status attainment, labor market structure, and segregation. At the national level, the changing occupational structure can be seen as a manifestation of the socioeconomic opportunities generated by the evolving economy and the distribution of labor and skills demanded. No other single type of evidence provides such a window on the economy and social structure as they intersect at the level of individuals.

The relative ubiquity of historical occupation data is not an accident. Contemporaries have always recognized that the work an individual performs is a singularly important fact about that person. The combined occupations of the population as a whole have long been seen as a measure of the evolution of the economy and the progress of the nation. Francis Amasa Walker – founding president of the American Economic Association and perhaps the most famous superintendent of the U.S. Census – made it clear how much value he placed on the census occupation question: "Whether the industrial or social character of a nation be considered, a true return of the occupations of the people constitutes the most important single feature of the census.... The habits of a people, their social tastes and moral standards, would be more truthfully depicted in a complete list of their daily occupations, than ever was done in any book of travels or of history" (U.S. Office of the Census 1872, pp. xxii–xxxiii). Although modern scholars might not wax on similarly, most would acknowledge the unique contributions that occupations have made to research in social and economic history.

Occupation, Industry, and Labor Force Participation

Occupations characterize the type of work performed by a person, such as carpenter, professor, or laborer. In government statistics, occupations are restricted to paid work or unpaid work in a family enterprise that contributes to the production of goods for market. Unpaid domestic labor for one's family does not constitute an occupation (see Folbre 1991). Occupation should be distinguished from industry, which describes the basic activity carried out by the establishment in which a person works (for example, construction or advertising). Industry is concerned with the kinds of goods and services produced, whereas occupation relates to the specific characteristics of the job a person performs, regardless of the product involved. For example, there are bookkeepers (an occupation) in the telecommunications, real estate, and educational industries. Industry and occupation are often confused, and many historical data sources purporting to record occupations very often report industry instead. The two were not always consistently distinguished even in published government statistics (Conk 1978).[1]

Occupation is also conceptually distinct from labor force participation. Labor force participation means working or seeking paid

[1] A series of tables on the industrial breakdown of the working population is also presented in this chapter. The essay, however, maintains its focus on occupations, which pose more complicated questions of measurement and interpretation. In contrast to occupations, the industrial classifications have not changed substantially over time, and their meanings have been little disputed.

work in a given week. Conceived to measure unemployment and total labor engaged in the economy, the modern labor force concept aims to record actual activity at a point in time. Occupation is a more flexible concept not subject to such precise criteria. All employed persons have an occupation, but a person may claim an occupation even though he or she is not a labor force participant (that is, not currently working or seeking work). The distinction between participation and occupation has particular salience for historical research. The labor force concept was introduced in the 1940 Census. Researchers must use "gainful employment" – whether or not a person claimed an occupation – as a proxy for labor force participation before that time. Because occupation reflects a person's social identity as well as his or her current work, some persons may have claimed an occupation although they were retired or otherwise not currently engaged in paid or market labor (Ransom and Sutch 1986). The issue of social identity was a particularly pointed one for married women, who may have had to choose between their role as housewife and the other work they performed on the family farm or business (Folbre and Abel 1989). Pre-1940 labor force measures based on occupation data are therefore likely to overestimate the overall labor force participation rate, especially among older workers, while undercounting the participation of married women and youth.[2]

Uses of Occupation Data

Occupation is a complex socioeconomic characteristic with a variety of potential applications. Not only are occupations the means through which most people earn a living – but also, to a large extent, they situate people within society. The concepts of social and occupational structures are so closely entwined that they tend to be used interchangeably by researchers. In many historical studies, occupation is the only information available that suggests the social standing and material situation of individuals and families. Nationally representative income data became available only beginning with the 1950 Census. Because of their intrinsic interest and the lack of viable alternatives, occupations have been widely used in studies ranging from conventional social histories to quantitative historical sociological and economic analyses. In modern society, occupation is the principal means by which most persons attain their economic and social status, and it is among the most potent determinants of the opportunities available to one's descendants.

As a multifaceted phenomenon suggestive of so many dimensions of social experience, there is no consensus among scholars concerning how best to employ occupations in historical research. Broadly speaking, there are two main approaches. One strategy is to group occupations into what are typically referred to as classes or strata. Such groupings frequently correspond to the familiar typology of upper, middle, and lower or working classes. Alternatively, classes are often defined to accentuate the manual–nonmanual divide, using groupings oriented to upper and lower, white and blue collars. Fewer studies apply a strict Marxist categorization of working class and capitalists. Most research by historians has tended to use one of these variants of the grouping or typology approach to occupational structure (see Thernstrom 1964, 1973).[3]

Rather than combining occupations into broad groupings, a second approach used by many quantitatively oriented researchers assigns a numerical score to each occupation. This method organizes occupations into a continuous hierarchy amenable to measurement and straightforward statistical analysis. These occupational measures are of three varieties. One type assigns occupational scores based on subjective determinations of prestige or social standing derived from modern surveys (Treiman 1976). A second measure gives each occupation a socioeconomic score purporting to reflect both income and social prestige (Duncan 1961). This is the favored approach of historical sociological research using occupations, and there is a supporting literature to validate its application at least several decades into the past (Hodge, Siegel, and Rossi 1964; Hauser 1982). The final approach is to ascribe economic status based on the average incomes of persons within occupations. This income-scoring method has been most often employed by economic historians lacking individual-level income data (Goldin 1986; Preston and Haines 1991). The income scores are usually not the focus of the analysis but are used to control for economic status while examining some other behavior or outcome. In addition to their use for inferring current income, occupations can also be interpreted as predictors of lifetime earnings because they suggest a person's career and work-life trajectory.

Most research focusing on occupations derives its theoretical grounding from sociological theory, to the extent that authors acknowledge such intellectual underpinnings. Marxist analyses aim to situate persons in terms of their relationship to the means of production. Weberian studies are more common and are content to define classes in terms of economic or social status. Many researchers in this tradition use the terminology of strata and stratification, rather than class. The connection of individual occupational standing to the class position of family members is a contentious issue in theorizing about occupations, and the interpretation of housewifery is a particularly thorny problem.[4]

Quantitative studies in which occupations are the actual focus of analysis tend to be explicitly or implicitly about inequality. Scholars can compare the attainment of population subgroups over time or to one another using either occupational scores or groupings. Such analyses typically aim to explore discrimination or social mobility. Mobility at the individual level, however, requires longitudinal data that follow persons over time or between generations (Blau and Duncan 1967; Featherman and Hauser 1978). Such data are rare, and the results depend a great deal on where the researcher draws boundaries between occupational groups in order to define upward and downward mobility. A final category of research aims to measure occupational segregation – usually along lines of race, sex, or ethnicity – through the use of an index of dissimilarity (Reskin and Hartmann 1986). Such indexes indicate the proportion of one group that would have to change occupations to replicate the distribution of the other (see Table Ba4207–4213). As with studies of social mobility, the results are sensitive to the number of occupational categories used in the analysis; thus, it is hard to make direct comparisons across studies by different researchers.

---

[2] On the potential bias with respect to married women's participation, see Abel and Folbre (1990). The effect of gainful employment as a measure of married women's participation is not straightforward and varies by occupation; see Goldin (1990), appendix to Chapter 2.

[3] On the application of Marxist class categories to occupation data, see Sobek (1991) and Wright (1980, 1985).

[4] Most research applies the husband's or primary breadwinner's status to all family members. See Acker (1973, 1980).

Availability of Historical Occupation Data

Occupation data are available in scattered sources as early as the colonial period, but national-level statistics depend on the U.S. Census, which first collected this information in 1850. Women were not asked the occupation question until the following census in 1860, and slaves were never asked, resulting in a lack of occupation data for most blacks until 1870.[5] These early qualifications aside, the census provides a continuous series of national occupation data for each decade from 1850 to the present.

The published census occupation statistics have three significant liabilities. The first problem is the lack of data for subgroups of the population. The Census Bureau has always been limited in what it could afford to tabulate and publish, and most censuses report separate statistics only for men and women. The second difficulty is the changing age limit of the persons to whom the occupation question was addressed. The minimum age for occupation responses began with age 15 in the mid-nineteenth century, dropped to age 10, and then rose in the twentieth century first to age 14 and finally to age 16. Occupations such as domestic servant and unpaid farm laborer are especially sensitive to such changes. The final problem with the published statistics concerns the differing classification systems employed from one census to the next. Each census used a different scheme, and at several points – the Censuses of 1870, 1910, 1940, and 1980 – there was a complete overhaul of the system, confounding long-term comparisons.

These limitations of the published census statistics can largely be overcome using the Integrated Public Use Microdata Series (IPUMS).[6] The IPUMS is a machine-readable database consisting of thirteen large random national samples drawn from the decennial U.S. Census from 1850 to 1990. All censuses over this period are included except for 1890, which was destroyed by fire, and 1930, which is not yet available to researchers. (The 2000 sample was not released in time to be included in this volume.) Containing more than 50 million person records, the IPUMS is large enough to provide detailed occupation statistics for subgroups of the population that were never tabulated by the historical censuses. Because all data are individual level, the population subject to the occupation statistics can be defined consistently across all census years.

The occupation statistics reported in this chapter are derived from the IPUMS database. The general method employed is described in Sobek (2001). The original published census statistics are not reported in this volume because they do not constitute a coherent statistical series. The greatest attribute of the IPUMS for the purposes of *Historical Statistics of the United States* is the common categorization of occupations for all census years into a single classification system (Sobek 1995). Occupation responses for all years are coded into the 1950 Census scheme, which presents occupations in a hierarchical arrangement of 268 categories, from professional workers through unskilled laborers, with a clear demarcation between manual and nonmanual work. The major occupational groupings in this classification are consistent with the scholarly understanding of occupational structure as reflected in the majority of historical and sociological research (Sobek 1996).

Of the occupation series in this chapter, only Tables Ba3688–4206 are not constructed using the IPUMS database, which represents the best available attempt at reconciling the differing published census occupation series from 1900 to 1970. Categories are collapsed together in some years, the data are acknowledged to be only approximate, and the basis for some of the decisions allocating the data among categories is unclear (U.S. Bureau of the Census 1975). Nevertheless, the extra detail offered and the lineage of the table warrant its inclusion.

Limitations of Historical Occupation Data

Despite the advantages conferred by the IPUMS for the purpose of creating consistent occupational series, researchers should be cognizant of a number of limitations affecting the use and interpretation of these data. One set of difficulties results from the quality of the occupation responses elicited from census interviewees as recorded on the manuscript returns. Some of the occupations written on the nineteenth-century census manuscripts are more industrial in character than occupational. Many persons responded with their place of employment (for example, grocery or steel mill), rather than giving their occupation within the establishment. The quality of the occupation data improved as the instructions to the census enumerators evolved in both clarity and precision, but this particular difficulty persisted to some degree until the introduction of separate industry and class-of-worker questions in the Census of 1910. The single greatest effect of this confusion of occupation and industry is to cast doubt on nineteenth-century statistics for managers and proprietors, since their status often had to be interpreted by application of simple rules (Sobek and Dillon 1995).

Another issue, alluded to previously, concerns changes over time in the wording of the occupation question. The census instructions steadily lengthened from one census to the next as the Bureau attempted to rectify perceived deficiencies in the enumeration. The relative smoothness of the data series suggests that most of these instruction changes had only a limited effect, for good or ill. Nevertheless, it is clear that the data generally improved over time, especially in the nineteenth century. Two overlapping groups, married women and unpaid family workers, received particular attention in the evolution of the occupation instructions. Data for these groups can be considered among the most problematic, particularly before the introduction of explicit labor force criteria in 1940. Paid domestic servants and farm laborers were sometimes counted as unpaid family workers or assigned to the nonoccupational labor category "keeping house." The occupation counts for women reported in this volume almost surely understate the number of employed married women before 1940 (Conk 1981; Folbre and Abel 1989; Goldin 1990).

The Census of 1910 is particularly anomalous. The enumerator instructions for 1910 contained strong language about the importance of recording occupations for women, even if they worked only occasionally and without pay in a family enterprise. The instructions produced much higher female occupational response rates in 1910, especially for married women on farms. The Census Bureau published but disavowed these results, and it altered the instructions in 1920 to yield response rates more in line with the previous historical trend. Scholars have long debated the proper interpretation of these 1910 occupation responses (Smuts 1960; Lebergott 1964; Oppenheimer 1970). No attempt has been made to alter the 1910 data for *Historical Statistics,* and so

[5] However, for what is known about the occupation of slaves, see Gutman and Sutch (1976).

[6] See the Guide to the Millennial Edition for information on the IPUMS.

researchers can draw their own conclusions from the unadulterated responses.[7]

Another perhaps more subtle difficulty with historical occupation data concerns the unavoidable costs associated with classification of any kind, regardless of the quality of the underlying data. The 1991 *Dictionary of Occupational Titles* contains more than 28,000 distinct occupations (U.S. Department of Labor 1991). No usable classification can accommodate such fine categorization. Even the detailed occupational schemes used by the various censuses never contained more than a few hundred categories. Therefore, virtually all detailed occupational categories are combinations of many distinct, though related, occupations (see Tables Ba1159–1439). The residual occupations at the end of each major occupational grouping (for example, operatives, not elsewhere classified) are especially heterogeneous and are sometimes very large. Conversely, one of the most important occupations for historical purposes – farmer – is unambiguous and consistent but includes persons of such differing means and life situations that it is of questionable value for making many kinds of inferences. In sum, the reliability of the data depends on the use to which they are put. If it is sufficient for a researcher's purposes to locate persons accurately within large occupational groupings, then the data are almost always sufficient; however, care must be taken when making finer distinctions.

The application of a consistent classification scheme to occupations spanning more than a century necessarily imposes some costs. Some difficulties are the result of changing terminology, such as the evolution of "engineers" from locomotive and stationary-engine tenders to white-collar professionals. "Clerks," "cashiers," and "secretaries" are likewise occupational terms that have persisted but whose meanings altered considerably over time. Because of technological change, nineteenth-century teamsters performed the same role as truck drivers in the twentieth century, although the more archaic occupational designation still persists in the 1950 classification. In the construction of the IPUMS database, the designers attempted to combine functionally equivalent occupations in a manner sensitive to such changes (Sobek 1995). The 1950 classification scheme can accommodate most changes in occupations over time, but in periods of transition in which multiple meanings of a term may have been in use, there is undoubtedly some blurring and slippage between categories. Researchers wishing to use occupations to infer economic status or class position must be especially sensitive to changes in the relative standing of specific occupations that may not be reflected in their static placement within the 1950 scheme (Sobek 1996).

A final consideration concerns the use of sample data to determine occupations for the population as a whole. The IPUMS database contains 1 percent samples of the population for most censuses before 1970 (up to 9 percent more recently). For smaller detailed occupations, the counts from such data may be subject to sampling error, especially when the data pertain to only a small subgroup of the whole population, such as nonwhite female workers.

Occupational Trends

The American occupational structure has changed markedly since 1850, with momentous consequences for the great majority of persons who earned their livelihoods through their position within this structure. The economy and occupational structure were dominated by agriculture in the mid-nineteenth century. From approximately half of the workforce in 1870, agriculture continued to engage a third of the nation's workers at the turn of the century (Table Ba1033–1046). The black population was especially concentrated in farming because of slavery and residence in the rural South. In the late nineteenth century, young single women in the labor force tended to work in domestic service and in semiskilled manufacturing jobs, such as seamstress. Most women withdrew from the labor force on marriage and did not return. Teaching was the only occupation of any size open to women that required much education. The large proportion of women in the "professional" occupational grouping in the nineteenth century is attributable solely to teaching – one of the poorest paid occupations at that end of the status hierarchy (Tables Ba1061–1074 and Ba1721–2001).

As the nation industrialized, farming declined in relative importance, although in absolute terms, the agricultural labor force continued to expand throughout the early twentieth century. The declining share of agriculture as a segment of the occupational structure was not counterbalanced by the growth of any one occupational grouping. The occupations most directly associated with the industrial economy – manufacturing jobs in the crafts and operatives grouping – grew in absolute and relative terms. The combined crafts and operative occupations grew more than 40 percent in the first decade of the twentieth century, and would peak at just over one third of the total workforce in 1950. What is evident from an examination of the original manuscripts is the increasing division of labor within manufacturing, as growing numbers of semiskilled operatives performed ever-more-specialized tasks as their contribution to the production process.

The most significant long-term change in the occupational structure was the growing share composed of nonmanual occupations – especially clerical and sales work, sometimes referred to as lower white collar. Figure Ba-G shows the growth of white-collar

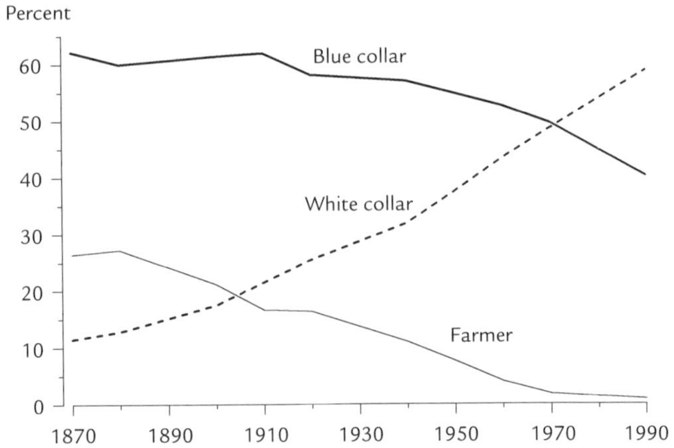

FIGURE Ba-G Occupational distribution – blue collar, white collar, and farmer as a percentage of the labor force: 1870–1990

Sources

Computed from the following: white collar, series Ba1034 and Ba1036–1039; farmer, series Ba1035; and blue collar, series Ba1040–1045. Percentages are based on the following denominator: series Ba1033 minus series Ba1046.

Documentation

The percentages graphed here sum to 100 percent.

[7] See Tables Ba1075–1088 and Ba1103–1130, and the labor force figures in Tables Ba340–354 and Ba425–469.

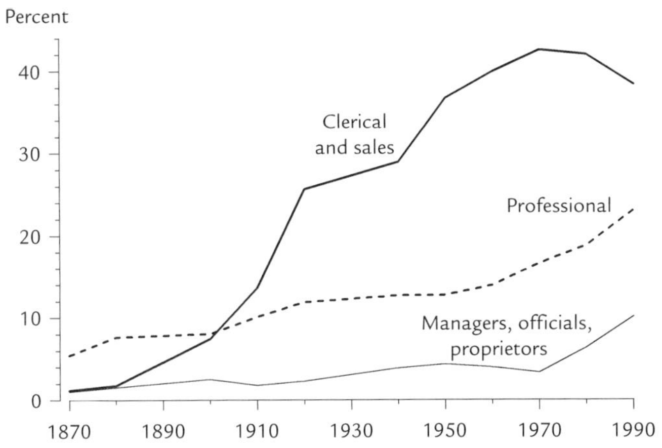

FIGURE Ba-H Women's white-collar employment as a percentage of the female labor force: 1870–1990

Sources

Computed from the following: professional, series Ba1062; managers, officials, and proprietors, series Ba1064–1065; and clerical and sales, series Ba1066–1067. Percentages are based on the following denominator: series Ba1061 minus series Ba1074.

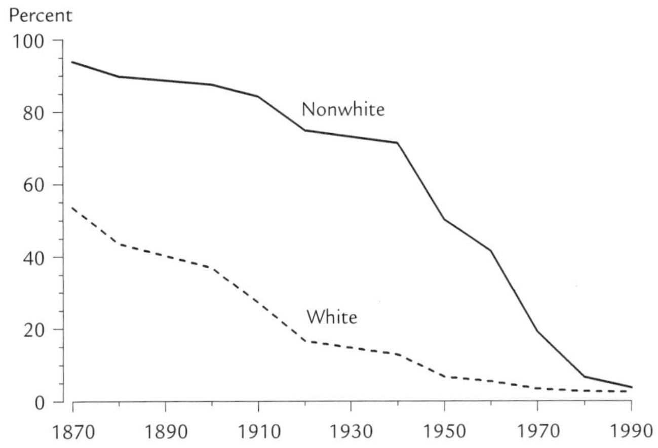

FIGURE Ba-I Women servants and laborers as a percentage of the female labor force, by race: 1870–1990

Sources

Computed from the following: white, series Ba1112 and Ba1114–1115; and nonwhite, series Ba1126 and Ba1128–1129. Percentages are based on the following denominators: white, series Ba1103 minus series Ba1116; and nonwhite, series Ba1117 minus series Ba1130.

employment among all workers. The steady shift out of manual work reflected the increasing importance of formal education in the labor market. The transition away from manual labor was particularly salient for women, who began entering clerical and sales work in large numbers around the turn of the century. Figure Ba-H shows the expansion of sales and clerical work and other white-collar employment among women. From less than 2 percent of the female workforce in 1880, clerical and sales workers accounted for over 25 percent of women workers by 1920. Improved transportation and communications spurred an expansion in firm size and corresponding demand for office labor. New office practices and technology – particularly the typewriter – reduced the specialized skills needed for such work so that more of the school-trained population became qualified for employment (Rotella 1977; Davies 1982). Sales and office work was less stigmatized than manual labor, and its growth would eventually help open the doors to greater participation by married women as the twentieth century progressed. The new and expanding occupations were urban in character and further spurred migration to the cities. By 1920, the majority of Americans lived in urban places.

Urbanization affected blacks most of all. Beginning during World War I, the "Great Migration" brought ever-increasing numbers of blacks northward to the urban centers of the Northeast and Midwest. The migrants were initially concentrated in unskilled occupations, with black women steadily taking over domestic service as white women moved on to more attractive and rewarding types of labor opened by educational qualifications (Table Ba1117–1130). The historical concentration of black women in the lower end of the occupational spectrum is evident in Figure Ba-I. Black men and women remained substantially occupationally segregated from their white counterparts until significant improvements stemming from the Civil Rights era and antidiscrimination laws in the late twentieth century opened previously closed doors (Table Ba4207–4213).

Until World War I and subsequent immigration laws largely cut the flow, immigrants made up as much as a quarter of the U.S. workforce. Immigrants were always predominantly urban, and they tended to enter nonagricultural manual occupations (Table Ba1145–1158). Farmers constituted 23.2 percent of native-born workers in 1900, but only 13.6 percent of employed immigrants. Although overrepresented in unskilled work, immigrant men were also skilled craft workers in percentages similar to those of native-born men. They were not generally subject to the levels of segregation faced by blacks of both sexes. Befitting their urban setting and backgrounds, immigrant men were actually more likely to be nonfarm proprietors than were the native-born. Of course, many immigrants were small proprietors, and the data on proprietorship before 1910 should be interpreted cautiously because of the ambiguity of many occupation responses.

The period since World War II witnessed the evolution to what has been characterized as a postindustrial or service economy, and this is certainly evident in the occupation statistics for the last few decades. Although the service-workers group proper has grown, the most noteworthy development in the occupational structure has been the rapid growth of professionals, managers, and officials – from 12 percent of the workforce in 1940 to 23 percent in 1990 (Table Ba1033–1046). This expansion among the most highly rewarded occupations reflects rising skill and educational levels in the workforce. At the same time, the demand for skilled labor has spurred a steady increase in college attendance. So striking has been the growth of the upper end of the occupational spectrum that some theorize the rise of a distinct new professional–managerial class. Perhaps most significantly, all major identifiable population subgroups have shared in the improved opportunities offered by the changing occupational structure, whether the measure is occupational segregation or socioeconomic status. And underlying the changing occupational distribution has been the rapid increase of married female participation in the workforce, with all the attendant ramifications for families, politics, and society (see Table Ba425–469).

Over the last century and a half, the economy has generated an ever-improving occupational structure in terms of status and material rewards. The entire structure has been shifted upward in terms of occupational desirability toward higher-skilled white-collar work. Clearly, inequality persists, and occupation statistics do not capture differences within occupations in the earnings of persons caused by discrimination or varying work experience. And there is no guarantee that past improvements will not plateau or reverse themselves. However, the evidence suggests that the economy has done well by the majority of Americans since the nineteenth century in terms of steadily improving and more equal occupational opportunity.

References

Abel, Marjorie, and Nancy Folbre. 1990. "A Methodology for Revising Estimates: Female Market Participation in the U.S. before 1940." *Historical Methods* 23: 167–76.

Acker, Joan. 1973. "Women and Social Stratification: A Case of Intellectual Sexism." *American Journal of Sociology* 78: 174–83.

Acker, Joan. 1980. "Women and Stratification: A Review of Recent Literature." *Contemporary Sociology* 9: 25–39.

Blau, Peter, and Otis D. Duncan. 1967. *The American Occupational Structure*. Free Press.

Conk, Margo. 1978. *The United States Census and Labor Force Change: A History of Occupation Statistics, 1870–1940*. UMI Research Press.

Conk, Margo. 1981. "Accuracy, Efficiency, and Bias: The Interpretation of Women's Work in the U.S. Census of Occupations, 1890–1940." *Historical Methods* 14: 65–72.

Davies, Margery W. 1982. *Woman's Place Is at the Typewriter: Office Work and Office Workers, 1870–1930*. Temple University Press.

Duncan, Otis D. 1961. "A Socioeconomic Index for All Occupations." In Albert Reiss Jr., editor. *Occupations and Social Status*. Free Press.

Featherman, David, and Robert Hauser. 1978. *Opportunity and Change*. Academic Press.

Folbre, Nancy. 1991. "The Unproductive Housewife: Her Evolution in Nineteenth-Century Economic Thought." *Signs* 16: 463–84.

Folbre, Nancy, and Marjorie Abel. 1989. "Women's Work and Women's Households: Gender Bias in the U.S. Census." *Social Research* 56: 545–70.

Goldin, Claudia. 1986. "The Female Labor Force and American Economic Growth, 1890–1980." In Stanley Engerman and Robert Gallman, editors. *Long-Term Factors in American Economic Growth*. University of Chicago Press.

Goldin, Claudia. 1990. *Understanding the Gender Gap: An Economic History of American Women*. Oxford University Press.

Gutman, Herbert, and Richard Sutch. 1976. "Sambo Makes Good, or Were Slaves Imbued with the Protestant Work Ethic?" In Paul A. David, Herbert G. Gutman, et al., editors. *Reckoning with Slavery: A Critical Study in the Quantitative History of American Negro Slavery*. Oxford University Press.

Hauser, Robert. 1982. "Occupational Status in the Nineteenth and Twentieth Centuries." *Historical Methods* 15: 111–26.

Hodge, Robert, Paul Siegel, and Peter Rossi. 1964. "Occupational Prestige in the United States, 1925–1963." *American Journal of Sociology* 70: 286–302.

Lebergott, Stanley. 1964. *Manpower in Economic Growth: The American Record since 1800*. McGraw-Hill.

Oppenheimer, Valerie Kincade. 1970. *The Female Labor Force in the United States: Demographic and Economic Factors Governing Its Growth and Changing Composition*. University of California Press.

Preston, Samuel, and Michael Haines. 1991. *Fatal Years: Child Mortality in Late Nineteenth-Century America*. Princeton University Press.

Ransom, Roger L., and Richard Sutch. 1986. "The Labor of Older Americans: Retirement of Men on and off the Job, 1870–1937." *Journal of Economic History* 46 (March): 1–30.

Reskin, Barbara, and Heidi Hartmann, editors. 1986. *Women's Work, Men's Work: Sex Segregation on the Job*. National Academy Press.

Rotella, Elyce J. 1977. *From Home to Office: U.S. Women at Work, 1870–1930*. UMI Research Press.

Smuts, Robert W. 1960. "The Female Labor Force: A Case Study in the Interpretation of Historical Statistics." *Journal of the American Statistical Association* 55: 71–9.

Sobek, Matthew. 1991. "Class Analysis and the U.S. Census Public Use Samples." *Historical Methods* 24: 171–81.

Sobek, Matthew. 1995. "The Comparability of Occupations and the Generation of Income Scores." *Historical Methods* 28: 47–51.

Sobek, Matthew. 1996. "Work, Status, and Income: Men in the American Occupational Structure since the Late Nineteenth Century." *Social Science History* 20: 169–207.

Sobek, Matthew. 2001. "New Statistics on the U.S. Labor Force, 1850–1990." *Historical Methods* 34: 71–87.

Sobek, Matthew, and Lisa Dillon. 1995. "Interpreting Work: Classifying Occupations in the Public Use Microdata Samples." *Historical Methods* 28: 70–3.

Thernstrom, Stephan. 1964. *Poverty and Progress: Social Mobility in a Nineteenth Century City*. Harvard University Press.

Thernstrom, Stephan. 1973. *The Other Bostonians: Poverty and Progress in the American Metropolis, 1880–1970*. Harvard University Press.

Treiman, Donald. 1976. "A Standard Occupational Prestige Scale for Use with Historical Data." *Journal of Interdisciplinary History* 7: 283–304.

U.S. Bureau of the Census. 1975. *Historical Statistics of the United States: Colonial Times to 1970*. U.S. Government Printing Office.

U.S. Department of Labor. 1991. *Dictionary of Occupational Titles*. 4th edition, revised. U.S. Government Printing Office.

U.S. Office of the Census. 1872. *Ninth Census of the United States, 1870*, volume 1, *Population*. U.S. Government Printing Office.

Wright, Erik O. 1980. "Class and Occupation." *Theory and Society* 9: 77–214.

Wright, Erik O. 1985. *Classes*. Verso.

WAGES AND WAGE INEQUALITY

Robert A. Margo

The price of labor – its "wage" – is a fundamental datum in economics and economic history. The most important by-product of economic growth is a rising standard of living, and the wage, relative to the prices of consumer goods – the "real" wage – is a summary statistic of progress: a high and rising value of wages relative to consumer prices is a sign of a high and rising standard of living. The reverse is equally true. The low wages relative to the price of consumer goods that have been paid throughout much of human history and to many of the world's workers even today is the very definition of poverty. Differences in wages – across occupations, industries, and locations, by educational level, between men and women, and so forth – can reveal much about the workings of an economy. For example, large differences in wages between different regions may be a sign of a poorly functioning labor market – too much labor in the region with relatively low wages and too little where wages are relatively high. However, just as a high rate of profit may induce firms to enter an industry, or a high return to capital (the interest rate) may spur investment, regional differentials may induce migration from the low- to the high-wage region, raising wages in the former and lowering wages in the latter, "integrating" the two regions into a single, common (and national) labor market. Changes in technology may alter the demand for one type of labor (for example, college graduates) versus another (for example, high school graduates), thereby affecting the ratio of wages of the two groups. If the effects are persistent, the relative supplies of the two types of labor may change – more college graduates if the "returns to education" have increased, or conversely, if they have fallen.

In an economy with competitive labor markets, the level of wages (and employment) is ultimately determined by the equilibration of the demand for, and supply of, labor. However, government may intervene, if it thinks that the price of labor is too low, by setting a minimum wage, or it may try to prevent wages from rising too high – for example, during war time – by imposing a maximum price or by regulating the pace at which wages increase.[1] Higher wages have always been an important goal of organized labor, and the success of unions in establishing a wage premium for their membership has waxed and waned throughout American history. Prejudice or social norms may influence the pattern of wages: wage "discrimination" is present whenever workers who are the same in terms of underlying productivity are paid differently because of their race, gender, or ethnic background.

This essay is a companion to the data series on wages and wage inequality. As such, it concentrates primarily on money or "nominal" wages – wages expressed in current, rather than "constant," dollars. One of the major uses of long-term series in nominal wages is that, with appropriate manipulation, they can be converted into real wages, which are indicators of the long-term change in the standard of living. The conversion of nominal to real wages is a subject in its own right and requires information on consumer and producer prices (for a discussion of the issues involved see the essay on prices and price indexes in Chapter Cc).

Measurement Issues

Wages are a payment for a flow of "labor services" – that is, they are the price that someone pays to the worker for "renting" the use of the worker's skills and energy for some period of time. Thus, wages are stated in terms of some unit of time, such as dollars per hour, day, week, month, or year. The method of quoting wages may not correspond to the time dimension of wage payment schemes. Thus, many workers paid on an hourly basis nonetheless have "steady" jobs. In the twentieth century, many wages are quoted on a "per hour" basis – for example, the hourly wages in manufacturing. In the nineteenth century (and earlier), the wage was often quoted "per day" or "per month." Conversion of series based on one time period to those based on another requires contemporaneous information on the number of hours worked per day, or days per month, and so forth.

For some types of economic analyses it may be important to distinguish between income from wages and salaries and income from self-employment. The census definition of individual and household "earnings" is the sum of wage and salary income plus income from self-employment.[2] Since 1950, one can distinguish between these two forms of income because the Census Bureau asked separate questions about these two types of income. It is important to note that in historical series, the distinction between wage and salary and self-employment income is rarely made. Thus, "wages" and "earnings" are often used interchangeably.

A time series of wages refers to annual values (or some other frequency, such as monthly or quarterly) of a measure of central tendency, such as the median, mode, midpoint of a range, or average. In interpreting wage series it is important to pay close attention to what the "average" (or median, etc.) really means. The "average hourly wage" may not be the literal average of rates of pay per hour across individuals but, instead, computed as total payments to labor divided by total hours worked, even if the workers in question were not hired by the hour.[3]

Throughout American history, some portion (or, on occasion, all) of wages were paid "in kind" – that is, in addition to (or in lieu of) monetary payments. That is, workers received part or all of their payments in goods or services. In-kind compensation in the form of goods may be literally that – as, for example, when farm labor in the nineteenth century received board (food), or when employees of large corporations in the late twentieth century received employer-paid health insurance or stock options. In addition, in-kind compensation may be in the form of characteristics of the work environment that workers generally value, for example, a cleaner facility, a better office, more vacation time, or a less stressful work pace. Alternatively, if the work environment were dangerous, workers might need a higher money wage to compensate for the increased personal risk. In such cases, economists speak of "compensating differentials" – to a first approximation, the difference in money wages between two jobs, one of which includes payment in-kind and the other does not, must equal the value of the in-kind payments. Thus, for example, the difference in monthly pay of farm labor with and without board should equal (approximately) the monthly cost of board. Unfortunately, there is little consistency across wage series in adjustments for in-kind compensation, typically because information on such compensation is often poor or lacking.

In principle, then, wage series are price series. Like all such series, wage changes over time reflect true changes in the level of prices combined with changes in the underlying "quality" of the good whose price is being measured, in this case, labor. Thus, time series of annual wages may fluctuate because the hourly wage rate changes or because annual hours worked changes. If one's interest is in understanding what has happened to the price of labor over time, then it is desirable to standardize as much as possible for the quality of the labor supply. Thus, for example, Table Ba4512–4520 reports earnings for full-time, year-round workers so as to remove from the series changes in earnings that derive from changes in the share of the labor force that works part-time. Over time, the average American worker has become healthier and much better educated. Most economists believe that such improvements in "human capital" are reflected in higher labor force "quality" and, therefore, in higher wages. Although it is possible to control for changes over time in labor force quality using the so-called hedonic price method, few historical wage series, in fact, are so adjusted.[4]

A related issue in interpreting longtime series of wages concerns the fact that, by definition, wage (or earnings) series pertain solely to persons in the labor force. Over time, however, there have been significant changes in labor force participation of various population groups. A well-known example concerns married women. Few married women worked outside the home in the early

[1] For data on the minimum wage, see Table Ba4422–4425.

[2] In modern data series, wage and salary income is pre–income tax, whereas self-employment income is net of business expenses, including business taxes.

[3] When series are computed by dividing total payments to labor by total time worked (for example, total hours) the convention (not always followed) is to refer to them as earnings (for example, see Table Ba4361–4366), rather than wages.

[4] The hedonic price method uses linear regression to control for worker (or other) characteristics; holding constant (via the regression) these characteristics, changes in the level of prices over time measure true change in prices. An example of an historical wage series constructed using the hedonic method is Table Ba4253–4267.

twentieth century; today, most do. As the labor force participation rate of married women increased, the characteristics of the typical female worker changed, affecting her wage relative to other groups, in particular, adult men (Goldin 1990).[5]

To convert a nominal into a real wage series, it is necessary first to convert the nominal series into index number form – that is, choose a base year (for example, 1900) or average for several years, and "deflate" (divide) the values in each year of the nominal series by the value in the base period, and then multiply by 100 – and then divide by an index of prices.[6] Because prices frequently have (and continue) to differ across locations, it is highly desirable that the price deflator and nominal wage series refer to the same geographic area, although this is not always feasible. From the standpoint of the economic welfare of workers, the appropriate price deflator is an index of consumer prices – the "cost of living." If the price deflator is an index of producer prices, the resulting real wage series is sometimes referred to as a "real labor cost" series. This is also a useful series because, under the assumption of a competitive labor market and profit maximization by employers, it traces out the "marginal product" of labor.[7]

"Wage inequality" refers to the extent of differences in wages across some unit of comparison – for example, individuals, firms, or locations. One of the most common ways to measure wage inequality is to examine differences in average wages – or more commonly, the ratio – between various population or labor market groups. When these groups are identified according to characteristics such as educational attainment, years of labor market experience, or occupation, the wage inequality measures are called "skill differentials." A high or rising value of the skill differential indicates a high or rising level of wage inequality; a low or falling value indicates wage equality or movement toward greater wage equality. A practical advantage of using skill differentials to measure inequality is that data on wages by occupations can be found for the United States for long periods of time. Occupational skill differentials can be constructed from some of the wage series presented in this chapter. For example, a national series of skill differentials for artisans relative to common laborers for the period 1825–1860 can be constructed by dividing series Ba4258 by series Ba4253. The level and trend of this skill differential so calculated are displayed in Figure Ba-J. It reveals an initial skill differential that is high, relative to the most comparable economy of the time – Britain. It also reveals a decline over time, suggesting that during the period of America's early industrialization, the real wages of artisans did not keep pace with the wages of common laborers. These data are consistent with the view of many labor historians who argue that the growth of the factory system of manufacturing

FIGURE Ba-J Occupational skill differential – ratio of wages for artisans to wages for common labor: 1825–1860

Sources

Series Ba4258 divided by series Ba4253.

led to a relative decline in the demand for artisan skills (see Margo 2000b, p. 156).[8]

Using the same technique, one can also calculate the degree of inequality between two or more labor market groups. Several series of female-to-male wage ratios may be found in Table Ba4224–4233. Additional measures of "gender differentials" can be readily constructed from data in Table Ba4512–4520. Wage ratios by race are shown in Table Ba4431–4439 or can be constructed, again, from data in Table Ba4512–4520.

One drawback to using skill, gender, or racial differentials to measure wage inequality is that overall wage inequality consists of two components: between-group inequality and within-group inequality. Wage differentials measure the between-group component of inequality. It is perfectly possible for between-group and within-group inequality to be moving in opposite directions. The behavior of wages in the 1970s offers an example: the ratio of wages of college graduates to high school graduates declined, but wage inequality within education groups rose. Caution should be exercised before drawing strong conclusions about changes in overall wage inequality from time series of wage differentials.

An alternative to wage differentials as measures of wage inequality is the so-called range statistic. A range statistic measures the differences between wages at two separate points in the wage distribution – for example, at the ninetieth and tenth percentiles. Before the range statistic is calculated, the data are usually converted to logarithms because otherwise, the size of the range will depend on the units of measurement. This statistic is called the "90–10" wage differential.

Estimation of range statistics requires enough information to identify exact points in the distribution of wages (for example, the wage at the tenth percentile). This means that economywide estimates of range statistics are difficult to produce prior to the 1940 Census, which was the first federal census to contain individual wage information for the entire labor force. The 90–10 wage differential calculated for the period beginning with the 1940 Census data are shown in Table Ba4426–4430. The 90–10 differential for men is displayed in Figure Ba-K. It reveals the sharp decline in wage inequality during the 1940s that Goldin and Margo (1992) have called "The Great Compression."

---

[5] Black men are another example. The earnings of black men relative to those of white men have been increasing since 1940 for full-time workers (see Tables Ba4431–4439 and Ba4512–4520). But, the black–white ratio has increased much less for the entire population because the labor force participation rate of black men has fallen over the same period, primarily among men whose wages would be low if they were in the labor force; see Donohue and Heckman (1991).

[6] Alternatively, a series may be presented in "constant dollars," meaning that current-dollar amounts are divided by the price index, with the base year set equal to unity. If the price index is known, it is straightforward to go back and forth between constant- and current-dollar amounts (for example, see Table Ba4512–4520).

[7] The marginal product of labor is $\Delta Q/\Delta L$, the change in output for a small change in the labor input.

[8] For an alternative view of the trend in the skill differential during early industrialization, see Williamson and Lindert (1980).

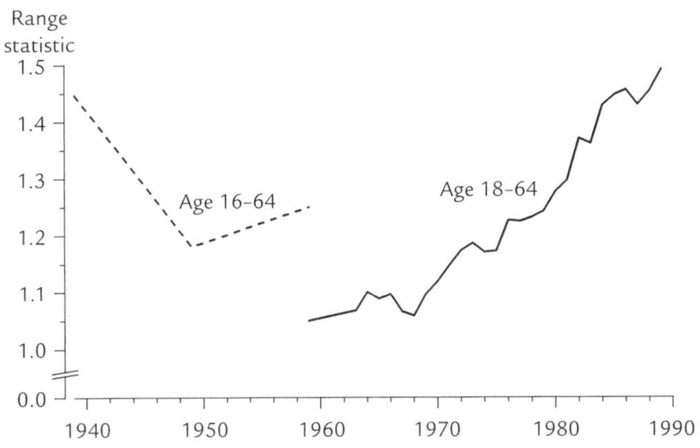

FIGURE Ba-K Wage inequality – the 90–10 wage differential in the male wage distribution: 1939–1989

Sources

Series Ba4426–4427.

Documentation

The range statistic shown here is the logarithm of the wage at the ninetieth percentile in the male wage distribution, minus the logarithm of the wage at the tenth percentile.

The range statistic is one of a large array of measures developed by economists and statisticians that attempt to summarize the extent of wage inequality. By far the most common such measure in general use is the standard deviation or the variance of the logarithm of wages. See series Ba4428–4430 for the trend in overall wage inequality according to this measure.

The level and, in some cases, even the trend in wage inequality will vary according to the measure used. For more detailed discussions of measures and trends in wage inequality, see Levy and Murnane (1992) and Katz and Autor (1999).

Sources of Wage Evidence in American History

As with many economic statistics, information on wages has changed markedly in availability over the course of American history. Before the Civil War, collection of wage data by state or federal government agencies was spotty, and most scholars have turned to archival sources to fill the void.

A variety of archival sources provide information on wages before 1860. Account books are very useful for extracting information on prices, in general, and wages, in particular. Account books are records of economic transactions, typically prepared by entrepreneurs or businesses. Account books survive in some abundance, especially for farmers, and thus have been used to track changes in farm wages over time. Drawbacks of account books are the lack of coverage of certain geographic regions, where surviving books are scarce, and the difficulty of valuing payment in kind (as opposed to wages). Examples of series that use account books as all or part of the data source are shown in Tables Ba4214–4217 and Ba4219–4223.

Payroll records are a second archival source. Payroll records are similar to account books in the sense that they record economic transactions; they differ, however, in that they pertain solely to the hiring of labor. Possibly the most extensive body of payroll data for the pre–Civil War period comes from the records of the U.S. Army. Officers called quartermasters stationed at army posts frequently would hire civilians from the local area to perform various tasks – for example, maintenance of horses, or constructing or repairing buildings, which required the services of carpenters, painters, masons, and other skilled artisans. Comparisons of wages paid to civilian employees of the army with wages paid in the local area suggest that the army rarely, if ever, overpaid its workers. Instead, it seems to have typically paid the "going wage" in the local area for labor of a specific type. Copies of the payrolls were sent to Washington, D.C., where they were later deposited at the National Archives. Unlike other such data for the nineteenth century, these records cover a wide variety of occupations in virtually all parts of the country. The series in Tables Ba4253–4270 are based on this source.

A few economic surveys collecting wage information were conducted by the federal government before the Civil War. Various census studies and other surveys can be used to estimate the annual earnings of manufacturing workers (see Table Ba4244–4249) at various dates between 1820 and 1860, as well as other compilations; for example, the 1850 and 1860 federal Censuses of Social Statistics provide evidence on wages in select occupations. These data are used in the construction of Table Ba4234–4243.

Two of the most important government surveys of wages in the nineteenth century are the so-called Weeks and Aldrich reports, named after the individuals in charge of the surveys. The Weeks report was conducted as part of the 1880 Census, whereas the Aldrich report was conducted in the early 1890s as part of a congressional inquiry into the effects of tariffs. Both reports were based on (nonrandom) samples of the payroll records of manufacturing firms in business operation at the time of the surveys. Wage series constructed from these records are retrospective, in the (important) sense that the firms had to be in existence prior to either survey. Firms that failed before the surveys were conducted are not included. The absence of failed firms introduces a systematic bias (of unknown direction) in these data. In both surveys, wage information is available by firm (and, hence, industry) and occupation. The Weeks report failed to include information on the number of observations underlying the wage averages reported by firms. This means that large and small firms must be given the same weight in analyses that make use of the data. If small and large firms pursue different wage-setting patterns, the results of analyses making use of these data will be biased.

Both the Weeks and Aldrich reports have been used in whole or part in the construction of wage series for the postbellum period; see, for example, Tables Ba4280–4297. The Massachusetts data have been used less often; however, they do figure prominently in the construction of series Ba4218. Because of deficiencies of both temporal and geographic coverage, the Weeks and Aldrich data are not particularly useful for constructing wage series for the antebellum period, except to a limited extent in the 1850s (see Table Ba4271–4279, which is based on the Weeks data).

The decennial federal censuses are another periodic source of wage information. The census first began collecting data on wages in 1850 (for manufacturing, and for various occupations included in the Census of Social Statistics, noted previously) and has continued to do so to the present day. The frequency of data collection, however, changed in the twentieth century as various special censuses (for example, the Censuses of Agriculture) began to be taken at nondecennial intervals. For the post–World War II period, the major source of annual earnings information is the Current Population Survey (CPS). The CPS is used to measure both annual earnings by various labor market groups (for example, college graduates) and earnings inequality. See, for example, Table Ba4426–4430.

During the second half of the nineteenth century, the collection of wage data became more routine as federal agencies expanded their operations and as states established their own bureaus of labor and industrial statistics.[9] These state agencies conducted numerous surveys of both individual workers and firms, sometimes publishing the original data in their annual reports, usually without any analysis. Carroll Wright, the first Commissioner of Labor Statistics in Massachusetts, and later chief of the U.S. Census Bureau, was a pioneer in such surveys. One such survey, published in 1885, provides wage evidence similar to that of the Aldrich and Weeks reports, and it is used in the construction of series Ba4218.

The U.S. Bureau of Labor Statistics (BLS), established in the late nineteenth century, is charged with the regular collection of wage and related labor market information. Prior to the 1930s, this was accomplished through the use of periodic surveys and special studies; see, for example, Tables Ba4253–4267, Ba4280–4282, and Ba4320–4334. Beginning in 1932, the Bureau surveyed firms on a monthly basis as to their employment and payroll; in March 1993, there were approximately 390,000 reporting units in the survey. These data are a fundamental source of wage information for the twentieth-century United States, and they are used in the construction of Tables Ba4361–4380. The BLS also produces Area Wage Surveys, which provide evidence on average wages in detailed occupations for various metropolitan areas.

In conjunction with the construction of the national income and product accounts (NIPA), the U.S. Bureau of Economic Analysis (BEA) publishes annual estimates of the average yearly wage and salary income of full-time employees by industry, beginning in 1929; see Tables Ba4397–4418 and Ba4490–4511. These have been extended backward in time; see Tables Ba4280–4282 and Ba4335–4360. Wage and salary income, of course, is not the only form of labor income: total compensation includes payments by firms into social insurance programs (for example, Social Security), employer-provided group health insurance, and so forth. Estimates of these average annual "supplements," in total for all industries, and by type of supplement, are provided in Tables Ba4419–4421 and Ba4484–4489. In addition to the BLS and BEA, there is an enormous number of specialty surveys that provide information on wages for specific groups.

Key Trends

The majority of series provided here pertain to the "nominal" wage. It is possible to construct a "real" wage series – that is, nominal wages adjusted for change in the cost of living – by dividing nominal wages by an appropriate price index. Table Ba4218 displays a nominal wage series for unskilled laborers. A real wage series, shown in Figure Ba-L, can be calculated using a consumer price index (CPI) developed by Paul David and Peter Solar that covers two full centuries.[10]

It is immediately evident that over this very long period, real wages have increased substantially; indeed, the average annual rate

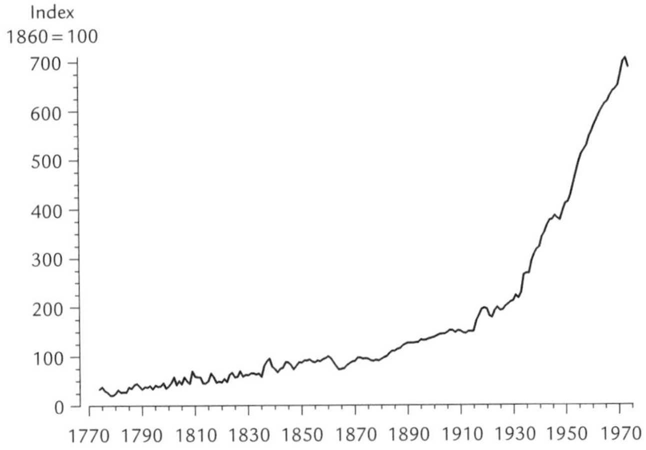

FIGURE Ba-L Index of real wages for unskilled labor: 1774–1974

Sources

Series Ba4218 divided by series Cc2, then multiplied by 100.

of growth of real wages is approximately 1.5 percent per annum.[11] A series growing at this rate will double in value every forty-six years, or approximately twice every three human generations. This particular series attempts to measure the price of "raw" (that is, unskilled) labor, and thus does not capture many improvements in labor force "quality" associated with higher wages. It is also evident from the values of both series underlying Figure Ba-L that the price level (the deflator) rose markedly over the two centuries, implying that growth in nominal wages not only kept up with growth in the price level but outpaced it.

Several other features of the graph are worthy of note. First, the growth rate of real wages accelerated: growth was slower during the nineteenth century than in the twentieth.[12] This acceleration in growth is also apparent in real per capita incomes and reflects fundamental shifts in the underlying sources of productivity growth over time. Second, it is apparent that year-to-year (or longer-term) variability in growth rates of real wages – volatility – was very considerable in the nineteenth century but was dampened in the twentieth century. This dampening in volatility is partly an artifact of improvements in the quality of the underlying data series, but it also reflects changes in labor market institutions that, to some extent, insulate wages from various real and nominal "shocks" – for example, wars or recessions.

The David-Solar data end shortly after the beginning of the so-called productivity slowdown, which began about 1973. A consequence of the slowdown in productivity growth was a marked slowdown in the rate of growth of real wages. The slowdown in real wage growth is clearly visible in Figure Ba-M. According to these data, the median annual earnings of men were lower in 1997 than in 1973 when adjusted for changes in the price level. Some of the stagnation may be more apparent than real if the conventional CPI

[9] For additional information on various nineteenth-century sources of wage statistics collected by the federal government, see Lebergott (1964).

[10] For additional real wage series covering the antebellum period, see Margo (2000b).

[11] Growth rates are estimated as the coefficient of a linear time trend in a regression of the log of the real wage index. A rate of 1.5 percent per annum is similar to the long-run growth rate of output per worker, and consistent with the view that, in the long run, labor is paid the value of its marginal product, as simple neoclassical models of the labor market predict.

[12] The (estimated) average annual growth rate from 1774 to 1900 is 1.2 percent per annum, compared with 2.5 percent per annum from 1900 to 1974.

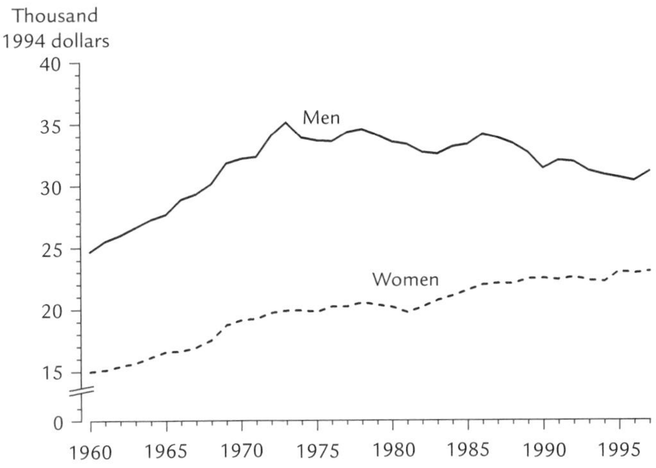

FIGURE Ba-M Median earnings of full-time workers, by sex: 1960–1997

Sources

Series Ba4512 and Ba4516.

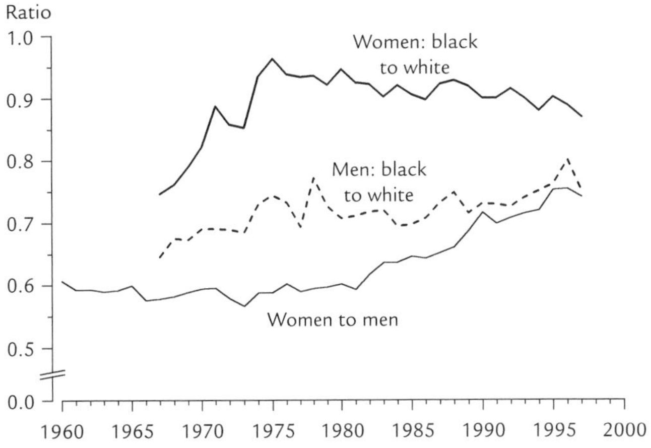

FIGURE Ba-N Earnings ratios for full-time workers, by sex and race: 1960–1997

Sources

Series Ba4512–4514 and Ba4516–4518.

used to adjust nominal wages overstates the true rate of inflation, as some observers charge. For a discussion of the accuracy of the CPI, see the essay on prices and price indexes in Chapter Cc.

Whether real wages on average have risen is not the only important question; it is equally important to determine if growth has favored one type of labor versus another – that is, whether there have been trends in wage inequality. Although much further work is needed, some basic features of the history of the American "wage structure" are evident. First, as shown previously in comparison with common labor, it appears that the wages of artisans were falling relative to those of other nonfarm occupations prior to the Civil War.[13] Second, it appears likely that the wages of skilled (or educated) labor were falling during the first part of the twentieth century, culminating in the so-called Great Compression of the 1940s (see Figure Ba-K) (Williamson and Lindert 1980; Goldin and Margo 1992.). Third, the United States has experienced a pronounced rise in wage inequality after 1970, which most economists attribute primarily to technological and other changes that have favored the demand for educated labor relative to other groups (Katz and Murphy 1992). The recent rise in wage inequality has taken place against the backdrop of little or no growth in the average real wage; thus, for some labor market groups (for example, high school dropouts) real wages were substantially lower at the end of the 1980s than in the early 1960s (Katz and Murphy 1992).

Other notable features of a changing wage structure include long-term increases in the earnings of men versus women, and African Americans relative to whites. Indeed, rather than being a constant, the series in Table Ba4224–4233 demonstrate that the wages of women relative to those of men have increased substantially over the past two centuries. Long-term increases in the relative earnings of African Americans are visible in Table Ba4431–4439, or by comparing changes over time in Table Ba4512–4520. For example, in 1967, the median African-American male worker earned 65 cents for every dollar earned by his white male counterpart when both worked full-time year-round; the corresponding figure for 1997 was 75 cents per dollar. The ratios of wages of women relative to men, African-American men relative to white men, and African-American women relative to white women calculated from Table Ba4512–4520 are plotted in Figure Ba-N. There is considerable debate among economists over the underlying sources for the rise in relative earnings of women and African Americans. Some stress the roles played by narrowing gender and racial differences in "human capital" (for example, the quantity and quality of schooling). Others focus on the role of government intervention in the form of antidiscrimination legislation (Smith and Welch 1989; Goldin 1990, 2000; Donohue and Heckman 1991).

Historically, regions were a defining feature of the American economy, and the integration of regional economies was an important part of the story of American economic development. It is apparent, for example, from Tables Ba4216–4217, Ba4234–4243, Ba4253–4267, and Ba4271–4279 that substantial regional differences in wages existed in the past.[14] These differences have narrowed in the twentieth century as regional economies have become better integrated and (to some extent) less specialized. Differences in average annual earnings across industries are also a feature of the historical (and contemporary) American wage structure. Although some of these can be explained by differences across industries in the skills (or other characteristics) of workers, to a surprising extent the "interindustry wage structure" has remained stable over time (see Allen 1995).

These observations merely scratch the surface of an extremely complex subject. For recent overviews of U.S. labor market

[13] Regressions of the log of the nominal wage on a time trend using series Ba4253, Ba4258, and Ba4263 indicate that nominal wages of common labor grew at about 1.1 percent per year over the 1825–1860 period, compared with 0.7 percent for artisans (1823–1860) and 1.4 percent for white-collar workers (1822–1860). The differences between the rates are statistically significant. The more rapid relative pace of growth among white-collar workers before the Civil War may be the first episode of a rising return to "educated" labor in American history; see Margo (2000b, p. 156).

[14] In thinking about regional differences, it is important to keep in mind that the data in these tables are not adjusted for regional differences in prices. However, adjusting for price level differences does not eliminate regional wage differentials and, in some cases, the differentials are even larger in real terms; see, for example, Margo (2000b, Chapter 5) for evidence on regional differences in real wages before the Civil War.

development, see Goldin (2000) and Margo (2000a, 2000b). For an overview of the American labor market in the colonial period, see Galenson (1996). Readers are invited to explore the ramifications of these series, whether in comparing trends of different types of labor, or in conjunction with series on consumer (or producer) prices or the prices of other factors of production.

References

Allen, Steven G. 1995. "Updated Notes on the Inter-Industry Wage Structure, 1890–1990." *Industrial and Labor Relations Review* 48: 305–20.

Donohue, John, and James Heckman. 1991. "Continuous versus Episodic Change: The Impact of Civil Rights Policy on the Economic Status of Blacks." *Journal of Economic Literature* 29: 1604–43.

Galenson, David W. 1996. "The Settlement and Growth of the Colonies: Population, Labor, and Economic Development." In Stanley L. Engerman and Robert E. Gallman, editors. *The Cambridge Economic History of the United States,* volume 1, *The Colonial Era*. Cambridge University Press.

Goldin, Claudia. 1990. *Understanding the Gender Gap: An Economic History of American Women*. Oxford University Press.

Goldin, Claudia. 2000. "Labor Markets in the Twentieth Century." In Stanley L. Engerman and Robert E. Gallman, editors. *The Cambridge Economic History of the United States,* volume 3, *The Twentieth Century*. Cambridge University Press.

Goldin, Claudia, and Robert A. Margo. 1992. "The Great Compression: The U.S. Wage Structure at Mid-Century." *Quarterly Journal of Economics* 107: 1–34.

Katz, Lawrence F., and David H. Autor. 1999. "Changes in the Wage Structure and Earnings Inequality." In Orley C. Ashenfelter and David Card, editors. *Handbook of Labor Economics*, volume 3A, Chapter 26. Elsevier.

Katz, Lawrence F., and Kevin M. Murphy. 1992. "Changes in Relative Wages, 1963–1987: Supply and Demand Factors." *Quarterly Journal of Economics* 107: 35–78.

Lebergott, Stanley. 1964. *Manpower in Economic Growth: The American Record since 1800*. McGraw-Hill.

Levy, Frank, and Richard J. Murnane. 1992. "U.S. Earnings Levels and Earnings Inequality: A Review of Recent Trends and Proposed Explanations." *Journal of Economic Literature* 30 (September): 1333–81.

Margo, Robert A. 2000a. "The Labor Force in the Nineteenth Century." In Stanley L. Engerman and Robert E. Gallman, editors. *The Cambridge Economic History of the United States,* volume 2, *The Long Nineteenth Century*. Cambridge University Press.

Margo, Robert A. 2000b. *Wages and Labor Markets in the United States, 1820–1860*. University of Chicago Press.

Smith, James P., and Finis Welch. 1989. "Black Progress after Myrdal." *Journal of Economic Literature* 27: 519–64.

Williamson, Jeffrey G., and Peter H. Lindert. 1980. *American Inequality: A Macroeconomic History*. Academic Press.

HOURS AND WORKING CONDITIONS

William A. Sundstrom

This essay discusses the tables containing statistics relating to nonpecuniary aspects of employment. Perhaps the most important of these, historically, has been the number of labor hours worked during a standard period, such as a day, week, or year. The long-term decline of work hours is an important component of long-term changes in economic welfare, as workers have, in effect, devoted part of their increased income to purchasing leisure time. Conventional estimates of national income per capita underestimate the growth of economic well-being to the extent that they fail to count the value of leisure.[1] Shortening the working day was a central demand of the labor movement until at least the early twentieth century. Labor hours are also a key component of measures of productivity (output per unit of input).

In addition to the hours series, historical statistics are available for some other indicators of working conditions. These include additional aspects of work schedules (such as vacations and other absences from work), nonwage benefits, occupational injuries and illnesses, and measures of job tenure and turnover.

This essay begins with a discussion of hours of work: some measurement issues; a brief user's guide to the various hours series; long-term trends drawn from the hours series, as well as business-cycle fluctuations in work hours over the past century and a half; and variations in the levels and trends of work hours by industry and worker demographic group. The second section examines another type of quantitative information related to working conditions – namely, turnover and job tenure. The last three sections consider series relating to other nonpecuniary aspects of work: occupational injuries, fringe benefits, and employer (workplace) size.

Hours of Work

Measurement Issues

The statistics on hours of work presented here typically report the number of work hours during a day or week. Information on hours of work has been obtained from two basic sources: employers (business establishments) and workers. All of the historical hours series for the period before 1940 presented here come from surveys or studies of business establishments. Beginning with the Population Census of 1940, the U.S. Bureau of the Census began asking workers about their hours of work in both its decennial censuses and the monthly Current Population Survey (CPS).

All of the hours statistics reported here refer to hours worked "for pay or profit," typically outside the home. They thus suffer from the fundamental problem that they do not capture hours of work spent at such productive but unremunerative activities as housework and caregiving. The resulting mismeasurement of work hours is especially severe when it comes to the work of women (see Wagman and Folbre 1996).

For the period before World War II, hours statistics cover primarily workers in manufacturing and a few other industries, such as railroads and mining. Hours data for other industries, such as services, are spotty. Even up to the present day, published hours statistics generally do not include agricultural workers.

The meaning of the term "hours of work" is not consistent across the various data series reported here. In most of the early establishment surveys, employers reported the regular or full-time hours at their establishment. For instance, a firm may report that its scheduled work hours were ten hours a day. Such regularly scheduled hours could and often did differ from actual hours of work. During seasonal or business-cycle downturns, for example, workers were often put on shortened workweeks, with the expectation that hours would return to their scheduled full-time level when business

[1] American workers today earn their incomes in about half the weekly hours they worked 150 years ago. If the hourly wage is considered a rough approximation of the value of a worker's time, then per capita wage and salary income underestimates the increase in workers' real well-being since then by a factor of 2.

recovered. Thus, the early series on work hours cannot be expected to pick up these fluctuations in actual hours worked.[2]

A dramatic illustration of the difference between scheduled and actual work hours is provided by the early years of the Great Depression. According to data collected by the National Industrial Conference Board, average *full-time* weekly hours in manufacturing firms fell from 49.6 in 1929 to 47.9 in 1932, whereas *actual* weekly hours fell from 48.3 to 34.8 (see Wolman 1938, p. 2, and Table Ba4592–4596). Because of this discrepancy, the various series on full-time hours are probably best interpreted as reflecting longer-run trends in scheduled work hours, rather than year-to-year fluctuations.

A second conceptual distinction is particularly important for the period since World War II. The hours statistics collected by the Bureau of Labor Statistics (BLS) Current Employment Statistics survey of establishments represent the average hours of work paid for by the employer. During the postwar period, the rise of paid time off in such forms as holidays, sick leave, and vacations has driven a wedge between reported hours paid for and actual hours worked. The estimated ratio of hours at work to hours paid provides a means of adjusting the standard BLS establishments series for this change (see Table Ba4647–4648). These ratios were calculated from a special BLS survey in order to improve measures of productivity. For example, for the entire nonfarm business sector, an estimate of average weekly hours worked is obtained by multiplying series Ba4576 and Ba4647.

A Brief User's Guide for the Work Hours Series

There are two major sources of information on hours of work before 1890: the Aldrich report and the Weeks report (see Table Ba4545–4551). The Weeks report was prepared by Joseph Weeks as part of the Census of 1880. The Aldrich report was prepared under the direction of the U.S. Commissioner of Labor, Carroll D. Wright, for the Senate Committee on Finance, chaired by Nelson W. Aldrich. Both reports are based on retrospective information from a cross section of manufacturing firms, and there are many doubts about their representativeness. A useful discussion of both reports and their limitations is provided by Clarence D. Long (1960, pp. 5–9).

Neither sample can be considered representative in its coverage by industry or region. Because of the retrospective nature of the samples, data from the earlier years in each survey come only from those surveyed establishments that had been in business continuously since those years. As one moves back in time, the samples tend to get smaller and smaller and, thus, probably less reliable. Still, the Weeks and Aldrich data seem to be in line with other sources on hours from the period. For example, using a much larger and more representative sample of establishments from the 1880 Census of Manufactures, Jeremy Atack and Fred Bateman (1992) found that a majority of workers in 1880 were scheduled to work exactly ten hours per day, which is consistent with the pattern reported by Aldrich and Weeks for that year. Both sources provide evidence on daily hours; to convert them to weekly hours, which are then roughly comparable with later series, one should multiply by 6, which was the typical number of working days per week in American manufacturing in the late nineteenth century.

Several annual hours series are available for 1890 and later. For the manufacturing sector as a whole, the most carefully constructed series are probably those of Albert Rees (series Ba4553) and Ethel Jones (series Ba4589), which together cover the period 1890–1957. Indeed, Jones uses Rees's numbers for the first part of her series. Her series makes use of a variety of sources to correct some problems in the standard BLS data (series Ba4580). Rees gives hours per day and Jones hours per week, but the Rees and Jones series can easily be linked as follows: for 1890–1899, multiply Rees's daily hours (series Ba4553) by days in operation per year (series Ba4552) and divide by 52.

To extend the manufacturing series forward in time from 1957, the user should append to Jones's series the BLS data in series Ba4580. Jones tried wherever possible to estimate hours actually worked, rather than hours paid for. Therefore, for comparability with the Jones series, the standard BLS hours series should be adjusted to hours worked as noted (by multiplying series Ba4580 and Ba4648). Piecing together these three components, one arrives at a reasonably consistent annual series of weekly hours in manufacturing for the entire period 1890–1996, which is exhibited and discussed in Figure Ba-O.

Data for some other sectors of the economy can also be constructed for a long run of years. For example, Jones provides hours for steam railroads and bituminous coal mining (series

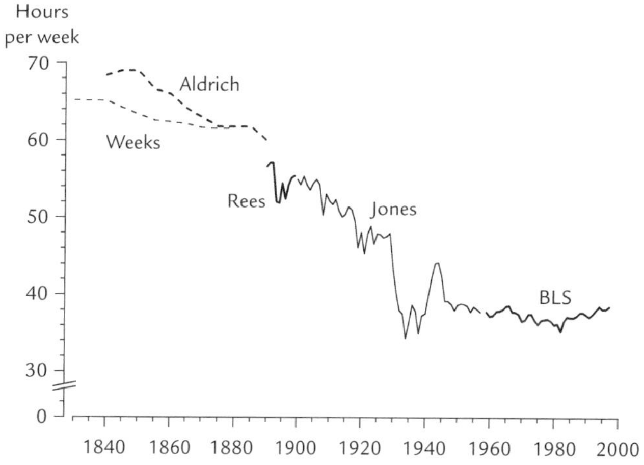

FIGURE Ba-O Average weekly work hours – manufacturing: 1830–1997

Sources

Based on series Ba4545–4553, Ba4580, Ba4589, and Ba4648.

Documentation

1830–1880 (Weeks report): average daily hours were obtained by computing a weighted average of series Ba4546–4551, using the data values as the weights and the lower bounds of the hour ranges as the figures to be averaged; the resulting average for daily hours was converted to weekly hours by multiplying by 6.

1840–1890 (Aldrich report): daily hours in series Ba4545 were multiplied by 6 to obtain weekly hours.

1890–1899 (Rees): daily hours in series Ba4552 were multiplied by average days in operation in series Ba4553 to obtain annual hours, which were then divided by 52.

1900–1957 (Jones): series Ba4589. Note that for the period 1900–1914, Jones relies on Rees's data, and so the computations described for series Ba4552–4553 would yield the same results.

1959–1997 (U.S. Bureau of Labor Statistics): hours paid, series Ba4580, were converted to hours worked by multiplying them by the ratio in series Ba4648.

[2] Series based at least in part on scheduled hours include those in Tables Ba4545–4574.

Ba4590–4591), which can be extended to the present day using series Ba4578 and Ba4584, respectively. Data collected by the National Industrial Conference Board provide hours by gender and skill level over the period 1914–1948 (Table Ba4592–4596).

For the period prior to 1940, obtaining a series for work hours in the economy as a whole is problematic, because annual statistics are generally lacking for several major sectors, such as trade and services. John Owen's series of weekly hours for private, nonagricultural workers (series Ba4575) is based on John Kendrick's estimates, which Kendrick (1961) built up from a large number of sources for different industries.[3] The series probably gives a good indication of the overall trend in hours during the first forty years of the twentieth century, but it is less reliable as an indication of year-to-year changes, as many of the underlying industry numbers are interpolated between a few benchmark years.

For the period since World War II, there are two major sources of annual data on work hours: the BLS survey of establishments or the Current Employment Statistics (CES) survey (Table Ba4576–4588), and the CPS, which surveys households (Tables Ba4597–4613). A key advantage of the CPS is that it permits one to examine hours levels and trends for different demographic groups (for example, by age, gender, or race).

The average weekly hours derived from the CPS are not comparable with those derived from the CES for several reasons. First, the CPS covers wage and salary workers (including domestics and other private household workers), self-employed persons, and unpaid workers in family-operated enterprises. The CES survey covers only production and nonsupervisory workers on the payrolls of private nonfarm establishments. Second, in the CPS survey, all persons with a job but not at work are excluded from the hours computations, whereas in the establishment survey, production or nonsupervisory employees on paid vacation, paid holiday, or paid sick leave are included and assigned the number of hours for which they were paid during the reporting period. Finally, the average hours in the CPS are the average hours per worker on all jobs held, whereas the average hours in the CES are the average hours per job. Thus, workers who hold multiple jobs ("moonlighting") have their total hours on all jobs combined counted in the CPS and their hours on each separate job counted separately in the CES.

Given these differences, it is hardly surprising that the CES and CPS estimates of weekly hours differ. What is perhaps less expected is that the two series have diverged substantially during the 1970s and 1980s. In 1966, the average workweek reported by the CES was about thirty-seven hours long, compared with about forty hours according to the CPS. By 1990, CES hours had fallen to just over 32, whereas CPS hours were just over 39. In other words, the gap between the average hours derived from these two sources had widened considerably (see also Figure Ba-P).

It can be shown that this increasing discrepancy is not merely the product of such technical differences between the sources as industry coverage and treatment of moonlighting.[4] Rather, a convincing case can be made that the average weekly hours derived from the CPS are biased upward because of an apparent tendency for individuals to overestimate their hours of work, and that this bias has grown. An independent source of information is time diary studies, in which respondents are asked to assign an activity to each minute of a twenty-four-hour period (see Table Ba4641–4646). These studies confirm that in 1985, individuals overestimated their work hours when responding to CPS-type questions, and that the bias was probably increasing over the period 1965–1985 (Robinson and Bostrom 1994). Although this conclusion remains controversial, the CPS hours series should be treated with skepticism.

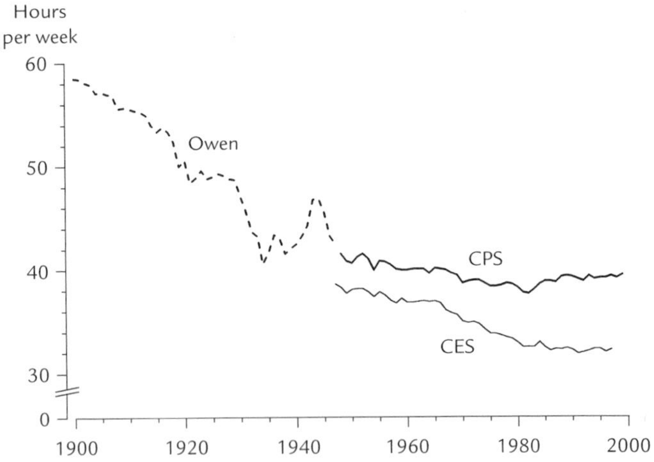

FIGURE Ba-P Average weekly work hours – private nonagricultural workers: 1900–1997

Sources

Based on series Ba4575–4576, Ba4597, and Ba4647–4648.

Documentation

1900–1947 (Owen): series Ba4575.

1948–1999 (Current Population Survey): series Ba4597.

1947–1997 (Current Employment Statistics): hours paid, series Ba4576, were converted to hours worked by multiplying them by the ratio in series Ba4647. Note that series Ba4647 was extrapolated back to 1947 by using the rate of change for 1959–1966 found in the manufacturing ratio, series Ba4648.

Another dimension of work time is the distribution of labor over the year. One simple summary measure is collected each March by the CPS: namely, how many weeks the respondent worked during the preceding year. Table Ba4614–4625 gives the number of workers within certain ranges of weeks worked, by gender and part-time status. Respondents are instructed to count the number of weeks during which they worked any number of hours, or received paid time off. Thus, the CPS measure of weeks worked includes paid time off for sick leave, vacations, and so forth.

For individuals who have a job but happen not to have worked during the CPS survey's reference week, the CPS asks them why they were not at work during that week: possible reasons include paid or unpaid leave for vacation, illness, bad weather, labor disputes, and so forth. Table Ba4649–4655 shows the number of employed workers who were absent from their jobs within these various categories of reasons. This table does not provide a complete picture of work absences, because workers who worked part of the week and were absent part of the week are counted as having been at work.

Trends and Cycles in Work Hours

The average American manufacturing worker in the mid to late nineteenth century worked between sixty and seventy hours per week. By the 1990s, weekly work hours in manufacturing had

[3] For the period after 1940, Owen's series is derived from decennial census and Current Population Survey data, and is restricted to nonstudent male workers.

[4] A useful discussion of the discrepancy between CPS and CES work hours can be found in Abraham, Spletzer, and Stewart (1998).

fallen to about forty, and considerably lower in the average nonmanufacturing industry. This decline occurred at an uneven pace. Figures Ba-O and Ba-P illustrate the long-term trends in weekly hours for manufacturing and all private nonagricultural workers, respectively.

During the second half of the nineteenth century, weekly hours in manufacturing trended downward – quite gradually (about one hour per decade) if one uses the estimates of the Weeks report, and more sharply (about two hours per decade) according to the Aldrich numbers. The pace of decline clearly accelerated during the early twentieth century, with a sharp dip following World War I and an especially large reduction during the Great Depression. According to Ethel Jones's figures, which are probably the most carefully prepared for the first half of the century, hours in manufacturing collapsed from 48 to 34 between 1929 and 1934. Weekly hours spiked nearly to pre-Depression levels during World War II, and then fell back to about 40 after the war. Overall, weekly hours fell on average by about 3.4 hours per decade between 1890 and 1950.

The postwar period shows a marked deceleration in the decline of work hours. Indeed, Figure Ba-O shows that weekly hours in manufacturing establishments fell only slightly between 1950 and 1980, and by the mid-1990s had returned to their 1950 level. For all private, nonfarm workers, shown in Figure Ba-P, the two major data sources tell dramatically different stories. According to the CPS survey, hours declined gradually between 1950 and 1980 and then increased a little thereafter. In contrast, the CES figures indicate that hours for all sectors declined much more significantly, albeit at only about half the rate of decline of the first half of the century. As noted previously, the CPS hours may be biased upward.

Why have work hours declined so much since the nineteenth century, and what accounts for the varying rate of decline? Perhaps the most obvious candidate for the overall trend is rising per capita income. According to the standard economic theory of labor supply, as workers' incomes rise, they may use some of this increased income to "buy back" increased leisure time in the form of shorter work hours. If workers tend to reduce their work hours in response to an increase in the real hourly wage, they exhibit what is known as a backward-bending labor supply curve. Indeed, the broad trend toward higher wages and shorter hours over the past 150 years can be taken as confirmation of the existence of backward-bending labor supply for most workers.

Of course, wages and incomes are not the only factors affecting work hours historically, and wage movements alone cannot account for the uneven timing of changes in hours. Other factors that have been cited by economists and historians include the impact of the business cycle, organized labor, government regulation of hours and other aspects of the employment relationship, and cultural changes affecting the value of leisure.

Weekly hours have tended to be procyclical – that is, hours move with the state of the economy over the business cycle. Examining the series for manufacturing in Figure Ba-O, one observes significant dips in hours during the recession years of the early 1890s, 1908, 1921, and, of course, the Great Depression of the 1930s. Evidently, employers cut hours during recessions – a practice known historically as worksharing – as an alternative to adjusting labor input through layoffs alone. The Owen series for all nonagricultural industries, shown in Figure Ba-P, is not as volatile as the manufacturing series, but it shows the same procyclical behavior. Although hours have continued to move with the business cycle during the post-Depression period, the importance of worksharing has declined relative to employment adjustment (see Bernanke and Powell 1986).

Unions and government intervention have also played a role in historical changes in work hours. During the nineteenth century, the eight-hour day was a potent rallying cry of the early labor movement. Strikes and union victories no doubt succeeded in reducing hours in certain industries and locations; still, hours declined in nonunion as well as heavily unionized sectors. By the early twentieth century, when the trend toward a shorter workweek accelerated, the demand for shorter hours was apparently no longer a top priority of the national unions (see Cahill 1932; Whaples 1990).

Legal restrictions on work hours directly affected only a small minority of American workers prior to the New Deal. With the National Industrial Recovery Act (NIRA) of 1933 and the Fair Labor Standards Act (FLSA) of 1938, the federal government began to regulate the hours of a large number of American workers. Although hours restrictions may help to explain why weekly hours have generally remained below forty during the postwar years, many view the anomaly of the postwar period to be not how low work hours have been but their failure to fall even further.

According to the historian Benjamin Hunnicutt (1988), both organized labor and the federal government abandoned the movement toward shorter work hours during the Great Depression. In part, this change reflected the rise of mass consumer culture – an underlying shift in Americans' cultural values toward consumption of purchased goods and services and away from leisure time. In addition, from the experience of the Depression, there emerged a political consensus favoring economic policies that promoted full employment at full-time hours, in place of the earlier emphasis on worksharing during economic bad times. During the postwar period, calls for shortening the workweek have garnered decidedly less political or popular support than in the past.

The Hunnicutt story meshes nicely with the evidence of the declining historical importance of worksharing, but there are other factors that could help account for the slowdown in the decline of hours and the reduced reliance on hours reduction over the business cycle. In particular, the rise of employee benefits – some of them legally mandated – has created increasing *quasi-fixed* employment costs during the postwar period. Quasi-fixed employment costs are per-worker costs that do not vary directly with how many hours the worker puts in on the job. Employer-provided medical insurance is an example of such a cost. The existence of quasi-fixed employment costs creates an incentive for employers to hire fewer workers at longer hours, and to vary labor input over the business cycle through employment variations rather than worksharing.

Finally, the slowing pace of the decline in hours could also reflect the declining relative value of leisure time to workers as they gained more of it over the past century. In the late nineteenth century, workers may have been more likely to sacrifice potential earnings for more leisure at a time when work hours were much longer and leisure relatively scarce. This trade-off looks less attractive to workers today. Interesting evidence consistent with this hypothesis is provided by Dora Costa. She shows that in the 1890s, the workers with the highest hourly wages tended to work the shortest hours. By the 1990s, this pattern had reversed, with higher-paid workers tending to put in longer hours (Costa 2000). These are precisely the patterns one would expect to observe if workers typically used wage increases to "purchase" more leisure in the nineteenth century but used them to purchase consumption goods in recent times.

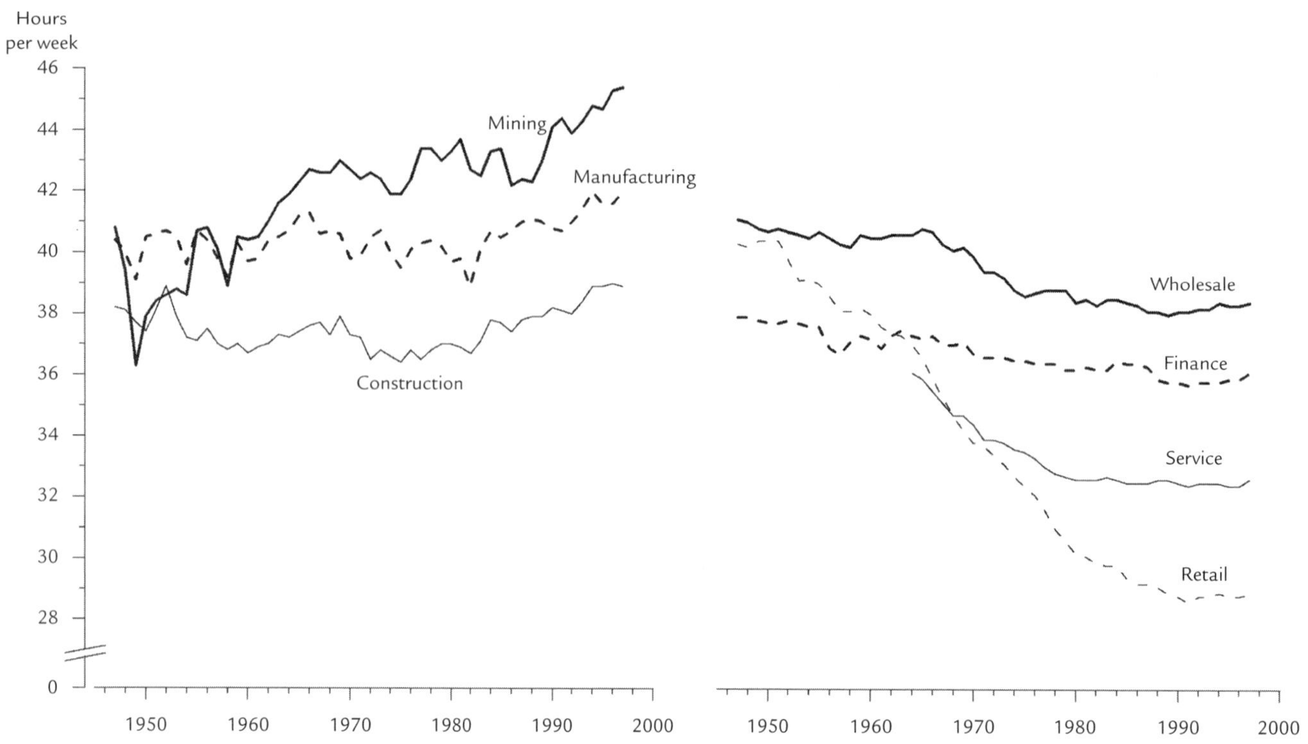

FIGURE Ba-Q Average weekly work hours – selected industries: 1947–1997

Sources

Series Ba4577, Ba4579–4580, and Ba4585–4588.

Variation in Work Hours by Industry and Worker Characteristics

In addition to the trends and cycles over time, hours of work vary in cross section by industry and demographic group. The most detailed information on this variation is available for the postwar period. Figure Ba-Q, for example, plots average weekly hours since 1950 from the CES establishments survey for selected broad industry groups. The plot reveals substantial divergence across industries over the postwar decades.[5] In 1950, the workweek in all these industry groups was between 37 and 41 hours. By the 1990s, the average workweek for a job in retail trade had fallen to less than 30 hours, whereas hours in manufacturing had crept upward to about 42.[6]

These industry-specific trends help explain why hours in manufacturing have remained quite stagnant during the second half of the twentieth century, although hours for the entire private nonfarm economy have fallen substantially. First, several of the important nonmanufacturing sectors have experienced diminishing workweeks. Second, the employment share of manufacturing has fallen over the same period, giving greater weight in the overall average to some of the industries with shorter workweeks. Why work hours have fallen in some industries and not in others is less clear, but it is undoubtedly related in part to the changing demographic composition of some of the industries (such as the entry of more married women into the paid workforce) and perhaps to institutional differences (such as unionization) between them.

Work hours vary by worker demographic group as well. Among men and women who have jobs outside the home, men typically work longer hours than women, and the gender gap in weekly hours has changed little since the 1950s: according to the CPS statistics in Table Ba4597–4607, the workweek of the average male worker has exceeded that of the average female worker by six to seven hours throughout the period covered. Of course, the labor force participation rate of women increased substantially during this period. Furthermore, those women who reported working were working more weeks per year. This can be seen in Figure Ba-R, which plots the percentage of male and female workers who reported being year-round, full-time workers. Evidently, the feminization of the paid workforce since World War II has involved increases in the proportion of women working outside the home and in the regularity of women's paid work over the year, but not increases in working women's weekly hours at paid employment relative to men's.

Turnover and Job Duration

The length of time a worker stays with a given employer provides important information about the nature of the employment relationship that is not captured by wages and hours. Job duration is in part an indicator of the quality of the match between an employer and employee and can be expected to vary with the characteristics of both workers (supply-side factors) and employers (demand-side factors). On the supply side, workers with short-term commitments to the labor market are likely to have shorter job durations. An

---

[5] The pattern of divergence is apparent across all industries, not just across the ones shown here.

[6] It should be remembered that these figures do not include the self-employed. The hours of small shopkeepers, not captured here, are presumably longer. It is interesting to note that during the nineteenth century, workers in trade and services probably had the longest workweek of any industry, according to the estimates of Kendrick (1961, p. 310). This may, presumably, have reflected the work hours of self-employed merchants.

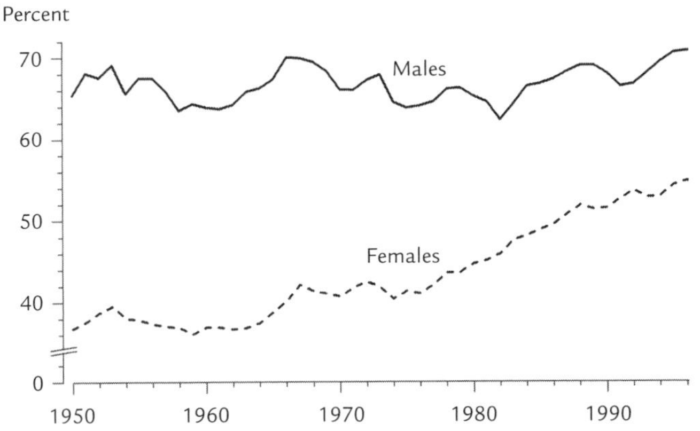

FIGURE Ba-R Percentage of workers working full-time year-round, by sex: 1950–1996

Sources

Table Ba4614–4625. Males: series Ba4614 as a percentage of the sum of series Ba4614–4619. Females: computed analogously.

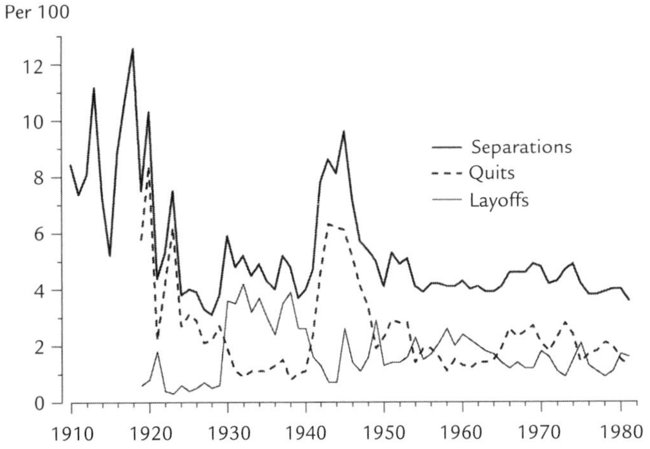

FIGURE Ba-S Monthly turnover rates in manufacturing – separations, quits, and layoffs per 100 workers: 1910–1981

Sources

Series Ba4684–4686.

example is immigrant workers who plan to return soon to their home country. On the demand side, employers may adopt strategies, such as fringe benefits or promotion plans, designed to increase the attachment of its workforce, perhaps to increase loyalty or hold down recruitment and training costs. Training costs may, in turn, be a reflection of the nature of the production technology. Of course, job duration is also affected by the exigencies of the business cycle: involuntary layoffs increase during cyclical downturns.

One source of quantitative information on workers' attachment to their employers is the rate of labor turnover, measured as the rate at which workers leave their current employer (separation rate) or are hired by a new employer (accession rate). Table Ba4682–4686 provides the available turnover series for the period 1910–1981, based on surveys of manufacturing employers. The separation rate is basically defined as the number of employees who left their job (employer) during a particular month, divided by the average total number of workers employed during that month; the accession rate is defined similarly.[7] For most of the years, the separation rate is decomposed into separations due to voluntary quits, due to layoffs, and due to other causes (such as disciplinary dismissals).

A plot of the separation rate and its quit and layoff components – shown in Figure Ba-S – reveals considerable change over time. Separation rates were very high before the mid-1920s and also climbed dramatically during World War II. Not surprisingly, quit rates and layoff rates tend to move in opposite directions over the business cycle: during recessions, workers are reluctant to quit their jobs, but layoffs escalate; during boom periods, when labor markets are tight, layoffs decline while quits rise.

Turnover rates provide an incomplete picture of employer–employee attachment, because movements in separations and accessions tend to be dominated by those workers and employers with the least attachment and the greatest sensitivity to the business cycle. It is quite possible that even during a period of very high labor turnover, most workers hold onto their jobs, while turnover increases dramatically for the more "footloose" workers and employers.[8]

To obtain a more complete picture, it is therefore important to examine data on the actual distribution of job durations, or the length of time each worker has been with her or his current employer. This measure captures the duration of job spells that have not yet been completed. In this sense, observed job duration underestimates how long a worker will ultimately be with her or his current employer. Job duration data come from questions asked intermittently by the Current Population Survey. There are various ways of summarizing the distribution of job durations. Three are included here: Table Ba4656–4667 provides the median duration; Table Ba4668–4675 gives the percentage of workers who had been working for their current employer for a year or less (very short jobs); and Table Ba4676–4681 gives the percentage with job durations of twenty years or more (very long jobs).

Scattered historical evidence on job duration during the late nineteenth and early twentieth centuries suggests that jobs tended to be shorter than they have been during the period since World War II, which is consistent with the evidence of high turnover rates. That jobs were shorter during earlier periods has been interpreted by some historians as evidence that "lifetime jobs" and strong employer–employee attachments are a product of the twentieth century, perhaps arising with the advent of modern personnel management practices. However, jobs of long duration were not uncommon even in the late nineteenth century, and so some dispute remains about the extent and nature of changes in the employment relationship.[9]

The evidence on job duration also sheds some light on concerns about the potential decline in job security during the 1980s and 1990s. Median job duration remained fairly stable for men between the 1960s and the mid-1990s: clearly, there is little evidence of an overall decline in job attachment for men during the last two decades of the twentieth century.[10] There is, however, a noticeable decline in men's median job tenure between 1993 and 1996. Among

---

[7] The precise calculation varies somewhat over the length of the series.

[8] This heterogeneity and its implications for interpreting turnover statistics are discussed in Woytinsky (1942).

[9] See Carter and Savoca (1990), Jacoby and Sharma (1992), and Owen (1995) for discussions of some of these issues.

[10] Careful studies of trends in job tenure during the late twentieth century can be found in Neumark (2000).

women, median job tenure has risen gradually over most of the period covered. In particular, the percentage of women with jobs of long duration (twenty years or more) has risen sharply since the late 1980s, a change that may reflect the increased regularity of married women's attachment to the labor force, as well as changes in women's occupational status.

Work-Related Injuries

Work-related injuries or illnesses are clearly another nonpecuniary aspect of work of considerable concern to workers. The risk of workplace injuries and fatalities gave rise to demands for government-sponsored workers' compensation programs during the early twentieth century, and they were implemented in a number of states. Even prior to the adoption of such programs, workers in risky occupations were often paid a compensating wage differential in contrast to workers of comparable skill in safer jobs.[11]

Work injuries are measured in terms of their frequency, either per worker or per worker-hour. Historical series for various industries are provided for the period before 1971 in Table Ba4742–4749 and after 1971 in Table Ba4750–4767. Unfortunately, major changes in the way work injury data were collected and analyzed make these two data sets largely noncomparable. Trends within each period, however, are suggestive. The period 1930–1960 witnessed a significant decline in injury rates in manufacturing and mining, particularly the latter. Injury rates appear to level off after 1960, and for the period since 1972, occupational injury rates have shown little overall trend. Not surprisingly, occupational injury and illness rates vary considerably across industries.

Employee Benefits

Fringe benefits became an important part of total worker compensation during the postwar period, but they are seldom counted in conventional wage and earnings statistics. The statistics on employee benefits included here come from two different Bureau of Labor Statistics programs, both of which survey establishments (employers). Information on the costs to employers of providing various benefits has been collected as part of the Employment Cost Index (ECI) and its predecessors, going back to 1959 (see Tables Ba4687–4702). Data on the incidence and provisions of selected employee benefits have been collected since 1979 under the Bureau of Labor Statistics Employee Benefits Survey (EBS; see Table Ba4712–4725).

The series in Tables Ba4687–4702 show the percentage of total employee compensation that was in the form of wages and salaries and various nonwage benefits, for manufacturing and all private-sector workers. These series provide a good picture of the overall economic importance of benefits over the past forty years. During the period covered, benefits have become an increasingly large fraction of total compensation, rising from about 19 percent in 1966 to 29 percent at their peak in 1994 (series Ba4696). This increase is largely accounted for by the rise in two components of benefit costs: insurance, which includes private medical insurance, and legally required benefits, which include employer contributions to Social Security, Medicare, and other mandated insurance programs.

The series for retirement benefits in these tables capture only employer contributions to private retirement plans. Another way of looking at retirement benefits is to combine the costs of employer contributions to both private plans and Social Security. Between 1977 and 1998, the cost of the Social Security tax to employers rose from 3.7 percent of total compensation to 4.7 percent, but contributions to private retirement plans fell from 4.3 percent to 3.8 percent of compensation. Thus overall, employer contributions to retirement plans on the whole were fairly stable, rising from 8.0 to 8.5 percent of total compensation (see Wiatrowski 1999, Table 5).

The employment-cost–based measures in Tables Ba4687–4702 do not provide information on how many workers are covered by different types of benefits. For this information, one can turn to the series from the EBS, shown in Table Ba4712–4725. Until 1987, this survey was restricted to "medium and large" private business establishments, and only the series for these establishments are included here.[12]

Before 1988, the industrial coverage of the EBS was incomplete (most service industries were excluded). After 1988, the survey becomes much more representative of the overall industrial composition of the private sector. Because of such changes in coverage, the series is not fully consistent over time, and trends over the approximately two decades covered by the EBS should be treated with caution. For example, between 1980 and 1997, the percentage of employees in surveyed establishments with defined benefit pensions fell from 84 to 50, and the percentage with medical benefits fell from 97 percent to 76 percent. In both cases, fairly large downward jumps in the series occur between 1986 and 1988, precisely when important changes in survey coverage were occurring. However, it is also the case that the downward trends in both series have continued since 1988, which can be taken as evidence that the trends overall are not merely the spurious effect of sample composition.

The case of medical coverage highlights the difference between looking at benefits in terms of employer compensation costs and in terms of incidence (employee coverage). According to series Ba4699, the cost of insurance benefits, of which medical insurance is the major component, rose dramatically as a percentage of total compensation between 1977 and 1994. During roughly the same period, the proportion of employees at medium and large establishments who had health benefits fell from nearly universal coverage to about three quarters (series Ba4714). A reasonable conclusion would be that the total costs of health benefits to employers rose as increases in medical insurance premiums during this period more than compensated for the declining percentage of the workforce covered.

Size of Workplace

The rise of the large business corporation is one of the central themes of U.S. economic history (Chandler 1977). One dimension of the scale of business enterprise is the impact of size on the nature of the employment relationship. Over the course of the twentieth

[11] For a summary of work by economic historians on workplace accidents and insurance, see Fishback (1998), pp. 734–40.

[12] Results for the recent surveys of smaller establishments and state and local government can be obtained from the BLS Web site.

century, that relationship tended to become more bureaucratic and subject to direct managerial control, as large firms created so-called internal labor markets (Jacoby 1985). In the late twentieth century, economists have found that large employers differ from smaller ones in a variety of ways. For example, controlling for worker characteristics, large firms tend to pay higher wages.

Historical series on the size distribution of the workplace are presented in Tables Ba4703–4711. The data come from the U.S. Census Bureau. These tables show the percentage of employees working in establishments of various sizes. An establishment is defined as a single physical location where business is conducted by a company. In manufacturing, for example, an establishment is a plant or production facility; in retailing, it is a store. Because a given business firm may operate at more than one location, average establishment size is typically smaller than average firm size. A large retail chain, for example, may own many small stores and employ thousands of workers, yet each establishment (store) may employ only a handful. In spite of this limitation, establishment size is important, as it is a measure of how many employees interact and are supervised at a given place of work.

For manufacturing, a consistent series of establishment size can be constructed from the Census of Manufactures beginning in 1904. Examination of Table Ba4703–4705 shows the remarkable constancy of establishment size in manufacturing during the twentieth century. As early as 1904, more than 60 percent of manufacturing employees worked in establishments with at least 100 employees. This figure rose to about 70 percent by 1919, and remained near this level through 1997. An alternative way of interpreting the same information is to note that rather small manufacturing facilities have held their own over the century, and since the late 1960s have actually increased in prominence (Granovetter 1984).

Consistent series on establishment size in manufacturing during the nineteenth century are harder to come by, but the available evidence suggests that increases in scale were substantial during the second half of the century (O'Brien 1988). In the aggregate, then, the economies of scale in production that accompanied the factory system and mechanization had largely been achieved by the turn of the century. Changes in the nature of the employment relationship in industry since then, by implication, cannot be attributed to the imperatives of growing workplaces, because establishment size simply has not changed much for the typical worker. This is not to rule out the possibility, however, that scale continued to increase at the level of the firm as a whole.

In trade and services, for which there are consistent series beginning in 1939, workplaces have tended to be much smaller, but the trend has been one of growth in size. The left panel of Figure Ba-T plots the proportion of workers in small establishments (fewer than 20 employees) for retail, wholesale, services, and manufacturing. The steady decline in the importance of small

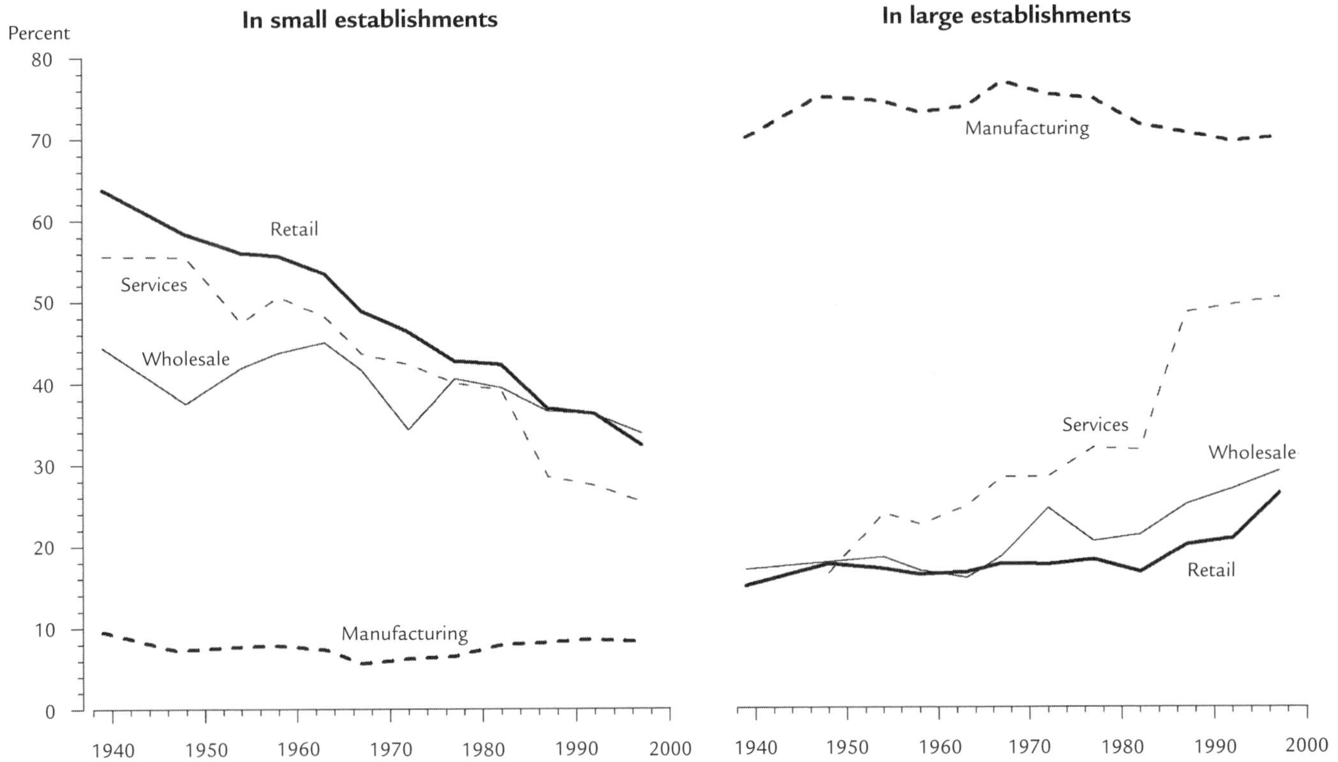

FIGURE Ba-T Percentage of manufacturing, retail, wholesale, and service employees working in small and large establishments: 1939–1997

Sources

Small establishments: series Ba4703, Ba4706, Ba4708, and Ba4710. Large establishments: computed as 100 percent minus series Ba4704, Ba4707, Ba4709, and Ba4711.

Documentation

Small establishments are those with fewer than 20 employees. Large establishments are those with at least 100 employees.

retailers and service establishments over the entire sixty years is evident. The right panel of Figure Ba-T does the same for the proportion of workers in large establishments (100 or more employees). Such establishments remain unusual in retail and wholesale trade, but there has been a notable increase in their share of employment since the 1970s.

References

Abraham, Katharine G., James R. Spletzer, and Jay C. Stewart. 1998."Divergent Trends in Alternative Wage Series." In John Haltiwanger, Marilyn E. Manser, and Robert Topel, editors. *Labor Statistics Measurement Issues.* University of Chicago Press.

Atack, Jeremy, and Fred Bateman. 1992. "How Long Was the Workday in 1880?" *Journal of Economic History* 52 (March): 129–60.

Bernanke, Ben S., and James L. Powell. 1986. "The Cyclical Behavior of Industrial Labor Markets: A Comparison of the Prewar and Postwar Eras." In Robert J. Gordon, editor. *The American Business Cycle: Continuity and Change.* University of Chicago Press.

Cahill, M. C. 1932. *Shorter Hours: A Study of the Movement since the Civil War.* Columbia University Press.

Carter, Susan B., and Elizabeth Savoca. 1990. "Labor Mobility and Lengthy Jobs in Nineteenth-Century America." *Journal of Economic History* 50 (1): 1–16.

Chandler, Alfred D., Jr. 1977. *The Visible Hand: The Managerial Revolution in American Business.* Harvard University Press.

Costa, Dora L. 2000. "The Wage and the Length of the Work Day: From the 1890s to 1991."*Journal of Labor Economics* 18 (1): 156–81.

Fishback, Price V. 1998. "Operations of 'Unfettered' Labor Markets: Exit and Voice in American Labor Markets at the Turn of the Century." *Journal of Economic Literature* 36 (2): 722–65.

Granovetter, Mark. 1984. "Small Is Bountiful: Labor Markets and Establishment Size." *American Sociological Review* 49 (June): 323–34.

Hunnicutt, Benjamin K. 1988. *Work without End: Abandoning Shorter Hours for the Right to Work.* Temple University Press.

Jacoby, Sanford M. 1985. *Employing Bureaucracy: Managers, Unions, and the Transformation of Work in American Industry, 1900–1945.* Columbia University Press.

Jacoby, Sanford M., and Sunil Sharma. 1992. "Employment Duration and Industrial Labor Mobility in the United States, 1880–1980." *Journal of Economic History* 52 (1): 161–79.

Kendrick, John W. 1961. *Productivity Trends in the United States.* Princeton University Press.

Long, Clarence D. 1960. *Wages and Earnings in the United States, 1860–1890.* Princeton University Press.

Neumark, David, editor. 2000. *On the Job: Is Long-Term Employment a Thing of the Past?* Russell Sage Foundation.

O'Brien, Anthony Patrick. 1988. "Factory Size, Economies of Scale, and the Great Merger Wave of 1898–1902."*Journal of Economic History* 48 (3): 639–49.

Owen, Laura J. 1995. "Worker Turnover in the 1920s: What Labor-Supply Arguments Don't Tell Us."*Journal of Economic History* 55 (4): 822–41.

Robinson, John P., and Ann Bostrom. 1994. "The Overestimated Workweek? What Time Diary Measures Suggest." *Monthly Labor Review* 117 (August): 11–23.

Wagman, Barnet, and Nancy Folbre. 1996. "Household Services and Economic Growth in the United States, 1870–1930." *Feminist Economics* 2 (1): 43–66.

Whaples, Robert M. 1990. "The Shortening of the American Work Week: An Economic and Historical Analysis of Its Context, Causes, and Consequences." Ph.D. dissertation, University of Pennsylvania.

Wiatrowski, William J. 1999. "Tracking Changes in Benefit Costs." *Compensation and Working Conditions* 4 (1): 32–7.

Wolman, Leo. 1938. *Hours of Work in American Industry.* National Bureau of Economic Research Bulletin number 71.

Woytinsky, W. S. 1942. *Three Aspects of Labor Dynamics.* Social Science Research Council.

Labor Unions

Joshua L. Rosenbloom

Labor unions are an important institution in U.S. labor markets today. Nearly 16.5 million workers, or 13.9 percent of all wage and salary workers, are members of unions, and more than 18 million, or 15.3 percent of workers, are represented by unions. Although the share of union workers in the economy has fallen from its peak in 1948, unions still affect almost every aspect of the employment relationship, and the presence of unions has effects on employment contracts for nonunionized as well as for unionized workers (Freeman and Medoff 1984). The tables presented here document changes in the size and character of unionization in the U.S. labor force since the beginnings of the modern labor movement in the 1880s, along with measures of selected effects of unionization. These include the impact of unionization on wages, the incidence of strikes, and public attitudes toward organized labor.

Historical Overview of Labor Organizing

The first reliable measures of union membership date from 1880, near the beginning of what may be called the modern era of organized labor. Although union progress was halting and irregular during most of the nineteenth century, there was a long history of organized labor prior to the 1880s. Skilled workers in a number of urban crafts formed organizations to pursue their interests as early as the 1780s. In addition to seeking higher wages and shorter hours, these organizations often provided fraternal benefits for sickness and burial. Among the challenges confronting these early labor organizations was their ambiguous legal status. Until the 1842 case of *Commonwealth v. Hunt*, in which Massachusetts Chief Justice Lemuel Shaw for the first time recognized the legality of unions, state courts had generally interpreted strikes as illegal conspiracies. Even after this ruling, however, employers continued to use the conspiracy argument with some success, and the passage of legislation repealing the conspiracy doctrine emerged as an important priority of organized labor in the late nineteenth century. Despite growing legislative support for labor in the late nineteenth century, striking workers continued to face the threat of injunctions issued to prevent injury to property.[1]

During the first half of the nineteenth century, the number of local craft unions proliferated, but most labor organizations remained transitory – forming during economic upswings and collapsing during business downturns. Growth in the number of labor organizations led to increased efforts at federation. In 1827, unions representing an array of different crafts in Philadelphia formed a trade council to pursue issues of common concern. Similar organizations soon appeared in most other major cities, and in 1834, the first national federation of labor organizations, the National Trades Union (NTU), was established in New York. This organization proved short-lived, however, vanishing, like many other labor organizations, in the depression that followed the panic of 1837.

[1] See Currie and Ferrie (2000) for a summary of the evolution of nineteenth-century labor law and for a careful elaboration of the extent of heterogeneity of state laws relating to labor organizations in the late nineteenth century.

By midcentury, the economy's growing geographic integration prompted the founding of the first national trade union, the National Typographical Union, in 1852 (Ulman 1955). It was followed by organizations of hat finishers (1854), journeyman stonecutters (1855), cigarmakers (1856), machinists, blacksmiths, and iron molders (1859). In 1866, another effort was made to form a national labor organization, the National Union, but like the NTU this effort soon collapsed. The depression that began in 1873 contributed to a substantial decline in union strength: membership declined sharply and fewer than ten of the thirty national unions in existence at the beginning of the decade survived into the second half of the 1870s.

As the economy rebounded at the end of the 1870s, labor organizations began to expand. Particularly successful was the Noble Order of the Knights of Labor. Founded in Philadelphia in 1869 by a group of garment cutters, the Knights of Labor remained a small organization until a series of successful railroad strikes in 1876–1877 attracted widespread attention to the group. In contrast to the craft-based organization of most previous unions, the Knights were organized into local and district assemblies, most of which welcomed workingmen regardless of craft or skill level. In addition to advocating the eight-hour day, the Knights promoted a variety of other social reforms, such as the graduated income tax and the prohibition of contract labor, and also sponsored consumer and producer cooperatives. In the first half of the 1880s, membership grew rapidly. By 1885, the organization had nearly 700,000 members nationwide. In the wake of several unsuccessful strikes and the backlash of public opinion following the 1886 Haymarket riot, however, the Knights were unable to sustain their previous momentum, and their membership collapsed as suddenly as it had expanded.

In the 1890s, a new, more narrowly focused organization, the American Federation of Labor (AFL), achieved considerable organizing success. Established in 1886 at a meeting of delegates from a number of national trade unions in Columbus, Ohio, the AFL was organized along craft lines, and its members limited their objectives to work-related issues, such as shorter hours, higher wages, and improved working conditions. With the emergence of the AFL, the modern era of labor organization may be said to have begun. Drawing on a per capita tax on all members to fund its activities, the AFL was able to successfully consolidate its position and expand its jurisdiction. Since the early twentieth century, several rival organizations have emerged to challenge the AFL's leadership of the labor movement. The most serious of these challenges occurred in the 1930s, when advocates of industrial unionism broke with the AFL leadership to establish the Committee for Industrial Organization (later renamed Congress of Industrial Organizations) (CIO). Eventually, however, differences with this group were bridged, and the two organizations merged to form the AFL–CIO, which remains the most important national labor organization in the United States today.

Union Membership

The growth of labor union membership from 1880 to the present is traced in Table Ba4783–4791. Several different series are available, reflecting different approaches to measuring union membership. Membership levels calculated from household interviews conducted as part of the Current Population Survey (CPS) (series Ba4788) are consistently below those in the series from Leo Troy and Neil Sheflin and the U.S. Bureau of Labor Statistics (BLS), which are based on union-reported data (series Ba4783–4786). The union-reported data may be higher because of double counting as a result of individuals holding membership in more than one union. However, it may also reflect a desire by these unions to inflate membership statistics for strategic reasons. Most scholars accept the individual survey data collected by the CPS to be a more accurate measure of union membership than earlier approaches based on union-reported data.

For 1897–1978, the BLS and Troy-Sheflin series provide alternative approaches to calculating union membership based on union-reported data. Whereas the Troy–Sheflin series relies consistently on the concept of dues-paying membership and makes use of union financial data, the BLS series is based on union-reported membership figures. Over the entire period, the two series reflect broadly the same patterns, but they differ more significantly over shorter subperiods. The divergence is especially great during the decade of the 1930s, with the BLS series showing a much sharper drop in membership in the early 1930s and a more rapid expansion of membership after 1933. On the face of it there is little basis for selecting one series over the other. Researchers must decide which concept of union membership is closest to the one they seek to measure. For 1897–1914, Gerald Friedman's recent revisions (series Ba4789) are clearly an improvement over both the Troy–Sheflin and BLS series, incorporating data from a broader and more consistent range of unions, as well as adjusting for Canadian membership in U.S. unions.

Despite the differences between the alternative series, all suggest a broadly similar chronology of union growth and decline. In absolute terms, union membership increased substantially between 1880 and the mid-1940s, when union density – the ratio of union membership to the nonagricultural labor force – reached a peak of around 35 percent (see Figure Ba-U). After 1945, the absolute number of union members continued to increase until 1976, when it began to decline. The growth of union membership after 1945 failed, however, to keep pace with the growth of the labor force, resulting in a decline in the relative number of union members beginning sometime in the early 1950s and continuing to the present.

An interesting feature of the membership data in Table Ba4783–4791 is that rather than increasing continuously, union membership and density have grown mainly during a small number of episodes of intense growth (see Freeman 1998, pp. 267–9). The first of these spurts occurred in the early 1880s, and it reflects the organizational successes scored in that decade by the Knights of Labor. Between 1883 and 1886, union membership more than tripled. The second spurt in union growth occurred from 1897 to 1904, when the AFL achieved significant gains in organizing skilled workers. During this period, membership more than doubled so that by 1904, more than one of every ten nonagricultural workers in the nation was a union member. After 1904, employer resistance stiffened, and union membership stagnated until World War I. Between 1916 and 1920, tight labor markets, together with government pressure to avoid interruptions of vital war production, combined to facilitate expanded organization, pushing the number of organized workers to new heights.

Perhaps the most unusual spurt in union membership is the one that began in 1933, at the height of the Great Depression. The rapid growth of union membership in an era of peacetime

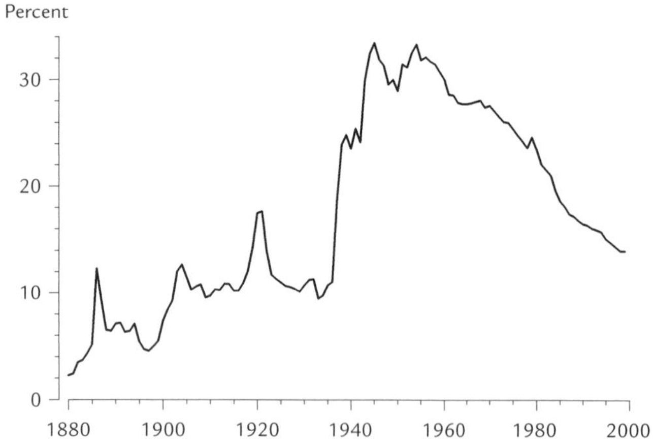

FIGURE Ba-U Union density – union membership as a percentage of nonagricultural employment: 1880–1999

Sources

Union membership: 1890–1914, series Ba4789; 1915–1976, series Ba4783; thereafter, series Ba4788.

Nonagricultural employment: 1890–1937, series Ba471 minus series Ba472; thereafter, series Ba481 minus series Ba482. For the years before 1890, figures are extrapolations based on data from Robert Margo, "The Labor Force in the Nineteenth Century," in *The Cambridge Economic History of the United States*, volume 2, *The Long Nineteenth Century*, edited by Stanley L. Engerman and Robert E. Gallman (Cambridge University Press, 2000), pp. 209, 213.

Documentation

For the years before 1890, the nonagricultural labor force was extrapolated on the basis of changes in population, adjusted for shifts in the sectoral distribution of the labor force and changes in the labor force participation rate. The Margo source reports unpublished figures from Thomas Weiss showing that the labor force as a share of total population increased from 34.7 percent in 1880 to 37.4 percent in 1890, while agriculture's share of the labor force fell from 47.7 percent in 1880 to 40.1 percent in 1890. Linear interpolations were used to create annual series for labor force participation and for the nonagricultural share of the labor force. Indexed versions of these series were multiplied together and then multiplied by an indexed version of the annual U.S. population figures from series Aa7 (with all indexes set to 1890 = 1). The result was a composite index that could be used to extrapolate the available 1890 value for the nonagricultural labor force (series Ba471 minus series Ba472) back to 1880.

high unemployment reflects the massive shift in the legal environment of organized labor. In 1932, the Norris–La Guardia Act curtailed the federal courts' power to issue injunctions against striking unions, and in 1933, workers' right to organize and bargain collectively through representatives of their own choosing was given legal recognition in section 7(a) of the National Industrial Recovery Act (NIRA). The National Labor Board, chaired by Senator Robert F. Wagner, was created to settle disputes arising under this act and was authorized to hold elections of employees to determine their bargaining representation. Although the NIRA was invalidated by the Supreme Court in 1935, the labor provisions of the act were reinstated in the same year as part of the Wagner–Connery National Labor Relations Act. Under this act, the National Labor Board became the National Labor Relations Board (NLRB).

The final spurt in union growth occurred during World War II. Following on the heels of labor's advances in the 1930s, union successes during the war meant that by 1945, more than one third of nonagricultural workers were represented by unions. At this time, it appeared that organized labor was an established force in the American labor market. Throughout the 1950s, unions won well over half of all NLRB representation elections (see series Ba4946–4947), and the public's views toward organized labor remained strongly favorable, with two thirds to three quarters of those polled expressing approval of organized labor (series Ba4995).

Beginning in the 1960s, however, union successes began to erode and membership declined, first in relative terms, and then in absolute numbers. One immediate cause of declining membership was declining success rates in representation elections. Table Ba4946–4949 reveals that by the mid-1970s, unions were winning less than half of all representation elections, and fewer than half of the workers were eligible for representation in each election.

Part of the explanation for this decline is the growth of employer opposition to unionization. Employers can attempt to block unionization efforts legally by offering unorganized workers greater benefits and attempting to convince workers that voting against unions is in their best interest. Or they can use illegal means, such as identifying and firing leading pro-union workers (Freeman 1985, p. 52). The series in Table Ba4950–4953 provide several indexes of the extent of such illegal employer opposition to unions. Complaints to the NLRB of unfair management practices (series Ba4950) more than doubled between the mid-1950s and the early 1960s, continuing to rise to a peak around 1980, and complaints about workers being fired for union activity followed a similar path. The number of workers awarded back pay (series Ba4952) and reinstated (series Ba4953) grew in tandem with complaints, providing confirmation of the validity of these union charges. Increased management opposition was paralleled by the erosion of public support for organized labor. Table Ba4995–4998 shows a decline in public approval of and confidence in organized labor after the mid-1960s.

Union Affiliation

The earliest spurts in union membership in the 1880s and at the turn of the century were associated with innovations in union organization. The growth of unionization in the 1880s was tied to the emergence of the Knights of Labor, whereas growth in the 1897–1904 period was tied to the success of the craft-oriented and narrowly focused goals advocated by the AFL. The success of the AFL's strategy of organizing craft workers and concentrating on improving wages and working conditions is mirrored in the growth of unions and union members affiliated with the Federation. Series Ba4792 shows that between 1897 and 1904, the number of AFL-affiliated unions more than doubled, rising from 58 to 120. At the same time, the AFL's share of all union members increased from around 60 percent to close to 80 percent (series Ba4793).

The AFL's opposition to widespread efforts to organize unskilled workers along industrial lines was a continuing source of tension within the labor movement in the early twentieth century. In 1905, this discontent led to the formation of the Industrial Workers of the World (IWW) as an alternative vehicle for labor organization along industrial lines. Despite some initial successes, however, the IWW did little to erode the AFL's dominant position. The issue again arose in 1935, when advocates of organization through industrial unions within the AFL formed the Committee for Industrial Organization, later renamed the Congress of Industrial Organizations (CIO). Following this split, both the AFL and the rival CIO staged massive organizing campaigns, which contributed to the expansion of unionization at this time.

Two alternative sets of membership estimates are reported in Table Ba4792–4804. The BLS series Ba4793 and Ba4795 attribute a much greater share of union membership to the CIO in the late 1930s than do the series constructed by Troy and Sheflin (series Ba4797–4798). The large discrepancies between these series illustrate some of the hazards in attempting to measure union membership in an era of substantial organizational changes. Even the head of the CIO, Philip Murray, was uncertain about the membership of the unions affiliated with his organization. In 1939, he indicated that per capita payments from affiliated unions implied a membership of 1.7 million, but he estimated that the actual membership figure may well have been as high as 3 million. Meanwhile, the BLS series Ba4795, which is based on reports from individual unions, indicates a figure of 4 million.

In 1955, the AFL and CIO agreed to merge, forming the American Federation of Labor–Congress of Industrial Organizations (AFL–CIO). Together, their membership accounted for close to 90 percent of union membership at the time. Table Ba4805–4813 shows that subsequently there has been some resurgence in independent or unaffiliated unions and a decline in the AFL–CIO share of union membership. Unfortunately, with the shift to reliance on individual survey data to measure union membership, the government ceased to collect data on membership of individual unions or their affiliations, and so these series end in the early 1980s.

Industrial and Demographic Characteristics of Union Membership

Additional insight into the growth and decline of organized labor can be gained by decomposing membership along industrial and demographic lines. Tables Ba4814–4883 report a number of series showing the breakdown of union membership along industrial lines for different subperiods. Because the sources for each table are different, and the industry definitions are not entirely consistent, it is not possible to construct a single continuous set of industry-level membership series.

At the turn of the twentieth century, the major centers of union strength were in the building trades (series Ba4816), mining (series Ba4815), and transportation and communications (series Ba4825), especially the railroads. Together, these three groups of unions accounted for over half of all unionized workers from 1900 through 1934. Although it is more difficult to calculate union density by industry, the proportion of workers belonging to unions in these industries was well above the national average (Wolman 1936, Chapter 8).

In the mid-1950s, when industry-level statistics are again available, the relative importance of manufacturing workers in the union movement had increased considerably. According to series Ba4832, manufacturing workers made up close to half of all union members in 1956. The share of unionized workers employed in manufacturing has fallen more or less continuously since 1956, however, so that by 1999, manufacturing workers accounted for less than 20 percent of the unionized workforce (series Ba4870). The decline of the relative importance of manufacturing has been paralleled by the increasing role of government employees in the union sector (series Ba4842 and Ba4880). This growth was facilitated by a series of actions greatly expanding the scope for organized labor in the public sector. In 1962, President John Kennedy granted federal employees the right to organize and bargain collectively. Similar actions by many state legislatures granted similar rights to state and municipal employees.

With the exception of data on union membership by sex, which was collected as early as 1954, there is little information about the demographic characteristics of union membership prior to 1983. Table Ba4906–4907 shows a rising proportion of women among organized workers. For the most part, this increase mirrors the rising participation of women in the paid labor force over this period. In 1954, women workers were substantially less likely than men to be members of a labor organization: 14.9 percent of women versus 31 percent of men were union members. Although the gap has narrowed, this imbalance still persists. In 1999, union density was 12.8 percent among women and 16.7 percent among men.

Beginning in 1983, data on union membership collected as part of the CPS provide a much richer picture of the characteristics of the unionized workforce. With the exception of the rise in women union members and some decline in the proportion of younger workers (series Ba4908), there are few pronounced trends in these series. These data are most interesting when set against the proportions of each group in the labor force as a whole. The greater rate of unionization among men has already been noted. It turns out as well that blacks are more likely to be union members than whites (17.2 percent of blacks versus 13.5 percent of whites in 1999), that full-time workers are more likely to belong to unions than part-time workers (15.4 percent versus 7.0 percent), and that younger workers, those under 25, are less likely than older workers to belong to unions (5.7 percent versus 15.5 percent).

The Impact of Unions on Wages

The presence of unions affects almost every facet of the employment relationship. Unions not only affect wages but also alter the compensation package, increasing the share of fringe benefits. They also affect the distribution of wages, the likelihood of quits and layoffs, the response of firms to cyclical fluctuations in demand, promotion practices, productivity, and firm profitability.[2] Disentangling the effects of unions per se from other characteristics in each of these cases is not simple, however, and most examinations of these impacts have relied on cross-sectional data and sophisticated econometric techniques to measure these impacts.

The one area that has been relatively well documented concerns unions' effects on wages. Even here, data are only available for a relatively short period.[3] Table Ba4928–4945 compares average hourly wages of union and nonunion workers within a variety of demographic groups. It is important to recognize that the comparisons possible with these data reflect a variety of different factors. First, because employers may raise wages of nonunion workers to deflect organizing drives – so-called union threat

[2] Freeman and Medoff (1984) is the most comprehensive examination of the extent and scope of unions' impacts.

[3] Gregg Lewis (1963) used highly aggregated macroeconomic data to draw inferences about the evolution of union wage differentials since 1920, but his estimates are inferences, not actual measurements. John Pencavel and Catherine E. Hartsog (1984) have extended Lewis's measurements as far as 1980.

effects – wage differentials may not fully capture the impact that unionization has on wage levels. Second, because workers are heterogeneous, unionized workers may differ systematically in characteristics from nonunion workers. Third, the industrial distribution of unionized and nonunionized workers may differ. As a result, these differentials may not accurately reflect the change in wages that would be achieved by an individual worker moving between the union and nonunion sectors. Bearing these caveats in mind, it is apparent that the presence of unions is associated with substantially higher wages, and that this effect is most pronounced for blacks and women. Indeed, whereas white male union members earn only a 10–15 percent premium, the union wage premium for black men is from 20 to 30 percent, and that for black women is from 30 to 40 percent.

Strikes

Strikes are one of the principal tools that workers can use to exert pressure on employers. In the early history of the union movement, strikes were an important vehicle used to gain employer recognition of organized labor's right to bargain. Today, they are used primarily as a means to enforce worker demands for better contract terms. By their nature, strikes are highly visible, and the apparent growth in labor conflict manifested in strikes during the 1880s was a major public policy concern. Consequently, data on strikes were one of the first kinds of economic statistics collected by the Federal Labor Statistics Bureau after its establishment in 1884. Table Ba4954–4964 summarizes a number of aggregate measures of strike activity beginning in 1881. Data on all strikes are available until 1981, but after that date, the U.S. Department of Labor began to collect data only for strikes involving 1,000 or more workers. Although only about 5–10 percent of strikes are so large, this subset of strikes accounts for two thirds to three quarters of all striking workers, and during the years when the two series overlap, their movements are highly correlated.

Figure Ba-V depicts two indexes of the number of workers involved in strikes, constructed by using changes in the number involved in large strikes to extrapolate the series for all strikes after 1981. The first index is simply a measure of the relative number of workers on strike in each year, whereas the second index shows changes in the ratio of workers on strike to nonagricultural employment in each year. Both indexes are characterized by large cyclical fluctuations in magnitude. Prior to World War II, episodes of rapid growth in union membership – the early 1880s, the late 1890s, World War I, and the late 1930s – were also typically characterized by sharp increases in strike volume. In the 1950s, both the number of strikes and the number of workers on strike were at historically unprecedented levels. Strike activity declined from its peak in the 1950s through the late 1960s, before experiencing another upsurge. Since the mid-1970s, the number of striking workers has fallen. In terms of absolute numbers of workers, strike activity follows something of an inverted-U shape, rising from relatively low levels in the 1880s to a peak immediately after World War II, and then trending downward. Relative to nonagricultural employment, however, there appears to be no long-term trend in worker involvement in strikes from 1881 through 1980. However, since 1980, strike activity has fallen off sharply.

Data on the industrial distribution of strikes from 1937 to 1981 are reported in Table Ba4971–4994. In the 1950s, the majority of striking workers were employed in manufacturing industries, but the share of striking workers employed in nonmanufacturing industries has grown consistently since 1955, with the result that by the mid-1960s, nonmanufacturing workers made up a majority of strikers. Information on the industrial distribution of union membership is incomplete for this period, but it is clear from the available data (Tables Ba4814–4844) that prior to 1968, the share of striking workers drawn from the manufacturing industry far exceeded manufacturing's share of unionized workers. From 1968 through 1978, the share of striking workers in manufacturing was more closely aligned with manufacturing's contributions to the unionized workforce.

For most of the period that data on strikes have been collected, government officials have attempted to identify the primary "causes" of each strike. Of course, strikes occur for a wide variety of reasons, and in many instances, there may be multiple factors involved. Nonetheless, some additional insights can be gained by classifying strikes into a small number of relatively broad categories on the basis of what appears to be their primary cause. Table Ba4965–4970 shows both the number of strikes and the number of workers involved, classified by three major categories of strike issues: (1) wages and hours, (2) union recognition, and (3) other issues. In the late nineteenth century, wages and hours issues were the predominant cause of strikes, but the proportion of strikes over union organization rose rapidly while wage and hours issues were declining in importance from 1880 through the 1910s. During the 1930s, when overall strike activity was relatively high, union organization was the chief cause of strikes. But between

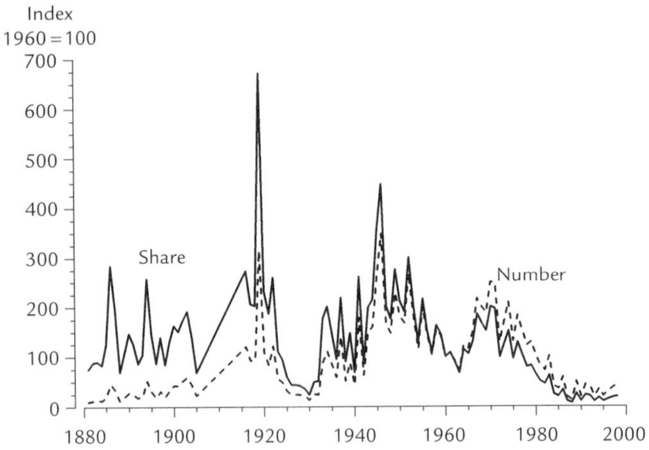

FIGURE Ba-V Indexes of workers involved in strikes – number and as a share of nonfarm employment: 1881–1998

Sources

Based on series Ba4955 and Ba4962, as well as the nonfarm employment data used in Figure Ba-U.

Documentation

The index for workers involved in strikes was computed by first indexing series Ba4955 and Ba4962 to 1960 = 100. Then the indexed series were linked at 1981–1982.

The index for workers involved in strikes as a share of nonfarm employment was computed by first expressing series Ba4955 and Ba4962 as a share of the nonfarm employment data used in Figure Ba-U. These ratio series were then indexed to 1960 = 100. Finally, the indexed series were linked at 1981–1982.

In both cases, the link was made so that the values based on series Ba4955 cover the years through 1981 and those based on series Ba4962 cover later years.

1940 and 1981, when the data end, wage and hours issues once again rose in importance, while strikes over union organization diminished in importance.

References

Currie, Janet, and Joseph Ferrie. 2000. "The Law and Labor Strife in the United States, 1881–1894." *Journal of Economic History* 60 (1): 42–66.

Freeman, Richard B. 1985. "Why Are Unions Faring Poorly in NLRB Representation Elections?" In Thomas A. Kochan, editor. *Challenges and Choices Facing American Labor*. MIT Press.

Freeman, Richard B. 1998. "Spurts in Union Growth: Defining Moments and Social Processes." In Michael D. Bordo, Claudia Goldin, and Eugene White, editors. *The Defining Moment: The Great Depression and the American Economy in the Twentieth Century*. University of Chicago Press.

Freeman, Richard B., and James L. Medoff. 1984. *What Do Unions Do?* Basic Books.

Lewis, H. Gregg. 1963. *Unionism and Relative Wages in the United States: An Empirical Inquiry*. University of Chicago Press.

Pencavel, John, and Catherine E. Hartsog. 1984. "A Reconsideration of the Effects of Unionism on Relative Wages and Employment in the United States, 1920–1980." *Journal of Labor Economics* 2 (2): 193–232.

Ulman, Lloyd. 1955. *The Rise of the National Trade Union*. Harvard University Press.

Wolman, Leo. 1936. *Ebb and Flow in Trade Unionism*. National Bureau of Economic Research, number 30.

HOUSEHOLD PRODUCTION

Lee A. Craig

Household production refers to the manufacture of goods and the provision of services for oneself and for members of one's household. Judged in terms of the way people spend their time, household production is arguably the largest sector of the U.S. economy. In a review article, F. Thomas Juster and Frank P. Stafford (1991) show that in recent decades, household production has accounted for more than half of the total working hours of adult women and almost a quarter of those of men. In the more distant past, household production consumed an even larger proportion of workers' time. Thus, the structure and change of the economics of the household are important components of long-term economic growth. Typically, economic data, such as prices and quantities, are the result of market transactions and are therefore relatively easy to observe. Unfortunately, this is frequently not the case with production conducted within the household, and it takes creative detective work to develop quantitative measures of change in household production over time.

The most important activities associated with household production typically include cooking, cleaning, child care, and home manufacturing. Cooking refers to the entire range of homemaking activities associated with meal preparation. These include shopping, putting food away, setting the table, preparing and serving food, washing the dishes, and other cleaning activities. Cleaning includes tasks such as caring for the house, doing the laundry, and mowing the lawn (Hill 1985). Child care, including education and training, has always been an important component of household production in households with children. Finally, although household manufacturing no longer plays an important role in the market economy, in the past, significant amounts of manufacturing, especially of textiles, were also part of household production.

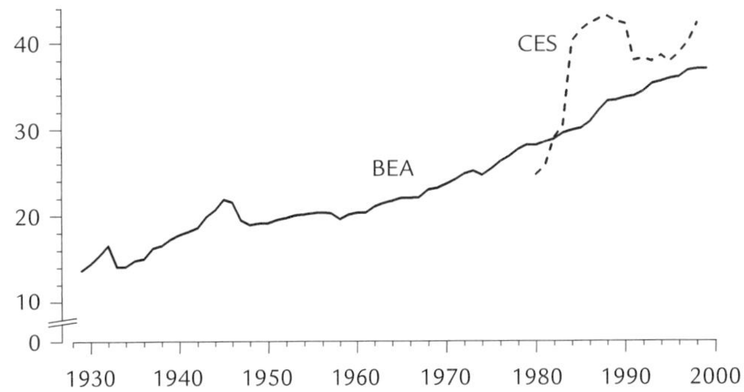

FIGURE Ba-W Consumption expenditures on food away from home as a percentage of total food expenditures: 1929–1999

Sources

Aggregate consumption expenditures, based on data from the U.S. Bureau of Economic Analysis (BEA): series Cd156 expressed as a percentage of series Cd154.

Expenditures of consumer units, based on the Consumer Expenditure Survey (CES): series Cd431 expressed as a percentage of series Cd429.

With the growth of the American economy, the production of many goods and services moved out of the household and into the market. Many of the goods and services that were once provided by mothers for themselves and their families in their own homes are today provided by highly specialized firms that produce for profit and distribute their goods for sale. One readily available measure of this movement is expenditures on food eaten away from home (see Figure Ba-W). In 1929, when these data were first compiled, such expenditures accounted for roughly 15 percent of all food expenditures. In the most recent years for which we have data, the share is between two and three times larger than this earlier figure. The care and feeding of boarders was another important household activity a century ago. Table Ba5082–5085 indicates that almost 12 percent of all households cared for one or more boarders or lodgers at that time.[1]

Over the same time period, other types of production moved away from the market and *into* the household. Some of this shift was associated with the move toward more extensive home ownership. Thus, as an increasing fraction of American households owned their own homes, the maintenance of residential property moved from the rental market sector to the household. Structural maintenance and home repairs, landscaping, and grounds maintenance increasingly became household rather than landlord activities. Data displayed in Table Dc653–669 illustrate the importance of this shift. The large decline in paid domestic help as a share of household expenditures represents another transfer into the home of goods and services that were previously produced in the market (see Figure Ba-X). Despite these changes, scholars generally conclude that on balance, the movement of production out of the household has overshadowed the movement of former market activities into the household.

Social trends also have a profound impact on household production. The long-term decline in fertility is a case in point. In 1800, total fertility for white women was above 7,000 per thousand,

[1] For a qualitative discussion of boarders, see Strasser (1982), Chapter 8.

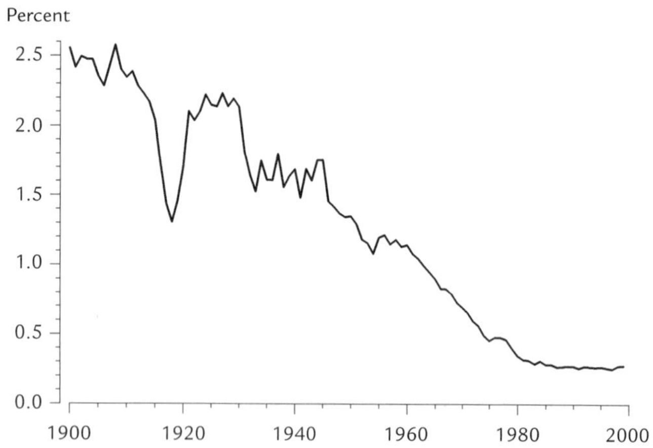

FIGURE Ba-X Consumption expenditures on domestic service as a percentage of total expenditures: 1900–1999

Sources

Through 1928: series Cd37 as a percentage of series Cd1; thereafter, series Cd192 as a percentage of series Cd153.

implying more than seven births per woman. Two hundred years later, total fertility for this group was about 2,000 (Table Ab52–117). The shift means that instead of fourteen years of pregnancy and nursing children (through the age of one year), the average woman now spends four years. She enjoys comparable reductions in the housework that attends the presence of young children in the home. Improved health and wealth of the older population has also lifted the burden of household production for mid-age adults. In 1850, 37 percent of males and 48 percent of females sixty-five years of age and older lived with their children or other relatives. Today the comparable rates are 4 percent and 6 percent, respectively (Table Ae245–319).

Inasmuch as household production does not pass through the market, its value is difficult to measure; it is not included in the standard statistical indicators of the performance of the economy. Gross domestic product (GDP), for example, includes only market-produced goods and services; it explicitly excludes the nonmarket production of the household. Household production is also excluded from most government output and trade statistics. Thus, for example, series Cd8 – consumption expenditures for clothing – measures only factory-produced clothing. Home-sewn clothing is omitted entirely. Similarly, the labor that goes into household production is omitted from official measures of the workforce. Thus, full-time homemakers, including those who report sixty-hour workweeks, are classified as "not in the labor force," according to the official statistics.

The omission of household production and household labor from official statistics means that the true output of the economy and the size of the workforce are underestimated. For example, Nancy Folbre and Barnet Wagman (1993) estimate that in 1800, the total output of the economy would have been somewhere between a fifth and a third larger than standard estimates had the value of household production been included. Moreover, when production and workers move out of the household and into the market, they move from the unmeasured to the measured realms. As the predominant transformation of the economy has been from household to market production, this finding, which has been confirmed by Lee Craig (1991, 1993), means that official statistics overstate the growth of the economy and of the labor force. Had household production and employment been properly included at earlier dates, the growth of the economy over time would look considerably less spectacular.

The statistics on household production displayed in this chapter measure the magnitude – as well as changes in the volume and value – of household production at different points in U.S. history. They are also attempts to indicate something of the significance of household production for the economic and social history of the United States. Unfortunately, they are often poor measures. They capture only a small portion of total household production, and they measure with wide margins of possible error. They omit important differences between home and market production in the nature and quality of the product and the conditions of work. For example, store-bought clothing, bread, and cookies differ from their home-sewn and home-baked counterparts, and home care of the elderly is different from that provided in a nursing home, yet these differences are not reflected here. Furthermore, cooking for one's family is different from cooking in a restaurant or from working in an office, earning money, and taking the family out to eat; yet the data are silent on these issues, too. Thus, the reader should use particular caution in handling these data.

Household Manufactures

In the eighteenth century, household production included a wide range of manufacturing activity in addition to the provision of services that predominate today. Historian Thomas Dublin, for example, conjectures that a typical New England farm housewife in this era probably

> milked the family cows, made butter and cheese, tended the family's garden plot, and sewed the children's clothes as they outgrew one set after another. She may also have spun woolen or linen yarn and woven cloth for her growing family, for the local historian remarks on the common appearance of spinning wheels and looms in the "homes of overworked farmers' wives" before the coming of textile factories. She may also have woven cloth or braided palm-leaf hats for local storekeepers or middlemen, for members of New Hampshire families in this period commonly pursued these outwork occupations to earn credits toward necessary store purchases. (Dublin 1994, p. 4)

The earliest systematic accounting of the quantity and value of goods produced in the home was conducted by Rolla Tryon. His primary objective was to illustrate the dramatic shift in the production of key goods and services from the home to the factory (Tryon 1966). Of the many goods and services that had been home produced for centuries, four remained quite prominent in the mid-nineteenth century: textiles, particularly clothing; food; boarding for nonhousehold members; and child care. Tables Ba4999–5090 contain data directly related to the household supply of these goods and services.

The data on home manufacturing in Table Ba4999–5078 reflect both industrialization and the westward migration. One can see the effect of industrialization in the decline of household production in both total and per capita terms in the older states. For example, in New Hampshire, the value of home manufactures per capita declined from $9.22 in 1810 to $1.89 in 1840 and then to $0.78 in 1860, which corresponds to an average annual decline of roughly 5 percent. To put this figure in perspective, consider that GDP per capita was growing by about 1 percent per annum over the same period. Although we do not know the overall size of the household sector, it is safe to conclude that a substantial proportion of the growth of market-produced goods was a result of the expansion of industries, such as textiles, which were displacing home-produced goods. Even by Tryon's narrow definition of household manufactures, the total value of household production remained relatively large, and stood at $1.18 per capita (more than 1 percent of per capita GDP) as late as 1850. A similar share of output today would amount to more than $100 billion.

The continuing importance of household production was related to the westward movement of population and economic activity. This migration is reflected in the fact that in states such as Tennessee and Mississippi, the total value of home manufactures increased substantially between 1810 and 1860 (by 3.5 percent annually in Tennessee and 1.3 percent in Mississippi). This increase occurred even as the per capita figures were falling, albeit at a much slower rate than those for the Eastern states. For example, during this period, per capita home manufactures were falling by 2.6 percent per year in Tennessee and by 1.6 percent in Mississippi.

Because of the prominence of the textile industry in early industrialization, Tryon paid particular attention to its shift from home to factory. The spinning of yarn and the weaving of cloth were among the first manufacturing activities to move out of the home and into the factory on a large scale. When the federal census collected statistics on the number of yards of different types of cloth spun in home manufactures throughout the United States in 1810, it found an average of 10.4 yards of cloth per person. However, the values varied widely across regions. In the largely urban District of Columbia, only 0.2 yard was produced per person; in largely rural New Hampshire, production totaled 19.9 yards per person.

By Tryon's definition of home manufactures, textiles composed 95 percent of the U.S. total for this category in 1810, although, as the previous example suggests, this percentage varied substantially from state to state (Tryon 1966, p. 166). Table Ba5079–5081 illustrates the relationship between the rise of the factory and the decline of household production. The table shows the overall home production of textiles, the per capita production, and the number of manufacturers in New York State between 1820 and 1855. Both overall and per capita production rose until 1825, but the subsequent growth of factories, and factory production, was so rapid that by 1855, the home-manufactured output per person was less than 3 percent of what it had been just thirty years earlier.

Clearly, this rapid decline in the quantity of home-manufactured textile products had much to do with the rise of factory-produced goods, and the regional differences previously noted were closely related to the regional character of industrialization in the United States. Not surprisingly, these two phenomena – the rise of the factory in certain regions and the transformation of the household economy – were inextricably linked. Studies of U.S. industrialization show that the early industrialization of the Northeast relative to the South resulted from the relatively low productivity of women and children in market production in the preindustrial (Northeastern) economy (Goldin and Sokoloff 1984; Craig and Field-Hendry 1993).

Despite the decline in home-produced textile products before the Civil War, particularly in the Northeast, as late as 1869 almost half (49 percent) of U.S. clothing was still home produced, and the vast majority (90 percent) of the total value of food consumed was produced in the home. Although the declines in the volume of home-produced food after that date were steady, they were not spectacular. With respect to textiles, by 1933, 15 percent of clothing was still home produced – an average annual compounded rate of decline after 1869 of roughly 2 percent. It is interesting to note that there was no acceleration in the decline of the home-produced share of overall clothing production, with the data showing almost exactly the same rate of decline from 1869 to 1900 and from 1900 to 1933. By comparison, the share of food produced in the home fell more slowly (1.3 percent per annum), but the decline accelerated over time, declining at less than 1 percent per annum before 1900 and by nearly 2 percent thereafter (calculated from Shaw 1947, pp. 30–52, 108, 174).

Causes and Consequences

Just as the decline in home manufacturing before the Civil War was related to economic developments both in and out of the household, the postbellum declines had causes that emanated from the market as well as from within the household. In particular, the evolving economic role of women (and, to a certain extent, of children) increasingly led women to be more prominent in the market economy. The most obvious indicator of this prominence is the increase in the labor force participation rate (LFPR) of women. Between 1890 and 1930, the LFPR of women rose by nearly one third, from 18.9 percent to 24.8 percent (Goldin 1990). Separating the causality from the consequences of such a conspicuous and multifaceted phenomenon as the rise of the female LFPR is beyond the scope of this essay. However, three related matters – evolving property rights, technological change, and the growth of child care outside the home – reveal a great deal about changes in household production.

One would expect that at the margin, the migration from home to market work would be influenced by the expected returns in the two activities. The returns to women from entering the market would increase as women increasingly came to possess the property right in their own personages – that is, they gained control over their own labor and earnings. In the past, the law did not always recognize the property rights of women. Table Ba5091–5095 contains three indicators of the evolution of women's property rights. These include the year each state passed legislation permitting women to (1) manage or otherwise control their own estates, (2) control their earnings, and (3) enter into business without their husband's consent. Note that prior to the Civil War, only a handful of states permitted women to control their own earnings, but by 1900, almost all states had done so.

In addition, the evolution of the economic roles of women was influenced by changes in both the capital intensity and technological change in household production. Mechanical appliances, particularly those powered by electricity, greatly increased the productivity of household workers, which in turn freed considerable amounts of time for other pursuits, including market work.[2]

Finally, since time immemorial, the economic role of women has been linked with that of children. However, in the nineteenth century, the economic roles of women and children began to diverge. As women increasingly left the household to enter the marketplace, children left the household to go to school (see Table Ba340–354 for employment and Table Bc7–18 for

[2] For a history of household technology and its impact on work both in and outside of the home, see Cowan (1976).

school enrollment trends). As the market activity of women accelerated in the twentieth century, even the care of preschool children became a market activity. Little statistical evidence concerning child care outside the home exists before the 1950s, but since that time we can document a relatively rapid development of this market. Table Ba5086–5090 contains data on child care arrangements for working mothers since 1959. The most striking feature of the data in the table is that between 1959 and 1994, the number of children who were receiving such care grew by 4.5 percent per year, while the population of children under five actually fell. Compared with the rates of change of other indicators discussed here, the shift in child care from the home to the market must be considered dramatic.

References

Cowan, Ruth Schwartz. 1976. "The 'Industrial Revolution' in the Home: Household Technology and Social Change in the 20th Century." *Technology and Culture* 17 (January): 58–72.

Craig, Lee A. 1991. "The Value of Household Labor in Antebellum Northern Agriculture." *Journal of Economic History* 51 (March): 67–82.

Craig, Lee A. 1993. *To Sow One Acre More: Childbearing and Farm Productivity in the Antebellum North.* Johns Hopkins University Press.

Craig, Lee A., and Elizabeth Field-Hendry. 1993. "Industrialization and the Earnings Gap." *Explorations in Economic History* 30 (1): 60–80.

Dublin, Thomas. 1994. *Transforming Women's Work: New England Lives in the Industrial Revolution.* Cornell University Press.

Folbre, Nancy, and Barnet Wagman. 1993. "Counting Housework: New Estimates of Real Product in the United States, 1800–1860." *Journal of Economic History* 53 (2): 275–88.

Goldin, Claudia. 1990. *Understanding the Gender Gap: An Economic History of American Women.* Oxford University Press.

Goldin, Claudia, and Kenneth Sokoloff. 1984. "The Relative Productivity Hypothesis of Industrialization: The American Case." *Quarterly Journal of Economics* 98 (3): 461–88.

Hill, Martha S. 1985. "Patterns of Time Use." In F. Thomas Juster and Frank P. Stafford, editors. *Time, Goods, and Well-Being.* Survey Research Center, Institute for Social Research, University of Michigan.

Juster, F. Thomas, and Frank P. Stafford. 1991. "The Allocation of Time: Empirical Findings, Behavioral Models, and Problems of Measurement." *Journal of Economic Literature* 29 (2): 471–522.

Shaw, William Howard. 1947. *Value of Commodity Output since 1869.* National Bureau of Economic Research.

Strasser, Susan. 1982. *Never Done: A History of American Housework.* Pantheon Books.

Tryon, Rolla Milton. 1966. "Household Manufactures in the United States, 1640–1860." Ph.D. dissertation, University of Chicago, 1916; reprinted by Augustus M. Kelley.

WORKFORCE

Thomas Weiss

TABLE Ba1–10 Male workforce, by age and race: 1800–1900 [Weiss]

Contributed by Thomas Weiss

	All races		White		Nonwhite					
					Total		Free		Slave	
	Age 10–15	Age 16 and older	Age 10–15	Age 16 and older	Age 10–15	Age 16 and older	Age 10–15	Age 16 and older	Age 10–15	Age 16 and older
	Ba1	Ba2	Ba3	Ba4	Ba5	Ba6	Ba7	Ba8	Ba9	Ba10
Year	Number	Number	Number	Number	Number	Number	Number	Number	Number	Number
1800	146,896	1,200,129	74,190	985,044	72,706	215,085	3,375	24,502	69,331	190,583
1810	195,622	1,641,798	97,393	1,343,875	98,229	297,923	5,764	41,278	92,465	256,644
1820	257,133	2,242,373	127,874	1,847,453	129,260	394,920	7,416	52,753	121,844	342,167
1830	329,886	3,048,122	163,610	2,542,086	166,276	506,035	10,383	68,535	155,893	437,500
1840	417,465	4,180,483	215,242	3,541,961	202,222	638,522	12,036	87,138	190,186	551,384
1850	550,369	5,988,149	303,862	5,131,128	246,508	857,022	11,621	105,422	234,886	751,600
1860	694,603	8,384,845	386,136	7,309,977	308,467	1,074,869	14,760	132,728	293,707	942,140
1870	571,208	10,340,205	419,585	9,075,643	151,623	1,264,562	151,623	1,264,562	—	—
1880	825,187	13,919,756	610,244	12,214,107	214,943	1,705,649	214,943	1,705,649	—	—
1890	1,093,586	18,447,234	805,758	16,402,821	287,828	2,044,413	287,828	2,044,413	—	—
1900	1,264,411	22,489,425	941,384	19,981,794	323,027	2,507,631	323,027	2,507,631	—	—

Source

Thomas Weiss, "Estimates of White and Nonwhite Gainful Workers in the United States by Age Group, Race, and Sex: Decennial Census Years, 1800–1900," *Historical Methods* 32 (1) (1999): 21–35.

Documentation

Gainful workers include individuals who reported an occupation to a U.S. Census worker, regardless of their state of employment. Thus, unemployed workers who were not actively looking for employment would be considered gainful workers, whereas new workers who had not established an occupation (that is, had not received their first job) would not be counted as gainful workers.

The series in this table were constructed from data collected and reported by the federal censuses of population.

The "Nonwhite" component includes blacks, Asians, and Native Americans.

Most of the estimation of industrial distribution of male and female workers was done at the state level and then aggregated to form the national estimates.

In 1800, 1810, and 1830, the census did not provide any workforce statistics. Hence, all data pertaining to the foregoing dates were estimated using population data reported by the censuses and estimated participation rates specific to the designated age/sex groups in the population. Although the census reported workforce statistics in 1820 and 1840, age and sex information was omitted. In 1850, slaves, all female workers, and male workers between the ages of 10 and 15 were excluded from census reports. In 1860, neither slaves nor free males and females age 10 to 15 were included in census reports. Hence, many antebellum workforce series were estimated.

In the postbellum period, there were other problems with census data. In 1870, underenumeration of the Southern states' population was a problem; in 1890, workers age 10 to 15 were undercounted

TABLE Ba11–24 Male workforce participation rate, by age and race: 1800–1900 [Weiss]

Contributed by Thomas Weiss

	All races			White			Nonwhite								
							Total			Free			Slave	
	Age 10 and older	Age 10–15	Age 16 and older	Age 10 and older	Age 10–15	Age 16 and older	Age 10 and older	Age 10–15	Age 16 and older	Age 10 and older	Age 10–15	Age 16 and older	Age 10–15	Age 16 and older
	Ba11	Ba12	Ba13	Ba14	Ba15	Ba16	Ba17	Ba18	Ba19	Ba20	Ba21 [1]	Ba22 [1]	Ba23 [2]	Ba24 [2]
Year	Percent	Percent	Percent	Percent	Percent	Percent	Percent	Percent	Percent	Percent	Percent	Percent	Percent	Percent
1800	76.3	33.5	90.4	73.5	21.0	90.6	88.5	84.6	89.8	76.2	37.9	88.6	90	90
1810	76.5	33.4	90.4	73.8	20.8	90.5	88.1	83.3	89.8	76.1	37.9	88.6	90	90
1820	76.9	33.5	90.4	74.4	20.8	90.6	88.1	83.4	89.8	76.0	37.9	88.6	90	90
1830	77.4	33.3	90.3	75.2	20.7	90.4	88.0	82.9	89.8	75.3	37.9	88.6	90	90
1840	77.8	32.6	90.3	75.8	20.8	90.4	88.1	83.2	89.8	76.2	37.9	88.6	90	90
1850	77.6	31.7	89.5	75.7	21.1	89.4	88.6	84.5	89.8	78.2	37.9	88.6	90	90
1860	78.8	31.0	90.3	77.2	20.6	90.3	88.6	84.4	89.8	78.1	37.9	88.6	90	90
1870	74.9	19.5	88.8	72.1	16.6	85.4	77.5	37.9	88.6	77.5	37.9	88.6	—	—
1880	78.7	24.4	90.6	78.1	21.2	90.2	83.1	43.4	94.0	83.1	43.4	94.0	—	—
1890	80.2	25.9	91.6	79.7	22.4	91.2	84.1	46.4	94.9	84.1	46.4	94.9	—	—
1900	79.7	26.1	90.2	79.2	22.5	89.9	83.7	48.6	92.3	83.7	48.6	92.3	—	—

[1] Values estimated prior to 1870.

[2] Estimated.

Source

Thomas Weiss, "Estimates of White and Nonwhite Gainful Workers in the United States by Age Group, Race, and Sex: Decennial Census Years, 1800–1900," *Historical Methods* 32 (1) (1999): 21–35.

Documentation

See the text for Table Ba1–10.

TABLE Ba25–39 Male workforce and workforce participation rate, by age and race: 1870–1900 [Census estimates]

Contributed by Thomas Weiss

	Male workforce						Workforce participation rate								
	All races		White		Nonwhite		All races			White			Nonwhite		
	Age 10–15	Age 16 and older	Age 10–15	Age 16 and older	Age 10–15	Age 16 and older	Age 10 and older	Age 10–15	Age 16 and older	Age 10 and older	Age 10–15	Age 16 and older	Age 10 and older	Age 10–15	Age 16 and older
	Ba25	Ba26	Ba27	Ba28	Ba29	Ba30	Ba31	Ba32	Ba33	Ba34	Ba35	Ba36	Ba37	Ba38	Ba39
Year	Number	Number	Number	Number	Number	Number	Percent	Percent	Percent	Percent	Percent	Percent	Percent	Percent	Percent
1870	741,475	11,068,130	544,655	9,714,546	196,820	1,353,584	81.0	25.3	95.1	77.9	21.5	91.4	84.8	49.2	94.8
1880	1,086,466	14,128,417	803,466	12,397,200	283,001	1,731,217	81.2	32.2	92.0	80.4	27.9	91.5	87.2	57.1	95.4
1890	1,244,939	18,373,471	917,275	16,337,233	327,664	2,036,238	80.6	29.5	91.3	80.0	25.5	90.9	85.2	52.8	94.5
1900	1,289,126	22,592,636	967,004	20,045,540	322,122	2,547,097	80.2	26.6	90.6	79.6	23.1	90.2	84.8	48.5	93.7

Source

Thomas Weiss, "Estimates of White and Nonwhite Gainful Workers in the United States by Age Group, Race, and Sex: Decennial Census Years, 1800–1900," *Historical Methods* 32 (1) (1999): 21–35.

Documentation

Tabulated from the Integrated Public Use Microdata Series; see the Guide to the Millennial Edition. Also see the text for Table Ba1–10.

TABLE Ba40–49 Female workforce, by age and race: 1800–1900 [Weiss]

Contributed by Thomas Weiss

	All races		White		Nonwhite					
					Total		Free		Slave	
	Age 10–15	Age 16 and older	Age 10–15	Age 16 and older	Age 10–15	Age 16 and older	Age 10–15	Age 16 and older	Age 10–15	Age 16 and older
	Ba40	Ba41	Ba42	Ba43	Ba44	Ba45	Ba46	Ba47	Ba48	Ba49
Year	Number	Number	Number	Number	Number	Number	Number	Number	Number	Number
1800	94,651	271,472	24,787	70,929	69,864	200,543	2,155	11,273	67,709	189,270
1810	125,741	374,203	31,696	99,277	94,045	274,926	3,695	19,239	90,351	255,687
1820	160,309	502,840	41,287	147,228	119,022	355,612	4,715	24,420	114,307	331,192
1830	205,737	688,088	48,828	222,273	156,909	465,815	6,718	32,307	150,191	433,508
1840	253,674	926,491	61,848	333,129	191,826	593,361	7,836	39,829	183,990	553,533
1850	325,499	1,328,791	88,693	531,015	236,806	797,775	7,810	47,378	228,996	750,397
1860	403,296	1,810,500	111,915	817,698	291,381	992,802	9,453	58,413	281,928	934,389
1870	200,821	1,672,947	104,047	1,149,206	96,774	523,741	96,774	523,741	—	—
1880	293,127	2,354,028	151,078	1,637,910	142,049	716,118	142,049	716,118	—	—
1890	409,418	3,596,621	223,951	2,704,917	185,467	891,704	185,467	891,704	—	—
1900	485,767	4,833,630	287,172	3,702,721	198,595	1,130,909	198,595	1,130,909	—	—

Source

Thomas Weiss, "Estimates of White and Nonwhite Gainful Workers in the United States by Age Group, Race, and Sex: Decennial Census Years, 1800–1900," *Historical Methods* 32 (1) (1999): 21–35.

Documentation

See the text for Table Ba1–10.

TABLE Ba50–63 Female workforce participation rate, by age and race: 1800–1900 [Weiss]

Contributed by Thomas Weiss

	All races			White			Nonwhite							
							Total			Free			Slave	
	Age 10 and older	Age 10–15	Age 16 and older	Age 10 and older	Age 10–15	Age 16 and older	Age 10 and older	Age 10–15	Age 16 and older	Age 10 and older	Age 10–15	Age 16 and older	Age 10–15	Age 16 and older
	Ba50	Ba51	Ba52	Ba53	Ba54	Ba55	Ba56	Ba57	Ba58	Ba59	Ba60 [1]	Ba61 [1]	Ba62 [2]	Ba63 [2]
Year	Percent	Percent	Percent	Percent	Percent	Percent	Percent	Percent	Percent	Percent	Percent	Percent	Percent	Percent
1800	21.4	23.3	20.8	6.9	7.7	6.7	82.9	83.4	82.7	33.0	25.2	35.1	90	90
1810	21.3	22.3	21.0	6.9	7.1	6.9	81.3	81.7	81.1	33.0	25.2	35.1	90	90
1820	20.9	21.3	20.8	7.3	6.8	7.4	81.4	81.7	81.3	33.0	25.2	35.1	90	90
1830	21.0	21.7	20.7	7.7	6.5	8.1	81.2	81.1	81.2	32.8	25.2	35.1	90	90
1840	20.7	20.7	20.6	8.3	6.3	8.9	81.4	81.4	81.4	32.9	25.2	35.1	90	90
1850	20.6	19.4	20.9	9.2	6.4	9.9	82.5	83.0	82.3	33.2	25.2	35.1	90	90
1860	20.3	18.7	20.7	9.9	6.2	10.8	82.6	83.1	82.4	33.2	25.2	35.1	90	90
1870	13.1	7.1	14.6	9.8	4.2	11.1	33.0	25.2	35.1	33.0	25.2	35.1	—	—
1880	14.7	9.0	16.0	11.4	5.4	12.7	37.5	29.8	39.5	37.5	29.8	39.5	—	—
1890	17.4	10.0	19.0	14.4	6.4	16.1	39.8	30.9	42.3	39.8	30.9	42.3	—	—
1900	18.8	10.2	20.6	16.0	7.0	17.8	40.0	30.1	42.5	40.0	30.1	42.5	—	—

[1] Values estimated prior to 1870.

[2] Estimated.

Source

Thomas Weiss, "Estimates of White and Nonwhite Gainful Workers in the United States by Age Group, Race, and Sex: Decennial Census Years, 1800–1900," *Historical Methods* 32 (1) (1999): 21–35.

Documentation

See the text for Table Ba1–10.

TABLE Ba64–78 Female workforce and workforce participation rate, by age and race: 1870–1900 [Decennial census estimates]

Contributed by Thomas Weiss

	Workforce						Workforce participation rate								
	All races		White		Nonwhite		All races			White			Nonwhite		
	Age 10–15	Age 16 and older	Age 10–15	Age 16 and older	Age 10–15	Age 16 and older	Age 10 and older	Age 10–15	Age 16 and older	Age 10 and older	Age 10–15	Age 16 and older	Age 10 and older	Age 10–15	Age 16 and older
	Ba64	Ba65	Ba66	Ba67	Ba68	Ba69	Ba70	Ba71	Ba72	Ba73	Ba74	Ba75	Ba76	Ba77	Ba78
Year	Number	Number	Number	Number	Number	Number	Percent	Percent	Percent	Percent	Percent	Percent	Percent	Percent	Percent
1870	291,483	1,650,986	151,020	1,134,120	140,463	516,866	13.6	10.2	14.4	10.0	6.1	10.9	35.0	36.6	34.6
1880	373,264	2,501,162	192,381	1,740,285	180,883	760,877	15.9	11.4	17.0	12.3	6.9	13.5	41.1	37.9	42.0
1890	452,744	3,629,573	247,651	2,729,699	205,094	899,874	17.7	11.0	19.1	14.6	7.1	16.2	40.8	34.2	42.7
1900	498,551	5,102,385	297,691	3,946,053	200,861	1,156,331	19.8	10.5	21.7	17.0	7.3	19.0	40.8	30.4	43.4

Source

Thomas Weiss, "Estimates of White and Nonwhite Gainful Workers in the United States by Age Group, Race, and Sex: Decennial Census Years, 1800–1900," *Historical Methods* 32 (1) (1999): 21–35.

Documentation

Tabulated from the Integrated Public Use Microdata Series; see the Guide to the Millennial Edition. Also see the text for Table Ba1–10.

TABLE Ba79–127 Free male gainful workers, by state: 1800–1900 [Age 16 and older]

Contributed by Thomas Weiss

	U.S. total	Alabama	Arizona	Arkansas	California	Colorado	Connecticut	Dakotas	Delaware	District of Columbia
	Ba79	Ba80	Ba81	Ba82	Ba83	Ba84	Ba85	Ba86	Ba87	Ba88
Year	Number	Number	Number	Number	Number	Number	Number	Number	Number	Number
1800	1,009,546	—	—	—	—	—	58,980	—	13,007	1,658
1810	1,385,154	—	—	—	—	—	63,089	—	15,476	2,829
1820	1,900,206	23,596	—	3,243	—	—	68,221	—	15,877	4,631
1830	2,610,622	45,161	—	6,595	—	—	78,708	—	17,289	6,422
1840	3,629,099	79,308	—	19,397	—	—	84,586	—	18,490	7,070
1850	5,236,550	97,534	—	39,283	77,567	—	106,251	—	21,712	11,283
1860	7,442,705	133,262	—	77,721	196,817	29,428	130,540	937	29,104	18,373
1870	10,340,206	260,812	5,646	132,431	223,283	16,901	155,803	5,708	32,126	34,559
1880	13,919,755	303,816	21,595	201,776	344,873	95,657	186,860	54,279	43,948	46,349
1890	18,447,225	389,796	24,624	300,064	478,615	171,262	238,968	160,707	52,212	67,339
1900	22,489,425	482,190	45,226	358,195	549,158	187,394	290,133	216,059	57,243	84,415

	Florida	Georgia	Idaho	Illinois	Indiana	Iowa	Kansas	Kentucky	Louisiana	Maine
	Ba89	Ba90	Ba91	Ba92	Ba93	Ba94	Ba95	Ba96	Ba97	Ba98
Year	Number	Number	Number	Number	Number	Number	Number	Number	Number	Number
1800	—	23,730	—	—	1,261	—	—	38,629	—	32,832
1810	—	33,466	—	2,958	5,197	—	—	69,743	15,452	50,011
1820	—	44,799	—	13,128	32,041	—	—	95,107	24,725	67,545
1830	5,438	69,668	—	34,732	72,584	—	—	120,099	29,988	96,215
1840	9,558	93,992	—	119,241	153,695	12,265	—	140,551	56,210	124,472
1850	12,793	117,578	—	209,754	242,656	48,252	—	184,099	79,307	159,738
1860	19,787	148,248	—	459,594	339,442	172,373	29,677	230,879	109,853	180,296
1870	47,615	285,724	10,721	656,990	415,860	308,962	114,513	333,838	207,262	175,465
1880	67,220	380,201	15,186	856,579	551,030	465,625	289,709	428,789	243,494	194,378
1890	110,687	474,611	33,054	1,145,463	657,516	560,159	415,892	501,647	288,563	209,356
1900	152,708	568,470	56,772	1,458,400	755,783	657,957	431,865	593,233	365,562	220,868

	Maryland	Massachusetts	Michigan	Minnesota	Mississippi	Missouri	Montana	Nebraska	Nevada	New Hampshire
	Ba99	Ba100	Ba101	Ba102	Ba103	Ba104	Ba105	Ba106	Ba107	Ba108
Year	Number	Number	Number	Number	Number	Number	Number	Number	Number	Number
1800	56,108	101,190	—	—	1,476	—	—	—	—	41,362
1810	64,238	116,527	1,566	—	6,496	—	—	—	—	48,780
1820	72,862	131,793	3,366	—	11,124	14,453	—	—	—	57,974
1830	86,047	162,763	9,640	—	18,210	26,449	—	—	—	67,139
1840	94,375	210,296	56,818	—	46,508	78,977	—	—	—	75,070
1850	129,110	288,274	106,628	2,315	70,785	150,127	—	—	—	92,342
1860	150,730	347,113	207,614	48,906	93,711	273,380	—	9,687	5,638	93,585
1870	203,678	439,363	339,672	119,579	226,633	447,033	13,876	41,324	26,427	93,820
1880	254,511	534,285	502,581	225,087	272,759	598,354	21,648	138,343	30,621	109,747
1890	296,535	703,196	652,598	398,895	321,128	764,733	67,282	321,478	21,448	125,044
1900	342,721	862,981	752,776	531,973	402,860	914,245	104,061	315,072	17,626	134,414

(continued)

TABLE Ba79–127 Free male gainful workers, by state: 1800–1900 [Age 16 and older] *Continued*

	New Jersey	New Mexico	New York	North Carolina	Ohio	Oklahoma	Oregon	Pennsylvania	Rhode Island	South Carolina
	Ba109	Ba110	Ba111	Ba112	Ba113	Ba114	Ba115	Ba116	Ba117	Ba118
Year	Number	Number	Number	Number	Number	Number	Number	Number	Number	Number
1800	45,491	—	132,431	75,727	10,358	—	—	141,458	16,142	44,000
1810	54,971	—	219,533	84,424	49,854	—	—	187,212	18,889	49,194
1820	64,752	—	327,638	95,396	129,891	—	—	247,328	20,394	56,319
1830	79,411	—	480,096	111,289	213,697	—	—	330,587	25,227	61,998
1840	94,664	—	645,238	114,141	364,763	—	—	426,733	29,497	62,932
1850	124,796	17,214	869,533	132,938	517,629	—	4,750	613,606	42,123	64,689
1860	178,747	23,097	1,112,524	166,768	604,513	—	17,880	773,766	50,019	76,584
1870	244,142	25,287	1,204,318	272,247	722,977	—	29,551	856,862	63,349	189,251
1880	320,146	36,615	1,485,730	337,588	850,554	—	63,598	1,185,189	83,516	240,250
1890	444,939	48,588	1,869,755	401,203	1,089,750	19,647	114,977	1,580,781	107,088	279,632
1900	584,780	56,723	2,269,211	478,595	1,265,716	223,673	148,869	1,932,857	134,686	333,282

	Tennessee	Texas	Utah	Vermont	Virginia	Washington	West Virginia	Wisconsin	Wyoming
	Ba119	Ba120	Ba121	Ba122	Ba123	Ba124	Ba125	Ba126	Ba127
Year	Number	Number	Number	Number	Number	Number	Number	Number	Number
1800	18,324	—	—	33,652	121,731	—	—	—	—
1810	44,346	—	—	47,561	133,339	—	—	—	—
1820	68,459	—	—	56,611	148,932	—	—	—	—
1830	113,501	—	—	69,205	172,465	—	—	—	—
1840	135,232	—	—	75,111	188,183	—	—	11,726	—
1850	165,255	41,743	3,099	89,740	221,278	—	—	80,768	—
1860	196,450	114,577	8,558	87,260	277,668	6,000	—	211,599	—
1870	288,479	232,119	19,845	94,018	335,548	9,487	109,957	260,801	6,344
1880	347,270	426,256	34,876	99,819	376,302	28,722	154,849	360,822	8,353
1890	461,439	608,580	61,349	107,199	429,567	152,663	202,301	486,307	28,589
1900	547,672	819,037	71,745	110,011	492,232	201,799	272,159	595,549	40,469

Source

Thomas Weiss, "Estimates of White and Nonwhite Gainful Workers in the United States by Age Group, Race, and Sex: Decennial Census Years, 1800–1900," *Historical Methods* 32 (1) (1999): 21–35.

Documentation

See the text for Table Ba1–10.

TABLE Ba128–176 Free female gainful workers, by state: 1800–1900 [Age 16 and older]

Contributed by Thomas Weiss

Year	U.S. total	Alabama	Arizona	Arkansas	California	Colorado	Connecticut	Dakotas	Delaware	District of Columbia
	Ba128	Ba129	Ba130	Ba131	Ba132	Ba133	Ba134	Ba135	Ba136	Ba137
	Number	Number	Number	Number	Number	Number	Number	Number	Number	Number
1800	82,206	—	—	—	—	—	5,918	—	692	138
1810	118,516	—	—	—	—	—	7,066	—	903	331
1820	171,648	2,115	—	77	—	—	8,725	—	1,051	603
1830	254,580	4,448	—	178	—	—	10,964	—	1,334	957
1840	372,958	8,111	—	626	—	—	13,318	—	1,596	1,310
1850	578,394	11,963	—	1,689	346	—	18,260	—	2,199	2,340
1860	876,111	15,511	—	4,053	6,171	63	25,738	75	3,132	3,922
1870	1,672,948	81,441	266	16,156	13,151	414	31,968	155	4,776	12,988
1880	2,353,988	98,566	451	23,200	27,159	4,608	44,660	2,672	7,088	19,064
1890	3,596,616	109,091	1,534	41,888	58,606	18,484	67,124	18,399	9,424	31,049
1900	4,833,630	158,345	6,162	62,532	85,790	27,369	83,898	27,498	11,894	40,382

Year	Florida	Georgia	Idaho	Illinois	Indiana	Iowa	Kansas	Kentucky	Louisiana	Maine
	Ba138	Ba139	Ba140	Ba141	Ba142	Ba143	Ba144	Ba145	Ba146	Ba147
	Number	Number	Number	Number	Number	Number	Number	Number	Number	Number
1800	—	2,239	—	—	15	—	—	1,513	—	1,794
1810	—	3,379	—	66	97	—	—	3,089	1,524	3,173
1820	—	4,651	—	364	747	—	—	4,898	2,195	5,112
1830	265	7,650	—	1,348	2,222	—	—	6,795	2,913	8,203
1840	420	10,734	—	5,265	5,762	426	—	8,762	5,092	12,027
1850	841	15,190	—	12,696	10,893	2,524	—	13,170	8,339	16,845
1860	1,604	18,607	—	33,281	19,360	11,184	1,444	18,106	12,245	22,251
1870	8,889	92,819	125	59,474	29,543	22,082	6,123	43,189	56,969	26,406
1880	14,472	120,628	274	99,005	47,872	42,383	18,129	49,035	75,011	31,881
1890	24,050	134,554	1,802	187,581	80,393	76,985	43,770	77,485	93,453	43,360
1900	33,459	182,037	4,375	275,105	111,024	102,037	53,386	98,181	109,484	49,917

Year	Maryland	Massachusetts	Michigan	Minnesota	Mississippi	Missouri	Montana	Nebraska	Nevada	New Hampshire
	Ba148	Ba149	Ba150	Ba151	Ba152	Ba153	Ba154	Ba155	Ba156	Ba157
	Number	Number	Number	Number	Number	Number	Number	Number	Number	Number
1800	3,920	16,075	—	—	115	—	—	—	—	5,124
1810	5,053	19,784	64	—	547	—	—	—	—	6,822
1820	6,426	24,856	135	—	1,015	313	—	—	—	9,089
1830	8,609	33,560	584	—	1,754	804	—	—	—	11,787
1840	10,908	44,774	5,036	—	4,543	2,908	—	—	—	14,146
1850	15,670	68,693	10,892	88	8,204	7,062	—	—	—	18,311
1860	21,856	93,887	23,864	3,586	10,631	17,713	—	399	30	21,162
1870	38,955	122,002	30,751	9,962	81,166	34,084	167	1,775	435	23,080
1880	54,094	165,121	51,534	23,573	92,855	58,180	482	9,725	1,461	28,419
1890	78,049	253,073	90,071	62,229	108,426	106,367	4,494	40,733	1,800	34,931
1900	91,097	317,558	126,517	90,887	144,254	145,498	9,539	44,121	1,969	39,807

(continued)

TABLE Ba128–176 Free female gainful workers, by state: 1800–1900 [Age 16 and older] *Continued*

	New Jersey	New Mexico	New York	North Carolina	Ohio	Oklahoma	Oregon	Pennsylvania	Rhode Island	South Carolina
	Ba158	Ba159	Ba160	Ba161	Ba162	Ba163	Ba164	Ba165	Ba166	Ba167
Year	Number	Number	Number	Number	Number	Number	Number	Number	Number	Number
1800	3,041	—	10,072	4,020	278	—	—	6,981	3,138	6,929
1810	4,172	—	18,815	5,140	1,832	—	—	10,992	3,806	8,041
1820	5,724	—	32,436	6,600	5,637	—	—	16,794	4,572	9,521
1830	7,774	—	54,107	8,801	11,428	—	—	25,912	5,979	11,199
1840	10,843	—	83,168	10,358	23,024	—	—	39,539	7,483	11,752
1850	16,921	1,054	127,587	13,916	37,569	—	49	62,768	10,990	13,460
1860	27,293	1,702	187,432	17,873	55,261	—	300	93,124	14,436	15,121
1870	40,925	2,779	242,112	51,988	79,475	—	644	124,695	19,691	80,475
1880	62,438	2,010	338,219	67,997	105,388	—	2,676	198,437	27,055	99,974
1890	102,877	3,639	482,239	97,842	173,540	1,014	10,394	301,226	38,018	105,807
1900	142,718	5,766	635,319	127,740	233,177	19,728	17,916	395,656	48,203	142,433

	Tennessee	Texas	Utah	Vermont	Virginia	Washington	West Virginia	Wisconsin	Wyoming
	Ba168	Ba169	Ba170	Ba171	Ba172	Ba173	Ba174	Ba175	Ba176
Year	Number	Number	Number	Number	Number	Number	Number	Number	Number
1800	407	—	—	1,623	8,174	—	—	—	—
1810	1,146	—	—	2,834	9,840	—	—	—	—
1820	2,177	—	—	3,964	11,854	—	—	—	—
1830	4,142	—	—	5,563	15,301	—	—	—	—
1840	5,941	—	—	6,864	17,874	—	—	347	—
1850	8,795	2,004	78	8,768	23,211	—	—	5,008	—
1860	11,460	6,334	372	10,556	29,364	59	—	15,552	—
1870	38,019	28,883	840	12,891	67,159	228	8,279	24,257	297
1880	46,352	48,153	2,576	15,113	71,339	1,009	10,266	42,945	439
1890	72,974	79,511	6,553	18,759	95,078	10,658	20,142	75,433	1,707
1900	103,553	122,425	10,334	21,852	114,438	20,203	28,680	106,474	2,893

Source

Thomas Weiss, "Estimates of White and Nonwhite Gainful Workers in the United States by Age Group, Race, and Sex: Decennial Census Years, 1800–1900," *Historical Methods* 32 (1) (1999): 21–35.

Documentation

See the text for Table Ba1–10.

TABLE Ba177–225 Free male gainful workers, by state: 1800–1900 [Age 10 to 15]

Contributed by Thomas Weiss

	U.S. total	Alabama	Arizona	Arkansas	California	Colorado	Connecticut	Dakotas	Delaware	District of Columbia
	Ba177	Ba178	Ba179	Ba180	Ba181	Ba182	Ba183	Ba184	Ba185	Ba186
Year	Number	Number	Number	Number	Number	Number	Number	Number	Number	Number
1800	77,565	—	—	—	—	—	2,452	—	1,181	28
1810	103,157	—	—	—	—	—	2,596	—	1,290	62
1820	135,289	3,839	—	411	—	—	2,632	—	1,279	98
1830	173,993	7,588	—	788	—	—	2,688	—	1,412	122
1840	227,279	14,213	—	2,458	—	—	2,606	—	1,336	161
1850	315,483	18,751	—	5,752	103	—	3,009	—	1,579	242
1860	400,896	23,324	—	11,367	907	23	3,518	48	1,936	342
1870	571,208	36,757	88	8,607	1,585	246	3,657	19	2,181	641
1880	825,187	64,918	205	28,300	3,430	815	5,803	714	2,704	617
1890	1,093,587	80,965	525	46,004	5,431	2,029	6,666	4,491	2,889	1,653
1900	1,264,411	80,989	1,358	49,747	7,187	2,903	6,838	9,001	2,781	1,365

	Florida	Georgia	Idaho	Illinois	Indiana	Iowa	Kansas	Kentucky	Louisiana	Maine
	Ba187	Ba188	Ba189	Ba190	Ba191	Ba192	Ba193	Ba194	Ba195	Ba196
Year	Number	Number	Number	Number	Number	Number	Number	Number	Number	Number
1800	—	3,788	—	—	63	—	—	4,695	—	1,080
1810	—	5,391	—	154	339	—	—	8,969	1,081	1,619
1820	—	6,634	—	657	1,998	—	—	12,066	1,341	2,148
1830	329	9,701	—	1,841	4,725	—	—	13,500	1,775	2,660
1840	485	14,138	—	5,675	9,531	454	—	15,493	2,737	3,300
1850	987	19,281	—	10,658	14,066	2,403	—	20,329	4,300	3,993
1860	1,723	21,630	—	18,680	17,808	7,487	1,018	23,628	6,063	4,014
1870	4,182	55,463	33	21,742	12,399	12,188	2,830	34,699	12,888	4,319
1880	6,532	65,329	101	37,100	32,628	17,832	13,225	36,643	24,682	4,087
1890	9,775	79,813	488	41,770	28,603	20,225	19,706	45,462	33,456	4,049
1900	11,281	77,462	1,395	50,994	26,454	24,564	20,304	53,676	39,620	3,979

	Maryland	Massachusetts	Michigan	Minnesota	Mississippi	Missouri	Montana	Nebraska	Nevada	New Hampshire
	Ba197	Ba198	Ba199	Ba200	Ba201	Ba202	Ba203	Ba204	Ba205	Ba206
Year	Number	Number	Number	Number	Number	Number	Number	Number	Number	Number
1800	3,456	3,676	—	—	151	—	—	—	—	1,367
1810	3,884	3,949	39	—	674	—	—	—	—	1,639
1820	4,061	4,353	63	—	1,323	903	—	—	—	1,806
1830	4,679	4,661	244	—	2,187	1,862	—	—	—	1,824
1840	4,896	5,105	1,636	—	5,472	5,282	—	—	—	1,844
1850	6,453	6,881	3,252	39	9,999	10,080	—	—	—	2,008
1860	7,769	8,211	5,559	1,111	11,778	16,819	—	195	5	1,932
1870	10,013	12,180	7,045	2,218	31,929	19,812	1	619	41	2,213
1880	11,121	12,306	11,610	4,961	32,330	31,662	100	3,816	109	2,593
1890	14,000	15,970	16,748	9,780	50,624	42,771	385	10,358	143	2,801
1900	17,034	16,393	19,523	16,973	63,906	52,621	929	12,282	183	2,547

(continued)

TABLE Ba177–225 Free male gainful workers, by state: 1800–1900 [Age 10 to 15] *Continued*

	New Jersey	New Mexico	New York	North Carolina	Ohio	Oklahoma	Oregon	Pennsylvania	Rhode Island	South Carolina
	Ba207	Ba208	Ba209	Ba210	Ba211	Ba212	Ba213	Ba214	Ba215	Ba216
Year	Number	Number	Number	Number	Number	Number	Number	Number	Number	Number
1800	2,214	—	6,422	14,015	530	—	—	8,147	1,165	6,490
1810	2,658	—	8,797	15,804	2,636	—	—	11,107	1,211	6,948
1820	2,875	—	12,397	17,330	6,673	—	—	13,724	1,275	7,450
1830	3,393	—	16,728	18,903	10,712	—	—	17,266	1,397	7,844
1840	3,746	—	19,682	19,603	16,678	—	—	21,276	1,542	7,919
1850	4,867	928	24,671	23,237	22,061	—	71	29,475	1,964	8,938
1860	6,163	1,400	29,491	26,081	24,523	—	268	35,811	2,370	9,303
1870	7,483	994	29,661	40,300	34,392	—	417	29,347	3,510	21,968
1880	9,957	1,945	38,534	55,623	31,282	—	966	53,895	3,604	31,765
1890	14,528	2,188	52,030	73,222	32,230	567	1,621	68,640	6,076	48,777
1900	18,457	2,987	55,218	77,986	34,165	20,259	2,331	84,195	5,143	56,363

	Tennessee	Texas	Utah	Vermont	Virginia	Washington	West Virginia	Wisconsin	Wyoming
	Ba217	Ba218	Ba219	Ba220	Ba221	Ba222	Ba223	Ba224	Ba225
Year	Number	Number	Number	Number	Number	Number	Number	Number	Number
1800	2,806	—	—	1,320	12,519	—	—	—	—
1810	6,723	—	—	2,009	13,580	—	—	—	—
1820	11,184	—	—	2,153	14,615	—	—	—	—
1830	16,526	—	—	2,292	16,350	—	—	—	—
1840	20,383	—	—	2,284	17,160	—	—	183	—
1850	24,881	3,504	111	2,469	21,698	—	—	2,441	—
1860	25,897	9,223	377	2,296	24,552	28	—	6,217	—
1870	34,091	16,115	597	1,615	37,532	37	6,082	6,472	1
1880	44,292	36,934	2,292	2,598	34,741	337	9,842	10,240	67
1890	57,519	58,518	2,354	2,667	42,914	1,500	15,741	14,574	340
1900	63,711	73,604	2,095	2,170	44,651	2,807	22,343	20,842	795

Source

Thomas Weiss, "Estimates of White and Nonwhite Gainful Workers in the United States by Age Group, Race, and Sex: Decennial Census Years, 1800–1900," *Historical Methods* 32 (1) (1999): 21–35.

Documentation

See the text for Table Ba1–10.

TABLE Ba226–274 Free female gainful workers, by state: 1800–1900 [Age 10 to 15]

Contributed by Thomas Weiss

Year	U.S. total	Alabama	Arizona	Arkansas	California	Colorado	Connecticut	Dakotas	Delaware	District of Columbia
	Ba226	Ba227	Ba228	Ba229	Ba230	Ba231	Ba232	Ba233	Ba234	Ba235
	Number	Number	Number	Number	Number	Number	Number	Number	Number	Number
1800	26,941	—	—	—	—	—	1,447	—	396	13
1810	35,390	—	—	—	—	—	1,508	—	439	29
1820	46,001	1,107	—	69	—	—	1,585	—	433	46
1830	55,545	2,026	—	133	—	—	1,588	—	458	59
1840	69,683	3,961	—	434	—	—	1,527	—	439	79
1850	96,503	5,279	—	994	25	—	1,850	—	522	117
1860	121,368	6,502	—	1,944	262	3	2,262	9	629	171
1870	200,821	15,182	30	2,322	629	22	1,993	5	1,231	853
1880	293,169	25,490	20	7,416	1,043	171	4,010	179	840	594
1890	409,421	36,261	172	13,028	1,937	663	4,256	874	924	1,078
1900	485,767	41,664	624	15,321	2,132	597	4,741	2,238	1,078	779

Year	Florida	Georgia	Idaho	Illinois	Indiana	Iowa	Kansas	Kentucky	Louisiana	Maine	Maryland
	Ba236	Ba237	Ba238	Ba239	Ba240	Ba241	Ba242	Ba243	Ba244	Ba245	Ba246
	Number	Number	Number	Number	Number	Number	Number	Number	Number	Number	Number
1800	—	1,086	—	—	9	—	—	694	—	368	1,501
1810	—	1,554	—	38	56	—	—	1,331	333	579	1,711
1820	0	2,060	—	181	318	—	—	1,817	470	778	1,894
1830	65	2,897	—	494	744	—	—	1,969	549	935	2,087
1840	95	4,177	—	1,512	1,513	64	—	2,287	836	1,167	2,172
1850	185	5,722	—	2,871	2,269	355	—	3,027	1,294	1,522	2,967
1860	331	6,380	—	5,116	2,887	1,136	121	3,557	1,787	1,530	3,620
1870	1,120	26,777	—	3,809	1,567	1,044	386	7,897	7,813	2,035	5,897
1880	3.312	31,704	17	7,096	3,550	2,462	1,222	5,387	20,041	1,647	4,706
1890	4,329	37,505	92	12,729	4,509	3,432	1,737	6,847	21,911	1,703	6,703
1900	4,122	36,502	141	19,541	5,692	4,846	2,185	7,441	21,427	2,013	7,886

Year	Massachusetts	Michigan	Minnesota	Mississippi	Missouri	Montana	Nebraska	Nevada	New Hampshire	New Jersey
	Ba247	Ba248	Ba249	Ba250	Ba251	Ba252	Ba253	Ba254	Ba255	Ba256
	Number	Number	Number	Number	Number	Number	Number	Number	Number	Number
1800	2,092	—	—	38	—	—	—	—	722	1,128
1810	2,260	13	—	153	—	—	—	—	878	1,362
1820	2,605	21	—	314	154	—	—	—	961	1,525
1830	2,712	76	—	480	310	—	—	—	944	1,715
1840	2,997	530	—	1,258	896	—	—	—	953	1,899
1850	4,213	1,082	12	2,302	1,759	—	—	—	1,089	2,573
1860	5,222	1,863	333	2,717	2,884	—	38	1	1,107	3,415
1870	6,299	2,296	898	15,352	4,627	4	119	8	1,055	3,486
1880	9,062	3,479	1,504	17,562	4,763	25	730	42	1,709	4,338
1890	10,205	5,877	3,396	27,011	6,458	142	1,911	24	1,927	8,394
1900	11,475	7,174	6,041	34,103	9,028	270	2,495	31	1,951	11,804

(continued)

TABLE Ba226–274 Free female gainful workers, by state: 1800–1900 [Age 10 to 15] *Continued*

	New Mexico	New York	North Carolina	Ohio	Oklahoma	Oregon	Pennsylvania	Rhode Island	South Carolina	Tennessee
	Ba257	Ba258	Ba259	Ba260	Ba261	Ba262	Ba263	Ba264	Ba265	Ba266
Year	Number	Number	Number	Number	Number	Number	Number	Number	Number	Number
1800	—	2,700	4,387	133	—	—	3,018	746	3,550	344
1810	—	4,734	5,125	669	—	—	4,210	800	3,745	800
1820	—	6,979	5,685	1,747	—	—	5,432	855	4,253	1,363
1830	—	9,395	5,879	2,790	—	—	6,569	922	4,174	1,934
1840	—	10,995	6,072	4,300	—	—	8,039	1,005	4,225	2,438
1850	159	14,548	7,262	5,810	—	11	11,199	1,395	4,813	2,978
1860	241	17,627	8,068	6,416	—	39	13,874	1,663	4,970	3,103
1870	301	14,927	10,752	4,045	—	41	9,640	2,024	13,257	7,365
1880	252	22,162	18,979	7,251	—	103	18,546	2,804	20,113	10,056
1890	295	31,701	27,851	10,637	43	399	26,617	4,696	32,000	12,068
1900	544	36,726	32,421	12,894	2,745	521	35,881	3,891	38,917	12,651

	Texas	Utah	Vermont	Virginia	Washington	West Virginia	Wisconsin	Wyoming
	Ba267	Ba268	Ba269	Ba270	Ba271	Ba272	Ba273	Ba274
Year	Number	Number	Number	Number	Number	Number	Number	Number
1800	—	—	501	2,070	—	—	—	—
1810	—	—	765	2,300	—	—	—	—
1820	—	—	837	2,511	—	—	—	—
1830	—	—	889	2,750	—	—	—	—
1840	—	—	878	2,865	—	—	70	—
1850	811	21	967	3,613	—	—	884	—
1860	2,200	65	911	4,058	7	—	2,300	—
1870	5,016	235	609	15,908	8	655	1,278	3
1880	10,790	311	1,054	11,858	54	1,242	3,448	25
1890	14,687	523	1,208	12,824	457	1,565	5,628	187
1900	17,967	430	900	11,094	578	2,481	9,673	111

Source

Thomas Weiss, "Estimates of White and Nonwhite Gainful Workers in the United States by Age Group, Race, and Sex: Decennial Census Years, 1800–1900," *Historical Methods* 32 (1) (1999): 21–35.

Documentation

See the text for Table Ba1–10.

TABLE Ba275–305 Male slave workers, by state: 1800–1860 [Age 10 and older]

Contributed by Thomas Weiss

	U.S. total	Alabama	Arkansas	Connecticut	Delaware	District of Columbia	Florida	Georgia	Illinois	Indiana	Iowa
	Ba275	Ba276	Ba277	Ba278	Ba279	Ba280	Ba281	Ba282	Ba283	Ba284	Ba285
Year	Number	Number	Number	Number	Number	Number	Number	Number	Number	Number	Number
1800	259,913	—	—	220	2,098	625	—	17,360	—	43	—
1810	349,117	—	—	72	1,424	1,071	—	30,749	62	76	—
1820	464,032	14,771	491	33	1,562	1,399	0	44,889	383	60	—
1830	593,393	33,600	1,303	6	1,103	1,383	4,936	63,405	224	—	—
1840	741,570	75,234	6,002	38	836	923	8,095	81,362	104	1	5
1850	986,486	104,955	14,547	—	692	917	12,251	114,482	—	—	—
1860	1,235,848	135,521	34,881	—	528	773	19,536	139,566	—	—	—

	Kentucky	Louisiana	Maryland	Michigan	Mississippi	Missouri	Nebraska	New Hampshire	New Jersey	New York
	Ba286	Ba287	Ba288	Ba289	Ba290	Ba291	Ba292	Ba293	Ba294	Ba295
Year	Number	Number	Number	Number	Number	Number	Number	Number	Number	Number
1800	10,804	—	32,261	—	1,059	—	—	3	3,617	5,923
1810	21,901	13,261	34,104	7	5,267	—	—	—	3,159	4,372
1820	35,549	24,715	33,739	—	10,100	2,922	—	—	3,036	3,352
1830	45,728	39,856	32,006	18	19,856	6,810	—	—	949	7
1840	52,626	57,443	27,978	—	59,640	16,082	—	—	272	—
1850	63,294	84,952	28,654	—	94,784	25,748	—	—	—	—
1860	68,561	116,258	27,842	—	140,625	33,784	5	—	—	—

	North Carolina	Ohio	Pennsylvania	Rhode Island	South Carolina	Tennessee	Texas	Utah	Virginia	Wisconsin
	Ba296	Ba297	Ba298	Ba299	Ba300	Ba301	Ba302	Ba303	Ba304	Ba305
Year	Number	Number	Number	Number	Number	Number	Number	Number	Number	Number
1800	37,735	—	497	86	43,149	3,673	—	—	100,761	—
1810	48,255	—	231	25	57,973	12,041	—	—	115,066	—
1820	60,126	—	76	15	78,323	21,642	—	—	126,849	—
1830	70,490	1	134	3	93,284	38,253	—	—	140,038	—
1840	70,823	2	21	1	95,432	51,626	—	—	137,023	3
1850	85,741	—	—	—	116,296	71,155	17,310	7	150,701	—
1860	100,889	—	—	—	122,213	82,057	55,468	11	157,329	—

Source

Thomas Weiss, "Estimates of White and Nonwhite Gainful Workers in the United States by Age Group, Race, and Sex: Decennial Census Years, 1800–1900," *Historical Methods* 32 (1) (1999): 21–35.

Documentation

See the text for Table Ba1–10.

TABLE Ba306–339 Female slave workers, by state: 1800–1860 [Age 10 and older]

Contributed by Thomas Weiss

	U.S. total	Alabama	Arkansas	Connecticut	Delaware	District of Columbia	Florida	Georgia	Illinois	Indiana	Iowa	Kansas
	Ba306	Ba307	Ba308	Ba309	Ba310	Ba311	Ba312	Ba313	Ba314	Ba315	Ba316	Ba317
Year	Number	Number	Number	Number	Number	Number	Number	Number	Number	Number	Number	Number
1800	256,979	—	—	359	1,681	743	—	17,739	—	41	—	—
1810	346,046	—	—	117	1,142	1,274	—	31,468	53	71	—	—
1820	445,518	13,538	520	54	1,208	1,582	—	44,332	242	57	—	—
1830	583,700	33,294	1,332	14	880	1,586	4,460	63,551	230	3	—	—
1840	737,505	74,258	5,863	11	773	1,270	7,818	83,848	99	2	8	—
1850	979,394	104,008	14,134	—	682	1,578	11,937	118,040	—	—	—	—
1860	1,216,317	134,035	33,754	—	605	1,451	18,887	142,052	—	—	—	1

	Kentucky	Louisiana	Maine	Maryland	Massachusetts	Michigan	Mississippi	Missouri	Nebraska	New Hampshire	New Jersey
	Ba318	Ba319	Ba320	Ba321	Ba322	Ba323	Ba324	Ba325	Ba326	Ba327	Ba328
Year	Number	Number	Number	Number	Number	Number	Number	Number	Number	Number	Number
1800	10,836	—	—	30,069	—	—	1,010	—	—	3	3,936
1810	22,001	11,811	—	31,934	—	8	5,016	—	—	—	3,438
1820	35,166	21,263	—	30,309	—	—	9,511	2,794	—	—	2,840
1830	46,736	34,191	2	29,295	1	8	19,530	7,237	—	3	1,068
1840	52,687	52,889	—	26,205	—	—	58,712	17,117	—	1	334
1850	63,481	77,869	—	27,520	—	—	94,058	26,168	—	—	—
1860	67,628	104,738	—	26,704	—	—	137,330	34,081	7	—	—

	New York	North Carolina	Ohio	Pennsylvania	Rhode Island	South Carolina	Tennessee	Texas	Utah	Virginia	Wisconsin
	Ba329	Ba330	Ba331	Ba332	Ba333	Ba334	Ba335	Ba336	Ba337	Ba338	Ba339
Year	Number	Number	Number	Number	Number	Number	Number	Number	Number	Number	Number
1800	6,445	36,467	—	541	145	45,722	3,877	—	—	97,366	—
1810	4,758	46,637	—	252	41	61,431	12,713	—	—	111,883	—
1820	3,479	55,831	—	112	26	78,799	22,884	—	—	120,973	—
1830	35	68,797	5	179	13	97,567	40,337	—	—	133,346	—
1840	3	70,273	1	19	4	102,450	52,089	—	—	130,768	5
1850	—	84,892	—	—	—	122,512	71,917	17,880	9	142,711	—
1860	—	98,400	—	—	—	128,206	83,418	55,315	9	149,697	—

Source

Thomas Weiss, "Estimates of White and Nonwhite Gainful Workers in the United States by Age Group, Race, and Sex: Decennial Census Years, 1800–1900," *Historical Methods* 32 (1) (1999): 21–35.

Documentation

See the text for Table Ba1–10.

EMPLOYMENT AND UNEMPLOYMENT

Susan B. Carter and Matthew Sobek

TABLE Ba340–354 Labor force participation, employment, and unemployment, by sex: 1850–1990[1] [Census estimates]

Contributed by Matthew Sobek

	Labor force participants			Labor force participation rate			Employed persons			Unemployed persons			Unemployment rate		
	Total	Male	Female	Total	Male	Female	Total	Male	Female	Total	Male	Female	Total	Male	Female
	Ba340	Ba341	Ba342	Ba343	Ba344	Ba345	Ba346	Ba347	Ba348	Ba349	Ba350	Ba351	Ba352	Ba353	Ba354
Year	Number	Number	Number	Percent	Percent	Percent	Number	Number	Number	Number	Number	Number	Percent	Percent	Percent
1850 [2]	—	5,227,198	—	—	89.7	—	—	—	—	—	—	—	—	—	—
1860 [2]	8,160,752	7,130,935	1,029,817	52.0	88.0	13.5	—	—	—	—	—	—	—	—	—
1870	12,004,238	10,225,890	1,778,348	53.6	91.5	15.8	—	—	—	—	—	—	—	—	—
1880	16,478,917	13,999,048	2,479,869	55.2	92.1	16.9	—	—	—	—	—	—	—	—	—
1900	27,554,086	22,388,264	5,165,822	57.7	91.7	22.1	—	—	—	—	—	—	—	—	—
1910 [3]	36,236,003	28,691,821	7,544,182	60.2	92.1	26.0	—	—	—	—	—	—	—	—	—
1920	40,196,595	31,980,647	8,215,948	57.8	90.4	24.1	—	—	—	—	—	—	—	—	—
1940	52,651,801	39,720,491	12,931,310	55.6	84.7	27.1	47,585,857	35,890,118	11,695,739	5,065,944	3,830,373	1,235,571	9.6	9.6	9.6
1950	59,325,379	42,847,530	16,477,849	56.0	83.2	30.3	56,983,272	41,108,562	15,874,710	2,342,107	1,738,968	603,139	3.9	4.1	3.7
1960	67,316,826	45,159,094	22,157,732	57.6	81.4	36.1	63,870,595	42,913,576	20,957,019	3,446,231	2,245,518	1,200,713	5.1	5.0	5.4
1970	79,764,936	49,180,233	30,584,703	56.7	77.0	42.0	76,270,849	47,281,244	28,989,605	3,494,087	1,898,989	1,595,098	4.4	3.9	5.2
1980	104,139,944	59,623,610	44,516,334	60.9	75.8	50.5	97,378,408	55,747,833	41,630,575	6,761,536	3,875,777	2,885,759	6.5	6.5	6.5
1990	122,806,586	66,350,709	56,455,877	64.2	75.3	57.5	115,083,092	62,109,922	52,973,170	7,723,493	4,240,787	3,482,706	6.3	6.4	6.2

[1] Data pertain to noninstitutionalized civilians age 16 and older.

[2] Excludes slaves.

[3] The wording of the 1910 Census occupation question elicited high participation rates for women.

Source

Matthew Sobek, "New Statistics on the U.S. Labor Force, 1850–1990," *Historical Methods* 34 (2001): 71–87, Tables 7 and 8.

Documentation

Tabulated from the Integrated Public Use Microdata Series; see the Guide to the Millennial Edition.

Before 1940, labor force participation means gainful employment (that is, whether a person claimed an occupation). Starting in 1940, labor force participation was formalized to mean working or seeking work in the week prior to the census. The switch from gainful employment to the labor force definition has implications for new, seasonal, part-time, and female workers.

Introduced as a feature of the labor force measure in 1940, unemployed status means that a person is currently without a job (at the time of the census) but is looking for work. The unemployment rate is the number of unemployed, divided by the total number of persons in the labor force.

The 1850 Census did not address the occupation question to women.

See the source for more discussion of the underlying data and methodology.

TABLE Ba355–390 Labor force participation of persons age 10 to 15, by sex: 1850–1970[1] [Census estimates]

Contributed by Matthew Sobek

Year	Age 10						Age 11					
	Labor force participants			Labor force participation rate			Labor force participants			Labor force participation rate		
	Total	Male	Female	Total	Male	Female	Total	Male	Female	Total	Male	Female
	Ba355	Ba356	Ba357	Ba358	Ba359	Ba360	Ba361	Ba362	Ba363	Ba364	Ba365	Ba366
	Number	Number	Number	Percent	Percent	Percent	Number	Number	Number	Percent	Percent	Percent
1850 [2]	—	—	—	—	—	—	—	—	—	—	—	—
1860 [2]	—	—	—	—	—	—	—	—	—	—	—	—
1870	81,784	57,671	24,113	7.5	10.0	4.7	73,223	53,350	19,873	8.5	12.3	4.7
1880	136,053	103,628	32,425	10.6	15.6	5.3	133,681	102,550	31,131	12.9	19.8	6.0
1900	151,021	111,558	39,463	8.6	12.4	4.6	173,788	128,254	45,534	11.1	16.6	5.8
1910	159,952	103,780	56,172	8.7	11.1	6.2	181,363	118,138	63,225	10.7	13.7	7.5
1920	62,983	39,364	23,619	2.8	3.5	2.1	67,813	46,019	21,794	3.3	4.4	2.1
1940	—	—	—	—	—	—	—	—	—	—	—	—
1950	—	—	—	—	—	—	—	—	—	—	—	—
1960	—	—	—	—	—	—	—	—	—	—	—	—
1970	—	—	—	—	—	—	—	—	—	—	—	—

Year	Age 12						Age 13					
	Labor force participants			Labor force participation rate			Labor force participants			Labor force participation rate		
	Total	Male	Female	Total	Male	Female	Total	Male	Female	Total	Male	Female
	Ba367	Ba368	Ba369	Ba370	Ba371	Ba372	Ba373	Ba374	Ba375	Ba376	Ba377	Ba378
	Number	Number	Number	Percent	Percent	Percent	Number	Number	Number	Percent	Percent	Percent
1850 [2]	—	—	—	—	—	—	—	—	—	—	—	—
1860 [2]	—	—	—	—	—	—	—	—	—	—	—	—
1870	155,420	110,646	44,774	14.9	21.1	8.7	154,955	110,908	44,047	18.2	25.5	10.5
1880	244,369	185,099	59,270	19.5	29.1	9.6	251,635	186,107	65,528	23.5	34.5	12.4
1900	249,678	179,100	70,578	14.7	20.5	8.6	244,365	178,341	66,024	16.4	23.8	8.9
1910	268,266	176,325	91,941	13.9	18.1	9.7	298,996	207,559	91,437	17.0	22.8	10.7
1920	121,697	80,520	41,177	5.5	7.2	3.7	133,313	93,150	40,163	6.6	9.1	4.0
1940	—	—	—	—	—	—	—	—	—	—	—	—
1950	—	—	—	—	—	—	—	—	—	—	—	—
1960	—	—	—	—	—	—	—	—	—	—	—	—
1970	—	—	—	—	—	—	—	—	—	—	—	—

Year	Age 14						Age 15					
	Labor force participants			Labor force participation rate			Labor force participants			Labor force participation rate		
	Total	Male	Female	Total	Male	Female	Total	Male	Female	Total	Male	Female
	Ba379	Ba380	Ba381	Ba382	Ba383	Ba384	Ba385	Ba386	Ba387	Ba388	Ba389	Ba390
	Number	Number	Number	Percent	Percent	Percent	Number	Number	Number	Percent	Percent	Percent
1850 [2]	—	—	—	—	—	—	—	91,081	—	—	43.2	—
1860 [2]	—	—	—	—	—	—	236,635	183,332	53,303	41.5	63.7	18.9
1870	243,693	175,669	68,024	26.4	37.7	14.9	274,906	197,279	77,627	33.0	46.9	18.9
1880	333,445	246,073	87,372	31.3	45.6	16.6	361,090	262,373	98,717	39.2	56.1	21.8
1900	420,430	302,800	117,629	27.2	38.9	15.4	546,407	389,315	157,092	36.0	50.1	21.3
1910	477,840	329,475	148,365	26.0	35.1	16.6	623,938	418,897	205,041	36.6	50.2	23.6
1920	264,315	179,830	84,485	12.9	17.4	8.3	410,519	270,158	140,361	21.9	29.0	14.9
1940	127,293	92,353	34,940	5.3	7.7	2.9	200,378	150,083	50,295	8.3	12.4	4.2
1950	182,829	137,928	44,901	8.7	12.9	4.4	241,102	177,779	63,323	11.7	17.0	6.2
1960	270,138	189,636	80,502	10.0	14.0	6.0	373,846	260,378	113,468	13.6	18.7	8.4
1970	371,769	252,089	119,679	9.0	12.1	5.9	486,001	325,492	160,509	12.1	15.9	8.1

[1] Data pertain to noninstitutionalized civilians.

[2] Excludes slaves.

Source

Tabulated from the Integrated Public Use Microdata Series (IPUMS); see the Guide to the Millennial Edition.

Documentation

Early censuses had varying lower-age limits for persons who were to answer the occupation and labor force questions. Other occupation and labor force tables calculated for the volume from the IPUMS are restricted to persons age 16 and older (the modern standard and lowest consistent age that can be applied in all years). This table calculates labor force statistics individually for each year of age under 16, to the extent that the relevant censuses allow. See Table Ba340–354 for comparable rates for the older population.

See the text for Table Ba340–354 for a discussion of labor force participation.

TABLE Ba391–403 Male labor force participation rate, by age: 1850–1990[1] [Census estimates]

Contributed by Matthew Sobek

	16–19	20–24	25–29	30–34	35–39	40–44	45–49	50–54	55–59	60–64	65–69	70–74	75 and older
	Ba391	Ba392	Ba393	Ba394	Ba395	Ba396	Ba397	Ba398	Ba399	Ba400	Ba401	Ba402	Ba403
Year	Percent	Percent	Percent	Percent	Percent	Percent	Percent	Percent	Percent	Percent	Percent	Percent	Percent
1850 [2]	75.59	87.65	93.01	94.30	95.35	95.29	95.79	93.99	94.31	92.23	87.86	77.01	65.87
1860 [2]	62.59	84.26	93.09	95.01	96.15	95.91	96.67	94.99	93.74	93.48	88.78	78.37	70.11
1870	68.68	90.13	96.16	97.48	97.95	97.93	97.44	97.48	97.12	94.59	92.00	83.89	68.74
1880	76.09	91.25	96.37	97.45	97.58	97.47	97.57	97.33	95.52	92.86	87.34	77.11	60.82
1900	74.91	91.72	96.74	97.96	97.96	97.91	97.20	96.02	94.25	90.69	84.20	67.90	48.20
1910	76.42	94.36	98.07	98.34	98.46	98.33	97.85	96.60	94.40	87.10	76.22	59.49	39.49
1920	66.33	90.77	96.80	97.96	98.16	98.01	97.52	95.72	92.67	87.91	78.83	59.81	35.79
1940	48.99	90.02	96.91	97.43	97.42	96.12	94.88	93.20	89.80	81.30	61.70	39.97	21.04
1950	48.83	82.93	92.07	95.66	96.64	96.37	95.09	92.44	88.96	81.32	60.87	39.99	20.68
1960	47.83	86.04	95.11	97.10	97.10	96.45	95.68	93.46	88.99	79.23	45.17	29.72	16.81
1970	45.90	79.80	94.00	96.10	96.10	95.50	94.40	92.30	87.80	74.00	39.70	23.10	12.90
1980	51.80	83.20	93.00	95.00	95.30	94.40	92.60	89.10	81.20	61.10	29.60	18.60	9.80
1990	51.40	81.90	92.50	94.00	93.90	93.40	92.20	89.00	79.40	55.80	28.30	17.00	8.60

[1] Data pertain to noninstitutionalized civilians.

[2] Excludes slaves.

Source

Matthew Sobek, "New Statistics on the U.S. Labor Force, 1850–1990," *Historical Methods* 34 (2001): 71–87, Table 9.

Documentation

Tabulated from the Integrated Public Use Microdata Series; see the Guide to the Millennial Edition. Also see the text for Table Ba340–354 for a discussion of labor force participation.

TABLE Ba404–416 Female labor force participation rate, by age: 1860–1990[1] [Census estimates]

Contributed by Matthew Sobek

	16–19	20–24	25–29	30–34	35–39	40–44	45–49	50–54	55–59	60–64	65–69	70–74	75 and older
	Ba404	Ba405	Ba406	Ba407	Ba408	Ba409	Ba410	Ba411	Ba412	Ba413	Ba414	Ba415	Ba416
Year	Percent	Percent	Percent	Percent	Percent	Percent	Percent	Percent	Percent	Percent	Percent	Percent	Percent
1860 [2]	21.50	18.55	12.12	9.79	8.52	10.48	10.15	11.69	9.68	9.72	10.45	8.91	8.30
1870	26.72	22.57	16.32	12.53	11.93	11.52	10.37	11.15	9.22	8.10	6.45	5.11	5.32
1880	28.92	25.18	16.84	13.33	12.71	12.29	10.90	11.64	9.38	9.43	7.52	6.74	4.58
1900	32.53	32.91	22.12	17.92	17.96	16.35	16.25	18.51	17.98	15.61	12.55	12.06	9.88
1910 [3]	38.77	39.02	27.36	22.88	22.44	21.39	20.85	19.04	17.26	15.70	11.16	8.55	6.04
1920	36.86	38.04	26.70	21.77	20.60	19.83	19.10	18.36	16.13	13.84	11.07	8.07	5.14
1940	27.84	45.82	35.60	30.52	28.62	25.53	23.57	20.88	18.44	15.15	9.77	5.17	2.93
1950	30.67	43.25	32.52	31.36	33.77	36.64	35.52	31.33	26.36	21.06	13.11	7.07	3.00
1960	32.65	45.02	34.80	35.37	40.48	45.60	47.82	46.17	40.37	29.66	16.68	9.86	4.78
1970	35.10	56.30	45.70	44.50	48.50	52.40	53.50	52.50	48.00	36.60	17.50	9.40	5.30
1980	45.70	67.70	66.30	63.30	64.50	65.20	61.70	56.40	48.70	34.20	15.20	8.10	3.60
1990	49.40	72.30	75.00	73.80	76.00	77.80	74.70	67.80	55.80	36.30	17.10	8.60	3.30

[1] Data pertain to noninstitutionalized civilians.

[2] Excludes slaves.

[3] The wording of the 1910 Census occupation question elicited high participation rates for women.

Source

Matthew Sobek, "New Statistics on the U.S. Labor Force, 1850–1990," *Historical Methods* 34 (2001): 71–87, Table 9.

Documentation

Tabulated from the Integrated Public Use Microdata Series; see the Guide to the Millennial Edition. Also see the text for Table Ba340–354 for a discussion of labor force participation.

TABLE Ba417–424 Labor force participation, by sex and race: 1850–1990[1] [Census estimates]

Contributed by Matthew Sobek

	Males				Females			
	Labor force participants		Labor force participation rate		Labor force participants		Labor force participation rate	
	White	Nonwhite	White	Nonwhite	White	Nonwhite	White	Nonwhite
	Ba417	Ba418	Ba419	Ba420	Ba421	Ba422	Ba423	Ba424
Year	Number	Number	Percent	Percent	Number	Number	Percent	Percent
1850 [2]	5,132,884	94,314	89.9	79.5	—	—	—	—
1860 [2]	7,010,712	120,223	88.1	82.8	978,452	51,365	13.1	35.7
1870	8,971,422	1,254,468	91.1	94.7	1,219,494	558,854	12.4	39.7
1880	12,281,729	1,717,319	91.7	95.4	1,715,918	763,951	13.4	42.0
1900	19,927,156	2,461,108	91.5	93.7	4,028,992	1,136,830	19.4	43.7
1910 [3]	25,658,279	3,033,542	91.7	96.0	5,731,815	1,812,367	22.1	58.1
1920	28,738,001	3,242,646	90.1	93.0	6,724,694	1,491,254	21.9	42.9
1940	36,024,636	3,695,855	84.5	86.6	11,107,844	1,823,466	25.7	39.8
1950	38,849,993	3,997,537	83.3	82.5	14,397,134	2,080,715	29.3	38.6
1960	40,835,448	4,323,646	81.7	78.1	19,319,941	2,837,791	35.1	44.0
1970	44,371,198	4,809,035	77.7	71.4	26,620,587	3,964,116	41.2	47.7
1980	52,871,662	6,751,948	76.7	69.3	38,058,938	6,457,396	50.0	53.8
1990	57,849,545	8,501,164	76.0	70.6	47,544,554	8,911,323	57.1	59.7

[1] Noninstitutionalized civilians age 16 and older.

[2] Excludes slaves.

[3] The wording of the 1910 Census occupation question elicited high participation rates for women.

Source

Matthew Sobek, "New Statistics on the U.S. Labor Force, 1850–1990," *Historical Methods* 34 (2001): 71–87, Tables 7 and 8.

Documentation

Tabulated from the Integrated Public Use Microdata Series; see the Guide to the Millennial Edition. Also see the text for Table Ba340–354 for a discussion of labor force participation.

TABLE Ba425–469 Female labor force participation rate, by race, marital status, and presence of children: 1880–1990[1] [Census estimates]

Contributed by Matthew Sobek

	All women									Women with no children		
	All races			White			Nonwhite			All races		
	Never married	Married	Separated, widowed, and divorced	Never married	Married	Separated, widowed, and divorced	Never married	Married	Separated, widowed, and divorced	Never married	Married	Separated, widowed, and divorced
	Ba425	Ba426	Ba427	Ba428	Ba429	Ba430	Ba431	Ba432	Ba433	Ba434	Ba435	Ba436
Year	Percent	Percent	Percent	Percent	Percent	Percent	Percent	Percent	Percent	Percent	Percent	Percent
1880	37.7	5.7	23.5	34.4	2.4	17.4	64.5	29.1	53.7	37.6	8.4	19.7
1900	48.6	5.7	37.4	46.6	3.4	32.2	65.9	25.6	65.8	48.5	8.7	31.2
1910 [2]	55.0	10.7	35.4	53.2	6.3	28.6	73.0	47.9	72.5	54.9	13.3	29.0
1920	57.2	9.1	33.7	57.1	6.6	28.6	57.9	32.0	66.7	57.1	13.0	28.0
1940	55.9	15.6	30.6	56.3	13.8	27.8	52.1	32.9	49.1	55.9	21.1	26.9
1950	57.0	22.0	37.2	58.4	21.1	35.1	44.7	32.4	48.1	57.1	28.3	33.6
1960	53.9	31.0	40.0	55.1	30.1	38.3	45.3	41.0	49.1	53.9	35.3	35.2
1970	51.8	39.5	40.7	53.0	38.5	39.6	44.8	49.9	46.4	51.8	41.4	34.4
1980	60.8	49.2	44.0	63.1	48.1	43.0	51.6	59.0	48.5	61.5	45.7	35.7
1990	66.8	58.3	47.2	68.7	57.6	46.2	60.6	64.9	51.6	67.8	51.1	39.5

Notes appear at end of table

TABLE Ba425–469 Female labor force participation rate, by race, marital status, and presence of children: 1880–1990 [Census estimates] *Continued*

	Women with no children						Women with children					
	White			Nonwhite			All races					
							With any children			With child age 6–17 (no child under age 6)		
	Never married	Married	Separated, widowed, and divorced	Never married	Married	Separated, widowed, and divorced	Never married	Married	Separated, widowed, and divorced	Never married	Married	Separated, widowed, and divorced
	Ba437	Ba438	Ba439	Ba440	Ba441	Ba442	Ba443	Ba444	Ba445	Ba446	Ba447	Ba448
Year	Percent	Percent	Percent	Percent	Percent	Percent	Percent	Percent	Percent	Percent	Percent	Percent
1880	34.6	4.7	15.1	64.5	34.4	46.3	43.0	4.7	31.4	37.5	4.7	28.2
1900	46.7	5.8	26.8	64.9	31.2	60.0	57.5	4.4	54.6	49.3	5.8	54.0
1910 [2]	53.2	8.3	23.0	72.2	50.4	67.0	61.9	9.3	55.0	59.8	10.3	53.0
1920	57.1	9.9	23.5	57.1	36.7	60.5	59.0	6.8	53.5	58.8	8.7	52.7
1940	56.3	18.8	24.3	52.0	39.9	45.5	52.4	10.9	48.9	60.6	13.9	49.3
1950	58.4	27.1	31.3	44.6	39.6	47.1	48.9	16.6	55.4	59.8	24.8	59.3
1960	55.1	34.3	33.3	45.0	45.5	46.3	52.2	27.9	61.7	63.9	39.0	67.6
1970	52.9	40.8	33.3	43.8	47.9	40.9	52.5	38.0	63.9	64.5	47.3	68.8
1980	63.5	45.1	35.1	51.4	51.5	39.7	51.9	52.7	70.7	67.2	60.1	75.4
1990	69.4	50.5	38.8	61.0	56.5	43.0	59.1	66.9	76.3	71.4	73.7	81.0

	Women with children											
	All races			White								
	With child under age 6			With any children			With child age 6–17 (no child under age 6)			With child under age 6		
	Never married	Married	Separated, widowed, and divorced	Never married	Married	Separated, widowed, and divorced	Never married	Married	Separated, widowed, and divorced	Never married	Married	Separated, widowed, and divorced
	Ba449	Ba450	Ba451	Ba452	Ba453	Ba454	Ba455	Ba456	Ba457	Ba458	Ba459	Ba460
Year	Percent	Percent	Percent	Percent	Percent	Percent	Percent	Percent	Percent	Percent	Percent	Percent
1880	46.1	4.7	38.1	20.8	1.6	22.5	23.6	2.1	22.1	17.8	1.4	23.5
1900	63.4	3.6	55.9	39.0	2.3	48.5	46.0	3.7	48.8	28.1	1.6	47.6
1910 [2]	63.5	8.7	60.8	42.1	5.3	47.3	44.8	6.4	46.5	39.0	4.6	50.2
1920	59.1	5.5	55.5	49.5	4.7	47.4	52.0	6.3	47.1	45.8	3.6	48.2
1940	43.3	7.8	47.1	51.0	9.6	46.3	58.9	12.4	46.8	39.3	6.7	43.8
1950	41.2	11.2	48.2	53.4	15.9	56.6	61.7	24.0	59.4	44.2	10.6	50.6
1960	46.9	19.4	51.9	59.0	27.0	63.9	67.8	38.2	68.5	53.2	18.1	54.2
1970	48.7	28.5	55.4	57.4	36.6	66.8	66.9	46.3	71.2	54.5	26.5	58.5
1980	45.7	44.0	60.4	51.5	51.2	73.1	69.0	59.1	78.1	45.9	41.8	61.9
1990	53.2	59.7	66.2	58.4	66.2	77.6	72.2	73.2	82.7	53.3	58.8	66.7

	Women with children								
	Nonwhite								
	With any children			With child age 6–17 (no child under age 6)			With child under age 6		
	Never married	Married	Separated, widowed, and divorced	Never married	Married	Separated, widowed, and divorced	Never married	Married	Separated, widowed, and divorced
	Ba461	Ba462	Ba463	Ba464	Ba465	Ba466	Ba467	Ba468	Ba469
Year	Percent	Percent	Percent	Percent	Percent	Percent	Percent	Percent	Percent
1880	64.3	27.1	64.1	68.5	27.1	61.9	63.2	27.0	66.2
1900	76.9	22.7	75.3	58.8	26.6	77.4	82.0	21.0	72.3
1910 [2]	84.3	46.2	83.2	89.7	48.1	83.1	82.0	45.3	83.3
1920	72.9	28.2	80.8	74.6	33.6	81.1	71.9	24.7	80.3
1940	54.6	25.2	61.6	64.3	32.8	63.1	47.5	19.0	57.5
1950	44.7	24.7	51.4	56.7	35.9	58.9	39.3	18.4	42.8
1960	48.7	37.6	55.7	60.8	49.8	63.9	44.2	31.2	47.8
1970	49.9	51.2	56.4	63.2	57.9	62.0	45.8	45.7	48.7
1980	52.1	64.3	64.2	66.4	68.6	67.8	45.6	59.8	56.7
1990	59.5	72.4	72.5	70.9	77.1	76.2	53.1	67.1	64.7

Notes appear on next page

(continued)

TABLE Ba425–469 Female labor force participation rate, by race, marital status, and presence of children: 1880–1990 [Census estimates] *Continued*

[1] Data pertain to noninstitutionalized civilians age 16 and older.

[2] The wording of the 1910 Census occupation question elicited high participation rates for women.

Source

Tabulated from the Integrated Public Use Microdata Series; see the Guide to the Millennial Edition.

Documentation

Married women with an absent spouse are interpreted as separated prior to 1950 in order to enhance comparability with the more modern census years. Presence of children for purposes of this table means a woman's own children who resided with her at the time of the census.

See the text for Table Ba340–354 for a discussion of labor force participation.

TABLE Ba470–477 Labor force, employment, and unemployment: 1890–1990[1] [Weir]

Contributed by Susan B. Carter

	Civilian labor force							
		Employed			Unemployed			
						As a percentage of		
	Total	Total	Farm	Government	Number	Civilian labor force	Civilian private nonfarm labor force	Federal "emergency" workers
	Ba470	Ba471	Ba472	Ba473 [2]	Ba474	Ba475	Ba476	Ba477
Year	Thousand	Thousand	Thousand	Thousand	Thousand	Percent	Percent	Number
1890	22,772	21,868	10,291	812	904	3.97	7.75	—
1891	23,382	22,332	10,367	840	1,050	4.49	8.62	—
1892	24,038	23,003	10,443	868	1,035	4.31	8.13	—
1893	24,649	22,981	10,519	897	1,668	6.77	12.60	—
1894	25,168	22,834	10,595	925	2,334	9.28	17.10	—
1895	25,679	23,501	10,671	953	2,178	8.48	15.50	—
1896	26,220	23,788	10,746	981	2,432	9.27	16.78	—
1897	26,712	24,439	10,822	1,009	2,273	8.51	15.27	—
1898	27,209	25,090	10,898	1,038	2,119	7.79	13.87	—
1899	27,753	26,130	10,974	1,066	1,623	5.85	10.33	—
1900	28,376	26,956	11,050	1,094	1,420	5.00	8.75	—
1901	29,153	27,947	10,916	1,129	1,206	4.14	7.05	—
1902	29,904	28,874	10,753	1,191	1,030	3.45	5.73	—
1903	30,698	29,616	10,869	1,229	1,082	3.53	5.82	—
1904	31,441	29,894	11,076	1,277	1,547	4.92	8.10	—
1905	32,299	31,042	11,187	1,335	1,257	3.89	6.36	—
1906	33,212	32,398	11,479	1,386	814	2.45	4.00	—
1907	34,183	33,135	11,493	1,448	1,048	3.07	4.93	—
1908	34,916	32,310	11,238	1,507	2,606	7.46	11.75	—
1909	35,721	33,704	11,163	1,564	2,017	5.65	8.77	—
1910	36,709	34,559	11,260	1,630	2,150	5.86	9.03	—
1911	37,478	34,845	11,107	1,672	2,633	7.02	10.66	—
1912	37,932	35,708	11,136	1,717	2,224	5.86	8.87	—
1913	38,675	36,454	10,974	1,757	2,221	5.74	8.56	—
1914	39,401	36,055	10,945	1,809	3,346	8.49	12.56	—
1915	39,600	36,020	10,953	1,861	3,580	9.04	13.37	—
1916	40,057	37,461	10,802	1,916	2,596	6.48	9.50	—
1917	40,023	37,951	10,788	2,000	2,072	5.18	7.61	—
1918	39,076	38,590	10,674	2,461	486	1.24	1.87	—
1919	39,696	38,769	10,498	2,449	927	2.34	3.47	—
1920	41,340	39,208	10,440	2,371	2,132	5.16	7.47	—
1921	41,979	37,221	10,443	2,397	4,758	11.33	16.33	—
1922	42,496	38,860	10,561	2,455	3,636	8.56	12.33	—
1923	43,444	41,569	10,621	2,524	1,875	4.32	6.19	—
1924	44,235	41,894	10,599	2,636	2,341	5.29	7.55	—
1925	45,169	43,054	10,662	2,765	2,115	4.68	6.66	—
1926	45,629	44,308	10,690	2,853	1,321	2.90	4.12	—
1927	46,375	44,567	10,529	2,945	1,808	3.90	5.50	—
1928	47,105	44,870	10,497	3,039	2,235	4.74	6.66	—
1929	47,757	46,374	10,541	3,065	1,383	2.89	4.05	—
1930	48,523	44,183	10,340	3,148	4,340	8.94	12.39	20
1931	49,325	41,604	10,240	3,563	7,721	15.65	21.74	299
1932	50,098	38,630	10,120	3,817	11,468	22.89	31.71	592
1933	50,882	40,247	10,092	5,361	10,635	20.90	30.02	2,195
1934	51,650	43,284	9,990	6,273	8,366	16.20	23.64	2,974

Notes appear at end of table

TABLE Ba470–477 Labor force, employment, and unemployment: 1890–1990 [Weir] *Continued*

	Civilian labor force							
		Employed			Unemployed			
						As a percentage of		
	Total	Total	Farm	Government	Number	Civilian labor force	Civilian private nonfarm labor force	Federal "emergency" workers
	Ba470	Ba471	Ba472	Ba473 [2]	Ba474	Ba475	Ba476	Ba477
Year	Thousand	Thousand	Thousand	Thousand	Thousand	Percent	Percent	Number
1935	52,283	44,760	10,110	6,568	7,523	14.39	21.13	3,087
1936	53,019	47,733	10,090	7,412	5,286	9.97	14.88	3,744
1937	53,768	48,831	10,000	6,519	4,937	9.18	13.25	2,763
1938	54,532	47,733	9,840	7,474	6,799	12.47	18.27	3,591
1939	55,218	48,993	9,710	7,250	6,225	11.27	16.27	3,255
1940	55,640	50,350	9,540	7,032	5,290	9.51	13.54	2,830
1941	55,910	52,559	9,100	6,869	3,351	5.99	8.39	2,209
1942	56,410	54,664	9,250	6,397	1,746	3.10	4.28	914
1943	55,540	54,555	9,080	6,165	985	1.77	2.44	85
1944	54,630	53,960	8,950	6,043	670	1.23	1.69	—
1945	53,860	52,820	8,580	5,944	1,040	1.93	2.64	—
1946	57,520	55,250	8,320	5,595	2,270	3.95	5.21	—
1947	59,682	57,053	7,891	5,474	2,629	4.41	5.68	—
1948	60,621	58,358	7,629	5,650	2,263	3.73	4.78	—
1949	61,315	57,683	7,658	5,856	3,632	5.92	7.60	—
1950	62,079	58,892	7,160	6,026	3,187	5.13	6.52	—
1951	61,649	59,967	6,726	6,389	1,682	2.73	3.47	—
1952	62,069	60,272	6,500	6,609	1,797	2.89	3.67	—
1953	63,470	61,206	6,260	6,645	2,264	3.57	4.48	—
1954	64,474	60,107	6,205	6,751	4,367	6.77	8.48	—
1955	65,551	62,131	6,450	6,914	3,420	5.22	6.56	—
1956	66,552	63,792	6,283	7,278	2,760	4.15	5.21	—
1957	67,160	64,065	5,947	7,616	3,095	4.61	5.78	—
1958	67,880	63,043	5,586	7,839	4,837	7.13	8.88	—
1959	68,669	64,629	5,565	8,083	4,040	5.88	7.34	—
1960	69,620	65,785	5,458	8,353	3,835	5.51	6.87	—
1961	70,309	65,744	5,200	8,594	4,565	6.49	8.08	—
1962	70,906	66,702	4,944	8,890	4,204	5.93	7.37	—
1963	72,074	67,760	4,687	9,225	4,314	5.99	7.42	—
1964	73,091	69,301	4,523	9,596	3,790	5.18	6.43	—
1965	74,548	71,070	4,361	10,074	3,478	4.66	5.78	—
1966	75,636	72,878	3,979	10,785	2,758	3.65	4.53	—
1967	76,911	74,376	3,844	11,391	2,535	3.30	4.11	—
1968	78,453	75,913	3,817	11,838	2,540	3.24	4.04	—
1969	80,111	77,875	3,606	12,195	2,236	2.79	3.48	—
1970	82,099	78,669	3,463	12,554	3,430	4.18	5.19	—
1971	84,346	79,355	3,394	12,880	4,991	5.92	7.33	—
1972	87,034	82,135	3,484	13,334	4,899	5.63	6.98	—
1973	89,408	85,051	3,470	13,732	4,357	4.87	6.03	—
1974	91,847	86,803	3,515	14,170	5,044	5.49	6.80	—
1975	94,299	85,830	3,408	14,686	8,469	8.98	11.11	—
1976	96,752	88,753	3,331	14,871	7,999	8.27	10.18	—
1977	99,161	92,017	3,283	15,127	7,144	7.20	8.85	—
1978	101,574	96,046	3,387	15,672	5,528	5.44	6.70	—
1979	104,062	98,825	3,347	15,947	5,237	5.03	6.18	—
1980	106,518	99,303	3,364	16,241	7,215	6.77	8.30	—
1981	108,670	100,400	3,368	16,031	8,270	7.61	9.26	—
1982	110,501	99,529	3,401	15,837	10,972	9.93	12.02	—
1983	112,237	100,822	3,383	15,869	11,415	10.17	12.28	—
1984	114,117	105,003	3,321	16,024	9,114	7.99	9.62	—
1985	115,774	107,154	3,179	16,394	8,620	7.45	8.96	—
1986	117,849	109,601	3,163	16,693	8,248	7.00	8.42	—
1987	119,766	112,439	3,208	17,010	7,327	6.12	7.36	—
1988	121,493	114,972	3,169	17,386	6,521	5.37	6.46	—
1989	123,173	117,327	3,199	17,779	5,846	4.75	5.72	—
1990	124,788	117,917	3,186	18,322	6,871	5.51	6.65	—

Notes appear at end of table **(continued)**

TABLE Ba470–477 Labor force, employment, and unemployment: 1890–1990 [Weir] *Continued*

[1] Civilian noninstitutional population. Through 1946, age 14 and older; thereafter, age 16 and older.

[2] Civilian employees only.

Sources

Series Ba470–476. David R. Weir, "A Century of U.S. Unemployment, 1890–1990," in Roger L. Ransom, Richard Sutch, and Susan B. Carter, editors, *Research in Economic History,* volume 14 (JAI Press, 1992), Table D3, pp. 341–3.

Series Ba477. Michael R. Darby, "Three-and-a-Half Million U.S. Employees Have Been Mislaid: Or, an Explanation of Unemployment, 1934–1941," *Journal of Political Economy* 84 (1) (1976): 7, Table 2.

Documentation

Since 1940, official annual statistics on the labor force, employment, unemployment, and persons not in the labor force have been based on the "labor force" concept. Specific concepts of the labor force, employment, and unemployment were developed in the later stages of the Great Depression of the 1930s. Before that time, aside from attempts in some of the decennial censuses, no direct measurements were made of the number of jobless persons. Mass unemployment in the early 1930s increased the need for statistics, and widely conflicting estimates based on a variety of indirect techniques began to appear. Most surveys in the 1930s counted as unemployed those persons not working but "willing and able to work." Willingness and ability, however, turned out to be extremely subjective concepts. Since they were dependent on the attitudes of the persons involved, it proved difficult to compile data on a comparable basis from place to place and from time to time. See Stanley L. Lebergott, "Labor," in U.S. Bureau of the Census, *Historical Statistics of the United States, Colonial Times to 1970,* Bicentennial Edition, 2 volumes (1975), Chapter D, p. 121.

A set of precise concepts was developed in the late 1930s to meet these various criticisms. The classification of an individual depended principally on his or her actual *activity* within a designated time period – that is, was the individual working, looking for work, or engaged in other activities? The official data collected in accordance with the labor force concept are presented in Table Ba478–486.

Prior to the 1930s, federal employment and unemployment statistics were based on the "gainful worker" concept. "Gainful workers" were individuals 10 years of age and older who reported an occupation. Census enumerators were instructed to find and enter the occupation of each person 10 years of age and over who followed an occupation in which he or she earned money or its equivalent, or in which he or she assisted in the production of marketable goods. Thus, the term "gainful workers" includes all persons who usually followed a gainful occupation, even those who were not employed when the census was taken. It does not include women doing housework in their own homes, without wages, and having no other employment, nor children working at home on general household work, or chores, or at odd times on other work. Beginning in 1900, those who were enumerated as "gainfully occupied" were asked to report their months (later, weeks) of unemployment during the previous year.

The gainful worker concept was originally developed to provide information on the American social structure and the distribution of employment across sectors. The question on unemployment was not added until after the severe industrial depression of the 1890s, and at first it was asked only of wage and salary workers. There were several problems in trying to measure unemployment rates using the gainful worker concept. As Stanley Lebergott noted: "First, the question about occupation, as posed by the census enumerator, made no reference to time. Responses thus varied substantially with the individual. In particular, many persons who were retired or permanently disabled and who had not worked for some time reported their former line of work and were counted as gainful workers. These individuals reported lengthy unemployment, in many cases unemployment for the full reference year. At the same time, many employed persons did not enter themselves as gainful workers, because they considered themselves as students or housewives and their current employment as only temporary" (Lebergott 1975, p. 121).

In addition, since young workers just beginning their job search were not counted as gainful workers until they became employed, the job search of new labor market entrants – which is classified as "unemployment," according to the labor force concept – was omitted entirely from the official statistics collected according to the gainful worker concept. For these and other reasons, the age and occupational groups are not strictly comparable from one decennial census to the next. For a more detailed discussion of the gainful worker concept and the data themselves, see John D. Durand, *The Labor Force in the United States, 1890–1940* (Social Science Research Council, 1948).

The shift of the official statistics from the gainful worker concept to the labor force concept made it difficult to compare the operation of the labor market and the economy before and after about 1940. To facilitate the study of long-term growth of the economy, Stanley Lebergott, in *Manpower in Economic Growth: The American Record since 1800* (McGraw-Hill, 1964), constructed estimates of employment and unemployment for the period 1890–1940, designed to be conceptually consistent with the labor force concept used by the government to collect such data for 1940 and later. He began by constructing annual estimates of the labor force. He did this by calculating the share of the population in the labor force for various age/sex groups at the decennial censuses. He then obtained annual population estimates for the same demographic groups and constructed annual labor force estimates based on linear interpolations. To estimate employment, Lebergott made use of employment and output data from a wide range of industries and sources. The precise procedures are described in Lebergott (1964, pp. 384–403) and in Weir (1992, pp. 307–11). The difference between Lebergott's labor force and employment estimates was unemployment. His employment estimation procedure for the years 1890–1900 relies entirely on manufacturing employment, a sector that accounted for just over 20 percent of the total at that time period (Weir 1992, p. 308).

Lebergott's employment and unemployment estimates were developed to facilitate the study of long-term growth of the economy. In the 1980s, when the rise of unemployment shifted the attention of scholars away from economic growth and toward cyclical instability, these data began to be used to study long-term change in unemployment dynamics. In an influential set of papers, Christina Romer ("Spurious Volatility in Historical Unemployment Data," *Journal of Political Economy* 94 (1) (1986): 1–37; and "New Estimates of Prewar Gross National Product and Unemployment," *Journal of Economic History* 46 (June 1986): 341–52) was sharply critical of Lebergott's pre-1940 estimates, arguing that the estimation methods produced systematic "excess volatility" of unemployment over the business cycle. In other words, in Romer's view, the Lebergott estimates suggested that unemployment was higher during depressions than was in fact the case.

The series presented in this table were produced by David Weir (1992). Weir systematically reexamined the data and method underlying Lebergott's estimates, modifying certain procedures and supplementing the sources where new ones were available. Overall, the Weir estimates are quite similar to Lebergott's, except in two cases. Weir's unemployment estimates for the depressions of the 1890s and for the 1930s are considerably lower than those of Lebergott's. For the 1890s, Weir's are lower because he estimated employment using data from the full range of industries in operation at the time, rather than relying solely on the manufacturing sector. For the 1930s, the difference stems from Weir's treatment of so-called Emergency Workers. Beginning in 1929 and continuing through 1943, the federal government created a series of employment programs for otherwise unemployed workers. The major programs included the Works Progress Administration (WPA) and the Civilian Conservation Corps (CCC). Together they employed several million workers during their peak years of operation during the depths of the Great Depression from 1933 through 1941. The numbers employed in such programs are shown in series Ba477. Standard practice by the U.S. Bureau of Labor Statistics (BLS) at the time was to count these workers as "unemployed." Subsequent long-term employment and unemployment estimates constructed by Stanley Lebergott continued this practice. For a defense of this classification see Lebergott (1964), pp. 184–5. Following Michael R. Darby, Weir considers these individuals as *employed*.

To provide a century's worth of conceptually consistent data on the labor force, employment, and unemployment, Weir linked his revisions of the Lebergott series with official federal data collected according to the labor force concept, which began in 1948. The federal data are reported in Table Ba478–486. The minor discrepancies between series in these two tables are the result of regular revisions of the data by the BLS since 1990.

TABLE Ba478–486 Labor force, employment, and unemployment: 1938–2000[1, 2]

Contributed by Susan B. Carter

		Labor force							
				Employed			Unemployed		
	Population	Total	As percentage of population	Total	Agriculture	Nonagriculture	Total	As percentage of labor force	Not in labor force
	Ba478	Ba479	Ba480	Ba481	Ba482	Ba483	Ba484	Ba485	Ba486
Year	Thousand	Thousand	Percent	Thousand	Thousand	Thousand	Thousand	Percent	Thousand
1938	—	54,610	—	44,220	9,690	34,530	10,390	19.0	—
1939	—	55,230	—	45,750	9,610	36,140	9,480	17.2	—
1940	—	55,640	—	47,520	9,540	37,980	8,120	14.6	—
1941	—	55,910	—	50,350	9,100	41,250	5,560	9.9	—
1942	—	56,410	—	53,750	9,250	44,500	2,660	4.7	—
1943	—	55,540	—	54,470	9,080	45,390	1,070	1.9	—
1944	93,220	54,630	58.6	53,960	8,950	45,010	670	1.2	38,590
1945	94,090	53,860	57.2	52,820	8,580	44,240	1,040	1.9	40,230
1946	103,070	57,520	55.8	55,250	8,320	46,930	2,270	3.9	45,550
1947	106,018	60,168	56.8	57,812	8,256	49,557	2,356	3.9	45,850
1947	101,827	59,350	58.3	57,038	7,890	49,148	2,311	3.9	42,477
1948	103,068	60,621	58.8	58,343	7,629	50,714	2,276	3.8	42,447
1949	103,994	61,286	58.9	57,651	7,658	49,993	3,637	5.9	42,708
1950	104,995	62,208	59.2	58,918	7,160	51,758	3,288	5.3	42,787
1951	104,621	62,017	59.2	59,961	6,726	53,235	2,055	3.3	42,604
1952	105,231	62,138	59.0	60,250	6,500	53,749	1,883	3.0	43,093
1953	107,056	63,015	58.9	61,179	6,260	54,919	1,834	2.9	44,041
1954	108,321	63,643	58.8	60,109	6,205	53,904	3,532	5.5	44,678
1955	109,683	65,023	59.3	62,170	6,450	55,722	2,852	4.4	44,660
1956	110,954	66,552	60.0	63,799	6,283	57,514	2,750	4.1	44,402
1957	112,265	66,929	59.6	64,071	5,947	58,123	2,859	4.3	45,336
1958	113,727	67,639	59.5	63,036	5,586	57,450	4,602	6.8	46,088
1959	115,329	68,369	59.3	64,630	5,565	59,065	3,740	5.5	46,960
1960	117,245	69,628	59.4	65,778	5,458	60,318	3,852	5.5	47,617
1961	118,771	70,459	59.3	65,746	5,200	60,546	4,714	6.7	48,312
1962	120,153	70,614	58.8	66,702	4,944	61,759	3,911	5.5	49,539
1963	122,416	71,833	58.7	67,762	4,687	63,076	4,070	5.7	50,583
1964	124,485	73,091	58.7	69,305	4,523	64,782	3,786	5.2	51,394
1965	126,513	74,455	58.9	71,088	4,361	66,726	3,366	4.5	52,058
1966	128,058	75,770	59.2	72,895	3,979	68,915	2,875	3.8	52,288
1967	129,874	77,347	59.6	74,372	3,844	70,527	2,975	3.8	52,527
1968	132,028	78,737	59.6	75,920	3,817	72,103	2,817	3.6	53,291
1969	134,335	80,734	60.1	77,902	3,606	74,296	2,832	3.5	53,602
1970	137,085	82,771	60.4	78,678	3,463	75,215	4,093	4.9	54,315
1971	140,216	84,382	60.2	79,367	3,394	75,972	5,016	5.9	55,834
1972	144,126	87,034	60.4	82,153	3,484	78,669	4,882	5.6	57,091
1973	147,096	89,429	60.8	85,064	3,470	81,594	4,365	4.9	57,667
1974	150,120	91,949	61.3	86,794	3,515	83,279	5,156	5.6	58,171
1975	153,153	93,775	61.2	85,846	3,408	82,438	7,929	8.5	59,377
1976	156,150	96,158	61.6	88,752	3,331	85,421	7,406	7.7	59,991
1977	159,033	99,009	62.3	92,017	3,283	88,734	6,991	7.1	60,025
1978	161,910	102,251	63.2	96,048	3,387	92,661	6,202	6.1	59,659
1979	164,863	104,962	63.7	98,824	3,347	95,477	6,137	5.8	59,900
1980	167,745	106,940	63.8	99,303	3,364	95,938	7,637	7.1	60,806
1981	170,130	108,670	63.9	100,397	3,368	97,030	8,273	7.6	61,460
1982	172,271	110,204	64.0	99,526	3,401	96,125	10,678	9.7	62,067
1983	174,215	111,550	64.0	100,834	3,383	97,450	10,717	9.6	62,665
1984	176,383	113,544	64.4	105,005	3,321	101,685	8,539	7.5	62,839
1985	178,206	115,461	64.8	107,150	3,179	103,971	8,312	7.2	62,744
1986	180,587	117,834	65.3	109,597	3,163	106,434	8,237	7.0	62,752
1987	182,753	119,865	65.6	112,440	3,208	109,232	7,425	6.2	62,888
1988	184,613	121,669	65.9	114,968	3,169	111,800	6,701	5.5	62,944
1989	186,393	123,869	66.5	117,342	3,199	114,142	6,528	5.3	62,523
1990	189,164	125,840	66.5	118,793	3,223	115,570	7,047	5.6	63,324
1991	190,925	126,346	66.2	117,718	3,269	114,449	8,628	6.8	64,578
1992	192,805	128,105	66.4	118,492	3,247	115,245	9,613	7.5	64,700
1993	194,838	129,200	66.3	120,259	3,115	117,144	8,940	6.9	65,638
1994	196,814	131,056	66.6	123,060	3,409	119,651	7,996	6.1	65,758

Notes appear at end of table

(continued)

TABLE Ba478–486 Labor force, employment, and unemployment: 1938–2000 *Continued*

		Labor force							
				Employed			Unemployed		
	Population	Total	As percentage of population	Total	Agriculture	Nonagriculture	Total	As percentage of labor force	Not in labor force
	Ba478	Ba479	Ba480	Ba481	Ba482	Ba483	Ba484	Ba485	Ba486
Year	Thousand	Thousand	Percent	Thousand	Thousand	Thousand	Thousand	Percent	Thousand
1995	198,584	132,304	66.6	124,900	3,440	121,460	7,404	5.6	66,280
1996	200,591	133,943	66.8	126,708	3,443	123,264	7,236	5.4	66,647
1997	203,133	136,297	67.1	129,558	3,399	126,159	6,739	4.9	66,837
1998	205,220	137,673	67.1	131,463	3,378	128,085	6,210	4.5	67,547
1999	207,753	139,368	67.1	133,488	3,281	130,207	5,880	4.2	68,385
2000	209,699	140,863	67.2	135,208	3,305	131,903	5,655	4.0	68,836

[1] Civilian noninstitutional population. Through the first set of values for 1947, age 14 and older; thereafter, age 16 and older.

[2] Data not strictly comparable over time; see text.

Sources

U.S. Bureau of Labor Statistics (BLS) Internet site and *BLS Handbook of Methods,* Bulletin number 2490 (April 1997). Monthly updates are available from the BLS periodical *Employment and Earnings.*

Documentation

This table presents official annual statistics on the labor force, employment, unemployment, and persons not in the labor force based on the "labor force concept," which was developed in the later years of the Great Depression of the 1930s. See the text for Table Ba470–477. This and related concepts were adopted for the national sample survey of households, called the *Monthly Report of Unemployment,* initiated in 1940 by the Works Progress Administration. See John N. Webb, "Concepts Used in Unemployment Surveys," *Journal of the American Statistical Association* (March 1939): 49–59.

The household survey was transferred to the U.S. Bureau of the Census in late 1942, and its name was changed to the *Monthly Report on the Labor Force.* The survey title was changed once more in 1948 to the present *Current Population Survey* (CPS) to reflect its expanding role as a source for a wide variety of demographic, social, and economic characteristics of the population. In 1959, responsibility for analyzing and publishing the CPS labor force data was transferred to the BLS; the Census Bureau continues to collect the data.

Since 1948, the CPS has been used for the regular collection of statistics on the labor force status of the civilian noninstitutional population 16 years of age and over. Persons under 16 years of age are excluded from the official definition of the labor force because child labor laws, compulsory school attendance, and general social custom prevent most of these children from working in the United States. The institutional population, which also is excluded from coverage, consists of inmates of penal and mental institutions, sanitariums, and homes for the aged, infirm, and needy.

The CPS is collected each month from a probability sample of approximately 50,000 occupied households. Respondents are assured that all information obtained is completely confidential and is used only for the purpose of statistical analysis. Although the survey is conducted on a strictly voluntary basis, refusals to cooperate amount to about 4 percent each month.

The time period covered in the monthly survey is a calendar week, selected as the survey reference period because the period used must be short enough so that the data obtained are "current," but not so short that the occurrence of holidays or other accidental events might cause erratic fluctuations in the information obtained. A calendar week fulfills these conditions as well as being a convenient and easily defined period of time. Since July 1955, the calendar week, Sunday through Saturday, that includes the twelfth day of the month has been defined as the reference week. The actual survey is conducted during the following week, which is the week containing the nineteenth day of the month.

Data presented in this and related tables are not strictly comparable over time. Of particular note are the changes in the CPS survey occurring in the years 1953, 1960, 1962, 1972, 1973, 1986, 1990, 1994, 1997, 1998, 1999, and 2000. For a discussion of these changes, see U.S. Bureau of Labor Statistics, "Design and Methodology," *Current Population Survey Technical Paper 63 (TP63)* (March 2000), Chapter 2, "History of the Current Population Survey."

The criteria used in classifying persons on the basis of their labor force activity and some of the major statistics obtained from the CPS are as follows.

Employed Persons

Employed persons are all those who, during the reference week, (1) did any work at all as paid employees, worked in their own business, profession, or on their own farm, or worked fifteen hours or more as unpaid workers in a family-operated enterprise and (2) all those who did not work but had jobs or businesses from which they were temporarily absent due to illness, bad weather, vacation, child care problems, labor dispute, maternity or paternity leave, or other family or personal obligations – whether or not they were paid by their employers for the time off and whether or not they were seeking other jobs. Each employed person is counted only once, even if he or she holds more than one job. Multiple jobholders are counted in the job at which they worked the greatest number of hours during the reference week. Included in the total are employed citizens of foreign countries who are residing in the United States, but are not living on the premises of an embassy. Excluded are persons whose only activity consisted of work around their own home (such as housework, painting, repairing, etc.) or volunteer work for religious, charitable, and similar organizations.

Unemployed Persons

Unemployed persons are all those who had no employment during the reference week, were available for work, except for temporary illness, and had made specific efforts, such as contacting employers, to find employment sometime during the four-week period ending with the reference week. Persons who were waiting to be recalled to a job from which they had been laid off need not have been looking for work to be classified as unemployed.

Civilian Labor Force

The civilian labor force comprises the total of all civilians classified as employed and unemployed.

Unemployment Rate

The unemployment rate represents the proportion of the civilian labor force that is unemployed.

Labor Force Participation Rate

This represents the proportion of the population that is in the labor force.

Not in the Labor Force

Included in this group are all persons in the civilian noninstitutional population who are neither employed nor unemployed. Information is collected on their desire for and availability to take a job at the time of the CPS interview, their job search activity in the prior year, and their reason for not looking in the four-week period ending with the reference week. This group includes persons marginally attached to the labor force, defined as persons not in the labor force who want and are available for a job and who have looked for work sometime in the past twelve months (or since the end of their last job, if they held one within the past twelve months), but are not currently looking. Those marginally attached to the labor force are divided into those not currently looking because they believe their search would be futile and those not currently looking for other reasons. For discouraged workers, the main reason for not recently looking for work was one of the following: believed no work available in their line of work or area; could not find any work; lacked necessary schooling, training, skills, or experience; thought by employers to be too young or too old; or other types of discrimination.

TABLE Ba487–506 Labor force, employment, and unemployment, by sex: 1969–2000[1, 2]

Contributed by Susan B. Carter

Male

		Labor force								
				Employed				Unemployed		
	Population	Total	As percentage of population	Total	As percentage of population	Agriculture	Nonagriculture	Total	As percentage of labor force	Not in labor force
	Ba487	Ba488	Ba489	Ba490	Ba491	Ba492	Ba493	Ba494	Ba495	Ba496
Year	Thousand	Thousand	Percent	Thousand	Percent	Thousand	Thousand	Thousand	Percent	Thousand
1969	62,898	50,221	79.8	48,818	77.6	2,963	45,855	1,403	2.8	12,677
1970	64,304	51,228	79.7	48,990	76.2	2,862	46,128	2,238	4.4	13,076
1971	65,942	52,180	79.1	49,390	74.9	2,795	46,595	2,789	5.3	13,762
1972	67,835	53,555	78.9	50,896	75.0	2,849	48,047	2,659	5.0	14,280
1973	69,292	54,624	78.8	52,349	75.5	2,847	49,502	2,275	4.2	14,667
1974	70,808	55,739	78.7	53,024	74.9	2,919	50,105	2,714	4.9	15,069
1975	72,291	56,299	77.9	51,857	71.7	2,824	49,032	4,442	7.9	15,993
1976	73,759	57,174	77.5	53,138	72.0	2,744	50,394	4,036	7.1	16,585
1977	75,193	58,396	77.7	54,728	72.8	2,671	52,057	3,667	6.3	16,797
1978	76,576	59,620	77.9	56,479	73.8	2,718	53,761	3,142	5.3	16,956
1979	78,020	60,726	77.8	57,607	73.8	2,686	54,921	3,120	5.1	17,293
1980	79,398	61,453	77.4	57,186	72.0	2,709	54,477	4,267	6.9	17,945
1981	80,511	61,974	77.0	57,397	71.3	2,700	54,697	4,577	7.4	18,537
1982	81,523	62,450	76.6	56,271	69.0	2,736	53,534	6,179	9.9	19,073
1983	82,531	63,047	76.4	56,787	68.8	2,704	54,083	6,260	9.9	19,484
1984	83,605	63,835	76.4	59,091	70.7	2,668	56,423	4,744	7.4	19,771
1985	84,469	64,411	76.3	59,891	70.9	2,535	57,356	4,521	7.0	20,058
1986	85,798	65,422	76.3	60,892	71.0	2,511	58,381	4,530	6.9	20,376
1987	86,899	66,207	76.2	62,107	71.5	2,543	59,564	4,101	6.2	20,692
1988	87,857	66,927	76.2	63,273	72.0	2,493	60,780	3,655	5.5	20,930
1989	88,762	67,840	76.4	64,315	72.5	2,513	61,802	3,525	5.2	20,923
1990	90,377	69,011	76.4	65,104	72.0	2,546	62,559	3,906	5.7	21,367
1991	91,278	69,168	75.8	64,223	70.4	2,589	61,634	4,946	7.2	22,110
1992	92,270	69,964	75.8	64,440	69.8	2,575	61,866	5,523	7.9	22,306
1993	93,332	70,404	75.4	65,349	70.0	2,478	62,871	5,055	7.2	22,927
1994	94,355	70,817	75.1	66,450	70.4	2,554	63,896	4,367	6.2	23,538
1995	95,178	71,360	75.0	67,377	70.8	2,559	64,818	3,983	5.6	23,818
1996	96,206	72,087	74.9	68,207	70.9	2,573	65,634	3,880	5.4	24,119
1997	97,715	73,261	75.0	69,685	71.3	2,552	67,133	3,577	4.9	24,454
1998	98,758	73,959	74.9	70,693	71.6	2,553	68,140	3,266	4.4	24,799
1999	99,722	74,512	74.7	71,446	71.6	2,432	69,014	3,066	4.1	25,210
2000	100,731	75,247	74.7	72,293	71.8	2,434	69,859	2,954	3.9	25,484

Female

		Labor force								
				Employed				Unemployed		
	Population	Total	As percentage of population	Total	As percentage of population	Agriculture	Nonagriculture	Total	As percentage of labor force	Not in labor force
	Ba497	Ba498	Ba499	Ba500	Ba501	Ba502	Ba503	Ba504	Ba505	Ba506
Year	Thousand	Thousand	Percent	Thousand	Percent	Thousand	Thousand	Thousand	Percent	Thousand
1969	71,436	30,513	42.7	29,084	40.7	643	28,441	1,429	4.7	40,924
1970	72,782	31,543	43.3	29,688	40.8	601	29,087	1,855	5.9	41,239
1971	74,274	32,202	43.4	29,976	40.4	599	29,377	2,227	6.9	42,072
1972	76,290	33,479	43.9	31,257	41.0	635	30,622	2,222	6.6	42,811
1973	77,804	34,804	44.7	32,715	42.0	622	32,093	2,089	6.0	43,000
1974	79,312	36,211	45.7	33,769	42.6	596	33,173	2,441	6.7	43,101
1975	80,860	37,475	46.3	33,989	42.0	584	33,404	3,486	9.3	43,386
1976	82,390	38,983	47.3	35,615	43.2	588	35,027	3,369	8.6	43,406
1977	83,840	40,613	48.4	37,289	44.5	612	36,677	3,324	8.2	43,227
1978	85,334	42,631	50.0	39,569	46.4	669	38,900	3,061	7.2	42,703
1979	86,843	44,235	50.9	41,217	47.5	661	40,556	3,018	6.8	42,608

Notes appear at end of table

(continued)

TABLE Ba487–506 Labor force, employment, and unemployment, by sex: 1969–2000 *Continued*

	Female									
		Labor force								
				Employed				Unemployed		
	Population	Total	As percentage of population	Total	As percentage of population	Agriculture	Nonagriculture	Total	As percentage of labor force	Not in labor force
	Ba497	Ba498	Ba499	Ba500	Ba501	Ba502	Ba503	Ba504	Ba505	Ba506
Year	Thousand	Thousand	Percent	Thousand	Percent	Thousand	Thousand	Thousand	Percent	Thousand
1980	88,348	45,487	51.5	42,117	47.7	656	41,461	3,370	7.4	42,861
1981	89,618	46,696	52.1	43,000	48.0	667	42,333	3,696	7.9	42,922
1982	90,748	47,755	52.6	43,256	47.7	665	42,591	4,499	9.4	42,993
1983	91,684	48,503	52.9	44,047	48.0	680	43,367	4,457	9.2	43,181
1984	92,778	49,709	53.6	45,915	49.5	653	45,262	3,794	7.6	43,068
1985	93,736	51,050	54.5	47,259	50.4	644	46,615	3,791	7.4	42,686
1986	94,789	52,413	55.3	48,706	51.4	652	48,054	3,707	7.1	42,376
1987	95,853	53,658	56.0	50,334	52.5	666	49,668	3,324	6.2	42,195
1988	96,756	54,742	56.6	51,696	53.4	676	51,020	3,046	5.6	42,014
1989	97,630	56,030	57.4	53,027	54.3	687	52,341	3,003	5.4	41,601
1990	98,787	56,829	57.5	53,689	54.3	678	53,011	3,140	5.5	41,957
1991	99,646	57,178	57.4	53,496	53.7	680	52,815	3,683	6.4	42,468
1992	100,535	58,141	57.8	54,052	53.8	672	53,380	4,090	7.0	42,394
1993	101,506	58,795	57.9	54,910	54.1	637	54,273	3,885	6.6	42,711
1994	102,460	60,239	58.8	56,610	55.3	855	55,755	3,629	6.0	42,221
1995	103,406	60,944	58.9	57,523	55.6	881	56,642	3,421	5.6	42,462
1996	104,385	61,857	59.3	58,501	56.0	871	57,630	3,356	5.4	42,528
1997	105,418	63,036	59.8	59,873	56.8	847	59,026	3,162	5.0	42,382
1998	106,462	63,714	59.8	60,771	57.1	825	59,945	2,944	4.6	42,748
1999	108,031	64,855	60.0	62,042	57.4	849	61,193	2,814	4.3	43,175
2000	108,968	65,616	60.2	62,915	57.7	871	62,044	2,701	4.1	43,352

[1] Civilian noninstitutional population, age 16 and older.

[2] Data not strictly comparable over time; see the text for Table Ba478–486.

Sources

U.S. Bureau of Labor Statistics (BLS) Internet site and *BLS Handbook of Methods,* Bulletin number 2490 (April 1997). Monthly updates are available from the BLS periodical *Employment and Earnings*.

Documentation

See the text for Table Ba478–486.

TABLE Ba507–518 Labor force participation rate, by sex and education: 1940–1990[1] [Census estimates]

Contributed by Matthew Sobek

	Both sexes				Males				Females			
	Fewer than 12 grades completed	12 grades completed	Fewer than 4 years of college	4 or more years of college	Fewer than 12 grades completed	12 grades completed	Fewer than 4 years of college	4 or more years of college	Fewer than 12 grades completed	12 grades completed	Fewer than 4 years of college	4 or more years of college
	Ba507	Ba508	Ba509	Ba510	Ba511	Ba512	Ba513	Ba514	Ba515	Ba516	Ba517	Ba518
Year	Percent	Percent	Percent	Percent	Percent	Percent	Percent	Percent	Percent	Percent	Percent	Percent
1940	59.2	59.9	62.4	76.5	94.0	96.6	95.3	95.8	22.9	32.5	35.8	49.0
1950	60.1	60.0	62.7	75.1	92.5	95.9	91.3	94.1	28.1	34.1	38.7	50.0
1960	64.3	64.1	68.3	81.0	91.6	96.9	95.3	96.9	37.3	41.2	44.2	56.1
1970	64.6	68.7	71.6	82.0	87.7	95.3	94.1	95.8	42.9	49.7	50.5	61.2
1980	61.8	73.0	78.8	86.0	79.9	91.1	92.4	94.9	45.3	59.7	65.7	73.5
1990 [2]	61.0	76.5	83.8	88.6	75.0	88.5	91.9	94.2	47.2	66.7	76.6	82.0

[1] Data pertain to noninstitutionalized civilians ages 25 to 64.

[2] Receipt of degree equated with number of years of college. See text.

Source

Tabulated from the Integrated Public Use Microdata Series; see the Guide to the Millennial Edition.

Documentation

Labor force participation means working or seeking work in the week prior to the census.

A person is recorded only in the category reflecting his or her highest level of educational attainment. Persons who received their schooling outside of the United States were to report the equivalent U.S. grade level in all years.

In 1980, persons with a general equivalency diploma (GED) were to be reported as having completed twelfth grade. In 1990, persons who completed twelfth grade but received no diploma or GED can be identified; these persons are considered graduates for the purposes of this table for the sake of compatibility with other years.

The 1990 Census recorded the receipt of college degrees, not the number of years of schooling. In this table, completion of a bachelor's or higher degree is equated with four or more years of college.

For a discussion of the source and general methodology employed, see Matthew Sobek, "New Statistics on the U.S. Labor Force, 1850–1990," *Historical Methods* 34 (2001): 71–87.

TABLE Ba519–534 Male labor force, by age: 1947–2000[1, 2]

Contributed by Susan B. Carter

	Labor force								Labor force participation rate							
		Age								Age						
	Total	16–19	20–24	25–34	35–44	45–54	55–64	65 and older	Overall	16–19	20–24	25–34	35–44	45–54	55–64	65 and older
	Ba519	Ba520	Ba521	Ba522	Ba523	Ba524	Ba525	Ba526	Ba527	Ba528	Ba529	Ba530	Ba531	Ba532	Ba533	Ba534
Year	Thousand	Thousand	Thousand	Thousand	Thousand	Thousand	Thousand	Thousand	Percent	Percent	Percent	Percent	Percent	Percent	Percent	Percent
1947	42,687	—	—	—	—	—	—	—	—	—	—	—	—	—	—	—
1948	43,284	2,600	4,673	10,327	9,596	7,943	5,764	2,384	86.6	63.8	84.6	95.9	98.0	95.8	89.4	46.8
1949	43,497	2,477	4,682	10,418	9,722	8,008	5,748	2,454	86.4	62.7	86.7	95.9	98.0	95.5	87.5	47.0
1950	43,817	2,504	4,632	10,527	9,793	8,117	5,794	2,453	86.4	63.2	87.9	96.1	97.6	95.8	87.0	45.8
1951	43,001	2,347	3,935	10,375	9,799	8,205	5,873	2,469	86.5	63.0	88.4	96.8	97.5	96.0	87.2	44.9
1952	42,867	2,312	3,338	10,585	9,945	8,326	5,949	2,416	86.3	61.3	88.1	97.5	97.9	96.2	87.5	42.6
1953	43,632	2,320	3,053	10,736	10,437	8,570	5,975	2,543	86.0	60.7	87.7	97.4	98.2	96.5	87.9	41.6
1954	43,963	2,295	3,051	10,771	10,513	8,702	6,105	2,526	85.6	58.0	86.9	97.4	98.1	96.5	88.7	40.5
1955	44,475	2,369	3,221	10,806	10,595	8,838	6,122	2,526	85.4	58.9	86.9	97.6	98.0	96.4	88.0	39.6
1956	45,090	2,433	3,485	10,685	10,663	9,002	6,220	2,602	85.5	60.5	87.7	97.3	98.0	96.6	88.5	40.0
1957	45,198	2,415	3,629	10,571	10,731	9,153	6,222	2,477	84.8	59.1	87.1	97.1	97.9	96.4	87.5	37.6
1958	45,521	2,428	3,771	10,475	10,843	9,320	6,304	2,378	84.2	56.6	86.9	97.2	97.9	96.3	87.9	35.6
1959	45,886	2,596	3,940	10,346	10,899	9,438	6,345	2,322	83.7	55.7	87.7	97.4	97.8	96.0	87.5	34.3
1960	46,390	2,787	4,123	10,251	10,967	9,574	6,399	2,287	83.4	56.2	88.1	97.5	97.7	95.7	86.8	33.1
1961	46,653	2,794	4,253	10,176	11,012	9,668	6,530	2,220	82.9	54.7	87.7	97.5	97.6	95.6	87.3	31.6
1962	46,600	2,770	4,279	9,920	11,115	9,715	6,560	2,241	82.0	53.8	86.8	97.2	97.5	95.6	86.2	30.3
1963	47,129	2,907	4,514	9,876	11,187	9,836	6,675	2,135	81.4	52.9	86.2	97.2	97.5	95.8	86.2	28.4
1964	47,679	3,074	4,754	9,876	11,156	9,956	6,741	2,124	81.0	52.4	86.2	97.4	97.3	95.7	85.6	28.0
1965	48,254	3,397	4,894	9,903	11,120	10,045	6,763	2,132	80.7	53.8	85.9	97.3	97.3	95.6	84.7	27.9
1966	48,470	3,685	4,820	9,948	10,983	10,100	6,847	2,089	80.5	55.4	85.1	97.3	97.2	95.4	84.5	27.0
1967	48,987	3,634	5,043	10,207	10,859	10,189	6,937	2,118	80.5	55.5	84.4	97.3	97.3	95.2	84.4	27.2
1968	49,533	3,681	5,070	10,610	10,725	10,267	7,025	2,154	80.1	55.1	82.7	97.0	97.1	94.9	84.3	27.3
1969	50,221	3,870	5,282	10,941	10,556	10,344	7,058	2,170	79.8	55.8	82.8	96.7	96.9	94.6	83.4	27.2
1970	51,228	4,008	5,717	11,327	10,469	10,417	7,126	2,165	79.7	56.1	83.3	96.4	96.8	94.2	82.9	26.8
1971	52,179	4,172	6,233	11,731	10,347	10,451	7,155	2,090	79.1	56.1	83.0	95.9	96.5	93.9	82.1	25.5
1972	53,555	4,476	6,766	12,350	10,372	10,412	7,155	2,026	78.9	58.1	83.9	95.6	96.3	93.2	80.5	24.3
1973	54,624	4,693	7,183	13,056	10,338	10,416	7,028	1,913	78.8	59.7	85.3	95.7	96.2	93.0	78.2	22.7
1974	55,738	4,861	7,387	13,665	10,401	10,431	7,063	1,932	78.7	60.6	86.0	95.8	96.0	92.2	77.3	22.3
1975	56,299	4,805	7,565	14,192	10,398	10,401	7,023	1,914	77.8	59.1	84.5	95.2	95.7	92.0	75.7	21.7
1976	57,174	4,886	7,866	14,784	10,500	10,293	7,020	1,826	77.5	59.3	85.2	95.2	95.3	91.6	74.3	20.1
1977	58,395	5,048	8,109	15,353	10,771	10,158	7,100	1,857	77.7	61.0	85.6	95.3	95.7	91.1	73.8	19.9
1978	59,621	5,149	8,327	15,814	11,159	10,083	7,151	1,936	77.9	62.0	85.9	95.3	95.7	91.3	73.3	20.4
1979	60,727	5,111	8,535	16,387	11,531	10,008	7,212	1,943	77.8	61.5	86.4	95.3	95.7	91.4	72.8	19.9
1980	61,453	4,999	8,607	16,971	11,836	9,905	7,242	1,893	77.4	60.6	85.8	95.2	95.5	91.2	72.1	19.0
1981	61,974	4,777	8,648	17,479	12,166	9,868	7,170	1,866	77.0	59.0	85.5	94.9	95.3	91.4	70.7	18.3
1982	62,450	4,470	8,604	17,793	12,781	9,784	7,174	1,845	76.6	56.7	84.9	94.7	95.4	91.2	70.2	17.8
1983	63,047	4,303	8,601	18,038	13,398	9,746	7,119	1,842	76.4	56.2	84.8	94.2	95.2	91.1	69.4	17.4
1984	63,835	4,134	8,594	18,488	14,037	9,776	7,050	1,755	76.4	56.0	85.0	94.3	95.3	91.2	68.6	16.3
1985	64,412	4,134	8,283	18,808	14,506	9,870	7,060	1,750	76.3	56.8	85.0	94.7	95.0	91.0	68.0	15.8
1986	65,422	4,102	8,148	19,383	15,029	9,994	6,954	1,811	76.3	56.4	85.8	94.6	94.8	91.0	67.3	15.9
1987	66,208	4,112	7,837	19,656	15,587	10,176	6,940	1,899	76.2	56.1	85.3	94.6	94.6	90.7	67.6	16.3
1988	66,928	4,159	7,594	19,742	16,074	10,566	6,831	1,960	76.2	56.9	85.1	94.3	94.5	91.0	67.1	16.5
1989	67,840	4,136	7,458	19,905	16,622	10,919	6,783	2,017	76.5	57.9	85.4	94.4	94.5	91.1	67.2	16.6
1990	69,010	4,094	7,866	19,872	17,481	11,103	6,627	1,967	76.3	55.7	84.4	94.1	94.3	90.7	67.7	16.3
1991	69,169	3,795	7,820	19,641	18,077	11,362	6,550	1,924	75.8	53.2	83.5	93.7	94.1	90.5	67.0	15.7
1992	69,963	3,751	7,770	19,495	18,347	12,040	6,551	2,010	75.8	53.4	83.3	93.8	93.7	90.7	67.0	16.0
1993	70,404	3,762	7,671	19,214	18,713	12,562	6,502	1,980	75.4	53.2	83.2	93.4	93.4	90.1	66.5	15.6
1994	70,817	3,896	7,540	18,854	18,966	12,962	6,423	2,176	75.0	54.1	83.1	92.6	92.8	89.1	65.5	16.9
1995	71,360	4,036	7,338	18,670	19,189	13,421	6,504	2,201	75.0	54.8	83.0	93.0	92.2	88.8	66.0	16.8
1996	72,087	4,043	7,104	18,430	19,602	13,967	6,693	2,247	74.9	53.3	82.5	93.2	92.4	89.1	66.9	16.9
1997	73,262	4,095	7,184	18,110	20,058	14,564	6,952	2,298	75.0	52.3	82.5	93.0	92.6	89.5	67.6	17.0
1998	73,959	4,244	7,221	17,796	20,242	14,963	7,253	2,240	74.9	53.3	82.0	93.2	92.6	89.2	68.1	16.4
1999	74,512	4,318	7,291	17,318	20,382	15,394	7,477	2,333	74.7	52.9	81.9	93.3	92.8	88.8	67.9	16.9
2000	75,247	4,317	7,558	17,073	20,334	15,951	7,574	2,439	74.7	53.0	82.6	93.4	92.6	88.6	67.3	17.5

[1] Civilian noninstitutional population, age 16 and older.

[2] Data not strictly comparable over time; see the text for Table Ba478–486.

Sources

U.S. Bureau of Labor Statistics (BLS) Internet site *BLS Handbook of Methods*, Bulletin number 2490 (April 1997). Monthly updates are available from the BLS periodical *Employment and Earnings*.

Documentation

See the text for Table Ba478–486.

TABLE Ba535-550 Female labor force, by age: 1947-2000[1, 2]

Contributed by Susan B. Carter

	Labor force								Labor force participation rate							
		Age								Age						
	Total	16-19	20-24	25-34	35-44	45-54	55-64	65 and older	Overall	16-19	20-24	25-34	35-44	45-54	55-64	65 and older
	Ba535	Ba536	Ba537	Ba538	Ba539	Ba540	Ba541	Ba542	Ba543	Ba544	Ba545	Ba546	Ba547	Ba548	Ba549	Ba550
Year	Thousand	Thousand	Thousand	Thousand	Thousand	Thousand	Thousand	Thousand	Percent	Percent	Percent	Percent	Percent	Percent	Percent	Percent
1947	16,664	—	—	—	—	—	—	—	—	—	—	—	—	—	—	—
1948	17,335	1,835	2,719	3,931	3,801	2,971	1,565	513	32.7	42.0	45.3	33.2	36.9	35.0	24.3	9.1
1949	17,788	1,811	2,658	3,997	3,989	3,099	1,678	556	33.1	42.4	45.0	33.4	38.1	35.9	25.3	9.6
1950	18,389	1,712	2,675	4,092	4,161	3,327	1,839	583	33.9	41.0	46.0	34.0	39.1	37.9	27.0	9.7
1951	19,016	1,756	2,659	4,293	4,301	3,534	1,923	551	34.6	42.4	46.5	35.4	39.8	39.7	27.6	8.9
1952	19,269	1,752	2,502	4,319	4,438	3,635	2,031	589	34.7	42.2	44.7	35.4	40.4	40.1	28.7	9.1
1953	19,382	1,707	2,428	4,162	4,662	3,679	2,049	693	34.4	40.7	44.3	34.0	41.3	40.4	29.1	10.0
1954	19,678	1,681	2,424	4,212	4,708	3,822	2,164	666	34.6	39.4	45.1	34.4	41.2	41.2	30.0	9.3
1955	20,548	1,723	2,445	4,252	4,805	4,154	2,391	779	35.7	39.7	45.9	34.9	41.6	43.8	32.5	10.6
1956	21,461	1,863	2,455	4,276	5,031	4,405	2,610	821	36.9	42.2	46.3	35.4	43.1	45.5	34.9	10.8
1957	21,732	1,860	2,442	4,255	5,116	4,615	2,631	813	36.9	41.1	45.9	35.6	43.3	46.5	34.5	10.5
1958	22,118	1,832	2,501	4,193	5,185	4,859	2,727	821	37.1	39.0	46.3	35.6	43.4	47.8	35.2	10.3
1959	22,483	1,896	2,473	4,089	5,228	5,080	2,882	836	37.1	38.2	45.1	35.3	43.4	49.0	36.6	10.2
1960	23,240	2,054	2,579	4,131	5,302	5,278	2,986	908	37.7	39.3	46.1	36.0	43.4	49.9	37.2	10.8
1961	23,806	2,142	2,697	4,143	5,390	5,403	3,106	926	38.1	39.7	47.0	36.4	43.8	50.1	37.9	10.7
1962	24,014	2,146	2,803	4,103	5,474	5,381	3,197	913	37.9	39.0	47.3	36.3	44.1	50.0	38.7	10.0
1963	24,704	2,232	2,959	4,174	5,601	5,502	3,331	906	38.3	38.0	47.5	37.2	44.9	50.6	39.7	9.6
1964	25,412	2,314	3,209	4,180	5,615	5,681	3,441	966	38.7	37.0	49.4	37.2	45.0	51.4	40.2	10.1
1965	26,200	2,513	3,365	4,330	5,720	5,711	3,587	976	39.3	38.0	49.9	38.5	46.1	50.9	41.1	10.0
1966	27,299	2,873	3,590	4,510	5,755	5,884	3,728	964	40.3	41.4	51.5	39.8	46.8	51.7	41.8	9.6
1967	28,360	2,887	3,966	4,848	5,844	5,983	3,855	979	41.1	41.6	53.3	41.9	48.1	51.8	42.4	9.6
1968	29,204	2,938	4,235	5,098	5,866	6,130	3,939	999	41.6	41.9	54.5	42.6	48.9	52.3	42.4	9.6
1969	30,513	3,100	4,597	5,395	5,902	6,386	4,077	1,057	42.7	43.2	56.7	43.7	49.9	53.8	43.1	9.9
1970	31,543	3,241	4,880	5,708	5,968	6,532	4,157	1,056	43.3	44.0	57.7	45.0	51.1	54.4	43.0	9.7
1971	32,202	3,298	5,098	5,983	5,957	6,573	4,234	1,059	43.4	43.4	57.7	45.6	51.6	54.3	42.9	9.5
1972	33,479	3,578	5,364	6,610	6,027	6,555	4,257	1,089	43.9	45.8	59.1	47.8	52.0	53.9	42.1	9.3
1973	34,804	3,814	5,663	7,320	6,154	6,567	4,228	1,061	44.7	47.8	61.1	50.4	53.3	53.7	41.1	8.9
1974	36,211	4,010	5,926	7,989	6,362	6,699	4,221	1,002	45.7	49.1	63.1	52.6	54.7	54.6	40.7	8.1
1975	37,475	4,065	6,185	8,673	6,505	6,683	4,323	1,042	46.3	49.1	64.1	54.9	55.8	54.6	40.9	8.2
1976	38,983	4,170	6,418	9,419	6,817	6,689	4,402	1,069	47.3	49.8	65.0	57.3	57.8	55.0	41.0	8.2
1977	40,613	4,303	6,717	10,149	7,171	6,720	4,477	1,078	48.4	51.2	66.5	59.7	59.6	55.8	40.9	8.1
1978	42,631	4,503	7,043	10,888	7,662	6,807	4,593	1,134	50.0	53.7	68.3	62.2	61.6	57.1	41.3	8.3
1979	44,235	4,527	7,234	11,551	8,154	6,889	4,719	1,161	50.9	54.2	69.0	63.9	63.6	58.3	41.7	8.3
1980	45,487	4,381	7,315	12,257	8,627	7,004	4,742	1,161	51.5	52.9	68.9	65.5	65.5	59.9	41.3	8.1
1981	46,696	4,211	7,451	12,912	9,045	7,101	4,799	1,176	52.1	51.8	69.6	66.7	66.8	61.1	41.4	8.0
1982	47,755	4,056	7,477	13,393	9,651	7,105	4,888	1,185	52.6	51.4	69.8	68.0	68.0	61.6	41.8	7.9
1983	48,503	3,868	7,451	13,796	10,213	7,105	4,873	1,198	52.9	50.8	69.9	69.0	68.7	61.9	41.5	7.8
1984	49,709	3,810	7,451	14,234	10,896	7,230	4,911	1,177	53.6	51.8	70.4	69.8	70.1	62.9	41.7	7.5
1985	51,050	3,767	7,434	14,742	11,567	7,452	4,932	1,156	54.5	52.1	71.8	70.9	71.8	64.4	42.0	7.3
1986	52,413	3,824	7,293	15,208	12,204	7,746	4,940	1,199	55.3	53.0	72.4	71.6	73.1	65.9	42.3	7.4
1987	53,658	3,875	7,140	15,577	12,873	8,034	4,937	1,221	56.0	53.3	73.0	72.4	74.5	67.1	42.7	7.4
1988	54,742	3,872	6,910	15,761	13,361	8,537	4,977	1,324	56.6	53.6	72.7	72.7	75.2	69.0	43.5	7.9
1989	56,030	3,818	6,721	15,990	13,980	8,997	5,095	1,429	57.4	53.9	72.4	73.5	76.0	70.5	45.0	8.4
1990	56,829	3,698	6,834	16,058	14,663	9,145	4,948	1,483	57.5	51.6	71.3	73.5	76.4	71.2	45.2	8.6
1991	57,178	3,470	6,728	15,867	15,235	9,465	4,924	1,489	57.4	50.0	70.1	73.1	76.5	72.0	45.2	8.5
1992	58,141	3,345	6,750	15,875	15,552	10,120	5,035	1,464	57.8	49.1	70.9	73.9	76.7	72.6	46.5	8.3
1993	58,795	3,408	6,683	15,566	15,849	10,733	5,097	1,459	57.9	49.7	70.9	73.4	76.6	73.5	47.2	8.1
1994	60,239	3,585	6,592	15,499	16,259	11,357	5,289	1,658	58.8	51.3	71.0	74.0	77.1	74.6	48.9	9.2
1995	60,944	3,729	6,349	15,528	16,562	11,801	5,356	1,618	58.9	52.2	70.3	74.9	77.2	74.4	49.2	8.8
1996	61,857	3,763	6,273	15,403	16,954	12,430	5,452	1,581	59.3	51.3	71.3	75.2	77.5	75.4	49.6	8.6
1997	63,036	3,837	6,348	15,271	17,268	13,010	5,713	1,590	59.8	51.0	72.7	76.0	77.7	76.0	50.9	8.6
1998	63,714	4,012	6,418	15,017	17,294	13,405	5,962	1,607	59.8	52.3	73.0	76.3	77.1	76.2	51.2	8.6
1999	64,855	4,015	6,643	14,826	17,501	13,994	6,204	1,673	60.0	51.0	73.2	76.4	77.2	76.7	51.5	8.9
2000	65,616	4,051	6,788	14,596	17,504	14,515	6,400	1,762	60.2	51.3	73.3	76.3	77.3	76.8	51.8	9.4

[1] Civilian noninstitutional population, age 16 and older.

[2] Data not strictly comparable over time; see the text for Table Ba478-486.

Sources

U.S. Bureau of Labor Statistics (BLS) Internet site and *BLS Handbook of Methods,* Bulletin number 2490 (April 1997). Monthly updates are available from the BLS periodical *Employment and Earnings*.

Documentation

See the text for Table Ba478-486.

TABLE Ba551–560 Male labor force, by race and Hispanic origin: 1954–2000[1, 2]

Contributed by Susan B. Carter

	Labor force					Labor force participation rate				
	Total	White	Nonwhite	Black	Hispanic	Overall	White	Nonwhite	Black	Hispanic
	Ba551	Ba552	Ba553	Ba554	Ba555	Ba556	Ba557	Ba558	Ba559	Ba560
Year	Thousand	Thousand	Thousand	Thousand	Thousand	Percent	Percent	Percent	Percent	Percent
1954	43,963	39,759	4,204	—	—	85.6	85.6	85.0	—	—
1955	44,475	40,197	4,280	—	—	85.4	85.3	85.6	—	—
1956	45,090	40,734	4,358	—	—	85.5	85.6	85.3	—	—
1957	45,198	40,826	4,370	—	—	84.8	84.9	83.7	—	—
1958	45,521	41,080	4,443	—	—	84.2	84.3	83.5	—	—
1959	45,886	41,397	4,488	—	—	83.7	83.7	83.4	—	—
1960	46,390	41,743	4,647	—	—	83.4	83.4	83.3	—	—
1961	46,653	41,986	4,667	—	—	82.9	82.9	82.8	—	—
1962	46,600	41,931	4,669	—	—	82.0	82.2	80.3	—	—
1963	47,129	42,404	4,725	—	—	81.4	81.5	80.2	—	—
1964	47,679	42,894	4,785	—	—	81.0	81.2	80.0	—	—
1965	48,254	43,400	4,856	—	—	80.7	80.8	79.9	—	—
1966	48,470	43,572	4,898	—	—	80.5	80.6	79.4	—	—
1967	48,987	44,041	4,946	—	—	80.5	80.6	79.3	—	—
1968	49,533	44,553	4,979	—	—	80.1	80.4	77.8	—	—
1969	50,221	45,185	5,037	—	—	79.8	80.2	76.5	—	—
1970	51,228	46,035	5,194	—	—	79.7	80.0	76.7	—	—
1971	52,179	46,904	5,276	—	—	79.1	79.6	75.0	—	—
1972	53,555	48,117	5,437	4,816	—	78.9	79.6	73.4	73.6	—
1973	54,624	48,921	5,705	4,924	2,356	78.8	79.5	73.2	73.4	—
1974	55,738	49,843	5,895	5,020	2,556	78.7	79.4	73.9	72.9	—
1975	56,299	50,324	5,976	5,016	2,597	77.8	78.7	71.5	70.9	—
1976	57,174	51,033	6,141	5,101	2,580	77.5	78.4	71.2	70.0	—
1977	58,395	52,033	6,362	5,263	2,817	77.7	78.4	71.6	70.6	—
1978	59,621	52,955	6,665	5,435	3,041	77.9	78.6	72.6	71.5	—
1979	60,727	53,857	6,870	5,559	3,184	77.8	78.6	72.5	71.3	—
1980	61,453	54,472	6,980	5,612	3,818	77.4	78.2	71.5	70.3	81.4
1981	61,974	54,895	7,079	5,685	4,005	77.0	77.9	70.6	70.0	80.6
1982	62,450	55,133	7,317	5,804	4,148	76.6	77.4	71.0	70.1	79.7
1983	63,047	55,480	7,567	5,966	4,362	76.4	77.2	71.3	70.6	80.3
1984	63,835	56,062	7,773	6,126	4,563	76.4	77.0	71.4	70.8	80.6
1985	64,412	56,472	7,940	6,220	4,729	76.3	77.0	71.6	70.8	80.3
1986	65,422	57,218	8,204	6,373	4,948	76.3	76.9	71.9	71.2	81.0
1987	66,208	57,779	8,428	6,486	5,163	76.2	76.9	72.0	71.1	81.0
1988	66,928	58,316	8,611	6,596	5,409	76.2	76.8	71.7	71.0	81.9
1989	67,840	58,988	8,852	6,701	5,595	76.5	77.1	72.0	71.0	82.0
1990	69,010	59,638	9,373	6,802	6,546	76.3	77.1	72.1	71.0	81.4
1991	69,169	59,656	9,512	6,851	6,664	75.8	76.6	71.5	70.4	80.3
1992	69,963	60,168	9,796	6,997	6,900	75.8	76.4	71.9	70.7	80.7
1993	70,404	60,484	9,920	7,019	7,076	75.4	76.2	71.1	69.6	80.2
1994	70,817	60,727	10,090	7,089	7,210	75.0	75.9	70.6	69.1	79.2
1995	71,360	61,145	10,215	7,183	7,376	75.0	75.7	70.7	69.0	79.1
1996	72,087	61,784	10,303	7,264	7,646	74.9	75.9	70.0	68.7	79.6
1997	73,262	62,639	10,622	7,354	8,309	75.0	75.9	70.2	68.3	80.1
1998	73,959	63,035	10,925	7,542	8,571	74.9	75.6	70.9	69.0	79.8
1999	74,512	63,413	11,099	7,652	8,546	74.7	75.5	70.3	68.7	79.8
2000	75,247	63,861	11,387	7,816	8,919	74.7	75.5	70.8	69.0	80.6

[1] Civilian noninstitutional population, age 16 and older.

[2] Data not strictly comparable over time; see the text for Table Ba478–486.

Sources

U.S. Bureau of Labor Statistics (BLS) Internet site and *BLS Handbook of Methods,* Bulletin number 2490 (April 1997). Monthly updates are available from the BLS periodical *Employment and Earnings*.

Documentation

See the text for Table Ba478–486.

Hispanics are included in both the white and the nonwhite population groups.

TABLE Ba561–570 Female labor force, by race and Hispanic origin: 1954–2000[1, 2]

Contributed by Susan B. Carter

	Labor force					Labor force participation rate				
	Total	White	Nonwhite	Black	Hispanic	Overall	White	Nonwhite	Black	Hispanic
	Ba561	Ba562	Ba563	Ba564	Ba565	Ba566	Ba567	Ba568	Ba569	Ba570
Year	Thousand	Thousand	Thousand	Thousand	Thousand	Percent	Percent	Percent	Percent	Percent
1954	19,678	17,057	2,621	—	—	34.6	33.3	46.4	—	—
1955	20,548	17,888	2,662	—	—	35.7	34.5	46.6	—	—
1956	21,461	18,694	2,767	—	—	36.9	35.7	47.7	—	—
1957	21,732	18,928	2,804	—	—	36.9	35.7	47.7	—	—
1958	22,118	19,213	2,903	—	—	37.1	35.8	48.8	—	—
1959	22,483	19,555	2,928	—	—	37.1	36.0	46.6	—	—
1960	23,240	20,172	3,069	—	—	37.7	36.5	48.1	—	—
1961	23,806	20,670	3,137	—	—	38.1	36.9	48.5	—	—
1962	24,014	20,819	3,195	—	—	37.9	36.7	48.2	—	—
1963	24,704	21,426	3,278	—	—	38.3	37.2	47.5	—	—
1964	25,412	22,027	3,385	—	—	38.7	37.5	48.9	—	—
1965	26,200	22,737	3,465	—	—	39.3	38.1	49.6	—	—
1966	27,299	23,704	3,601	—	—	40.3	39.2	49.5	—	—
1967	28,360	24,658	3,703	—	—	41.1	40.1	49.3	—	—
1968	29,204	25,423	3,780	—	—	41.6	40.7	48.9	—	—
1969	30,513	26,593	3,918	—	—	42.7	41.8	50.0	—	—
1970	31,543	27,521	4,024	—	—	43.3	42.6	48.8	—	—
1971	32,202	28,060	4,142	—	—	43.4	42.6	49.7	—	—
1972	33,479	29,157	4,323	4,816	—	43.9	43.2	49.3	73.6	—
1973	34,804	30,231	4,575	4,924	1,317	44.7	44.1	49.1	73.4	—
1974	36,211	31,437	4,772	5,020	1,456	45.7	45.2	49.3	72.9	—
1975	37,475	32,508	4,967	5,016	1,574	46.3	45.9	49.1	70.9	—
1976	38,983	33,735	5,250	5,101	1,625	47.3	46.9	50.4	70.0	—
1977	40,613	35,108	5,505	5,263	1,720	48.4	48.0	51.1	70.6	—
1978	42,631	36,679	5,951	5,435	1,938	50.0	49.4	53.5	71.5	—
1979	44,235	38,067	6,168	5,559	2,035	50.9	50.5	53.7	71.3	—
1980	45,487	39,127	6,359	5,612	2,328	51.5	51.2	53.6	70.3	47.4
1981	46,696	40,157	6,539	5,685	2,486	52.1	51.9	53.6	70.0	48.3
1982	47,755	41,010	6,745	5,804	2,586	52.6	52.4	53.9	70.1	48.1
1983	48,503	41,541	6,962	5,966	2,671	52.9	52.7	54.4	70.6	47.7
1984	49,709	42,431	7,279	6,126	2,888	53.6	53.3	55.3	70.8	49.6
1985	51,050	43,455	7,595	6,220	2,970	54.5	54.1	56.6	70.8	49.3
1986	52,413	44,584	7,829	6,373	3,128	55.3	55.0	57.0	71.2	50.1
1987	53,658	45,510	8,148	6,486	3,377	56.0	55.7	57.8	71.1	52.0
1988	54,742	46,439	8,303	6,596	3,573	56.6	56.4	57.6	71.0	53.2
1989	56,030	47,367	8,663	6,701	3,728	57.4	57.2	58.7	71.0	53.5
1990	56,829	47,809	9,020	6,802	4,174	57.5	57.4	58.1	71.0	53.1
1991	57,178	48,087	9,092	6,851	4,256	57.4	57.4	57.3	70.4	52.3
1992	58,141	48,669	9,472	6,997	4,439	57.8	57.7	58.4	70.7	52.8
1993	58,795	49,216	9,579	7,019	4,534	57.9	58.0	57.7	69.6	52.1
1994	60,239	50,356	9,884	7,089	4,765	58.8	58.9	58.3	69.1	52.9
1995	60,944	50,804	10,140	7,183	4,891	58.9	59.0	58.9	69.0	52.6
1996	61,857	51,325	10,532	7,264	5,128	59.3	59.1	60.0	68.7	53.4
1997	63,036	52,054	10,982	7,354	5,486	59.8	59.5	61.0	68.3	55.1
1998	63,714	52,380	11,334	7,542	5,746	59.8	59.4	61.8	69.0	55.6
1999	64,855	53,096	11,760	7,652	6,119	60.0	59.6	62.3	68.7	55.9
2000	65,616	53,714	11,902	7,816	6,449	60.2	59.8	62.0	69.0	56.9

[1] Civilian noninstitutional population, age 16 and older.

[2] Data not strictly comparable over time; see the text for Table Ba478–486.

Sources

U.S. Bureau of Labor Statistics (BLS) Internet site and *BLS Handbook of Methods*, Bulletin number 2490 (April 1997). Monthly updates are available from the BLS periodical *Employment and Earnings*.

Documentation

See the text for Table Ba478–486.

Hispanics are included in both the white and the nonwhite population groups.

TABLE Ba571–578 Female labor force, by marital status: 1955–1999[1, 2]

Contributed by Susan B. Carter

	Labor force				Labor force participation rate			
	Total	Single	Married, spouse present	Widowed, separated, or divorced	Overall	Single	Married, spouse present	Widowed, separated, or divorced
	Ba571	Ba572	Ba573	Ba574	Ba575	Ba576	Ba577	Ba578
Year	Thousand	Thousand	Thousand	Thousand	Percent	Percent	Percent	Percent
1955	20,548	5,281	10,809	4,458	35.7	61.1	28.5	40.7
1956	21,461	5,420	11,522	4,520	36.9	62.2	29.9	41.2
1957	21,732	5,361	11,795	4,576	36.9	61.4	30.1	41.3
1958	22,118	5,269	12,164	4,683	37.1	59.8	30.7	41.6
1959	22,483	5,194	12,510	4,781	37.1	57.8	31.2	41.6
1960	23,240	5,410	12,893	4,937	37.7	58.6	31.9	41.6
1961	23,806	5,419	13,259	5,129	38.1	57.9	32.5	41.7
1962	24,014	5,363	13,556	5,096	37.9	56.5	32.9	40.6
1963	24,704	5,597	13,812	5,294	38.3	55.2	33.4	40.9
1964	25,412	5,790	14,345	5,277	38.7	54.5	34.1	40.6
1965	26,200	5,976	14,829	5,396	39.3	54.5	34.9	40.7
1966	27,299	6,279	15,425	5,593	40.3	55.7	35.9	41.3
1967	28,360	6,485	16,247	5,630	41.1	55.3	37.3	41.0
1968	29,204	6,714	16,937	5,553	41.6	55.6	38.2	40.4
1969	30,513	7,015	17,768	5,732	42.7	56.7	35.6	40.7
1970	31,543	7,265	18,475	5,804	43.3	56.8	40.5	40.3
1971	32,202	7,460	18,764	5,976	43.4	56.4	40.6	40.3
1972	33,479	7,889	19,352	6,239	43.9	57.5	41.2	40.0
1973	34,804	8,272	20,172	6,361	44.7	58.6	42.3	39.7
1974	36,211	8,671	20,869	6,672	45.7	59.5	43.3	40.2
1975	37,475	9,125	21,484	6,866	46.3	59.8	44.3	40.1
1976	38,983	9,689	22,139	7,156	47.3	61.0	45.3	40.5
1977	40,613	10,311	22,776	7,526	48.4	62.1	46.4	41.5
1978	42,631	11,067	23,539	8,025	50.0	63.7	47.8	42.8
1979	44,235	11,597	24,378	8,260	50.9	64.6	49.0	43.1
1980	45,487	11,865	24,980	8,643	51.5	64.4	49.9	43.6
1981	46,696	12,124	25,428	9,144	52.1	64.5	50.5	44.6
1982	47,755	12,460	25,971	9,324	52.6	65.1	51.1	44.8
1983	48,503	12,659	26,468	9,376	52.9	65.0	51.8	44.4
1984	49,709	12,867	27,199	9,644	53.6	65.6	52.8	44.7
1985	51,050	13,163	27,894	9,993	54.5	66.6	53.8	45.1
1986	52,413	13,512	28,623	10,277	55.3	67.2	54.9	45.6
1987	53,658	13,885	29,381	10,393	56.0	67.4	55.9	45.7
1988	54,742	14,194	29,921	10,627	56.6	67.7	56.7	46.2
1989	56,030	14,377	30,548	11,104	57.4	68.0	57.8	47.0
1990	56,829	14,612	30,901	11,315	57.5	66.7	58.4	47.2
1991	57,178	14,681	31,112	11,385	57.4	66.2	58.5	46.8
1992	58,141	14,872	31,700	11,570	57.8	66.2	59.3	47.1
1993	58,795	15,031	31,980	11,784	57.9	66.2	59.4	47.2
1994	60,239	15,333	32,888	12,018	58.8	66.7	60.7	47.5
1995	60,944	15,467	33,359	12,118	58.9	66.8	61.0	47.4
1996	61,857	15,842	33,618	12,397	59.3	67.1	61.2	48.1
1997	63,036	16,492	33,802	12,742	59.8	67.9	61.6	48.6
1998	63,714	17,087	33,857	12,771	59.8	68.5	61.2	48.8
1999	64,855	17,575	34,372	12,909	60.0	68.7	61.2	49.1

[1] Civilian noninstitutional population, age 16 and older.

[2] Data not strictly comparable over time; see the text for Table Ba478–486.

Sources

U.S. Bureau of Labor Statistics, *Handbook of Labor Statistics,* Bulletin number 2340 (August 1989), Table 6, with updates calculated from the Bureau of Labor Statistics Internet site.

Documentation

See the text for Table Ba478–486.

TABLE Ba579–582 Labor force participation rate for married women, by age and presence of children: 1948–1999[1,2]

Contributed by Susan B. Carter

		Presence and age of children		
	Overall	With no children under 18	With children under 6	With children under 3
	Ba579	Ba580	Ba581	Ba582
Year	Percent	Percent	Percent	Percent
1948	22.0	28.4	10.8	—
1949	22.5	28.7	11.0	—
1950	23.8	30.3	11.9	—
1951	25.2	31.0	14.0	—
1952	25.3	30.9	13.9	—
1953	26.3	31.2	15.5	—
1954	26.6	31.6	14.9	—
1955	27.7	32.7	16.2	—
1956	29.0	35.3	15.9	—
1957	29.6	35.6	17.0	—
1958	30.2	35.4	18.2	—
1959	30.9	35.2	18.7	—
1960	30.5	34.7	18.6	—
1961	32.7	37.3	20.0	—
1962	32.7	36.1	21.3	—
1963	33.7	37.4	22.5	—
1964	34.4	37.8	22.7	—
1965	34.7	38.3	23.3	—
1966	35.4	38.4	24.2	—
1967	36.8	38.9	26.5	—
1968	38.3	40.1	27.6	—
1969	39.6	41.0	28.5	—
1970	40.8	42.2	30.3	—
1971	40.8	42.1	29.6	—
1972	41.5	42.7	30.1	—
1973	42.2	42.8	32.7	—
1974	43.1	43.0	34.4	—
1975	44.4	43.8	36.7	32.7
1976	45.1	43.7	37.5	32.7
1977	46.6	44.8	39.4	34.7
1978	47.5	44.6	41.7	37.9
1979	49.3	46.6	43.3	39.6
1980	50.1	46.0	45.1	41.3
1981	51.0	46.3	47.8	43.7
1982	51.2	46.2	48.7	45.3
1983	51.8	46.6	49.9	46.0
1984	52.8	47.2	51.8	48.2
1985	54.2	48.2	53.4	50.5
1986	54.6	48.2	53.8	50.9
1987	55.8	48.4	56.8	54.2
1988	56.6	48.9	57.1	54.5
1989	57.6	50.5	57.4	53.9
1990	58.2	51.1	58.9	55.5
1991	58.5	51.2	59.9	56.8
1992	59.3	51.9	59.9	57.5
1993	59.4	52.4	59.6	57.3
1994	60.6	53.2	61.7	59.7
1995	61.1	53.2	63.5	60.9
1996	61.1	53.4	62.7	60.5
1997	62.1	54.2	63.6	61.3
1998	61.8	54.1	63.7	61.4
1999	61.6	54.4	61.8	59.2

[1] Civilian noninstitutional population, age 16 and older.

[2] Data not strictly comparable over time; see the text for Table Ba478–486.

Sources

For 1948–1970: U.S. Department of Commerce, *Historical Statistics of the United States* (1975), Series D69 and D70. For 1971–1988: U.S Bureau of Labor Statistics, *Handbook of Labor Statistics* (August 1989), Tables 55 and 57. For 1989–1999: U.S. Bureau of the Census, *Statistical Abstract of the United States: 1998*, CD-ROM, Table 654; *Statistical Abstract of the United States: 1999*, Table 660; and *Statistical Abstract of the United States: 2000*, Table 654.

Documentation

See the text for Table Ba478–486.

Data cover married women with spouse present.

TABLE Ba583–596 Unemployment rate, by age, sex, race, and Hispanic origin: 1947–2000[1, 2]

Contributed by Susan B. Carter

	All races					White			Nonwhite			Hispanic		
				Age										
	All persons	Male	Female	16–19	20 and older	All	Male	Female	All	Male	Female	All	Male	Female
	Ba583	Ba584	Ba585	Ba586	Ba587	Ba588	Ba589	Ba590	Ba591	Ba592	Ba593	Ba594	Ba595	Ba596
Year	Percent	Percent	Percent	Percent	Percent	Percent	Percent	Percent	Percent	Percent	Percent	Percent	Percent	Percent
1947	3.9	4.0	3.7	—	—	—	—	—	—	—	—	—	—	—
1948	3.8	3.6	4.1	9.2	3.3	—	—	—	—	—	—	—	—	—
1949	5.9	5.9	6.0	13.4	5.4	—	—	—	—	—	—	—	—	—
1950	5.3	5.1	5.7	12.2	4.8	—	—	—	—	—	—	—	—	—
1951	3.3	2.8	4.4	8.2	3.0	—	—	—	—	—	—	—	—	—
1952	3.0	2.8	3.6	8.5	2.7	—	—	—	—	—	—	—	—	—
1953	2.9	2.8	3.3	7.6	2.6	—	—	—	—	—	—	—	—	—
1954	5.5	5.3	6.0	12.6	5.1	5.0	4.8	5.5	9.9	10.3	9.2	—	—	—
1955	4.4	4.2	4.9	11.0	3.9	3.9	3.7	4.3	8.7	8.8	8.5	—	—	—
1956	4.1	3.8	4.8	11.1	3.7	3.6	3.4	4.2	8.3	7.9	8.9	—	—	—
1957	4.3	4.1	4.7	11.6	3.8	3.8	3.6	4.3	7.9	8.3	7.3	—	—	—
1958	6.8	6.8	6.8	15.9	6.2	6.1	6.1	6.2	12.6	13.7	10.8	—	—	—
1959	5.5	5.2	5.9	14.6	4.8	4.8	4.6	5.3	10.7	11.5	9.4	—	—	—
1960	5.5	5.4	5.9	14.7	4.8	5.0	4.8	5.3	10.2	10.7	9.4	—	—	—
1961	6.7	6.4	7.2	16.8	5.9	6.0	5.7	6.5	12.4	12.8	11.9	—	—	—
1962	5.5	5.2	6.2	14.7	4.9	4.9	4.6	5.5	10.9	10.9	11.0	—	—	—
1963	5.7	5.2	6.5	17.2	4.8	5.0	4.7	5.8	10.8	10.5	11.2	—	—	—
1964	5.2	4.6	6.2	16.2	4.3	4.6	4.1	5.5	9.6	8.9	10.7	—	—	—
1965	4.5	4.0	5.5	14.8	3.6	4.1	3.6	5.0	8.1	7.4	9.2	—	—	—
1966	3.8	3.2	4.8	12.8	2.9	3.4	2.8	4.3	7.3	6.3	8.7	—	—	—
1967	3.8	3.1	5.2	12.9	3.0	3.4	2.7	4.6	7.4	6.0	9.1	—	—	—
1968	3.6	2.9	4.8	12.7	2.7	3.2	2.6	4.3	6.7	5.6	8.3	—	—	—
1969	3.5	2.8	4.7	12.2	2.7	3.1	2.5	4.2	6.4	5.3	7.8	—	—	—
1970	4.9	4.4	5.9	15.3	4.0	4.5	4.0	5.4	8.2	7.3	9.3	—	—	—
1971	5.9	5.3	6.9	16.9	4.9	5.4	4.9	6.3	9.9	9.1	10.9	—	—	—
1972	5.6	5.0	6.6	16.2	4.5	5.1	4.5	5.9	10.0	8.9	11.4	—	—	—
1973	4.9	4.2	6.0	14.5	3.9	4.3	3.8	5.3	9.0	7.7	10.6	7.5	6.7	9.0
1974	5.6	4.9	6.7	16.0	4.5	5.0	4.4	6.1	9.9	9.2	10.8	8.1	7.3	9.4
1975	8.5	7.9	9.3	19.9	7.3	7.8	7.2	8.6	13.8	13.6	13.9	12.2	11.4	13.5
1976	7.7	7.1	8.6	19.0	6.5	7.0	6.4	7.9	13.1	12.7	13.6	11.5	10.8	12.7
1977	7.1	6.3	8.2	17.8	5.9	6.2	5.5	7.3	13.1	12.3	13.9	10.1	9.0	11.9
1978	6.1	5.3	7.2	16.4	5.0	5.2	4.6	6.2	11.9	11.0	13.0	9.1	7.7	11.3
1979	5.8	5.1	6.8	16.1	4.8	5.1	4.5	5.9	11.3	10.4	12.3	8.3	7.0	10.3
1980	7.1	6.9	7.4	17.8	6.1	6.3	6.1	6.5	13.1	13.2	13.1	10.1	9.7	10.7
1981	7.6	7.4	7.9	19.6	6.5	6.7	6.5	6.9	14.2	14.1	14.3	10.4	10.2	10.8
1982	9.7	9.9	9.4	23.2	8.6	8.6	8.8	8.3	17.3	18.2	16.4	13.8	13.6	14.1
1983	9.6	9.9	9.2	22.4	8.6	8.4	8.8	7.9	17.8	18.5	17.1	13.7	13.6	13.8
1984	7.5	7.4	7.6	18.9	6.7	6.5	6.4	6.5	14.4	14.7	14.0	10.7	10.5	11.1
1985	7.2	7.0	7.4	18.6	6.4	6.2	6.1	6.4	13.7	13.8	13.5	10.5	10.2	11.0
1986	7.0	6.9	7.1	18.3	6.2	6.0	6.0	6.1	13.1	13.4	12.8	10.6	10.5	10.8
1987	6.2	6.2	6.2	16.9	5.4	5.3	5.4	5.2	11.6	11.5	11.7	8.8	8.7	8.9
1988	5.5	5.5	5.6	15.3	4.8	4.7	4.7	4.7	10.4	10.3	10.5	8.2	8.1	8.3
1989	5.3	5.2	5.4	15.0	4.6	4.5	4.5	4.5	10.0	10.0	10.0	8.0	7.6	8.8
1990	5.6	5.7	5.5	15.5	4.9	4.8	4.9	4.7	10.1	10.4	9.9	8.2	8.0	8.4
1991	6.8	7.2	6.4	18.7	6.1	6.1	6.5	5.6	11.1	11.4	10.8	10.0	10.3	9.6
1992	7.5	7.9	7.0	20.1	6.8	6.6	7.0	6.1	12.7	13.4	11.9	11.6	11.7	11.4
1993	6.9	7.2	6.6	19.0	6.2	6.1	6.3	5.7	11.7	12.4	11.0	10.8	10.6	11.0
1994	6.1	6.2	6.0	17.6	5.4	5.3	5.4	5.2	10.5	10.8	10.2	9.9	9.4	10.7
1995	5.6	5.6	5.6	17.3	4.9	4.9	4.9	4.8	9.6	9.6	9.5	9.3	8.8	10.0
1996	5.4	5.4	5.4	16.7	4.7	4.7	4.7	4.7	9.3	9.5	9.0	8.9	7.9	10.2
1997	4.9	4.9	5.0	16.0	4.3	4.2	4.2	4.2	8.8	8.8	8.8	7.7	7.0	8.9
1998	4.5	4.4	4.6	14.6	3.9	3.9	3.9	3.9	7.8	7.6	7.9	7.2	6.4	8.2
1999	4.2	4.1	4.3	13.9	3.6	3.7	3.6	3.8	7.0	7.1	6.9	6.4	5.6	7.6
2000	4.0	3.9	4.1	13.1	3.4	3.5	3.4	3.6	6.7	6.9	6.4	5.7	4.9	6.7

[1] Civilian noninstitutional population, age 16 and older.

[2] Data not strictly comparable over time; see the text for Table Ba478–486.

Sources

Calculations based on U.S. Bureau of Labor Statistics (BLS) Internet site and *BLS Handbook of Methods,* Bulletin number 2490 (April 1997). Monthly updates are available from the BLS periodical *Employment and Earnings*.

Documentation

See the text for Table Ba478–486.

Hispanics are included in both the white and the nonwhite population groups.

TABLE Ba597–626 Duration of unemployment, by sex and race: 1948–2000[1, 2]

Contributed by Susan B. Carter

	All unemployed persons						Male					
	Weeks of unemployment		Percentage distribution, by weeks of unemployment				Weeks of unemployment		Percentage distribution, by weeks of unemployment			
	Mean	Median	Fewer than 5	5 to 14	15 to 26	27 or more	Mean	Median	Fewer than 5	5 to 14	15 to 26	27 or more
	Ba597	Ba598	Ba599	Ba600	Ba601	Ba602	Ba603	Ba604	Ba605	Ba606	Ba607	Ba608
Year	Weeks	Weeks	Percent	Percent	Percent	Percent	Weeks	Weeks	Percent	Percent	Percent	Percent
1948	8.6	—	57.1	29.4	8.5	5.1	—	—	—	—	—	—
1949	10.0	—	48.3	32.8	11.8	7.0	—	—	—	—	—	—
1950	12.1	—	44.1	32.1	12.9	10.9	—	—	—	—	—	—
1951	9.7	—	57.3	27.9	8.1	6.7	—	—	—	—	—	—
1952	8.4	—	60.3	27.4	7.9	4.5	—	—	—	—	—	—
1953	8.0	—	62.3	26.3	7.2	4.3	—	—	—	—	—	—
1954	11.8	—	45.4	31.6	14.0	9.0	—	—	—	—	—	—
1955	13.0	—	46.8	28.6	12.8	11.8	—	—	—	—	—	—
1956	11.3	—	51.3	29.3	10.9	8.4	—	—	—	—	—	—
1957	10.5	—	49.2	31.2	11.2	8.4	—	—	—	—	—	—
1958	13.9	—	38.1	30.3	17.1	14.5	—	—	—	—	—	—
1959	14.4	—	42.4	29.8	12.5	15.3	—	—	—	—	—	—
1960	12.8	—	44.6	30.5	13.1	11.8	—	—	—	—	—	—
1961	15.6	—	38.3	29.2	15.4	17.1	—	—	—	—	—	—
1962	14.7	—	42.5	29.0	13.7	15.0	—	—	—	—	—	—
1963	14.0	—	43.0	30.2	13.1	13.6	—	—	—	—	—	—
1964	13.3	—	44.8	29.5	13.0	12.7	—	—	—	—	—	—
1965	11.8	—	48.4	29.2	12.0	10.4	—	—	—	—	—	—
1966	10.4	—	54.7	27.1	10.0	8.3	—	—	—	—	—	—
1967	8.7	2.3	54.9	30.0	9.1	5.9	11.9	4.7	—	30.2	9.6	7.2
1968	8.4	4.5	56.6	28.8	9.1	5.5	9.4	4.7	—	30.6	9.3	6.8
1969	7.8	4.4	57.5	29.2	8.5	4.7	8.5	4.5	—	30.4	9.1	5.3
1970	8.6	4.9	52.3	31.5	10.4	5.8	9.5	5.2	—	33.4	11.2	6.6
1971	11.3	6.3	44.8	31.6	13.3	10.4	12.3	6.9	—	32.5	14.8	11.6
1972	12.0	6.2	45.9	30.2	12.3	11.6	13.4	6.9	—	31.3	13.8	13.3
1973	10.0	5.2	51.0	30.1	11.1	7.9	11.2	5.6	—	31.5	12.3	9.2
1974	9.8	5.2	50.5	31.0	11.1	7.4	10.9	5.7	—	32.0	12.4	8.9
1975	14.2	8.4	37.1	31.3	16.4	15.2	15.3	9.4	—	31.9	17.6	17.0
1976	15.8	8.2	38.4	29.6	13.8	18.2	17.3	9.3	34.7	29.9	14.9	22.1
1977	14.3	7.0	41.8	30.5	13.1	14.7	15.9	8.0	38.2	30.7	14.0	17.1
1978	11.9	5.9	46.2	31.0	12.3	10.5	13.4	6.8	42.4	31.4	13.8	12.3
1979	10.8	5.4	48.1	31.7	11.5	8.7	12.0	6.1	44.5	32.4	12.8	10.3
1980	11.9	6.5	43.2	32.3	13.8	10.7	13.2	7.6	39.0	33.0	15.5	12.5
1981	13.7	6.9	41.7	30.7	13.6	14.0	15.4	8.1	37.8	30.8	14.5	16.8
1982	15.6	8.7	36.4	31.0	16.0	16.6	17.3	9.8	32.5	31.2	17.2	19.1
1983	20.0	10.1	33.3	27.4	15.4	23.9	22.7	12.4	28.3	27.1	16.4	28.2
1984	18.2	7.9	39.2	28.7	12.9	19.1	21.1	9.3	35.2	28.4	13.7	22.7
1985	15.6	6.8	42.1	30.2	12.3	15.4	18.0	8.2	37.5	30.2	13.9	18.4
1986	15.0	6.9	41.9	31.0	12.7	14.4	17.2	8.1	37.8	31.1	13.8	17.3
1987	14.5	6.5	43.7	29.6	12.7	14.0	16.7	7.7	39.4	29.7	13.9	17.1
1988	13.5	5.9	46.0	30.0	12.0	12.1	15.6	7.0	41.2	30.8	13.3	14.7
1989	11.9	4.8	48.6	30.3	11.2	9.9	13.7	5.7	44.7	30.5	12.3	12.5
1990	12.0	5.3	46.3	32.0	11.7	10.0	13.6	6.1	42.7	32.5	12.7	12.1
1991	13.7	6.8	40.3	32.4	14.4	12.9	15.2	7.8	36.8	32.5	15.8	14.9
1992	17.7	8.7	35.1	29.4	15.1	20.3	19.5	9.7	32.1	29.2	15.9	22.7
1993	18.0	8.3	36.5	28.9	14.5	20.1	19.8	9.4	33.3	28.7	15.5	22.5
1994	18.8	9.2	34.1	30.1	15.5	20.3	20.3	9.8	32.3	29.8	15.7	22.1
1995	16.6	8.3	36.5	31.6	14.6	17.3	17.7	8.7	35.0	31.5	14.8	18.7
1996	16.7	8.3	36.4	31.6	14.6	17.4	17.7	8.7	35.1	31.4	14.9	18.5
1997	15.8	8.0	37.7	31.7	14.8	15.8	16.4	8.3	36.7	31.3	15.3	16.6
1998	14.5	6.7	42.2	31.4	12.3	14.1	15.2	7.0	41.1	31.5	12.2	15.2
1999	13.4	6.4	43.7	31.2	12.8	12.3	14.0	6.7	42.7	31.2	13.1	13.0
2000	12.6	5.9	45.0	31.9	11.8	11.4	13.2	6.1	44.2	32.0	11.6	12.2

Notes appear at end of table

TABLE Ba597–626 Duration of unemployment, by sex and race: 1948–2000 *Continued*

	Female						White	
	Weeks of unemployment		Percentage distribution, by weeks of unemployment				Weeks of unemployment	
	Mean	Median	Fewer than 5	5 to 14	15 to 26	27 or more	Mean	Median
	Ba609	Ba610	Ba611	Ba612	Ba613	Ba614	Ba615	Ba616
Year	Weeks	Weeks	Percent	Percent	Percent	Percent	Weeks	Weeks
1948	—	—	—	—	—	—	—	—
1949	—	—	—	—	—	—	—	—
1950	—	—	—	—	—	—	—	—
1951	—	—	—	—	—	—	—	—
1952	—	—	—	—	—	—	—	—
1953	—	—	—	—	—	—	—	—
1954	—	—	—	—	—	—	—	—
1955	—	—	—	—	—	—	—	—
1956	—	—	—	—	—	—	—	—
1957	—	—	—	—	—	—	—	—
1958	—	—	—	—	—	—	—	—
1959	—	—	—	—	—	—	—	—
1960	—	—	—	—	—	—	—	—
1961	—	—	—	—	—	—	—	—
1962	—	—	—	—	—	—	—	—
1963	—	—	—	—	—	—	—	—
1964	—	—	—	—	—	—	—	—
1965	—	—	—	—	—	—	—	—
1966	—	—	—	—	—	—	—	—
1967	9.8	4.4	—	—	30.4	—	10.7	4.4
1968	7.5	4.2	—	—	26.9	—	8.4	4.4
1969	7.3	4.2	—	—	28.0	—	7.8	4.3
1970	7.9	4.4	—	—	29.3	—	8.7	4.7
1971	10.1	5.2	—	—	30.4	—	11.3	6.1
1972	10.6	4.9	—	—	28.8	—	12.1	5.8
1973	8.8	4.5	—	—	28.6	—	9.8	4.8
1974	8.4	4.6	—	—	29.8	—	9.4	4.8
1975	12.6	7.0	—	—	30.6	—	14.0	8.2
1976	14.0	6.8	42.9	42.9	29.4	3.9	15.6	8.0
1977	12.5	6.1	45.7	45.7	30.3	3.9	14.0	6.8
1978	10.5	5.0	50.1	50.1	30.6	3.7	11.3	5.5
1979	9.6	4.8	51.7	51.7	31.0	3.6	10.3	5.1
1980	10.3	5.4	48.4	48.4	31.5	3.7	11.5	6.3
1981	11.7	5.8	46.5	46.5	30.5	4.4	13.0	6.7
1982	13.3	7.1	41.6	41.6	30.8	5.2	15.0	8.5
1983	16.1	7.7	40.3	40.3	27.8	4.7	19.4	9.9
1984	14.6	6.4	44.3	44.3	29.1	4.1	17.5	7.6
1985	12.8	5.6	47.5	47.5	30.1	3.2	15.0	6.6
1986	12.4	5.7	46.8	46.8	30.9	3.8	14.5	6.6
1987	11.8	5.2	49.1	49.1	29.4	3.8	14.0	6.2
1988	11.0	4.8	51.8	51.8	29.0	3.3	12.9	5.6
1989	9.7	4.2	53.3	53.3	30.1	3.4	11.4	4.6
1990	10.0	4.4	50.8	50.8	31.5	3.3	11.6	5.1
1991	11.7	5.6	45.1	45.1	32.2	4.2	13.4	6.7
1992	15.4	7.3	39.2	39.2	29.7	4.9	17.6	8.6
1993	15.6	6.9	40.7	40.7	29.2	4.4	17.6	8.1
1994	17.0	8.5	36.3	36.3	30.4	5.8	18.0	8.6
1995	15.4	7.7	38.2	38.2	31.8	5.4	15.7	7.6
1996	15.6	7.8	37.9	37.9	31.8	5.9	15.8	7.8
1997	15.1	7.6	38.7	38.7	32.2	5.9	14.5	7.3
1998	13.7	6.3	43.5	43.5	31.3	5.1	13.1	5.8
1999	12.7	6.1	44.7	44.7	31.1	5.3	12.2	5.6
2000	12.0	5.8	45.8	45.8	31.8	4.8	11.6	5.2

(continued)

TABLE Ba597–626 Duration of unemployment, by sex and race: 1948–2000 *Continued*

	White				Nonwhite					
	Percentage distribution, by weeks of unemployment				Weeks of unemployment		Percenage distribution, by weeks of unemployment			
	Fewer than 5	5 to 14	15 to 26	27 or more	Mean	Median	Fewer than 5	5 to 14	15 to 26	27 or more
	Ba617	Ba618	Ba619	Ba620	Ba621	Ba622	Ba623	Ba624	Ba625	Ba626
Year	Percent	Percent	Percent	Percent	Weeks	Weeks	Percent	Percent	Percent	Percent
1948	—	—	—	—	—	—	—	—	—	—
1949	—	—	—	—	—	—	—	—	—	—
1950	—	—	—	—	—	—	—	—	—	—
1951	—	—	—	—	—	—	—	—	—	—
1952	—	—	—	—	—	—	—	—	—	—
1953	—	—	—	—	—	—	—	—	—	—
1954	—	—	—	—	—	—	—	—	—	—
1955	—	—	—	—	—	—	—	—	—	—
1956	—	—	—	—	—	—	—	—	—	—
1957	—	—	—	—	—	—	—	—	—	—
1958	—	—	—	—	—	—	—	—	—	—
1959	—	—	—	—	—	—	—	—	—	—
1960	—	—	—	—	—	—	—	—	—	—
1961	—	—	—	—	—	—	—	—	—	—
1962	—	—	—	—	—	—	—	—	—	—
1963	—	—	—	—	—	—	—	—	—	—
1964	—	—	—	—	—	—	—	—	—	—
1965	—	—	—	—	—	—	—	—	—	—
1966	—	—	—	—	—	—	—	—	—	—
1967	—	29.6	9.1	5.6	11.4	4.9	—	32.9	9.2	6.9
1968	—	28.4	9.1	5.5	8.7	4.5	—	30.2	9.0	5.6
1969	—	28.8	8.5	4.6	8.5	4.5	—	30.8	8.8	5.1
1970	—	31.2	10.5	5.6	9.0	5.0	—	33.0	10.2	6.2
1971	—	31.6	13.1	10.3	11.6	6.4	—	31.7	14.1	10.5
1972	—	29.6	12.2	11.7	12.1	6.3	—	32.2	12.7	11.1
1973	—	29.6	10.7	7.6	10.8	5.6	—	31.9	12.3	8.8
1974	—	30.4	10.8	7.1	10.6	5.8	—	33.2	12.5	8.5
1975	—	31.5	16.3	15.0	14.8	8.9	—	30.8	17.2	16.1
1976	38.7	29.4	13.9	18.0	16.7	8.5	37.2	30.6	13.2	18.9
1977	42.7	29.9	13.0	14.4	15.4	7.8	38.3	32.6	13.1	15.9
1978	47.9	30.6	12.0	9.5	14.0	7.2	40.7	32.3	13.6	13.4
1979	49.5	31.4	11.3	7.8	12.7	6.4	43.6	32.7	12.1	11.6
1980	43.9	32.4	13.7	10.1	13.4	7.3	40.8	32.1	14.1	13.1
1981	42.6	31.0	13.4	13.0	16.0	8.0	38.6	29.7	14.2	17.5
1982	36.7	31.6	16.0	15.7	17.8	9.4	35.2	28.9	16.0	19.9
1983	33.6	27.8	15.6	23.0	21.8	10.7	32.5	26.2	14.8	26.6
1984	40.2	28.7	13.0	18.0	20.1	8.8	36.5	28.6	12.6	22.3
1985	43.2	30.2	12.1	14.5	17.4	7.8	38.8	30.1	13.1	18.0
1986	42.8	31.0	12.6	13.6	16.7	7.8	39.1	31.0	13.0	16.8
1987	44.9	29.5	12.4	13.2	16.1	7.5	40.4	29.9	13.5	16.2
1988	47.2	29.7	11.9	11.2	15.2	6.8	42.8	30.6	12.1	14.5
1989	49.5	30.3	11.0	9.2	—	—	—	—	—	—
1990	47.4	31.5	11.7	9.4	—	—	—	—	—	—
1991	40.6	32.5	14.4	12.5	—	—	—	—	—	—
1992	35.3	29.3	15.1	20.3	—	—	—	—	—	—
1993	37.1	29.0	14.5	19.5	—	—	—	—	—	—
1994	35.9	30.0	14.9	19.3	—	—	—	—	—	—
1995	38.6	31.6	13.9	15.8	—	—	—	—	—	—
1996	38.4	31.4	14.2	16.0	—	—	—	—	—	—
1997	40.1	31.9	13.9	14.1	—	—	—	—	—	—
1998	45.1	31.1	11.7	12.1	—	—	—	—	—	—
1999	46.3	31.0	12.2	10.6	—	—	—	—	—	—
2000	47.5	31.4	11.1	10.0	—	—	—	—	—	—

[1] Civilian noninstitutional population, age 16 and older.

[2] Data not strictly comparable over time; see the text for Table Ba478–486.

Sources

U.S. Bureau of Labor Statistics (BLS) Internet site and *BLS Handbook of Methods,* Bulletin number 2490 (April 1997). Monthly updates are available from the BLS periodical *Employment and Earnings*.

Documentation

See the text for Table Ba478–486.

Duration of unemployment represents the length of time (through the current reference week) that persons classified as unemployed had been continuously looking for work and, thus, is a measure of an in-progress spell of joblessness. For persons on layoff, duration of unemployment represents the number of full weeks since the end of their most recent period of employment. Two useful measures of the duration of unemployment are the mean and the median. Mean duration is the arithmetic average computed from single weeks of unemployment. Median duration is the midpoint of a distribution of weeks of unemployment.

TABLE Ba627–651 Unemployed persons as a percent of the labor force, by sex, race, and reason for unemployment: 1967–2000[1, 2]

Contributed by Susan B. Carter

	Both sexes					Male					Female	
	Total	Job losers	Job leavers	Labor market reentrants	New labor market entrants	Total	Job losers	Job leavers	Labor market reentrants	New labor market entrants	Total	Job losers
	Ba627	Ba628	Ba629	Ba630	Ba631	Ba632	Ba633	Ba634	Ba635	Ba636	Ba637	Ba638
Year	Percent	Percent	Percent	Percent	Percent	Percent	Percent	Percent	Percent	Percent	Percent	Percent
1967	3.8	1.6	0.6	1.2	0.5	3.1	—	—	—	—	5.2	—
1968	3.6	1.4	0.5	1.2	0.5	2.9	—	—	—	—	4.8	—
1969	3.5	1.3	0.5	1.2	0.5	2.8	—	—	—	—	4.7	—
1970	4.9	2.2	0.7	1.5	0.6	4.4	—	—	—	—	5.9	—
1971	5.9	2.8	0.7	1.7	0.7	5.3	—	—	—	—	6.9	—
1972	5.6	2.4	0.7	1.7	0.8	5.0	—	—	—	—	6.6	—
1973	4.9	1.9	0.8	1.5	0.7	4.2	—	—	—	—	6.0	—
1974	5.6	2.4	0.8	1.6	0.7	4.9	—	—	—	—	6.7	—
1975	8.5	4.7	0.9	2.0	0.9	7.9	—	—	—	—	9.3	—
1976	7.7	3.8	0.9	2.0	0.9	7.1	4.2	0.7	1.4	0.7	8.6	3.2
1977	7.1	3.2	0.9	2.0	1.0	6.3	3.5	0.7	1.4	0.8	8.2	2.8
1978	6.1	2.5	0.9	1.8	0.9	5.3	2.7	0.7	1.2	0.7	7.2	2.3
1979	5.8	2.5	0.8	1.7	0.8	5.1	2.7	0.7	1.1	0.6	6.8	2.2
1980	7.1	3.7	0.8	1.8	0.8	6.9	4.3	0.7	1.3	0.7	7.4	2.9
1981	7.6	3.9	0.8	1.9	0.9	7.4	4.6	0.7	1.4	0.8	7.9	3.1
1982	9.7	5.7	0.8	2.2	1.1	9.9	6.9	0.6	1.5	0.9	9.4	4.2
1983	9.6	5.6	0.7	2.2	1.1	9.9	6.9	0.6	1.5	0.9	9.2	4.0
1984	7.5	3.9	0.7	1.9	1.0	7.4	4.7	0.6	1.4	0.8	7.6	2.9
1985	7.2	3.6	0.8	2.0	0.9	7.0	4.3	0.6	1.4	0.8	7.4	2.7
1986	7.0	3.4	0.9	1.8	0.9	6.9	4.2	0.8	1.2	0.7	7.1	2.5
1987	6.2	3.0	0.8	1.6	0.8	6.2	3.7	0.7	1.1	0.6	6.2	2.1
1988	5.5	2.5	0.8	1.5	0.7	5.5	3.1	0.8	1.0	0.6	5.6	1.9
1989	5.3	2.4	0.8	1.5	0.5	5.2	2.9	0.7	1.1	0.5	5.4	1.8
1990	5.6	2.7	0.8	1.5	0.5	5.7	3.3	0.8	1.2	0.5	5.5	2.0
1991	6.8	3.7	0.8	1.7	0.6	7.2	4.6	0.7	1.3	0.5	6.4	2.7
1992	7.5	4.2	0.8	1.8	0.7	7.9	5.1	0.7	1.4	0.7	7.0	3.1
1993	6.9	3.8	0.8	1.7	0.7	7.2	4.5	0.7	1.3	0.7	6.6	2.9
1994	6.1	2.9	0.6	2.1	0.5	6.2	3.4	0.6	1.8	0.4	6.0	2.3
1995	5.6	2.6	0.6	1.9	0.4	5.6	3.1	0.6	1.6	0.4	5.6	2.1
1996	5.4	2.5	0.6	1.9	0.4	5.4	3.0	0.5	1.5	0.4	5.4	2.0
1997	4.9	2.2	0.6	1.7	0.4	4.9	2.6	0.6	1.4	0.4	5.0	1.8
1998	4.5	2.1	0.5	1.5	0.4	4.4	2.3	0.5	1.3	0.4	4.6	1.8
1999	4.2	1.9	0.6	1.4	0.3	4.1	2.1	0.5	1.2	0.3	4.3	1.6
2000	4.0	1.8	0.6	1.4	0.3	3.9	2.0	0.5	1.1	0.3	4.1	1.5

Notes appear at end of table

(continued)

TABLE Ba627–651 Unemployed persons as a percent of the labor force, by sex, race, and reason for unemployment: 1967–2000 *Continued*

	Female			White					Nonwhite				
	Job leavers	Labor market reentrants	New labor market entrants	Total	Job losers	Job leavers	Labor market reentrants	New labor market entrants	Total	Job losers	Job leavers	Labor market reentrants	New labor market entrants
	Ba639	Ba640	Ba641	Ba642	Ba643	Ba644	Ba645	Ba646	Ba647	Ba648	Ba649	Ba650	Ba651
Year	Percent	Percent	Percent	Percent	Percent	Percent	Percent	Percent	Percent	Percent	Percent	Percent	Percent
1967	—	—	—	3.4	1.4	0.5	1.1	0.4	7.4	—	—	—	—
1968	—	—	—	3.2	1.2	0.5	1.0	0.5	6.7	—	—	—	—
1969	—	—	—	3.1	1.1	0.5	1.1	0.4	6.4	—	—	—	—
1970	—	—	—	4.5	2.0	0.6	1.3	0.5	8.2	—	—	—	—
1971	—	—	—	5.4	2.6	0.6	1.6	0.7	9.9	—	—	—	—
1972	—	—	—	5.1	2.2	0.7	1.5	0.7	10.0	—	—	—	—
1973	—	—	—	4.3	1.7	0.7	1.3	0.6	9.0	—	—	—	—
1974	—	—	—	5.0	2.2	0.8	1.4	0.6	9.9	—	—	—	—
1975	—	—	—	7.8	4.3	0.9	1.8	0.7	13.8	—	—	—	—
1976	1.3	2.9	1.2	7.0	3.5	0.9	1.8	0.8	13.1	6.0	1.2	3.9	2.0
1977	1.2	2.9	1.3	6.2	2.9	0.9	1.7	0.8	13.1	5.4	1.2	4.2	2.3
1978	1.1	2.7	1.2	5.2	2.2	0.8	1.5	0.7	11.9	4.6	1.2	3.9	2.3
1979	1.0	2.6	1.1	5.1	2.2	0.8	1.5	0.6	11.3	4.6	1.1	3.6	2.0
1980	1.0	2.5	1.0	6.3	3.3	0.8	1.5	0.6	13.1	6.3	1.2	3.6	2.0
1981	1.0	2.7	1.1	6.7	3.5	0.8	1.6	0.7	14.2	6.8	1.2	3.9	2.2
1982	0.9	3.0	1.3	8.6	5.2	0.7	1.9	0.8	17.3	9.4	1.0	4.3	2.7
1983	0.9	3.0	1.3	8.4	5.1	0.7	1.8	0.9	17.8	9.3	1.0	4.7	2.7
1984	0.9	2.6	1.2	6.5	3.4	0.7	1.6	0.7	14.4	6.7	1.0	4.1	2.6
1985	0.9	2.7	1.1	6.2	3.2	0.7	1.6	0.7	13.7	6.4	1.0	4.0	2.3
1986	0.9	2.6	1.0	6.0	3.0	0.8	1.5	0.7	13.1	5.9	1.2	3.7	2.2
1987	0.9	2.3	0.9	5.3	2.7	0.8	1.4	0.6	11.6	5.2	1.1	3.5	1.9
1988	0.9	2.0	0.8	4.7	2.3	0.7	1.2	0.5	10.4	4.5	1.2	3.0	1.7
1989	0.9	2.0	0.6	4.5	2.1	0.8	1.2	0.4	10.0	—	—	—	—
1990	0.9	2.0	0.7	4.8	2.4	0.7	1.3	0.4	10.1	—	—	—	—
1991	0.9	2.2	0.7	6.1	3.4	0.8	1.4	0.5	11.1	—	—	—	—
1992	0.9	2.2	0.8	6.6	3.8	0.7	1.5	0.6	12.7	—	—	—	—
1993	0.8	2.1	0.8	6.1	3.4	0.7	1.4	0.6	11.7	—	—	—	—
1994	0.6	2.5	0.5	5.3	2.7	0.6	1.7	0.3	10.5	—	—	—	—
1995	0.7	2.3	0.5	4.9	2.4	0.6	1.5	0.3	9.6	—	—	—	—
1996	0.6	2.3	0.5	4.7	2.3	0.5	1.5	0.3	9.3	—	—	—	—
1997	0.6	2.1	0.5	4.2	2.0	0.5	1.4	0.3	8.8	—	—	—	—
1998	0.6	1.9	0.4	3.9	1.8	0.5	1.3	0.3	7.8	—	—	—	—
1999	0.6	1.7	0.4	3.7	1.7	0.5	1.2	0.3	7.0	—	—	—	—
2000	0.6	1.7	0.3	3.5	1.6	0.5	1.2	0.2	6.7	—	—	—	—

[1] Civilian noninstitutional population, age 16 and older.

[2] Data not strictly comparable over time; see the text for Table Ba478–486.

Sources

U.S. Bureau of Labor Statistics (BLS) Internet site and *BLS Handbook of Methods*, Bulletin number 2490 (April 1997). Monthly updates are available from the BLS periodical *Employment and Earnings*.

Documentation

See the text for Table Ba478–486.

These data show the number of unemployed, classified according to the reason for their unemployment and expressed as a share of the labor force. There are four major categories. The first is "job losers." These include persons whose employment ended involuntarily and who have begun looking for work, persons on temporary layoff who have been given a date to return to work or expect to return within six months, and persons who completed temporary jobs and began looking for work after the jobs ended. The second group is "job leavers," defined as persons who quit or otherwise terminated their employment voluntarily and immediately began looking for work. The third category is "reentrants," persons who previously worked but spent some time out of the labor force prior to beginning their job search. The final category, "new entrants," includes persons who never worked before but are now searching for work.

EMPLOYMENT, BY INDUSTRY

Susan B. Carter and Matthew Sobek

TABLE Ba652–669 Major industrial groups of labor force participants – all persons: 1910–1990[1]

Contributed by Matthew Sobek

	Total	Agriculture	Forestry and fisheries	Mining	Construction	Manufacturing		Transportation and communications	Trade	
						Durable	Nondurable		Wholesale	Retail
	Ba652	Ba653	Ba654	Ba655	Ba656	Ba657	Ba658	Ba659	Ba660	Ba661
Year	Number	Number	Number	Number	Number	Number	Number	Number	Number	Number
1910	36,214,087	11,130,376	115,871	1,072,307	2,154,941	3,691,233	3,857,734	3,217,172	638,296	3,515,412
1920	39,896,324	10,037,798	76,482	1,256,767	1,924,780	5,278,417	4,687,223	3,793,266	864,346	4,017,713
1940	47,508,794	8,397,714	179,347	979,477	3,458,030	5,200,120	5,694,035	3,162,801	1,192,505	6,499,057
1950	56,920,536	6,851,096	120,624	963,013	3,491,549	8,020,371	6,982,953	4,487,076	2,072,591	8,799,752
1960	63,870,298	4,141,121	94,259	644,683	3,795,494	9,947,934	7,436,477	4,335,368	2,195,813	9,414,645
1970	76,270,514	2,733,374	90,152	626,676	4,558,825	11,924,580	7,799,799	5,032,000	3,101,030	12,194,466
1980	97,378,409	2,754,146	152,063	1,022,392	5,695,444	13,635,441	8,227,447	6,137,801	4,084,482	15,801,589
1990	115,083,095	2,912,813	170,950	720,712	7,145,692	12,070,623	8,275,640	6,897,823	4,920,435	19,485,287

	Finance, insurance, and real estate	Business service	Personal service	Education service	Other professional service	Entertainment	Government	Industry unknown
	Ba662	Ba663	Ba664	Ba665	Ba666	Ba667	Ba668	Ba669
Year	Number	Number	Number	Number	Number	Number	Number	Number
1910	614,114	400,761	3,459,744	810,086	864,747	172,798	498,495	—
1920	851,917	1,127,628	3,029,417	970,343	975,800	225,519	778,908	—
1940	1,484,774	885,711	4,045,551	1,716,967	1,757,996	481,805	1,648,953	723,951
1950	1,950,644	1,464,664	3,524,513	2,145,444	2,669,398	552,044	2,561,738	263,066
1960	2,714,836	1,752,304	3,759,322	3,386,909	3,993,962	559,652	3,197,638	2,499,881
1970	3,831,428	2,673,536	3,547,755	6,927,243	6,288,564	762,681	4,178,405	—
1980	5,883,281	4,493,443	3,075,975	8,781,652	10,575,827	1,209,583	5,847,843	—
1990	7,957,539	6,839,897	3,655,927	10,786,155	14,849,119	2,028,650	6,365,833	—

[1] Data pertain to noninstitutionalized civilians age 16 and older; in the labor force 1940–1990, or with an occupation 1910–1920.

Source

Matthew Sobek, "New Statistics on the U.S. Labor Force, 1850–1990," *Historical Methods* 34 (2001): 71–87, Table 4.

Documentation

Tabulated from the Integrated Public Use Microdata Series; see the Guide to the Millennial Edition.

Industries are grouped according to the 1950 Census classification. See the source for discussion of the underlying data and methodology.

The wording of the 1910 Census instructions led to large numbers of women counted as having occupations, especially in agriculture. The 1920 Census was taken in January, depressing agricultural employment.

TABLE Ba670–687 Major industrial groups of labor force participants – males: 1910–1990[1]

Contributed by Matthew Sobek

	Total	Agriculture	Forestry and fisheries	Mining	Construction	Manufacturing		Transportation and communications	Trade	
						Durable	Nondurable		Wholesale	Retail
	Ba670	Ba671	Ba672	Ba673	Ba674	Ba675	Ba676	Ba677	Ba678	Ba679
Year	Number	Number	Number	Number	Number	Number	Number	Number	Number	Number
1910	28,670,661	9,681,238	115,115	1,061,979	2,134,034	3,508,611	2,704,066	3,058,983	581,116	2,739,331
1920	31,708,994	9,137,722	75,776	1,243,549	1,898,659	4,822,512	3,300,550	3,450,245	773,016	2,974,590
1940	35,838,736	7,876,151	175,236	963,311	3,404,610	4,613,609	3,740,104	2,808,043	1,013,808	4,543,125
1950	41,071,091	6,279,350	115,102	935,867	3,397,878	6,736,572	4,519,724	3,794,624	1,675,026	5,564,742
1960	42,913,576	3,734,745	87,786	612,616	3,645,474	8,183,431	4,811,384	3,595,764	1,748,230	5,512,714
1970	47,280,976	2,421,682	79,289	575,601	4,289,997	9,330,654	4,727,542	3,944,488	2,370,828	6,586,495
1980	55,747,834	2,256,818	124,030	898,866	5,217,327	10,059,718	4,806,004	4,636,850	2,977,110	7,770,026
1990	62,109,924	2,305,645	134,849	613,961	6,419,846	8,757,901	4,802,344	4,946,762	3,409,890	9,506,290

	Finance, insurance, and real estate	Business service	Personal service	Education service	Other professional service	Entertainment	Government	Industry unknown
	Ba680	Ba681	Ba682	Ba683	Ba684	Ba685	Ba686	Ba687
Year	Number	Number	Number	Number	Number	Number	Number	Number
1910	514,113	344,589	823,941	207,056	597,741	140,052	458,696	—
1920	636,869	849,530	844,387	224,513	648,524	173,460	655,092	—
1940	1,027,536	795,982	1,199,261	610,120	951,465	382,765	1,254,929	478,681
1950	1,168,034	1,271,178	1,162,092	756,735	1,243,694	407,631	1,869,045	173,797
1960	1,473,732	1,378,344	1,064,324	1,244,781	1,632,317	383,625	2,294,161	1,510,148
1970	1,916,794	1,872,676	999,507	2,535,838	2,228,035	504,016	2,897,534	—
1980	2,465,123	2,904,515	907,322	2,971,031	3,448,009	730,345	3,574,740	—
1990	3,192,179	4,103,137	1,143,717	3,226,015	4,673,631	1,183,757	3,690,000	—

[1] Data pertain to noninstitutionalized civilians age 16 and older; in the labor force 1940–1990, or with an occupation 1910–1920.

Source

Tabulated from the Integrated Public Use Microdata Series; see the Guide to the Millennial Edition.

Documentation

Industries are grouped according to the 1950 Census classification. For a discussion of the source and general methodology employed, see Matthew Sobek, "New Statistics on the U.S. Labor Force, 1850–1990," *Historical Methods* 34 (2001): 71–87.

The 1920 Census was taken in January, depressing agricultural employment.

TABLE Ba688–705 Major industrial groups of labor force participants – females: 1910–1990[1]

Contributed by Matthew Sobek

	Total	Agriculture	Forestry and fisheries	Mining	Construction	Manufacturing		Transportation and communications	Trade	
						Durable	Nondurable		Wholesale	Retail
	Ba688	Ba689	Ba690	Ba691	Ba692	Ba693	Ba694	Ba695	Ba696	Ba697
Year	Number	Number	Number	Number	Number	Number	Number	Number	Number	Number
1910	7,543,428	1,449,138	756	10,328	20,907	182,622	1,153,668	158,189	57,180	777,081
1920	8,187,330	900,076	706	13,218	26,121	455,905	1,386,673	343,021	91,330	1,043,123
1940	11,670,058	521,563	4,111	16,166	53,420	586,511	1,953,931	354,758	178,697	1,955,932
1950	15,849,445	571,746	5,522	27,146	93,671	1,283,799	2,463,229	692,452	397,565	3,235,010
1960	20,956,722	406,376	6,473	32,067	150,020	1,764,503	2,625,093	739,604	447,583	3,901,931
1970	28,989,537	311,692	10,863	51,075	268,828	2,593,926	3,072,257	1,087,512	730,202	5,607,971
1980	41,630,576	497,329	28,033	123,526	478,117	3,575,723	3,421,442	1,500,951	1,107,372	8,031,562
1990	52,973,171	607,168	36,101	106,750	725,846	3,312,722	3,473,296	1,951,061	1,510,545	9,978,998

	Finance, insurance, and real estate	Business service	Personal service	Education service	Other professional service	Entertainment	Government	Industry unknown
	Ba698	Ba699	Ba700	Ba701	Ba702	Ba703	Ba704	Ba705
Year	Number	Number	Number	Number	Number	Number	Number	Number
1910	100,001	56,172	2,635,804	603,031	267,006	32,746	39,799	—
1920	215,048	278,098	2,185,030	745,830	327,276	52,059	123,816	—
1940	457,238	89,729	2,846,290	1,106,847	806,531	99,040	394,024	245,270
1950	782,610	193,486	2,362,421	1,388,709	1,425,704	144,413	692,693	89,269
1960	1,241,104	373,960	2,694,998	2,142,128	2,361,645	176,027	903,477	989,733
1970	1,914,635	800,861	2,548,248	4,391,404	4,060,528	258,665	1,280,870	—
1980	3,418,158	1,588,928	2,168,653	5,810,621	7,127,819	479,239	2,273,103	—
1990	4,765,360	2,736,760	2,512,210	7,560,139	10,175,488	844,893	2,675,834	—

[1] Data pertain to noninstitutionalized civilians age 16 and older; in the labor force 1940–1990, or with an occupation 1910–1920.

Source

Tabulated from the Integrated Public Use Microdata Series; see the Guide to the Millennial Edition.

Documentation

Industries are grouped according to the 1950 Census classification. For a discussion of the source and general methodology employed, see Matthew Sobek, "New Statistics on the U.S. Labor Force, 1850–1990," *Historical Methods* 34 (2001): 71–87.

The wording of the 1910 Census instructions led to large numbers of women counted as having occupations, especially in agriculture. The 1920 Census was taken in January, depressing agricultural employment.

TABLE Ba706–723 Major industrial groups of labor force participants – white males: 1910–1990[1]

Contributed by Matthew Sobek

	Total	Agriculture	Forestry and fisheries	Mining	Construction	Manufacturing		Transportation and communications	Trade	
						Durable	Nondurable		Wholesale	Retail
	Ba706	Ba707	Ba708	Ba709	Ba710	Ba711	Ba712	Ba713	Ba714	Ba715
Year	Number	Number	Number	Number	Number	Number	Number	Number	Number	Number
1910	25,643,417	8,126,054	75,064	984,144	1,981,639	3,229,262	2,576,105	2,749,911	566,758	2,583,914
1920	28,571,501	7,718,264	51,355	1,165,544	1,739,029	4,448,101	3,093,139	3,124,756	750,810	2,814,026
1940	32,541,839	6,607,200	147,705	903,719	3,057,443	4,330,303	3,560,474	2,608,455	970,169	4,265,963
1950	37,340,606	5,377,288	98,662	889,812	3,092,960	6,166,749	4,211,581	3,457,072	1,578,420	5,166,524
1960	38,963,896	3,235,264	76,918	593,977	3,300,256	7,562,112	4,463,288	3,279,662	1,625,913	5,075,810
1970	42,767,632	2,170,672	72,277	550,148	3,872,120	8,443,710	4,259,818	3,518,419	2,189,115	6,057,095
1980	49,748,053	2,080,613	113,342	851,101	4,743,642	9,015,570	4,207,380	4,060,980	2,731,564	7,019,351
1990	54,620,201	2,144,248	121,436	579,369	5,850,301	7,822,194	4,168,175	4,243,424	3,087,564	8,304,697

	Finance, insurance, and real estate	Business service	Personal service	Education service	Other professional service	Entertainment	Government	Industry unknown
	Ba716	Ba717	Ba718	Ba719	Ba720	Ba721	Ba722	Ba723
Year	Number	Number	Number	Number	Number	Number	Number	Number
1910	491,694	326,453	626,709	191,438	564,239	128,465	441,568	—
1920	617,797	810,077	648,614	207,759	611,995	160,038	610,197	—
1940	972,434	749,964	928,536	567,416	894,005	351,824	1,198,851	427,378
1950	1,102,877	1,187,964	917,863	695,449	1,145,129	373,695	1,730,722	147,839
1960	1,400,738	1,279,041	836,891	1,129,745	1,478,119	341,182	2,057,363	1,227,617
1970	1,795,928	1,715,565	819,362	2,283,527	1,998,308	457,134	2,564,434	—
1980	2,246,997	2,621,757	754,320	2,607,933	2,987,637	655,045	3,050,821	—
1990	2,855,455	3,618,621	929,134	2,765,677	3,995,917	1,050,723	3,083,266	—

[1] Data pertain to noninstitutionalized civilians age 16 and older; in the labor force 1940–1990, or with an occupation 1910–1920.

Source

Matthew Sobek, "New Statistics on the U.S. Labor Force, 1850–1990," *Historical Methods* 34 (2001): 71–87, Table 5.

Documentation

Tabulated from the Integrated Public Use Microdata Series; see the Guide to the Millennial Edition.

Industries are grouped according to the 1950 Census classification. See the source for more discussion of the underlying data and methodology.

The 1920 Census was taken in January, depressing agricultural employment.

TABLE Ba724–741 Major industrial groups of labor force participants – nonwhite males: 1910–1990[1]

Contributed by Matthew Sobek

Year	Total	Agriculture	Forestry and fisheries	Mining	Construction	Manufacturing: Durable	Manufacturing: Nondurable	Transportation and communications
	Ba724	Ba725	Ba726	Ba727	Ba728	Ba729	Ba730	Ba731
	Number	Number	Number	Number	Number	Number	Number	Number
1910	3,027,245	1,555,185	40,051	77,835	152,395	279,349	127,961	309,072
1920	3,137,493	1,419,458	24,421	78,005	159,630	374,411	207,411	325,489
1940	3,296,897	1,268,951	27,531	59,592	347,167	283,306	179,630	199,588
1950	3,730,485	902,062	16,440	46,055	304,918	569,823	308,143	337,552
1960	3,949,680	499,481	10,868	18,639	345,218	621,319	348,096	316,102
1970	4,513,346	251,011	7,012	25,453	417,877	886,944	467,724	426,069
1980	5,999,780	176,204	10,687	47,764	473,686	1,044,148	598,624	575,870
1990	7,489,723	161,397	13,412	34,592	569,545	935,707	634,170	703,338

Year	Trade: Wholesale	Trade: Retail	Finance, insurance, and real estate	Business service	Personal service	Education service	Other professional service	Entertainment	Government	Industry unknown
	Ba732	Ba733	Ba734	Ba735	Ba736	Ba737	Ba738	Ba739	Ba740	Ba741
	Number	Number	Number	Number	Number	Number	Number	Number	Number	Number
1910	14,358	155,418	22,418	18,136	197,232	15,617	33,502	11,587	17,129	—
1920	22,206	160,564	19,072	39,453	195,773	16,754	36,529	13,422	44,895	—
1940	43,639	277,162	55,102	46,018	270,725	42,704	57,460	30,941	56,078	51,303
1950	96,606	398,218	65,157	83,214	244,229	61,286	98,565	33,936	138,323	25,958
1960	122,317	436,904	72,994	99,303	227,433	115,036	154,198	42,443	236,798	282,531
1970	181,713	529,400	120,866	157,111	180,145	252,311	229,727	46,882	333,101	—
1980	245,547	750,676	218,126	282,758	153,002	363,098	460,372	75,299	523,919	—
1990	322,326	1,201,593	336,723	484,516	214,583	460,339	677,714	133,034	606,734	—

[1] Data pertain to noninstitutionalized civilians age 16 and older; in the labor force 1940–1990, or with an occupation 1910–1920.

Source

Matthew Sobek, "New Statistics on the U.S. Labor Force, 1850–1990," *Historical Methods* 34 (2001): 71–87, Table 5.

Documentation

Tabulated from the Integrated Public Use Microdata Series; see the Guide to the Millennial Edition.

Industries are grouped according to the 1950 Census classification. See the source for more discussion of the underlying data and methodology.

The 1920 Census was taken in January, depressing agricultural employment.

TABLE Ba742–759 Major industrial groups of labor force participants – white females: 1910–1990[1]

Contributed by Matthew Sobek

	Total	Agriculture	Forestry and fisheries	Mining	Construction	Manufacturing		Transportation and communications
						Durable	Nondurable	
	Ba742	Ba743	Ba744	Ba745	Ba746	Ba747	Ba748	Ba749
Year	Number	Number	Number	Number	Number	Number	Number	Number
1910	5,731,059	599,504	504	10,328	18,640	176,325	1,123,189	155,418
1920	6,724,062	390,778	403	12,713	22,893	442,583	1,327,544	336,962
1940	10,050,414	248,258	3,628	15,471	49,890	576,799	1,889,922	350,439
1950	13,907,452	394,257	4,939	26,928	91,365	1,235,873	2,327,175	674,390
1960	18,362,602	311,843	5,876	31,373	142,652	1,686,323	2,458,134	712,301
1970	25,326,142	256,986	9,678	48,972	252,437	2,356,202	2,735,033	979,067
1980	35,849,765	457,752	24,348	111,926	441,329	3,103,330	2,872,587	1,278,137
1990	45,029,920	566,097	31,872	97,223	661,257	2,826,933	2,849,788	1,619,639

	Trade		Finance, insurance, and real estate	Business service	Personal service	Education service	Other professional service	Entertainment	Government	Industry unknown
	Wholesale	Retail								
	Ba750	Ba751	Ba752	Ba753	Ba754	Ba755	Ba756	Ba757	Ba758	Ba759
Year	Number	Number	Number	Number	Number	Number	Number	Number	Number	Number
1910	55,668	756,937	95,719	53,401	1,781,636	576,582	256,930	30,983	39,295	—
1920	90,017	1,001,147	211,115	272,648	1,424,812	709,403	313,244	49,334	118,466	—
1940	174,851	1,886,555	444,649	86,598	1,811,599	1,033,518	774,410	92,356	380,474	230,997
1950	381,585	3,039,640	755,952	186,751	1,341,552	1,274,914	1,312,109	134,582	642,696	82,744
1960	426,761	3,647,263	1,199,554	357,216	1,568,981	1,947,771	2,095,890	163,374	804,962	802,328
1970	677,925	5,182,665	1,777,184	734,136	1,678,266	3,852,915	3,478,766	238,250	1,067,660	—
1980	1,012,677	7,307,813	3,047,222	1,409,591	1,638,500	4,986,306	5,947,157	432,732	1,778,358	—
1990	1,344,685	8,763,628	4,155,565	2,383,109	1,994,055	6,516,313	8,431,638	750,244	2,037,874	—

[1] Data pertain to noninstitutionalized civilians age 16 and older; in the labor force 1940–1990, or with an occupation 1910–1920.

Source

Matthew Sobek, "New Statistics on the U.S. Labor Force, 1850–1990," *Historical Methods* 34 (2001): 71–87, Table 6.

Documentation

Tabulated from the Integrated Public Use Microdata Series; see the Guide to the Millennial Edition.

Industries are grouped according to the 1950 Census classification. See the source for more discussion of the underlying data and methodology.

The wording of the 1910 Census instructions led to large numbers of women counted as having occupations, especially in agriculture. The 1920 Census was taken in January, depressing agricultural employment.

TABLE Ba760–777 Major industrial groups of labor force participants – nonwhite females: 1910–1990[1]

Contributed by Matthew Sobek

	Total	Agriculture	Forestry and fisheries	Mining	Construction	Manufacturing		Transportation and communications
						Durable	Nondurable	
	Ba760	Ba761	Ba762	Ba763	Ba764	Ba765	Ba766	Ba767
Year	Number	Number	Number	Number	Number	Number	Number	Number
1910	1,812,368	849,634	252	0	2,267	6,297	30,479	2,771
1920	1,463,268	509,298	303	505	3,228	13,322	59,129	6,059
1940	1,619,644	273,305	483	695	3,530	9,712	64,009	4,319
1950	1,941,993	177,489	583	218	2,306	47,926	136,054	18,062
1960	2,594,120	94,533	597	694	7,368	78,180	166,959	27,303
1970	3,663,396	54,706	1,185	2,103	16,391	237,724	337,224	108,445
1980	5,780,813	39,577	3,685	11,600	36,787	472,394	548,856	222,814
1990	7,943,249	41,071	4,228	9,528	64,589	485,788	623,508	331,422

	Trade		Finance, insurance, and real estate	Business service	Personal service	Education service	Other professional service	Entertainment	Government	Industry unknown
	Wholesale	Retail								
	Ba768	Ba769	Ba770	Ba771	Ba772	Ba773	Ba774	Ba775	Ba776	Ba777
Year	Number	Number	Number	Number	Number	Number	Number	Number	Number	Number
1910	1,511	19,144	4,282	2,771	854,168	26,449	10,076	1,763	504	—
1920	1,313	41,976	3,933	5,450	760,218	36,427	14,032	2,725	5,350	—
1940	3,846	69,377	12,589	3,131	1,034,691	73,329	32,121	6,684	13,550	14,273
1950	15,980	195,370	26,658	6,735	1,020,869	113,795	113,595	9,831	49,997	6,525
1960	20,822	254,668	41,550	16,744	1,126,017	194,357	265,755	12,653	98,515	187,405
1970	52,277	425,306	137,451	66,724	869,982	538,490	581,763	20,415	213,210	—
1980	94,695	723,749	370,936	179,337	530,154	824,315	1,180,662	46,507	494,745	—
1990	165,860	1,215,369	609,795	353,651	518,155	1,043,826	1,743,850	94,649	637,960	—

[1] Data pertain to noninstitutionalized civilians age 16 and older; in the labor force 1940–1990, or with an occupation 1910–1920.

Source

Matthew Sobek, "New Statistics on the U.S. Labor Force, 1850–1990," *Historical Methods* 34 (2001): 71–87, Table 6.

Documentation

Tabulated from the Integrated Public Use Microdata Series; see the Guide to the Millennial Edition.

Industries are grouped according to the 1950 Census classification. See the source for more discussion of the underlying data and methodology.

The wording of the 1910 Census instructions led to large numbers of women counted as having occupations, especially in agriculture. The 1920 Census was taken in January, depressing agricultural employment.

TABLE Ba778–795 Major industrial groups of labor force participants – native-born persons: 1910–1990[1]

Contributed by Matthew Sobek

	Total	Agriculture	Forestry and fisheries	Mining	Construction	Manufacturing		Transportation and communications
						Durable	Nondurable	
	Ba778	Ba779	Ba780	Ba781	Ba782	Ba783	Ba784	Ba785
Year	Number	Number	Number	Number	Number	Number	Number	Number
1910	28,251,512	10,025,827	92,696	597,741	1,495,486	2,484,668	2,551,168	2,432,023
1920	32,082,704	9,136,372	64,471	852,633	1,459,430	3,818,305	3,309,330	3,109,799
1940	41,833,538	7,877,764	159,559	852,317	3,038,313	4,369,792	4,829,417	2,806,460
1950	51,617,541	6,485,606	108,365	898,695	3,163,940	7,155,720	6,132,071	4,142,154
1960	59,380,565	3,913,117	88,179	627,352	3,557,492	9,184,020	6,719,205	4,103,460
1970	71,567,578	2,601,712	85,663	612,956	4,319,795	11,143,766	7,155,147	4,806,302
1980	90,067,543	2,533,572	145,549	992,098	5,341,526	12,468,780	7,360,747	5,792,815
1990	103,217,455	2,491,365	158,213	689,311	6,411,338	10,734,642	7,175,442	6,339,260

	Trade		Finance, insurance, and real estate	Business service	Personal service	Education service	Other professional service	Entertainment	Government	Industry unknown
	Wholesale	Retail								
	Ba786	Ba787	Ba788	Ba789	Ba790	Ba791	Ba792	Ba793	Ba794	Ba795
Year	Number	Number	Number	Number	Number	Number	Number	Number	Number	Number
1910	507,060	2,563,510	523,936	305,546	2,634,292	743,335	710,337	143,075	440,812	—
1920	705,510	2,986,770	744,440	956,807	2,345,978	904,546	825,854	177,799	684,660	—
1940	1,040,887	5,491,632	1,302,311	789,150	3,482,412	1,615,638	1,558,192	425,777	1,544,843	649,074
1950	1,867,961	7,839,434	1,771,156	1,357,053	3,086,962	2,028,275	2,413,581	499,962	2,432,126	234,480
1960	2,036,822	8,679,871	2,532,726	1,635,844	3,391,350	3,231,910	3,677,696	514,418	3,086,752	2,400,351
1970	2,906,025	11,410,909	3,579,701	2,498,425	3,246,093	6,611,816	5,831,792	710,934	4,046,542	—
1980	3,788,727	14,610,154	5,436,352	4,134,401	2,711,753	8,319,135	9,715,893	1,121,104	5,594,937	—
1990	4,397,599	17,332,932	7,218,840	6,065,779	2,988,386	9,982,515	13,396,521	1,846,506	5,988,806	—

[1] Data pertain to noninstitutionalized civilians age 16 and older; in the labor force 1940–1990, or with an occupation 1910–1920.

Source

Tabulated from the Integrated Public Use Microdata Series; see the Guide to the Millennial Edition.

Documentation

Industries are grouped according to the 1950 Census classification. For a discussion of the source and general methodology employed, see Matthew Sobek, "New Statistics on the U.S. Labor Force, 1850–1990," *Historical Methods* 34 (2001): 71–87.

The wording of the 1910 Census instructions led to large numbers of women counted as having occupations, especially in agriculture. The 1920 Census was taken in January, depressing agricultural employment.

TABLE Ba796–813 Major industrial groups of labor force participants – foreign-born persons: 1910–1990[1]

Contributed by Matthew Sobek

	Total	Agriculture	Forestry and fisheries	Mining	Construction	Manufacturing		Transportation and communications
						Durable	Nondurable	
	Ba796	Ba797	Ba798	Ba799	Ba800	Ba801	Ba802	Ba803
Year	Number	Number	Number	Number	Number	Number	Number	Number
1910	7,962,576	1,104,549	23,174	474,566	659,455	1,206,565	1,306,567	785,149
1920	7,813,620	901,426	12,011	404,134	465,350	1,460,112	1,377,893	683,467
1940	5,672,886	519,588	19,788	127,059	419,616	830,126	864,113	356,139
1950	4,960,353	337,356	12,031	59,184	306,388	820,160	813,486	316,602
1960	4,489,733	228,004	6,080	17,331	238,002	763,914	717,272	231,908
1970	4,702,938	131,662	4,490	13,720	239,030	780,814	644,652	225,698
1980	7,310,869	220,575	6,514	30,294	353,918	1,166,661	866,700	344,986
1990	11,865,640	421,448	12,737	31,401	734,354	1,335,981	1,100,198	558,563

	Trade		Finance, insurance, and real estate	Business service	Personal service	Education service	Other professional service	Entertainment	Government	Industry unknown
	Wholesale	Retail								
	Ba804	Ba805	Ba806	Ba807	Ba808	Ba809	Ba810	Ba811	Ba812	Ba813
Year	Number	Number	Number	Number	Number	Number	Number	Number	Number	Number
1910	131,236	951,902	90,178	95,215	825,452	66,752	154,410	29,723	57,683	—
1920	158,836	1,030,943	107,477	170,821	683,439	65,797	149,946	47,720	94,248	—
1940	151,618	1,007,223	182,463	96,561	562,747	101,127	199,703	56,028	104,110	74,877
1950	191,010	907,865	166,829	98,221	413,679	103,732	232,445	47,593	111,683	22,089
1960	158,991	734,774	182,110	116,460	367,972	154,999	316,266	45,234	110,886	99,530
1970	195,005	783,557	251,728	175,111	301,662	315,427	456,772	51,747	131,863	—
1980	295,756	1,191,435	446,929	359,042	364,223	462,516	859,935	88,479	252,906	—
1990	522,836	2,152,355	738,698	774,118	667,541	803,640	1,452,598	182,144	377,028	—

[1] Data pertain to noninstitutionalized civilians age 16 and older; in the labor force 1940–1990, or with an occupation 1910–1920.

Source

Tabulated from the Integrated Public Use Microdata Series; see the Guide to the Millennial Edition.

Documentation

Industries are grouped according to the 1950 Census classification. For a discussion of the source and general methodology employed, see Matthew Sobek, "New Statistics on the U.S. Labor Force, 1850–1990," *Historical Methods* 34 (2001): 71–87.

The wording of the 1910 Census instructions led to large numbers of women counted as having occupations, especially in agriculture. The 1920 Census was taken in January, depressing agricultural employment.

TABLE Ba814–830 The labor force, by industry: 1800–1960[1] [Lebergott and Weiss]

Contributed by Susan B. Carter

	Lebergott									
		Free or slave status		Industry						
								Manufacturing		
									Wage earners	
	Total	Free	Slave	Agriculture	Fishing	Mining	Construction	Total	Cotton textile	Primary iron and steel
	Ba814	Ba815	Ba816	Ba817	Ba818	Ba819	Ba820	Ba821	Ba822	Ba823
Year	Thousand	Thousand	Thousand	Thousand	Thousand	Thousand	Thousand	Thousand	Thousand	Thousand
1800	1,680	1,150	530	1,400	5	10	—	—	1	1
1810	2,330	1,590	740	1,950	6	11	—	75	10	5
1820	3,135	2,185	950	2,470	14	13	—	—	12	5
1830	4,200	3,020	1,180	2,965	15	22	—	—	55	20
1840	5,660	4,180	1,480	3,570	24	32	290	500	72	24
1850	8,250	6,280	1,970	4,520	30	102	410	1,200	92	35
1860	11,110	8,770	2,340	5,880	31	176	520	1,530	122	43
1870	12,930	12,930	—	6,790	28	180	780	2,470	135	78
1880	17,390	17,390	—	8,920	41	280	900	3,290	175	130
1890	23,320	23,320	—	9,960	60	440	1,510	4,390	222	149
1900	29,070	29,070	—	11,680	69	637	1,665	5,895	303	222
1910	37,480	37,480	—	11,770	68	1,068	1,949	8,332	370	306
1920	41,610	41,610	—	10,790	53	1,180	1,233	11,190	450	460
1930	48,830	48,830	—	10,560	73	1,009	1,988	9,884	372	375
1940	56,290	56,290	—	9,575	60	925	1,876	11,309	400	485
1950	65,470	65,470	—	7,870	77	901	3,029	15,648	350	550
1960	74,060	74,060	—	5,970	45	709	3,640	17,145	300	530

	Lebergott					Weiss	
	Industry						
		Transportation		Service			
	Trade	Ocean vessels	Railway	Teachers	Domestics	Total	Farm
	Ba824	Ba825	Ba826	Ba827	Ba828	Ba829	Ba830
Year	Thousand	Thousand	Thousand	Thousand	Thousand	Thousand	Thousand
1800	—	40	—	5	40	1,713	1,274
1810	—	60	—	12	70	2,337	1,690
1820	—	50	—	20	110	3,163	2,249
1830	—	70	—	30	160	4,272	2,982
1840	350	95	7	45	240	5,778	3,882
1850	530	135	20	80	350	8,193	4,889
1860	890	145	80	115	600	11,293	6,299
1870	1,310	135	230	170	1,000	12,785	6,378
1880	1,930	125	416	230	1,130	17,392	8,302
1890	2,960	120	750	350	1,580	23,547	9,433
1900	3,970	105	1,040	436	1,800	29,073	10,496
1910	5,320	150	1,855	595	2,090	—	—
1920	5,845	205	2,236	752	1,660	—	—
1930	8,122	160	1,659	1,044	2,270	—	—
1940	9,328	150	1,160	1,086	2,300	—	—
1950	12,152	130	1,373	1,270	1,995	—	—
1960	14,051	135	883	1,850	2,489	—	—

[1] Persons age 10 and older.

Sources

Stanley Lebergott, *The Americans: An Economic Record* (Norton, 1984), p. 66. Thomas Weiss, "U.S. Labor Force Estimates and Economic Growth," in Robert E. Gallman and John Joseph Wallis, editors, *American Economic Growth and Standards of Living before the Civil War* (University of Chicago Press, 1992), p. 22. Thomas Weiss, "Long-term Changes in U.S. Agricultural Output per Worker, 1800–1900," *Economic History Review* 46 (2) (1993): 324–41 (and unpublished appendix).

Documentation

Stanley Lebergott developed his labor force estimates to be conceptually comparable to those of the U.S. Bureau of Labor Statistics (BLS) Current Population Survey (CPS). The CPS data are first available in 1938; see Table Ba478–486. Subsequent revisions of the CPS data have led to differences between the CPS and the Lebergott estimates in overlapping years. The CPS figures are not directly comparable with census figures, nor with those of the BLS Current Employment Survey.

For a detailed discussion of the derivation of the Lebergott estimates, see Stanley Lebergott, "Labor Force and Employment, 1800–1960," in *Conference on Research in Income and Wealth, Output, Employment, and Productivity in the United States after 1800,* Studies in Income and Wealth, volume 30 (National Bureau of Economic Research, 1966), pp. 134–204.

The data presented in series Ba814–829 reflect subsequent revisions suggested by Paul David and described in Lebergott (1984).

Thomas Weiss's estimates were also designed to be comparable to those in the CPS. His approach was to build national estimates of the total and the

TABLE Ba814–830 The labor force, by industry: 1800–1960 [Lebergott and Weiss] *Continued*

agricultural labor force for the period 1800–1900 from state-level estimates. For a detailed discussion of his methods, along with the state-by-state estimates for 1800–1860, see Weiss (1992), pp. 36–72. The total labor force figures shown here for 1800–1860 differ slightly from those shown in the original publication. Differences between the previously published and current estimates are, for the most part, due to rounding errors. They amount to less than 0.07 percent in all years except 1820. The 1820 figures for the total labor force were adjusted to reflect revisions in the underlying total population data for Alabama. The 1820 Alabama population adjustments had no effect on the 1820 Alabama farm labor force estimates.

For the period of overlap between the Lebergott and Weiss total and farm labor force estimates – 1800 to 1900 – the Weiss estimates are the preferred ones. For a comparison of the Lebergott and Weiss estimates for the years 1800–1860, see Claudia Goldin, "Comment," in Robert E. Gallman and John Joseph Wallis, editors, *American Economic Growth and Standards of Living before the Civil War* (University of Chicago Press, 1992), pp. 75–8.

TABLE Ba831–839 Employees on nonagricultural payrolls, by industry: 1900–1940 [Lebergott]

Contributed by Richard Sutch

	Total	Mining	Contract construction	Manufacturing	Transportation, communications, and public utilities	Wholesale and retail trade	Finance, insurance, and real estate services	Other private services	Governmental occupations
	Ba831	Ba832	Ba833	Ba834	Ba835	Ba836	Ba837	Ba838	Ba839
Year	Thousand	Thousand	Thousand	Thousand	Thousand	Thousand	Thousand	Thousand	Thousand
1900	15,178	637	1,147	5,468	2,282	2,502	308	1,740	1,094
1901	16,294	703	1,274	5,817	2,404	2,765	322	1,880	1,129
1902	17,395	685	1,393	6,305	2,754	2,827	337	1,903	1,191
1903	17,858	834	1,290	6,527	2,666	2,979	351	1,982	1,229
1904	17,640	801	1,257	6,199	2,743	2,992	369	2,002	1,277
1905	18,707	889	1,208	6,739	2,905	3,170	385	2,076	1,335
1906	20,069	894	1,391	7,226	3,110	3,442	405	2,215	1,386
1907	20,523	1,051	1,436	7,322	3,114	3,486	423	2,243	1,448
1908	19,259	900	1,308	6,570	3,069	3,299	442	2,164	1,507
1909	21,203	998	1,376	7,661	3,229	3,585	464	2,326	1,564
1910	21,697	1,068	1,342	7,828	3,366	3,570	483	2,410	1,630
1911	22,093	1,052	1,249	7,870	3,426	3,813	520	2,491	1,672
1912	23,191	1,083	1,337	8,322	3,552	4,073	568	2,539	1,717
1913	24,143	1,182	1,412	8,751	3,570	4,232	613	2,626	1,757
1914	23,190	1,027	1,267	8,210	3,445	4,128	657	2,647	1,809
1915	23,149	1,022	1,195	8,210	3,439	4,091	694	2,637	1,861
1916	25,510	1,168	1,208	9,629	3,579	4,476	738	2,796	1,916
1917	25,762	1,267	1,027	9,872	3,722	4,320	771	2,783	2,000
1918	26,432	1,311	928	10,167	3,877	4,110	809	2,769	2,461
1919	27,270	1,067	1,011	10,702	4,055	4,213	868	2,905	2,449
1920	27,434	1,180	850	10,702	4,317	4,012	902	3,100	2,371
1921	24,542	906	1,035	8,262	3,929	3,960	968	3,085	2,397
1922	26,616	880	1,315	9,129	3,897	4,708	1,081	3,151	2,455
1923	29,231	1,181	1,408	10,317	4,185	5,194	1,175	3,247	2,524
1924	28,577	1,091	1,556	9,675	4,063	5,047	1,211	3,298	2,636
1925	29,751	1,065	1,680	9,942	4,018	5,717	1,264	3,300	2,765
1926	30,599	1,168	1,756	10,156	4,077	5,864	1,328	3,397	2,853
1927	30,481	1,100	1,761	9,996	3,997	5,942	1,380	3,360	2,945
1928	30,539	1,038	1,704	9,942	3,886	6,047	1,484	3,399	3,039
1929	31,339	1,087	1,497	10,702	3,916	6,123	1,509	3,440	3,065
1930	29,424	1,009	1,372	9,562	3,685	5,797	1,475	3,376	3,148
1931	26,649	873	1,214	8,170	3,254	5,284	1,407	3,183	3,264
1932	23,628	731	970	6,931	2,816	4,683	1,341	2,931	3,225
1933	23,711	744	809	7,397	2,672	4,755	1,295	2,873	3,166
1934	25,953	883	862	8,501	2,750	5,281	1,319	3,058	3,299
1935	27,053	897	912	9,069	2,786	5,431	1,335	3,142	3,481
1936	29,082	946	1,145	9,827	2,973	5,809	1,388	3,326	3,668
1937	31,026	1,015	1,112	10,794	3,134	6,265	1,432	3,518	3,756
1938	29,209	891	1,055	9,440	2,863	6,179	1,425	3,473	3,883
1939	30,618	854	1,150	10,278	2,936	6,426	1,462	3,517	3,995
1940	32,376	925	1,294	10,985	3,038	6,750	1,502	3,681	4,202

Sources

Stanley Lebergott, *Manpower in Economic Growth: The American Record since 1800* (McGraw-Hill, 1964), Table A-5. Also see for 1929–1940: U.S. Bureau of Labor Statistics (BLS), *Handbook of Labor Statistics* (1972), p. 89.

Documentation

Lebergott's estimates for the period 1900–1928 were designed to be comparable with those of the BLS establishment employment data published in 1972. Lebergott linked his estimates directly to the BLS estimates for 1929–1960, taken from the BLS source cited in the source. At that time, the BLS also published estimates for the period 1919–1928, but Lebergott preferred his estimates to the "official ones" – a preference to be taken seriously because he was himself the author of the official statistics that he later decided to revise (Lebergott 1964, p. 363). Since 1972, the BLS has revised its own series to 1919 several times (see Table Ba840–848). Thus, Lebergott's data no

(continued)

TABLE Ba831–839 Employees on nonagricultural payrolls, by industry: 1900–1940 [Lebergott] *Continued*

longer make a clean splice at 1919, 1929, or any other date. Note that the BLS data for 1929–1940 reproduced here from Lebergott are now considered obsolete. They are given here to assist the user in linking his 1900–1929 estimates to subsequent data.

Employment data refer to persons on establishment payrolls who receive pay for any part of the reference pay period. Proprietors, the self-employed, unpaid family workers, farm workers, and domestic workers in households are excluded. Government employment covers civilian employees only.

For a more detailed description of the BLS data, see U.S. Bureau of Labor Statistics, *Employment, Hours, and Earnings, United States, 1909–1971*, Bulletin number 1312-8 (1971). For an analysis of historical trends, see Lebergott (1964).

TABLE Ba840–848 Employees on nonagricultural payrolls, by industry: 1919–1999 [Bureau of Labor Statistics]

Contributed by Richard Sutch

	Total	Mining	Construction	Manufacturing	Transportation, communication, and public utilities	Wholesale and retail trade	Finance, insurance, and real estate services	Other private services	Governmental occupations
	Ba840	Ba841	Ba842	Ba843	Ba844	Ba845	Ba846	Ba847	Ba848
Year	Thousand	Thousand	Thousand	Thousand	Thousand	Thousand	Thousand	Thousand	Thousand
1919	27,078	1,133	1,036	10,659	3,711	4,514	—	—	2,676
1920	27,340	1,239	863	10,658	3,998	4,467	—	—	2,603
1921	24,372	962	1,027	8,257	3,459	4,589	—	—	2,528
1922	25,816	929	1,200	9,120	3,505	4,903	—	—	2,538
1923	28,382	1,212	1,244	10,300	3,882	5,290	—	—	2,607
1924	28,028	1,101	1,336	9,671	3,807	5,407	—	—	2,720
1925	28,766	1,089	1,461	9,939	3,826	5,576	—	—	2,800
1926	29,806	1,185	1,570	10,156	3,942	5,784	—	—	2,846
1927	29,962	1,114	1,623	10,001	3,895	5,908	—	—	2,915
1928	29,986	1,050	1,621	9,947	3,828	5,874	—	—	2,995
1929	31,324	1,087	1,512	10,702	3,916	6,123	—	—	3,065
1930	29,409	1,009	1,387	9,562	3,685	5,797	—	—	3,148
1931	26,635	873	1,229	8,170	3,254	5,284	—	—	3,264
1932	23,615	731	985	6,931	2,816	4,683	—	—	3,225
1933	23,699	744	824	7,397	2,672	4,755	—	—	3,166
1934	25,940	883	877	8,501	2,750	5,281	—	—	3,299
1935	27,039	897	927	9,069	2,786	5,431	—	—	3,481
1936	29,068	946	1,160	9,827	2,973	5,809	—	—	3,668
1937	31,011	1,015	1,127	10,794	3,134	6,265	—	—	3,756
1938	29,194	891	1,070	9,440	2,863	6,179	—	—	3,883
1939	30,603	854	1,165	10,278	2,936	6,426	1,447	3,502	3,995
1940	32,361	925	1,311	10,985	3,038	6,750	1,485	3,665	4,202
1941	36,537	957	1,814	13,192	3,274	7,210	1,525	3,905	4,660
1942	40,106	992	2,198	15,280	3,460	7,118	1,509	4,066	5,483
1943	42,434	925	1,587	17,602	3,647	6,982	1,481	4,130	6,080
1944	41,864	892	1,108	17,328	3,829	7,058	1,461	4,145	6,043
1945	40,374	836	1,147	15,524	3,906	7,314	1,481	4,222	5,944
1946	41,652	862	1,683	14,703	4,061	8,376	1,675	4,697	5,595
1947	43,857	955	2,009	15,545	4,166	8,955	1,728	5,025	5,474
1948	44,866	994	2,198	15,582	4,189	9,272	1,800	5,181	5,650
1949	43,754	930	2,194	14,441	4,001	9,264	1,828	5,239	5,856
1950	45,197	901	2,364	15,241	4,034	9,386	1,888	5,356	6,026
1951	47,819	929	2,637	16,393	4,226	9,742	1,956	5,547	6,389
1952	48,793	898	2,668	16,632	4,248	10,004	2,035	5,699	6,609
1953	50,202	866	2,659	17,549	4,290	10,247	2,111	5,835	6,645
1954	48,990	791	2,646	16,314	4,084	10,235	2,200	5,969	6,751
1955	50,641	792	2,839	16,882	4,141	10,535	2,298	6,240	6,914
1956	52,369	822	3,039	17,243	4,244	10,858	2,389	6,497	7,278
1957	52,855	828	2,962	17,176	4,241	10,886	2,438	6,708	7,616
1958	51,322	751	2,817	15,945	3,976	10,750	2,481	6,765	7,839
1959	53,270	732	3,004	16,675	4,011	11,127	2,549	7,087	8,083
1960	54,189	712	2,926	16,796	4,004	11,391	2,628	7,378	8,353
1961	53,999	672	2,859	16,326	3,903	11,337	2,688	7,619	8,594
1962	55,549	650	2,948	16,853	3,906	11,566	2,754	7,982	8,890
1963	56,653	635	3,010	16,995	3,903	11,778	2,830	8,277	9,225
1964	58,283	634	3,097	17,274	3,951	12,160	2,911	8,660	9,596

TABLE Ba840–848 Employees on nonagricultural payrolls, by industry: 1919–1999 [Bureau of Labor Statistics] *Continued*

	Total	Mining	Construction	Manufacturing	Transportation, communication, and public utilities	Wholesale and retail trade	Finance, insurance, and real estate services	Other private services	Governmental occupations
	Ba840	Ba841	Ba842	Ba843	Ba844	Ba845	Ba846	Ba847	Ba848
Year	Thousand	Thousand	Thousand	Thousand	Thousand	Thousand	Thousand	Thousand	Thousand
1965	60,763	632	3,232	18,062	4,036	12,716	2,977	9,036	10,074
1966	63,901	627	3,317	19,214	4,158	13,245	3,058	9,498	10,784
1967	65,803	613	3,248	19,447	4,268	13,606	3,185	10,045	11,391
1968	67,897	606	3,350	19,781	4,318	14,099	3,337	10,567	11,839
1969	70,384	619	3,575	20,167	4,442	14,705	3,512	11,169	12,195
1970	70,880	623	3,588	19,367	4,515	15,040	3,645	11,548	12,554
1971	71,211	609	3,704	18,623	4,476	15,352	3,772	11,797	12,881
1972	73,675	628	3,889	19,151	4,541	15,949	3,908	12,276	13,334
1973	76,790	642	4,097	20,154	4,656	16,607	4,046	12,857	13,732
1974	78,265	697	4,020	20,077	4,725	16,987	4,148	13,441	14,170
1975	76,945	752	3,525	18,323	4,542	17,060	4,165	13,892	14,686
1976	79,382	779	3,576	18,997	4,582	17,755	4,271	14,551	14,871
1977	82,471	813	3,851	19,682	4,713	18,516	4,467	15,302	15,127
1978	86,697	851	4,229	20,505	4,923	19,542	4,724	16,252	15,672
1979	89,823	958	4,463	21,040	5,136	20,192	4,975	17,112	15,947
1980	90,406	1,027	4,346	20,285	5,146	20,310	5,160	17,890	16,241
1981	91,152	1,139	4,188	20,170	5,165	20,547	5,298	18,615	16,031
1982	89,544	1,128	3,904	18,780	5,081	20,453	5,340	19,021	15,837
1983	90,152	952	3,946	18,432	4,952	20,871	5,466	19,664	15,869
1984	94,408	966	4,380	19,372	5,156	22,080	5,684	20,746	16,024
1985	97,387	927	4,668	19,248	5,233	23,042	5,948	21,927	16,394
1986	99,344	777	4,810	18,947	5,247	23,641	6,273	22,957	16,693
1987	101,958	717	4,958	18,999	5,362	24,269	6,533	24,110	17,010
1988	105,209	713	5,098	19,314	5,512	25,053	6,630	25,504	17,386
1989	107,884	692	5,171	19,391	5,614	25,662	6,668	26,907	17,779
1990	109,403	709	5,120	19,076	5,777	25,774	6,709	27,934	18,304
1991	108,249	689	4,650	18,406	5,755	25,365	6,646	28,336	18,402
1992	108,601	635	4,492	18,104	5,718	25,353	6,602	29,052	18,645
1993	110,713	610	4,668	18,075	5,811	25,755	6,757	30,197	18,841
1994	114,163	601	4,986	18,321	5,984	26,670	6,896	31,579	19,128
1995	117,191	581	5,160	18,524	6,132	27,565	6,806	33,117	19,305
1996	119,608	580	5,418	18,495	6,253	28,079	6,911	34,454	19,419
1997	122,690	596	5,691	18,675	6,408	28,614	7,109	36,040	19,557
1998	125,826	590	6,020	18,805	6,611	29,095	7,389	37,533	19,823
1999	128,786	535	6,404	18,543	6,826	29,712	7,569	39,027	20,170

Sources

U.S. Bureau of Labor Statistics (BLS), *Employment, Hours, and Earnings: United States, 1909–94,* Bulletin number 2445, 2 volumes (1994); *Employment, Hours, and Earnings: United States, 1990–95,* Bulletin number 2465 (1995); *National Employment, Hours, and Earnings,* BLS Internet site. Also see the periodical *Employment and Earnings,* published monthly by the BLS. For 1919–1938 for series Ba846–847: *Employment, Hours, and Earnings: United States, 1909–90,* Bulletin number 2370 (1990). These data are also available at the BLS Internet site.

Documentation

Data are annual averages of monthly figures.

These data are collected by the BLS Current Employment Statistics program, a federal-state cooperative effort undertaken monthly from the payroll records of a sample of nonfarm business establishments. The firms submit the data voluntarily. In 1999, the sample surveyed 400,000 establishments employing about a third of all wage and salary workers.

Employment data refer to persons on establishments' payrolls who receive pay for any part of the reference pay period. These numbers include workers on paid sick leave (when pay is received directly from the firm), paid holiday, or paid vacation, and those who work during a part of the pay period and are unemployed or on strike during the rest of the period. Proprietors, the self-employed, unpaid family workers, farm workers, and domestic workers in households are excluded. Government employment covers civilian employees only.

Periodically, the industry employment series are adjusted to recent benchmarks to improve their accuracy. These adjustments may also affect the hours, earnings, and labor turnover series since employment levels are used as weights. Industry data for these series have been adjusted to March 1993 benchmarks. For a more detailed description of the methods used to measure nonfarm payroll employment, see Appendix A of BLS Bulletin number 2465. The data summarized in these series are available in considerable detail (estimates are provided for more than 600 different industries each month). For a discussion of available historical data, see BLS, *Employment and Earnings, United States, 1909–1971,* Bulletin number 1312-8 (1971).

Total employment in nonagricultural establishments from the "payroll" survey is not directly comparable with the estimates of nonagricultural employment obtained from the monthly "household" survey (Current Population Survey). The household survey includes the self-employed, unpaid family workers, and private household workers and is basically a count of persons. The payroll series, in contrast, excludes these workers and is basically a count of jobs. Thus, the multiple jobholder, counted only once in the household survey, would be counted once for each job by the payroll survey. Employment estimates developed by quinquennial censuses may differ from payroll estimates due, primarily, to the reporting practices of multiproduct establishments and administrative handling of central offices and auxiliary units.

The data summarized in these series are available in considerable detail; see the tables mentioned in the following list and the original sources.

Series Ba840. The sum of series Ba841–848.

Series Ba841. Standard Industrial Classification (SIC) codes are: 10, 12, 13, and 14. See the Introduction to Part D for a discussion of SIC codes. For a disaggregation of this series, see Table Db12–24.

(continued)

TABLE Ba840–848 Employees on nonagricultural payrolls, by industry: 1919–1999 [Bureau of Labor Statistics] *Continued*

Series Ba842. Total employees in construction, SIC codes 15, 16, and 17. For a disaggregation of this series, see Table Dc241–255.

Series Ba843. Total employees in manufacturing, SIC codes 20–39. For a disaggregation of this series, see Table Dd661–683.

Series Ba844. SIC codes 40–42 and 44–49. Excludes the U.S. Postal Service. For a disaggregation of this series, see Tables Df72–80, Dg1–7, Dh198–218, and Dh230–235.

Series Ba845. SIC codes 50–59. For a disaggregation of this series, see Table De14–25.

Series Ba846. SIC codes 60–65 and 67. For a disaggregation of this series, see Table Cj423–431.

Series Ba847. SIC codes 07, 70–87, plus SIC 99, unclassifiable industries. For a disaggregation of this series, see Table Dh198–214.

Series Ba848. For a disaggregation of this series, see Table Ea966–985.

TABLE Ba849–857 Female employees on nonagricultural payrolls, by industry: 1959–1999[1] [Bureau of Labor Statistics]

Contributed by Susan B. Carter

	Total	Mining	Construction	Manufacturing	Transportation, communication, and public utilities	Wholesale and retail trade	Finance, insurance, and real estate services	Other private services	Governmental occupations
	Ba849	Ba850	Ba851	Ba852	Ba853	Ba854	Ba855	Ba856	Ba857
Year	Thousand	Thousand	Thousand	Thousand	Thousand	Thousand	Thousand	Thousand	Thousand
1959	—	—	—	4,358	—	—	—	—	—
1960	—	36	—	4,371	—	4,295	—	—	—
1961	—	35	—	4,292	—	4,267	—	—	—
1962	—	35	—	4,474	—	4,355	—	—	—
1963	—	35	—	4,482	—	4,428	—	—	—
1964	19,662	34	152	4,537	723	4,618	1,464	4,415	3,718
1965	20,660	34	152	4,768	748	4,881	1,496	4,611	3,970
1966	22,168	34	156	5,213	786	5,124	1,549	4,931	4,375
1967	23,272	35	158	5,353	835	5,297	1,624	5,267	4,703
1968	24,395	36	164	5,490	860	5,526	1,709	5,632	4,979
1969	25,595	37	174	5,667	911	5,841	1,819	5,994	5,153
1970	26,132	37	186	5,448	957	6,007	1,907	6,224	5,365
1971	26,466	37	199	5,229	955	6,128	1,978	6,438	5,502
1972	27,541	40	219	5,470	953	6,350	2,032	6,718	5,759
1973	28,988	43	241	5,865	987	6,682	2,138	7,023	6,010
1974	30,124	49	262	5,849	1,018	6,978	2,245	7,454	6,270
1975	30,178	55	256	5,257	996	7,051	2,287	7,822	6,454
1976	31,570	60	281	5,607	1,010	7,400	2,371	8,256	6,586
1977	33,252	65	304	5,880	1,051	7,764	2,511	8,771	6,907
1978	35,349	76	331	6,237	1,133	8,280	2,708	9,368	7,216
1979	37,096	91	355	6,466	1,237	8,697	2,882	9,919	7,450
1980	38,186	105	372	6,317	1,292	8,851	3,039	10,452	7,759
1981	39,035	129	380	6,341	1,340	8,989	3,158	10,969	7,730
1982	39,041	134	377	5,990	1,339	9,077	3,198	11,330	7,595
1983	39,826	117	388	5,964	1,313	9,375	3,277	11,755	7,637
1984	42,022	118	427	6,295	1,386	10,076	3,430	12,413	7,878
1985	43,851	120	463	6,230	1,448	10,668	3,634	13,129	8,159
1986	45,476	106	495	6,181	1,480	11,088	3,886	13,819	8,420
1987	47,188	95	523	6,242	1,532	11,500	4,076	14,549	8,672
1988	49,053	96	539	6,352	1,619	11,928	4,134	15,454	8,931
1989	50,690	94	547	6,399	1,643	12,275	4,188	16,296	9,248
1990	51,894	95	552	6,285	1,714	12,336	4,239	16,958	9,714
1991	52,016	97	532	6,067	1,722	12,168	4,215	17,352	9,862
1992	52,483	93	511	5,964	1,711	12,150	4,192	17,830	10,033
1993	53,560	88	521	5,933	1,740	12,297	4,279	18,507	10,197
1994	55,164	85	546	5,987	1,799	12,724	4,354	19,271	10,397
1995	56,643	81	573	6,010	1,857	13,128	4,295	20,131	10,568
1996	57,855	80	605	5,950	1,908	13,372	4,359	20,883	10,699
1997	59,388	82	632	5,992	1,940	13,624	4,478	21,787	10,853
1998	60,846	84	666	6,001	1,989	13,845	4,639	22,559	11,064
1999	62,318	79	711	5,888	2,087	14,132	4,734	23,366	11,321

[1] Data are annual averages of monthly figures.

Source

U.S. Bureau of Labor Statistics (BLS), Current Employment Statistics program, BLS Internet site.

Documentation

See the text for Table Ba840–848 for information on the data source and series-specific details.

TABLE Ba858–865 Production employees on nonagricultural payrolls, by industry: 1919–1999[1] [Bureau of Labor Statistics]

Contributed by Susan B. Carter

Year	Total	Mining	Construction	Manufacturing	Transportation, communication, and public utilities	Wholesale and retail trade	Finance, insurance, and real estate services	Other private services
	Ba858	Ba859	Ba860	Ba861	Ba862	Ba863	Ba864	Ba865
	Thousand	Thousand	Thousand	Thousand	Thousand	Thousand	Thousand	Thousand
1919	—	—	—	8,617	—	—	—	—
1920	—	—	—	8,652	—	—	—	—
1921	—	—	—	6,622	—	—	—	—
1922	—	—	—	7,327	—	—	—	—
1923	—	—	—	8,388	—	—	—	—
1924	—	—	—	7,789	—	—	—	—
1925	—	—	—	8,061	—	—	—	—
1926	—	—	—	8,214	—	—	—	—
1927	—	—	—	8,037	—	—	—	—
1928	—	—	—	8,051	—	—	—	—
1929	—	—	—	8,567	—	—	—	—
1930	—	—	—	7,464	—	—	—	—
1931	—	—	—	6,301	—	—	—	—
1932	—	—	—	5,351	—	—	—	—
1933	—	—	—	5,924	—	—	—	—
1934	—	—	—	6,909	—	—	—	—
1935	—	—	—	7,374	—	—	—	—
1936	—	—	—	8,014	—	—	—	—
1937	—	—	—	8,791	—	—	—	—
1938	—	—	—	7,478	—	—	—	—
1939	—	—	—	8,318	—	—	—	—
1940	—	—	—	8,940	—	—	—	—
1941	—	—	—	11,016	—	—	—	—
1942	—	—	—	12,996	—	—	—	—
1943	—	—	—	15,147	—	—	—	—
1944	—	—	—	14,740	—	—	—	—
1945	—	—	—	13,009	—	—	—	—
1946	—	—	—	12,274	—	—	—	—
1947	33,747	871	1,786	12,990	—	8,241	1,436	—
1948	34,489	906	1,954	12,910	—	8,629	1,496	—
1949	33,159	839	1,949	11,790	—	8,595	1,517	—
1950	34,349	816	2,101	12,523	—	8,742	1,565	—
1951	36,225	840	2,343	13,368	—	9,091	1,622	—
1952	36,643	801	2,360	13,359	—	9,333	1,683	—
1953	37,694	765	2,341	14,055	—	9,510	1,742	—
1954	36,276	686	2,316	12,817	—	9,456	1,807	—
1955	37,500	680	2,477	13,288	—	9,675	1,889	—
1956	38,495	702	2,653	13,436	—	9,933	1,961	—
1957	38,384	695	2,577	13,189	—	9,923	1,998	—
1958	36,608	611	2,420	11,997	—	9,736	2,029	—
1959	38,080	590	2,577	12,603	—	10,087	2,086	—
1960	38,516	570	2,497	12,586	—	10,315	2,145	—
1961	37,989	532	2,426	12,083	—	10,234	2,189	—
1962	38,979	512	2,500	12,488	—	10,400	2,237	—
1963	39,553	498	2,562	12,555	—	10,560	2,291	—
1964	40,560	497	2,637	12,781	3,490	10,869	2,346	7,939
1965	42,278	494	2,749	13,434	3,561	11,358	2,388	8,295
1966	44,249	487	2,818	14,296	3,638	11,820	2,441	8,749
1967	45,137	469	2,741	14,308	3,718	12,121	2,533	9,246
1968	46,473	461	2,822	14,514	3,757	12,542	2,651	9,727
1969	48,208	472	3,012	14,767	3,863	13,094	2,797	10,205
1970	48,156	473	2,990	14,044	3,914	13,375	2,879	10,481
1971	48,148	455	3,071	13,544	3,872	13,615	2,936	10,655
1972	49,939	475	3,257	14,045	3,943	14,135	3,024	11,059
1973	52,201	486	3,405	14,838	4,034	14,712	3,121	11,606
1974	52,809	530	3,294	14,638	4,079	14,999	3,169	12,100

Note appears at end of table

(continued)

TABLE Ba858–865 Production employees on nonagricultural payrolls, by industry: 1919–1999 [Bureau of Labor Statistics] *Continued*

	Total	Mining	Construction	Manufacturing	Transportation, communication, and public utilities	Wholesale and retail trade	Finance, insurance, and real estate services	Other private services
	Ba858	Ba859	Ba860	Ba861	Ba862	Ba863	Ba864	Ba865
Year	Thousand	Thousand	Thousand	Thousand	Thousand	Thousand	Thousand	Thousand
1975	50,991	571	2,808	13,043	3,894	15,023	3,173	12,479
1976	52,897	592	2,814	13,638	3,918	15,649	3,243	13,043
1977	55,179	618	3,021	14,135	4,008	16,316	3,397	13,683
1978	58,156	638	3,354	14,734	4,142	17,219	3,593	14,476
1979	60,367	719	3,565	15,068	4,299	17,748	3,776	15,193
1980	60,331	762	3,421	14,214	4,293	17,812	3,907	15,921
1981	60,923	841	3,261	14,020	4,283	17,958	3,999	16,562
1982	59,468	821	2,998	12,742	4,190	17,855	3,996	16,867
1983	60,028	673	3,031	12,528	4,072	18,228	4,066	17,429
1984	63,339	686	3,404	13,280	4,258	19,202	4,226	18,284
1985	65,475	658	3,655	13,084	4,335	20,028	4,410	19,305
1986	66,866	545	3,770	12,864	4,339	20,548	4,637	20,163
1987	68,771	511	3,870	12,952	4,446	21,063	4,797	21,132
1988	71,099	512	3,980	13,193	4,555	21,726	4,811	22,323
1989	73,017	493	4,035	13,230	4,655	22,243	4,829	23,532
1990	73,774	509	3,974	12,947	4,781	22,317	4,860	24,387
1991	72,631	489	3,549	12,434	4,774	21,879	4,795	24,712
1992	72,918	448	3,431	12,287	4,768	21,865	4,772	25,347
1993	74,761	431	3,589	12,341	4,862	22,251	4,908	26,380
1994	77,607	427	3,858	12,632	5,012	23,028	5,018	27,632
1995	80,125	424	3,993	12,826	5,140	23,802	4,961	28,979
1996	82,092	430	4,199	12,776	5,260	24,240	5,043	30,144
1997	84,541	450	4,415	12,907	5,366	24,692	5,193	31,518
1998	86,805	447	4,669	12,952	5,481	25,041	5,429	32,786
1999	88,911	402	4,953	12,739	5,660	25,584	5,546	34,027

[1] Data are annual averages of monthly figures.

Source

U.S. Bureau of Labor Statistics (BLS), Current Employment Statistics Program, BLS Internet site: series Ba858, eeu00500003; series Ba859, eeu10000003; series Ba860, eeu20000003; series Ba861, eeu30000003; series Ba862, eeu40000003; series Ba863, eeu50000003; series Ba864, eeu80000003; series Ba865, eeu80000003.

Documentation

See the text for Table Ba840–848 for information on the data source and series-specific details.

TABLE Ba866–879 Full-time equivalent employees, by industry: 1929–1948 [Bureau of Economic Analysis]

Contributed by Richard Sutch

					Manufacturing									
	Total	Agriculture, forestry, and fisheries	Mining	Contract construction	Durable goods	Nondurable goods	Transportation	Communications	Electric, gas, and sanitary services	Wholesale trade	Retail trade and automobile services	Finance, insurance, and real estate	Services	Government
	Ba866	Ba867	Ba868	Ba869	Ba870	Ba871	Ba872	Ba873	Ba874	Ba875	Ba876	Ba877	Ba878	Ba879
Year	Thousand	Thousand	Thousand	Thousand	Thousand	Thousand	Thousand	Thousand	Thousand	Thousand	Thousand	Thousand	Thousand	Thousand
1929	35,338	2,952	993	1,484	5,238	5,190	2,873	538	493	1,631	4,215	1,415	5,112	3,204
1930	33,249	2,770	932	1,366	4,457	4,852	2,632	530	501	1,571	3,980	1,390	4,928	3,340
1931	30,186	2,698	813	1,198	3,497	4,398	2,280	467	463	1,418	3,656	1,328	4,547	3,422
1932	26,746	2,512	672	907	2,724	3,954	1,934	421	407	1,279	3,217	1,266	4,068	3,384
1933	27,215	2,486	693	703	2,893	4,311	1,841	391	393	1,275	3,197	1,219	3,919	3,893
1934	30,440	2,482	822	806	3,587	4,777	1,910	390	409	1,406	3,576	1,242	4,280	4,752
1935	31,797	2,501	840	866	3,941	4,963	1,933	389	414	1,443	3,743	1,261	4,448	5,054
1936	34,933	2,579	897	1,104	4,460	5,185	2,046	408	442	1,550	4,034	1,305	4,748	6,174
1937	36,193	2,557	955	1,082	5,130	5,461	2,159	440	458	1,706	4,340	1,346	5,000	5,558
1938	34,499	2,445	859	1,055	4,085	5,046	1,897	418	444	1,707	4,216	1,342	4,800	6,184
1939	35,915	2,368	832	1,219	4,609	5,358	1,990	423	445	1,776	4,389	1,376	4,957	6,172
1940	37,924	2,326	927	1,285	5,367	5,515	2,072	433	465	1,840	4,686	1,422	5,274	6,310
1941	42,575	2,300	975	1,774	6,999	6,138	2,257	476	476	1,952	5,075	1,462	5,347	7,341
1942	47,538	2,226	985	2,131	8,846	6,438	2,410	501	443	1,857	4,966	1,439	5,518	9,773
1943	53,686	2,121	917	1,566	10,924	6,478	2,631	518	391	1,752	4,926	1,389	5,226	14,868
1944	54,982	1,961	879	1,110	10,722	6,328	2,817	516	371	1,771	4,896	1,364	5,165	17,137
1945	53,282	1,869	829	1,135	8,933	6,253	2,894	533	378	1,868	5,070	1,393	5,181	17,012
1946	47,068	1,937	871	1,739	7,742	6,751	2,886	649	451	2,215	6,011	1,594	5,510	8,759
1947	47,121	2,007	933	2,062	8,330	6,875	2,867	683	492	2,403	6,280	1,641	5,791	6,762
1948	48,097	2,065	981	2,278	8,309	6,967	2,854	739	528	2,428	6,477	1,670	5,982	6,812

Source

U.S. Bureau of Economic Analysis (BEA), *National Income and Product Accounts of the United States,* volume 1, *1929–58* (February 1993), Table 6.5A, pp. 115–16.

Documentation

For more recent data, see Tables Ba880–909.

These data are a by-product of the BEA program to estimate the gross domestic product of the United States. The definitions of the industries accord with the 1942 Standard Industrial Classification (SIC) system. See the Introduction to Part D for a discussion of SIC codes. Beginning with 1949, the data are based on the 1972 SIC system. Users may judge the extent of the definitional change, because the data for 1948 are given in this table using the 1942 SIC system and in Table Ba880–894 using the 1972 system. The two major changes involved moving artisan construction from services (in the 1942 system) to construction (in the 1972 system) and moving automobile services from retail trade and automobile services (in the 1942 system) to the services sector. The original sources provide finer industrial detail.

The number of full-time equivalent employees equals the number of employees on full-time schedules plus the number of employees on part-time schedules, converted to a full-time basis. The number of full-time equivalent employees in each industry is the product of the total number of employees and the ratio of average weekly hours per employee for all employees to average weekly hours per employee on full-time schedules. For each industry, only wage and salary workers are included. Proprietors, the self-employed, and unpaid family workers are excluded. Government workers (including individuals on work relief during the Great Depression) are included in series Ba878, regardless of the economic sector to which they contributed. The original source also presents data on the number of full-time and part-time workers by industry.

The SIC codes corresponding to each series are as follows: series Ba867: SIC codes 1–9; series Ba868: SIC codes 10–14; series Ba869: SIC codes 15–17; series Ba870: SIC codes 24, 25, 32–39; series Ba871: SIC codes 20–23 and 26–31; series Ba872: SIC codes 40, 42, 44–49; series Ba873: SIC code 48; series Ba874: SIC code 49; series Ba875: SIC codes 50–51; series Ba876: SIC codes 52–59; series Ba877: SIC codes 60–67; series Ba878: SIC codes 70–89; series Ba879: SIC codes 43, 91–97.

Series Ba866. Equals the sum of series Ba867–878 plus a small residual category (not shown) that is sometimes negative, representing workers in unclassifiable industries and a statistical discrepancy.

TABLE Ba880–894 Full-time equivalent employees, by industry: 1948–1987 [Bureau of Economic Analysis]

Contributed by Richard Sutch

	Total	Agriculture, forestry, and fisheries	Mining	Construction	Manufacturing: Durable goods	Manufacturing: Nondurable goods	Transportation	Communications	Electric, gas, and sanitary services	Trade: Wholesale	Trade: Retail	Finance, insurance, and real estate	Services	Government	Auto repair, services, and parking
	Ba880	Ba881	Ba882	Ba883	Ba884	Ba885	Ba886	Ba887	Ba888	Ba889	Ba890	Ba891	Ba892	Ba893	Ba894
Year	Thousand	Thousand	Thousand	Thousand	Thousand	Thousand	Thousand	Thousand	Thousand	Thousand	Thousand	Thousand	Thousand	Thousand	Thousand
1948	48,029	2,072	993	2,321	8,343	7,178	2,854	739	528	2,586	5,852	1,635	6,177	6,744	223
1949	46,769	2,000	923	2,194	7,494	6,874	2,662	736	541	2,528	5,805	1,663	6,157	7,207	208
1950	48,527	2,067	924	2,411	8,087	7,023	2,710	717	545	2,559	5,942	1,742	6,372	7,432	196
1951	52,537	1,999	937	2,668	9,090	7,162	2,868	747	555	2,715	6,275	1,826	6,483	9,267	191
1952	53,673	1,933	914	2,683	9,391	7,091	2,849	773	560	2,784	6,384	1,902	6,434	10,043	194
1953	54,612	1,882	872	2,643	10,047	7,194	2,856	801	571	2,830	6,482	1,986	6,513	10,013	193
1954	52,782	1,902	794	2,611	9,088	6,911	2,654	799	572	2,821	6,405	2,060	6,437	9,855	189
1955	53,988	1,847	798	2,734	9,487	7,003	2,699	811	577	2,891	6,570	2,163	6,801	9,745	198
1956	55,303	1,769	837	2,853	9,741	7,033	2,755	857	583	3,031	6,781	2,268	7,097	9,840	211
1957	55,724	1,747	833	2,801	9,731	7,014	2,717	876	589	3,041	6,811	2,339	7,323	10,035	219
1958	53,919	1,780	742	2,705	8,588	6,703	2,481	826	601	3,017	6,698	2,377	7,452	10,077	226
1959	55,574	1,771	710	2,838	9,160	6,900	2,504	799	594	3,069	6,900	2,426	7,694	10,343	243
1960	56,581	1,755	692	2,805	9,246	6,943	2,507	807	600	3,132	7,100	2,511	8,005	10,621	258
1961	56,479	1,763	657	2,777	8,908	6,864	2,412	796	600	3,130	7,040	2,541	8,133	10,983	260
1962	58,034	1,723	640	2,855	9,358	7,002	2,418	792	597	3,161	7,198	2,592	8,398	11,391	265
1963	58,907	1,677	623	2,939	9,473	7,011	2,407	791	597	3,193	7,364	2,666	8,639	11,599	277
1964	60,208	1,552	619	3,049	9,650	7,072	2,421	808	598	3,268	7,643	2,729	8,923	11,939	291
1965	62,633	1,476	624	3,221	10,289	7,335	2,472	844	610	3,372	7,941	2,837	9,317	12,316	306
1966	66,071	1,382	621	3,327	11,224	7,628	2,556	890	617	3,501	8,301	2,924	9,822	13,293	320
1967	67,992	1,314	604	3,301	11,332	7,736	2,593	924	628	3,585	8,541	3,074	10,369	14,006	331
1968	69,859	1,298	599	3,418	11,510	7,876	2,633	936	640	3,668	8,867	3,233	10,741	14,456	340
1969	71,718	1,274	611	3,562	11,786	8,003	2,650	1,002	651	3,782	9,180	3,387	11,136	14,716	353
1970	71,225	1,280	615	3,481	11,064	7,842	2,608	1,066	667	3,864	9,329	3,491	11,247	14,691	365
1971	70,846	1,276	602	3,538	10,445	7,642	2,553	1,065	678	3,891	9,524	3,564	11,428	14,659	379
1972	72,674	1,293	612	3,739	10,824	7,747	2,566	1,080	693	4,005	9,764	3,692	12,003	14,677	397
1973	76,034	1,368	626	4,011	11,666	7,939	2,659	1,105	711	4,230	10,281	3,896	12,680	14,886	433
1974	77,142	1,458	685	3,928	11,729	7,809	2,684	1,119	721	4,342	10,465	4,020	13,045	15,158	440
1975	75,376	1,440	739	3,442	10,488	7,295	2,547	1,099	711	4,260	10,501	4,064	13,351	15,464	444
1976	77,712	1,532	767	3,510	10,916	7,630	2,573	1,086	714	4,408	10,975	4,178	13,906	15,542	474
1977	80,417	1,490	811	3,772	11,450	7,795	2,663	1,103	729	4,574	11,481	4,361	14,541	15,670	509
1978	84,523	1,496	864	4,206	12,142	7,952	2,793	1,146	757	4,826	12,213	4,651	15,496	16,009	566
1979	87,313	1,546	937	4,459	12,613	8,000	2,898	1,207	785	5,065	12,527	4,882	16,272	16,144	600
1980	87,236	1,593	1,020	4,231	12,015	7,802	2,846	1,241	804	5,112	12,425	5,034	16,849	16,288	591
1981	88,000	1,582	1,137	4,074	11,955	7,799	2,820	1,280	832	5,237	12,541	5,163	17,477	16,165	598
1982	86,217	1,523	1,106	3,751	10,849	7,423	2,677	1,310	854	5,139	12,458	5,154	17,866	16,171	619
1983	86,774	1,636	936	3,802	10,564	7,402	2,636	1,254	861	5,104	12,821	5,295	18,478	16,055	638
1984	91,206	1,565	954	4,281	11,361	7,564	2,802	1,245	874	5,388	13,788	5,523	19,670	16,264	707
1985	93,697	1,483	910	4,592	11,325	7,462	2,873	1,218	890	5,508	14,526	5,741	20,624	16,617	780
1986	95,418	1,476	759	4,767	11,052	7,440	2,919	1,191	896	5,549	14,922	6,036	21,523	16,955	796
1987	98,190	1,564	699	4,854	11,026	7,568	3,039	1,183	902	5,687	15,490	6,294	22,708	17,242	849

Sources

U.S. Bureau of Economic Analysis (BEA), National Income and Product Accounts of the United States Internet site. The data on government employees for the years 1948 to 1958 are in error. They have been corrected by summing the component series after consultation with Robert Yuskavage at the Industry Economics Division of the BEA. Also see *National Income and Product Accounts of the United States,* volume 1, *1929–58* (February 1993), Table 6.5B, p. 117, and *National Income and Product Accounts of the United States,* volume 2, *1959–88* (September 1992), Table 6.5B, pp. 212–13.

Documentation

For more recent data, see Table Ba895–909. See also Table Ba866–879.

See the text for Table Ba866–879 for a definition and further description of these data. In this table, the definitions of the industries accord with the 1972 Standard Industrial Classification (SIC) system. See the Introduction to Part D for a discussion of SIC codes. Beginning with 1987, the data are based on the 1987 SIC system. Users may judge the extent of the definitional change, because the data for 1987 are given in this table using the 1972 SIC system and in Table Ba895–909 using the 1987 system. The original sources provide finer industrial detail.

Series Ba880. Equals the sum of series Ba881–892 plus a small residual category (not shown), which is sometimes negative, representing workers in unclassifiable industries and a statistical discrepancy.

The SIC codes corresponding to each series are as follows: series Ba881: SIC72 codes 1–9; series Ba882: SIC72 codes 10–14; series Ba883: SIC72 codes 15–17; series Ba884: SIC72 codes 24, 25, and 32–39; series Ba885: SIC72 codes 20–23 and 26–31; series Ba886: SIC72 codes 40–42 and 44–47; series Ba887: SIC72 code 48; series Ba888: SIC72 code 49; series Ba889: SIC72 codes 50 and 51; series Ba890: SIC72 codes 52–59; series Ba891: SIC72 codes 60–67; series Ba892: SIC72 codes 70–89, including SIC72 code 75, auto repair, services, and parking (Series Ba894); series Ba893: SIC72 codes 43 and 91–97.

Series Ba894. This industry – auto repair, services, and parking (SIC72 code 75) – is included as an addendum so that users who wish to link data in this table with the data in Table Ba866–879 may remove auto services from the services industry and add it to the retail trade industry, thus making the data more directly comparable with that for 1929–1947.

TABLE Ba895–909 Full-time equivalent employees, by industry: 1987–1998 [Bureau of Economic Analysis]

Contributed by Richard Sutch

					Manufacturing						Trade					
	Total	Agriculture, forestry, and fisheries	Mining	Construction	Durable goods	Nondurable goods	Trans-portation	Communi-cations	Electric, gas, and sanitary services	Wholesale	Retail	Finance, insurance, and real estate	Services	Government	Auto repair, services, and parking
	Ba895	Ba896	Ba897	Ba898	Ba899	Ba900	Ba901	Ba902	Ba903	Ba904	Ba905	Ba906	Ba907	Ba908	Ba909
Year	Thousand	Thousand	Thousand	Thousand	Thousand	Thousand	Thousand	Thousand	Thousand	Thousand	Thousand	Thousand	Thousand	Thousand	Thousand
1987	98,178	1,564	699	4,854	10,993	7,597	3,037	1,183	904	5,707	15,468	6,302	22,699	17,237	849
1988	101,047	1,665	709	5,015	11,233	7,702	3,169	1,181	912	5,841	15,981	6,382	23,690	17,642	886
1989	103,754	1,625	684	5,093	11,239	7,749	3,272	1,163	916	6,064	16,472	6,422	25,093	18,045	922
1990	104,908	1,618	701	5,040	10,959	7,720	3,305	1,208	937	6,013	16,560	6,496	26,093	18,340	955
1991	103,356	1,614	680	4,578	10,417	7,589	3,278	1,187	944	5,851	16,124	6,446	26,347	18,383	909
1992	103,540	1,581	626	4,405	10,129	7,542	3,268	1,159	942	5,856	16,258	6,369	27,166	18,327	911
1993	105,096	1,623	601	4,563	10,077	7,585	3,408	1,163	931	5,787	16,692	6,501	28,311	18,261	962
1994	107,977	1,679	593	4,883	10,335	7,675	3,556	1,182	918	5,971	17,308	6,620	29,461	18,248	1,005
1995	111,017	1,760	575	5,180	10,561	7,629	3,684	1,197	896	6,201	18,030	6,552	30,868	18,335	1,061
1996	113,300	1,789	571	5,444	10,664	7,504	3,783	1,229	872	6,280	18,383	6,637	32,232	18,328	1,136
1997	116,213	1,839	589	5,752	10,880	7,470	3,886	1,293	858	6,458	18,759	6,796	33,674	18,415	1,182
1998	119,317	1,972	581	6,074	11,100	7,413	4,034	1,341	844	6,627	19,065	7,027	35,151	18,550	1,214

Sources

U.S. Bureau of Economic Analysis (BEA), National Income and Product Accounts of the United States Internet site. Also see BEA, *National Income and Product Accounts of the United States,* volume 2, *1959–88* (September 1992), Table 6.5C, p. 212.

Updated from time to time in the BEA's *Survey of Current Business* (monthly periodical).

Documentation

See the text to Table Ba866–879 for a definition and further description of these data. In this table, the definitions of the industries accord with the 1987 Standard Industrial Classification (SIC) system. See the Introduction to Part D for a discussion of SIC codes. The data in Table Ba880–894 define the industries using the 1972 SIC system. Users may judge the extent of the definitional change by comparing the tables, because the data for 1987 is given in this table using the 1987 SIC system and in Table Ba895–909 using the 1972 system. The original sources provide finer industrial detail.

The SIC codes corresponding to each series are as follows: series Ba896: SIC87 codes 1–9; series Ba897: SIC87 codes 10–14; series Ba898: SIC87 codes 15–17; series Ba899: SIC87 codes 24, 25, and 32–39; series Ba900: SIC87 codes 20–23 and 26–31; series Ba901: SIC87 codes 40–42 and 44–47; series Ba902: SIC87 code 48; series Ba903: SIC87 code 49; series Ba904: SIC87 codes 50 and 51; series Ba905: SIC87 codes 52–59; series Ba906: SIC87 codes 60–67; series Ba907: SIC87 codes 70–89, including code 75, auto repair, services, and parking (series Ba909); series Ba908: SIC87 codes 43 and 91–97.

Series Ba895. Equals the sum of series Ba896–908 plus a residual (not shown).

Series Ba909. This industry – auto repair, services, and parking (SIC87 code 75) – is included as an addendum so that users who wish to link data in this table with the data in Table Ba866–879 may remove auto services from the services industry and add it to the retail trade industry, thus making the data more directly comparable with that for 1929–1947.

TABLE Ba910–921 Self-employed persons, unpaid family workers, and domestic service employees by industry: 1900–1960[1] [Lebergott]

Contributed by Susan B. Carter and Richard Sutch

	Self-employed persons								Unpaid family workers			
	Total	Farm	Nonfarm	Construction	Manufacturing	Trade	Service	Nonfarm not elsewhere classified	Total	Farm	Nonfarm	Domestic service employees
	Ba910	Ba911	Ba912	Ba913	Ba914	Ba915	Ba916	Ba917	Ba918	Ba919	Ba920	Ba921
Year	Thousand	Thousand	Thousand	Thousand	Thousand	Thousand	Thousand	Thousand	Thousand	Thousand	Thousand	Thousand
1900	9,642	5,830	3,812	481	427	1,337	1,132	435	3,011	2,840	171	1,800
1901	9,854	5,906	3,948	543	437	1,360	1,170	438	2,968	2,784	184	1,829
1902	10,031	5,942	4,089	608	447	1,384	1,208	442	2,913	2,728	185	1,858
1903	10,127	5,978	4,149	597	456	1,409	1,243	444	2,864	2,672	192	1,886
1904	10,207	6,014	4,193	570	466	1,433	1,277	447	2,805	2,616	189	1,915
1905	10,323	6,050	4,273	580	476	1,458	1,311	448	2,756	2,560	196	1,944
1906	10,467	6,086	4,381	619	485	1,484	1,341	452	2,714	2,504	210	1,973
1907	10,609	6,122	4,487	656	495	1,510	1,371	455	2,656	2,448	208	2,002
1908	10,683	6,158	4,525	626	504	1,537	1,398	460	2,585	2,392	193	2,030
1909	10,772	6,194	4,578	624	504	1,564	1,425	461	2,544	2,336	208	2,059
1910	10,873	6,230	4,643	634	504	1,591	1,450	464	2,483	2,280	203	2,090
1911	10,912	6,266	4,646	608	504	1,598	1,472	464	2,422	2,206	216	2,090
1912	10,987	6,302	4,685	619	505	1,606	1,486	469	2,371	2,142	229	2,090
1913	11,101	6,338	4,763	667	505	1,613	1,510	468	2,308	2,072	236	2,090
1914	11,143	6,374	4,769	644	505	1,621	1,530	469	2,233	2,004	229	2,090
1915	11,117	6,410	4,707	591	504	1,628	1,512	472	2,162	1,937	225	1,982
1916	11,137	6,446	4,691	586	498	1,636	1,493	478	2,111	1,867	244	1,875
1917	11,128	6,475	4,653	580	494	1,643	1,471	465	2,024	1,790	234	1,768
1918	11,069	6,504	4,565	531	489	1,651	1,447	447	1,911	1,690	221	1,660
1919	10,986	6,533	4,453	446	488	1,658	1,431	430	1,807	1,582	225	1,660
1920	11,021	6,560	4,461	487	488	1,666	1,407	413	1,763	1,550	213	1,660
1921	10,956	6,509	4,447	478	429	1,706	1,420	414	1,756	1,550	206	1,736
1922	11,010	6,455	4,555	524	406	1,747	1,420	458	1,787	1,547	240	1,813
1923	11,125	6,403	4,722	617	383	1,789	1,436	497	1,805	1,545	260	1,889
1924	11,149	6,348	4,801	654	361	1,833	1,456	497	1,810	1,542	268	1,965
1925	11,178	6,296	4,882	685	338	1,877	1,475	507	1,819	1,545	274	2,042
1926	11,229	6,244	4,985	717	338	1,922	1,498	510	1,791	1,515	276	2,118
1927	11,243	6,197	5,046	718	339	1,968	1,506	515	1,749	1,475	274	2,194
1928	11,254	6,165	5,089	688	339	2,016	1,519	527	1,758	1,485	273	2,270
1929	11,298	6,162	5,136	677	341	2,064	1,541	513	1,758	1,488	270	2,423
1930	11,203	6,150	5,053	561	322	2,114	1,534	522	1,750	1,480	270	2,270
1931	11,119	6,160	4,959	531	286	2,073	1,556	513	1,788	1,520	268	2,043
1932	10,910	6,180	4,730	395	235	1,942	1,671	487	1,829	1,560	269	1,762
1933	10,864	6,180	4,684	303	224	2,036	1,654	467	1,854	1,580	274	1,677
1934	10,858	6,160	4,698	349	237	2,067	1,544	501	1,848	1,580	268	1,897
1935	10,895	6,140	4,755	377	246	2,081	1,539	512	1,910	1,640	270	1,989
1936	11,014	6,020	4,994	489	265	2,160	1,552	528	1,889	1,610	279	2,132
1937	11,021	5,880	5,141	479	296	2,239	1,585	542	1,886	1,590	296	2,262
1938	10,861	5,730	5,131	467	287	2,270	1,574	533	1,879	1,590	289	2,093
1939	10,913	5,610	5,303	548	316	2,328	1,590	521	1,895	1,600	295	2,227
1940	10,870	5,480	5,390	582	324	2,344	1,589	551	1,880	1,580	300	2,300
1941	10,460	5,160	5,300	526	339	2,333	1,566	536	2,050	1,710	340	2,100
1942	9,690	4,580	5,110	485	346	2,224	1,560	495	2,450	2,080	370	2,150
1943	9,212	4,530	4,682	416	353	1,966	1,440	507	2,700	2,300	400	1,820
1944	9,398	4,740	4,658	392	360	1,935	1,440	531	2,610	2,210	400	1,730
1945	9,669	4,680	4,989	439	372	2,049	1,570	559	2,540	2,140	400	1,680
1946	10,393	4,810	5,583	583	415	2,266	1,750	569	2,240	1,840	400	1,575
1947	11,017	4,973	6,044	695	447	2,377	1,960	565	2,043	1,616	427	1,714
1948	10,810	4,671	6,139	695	466	2,490	1,921	567	1,957	1,556	401	1,731
1949	10,826	4,618	6,208	687	425	2,657	1,908	531	1,959	1,563	396	1,772
1950	10,415	4,346	6,069	696	407	2,562	1,883	521	1,831	1,427	404	1,995
1951	9,890	4,022	5,868	691	417	2,445	1,765	550	1,786	1,386	400	2,055
1952	9,606	3,936	5,670	687	390	2,359	1,759	475	1,773	1,342	431	1,922
1953	9,568	3,821	5,747	655	385	2,409	1,761	537	1,696	1,273	423	1,920
1954	9,701	3,821	5,880	699	424	2,481	1,745	531	1,675	1,230	445	1,919

Note appears at end of table

TABLE Ba910–921 Self-employed persons, unpaid family workers, and domestic service employees by industry: 1900–1960 [Lebergott] *Continued*

	Self-employed persons								Unpaid family workers			
	Total	Farm	Nonfarm	Construction	Manufacturing	Trade	Service	Nonfarm not elsewhere classified	Total	Farm	Nonfarm	Domestic service employees
	Ba910	Ba911	Ba912	Ba913	Ba914	Ba915	Ba916	Ba917	Ba918	Ba919	Ba920	Ba921
Year	Thousand	Thousand	Thousand	Thousand	Thousand	Thousand	Thousand	Thousand	Thousand	Thousand	Thousand	Thousand
1955	9,617	3,731	5,886	727	423	2,378	1,784	574	1,823	1,299	524	2,216
1956	9,506	3,570	5,936	708	435	2,403	1,806	584	1,904	1,323	581	2,359
1957	9,394	3,304	6,090	736	430	2,465	1,875	584	1,857	1,231	626	2,328
1958	9,272	3,087	6,185	745	408	2,449	1,984	599	1,691	1,086	605	2,456
1959	9,325	3,027	6,298	769	393	2,431	2,083	622	1,718	1,121	597	2,520
1960	9,169	2,802	6,367	758	383	2,443	2,175	608	1,669	1,054	615	2,489

[1] Persons age 14 and older.

Sources

Stanley Lebergott, *Manpower in Economic Growth: The American Record since 1800* (McGraw-Hill, 1964), Tables A-4 and A-7. David R. Weir, "A Century of U.S. Unemployment, 1890–1990: Revised Estimates and Evidence for Stabilization," in Roger L. Ransom, Richard Sutch, et al., editors, *Research in Economic History*, volume 14 (JAI Press, 1992), Table C1.

Documentation

The self-employed are persons who work for profit or fees in their own business, farm, profession, or trade. Only unincorporated self-employed persons are included because technically, self-employed persons who have incorporated their businesses are employees of their corporation. Unpaid family workers are persons working without pay for fifteen hours a week or more on a farm or in a business operated by a member of the household to whom they are related by birth or marriage. Domestic service employees are wage or salary employees of private nonfarm households, such as housecleaners, chauffeurs, gardeners, and servants.

Employed civilians are partitioned into four subcategories: employees of establishments, the self-employed, unpaid family workers, and domestic service employees. This table provides data on the last three categories. For employees of establishments, see Table Ba840–848.

The original estimates of these series were made by Lebergott (1964, pp. 364–84, 419–20). They were intended to be comparable with the concepts used by the Current Population Survey (CPS). See Table Ba922–933. Lebergott's self-employment figures for construction and trade from 1900 to 1930 were revised by Weir, who accepted the estimates made by Lebergott for the other sectors. Because of Weir's revision to construction and trade, the total given here for 1900–1930 is his. Lebergott's estimates for the period 1900–1946 were designed to be comparable with those of the U.S. Bureau of Labor Statistics (BLS) CPS data. He linked his estimates directly to unpublished BLS estimates for 1947–1960. Since the time that Lebergott prepared his estimates, the BLS has revised its own series and now reports data for those age 16 and older instead of 14 and older. See Tables Ba922–969 for the latest BLS estimates. Because of changes by the BLS, Lebergott's data no longer make a clean splice at 1947.

Lebergott defines the farm sector, construction, and manufacturing in a manner consistent with the BLS's CPS estimates. He defines "trade" as the sum of wholesale and retail trade (excluding automobile services). His definition of the service sector departs from the BLS practice by excluding the self-employed in forestry and fisheries.

TABLE Ba922–933 Self-employed persons, unpaid family workers, and private household employees, by industry: 1948–1999[1] [Current Population Survey]

Contributed by Richard Sutch

	Self-employed persons								Unpaid family workers			
			Nonagriculture									
	Total	Agriculture	Total	Construction	Manufacturing	Trade	Service except private households	Private household service	Total	Agriculture	Nonagriculture	Private household employees
	Ba922	Ba923 [2]	Ba924	Ba925	Ba926	Ba927	Ba928	Ba929	Ba930	Ba931	Ba932	Ba933
Year	Thousand	Thousand	Thousand	Thousand	Thousand	Thousand	Thousand	Thousand	Thousand	Thousand	Thousand	Thousand
1948	10,775	4,665	6,110	—	—	—	—	—	1,701	1,317	384	1,619
1949	10,776	4,609	6,167	—	—	—	—	—	1,700	1,321	379	1,657
1950	10,359	4,340	6,019	—	—	—	—	—	1,573	1,190	383	1,862
1951	9,821	4,017	5,804	—	—	—	—	—	1,546	1,163	383	1,911
1952	9,547	3,933	5,614	—	—	—	—	—	1,546	1,129	417	1,785
1953	9,556	3,816	5,740	—	—	—	—	—	1,478	1,069	409	1,868
1954	9,656	3,817	5,839	—	—	—	—	—	1,475	1,044	431	1,791
1955	9,577	3,726	5,851	—	—	—	—	—	1,634	1,123	511	2,054
1956	9,459	3,563	5,896	—	—	—	—	—	1,701	1,142	559	2,153
1957	9,312	3,301	6,011	—	—	—	—	—	1,667	1,065	602	2,102
1958	9,184	3,082	6,102	—	—	—	—	—	1,528	941	587	2,200
1959	9,242	3,020	6,222	—	—	—	—	—	1,542	963	579	2,228

Notes appear at end of table

(continued)

TABLE Ba922–933 Self-employed persons, unpaid family workers, and private household employees, by industry: 1948–1999 [Current Population Survey] *Continued*

	Self-employed persons								Unpaid family workers			
			Nonagriculture									
	Total	Agriculture	Total	Construction	Manufacturing	Trade	Service except private households	Private household service	Total	Agriculture	Nonagriculture	Private household employees
	Ba922	Ba923 [2]	Ba924	Ba925	Ba926	Ba927	Ba928	Ba929	Ba930	Ba931	Ba932	Ba933
Year	Thousand	Thousand	Thousand	Thousand	Thousand	Thousand	Thousand	Thousand	Thousand	Thousand	Thousand	Thousand
1960	9,098	2,795	6,303	—	—	—	—	—	1,499	901	598	2,183
1961	9,045	2,737	6,308	—	—	—	—	—	1,472	833	639	2,233
1962	8,802	2,609	6,193	—	—	—	—	—	1,376	773	603	2,216
1963	8,541	2,427	6,114	—	—	—	—	—	1,269	696	573	2,226
1964	8,536	2,357	6,179	—	—	—	—	—	1,272	696	576	2,262
1965	8,394	2,297	6,097	—	—	—	—	—	1,278	678	600	2,165
1966	8,127	2,136	5,991	—	—	—	—	—	1,142	578	564	2,069
1967	7,170	1,996	5,174	—	—	—	—	—	1,052	547	505	1,966
1968	7,087	1,985	5,102	—	—	—	—	—	1,035	550	485	1,916
1969	7,148	1,896	5,252	—	—	—	—	—	1,048	531	517	1,826
1970	7,031	1,810	5,221	—	—	—	—	—	1,001	499	502	1,755
1971	7,077	1,750	5,327	—	—	—	—	—	1,001	479	522	1,696
1972	7,157	1,792	5,365	746	244	1,688	2,178	30	986	467	519	1,660
1973	7,255	1,780	5,474	810	260	1,669	2,184	41	962	422	540	1,551
1974	7,455	1,758	5,697	874	261	1,728	2,254	38	880	391	489	1,403
1975	7,427	1,722	5,705	839	273	1,709	2,280	30	869	386	483	1,362
1976	7,428	1,646	5,783	877	286	1,688	2,338	25	806	342	464	1,374
1977	7,694	1,580	6,114	950	305	1,758	2,487	31	841	343	498	1,395
1978	8,047	1,618	6,429	1,091	322	1,765	2,547	34	795	316	479	1,384
1979	8,384	1,593	6,791	1,152	339	1,853	2,642	62	767	304	463	1,264
1980	8,643	1,642	7,000	1,173	358	1,899	2,741	64	711	297	413	1,192
1981	8,735	1,638	7,097	1,152	362	1,885	2,860	66	656	266	390	1,208
1982	8,898	1,636	7,262	1,117	353	1,870	3,032	61	661	261	401	1,207
1983	9,143	1,565	7,575	1,158	371	1,932	3,224	9	616	240	376	1,247
1984	9,338	1,553	7,785	1,235	360	1,920	3,379	4	548	213	335	1,238
1985	9,269	1,458	7,811	1,301	347	1,792	3,471	6	474	185	289	1,249
1986	9,327	1,447	7,881	1,369	371	1,787	3,449	6	423	169	255	1,235
1987	9,624	1,423	8,201	1,384	354	1,841	3,655	8	413	153	260	1,208
1988	9,917	1,398	8,519	1,427	394	1,823	3,868	10	409	150	260	1,153
1989	10,008	1,403	8,605	1,423	406	1,882	3,917	8	410	131	279	1,101
1990	10,097	1,378	8,719	1,457	427	1,851	4,021	9	358	105	253	1,027
1991	10,274	1,423	8,851	1,442	418	1,873	4,160	6	343	118	226	1,010
1992	9,960	1,385	8,575	1,460	390	1,770	3,965	10	345	112	233	1,135
1993	10,280	1,320	8,959	1,549	439	1,886	4,033	8	324	106	218	1,126
1994	10,648	1,645	9,003	1,506	426	1,906	4,132	10	180	49	131	966
1995	10,482	1,580	8,902	1,460	433	1,772	4,158	8	156	45	110	963
1996	10,490	1,518	8,971	1,496	406	1,760	4,182	7	178	56	122	928
1997	10,513	1,457	9,056	1,492	422	1,761	4,294	6	171	51	120	915
1998	10,303	1,341	8,962	1,519	428	1,640	4,311	5	141	38	103	962
1999	10,087	1,297	8,790	1,545	380	1,621	4,131	7	135	40	95	933

[1] Persons age 16 and over.

[2] Excludes forestry and fishing.

Sources

U.S. Bureau of Labor Statistics (BLS), "Labor Force Statistics from the Current Population Survey," and the BLS Internet site. See also the periodical *Employment and Earnings*, published monthly with updates by the BLS.

Documentation

Employed civilians are partitioned into four subcategories: employees of establishments, the self-employed, unpaid family workers, and domestic service employees. This table provides data on the last three categories. For employees of establishments, see Table Ba840–848. See Table Ba910–921 for the definitions and description of the data. This table is organized to facilitate the linkage with Table Ba910–921 that is based on work by Stanley Lebergott. Agriculture and nonagriculture are comparable to Lebergott's farm and nonfarm sectors. The service sector reported here, however, departs from the BLS practice by excluding the self-employed in forestry and fisheries, who are included instead in other nonagriculture self-employment. Industrial detail for the self-employed and the series on wage and salary workers in private households are not available for the period before 1972.

TABLE Ba934–945 Self-employed persons, by industry: 1929–1948 [Bureau of Economic Analysis]

Contributed by Richard Sutch

	Total	Farms	Agricultural services, forestry, and fisheries	Mining	Contract construction	Manufacturing		Transportation, communications, and public utilities	Wholesale trade	Retail trade and automobile services	Finance, insurance, and real estate	Services
						Durable goods	Nondurable goods					
	Ba934	Ba935	Ba936	Ba937	Ba938	Ba939	Ba940	Ba941	Ba942	Ba943	Ba944	Ba945
Year	Thousand	Thousand	Thousand	Thousand	Thousand	Thousand	Thousand	Thousand	Thousand	Thousand	Thousand	Thousand
1929	10,320	5,566	109	24	822	44	84	164	113	1,862	160	1,372
1930	10,311	5,566	105	24	817	34	75	166	114	1,859	161	1,390
1931	10,352	5,663	110	26	785	24	64	167	115	1,851	160	1,387
1932	10,350	5,760	98	29	737	18	50	169	116	1,841	157	1,375
1933	10,371	5,857	95	31	680	19	50	170	118	1,841	154	1,356
1934	10,493	5,954	87	35	654	23	54	170	124	1,855	159	1,378
1935	10,645	6,051	99	36	648	26	53	172	129	1,865	164	1,402
1936	10,567	5,871	94	37	659	28	59	175	140	1,915	170	1,419
1937	10,495	5,691	119	38	656	28	67	177	151	1,965	174	1,429
1938	10,338	5,511	110	38	631	28	70	179	150	2,002	178	1,441
1939	10,266	5,331	111	38	645	39	80	182	166	2,051	184	1,439
1940	10,150	5,153	110	38	656	45	82	187	175	2,082	189	1,433
1941	10,090	5,078	108	40	675	52	85	195	184	2,051	185	1,437
1942	9,947	5,003	112	36	728	56	90	183	184	1,950	197	1,408
1943	9,431	4,928	105	32	606	60	94	166	160	1,722	186	1,372
1944	9,273	4,853	117	26	536	65	103	152	165	1,702	197	1,357
1945	9,349	4,780	117	26	565	75	99	134	184	1,792	209	1,368
1946	9,913	4,649	127	30	812	84	104	164	204	1,962	219	1,558
1947	10,199	4,518	132	35	945	92	99	189	217	2,096	223	1,653
1948	10,211	4,410	143	35	984	248	192	197	253	1,999	220	1,530

Source

U.S. Bureau of Economic Analysis (BEA), *National Income and Product Accounts of the United States,* volume 1, *1929–58* (February 1993), Table 6.7A, p. 121.

Documentation

For more recent data, see Tables Ba946–969.

Self-employed persons are active proprietors or partners who devote a majority of their working hours to their unincorporated business. Unpaid family workers are excluded. These data are by-products of the BEA program to estimate the gross domestic product of the United States. The definitions of the industries accord with the 1942 Standard Industrial Classification (SIC) system. See the Introduction to Part D for a discussion of SIC codes. Beginning with 1949, the data are based on the 1972 SIC system. Users may judge the extent of the definitional change, because the data for 1948 given in this table use the 1942 SIC system and in Table Ba946–957 use the 1972 system. The two major changes involved moving artisan construction from services (in the 1942 system) to construction (in the 1972 system) and moving automobile services from retail trade and automobile services (in the 1942 system) to the services sector (in the 1972 system).

TABLE Ba946–957 Self-employed persons, by industry: 1948–1987 [Bureau of Economic Analysis]

Contributed by Richard Sutch

	Total	Farms	Agricultural services, forestry, and fisheries	Mining	Construction	Manufacturing: Durable goods	Manufacturing: Nondurable goods	Transportation	Wholesale trade	Retail trade	Finance, insurance, and real estate	Services
	Ba946	Ba947	Ba948	Ba949	Ba950	Ba951	Ba952	Ba953	Ba954	Ba955	Ba956	Ba957
Year	Thousand	Thousand	Thousand	Thousand	Thousand	Thousand	Thousand	Thousand	Thousand	Thousand	Thousand	Thousand
1948	10,211	4,410	143	35	984	248	192	197	253	1,999	220	1,530
1949	10,064	4,302	138	33	961	233	176	196	255	2,034	205	1,531
1950	9,996	4,194	141	33	1,004	230	168	200	259	2,029	199	1,539
1951	9,699	3,879	144	35	960	246	167	207	265	2,027	219	1,550
1952	9,637	3,794	152	35	918	254	168	208	272	2,025	239	1,572
1953	9,475	3,660	154	36	885	253	158	210	273	2,001	261	1,584
1954	9,329	3,658	153	39	783	231	148	201	271	1,974	289	1,582
1955	9,149	3,530	148	37	729	222	140	196	273	2,023	270	1,581
1956	8,981	3,336	146	36	727	213	134	194	276	2,039	257	1,623
1957	8,821	3,120	143	36	724	204	128	195	277	2,056	255	1,683
1958	8,611	2,928	140	33	692	195	120	191	278	2,077	251	1,706
1959	8,428	2,795	138	32	695	191	120	186	282	2,011	242	1,736
1960	8,305	2,639	137	29	686	190	119	186	289	1,975	243	1,812
1961	8,177	2,542	137	28	684	186	117	185	289	1,894	243	1,872
1962	8,009	2,450	137	26	686	181	117	182	287	1,787	244	1,912
1963	7,722	2,264	138	24	680	176	116	181	287	1,655	243	1,958
1964	7,652	2,171	139	23	679	171	113	181	287	1,651	240	1,997
1965	7,526	2,096	141	20	682	169	109	182	276	1,624	238	1,989
1966	7,271	1,909	141	19	658	165	95	177	281	1,532	242	2,052
1967	7,188	1,885	139	20	664	172	95	185	264	1,432	258	2,074
1968	7,115	1,866	139	19	666	162	94	185	252	1,392	260	2,080
1969	7,199	1,778	141	15	694	166	102	185	259	1,416	266	2,177
1970	7,097	1,692	146	14	698	172	99	189	259	1,437	258	2,133
1971	7,142	1,638	151	15	723	168	81	202	263	1,480	272	2,149
1972	7,234	1,662	161	13	760	167	81	207	247	1,472	267	2,197
1973	7,316	1,646	167	15	824	167	99	195	262	1,436	306	2,199
1974	7,527	1,627	170	16	888	175	91	220	275	1,483	314	2,268
1975	7,506	1,571	180	16	854	177	102	227	261	1,478	341	2,299
1976	7,495	1,498	180	24	890	183	110	221	282	1,432	329	2,346
1977	7,758	1,439	176	20	963	201	111	222	258	1,527	347	2,494
1978	8,118	1,455	207	21	1,107	206	124	248	248	1,545	408	2,549
1979	8,416	1,419	218	21	1,167	213	133	278	280	1,597	451	2,639
1980	8,658	1,458	224	28	1,186	221	142	282	294	1,628	463	2,732
1981	8,753	1,456	222	26	1,166	221	145	298	297	1,612	456	2,854
1982	8,923	1,414	263	34	1,131	215	143	308	284	1,610	496	3,025
1983	9,213	1,333	264	29	1,171	220	155	325	320	1,634	539	3,223
1984	9,412	1,318	268	25	1,248	217	147	321	326	1,614	550	3,378
1985	9,327	1,214	281	20	1,312	214	137	318	308	1,499	563	3,461
1986	9,369	1,185	303	26	1,370	223	161	319	297	1,512	557	3,416
1987	9,665	1,142	335	27	1,386	213	155	336	315	1,549	598	3,609

Sources

U.S. Bureau of Economic Analysis (BEA), National Income and Product Accounts of the United States Internet site. Also see BEA, *National Income and Product Accounts of the United States,* volume 1, *1929–58* (February 1993), Table 6.7B, p. 121, and *National Income and Product Accounts of the United States,* volume 2, *1959–88* (September 1992), Table 6.7B, p. 218.

Documentation

For more recent data, see Table Ba958-969. Also see Table Ba934-945.

See the text for Table Ba934-945 for a definition and further description of these data. In this table, the definitions of the industries accord with the 1972 Standard Industrial Classification (SIC) system. See the Introduction to Part D for a discussion of SIC codes. Beginning with 1987, the data are based on the 1987 SIC system. Users may judge the extent of the definitional change, because the data for 1987 given in this table use the 1972 SIC system and in Table Ba958-969 use the 1987 system. The original source provides finer industrial detail.

The SIC codes corresponding to each series are as follows: series Ba947: SIC72 codes 1 and 2; series Ba948: SIC72 codes 7–9; series Ba949: SIC72 codes 10–14; series Ba950: SIC72 codes 15–17; series Ba951: SIC72 codes 24, 25, and 32–39; series Ba952: SIC72 codes 20–23 and 26–31; series Ba953: SIC72 codes 40–42 and 44–47; series Ba954: SIC72 codes 50 and 51; series Ba955: SIC72 codes 52–59; series Ba956: SIC72 codes 60–67; series Ba957: SIC72 codes 70–89, including SIC72 code 75, auto repair, services, and parking.

Series Ba946. Equals the sum of series Ba947–957 plus a small residual category (not shown), which is sometimes negative, representing workers in unclassifiable industries and a statistical discrepancy.

TABLE Ba958–969 Self-employed persons, by industry: 1987–1998 [Bureau of Economic Analysis]

Contributed by Richard Sutch

						Manufacturing			Trade			
	Total	Farms	Agricultural services, forestry, and fisheries	Mining	Construction	Durable goods	Nondurable goods	Transportation	Wholesale	Retail	Finance, insurance, and real estate	Services
	Ba958	Ba959	Ba960	Ba961	Ba962	Ba963	Ba964	Ba965	Ba966	Ba967	Ba968	Ba969
	Thousand	Thousand	Thousand	Thousand	Thousand	Thousand	Thousand	Thousand	Thousand	Thousand	Thousand	Thousand
1987	9,665	1,142	335	27	1,386	213	155	336	315	1,549	598	3,609
1988	9,956	1,118	320	29	1,438	231	167	344	337	1,498	624	3,850
1989	10,041	1,085	349	25	1,433	246	163	323	349	1,548	621	3,899
1990	10,132	1,058	379	24	1,473	258	174	304	334	1,539	634	3,955
1991	10,373	1,082	397	23	1,457	253	168	318	350	1,544	618	4,163
1992	10,040	1,061	371	23	1,471	247	151	335	349	1,439	630	3,963
1993	10,505	1,066	387	17	1,566	264	183	373	354	1,569	661	4,065
1994	10,564	1,071	403	14	1,523	247	185	381	353	1,590	631	4,166
1995	10,514	1,224	396	16	1,470	255	181	395	354	1,432	659	4,132
1996	10,524	1,114	435	15	1,506	247	161	434	307	1,468	673	4,164
1997	10,544	1,063	419	14	1,502	254	170	436	277	1,499	628	4,282
1998	10,232	951	415	20	1,529	255	176	429	292	1,354	609	4,202

Sources

U.S. Bureau of Economic Analysis (BEA), National Income and Product Accounts of the United States Internet site. Also see *National Income and Product Accounts of the United States,* volume 2, *1959–88* (September 1992), Table 6.7B, p. 218.

Series are updated from time to time in the BEA's *Survey of Current Business* (monthly periodical).

Documentation

For earlier data, see Tables Ba934–957.

See the notes to Table Ba934–945 for a definition and further description of these data. In this table, the definitions of the industries accord with the 1987 Standard Industrial Classification (SIC) system. See the Introduction to Part D for a discussion of SIC codes. Before 1987, the data were based on the 1972 SIC system. Users may judge the extent of the definitional change, because the data for 1987 given in this table use the 1987 SIC system and in Table Ba946–957 use the 1972 system. The original source provides finer industrial detail.

The SIC codes corresponding to each series are as follows: series Ba959: SIC87 codes 1 and 2; series Ba960: SIC87 codes 7–9; series Ba961: SIC87 codes 10–14; series Ba962: SIC87 codes 15–17; series Ba963: SIC87 codes 24, 25, and 32–39; series Ba964: SIC87 codes 20–23 and 26–31; series Ba965: SIC87 codes 40–42 and 44–47; series Ba966: SIC87 codes 50 and 51; series Ba967: SIC87 codes 52–59; series Ba968: SIC87 codes 60–67; series Ba969: SIC87 codes 70–89.

Series Ba958. Equals the sum of series Ba959–969 plus a small residual category (not shown), which is sometimes negative, representing workers in unclassifiable industries and a statistical discrepancy.

TABLE Ba970–983 Self-employed workers, by sex and industry: 1948–2000[1, 2]

Contributed by Susan B. Carter

	Self-employed workers											Self-employment rate		
				Industry										
	Total	Male	Female	Agricultural	Nonagricultural	Construction	Manufacturing	Transportation, communications, and other public utilities	Trade	Finance, insurance, and real estate	Services	Overall	Male	Female
	Ba970	Ba971	Ba972	Ba973	Ba974	Ba975	Ba976	Ba977	Ba978	Ba979	Ba980	Ba981	Ba982	Ba983
Year	Thousand	Thousand	Thousand	Thousand	Thousand	Thousand	Thousand	Thousand	Thousand	Thousand	Thousand	Percent	Percent	Percent
1948	10,775	—	—	4,665	6,110	—	—	—	—	—	—	17.8	—	—
1949	10,776	—	—	4,609	6,167	—	—	—	—	—	—	18.7	—	—
1950	10,359	—	—	4,340	6,019	—	—	—	—	—	—	17.6	—	—
1951	9,821	—	—	4,017	5,804	—	—	—	—	—	—	16.4	—	—
1952	9,547	—	—	3,933	5,614	—	—	—	—	—	—	15.8	—	—
1953	9,556	—	—	3,816	5,740	—	—	—	—	—	—	15.6	—	—
1954	9,656	—	—	3,817	5,839	—	—	—	—	—	—	16.1	—	—
1955	9,577	—	—	3,726	5,851	—	—	—	—	—	—	15.4	—	—
1956	9,459	—	—	3,563	5,896	—	—	—	—	—	—	14.8	—	—
1957	9,312	—	—	3,301	6,011	—	—	—	—	—	—	14.5	—	—
1958	9,184	—	—	3,082	6,102	—	—	—	—	—	—	14.6	—	—
1959	9,242	—	—	3,020	6,222	—	—	—	—	—	—	14.3	—	—
1960	9,098	—	—	2,795	6,303	—	—	—	—	—	—	13.8	—	—
1961	9,045	—	—	2,737	6,308	—	—	—	—	—	—	13.8	—	—
1962	8,802	—	—	2,609	6,193	—	—	—	—	—	—	13.2	—	—
1963	8,541	—	—	2,427	6,114	—	—	—	—	—	—	12.6	—	—
1964	8,536	—	—	2,357	6,179	—	—	—	—	—	—	12.3	—	—
1965	8,394	—	—	2,297	6,097	—	—	—	—	—	—	11.8	—	—
1966	8,127	—	—	2,136	5,991	—	—	—	—	—	—	11.1	—	—
1967	7,170	—	—	1,996	5,174	—	—	—	—	—	—	9.6	—	—
1968	7,087	—	—	1,985	5,102	—	—	—	—	—	—	9.3	—	—
1969	7,148	—	—	1,896	5,252	—	—	—	—	—	—	9.2	—	—
1970	7,031	—	—	1,810	5,221	—	—	—	—	—	—	8.9	—	—
1971	7,077	—	—	1,750	5,327	—	—	—	—	—	—	8.9	—	—
1972	7,157	—	—	1,792	5,365	746	244	203	1,688	262	2,209	8.7	—	—
1973	7,255	—	—	1,780	5,474	810	260	193	1,669	301	2,224	8.5	—	—
1974	7,455	—	—	1,758	5,697	874	261	217	1,728	309	2,291	8.6	—	—
1975	7,427	—	—	1,722	5,705	839	273	223	1,709	335	2,310	8.7	—	—
1976	7,428	5,766	1,662	1,646	5,783	877	286	219	1,688	324	2,363	8.4	10.1	4.3
1977	7,694	5,885	1,809	1,580	6,114	950	305	220	1,758	342	2,518	8.4	10.1	4.5
1978	8,047	6,078	1,969	1,618	6,429	1,091	322	246	1,765	402	2,581	8.4	10.2	4.6
1979	8,384	6,238	2,146	1,593	6,791	1,152	339	276	1,853	445	2,704	8.5	10.3	4.9
1980	8,643	6,362	2,280	1,642	7,000	1,173	358	282	1,899	458	2,804	8.7	10.4	5.0
1981	8,735	6,347	2,388	1,638	7,097	1,152	362	294	1,885	451	2,926	8.7	10.2	5.1
1982	8,898	6,386	2,512	1,636	7,262	1,117	353	304	1,870	490	3,093	8.9	10.2	5.3
1983	9,143	6,494	2,649	1,565	7,575	1,158	371	322	1,932	532	3,233	9.1	10.3	5.5
1984	9,338	6,568	2,770	1,553	7,785	1,235	360	318	1,920	544	3,383	8.9	10.3	5.6

	Self-employed workers											Self-employment rate		
				Industry										
	Total	Male	Female	Agricultural	Nonagricultural	Construction	Manufacturing	Transportation, communications, and other public utilities	Trade	Finance, insurance, and real estate	Services	Overall	Male	Female
	Ba970	Ba971	Ba972	Ba973	Ba974	Ba975	Ba976	Ba977	Ba978	Ba979	Ba980	Ba981	Ba982	Ba983
Year	Thousand	Thousand	Thousand	Thousand	Thousand	Thousand	Thousand	Thousand	Thousand	Thousand	Thousand	Percent	Percent	Percent
1985	9,269	6,452	2,817	1,458	7,811	1,301	347	315	1,792	558	3,477	8.7	10.0	5.5
1986	9,327	6,498	2,829	1,447	7,881	1,369	371	318	1,787	556	3,455	8.5	9.9	5.4
1987	9,624	6,617	3,007	1,423	8,201	1,384	354	335	1,841	597	3,663	8.6	10.0	5.6
1988	9,917	6,738	3,179	1,398	8,519	1,427	394	345	1,823	624	3,878	8.6	10.1	5.8
1989	10,008	6,729	3,279	1,403	8,605	1,423	406	323	1,882	621	3,924	8.5	9.9	5.9
1990	10,097	6,749	3,349	1,378	8,719	1,457	427	301	1,851	630	4,030	8.5	9.8	5.9
1991	10,274	6,886	3,388	1,423	8,851	1,442	418	317	1,873	611	4,166	8.7	10.0	5.9
1992	9,960	6,777	3,184	1,385	8,575	1,460	390	337	1,770	622	3,975	8.4	9.7	5.5
1993	10,280	7,011	3,269	1,320	8,959	1,549	439	372	1,886	655	4,041	8.5	10.0	5.6
1994	10,648	6,756	3,891	1,645	9,003	1,506	426	385	1,906	625	4,142	8.7	9.5	6.5
1995	10,482	6,599	3,883	1,580	8,902	1,460	433	396	1,772	660	4,166	8.4	9.2	6.4
1996	10,490	6,590	3,900	1,518	8,971	1,496	406	432	1,760	674	4,189	8.3	9.1	6.3
1997	10,513	6,591	3,923	1,457	9,056	1,492	422	438	1,761	629	4,300	8.1	9.0	6.2
1998	10,303	6,485	3,818	1,341	8,962	1,519	428	430	1,640	609	4,317	7.8	8.8	6.0
1999	10,087	6,328	3,759	1,297	8,790	1,545	380	429	1,621	661	4,138	7.6	8.5	5.8
2000	9,907	6,154	3,753	1,233	8,674	1,581	343	399	1,498	693	4,145	7.3	8.2	5.7

[1] Civilian noninstitutional population, age 16 and older.

[2] Data not strictly comparable over time; see the text for Table Ba478–486.

Sources

Calculations based on U.S. Bureau of Labor Statistics (BLS) Internet site and *BLS Handbook of Methods,* Bulletin number 2490 (April 1997). Monthly updates are available from the BLS periodical *Employment and Earnings*.

Documentation

See the text for Table Ba478–486.

Self-employed persons are those who work for profit or fees in their own business, profession, or trade, or who operate a farm. The self-employment rate is calculated by dividing the number of self-employed by the number in the labor force.

TABLE Ba984–987 Unpaid family workers, by sex: 1948–2000[1, 2]

Contributed by Susan B. Carter

			Female	
	Total	As percentage of labor force	Total	As percentage of female labor force
	Ba984	Ba985	Ba986	Ba987
Year	Thousand	Percent	Thousand	Percent
1948	1,701	2.81	—	—
1949	1,700	2.77	—	—
1950	1,573	2.53	—	—
1951	1,546	2.49	—	—
1952	1,546	2.49	—	—
1953	1,478	2.35	—	—
1954	1,475	2.32	—	—
1955	1,634	2.51	—	—
1956	1,701	2.56	—	—
1957	1,667	2.49	—	—
1958	1,528	2.26	—	—
1959	1,542	2.26	—	—
1960	1,499	2.15	—	—
1961	1,472	2.09	—	—
1962	1,376	1.95	—	—
1963	1,269	1.77	—	—
1964	1,272	1.74	—	—
1965	1,278	1.72	—	—
1966	1,142	1.51	—	—
1967	1,052	1.36	—	—
1968	1,035	1.31	—	—
1969	1,048	1.30	—	—
1970	1,001	1.21	—	—
1971	1,001	1.19	—	—
1972	986	1.13	—	—
1973	962	1.08	—	—
1974	880	0.96	—	—
1975	869	0.93	—	—
1976	806	0.84	638	1.64
1977	841	0.85	678	1.67
1978	795	0.78	660	1.55
1979	767	0.73	625	1.41
1980	711	0.66	553	1.22
1981	656	0.60	518	1.11
1982	661	0.60	514	1.08
1983	616	0.55	480	0.99
1984	548	0.48	431	0.87
1985	474	0.41	376	0.74
1986	423	0.36	335	0.64
1987	413	0.34	316	0.59
1988	409	0.34	320	0.58
1989	410	0.33	328	0.59
1990	358	0.28	271	0.48
1991	343	0.27	264	0.46
1992	345	0.27	264	0.45
1993	324	0.25	235	0.40
1994	180	0.14	117	0.19
1995	156	0.12	105	0.17
1996	178	0.13	112	0.18
1997	171	0.13	111	0.18
1998	141	0.10	89	0.14
1999	135	0.10	90	0.14
2000	139	0.10	87	0.13

[1] Civilian noninstitutional population, age 16 and older.

[2] Data not strictly comparable over time; see the text for Table Ba478–486.

Sources

U.S. Bureau of Labor Statistics (BLS) Internet site and *BLS Handbook of Methods*, Bulletin number 2490 (April 1997). Monthly updates are available from the BLS periodical *Employment and Earnings*.

Documentation

See the text for Table Ba478–486.

Unpaid family workers are persons working without pay for fifteen hours a week or more on a farm or in a business operated by a member of the household to whom they are related by birth or marriage. Unpaid family workers are included in the total of employed persons.

TABLE Ba988–1002 Persons engaged in production, by industry: 1929–1948 [Bureau of Economic Analysis]

Contributed by Richard Sutch

						Manufacturing									
	Total	Farms	Agricultural services, forestry, and fisheries	Mining	Contract construction	Durable goods	Nondurable goods	Transportation	Communications	Gas, electric, and sanitary services	Wholesale trade	Retail trade and automobile services	Finance, insurance, and real estate	Services	Government
	Ba988	Ba989	Ba990	Ba991	Ba992	Ba993	Ba994	Ba995	Ba996	Ba997	Ba998	Ba999	Ba1000	Ba1001	Ba1002
Year	Thousand	Thousand	Thousand	Thousand	Thousand	Thousand	Thousand	Thousand	Thousand	Thousand	Thousand	Thousand	Thousand	Thousand	Thousand
1929	45,606	8,391	236	1,017	2,306	5,282	5,274	3,034	539	495	1,744	6,077	1,575	6,484	3,152
1930	43,507	8,214	227	956	2,183	4,491	4,927	2,795	531	503	1,685	5,839	1,551	6,318	3,287
1931	40,485	8,239	232	839	1,983	3,521	4,462	2,444	468	465	1,533	5,507	1,488	5,934	3,369
1932	37,043	8,162	208	701	1,644	2,742	4,004	2,100	422	409	1,395	5,058	1,423	5,443	3,331
1933	37,534	8,235	203	724	1,383	2,912	4,361	2,008	392	395	1,393	5,038	1,373	5,275	3,841
1934	40,881	8,330	193	857	1,460	3,610	4,831	2,077	391	411	1,530	5,431	1,401	5,658	4,700
1935	42,389	8,440	211	876	1,514	3,967	5,016	2,102	390	416	1,572	5,608	1,425	5,850	5,001
1936	45,446	8,346	198	934	1,763	4,488	5,244	2,218	409	444	1,690	5,949	1,475	6,167	6,120
1937	46,633	8,118	249	993	1,738	5,158	5,528	2,333	441	460	1,857	6,305	1,520	6,429	5,503
1938	44,780	7,841	225	897	1,686	4,113	5,116	2,073	419	446	1,857	6,218	1,520	6,241	6,127
1939	46,123	7,595	215	870	1,864	4,648	5,438	2,169	424	447	1,942	6,440	1,560	6,396	6,114
1940	48,015	7,377	212	965	1,941	5,412	5,597	2,256	434	467	2,015	6,768	1,611	6,707	6,251
1941	52,606	7,279	207	1,015	2,449	7,051	6,223	2,447	478	479	2,136	7,126	1,647	6,784	7,282
1942	57,418	7,124	217	1,021	2,859	8,902	6,528	2,586	504	447	2,041	6,916	1,636	6,926	9,714
1943	63,059	6,950	204	949	2,172	10,984	6,572	2,789	521	396	1,912	6,648	1,575	6,598	14,810
1944	64,197	6,705	226	905	1,646	10,787	6,431	2,960	519	377	1,936	6,598	1,561	6,522	17,079
1945	62,573	6,539	227	855	1,700	9,008	6,352	3,018	536	385	2,052	6,862	1,602	6,549	16,954
1946	56,920	6,466	247	901	2,551	7,826	6,855	3,039	652	459	2,419	7,973	1,813	7,068	8,698
1947	57,255	6,400	257	968	3,007	8,422	6,974	3,043	687	501	2,620	8,376	1,864	7,444	6,697
1948	58,240	6,350	260	1,019	3,262	8,397	7,062	3,039	742	537	2,642	8,639	1,890	7,650	6,744

Source

U.S. Bureau of Economic Analysis (BEA), *National Income and Product Accounts of the United States*, volume 1, *1929–58* (February 1993), Table 6.8A, p. 122.

Documentation

For more recent data, see Tables Ba1003–1032.

Persons engaged in production equals the number of full-time equivalent employees (Tables Ba866–909) plus the number of self-employed persons (Tables Ba934–969). Unpaid family workers are excluded. These data are a by-product of the BEA program to estimate the gross domestic product of the United States. Beginning in 1949, BEA data on persons engaged in production by industry are organized according to the 1972 Standard Industrial Classification (SIC) system. The two major changes involved moving artisan construction from services (in the 1942 system) to construction (in the 1972 system) and moving automobile services from retail trade and automobile services (in the 1942 system) to the services sector (in the 1972 system). Users may judge the quantitative significance of these definitional changes by comparing data for 1948 shown in this table with data for the same year shown in Table Ba988–1002.

TABLE Ba1003–1017 Persons engaged in production, by industry: 1948–1987 [Bureau of Economic Analysis]

Contributed by Susan B. Carter and Richard Sutch

	Total	Farms	Agricultural services, forestry, and fisheries	Mining	Construction	Manufacturing		Transportation	Communications	Electric, gas, and sanitary services	Trade		Finance, insurance, and real estate	Services	Auto repair, services, and parking
						Durable goods	Nondurable goods				Wholesale	Retail			
	Ba1003	Ba1004	Ba1005	Ba1006	Ba1007	Ba1008	Ba1009	Ba1010	Ba1011	Ba1012	Ba1013	Ba1014	Ba1015	Ba1016	Ba1017
Year	Thousand	Thousand	Thousand	Thousand	Thousand	Thousand	Thousand	Thousand	Thousand	Thousand	Thousand	Thousand	Thousand	Thousand	Thousand
1948	58,240	6,350	275	1,028	3,305	8,591	7,370	3,039	742	537	2,839	7,851	1,855	7,707	340
1949	56,833	6,171	269	956	3,155	7,727	7,050	2,847	739	549	2,783	7,839	1,868	7,688	325
1950	58,523	6,127	275	957	3,415	8,317	7,191	2,899	720	553	2,818	7,971	1,941	7,911	312
1951	62,236	5,735	287	972	3,628	9,336	7,329	3,063	750	564	2,980	8,302	2,045	8,033	305
1952	63,310	5,580	299	949	3,601	9,645	7,259	3,046	776	568	3,056	8,409	2,141	8,006	307
1953	64,087	5,402	294	908	3,528	10,300	7,352	3,054	804	580	3,103	8,483	2,247	8,097	305
1954	62,111	5,420	293	833	3,394	9,319	7,059	2,841	802	583	3,092	8,379	2,349	8,019	301
1955	63,137	5,237	288	835	3,463	9,709	7,143	2,882	814	587	3,164	8,593	2,433	8,382	311
1956	64,284	4,962	289	873	3,580	9,954	7,167	2,936	860	593	3,307	8,820	2,525	8,720	324
1957	64,545	4,724	286	869	3,525	9,935	7,142	2,900	879	598	3,318	8,867	2,594	9,006	336
1958	62,530	4,567	281	775	3,397	8,783	6,823	2,661	828	610	3,295	8,775	2,628	9,158	351
1959	64,002	4,426	278	742	3,533	9,351	7,020	2,679	801	603	3,351	8,911	2,668	9,430	361
1960	64,886	4,243	288	721	3,491	9,436	7,062	2,682	809	609	3,421	9,075	2,754	9,817	391
1961	64,656	4,144	298	685	3,461	9,094	6,981	2,586	798	609	3,419	8,934	2,784	10,005	398
1962	66,043	4,001	309	666	3,541	9,539	7,119	2,590	794	605	3,448	8,985	2,836	10,310	404
1963	66,629	3,762	317	647	3,619	9,649	7,127	2,578	793	605	3,480	9,019	2,909	10,597	423
1964	67,860	3,532	330	642	3,728	9,821	7,185	2,592	810	606	3,555	9,294	2,969	10,920	440
1965	70,159	3,366	347	644	3,903	10,458	7,444	2,643	846	619	3,648	9,565	3,075	11,306	450
1966	73,342	3,077	355	640	3,985	11,389	7,723	2,722	892	626	3,782	9,833	3,166	11,874	465
1967	75,180	2,973	365	624	3,965	11,504	7,831	2,766	926	638	3,849	9,973	3,332	12,443	487
1968	76,974	2,929	374	618	4,084	11,672	7,970	2,807	938	649	3,920	10,259	3,493	12,821	492
1969	78,917	2,810	383	626	4,256	11,952	8,105	2,822	1,004	662	4,041	10,596	3,653	13,313	504
1970	78,322	2,733	385	629	4,179	11,236	7,941	2,785	1,068	677	4,123	10,766	3,749	13,380	508
1971	77,988	2,672	393	617	4,261	10,613	7,723	2,743	1,067	688	4,154	11,004	3,836	13,577	546
1972	79,908	2,694	422	625	4,499	10,991	7,828	2,762	1,082	702	4,252	11,236	3,959	14,200	574
1973	83,350	2,716	465	641	4,835	11,833	8,038	2,845	1,107	718	4,492	11,717	4,202	14,879	607
1974	84,669	2,773	482	701	4,816	11,904	7,900	2,893	1,122	729	4,617	11,948	4,334	15,313	617
1975	82,882	2,723	468	755	4,296	10,665	7,397	2,764	1,101	719	4,521	11,979	4,405	15,650	638
1976	85,207	2,704	506	791	4,400	11,099	7,740	2,788	1,087	719	4,690	12,407	4,507	16,252	681
1977	88,175	2,580	525	831	4,735	11,651	7,906	2,879	1,105	733	4,832	13,008	4,708	17,035	724
1978	92,638	2,536	622	885	5,313	12,348	8,073	3,034	1,148	762	5,074	13,758	5,059	18,045	788
1979	95,726	2,507	676	958	5,626	12,826	8,130	3,160	1,211	797	5,345	14,124	5,333	18,911	842
1980	95,889	2,574	701	1,048	5,417	12,236	7,939	3,115	1,245	813	5,406	14,053	5,497	19,581	847
1981	96,747	2,532	728	1,163	5,240	12,176	7,938	3,099	1,286	845	5,534	14,153	5,619	20,331	876
1982	95,138	2,436	764	1,140	4,882	11,064	7,560	2,972	1,316	863	5,424	14,067	5,652	20,891	926
1983	95,986	2,439	794	964	4,973	10,786	7,551	2,945	1,266	868	5,423	14,455	5,834	21,703	935
1984	100,614	2,313	838	979	5,529	11,579	7,705	3,105	1,255	884	5,714	15,402	6,073	23,047	1,032

	Total	Farms	Agricultural services, forestry, and fisheries	Mining	Construction	Manufacturing		Transportation	Communications	Electric, gas, and sanitary services	Trade		Finance, insurance, and real estate	Services	Auto repair, services, and parking
						Durable goods	Nondurable goods				Wholesale	Retail			
	Ba1003	Ba1004	Ba1005	Ba1006	Ba1007	Ba1008	Ba1009	Ba1010	Ba1011	Ba1012	Ba1013	Ba1014	Ba1015	Ba1016	Ba1017
Year	Thousand	Thousand	Thousand	Thousand	Thousand	Thousand	Thousand	Thousand	Thousand	Thousand	Thousand	Thousand	Thousand	Thousand	Thousand
1985	103,027	2,077	902	930	5,904	11,539	7,593	3,178	1,225	897	5,816	16,026	6,305	24,090	1,122
1986	104,785	2,001	964	786	6,138	11,274	7,598	3,217	1,205	903	5,847	16,433	6,592	24,939	1,146
1987	107,843	1,968	1,073	726	6,240	11,236	7,722	3,360	1,192	908	6,001	17,038	6,892	26,316	1,187

Sources

U.S. Bureau of Economic Analysis (BEA), National Income and Product Accounts of the United States (NIPA) Internet site.

Data are updated from time to time in the BEA's *Survey of Current Business* (monthly periodical).

Documentation

For comparable data, see Tables Ba988–1002 and Ba1018–1032.

See the notes to Table Ba988–1002 for definitions and further description. In this table, industries accord with the 1972 Standard Industrial Classification (SIC) system. See the Introduction to Part D for a discussion of SIC codes. In Table Ba1018–1032, the data are based on the 1987 SIC system. Users may judge the extent of the definitional change by comparing data for 1987 in this table with that given in Table Ba1018–1032. The original source provides finer industrial detail than is shown here.

The SIC codes corresponding to each series are as follows: series Ba1004: SIC72 codes 1 and 2; series Ba1005: SIC72 codes 7–9; series Ba1006: SIC72 codes 10–14; series Ba1007: SIC72 codes 15–17; series Ba1008: SIC72 codes 24, 25, and 32–39; series Ba1009: SIC72 codes 20–23 and 26–31; series Ba1010: SIC72 codes 40–42 and 44–47; series Ba1011: SIC72 code 48; series Ba1012: SIC72 code 49; series Ba1013: SIC72 codes 50 and 51; series Ba1014: SIC72 codes 52–59; series Ba1015: SIC72 codes 60–67; series Ba1016: SIC72 codes 70–89, including SIC72 code 75, auto repair, services, and parking (series Ba1017).

Series Ba1003. The sum of series Ba1004–1016 plus total persons engaged in governmental production and a small residual category (not shown), which is sometimes negative, representing workers in unclassifiable industries and a statistical discrepancy.

Series Ba1017, auto repair, services, and parking (SIC72 code 75). Included as an addendum so that users who wish to link data in this table with the data in Table Ba988–1002 may remove auto services from the services industry and add it to the retail trade industry, thus making the data more directly comparable with that for 1929–1947.

TABLE Ba1018–1032 Persons engaged in production, by industry: 1987–1998 [Bureau of Economic Analysis]

Contributed by Susan B. Carter and Richard Sutch

	Total	Farms	Agricultural services, forestry, and fisheries	Mining	Construction	Manufacturing: Durable goods	Manufacturing: Nondurable goods	Transportation	Communications	Electric, gas, and sanitary services	Wholesale trade	Retail trade	Finance, insurance, and real estate	Services	Auto repair, services, and parking
	Ba1018	Ba1019	Ba1020	Ba1021	Ba1022	Ba1023	Ba1024	Ba1025	Ba1026	Ba1027	Ba1028	Ba1029	Ba1030	Ba1031	Ba1032
Year	Thousand	Thousand	Thousand	Thousand	Thousand	Thousand	Thousand	Thousand	Thousand	Thousand	Thousand	Thousand	Thousand	Thousand	Thousand
1987	107,843	1,968	1,073	726	6,240	11,206	7,752	3,358	1,192	910	6,022	17,017	6,900	26,308	1,187
1988	111,003	1,977	1,126	738	6,453	11,464	7,869	3,497	1,189	920	6,178	17,479	7,006	27,540	1,234
1989	113,824	1,880	1,179	709	6,526	11,485	7,912	3,580	1,172	922	6,413	18,020	7,043	29,021	1,254
1990	115,040	1,846	1,209	725	6,513	11,217	7,894	3,591	1,219	944	6,347	18,099	7,130	30,048	1,277
1991	113,729	1,862	1,231	703	6,035	10,670	7,757	3,577	1,198	952	6,201	17,668	7,064	30,510	1,245
1992	113,580	1,803	1,210	649	5,876	10,376	7,693	3,583	1,171	950	6,205	17,697	6,999	31,129	1,266
1993	115,601	1,800	1,276	618	6,129	10,341	7,768	3,753	1,180	942	6,141	18,261	7,162	32,376	1,325
1994	118,541	1,791	1,362	607	6,406	10,582	7,860	3,914	1,192	931	6,324	18,898	7,251	33,627	1,338
1995	121,531	1,968	1,412	591	6,650	10,816	7,810	4,041	1,221	910	6,555	19,462	7,211	35,000	1,363
1996	123,824	1,827	1,511	586	6,950	10,911	7,665	4,181	1,259	878	6,587	19,851	7,310	36,396	1,481
1997	126,757	1,814	1,507	603	7,254	11,134	7,640	4,284	1,324	865	6,735	20,258	7,424	37,956	1,511
1998	129,549	1,705	1,633	601	7,603	11,355	7,589	4,433	1,365	850	6,919	20,419	7,636	39,353	1,522

Sources

U.S. Bureau of Economic Analysis (BEA), National Income and Product Accounts of the United States (NIPA) Internet site.

Data are updated from time to time in the BEA's *Survey of Current Business* (monthly periodical).

Documentation

For comparable data, see also Tables Ba988–1017.

See the notes to Table Ba988–1002 for definitions and further description. In this table, industries accord with the 1987 Standard Industrial Classification (SIC) system. See the Introduction to Part D for a discussion of SIC codes. Before 1987, the data were based on the 1972 SIC system. Users may judge the extent of the definitional change, because the data for 1987 given in this table use the 1987 SIC system and in Table Ba1003–1017 use the 1972 system. The original source provides finer industrial detail.

The SIC codes corresponding to each series are as follows: series Ba1019: SIC87 codes 1 and 2; series Ba1020: SIC87 codes 7–9; series Ba1021: SIC87 codes 10–14; series Ba1022: SIC87 codes 15–17; series Ba1023: SIC87 codes 24, 25, and 32–39; series Ba1024: SIC87 codes 20–23 and 26–31; series Ba1025: SIC87 codes 40–42 and 44–47; series Ba1026: SIC87 code 48; series Ba1027: SIC87 code 49; series Ba1028: SIC87 codes 50 and 51; series Ba1029: SIC87 codes 52–59; series Ba1030: SIC87 codes 60–67; series Ba1031: SIC87 codes 70–89, including SIC87 code 75, auto repair, services, and parking (series Ba1032).

Series Ba1018. Equals the sum of series Ba1019–1031 plus total persons engaged in governmental production and a small residual category (not shown), which is sometimes negative, representing workers in unclassifiable industries and a statistical discrepancy.

Series Ba1032, auto repair, services, and parking (SIC87 code 75). Included as an addendum so that users who wish to link data in this table with the data in Table Ba988–1002 may remove auto services from the services industry and add it to the retail trade industry, thus making the data more directly comparable with that for 1929–1947.

OCCUPATIONS

Matthew Sobek

TABLE Ba1033–1046 Major occupational groups – all persons: 1860–1990[1]

Contributed by Matthew Sobek

	Total	Professionals	Farmers	Proprietors	Managers and officials	Clerical workers	Sales workers	Craft workers	Operatives	Domestic service workers	Other service workers	Farm laborers	Laborers	Unclassified
	Ba1033	Ba1034	Ba1035	Ba1036	Ba1037	Ba1038	Ba1039	Ba1040	Ba1041	Ba1042	Ba1043	Ba1044	Ba1045	Ba1046
Year	Number	Number	Number	Number	Number	Number	Number	Number	Number	Number	Number	Number	Number	Number
1860 [2]	8,160,752	293,604	2,707,274	312,085	115,513	45,683	190,432	1,154,336	975,641	509,569	96,189	937,725	822,701	—
1870	12,004,238	356,985	3,175,839	409,807	195,854	129,141	281,778	1,362,750	1,527,567	930,704	168,507	2,338,046	1,127,260	—
1880	16,478,917	584,940	4,490,111	553,492	269,291	263,931	436,293	1,703,847	2,273,682	1,094,249	274,238	2,554,056	1,980,787	—
1900	27,554,085	1,126,205	5,824,546	1,039,691	591,941	1,054,110	1,000,987	3,141,081	3,824,089	2,105,943	876,528	3,465,130	3,503,834	—
1910	36,236,003	1,699,267	6,029,300	1,598,762	891,448	1,944,359	1,639,065	4,177,386	5,809,146	1,980,127	1,524,454	5,077,650	3,865,039	—
1920	40,113,274	2,261,078	6,569,911	1,586,186	1,121,201	3,263,382	2,001,550	5,681,928	6,352,824	1,490,405	1,778,456	3,398,866	4,607,487	—
1940	47,584,238	3,398,320	5,216,903	2,029,575	1,748,823	4,927,067	2,968,019	5,476,776	8,586,887	2,113,392	3,377,546	3,003,540	4,373,802	363,588
1950	56,973,749	5,047,198	4,350,507	2,544,012	2,557,926	7,139,285	3,979,498	7,954,410	11,489,205	1,400,662	4,446,612	2,298,610	3,540,518	225,306
1960	63,870,595	7,223,009	2,476,905	1,897,753	3,465,821	9,208,407	4,557,175	8,708,246	11,843,724	1,636,080	5,410,950	1,365,786	3,020,026	3,056,713
1970	76,270,515	11,859,938	1,402,232	1,511,976	4,500,219	13,690,216	5,520,037	10,351,231	13,601,511	1,159,022	8,379,433	947,136	3,347,564	—
1980	97,378,407	17,007,194	1,284,364	1,970,292	8,128,630	18,744,101	6,543,063	11,717,408	14,334,201	592,727	11,974,361	889,294	4,192,772	—
1990	115,083,094	23,561,866	1,040,236	2,128,820	12,536,174	21,560,507	7,870,883	12,062,085	13,373,392	521,839	14,724,463	771,036	4,931,793	—

[1] Data pertain to noninstitutionalized civilians age 16 and older who reported an occupation; employed persons only beginning 1940.

[2] Excludes slaves.

Source

Matthew Sobek, "New Statistics on the U.S. Labor Force, 1850–1990," *Historical Methods* 34 (2001): 71–87, Table 1.

Documentation

Tabulated from the Integrated Public Use Microdata Series (IPUMS). See the Guide to the Millennial Edition for information on the IPUMS.

Occupations are grouped according to the 1950 Census classification, a hierarchical system intended to reflect relative socioeconomic status. The individual, detailed occupation responses for all censuses were classified into the 1950 system in the IPUMS database. The groupings in this table are aggregations of those 268 detailed 1950 occupations. The one divergence from the 1950 categorization is the identification of proprietors separately from managers and officials.

See Tables Ba1159–3687 for statistics on and discussion of the detailed occupational categories underlying the groupings.

Only currently employed persons are included beginning in 1940. In prior years, varying instructions governed legitimate occupation responses, but employment status was not a condition.

See the source for more discussion of the underlying data and methodology.

Series Ba1034. The professionals group includes teachers and medical nurses, two professions that employed large numbers of women in all census years.

Series Ba1036. Excludes farmers, self-employed professionals, and craft workers. Proprietors are identified with the aid of a self-employment question beginning in 1910; in prior years, detailed occupation title alone is used.

Series Ba1041. Operatives are semiskilled workers not classified elsewhere.

TABLE Ba1047–1060 Major occupational groups – males: 1850–1990[1]

Contributed by Matthew Sobek

Year	Total	Professionals	Farmers	Proprietors	Managers and officials	Clerical workers	Sales workers	Craft workers	Operatives	Domestic service workers	Other service workers	Farm laborers	Laborers	Unclassified
	Ba1047	Ba1048	Ba1049	Ba1050	Ba1051	Ba1052	Ba1053	Ba1054	Ba1055	Ba1056	Ba1057	Ba1058	Ba1059	Ba1060
	Number	Number	Number	Number	Number	Number	Number	Number	Number	Number	Number	Number	Number	Number
1850 [2]	5,227,198	151,425	2,367,261	192,066	58,532	13,846	113,543	869,878	475,780	13,046	44,685	296,648	630,488	—
1860 [2]	7,130,935	222,983	2,611,306	292,546	114,511	45,082	186,421	1,116,180	701,935	41,983	69,537	921,682	806,769	—
1870	10,225,890	260,322	3,125,692	393,973	193,548	122,631	267,347	1,326,281	1,188,669	69,695	129,402	2,050,300	1,098,030	—
1880	13,999,048	396,127	4,400,647	522,474	262,015	254,158	403,281	1,651,200	1,702,545	149,326	210,483	2,198,675	1,848,117	—
1900	22,388,264	711,847	5,496,702	944,829	557,790	832,512	840,101	3,033,317	2,802,612	208,697	573,727	3,018,139	3,367,991	—
1910	28,691,820	940,063	5,751,714	1,510,600	845,099	1,276,340	1,282,385	4,075,873	4,204,842	169,272	968,275	3,917,181	3,750,176	—
1920	31,921,604	1,290,199	6,285,024	1,481,427	1,038,350	1,675,061	1,493,271	5,538,440	4,705,175	85,374	1,131,892	2,786,908	4,410,483	—
1940	35,888,499	1,935,745	5,056,508	1,784,179	1,547,339	2,403,009	2,154,778	5,324,179	6,319,653	147,322	2,068,378	2,660,676	4,257,790	228,943
1950	41,099,339	3,041,618	4,235,610	2,226,496	2,195,474	2,695,600	2,632,180	7,718,881	8,382,917	61,423	2,474,194	1,863,833	3,417,346	153,767
1960	42,913,576	4,475,034	2,365,007	1,644,501	2,938,860	2,963,416	2,908,122	8,461,992	8,595,629	53,998	2,571,380	1,122,118	2,912,841	1,900,678
1970	47,280,979	7,055,057	1,330,761	1,304,051	3,746,571	3,543,375	3,353,567	9,844,294	9,419,627	36,151	3,777,302	790,828	3,079,395	—
1980	55,747,832	9,200,342	1,157,585	1,616,711	5,839,938	4,129,631	3,689,742	10,925,989	9,770,276	26,138	5,060,177	686,846	3,644,457	—
1990	62,109,921	11,372,403	896,928	1,652,516	7,658,588	4,811,482	4,293,790	11,113,939	9,252,218	25,366	6,241,551	600,122	4,191,018	—

[1] Data pertain to noninstitutionalized civilians age 16 and older who reported an occupation; employed persons only beginning 1940.

[2] Excludes slaves.

Source

Tabulated from the Integrated Public Use Microdata Series (IPUMS). See the Guide to the Millennial Edition for information on the IPUMS.

Documentation

See the text for Table Ba1033–1046.

TABLE Ba1061–1074 Major occupational groups – females: 1860–1990[1]

Contributed by Matthew Sobek

	Total	Professionals	Farmers	Proprietors	Managers and officials	Clerical workers	Sales workers	Craft workers	Operatives	Domestic service workers	Other service workers	Farm laborers	Laborers	Unclassified
	Ba1061	Ba1062	Ba1063	Ba1064	Ba1065	Ba1066	Ba1067	Ba1068	Ba1069	Ba1070	Ba1071	Ba1072	Ba1073	Ba1074
Year	Number	Number	Number	Number	Number	Number	Number	Number	Number	Number	Number	Number	Number	Number
1860 [2]	1,029,817	70,621	95,968	19,539	1,002	601	4,011	38,156	273,706	467,586	26,652	16,043	15,932	—
1870	1,778,348	96,663	50,147	15,834	2,306	6,510	14,431	36,469	338,898	861,009	39,105	287,746	29,230	—
1880	2,479,869	188,813	89,464	31,018	7,276	9,773	33,012	52,647	571,137	944,923	63,755	355,381	132,670	—
1900	5,165,820	414,359	327,844	94,862	34,150	221,598	160,886	107,764	1,021,477	1,897,246	302,800	446,991	135,843	—
1910 [3]	7,544,183	759,204	277,586	88,162	46,348	668,019	356,680	101,513	1,604,304	1,810,856	556,179	1,160,469	114,863	—
1920	8,191,670	970,879	284,887	104,759	82,851	1,588,321	508,279	143,488	1,647,649	1,405,031	646,564	611,958	197,004	—
1940	11,695,739	1,462,575	160,395	245,396	201,484	2,524,058	813,241	152,597	2,267,234	1,966,070	1,309,168	342,864	116,012	134,645
1950	15,874,410	2,005,580	114,897	317,516	362,452	4,443,685	1,347,318	235,529	3,106,288	1,339,239	1,972,418	434,777	123,172	71,539
1960	20,957,019	2,747,975	111,898	253,252	526,961	6,244,991	1,649,053	246,254	3,248,095	1,582,082	2,839,570	243,668	107,185	1,156,035
1970	28,989,537	4,804,882	71,471	207,925	753,648	10,146,841	2,166,470	506,937	4,181,884	1,122,871	4,602,131	156,308	268,169	—
1980	41,630,576	7,806,852	126,779	353,581	2,288,692	14,614,471	2,853,321	791,419	4,563,925	566,589	6,914,185	202,447	548,315	—
1990	52,973,172	12,189,463	143,307	476,305	4,877,586	16,749,025	3,577,093	948,145	4,121,174	496,473	8,482,912	170,914	740,775	—

[1] Data pertain to noninstitutionalized civilians age 16 and older who reported an occupation; employed persons only beginning 1940.

[2] Excludes slaves.

[3] The wording of the 1910 Census occupation question elicited high response rates for women, especially in agriculture.

Source

Tabulated from the Integrated Public Use Microdata Series (IPUMS). See the Guide to the Millennial Edition for information on the IPUMS.

Documentation

See the text for Table Ba1033–1046.

TABLE Ba1075–1088 Major occupational groups – white males: 1850–1990[1]

Contributed by Matthew Sobek

Year	Total	Professionals	Farmers	Proprietors	Managers and officials	Clerical workers	Sales workers	Craft workers	Operatives	Domestic service workers	Other service workers	Farm laborers	Laborers	Unclassified
	Ba1075	Ba1076	Ba1077	Ba1078	Ba1079	Ba1080	Ba1081	Ba1082	Ba1083	Ba1084	Ba1085	Ba1086	Ba1087	Ba1088
	Number	Number	Number	Number	Number	Number	Number	Number	Number	Number	Number	Number	Number	Number
1850	5,132,884	150,718	2,355,845	191,155	58,330	13,744	113,543	862,194	465,166	9,508	35,787	286,842	590,052	—
1860	7,010,712	221,576	2,600,552	291,740	114,410	44,880	186,019	1,108,544	679,384	32,844	58,392	898,462	773,909	—
1870	8,971,422	254,796	2,929,834	390,059	192,543	120,719	265,136	1,283,160	1,107,759	31,756	102,682	1,404,558	888,420	—
1880	12,281,729	380,064	3,984,119	515,089	258,922	251,372	397,302	1,603,238	1,586,904	75,719	161,288	1,664,163	1,403,549	—
1900	19,927,156	681,491	4,795,479	924,338	550,201	826,440	833,271	2,946,803	2,625,789	116,870	465,205	2,410,262	2,751,007	—
1910	25,658,280	899,760	4,916,187	1,474,579	835,276	1,257,448	1,271,302	3,964,285	3,919,196	96,223	767,013	3,175,609	3,081,402	—
1920	28,744,956	1,247,409	5,402,751	1,449,024	1,029,266	1,648,010	1,477,629	5,386,377	4,398,590	42,086	888,256	2,262,239	3,513,319	—
1940	32,588,404	1,869,209	4,388,726	1,743,649	1,535,098	2,360,685	2,123,662	5,177,732	5,926,001	55,200	1,695,714	2,078,783	3,425,344	208,601
1950	37,366,840	2,959,362	3,741,063	2,164,623	2,163,092	2,576,706	2,585,850	7,423,285	7,591,594	28,030	1,976,172	1,488,005	2,537,130	131,928
1960	38,963,896	4,318,742	2,193,680	1,597,581	2,899,016	2,758,295	2,848,053	8,063,956	7,669,383	24,204	2,020,007	845,070	2,152,488	1,573,421
1970	42,767,634	6,695,140	1,286,731	1,262,912	3,640,313	3,182,246	3,250,065	9,160,478	8,143,933	17,373	3,088,442	629,819	2,410,182	—
1980	49,748,051	8,435,292	1,125,928	1,543,481	5,510,397	3,540,543	3,511,914	10,023,530	8,337,631	15,792	4,107,750	593,964	3,001,829	—
1990	54,620,200	10,171,817	874,461	1,541,581	7,077,905	3,968,173	4,007,694	10,107,144	7,836,403	18,665	4,958,277	542,387	3,515,693	—

[1] Data pertain to noninstitutionalized civilians age 16 and older who reported an occupation; employed persons only beginning 1940.

Source

Matthew Sobek, "New Statistics on the U.S. Labor Force, 1850–1990," *Historical Methods* 34 (2001): 71–87, Table 2.

Documentation

Tabulated from the Integrated Public Use Microdata Series (IPUMS). See the Guide to the Millennial Edition for information on the IPUMS. Also see the text for Table Ba1033–1046.

TABLE Ba1089–1102 Major occupational groups – nonwhite males: 1850–1990[1]

Contributed by Matthew Sobek

	Total	Professionals	Farmers	Proprietors	Managers and officials	Clerical workers	Sales workers	Craft workers	Operatives	Domestic service workers	Other service workers	Farm laborers	Laborers	Unclassified
	Ba1089	Ba1090	Ba1091	Ba1092	Ba1093	Ba1094	Ba1095	Ba1096	Ba1097	Ba1098	Ba1099	Ba1100	Ba1101	Ba1102
Year	Number	Number	Number	Number	Number	Number	Number	Number	Number	Number	Number	Number	Number	Number
1850 [2]	94,314	707	11,416	911	202	102	0	7,684	10,614	3,538	8,898	9,806	40,436	—
1860 [2]	120,223	1,407	10,754	806	101	202	402	7,636	22,551	9,139	11,145	23,220	32,860	—
1870	1,254,468	5,526	195,858	3,914	1,005	1,912	2,211	43,121	80,910	37,939	26,720	645,742	209,610	—
1880	1,717,319	16,063	416,528	7,385	3,093	2,786	5,979	47,962	115,641	73,607	49,195	534,512	444,568	—
1900	2,461,106	30,356	701,222	20,490	7,589	6,071	6,830	86,514	176,823	91,827	108,522	607,878	616,984	—
1910	3,033,543	40,303	835,528	36,021	9,824	18,892	11,083	111,588	285,646	73,049	201,262	741,572	668,775	—
1920	3,176,648	42,790	882,273	32,403	9,084	27,051	15,642	152,063	306,585	43,288	243,636	524,669	897,164	—
1940	3,300,095	66,536	667,782	40,530	12,241	42,324	31,116	146,447	393,652	92,122	372,664	581,893	832,446	20,342
1950	3,732,499	82,256	494,547	61,873	32,382	118,894	46,330	295,596	791,323	33,393	498,022	375,828	880,216	21,839
1960	3,949,680	156,292	171,327	46,920	39,844	205,121	60,069	398,036	926,246	29,794	551,373	277,048	760,353	327,257
1970	4,513,344	359,917	44,030	41,138	106,258	361,129	103,502	683,816	1,275,694	18,778	688,860	161,009	669,213	—
1980	5,999,781	765,050	31,657	73,230	329,542	589,088	177,828	902,459	1,432,645	10,346	952,426	92,882	642,628	—
1990	7,489,722	1,200,586	22,467	110,935	580,683	843,310	286,096	1,006,795	1,415,815	6,702	1,283,274	57,735	675,324	—

[1] Data pertain to noninstitutionalized civilians age 16 and older who reported an occupation; employed persons only beginning 1940.

[2] Excludes slaves.

Source

Matthew Sobek, "New Statistics on the U.S. Labor Force, 1850–1990," *Historical Methods* 34 (2001): 71–87, Table 2.

Documentation

Tabulated from the Integrated Public Use Microdata Series (IPUMS). See the Guide to the Millennial Edition for information on the IPUMS. Also see the text for Table Ba1033–1046.

TABLE Ba1103–1116 Major occupational groups – white females: 1860–1990[1]

Contributed by Matthew Sobek

	Total	Professionals	Farmers	Proprietors	Managers and officials	Clerical workers	Sales workers	Craft workers	Operatives	Domestic service workers	Other service workers	Farm laborers	Laborers	Unclassified
	Ba1103	Ba1104	Ba1105	Ba1106	Ba1107	Ba1108	Ba1109	Ba1110	Ba1111	Ba1112	Ba1113	Ba1114	Ba1115	Ba1116
Year	Number	Number	Number	Number	Number	Number	Number	Number	Number	Number	Number	Number	Number	Number
1860	978,452	70,421	95,162	19,539	1,002	601	4,011	38,055	268,274	429,194	24,846	13,427	13,920	—
1870	1,219,494	95,458	35,269	15,532	2,205	6,410	13,930	36,469	329,853	617,954	31,263	27,538	7,613	—
1880	1,715,918	184,620	63,939	30,220	7,276	9,575	32,614	51,649	535,710	658,954	53,477	58,051	29,833	—
1900	4,028,994	399,181	254,231	91,068	34,150	219,322	160,128	107,764	1,002,505	1,330,349	275,480	92,586	62,230	—
1910 [2]	5,731,814	732,000	198,239	84,384	44,585	663,233	353,909	99,749	1,532,766	1,074,825	463,230	392,449	92,445	—
1920	6,725,778	934,750	197,098	98,399	81,035	1,578,936	503,735	140,763	1,554,003	771,480	520,008	190,752	154,819	—
1940	10,073,883	1,391,016	109,230	233,859	197,573	2,501,782	801,265	146,137	2,146,374	1,053,611	1,147,296	124,022	100,163	121,555
1950	13,928,559	1,890,877	79,316	299,480	352,567	4,354,471	1,316,825	225,555	2,820,180	542,845	1,600,635	294,811	89,476	61,521
1960	18,362,800	2,551,936	94,463	238,608	512,115	6,023,890	1,604,025	228,418	2,915,387	688,817	2,300,721	170,858	82,573	950,989
1970	25,326,143	4,332,102	64,426	196,825	714,842	9,361,761	2,061,746	455,376	3,575,830	514,016	3,716,684	115,421	217,114	—
1980	35,849,763	6,819,719	121,921	331,165	2,101,317	12,935,074	2,653,768	688,814	3,706,417	317,902	5,551,809	178,015	443,842	—
1990	45,029,921	10,562,118	139,116	432,778	4,375,073	14,396,693	3,225,340	809,520	3,221,072	349,392	6,748,708	151,277	618,834	—

[1] Data pertain to noninstitutionalized civilians age 16 and older who reported an occupation; employed persons only beginning 1940.

[2] The wording of the 1910 Census occupation question elicited high response rates for women, especially in agriculture.

Source

Matthew Sobek, "New Statistics on the U.S. Labor Force, 1850–1990," *Historical Methods* 34 (2001): 71–87, Table 3.

Documentation

Tabulated from the Integrated Public Use Microdata Series (IPUMS). See the Guide to the Millennial Edition for information on IPUMS. Also see the text for Table Ba1033–1046.

TABLE Ba1117–1130 Major occupational groups – nonwhite females: 1860–1990[1]

Contributed by Matthew Sobek

	Total	Professionals	Farmers	Proprietors	Managers and officials	Clerical workers	Sales workers	Craft workers	Operatives	Domestic service workers	Other service workers	Farm laborers	Laborers	Unclassified
	Ba1117	Ba1118	Ba1119	Ba1120	Ba1121	Ba1122	Ba1123	Ba1124	Ba1125	Ba1126	Ba1127	Ba1128	Ba1129	Ba1130
Year	Number	Number	Number	Number	Number	Number	Number	Number	Number	Number	Number	Number	Number	Number
1860 [2]	51,365	200	806	0	0	0	0	101	5,432	38,392	1,806	2,616	2,012	—
1870	558,854	1,205	14,878	302	101	100	501	0	9,045	243,055	7,842	260,208	21,617	—
1880	763,951	4,193	25,525	798	0	198	398	998	35,427	285,969	10,278	297,330	102,837	—
1900	1,136,829	15,178	73,613	3,794	0	2,277	759	0	18,972	566,897	27,320	354,406	73,613	—
1910 [3]	1,812,364	27,204	79,346	3,778	1,763	4,786	2,771	1,763	71,537	736,030	92,948	768,020	22,418	—
1920	1,465,892	36,129	87,789	6,360	1,816	9,385	4,544	2,725	93,646	633,551	126,556	421,206	42,185	—
1940	1,621,856	71,559	51,165	11,537	3,911	22,276	11,976	6,460	120,860	912,459	161,872	218,842	15,849	13,090
1950	1,945,851	114,703	35,581	18,036	9,885	89,214	30,493	9,974	286,108	796,394	371,783	139,966	33,696	10,018
1960	2,594,219	196,039	17,435	14,644	14,846	221,101	45,028	17,836	332,708	893,265	538,849	72,810	24,612	205,046
1970	3,663,395	472,780	7,045	11,100	38,806	785,081	104,724	51,561	606,055	608,855	885,447	40,886	51,055	—
1980	5,780,812	987,132	4,858	22,416	187,374	1,679,397	199,553	102,605	857,508	248,687	1,362,376	24,433	104,473	—
1990	7,943,250	1,627,345	4,192	43,527	502,513	2,352,332	351,752	138,625	900,101	147,081	1,734,204	19,637	121,941	—

[1] Data pertain to noninstitutionalized civilians age 16 and older who reported an occupation; employed persons only beginning 1940.

[2] Excludes slaves.

[3] The wording of the 1910 Census occupation question elicited high response rates for women, especially in agriculture.

Source

Matthew Sobek, "New Statistics on the U.S. Labor Force, 1850–1990," *Historical Methods* 34 (2001): 71–87, Table 3.

Documentation

Tabulated from the Integrated Public Use Microdata Series (IPUMS). See the Guide to the Millennial Edition for information on the IPUMS. Also see the text for Table Ba1033–1046.

TABLE Ba1131–1144 Major occupational groups – native-born persons: 1850–1990[1]

Contributed by Matthew Sobek

	Total	Professionals	Farmers	Proprietors	Managers and officials	Clerical workers	Sales workers	Craft workers	Operatives	Domestic service workers	Other service workers	Farm laborers	Laborers	Unclassified
	Ba1131	Ba1132	Ba1133	Ba1134	Ba1135	Ba1136	Ba1137	Ba1138	Ba1139	Ba1140	Ba1141	Ba1142	Ba1143	Ba1144
Year	Number	Number	Number	Number	Number	Number	Number	Number	Number	Number	Number	Number	Number	Number
1850 [2,3]	4,330,033	138,387	2,212,601	155,874	49,034	11,519	91,102	664,684	333,152	10,614	30,231	246,198	386,637	—
1860 [3]	6,066,283	256,529	2,375,590	227,929	89,369	37,575	141,952	782,299	613,174	285,658	56,419	786,359	413,430	—
1870	9,067,672	304,211	2,709,112	278,579	139,159	107,708	214,839	897,093	913,332	640,063	100,186	2,139,401	623,989	—
1880	12,810,115	507,748	3,814,670	392,117	185,815	224,529	344,919	1,137,703	1,494,556	797,165	184,776	2,348,229	1,377,888	—
1900	21,642,267	977,461	5,023,149	749,792	466,723	921,303	813,539	2,185,628	2,697,125	1,551,947	648,099	3,176,749	2,430,752	—
1910	28,267,634	1,488,937	5,363,800	1,079,863	716,131	1,752,920	1,397,500	2,959,486	3,985,192	1,525,461	1,080,367	4,645,654	2,272,323	—
1920	32,259,908	2,013,450	5,935,501	1,091,891	958,222	2,986,389	1,701,349	4,203,714	4,525,996	1,196,627	1,307,667	3,139,621	3,199,481	—
1940	41,906,616	3,102,167	4,875,276	1,557,510	1,561,453	4,634,952	2,673,059	4,498,309	7,351,981	1,902,302	2,804,792	2,842,755	3,771,976	330,084
1950	51,655,571	4,682,648	4,160,706	2,100,609	2,343,351	6,796,069	3,680,116	7,042,794	10,268,683	1,264,376	3,827,511	2,141,822	3,157,707	189,179
1960	59,380,862	6,789,917	2,393,915	1,683,048	3,261,872	8,783,780	4,264,641	8,033,431	10,838,296	1,512,959	4,864,194	1,238,002	2,797,280	2,919,527
1970	71,567,577	11,132,209	1,374,444	1,395,309	4,277,406	13,011,296	5,217,408	9,722,911	12,600,965	1,074,640	7,735,700	870,603	3,154,686	—
1980	90,067,541	15,780,573	1,259,806	1,791,980	7,643,649	17,609,491	6,167,756	10,893,803	12,905,996	514,376	10,886,278	750,610	3,863,223	—
1990	103,217,455	21,383,134	1,005,295	1,861,480	11,561,956	19,774,203	7,267,483	10,868,087	11,523,739	375,952	12,749,475	550,504	4,296,147	—

[1] Data pertain to noninstitutionalized civilians age 16 and older who reported an occupation; employed persons only beginning 1940.

[2] Excludes women.

[3] Excludes slaves.

Source

Tabulated from the Integrated Public Use Microdata Series (IPUMS). See the Guide to the Millennial Edition for information on the IPUMS.

Documentation

See the text for Table Ba1033–1046.

TABLE Ba1145–1158 Major occupational groups – foreign-born persons: 1850–1990[1]

Contributed by Matthew Sobek

	Total	Professionals	Farmers	Proprietors	Managers and officials	Clerical workers	Sales workers	Craft workers	Operatives	Domestic service workers	Other service workers	Farm laborers	Laborers	Unclassified
	Ba1145	Ba1146	Ba1147	Ba1148	Ba1149	Ba1150	Ba1151	Ba1152	Ba1153	Ba1154	Ba1155	Ba1156	Ba1157	Ba1158
Year	Number	Number	Number	Number	Number	Number	Number	Number	Number	Number	Number	Number	Number	Number
1850 [2,3]	946,986	15,867	171,839	37,303	10,206	2,327	22,745	208,630	148,896	13,749	16,374	51,763	247,287	—
1860 [3]	2,094,469	37,075	331,684	84,156	26,144	8,108	48,480	372,037	362,467	223,911	39,770	151,366	409,271	—
1870	2,936,566	52,774	466,727	131,228	56,695	21,433	66,939	465,657	614,235	290,641	68,321	198,645	503,271	—
1880	3,668,802	77,192	675,441	161,375	83,476	39,402	91,374	566,144	779,126	297,084	89,462	205,827	602,899	—
1900	5,911,817	148,744	801,397	289,899	125,218	132,807	187,448	955,453	1,126,964	553,996	228,428	288,381	1,073,082	—
1910	7,968,369	210,330	665,500	518,899	175,317	191,438	241,565	1,217,900	1,823,954	454,666	444,087	431,996	1,592,717	—
1920	7,853,366	247,628	634,410	494,295	162,979	276,993	300,201	1,478,214	1,826,828	293,778	470,789	259,245	1,408,006	—
1940	5,675,252	295,951	341,526	471,863	187,269	292,014	294,859	978,265	1,234,401	210,799	572,653	160,524	601,624	33,504
1950	4,961,847	324,154	175,264	427,447	202,519	304,319	274,679	866,895	1,160,465	128,550	582,068	145,029	357,601	12,857
1960	4,489,733	433,092	82,990	214,705	203,949	424,627	292,534	674,815	1,005,428	123,121	546,756	127,784	222,746	137,186
1970	4,702,937	727,729	27,788	116,668	222,813	678,921	302,629	628,320	1,000,545	84,382	643,733	76,532	192,877	—
1980	7,310,866	1,226,621	24,558	178,312	484,981	1,134,610	375,308	823,604	1,428,204	78,351	1,088,084	138,684	329,549	—
1990	11,865,636	2,178,732	34,941	267,340	974,217	1,786,304	603,400	1,193,997	1,849,652	145,887	1,974,988	220,532	635,646	—

[1] Data pertain to noninstitutionalized civilians age 16 and older who reported an occupation; employed persons only beginning 1940.

[2] Excludes women.

[3] Excludes slaves.

Source

Tabulated from the Integrated Public Use Microdata Series (IPUMS). See the Guide to the Millennial Edition for information on the IPUMS.

Documentation

See the text for Table Ba1033–1046.

TABLE Ba1159–1395 Detailed occupations – all persons: 1850–1990[1] [Part 1]

Contributed by Matthew Sobek

		Professional, technical, and kindred workers														
															College professors and instructors	
Year	Total	Total	Accountants and auditors	Actors and actresses	Airplane pilots and navigators	Architects	Artists and art teachers	Athletes	Authors	Chemists	Chiropractors	Clergymen	College presidents and deans	Agricultural sciences	Biological sciences
	Ba1159	Ba1160	Ba1161	Ba1162	Ba1163	Ba1164	Ba1165	Ba1166	Ba1167	Ba1168	Ba1169	Ba1170	Ba1171	Ba1172	Ba1173
	Hundred	Hundred	Hundred	Hundred	Hundred	Hundred	Hundred	Hundred	Hundred	Hundred	Hundred	Hundred	Hundred	Hundred	Hundred
1850 [2,3]	52,770	1,603	7	5	0	4	21	2	1	8	0	289	1	0	0
1860 [2]	81,608	3,049	17	4	0	14	48	5	4	4	0	352	4	0	0
1870	120,042	3,780	12	8	0	22	50	0	6	17	0	490	0	0	0
1880	164,789	6,192	23	60	0	38	88	7	9	26	0	694	4	0	0
1900	275,541	11,771	76	175	0	61	228	30	30	83	0	971	0	0	0
1910	362,360	18,023	395	295	0	166	355	0	20	151	0	1,239	0	0	0
1920	401,133	22,611	1,257	250	8	155	338	36	68	331	56	1,310	9	3	0
1940	475,842	33,983	0	144	57	190	558	88	143	555	105	1,350	0	0	0
1950	569,737	50,472	3,787	160	161	252	788	83	150	780	138	1,755	57	51	62
1960	638,706	72,230	4,757	82	279	296	985	32	268	804	140	2,030	71	30	79
1970	762,705	118,599	6,997	97	496	561	1,008	0	248	1,091	139	2,189	397	49	207
1980	973,784	170,072	9,864	0	735	1,062	1,452	0	448	988	211	2,828	0	33	97
1990	1,150,831	235,619	15,457	0	1,064	1,525	2,033	0	1,036	1,353	457	3,185	0	10	61

	Professional, technical, and kindred workers														
	College professors and instructors														
Year	Chemistry	Economics	Engineering	Geology and geophysics	Mathematics	Medical sciences	Physics	Psychology	Statistics	Natural sciences not elsewhere classified	Social sciences not elsewhere classified	Nonscientific subjects	Subject not specified	Dancers and dancing teachers	Dentists
	Ba1174	Ba1175	Ba1176	Ba1177	Ba1178	Ba1179	Ba1180	Ba1181	Ba1182	Ba1183	Ba1184	Ba1185	Ba1186	Ba1187	Ba1188
	Hundred	Hundred	Hundred	Hundred	Hundred	Hundred	Hundred	Hundred	Hundred	Hundred	Hundred	Hundred	Hundred	Hundred	Hundred
1850 [2,3]	0	0	0	0	1	0	0	0	0	0	0	3	8	1	20
1860 [2]	0	0	0	0	2	1	0	0	0	0	0	9	6	7	65
1870	0	0	0	2	2	0	0	0	0	0	0	2	10	2	67
1880	1	0	0	1	2	0	0	0	0	1	0	18	14	1	122
1900	0	0	0	0	0	0	0	0	0	0	0	0	91	15	250
1910	0	0	0	0	0	0	0	0	0	0	0	0	257	0	426
1920	4	0	7	0	2	5	2	0	0	1	6	10	258	39	570
1940	0	0	0	0	0	0	0	0	0	0	0	0	739	126	707
1950	70	36	85	9	50	24	41	38	5	1	194	237	256	132	729
1960	66	40	96	17	95	64	52	28	1	3	251	302	526	196	832
1970	154	99	164	0	257	280	141	127	0	45	347	937	1,555	58	913
1980	83	51	111	0	189	278	56	56	0	23	130	508	4,262	115	1,258
1990	51	36	74	0	207	183	39	43	0	13	78	466	6,177	206	1,538

	Professional, technical, and kindred workers														
	Designers	Dietitians and nutritionists	Draftsmen	Editors and reporters	Engineers, aeronautical	Engineers, chemical	Engineers, civil	Engineers, electrical	Engineers, industrial	Engineers, mechanical	Engineers, metallurgical, metallurgists	Engineers, mining	Engineers not elsewhere classified	Entertainers not elsewhere classified	Farm and home management advisors
	Ba1189	Ba1190	Ba1191	Ba1192	Ba1193	Ba1194	Ba1195	Ba1196	Ba1197	Ba1198	Ba1199	Ba1200	Ba1201	Ba1202	Ba1203
Year	Hundred	Hundred	Hundred	Hundred	Hundred	Hundred	Hundred	Hundred	Hundred	Hundred	Hundred	Hundred	Hundred	Hundred	Hundred
1850 [2, 3]	2	0	1	23	0	0	6	0	0	1	0	0	0	9	0
1860 [2]	0	0	2	38	0	0	22	0	0	2	0	2	0	5	6
1870	2	0	8	55	0	0	32	0	0	0	0	8	0	14	2
1880	8	0	24	123	0	0	64	0	0	4	0	10	0	39	0
1900	46	0	114	288	0	0	114	46	0	106	0	38	0	91	0
1910	103	0	325	350	0	0	433	0	0	144	0	103	0	212	0
1920	167	16	528	342	4	13	682	294	33	266	11	62	99	39	33
1940	230	0	894	592	0	116	842	542	136	782	109	0	0	62	120
1950	429	230	1,153	888	185	317	1,284	1,098	463	1,154	123	108	774	151	141
1960	698	262	2,169	1,296	521	411	1,576	1,757	1,019	1,565	178	114	1,441	101	130
1970	1,080	407	2,845	2,212	656	521	1,733	2,820	1,840	1,807	159	154	2,416	609	132
1980	3,233	653	3,178	3,181	856	569	2,006	3,203	3,057	2,114	237	328	2,943	951	0
1990	5,756	892	3,114	4,219	1,379	637	2,455	4,535	4,469	1,949	174	304	3,826	1,597	0

	Professional, technical, and kindred workers														
								Natural scientists not elsewhere classified							
	Foresters and conservationists	Funeral directors and embalmers	Lawyers and judges	Librarians	Musicians and music teachers	Nurses, professional	Nurses, student professional	Agricultural scientists	Biological scientists	Geologists and geophysicists	Mathematicians	Physicists	Miscellaneous natural scientists	Optometrists	Osteopaths
	Ba1204	Ba1205	Ba1206	Ba1207	Ba1208	Ba1209	Ba1210	Ba1211	Ba1212	Ba1213	Ba1214	Ba1215	Ba1216	Ba1217	Ba1218
Year	Hundred	Hundred	Hundred	Hundred	Hundred	Hundred	Hundred	Hundred	Hundred	Hundred	Hundred	Hundred	Hundred	Hundred	Hundred
1850 [2, 3]	0	6	244	0	33	0	0	0	0	0	0	0	1	0	0
1860 [2]	0	10	343	2	116	2	0	0	1	0	0	0	0	0	0
1870	0	24	443	4	162	2	0	0	2	0	0	0	0	0	0
1880	0	58	655	7	340	2	0	0	2	3	0	0	0	0	0
1900	8	137	1,025	61	918	99	0	0	0	0	0	8	8	0	0
1910	43	174	1,116	73	1,416	945	0	0	0	0	0	0	0	0	0
1920	73	227	1,223	140	1,210	1,143	187	5	18	21	0	2	3	34	37
1940	0	349	1,713	351	1,309	3,273	0	0	0	0	0	0	0	125	68
1950	269	387	1,786	610	1,630	4,046	674	57	91	107	23	75	21	170	70
1960	326	368	2,094	856	1,856	5,791	571	81	126	198	71	134	29	173	43
1970	398	409	2,778	1,332	2,712	9,179	180	130	290	227	77	224	13	177	0
1980	537	403	5,245	1,990	5,022	14,060	0	245	652	461	63	318	87	247	0
1990	489	456	7,631	2,510	7,763	21,145	0	327	870	518	57	376	182	271	0

Notes appear at end of table

(continued)

TABLE Ba1159–1395 Detailed occupations – all persons: 1850–1990 [Part 1] *Continued*

Year	Professional, technical, and kindred workers: Personnel and labor-relations workers	Pharmacists	Photographers	Physicians and surgeons	Radio operators	Recreation and group workers	Religious workers	Social and welfare workers, except group	Social scientists: Economists	Social scientists: Psychologists	Social scientists: Statisticians and actuaries	Social scientists: Miscellaneous social scientists	Sports instructors and officials	Surveyors	Teachers not elsewhere classified
	Ba1219	Ba1220	Ba1221	Ba1222	Ba1223	Ba1224	Ba1225	Ba1226	Ba1227	Ba1228	Ba1229	Ba1230	Ba1231	Ba1232	Ba1233
	Hundred	Hundred	Hundred	Hundred	Hundred	Hundred	Hundred	Hundred	Hundred	Hundred	Hundred	Hundred	Hundred	Hundred	Hundred
1850 [2,3]	0	55	7	432	0	0	1	0	0	0	0	0	0	13	326
1860 [2]	0	99	54	622	0	0	26	0	0	0	0	0	0	28	1,117
1870	0	188	61	672	0	0	12	4	0	0	0	0	12	32	1,293
1880	0	285	112	888	0	0	57	0	0	0	0	0	0	39	2,292
1900	0	501	258	1,313	0	0	137	0	0	0	0	15	8	68	4,090
1910	0	640	315	1,542	0	0	196	5	0	0	0	0	0	45	6,197
1920	21	720	277	1,353	30	74	315	126	2	1	26	3	96	95	7,366
1940	0	801	349	1,723	90	0	324	739	0	0	0	0	244	179	10,561
1950	539	975	541	1,975	190	158	431	847	99	42	235	40	445	268	11,525
1960	1,006	966	509	2,253	265	386	579	1,001	166	138	203	31	714	425	16,866
1970	2,918	1,095	644	2,784	534	499	344	2,179	643	292	271	126	653	592	27,648
1980	6,247	1,435	905	4,305	1,083	339	478	4,468	947	913	401	304	575	780	37,003
1990	7,647	1,811	1,359	5,731	777	457	969	6,414	1,471	1,892	481	490	825	985	44,657

Year	Professional, technical, and kindred workers: Technicians – medical and dental	Technicians – testing	Technicians not elsewhere classified	Therapists and healers not elsewhere classified	Veterinarians	Professional, technical, and kindred workers not elsewhere classified	Farmers: Total	Farmers – owners and tenants	Farm managers	Managers, officials, and proprietors: Total	Buyers and department heads – store	Buyers and shippers – farm products	Conductors – railroad	Credit men	Floormen and floor managers – store
	Ba1234	Ba1235	Ba1236	Ba1237	Ba1238	Ba1239	Ba1240	Ba1241	Ba1242	Ba1243	Ba1244	Ba1245	Ba1246	Ba1247	Ba1248
	Hundred	Hundred	Hundred	Hundred	Hundred	Hundred	Hundred	Hundred	Hundred	Hundred	Hundred	Hundred	Hundred	Hundred	Hundred
1850 [2,3]	0	0	0	0	0	71	23,844	23,837	7	2,455	0	3	4	0	0
1860 [2]	0	0	0	1	2	7	27,073	27,017	56	4,125	0	59	66	0	0
1870	0	2	1	4	8	41	31,758	31,736	22	5,681	0	119	99	0	0
1880	0	0	0	7	29	38	44,901	44,875	26	7,645	1	236	185	0	0
1900	0	0	8	61	106	91	58,245	58,116	129	15,436	38	531	402	8	23
1910	0	0	0	76	123	144	60,688	60,278	411	23,418	0	506	607	0	181
1920	48	69	13	64	151	120	65,699	64,749	951	27,074	415	606	827	90	49
1940	0	608	81	200	114	1,597	52,169	51,822	347	37,784	693	368	476	310	106
1950	807	835	310	250	173	1,141	43,505	43,183	322	51,019	1,361	283	551	364	104
1960	1,376	2,495	961	348	165	3,003	24,769	24,525	244	53,636	2,324	197	464	505	108
1970	2,751	3,301	1,567	815	191	12,681	14,022	13,437	585	60,122	6,292	205	391	597	0
1980	5,686	8,032	2,606	1,995	341	10,556	12,844	11,469	1,375	100,989	8,373	185	450	0	0
1990	9,726	9,776	3,781	3,354	485	19,337	10,402	8,127	2,275	146,650	8,100	159	357	0	0

Year	Managers, officials, and proprietors								Clerical and kindred workers						
	Inspectors – public administration	Managers and superintendents – building	Officers, pilots, pursers, and engineers – ship	Officials and administrators not elsewhere classified – public administration	Officials – lodge, society, union, and so forth	Postmasters	Purchasing agents and buyers not elsewhere classified	Managers, officials, and proprietors not elsewhere classified	Total	Agents not elsewhere classified	Attendants and assistants – library	Attendants – physician's and dentist's office	Baggagemen – transportation	Bank tellers	Bookkeepers
	Ba1249	Ba1250	Ba1251	Ba1252	Ba1253	Ba1254	Ba1255	Ba1256	Ba1257	Ba1258	Ba1259	Ba1260	Ba1261	Ba1262	Ba1263
	Hundred	Hundred	Hundred	Hundred	Hundred	Hundred	Hundred	Hundred	Hundred	Hundred	Hundred	Hundred	Hundred	Hundred	Hundred
1850 [2,3]	11	22	78	70	0	19	0	2,248	138	25	0	1	8	4	22
1860 [2]	6	38	166	114	0	46	0	3,629	457	53	0	0	14	12	143
1870	21	12	165	138	0	31	0	5,095	1,291	40	10	0	18	10	304
1880	37	17	180	282	11	63	11	6,622	2,641	211	0	0	51	14	649
1900	76	0	175	228	30	250	0	13,675	10,541	311	15	0	76	61	2,391
1910	0	0	247	846	60	290	0	20,680	19,053	496	0	0	131	76	3,882
1920	200	187	435	554	104	301	163	23,143	32,634	337	33	127	112	211	5,245
1940	433	771	301	1,303	223	382	416	32,002	49,271	1,007	337	382	54	0	8,677
1950	566	755	478	1,294	247	366	683	43,966	71,393	1,353	149	408	77	669	7,494
1960	719	510	352	1,934	317	378	1,032	44,796	92,084	1,592	332	752	56	1,314	9,243
1970	983	850	236	2,706	491	350	1,611	45,410	136,902	217	1,228	2,072	0	2,512	15,346
1980	1,496	1,940	369	3,653	0	308	2,598	81,616	187,441	0	1,387	4,305	0	4,953	18,249
1990	1,572	3,992	363	8,859	0	406	3,561	119,281	215,605	0	1,462	3,868	0	4,892	18,464

Year	Clerical and kindred workers													
	Cashiers	Collectors, bill and account	Dispatchers and starters – vehicle	Express messengers and railway mail clerks	Mail carriers	Messengers and office boys	Office machine operators	Shipping and receiving clerks	Stenographers, typists, and secretaries	Telegraph messengers	Telegraph operators	Telephone operators	Ticket, station, and express agents	Clerical and kindred workers not elsewhere classified
	Ba1264	Ba1265	Ba1266	Ba1267	Ba1268	Ba1269	Ba1270	Ba1271	Ba1272	Ba1273	Ba1274	Ba1275	Ba1276	Ba1277
	Hundred	Hundred	Hundred	Hundred	Hundred	Hundred	Hundred	Hundred	Hundred	Hundred	Hundred	Hundred	Hundred	Hundred
1850 [2,3]	1	12	0	0	8	5	0	3	0	1	5	0	13	29
1860 [2]	6	28	0	8	28	12	0	2	2	0	8	0	50	90
1870	10	17	2	22	20	22	0	14	0	1	53	0	118	630
1880	30	37	12	16	90	57	0	75	12	4	161	10	213	1,001
1900	281	228	23	68	220	296	8	281	1,002	30	584	220	334	4,113
1910	655	322	0	184	844	539	0	773	3,063	35	683	924	287	6,159
1920	832	327	30	264	977	477	154	1,260	6,603	48	787	1,879	535	12,395
1940	0	389	0	244	1,237	527	732	2,263	11,097	129	521	1,974	435	19,266
1950	2,348	211	339	195	1,680	635	1,516	2,936	16,300	79	357	3,801	593	30,253
1960	4,708	321	556	70	1,895	560	3,014	2,751	22,470	35	194	3,544	728	37,950
1970	8,182	511	602	0	2,503	508	5,492	4,089	38,060	21	128	4,106	983	50,342
1980	17,120	832	947	0	2,545	817	9,388	6,398	46,487	0	78	3,585	993	69,358
1990	25,346	1,548	1,952	0	3,191	1,325	13,782	7,939	45,945	0	0	2,249	2,609	81,033

Notes appear at end of table

(continued)

TABLE Ba1159–1395 Detailed occupations – all persons: 1850–1990 [Part 1] *Continued*

	Sales workers										Craft workers, foremen, and kindred workers				
	Total	Advertising agents and salesmen	Auctioneers	Demonstrators	Hucksters and peddlers	Insurance agents and brokers	Newsboys	Real estate agents and brokers	Stock and bond salesmen	Salesmen and sales clerks not elsewhere classified	Total	Bakers	Blacksmiths	Bookbinders	Boilermakers
	Ba1278	Ba1279	Ba1280	Ba1281	Ba1282	Ba1283	Ba1284	Ba1285	Ba1286	Ba1287	Ba1288	Ba1289	Ba1290	Ba1291	Ba1292
Year	Hundred	Hundred	Hundred	Hundred	Hundred	Hundred	Hundred	Hundred	Hundred	Hundred	Hundred	Hundred	Hundred	Hundred	Hundred
1850 [2,3]	1,144	0	8	0	112	6	5	4	1	1,007	8,733	146	952	32	19
1860 [2]	1,938	0	18	0	215	10	12	20	0	1,663	11,543	203	1,132	62	20
1870	2,970	6	16	0	381	134	22	98	0	2,313	13,636	259	1,420	66	56
1880	4,581	5	26	0	557	134	22	137	6	3,695	17,045	364	1,764	98	106
1900	10,010	30	15	0	751	683	23	546	0	7,961	31,760	706	2,170	395	304
1910	17,172	0	25	38	877	778	106	1,290	161	13,897	42,472	695	2,363	320	395
1920	20,016	169	57	39	465	1,248	79	1,245	173	16,541	56,819	1,029	2,010	227	716
1940	29,680	363	72	87	526	2,390	386	1,164	231	24,461	54,768	1,357	823	0	303
1950	39,795	301	157	179	226	3,091	431	1,562	140	33,708	79,544	1,166	434	302	348
1960	45,572	345	40	262	492	4,314	792	1,985	310	37,033	87,082	1,085	205	277	206
1970	55,200	635	49	387	1,183	5,492	621	2,605	967	43,261	103,512	1,079	166	336	287
1980	65,431	1,103	66	113	2,050	7,370	971	6,447	1,311	46,000	117,174	1,176	0	283	334
1990	78,709	1,658	77	401	2,083	10,538	1,049	7,818	2,879	52,206	120,621	1,519	0	276	208

	Craft workers, foremen, and kindred workers														
	Brickmasons, stonemasons, and tile setters	Cabinetmakers	Carpenters	Cement and concrete finishers	Compositors and typesetters	Cranemen, derrickmen, and hoistmen	Decorators and window dressers	Electricians	Electrotypers and stereotypers	Engravers, except photoengravers	Excavating, grading, and road machinery operators	Foremen not elsewhere classified	Forgemen and hammermen	Furriers	Glaziers
	Ba1293	Ba1294	Ba1295	Ba1296	Ba1297	Ba1298	Ba1299	Ba1300	Ba1301	Ba1302	Ba1303	Ba1304	Ba1305	Ba1306	Ba1307
Year	Hundred	Hundred	Hundred	Hundred	Hundred	Hundred	Hundred	Hundred	Hundred	Hundred	Hundred	Hundred	Hundred	Hundred	Hundred
1850 [2,3]	507	377	2,194	1	158	0	0	0	0	18	14	24	10	2	1
1860 [2]	647	338	2,919	0	204	0	0	0	0	28	4	242	13	8	8
1870	876	332	3,526	0	282	2	4	0	2	37	13	118	12	12	8
1880	952	354	3,858	5	555	0	0	4	10	55	7	235	6	16	7
1900	1,571	387	6,246	0	1,260	8	0	501	46	53	0	1,222	0	23	23
1910	1,821	416	8,131	0	1,267	0	58	1,297	63	136	0	2,945	68	0	0
1920	1,253	538	8,374	80	1,482	306	82	2,063	40	106	106	4,818	90	88	37
1940	1,156	707	6,062	238	1,672	1,091	317	1,964	90	76	0	5,919	0	164	123
1950	1,595	692	9,027	338	1,797	1,057	414	3,128	197	109	1,086	8,465	174	138	147
1960	1,829	624	8,160	391	1,805	1,217	501	3,380	91	126	1,953	11,705	105	43	165
1970	1,880	659	8,300	651	1,539	1,495	689	4,485	68	80	3,084	15,741	150	28	247
1980	1,954	719	11,169	568	683	1,487	0	6,035	0	140	3,421	21,709	140	84	306
1990	2,320	689	12,353	626	706	956	0	6,602	0	165	3,658	17,397	162	152	429

Craft workers, foremen, and kindred workers

Year	Heat treaters, annealers, temperers	Inspectors, scalers, and graders – log and lumber	Inspectors not elsewhere classified	Jewelers, watchmakers, goldsmiths, silversmiths	Job setters – metal	Linemen and servicemen	Locomotive engineers	Locomotive firemen	Loom fixers	Machinists	Mechanics and repairmen – airplane	Mechanics and repairmen – automobile	Mechanics and repairmen – office machine	Mechanics and repairmen – radio and television	Mechanics and repairmen – railroad and car shop
	Ba1308	Ba1309	Ba1310	Ba1311	Ba1312	Ba1313	Ba1314	Ba1315	Ba1316	Ba1317	Ba1318	Ba1319	Ba1320	Ba1321	Ba1322
	Hundred	Hundred	Hundred	Hundred	Hundred	Hundred	Hundred	Hundred	Hundred	Hundred	Hundred	Hundred	Hundred	Hundred	Hundred
1850 [2, 3]	0	1	5	119	0	0	5	0	0	234	0	0	0	0	1
1860 [2]	0	2	8	130	0	0	18	10	0	373	0	0	0	0	4
1870	0	13	11	157	0	0	114	78	0	533	0	0	0	0	18
1880	5	4	33	223	0	11	165	109	3	837	0	0	0	0	23
1900	0	61	212	357	0	83	539	486	46	2,550	0	0	0	0	152
1910	13	0	499	280	0	244	1,053	713	123	4,496	0	0	0	0	338
1920	37	124	903	357	25	577	1,130	929	182	8,209	10	1,976	29	1	746
1940	130	172	775	457	0	1,112	682	463	210	4,689	236	3,744	0	0	380
1950	174	195	1,015	498	246	2,140	783	580	329	5,096	708	6,737	183	773	520
1960	199	175	989	377	378	2,730	584	358	272	4,976	1,142	6,679	291	1,072	402
1970	204	174	1,159	367	840	3,909	477	127	207	3,678	1,479	9,044	713	1,360	557
1980	227	0	489	726	543	4,165	705	0	0	4,991	1,084	12,366	825	1,604	0
1990	177	0	671	882	273	3,537	444	0	0	5,424	1,626	13,633	1,262	1,668	0

Craft workers, foremen, and kindred workers

Year	Mechanics and repairmen not elsewhere classified	Millers – grain, flour, feed, and so forth	Millwrights	Molders – metal	Motion picture projectionists	Opticians and lens grinders and polishers	Painters – construction and maintenance	Paperhangers	Pattern and model makers, except paper	Photoengravers and lithographers	Piano and organ tuners and repairmen	Plasterers	Plumbers and pipe fitters	Pressmen and plate printers – printing	Rollers and roll hands – metal
	Ba1323	Ba1324	Ba1325	Ba1326	Ba1327	Ba1328	Ba1329	Ba1330	Ba1331	Ba1332	Ba1333	Ba1334	Ba1335	Ba1336	Ba1337
	Hundred	Hundred	Hundred	Hundred	Hundred	Hundred	Hundred	Hundred	Hundred	Hundred	Hundred	Hundred	Hundred	Hundred	Hundred
1850 [2, 3]	288	318	91	89	0	2	213	6	16	8	0	94	15	1	10
1860 [2]	384	394	54	179	0	2	503	16	20	8	2	154	65	0	18
1870	260	381	114	281	0	3	732	19	30	8	8	156	126	0	68
1880	297	433	92	400	0	14	1,092	39	57	33	14	271	179	7	28
1900	569	296	114	896	0	61	2,262	205	159	76	15	379	964	288	0
1910	388	217	217	1,217	0	96	2,753	239	237	71	91	458	1,524	262	166
1920	1,203	241	383	1,315	101	126	2,695	193	300	118	69	382	2,157	244	263
1940	4,105	158	406	710	298	137	3,348	298	317	257	97	458	1,779	371	266
1950	8,426	122	584	576	250	209	4,070	243	529	308	140	648	2,747	577	341
1960	12,460	95	602	507	169	193	3,692	101	430	282	49	475	3,081	741	294
1970	10,945	71	794	531	165	276	3,533	0	386	322	67	281	3,645	1,520	196
1980	15,115	0	1,249	342	135	451	4,243	0	333	250	0	254	4,652	2,827	177
1990	15,879	0	891	195	97	727	5,688	0	290	470	0	379	4,670	3,368	120

Notes appear at end of table

(continued)

TABLE Ba1159–1395 Detailed occupations – all persons: 1850–1990 [Part 1] *Continued*

	Craft workers, foremen, and kindred workers										Operatives and kindred workers				
	Roofers and slaters	Shoemakers and repairers, except factory	Stationary engineers	Stonecutters and stone carvers	Structural metal workers	Tailors and tailoresses	Tinsmiths, coppersmiths, sheet metal workers	Toolmakers, die makers, and setters	Upholsterers	Craftsmen and kindred workers not elsewhere classified	Total	Apprentice auto mechanics	Apprentice bricklayers and masons	Apprentice carpenters	Apprentice electricians
	Ba1338	Ba1339	Ba1340	Ba1341	Ba1342	Ba1343	Ba1344	Ba1345	Ba1346	Ba1347	Ba1348	Ba1349	Ba1350	Ba1351	Ba1352
Year	Hundred	Hundred	Hundred	Hundred	Hundred	Hundred	Hundred	Hundred	Hundred	Hundred	Hundred	Hundred	Hundred	Hundred	Hundred
1850 [2, 3]	1	1,363	103	112	0	561	112	5	24	477	4,823	0	0	3	0
1860 [2]	13	1,308	226	148	2	913	193	6	26	533	9,756	0	6	84	0
1870	38	1,130	299	194	0	846	268	12	47	665	15,278	0	25	70	0
1880	45	1,055	617	286	1	1,185	397	10	93	592	22,745	0	5	46	0
1900	99	949	1,442	440	15	1,859	592	0	258	425	38,241	0	0	8	15
1910	149	650	2,237	322	106	1,950	650	118	184	438	57,409	0	0	0	0
1920	116	714	2,054	218	854	2,106	703	611	217	753	66,376	33	1	13	35
1940	299	656	1,897	190	423	1,076	792	930	392	0	85,869	0	0	128	63
1950	505	562	2,248	115	489	1,029	1,271	1,575	646	743	114,892	65	76	111	118
1960	488	348	2,750	45	575	379	1,371	1,838	570	1,057	118,437	14	21	53	87
1970	572	767	1,721	68	847	673	1,471	1,914	620	6,865	136,015	33	40	78	205
1980	998	1,096	1,616	0	980	565	1,474	1,843	641	0	143,342	35	23	82	174
1990	1,633	1,265	2,147	0	782	529	1,570	1,404	701	0	133,734	16	8	42	141

	Operatives and kindred workers														
	Apprentice machinists and toolmakers	Apprentice mechanics, except auto	Apprentice plumbers and pipe fitters	Apprentices – building trades not elsewhere classified	Apprentices – metalworking trades not elsewhere classified	Apprentices – printing trades	Apprentices – other specified trades	Apprentices – trade not specified	Asbestos and insulation workers	Attendants – auto service and parking	Blasters and powdermen	Boatmen, canalmen, and lock keepers	Brakemen – railroad	Bus drivers	Chainmen, rodmen, and axmen – surveying
	Ba1353	Ba1354	Ba1355	Ba1356	Ba1357	Ba1358	Ba1359	Ba1360	Ba1361	Ba1362	Ba1363	Ba1364	Ba1365	Ba1366	Ba1367
Year	Hundred	Hundred	Hundred	Hundred	Hundred	Hundred	Hundred	Hundred	Hundred	Hundred	Hundred	Hundred	Hundred	Hundred	Hundred
1850 [2, 3]	0	0	0	2	0	0	9	21	0	0	0	277	4	38	0
1860 [2]	14	8	8	24	110	20	128	80	0	0	0	260	30	32	0
1870	35	14	10	39	119	31	163	29	0	0	6	212	125	36	0
1880	40	0	11	12	68	16	161	19	0	0	0	211	230	40	0
1900	129	0	30	0	114	15	159	46	0	0	0	91	835	0	8
1910	0	0	0	191	0	0	53	592	0	0	0	53	942	0	0
1920	166	12	54	6	72	45	79	94	26	37	23	57	1,215	111	20
1940	171	0	104	169	0	165	260	122	104	2,291	64	130	720	0	125
1950	171	45	205	54	86	219	149	149	181	2,442	116	151	781	1,580	124
1960	137	41	88	26	46	116	90	105	209	3,450	59	67	586	1,825	90
1970	189	68	139	19	61	88	117	33	251	4,467	75	47	470	2,341	106
1980	152	0	107	0	8	0	45	0	482	3,333	95	0	768	3,746	93
1990	37	0	67	0	9	0	20	0	623	2,817	82	0	314	4,285	41

Year	Operatives and kindred workers													
	Conductors – bus and street railway	Deliverymen and routemen	Dressmakers and seamstresses, except factory	Dyers	Filers, grinders, and polishers – metal	Fruit, nut, vegetable graders, packers, not factory	Furnacemen, smeltermen, and pourers	Heaters – metal	Laundry and dry cleaning operatives	Meat cutters, except slaughter and packing houses	Milliners	Mine operatives and laborers	Motormen, mine, factory, logging camp, and so forth	Motormen, street, subway, and elevated railway
	Ba1368	Ba1369	Ba1370	Ba1371	Ba1372	Ba1373	Ba1374	Ba1375	Ba1376	Ba1377	Ba1378	Ba1379	Ba1380	Ba1381
	Hundred	Hundred	Hundred	Hundred	Hundred	Hundred	Hundred	Hundred	Hundred	Hundred	Hundred	Hundred	Hundred	Hundred
1850 [2,3]	0	13	24	23	2	0	97	1	3	189	7	872	0	1
1860 [2]	5	27	1,327	26	33	0	60	12	10	327	272	1,197	0	16
1870	8	57	1,454	24	48	0	118	8	131	424	258	1,721	0	27
1880	17	123	2,261	51	73	0	405	22	539	753	392	2,564	0	106
1900	152	243	4,273	0	410	15	212	38	137	873	865	5,585	0	364
1910	610	2,134	4,008	164	418	45	297	71	1,088	151	1,290	8,887	0	668
1920	597	1,523	2,822	187	625	90	283	145	1,443	1,256	653	10,133	90	586
1940	164	3,708	1,484	222	1,040	363	280	205	2,117	1,348	111	6,790	158	355
1950	128	2,327	1,424	289	1,552	461	570	116	4,264	1,719	174	5,639	242	250
1960	42	4,045	1,183	181	1,474	190	537	81	3,887	1,807	40	2,887	129	74
1970	94	6,091	984	239	2,476	274	657	68	3,527	2,022	23	2,126	94	0
1980	0	6,797	957	0	2,708	0	0	0	2,693	2,762	0	2,892	0	0
1990	0	1,356	893	0	1,358	0	0	0	3,303	2,562	0	1,919	0	0

Year	Operatives and kindred workers													
	Oilers and greasers, except auto	Painters, except construction or maintenance	Photographic process workers	Power station operators	Sailors and deckhands	Sawyers	Spinners – textile	Stationary firemen	Switchmen – railroad	Taxicab drivers and chauffeurs	Truck and tractor drivers	Weavers – textile	Welders and flame cutters	Operatives and kindred workers not elsewhere classified
	Ba1382	Ba1383	Ba1384	Ba1385	Ba1386	Ba1387	Ba1388	Ba1389	Ba1390	Ba1391	Ba1392	Ba1393	Ba1394	Ba1395
	Hundred	Hundred	Hundred	Hundred	Hundred	Hundred	Hundred	Hundred	Hundred	Hundred	Hundred	Hundred	Hundred	Hundred
1850 [2,3]	0	22	0	0	656	97	53	17	1	12	317	167	1	1,892
1860 [2]	0	66	0	0	629	143	254	30	2	28	556	441	4	3,485
1870	0	112	2	0	605	99	55	38	16	47	1,095	238	4	7,772
1880	0	189	1	0	707	91	22	146	30	65	1,537	264	2	11,527
1900	23	250	0	0	425	288	607	531	175	516	4,470	1,442	8	14,890
1910	154	584	0	0	481	456	544	1,035	645	804	4,249	2,053	28	24,716
1920	260	656	66	40	521	392	808	1,339	686	1,620	5,795	1,851	261	29,546
1940	363	839	235	333	364	432	0	1,144	436	0	11,739	0	1,256	45,766
1950	603	1,460	318	235	466	973	784	1,342	661	2,038	13,439	1,037	2,750	62,805
1960	499	1,407	398	271	333	876	543	865	574	1,595	15,484	633	3,648	67,650
1970	453	1,350	603	186	255	977	0	955	529	1,541	13,704	481	5,337	82,143
1980	416	1,801	836	278	283	935	0	1,435	92	1,750	17,077	687	7,048	82,753
1990	234	1,556	939	370	220	849	0	902	52	1,926	26,672	563	5,868	73,689

[1] Data pertain to noninstitutionalized civilians age 16 and older who reported an occupation; employed persons only beginning 1940.

[2] Excludes slaves.

[3] Excludes women.

Source

Matthew Sobek, "New Statistics on the U.S. Labor Force, 1850–1990," *Historical Methods* 34 (2001): 71–87, Table A1.

Documentation

Tabulated from the Integrated Public Use Microdata Series (IPUMS). See the Guide to the Millennial Edition for information on the IPUMS.

Occupations are classified according to the 1950 Census scheme, a hierarchical system intended to reflect relative socioeconomic status. The major groupings in the table are organized from highest to lowest status as conceived by government statisticians at the time. Differing census years were coded

(continued)

TABLE Ba1159–1395 Detailed occupations – all persons: 1850–1990 [Part 1] *Continued*

into the 1950 classification in the source. The underlying data were less detailed in some years than others; therefore, select occupational categories disappear in some years. They may have been combined with other similar occupations or relegated to the residual categories at the end of each major grouping. See the source for more discussion of the underlying data and methodology.

The census occupational classification changed markedly between 1970 and 1980. Application of the 1950 classification to 1980 and 1990 imposed some costs. Users should be cognizant of the imperfect translations of many of the occupational categories for these years.

Only currently employed persons are included in this table, beginning in 1940. In prior years, varying instructions governed legitimate occupation responses, but employment status was not a condition.

See Tables Ba1033–1158 for comparable statistics limited to the major occupational groupings.

Series Ba1396–1399 (service workers in private households). Difficulties with terminology (for example, housekeeper, keeping house, nurse) makes the classification of domestic service workers problematic in many cases, particularly in the nineteenth century. The figures should be used with some caution.

Series Ba1420 (practical nurses). In early censuses, it is often difficult to distinguish medical nurses from domestic servants (nurses).

Series Ba1428–1429 (farm laborers). Unpaid family farm laborers are combined with wage-work farm laborers in many years. In practice, they are not consistently distinguished before 1920. The 1910 Census instructions led to many more responses from female farm laborers than in surrounding censuses. The 1920 Census was the only one taken in January, depressing farm labor counts to some degree.

Series Ba1437 (teamsters). For consistency over time, persons identified as teamsters before 1940 are coded to truck and tractor drivers, series Ba1392, which was the functional equivalent for later years.

TABLE Ba1396–1439 Detailed occupations – all persons: 1850–1990[1] [Part 2]

Contributed by Matthew Sobek

	Service workers, private household				Service workers, not household										
	Total	Housekeepers – private household	Laundresses – private household	Private household workers not elsewhere classified	Total	Attendants – hospital and other institution	Attendants – professional and personal service not elsewhere classified	Attendants – recreation and amusement	Barbers, beauticians, and manicurists	Bartenders	Bootblacks	Boarding and lodging house keepers	Charwomen and cleaners	Cooks, except private household	Counter and fountain workers
	Ba1396	Ba1397	Ba1398	Ba1399	Ba1400	Ba1401	Ba1402	Ba1403	Ba1404	Ba1405	Ba1406	Ba1407	Ba1408	Ba1409	Ba1410
Year	Hundred	Hundred	Hundred	Hundred	Hundred	Hundred	Hundred	Hundred	Hundred	Hundred	Hundred	Hundred	Hundred	Hundred	Hundred
1850 [2,3]	244	1	3	240	466	1	0	1	78	55	0	30	0	0	0
1860 [2]	5,096	4	385	4,707	966	2	21	2	87	101	3	147	5	2	0
1870	9,307	16	572	8,719	1,688	12	74	2	220	187	3	122	1	48	0
1880	10,942	619	785	9,539	2,745	15	96	7	450	249	12	245	6	102	0
1900	21,059	584	3,764	16,711	8,765	0	8	0	1,229	1,025	76	637	15	167	0
1910	19,801	1,955	5,189	12,658	15,333	0	229	0	1,932	1,101	164	1,597	315	1,615	0
1920	14,904	1,978	3,831	9,095	17,785	196	123	66	2,174	233	135	1,266	322	1,772	76
1940	21,134	3,383	1,934	15,816	33,775	1,145	368	588	4,210	1,202	146	632	754	3,088	0
1950	14,007	1,424	705	11,877	44,466	2,053	521	551	3,902	2,081	140	278	1,199	4,538	918
1960	16,361	1,449	403	14,508	54,110	3,883	714	455	4,800	1,744	81	299	1,686	5,579	1,522
1970	11,590	1,020	116	10,454	83,794	7,196	2,146	682	6,411	1,870	38	71	4,351	8,295	1,492
1980	5,927	660	19	5,248	119,744	12,955	7,754	1,548	6,432	2,874	0	0	6,115	15,450	1,879
1990	5,218	321	17	4,881	147,245	17,194	11,791	2,306	7,920	3,008	0	0	6,396	21,065	2,055

	Service workers, not household														
	Elevator operators	Firemen (fire protection)	Guards, watchmen, and doorkeepers	Housekeepers and stewards, except household	Janitors and sextons	Marshals and constables	Midwives	Policemen and detectives	Porters	Practical nurses	Sheriffs and bailiffs	Ushers – recreation and amusement	Waiters and waitresses	Watchmen (crossing) and bridge tenders	Service workers (not private household) not elsewhere classified
	Ba1411	Ba1412	Ba1413	Ba1414	Ba1415	Ba1416	Ba1417	Ba1418	Ba1419	Ba1420	Ba1421	Ba1422	Ba1423	Ba1424	Ba1425
Year	Hundred	Hundred	Hundred	Hundred	Hundred	Hundred	Hundred	Hundred	Hundred	Hundred	Hundred	Hundred	Hundred	Hundred	Hundred
1850 [2,3]	0	0	30	12	2	34	0	29	60	7	15	0	70	18	23
1860 [2]	0	2	70	56	7	43	16	36	132	75	21	2	93	16	25
1870	0	8	125	33	59	36	16	135	173	75	39	0	220	39	59
1880	0	18	223	38	80	57	26	149	206	173	69	0	312	47	167
1900	121	159	531	425	607	83	46	402	600	1,616	68	0	873	76	0
1910	186	317	809	647	1,103	98	50	683	849	1,310	108	0	2,025	35	159
1920	365	562	1,266	479	1,541	57	48	929	1,104	1,256	98	47	2,053	101	1,515
1940	790	750	2,225	932	3,659	100	0	1,496	1,588	956	150	193	5,424	167	3,213
1950	917	1,129	2,552	1,085	4,621	77	11	2,031	1,665	1,433	194	220	6,795	127	5,430
1960	751	1,321	2,473	1,469	6,010	78	12	2,610	1,404	2,070	261	120	8,154	270	6,344
1970	363	1,749	3,177	1,360	12,081	52	8	3,718	189	2,357	344	146	10,281	414	15,006
1980	202	2,097	6,418	664	20,589	0	0	4,916	196	4,251	608	218	13,617	489	10,474
1990	102	2,484	9,458	1,025	24,127	0	0	6,144	353	4,185	1,194	269	13,496	508	12,166

	Farm laborers					Laborers									
	Total	Farm foremen	Farm laborers, wage workers	Farm laborers, unpaid family workers	Farm service laborers, self-employed	Total	Fishermen and oystermen	Garage laborers, car washers, and greasers	Gardeners, except farm, and groundskeepers	Longshoremen and stevedores	Lumbermen, raftsmen, and woodchoppers	Teamsters	Laborers not elsewhere classified	Unknown occupation
	Ba1426	Ba1427	Ba1428	Ba1429	Ba1430	Ba1431	Ba1432	Ba1433	Ba1434	Ba1435	Ba1436	Ba1437	Ba1438	Ba1439
Year	Hundred	Hundred	Hundred	Hundred	Hundred	Hundred	Hundred	Hundred	Hundred	Hundred	Hundred	Hundred	Hundred	Hundred
1850 [2,3]	2,980	164	2,816	0	0	6,340	126	0	85	13	80	0	6,036	—
1860 [2]	9,377	143	9,222	12	0	8,227	246	0	184	16	137	0	7,643	—
1870	23,380	32	23,317	31	0	11,273	207	0	326	78	258	0	10,404	—
1880	25,541	40	25,501	0	0	19,810	334	0	413	104	502	0	18,457	—
1900	34,651	38	19,724	14,890	0	35,061	668	8	175	319	911	0	32,982	—
1910	50,389	242	50,147	0	0	38,603	668	0	992	698	1,416	0	34,829	—
1920	33,989	156	20,348	13,427	58	43,227	467	271	403	831	1,750	0	39,506	—
1940	30,035	238	18,744	11,053	0	43,738	615	490	1,626	605	1,330	250	38,822	3,636
1950	22,986	182	14,704	8,019	81	35,405	762	896	1,478	655	1,840	239	29,536	2,253
1960	13,658	253	10,900	2,451	54	30,200	367	843	1,754	501	1,168	194	25,373	30,567
1970	9,471	321	8,168	942	41	33,476	271	0	2,972	442	793	71	28,928	—
1980	8,893	498	8,394	0	0	41,928	493	0	3,508	242	933	0	36,752	—
1990	7,710	397	7,313	0	0	49,318	477	0	6,310	138	989	0	41,403	—

[1] Data pertain to noninstitutionalized civilians age 16 and older who reported an occupation; employed persons only beginning 1940.

[2] Excludes slaves.

[3] Excludes women.

Source

See the source for Table Ba1159–1395.

Documentation

See the text for Table Ba1159–1395.

TABLE Ba1440–1676 Detailed occupations – males: 1850–1990[1] [Part 1]

Contributed by Matthew Sobek

		Professional, technical, and kindred workers													
														College professors and instructors	
	Total	Total	Accountants and auditors	Actors and actresses	Airplane pilots and navigators	Architects	Artists and art teachers	Athletes	Authors	Chemists	Chiropractors	Clergymen	College presidents and deans	Agricultural sciences	Biological sciences
	Ba1440	Ba1441	Ba1442	Ba1443	Ba1444	Ba1445	Ba1446	Ba1447	Ba1448	Ba1449	Ba1450	Ba1451	Ba1452	Ba1453	Ba1454
Year	Hundred	Hundred	Hundred	Hundred	Hundred	Hundred	Hundred	Hundred	Hundred	Hundred	Hundred	Hundred	Hundred	Hundred	Hundred
1850 [2]	52,272	1,575	7	5	0	4	21	2	1	8	0	288	1	0	0
1860 [2]	71,309	2,343	17	2	0	14	42	5	2	4	0	350	2	0	0
1870	102,259	2,814	12	6	0	22	46	0	2	17	0	487	0	0	0
1880	139,990	4,301	23	40	0	38	55	5	8	26	0	685	4	0	0
1900	223,883	7,627	61	106	0	61	152	30	8	83	0	964	61	0	0
1910	286,918	9,401	0	159	0	166	202	0	13	149	0	1,219	0	0	0
1920	319,806	13,078	1,132	150	10	176	207	43	37	310	34	1,268	6	4	0
1940	358,885	19,357	0	85	54	187	385	81	106	537	87	1,311	0	0	0
1950	410,993	30,416	3,232	95	161	247	499	82	98	704	120	1,675	41	50	48
1960	429,136	44,750	3,989	54	276	288	643	30	188	746	128	1,976	59	29	63
1970	472,810	70,551	5,192	56	489	540	644	0	171	964	128	2,129	303	47	161
1980	557,478	92,003	6,090	0	724	974	757	0	244	788	187	2,665	0	28	65
1990	621,099	113,724	7,288	0	1,026	1,295	957	0	529	990	319	2,849	0	7	39

	Professional, technical, and kindred workers														
	College professors and instructors														
	Chemistry	Economics	Engineering	Geology and geophysics	Mathematics	Medical sciences	Physics	Psychology	Statistics	Natural sciences not elsewhere classified	Social sciences not elsewhere classified	Nonscientific subjects	Subject not specified	Dancers and dancing teachers	Dentists
	Ba1455	Ba1456	Ba1457	Ba1458	Ba1459	Ba1460	Ba1461	Ba1462	Ba1463	Ba1464	Ba1465	Ba1466	Ba1467	Ba1468	Ba1469
Year	Hundred	Hundred	Hundred	Hundred	Hundred	Hundred	Hundred	Hundred	Hundred	Hundred	Hundred	Hundred	Hundred	Hundred	Hundred
1850 [2]	0	0	0	0	1	0	0	0	0	0	0	3	8	1	20
1860 [2]	0	0	0	0	2	1	0	0	0	0	0	9	6	5	65
1870	0	0	0	2	2	0	0	0	0	0	0	2	10	2	67
1880	1	0	0	1	2	0	0	0	0	1	0	18	14	1	122
1900	0	0	0	0	0	0	0	0	0	0	0	0	0	8	250
1910	0	0	0	0	0	0	0	0	0	0	0	0	217	0	418
1920	8	0	2	0	2	4	0	0	0	2	6	6	148	18	556
1940	0	0	0	0	0	0	0	0	0	0	0	0	536	28	693
1950	59	31	85	9	40	22	30	23	5	1	132	148	169	29	709
1960	55	38	94	16	84	48	50	19	1	2	166	209	416	44	811
1970	136	91	153	0	205	132	134	92	0	41	279	567	1,072	10	883
1980	65	40	98	0	131	90	51	34	0	19	92	251	2,812	26	1,175
1990	38	27	63	0	127	59	35	21	0	8	53	196	3,737	48	1,344

	Professional, technical, and kindred workers														
	Designers	Dietitians and nutritionists	Draftsmen	Editors and reporters	Engineers, aeronautical	Engineers, chemical	Engineers, civil	Engineers, electrical	Engineers, industrial	Engineers, mechanical	Engineers, metallurgical, metallurgists	Engineers, mining	Engineers not elsewhere classified	Entertainers not elsewhere classified	Farm and home management advisors
	Ba1470	Ba1471	Ba1472	Ba1473	Ba1474	Ba1475	Ba1476	Ba1477	Ba1478	Ba1479	Ba1480	Ba1481	Ba1482	Ba1483	Ba1484
Year	Hundred	Hundred	Hundred	Hundred	Hundred	Hundred	Hundred	Hundred	Hundred	Hundred	Hundred	Hundred	Hundred	Hundred	Hundred
1850 [2]	2	0	1	23	0	0	6	0	0	1	0	0	0	9	0
1860 [2]	0	0	2	38	0	0	22	0	0	2	0	2	0	5	6
1870	2	0	8	53	0	0	32	0	0	0	0	8	0	12	2
1880	8	0	24	119	0	0	64	0	0	4	0	10	0	35	0
1900	38	0	114	266	0	0	114	46	0	106	0	38	0	83	0
1910	73	0	322	315	0	0	466	0	0	144	0	103	0	214	0
1920	112	0	546	296	2	26	671	280	24	300	14	63	116	49	22
1940	149	0	874	452	0	114	839	540	128	779	95	0	0	53	76
1950	327	11	1,085	641	179	302	1,243	1,087	455	1,147	116	104	771	93	64
1960	571	17	2,034	865	516	405	1,570	1,740	996	1,561	174	114	1,433	76	67
1970	825	35	2,620	1,414	645	514	1,710	2,769	1,788	1,790	157	152	2,385	452	66
1980	1,621	68	2,671	1,626	828	541	1,945	3,045	2,577	2,071	225	315	2,828	591	0
1990	2,570	92	2,546	1,937	1,266	569	2,283	4,092	3,302	1,851	155	285	3,471	794	0

	Professional, technical, and kindred workers														
								Natural scientists not elsewhere classified							
	Foresters and conservationists	Funeral directors and embalmers	Lawyers and judges	Librarians	Musicians and music teachers	Nurses, professional	Nurses, student professional	Agricultural scientists	Biological scientists	Geologists and geophysicists	Mathematicians	Physicists	Miscellaneous natural scientists	Optometrists	Osteopaths
	Ba1485	Ba1486	Ba1487	Ba1488	Ba1489	Ba1490	Ba1491	Ba1492	Ba1493	Ba1494	Ba1495	Ba1496	Ba1497	Ba1498	Ba1499
Year	Hundred	Hundred	Hundred	Hundred	Hundred	Hundred	Hundred	Hundred	Hundred	Hundred	Hundred	Hundred	Hundred	Hundred	Hundred
1850 [2]	0	6	244	0	32	0	0	0	0	0	0	0	1	0	0
1860 [2]	0	10	343	2	71	0	0	0	1	0	0	0	0	0	0
1870	0	24	441	2	90	2	0	0	2	0	0	0	0	0	0
1880	0	57	655	3	177	0	0	0	2	3	0	0	0	0	0
1900	8	129	1,009	0	508	0	0	0	0	0	0	8	8	0	0
1910	43	161	1,103	0	572	55	0	0	0	0	0	0	0	0	0
1920	67	219	1,229	8	497	41	0	4	10	24	0	2	0	37	20
1940	0	331	1,668	48	708	118	0	0	0	0	0	0	0	112	57
1950	251	347	1,729	61	749	94	23	55	64	102	16	68	20	161	64
1960	317	345	2,022	113	786	126	11	76	95	188	52	130	25	166	38
1970	382	383	2,645	231	1,216	690	12	120	191	218	60	215	10	170	0
1980	490	370	4,520	332	2,356	1,238	0	186	423	409	52	302	70	228	0
1990	426	399	5,785	414	3,218	1,913	0	240	500	443	41	329	128	232	0

Notes appear at end of table

(continued)

TABLE Ba1440–1676 Detailed occupations – males: 1850–1990 [Part 1] *Continued*

	Professional, technical, and kindred workers								Social scientists						
	Personnel and labor-relations workers	Pharmacists	Photographers	Physicians and surgeons	Radio operators	Recreation and group workers	Religious workers	Social and welfare workers, except group	Economists	Psychologists	Statisticians and actuaries	Miscellaneous social scientists	Sports instructors and officials	Surveyors	Teachers not elsewhere classified
	Ba1500	Ba1501	Ba1502	Ba1503	Ba1504	Ba1505	Ba1506	Ba1507	Ba1508	Ba1509	Ba1510	Ba1511	Ba1512	Ba1513	Ba1514
Year	Hundred	Hundred	Hundred	Hundred	Hundred	Hundred	Hundred	Hundred	Hundred	Hundred	Hundred	Hundred	Hundred	Hundred	Hundred
1850 [2]	0	55	7	432	0	0	0	0	0	0	0	0	0	13	303
1860 [2]	0	99	52	622	0	0	24	0	0	0	0	0	0	28	478
1870	0	188	59	659	0	0	2	4	0	0	0	0	12	32	449
1880	0	283	105	862	0	0	1	0	0	0	0	0	0	38	741
1900	0	501	235	1,283	0	0	8	0	0	0	0	15	8	68	1,009
1910	0	0	257	1,466	0	0	93	5	0	0	0	0	0	0	1,207
1920	20	734	239	1,343	22	37	57	34	2	0	22	2	93	91	1,223
1940	0	746	317	1,646	86	0	88	285	0	0	0	0	196	168	2,649
1950	383	837	444	1,859	164	99	152	264	67	17	153	28	326	240	2,939
1960	712	896	446	2,114	242	234	231	365	144	97	135	24	476	407	4,841
1970	2,004	956	556	2,525	447	295	155	804	569	180	168	89	464	574	8,928
1980	3,538	1,087	687	3,724	715	106	206	1,551	669	477	235	172	421	732	11,767
1990	3,444	1,154	948	4,547	600	124	412	1,981	835	776	268	238	588	889	11,945

	Professional, technical, and kindred workers						Farmers			Managers, officials, and proprietors					
	Technicians – medical and dental	Technicians – testing	Technicians not elsewhere classified	Therapists and healers not elsewhere classified	Veterinarians	Professional, technical, and kindred workers not elsewhere classified	Total	Farmers – owners and tenants	Farm managers	Total	Buyers and department heads – store	Buyers and shippers – farm products	Conductors – railroad	Credit men	Floormen and floor managers – store
	Ba1515	Ba1516	Ba1517	Ba1518	Ba1519	Ba1520	Ba1521	Ba1522	Ba1523	Ba1524	Ba1525	Ba1526	Ba1527	Ba1528	Ba1529
Year	Hundred	Hundred	Hundred	Hundred	Hundred	Hundred	Hundred	Hundred	Hundred	Hundred	Hundred	Hundred	Hundred	Hundred	Hundred
1850 [2]	0	0	0	0	0	69	23,673	23,666	7	2,437	0	3	4	0	0
1860 [2]	0	0	0	1	2	7	26,113	26,070	43	3,925	0	59	66	0	0
1870	0	2	1	4	8	37	31,257	31,235	22	5,508	0	119	99	0	0
1880	0	0	0	7	29	33	44,006	43,985	22	7,276	1	236	184	0	0
1900	0	0	8	46	106	83	54,967	54,846	121	14,169	38	531	402	8	23
1910	0	0	0	25	123	111	57,517	57,517	0	23,557	0	0	607	0	141
1920	24	55	12	24	152	79	64,337	63,522	815	25,312	276	594	826	85	41
1940	0	410	70	114	108	1,243	50,565	50,228	337	33,315	509	365	471	269	72
1950	353	626	273	116	146	955	42,356	42,055	301	44,220	1,014	282	551	279	51
1960	532	2,115	909	156	162	2,361	23,650	23,413	237	45,834	1,820	193	462	385	59
1970	987	2,709	1,474	331	179	7,672	13,308	12,746	561	50,506	5,204	199	386	433	0
1980	1,716	5,828	2,300	591	295	5,852	11,576	10,322	1,254	74,567	6,475	170	442	0	0
1990	2,603	6,890	3,241	821	358	10,725	8,969	6,977	1,992	93,111	5,048	134	335	0	0

Year	Managers, officials, and proprietors: Inspectors – public administration	Managers and superintendents – building	Officers, pilots, pursers, and engineers – ship	Officials and administrators not elsewhere classified – public administration	Officials – lodge, society, union, and so forth	Postmasters	Purchasing agents and buyers not elsewhere classified	Managers, officials, and proprietors not elsewhere classified	Clerical and kindred workers: Total	Agents not elsewhere classified	Attendants and assistants – library	Attendants – physician's and dentist's office	Baggagemen – transportation	Bank tellers	Bookkeepers
	Ba1530	Ba1531	Ba1532	Ba1533	Ba1534	Ba1535	Ba1536	Ba1537	Ba1538	Ba1539	Ba1540	Ba1541	Ba1542	Ba1543	Ba1544
	Hundred	Hundred	Hundred	Hundred	Hundred	Hundred	Hundred	Hundred	Hundred	Hundred	Hundred	Hundred	Hundred	Hundred	Hundred
1850 [2]	11	21	78	69	0	19	0	2,232	138	25	0	1	8	4	22
1860 [2]	6	38	166	114	0	46	0	3,429	451	51	0	0	14	12	141
1870	21	12	165	138	0	29	0	4,923	1,226	40	4	0	18	9	292
1880	37	17	180	276	9	55	10	6,271	2,544	206	0	0	51	14	622
1900	76	0	175	220	30	205	0	12,461	8,325	296	8	0	76	61	1,890
1910	0	0	247	1,025	45	0	0	21,491	12,763	516	0	0	128	0	2,919
1920	213	154	428	469	43	179	205	21,801	16,979	327	6	8	105	207	2,467
1940	424	444	298	1,140	196	216	334	28,575	24,030	884	70	79	54	0	4,197
1950	554	488	422	1,086	220	220	618	38,436	26,956	1,128	28	23	73	352	1,709
1960	680	308	350	1,522	285	231	928	38,612	29,634	1,329	79	23	53	415	1,477
1970	923	514	231	2,151	412	240	1,392	38,420	35,434	208	259	200	0	356	2,750
1980	1,239	1,144	361	2,405	0	174	1,848	60,308	41,296	0	263	455	0	438	1,846
1990	1,088	2,142	350	3,688	0	214	2,091	78,022	48,115	0	304	470	0	483	1,898

Year	Clerical and kindred workers: Cashiers	Collectors, bill and account	Dispatchers and starters – vehicle	Express messengers and railway mail clerks	Mail carriers	Messengers and office boys	Office machine operators	Shipping and receiving clerks	Stenographers, typists, and secretaries	Telegraph messengers	Telegraph operators	Telephone operators	Ticket, station, and express agents	Clerical and kindred workers not elsewhere classified
	Ba1545	Ba1546	Ba1547	Ba1548	Ba1549	Ba1550	Ba1551	Ba1552	Ba1553	Ba1554	Ba1555	Ba1556	Ba1557	Ba1558
	Hundred	Hundred	Hundred	Hundred	Hundred	Hundred	Hundred	Hundred	Hundred	Hundred	Hundred	Hundred	Hundred	Hundred
1850 [2]	1	12	0	0	8	5	0	3	0	1	5	0	13	29
1860 [2]	6	28	0	8	28	12	0	2	2	0	8	0	50	88
1870	8	17	2	22	20	20	0	14	0	1	51	0	116	592
1880	24	36	12	16	90	57	0	75	12	4	152	9	209	956
1900	152	228	23	68	212	281	0	273	296	30	531	23	334	3,544
1910	0	302	0	184	839	489	0	761	469	33	615	91	285	5,134
1920	270	302	24	266	986	359	16	1,191	783	59	657	101	521	8,323
1940	0	357	0	244	1,216	501	162	2,102	767	127	408	128	413	12,320
1950	457	173	307	194	1,653	483	255	2,760	871	74	296	280	521	15,317
1960	1,020	270	500	67	1,863	468	750	2,517	761	31	137	139	580	17,157
1970	1,319	330	497	0	2,304	403	1,450	3,504	1,265	18	93	226	617	19,634
1980	2,882	328	649	0	2,210	615	2,502	4,956	762	0	47	698	431	22,215
1990	5,382	519	1,027	0	2,341	990	3,772	5,583	907	0	0	298	771	23,369

Notes appear at end of table

(continued)

TABLE Ba1440–1676 Detailed occupations – males: 1850–1990 [Part 1] *Continued*

	Sales workers										Craft workers, foremen, and kindred workers				
	Total	Advertising agents and salesmen	Auctioneers	Demonstrators	Hucksters and peddlers	Insurance agents and brokers	Newsboys	Real estate agents and brokers	Stock and bond salesmen	Salesmen and sales clerks not elsewhere classified	Total	Bakers	Blacksmiths	Bookbinders	Boilermakers
	Ba1559	Ba1560	Ba1561	Ba1562	Ba1563	Ba1564	Ba1565	Ba1566	Ba1567	Ba1568	Ba1569	Ba1570	Ba1571	Ba1572	Ba1573
Year	Hundred	Hundred	Hundred	Hundred	Hundred	Hundred	Hundred	Hundred	Hundred	Hundred	Hundred	Hundred	Hundred	Hundred	Hundred
1850 [2]	1,140	0	8	0	112	6	5	4	1	1,004	8,699	145	951	32	19
1860 [2]	1,896	0	18	0	201	10	12	20	0	1,635	11,162	203	1,128	36	20
1870	2,820	6	16	0	361	134	22	98	0	2,182	13,271	255	1,418	38	56
1880	4,246	5	26	0	524	134	22	137	6	3,394	16,516	356	1,764	65	106
1900	8,401	30	15	0	729	660	23	546	0	6,398	30,659	675	2,170	243	304
1910	12,824	0	25	10	0	748	106	1,257	164	10,514	40,759	678	2,363	0	393
1920	14,942	134	51	10	430	1,162	75	1,250	164	11,666	55,633	925	2,126	116	684
1940	21,548	317	48	19	492	2,236	375	1,068	197	16,796	53,242	1,244	821	0	301
1950	26,322	259	132	45	196	2,850	407	1,322	117	20,993	77,189	1,069	433	145	344
1960	29,081	293	39	14	195	3,889	736	1,510	294	22,111	84,620	915	204	133	206
1970	33,536	506	46	35	239	4,671	521	1,784	878	24,855	98,443	759	160	146	283
1980	36,897	648	56	25	430	4,881	638	3,531	1,071	25,617	109,260	713	0	126	328
1990	42,938	801	66	71	696	5,416	624	3,853	2,090	29,321	111,139	834	0	130	203

	Craft workers, foremen, and kindred workers														
	Brickmasons, stonemasons, and tile setters	Cabinetmakers	Carpenters	Cement and concrete finishers	Compositors and typesetters	Cranemen, derrickmen, and hoistmen	Decorators and window dressers	Electricians	Electrotypers and stereotypers	Engravers, except photoengravers	Excavating, grading, and road machinery operators	Foremen not elsewhere classified	Forgemen and hammermen	Furriers	Glaziers
	Ba1574	Ba1575	Ba1576	Ba1577	Ba1578	Ba1579	Ba1580	Ba1581	Ba1582	Ba1583	Ba1584	Ba1585	Ba1586	Ba1587	Ba1588
Year	Hundred	Hundred	Hundred	Hundred	Hundred	Hundred	Hundred	Hundred	Hundred	Hundred	Hundred	Hundred	Hundred	Hundred	Hundred
1850 [2]	507	376	2,187	1	157	0	0	0	0	18	14	24	10	2	1
1860 [2]	643	336	2,909	0	202	0	0	0	0	28	4	240	13	2	8
1870	871	330	3,524	0	274	2	4	0	2	37	13	118	12	10	8
1880	949	353	3,851	5	533	0	0	4	10	55	7	229	6	9	7
1900	1,571	387	6,246	0	1,108	8	0	501	46	46	0	1,123	0	15	23
1910	1,819	406	8,106	0	1,146	0	53	1,295	55	134	0	2,746	76	0	0
1920	1,237	499	8,461	79	1,345	312	79	2,087	49	120	91	4,390	106	55	35
1940	1,151	664	6,048	237	1,558	1,087	262	1,948	85	69	0	5,462	0	141	120
1950	1,590	687	8,975	336	1,682	1,043	305	3,106	183	96	1,077	7,816	171	117	139
1960	1,822	616	8,138	390	1,647	1,209	265	3,352	89	110	1,949	10,912	102	32	164
1970	1,856	625	8,189	643	1,302	1,476	298	4,400	66	59	3,049	14,471	142	23	238
1980	1,930	661	10,999	562	306	1,457	0	5,922	0	88	3,374	18,887	129	28	293
1990	2,288	649	12,146	619	209	933	0	6,441	0	104	3,593	14,769	152	55	407

Craft workers, foremen, and kindred workers

Year	Heat treaters, annealers, temperers	Inspectors, scalers, and graders – log and lumber	Inspectors not elsewhere classified	Jewelers, watchmakers, goldsmiths, silversmiths	Job setters – metal	Linemen and servicemen	Locomotive engineers	Locomotive firemen	Loom fixers	Machinists	Mechanics and repairmen – airplane	Mechanics and repairmen – automobile	Mechanics and repairmen – office machine	Mechanics and repairmen – radio and television	Mechanics and repairmen – railroad and car shop
	Ba1589	Ba1590	Ba1591	Ba1592	Ba1593	Ba1594	Ba1595	Ba1596	Ba1597	Ba1598	Ba1599	Ba1600	Ba1601	Ba1602	Ba1603
Year	Hundred	Hundred	Hundred	Hundred	Hundred	Hundred	Hundred	Hundred	Hundred	Hundred	Hundred	Hundred	Hundred	Hundred	Hundred
1850 [2]	0	1	5	118	0	0	5	0	0	234	0	0	0	0	1
1860 [2]	0	2	8	128	0	0	18	10	0	373	0	0	0	0	4
1870	0	13	11	157	0	0	114	78	0	533	0	0	0	0	18
1880	4	4	33	217	0	11	165	109	3	836	0	0	0	0	23
1900	0	61	197	334	0	83	539	486	46	2,542	0	0	0	0	152
1910	10	0	486	270	0	239	1,058	710	123	4,668	0	0	0	0	0
1920	32	134	901	357	22	598	1,138	933	205	8,160	6	1,998	36	2	759
1940	126	164	715	413	0	1,094	681	463	210	4,649	233	3,735	0	0	380
1950	173	186	931	470	241	2,089	781	580	320	5,026	697	6,673	181	754	520
1960	196	167	938	359	375	2,687	584	358	269	4,908	1,129	6,654	291	1,058	401
1970	199	156	1,071	319	818	3,802	474	125	204	3,562	1,438	8,916	699	1,309	551
1980	213	0	465	575	507	3,826	694	0	0	4,758	1,047	12,230	770	1,525	0
1990	166	0	614	655	247	3,219	432	0	0	5,193	1,549	13,400	1,125	1,520	0

Craft workers, foremen, and kindred workers

Year	Mechanics and repairmen not elsewhere classified	Millers – grain, flour, feed, and so forth	Millwrights	Molders – metal	Motion picture projectionists	Opticians and lens grinders and polishers	Painters – construction and maintenance	Paperhangers	Pattern and model makers, except paper	Photoengravers and lithographers	Piano and organ tuners and repairmen	Plasterers	Plumbers and pipe fitters	Pressmen and plate printers – printing	Rollers and roll hands – metal
	Ba1604	Ba1605	Ba1606	Ba1607	Ba1608	Ba1609	Ba1610	Ba1611	Ba1612	Ba1613	Ba1614	Ba1615	Ba1616	Ba1617	Ba1618
Year	Hundred	Hundred	Hundred	Hundred	Hundred	Hundred	Hundred	Hundred	Hundred	Hundred	Hundred	Hundred	Hundred	Hundred	Hundred
1850 [2]	287	317	90	89	0	2	212	6	16	8	0	94	15	1	10
1860 [2]	384	390	54	179	0	2	501	16	20	8	2	150	65	0	18
1870	260	379	114	281	0	3	726	19	30	8	8	156	126	0	68
1880	297	430	92	400	0	14	1,087	39	57	33	14	271	179	7	28
1900	569	296	114	888	0	61	2,262	197	159	76	15	379	964	273	0
1910	401	214	0	1,217	0	0	2,738	229	234	68	91	458	1,519	252	164
1920	1,227	229	373	1,213	99	128	2,641	160	296	132	69	345	2,146	235	245
1940	4,017	157	406	703	286	128	3,310	262	313	253	97	452	1,771	365	264
1950	8,305	122	582	572	246	191	3,979	214	505	298	137	638	2,726	558	336
1960	12,276	94	602	492	167	164	3,615	88	418	270	49	474	3,074	707	287
1970	10,695	70	785	471	160	212	3,373	0	367	283	64	276	3,606	1,387	183
1980	14,622	0	1,207	295	122	266	3,913	0	291	204	0	250	4,596	2,350	158
1990	15,287	0	864	166	82	318	5,121	0	233	344	0	371	4,603	2,756	103

Notes appear at end of table

(continued)

TABLE Ba1440–1676 Detailed occupations – males: 1850–1990 [Part 1] *Continued*

	Craft workers, foremen, and kindred workers										Operatives and kindred workers				
	Roofers and slaters	Shoemakers and repairers, except factory	Stationary engineers	Stonecutters and stone carvers	Structural metal workers	Tailors and tailoresses	Tinsmiths, coppersmiths, sheet metal workers	Toolmakers, die makers, and setters	Upholsterers	Craftsmen and kindred workers not elsewhere classified	Total	Apprentice auto mechanics	Apprentice bricklayers and masons	Apprentice carpenters	Apprentice electricians
	Ba1619	Ba1620	Ba1621	Ba1622	Ba1623	Ba1624	Ba1625	Ba1626	Ba1627	Ba1628	Ba1629	Ba1630	Ba1631	Ba1632	Ba1633
Year	Hundred	Hundred	Hundred	Hundred	Hundred	Hundred	Hundred	Hundred	Hundred	Hundred	Hundred	Hundred	Hundred	Hundred	Hundred
1850 [2]	1	1,362	102	112	0	547	112	5	24	475	4,760	0	0	3	0
1860 [2]	13	1,300	224	148	0	618	193	6	24	529	7,019	0	6	84	0
1870	38	1,122	299	192	0	556	266	12	45	665	11,887	0	25	70	0
1880	45	1,053	616	286	1	771	394	10	88	590	17,033	0	5	46	0
1900	99	941	1,434	440	15	1,313	592	0	243	425	28,026	0	0	8	15
1910	149	647	2,232	322	106	1,521	650	116	169	431	42,048	0	0	0	0
1920	116	692	2,083	272	828	1,728	714	631	223	728	46,352	26	0	8	37
1940	292	648	1,884	172	392	924	787	929	370	0	63,197	0	0	118	63
1950	505	549	2,232	113	486	793	1,256	1,572	601	737	83,829	54	76	110	118
1960	488	339	2,730	44	570	311	1,349	1,823	521	1,039	85,956	14	21	53	86
1970	564	705	1,693	62	837	467	1,439	1,873	520	6,521	94,196	32	38	78	202
1980	988	994	1,565	0	947	337	1,425	1,807	510	0	97,703	34	22	76	164
1990	1,610	1,165	2,046	0	749	278	1,490	1,367	536	0	92,522	16	7	40	135

	Operatives and kindred workers														
	Apprentice machinists and toolmakers	Apprentice mechanics, except auto	Apprentice plumbers and pipe fitters	Apprentices – building trades not elsewhere classified	Apprentices – metalworking trades not elsewhere classified	Apprentices – printing trades	Apprentices – other specified trades	Apprentices – trade not specified	Asbestos and insulation workers	Attendants – auto service and parking	Blasters and powdermen	Boatmen, canalmen, and lock keepers	Brakemen – railroad	Bus drivers	Chainmen, rodmen, and axmen – surveying
	Ba1634	Ba1635	Ba1636	Ba1637	Ba1638	Ba1639	Ba1640	Ba1641	Ba1642	Ba1643	Ba1644	Ba1645	Ba1646	Ba1647	Ba1648
Year	Hundred	Hundred	Hundred	Hundred	Hundred	Hundred	Hundred	Hundred	Hundred	Hundred	Hundred	Hundred	Hundred	Hundred	Hundred
1850 [2]	0	0	0	2	0	0	8	21	0	0	0	274	4	38	0
1860 [2]	14	8	8	24	110	20	126	72	0	0	0	258	30	32	0
1870	35	14	10	39	119	31	151	29	0	0	6	212	125	36	0
1880	40	0	11	12	68	15	125	18	0	0	0	208	230	40	0
1900	129	0	30	0	114	15	137	46	0	0	0	91	835	0	8
1910	0	0	0	191	0	0	3	605	0	0	0	53	942	0	0
1920	146	26	57	0	83	51	61	87	26	34	12	35	1,189	87	20
1940	171	0	79	168	0	143	240	118	96	2,186	62	120	715	0	125
1950	170	45	173	54	84	199	145	145	165	2,387	116	143	777	1,527	116
1960	133	40	88	25	46	114	81	98	203	3,385	59	65	585	1,650	88
1970	187	65	138	18	61	84	107	30	246	4,340	72	44	464	1,672	104
1980	144	0	104	0	6	0	34	0	464	3,058	91	0	760	2,030	88
1990	35	0	65	0	8	0	17	0	601	2,507	78	0	309	2,192	36

	Operatives and kindred workers													
	Conductors – bus and street railway	Deliverymen and routemen	Dressmakers and seamstresses, except factory	Dyers	Filers, grinders, and polishers – metal	Fruit, nut, vegetable graders, packers, not factory	Furnacemen, smeltermen, and pourers	Heaters – metal	Laundry and dry cleaning operatives	Meat cutters, except slaughter and packing houses	Milliners	Mine operatives and laborers	Motormen, mine, factory, logging camp, and so forth	Motormen, street, subway, and elevated railway
	Ba1649	Ba1650	Ba1651	Ba1652	Ba1653	Ba1654	Ba1655	Ba1656	Ba1657	Ba1658	Ba1659	Ba1660	Ba1661	Ba1662
Year	Hundred	Hundred	Hundred	Hundred	Hundred	Hundred	Hundred	Hundred	Hundred	Hundred	Hundred	Hundred	Hundred	Hundred
1850 [2]	0	13	2	23	2	0	97	1	3	189	2	869	0	1
1860 [2]	5	25	15	26	31	0	60	12	6	323	13	1,193	0	16
1870	8	55	15	24	46	0	118	8	66	424	7	1,717	0	27
1880	17	119	10	50	71	0	405	22	149	749	15	2,563	0	106
1900	152	243	61	0	402	15	212	30	76	865	23	5,570	0	364
1910	610	2,111	40	161	390	25	292	71	383	151	65	8,857	0	662
1920	619	1,759	79	185	657	67	264	134	491	1,278	24	9,907	93	566
1940	163	3,684	66	214	968	192	279	158	500	1,338	14	6,755	157	355
1950	128	2,284	46	267	1,487	220	562	103	1,358	1,684	34	5,633	242	245
1960	42	3,935	43	178	1,387	58	529	80	1,096	1,753	5	2,876	128	74
1970	91	5,899	47	222	2,163	74	632	65	1,075	1,906	3	2,053	93	0
1980	0	6,332	63	0	2,259	0	0	0	845	2,366	0	2,800	0	0
1990	0	1,215	59	0	1,158	0	0	0	1,205	2,075	0	1,848	0	0

	Operatives and kindred workers													
	Oilers and greasers, except auto	Painters, except construction or maintenance	Photographic process workers	Power station operators	Sailors and deckhands	Sawyers	Spinners – textile	Stationary firemen	Switchmen – railroad	Taxicab drivers and chauffeurs	Truck and tractor drivers	Weavers – textile	Welders and flame cutters	Operatives and kindred workers not elsewhere classified
	Ba1663	Ba1664	Ba1665	Ba1666	Ba1667	Ba1668	Ba1669	Ba1670	Ba1671	Ba1672	Ba1673	Ba1674	Ba1675	Ba1676
Year	Hundred	Hundred	Hundred	Hundred	Hundred	Hundred	Hundred	Hundred	Hundred	Hundred	Hundred	Hundred	Hundred	Hundred
1850 [2]	0	22	0	0	655	97	46	17	1	12	316	159	1	1,880
1860 [2]	0	54	0	0	629	143	84	30	2	28	556	158	4	2,812
1870	0	112	0	0	603	99	44	38	16	47	1,093	130	4	6,281
1880	0	187	0	0	705	91	13	145	30	64	1,535	158	2	9,011
1900	23	243	0	0	425	281	296	531	175	516	4,462	751	8	10,875
1910	154	572	0	0	479	456	207	1,033	680	801	4,229	1,078	0	16,748
1920	284	627	22	43	414	422	298	1,367	647	1,647	2,708	990	276	18,498
1940	357	775	141	323	360	430	0	1,135	436	0	11,668	0	1,233	27,089
1950	597	1,252	176	225	457	950	181	1,307	660	2,018	13,392	624	2,661	38,431
1960	495	1,266	228	251	328	859	108	860	571	1,552	15,419	367	3,495	41,146
1970	438	1,148	323	181	249	894	0	892	520	1,450	13,499	220	5,029	47,050
1980	401	1,479	394	264	275	824	0	1,373	90	1,554	16,687	243	6,662	45,715
1990	224	1,296	449	350	213	737	0	847	48	1,716	25,094	197	5,597	42,146

[1] Data pertain to noninstitutionalized civilians age 16 and older who reported an occupation; employed persons only beginning 1940.

[2] Excludes slaves.

Source

See the source for Table Ba1159–1395.

Documentation

See the text for Table Ba1159–1395.

TABLE Ba1677–1720 Detailed occupations – males: 1850–1990[1] [Part 2]

Contributed by Matthew Sobek

	Service workers, private household				Service workers, not household										
	Total	Housekeepers – private household	Laundresses – private household	Private household workers not elsewhere classified	Total	Attendants – hospital and other institution	Attendants – professional and personal service not elsewhere classified	Attendants – recreation and amusement	Barbers, beauticians, and manicurists	Bartenders	Bootblacks	Boarding and lodging house keepers	Charwomen and cleaners	Cooks, except private household	Counter and fountain workers
	Ba1677	Ba1678	Ba1679	Ba1680	Ba1681	Ba1682	Ba1683	Ba1684	Ba1685	Ba1686	Ba1687	Ba1688	Ba1689	Ba1690	Ba1691
Year	Hundred	Hundred	Hundred	Hundred	Hundred	Hundred	Hundred	Hundred	Hundred	Hundred	Hundred	Hundred	Hundred	Hundred	Hundred
1850 [2]	130	0	1	129	447	1	0	1	76	55	0	21	0	0	0
1860 [2]	420	0	7	413	695	0	0	2	85	101	3	46	2	2	0
1870	697	0	36	661	1,297	4	17	2	206	187	3	38	1	27	0
1880	1,493	5	37	1,451	2,105	11	14	7	423	248	12	76	5	56	0
1900	1,799	0	61	1,738	6,026	0	8	0	1,154	1,025	76	99	15	106	0
1910	2,579	174	81	2,325	8,796	0	141	0	1,738	1,098	164	191	93	0	0
1920	860	20	95	744	11,391	112	73	53	1,844	243	112	168	134	1,091	63
1940	1,473	45	59	1,369	20,684	620	148	499	2,096	1,136	132	86	335	1,738	0
1950	614	20	4	591	24,742	839	179	506	1,953	1,915	122	68	470	2,090	461
1960	540	17	6	517	25,714	1,007	205	387	2,078	1,547	80	27	520	1,972	394
1970	362	37	5	320	37,773	1,094	334	518	2,049	1,477	33	17	1,830	3,039	346
1980	261	22	3	237	50,602	1,579	958	917	1,542	1,621	0	0	1,473	6,639	355
1990	254	14	2	238	62,415	2,187	1,220	1,198	1,375	1,516	0	0	1,248	10,588	572

	Service workers, not household														
	Elevator operators	Firemen (fire protection)	Guards, watchmen, and doorkeepers	Housekeepers and stewards, except household	Janitors and sextons	Marshals and constables	Midwives	Policemen and detectives	Porters	Practical nurses	Sheriffs and bailiffs	Ushers – recreation and amusement	Waiters and waitresses	Watchmen (crossing) and bridge tenders	Service workers (not private household) not elsewhere classified
	Ba1692	Ba1693	Ba1694	Ba1695	Ba1696	Ba1697	Ba1698	Ba1699	Ba1700	Ba1701	Ba1702	Ba1703	Ba1704	Ba1705	Ba1706
Year	Hundred	Hundred	Hundred	Hundred	Hundred	Hundred	Hundred	Hundred	Hundred	Hundred	Hundred	Hundred	Hundred	Hundred	Hundred
1850 [2]	0	0	30	12	2	34	0	29	60	1	15	0	68	18	23
1860 [2]	0	2	68	27	7	43	0	36	132	2	21	2	81	14	18
1870	0	8	125	20	48	36	0	135	173	0	39	0	152	37	36
1880	0	18	223	36	74	57	0	149	206	4	69	0	250	40	128
1900	114	159	531	106	478	83	0	402	600	15	68	0	554	68	364
1910	189	317	799	0	924	98	3	683	851	116	108	0	1,136	0	146
1920	316	560	1,235	134	1,268	55	0	994	1,073	39	99	22	1,065	99	538
1940	659	748	2,192	196	3,257	100	0	1,476	1,554	62	146	155	1,783	167	1,399
1950	639	1,126	2,498	253	4,014	75	1	1,986	1,611	53	183	145	1,170	126	2,260
1960	506	1,317	2,407	255	5,220	72	5	2,530	1,383	98	249	82	1,082	154	2,139
1970	266	1,731	3,013	303	10,529	50	2	3,581	185	87	323	102	1,111	169	5,584
1980	158	2,078	5,558	139	15,668	0	0	4,635	182	145	532	146	1,659	170	4,447
1990	87	2,423	7,863	204	16,513	0	0	5,335	316	265	973	179	2,662	182	5,509

	Farm laborers					Laborers								
	Total	Farm foremen	Farm laborers, wage workers	Farm laborers, unpaid family workers	Farm service laborers, self-employed	Total	Fishermen and oystermen	Garage laborers, car washers, and greasers	Gardeners, except farm, and groundskeepers	Longshoremen and stevedores	Lumbermen, raftsmen, and woodchoppers	Teamsters	Laborers not elsewhere classified	Unknown occupation
	Ba1707	Ba1708	Ba1709	Ba1710	Ba1711	Ba1712	Ba1713	Ba1714	Ba1715	Ba1716	Ba1717	Ba1718	Ba1719	Ba1720
Year	Hundred	Hundred	Hundred	Hundred	Hundred	Hundred	Hundred	Hundred	Hundred	Hundred	Hundred	Hundred	Hundred	Hundred
1850 [2]	2,966	163	2,804	0	0	6,306	126	0	85	13	80	0	6,002	—
1860 [2]	9,217	143	9,062	12	0	8,068	245	0	174	16	137	0	7,495	—
1870	20,503	32	20,444	27	0	10,980	205	0	324	78	258	0	10,115	—
1880	21,987	38	21,949	0	0	18,483	329	0	404	104	497	0	17,150	—
1900	30,181	38	17,599	12,545	0	33,703	668	8	167	319	911	0	31,631	—
1910	39,172	501	38,671	0	0	37,502	668	0	937	695	1,413	0	33,789	—
1920	26,793	158	18,783	7,807	45	44,128	444	264	420	856	1,879	2,700	37,566	—
1940	26,607	236	17,727	8,643	0	42,578	588	485	1,603	601	1,325	247	37,728	2,289
1950	18,638	180	13,433	4,945	80	34,173	748	817	1,446	643	1,825	234	28,461	1,538
1960	11,221	247	9,692	1,228	54	29,128	362	812	1,722	500	1,160	193	24,379	19,007
1970	7,908	302	7,010	562	35	30,794	259	0	2,883	434	772	68	26,378	—
1980	6,868	414	6,455	0	0	36,445	461	0	3,258	239	910	0	31,577	—
1990	6,001	343	5,658	0	0	41,910	446	0	5,827	135	959	0	34,544	—

[1] Data pertain to noninstitutionalized civilians age 16 and older who reported an occupation; employed persons only beginning 1940.

[2] Excludes slaves.

Source

See the source for Table Ba1159–1395.

Documentation

See the text for Table Ba1159–1395.

TABLE Ba1721–1957 Detailed occupations – females: 1860–1990[1] [Part 1]

Contributed by Matthew Sobek

		Professional, technical, and kindred workers												College professors and instructors	
	Total	Total	Accountants and auditors	Actors and actresses	Airplane pilots and navigators	Architects	Artists and art teachers	Athletes	Authors	Chemists	Chiropractors	Clergymen	College presidents and deans	Agricultural sciences	Biological sciences
	Ba1721	Ba1722	Ba1723	Ba1724	Ba1725	Ba1726	Ba1727	Ba1728	Ba1729	Ba1730	Ba1731	Ba1732	Ba1733	Ba1734	Ba1735
Year	Hundred	Hundred	Hundred	Hundred	Hundred	Hundred	Hundred	Hundred	Hundred	Hundred	Hundred	Hundred	Hundred	Hundred	Hundred
1860 [2]	10,298	706	0	2	0	0	6	0	2	0	0	2	2	0	0
1870	17,783	967	0	2	0	0	4	0	4	0	0	3	0	0	0
1880	24,799	1,891	0	20	0	0	33	2	1	0	0	9	0	0	0
1900	51,658	4,144	15	68	0	0	76	0	23	0	0	8	30	0	0
1910 [3]	75,442	7,592	0	136	0	0	154	0	8	3	0	20	0	0	0
1920	82,159	10,076	148	93	0	0	144	0	37	14	6	26	4	0	0
1940	116,957	14,626	0	59	3	3	173	6	36	18	18	38	0	0	0
1950	158,744	20,056	554	65	0	4	289	2	52	76	18	80	15	1	14
1960	209,570	27,480	768	28	3	8	343	2	80	58	12	54	12	1	16
1970	289,896	48,049	1,804	42	7	21	365	0	77	127	11	59	94	3	46
1980	416,306	78,069	3,775	0	11	87	695	0	204	200	24	162	0	5	31
1990	529,732	121,895	8,170	0	38	230	1,076	0	507	363	138	335	0	3	22

	Professional, technical, and kindred workers														
	College professors and instructors														
	Chemistry	Economics	Engineering	Geology and geophysics	Mathematics	Medical sciences	Physics	Psychology	Statistics	Natural sciences not elsewhere classified	Social sciences not elsewhere classified	Nonscientific subjects	Subject not specified	Dancers and dancing teachers	Dentists
	Ba1736	Ba1737	Ba1738	Ba1739	Ba1740	Ba1741	Ba1742	Ba1743	Ba1744	Ba1745	Ba1746	Ba1747	Ba1748	Ba1749	Ba1750
Year	Hundred	Hundred	Hundred	Hundred	Hundred	Hundred	Hundred	Hundred	Hundred	Hundred	Hundred	Hundred	Hundred	Hundred	Hundred
1860 [2]	0	0	0	0	0	0	0	0	0	0	0	0	0	2	0
1870	0	0	0	0	0	0	0	0	0	0	0	0	0	0	0
1880	0	0	0	0	0	0	0	0	0	0	0	0	0	0	0
1900	0	0	0	0	0	0	0	0	0	0	0	0	0	8	0
1910 [3]	0	0	0	0	0	0	0	0	0	0	0	0	40	0	8
1920	0	0	0	0	0	0	0	0	0	0	2	0	51	32	4
1940	0	0	0	0	0	0	0	0	0	0	0	0	203	98	14
1950	10	5	0	0	10	2	11	15	0	0	62	89	87	103	20
1960	11	2	2	1	11	16	2	9	0	1	85	93	110	152	21
1970	18	8	11	0	52	148	7	34	0	4	68	370	483	48	30
1980	18	11	13	0	58	188	5	22	0	4	38	257	1,450	89	83
1990	13	10	11	0	80	124	4	22	0	4	25	270	2,440	158	194

	Professional, technical, and kindred workers														
	Designers	Dietitians and nutritionists	Draftsmen	Editors and reporters	Engineers, aeronautical	Engineers, chemical	Engineers, civil	Engineers, electrical	Engineers, industrial	Engineers, mechanical	Engineers, metallurgical, metallurgists	Engineers, mining	Engineers not elsewhere classified	Entertainers not elsewhere classified	Farm and home management advisors
	Ba1751	Ba1752	Ba1753	Ba1754	Ba1755	Ba1756	Ba1757	Ba1758	Ba1759	Ba1760	Ba1761	Ba1762	Ba1763	Ba1764	Ba1765
Year	Hundred	Hundred	Hundred	Hundred	Hundred	Hundred	Hundred	Hundred	Hundred	Hundred	Hundred	Hundred	Hundred	Hundred	Hundred
1860 [2]	0	0	0	0	0	0	0	0	0	0	0	0	0	0	0
1870	0	0	0	2	0	0	0	0	0	0	0	0	0	2	0
1880	0	0	0	4	0	0	0	0	0	0	0	0	0	4	0
1900	8	0	0	23	0	0	0	0	0	0	0	0	0	8	0
1910 [3]	30	0	3	35	0	0	13	0	0	0	0	0	0	3	0
1920	45	18	16	75	0	0	0	2	0	0	0	0	0	6	0
1940	80	0	20	141	0	2	3	2	8	2	14	0	0	9	44
1950	103	219	67	247	5	15	41	10	8	7	7	4	3	58	77
1960	127	245	134	431	5	6	6	17	23	4	4	0	8	25	63
1970	256	372	225	798	11	7	23	50	52	16	2	2	31	157	66
1980	1,612	585	507	1,556	27	27	60	158	480	42	12	13	115	360	0
1990	3,186	800	568	2,281	113	67	172	444	1,167	97	19	19	356	802	0

	Professional, technical, and kindred workers														
								Natural scientists not elsewhere classified							
	Foresters and conservationists	Funeral directors and embalmers	Lawyers and judges	Librarians	Musicians and music teachers	Nurses, professional	Nurses, student professional	Agricultural scientists	Biological scientists	Geologists and geophysicists	Mathematicians	Physicists	Miscellaneous natural scientists	Optometrists	Osteopaths
	Ba1766	Ba1767	Ba1768	Ba1769	Ba1770	Ba1771	Ba1772	Ba1773	Ba1774	Ba1775	Ba1776	Ba1777	Ba1778	Ba1779	Ba1780
Year	Hundred	Hundred	Hundred	Hundred	Hundred	Hundred	Hundred	Hundred	Hundred	Hundred	Hundred	Hundred	Hundred	Hundred	Hundred
1860 [2]	0	0	0	0	45	2	0	0	0	0	0	0	0	0	0
1870	0	0	2	2	72	0	0	0	0	0	0	0	0	0	0
1880	0	1	0	4	164	2	0	0	0	0	0	0	0	0	0
1900	0	8	15	61	410	99	0	0	0	0	0	0	0	0	0
1910 [3]	0	13	13	0	844	889	0	0	0	0	0	0	0	0	0
1920	0	4	10	148	751	1,311	166	2	10	0	0	0	0	0	6
1940	0	17	45	303	601	3,156	0	0	0	0	0	0	0	13	11
1950	18	40	57	549	882	3,952	651	2	27	4	7	6	1	9	6
1960	9	23	72	743	1,070	5,665	560	5	31	10	19	4	4	7	5
1970	16	26	133	1,101	1,496	8,489	169	10	99	8	17	9	3	7	0
1980	47	33	726	1,659	2,666	12,822	0	58	229	52	11	16	17	19	0
1990	63	57	1,846	2,096	4,544	19,232	0	88	369	75	16	47	53	40	0

Notes appear at end of table

(continued)

TABLE Ba1721–1957 Detailed occupations – females: 1860–1990 [Part 1] *Continued*

	Professional, technical, and kindred workers														
									Social scientists						
	Personnel and labor-relations workers	Pharmacists	Photographers	Physicians and surgeons	Radio operators	Recreation and group workers	Religious workers	Social and welfare workers, except group	Economists	Psychologists	Statisticians and actuaries	Miscellaneous social scientists	Sports instructors and officials	Surveyors	Teachers not elsewhere classified
	Ba1781	Ba1782	Ba1783	Ba1784	Ba1785	Ba1786	Ba1787	Ba1788	Ba1789	Ba1790	Ba1791	Ba1792	Ba1793	Ba1794	Ba1795
Year	Hundred	Hundred	Hundred	Hundred	Hundred	Hundred	Hundred	Hundred	Hundred	Hundred	Hundred	Hundred	Hundred	Hundred	Hundred
1860 [2]	0	0	2	0	0	0	2	0	0	0	0	0	0	0	639
1870	0	0	2	13	0	0	10	0	0	0	0	0	0	0	844
1880	0	2	7	26	0	0	56	0	0	0	0	0	0	1	1,551
1900	0	0	23	30	0	0	129	0	0	0	0	0	0	0	3,081
1910 [3]	0	0	58	76	0	0	103	0	0	0	0	0	0	0	4,990
1920	2	34	51	57	2	8	256	89	0	2	8	0	14	0	6,317
1940	0	55	31	77	4	0	237	454	0	0	0	0	47	11	7,912
1950	156	139	97	116	26	60	279	583	33	25	82	12	120	28	8,586
1960	294	70	63	139	23	151	348	637	22	42	69	7	238	18	12,024
1970	914	139	88	258	87	204	190	1,375	74	112	103	37	189	18	18,720
1980	2,709	348	218	581	368	233	272	2,917	278	436	166	133	154	49	25,236
1990	4,204	656	411	1,184	177	333	557	4,433	636	1,116	213	252	237	96	32,711

	Professional, technical, and kindred workers						Farmers			Managers, officials, and proprietors					
	Technicians – medical and dental	Technicians – testing	Technicians not elsewhere classified	Therapists and healers not elsewhere classified	Veterinarians	Professional, technical, and kindred workers not elsewhere classified	Total	Farmers – owners and tenants	Farm managers	Total	Buyers and department heads – store	Buyers and shippers – farm products	Conductors – railroad	Credit men	Floormen and floor managers – store
	Ba1796	Ba1797	Ba1798	Ba1799	Ba1800	Ba1801	Ba1802	Ba1803	Ba1804	Ba1805	Ba1806	Ba1807	Ba1808	Ba1809	Ba1810
Year	Hundred	Hundred	Hundred	Hundred	Hundred	Hundred	Hundred	Hundred	Hundred	Hundred	Hundred	Hundred	Hundred	Hundred	Hundred
1860 [2]	0	0	0	0	0	0	960	947	13	199	0	0	0	0	0
1870	0	0	0	0	0	4	501	501	0	173	0	0	0	0	0
1880	0	0	0	0	0	5	895	891	4	369	0	0	1	0	0
1900	0	0	0	15	0	8	3,278	3,271	8	1,267	0	0	0	0	0
1910 [3]	0	0	0	50	0	106	2,776	2,776	0	1,345	0	0	0	0	40
1920	14	16	2	39	2	30	2,933	2,783	150	1,795	57	4	2	2	16
1940	0	198	11	87	6	354	1,604	1,594	10	4,469	184	3	5	41	34
1950	454	208	37	134	27	186	1,149	1,129	20	6,800	348	2	1	85	53
1960	845	381	52	191	3	642	1,119	1,112	7	7,802	504	4	2	121	49
1970	1,764	592	92	484	12	5,010	715	691	24	9,616	1,087	6	5	164	0
1980	3,971	2,205	306	1,404	46	4,703	1,268	1,147	121	26,423	1,898	15	8	0	0
1990	7,123	2,886	540	2,534	127	8,611	1,433	1,150	283	53,539	3,052	25	22	0	0

Year	Managers, officials, and proprietors: Inspectors – public administration	Managers and superintendents – building	Officers, pilots, pursers, and engineers – ship	Officials and administrators not elsewhere classified – public administration	Officials – lodge, society, union, and so forth	Postmasters	Purchasing agents and buyers not elsewhere classified	Managers, officials, and proprietors not elsewhere classified	Clerical and kindred workers: Total	Agents not elsewhere classified	Attendants and assistants – library	Attendants – physician's and dentist's office	Baggagemen – transportation	Bank tellers	Bookkeepers
	Ba1811	Ba1812	Ba1813	Ba1814	Ba1815	Ba1816	Ba1817	Ba1818	Ba1819	Ba1820	Ba1821	Ba1822	Ba1823	Ba1824	Ba1825
	Hundred	Hundred	Hundred	Hundred	Hundred	Hundred	Hundred	Hundred	Hundred	Hundred	Hundred	Hundred	Hundred	Hundred	Hundred
1860 [2]	0	0	0	0	0	0	0	199	6	2	0	0	0	0	2
1870	0	0	0	0	0	2	0	171	65	0	6	0	0	1	12
1880	0	0	0	6	2	8	1	351	98	5	0	0	0	0	27
1900	0	0	0	8	0	46	0	1,214	2,216	15	8	0	0	0	501
1910 [3]	0	0	0	121	15	0	0	1,169	6,680	20	0	0	3	0	1,869
1920	8	57	0	45	8	124	10	1,463	16,206	30	20	108	2	18	2,939
1940	8	327	3	163	27	165	82	3,427	25,241	123	267	303	0	0	4,481
1950	13	267	56	207	28	146	65	5,530	44,437	226	121	385	4	317	5,785
1960	40	202	2	411	32	146	105	6,184	62,450	263	253	729	3	899	7,766
1970	60	336	5	555	79	110	219	6,990	101,468	9	969	1,872	0	2,156	12,596
1980	258	797	8	1,248	0	134	750	21,308	146,145	0	1,124	3,849	0	4,515	16,403
1990	484	1,850	12	5,172	0	192	1,471	41,259	167,490	0	1,158	3,398	0	4,409	16,566

Year	Clerical and kindred workers: Cashiers	Collectors, bill and account	Dispatchers and starters – vehicle	Express messengers and railway mail clerks	Mail carriers	Messengers and office boys	Office machine operators	Shipping and receiving clerks	Stenographers, typists, and secretaries	Telegraph messengers	Telegraph operators	Telephone operators	Ticket, station, and express agents	Clerical and kindred workers not elsewhere classified
	Ba1826	Ba1827	Ba1828	Ba1829	Ba1830	Ba1831	Ba1832	Ba1833	Ba1834	Ba1835	Ba1836	Ba1837	Ba1838	Ba1839
	Hundred	Hundred	Hundred	Hundred	Hundred	Hundred	Hundred	Hundred	Hundred	Hundred	Hundred	Hundred	Hundred	Hundred
1860 [2]	0	0	0	0	0	0	0	0	0	0	0	0	0	2
1870	2	0	0	0	0	2	0	0	0	0	2	0	2	38
1880	6	1	0	0	0	0	0	0	0	0	9	1	4	45
1900	129	0	0	0	8	15	8	8	706	0	53	197	0	569
1910 [3]	0	20	0	0	5	63	0	13	2,594	3	68	834	13	1,176
1920	596	37	2	2	12	73	112	51	6,286	2	144	1,734	14	4,023
1940	0	32	0	0	21	26	570	161	10,329	2	113	1,846	21	6,946
1950	1,891	37	32	1	26	152	1,261	176	15,429	5	60	3,521	73	14,936
1960	3,688	51	56	3	32	92	2,264	234	21,709	4	58	3,406	148	20,793
1970	6,863	181	105	0	199	104	4,042	586	36,795	3	35	3,880	365	30,708
1980	14,238	504	298	0	335	203	6,886	1,442	45,726	0	31	2,887	562	47,143
1990	19,965	1,030	925	0	849	335	10,010	2,357	45,037	0	0	1,951	1,838	57,663

Notes appear at end of table

(continued)

TABLE Ba1721–1957 Detailed occupations – females: 1860–1990 [Part 1] *Continued*

	Sales workers										Craft workers, foremen, and kindred workers				
	Total	Advertising agents and salesmen	Auctioneers	Demonstrators	Hucksters and peddlers	Insurance agents and brokers	Newsboys	Real estate agents and brokers	Stock and bond salesmen	Salesmen and sales clerks not elsewhere classified	Total	Bakers	Blacksmiths	Bookbinders	Boilermakers
	Ba1840	Ba1841	Ba1842	Ba1843	Ba1844	Ba1845	Ba1846	Ba1847	Ba1848	Ba1849	Ba1850	Ba1851	Ba1852	Ba1853	Ba1854
Year	Hundred	Hundred	Hundred	Hundred	Hundred	Hundred	Hundred	Hundred	Hundred	Hundred	Hundred	Hundred	Hundred	Hundred	Hundred
1860 [2]	42	0	0	0	14	0	0	0	0	28	382	0	4	26	0
1870	150	0	0	0	20	0	0	0	0	130	365	4	2	28	0
1880	335	0	0	0	34	0	0	0	0	301	529	8	0	33	0
1900	1,609	0	0	0	23	23	0	0	0	1,563	1,100	30	0	152	0
1910 [3]	3,567	0	0	28	0	30	0	33	0	3,476	1,015	48	5	0	3
1920	5,135	16	0	32	12	53	2	41	6	4,972	1,412	39	8	118	2
1940	8,132	46	24	68	34	155	11	97	34	7,664	1,526	113	2	0	2
1950	13,473	42	25	134	30	240	24	240	23	12,715	2,355	97	1	157	3
1960	16,491	52	1	248	297	424	56	474	16	14,922	2,463	169	1	144	0
1970	21,665	129	3	352	943	821	100	820	89	18,406	5,069	321	6	190	4
1980	28,533	455	9	88	1,620	2,489	333	2,916	241	20,382	7,914	463	0	157	6
1990	35,771	857	11	330	1,387	5,123	425	3,964	789	22,885	9,481	684	0	146	5

	Craft workers, foremen, and kindred workers														
	Brickmasons, stonemasons, and tile setters	Cabinetmakers	Carpenters	Cement and concrete finishers	Compositors and typesetters	Cranemen, derrickmen, and hoistmen	Decorators and window dressers	Electricians	Electrotypers and stereotypers	Engravers, except photoengravers	Excavating, grading, and road machinery operators	Foremen not elsewhere classified	Forgemen and hammermen	Furriers	Glaziers
	Ba1855	Ba1856	Ba1857	Ba1858	Ba1859	Ba1860	Ba1861	Ba1862	Ba1863	Ba1864	Ba1865	Ba1866	Ba1867	Ba1868	Ba1869
Year	Hundred	Hundred	Hundred	Hundred	Hundred	Hundred	Hundred	Hundred	Hundred	Hundred	Hundred	Hundred	Hundred	Hundred	Hundred
1860 [2]	4	2	10	0	2	0	0	0	0	0	0	2	0	6	0
1870	5	2	2	0	8	0	0	0	0	0	0	0	0	2	0
1880	3	1	7	0	22	0	0	0	0	0	0	6	0	7	0
1900	0	0	0	0	152	0	0	0	0	8	0	99	0	8	0
1910 [3]	3	10	25	0	121	0	5	3	8	3	0	202	0	0	0
1920	6	4	24	0	116	0	10	10	0	8	2	381	4	12	2
1940	5	43	14	1	114	4	55	16	5	7	0	457	0	23	3
1950	5	6	51	2	115	14	109	22	14	13	9	648	3	20	8
1960	7	8	22	1	158	8	236	28	2	16	4	793	3	11	1
1970	24	34	111	9	237	19	392	84	2	21	35	1,270	8	5	9
1980	24	58	170	6	377	30	0	113	0	52	47	2,822	10	55	13
1990	32	41	207	7	497	24	0	162	0	61	65	2,628	11	97	22

Craft workers, foremen, and kindred workers

Year	Heat treaters, annealers, temperers	Inspectors, scalers, and graders – log and lumber	Inspectors not elsewhere classified	Jewelers, watchmakers, goldsmiths, silversmiths	Job setters – metal	Linemen and servicemen	Locomotive engineers	Locomotive firemen	Loom fixers	Machinists	Mechanics and repairmen – airplane	Mechanics and repairmen – automobile	Mechanics and repairmen – office machine	Mechanics and repairmen – radio and television	Mechanics and repairmen – railroad and car shop
	Ba1870	Ba1871	Ba1872	Ba1873	Ba1874	Ba1875	Ba1876	Ba1877	Ba1878	Ba1879	Ba1880	Ba1881	Ba1882	Ba1883	Ba1884
	Hundred	Hundred	Hundred	Hundred	Hundred	Hundred	Hundred	Hundred	Hundred	Hundred	Hundred	Hundred	Hundred	Hundred	Hundred
1860 [2]	0	0	0	2	0	0	0	0	0	0	0	0	0	0	0
1870	0	0	0	0	0	0	0	0	0	0	0	0	0	0	0
1880	1	0	0	6	0	0	0	0	0	1	0	0	0	0	0
1900	0	0	15	23	0	0	0	0	0	8	0	0	0	0	0
1910 [3]	3	0	13	10	0	5	3	3	0	33	0	0	0	0	0
1920	0	0	39	24	0	20	0	0	0	71	0	4	0	0	0
1940	4	7	59	44	0	18	1	0	0	40	3	9	0	0	0
1950	2	9	84	28	6	51	2	0	9	70	10	64	2	19	0
1960	3	8	52	18	3	43	0	0	3	69	13	25	0	14	1
1970	5	18	87	48	23	107	4	2	3	116	41	128	14	51	6
1980	14	0	24	151	36	339	12	0	0	233	38	136	55	79	0
1990	11	0	57	226	26	318	12	0	0	232	76	234	137	148	0

Craft workers, foremen, and kindred workers

Year	Mechanics and repairmen not elsewhere classified	Millers – grain, flour, feed, and so forth	Millwrights	Molders – metal	Motion picture projectionists	Opticians and lens grinders and polishers	Painters – construction and maintenance	Paperhangers	Pattern and model makers, except paper	Photoengravers and lithographers	Piano and organ tuners and repairmen	Plasterers	Plumbers and pipe fitters	Pressmen and plate printers – printing	Rollers and roll hands – metal
	Ba1885	Ba1886	Ba1887	Ba1888	Ba1889	Ba1890	Ba1891	Ba1892	Ba1893	Ba1894	Ba1895	Ba1896	Ba1897	Ba1898	Ba1899
	Hundred	Hundred	Hundred	Hundred	Hundred	Hundred	Hundred	Hundred	Hundred	Hundred	Hundred	Hundred	Hundred	Hundred	Hundred
1860 [2]	0	4	0	0	0	0	2	0	0	0	0	4	0	0	0
1870	0	2	0	0	0	0	6	0	0	0	0	0	0	0	0
1880	0	3	0	0	0	0	5	0	0	0	0	0	0	0	0
1900	0	0	0	8	0	0	0	8	0	0	0	0	0	15	0
1910 [3]	3	3	0	0	0	0	15	10	3	3	0	0	5	10	3
1920	14	4	2	6	0	4	22	6	2	4	0	0	8	6	4
1940	88	1	0	7	11	9	38	36	4	4	0	6	9	6	2
1950	122	0	3	4	4	18	90	29	24	11	3	10	21	19	5
1960	184	1	0	15	2	29	77	13	12	12	0	1	7	34	7
1970	250	2	9	60	6	64	160	0	18	39	4	5	39	133	14
1980	493	0	42	48	13	186	330	0	42	45	0	4	56	477	19
1990	592	0	27	29	15	409	567	0	57	126	0	8	67	612	17

Notes appear at end of table

(continued)

TABLE Ba1721–1957 Detailed occupations – females: 1860–1990 [Part 1] *Continued*

	Craft workers, foremen, and kindred workers										Operatives and kindred workers				
	Roofers and slaters	Shoemakers and repairers, except factory	Stationary engineers	Stonecutters and stone carvers	Structural metal workers	Tailors and tailoresses	Tinsmiths, coppersmiths, sheet metal workers	Toolmakers, die makers, and setters	Upholsterers	Craftsmen and kindred workers not elsewhere classified	Total	Apprentice auto mechanics	Apprentice bricklayers and masons	Apprentice carpenters	Apprentice electricians
	Ba1900	Ba1901	Ba1902	Ba1903	Ba1904	Ba1905	Ba1906	Ba1907	Ba1908	Ba1909	Ba1910	Ba1911	Ba1912	Ba1913	Ba1914
Year	Hundred	Hundred	Hundred	Hundred	Hundred	Hundred	Hundred	Hundred	Hundred	Hundred	Hundred	Hundred	Hundred	Hundred	Hundred
1860 [2]	0	8	2	0	2	295	0	0	2	4	2,737	0	0	0	0
1870	0	8	0	2	0	290	2	0	2	0	3,391	0	0	0	0
1880	0	2	1	0	0	414	3	0	5	2	5,711	0	0	0	0
1900	0	8	8	0	0	546	0	0	15	0	10,215	0	0	0	0
1910 [3]	0	3	5	0	0	428	0	3	15	8	16,043	0	0	0	0
1920	0	37	4	4	4	353	4	2	8	8	16,348	0	0	0	0
1940	7	8	13	18	31	152	4	1	22	0	22,672	0	0	10	0
1950	0	13	15	2	3	236	15	3	45	6	31,063	11	0	1	0
1960	0	9	20	1	5	68	22	15	49	18	32,481	0	0	0	1
1970	8	62	27	6	10	206	32	41	99	344	41,819	1	2	1	3
1980	10	102	50	0	33	228	49	36	130	0	45,639	1	1	5	9
1990	23	100	101	0	34	252	80	37	165	0	41,212	1	(Z)	2	7

	Operatives and kindred workers														
	Apprentice machinists and toolmakers	Apprentice mechanics, except auto	Apprentice plumbers and pipe fitters	Apprentices – building trades not elsewhere classified	Apprentices – metalworking trades not elsewhere classified	Apprentices – printing trades	Apprentices – other specified trades	Apprentices – trade not specified	Asbestos and insulation workers	Attendants – auto service and parking	Blasters and powdermen	Boatmen, canalmen, and lock keepers	Brakemen – railroad	Bus drivers	Chainmen, rodmen, and axmen – surveying
	Ba1915	Ba1916	Ba1917	Ba1918	Ba1919	Ba1920	Ba1921	Ba1922	Ba1923	Ba1924	Ba1925	Ba1926	Ba1927	Ba1928	Ba1929
Year	Hundred	Hundred	Hundred	Hundred	Hundred	Hundred	Hundred	Hundred	Hundred	Hundred	Hundred	Hundred	Hundred	Hundred	Hundred
1860 [2]	0	0	0	0	0	0	2	8	0	0	0	2	0	0	0
1870	0	0	0	0	0	0	12	0	0	0	0	0	0	0	0
1880	0	0	0	0	0	1	36	1	0	0	0	3	0	0	0
1900	0	0	0	0	0	0	23	0	0	0	0	0	0	0	0
1910 [3]	0	0	0	0	0	0	50	13	0	0	0	0	3	0	0
1920	0	0	0	0	0	2	10	6	0	4	0	0	4	4	0
1940	0	0	25	1	0	22	20	4	8	104	2	11	5	0	0
1950	2	0	32	0	2	20	4	4	16	55	0	8	5	53	9
1960	5	1	0	1	0	2	9	7	6	65	0	2	1	175	2
1970	2	3	2	1	(Z)	5	10	3	5	127	3	3	6	670	1
1980	8	0	3	0	1	0	11	0	18	275	3	0	8	1,716	5
1990	2	0	2	0	1	0	3	0	22	310	4	0	5	2,093	5

Year	Operatives and kindred workers													
	Conductors – bus and street railway	Deliverymen and routemen	Dressmakers and seamstresses, except factory	Dyers	Filers, grinders, and polishers – metal	Fruit, nut, vegetable graders, packers, not factory	Furnacemen, smeltermen, and pourers	Heaters – metal	Laundry and dry cleaning operatives	Meat cutters, except slaughter and packing houses	Milliners	Mine operatives and laborers	Motormen, mine, factory, logging camp, and so forth	Motormen, street, subway, and elevated railway
	Ba1930	Ba1931	Ba1932	Ba1933	Ba1934	Ba1935	Ba1936	Ba1937	Ba1938	Ba1939	Ba1940	Ba1941	Ba1942	Ba1943
	Hundred	Hundred	Hundred	Hundred	Hundred	Hundred	Hundred	Hundred	Hundred	Hundred	Hundred	Hundred	Hundred	Hundred
1860 [2]	0	2	1,312	0	2	0	0	0	4	4	259	4	0	0
1870	0	2	1,439	0	2	0	0	0	65	0	251	4	0	0
1880	0	4	2,251	1	2	0	0	0	390	4	377	1	0	0
1900	0	0	4,212	0	8	0	0	8	61	8	842	15	0	0
1910 [3]	0	23	3,967	3	28	20	5	0	705	0	1,224	33	0	5
1920	2	16	2,822	6	37	57	2	0	949	18	580	24	0	2
1940	1	24	1,418	8	72	171	1	47	1,616	10	97	35	1	0
1950	0	43	1,379	23	65	241	8	13	2,906	34	140	6	0	5
1960	0	110	1,140	3	87	132	8	1	2,791	55	35	11	1	0
1970	3	192	936	17	313	200	25	3	2,452	116	20	73	1	0
1980	0	465	894	0	449	0	0	0	1,848	397	0	91	0	0
1990	0	141	835	0	200	0	0	0	2,098	487	0	71	0	0

Year	Operatives and kindred workers													
	Oilers and greasers, except auto	Painters, except construction or maintenance	Photographic process workers	Power station operators	Sailors and deckhands	Sawyers	Spinners – textile	Stationary firemen	Switchmen – railroad	Taxicab drivers and chauffeurs	Truck and tractor drivers	Weavers – textile	Welders and flame cutters	Operatives and kindred workers not elsewhere classified
	Ba1944	Ba1945	Ba1946	Ba1947	Ba1948	Ba1949	Ba1950	Ba1951	Ba1952	Ba1953	Ba1954	Ba1955	Ba1956	Ba1957
	Hundred	Hundred	Hundred	Hundred	Hundred	Hundred	Hundred	Hundred	Hundred	Hundred	Hundred	Hundred	Hundred	Hundred
1860 [2]	0	12	0	0	0	0	170	0	0	0	0	282	0	673
1870	0	0	2	0	2	0	11	0	0	0	2	107	0	1,492
1880	0	2	1	0	2	0	9	1	0	1	2	107	0	2,516
1900	0	8	0	0	0	8	311	0	0	0	8	691	0	4,015
1910 [3]	0	13	0	0	3	0	338	3	0	3	20	975	0	8,612
1920	2	37	45	0	2	2	562	0	6	8	18	858	6	10,256
1940	7	64	94	10	4	2	0	9	0	0	71	0	23	18,677
1950	6	208	142	10	9	22	603	35	1	20	48	413	89	24,374
1960	4	142	170	20	5	17	435	5	3	43	65	266	152	26,504
1970	15	201	281	5	7	83	0	62	9	90	205	261	308	35,092
1980	15	322	443	14	9	111	0	62	3	196	390	443	386	37,038
1990	10	259	490	20	7	112	0	56	3	210	1,579	366	271	31,543

(Z) Fewer than 50.

[1] Data pertain to noninstitutionalized civilians age 16 and older who reported an occupation; employed persons only beginning 1940.

[2] Excludes slaves.

[3] The wording of the 1910 Census occupation question elicited more female occupation responses than in surrounding censuses, especially in agriculture.

Source

See the source for Table Ba1159–1395.

Documentation

See the text for Table Ba1159–1395.

TABLE Ba1958–2001 Detailed occupations – females: 1860–1990[1] [Part 2]

Contributed by Matthew Sobek

	Service workers, private household				Service workers, not household										
	Total	Housekeepers – private household	Laundresses – private household	Private household workers not elsewhere classified	Total	Attendants – hospital and other institution	Attendants – professional and personal service not elsewhere classified	Attendants – recreation and amusement	Barbers, beauticians, and manicurists	Bartenders	Bootblacks	Boarding and lodging house keepers	Charwomen and cleaners	Cooks, except private household	Counter and fountain workers
	Ba1958	Ba1959	Ba1960	Ba1961	Ba1962	Ba1963	Ba1964	Ba1965	Ba1966	Ba1967	Ba1968	Ba1969	Ba1970	Ba1971	Ba1972
Year	Hundred	Hundred	Hundred	Hundred	Hundred	Hundred	Hundred	Hundred	Hundred	Hundred	Hundred	Hundred	Hundred	Hundred	Hundred
1860 [2]	4,676	4	378	4,294	271	2	21	0	2	0	0	101	3	0	0
1870	8,610	16	536	8,058	391	8	57	0	13	0	0	84	0	21	0
1880	9,449	614	748	8,087	641	4	82	0	27	1	0	169	1	46	0
1900	17,151	584	8	16,559	4,849	15	0	0	76	0	0	539	0	61	0
1910 [3]	19,371	1,892	5,108	12,370	4,300	0	91	0	194	3	0	1,411	244	0	0
1920	13,762	1,771	3,785	8,206	6,408	81	95	2	337	0	2	1,104	193	777	14
1940	19,661	3,338	1,875	14,448	13,092	525	220	89	2,114	66	14	545	419	1,350	0
1950	13,392	1,404	702	11,286	19,724	1,214	341	45	1,949	166	18	210	729	2,448	457
1960	15,821	1,432	397	13,991	28,396	2,876	509	68	2,722	197	1	272	1,166	3,607	1,129
1970	11,229	983	111	10,135	46,021	6,102	1,811	164	4,362	393	4	54	2,521	5,256	1,146
1980	5,666	638	16	5,012	69,142	11,375	6,796	631	4,890	1,253	0	0	4,642	8,811	1,524
1990	4,965	307	15	4,643	84,829	15,006	10,571	1,108	6,545	1,492	0	0	5,148	10,477	1,483

	Service workers, not household														
	Elevator operators	Firemen (fire protection)	Guards, watchmen, and doorkeepers	Housekeepers and stewards, except household	Janitors and sextons	Marshals and constables	Midwives	Policemen and detectives	Porters	Practical nurses	Sheriffs and bailiffs	Ushers – recreation and amusement	Waiters and waitresses	Watchmen (crossing) and bridge tenders	Service workers (not private household) not elsewhere classified
	Ba1973	Ba1974	Ba1975	Ba1976	Ba1977	Ba1978	Ba1979	Ba1980	Ba1981	Ba1982	Ba1983	Ba1984	Ba1985	Ba1986	Ba1987
Year	Hundred	Hundred	Hundred	Hundred	Hundred	Hundred	Hundred	Hundred	Hundred	Hundred	Hundred	Hundred	Hundred	Hundred	Hundred
1860 [2]	0	0	2	29	0	0	16	0	0	73	0	0	12	2	7
1870	0	0	0	13	11	0	16	0	0	75	0	0	67	2	23
1880	0	0	1	2	6	0	26	0	0	169	0	0	62	7	39
1900	8	0	0	319	129	0	46	0	0	0	0	0	319	8	3,332
1910 [3]	0	0	10	0	181	0	48	0	8	1,207	0	0	892	0	13
1920	55	2	12	286	209	2	43	14	10	1,079	4	30	1,031	4	1,022
1940	131	2	33	736	403	0	0	19	34	894	4	38	3,641	0	1,814
1950	278	3	54	832	606	2	10	45	54	1,380	11	75	5,624	1	3,170
1960	245	4	66	1,214	790	6	7	81	21	1,972	12	39	7,072	115	4,205
1970	97	17	164	1,058	1,553	2	6	138	4	2,270	21	44	9,170	245	9,422
1980	43	19	860	525	4,920	0	0	281	15	4,106	75	71	11,958	319	6,027
1990	15	61	1,595	821	7,614	0	0	809	37	3,920	221	90	10,834	326	6,656

Year	Farm laborers: Total	Farm laborers: Farm foremen	Farm laborers: Farm laborers, wage workers	Farm laborers: Farm laborers, unpaid family workers	Farm laborers: Farm service laborers, self-employed	Laborers: Total	Laborers: Fishermen and oystermen	Laborers: Garage laborers, car washers, and greasers	Laborers: Gardeners, except farm, and groundskeepers	Laborers: Longshoremen and stevedores	Laborers: Lumbermen, raftsmen, and woodchoppers	Laborers: Teamsters	Laborers: Laborers not elsewhere classified	Unknown occupation
	Ba1988	Ba1989	Ba1990	Ba1991	Ba1992	Ba1993	Ba1994	Ba1995	Ba1996	Ba1997	Ba1998	Ba1999	Ba2000	Ba2001
	Hundred	Hundred	Hundred	Hundred	Hundred	Hundred	Hundred	Hundred	Hundred	Hundred	Hundred	Hundred	Hundred	Hundred
1860 [2]	160	0	160	0	0	159	1	0	10	0	0	0	148	—
1870	2,877	0	2,873	4	0	292	2	0	2	0	0	0	288	—
1880	3,554	2	3,552	0	0	1,327	5	0	9	0	5	0	1,308	—
1900	4,470	0	2,125	2,345	0	1,358	0	0	8	0	0	0	1,351	—
1910 [3]	11,605	58	11,547	0	0	1,149	0	0	55	3	5	0	1,086	—
1920	6,072	16	2,246	3,808	2	2,012	2	0	12	4	8	18	1,968	—
1940	3,429	2	1,017	2,410	0	1,160	26	5	23	4	4	3	1,094	1,346
1950	4,348	2	1,271	3,074	1	1,232	15	78	32	13	15	4	1,075	715
1960	2,437	6	1,208	1,222	0	1,072	5	31	32	1	8	1	994	11,560
1970	1,563	19	1,158	380	6	2,682	12	0	89	8	21	2	2,550	—
1980	2,024	85	1,940	0	0	5,483	32	0	250	3	22	0	5,175	—
1990	1,709	54	1,655	0	0	7,408	31	0	484	3	31	0	6,860	—

[1] Data pertain to noninstitutionalized civilians age 16 and older who reported an occupation; employed persons only beginning 1940.

[2] Excludes slaves.

[3] The wording of the 1910 Census occupation question elicited more female occupation responses than in surrounding censuses, especially in agriculture.

Source

See the source for Table Ba1159–1395.

Documentation

See the text for Table Ba1159–1395.

TABLE Ba2002–2238 Detailed occupations – white males: 1850–1990[1] [Part 1]

Contributed by Matthew Sobek

		Professional, technical, and kindred workers													
														College professors and instructors	
	Total	Total	Accountants and auditors	Actors and actresses	Airplane pilots and navigators	Architects	Artists and art teachers	Athletes	Authors	Chemists	Chiropractors	Clergymen	College presidents and deans	Agricultural sciences	Biological sciences
	Ba2002	Ba2003	Ba2004	Ba2005	Ba2006	Ba2007	Ba2008	Ba2009	Ba2010	Ba2011	Ba2012	Ba2013	Ba2014	Ba2015	Ba2016
Year	Hundred	Hundred	Hundred	Hundred	Hundred	Hundred	Hundred	Hundred	Hundred	Hundred	Hundred	Hundred	Hundred	Hundred	Hundred
1850	51,329	1,568	7	5	0	4	21	2	1	8	0	286	1	0	0
1860	70,107	2,329	17	2	0	14	42	4	2	4	0	345	2	0	0
1870	89,714	2,757	12	6	0	22	46	0	2	17	0	461	0	0	0
1880	122,817	4,140	23	39	0	38	55	4	8	26	0	608	4	0	0
1900	199,272	7,323	61	106	0	61	152	23	8	83	0	835	61	0	0
1910	256,583	8,998	0	156	0	164	202	0	10	149	0	1,048	0	0	0
1920	287,380	12,660	1,132	136	10	176	203	43	37	310	34	1,081	6	4	0
1940	325,884	18,692	0	82	54	184	375	76	105	531	83	1,145	0	0	0
1950	373,668	29,594	3,223	93	160	246	489	78	98	696	119	1,504	38	41	48
1960	389,639	43,187	3,923	52	276	283	624	29	186	721	126	1,821	53	29	61
1970	427,676	66,951	5,033	52	486	514	612	0	167	899	126	1,992	288	45	154
1980	497,480	84,353	5,644	0	711	905	697	0	234	698	179	2,478	0	27	62
1990	546,202	101,718	6,558	0	997	1,191	878	0	504	845	303	2,581	0	7	38

	Professional, technical, and kindred workers														
	College professors and instructors														
	Chemistry	Economics	Engineering	Geology and geophysics	Mathematics	Medical sciences	Physics	Psychology	Statistics	Natural sciences not elsewhere classified	Social sciences not elsewhere classified	Nonscientific subjects	Subject not specified	Dancers and dancing teachers	Dentists
	Ba2017	Ba2018	Ba2019	Ba2020	Ba2021	Ba2022	Ba2023	Ba2024	Ba2025	Ba2026	Ba2027	Ba2028	Ba2029	Ba2030	Ba2031
Year	Hundred	Hundred	Hundred	Hundred	Hundred	Hundred	Hundred	Hundred	Hundred	Hundred	Hundred	Hundred	Hundred	Hundred	Hundred
1850	0	0	0	0	1	0	0	0	0	0	0	3	8	1	20
1860	0	0	0	0	2	1	0	0	0	0	0	9	6	5	65
1870	0	0	0	2	2	0	0	0	0	0	0	1	10	2	67
1880	1	0	0	1	2	0	0	0	0	1	0	18	14	1	122
1900	0	0	0	0	0	0	0	0	0	0	0	0	0	8	243
1910	0	0	0	0	0	0	0	0	0	0	0	0	214	0	406
1920	8	0	2	0	2	4	0	0	0	2	6	6	144	18	548
1940	0	0	0	0	0	0	0	0	0	0	0	0	518	25	678
1950	59	31	85	9	40	21	29	22	5	1	128	145	159	26	691
1960	53	37	89	16	83	45	47	19	1	2	160	200	396	42	787
1970	130	88	142	0	193	125	126	89	0	39	265	547	1,012	8	848
1980	59	37	92	0	118	83	46	32	0	19	87	236	2,577	23	1,115
1990	34	24	57	0	110	53	30	19	0	7	48	182	3,239	41	1,243

	Professional, technical, and kindred workers														
	Designers	Dietitians and nutritionists	Draftsmen	Editors and reporters	Engineers, aeronautical	Engineers, chemical	Engineers, civil	Engineers, electrical	Engineers, industrial	Engineers, mechanical	Engineers, metallurgical, metallurgists	Engineers, mining	Engineers not elsewhere classified	Entertainers not elsewhere classified	Farm and home management advisors
	Ba2032	Ba2033	Ba2034	Ba2035	Ba2036	Ba2037	Ba2038	Ba2039	Ba2040	Ba2041	Ba2042	Ba2043	Ba2044	Ba2045	Ba2046
Year	Hundred	Hundred	Hundred	Hundred	Hundred	Hundred	Hundred	Hundred	Hundred	Hundred	Hundred	Hundred	Hundred	Hundred	Hundred
1850	2	0	1	23	0	0	6	0	0	1	0	0	0	9	0
1860	0	0	2	38	0	0	22	0	0	2	0	2	0	5	6
1870	2	0	8	53	0	0	32	0	0	0	0	8	0	12	2
1880	8	0	23	118	0	0	64	0	0	3	0	9	0	35	0
1900	38	0	114	266	0	0	114	46	0	106	0	38	0	68	0
1910	73	0	322	315	0	0	466	0	0	141	0	103	0	194	0
1920	112	0	546	294	2	26	663	280	24	300	14	63	112	47	22
1940	148	0	869	440	0	114	836	539	125	776	94	0	0	46	72
1950	323	8	1,080	636	179	301	1,234	1,084	455	1,144	116	104	767	81	61
1960	561	11	1,985	858	504	403	1,538	1,711	987	1,547	174	113	1,412	69	59
1970	797	27	2,499	1,372	625	502	1,637	2,669	1,762	1,742	154	149	2,326	420	61
1980	1,516	46	2,448	1,531	772	499	1,771	2,799	2,445	1,936	212	303	2,618	549	0
1990	2,346	60	2,308	1,801	1,132	514	2,036	3,623	3,078	1,691	144	269	3,133	722	0

	Professional, technical, and kindred workers														
								Natural scientists not elsewhere classified							
	Foresters and conservationists	Funeral directors and embalmers	Lawyers and judges	Librarians	Musicians and music teachers	Nurses, professional	Nurses, student professional	Agricultural scientists	Biological scientists	Geologists and geophysicists	Mathematicians	Physicists	Miscellaneous natural scientists	Optometrists	Osteopaths
	Ba2047	Ba2048	Ba2049	Ba2050	Ba2051	Ba2052	Ba2053	Ba2054	Ba2055	Ba2056	Ba2057	Ba2058	Ba2059	Ba2060	Ba2061
Year	Hundred	Hundred	Hundred	Hundred	Hundred	Hundred	Hundred	Hundred	Hundred	Hundred	Hundred	Hundred	Hundred	Hundred	Hundred
1850	0	6	244	0	32	0	0	0	0	0	0	0	1	0	0
1860	0	10	343	2	67	0	0	0	1	0	0	0	0	0	0
1870	0	24	441	2	89	2	0	0	2	0	0	0	0	0	0
1880	0	56	651	2	167	0	0	0	2	3	0	0	0	0	0
1900	8	129	994	0	493	0	0	0	0	0	0	8	8	0	0
1910	43	154	1,093	0	524	53	0	0	0	0	0	0	0	0	0
1920	67	205	1,223	8	467	39	0	4	10	24	0	2	0	37	20
1940	0	304	1,655	47	644	117	0	0	0	0	0	0	0	112	56
1950	250	316	1,709	61	697	87	23	50	64	102	16	66	19	157	60
1960	307	318	1,992	109	733	106	11	71	85	188	51	130	25	163	38
1970	372	352	2,600	215	1,136	632	10	114	172	214	56	206	9	166	0
1980	465	336	4,380	294	2,149	1,093	0	172	385	396	47	279	65	220	0
1990	398	361	5,556	354	2,854	1,644	0	221	433	431	36	304	119	221	0

Note appears at end of table

(continued)

TABLE Ba2002–2238 Detailed occupations – white males: 1850–1990 [Part 1] *Continued*

	Professional, technical, and kindred workers								Social scientists						
	Personnel and labor-relations workers	Pharmacists	Photographers	Physicians and surgeons	Radio operators	Recreation and group workers	Religious workers	Social and welfare workers, except group	Economists	Psychologists	Statisticians and actuaries	Miscellaneous social scientists	Sports instructors and officials	Surveyors	Teachers not elsewhere classified
	Ba2062	Ba2063	Ba2064	Ba2065	Ba2066	Ba2067	Ba2068	Ba2069	Ba2070	Ba2071	Ba2072	Ba2073	Ba2074	Ba2075	Ba2076
Year	Hundred	Hundred	Hundred	Hundred	Hundred	Hundred	Hundred	Hundred	Hundred	Hundred	Hundred	Hundred	Hundred	Hundred	Hundred
1850	0	55	7	432	0	0	0	0	0	0	0	0	0	13	301
1860	0	99	52	619	0	0	24	0	0	0	0	0	0	28	478
1870	0	187	58	655	0	0	2	4	0	0	0	0	11	32	430
1880	0	283	105	856	0	0	0	0	0	0	0	0	0	38	690
1900	0	501	228	1,267	0	0	8	0	0	0	0	15	8	68	918
1910	0	0	254	1,438	0	0	93	5	0	0	0	0	0	0	1,131
1920	20	724	235	1,311	22	30	51	34	2	0	22	2	93	91	1,162
1940	0	727	310	1,597	85	0	81	277	0	0	0	0	191	164	2,498
1950	381	821	432	1,817	164	91	147	241	67	17	148	27	312	240	2,742
1960	699	872	433	2,033	237	220	220	320	143	96	129	21	453	398	4,479
1970	1,909	923	527	2,368	430	253	149	683	551	172	161	84	433	557	8,312
1980	3,206	1,013	632	3,293	660	79	193	1,249	630	447	216	158	378	697	10,743
1990	3,041	1,047	867	3,974	536	96	371	1,552	775	717	242	216	514	840	10,758

	Professional, technical, and kindred workers						Farmers			Managers, officials, and proprietors					
	Technicians – medical and dental	Technicians – testing	Technicians not elsewhere classified	Therapists and healers not elsewhere classified	Veterinarians	Professional, technical, and kindred workers not elsewhere classified	Total	Farmers – owners and tenants	Farm managers	Total	Buyers and department heads – store	Buyers and shippers – farm products	Conductors – railroad	Credit men	Floormen and floor managers – store
	Ba2077	Ba2078	Ba2079	Ba2080	Ba2081	Ba2082	Ba2083	Ba2084	Ba2085	Ba2086	Ba2087	Ba2088	Ba2089	Ba2090	Ba2091
Year	Hundred	Hundred	Hundred	Hundred	Hundred	Hundred	Hundred	Hundred	Hundred	Hundred	Hundred	Hundred	Hundred	Hundred	Hundred
1850	0	0	0	0	0	66	23,558	23,551	7	2,426	0	3	4	0	0
1860	0	0	0	0	2	7	26,006	25,963	42	3,916	0	59	66	0	0
1870	0	2	1	4	8	35	29,298	29,277	21	5,462	0	119	99	0	0
1880	0	0	0	6	28	30	39,841	39,819	22	7,172	1	234	184	0	0
1900	0	0	8	46	106	83	47,955	47,833	121	13,895	38	524	402	8	23
1910	0	0	0	25	123	98	49,162	49,162	0	23,099	0	0	607	0	141
1920	20	53	12	20	152	77	55,034	54,254	781	24,884	276	592	826	85	41
1940	0	405	69	106	104	1,226	43,887	43,560	327	32,787	507	365	471	268	70
1950	339	604	272	112	143	941	37,411	37,113	298	43,277	1,005	281	550	278	51
1960	490	2,054	882	144	159	2,286	21,937	21,711	226	44,966	1,806	192	460	382	59
1970	873	2,567	1,401	299	176	7,147	12,867	12,330	537	49,032	5,110	196	376	427	0
1980	1,428	5,284	2,081	517	286	5,280	11,259	10,099	1,160	70,539	6,278	164	417	0	0
1990	2,128	5,957	2,845	703	341	9,423	8,745	6,847	1,898	86,195	4,796	126	308	0	0

Year	Managers, officials, and proprietors								Clerical and kindred workers							
	Inspectors – public administration	Managers and superintendents – building	Officers, pilots, pursers, and engineers – ship	Officials and administrators not elsewhere classified – public administration	Officials – lodge, society, union, and so forth	Postmasters	Purchasing agents and buyers not elsewhere classified	Managers, officials, and proprietors not elsewhere classified	Total	Agents not elsewhere classified	Attendants and assistants – library	Attendants – physician's and dentist's office	Baggagemen – transportation	Bank tellers	Bookkeepers
	Ba2092	Ba2093	Ba2094	Ba2095	Ba2096	Ba2097	Ba2098	Ba2099	Ba2100	Ba2101	Ba2102	Ba2103	Ba2104	Ba2105	Ba2106
	Hundred	Hundred	Hundred	Hundred	Hundred	Hundred	Hundred	Hundred	Hundred	Hundred	Hundred	Hundred	Hundred	Hundred	Hundred
1850	11	21	78	69	0	19	0	2,221	137	24	0	1	8	4	22
1860	6	38	166	114	0	46	0	3,420	449	51	0	0	13	12	141
1870	21	12	163	138	0	29	0	4,880	1,207	39	4	0	17	9	292
1880	36	17	178	271	8	55	10	6,178	2,516	203	0	0	51	14	620
1900	76	0	159	220	30	205	0	12,211	8,264	296	8	0	76	61	1,890
1910	0	0	244	1,023	43	0	0	21,041	12,574	514	0	0	123	0	2,902
1920	209	146	428	467	41	179	201	21,395	16,701	327	6	6	101	207	2,461
1940	421	412	297	1,138	193	215	333	28,096	23,607	877	68	75	53	0	4,167
1950	544	438	411	1,080	215	218	611	37,596	25,767	1,123	23	17	62	352	1,697
1960	663	267	344	1,488	276	229	924	37,877	27,583	1,313	75	22	44	409	1,445
1970	871	476	226	2,050	387	236	1,365	37,312	31,822	205	232	156	0	327	2,619
1980	1,126	1,048	343	2,173	0	166	1,761	57,062	35,405	0	217	334	0	366	1,643
1990	948	1,967	335	3,234	0	192	1,949	72,341	39,682	0	239	323	0	390	1,606

Year	Clerical and kindred workers													
	Cashiers	Collectors, bill and account	Dispatchers and starters – vehicle	Express messengers and railway mail clerks	Mail carriers	Messengers and office boys	Office machine operators	Shipping and receiving clerks	Stenographers, typists, and secretaries	Telegraph messengers	Telegraph operators	Telephone operators	Ticket, station, and express agents	Clerical and kindred workers not elsewhere classified
	Ba2107	Ba2108	Ba2109	Ba2110	Ba2111	Ba2112	Ba2113	Ba2114	Ba2115	Ba2116	Ba2117	Ba2118	Ba2119	Ba2120
	Hundred	Hundred	Hundred	Hundred	Hundred	Hundred	Hundred	Hundred	Hundred	Hundred	Hundred	Hundred	Hundred	Hundred
1850	1	12	0	0	8	5	0	3	0	1	5	0	13	29
1860	6	28	0	8	28	12	0	2	2	0	8	0	50	87
1870	8	17	2	21	19	16	0	14	0	0	51	0	116	582
1880	24	36	12	16	85	49	0	74	12	4	152	9	209	948
1900	144	228	23	68	197	250	0	273	296	30	531	23	334	3,536
1910	0	292	0	184	804	436	0	753	469	30	615	91	285	5,078
1920	270	296	24	260	949	308	16	1,171	777	59	657	99	519	8,187
1940	0	350	0	238	1,150	443	160	2,058	762	125	404	126	413	12,139
1950	446	166	299	185	1,517	407	238	2,565	843	68	296	272	519	14,672
1960	971	259	489	58	1,660	393	713	2,244	716	25	136	129	566	15,917
1970	1,203	314	476	0	2,030	339	1,305	3,012	1,152	13	90	207	577	17,565
1980	2,487	291	606	0	1,912	488	2,102	4,206	646	0	42	628	373	19,064
1990	4,423	441	930	0	1,945	783	3,032	4,674	721	0	0	238	647	19,291

(continued)

TABLE Ba2002–2238 Detailed occupations – white males: 1850–1990 [Part 1] *Continued*

	Sales workers										Craft workers, foremen, and kindred workers				
	Total	Advertising agents and salesmen	Auctioneers	Demonstrators	Hucksters and peddlers	Insurance agents and brokers	Newsboys	Real estate agents and brokers	Stock and bond salesmen	Salesmen and sales clerks not elsewhere classified	Total	Bakers	Blacksmiths	Bookbinders	Boilermakers
	Ba2121	Ba2122	Ba2123	Ba2124	Ba2125	Ba2126	Ba2127	Ba2128	Ba2129	Ba2130	Ba2131	Ba2132	Ba2133	Ba2134	Ba2135
Year	Hundred	Hundred	Hundred	Hundred	Hundred	Hundred	Hundred	Hundred	Hundred	Hundred	Hundred	Hundred	Hundred	Hundred	Hundred
1850	1,140	0	8	0	112	6	5	4	1	1,004	8,622	144	935	32	19
1860	1,892	0	18	0	199	10	12	20	0	1,633	11,085	203	1,113	36	20
1870	2,796	6	16	0	352	134	20	97	0	2,170	12,840	250	1,307	38	56
1880	4,186	5	26	0	488	134	21	137	6	3,371	16,036	351	1,650	65	105
1900	8,333	30	15	0	706	660	23	546	0	6,352	29,787	668	2,057	243	304
1910	12,713	0	25	10	0	741	103	1,247	164	10,423	39,643	655	2,267	0	383
1920	14,804	132	51	10	410	1,144	73	1,242	164	11,579	54,087	895	2,031	116	667
1940	21,237	315	47	18	454	2,193	360	1,049	196	16,604	51,777	1,214	781	0	295
1950	25,859	258	130	39	184	2,789	387	1,274	111	20,686	74,233	1,004	407	141	340
1960	28,481	289	39	14	176	3,809	679	1,476	289	21,710	80,640	836	198	121	203
1970	32,501	495	46	34	230	4,535	500	1,742	861	24,058	91,605	663	146	132	269
1980	35,119	624	56	23	401	4,600	594	3,394	1,035	24,392	100,235	610	0	113	301
1990	40,077	748	65	64	627	5,024	561	3,603	1,978	27,407	101,071	688	0	115	180

	Craft workers, foremen, and kindred workers														
	Brickmasons, stonemasons, and tile setters	Cabinetmakers	Carpenters	Cement and concrete finishers	Compositors and typesetters	Cranemen, derrickmen, and hoistmen	Decorators and window dressers	Electricians	Electrotypers and stereotypers	Engravers, except photoengravers	Excavating, grading, and road machinery operators	Foremen not elsewhere classified	Forgemen and hammermen	Furriers	Glaziers
	Ba2136	Ba2137	Ba2138	Ba2139	Ba2140	Ba2141	Ba2142	Ba2143	Ba2144	Ba2145	Ba2146	Ba2147	Ba2148	Ba2149	Ba2150
Year	Hundred	Hundred	Hundred	Hundred	Hundred	Hundred	Hundred	Hundred	Hundred	Hundred	Hundred	Hundred	Hundred	Hundred	Hundred
1850	502	375	2,167	1	157	0	0	0	0	18	14	24	10	2	1
1860	633	336	2,891	0	202	0	0	0	0	28	4	240	13	2	8
1870	819	325	3,390	0	272	2	4	0	2	37	12	113	12	10	8
1880	900	348	3,706	5	530	0	0	4	10	55	7	228	6	9	7
1900	1,487	379	5,980	0	1,100	8	0	501	46	46	0	1,100	0	15	23
1910	1,675	401	7,869	0	1,134	0	53	1,292	55	134	0	2,688	73	0	0
1920	1,144	489	8,151	67	1,337	308	79	2,071	49	120	89	4,311	101	55	35
1940	1,060	646	5,802	190	1,546	1,065	258	1,932	85	69	0	5,391	0	138	116
1950	1,401	669	8,620	251	1,658	976	295	3,069	179	96	1,037	7,711	164	116	131
1960	1,597	603	7,712	280	1,615	1,081	251	3,294	89	107	1,872	10,717	99	31	160
1970	1,559	592	7,659	441	1,226	1,280	280	4,239	64	57	2,793	13,864	130	23	225
1980	1,637	622	10,251	415	289	1,257	0	5,557	0	83	3,083	17,534	115	25	276
1990	1,989	611	11,348	486	194	810	0	5,957	0	98	3,269	13,489	133	48	384

	Craft workers, foremen, and kindred workers														
	Heat treaters, annealers, temperers	Inspectors, scalers, and graders – log and lumber	Inspectors not elsewhere classified	Jewelers, watchmakers, goldsmiths, silversmiths	Job setters – metal	Linemen and servicemen	Locomotive engineers	Locomotive firemen	Loom fixers	Machinists	Mechanics and repairmen – airplane	Mechanics and repairmen – automobile	Mechanics and repairmen – office machine	Mechanics and repairmen – radio and television	Mechanics and repairmen – railroad and car shop
	Ba2151	Ba2152	Ba2153	Ba2154	Ba2155	Ba2156	Ba2157	Ba2158	Ba2159	Ba2160	Ba2161	Ba2162	Ba2163	Ba2164	Ba2165
Year	Hundred	Hundred	Hundred	Hundred	Hundred	Hundred	Hundred	Hundred	Hundred	Hundred	Hundred	Hundred	Hundred	Hundred	Hundred
1850	0	1	5	118	0	0	5	0	0	234	0	0	0	0	1
1860	0	2	8	128	0	0	18	10	0	373	0	0	0	0	4
1870	0	13	11	157	0	0	114	77	0	532	0	0	0	0	17
1880	4	4	33	216	0	11	165	105	3	833	0	0	0	0	23
1900	0	61	197	326	0	83	539	471	46	2,542	0	0	0	0	144
1910	10	0	469	267	0	232	1,053	650	123	4,635	0	0	0	0	0
1920	30	130	895	353	22	588	1,130	858	205	8,067	6	1,939	36	2	757
1940	122	152	710	406	0	1,076	674	444	210	4,603	230	3,546	0	0	370
1950	163	163	922	463	238	2,063	772	553	319	4,945	685	6,260	177	727	492
1960	189	149	920	349	369	2,652	584	350	269	4,760	1,077	6,194	285	1,006	386
1970	180	136	1,017	305	770	3,631	466	120	200	3,373	1,354	8,149	674	1,225	508
1980	183	0	429	533	473	3,540	624	0	0	4,341	950	11,162	713	1,409	0
1990	148	0	555	580	225	2,916	384	0	0	4,725	1,371	12,135	999	1,348	0

	Craft workers, foremen, and kindred workers														
	Mechanics and repairmen not elsewhere classified	Millers – grain, flour, feed, and so forth	Millwrights	Molders – metal	Motion picture projectionists	Opticians and lens grinders and polishers	Painters – construction and maintenance	Paperhangers	Pattern and model makers, except paper	Photoengravers and lithographers	Piano and organ tuners and repairmen	Plasterers	Plumbers and pipe fitters	Pressmen and plate printers – printing	Rollers and roll hands – metal
	Ba2166	Ba2167	Ba2168	Ba2169	Ba2170	Ba2171	Ba2172	Ba2173	Ba2174	Ba2175	Ba2176	Ba2177	Ba2178	Ba2179	Ba2180
Year	Hundred	Hundred	Hundred	Hundred	Hundred	Hundred	Hundred	Hundred	Hundred	Hundred	Hundred	Hundred	Hundred	Hundred	Hundred
1850	285	316	90	89	0	2	210	6	16	8	0	92	15	1	10
1860	383	387	53	179	0	2	497	16	20	8	2	146	65	0	18
1870	255	370	113	281	0	2	714	18	30	8	8	148	126	0	66
1880	290	426	91	399	0	14	1,069	38	57	33	14	251	179	7	27
1900	554	288	114	865	0	61	2,201	190	159	76	15	311	964	266	0
1910	395	207	0	1,199	0	0	2,645	227	234	68	91	408	1,486	249	161
1920	1,171	227	371	1,142	99	128	2,542	152	296	132	69	298	2,104	233	241
1940	3,947	150	404	658	280	126	3,183	246	313	249	93	401	1,727	364	251
1950	7,990	118	573	466	240	187	3,773	195	487	290	132	544	2,653	546	296
1960	11,573	88	586	382	164	163	3,326	78	416	268	48	394	2,961	686	253
1970	10,143	62	763	369	154	203	3,040	0	360	277	61	225	3,413	1,307	158
1980	13,460	0	1,143	246	113	250	3,470	0	278	195	0	207	4,234	2,123	136
1990	13,958	0	813	154	77	287	4,564	0	222	324	0	318	4,204	2,460	93

Note appears at end of table

(continued)

TABLE Ba2002–2238 Detailed occupations – white males: 1850–1990 [Part 1] *Continued*

	Craft workers, foremen, and kindred workers										Operatives and kindred workers				
	Roofers and slaters	Shoemakers and repairers, except factory	Stationary engineers	Stonecutters and stone carvers	Structural metal workers	Tailors and tailoresses	Tinsmiths, coppersmiths, sheet metal workers	Toolmakers, die makers, and setters	Upholsterers	Craftsmen and kindred workers not elsewhere classified	Total	Apprentice auto mechanics	Apprentice bricklayers and masons	Apprentice carpenters	Apprentice electricians
	Ba2181	Ba2182	Ba2183	Ba2184	Ba2185	Ba2186	Ba2187	Ba2188	Ba2189	Ba2190	Ba2191	Ba2192	Ba2193	Ba2194	Ba2195
Year	Hundred	Hundred	Hundred	Hundred	Hundred	Hundred	Hundred	Hundred	Hundred	Hundred	Hundred	Hundred	Hundred	Hundred	Hundred
1850	1	1,349	101	112	0	545	110	5	24	466	4,654	0	0	3	0
1860	13	1,291	223	148	0	613	192	6	24	525	6,794	0	6	84	0
1870	34	1,087	296	190	0	549	265	12	45	640	11,078	0	24	69	0
1880	44	1,013	607	286	1	753	389	9	88	571	15,877	0	5	46	0
1900	83	903	1,404	433	15	1,283	577	0	243	417	26,258	0	0	8	15
1910	144	620	2,179	320	106	1,474	642	113	164	395	39,192	0	0	0	0
1920	112	637	2,059	268	765	1,663	704	629	223	690	43,358	26	0	8	37
1940	278	604	1,859	166	379	893	779	927	368	0	59,260	0	0	117	51
1950	476	477	2,185	108	476	734	1,234	1,566	585	698	75,916	53	70	107	116
1960	434	300	2,682	43	537	283	1,308	1,806	492	968	76,694	14	20	50	84
1970	494	637	1,603	59	797	422	1,384	1,838	472	5,614	81,439	31	33	73	193
1980	852	914	1,404	0	864	286	1,339	1,739	458	0	83,376	30	19	69	153
1990	1,436	1,060	1,832	0	683	221	1,381	1,317	483	0	78,364	14	6	37	124

	Operatives and kindred workers														
	Apprentice machinists and toolmakers	Apprentice mechanics, except auto	Apprentice plumbers and pipe fitters	Apprentices – building trades not elsewhere classified	Apprentices – metalworking trades not elsewhere classified	Apprentices – printing trades	Apprentices – other specified trades	Apprentices – trade not specified	Asbestos and insulation workers	Attendants – auto service and parking	Blasters and powdermen	Boatmen, canalmen, and lock keepers	Brakemen – railroad	Bus drivers	Chainmen, rodmen, and axmen – surveying
	Ba2196	Ba2197	Ba2198	Ba2199	Ba2200	Ba2201	Ba2202	Ba2203	Ba2204	Ba2205	Ba2206	Ba2207	Ba2208	Ba2209	Ba2210
Year	Hundred	Hundred	Hundred	Hundred	Hundred	Hundred	Hundred	Hundred	Hundred	Hundred	Hundred	Hundred	Hundred	Hundred	Hundred
1850	0	0	0	2	0	0	8	21	0	0	0	266	4	38	0
1860	14	8	8	24	108	20	126	71	0	0	0	254	28	32	0
1870	35	14	10	38	116	31	151	28	0	0	6	194	123	35	0
1880	40	0	11	12	68	13	118	18	0	0	0	194	227	38	0
1900	129	0	30	0	114	15	137	46	0	0	0	91	820	0	8
1910	0	0	0	191	0	0	3	600	0	0	0	50	899	0	0
1920	146	26	57	0	81	49	61	87	26	32	12	35	1,146	83	20
1940	167	0	77	162	0	138	236	114	92	2,023	57	113	692	0	120
1950	167	43	167	53	83	191	144	144	159	2,118	109	135	754	1,477	113
1960	129	38	88	21	43	111	79	97	198	3,059	54	63	567	1,462	81
1970	179	61	132	16	59	78	99	27	235	3,930	66	41	442	1,367	98
1980	134	0	97	0	6	0	31	0	425	2,694	81	0	684	1,495	82
1990	34	0	61	0	7	0	15	0	536	2,134	69	0	277	1,536	34

Year	Conductors – bus and street railway	Deliverymen and routemen	Dressmakers and seamstresses, except factory	Dyers	Filers, grinders, and polishers – metal	Fruit, nut, vegetable graders, packers, not factory	Furnacemen, smeltermen, and pourers	Heaters – metal	Laundry and dry cleaning operatives	Meat cutters, except slaughter and packing house	Milliners	Mine operatives and laborers	Motormen, mine, factory, logging camp, and so forth	Motormen, street, subway, and elevated railway
	Operatives and kindred workers													
	Ba2211	Ba2212	Ba2213	Ba2214	Ba2215	Ba2216	Ba2217	Ba2218	Ba2219	Ba2220	Ba2221	Ba2222	Ba2223	Ba2224
	Hundred	Hundred	Hundred	Hundred	Hundred	Hundred	Hundred	Hundred	Hundred	Hundred	Hundred	Hundred	Hundred	Hundred
1850	0	13	2	23	1	0	97	1	3	189	2	862	0	1
1860	5	25	14	26	31	0	60	12	6	322	13	1,059	0	16
1870	8	54	14	24	46	0	112	8	6	415	7	1,461	0	26
1880	17	117	10	47	71	0	399	22	53	737	15	2,296	0	105
1900	152	205	61	0	402	8	197	30	53	842	23	5,145	0	357
1910	610	1,836	40	159	385	20	262	68	222	144	65	8,116	0	662
1920	617	1,524	79	183	649	63	247	130	294	1,254	22	9,244	91	566
1940	163	3,283	55	204	938	171	249	149	363	1,301	14	6,234	149	354
1950	117	2,058	37	251	1,386	191	446	98	925	1,619	29	5,254	219	236
1960	31	3,622	35	168	1,284	53	403	72	674	1,660	5	2,762	109	63
1970	51	5,287	39	185	1,941	64	486	55	744	1,770	3	1,926	79	0
1980	0	5,636	49	0	1,969	0	0	0	621	2,109	0	2,603	0	0
1990	0	1,130	46	0	1,028	0	0	0	895	1,823	0	1,705	0	0

Year	Oilers and greasers, except auto	Painters, except construction or maintenance	Photographic process workers	Power station operators	Sailors and deckhands	Sawyers	Spinners – textile	Stationary firemen	Switchmen – railroad	Taxicab drivers and chauffeurs	Truck and tractor drivers	Weavers – textile	Welders and flame cutters	Operatives and kindred workers not elsewhere classified
	Operatives and kindred workers													
	Ba2225	Ba2226	Ba2227	Ba2228	Ba2229	Ba2230	Ba2231	Ba2232	Ba2233	Ba2234	Ba2235	Ba2236	Ba2237	Ba2238
	Hundred	Hundred	Hundred	Hundred	Hundred	Hundred	Hundred	Hundred	Hundred	Hundred	Hundred	Hundred	Hundred	Hundred
1850	0	22	0	0	615	94	46	17	1	10	297	159	1	1,854
1860	0	54	0	0	615	140	84	24	2	26	542	158	4	2,771
1870	0	111	0	0	561	91	44	35	16	36	982	130	4	6,010
1880	0	187	0	0	612	82	13	131	30	49	1,378	158	2	8,560
1900	15	243	0	0	357	235	296	471	175	364	4,121	751	8	10,336
1910	144	567	0	0	353	428	207	889	662	708	3,685	1,073	0	16,144
1920	268	621	22	43	343	398	292	1,168	629	1,298	2,404	990	276	17,711
1940	341	749	138	297	327	382	0	1,019	429	0	10,648	0	1,218	25,925
1950	558	1,151	166	220	394	736	179	1,121	647	1,709	11,818	622	2,553	34,971
1960	442	1,109	213	245	277	696	107	749	553	1,268	13,171	362	3,306	37,000
1970	390	974	294	177	215	728	0	786	484	1,132	11,630	196	4,541	40,103
1980	348	1,282	342	242	240	695	0	1,158	81	1,143	14,343	192	5,860	38,464
1990	195	1,144	379	320	185	638	0	727	43	1,190	21,596	151	4,991	35,295

[1] Data pertain to noninstitutionalized civilians age 16 and older who reported an occupation; employed persons only beginning 1940.

Source

See the source for Table Ba1159–1395.

Documentation

See the text for Table Ba1159–1395.

TABLE Ba2239–2282 Detailed occupations – white males: 1850–1990[1] [Part 2]

Contributed by Matthew Sobek

	Service workers, private household				Service workers, not household										
	Total	Housekeepers – private household	Laundresses – private household	Private household workers not elsewhere classified	Total	Attendants – hospital and other institution	Attendants – professional and personal service not elsewhere classified	Attendants – recreation and amusement	Barbers, beauticians, and manicurists	Bartenders	Bootblacks	Boarding and lodging house keepers	Charwomen and cleaners	Cooks, except private household	Counter and fountain workers
	Ba2239	Ba2240	Ba2241	Ba2242	Ba2243	Ba2244	Ba2245	Ba2246	Ba2247	Ba2248	Ba2249	Ba2250	Ba2251	Ba2252	Ba2253
Year	Hundred	Hundred	Hundred	Hundred	Hundred	Hundred	Hundred	Hundred	Hundred	Hundred	Hundred	Hundred	Hundred	Hundred	Hundred
1850	95	0	1	94	358	1	0	1	33	55	0	21	0	0	0
1860	328	0	5	323	584	0	0	2	44	100	0	46	0	0	0
1870	318	0	2	316	1,029	4	14	2	135	184	0	37	0	14	0
1880	757	4	3	750	1,613	10	13	6	295	238	8	71	2	32	0
1900	1,017	0	0	1,017	4,804	0	0	0	1,002	994	53	91	15	76	0
1910	1,552	159	30	1,363	7,081	0	128	0	1,564	1,071	139	174	76	0	0
1920	434	20	49	365	8,889	105	65	45	1,613	237	83	154	130	755	63
1940	552	27	30	495	16,957	557	137	442	1,949	1,109	54	80	289	1,328	0
1950	280	15	2	263	19,762	674	152	440	1,773	1,815	40	68	366	1,517	438
1960	242	12	0	230	20,200	703	171	328	1,897	1,464	24	26	399	1,393	350
1970	174	20	4	150	30,884	787	271	479	1,863	1,389	11	16	1,187	2,384	323
1980	158	13	2	143	41,077	1,070	725	806	1,377	1,500	0	0	962	5,270	305
1990	187	9	2	176	49,583	1,507	959	1,029	1,171	1,406	0	0	786	8,008	473

	Service workers, not household														
	Elevator operators	Firemen (fire protection)	Guards, watchmen, and doorkeepers	Housekeepers and stewards, except household	Janitors and sextons	Marshals and constables	Midwives	Policemen and detectives	Porters	Practical nurses	Sheriffs and bailiffs	Ushers – recreation and amusement	Waiters and waitresses	Watchmen (crossing) and bridge tenders	Service workers (not private household) not elsewhere classified
	Ba2254	Ba2255	Ba2256	Ba2257	Ba2258	Ba2259	Ba2260	Ba2261	Ba2262	Ba2263	Ba2264	Ba2265	Ba2266	Ba2267	Ba2268
Year	Hundred	Hundred	Hundred	Hundred	Hundred	Hundred	Hundred	Hundred	Hundred	Hundred	Hundred	Hundred	Hundred	Hundred	Hundred
1850	0	0	30	8	2	34	0	29	47	0	15	0	39	18	23
1860	0	2	68	17	6	43	0	36	108	2	21	2	54	14	18
1870	0	8	122	16	34	32	0	128	114	0	39	0	79	37	28
1880	0	18	219	28	56	56	0	148	116	3	68	0	78	40	110
1900	91	159	516	106	395	83	0	395	159	8	68	0	304	68	220
1910	141	310	753	0	652	93	3	678	290	113	106	0	660	0	131
1920	247	544	1,203	112	935	53	0	980	276	32	99	18	674	99	367
1940	555	743	2,087	176	2,439	100	0	1,462	452	53	146	154	1,433	159	1,054
1950	520	1,114	2,403	229	2,812	73	0	1,945	400	48	180	141	811	122	1,682
1960	382	1,289	2,260	207	3,674	72	3	2,428	320	80	242	78	774	146	1,491
1970	202	1,678	2,687	252	8,078	47	2	3,339	115	66	307	97	854	159	4,292
1980	120	1,930	4,514	102	12,210	0	0	4,220	109	113	482	132	1,357	150	3,624
1990	67	2,183	6,076	147	12,913	0	0	4,721	211	195	854	150	2,201	153	4,372

	Farm laborers					Laborers								
	Total	Farm foremen	Farm laborers, wage workers	Farm laborers, unpaid family workers	Farm service laborers, self-employed	Total	Fishermen and oystermen	Garage laborers, car washers, and greasers	Gardeners, except farm, and groundskeepers	Longshoremen and stevedores	Lumbermen, raftsmen, and woodchoppers	Teamsters	Laborers not elsewhere classified	Unknown occupation
	Ba2269	Ba2270	Ba2271	Ba2272	Ba2273	Ba2274	Ba2275	Ba2276	Ba2277	Ba2278	Ba2279	Ba2280	Ba2281	Ba2282
Year	Hundred	Hundred	Hundred	Hundred	Hundred	Hundred	Hundred	Hundred	Hundred	Hundred	Hundred	Hundred	Hundred	Hundred
1850	2,868	163	2,706	0	0	5,902	116	0	80	13	80	0	5,612	—
1860	8,985	143	8,829	12	0	7,739	237	0	173	14	135	0	7,179	—
1870	14,046	27	13,992	26	0	8,884	173	0	260	72	215	0	8,163	—
1880	16,642	37	16,605	0	0	14,037	269	0	339	87	448	0	12,894	—
1900	24,103	38	13,281	10,784	0	27,533	584	8	152	235	729	0	25,825	—
1910	31,756	474	31,283	0	0	30,814	574	0	869	524	1,111	0	27,736	—
1920	21,353	146	14,722	6,440	45	35,174	359	211	373	532	1,615	2,262	29,823	—
1940	20,788	218	13,494	7,076	0	34,253	537	310	1,340	409	1,063	208	30,388	2,086
1950	14,880	169	10,663	3,972	76	25,371	663	442	1,155	424	1,350	168	21,169	1,319
1960	8,451	232	7,129	1,040	50	21,525	322	472	1,322	325	803	131	18,150	15,734
1970	6,298	270	5,463	533	31	24,102	233	0	2,266	267	565	54	20,717	—
1980	5,940	373	5,567	0	0	30,018	420	0	2,689	150	744	0	26,016	—
1990	5,424	319	5,104	0	0	35,157	389	0	4,992	88	817	0	28,871	—

[1] Data pertain to noninstitutionalized civilians age 16 and older who reported an occupation; employed persons only beginning 1940.

Source

See the source for Table Ba1159–1395.

Documentation

See the text for Table Ba1159–1395.

TABLE Ba2283–2519 Detailed occupations – nonwhite males: 1850–1990[1] [Part 1]

Contributed by Matthew Sobek

		Professional, technical, and kindred workers												College professors and instructors	
	Total	Total	Accountants and auditors	Actors and actresses	Airplane pilots and navigators	Architects	Artists and art teachers	Athletes	Authors	Chemists	Chiropractors	Clergymen	College presidents and deans	Agricultural sciences	Biological sciences
	Ba2283	Ba2284	Ba2285	Ba2286	Ba2287	Ba2288	Ba2289	Ba2290	Ba2291	Ba2292	Ba2293	Ba2294	Ba2295	Ba2296	Ba2297
Year	Hundred	Hundred	Hundred	Hundred	Hundred	Hundred	Hundred	Hundred	Hundred	Hundred	Hundred	Hundred	Hundred	Hundred	Hundred
1850 [2]	943	7	0	0	0	0	0	0	0	0	0	2	0	0	0
1860 [2]	1,202	14	0	0	0	0	0	1	0	0	0	5	0	0	0
1870	12,545	56	0	0	0	0	0	0	0	0	0	26	0	0	0
1880	17,173	162	0	1	0	0	0	1	0	0	0	77	0	0	0
1900	24,611	304	0	0	0	0	0	8	0	0	0	129	0	0	0
1910	30,336	403	0	3	0	3	0	0	3	0	0	171	0	0	0
1920	32,426	418	0	14	0	0	4	0	0	0	0	187	0	0	0
1940	33,001	665	0	3	0	3	10	5	1	6	4	166	0	0	0
1950	37,325	823	9	2	1	2	10	4	0	8	1	171	4	9	0
1960	39,497	1,563	67	2	0	5	19	1	2	25	2	155	6	0	2
1970	45,133	3,599	160	4	3	26	32	0	5	65	2	137	15	2	7
1980	59,998	7,650	445	0	13	70	60	0	9	89	7	187	0	2	3
1990	74,897	12,006	730	0	29	104	79	0	25	144	16	269	0	(Z)	1

	Professional, technical, and kindred workers														
	College professors and instructors														
	Chemistry	Economics	Engineering	Geology and geophysics	Mathematics	Medical sciences	Physics	Psychology	Statistics	Natural sciences not elsewhere classified	Social sciences not elsewhere classified	Nonscientific subjects	Subject not specified	Dancers and dancing teachers	Dentists
	Ba2298	Ba2299	Ba2300	Ba2301	Ba2302	Ba2303	Ba2304	Ba2305	Ba2306	Ba2307	Ba2308	Ba2309	Ba2310	Ba2311	Ba2312
Year	Hundred	Hundred	Hundred	Hundred	Hundred	Hundred	Hundred	Hundred	Hundred	Hundred	Hundred	Hundred	Hundred	Hundred	Hundred
1850 [2]	0	0	0	0	0	0	0	0	0	0	0	0	0	0	0
1860 [2]	0	0	0	0	0	0	0	0	0	0	0	0	0	0	0
1870	0	0	0	0	0	0	0	0	0	0	0	1	0	0	0
1880	0	0	0	0	0	0	0	0	0	0	0	0	0	0	0
1900	0	0	0	0	0	0	0	0	0	0	0	0	0	0	8
1910	0	0	0	0	0	0	0	0	0	0	0	0	3	0	13
1920	0	0	0	0	0	0	0	0	0	0	0	0	4	0	8
1940	0	0	0	0	0	0	0	0	0	0	0	0	18	3	15
1950	1	0	(Z)	0	0	1	1	1	0	0	4	3	10	4	18
1960	2	1	5	0	1	3	3	0	0	0	6	9	20	2	24
1970	6	4	11	0	12	6	8	3	0	1	14	20	61	2	35
1980	7	2	7	0	13	7	5	2	0	1	6	15	235	3	59
1990	5	3	6	0	17	6	5	2	0	1	5	14	497	7	101

Year	Designers	Dietitians and nutritionists	Draftsmen	Editors and reporters	Engineers, aeronautical	Engineers, chemical	Engineers, civil	Engineers, electrical	Engineers, industrial	Engineers, mechanical	Engineers, metallurgical, metallurgists	Engineers, mining	Engineers not elsewhere classified	Entertainers not elsewhere classified	Farm and home management advisors
	Professional, technical, and kindred workers														
	Ba2313	Ba2314	Ba2315	Ba2316	Ba2317	Ba2318	Ba2319	Ba2320	Ba2321	Ba2322	Ba2323	Ba2324	Ba2325	Ba2326	Ba2327
	Hundred	Hundred	Hundred	Hundred	Hundred	Hundred	Hundred	Hundred	Hundred	Hundred	Hundred	Hundred	Hundred	Hundred	Hundred
1850 [2]	0	0	0	0	0	0	0	0	0	0	0	0	0	0	0
1860 [2]	0	0	0	0	0	0	0	0	0	0	0	0	0	0	0
1870	0	0	0	0	0	0	0	0	0	0	0	0	0	0	0
1880	0	0	1	1	0	0	0	0	0	1	0	1	0	0	0
1900	0	0	0	0	0	0	0	0	0	0	0	0	0	15	0
1910	0	0	0	0	0	0	0	0	0	3	0	0	0	20	0
1920	0	0	0	2	0	0	8	0	0	0	0	0	4	2	0
1940	1	0	5	12	0	0	4	1	3	3	1	0	0	7	4
1950	4	3	5	5	(Z)	1	10	3	0	2	0	0	4	11	2
1960	10	6	49	7	12	2	32	29	9	14	0	1	21	7	8
1970	28	9	122	42	20	12	74	100	26	48	3	3	58	32	5
1980	105	22	223	95	56	42	175	246	132	135	14	12	210	42	0
1990	224	32	238	136	134	55	247	469	224	160	12	15	338	72	0

Year	Foresters and conservationists	Funeral directors and embalmers	Lawyers and judges	Librarians	Musicians and music teachers	Nurses, professional	Nurses, student professional	Natural scientists not elsewhere classified: Agricultural scientists	Biological scientists	Geologists and geophysicists	Mathematicians	Physicists	Miscellaneous natural scientists	Optometrists	Osteopaths
	Professional, technical, and kindred workers														
	Ba2328	Ba2329	Ba2330	Ba2331	Ba2332	Ba2333	Ba2334	Ba2335	Ba2336	Ba2337	Ba2338	Ba2339	Ba2340	Ba2341	Ba2342
	Hundred	Hundred	Hundred	Hundred	Hundred	Hundred	Hundred	Hundred	Hundred	Hundred	Hundred	Hundred	Hundred	Hundred	Hundred
1850 [2]	0	0	0	0	0	0	0	0	0	0	0	0	0	0	0
1860 [2]	0	0	0	0	4	0	0	0	0	0	0	0	0	0	0
1870	0	0	0	0	1	0	0	0	0	0	0	0	0	0	0
1880	0	1	4	1	10	0	0	0	0	0	0	0	0	0	0
1900	0	0	15	0	15	0	0	0	0	0	0	0	0	0	0
1910	0	8	10	0	48	3	0	0	0	0	0	0	0	0	0
1920	0	14	6	0	30	2	0	0	0	0	0	0	0	0	0
1940	0	28	12	1	64	1	0	0	0	0	0	0	0	0	1
1950	1	31	19	0	52	7	0	5	1	0	0	2	1	4	4
1960	10	27	30	4	53	20	0	5	10	0	1	0	0	3	0
1970	10	32	45	16	80	58	2	6	19	4	4	8	1	3	0
1980	25	34	140	38	207	145	0	15	38	13	4	23	4	8	0
1990	28	38	229	60	365	269	0	19	68	13	5	25	9	11	0

Notes appear at end of table

(continued)

TABLE Ba2283–2519 Detailed occupations – nonwhite males: 1850–1990 [Part 1] *Continued*

	Professional, technical, and kindred workers														
									Social scientists						
	Personnel and labor-relations workers	Pharmacists	Photographers	Physicians and surgeons	Radio operators	Recreation and group workers	Religious workers	Social and welfare workers, except group	Economists	Psychologists	Statisticians and actuaries	Miscellaneous social scientists	Sports instructors and officials	Surveyors	Teachers not elsewhere classified
	Ba2343	Ba2344	Ba2345	Ba2346	Ba2347	Ba2348	Ba2349	Ba2350	Ba2351	Ba2352	Ba2353	Ba2354	Ba2355	Ba2356	Ba2357
Year	Hundred	Hundred	Hundred	Hundred	Hundred	Hundred	Hundred	Hundred	Hundred	Hundred	Hundred	Hundred	Hundred	Hundred	Hundred
1850 [2]	0	0	0	0	0	0	0	0	0	0	0	0	0	0	2
1860 [2]	0	0	0	3	0	0	0	0	0	0	0	0	0	0	0
1870	0	1	1	4	0	0	0	0	0	0	0	0	1	0	19
1880	0	0	0	6	0	0	1	0	0	0	0	0	0	0	51
1900	0	0	8	15	0	0	0	0	0	0	0	0	0	0	91
1910	0	0	3	28	0	0	0	0	0	0	0	0	0	0	76
1920	0	10	4	32	0	6	6	0	0	0	0	0	0	0	61
1940	0	19	7	48	1	0	6	8	0	0	0	0	5	4	151
1950	2	16	12	42	0	8	5	23	0	0	5	1	13	0	197
1960	13	25	13	81	5	14	11	45	1	1	6	3	23	9	363
1970	95	33	28	157	17	41	6	121	18	8	7	6	31	17	616
1980	332	74	56	431	54	27	13	302	40	30	19	13	43	34	1,024
1990	403	107	81	573	64	28	41	429	60	59	26	21	74	50	1,188

	Professional, technical, and kindred workers						Farmers			Managers, officials, and proprietors					
	Technicians – medical and dental	Technicians – testing	Technicians not elsewhere classified	Therapists and healers not elsewhere classified	Veterinarians	Professional, technical, and kindred workers not elsewhere classified	Total	Farmers – owners and tenants	Farm managers	Total	Buyers and department heads – store	Buyers and shippers – farm products	Conductors – railroad	Credit men	Floormen and floor managers – store
	Ba2358	Ba2359	Ba2360	Ba2361	Ba2362	Ba2363	Ba2364	Ba2365	Ba2366	Ba2367	Ba2368	Ba2369	Ba2370	Ba2371	Ba2372
Year	Hundred	Hundred	Hundred	Hundred	Hundred	Hundred	Hundred	Hundred	Hundred	Hundred	Hundred	Hundred	Hundred	Hundred	Hundred
1850 [2]	0	0	0	0	0	3	114	114	0	11	0	0	0	0	0
1860 [2]	0	0	0	1	0	0	108	107	1	9	0	0	0	0	0
1870	0	0	0	0	0	2	1,959	1,958	1	45	0	0	0	0	0
1880	0	0	0	1	1	3	4,165	4,165	0	104	0	2	0	0	0
1900	0	0	0	0	0	0	7,012	7,012	0	273	0	8	0	0	0
1910	0	0	0	0	0	13	8,355	8,355	0	458	0	0	0	0	0
1920	4	2	0	4	0	2	9,303	9,268	34	428	0	2	0	0	0
1940	0	5	1	8	4	17	6,678	6,668	10	528	2	0	0	1	2
1950	14	23	(Z)	4	2	14	4,945	4,942	4	943	9	1	1	1	0
1960	42	61	27	13	3	76	1,713	1,702	11	868	14	1	2	3	0
1970	114	142	74	32	3	525	440	416	25	1,474	94	3	11	6	0
1980	288	544	220	74	9	572	317	223	94	4,028	197	6	25	0	0
1990	475	933	396	118	18	1,303	225	130	95	6,916	252	8	27	0	0

	Managers, officials, and proprietors								Clerical and kindred workers					
	Inspectors – public administration	Managers and superintendents – building	Officers, pilots, pursers, and engineers – ship	Officials and administrators not elsewhere classified – public administration	Officials – lodge, society, union, and so forth	Postmasters	Purchasing agents and buyers not elsewhere classified	Managers, officials, and proprietors not elsewhere classified	Total	Agents not elsewhere classified	Attendants and assistants – library	Attendants – physician's and dentist's office	Baggagemen – transportation	Bank tellers
	Ba2373	Ba2374	Ba2375	Ba2376	Ba2377	Ba2378	Ba2379	Ba2380	Ba2381	Ba2382	Ba2383	Ba2384	Ba2385	Ba2386
Year	Hundred	Hundred	Hundred	Hundred	Hundred	Hundred	Hundred	Hundred	Hundred	Hundred	Hundred	Hundred	Hundred	Hundred
1850 [2]	0	0	0	0	0	0	0	11	1	1	0	0	0	0
1860 [2]	0	0	0	0	0	0	0	9	2	0	0	0	1	0
1870	0	0	2	0	0	0	0	43	19	1	0	0	1	0
1880	1	0	2	5	1	0	0	93	28	3	0	0	0	0
1900	0	0	15	0	0	0	0	250	61	0	0	0	0	0
1910	0	0	3	3	3	0	0	451	189	3	0	0	5	0
1920	4	8	0	2	2	0	4	406	278	0	0	2	4	0
1940	3	32	1	2	4	1	1	479	423	7	2	4	1	0
1950	10	50	11	7	5	2	7	840	1,189	4	5	6	11	0
1960	17	41	6	34	9	2	4	735	2,051	16	4	1	9	6
1970	52	38	6	101	25	5	27	1,108	3,611	3	27	43	0	29
1980	112	96	19	232	0	7	88	3,246	5,891	0	46	121	0	72
1990	140	175	16	454	0	22	142	5,680	8,433	0	65	146	0	93

	Clerical and kindred workers														
	Bookkeepers	Cashiers	Collectors, bill and account	Dispatchers and starters – vehicle	Express messengers and railway mail clerks	Mail carriers	Messengers and office boys	Office machine operators	Shipping and receiving clerks	Stenographers, typists, and secretaries	Telegraph messengers	Telegraph operators	Telephone operators	Ticket, station, and express agents	Clerical and kindred workers not elsewhere classified
	Ba2387	Ba2388	Ba2389	Ba2390	Ba2391	Ba2392	Ba2393	Ba2394	Ba2395	Ba2396	Ba2397	Ba2398	Ba2399	Ba2400	Ba2401
Year	Hundred	Hundred	Hundred	Hundred	Hundred	Hundred	Hundred	Hundred	Hundred	Hundred	Hundred	Hundred	Hundred	Hundred	Hundred
1850 [2]	0	0	0	0	0	0	0	0	0	0	0	0	0	0	0
1860 [2]	0	0	0	0	0	0	0	0	0	0	0	0	0	0	1
1870	0	0	0	0	1	1	4	0	0	0	1	0	0	0	10
1880	2	0	0	0	0	5	8	0	1	0	0	0	0	0	9
1900	0	8	0	0	0	15	30	0	0	0	0	0	0	0	8
1910	18	0	10	0	0	35	53	0	8	0	3	0	0	0	55
1920	6	0	6	0	6	37	51	0	20	6	0	0	2	2	136
1940	30	0	7	0	6	66	58	2	45	5	2	4	2	0	182
1950	12	11	8	8	9	136	76	17	195	28	6	1	8	2	645
1960	32	49	11	11	9	202	76	37	273	45	6	1	10	14	1,240
1970	131	116	16	21	0	274	65	145	492	113	5	3	18	41	2,069
1980	203	395	37	43	0	298	126	399	750	116	0	5	70	58	3,151
1990	292	959	78	97	0	397	207	740	909	186	0	0	60	124	4,079

Notes appear at end of table

(continued)

TABLE Ba2283–2519 Detailed occupations – nonwhite males: 1850–1990 [Part 1] *Continued*

	Sales workers										Craft workers, foremen, and kindred workers				
	Total	Advertising agents and salesmen	Auctioneers	Demonstrators	Hucksters and peddlers	Insurance agents and brokers	Newsboys	Real estate agents and brokers	Stock and bond salesmen	Salesmen and sales clerks not elsewhere classified	Total	Bakers	Blacksmiths	Bookbinders	Boilermakers
	Ba2402	Ba2403	Ba2404	Ba2405	Ba2406	Ba2407	Ba2408	Ba2409	Ba2410	Ba2411	Ba2412	Ba2413	Ba2414	Ba2415	Ba2416
Year	Hundred	Hundred	Hundred	Hundred	Hundred	Hundred	Hundred	Hundred	Hundred	Hundred	Hundred	Hundred	Hundred	Hundred	Hundred
1850 [2]	0	0	0	0	0	0	0	0	0	0	77	1	16	0	0
1860 [2]	4	0	0	0	2	0	0	0	0	2	76	0	15	0	0
1870	24	0	0	0	9	0	2	1	0	12	431	5	111	0	0
1880	60	0	0	0	36	0	1	0	0	23	480	5	115	0	1
1900	68	0	0	0	23	0	0	0	0	46	873	8	114	0	0
1910	111	0	0	0	0	8	3	10	0	91	1,116	23	96	0	10
1920	138	2	0	0	20	18	2	8	0	87	1,546	30	95	0	16
1940	311	2	1	1	37	43	15	19	1	193	1,464	30	39	0	5
1950	463	1	2	5	12	61	20	48	6	308	2,956	65	26	5	5
1960	601	4	0	0	19	81	57	35	5	401	3,980	80	6	13	3
1970	1,035	11	(Z)	1	10	136	21	42	17	797	6,838	96	13	14	14
1980	1,778	24	1	2	29	280	44	137	36	1,225	9,025	104	0	14	27
1990	2,861	53	2	7	69	392	63	250	112	1,914	10,068	146	0	15	22

	Craft workers, foremen, and kindred workers														
	Brickmasons, stonemasons, and tile setters	Cabinetmakers	Carpenters	Cement and concrete finishers	Compositors and typesetters	Cranemen, derrickmen, and hoistmen	Decorators and window dressers	Electricians	Electrotypers and stereotypers	Engravers, except photoengravers	Excavating, grading, and road machinery operators	Foremen not elsewhere classified	Forgemen and hammermen	Furriers	Glaziers
	Ba2417	Ba2418	Ba2419	Ba2420	Ba2421	Ba2422	Ba2423	Ba2424	Ba2425	Ba2426	Ba2427	Ba2428	Ba2429	Ba2430	Ba2431
Year	Hundred	Hundred	Hundred	Hundred	Hundred	Hundred	Hundred	Hundred	Hundred	Hundred	Hundred	Hundred	Hundred	Hundred	Hundred
1850 [2]	5	1	20	0	0	0	0	0	0	0	0	0	0	0	0
1860 [2]	10	0	18	0	0	0	0	0	0	0	0	0	0	0	0
1870	51	4	134	0	2	0	0	0	0	0	1	5	0	0	0
1880	50	5	146	0	3	0	0	0	0	0	0	1	0	0	0
1900	83	8	266	0	8	0	0	0	0	0	0	23	0	0	0
1910	144	5	237	0	13	0	0	3	0	0	0	58	3	0	0
1920	93	10	310	12	8	4	0	16	0	0	2	79	4	0	0
1940	91	18	246	47	12	22	4	16	0	0	0	71	0	3	3
1950	189	18	356	85	24	67	9	37	4	(Z)	40	105	7	1	8
1960	225	13	426	110	32	128	14	58	0	3	78	194	4	1	4
1970	297	33	531	202	77	196	17	161	2	2	256	607	12	1	13
1980	292	39	748	147	17	200	0	364	0	6	291	1,353	14	3	18
1990	299	38	798	133	15	123	0	484	0	6	325	1,279	19	7	24

	Craft workers, foremen, and kindred workers														
	Heat treaters, annealers, temperers	Inspectors, scalers, and graders – log and lumber	Inspectors not elsewhere classified	Jewelers, watchmakers, goldsmiths, silversmiths	Job setters – metal	Linemen and servicemen	Locomotive engineers	Locomotive firemen	Loom fixers	Machinists	Mechanics and repairmen – airplane	Mechanics and repairmen – automobile	Mechanics and repairmen – office machine	Mechanics and repairmen – radio and television	Mechanics and repairmen – railroad and car shop
	Ba2432	Ba2433	Ba2434	Ba2435	Ba2436	Ba2437	Ba2438	Ba2439	Ba2440	Ba2441	Ba2442	Ba2443	Ba2444	Ba2445	Ba2446
Year	Hundred	Hundred	Hundred	Hundred	Hundred	Hundred	Hundred	Hundred	Hundred	Hundred	Hundred	Hundred	Hundred	Hundred	Hundred
1850 [2]	0	0	0	0	0	0	0	0	0	0	0	0	0	0	0
1860 [2]	0	0	0	0	0	0	0	0	0	0	0	0	0	0	0
1870	0	0	0	0	0	0	0	1	0	1	0	0	0	0	1
1880	0	0	0	1	0	0	0	4	0	3	0	0	0	0	0
1900	0	0	0	8	0	0	0	15	0	0	0	0	0	0	8
1910	0	0	18	3	0	8	5	60	0	33	0	0	0	0	0
1920	2	4	6	4	0	10	8	75	0	93	0	59	0	0	2
1940	4	12	5	6	0	18	7	19	0	46	3	189	0	0	10
1950	10	23	9	8	3	26	9	26	1	81	12	413	4	28	28
1960	7	18	18	10	7	35	0	8	0	147	52	460	6	52	15
1970	19	20	54	14	47	171	8	5	5	189	84	766	25	84	43
1980	30	0	36	42	34	285	70	0	0	417	97	1,068	57	116	0
1990	19	0	59	75	21	303	48	0	0	467	178	1,264	126	171	0

	Craft workers, foremen, and kindred workers														
	Mechanics and repairmen not elsewhere classified	Millers – grain, flour, feed, and so forth	Millwrights	Molders – metal	Motion picture projectionists	Opticians and lens grinders and polishers	Painters – construction and maintenance	Paperhangers	Pattern and model makers, except paper	Photoengravers and lithographers	Piano and organ tuners and repairmen	Plasterers	Plumbers and pipe fitters	Pressmen and plate printers – printing	Rollers and roll hands – metal
	Ba2447	Ba2448	Ba2449	Ba2450	Ba2451	Ba2452	Ba2453	Ba2454	Ba2455	Ba2456	Ba2457	Ba2458	Ba2459	Ba2460	Ba2461
Year	Hundred	Hundred	Hundred	Hundred	Hundred	Hundred	Hundred	Hundred	Hundred	Hundred	Hundred	Hundred	Hundred	Hundred	Hundred
1850 [2]	2	1	0	0	0	0	2	0	0	0	0	2	0	0	0
1860 [2]	1	3	1	0	0	0	4	0	0	0	0	4	0	0	0
1870	4	9	1	0	0	1	12	1	0	0	0	8	0	0	2
1880	7	4	1	1	0	0	18	1	0	0	0	20	0	0	1
1900	15	8	0	23	0	0	61	8	0	0	0	68	0	8	0
1910	5	8	0	18	0	0	93	3	0	0	0	50	33	3	3
1920	57	2	2	71	0	0	99	8	0	0	0	47	43	2	4
1940	69	8	2	46	6	2	127	16	0	4	3	51	44	1	13
1950	315	4	8	106	6	4	206	19	17	7	5	94	73	12	40
1960	703	6	17	111	3	1	289	10	2	2	1	81	114	21	34
1970	552	7	22	102	6	10	333	0	7	6	3	52	193	80	24
1980	1,162	0	65	49	9	16	443	0	13	9	0	43	362	227	22
1990	1,328	0	52	12	6	31	556	0	11	20	0	52	399	297	10

Notes appear at end of table

(continued)

TABLE Ba2283–2519 Detailed occupations – nonwhite males: 1850–1990 [Part 1] *Continued*

	Craft workers, foremen, and kindred workers										Operatives and kindred workers				
	Roofers and slaters	Shoemakers and repairers, except factory	Stationary engineers	Stonecutters and stone carvers	Structural metal workers	Tailors and tailoresses	Tinsmiths, coppersmiths, sheet metal workers	Toolmakers, die makers, and setters	Upholsterers	Craftsmen and kindred workers not elsewhere classified	Total	Apprentice auto mechanics	Apprentice bricklayers and masons	Apprentice carpenters	Apprentice electricians
	Ba2462	Ba2463	Ba2464	Ba2465	Ba2466	Ba2467	Ba2468	Ba2469	Ba2470	Ba2471	Ba2472	Ba2473	Ba2474	Ba2475	Ba2476
Year	Hundred	Hundred	Hundred	Hundred	Hundred	Hundred	Hundred	Hundred	Hundred	Hundred	Hundred	Hundred	Hundred	Hundred	Hundred
1850 [2]	0	12	1	0	0	2	2	0	0	9	106	0	0	0	0
1860 [2]	0	9	1	0	0	5	1	0	0	4	226	0	0	0	0
1870	4	35	3	2	0	7	1	0	0	25	809	0	1	1	0
1880	1	40	9	0	0	18	5	1	0	20	1,156	0	0	0	0
1900	15	38	30	8	0	30	15	0	0	8	1,768	0	0	0	0
1910	5	28	53	3	0	48	8	3	5	35	2,856	0	0	0	0
1920	4	55	24	4	63	65	10	2	0	39	2,994	0	0	0	0
1940	13	44	25	6	13	31	9	2	2	0	3,937	0	0	1	12
1950	29	72	47	5	10	59	22	6	16	40	7,913	2	6	3	2
1960	54	39	48	1	33	28	42	17	29	71	9,262	0	1	3	2
1970	70	68	91	4	40	45	55	35	49	907	12,757	1	5	5	9
1980	136	79	161	0	82	51	87	68	52	0	14,326	4	2	7	12
1990	174	106	213	0	66	56	109	51	53	0	14,158	2	1	3	11

	Operatives and kindred workers														
	Apprentice machinists and toolmakers	Apprentice mechanics, except auto	Apprentice plumbers and pipe fitters	Apprentices – building trades not elsewhere classified	Apprentices – metalworking trades not elsewhere classified	Apprentices – printing trades	Apprentices – other specified trades	Apprentices – trade not specified	Asbestos and insulation workers	Attendants – auto service and parking	Blasters and powdermen	Boatmen, canalmen, and lock keepers	Brakemen – railroad	Bus drivers	Chainmen, rodmen, and axmen – surveying
	Ba2477	Ba2478	Ba2479	Ba2480	Ba2481	Ba2482	Ba2483	Ba2484	Ba2485	Ba2486	Ba2487	Ba2488	Ba2489	Ba2490	Ba2491
Year	Hundred	Hundred	Hundred	Hundred	Hundred	Hundred	Hundred	Hundred	Hundred	Hundred	Hundred	Hundred	Hundred	Hundred	Hundred
1850 [2]	0	0	0	0	0	0	0	0	0	0	0	8	0	0	0
1860 [2]	0	0	0	0	2	0	0	1	0	0	0	4	2	0	0
1870	0	0	0	1	3	0	0	1	0	0	0	17	2	1	0
1880	0	0	0	0	0	2	7	0	0	0	0	15	3	2	0
1900	0	0	0	0	0	0	0	0	0	0	0	0	15	0	0
1910	0	0	0	0	0	0	0	5	0	0	0	3	43	0	0
1920	0	0	0	0	2	2	0	0	0	2	0	0	43	4	0
1940	4	0	2	6	0	5	4	4	4	163	4	7	23	0	5
1950	2	3	7	1	1	7	1	1	6	269	7	9	23	50	3
1960	4	2	0	4	3	3	2	1	5	326	5	2	18	187	7
1970	8	4	6	2	3	6	8	3	11	410	6	3	22	305	6
1980	9	0	7	0	1	0	3	0	39	365	10	0	76	535	6
1990	1	0	4	0	1	0	2	0	65	373	9	0	32	657	2

Year	Conductors – bus and street railway	Deliverymen and routemen	Dressmakers and seamstresses, except factory	Dyers	Filers, grinders, and polishers – metal	Fruit, nut, vegetable graders, packers, not factory	Furnacemen, smeltermen, and pourers	Heaters – metal	Laundry and dry cleaning operatives	Meat cutters, except slaughter and packing houses	Milliners	Mine operatives and laborers	Motormen, mine, factory, logging camp, and so forth	Motormen, street, subway, and elevated railway
	Operatives and kindred workers													
	Ba2492	Ba2493	Ba2494	Ba2495	Ba2496	Ba2497	Ba2498	Ba2499	Ba2500	Ba2501	Ba2502	Ba2503	Ba2504	Ba2505
	Hundred	Hundred	Hundred	Hundred	Hundred	Hundred	Hundred	Hundred	Hundred	Hundred	Hundred	Hundred	Hundred	Hundred
1850 [2]	0	0	0	0	1	0	0	0	0	0	0	7	0	0
1860 [2]	0	0	1	0	0	0	0	0	0	1	0	134	0	0
1870	0	1	1	0	0	0	6	0	60	9	0	257	0	1
1880	0	2	0	3	0	0	6	0	96	12	0	267	0	1
1900	0	38	0	0	0	8	15	0	23	23	0	425	0	8
1910	0	275	0	3	5	5	30	3	161	8	0	741	0	0
1920	2	235	0	2	8	4	16	4	197	24	2	663	2	0
1940	0	402	11	10	30	21	31	10	137	37	0	522	8	1
1950	11	226	9	15	101	30	116	5	433	66	5	379	23	9
1960	11	313	8	10	103	5	125	8	422	93	0	115	19	11
1970	39	612	9	37	222	10	146	10	331	136	(Z)	127	14	0
1980	0	696	14	0	290	0	0	0	224	256	0	198	0	0
1990	0	86	13	0	130	0	0	0	310	252	0	144	0	0

Year	Oilers and greasers, except auto	Painters, except construction or maintenance	Photographic process workers	Power station operators	Sailors and deckhands	Sawyers	Spinners – textile	Stationary firemen	Switchmen – railroad	Taxicab drivers and chauffeurs	Truck and tractor drivers	Weavers – textile	Welders and flame cutters	Operatives and kindred workers not elsewhere classified
	Operatives and kindred workers													
	Ba2506	Ba2507	Ba2508	Ba2509	Ba2510	Ba2511	Ba2512	Ba2513	Ba2514	Ba2515	Ba2516	Ba2517	Ba2518	Ba2519
	Hundred	Hundred	Hundred	Hundred	Hundred	Hundred	Hundred	Hundred	Hundred	Hundred	Hundred	Hundred	Hundred	Hundred
1850 [2]	0	0	0	0	40	3	0	0	0	2	18	0	0	26
1860 [2]	0	0	0	0	14	3	0	6	0	2	14	0	0	41
1870	0	1	0	0	42	8	0	3	0	11	112	0	0	270
1880	0	1	0	0	93	9	0	14	0	15	158	0	0	451
1900	8	0	0	0	68	46	0	61	0	152	342	0	0	539
1910	10	5	0	0	126	28	0	144	18	93	544	5	0	605
1920	16	6	0	0	71	24	6	199	18	349	304	0	0	787
1940	16	27	3	26	33	49	0	116	7	0	1,020	0	15	1,164
1950	39	100	9	5	63	214	2	186	14	310	1,574	2	108	3,460
1960	53	156	15	6	51	162	1	110	18	284	2,248	5	189	4,147
1970	48	174	29	4	34	166	0	106	37	319	1,869	25	488	6,947
1980	53	198	51	22	35	130	0	215	9	411	2,345	51	801	7,251
1990	29	153	70	30	28	99	0	120	6	526	3,498	46	606	6,850

(Z) Fewer than 50.

[1] Data pertain to noninstitutionalized civilians age 16 and older who reported an occupation; employed persons only beginning 1940.

[2] Excludes slaves.

Source

See the source for Table Ba1159–1395.

Documentation

See the text for Table Ba1159–1395.

TABLE Ba2520–2563 Detailed occupations – nonwhite males: 1850–1990[1] [Part 2]

Contributed by Matthew Sobek

	Service workers, private household				Service workers, not household										
	Total	Housekeepers – private household	Laundresses – private household	Private household workers not elsewhere classified	Total	Attendants – hospital and other institution	Attendants – professional and personal service not elsewhere classified	Attendants – recreation and amusement	Barbers, beauticians, and manicurists	Bartenders	Bootblacks	Boarding and lodging house keepers	Charwomen and cleaners	Cooks, except private household	Counter and fountain workers
	Ba2520	Ba2521	Ba2522	Ba2523	Ba2524	Ba2525	Ba2526	Ba2527	Ba2528	Ba2529	Ba2530	Ba2531	Ba2532	Ba2533	Ba2534
Year	Hundred	Hundred	Hundred	Hundred	Hundred	Hundred	Hundred	Hundred	Hundred	Hundred	Hundred	Hundred	Hundred	Hundred	Hundred
1850 [2]	35	0	0	35	89	0	0	0	42	0	0	0	0	0	0
1860 [2]	91	0	2	89	111	0	0	0	41	1	3	0	2	2	0
1870	379	0	34	345	268	0	3	0	71	3	3	1	1	13	0
1880	736	1	34	701	492	1	1	1	128	10	4	5	3	24	0
1900	782	0	61	721	1,222	0	8	0	152	30	23	8	0	30	0
1910	1,028	15	50	962	1,715	0	13	0	174	28	25	18	18	0	0
1920	426	0	47	379	2,501	6	8	8	231	6	28	14	4	337	0
1940	921	18	29	874	3,727	64	11	57	147	27	79	6	46	411	0
1950	334	5	1	328	4,980	165	27	66	180	100	82	0	104	573	23
1960	298	5	6	287	5,514	304	34	60	181	83	56	1	120	579	44
1970	188	17	2	169	6,889	307	64	39	186	88	22	1	643	656	23
1980	103	9	1	93	9,524	509	233	111	165	121	0	0	511	1,369	51
1990	67	5	(Z)	62	12,833	680	261	169	204	110	0	0	462	2,580	99

	Service workers, not household														
	Elevator operators	Firemen (fire protection)	Guards, watchmen, and doorkeepers	Housekeepers and stewards, except household	Janitors and sextons	Marshals and constables	Midwives	Policemen and detectives	Porters	Practical nurses	Sheriffs and bailiffs	Ushers – recreation and amusement	Waiters and waitresses	Watchmen (crossing) and bridge tenders	Service workers (not private household) not elsewhere classified
	Ba2535	Ba2536	Ba2537	Ba2538	Ba2539	Ba2540	Ba2541	Ba2542	Ba2543	Ba2544	Ba2545	Ba2546	Ba2547	Ba2548	Ba2549
Year	Hundred	Hundred	Hundred	Hundred	Hundred	Hundred	Hundred	Hundred	Hundred	Hundred	Hundred	Hundred	Hundred	Hundred	Hundred
1850 [2]	0	0	0	4	0	0	0	0	13	1	0	0	28	0	0
1860 [2]	0	0	0	10	1	0	0	0	24	0	0	0	27	0	0
1870	0	0	3	4	14	4	0	7	59	0	0	0	73	0	8
1880	0	0	4	8	18	1	0	1	91	1	1	0	173	0	18
1900	23	0	15	0	83	0	0	8	440	8	0	0	250	0	144
1910	48	8	45	0	272	5	0	5	562	3	3	0	476	0	15
1920	69	16	32	22	333	2	0	14	797	6	0	4	392	0	170
1940	104	5	105	20	818	0	0	14	1,103	9	0	1	349	8	345
1950	119	13	95	23	1,202	2	1	41	1,211	5	3	4	359	4	578
1960	124	28	146	48	1,546	0	2	102	1,063	18	7	4	308	8	649
1970	64	53	326	50	2,450	3	1	242	69	21	16	5	258	10	1,292
1980	38	148	1,044	37	3,458	0	0	415	73	32	50	14	302	20	824
1990	20	241	1,787	57	3,600	0	0	614	105	70	119	29	461	29	1,137

	Farm laborers					Laborers								
	Total	Farm foremen	Farm laborers, wage workers	Farm laborers, unpaid family workers	Farm service laborers, self-employed	Total	Fishermen and oystermen	Garage laborers, car washers, and greasers	Gardeners, except farm, and groundskeepers	Longshoremen and stevedores	Lumbermen, raftsmen, and woodchoppers	Teamsters	Laborers not elsewhere classified	Unknown occupation
	Ba2550	Ba2551	Ba2552	Ba2553	Ba2554	Ba2555	Ba2556	Ba2557	Ba2558	Ba2559	Ba2560	Ba2561	Ba2562	Ba2563
Year	Hundred	Hundred	Hundred	Hundred	Hundred	Hundred	Hundred	Hundred	Hundred	Hundred	Hundred	Hundred	Hundred	Hundred
1850 [2]	98	0	98	0	0	404	10	0	5	0	0	0	389	—
1860 [2]	232	0	232	0	0	329	8	0	1	2	2	0	316	—
1870	6,457	5	6,451	1	0	2,096	32	0	63	6	42	0	1,952	—
1880	5,345	1	5,344	0	0	4,446	60	0	65	17	49	0	4,255	—
1900	6,079	0	4,318	1,761	0	6,170	83	0	15	83	182	0	5,806	—
1910	7,416	28	7,388	0	0	6,688	93	0	68	171	302	0	6,053	—
1920	5,441	12	4,061	1,367	0	8,954	85	53	47	325	264	438	7,743	—
1940	5,819	18	4,234	1,567	0	8,324	52	175	264	192	263	39	7,340	203
1950	3,758	11	2,769	973	5	8,802	84	375	292	219	475	66	7,292	218
1960	2,770	15	2,563	188	4	7,604	40	340	401	175	357	62	6,229	3,273
1970	1,610	32	1,546	28	4	6,692	26	0	617	167	208	14	5,661	—
1980	929	41	888	0	0	6,426	41	0	569	89	166	0	5,561	—
1990	577	24	554	0	0	6,753	57	0	835	47	141	0	5,672	—

(Z) Fewer than 50.

[1] Data pertain to noninstitutionalized civilians age 16 and older who reported an occupation; employed persons only beginning 1940.

[2] Excludes slaves.

Source

See the source for Table Ba1159–1395.

Documentation

See the text for Table Ba1159–1395.

TABLE Ba2564–2800 Detailed occupations – white females: 1860–1990[1] [Part 1]

Contributed by Matthew Sobek

		Professional, technical, and kindred workers												College professors and instructors	
	Total	Total	Accountants and auditors	Actors and actresses	Airplane pilots and navigators	Architects	Artists and art teachers	Athletes	Authors	Chemists	Chiropractors	Clergymen	College presidents and deans	Agricultural sciences	Biological sciences
	Ba2564	Ba2565	Ba2566	Ba2567	Ba2568	Ba2569	Ba2570	Ba2571	Ba2572	Ba2573	Ba2574	Ba2575	Ba2576	Ba2577	Ba2578
Year	Hundred	Hundred	Hundred	Hundred	Hundred	Hundred	Hundred	Hundred	Hundred	Hundred	Hundred	Hundred	Hundred	Hundred	Hundred
1860	9,785	704	0	2	0	0	6	0	2	0	0	2	2	0	0
1870	12,195	955	0	2	0	0	4	0	4	0	0	3	0	0	0
1880	17,159	1,849	0	19	0	0	33	2	1	0	0	9	0	0	0
1900	40,290	3,992	15	68	0	0	76	0	23	0	0	8	30	0	0
1910 [2]	57,318	7,320	0	134	0	0	154	0	8	3	0	20	0	0	0
1920	67,247	9,680	148	89	0	0	144	0	37	14	6	22	4	0	0
1940	100,739	13,910	0	57	3	3	171	5	36	18	18	36	0	0	0
1950	139,286	18,909	549	64	0	4	280	2	52	74	18	71	14	1	14
1960	183,628	25,519	744	27	3	6	333	2	79	55	12	48	12	1	14
1970	253,261	43,321	1,705	39	7	19	355	0	75	111	11	54	88	2	42
1980	358,498	68,197	3,296	0	10	81	665	0	193	160	22	149	0	4	29
1990	450,299	105,621	6,959	0	35	211	1,017	0	481	291	127	304	0	2	20

	Professional, technical, and kindred workers														
	College professors and instructors														
	Chemistry	Economics	Engineering	Geology and geophysics	Mathematics	Medical sciences	Physics	Psychology	Statistics	Natural sciences not elsewhere classified	Social sciences not elsewhere classified	Nonscientific subjects	Subject not specified	Dancers and dancing teachers	Dentists
	Ba2579	Ba2580	Ba2581	Ba2582	Ba2583	Ba2584	Ba2585	Ba2586	Ba2587	Ba2588	Ba2589	Ba2590	Ba2591	Ba2592	Ba2593
Year	Hundred	Hundred	Hundred	Hundred	Hundred	Hundred	Hundred	Hundred	Hundred	Hundred	Hundred	Hundred	Hundred	Hundred	Hundred
1860	0	0	0	0	0	0	0	0	0	0	0	0	0	2	0
1870	0	0	0	0	0	0	0	0	0	0	0	0	0	0	0
1880	0	0	0	0	0	0	0	0	0	0	0	0	0	0	0
1900	0	0	0	0	0	0	0	0	0	0	0	0	0	8	0
1910 [2]	0	0	0	0	0	0	0	0	0	0	0	0	38	0	8
1920	0	0	0	0	0	0	0	0	0	0	2	0	49	32	4
1940	0	0	0	0	0	0	0	0	0	0	0	0	194	93	14
1950	10	5	0	0	8	2	11	15	0	0	57	85	82	99	15
1960	11	2	2	1	11	15	1	9	0	1	77	91	88	143	20
1970	17	7	10	0	48	138	7	33	0	4	62	346	441	43	29
1980	16	10	12	0	51	173	4	20	0	4	35	237	1,303	77	73
1990	11	9	11	0	72	112	3	21	0	4	23	247	2,150	139	160

	Professional, technical, and kindred workers														
	Designers	Dietitians and nutritionists	Draftsmen	Editors and reporters	Engineers, aeronautical	Engineers, chemical	Engineers, civil	Engineers, electrical	Engineers, industrial	Engineers, mechanical	Engineers, metallurgical, metallurgists	Engineers, mining	Engineers not elsewhere classified	Entertainers not elsewhere classified	Farm and home management advisors
	Ba2594	Ba2595	Ba2596	Ba2597	Ba2598	Ba2599	Ba2600	Ba2601	Ba2602	Ba2603	Ba2604	Ba2605	Ba2606	Ba2607	Ba2608
Year	Hundred	Hundred	Hundred	Hundred	Hundred	Hundred	Hundred	Hundred	Hundred	Hundred	Hundred	Hundred	Hundred	Hundred	Hundred
1860	0	0	0	0	0	0	0	0	0	0	0	0	0	0	0
1870	0	0	0	2	0	0	0	0	0	0	0	0	0	2	0
1880	0	0	0	4	0	0	0	0	0	0	0	0	0	4	0
1900	8	0	0	23	0	0	0	0	0	0	0	0	0	8	0
1910 [2]	30	0	3	35	0	0	13	0	0	0	0	0	0	3	0
1920	45	18	16	75	0	0	0	2	0	0	0	0	0	6	0
1940	79	0	20	141	0	2	3	2	8	2	13	0	0	7	42
1950	100	203	66	242	5	15	34	10	8	7	7	4	3	56	71
1960	125	208	131	424	5	6	5	17	21	4	4	0	8	22	59
1970	240	289	213	770	11	6	22	48	50	15	2	2	31	147	58
1980	1,533	436	462	1,457	24	24	53	136	432	37	10	11	100	336	0
1990	2,974	612	509	2,077	95	57	141	360	1,041	85	16	18	311	728	0

	Professional, technical, and kindred workers														
								Natural scientists not elsewhere classified							
	Foresters and conservationists	Funeral directors and embalmers	Lawyers and judges	Librarians	Musicians and music teachers	Nurses, professional	Nurses, student professional	Agricultural scientists	Biological scientists	Geologists and geophysicists	Mathematicians	Physicists	Miscellaneous natural scientists	Optometrists	Osteopaths
	Ba2609	Ba2610	Ba2611	Ba2612	Ba2613	Ba2614	Ba2615	Ba2616	Ba2617	Ba2618	Ba2619	Ba2620	Ba2621	Ba2622	Ba2623
Year	Hundred	Hundred	Hundred	Hundred	Hundred	Hundred	Hundred	Hundred	Hundred	Hundred	Hundred	Hundred	Hundred	Hundred	Hundred
1860	0	0	0	0	44	2	0	0	0	0	0	0	0	0	0
1870	0	0	2	2	72	0	0	0	0	0	0	0	0	0	0
1880	0	1	0	4	162	2	0	0	0	0	0	0	0	0	0
1900	0	8	15	61	387	99	0	0	0	0	0	0	0	0	0
1910 [2]	0	13	10	0	826	872	0	0	0	0	0	0	0	0	0
1920	0	4	10	146	724	1,280	164	2	10	0	0	0	0	0	6
1940	0	14	45	296	587	3,079	0	0	0	0	0	0	0	13	11
1950	17	30	57	538	852	3,815	628	1	25	4	6	6	1	9	5
1960	8	22	70	710	1,032	5,289	539	5	30	10	18	4	4	7	4
1970	15	20	127	1,017	1,431	7,724	156	10	90	8	15	9	3	7	0
1980	42	25	666	1,495	2,453	11,341	0	51	199	49	9	15	14	18	0
1990	57	48	1,691	1,828	4,097	16,614	0	76	317	71	13	42	47	34	0

Notes appear at end of table

(continued)

TABLE Ba2564–2800 Detailed occupations – white females: 1860–1990 [Part 1] *Continued*

	Professional, technical, and kindred workers														
									Social scientists						
	Personnel and labor-relations workers	Pharmacists	Photographers	Physicians and surgeons	Radio operators	Recreation and group workers	Religious workers	Social and welfare workers, except group	Economists	Psychologists	Statisticians and actuaries	Miscellaneous social scientists	Sports instructors and officials	Surveyors	Teachers not elsewhere classified
	Ba2624	Ba2625	Ba2626	Ba2627	Ba2628	Ba2629	Ba2630	Ba2631	Ba2632	Ba2633	Ba2634	Ba2635	Ba2636	Ba2637	Ba2638
Year	Hundred	Hundred	Hundred	Hundred	Hundred	Hundred	Hundred	Hundred	Hundred	Hundred	Hundred	Hundred	Hundred	Hundred	Hundred
1860	0	0	2	0	0	0	2	0	0	0	0	0	0	0	638
1870	0	0	2	13	0	0	10	0	0	0	0	0	0	0	832
1880	0	2	7	23	0	0	55	0	0	0	0	0	0	1	1,518
1900	0	0	23	30	0	0	129	0	0	0	0	0	0	0	2,952
1910 [2]	0	0	55	73	0	0	103	0	0	0	0	0	0	0	4,768
1920	2	34	51	55	2	8	254	89	0	2	8	0	14	0	6,004
1940	0	54	29	76	4	0	234	440	0	0	0	0	46	9	7,365
1950	155	128	93	115	26	54	270	525	31	25	80	8	117	21	7,899
1960	286	67	63	130	23	135	337	563	21	41	67	7	230	15	10,967
1970	839	127	84	217	82	172	184	1,123	69	104	95	33	185	17	16,839
1980	2,327	309	205	429	325	199	255	2,252	257	387	141	120	148	44	21,978
1990	3,587	558	378	934	151	291	519	3,380	587	1,024	174	229	220	86	28,601

	Professional, technical, and kindred workers						Farmers			Managers, officials, and proprietors					
	Technicians – medical and dental	Technicians – testing	Technicians not elsewhere classified	Therapists and healers not elsewhere classified	Veterinarians	Professional, technical, and kindred workers not elsewhere classified	Total	Farmers – owners and tenants	Farm managers	Total	Buyers and department heads – store	Buyers and shippers – farm products	Conductors – railroad	Credit men	Floormen and floor managers – store
	Ba2639	Ba2640	Ba2641	Ba2642	Ba2643	Ba2644	Ba2645	Ba2646	Ba2647	Ba2648	Ba2649	Ba2650	Ba2651	Ba2652	Ba2653
Year	Hundred	Hundred	Hundred	Hundred	Hundred	Hundred	Hundred	Hundred	Hundred	Hundred	Hundred	Hundred	Hundred	Hundred	Hundred
1860	0	0	0	0	0	0	952	939	13	199	0	0	0	0	0
1870	0	0	0	0	0	4	353	353	0	169	0	0	0	0	0
1880	0	0	0	0	0	3	639	635	4	361	0	0	1	0	0
1900	0	0	0	15	0	8	2,542	2,535	8	1,229	0	0	0	0	0
1910 [2]	0	0	0	50	0	103	1,982	1,982	0	1,290	0	0	0	0	40
1920	14	16	2	37	2	24	1,962	1,818	144	1,722	57	4	2	2	16
1940	0	197	10	84	6	342	1,092	1,082	10	4,314	184	3	5	41	34
1950	438	196	35	125	25	180	793	773	20	6,520	344	2	1	85	53
1960	777	360	48	179	3	606	945	938	7	7,507	500	4	2	121	48
1970	1,564	542	85	448	12	4,271	644	623	21	9,117	1,051	6	4	160	0
1980	3,415	1,891	252	1,267	45	3,896	1,219	1,116	103	24,325	1,795	14	7	0	0
1990	6,120	2,365	427	2,314	120	7,187	1,391	1,127	264	48,079	2,852	19	16	0	0

Year	Managers, officials, and proprietors: Inspectors – public administration	Managers and superintendents – building	Officers, pilots, pursers, and engineers – ship	Officials and administrators not elsewhere classified – public administration	Officials – lodge, society, union, and so forth	Postmasters	Purchasing agents and buyers not elsewhere classified	Managers, officials, and proprietors not elsewhere classified	Clerical and kindred workers: Total	Agents not elsewhere classified	Attendants and assistants – library	Attendants – physician's and dentist's office	Baggagemen – transportation	Bank tellers	Bookkeepers
	Ba2654	Ba2655	Ba2656	Ba2657	Ba2658	Ba2659	Ba2660	Ba2661	Ba2662	Ba2663	Ba2664	Ba2665	Ba2666	Ba2667	Ba2668
	Hundred	Hundred	Hundred	Hundred	Hundred	Hundred	Hundred	Hundred	Hundred	Hundred	Hundred	Hundred	Hundred	Hundred	Hundred
1860	0	0	0	0	0	0	0	199	6	2	0	0	0	0	2
1870	0	0	0	0	0	2	0	167	64	0	6	0	0	0	12
1880	0	0	0	6	2	8	1	343	96	5	0	0	0	0	27
1900	0	0	0	8	0	46	0	1,176	2,193	15	8	0	0	0	501
1910 [2]	0	0	0	118	13	0	0	1,118	6,632	18	0	0	3	0	1,846
1920	8	57	0	45	8	124	10	1,390	16,101	28	20	103	2	18	2,927
1940	8	317	3	160	26	165	82	3,287	25,018	120	260	291	0	0	4,450
1950	12	256	52	205	28	146	64	5,273	43,545	220	108	368	3	315	5,750
1960	36	190	1	396	30	145	102	5,934	60,239	257	234	699	3	887	7,671
1970	49	322	5	511	74	108	207	6,620	93,618	8	881	1,631	0	2,050	12,154
1980	207	732	6	1,072	0	131	688	19,673	129,351	0	974	3,302	0	4,088	15,402
1990	365	1,692	10	4,371	0	180	1,314	37,259	143,967	0	972	2,867	0	3,859	15,218

Year	Clerical and kindred workers: Cashiers	Collectors, bill and account	Dispatchers and starters – vehicle	Express messengers and railway mail clerks	Mail carriers	Messengers and office boys	Office machine operators	Shipping and receiving clerks	Stenographers, typists, and secretaries	Telegraph messengers	Telegraph operators	Telephone operators	Ticket, station, and express agents	Clerical and kindred workers not elsewhere classified
	Ba2669	Ba2670	Ba2671	Ba2672	Ba2673	Ba2674	Ba2675	Ba2676	Ba2677	Ba2678	Ba2679	Ba2680	Ba2681	Ba2682
	Hundred	Hundred	Hundred	Hundred	Hundred	Hundred	Hundred	Hundred	Hundred	Hundred	Hundred	Hundred	Hundred	Hundred
1860	0	0	0	0	0	0	0	0	0	0	0	0	0	2
1870	2	0	0	0	0	2	0	0	0	0	2	0	2	38
1880	6	1	0	0	0	0	0	0	0	0	9	1	4	43
1900	129	0	0	0	0	15	8	8	698	0	53	197	0	562
1910 [2]	0	18	0	0	5	60	0	13	2,579	3	68	834	13	1,174
1920	590	37	2	2	12	69	112	49	6,254	2	144	1,728	14	3,986
1940	0	32	0	0	21	25	568	158	10,268	2	112	1,837	20	6,854
1950	1,838	36	31	1	26	149	1,231	162	15,183	4	60	3,492	73	14,495
1960	3,564	48	51	2	30	81	2,161	207	21,009	4	57	3,313	145	19,817
1970	6,355	169	95	0	164	89	3,557	516	34,656	3	31	3,445	331	27,483
1980	12,528	440	263	0	292	170	5,626	1,248	41,635	0	26	2,418	479	40,460
1990	16,384	872	801	0	719	288	8,004	2,007	40,212	0	0	1,558	1,615	48,591

Notes appear at end of table

(continued)

TABLE Ba2564–2800 Detailed occupations – white females: 1860–1990 [Part 1] *Continued*

	Sales workers										Craft workers, foremen, and kindred workers				
	Total	Advertising agents and salesmen	Auctioneers	Demonstrators	Hucksters and peddlers	Insurance agents and brokers	Newsboys	Real estate agents and brokers	Stock and bond salesmen	Salesmen and sales clerks not elsewhere classified	Total	Bakers	Blacksmiths	Bookbinders	Boilermakers
	Ba2683	Ba2684	Ba2685	Ba2686	Ba2687	Ba2688	Ba2689	Ba2690	Ba2691	Ba2692	Ba2693	Ba2694	Ba2695	Ba2696	Ba2697
Year	Hundred	Hundred	Hundred	Hundred	Hundred	Hundred	Hundred	Hundred	Hundred	Hundred	Hundred	Hundred	Hundred	Hundred	Hundred
1860	42	0	0	0	14	0	0	0	0	28	381	0	4	26	0
1870	145	0	0	0	16	0	0	0	0	129	365	4	2	28	0
1880	331	0	0	0	30	0	0	0	0	301	519	8	0	33	0
1900	1,601	0	0	0	15	23	0	0	0	1,563	1,100	30	0	152	0
1910 [2]	3,539	0	0	28	0	28	0	30	0	3,453	998	45	5	0	3
1920	5,088	16	0	32	12	51	2	41	6	4,928	1,384	37	8	118	2
1940	8,013	42	23	68	29	148	11	92	34	7,566	1,461	106	2	0	2
1950	13,168	42	25	115	26	216	21	238	23	12,462	2,256	86	1	154	3
1960	16,040	51	1	245	286	402	53	463	16	14,523	2,284	147	1	129	0
1970	20,617	126	3	342	921	755	99	804	86	17,482	4,554	276	6	168	4
1980	26,538	433	8	84	1,536	2,182	314	2,826	223	18,931	6,888	412	0	139	4
1990	32,253	792	11	312	1,259	4,418	395	3,736	709	20,621	8,095	588	0	122	4

	Craft workers, foremen, and kindred workers														
	Brickmasons, stonemasons, and tile setters	Cabinetmakers	Carpenters	Cement and concrete finishers	Compositors and typesetters	Cranemen, derrickmen, and hoistmen	Decorators and window dressers	Electricians	Electrotypers and stereotypers	Engravers, except photoengravers	Excavating, grading, and road machinery operators	Foremen not elsewhere classified	Forgemen and hammermen	Furriers	Glaziers
	Ba2698	Ba2699	Ba2700	Ba2701	Ba2702	Ba2703	Ba2704	Ba2705	Ba2706	Ba2707	Ba2708	Ba2709	Ba2710	Ba2711	Ba2712
Year	Hundred	Hundred	Hundred	Hundred	Hundred	Hundred	Hundred	Hundred	Hundred	Hundred	Hundred	Hundred	Hundred	Hundred	Hundred
1860	4	2	10	0	2	0	0	0	0	0	0	2	0	6	0
1870	5	2	2	0	8	0	0	0	0	0	0	0	0	2	0
1880	3	1	5	0	22	0	0	0	0	0	0	6	0	7	0
1900	0	0	0	0	152	0	0	0	0	8	0	99	0	8	0
1910 [2]	3	10	23	0	118	0	5	3	8	3	0	199	0	0	0
1920	4	4	22	0	116	0	10	10	0	8	2	381	4	10	2
1940	5	40	13	1	108	4	53	16	5	7	0	447	0	23	3
1950	5	5	51	2	113	14	106	21	12	13	9	635	3	19	8
1960	6	7	20	1	150	7	220	25	2	14	4	769	3	11	1
1970	18	31	98	5	221	15	368	76	2	20	30	1,174	7	4	8
1980	19	52	147	3	360	22	0	95	0	48	37	2,476	8	43	12
1990	25	38	186	5	465	18	0	134	0	55	53	2,243	9	79	17

Craft workers, foremen, and kindred workers

Year	Heat treaters, annealers, temperers	Inspectors, scalers, and graders – log and lumber	Inspectors not elsewhere classified	Jewelers, watchmakers, goldsmiths, silversmiths	Job setters – metal	Linemen and servicemen	Locomotive engineers	Locomotive firemen	Loom fixers	Machinists	Mechanics and repairmen – airplane	Mechanics and repairmen – automobile	Mechanics and repairmen – office machine	Mechanics and repairmen – radio and television	Mechanics and repairmen – railroad and car shop
	Ba2713	Ba2714	Ba2715	Ba2716	Ba2717	Ba2718	Ba2719	Ba2720	Ba2721	Ba2722	Ba2723	Ba2724	Ba2725	Ba2726	Ba2727
	Hundred	Hundred	Hundred	Hundred	Hundred	Hundred	Hundred	Hundred	Hundred	Hundred	Hundred	Hundred	Hundred	Hundred	Hundred
1860	0	0	0	2	0	0	0	0	0	0	0	0	0	0	0
1870	0	0	0	0	0	0	0	0	0	0	0	0	0	0	0
1880	1	0	0	6	0	0	0	0	0	1	0	0	0	0	0
1900	0	0	15	23	0	0	0	0	0	8	0	0	0	0	0
1910 [2]	3	0	13	10	0	5	3	3	0	33	0	0	0	0	0
1920	0	0	34	24	0	20	0	0	0	67	0	4	0	0	0
1940	4	7	58	27	0	18	1	0	0	36	3	9	0	0	0
1950	1	7	78	26	6	49	2	0	3	67	9	58	2	18	0
1960	3	8	38	17	2	43	0	0	3	60	12	20	0	14	1
1970	4	13	68	43	22	95	3	1	3	102	36	114	13	46	6
1980	11	0	19	129	32	281	9	0	0	184	30	115	48	67	0
1990	9	0	45	188	21	245	9	0	0	185	59	200	118	123	0

Craft workers, foremen, and kindred workers

Year	Mechanics and repairmen not elsewhere classified	Millers – grain, flour, feed, and so forth	Millwrights	Molders – metal	Motion picture projectionists	Opticians and lens grinders and polishers	Painters – construction and maintenance	Paperhangers	Pattern and model makers, except paper	Photoengravers and lithographers	Piano and organ tuners and repairmen	Plasterers	Plumbers and pipe fitters	Pressmen and plate printers – printing	Rollers and roll hands – metal
	Ba2728	Ba2729	Ba2730	Ba2731	Ba2732	Ba2733	Ba2734	Ba2735	Ba2736	Ba2737	Ba2738	Ba2739	Ba2740	Ba2741	Ba2742
	Hundred	Hundred	Hundred	Hundred	Hundred	Hundred	Hundred	Hundred	Hundred	Hundred	Hundred	Hundred	Hundred	Hundred	Hundred
1860	0	4	0	0	0	0	2	0	0	0	0	4	0	0	0
1870	0	2	0	0	0	0	6	0	0	0	0	0	0	0	0
1880	0	3	0	0	0	0	5	0	0	0	0	0	0	0	0
1900	0	0	0	8	0	0	0	8	0	0	0	0	0	15	0
1910 [2]	3	3	0	0	0	0	15	10	3	3	0	0	5	10	3
1920	14	4	2	6	0	4	22	6	2	4	0	0	8	6	4
1940	85	1	0	7	9	9	34	36	4	4	0	5	8	5	2
1950	117	0	1	4	4	18	90	29	23	11	3	9	20	17	4
1960	160	1	0	13	2	26	70	13	12	12	0	1	7	33	7
1970	228	2	8	53	5	57	148	0	17	37	3	4	34	117	13
1980	424	0	34	41	12	170	288	0	37	41	0	3	48	416	17
1990	494	0	23	24	13	365	519	0	46	115	0	7	58	528	15

Notes appear at end of table

(continued)

TABLE Ba2564–2800 Detailed occupations – white females: 1860–1990 [Part 1] *Continued*

	Craft workers, foremen, and kindred workers										Operatives and kindred workers				
	Roofers and slaters	Shoemakers and repairers, except factory	Stationary engineers	Stonecutters and stone carvers	Structural metal workers	Tailors and tailoresses	Tinsmiths, coppersmiths, sheet metal workers	Toolmakers, die makers, and setters	Upholsterers	Craftsmen and kindred workers not elsewhere classified	Total	Apprentice auto mechanics	Apprentice bricklayers and masons	Apprentice carpenters	Apprentice electricians
	Ba2743	Ba2744	Ba2745	Ba2746	Ba2747	Ba2748	Ba2749	Ba2750	Ba2751	Ba2752	Ba2753	Ba2754	Ba2755	Ba2756	Ba2757
Year	Hundred	Hundred	Hundred	Hundred	Hundred	Hundred	Hundred	Hundred	Hundred	Hundred	Hundred	Hundred	Hundred	Hundred	Hundred
1860	0	8	2	0	2	294	0	0	2	4	2,683	0	0	0	0
1870	0	8	0	2	0	290	2	0	2	0	3,301	0	0	0	0
1880	0	2	1	0	0	407	3	0	5	1	5,357	0	0	0	0
1900	0	8	8	0	0	546	0	0	15	0	10,025	0	0	0	0
1910 [2]	0	3	5	0	0	426	0	3	15	3	15,328	0	0	0	0
1920	0	35	4	4	4	343	4	2	8	8	15,385	0	0	0	0
1940	6	8	13	17	30	152	4	1	22	0	21,464	0	0	8	0
1950	0	13	15	2	3	222	15	3	41	5	28,202	11	0	1	0
1960	0	8	18	1	5	61	21	15	44	18	29,154	0	0	0	1
1970	6	57	24	6	9	180	28	39	88	291	35,758	1	2	1	3
1980	7	92	44	0	27	191	43	31	118	0	37,064	1	1	5	8
1990	19	85	85	0	28	190	65	30	147	0	32,211	1	(Z)	1	6

	Operatives and kindred workers														
	Apprentice machinists and toolmakers	Apprentice mechanics, except auto	Apprentice plumbers and pipe fitters	Apprentices – building trades not elsewhere classified	Apprentices – metalworking trades not elsewhere classified	Apprentices – printing trades	Apprentices – other specified trades	Apprentices – trade not specified	Asbestos and insulation workers	Attendants – auto service and parking	Blasters and powdermen	Boatmen, canalmen, and lock keepers	Brakemen – railroad	Bus drivers	Chainmen, rodmen, and axmen – surveying
	Ba2758	Ba2759	Ba2760	Ba2761	Ba2762	Ba2763	Ba2764	Ba2765	Ba2766	Ba2767	Ba2768	Ba2769	Ba2770	Ba2771	Ba2772
Year	Hundred	Hundred	Hundred	Hundred	Hundred	Hundred	Hundred	Hundred	Hundred	Hundred	Hundred	Hundred	Hundred	Hundred	Hundred
1860	0	0	0	0	0	0	2	8	0	0	0	2	0	0	0
1870	0	0	0	0	0	0	12	0	0	0	0	0	0	0	0
1880	0	0	0	0	0	1	35	1	0	0	0	3	0	0	0
1900	0	0	0	0	0	0	23	0	0	0	0	0	0	0	0
1910 [2]	0	0	0	0	0	0	48	13	0	0	0	0	0	0	0
1920	0	0	0	0	0	2	8	6	0	4	0	0	4	4	0
1940	0	0	25	0	0	18	19	4	8	101	1	10	4	0	0
1950	1	0	29	0	2	18	4	4	13	55	0	8	5	52	7
1960	5	1	0	1	0	2	6	7	5	59	0	2	1	168	1
1970	2	3	1	1	(Z)	4	9	3	4	115	3	3	5	627	1
1980	7	0	3	0	1	0	9	0	14	249	2	0	7	1,496	5
1990	2	0	2	0	1	0	3	0	17	265	3	0	3	1,700	5

Year	Conductors – bus and street railway	Deliverymen and routemen	Dressmakers and seamstresses, except factory	Dyers	Filers, grinders, and polishers – metal	Fruit, nut, vegetable graders, packers, not factory	Furnacemen, smeltermen, and pourers	Heaters – metal	Laundry and dry cleaning operatives	Meat cutters, except slaughter and packing houses	Milliners	Mine operatives and laborers	Motormen, mine, factory, logging camp, and so forth	Motormen, street, subway, and elevated railway
	Operatives and kindred workers													
	Ba2773	Ba2774	Ba2775	Ba2776	Ba2777	Ba2778	Ba2779	Ba2780	Ba2781	Ba2782	Ba2783	Ba2784	Ba2785	Ba2786
	Hundred	Hundred	Hundred	Hundred	Hundred	Hundred	Hundred	Hundred	Hundred	Hundred	Hundred	Hundred	Hundred	Hundred
1860	0	2	1,271	0	2	0	0	0	4	4	259	4	0	0
1870	0	2	1,374	0	2	0	0	0	62	0	251	4	0	0
1880	0	3	2,148	1	2	0	0	0	177	4	377	1	0	0
1900	0	0	4,068	0	8	0	0	8	53	8	835	15	0	0
1910 [2]	0	18	3,602	3	28	20	3	0	572	0	1,217	33	0	5
1920	2	14	2,503	6	37	57	2	0	682	16	572	22	0	2
1940	1	21	1,301	8	69	158	1	46	1,269	10	95	32	1	0
1950	0	38	1,263	22	59	222	6	7	1,914	34	124	6	0	5
1960	0	101	1,046	3	85	121	8	0	1,760	48	34	9	0	0
1970	2	175	825	15	267	180	21	3	1,544	93	17	65	1	0
1980	0	416	733	0	378	0	0	0	1,244	297	0	77	0	0
1990	0	130	657	0	166	0	0	0	1,453	330	0	59	0	0

Year	Oilers and greasers, except auto	Painters, except construction or maintenance	Photographic process workers	Power station operators	Sailors and deckhands	Sawyers	Spinners – textile	Stationary firemen	Switchmen – railroad	Taxicab drivers and chauffeurs	Truck and tractor drivers	Weavers – textile	Welders and flame cutters	Operatives and kindred workers not elsewhere classified
	Operatives and kindred workers													
	Ba2787	Ba2788	Ba2789	Ba2790	Ba2791	Ba2792	Ba2793	Ba2794	Ba2795	Ba2796	Ba2797	Ba2798	Ba2799	Ba2800
	Hundred	Hundred	Hundred	Hundred	Hundred	Hundred	Hundred	Hundred	Hundred	Hundred	Hundred	Hundred	Hundred	Hundred
1860	0	12	0	0	0	0	164	0	0	0	0	278	0	669
1870	0	0	2	0	2	0	10	0	0	0	2	107	0	1,469
1880	0	2	1	0	2	0	7	1	0	1	2	105	0	2,484
1900	0	8	0	0	0	8	311	0	0	0	8	691	0	3,984
1910 [2]	0	13	0	0	0	0	338	0	0	3	15	945	0	8,456
1920	2	35	45	0	2	2	560	0	4	8	18	836	6	9,924
1940	7	63	92	8	3	2	0	8	0	0	53	0	22	17,997
1950	6	194	135	10	7	19	601	29	1	17	34	396	86	22,757
1960	4	126	163	20	5	15	433	5	3	34	55	260	144	24,413
1970	14	172	255	5	5	73	0	54	8	74	169	240	270	30,424
1980	13	270	392	12	7	93	0	52	2	160	328	330	316	30,134
1990	8	211	432	15	5	93	0	45	1	162	1,361	267	219	24,587

(Z) Fewer than 50.

[1] Data pertain to noninstitutionalized civilians age 16 and older who reported an occupation; employed persons only beginning 1940.

[2] The wording of the 1910 Census occupation question elicited more female occupation responses than in surrounding censuses, especially in agriculture.

Source

See the source for Table Ba1159–1395.

Documentation

See the text for Table Ba1159–1395.

TABLE Ba2801–2844 Detailed occupations – white females: 1860–1990[1] [Part 2]

Contributed by Matthew Sobek

	Service workers, private household				Service workers, not household										
	Total	Housekeepers – private household	Laundresses – private household	Private household workers not elsewhere classified	Total	Attendants – hospital and other institution	Attendants – professional and personal service not elsewhere classified	Attendants – recreation and amusement	Barbers, beauticians, and manicurists	Bartenders	Bootblacks	Boarding and lodging house keepers	Charwomen and cleaners	Cooks, except private household	Counter and fountain workers
	Ba2801	Ba2802	Ba2803	Ba2804	Ba2805	Ba2806	Ba2807	Ba2808	Ba2809	Ba2810	Ba2811	Ba2812	Ba2813	Ba2814	Ba2815
Year	Hundred	Hundred	Hundred	Hundred	Hundred	Hundred	Hundred	Hundred	Hundred	Hundred	Hundred	Hundred	Hundred	Hundred	Hundred
1860	4,292	4	238	4,050	252	2	20	0	0	0	0	97	0	0	0
1870	6,180	15	193	5,971	313	8	24	0	8	0	0	84	0	16	0
1880	6,590	566	210	5,813	538	4	69	0	23	1	0	166	1	33	0
1900	13,440	501	0	12,939	2,618	15	0	0	53	0	0	486	0	53	0
1910 [2]	11,630	1,766	1,547	8,317	3,751	0	86	0	166	3	0	1,300	202	0	0
1920	7,406	1,657	891	4,858	5,138	77	59	2	239	0	0	1,023	118	521	12
1940	10,536	2,866	367	7,303	11,473	492	207	77	1,951	61	12	500	339	1,041	0
1950	5,428	1,054	219	4,156	16,006	976	213	39	1,687	145	14	196	523	1,860	399
1960	6,888	996	198	5,694	23,007	2,220	338	66	2,381	182	1	251	856	2,839	1,004
1970	5,140	567	63	4,510	37,167	4,516	1,535	151	3,968	376	3	50	1,572	4,084	1,023
1980	3,179	370	10	2,798	55,518	8,066	5,588	561	4,433	1,192	0	0	2,880	6,986	1,365
1990	3,494	190	11	3,293	67,487	10,205	9,099	936	5,758	1,418	0	0	3,449	8,197	1,293

	Service workers, not household														
	Elevator operators	Firemen (fire protection)	Guards, watchmen, and doorkeepers	Housekeepers and stewards, except household	Janitors and sextons	Marshals and constables	Midwives	Policemen and detectives	Porters	Practical nurses	Sheriffs and bailiffs	Ushers – recreation and amusement	Waiters and waitresses	Watchmen (crossing) and bridge tenders	Service workers (not private household) not elsewhere classified
	Ba2816	Ba2817	Ba2818	Ba2819	Ba2820	Ba2821	Ba2822	Ba2823	Ba2824	Ba2825	Ba2826	Ba2827	Ba2828	Ba2829	Ba2830
Year	Hundred	Hundred	Hundred	Hundred	Hundred	Hundred	Hundred	Hundred	Hundred	Hundred	Hundred	Hundred	Hundred	Hundred	Hundred
1860	0	0	2	28	0	0	15	0	0	69	0	0	11	2	6
1870	0	0	0	11	10	0	14	0	0	50	0	0	63	2	22
1880	0	0	1	2	6	0	19	0	0	117	0	0	55	7	35
1900	0	0	0	296	129	0	46	0	0	0	0	0	296	8	1,237
1910 [2]	0	0	10	0	149	0	38	0	3	987	0	0	799	0	10
1920	30	0	10	270	162	2	24	14	10	913	4	26	911	4	706
1940	102	2	31	699	354	0	0	19	29	805	4	37	3,483	0	1,227
1950	158	3	47	748	440	2	(Z)	44	27	1,231	11	74	5,193	1	1,974
1960	141	4	59	1,083	590	6	1	73	10	1,664	11	37	6,563	101	2,530
1970	53	16	134	943	1,130	2	3	120	3	1,753	19	41	8,582	211	6,879
1980	22	17	650	460	3,415	0	0	224	10	3,273	63	61	11,122	267	4,863
1990	7	52	1,125	706	5,638	0	0	623	26	3,081	178	75	9,955	261	5,406

	Farm laborers					Laborers								
	Total	Farm foremen	Farm laborers, wage workers	Farm laborers, unpaid family workers	Farm service laborers, self-employed	Total	Fishermen and oystermen	Garage laborers, car washers and greasers	Gardeners, except farm, and groundskeepers	Longshoremen and stevedores	Lumbermen, raftsmen, and woodchoppers	Teamsters	Laborers not elsewhere classified	Unknown occupation
	Ba2831	Ba2832	Ba2833	Ba2834	Ba2835	Ba2836	Ba2837	Ba2838	Ba2839	Ba2840	Ba2841	Ba2842	Ba2843	Ba2844
Year	Hundred	Hundred	Hundred	Hundred	Hundred	Hundred	Hundred	Hundred	Hundred	Hundred	Hundred	Hundred	Hundred	Hundred
1860	134	0	134	0	0	139	0	0	9	0	0	0	130	—
1870	275	0	271	4	0	76	2	0	0	0	0	0	74	—
1880	581	2	579	0	0	298	3	0	7	0	3	0	285	—
1900	926	0	417	508	0	622	0	0	8	0	0	0	615	—
1910 [2]	3,924	55	3,869	0	0	924	0	0	55	0	5	0	864	—
1920	1,785	16	527	1,240	2	1,596	2	0	12	0	8	14	1,560	—
1940	1,240	2	276	962	0	1,002	25	3	15	1	4	3	951	1,216
1950	2,948	1	614	2,332	1	895	5	22	24	12	14	4	816	615
1960	1,709	6	627	1,075	0	826	5	18	26	0	4	0	773	9,510
1970	1,154	15	773	361	5	2,171	9	0	68	5	15	2	2,072	—
1980	1,780	67	1,713	0	0	4,438	27	0	212	2	16	0	4,181	—
1990	1,513	45	1,467	0	0	6,188	28	0	431	2	24	0	5,703	—

(Z) Fewer than 50.

[1] Data pertain to noninstitutionalized civilians age 16 and older who reported an occupation; employed persons only beginning 1940.

[2] The wording of the 1910 Census occupation question elicited more female occupation responses than in surrounding censuses, especially in agriculture.

Source

See the source for Table Ba1159–1395.

Documentation

See the text for Table Ba1159–1395.

TABLE Ba2845–3081 Detailed occupations – nonwhite females: 1860–1990[1] [Part 1]

Contributed by Matthew Sobek

		Professional, technical, and kindred workers												College professors and instructors	
	Total	Total	Accountants and auditors	Actors and actresses	Airplane pilots and navigators	Architects	Artists and art teachers	Athletes	Authors	Chemists	Chiropractors	Clergymen	College presidents and deans	Agricultural sciences	Biological sciences
	Ba2845	Ba2846	Ba2847	Ba2848	Ba2849	Ba2850	Ba2851	Ba2852	Ba2853	Ba2854	Ba2855	Ba2856	Ba2857	Ba2858	Ba2859
Year	Hundred	Hundred	Hundred	Hundred	Hundred	Hundred	Hundred	Hundred	Hundred	Hundred	Hundred	Hundred	Hundred	Hundred	Hundred
1860 [2]	514	2	0	0	0	0	0	0	0	0	0	0	0	0	0
1870	5,589	12	0	0	0	0	0	0	0	0	0	0	0	0	0
1880	7,640	42	0	1	0	0	0	0	0	0	0	0	0	0	0
1900	11,368	152	0	0	0	0	0	0	0	0	0	0	0	0	0
1910 [3]	18,124	272	0	3	0	0	0	0	0	0	0	0	0	0	0
1920	14,913	396	0	4	0	0	0	0	0	0	0	4	0	0	0
1940	16,219	716	0	2	0	0	3	1	0	0	0	2	0	0	0
1950	19,459	1,147	5	1	0	0	9	0	0	2	0	10	1	0	0
1960	25,942	1,960	24	1	0	2	10	0	1	3	0	6	0	0	2
1970	36,634	4,728	100	3	0	2	10	0	2	16	0	6	6	(Z)	4
1980	57,808	9,871	479	0	1	6	30	0	11	40	2	14	0	(Z)	3
1990	79,433	16,273	1,210	0	3	19	59	0	26	72	11	31	0	(Z)	2

	Professional, technical, and kindred workers														
	College professors and instructors														
	Chemistry	Economics	Engineering	Geology and geophysics	Mathematics	Medical sciences	Physics	Psychology	Statistics	Natural sciences not elsewhere classified	Social sciences not elsewhere classified	Nonscientific subjects	Subject not specified	Dancers and dancing teachers	Dentists
	Ba2860	Ba2861	Ba2862	Ba2863	Ba2864	Ba2865	Ba2866	Ba2867	Ba2868	Ba2869	Ba2870	Ba2871	Ba2872	Ba2873	Ba2874
Year	Hundred	Hundred	Hundred	Hundred	Hundred	Hundred	Hundred	Hundred	Hundred	Hundred	Hundred	Hundred	Hundred	Hundred	Hundred
1860 [2]	0	0	0	0	0	0	0	0	0	0	0	0	0	0	0
1870	0	0	0	0	0	0	0	0	0	0	0	0	0	0	0
1880	0	0	0	0	0	0	0	0	0	0	0	0	0	0	0
1900	0	0	0	0	0	0	0	0	0	0	0	0	0	0	0
1910 [3]	0	0	0	0	0	0	0	0	0	0	0	0	3	0	0
1920	0	0	0	0	0	0	0	0	0	0	0	0	2	0	0
1940	0	0	0	0	0	0	0	0	0	0	0	0	9	5	0
1950	0	0	0	0	2	0	0	0	0	0	5	4	4	4	5
1960	0	0	0	0	0	1	1	0	0	0	8	2	22	9	1
1970	1	1	1	0	4	10	1	2	0	(Z)	6	23	42	5	1
1980	1	1	1	0	7	15	1	2	0	(Z)	3	20	147	12	10
1990	1	(Z)	1	0	8	13	1	1	0	(Z)	2	23	291	19	34

Year	Designers	Dietitians and nutritionists	Draftsmen	Editors and reporters	Engineers, aeronautical	Engineers, chemical	Engineers, civil	Engineers, electrical	Engineers, industrial	Engineers, mechanical	Engineers, metallurgical, metallurgists	Engineers, mining	Engineers not elsewhere classified	Entertainers not elsewhere classified	Farm and home management advisors
	Professional, technical, and kindred workers														
	Ba2875	Ba2876	Ba2877	Ba2878	Ba2879	Ba2880	Ba2881	Ba2882	Ba2883	Ba2884	Ba2885	Ba2886	Ba2887	Ba2888	Ba2889
	Hundred	Hundred	Hundred	Hundred	Hundred	Hundred	Hundred	Hundred	Hundred	Hundred	Hundred	Hundred	Hundred	Hundred	Hundred
1860 [2]	0	0	0	0	0	0	0	0	0	0	0	0	0	0	0
1870	0	0	0	0	0	0	0	0	0	0	0	0	0	0	0
1880	0	0	0	0	0	0	0	0	0	0	0	0	0	0	0
1900	0	0	0	0	0	0	0	0	0	0	0	0	0	0	0
1910 [3]	0	0	0	0	0	0	0	0	0	0	0	0	0	0	0
1920	0	0	0	0	0	0	0	0	0	0	0	0	0	0	0
1940	1	0	0	0	0	0	0	0	0	0	1	0	0	2	2
1950	3	16	1	5	0	0	6	0	1	0	0	0	0	2	7
1960	2	37	3	7	0	0	1	0	2	0	0	0	0	3	4
1970	15	82	12	28	(Z)	(Z)	2	2	2	1	0	0	1	11	8
1980	79	149	45	98	4	4	8	22	48	5	1	2	15	24	0
1990	212	187	59	204	18	10	31	84	126	12	3	2	45	74	0

Year	Foresters and conservationists	Funeral directors and embalmers	Lawyers and judges	Librarians	Musicians and music teachers	Nurses, professional	Nurses, student professional	Agricultural scientists	Biological scientists	Geologists and geophysicists	Mathematicians	Physicists	Miscellaneous natural scientists	Optometrists	Osteopaths
	Professional, technical, and kindred workers							Natural scientists not elsewhere classified							
	Ba2890	Ba2891	Ba2892	Ba2893	Ba2894	Ba2895	Ba2896	Ba2897	Ba2898	Ba2899	Ba2900	Ba2901	Ba2902	Ba2903	Ba2904
	Hundred	Hundred	Hundred	Hundred	Hundred	Hundred	Hundred	Hundred	Hundred	Hundred	Hundred	Hundred	Hundred	Hundred	Hundred
1860 [2]	0	0	0	0	1	0	0	0	0	0	0	0	0	0	0
1870	0	0	0	0	0	0	0	0	0	0	0	0	0	0	0
1880	0	0	0	0	2	0	0	0	0	0	0	0	0	0	0
1900	0	0	0	0	23	0	0	0	0	0	0	0	0	0	0
1910 [3]	0	0	3	0	18	18	0	0	0	0	0	0	0	0	0
1920	0	0	0	2	26	30	2	0	0	0	0	0	0	0	0
1940	0	3	0	7	14	76	0	0	0	0	0	0	0	0	0
1950	1	9	1	11	30	137	24	1	2	0	(Z)	0	0	1	(Z)
1960	1	1	2	33	38	376	21	0	1	0	1	0	0	0	1
1970	1	6	6	84	65	765	12	1	9	1	1	1	(Z)	1	0
1980	4	8	60	164	213	1,481	0	7	29	4	2	1	3	1	0
1990	6	9	155	269	447	2,618	0	12	52	4	3	5	6	5	0

Notes appear at end of table

(continued)

TABLE Ba2845–3081 Detailed occupations – nonwhite females: 1860–1990 [Part 1] *Continued*

	Professional, technical, and kindred workers														
									Social scientists						
	Personnel and labor-relations workers	Pharmacists	Photographers	Physicians and surgeons	Radio operators	Recreation and group workers	Religious workers	Social and welfare workers, except group	Economists	Psychologists	Statisticians and actuaries	Miscellaneous social scientists	Sports instructors and officials	Surveyors	Teachers not elsewhere classified
	Ba2905	Ba2906	Ba2907	Ba2908	Ba2909	Ba2910	Ba2911	Ba2912	Ba2913	Ba2914	Ba2915	Ba2916	Ba2917	Ba2918	Ba2919
Year	Hundred	Hundred	Hundred	Hundred	Hundred	Hundred	Hundred	Hundred	Hundred	Hundred	Hundred	Hundred	Hundred	Hundred	Hundred
1860 [2]	0	0	0	0	0	0	0	0	0	0	0	0	0	0	1
1870	0	0	0	0	0	0	0	0	0	0	0	0	0	0	12
1880	0	0	0	3	0	0	1	0	0	0	0	0	0	0	33
1900	0	0	0	0	0	0	0	0	0	0	0	0	0	0	129
1910 [3]	0	0	3	3	0	0	0	0	0	0	0	0	0	0	222
1920	0	0	0	2	0	0	2	0	0	0	0	0	0	0	312
1940	0	1	2	1	0	0	3	14	0	0	0	0	1	2	547
1950	1	11	4	1	0	6	9	58	1	0	2	4	3	7	687
1960	8	3	0	10	0	16	11	74	1	1	2	0	8	3	1,057
1970	75	12	5	41	4	32	6	252	5	7	8	4	5	2	1,881
1980	382	39	12	152	42	34	17	665	21	49	24	12	6	5	3,257
1990	617	98	33	250	26	42	38	1,053	49	92	39	23	17	11	4,111

	Professional, technical, and kindred workers						Farmers			Managers, officials, and proprietors					
	Technicians – medical and dental	Technicians – testing	Technicians not elsewhere classified	Therapists and healers not elsewhere classified	Veterinarians	Professional, technical, and kindred workers not elsewhere classified	Total	Farmers – owners and tenants	Farm managers	Total	Buyers and department heads – store	Buyers and shippers – farm products	Conductors – railroad	Credit men	Floormen and floor managers – store
	Ba2920	Ba2921	Ba2922	Ba2923	Ba2924	Ba2925	Ba2926	Ba2927	Ba2928	Ba2929	Ba2930	Ba2931	Ba2932	Ba2933	Ba2934
Year	Hundred	Hundred	Hundred	Hundred	Hundred	Hundred	Hundred	Hundred	Hundred	Hundred	Hundred	Hundred	Hundred	Hundred	Hundred
1860 [2]	0	0	0	0	0	0	8	8	0	0	0	0	0	0	0
1870	0	0	0	0	0	0	149	149	0	4	0	0	0	0	0
1880	0	0	0	0	0	2	255	255	0	8	0	0	0	0	0
1900	0	0	0	0	0	0	736	736	0	38	0	0	0	0	0
1910 [3]	0	0	0	0	0	3	793	793	0	55	0	0	0	0	0
1920	0	0	0	2	0	6	972	966	6	73	0	0	0	0	0
1940	0	1	1	3	0	12	512	512	0	154	0	0	0	0	0
1950	16	12	2	9	2	7	356	356	0	279	4	0	0	0	0
1960	68	21	4	12	0	36	174	174	0	295	4	0	0	0	1
1970	199	50	7	36	(Z)	739	70	67	3	499	36	(Z)	1	4	0
1980	556	313	54	137	1	807	49	31	17	2,098	103	1	1	0	0
1990	1,003	521	113	220	7	1,424	42	23	18	5,460	200	6	6	0	0

Year	Managers, officials, and proprietors: Inspectors – public administration	Managers and superintendents – building	Officers, pilots, pursers, and engineers – ship	Officials and administrators not elsewhere classified – public administration	Officials – lodge, society, union, and so forth	Postmasters	Purchasing agents and buyers not elsewhere classified	Managers, officials, and proprietors not elsewhere classified	Clerical and kindred workers: Total	Agents not elsewhere classified	Attendants and assistants – library	Attendants – physician's and dentist's office	Baggagemen – transportation	Bank tellers	Bookkeepers
	Ba2935	Ba2936	Ba2937	Ba2938	Ba2939	Ba2940	Ba2941	Ba2942	Ba2943	Ba2944	Ba2945	Ba2946	Ba2947	Ba2948	Ba2949
	Hundred	Hundred	Hundred	Hundred	Hundred	Hundred	Hundred	Hundred	Hundred	Hundred	Hundred	Hundred	Hundred	Hundred	Hundred
1860 [2]	0	0	0	0	0	0	0	0	0	0	0	0	0	0	0
1870	0	0	0	0	0	0	0	4	1	0	0	0	0	1	0
1880	0	0	0	0	0	0	0	8	2	0	0	0	0	0	0
1900	0	0	0	0	0	0	0	38	23	0	0	0	0	0	0
1910 [3]	0	0	0	3	3	0	0	50	48	3	0	0	0	0	23
1920	0	0	0	0	0	0	0	73	106	2	0	4	0	0	12
1940	0	10	0	3	1	0	0	140	223	3	7	12	0	0	31
1950	(Z)	11	4	2	0	0	2	256	892	6	13	17	1	2	36
1960	4	12	1	16	2	2	3	250	2,211	6	19	30	0	12	96
1970	11	14	(Z)	45	5	2	13	370	7,851	1	88	241	0	105	442
1980	51	64	1	176	0	4	62	1,635	16,794	0	150	547	0	427	1,001
1990	119	158	2	800	0	12	157	4,000	23,523	0	186	531	0	550	1,347

Clerical and kindred workers

Year	Cashiers	Collectors, bill and account	Dispatchers and starters – vehicle	Express messengers and railway mail clerks	Mail carriers	Messengers and office boys	Office machine operators	Shipping and receiving clerks	Stenographers, typists, and secretaries	Telegraph messengers	Telegraph operators	Telephone operators	Ticket, station, and express agents	Clerical and kindred workers not elsewhere classified
	Ba2950	Ba2951	Ba2952	Ba2953	Ba2954	Ba2955	Ba2956	Ba2957	Ba2958	Ba2959	Ba2960	Ba2961	Ba2962	Ba2963
	Hundred	Hundred	Hundred	Hundred	Hundred	Hundred	Hundred	Hundred	Hundred	Hundred	Hundred	Hundred	Hundred	Hundred
1860 [2]	0	0	0	0	0	0	0	0	0	0	0	0	0	0
1870	0	0	0	0	0	0	0	0	0	0	0	0	0	0
1880	0	0	0	0	0	0	0	0	0	0	0	0	0	2
1900	0	0	0	0	8	0	0	0	8	0	0	0	0	8
1910 [3]	0	3	0	0	0	3	0	0	15	0	0	0	0	3
1920	6	0	0	0	0	4	0	2	32	0	0	6	0	37
1940	0	0	0	0	0	1	2	3	61	0	1	9	1	92
1950	53	2	1	0	0	3	30	14	247	1	0	29	0	442
1960	125	3	5	1	2	11	103	27	701	0	1	93	3	976
1970	508	13	10	0	35	15	485	70	2,139	1	4	436	35	3,225
1980	1,710	65	35	0	43	33	1,261	194	4,091	0	5	469	82	6,683
1990	3,581	158	124	0	130	46	2,006	349	4,826	0	0	393	223	9,072

Notes appear at end of table

(continued)

TABLE Ba2845–3081 Detailed occupations – nonwhite females: 1860–1990 [Part 1] *Continued*

	Sales workers										Craft workers, foremen, and kindred workers				
	Total	Advertising agents and salesmen	Auctioneers	Demonstrators	Hucksters and peddlers	Insurance agents and brokers	Newsboys	Real estate agents and brokers	Stock and bond salesmen	Salesmen and sales clerks not elsewhere classified	Total	Bakers	Blacksmiths	Bookbinders	Boilermakers
	Ba2964	Ba2965	Ba2966	Ba2967	Ba2968	Ba2969	Ba2970	Ba2971	Ba2972	Ba2973	Ba2974	Ba2975	Ba2976	Ba2977	Ba2978
Year	Hundred	Hundred	Hundred	Hundred	Hundred	Hundred	Hundred	Hundred	Hundred	Hundred	Hundred	Hundred	Hundred	Hundred	Hundred
1860 [2]	0	0	0	0	0	0	0	0	0	0	1	0	0	0	0
1870	5	0	0	0	4	0	0	0	0	1	0	0	0	0	0
1880	4	0	0	0	4	0	0	0	0	0	10	0	0	0	0
1900	8	0	0	0	8	0	0	0	0	0	0	0	0	0	0
1910 [3]	28	0	0	0	0	3	0	3	0	23	18	3	0	0	0
1920	47	0	0	0	0	2	0	0	0	45	28	2	0	0	0
1940	120	4	1	0	5	7	0	4	0	99	65	7	0	0	0
1950	305	(Z)	(Z)	19	4	24	3	2	0	252	100	11	0	3	0
1960	450	1	0	3	11	22	3	11	0	399	178	22	0	15	0
1970	1,047	3	(Z)	10	22	66	2	17	3	924	516	44	1	22	(Z)
1980	1,996	21	1	4	84	307	19	90	18	1,451	1,026	50	0	17	2
1990	3,518	65	1	18	128	705	30	228	80	2,264	1,386	97	0	24	1

	Craft workers, foremen, and kindred workers														
	Brickmasons, stonemasons, and tile setters	Cabinetmakers	Carpenters	Cement and concrete finishers	Compositors and typesetters	Cranemen, derrickmen, and hoistmen	Decorators and window dressers	Electricians	Electrotypers and stereotypers	Engravers, except photoengravers	Excavating, grading, and road machinery operators	Foremen not elsewhere classified	Forgemen and hammermen	Furriers	Glaziers
	Ba2979	Ba2980	Ba2981	Ba2982	Ba2983	Ba2984	Ba2985	Ba2986	Ba2987	Ba2988	Ba2989	Ba2990	Ba2991	Ba2992	Ba2993
Year	Hundred	Hundred	Hundred	Hundred	Hundred	Hundred	Hundred	Hundred	Hundred	Hundred	Hundred	Hundred	Hundred	Hundred	Hundred
1860 [2]	0	0	0	0	0	0	0	0	0	0	0	0	0	0	0
1870	0	0	0	0	0	0	0	0	0	0	0	0	0	0	0
1880	0	0	2	0	0	0	0	0	0	0	0	0	0	0	0
1900	0	0	0	0	0	0	0	0	0	0	0	0	0	0	0
1910 [3]	0	0	3	0	3	0	0	0	0	0	0	3	0	0	0
1920	2	0	2	0	0	0	0	0	0	0	0	0	0	2	0
1940	(Z)	3	1	0	6	0	2	0	0	0	0	9	0	0	0
1950	0	1	0	0	2	0	3	1	2	0	0	13	0	1	0
1960	1	1	2	0	8	1	16	3	0	2	0	24	0	0	0
1970	5	4	13	4	16	4	24	8	(Z)	1	5	96	1	1	1
1980	5	6	23	3	17	8	0	18	0	4	9	346	3	13	1
1990	7	3	21	2	32	6	0	28	0	7	12	385	2	18	4

Craft workers, foremen, and kindred workers

Year	Heat treaters, annealers, temperers	Inspectors, scalers, and graders – log and lumber	Inspectors not elsewhere classified	Jewelers, watchmakers, goldsmiths, silversmiths	Job setters – metal	Linemen and servicemen	Locomotive engineers	Locomotive firemen	Loom fixers	Machinists	Mechanics and repairmen – airplane	Mechanics and repairmen – automobile	Mechanics and repairmen – office machine	Mechanics and repairmen – radio and television	Mechanics and repairmen – railroad and car shop
	Ba2994	Ba2995	Ba2996	Ba2997	Ba2998	Ba2999	Ba3000	Ba3001	Ba3002	Ba3003	Ba3004	Ba3005	Ba3006	Ba3007	Ba3008
	Hundred	Hundred	Hundred	Hundred	Hundred	Hundred	Hundred	Hundred	Hundred	Hundred	Hundred	Hundred	Hundred	Hundred	Hundred
1860 [2]	0	0	0	0	0	0	0	0	0	0	0	0	0	0	0
1870	0	0	0	0	0	0	0	0	0	0	0	0	0	0	0
1880	0	0	0	0	0	0	0	0	0	0	0	0	0	0	0
1900	0	0	0	0	0	0	0	0	0	0	0	0	0	0	0
1910 [3]	0	0	0	0	0	0	0	0	0	0	0	0	0	0	0
1920	0	0	4	0	0	0	0	0	0	4	0	0	0	0	0
1940	0	0	1	17	0	0	0	0	0	4	0	0	0	0	0
1950	1	2	6	2	0	2	0	0	6	3	1	7	0	1	0
1960	0	0	14	1	1	0	0	0	0	9	1	5	0	0	0
1970	(Z)	5	19	5	1	12	(Z)	(Z)	(Z)	14	5	14	2	6	0
1980	3	0	5	21	4	58	2	0	0	49	8	21	7	12	0
1990	2	0	12	39	5	72	4	0	0	47	17	34	19	25	0

Craft workers, foremen, and kindred workers

Year	Mechanics and repairmen not elsewhere classified	Millers – grain, flour, feed, and so forth	Millwrights	Molders – metal	Motion picture projectionists	Opticians and lens grinders and polishers	Painters – construction and maintenance	Paperhangers	Pattern and model makers, except paper	Photoengravers and lithographers	Piano and organ tuners and repairmen	Plasterers	Plumbers and pipe fitters	Pressmen and plate printers – printing	Rollers and roll hands – metal
	Ba3009	Ba3010	Ba3011	Ba3012	Ba3013	Ba3014	Ba3015	Ba3016	Ba3017	Ba3018	Ba3019	Ba3020	Ba3021	Ba3022	Ba3023
	Hundred	Hundred	Hundred	Hundred	Hundred	Hundred	Hundred	Hundred	Hundred	Hundred	Hundred	Hundred	Hundred	Hundred	Hundred
1860 [2]	0	0	0	0	0	0	0	0	0	0	0	0	0	0	0
1870	0	0	0	0	0	0	0	0	0	0	0	0	0	0	0
1880	0	0	0	0	0	0	0	0	0	0	0	0	0	0	0
1900	0	0	0	0	0	0	0	0	0	0	0	0	0	0	0
1910 [3]	0	0	0	0	0	0	0	0	0	0	0	0	0	0	0
1920	0	0	0	0	0	0	0	0	0	0	0	0	0	0	0
1940	3	0	0	0	2	0	4	0	0	0	0	1	1	1	0
1950	4	0	2	0	0	1	(Z)	0	1	0	0	2	1	2	1
1960	24	0	0	2	0	3	7	0	0	0	0	0	0	1	0
1970	22	0	(Z)	7	(Z)	7	12	0	1	3	1	1	5	15	1
1980	69	0	7	7	1	16	42	0	5	4	0	1	9	60	3
1990	98	0	4	4	2	43	48	0	12	11	0	1	9	83	2

Notes appear at end of table

(continued)

TABLE Ba2845–3081 Detailed occupations – nonwhite females: 1860–1990 [Part 1] *Continued*

	Craft workers, foremen, and kindred workers										Operatives and kindred workers				
	Roofers and slaters	Shoemakers and repairers, except factory	Stationary engineers	Stonecutters and stone carvers	Structural metal workers	Tailors and tailoresses	Tinsmiths, coppersmiths, sheet metal workers	Toolmakers, die makers, and setters	Upholsterers	Craftsmen and kindred workers not elsewhere classified	Total	Apprentice auto mechanics	Apprentice bricklayers and masons	Apprentice carpenters	Apprentice electricians
	Ba3024	Ba3025	Ba3026	Ba3027	Ba3028	Ba3029	Ba3030	Ba3031	Ba3032	Ba3033	Ba3034	Ba3035	Ba3036	Ba3037	Ba3038
Year	Hundred	Hundred	Hundred	Hundred	Hundred	Hundred	Hundred	Hundred	Hundred	Hundred	Hundred	Hundred	Hundred	Hundred	Hundred
1860 [2]	0	0	0	0	0	1	0	0	0	0	54	0	0	0	0
1870	0	0	0	0	0	0	0	0	0	0	90	0	0	0	0
1880	0	0	0	0	0	7	0	0	0	1	354	0	0	0	0
1900	0	0	0	0	0	0	0	0	0	0	190	0	0	0	0
1910 [3]	0	0	0	0	0	3	0	0	0	5	715	0	0	0	0
1920	0	2	0	0	0	10	0	0	0	0	964	0	0	0	0
1940	1	0	0	1	1	0	0	0	0	0	1,209	0	0	2	0
1950	0	(Z)	1	1	0	15	0	0	4	1	2,861	0	0	0	0
1960	0	1	2	0	0	7	1	0	5	0	3,327	0	0	0	0
1970	2	5	4	(Z)	1	27	4	2	11	53	6,061	0	0	0	0
1980	3	11	6	0	6	37	6	5	12	0	8,575	0	0	1	1
1990	4	15	16	0	6	62	15	7	18	0	9,001	0	(Z)	1	1

	Operatives and kindred workers														
	Apprentice machinists and toolmakers	Apprentice mechanics, except auto	Apprentice plumbers and pipe fitters	Apprentices – building trades not elsewhere classified	Apprentices – metalworking trades not elsewhere classified	Apprentices – printing trades	Apprentices – other specified trades	Apprentices – trade not specified	Asbestos and insulation workers	Attendants – auto service and parking	Blasters and powdermen	Boatmen, canalmen, and lock keepers	Brakemen – railroad	Bus drivers	Chainmen, rodmen, and axmen – surveying
	Ba3039	Ba3040	Ba3041	Ba3042	Ba3043	Ba3044	Ba3045	Ba3046	Ba3047	Ba3048	Ba3049	Ba3050	Ba3051	Ba3052	Ba3053
Year	Hundred	Hundred	Hundred	Hundred	Hundred	Hundred	Hundred	Hundred	Hundred	Hundred	Hundred	Hundred	Hundred	Hundred	Hundred
1860 [2]	0	0	0	0	0	0	0	0	0	0	0	0	0	0	0
1870	0	0	0	0	0	0	0	0	0	0	0	0	0	0	0
1880	0	0	0	0	0	0	1	0	0	0	0	0	0	0	0
1900	0	0	0	0	0	0	0	0	0	0	0	0	0	0	0
1910 [3]	0	0	0	0	0	0	3	0	0	0	0	0	3	0	0
1920	0	0	0	0	0	0	2	0	0	0	0	0	0	0	0
1940	0	0	0	1	0	4	1	0	0	3	1	1	1	0	0
1950	1	0	2	0	0	2	0	0	3	0	0	0	0	(Z)	2
1960	0	0	0	0	0	0	3	0	1	6	0	0	0	7	1
1970	(Z)	(Z)	(Z)	0	0	(Z)	1	0	1	12	(Z)	(Z)	1	43	1
1980	1	0	(Z)	0	(Z)	0	1	0	3	26	1	0	(Z)	220	(Z)
1990	1	0	0	0	(Z)	0	(Z)	0	5	45	1	0	2	392	(Z)

	Operatives and kindred workers													
	Conductors – bus and street railway	Deliverymen and routemen	Dressmakers and seamstresses, except factory	Dyers	Filers, grinders, and polishers – metal	Fruit, nut, vegetable graders, packers, not factory	Furnacemen, smeltermen, and pourers	Heaters – metal	Laundry and dry cleaning operatives	Meat cutters, except slaughter and packing houses	Milliners	Mine operatives and laborers	Motormen, mine, factory, logging camp, and so forth	Motormen, street, subway, and elevated railway
	Ba3054	Ba3055	Ba3056	Ba3057	Ba3058	Ba3059	Ba3060	Ba3061	Ba3062	Ba3063	Ba3064	Ba3065	Ba3066	Ba3067
Year	Hundred	Hundred	Hundred	Hundred	Hundred	Hundred	Hundred	Hundred	Hundred	Hundred	Hundred	Hundred	Hundred	Hundred
1860 [2]	0	0	40	0	0	0	0	0	0	0	0	0	0	0
1870	0	0	64	0	0	0	0	0	3	0	0	0	0	0
1880	0	1	103	0	0	0	0	0	214	0	0	0	0	0
1900	0	0	144	0	0	0	0	0	8	0	8	0	0	0
1910 [3]	0	5	365	0	0	0	3	0	134	0	8	0	0	0
1920	0	2	318	0	0	0	0	0	268	2	8	2	0	0
1940	0	3	117	0	3	12	0	1	347	0	2	3	0	0
1950	0	5	115	1	6	19	2	6	992	1	16	0	0	0
1960	0	9	94	0	2	11	0	1	1,031	7	1	2	1	0
1970	1	17	111	3	46	20	5	(Z)	908	23	3	7	0	0
1980	0	48	161	0	72	0	0	0	604	99	0	15	0	0
1990	0	11	177	0	33	0	0	0	645	157	0	11	0	0

	Operatives and kindred workers													
	Oilers and greasers, except auto	Painters, except construction or maintenance	Photographic process workers	Power station operators	Sailors and deckhands	Sawyers	Spinners – textile	Stationary firemen	Switchmen – railroad	Taxicab drivers and chauffeurs	Truck and tractor drivers	Weavers – textile	Welders and flame cutters	Operatives and kindred workers not elsewhere classified
	Ba3068	Ba3069	Ba3070	Ba3071	Ba3072	Ba3073	Ba3074	Ba3075	Ba3076	Ba3077	Ba3078	Ba3079	Ba3080	Ba3081
Year	Hundred	Hundred	Hundred	Hundred	Hundred	Hundred	Hundred	Hundred	Hundred	Hundred	Hundred	Hundred	Hundred	Hundred
1860 [2]	0	0	0	0	0	0	6	0	0	0	0	4	0	4
1870	0	0	0	0	0	0	1	0	0	0	0	0	0	22
1880	0	0	0	0	0	0	2	0	0	0	0	2	0	32
1900	0	0	0	0	0	0	0	0	0	0	0	0	0	30
1910 [3]	0	0	0	0	3	0	0	3	0	0	5	30	0	156
1920	0	2	0	0	0	0	2	0	2	0	0	22	0	333
1940	0	1	2	2	1	0	0	1	0	0	18	0	1	680
1950	0	14	7	0	3	4	3	6	0	3	13	17	2	1,617
1960	0	16	7	0	0	2	2	0	0	9	10	6	8	2,091
1970	1	30	26	(Z)	2	11	0	8	(Z)	17	36	21	39	4,668
1980	2	52	50	2	2	18	0	10	(Z)	36	62	113	70	6,904
1990	2	48	58	5	1	19	0	10	2	48	218	99	52	6,956

(Z) Fewer than 50.

[1] Data pertain to noninstitutionalized civilians age 16 and older who reported an occupation; employed persons only beginning 1940.

[2] Excludes slaves.

[3] The wording of the 1910 Census occupation question elicited more female occupation responses than in surrounding censuses, especially in agriculture.

Source

See the source for Table Ba1159–1395.

Documentation

See the text for Table Ba1159–1395.

TABLE Ba3082–3125 Detailed occupations – nonwhite females: 1860–1990[1] [Part 2]

Contributed by Matthew Sobek

	Service workers, private household				Service workers, not household										
	Total	Housekeepers – private household	Laundresses – private household	Private household workers not elsewhere classified	Total	Attendants – hospital and other institution	Attendants – professional and personal service not elsewhere classified	Attendants – recreation and amusement	Barbers, beauticians, and manicurists	Bartenders	Bootblacks	Boarding and lodging house keepers	Charwomen and cleaners	Cooks, except private household	Counter and fountain workers
	Ba3082	Ba3083	Ba3084	Ba3085	Ba3086	Ba3087	Ba3088	Ba3089	Ba3090	Ba3091	Ba3092	Ba3093	Ba3094	Ba3095	Ba3096
Year	Hundred	Hundred	Hundred	Hundred	Hundred	Hundred	Hundred	Hundred	Hundred	Hundred	Hundred	Hundred	Hundred	Hundred	Hundred
1860 [2]	384	0	140	244	18	0	1	0	2	0	0	4	3	0	0
1870	2,431	1	343	2,087	78	0	33	0	5	0	0	0	0	5	0
1880	2,860	48	538	2,274	103	0	13	0	4	0	0	3	0	13	0
1900	3,711	83	8	3,620	2,231	0	0	0	23	0	0	53	0	8	0
1910 [3]	7,741	126	3,562	4,053	549	0	5	0	28	0	0	111	43	0	0
1920	6,356	114	2,895	3,347	1,270	4	37	0	97	0	2	81	75	256	2
1940	9,125	472	1,508	7,145	1,619	33	13	13	163	5	2	45	80	309	0
1950	7,964	351	483	7,130	3,718	238	129	5	262	21	4	15	206	589	58
1960	8,933	436	199	8,297	5,388	656	171	2	341	15	0	21	311	768	125
1970	6,089	416	48	5,625	8,854	1,586	276	13	394	17	1	4	949	1,172	123
1980	2,487	267	6	2,214	13,624	3,309	1,208	70	457	61	0	0	1,762	1,825	159
1990	1,471	117	3	1,350	17,342	4,802	1,472	172	787	73	0	0	1,699	2,280	189

	Service workers, not household														
	Elevator operators	Firemen (fire protection)	Guards, watchmen, and doorkeepers	Housekeepers and stewards, except household	Janitors and sextons	Marshals and constables	Midwives	Policemen and detectives	Porters	Practical nurses	Sheriffs and bailiffs	Ushers – recreation and amusement	Waiters and waitresses	Watchmen (crossing) and bridge tenders	Service workers (not private household) not elsewhere classified
	Ba3097	Ba3098	Ba3099	Ba3100	Ba3101	Ba3102	Ba3103	Ba3104	Ba3105	Ba3106	Ba3107	Ba3108	Ba3109	Ba3110	Ba3111
Year	Hundred	Hundred	Hundred	Hundred	Hundred	Hundred	Hundred	Hundred	Hundred	Hundred	Hundred	Hundred	Hundred	Hundred	Hundred
1860 [2]	0	0	0	1	0	0	1	0	0	4	0	0	1	0	1
1870	0	0	0	2	1	0	2	0	0	25	0	0	4	0	1
1880	0	0	0	0	0	0	7	0	0	52	0	0	7	0	4
1900	8	0	0	23	0	0	0	0	0	0	0	0	23	0	2,095
1910 [3]	0	0	0	0	33	0	10	0	5	219	0	0	93	0	3
1920	24	2	2	16	47	0	18	0	0	166	0	4	120	0	316
1940	29	0	2	37	49	0	0	0	5	88	0	1	158	0	587
1950	120	0	7	84	166	0	10	1	28	148	0	1	431	1	1,196
1960	105	0	7	132	200	0	6	8	11	309	1	2	509	15	1,675
1970	44	1	29	115	422	(Z)	2	18	1	517	2	3	588	34	2,542
1980	21	2	210	66	1,505	0	0	56	5	833	12	10	836	53	1,164
1990	8	9	470	115	1,976	0	0	186	11	838	44	15	880	65	1,250

	Farm laborers					Laborers								
	Total	Farm foremen	Farm laborers, wage workers	Farm laborers, unpaid family workers	Farm service laborers, self-employed	Total	Fishermen and oystermen	Garage laborers, car washers, and greasers	Gardeners, except farm, and groundskeepers	Longshoremen and stevedores	Lumbermen, raftsmen, and woodchoppers	Teamsters	Laborers not elsewhere classified	Unknown occupation
	Ba3112	Ba3113	Ba3114	Ba3115	Ba3116	Ba3117	Ba3118	Ba3119	Ba3120	Ba3121	Ba3122	Ba3123	Ba3124	Ba3125
Year	Hundred	Hundred	Hundred	Hundred	Hundred	Hundred	Hundred	Hundred	Hundred	Hundred	Hundred	Hundred	Hundred	Hundred
1860 [2]	26	0	26	0	0	20	1	0	1	0	0	0	18	—
1870	2,602	0	2,602	0	0	216	0	0	2	0	0	0	214	—
1880	2,973	0	2,973	0	0	1,028	2	0	2	0	2	0	1,022	—
1900	3,544	0	1,708	1,837	0	736	0	0	0	0	0	0	736	—
1910 [3]	7,680	3	7,678	0	0	224	0	0	0	3	0	0	222	—
1920	4,287	0	1,718	2,568	0	416	0	0	0	4	0	4	408	—
1940	2,188	0	741	1,447	0	158	1	2	8	3	1	0	143	131
1950	1,400	1	657	741	0	337	10	57	8	1	2	1	259	100
1960	728	0	581	147	0	246	0	13	6	1	4	1	221	2,050
1970	409	4	385	19	1	511	3	0	21	3	6	(Z)	478	—
1980	244	17	227	0	0	1,045	5	0	38	1	6	0	994	—
1990	196	9	188	0	0	1,219	3	0	52	(Z)	6	0	1,157	—

(Z) Fewer than 50.

[1] Data pertain to noninstitutionalized civilians age 16 and older who reported an occupation; employed persons only beginning 1940.

[2] Excludes slaves.

[3] The wording of the 1910 Census occupation question elicited more female occupation responses than in surrounding censuses, especially in agriculture.

Source

See the source for Table Ba1159–1395.

Documentation

See the text for Table Ba1159–1395.

TABLE Ba3126–3362 Detailed occupations – native-born persons: 1850–1990[1] [Part 1]

Contributed by Matthew Sobek

Year	Total	Professional, technical, and kindred workers: Total	Accountants and auditors	Actors and actresses	Airplane pilots and navigators	Architects	Artists and art teachers	Athletes	Authors	Chemists	Chiropractors	Clergymen	College presidents and deans	College professors and instructors: Agricultural sciences	College professors and instructors: Biological sciences
	Ba3126	Ba3127	Ba3128	Ba3129	Ba3130	Ba3131	Ba3132	Ba3133	Ba3134	Ba3135	Ba3136	Ba3137	Ba3138	Ba3139	Ba3140
	Hundred	Hundred	Hundred	Hundred	Hundred	Hundred	Hundred	Hundred	Hundred	Hundred	Hundred	Hundred	Hundred	Hundred	Hundred
1850 [2, 3]	43,300	1,434	7	4	0	2	17	2	1	7	0	259	0	0	0
1860 [2]	60,663	2,652	15	2	0	10	36	5	4	2	0	302	4	0	0
1870	90,677	3,203	12	6	0	14	30	0	6	13	0	368	0	0	0
1880	128,101	5,363	21	49	0	23	69	6	7	14	0	527	4	0	0
1900	216,423	10,245	68	144	0	46	182	30	30	61	0	744	76	0	0
1910	282,676	14,889	0	252	0	126	262	0	10	121	0	992	0	0	0
1920	324,656	20,602	1,132	207	8	144	266	43	61	276	30	1,002	10	4	0
1940	419,066	31,022	0	121	54	173	465	76	124	491	90	1,113	0	0	0
1950	516,556	46,826	3,556	130	148	230	695	78	128	736	119	1,556	51	50	57
1960	593,809	67,899	4,511	75	269	261	907	30	248	713	130	1,876	71	27	75
1970	715,676	111,322	6,598	88	477	495	919	0	234	947	131	2,039	381	46	186
1980	900,675	157,806	9,080	0	701	947	1,330	0	410	841	199	2,642	0	32	87
1990	1,032,175	213,831	13,863	0	1,004	1,312	1,839	0	961	1,108	421	2,943	0	9	54

Professional, technical, and kindred workers

Year	College professors and instructors: Chemistry	Economics	Engineering	Geology and geophysics	Mathematics	Medical sciences	Physics	Psychology	Statistics	Natural sciences not elsewhere classified	Social sciences not elsewhere classified	Nonscientific subjects	Subject not specified	Dancers and dancing teachers	Dentists
	Ba3141	Ba3142	Ba3143	Ba3144	Ba3145	Ba3146	Ba3147	Ba3148	Ba3149	Ba3150	Ba3151	Ba3152	Ba3153	Ba3154	Ba3155
	Hundred	Hundred	Hundred	Hundred	Hundred	Hundred	Hundred	Hundred	Hundred	Hundred	Hundred	Hundred	Hundred	Hundred	Hundred
1850 [2, 3]	0	0	0	0	1	0	0	0	0	0	0	3	6	1	19
1860 [2]	0	0	0	0	2	1	0	0	0	0	0	7	6	7	58
1870	0	0	0	2	2	0	0	0	0	0	0	2	6	2	63
1880	1	0	0	1	2	0	0	0	0	0	0	6	10	1	113
1900	0	0	0	0	0	0	0	0	0	0	0	0	0	15	228
1910	0	0	0	0	0	0	0	0	0	0	0	0	237	0	395
1920	8	0	2	0	2	4	0	0	0	2	8	2	183	43	499
1940	0	0	0	0	0	0	0	0	0	0	0	0	668	117	647
1950	64	33	82	8	48	22	40	35	4	1	182	213	235	128	667
1960	61	35	87	15	86	52	46	25	1	3	235	255	472	177	770
1970	131	86	137	0	225	248	117	117	0	39	312	820	1,396	53	868
1980	71	43	97	0	165	256	45	52	0	21	120	450	3,777	102	1,181
1990	43	30	63	0	176	165	28	37	0	10	68	394	5,154	186	1,401

	Professional, technical, and kindred workers														
	Designers	Dietitians and nutritionists	Draftsmen	Editors and reporters	Engineers, aeronautical	Engineers, chemical	Engineers, civil	Engineers, electrical	Engineers, industrial	Engineers, mechanical	Engineers, metallurgical, metallurgists	Engineers, mining	Engineers not elsewhere classified	Entertainers not elsewhere classified	Farm and home management advisors
	Ba3156	Ba3157	Ba3158	Ba3159	Ba3160	Ba3161	Ba3162	Ba3163	Ba3164	Ba3165	Ba3166	Ba3167	Ba3168	Ba3169	Ba3170
Year	Hundred	Hundred	Hundred	Hundred	Hundred	Hundred	Hundred	Hundred	Hundred	Hundred	Hundred	Hundred	Hundred	Hundred	Hundred
1850 [2, 3]	1	0	1	21	0	0	5	0	0	1	0	0	0	7	0
1860 [2]	0	0	0	32	0	0	20	0	0	0	0	2	0	5	2
1870	0	0	6	36	0	0	29	0	0	0	0	8	0	12	0
1880	4	0	16	100	0	0	53	0	0	4	0	9	0	29	0
1900	30	0	99	243	0	0	76	30	0	99	0	30	0	61	0
1910	60	0	280	320	0	0	416	0	0	116	0	81	0	196	0
1920	95	16	481	339	2	22	588	252	22	246	10	55	97	47	20
1940	171	0	801	543	0	98	769	490	115	678	102	0	0	57	118
1950	325	210	1,074	832	176	300	1,198	1,015	443	1,042	119	106	698	135	139
1960	580	244	1,980	1,235	486	377	1,486	1,652	967	1,416	163	109	1,351	88	129
1970	932	376	2,599	2,089	595	472	1,578	2,592	1,739	1,629	147	145	2,232	542	130
1980	2,934	599	2,881	2,955	761	500	1,771	2,877	2,867	1,876	213	304	2,613	885	0
1990	5,124	791	2,791	3,940	1,207	543	2,070	3,902	4,105	1,697	159	278	3,318	1,383	0

	Professional, technical, and kindred workers														
								Natural scientists not elsewhere classified							
	Foresters and conservationists	Funeral directors and embalmers	Lawyers and judges	Librarians	Musicians and music teachers	Nurses, professional	Nurses, student professional	Agricultural scientists	Biological scientists	Geologists and geophysicists	Mathematicians	Physicists	Miscellaneous natural scientists	Optometrists	Osteopaths
	Ba3171	Ba3172	Ba3173	Ba3174	Ba3175	Ba3176	Ba3177	Ba3178	Ba3179	Ba3180	Ba3181	Ba3182	Ba3183	Ba3184	Ba3185
Year	Hundred	Hundred	Hundred	Hundred	Hundred	Hundred	Hundred	Hundred	Hundred	Hundred	Hundred	Hundred	Hundred	Hundred	Hundred
1850 [2, 3]	0	6	230	0	16	0	0	0	0	0	0	0	0	0	0
1860 [2]	0	8	316	2	58	2	0	0	1	0	0	0	0	0	0
1870	0	20	420	4	96	0	0	0	2	0	0	0	0	0	0
1880	0	48	607	7	243	1	0	0	1	2	0	0	0	0	0
1900	8	129	949	61	698	76	0	0	0	0	0	8	8	0	0
1910	30	141	1,058	0	1,161	705	0	0	0	0	0	0	0	0	0
1920	61	207	1,146	150	1,063	1,146	156	6	20	20	0	2	0	26	26
1940	0	326	1,590	332	1,130	2,984	0	0	0	0	0	0	0	113	66
1950	257	368	1,662	582	1,462	3,746	640	51	85	105	20	56	20	161	67
1960	320	361	1,991	815	1,744	5,409	562	77	115	194	66	124	28	162	41
1970	393	403	2,682	1,255	2,539	8,530	174	123	253	216	72	194	11	168	0
1980	526	396	5,066	1,870	4,700	12,892	0	231	565	434	57	274	81	234	0
1990	475	447	7,303	2,320	7,135	19,122	0	303	709	477	49	321	168	257	0

Notes appear at end of table

(continued)

TABLE Ba3126–3362 Detailed occupations – native-born persons: 1850–1990 [Part 1] *Continued*

	Professional, technical, and kindred workers														
									Social scientists						
	Personnel and labor-relations workers	Pharmacists	Photographers	Physicians and surgeons	Radio operators	Recreation and group workers	Religious workers	Social and welfare workers, except group	Economists	Psychologists	Statisticians and actuaries	Miscellaneous social scientists	Sports instructors and officials	Surveyors	Teachers not elsewhere classified
	Ba3186	Ba3187	Ba3188	Ba3189	Ba3190	Ba3191	Ba3192	Ba3193	Ba3194	Ba3195	Ba3196	Ba3197	Ba3198	Ba3199	Ba3200
Year	Hundred	Hundred	Hundred	Hundred	Hundred	Hundred	Hundred	Hundred	Hundred	Hundred	Hundred	Hundred	Hundred	Hundred	Hundred
1850 [2, 3]	0	45	6	397	0	0	1	0	0	0	0	0	0	9	297
1860 [2]	0	75	40	555	0	0	4	0	0	0	0	0	0	24	1,038
1870	0	141	44	592	0	0	8	4	0	0	0	0	11	30	1,173
1880	0	237	92	807	0	0	28	0	0	0	0	0	0	35	2,130
1900	0	463	235	1,123	0	0	68	0	0	0	0	15	8	61	3,863
1910	0	0	257	1,368	0	0	154	5	0	0	0	0	0	0	5,796
1920	22	676	252	1,256	18	45	223	105	2	2	28	2	89	83	7,167
1940	0	680	296	1,532	84	0	243	671	0	0	0	0	224	166	10,157
1950	516	873	498	1,687	186	153	354	794	87	41	215	28	422	262	11,084
1960	959	893	458	1,899	256	375	515	940	160	125	193	28	700	413	16,417
1970	2,812	1,028	593	2,253	522	482	314	2,066	589	271	250	117	617	578	26,871
1980	5,905	1,334	843	3,352	1,050	323	447	4,209	860	846	366	285	535	750	35,740
1990	7,082	1,636	1,244	4,510	734	433	889	5,953	1,342	1,753	424	449	763	936	42,540

	Professional, technical, and kindred workers						Farmers			Managers, officials, and proprietors					
	Technicians – medical and dental	Technicians – testing	Technicians not elsewhere classified	Therapists and healers not elsewhere classified	Veterinarians	Professional, technical, and kindred workers not elsewhere classified	Total	Farmers – owners and tenants	Farm managers	Total	Buyers and department heads – store	Buyers and shippers – farm products	Conductors – railroad	Credit men	Floormen and floor managers – store
	Ba3201	Ba3202	Ba3203	Ba3204	Ba3205	Ba3206	Ba3207	Ba3208	Ba3209	Ba3210	Ba3211	Ba3212	Ba3213	Ba3214	Ba3215
Year	Hundred	Hundred	Hundred	Hundred	Hundred	Hundred	Hundred	Hundred	Hundred	Hundred	Hundred	Hundred	Hundred	Hundred	Hundred
1850 [2, 3]	0	0	0	0	0	62	22,126	22,119	7	1,994	0	3	3	0	0
1860 [2]	0	0	0	1	0	6	23,756	23,702	54	3,056	0	47	50	0	0
1870	0	0	1	2	4	33	27,091	27,069	22	3,891	0	101	77	0	0
1880	0	0	0	6	21	30	38,147	38,123	24	5,291	1	186	156	0	0
1900	0	0	8	53	83	3 8	50,231	50,102	129	11,459	38	478	349	0	15
1910	0	0	0	58	106	186	53,638	53,638	0	17,960	0	0	557	0	139
1920	34	63	10	30	148	87	60,840	59,984	856	20,519	254	521	779	77	49
1940	0	549	74	148	105	1,473	48,753	48,439	314	31,190	619	337	447	295	89
1950	733	778	294	218	162	1,053	41,607	41,302	305	44,440	1,262	264	526	349	91
1960	1,262	2,389	913	303	158	2,760	23,939	23,707	232	49,449	2,169	191	452	484	99
1970	2,499	3,112	1,491	763	182	12,013	13,744	13,182	562	56,727	5,968	196	383	576	0
1980	5,164	7,349	2,396	1,889	323	9,826	12,598	11,280	1,318	94,356	7,933	179	442	0	0
1990	8,737	8,541	3,378	3,107	452	17,263	10,053	7,936	2,117	134,234	7,556	148	347	0	0

	Managers, officials, and proprietors								Clerical and kindred workers						
	Inspectors – public administration	Managers and superintendents – building	Officers, pilots, pursers, and engineers – ship	Officials and administrators not elsewhere classified – public administration	Officials – lodge, society, union, and so forth	Postmasters	Purchasing agents and buyers not elsewhere classified	Managers, officials, and proprietors not elsewhere classified	Total	Agents not elsewhere classified	Attendants and assistants – library	Attendants – physician's and dentist's office	Baggagemen – transportation	Bank tellers	Bookkeepers
	Ba3216	Ba3217	Ba3218	Ba3219	Ba3220	Ba3221	Ba3222	Ba3223	Ba3224	Ba3225	Ba3226	Ba3227	Ba3228	Ba3229	Ba3230
Year	Hundred	Hundred	Hundred	Hundred	Hundred	Hundred	Hundred	Hundred	Hundred	Hundred	Hundred	Hundred	Hundred	Hundred	Hundred
1850 [2,3]	10	20	66	65	0	19	0	1,808	115	20	0	1	7	4	18
1860 [2]	6	32	130	105	0	42	0	2,643	376	40	0	0	14	8	113
1870	12	8	142	126	0	30	0	3,394	1,077	26	10	0	14	8	235
1880	32	13	144	241	9	58	9	4,442	2,247	166	0	0	43	13	529
1900	53	0	137	197	23	212	0	9,957	9,213	266	15	0	61	61	2,064
1910	0	0	171	1,045	48	0	0	16,000	17,529	476	0	0	126	0	4,247
1920	189	150	308	469	39	286	189	17,210	30,435	308	26	112	103	209	4,885
1940	406	539	232	1,232	190	369	383	26,050	46,350	931	324	358	53	0	8,127
1950	548	535	407	1,233	226	355	630	38,014	67,961	1,279	144	391	71	645	7,161
1960	687	398	304	1,849	290	373	991	41,164	87,838	1,516	318	718	53	1,264	8,817
1970	949	747	217	2,606	464	345	1,551	42,727	130,113	212	1,165	1,950	0	2,381	14,520
1980	1,437	1,753	346	3,490	0	304	2,491	75,981	176,095	0	1,291	3,997	0	4,621	17,154
1990	1,476	3,626	343	8,327	0	398	3,355	108,657	197,742	0	1,322	3,510	0	4,412	17,042

	Clerical and kindred workers													
	Cashiers	Collectors, bill and account	Dispatchers and starters – vehicle	Express messengers and railway mail clerks	Mail carriers	Messengers and office boys	Office machine operators	Shipping and receiving clerks	Stenographers, typists, and secretaries	Telegraph messengers	Telegraph operators	Telephone operators	Ticket, station, and express agents	Clerical and kindred workers not elsewhere classified
	Ba3231	Ba3232	Ba3233	Ba3234	Ba3235	Ba3236	Ba3237	Ba3238	Ba3239	Ba3240	Ba3241	Ba3242	Ba3243	Ba3244
Year	Hundred	Hundred	Hundred	Hundred	Hundred	Hundred	Hundred	Hundred	Hundred	Hundred	Hundred	Hundred	Hundred	Hundred
1850 [2,3]	1	9	0	0	8	2	0	2	0	1	5	0	10	26
1860 [2]	4	24	0	8	20	8	0	2	2	0	8	0	48	76
1870	6	14	2	22	14	16	0	12	0	1	47	0	105	544
1880	23	26	10	16	75	43	0	64	10	4	144	10	193	881
1900	258	167	15	68	190	235	8	182	941	30	562	197	288	3,605
1910	0	277	0	174	773	494	0	607	2,877	25	662	882	262	5,647
1920	805	272	22	256	933	373	124	1,031	6,619	53	761	1,753	505	11,285
1940	0	353	0	233	1,182	494	694	2,025	10,599	123	486	1,903	400	18,065
1950	2,221	203	322	190	1,622	603	1,449	2,640	15,678	66	343	3,676	568	28,689
1960	4,495	305	539	69	1,858	514	2,869	2,512	21,557	34	184	3,420	674	36,123
1970	7,756	489	583	0	2,449	449	5,129	3,796	36,307	20	122	3,977	902	47,907
1980	15,949	787	911	0	2,466	740	8,642	5,895	44,169	0	75	3,436	886	65,076
1990	22,668	1,438	1,862	0	3,013	1,182	12,462	7,074	43,100	0	0	2,142	2,245	74,270

Notes appear at end of table

(continued)

TABLE Ba3126–3362 Detailed occupations – native-born persons: 1850–1990 [Part 1] *Continued*

	Sales workers										Craft workers, foremen, and kindred workers				
	Total	Advertising agents and salesmen	Auctioneers	Demonstrators	Hucksters and peddlers	Insurance agents and brokers	Newsboys	Real estate agents and brokers	Stock and bond salesmen	Salesmen and sales clerks not elsewhere classified	Total	Bakers	Blacksmiths	Bookbinders	Boilermakers
	Ba3245	Ba3246	Ba3247	Ba3248	Ba3249	Ba3250	Ba3251	Ba3252	Ba3253	Ba3254	Ba3255	Ba3256	Ba3257	Ba3258	Ba3259
Year	Hundred	Hundred	Hundred	Hundred	Hundred	Hundred	Hundred	Hundred	Hundred	Hundred	Hundred	Hundred	Hundred	Hundred	Hundred
1850 [2, 3]	915	0	6	0	65	6	5	3	0	830	6,647	54	772	23	6
1860 [2]	1,446	0	18	0	102	8	2	14	0	1,301	7,823	49	833	40	4
1870	2,271	4	11	0	197	120	14	74	0	1,850	8,971	88	975	46	29
1880	3,638	4	25	0	325	116	14	121	3	3,030	11,379	151	1,239	76	57
1900	8,135	23	8	0	379	546	23	440	0	6,716	22,092	319	1,480	296	220
1910	13,975	0	25	33	0	665	88	1,071	159	11,935	29,595	270	1,725	0	295
1920	17,150	142	47	41	166	1,033	57	1,069	156	14,439	42,502	426	1,596	193	519
1940	26,731	332	66	81	326	2,175	368	1,021	222	22,140	44,983	849	642	0	245
1950	36,801	279	136	164	175	2,882	415	1,413	129	31,210	70,428	839	353	256	308
1960	42,646	328	39	250	458	4,151	762	1,829	293	34,536	80,334	840	179	240	192
1970	52,174	610	48	372	1,133	5,287	601	2,452	914	40,757	97,229	880	156	307	270
1980	61,678	1,056	64	108	1,948	7,019	929	6,064	1,225	43,266	108,938	977	0	257	317
1990	72,675	1,575	75	374	1,934	9,915	965	7,115	2,654	48,069	108,681	1,172	0	243	199

	Craft workers, foremen, and kindred workers														
	Brickmasons, stonemasons, and tile setters	Cabinetmakers	Carpenters	Cement and concrete finishers	Compositors and typesetters	Cranemen, derrickmen, and hoistmen	Decorators and window dressers	Electricians	Electrotypers and stereotypers	Engravers, except photoengravers	Excavating, grading, and road machinery operators	Foremen not elsewhere classified	Forgemen and hammermen	Furriers	Glaziers
	Ba3260	Ba3261	Ba3262	Ba3263	Ba3264	Ba3265	Ba3266	Ba3267	Ba3268	Ba3269	Ba3270	Ba3271	Ba3272	Ba3273	Ba3274
Year	Hundred	Hundred	Hundred	Hundred	Hundred	Hundred	Hundred	Hundred	Hundred	Hundred	Hundred	Hundred	Hundred	Hundred	Hundred
1850 [2, 3]	354	278	1,884	1	120	0	0	0	0	11	2	18	10	1	1
1860 [2]	423	219	2,368	0	156	0	0	0	0	12	4	214	9	8	0
1870	551	190	2,734	0	208	2	2	0	2	17	5	80	8	8	0
1880	563	176	2,903	4	463	0	0	4	9	32	2	138	4	11	2
1900	1,070	182	4,652	0	979	0	0	402	23	30	0	903	0	8	15
1910	1,164	189	5,909	0	1,091	0	38	1,106	58	118	0	2,219	60	0	0
1920	819	239	6,467	57	1,217	221	65	1,824	41	108	83	3,733	81	30	14
1940	864	452	5,057	183	1,455	959	285	1,757	81	61	0	5,192	0	71	99
1950	1,305	557	8,033	291	1,631	898	387	2,915	181	97	1,047	7,563	139	83	138
1960	1,637	509	7,536	361	1,685	1,116	471	3,196	89	106	1,918	10,959	101	26	152
1970	1,707	550	7,721	593	1,431	1,433	645	4,275	66	72	3,016	14,964	142	14	235
1980	1,771	626	10,388	517	644	1,423	0	5,733	0	128	3,322	20,342	130	59	292
1990	1,978	601	11,094	536	666	904	0	6,117	0	146	3,516	15,937	148	100	401

Craft workers, foremen, and kindred workers

Year	Heat treaters, annealers, temperers	Inspectors, scalers, and graders – log and lumber	Inspectors not elsewhere classified	Jewelers, watchmakers, goldsmiths, silversmiths	Job setters – metal	Linemen and servicemen	Locomotive engineers	Locomotive firemen	Loom fixers	Machinists	Mechanics and repairmen – airplane	Mechanics and repairmen – automobile	Mechanics and repairmen – office machine	Mechanics and repairmen – radio and television	Mechanics and repairmen – railroad and car shop
	Ba3275	Ba3276	Ba3277	Ba3278	Ba3279	Ba3280	Ba3281	Ba3282	Ba3283	Ba3284	Ba3285	Ba3286	Ba3287	Ba3288	Ba3289
	Hundred	Hundred	Hundred	Hundred	Hundred	Hundred	Hundred	Hundred	Hundred	Hundred	Hundred	Hundred	Hundred	Hundred	Hundred
1850 [2,3]	0	1	5	81	0	0	5	0	0	181	0	0	0	0	1
1860 [2]	0	2	2	82	0	0	14	4	0	262	0	0	0	0	0
1870	0	9	5	94	0	0	102	64	0	353	0	0	0	0	12
1880	2	3	17	144	0	7	137	93	3	544	0	0	0	0	12
1900	0	46	152	266	0	53	478	455	30	1,837	0	0	0	0	99
1910	8	0	406	171	0	232	937	645	63	3,423	0	0	0	0	0
1920	16	101	769	235	18	578	1,022	856	89	6,382	6	1,789	36	2	531
1940	106	154	684	359	0	1,043	616	428	161	3,794	215	3,436	0	0	306
1950	152	173	915	394	211	2,050	732	547	282	4,371	686	6,416	179	734	452
1960	188	165	934	297	343	2,674	562	349	266	4,468	1,094	6,348	279	1,028	374
1970	193	171	1,108	280	783	3,814	468	124	203	3,375	1,407	8,587	682	1,285	528
1980	214	0	470	574	496	4,020	688	0	0	4,492	1,006	11,476	778	1,509	0
1990	164	0	619	639	239	3,389	429	0	0	4,810	1,469	12,175	1,151	1,517	0

Craft workers, foremen, and kindred workers

Year	Mechanics and repairmen not elsewhere classified	Millers – grain, flour, feed, and so forth	Millwrights	Molders – metal	Motion picture projectionists	Opticians and lens grinders and polishers	Painters – construction and maintenance	Paperhangers	Pattern and model makers, except paper	Photoengravers and lithographers	Piano and organ tuners and repairmen	Plasterers	Plumbers and pipe fitters	Pressmen and plate printers – printing	Rollers and roll hands – metal
	Ba3290	Ba3291	Ba3292	Ba3293	Ba3294	Ba3295	Ba3296	Ba3297	Ba3298	Ba3299	Ba3300	Ba3301	Ba3302	Ba3303	Ba3304
	Hundred	Hundred	Hundred	Hundred	Hundred	Hundred	Hundred	Hundred	Hundred	Hundred	Hundred	Hundred	Hundred	Hundred	Hundred
1850 [2,3]	245	283	80	61	0	2	152	4	15	2	0	74	10	0	9
1860 [2]	283	340	50	87	0	0	360	10	16	2	2	102	33	0	12
1870	175	333	98	144	0	3	477	17	26	2	4	121	82	0	32
1880	227	358	74	258	0	5	832	33	43	19	12	203	127	5	21
1900	402	281	99	584	0	30	1,723	197	99	68	15	296	774	235	0
1910	297	169	0	718	0	0	2,086	189	169	58	65	317	1,267	227	96
1920	947	203	276	716	83	112	2,000	140	233	108	57	256	1,793	221	185
1940	3,557	144	310	503	263	121	2,711	275	252	203	85	356	1,539	339	210
1950	7,565	112	501	476	237	187	3,506	221	474	276	123	572	2,529	543	285
1960	11,533	92	561	470	159	173	3,316	92	372	258	47	416	2,922	703	267
1970	10,399	70	765	494	153	252	3,199	0	347	298	62	254	3,488	1,426	184
1980	14,226	0	1,192	304	126	407	3,774	0	295	234	0	227	4,422	2,615	166
1990	14,599	0	858	166	91	645	4,754	0	244	438	0	283	4,335	3,028	110

Notes appear at end of table

(continued)

TABLE Ba3126–3362 Detailed occupations – native-born persons: 1850–1990 [Part 1] *Continued*

	Craft workers, foremen, and kindred workers										Operatives and kindred workers				
	Roofers and slaters	Shoemakers and repairers, except factory	Stationary engineers	Stonecutters and stone carvers	Structural metal workers	Tailors and tailoresses	Tinsmiths, coppersmiths, sheet metal workers	Toolmakers, die makers, and setters	Upholsterers	Craftsmen and kindred workers not elsewhere classified	Total	Apprentice auto mechanics	Apprentice bricklayers and masons	Apprentice carpenters	Apprentice electricians
	Ba3305	Ba3306	Ba3307	Ba3308	Ba3309	Ba3310	Ba3311	Ba3312	Ba3313	Ba3314	Ba3315	Ba3316	Ba3317	Ba3318	Ba3319
Year	Hundred	Hundred	Hundred	Hundred	Hundred	Hundred	Hundred	Hundred	Hundred	Hundred	Hundred	Hundred	Hundred	Hundred	Hundred
1850 [2, 3]	0	1,027	75	64	0	275	77	4	15	365	3,332	0	0	3	0
1860 [2]	8	776	137	60	2	384	116	4	10	321	6,132	0	2	74	0
1870	23	644	205	81	0	374	169	4	16	354	9,133	0	23	68	0
1880	26	531	459	159	0	497	278	6	56	358	14,953	0	5	40	0
1900	91	364	1,085	212	15	577	455	0	220	273	26,971	0	0	0	15
1910	106	176	1,736	164	73	579	469	91	116	302	39,852	0	0	0	0
1920	83	256	1,680	130	623	590	538	463	162	483	45,180	24	0	6	37
1940	260	311	1,604	151	331	305	647	657	293	0	73,520	0	0	114	60
1950	472	337	2,013	95	433	548	1,137	1,292	542	639	102,687	59	74	106	111
1960	466	204	2,550	40	529	134	1,300	1,567	492	989	108,383	13	20	52	85
1970	552	670	1,635	61	806	412	1,405	1,693	547	6,570	126,010	31	39	77	199
1980	936	978	1,514	0	931	324	1,403	1,665	551	0	129,060	34	22	79	168
1990	1,423	1,095	1,994	0	728	247	1,453	1,252	580	0	115,237	16	7	38	135

	Operatives and kindred workers														
	Apprentice machinists and toolmakers	Apprentice mechanics, except auto	Apprentice plumbers and pipe fitters	Apprentices – building trades not elsewhere classified	Apprentices – metalworking trades not elsewhere classified	Apprentices – printing trades	Apprentices – other specified trades	Apprentices – trade not specified	Asbestos and insulation workers	Attendants – auto service and parking	Blasters and powdermen	Boatmen, canalmen, and lock keepers	Brakemen – railroad	Bus drivers	Chainmen, rodmen, and axmen – surveying
	Ba3320	Ba3321	Ba3322	Ba3323	Ba3324	Ba3325	Ba3326	Ba3327	Ba3328	Ba3329	Ba3330	Ba3331	Ba3332	Ba3333	Ba3334
Year	Hundred	Hundred	Hundred	Hundred	Hundred	Hundred	Hundred	Hundred	Hundred	Hundred	Hundred	Hundred	Hundred	Hundred	Hundred
1850 [2, 3]	0	0	0	2	0	0	7	19	0	0	0	215	1	36	0
1860 [2]	12	6	6	20	84	18	104	64	0	0	0	214	26	30	0
1870	35	12	8	31	111	19	129	23	0	0	2	191	92	34	0
1880	39	0	10	12	64	16	138	18	0	0	0	175	200	37	0
1900	106	0	30	0	91	15	129	46	0	0	0	83	759	0	8
1910	0	0	0	184	0	0	53	564	0	0	0	48	894	0	0
1920	136	24	53	0	71	53	67	91	22	37	4	28	1,118	85	16
1940	162	0	85	164	0	154	246	116	94	2,183	56	117	683	0	121
1950	166	44	193	53	84	207	137	148	174	2,371	104	126	750	1,500	119
1960	133	39	88	26	46	113	86	100	201	3,392	54	63	565	1,748	88
1970	183	67	136	18	60	84	112	32	244	4,323	73	45	463	2,264	103
1980	144	0	103	0	7	0	41	0	461	3,145	92	0	754	3,588	91
1990	36	0	63	0	9	0	18	0	533	2,490	79	0	310	4,046	40

Year	Operatives and kindred workers													
	Conductors – bus and street railway	Deliverymen and routemen	Dressmakers and seamstresses, except factory	Dyers	Filers, grinders, and polishers – metal	Fruit, nut, vegetable graders, packers, not factory	Furnacemen, smeltermen, and pourers	Heaters – metal	Laundry and dry cleaning operatives	Meat cutters, except slaughter and packing houses	Milliners	Mine operatives and laborers	Motormen, mine, factory, logging camp, and so forth	Motormen, street, subway, and elevated railway
	Ba3335	Ba3336	Ba3337	Ba3338	Ba3339	Ba3340	Ba3341	Ba3342	Ba3343	Ba3344	Ba3345	Ba3346	Ba3347	Ba3348
	Hundred	Hundred	Hundred	Hundred	Hundred	Hundred	Hundred	Hundred	Hundred	Hundred	Hundred	Hundred	Hundred	Hundred
1850 [2,3]	0	3	19	5	2	0	55	1	3	101	5	527	0	1
1860 [2]	4	13	1,080	4	15	0	40	8	2	159	219	446	0	8
1870	6	29	1,119	6	22	0	53	2	30	217	231	603	0	15
1880	17	83	1,829	21	36	0	247	12	319	422	331	1,184	0	66
1900	114	212	3,499	0	212	8	137	30	99	584	751	3,081	0	235
1910	456	1,733	3,363	73	285	38	123	53	768	128	1,116	4,605	0	476
1920	532	1,483	2,363	89	464	105	136	108	1,104	812	521	6,526	77	448
1940	125	3,379	1,204	157	808	304	213	170	1,794	1,043	85	5,764	131	274
1950	95	2,199	1,154	242	1,336	398	484	102	3,853	1,427	140	5,189	225	210
1960	34	3,872	921	159	1,311	164	488	72	3,529	1,570	24	2,811	125	59
1970	85	5,855	752	219	2,269	236	629	65	3,140	1,809	17	2,077	91	0
1980	0	6,465	696	0	2,430	0	0	0	2,296	2,443	0	2,812	0	0
1990	0	1,276	568	0	1,183	0	0	0	2,594	2,131	0	1,827	0	0

Year	Operatives and kindred workers													
	Oilers and greasers, except auto	Painters, except construction or maintenance	Photographic process workers	Power station operators	Sailors and deckhands	Sawyers	Spinners – textile	Stationary firemen	Switchmen – railroad	Taxicab drivers and chauffeurs	Truck and tractor drivers	Weavers – textile	Welders and flame cutters	Operatives and kindred workers not elsewhere classified
	Ba3349	Ba3350	Ba3351	Ba3352	Ba3353	Ba3354	Ba3355	Ba3356	Ba3357	Ba3358	Ba3359	Ba3360	Ba3361	Ba3362
	Hundred	Hundred	Hundred	Hundred	Hundred	Hundred	Hundred	Hundred	Hundred	Hundred	Hundred	Hundred	Hundred	Hundred
1850 [2,3]	0	16	0	0	521	77	33	4	1	5	212	55	0	1,402
1860 [2]	0	48	0	0	402	117	180	22	0	18	327	212	4	2,141
1870	0	62	2	0	404	69	25	28	6	29	714	109	0	4,571
1880	0	140	1	0	502	66	10	97	17	40	1,109	131	2	7,518
1900	23	190	0	0	288	228	379	364	91	379	3,468	820	8	10,488
1910	123	423	0	0	310	368	330	680	524	657	3,446	1,179	0	16,852
1920	199	473	57	37	296	355	546	968	588	1,404	2,383	1,025	227	19,983
1940	312	670	209	299	272	399	0	912	402	0	10,888	0	1,097	38,256
1950	534	1,263	292	221	366	937	734	1,162	628	1,824	12,911	893	2,544	54,796
1960	466	1,252	363	262	266	850	515	800	556	1,460	15,053	587	3,437	60,470
1970	429	1,224	547	182	222	940	0	899	517	1,397	13,358	457	5,047	74,994
1980	399	1,618	759	271	256	890	0	1,364	89	1,487	16,476	633	6,502	72,445
1990	220	1,317	829	358	203	783	0	850	50	1,380	24,760	508	5,249	61,331

[1] Data pertain to noninstitutionalized civilians age 16 and older who reported an occupation; employed persons only beginning 1940.

[2] Excludes slaves.

[3] Excludes women.

Source

See the source for Table Ba1159–1395.

Documentation

See the text for Table Ba1159–1395.

TABLE Ba3363–3406 Detailed occupations – native-born persons: 1850–1990[1] [Part 2]

Contributed by Matthew Sobek

Year	Service workers, private household: Total	Housekeepers – private household	Laundresses – private household	Private household workers not elsewhere classified	Service workers, not household: Total	Attendants – hospital and other institution	Attendants – professional and personal service not elsewhere classified	Attendants – recreation and amusement	Barbers, beauticians, and manicurists	Bartenders	Bootblacks	Boarding and lodging house keepers	Charwomen and cleaners	Cooks, except private household	Counter and fountain workers
	Ba3363	Ba3364	Ba3365	Ba3366	Ba3367	Ba3368	Ba3369	Ba3370	Ba3371	Ba3372	Ba3373	Ba3374	Ba3375	Ba3376	Ba3377
	Hundred	Hundred	Hundred	Hundred	Hundred	Hundred	Hundred	Hundred	Hundred	Hundred	Hundred	Hundred	Hundred	Hundred	Hundred
1850 [2,3]	106	0	1	105	302	0	0	1	63	28	0	17	0	0	0
1860 [2]	2,857	4	204	2,649	568	2	13	0	55	47	2	97	5	2	0
1870	6,401	14	412	5,975	1,005	8	31	0	135	93	2	65	1	26	0
1880	7,972	500	598	6,874	1,851	10	80	3	292	159	10	155	3	67	0
1900	13,645	395	15	13,235	8,355	15	8	0	971	706	53	471	8	99	0
1910	16,711	1,615	4,627	10,469	9,348	0	191	0	1,358	763	40	1,202	202	0	0
1920	11,778	1,438	3,526	6,814	13,178	146	132	38	1,582	128	37	992	158	1,349	63
1940	19,023	3,016	1,830	14,178	28,048	1,036	338	546	3,479	935	128	523	506	2,409	0
1950	12,644	1,235	673	10,736	38,275	1,899	491	517	3,274	1,761	117	222	866	3,721	765
1960	15,130	1,238	383	13,508	48,642	3,633	664	432	4,234	1,531	71	273	1,364	4,856	1,340
1970	10,746	873	110	9,764	77,357	6,808	2,003	642	5,834	1,710	34	61	3,814	7,429	1,379
1980	5,144	489	15	4,639	108,863	11,876	7,148	1,437	5,834	2,657	0	0	5,205	13,658	1,753
1990	3,760	181	14	3,565	127,495	15,019	10,555	2,077	6,974	2,755	0	0	4,900	17,269	1,870

Year	Service workers, not household: Elevator operators	Firemen (fire protection)	Guards, watchmen, and doorkeepers	Housekeepers and stewards, except household	Janitors and sextons	Marshals and constables	Midwives	Policemen and detectives	Porters	Practical nurses	Sheriffs and bailiffs	Ushers – recreation and amusement	Waiters and waitresses	Watchmen (crossing) and bridge tenders	Service workers (not private household) not elsewhere classified
	Ba3378	Ba3379	Ba3380	Ba3381	Ba3382	Ba3383	Ba3384	Ba3385	Ba3386	Ba3387	Ba3388	Ba3389	Ba3390	Ba3391	Ba3392
	Hundred	Hundred	Hundred	Hundred	Hundred	Hundred	Hundred	Hundred	Hundred	Hundred	Hundred	Hundred	Hundred	Hundred	Hundred
1850 [2,3]	0	0	21	7	0	32	0	24	26	6	14	0	39	7	15
1860 [2]	0	2	46	43	5	41	12	24	34	48	21	2	42	14	10
1870	0	6	70	23	41	33	8	81	72	67	37	0	127	31	45
1880	0	11	123	26	44	48	14	102	130	134	62	0	236	39	105
1900	99	121	349	334	372	83	8	281	501	15	61	0	683	53	3,066
1910	131	264	524	0	733	93	15	549	657	1,008	103	0	1,388	0	126
1920	270	479	866	290	1,057	53	32	850	899	911	93	51	1,477	79	1,146
1940	609	707	1,770	781	2,865	93	0	1,384	1,371	829	142	181	4,700	148	2,566
1950	715	1,066	2,178	923	3,814	76	11	1,937	1,448	1,271	186	216	6,149	109	4,543
1960	611	1,297	2,262	1,277	5,350	75	11	2,547	1,239	1,930	253	114	7,492	239	5,546
1970	292	1,724	2,985	1,224	11,027	51	7	3,642	166	2,243	338	135	9,460	383	13,966
1980	147	2,056	5,998	601	18,601	0	0	4,794	173	4,046	593	204	12,411	459	9,212
1990	72	2,425	8,675	929	20,291	0	0	5,923	289	3,890	1,159	247	11,813	474	9,888

	Farm laborers					Laborers								
	Total	Farm foremen	Farm laborers, wage workers	Farm laborers, unpaid family workers	Farm service laborers, self-employed	Total	Fishermen and oystermen	Garage laborers, car washers, and greasers	Gardeners, except farm, and groundskeepers	Longshoremen and stevedores	Lumbermen, raftsmen, and woodchoppers	Teamsters	Laborers not elsewhere classified	Unknown occupation
	Ba3393	Ba3394	Ba3395	Ba3396	Ba3397	Ba3398	Ba3399	Ba3400	Ba3401	Ba3402	Ba3403	Ba3404	Ba3405	Ba3406
Year	Hundred	Hundred	Hundred	Hundred	Hundred	Hundred	Hundred	Hundred	Hundred	Hundred	Hundred	Hundred	Hundred	Hundred
1850 [2,3]	2,462	158	2,304	0	0	3,866	109	0	25	8	70	0	3,654	—
1860 [2]	7,864	141	7,710	12	0	4,134	148	0	64	2	101	0	3,819	—
1870	21,394	31	21,332	31	0	6,240	161	0	131	24	196	0	5,728	—
1880	23,482	34	23,448	0	0	13,780	247	0	196	46	324	0	12,967	—
1900	31,767	30	17,326	14,411	0	24,308	516	8	114	152	683	0	22,835	—
1910	46,457	486	45,970	0	0	22,723	461	0	710	302	1,040	0	20,209	—
1920	30,074	136	18,516	11,376	47	32,399	371	237	241	517	1,450	2,359	27,222	—
1940	28,428	221	17,356	10,850	0	37,720	483	454	1,205	428	1,221	231	33,699	3,301
1950	21,418	163	13,387	7,792	76	31,577	670	844	1,161	520	1,762	229	26,391	1,892
1960	12,380	237	9,711	2,379	53	27,973	330	815	1,531	391	1,153	193	23,560	29,195
1970	8,706	297	7,450	920	39	31,547	246	0	2,669	389	779	69	27,394	—
1980	7,506	438	7,068	0	0	38,632	460	0	3,061	198	914	0	34,000	—
1990	5,505	310	5,196	0	0	42,961	425	0	4,996	123	957	0	36,461	—

[1] Data pertain to noninstitutionalized civilians age 16 and older who reported an occupation; employed persons only beginning 1940.

[2] Excludes slaves.

[3] Excludes women.

Source

See the source for Table Ba1159–1395.

Documentation

See the text for Table Ba1159–1395.

TABLE Ba3407–3643 Detailed occupations – foreign-born persons: 1850–1990[1] [Part 1]

Contributed by Matthew Sobek

			Professional, technical, and kindred workers												College professors and instructors	
	Total	Total	Accountants and auditors	Actors and actresses	Airplane pilots and navigators	Architects	Artists and art teachers	Athletes	Authors	Chemists	Chiropractors	Clergymen	College presidents and deans	Agricultural sciences	Biological sciences
	Ba3407	Ba3408	Ba3409	Ba3410	Ba3411	Ba3412	Ba3413	Ba3414	Ba3415	Ba3416	Ba3417	Ba3418	Ba3419	Ba3420	Ba3421
Year	Hundred	Hundred	Hundred	Hundred	Hundred	Hundred	Hundred	Hundred	Hundred	Hundred	Hundred	Hundred	Hundred	Hundred	Hundred
1850 [2,3]	9,470	169	0	1	0	2	4	0	0	1	0	30	1	0	0
1860 [2]	20,945	397	2	2	0	4	12	0	0	2	0	50	0	0	0
1870	29,366	577	0	2	0	8	20	0	0	4	0	122	0	0	0
1880	36,688	830	2	11	0	15	19	1	2	12	0	167	0	0	0
1900	59,118	1,525	8	30	0	15	46	0	0	23	0	228	15	0	0
1910	79,684	2,103	0	43	0	40	93	0	10	30	0	247	0	0	0
1920	77,310	2,552	148	37	2	32	85	0	12	49	10	292	0	0	0
1940	56,753	2,960	0	23	3	18	93	11	19	64	15	236	0	0	0
1950	49,618	3,242	213	26	6	19	88	1	18	42	10	194	4	2	5
1960	44,897	4,331	246	7	10	35	79	2	20	91	10	154	0	3	4
1970	47,029	7,277	399	9	19	66	89	0	14	144	8	150	16	3	21
1980	73,109	12,266	784	0	33	115	121	0	38	147	13	185	0	1	9
1990	118,656	21,787	1,594	0	61	213	195	0	75	245	36	242	0	1	7

	Professional, technical, and kindred workers														
	College professors and instructors														
	Chemistry	Economics	Engineering	Geology and geophysics	Mathematics	Medical sciences	Physics	Psychology	Statistics	Natural sciences not elsewhere classified	Social sciences not elsewhere classified	Nonscientific subjects	Subject not specified	Dancers and dancing teachers	Dentists
	Ba3422	Ba3423	Ba3424	Ba3425	Ba3426	Ba3427	Ba3428	Ba3429	Ba3430	Ba3431	Ba3432	Ba3433	Ba3434	Ba3435	Ba3436
Year	Hundred	Hundred	Hundred	Hundred	Hundred	Hundred	Hundred	Hundred	Hundred	Hundred	Hundred	Hundred	Hundred	Hundred	Hundred
1850 [2,3]	0	0	0	0	0	0	0	0	0	0	0	0	2	0	1
1860 [2]	0	0	0	0	0	0	0	0	0	0	0	2	0	0	7
1870	0	0	0	0	0	0	0	0	0	0	0	0	4	0	4
1880	0	0	0	0	0	0	0	0	0	1	0	12	4	0	9
1900	0	0	0	0	0	0	0	0	0	0	0	0	0	0	23
1910	0	0	0	0	0	0	0	0	0	0	0	0	20	0	30
1920	0	0	0	0	0	0	0	0	0	0	0	4	16	8	61
1940	0	0	0	0	0	0	0	0	0	0	0	0	70	9	60
1950	5	2	3	2	2	2	1	3	1	0	11	21	20	4	60
1960	5	5	9	2	9	12	6	3	0	0	16	47	54	19	62
1970	23	13	27	0	32	32	24	9	0	6	35	116	159	5	45
1980	12	8	14	0	24	22	11	4	0	2	10	58	484	13	77
1990	8	7	11	0	31	18	11	6	0	2	10	72	1,023	20	137

Professional, technical, and kindred workers

Year	Designers	Dietitians and nutritionists	Draftsmen	Editors and reporters	Engineers, aeronautical	Engineers, chemical	Engineers, civil	Engineers, electrical	Engineers, industrial	Engineers, mechanical	Engineers, metallurgical, metallurgists	Engineers, mining	Engineers not elsewhere classified	Entertainers not elsewhere classified	Farm and home management advisors
	Ba3437	Ba3438	Ba3439	Ba3440	Ba3441	Ba3442	Ba3443	Ba3444	Ba3445	Ba3446	Ba3447	Ba3448	Ba3449	Ba3450	Ba3451
	Hundred	Hundred	Hundred	Hundred	Hundred	Hundred	Hundred	Hundred	Hundred	Hundred	Hundred	Hundred	Hundred	Hundred	Hundred
1850 [2,3]	1	0	0	2	0	0	1	0	0	0	0	0	0	2	0
1860 [2]	0	0	2	6	0	0	2	0	0	2	0	0	0	0	4
1870	2	0	2	19	0	0	3	0	0	0	0	0	0	2	2
1880	4	0	8	23	0	0	11	0	0	0	0	1	0	10	0
1900	15	0	15	46	0	0	38	15	0	8	0	8	0	30	0
1910	43	0	45	30	0	0	63	0	0	28	0	23	0	20	0
1920	61	2	81	32	0	4	83	30	2	55	4	8	18	8	2
1940	59	0	93	50	0	18	73	53	21	104	7	0	0	5	2
1950	101	16	76	46	8	16	75	67	17	107	4	2	67	15	1
1960	118	18	188	61	35	34	90	106	52	148	15	5	91	13	1
1970	148	31	247	122	62	49	156	227	101	178	13	9	184	67	2
1980	299	55	297	227	95	68	234	326	190	238	24	24	330	66	0
1990	632	101	323	279	173	93	385	633	364	252	15	26	509	213	0

Professional, technical, and kindred workers

Year	Foresters and conservationists	Funeral directors and embalmers	Lawyers and judges	Librarians	Musicians and music teachers	Nurses, professional	Nurses, student professional	Natural scientists not elsewhere classified: Agricultural scientists	Biological scientists	Geologists and geophysicists	Mathematicians	Physicists	Miscellaneous natural scientists	Optometrists	Osteopaths
	Ba3452	Ba3453	Ba3454	Ba3455	Ba3456	Ba3457	Ba3458	Ba3459	Ba3460	Ba3461	Ba3462	Ba3463	Ba3464	Ba3465	Ba3466
	Hundred	Hundred	Hundred	Hundred	Hundred	Hundred	Hundred	Hundred	Hundred	Hundred	Hundred	Hundred	Hundred	Hundred	Hundred
1850 [2,3]	0	0	14	0	17	0	0	0	0	0	0	0	1	0	0
1860 [2]	0	2	26	0	58	0	0	0	0	0	0	0	0	0	0
1870	0	4	23	0	66	2	0	0	0	0	0	0	0	0	0
1880	0	10	48	0	97	1	0	0	1	1	0	0	0	0	0
1900	0	8	76	0	220	23	0	0	0	0	0	0	0	0	0
1910	13	33	58	0	254	239	0	0	0	0	0	0	0	0	0
1920	6	16	93	6	185	205	10	0	0	4	0	0	0	10	0
1940	0	23	123	19	178	290	0	0	0	0	0	0	0	11	2
1950	9	15	108	23	157	268	24	6	5	2	3	16	1	9	3
1960	6	7	104	41	112	381	9	4	11	4	5	11	1	11	2
1970	6	6	96	77	174	649	6	7	37	11	5	30	2	9	0
1980	11	6	180	121	322	1,168	0	14	87	27	6	44	5	12	0
1990	14	9	328	191	628	2,023	0	24	161	41	8	54	14	14	0

Notes appear at end of table

(continued)

TABLE Ba3407–3643 Detailed occupations – foreign-born persons: 1850–1990 [Part 1] *Continued*

	Professional, technical, and kindred workers														
									Social scientists						
	Personnel and labor-relations workers	Pharmacists	Photographers	Physicians and surgeons	Radio operators	Recreation and group workers	Religious workers	Social and welfare workers, except group	Economists	Psychologists	Statisticians and actuaries	Miscellaneous social scientists	Sports instructors and officials	Surveyors	Teachers not elsewhere classified
	Ba3467	Ba3468	Ba3469	Ba3470	Ba3471	Ba3472	Ba3473	Ba3474	Ba3475	Ba3476	Ba3477	Ba3478	Ba3479	Ba3480	Ba3481
Year	Hundred	Hundred	Hundred	Hundred	Hundred	Hundred	Hundred	Hundred	Hundred	Hundred	Hundred	Hundred	Hundred	Hundred	Hundred
1850 [2,3]	0	10	1	34	0	0	0	0	0	0	0	0	0	4	29
1860 [2]	0	24	14	67	0	0	22	0	0	0	0	0	0	4	79
1870	0	47	17	80	0	0	4	0	0	0	0	0	1	2	120
1880	0	48	20	81	0	0	29	0	0	0	0	0	0	4	162
1900	0	38	23	190	0	0	68	0	0	0	0	0	0	8	228
1910	0	0	58	174	0	0	43	0	0	0	0	0	0	0	401
1920	0	93	39	144	6	0	89	18	0	0	2	0	18	8	373
1940	0	121	53	191	6	0	81	68	0	0	0	0	20	13	404
1950	21	90	41	257	4	4	64	45	12	(Z)	19	2	18	6	368
1960	47	74	51	355	9	11	64	61	6	14	10	3	14	12	448
1970	106	67	51	531	12	17	30	112	54	21	21	9	36	14	777
1980	342	101	62	953	33	15	31	259	87	67	35	19	40	30	1,263
1990	565	175	115	1,221	43	23	80	460	130	140	57	41	62	49	2,117

	Professional, technical, and kindred workers						Farmers			Managers, officials, and proprietors					
	Technicians – medical and dental	Technicians – testing	Technicians not elsewhere classified	Therapists and healers not elsewhere classified	Veterinarians	Professional, technical, and kindred workers not elsewhere classified	Total	Farmers – owners and tenants	Farm managers	Total	Buyers and department heads – store	Buyers and shippers – farm products	Conductors – railroad	Credit men	Floormen and floor managers – store
	Ba3482	Ba3483	Ba3484	Ba3485	Ba3486	Ba3487	Ba3488	Ba3489	Ba3490	Ba3491	Ba3492	Ba3493	Ba3494	Ba3495	Ba3496
Year	Hundred	Hundred	Hundred	Hundred	Hundred	Hundred	Hundred	Hundred	Hundred	Hundred	Hundred	Hundred	Hundred	Hundred	Hundred
1850 [2,3]	0	0	0	0	0	9	1,718	1,718	0	461	0	0	1	0	0
1860 [2]	0	0	0	0	2	1	3,317	3,315	2	1,069	0	12	16	0	0
1870	0	2	0	2	4	8	4,667	4,667	0	1,790	0	18	22	0	0
1880	0	0	0	1	8	8	6,754	6,752	2	2,354	0	50	29	0	0
1900	0	0	0	8	23	53	8,014	8,014	0	3,977	0	53	53	8	8
1910	0	0	0	18	18	30	6,655	6,655	0	6,942	0	0	50	0	43
1920	4	8	4	32	6	22	6,431	6,321	110	6,589	79	77	49	10	8
1940	0	59	7	53	10	124	3,415	3,382	33	6,591	74	31	29	15	17
1950	69	52	16	30	10	78	1,753	1,737	16	6,300	94	19	22	13	10
1960	115	107	48	45	7	243	830	818	12	4,187	155	6	12	21	9
1970	252	189	76	52	9	669	278	255	23	3,395	324	9	8	22	0
1980	522	683	210	106	18	730	246	189	57	6,633	440	6	8	0	0
1990	989	1,235	403	247	33	2,074	349	191	158	12,416	543	11	10	0	0

Year	Managers, officials, and proprietors								Clerical and kindred workers						
	Inspectors – public administration	Managers and superintendents – building	Officers, pilots, pursers, and engineers – ship	Officials and administrators not elsewhere classified – public administration	Officials – lodge, society, union, and so forth	Postmasters	Purchasing agents and buyers not elsewhere classified	Managers, officials, and proprietors not elsewhere classified	Total	Agents not elsewhere classified	Attendants and assistants – library	Attendants – physician's and dentist's office	Baggagemen – transportation	Bank tellers	Bookkeepers
	Ba3497	Ba3498	Ba3499	Ba3500	Ba3501	Ba3502	Ba3503	Ba3504	Ba3505	Ba3506	Ba3507	Ba3508	Ba3509	Ba3510	Ba3511
	Hundred	Hundred	Hundred	Hundred	Hundred	Hundred	Hundred	Hundred	Hundred	Hundred	Hundred	Hundred	Hundred	Hundred	Hundred
1850 [2,3]	1	2	12	5	0	0	0	440	23	5	0	0	1	0	4
1860 [2]	0	6	36	9	0	4	0	986	81	13	0	0	0	4	30
1870	9	4	23	12	0	1	0	1,701	214	14	0	0	4	2	68
1880	5	4	36	41	2	5	2	2,180	394	45	0	0	8	1	121
1900	23	0	38	30	8	38	0	3,719	1,328	46	0	0	15	0	326
1910	0	0	76	101	13	0	0	6,660	1,914	60	0	0	5	0	542
1920	32	61	120	45	12	16	26	6,053	2,750	49	0	4	4	16	521
1940	26	232	69	71	33	12	31	5,950	2,920	76	12	24	1	0	551
1950	15	219	69	55	18	11	51	5,702	3,043	71	4	16	6	22	298
1960	33	113	48	85	27	5	41	3,633	4,246	76	14	34	3	51	426
1970	35	103	19	100	27	5	60	2,683	6,789	5	63	122	0	131	826
1980	59	188	23	163	0	4	107	5,635	11,346	0	95	307	0	332	1,095
1990	95	367	19	532	0	9	206	10,624	17,863	0	141	358	0	479	1,422

Year	Clerical and kindred workers													
	Cashiers	Collectors, bill and account	Dispatchers and starters – vehicle	Express messengers and railway mail clerks	Mail carriers	Messengers and office boys	Office machine operators	Shipping and receiving clerks	Stenographers, typists, and secretaries	Telegraph messengers	Telegraph operators	Telephone operators	Ticket, station, and express agents	Clerical and kindred workers not elsewhere classified
	Ba3512	Ba3513	Ba3514	Ba3515	Ba3516	Ba3517	Ba3518	Ba3519	Ba3520	Ba3521	Ba3522	Ba3523	Ba3524	Ba3525
	Hundred	Hundred	Hundred	Hundred	Hundred	Hundred	Hundred	Hundred	Hundred	Hundred	Hundred	Hundred	Hundred	Hundred
1850 [2,3]	0	3	0	0	0	3	0	1	0	0	0	0	3	3
1860 [2]	2	4	0	0	8	4	0	0	0	0	0	0	2	14
1870	4	3	0	0	6	6	0	2	0	0	6	0	13	86
1880	7	11	2	0	15	14	0	11	2	0	17	0	20	121
1900	23	61	8	0	30	61	0	99	61	0	23	23	46	508
1910	0	45	0	10	71	58	0	166	186	10	20	43	35	662
1920	61	67	4	12	65	59	4	211	450	8	41	83	30	1,061
1940	0	37	0	11	55	33	39	238	497	6	35	71	34	1,200
1950	112	8	16	3	51	28	51	286	505	13	11	111	23	1,407
1960	213	16	17	1	37	46	145	239	913	1	10	125	54	1,827
1970	426	22	19	0	54	59	362	293	1,753	2	6	129	81	2,435
1980	1,171	46	36	0	78	77	746	503	2,319	0	3	149	107	4,282
1990	2,679	111	90	0	178	143	1,320	865	2,845	0	0	107	364	6,762

Notes appear at end of table

(continued)

TABLE Ba3407–3643 Detailed occupations – foreign-born persons: 1850–1990 [Part 1] *Continued*

	Sales workers										Craft workers, foremen, and kindred workers				
	Total	Advertising agents and salesmen	Auctioneers	Demonstrators	Hucksters and peddlers	Insurance agents and brokers	Newsboys	Real estate agents and brokers	Stock and bond salesmen	Salesmen and sales clerks not elsewhere classified	Total	Bakers	Blacksmiths	Bookbinders	Boilermakers
	Ba3526	Ba3527	Ba3528	Ba3529	Ba3530	Ba3531	Ba3532	Ba3533	Ba3534	Ba3535	Ba3536	Ba3537	Ba3538	Ba3539	Ba3540
Year	Hundred	Hundred	Hundred	Hundred	Hundred	Hundred	Hundred	Hundred	Hundred	Hundred	Hundred	Hundred	Hundred	Hundred	Hundred
1850 [2, 3]	228	0	2	0	48	0	0	1	1	177	2,086	92	180	9	13
1860 [2]	493	0	0	0	113	2	10	6	0	362	3,720	154	299	22	16
1870	699	2	5	0	183	14	8	24	0	463	4,665	171	445	20	27
1880	944	1	1	0	232	18	8	16	3	664	5,666	213	526	22	49
1900	1,874	8	8	0	372	137	0	106	0	1,245	9,668	387	691	99	83
1910	2,416	0	0	5	0	113	18	219	5	2,055	12,179	456	642	0	101
1920	2,927	8	4	2	276	183	20	221	14	2,199	14,543	538	538	41	166
1940	2,949	31	6	6	200	216	19	143	9	2,319	9,783	507	181	0	57
1950	2,747	17	18	10	51	186	14	139	11	2,302	8,669	319	79	44	38
1960	2,925	17	1	12	34	162	30	155	17	2,497	6,748	245	26	37	14
1970	3,026	26	1	15	50	206	20	152	52	2,504	6,283	199	10	29	17
1980	3,753	47	2	6	103	350	42	384	86	2,734	8,236	199	0	26	16
1990	6,034	83	2	26	149	624	84	703	225	4,137	11,940	346	0	33	9

	Craft workers, foremen, and kindred workers														
	Brickmasons, stonemasons, and tile setters	Cabinetmakers	Carpenters	Cement and concrete finishers	Compositors and typesetters	Cranemen, derrickmen, and hoistmen	Decorators and window dressers	Electricians	Electrotypers and stereotypers	Engravers, except photoengravers	Excavating, grading, and road machinery operators	Foremen not elsewhere classified	Forgemen and hammermen	Furriers	Glaziers
	Ba3541	Ba3542	Ba3543	Ba3544	Ba3545	Ba3546	Ba3547	Ba3548	Ba3549	Ba3550	Ba3551	Ba3552	Ba3553	Ba3554	Ba3555
Year	Hundred	Hundred	Hundred	Hundred	Hundred	Hundred	Hundred	Hundred	Hundred	Hundred	Hundred	Hundred	Hundred	Hundred	Hundred
1850 [2, 3]	154	99	310	0	37	0	0	0	0	7	12	6	0	1	0
1860 [2]	224	118	551	0	48	0	0	0	0	16	0	28	4	0	8
1870	325	141	792	0	73	0	2	0	0	20	8	38	4	4	8
1880	389	179	956	1	92	0	0	0	1	23	5	98	2	5	5
1900	501	205	1,594	0	281	8	0	99	23	23	0	319	0	15	8
1910	657	227	2,222	0	176	0	20	191	5	18	0	728	15	0	0
1920	424	264	2,018	22	243	91	24	274	8	20	10	1,039	28	37	22
1940	292	255	1,005	54	216	132	32	207	9	15	0	727	0	93	24
1950	281	132	957	45	155	145	25	198	16	12	32	850	33	55	8
1960	191	115	624	30	121	102	30	183	2	20	35	745	5	17	13
1970	173	109	580	58	108	62	44	209	3	8	68	777	9	14	12
1980	183	93	782	51	39	64	0	302	0	12	99	1,367	9	25	15
1990	342	89	1,259	90	41	52	0	485	0	19	142	1,460	15	52	28

	Craft workers, foremen, and kindred workers														
	Heat treaters, annealers, temperers	Inspectors, scalers, and graders – log and lumber	Inspectors not elsewhere classified	Jewelers, watchmakers, goldsmiths, silversmiths	Job setters – metal	Linemen and servicemen	Locomotive engineers	Locomotive firemen	Loom fixers	Machinists	Mechanics and repairmen – airplane	Mechanics and repairmen – automobile	Mechanics and repairmen – office machine	Mechanics and repairmen – radio and television	Mechanics and repairmen – railroad and car shop
	Ba3556	Ba3557	Ba3558	Ba3559	Ba3560	Ba3561	Ba3562	Ba3563	Ba3564	Ba3565	Ba3566	Ba3567	Ba3568	Ba3569	Ba3570
Year	Hundred	Hundred	Hundred	Hundred	Hundred	Hundred	Hundred	Hundred	Hundred	Hundred	Hundred	Hundred	Hundred	Hundred	Hundred
1850 [2,3]	0	0	0	38	0	0	0	0	0	54	0	0	0	0	0
1860 [2]	0	0	6	48	0	0	4	6	0	110	0	0	0	0	4
1870	0	4	6	63	0	0	12	14	0	180	0	0	0	0	6
1880	3	1	16	79	0	4	28	16	0	293	0	0	0	0	11
1900	0	15	61	91	0	30	61	30	15	713	0	0	0	0	53
1910	5	0	93	108	0	13	123	68	60	1,277	0	0	0	0	0
1920	16	32	170	146	4	41	116	77	116	1,850	0	213	0	0	227
1940	24	17	90	98	0	69	66	35	49	895	21	308	0	0	74
1950	22	20	97	94	35	74	45	26	46	703	21	284	4	36	67
1960	11	10	56	80	36	56	22	9	6	508	48	331	12	44	29
1970	11	3	51	87	58	95	9	3	4	303	73	457	31	75	29
1980	13	0	19	151	47	145	17	0	0	499	78	890	47	95	0
1990	13	0	52	243	34	147	15	0	0	615	157	1,459	111	151	0

	Craft workers, foremen, and kindred workers														
	Mechanics and repairmen not elsewhere classified	Millers – grain, flour, feed, and so forth	Millwrights	Molders – metal	Motion picture projectionists	Opticians and lens grinders and polishers	Painters – construction and maintenance	Paperhangers	Pattern and model makers, except paper	Photoengravers and lithographers	Piano and organ tuners and repairmen	Plasterers	Plumbers and pipe fitters	Pressmen and plate printers – printing	Rollers and roll hands – metal
	Ba3571	Ba3572	Ba3573	Ba3574	Ba3575	Ba3576	Ba3577	Ba3578	Ba3579	Ba3580	Ba3581	Ba3582	Ba3583	Ba3584	Ba3585
Year	Hundred	Hundred	Hundred	Hundred	Hundred	Hundred	Hundred	Hundred	Hundred	Hundred	Hundred	Hundred	Hundred	Hundred	Hundred
1850 [2,3]	43	35	11	28	0	0	62	2	1	6	0	20	5	1	1
1860 [2]	100	54	4	92	0	2	143	6	4	6	0	52	32	0	6
1870	84	48	16	137	0	0	255	2	4	6	4	35	44	0	36
1880	70	75	18	142	0	9	260	6	14	14	2	69	52	2	7
1900	167	15	15	311	0	30	539	8	61	8	0	83	190	53	0
1910	106	48	0	499	0	0	668	50	68	13	25	141	257	35	71
1920	294	30	99	503	16	20	663	26	65	28	12	89	361	20	65
1940	547	14	96	207	35	16	637	23	65	53	11	102	241	32	56
1950	812	6	80	99	13	22	540	21	55	31	13	71	202	32	56
1960	928	3	42	37	10	20	376	9	58	24	2	59	159	38	27
1970	546	1	29	37	12	24	335	0	39	24	5	28	158	93	12
1980	889	0	57	38	9	45	469	0	38	16	0	28	230	212	11
1990	1,280	0	33	29	6	82	934	0	46	33	0	95	335	340	10

Notes appear at end of table

(continued)

TABLE Ba3407–3643 Detailed occupations – foreign-born persons: 1850–1990 [Part 1] *Continued*

	Craft workers, foremen, and kindred workers										Operatives and kindred workers				
	Roofers and slaters	Shoemakers and repairers, except factory	Stationary engineers	Stonecutters and stone carvers	Structural metal workers	Tailors and tailoresses	Tinsmiths, coppersmiths, sheet metal workers	Toolmakers, die makers, and setters	Upholsterers	Craftsmen and kindred workers not elsewhere classified	Total	Apprentice auto mechanics	Apprentice bricklayers and masons	Apprentice carpenters	Apprentice electricians
	Ba3586	Ba3587	Ba3588	Ba3589	Ba3590	Ba3591	Ba3592	Ba3593	Ba3594	Ba3595	Ba3596	Ba3597	Ba3598	Ba3599	Ba3600
Year	Hundred	Hundred	Hundred	Hundred	Hundred	Hundred	Hundred	Hundred	Hundred	Hundred	Hundred	Hundred	Hundred	Hundred	Hundred
1850 [2,3]	1	336	28	49	0	286	35	1	9	112	1,491	0	0	0	0
1860 [2]	5	532	89	88	0	530	77	2	16	212	3,625	0	4	10	0
1870	15	486	93	113	0	472	99	8	31	311	6,144	0	2	2	0
1880	19	524	159	128	1	688	119	4	37	234	7,792	0	0	6	0
1900	8	584	357	228	0	1,283	137	0	38	152	11,270	0	0	8	0
1910	43	474	501	159	33	1,370	181	28	68	136	18,240	0	0	0	0
1920	32	473	408	146	209	1,491	180	170	69	254	17,521	2	0	2	0
1940	39	345	294	39	92	770	145	273	98	0	12,344	0	0	14	3
1950	32	219	220	20	56	474	126	272	101	98	11,605	6	1	3	5
1960	22	143	199	5	46	245	72	271	78	68	10,054	1	1	1	2
1970	20	96	86	7	41	261	66	220	72	294	10,005	2	1	1	5
1980	61	118	102	0	49	241	71	178	89	0	14,282	2	1	3	5
1990	211	170	153	0	54	283	117	152	122	0	18,497	1	1	4	6

	Operatives and kindred workers														
	Apprentice machinists and toolmakers	Apprentice mechanics, except auto	Apprentice plumbers and pipe fitters	Apprentices – building trades not elsewhere classified	Apprentices – metalworking trades not elsewhere classified	Apprentices – printing trades	Apprentices – other specified trades	Apprentices – trade not specified	Asbestos and insulation workers	Attendants – auto service and parking	Blasters and powdermen	Boatmen, canalmen, and lock keepers	Brakemen – railroad	Bus drivers	Chainmen, rodmen, and axmen – surveying
	Ba3601	Ba3602	Ba3603	Ba3604	Ba3605	Ba3606	Ba3607	Ba3608	Ba3609	Ba3610	Ba3611	Ba3612	Ba3613	Ba3614	Ba3615
Year	Hundred	Hundred	Hundred	Hundred	Hundred	Hundred	Hundred	Hundred	Hundred	Hundred	Hundred	Hundred	Hundred	Hundred	Hundred
1850 [2,3]	0	0	0	0	0	0	2	2	0	0	0	62	3	2	0
1860 [2]	2	2	2	4	26	2	24	16	0	0	0	45	4	2	0
1870	0	2	2	8	8	12	34	6	0	0	4	20	33	2	0
1880	1	0	1	0	4	0	23	1	0	0	0	37	30	3	0
1900	23	0	0	0	23	0	30	0	0	0	0	8	76	0	0
1910	0	0	0	8	0	0	0	53	0	0	0	5	50	0	0
1920	10	2	4	0	12	0	4	2	4	2	8	6	75	6	4
1940	9	0	19	5	0	11	15	7	10	108	8	13	37	0	4
1950	5	2	11	1	2	11	10	2	6	58	12	23	26	73	6
1960	5	2	0	0	0	3	4	5	8	58	5	4	21	77	2
1970	6	1	3	2	1	5	5	(Z)	7	144	2	3	8	78	2
1980	8	0	4	0	(Z)	0	4	0	22	189	3	0	14	159	2
1990	1	0	4	0	(Z)	0	2	0	90	326	4	0	4	240	1

	Operatives and kindred workers													
	Conductors – bus and street railway	Deliverymen and routemen	Dressmakers and seamstresses, except factory	Dyers	Filers, grinders, and polishers – metal	Fruit, nut, vegetable graders, packers, not factory	Furnacemen, smeltermen, and pourers	Heaters – metal	Laundry and dry cleaning operatives	Meat cutters, except slaughter and packing houses	Milliners	Mine operatives and laborers	Motormen, mine, factory, logging camp, and so forth	Motormen, street, subway, and elevated railway
	Ba3616	Ba3617	Ba3618	Ba3619	Ba3620	Ba3621	Ba3622	Ba3623	Ba3624	Ba3625	Ba3626	Ba3627	Ba3628	Ba3629
Year	Hundred	Hundred	Hundred	Hundred	Hundred	Hundred	Hundred	Hundred	Hundred	Hundred	Hundred	Hundred	Hundred	Hundred
1850 [2,3]	0	10	5	18	0	0	43	0	0	88	2	346	0	0
1860 [2]	1	14	246	22	18	0	20	4	8	167	53	751	0	8
1870	2	28	335	18	26	0	65	6	101	206	27	1,118	0	12
1880	0	40	432	30	37	0	158	10	220	331	61	1,380	0	40
1900	38	30	774	0	197	8	76	8	38	288	114	2,504	0	129
1910	154	401	645	91	134	8	174	18	320	23	174	4,285	0	191
1920	89	292	538	101	229	18	130	26	337	485	83	3,406	16	120
1940	39	329	280	65	230	59	67	35	323	305	26	1,025	26	81
1950	31	116	263	47	211	63	85	14	376	275	32	421	17	39
1960	8	172	262	22	162	26	49	9	358	237	16	76	4	15
1970	9	236	231	20	207	38	29	3	388	213	6	49	3	0
1980	0	332	261	0	278	0	0	0	397	319	0	80	0	0
1990	0	80	325	0	175	0	0	0	710	431	0	92	0	0

	Operatives and kindred workers													
	Oilers and greasers, except auto	Painters, except construction or maintenance	Photographic process workers	Power station operators	Sailors and deckhands	Sawyers	Spinners – textile	Stationary firemen	Switchmen – railroad	Taxicab drivers and chauffeurs	Truck and tractor drivers	Weavers – textile	Welders and flame cutters	Operatives and kindred workers not elsewhere classified
	Ba3630	Ba3631	Ba3632	Ba3633	Ba3634	Ba3635	Ba3636	Ba3637	Ba3638	Ba3639	Ba3640	Ba3641	Ba3642	Ba3643
Year	Hundred	Hundred	Hundred	Hundred	Hundred	Hundred	Hundred	Hundred	Hundred	Hundred	Hundred	Hundred	Hundred	Hundred
1850 [2,3]	0	6	0	0	135	20	19	13	0	7	104	112	1	490
1860 [2]	0	18	0	0	228	26	74	8	2	10	230	229	0	1,344
1870	0	50	0	0	201	30	30	10	10	18	382	128	4	3,201
1880	0	50	0	0	205	25	12	49	13	25	428	134	0	4,008
1900	0	61	0	0	137	61	228	167	83	137	1,002	622	0	4,402
1910	30	161	0	0	171	88	214	355	156	146	804	874	0	8,509
1920	87	191	10	6	120	69	314	400	65	252	343	824	55	8,772
1940	52	170	26	34	93	33	0	232	34	0	851	0	159	7,507
1950	67	190	21	14	100	31	46	169	29	191	469	137	189	7,698
1960	33	155	36	9	67	26	28	65	18	135	431	46	211	7,181
1970	24	126	56	4	34	37	0	56	13	144	346	24	290	7,149
1980	17	183	77	6	27	45	0	71	3	263	601	54	545	10,308
1990	14	239	109	12	16	66	0	52	2	546	1,912	55	619	12,358

(Z) Fewer than 50.

[1] Data pertain to noninstitutionalized civilians age 16 and older who reported an occupation; employed persons only beginning 1940.

[2] Excludes slaves.

[3] Excludes women.

Source

See the source for Table Ba1159–1395.

Documentation

See the text for Table Ba1159–1395.

TABLE Ba3644–3687 Detailed occupations – foreign-born persons: 1850–1990[1] [Part 2]

Contributed by Matthew Sobek

	Service workers, private household				Service workers, not household										
Year	Total	Housekeepers – private household	Laundresses – private household	Private household workers not elsewhere classified	Total	Attendants – hospital and other institution	Attendants – professional and personal service not elsewhere classified	Attendants – recreation and amusement	Barbers, beauticians, and manicurists	Bartenders	Bootblacks	Boarding and lodging house keepers	Charwomen and cleaners	Cooks, except private household	Counter and fountain workers
	Ba3644	Ba3645	Ba3646	Ba3647	Ba3648	Ba3649	Ba3650	Ba3651	Ba3652	Ba3653	Ba3654	Ba3655	Ba3656	Ba3657	Ba3658
	Hundred	Hundred	Hundred	Hundred	Hundred	Hundred	Hundred	Hundred	Hundred	Hundred	Hundred	Hundred	Hundred	Hundred	Hundred
1850 [2,3]	137	1	2	134	164	1	0	0	15	26	0	13	0	0	0
1860 [2]	2,239	0	181	2,058	398	0	8	2	32	54	1	50	0	0	0
1870	2,906	2	160	2,744	683	4	43	2	84	94	1	57	0	22	0
1880	2,971	119	187	2,665	895	5	16	4	157	91	2	90	3	35	0
1900	5,305	190	53	5,062	2,520	0	0	0	258	319	23	167	8	68	0
1910	5,239	451	562	4,227	3,748	0	40	0	574	338	123	401	136	0	0
1920	2,844	353	355	2,136	4,621	47	37	16	598	116	77	280	168	519	14
1940	2,108	368	103	1,637	5,727	109	30	42	731	267	18	108	249	678	0
1950	1,286	182	28	1,075	5,821	137	28	29	589	298	22	56	316	765	146
1960	1,231	211	20	1,000	5,468	250	51	23	566	213	10	26	322	723	182
1970	844	147	6	691	6,437	388	143	40	577	160	3	10	537	866	113
1980	784	171	4	609	10,881	1,079	606	111	597	216	0	0	909	1,792	126
1990	1,459	140	2	1,316	19,750	2,175	1,236	229	945	252	0	0	1,496	3,796	185

	Service workers, not household														
Year	Elevator operators	Firemen (fire protection)	Guards, watchmen, and doorkeepers	Housekeepers and stewards, except household	Janitors and sextons	Marshals and constables	Midwives	Policemen and detectives	Porters	Practical nurses	Sheriffs and bailiffs	Ushers – recreation and amusement	Waiters and waitresses	Watchmen (crossing) and bridge tenders	Service workers (not private household) not elsewhere classified
	Ba3659	Ba3660	Ba3661	Ba3662	Ba3663	Ba3664	Ba3665	Ba3666	Ba3667	Ba3668	Ba3669	Ba3670	Ba3671	Ba3672	Ba3673
	Hundred	Hundred	Hundred	Hundred	Hundred	Hundred	Hundred	Hundred	Hundred	Hundred	Hundred	Hundred	Hundred	Hundred	Hundred
1850 [2,3]	0	0	9	5	2	2	0	5	33	1	1	0	30	11	8
1860 [2]	0	0	24	13	2	2	4	12	98	27	0	0	51	2	15
1870	0	2	55	10	18	3	8	54	101	8	2	0	92	8	14
1880	0	7	101	12	36	9	12	47	77	39	7	0	76	8	62
1900	23	38	182	91	235	0	38	121	99	0	8	0	190	23	630
1910	58	53	285	0	373	5	35	134	202	315	5	0	640	0	33
1920	101	83	381	130	420	4	10	158	185	207	10	2	619	24	414
1940	180	43	455	151	794	6	0	112	217	127	8	12	724	20	647
1950	197	52	349	148	785	1	(Z)	85	207	152	7	4	586	18	843
1960	140	24	210	192	660	3	1	63	164	140	8	6	662	31	798
1970	71	25	192	137	1,054	1	1	76	23	113	6	11	821	31	1,040
1980	55	41	420	63	1,988	0	0	122	24	205	15	14	1,206	30	1,262
1990	30	59	783	96	3,836	0	0	221	63	294	36	22	1,683	34	2,277

	Farm laborers					Laborers								
	Total	Farm foremen	Farm laborers, wage workers	Farm laborers, unpaid family workers	Farm service laborers, self-employed	Total	Fishermen and oystermen	Garage laborers, car washers, and greasers	Gardeners, except farm, and groundskeepers	Longshoremen and stevedores	Lumbermen, raftsmen, and woodchoppers	Teamsters	Laborers not elsewhere classified	Unknown occupation
	Ba3674	Ba3675	Ba3676	Ba3677	Ba3678	Ba3679	Ba3680	Ba3681	Ba3682	Ba3683	Ba3684	Ba3685	Ba3686	Ba3687
Year	Hundred	Hundred	Hundred	Hundred	Hundred	Hundred	Hundred	Hundred	Hundred	Hundred	Hundred	Hundred	Hundred	Hundred
1850 [2,3]	518	6	512	0	0	2,474	17	0	60	5	10	0	2,382	—
1860 [2]	1,514	2	1,512	0	0	4,093	98	0	120	14	36	0	3,824	—
1870	1,986	1	1,985	0	0	5,033	46	0	194	54	62	0	4,676	—
1880	2,058	6	2,052	0	0	6,030	87	0	217	58	178	0	5,490	—
1900	2,884	8	2,398	478	0	10,754	152	0	61	167	228	0	10,146	—
1910	4,320	73	4,247	0	0	15,927	207	0	282	395	378	0	14,665	—
1920	2,791	39	2,514	239	0	13,741	75	26	191	343	436	359	12,311	—
1940	1,605	17	1,386	202	0	6,016	132	36	421	177	109	19	5,122	335
1950	1,450	16	1,238	193	4	3,576	91	42	309	131	64	8	2,932	129
1960	1,278	16	1,189	72	1	2,227	37	28	223	111	15	1	1,813	1,372
1970	765	24	718	21	2	1,929	24	0	303	52	14	1	1,534	—
1980	1,387	61	1,326	0	0	3,295	34	0	447	43	19	0	2,752	—
1990	2,205	87	2,118	0	0	6,356	52	0	1,314	15	32	0	4,943	—

(Z) Fewer than 50.

1 Data pertain to noninstitutionalized civilians age 16 and older who reported an occupation; employed persons only beginning 1940.

2 Excludes slaves.

3 Excludes women.

Source

See the source for Table Ba1159–1395.

Documentation

See the text for Table Ba1159–1395.

TABLE Ba3688–3832 Detailed occupations – the economically active population: 1900–1970[1] [Part 1]

Contributed by Matthew Sobek

		Professional, technical, and kindred workers												
	Total	Total	Accountants and auditors	Actors and actresses	Athletes	Dancers and dancing teachers	Sports instructors and officials	Entertainers not elsewhere classified	Airplane pilots and navigators	Architects	Artists and art teachers	Authors	Chemists	Clergymen
	Ba3688	Ba3689	Ba3690	Ba3691	Ba3692	Ba3693	Ba3694	Ba3695	Ba3696	Ba3697	Ba3698	Ba3699	Ba3700	Ba3701
Year	Thousand	Thousand	Thousand	Thousand	Thousand	Thousand	Thousand	Thousand	Thousand	Thousand	Thousand	Thousand	Thousand	Thousand
1900	29,030	1,234	23	—	—	—	—	31 [29]	—	11	25	3	9	—
1910	37,291	1,758	39	—	—	—	—	48 [29]	—	16	34	4	16	118
1920	42,206	2,283	118	—	—	—	—	48 [29]	1	17	35	7	28	127
1930	48,686	3,311	192	—	—	—	—	76 [29]	6	23	57	12	45	149
1940	51,742	3,879	238	21	9	14	25	12	5	22	66	14	57	141
1950 [22]	58,999	5,081	390	20	13	18	47	17	14	25	83	17	77	171
1950 [23]	59,230 [27]	5,000	385	18	12	17	46	16	15	24	81	16	76	169
1960 [23]	67,990 [27]	7,336	477	13	5	22	78	12	28	31	105	29	84	202
1960 [24]	67,990 [27]	7,090 [28]	496	12	—	—	—	—	28	38	—	29	96	202
1970 [25]	80,603 [27]	11,018 [28]	713	15	—	—	—	—	52	57	—	26	110	219
1970 [26]	79,802 [27]	11,561 [28]	712	15	—	—	—	—	52	57	—	26	110	219

	Professional, technical, and kindred workers												Engineers, technical	
	Religious workers	Recreation and group workers	Social and welfare workers, except group	Recreation and social workers	Religious, recreation, and social workers	Clergymen, and religious, recreation, and social workers	College presidents, professors, and instructors not elsewhere classified	Dentists	Designers	Draftsmen	Designers and draftsmen	Editors and reporters	Total	Civil
	Ba3702	Ba3703	Ba3704	Ba3705 [2]	Ba3706 [3]	Ba3707 [4]	Ba3708	Ba3709	Ba3710	Ba3711	Ba3712 [5]	Ba3713	Ba3714	Ba3715
Year	Thousand	Thousand	Thousand	Thousand	Thousand	Thousand	Thousand	Thousand	Thousand	Thousand	Thousand	Thousand	Thousand	Thousand
1900	—	—	—	—	—	114	7	30	—	—	18	32	38	20
1910	—	—	—	—	19	—	16	40	—	—	45	36	77	40
1920	—	—	—	—	46	—	33	56	—	—	67	39	134	56
1930	—	—	—	—	71	—	62	71	—	—	98	61	217	88
1940	42	—	—	77	—	—	77	71	32	82	—	66	297	97
1950 [22]	42	—	—	95	—	—	127	76	41	127	—	93	543	128
1950 [23]	42	17	77	—	—	—	126	76	29	136	—	73	535	126
1960 [23]	57	38	98	—	—	—	179	83	68	219	—	103	872	158
1960 [24]	61	29	95	—	—	—	—	83	69	219	—	106	871	158
1970 [25]	36	54	221	—	—	—	—	91	112	295	—	151	1,231	175
1970 [26]	36	53	221	—	—	—	—	91	112	294	—	151	1,230	175

Year	Professional, technical, and kindred workers													
	Engineers, technical													
	Chemical	Metallurgical and metallurgists	Mining	Metallurgical and mining	Chemical, metallurgical, and mining	Electrical	Industrial	Aeronautical	Mechanical	Engineers not elsewhere classified	Farm and home management advisors	Funeral directors and embalmers	Lawyers and judges	Librarians
	Ba3716	Ba3717	Ba3718	Ba3719 [6]	Ba3720 [7]	Ba3721	Ba3722	Ba3723	Ba3724	Ba3725	Ba3726	Ba3727	Ba3728	Ba3729
	Thousand	Thousand	Thousand	Thousand	Thousand	Thousand	Thousand	Thousand	Thousand	Thousand	Thousand	Thousand	Thousand	Thousand
1900	—	—	—	—	3	—	—	—	—	14 [30]	—	16	108	3
1910	—	—	—	—	7	15	—	—	—	15 [31]	1	21	115	7
1920	—	—	—	—	11	27	—	—	—	39 [31]	3	24	123	15
1930	—	—	—	—	14	58	—	—	—	58 [31]	4	34	161	30
1940	13	—	—	12	—	65	13	—	—	97 [32]	12	40	182	39
1950 [22]	34	—	—	23	—	110	42	—	—	207 [32]	13	41	184	57
1950 [23]	33	12	14	—	—	108	41	18	115	67	12	40	182	56
1960 [23]	41	19	12	—	—	185	98	53	160	145	14	37	213	85
1960 [24]	42	9	7	—	—	188	115	53	162	137	14	39	218	76
1970 [25]	53	16	5	—	—	286	188	69	181	259	13	41	274	124
1970 [26]	53	16	5	—	—	286	188	69	181	259	13	41	273	124

Year	Professional, technical, and kindred workers													
	Musicians and music teachers	Nurses, professional	Nurses, student professional	Nurses, professional and student	Optometrists	Pharmacists	Photographers	Physicians and surgeons	Osteopaths	Physicians, surgeons, and osteopaths	Chiropractors	Therapists and healers not elsewhere classified	Chiropractors, therapists, and healers	Physicians, surgeons, osteopaths, chiropractors, and therapists
	Ba3730	Ba3731	Ba3732	Ba3733 [8]	Ba3734	Ba3735	Ba3736	Ba3737	Ba3738	Ba3739 [9]	Ba3740	Ba3741	Ba3742 [10]	Ba3743 [11]
	Thousand	Thousand	Thousand	Thousand	Thousand	Thousand	Thousand	Thousand	Thousand	Thousand	Thousand	Thousand	Thousand	Thousand
1900	92	—	—	12	—	46	25	—	—	—	—	—	—	131
1910	139	—	—	82	1	54	30	—	—	152	—	—	5	—
1920	130	—	—	149	7	64	29	146	5	—	—	—	12	—
1930	165	—	—	294	8	84	33	157	6	—	12	14	—	—
1940	167	—	—	377	10	83	38	168	6	—	11	18	—	—
1950 [22]	166	—	—	491	15	90	56	195	5	—	13	25	—	—
1950 [23]	162	406	77	—	15	89	55	193	5	—	13	25	—	—
1960 [23]	198	592	58	—	16	93	53	230	4	—	14	37	—	—
1960 [24]	—	630	—	—	16	96	53	—	—	233	14	—	—	—
1970 [25]	—	842	—	—	17	110	67	—	—	282	14	—	—	—
1970 [26]	—	841	—	—	17	110	67	—	—	282	14	—	—	—

Notes appear at end of table

(continued)

TABLE Ba3688–3832 Detailed occupations – the economically active population: 1900–1970 [Part 1] *Continued*

	Professional, technical, and kindred workers													
	Radio operators	Surveyors	Teachers not elsewhere classified	Technicians, medical and dental	Technicians, testing	Technicians, medical, dental, and testing	Technicians not elsewhere classified	Veterinarians	Dietitians and nutritionists	Foresters and conservationists	Natural scientists not elsewhere classified	Personnel and labor-relations workers	Social scientists	Professional and kindred workers not elsewhere classified
	Ba3744	Ba3745	Ba3746	Ba3747	Ba3748	Ba3749 [12]	Ba3750	Ba3751	Ba3752	Ba3753	Ba3754	Ba3755	Ba3756	Ba3757
Year	Thousand	Thousand	Thousand	Thousand	Thousand	Thousand	Thousand	Thousand	Thousand	Thousand	Thousand	Thousand	Thousand	Thousand
1900	—	6	436	—	—	—	—	8	—	—	—	—	—	12
1910	4	8	595	—	—	—	—	12	—	—	—	—	—	20
1920	5	9	752	—	—	—	4 [33]	13	—	—	—	—	—	32
1930	5	15	1,044	—	—	—	20 [33]	12	—	—	—	—	—	73
1940	7	17	1,086	—	—	73	11	11	—	—	—	—	—	153
1950 [22]	17	27	1,149	—	—	158	28	14	—	—	—	—	—	302
1950 [23]	17	27	1,133	78	104	—	19	14	23	27	43	53	36	108
1960 [23]	29	46	1,684	141	281	—	67	15	27	34	67	99	57	345
1960 [24]	18	47	—	129	346	—	73	15	27	34	62	103	42	—
1970 [25]	29	62	—	264	471	—	74	20	41	42	95	296	110	—
1970 [26]	29	62	—	264	471	—	74	20	41	42	95	296	110	—

	Farmers and farm managers			Managers, officials, and proprietors, except farm											
										Inspectors and officials not elsewhere classified, public administration					
										All levels of government			Federal, including postal service		
	Total	Farmers (owners and tenants)	Farm managers	Total	Buyers and department heads, store	Buyers and shippers, farm products	Conductors, railroad	Credit men	Floormen and floor managers, store	Inspectors	Officials and administrators	Inspectors, officials, and administrators	Inspectors	Officials and administrators	Inspectors, officials, and administrators
	Ba3758	Ba3759	Ba3760	Ba3761	Ba3762	Ba3763	Ba3764	Ba3765	Ba3766	Ba3767	Ba3768	Ba3769 [13]	Ba3770	Ba3771	Ba3772 [14]
Year	Thousand	Thousand	Thousand	Thousand	Thousand	Thousand	Thousand	Thousand	Thousand	Thousand	Thousand	Thousand	Thousand	Thousand	Thousand
1900	5,763	5,752	10	1,697	—	12	43	2	2	—	—	58	—	—	18
1910	6,163	6,132	31	2,462	15	51	66	2	4	—	—	72	—	—	20
1920	6,442	6,384	58	2,803	20	48	75	14	4	—	—	100	—	—	42
1930	6,032	5,992	40	3,614	35	42	73	22	6	—	—	124	—	—	40
1940	5,362	5,324	38	3,770	74	43	48	30	7	43	122	—	20	40	—
1950 [22]	4,375	4,339	36	5,155	147	29	57	34	11	58	158	—	28	51	—
1950 [23]	4,325	4,290	35	5,096	145	29	56	33	11	58	156	—	29	51	—
1960 [23]	2,526	2,501	25	5,489	238	18	45	48	11	77	201	—	41	69	—
1960 [24]	2,528	2,503	25	5,708 [28]	210	31	45	48	—	62	195	—	43	79	—
1970 [25]	1,350	1,289	61	6,224 [28]	387	20	40	60	—	82	248	—	51	120	—
1970 [26]	1,428 [27]	1,286	61	6,463 [28]	387	20	40	60	—	81	248	—	51	120	—

	Managers, officials, and proprietors, except farm														
	Inspectors and officials not elsewhere classified, public administration											Managers, officials, and proprietors not elsewhere classified			
	State			Local											
	Inspectors	Officials and administrators	Inspectors, officials, and administrators	Inspectors	Officials and administrators	Inspectors, officials, and administrators	Managers and superintendants, building	Officers, pilots, pursers, and engineers, ship	Officials, lodge, society, union, and so forth	Postmasters	Purchasing agents and buyers not elsewhere classified	Total	Construction	Manufacturing	Transportation
	Ba3773	Ba3774	Ba3775 [15]	Ba3776	Ba3777	Ba3778 [16]	Ba3779	Ba3780	Ba3781	Ba3782	Ba3783	Ba3784	Ba3785	Ba3786	Ba3787
Year	Thousand	Thousand	Thousand	Thousand	Thousand	Thousand	Thousand	Thousand	Thousand	Thousand	Thousand	Thousand	Thousand	Thousand	Thousand
1900	—	—	4	—	—	35	—	43	—	19	7	1,511	58	174	66
1910	—	—	7	—	—	44	32	45	8	25	8	2,135	183	350	82
1920	—	—	9	—	—	49	43	49	12	29	18	2,390	107	406	83
1930	—	—	15	—	—	70	71	49	15	34	29	3,113	199	447	98
1940	11	21	—	12	61	—	72	35	26	40	34	3,197	175	432	90
1950 [22]	10	24	—	20	83	—	68	43	28	39	65	4,419	296	665	151
1950 [23]	10	23	—	20	82	—	67	42	27	39	64	4,368	293	669	150
1960 [23]	14	37	—	22	96	—	54	37	34	37	105	4,586	378	826	159
1960 [24]	10	37	—	9	79	—	46	31	43	38	111	4,268	378	801	167
1970 [25]	20	49	—	10	79	—	85	26	51	36	164	3,756	397	752	164
1970 [26]	20	49	—	10	79	—	85	26	51	35	164	3,753	399	760	164

	Managers, officials, and proprietors, except farm														
	Managers, officials, and proprietors not elsewhere classified														
			Retail trade												
	Telecommunications, utilities, and sanitary services	Wholesale trade	Total	Eating and drinking places	Food and dairy stores, and milk retailing	General merchandise and 5-and-10-cent stores	Apparel and accessories stores	Motor vehicles and accessories, retailing	Gasoline service stations	Furniture, home furnishings, and equipment stores	Hardware, farm implement, and building materials	Other retail trade	Banking and other finance	Insurance and real estate	Banking, insurance, and real estate
	Ba3788	Ba3789	Ba3790	Ba3791	Ba3792	Ba3793	Ba3794	Ba3795	Ba3796	Ba3797	Ba3798	Ba3799	Ba3800	Ba3801	Ba3802 [17]
Year	Thousand	Thousand	Thousand	Thousand	Thousand	Thousand	Thousand	Thousand	Thousand	Thousand	Thousand	Thousand	Thousand	Thousand	Thousand
1900	6	78	930	110	—	—	—	—	—	—	—	820 [34]	76	14	—
1910	19	104	1,119	129	395	167	85	5	2	—	—	336 [35]	75	29	—
1920	25	143	1,220	106	444	162	97	29	15	—	—	368 [35]	122	38	—
1930	39	152	1,592	165	540	184	96	62	89	—	—	456 [35]	174	66	—
1940	54	225	1,620	270	469	111	99	65	183	57	95	271	126	65	—
1950 [22]	68	343	1,977	370	512	128	130	119	186	98	131	305	143	117	—
1950 [23]	86	338	1,943	365	495	139	128	117	184	97	129	288	142	116	—
1960 [23]	108	338	1,628	287	327	135	108	143	197	81	122	229	227	191	—
1960 [24]	108	340	1,341	—	327	136	108	143	197	81	122	228	—	—	397
1970 [25]	115	310	1,119	—	255	128	82	130	170	71	81	202	—	—	212
1970 [26]	117	312	1,122	—	255	128	82	130	169	71	81	206	—	—	214

Notes appear at end of table

(continued)

TABLE Ba3688–3832 Detailed occupations – the economically active population: 1900–1970 [Part 1] *Continued*

	Managers, officials, and proprietors, except farm — Managers, officials, and proprietors not elsewhere classified						Clerical and kindred workers								
	Automobile repair services and garages	Miscellaneous repair services	Automobile and miscellaneous repair services	Personal business services	Business services	All other industries (including not reported)	Total	Agents not elsewhere classified	Collectors, bill and account	Agents not elsewhere classified and collectors	Attendants and assistants, library	Attendants, physician's and dentist's office	Baggagemen, transportation	Bookkeepers	Cashiers
	Ba3803	Ba3804	Ba3805 [18]	Ba3806	Ba3807	Ba3808	Ba3809	Ba3810	Ba3811	Ba3812 [19]	Ba3813	Ba3814	Ba3815	Ba3816	Ba3817
Year	Thousand	Thousand	Thousand	Thousand	Thousand	Thousand	Thousand	Thousand	Thousand	Thousand	Thousand	Thousand	Thousand	Thousand	Thousand
1900	—	—	—	72	—	36 [36]	877	—	—	59	1	—	19	—	—
1910	5	7	—	88	—	74 [36]	1,987	28	36	—	3	6	12	—	—
1920	56	8	—	76	—	107 [36]	3,385	64	31	—	2	14	12	—	—
1930	93	9	—	105	—	140 [36]	4,336	102	43	—	2	28	9	—	—
1940	66	14	—	129	33	169	4,982	73	45	—	24	35	6	—	—
1950 [22]	86	35	—	216	63	259	7,232	128	24	—	13	43	8	—	—
1950 [23]	85	34	—	213	59	241	7,132	126	24	—	13	42	8	739	239
1960 [23]	60	28	—	211	103	330	9,617	163	32	—	33	73	6	936	492
1960 [24]	—	—	191	212	—	332	9,431	—	34	—	37	—	—	951	510
1970 [25]	—	—	195	223	—	270	13,457	—	53	—	129	—	—	1,574	878
1970 [26]	—	—	196	225	—	245	14,208	—	53	—	126	—	—	1,572	869

	Clerical and kindred workers														
	Bookkeepers and cashiers	Express messengers and railway mail clerks	Mail carriers	Stenographers, typists, and secretaries	Messenger and office boys	Telegraph messengers	Messengers, including telegraph	Telegraph operators	Telephone operators	Ticket, station, and express agents	Office machine operators	Shipping and receiving clerks	Bank tellers	Dispatchers and starters, vehicle	Clerical and kindred workers not elsewhere classified
	Ba3818 [20]	Ba3819	Ba3820	Ba3821	Ba3822	Ba3823	Ba3824 [21]	Ba3825	Ba3826	Ba3827	Ba3828	Ba3829	Ba3830	Ba3831	Ba3832
Year	Thousand	Thousand	Thousand	Thousand	Thousand	Thousand	Thousand	Thousand	Thousand	Thousand	Thousand	Thousand	Thousand	Thousand	Thousand
1900	232	—	28	134	—	—	66	56	19	27	—	—	—	—	235 [37]
1910	447	22	81	387	103	9	—	66	98	35	—	—	—	—	654 [37]
1920	616	25	91	786	110	9	—	75	190	37	—	—	—	—	1,323 [37]
1930	738	26	121	1,097	80	16	—	68	249	38	38	—	—	—	1,681 [38]
1940	721	23	124	1,223	64	17	—	42	214	47	66	233	—	—	2,026 [39]
1950 [22]	994	19	171	1,661	60	8	—	36	375	61	150	304	—	—	3,178 [39]
1950 [23]	—	19	168	1,629	59	8	—	35	367	68	146	297	65	32	3,047
1960 [23]	—	7	202	2,313	63	5	—	21	372	73	318	295	131	59	4,026
1960 [24]	—	—	199	2,316	—	—	63	21	372	75	322	325	135	48	4,025
1970 [25]	—	—	256	3,920	—	—	61	13	421	100	572	427	254	61	4,737
1970 [26]	—	—	256	3,914	—	—	59	13	420	100	571	427	253	61	5,514

[1] Persons age 14 years and over, except as indicated for 1970.
[2] Combines series Ba3703–3704.
[3] Combines series Ba3702–3704.
[4] Combines series Ba3701–3704.
[5] Combines series Ba3710–3711.
[6] Combines series Ba3717–3718.
[7] Combines series Ba3716–3718.
[8] Combines series Ba3731–3732.
[9] Combines series Ba3737–3738.
[10] Combines series Ba3740–3741.
[11] Combines series Ba3737–3741.
[12] Combines series Ba3747–3748.
[13] Combines series Ba3767–3768.
[14] Combines series Ba3770–3771.
[15] Combines series Ba3773–3774.
[16] Combines series Ba3776–3777.
[17] Combines series Ba3800–3801.
[18] Combines series Ba3803–3804 and Ba3807.
[19] Combines series Ba3810–3811.
[20] Combines series Ba3816–3817.
[21] Combines series Ba3822–3823.
[22] 1950 classification.
[23] 1960 classification.
[24] 1970 classification.
[25] Age 14 and older.
[26] Age 16 and older.
[27] Includes persons for whom occupations were not reported.
[28] Includes occupations not shown separately.
[29] Includes series Ba3691–3694.
[30] Includes series Ba3721–3724.
[31] Includes series Ba3722–3724.
[32] Includes series Ba3723–3724.
[33] Includes series Ba3747–3748.
[34] Includes series Ba3792–3798.
[35] Includes series Ba3797–3798.
[36] Includes series Ba3807.
[37] Includes series Ba3828–3831.
[38] Includes series Ba3829–3831.
[39] Includes series Ba3830–3831.

Sources

U.S. Bureau of the Census. For 1900–1950 (1950 classification): David L. Kaplan and M. Claire Casey, *Occupational Trends in the United States, 1900–1950,* Working Paper number 5, 1958; for 1950–1960 (1960 classification): *U.S. Census of Population: 1960,* volume I, part 1, Table 201; for 1960–1970 (1970 classification): *U.S. Census of Population: 1970,* volume I, part 1, Table 221.

Documentation

The data for 1900–1950 (1950 classification) constitute primarily an updating by Kaplan and Casey of the material in *Sixteenth Census Reports, Comparative Occupation Statistics in the United States, 1870–1940.* Separate series developed by Alba M. Edwards in that report were brought together, and a number of new estimates were prepared to fill the gaps. The appropriate figures were then adjusted to conform to the definitions used in the 1950 occupational classification system. Except where firm evidence supported a change, Edwards's basic assumptions and estimates were utilized throughout.

The source cautions that the data, particularly those for 1900, are approximations only. The estimates for 1900 "were included mainly for the purpose of rounding out a half-century of information, despite some obvious deficiencies. Particularly prior to 1910, there is little information available on the exact definitions used for the several occupational categories. And, even for fairly recent years, there is often only meager statistical intelligence on which to base adjustments for comparability with the 1950 definitions."

The universe covered in the Kaplan and Casey series is described as the "economically active population." Prior to 1940, this refers to civilian gainful workers 10 years old and over; for 1940 and 1950, it refers to persons 14 years old and over in the experienced civilian labor force (all employed and unemployed workers with previous work experience). Two differences should be noted. First, there are important differences between the gainful-worker and labor force concepts (see essay on occupations in this chapter). Second, there is the difference in age limitation. The inclusion of the 10–13 group prior to 1940, and their exclusion in 1940 and 1950, follows the census practice in those years.

The occupation classification system used in the 1970 Census is similar to that used in each decennial census since 1940. However, the changes made for each of the censuses affect the comparability of data from one census to another. For example, many of the larger 1960 occupation categories were divided into several smaller categories, increasing the number of categories in the 1970 system to 441, compared with 297 in 1960.

A new major group, "transport equipment operatives," which was added to the occupation classification in 1970, includes occupations that were formerly part of the "operatives" major group. The arrangement of some major groups was changed to form more "families" of occupations. This applies especially to the "professional" and "service" major groups. Although there was an effort to limit changes between major groups, there were many cases for which such changes were necessary. One such change is the treatment of apprentices. They were moved from "operatives" to "craftsmen" and are classified as a subcategory of their craft.

Two other changes in the census have an important effect on comparability: (1) the allocation of "not reported" cases to the major groups in 1970, which increased the size of those totals relative to the totals for 1950 and 1960, when there was no allocation of these characteristics; and (2) the age coverage for statistics on these subjects to accord with past and current definitions of the labor force.

The Census of Population occupational classification system is generally comparable with the system used in U.S. Bureau of Employment Security, *Dictionary of Occupational Titles* (DOT), 3d edition (1965), with the exception of the blue collar workers (that is, manual and service workers). The DOT structure for these occupations is quite different from that used by the Census Bureau. An important reason is that the two systems are designed to meet different needs and to be used under different circumstances. The DOT system is designed primarily for employment service needs, such as placement and counseling, and is ordinarily used to classify very detailed occupational information obtained in an interview with the worker. The census system, on the other hand, is designed for statistical purposes and is ordinarily used in the classification of limited occupational descriptions obtained in a self-enumeration questionnaire or in an interview with a member of the worker's family.

TABLE Ba3833–3936 Detailed occupations – the economically active population: 1900–1970[1] [Part 2]

Contributed by Matthew Sobek

	Salesworkers													
										Salesmen and sales clerks not elsewhere classified				
	Total	Advertising agents and salesmen	Auctioneers	Demonstrators	Hucksters and peddlers	Insurance agents and brokers	Newsboys	Real estate agents and brokers	Stock and bond salesmen	Total	Manufacturing	Wholesale trade	Retail trade	Other industries (including not reported)
	Ba3833	Ba3834	Ba3835	Ba3836	Ba3837	Ba3838	Ba3839	Ba3840	Ba3841	Ba3842 [2]	Ba3843	Ba3844	Ba3845	Ba3846
Year	Thousand	Thousand	Thousand	Thousand	Thousand	Thousand	Thousand	Thousand	Thousand	Thousand	Thousand	Thousand	Thousand	Thousand
1900	1,307	12	3	3	77	78	7	34	4	1,089	—	—	—	—
1910	1,755	11	4	4	80	88	30	78	6	1,454	—	—	—	—
1920	2,058	25	5	5	50	120	28	89	11	1,724	—	—	—	—
1930	3,059	40	4	8	57	257	39	150	22	2,482	—	—	—	—
1940	3,450	41	4	10	55	253	58	119	18	2,893	—	—	—	—
1950 [17]	4,133	35	6	14	24	312	101	145	11	3,485	—	—	—	—
1950 [18]	4,025	34	5	14	24	276	100	143	11	—	334	413	2,536	136
1960 [18]	4,801	35	4	26	57	369	197	196	29	—	474	504	2,724	186
1960 [19]	4,799	35	4	29	62	371	197	196	35	—	475	508	2,669	217
1970 [20]	5,433	65	5	40	122	461	188	266	99	—	420	651	2,868	247
1970 [21]	5,625 [22]	64	5	40	122	460	65	266	99	—	419	650	2,845	244

	Craftsmen, foremen, and kindred workers														
	Total	Bakers	Boilermakers	Bookbinders	Brickmasons, stonemasons, and tile setters	Cabinetmakers	Carpenters	Cement and concrete finishers	Electrotypers and stereotypers	Engravers, except photoengravers	Photoengravers and lithographers	Engravers, photoengravers, and lithographers	Compositors and typesetters	Pressmen and plate printers, printing	Engravers, photoengravers, compositors, and pressmen
	Ba3847	Ba3848	Ba3849	Ba3850	Ba3851	Ba3852	Ba3853	Ba3854	Ba3855	Ba3856	Ba3857	Ba3858 [3]	Ba3859	Ba3860	Ba3861 [4]
Year	Thousand	Thousand	Thousand	Thousand	Thousand	Thousand	Thousand	Thousand	Thousand	Thousand	Thousand	Thousand	Thousand	Thousand	Thousand
1900	3,062	70	31	26	149	36	596	—	3	—	—	—	—	—	136
1910	4,315	90	45	17	160	43	815	9	4	—	—	22	128	20	—
1920	5,482	98	74	19	135	50	885	8	5	—	—	23	140	19	—
1930	6,246	141	50	19	171	63	917	15	8	—	—	28	184	31	—
1940	6,203	139	33	19	141	60	776	32	8	9	23	—	181	36	—
1950 [17]	8,350	128	40	33	181	78	1,016	34	12	10	29	—	182	51	—
1950 [18]	8,205	125	39	32	177	77	993	33	12	10	29	—	179	50	—
1960 [18]	9,241	113	27	28	208	69	924	48	9	12	25	—	183	75	—
1960 [19]	9,465 [16]	117	28	30	222	71	936	48	9	12	28	—	193	85	—
1970 [20]	10,435 [16]	113	31	36	213	70	923	75	7	9	33	—	163	160	—
1970 [21]	11,082 [16]	112	31	36	213	70	922	75	7	9	33	—	163	160	—

	Craftsmen, foremen, and kindred workers														
											Foremen				
													Manufacturing		
	Decorators and window dressers	Electricians	Cranemen, derrickmen, and hoistmen	Excavating, grading, and road machinery operators	Cranemen and excavating machinery operators	Stationary engineers	Cranemen, excavating machinery operators, and stationary engineers	Blacksmiths	Forgemen and hammermen	Blacksmiths, forgemen, and hammermen	Foremen not elsewhere classified	Construction	Total	Metal industries	Metal, machinery, and transportation equipment
	Ba3862	Ba3863	Ba3864	Ba3865	Ba3866 [5]	Ba3867	Ba3868 [6]	Ba3869	Ba3870	Ba3871 [7]	Ba3872	Ba3873	Ba3874	Ba3875	Ba3876
Year	Thousand	Thousand	Thousand	Thousand	Thousand	Thousand	Thousand	Thousand	Thousand	Thousand	Thousand	Thousand	Thousand	Thousand	Thousand
1900	3	51	—	—	—	—	134	—	—	220	162	—	90	—	—
1910	5	108	—	—	—	—	219	—	—	238	318	15	164	—	—
1920	9	192	—	—	—	—	258	—	—	209	485	14	296	—	—
1930	20	253	—	—	—	—	294	—	—	136	551	43	293	—	—
1940	30	221	—	—	123	201	—	—	—	99	585	79	310	—	—
1950 [17]	46	332	—	—	223	222	—	—	—	60	867	62	525	—	—
1950 [18]	45	326	108	111	—	219	—	45	14	—	856	61	520	84	81
1960 [18]	53	356	132	226	—	276	—	21	12	—	1,199	103	756	131	134
1960 [19]	53	365	133	284	—	293	—	20	13	—	1,186	103	662	—	—
1970 [20]	73	483	159	346	—	173	—	10	16	—	1,618	158	934	—	—
1970 [21]	72	483	159	345	—	173	—	10	16	—	1,617	159	938	—	—

	Craftsmen, foremen, and kindred workers														
	Foremen														
	Manufacturing														
	Machinery, including electrical	Transportation equipment	Textiles, textile products, and apparel	Other durable goods	Other nondurable goods (including not specified manufacturing)	Other goods (including not specified manufacturing)	Railroads and railway express service	Transportation, except railroads	Telecommunications, utilities, and sanitary services	Transportation (except railroads), and telecommunications	Railroads, other transportation, and telecommunications	Other industries (including not reported)	Furriers	Painters, construction and maintenance	Glaziers
	Ba3877	Ba3878 [8]	Ba3879	Ba3880	Ba3881	Ba3882 [9]	Ba3883	Ba3884	Ba3885	Ba3886 [10]	Ba3887 [11]	Ba3888	Ba3889	Ba3890	Ba3891
Year	Thousand	Thousand	Thousand	Thousand	Thousand	Thousand	Thousand	Thousand	Thousand	Thousand	Thousand	Thousand	Thousand	Thousand	Thousand
1900	—	—	—	—	—	—	38	—	—	10	—	24	7	—	—
1910	—	—	—	—	—	—	69	—	—	24	—	45	8	—	—
1920	—	—	—	—	—	—	81	—	—	31	—	63	9	—	—
1930	—	—	—	—	—	—	83	—	—	44	—	88	12	—	—
1940	—	112	53	—	—	144	51	15	27	—	—	104	16	451	8
1950 [17]	—	218	72	—	—	235	55	20	41	—	—	164	14	447	11
1950 [18]	51	—	70	77	157	—	54	20	41	—	—	161	13	433	11
1960 [18]	82	—	76	102	230	—	36	28	58	—	—	218	4	416	16
1960 [19]	—	—	—	—	—	—	—	—	—	—	202	218	5	384	18
1970 [20]	—	—	—	—	—	—	—	—	—	—	156	369	3	361	26
1970 [21]	—	—	—	—	—	—	—	—	—	—	157	363	3	359	26

Notes appear at end of table

(continued)

TABLE Ba3833–3936 Detailed occupations – the economically active population: 1900–1970 [Part 2] *Continued*

	Craftsmen, foremen, and kindred workers														
				Inspectors not elsewhere classified											
	Painters and glaziers	Heat treaters, annealers, and temperers	Inspectors, scalers, and graders, log and lumber	Total	Construction	Railroads and railway express service	Transportation except railroad, communications, and other public utilities	Other industries (including not reported)	Jewelers, watchmakers, goldsmiths, and silversmiths	Linemen and servicemen, telegraph, telephone, and power	Locomotive engineers	Locomotive firemen	Locomotive engineers and firemen	Loom fixers	Job setters, metal
	Ba3892 [12]	Ba3893	Ba3894	Ba3895	Ba3896	Ba3897	Ba3898	Ba3899	Ba3900	Ba3901	Ba3902	Ba3903	Ba3904 [13]	Ba3905	Ba3906
Year	Thousand	Thousand	Thousand	Thousand	Thousand	Thousand	Thousand	Thousand	Thousand	Thousand	Thousand	Thousand	Thousand	Thousand	Thousand
1900	221	—	2	22	1	20	1	—	23	18	—	—	107	9	—
1910	288	2	7	53	4	28	8	14	33	35	99	76	—	13	—
1920	265	3	7	77	3	43	10	21	40	51	113	91	—	16	—
1930	446	6	7	78	7	39	14	17	39	106	104	67	—	19	—
1940	—	11	17	82	9	30	14	30	36	116	67	50	—	25	—
1950 [17]	—	19	18	99	8	37	13	40	49	219	74	57	—	32	—
1950 [18]	—	18	20	98	8	37	13	40	48	217	73	56	—	31	25
1960 [18]	—	20	21	102	15	30	15	42	38	278	58	39	—	24	41
1960 [19]	—	22	22	101	15	30	—	56 [23]	38	273	60	39	—	24	—
1970 [20]	—	21	18	121	23	25	—	73 [23]	38	397	50	14	—	21	—
1970 [21]	—	21	18	121	23	25	—	72 [23]	38	397	50	14	—	21	—

	Craftsmen, foremen, and kindred workers														
			Mechanics and repairmen												
	Machinists	Job setters and machinists	Airplane	Automobile	Railroad and car shop	Office machine	Radio and television	Mechanics and repairmen not elsewhere classified	Toolmakers, die makers, and die setters	Job setters, machinists, mechanics, and toolmakers	Millers, grain, flour, feed, and so forth	Millwrights	Molders, metal	Motion picture projectionists	Opticians, and lens grinders and polishers
	Ba3907	Ba3908 [14]	Ba3909	Ba3910	Ba3911	Ba3912	Ba3913	Ba3914	Ba3915	Ba3916 [15]	Ba3917	Ba3918	Ba3919	Ba3920	Ba3921
Year	Thousand	Thousand	Thousand	Thousand	Thousand	Thousand	Thousand	Thousand	Thousand	Thousand	Thousand	Thousand	Thousand	Thousand	Thousand
1900	—	—	—	—	—	—	—	—	—	304	25	8	97	—	6
1910	—	—	—	—	—	—	—	—	—	520	23	17	121	4	9
1920	—	—	—	—	—	—	—	—	—	1,168	23	38	124	10	11
1930	—	—	—	—	—	—	—	—	—	1,387	16	42	105	20	13
1940	—	535	28	448	46	—	—	436 [24]	100	—	16	44	86	24	12
1950 [17]	—	571	75	693	49	—	—	987 [24]	160	—	10	61	65	27	20
1950 [18]	535	—	74	682	48	31	79	875	157	—	10	60	64	27	20
1960 [18]	516	—	119	703	41	30	106	1,302	187	—	9	68	52	18	21
1960 [19]	521	—	116	684	62	30	105	1,188	188	—	9	69	53	18	21
1970 [20]	390	—	146	938	57	40	141	1,165	207	—	7	81	57	16	28
1970 [21]	390	—	146	936	56	40	140	1,135	207	—	7	81	57	16	28

	Craftsmen, foremen, and kindred workers														
	Paperhangers	Pattern and model makers, except paper	Piano and organ tuners and repairmen	Plasterers	Plumbers and pipe fitters	Rollers and roll hands, metal	Roofers and slaters	Shoemakers and repairers, except factory	Stonecutters and stone carvers	Structural metalworkers	Tailors and tailoresses	Tinsmiths, coppersmiths, and sheet metal workers	Upholsterers	Craftsmen and kindred workers not elsewhere classified	Members of the armed forces
	Ba3922	Ba3923	Ba3924	Ba3925	Ba3926	Ba3927	Ba3928	Ba3929	Ba3930	Ba3931	Ba3932	Ba3933	Ba3934	Ba3935	Ba3936 [16]
Year	Thousand	Thousand	Thousand	Thousand	Thousand	Thousand	Thousand	Thousand	Thousand	Thousand	Thousand	Thousand	Thousand	Thousand	Thousand
1900	22	15	4	35	92	6	9	102	37	4	134	49	26	60	—
1910	26	24	7	48	148	18	14	70	36	18	205	60	20	73	—
1920	19	28	7	38	207	25	12	79	23	31	192	75	24	66	—
1930	28	30	7	70	238	31	24	76	23	33	169	83	42	43	—
1940	31	30	5	53	211	33	33	68	15	47	120	91	43	47	3
1950 [17]	23	38	8	66	304	32	50	60	9	57	88	133	65	76	38
1950 [18]	23	37	8	64	298	31	49	59	9	55	86	130	64	74	30
1960 [18]	11	40	6	53	331	31	55	37	7	66	43	145	62	112	18
1960 [19]	27	42	6	54	340	20	57	43	7	66	87	150	63	281	18
1970 [20]	11	40	7	31	398	20	65	32	7	79	71	162	65	335	36
1970 [21]	11	40	7	31	398	20	65	32	7	79	71	162	65	996	36

[1] Persons age 14 years and over, except as indicated for 1970.
[2] Combines series Ba3843–3846.
[3] Combines series Ba3856–3857.
[4] Combines series Ba3856–3860.
[5] Combines series Ba3864–3865.
[6] Combines series Ba3864–3867.
[7] Combines series Ba3869–3870.
[8] Combines series Ba3875–3877.
[9] Combines series Ba3880–3881.
[10] Combines series Ba3884–3885.
[11] Combines series Ba3883–3885.
[12] Combines series Ba3890–3891.
[13] Combines series Ba3902–3903.
[14] Combines series Ba3906–3907.
[15] Combines series Ba3906–3915.
[16] Includes occupations not shown separately.
[17] 1950 classification.
[18] 1960 classification.
[19] 1970 classification.
[20] Age 14 and older.
[21] Age 16 and older.
[22] Includes persons for whom occupations were not reported.
[23] Includes series Ba3898.
[24] Includes series Ba3912–3913.

Sources

See the sources for Table Ba3688–3832.

Documentation

See the text for Table Ba3688–3832.

TABLE Ba3937–4110 Detailed occupations – the economically active population: 1900–1970[1] [Part 3]

Contributed by Matthew Sobek

	Operatives and kindred workers														
		Apprentices													
	Total	Carpenters	Electricians	Plumbers and pipe fitters	Printing trades	Machinists and toolmakers	Auto mechanics	Bricklayers and masons	Mechanics, except auto	Building trades not elsewhere classified	Metalworking trades not elsewhere classified	Other specified trades	Trade not specified	Asbestos and insulation workers	Attendants, auto service and parking
	Ba3937	Ba3938	Ba3939	Ba3940	Ba3941	Ba3942	Ba3943	Ba3944	Ba3945	Ba3946	Ba3947	Ba3948	Ba3949	Ba3950	Ba3951
Year	Thousand	Thousand	Thousand	Thousand	Thousand	Thousand	Thousand	Thousand	Thousand	Thousand	Thousand	Thousand	Thousand	Thousand	Thousand
1900	3,720	2	—	3	4	—	—	—	—	—	—	—	57 [31]	—	—
1910	5,441	6	3	10	12	—	—	—	—	—	—	—	86 [31]	2	—
1920	6,587	5	10	7	12	39	—	—	—	—	—	—	66 [32]	1	18
1930	7,691	4	5	6	11	14	—	—	—	—	—	—	49 [32]	3	144
1940	9,518	8	3	5	10	20	—	—	—	—	—	33 [30]	12	6	245
1950 [24]	12,030	11	9	13	16	16	—	—	—	—	—	42 [30]	15	17	253
1950 [25]	11,754 [29]	11	9	12	16	16	4	6	7	4	7	13	15	15	248
1960 [25]	12,846 [29]	6	10	8	12	16	2	3	4	3	6	9	10	20	378
1960 [26]	12,254 [29]	—	—	—	—	—	—	—	—	—	—	—	—	20	—
1970 [27]	13,406 [29]	—	—	—	—	—	—	—	—	—	—	—	—	26	—
1970 [28]	14,335 [29]	—	—	—	—	—	—	—	—	—	—	—	—	26	—

	Operatives and kindred workers														
	Blasters and powdermen	Boatmen, canalmen, and lock keepers	Brakemen, railroad	Switchmen, railroad	Brakemen and switchmen, railroad	Chainmen, rodmen, and axmen, surveying	Conductors, bus and street railway	Deliverymen and routemen	Dressmakers and seamstresses, except factory	Dyers	Filers, grinders, and polishers, metal	Fruit, nut, and vegetable graders and packers, except factory	Furnacemen, smeltermen, and pourers	Heaters, metal	Laundry and dry cleaning operatives
	Ba3952	Ba3953	Ba3954	Ba3955	Ba3956 [2]	Ba3957	Ba3958	Ba3959	Ba3960	Ba3961	Ba3962	Ba3963	Ba3964	Ba3965	Ba3966
Year	Thousand	Thousand	Thousand	Thousand	Thousand	Thousand	Thousand	Thousand	Thousand	Thousand	Thousand	Thousand	Thousand	Thousand	Thousand
1900	1	13	—	—	107	—	24	167	413	5	17	—	13	5	91
1910	2	5	—	—	160	4	57	230	467	14	50	5	26	10	132
1920	7	6	—	—	208	3	64	170	259	15	60	8	24	16	142
1930	7	6	—	—	173	4	37	187	198	18	79	10	20	15	265
1940	7	6	77	50	—	11	18	294	172	28	117	25	33	10	314
1950 [24]	12	9	82	63	—	8	12	253	147	26	160	37	59	10	462
1950 [25]	12	8	81	62	—	8	11	249	147	25	156	34	58	10	451
1960 [25]	7	7	65	60	—	11	4	438	124	19	159	28	57	8	412
1960 [26]	6	—	65	60	—	11	12	462	126	19	152	—	56	8	—
1970 [27]	8	—	49	53	—	12	10	649	102	25	123	—	68	7	—
1970 [28]	8	—	49	53	—	12	10	643	102	25	123	—	67	7	—

	Operatives and kindred workers														
			Mine operatives and laborers not elsewhere classified												
	Meatcutters, except slaughter and packing houses	Milliners	Total	Coal mining	Crude petroleum and natural gas extraction	Mining and quarrying, except fuel	Motormen, mine, factory, logging camp, and so forth	Motormen, street, subway, and elevated railway	Oilers and greasers, except auto	Painters, except construction and maintenance	Photographic process workers	Power station operators	Sailors and deckhands	Sawyers	Spinners, textile
	Ba3967	Ba3968	Ba3969 [3]	Ba3970	Ba3971	Ba3972	Ba3973	Ba3974	Ba3975	Ba3976	Ba3977	Ba3978	Ba3979	Ba3980	Ba3981
Year	Thousand	Thousand	Thousand	Thousand	Thousand	Thousand	Thousand	Thousand	Thousand	Thousand	Thousand	Thousand	Thousand	Thousand	Thousand
1900	33	75	660	—	—	—	—	37	—	55	2	—	40	18	56
1910	41	100	907	—	—	—	3	56	14	49	2	12	47	43	74
1920	61	50	995	—	—	—	12	63	25	61	3	21	55	34	83
1930	120	25	892	—	—	—	17	58	31	83	8	29	65	36	81
1940	160	15	845	—	—	—	20	39	40	104	15	22	47	50	113
1950 [24]	180	13	620	—	—	—	25	27	63	126	30	22	55	100	88
1950 [25]	177	13	605	381	108	116	24	27	62	123	29	22	52	99	85
1960 [25]	186	4	331	140	102	89	15	8	57	148	44	27	41	95	52
1960 [26]	189	4	247	—	—	—	15	—	57	—	47	27	41	104	—
1970 [27]	206	2	164	—	—	—	10	—	49	—	67	18	29	108	—
1970 [28]	205	2	164	—	—	—	10	—	49	—	67	18	29	108	—

	Operatives and kindred workers														
								Operatives and kindred workers not elsewhere classified							
									Manufacturing						
	Stationary firemen	Bus drivers	Taxicab drivers and chauffeurs	Truck and tractor drivers	Bus, taxicab, and truck drivers	Weavers, textile	Welders and flame-cutters	Total	Total	Sawmills, planing mills, and millwork	Miscellaneous wood products	Sawmills and miscellaneous wood products	Furniture and fixtures	Glass and glass products	Cement and concrete, gypsum, and plaster products
	Ba3982	Ba3983	Ba3984	Ba3985	Ba3986 [4]	Ba3987	Ba3988	Ba3989	Ba3990	Ba3991	Ba3992	Ba3993 [5]	Ba3994	Ba3995	Ba3996
Year	Thousand	Thousand	Thousand	Thousand	Thousand	Thousand	Thousand	Thousand	Thousand	Thousand	Thousand	Thousand	Thousand	Thousand	Thousand
1900	73	—	—	—	—	155	—	1,592	1,443	—	—	75	19	25	5
1910	111	—	—	—	46	202	3	2,451	2,318	—	—	105	44	42	9
1920	144	—	—	—	285	219	54	3,284	3,076	—	—	92	52	45	8
1930	127	—	—	—	972	225	37	3,634	3,189	—	—	91	72	41	11
1940	128	—	—	—	1,515	109	137	4,654	4,225	63	36	—	82	54	13
1950 [24]	130	—	—	—	1,808	105	283	6,627	5,847	151	46	—	132	76	30
1950 [25]	128	158	214	1,397	—	103	277	4,752	4,079	144	39	—	112	56	28
1960 [25]	93	185	171	1,663	—	66	387	4,993	4,305	104	38	—	107	55	35
1960 [26]	106	185	171	1,550 [33]	—	69	388	—	—	—	—	—	—	—	—
1970 [27]	97	239	158	1,455 [33]	—	52	566	—	—	—	—	—	—	—	—
1970 [28]	97	239	158	1,453 [33]	—	52	566	—	—	—	—	—	—	—	—

Notes appear at end of table

(continued)

TABLE Ba3937–4110 Detailed occupations – the economically active population: 1900–1970 [Part 3] *Continued*

	Operatives and kindred workers														
	Operatives and kindred workers not elsewhere classified														
	Manufacturing														
	Structural clay products	Pottery and related products	Miscellaneous nonmetallic mineral and stone products	Motor vehicles and motor vehicle equipment	Ship and boat building and repairing	Blast furnaces, steelworks, and rolling mills	Other primary iron and steel industries	Fabricated steel products	Other primary iron and steel, and steel products	Office and store machines and devices	Miscellaneous machinery	Not specified metal industries	Agricultural machinery and tractors	Aircraft and parts	Railroad and miscellaneous transportation equipment
	Ba3997	Ba3998	Ba3999	Ba4000	Ba4001	Ba4002	Ba4003	Ba4004	Ba4005 [6]	Ba4006	Ba4007	Ba4008	Ba4009	Ba4010	Ba4011
Year	Thousand	Thousand	Thousand	Thousand	Thousand	Thousand	Thousand	Thousand	Thousand	Thousand	Thousand	Thousand	Thousand	Thousand	Thousand
1900	7	10	9	—	—	—	—	—	—	—	—	—	—	—	—
1910	13	16	9	21	6	—	—	—	—	—	—	—	—	—	—
1920	10	17	6	125	53	—	—	—	—	—	—	—	—	—	—
1930	13	23	8	170	11	—	—	—	—	—	—	—	—	—	—
1940	16	25	18	208	19	105	—	—	209	24	123	12	21	27	11
1950 [24]	23	35	28	371	15	133	—	—	324	40	273	4	52	67	19
1950 [25]	21	32	24	216	15	120	65	216	—	28	165	4	36	31	17
1960 [25]	21	21	38	174	20	100	65	288	—	26	231	2	24	78	18
1960 [26]	—	—	—	—	—	—	—	—	—	—	—	—	—	—	—
1970 [27]	—	—	—	—	—	—	—	—	—	—	—	—	—	—	—
1970 [28]	—	—	—	—	—	—	—	—	—	—	—	—	—	—	—

	Operatives and kindred workers														
	Operatives and kindred workers not elsewhere classified														
	Manufacturing														
	Metal industry and machinery not elsewhere classified	Metal industry and machinery not elsewhere classified, including motor vehicles	Primary nonferrous industries	Nonferrous metal industries and products	Electrical machinery, equipment, and supplies	Professional equipment and supplies	Photographic equipment and supplies	Professional and photographic equipment and supplies	Watches, clocks, and clockwork-operated devices	Miscellaneous manufacturing industries	Meat products	Canning and preserving of fruits, vegetables, and seafood	Meat products and fruit and vegetable canning	Dairy products	Grain-mill products
	Ba4012 [7]	Ba4013 [8]	Ba4014	Ba4015 [9]	Ba4016	Ba4017	Ba4018	Ba4019 [10]	Ba4020	Ba4021	Ba4022	Ba4023	Ba4024 [11]	Ba4025	Ba4026
Year	Thousand	Thousand	Thousand	Thousand	Thousand	Thousand	Thousand	Thousand	Thousand	Thousand	Thousand	Thousand	Thousand	Thousand	Thousand
1900	—	121	—	11	18	—	—	—	—	102 [34]	—	—	11	13	4
1910	286	—	—	27	25	—	—	—	—	133 [34]	26	8	—	12	4
1920	370	—	—	32	65	—	—	—	—	192 [34]	50	18	—	19	8
1930	397	—	—	34	117	—	—	—	—	172 [34]	53	26	—	26	7
1940	—	—	—	48	150	—	—	29	—	172 [35]	91	52	—	36	17
1950 [24]	—	—	—	98	356	—	—	60	—	258 [35]	132	95	—	62	33
1950 [25]	—	—	66	—	218	30	10	—	16	141	93	65	—	58	29
1960 [25]	—	—	85	—	313	44	11	—	10	140	134	92	—	57	30
1960 [26]	—	—	—	—	—	—	—	—	—	—	—	—	—	—	—
1970 [27]	—	—	—	—	—	—	—	—	—	—	—	—	—	—	—
1970 [28]	—	—	—	—	—	—	—	—	—	—	—	—	—	—	—

Year	Operatives and kindred workers — Operatives and kindred workers not elsewhere classified — Manufacturing													
	Bakery products	Confectionery and related products	Beverage industries	Miscellaneous food preparations and kindred products	Not specified food industries	Tobacco manufactures	Knitting mills	Dyeing and finishing textiles, except knit goods	Carpets, rugs, and other floor covering	Yarn, thread, and fabric mills	Miscellaneous textile mill products	Apparel and accessories	Miscellaneous fabricated textile products	Pulp, paper, and paperboard mills
	Ba4027	Ba4028	Ba4029	Ba4030	Ba4031	Ba4032	Ba4033	Ba4034	Ba4035	Ba4036	Ba4037	Ba4038	Ba4039	Ba4040
Year	Thousand	Thousand	Thousand	Thousand	Thousand	Thousand	Thousand	Thousand	Thousand	Thousand	Thousand	Thousand	Thousand	Thousand
1900	5	27	13	—	2 [36]	116	41	13	10	202	31	225	21	—
1910	9	31	20	—	16 [36]	152	85	16	15	269	48	336	18	36
1920	20	52	10	—	21 [36]	145	104	18	14	323	46	365	21	55
1930	28	44	7	—	30 [36]	104	129	20	17	324	35	422	15	64
1940	45	49	36	—	29 [36]	86	192	24	21	426	35	734	53	87
1950 [24]	68	51	57	—	51 [36]	70	154	26	26	477	32	824	58	106
1950 [25]	33	27	51	32	5	54	26	25	20	373	28	384	37	99
1960 [25]	44	26	48	35	5	41	62	24	12	251	21	395	42	110
1960 [26]	—	—	—	—	—	—	—	—	—	—	—	—	—	—
1970 [27]	—	—	—	—	—	—	—	—	—	—	—	—	—	—
1970 [28]	—	—	—	—	—	—	—	—	—	—	—	—	—	—

Year	Operatives and kindred workers — Operatives and kindred workers not elsewhere classified — Manufacturing												
	Miscellaneous paper and pulp products	Paperboard containers and boxes	Printing, publishing, and allied industries	Synthetic fibers	Paints, varnishes, and related products	Drugs and medicines	Miscellaneous chemicals and allied products	Drugs and miscellaneous chemicals	Petroleum refining	Miscellaneous petroleum and coal products	Rubber products	Leather – tanned, curried, and finished	Footwear, except rubber
	Ba4041	Ba4042	Ba4043	Ba4044	Ba4045	Ba4046	Ba4047	Ba4048 [12]	Ba4049	Ba4050	Ba4051	Ba4052	Ba4053
Year	Thousand	Thousand	Thousand	Thousand	Thousand	Thousand	Thousand	Thousand	Thousand	Thousand	Thousand	Thousand	Thousand
1900	21 [37]	19	16	—	3	—	—	9	1	2	15	26	98
1910	10	18	42	—	4	—	—	33	4	2	32	34	181
1920	14	20	48	—	6	—	—	51	14	2	86	32	206
1930	17	14	51	21	8	—	—	53	27	2	81	29	210
1940	28	41	59	31	12	—	—	72	30	5	85	35	228
1950 [24]	61	64	80	27	18	—	—	149	48	7	127	32	226
1950 [25]	50	58	71	26	16	13	113	—	43	7	136	30	169
1960 [25]	48	69	97	23	17	17	136	—	44	6	162	18	148
1960 [26]	—	—	—	—	—	—	—	—	—	—	—	—	—
1970 [27]	—	—	—	—	—	—	—	—	—	—	—	—	—
1970 [28]	—	—	—	—	—	—	—	—	—	—	—	—	—

Notes appear at end of table

(continued)

TABLE Ba3937–4110 Detailed occupations – the economically active population: 1900–1970 [Part 3] *Continued*

	Operatives and kindred workers													
	Operatives and kindred workers not elsewhere classified													
	Manufacturing		Nonmanufacturing industries (including not reported)											
	Leather products, except footwear	Not specified manufacturing industries	Total	Construction	Railroads and railway express service	Transportation, except railroad	Telecommunications, utilities, and sanitary services	Transportation (except railroad) and telecommunications	Wholesale and retail trade	Business and repair services	Transportation, telecommunications, trade, and business services	Public administration	Personal services	All other industries (including not reported)
	Ba4054	Ba4055	Ba4056	Ba4057	Ba4058	Ba4059	Ba4060	Ba4061 [13]	Ba4062	Ba4063	Ba4064 [14]	Ba4065	Ba4066	Ba4067
Year	Thousand	Thousand	Thousand	Thousand	Thousand	Thousand	Thousand	Thousand	Thousand	Thousand	Thousand	Thousand	Thousand	Thousand
1900	31	67	149	7	—	—	—	—	—	—	137	—	—	5 [38]
1910	29	93	132	8	61	—	—	19	27	6	—	3	—	9 [38]
1920	33	207	208	4	111	—	—	30	40	8	—	4	—	12 [38]
1930	26	139	445	15	98	—	—	57	74	30	—	6	—	165 [38]
1940	44	74	429	40	73	24	24	—	145	38	—	11	—	75 [38]
1950 [24]	50	43	780	71	96	37	52	—	311	54	—	54	—	105 [38]
1950 [25]	39	19	673	72	94	31	52	—	224	50	—	51	20	80
1960 [25]	31	10	688	102	56	36	50	—	220	72	—	46	15	90
1960 [26]	—	—	—	—	—	—	—	—	—	—	—	—	—	—
1970 [27]	—	—	—	—	—	—	—	—	—	—	—	—	—	—
1970 [28]	—	—	—	—	—	—	—	—	—	—	—	—	—	—

	Private household workers										Service workers, except private household				
		Laundresses			Housekeepers			Private household workers not elsewhere classified							
	Total	Total	Living in	Living out	Total	Living in	Living out	Total	Living in	Living out	Total	Attendants, hospital and other institution	Midwives	Practical nurses	Midwives and practical nurses
	Ba4068	Ba4069 [15]	Ba4070	Ba4071	Ba4072 [16]	Ba4073	Ba4074	Ba4075 [17]	Ba4076	Ba4077	Ba4078	Ba4079	Ba4080	Ba4081	Ba4082 [18]
Year	Thousand	Thousand	Thousand	Thousand	Thousand	Thousand	Thousand	Thousand	Thousand	Thousand	Thousand	Thousand	Thousand	Thousand	Thousand
1900	1,579	280	—	—	—	—	—	1,299 [40]	—	—	1,047	—	—	—	—
1910	1,851	513	—	—	—	—	—	1,338 [40]	—	—	1,711	—	—	—	—
1920	1,411	375	—	—	—	—	—	1,036 [40]	—	—	1,901	—	—	—	—
1930	1,998	344	—	—	—	—	—	1,654 [40]	—	—	2,774	—	—	—	—
1940	2,412	203	—	—	410	—	—	1,799	—	—	3,657	102	—	—	115
1950 [24]	1,539	76	—	—	150	—	—	1,313	—	—	4,641	216	—	—	151
1950 [25]	1,492 [39]	—	1	73	—	53	93	—	163	1,034	4,524	212	2	145	—
1960 [25]	1,825 [39]	—	(Z)	41	—	56	96	—	104	1,178	5,765	409	1	217	—
1960 [26]	1,817	41	—	—	156	—	—	1,619	—	—	6,086	420	1	175	—
1970 [27]	1,143	13	—	—	105	—	—	1,025	—	—	8,449	749	1	242	—
1970 [28]	1,204	12	—	—	105	—	—	1,087	—	—	9,047	746	1	242	—

	Service workers, except private household													
	Attendants, midwives, and practical nurses	Attendants (professional and personal service) not elsewhere classified	Attendants, recreation and amusement	Ushers, recreation and amusement	Attendants and ushers, recreation and amusement	Barbers, beauticians, and manicurists	Bartenders	Boarding and lodging house keepers	Bootblacks	Charwomen and cleaners	Cooks, except private household	Elevator operators	Firemen (fire protection)	Guards, watchmen, and doorkeepers
	Ba4083 [19]	Ba4084	Ba4085	Ba4086	Ba4087 [20]	Ba4088	Ba4089	Ba4090	Ba4091	Ba4092	Ba4093	Ba4094	Ba4095	Ba4096
Year	Thousand	Thousand	Thousand	Thousand	Thousand	Thousand	Thousand	Thousand	Thousand	Thousand	Thousand	Thousand	Thousand	Thousand
1900	109	—	—	—	6	133	89	71	8	29	117	13	15	—
1910	133	2	—	—	9	193	101	165	14	29	174	25	36	78
1920	157	3	—	—	13	214	26	133	15	31	200	41	51	116
1930	198	4	—	—	29	371	—	144	19	52	292	68	73	148
1940	—	42	64	22	—	449	131	74	16	72	349	87	82	216
1950 [24]	—	52	66	26	—	396	214	30	15	128	478	97	112	255
1950 [25]	—	43	65	25	—	391	209	29	15	124	466	94	112	250
1960 [25]	—	75	63	16	—	487	184	30	10	192	597	77	139	258
1960 [26]	—	84	74	16	—	489	184	30	10	402	603	77	139	259
1970 [27]	—	65	83	16	—	651	199	8	5	470	886	37	178	329
1970 [28]	—	64	76	15	—	650	199	7	4	461	873	37	178	329

	Service workers, except private household													
	Policemen and detectives, government	Policemen and detectives, private	Policemen and detectives	Marshals and constables	Guards, policemen, and marshals	Housekeepers and stewards, except private household	Janitors and sextons	Porters	Sheriffs and bailiffs	Counter and fountain workers	Waiters and waitresses	Counter workers and waiters	Watchmen (crossing) and bridge tenders	Service workers (except private household) not elsewhere classified
	Ba4097	Ba4098	Ba4099 [21]	Ba4100	Ba4101 [22]	Ba4102	Ba4103	Ba4104	Ba4105	Ba4106	Ba4107	Ba4108 [23]	Ba4109	Ba4110
Year	Thousand	Thousand	Thousand	Thousand	Thousand	Thousand	Thousand	Thousand	Thousand	Thousand	Thousand	Thousand	Thousand	Thousand
1900	—	—	—	—	116	34	57	42	5	—	—	107	4	93
1910	—	—	68	9	—	45	113	96	7	—	—	200	10	203
1920	—	—	94	7	—	52	179	102	11	—	—	242	13	203
1930	—	—	145	9	—	61	310	151	15	—	—	415	13	259
1940	135	21	—	9	—	90	377	182	16	—	—	636	10	360
1950 [24]	176	21	—	7	—	112	482	179	19	—	—	836	12	561
1950 [25]	175	21	—	7	—	110	475	174	19	93	717	—	9	544
1960 [25]	238	17	—	6	—	152	621	155	24	167	896	—	26	709
1960 [26]	—	—	262	6	—	—	785	—	24	168	899	—	29	950
1970 [27]	—	—	378	5	—	—	1,301	—	35	168	1,127	—	42	1,472
1970 [28]	—	—	378	5	—	—	1,274	—	35	161	1,100	—	42	2,168

Notes appear on next page

(continued)

TABLE Ba3937–4110 Detailed occupations – the economically active population: 1900–1970 [Part 3] *Continued*

(Z) Fewer than 500.

[1] Persons age 14 years and older, except as indicated for 1970.
[2] Combines series Ba3954–3955.
[3] Combines series Ba3970–3972.
[4] Combines series Ba3983–3985.
[5] Combines series Ba3991–3992.
[6] Combines series Ba4003–4004.
[7] Combines series Ba4002–4011.
[8] Combines series Ba4000–4011.
[9] Includes series Ba4014.
[10] Combines series Ba4017–4018.
[11] Combines series Ba4022–4023.
[12] Combines series Ba4046–4047.
[13] Combines series Ba4059–4060.
[14] Combines series Ba4058–4063.
[15] Combines series Ba4070–4071.
[16] Combines series Ba4073–4074.
[17] Combines series Ba4076–4077.
[18] Combines series Ba4080–4081.
[19] Combines series Ba4079–4081.
[20] Combines series Ba4085–4086.
[21] Combines series Ba4097–4098.
[22] Combines series Ba4096–4100.
[23] Combines series Ba4106–4107.
[24] 1950 classification.
[25] 1960 classification.
[26] 1970 classification.
[27] Age 14 and older.
[28] Age 16 and older.
[29] Includes occupations not shown separately.
[30] Includes series Ba3943–3947.
[31] Includes series Ba3942–3948.
[32] Includes series Ba3943–3948.
[33] Excludes tractor drivers.
[34] Includes series Ba4017–4020.
[35] Includes series Ba4020.
[36] Includes series Ba4030.
[37] Includes series Ba4040.
[38] Includes series Ba4066.
[39] Includes babysitters, not shown separately.
[40] Includes series Ba4072–4074.

Sources

See the sources for Table Ba3688–3832.

Documentation

See the text for Table Ba3688–3832.

TABLE Ba4111–4206 Detailed occupations – the economically active population: 1900–1970[1] [Part 4]

Contributed by Matthew Sobek

	Farm laborers and foremen						Laborers, except farm and mine						
	Total	Farm foremen	Farm laborers, wage workers	Farm laborers, unpaid family workers	Farm laborers	Farm service laborers, self-employed	Total	Fishermen and oystermen	Garage laborers, and car washers and greasers	Gardeners, except farm, and groundskeepers	Longshoremen and stevedores	Lumbermen, raftsmen, and woodchoppers	Teamsters
	Ba4111	Ba4112	Ba4113	Ba4114	Ba4115 [2]	Ba4116	Ba4117	Ba4118	Ba4119	Ba4120	Ba4121	Ba4122	Ba4123
Year	Thousand	Thousand	Thousand	Thousand	Thousand	Thousand	Thousand	Thousand	Thousand	Thousand	Thousand	Thousand	Thousand
1900	5,125	7	—	—	5,115	4	3,620	69	—	24	29	117	374
1910	5,370	19	2,832	2,514	—	6	4,478	68	4	65	63	139	441
1920	4,948	35	2,271	2,633	—	10	4,905	53	33	71	86	180	412
1930	4,290	28	2,597	1,660	—	5	5,335	73	77	168	74	147	120
1940	3,632	17	2,405	1,208	—	3	4,875	64	63	163	74	169	31
1950 [17]	2,578	17	1,617	934	—	10	3,885	75	72	159	73	196	23
1950 [18]	2,533	18	1,584	921	—	10	3,774 [23]	78	70	156	73	189	22
1960 [18]	1,560	25	1,244	284	—	5	3,530 [23]	41	93	216	61	136	22
1960 [19]	1,604	25	1,288	286	—	5	3,755 [23]	41	—	—	61	132	22
1970 [20]	995	34	848	109	—	4	3,515 [23]	31	—	—	47	90	8
1970 [21]	1,022 [22]	33	808	94	—	4	3,751 [23]	31	—	—	47	89	8

	Laborers not elsewhere classified												
		Manufacturing											
	Total	Total	Sawmills, planing mills, and millwork	Miscellaneous wood products	Sawmills and miscellaneous wood products	Furniture and fixtures	Glass and glass products	Cement and concrete, gypsum, and plaster products	Structural clay products	Glass, cement, and structural clay products	Pottery and related products	Miscellaneous nonmetallic mineral and stone products	Motor vehicles and motor vehicle equipment
	Ba4124	Ba4125	Ba4126	Ba4127	Ba4128 [3]	Ba4129	Ba4130	Ba4131	Ba4132	Ba4133 [4]	Ba4134	Ba4135	Ba4136
Year	Thousand	Thousand	Thousand	Thousand	Thousand	Thousand	Thousand	Thousand	Thousand	Thousand	Thousand	Thousand	Thousand
1900	3,007	723	—	—	139	7	15	13	42	—	6	7	—
1910	3,696	1,487	—	—	289	24	25	36	78	—	9	7	16
1920	4,070	2,169	—	—	280	35	29	30	49	—	12	5	83
1930	4,675	1,960	—	—	292	40	28	39	60	—	11	8	124
1940	4,312	1,598	230	27	—	35	21	26	39	—	7	14	71
1950 [17]	3,288	1,209	152	18	—	21	16	24	29	—	7	9	51
1950 [18]	2,997	1,154	147	18	—	20	14	24	28	—	7	9	50
1960 [18]	2,763	961	97	13	—	18	14	28	26	—	5	10	36
1960 [19]	1,165	662	47	47	—	13	—	—	—	53	—	—	20
1970 [20]	688	347	26	26	—	7	—	—	—	24	—	—	13
1970 [21]	675	349	26	26	—	7	—	—	—	24	—	—	13

Notes appear at end of table

(continued)

TABLE Ba4111–4206 Detailed occupations – the economically active population: 1900–1970 [Part 4] *Continued*

	Laborers not elsewhere classified											
	Manufacturing											
	Ship and boat building and repairing	Blast furnaces, steelworks, and rolling mills	Other primary iron and steel industries	Fabricated steel products	Other primary iron and steel, and steel products	Office and store machines and devices	Miscellaneous machinery	Not specified metal industries	Agricultural machinery and tractors	Aircraft and parts	Railroad and miscellaneous transportation equipment	Metal industry and machinery not elsewhere classified
	Ba4137	Ba4138	Ba4139	Ba4140	Ba4141 [5]	Ba4142	Ba4143	Ba4144	Ba4145	Ba4146	Ba4147	Ba4148 [6]
Year	Thousand	Thousand	Thousand	Thousand	Thousand	Thousand	Thousand	Thousand	Thousand	Thousand	Thousand	Thousand
1900	—	—	—	—	—	—	—	—	—	—	—	—
1910	12	—	—	—	—	—	—	—	—	—	—	419
1920	69	—	—	—	—	—	—	—	—	—	—	544
1930	17	—	—	—	—	—	—	—	—	—	—	492
1940	23	201	—	—	128	2	46	6	11	4	8	—
1950 [17]	16	145	—	—	111	2	43	1	14	4	6	—
1950 [18]	16	141	52	60	—	2	39	1	13	4	6	—
1960 [18]	14	119	42	62	—	2	37	(Z)	7	6	6	—
1960 [19]	—	109	—	—	—	—	—	—	—	—	—	—
1970 [20]	—	43	—	—	—	—	—	—	—	—	—	—
1970 [21]	—	43	—	—	—	—	—	—	—	—	—	—

	Laborers not elsewhere classified											
	Manufacturing											
	Metal industry and machinery not elsewhere classified, including motor vehicles	Nonferrous metal industries and products	Electrical machinery, equipment, and supplies	Professional equipment and supplies	Photographic equipment and supplies	Professional and photographic equipment and supplies	Watches, clocks, and clockwork-operated devices	Professional and photographic equipment, and watches	Miscellaneous manufacturing industries	Meat products	Canning and preserving of fruits, vegetables, and seafood	Meat products and fruit and vegetable canning
	Ba4149 [7]	Ba4150	Ba4151	Ba4152	Ba4153	Ba4154 [8]	Ba4155	Ba4156 [9]	Ba4157	Ba4158	Ba4159	Ba4160 [10]
Year	Thousand	Thousand	Thousand	Thousand	Thousand	Thousand	Thousand	Thousand	Thousand	Thousand	Thousand	Thousand
1900	145	15	8	—	—	—	—	—	30 [24]	—	—	12
1910	—	33	11	—	—	—	—	—	43 [24]	34	10	—
1920	—	43	27	—	—	—	—	—	101 [24]	60	19	—
1930	—	39	37	—	—	—	—	—	74 [24]	43	26	—
1940	—	43	30	—	—	4	—	—	27 [25]	47	34	—
1950 [17]	—	33	33	—	—	4	—	—	18 [25]	37	27	—
1950 [18]	—	27	34	3	1	—	1	—	15	36	23	—
1960 [18]	—	25	33	3	1	—	(Z)	—	12	30	24	—
1960 [19]	—	—	23	—	—	—	—	3	13	—	—	—
1970 [20]	—	—	13	—	—	—	—	2	11	—	—	—
1970 [21]	—	—	13	—	—	—	—	2	11	—	—	—

Year	Laborers not elsewhere classified											
	Manufacturing											
	Dairy products	Grain-mill products	Bakery products	Confectionery and related products	Beverage industries	Miscellaneous food preparations and kindred products	Not specified food industries	Tobacco manufacturers	Knitting mills	Dyeing and finishing textiles, except knit goods	Carpets, rugs, and other floor coverings	Yarn, thread, and fabric mills
	Ba4161	Ba4162	Ba4163	Ba4164	Ba4165	Ba4166	Ba4167	Ba4168	Ba4169	Ba4170	Ba4171	Ba4172
	Thousand	Thousand	Thousand	Thousand	Thousand	Thousand	Thousand	Thousand	Thousand	Thousand	Thousand	Thousand
1900	5	10	3	3	12	—	3 [26]	14	4	9	2	44
1910	5	9	5	3	19	—	17 [26]	16	8	10	4	59
1920	15	18	8	7	11	—	32 [26]	35	12	11	4	120
1930	17	16	12	6	9	—	26 [26]	21	9	8	5	94
1940	17	21	8	8	22	—	29 [26]	17	5	5	7	71
1950 [17]	15	20	10	4	25	—	24 [26]	10	3	3	6	50
1950 [18]	23	18	5	4	21	29	2	7	—	—	—	45
1960 [18]	18	17	9	3	17	17	2	7	—	—	—	30
1960 [19]	—	—	—	—	—	—	90 [27]	4	—	—	—	—
1970 [20]	—	—	—	—	—	—	44 [27]	2	—	—	—	—
1970 [21]	—	—	—	—	—	—	44 [27]	2	—	—	—	—

Year	Laborers not elsewhere classified											
	Manufacturing											
	Miscellaneous textile mill products	Apparel and accessories	Miscellaneous fabricated textile products	Pulp, paper, and paperboard mills	Miscellaneous paper and pulp products	Pulp and paper mills, and paper products	Paperboard containers and boxes	Pulp and paper mills, paperboard, and paper products	Printing, publishing, and allied industries	Synthetic fibers	Paints, varnishes, and related products	Drugs and medicines
	Ba4173	Ba4174	Ba4175	Ba4176	Ba4177	Ba4178 [11]	Ba4179	Ba4180 [12]	Ba4181	Ba4182	Ba4183	Ba4184
	Thousand	Thousand	Thousand	Thousand	Thousand	Thousand	Thousand	Thousand	Thousand	Thousand	Thousand	Thousand
1900	5	5	1	—	—	14	1	—	4	—	2	—
1910	8	8	1	31	2	—	1	—	5	—	3	—
1920	8	12	1	52	3	—	3	—	8	—	5	—
1930	5	14	1	52	4	—	3	—	11	5	6	—
1940	7	10	3	44	6	—	10	—	10	5	6	—
1950 [17]	4	9	3	29	9	—	10	—	12	3	5	—
1950 [18]	14	—	11 [29]	28	8	—	10	—	12	3	5	2
1960 [18]	10	—	11 [29]	25	5	—	9	—	13	3	3	2
1960 [19]	14 [28]	—	4 [29]	—	—	—	—	29	7	—	—	—
1970 [20]	12 [28]	—	4 [29]	—	—	—	—	15	5	—	—	—
1970 [21]	12 [28]	—	4 [29]	—	—	—	—	15	5	—	—	—

Notes appear at end of table

(continued)

TABLE Ba4111–4206 Detailed occupations – the economically active population: 1900–1970 [Part 4] *Continued*

	Laborers not elsewhere classified											
	Manufacturing										Nonmanufacturing industries (including not reported)	
	Miscellaneous chemical and allied products	Drugs and chemical products	Petroleum, refining	Miscellaneous petroleum and coal products	Rubber products	Leather – tanned, curried, and finished	Footwear, except rubber	Leather products, except footwear	Leather and footwear	Not specified manufacturing industries	Total	Construction
	Ba4185	Ba4186 [13]	Ba4187	Ba4188	Ba4189	Ba4190	Ba4191	Ba4192	Ba4193 [14]	Ba4194	Ba4195	Ba4196
Year	Thousand	Thousand	Thousand	Thousand	Thousand	Thousand	Thousand	Thousand	Thousand	Thousand	Thousand	Thousand
1900	—	15	5	11	6	16	5	3	—	79	2,284	20
1910	—	45	11	11	14	21	10	4	—	109	2,210	531
1920	—	79	32	9	51	27	19	8	—	191	1,901	391
1930	—	80	41	5	29	17	18	3	—	114	2,715	710
1940	—	77	28	8	20	11	12	3	—	44	2,714	1,340
1950 [17]	—	61	25	6	17	8	6	2	—	11	2,079	788
1950 [18]	45	—	24	3	21	—	—	—	15	11	1,843	699
1960 [18]	41	—	14	3	18	—	—	—	11	2	1,802	751
1960 [19]	—	—	—	—	—	—	—	—	8	2	—	802
1970 [20]	—	—	—	—	—	—	—	—	4	3	—	649
1970 [21]	—	—	—	—	—	—	—	—	4	3	—	645

	Laborers not elsewhere classified									
	Nonmanufacturing industries (including not reported)									
	Railroads and railway express service	Transportation, except railroads	Telecommunications, utilities, and sanitary services	Transportation (except railroad) and telecommunications	Railroads, other transportation, and telecommunications	Wholesale and retail trade	Business and repair services	Public administration	Personal services	All other industries (including not reported)
	Ba4197	Ba4198	Ba4199	Ba4200 [15]	Ba4201 [16]	Ba4202	Ba4203	Ba4204	Ba4205	Ba4206
Year	Thousand	Thousand	Thousand	Thousand	Thousand	Thousand	Thousand	Thousand	Thousand	Thousand
1900	284	—	—	86	—	68	1	—	—	1,825 [30]
1910	599	—	—	195	—	152	2	56	—	675 [30]
1920	543	—	—	199	—	182	2	93	—	490 [30]
1930	490	—	—	249	—	253	15	134	—	864 [30]
1940	278	98	103	—	—	250	7	52	64	520
1950 [17]	293	119	135	—	—	345	15	107	83	194
1950 [18]	284	87	132	—	—	270	16	98	79	179
1960 [18]	136	91	123	—	—	372	24	77	77	151
1960 [19]	—	—	—	—	191	130	15	74	—	128
1970 [20]	—	—	—	—	105	98	23	95	—	95
1970 [21]	—	—	—	—	105	96	22	95	—	83

TABLE Ba4111–4206 Detailed occupations – the economically active population: 1900–1970 [Part 4] *Continued*

(Z) Fewer than 500.

[1] Persons age 14 years and over, except as indicated for 1970.

[2] Combines series Ba4113–4114.

[3] Combines series Ba4126–4127.

[4] Combines series Ba4130–4132.

[5] Combines series Ba4139–4140.

[6] Combines series Ba4138–4147.

[7] Combines series Ba4136–4148.

[8] Combines series Ba4152–4153.

[9] Combines series Ba4152–4155.

[10] Combines series Ba4158–4159.

[11] Combines series Ba4176–4177.

[12] Combines series Ba4176–4179.

[13] Combines series Ba4184–4185.

[14] Combines series Ba4190–4192.

[15] Combines series Ba4198–4199.

[16] Combines series Ba4197–4199.

[17] 1950 classification.

[18] 1960 classification.

[19] 1970 classification.

[20] Age 14 and older.

[21] Age 16 and older.

[22] Includes persons for whom occupations were not reported.

[23] Includes carpenters' helpers, truck drivers, helpers, and warehousemen, not shown separately.

[24] Includes series Ba4152–4155.

[25] Includes series Ba4155.

[26] Includes series Ba4166.

[27] Includes series Ba4158–4166.

[28] Includes series Ba4169–4172.

[29] Includes series Ba4174.

[30] Includes series Ba4205.

Sources

See the sources for Table Ba3688–3832.

Documentation

See the text for Table Ba3688–3832.

TABLE Ba4207–4213 Occupational segregation indexes, by sex, race, and nativity: 1850–1990

Contributed by Matthew Sobek

	Men and women compared			White and nonwhite compared		Native-born and foreign-born compared	
	All men and women compared	White men and white women compared	Nonwhite men and nonwhite women compared	White men and nonwhite men compared	White women and nonwhite women compared	Native-born and foreign-born compared	Native-born white men and foreign-born men compared
	Ba4207	Ba4208	Ba4209	Ba4210	Ba4211	Ba4212	Ba4213
Year	Index	Index	Index	Index	Index	Index	Index
1850 [1]	—	—	—	55.0	—	37.3	38.2
1860 [1]	68.6	77.3	79.7	51.0	38.4	36.1	36.8
1870	63.9	81.5	42.8	47.8	52.6	35.5	36.5
1880	70.2	75.9	45.7	38.6	54.9	28.9	30.5
1900	67.1	70.5	59.5	35.7	49.7	27.4	27.9
1910	66.0	66.2	63.0	39.0	61.5	33.9	34.2
1920	68.7	68.4	65.3	43.3	67.5	31.0	31.4
1940	65.5	65.3	70.9	44.4	65.3	24.5	25.6
1950	63.3	62.8	66.0	41.2	58.3	24.0	24.8
1960	62.3	62.5	66.7	40.6	51.0	19.9	22.0
1970	56.7	58.3	56.8	33.5	31.5	17.1	20.0
1980	51.7	53.1	48.7	24.7	21.6	17.3	20.1
1990	47.7	48.5	43.5	21.2	18.2	18.2	20.6

[1] Free persons only; slaves excluded.

Source

Tabulated from the Integrated Public Use Microdata Series (IPUMS). See the Guide to the Millennial Edition for information on the IPUMS.

Documentation

These data pertain to noninstitutionalized civilians age 16 and older; persons with an occupation 1850–1920, or employed persons 1940–1990.

Segregation indexes were calculated using the 268 detailed occupational categories of the 1950 Census classification system.

The index numbers represent the percentage of persons in one group who would have to change occupations to match the distribution of the other group. Mathematically, the index equals one half the sum of the absolute percentage differences in each occupation for the two groups. The magnitude of the index is sensitive to the number of categories used (as well as the size of the differences). Consequently, it is difficult to make direct comparisons to other studies that used only broad groupings of occupations in calculating such measures.

WAGES

Robert A. Margo

TABLE Ba4214–4215 Indexes of wages in Massachusetts agriculture: 1750–1855

Contributed by Robert A. Margo

	Unweighted	Weighted
	Ba4214	Ba4215
Year	Index 1795–1805 = 100	Index 1795–1805 = 100
1750	72.8	70.1
1751	63.8	74.4
1752	62.3	69.8
1753	100.0	79.2
1754	65.3	59.6
1755	63.4	69.9
1756	72.5	71.5
1757	71.9	73.0
1758	73.2	59.7
1759	76.6	76.1
1760	71.9	63.3
1761	80.6	75.0
1762	87.5	75.7
1763	78.5	79.1
1764	82.1	76.5
1765	93.4	80.4
1766	75.8	70.8
1767	76.4	74.5
1768	88.3	71.6
1769	70.0	75.0
1770	68.3	69.1
1771	89.4	79.0
1772	83.2	78.9
1773	75.1	80.2
1774	70.0	77.0
1775	80.9	74.6
1776	79.4	81.5
1777	86.0	104.8
1778	119.2	71.2
1779	75.7	68.6
1780	98.1	73.3
1781	83.0	81.4
1782	99.8	63.7
1783	74.2	81.9
1784	87.4	98.6
1785	86.0	80.8
1786	93.0	70.9
1787	77.9	77.3
1788	97.2	77.8
1789	83.4	79.4
1790	89.4	78.7
1791	88.5	77.7
1792	90.8	78.3
1793	82.8	76.0
1794	91.7	79.3
1795	82.3	87.2
1796	86.0	95.8
1797	91.1	103.1
1798	99.2	115.3
1799	86.2	103.6
1800	96.4	85.0
1801	113.8	120.2
1802	113.6	90.2
1803	93.4	105.7
1804	116.0	90.0
1805	120.9	104.4
1806	115.8	126.9
1807	129.8	128.1
1808	136.2	114.0
1809	144.5	128.6
1810	122.8	126.4
1811	137.9	122.8
1812	130.0	121.2
1813	124.9	135.9
1814	150.6	156.7
1815	136.6	153.7
1816	124.3	153.5
1817	129.6	138.6
1818	133.8	150.1
1819	136.2	152.4
1820	140.6	132.0
1821	101.1	136.9
1822	149.6	121.2
1823	126.0	136.5
1824	121.7	130.4
1825	153.6	119.6
1826	132.3	149.9
1827	142.3	141.2
1828	141.7	141.9
1829	118.1	142.0
1830	153.2	139.7
1831	158.7	145.3
1832	146.8	141.4
1833	141.1	139.9
1834	124.0	140.8
1835	152.3	137.2
1836	169.4	155.5
1837	163.8	178.9
1838	169.8	157.0
1839	154.2	166.8
1840	173.2	167.8
1841	167.7	147.5
1842	164.0	143.1
1843	127.7	142.7
1844	168.5	139.8
1845	167.4	155.7
1846	160.0	145.1
1847	204.9	177.4
1848	191.9	164.0
1849	174.3	159.0
1850	141.5	176.0
1851	157.4	151.7
1852	188.7	161.5
1853	185.7	165.4
1854	220.2	188.2
1855	283.0	197.9

Source

Winifred Barr Rothenberg, *From Market-Places to a Market Economy: The Transformation of Rural Massachusetts, 1750–1850* (University of Chicago Press, 1992), pp. 176–9.

Documentation

The indexes were derived from a sample of farm account books collected by the author. The account books record various transactions, including labor

TABLE Ba4214–4215 Indexes of wages in Massachusetts agriculture: 1750–1855 *Continued*

hired daily or for longer periods (monthly or annually). Labor was hired either by the task, which varied across crops, or for tasks that were not crop-specific (such as building, or "unspecified work").

The unweighted index was constructed by first grouping observations for building, miscellaneous, or unspecified work by year. Average values were next computed for each year, and the series indexed at the average value over the 1795–1805 period. For the weighted index, daily wage rates were used. Observations were grouped by crop, based on tasks specific to the production of each crop (for example, observations pertaining to mowing, raking, and haying were assigned to hay production). Average values were computed for each year, and the crop-specific series were indexed relative to their 1795–1805 averages. The crop-specific series were then aggregated into an overall series by weighting each crop by the percentage of each crop's share of the aggregate value of output produced in a sample of Massachusetts and Maine towns in 1801. For further details, consult Rothenberg (1992), Appendix B of Chapter 6.

TABLE Ba4216–4217 Daily wages for farm labor in Maryland and West Virginia: 1753–1860

Contributed by Robert A. Margo

	Maryland	West Virginia
	Ba4216	Ba4217
Year	Index 1753 = 100	Dollars
1753	100	—
1756	135	—
1757	101	—
1758	100	—
1759	125	—
1760	125	—
1761	100	—
1762	125	—
1763	125	—
1764	125	—
1765	100	—
1767	100	—
1768	100	—
1769	100	—
1770	100	—
1771	100	—
1772	100	—
1773	100	—
1774	100	—
1775	100	—
1776	100	—
1777	100	—
1778	100	—
1779	100	—
1780	100	—
1781	75	—
1782	75	—
1783	87	—
1784	100	—
1785	75	—
1786	75	—
1787	75	—
1788	—	0.417
1789	—	0.500
1790	—	0.583
1791	150	0.625
1792	125	0.666
1793	125	0.666
1794	188	—
1795	—	0.718
1796	188	0.782
1797	—	0.667
1798	—	0.666
1800	—	0.500
1801	—	0.450
1802	—	0.663
1803	—	0.400
1804	—	0.500
1805	—	0.733
1806	180	0.625
1807	—	0.607
1808	150	0.500
1809	125	—
1810	125	—
1811	150	—
1812	150	—
1813	150	0.813
1814	150	0.650
1815	150	0.750
1816	150	0.625
1817	150	0.755
1818	150	—
1819	150	—
1820	150	0.750
1821	150	0.500
1822	150	0.500
1823	—	0.608
1824	—	0.563
1825	141	0.563
1826	128	0.563
1827	—	0.708
1828	188	0.508
1829	188	0.500
1830	188	0.500
1831	188	—
1832	188	0.500
1833	150	0.425
1834	150	0.438
1835	141	0.459
1836	141	0.438
1837	—	0.691
1838	—	0.563
1839	188	0.654

(continued)

TABLE Ba4216–4217 Daily wages for farm labor in Maryland and West Virginia: 1753–1860 *Continued*

Year	Maryland Ba4216 Index 1753 = 100	West Virginia Ba4217 Dollars
1840	—	0.602
1841	150	0.438
1842	150	0.500
1843	150	0.426
1844	150	0.425
1845	150	0.425
1846	150	0.425
1847	150	0.425
1848	150	0.473
1849	150	0.506
1850	150	0.425
1851	—	0.506
1852	—	0.433
1853	—	0.506
1854	—	0.450
1855	—	0.500
1856	—	0.500
1857	—	0.878
1858	—	0.550
1859	—	0.670
1860	—	0.875

Sources

Donald R. Adams Jr., "Prices and Wages in Maryland 1750–1850," *Journal of Economic History* 46 (September 1986): 630–1; "Prices and Wages in Antebellum America: The West Virginia Experience," *Journal of Economic History* 52 (March 1992): 215–16.

Documentation

Series Ba4216. Figures are based on unweighted averages of daily wage rates paid to male agricultural laborers for unspecified work. Monthly wage rates were used by the author to estimate changes in wages for certain years. Sources of wage quotations include Chancery Court Records and account books.

Series Ba4217. Figures are unweighted averages. Monthly wage rates were converted to daily wage rates by dividing by twenty-six days. Manuscript sources from the West Virginia Collection at the West Virginia University Library were used.

TABLE Ba4218 Index of money wages for unskilled labor: 1774–1974

Contributed by Robert A. Margo

Year	Money wages for unskilled labor Ba4218 Index 1860 = 100
1774	33
1775	35
1776	32
1777	35
1778	36
1779	31
1780	41
1781	43
1782	39
1783	36
1784	34
1785	44
1786	40
1787	48
1788	48
1789	42
1790	37
1791	43
1792	43
1793	48
1794	45
1795	63
1796	62
1797	61
1798	69
1799	52
1800	60
1801	71
1802	75
1803	57
1804	72
1805	62
1806	86
1807	69
1808	68
1809	104
1810	88
1811	91
1812	92
1813	87
1814	97
1815	92
1816	111
1817	93
1818	72
1819	75
1820	67
1821	74
1822	68
1823	80
1824	78
1825	68
1826	70
1827	84
1828	67
1829	70
1830	68
1831	68
1832	68
1833	64
1834	67
1835	62
1836	91
1837	104
1838	107
1839	89
1840	77
1841	71
1842	73
1843	68
1844	80
1845	80
1846	76
1847	73
1848	76
1849	81
1850	82
1851	84
1852	85
1853	87
1854	90
1855	91
1856	93
1857	94
1858	93
1859	96
1860	100
1861	102
1862	106
1863	121
1864	138
1865	145
1866	145
1867	145
1868	146
1869	146
1870	142
1871	142
1872	143
1873	136
1874	131

TABLE Ba4218 Index of money wages for unskilled labor: 1774–1974 *Continued*

Year	Money wages for unskilled labor Ba4218 Index 1860 = 100	Year	Money wages for unskilled labor Ba4218 Index 1860 = 100	Year	Money wages for unskilled labor Ba4218 Index 1860 = 100	Year	Money wages for unskilled labor Ba4218 Index 1860 = 100
1875	125	1900	140	1925	404	1950	1,184
1876	118	1901	144	1926	409	1951	1,283
1877	114	1902	148	1927	418	1952	1,358
1878	111	1903	154	1928	420	1953	1,450
1879	109	1904	155	1929	431	1954	1,521
1880	116	1905	157	1930	424	1955	1,584
1881	120	1906	165	1931	407	1956	1,662
1882	123	1907	172	1932	355	1957	1,745
1883	128	1908	164	1933	356	1958	1,830
1884	130	1909	166	1934	424	1959	1,903
1885	128	1910	172	1935	439	1960	1,976
1886	129	1911	168	1936	445	1961	2,047
1887	132	1912	171	1937	506	1962	2,114
1888	138	1913	179	1938	520	1963	2,181
1889	138	1914	180	1939	527	1964	2,245
1890	138	1915	182	1940	542	1965	2,314
1891	138	1916	224	1941	604	1966	2,399
1892	138	1917	279	1942	686	1967	2,515
1893	138	1918	351	1943	757	1968	2,660
1894	132	1919	409	1944	791	1969	2,822
1895	135	1920	469	1945	813	1970	3,021
1896	133	1921	388	1946	900	1971	3,265
1897	133	1922	357	1947	1,017	1972	3,499
1898	135	1923	393	1948	1,087	1973	3,753
1899	137	1924	406	1949	1,131	1974	4,059

Source

Paul A. David and Peter Solar, "A Bicentenary Contribution to the History of the Cost of Living in America," *Research in Economic History* 2 (1977): 16, 59.

Documentation

To construct their index of money wages, the authors relied on a variety of published sources. The goal was to compute an index based on daily or (preferably) hourly wage rates for "common" or unskilled labor. For 1774–1830, data pertaining to Philadelphia and for nonfarm laborers collected by the Massachusetts Bureau of Statistics of Labor and published in its *Sixteenth Annual Report* in 1885 were used. For 1830–1890, the authors used benchmark observations prepared by Stanley Lebergott for the Census years 1830–1880, interpolating between Census dates based on various annual series. An interpolating series for 1860–1880 was also drawn from Lebergott, based on quotations from the Weeks report of the 1880 Census. For 1830–1832, the authors assumed no change in wage rates. For 1832–1840, annual interpolation was based on a geometric average of wages from the Weeks report and from the Erie Canal. From 1840 to 1860, interpolation was based entirely on wage observations from the Weeks report. For 1880–1890, interpolation was based on wage observations from the Aldrich report of 1893.

For 1890–1914, the authors relied on series compiled by Whitney Coombs, *The Wages of Unskilled Labor in Manufacturing Industries in the United States, 1890–1924* (Columbia University Press, 1926), who produced a series of weekly wage rates of unskilled laborers in manufacturing, which the authors converted to hourly by dividing by the length of the average workweek in hours. The original sources for the wage data were studies conducted by the U.S. Bureau of Labor Statistics (BLS). For 1914–1948, the index was based on data collected by the National Industrial Conference Board (NICB), pertaining to unskilled production workers in twenty-five manufacturing industries. The NICB reported data for 1914 and 1920–1948. Figures for 1915–1919 were interpolated on the basis of a weekly earnings series also constructed by Coombs.

The estimates for 1948–1974 were prepared in three stages. In the first stage, annual indexes of hourly wage rates for "janitors, porters, and cleaners (men)" and "laborers, material handling" were computed for the four major census regions (East, South, Midwest, and West) on the basis of data from the BLS Area Wage Surveys for 1952–1973. In the second stage, the authors compiled a national index of hourly wage rates of unskilled plant workers for 1961–1973 from BLS data. The ratio of the national index to the Eastern index (from Stage 1) was regressed on the ratios of the Southern, Midwestern, and Western series to the Eastern series (all from Stage 1). Using the regression coefficients, and the values of the Stage 1 series, the national index was extended backward from 1961 to 1952. Additional BLS data were used to interpolate over the 1948–1951 and 1973–1974 periods. Further details may be found in the original article.

The source also provides a consumer price index for these years. See series Cc2.

TABLE Ba4219–4223 Daily and monthly wages in the Philadelphia and Brandywine regions: 1785–1860

Contributed by Robert A. Margo

	Daily wages, Philadelphia region		Monthly wages, Brandywine region		
				Manufacturing workers	
	Laborers	Artisans	Farm labor (including board)	Male	Female
	Ba4219	Ba4220	Ba4221	Ba4222	Ba4223
Year	Dollars	Dollars	Dollars	Dollars	Dollars
1785	0.70 [1]	1.33	—	—	—
1786	—	1.00	—	—	—
1787	0.52 [1]	1.00	—	—	—
1788	—	0.97	—	—	—
1789	0.52	1.00	—	—	—
1790	0.50	1.01	—	—	—
1791	0.53	1.05	—	—	—
1792	0.66	1.00	—	—	—
1793	0.80	1.25	—	—	—
1794	1.00	1.39	—	—	—
1795	1.00	1.66	—	—	—
1796	1.00	1.74	—	—	—
1797	1.00	1.83	—	—	—
1798	1.00	1.57	—	—	—
1799	1.00	1.62	—	—	—
1800	1.00	1.64	16.00	—	—
1801	1.00	1.55	17.25	—	—
1802	0.75	1.31	17.25	17.00	—
1803	0.75	1.43	16.00	17.00	—
1804	1.00	1.60	16.50	18.00	—
1805	1.00	1.57	17.00	18.50	—
1806	1.00	1.66	17.00	18.00	—
1807	1.00	1.68	17.00	18.00	—
1808	0.75	1.47	16.50	18.00	—
1809	1.00	1.56	17.00	19.00	—
1810	1.00	1.72	17.00	18.50	—
1811	1.00	1.77	17.50	21.50	—
1812	1.00	1.58	18.00	22.25	—
1813	1.00	1.52	19.50	21.50	—
1814	1.00	1.63	18.25	21.50	—
1815	1.00	1.91	—	22.25	9.50 [1]
1816	1.00	1.89	19.00	21.00	9.00 [1]
1817	1.00	1.71	19.00	20.50	—
1818	1.00	1.86	18.00	20.75	9.00 [1]
1819	1.00	1.63	18.50	20.13	10.50 [1]
1820	—	1.55	18.00	20.33	8.00
1821	0.75	1.37	18.25	19.71	8.00
1822	0.75	1.65	16.75	18.38	8.00
1823	1.00	1.47	16.25	18.63	8.00
1824	1.00	1.55	17.75	19.38	—
1825	1.00	1.74	17.50	18.67	—
1826	1.00	1.70	16.75	18.99	—
1827	1.00	1.73	17.00	17.94	—
1828	1.00	1.74	16.00	16.67	—
1829	1.00	1.80	17.25	19.25	—
1830	1.00	1.73	16.50	19.81	—
1831	—	—	16.50	18.93	—
1832	—	—	16.00	17.75	—
1833	—	—	17.25	19.38	—
1834	—	—	17.25	18.46	8.50 [1]
1835	—	—	17.25	19.25	9.00 [1]
1836	—	—	18.75	18.63	—
1837	—	—	19.00	20.84	9.75 [1]
1838	—	—	19.25	20.81	10.50 [1]
1839	—	—	18.75	20.46	10.50 [1]
1840	—	—	17.75	19.42	9.63 [1]
1841	—	—	17.75	20.05	10.50 [1]
1842	—	—	17.75	21.52	9.00 [1]
1843	—	—	16.50	19.70	8.00 [1]
1844	—	—	16.75	19.36	8.00
1845	—	—	17.75	19.99	9.50 [1]
1846	—	—	17.00	19.80	9.25 [1]
1847	—	—	16.50	20.51	11.75 [1]
1848	—	—	16.50	21.47	11.25 [1]
1849	—	—	16.00	20.53	11.50 [1]
1850	—	—	16.75	19.78	10.25 [1]
1851	—	—	16.75	19.67	10.00 [1]
1852	—	—	18.25	20.03	12.00 [1]
1853	—	—	18.00	20.16	12.00 [1]
1854	—	—	18.00	19.88	10.50 [1]
1855	—	—	19.50	19.77	10.75 [1]
1856	—	—	19.50	19.60	10.00 [1]
1857	—	—	19.00	19.80	10.00 [1]
1858	—	—	19.75	21.15	12.00 [1]
1859	—	—	19.25	21.49	10.50 [1]
1860	—	—	20.25	22.98	—

[1] Midpoint of range reported in original source.

Sources

Series Ba4219–4220. Donald R. Adams Jr., "Wage Rates in the Early National Period: Philadelphia, 1785–1830," *Journal of Economic History* 28 (September 1968): 404–26.

Series Ba4221–4223. Donald R. Adams Jr., "The Standard of Living during American Industrialization: Evidence from the Brandywine Region," *Journal of Economic History* 42 (December 1982): 903–17.

Documentation

Series Ba4219–4220. The principal manuscript sources utilized in constructing these series are as follows: Pennsylvania Historical Society, Joshua Humphreys Shipyard Accounts, and Moses Lancaster Account Book; American Philosophical Society, Treasurer's Account Book; Records of the Ship *North Carolina,* American State Papers, I, Class VI (Gales and Seaton, 1834), p. 836; Stephen Girard Collection: Ship Disbursements and Repair Records (Ship *Good Friends,* Ship *Liberty,* Brig *Polly,* Brig *Kitty,* Ship *Two Brothers,* Ship *North America,* Ship *Helvetius,* and Ship *Superb*); Bills and Receipts; Bills and Receipts Alphabetically; Place Accounts; New Houses and Stores in Water Street No. 2; and Real Estate Accounts. Wage rates were obtained from the actual receipts, bills, day books, and account books. For further details, consult Adams (1968).

Series Ba4219–4220. A large number of archival records of business firms and farms were used in the construction of the series. Various sources were more complete than others and were relied on more heavily by Adams. The most important sources of manufacturing wages were those of E. I. DuPont and Company; Charles I. DuPont and Company; and Bancroft, Simpson, and Eddystone Company. Averages were represented in all cases by midrange values. Where possible, samples were taken in January and June and averages computed. For a complete listing of primary sources and their location, consult Adams (1982).

TABLE Ba4224–4233 Female-to-male earnings ratios: 1815–1987

Contributed by Robert A. Margo

			Full-time earnings, twenty-one industries		Manufacturing		All occupations			
								Median weekly wage and salary income		
									Hours adjusted	
	Agriculture	Manufacturing	Weekly	Hourly	Full-time	Total	Median year-round earnings	Actual	All workers	Workers age 25–34
	Ba4224	Ba4225	Ba4226	Ba4227	Ba4228	Ba4229	Ba4230	Ba4231	Ba4232	Ba4233
Year	Ratio	Ratio	Ratio	Ratio	Ratio	Ratio	Ratio	Ratio	Ratio	Ratio
1815	0.288	—	—	—	—	—	—	—	—	—
1820	—	0.337	—	—	—	—	—	—	—	—
1832	—	0.437	—	—	—	—	—	—	—	—
1850	—	0.485	—	—	—	—	—	—	—	—
1885	—	0.559	—	—	—	—	—	—	—	—
1890	—	0.539	—	—	—	—	—	—	—	—
1900	—	0.554	—	—	—	—	—	—	—	—
1905	—	0.556	—	—	—	—	—	—	—	—
1914	—	—	0.568	0.592	—	—	—	—	—	—
1920	—	—	0.559	0.645	—	—	—	—	—	—
1921	—	—	0.617	0.653	—	—	—	—	—	—
1922	—	—	0.612	0.677	—	—	—	—	—	—
1923	—	—	0.607	0.672	—	—	—	—	—	—
1924	—	—	0.593	0.664	—	—	—	—	—	—
1925	—	—	0.592	0.657	—	—	—	—	—	—
1926	—	—	0.585	0.662	—	—	—	—	—	—
1927	—	—	0.587	0.652	—	—	—	—	—	—
1928	—	—	0.573	0.645	—	—	—	—	—	—
1929	—	—	0.575	0.637	—	—	—	—	—	—
1930	—	—	0.578	0.635	—	—	—	—	—	—
1931	—	—	0.612	0.621	—	—	—	—	—	—
1932	—	—	0.653	0.618	—	—	—	—	—	—
1933	—	—	0.661	0.656	—	—	—	—	—	—
1934	—	—	0.688	0.704	—	—	—	—	—	—
1935	—	—	0.653	0.700	—	—	—	—	—	—
1939	—	—	—	—	0.539	0.513	—	—	—	—
1950	—	—	—	—	—	0.537	—	—	—	—
1951	—	—	—	—	—	0.532	—	—	—	—
1952	—	—	—	—	—	0.558	—	—	—	—
1953	—	—	—	—	—	0.512	—	—	—	—
1954	—	—	—	—	—	0.497	—	—	—	—
1955	—	—	—	—	0.580	0.526	0.639	—	—	—
1957	—	—	—	—	0.554	0.496	0.638	—	—	—
1959	—	—	—	—	0.580	—	0.613	—	—	—
1961	—	—	—	—	0.534	—	0.592	—	—	—
1963	—	—	—	—	0.544	—	0.589	—	—	—
1965	—	—	—	—	0.532	—	0.599	—	—	—
1967	—	—	—	—	0.563	—	0.578	—	—	—
1969	—	—	—	—	0.544	—	0.605	—	—	—
1971	—	—	—	—	—	—	0.595	0.617	0.68	0.73
1973	—	—	—	—	—	—	0.566	0.617	0.68	0.72
1975	—	—	—	—	—	—	0.588	0.620	0.68	0.73
1977	—	—	—	—	—	—	0.589	0.619	0.67	0.72
1979	—	—	—	—	—	—	0.596	0.625	0.68	0.73
1981	—	—	—	—	—	—	0.592	—	—	—
1982	—	—	—	—	—	—	0.617	0.654	0.71	0.79
1983	—	—	—	—	—	—	0.636	0.667	0.72	0.80
1984	—	—	—	—	—	—	0.637	0.678	0.71	—
1985	—	—	—	—	—	—	0.646	0.682	0.74	—
1986	—	—	—	—	—	—	0.643	0.692	0.75	—
1987	—	—	—	—	—	—	0.655	0.700	0.76	—

Source

Claudia Goldin, *Understanding the Gender Gap: An Economic History of American Women* (Oxford University Press, 1990), Table 3.1.

Documentation

Except where otherwise indicated, figures refer to year-round full-time employees. Detailed notes to these series may be found in the original source.

Series Ba4226–4227. From the National Industrial Conference Board.

Series Ba4232–4233. Series adjusted to hold constant the number of hours worked per week.

TABLE Ba4234–4243 Monthly earnings with board of farm laborers, by region: 1818–1948

Contributed by Robert A. Margo

	United States	New England	Middle Atlantic	East North Central	West North Central	South Atlantic	East South Central	West South Central	Mountain	Pacific
	Ba4234	Ba4235	Ba4236	Ba4237	Ba4238	Ba4239	Ba4240	Ba4241	Ba4242	Ba4243
Year	Dollars	Dollars	Dollars	Dollars	Dollars	Dollars	Dollars	Dollars	Dollars	Dollars
1818	9.45	11.90	9.82	8.86	10.15	8.10	10.36	—	—	—
1826	8.83	11.65	8.38	8.73	10.15	7.18	9.39	—	—	—
1830	8.85	11.60	8.52	8.73	10.15	7.16	9.37	—	—	—
1850	10.85	12.98	11.17	11.44	12.00	8.20	9.60	11.28	—	68.00
1860	13.66	14.73	12.75	13.79	13.76	11.08	14.06	15.53	—	34.16
1870	16.57	19.84	17.89	16.94	17.10	9.95	12.78	14.05	—	29.19
1880	11.70	13.94	13.71	15.48	14.88	8.81	10.16	12.90	24.74	24.77
1890	13.93	17.78	15.76	15.92	15.84	9.46	10.58	12.84	21.67	22.64
1899	14.56	18.20	15.98	16.90	18.04	9.32	10.72	11.86	26.33	25.10
1909	21.30	25.82	22.21	23.59	26.47	14.64	15.05	17.33	34.34	34.28
1919	41.52	46.16	41.17	42.21	50.81	30.23	29.09	36.19	59.20	65.30
1929	40.40	50.93	45.72	41.73	42.10	25.23	23.28	27.67	49.96	59.90
1940	28.05	33.54	30.00	29.40	28.12	17.46	16.34	19.61	36.11	42.84
1948	91.00	104.00	99.00	101.00	107.00	57.00	49.00	73.00	129.00	158.00

Source

Stanley Lebergott, *Manpower in Economic Growth: The American Record since 1800* (McGraw-Hill, 1964), Tables A-23 and A-24, pp. 257ff.

Documentation

For most of the nineteenth century and well into the twentieth, the common method of wage payment in agriculture was monthly, with board included. Reasonably satisfactory data for individual states are available at something like decennial intervals for the entire period beginning with 1818. These figures have been supplemented with partial information to provide national estimates for the years for which this is not so. State data for 1818–1819 were combined into divisions and U.S. averages using weights from the population census. For 1909 and 1919, they differ from U.S. Department of Agriculture (USDA) division totals.

For 1818, 1826, and 1830, estimates were made in 1832 by Senator John Holmes of Maine and reported by him in the Congressional *Register of Debates*. For certain states there are, in addition, the results of a survey in 1832–1834 on 1832 farm wages made by Secretary of State Edward Livingstone, drawing on returns from many individual towns in these states (that is, 59 of 134 towns in Connecticut, 101 of 444 in Maine, 109 of 230 in New Hampshire, and so forth). Given the broader basis of the Secretary's survey, his figures were used to represent the 1830 average (other data indicate virtually no 1830–1832 change), with the Holmes series used to extrapolate these values to 1818 and 1826. For 1818, 1826, and 1830, the total number of persons reported by the 1820 Census as having agricultural occupations was used for weighting.

For 1850 and 1860, special wage-rate inquiries made in conjunction with census reports on social statistics gave monthly rates paid to farmhands (with board) and were used here.

For 1850, the number of free, white male farmers age 15 and over was used for weighting, and for 1860, the number of farm laborers. Examination of the ratios of farmers to farm laborers in 1860 indicated a marked degree of intrastate uniformity, and so the shift from one type of weights to the other would not make a marked difference.

The source used for 1870 was a study made by Edward Young, Chief of the Bureau of the Statistics of the Treasury Department, in which figures on wage rates in a host of occupations were collected. Because of the timing, it is possible that these data were collected in connection with the 1870 Census. The data were more probably developed, as the other materials in the volume were, from information secured by the assistant assessors of internal revenue in the various states. Their issuance, however, under the sponsorship of a competent statistician who was experienced in data evaluation and presentation and had worked under David A. Wells entitles them to serious consideration.

For 1880 and 1890, the crop-reporter surveys of the USDA were used to provide state estimates.

For 1899, the USDA survey reported rates for men hired not "by the year"– as do the reports used for earlier periods – but "by the year or season." In examining the extent of noncomparability, Lebergott was limited to a comparison between the two types of rates for 1909, that being the only year for which the USDA reported both types of rates.

Day rates (other than harvest) were charted against monthly rates by the year and season for the years 1891–1909. The scatter showed a close and simple correlation for all years except 1909. Given the scatter and the day rate for 1909, Lebergott deduced a 1909 rate for the year and season that is virtually the same as the enumerated "year" rate for that date. On this basis, he took the year-season rate for 1899 as roughly identical with the desired year rate for that date. He secured the same result by charting the year rates for 1866–1890 and 1909 against the daily rate (other than harvest) and interpolating for 1899 by the daily rate. It was therefore concluded that the "year-season" state rates for 1899 as actually reported could be used as satisfactory approximations of the year rates for that date.

For 1870 and 1880, the Census of Population counts of agricultural laborers ages 16 to 59 were used as weights. For 1890 and 1899, the census count of male agricultural laborers age 16 and over in 1900 was used. For 1909 and 1919, the division estimates of the USDA were not used because they were weighted by the number of farms employing hired labor at any time during the year. Such weights will distort the relative importance of states that characteristically hired above (or below) average proportions of migrant labor, or short-term labor. Thus, while New Jersey reported roughly as many farms with hired labor in the Agricultural Census as it did hired laborers in the Census of Populations, North Dakota reported almost twice as many. The population count of farm laborers (working off-farm) was therefore used to compute regional and U.S. averages.

For 1929 and 1940, the USDA division figures were used, these having been weighted by the count of hired farm workers derived from the surveys themselves. For 1948, the 1950 Census of Agriculture count of hired farm workers was used.

See Appendix 2 regarding the composition of census regions and divisions.

TABLE Ba4244–4249 Annual earnings of male manufacturing workers in New England and the Middle Atlantic, by urban–rural location: 1820–1860

Contributed by Robert A. Margo

	Middle Atlantic			New England		
	All	Rural	Urban	All	Rural	Urban
	Ba4244	Ba4245	Ba4246	Ba4247	Ba4248	Ba4249
Year	Dollars	Dollars	Dollars	Dollars	Dollars	Dollars
1820	265.9	238.3	295.5	269.7	252.2	293.6
1832	278.0	270.1	342.0	299.9	303.4	296.8
1850	350.5	287.2	362.1	326.9	313.5	329.9
1860	354.3	374.7	348.8	371.1	351.9	372.7

Source

Kenneth L. Sokoloff and Georgia C. Villaflor, "The Market for Manufacturing Workers during Early Industrialization: The American Northeast, 1820 to 1860," in C. Goldin and H. Rockoff, editors, *Strategic Factors in Nineteenth Century American Economic History: A Volume to Honor Robert W. Fogel* (University of Chicago Press, 1992), p. 36.

Documentation

All figures pertain to adult males. The estimates were computed from firm-level data on wages and employees, as drawn from the manuscript censuses of manufacturing of 1820, 1850, and 1860, and the Treasury Department's McLane Report of 1832. Figures for 1820, 1850, and 1860 pertain to 1819, 1849, and 1859.

In 1850 and 1860, the Census did not separate out wages paid to adult men and boys. The authors assumed that the proportion of boys among male employees in 1850 and 1860 were the same, by industry, as in 1820, if the fraction was less than or equal to 33 percent in 1820; if greater than 33 percent in 1820, the fraction was reduced to 33 percent. The average male wage was then estimated by assuming that the boy wage was 50 percent of the adult male wage.

Eighteen industries were included in the sample. In 1820, the bottom 30 percent of firms (as measured by the average wage) were excluded on the presumption that such firms were operating only part of the year.

Urban firms were located in a county with at least one city of population 10,000 or more, or in a county adjacent to such a county. Rural firms are those located in counties not meeting the urban criterion.

TABLE Ba4250–4252 Annual earnings of civil engineers: 1820–1859

Contributed by Robert A. Margo

	First rank	Second rank	Third rank
	Ba4250	Ba4251	Ba4252
Year	Dollars	Dollars	Dollars
1820	2,967	1,288	—
1821	2,967	1,226	—
1822	2,917	1,229	—
1823	2,917	1,226	—
1824	2,911	1,246	—
1825	2,911	1,280	620
1826	2,919	1,358	633
1827	2,675	1,360	716
1828	2,550	1,333	722
1829	2,675	1,314	716
1830	2,616	1,377	716
1831	2,650	1,260	704
1832	3,069	1,239	678
1833	2,857	1,264	642
1834	2,993	1,292	676
1835	2,744	1,398	632
1836	3,040	1,357	749
1837	3,199	1,428	713
1838	2,986	1,396	746
1839	2,979	1,373	780
1840	2,888	1,281	737
1841	2,833	1,267	729
1842	2,852	1,303	754
1843	2,865	1,371	662
1844	2,882	1,398	670
1845	3,272	1,115	715
1846	3,136	1,148	760
1847	3,208	1,213	842
1848	3,135	1,300	836
1849	3,306	1,410	742
1850	3,290	1,445	749
1851	3,331	1,403	747
1852	3,308	1,347	782
1853	3,176	1,344	773
1854	3,260	1,299	749
1855	3,729	1,341	728
1856	3,461	1,400	687
1857	2,925	1,316	812
1858	2,865	1,369	776
1859	3,047	1,409	782

Source

Mark Aldrich, "Earnings of American Civil Engineers," *Journal of Economic History* 31 (June 1971): 409–10.

Documentation

These series present average annual earnings of civil engineers, by rank, employed on construction of canals and railroads. Lower ranks (first) indicate higher levels of skill, experience, and supervisory responsibility. Data consist of more than 4,000 observations of annual earnings. Sources include manuscript records of individuals, firms, and government agencies; published reports of firms and government agencies; and state and federal documents. For further details on sources, see Mark Aldrich, "Rates of Return on Investment in Technical Education in the Ante-bellum American Economy" (Ph.D. dissertation, University of Texas at Austin, 1969).

TABLE Ba4253–4267 Daily and monthly wages for common labor, artisans, and clerks, by region: 1821–1860

Contributed by Robert A. Margo

	Common labor, daily					Artisans, daily					Clerks, monthly				
	United States	Northeast	Midwest	South Atlantic	South Central	United States	Northeast	Midwest	South Atlantic	South Central	United States	Northeast	Midwest	South Atlantic	South Central
	Ba4253	Ba4254	Ba4255	Ba4256	Ba4257	Ba4258	Ba4259	Ba4260	Ba4261	Ba4262	Ba4263	Ba4264	Ba4265	Ba4266	Ba4267
Year	Dollars	Dollars	Dollars	Dollars	Dollars	Dollars	Dollars	Dollars	Dollars	Dollars	Dollars	Dollars	Dollars	Dollars	Dollars
1821	—	0.78	—	—	0.74	—	1.00	—	—	1.67	—	40.07	34.63	—	44.35
1822	—	0.69	—	—	0.76	—	1.26	1.31	—	1.75	32.65	29.42	33.20	34.06	47.20
1823	—	0.75	0.51	—	0.77	1.40	1.35	1.25	1.42	1.84	32.77	31.53	34.28	32.15	41.77
1824	—	0.75	0.65	—	0.75	1.26	1.20	1.20	1.27	1.79	32.84	32.56	31.24	30.35	40.44
1825	0.71	0.78	0.54	0.64	0.74	1.28	1.18	1.22	1.41	1.75	36.16	33.34	36.44	38.68	45.32
1826	0.71	0.77	0.56	0.65	0.76	1.37	1.22	1.40	1.52	2.02	34.07	29.97	37.10	37.14	48.17
1827	0.70	0.72	0.59	0.65	0.83	1.46	1.32	1.45	1.61	2.21	34.43	31.37	34.25	35.33	48.52
1828	0.69	0.67	0.65	0.65	0.91	1.39	1.26	1.50	1.47	2.02	34.43	30.43	39.08	34.17	52.63
1829	0.70	0.70	0.65	0.60	0.91	1.37	1.21	1.49	1.62	1.85	36.93	35.30	36.33	33.25	51.79
1830	0.69	0.69	0.65	0.58	0.92	1.33	1.15	1.48	1.64	1.77	35.76	32.16	34.73	32.01	60.70
1831	0.67	0.65	0.65	0.58	0.88	1.36	1.17	1.67	1.65	1.78	33.38	32.35	29.72	30.81	44.62
1832	0.69	0.72	0.65	0.56	0.88	1.40	1.21	1.63	1.65	1.88	35.08	33.81	35.36	33.00	43.99
1833	0.71	0.72	0.75	0.55	0.86	1.41	1.23	1.49	1.66	2.08	35.77	33.64	35.51	35.34	46.71
1834	0.78	0.85	0.81	0.54	0.89	1.52	1.37	1.47	1.70	2.23	36.39	33.64	39.63	35.78	47.47
1835	0.78	0.85	0.82	0.54	0.84	1.56	1.42	1.42	1.74	2.30	35.54	33.71	34.56	34.24	46.29
1836	0.81	0.89	0.66	0.70	0.95	1.65	1.52	1.56	1.81	2.28	36.98	33.57	33.40	40.18	50.05
1837	0.95	0.98	1.04	0.77	0.94	1.63	1.44	1.95	1.67	2.13	44.31	39.95	39.67	42.57	68.50
1838	0.80	0.88	0.78	0.70	0.73	1.48	1.40	1.57	1.55	1.72	43.24	36.66	42.25	45.03	69.19
1839	0.84	0.81	0.96	0.71	0.90	1.54	1.47	1.42	1.55	2.08	48.56	42.00	42.51	47.71	81.24
1840	0.72	0.67	0.75	0.67	0.88	1.50	1.39	1.35	1.55	2.33	45.64	41.25	38.46	42.33	69.47
1841	0.76	0.81	0.66	0.61	0.95	1.50	1.41	1.24	1.56	2.38	40.24	38.58	37.66	39.73	63.49
1842	0.78	0.84	0.76	0.54	0.94	1.41	1.27	1.24	1.58	2.22	40.83	39.91	39.12	37.55	61.88
1843	0.81	0.91	0.74	0.54	0.92	1.35	1.34	1.05	1.52	1.73	44.46	44.96	47.12	40.60	55.20
1844	0.80	0.95	0.71	0.55	0.78	1.28	1.21	1.15	1.52	1.65	42.60	40.44	45.64	43.90	57.15
1845	0.78	0.95	0.69	0.56	0.73	1.44	1.45	1.23	1.51	1.73	44.00	40.76	46.70	47.46	59.45
1846	0.77	0.91	0.69	0.63	0.70	1.35	1.37	1.02	1.43	1.83	43.12	37.97	49.19	45.89	62.33
1847	0.72	0.77	0.67	0.70	0.68	1.41	1.42	1.17	1.36	1.96	45.55	43.37	42.13	44.37	65.50
1848	0.86	1.03	0.77	0.69	0.74	1.38	1.34	1.25	1.41	1.93	44.59	41.58	45.48	42.90	61.74
1849	0.84	0.93	0.79	0.68	0.85	1.48	1.46	1.38	1.44	1.88	44.71	41.38	47.12	41.47	61.33
1850	0.85	0.94	0.80	0.68	0.85	1.44	1.42	1.35	1.44	1.81	45.54	42.17	47.12	42.95	60.84
1851	0.84	0.87	0.81	0.67	0.95	1.46	1.35	1.54	1.45	1.92	51.93	49.14	59.01	44.48	62.23
1852	0.89	0.96	0.81	0.65	1.06	1.50	1.42	1.50	1.46	2.04	51.63	48.36	56.64	45.95	64.46
1853	0.88	0.95	0.81	0.68	1.02	1.57	1.49	1.59	1.47	2.09	49.19	46.70	48.56	45.54	64.25
1854	0.93	1.00	0.91	0.71	0.97	1.63	1.57	1.62	1.49	2.14	50.86	49.85	49.19	43.29	63.62
1855	0.96	1.04	0.92	0.76	0.98	1.71	1.67	1.69	1.50	2.19	51.41	52.08	46.33	43.16	62.51
1856	0.97	1.08	0.90	0.84	0.96	1.75	1.78	1.69	1.52	2.02	52.87	53.61	49.39	45.80	60.21
1857	1.02	1.11	0.98	0.87	0.99	1.84	1.80	1.79	1.84	2.22	55.25	51.82	52.23	43.72	84.30
1858	0.96	0.93	0.99	0.91	1.02	1.87	1.86	1.74	1.65	2.50	52.81	52.65	51.61	42.19	64.18
1859	1.05	1.11	1.02	0.90	1.09	1.87	1.87	1.74	1.74	2.36	48.41	46.70	43.15	41.65	68.57
1860	1.03	1.09	1.00	0.88	1.10	1.83	1.80	1.75	1.85	2.25	52.10	49.19	53.34	43.76	69.61

TABLE Ba4253–4267 Daily and monthly wages for common labor, artisans, and clerks, by region: 1821–1860 *Continued*

Source

Robert A. Margo, *Wages and Labor Markets before the Civil War* (University of Chicago Press, 2000), Tables 3A.5, 3A.6, 3A.7, and 5B.4.

Documentation

These series were constructed from benchmark estimates for 1860 and nominal wage indexes spanning the 1821–1860 period. Figures are without board. Data underlying the indexes were drawn from payroll records of civilian employees of the U.S. Army at various army posts throughout the United States. The indexes (1850 = 100) were derived from hedonic regressions of wage rates, in which the dependent variable was the log of the per diem wage, and the independent variables were characteristics of the worker or the job, the post location, and the time period (for example, 1836). Separate regressions were estimated for each occupational group (for example, artisans) for each of the four major census regions (Northeast, Midwest, South Atlantic, and South Central), a total of twelve regressions.

For common labor and artisans, the benchmark wage estimates were derived from figures published in the 1850 federal Census of Social Statistics. For clerks, the benchmark wage estimates were derived by multiplying the regression coefficients by an assumed set of weights meant to reflect the geographic distribution of population within each census region. For common labor and artisans, daily wages rates are shown; for clerks, monthly wage rates.

The "United States" figures are weighted averages of the regional figures; the weights are regional estimates of occupational shares.

TABLE Ba4268–4270 Daily and monthly wages in California for common labor, artisans, and clerks: 1847–1860

Contributed by Robert A. Margo

Year	Common labor, daily	Artisans, daily	Clerks, monthly
	Ba4268	Ba4269	Ba4270
	Dollars	Dollars	Dollars
1847	1.00 [1]	—	—
1848	4.00 [2]	3.83 [3]	111.11 [4]
1849	7.17	12.01	210.33
1850	4.20	6.42	194.35
1851	3.48	6.18	173.07
1852	3.32	5.06	143.41
1853	3.00	4.99	138.11
1854	2.59	4.85	131.68
1855	2.40	4.70	136.79
1856	2.32	4.77	139.65
1857	2.57	3.93	143.24
1858	2.54	3.74	143.10
1859	2.37	3.83	135.01
1860	2.62	4.08	121.11

[1] 1847 through February 1848.

[2] June 1848 through December 1848.

[3] March 1848 through May 1848.

[4] Weighted average of estimates for March–May 1848 and June–December 1848; weights are one third (March–May) and two thirds (June–December).

Source

Robert A. Margo, *Wages and Labor Markets before the Civil War* (University of Chicago Press, 2000), Table 6C.2.

Documentation

These series were constructed from benchmark estimates for 1860 and nominal wage indexes spanning the 1847–1860 period. Data underlying the indexes were drawn from payroll records of civilian employees of the U.S. Army at various army posts in California. The indexes (1860 = 100) were derived from hedonic regressions of wage rates, in which the dependent variable was the log of the per diem wage, and the independent variables were characteristics of the worker or the job, and the time period (for example, 1852). For common labor and artisans, the benchmark wage estimates were derived from figures published in the 1860 federal Census of Social Statistics. For clerks, the benchmark wage estimate was derived by multiplying the regression coefficients by an assumed set of weights meant to reflect the geographic distribution of population. For further details, see Margo (2000), Chapters 3 and 6.

Wages do not include board.

TABLE Ba4271–4279 Daily wages for common labor, by region: 1851–1880

Contributed by Robert A. Margo

	New England	Middle Atlantic	East North Central	West North Central	East South Central	South Atlantic	West South Central	Mountain	Pacific
	Ba4271	Ba4272	Ba4273	Ba4274	Ba4275	Ba4276	Ba4277	Ba4278	Ba4279
Year	Dollars	Dollars	Dollars	Dollars	Dollars	Dollars	Dollars	Dollars	Dollars
1851	0.965	0.867	0.908	1.170	0.900	0.770	—	—	—
1852	1.000	0.859	0.859	1.195	0.900	0.770	—	—	—
1853	1.119	0.909	0.869	1.195	1.000	0.770	—	—	—
1854	1.116	0.953	0.884	1.226	1.000	0.650	—	—	—
1855	1.085	0.945	0.895	1.226	1.000	0.650	—	—	—
1856	1.119	0.937	0.901	1.276	0.817	0.683	—	—	—
1857	1.188	0.954	0.941	1.225	0.817	0.663	—	—	—
1858	1.169	0.922	0.908	1.219	0.827	0.670	—	—	—
1859	1.150	0.936	0.923	1.071	0.827	0.870	—	—	—
1860	1.136	0.983	0.936	1.083	0.827	0.683	—	—	—
1861	1.126	0.987	0.980	1.040	0.910	0.677	—	—	—
1862	1.138	1.031	1.028	1.196	1.125	0.700	—	1.500	2.750
1863	1.159	1.158	1.269	1.301	1.375	1.250	—	1.500	2.750
1864	1.343	1.334	1.466	1.544	1.540	2.375	—	1.500	2.750
1865	1.448	1.471	1.499	1.717	1.541	0.880	—	1.375	2.750
1866	1.497	1.512	1.520	1.665	1.484	0.777	1.045	1.375	2.750
1867	1.523	1.496	1.522	1.550	1.463	0.745	1.295	1.250	2.750
1868	1.535	1.495	1.503	1.531	1.470	0.745	0.960	1.500	2.750
1869	1.568	1.496	1.496	1.491	1.437	0.745	0.905	1.333	2.750
1870	1.569	1.483	1.509	1.456	1.346	0.824	0.980	1.333	2.625
1871	1.582	1.470	1.485	1.433	1.356	0.867	1.070	1.333	2.583
1872	1.579	1.478	1.510	1.424	1.332	0.860	1.113	1.333	2.583
1873	1.576	1.467	1.488	1.433	1.311	0.855	0.923	1.333	2.583
1874	1.533	1.368	1.403	1.359	1.258	0.805	1.087	1.438	2.583
1875	1.455	1.305	1.342	1.350	1.231	0.878	1.098	1.438	2.196
1876	1.405	1.242	1.285	1.302	1.185	0.849	1.018	1.438	2.096
1877	1.340	1.204	1.237	1.254	1.148	0.841	1.103	1.700	2.096
1878	1.291	1.184	1.208	1.205	1.130	0.809	1.170	1.700	2.100
1879	1.279	1.180	1.247	1.195	1.153	0.809	1.253	1.650	2.100
1880	1.327	1.250	1.310	1.322	1.160	0.852	1.296	1.650	2.100

Source

Philip R. P. Coelho and James F. Shepherd, "Regional Differences in Real Wages: The United States, 1851–1880," *Explorations in Economic History* 13 (April 1976): 229–30.

Documentation

Data on wages were obtained from the Weeks report, published as part of the 1880 Census. Joseph D. Weeks and his staff collected observations on wages from payroll records of 627 manufacturing, mechanical, and mining firms, 77 percent of which were located in New England, the Middle Atlantic, and East North Central states. The report listed wages for six occupations (engineers, blacksmiths, machinists, painters, carpenters, and common laborers) by industry, state, and city. The number of wage observations per firm in each occupation is not known. The authors grouped the data for common laborers – the largest occupation – by census region and computed average daily wages by year.

Weekly wages were converted to daily wages assuming a 5.5-day workweek. Monthly wages were converted to daily wages assuming a 22-day work month, and annual wages were converted to daily wages assuming a 286-day work year. The vast majority of observations pertained to daily wage rates, however, and exclusion of nondaily wages did not alter any of the major findings.

Because of the small number of firms in the Weeks sample outside the Northeast and East North Central regions, the figures for the West North Central, South, Mountain, and Pacific regions should be used with caution.

See Appendix 2 regarding the composition of census regions and divisions.

TABLE Ba4280–4282 Daily and annual earnings of employees – all and nonfarm: 1860–1929

Contributed by Robert A. Margo

Year	All employees, annual	Nonfarm employees: Daily	Nonfarm employees: Annual	Year	All employees, annual	Nonfarm employees: Daily	Nonfarm employees: Annual
	Ba4280	Ba4281	Ba4282		Ba4280	Ba4281	Ba4282
	Dollars	Dollars	Dollars		Dollars	Dollars	Dollars
1860	—	1.09	363	1895	—	—	438
1861	—	1.11	370	1896	—	—	439
1862	—	1.15	383	1897	—	—	442
1863	—	1.38	459	1898	—	—	440
1864	—	1.52	506	1899	—	—	470
1865	—	1.54	512	1900	418	—	483
1866	—	1.47	489	1901	438	—	497
1867	—	1.44	479	1902	472	—	528
1868	—	1.50	499	1903	477	—	534
1869	—	1.49	496	1904	482	—	538
1870	—	1.47	489	1905	490	—	550
1871	—	1.45	482	1906	504	—	566
1872	—	1.46	486	1907	529	—	592
1873	—	1.40	466	1908	519	—	577
1874	—	1.32	439	1909	545	—	600
1875	—	1.27	423	1910	575	—	634
1876	—	1.21	403	1911	587	—	644
1877	—	1.17	389	1912	601	—	657
1878	—	1.14	379	1913	633	—	687
1879	—	1.12	373	1914	639	—	696
1880	—	1.16	386	1915	635	—	692
1881	—	—	409	1916	705	—	760
1882	—	—	428	1917	807	—	866
1883	—	—	438	1918	994	—	1,063
1884	—	—	441	1919	1,142	—	1,215
1885	—	—	446	1920	1,342	—	1,426
1886	—	—	453	1921	1,227	—	1,330
1887	—	—	462	1922	1,190	—	1,289
1888	—	—	466	1923	1,278	—	1,376
1889	—	—	471	1924	1,293	—	1,396
1890	—	—	475	1925	1,317	—	1,420
1891	—	—	480	1926	1,346	—	1,452
1892	—	—	482	1927	1,380	—	1,487
1893	—	—	458	1928	1,384	—	1,490
1894	—	—	420	1929	1,425	—	1,534

Source

Stanley Lebergott, *Manpower in Economic Growth: The American Record since 1800* (McGraw-Hill, 1964), pp. 523, 524, 528.

Documentation

Series Ba4280

This series is computed as weighted averages of the series for individual industries. The weights were the numbers employed by industry. The earnings figures for 1900–1928 were computed to link to those of the U.S. Department of Commerce national income accounts that begin in 1929. In constructing his estimates, Lebergott made use of a wide variety of sources, including special census reports and the detailed studies of Simon Kuznets, *National Income and Its Composition, 1919 to 1938* (National Bureau of Economic Research, number 40, 1941); and Paul Douglas, *Real Wages in the United States, 1890–1926* (Houghton Mifflin, 1930). For additional information on the construction of these series consult Lebergott (1964), pp. 479–506.

Estimates exclude the armed forces.

Series Ba4281–4282

These series are based on data collected under the direction of Joseph Weeks as part of the 1880 Census and benchmarks for various years. Lebergott used the Weeks Report to interpolate between census-year benchmarks which he derived from the Census of Population and other reports. He checked the movement of his series against an extensive set of contemporary investigations made by David A. Wells as Special Commissioner of the Revenue. See Lebergott (1964), pp. 295–303, for details regarding their construction.

TABLE Ba4283–4289 Daily wages in manufacturing establishments, by occupation: 1860–1880

Contributed by Robert A. Margo

	Skilled						
	All	Blacksmiths	Carpenters	Engineers	Machinists	Painters	Laborers
	Ba4283	Ba4284	Ba4285	Ba4286	Ba4287	Ba4288	Ba4289
Year	Dollars	Dollars	Dollars	Dollars	Dollars	Dollars	Dollars
1860	1.62	1.64	1.65	1.61	1.61	1.62	1.03
1861	1.67	1.65	1.80	1.65	1.66	1.64	1.04
1862	1.78	1.77	1.97	1.72	1.77	1.76	1.08
1863	2.00	2.07	2.09	1.87	2.05	2.02	1.20
1864	2.33	2.42	2.58	2.19	2.28	2.25	1.39
1865	2.50	2.61	2.68	2.33	2.56	2.31	1.48
1866	2.62	2.74	2.77	2.44	2.73	2.40	1.53
1867	2.59	2.69	2.75	2.38	2.73	2.47	1.53
1868	2.58	2.73	2.67	2.35	2.66	2.52	1.51
1869	2.60	2.73	2.68	2.40	2.66	2.61	1.53
1870	2.61	2.68	2.64	2.47	2.67	2.67	1.52
1871	2.58	2.66	2.57	2.38	2.72	2.67	1.50
1872	2.64	2.69	2.59	2.53	2.72	2.70	1.52
1873	2.62	2.70	2.52	2.50	2.73	2.68	1.52
1874	2.48	2.62	2.42	2.40	2.53	2.60	1.43
1875	2.39	2.41	2.42	2.33	2.47	2.35	1.39
1876	2.24	2.32	2.12	2.17	2.34	2.20	1.33
1877	2.18	2.27	2.06	2.11	2.29	2.09	1.28
1878	2.15	2.23	2.03	2.06	2.29	2.04	1.26
1879	2.16	2.21	2.05	2.08	2.35	2.08	1.27
1880	2.26	2.31	2.15	2.17	2.45	2.21	1.32

Source

Clarence D. Long, *Wages and Earnings in the United States, 1860–1890* (National Bureau of Economic Research, 1960), p. 144.

Documentation

These series were compiled from Tenth Census Reports, *Report on the Statistics of Wages in the Manufacturing Industries with Supplementary Reports on the Average Retail Prices of Necessaries of Life and on Trade Societies, and Strikes and Lockouts,* volume 20 (1886), by Joseph D. Weeks, editor.

Weeks gathered his data from payroll records to give a continuous wage history of the same occupations in the same firms. In each of the more prominent manufacturing, mechanical, and mining industries in various sections of the country, "typical" establishments were selected on the basis of their age, standing, productive capacity, and general reputation. The mailing list of firms was said to be prepared after much correspondence with experts in each industry and recourse to trade directories and publications. No important branch of manufacturing was overlooked, but information on some was not returned or was judged unsatisfactory. Of the more than fifty industries with satisfactory returns, fewer than twenty could be used in Weeks's investigation, for only that many had wage data covering the entire period 1860–1880. Reported earnings do not usually include overtime, holiday and Sunday work, and other extra earnings. Any payments to helpers and underhands have been deducted, so that the worker's wage covers only what he received for his own work. Weeks attempted to convert piece rates into daily wages wherever the firms could furnish information on time put in by pieceworkers.

Series Ba4283. Weighted by the number of establishments; unweighted within each occupation.

TABLE Ba4290–4297 Hourly wages in manufacturing, by industry: 1865–1914

Contributed by Robert A. Margo

	All trades	Cotton textile	Foundries and machine shops	Leather	Paper	Printing (books and newspapers)	Stone industry	Woolen textile
	Ba4290	Ba4291	Ba4292	Ba4293	Ba4294	Ba4295	Ba4296	Ba4297
Year	Dollars	Dollars	Dollars	Dollars	Dollars	Dollars	Dollars	Dollars
1865	0.1841	0.1101	0.2239	0.2165	0.1368	0.2362	0.2479	0.1323
1866	0.1897	0.1247	0.2273	0.2803	0.1510	0.2326	0.2596	0.1395
1867	0.2025	0.1263	0.2410	0.1918	0.1563	0.2751	0.2831	0.1294
1868	0.2009	0.1266	0.2280	0.1918	0.1719	0.2833	0.2892	0.1264
1869	0.2022	0.1309	0.2270	0.1918	0.1667	0.2850	0.3033	0.1229
1870	0.1999	0.1324	0.2215	0.1708	0.1719	0.2867	0.2798	0.1265
1871	0.2029	0.1369	0.2253	0.1665	0.1860	0.2861	0.2873	0.1277
1872	0.2074	0.1374	0.2335	0.1665	0.1840	0.2953	0.2890	0.1276
1873	0.2110	0.1378	0.2437	0.1750	0.1855	0.2945	0.2805	0.1326
1874	0.2095	0.1320	0.2419	0.1750	0.2020	0.2933	0.2810	0.1356
1875	0.2041	0.1316	0.2256	0.1668	0.2002	0.2945	0.2803	0.1340
1876	0.1930	0.1196	0.2045	0.1583	0.1681	0.2965	0.2753	0.1335
1877	0.1850	0.1196	0.1987	0.1583	0.1389	0.2851	0.2245	0.1273
1878	0.1823	0.1204	0.1945	0.1603	0.1483	0.2727	0.2253	0.1318
1879	0.1770	0.1146	0.1937	0.1520	0.1385	0.2598	0.2309	0.1268
1880	0.1810	0.1201	0.2029	0.1520	0.1629	0.2573	0.2091	0.1301
1881	0.1804	0.1189	0.2085	0.1438	0.1627	0.2458	0.2244	0.1305
1882	0.1868	0.1235	0.2157	0.1438	0.1723	0.2493	0.2507	0.1379
1883	0.1888	0.1194	0.2211	0.1398	0.1939	0.2554	0.2426	0.1377
1884	0.1855	0.1161	0.2189	0.1355	0.1707	0.2517	0.2519	0.1346
1885	0.1830	0.1135	0.2142	0.1403	0.1700	0.2481	0.2523	0.1359
1886	0.1893	0.1214	0.2140	0.1555	0.1784	0.2563	0.2624	0.1474
1887	0.1926	0.1285	0.2230	0.1515	0.1684	0.2536	0.2658	0.1434
1888	0.1930	0.1300	0.2196	0.1528	0.1629	0.2551	0.2736	0.1483
1889	0.1950	0.1311	0.2233	0.1528	0.1583	0.2533	0.2931	0.1510
1890	0.1973	0.1316	0.2243	0.1583	0.1696	0.2555	0.3093	0.1517
1891	0.1989	0.1311	0.2272	0.1559	0.1723	0.2581 [1]	0.3148	0.1524
1892	0.1999	0.1327	0.2293	0.1542	0.1717	0.2587	0.3150	0.1514
1893	0.2033	0.1409	0.2283	0.1620	0.1747	0.2598	0.3156	0.1601
1894	0.1976	0.1316	0.2228	0.1517	0.1720	0.2585	0.3097	0.1547
1895	0.1975	0.1289	0.2244	0.1527	0.1719	0.2596	0.3103	0.1530
1896	0.2039	0.1373	0.2286	0.1525	0.1706	0.2684	0.3251	0.1584
1897	0.2036	0.1368	0.2257	0.1506	0.1689	0.2701	0.3301	0.1614
1898	0.2025	0.1340	0.2246	0.1484	0.1682	0.2720	0.3305	0.1580
1899	0.2036	0.1287	0.2284	0.1593	0.1781	0.2752	0.3300	0.1577
1900	0.2144	0.1486	0.2370	0.1580	0.1768	0.2796	0.3382	0.1744
1901	0.2184	0.1486	0.2435	0.1597	0.1842	0.2828	0.3619	0.1742
1902	0.2235	0.1498	0.2507	0.1577	0.1844	0.2884	0.3874	0.1781
1903	0.2294	0.1542	0.2578	0.1611	0.1946	0.2955	0.4014	0.1779
1904	0.2290	0.1504	0.2562	0.1635	0.1966	0.3023	0.3931	0.1772
1905	0.2325	0.1510	0.2604	0.1660	0.2006	0.3084	0.4007	0.1793
1906	0.2410	0.1633	0.2669	0.1668	0.2008	0.3180	0.3947	0.1943
1907	0.2562	0.1877	0.2741	0.1695	0.2180	0.3372	0.4044	0.2076
1908	—	0.2445	—	—	—	—	—	0.2045
1909	—	0.2260	—	—	—	—	—	0.2056
1910	—	0.2279	—	—	—	—	—	0.1991
1911	—	0.2306	—	—	—	—	—	0.1988
1912	—	0.2545	—	—	—	—	—	0.2266
1913	—	0.2585	—	—	—	—	—	0.2142
1914	—	0.2619	—	—	—	—	—	0.2257

[1] Fixed-weight average of two industries, "Printing, Books" and "Printing, Newspapers." The weights are 0.33 and 0.67, respectively; see the source, p. 279.

Source

Christopher Hanes, "Comparable Indices of Wholesale Prices and Manufacturing Wage Rates in the United States, 1865–1914," *Research in Economic History* 14 (1992): 269–92.

Documentation

The original data sources for these series are the following: Nelson Aldrich, *Aldrich Report*, in *Wholesale Prices, Wages, and Transportation* (1893); U.S. Bureau of Labor, *Nineteenth Annual Report of the Commissioner, 1904: Wages and Hours of Labor*; and various U.S. Bureau of Labor Statistics (BLS) bulletins. The Aldrich report and BLS sources record average daily or hourly wage rates for selected jobs for fixed samples of firms, typically at the firm level or averaged across firms within a given geographic area. The Aldrich report and the BLS sources overlap in 1890. An overall sample for the 1865–1914 period was constructed by matching industries and occupations within states or census regions from the various sources. The bulk of the data pertain to the Northeast. Averages by occupation within industries were computed by weighting by employment in the firm (for observations from the Aldrich report) or group of firms (BLS sources). Series computed from the BLS sources were linked to the Aldrich series by using the change in wage rates from 1890 to 1891. Industry averages are unweighted averages of the industry/occupation series.

Series Ba4290. Equals the weighted average of series Ba4291–4297. The weights are industry and employment totals reported in the 1890 Census.

TABLE Ba4298–4313 Annual and hourly earnings in manufacturing, by industry: 1889–1914

Contributed by Robert A. Margo

	Annual earnings, all industries	Hourly earnings	Textiles													
		All industries	All	Cotton	Wool	Silk	Hosiery and knit goods	Dyeing and finishing	Boots and shoes	Leather	Electrical machinery	Paper and paper products	Rubber	Glass	Foundry and machine shops	Iron and steel
	Ba4298	Ba4299	Ba4300	Ba4301	Ba4302	Ba4303	Ba4304	Ba4305	Ba4306	Ba4307	Ba4308	Ba4309	Ba4310	Ba4311	Ba4312	Ba4313
Year	Dollars	Dollars	Dollars	Dollars	Dollars	Dollars	Dollars	Dollars	Dollars	Dollars	Dollars	Dollars	Dollars	Dollars	Dollars	Dollars
1889	417	—	—	—	—	—	—	—	—	—	—	—	—	—	—	—
1890	425	0.144	0.106	0.099	0.116	0.120	0.094	0.154	0.161	0.169	—	0.120	0.158	—	0.185	—
1891	425	0.144	0.107	0.099	0.118	0.122	0.096	0.157	0.159	0.175	—	0.119	0.155	—	0.190	—
1892	431	0.145	0.107	0.098	0.119	0.117	0.101	0.155	0.161	0.173	—	0.122	0.153	—	0.186	0.170
1893	410	0.151	0.117	0.104	0.133	0.132	0.106	0.168	0.164	0.171	—	0.125	0.163	—	0.188	0.172
1894	376	0.139	0.110	0.104	0.117	0.123	0.103	0.162	0.160	0.159	—	0.123	0.154	—	0.186	0.158
1895	392	0.138	0.105	0.095	0.118	0.112	0.099	0.154	0.154	0.161	—	0.119	0.152	—	0.180	0.153
1896	393	0.144	0.108	0.097	0.123	0.123	0.100	0.158	0.150	0.162	0.163	0.121	0.160	—	0.178	0.158
1897	395	0.140	0.105	0.097	0.120	0.155	0.095	0.150	0.147	0.160	0.165	0.119	0.157	—	0.173	0.154
1898	394	0.137	0.104	0.091	0.123	0.113	0.096	0.151	0.142	0.155	0.174	0.112	0.159	—	0.175	0.158
1899	420	0.146	0.106	0.092	0.124	0.114	0.102	0.148	0.145	0.151	0.172	0.123	0.158	0.181	0.173	0.179
1900	432	0.151	0.110	0.100	0.130	0.109	0.102	0.149	0.148	0.152	0.174	0.127	0.157	0.195	0.180	0.187
1901	446	0.158	0.112	0.101	0.132	0.108	0.102	0.150	0.151	0.153	0.183	0.130	0.163	0.204	0.183	0.196
1902	474	0.165	0.116	0.104	0.135	0.116	0.104	0.157	0.154	0.154	0.187	0.136	0.160	0.210	0.194	0.203
1903	481	0.170	0.122	0.109	0.139	0.123	0.110	0.157	0.165	0.157	0.205	0.133	0.161	0.199	0.202	0.202
1904	471	0.169	0.118	0.107	0.137	0.120	0.107	0.154	0.163	0.161	0.196	0.141	0.164	0.214	0.200	0.192
1905	487	0.172	0.119	0.103	0.139	0.130	0.112	0.164	0.172	0.159	0.198	0.142	0.166	0.225	0.202	0.194
1906	526	0.184	0.127	0.110	0.149	0.130	0.127	0.168	0.176	0.172	0.206	0.142	0.181	0.221	0.213	0.203
1907	538	0.191	0.134	0.124	0.154	0.138	0.123	0.166	0.185	0.178	0.209	0.158	0.180	0.228	0.218	0.215
1908	482	0.184	0.132	0.121	0.155	0.124	0.122	0.167	0.184	0.178	0.210	0.177	0.196	0.235	0.219	0.214
1909	512	0.186	0.134	0.118	0.156	0.138	0.124	0.174	0.184	0.182	0.208	0.167	0.195	0.223	0.220	0.220
1910	538	0.198	0.141	0.130	0.161	0.143	0.130	0.180	0.194	0.188	0.221	0.173	0.208	0.239	0.230	0.232
1911	545	0.202	0.143	0.130	0.161	0.150	0.133	0.175	0.198	0.194	0.223	0.181	0.210	0.244	0.235	0.247
1912	564	0.207	0.150	0.136	0.171	0.155	0.140	0.182	0.204	0.189	0.235	0.189	0.217	0.250	0.241	0.248
1913	585	0.221	0.159	0.141	0.173	0.179	0.146	0.191	0.210	0.223	0.241	0.195	0.222	0.262	0.251	0.274
1914	574	0.220	0.160	0.141	0.190	0.169	0.160	0.201	0.212	0.214	0.240	0.205	0.239	0.263	0.253	0.266

Source

Albert Rees, *Real Wages in Manufacturing, 1890–1914* (Princeton University Press, for the National Bureau of Economic Research, 1961), Tables 10 and 13.

Documentation

Rees's estimates of hourly earnings of wage earners in all manufacturing begin with estimates of average annual earnings in Census years (1889, 1899, 1904, 1909, and 1914 are considered Census years). To obtain average annual earnings, he divided total wage payments by the average number of wage earners after adjusting the data to conform to the definition of manufacturing in effect for the 1958 Census. This meant deducting industries no longer considered manufacturing, the most important of which are railroad repair shop products, with 366,000 workers in 1914, and illuminating gas, with 44,000 workers. The effect of the adjustment was to reduce average annual earnings by $6 in each census year, except in 1889, when it reduced annual earnings by $4.

For 1889, Rees also had to adjust the original Census figures to eliminate the hand and custom trades. This adjustment was made for each industry and was based on separate data on factory industries for 1899 given in the Census of Manufactures of 1904. When the 1899 data showed that an industry was partly a factory industry and partly a hand or custom trade, Rees applied the 1899 proportions to the 1889 figures.

The nature of the Census employment concepts have an important effect on annual earnings figures for Census years. The figures Rees would have preferred were total payrolls divided by the number of workers in average daily attendance when the plant was in operation because, at a later step, he divided annual earnings by the number of days in operation to get average daily earnings. The nature of the appropriate average employment concept can be seen more easily by reversing the order of the division: total payrolls divided by days in operation would give average daily payrolls, which, divided by the number of workers in average daily attendance, would give average daily earnings.

The actual Census employment figures differ from this ideal in two opposite ways. In 1914 and 1909, employers were asked to report, from time or payroll records, the number of workers employed on the fifteenth day of each month or the nearest representative day. The employment figures for the twelve months were then added, employment in any month in which the plant was not in operation was counted as zero, and the sum was divided by 12. The first source of error was the inclusion of these zero figures, which resulted in too low an average employment and too high a daily earnings figure.

In effect, time lost during whole months in which an establishment was not in operation was counted twice: once in employment and once in the number of days worked. In seasonal industries such as glass, where the error on this account is large, Rees made special corrections to allow for it.

The second source of error was that employers probably included in their count some workers who were on the payroll on the fifteenth day of the month but were not at work or receiving pay on that day. This source of error resulted in too high an average employment and too low an average daily wage. Checks of the hourly earnings figures against data built up from hourly wage rates did not suggest any consistent bias in the estimates and, thus, led Rees to conclude that the two sources of error were, in general, roughly offsetting.

Prior to 1909, the Census employment concepts were somewhat different. In 1899 and 1904, employers reported average employment for each month without reference to a particular day. In 1889, the average employment concept was essentially average employment during the time the plant was in operation. Thus, the first of the two sources of error is absent in 1889 while the second is not. For this reason, the earnings estimates for the early 1890s may be slightly too low.

For the intercensal years, Rees used data for Massachusetts, New Jersey, and Pennsylvania as interpolators. The Massachusetts series covers the full period, the Pennsylvania series begins in 1892, and the New Jersey series begins in 1895. He linked the series at these points to prevent the changes in coverage from affecting the movement of the series.

Rees computed the average number of days per year that establishments were in operation as a weighted average of data for the same states used in interpolating annual earnings. Within each state, Rees computed employment-weighted averages of days in operation by industries; the all-manufacturing averages published by some of the states are weighted by the number of establishments. The weights for combining states in Census years were Census employment in manufacturing; for other years, linear interpolations of the Census weights were used. The full-time work year during the period 1889–1914 was 312 days (365 minus 52 Sundays and 1 holiday).

Rees used the series on average full-time hours per day in all manufacturing in deriving some of his industry data on hourly earnings, referring to it as the "general hours series." Throughout the study, he converted weekly hours to daily hours by dividing by 6. The daily hours figures for 1914 and 1909 were computed from the frequency distributions of full-time hours per week in the Census of Manufactures.

From 1903 to 1914, the movement of the general hours series was based on U.S. Bureau of Labor Statistics (BLS) data for seven industries, using Paul Douglas's processing for six of them; see Douglas, *Real Wages in the United States, 1890–1926* (Houghton Mifflin, 1930). The industries are cotton, silk, hosiery and knit goods, woolen and worsted, boots and shoes, lumber, and iron and steel. These were combined by Census employment weights, using linear interpolation of these weights for intercensal years. The resulting series was then adjusted to pass through the points computed from Census data for 1909 and 1914.

This segment of the general hours series used the hours data for all of Douglas's payroll industries except clothing (for which Douglas interpolated the data for 1907–1912) and slaughtering and meatpacking (for which he assumed a constant sixty-hour week on the basis of information other than the BLS data). Rees added the silk industry, for which he computed average hours from the BLS bulletins following Douglas's method.

For 1890–1902, the movement of the general hours series was taken from Leo Wolman's series for all manufacturing (*Hours of Work in American Industry*, National Bureau of Economic Research Bulletin number 71 (1938)). This was linked to the segment of the general hours series for 1903–1909 by means of an overlap of one year at 1903. The resulting change in the level of Wolman's series was an increase of 0.2 hour per week. Wolman's series uses all the hours data for manufacturing given in the *Nineteenth Annual Report of the Commissioner of Labor*; it thus has much broader coverage (forty-eight industries) than Douglas's series, which was derived from the same source for this period but is confined to fourteen industries.

Rees's estimates of money earnings for individual industries were derived in essentially the same way as the estimates for all manufacturing. However, he used data from several additional states to estimate the number of days in operation per year, and to interpolate annual earnings between Census years. These states provided usable data only for some industries or only for short periods of time. See the source for additional detail.

The choice of industries was dictated by the availability of state data. None of the state sources provides definitions or descriptions of the industries to which its industry series refer, and the industry titles at times proved quite misleading. Large differences between state and Census data in the movement of annual earnings from one Census year to the next were often grounds for not using a series. Because it was possible for Rees to combine series given separately in his sources, but not to break them down, the industry coverage of his series is always that of the broadest of their components.

The levels of average daily hours for individual industries for 1909 and 1914 were computed from Census data. In two industries, Rees made special assumptions about the means of the open-end classes in the Census distributions. For glass, short workweeks were common for part of the workforce, apparently because of the heat and physical strain of some jobs. In this industry, he assumed that the mean of the weekly-hours class "48 hours and under" was forty-four hours. For iron and steel, the means of the open-end class "over 72 hours" were computed from BLS data.

The movement of hours, except for the trend from 1909 to 1914, was based ultimately on BLS data that were combined in several different ways. In five industries (cotton, woolens, hosiery and knit goods, boots and shoes, and iron and steel), Rees used the Douglas payroll series adjusted to the Census levels of 1909 and 1914. For silk, he computed an hours series using Douglas's methods; this was then adjusted to Census levels. The hours series for "all textiles" is the weighted averages of the series for cotton, woolen, silk, and hosiery and knit goods, with no new adjustment to Census levels. In the remaining industries, except dyeing and finishing textiles, he used the general hours series to estimate the movement of hours from 1903 to 1914, adjusting it to the census levels of each industry. For dyeing and finishing textiles, he used the series for all textiles.

In five industries (dyeing and finishing textiles, leather, paper, glass, and foundries and machine shops) for the period before 1903, Rees used the data for individual industries in the *Nineteenth Annual Report of the Commissioner of Labor*. For the two remaining industries (rubber and electrical machinery), the data in that report covered four establishments or fewer, and were considered too unreliable to use. Therefore, he used the general hours series in these industries before 1903 as well as after.

Hourly earnings is average annual earnings divided by average annual hours. Average annual hours is average days in operation per year times average hours per day.

Series Ba4298. Data are expressed per full-time equivalent worker.

TABLE Ba4314–4319 Hourly and weekly earnings in selected industries and for lower skilled labor: 1890–1926

Contributed by Robert A. Margo

Year	Manufacturing industries, hourly	Bituminous coal mining, hourly	Railroads, weekly	Building trades (union), hourly	Postal employees, hourly	Lower-skilled labor, weekly
	Ba4314	Ba4315	Ba4316	Ba4317	Ba4318	Ba4319
	Dollars	Dollars	Dollars	Dollars	Dollars	Dollars
1890	0.199	0.180	11.38	0.341	0.352	8.71
1891	0.202	0.169	11.27	0.341	0.358	9.74
1892	0.203	0.179	11.46	0.348	0.360	8.75
1893	0.205	0.188	11.37	0.347	0.361	8.73
1894	0.200	0.171	11.25	0.339	0.368	8.34
1895	0.200	0.158	11.22	0.341	0.375	7.45
1896	0.205	0.147	11.22	0.343	0.378	8.46
1897	0.203	0.138	11.25	0.346	0.381	8.40
1898	0.204	0.170	11.31	0.348	0.376	8.53
1899	0.209	0.185	11.37	0.361	0.370	8.70
1900	0.216	0.204	11.43	0.374	0.371	8.83
1901	0.219	0.231	11.49	0.391	0.375	9.05
1902	0.227	0.244	11.73	0.413	0.374	9.25
1903	0.236	0.267	12.12	0.436	0.372	9.64
1904	0.236	0.271	12.56	0.443	0.373	9.84
1905	0.239	0.276	12.45	0.454	0.375	9.91
1906	0.248	0.293	12.84	0.481	0.369	10.34
1907	0.257	0.288	13.35	0.498	0.378	10.76
1908	0.250	0.293	13.47	0.505	0.395	10.22
1909	0.252	0.292	13.59	0.510	0.409	10.37
1910	0.260	0.299	14.07	0.520	0.420	10.65
1911	0.263	0.305	14.49	0.531	0.429	10.13
1912	0.274	0.320	14.79	0.544	0.437	10.32
1913	0.285	0.316	15.12	0.557	0.450	10.84
1914	0.287	0.323	15.36	0.567	0.464	10.78
1915	0.287	0.337	15.78	0.569	0.466	10.65
1916	0.320	0.379	16.62	0.587	0.471	13.78
1917	0.364	0.484	18.84	0.624	0.484	17.18
1918	0.448	0.599	26.40	0.684	0.536	21.69
1919	0.529	0.699	27.66	0.780	0.648	23.83
1920	0.663	0.784	34.14	1.052	0.739	25.98
1921	0.607	0.846	31.14	1.076	0.759	—
1922	0.574	0.834	30.30	1.006	0.748	—
1923	0.620	0.864	30.24	1.107	0.762	—
1924	0.636	0.811	30.66	1.188	0.788	—
1925	0.645	0.724	31.80	1.229	0.836	—
1926	0.647	0.719	32.16	1.313	0.867	—

Sources

For series Ba4314–4318: Paul H. Douglas, *Real Wages in the United States, 1890–1926* (Houghton Mifflin, 1930). For series Ba4319: Whitney Coombs, *The Wages of Unskilled Labor in Manufacturing Industries in the United States 1890–1924* (Columbia University Press, 1926), p. 99.

Documentation

Series Ba4314. These data on hourly earnings are weighted averages for union and payroll employees. The union scales of wages are substantially higher and less flexible than the wages of all workers in the "union" industries. Since the weight of the union industries in the all-manufacturing average is based on the total number of skilled and semiskilled workers in the industries, the total manufacturing average is too high (see Leo Wolman, "American Wages," *Quarterly Journal of Economics* 46 (1932): 398–406). Beginning in 1907, the union series is a weighted average of trade union scales for occupations. The weights are union membership by crafts. The series are extrapolated back to 1890 by use of payroll data from the sources of the payroll employee series. Average earnings for "payroll" manufacturing industries are averages weighted by employment data from employer payrolls given in various U.S. Bureau of Labor Statistics (BLS) bulletins and in the *Nineteenth Annual Report of the Commissioner of Labor*. Until 1913, the original data are for selected occupations only, and they exclude most laborers and some other unskilled workers. Therefore, for 1890–1913, the series are extrapolations backward from the 1914 level.

Series Ba4315. Average hourly earnings are obtained by dividing average annual earnings by average days worked, as reported by the U.S. Geological Survey; the resulting series was divided by daily hours worked.

Series Ba4316. For 1895–1914, average full-time weekly earnings on railroads is based on average daily wages by occupations; for 1914–1926, it is based on average hourly wages as reported by the U.S. Interstate Commerce Commission and estimated daily hours.

Series Ba4317. Average hourly earnings in the building trades are weighted averages of trade union scales for occupations. The weights are union membership by crafts.

Series Ba4318. Estimated by dividing average annual earnings by 52 to obtain weekly earnings, and then dividing again by average weekly hours to obtain hourly earnings.

Series Ba4319. Data on full-time weekly earnings are based on the wages of the least-skilled or lowest-paid occupations reported for each industry in BLS bulletins and in the *Nineteenth Annual Report of the Commissioner of Labor*, except that the figure for 1920 is based on the data of the National Industrial Conference Board. Since these sources exclude most laborers before 1914, the series is labeled here as "lower-skilled," though it is called "unskilled" by Coombs and by Douglas.

TABLE Ba4320–4334 Annual earnings in selected industries and occupations: 1890–1926

Contributed by Robert A. Margo

	All industries		Manufacturing and steam railroads												
				Wage earners											
	Includes farm labor	Excludes farm labor	Clerical workers	Manufacturing	Steam railroads	Street railways	Telephones	Telegraphs	Gas and electricity	Bituminous coal mining	Farm labor	Federal employees	Postal employees	Public school teachers	Ministers
	Ba4320	Ba4321	Ba4322	Ba4323	Ba4324	Ba4325	Ba4326	Ba4327	Ba4328	Ba4329	Ba4330	Ba4331	Ba4332	Ba4333	Ba4334
Year	Dollars	Dollars	Dollars	Dollars	Dollars	Dollars	Dollars	Dollars	Dollars	Dollars	Dollars	Dollars	Dollars	Dollars	Dollars
1890	438	486	848	439	560	557	—	—	687	406	233	—	878	256	794
1891	438	487	882	442	554	529	—	—	587	377	236	—	894	264	786
1892	445	495	885	446	563	535	—	—	625	393	238	1,096	899	270	793
1893	430	480	923	420	563	526	—	—	627	383	232	1,101	902	276	809
1894	400	448	928	386	546	508	—	—	670	292	214	1,110	919	283	824
1895	415	468	941	416	546	509	—	—	640	307	216	1,104	935	289	787
1896	411	462	954	406	544	531	—	—	665	282	220	1,084	944	294	764
1897	411	462	970	408	543	552	—	—	703	270	224	1,057	950	298	750
1898	417	468	1,010	412	542	558	—	—	698	316	228	1,025	939	306	739
1899	428	480	1,004	426	543	591	—	—	612	379	239	1,017	924	318	722
1900	438	490	1,011	435	548	604	—	—	620	438	247	1,033	925	328	731
1901	454	508	1,009	456	549	601	—	—	615	465	255	1,047	936	337	730
1902	467	519	1,025	473	562	576	408	544	—	490	264	1,061	934	346	737
1903	489	543	1,037	486	593	582	397	573	—	522	277	1,067	928	358	761
1904	490	540	1,056	477	600	610	392	601	556	470	290	1,066	931	377	759
1905	503	554	1,076	494	589	646	401	581	543	500	302	1,072	935	392	759
1906	520	569	1,074	506	607	662	412	592	581	537	315	1,084	921	409	773
1907	542	595	1,091	522	661	658	412	635	623	580	319	1,094	944	431	831
1908	516	563	1,111	475	667	650	420	639	595	487	324	1,102	987	455	833
1909	543	594	1,136	518	644	671	430	622	618	524	328	1,106	1,021	476	831
1910	574	630	1,156	558	677	681	417	649	622	558	336	1,108	1,049	492	802
1911	575	629	1,213	537	705	685	419	670	648	553	338	1,116	1,071	509	856
1912	592	646	1,209	550	721	674	438	669	641	614	348	1,128	1,091	529	879
1913	621	675	1,236	578	760	704	438	717	661	631	360	1,136	1,124	547	899
1914	627	682	1,257	580	795	737	476	742	651	543	351	1,140	1,157	564	938
1915	633	687	1,267	568	815	748	529	792	644	589	355	1,152	1,162	578	984
1916	708	765	1,359	651	867	798	567	806	679	750	388	1,211	1,175	605	1,017
1917	830	887	1,477	774	989	872	616	769	853	976	481	1,295	1,207	648	1,069
1918	1,047	1,115	1,697	980	1,424	1,111	690	831	1,092	1,211	604	1,380	1,339	689	1,186
1919	1,201	1,272	1,914	1,158	1,509	1,387	844	967	1,291	1,097	706	1,520	1,618	810	1,238
1920	1,407	1,489	2,160	1,358	1,817	1,608	980	1,145	1,432	1,386	810	1,648	1,844	936	1,428
1921	1,233	1,349	2,134	1,180	1,632	1,539	1,038	1,159	1,364	1,013	522	1,593	1,870	1,082	1,556
1922	1,201	1,305	2,067	1,149	1,591	1,436	1,064	1,110	1,343	954	508	1,625	1,844	1,188	1,622
1923	1,299	1,393	2,126	1,254	1,585	1,493	1,069	1,133	1,355	1,246	572	1,658	1,870	1,224	1,620
1924	1,303	1,402	2,196	1,240	1,570	1,544	1,104	1,150	1,436	1,120	574	1,708	1,934	1,247	1,678
1925	1,336	1,434	2,239	1,280	1,597	1,565	1,108	1,161	1,448	1,141	587	1,776	2,051	1,263	1,769
1926	1,376	1,473	2,310	1,309	1,613	1,566	1,117	1,215	1,477	1,247	593	1,809	2,128	1,277	1,826

Source

Paul H. Douglas, *Real Wages in the United States, 1890–1926* (Houghton Mifflin, 1930).

Documentation

Series Ba4320–4321. These are weighted averages of series Ba4322–4334 and an additional series beginning in 1902 for anthracite coal. The weights are based on decennial census employment estimates interpolated for intercensal years based on state employment data when available; elsewhere they are linear. The weights for decennial census years and for 1926 are shown in the source on page 390.

Series Ba4322. The series is based on average earnings of salaried workers in manufacturing, computed from the Censuses of Manufactures for Census years, with data from three states used to interpolate

(continued)

TABLE Ba4320–4334 Annual earnings in selected industries and occupations: 1890–1926 *Continued*

for intercensal years based on state employment data when available; elsewhere they are linear. The weights for decennial census years and for 1926 are shown in the source on page 390.

Series Ba4322. The series is based on average earnings of salaried workers in manufacturing, computed from the Censuses of Manufactures for Census years, with data from three states used to interpolate for other years; and, beginning in 1895, earnings of salaried workers in railroads from the Interstate Commerce Commission (ICC), with data from two state railway commissions and one railroad used to extrapolate back to 1890.

Series Ba4323. The series is based on data from the Census of Manufactures for Census years (total wages paid and wage earners). Figures for intercensal years are interpolated using similar data from the labor bureaus of a number of states. Census data for 1890 are adjusted to eliminate the hand trades.

Series Ba4324. The series is based on ICC data since 1905 and extrapolated back to 1890 by using data from several state railroad commissions.

Series Ba4325. The series is based on the Eleventh Census (1890) and the Censuses of Electrical Industries. Figures for intercensal years are interpolations based on data from several state railroad and public utility commissions and state labor bureaus.

Series Ba4326–4327. The series is based on Censuses of Electrical Industries. Figures for intercensal years are interpolations based on data published by the Pennsylvania Department of Internal Affairs.

Series Ba4328. The series is based on the Censuses of Electrical Industries (electricity) and on the Censuses of Manufactures (gas) for Census years. Figures for intercensal years are interpolations based on data for New York City, Wisconsin, Illinois, and Pennsylvania, from state sources.

Series Ba4329. The series is based on aggregate wage payments from the Census of Mines and Quarries of 1889, 1902, 1909, and 1919 as revised in the Fourteenth Census (1920), divided by employment figures reported by the U.S. Geological Survey. Figures for intercensal years are interpolations based on data from the state labor bureaus or departments of mines of five major coal-producing states.

Series Ba4330. The series is based on the U.S. Department of Agriculture series of daily wages of farm labor without board and of monthly wages of farm labor without board. Data for 1900–1909 are linear interpolations covering from one to three years each.

Series Ba4331. Covers employees of federal executive departments in Washington, D.C., only. The data are from the Official Register, adjusted to include bonuses paid during 1917–1924.

Series Ba4332. Covers letter carriers and, beginning in 1906, postal clerks in first- and second-class post offices. The data are from the Annual Reports of the Postmaster General, adjusted to calendar years.

Series Ba4333. Covers teachers, principals, and supervisors in public elementary and secondary schools. The data are from the Annual Reports of the U.S. Commissioner of Education, adjusted to a calendar year basis. Data for some years after 1915 are interpolations based on studies of the National Education Association.

Series Ba4334. Covers salaries of Methodist and Congregational ministers as reported in the Methodist Year Book and the Annual Congregational Gray Book.

TABLE Ba4335–4360 Annual earnings of full-time employees, by industry: 1900–1928

Contributed by Robert A. Margo

			Mining					Transportation				Communications and public utilities		
	Agriculture	Manufacturing	Total	Anthracite coal	Bituminous coal	Metal	Construction	Total	Railroad	Water	Local	Total	Gas and electric	Telephone and telegraph
	Ba4335	Ba4336	Ba4337	Ba4338	Ba4339	Ba4340	Ba4341	Ba4342	Ba4343	Ba4344	Ba4345	Ba4346	Ba4347	Ba4348
Year	Dollars	Dollars	Dollars	Dollars	Dollars	Dollars	Dollars	Dollars	Dollars	Dollars	Dollars	Dollars	Dollars	Dollars
1900	178	487	479	340	516	—	593	505	536	390	510	470	506	433
1901	182	511	531	420	548	—	590	505	537	393	508	496	506	433
1902	191	537	532	289	577	794	611	472	550	400	487	473	518	444
1903	191	548	619	544	615	—	637	528	580	403	492	483	544	443
1904	221	538	599	638	554	—	644	540	587	407	516	487	550	448
1905	199	561	610	579	589	—	659	543	576	410	546	477	538	450
1906	219	577	636	550	633	—	693	560	594	417	559	497	575	460
1907	220	598	697	633	683	—	714	592	646	427	556	521	617	471
1908	220	548	590	553	574	—	721	591	652	427	549	516	589	482
1909	221	599	625	556	617	865	731	583	630	423	567	531	612	488
1910	223	651	668	604	657	—	804	607	662	420	575	516	616	461
1911	225	632	671	633	652	—	779	624	690	417	579	658	641	488
1912	232	651	723	616	723	—	791	634	705	437	570	527	635	467
1913	236	689	749	659	743	—	827	667	743	467	595	560	654	515
1914	234	696	666	636	640	923	838	695	778	484	623	579	644	557
1915	236	661	716	671	694	976	827	711	797	531	632	607	637	614
1916	259	751	889	711	884	1,152	882	768	848	669	674	640	672	647
1917	327	883	1,138	1,019	1,150	1,352	1,001	885	968	851	737	727	844	675
1918	401	1,107	1,399	1,426	1,427	1,499	1,191	1,265	1,393	1,086	938	866	1,081	753
1919	463	1,293	1,370	1,508	1,276	1,611	1,387	1,352	1,477	1,305	1,172	1,035	1,278	906

TABLE Ba4335–4360 Annual earnings of full-time employees, by industry: 1900–1928 *Continued*

			Mining					Transportation				Communications and public utilities		
	Agriculture	Manufacturing	Total	Anthracite coal	Bituminous coal	Metal	Construction	Total	Railroad	Water	Local	Total	Gas and electric	Telephone and telegraph
	Ba4335	Ba4336	Ba4337	Ba4338	Ba4339	Ba4340	Ba4341	Ba4342	Ba4343	Ba4344	Ba4345	Ba4346	Ba4347	Ba4348
Year	Dollars	Dollars	Dollars	Dollars	Dollars	Dollars	Dollars	Dollars	Dollars	Dollars	Dollars	Dollars	Dollars	Dollars
1920	528	1,532	1,684	1,777	1,633	1,639	1,710	1,645	1,807	1,499	1,435	1,238	1,489	1,115
1921	344	1,346	1,757	1,868	1,808	1,482	1,380	1,533	1,664	1,339	1,470	1,276	1,497	1,161
1922	331	1,283	1,300	1,814	1,165	1,345	1,297	1,461	1,630	1,088	1,394	1,265	1,423	1,176
1923	372	1,403	1,822	2,014	1,848	1,497	1,614	1,484	1,631	1,132	1,413	1,292	1,429	1,199
1924	375	1,427	1,703	2,117	1,621	1,378	1,620	1,509	1,627	1,219	1,472	1,371	1,544	1,250
1925	382	1,450	1,580	2,129	1,427	1,455	1,655	1,539	1,655	1,227	1,502	1,378	1,552	1,257
1926	386	1,476	1,597	2,124	1,434	1,463	1,664	1,562	1,671	1,238	1,530	1,427	1,571	1,317
1927	387	1,502	1,590	1,851	1,446	1,485	1,708	1,579	1,687	1,220	1,549	1,440	1,558	1,343
1928	385	1,534	1,478	1,825	1,342	1,516	1,719	1,607	1,720	1,255	1,553	1,474	1,591	1,378

			Services						Government			
	Wholesale and retail trade	Finance, insurance, and real estate	Total	Personal	Medical and other health	Domestic	Nonprofit	Educational	Total	State and local	Public education	Federal civilian
	Ba4349	Ba4350	Ba4351	Ba4352 [1]	Ba4353	Ba4354	Ba4355	Ba4356	Ba4357	Ba4358 [2]	Ba4359	Ba4360 [3]
Year	Dollars	Dollars	Dollars	Dollars	Dollars	Dollars	Dollars	Dollars	Dollars	Dollars	Dollars	Dollars
1900	508	1,040	340	330	256	240	652	469	584	590	345	940
1901	510	1,037	344	332	258	243	651	483	572	605	354	974
1902	521	1,051	361	344	267	264	657	489	584	612	364	967
1903	537	1,078	370	354	275	270	679	532	602	621	377	1,009
1904	551	1,099	379	364	283	277	677	509	614	640	397	971
1905	561	1,115	385	376	292	278	677	511	628	646	412	976
1906	569	1,146	393	381	296	286	689	528	651	664	430	999
1907	580	1,180	420	394	306	316	741	544	675	694	453	1,014
1908	593	1,218	429	403	313	328	743	545	683	695	479	1,001
1909	609	1,263	439	420	326	331	741	546	710	696	501	1,071
1910	630	1,301	447	435	338	337	715	549	725	699	518	1,096
1911	666	1,355	462	453	352	343	763	560	739	712	535	1,113
1912	666	1,338	469	453	352	350	784	568	757	724	556	1,140
1913	685	1,349	479	459	357	357	802	603	788	779	575	1,169
1914	706	1,368	487	471	366	355	837	610	798	788	593	1,197
1915	720	1,399	493	490	381	342	876	623	753	804	608	1,224
1916	760	1,406	523	524	407	357	907	631	844	826	636	1,273
1917	828	1,439	571	580	451	389	953	679	880	832	682	1,318
1918	941	1,438	646	669	520	432	1,058	721	1,023	902	725	1,415
1919	1,070	1,589	757	780	606	538	1,104	784	1,156	1,022	852	1,609
1920	1,270	1,758	912	940	752	665	1,286	894	1,245	1,164	970	1,707
1921	1,260	1,860	905	932	983	649	1,392	1,022	1,317	1,296	1,109	1,683
1922	1,261	1,932	908	933	912	649	1,446	1,109	1,358	1,316	1,206	1,694
1923	1,272	1,896	942	941	845	711	1,454	1,130	1,378	1,336	1,239	1,704
1924	1,314	1,944	965	972	845	732	1,507	1,148	1,400	1,346	1,269	1,747
1925	1,359	1,997	984	1,006	916	741	1,578	1,173	1,425	1,377	1,299	1,762
1926	1,416	2,008	1,005	1,048	857	748	1,607	1,214	1,482	1,422	1,342	1,888
1927	1,480	2,019	1,046	1,095	931	756	1,647	1,252	1,531	1,488	1,393	1,907
1928	1,573	2,043	1,065	1,164	930	725	1,675	1,284	1,550	1,500	1,433	1,916

[1] Data for 1900–1928 not comparable with data for 1929–1948 or 1949–1994, which are shown in Tables Ba4397–4418 and Ba4490–4511.

[2] General government only.

[3] Includes work relief.

Source

Stanley Lebergott, *Manpower in Economic Growth: The American Record since 1800* (McGraw-Hill, 1964), pp. 480–506, Table A-18.

Documentation

The earnings figures for 1900–1928 were computed to link to those of the U.S. Department of Commerce national income accounts that begin in 1929 (with the exception of personal services, as noted). In constructing his estimates, Lebergott made use of a wide variety of sources, including special census reports and the detailed studies of Simon Kuznets, *National Income and Its Composition, 1919 to 1938* (National Bureau of Economic Research, 1941); and Paul Douglas, *Real Wages in the United States, 1890–1926* (Houghton Mifflin, 1930).

The following summaries from Lebergott's book describe the derivation of estimates for certain individual industries for the 1900–1928 period.

Series Ba4335. For 1910–1928, average earnings were computed from estimates of wages of hired labor (including the value of perquisites) and the average employment of such labor. For 1899, the total cost of hired labor as reported in the Agricultural Census and total employment of hired labor as reported in the Census of Population were used for computing an earnings figure. For 1902, 1906, and 1909, figures were interpolated between 1899 and 1910 averages by the average monthly farm wage rates as derived from the surveys of the U.S. Department of Agriculture.

(continued)

TABLE Ba4335–4360 Annual earnings of full-time employees, by industry: 1900–1928 *Continued*

Series Ba4335. Since analysis by Louis Ducoff indicates a close relationship over the 1910–1943 period between farm wage-rate changes and prices received by farmers, Lebergott used the U.S. Bureau of Labor Statistics wholesale price index component for farm prices to interpolate farm wage rates between the U.S. Department of Agriculture survey dates.

Series Ba4336. For manufacturing employees, Lebergott relied on the Census of Manufactures series for Census years, interpolating for the pre-1919 years by the state data as combined by Paul Douglas, and for the post-1919 years by similar data as combined by Simon Kuznets.

Series Ba4337. The estimates for all mining were computed as the weighted sum of series for anthracite, bituminous, metal, and oil mining for 1902, 1909, and the years 1914–1928. For the remaining years in the 1900–1913 period, total mining was estimated from the trend in coal mining, the ratio of one average to the other being much the same in 1902, 1909, and 1914. All mining earnings were 108.5 percent of coal mining in 1914 and 107.8 percent in 1909. For 1902, they were 11.3 percent, a difference explained by the anthracite strike of that year. The 1909 ratio was therefore used for 1900–1913.

Series Ba4338–4339. Separate estimates were computed for each industry for the years 1900–1928. For 1919–1928, the averages can be readily derived from Kuznets's estimates. For earlier years, the Census data were interpolated by Paul Douglas on the basis of the relevant state series; his figures were used for extrapolation after some adjustments. For both the anthracite coal strike of 1902 and the bituminous coal strike of 1919, Lebergott followed Douglas in showing a decline in earnings, relating total payrolls to the average number customarily employed in the nonstrike months. As this decline is also reflected in employment data, the two may not be multiplied together for these years to give total payrolls.

Series Ba4340. For metal mining, Lebergott interpolated between Census benchmark data by the weighted trend of earnings in copper and iron mining. Because the precious metals, lead, and zinc were mined primarily in the West during this period, the employment weight for these industries was given to the series for copper, which is primarily one for the Mountain States.

Series Ba4341. For the construction sector, Lebergott began with the 1929 average wage as reported by the Department of Commerce and extrapolated back to 1919 by Kuznets's estimate of implicit full-time earnings. He then extrapolated back to 1900 using Douglas's adjusted index of weekly earnings for building tradesmen and for unskilled laborers weighted by Census of Population weights. To adjust this series for the varying volume of employment from year to year, Lebergott multiplied by an adjustment ratio – computed as the ratio of an index of weekly to annual earnings in manufacturing.

Series Ba4342–4348. The group averages, as those for utilities and for communications, represent weighted averages of earnings in each industry sector. The weights used were the employment estimates displayed in Lebergott's Appendix Table A-5, p. 514. The average earnings were, in general, the Department of Commerce's 1929 figure extrapolated to 1919 by Kuznets's series, and to 1900 by Douglas's series. There were three partial exceptions to this primary procedure: (1) for gas and electricity, alternative estimates of the 1900–1904 trend were made because Lebergott felt that Douglas's figures, based on Wisconsin reports, show an unreasonable trend; (2) for the telephone and telegraph industries the 1902 estimate was extrapolated to 1900 by the trend for street railways earnings, the two showing similar trends in immediately subsequent years; and (3) for water transport, the 1900–1918 trend of average weekly earnings of seamen was adjusted to the trend for annual earnings by the ratios of weekly to annual series for earnings on steam railroads.

Series Ba4349. Lebergott made direct estimates for trade by using, as basic sources, a variety of direct studies of earnings made in the period 1900–1919. He constructed his benchmark estimates for 1900 using the 1901 Cost of Living Survey (of 24,000 families), an 1895–1896 study by the Commissioner of Labor on earnings in the various industries of thirty states, and the 1899 Census of Manufactures. He developed his benchmark estimates for 1909 and 1919 from the Censuses of Manufactures conducted in those years, in particular the special studies of the steam laundry and telephone industries, from a massive 1909 Bureau of Labor study of women's earnings, and from a 1921 study by the National Bureau of Economic Research and the Census Bureau. Interpolations were then made between these benchmark averages.

Series Ba4350. Earnings were computed as the weighted sum of earnings in the two major occupational categories, agents and clerical personnel. Estimates of the number of agents who were employees were made from Census of Population data. Average earnings of agents in 1900, 1905, 1910, and 1920 were available for Metropolitan Life Insurance Company agents, the largest company in the field. Interpolation for 1901–1904 and 1910–1920 was by the movement of earnings in trade. For 1906–1909, a linear trend was used to reflect the readjustment of agents' earnings after the Armstrong Investigation, leading to a much greater 1905–1910 growth than appears in trade earnings. Unpublished figures on earnings of salaried clerical employees in one of the five largest insurance companies were used for the years 1909 and 1914–1919. These were extrapolated to 1900 and interpolated for 1910–1913 by the trend in earnings of salaried clerical personnel in manufacturing. The two series thus estimated were combined with employment weights derived from the 1910 Census, giving a trend series for 1900–1919. This series was used to extrapolate the 1919–1929 figures derived from Kuznets's estimates.

Series Ba4352

The first step in developing this series was to make a benchmark earnings estimate for 1900, by estimating averages for key occupations and industries, then weighting them together by the number of employees in each. (Consistent weights were available from the special class-of-worker tabulations from the 1910 Census.)

For 1920 and 1921, the results of a U.S. Census Bureau–National Bureau of Economic Research nationwide survey for the President's Conference on Unemployment were used.

The personal-service earnings figures, thus derived for 1900 and 1920, as well as that for 1929 shown in Department of Commerce estimates, are virtually identical with the average earnings in laundries for those years. Therefore, the Census of Manufactures data on laundry earnings in 1909, 1914, 1919, 1925, and 1927 were used to extrapolate the 1919 service earnings figure to these additional years.

Ratios of personal-service earnings to those for trade, a segment for which yearly estimates had already been made and which is similar in certain key respects to that of service, were computed. The ratios were as follows: 1900, 0.65 (or 65 percent); 1909, 0.69; 1914, 0.67; 1921, 0.73; 1925, 0.69; 1927, 0.70. The relationship appears to be quite reasonable and steady, even to the extent of indicating a relatively greater rise for the lower-paid industry than the higher-paid one during World War I and after – a phenomenon apparent in other series based on very solid annual or biennial reports. These ratios were, therefore, interpolated and applied to the trade series to give the estimates of earnings in personal service.

Series Ba4358

An initial benchmark for earnings in 1905 was established as follows. (1) For policemen and firemen, the largest single group, averages of earnings data available for cities with population of 30,000 or more in 1905 were adjusted to apply to all cities on the basis of the ratio of teachers' earnings in larger and smaller cities. (2) For the next-largest occupation group, city labor, the 1905 Census data for employees of street-cleaning departments were used, after an adjustment similar to that noted for averages of policemen and firemen, to make the figures apply to the United States as a whole. (3) For city officials and other city employees, the average for policemen and firemen was used. (4) For state and county officials, the Office of Education data on average earnings of teachers were used since the two were very similar in level during stable periods in the 1920s. (5) In addition, an estimate of the number employed in state mental hospitals and institutions for the feebleminded was prepared as part of the employment estimates. The average salary for this group was assumed to be the same for all hospitals, computed as part of the estimates for service. These live earnings averages were then weighted together by the occupation data for local government in 1910, as shown by the Census of Population.

TABLE Ba4335–4360 Annual earnings of full-time employees, by industry: 1900–1928 *Continued*

For 1919–1928, Kuznets's estimates based on a review of available reports for individual cities and states were used. The 1905–1919–1928 data show a close similarity of trend to that for the earnings of urban teachers, suggesting that the data could be used for interpolation. In the critical overlap period of 1919–1921, however, the rate of change in teachers' salaries was not proportionate to that for other state employees, with salaries of the former lagging behind increases previously granted to other local employees and, in addition, reflecting the impact of heavy postwar enrollments. The procedure used, therefore, was to extrapolate the 1919 estimate to 1916 by the movement of earnings for policemen and firemen in selected cities, as estimated by Willford I. King, *The National Income and Its Purchasing Power* (National Bureau of Economic Research, 1930). The resultant estimate of local government earnings in 1916 was 91 percent of the average salary of urban teachers, a ratio almost identical with the 88 percent implicit in the 1905 figures estimated earlier. By extrapolating and interpolating these percentages, and those for 1905 and 1919, and applying them to the urban teachers' salary estimates, the final series for local government was derived.

Series Ba4359

For this series, the biennial surveys of the Office of Education provide the basic raw materials. These were developed into consistent estimates by Douglas and Kuznets; their series were used to extrapolate the 1929 Department of Commerce benchmark.

Series Ba4360

Separate earnings series were derived for postal and for nonpostal civilian employees of the federal government, the two series being weighted together and then used to interpolate between benchmark estimates for 1899 and 1929. The 1899 benchmark was derived by sampling the complete list of federal employees and their salaries as recorded in the U.S. Official Register for 1899. For 1929, Department of Commerce data were used.

A benchmark estimate for 1899 earnings in postal service was computed by sampling from the Official Register for that year, with interpolation between that figure and the implicit Department of Commerce 1929 average by a series for all postal employees. Benchmark averages for all federal employees outside the postal service were computed for 1899 and 1919 by sampling from the complete list of employees shown in the Official Register for those years. The procedure was identical with that used for postal employees. Interpolation from 1899 to 1919 was by the trend of salaries of government employees in the District of Columbia. For 1920–1928, Lebergott interpolated between the 1919 figure and Kuznets's 1929 figure.

TABLE Ba4361–4366 Hourly and weekly earnings of production workers in manufacturing: 1909–1995

Contributed by Robert A. Margo

	All manufacturing		Durable goods manufacturing		Nondurable goods manufacturing	
	Hourly	Weekly	Hourly	Weekly	Hourly	Weekly
	Ba4361	Ba4362	Ba4363	Ba4364	Ba4365	Ba4366
Year	Dollars	Dollars	Dollars	Dollars	Dollars	Dollars
1909	0.19	9.74	—	—	—	—
1914	0.22	10.92	—	—	—	—
1915	—	11.22	—	—	—	—
1916	—	12.63	—	—	—	—
1917	—	14.97	—	—	—	—
1918	—	19.12	—	—	—	—
1919	0.47	21.84	—	—	—	—
1920	0.55	26.02	—	—	—	—
1921	0.51	21.94	—	—	—	—
1922	0.48	21.28	—	—	—	—
1923	0.52	23.56	—	25.42	—	21.50
1924	0.54	23.67	—	25.48	—	21.63
1925	0.54	24.11	—	26.02	—	21.99
1926	0.54	24.38	—	26.23	—	22.29
1927	0.54	24.47	—	26.28	—	22.55
1928	0.56	24.70	—	26.86	—	22.42
1929	0.56	24.76	—	26.84	—	22.47
1930	0.55	23.00	—	24.42	—	21.40
1931	0.51	20.64	—	20.98	—	20.09
1932	0.44	16.89	0.49	15.99	0.41	17.26
1933	0.44	16.65	0.47	16.20	0.42	16.76
1934	0.53	18.20	0.55	18.59	0.51	17.73
1935	0.54	19.91	0.57	21.24	0.52	18.77
1936	0.55	21.56	0.58	23.72	0.52	19.57
1937	0.62	23.82	0.67	26.61	0.57	21.17
1938	0.62	22.07	0.68	23.70	0.57	20.65
1939	0.63	23.64	0.69	26.19	0.57	21.36
1940	0.66	24.96	0.72	28.07	0.59	21.83
1941	0.73	29.48	0.80	33.56	0.63	24.39
1942	0.85	36.68	0.94	42.17	0.71	28.57
1943	0.96	43.07	1.05	48.73	0.79	33.45
1944	1.01	45.70	1.11	51.38	0.84	36.38
1945	1.02	44.20	1.10	48.36	0.89	37.48
1946	1.08	43.32	1.14	46.22	1.00	40.30
1947	1.22	49.17	1.28	51.76	1.15	46.03
1948	1.33	53.12	1.40	56.36	1.25	49.50
1949	1.38	53.88	1.45	57.25	1.30	50.38
1950	1.44	58.32	1.52	62.43	1.35	53.48
1951	1.56	63.34	1.65	68.48	1.44	56.88
1952	1.65	67.16	1.75	72.63	1.51	59.95
1953	1.74	70.47	1.86	76.63	1.58	62.57
1954	1.78	70.49	1.90	76.19	1.62	63.18
1955	1.86	75.70	1.99	82.19	1.67	66.63
1956	1.95	78.78	2.08	85.28	1.77	70.09
1957	2.05	81.59	2.19	88.26	1.85	72.52
1958	2.11	82.71	2.26	89.27	1.91	74.11
1959	2.19	88.26	2.36	96.05	1.98	78.61
1960	2.26	89.72	2.43	97.44	2.05	80.36
1961	2.32	92.34	2.49	100.35	2.11	82.92
1962	2.39	96.56	2.56	104.70	2.17	85.93
1963	2.46	99.63	2.63	108.09	2.22	87.91
1964	2.53	102.97	2.71	112.19	2.29	90.91

(continued)

TABLE Ba4361–4366 Hourly and weekly earnings of production workers in manufacturing: 1909–1995 *Continued*

	All manufacturing		Durable goods manufacturing		Nondurable goods manufacturing	
	Hourly	Weekly	Hourly	Weekly	Hourly	Weekly
	Ba4361	Ba4362	Ba4363	Ba4364	Ba4365	Ba4366
Year	Dollars	Dollars	Dollars	Dollars	Dollars	Dollars
1965	2.61	107.53	2.79	117.18	2.36	94.64
1966	2.72	112.34	2.90	122.09	2.45	98.49
1967	2.83	114.90	3.00	123.60	2.57	102.03
1968	3.01	122.51	3.19	132.07	2.74	109.05
1969	3.19	129.51	3.38	139.59	2.91	115.53
1970	3.35	133.33	3.55	143.07	3.08	120.43
1971	3.57	142.44	3.79	152.74	3.27	128.51
1972	3.82	154.71	4.07	167.68	3.48	138.16
1973	4.09	166.46	4.35	180.09	3.70	146.52
1974	4.42	176.80	4.70	190.82	4.01	156.79
1975	4.83	190.79	5.15	205.49	4.37	169.56
1976	5.22	209.32	5.57	226.14	4.71	185.57
1977	5.68	228.90	6.06	248.46	5.11	201.33
1978	6.17	249.27	6.58	270.44	5.54	218.28
1979	6.70	269.34	7.12	290.50	6.01	236.19
1980	7.27	288.62	7.75	310.78	6.56	255.84
1981	7.99	318.00	8.53	342.91	7.19	281.85
1982	8.49	330.26	9.03	354.88	7.75	297.60
1983	8.83	354.08	9.38	381.77	8.09	318.75
1984	9.19	374.03	9.73	402.82	8.39	333.08
1985	9.54	386.37	10.09	415.71	8.72	345.31
1986	9.73	396.01	10.28	424.56	8.95	357.11
1987	9.91	406.31	10.43	432.85	9.19	369.44
1988	10.19	418.81	10.71	447.68	9.45	379.89
1989	10.48	429.68	11.01	458.02	9.75	391.95
1990	10.83	441.86	11.35	468.76	10.12	404.80
1991	11.18	455.03	11.75	482.93	10.44	419.69
1992	11.46	469.86	12.02	498.83	10.73	433.49
1993	11.74	486.04	12.33	519.09	10.98	455.79
1994	12.07	506.94	12.68	543.97	11.24	459.72
1995	12.37	514.49	12.93	548.23	11.58	468.99

Sources

For 1909-1992: U.S. Bureau of Labor Statistics (BLS), *Employment, Hours, and Earnings, United States, 1909–1994*, volumes 1 and 2, Bulletin number 2445 (September 1994). For 1993-1995: *Employment, Hours, and Earnings, United States, 1988–1996*, Bulletin number 2481 (August 1996).

The specific page numbers are as follows. For series Ba4361-4362: *Employment, Hours, and Earnings, 1909–1994*, pp. 69-71; *Employment, Hours, and Earnings, 1988–1996*, p. 22. For series Ba4363-4364: *Employment, Hours, and Earnings, 1909–1994*, pp. 74-5; *Employment, Hours, and Earnings, 1988–1996*, p. 23. For series Ba4365-4366: *Employment, Hours, and Earnings, 1909–1994*, pp. 472-4; *Employment, Hours and Earnings, 1988–1996*, p. 160.

These data are updated periodically by the BLS; check its bulletin series.

Documentation

The figures for 1909-1931 represent estimates based largely on periodic wage and hour surveys conducted by the BLS during that period for a narrow list of manufacturing industries. These figures are an extension of, and are adjusted for comparability with, the figures for 1932-1957. For a discussion of the methods and data used to derive the figures for 1909-1931, see BLS, *Monthly Labor Review* (July 1955): 801-6. The estimates of average weekly earnings for 1909-1931, based primarily on census data, tend to be more accurate than those for average hourly earnings. It is likely that the hourly earnings figures are overstated because the BLS surveys of wages tended to sample large firms more heavily than small firms.

For 1932-1995, the underlying employment, payroll, and person-hour figures were obtained by means of a monthly mail questionnaire survey of establishments conducted in cooperation with state employment agencies. As of March 1993, there were approximately 390,000 reporting units included in the survey. Each establishment reported the following information: (1) the number of production workers or nonsupervisory employees who worked or received pay for any part of the payroll period that includes the twelfth of the month; (2) the total gross payrolls for these employees before such deductions as Social Security taxes, withholding taxes, union dues, and so forth (the payroll figures include pay for overtime, shift premiums, sick leave, holidays, vacations, and production bonuses, but exclude payments in kind, retroactive pay, nonproduction bonuses, employer contributions to private welfare funds, insurance and pension plans, and similar fringe payments); and (3) total person-hours paid for these employees, including hours paid for vacations, holidays, sick leave, travel time, lunchtime, and so forth. Within each detailed industry, the payroll, employment, and person-hour figures for reporting establishments are aggregated, and average hourly earnings, average weekly hours, and average weekly earnings are computed. The average hourly earnings for a group of industries are weighted arithmetic means of the corresponding averages for the industries within the group. The weights used for earnings are estimates of aggregate production-worker person-hours. Average weekly earnings for the group is the product of the average hourly earnings and the average weekly hours for the group. Average hourly earnings figures exclude such fringe payments as employer contributions to private health, welfare, and insurance funds, and they include premium payments for overtime and for night work. For further details on the survey, consult Appendix A of *Employment, Hours, and Earnings*.

TABLE Ba4367–4380 Hourly and weekly earnings of production and nonsupervisory workers in selected industries: 1909–1995

Contributed by Robert A. Margo

	Bituminous coal and lignite mining		Class I steam railroads		Nonsupervisory workers									
					Construction		Wholesale trade		Retail trade		Electric services		Finance, insurance, and real estate	
	Hourly	Weekly	Hourly	Weekly	Hourly	Weekly	Hourly	Weekly	Hourly	Weekly	Hourly	Weekly	Hourly	Weekly
	Ba4367 [1]	Ba4368	Ba4369 [2]	Ba4370 [2]	Ba4371 [3]	Ba4372 [3]	Ba4373	Ba4374	Ba4375 [4]	Ba4376 [4]	Ba4377 [5]	Ba4378 [5]	Ba4379	Ba4380
Year	Dollars	Dollars	Dollars	Dollars	Dollars	Dollars	Dollars	Dollars	Dollars	Dollars	Dollars	Dollars	Dollars	Dollars
1909	0.31	11.70	—	—	—	—	—	—	—	—	—	—	—	—
1914	0.35	12.11	—	—	—	—	—	—	—	—	—	—	—	—
1919	0.73	25.84	—	—	—	—	—	—	—	—	—	—	—	—
1923	0.82	25.41	—	—	—	—	—	—	—	—	—	—	—	—
1924	0.79	23.42	—	—	—	—	—	—	—	—	—	—	—	—
1925	0.77	26.24	—	—	—	—	—	—	—	—	—	—	—	—
1926	0.76	28.42	—	—	—	—	—	—	—	—	—	—	—	—
1927	0.73	24.18	—	—	—	—	—	—	—	—	—	—	—	—
1928	0.69	24.46	—	—	—	—	—	—	—	—	—	—	—	—
1929	0.66	25.11	—	—	—	—	—	—	—	—	—	—	—	—
1930	0.66	22.04	—	—	—	—	—	—	—	—	—	—	—	—
1931	0.63	17.59	—	—	—	—	—	—	—	—	—	—	—	—
1932	0.50	13.58	—	—	—	—	—	26.75	—	—	0.70	30.78	—	—
1933	0.49	14.21	—	—	—	—	—	25.19	—	—	0.69	29.23	—	—
1934	0.65	17.45	—	—	0.80	22.97	—	25.44	—	—	0.78	29.98	—	—
1935	0.72	18.86	—	—	0.82	24.51	0.61	25.38	—	—	0.79	31.07	—	—
1936	0.77	21.89	—	—	0.82	27.01	0.63	26.96	—	—	0.80	32.22	—	—
1937	0.83	22.94	—	—	0.90	30.14	0.66	28.36	—	—	0.85	34.22	—	—
1938	0.85	19.78	—	—	0.91	29.19	0.67	28.51	—	—	0.86	34.15	—	—
1939	0.86	22.99	0.73	31.90	0.93	30.39	0.69	28.76	0.48	21.01	0.87	34.38	—	—
1940	0.85	23.74	0.73	32.47	0.96	31.70	0.71	29.36	0.49	21.34	0.88	35.10	—	—
1941	0.96	29.47	0.74	34.03	1.01	35.14	0.76	31.36	0.52	22.17	0.92	36.54	—	—
1942	1.03	33.37	0.84	39.34	1.15	41.80	0.83	34.28	0.56	23.37	0.98	39.60	—	—
1943	1.10	39.97	0.85	41.49	1.25	48.13	0.90	37.99	0.61	24.79	1.05	44.16	—	—
1944	1.15	49.32	0.95	46.46	1.32	52.18	0.95	40.76	0.65	26.77	1.11	48.04	—	—
1945	1.20	50.36	0.96	46.32	1.38	53.73	0.99	42.37	0.70	28.59	1.14	50.05	—	—
1946	1.36	56.04	1.09	50.00	1.48	56.24	1.11	46.05	0.80	32.92	1.26	52.04	—	—
1947	1.58	63.75	1.19	55.03	1.54	58.87	1.22	50.14	0.84	33.77	1.34	56.41	1.14	43.21
1948	1.84	69.18	1.30	60.11	1.71	65.27	1.31	53.63	0.90	36.22	1.44	60.54	1.20	45.48
1949	1.88	60.63	1.43	62.36	1.79	67.56	1.36	55.49	0.95	38.42	1.53	63.73	1.26	47.63
1950	1.94	67.46	1.57	64.14	1.86	69.68	1.43	58.08	0.98	39.71	1.58	65.85	1.34	50.52
1951	2.14	74.69	1.73	70.93	2.02	76.96	1.52	62.02	1.06	42.82	1.70	71.40	1.45	54.67
1952	2.22	75.04	1.83	74.30	2.13	82.86	1.61	65.53	1.09	43.38	1.80	74.70	1.51	57.08
1953	2.40	81.84	1.88	76.33	2.28	86.41	1.70	69.02	1.16	45.36	1.93	80.10	1.58	59.57
1954	2.40	77.52	1.93	78.74	2.39	88.91	1.76	71.28	1.20	47.04	2.01	83.21	1.65	62.04
1955	2.47	92.13	1.96	82.12	2.45	90.90	1.83	74.48	1.25	48.75	2.09	86.32	1.70	63.92
1956	2.72	102.00	2.12	88.40	2.57	96.38	1.94	78.57	1.30	50.18	2.20	91.52	1.78	65.68
1957	2.92	106.00	2.26	94.24	2.71	100.27	2.02	81.41	1.37	52.20	2.30	95.22	1.84	67.53
1958	2.93	97.57	2.44	101.50	2.82	103.78	2.09	84.02	1.42	54.10	2.43	99.63	1.89	70.12
1959	3.11	111.34	2.54	106.43	2.93	108.41	2.18	88.51	1.47	56.15	2.55	104.81	1.95	72.74
1960	3.14	112.41	2.61	108.84	3.08	113.04	2.24	90.72	1.52	57.76	2.66	109.86	2.02	75.14
1961	3.12	112.01	2.67	112.94	3.20	118.08	2.31	93.56	1.56	58.66	2.75	112.75	2.09	77.12
1962	3.12	114.46	2.72	115.87	3.31	122.47	2.37	96.22	1.63	60.96	2.87	118.24	2.17	80.94
1963	3.15	121.43	2.76	118.40	3.41	127.19	2.45	99.47	1.68	62.66	2.97	122.36	2.25	84.38
1964	3.30	128.91	2.80	121.80	3.55	132.06	2.52	102.31	1.75	64.75	3.09	127.62	2.30	85.79
1965	3.49	140.26	3.00	130.80	3.70	138.38	2.61	106.49	1.82	66.61	3.22	133.31	2.39	88.91
1966	3.66	149.74	3.09	135.65	3.89	146.26	2.73	111.11	1.91	68.57	3.35	139.70	2.47	92.13
1967	3.75	153.28	3.24	139.97	4.11	154.95	2.88	116.06	2.01	70.95	3.50	145.25	2.58	95.46
1968	3.86	155.17	3.44	151.02	4.41	164.93	3.05	122.31	2.16	74.95	3.71	154.34	2.75	101.75
1969	4.24	169.18	3.68	162.66	4.79	181.54	3.23	129.85	2.30	78.66	3.95	165.51	2.93	108.70
1970	4.58	186.41	3.89	171.94	5.24	195.45	3.43	136.86	2.44	82.47	4.22	176.40	3.07	112.67
1971	4.83	194.17	4.36	188.35	5.69	211.67	3.64	143.42	2.60	87.62	4.51	188.52	3.22	117.85
1972	5.31	216.12	4.89	214.67	6.06	221.19	3.85	151.69	2.75	91.85	4.81	200.58	3.36	122.98
1973	5.75	228.28	5.40	240.30	6.41	235.89	4.07	159.54	2.91	96.32	5.11	216.15	3.53	129.20
1974	6.26	234.75	5.68	249.92	6.81	249.25	4.38	169.94	3.14	102.68	5.51	231.42	3.17	137.61

Notes appear at end of table

(continued)

TABLE Ba4367–4380 Hourly and weekly earnings of production and nonsupervisory workers in selected industries: 1909–1995 *Continued*

	Bituminous coal and lignite mining		Class I steam railroads		Nonsupervisory workers									
					Construction		Wholesale trade		Retail trade		Electric services		Finance, insurance, and real estate	
	Hourly	Weekly	Hourly	Weekly	Hourly	Weekly	Hourly	Weekly	Hourly	Weekly	Hourly	Weekly	Hourly	Weekly
	Ba4367 [1]	Ba4368	Ba4369 [2]	Ba4370 [2]	Ba4371 [3]	Ba4372 [3]	Ba4373	Ba4374	Ba4375 [4]	Ba4376 [4]	Ba4377 [5]	Ba4378 [5]	Ba4379	Ba4380
Year	Dollars	Dollars	Dollars	Dollars	Dollars	Dollars	Dollars	Dollars	Dollars	Dollars	Dollars	Dollars	Dollars	Dollars
1975	7.24	285.98	6.05	261.97	7.31	266.08	4.72	182.19	3.36	108.86	6.06	249.07	4.06	148.19
1976	7.77	309.25	6.88	300.66	7.71	283.73	5.02	194.27	3.57	114.60	6.59	272.83	4.27	155.43
1977	8.27	346.51	7.39	321.47	8.10	295.65	5.39	209.13	3.85	121.66	7.15	298.16	4.54	165.26
1978	9.55	387.73	7.87	343.92	8.66	318.58	5.88	228.14	4.20	130.20	7.71	326.13	4.89	178.00
1979	10.31	419.62	8.94	392.47	9.27	342.99	6.39	247.93	4.53	138.62	8.34	351.95	5.27	190.77
1980	10.90	437.09	9.92	426.56	9.94	367.78	6.95	266.88	4.88	147.38	9.12	387.60	5.79	209.60
1981	11.95	483.98	10.65	457.95	10.82	399.26	7.55	290.68	5.25	158.03	10.02	418.84	6.31	229.05
1982	12.73	507.93	11.50	484.15	11.63	426.82	8.08	309.46	5.48	163.85	10.88	454.78	6.78	254.44
1983	13.78	551.20	12.84	541.85	11.94	442.97	8.54	328.79	5.74	171.05	11.57	481.31	7.29	264.90
1984	14.87	606.70	13.33	573.19	12.13	458.51	8.88	341.88	5.85	174.33	12.28	510.85	7.63	278.50
1985	15.30	630.36	13.64	594.70	12.32	464.46	9.15	351.36	5.94	174.64	12.94	540.89	7.94	289.02
1986	15.46	627.68	13.89	608.38	12.48	466.75	9.34	357.72	6.03	176.08	13.46	562.63	8.36	304.30
1987	15.81	665.60	14.29	627.33	12.71	480.44	9.59	365.38	6.12	178.70	13.85	570.62	8.73	316.90
1988	16.26	686.17	15.00	673.50	13.08	495.73	9.98	380.24	6.31	183.62	14.38	598.21	9.06	325.25
1989	16.39	709.69	15.68	693.06	13.54	513.17	10.39	394.82	6.53	188.72	15.04	631.68	9.53	341.17
1990	16.85	741.40	16.08	726.82	13.77	526.01	10.79	411.10	6.75	194.40	15.80	658.86	9.97	356.93
1991	17.21	769.29	15.68	707.17	14.00	533.40	11.15	424.82	6.94	198.48	16.28	675.62	10.39	370.92
1992	17.29	762.49	16.66	736.37	14.15	537.70	11.39	435.10	7.12	205.06	16.68	695.56	10.82	387.36
1993	17.46	778.72	16.93	782.17	14.38	553.63	11.74	448.47	7.29	209.95	17.34	728.28	11.35	406.33
1994	17.97	812.24	16.76	786.04	14.73	573.00	12.06	463.10	7.49	216.46	18.04	764.90	11.83	423.51
1995	18.68	840.60	17.48	811.07	15.08	585.10	12.43	476.07	7.69	221.47	18.54	786.10	12.33	442.65

[1] Data based on eleven-month average for 1962–1970.

[2] For 1939–1955, data for railroads with operating revenues of $1 million or more; for 1956–1964, $3 million or more; for 1965–1975, $5 million or more; for 1976–1977, $10 million or more; thereafter, $50 million or more. Includes Amtrak beginning in 1993.

[3] Beginning 1947, data cover both on-site and off-site workers on both private and public projects; prior to 1947, data refer only to on-site workers on privately financed construction.

[4] Beginning 1947, includes eating and drinking places.

[5] Beginning 1947, includes only companies engaged exclusively in producing and distributing electricity; prior to 1947, includes combined gas and electric utilities whose income results primarily from sale of electricity.

Sources

For 1909–1992: U.S. Bureau of Labor Statistics (BLS), *Employment, Hours, and Earnings, United States, 1909–1994*, volumes 1 and 2, Bulletin number 2445 (September 1994). For 1993–1995: *Employment, Hours, and Earnings, United States, 1988–1996*, Bulletin number 2481 (August 1996).

The specific page numbers are as follows. For series Ba4367–4368: *Employment, Hours, and Earnings, 1909–1994*, pp. 24–25; *Employment, Hours, and Earnings, 1988–1996*, p. 7. For series Ba4369–4370: *Employment, Hours, and Earnings, 1909–1994*, p. 795; *Employment, Hours, and Earnings, 1988–1996*, p. 257. For series Ba4371–4372: *Employment, Hours, and Earnings, 1909–1994*, pp. 41–43; *Employment, Hours and Earnings, 1988–1996*, p. 12. For series Ba4373–4374: *Employment, Hours, and Earnings, 1909–1994*, pp. 844–46; *Employment, Hours, and Earnings, 1988–1996*, p. 275. For series Ba4375–4376: *Employment, Hours, and Earnings, 1909–1994*, pp. 884–6; *Employment, Hours, and Earnings, 1988–1996*, p. 296. For series Ba4377–4378: *Employment, Hours, and Earnings, 1909–1994*, pp. 830–1; *Employment, Hours, and Earnings, 1988–1996*, p. 271. For series Ba4379–4380: *Employment, Hours, and Earnings, 1909–1994*, pp. 950–1; *Employment, Hours, and Earnings, 1988–1996*, p. 324.

These data are updated periodically by the BLS; check its bulletin series.

Documentation

Series Ba4367–4368

Data relate to production workers.

For 1909–1931, estimates are based on a variety of sources, including special studies by the BLS and data collected by the U.S. Bureau of the Census, the U.S. Bureau of Mines, and reports of state coal commissions. For 1932–1995, figures are strictly comparable in concept and method of estimation with those for manufacturing (Table Ba4361–4366).

Before 1945, lunchtime was not paid for in the mines. Beginning April 1945, mine operators paid for fifteen minutes of lunchtime per day; in July 1947, the paid lunchtime was increased to one-half hour. Similarly, before November 1943, working time was computed on a "face-to-face" basis. From November 1943 to April 1945, inside mine workers were paid for forty-five minutes of travel time per day at two thirds of the regular rate.

Since April 1945, inside workers have been paid for all travel time at the applicable hourly rate. Data published by the Bureau of Mines (*Minerals Yearbook*, 1946, p. 81) show that in 1944, travel time amounted, on the average, to 10–15 percent of total time paid for. Therefore, average hourly earnings figures may have a correspondingly serious downward bias if used to measure average earnings per hour actually worked.

Average hourly earnings figures exclude contributions of coal mine employers to the miners' welfare and retirement fund, established in 1946. This fund was financed by mine operators through contributions of 5 cents for each ton of coal produced. In 1947, the contribution was raised to 10 cents. The medical and hospital fund, previously financed by miners, was combined with the welfare and retirement fund, and the rate of contribution was raised several more times until, in 1952, it reached the current (1970) rate of 40 cents a ton. In 1969, wage supplements in bituminous coal mining, chiefly employer contributions to the welfare and retirement fund, amounted to 20 percent of total compensation.

For an alternative source of hourly earnings data for bituminous coal mining covering the period 1890–1957, see H. G. Lewis, *Unionism and Relative Wages in the United States* (University of Chicago Press, 1963).

Series Ba4369–4370

The series is based on monthly data and relate to all employees except executives, officials, and staff assistants.

Figures for Class I railroads are based on their monthly reports to the U.S. Interstate Commerce Commission. Until 1951, the figures covered all hourly

TABLE Ba4367–4380 Hourly and weekly earnings of production and nonsupervisory workers in selected industries: 1909–1995 *Continued*

rated employees of Class I railroads, excluding Class I switching and terminal companies. Since 1951, the figures cover all employees (excluding switching and terminal companies) except executives, officials, and staff assistants. Although the figures since 1951 are not strictly comparable with those for earlier years, the difference is not large.

Average hourly earnings are computed by dividing the total compensation of covered employees by total man-hours paid for. Average weekly earnings are derived by multiplying average weekly hours by average hourly earnings. Average weekly hours equal total man-hours paid for (during a month) reduced to a weekly basis, divided by the full-month count of employees on the payroll. The full-month count generally tends to be somewhat larger than a count for the payroll period that includes the twelfth of the month, which is used for other industries. For this reason, the weekly earnings tend to be slightly lower than they would be if computed on the latter basis.

Series Ba4371–4380. See the text for Table Ba4361–4366.

Series Ba4379–4380. Excludes nonoffice commissioned agents.

TABLE Ba4381–4390 Hourly and weekly earnings of production workers in manufacturing, by sex and degree of skill: 1914–1948

Contributed by Robert A. Margo

	All		Male		Female		Unskilled male		Skilled and semiskilled male	
	Hourly	Weekly	Hourly	Weekly	Hourly	Weekly	Hourly	Weekly	Hourly	Weekly
	Ba4381	Ba4382	Ba4383	Ba4384	Ba4385	Ba4386	Ba4387	Ba4388	Ba4389	Ba4390
Year	Dollars	Dollars	Dollars	Dollars	Dollars	Dollars	Dollars	Dollars	Dollars	Dollars
1914	0.247 [1]	12.68	0.262	13.65	0.155	7.75	0.203	10.71	0.291	14.99
1920	0.606 [2]	29.39	0.642	31.69	0.414	17.71	0.529	26.06	0.687	34.10
1921	0.524	23.77	0.554	25.35	0.362	15.63	0.437	20.28	0.599	27.36
1922	0.494 [3]	24.29	0.520	25.90	0.352	15.84	0.402	20.30	0.566	28.11
1923	0.541	26.61	0.570	28.39	0.383	17.24	0.443	22.28	0.619	30.81
1924	0.562	26.43	0.592	28.27	0.393	16.75	0.458	22.41	0.644	30.55
1925	0.561	27.08	0.592	29.00	0.389	17.17	0.455	22.93	0.644	31.29
1926	0.568	27.42	0.601	29.51	0.398	17.27	0.461	23.21	0.652	31.61
1927	0.576	27.53	0.610	29.59	0.398	17.37	0.471	23.54	0.656	31.51
1928	0.579	27.80	0.614	29.95	0.396	17.15	0.474	23.89	0.659	31.94
1929	0.590	28.55	0.625	30.64	0.398	17.61	0.486	24.40	0.668	32.60
1930	0.589	25.84	0.622	27.66	0.395	15.98	0.478	21.90	0.663	29.17
1931	0.564	22.62	0.597	24.00	0.371	14.69	0.460	19.18	0.634	25.05
1932	0.498	17.05	0.526	17.96	0.325	11.73	0.400	14.48	0.559	19.48
1933	0.491	17.71	0.518	18.69	0.340	12.35	0.401	14.91	0.550	20.27
1934	0.580	20.06	0.607	21.07	0.427	14.50	0.479	16.46	0.643	22.45
1935	0.599	22.23	0.628	23.49	0.437	15.37	0.495	18.22	0.665	24.98
1936	0.619	24.39	0.651	26.02	0.434	15.74	0.501	20.00	0.689	27.58
1937	0.695	26.80	0.735	28.72	0.473	17.02	0.570	22.41	0.777	30.39
1938	0.716	24.43	0.758	26.07	0.482	15.69	0.586	20.67	0.802	27.49
1939	0.720	27.05	0.765	28.96	0.475	17.02	0.594	22.82	0.808	30.53
1940	0.739	28.54	0.784	30.64	0.491	17.43	0.611	23.91	0.827	32.41
1941	0.814	33.62	0.867	36.18	0.533	20.29	0.682	28.19	0.914	38.32
1942	0.924	40.03	0.987	43.46	0.609	23.95	0.773	33.49	1.043	46.31
1943	1.014	45.88	1.103	51.05	0.699	28.83	0.854	38.86	1.164	54.10
1944	1.067	48.83	1.164	54.65	0.752	31.21	0.892	41.07	1.227	57.85
1945	1.097	48.46	1.185	53.47	0.787	32.18	0.917	41.03	1.248	56.39
1946	1.190	47.55	1.260	50.72	0.876	34.14	1.015	40.86	1.320	53.10
1947	1.342	54.27	1.414	57.77	1.007	38.99	1.147	46.80	1.478	60.35
1948	1.431 [4]	57.22	1.503	60.98	1.090	41.86	1.227	49.88	1.567	63.52

[1] July.

[2] June–December.

[3] July–December.

[4] January–July.

Source

National Industrial Conference Board (NICB), *The Economic Almanac for 1950* (1950), pp. 336–44.

Documentation

The underlying data were collected by the NICB from a sample of companies representing twenty-five industries (durable and nondurable goods) by means of a monthly mail questionnaire. The number of firms included in the sample, as well as the distribution of these firms by size and geographical location, varied somewhat from time to time. In 1936, the sample included 1,886 firms employing about one third of all wage earners in the twenty-five industries covered and about one fifth of all wage earners in all manufacturing industries. The average firm in the sample (in most of the twenty-five industries) was substantially larger (in terms of employment) than the average firm in the population from which the sample was taken. Although some tendency toward an upward bias in the level of earnings of the sample firms may exist, it is not clear if this bias also had a trend or varied with the business cycle.

Within each industry, average hourly earnings was obtained by dividing the aggregate payroll for reporting companies by the aggregate man-hours. Average weekly earnings was obtained in a similar manner. The averages for all industries taken together were weighted means of the separate industry averages, with fixed employment weights estimated for each industry from the 1923 Census of Manufactures.

The distinction in classification between unskilled males and other male workers was not precisely stated by the NICB, and the classification was made by the reporting firms.

TABLE Ba4391–4395 Earnings of male clerical workers and clerical-to-unskilled earnings ratios – railroads and New York factories: 1922–1952

Contributed by Robert A. Margo

		Class I steam railroads			
				As a ratio to unskilled earnings	
	Employed in factories, New York State, weekly	Monthly	Hourly	Monthly	Hourly
	Ba4391	Ba4392	Ba4393	Ba4394	Ba4395
Year	Dollars	Dollars	Dollars	Ratio	Ratio
1922	—	124.54	0.617	1.522	1.574
1923	42.18	125.17	0.617	1.532	1.570
1924	43.60	127.41	0.635	1.585	1.584
1925	44.38	128.35	0.640	1.596	1.592
1926	45.54	129.78	0.646	1.600	1.599
1927	46.73	133.01	0.664	1.638	1.631
1928	46.70	136.94	0.686	1.687	1.677
1929	48.24	138.66	0.692	1.687	1.684
1930	49.34	138.92	0.703	1.789	1.710
1931	46.22	137.96	0.711	1.929	1.738
1932	42.14	126.07	0.655	2.144	1.770
1933	41.52	124.50	0.654	2.064	1.812
1934	42.71	130.16	0.666	1.985	1.815
1935	42.04	142.11	0.722	1.968	1.819
1936	42.67	145.08	0.726	1.848	1.793
1937	44.76	149.41	0.746	1.809	1.747
1938	43.52	155.03	0.784	1.809	1.723
1939	45.90	155.97	0.786	1.750	1.712
1940	45.25	156.76	0.783	1.728	1.698
1941	49.99	164.62	0.813	1.646	1.633
1942	56.17	182.28	0.887	1.569	1.540
1943	57.83	202.00	0.958	1.436	1.430
1944	—	209.16	0.996	1.393	1.419
1945	—	209.26	1.007	1.387	1.410
1946	—	243.43	1.196	1.384	1.347
1947	—	253.14	1.260	1.352	1.328
1948	—	279.48	1.393	1.309	1.290
1949	—	289.05	1.528	1.318	1.279
1950	—	293.69	1.698	1.343	1.272
1951	—	322.47	1.875	1.322	1.245
1952	—	337.05	1.961	1.311	1.232

Source

Claudia Goldin and Robert A. Margo, "The Great Compression: The Wage Structure in the United States at Mid-Century," *Quarterly Journal of Economics* 107 (February 1992): 18; and accompanying appendix, "Skill Ratios and Wage Distributions: 1920's to 1950's," NBER Working Paper number 3817 (National Bureau of Economic Research, August 1991), pp. 7–9.

Documentation

The original data for series Ba4391 were collected by the New York State Bureau of Labor Statistics. Data for other series were originally collected by the U.S. Interstate Commerce Commission.

Series Ba4394–4395. These ratios compare the earnings of male clerical workers to male common laborers, both employed in Class I steam railroads.

TABLE Ba4396 Hourly earnings in manufacturing: 1923–1990

Contributed by Robert A. Margo

Year	Hourly earnings Ba4396 Dollars	Year	Hourly earnings Ba4396 Dollars
1923	0.537	1960	2.367
1924	0.560	1961	2.429
1925	0.562	1962	2.502
1926	0.568	1963	2.565
1927	0.574	1964	2.642
1928	0.577	1965	2.725
1929	0.588	1966	2.825
1930	0.591	1967	2.929
1931	0.569	1968	3.120
1932	0.512	1969	3.308
1933	0.497	1970	3.481
1934	0.583	1971	3.728
1935	0.603	1972	3.997
1936	0.611	1973	4.254
1937	0.688	1974	4.585
1938	0.711	1975	5.003
1939	0.714	1976	5.407
1940	0.731	1977	5.882
1947	1.271	1978	6.367
1948	1.386	1979	6.891
1949	1.444	1980	7.515
1950	1.503	1981	8.257
1951	1.629	1982	8.784
1952	1.722	1983	9.120
1953	1.815	1984	9.464
1954	1.862	1985	9.834
1955	1.939	1986	10.054
1956	2.034	1987	10.217
1957	2.125	1988	10.454
1958	2.201	1989	10.743
1959	2.300	1990	11.065

Source

Christopher Hanes, "Changes in the Cyclical Behavior of Real Wage Rates 1870–1990," *Journal of Economic History* 56 (December 1996): 856–7.

Documentation

This series was constructed from data collected originally by the National Industrial Conference Board and the U.S. Bureau of Labor Statistics. Data from twenty-one industries were matched by industry across the various data sources. Industry series were weighted by 1989 employment to form the aggregate series reported in the table.

TABLE Ba4397–4418 Wage and salary accruals per full-time equivalent employee, by industry: 1929–1948

Contributed by Robert A. Margo

	Agriculture, forestry, and fisheries	Mining	Contract construction	Manufacturing			Transportation	Communications	Electric, gas, and sanitary services	Wholesale trade	Retail trade and automobile services
				All	Durable goods	Nondurable goods					
	Ba4397	Ba4398	Ba4399	Ba4400	Ba4401	Ba4402	Ba4403	Ba4404	Ba4405	Ba4406	Ba4407
Year	Dollars	Dollars	Dollars	Dollars	Dollars	Dollars	Dollars	Dollars	Dollars	Dollars	Dollars
1929	479	1,526	1,674	1,543	1,630	1,455	1,643	1,394	1,562	2,072	1,409
1930	464	1,424	1,526	1,488	1,556	1,425	1,610	1,423	1,575	2,039	1,384
1931	377	1,221	1,233	1,369	1,391	1,352	1,549	1,456	1,572	1,934	1,324
1932	299	1,016	907	1,150	1,127	1,166	1,373	1,363	1,516	1,672	1,173
1933	278	990	869	1,086	1,087	1,086	1,334	1,274	1,427	1,477	1,066
1934	303	1,108	942	1,153	1,171	1,139	1,393	1,364	1,484	1,550	1,102
1935	344	1,154	1,027	1,216	1,264	1,178	1,492	1,401	1,565	1,640	1,139
1936	368	1,263	1,178	1,287	1,376	1,210	1,582	1,451	1,588	1,652	1,159
1937	430	1,366	1,278	1,376	1,491	1,267	1,644	1,516	1,683	1,693	1,218
1938	441	1,282	1,193	1,296	1,365	1,241	1,676	1,622	1,723	1,686	1,217
1939	460	1,367	1,268	1,363	1,479	1,263	1,723	1,643	1,739	1,698	1,224
1940	487	1,388	1,330	1,432	1,568	1,299	1,756	1,661	1,772	1,754	1,236
1941	593	1,579	1,635	1,653	1,840	1,440	1,885	1,685	1,847	1,943	1,299
1942	799	1,796	2,191	2,023	2,292	1,654	2,183	1,766	2,016	2,177	1,395
1943	1,031	2,162	2,503	2,349	2,619	1,895	2,493	1,934	2,261	2,416	1,555
1944	1,220	2,499	2,602	2,517	2,774	2,081	2,679	2,110	2,439	2,600	1,709
1945	1,339	2,621	2,600	2,517	2,732	2,211	2,734	2,325	2,566	2,751	1,879
1946	1,428	2,719	2,537	2,517	2,615	2,404	2,973	2,499	2,665	3,021	2,141
1947	1,518	3,113	2,829	2,793	2,883	2,683	3,168	2,672	2,959	3,322	2,368
1948	1,594	3,387	3,126	3,038	3,159	2,895	3,428	2,869	3,189	3,661	2,530

	Finance, insurance, and real estate	Services						Government			
		All	Personal	Health	Educational not elsewhere classified	Membership organizations	Private household	All	Federal civilian	State and local	Public education
	Ba4408	Ba4409 [1]	Ba4410	Ba4411	Ba4412	Ba4413	Ba4414	Ba4415	Ba4416 [2]	Ba4417	Ba4418
Year	Dollars	Dollars	Dollars	Dollars	Dollars	Dollars	Dollars	Dollars	Dollars	Dollars	Dollars
1929	2,062	1,079	1,219	925	1,313	1,712	731	1,574	1,933	1,538	1,517
1930	1,973	1,066	1,200	933	1,329	1,698	676	1,576	1,768	1,555	1,528
1931	1,858	1,008	1,136	919	1,323	1,653	584	1,568	1,895	1,532	1,536
1932	1,652	918	996	865	1,279	1,545	497	1,499	1,824	1,462	1,470
1933	1,555	854	889	810	1,189	1,442	460	1,344	1,673	1,364	1,365
1934	1,601	857	905	801	1,175	1,440	473	1,297	1,717	1,317	1,329
1935	1,632	873	915	829	1,163	1,435	485	1,305	1,759	1,311	1,358
1936	1,713	898	940	851	1,180	1,465	506	1,290	1,896	1,431	1,395
1937	1,788	938	978	876	1,211	1,497	558	1,367	1,797	1,471	1,435
1938	1,731	943	992	899	1,228	1,529	527	1,348	1,832	1,502	1,476
1939	1,729	952	1,034	908	1,234	1,546	544	1,348	1,843	1,506	1,473
1940	1,725	953	1,042	927	1,240	1,408	554	1,354	1,894	1,534	1,507
1941	1,777	1,020	1,075	955	1,264	1,379	601	1,399	1,970	1,565	1,534
1942	1,885	1,132	1,196	1,036	1,344	1,482	706	1,645	2,226	1,626	1,588
1943	2,041	1,347	1,384	1,127	1,469	1,679	919	1,797	2,628	1,749	1,688
1944	2,191	1,538	1,570	1,262	1,562	1,795	1,140	1,930	2,677	1,861	1,817
1945	2,347	1,688	1,709	1,401	1,641	1,876	1,313	2,059	2,646	2,004	1,975
1946	2,570	1,863	1,854	1,605	1,802	1,984	1,411	2,380	2,904	2,162	2,127
1947	2,740	1,996	1,978	1,821	2,113	2,077	1,463	2,615	3,180	2,375	2,374
1948	3,010	2,074	2,087	1,825	2,009	2,090	1,500	2,818	3,256	2,673	2,666

[1] Does not include automobile services.

[2] Excludes work relief.

Source

U.S. Department of Commerce, *National Income and Product Accounts of the United States, 1929–1994*, volume 2 (April 1998), pp. 31–2.

Documentation

These estimates are ratios of aggregate wage and salary payments, by industry, to the aggregate number of full-time equivalent employees, by industry.

Wages and salaries include executives' compensation, bonuses, tips, and payments in kind, and exclude those sources of labor income as supplements to wages and salaries.

Full-time equivalent employment measures man-years of full-time employment of wage and salary earners, and its equivalent in work performed by part-time workers. For a discussion of the concept of full-time equivalent employment and the methods of estimation involved in converting part-time work to its full-time equivalent, see the *Survey of Current Business* (June 1945): 17–18.

TABLE Ba4397–4418 Wage and salary accruals per full-time equivalent employee, by industry: 1929–1948 *Continued*

Since 1939, private industry employment and payrolls have been based principally on records of the Social Security programs. For 1929–1938, the employment and payroll figures are extrapolations backward from 1939, based on sources and methods similar to those used by Stanley Lebergott, *Manpower in Economic Growth: The American Record since 1800* (McGraw-Hill, 1964). The mainstay of the private industry estimates has been data of the state unemployment insurance (UI) programs, as compiled by the U.S. Department of Labor. Additions were made for employment covered by Old-Age, Survivors, Disability, and Health Insurance (OASDHI), but not by UI (for example, employment in small firms omitted from UI coverage under some state laws). Railroad Retirement Act coverage came from the U.S. Interstate Commerce Commission's (ICC) Transport Statistics, except that certain employments covered by the Railroad Retirement Act, but not reported to the ICC, were estimated from Railroad Retirement Board data.

This general method was followed except for categories for which more reliable data were available from other sources, or where the proportion of firms not covered by Social Security programs was large: agriculture, forestry, and fisheries; hospitals; private higher education; religious organizations; and private households. Data for these categories were obtained from the U.S. Department of Agriculture, the American Hospital Association, the Office of Education, and various governmental censuses and surveys.

Employment and payroll figures used as a basis for earnings in government and in private households were as follows: (1) for the federal government, reports of the Civil Service Commission, records of the armed services, and (for 1933–1943) records of the federal work relief projects; (2) for state and local governments, reports of the U.S. Bureau of the Census, the Office of Education, and so forth; and (3) for private households, the Census of Population and the Current Population Survey of the Census Bureau.

TABLE Ba4419–4421 Compensation per full-time equivalent employee in all industries – wage and salary accruals and supplements: 1929–1994

Contributed by Robert A. Margo

	Total compensation	Wage and salary accruals	Supplements
	Ba4419	Ba4420	Ba4421
Year	Dollars	Dollars	Dollars
1929	1,448	1,430	18
1930	1,411	1,392	19
1931	1,319	1,299	20
1932	1,164	1,143	21
1933	1,089	1,069	20
1934	1,129	1,110	19
1935	1,177	1,157	20
1936	1,231	1,203	28
1937	1,327	1,277	50
1938	1,307	1,249	58
1939	1,342	1,282	60
1940	1,377	1,317	60
1941	1,523	1,460	63
1942	1,795	1,729	66
1943	2,042	1,973	69
1944	2,207	2,126	81
1945	2,312	2,208	104
1946	2,506	2,383	123
1947	2,740	2,616	124
1948	2,958	2,822	136
1949	3,037	2,881	156
1950	3,203	3,034	169
1951	3,456	3,266	190
1952	3,658	3,458	200
1953	3,853	3,643	210
1954	3,967	3,737	230
1955	4,184	3,929	255
1956	4,426	4,141	285
1957	4,626	4,306	320
1958	4,817	4,475	342
1959	5,061	4,675	386
1960	5,243	4,822	421
1961	5,410	4,966	444
1962	5,642	5,158	484
1963	5,865	5,344	521
1964	6,162	5,610	552
1965	6,384	5,807	577
1966	6,704	6,058	646
1967	6,994	6,309	685
1968	7,511	6,755	756
1969	8,063	7,226	837
1970	8,679	7,743	936
1971	9,317	8,250	1,067
1972	10,001	8,788	1,213
1973	10,694	9,320	1,374
1974	11,568	10,009	1,559
1975	12,620	10,808	1,812
1976	13,660	11,576	2,084
1977	14,709	12,360	2,349
1978	15,836	13,264	2,572
1979	17,217	14,382	2,835
1980	18,959	15,792	3,167
1981	20,771	17,246	3,525
1982	22,357	18,487	3,870
1983	23,558	19,416	4,142
1984	24,747	20,342	4,405
1985	25,888	21,299	4,589
1986	26,960	22,182	4,778
1987	28,086	23,146	4,940
1988	29,428	24,279	5,149
1989	30,373	25,039	5,334
1990	32,117	26,415	5,702
1991	33,456	27,357	6,099
1992	35,202	28,690	6,512
1993	36,286	29,430	6,856
1994	37,150	30,131	7,019

(continued)

TABLE Ba4419–4421 Compensation per full-time equivalent employee in all industries – wage and salary accruals and supplements: 1929–1994 *Continued*

Source

Computed from U.S. Department of Commerce, *National Income and Product Accounts of the United States, 1929–1994*, volume 2 (April 1998), pp. 7–12, 25–30, 47–50.

Documentation

Annual supplements per full-time equivalent employee were computed by dividing estimates of aggregate supplements to wages and salaries, by industry, by the corresponding estimates of the aggregate number of full-time equivalent employees. Aggregate supplements are the sum of "employer contributions for social insurance" and "other labor income." Data for employer contributions for social insurance have a high degree of reliability because they are obtained almost exclusively from the accounting records of the agencies administering the programs. Estimates for other labor income are less reliable.

Data on supplements to wages and salaries are obtained from a variety of sources. Reports filed by employers with the administrative agencies or with the U.S. Treasury are the sources of figures for employer contributions under old-age and survivors insurance, state unemployment insurance and cash sickness compensation, railroad retirement and unemployment insurance, and the federal unemployment tax. Payments made by the federal government to its civilian employee retirement systems are obtained from Treasury records and the records of the administrative agencies. Estimates of federal government contributions made to government life insurance programs are based on monthly reports of the Veterans Administration.

Contributions to state and local retirement systems shown in this table are based on data supplied between 1936 and 1980 by the U.S. Department of Health, Education, and Welfare (HEW) and since then by the U.S. Department of Health and Human Services (HHS). Estimates for 1929–1935 are extrapolations from the 1936 figure based on a sample survey of state and local government units.

Estimates of compensation for injuries are based on data in the annual *Insurance Yearbook* (Spectator Company), on reports of state insurance funds, and on information furnished by state accident compensation commissions.

Employer contributions to private pension plans are estimated chiefly from tabulations prepared by the Internal Revenue Service. Contributions to health and welfare funds are estimated from data obtained from the Amalgamated Clothing Workers of America, the International Ladies' Garment Workers' Union, the United Mine Workers of America, and the American Telephone and Telegraph Company. Employer contributions for group insurance are based on studies made by HHS and on reports from the Institute of Life Insurance.

Data on the pay of military reservists were obtained from the armed services or from the annual budget of the U.S. government. Data on federal payments to enemy prisoners of war were obtained from the U.S. Department of Defense. Other items in "other labor income" have always been small in amount.

Series Ba4419. Equals the sum of series Ba4420–4421.

TABLE Ba4422–4425 Federal minimum wage rates under the Fair Labor Standards Act and amendments: 1938–1997

Contributed by Susan B. Carter

		1938 Fair Labor Standards Act	1961 amendments	1966 and subsequent amendments	
				Nonfarm workers	Farm workers
		Ba4422	Ba4423	Ba4424	Ba4425
Year	Date	Dollars per hour	Dollars per hour	Dollars per hour	Dollars per hour
1938	Oct 24	0.25	—	—	—
1939	Oct 24	0.30	—	—	—
1949	Oct 24	0.40	—	—	—
1950	Jan 25	0.75	—	—	—
1956	Mar 1	1.00	—	—	—
1961	Sep 3	1.15	1.00	—	—
1963	Sep 3	1.25	—	—	—
1964	Sep 3	—	1.15	—	—
1965	Sep 3	—	1.25	—	—
1967	Feb 1	1.40	1.40	1.00	1.00
1968	Feb 1	1.60	1.60	1.15	1.15
1969	Feb 1	—	—	1.30	1.30
1970	Feb 1	—	—	1.45	—
1971	Feb 1	—	—	1.60	—
1974	May 1	2.00	2.00	1.90	1.60
1975	Jan 1	2.10	2.10	2.00	1.80
1976	Jan 1	2.30	2.30	2.20	2.00
1977	Jan 1	—	—	2.30	2.20
1978	Jan 1	2.65	2.65	2.65	2.65
1979	Jan 1	2.90	2.90	2.90	2.90
1980	Jan 1	3.10	3.10	3.10	3.10
1981	Jan 1	3.35	3.35	3.35	3.35
1990	Apr 1	3.80	3.80	3.80	3.80
1991	Apr 1	4.25	4.25	4.25	4.25
1996	Oct 1	4.75	4.75	4.75	4.75
1997	Sep 1 [1]	5.15	5.15	5.15	5.15

TABLE Ba4422–4425 Federal minimum wage rates under the Fair Labor Standards Act and amendments: 1938–1997 *Continued*

[1] A subminimum wage of $4.25 per hour applies to employees under 20 years of age, during their first ninety consecutive calendar days of employment.

Source

U.S. Employment Standards Administration minimum wage chart posted on the Department of Labor Web site.

Documentation

The federal minimum wage was established with the passage of the Fair Labor Standards Act (FLSA) of 1938. The FSLA was a cornerstone of New Deal legislation designed to end the Great Depression of the 1930s. The 1938 Act applied to workers engaged in interstate commerce or in the production of goods for interstate commerce.

Series Ba4422. Indicates the new minimum level at each successive change. All increases in the minimum wage rate beginning in 1978 covered all nonexempt workers.

Series Ba4423. The 1961 amendments to the FLSA extended coverage to employees in large retail and service enterprises as well as to local transit, construction, and gasoline service station employees. The level of the minimum for these workers is shown in this series. In 1990, a grandfather clause was established to protect employees who did not meet the tests for individual coverage (whose employers were covered as of March 31, 1990) but would have become exempt from coverage when a new law raised the annual dollar volume (ADV) test for enterprise coverage.

Series Ba4424–4425. The 1966 amendments to the FSLA extended coverage to state and local government employees of hospitals, nursing homes, and schools, and to laundries, dry cleaners, and large hotels, motels, restaurants, and farms. Subsequent amendments extended coverage to the remaining federal, state, and local government employees who were not protected in 1966, to certain workers in retail and service trades previously exempted, and to certain domestic workers in private household employment.

TABLE Ba4426–4430 Summary measures of wage inequality: 1939–1989

Contributed by Robert A. Margo

	Difference between 90th and 10th percentiles, log of weekly wage		Standard deviation, log of the hourly wage, males, age 18–65	Variance, log of annual wage and salary income	
	Males, age 18–64	Males, age 18–65		Males, age 16 and older	Females, age 16 and older
	Ba4426	Ba4427	Ba4428	Ba4429	Ba4430
Year	Number	Number	Number	Number	Number
1939	1.447	—	—	—	—
1949	1.181	—	—	—	—
1959	1.250	1.050	0.450	—	—
1963	—	1.068	0.453	1.471	2.125
1964	—	1.101	0.456	1.494	2.143
1965	—	1.089	0.459	1.408	2.021
1966	—	1.097	0.453	1.342	1.921
1967	—	1.066	0.446	1.354	1.867
1968	—	1.059	0.446	1.343	1.847
1969	—	1.097	0.448	1.357	1.858
1970	—	1.120	0.455	1.428	1.890
1971	—	1.148	0.467	1.408	1.838
1972	—	1.174	0.483	1.397	1.821
1973	—	1.187	0.477	1.402	1.770
1974	—	1.171	0.481	1.401	1.754
1975	—	1.173	0.479	1.380	1.729
1976	—	1.227	0.490	1.411	1.717
1977	—	1.225	0.495	1.426	1.700
1978	—	1.232	0.499	1.395	1.685
1979	—	1.243	0.504	1.430	1.852
1980	—	1.277	0.509	1.471	1.814
1981	—	1.297	0.520	1.536	1.755
1982	—	1.371	0.530	1.471	1.814
1983	—	1.362	0.540	1.724	1.917
1984	—	1.429	0.550	1.624	1.910
1985	—	1.447	0.560	1.579	1.867
1986	—	1.456	0.563	1.606	1.872
1987	—	1.430	0.562	1.641	1.902
1988	—	1.454	0.567	—	—
1989	—	1.491	0.578	—	—

(continued)

TABLE Ba4426–4430 Summary measures of wage inequality: 1939–1989 *Continued*

Sources

Series Ba4426. Claudia Goldin and Robert A. Margo, "The Great Compression: The Wage Structure in the United States at Mid-Century," *Quarterly Journal of Economics* 107 (February 1992): 2.

Series Ba4427–4428. Chinhui Juhn, Kevin M. Murphy, and Brooks Pierce, "Wage Inequality and the Rise in Returns to Skill," *Journal of Political Economy* 101 (June 1993): 420; and personal communication, Chinhui Juhn.

Series Ba4429–4430. Barry Bluestone, "The Changing Nature of Employment and Earnings in the U.S. Economy, 1963–1987," conference paper, as published in Frank Levy and Richard J. Murnane, "U.S. Earnings Levels and Earnings Inequality: A Review of Recent Trends and Proposed Explanations," *Journal of Economic Literature* 30 (September 1992): 1344–5.

Documentation

Series Ba4426. The data sources are the public use microdata samples of the 1940, 1950, and 1960 Censuses. The sample used includes males, ages 18 to 64, who were wage and salary workers working more than thirty-nine weeks in 1939 and earning more than 50 percent of the minimum wage on a full-time basis. Wage and salary earnings refer to the calendar year prior to the date of the survey.

Series Ba4427. The data sources are the annual microdata files of the Current Population Survey (March). The sample used includes males, ages 18 to 65, who worked thirty-five or more hours per week, were not self-employed or working without pay, did not live in group quarters, worked at least fourteen weeks, had a positive number of years of potential work experience (i.e., age minus years of schooling minus 6 greater than 0), did not work part of the year because of retirement or schooling, and earned at least $67.00 per week in 1982 dollars, that is, 50 percent of the 1982 real full-time (forty hours per week) weekly minimum wage. Wage and salary income refers to the calendar year prior to the survey.

Series Ba4428. Has the same source and sample definition as series Ba4427. Hourly wage is weekly wage divided by usual weekly hours.

Series Ba4429–4430. These data are also drawn from the annual microdata files of the Current Population Survey. The sample for series Ba4429 includes males, age 16 and older, with positive wage and salary income. The sample for series Ba4430 includes females, age 16 and older, with positive wage and salary income.

TABLE Ba4431–4439 Black-to-white wage ratios for males, by years of labor market experience: 1940–1980

Contributed by Robert A. Margo

	All	1–5 years	6–10 years	11–15 years	16–20 years	21–25 years	26–30 years	31–35 years	36–40 years
	Ba4431	Ba4432	Ba4433	Ba4434	Ba4435	Ba4436	Ba4437	Ba4438	Ba4439
Year	Ratio	Ratio	Ratio	Ratio	Ratio	Ratio	Ratio	Ratio	Ratio
1940	0.433	0.467	0.475	0.444	0.444	0.423	0.417	0.402	0.398
1950	0.552	0.618	0.610	0.583	0.566	0.541	0.532	0.503	0.469
1960	0.575	0.602	0.591	0.594	0.584	0.576	0.562	0.538	0.559
1970	0.644	0.751	0.701	0.662	0.628	0.627	0.606	0.600	0.603
1980	0.726	0.842	0.766	0.735	0.712	0.678	0.669	0.665	0.685

Source

James P. Smith and Finis R. Welch, "Black Progress after Myrdal," *Journal of Economic Literature* 27 (June 1989): 522.

Documentation

Except in 1940, figures are ratios of arithmetic means of the sum of weekly wage and salary income and self-employment income. The 1940 values are ratios of arithmetic means of weekly wage and salary income only.

Figures are based on samples from the public use microdata files of the 1940 to 1980 Censuses. The samples consist of men, ages 16 to 64, who were U.S. citizens and did not live in group quarters. Individuals were excluded from the computation if any of the following conditions were true: (1) worked fewer than fifty weeks in the previous year and attended school; (2) worked fewer than twenty-seven weeks in the previous year; (3) in military service; (4) reported labor force status as self-employed or working without pay if not in agriculture; (5) weekly wages below $1.50 in 1940, $3.25 in 1950, $6.25 in 1960, $10.00 in 1970, or $19.80 in 1980; (6) weekly wages exceeded $125 in 1940, $250 in 1950, $625 in 1960, $1,250 in 1970, or $1,875 in 1980; or (7) income exceeded the maximum reported in the census and did not work at least forty weeks in the previous year.

Years of labor market experience is current age minus age at end of schooling. This age is 17 for persons with zero to eleven years of schooling, 18 for persons with exactly twelve years of schooling, 20 for persons with thirteen to fifteen years of schooling, and 23 for persons with sixteen or more years of schooling.

TABLE Ba4440–4483 Hourly and weekly earnings of production workers in manufacturing, by industry: 1947–1999

Contributed by Susan B. Carter

	Hourly earnings										
		Durable goods									
	Total	Total	Lumber and wood products	Furniture and fixtures	Paper and allied products	Printing and publishing	Chemicals and allied products	Petroleum and coal products	Rubber and miscellaneous plastics products	Leather and leather products	Stone, clay, and glass products
	Ba4440	Ba4441	Ba4442	Ba4443	Ba4444	Ba4445	Ba4446	Ba4447	Ba4448	Ba4449	Ba4450
Year	Dollars	Dollars	Dollars	Dollars	Dollars	Dollars	Dollars	Dollars	Dollars	Dollars	Dollars
1947	1.22	1.28	1.09	1.10	1.15	1.48	1.22	1.50	1.29	1.04	1.19
1948	1.33	1.39	1.19	1.19	1.28	1.65	1.34	1.71	1.36	1.11	1.31
1949	1.38	1.45	1.23	1.23	1.33	1.77	1.42	1.80	1.41	1.12	1.37
1950	1.44	1.45	1.30	1.28	1.40	1.83	1.50	1.84	1.47	1.17	1.44
1951	1.56	1.65	1.41	1.39	1.51	1.91	1.62	1.99	1.58	1.25	1.54
1952	1.65	1.74	1.49	1.47	1.59	2.02	1.69	2.10	1.70	1.30	1.61
1953	1.74	1.85	1.56	1.54	1.67	2.11	1.81	2.22	1.79	1.35	1.72
1954	1.78	1.89	1.57	1.57	1.73	2.18	1.89	2.29	1.83	1.36	1.77
1955	1.86	1.98	1.62	1.62	1.81	2.26	1.97	2.37	1.95	1.39	1.86
1956	1.95	2.08	1.69	1.69	1.92	2.33	2.09	2.54	2.02	1.48	1.96
1957	2.05	2.18	1.74	1.75	2.02	2.40	2.20	2.66	2.11	1.52	2.05
1958	2.11	2.25	1.80	1.78	2.10	2.49	2.29	2.73	2.18	1.56	2.12
1959	2.19	2.35	1.87	1.83	2.18	2.59	2.40	2.85	2.27	1.59	2.22
1960	2.26	2.42	1.90	1.88	2.26	2.68	2.50	2.89	2.32	1.64	2.28
1961	2.32	2.48	1.95	1.91	2.34	2.75	2.58	3.01	2.38	1.68	2.34
1962	2.39	2.55	1.99	1.95	2.40	2.82	2.65	3.05	2.44	1.72	2.41
1963	2.46	2.63	2.05	2.00	2.48	2.89	2.72	3.16	2.47	1.76	2.48
1964	2.53	2.70	2.12	2.05	2.56	2.97	2.80	3.20	2.54	1.83	2.53
1965	2.61	2.78	2.18	2.12	2.65	3.06	2.89	3.28	2.61	1.88	2.62
1966	2.72	2.89	2.26	2.21	2.75	3.16	2.98	3.41	2.68	1.94	2.72
1967	2.83	2.99	2.38	2.33	2.87	3.28	3.10	3.58	2.75	2.07	2.82
1968	3.01	3.18	2.58	2.47	3.05	3.48	3.26	3.75	2.93	2.23	2.99
1969	3.19	3.38	2.75	2.62	3.24	3.69	3.47	4.00	3.08	2.36	3.19
1970	3.35	3.55	2.97	2.77	3.44	3.92	3.69	4.28	3.21	2.49	3.40
1971	3.57	3.79	3.18	2.90	3.67	4.20	3.97	4.57	3.41	2.59	3.67
1972	3.82	4.07	3.34	3.08	3.95	4.51	4.26	4.96	3.63	2.68	3.94
1973	4.09	4.35	3.62	3.29	4.20	4.75	4.51	5.28	3.84	2.79	4.22
1974	4.42	4.70	3.90	3.53	4.53	5.03	4.88	5.68	4.09	2.99	4.54
1975	4.83	5.15	4.28	3.78	5.01	5.38	5.39	6.48	4.42	3.21	4.92
1976	5.22	5.57	4.74	3.99	5.47	5.71	5.91	7.21	4.71	3.40	5.33
1977	5.68	6.06	5.11	4.34	5.96	6.12	6.43	7.83	5.21	3.61	5.81
1978	6.17	6.58	5.62	4.68	6.52	6.51	7.02	8.63	5.57	3.89	6.32
1979	6.70	7.12	6.08	5.06	7.13	6.94	7.60	9.36	6.02	4.22	6.85
1980	7.27	7.75	6.57	5.49	7.84	7.53	8.30	10.10	6.58	4.58	7.50
1981	7.99	8.53	7.02	5.91	8.60	8.19	9.12	11.38	7.22	4.99	8.27
1982	8.49	9.03	7.46	6.31	9.32	8.74	9.96	12.46	7.70	5.33	8.87
1983	8.83	9.38	7.82	6.62	9.93	9.11	10.58	13.28	8.06	5.54	9.27
1984	9.19	9.73	8.05	6.84	10.41	9.41	11.07	13.44	8.35	5.71	9.57
1985	9.54	10.09	8.25	7.17	10.83	9.71	11.56	14.06	8.60	5.83	9.84
1986	9.73	10.28	8.37	7.46	11.18	9.99	11.98	14.19	8.79	5.92	10.04
1987	9.91	10.43	8.43	7.67	11.43	10.28	12.37	14.58	8.98	6.08	10.25
1988	10.19	10.71	8.59	7.95	11.69	10.53	12.71	14.97	9.19	6.28	10.56
1989	10.48	11.01	8.84	8.25	11.96	10.88	13.09	15.41	9.46	6.59	10.82
1990	10.83	11.35	9.08	8.52	12.31	11.24	13.54	16.24	9.76	6.91	11.12
1991	11.18	11.75	9.24	8.76	12.72	11.48	14.04	17.04	10.07	7.18	11.36
1992	11.46	12.02	9.44	9.01	13.07	11.74	14.51	17.90	10.36	7.42	11.60
1993	11.74	12.33	9.61	9.27	13.42	11.93	14.82	18.53	10.57	7.63	11.85
1994	12.07	12.68	9.84	9.55	13.77	12.14	15.13	19.07	10.70	7.97	12.13
1995	12.37	12.94	10.12	9.82	14.23	12.33	15.62	19.36	10.91	8.17	12.41
1996	12.77	13.33	10.44	10.15	14.67	12.65	16.17	19.32	11.24	8.57	12.82
1997	13.17	13.73	10.76	10.55	15.05	13.06	16.57	20.20	11.57	8.97	13.18
1998	13.49	13.98	11.10	10.90	15.50	13.46	17.09	20.91	11.89	9.35	13.59
1999	13.91	14.40	11.47	11.23	15.94	13.84	17.38	21.39	12.36	9.77	13.87

(continued)

TABLE Ba4440–4483 Hourly and weekly earnings of production workers in manufacturing, by industry: 1947–1999 *Continued*

	Hourly earnings										
	Durable goods						Nondurable goods				
	Primary metal industries	Fabricated metal products	Industrial machinery and equipment	Electronic and other electrical equipment	Transportation equipment	Instruments and related products	Total	Food and kindred products	Tobacco products	Textile mill products	Apparel and other textile products
	Ba4451	Ba4452	Ba4453	Ba4454	Ba4455	Ba4456	Ba4457	Ba4458	Ba4459	Ba4460	Ba4461
Year	Dollars	Dollars	Dollars	Dollars	Dollars	Dollars	Dollars	Dollars	Dollars	Dollars	Dollars
1947	1.39	1.27	1.34	—	1.44	—	1.15	1.06	0.90	1.04	1.16
1948	1.52	1.39	1.46	—	1.57	—	1.25	1.15	0.96	1.16	1.22
1949	1.59	1.45	1.52	—	1.64	—	1.30	1.21	1.00	1.18	1.21
1950	1.65	1.52	1.60	—	1.72	—	1.30	1.26	1.08	1.23	1.24
1951	1.81	1.64	1.75	—	1.84	—	1.45	1.35	1.14	1.32	1.31
1952	1.90	1.72	1.85	—	1.95	—	1.51	1.44	1.18	1.34	1.32
1953	2.06	1.83	1.95	—	2.05	—	1.58	1.53	1.25	1.36	1.35
1954	2.10	1.88	2.00	—	2.11	—	1.62	1.59	1.30	1.36	1.37
1955	2.24	1.96	2.08	—	2.21	—	1.68	1.66	1.34	1.38	1.37
1956	2.37	2.05	2.20	—	2.29	—	1.77	1.76	1.45	1.44	1.47
1957	2.50	2.16	2.29	—	2.39	—	1.85	1.85	1.53	1.49	1.51
1958	2.64	2.26	2.37	—	2.51	—	1.92	1.94	1.59	1.49	1.54
1959	2.77	2.35	2.48	—	2.64	—	1.98	2.02	1.65	1.56	1.56
1960	2.81	2.43	2.55	—	2.74	—	2.05	2.11	1.70	1.61	1.59
1961	2.90	2.49	2.62	—	2.80	—	2.11	2.17	1.78	1.63	1.64
1962	2.98	2.55	2.71	—	2.91	—	2.17	2.24	1.85	1.68	1.69
1963	3.04	2.61	2.78	—	3.01	—	2.22	2.30	1.91	1.71	1.73
1964	3.11	2.68	2.87	—	3.09	—	2.29	2.37	1.95	1.79	1.79
1965	3.18	2.76	2.95	—	3.21	—	2.36	2.44	2.09	1.87	1.83
1966	3.28	2.88	3.08	—	3.33	—	2.45	2.52	2.19	1.96	1.89
1967	3.34	2.98	3.19	—	3.44	—	2.57	2.64	2.27	2.06	2.03
1968	3.55	3.16	3.36	—	3.69	—	2.74	2.80	2.48	2.21	2.21
1969	3.79	3.34	3.58	—	3.89	—	2.91	2.96	2.62	2.35	2.31
1970	3.93	3.53	3.77	—	4.06	—	3.08	3.16	2.91	2.45	2.39
1971	4.23	3.77	4.02	—	4.45	—	3.27	3.38	3.16	2.57	2.49
1972	4.66	4.05	4.32	—	4.81	—	3.48	3.60	3.47	2.75	2.60
1973	5.04	4.29	4.60	—	5.15	—	3.70	3.85	3.76	2.95	2.76
1974	5.60	4.61	4.94	—	5.54	—	4.01	4.19	4.12	3.20	2.97
1975	6.18	5.05	5.37	—	6.07	—	4.37	4.61	4.55	3.42	3.17
1976	6.77	5.50	5.79	—	6.62	—	4.71	4.98	4.98	3.69	3.40
1977	7.40	5.91	6.26	—	7.29	—	5.11	5.37	5.54	3.99	3.62
1978	8.20	6.35	6.78	—	7.91	—	5.54	5.80	6.13	4.30	3.94
1979	8.98	6.85	7.32	—	8.53	—	6.01	6.27	6.67	4.66	4.23
1980	9.77	7.45	8.00	—	9.35	—	6.56	6.85	7.74	5.07	4.56
1981	10.81	8.20	8.81	—	10.39	—	7.19	7.44	8.88	5.52	4.97
1982	11.33	8.77	9.26	—	11.11	—	7.75	7.92	9.79	5.83	5.20
1983	11.35	9.12	9.56	—	11.67	—	8.09	8.19	10.38	6.18	5.38
1984	11.47	9.40	9.97	—	12.20	—	8.39	8.39	11.22	6.46	5.55
1985	11.67	9.71	10.30	—	12.71	—	8.72	8.57	11.96	6.70	5.73
1986	11.86	9.89	10.58	—	12.81	—	8.95	8.75	12.88	6.93	5.84
1987	11.94	10.01	10.73	—	12.94	—	9.19	8.93	14.07	7.17	5.94
1988	12.16	10.29	11.08	9.79	13.29	10.60	9.45	9.12	14.67	7.38	6.12
1989	12.43	10.57	11.40	10.05	13.67	10.83	9.75	9.38	15.31	7.67	6.35
1990	12.92	10.83	11.77	10.30	14.08	11.29	10.12	9.62	16.23	8.02	6.57
1991	13.33	11.19	12.15	10.70	14.75	11.64	10.44	9.90	16.77	8.30	6.77
1992	13.66	11.42	12.41	11.00	15.20	11.89	10.73	10.20	16.92	8.60	6.95
1993	13.99	11.69	12.73	11.24	15.80	12.23	10.98	10.45	16.89	8.88	7.09
1994	14.34	11.93	13.00	11.50	16.51	12.47	11.24	10.66	19.07	9.13	7.34
1995	14.62	12.13	13.24	11.69	16.74	12.71	11.58	10.93	19.41	9.41	7.64
1996	14.97	12.50	13.59	12.18	17.19	13.13	11.97	11.20	19.35	9.69	7.96
1997	15.22	12.78	14.07	12.70	17.55	13.52	12.34	11.48	19.24	10.03	8.25
1998	15.48	13.07	14.47	13.10	17.51	13.81	12.76	11.80	18.56	10.39	8.52
1999	15.83	13.48	15.02	13.46	18.04	14.17	13.16	12.09	19.07	10.71	8.86

TABLE Ba4440–4483 Hourly and weekly earnings of production workers in manufacturing, by industry: 1947–1999 *Continued*

	Weekly earnings										
		Durable goods									
	Total	Total	Lumber and wood products	Furniture and fixtures	Paper and allied products	Printing and publishing	Chemicals and allied products	Petroleum and coal products	Rubber and miscellaneous plastics products	Leather and leather products	Stone, clay, and glass products
	Ba4462	Ba4463	Ba4464	Ba4465	Ba4466	Ba4467	Ba4468	Ba4469	Ba4470	Ba4471	Ba4472
Year	Dollars	Dollars	Dollars	Dollars	Dollars	Dollars	Dollars	Dollars	Dollars	Dollars	Dollars
1947	49.13	51.64	43.93	45.53	49.69	59.30	50.26	60.94	51.60	40.07	48.95
1948	53.08	56.24	47.64	48.83	54.70	65.13	55.29	69.30	53.29	41.11	53.20
1949	53.80	57.13	48.10	49.36	55.42	68.60	57.67	72.42	54.13	41.03	54.27
1950	58.28	59.60	51.31	53.55	60.53	71.23	61.64	75.11	60.27	43.95	59.06
1951	63.34	68.48	55.41	57.13	65.08	74.30	66.91	81.19	64.46	46.13	63.76
1952	66.75	72.04	59.15	60.86	68.05	78.58	69.12	85.05	69.53	49.92	66.17
1953	70.47	76.22	61.31	62.99	71.81	82.29	74.21	90.35	72.32	50.90	70.18
1954	70.49	75.79	61.39	62.80	73.18	83.93	77.11	93.20	72.83	50.18	71.69
1955	75.30	81.77	63.99	67.07	78.01	87.91	80.97	96.93	81.32	52.68	77.00
1956	78.78	85.28	65.74	68.78	82.18	90.64	85.90	104.14	81.61	55.65	80.56
1957	81.19	87.85	66.82	69.83	85.45	92.64	89.98	108.53	85.67	56.85	82.82
1958	82.32	88.88	69.48	69.95	87.99	94.62	93.20	111.66	85.67	57.25	84.80
1959	88.26	95.65	74.24	74.48	93.30	99.72	99.36	117.42	93.75	60.26	91.46
1960	89.72	97.04	74.29	75.20	95.15	102.91	103.25	118.78	92.80	60.52	92.57
1961	92.34	99.70	77.03	76.40	99.45	105.05	106.81	124.01	96.15	62.83	95.24
1962	96.56	104.30	79.20	79.37	102.24	108.01	110.24	126.88	100.04	64.67	98.81
1963	99.23	108.09	82.41	81.80	105.90	110.69	113.15	131.77	101.02	66.00	102.67
1964	102.97	112.05	85.65	84.46	109.57	114.35	116.48	133.76	104.90	69.36	105.50
1965	107.53	116.76	89.16	87.98	114.22	118.12	121.09	138.42	109.62	71.82	110.04
1966	112.19	121.67	92.21	91.72	119.35	122.61	125.16	144.58	112.56	74.88	114.24
1967	114.49	123.19	95.91	94.13	122.84	125.95	128.96	152.87	113.85	79.07	117.31
1968	122.51	131.65	104.75	100.28	130.85	133.28	136.27	159.38	121.60	85.41	124.98
1969	129.51	139.59	110.55	105.85	139.32	141.33	145.05	170.40	126.90	87.79	133.66
1970	133.33	143.07	117.61	108.58	144.14	147.78	153.50	183.18	129.36	92.63	140.08
1971	142.44	152.74	126.56	115.42	154.51	157.50	165.15	195.60	137.76	97.64	152.67
1972	154.71	167.68	134.94	123.82	169.06	170.03	177.64	211.79	149.56	102.64	165.48
1973	166.46	180.09	144.80	131.60	180.18	179.08	188.52	223.87	158.21	105.46	176.82
1974	176.80	190.82	152.88	138.02	191.17	188.63	202.52	239.13	166.05	110.33	187.50
1975	190.79	205.49	166.06	143.64	208.42	198.52	220.99	266.98	176.36	119.09	198.77
1976	209.32	226.14	189.13	154.81	232.48	214.13	245.86	303.54	191.70	127.16	219.06
1977	228.90	248.46	203.89	169.26	255.68	230.72	268.13	334.34	214.13	133.21	239.95
1978	249.27	270.44	223.68	183.92	279.71	244.78	294.14	376.27	227.81	144.32	262.91
1979	269.34	290.50	240.16	195.82	303.74	260.25	318.44	409.97	244.41	154.03	284.28
1980	288.62	310.78	253.60	209.17	330.85	279.36	344.45	422.18	263.20	168.09	306.00
1981	318.00	342.91	271.67	226.94	365.50	305.49	379.39	491.62	290.97	183.13	335.76
1982	330.26	354.88	284.23	234.73	389.58	324.25	407.36	546.99	304.92	189.75	355.69
1983	354.08	381.77	313.58	260.83	423.02	342.54	440.13	582.99	332.07	203.87	384.71
1984	374.03	402.82	321.20	271.55	448.67	356.64	463.83	587.33	348.20	210.13	401.94
1985	386.37	415.71	329.18	282.50	466.77	367.04	484.36	604.58	353.46	216.88	412.30
1986	396.01	424.56	338.15	296.91	482.98	379.62	501.96	621.52	363.91	218.45	423.69
1987	406.31	432.85	342.26	306.80	496.06	390.64	523.25	641.52	373.57	232.26	433.58
1988	418.81	447.68	344.46	313.23	506.18	400.14	536.36	664.67	383.22	235.50	446.69
1989	429.68	458.02	354.48	325.88	517.87	412.35	555.02	682.66	391.64	249.76	457.69
1990	441.86	468.76	365.02	333.13	533.02	426.00	576.80	724.30	401.14	258.43	467.04
1991	455.03	482.93	369.60	340.76	550.78	432.80	602.32	751.46	413.88	269.25	473.71
1992	469.86	498.83	383.26	357.70	569.85	447.29	625.38	784.02	432.01	281.96	489.52
1993	486.04	519.09	392.09	371.73	585.11	456.92	638.74	819.03	441.83	294.52	506.00
1994	506.94	543.97	405.41	385.82	604.50	468.60	653.62	846.71	451.54	306.85	526.44
1995	514.59	548.66	410.87	388.87	613.31	471.01	674.78	846.03	452.77	310.46	533.63
1996	531.23	565.19	425.95	399.91	635.21	483.23	698.54	842.35	466.46	326.52	555.11
1997	553.14	587.64	441.16	424.11	657.69	502.81	715.82	870.62	483.63	344.45	569.38
1998	562.53	591.35	456.21	441.45	672.70	515.52	738.29	911.68	495.81	351.56	591.17
1999	580.05	607.68	472.56	452.57	693.39	528.69	747.34	921.91	515.41	369.31	603.35

(continued)

TABLE Ba4440–4483 Hourly and weekly earnings of production workers in manufacturing, by industry: 1947–1999 *Continued*

	Weekly earnings										
	Durable goods						Nondurable goods				
	Primary metal industries	Fabricated metal products	Industrial machinery and equipment	Electronic and other electrical equipment	Transportation equipment	Instruments and related products	Total	Food and kindred products	Tobacco products	Textile mill products	Apparel and other textile products
	Ba4473	Ba4474	Ba4475	Ba4476	Ba4477	Ba4478	Ba4479	Ba4480	Ba4481	Ba4482	Ba4483
Year	Dollars	Dollars	Dollars	Dollars	Dollars	Dollars	Dollars	Dollars	Dollars	Dollars	Dollars
1947	55.38	51.74	55.78	—	56.97	—	46.03	45.92	35.17	40.99	41.80
1948	61.14	56.37	60.38	—	61.70	—	49.54	48.84	36.58	45.28	43.68
1949	60.90	57.45	60.27	—	65.10	—	50.41	50.49	37.26	44.52	42.76
1950	67.36	63.04	67.04	—	71.29	—	51.45	52.88	41.00	48.59	44.60
1951	75.30	68.55	76.13	—	75.81	—	57.42	56.84	43.89	51.22	46.64
1952	77.52	71.72	79.55	—	81.51	—	59.95	60.34	45.31	52.39	47.92
1953	84.46	76.49	82.68	—	85.28	—	62.57	63.50	47.63	53.18	48.74
1954	81.48	76.70	81.40	—	86.30	—	63.18	65.67	48.88	52.09	48.36
1955	92.51	81.73	87.15	—	93.48	—	67.03	68.89	51.86	55.34	49.73
1956	97.17	84.67	93.06	—	94.81	—	70.09	72.69	56.26	57.17	52.92
1957	99.00	88.34	94.12	—	97.51	—	72.52	75.48	58.75	57.96	53.91
1958	101.11	90.17	94.33	—	100.40	—	74.50	79.15	62.17	57.51	54.05
1959	112.19	96.12	102.92	—	107.45	—	78.61	82.82	64.52	63.02	56.63
1960	109.59	98.42	104.55	—	111.52	—	80.36	86.09	64.94	63.60	56.45
1961	114.55	100.85	107.16	—	113.40	—	82.92	88.75	69.42	65.04	58.06
1962	119.80	104.81	113.01	—	122.22	—	86.15	91.84	71.41	68.21	61.18
1963	124.64	107.79	116.20	—	126.42	—	87.91	94.30	73.92	69.43	62.45
1964	129.69	111.76	121.69	—	130.09	—	90.91	97.17	75.66	73.39	64.26
1965	133.88	116.20	127.15	—	137.71	—	94.64	100.28	79.21	77.98	66.61
1966	138.09	122.11	134.90	—	141.86	—	98.49	103.82	85.19	82.12	68.80
1967	137.27	123.67	135.58	—	142.42	—	102.03	107.98	87.62	84.25	73.08
1968	147.68	131.77	141.12	—	155.72	—	109.05	114.24	93.99	91.05	79.78
1969	158.42	138.94	152.15	—	161.44	—	115.53	120.77	97.99	95.88	82.93
1970	158.77	143.67	154.95	—	163.62	—	120.43	127.98	110.00	97.76	84.37
1971	169.62	152.31	163.21	—	181.12	—	128.51	136.21	119.45	104.34	88.64
1972	192.92	166.86	181.87	—	200.58	—	138.16	145.80	130.47	113.58	93.60
1973	213.19	178.46	196.88	—	216.82	—	146.52	155.54	145.14	120.66	99.08
1974	232.96	188.09	207.97	—	224.37	—	156.79	169.28	157.80	126.40	104.54
1975	247.20	202.51	219.10	—	245.23	—	169.56	185.78	173.81	134.41	111.58
1976	276.22	224.40	238.55	—	276.05	—	185.57	201.69	186.75	147.97	121.72
1977	305.62	242.31	259.79	—	309.83	—	201.33	214.80	209.41	161.20	128.87
1978	342.76	260.35	284.76	—	333.80	—	218.28	230.26	233.55	173.72	140.26
1979	371.77	278.80	305.24	—	350.58	—	236.19	250.17	253.46	188.26	149.32
1980	391.78	300.98	328.00	—	379.61	—	255.84	271.95	294.89	203.31	161.42
1981	437.81	330.46	360.33	—	424.95	—	281.85	295.37	344.54	218.59	177.43
1982	437.34	343.78	367.62	—	449.96	—	297.60	312.05	370.06	218.63	180.44
1983	459.68	370.27	387.18	—	491.31	—	318.75	323.51	388.21	249.67	194.76
1984	478.30	389.16	417.74	—	520.94	—	333.08	333.92	436.46	257.75	202.02
1985	484.31	401.02	427.45	—	541.45	—	345.31	342.80	444.91	265.99	208.57
1986	496.93	408.46	440.13	—	541.86	—	357.11	350.00	481.71	284.82	214.33
1987	514.61	416.42	452.81	—	543.48	—	369.44	358.99	548.73	299.71	219.78
1988	528.96	431.15	473.12	401.39	567.48	438.84	379.89	367.54	583.87	302.58	226.44
1989	534.49	439.71	483.36	410.04	579.61	445.11	391.95	381.77	590.97	313.70	234.32
1990	551.68	447.28	493.16	420.24	591.36	464.02	404.80	392.50	636.22	320.00	239.15
1991	562.53	461.03	506.66	435.49	618.03	477.24	419.69	401.94	655.71	336.98	250.49
1992	587.38	475.07	523.70	453.20	635.36	488.68	433.49	414.12	653.11	353.46	258.54
1993	611.36	492.15	547.39	469.83	679.40	502.65	445.79	425.32	631.69	367.63	263.75
1994	641.00	511.80	568.10	485.30	731.39	520.00	459.72	440.26	749.45	379.81	275.25
1995	643.28	514.31	574.62	486.30	733.21	526.19	468.99	449.22	768.64	383.93	282.68
1996	661.67	530.00	585.73	505.47	756.36	547.52	484.79	459.20	774.00	393.41	294.52
1997	683.38	544.43	613.45	533.40	780.98	567.84	504.71	474.12	748.44	415.24	307.73
1998	684.22	552.86	619.32	542.34	759.93	570.35	521.88	492.06	710.85	425.99	317.80
1999	699.69	568.86	633.84	557.24	790.15	588.06	538.24	505.36	762.80	438.04	332.25

Source

U.S. Bureau of Labor Statistics (BLS), *Nonfarm Payroll Statistics from the Current Employment Statistics: National Employment, Hours, and Earnings*, retrieved at BLS Internet site, August 18, 2000.

Documentation

See the text for Table Ba831–839.

This table excludes miscellaneous manufacturing industries not elsewhere classified.

The following pairs of series are the same: series Ba4361 and Ba4440; series Ba4363 and Ba4441; series Ba4365 and Ba4457; series Ba4362 and Ba4462; series Ba4364 and Ba4463; series Ba4366 and Ba4479.

TABLE Ba4484–4489 Supplements per full-time equivalent employee in all industries, by type: 1948–1994

Contributed by Robert A. Margo

	Total	Social insurance	Private pensions and profit sharing	Group health insurance	Workers' compensation	Other
	Ba4484	Ba4485	Ba4486	Ba4487	Ba4488	Ba4489
Year	Dollars	Dollars	Dollars	Dollars	Dollars	Dollars
1948	136	80	25	9	17	6
1949	156	93	27	12	17	7
1950	169	94	35	15	16	8
1951	190	102	43	19	17	9
1952	200	103	47	21	19	9
1953	210	100	53	25	21	11
1954	230	114	55	28	21	12
1955	255	125	63	32	21	14
1956	285	139	68	37	23	18
1957	320	158	75	44	24	20
1958	342	168	77	50	24	23
1959	386	196	86	55	26	24
1960	421	229	86	60	27	26
1961	441	233	87	66	28	27
1962	484	259	94	72	30	29
1963	521	284	98	77	32	30
1964	552	291	109	86	34	32
1965	577	292	122	94	35	34
1966	646	345	131	97	37	36
1967	685	367	139	101	40	38
1968	756	395	153	120	45	43
1969	837	440	165	139	48	45
1970	936	479	183	170	53	50
1971	1,067	549	213	193	56	56
1972	1,213	621	246	222	61	63
1973	1,374	727	275	241	68	63
1974	1,559	826	317	274	77	66
1975	1,812	937	372	338	89	76
1976	2,084	1,058	430	412	106	78
1977	2,349	1,171	486	482	127	83
1978	2,572	1,269	529	544	143	87
1979	2,835	1,411	571	602	162	88
1980	3,167	1,564	634	699	177	92
1981	3,525	1,786	650	815	183	91
1982	3,870	1,952	683	958	184	93
1983	4,142	2,100	707	1,054	186	95
1984	4,405	2,334	688	1,100	193	91
1985	4,589	2,422	690	1,174	211	93
1986	4,778	2,515	694	1,230	244	96
1987	4,940	2,543	689	1,334	277	97
1988	5,149	2,658	629	1,456	302	104
1989	5,334	2,702	584	1,622	323	103
1990	5,702	2,822	606	1,807	359	109
1991	6,099	2,977	638	1,987	384	113
1992	6,512	3,119	698	2,204	380	111
1993	6,856	3,193	797	2,355	396	116
1994	7,019	3,269	851	2,406	378	116

Source

Computed from U.S. Department of Commerce, *National Income and Product Accounts of the United States, 1929–1994,* volume 2 (April 1998), pp. 47–50.

Documentation

These data give annual employer contributions per full-time equivalent employee.

Series Ba4484. May not equal the sum of series Ba4485–4489 because of rounding error.

Series Ba4485. Includes Old-age, Survivors, and Disability Insurance; Railroad Retirement insurance; federal Civilian Employee Retirement Systems; state and local employee retirement systems; state unemployment insurance; federal unemployment tax; railroad unemployment insurance; cash sickness compensation funds; and government life insurance.

Series Ba4489. Includes group life insurance, supplemental unemployment insurance, pay of military reservists, directors' fees, jury and witness fees, compensation of prison inmates, and marriage fees to justices of the peace.

TABLE Ba4490–4511 Wage and salary accruals per full-time equivalent employee, by industry: 1949–1994

Contributed by Robert A. Margo

	Agriculture, forestry, and fisheries	Mining	Construction	Manufacturing			Transportation	Communications	Electric, gas, and sanitary services	Wholesale trade
				Total	Durable goods	Nondurable goods				
	Ba4490	Ba4491	Ba4492	Ba4493	Ba4494	Ba4495	Ba4496	Ba4497	Ba4498	Ba4499
Year	Dollars	Dollars	Dollars	Dollars	Dollars	Dollars	Dollars	Dollars	Dollars	Dollars
1949	1,564	3,215	3,229	3,107	3,240	2,961	3,512	3,019	3,353	3,621
1950	1,531	3,465	3,377	3,330	3,483	3,154	3,639	3,180	3,556	3,806
1951	1,656	3,889	3,774	3,652	3,862	3,386	3,947	3,390	3,827	4,028
1952	1,697	4,067	4,086	3,894	4,126	3,587	4,153	3,642	4,130	4,134
1953	1,688	4,374	4,354	4,133	4,383	3,784	4,334	3,881	4,408	4,320
1954	1,607	4,402	4,484	4,224	4,452	3,923	4,436	4,093	4,610	4,442
1955	1,640	4,721	4,607	4,481	4,737	4,134	4,623	4,339	4,783	4,616
1956	1,734	5,033	4,914	4,739	4,993	4,387	4,886	4,501	5,072	4,883
1957	1,811	5,235	5,120	4,928	5,207	4,540	5,163	4,675	5,307	5,119
1958	1,854	5,252	5,305	5,148	5,478	4,725	5,405	4,931	5,552	5,294
1959	1,905	5,573	5,498	5,413	5,763	4,950	5,680	5,305	5,916	5,558
1960	2,010	5,725	5,750	5,545	5,894	5,081	5,835	5,532	6,150	5,756
1961	2,106	5,900	5,938	5,701	6,048	5,250	5,994	5,793	6,390	5,932
1962	2,239	6,095	6,174	5,916	6,291	5,416	6,228	6,078	6,655	6,172
1963	2,374	6,324	6,364	6,111	6,512	5,570	6,428	6,335	6,941	6,419
1964	2,641	6,624	6,709	6,417	6,842	5,836	6,740	6,687	7,303	6,703
1965	2,907	6,904	6,921	6,564	7,001	5,950	6,989	6,823	7,480	6,981
1966	3,186	7,253	7,363	6,801	7,228	6,172	7,269	7,084	7,801	7,345
1967	3,405	7,672	7,738	7,044	7,475	6,413	7,603	7,289	8,191	7,690
1968	3,639	8,117	8,332	7,534	8,002	6,849	8,107	7,752	8,666	8,142
1969	3,992	8,799	9,049	7,970	8,454	7,257	8,746	8,282	9,316	8,685
1970	4,196	9,457	9,810	8,378	8,865	7,691	9,396	8,755	10,028	9,193
1971	4,280	10,038	10,473	8,883	9,407	8,167	10,266	9,526	10,696	9,671
1972	4,460	10,861	10,747	9,450	10,032	8,636	10,991	10,643	11,420	10,245
1973	4,995	11,701	11,251	10,027	10,658	9,099	11,980	11,489	12,156	10,897
1974	5,380	12,950	12,192	10,843	11,453	9,925	12,677	12,536	13,031	11,992
1975	5,789	14,728	13,447	11,899	12,594	10,901	13,550	13,887	14,231	12,930
1976	6,153	15,962	14,242	12,835	13,622	11,710	14,944	15,615	15,653	13,684
1977	6,746	17,356	14,639	13,859	14,730	12,578	16,151	17,060	16,916	14,584
1978	7,511	19,078	15,396	14,937	15,837	13,563	17,504	18,739	18,279	15,714
1979	8,169	21,027	16,784	16,268	17,227	14,755	19,036	20,350	19,745	17,118
1980	8,540	23,476	18,577	17,894	19,043	16,352	20,818	22,157	21,782	18,825
1981	8,887	26,298	20,361	19,641	20,856	17,779	22,492	24,549	24,091	20,328
1982	10,154	28,341	21,879	21,138	22,360	19,353	23,465	26,724	26,382	21,693
1983	9,559	29,629	21,995	22,330	23,618	20,491	24,293	28,925	28,386	22,589
1984	10,569	30,926	22,111	23,560	24,910	21,532	24,774	29,879	30,437	23,901
1985	11,864	32,202	22,836	24,960	26,432	22,726	25,333	32,012	32,443	25,042
1986	12,115	33,514	23,660	26,024	27,587	23,703	25,766	33,356	33,943	26,158
1987	12,262	34,210	24,749	26,739	28,272	24,506	26,465	35,111	35,439	27,311
1988	12,977	35,212	25,987	27,986	29,542	25,719	27,031	36,331	36,700	29,243
1989	14,151	36,548	26,778	28,860	30,457	26,541	27,623	37,260	38,422	30,078
1990	16,014	38,081	27,832	30,148	31,739	27,890	29,019	38,930	39,538	31,810
1991	16,165	39,749	28,556	31,241	32,890	28,980	29,951	40,161	41,243	32,819
1992	16,748	42,242	29,347	32,813	34,506	30,542	31,514	42,212	43,160	34,352
1993	17,359	43,569	29,405	33,695	35,521	31,271	31,313	43,862	45,480	35,358
1994	17,833	44,482	30,191	34,725	36,724	32,032	31,882	46,802	46,725	36,504

TABLE Ba4490–4511 Wage and salary accruals per full-time equivalent employee, by industry: 1949–1994 *Continued*

			Services						Government			
	Retail trade	Finance, insurance, and real estate	Total	Personal	Health	Educational	Social and membership organizations	Private household	Total	Federal civilian	State and local	Public education
	Ba4500	Ba4501	Ba4502	Ba4503	Ba4504	Ba4505	Ba4506	Ba4507	Ba4508	Ba4509	Ba4510	Ba4511
Year	Dollars	Dollars	Dollars	Dollars	Dollars	Dollars	Dollars	Dollars	Dollars	Dollars	Dollars	Dollars
1949	2,596	3,095	2,156	2,163	1,935	2,063	2,384	1,498	2,888	3,481	2,754	2,805
1950	2,711	3,262	2,213	2,246	2,045	2,135	2,495	1,502	3,043	3,632	2,841	2,934
1951	2,785	3,418	2,368	2,375	2,177	2,240	2,617	1,588	3,152	3,924	3,041	3,147
1952	2,891	3,552	2,554	2,526	2,344	2,320	2,746	1,707	3,322	4,202	3,241	3,327
1953	3,035	3,708	2,708	2,682	2,486	2,419	2,914	1,805	3,427	4,412	3,385	3,478
1954	3,136	3,874	2,844	2,817	2,592	2,535	3,055	1,874	3,540	4,508	3,551	3,685
1955	3,267	4,005	2,958	2,957	2,727	2,646	3,126	1,956	3,753	4,804	3,675	3,788
1956	3,374	4,168	3,115	3,129	2,789	2,866	3,216	2,017	3,941	5,024	3,855	4,018
1957	3,514	4,314	3,249	3,250	2,919	2,959	3,352	2,075	4,085	5,205	4,064	4,288
1958	3,626	4,523	3,378	3,369	3,077	3,080	3,498	2,154	4,376	5,779	4,260	4,561
1959	3,785	4,791	3,539	3,555	3,210	3,371	3,559	2,214	4,450	5,851	4,299	4,453
1960	3,911	4,910	3,688	3,665	3,414	3,529	3,584	2,356	4,628	6,072	4,511	4,687
1961	4,001	5,203	3,854	3,810	3,636	3,764	3,684	2,364	4,774	6,453	4,698	4,914
1962	4,156	5,353	4,023	3,968	3,831	4,010	3,787	2,418	4,943	6,644	4,962	5,209
1963	4,297	5,522	4,171	4,063	4,051	4,210	3,896	2,471	5,171	6,993	5,131	5,361
1964	4,454	5,797	4,383	4,267	4,277	4,528	4,000	2,557	5,434	7,518	5,317	5,565
1965	4,623	5,962	4,562	4,375	4,410	4,741	4,138	2,657	5,672	7,858	5,538	5,757
1966	4,776	6,239	4,785	4,551	4,565	5,020	4,280	2,780	5,893	8,170	5,818	6,046
1967	4,970	6,516	5,005	4,705	4,861	5,182	4,402	2,961	6,170	8,259	6,262	6,503
1968	5,275	6,994	5,377	4,960	5,292	5,664	4,655	3,254	6,684	9,002	6,749	7,019
1969	5,591	7,400	5,885	5,254	5,845	6,395	5,138	3,543	7,171	9,690	7,227	7,504
1970	5,914	7,823	6,406	5,636	6,593	7,013	5,449	3,847	7,974	10,921	7,852	8,170
1971	6,234	8,347	6,840	5,892	7,043	7,642	5,924	4,159	8,642	11,769	8,405	8,676
1972	6,607	8,861	7,243	6,268	7,499	8,389	6,088	4,478	9,387	12,597	8,866	9,139
1973	6,902	9,270	7,710	6,585	7,980	8,654	6,645	4,833	9,988	13,464	9,443	9,623
1974	7,381	9,853	8,354	7,079	8,727	8,926	7,130	5,260	10,581	14,083	9,994	10,089
1975	7,918	10,609	9,010	7,459	9,624	9,099	7,407	5,744	11,387	15,201	10,794	11,007
1976	8,439	11,386	9,642	7,943	10,465	9,402	7,701	6,479	12,144	16,238	11,549	11,849
1977	8,873	12,184	10,296	8,322	11,248	9,675	8,297	6,844	12,917	17,474	12,031	12,539
1978	9,404	13,140	11,146	9,034	12,181	9,933	8,934	7,543	13,732	18,909	13,005	13,207
1979	10,104	14,300	12,172	9,710	13,276	10,566	9,557	7,809	14,676	19,903	13,964	14,415
1980	10,961	15,881	13,492	10,621	14,763	11,713	10,395	7,946	16,039	21,227	15,315	15,788
1981	11,736	17,390	14,818	11,184	16,295	12,698	11,147	8,157	17,668	23,032	16,770	17,136
1982	12,365	19,111	16,085	11,548	17,889	13,563	11,856	8,439	19,002	24,434	18,036	18,539
1983	12,920	20,978	17,077	12,255	19,055	14,477	12,486	8,636	20,213	25,322	19,356	19,479
1984	13,291	22,322	17,925	12,589	19,974	15,052	13,183	9,504	21,386	26,412	20,551	20,770
1985	13,626	24,132	18,748	12,888	20,830	15,849	13,530	9,564	22,479	27,327	21,641	21,846
1986	14,149	26,197	19,655	13,382	21,780	16,608	14,319	10,115	23,391	28,092	22,647	22,868
1987	14,602	28,113	21,000	13,738	23,911	17,360	14,814	10,331	24,541	28,996	23,815	24,291
1988	15,161	29,979	22,363	14,674	25,889	18,724	15,630	11,433	25,531	30,498	24,768	24,911
1989	15,500	30,690	23,218	15,267	27,071	19,691	16,150	10,592	26,565	31,444	25,896	26,022
1990	16,065	32,071	24,996	16,129	28,923	20,990	16,788	11,312	28,195	32,602	27,431	27,613
1991	16,722	33,331	25,581	16,344	30,304	22,022	16,727	11,093	29,699	34,876	28,720	28,989
1992	17,430	36,403	26,943	17,001	31,809	22,349	18,310	11,505	30,976	36,607	29,696	29,868
1993	17,637	38,794	27,439	17,218	32,198	22,965	18,788	12,273	31,933	38,953	30,524	30,605
1994	18,130	39,282	27,886	17,337	32,780	23,637	19,266	13,143	32,921	41,357	31,456	31,269

Source

U.S. Department of Commerce, *National Income and Product Accounts of the United States, 1929–1994*, volume 2 (April 1998), pp. 33–6.

Documentation

See the text for Table Ba4397–4418.

TABLE Ba4512–4520 Median earnings of full-time workers, by sex and race: 1960–1997

Contributed by Robert A. Margo

	Male				Female				
	All	White	Black	Hispanic	All	White	Black	Hispanic	Consumer price index
	Ba4512	Ba4513	Ba4514	Ba4515	Ba4516	Ba4517	Ba4518	Ba4519	Ba4520
Year	1994 dollars	1994 dollars	1994 dollars	1994 dollars	1994 dollars	1994 dollars	1994 dollars	1994 dollars	Index 1994 = 1.00
1960	24,706	—	—	—	14,990	—	—	—	0.217
1961	25,513	—	—	—	15,116	—	—	—	0.219
1962	25,998	—	—	—	15,416	—	—	—	0.221
1963	26,614	—	—	—	15,688	—	—	—	0.225
1964	27,278	—	—	—	16,135	—	—	—	0.227
1965	27,681	—	—	—	16,588	—	—	—	0.231
1966	28,865	—	—	—	16,614	—	—	—	0.238
1967	29,322	30,195	19,503	—	16,943	17,470	13,040	—	0.245
1968	30,127	30,937	20,890	—	17,521	18,004	13,708	—	0.254
1969	31,803	32,860	22,117	—	18,721	19,100	15,080	—	0.266
1970	32,173	33,096	22,851	—	19,101	19,420	15,958	—	0.279
1971	32,319	33,213	22,931	—	19,232	19,431	17,241	—	0.291
1972	34,053	35,358	24,370	—	19,703	20,020	17,180	—	0.300
1973	35,122	36,158	24,742	—	19,891	20,202	17,228	—	0.318
1974	33,875	34,063	24,894	25,371	19,903	20,046	18,741	16,919	0.350
1975	33,643	34,424	25,597	24,822	19,788	19,812	19,084	16,959	0.379
1976	33,570	34,463	25,229	25,616	20,207	20,344	19,086	17,410	0.401
1977	34,297	35,315	24,493	25,300	20,209	20,335	18,987	17,625	0.426
1978	34,536	35,118	27,102	25,765	20,528	20,693	19,367	17,729	0.455
1979	34,074	34,855	25,310	24,793	20,329	20,488	18,873	16,909	0.499
1980	33,515	34,497	24,394	24,414	20,163	20,307	19,217	17,429	0.555
1981	33,324	34,058	24,224	24,212	19,740	19,916	18,421	17,647	0.608
1982	32,674	33,488	24,033	23,845	20,174	20,401	18,807	17,226	0.645
1983	32,558	33,355	24,035	24,059	20,705	20,930	18,882	17,355	0.672
1984	33,118	34,179	23,729	24,163	21,082	21,259	19,570	17,894	0.701
1985	33,324	34,518	24,074	23,485	21,519	21,756	19,707	17,996	0.726
1986	34,151	35,058	24,798	22,737	21,949	22,206	19,923	18,709	0.740
1987	33,849	34,069	24,947	22,744	22,062	22,276	20,548	18,949	0.766
1988	33,393	34,110	25,520	22,363	22,056	22,323	20,718	18,597	0.798
1989	32,665	34,111	24,412	21,941	22,432	22,615	20,783	18,719	0.837
1990	31,384	32,748	23,941	21,698	22,476	22,732	20,455	17,770	0.882
1991	32,013	32,933	24,020	21,513	22,364	22,626	20,369	17,675	0.919
1992	31,897	32,593	23,658	20,641	22,579	22,810	20,877	18,048	0.947
1993	31,186	31,885	23,608	20,665	22,304	22,587	20,323	17,187	0.975
1994	30,854	31,598	23,742	20,314	22,205	22,623	19,910	17,569	1.000
1995	30,628	31,285	23,849	19,817	23,048	22,280	20,095	16,704	1.028
1996	30,362	31,138	24,940	19,888	22,903	22,820	20,283	17,630	1.059
1997	31,093	32,495	24,407	19,959	23,059	23,390	20,346	17,519	1.083

Source

Figures are derived from the Current Population Survey (CPS) by the Census Bureau and are updated periodically. For details on the CPS, see U.S. Bureau of the Census, "Measuring 50 Years of Economic Change Using the March Current Population Survey," *Current Population Reports* P60-203, available at the Census Bureau Internet site.

Documentation

The data pertain to full-time, year-round workers, age 15 and over. Earnings includes pretax wage and salary income, net income from nonfarm self-employment, and net income from farm self-employment.

Series Ba4520. The consumer price index (CPI) is that used by the Census Bureau in its publications, the so-called experimental CPI-U-X1 for 1967–1982 and the CPI-U for 1983–1997. Index values prior to 1967 are derived by applying the 1967 CPI-U-X1-to-CPI-U ratio to the 1960–1966 CPI-U index. Earnings in current dollars can be computed by multiplying the constant dollar figures by the value of the CPI.

TABLE Ba4521–4528 Employment cost indexes, by type of occupation and industry: 1975–1999[1] [Wages and salaries]

Contributed by Susan B. Carter

		Private-industry employees						
			Occupation			Industry		
	All civilian employees	All	White-collar	Blue-collar	Service	Goods	Service	Employees of state and local governments
	Ba4521	Ba4522	Ba4523	Ba4524	Ba4525	Ba4526	Ba4527	Ba4528
Year: quarter	Index	Index	Index	Index	Index	Index	Index	Index
1975: 3	—	45.0	44.3	46.2	45.1	45.9	44.3	—
1975: 4	—	45.9	44.9	47.0	46.6	46.9	45.1	—
1976: 1	—	46.7	45.8	48.1	47.5	47.7	46.0	—
1976: 2	—	47.5	46.4	49.0	49.0	48.5	46.8	—
1976: 3	—	48.2	47.0	49.9	49.2	49.5	47.3	—
1976: 4	—	49.2	47.9	50.8	50.2	50.4	48.2	—
1977: 1	—	49.9	48.5	51.7	50.9	51.3	48.8	—
1977: 2	—	50.8	49.3	52.8	52.0	52.3	49.7	—
1977: 3	—	51.7	50.2	53.8	52.9	53.4	50.5	—
1977: 4	—	52.6	51.1	54.7	53.4	54.3	51.4	—
1978: 1	—	53.6	52.0	55.7	55.4	55.3	52.3	—
1978: 2	—	54.7	53.1	56.9	56.4	56.3	53.6	—
1978: 3	—	55.8	54.1	58.1	57.7	57.4	54.7	—
1978: 4	—	56.6	54.7	59.2	58.1	58.8	55.1	—
1979: 1	—	57.7	55.8	60.3	60.0	59.8	56.3	—
1979: 2	—	58.9	56.8	61.7	60.5	60.9	57.4	—
1979: 3	—	60.1	58.0	62.9	61.2	62.0	58.8	—
1979: 4	—	61.5	59.5	64.5	62.2	63.7	60.0	—
1980: 1	—	63.0	60.9	66.0	64.4	65.3	61.5	—
1980: 2	—	64.3	62.1	67.7	65.2	66.7	62.6	—
1980: 3	—	65.8	63.3	69.3	66.3	68.2	64.1	—
1980: 4	—	67.1	64.6	70.7	67.3	69.7	65.3	—
1981: 1	—	68.9	66.6	72.2	70.4	71.2	67.4	—
1981: 2	69.2	70.3	67.9	73.9	71.0	72.8	68.6	63.9
1981: 3	70.9	71.7	69.1	75.6	72.2	74.4	69.8	67.0
1981: 4	72.2	73.0	70.5	76.7	72.9	75.7	71.1	68.3
1982: 1	73.5	74.5	72.1	77.8	75.7	77.1	72.6	69.1
1982: 2	74.2	75.3	72.8	78.7	76.6	77.9	73.4	69.4
1982: 3	75.9	76.7	74.3	80.1	77.6	79.3	74.8	72.5
1982: 4	76.7	77.6	75.1	81.0	79.1	80.0	75.9	72.8
1983: 1	77.6	78.5	76.2	81.8	80.1	80.8	76.9	73.5
1983: 2	78.4	79.4	77.1	82.6	80.6	81.6	77.8	73.9
1983: 3	79.7	80.5	78.7	83.4	80.7	82.4	79.2	76.1
1983: 4	80.6	81.4	79.6	84.1	82.7	83.2	80.2	76.6
1984: 1	81.5	82.4	80.4	85.0	85.0	84.1	81.3	77.7
1984: 2	82.2	83.1	81.4	85.6	84.7	84.7	82.1	77.9
1984: 3	83.2	83.8	82.1	86.2	86.0	85.5	82.7	80.5
1984: 4	84.2	84.8	83.0	87.1	87.8	86.4	83.7	81.2
1985: 1	85.1	85.8	84.2	88.0	87.9	87.5	84.6	82.0
1985: 2	85.9	86.7	85.2	88.8	88.3	88.4	85.6	82.2
1985: 3	87.3	87.8	86.4	89.9	89.6	89.0	87.1	85.1
1985: 4	87.8	88.3	87.1	90.1	89.9	89.4	87.7	85.7
1986: 1	88.7	89.2	88.0	90.9	90.8	90.4	88.5	86.5
1986: 2	89.4	89.9	89.0	91.4	90.8	91.3	89.1	86.8
1986: 3	90.4	90.6	89.6	91.9	91.5	91.8	89.8	89.7
1986: 4	90.9	91.1	90.1	92.4	92.3	92.3	90.3	90.3
1987: 1	91.8	92.0	91.4	92.8	93.3	92.8	91.5	91.0
1987: 2	92.3	92.6	91.9	93.5	93.6	93.4	92.1	91.2
1987: 3	93.5	93.5	93.0	94.3	94.1	94.3	93.1	93.3
1987: 4	94.1	94.1	93.4	95.2	94.5	95.2	93.4	94.1
1988: 1	95.0	95.0	94.4	95.9	95.5	96.1	94.3	95.0
1988: 2	95.9	96.1	95.6	96.8	96.4	96.9	95.5	95.2
1988: 3	97.2	97.0	96.7	97.4	97.7	97.5	96.7	97.7
1988: 4	98.1	98.0	97.8	98.2	98.7	98.2	97.8	98.7

Note appears at end of table

(continued)

TABLE Ba4521–4528 Employment cost indexes, by type of occupation and industry: 1975–1999 [Wages and salaries] *Continued*

		Private-industry employees						
			Occupation			Industry		
	All civilian employees	All	White-collar	Blue-collar	Service	Goods	Service	Employees of state and local governments
	Ba4521	Ba4522	Ba4523	Ba4524	Ba4525	Ba4526	Ba4527	Ba4528
Year: quarter	Index	Index	Index	Index	Index	Index	Index	Index
1989: 1	99.2	99.0	99.0	99.0	99.4	99.1	99.1	99.5
1989: 2	100.0	100.0	100.0	100.0	100.0	100.0	100.0	100.0
1989: 3	101.6	101.2	101.4	101.0	100.9	101.0	101.4	103.1
1989: 4	102.4	102.0	102.4	101.6	102.3	102.0	102.2	103.9
1990: 1	103.6	103.2	103.6	102.7	103.1	103.1	103.3	105.1
1990: 2	104.7	104.5	104.9	103.8	104.2	104.2	104.6	105.7
1990: 3	106.0	105.4	106.0	104.6	104.9	105.1	105.7	108.6
1990: 4	106.8	106.1	106.6	105.2	106.4	105.8	106.3	109.4
1991: 1	108.0	107.3	107.9	106.4	106.9	107.0	107.5	110.6
1991: 2	108.9	108.4	109.1	107.3	108.3	108.0	108.7	110.9
1991: 3	110.0	109.3	110.1	108.0	109.8	108.7	109.7	112.8
1991: 4	110.6	110.0	110.7	108.8	110.6	109.7	110.2	113.2
1992: 1	111.5	110.9	111.7	109.7	111.2	110.7	111.1	113.8
1992: 2	112.1	111.6	112.3	110.4	111.6	111.4	111.7	114.2
1992: 3	113.0	112.2	112.9	111.1	112.5	112.1	112.3	115.9
1992: 4	113.6	112.9	113.7	111.6	112.9	112.8	113.0	116.6
1993: 1	114.5	113.9	114.7	112.5	113.5	113.8	113.9	117.2
1993: 2	115.2	114.6	115.5	113.2	114.1	114.5	114.7	117.4
1993: 3	116.4	115.7	116.7	114.1	114.9	115.3	115.9	119.3
1993: 4	117.1	116.4	117.5	114.8	115.3	116.1	116.6	119.7
1994: 1	117.8	117.2	118.3	115.6	116.3	116.9	117.3	120.4
1994: 2	118.6	118.1	119.3	116.5	116.8	118.0	118.2	120.7
1994: 3	119.8	119.1	120.2	117.5	117.6	118.9	119.2	122.8
1994: 4	120.4	119.7	120.8	118.0	118.8	119.6	119.7	123.4
1995: 1	121.3	120.6	121.7	119.0	119.4	120.4	120.7	124.3
1995: 2	122.2	121.5	122.7	120.1	120.0	121.4	121.6	124.6
1995: 3	123.2	122.4	123.6	120.8	120.8	122.1	122.6	126.6
1995: 4	123.9	123.1	124.3	121.4	121.4	122.9	123.2	127.3
1996: 1	125.1	124.4	125.8	122.5	122.2	123.9	124.7	127.8
1996: 2	126.1	125.6	127.0	123.7	123.0	125.1	125.8	128.1
1996: 3	127.2	126.5	128.0	124.3	124.1	126.1	126.7	130.1
1996: 4	128.0	127.3	128.7	125.1	125.7	126.8	127.5	130.9
1997: 1	129.2	128.6	130.2	126.0	126.6	127.5	129.0	131.4
1997: 2	130.1	129.7	131.3	127.3	127.6	128.9	130.1	131.5
1997: 3	131.6	131.0	132.7	128.3	129.9	129.9	131.5	133.6
1997: 4	132.8	132.3	134.2	129.1	131.1	130.6	133.1	134.4
1998: 1	134.0	133.7	135.7	130.2	132.1	132.0	134.4	135.1
1998: 2	135.0	134.9	137.0	131.3	133.0	133.2	135.6	135.4
1998: 3	136.8	136.6	139.0	132.4	134.4	134.3	137.6	137.6
1998: 4	137.7	137.4	139.9	133.2	135.3	135.2	138.4	138.5
1999: 1	138.4	138.1	140.3	134.3	136.7	136.3	138.9	139.0
1999: 2	139.8	139.7	142.1	135.6	137.8	137.3	140.8	139.6
1999: 3	141.3	141.0	143.5	136.8	138.0	138.5	142.1	142.2
1999: 4	142.5	142.2	144.8	137.7	139.6	139.7	143.3	143.5

[1] See source for discussion of changing distribution weights and index base over time.

Source

U.S. Bureau of Labor Statistics, *News, Employment Cost Index* (published quarterly).

Documentation

See the text for Table Ba4529–4536.

TABLE Ba4529–4536 Employment cost indexes, by type of occupation and industry: 1979–1999[1] [Total compensation]

Contributed by Susan B. Carter

		Private-industry employees						
			Occupation			Industry		
	All civilian employees	All	White-collar	Blue-collar	Service	Goods	Service	Employees of state and local governments
	Ba4529	Ba4530	Ba4531	Ba4532	Ba4533	Ba4534	Ba4535	Ba4536
Year: quarter	Index	Index	Index	Index	Index	Index	Index	Index
1979: 4	—	59.1	57.4	61.3	58.8	60.7	57.7	—
1980: 1	—	60.6	59.0	62.8	61.4	62.3	59.3	—
1980: 2	—	62.1	60.4	64.4	62.0	63.7	60.7	—
1980: 3	—	63.5	61.6	66.1	63.3	65.3	62.1	—
1980: 4	—	64.8	62.9	67.5	64.4	66.7	63.3	—
1981: 1	—	67.1	65.4	69.6	67.8	68.9	65.8	—
1981: 2	67.2	68.4	66.5	71.1	68.3	70.4	66.9	61.5
1981: 3	68.9	69.8	67.7	72.7	69.6	72.0	68.1	64.8
1981: 4	70.2	71.2	69.2	74.0	70.4	73.3	69.5	66.1
1982: 1	71.4	72.4	70.4	75.1	72.8	74.7	70.6	67.0
1982: 2	72.2	73.4	71.3	76.1	73.7	75.6	71.5	67.3
1982: 3	73.9	74.8	72.9	77.5	74.8	77.1	73.0	70.3
1982: 4	74.8	75.8	73.7	78.4	76.3	77.8	74.1	70.8
1983: 1	76.0	77.1	75.0	79.7	77.7	79.2	75.4	71.7
1983: 2	76.9	78.0	76.0	80.7	78.2	80.0	76.4	72.1
1983: 3	78.2	79.1	77.5	81.5	78.6	80.9	77.7	74.3
1983: 4	79.1	80.1	78.4	82.3	80.5	81.6	78.9	75.1
1984: 1	80.5	81.5	79.8	83.6	82.9	82.9	80.3	76.2
1984: 2	81.1	82.2	80.8	84.2	82.7	83.7	81.1	76.6
1984: 3	82.2	82.9	81.4	84.9	84.1	84.4	81.7	79.3
1984: 4	83.2	84.0	82.4	85.8	85.8	85.4	82.9	80.1
1985: 1	84.3	85.0	83.7	86.7	86.2	86.6	83.7	81.0
1985: 2	84.9	85.7	84.6	87.3	86.3	87.2	84.5	81.2
1985: 3	86.2	86.8	85.7	88.2	87.9	87.7	86.1	84.0
1985: 4	86.8	87.3	86.4	88.5	88.4	88.2	86.6	84.6
1986: 1	87.7	88.2	87.4	89.4	89.4	89.2	87.5	85.5
1986: 2	88.3	88.9	88.2	89.8	89.5	90.0	88.0	86.0
1986: 3	89.3	89.5	88.8	90.5	90.3	90.6	88.8	88.4
1986: 4	89.9	90.1	89.4	90.9	91.1	91.0	89.3	89.0
1987: 1	90.7	91.0	90.6	91.3	91.9	91.5	90.5	89.8
1987: 2	91.3	91.6	91.2	92.1	92.3	92.1	91.2	90.0
1987: 3	92.3	92.5	92.1	92.9	92.8	92.9	92.1	92.1
1987: 4	93.1	93.1	92.7	93.7	93.3	93.8	92.6	93.0
1988: 1	94.4	94.5	93.9	95.4	94.6	95.5	93.8	94.2
1988: 2	95.4	95.7	95.1	96.4	95.6	96.5	95.1	94.5
1988: 3	96.7	96.6	96.2	97.1	97.1	97.1	96.2	97.1
1988: 4	97.7	97.6	97.3	97.9	98.2	97.9	97.3	98.2
1989: 1	98.9	98.8	98.9	98.8	99.2	98.9	98.8	99.4
1989: 2	100.0	100.0	100.0	100.0	100.0	100.0	100.0	100.0
1989: 3	101.6	101.2	101.4	101.1	101.1	101.1	101.3	103.3
1989: 4	102.6	102.3	102.4	101.9	102.5	102.1	102.3	104.3
1990: 1	104.3	103.9	104.1	103.5	103.9	103.9	103.8	105.8
1990: 2	105.4	105.2	105.5	104.7	104.9	105.2	105.2	106.5
1990: 3	106.9	106.2	106.7	105.6	105.7	106.2	106.2	109.4
1990: 4	107.6	107.0	107.4	106.4	107.3	107.0	107.0	110.4
1991: 1	109.1	108.5	109.0	107.9	108.3	108.5	108.5	111.8
1991: 2	110.2	109.8	110.3	109.0	109.9	109.8	109.8	112.0
1991: 3	111.5	111.0	111.4	110.2	111.5	111.0	111.0	113.9
1991: 4	112.2	111.7	112.2	111.0	112.4	111.9	111.6	114.4
1992: 1	113.5	113.1	113.4	112.5	113.5	113.5	112.8	115.2
1992: 2	114.2	113.9	114.2	113.4	114.2	114.3	113.6	115.7
1992: 3	115.4	114.8	115.1	114.3	115.4	115.3	114.4	117.9
1992: 4	116.1	115.6	115.9	115.0	115.9	116.1	115.2	118.6
1993: 1	117.5	117.1	117.4	116.6	117.2	118.0	116.4	119.3
1993: 2	118.3	118.0	118.3	117.7	118.0	119.1	117.3	119.6
1993: 3	119.5	119.1	119.4	118.7	118.9	119.9	118.5	121.4
1993: 4	120.2	119.8	120.2	119.3	119.5	120.6	119.3	121.9

Note appears at end of table

(continued)

TABLE Ba4529–4536 Employment cost indexes, by type of occupation and industry: 1979–1999 [Total compensation] *Continued*

		Private-industry employees						
			Occupation			Industry		
	All civilian employees	All	White-collar	Blue-collar	Service	Goods	Service	Employees of state and local governments
	Ba4529	Ba4530	Ba4531	Ba4532	Ba4533	Ba4534	Ba4535	Ba4536
Year: quarter	Index	Index	Index	Index	Index	Index	Index	Index
1994: 1	121.3	121.0	121.5	120.3	120.6	121.8	120.4	122.6
1994: 2	122.1	122.0	122.5	121.2	121.0	123.0	121.2	123.1
1994: 3	123.3	123.0	123.5	122.3	121.8	123.9	122.3	125.0
1994: 4	123.8	123.5	124.1	122.6	122.9	124.3	122.8	125.6
1995: 1	124.8	124.5	125.3	123.5	123.4	125.3	123.9	126.4
1995: 2	125.6	125.4	126.2	124.4	124.0	125.9	124.9	126.9
1995: 3	126.6	126.2	127.0	125.1	124.7	126.5	125.8	128.7
1995: 4	127.2	126.7	127.6	125.6	125.2	127.3	126.2	129.3
1996: 1	128.3	127.9	129.0	126.6	125.8	128.2	127.6	129.9
1996: 2	129.2	129.0	130.0	127.6	126.5	129.3	128.6	130.2
1996: 3	130.2	129.8	131.1	128.1	127.4	130.1	129.5	131.9
1996: 4	130.9	130.6	131.7	129.0	128.9	130.9	130.2	132.7
1997: 1	132.0	131.7	133.1	129.6	129.8	131.4	131.6	133.2
1997: 2	132.8	132.8	134.1	130.8	130.9	132.7	132.5	133.3
1997: 3	134.1	133.9	135.2	131.7	133.1	133.6	133.8	135.0
1997: 4	135.2	135.1	136.7	132.3	134.1	134.1	135.3	135.7
1998: 1	136.3	136.3	138.1	133.1	135.3	135.1	136.7	136.5
1998: 2	137.4	137.5	139.4	134.3	136.0	136.2	137.8	136.9
1998: 3	139.0	139.0	141.1	135.2	137.3	137.1	139.6	139.0
1998: 4	139.8	139.8	142.0	135.9	138.0	137.8	140.5	139.8
1999: 1	140.4	140.4	142.4	136.9	139.5	138.9	140.9	140.5
1999: 2	141.8	142.0	144.1	138.2	140.6	139.9	142.8	141.0
1999: 3	143.3	143.3	145.6	139.4	141.0	141.1	144.1	143.1
1999: 4	144.6	144.6	146.9	140.5	142.6	142.5	145.3	144.6

[1] See text for discussion of changing distribution weights and index base over time.

Source

U.S. Bureau of Labor Statistics (BLS), *News, Employment Cost Index* (published quarterly).

Documentation

The Employment Cost Index (ECI) was developed in the early 1970s in response to policymakers' need for a timely, accurate, and comprehensive indicator of changes in employers' labor costs that was free from the influence of employment shifts among industries and occupations. It differs from the average hourly earnings data presented in Tables Ba4361–4380 in two ways. First, it covers not only nonsupervisory workers but also all occupations and establishments in the private nonfarm sector plus state and local government. The ECI, however, does not include data for the self-employed or for farm, private household, and federal government employees. Second, it includes employers' costs for employee benefits in addition to wages and salaries. The benefits are paid leave, supplemental pay, life insurance, short-term and long-term disability benefits, health benefits, retirement and savings benefits, legally required benefits, and other benefits (severance pay and supplemental unemployment insurance). It does not include employer training costs or bonuses.

In order to remove the effects of occupation and industry shifts, the ECI is calculated by using a fixed basket of occupations. This basket is constructed by holding the distribution of employment among industries and occupations fixed over time. The purpose of this standardization is to prevent, for example, a more rapid growth in the number of high-paying technical jobs from appearing as an employment cost increase. The job categories/occupations used to calculate the ECI are narrowly defined, so that all workers in a given category perform their employment tasks at roughly the same skill level. The ECI periodically changes its weights to reflect structure shifts in the economy's employment. The shift of jobs out of goods-producing industries into the service sector is an example of a structural shift. Three different distribution weights have been used to calculate the ECI. ECI figures published from 1975 to May 1986 were based on employment count data from the 1970 Census. In June 1986, employment count data from the 1980 Census was used to recalculate the ECI distribution weights. In March 1995, the 1990 Census employment count was used.

Beginning in the March 1990 ECI news release, the base for index numbers is June 1989 = 100, rather than June 1981 = 100. The change is explained in the technical note, "Employment Cost Index Rebased to June 1989," in the April 1990 issue of the *Monthly Labor Review*.

ECI statistics were first published for September–December 1975, at which time they were limited to private industry wage and salary changes by major occupational and industry groups, region, union status, and area size. Over time, new series were added and coverage was expanded.

The ECI was developed primarily to aid in economic analysis, and that remains its most important use. Analysts and policymakers, including the Federal Reserve Board, use the ECI to form monetary policies and to monitor the effects of those policies. The ECI is also used to forecast wage trends and facilitate wage and benefit cost planning. The ECI serves as a guide in negotiations in collective bargaining. Several health cost containment laws, including one for Medicare, use the ECI as an adjustment factor to determine the allowable increases in hospital and physician charges. Increasingly, the ECI is being used as a labor cost escalator in long-term purchasing and service contracts in both the private and the public sectors in the United States, as well as in other countries. The ECI is used in the federal pay-setting process and to develop measures of national economic performance and welfare.

Because the ECI is based on a probability sample, the ECI survey is subject to sampling errors that may cause the estimates to deviate from the results that would be obtained if the records of all establishments could be used in the calculations. Because probability samples are used, standard errors can be calculated and are available from the BLS. See BLS, *Employment Cost Indexes: 1975–1998*, Bulletin number 2514 (1998).

Series Ba4521, Ba4529, and Ba4537. Include private industry and state and local government workers, and exclude farm, household, and federal government workers.

Series Ba4527, Ba4535, and Ba4543. Include transportation, communication, and public utilities; wholesale and retail trade; finance, insurance, and real estate; and service industries.

TABLE Ba4537–4544 Employment cost indexes, by type of occupation and industry: 1979–1999[1] [Benefits]

Contributed by Susan B. Carter

		Private industry employees						
			Occupation			Industry		
	All civilian employees	All	White-collar	Blue-collar	Service	Goods	Service	Employees of state and local governments
	Ba4537	Ba4538	Ba4539	Ba4540	Ba4541	Ba4542	Ba4543	Ba4544
Year: quarter	Index	Index	Index	Index	Index	Index	Index	Index
1979: 4	—	53.2	52.1	54.8	—	54.6	51.9	—
1980: 1	—	55.0	54.2	56.3	—	56.2	54.0	—
1980: 2	—	56.7	56.1	57.7	—	57.5	56.0	—
1980: 3	—	58.1	57.2	59.6	—	59.3	57.2	—
1980: 4	—	59.4	58.4	60.9	—	60.5	58.4	—
1981: 1	—	62.9	62.2	64.2	—	64.2	61.8	—
1981: 2	62.5	63.9	63.0	65.4	—	65.5	62.5	—
1981: 3	64.1	65.2	64.2	66.8	—	67.0	63.6	—
1981: 4	65.5	66.6	65.7	68.1	—	68.2	65.1	—
1982: 1	66.3	67.3	66.0	69.3	—	69.5	65.3	—
1982: 2	67.5	68.6	67.4	70.5	—	70.8	66.6	—
1982: 3	69.4	70.4	69.3	72.1	—	72.5	68.5	—
1982: 4	70.4	71.4	70.2	73.1	—	73.2	69.6	—
1983: 1	72.3	73.4	71.9	75.6	—	75.8	71.3	—
1983: 2	73.3	74.5	73.0	76.7	—	76.7	72.5	—
1983: 3	74.7	75.7	74.5	77.6	—	77.8	73.8	—
1983: 4	75.7	76.7	75.5	78.4	—	78.3	75.2	—
1984: 1	77.8	78.9	77.8	80.5	—	80.4	77.6	—
1984: 2	78.6	79.9	79.0	81.2	—	81.3	78.6	—
1984: 3	79.8	80.6	79.7	81.9	—	82.1	79.2	—
1984: 4	80.9	81.7	80.9	83.0	—	83.2	80.4	—
1985: 1	82.3	83.1	82.3	84.1	—	84.9	81.4	—
1985: 2	82.4	83.2	82.7	84.1	—	84.7	81.9	—
1985: 3	83.6	84.2	83.8	84.7	82.7	85.2	83.2	—
1985: 4	84.1	84.6	84.3	85.1	84.0	85.7	83.6	—
1986: 1	85.3	85.8	85.5	86.3	84.9	86.8	84.9	—
1986: 2	85.7	86.1	86.0	86.5	85.4	87.4	85.1	—
1986: 3	86.6	87.0	86.6	87.4	86.6	87.9	86.1	—
1986: 4	87.3	87.5	87.3	87.7	87.6	88.3	86.8	—
1987: 1	88.0	88.2	88.2	88.2	88.2	88.7	87.8	—
1987: 2	88.6	89.0	88.9	89.1	88.4	89.4	88.6	—
1987: 3	89.6	89.6	89.7	89.8	88.7	90.0	89.4	—
1987: 4	90.5	90.5	90.5	90.7	89.7	90.9	90.2	—
1988: 1	93.2	93.4	92.8	94.2	92.1	94.4	92.5	—
1988: 2	94.3	94.7	94.0	95.7	93.4	95.7	93.8	—
1988: 3	95.7	95.7	95.0	96.5	95.1	96.5	94.9	—
1988: 4	96.8	96.7	96.2	97.4	96.8	97.3	96.1	—
1989: 1	98.6	98.4	98.3	98.6	98.7	98.7	98.2	—
1989: 2	100.0	100.0	100.0	100.0	100.0	100.0	100.0	100.0
1989: 3	101.9	101.4	101.4	101.4	101.6	101.5	101.4	103.9
1989: 4	103.2	102.6	102.6	102.6	103.0	102.6	102.6	105.3
1990: 1	105.9	105.5	105.6	105.2	106.0	105.7	105.3	107.5
1990: 2	107.2	106.9	107.1	106.6	107.0	107.2	106.6	108.3
1990: 3	108.9	108.3	108.6	107.9	108.1	108.7	107.9	111.3
1990: 4	110.1	109.4	109.7	109.0	109.9	109.9	109.0	112.7
1991: 1	112.2	111.6	112.1	111.0	112.3	111.9	111.4	114.6
1991: 2	113.6	113.5	113.8	112.8	114.5	113.9	113.0	114.4
1991: 3	115.4	115.2	115.3	114.9	116.5	115.8	114.6	116.4
1991: 4	116.3	116.2	116.4	115.7	117.8	116.7	115.7	117.1
1992: 1	118.6	118.6	118.4	118.7	120.0	119.7	117.7	118.5
1992: 2	119.6	119.7	119.4	119.7	121.6	120.6	118.8	119.3
1992: 3	121.4	121.2	121.0	121.2	123.7	122.3	120.4	122.3
1992: 4	122.5	122.2	122.0	122.2	124.6	123.4	121.2	123.4
1993: 1	125.0	125.2	124.7	125.5	127.7	127.3	123.4	124.2
1993: 2	126.2	126.7	125.9	127.3	129.3	129.0	124.6	124.5
1993: 3	127.4	127.7	126.8	128.4	130.5	130.0	125.7	126.2
1993: 4	128.1	128.3	127.6	128.9	131.5	130.3	126.7	127.0

Note appears at end of table

(continued)

TABLE Ba4537–4544 Employment cost indexes, by type of occupation and industry: 1979–1999 [Benefits] *Continued*

	All civilian employees	Private industry employees						Employees of state and local governments
			Occupation			Industry		
		All	White-collar	Blue-collar	Service	Goods	Service	
	Ba4537	Ba4538	Ba4539	Ba4540	Ba4541	Ba4542	Ba4543	Ba4544
Year: quarter	Index	Index	Index	Index	Index	Index	Index	Index
1994: 1	130.1	130.7	130.5	130.5	132.9	132.7	128.9	127.9
1994: 2	131.0	131.7	131.6	131.5	133.1	133.9	129.7	128.5
1994: 3	132.3	132.8	132.8	132.7	134.2	134.8	131.2	130.3
1994: 4	132.5	133.0	133.3	132.5	134.7	134.8	131.5	130.5
1995: 1	133.8	134.5	135.2	133.3	135.0	135.9	133.2	131.1
1995: 2	134.5	135.1	136.0	133.6	135.6	135.9	134.1	132.2
1995: 3	135.2	135.6	136.6	134.1	135.7	136.2	134.8	133.6
1995: 4	135.5	135.9	136.7	134.7	136.0	137.1	134.7	133.9
1996: 1	136.2	136.6	137.7	135.2	135.7	137.7	135.5	134.7
1996: 2	136.9	137.4	138.4	136.1	136.3	138.6	136.2	135.1
1996: 3	137.7	138.1	139.5	136.2	136.2	138.8	137.2	136.1
1996: 4	138.2	138.6	139.7	137.0	137.4	139.7	137.4	136.8
1997: 1	138.9	139.4	140.8	137.2	138.3	139.9	138.5	137.4
1997: 2	139.6	140.1	141.5	138.0	139.6	140.9	139.2	137.4
1997: 3	140.3	140.8	142.0	138.8	141.4	141.5	139.8	138.2
1997: 4	141.1	141.8	143.4	139.0	142.0	141.5	141.4	138.6
1998: 1	142.0	142.6	144.7	139.1	143.3	141.5	142.7	139.7
1998: 2	143.0	143.7	145.6	140.4	143.7	142.5	143.8	140.3
1998: 3	144.0	144.5	146.6	141.0	144.7	143.0	144.9	142.1
1998: 4	144.7	145.2	147.4	141.6	144.8	143.2	145.7	142.7
1999: 1	145.3	145.8	147.9	142.2	146.3	144.3	146.1	143.6
1999: 2	146.6	147.3	149.4	143.6	147.6	145.2	147.9	144.0
1999: 3	147.9	148.6	151.0	144.8	148.4	146.3	149.4	145.0
1999: 4	149.5	150.2	152.5	146.2	149.9	148.2	150.7	146.7

[1] See source for discussion of changing distribution weights and index base over time.

Source

U.S. Bureau of Labor Statistics, *News, Employment Cost Index* (published quarterly).

Documentation

See the discussion for Table Ba4529–4536.

HOURS AND WORKING CONDITIONS

William A. Sundstrom

TABLE Ba4545–4551 Average daily hours worked in manufacturing, and the distribution of manufacturing establishments, by hours worked: 1830–1890

Contributed by William A. Sundstrom

		Establishments in which some employees worked					
	Average daily hours of work	8–9 hours per day	9–10 hours per day	10–11 hours per day	11–12 hours per day	12–13 hours per day	13–14 hours per day
	Ba4545	Ba4546	Ba4547	Ba4548	Ba4549	Ba4550	Ba4551
Year	Hours	Number	Number	Number	Number	Number	Number
1830	—	2	5	11	2	12	5
1835	—	2	5	17	4	14	6
1840	11.4	2	6	28	5	20	8
1845	11.5	4	7	49	9	24	10
1850	11.5	7	10	87	23	40	6
1855	11.1	11	17	133	36	48	5
1860	11.0	13	22	200	49	58	8
1865	10.7	20	34	290	64	77	11
1870	10.5	37	58	447	80	105	17
1875	10.3	49	77	561	88	136	19
1880	10.3	53	91	619	100	152	24
1885	10.3	—	—	—	—	—	—
1890	10.0	—	—	—	—	—	—

Sources

Series Ba4545. U.S. Congress, Senate Committee on Finance, *Wholesale Prices, Wages, and Transportation*, Part 1, Senate Report number 1394 (U.S. Government Printing Office, 1893), p. 179.

Series Ba4546–4551. U.S. Department of the Interior, Census Office, *Report on the Statistics of Wages in Manufacturing Industries* (1886), p. xxviii.

Documentation

The two most important sources for time series on hours of work in manufacturing during the nineteenth century are the so-called Aldrich and Weeks reports. The Weeks report was prepared by Joseph Weeks as part of the Census of 1880. The Aldrich report was prepared under the direction of the Commissioner of Labor, Carroll D. Wright, for the Senate Committee on Finance, chaired by Nelson W. Aldrich. The data underlying both reports were collected from manufacturing establishments, which apparently used their payroll records to answer retrospective questions about wages, hours, and employment. A useful discussion of both reports and their limitations is provided by Clarence D. Long, *Wages and Earnings in the United States, 1860–1890* (Princeton University Press, 1960), pp. 5–9.

Neither sample can be considered representative in its coverage by industry or region. Due to the retrospective nature of the samples, data from the earlier years in each survey come only from those surveyed establishments that had been in business continuously since those years. This may introduce selection bias if older, surviving firms differ systematically from younger firms. The text of the Aldrich report, for example, notes: "It must be remembered that our figures refer to certain picked establishments, where, in view of the complete organization at an early date, it is probable that shorter hours made an earlier appearance than in the mass of work-shops" (pp. 179–80).

The text of the Weeks report provides a sample questionnaire. The question on hours asks the firm to provide "the regular hours of labor per day of several of the most important classes" of employees for the years covered. Thus, the hours reported by Weeks are probably best thought of as the normal or scheduled hours of work, rather than actual hours worked or paid for. No such detail about the hours question is provided in the Aldrich report.

In spite of their differences and known deficiencies, the Weeks and Aldrich samples both suggest broadly similar downward trends in work hours over the period, and both are roughly consistent with findings derived from more representative samples from the late nineteenth century. For example, using a much larger and more representative sample of establishments from the 1880 Census of Manufactures, Jeremy Atack and Fred Bateman find that a majority of workers in 1880 were scheduled to work exactly ten hours per day, which is consistent with the pattern reported by Weeks for that year; see Atack and Bateman, "How Long Was the Workday in 1880?" *Journal of Economic History* 52 (March 1992): 129–60.

Rather than reporting average hours, the Weeks report provides a table of the number of "statements" from reporting establishments within each range of hours, which are reproduced in series Ba4546–4551. Because employers were asked to report hours for "several" important classes of workers (presumably the most numerous occupations), a single establishment could supply more than one statement. It appears that the typical establishment reported a single hours figure for all employees. For the year 1880, for example, there were 769 reporting establishments, and a total of 1,039 statements regarding hours, or about 1.35 statements per establishment. As can be seen, the number of establishments that reported hours for the Weeks report at each date decreases dramatically as one moves back in time; the sample consists of fewer than 100 statements for the years 1830–1840.

The hours distributions from the Weeks report may be aggregated into an average hours series in various ways. Long (1960, p. 35), for example, presents an average of the midpoints of each hours interval, weighted by the number of statements. Given the widespread tendency to set hours at whole numbers, however, a better average is probably obtained by taking the average of the lower bound of each interval, again weighted by the number of statements. This procedure yields average hours that fall from 10.9 in 1830 to 10.3 in 1880. The structure of the Weeks data makes it impossible to create averages weighted by number of workers.

Series Ba4545. Based on the Aldrich report.

Series Ba4546–4551. Based on the Weeks report. Series Ba4546 covers establishments in which some employees worked at least eight hours and less than nine hours per day. Hour ranges for the other series follow the same pattern.

TABLE Ba4552–4567 Average daily hours worked and annual operating days, by manufacturing industry: 1890–1914

Contributed by William A. Sundstrom

Year	Average days in operation	Average daily hours worked: Total	Textiles	Cotton	Wool	Silk	Hosiery and knit goods	Dyeing and finishing textiles	Boots and shoes	Leather	Electrical machinery	Paper and paper products	Rubber	Glass	Foundry and machine shops	Iron and steel
	Ba4552	Ba4553	Ba4554	Ba4555	Ba4556	Ba4557	Ba4558	Ba4559	Ba4560	Ba4561	Ba4562	Ba4563	Ba4564	Ba4565	Ba4566	Ba4567
	Days	Hours	Hours	Hours	Hours	Hours	Hours	Hours	Hours	Hours	Hours	Hours	Hours	Hours	Hours	Hours
1890	294	10.02	10.16	10.31	9.98	9.95	10.13	9.96	9.81	9.67	—	10.90	9.88	—	10.10	—
1891	297	10.01	10.19	10.37	9.96	10.02	10.13	9.96	9.84	9.67	—	10.87	9.87	—	10.10	—
1892	296	10.04	10.20	10.40	9.96	9.92	10.13	9.89	9.81	9.65	—	10.87	9.90	—	10.06	10.67
1893	271	9.99	10.06	10.26	9.83	9.63	10.07	9.74	9.79	9.67	—	10.83	9.85	—	10.03	10.67
1894	272	9.92	9.83	10.01	9.78	9.60	9.47	9.57	9.79	9.67	—	10.89	9.78	—	10.01	10.75
1895	284	9.97	10.06	10.25	9.88	9.60	10.05	9.75	9.79	9.69	—	10.89	9.83	—	10.05	10.74
1896	274	9.96	10.05	10.21	9.88	9.65	10.05	9.75	9.79	9.69	9.62	10.87	9.82	—	10.03	10.59
1897	284	9.94	9.99	10.16	9.73	9.67	10.05	9.60	9.76	9.72	9.60	10.94	9.80	—	10.01	10.66
1898	288	9.97	10.09	10.30	9.86	9.68	10.05	9.77	9.76	9.74	9.63	10.99	9.83	—	10.05	10.69
1899	290	9.94	10.10	10.30	9.86	9.70	10.05	9.77	9.76	9.70	9.60	10.38	9.80	9.00	10.01	10.57
1900	289	9.89	10.06	10.26	9.86	9.70	9.92	9.77	9.72	9.71	9.55	10.38	9.75	9.01	9.96	10.74
1901	287	9.84	10.05	10.25	9.86	9.68	9.92	9.77	9.74	9.71	9.50	10.20	9.70	8.94	9.81	10.66
1902	294	9.79	9.99	10.20	9.75	9.65	9.92	9.77	9.62	9.71	9.45	10.13	9.65	8.92	9.69	10.66
1903	291	9.71	9.95	10.18	9.73	9.63	9.82	9.77	9.51	9.70	9.38	10.22	9.57	9.11	9.57	10.67
1904	288	9.68	9.92	10.16	9.66	9.55	9.82	9.79	9.52	9.67	9.35	10.17	9.55	9.15	9.52	10.57
1905	292	9.70	9.93	10.16	9.73	9.57	9.80	9.82	9.51	9.70	9.37	10.27	9.57	9.23	9.54	10.69
1906	297	9.63	9.89	10.11	9.70	9.57	9.75	9.76	9.46	9.70	9.30	10.23	9.50	9.26	9.50	10.67
1907	294	9.60	9.83	10.01	9.66	9.57	9.73	9.73	9.44	9.71	9.27	9.81	9.46	9.21	9.47	10.67
1908	274	9.55	9.75	9.90	9.63	9.55	9.68	9.65	9.44	9.66	9.22	9.76	9.41	9.16	9.42	10.53
1909	289	9.56	9.76	9.90	9.63	9.53	9.70	9.66	9.42	9.67	9.23	9.78	9.42	9.17	9.43	10.64
1910	286	9.49	9.60	9.69	9.48	9.51	9.54	9.52	9.40	9.62	9.18	9.71	9.36	9.09	9.37	10.58
1911	284	9.47	9.63	9.72	9.51	9.48	9.57	9.56	9.39	9.63	9.18	9.70	9.35	9.08	9.36	10.39
1912	290	9.39	9.49	9.57	9.38	9.40	9.43	9.43	9.27	9.56	9.10	9.61	9.27	9.01	9.29	10.31
1913	283	9.36	9.48	9.60	9.37	9.36	9.27	9.43	9.21	9.56	9.09	9.59	9.25	8.99	9.27	10.29
1914	281	9.28	9.35	9.50	9.23	9.18	9.18	9.31	9.15	9.50	9.03	9.51	9.18	8.91	9.20	10.12

Source

Albert Rees, *Real Wages in Manufacturing, 1890–1914* (Princeton University Press, 1961), Tables 10 and 13.

Documentation

The average number of days per year that establishments were in operation is a weighted average of data from the three states that published annual data on days in operation for most of the sample period: Massachusetts, New Jersey, and Pennsylvania. The Massachusetts series covers the full period, the Pennsylvania series begins in 1892, and the New Jersey series begins in 1895. Rees linked the series at these points to prevent the changes in coverage from affecting the movement of the series. Within each state, he computed employment-weighted averages of days in operation by industries; the all-manufacturing averages published by some of the states are weighted by the number of establishments. The weights for combining states in census years were census employment in manufacturing; for other years, linear interpolations of the census weights. The full-time work year during the period 1889–1914 was apparently 312 days - 365 minus 52 Sundays and 1 holiday.

To derive his series of daily hours in all manufacturing, Rees started with hours data for all manufacturing from the 1909 and 1914 Census of Manufactures, and then linked annual U.S. Bureau of Labor Statistics (BLS) data for selected industries to the 1909 and 1914 levels to capture year-to-year movements in hours around those two dates.

The daily hours in 1909 and 1914 were computed from the frequency distributions of full-time hours per week in the Census of Manufactures. Rees converted weekly hours to daily hours by dividing by 6. He notes that the census hours figures are full-time or prevailing hours, and thus refer to the "normal workweek" of the establishment or occupation, rather than actual hours worked or paid for (Rees 1961, p. 27).

From 1903 to 1914, the movement of hours was based on BLS data for seven industries, using Paul Douglas's processing for six of them (see Table Ba4568–4574); Douglas, *Real Wages in the United States, 1890–1926* (Houghton Mifflin, 1930). The industries are cotton, silk, hosiery and knit goods, woolen and worsted, boots and shoes, lumber, and iron and steel. These were combined by census employment weights, using linear interpolation of these weights for intercensal years. The resulting series was then adjusted to pass through the points computed from census data for 1909 and 1914. This segment of the hours series used the hours data for all of Douglas's payroll industries except clothing (for which Douglas interpolated the data for 1907–1912) and slaughtering and meatpacking (for which he assumed a constant sixty-hour week on the basis of information other than the BLS data). Rees added the silk industry, for which he computed average hours from the BLS Bulletins following Douglas's method.

For 1890–1902, the movement of the manufacturing hours series was taken from Leo Wolman's series for all manufacturing; Wolman, *Hours of Work in American Industry*, National Bureau of Economic

TABLE Ba4552–4567 Average daily hours worked and annual operating days, by manufacturing industry: 1890–1914 *Continued*

Research, Bulletin number 71 (1938). This was linked to the segment of the hours series for 1903–1909 by means of an overlap of one year at 1903. The resulting change in the level of Wolman's series was an increase of 0.2 hour per week. Wolman's series uses all the hours data for manufacturing in the *Nineteenth Annual Report of the Commissioner of Labor*; it thus has much broader coverage (forty-eight industries) than Douglas's series, which was derived from the same source for this period but is confined to fourteen industries.

The levels of average daily hours for individual industries for 1909 and 1914 were again computed from census data. In two industries, Rees made special assumptions about the means of the open-end classes in the census hours distributions. For glass, short workweeks were common for part of the workforce, apparently because of the heat and physical strain of some jobs. In this industry, he assumed that the mean of the weekly hours class "48 hours and under" was forty-four hours. For iron and steel, the means of the open-end class "over 72 hours" were computed from BLS data.

The movement of hours, except for the trend from 1909 to 1914, was based ultimately on BLS data, combined in several different ways. In five industries (cotton, woolens, hosiery and knit goods, boots and shoes, and iron and steel), Rees used the Douglas payroll series adjusted to the census levels of 1909 and 1914. For silk, he computed an hours series using Douglas's methods; this was then adjusted to census levels. The hours series for "all textiles" is the weighted averages of the series for cotton, woolen, silk, and hosiery and knit goods, with no new adjustment to census levels. In the remaining industries, except dyeing and finishing textiles, he used the hours series for all manufacturing to estimate the movement of hours from 1903 to 1914, adjusting it to the census levels of each industry. For dyeing and finishing textiles, he used the series for all textiles.

In five industries (dyeing and finishing textiles, leather, paper, glass, and foundries and machine shops) for the period before 1903, Rees used the data for individual industries in the *Nineteenth Annual Report of the Commissioner of Labor*. For the two remaining industries (rubber and electrical machinery), the data in that report covered four establishments or fewer and were considered too unreliable to use. Therefore, he used the manufacturing series in these industries before 1903 as well as after.

TABLE Ba4568–4574 Average weekly hours worked in manufacturing and selected other industries: 1890–1926

Contributed by William A. Sundstrom

	Manufacturing					Building trades	
	Total	Union industries	Payroll industries	Bituminous coal mining	Postal employees	Union	Full-time (Wolman)
	Ba4568	Ba4569	Ba4570	Ba4571	Ba4572	Ba4573	Ba4574
Year	Hours	Hours	Hours	Hours	Hours	Hours	Hours
1890	60.0	54.4	62.2	60.0	48.0	51.3	55.2
1891	59.7	54.0	62.1	60.0	48.0	51.0	54.8
1892	59.8	54.0	62.3	60.0	48.0	50.6	54.3
1893	59.7	53.9	62.2	60.0	48.0	50.4	54.2
1894	59.1	53.6	61.7	60.0	48.0	50.5	54.3
1895	59.5	53.5	62.3	60.0	48.0	50.3	54.0
1896	59.2	53.5	62.1	60.0	48.0	50.1	53.8
1897	59.1	53.4	61.9	60.0	48.0	49.8	53.6
1898	59.3	53.4	62.2	52.8	48.0	49.5	53.3
1899	59.1	53.0	62.1	52.7	48.0	48.9	52.6
1900	59.0	53.0	62.1	52.6	48.0	48.3	52.0
1901	58.7	52.4	61.9	52.4	48.0	47.5	51.0
1902	58.3	51.8	61.5	52.3	48.0	46.7	50.2
1903	57.9	51.4	61.2	52.2	48.0	46.3	50.3
1904	57.7	51.1	61.1	51.6	48.0	46.1	—
1905	57.7	51.1	61.1	51.6	48.0	46.1	—
1906	57.3	51.0	60.7	51.6	48.0	45.9	—
1907	57.3	50.8	60.6	51.6	48.0	45.7	—
1908	56.8	50.4	60.3	51.6	48.0	45.6	—
1909	56.8	50.3	60.2	51.6	48.0	45.6	—
1910	56.6	50.1	59.8	51.6	48.0	45.2	—
1911	56.4	49.8	59.6	51.6	48.0	45.0	—
1912	56.0	49.5	59.3	51.6	48.0	45.0	—
1913	55.5	49.2	58.8	51.6	48.0	44.9	—
1914	55.2	48.8	58.3	51.6	48.0	44.7	—
1915	55.0	48.6	58.2	51.6	48.0	44.8	—
1916	54.9	48.0	58.2	51.6	48.0	44.5	—
1917	54.6	47.6	57.9	49.8	48.0	44.4	—
1918	53.6	47.2	56.6	48.7	48.0	44.1	—
1919	52.3	46.2	55.1	48.4	48.0	44.0	—
1920	51.0	45.7	53.5	48.2	48.0	43.8	—
1921	50.7	46.1	52.7	48.2	47.4	43.8	—
1922	51.2	46.2	53.4	48.4	47.4	43.8	—
1923	51.0	46.3	53.0	48.4	47.2	43.9	—
1924	50.4	46.1	52.1	48.5	47.2	43.8	—
1925	50.3	45.9	52.2	48.5	47.2	43.9	—
1926	50.3	45.9	52.2	48.4	47.2	43.8	—

(continued)

TABLE Ba4568–4574 Average weekly hours worked in manufacturing and selected other industries: 1890–1926 *Continued*

Sources

Series Ba4568–4573. Paul H. Douglas, *Real Wages in the United States, 1890–1926* (Houghton Mifflin, 1930).

Series Ba4574. Leo Wolman, *Hours of Work in American Industry,* National Bureau of Economic Research, Bulletin number 71 (1938): 2.

Documentation

The average hours for total manufacturing industries is a weighted average of the hours in what Douglas referred to as "union" and "payroll" manufacturing industries. Since the weight of the union industries in the all-manufacturing average is based on the total number of skilled and semiskilled workers in the industries, the average for total manufacturing probably over-represents union hours.

Beginning in 1907, weekly hours in the so-called union manufacturing industries are weighted averages of trade union scales for occupations. The weights are union membership by crafts. The series are extrapolated back to 1890 by use of payroll data from the sources used for the payroll manufacturing industries.

Average hours in the payroll industries are averages weighted by employment data from employer payrolls given in various U.S. Bureau of Labor Statistics (BLS) Bulletins and in the *Nineteenth Annual Report of the Commissioner of Labor.* Until 1913, the original data are for selected occupations only, and exclude most laborers and some other unskilled workers. Therefore, for 1890–1913, the series are extrapolations backward from the 1914 level.

Differences between the union and payroll series are not necessarily reliable indicators of differences in hours between workers in union and nonunion industries. Because the biases in the union series are probably much greater than those in the payroll series, it may sometimes be desirable to use only the latter to represent all manufacturing.

Douglas's average hours (standard) in bituminous coal mining are estimated from union contracts and their coverage for 1890–1903; after 1903, they are based on data from the U.S. Geological Survey. Average hours for postal employees are based on nominal hours as set by law, adjusted (after 1920) for sick leave. Average hours in the building trades were obtained in the same way as the series for union manufacturing industries, using trade union scales.

Series Ba4574. Figures are Wolman's estimate of average full-time weekly hours in the building trades, based on his reworking of hours data presented in the *Nineteenth Annual Report of the Commissioner of Labor.* His series is the weighted average of hours in nineteen building trades occupations, where the weight for each occupation in each year is the number of employees covered in the survey of that occupation in the year. For the building trades, Wolman expressed the opinion that the hours data in the *Nineteenth Annual Report* were those established by unions, although it can be seen that his hours figures for the building trades are considerably greater than those generated by Douglas from union contracts.

All the hours series in this table should be interpreted as standard or "normal" full-time weekly hours, rather than actual hours worked or paid for.

TABLE Ba4575 Average weekly hours of workers in private, nonagricultural jobs: 1900–1986[1]

Contributed by William A. Sundstrom

Year	Average weekly hours Ba4575 Hours	Year	Average weekly hours Ba4575 Hours	Year	Average weekly hours Ba4575 Hours
1900	58.5	1925	49.0	1950	41.1
1901	58.4	1926	49.3	1951	41.7
1902	58.1	1927	49.1	1952	42.0
1903	57.9	1928	48.8	1953	41.5
1904	57.1	1929	48.7	1954	40.4
1905	57.2	1930	47.1	1955	41.6
1906	57.0	1931	45.6	1956	41.9
1907	56.9	1932	43.7	1957	41.2
1908	55.6	1933	43.3	1958	40.9
1909	55.7	1934	40.6	1959	40.8
1910	55.6	1935	41.7	1960	41.0
1911	55.4	1936	43.4	1961	41.2
1912	55.3	1937	43.1	1962	41.7
1913	55.0	1938	41.6	1966	42.1
1914	54.0	1939	42.1	1969	42.0
1915	53.4	1940	42.5	1972	41.4
1916	53.8	1941	43.3	1975	40.8
1917	53.4	1942	44.3	1976	40.9
1918	52.4	1943	46.8	1977	41.3
1919	50.0	1944	46.9	1978	41.3
1920	50.6	1945	45.6	1981	40.8
1921	48.4	1946	43.3	1984	41.2
1922	48.9	1947	42.4	1986	41.6
1923	49.6	1948	41.7		
1924	48.8	1949	41.0		

TABLE Ba4575 Average weekly hours of workers in private, nonagricultural jobs: 1900–1986 *Continued*

[1] Beginning in 1940, average weekly hours of nonstudent male wage and salary workers in private, nonagricultural jobs, adjusted to exclude vacation and holiday time; for 1900–1939, includes students and women, with no adjustment for paid vacation and holiday time.

Sources

For 1900–1961: John D. Owen, *The Price of Leisure: An Economic Analysis of the Demand for Leisure Time* (Rotterdam University Press, 1969), p. 67; for 1962–1977: John D. Owen, *Working Hours: An Economic Analysis* (Lexington Books, 1979), p. 10; for 1978–1986: John D. Owen, "Work-Time Reduction in the U.S. and Western Europe," *Monthly Labor Review* 111 (12) (1988): 42–3.

Documentation

John Owen's series for 1900–1940 is derived from unpublished materials on employment and worker hours supplied to Owen by John W. Kendrick, who prepared them for his book *Productivity Trends in the United States* (Princeton University Press, 1961). For these years, the series covers wage and salary employees, excluding farm and general government workers. Kendrick's hours data were based on a variety of sources, including the U.S. Bureau of Labor Statistics, various state labor reports, and other establishment-level sources. For some important nonmanufacturing industries, such as wholesale and retail trade, few sources were available, and Kendrick relied on interpolation between a few benchmark years. For this reason, the Kendrick–Owen series does not adequately capture year-to-year fluctuations in hours and is best thought of as indicating longer-run trends in work hours for the nonagricultural economy as a whole.

For the period 1940–1986, Owen used hours data from the decennial Census of Population and the Current Population Survey (CPS). For these years, he estimated the weekly hours of nonstudent males only and adjusted the hours to remove estimated vacation and holiday time. The hours estimates are subject to the same caveats that apply to the standard CPS hours series, Table Ba4597–4607. The earlier and later series overlap in 1940, and Owen linked them by raising the 1900–1940 hours to equal the level of the later series in 1940.

For the years 1940–1956, the average hours of men and women separately were available only for 1940 and 1950. To obtain the hours of males in the other years, Owen used an estimate of the male–female hours differential in each year and employment weights by sex to adjust the overall hours figures. The male–female hours differential was calculated by linear interpolation for the years between 1940 and 1950 and between 1950 and 1956. To calculate the hours of nonstudent males, he used average hours for all males and removed from the average the hours of employed male students, again using employment weights. Work hours of students had to be estimated for some years on the basis of the hours of male students by age at certain benchmarks.

Owen's (1988, p. 43) adjustment for vacation and holiday time is based on estimates derived from the CPS, and it includes an adjustment for the underestimation of holidays due to the time of month when the CPS is conducted. For the 1900–1940 hours estimates, there is no adjustment for vacations and holidays. For the 1941–1977 estimates, Owen used an index of vacation and holiday time constructed to reflect relative changes in such time off since 1940. The adjusted hours for 1978, 1981, 1984, and 1986 presented here use the methodology from Owen (1969, 1979) to extend the adjustment for vacation and holiday time through 1986. Recalculation of these figures was necessary because in his 1988 article, Owen changed his adjustment calculation in a way that was incompatible with estimates in his previous publications. The calculation used here works as follows. First, values of Owen's index for vacation and holiday time are calculated for the years 1978, 1981, and 1984 by using linear interpolation between his index values for 1975, 1980, 1983, and 1986 (see Owen 1988, p. 43). The number of hours represented by one unit of the index number is calculated for the year 1975, for which the unadjusted hours (42.2), adjusted hours (40.8), and index number value (202) are all available. Thus, the number of vacation hours represented by one unit of the index number is $(42.2 - 40.8)/202 = 0.00693$. Finally, hours for other years are adjusted by using that year's index number. For example, in 1978, the unadjusted average hours of nonstudent males was 42.7, and the value of the vacation index was 203.2. Therefore, the adjusted hours are given by $42.7 - 0.00693*203.2 = 41.3$.

Owen's objective in restricting the average hours to male nonstudents during the post-1940 period was to control for changes in the composition of the labor force – in particular, the entry of married women – that would alter work hours. Because of the changes in sources, sample composition, and treatment of vacation and holiday time in 1940, the comparability of Owen's series before and after that date must be questioned. The pre-1940 estimates are more comparable with the later estimates to the extent that the gender composition of the workforce and gender differences in hours of work were fairly constant over the period 1900–1940, and to the extent that the incidence of vacations and holidays did not change much.

TABLE Ba4576–4588 Average weekly hours of production or nonsupervisory workers on private nonagricultural payrolls, by industry: 1909–1997

Contributed by William A. Sundstrom

		Mining			Manufacturing			Transportation and public utilities		Trade			
	Total nonagricultural	Total	Bituminous coal–lignite	Construction	Total	Durable	Nondurable	Total	Class I railroad	Wholesale	Retail	Finance, insurance, and real estate	Services
	Ba4576	Ba4577	Ba4578	Ba4579	Ba4580	Ba4581	Ba4582	Ba4583	Ba4584	Ba4585	Ba4586	Ba4587	Ba4588
Year	Hours	Hours	Hours	Hours	Hours	Hours	Hours	Hours	Hours	Hours	Hours	Hours	Hours
1909	—	—	37.5	—	51.0	—	—	—	—	—	—	—	—
1914	—	—	34.9	—	49.4	—	—	—	—	—	—	—	—
1919	—	—	35.2	—	46.3	—	—	—	—	—	—	—	—
1920	—	—	—	—	47.4	—	—	—	—	—	—	—	—
1921	—	—	—	—	43.1	—	—	—	—	—	—	—	—
1922	—	—	—	—	44.2	—	—	—	—	—	—	—	—
1923	—	—	31.1	—	45.6	—	—	—	—	—	—	—	—
1924	—	—	29.8	—	43.7	—	—	—	—	—	—	—	—
1925	—	—	33.9	—	44.5	—	—	—	—	—	—	—	—
1926	—	—	37.4	—	45.0	—	—	—	—	—	—	—	—
1927	—	—	33.3	—	45.0	—	—	—	—	—	—	—	—
1928	—	—	35.3	—	44.4	—	—	—	—	—	—	—	—
1929	—	—	38.1	—	44.2	—	—	—	—	—	—	—	—

(continued)

TABLE Ba4576–4588 Average weekly hours of production or nonsupervisory workers on private nonagricultural payrolls, by industry: 1909–1997 *Continued*

		Mining			Manufacturing			Transportation and public utilities		Trade			
	Total nonagricultural	Total	Bituminous coal–lignite	Construction	Total	Durable	Nondurable	Total	Class I railroad	Wholesale	Retail	Finance, insurance, and real estate	Services
	Ba4576	Ba4577	Ba4578	Ba4579	Ba4580	Ba4581	Ba4582	Ba4583	Ba4584	Ba4585	Ba4586	Ba4587	Ba4588
Year	Hours	Hours	Hours	Hours	Hours	Hours	Hours	Hours	Hours	Hours	Hours	Hours	Hours
1930	—	—	33.3	—	42.1	—	—	—	—	—	—	—	—
1931	—	—	28.1	—	40.5	—	—	—	—	—	—	—	—
1932	—	—	27.0	—	38.3	32.5	41.9	—	—	—	—	—	—
1933	—	—	29.3	—	38.1	34.7	40.0	—	—	—	—	—	—
1934	—	—	26.8	28.9	34.6	33.8	35.1	—	—	—	—	—	—
1935	—	—	26.2	30.1	36.6	37.2	36.1	—	—	41.6	—	—	—
1936	—	—	28.5	32.8	39.2	40.9	37.7	—	—	42.9	—	—	—
1937	—	—	27.7	33.4	38.6	39.9	37.4	—	—	43.1	—	—	—
1938	—	—	23.3	32.1	35.6	34.9	36.1	—	—	42.3	—	—	—
1939	—	—	26.8	32.6	37.7	37.9	37.4	—	43.7	41.8	43.4	—	—
1940	—	—	27.8	33.1	38.1	39.2	37.0	—	44.3	41.3	43.2	—	—
1941	—	—	30.7	34.8	40.6	42.0	38.9	—	45.8	41.1	42.8	—	—
1942	—	—	32.4	36.4	43.1	45.0	40.3	—	47.0	41.4	41.8	—	—
1943	—	—	36.3	38.4	45.0	46.5	42.5	—	48.7	42.3	40.9	—	—
1944	—	—	43.0	39.6	45.2	46.5	43.1	—	48.9	43.0	41.0	—	—
1945	—	—	42.0	39.0	43.5	44.0	42.3	—	48.5	42.8	40.9	—	—
1946	—	—	41.3	38.1	40.3	40.4	40.5	—	46.0	41.6	41.3	—	—
1947	40.3	40.8	40.3	38.2	40.4	40.5	40.2	—	46.4	41.1	40.3	37.9	—
1948	40.0	39.4	37.7	38.1	40.0	40.4	39.6	—	46.2	41.0	40.2	37.9	—
1949	39.4	36.3	32.3	37.7	39.1	39.4	38.9	—	43.7	40.8	40.4	37.8	—
1950	39.8	37.9	34.7	37.4	40.5	41.1	39.7	—	40.8	40.7	40.4	37.7	—
1951	39.9	38.4	34.9	38.1	40.6	41.5	39.5	—	41.0	40.8	40.4	37.7	—
1952	39.9	38.6	33.8	38.9	40.7	41.5	39.7	—	40.6	40.7	39.8	37.8	—
1953	39.6	38.8	34.1	37.9	40.5	41.2	39.6	—	40.6	40.6	39.1	37.7	—
1954	39.1	38.6	32.3	37.2	39.6	40.1	39.0	—	40.8	40.5	39.2	37.6	—
1955	39.6	40.7	37.3	37.1	40.7	41.3	39.9	—	41.9	40.7	39.0	37.6	—
1956	39.3	40.8	37.5	37.5	40.4	41.0	39.6	—	41.7	40.5	38.6	36.9	—
1957	38.8	40.1	36.3	37.0	39.8	40.3	39.2	—	41.7	40.3	38.1	36.7	—
1958	38.5	38.9	33.3	36.8	39.2	39.5	38.8	—	41.6	40.2	38.1	37.1	—
1959	39.0	40.5	35.8	37.0	40.3	40.7	39.7	—	41.9	40.6	38.2	37.3	—
1960	38.6	40.4	35.8	36.7	39.7	40.1	39.2	—	41.7	40.5	38.0	37.2	—
1961	38.6	40.5	35.9	36.9	39.8	40.3	39.3	—	42.3	40.5	37.6	36.9	—
1962	38.7	41.0	36.7	37.0	40.4	40.9	39.6	—	42.6	40.6	37.4	37.3	—
1963	38.8	41.6	38.6	37.3	40.5	41.1	39.6	—	42.9	40.6	37.3	37.5	—
1964	38.7	41.9	39.0	37.2	40.7	41.4	39.7	41.1	43.5	40.6	37.0	37.3	36.1
1965	38.8	42.3	40.2	37.4	41.2	42.0	40.1	41.3	43.6	40.8	36.6	37.2	35.9
1966	38.6	42.7	40.8	37.6	41.3	42.1	40.2	41.2	43.9	40.7	35.9	37.3	35.5
1967	38.0	42.6	40.8	37.7	40.6	41.2	39.7	40.5	43.2	40.3	35.3	37.0	35.1
1968	37.8	42.6	40.2	37.3	40.7	41.4	39.8	40.6	43.9	40.1	34.7	37.0	34.7
1969	37.7	43.0	39.9	37.9	40.6	41.3	39.7	40.7	44.2	40.2	34.2	37.1	34.7
1970	37.1	42.7	40.7	37.3	39.8	40.3	39.1	40.5	44.2	39.9	33.8	36.7	34.4
1971	36.9	42.4	40.2	37.2	39.9	40.3	39.3	40.1	43.2	39.4	33.7	36.6	33.9
1972	37.0	42.6	40.7	36.5	40.5	41.2	39.7	40.4	43.9	39.4	33.4	36.6	33.9
1973	36.9	42.4	39.7	36.8	40.7	41.4	39.6	40.5	44.5	39.2	33.1	36.6	33.8
1974	36.5	41.9	37.5	36.6	40.0	40.6	39.1	40.2	44.0	38.8	32.7	36.5	33.6
1975	36.1	41.9	39.5	36.4	39.5	39.9	38.8	39.7	43.3	38.6	32.4	36.5	33.5
1976	36.1	42.4	39.8	36.8	40.1	40.6	39.4	39.8	43.7	38.7	32.1	36.4	33.3
1977	36.0	43.4	41.9	36.5	40.3	41.0	39.4	39.9	43.5	38.8	31.6	36.4	33.0
1978	35.8	43.4	40.6	36.8	40.4	41.1	39.4	40.0	43.7	38.8	31.0	36.4	32.8
1979	35.7	43.0	40.7	37.0	40.2	40.8	39.3	39.9	43.9	38.8	30.6	36.2	32.7
1980	35.3	43.3	40.1	37.0	39.7	40.1	39.0	39.6	43.0	38.4	30.2	36.2	32.6
1981	35.2	43.7	40.5	36.9	39.8	40.2	39.2	39.4	43.0	38.5	30.1	36.3	32.6
1982	34.8	42.7	39.9	36.7	38.9	39.3	38.4	39.0	42.1	38.3	29.9	36.2	32.6
1983	35.0	42.5	40.0	37.1	40.1	40.7	39.4	39.0	42.2	38.5	29.8	36.2	32.7
1984	35.2	43.3	40.8	37.8	40.7	41.4	39.7	39.4	43.0	38.5	29.8	36.5	32.6
1985	34.9	43.4	41.2	37.7	40.5	41.2	39.6	39.5	43.6	38.4	29.4	36.4	32.5
1986	34.8	42.2	40.6	37.4	40.7	41.3	39.9	39.2	43.8	38.3	29.2	36.4	32.5
1987	34.8	42.4	42.1	37.8	41.0	41.5	40.2	39.2	43.9	38.1	29.2	36.3	32.5
1988	34.7	42.3	42.2	37.9	41.1	41.8	40.2	38.8	44.9	38.1	29.1	35.9	32.6
1989	34.6	43.0	43.3	37.9	41.0	41.6	40.2	38.9	44.2	38.0	28.9	35.8	32.6

TABLE Ba4576–4588 Average weekly hours of production or nonsupervisory workers on private nonagricultural payrolls, by industry: 1909–1997 *Continued*

		Mining			Manufacturing			Transportation and public utilities		Trade			
	Total nonagricultural	Total	Bituminous coal–lignite	Construction	Total	Durable	Nondurable	Total	Class I railroad	Wholesale	Retail	Finance, insurance, and real estate	Services
	Ba4576	Ba4577	Ba4578	Ba4579	Ba4580	Ba4581	Ba4582	Ba4583	Ba4584	Ba4585	Ba4586	Ba4587	Ba4588
Year	Hours	Hours	Hours	Hours	Hours	Hours	Hours	Hours	Hours	Hours	Hours	Hours	Hours
1990	34.5	44.1	44.0	38.2	40.8	41.3	40.0	38.9	45.2	38.1	28.8	35.8	32.5
1991	34.3	44.4	44.7	38.1	40.7	41.1	40.2	38.7	45.1	38.1	28.6	35.7	32.4
1992	34.4	43.9	44.1	38.0	41.0	41.5	40.4	38.9	44.2	38.2	28.8	35.8	32.5
1993	34.5	44.3	44.6	38.4	41.4	42.1	40.6	38.6	46.2	38.2	28.8	35.8	32.5
1994	34.7	44.8	45.3	38.9	42.0	42.9	40.9	39.7	46.9	38.4	28.9	35.8	32.5
1995	34.5	44.7	45.1	38.9	41.6	42.4	40.5	39.4	46.4	38.3	28.8	35.9	32.4
1996	34.4	45.3	45.9	39.0	41.6	42.4	40.5	39.6	48.0	38.3	28.8	35.9	32.4
1997	34.6	45.4	45.5	38.9	42.0	42.8	40.9	39.7	49.3	38.4	28.9	36.1	32.6

Sources

For 1909–1993: U.S. Bureau of Labor Statistics (BLS), *Employment, Hours, and Earnings, United States, 1909–94*, volumes 1 and 2, Bulletin number 2445 (September 1994), various tables. This source includes hours data for construction beginning in 1947. Hours in construction for the years 1934–1946 are from *Historical Statistics of the United States* (1975), series D878. For 1994–1997: BLS, *Employment and Earnings*, January and March issues.

For more recent data: annual updates in the January and March issues of *Employment and Earnings*.

Documentation

For manufacturing, hours estimates for the years 1909–1931 are based largely on periodic wage and hour surveys conducted by the BLS during that period for a narrow list of manufacturing industries. These figures are an extension of, and are adjusted for comparability with, the figures for 1932–1957. For a discussion of the methods and data used to derive the figures for 1909–1931, see BLS, *Monthly Labor Review* (July 1955): 801–6. The estimates of average weekly hours for 1909–1931 are likely to be understated because the BLS surveys tended to sample large firms more heavily than small firms. For coal mining, hours estimates for 1909–1931 are based on a variety of sources, including special studies by the BLS and data collected by the Bureau of the Census, by the Bureau of Mines, and in reports of state coal commissions.

For 1932–1997, the underlying employment, payroll, and man-hour figures for the various industries were obtained by means of a monthly survey of cooperating establishments (now known as the Current Employment Statistics survey). Responses are to be extracted from actual payroll records. The survey is conducted primarily by mail, but phone collection is used to obtain higher response rates from selected respondents. In 1997, the sample consisted of about 390,000 establishments employing about 48 million nonfarm wage and salary workers. The average weekly hours series are constructed from the following information collected by the survey: (1) the number of production workers or nonsupervisory employees who worked or received pay for any part of the payroll period that includes the twelfth of the month; and (2) total hours paid for these employees, including hours paid for vacations, holidays, sick leave, travel time, lunchtime, and so forth.

The series refer to the hours of production workers in mining and manufacturing, construction workers, and nonsupervisory employees in all other industries. Production workers include working supervisors and all nonsupervisory workers engaged in production and services closely associated with production operations (such as record keeping). Construction workers are defined similarly for the construction industry. Nonsupervisory employees include service-sector workers not above the working supervisory level.

Within each detailed industry, the employment and hours figures for reporting establishments are aggregated, and average weekly hours are computed. The average weekly hours for a group of industries are weighted arithmetic means of the corresponding averages for the industries within the group. The weights used for hours are estimates of aggregate production-worker employment.

Average weekly hours worked or paid for differ from average full-time or standard hours (before payment at overtime-premium rates) and from average hours worked per week. During periods of substantial unemployment, average weekly hours paid for often may be considerably below the full-time level of hours or the level at which premium payments for overtime begin. On the other hand, during periods of relatively full employment, overtime hours tend to raise the average weekly hours above the full-time level.

Until the 1940s, the distinction in most industries between hours paid for and hours actually worked was relatively unimportant. The widespread adoption of paid vacations of increasing length and of an increasing number of paid holidays (and in some industries paid travel time, lunchtime, etc.), however, has raised average weekly hours (which are hours paid for) above average hours worked by increasing amounts. In the coal mines, for example, lunchtime was not paid for in the mines until 1945. Beginning April 1945, mine operators paid for fifteen minutes of lunchtime per day; in July 1947, the lunchtime paid for was increased to one-half hour. Pay for travel time within mines was also initiated during the 1940s. Periodic surveys of hours at work conducted by the BLS since the 1950s make it possible to estimate average weekly hours at work from the hours paid for series. The BLS estimates of the ratio of hours at work to hours paid for are provided in Table Ba4647–4648.

Hours figures for Class I railroads are based on their monthly reports to the U.S. Interstate Commerce Commission. Until 1951, the figures covered all hourly rated employees of Class I railroads, excluding Class I switching and terminal companies. Since 1951, the figures cover all employees (excluding switching and terminal companies) except executives, officials, and staff assistants. Although the figures since 1951 are not strictly comparable with those for earlier years, the difference is not large. For 1939–1955, data are for railroads with operating revenues of $1 million or more; for 1956–1964, $3 million or more; for 1965–1975, $5 million or more; for 1976–1977, $10 million or more; for 1978–1994, $50 million or more; and from 1995 on, 1993 operating revenues of $253.7 million or more. Figures for 1995 and thereafter include Amtrak.

Average weekly hours on Class I railroads equal total man-hours paid for (during a month) reduced to a weekly basis, divided by the full-month count of employees on the payroll. The full-month count generally tends to be somewhat larger than a count for the payroll period that includes the twelfth of the month, which is used for other industries. For this reason, the weekly hours figures tend to be slightly lower than they would be if computed on the latter basis.

TABLE Ba4589–4591 Average weekly hours worked in manufacturing, railroads, and bituminous coal mining: 1900–1957

Contributed by William A. Sundstrom

Year	Manufacturing	Class I steam railroads	Bituminous coal mining
	Ba4589	Ba4590	Ba4591
	Hours	Hours	Hours
1900	55.0	52.3	42.8
1901	54.3	52.0	41.0
1902	55.4	51.3	41.9
1903	54.3	52.3	40.8
1904	53.6	52.7	36.2
1905	54.5	50.6	38.0
1906	55.0	50.4	38.3
1907	54.3	53.7	42.0
1908	50.3	53.9	34.7
1909	53.1	51.5	37.5
1910	52.2	52.3	38.9
1911	51.7	53.1	37.8
1912	52.4	53.1	40.0
1913	50.9	54.8	41.6
1914	50.1	55.6	34.9
1915	50.4	55.1	36.9
1916	51.4	56.0	42.4
1917	51.0	55.2	43.9
1918	49.6	54.3	44.7
1919	46.1	46.8	35.2
1920	48.1	48.0	39.3
1921	45.3	43.8	26.3
1922	47.9	46.1	24.9
1923	48.9	46.2	31.1
1924	46.6	44.9	29.8
1925	47.9	45.0	33.9
1926	47.8	45.1	37.4
1927	47.4	44.7	33.3
1928	47.6	44.6	35.3
1929	48.0	44.8	38.1
1930	43.6	42.9	33.3
1931	40.2	40.7	28.1
1932	38.0	38.5	27.0
1933	37.6	38.4	29.3
1934	34.4	39.7	26.8
1935	36.4	40.2	26.2
1936	38.7	42.1	28.5
1937	37.9	42.1	27.7
1938	35.0	41.3	23.3
1939	37.3	42.1	26.8
1940	37.6	42.5	27.8
1941	40.0	44.0	30.7
1942	42.3	45.2	32.4
1943	44.1	47.2	35.8
1944	44.2	47.1	40.1
1945	42.4	46.4	38.4
1946	39.2	43.8	37.5
1947	39.2	43.8	35.7
1948	38.8	43.7	32.6
1949	38.0	41.0	27.9
1950	38.7	38.1	30.0
1951	38.9	37.9	30.2
1952	38.8	37.4	29.2
1953	38.6	37.1	29.5
1954	37.8	36.4	28.0
1955	38.5	37.1	32.4
1956	38.2	36.9	32.6
1957	37.8	36.5	31.5

Source

Ethel B. Jones, "New Estimates of Hours of Work per Week and Hourly Earnings, 1900–1957," *Review of Economics and Statistics* 45 (4) (1963): 375–85.

Documentation

The annual series of average weekly hours generated by Jones represent an attempt to improve on the standard U.S. Bureau of Labor Statistics (BLS) historical hours series (see Table Ba4576–4588) in three ways. First, Jones attempted to adjust weekly hours to reflect actual hours worked, rather than hours paid for. Second, she extended the annual series back in time to 1900 by linking the BLS series to various other sources. Third, she attempted to correct the BLS data when superior data were available from other sources.

Jones's series for hours in manufacturing for 1947–1957 are from the Census of Manufactures and the Census Bureau's annual survey of manufactures, and represent hours worked rather than hours paid for. The manufacturing hours for 1933–1946 are based on the BLS series but adjusted at benchmark years to hours data from the Census of Manufactures in 1933, 1935, 1937, and 1939. The series for 1920–1932 is based on the year-to-year movements of the National Industrial Conference Board (NICB) hours series (see Table Ba4592–4596). This series is linked to a benchmark level for the year 1929, which is a weighted mean of hours in various industries, drawn largely from NICB and BLS industry surveys. For 1900–1919, the manufacturing hours series is based on estimates by Albert Rees.

A logical way to extend the Jones series for manufacturing beyond 1957 is to use the BLS manufacturing hours, series Ba4580, for subsequent years, multiplied by the ratio of hours worked to hours paid for in manufacturing, series Ba4648.

Jones's series for the railroads – like the BLS railroad series – is derived from reports of the U.S. Interstate Commerce Commission (ICC), but Jones excludes from her estimates "time paid for but not worked," as well as "constructive allowances" for train and engine service employees. The latter includes the paid vacation time of those employees. The ICC reported total hours; Jones converts these to average weekly hours per worker by dividing by an estimate of the average number of workers employed during a week. Prior to 1915, the ICC did not collect information on hours of work, but she was able to construct average weekly hours using information on average days worked per year and an estimate of average daily hours. She claims that scheduled daily hours on the railroads varied little between 1900 and 1915.

The Jones series for mining uses the BLS series up to 1943. After that date, mines began paying workers for hours spent traveling from the mineshaft opening to their place of work within the mine. In addition, bituminous mines began paying workers for their lunch break beginning in 1945. Jones deducts these hours paid for but not worked in order to make the hours series reflect hours at work, defined on a consistent basis before and after the changes in pay policy. The Jones article also includes a series for hours in anthracite coal mining.

TABLE Ba4592–4596 Average weekly hours of production workers in manufacturing, by sex and degree of skill: 1914–1948

Contributed by William A. Sundstrom

		Male			
	All	All	Unskilled	Skilled and semiskilled	Female
	Ba4592	Ba4593	Ba4594	Ba4595	Ba4596
Year	Hours	Hours	Hours	Hours	Hours
1914 [1]	51.5	52.2	52.9	51.7	50.1
1920 [2]	48.2	49.2	49.2	49.4	43.0
1921	45.6	46.0	46.5	45.9	43.2
1922 [3]	49.2	50.0	50.5	49.8	45.0
1923	49.2	50.0	50.3	49.9	45.0
1924	46.9	47.8	48.9	47.5	42.6
1925	48.2	49.0	50.3	48.6	44.1
1926	48.1	49.1	50.2	48.5	43.5
1927	47.7	48.5	49.9	48.1	43.7
1928	47.9	48.8	50.4	48.5	43.4
1929	48.3	49.1	50.2	48.8	44.2
1930	43.9	44.5	45.9	44.0	40.5
1931	40.4	40.4	41.8	39.7	39.8
1932	34.8	34.4	36.4	35.1	36.3
1933	36.4	36.3	37.4	37.1	36.6
1934	34.7	34.8	34.4	35.0	34.0
1935	37.2	37.5	37.0	37.7	35.2
1936	39.5	40.1	40.0	40.1	36.2
1937	38.7	39.3	39.6	39.3	36.1
1938	34.3	34.6	35.5	34.4	32.6
1939	37.6	38.0	38.6	37.9	35.8
1940	38.6	39.2	39.3	39.2	35.5
1941	41.2	41.8	41.4	42.0	38.0
1942	43.0	43.9	43.1	44.3	39.2
1943	45.0	46.2	45.4	46.4	41.1
1944	45.6	46.9	46.0	47.1	41.3
1945	44.2	45.2	44.8	45.2	40.8
1946	40.1	40.4	40.4	40.3	39.0
1947	40.4	40.9	40.9	40.9	38.7
1948 [4]	40.3	40.7	40.7	40.6	38.4

[1] Month of July.

[2] Average of seven months, June–December.

[3] Average of six months, July–December.

[4] Average of seven months, January–July.

Source

National Industrial Conference Board, *The Economic Almanac for 1950* (National Industrial Conference Board, 1950), pp. 336–44.

Documentation

The underlying data were collected by the National Industrial Conference Board (NICB) from a sample of companies representing twenty-five industries (durable and nondurable goods) by means of a monthly mail questionnaire. The number of firms included in the sample, as well as the distribution of these firms by size and geographical location, varied somewhat from time to time. In 1936, the sample included 1,886 firms employing about one third of all wage earners in the twenty-five industries covered and about one fifth of all wage earners in all manufacturing industries. The average firm in the sample (in most of the twenty-five industries) was substantially larger (in terms of employment) than the average firm in the population from which the sample was taken.

Within each industry, average weekly hours were obtained by dividing the total number of hours worked by the total number of wage earners. The averages for all industries taken together were weighted means of the separate industry averages, with fixed employment weights estimated for each industry with the help of the 1923 Census of Manufactures.

The distinction in classification between unskilled males and other male workers was not precisely stated by the NICB, and the classification was made by the reporting firms.

TABLE Ba4597–4607 Average weekly hours worked in nonagricultural industries, by age, sex, and race: 1948–1999[1]

Contributed by William A. Sundstrom

				White			Nonwhite				
	All	Male	Female	All	Male	Female	All	Male	Female	Age 16–19	Age 20 and older
	Ba4597	Ba4598	Ba4599	Ba4600	Ba4601	Ba4602	Ba4603 [2]	Ba4604 [2]	Ba4605 [2]	Ba4606	Ba4607
Year	Hours	Hours	Hours	Hours	Hours	Hours	Hours	Hours	Hours	Hours	Hours
1948	41.6	—	—	—	—	—	—	—	—	—	—
1949	40.9	—	—	—	—	—	—	—	—	—	—
1950	40.7	—	—	—	—	—	—	—	—	—	—
1951	41.3	—	—	—	—	—	—	—	—	—	—
1952	41.6	—	—	—	—	—	—	—	—	—	—
1953	41.1	—	—	—	—	—	—	—	—	—	—
1954	40.0	—	—	—	—	—	—	—	—	—	—
1955	40.9	—	—	—	—	—	—	—	—	—	—
1956	40.8	43.0	36.7	40.3	43.3	34.9	37.3	39.7	33.8	—	—
1957	40.5	42.6	36.4	40.9	42.9	36.7	37.3	39.6	34.1	—	—
1958	40.1	42.2	36.0	40.5	42.5	36.3	36.9	39.1	34.0	—	—
1959	40.0	42.2	35.7	40.4	42.5	36.1	36.8	38.9	33.9	—	—
1960	40.0	42.2	35.6	40.4	42.7	35.9	37.0	39.2	33.8	—	—
1961	40.1	42.5	35.5	40.4	42.8	35.7	37.1	39.5	33.9	—	—
1962	40.1	42.6	35.4	40.4	42.9	35.6	37.1	39.5	33.8	—	—
1963	40.1	42.7	35.2	40.4	43.0	35.4	37.5	39.9	34.0	—	—
1964	39.7	42.3	34.8	40.0	42.6	34.9	37.2	39.6	33.9	—	—
1965	40.2	42.9	35.2	40.4	43.2	35.3	37.8	40.2	34.5	—	—
1966	40.1	42.9	35.2	40.7	43.6	35.3	37.6	39.9	34.4	—	—
1967	40.0	42.8	35.2	40.3	43.1	35.3	37.7	40.1	34.4	28.2	40.9
1968	39.7	42.6	34.8	39.9	42.9	34.9	37.6	39.9	34.5	28.0	40.6
1969	39.5	42.5	34.8	39.8	42.7	34.8	37.5	39.8	34.6	27.7	40.5
1970	38.7	41.6	34.0	38.9	41.9	34.0	37.0	39.2	34.2	27.0	39.7
1971	38.9	41.8	34.2	39.1	42.1	34.2	37.1	39.3	34.3	26.9	40.0
1972	39.0	42.0	34.4	39.3	42.2	34.4	37.2	39.3	34.5	27.4	40.1
1973	39.0	42.0	34.3	39.3	42.3	34.3	37.3	39.3	34.7	28.4	40.1
1974	38.7	41.6	34.2	38.9	41.9	34.1	37.0	39.0	34.6	28.3	39.7
1975	38.4	41.3	34.0	38.6	41.6	34.0	36.7	38.7	34.3	27.0	39.4
1976	38.4	41.4	34.1	38.6	41.6	33.9	37.0	38.9	34.8	27.2	39.3 [3]
1977	38.5	41.6	34.2	38.7	41.9	34.1	37.0	39.0	34.8	27.7	39.5
1978	38.7	41.8	34.4	38.9	42.1	34.3	37.2	39.2	35.0	27.9	39.7
1979	38.6	41.7	34.4	38.8	41.9	34.3	37.3	39.2	35.2	27.9	39.6
1980	38.3	41.2	34.4	38.4	41.4	34.3	37.2	39.0	35.3	27.2	39.2
1981	37.8	40.7	34.1	38.0	41.0	33.9	37.0	38.8	35.1	26.5	38.7
1982	37.7	40.6	34.0	37.9	40.9	33.9	36.8	38.5	35.0	25.2	38.6
1983	38.1	41.0	34.4	38.2	41.2	34.3	37.1	38.8	35.2	25.2	39.0
1984	38.6	41.5	34.9	38.7	41.8	34.8	37.6	39.3	35.7	26.0	39.4
1985	38.9	41.8	35.2	39.0	42.1	35.0	37.9	39.7	36.1	26.0	39.7
1986	38.9	41.9	35.3	39.1	42.2	35.2	37.9	39.5	36.2	25.6	39.8
1987	38.8	41.8	35.3	39.0	42.1	35.1	38.0	39.8	36.2	25.5	39.7
1988	39.3	42.2	35.7	39.4	42.5	35.5	38.4	40.2	36.6	26.0	40.1
1989	39.4	42.4	35.8	39.6	42.7	35.7	—	—	—	25.9	40.2
1990	39.3	42.1	35.8	39.4	42.4	35.7	—	—	—	25.9	40.1
1991	39.1	41.9	35.8	39.2	42.1	35.6	—	—	—	24.7	39.9
1992	38.9	41.6	35.6	38.9	41.8	35.4	—	—	—	24.4	39.5
1993	39.4	42.1	36.0	39.4	42.4	35.8	—	—	—	24.4	40.1
1994	39.1	42.1	35.6	39.2	42.4	35.4	—	—	—	24.7	39.9
1995	39.2	42.2	35.7	39.3	42.5	35.5	—	—	—	25.0	39.9
1996	39.2	42.2	35.7	39.3	42.5	35.5	—	—	—	24.8	40.0
1997	39.4	42.3	36.0	39.5	42.5	35.8	—	—	—	25.0	40.2
1998	39.2	42.2	35.9	39.3	42.4	35.6	—	—	—	25.2	40.0
1999	39.5	42.4	36.2	39.6	42.6	36.0	—	—	—	25.2	40.3

[1] Through 1966, age 14 and older; thereafter, age 16 and older.

[2] Beginning 1983, "nonwhite" refers to blacks only.

[3] 29.3 in the original source (assumed to be in error).

Sources

For 1948–1955: U.S. Bureau of Labor Statistics (BLS), *Labor Force Statistics Derived from the Current Population Survey, 1948–87*, Bulletin number 2307 (August 1988), Table A-23. For 1956–1958: U.S. Bureau of the Census, *Current Population Reports, Labor Force* (series P-57), various issues. For 1959–1999: BLS, *Employment and Earnings*, various issues.

For more recent data: annual updates in the January issue of *Employment and Earnings*.

Documentation

These series are based on data from household interviews conducted by the Current Population Survey (CPS), a sample survey of the population 16 years of age and over. The survey is conducted each month by the Census Bureau for the BLS. The information is collected by trained interviewers from a sample that as of 1996 consisted of about 50,000 households located in 754 sample areas. These areas are chosen to represent all counties and

TABLE Ba4597–4607 Average weekly hours worked in nonagricultural industries, by age, sex, and race: 1948–1999 *Continued*

independent cities in the United States, with coverage in fifty states and the District of Columbia. The data collected are based on the activity or status reported for the calendar week, including the twelfth of the month. The questionnaire and sample design of the CPS have been changed at various points over time; major changes are summarized in the January issue of *Employment and Earnings* each year. These changes do not appear to have had a large impact on the hours of work series.

Hours of work in the CPS data refer to the actual number of hours worked during the survey week, and thus do not include paid time off for holidays, vacation, sick leave, or the like. For persons working in more than one job, the figures relate to the total number of hours worked in all jobs during the week. Average hours worked are calculated only for those workers who report having worked at least one hour during the survey week; the figures thus exclude those individuals who are considered "employed" by the Census but who were absent from their jobs for the entire survey week due to illness, bad weather, vacation (for the entire week), labor-management disputes, or personal reasons. Annual averages are calculated as the arithmetic mean of the twelve monthly average hours figures.

The average weekly hours derived from the household survey (CPS) are not comparable with those derived from the BLS establishment survey, Table Ba4576–4588, for various reasons. First, the household survey covers wage and salary workers (including domestics and other private household workers), self-employed persons, and unpaid workers in family-operated enterprises. The establishment survey covers only production and nonsupervisory workers on the payrolls of nonfarm establishments. Second, in the household survey, all persons with a job, but not at work, are excluded from the hours computations, whereas in the establishment survey, production or nonsupervisory employees on paid vacation, paid holiday, or paid sick leave are included and assigned the number of hours for which they were paid during the reporting period. Finally, the average hours from the household survey are the average hours per worker on all jobs held, whereas the average hours from the establishment survey are the average per job. Thus, workers who hold multiple jobs have their total hours on all jobs counted in the household survey and their separate jobs counted separately in the establishment survey.

The average weekly hours derived from the CPS may be biased upward because of an apparent tendency for individuals to overestimate their hours of work. Time diary studies, in which respondents are asked to assign an activity to each minute of a twenty-four-hour period, suggest that the overestimate of hours may be large and was probably increasing over the period 1965–1985; see John P. Robinson and Ann Bostrom, "The Overestimated Workweek? What Time Diary Measures Suggest," *Monthly Labor Review* 117 (August 1994): 11–23. Thus, care should be taken in using the CPS hours data to infer trends in work hours over that period.

TABLE Ba4608–4613 Average weekly hours worked in nonagricultural industries, by sex and marital status: 1956–1999[1]

Contributed by William A. Sundstrom

	Male			Female		
	Married, spouse present	Widowed, divorced, or separated	Never married	Married, spouse present	Widowed, divorced, or separated	Never married
	Ba4608	Ba4609	Ba4610	Ba4611	Ba4612	Ba4613
Year	Hours	Hours	Hours	Hours	Hours	Hours
1956	44.3	41.4	36.9	36.4	38.4	36.1
1957	44.0	41.1	36.2	36.2	37.9	35.6
1958	43.6	40.7	35.3	35.8	37.7	35.3
1959	43.6	40.6	35.3	35.7	37.5	34.4
1960	43.8	40.6	35.8	35.3	37.5	34.7
1961	44.1	41.1	35.1	35.3	37.6	33.9
1962	44.2	41.4	34.8	35.2	37.8	33.6
1963	44.4	41.6	34.7	35.2	37.5	33.2
1964	44.1	41.3	34.2	35.0	36.9	32.6
1965	44.7	42.1	34.5	35.3	37.5	32.8
1966	44.8	42.2	34.0	35.5	37.7	32.6
1967	44.4	41.7	35.3	35.1	37.2	33.7
1968	44.2	41.2	35.2	34.8	36.7	33.4
1969	44.1	41.4	35.0	34.8	36.7	33.1
1970	43.2	40.9	34.5	34.0	36.4	32.2
1971	43.5	40.9	34.6	34.4	36.5	32.1
1972	43.7	41.3	34.8	34.5	36.5	32.3
1973	43.7	41.6	35.5	34.4	36.5	32.4
1974	43.3	41.4	35.4	34.3	36.2	32.3
1975	43.0	41.1	34.9	34.2	36.2	31.9
1976	43.1	41.5	35.2	34.2	36.3	32.1
1977	43.4	41.6	35.6	34.2	36.3	32.5
1978	43.6	42.1	36.1	34.4	36.7	32.7
1979	43.4	42.1	36.3	34.3	36.7	32.9
1980	42.9	41.7	36.0	34.3	36.9	32.9
1981	42.4	41.4	35.9	33.9	36.5	32.6
1982	42.4	41.2	35.5	33.8	36.5	32.6
1983	42.9	41.4	35.7	34.3	36.9	32.9
1984	43.3	42.0	36.6	34.7	37.3	33.4

Note appears at end of table **(continued)**

TABLE Ba4608–4613 Average weekly hours worked in nonagricultural industries, by sex and marital status: 1956–1999 *Continued*

	Male			Female		
	Married, spouse present	Widowed, divorced, or separated	Never married	Married, spouse present	Widowed, divorced, or separated	Never married
	Ba4608	Ba4609	Ba4610	Ba4611	Ba4612	Ba4613
Year	Hours	Hours	Hours	Hours	Hours	Hours
1985	43.6	42.6	36.9	34.9	37.4	33.9
1986	43.7	42.4	37.0	35.1	37.6	34.0
1987	43.6	42.5	37.0	35.1	37.5	34.0
1988	44.0	42.9	37.6	35.4	38.1	34.4
1989	44.2	43.1	37.8	35.7	38.3	34.4
1990	43.9	42.8	37.6	35.6	38.2	34.4
1991	43.7	42.5	37.3	35.7	38.0	34.1
1992	43.4	42.1	36.9	35.5	37.7	34.0
1993	44.1	42.9	37.2	36.0	38.1	34.2
1994	44.0	42.6	37.6	35.5	37.7	34.0
1995	43.9	42.6	37.9	35.6	37.8	34.1
1996	44.0	42.7	37.7	35.7	37.8	34.0
1997	44.2	42.7	37.9	36.0	38.2	34.3
1998	44.0	42.8	37.8	35.8	38.0	34.2
1999	44.2	42.9	38.1	36.3	38.5	34.5

[1] Through 1966, age 14 and older; thereafter, age 16 and older.

Sources

For 1956–1958: U.S. Bureau of the Census, *Current Population Reports, Labor Force* (series P-57), various issues. For 1959–1999: U.S. Bureau of Labor Statistics, *Employment and Earnings*, various issues.

For more recent data: annual updates in the January issue of *Employment and Earnings*.

Documentation

These series are based on hours data from household interviews conducted by the Current Population Survey. For a discussion of the source, see the text for Table Ba4597–4607.

TABLE Ba4614–4625 Persons at work, by sex, full-time status, and weeks worked during the year: 1950–1996[1]

Contributed by William A. Sundstrom

	Male						Female					
	Usually full-time			Usually part-time			Usually full-time			Usually part-time		
	50–52 weeks	27–49 weeks	1–26 weeks	50–52 weeks	27–49 weeks	1–26 weeks	50–52 weeks	27–49 weeks	1–26 weeks	50–52 weeks	27–49 weeks	1–26 weeks
	Ba4614	Ba4615	Ba4616	Ba4617	Ba4618	Ba4619	Ba4620	Ba4621	Ba4622	Ba4623	Ba4624	Ba4625
Year	Thousand	Thousand	Thousand	Thousand	Thousand	Thousand	Thousand	Thousand	Thousand	Thousand	Thousand	Thousand
1950	29,783	7,624	3,636	1,406	1,004	2,074	8,592	4,171	4,377	1,916	1,210	3,088
1951	30,894	7,518	2,926	1,310	918	1,798	9,248	4,500	4,458	1,834	1,322	3,236
1952	30,878	7,922	3,016	1,178	896	1,814	9,608	4,452	4,418	1,914	1,398	3,018
1953	31,902	7,317	2,840	1,341	1,055	1,691	9,699	4,686	4,088	1,929	1,278	2,856
1954	30,389	7,567	3,448	1,552	1,227	2,135	9,691	4,458	4,506	2,149	1,436	3,239
1955	32,137	7,356	3,331	1,930	1,066	1,814	10,497	4,596	4,674	2,843	1,507	3,612
1956	32,342	7,218	3,144	1,920	1,074	2,206	10,436	4,573	4,724	2,840	1,619	3,756
1957	32,089	7,350	3,447	2,135	1,115	2,573	10,729	4,631	4,628	2,854	1,757	4,356
1958	30,727	7,233	4,091	2,348	1,259	2,721	10,602	4,313	4,708	3,054	1,766	4,293
1959	31,502	7,830	3,665	2,211	1,224	2,541	10,528	4,685	4,794	2,962	1,880	4,340
1960	31,966	7,653	3,857	2,247	1,267	3,043	11,299	4,479	4,899	3,060	2,023	4,825
1961	31,769	7,434	4,264	2,240	1,165	2,984	11,237	4,608	4,906	2,951	1,905	4,826
1962	32,513	7,185	4,289	2,114	1,305	3,233	11,506	4,917	4,857	3,016	2,063	4,999
1963	33,587	6,686	4,021	2,098	1,274	3,373	11,862	4,879	5,132	3,131	2,079	5,105
1964	34,428	6,723	4,162	2,164	1,220	3,281	12,418	4,968	5,126	3,104	2,154	5,376
1965	35,300	6,306	3,946	2,326	1,197	3,344	13,092	4,865	5,188	3,092	2,071	5,459
1966	36,191	5,802	3,916	2,091	1,162	2,546	13,858	4,845	5,528	3,316	2,218	4,793
1967	36,621	6,051	3,986	2,096	1,202	2,436	15,084	4,651	5,516	3,545	2,228	4,763
1968	37,014	6,111	4,188	2,237	1,227	2,535	15,271	5,004	5,678	3,532	2,493	4,940
1969	37,160	6,383	4,207	2,366	1,449	2,825	15,636	4,998	5,769	3,916	2,663	5,105

TABLE Ba4614–4625 Persons at work, by sex, full-time status, and weeks worked during the year: 1950–1996 *Continued*

	Male						Female					
	Usually full-time			Usually part-time			Usually full-time			Usually part-time		
	50–52 weeks	27–49 weeks	1–26 weeks	50–52 weeks	27–49 weeks	1–26 weeks	50–52 weeks	27–49 weeks	1–26 weeks	50–52 weeks	27–49 weeks	1–26 weeks
	Ba4614	Ba4615	Ba4616	Ba4617	Ba4618	Ba4619	Ba4620	Ba4621	Ba4622	Ba4623	Ba4624	Ba4625
Year	Thousand	Thousand	Thousand	Thousand	Thousand	Thousand	Thousand	Thousand	Thousand	Thousand	Thousand	Thousand
1970	36,361	7,176	4,647	2,441	1,455	2,962	15,782	4,982	5,574	3,882	2,911	5,679
1971	37,138	6,942	4,975	2,535	1,577	3,089	16,398	4,760	5,553	4,293	2,879	5,341
1972	38,596	6,808	4,922	2,403	1,532	3,160	17,112	4,886	5,834	4,159	2,802	5,441
1973	39,956	6,736	4,729	2,532	1,639	3,266	17,691	5,163	5,922	4,497	3,199	5,781
1974	38,310	8,056	5,460	2,545	1,877	3,142	17,445	5,566	5,876	4,589	3,685	6,060
1975	37,693	7,908	6,104	2,578	1,772	3,035	17,997	5,317	5,886	5,109	3,619	5,583
1976	38,669	8,014	6,107	2,541	1,796	3,234	18,676	5,627	5,930	5,071	3,884	6,262
1977	39,835	8,239	5,847	2,525	1,910	3,337	19,889	5,914	5,881	5,247	3,937	6,352
1978	41,656	8,005	5,689	2,544	1,913	3,206	21,517	6,038	5,935	5,346	4,201	6,282
1979	42,464	8,259	5,355	2,699	1,999	3,288	22,242	6,645	5,824	5,491	4,293	6,434
1980	41,915	8,284	5,831	2,814	1,901	3,515	23,021	6,182	5,686	6,124	4,127	6,352
1981	41,806	8,338	5,665	2,946	2,085	3,930	23,486	6,098	5,277	6,187	4,512	6,465
1982	40,129	8,334	6,454	3,118	2,375	3,955	23,844	5,772	5,042	6,694	4,318	6,242
1983	41,469	7,645	6,018	3,210	2,018	4,153	25,275	5,399	4,801	7,087	4,188	6,313
1984	43,833	7,549	5,545	3,099	2,065	3,868	26,585	6,021	4,778	6,734	4,305	6,765
1985	44,952	7,757	5,497	3,262	2,152	3,680	27,470	5,858	4,938	6,926	4,401	6,572
1986	45,934	7,668	5,537	3,176	2,117	3,801	28,493	5,954	4,835	7,334	4,334	6,579
1987	47,106	7,489	5,143	3,175	2,165	3,940	29,882	5,788	4,727	7,774	4,301	6,463
1988	48,299	7,329	4,876	3,468	2,198	3,849	31,328	5,546	4,753	7,916	4,425	6,462
1989	48,840	7,622	4,768	3,611	2,253	3,656	31,374	6,623	4,713	7,653	4,731	6,020
1990	48,354	8,151	4,952	3,637	2,320	3,654	31,681	6,565	4,673	7,856	4,688	6,031
1991	47,124	8,308	5,410	3,818	2,342	3,898	32,450	6,168	4,179	8,126	4,661	6,087
1992	47,547	7,955	5,451	3,862	2,349	4,064	33,174	5,621	4,245	8,462	4,487	5,865
1993	49,059	7,297	5,357	3,997	2,134	4,205	33,489	5,736	4,495	8,813	4,632	6,250
1994	50,796	7,075	4,945	3,945	2,356	4,016	34,134	5,956	4,367	8,984	4,597	6,414
1995	51,976	6,970	4,501	4,023	2,255	3,942	35,471	5,995	4,416	8,688	4,573	6,160
1996	53,101	6,877	4,646	4,318	2,135	3,932	36,390	6,105	4,392	9,061	4,507	5,916

[1] Through 1966, age 14 and older; thereafter, age 16 and older.

Sources

For 1950–1986: U.S. Bureau of Labor Statistics (BLS), *Labor Force Statistics Derived from the Current Population Survey, 1948–87,* Bulletin number 2307 (August 1988), Table C-2; for 1987–1996: BLS news releases on "Work Experience of the Population," various dates.

For more recent data: annual data in a BLS news release.

Documentation

Data on weeks worked during the previous calendar year are collected each March in a supplement to the Current Population Survey (CPS). "Full-time" is defined as working thirty-five hours or more per week. In this table, workers are classified as full- or part-time according to their self-reported *usual* weekly hours; this contrasts with the full- and part-time classifications in Table Ba4626–4639, which are based on what the worker reports as her or his *actual* hours worked during the survey week.

Over the years, the CPS has undergone various changes that affect the historical comparability of employment and labor force statistics. For example, the employment figures are estimates based on the CPS sample; the weights used to arrive at the estimates are adjusted periodically to reflect population changes revealed in each decennial census. The impact of these adjustments and other changes in CPS procedures are summarized in the notes accompanying the statistics in the BLS publication *Employment and Earnings*. The adjustments are usually not large relative to the total population, but sometimes they have a more significant impact on the estimates for particular demographic groups. In general, these changes are thought to have smaller effects on ratios derived from the data than on levels. For example, a series of the percentage of workers who worked year-round and full-time would be more comparable from decade to decade than the underlying series on the actual number of such workers.

TABLE Ba4626–4639 Persons at work and working full-time, by age, sex, and race: 1956–1997[1]

Contributed by William A. Sundstrom

	Total		Total		Female		White		Nonwhite		Age 16–19		Age 20 and older	
	At work	Working full-time	At work	Working full-time	At work	Working full-time	At work	Working full-time	At work	Working full-time	At work	Working full-time	At work	Working full-time
	Ba4626	Ba4627	Ba4628	Ba4629	Ba4630	Ba4631	Ba4632	Ba4633	Ba4634 [2]	Ba4635 [2]	Ba4636	Ba4637	Ba4638	Ba4639
Year	Thousand	Thousand	Thousand	Thousand	Thousand	Thousand	Thousand	Thousand	Thousand	Thousand	Thousand	Thousand	Thousand	Thousand
1956	54,808	48,511	—	—	—	—	—	—	—	—	—	—	—	—
1957	55,301	48,617	—	—	—	—	—	—	—	—	—	—	—	—
1958	54,573	47,078	—	—	—	—	—	—	—	—	—	—	—	—
1959	56,090	48,865	—	—	—	—	—	—	—	—	—	—	—	—
1960	57,277	49,542	—	—	—	—	—	—	—	—	—	—	—	—
1961	57,601	49,427	—	—	—	—	—	—	—	—	—	—	—	—
1962	58,656	50,619	—	—	—	—	—	—	—	—	—	—	—	—
1963	59,752	51,440	—	—	—	—	—	—	—	—	—	—	—	—
1964	61,456	52,871	—	—	—	—	—	—	—	—	—	—	—	—
1965	63,358	54,690	—	—	—	—	—	—	—	—	—	—	—	—
1966	65,453	56,348	—	—	—	—	—	—	—	—	—	—	—	—
1967	66,827	56,865	42,170	38,536	24,657	18,331	59,672	51,039	7,156	5,827	5,137	2,553	61,690	54,314
1968	68,044	57,877	42,632	39,066	25,412	18,810	60,781	51,858	7,263	6,019	5,218	2,553	62,826	55,322
1969	70,018	59,181	43,387	39,541	26,631	19,640	62,502	52,954	7,516	6,228	5,571	2,653	64,447	56,528
1970	70,684	59,101	43,579	39,453	27,105	19,650	63,112	52,888	7,572	6,213	5,566	2,548	65,117	56,555
1971	71,146	59,203	43,922	39,651	27,224	19,553	63,607	53,000	7,539	6,203	5,590	2,469	65,556	56,734
1972	73,662	61,317	45,278	40,878	28,384	20,439	65,868	54,895	7,794	6,424	6,117	2,768	67,545	58,548
1973	76,182	63,560	46,544	42,183	29,639	21,377	67,931	56,669	8,251	6,891	6,610	3,201	69,572	60,358
1974	77,282	64,083	46,783	42,185	30,499	21,898	68,855	57,132	8,427	6,951	6,711	3,226	70,571	60,856
1975	76,396	62,325	45,708	40,663	30,688	21,663	68,168	55,689	8,227	6,634	6,359	2,757	70,036	59,567
1976	79,024	64,810	46,945	41,983	32,079	22,827	70,429	57,741	8,595	7,068	6,608	2,883	72,417	61,929
1977	81,999	67,263	48,365	43,247	33,633	24,015	73,047	59,872	8,951	7,390	6,975	3,118	75,024	64,146
1978	85,693	70,543	49,954	44,857	35,738	25,686	76,096	62,600	9,597	7,943	7,328	3,333	78,365	67,210
1979	88,133	72,647	50,947	45,811	37,186	26,835	78,184	64,353	9,950	8,294	7,338	3,359	80,795	69,287
1980	88,325	72,022	50,394	44,774	37,931	27,248	78,377	63,810	9,948	8,213	6,956	2,963	81,370	69,060
1981	89,445	72,732	50,714	45,052	38,730	27,677	79,381	64,414	10,063	8,316	6,503	2,635	82,941	70,095
1982	90,552	72,245	50,757	44,323	39,795	27,922	79,887	63,595	10,665	8,650	5,937	2,117	84,615	70,128
1983	92,038	73,624	51,396	44,948	40,642	28,675	81,023	64,706	8,620	6,961	5,817	2,029	86,221	71,595
1984	96,246	78,030	53,779	47,529	42,467	30,499	84,315	68,281	9,356	7,616	5,939	2,171	90,307	75,859
1985	98,303	79,931	54,599	48,383	43,704	31,549	85,857	69,713	9,711	7,951	5,914	2,181	92,389	77,751
1986	100,821	81,974	55,655	49,238	45,166	32,736	87,806	71,246	10,073	8,284	6,008	2,095	94,813	79,878
1987	103,448	84,398	56,823	50,359	46,625	34,039	89,787	73,052	10,517	8,718	6,161	2,145	97,287	82,253
1988	106,101	86,627	58,063	51,448	48,038	35,180	91,929	74,881	10,869	9,022	6,319	2,258	99,783	84,370
1989	108,101	88,482	58,948	52,398	49,153	36,084	93,380	76,237	11,143	9,279	6,270	2,261	101,831	86,220
1990	108,697	89,081	59,146	52,484	49,551	36,598	93,886	76,697	11,184	9,358	5,791	2,031	102,906	87,050
1991	107,865	87,513	58,366	51,264	49,499	36,248	93,032	75,238	11,094	9,194	5,210	1,625	102,655	85,888
1992	108,457	88,012	58,562	51,326	49,895	36,687	93,383	75,604	11,142	9,194	4,987	1,511	103,470	86,502
1993	110,340	89,597	59,568	52,218	50,772	37,379	94,835	76,814	11,408	9,428	5,134	1,541	105,206	88,056
1994	114,233	92,812	61,536	54,266	52,697	38,546	97,375	78,832	12,131	10,090	5,692	1,751	108,541	91,060
1995	116,071	94,700	62,530	55,408	53,541	39,291	98,653	80,106	12,621	10,629	5,906	1,885	110,166	92,815
1996	117,678	96,405	63,274	56,185	54,404	40,220	99,745	81,325	12,836	10,845	5,986	1,908	111,693	94,497
1997	120,770	91,021	64,821	53,683	55,949	37,338	102,063	76,478	13,247	10,287	6,183	1,790	114,587	89,231

TABLE Ba4626–4639 Persons at work and working full-time, by age, sex, and race: 1956–1997 *Continued*

[1] Through 1966, age 14 and older; thereafter, age 16 and older.

[2] Beginning 1983, "nonwhite" refers to blacks only.

Sources

For 1956–1958: U.S. Bureau of the Census, *Current Population Reports, Labor Force* (series P-57), various issues. For 1959–1997: U.S. Bureau of Labor Statistics, *Employment and Earnings*, various issues.

For more recent data: annual updates in the January issue of *Employment and Earnings*.

Documentation

These series are based on the distribution of reported weekly hours at work from the Current Population Survey (CPS). For a discussion of hours data from the CPS, see the text for Table Ba4597–4607. Full-time is defined as having worked thirty-five hours or more during the survey week. Hours of work refer to the actual number of hours worked during the week, and thus do not include paid time off for holidays, vacation, sick leave, or the like. Consequently, the designation "full-time" is not necessarily indicative of an individual worker's "usual" work schedule. For persons working at more than one job, the weekly hours are the total number of hours worked in all jobs during the week. Thus, a person working two part-time jobs of twenty hours each would be counted as working full-time.

Over the years, the CPS has undergone various changes that affect the historical comparability of employment and labor force statistics. For example, the employment figures presented here are estimates based on the CPS sample; the weights used to arrive at the estimates are adjusted periodically to reflect population changes revealed in each decennial census. The impact of these adjustments and other changes in CPS procedures are summarized in the notes accompanying the statistics in the BLS publication *Employment and Earnings*. The adjustments are usually not large relative to the total population, but sometimes they have a more significant impact on the estimates for particular demographic groups. In general, these changes are thought to have smaller effects on ratios derived from the data than on levels. For example, a series of the percentage of workers who worked full-time would be more comparable from decade to decade than the underlying series on the actual number of such workers.

TABLE Ba4640 Average weekly overtime hours of production workers in manufacturing: 1956–1999

Contributed by William A. Sundstrom

	Average weekly overtime hours		Average weekly overtime hours		Average weekly overtime hours
	Ba4640		Ba4640		Ba4640
Year	Hours	Year	Hours	Year	Hours
1956	2.8	1970	3.0	1985	3.3
1957	2.3	1971	2.9	1986	3.4
1958	2.0	1972	3.5	1987	3.7
1959	2.7	1973	3.8	1988	3.9
1960	2.5	1974	3.3	1989	3.8
1961	2.4	1975	2.6	1990	3.6
1962	2.8	1976	3.1	1991	3.6
1963	2.8	1977	3.5	1992	3.8
1964	3.1	1978	3.6	1993	4.1
1965	3.6	1979	3.3	1994	4.7
1966	3.9	1980	2.8	1995	4.4
1967	3.4	1981	2.8	1996	4.5
1968	3.6	1982	2.3	1997	4.8
1969	3.6	1983	3.0	1998	4.6
		1984	3.4	1999	4.6

Source

U.S. Bureau of Labor Statistics (BLS) Internet site, series ID EEU30000007, August 4, 2000.

Documentation

Data on overtime hours per week in manufacturing are collected by the BLS's monthly Current Employment Statistics survey of business establishments. See the text for Table Ba4576–4588 for more details on the survey.

Production workers include working supervisors and all nonsupervisory workers (including group leaders and trainees) engaged in fabricating, processing, assembling, inspecting, receiving, storing, handling, packing, warehousing, shipping, trucking, hauling, maintenance, repair, janitorial, guard services, product development, auxiliary production for a plant's own use (for example, power plant), record keeping, and other services closely associated with the aforementioned production operations.

Overtime hours are hours worked by production or related workers for which overtime premiums were paid because the hours were in excess of the number of hours of either the straight-time workday or the workweek during the pay period that included the twelfth of the month. Weekend and holiday hours are included only if overtime premiums were paid. Hours for which only shift differential, hazard, incentive, or other similar types of premiums were paid are excluded.

TABLE Ba4641–4646 Time spent at paid work, by sex and employment status: 1965–1985

Contributed by Susan B. Carter

	Women			Men		
	All	Employed	Nonemployed	All	Employed	Nonemployed
	Ba4641	Ba4642	Ba4643	Ba4644	Ba4645	Ba4646
Year	Hours	Hours	Hours	Hours	Hours	Hours
1965	17.5	36.8	2.0	43.0	46.5	10.5
1975	17.8	35.8	3.0	37.8	42.9	8.7
1985	20.3	30.8	3.8	33.6	39.7	10.6

Source

John P. Robinson and Geoffrey Godbey, *Time for Life: The Surprising Ways Americans Use Their Time* (Pennsylvania State University Press, 1997), Table 2, p. 95.

Documentation

These estimates of time spent at paid work were derived from time diaries collected from a scientifically selected, representative sample of adults ages 18–64. These individuals were asked to focus on a single day and to describe the day's activities in their own words, recording the time the activity was begun and the time it was ended.

Time spent at paid work includes coffee breaks and second jobs but excludes the work commute, lunch breaks, and paid vacations.

The "employed" are defined as those "working 20 hours or more, the cutoff used in certain government analyses to define the respondent as employed" (Robinson and Godbey 1997, p. 90).

TABLE Ba4647–4648 Ratio of hours at work to hours paid: 1959–1998[1]

Contributed by William A. Sundstrom

	Nonfarm	Manufacturing
	Ba4647	Ba4648
Year	Ratio	Ratio
1959	—	0.938
1960	—	0.938
1961	—	0.938
1962	—	0.937
1963	—	0.937
1964	—	0.937
1965	—	0.936
1966	0.953	0.936
1967	0.950	0.932
1968	0.948	0.928
1969	0.946	0.924
1970	0.944	0.921
1971	0.945	0.922
1972	0.945	0.926
1973	0.942	0.922
1974	0.939	0.918
1975	0.938	0.917
1976	0.937	0.916
1977	0.935	0.915
1978	0.935	0.914
1979	0.934	0.913
1980	0.934	0.912
1981	0.924	0.912
1982	0.936	0.908
1983	0.930	0.914
1984	0.939	0.914
1985	0.932	0.916
1986	0.925	0.912
1987	0.930	0.910
1988	0.931	0.918
1989	0.938	0.920
1990	0.935	0.918
1991	0.930	0.913
1992	0.931	0.916
1993	0.933	0.919
1994	0.933	0.918
1995	0.938	0.918
1996	0.932	0.918
1997	0.934	0.917
1998	0.934	0.912

[1] Before 1981, ratios are for all employees; thereafter, for production and nonsupervisory workers.

Sources

For 1959–1980: Mary Jablonski, Kent Kunze, et al., "Hours at Work: A New Base for BLS Productivity Statistics," *Monthly Labor Review* 113 (2) (1990), Table 5. For 1981–1995: U.S. Bureau of Labor Statistics (BLS), Office of Productivity and Technology, "1995 Hours at Work Survey" (December 1996), Table 1; for 1996–1998: BLS, Office of Productivity and Technology, "2000 Hours at Work Survey" (December 2001), Table 1.

For more recent data: The Hours at Work Survey is conducted annually. Summary reports can be found at the BLS Internet Site.

Documentation

Data on average weekly hours collected by the BLS Current Employment Statistics program (see Table Ba4576–4588) represent hours paid. Hours paid include paid leave for holidays, vacations, and sick and personal, or administrative, leave (for example, personal business, funeral leave, and jury duty). These forms of paid leave represent time not devoted to production. Hours at work exclude paid leave while hours paid do not.

Since 1982, the BLS has conducted an annual Hours at Work Survey of a stratified random sample of establishments in the unemployment insurance reporting system. Stratification is both by industry and by number of employees at the establishment. During the first six years of the survey, approximately 4,500 establishments were sampled. The sample size has increased somewhat since then, but the response rate dropped during 1995 and 1996, increasing the sampling error associated with the ratios. The surveyed establishments are asked to provide annual and quarterly data on hours at work and hours paid for the previous year. The survey defines hours at work as time spent actually working, as well as short rest periods, coffee breaks, standby and down time, travel time from job site to job site within the working day, and the like.

TABLE Ba4647–4648 Ratio of hours at work to hours paid: 1959–1998 *Continued*

The historical series for years prior to 1981 were constructed from two earlier BLS surveys that collected information on hours paid and hours of paid leave: the Survey of Employer Expenditures for Selected Supplementary Compensation Practices for Production and Related Workers in Manufacturing Industries (conducted in 1959 and 1962) and the Survey of Employer Expenditures for Employee Compensation (conducted biennially from 1966 to 1974 and in 1977). Linear interpolation was used to fill gaps in the coverage (see Jablonski, Kunze, et al. 1990, pp. 21–2). Mary Jablonski, Kent Kunze, and their colleagues also extended both series back to 1947 by assuming that the industry-specific ratios were constant prior to the date of the first survey – as there was no justification for assuming the ratios were constant, these earlier numbers have not been included in the series here. The historical estimates are for all employees, whereas the series for 1981 on are for production and nonsupervisory workers. Comparison of the two series, where they overlap during the 1980s, reveals that the ratios for all employees and for production and nonsupervisory workers are very similar.

The ratios in this table can be used to obtain estimates of average weekly hours spent at work by multiplying the relevant hours series from Table Ba4576–4588 by the associated ratio of hours at work to hours paid. For example, for the entire nonfarm business sector, an estimate of average weekly hours worked is obtained by multiplying together series Ba4576 and Ba4647.

TABLE Ba4649–4655 Persons employed but not at work, by cause of absence: 1976–1999

Contributed by William A. Sundstrom

		Persons employed but not at work					
			Cause				
	Persons employed	Total	Own illness	Vacation	Bad weather	Labor dispute	Other reasons
	Ba4649	Ba4650	Ba4651	Ba4652	Ba4653	Ba4654	Ba4655
Year	Thousand	Thousand	Thousand	Thousand	Thousand	Thousand	Thousand
1976	88,752	5,367	1,401	2,930	100	116	820
1977	92,017	5,519	1,426	2,951	237	120	786
1978	96,048	5,572	1,436	2,985	237	100	815
1979	98,824	5,747	1,420	3,191	198	123	816
1980	99,303	5,881	1,426	3,320	155	105	876
1981	100,397	5,790	1,413	3,247	112	64	953
1982	99,526	5,712	1,331	3,153	202	36	988
1983	100,834	5,563	1,291	3,096	124	91	962
1984	105,005	5,575	1,322	3,147	118	40	947
1985	107,150	5,789	1,308	3,338	141	42	960
1986	109,597	5,741	1,292	3,234	128	56	1,030
1987	112,440	5,910	1,320	3,421	92	34	1,043
1988	114,968	5,831	1,364	3,236	122	30	1,080
1989	117,342	6,170	1,405	3,437	133	63	1,132
1990	118,793	6,160	1,341	3,529	90	24	1,177
1991	117,718	5,915	1,305	3,291	119	17	1,182
1992	118,492	6,088	1,259	3,409	128	19	1,272
1993	120,259	6,041	1,295	3,328	153	24	1,241
1994	123,060	5,619	1,184	2,877	165	15	1,378
1995	124,900	5,582	1,084	2,982	122	21	1,372
1996	126,708	5,768	1,090	3,085	256	11	1,325
1997	129,558	5,555	1,114	2,942	146	20	1,333
1998	131,463	5,586	1,095	3,033	130	10	1,318
1999	133,488	5,407	1,096	2,899	104	7	1,301

Sources

U.S. Bureau of Labor Statistics (BLS) Internet site, July 31, 2000. For series Ba4649: see the sources for series Ba481. Series Ba4650–4655 are from the following BLS series: LFU14000000, LFU14010000, LFU14020000, LFU14030000, LFU14040000, and LFU14050000, respectively.

Documentation

These data are collected monthly in the Current Population Survey (CPS). Annual figures are averages of the monthly figures. Data are for employed civilians age 16 and older.

Individuals are counted as employed if, during the CPS reference week, they: (a) did any work at all (at least one hour) as paid employees, worked in their own business, profession, or on their own farm, or worked fifteen hours or more as unpaid workers in an enterprise operated by a member of the family; or (b) were not working but had jobs or businesses from which they were temporarily absent because of vacation, illness, bad weather, child care problems, maternity or paternity leave, labor-management dispute, job training, or other family or personal reasons, whether or not they were paid for the time off or were seeking other jobs. The persons in the latter category (b) are considered to be employed but not at work. Only those who do not work for the entire week are counted as not at work; workers who are absent only part of the week but work some hours are counted as employed and at work. Consequently, the figures given in this table underestimate the total number of workers who experience an absence from work during a given week.

Series Ba4649. Equals series Ba481.

TABLE Ba4656–4667 Median job duration for employed persons, by age and sex: 1951–1998

Contributed by William A. Sundstrom

	Both sexes				Males				Females			
	Age, 25–34	Age, 35–44	Age, 45–54	Age, 55–64	Age, 25–34	Age, 35–44	Age, 45–54	Age, 55–64	Age, 25–34	Age, 35–44	Age, 45–54	Age, 55–64
	Ba4656	Ba4657	Ba4658	Ba4659	Ba4660	Ba4661	Ba4662	Ba4663	Ba4664	Ba4665	Ba4666	Ba4667
Year	Years	Years	Years	Years	Years	Years	Years	Years	Years	Years	Years	Years
1951	2.6	3.2	6.3	8.0	2.8	4.5	7.6	9.3	1.8	3.1	4.0	4.5
1963	3.0	6.0	9.0	11.8	3.5	7.6	11.4	14.7	2.0	3.6	6.1	7.8
1966	2.7	6.0	8.8	13.0	3.2	7.8	11.5	15.8	1.9	3.5	5.1	9.0
1968	2.5	5.2	8.6	12.3	2.8	6.9	10.2	14.8	1.6	2.9	5.1	8.7
1973	2.8	5.2	8.4	11.4	3.1	6.5	11.3	14.4	2.2	3.4	5.7	8.5
1978	2.5	4.9	8.3	11.1	2.8	6.8	11.1	14.6	2.0	3.3	5.8	8.6
1979	2.8	5.4	9.7	12.7	3.3	7.6	12.5	15.8	2.2	3.3	6.4	9.6
1981	3.1	5.1	9.1	12.1	3.1	7.1	11.1	15.1	3.0	4.1	6.1	10.1
1983	3.0	5.3	9.7	13.0	3.3	7.3	12.7	16.4	2.7	4.1	6.4	9.9
1987	3.0	5.6	9.2	12.2	3.2	7.1	11.8	15.1	2.6	4.4	6.9	9.9
1991	3.0	5.5	9.5	11.9	3.2	6.8	11.6	15.0	2.7	4.5	6.8	9.8
1993	3.2	5.8	9.5	12.4	3.5	6.9	11.7	14.0	3.0	5.0	7.6	10.3
1996	2.8	5.3	8.3	10.2	3.0	6.1	10.1	10.5	2.7	4.8	7.0	10.0
1998	2.7	5.0	8.1	10.1	2.8	5.5	9.4	11.2	2.5	4.5	7.2	9.6

Sources

For 1951–1993: Henry S. Farber, "Are Lifetime Jobs Disappearing? Job Duration in the United States, 1973–1993," in John Haltiwanger, Marilyn E. Manser, and Robert Topel, editors, *Labor Statistics Measurement Issues*, volume 60, National Bureau of Economic Research, Studies in Income and Wealth (University of Chicago Press, 1998), Table 5A.1, pp. 157–206. For 1996: U.S. Bureau of Labor Statistics (BLS), "Employee Tenure in the Mid-1990s," U.S. Department of Labor press release USDL 97-25 (January 30, 1997), Table 1. For 1998: BLS, "Employee Tenure in 1998," U.S. Department of Labor press release USDL 98-387 (September 23, 1998), Table 1.

Documentation

Job duration refers to the length of time workers have been continuously employed by their current employer. The data underlying the estimates in Tables Ba4656–4681 were collected at irregular intervals by the U.S. Bureau of the Census as part of its Current Population Survey (CPS). The figures for 1951–1968 are taken directly from BLS publications and are reproduced in the article by Henry Farber (1998). The figures for 1973–1993 are calculated by Farber from samples drawn from the CPS. The figures for 1996–1998 are taken directly from BLS press releases.

For the years 1951–1981 (except 1979), the CPS survey asked workers what year they started working at their present job. For 1979, 1983, and later, the survey asked workers how many years they had worked for their current employer. Until 1996, job durations longer than one year were coded to the nearest integer year. Beginning in 1996, workers who responded "1 year" or "2 years" were asked a follow-up question to obtain the exact number of months, and partial years were coded. In calculating the median job duration from integer responses (pre-1996), some assumption must be made about the rounding rule respondents used in answering the question. For details on his treatment of this issue, see Farber (1998), pp. 160–1.

The change in the wording of the survey question between the 1970s and 1980s creates two potential sources of noncomparability. First, for the earlier surveys, workers may have interpreted the question as referring to how long they had been at their present position (occupation), rather than with their present employer. Thus, a worker who had been with the same employer for ten years but had been promoted to a new position one year before the survey might have given a job duration of either ten years or one year, depending on her or his interpretation of the meaning of "job." This ambiguity is eliminated in the later surveys. A second problem is that individual responses tend to heap on "round numbers," such as the year 1980 (as opposed to 1981) or the job duration ten years (as opposed to eleven); see Farber (1998), p. 160. This heaping will have different effects, depending on which way the job-duration question is asked. For these reasons, changes in measured job tenure before and after 1981 should be treated with caution.

TABLE Ba4668–4675 Percentage of employed persons with job duration of one year or less, by age and sex: 1973–1998

Contributed by William A. Sundstrom

	Males				Females			
	Age, 25–34	Age, 35–44	Age, 45–54	Age, 55–64	Age, 25–34	Age, 35–44	Age, 45–54	Age, 55–64
	Ba4668	Ba4669	Ba4670	Ba4671	Ba4672	Ba4673	Ba4674	Ba4675
Year	Percent	Percent	Percent	Percent	Percent	Percent	Percent	Percent
1973	24.9	13.7	9.7	7.0	32.8	22.3	13.7	9.6
1978	28.3	16.6	11.0	9.5	35.1	25.9	17.6	12.3
1979	30.9	17.3	11.3	8.9	39.8	30.1	19.0	13.1
1981	26.7	17.2	11.1	9.4	34.5	23.7	16.7	11.2
1983	27.6	16.8	11.2	8.9	33.1	24.2	15.5	10.8
1987	28.2	17.4	12.7	9.6	34.3	24.5	17.2	12.1
1991	28.0	16.7	12.9	10.6	33.1	22.9	16.4	12.2
1993	26.8	16.1	13.0	9.9	29.4	20.7	13.7	10.0
1996	28.2	16.3	11.9	10.3	30.9	19.6	14.1	11.0
1998	30.6	19.2	14.3	11.3	32.2	21.9	15.2	11.9

Sources

For 1973–1993: Henry S. Farber, "Are Lifetime Jobs Disappearing? Job Duration in the United States, 1973–1993," in John Haltiwanger, Marilyn E. Manser, and Robert Topel, editors, *Labor Statistics Measurement Issues*, National Bureau of Economic Research, Studies in Income and Wealth, volume 60 (University of Chicago Press, 1998), Table 5A.5, pp. 157–206. For 1996: U.S. Bureau of Labor Statistics (BLS), "Employee Tenure in the Mid-1990s," U.S. Department of Labor press release USDL 97-25 (January 30, 1997), Table 3. For 1998: BLS, "Employee Tenure in 1998," U.S. Department of Labor press release USDL 98-387 (September 23, 1998), Table 3.

Documentation

See the text for Table Ba4656–4667.

TABLE Ba4676–4681 Percentage of employed persons with job duration of more than twenty years, by age and sex: 1973–1998

Contributed by William A. Sundstrom

	Males			Females		
	Age, 35–44	Age, 45–54	Age, 55–64	Age, 35–44	Age, 45–54	Age, 55–64
	Ba4676	Ba4677	Ba4678	Ba4679	Ba4680	Ba4681
Year	Percent	Percent	Percent	Percent	Percent	Percent
1973	6.0	28.3	38.8	3.3	9.7	17.7
1978	5.7	28.8	39.8	2.1	9.0	18.3
1979	4.3	29.6	41.0	1.8	9.7	18.1
1981	5.8	27.1	39.4	2.2	9.6	18.3
1983	4.1	27.9	40.3	1.6	7.8	17.2
1987	3.9	25.6	36.5	1.3	8.1	16.4
1991	4.7	26.8	36.7	2.8	10.6	19.4
1993	4.1	27.1	36.0	3.0	13.2	19.1
1996 [1]	7.1	29.3	34.4	4.4	15.2	23.1
1998 [1]	6.8	27.5	35.8	4.2	15.8	21.6

[1] Refers to percentage with job duration of twenty years or more.

Sources

For 1973–1993: Henry S. Farber, "Are Lifetime Jobs Disappearing? Job Duration in the United States, 1973–1993," in John Haltiwanger, Marilyn E. Manser, and Robert Topel, editors, *Labor Statistics Measurement Issues*, National Bureau of Economic Research, Studies in Income and Wealth, volume 60 (University of Chicago Press, 1998), Table 5A.7, pp. 157–206. For 1996: U.S. Bureau of Labor Statistics (BLS), "Employee Tenure in the Mid-1990s," U.S. Department of Labor press release USDL 97-25 (January 30, 1997), Table 3. For 1998: BLS, "Employee Tenure in 1998," U.S. Department of Labor press release USDL 98-387 (September 23, 1998), Table 3.

Documentation

See the text for Table Ba4656–4667.

TABLE Ba4682–4686 Monthly turnover rates in manufacturing, by type of turnover: 1910–1981[1,2,3]

Contributed by William A. Sundstrom

Year	Accession (hire) rate	Rate of new hires	Separation rate	Quit rate	Layoff rate
	Ba4682	Ba4683	Ba4684	Ba4685 [4]	Ba4686
	Per 100	Per 100	Per 100	Per 100	Per 100
1910	8.8	—	8.4	—	—
1911	7.1	—	7.4	—	—
1912	9.3	—	8.1	—	—
1913	11.3	—	11.2	—	—
1914 [5]	6.7	—	7.3	—	—
1915	6.4	—	5.2	—	—
1916	11.5	—	8.9	—	—
1917	11.4	—	10.8	—	—
1918 [5]	14.5	—	12.6	—	—
1919	10.1	—	7.5	5.8	0.6
1920	10.1	—	10.3	8.4	0.8
1921	2.8	—	4.4	2.2	1.8
1922	8.0	—	5.3	4.2	0.4
1923	9.0	—	7.5	6.2	0.3
1924	3.3	—	3.8	2.7	0.6
1925	5.2	—	4.0	3.1	0.4
1926	4.5	—	3.9	2.9	0.5
1927	3.3	—	3.3	2.1	0.7
1928	3.7	—	3.1	2.2	0.5
1929	4.4	—	3.8	2.7	0.6
1930	3.8	—	5.9	1.9	3.6
1931	3.7	—	4.8	1.1	3.5
1932	4.1	—	5.2	0.9	4.2
1933	6.5	—	4.5	1.1	3.2
1934	5.7	—	4.9	1.1	3.7
1935	5.1	—	4.3	1.1	3.0
1936	5.3	—	4.0	1.3	2.4
1937	4.3	—	5.2	1.5	3.5
1938	4.7	—	4.8	0.8	3.9
1939	5.0	—	3.7	1.0	2.6
1940	5.4	—	4.0	1.1	2.6
1941	6.5	—	4.7	2.4	1.6
1942	9.3	—	7.8	4.6	1.3
1943	9.1	—	8.6	6.3	0.7
1944	7.4	—	8.1	6.2	0.7
1945	7.7	—	9.6	6.1	2.6
1946	8.1	—	7.2	5.2	1.4
1947	6.2	—	5.7	4.1	1.1
1948	5.4	—	5.4	3.4	1.6
1949	4.3	—	5.0	1.9	2.9
1950	5.3	—	4.1	2.3	1.3
1951	5.3	4.1	5.3	2.9	1.4
1952	5.4	4.1	4.9	2.8	1.4
1953	4.8	3.6	5.1	2.8	1.6
1954	3.6	1.9	4.1	1.4	2.3
1955	4.5	3.0	3.9	1.9	1.5
1956	4.2	2.8	4.2	1.9	1.7
1957	3.6	2.2	4.2	1.6	2.1
1958	3.6	1.7	4.1	1.1	2.6
1959	4.2	2.6	4.1	1.5	2.0
1960	3.8	2.2	4.3	1.3	2.4
1961	4.1	2.2	4.0	1.2	2.2
1962	4.1	2.5	4.1	1.4	2.0
1963	3.9	2.4	3.9	1.4	1.8
1964	4.0	2.6	3.9	1.5	1.7
1965	4.3	3.1	4.1	1.9	1.4
1966	5.0	3.8	4.6	2.6	1.2
1967	4.4	3.3	4.6	2.3	1.4
1968	4.6	3.5	4.6	2.5	1.2
1969	4.7	3.7	4.9	2.7	1.2

Notes appear at end of table

TABLE Ba4682–4686 Monthly turnover rates in manufacturing, by type of turnover: 1910–1981 *Continued*

	Accession (hire) rate	Rate of new hires	Separation rate	Quit rate	Layoff rate
	Ba4682	Ba4683	Ba4684	Ba4685 [4]	Ba4686
Year	Per 100	Per 100	Per 100	Per 100	Per 100
1970	4.0	2.8	4.8	2.1	1.8
1971	3.9	2.6	4.2	1.8	1.6
1972	4.5	3.3	4.3	2.3	1.1
1973	4.8	3.9	4.7	2.8	0.9
1974	4.2	3.2	4.9	2.4	1.5
1975	3.7	2.0	4.2	1.4	2.1
1976	3.9	2.6	3.8	1.7	1.3
1977	4.0	2.8	3.8	1.8	1.1
1978	4.1	3.1	3.9	2.1	0.9
1979	4.0	2.9	4.0	2.0	1.1
1980	3.5	2.1	4.0	1.5	1.7
1981	3.2	2.0	3.6	1.3	1.6

[1] Beginning 1943, labor turnover rates refer to all employees; previously, to production workers only.

[2] Beginning 1959, transfers between establishments of the same firm are included in total accessions and total separations; 1959–1981 figures, therefore, are not strictly comparable with earlier data.

[3] For 1919–1929, averages are unweighted medians; in all other years, arithmetic means.

[4] Prior to 1940, quits include miscellaneous separations.

[5] Additional data value available for twelve-month period ending at the middle of year. See text.

Sources

For 1910–1918: Paul F. Brissenden and Emil Frankel, "Mobility of Labor in American Industry," *Monthly Labor Review* 10 (6) (1920): 41.

For 1919–1928: W. A. Berridge, "Labor Turnover in American Factories," *Monthly Labor Review* 29 (1) (1929): 64–5.

For 1929: "Labor Turnover in American Factories, December, 1930," *Monthly Labor Review* 32 (2) (1931): 105.

For 1930–1970: U.S. Bureau of Labor Statistics (BLS), *Employment and Earnings, United States, 1909–71*, Bulletin number 1312-8 (1972), Table 8.

For 1971–1981: BLS, *Employment and Earnings* 29 (3) (1982), Table D-1.

Documentation

Data in this table are expressed as monthly rates per 100 employees.

BLS turnover statistics are based on surveys of business establishments. The figures for 1910–1918 are based on two field investigations undertaken by agents of the BLS, the first during 1915 and 1916 and the second during 1918. The sample sizes are small: fewer than fifty establishments were surveyed in five of the calendar years during this period, with a low of sixteen establishments surveyed in 1910. Although firms from a variety of manufacturing industries were surveyed, the sample is not a random sample of manufacturing establishments. Furthermore, the establishments surveyed tended to be larger than average and to have centralized employment systems. The latter fact may bias the turnover rates down, relative to the full population of firms.

The accession rates for 1910–1918 reported here were computed by dividing the total number of accessions (hires) for the year in question (reported by all establishments) by the total number of full-time equivalent workers. The survey actually recorded total labor hours for the year; the number of full-time equivalents was calculated by dividing the total annual hours by 3,000. To the extent that the typical employee worked fewer than 3,000 hours per year, the number of workers is understated, lending a source of upward bias to the accession rate. The separation rates were calculated similarly.

The figures for 1919–1929 are those of the Metropolitan Life Insurance Company, which pioneered in collecting labor turnover data on a regular basis beginning in January 1926. Subsequently, the company secured data that enabled it to estimate turnover rates monthly back to January 1919.

The company obtained its turnover data by means of a mail questionnaire sent monthly to reporting firms. (The sample of reporting firms, 160 in November 1926, had grown to 350 by mid-1929.) Each firm was asked to report each month: (1) the daily average number of employees on the payroll, and the total number of (2) accessions, (3) voluntary quits, (4) discharges, and (5) layoffs during the month. The accession rate for each company was computed by dividing the total number of accessions during the month by the daily average number on the payroll during the month. The composite or average accession rate for all reporting firms was the unweighted median of the accession rates computed for individual firms. The annual average was the arithmetic mean of the twelve monthly median accession rates. Quits and layoffs were handled in a similar fashion. (The total separation rate, however, was computed as the sum of the median discharge rate, the median quit rate, and the median layoff rate.) The figures for 1919–1929 were originally stated as equivalent annual rates rather than monthly rates. They have been converted to monthly rates by dividing by 12.

In July 1929, the BLS took over the work of the Metropolitan Life Insurance Company. At that time, approximately 350 large manufacturers employed 700,000 workers in the sample of reporting firms. In 1954, the BLS began enlisting the cooperation of various state employment agencies in the collection of turnover statistics. This cooperative program continued until the collection of turnover data by the BLS was terminated at the end of 1981. In 1980, the establishments in the manufacturing sample employed nearly 8.5 million workers.

BLS turnover rate estimates were based on reports made monthly on a mail questionnaire by a sample of cooperating firms. The reporting firms tended to be considerably larger, on average, than all firms within the population sampled. This large-firm bias may cause underestimation of turnover rates. Before 1958, the BLS turnover rates for "all manufacturing" actually excluded from the sample certain highly seasonal industries, such as canning and preserving, as well as printing and publishing. The rates for 1930–1958 were subsequently revised by the BLS to reflect the influence of the formerly excluded industries; the revised rates are reported here. Plants experiencing work stoppages are excluded.

Throughout the period 1930–1981, cooperating firms were asked to report each month their total accessions, total separations, quits, layoffs, and discharges, as well as the total number of employees. Quits are defined as terminations of employment initiated by employees; they include unauthorized absences of more than a week. Layoffs are terminations of employment for more than a week, initiated by management, without prejudice to the worker. Discharges are terminations of employment by management for cause (incompetence, laziness, etc.). The revised turnover series published by the BLS after 1958 do not provide separate figures for discharges. Prior to 1940, quits included "miscellaneous" separations; beginning in 1940, quits do not include the miscellaneous category. Miscellaneous separations are defined as terminations of employment for military duty of more than thirty days and separations other than those itemized (thus, miscellaneous includes separations due to worker deaths, for example). During the 1940s and 1950s, the ratio of miscellaneous separations to quits typically ranged from less than 5 percent to about 40 percent.

(continued)

TABLE Ba4682–4686 Monthly turnover rates in manufacturing, by type of turnover: 1910–1981 *Continued*

Beginning with 1943, the labor turnover rates pertain to all employees; before that date, the rates were for production workers only. Before October 1945, the employment base used to calculate turnover rates was the average of the number of employees on the payroll the last day of the preceding month and the last day of the current month. Subsequently, employment was measured as the number of employees who worked during or received pay for any part of the pay period that included the twelfth of the month. The effect of this change in the employment base was negligible.

Beginning with 1959, transfers between establishments of the same firm are included in total accessions and total separations; 1959–1981 figures therefore are not strictly comparable with prior data.

Series Ba4682 and Ba4684. Additional data points calculated for a twelve-month period ending "about the middle" of the second year are available for 1913–1914 and 1917–1918. The values for hires are 7.727 and 17.194 for 1913–1914 and 1917–1918, respectively; the values for separations are 8.296 and 16.712.

TABLE Ba4687–4694 Employer compensation costs for production and related workers – percentage distribution, by type of compensation: 1959–1998 [Private manufacturing establishments]

Contributed by William A. Sundstrom

		Benefits						
	Wages and salaries	Total	Paid leave	Supplemental pay	Insurance	Retirement	Legally required	Other
	Ba4687	Ba4688	Ba4689	Ba4690	Ba4691	Ba4692	Ba4693	Ba4694
Year	Percent	Percent	Percent	Percent	Percent	Percent	Percent	Percent
1959	81.5	18.3	5.4	4.4	2.0	2.2	4.1	0.2
1962	80.1	20.0	5.5	4.4	2.4	2.3	5.1	0.3
1966	77.7	22.5	5.8	5.3	2.8	2.6	5.8	0.2
1968	77.4	22.5	6.2	4.9	3.1	2.7	5.4	0.2
1970	76.2	23.9	6.9	4.4	3.9	3.0	5.5	0.2
1972	74.8	25.2	6.5	4.6	4.2	3.4	6.2	0.3
1974	73.0	26.9	7.2	4.3	4.7	3.6	6.9	0.2
1977	70.9	29.1	7.3	4.1	5.5	4.3	7.4	—
1986	69.7	30.3	6.2	3.6	6.5	3.8	10.0	0.2
1988	67.0	33.0	7.0	4.7	8.1	3.1	9.7	0.4
1990	66.4	33.6	6.8	4.8	8.5	3.1	10.1	0.3
1992	65.0	35.0	6.9	4.6	9.7	3.5	10.0	0.4
1994	63.7	36.3	6.8	4.4	10.3	4.2	10.1	0.5
1996	65.2	34.8	6.8	5.0	9.3	3.4	9.9	0.4
1998	66.2	33.8	6.7	5.2	8.6	3.4	9.6	0.4

Source

William J. Wiatrowski, "Tracking Changes in Benefit Costs," *Compensation and Working Conditions* 4 (1) (1999), Table 3.

Documentation

The data on employer compensation costs for Tables Ba4687–4702 come from two U.S. Bureau of Labor Statistics (BLS) surveys. The data for 1959–1977 are from the Employer Expenditures for Employee Compensation (EEEC) survey. For 1986–1998, the data are from the Employer Costs for Employee Compensation (ECEC) index, which is generated from BLS data collected for the Employment Cost Index.

The EEEC and ECEC indexes vary in two important respects. First, the (earlier) EEEC is based on expenditures for employee compensation for the entire year preceding the survey. The (later) ECEC is calculated from the price of each specific benefit plan in March of each year multiplied by the number of workers receiving that benefit. Second, components of compensation are grouped differently by the two surveys. For the series included here, the benefits have been grouped to provide a reasonable level of comparability between the earlier and later surveys.

In Tables Ba4687–4702, the series for wages and salaries plus the series for total benefits add up to 100 percent, within rounding error. Also, the series for total benefits equal the sum of the remaining series.

The series on wages and salaries are for straight-time pay only. Overtime, shift differentials, and nonproduction bonuses are included as part of benefits in the category "supplemental pay."

Paid leave includes paid vacation, holidays, personal leave, sick leave, and so forth.

Insurance benefits include health, life, and disability insurance.

Retirement benefits include the cost of employer contributions to worker retirement plans, not including Social Security. The employer's share of Social Security, Medicare, workers' compensation, and unemployment insurance are aggregated under the heading "legally required" benefits, which does not include the employee's contribution to these programs (for example, employee's Social Security tax).

TABLE Ba4695–4702 Employer compensation costs for production and related workers – percentage distribution, by type of compensation: 1966–1998 [Private establishments]

Contributed by William A. Sundstrom

		Benefits						
	Wages and salaries	Total	Paid leave	Supplemental pay	Insurance	Retirement	Legally required	Other
	Ba4695	Ba4696	Ba4697	Ba4698	Ba4699	Ba4700	Ba4701	Ba4702
Year	Percent	Percent	Percent	Percent	Percent	Percent	Percent	Percent
1966	80.6	19.2	5.7	3.6	2.1	2.6	5.1	0.1
1968	80.4	19.5	5.9	3.4	2.2	2.9	5.0	0.1
1970	79.8	20.2	6.3	3.0	2.6	3.2	5.0	0.1
1972	78.5	21.5	6.3	3.0	3.0	3.5	5.5	0.2
1974	76.3	23.7	6.7	3.4	3.3	3.9	6.3	0.1
1977	74.8	25.1	6.9	3.0	4.0	4.3	6.8	0.1
1986	73.0	27.0	7.0	2.3	5.5	3.8	8.4	0.1
1988	72.7	27.3	7.0	2.4	5.6	3.3	8.8	0.2
1990	72.4	27.6	6.9	2.5	6.1	3.0	9.0	0.0
1992	71.8	28.2	6.8	2.4	6.9	2.9	9.1	0.1
1994	71.1	28.9	6.5	2.6	7.2	3.0	9.4	0.2
1996	71.9	28.1	6.4	2.8	6.5	3.1	9.1	0.2
1998	72.4	27.7	6.6	2.6	6.3	3.8	8.2	0.2

Source

William J. Wiatrowski, "Tracking Changes in Benefit Costs," *Compensation and Working Conditions* 4 (1) (1999), Table 3.

Documentation

See the text for Table Ba4687–4694.

TABLE Ba4703–4705 Percentage of manufacturing employees in establishments of selected sizes: 1904–1997[1]

Contributed by William A. Sundstrom

	Fewer than 20 employees	Fewer than 100 employees	Fewer than 1,000 employees
	Ba4703	Ba4704	Ba4705
Year	Percent	Percent	Percent
1904 [2]	13.6	39.2	88.1
1909	14.4	37.8	84.7
1914	13.1	35.0	82.2
1919	10.3	29.2	73.6
1921	11.8	34.3	80.3
1923	9.4	28.8	75.9
1929	9.8	29.1	—
1933	10.0	30.8	—
1935	9.5	28.9	—
1937	8.0	26.7	73.6
1939	9.5	30.0	77.6
1947	7.2	25.0	—
1954	7.7	25.6	67.4
1958	7.8	27.0	—
1963	7.3	26.2	69.5
1967	5.6	23.2	67.2
1972	6.2	24.8	71.3
1977	6.5	25.3	72.5
1982	7.9	28.4	74.8
1987	8.2	29.5	76.3
1992	8.5	30.6	78.8
1997	8.2	30.0	79.5

[1] For 1904–1939, figures refer to wage earners and include upper bound. For 1947–1997, figures refer to all employees and exclude upper bound. See text.

[2] Estimated; see text.

Sources

For 1904–1977: Mark Granovetter, "Small Is Bountiful: Labor Markets and Establishment Size," *American Sociological Review* 49 (1984): 326.

For 1982–1992: U.S. Bureau of the Census, Census of Manufactures for 1982, 1987, and 1992, *Subject Series General Summary*, publication numbers MC82-S-1 (Part 2), MC87-S-1, and MC92-S-1.

For 1997: U.S. Bureau of the Census, *County Business Patterns 1997*, CBP/97-1 (September 1999), p. 8.

Documentation

Granovetter's series comes from the Census of Manufactures for various years.

An establishment is defined as a single physical location where manufacturing is performed. Consequently, the figures here refer to the number of employees working at a given location, not for a given company: companies

(continued)

TABLE Ba4703–4705 Percentage of manufacturing employees in establishments of selected sizes: 1904–1997 *Continued*

with multiple production locations have each establishment counted separately in these data.

The figures for 1904–1939 refer only to "wage earners" (essentially production workers), whereas those beginning in 1947 refer to all employees. Because wage earners are a subset of total employees, this change should tend to bias upward the percentage of employees in smaller firms for 1904–1939 relative to later years. For example, an establishment employing 90 wage earners and 15 other employees would be counted as having fewer than 100 wage earners before 1940, but more than 100 employees thereafter. Also for 1904–1939, the percentages include the upper bound (for example, twenty or fewer), whereas for 1947 on they do not (for example, fewer than twenty). This should also bias upward the percentage in smaller firms during the early years, though by a small amount.

The Census of Manufactures for 1904 gave only the number of establishments in each size class, not the number of wage earners, and so Granovetter estimated the number of wage earners in each class by assuming that the average number of wage earners per establishment in each size category was the same in 1904 as it was in 1909.

The figures for 1997 come from the Census Bureau's County Business Patterns, based on an annual survey. Although there are differences in definitions and coverage between the Census of Manufactures and the County Business Patterns data, the two sources appear to be quite comparable at the level of aggregation used here. For example, the following table gives establishment size information based on the two sources for 1992. The figures are quite similar.

Percentage of employees in establishments employing:

	Fewer than 20	Fewer than 100	Fewer than 1,000
Census of Manufactures	8.5	30.6	78.8
County Business Patterns	8.4	29.9	77.7

TABLE Ba4706–4711 Percentage of retail, wholesale, and service employees in establishments of selected sizes: 1939–1997

Contributed by William A. Sundstrom

	Retail		Wholesale		Service	
	Fewer than 20 employees	Fewer than 100 employees	Fewer than 20 employees	Fewer than 100 employees	Fewer than 20 employees	Fewer than 100 employees
	Ba4706	Ba4707	Ba4708	Ba4709	Ba4710	Ba4711
Year	Percent	Percent	Percent	Percent	Percent	Percent
1939	63.8	85.0	44.4	83.0	55.6	—
1948	58.3	82.4	37.6	—	55.5	83.5
1954	56.0	83.0	41.9	81.5	47.4	76.1
1958	55.6	83.7	43.7	83.2	50.6	77.5
1963	53.4	83.4	45.0	84.1	48.2	75.2
1967	48.8	82.4	41.6	81.4	43.6	71.7
1972	46.3	82.5	34.4	75.5	42.3	71.7
1977	42.7	81.9	40.6	79.6	40.0	68.1
1982	42.2	83.4	39.5	78.8	39.1	68.4
1987	36.9	80.1	36.6	75.0	28.5	51.6
1992	36.2	79.3	36.1	73.2	27.4	50.6
1997	32.4	73.8	33.8	71.0	25.4	49.7

Sources

For retail trade and services, 1939–1977, and wholesale trade, 1939–1967: Mark Granovetter, "Small Is Bountiful: Labor Markets and Establishment Size," *American Sociological Review* 49 (June 1984): 326.

For retail trade and services, 1982–1992: U.S. Bureau of the Census, Census of Retail Trade and Census of Service Industries for 1982, 1987, and 1992, subject reports on Establishment and Firm Size for each year.

For retail trade and services, 1997, and wholesale trade, 1972–1997: U.S. Bureau of the Census, *County Business Patterns*, summary for the United States for each year.

Documentation

Granovetter's series come from the Census of Retail Trade, Census of Wholesale Trade, and Census of Selected Services, collectively known as the Census of Business in the earlier years.

Since 1972, the Census of Wholesale Trade has published employment by size class only for merchant wholesalers. To maintain consistency in industry coverage, the size distributions reported here for wholesale trade, beginning in 1972, are from the Census Bureau's *County Business Patterns* reports. *County Business Patterns* data are also used for the 1997 figures in retail and services.

Although there are differences in definitions and coverage between the Census of Manufactures and the County Business Patterns data, the two sources appear to be quite comparable at the level of aggregation used here. For example, the following table gives establishment size information based on the two sources for 1992. The figures are quite similar.

Percentage of employees, by establishment size (employment)

	Retail trade		Service industries	
	Fewer than 20	Fewer than 100	Fewer than 20	Fewer than 100
Census of Manufactures	36.2	79.3	27.4	50.6
County Business Patterns	35.9	78.0	27.5	51.5

An establishment is defined as a single physical location at which business is conducted. Consequently, the figures here refer to the number of employees working at a given location, not for a given company: companies with multiple locations have each establishment counted separately in these data.

The Census of Service Industries reports establishment size distributions separately for firms subject to federal income tax and those exempt from it. The figures here are for both types combined.

TABLE Ba4712–4725 Employee benefits in medium and large private-sector establishments – coverage and paid days off per year: 1979–1997

Contributed by William A. Sundstrom

	Percentage of employees with										Average number of paid days per year			
													Vacation	
	Defined-benefit pension	Defined-contribution retirement plan	Medical care benefits	Dental care benefits	Long-term disability insurance	Life insurance benefits	Paid sick leave	Paid personal leave	Paid holidays	Paid vacations	Personal leave	Holidays	At 5 years of service	At 20 years of service
	Ba4712	Ba4713	Ba4714	Ba4715	Ba4716	Ba4717	Ba4718	Ba4719	Ba4720	Ba4721	Ba4722	Ba4723	Ba4724	Ba4725
Year	Percent	Percent	Percent	Percent	Percent	Percent	Percent	Percent	Percent	Percent	Days	Days	Days	Days
1979	—	—	—	—	—	—	—	—	—	100	—	—	—	—
1980	84	—	97	54	40	96	62	20	99	100	—	10.1	12.4	20.6
1981	84	—	97	59	41	96	65	23	99	99	—	10.2	12.5	20.5
1982	84	—	97	66	43	96	67	24	99	99	3.8	10.0	12.4	20.5
1983	82	—	96	71	45	96	67	25	99	100	3.7	9.8	12.5	20.5
1984	82	—	97	75	47	96	67	23	99	99	3.6	9.8	12.5	20.5
1985	80	53	96	73	48	96	67	26	98	99	3.7	10.1	12.7	20.7
1986	76	60	95	67	48	96	70	25	99	100	3.7	10.0	12.7	20.6
1988	63	45	90	60	42	92	69	24	96	98	3.3	9.4	13.1	20.1
1989	63	48	92	66	45	94	68	22	97	97	3.1	9.2	13.4	20.4
1991	59	48	83	60	40	94	67	21	92	96	3.3	10.2	13.4	20.4
1993	56	49	82	62	41	91	65	21	91	97	3.1	10.2	13.6	20.4
1995	52	55	77	—	42	87	58	22	89	96	3.3	9.1	—	—
1997	50	57	76	—	43	87	56	20	89	95	3.5	9.3	—	—

Source

U.S. Bureau of Labor Statistics (BLS) Internet site, August 2, 2000, the following BLS series: EBUDBINC000000ML, EBUDCINC000000ML, EBUMEDINC00000ML, EBUDENTINC0000ML, EBULTDINC00000ML, EBULIFEINC0000ML, EBUSICKINC0000ML, EBUPERSINC0000ML, EBUPERSAVE0000ML, EBUHOLINC00000ML, EBUHOLAVE00000ML, EBUVACINC00000ML, EBUVACAVG5YRS0ML, and EBUVACAVG20YRSML.

Documentation

Benefits data come from the BLS's Employee Benefits Survey (EBS), an annual survey of the incidence and provisions of selected benefits provided by employers to their employees. The survey currently collects data from a sample of approximately 6,000 private-sector and state and local government establishments. The data are presented as a percentage of employees who participate in a certain benefit, or as an average benefit provision.

The series included here all refer to employees of medium and large private business establishments. For the surveys conducted during the period 1979–1986, medium and large establishments were defined as those that employed at least 50, 100, or 250 workers, depending on the industry (most service industries were excluded). The surveys conducted in 1988 and 1989 included medium and large establishments with 100 workers or more in all private industries. The 1988 survey represented a significant expansion in the employment coverage over the 1979–1986 surveys. The expansion increased the private-sector employment coverage of the survey by nearly 50 percent. All surveys conducted over the 1979–1989 period excluded establishments in Alaska and Hawai'i, as well as part-time employees. Because of these changes, the comparability of the series before and after the late 1980s must be questioned.

Since 1990, the EBS has continued to survey medium and large establishments (those employing 100 or more workers) during odd-numbered reference years; small private establishments (those employing fewer than 100 workers) and state and local governments (regardless of employment size) are surveyed for even-numbered reference years.

Definitions of Benefit Terms

Series Ba4712. Defined benefit pension: a retirement plan that calculates retirement benefits using specific formulas, generally based on salary, years of service, or both. Employers are obligated to provide to their employees the benefits derived from these calculations.

Series Ba4713. Defined contribution retirement plan: a retirement benefit plan in which the amount of the employer's annual contribution is specified. Individual accounts are set up for participants, and benefits are based on the amounts credited to these accounts (through employer contributions and, if applicable, employee contributions), plus any investment earnings on the money in the account.

Series Ba4714. Medical care: a type of insurance coverage that provides for the payment of benefits as a result of sickness or injury. Medical care coverage can be provided in a hospital or a doctor's office.

Series Ba4716. Long-term disability insurance: provides a monthly benefit to employees who, due to injury or illness, are unable to perform the duties of their normal occupation or any other, for periods of time extending beyond their short-term disability and/or sickness and accident insurance.

Series Ba4717. Life insurance: a contract that pays the beneficiary a set sum of money on the death of the policyholder. These plans pay benefits as a lump sum.

TABLE Ba4726–4741 Injuries and fatalities in mining, quarrying, and related industries: 1870–1970

Contributed by Susan B. Carter

	Coal mining						Quarrying and related industries				Metal and nonmetal mining					
	Number		Per million man-hours		Fatalities per 1,000 300-day workers	Fatalities per 1,000 employed	Number		Per million man-hours		Number		Per million man-hours		Per 1,000 300-day workers	
	Fatal	Nonfatal	Fatal	Nonfatal			Fatal	Nonfatal	Fatal	Nonfatal	Fatal	Nonfatal	Fatal	Nonfatal	Fatal	Nonfatal
	Ba4726	Ba4727	Ba4728 [1]	Ba4729	Ba4730	Ba4731	Ba4732	Ba4733	Ba4734 [2]	Ba4735 [2,3]	Ba4736 [4]	Ba4737 [5]	Ba4738	Ba4739	Ba4740	Ba4741 [5]
Year	Number	Number	Per million hours	Per million hours	Per 1,000	Per 1,000	Number	Number	Per million hours	Per million hours	Number	Number	Per million hours	Per million hours	Per 1,000	Per 1,000
1870	211 [6]	—	—	—	—	5.93	—	—	—	—	—	—	—	—	—	—
1871	210 [6]	—	—	—	—	5.60	—	—	—	—	—	—	—	—	—	—
1872	223 [6]	—	—	—	—	4.98	—	—	—	—	—	—	—	—	—	—
1873	263 [6]	—	—	—	—	5.46	—	—	—	—	—	—	—	—	—	—
1874	260	—	—	—	—	3.87	—	—	—	—	—	—	—	—	—	—
1875	260	—	—	—	—	3.06	—	—	—	—	—	—	—	—	—	—
1876	256	—	—	—	—	2.83	—	—	—	—	—	—	—	—	—	—
1877	244	—	—	—	—	2.77	—	—	—	—	—	—	—	—	—	—
1878	260	—	—	—	—	2.62	—	—	—	—	—	—	—	—	—	—
1879	329	—	—	—	—	3.30	—	—	—	—	—	—	—	—	—	—
1880	280	—	—	—	—	2.21	—	—	—	—	—	—	—	—	—	—
1881	416	—	—	—	—	2.93	—	—	—	—	—	—	—	—	—	—
1882	502	—	—	—	—	2.75	—	—	—	—	—	—	—	—	—	—
1883	593	—	—	—	—	3.34	—	—	—	—	—	—	—	—	—	—
1884	762	—	—	—	—	2.80	—	—	—	—	—	—	—	—	—	—
1885	574	—	—	—	—	2.58	—	—	—	—	—	—	—	—	—	—
1886	530	—	—	—	—	2.25	—	—	—	—	—	—	—	—	—	—
1887	535	—	—	—	—	2.20	—	—	—	—	—	—	—	—	—	—
1888	728	—	—	—	—	2.55	—	—	—	—	—	—	—	—	—	—
1889	668	—	—	—	—	2.36	—	—	—	—	—	—	—	—	—	—
1890	733	—	—	—	3.50	2.52	—	—	—	—	—	—	—	—	—	—
1891	956	—	—	—	4.30	3.08	—	—	—	—	—	—	—	—	—	—
1892	991	—	—	—	4.42	3.12	—	—	—	—	—	—	—	—	—	—
1893	958	—	—	—	4.03	2.70	—	—	—	—	—	—	—	—	—	—
1894	958	—	—	—	4.50	2.67	—	—	—	—	—	—	—	—	—	—
1895	1,142	—	—	—	4.68	3.04	—	—	—	—	—	—	—	—	—	—
1896	1,083	—	—	—	4.62	2.85	—	—	—	—	—	—	—	—	—	—
1897	990	—	—	—	4.27	2.55	—	—	—	—	—	—	—	—	—	—
1898	1,062	—	—	—	4.28	2.71	—	—	—	—	—	—	—	—	—	—
1899	1,241	—	—	—	4.40	3.14	—	—	—	—	—	—	—	—	—	—
1900	1,489	—	—	—	4.87	3.44	—	—	—	—	—	—	—	—	—	—
1901	1,574	—	—	—	4.54	3.27	—	—	—	—	—	—	—	—	—	—
1902	1,724	—	—	—	5.15	3.38	—	—	—	—	—	—	—	—	—	—
1903	1,926	—	1.9 [7]	—	4.72	3.46	—	—	—	—	—	—	—	—	—	—
1904	1,995	—	2.1 [7]	—	5.17	3.48	—	—	—	—	—	—	—	—	—	—
1905	2,232	—	2.0 [7]	—	5.14	3.63	—	—	—	—	—	—	—	—	—	—
1906	2,138	—	1.6 [8]	—	4.87	3.39	—	—	—	—	—	—	—	—	—	—
1907	3,242	—	2.6 [8]	—	6.25	4.81	—	—	—	—	—	—	—	—	—	—
1908	2,445	—	2.1 [8]	—	5.54	3.60	—	—	—	—	—	—	—	—	—	—
1909	2,642	—	2.3 [8]	—	5.35	3.96	—	—	—	—	—	—	—	—	—	—

	Coal mining						Quarrying and related industries				Metal and nonmetal mining					
	Number		Per million man-hours		Fatalities per 1,000 300-day workers	Fatalities per 1,000 employed	Number		Per million man-hours		Number		Per million man-hours		Per 1,000 300-day workers	
	Fatal	Nonfatal	Fatal	Nonfatal			Fatal	Nonfatal	Fatal	Nonfatal	Fatal	Nonfatal	Fatal	Nonfatal	Fatal	Nonfatal
	Ba4726	Ba4727	Ba4728 [1]	Ba4729	Ba4730	Ba4731	Ba4732	Ba4733	Ba4734 [2]	Ba4735 [2,3]	Ba4736 [4]	Ba4737 [5]	Ba4738	Ba4739	Ba4740	Ba4741 [5]
Year	Number	Number	Per million hours	Per million hours	Per 1,000	Per 1,000	Number	Number	Per million hours	Per million hours	Number	Number	Per million hours	Per million hours	Per 1,000	Per 1,000
1910	2,821	—	2.6 [8]	—	5.30	3.89	—	—	—	—	—	—	—	—	—	—
1911	2,656	—	1.9	—	4.97	3.65	188	5,390	0.8	23	695	26,577	—	—	4.4	170
1912	2,419	—	1.7	—	4.46	3.35	213	6,552	0.8	25	661	30,724	—	—	4.1	190
1913	2,785	—	1.8	—	4.70	3.73	183	7,739	0.8	32	683	32,971	—	—	3.7	180
1914	2,454	—	1.8	—	4.66	3.22	180	7,836	0.9	41	559	30,216	—	—	3.9	212
1915	2,269	—	1.7	—	4.44	3.09	148	9,671	0.6	42	553	35,295	—	—	3.9	249
1916	2,226	—	1.5	—	3.93	3.09	173	13,427	0.8	63	697	48,237	—	—	3.6	251
1917	2,696	—	1.7	—	4.25	3.56	131	13,242	0.6	66	852	46,286	—	—	4.4	241
1918	2,580	—	1.6	—	3.94	3.38	125	8,719	0.8	52	646	42,915	—	—	3.6	237
1919	2,323	—	1.8	—	4.28	2.99	123	9,199	0.7	51	468	31,506	—	—	3.5	234
1920	2,272	—	1.6	—	3.78	2.90	178	11,217	0.8	52	425	32,562	—	—	3.2	242
1921	1,995	—	1.7	—	4.20	2.42	120	10,465	0.7	62	230	18,604	—	—	3.1	250
1922	1,984	—	2.0	—	4.90	2.35	132	11,839	0.7	61	344	26,080	—	—	3.5	268
1923	2,462	—	1.8	—	4.39	2.85	143	14,990	0.6	63	367	33,563	—	—	3.0	275
1924	2,402	—	2.0	—	4.80	3.08	138	14,777	0.6	62	418	33,118	—	—	3.5	278
1925	2,234	—	1.9	—	4.65	2.98	149	14,165	0.6	61	371	35,132	—	—	3.0	284
1926	2,518	—	1.9	—	4.50	3.32	154	13,201	0.7	57	430	30,350	—	—	3.5	245
1927	2,231	—	1.8	—	4.43	2.94	135	13,459	0.6	59	352	25,133	—	—	3.1	222
1928	2,176	—	1.9	—	4.64	3.19	119	10,568	0.5	47	273	22,483	—	—	2.5	206
1929	2,187	—	1.9	—	4.54	3.34	126	9,810	0.6	46	350	23,092	—	—	3.0	200
1930	2,063	99,981	1.9	91	5.00	3.20	105	7,417	0.6	40	271	15,594	—	—	2.9	168
1931	1,463	77,958	1.7	88	4.42	2.48	61	5,427	0.5	41	158	8,709	1.0	56	2.5	140
1932	1,207	56,283	1.7	80	4.60	2.29	32	3,574	0.3	38	107	5,014	1.2	54	2.9	136
1933	1,064	59,129	1.3	75	3.58	2.03	59	3,637	0.7	41	95	5,925	1.0	63	2.4	153
1934	1,226	65,559	1.4	77	3.54	2.16	60	3,924	0.6	41	116	7,892	1.0	68	2.4	161
1935	1,242	63,426	1.5	77	3.67	2.20	51	4,152	0.5	38	164	10,206	1.0	63	2.4	150
1936	1,342	67,540	1.4	73	3.50	2.30	91	5,717	0.6	39	199	14,650	1.0	72	2.4	174
1937	1,413	66,259	1.6	73	3.69	2.40	77	6,348	0.5	40	219	18,055	0.9	75	2.2	181
1938	1,105	49,636	1.6	71	3.76	2.04	82	5,027	0.6	38	156	12,722	0.8	68	2.0	162
1939	1,078	51,773	1.4	68	3.35	2.00	48	5,204	0.3	36	173	13,710	0.8	66	2.0	158
1940	1,388	57,776	1.6	69	3.92	2.60	72	5,188	0.5	35	223	14,766	1.0	64	2.3	153
1941	1,266	61,057	1.4	66	3.26	2.32	76	6,870	0.4	40	230	15,772	0.9	62	2.2	148
1942	1,471	66,774	1.4	65	3.42	2.77	112	6,349	0.6	35	237	13,957	0.9	56	2.3	133
1943	1,451	64,594	1.4	62	3.39	2.98	80	5,199	0.5	33	220	13,004	0.9	56	2.3	134
1944	1,298	63,691	1.2	59	3.05	2.86	73	4,437	0.6	34	147	10,177	0.8	54	1.9	130
1945	1,068	57,117	1.1	60	2.82	2.44	53	4,121	0.4	32	121	9,099	0.6	45	1.4	107
1946	968	55,350	1.1	63	2.80	2.09	55	5,137	0.4	32	126	9,580	0.7	51	1.6	122
1947	1,158	57,660	1.2	61	2.96	2.36	75	5,504	0.4	32	145	10,472	0.7	47	1.6	114
1948	999	53,472	1.1	60	2.60	1.97	75	4,994	0.4	28	128	9,641	0.6	43	1.4	103
1949	585	35,405	0.9	55	1.13	1.21	66	4,826	0.4	26	86	8,863	0.4	43	1.0	103

Notes appear at end of table

(continued)

TABLE Ba4726–4741 Injuries and fatalities in mining, quarrying, and related industries: 1870–1970 *Continued*

	Coal mining						Quarrying and related industries				Metal and nonmetal mining					
	Number		Per million man-hours		Fatalities per 1,000 300-day workers	Fatalities per 1,000 employed	Number		Per million man-hours		Number		Per million man-hours		Per 1,000 300-day workers	
	Fatal	Nonfatal	Fatal	Nonfatal			Fatal	Nonfatal	Fatal	Nonfatal	Fatal	Nonfatal	Fatal	Nonfatal	Fatal	Nonfatal
	Ba4726	Ba4727	Ba4728 [1]	Ba4729	Ba4730	Ba4731	Ba4732	Ba4733	Ba4734 [2]	Ba4735 [2,3]	Ba4736 [4]	Ba4737 [5]	Ba4738	Ba4739	Ba4740	Ba4741 [5]
Year	Number	Number	Per million hours	Per million hours	Per 1,000	Per 1,000	Number	Number	Per million hours	Per million hours	Number	Number	Per million hours	Per million hours	Per 1,000	Per 1,000
1950	643	37,264	0.9	52	2.11	1.33	54	4,762	0.3	25	110	8,634	0.5	41	1.3	98
1951	785	35,553	1.1	51	2.64	1.78	57	4,945	0.3	26	118	8,953	0.5	39	1.2	94
1952	548	30,074	0.9	51	2.16	1.37	74	4,503	0.4	24	135	8,707	0.6	38	1.4	92
1953	461	24,258	0.9	47	2.11	1.31	43	4,450	0.2	23	118	8,409	0.5	36	1.2	87
1954	396	17,718	1.0	46	2.40	1.40	34	3,834	0.2	22	105	6,780	0.5	34	1.3	81
1955	420	18,885	1.0	45	2.35	1.61	53	3,811	0.3	22	104	8,239	0.5	36	1.1	87
1956	448	19,816	1.0	46	2.43	1.72	50	3,754	0.3	21	122	8,347	0.5	32	1.1	76
1957	478	18,792	1.2	46	2.75	1.88	53	4,210	0.3	23	99	7,921	0.3	27	0.8	66
1958	358	14,160	1.1	44	2.61	1.59	45	4,572	0.2	24	97	6,411	0.4	25	0.9	60
1959	293	12,163	1.0	41	2.33	1.44	52	4,790	0.3	24	100	6,862	0.4	26	0.9	62
1960	325	11,902	1.2	42	2.73	1.71	39	4,668	0.2	23	121	7,132	0.4	24	1.0	58
1961	294	11,197	1.2	44	2.71	1.75	32	4,280	0.2	22	74	6,668	0.3	24	0.6	58
1962	289	10,944	1.1	45	2.73	1.79	67	3,299	0.4	17	98	6,072	0.4	23	0.9	57
1963	284	11,133	1.1	44	2.65	1.81	61	3,468	0.3	18	79	5,818	0.3	23	0.8	56
1964	242	11,070	1.0	44	2.27	1.61	61	3,367	0.3	18	84	6,158	0.3	24	0.8	58
1965	259	11,138	1.0	45	2.47	1.74	48	3,305	0.3	17	92	6,236	0.3	23	0.8	56
1966	233	10,446	1.0	43	2.27	1.60	51	3,583	0.3	19	109	6,632	0.4	24	1.0	58
1967	222	10,115	0.9	42	2.18	1.59	46	3,267	0.3	18	103	6,019	0.4	24	1.0	58
1968	311	9,639	1.3	41	3.15	2.31	58	3,260	0.3	17	98	5,847	0.4	24	1.0	57
1969	203	9,917	0.9	42	2.03	1.52	53	3,389	0.3	18	95	6,092	0.4	24	0.9	57
1970	260	11,552	1.0	44	2.42	1.86	43	3,666	0.2	20	93	6,637	0.4	26	0.9	62

[1] Figures for 1930–1970 are on a portal-to-portal basis; earlier years are on a working-time basis. The 1930 frequency rate for fatalities per million man-hours on a portal-to-portal basis was 1.9; the working-time rate was 2.1.

[2] Man-hours for 1911–1923 computed on assumption that weighted average length of workday was 9.36 hours, as shown by reports from representative operating companies for 1924.

[3] Injury rate for years before 1916 are believed not to be representative, owing to probable incompleteness of reports of slight or minor injuries.

[4] Beginning 1945, metal mill data are included; nonmetal mill data included beginning 1955; clay mill data included beginning 1956.

[5] Prior to 1916, accident reports for mines in the gold, silver, and miscellaneous metal groups are not complete as to nonfatal injuries.

[6] Data reflect only Pennsylvania anthracite fatalities; data for bituminous coal mining are not available prior to 1874.

[7] Anthracite coal mining only.

[8] Bituminous and anthracite coal mining. Data for bituminous coal cover only states that maintained complete records of fatal accidents, representing 98–99 percent of total coal production.

Sources

U.S. Bureau of the Census, *Historical Statistics of the United States, Colonial Times to 1970*, Bicentennial Edition (1975), Series M 271 through M 286.

Original sources are from the U.S. Bureau of Mines: for series Ba4726–4729, 1870–1929, Injury Experience in Coal Mining and its predecessor, Coal-Mine Accidents in the United States; for series Ba4726–4729, 1930–1966, and series Ba4730–4731, 1870–1966, Injury Experience in Coal Mining, Information Circular number 8419 (1966); for series Ba4726–4731, 1967–1970, *Minerals Yearbook*, annual volumes and unpublished data. For series Ba4732–4735, 1911–1960, Injury Experience in the Quarry Industry, Information Circular number 8171 (1960); 1961–1970, *Minerals Yearbook*, annual volumes and unpublished data. For series Ba4736–4741, 1911–1954, Injury Experience in the Metal and Nonmetal Industries, and its predecessors: Metal and Non-metal Mine Accidents in the United States and Metal Mine Accidents in the United States; 1955–1970, *Minerals Yearbook*, annual volumes and unpublished data.

Documentation

The Bureau of Mines began gathering information on nonfatal injuries in 1930. Data on number of fatalities go back to 1870 for anthracite and to 1874 for bituminous coal. Availability of information on fatalities for the nineteenth century and the early years of the twentieth century depended on the existence of state records, which, in turn, depended mainly on whether the states had mine inspection services.

For 1870–1909, the record of fatalities is incomplete for bituminous coal. Incompleteness since 1870 applies only to bituminous coal. Pennsylvania anthracite records are complete since 1870, with partial data available for 1847 and 1869 (Bureau of Mines Bulletin number 115, pp. 7, 9, 105). By 1890, the fatality records cover almost 90 percent of all production; between 1895 and 1900, about 95 percent; and between 1901 and 1909, in the neighborhood of 98–99 percent.

The employment statistics used in deriving the injury and fatality frequency measures since 1890 are based on canvasses conducted by the Bureau of Mines (or the Geological Survey), with occasional figures from the Census of Mineral Industries. Although these underlying employment data are not presented here, they are available in the source bulletins. In subsequent years, separate employment figures, collected on accident canvasses, were used for deriving the frequency.

The figures on man-hours of employment, on which the frequency rates per million man-hours are based, were derived as follows: Producers began reporting man-hours of employment to the Bureau of Mines in 1930, but during the early 1930s, many mines left the man-hours question unanswered, and even in the 1940s, the man-hours were not always reported. For mines not reporting man-hours, the Bureau estimated the figure by multiplying the average number of employees (active period average) by the number of days on which the mine was active, and then multiplying the product by the number of hours constituting a standard work shift in the particular mine. This method, with certain variations, was used by the Bureau to estimate man-hours in all years prior to 1930 when no direct information on man-hours was collected. Estimated man-hours, though reasonably accurate, suffered from two major shortcomings: (1) the number of active days was generally determined by the number of days on which the tipple, that is, the machinery employed in screening coal and loading it onto trucks or railroad cars, was active, omitting days on which no coal was brought to the surface, although on such days, men were often employed underground in loading coal or in repair or maintenance work; and (2) the standard work shift did not apply to all occupations, and many miners were irregular in observing standard working hours (see Bureau of Mines *Bulletin* number 380, pp. 8–9; and *Bulletin* 283, p. 64).

The 1943 bituminous coal mine wage agreement made portal-to-portal time, rather than face or working time hours, the basis for pay. Since 1944, only portal-to-portal man-hours have been reported. Conversion factors were applied to man-hour data for underground bituminous coal employees back to 1930. No such adjustment was made, however, for surfacemen at underground mines or strip mine employees in the bituminous coal industry. No adjustment was deemed necessary in the anthracite industry.

The 300-day worker basis was derived by converting the average number of employees (active period average) according to the ratio between active mine days and 300 days. For the very early years, information on active days was not available; therefore, the simple measure of fatalities per 1,000 was used.

For 1888 and earlier years, corresponding employment data are not available for all recorded fatalities. The rates are based on fatalities for which corresponding employment data do exist. Apparently, comparable fatality and employment data exist for all Pennsylvania anthracite back through 1870.

For series related to quarrying and related industries, separate figures are shown in the basic source, according to the kind of rock produced and also for stone classified as dimension and nondimension. Nondimension stone includes all stone used in unshaped or irregular form, as for road building and cement and lime manufacture; dimension stone includes all stone that is cut or shaped for building or monumental purposes. By far, the major share of employment is in nondimension stone. The figures also cover crushing, screening, rock dressing, and the manufacture of cement and lime, insofar as these operations are conducted by the quarry companies; except for crushing and screening, these operations are classified as manufacturing in the *Standard Industrial Classification Manual*. On the other hand, quarries producing sand, gravel, and clay are excluded.

The source states that the data are comparable only since 1916 because information reported for prior years was obviously incomplete as to number of injuries, especially those causing disability for only one or two days. Also included is the classification of nonfatal injuries in the categories of "permanent total," "permanent partial," and "temporary total." The last category is further divided, for 1915–1929, into the subclasses "temporary disabilities lasting more than 14 days" and "temporary disabilities lasting more than the remainder of the day on which the accident occurred, but not exceeding 14 days."

The employment data used in deriving the injury and fatality frequency measures are comparable with the injury data. However, they must be carefully evaluated before they are used for other purposes.

Employment and injury data for metal and nonmetal mines have been compiled from voluntary reports collected by the Bureau of Mines annually since 1911. Separate figures are shown in the basic source by type of mining method. Over the entire period, there have been numerous changes in the classification systems used. In addition, data are given by kind of mine, as follows: copper, iron ore, lead–zinc, gold–silver lode, gold placer, miscellaneous metal mines, and nonmetal mines. Included under miscellaneous metal mines are those working ores of quicksilver, manganese, tungsten, vanadium, chromium, and other metals, plus pyrite mines (the cinder is used in metallurgical works for its iron and copper content) and bauxite mines (the primary source of aluminum). The nonmetallic group includes mines that produce asbestos, asphaltum, barite, borax, emery, feldspar, fluorspar, garnet, graphite, gypsum, lithium, magnesite, mica, mineral paint, phosphate rock, potash, quartz, salt, soapstone, sulfur, talc, and tripoli.

For 1911–1914, nonfatalities were simply divided into "serious," of more than twenty days, duration, and "slight," of more than one but less than twenty days, duration. For 1915–1919, temporary injuries were separated into "serious," of more than fourteen days, duration, and "slight," of more than one but less than fourteen days, duration. For 1930–1970, nonfatalities have been recorded as temporary or permanent, with the latter subdivided into total and partial disability.

Injury data for 1931–1965 have been published in Injury Experience in the Metallic Mineral Industries, 1965, Information Circular number 8433, and Injury Experience in the Nonmetallic Mineral Industries (except stone and coal), 1964–1965, Information Circular number 8481. These sources show data for men employed, average days active, and man-days and man-hours worked, as well as for fatal and nonfatal injuries and for frequency rates at mines and mills.

Frequency rate measures were originally expressed per 1,000 men employed. Shortly thereafter, in an attempt to secure a uniform time basis for comparison, the Bureau of Mines began to express all frequency rates on a 300-day worker basis (derived by converting the average number of employees on active days according to the ratio between active mine days and 300 days). These rates were extended back through 1911. Rates per million man-hours of exposure are not available prior to 1931 in the reports, although partial man-hour data by length of shift are available from 1921 to 1930.

The employment data used in deriving the injury frequency measures are comparable with the fatality and injury records. However, they do not necessarily reflect total employment within the industry. Despite incomplete coverage, the data are considered by the Bureau to be representative of hazard exposure.

Series Ba4732–4735. Includes manufacture of cement and lime.

TABLE Ba4742–4749 Injury rates in manufacturing, mining, and railroads: 1922–1970[1]

Contributed by William A. Sundstrom

		Mining					Class I railroads	
	Manufacturing	Total	Coal	Metals	Nonmetals	Stone quarries	All injuries	Excluding 1- to 3-day injuries
	Ba4742 [2]	Ba4743 [3]	Ba4744	Ba4745	Ba4746	Ba4747	Ba4748 [4]	Ba4749
Year	Per million hours	Per million hours	Per million hours	Per million hours	Per million hours	Per million hours	Per million hours	Per million hours
1922	—	—	—	—	—	—	—	27.1
1923	—	—	—	—	—	—	—	30.9
1924	—	—	—	—	—	62.9	—	27.3
1925	—	—	—	—	—	61.4	—	26.1
1926	24.2	—	—	—	—	58.0	—	23.9
1927	22.6	—	—	—	—	59.2	—	19.4
1928	22.5	—	—	—	—	47.5	—	16.2
1929	24.0	—	—	—	—	46.9	—	13.8
1930	23.1	—	—	—	—	40.3	—	9.4
1931	18.9	79.9	89.9	58.0	47.5	41.0	—	7.5
1932	19.6	74.8	82.2	57.2	45.2	38.5	—	7.4
1933	19.3	71.7	75.9	65.8	53.3	42.1	—	6.9
1934	20.2	73.8	78.1	71.5	52.4	41.8	—	7.0
1935	17.9	72.7	79.0	65.8	50.7	38.2	—	6.7
1936	16.6	70.2	74.4	76.3	48.6	39.5	13.7	8.3
1937	17.8	70.5	74.2	78.9	48.7	40.6	13.6	8.2
1938	15.1	67.5	73.0	71.3	41.1	38.2	11.1	6.8
1939	14.9	64.8	69.5	69.4	42.2	36.5	11.1	6.7
1940	15.3	65.2	70.4	66.8	44.2	35.7	11.5	6.7
1941	18.1	63.2	67.6	64.2	51.6	40.1	14.6	8.3
1942	19.9	61.2	66.8	56.6	55.5	35.7	17.6	10.2
1943	20.0	59.4	63.8	56.9	53.4	34.0	20.3	11.9
1944	18.4	57.2	60.3	55.4	50.5	34.9	20.6	11.8
1945	18.6	55.5	60.7	44.9	47.2	32.8	20.5	11.9
1946	19.9	58.0	64.0	51.2	51.9	32.8	19.0	10.5
1947	18.8	55.8	61.9	48.1	45.8	32.4	18.2	9.7
1948	17.2	53.2	60.6	43.4	42.9	28.3	16.2	8.5
1949	14.5	48.3	56.0	43.6	42.1	26.8	13.7	7.0
1950	14.7	46.3	53.3	41.0	44.2	25.4	14.2	7.3
1951	15.5	45.1	52.1	38.8	45.4	26.2	14.7	7.5
1952	14.3	43.6	51.6	38.3	40.9	24.5	13.7	7.0
1953	13.4	40.3	48.1	34.8	47.3	23.7	13.6	6.7
1954	11.9	37.7	46.7	34.3	32.6	22.0	12.6	6.5
1955	12.1	38.3	46.0	38.0	32.0	22.0	13.9	7.2
1956	12.0	37.1	46.7	32.9	29.7	21.3	14.7	7.7
1957	11.4	35.8	47.2	28.0	27.1	23.3	5.3	—
1958	11.4	31.9	45.1	26.7	23.3	24.7	6.7	—
1959	12.4	29.2	42.1	26.7	25.6	24.3	7.2	—
1960	12.0	29.8	43.4	25.2	23.4	23.3	7.3	—
1961	11.8	29.5	45.0	26.6	21.5	22.4	12.0	—
1962	11.9	28.6	45.1	25.0	21.9	17.4	11.7	—
1963	11.9	28.8	45.1	25.1	21.8	18.2	12.0	—
1964	12.3	28.8	44.8	25.0	23.4	18.2	12.6	—
1965	12.8	28.3	45.8	23.8	23.0	17.3	12.1	—
1966	13.6	28.4	43.8	25.1	23.3	19.1	12.0	—
1967	14.0	28.0	42.8	24.8	24.0	17.8	12.2	—
1968	14.0	27.8	42.5	23.1	25.3	17.8	12.5	—
1969	14.8	28.0	42.6	23.9	24.2	18.4	12.2	—
1970	15.2	28.9	42.6	25.6	26.1	19.8	11.5	—

[1] Rates are average number of disabling injuries per million person-hours worked.

[2] Beginning 1958, industry definition revised to conform to the 1957 edition of the *Standard Industrial Classification Manual*. Comparisons to prior years should be made with caution.

[3] Beginning 1958, includes sand and gravel operations.

[4] Beginning 1957, accidents reported on different basis; data not comparable with prior years.

Sources

Series Ba4742. For 1926–1949 and 1958–1970: U.S. Bureau of Labor Statistics (BLS), *Handbook of Labor Statistics*, 1950 and 1972 editions; for 1950–1952: BLS, *Work Injuries in the United States, 1950*, and subsequent annual issues. For 1953–1957: U.S. Department of Labor, news releases.

Series Ba4743–4747. U.S. Bureau of Mines, *Minerals Yearbook, 1970*, and earlier annual issues.

Series Ba4748–4749. U.S. Federal Railroad Administration (prior to 1966, U.S. Interstate Commerce Commission), *Accident Bulletin*, various issues.

TABLE Ba4742–4749 Injury rates in manufacturing, mining, and railroads: 1922–1970 *Continued*

Documentation

Series Ba4742

The BLS's first continuing compilation of injury-rate statistics began in 1910 for the iron and steel industry. In 1925, the injury-rate compilations were expanded to cover twenty-four industries. In 1952, the compilations covered more than 200 manufacturing and nonmanufacturing industry classifications. In 1970, the survey provided injury-frequency rates for 490 manufacturing and 180 nonmanufacturing categories. Since 1970, statistics on work injuries in manufacturing and most other industries have been collected from the Survey of Occupational Injuries and Illnesses, based on employer records maintained under the Occupational Safety and Health Act of 1970 (see Table Ba4750–4767). The pre- and post-1970 work accident statistics are not considered comparable.

Efforts to standardize the compilation of work-injury statistics were initiated by BLS in 1911, resulting in the first standardized procedures in 1920. In 1926, the American Engineering Standards Committee, later the American Standards Association, undertook a revision of these procedures. Their work led to the publication of the first American Standard Method of Compiling Industrial Injury Rates in 1937. This standard was revised in 1954 and again in 1967.

The standard injury-frequency rate is the average number of disabling injuries per million person-hours worked. A disabling injury is an injury incurred in the course of and arising out of employment, which results in death or permanent physical impairment, or renders the injured person unable to perform any regularly established job, open and available to him or her, during the entire time interval corresponding to the hours of his or her regular shift on one or more days after the injury.

The BLS annual injury-rate estimates here are based on a sample mail survey conducted once a year. Cooperating firms were asked to report for all employees (1) average employment, (2) aggregate man-hours worked by all employees, (3) aggregate number of disabling work injuries by extent of disability, and (4) time lost because of disabilities. As of 1970, the manufacturing sample covered approximately 50,000 establishments. The injury-rate series for manufacturing excludes petroleum refining, smelting and refining of nonferrous metals, cement and lime manufacturing, and coke production, which were covered in similar surveys conducted by the Bureau of Mines (see Table Ba4726–4741).

Prior to 1936, the data are based on surveys covering only wage earners in thirty manufacturing industries. Since 1936, the data refer to all employees in all manufacturing industries. Since 1936, separate injury-frequency rates have been computed for component industries by dividing aggregate injuries by aggregate man-hours in reporting establishments. In computing the average rate for all manufacturing, the separate averages for the component industries are weighted by estimated total employment in these industries. Before 1936, the weights implicitly were aggregate man-hours in the reporting firms in each industry.

The data series exclude petroleum refining, smelting and refining of nonferrous metals, cement and lime manufacturing, and coke production.

Series Ba4743–4747. Except for coal mining since 1941, the Bureau of Mines estimates of work-injury frequency rates in "mining" industries were based on reports made voluntarily by mining establishments. Beginning in 1941, coal-mining firms were obliged by federal law to report work-injury and related data to the Bureau of Mines.

Series Ba4744. Includes data on coal-mine mechanical-cleaning plants and mill data for metal, nonmetal, and stone quarries. Excludes coke production.

Series Ba4745. Copper, gold-silver, iron, lead-zinc, uranium, and miscellaneous.

Series Ba4746. Clay-shale, gypsum, phosphate rock, potash, salt, sulfur, and miscellaneous.

Series Ba4747. Cement, granite, lime, limestone, marble, sandstone, slate, traprock, and miscellaneous.

Series Ba4748–4749. Both series for railroads exclude work injuries suffered by employees of Class I switching and terminal companies after 1932. They are based on monthly accident reports that the Class I railroads are required by federal law to make to the Federal Railroad Administration. The two series thus result from essentially complete censuses of man-hours worked and of reportable work injuries.

Before 1936, a reportable work injury was either a fatality or a nonfatal injury to an employee "sufficient to incapacitate him from performing his ordinary duties for more than 3 days in the aggregate in the 10 days immediately following the accident." Series Ba4744 includes only such work injuries. From 1936 through 1956, the railroads were required to report work injuries incapacitating employees for one to three days immediately following an accident, as well as more serious injuries. Series Ba4748 equals series Ba4749 plus the average work-injury frequency rate for "1–3 day" injuries.

In an effort to narrow the field of reportable accidents while conforming with the intent of the Accident Reports Act, significant changes affecting the reportability of certain types of railroad accidents were made in Rules Governing Monthly Reports of Railroad Accidents, effective January 1, 1957. Minor revisions of these rules have been made from time to time. Therefore, data for accidents occurring prior to 1957 are not necessarily comparable with those for later years.

The concept of "disabling injury" underlying the manufacturing series (series Ba4742) is essentially the same as that underlying series Ba4748. Series Ba4749, which excludes "1–3 day" injuries, is not comparable to series Ba4742 in level; and series Ba4748 also tends to have a downward bias in trend relative to series Ba4742. Series Ba4749 has been included to indicate, at least crudely, the trend in the average injury-frequency rates on Class I railroads before 1936.

Both series cover all employees of Class I railroads. The person-hour base of both series is the aggregate number of straight-time hours actually worked and overtime hours paid for in millions of person-hours. Days worked by daily-rated employees have been converted to person-hours worked by multiplying days worked by 8. The average injury-frequency rate is the ratio of the aggregate number of work injuries to the person-hour base.

TABLE Ba4750–4767 Occupational injury and illness rates, by industry: 1972–1998[1,2]

Contributed by William A. Sundstrom

	Total private sector		Agriculture, forestry, and fishing		Mining		Construction		Manufacturing		Transportation and public utilities		Wholesale and retail trade		Finance, insurance, and real estate		Services	
	Total cases	Lost workday cases	Total cases	Lost workday cases	Total cases	Lost workday cases	Total cases	Lost workday cases	Total cases	Lost workday cases	Total cases	Lost workday cases	Total cases	Lost workday cases	Total cases	Lost workday cases	Total cases	Lost workday cases
	Ba4750	Ba4751	Ba4752	Ba4753	Ba4754	Ba4755	Ba4756	Ba4757	Ba4758	Ba4759	Ba4760	Ba4761	Ba4762	Ba4763	Ba4764	Ba4765	Ba4766	Ba4767
Year	Per 100	Per 100	Per 100	Per 100	Per 100	Per 100	Per 100	Per 100	Per 100	Per 100	Per 100	Per 100	Per 100	Per 100	Per 100	Per 100	Per 100	Per 100
1972	10.9	3.3	—	—	—	—	19.0	6.0	15.6	4.2	10.8	4.5	8.4	2.8	2.5	0.8	6.1	2.0
1973	11.0	3.4	11.6	4.6	12.5	5.8	19.8	6.1	15.3	4.5	10.3	4.4	8.6	2.7	2.4	0.8	6.2	1.9
1974	10.4	3.5	9.9	4.5	10.2	5.1	18.3	5.9	14.6	4.7	10.5	4.8	8.4	2.8	2.4	0.8	5.8	1.9
1975	9.1	3.3	8.5	3.7	11.0	5.7	16.0	5.5	13.0	4.5	9.4	4.6	7.3	2.6	2.2	0.8	5.4	2.0
1976	9.2	3.5	11.0	4.7	11.0	5.8	15.3	5.5	13.2	4.8	9.8	5.0	7.5	2.8	2.0	0.7	5.3	2.0
1977	9.3	3.8	11.5	5.1	10.9	6.0	15.5	5.9	13.1	5.1	9.7	5.3	7.7	2.9	2.0	0.8	5.5	2.2
1978	9.4	4.1	11.6	5.4	11.5	6.4	16.0	6.4	13.2	5.6	10.1	5.7	7.9	3.2	2.1	0.8	5.5	2.4
1979	9.5	4.3	11.7	5.7	11.4	6.8	16.2	6.8	13.3	5.9	10.2	5.9	8.0	3.4	2.1	0.9	5.5	2.5
1980	8.7	4.0	11.9	5.8	11.2	6.5	15.7	6.5	12.2	5.4	9.4	5.5	7.4	3.2	2.0	0.8	5.2	2.3
1981	8.3	3.8	12.3	5.9	11.6	6.2	15.1	6.3	11.5	5.1	9.0	5.3	7.3	3.1	1.9	0.8	5.0	2.3
1982	7.7	3.5	11.8	5.9	10.5	5.4	14.6	6.0	10.2	4.4	8.5	4.9	7.2	3.1	2.0	0.9	4.9	2.3
1983	7.6	3.4	11.9	6.1	8.4	4.5	14.8	6.3	10.0	4.3	8.2 [3]	4.7 [3]	7.2 [3]	3.1 [3]	2.0 [3]	0.9 [3]	5.1 [3]	2.4 [3]
1984	8.0	3.7	12.0	6.1	9.7	5.3	15.5	6.9	10.6	4.7	8.8 [3]	5.2 [3]	7.4 [3]	3.3 [3]	1.9 [3]	0.9 [3]	5.2 [3]	2.5 [3]
1985	7.9	3.6	11.4	5.7	8.4	4.8	15.2	6.8	10.4	4.6	8.6	5.0	7.4	3.2	2.0	0.9	5.4	2.6
1986	7.9	3.6	11.2	5.6	7.4	4.1	15.2	6.9	10.6	4.7	8.2	4.8	7.7	3.3	2.0	0.9	5.3	2.5
1987	8.3	3.8	11.2	5.7	8.5	4.9	14.7	6.8	11.9	5.3	8.4	4.9	7.7	3.4	2.0	0.9	5.5	2.7
1988	8.6	4.0	10.9	5.6	8.8	5.1	14.6	6.8	13.1	5.7	8.9	5.1	7.8	3.5	2.0	0.9	5.4	2.6
1989	8.6	4.0	10.9	5.7	8.5	4.8	14.3	6.8	13.1	5.8	9.2	5.3	8.0	3.6	2.0	0.9	5.5	2.7
1990	8.8	4.1	11.6	5.9	8.3	5.0	14.2	6.7	13.2	5.8	9.6	5.5	7.9	3.5	2.4	1.1	6.0	2.8
1991	8.4	3.9	10.8	5.4	7.4	4.5	13.0	6.1	12.7	5.6	9.3	5.4	7.6	3.4	2.4	1.1	6.2	2.8
1992	8.9	3.9	11.6	5.4	7.3	4.1	13.1	5.8	12.5	5.4	9.1	5.1	8.4	3.5	2.9	1.2	7.1	3.0
1993	8.5	3.8	11.2	5.0	6.8	3.9	12.2	5.5	12.1	5.3	9.5	5.4	8.1	3.4	2.9	1.2	6.7	2.8
1994	8.4	3.8	10.0	4.7	6.3	3.9	11.8	5.5	12.2	5.5	9.3	5.5	7.9	3.4	2.7	1.1	6.5	2.8
1995	8.1	3.6	9.7	4.3	6.2	3.9	10.6	4.9	11.6	5.3	9.1	5.2	7.5	3.2	2.6	1.0	6.4	2.8
1996	7.4	3.4	8.7	3.9	5.4	3.2	9.9	4.5	10.6	4.9	8.7	5.1	6.8	2.9	2.4	0.9	6.0	2.6
1997	7.1	3.3	8.4	4.1	5.9	3.7	9.5	4.4	10.3	4.8	8.2	4.8	6.7	3.0	2.2	0.9	5.6	2.5
1998	6.7	3.1	7.9	3.9	4.9	2.9	8.8	4.0	9.7	4.7	7.3	4.3	6.5	2.8	1.9	0.7	5.2	2.4

[1] Rates are expressed per 100 full-time equivalent workers; see text. Beginning 1992, rates do not include fatalities.

[2] Data for 1989 and subsequent years are based on revised Standard Industrial Classification codes, and thus are not strictly comparable with earlier years.

[3] Data corrected for apparent error in source document (numbers displaced by one column).

Sources

For 1972–1982: U.S. Bureau of Labor Statistics (BLS), *Handbook of Labor Statistics*, Bulletin number 2217 (June 1985), pp. 411–14; for 1983–1984: BLS, *Handbook of Labor Statistics*, Bulletin number 2340 (August 1989), pp. 546–9; for 1985–1998: BLS, *Monthly Labor Review* 123 (1) (2000) Table 46, p. 117.

For more recent data: annual updates in *Monthly Labor Review*.

Documentation

With the exceptions of mining and railroads, these data are from the Survey of Occupational Injuries and Illnesses, which collects data from employers about their workers' job-related injuries and illnesses, based on records they maintain under the Occupational Safety and Health Act of 1970. Self-employed individuals and farms with fewer than eleven employees are excluded from the survey. The survey is based on a federal–state cooperative program, with an independent sample selected for each participating state. Sampling is stratified by Standard Industrial Classification code and size of employment. Mining and railroad data are furnished to the BLS by the Mine Safety and Health Administration and the Federal Railroad Administration, respectively. Work accident data collected under the Survey of Occupational Injuries and Illnesses are not considered comparable with earlier data (for example, series Ba4742).

An occupational injury is any injury that results from a work-related event or a single, instantaneous exposure in the work environment. An occupational illness is an abnormal condition or disorder, other than one resulting from an occupational injury, caused by exposure to factors associated with employment. Lost workday cases involve days away from work or days of restricted work activity, or both. Incidence rates are computed as the number of injuries and/or illnesses per 100 full-time workers. The

TABLE Ba4750–4767 Occupational injury and illness rates, by industry: 1972–1998 *Continued*

formula for the rate is 200,000*N/(EH), where *N* is the number of injuries and illnesses, EH is the total hours worked by all employees during the calendar year, and 200,000 represents the base for 100 full-time equivalent workers (full-time is assumed to be forty hours per week, fifty weeks per year).

Beginning with 1992, the data measure only nonfatal injuries and illnesses. Data on fatal occupational injuries from the Census of Fatal Occupational Injuries are summarized and updated in the BLS publication *Monthly Labor Review*. Fatalities constitute a very small percentage of occupational injuries and illnesses. In 1992, for example, there were approximately 6.8 million total cases of occupational injuries and illnesses reported in the private sector, but only about 5,000 fatalities.

TABLE Ba4768–4777 Railroad injuries and fatalities: 1890–1996[1, 2]

Contributed by Louis P. Cain

			Passengers		Employees		Trespassers		Other persons	
	Killed	Injured	Killed	Injured	Killed	Injured	Killed	Injured	Killed	Injured
	Ba4768	Ba4769	Ba4770	Ba4771	Ba4772	Ba4773	Ba4774	Ba4775	Ba4776 [3]	Ba4777 [3]
Year	Number	Number	Number	Number	Number	Number	Number	Number	Number	Number
1890	6,335	29,027	286	2,425	2,451	22,396	—	—	3,598	4,206
1891	7,029	33,881	293	2,972	2,660	26,140	—	—	4,076	4,769
1892	7,147	36,652	376	3,227	2,554	28,267	—	—	4,217	5,158
1893	7,346	40,393	299	3,229	2,727	31,729	—	—	4,320	5,435
1894	6,447	31,889	824	3,034	1,823	23,422	—	—	4,300	5,433
1895	6,136	33,748	170	2,375	1,811	25,696	—	—	4,155	6,677
1896	6,448	38,687	181	2,873	1,861	29,969	—	—	4,406	5,845
1897	6,437	36,731	222	2,795	1,693	27,667	—	—	4,522	6,269
1898	6,859	40,882	221	2,945	1,958	31,761	—	—	4,680	6,176
1899	7,123	44,620	239	3,442	2,210	34,923	—	—	4,674	6,255
1900	7,865	50,320	249	4,128	2,550	39,643	—	—	5,066	6,549
1901	8,455	53,339	282	4,988	2,675	41,142	—	—	5,498	7,209
1902	8,588	64,662	345	6,683	2,969	50,524	—	—	5,274	7,455
1903	9,840	76,553	355	8,231	3,606	60,481	—	—	5,879	7,841
1904	10,046	84,155	441	9,111	3,632	67,067	—	—	5,973	7,977
1905	9,703	86,008	537	10,457	3,361	66,833	—	—	5,805	8,718
1906	10,618	97,706	359	10,764	3,929	76,701	—	—	6,330	10,241
1907	11,839	111,016	610	13,041	4,534	87,644	—	—	6,695	10,331
1908	10,188	104,230	381	11,556	3,405	82,487	—	—	6,402	10,187
1909	8,722	95,626	253	10,311	2,610	75,006	—	—	5,859	10,309
1910	9,682	119,507	324	12,451	3,382	95,671	—	—	5,976	11,385
1911	10,396	150,159	299	12,042	3,602	126,039	—	—	6,495	12,078
1912	10,585	169,538	283	14,938	3,635	142,442	—	—	6,667	12,158
1913	10,964	200,308	350	15,130	3,715	171,417	—	—	6,899	13,761
1914	10,302	192,662	232	13,887	3,259	165,212	—	—	6,811	13,563
1915	8,621	162,040	199	10,914	2,152	138,092	—	—	6,270	13,034
1916 [4]	9,364	180,375	239	7,488	2,687	160,663	—	—	6,438	12,224
1916 [4]	10,001	196,722	246	7,152	2,941	176,923	—	—	6,814	12,647
1917	10,087	194,805	301	7,582	3,199	174,247	—	—	6,587	12,976
1918	9,286	174,575	471	7,316	3,419	156,013	—	—	5,396	11,246
1919	6,978	149,053	273	7,456	2,138	131,018	—	—	4,567	10,579
1920	6,958	168,309	229	7,591	2,578	149,414	—	—	4,151	11,304
1921	5,996	120,685	205	5,584	1,446	104,530	—	—	4,345	10,571
1922	6,325	134,871	200	6,153	1,657	117,197	2,430	2,844	2,038	8,677
1923	7,385	171,712	138	5,847	2,026	152,678	2,779	3,047	2,442	10,140
1924	6,617	143,739	149	5,354	1,543	125,319	2,556	2,853	2,369	10,213
1925	6,766	137,435	171	4,952	1,599	119,224	2,584	2,688	2,412	10,571
1926	7,090	130,235	152	4,461	1,672	111,903	2,561	2,545	2,705	11,326
1927	6,992	104,817	88	3,893	1,570	88,223	2,726	2,725	2,608	9,976
1928	6,680	86,205	91	3,468	1,329	70,873	2,487	2,367	2,773	9,497
1929	6,690	77,013	114	3,846	1,428	60,739	2,424	2,346	2,724	10,082
1930	5,665	49,443	61	2,666	977	35,872	2,409	2,675	2,218	8,230
1931	5,271	35,671	46	2,104	677	23,358	2,489	2,977	2,059	7,232
1932	4,905	29,232	27	1,912	579	17,742	2,577	3,364	1,722	6,214
1933	5,180	27,516	51	2,067	533	15,932	2,892	3,602	1,704	5,915
1934	5,020	28,641	38	1,945	556	17,338	2,697	2,785	1,729	6,573
1935	5,258	28,108	30	1,949	600	16,742	2,786	2,706	1,842	6,711
1936	5,550	34,723	41	2,548	720	22,409	2,801	2,418	1,988	7,348
1937	5,502	36,713	34	2,594	712	24,114	2,654	2,302	2,102	7,703
1938	4,649	27,275	81	2,345	513	16,569	2,360	2,108	1,695	6,253
1939	4,492	28,144	40	2,580	536	17,383	2,352	1,956	1,564	6,225

Notes appear at end of table

(continued)

TABLE Ba4768–4777 Railroad injuries and fatalities: 1890–1996 *Continued*

			Passengers		Employees		Trespassers		Other persons	
	Killed	Injured	Killed	Injured	Killed	Injured	Killed	Injured	Killed	Injured
	Ba4768	Ba4769	Ba4770	Ba4771	Ba4772	Ba4773	Ba4774	Ba4775	Ba4776 [3]	Ba4777 [3]
Year	Number	Number	Number	Number	Number	Number	Number	Number	Number	Number
1940	4,740	29,606	83	2,597	583	18,350	2,095	1,773	1,979	6,886
1941	5,191	37,829	48	3,009	807	25,866	2,195	1,576	2,141	7,378
1942	5,337	48,123	122	3,501	1,005	36,032	2,013	1,353	2,197	7,237
1943	5,051	60,348	278	5,166	1,072	46,971	1,755	1,135	1,946	7,076
1944	4,908	61,251	267	4,854	1,087	48,613	1,550	964	2,004	6,820
1945	4,812	61,515	156	4,840	972	48,632	1,592	1,012	2,092	7,031
1946	4,508	52,026	128	4,714	738	39,472	1,635	987	2,007	6,853
1947	4,285	48,819	79	4,246	791	36,880	1,480	1,018	1,935	6,675
1948	3,883	43,107	59	3,607	622	31,961	1,445	964	1,757	6,575
1949	3,426	32,123	37	2,545	450	22,993	1,287	921	1,652	5,664
1950	3,486	33,267	180	3,419	392	22,586	1,215	942	1,699	6,320
1951	3,459	34,454	150	3,184	432	24,266	1,142	826	1,735	6,178
1952	3,011	30,001	24	2,049	386	21,339	1,043	807	1,558	5,806
1953	3,039	29,214	49	2,503	343	20,170	1,044	796	1,603	5,745
1954	2,575	25,547	30	2,247	235	17,219	870	727	1,440	5,354
1955	2,761	27,840	24	2,253	282	19,011	867	680	1,588	5,896
1956	2,578	28,676	57	2,756	288	19,608	818	724	1,415	5,588
1957	2,393	18,688	15	1,566	195	12,246	742	617	1,441	4,259
1958	2,311	19,343	61	1,628	187	13,305	711	660	1,352	3,750
1959	2,094	19,909	10	1,352	178	14,198	641	619	1,265	3,740
1960	2,248	19,577	32	1,463	198	13,710	617	564	1,401	3,840
1961	2,127	27,118	17	1,887	145	20,194	624	678	1,341	4,359
1962	2,106	26,880	27	2,109	190	19,733	617	678	1,272	4,360
1963	2,141	27,456	13	2,135	173	19,992	571	658	1,384	4,671
1964	2,423	27,614	8	1,489	188	20,499	619	711	1,608	4,915
1965	2,399	25,789	11	1,189	184	19,133	634	668	1,570	4,799
1966	2,684	25,552	23	1,244	168	18,651	678	702	1,815	4,955
1967	2,483	24,523	12	1,054	176	18,055	646	696	1,649	4,718
1968	2,359	24,608	11	1,329	150	18,116	628	663	1,570	4,500
1969	2,299	23,356	6	862	190	17,255	627	674	1,476	4,565
1970	2,225	21,327	8	489	172	16,285	593	646	1,452	3,907
1971	2,010	18,972	16	536	123	14,191	551	607	1,320	3,638
1972	1,945	17,930	47	680	133	12,973	537	586	1,228	3,691
1975	1,560	—	8	—	113	—	524	—	915	—
1976	1,630	65,331	5	998	109	58,477	457	766	1,059	5,090
1977	1,530	67,867	4	503	116	61,643	458	689	952	5,032
1978	1,646	72,545	13	1,252	131	65,794	492	746	1,010	4,753
1979	1,429	74,126	6	999	102	65,955	516	805	805	4,496
1980	1,417	62,246	4	593	101	57,002	566	728	746	3,923
1981	1,284	53,003	4	409	67	48,483	582	761	631	3,350
1982	1,119	40,275	9	387	80	36,541	501	671	529	2,676
1983	1,073	34,819	4	502	64	30,811	472	683	533	2,823
1984	1,247	38,570	12	1,000	64	33,808	588	773	583	2,989
1985	1,036	34,304	3	657	48	30,479	474	734	511	2,672
1986	1,091	26,923	4	686	59	22,771	519	706	509	2,760
1987	1,165	26,033	16	475	56	22,378	584	673	509	2,507
1988	1,199	27,054	2	337	44	23,000	598	920	555	2,796
1989	—	29,269	8	399	50	22,590	641	898	625	2,828
1990	—	27,707	3	473	40	21,296	700	793	554	2,581
1991	—	25,911	8	382	36	19,988	663	769	487	2,329
1992	—	23,849	3	411	35	18,065	646	772	486	2,135
1993	—	21,730	58	559	51	15,711	675	733	495	2,116
1994	—	19,455	5	497	31	13,386	682	764	508	2,165
1995	—	16,779	0	573	36	11,029	660	700	450	2,137
1996	—	15,074	12	513	33	9,427	620	750	374	1,868

[1] Statistics on accidents and fatalities not strictly comparable because of changing definition of a reportable accident.

[2] Fiscal years ending June 30 through the first set of values shown for 1916; calendar years thereafter.

[3] Treatment of nontrain and trespasser accidents varies over time. See text.

[4] First set of 1916 figures is comparable to earlier data; second set is comparable to later data.

Sources

U.S. Federal Railroad Administration, *Accident Bulletin*, published annually (formerly issued by U.S. Interstate Commerce Commission), and related monthly reports.

Documentation

Reportable railroad accidents are divided into three groups: (1) train accidents, (2) train-service accidents, and (3) nontrain accidents. Train

TABLE Ba4768–4777 Railroad injuries and fatalities: 1890–1996 *Continued*

accidents are those arising from the operation or movement of trains, locomotives, or cars that result in a reportable death or injury and more than $750 damage to equipment, track, or roadbed; or a collision, derailment, or other train accident, with more than $750 damage to equipment, track, or roadbed. Train-service accidents are those arising from the operation or movement of trains, locomotives, or cars that result in a reportable death or injury but not more than $750 damage to equipment, track, or roadbed. Nontrain accidents are those that do not result from the operation or movement of trains, locomotives, or cars but are attributable to shop machinery or the use of tools and apparatus and that result in reportable casualties.

Series Ba4770–4771. Includes both passengers on trains and travelers not on trains.

Series Ba4776–4777. Includes passenger casualties sustained in nontrain accidents. The series also include trespassers prior to 1922. Prior to 1921, they include casualties sustained by employees not on duty in nontrain accidents; after that date, such casualties are included in the employees series.

TABLE Ba4778–4782 Underground accidents in the bituminous coal industry: 1906–1930

Contributed by Price V. Fishback

	Persons killed in accidents		Accident rate		
	All	Large-scale	Total	Small-scale	Large-scale
	Ba4778	Ba4779	Ba4780	Ba4781	Ba4782
Year	Number	Number	Per 10 million hours	Per 10 million hours	Per 10 million hours
1906	1,431	211	19.28	16.44	2.84
1907	2,364	899	26.60	16.48	10.12
1908	1,637	319	22.60	18.20	4.40
1909	1,965	476	23.50	17.81	5.69
1910	2,068	471	22.75	17.57	5.18
1911	1,840	318	20.83	17.23	3.60
1912	1,683	248	18.34	15.64	2.70
1913	2,039	445	20.64	16.14	4.50
1914	1,714	284	20.12	16.79	3.33
1915	1,553	249	18.36	15.42	2.94
1916	1,553	142	16.44	14.94	1.50
1917	1,908	257	18.84	16.30	2.54
1918	1,839	54	18.23	17.70	0.54
1919	1,537	101	19.17	17.91	1.26
1920	1,627	53	17.34	16.78	0.56
1921	1,340	29	19.68	19.25	0.43
1922	1,546	269	23.17	19.14	4.03
1923	1,825	286	21.03	17.73	3.30
1924	1,805	444	24.55	18.51	6.04
1925	1,727	253	21.61	18.44	3.17
1926	1,953	327	22.00	18.32	3.68
1927	1,632	153	20.63	18.70	1.93
1928	1,662	316	22.43	18.17	4.26
1929	1,615	150	20.97	19.02	1.95
1930	1,517	214	23.72	20.37	3.35

Sources

Price V. Fishback, *Soft Coal, Hard Choices: The Economic Welfare of Bituminous Coal Miners, 1890–1930* (Oxford University Press, 1992), pp. 103, 234–5, based on data reported by Keith Dix, *Work Relations in the Coal Industry: The Hand-Loading Era, 1880–1930*, West Virginia Bulletin, series 78, number 7-2 (1978), p. 79, and by W. W. Adams, L. E. Geyer, et al., "Coal-Mine Accidents in the United States, 1930," U.S. Bureau of Mines Bulletin number 355 (1930): 94–100.

Documentation

Accident rates were calculated by dividing the measure of fatalities by a measure of hours worked. Fishback reported information on all underground deaths, deaths in large-scale accidents (accidents in which five or more miners were killed), and deaths in small-scale accidents (accidents in which fewer than five miners were killed).

Underground hours worked are calculated as the product of total average underground workers and days worked and average hours worked per day. Days worked is defined as the average number of days the mines were open.

Series Ba4780–4782. Rates expressed per 10 million person-hours worked.

LABOR UNIONS

Joshua L. Rosenbloom

TABLE Ba4783–4791 Union membership: 1880–1999

Contributed by Joshua L. Rosenbloom

	Bureau of Labor Statistics		Troy–Sheflin		Current Population Survey				
	Union members	Canadian members of U.S. unions	Union members	Canadian members of U.S. unions	Union members among wage and salary workers	Wage and salary workers covered by union contracts	Friedman – union members	Wolman – union members	Troy – union members
	Ba4783	Ba4784	Ba4785	Ba4786	Ba4787	Ba4788	Ba4789	Ba4790	Ba4791
Year	Thousand	Thousand	Thousand	Thousand	Thousand	Thousand	Thousand	Thousand	Thousand
1880	—	—	—	—	—	—	169.9	—	—
1881	—	—	—	—	—	—	190.4	—	—
1882	—	—	—	—	—	—	287.6	—	—
1883	—	—	—	—	—	—	316.9	—	—
1884	—	—	—	—	—	—	391.0	—	—
1885	—	—	—	—	—	—	486.3	—	—
1886	—	—	—	—	—	—	1,206.6	—	—
1887	—	—	—	—	—	—	942.8	—	—
1888	—	—	—	—	—	—	697.2	—	—
1889	—	—	—	—	—	—	713.5	—	—
1890	—	—	—	—	—	—	822.1	—	—
1891	—	—	—	—	—	—	857.8	—	—
1892	—	—	—	—	—	—	793.3	—	—
1893	—	—	—	—	—	—	800.8	—	—
1894	—	—	—	—	—	—	867.4	—	—
1895	—	—	—	—	—	—	699.2	—	—
1896	—	—	—	—	—	—	613.9	—	—
1897	440	—	463.6	8.2	—	—	619.6	447.0	—
1898	467	—	533.4	9.4	—	—	710.2	500.7	—
1899	550	—	693.0	12.2	—	—	831.4	611.0	—
1900	791	—	949.2	16.8	—	—	1,170.2	868.5	—
1901	1,058	—	1,205.7	21.3	—	—	1,440.7	1,124.7	—
1902	1,335	—	1,546.5	27.3	—	—	1,681.0	1,375.9	—
1903	1,824	—	1,964.7	34.7	—	—	2,256.5	1,913.9	—
1904	2,067	—	2,054.9	36.3	—	—	2,383.4	2,072.7	—
1905	1,918	—	1,982.1	35.0	—	—	2,277.9	2,022.3	—
1906	1,892	—	1,965.3	34.7	—	—	2,156.9	1,907.3	—
1907	2,077	—	2,097.1	37.1	—	—	2,300.5	2,080.4	—
1908	2,092	—	2,088.6	36.9	—	—	2,277.0	2,130.6	—
1909	1,965	—	2,030.8	35.9	—	—	2,157.1	2,005.6	—
1910	2,116	—	2,207.5	39.0	—	—	2,268.7	2,140.5	—
1911	2,318	—	2,375.9	42.0	—	—	2,451.5	2,343.4	—
1912	2,405	—	2,533.2	44.8	—	—	2,519.1	2,452.4	—
1913	2,661	—	2,713.6	47.9	—	—	2,773.2	2,716.3	—
1914	2,647	—	2,658.4	47.0	—	—	2,724.6	2,687.1	—
1915	2,560	—	2,644.3	46.7	—	—	—	2,582.6	—
1916	2,722	—	2,869.8	96.5	—	—	—	2,772.7	—
1917	2,976	—	3,198.0	107.5	—	—	—	3,061.4	—
1918	3,368	—	3,685.3	123.9	—	—	—	3,467.3	—
1919	4,046	—	4,407.4	148.2	—	—	—	4,125.2	—
1920	5,034	—	4,991.0	167.8	—	—	—	5,047.8	—
1921	4,722	—	4,542.0	152.7	—	—	—	4,781.3	—
1922	3,950	—	3,884.8	130.6	—	—	—	4,027.4	—
1923	3,629	—	3,597.1	120.9	—	—	—	3,622.0	—
1924	3,549	—	3,530.4	118.7	—	—	—	3,536.1	—
1925	3,566	—	3,813.3	128.2	—	—	—	3,519.4	—
1926	3,592	—	4,016.6	274.4	—	—	—	3,502.4	—
1927	3,600	—	4,126.8	281.9	—	—	—	3,546.5	—
1928	3,567	—	4,068.1	277.9	—	—	—	3,479.8	—
1929	3,625	—	4,025.5	275.0	—	—	—	3,442.6	—

TABLE Ba4783–4791 Union membership: 1880–1999 *Continued*

	Bureau of Labor Statistics		Troy–Sheflin		Current Population Survey				
	Union members	Canadian members of U.S. unions	Union members	Canadian members of U.S. unions	Union members among wage and salary workers	Wage and salary workers covered by union contracts	Friedman – union members	Wolman – union members	Troy – union members
	Ba4783	Ba4784	Ba4785	Ba4786	Ba4787	Ba4788	Ba4789	Ba4790	Ba4791
Year	Thousand	Thousand	Thousand	Thousand	Thousand	Thousand	Thousand	Thousand	Thousand
1930	3,632	231	3,980.6	231.0	—	—	—	3,392.8	—
1931	3,526	216	3,775.7	216.0	—	—	—	3,358.1	—
1932	3,226	176	3,576.2	176.0	—	—	—	3,144.3	—
1933	2,857	168	3,659.0	168.0	—	—	—	2,973.0	—
1934	3,249	161	4,163.7	161.0	—	—	—	3,608.6	—
1935	3,728	144	3,793.6	144.0	—	—	—	—	3,753
1936	4,164	175	4,315.7	175.0	—	—	—	—	4,107
1937	7,218	217	5,923.1	217.0	—	—	—	—	5,780
1938	8,265	231	6,192.7	231.0	—	—	—	—	6,081
1939	8,980	217	6,708.2	217.0	—	—	—	—	6,556
1940	8,944	227	7,523.7	227.0	—	—	—	—	7,282
1941	10,489	288	9,016.6	288.0	—	—	—	—	8,698
1942	10,762	382	10,569.1	382.0	—	—	—	—	10,200
1943	13,642	429	12,102.6	429.0	—	—	—	—	11,812
1944	14,621	475	12,604.8	475.0	—	—	—	—	12,628
1945	14,796	474	12,728.2	474.0	—	—	—	—	12,562
1946	14,974	579	13,514.7	579.0	—	—	—	—	13,263
1947	15,414	627	14,694.1	627.0	—	—	—	—	14,595
1948	15,000 [1]	681	14,952.9	681.0	—	—	—	—	15,020
1949	15,000 [1]	718	14,653.8	718.0	—	—	—	—	14,695
1950	15,000 [1]	733	15,027.2	733.0	—	—	—	—	14,823
1951	16,750 [2]	804	15,893.4	754.0	—	—	—	—	15,772
1952	16,750 [2]	858	16,490.0	858.0	—	—	—	—	16,310
1953	17,860	912	17,222.0	912.0	—	—	—	—	17,316
1954	17,955	933	16,741.5	933.0	—	—	—	—	16,612
1955	17,749	947	17,073.9	947.0	—	—	—	—	16,990
1956	18,477	987	17,433.0	987.0	—	—	—	—	17,383
1957	18,431	1,062	17,559.7	1,062.0	—	—	—	—	17,687
1958	18,081	1,052	16,622.5	1,052.0	—	—	—	—	16,702
1959	18,169	1,052	16,490.3	1,052.0	—	—	—	—	16,501
1960	18,117	1,068	16,584.1	1,068.0	—	—	—	—	16,607
1961	17,328	1,025	16,425.5	1,025.0	—	—	—	—	16,143
1962	17,630	1,044	17,936.7	1,042.9	—	—	—	—	15,928
1963	17,586	1,062	18,187.9	1,054.5	—	—	—	—	—
1964	17,976	1,135	18,693.2	1,095.9	—	—	—	—	—
1965	18,519	1,220	19,443.4	1,174.6	—	—	—	—	—
1966	19,181	1,241	20,171.6	1,249.3	—	—	—	—	—
1967	19,712	1,345	20,986.6	1,318.8	—	—	—	—	—
1968	20,258	1,342	21,379.8	1,362.4	—	—	—	—	—
1969	20,382	1,346	21,565.8	1,380.1	—	—	—	—	—
1970	20,751	1,371	22,348.5	1,358.1	—	—	—	—	—
1971	20,582	1,371	22,098.9	1,387.8	—	—	—	—	—
1972	20,893	1,458	22,640.3	1,434.5	—	—	—	—	—
1973	21,294	1,443	23,370.8	1,489.5	18,088.6	—	—	—	—
1974	21,643	1,444	23,660.8	1,495.5	18,176.5	—	—	—	—
1975	—	—	23,701.4	1,494.4	16,778.3	—	—	—	—
1976	21,171	1,537	23,686.1	1,533.1	17,403.0	—	—	—	—
1977	—	—	23,178.3	1,546.1	19,335.1	21,534.6	—	—	—
1978	21,784	1,538	23,353.0	1,596.6	19,548.4	21,897.5	—	—	—
1979	—	—	23,672.4	1,647.0	20,986.1	23,540.1	—	—	—
1980	—	—	22,556.3	1,588.0	20,095.3	22,493.4	—	—	—
1981	—	—	22,204.1	1,557.3	19,123.4	21,434.4	—	—	—
1982	—	—	21,130.5	1,559.1	—	—	—	—	—
1983	—	—	20,185.1	1,551.5	17,717.4	20,532.1	—	—	—
1984	—	—	—	—	17,339.8	19,931.5	—	—	—

Notes appear at end of table

(continued)

TABLE Ba4783–4791 Union membership: 1880–1999 *Continued*

	Bureau of Labor Statistics		Troy–Sheflin		Current Population Survey				
	Union members	Canadian members of U.S. unions	Union members	Canadian members of U.S. unions	Union members among wage and salary workers	Wage and salary workers covered by union contracts	Friedman – union members	Wolman – union members	Troy – union members
	Ba4783	Ba4784	Ba4785	Ba4786	Ba4787	Ba4788	Ba4789	Ba4790	Ba4791
Year	Thousand	Thousand	Thousand	Thousand	Thousand	Thousand	Thousand	Thousand	Thousand
1985	—	—	—	—	16,996.1	19,358.1	—	—	—
1986	—	—	—	—	16,975.2	19,277.8	—	—	—
1987	—	—	—	—	16,913.1	19,051.0	—	—	—
1988	—	—	—	—	17,001.7	19,241.3	—	—	—
1989	—	—	—	—	16,960.5	19,197.6	—	—	—
1990	—	—	—	—	16,739.8	19,057.8	—	—	—
1991	—	—	—	—	16,568.4	18,733.8	—	—	—
1992	—	—	—	—	16,390.3	18,540.1	—	—	—
1993	—	—	—	—	16,598.1	18,646.4	—	—	—
1994	—	—	—	—	16,740.3	18,842.5	—	—	—
1995	—	—	—	—	16,359.6	18,346.3	—	—	—
1996	—	—	—	—	16,109.9	18,158.1	—	—	—
1997	—	—	—	—	16,109.9	18,158.1	—	—	—
1998	—	—	—	—	16,211.4	17,918.3	—	—	—
1999	—	—	—	—	16,476.7	18,182.3	—	—	—

[1] Midpoint of range 14–16 million.

[2] Midpoint of range 16.5–17 million.

Sources

U.S. Bureau of Labor Statistics (BLS), *Handbook of Labor Statistics*, Bulletin number 1016 (1950), Table E-1; Bulletin number 2000 (1978), Table 150; and *Directory of National Unions and Employee Associations* (1979). Leo Troy and Neil Sheflin, *U.S. Union Sourcebook: Membership, Finances, Structure, Directory*, 1st edition (Industrial Relations Data and Information Services, 1985), Appendix A. Barry T. Hirsch and David A. Macpherson, *Union Membership and Earnings Data Book: Compilations from the Current Population Survey*, 2000 edition (Bureau of National Affairs, 2000), Table 1. Gerald Friedman, "New Estimates of Union Membership: The United States, 1880–1914," *Historical Methods* 32 (2) (1999). Leo Wolman, *The Ebb and Flow of Trade Unionism*, NBER publication number 30 (National Bureau of Economic Research, 1936); from Leo Troy, *Trade Union Membership, 1897–1962*, NBER Occasional Paper number 92 (Columbia University Press for the National Bureau of Economic Research, 1965).

The only *currently updated* series of union membership statistics available for the United States is derived from the Current Population Survey (CPS). These statistics are reported in Hirsch and Macpherson (2000), which is updated annually, as well as in the January issue of BLS's *Employment and Earnings*.

Documentation

This table provides several alternative estimates of union membership. The series cover different, but overlapping, periods of time and employ somewhat different methods of measuring union membership. Three distinct approaches to measuring union membership can be identified. The first relies on official membership figures reported directly by the various trade unions. The second infers membership information on the basis of financial data reported by unions. The third uses surveys of samples of households.

Official membership statistics are problematic because unions may differ in their definition and reporting of membership, in the accuracy and availability of membership data at their headquarters, and in their willingness to make these data available to outsiders. Unions define eligibility for membership in a variety of ways. In particular, dues payments may be waived or reduced for workers who are unemployed or on strike. Similarly, members who are apprentices, retired, or in the armed forces may not be obliged to pay the full-time dues. Unions and union locals may also seek, for strategic reasons, to either over- or understate the extent of their membership. Although the Bureau of Labor Statistics has attempted to gather information about variation in union membership reports, these efforts have been largely unsuccessful. See Harry P. Cohany, "Union Membership," in *BLS Handbook of Methods for Surveys and Studies*, Bulletin number 1711 (U.S. Government Printing Office, 1971), Chapter 21.

Union financial data provide an alternative route to measuring membership that avoids potential inconsistencies in union reporting practices. In the simplest case, dividing union dues revenue by the full-time dues rate provides a measure of the "average annual, dues-paying, full-time equivalent membership." While official membership figures appear likely to overstate actual membership, the dues-paying-member concept may result in an undercount of membership to the extent that some active members are not obliged to pay full-time dues for one reason or another. Where unions have multiple dues rates, or where dues are calculated as a percentage of income, the use of financial data becomes more complicated and may result in inaccurate measurements of membership. In some instances, it is possible to calculate membership for different membership classes, or to use other payments that are apportioned on a strictly per capita basis to make the calculations. See Troy (1965), pp. 10–14.

A third approach to measuring union membership relies on household surveys conducted by the U.S. Bureau of the Census for its monthly Current Population Survey. The CPS has included questions on union status in the survey since 1973. The survey approach has the virtue of avoiding the ambiguities involved in using either official figures or union financial data, but the CPS survey data refer only to wage and salary workers, and thus exclude self-employed union members. They are also limited to the sole or principal job of full- and part-time workers, and will undercount the small number of individuals (mainly in the performing arts) who hold membership in more than one union.

Series Ba4783–4784. The BLS series on union membership are a combination of two distinct approaches to the measurement problem. From 1951 through 1978, when the practice was discontinued, the Bureau compiled comprehensive membership statistics on the basis of biennial questionnaires that asked unions to report the average number of dues-paying members or the number of members in good standing for the two most recent years. Where unions failed to respond, the Bureau filled this gap with estimates from other sources, such as union periodicals, convention proceedings, financial statements, and collective bargaining agreements. In addition to total membership data, the survey also collected data on the number of women members (first reported in 1953), membership outside the United States (first reported in 1955), membership by occupational category and industry (first reported in 1957), and membership by state (first reported in 1959). To be included in the survey, a union had either to be affiliated with the

TABLE Ba4783–4791 Union membership: 1880–1999 *Continued*

American Federation of Labor–Congress of Industrial Organizations (AFL–CIO) or (if it was unaffiliated) to be a party to collective bargaining agreements with different employers in more than one state. In addition, unions of federal government employees that have received "exclusive recognition" under Executive Order 11491 were also included in the survey beginning in 1968.

Series Ba4783–4784. Prior to 1951, BLS estimates of union membership were built up by aggregating reports of the AFL and the CIO, to which were added estimates of independent membership derived from a variety of sources. Membership figures for the AFL were derived from Lewis Lorwin, *The American Federation of Labor* (Brookings Institution Press, 1935), p. 488, and from "Proceedings" of the AFL's annual convention. These sources report membership based on the per capita payments of affiliated unions that the AFL used to allocate voting rights at its convention. The CIO never published a consecutive membership series. Therefore, figures shown are based on reports or statements of CIO officials. See BLS (1950), pp. 137–9, for specific sources. Independent union membership data for 1897–1934 were derived from Wolman (1936). For 1929–1934, these data have been adjusted to include membership in the Trade Union Unity League. Wolman's estimates of independent trade union membership are reported in series Ba4801. Data on unaffiliated unions from 1934 through 1950 are fragmentary, and the Bureau estimated them from a variety of available sources.

Series Ba4785–4786. Leo Troy and Neil Sheflin used union financial data to construct a consistent set of estimates of full-time dues-paying membership. For 1962–1983, they obtained their data from annual financial reports filed under the Labor Management Reporting and Disclosure Act of 1959 (LMRDA). Under LMRDA as supplemented by Executive Order 11491 of 1970, Section 7120 of the Civil Service Reform Act of 1978, and the Postal Reorganization Act of 1970, essentially all multistate unions, as well as unions representing federal employees and postal unions, file such reports. Unions of state, county, and municipal employees are also included in the post-1962 data, although they do not file under the LMRDA. To construct their estimates, Troy and Sheflin began with the annual per capita revenues received by the parent regional, national, or international organization from local unions and divided these sums by the organization's per capita dues rate. The result is the average annual, full-time equivalent dues-paying membership. See Troy and Sheflin (1985) for additional details. Their estimates of Canadian union membership are from the directories of labor organizations in Canada published by Labour Canada.

Series Ba4785–4786. Membership figures for 1935–1961 were derived from Troy (1965) (reported in series Ba4790) after revision, extension of coverage, and conversion to a calendar-year basis, using a simple weighted average of the current and next-year membership, with the percentage of the current calendar year included in the fiscal year used as the weight. For 1897–1934, data on union membership are derived from Wolman (1936) (reported in series Ba4791), adjusted to a calendar-year basis. The AFL's annual convention reported membership as of the August fiscal year closing date during this period; this was done by applying weights of 0.667 and 0.333 for the current and one-year-ahead figures reported by Wolman for the AFL (series Ba4800).

Series Ba4787–4788. The following description of the measurement of union membership and coverage based on the Current Population Survey is excerpted with minor editorial changes from Barry T. Hirsch and David A. Macpherson, *Union Membership and Earnings Data Book: Compilations from the Current Population Survey*, 1996 edition (BNAPlus, 1996). CPS unionization estimates are based on calculations from a monthly survey of households conducted by the Census Bureau. Currently, the CPS sample includes interviews each month with about 57,000 households, containing an average of roughly two persons age 16 and over per household. These households include approximately 60,000 employed *wage and salary* workers (earnings and union status are not reported for self-employed workers). Households are selected by the Census Bureau primarily on the basis of area of residence, so that accurate estimates of employment and the labor force can be obtained. The CPS sampling design is such that households are interviewed for four months, followed by eight months out of the sample and an additional four months in the sample.

Series Ba4787–4788. Questions on union status are included in an earnings supplement that is administered each month to a quarter sample of the CPS that comprises those households leaving the sample. Annual figures are compiled from each year's twelve monthly CPS Outgoing Rotation Group (ORG) files. Individuals are included in the ORG files in the same month in consecutive years. But within each year, all observations are for unique individuals. Monthly sample sizes are approximately 15,000, and annual sample sizes are roughly 180,000. Union membership and contract coverage information are based on responses to two survey questions. There have been no changes in the union status questions since 1977. Individuals are counted as union members if they respond yes to the question: "On this job, is [respondent] a member of a labor union or of an employee association similar to a union?" Those who answer no to the union membership question are then asked: "On this job, is [respondent] covered by a union or employee association contract?" Workers are counted as covered if they are union members, or if they are not union members but say they are covered by a union contract. Union status is recorded for all workers. The Census Bureau assigns responses for individuals unable to provide answers (approximately 2 percent), based on characteristics such as industry, occupation, age, race, and sex. For the years 1973–1976, there was a membership question but no question to nonmembers about coverage. The union membership question in this period read: "Does [respondent] belong to a labor union on this job?" In 1977, the phrase "or employee association similar to a union" was added, along with the follow-up question on coverage.

Series Ba4787–4788. Union status questions were not asked monthly in the CPS until January 1983. Prior to 1983, union information was collected for the years 1966 and 1970, and then became available on a regular basis in the CPS for May 1973 through May 1981. Sample sizes for these earlier years are substantially smaller than those since 1983 and are consequently subject to greater sampling error. There were no union questions asked in the 1982 CPS.

Series Ba4789. Gerald Friedman's estimates of union membership in the years 1880–1914 are constructed from a wide variety of secondary and primary sources. For 1897–1914, Friedman's figures modify Wolman's estimates by (1) including membership data for the Knights of Labor, and at least twelve national trade unions omitted by Wolman; (2) including members of local unions unaffiliated with national unions; (3) deducting Canadian members of U.S.-based unions; and (4) correcting some transcription errors in collecting data on membership in the AFL federal labor unions. See Friedman (1999), pp. 75–8, for further discussion of these corrections, and of methods used to reconstruct union membership before 1897.

Series Ba4790–4791. These union membership estimates are derived primarily from financial data. Consequently, they are measures of the annual average number of dues-paying members.

TABLE Ba4792–4804 Union membership, by affiliation: 1897–1955

Contributed by Joshua L. Rosenbloom

	Bureau of Labor Statistics					Troy–Sheflin			Wolman		Troy		
	Unions affiliated with the AFL		Unions affiliated with the CIO		Membership in independent or unaffiliated unions	AFL-affiliated unions	CIO-affiliated unions	Independent or unaffiliated unions	AFL-affiliated unions	Independent or unaffiliated unions	AFL-affiliated unions	CIO-affiliated unions	Independent or unaffiliated unions
	Unions	Membership	Unions	Membership									
	Ba4792	Ba4793	Ba4794	Ba4795	Ba4796 [1]	Ba4797	Ba4798	Ba4799	Ba4800	Ba4801	Ba4802	Ba4803	Ba4804
Year	Number	Thousand	Number	Thousand	Thousand	Thousand	Thousand	Thousand	Thousand	Thousand	Thousand	Thousand	Thousand
1897	58	265	—	—	—	283.1	—	180.5	272	175	—	—	—
1898	67	278	—	—	—	337.2	—	196.2	312	189	—	—	—
1899	73	349	—	—	—	480.4	—	212.5	410	201	—	—	—
1900	82	548	—	—	—	697.7	—	251.5	625	243	—	—	—
1901	87	788	—	—	—	919.9	—	285.9	854	270	—	—	—
1902	97	1,024	—	—	—	1,230.3	—	316.2	1,065	311	—	—	—
1903	113	1,466	—	—	—	1,595.3	—	369.4	1,556	358	—	—	—
1904	120	1,676	—	—	—	1,659.5	—	395.3	1,682	391	—	—	—
1905	118	1,494	—	—	—	1,548.4	—	433.7	1,598	424	—	—	—
1906	119	1,454	—	—	—	1,504.1	—	461.2	1,469	438	—	—	—
1907	117	1,539	—	—	—	1,599.2	—	497.9	1,542	538	—	—	—
1908	116	1,587	—	—	—	1,584.5	—	504.2	1,625	505	—	—	—
1909	119	1,483	—	—	—	1,536.7	—	494.1	1,524	482	—	—	—
1910	120	1,562	—	—	—	1,642.3	—	565.2	1,587	554	—	—	—
1911	115	1,762	—	—	—	1,813.4	—	562.5	1,787	556	—	—	—
1912	112	1,770	—	—	—	1,908.5	—	624.8	1,818	635	—	—	—
1913	111	1,996	—	—	—	2,062.6	—	651.0	2,051	665	—	—	—
1914	110	2,021	—	—	—	2,040.5	—	617.9	2,061	626	—	—	—
1915	110	1,946	—	—	—	2,027.1	—	617.2	1,968	614	—	—	—
1916	111	2,073	—	—	—	2,209.1	—	660.6	2,124	649	—	—	—
1917	111	2,371	—	—	—	2,586.0	—	611.9	2,457	605	—	—	—
1918	111	2,726	—	—	—	2,997.2	—	688.0	2,825	642	—	—	—
1919	111	3,260	—	—	—	3,606.8	—	800.6	3,339	786	—	—	—
1920	110	4,079	—	—	—	4,052.9	—	938.1	4,093	955	—	—	—
1921	110	3,907	—	—	—	3,734.9	—	807.2	3,967	815	—	—	—
1922	112	3,196	—	—	—	3,147.0	—	737.9	3,273	754	—	—	—
1923	108	2,926	—	—	—	2,897.0	—	700.1	2,919	703	—	—	—
1924	107	2,866	—	—	—	2,842.4	—	688.0	2,853	683	—	—	—
1925	107	2,877	—	—	—	2,823.5	—	989.8	2,831	689	—	—	—
1926	107	2,804	—	—	—	2,824.6	—	1,192.0	2,715	788	—	—	—
1927	106	2,813	—	—	—	2,839.9	—	1,286.9	2,759	787	—	—	—
1928	107	2,896	—	—	—	2,800.7	—	1,267.4	2,809	671	—	—	—
1929	105	2,934	—	—	—	2,761.7	—	1,263.8	2,770	691	—	—	—
1930	104	2,961	—	—	—	2,744.5	—	1,236.1	2,745	671	—	—	—
1931	105	2,890	—	—	—	2,680.0	—	1,095.7	2,743	636	—	—	—
1932	106	2,532	—	—	—	2,435.8	—	1,140.5	2,497	694	—	—	—
1933	108	2,127	—	—	—	2,504.3	—	1,154.8	2,318	730	—	—	—
1934	109	2,608	—	—	—	3,090.6	—	1,073.1	3,030	683	—	—	—

Year	Bureau of Labor Statistics: Unions affiliated with the AFL: Unions	Bureau of Labor Statistics: Unions affiliated with the AFL: Membership	Bureau of Labor Statistics: Unions affiliated with the CIO: Unions	Bureau of Labor Statistics: Unions affiliated with the CIO: Membership	Bureau of Labor Statistics: Membership in independent or unaffiliated unions	Troy–Sheflin: AFL-affiliated unions	Troy–Sheflin: CIO-affiliated unions	Troy–Sheflin: Independent or unaffiliated unions	Wolman: AFL-affiliated unions	Wolman: Independent or unaffiliated unions	Troy: AFL-affiliated unions	Troy: CIO-affiliated unions	Troy: Independent or unaffiliated unions
	Ba4792	Ba4793	Ba4794	Ba4795	Ba4796 [1]	Ba4797	Ba4798	Ba4799	Ba4800	Ba4801	Ba4802	Ba4803	Ba4804
	Number	Thousand	Number	Thousand	Thousand	Thousand	Thousand	Thousand	Thousand	Thousand	Thousand	Thousand	Thousand
1935	109	3,045	—	—	683	3,255.8	—	537.8	—	—	3,218	—	535
1936	111	3,422	—	—	742	3,701.0	—	614.6	—	—	3,516	—	591
1937	100	2,861	32	3,718	639	3,296.1	2,015.5	611.5	—	—	3,180	1,991	609
1938	102	3,623	42	4,038	604	3,641.9	1,972.7	578.1	—	—	3,547	1,958	575
1939	104	4,006	45	4,000	974	3,961.8	1,875.9	870.5	—	—	3,878	1,838	840
1940	105	4,247	42	3,625	1,072	4,475.8	2,242.8	805.1	—	—	4,343	2,154	785
1941	106	4,569	41	5,000	920	5,381.4	2,739.7	895.4	—	—	5,179	2,654	865
1942	102	5,483	39	4,195	1,084	6,279.4	2,602.6	1,687.1	—	—	6,076	2,493	1,631
1943	99	6,564	40	5,285	1,793	6,859.5	3,448.4	1,794.7	—	—	6,779	3,303	1,729
1944	100	6,807	41	5,935	1,879	6,866.5	3,983.9	1,754.4	—	—	6,877	3,937	1,814
1945	102	6,931	40	6,000	1,865	7,003.4	3,947.2	1,777.6	—	—	6,890	3,928	1,744
1946	102	7,152	40	6,000	1,822	7,857.9	3,935.9	1,720.9	—	—	7,652	3,847	1,764
1947	105	7,578	40	6,000	1,836	8,545.5	4,471.6	1,677.0	—	—	8,467	4,451	1,677
1948	105	7,221	40	—	2,350 [2]	8,064.2	4,382.7	2,506.0	—	—	8,095	4,451	2,474
1949	107	7,241	39	—	2,150 [2]	8,189.1	4,216.2	2,248.5	—	—	8,143	4,314	2,238
1950	107	7,143	30	—	2,600 [2]	8,598.0	3,765.9	2,663.2	—	—	8,494	3,713	2,616
1951	108	9,500	33	5,000	2,250 [2]	9,610.1	4,192.6	2,090.7	—	—	9,497	4,183	2,092
1952	109	9,500	33	5,000	2,250 [2]	10,091.2	4,325.1	2,073.7	—	—	9,977	4,261	2,071
1953	110	10,778	35	5,252	1,830	10,392.3	4,804.0	2,025.7	—	—	10,438	4,838	2,040
1954	109	10,929	32	5,200	1,826	10,366.7	4,539.9	1,834.9	—	—	10,258	4,494	1,860
1955	—	—	—	—	—	10,664.3	4,630.6	1,770.9	—	—	10,593	4,608	1,788

[1] For 1897–1934, the U.S. Bureau of Labor Statistics (BLS) accepted Wolman's estimates of membership in independent or unaffiliated unions, series Ba4801.

[2] Figures for 1948–1952 are midpoints of the following estimated ranges: 2.2–2.5 million, 2.0–2.3 million, 2.4–2.8 million, 2.0–2.5 million, and 2.0–2.5 million, respectively.

Sources

BLS, *Handbook of Labor Statistics,* Bulletin number 1016 (1950), Table E-1, and Bulletin number 2000 (1978), Table 149. Leo Troy and Neil Sheflin, *U.S. Union Sourcebook: Membership, Finances, Structure, Directory* (Industrial Relations Data and Information Services, 1985), Appendix Table A-1. Leo Wolman, *The Ebb and Flow of Trade Unionism*, NBER publication number 30 (National Bureau of Economic Research, 1936), from Leo Troy, *Trade Union Membership, 1897–1962*, NBER Occasional Paper number 92 (Columbia University Press for the National Bureau of Economic Research, 1965).

Documentation

See also the text for Table Ba4783–4791 for a discussion of the methods used in constructing the series in this table.

The Committee for Industrial Organization, later renamed Congress of Industrial Organizations (CIO), was formed in November 1935 by eight unions affiliated with the American Federation of Labor (AFL) and maintained its identity until it merged with the AFL in December 1955. The new organization was named the American Federation of Labor and Congress of Industrial Organizations (AFL–CIO). For 1955, the BLS reports the combined membership of the AFL and CIO under the heading AFL–CIO (see series Ba4806). Leo Troy and Neil Sheflin have adjusted the data to a calendar-year basis. Consequently, they assign most membership to the AFL and CIO separately, reporting only a small figure for the newly created AFL–CIO in 1955 (see series Ba4808).

Treatment of unions in the independent and unaffiliated category is subject to a variety of limitations. Several important developments should be noted. In December 1947, the United Mine Workers disaffiliated from the AFL and are included in the independent category in subsequent years. In 1949, the Communications Workers of America affiliated with the CIO. In 1950, the expulsion of eleven unions from the CIO placed these organizations in the Independent Unions category.

Series Ba4800–4804. These union membership estimates are derived primarily from financial data. Consequently, they are measures of the annual average number of dues-paying members. See the text for Table Ba4783–4791 for further discussion of this method.

TABLE Ba4805–4813 Union membership, by affiliation: 1955–1983

Contributed by Joshua L. Rosenbloom

	Bureau of Labor Statistics			Troy–Sheflin				Troy	
	Unions affiliated with AFL–CIO								
	Unions	Membership	Membership in independent or unaffiliated unions	Unions affiliated with AFL–CIO	Independent or unaffiliated unions	Assembly of Governmental Employees	American Association of Classified School Employees	Unions affiliated with the AFL–CIO	Independent or unaffiliated unions
	Ba4805	Ba4806	Ba4807	Ba4808	Ba4809	Ba4810	Ba4811	Ba4812	Ba4813
Year	Number	Thousand	Thousand	Thousand	Thousand	Thousand	Thousand	Thousand	Thousand
1955	139	16,062	1,688	8.1 [1]	1,770.9	—	—	—	—
1956	137	16,904	1,573	15,707.5	1,725.5	—	—	15,639	1,744
1957	139	16,954	1,476	15,965.1	1,594.6	—	—	16,078	1,609
1958	137	14,993	3,088	13,849.3	2,773.2	—	—	13,891	2,812
1959	135	15,124	3,044	13,701.4	2,788.9	—	—	13,715	2,787
1960	134	15,072	3,045	13,866.6	2,717.5	—	—	13,881	2,726
1961	131	14,572	2,756	13,618.2	2,807.2	—	—	13,568	2,575
1962	130	14,835	2,794	13,784.8	4,152.0	—	—	13,576	2,352
1963	130	14,818	2,768	13,904.2	4,283.8	—	—	—	—
1964	129	15,150	2,825	14,235.3	4,457.9	—	—	—	—
1965	128	15,604	2,915	14,815.9	4,627.5	—	—	—	—
1966	129	16,198	2,983	15,372.1	4,799.5	—	—	—	—
1967	128	16,638	3,074	15,960.6	5,025.9	—	—	—	—
1968	126	15,608	4,650	16,625.8	5,114.1	—	—	—	—
1969	120	15,642	4,740	14,982.8	6,582.9	—	—	—	—
1970	120	15,978	4,773	14,988.5	6,929.0	430.9	—	—	—
1971	115	16,183	4,399	15,238.6	6,398.9	461.3	—	—	—
1972	113	16,507	4,386	15,241.1	6,842.5	556.7	—	—	—
1973	112	16,726	4,568	15,662.3	7,010.2	606.5	91.7	—	—
1974	111	16,938	4,705	15,673.5	7,241.5	653.8	91.9	—	—
1975	—	—	—	15,666.7	7,273.5	660.8	100.4	—	—
1976	112	16,699	4,472	15,610.6	7,297.5	669.5	108.5	—	—
1977	—	—	—	15,210.2	7,219.4	635.8	112.9	—	—
1978	108	17,024	4,760	15,523.7	7,284.9	427.4	117.1	—	—
1979	—	—	—	15,831.3	7,301.4	413.7	125.9	—	—
1980	—	—	—	14,997.3	7,035.9	397.1	125.9	—	—
1981	—	—	—	16,241.4	5,492.8	344.0	125.9	—	—
1982	—	—	—	15,435.9	5,227.5	341.1	125.9	—	—
1983	—	—	—	14,829.7	4,889.3	340.2	125.9	—	—

[1] Most membership were assigned to the American Federation of Labor and Congress of Industrial Organizations separately; see the text for Table Ba4792–4804.

Sources

U.S. Bureau of Labor Statistics (BLS), *Handbook of Labor Statistics*, Bulletin number 2000 (1978), Table 150, and *Directory of National Unions and Employee Associations* (1979). Leo Troy and Neil Sheflin, *Union Sourcebook: Membership, Finances, Structure, Directory*, 1st edition (Industrial Relations Data and Information Services, 1985), Appendix A. Leo Troy, *Trade Union Membership, 1897–1962*, NBER Occasional Paper 92 (Columbia University Press for the National Bureau of Economic Research, 1965).

Documentation

See the text for Tables Ba4783–4804 for additional discussion.

Series Ba4807. Excludes members of single-firm and local unaffiliated unions.

TABLE Ba4814–4831 Union membership, by industry: 1897–1934

Contributed by Joshua L. Rosenbloom

	Total	Mining, quarrying, and oil	Building construction	Metals, machinery, and shipbuilding	Textiles	Leather and shoes	Clothing	Lumber and woodworking	Paper, printing, and bookbinding
	Ba4814	Ba4815	Ba4816	Ba4817	Ba4818	Ba4819	Ba4820	Ba4821	Ba4822
Year	Thousand	Thousand	Thousand	Thousand	Thousand	Thousand	Thousand	Thousand	Thousand
1897	447	21	67	50	8	15	15	6	38
1898	501	44	74	46	8	12	15	12	39
1899	611	75	97	59	7	8	15	16	43
1900	868	131	153	81	8	10	25	26	48
1901	1,125	218	192	104	7	15	38	32	55
1902	1,376	197	263	137	15	24	59	34	70
1903	1,914	280	369	205	19	42	77	48	88
1904	2,073	279	392	213	15	43	78	52	92
1905	2,022	297	373	166	14	41	63	42	91
1906	1,907	265	389	187	14	40	54	36	88
1907	2,080	312	433	212	16	40	65	27	86
1908	2,131	290	445	200	17	40	73	20	87
1909	2,006	307	426	178	14	40	80	19	83
1910	2,140	275	459	196	21	47	98	28	90
1911	2,343	311	479	210	21	50	145	29	97
1912	2,452	343	509	204	23	56	131	26	102
1913	2,716	432	553	219	29	55	164	25	107
1914	2,687	380	542	226	30	58	158	25	111
1915	2,583	332	533	224	22	53	174	21	116
1916	2,773	338	553	267	29	61	210	18	126
1917	3,061	373	606	310	41	73	222	18	137
1918	3,467	433	701	396	49	75	258	14	144
1919	4,125	419	802	618	60	104	324	16	148
1920	5,048	439	888	859	149	113	374	24	164
1921	4,781	470	869	728	88	96	323	20	182
1922	4,027	387	826	506	37	90	310	12	160
1923	3,622	530	790	257	37	56	295	11	151
1924	3,536	493	814	218	38	47	282	11	154
1925	3,519	439	837	205	36	54	292	10	156
1926	3,502	386	867	202	36	55	292	11	158
1927	3,546	397	903	204	35	49	267	13	162
1928	3,480	333	905	205	35	45	239	13	162
1929	3,443	271	919	211	35	47	218	13	162
1930	3,393	230	904	203	35	44	230	13	165
1931	3,358	309	890	191	34	38	224	12	166
1932	3,144	357	806	173	29	29	211	8	160
1933	2,973	355	583	180	16	76	336	8	153
1934	3,609 [1]	579	605	222	40	117	405	10	162

Note appears at end of table

(continued)

TABLE Ba4814–4831 Union membership, by industry: 1897–1934 *Continued*

Year	Chemicals, clay, glass, stone	Food, liquor, tobacco	Transportation and communications	Public service	Theaters and music	Trade	Hotel and restaurant service	Domestic and personal service	Miscellaneous industries
	Ba4823	Ba4824	Ba4825	Ba4826	Ba4827	Ba4828	Ba4829	Ba4830	Ba4831
	Thousand	Thousand	Thousand	Thousand	Thousand	Thousand	Thousand	Thousand	Thousand
1897	23	46	116	11	7	4	2	2	17
1898	25	46	130	11	8	6	2	3	18
1899	27	51	158	11	9	8	2	4	22
1900	30	69	189	15	9	20	5	7	42
1901	33	77	216	18	13	25	10	14	59
1902	39	93	258	19	15	30	19	20	84
1903	46	122	339	22	20	50	39	29	119
1904	49	136	444	23	28	50	49	30	100
1905	51	104	446	24	38	50	39	27	158
1906	55	103	422	26	43	50	34	29	72
1907	55	110	460	31	45	50	36	27	73
1908	55	112	470	39	47	50	39	30	118
1909	57	119	438	44	52	15	37	29	66
1910	60	128	480	53	60	15	37	29	64
1911	59	128	513	66	69	15	43	31	76
1912	60	137	530	67	77	15	48	32	94
1913	56	141	557	86	82	15	69	34	92
1914	58	145	562	91	92	15	72	37	86
1915	53	119	576	90	87	15	61	38	69
1916	52	117	623	96	87	15	59	40	82
1917	52	120	695	102	82	15	65	44	105
1918	51	137	777	105	87	15	65	44	114
1919	48	168	959	137	88	15	61	42	119
1920	52	181	1,256	161	99	21	60	51	157
1921	53	146	1,240	172	106	21	69	55	143
1922	50	99	1,039	171	107	17	60	61	95
1923	50	76	907	180	104	10	45	56	67
1924	45	76	893	185	108	10	46	57	61
1925	42	75	893	193	110	10	46	60	60
1926	42	75	884	204	112	10	46	63	61
1927	41	70	889	212	113	10	47	66	68
1928	39	66	890	224	132	10	46	66	69
1929	38	65	892	247	135	10	45	67	67
1930	35	62	882	264	134	10	44	73	64
1931	33	60	816	276	132	10	38	70	60
1932	29	56	699	300	128	9	31	63	57
1933	27	58	609	296	127	5	32	55	57
1934	47	82	645	299	127	6	53	64	137

[1] Includes 11,000 union members in the professional service industry, not shown separately.

Source

Leo Wolman, *Ebb and Flow in Trade Unionism*, NBER publication number 30 (National Bureau of Economic Research, 1936), pp. 172–93.

Documentation

These figures were obtained by classifying national and international unions into industrial categories and totaling membership of the unions in each category in each year. Some errors of classification arise when a union has membership in more than one category. For example, the Meat Cutters and Butcher Workmen, classified in food, liquor, and tobacco, had many members in retail meat stores; the Operating Engineers, classified as miscellaneous, had many members in building construction. These problems are less important in 1897–1934 than in recent years.

The source also reports estimates of union density by industry in 1910, 1920, and 1930 for the categories shown here and for more detailed categories.

Series Ba4814. For 1897–1928, this total equals that reported by Wolman for all unions, series Ba4790. But for 1929–1934, the totals differ because unions affiliated with the Trade Union Unity League in 1929–1934 are excluded.

Series Ba4831. In the later part of the period, the "Miscellaneous industries" column consists largely of two unions, the Firemen and Oilers and the Operating Engineers. The Industrial Workers of the World is included from 1905 to 1914 and is the largest union in the series for some years. The Horseshoers are important in the early years, declining rapidly in the 1920s.

TABLE Ba4832–4844 Union membership, by industry: 1956–1978

Contributed by Joshua L. Rosenbloom

		Nonmanufacturing									Government		
	Manufacturing	Total	Mining and quarrying	Contract construction	Transportation services	Telephone and telegraph services	Electric, gas, and sanitary services (including water)	Wholesale and retail trade	Service industries	Miscellaneous industries not elsewhere classified	Total	Federal	State and local
	Ba4832	Ba4833	Ba4834	Ba4835	Ba4836	Ba4837	Ba4838	Ba4839	Ba4840	Ba4841	Ba4842	Ba4843	Ba4844
Year	Thousand	Thousand	Thousand	Thousand	Thousand	Thousand	Thousand	Thousand	Thousand	Thousand	Thousand	Thousand	Thousand
1956	8,839	8,350	518	2,123	2,727	428	323	883	1,222	126	915	—	—
1958	8,359	8,574	622	2,324	2,712	409	259	852	1,240	156	1,035	—	—
1960	8,591	8,375	593	2,271	2,566	412	275	846	1,281	131	1,070	—	—
1962	8,050	8,289	352	2,417	2,572	416	327	1,129	996	80	1,225	—	—
1964	8,342	8,125	321	2,323	2,429	437	305	1,217	968	125	1,453	897	556
1968	9,218	8,837	342	2,541	2,503	476	324	1,392	1,093	166	2,155	1,351	804
1970	9,173	9,198	369	2,576	2,441	533	312	1,549	1,287	131	2,318	1,370	948
1972	8,920	9,458	331	2,752	2,358	549	304	1,284	1,649	231	2,460	1,369	1,091
1974	9,144	9,520	372	2,738	2,343	672	243	1,329	1,665	158	2,920	1,392	1,529
1976	8,567	9,549	401	2,694	2,330	573	310	1,314	1,665	262	3,012	1,301	1,711
1978	8,119	9,998	428	2,884	1,748	547	356	1,713	1,824	498	3,626	1,596	2,030

Sources

U.S. Bureau of Labor Statistics, *Handbook of Labor Statistics 1979,* Bulletin number 2000 (1979), Table 147, and U.S. Department of Labor, *Directory of National Unions and Employee Associations*, various years.

Documentation

Union membership by industry is calculated on the basis of percentage allocations of membership reported by individual unions in the Bureau of Labor Statistics biennial survey of national and international unions. Note that figures include members outside the continental United States. To be included in the survey, unions must be an affiliate of the American Federation of Labor–Congress of Industrial Organizations or, in the case of unaffiliated unions, a party to collective bargaining agreements with different employers in more than one state. Unions whose activity is confined to a single locality or to a single employer are thus excluded.

TABLE Ba4845–4869 Union membership in manufacturing industries: 1956–1978

Contributed by Joshua L. Rosenbloom

		Food, beverages, and tobacco			Clothing, textiles, and leather				Furniture, lumber, wood products, and paper			
	Total	Total	Food and kindred, including beverages	Tobacco	Total	Textile mill	Apparel and related	Leather	Total	Lumber and wood, excluding furniture	Furniture and fixtures	Paper and allied products
	Ba4845	Ba4846 [1]	Ba4847	Ba4848	Ba4849 [1]	Ba4850	Ba4851	Ba4852	Ba4853 [1]	Ba4854	Ba4855	Ba4856
Year	Thousand	Thousand	Thousand	Thousand	Thousand	Thousand	Thousand	Thousand	Thousand	Thousand	Thousand	Thousand
1956	8,839	—	—	—	—	—	—	—	—	—	—	—
1958	8,359	1,029	—	—	1,228	—	—	—	775	—	—	—
1960	8,591	1,043	—	—	1,219	—	—	—	822	—	—	—
1962	8,050	1,045	—	—	1,226	—	—	—	766	—	—	—
1964	8,342	1,063	—	—	1,216	—	—	—	811	—	—	—
1968	9,218	919	880	39	1,192	191	870	131	915	310	157	448
1970	9,173	944	906	38	1,183	191	852	140	882	215	214	453
1972	8,920	973	933	40	1,095	176	788	131	903	228	205	470
1974	9,144	951	908	43	1,047	169	750	128	847	261	220	366
1976	8,567	975	934	41	989	166	707	116	789	266	205	318
1978	8,119	632	595	37	958	156	683	119	825	262	174	389

		Petroleum, chemicals, and rubber					Metals, machinery, and equipment, except transportation equipment						
	Printing and publishing	Total	Chemicals and related	Petroleum refining and related	Rubber and miscellaneous plastic	Stone, clay, glass, and concrete	Total	Primary metals industries	Fabricated metal products	Machinery, except electrical	Electrical machinery, equipment, and supplies	Transportation equipment	Miscellaneous manufacturing industries
	Ba4857	Ba4858 [1]	Ba4859	Ba4860	Ba4861	Ba4862	Ba4863 [1]	Ba4864	Ba4865	Ba4866	Ba4867	Ba4868	Ba4869
Year	Thousand	Thousand	Thousand	Thousand	Thousand	Thousand	Thousand	Thousand	Thousand	Thousand	Thousand	Thousand	Thousand
1956	—	—	—	—	—	—	—	—	—	—	—	—	—
1958	346	540	—	—	—	251	2,700	—	—	—	—	1,255	235
1960	350	546	—	—	—	249	2,891	—	—	—	—	1,323	148
1962	359	491	—	—	—	269	2,583	—	—	—	—	1,187	124
1964	355	562	—	—	—	253	2,646	—	—	—	—	1,197	239
1968	375	724	382	96	246	295	3,022	773	543	692	1,014	1,333	443
1970	370	713	361	80	272	284	3,290	788	918	550	1,034	1,109	398
1972	353	631	284	77	270	317	3,125	794	671	608	1,052	1,032	491
1974	359	625	268	82	275	325	3,343	817	726	726	1,074	1,144	503
1976	356	646	248	115	283	328	3,119	789	703	713	914	1,040	325
1978	281	565	219	77	269	293	2,772	774	613	670	715	1,110	683

[1] The source supplies aggregated data for these industries only through 1964. For subsequent years, it only reports more disaggregated figures. After 1964, the values given are summations of the relevant subtotal series.

Sources

U.S. Bureau of Labor Statistics (BLS), *Handbook of Labor Statistics 1979*, Bulletin number 2000 (1979), Table 147, and BLS, *Directory of National Unions and Employee Associations*, various years.

Documentation

See the text for Table Ba4832–4844 for a discussion of methods.

Series Ba4865. Excludes ordnance, machinery, and transportation equipment.

TABLE Ba4870–4883 Union membership, by industry: 1973–1999[1]

Contributed by Joshua L. Rosenbloom

		Nonmanufacturing									Government			
	Manufacturing	Total	Mining and quarrying	Contract construction	Transportation services	Telephone and telegraph	Electric, gas, and sanitary utilities	Wholesale and retail trade	Service industries	Agriculture, forestry, and fisheries	Total	Federal	State	Local
	Ba4870	Ba4871	Ba4872	Ba4873	Ba4874	Ba4875	Ba4876	Ba4877	Ba4878	Ba4879	Ba4880	Ba4881	Ba4882	Ba4883
Year	Thousand	Thousand	Thousand	Thousand	Thousand	Thousand	Thousand	Thousand	Thousand	Thousand	Thousand	Thousand	Thousand	Thousand
1973	7,866.5	10,222.1	236.2	1,774.9	1,469.1	595.5	470.1	1,781.7	2,584.0	70.5	1,240.1	709.4	133.2	397.5
1974	7,803.8	10,372.7	220.5	1,641.8	1,566.7	667.4	433.9	1,715.3	2,810.6	40.9	1,275.6	720.9	132.7	422.0
1975	6,696.8	10,081.5	239.6	1,435.0	1,447.6	598.6	408.8	1,636.8	2,934.5	46.2	1,334.4	732.5	144.4	457.5
1976	6,991.0	10,412.0	232.6	1,457.4	1,487.7	507.9	474.0	1,725.1	3,104.0	32.2	1,391.1	760.6	171.3	459.2
1977	7,159.4	12,175.7	255.8	1,606.2	1,528.9	568.7	498.0	1,774.5	4,289.0	57.1	1,597.5	750.2	226.2	621.1
1978	7,107.1	12,441.3	254.2	1,613.7	1,570.8	625.5	548.5	1,701.4	4,442.1	68.8	1,616.3	761.8	266.3	588.2
1979	7,567.6	13,418.5	276.9	1,660.1	1,686.5	702.3	522.2	1,812.8	4,825.7	79.1	1,852.9	809.0	300.7	743.2
1980	6,770.9	13,324.4	286.3	1,573.8	1,595.3	713.9	593.9	1,752.8	4,933.0	62.9	1,812.5	856.6	252.6	703.3
1981	6,700.9	12,422.5	181.9	1,618.4	1,425.3	698.0	504.0	1,721.8	4,587.3	20.1	1,665.7	755.7	228.1	681.9
1983	5,346.1	12,371.3	185.7	1,292.7	1,287.9	648.7	574.1	1,589.1	4,819.6	62.6	1,910.9	785.8	401.2	723.9
1984	5,291.8	12,048.0	165.7	1,216.8	1,253.0	626.3	572.4	1,503.6	4,802.3	47.9	1,860.0	741.2	399.8	719.0
1985	5,028.7	11,967.4	158.9	1,202.6	1,274.8	625.5	522.5	1,412.2	4,793.1	47.2	1,930.6	770.7	444.4	715.5
1986	4,904.6	12,070.6	148.8	1,271.4	1,223.3	614.9	498.7	1,439.3	4,756.7	52.1	2,065.4	831.1	455.0	779.3
1987	4,727.0	12,186.1	148.7	1,230.8	1,188.1	544.7	536.3	1,451.2	4,872.8	42.5	2,171.0	888.4	488.1	794.5
1988	4,554.2	12,447.5	137.7	1,250.6	1,245.1	535.0	537.5	1,397.0	5,039.8	36.6	2,268.2	925.5	540.0	802.7
1989	4,498.8	12,461.7	121.1	1,320.5	1,171.8	540.4	501.2	1,332.6	5,150.3	24.7	2,299.1	881.1	590.6	827.4
1990	4,219.7	12,520.1	126.6	1,272.9	1,171.0	532.8	532.9	1,348.7	5,182.3	35.3	2,317.6	914.0	554.1	849.5
1991	4,001.6	12,566.8	108.5	1,143.7	1,189.0	510.8	526.8	1,414.9	5,259.3	37.0	2,376.8	896.2	598.6	882.0
1992	3,798.9	12,591.4	96.1	1,088.4	1,181.5	530.9	545.4	1,420.1	5,389.8	44.2	2,295.0	866.0	582.5	846.5
1993	3,610.3	12,987.8	109.1	1,105.8	1,232.6	513.6	524.2	1,380.3	5,650.7	34.0	2,437.5	884.8	640.7	912.0
1994	3,525.7	13,214.6	107.6	1,109.7	1,259.6	425.8	488.6	1,391.9	5,784.8	49.4	2,597.2	997.8	642.2	957.2
1995	3,465.2	12,894.4	87.0	1,071.6	1,222.6	406.6	482.5	1,410.5	5,657.1	45.3	2,511.2	955.7	629.3	926.2
1996	3,408.8	12,860.6	78.7	1,157.6	1,233.1	371.4	466.4	1,343.2	5,750.4	37.1	2,422.7	875.7	631.8	915.2
1997	3,266.9	12,842.9	87.6	1,223.0	1,265.1	366.7	471.5	1,329.4	5,645.7	43.1	2,410.8	879.7	595.0	936.1
1998	3,126.9	13,084.5	82.8	1,212.3	1,256.8	407.1	474.5	1,295.2	5,759.2	35.7	2,560.9	951.5	574.8	1,034.6
1999	3,034.2	13,442.1	60.3	1,362.0	1,279.5	437.2	455.0	1,291.0	6,064.9	56.1	2,436.1	890.9	552.4	992.8

[1] Data pertain to wage and salary workers.

Source

Unpublished calculations from Current Population Survey (CPS) data performed by Barry T. Hirsch and David A. Macpherson.

Documentation

These figures are obtained by summing union membership using industry affiliation as given in the CPS. For a discussion of issues related to the calculation of union membership using the CPS data, see the text for Table Ba4783–4791.

TABLE Ba4884–4905 Union membership in manufacturing industries: 1973–1999[1]

Contributed by Joshua L. Rosenbloom

	Total	Ordnance and accessories	Food and kindred products	Tobacco manufactures	Textile mill products	Apparel and related products	Lumber and wood products, except furniture	Furniture and fixtures	Paper and allied products	Printing, publishing, and allied industries	Chemicals and allied products
	Ba4884	Ba4885	Ba4886	Ba4887	Ba4888	Ba4889	Ba4890	Ba4891	Ba4892	Ba4893	Ba4894
Year	Thousand	Thousand	Thousand	Thousand	Thousand	Thousand	Thousand	Thousand	Thousand	Thousand	Thousand
1973	7,866.5	92.6	695.2	24.7	142.0	478.0	180.3	120.4	423.3	295.0	288.1
1974	7,803.8	71.4	701.6	30.6	134.8	435.3	181.4	138.4	380.2	288.5	326.4
1975	6,696.8	71.3	701.4	16.9	92.7	359.5	149.2	112.8	325.5	267.2	283.3
1976	6,991.0	62.5	670.3	26.4	108.7	335.6	156.5	113.7	355.1	256.9	319.3
1977	7,159.4	65.0	733.8	16.5	96.3	342.5	153.3	122.8	354.7	254.4	324.9
1978	7,107.1	56.9	710.1	13.6	84.9	353.5	158.5	132.6	364.5	258.0	334.3
1979	7,567.6	41.8	713.2	19.8	91.3	402.9	141.5	158.0	400.9	310.3	339.9
1980	6,770.9	73.8	627.8	19.1	116.8	326.5	102.7	124.2	368.8	289.6	319.6
1981	6,700.9	128.4	697.7	34.4	56.6	340.8	138.9	121.7	303.3	270.9	399.4
1983	5,346.1	63.3	548.6	23.9	75.7	290.7	101.4	82.4	326.8	241.4	233.0
1984	5,291.8	75.8	547.4	19.7	72.9	253.6	102.7	87.9	308.1	235.8	197.2
1985	5,028.7	78.5	561.9	22.2	77.5	254.0	87.7	90.1	299.0	212.3	186.5
1986	4,904.6	63.4	532.1	17.8	70.4	223.4	78.6	99.1	302.0	209.1	182.1
1987	4,727.0	69.6	467.7	17.9	59.4	210.8	86.6	106.8	303.8	217.6	206.0
1988	4,554.2	65.3	438.0	18.6	69.5	200.6	91.7	113.5	289.1	195.5	199.4
1989	4,498.8	59.4	492.6	14.3	60.1	190.1	95.8	93.9	277.8	196.2	212.3
1990	4,219.7	59.2	463.2	7.9	62.2	157.5	87.4	80.4	274.8	192.4	198.4
1991	4,001.6	54.6	414.8	16.0	46.5	146.7	83.2	83.9	282.2	190.8	183.0
1992	3,798.9	54.5	404.8	19.1	40.6	127.3	63.7	58.8	278.5	177.5	174.2
1993	3,610.3	30.7	405.1	20.8	49.7	112.0	70.7	66.8	284.9	153.5	152.2
1994	3,525.7	34.6	381.6	18.4	38.9	129.4	63.7	68.1	266.3	157.0	171.3
1995	3,465.2	30.9	389.8	10.5	34.7	125.4	87.2	56.8	220.9	141.2	176.5
1996	3,408.8	21.8	402.2	8.5	35.1	87.6	85.2	55.8	231.5	133.7	149.5
1997	3,266.9	35.2	382.4	11.6	38.0	76.6	75.0	43.4	187.8	134.3	149.1
1998	3,126.9	29.4	363.8	12.3	30.8	57.7	78.0	45.1	201.6	141.4	144.0
1999	3,034.2	30.2	361.7	11.8	26.3	58.1	61.7	43.6	169.7	136.3	127.0

	Petroleum refining and related industries	Rubber and miscellaneous plastic products	Leather and leather products	Stone, clay, glass, and concrete products	Primary metals industries	Fabricated metal products	Machinery, except electrical	Electrical machinery	Transportation equipment	Professional scientific and controlling instruments	Miscellaneous manufacturing industries
	Ba4895	Ba4896	Ba4897	Ba4898	Ba4899	Ba4900	Ba4901	Ba4902	Ba4903	Ba4904	Ba4905
Year	Thousand	Thousand	Thousand	Thousand	Thousand	Thousand	Thousand	Thousand	Thousand	Thousand	Thousand
1973	102.9	283.0	79.3	302.9	844.1	605.8	725.3	718.4	1,216.4	93.4	155.4
1974	75.2	282.1	88.8	302.7	911.3	624.3	746.9	751.1	1,107.1	95.2	130.5
1975	72.2	192.0	68.9	274.6	745.8	487.8	654.9	575.3	1,012.9	98.5	134.1
1976	71.0	231.6	76.4	270.8	741.0	529.7	724.2	632.5	1,103.9	86.1	118.8
1977	88.0	249.5	83.2	276.0	738.0	559.1	695.7	644.8	1,153.9	98.3	108.7
1978	73.3	231.0	73.9	297.6	647.6	545.3	747.8	626.1	1,165.6	108.6	123.4
1979	81.4	237.0	77.0	308.7	725.3	559.1	787.5	653.4	1,313.6	97.4	107.6
1980	75.0	204.6	55.1	291.6	686.4	490.7	797.9	599.1	1,038.4	78.5	84.7
1981	83.4	145.7	43.5	252.3	614.1	554.7	688.3	583.2	1,059.5	122.9	61.2
1983	65.3	182.7	56.8	201.3	432.3	328.5	476.2	498.8	971.5	61.7	83.8
1984	66.0	190.5	42.1	179.1	425.2	326.1	474.1	474.4	1,083.1	56.2	73.9
1985	60.8	171.7	31.7	150.4	394.1	297.8	456.8	441.2	1,040.0	58.9	55.6
1986	56.6	146.3	28.4	180.1	384.3	302.6	409.3	403.7	1,091.1	61.2	63.0
1987	55.1	158.9	27.5	165.1	385.1	276.1	383.6	408.3	1,005.7	52.7	62.7
1988	58.4	154.9	22.7	154.0	380.3	267.1	382.6	346.1	1,013.9	42.1	50.9
1989	57.7	133.0	15.8	173.9	396.4	246.9	346.4	383.5	941.8	50.0	60.9
1990	44.2	115.0	15.5	172.7	367.6	254.0	346.8	322.7	895.2	47.7	54.9
1991	54.1	115.5	22.1	146.1	323.3	247.0	334.2	302.6	853.3	48.3	53.4
1992	56.1	127.2	25.5	150.1	314.6	217.5	282.3	293.5	847.7	52.5	32.9
1993	52.3	104.7	25.3	147.4	327.1	206.7	257.6	256.8	798.3	40.3	47.4
1994	47.4	122.7	22.9	133.1	303.8	209.6	279.6	220.9	766.3	46.1	44.0

Note appears at end of table

TABLE Ba4884–4905 Union membership in manufacturing industries: 1973–1999 *Continued*

Year	Petroleum refining and related industries	Rubber and miscellaneous plastic products	Leather and leather products	Stone, clay, glass, and concrete products	Primary metals industries	Fabricated metal products	Machinery, except electrical	Electrical machinery	Transportation equipment	Professional scientific and controlling instruments	Miscellaneous manufacturing industries
	Ba4895	Ba4896	Ba4897	Ba4898	Ba4899	Ba4900	Ba4901	Ba4902	Ba4903	Ba4904	Ba4905
	Thousand	Thousand	Thousand	Thousand	Thousand	Thousand	Thousand	Thousand	Thousand	Thousand	Thousand
1995	43.1	121.1	27.5	123.4	313.0	214.7	291.6	195.4	778.3	38.7	44.5
1996	37.1	120.4	27.2	135.1	320.6	214.3	251.1	241.0	777.9	30.7	42.5
1997	40.2	123.0	24.3	134.3	297.4	219.0	287.3	220.2	705.2	38.2	44.4
1998	32.8	127.3	18.4	136.5	256.9	182.6	288.5	219.1	684.0	33.0	43.7
1999	41.5	141.0	10.8	123.4	266.9	175.2	248.0	211.4	697.3	32.2	60.1

[1] Data pertain to wage and salary workers.

Source

Unpublished calculations from Current Population Survey (CPS) data provided by Barry T. Hirsch and David A. Macpherson.

Documentation

For a discussion of issues related to the calculation of union membership using the CPS data, see the text for Table Ba4783–4791.

Series Ba4900. Excludes ordnance, machinery, and transportation equipment.

Series Ba4904. Includes photographic and optical goods, watches, and clocks.

TABLE Ba4906–4907 Union membership, by sex: 1954–1978

Contributed by Joshua L. Rosenbloom

Year	Male	Female
	Ba4906	Ba4907
	Thousand	Thousand
1954	15,005	2,950
1956	15,077	3,400
1958	14,807	3,274
1960	14,813	3,304
1962	14,358	3,272
1964	14,563	3,413
1966	15,492	3,689
1968	16,318	3,940
1970	16,469	4,282
1972	16,369	4,524
1974	17,043	4,600
1976	16,523	4,648
1978	16,517	5,267

Source

U.S. Bureau of Labor Statistics, *National Unions and Employee Associations*, Bulletin number 2079 (1979), Table 10.

Documentation

This table reports union membership broken down by sex, based on the responses to biennial questionnaires distributed by the Bureau of Labor Statistics. See the text for Table Ba4783–4791 for further discussion of this method of measuring union membership.

TABLE Ba4908–4917 Union membership, by age, sex, race, and full-time status: 1983–1999[1]

Contributed by Joshua L. Rosenbloom

	Age			Sex		Race or ethnicity			Employment status	
	16–24	25–54	55 or older	Male	Female	White	Black	Hispanic	Full-time	Part-time
	Ba4908	Ba4909	Ba4910	Ba4911	Ba4912	Ba4913	Ba4914	Ba4915	Ba4916	Ba4917
Year	Thousand	Thousand	Thousand	Thousand	Thousand	Thousand	Thousand	Thousand	Thousand	Thousand
1983	1,749	13,299	2,670	11,809	5,908	14,844	2,440	—	16,271	1,446
1984	1,576	13,253	2,510	11,511	5,829	14,380	2,514	—	16,074	1,266
1985	1,440	13,062	2,495	11,264	5,732	14,124	2,445	1,174	15,717	1,280
1986	1,385	13,171	2,419	11,173	5,802	14,061	2,436	1,193	15,698	1,277
1987	1,299	13,274	2,340	11,071	5,842	13,972	2,445	1,234	15,670	1,243
1988	1,206	13,462	2,333	11,019	5,982	13,932	2,559	1,220	15,773	1,229
1989	1,203	13,482	2,276	10,820	6,141	13,894	2,549	1,196	15,701	1,259
1990	1,178	13,344	2,217	10,564	6,175	13,798	2,410	1,209	15,422	1,318
1991	1,142	13,310	2,117	10,430	6,138	13,587	2,425	1,275	15,179	1,390
1992	982	13,308	2,101	10,013	6,277	13,416	2,433	1,244	14,975	1,415
1993	1,010	13,503	2,086	10,083	6,515	13,612	2,435	1,291	15,171	1,427
1994	1,126	13,598	2,024	10,106	6,642	13,520	2,513	1,420	15,093	1,623
1995	1,022	13,333	2,004	9,929	6,430	13,149	2,519	1,357	14,790	1,537
1996	991	13,294	1,984	9,859	6,410	13,232	2,441	1,394	14,762	1,477
1997	968	13,066	2,076	9,763	6,347	13,088	2,394	1,407	14,619	1,449
1998	1,014	13,082	2,116	9,850	6,362	13,118	2,460	1,471	14,825	1,354
1999	1,110	13,214	2,153	9,949	6,528	13,349	2,463	1,525	14,974	1,459

[1] Data pertain to employed wage and salary workers.

Source

U.S. Bureau of Labor Statistics, *Employment and Earnings*, January issues, various years.

Documentation

See the text for Table Ba4783–4791.

Series Ba4916–4917. The distinction between full- and part-time workers is based on hours usually worked in the principal job. Because the status of the principal job is not identifiable for a small number of multiple job holders, the total of these columns may not equal total union membership in all years.

TABLE Ba4918–4927 Workers covered by union contracts, by age, sex, race, and full-time status: 1983–1999[1]

Contributed by Joshua L. Rosenbloom

	Age			Sex		Race or ethnicity			Employment status	
	16–24	25–54	55 or older	Male	Female	White	Black	Hispanic	Full-time	Part-time
	Ba4918	Ba4919	Ba4920	Ba4921	Ba4922	Ba4923	Ba4924	Ba4925	Ba4926	Ba4927
Year	Thousand	Thousand	Thousand	Thousand	Thousand	Thousand	Thousand	Thousand	Thousand	Thousand
1983	2,145	15,366	3,022	13,270	7,262	17,182	2,850	—	18,745	1,787
1984	1,901	15,237	2,793	12,832	7,100	16,547	2,865	1,210	18,376	1,556
1985	1,725	14,852	2,782	12,448	6,910	16,083	2,775	—	17,816	1,542
1986	1,655	14,940	2,682	12,317	6,961	15,955	2,773	1,339	17,748	4,213
1987	1,538	14,921	2,591	12,144	6,907	15,712	2,769	1,371	17,567	4,286
1988	1,457	15,188	2,596	12,132	7,109	15,759	2,898	1,353	17,753	1,488
1989	1,424	15,259	2,515	11,955	7,243	15,689	2,912	1,330	17,683	1,515
1990	1,410	15,152	2,497	11,731	7,327	15,669	2,771	1,348	17,469	1,589
1991	1,341	15,028	2,366	11,494	7,240	15,331	2,759	1,447	17,095	1,639
1992	1,176	15,031	2,334	11,128	7,412	15,148	2,763	1,415	16,886	1,654
1993	1,165	15,172	2,309	11,039	7,607	15,262	2,772	1,427	16,999	1,647
1994	1,302	15,268	2,279	11,110	7,740	15,213	2,844	1,592	16,933	1,879
1995	1,199	14,937	2,211	10,868	7,479	14,747	2,819	1,535	16,531	1,781
1996	1,146	14,816	2,195	10,761	7,397	14,761	2,733	1,573	16,429	1,697
1997	1,140	14,533	2,250	10,619	7,304	14,538	2,688	1,602	16,227	1,653
1998	1,151	14,442	2,324	10,638	7,280	14,460	2,739	1,634	16,323	1,559
1999	1,239	14,590	2,354	10,758	7,425	14,668	2,757	1,684	16,501	1,634

[1] Data pertain to employed wage and salary workers.

Source

U.S. Bureau of Labor Statistics, *Employment and Earnings*, January issues, various years.

Documentation

See the text for Tables Ba4783–4791 and Ba4908–4917.

TABLE Ba4928–4945 Hourly wages of union and nonunion workers, by sector, sex, and race: 1973–1999[1]

Contributed by Joshua L. Rosenbloom

	All workers		Private-sector workers		Public-sector workers		Male						Female					
							Total		White		Black		Total		White		Black	
	Union	Nonunion	Union	Nonunion	Union	Nonunion	Union	Nonunion	Union	Nonunion	Union	Nonunion	Union	Nonunion	Union	Nonunion	Union	Nonunion
	Ba4928	Ba4929	Ba4930	Ba4931	Ba4932	Ba4933	Ba4934	Ba4935	Ba4936	Ba4937	Ba4938	Ba4939	Ba4940	Ba4941	Ba4942	Ba4943	Ba4944	Ba4945
Year	Dollars	Dollars	Dollars	Dollars	Dollars	Dollars	Dollars	Dollars	Dollars	Dollars	Dollars	Dollars	Dollars	Dollars	Dollars	Dollars	Dollars	Dollars
1973	4.69	3.74	4.64	3.70	4.92	4.46	5.05	4.56	5.11	4.66	4.62	3.45	3.52	3.02	3.52	3.05	3.55	2.63
1974	5.11	3.99	5.03	3.98	5.44	4.65	5.45	4.86	5.54	4.98	4.77	3.49	4.00	3.23	3.99	3.27	4.13	2.90
1975	5.50	4.34	5.41	4.33	5.82	5.02	5.85	5.28	5.94	5.40	5.19	3.88	4.46	3.51	4.45	3.55	4.53	3.09
1976	5.93	4.59	5.86	4.59	6.17	5.29	6.37	5.56	6.43	5.69	5.95	3.93	4.67	3.78	4.68	3.80	4.68	3.52
1977	6.47	4.76	6.41	4.78	6.62	5.47	6.98	5.82	7.10	5.97	5.99	4.14	5.15	3.87	5.19	3.90	5.00	3.57
1978	6.82	5.08	6.82	5.14	6.82	5.65	7.34	6.22	7.45	6.35	6.50	4.67	5.52	4.14	5.54	4.17	5.41	3.77
1979	7.26	5.76	7.27	5.85	7.26	6.32	7.88	7.11	8.03	7.24	6.80	5.57	5.73	4.58	5.78	4.60	5.52	4.27
1980	7.87	6.29	7.89	6.39	7.82	6.92	8.54	7.82	8.68	8.01	7.46	5.75	6.30	5.02	6.31	5.06	6.27	4.60
1981	8.49	6.56	8.59	6.64	8.25	7.32	9.22	8.10	9.32	8.23	8.53	6.91	6.85	5.30	6.82	5.35	6.96	4.81
1983	9.80	7.63	9.79	7.73	9.81	8.54	10.63	9.37	10.81	9.60	9.37	7.00	8.11	6.25	8.20	6.31	7.79	5.63
1984	10.27	8.24	10.21	8.11	10.40	9.02	11.12	9.81	11.31	10.06	9.85	7.29	8.58	6.57	8.68	6.64	8.22	5.91
1985	10.78	8.68	10.72	8.54	10.90	9.63	11.67	10.34	11.92	10.63	9.99	7.63	9.03	6.93	9.12	7.00	8.71	6.23
1986	11.25	9.08	11.14	8.93	11.46	10.01	12.16	10.82	12.35	11.12	10.88	7.73	9.51	7.26	9.59	7.34	9.16	6.52
1987	11.73	9.54	11.47	9.41	12.18	10.41	12.60	11.37	12.84	11.69	11.03	8.21	10.06	7.65	10.15	7.74	9.67	6.76
1988	12.40	10.04	12.03	9.88	13.02	11.12	13.39	11.95	13.61	12.30	12.04	8.69	10.57	8.06	10.66	8.16	10.18	7.16
1989	12.58	9.98	12.27	9.82	13.08	11.03	13.42	11.52	13.64	11.88	11.88	8.41	11.10	8.38	11.27	8.47	10.37	7.49
1990	13.16	10.55	12.71	10.39	13.86	11.58	13.94	12.17	14.24	12.52	12.00	8.87	11.81	8.88	11.92	9.00	11.07	7.73
1991	13.56	11.12	13.07	10.80	14.30	12.17	14.32	12.58	14.65	12.93	12.29	9.25	12.27	9.34	12.39	9.44	11.54	8.33
1992	14.00	11.29	13.46	11.10	14.78	12.54	14.78	12.82	15.11	13.18	12.66	9.37	12.74	9.74	12.95	9.86	11.64	8.64
1993	14.50	11.66	13.89	11.44	15.33	13.08	15.27	13.21	15.59	13.59	13.17	9.79	13.30	10.08	13.47	10.22	12.40	8.89
1994	15.09	11.96	14.32	11.77	16.15	13.30	15.80	13.52	16.17	13.89	13.68	10.46	14.03	10.33	14.36	10.48	12.53	9.13
1995	15.40	12.26	14.61	12.08	16.47	13.52	16.17	13.92	16.56	14.36	13.94	10.44	14.21	10.52	14.49	10.70	13.19	9.32
1996	15.71	12.62	14.89	12.45	16.84	13.95	16.46	14.31	16.93	14.70	13.50	10.62	14.54	10.88	14.84	11.08	13.31	9.38
1997	16.36	13.15	15.49	13.00	17.55	14.32	17.12	14.91	17.51	15.30	14.51	11.22	15.16	11.33	15.54	11.54	13.62	9.71
1998	16.81	13.74	16.02	13.61	17.86	14.81	17.62	15.54	18.04	15.96	15.23	11.87	15.54	11.88	15.88	12.06	14.23	10.48
1999	17.31	14.44	16.47	14.30	18.43	15.52	18.08	16.44	18.56	16.85	15.16	12.59	16.14	12.38	16.40	12.58	15.16	12.59

[1] Data pertain to employed wage and salary workers.

Source

Barry T. Hirsch and David A. Macpherson, *Union Membership and Earnings Data Book: Compilations from the Current Population Survey*, 2000 edition (Bureau of National Affairs, 2000), Tables 2a, 2b.

Documentation

Mean hourly earnings are calculated from Current Population Survey (CPS) data. See the text for Table Ba4783–4791 for further discussion of the CPS. The data refer to each worker's principal job and include "usual" pay for overtime, commissions, and tips, but do not include bonuses and nonwage benefits (health insurance, pensions, and so forth). For years prior to 1994, the hourly earnings measure is constructed by dividing "usual weekly earnings" by "usual hours worked per week." The census allocates weekly earnings to those who choose not to report or are unable to report earnings by matching such cases to other individuals with the same characteristics. Changes in the CPS beginning in 1994 make it possible to use an explicit measure of hourly earnings for all hourly workers and for salaried workers who choose to report earnings on an hourly basis.

A serious limitation of the CPS for constructing earnings distributions is that earnings are "top coded" or "capped" at a maximum value. The CPS Outgoing Rotation Group files have top codes of $999 per week through 1988 and $1,923 per week beginning in 1989 (about $100,000 in annual earnings). The problem of top coding is of particular concern prior to 1989, when the top code was very low. If one were to try to compute average weekly earnings, attributing all wage-earnings in the highest earnings category with earnings of $999 per week, the result would understate the true average since many wage earners earned far more than $999 per week. One approach to the problem is to report median earnings, as the U.S. Bureau of Labor Statistics does in *Employment and Earnings*, January issues. Unfortunately, the median can diverge substantially from the mean value, and it may be insensitive to modest changes in earnings or highly sensitive to small changes. An alternative is to make some assumption about the shape of the upper tail of the wage distribution. Here it is assumed that the upper tail of the earnings distribution follows a Pareto distribution. For each year, Hirsch and Macpherson estimate the parameters of this distribution separately by gender for workers above the median wage in that year.

The source reports mean wages deflated by the CPI-U (consumer price index for all urban consumers) cost of living index. Data in the table have been converted back to current dollars by multiplying real values by the corresponding price index for each year.

TABLE Ba4946–4949 National Labor Relations Board elections and results: 1936–1998[1]

Contributed by Joshua L. Rosenbloom

	Elections held	Elections won by unions	Employees eligible to vote	
			Total	In elections won by unions
	Ba4946	Ba4947	Ba4948	Ba4949
Fiscal year	Number	Number	Number	Number
1936	31	18	9,512	—
1937	265	214	181,424	—
1938	1,152	945	394,558	—
1939	746	574	207,597	—
1940	1,192	921	595,544	—
1941	2,568	2,127	729,915	—
1942	4,212	3,636	1,296,567	—
1943	4,153	3,580	1,126,501	—
1944	4,712	3,983	1,322,225	—
1945	4,919	4,078	1,087,177	—
1946	5,589	4,446	846,431	—
1947	6,920	5,194	934,553	—
1948	3,222	2,337	384,565	—
1949	5,514	3,889	588,761	—
1950	5,619	4,186	890,374	753,598
1951	6,432	4,758	666,556	505,322
1952	6,765	4,933	771,346	—
1953	6,050	4,350	737,998	584,450
1954	4,663	3,060	511,430	343,092
1955	4,215	2,489	515,995	378,962
1956	4,946	3,230	462,712	291,292
1957	4,729	2,942	458,904	264,920
1958	4,337	2,636	351,217	196,334
1959	5,428	3,410	430,023	257,028
1960	6,380	3,740	483,964	286,048
1961	6,354	3,563	450,930	229,283
1962	7,355	4,305	536,047	305,976
1963	6,871	4,052	489,365	265,747
1964	7,529	4,296	551,751	295,230
1965	7,776	4,680	544,536	333,545
1966	8,324	5,059	592,722	339,407
1967	8,116	4,791	623,711	357,114
1968	7,857	4,495	566,164	292,053
1969	7,993	4,367	592,761	299,979
1970	8,074	4,458	608,558	318,890
1971	8,362	4,445	586,155	274,700
1972	8,923	4,787	591,636	297,127
1973	9,369	4,786	541,445	233,874
1974	8,858	4,425	544,331	203,265
1975	8,577	4,138	568,920	218,281
1976	8,638	4,159	475,404	173,385
(TQ)	2,277	1,037	144,042	57,345
1977	9,484	4,363	570,716	223,689
1978	8,240	3,791	471,819	177,256
1979	8,043	3,623	577,942	212,027
1980	8,198	3,744	521,602	196,515
1981	7,512	3,234	449,243	165,232
1982	5,116	2,064	297,764	103,534
1983	4,405	1,895	209,918	91,311
1984	4,436	1,861	249,512	105,919
1985	4,614	1,956	254,220	91,161
1986	4,520	1,951	259,239	91,999
1987	4,069	1,788	241,825	96,384
1988	4,153	1,921	243,692	97,043
1989	4,413	2,059	273,775	110,037
1990	4,210	1,965	261,385	93,789
1991	3,752	1,663	225,842	90,051
1992	3,599	1,673	219,730	83,379
1993	3,586	1,706	231,187	97,166
1994	3,572	1,665	210,834	85,603
1995	3,399	1,611	215,137	86,678
1996	3,277	1,469	219,073	82,947
1997	3,480	1,677	236,016	101,646
1998	3,795	1,856	250,726	100,535

(TQ) means transitional quarter.

[1] For 1936–1976, fiscal years ending June 30; for 1977–1998, fiscal years ending September 30.

Source

National Labor Relations Board, *Annual Report* (annual issues), Table 13. Current data are reported in these annual reports.

Documentation

Although labor's right to bargain collectively was first specified legislatively in Section 7a of the National Industrial Recovery Act of 1933, no enforcement machinery was created at that time. After this Act was found unconstitutional in 1935, Congress replaced Section 7a with a much more elaborate law, the National Labor Relations Act, usually called the Wagner Act after its sponsor, Senator Robert F. Wagner of New York. The new Act prohibited employers from (1) interfering with, restraining or coercing employees in the exercise of their rights of self-organization and collective bargaining; (2) dominating or interfering with the formation or administration of any labor organization or contributing financial or other support to it; (3) encouraging or discouraging union membership by discrimination in regard to hiring or tenure of employment or condition of work, except such discrimination as might be involved in a closed-shop agreement with a bona fide union enjoying majority status; (4) discharging or otherwise discriminating against an employee for filing charges or testifying under the Act; and (5) refusing to bargain collectively. In addition, it created the National Labor Relations Board (NLRB) with powers to enforce these principles.

Among the powers granted to the NLRB was the authority, on its own initiative or at the request of a union, to supervise a free, secret election to determine which union, if any, should represent a particular group of workers. In its annual reports, the Board provides information on the number and results of these union-representation elections held during each fiscal year.

Since the NLRB was not appointed until August 27, data for 1936 are for a period of less than twelve months.

Series Ba4947 and Ba4949. Data are the totals of figures reported separately for "trade unions," "unaffiliated national unions," and "unaffiliated local unions."

TABLE Ba4950–4953 Complaints of unfair practices received and remedial actions taken by the National Labor Relations Board: 1936–1998[1]

Contributed by Joshua L. Rosenbloom

	Complaints filed against employers			
	Unfair practices	Section 8(3)	Workers awarded back pay	Workers offered reinstatement
	Ba4950	Ba4951	Ba4952	Ba4953
Fiscal year	Number	Number	Number	Number
1936	865	594	—	—
1937	3,124	2,130	—	—
1938	6,807	4,463	—	—
1939	4,618	3,012	—	—
1940	3,934	2,671	4,800	31,000 [3]
1941	4,817	2,995	—	23,475
1942	4,967	3,221	5,925	8,251
1943	3,403	2,256	5,115	7,111
1944	2,573	1,761	3,734	2,972
1945	2,427	1,639	1,973	1,919
1946	3,815	2,434	2,779	3,184
1947	4,232	2,794	2,656	4,114
1948	2,849	2,038	1,196	981 [4]
1949	4,154	2,863	463	280
1950	4,472	3,213	2,259	2,111
1951	4,164	2,899	4,429	3,864
1952	4,306	2,972	2,734	1,801
1953	4,409	3,023	2,987	1,754
1954	4,373	3,072	2,292	1,438
1955	4,362	3,089	1,836	1,275
1956	3,522	2,661	1,955	1,841
1957	3,655	2,789	1,457	922
1958	6,068	4,649	1,368	1,067
1959	8,266	6,775	1,521	42,078 [5]
1960	7,723	6,044	3,110	1,885
1961	8,136	6,240	3,448	2,507
1962	9,231	6,953	3,223	2,465
1963	9,550	6,840	6,890	3,478
1964	10,695	7,654	5,044	4,044
1965	10,931	7,367	4,477	5,875
1966	10,902	7,203	15,361	6,187
1967	11,259	7,463	13,815	4,274
1968	11,892	8,129	6,144	3,107
1969	12,002	8,122	6,166	3,748
1970	13,601	9,290	6,679	3,779
1971	15,467	10,368	6,423	4,068
1972	17,733	11,164	5,822	3,555
1973	17,361	10,979	6,215	5,407
1974	17,978	11,620	6,794	4,778
1975	20,311	13,426	6,948	3,816
1976	23,496	15,090	6,822	4,440
(TQ)	6,223	3,982	1,582	1,057
1977	26,105	16,697	7,220	4,458
1978	27,056	17,125	8,270	5,533
1979	29,026	17,220	14,320	5,837
1980	31,281	18,315	15,357	10,033
1981	31,273	17,571	25,631	6,463
1982	27,749	14,732	— [2]	— [2]
1983	28,995	14,866	17,888	6,029
1984	24,852	13,172	34,532	5,363
1985	22,545	11,824	18,280	10,905
1986	24,084	12,714	17,588	3,196
1987	22,475	11,548	16,973	4,307
1988	22,266	11,196	17,487	4,179
1989	22,345	11,567	18,888	4,508
1990	24,075	11,886	16,073	4,026
1991	23,005	11,265	17,661	3,023
1992	23,119	11,310	21,193	3,811
1993	24,500	11,678	21,106	4,177
1994	26,058	13,316	20,248	4,165
1995	26,244	13,298	26,042	6,603
1996	25,752	13,305	17,505	2,760
1997	25,809	13,127	20,673	2,266
1998	23,630	11,673	23,682	2,528

(TQ) means transitional quarter.

[1] For 1936–1976, fiscal years ending June 30; for 1977–1998, fiscal years ending September 30.

[2] Data on back pay and employee reinstatements were not available because of "technical problems."

[3] According to the National Labor Relations Board (*Annual Report,* 1940, p. 17) "the statistical record of remedies in unfair labor practice cases is not so complete as the record of cases received and closed." The figures here are described as approximate.

[4] The Labor Management Relations Act was passed on June 23, 1947. Section 8(A) restates the provisions of Section 8 of the National Labor Relations Act. The data for fiscal year 1948 include charges brought under both acts.

[5] Figures include 32 West Coast trucking industry cases involving 41,200 workers.

Source

National Labor Relations Board, *Annual Report* (various years), Tables 2 and 3. Current data are reported in these annual reports.

Documentation

Section 8 of the National Labor Relations Act prohibited employers from discharging or otherwise punishing employees for union organizing. These provisions were restated in Section 8(A) of the Labor Management Relations Act passed on June 23, 1947. The National Labor Relations Board is empowered to investigate allegations of such unfair practices and to impose remedial actions, such as reinstatement, in cases where it finds the allegations to be justified.

TABLE Ba4954–4964 Work stoppages, workers involved, average duration, and person-days idle: 1881–1998

Contributed by Joshua L. Rosenbloom

		Workers involved		Person-days idle				Involving 1,000 or more workers			
										Person-days idle	
	Stoppages	Number	As a percentage of total employment	Number	As a percentage of estimated total working time	Per worker involved	Average duration	Number	Workers involved	Number	As a percentage of estimated total working time
	Ba4954	Ba4955	Ba4956	Ba4957	Ba4958	Ba4959	Ba4960	Ba4961	Ba4962	Ba4963	Ba4964
Year	Number	Thousand	Percent	Thousand	Percent	Number	Days	Number	Thousand	Thousand	Percent
1881	477	130	—	—	—	—	—	—	—	—	—
1882	476	159	—	—	—	—	—	—	—	—	—
1883	506	170	—	—	—	—	—	—	—	—	—
1884	485	165	—	—	—	—	—	—	—	—	—
1885	695	258	—	—	—	—	—	—	—	—	—
1886	1,572	610	—	—	—	—	—	—	—	—	—
1887	1,503	439	—	—	—	—	—	—	—	—	—
1888	946	163	—	—	—	—	—	—	—	—	—
1889	1,111	260	—	—	—	—	—	—	—	—	—
1890	1,897	373	4.2	—	—	—	—	—	—	—	—
1891	1,786	330	3.6	—	—	—	—	—	—	—	—
1892	1,359	239	2.5	—	—	—	—	—	—	—	—
1893	1,375	288	3.2	—	—	—	—	—	—	—	—
1894	1,404	690	8.3	—	—	—	—	—	—	—	—
1895	1,255	407	4.4	—	—	—	—	—	—	—	—
1896	1,066	249	2.8	—	—	—	—	—	—	—	—
1897	1,110	416	4.3	—	—	—	—	—	—	—	—
1898	1,098	263	2.6	—	—	—	—	—	—	—	—
1899	1,838	432	3.9	—	—	—	—	—	—	—	—
1900	1,839	568	4.9	—	—	—	—	—	—	—	—
1901	3,012	564	4.6	—	—	—	—	—	—	—	—
1902	3,240	692	5.4	—	—	—	—	—	—	—	—
1903	3,648	788	5.9	—	—	—	—	—	—	—	—
1904	2,419	574	4.3	—	—	—	—	—	—	—	—
1905	2,186	302	2.1	—	—	—	—	—	—	—	—
1914	1,204	—	—	—	—	—	—	—	—	—	—
1915	1,593	—	—	—	—	—	—	—	—	—	—
1916	3,789	1,600	8.4	—	—	—	—	—	—	—	—
1917	4,450	1,227	6.3	—	—	—	—	—	—	—	—
1918	3,353	1,240	6.2	—	—	—	—	—	—	—	—
1919	3,630	4,160	20.8	—	—	—	—	—	—	—	—
1920	3,411	1,463	7.2	—	—	—	—	—	—	—	—
1921	2,385	1,099	6.4	—	—	—	—	—	—	—	—
1922	1,112	1,613	8.7	—	—	—	—	—	—	—	—
1923	1,553	757	3.5	—	—	—	—	—	—	—	—
1924	1,249	655	3.1	—	—	—	—	—	—	—	—
1925	1,301	428	2.0	—	—	—	—	—	—	—	—
1926	1,035	330	1.5	—	—	—	—	—	—	—	—
1927	666	330	1.4	26,200	—	79.5	26.5	—	—	—	—
1928	620	314	1.3	12,600	—	40.2	27.6	—	—	—	—
1929	924	286	1.2	5,350	—	18.5	22.6	—	—	—	—
1930	651	183	0.8	3,320	—	18.1	22.3	—	—	—	—
1931	796	342	1.6	6,890	—	20.2	18.8	—	—	—	—
1932	852	324	1.8	10,500	—	32.4	19.6	—	—	—	—
1933	1,672	1,170	6.3	16,900	—	14.4	16.9	—	—	—	—
1934	1,817	1,470	7.2	19,600	—	13.4	19.5	—	—	—	—
1935	2,003	1,120	5.2	15,500	—	13.8	23.8	—	—	—	—
1936	2,156	789	3.1	13,900	—	17.6	23.3	—	—	—	—
1937	4,720	1,860	7.2	28,400	—	15.3	20.3	—	—	—	—
1938	2,772	688	2.8	9,150	—	13.3	23.6	—	—	—	—
1939	2,639	1,170	3.5	17,800	0.21	15.2	23.4	—	—	—	—
1940	2,493	577	1.7	6,700	0.08	11.6	20.9	—	—	—	—
1941	4,314	2,360	6.1	23,000	0.23	9.8	18.3	—	—	—	—
1942	3,036	840	2.0	4,180	0.04	5.0	11.7	—	—	—	—
1943	3,734	1,980	4.6	13,500	0.10	6.8	5.0	—	—	—	—
1944	4,958	2,120	4.8	8,720	0.07	4.1	5.6	—	—	—	—

TABLE Ba4954–4964 Work stoppages, workers involved, average duration, and person-days idle: 1881–1998 *Continued*

		Workers involved		Person-days idle				Involving 1,000 or more workers			
										Person-days idle	
	Stoppages	Number	As a percentage of total employment	Number	As a percentage of estimated total working time	Per worker involved	Average duration	Number	Workers involved	Number	As a percentage of estimated total working time
	Ba4954	Ba4955	Ba4956	Ba4957	Ba4958	Ba4959	Ba4960	Ba4961	Ba4962	Ba4963	Ba4964
Year	Number	Thousand	Percent	Thousand	Percent	Number	Days	Number	Thousand	Thousand	Percent
1945	4,616	3,470	8.2	38,000	0.31	11.0	9.9	—	—	—	—
1946	4,990	4,600	10.5	116,000	1.04	25.2	24.2	—	—	—	—
1947	3,693	2,170	4.7	34,600	0.30	15.9	25.6	270	1,629	25,720	—
1948	3,419	1,960	4.2	34,100	0.28	17.4	21.8	245	1,435	26,127	0.22
1949	3,606	3,030	6.7	50,500	0.44	16.7	22.5	262	2,537	43,420	0.38
1950	4,843	2,410	5.1	38,800	0.33	16.1	19.2	424	1,698	30,390	0.26
1951	4,737	2,220	4.5	22,900	0.18	10.3	17.4	415	1,462	15,070	0.12
1952	5,117	3,540	7.3	59,100	0.48	16.7	19.6	470	2,746	48,820	0.38
1953	5,091	2,400	4.7	28,300	0.22	11.8	20.3	437	1,623	18,130	0.14
1954	3,468	1,530	3.1	22,600	0.18	14.7	22.5	265	1,075	16,630	0.13
1955	4,320	2,650	5.2	28,200	0.22	10.7	18.5	363	2,055	21,180	0.16
1956	3,825	1,900	3.6	33,100	0.24	17.4	18.9	287	1,370	26,840	0.20
1957	3,673	1,390	2.6	16,500	0.12	11.4	19.2	279	887	10,340	0.07
1958	3,694	2,060	3.9	23,900	0.18	11.6	19.7	332	1,587	17,900	0.13
1959	3,708	1,880	3.3	69,000	0.50	36.7	24.6	245	1,381	60,850	0.43
1960	3,333	1,320	2.4	19,100	0.14	14.5	23.4	222	896	13,260	0.09
1961	3,367	1,450	2.6	16,300	0.11	11.2	23.7	195	1,031	10,140	0.07
1962	3,614	1,230	2.2	18,600	0.13	15.0	24.6	211	793	11,760	0.08
1963	3,362	941	1.1	16,100	0.11	17.1	23.0	181	512	10,020	0.07
1964	3,655	1,640	2.7	22,900	0.15	14.0	22.9	246	1,183	16,220	0.11
1965	3,963	1,550	2.5	23,300	0.15	15.1	25.0	268	999	15,140	0.10
1966	4,405	1,960	3.0	25,400	0.15	12.9	22.2	321	1,300	16,000	0.10
1967	4,595	2,870	4.3	42,100	0.25	14.7	22.8	381	2,192	31,320	0.18
1968	5,045	2,649	3.8	49,018	0.28	18.5	24.5	392	1,855	35,567	0.20
1969	5,700	2,481	3.5	42,869	0.24	17.3	22.5	412	1,576	29,397	0.16
1970	5,716	3,305	4.7	66,414	0.37	20.1	25.0	381	2,468	52,761	0.29
1971	5,138	3,280	4.5	47,589	0.26	14.5	27.0	298	2,516	35,538	0.19
1972	5,010	1,714	2.3	27,066	0.15	15.8	24.0	250	975	16,764	0.09
1973	5,353	2,251	2.9	27,948	0.14	12.4	24.0	317	1,400	16,260	0.08
1974	6,074	2,778	3.5	47,991	0.24	17.3	27.1	424	1,796	31,809	0.16
1975	5,031	1,746	2.2	31,237	0.16	17.9	26.8	235	965	17,563	0.09
1976	5,648	2,420	3.0	37,859	0.19	15.6	28.0	231	1,519	23,962	0.12
1977	5,506	2,040	2.4	35,822	0.17	17.6	29.3	298	1,212	21,258	0.10
1978	4,230	1,623	1.9	36,922	0.17	22.8	33.2	219	1,006	23,774	0.11
1979	4,827	1,727	1.9	34,754	0.15	20.1	32.1	235	1,021	20,409	0.09
1980	3,885	1,366	1.5	33,289	0.14	24.4	35.4	187	795	20,844	0.09
1981	2,568	1,081	1.2	24,730	0.11	22.9	—	145	729	16,908	0.07
1982	—	—	—	—	—	—	—	96	656	9,061	0.04
1983	—	—	—	—	—	—	—	81	909	17,461	0.08
1984	—	—	—	—	—	—	—	62	376	8,499	0.04
1985	—	—	—	—	—	—	—	54	324	7,079	0.03
1986	—	—	—	—	—	—	—	69	533	11,861	0.05
1987	—	—	—	—	—	—	—	46	174	4,481	0.02
1988	—	—	—	—	—	—	—	40	118	4,381	0.02
1989	—	—	—	—	—	—	—	51	452	16,996	0.07
1990	—	—	—	—	—	—	—	44	185	5,926	0.02
1991	—	—	—	—	—	—	—	40	392	4,584	0.02
1992	—	—	—	—	—	—	—	35	364	3,989	0.01
1993	—	—	—	—	—	—	—	35	182	3,981	0.01
1994	—	—	—	—	—	—	—	45	322	5,021	0.02
1995	—	—	—	—	—	—	—	31	192	5,771	0.02
1996	—	—	—	—	—	—	—	37	273	4,889	0.02
1997	—	—	—	—	—	—	—	29	339	4,497	0.01
1998	—	—	—	—	—	—	—	34	387	5,116	0.02

(continued)

TABLE Ba4954–4964 Work stoppages, workers involved, average duration, and person-days idle: 1881–1998 *Continued*

Sources

U.S. Bureau of Labor Statistics (BLS): *Handbook of Labor Statistics, 1975*, Bulletin number 1865, Table 159; *Handbook of Labor Statistics, 1983*, Bulletin number 2175, Table 128; *Handbook of Labor Statistics, 1989*, Bulletin number 2340; BLS Internet site.

Current work stoppage data may be obtained from the BLS Internet site.

Documentation

Work stoppages include both strikes and lockouts. A strike is defined as a temporary stoppage of work by a group of employees to express a grievance or enforce a demand. A lockout is defined as a temporary withholding of work from a group of employees by an employer (or group of employers) to enforce acceptance of the employer's terms. Most stoppages are strikes rather than lockouts.

All stoppages, whether or not authorized by the union, legal or illegal, are counted. The data exclude strikes lasting less than a full shift or involving fewer than six workers, all strikes of American seamen in foreign ports, and strikes of foreign crews on foreign ships in American ports. After 1981, data are available only for strikes involving 1,000 or more workers.

Data collection methods have varied over time. In 1887, the Bureau of Labor used newspaper and periodical reports to identify work stoppages. Staff members then visited the areas where strikes were reported, and they collected detailed information. Similar procedures were followed in subsequent studies conducted in 1894, 1901, and 1906. From 1906 to 1913, no federal agency collected data on work stoppages. Beginning in 1914, the Bureau of Labor Statistics attempted to collect data, relying solely on printed sources. In the following year, it adopted a new procedure that, with modifications, continued until 1981. In this approach, once information about a strike was obtained from press and/or other sources, questionnaires were sent to the parties involved. In 1927, procedures were improved to ensure the procurement of data on the number of workers involved in all stoppages and the computation of days of idleness. Since 1981, the principal source of data has been newspaper accounts.

Figures for workers involved include all workers made idle in the establishment where the stoppage occurs, even though they may not all be participants in the controversy. The figures exclude indirect or secondary idleness in other establishments that suspend or curtail operations because of shortages of materials or services resulting from a stoppage. The number of workers involved is the number on the day of maximum idleness.

Estimated working time is computed by multiplying the average number of workers employed each year by the days worked by most employees during the year.

Series Ba4954–4955 and Ba4961–4962. The number of stoppages and numbers of workers involved relates to stoppages beginning during the calendar year.

Series Ba4957–4959 and Ba4963–4964. The number of person-days idle and percentage of working time idle relates to all stoppages in effect during the calendar year.

Series Ba4960. The average duration relates to stoppages ending during the calendar year. Data are simple averages; each stoppage is given equal weight.

TABLE Ba4965–4970 Work stoppages and workers involved, by major issue: 1881–1981[1]

Contributed by Joshua L. Rosenbloom

	Work stoppages, by issue			Workers involved, by issue		
	Wages and hours	Union organization	Other and not reported	Wages and hours	Union organization	Other and not reported
	Ba4965	Ba4966	Ba4967	Ba4968	Ba4969	Ba4970
Year	Number	Number	Number	Thousand	Thousand	Thousand
1881	382	32	63	118	5	7
1882	353	38	85	133	12	14
1883	372	55	79	131	28	12
1884	341	50	94	145	4	16
1885	486	67	142	214	14	30
1886	1,073	210	289	445	79	87
1887	836	299	368	249	91	99
1888	540	163	243	100	23	41
1889	662	173	276	207	29	24
1890	1,039	318	540	276	32	66
1891	867	334	585	221	55	54
1892	693	261	405	122	59	57
1893	783	257	335	162	59	66
1894	865	206	333	469	25	196
1895	810	217	228	305	51	51
1896	547	297	222	160	53	36
1897	680	193	237	335	36	45
1898	645	236	217	184	30	49
1899	1,014	471	353	288	66	79
1900	931	414	494	210	282	76
1901	1,413	1,016	583	288	161	115
1902	1,604	1,051	585	279	279	134
1903	1,778	1,200	670	396	235	156
1904	944	964	511	272	210	92
1905	942	800	444	191	57	54
1914	403	253	548	—	—	—
1915	770	312	511	—	—	—
1916	2,036	721	1,032	—	—	—
1917	2,268	799	1,383	—	—	—
1918	1,869	584	900	—	—	—
1919	2,036	869	725	—	—	—
1920	2,038	622	751	—	—	—
1921	1,501	373	511	—	—	—
1922	583	208	321	—	—	—
1923	721	308	524	—	—	—
1924	537	244	468	—	—	—
1925	537	219	545	—	—	—
1926	478	206	351	—	—	—
1927	273	240	153	232	45	43
1928	222	226	172	140	95	88
1929	373	382	169	104	102	80
1930	284	207	160	73	76	33
1931	447	221	128	155	116	74
1932	560	162	130	234	73	18
1933	926	533	213	544	465	135
1934	717	835	265	346	762	372
1935	760	945	298	663	288	151
1936	756	1,083	317	251	365	94
1937	1,410	2,728	582	436	1,160	347
1938	776	1,385	611	252	224	211
1939	699	1,411	529	352	641	185
1940	753	1,243	497	235	190	148
1941	1,535	2,138	641	1,110	744	512
1942	1,423	943	670	429	191	232
1943	1,906	585	1,243	1,220	226	523
1944	2,146	808	2,004	810	395	922

Note appears at end of table

(continued)

TABLE Ba4965–4970 Work stoppages and workers involved, by major issue: 1881–1981 *Continued*

	Work stoppages, by issue			Workers involved, by issue		
	Wages and hours	Union organization	Other and not reported	Wages and hours	Union organization	Other and not reported
	Ba4965	Ba4966	Ba4967	Ba4968	Ba4969	Ba4970
Year	Number	Number	Number	Thousand	Thousand	Thousand
1945	1,956	946	1,714	1,340	671	1,060
1946	2,238	1,617	1,135	3,710	568	663
1947	1,707	1,102	884	805	931	431
1948	1,737	780	902	1,210	228	518
1949	1,682	781	1,143	1,540	82	1,410
1950	2,559	919	1,365	1,460	130	819
1951	2,102	888	1,747	1,180	136	904
1952	2,447	839	1,831	1,450	841	1,244
1953	2,825	745	1,521	1,460	162	781
1954	1,726	588	1,154	886	54	591
1955	2,154	844	1,322	1,780	244	625
1956	1,821	774	1,230	1,270	183	447
1957	1,730	751	1,192	752	72	563
1958	1,875	583	1,236	1,380	73	603
1959	1,872	664	1,172	1,320	154	400
1960	1,592	538	1,203	568	246	504
1961	1,664	518	1,185	565	92	795
1962	1,824	582	1,208	725	106	403
1963	1,573	531	1,258	470	94	376
1964	1,700	556	1,399	699	87	854
1965	1,923	594	1,446	821	154	571
1966	2,259	596	1,550	1,114	130	718
1967	2,433	586	1,576	1,966	114	790
1968	2,891	513	1,641	1,676	112	861
1969	3,199	593	1,908	1,425	250	806
1970	3,132	587	1,997	2,147	106	1,053
1971	2,804	482	1,852	2,310	179	791
1972	2,363	511	2,136	795	98	821
1973	2,844	446	2,063	1,255	117	876
1974	3,863	348	1,863	2,064	47	668
1975	2,805	268	1,958	872	92	781
1976	3,058	325	2,265	1,276	127	1,018
1977	3,369	252	1,885	990	41	1,008
1978	2,957	272	1,001	919	39	665
1979	3,362	250	1,215	1,197	48	482
1980	2,741	205	939	912	35	420
1981	1,804	170	594	792	32	257

[1] Prior to 1961, strikes over other contractual matters are included under "Wages and hours." Beginning in 1961, however, this category of strikes is included under "Other and not reported."

Sources

U.S. Bureau of Labor Statistics, *Handbook of Labor Statistics, 1972*, and *Handbook of Labor Statistics, 1983*, Table 131.

Documentation

The methods used to compile data on work stoppages are discussed in the text for Table Ba4954–4964. The classification of causes of strikes necessarily lacks precision because many strikes involve more than one issue. In particular, strikes for union organization often involve demands concerning wages or hours as well. The major causes listed in this table reflect an aggregation of more detailed classification of strike causes. The category of wage and hours issues includes strikes over general wage changes; supplementary benefits; wage adjustments; hours of work; and, prior to 1961, other contractual matters. Beginning in 1961, other contractual matters were included in the "other and not reported" category. Other separately enumerated causes included in the "other and not reported" category are job security, plant administration, other working conditions, interunion and intraunion matters, and strikes where causes were not reported.

TABLE Ba4971–4994 Work stoppages, workers involved, person-days idle, and working time lost, by industry: 1937–1981

Contributed by Joshua L. Rosenbloom

	Manufacturing industries				Nonmanufacturing industries			
	Number	Workers involved	Person-days idle	Estimated working time lost	Number	Workers involved	Person-days idle	Estimated working time lost
	Ba4971	Ba4972	Ba4973	Ba4974	Ba4975	Ba4976	Ba4977	Ba4978
Year	Number	Thousand	Thousand	Percent	Number	Thousand	Thousand	Percent
1937	2,779	1,230	20,000	0.79	1,961	663	8,450	0.20
1938	1,436	410	5,820	0.27	1,336	278	3,330	0.08
1939	1,389	394	7,180	0.31	1,224	777	10,600	0.25
1940	1,410	352	4,400	0.17	1,098	225	2,300	0.05
1941	2,652	1,270	12,500	0.49	1,642	1,090	10,600	0.23
1942	1,879	616	2,680	0.08	1,089	224	1,500	0.03
1943	2,491	1,220	3,430	0.07	1,261	763	10,100	0.21
1944	3,257	1,680	6,150	0.14	1,700	434	2,570	0.05
1945	3,185	2,510	28,800	0.78	1,569	958	9,270	0.21
1946	2,887	2,210	81,700	2.42	2,108	2,360	34,100	0.72
1947	1,993	801	15,700	0.43	1,700	1,370	18,900	0.39
1948	1,675	959	17,600	0.46	1,744	996	16,500	0.31
1949	1,661	1,220	24,200	0.73	1,945	1,820	26,300	0.39
1950	2,705	1,450	22,900	0.66	2,138	959	15,900	0.30
1951	2,548	1,370	17,500	0.43	2,189	844	5,470	0.11
1952	2,665	1,880	42,300	1.03	2,452	1,660	16,800	0.27
1953	2,612	1,320	15,600	0.36	2,479	1,090	12,700	0.19
1954	1,703	772	13,700	0.33	1,762	761	8,900	0.14
1955	2,406	2,000	18,800	0.45	1,913	646	9,390	0.14
1956	1,986	1,360	12,700	0.63	1,856	544	6,020	0.09
1957	1,965	778	9,390	0.22	1,711	610	7,080	0.10
1958	1,955	1,490	15,400	0.39	1,739	574	8,520	0.12
1959	2,043	1,280	55,500	1.34	1,672	600	13,500	0.19
1960	1,598	707	11,200	0.27	1,740	610	7,900	0.11
1961	1,677	897	9,780	0.24	1,694	555	6,500	0.08
1962	1,789	638	10,100	0.24	1,825	596	8,460	0.11
1963	1,685	555	10,400	0.24	1,678	386	5,730	0.07
1964	1,794	994	15,700	0.35	1,865	646	7,210	0.09
1965	2,080	913	14,300	0.31	1,886	633	9,020	0.11
1966	2,296	922	13,700	0.28	2,110	1,040	11,700	0.14
1967	2,328	1,350	27,800	0.57	2,267	1,530	14,300	0.15
1968	2,664	1,180	24,000	0.47	2,396	1,470	25,000	0.20
1969	2,822	1,308	24,107	0.47	2,893	1,174	18,763	0.14
1970	2,481	1,128	38,006	0.77	3,241	2,177	28,407	0.21
1971	2,391	863	18,485	0.39	2,762	2,417	29,104	0.22
1972	2,056	646	12,283	0.26	2,954	1,068	14,784	0.11
1973	2,282	963	14,319	0.29	3,072	1,287	13,630	0.09
1974	2,823	1,145	23,599	0.47	3,253	1,632	24,392	0.16
1975	1,897	464	14,876	0.32	3,134	1,282	16,361	0.11
1976	2,245	975	24,263	0.51	3,406	1,446	13,596	0.09
1977	2,537	788	18,331	0.37	2,970	1,252	17,486	0.11
1978	2,121	568	15,602	0.31	2,110	1,055	21,320	0.13
1979	2,296	681	20,291	0.39	2,536	1,047	14,462	0.08
1980	1,809	453	17,154	0.34	2,080	913	16,135	0.09
1981	1,192	263	6,132	0.12	1,377	818	18,598	0.10

(continued)

TABLE Ba4971–4994 Work stoppages, workers involved, person-days idle, and working time lost, by industry: 1937–1981 *Continued*

	Mining				Contract construction			
	Number	Workers involved	Person-days idle	Estimated working time lost	Number	Workers involved	Person-days idle	Estimated working time lost
	Ba4979	Ba4980	Ba4981	Ba4982	Ba4983	Ba4984	Ba4985	Ba4986
Year	Number	Thousand	Thousand	Percent	Number	Thousand	Thousand	Percent
1937	111	163	2,620	—	328	72	848	—
1938	63	38	529	—	315	44	405	—
1939	64	383	7,460	—	320	70	633	—
1940	65	42	269	—	310	71	493	—
1941	143	737	7,230	—	395	186	923	—
1942	156	83	516	0.31	239	31	164	0.04
1943	463	610	9,370	4.25	188	36	141	0.04
1944	893	278	1,410	0.56	168	23	120	0.06
1945	670	678	6,230	2.88	206	46	447	0.20
1946	570	974	21,400	10.35	351	146	1,450	0.40
1947	478	517	2,440	1.12	382	175	2,770	0.66
1948	614	651	10,400	4.51	380	108	1,430	0.29
1949	476	1,380	19,200	8.39	615	197	2,760	0.53
1950	508	196	9,700	4.37	611	237	2,460	0.44
1951	622	284	1,290	0.55	651	232	1,190	0.18
1952	650	547	4,310	1.92	794	634	6,700	1.03
1953	460	156	846	0.40	1,039	574	8,000	1.22
1954	248	111	845	0.44	804	437	4,800	0.71
1955	343	114	1,080	0.57	733	204	1,810	0.28
1956	321	129	1,320	0.65	784	231	2,680	0.35
1957	198	56	240	0.11	785	308	3,970	0.51
1958	168	39	302	0.16	844	326	4,790	0.71
1959	187	120	5,650	3.26	771	251	4,120	0.58
1960	154	49	700	0.41	773	269	4,470	0.63
1961	154	38	310	0.18	824	217	3,490	0.50
1962	159	52	983	0.60	913	284	4,150	0.60
1963	153	46	481	0.30	840	208	1,930	0.25
1964	155	83	808	0.49	944	248	2,790	0.35
1965	188	72	431	0.27	943	301	4,630	0.57
1966	194	96	794	0.50	977	455	6,140	0.73
1967	254	102	3,030	1.95	867	305	5,160	0.62
1968	301	213	2,550	1.60	912	364	8,720	1.05
1969	495	220	1,157	0.72	973	433	10,386	1.19
1970	544	211	850	0.54	1,137	621	15,240	1.79
1971	657	383	4,934	3.23	751	451	6,850	0.83
1972	1,000	267	724	0.47	701	454	7,844	0.88
1973	1,079	301	865	0.55	539	367	3,663	0.40
1974	1,050	501	4,061	2.40	688	630	12,721	1.27
1975	1,165	392	1,643	0.88	600	308	7,307	0.84
1976	1,425	515	2,220	1.13	503	172	3,240	0.36
1977	999	676	7,281	3.48	486	218	3,284	0.34
1978	275	114	10,261	4.89	385	169	2,272	0.21
1979	441	141	511	0.20	273	121	1,646	0.14
1980	297	117	1,952	0.73	287	320	4,753	0.43
1981	196	298	8,866	3.19	243	210	4,440	0.41

TABLE Ba4971–4994 Work stoppages, workers involved, person-days idle, and working time lost, by industry: 1937–1981 *Continued*

	Transportation, communications, electric, gas, and sanitary services				Wholesale and retail trade			
	Number	Workers involved	Person-days idle	Estimated working time lost	Number	Workers involved	Person-days idle	Estimated working time lost
	Ba4987	Ba4988	Ba4989	Ba4990	Ba4991	Ba4992	Ba4993	Ba4994
Year	Number	Thousand	Thousand	Percent	Number	Thousand	Thousand	Percent
1937	379	138	1,890	—	—	—	—	—
1938	216	77	730	—	—	—	—	—
1939	256	87	867	—	—	—	—	—
1940	185	45	596	—	—	—	—	—
1941	280	52	433	—	—	—	—	—
1942	221	42	171	—	260	30	304	—
1943	284	56	183	—	119	26	90	—
1944	335	73	345	0.03	139	32	270	0.01
1945	342	157	1,550	0.15	182	35	336	0.02
1946	479	1,020	9,020	0.94	385	64	882	0.05
1947	282	468	11,500	1.19	336	61	1,010	0.05
1948	293	160	3,290	0.34	241	30	557	0.03
1949	347	154	2,320	0.25	329	46	1,440	0.07
1950	386	405	2,380	0.25	381	70	927	0.04
1951	387	231	1,790	0.17	277	40	289	0.01
1952	406	372	4,170	0.39	397	76	1,050	0.04
1953	372	256	2,380	0.22	408	71	1,050	0.04
1954	282	146	1,410	0.14	298	53	1,690	0.06
1955	275	253	4,860	0.47	409	52	1,090	0.04
1956	243	130	1,170	0.11	336	37	558	0.02
1957	209	169	2,010	0.19	372	63	654	0.02
1958	242	132	2,270	0.23	358	57	942	0.03
1959	233	140	1,910	0.19	311	72	1,570	0.05
1960	266	200	1,750	0.18	290	33	451	0.02
1961	243	211	1,710	0.17	308	62	716	0.02
1962	213	182	2,490	0.25	364	30	535	0.02
1963	205	63	2,540	0.25	293	34	498	0.02
1964	257	205	1,900	0.19	309	62	1,340	0.04
1965	216	185	3,000	0.29	336	43	570	0.02
1966	240	312	3,390	0.32	365	42	508	0.02
1967	345	866	3,450	0.32	431	87	994	0.03
1968	303	571	9,310	0.84	417	75	972	0.03
1969	320	212	4,031	0.36	470	93	1,310	0.04
1970	400	858	7,208	0.63	487	74	1,876	0.05
1971	316	1,267	13,420	1.18	502	134	2,086	0.05
1972	256	115	3,245	0.29	389	52	132	0.03
1973	324	193	3,297	0.28	499	136	2,124	0.05
1974	320	140	3,226	0.27	549	137	1,758	0.04
1975	268	167	3,089	0.27	371	63	1,426	0.03
1976	354	386	3,461	0.30	467	56	1,311	0.03
1977	303	56	2,157	0.19	486	86	1,988	0.04
1978	259	395	4,453	0.37	445	117	1,758	0.04
1979	376	387	5,643	0.44	511	64	1,368	0.03
1980	243	96	1,741	0.14	411	61	1,403	0.03
1981	181	86	640	0.05	247	47	669	0.01

Sources

U.S. Bureau of Labor Statistics, *Analysis of Work Stoppages* (published annually), and *Handbook of Labor Statistics, 1983*, Table 132.

Documentation

Data on number of stoppages and number of workers involved are for stoppages beginning during the year. Data on person-days idle and percentage of working time lost are totals during the year.

TABLE Ba4995–4998 Public opinion regarding labor unions: 1936–1999

Contributed by Joshua L. Rosenbloom

	Percentage expressing approval or disapproval			Percentage expressing a great deal of confidence
	Approval	Disapproval	No opinion	
	Ba4995	Ba4996	Ba4997	Ba4998
Year	Percent	Percent	Percent	Percent
1936	72	20	8	—
1939	68	24	8	—
1941	61	30	9	—
1947	64	25	11	—
1948	64	21	15	—
1953	75	18	7	—
1957	75	14	11	—
1958	64	21	15	—
1959	68	19	13	—
1961	70	18	12	—
1962	64	24	11	—
1963	68	22	10	—
1965	71	19	11	—
1967	66	23	11	—
1972	60	27	13	—
1973	—	—	—	30
1975	—	—	—	38
1977	—	—	—	39
1978	59	31	10	—
1979	55	33	12	36
1981	—	—	—	28
1983	—	—	—	26
1984	—	—	—	30
1985	58	27	15	28
1986	59	30	11	29
1987	—	—	—	26
1988	—	—	—	26
1990	—	—	—	27
1991	60	30	10	25
1992	—	—	—	26
1993	—	—	—	26
1994	—	—	—	26
1995	—	—	—	26
1996	—	—	—	25
1997	60	31	9	23
1998	—	—	—	26
1999	66	29	5	28

Sources

1936–1967: George H. Gallup, *The Gallup Poll: Public Opinion, 1935–1971*, 3 volumes (Random House, 1972); *The Gallup Poll: Public Opinion, 1972–1977*, 2 volumes (Scholarly Resources, 1978); and *The Gallup Poll: Public Opinion*, annual volumes (Scholarly Resources, 1979–1996).

Current poll results are available from the Gallup Organization's Internet site.

Documentation

This table reports responses to public opinion surveys conducted by the Gallup Poll. Among the questions regularly included in its public opinion polls are two that relate to attitudes toward labor unions. The percentage expressing approval, disapproval, or no opinion regarding labor unions (series Ba4995–4997) are derived from response to the question "Do you approve or disapprove of labor unions?" The percentage expressing quite a lot or a great deal of confidence in labor unions (series Ba4998) is derived from responses to the question "How much respect and confidence do you, yourself, have in labor unions?" This latter question is generally included in a much broader survey of public confidence in a large number of social, political, and economic institutions.

All responses result from surveying selected samples of the population. Prior to 1950, the sampling procedure was designed to produce an approximation of the adult civilian population living in the United States, except for those persons in institutions such as prisons or hospitals. The sampling procedure began by drawing a nationally representative selection of places distributed by region- and city-size strata. Within each location, respondents were then selected by age, sex, and socioeconomic quotas. Since 1950, all Gallup Polls have been based on a national probability sample of interviewing areas.

HOUSEHOLD PRODUCTION

Lee A. Craig

TABLE Ba4999–5078 Value of home manufacturing, by state: 1810–1860

Contributed by Lee A. Craig

	Value															
	Alabama	Arkansas	California	Connecticut	Delaware	District of Columbia	Florida	Georgia	Illinois	Indiana	Iowa	Kansas	Kentucky	Louisiana	Maine	Maryland
	Ba4999	Ba5000	Ba5001	Ba5002	Ba5003	Ba5004	Ba5005	Ba5006	Ba5007	Ba5008	Ba5009	Ba5010	Ba5011	Ba5012	Ba5013	Ba5014
Year	Dollars	Dollars	Dollars	Dollars	Dollars	Dollars	Dollars	Dollars	Dollars	Dollars	Dollars	Dollars	Dollars	Dollars	Dollars	Dollars
1810	—	—	—	2,241,847	212,581	39,500	—	2,149,033	55,973	177,813	—	—	2,366,013	107,241	1,067,703	1,036,866
1840	1,656,119	489,750	—	226,162	62,116	1,500	20,205	1,467,630	993,567	1,289,802	25,966	—	2,622,462	65,190	804,397	176,050
1850	1,934,120	638,217	7,000	192,252	38,121	2,075	75,582	1,838,968	1,155,902	1,631,039	221,292	—	2,459,128	139,232	513,599	111,828
1860	1,817,520	1,019,240	255,653	48,954	17,591	440	63,259	1,431,413	923,220	986,393	317,690	24,748	2,095,578	502,100	490,786	67,003

	Value															
	Massachusetts	Michigan	Minnesota	Mississippi	Missouri	Nebraska	Nevada	New Hampshire	New Jersey	New Mexico	New York	North Carolina	Ohio	Oregon	Pennsylvania	Rhode Island
	Ba5015	Ba5016	Ba5017	Ba5018	Ba5019	Ba5020	Ba5021	Ba5022	Ba5023	Ba5024	Ba5025	Ba5026	Ba5027	Ba5028	Ba5029	Ba5030
Year	Dollars	Dollars	Dollars	Dollars	Dollars	Dollars	Dollars	Dollars	Dollars	Dollars	Dollars	Dollars	Dollars	Dollars	Dollars	Dollars
1810	2,155,029	3,470	—	266,493	—	—	—	1,976,714	1,294,180	—	5,029,895	2,989,140	1,334,515	—	4,612,979	900,019
1840	231,942	113,955	—	682,945	1,149,544	—	—	538,303	201,625	—	4,636,547	1,413,242	1,853,937	—	1,303,093	51,180
1850	205,333	340,947	—	1,164,020	1,674,705	—	—	393,455	112,781	6,033	1,280,333	2,086,522	1,712,196	—	749,132	26,495
1860	245,886	142,756	7,981	1,382,144	1,984,262	15,995	300	251,052	27,588	26,406	717,898	2,045,372	596,197	46,278	544,728	7,824

	Value								Per capita value							
	South Carolina	Tennessee	Texas	Utah	Vermont	Virginia	Washington	Wisconsin	Alabama	Arkansas	California	Connecticut	Delaware	District of Columbia	Florida	Georgia
	Ba5031	Ba5032	Ba5033	Ba5034	Ba5035	Ba5036	Ba5037	Ba5038	Ba5039	Ba5040	Ba5041	Ba5042	Ba5043	Ba5044	Ba5045	Ba5046
Year	Dollars	Dollars	Dollars	Dollars	Dollars	Dollars	Dollars	Dollars	Dollars	Dollars	Dollars	Dollars	Dollars	Dollars	Dollars	Dollars
1810	1,677,228	1,691,548	—	—	1,321,427	4,885,602	—	—	—	—	—	8.52	2.92	1.64	—	8.65
1840	930,703	2,886,661	—	—	674,548	2,441,672	—	12,567	2.80	5.02	—	0.73	0.79	0.03	0.37	2.12
1850	909,525	3,137,790	266,984	1,392	267,710	2,156,312	—	43,624	2.51	3.04	0.07	0.52	0.42	0.04	0.86	2.03
1860	815,117	3,174,977	584,217	66,851	63,334	1,576,627	33,506	127,992	1.88	2.34	0.67	0.11	0.16	0.00	0.45	1.35

(continued)

TABLE Ba4999–5078 Value of home manufacturing, by state: 1810–1860 *Continued*

	Per capita value															
	Illinois	Indiana	Iowa	Kansas	Kentucky	Louisiana	Maine	Maryland	Massachusetts	Michigan	Minnesota	Mississippi	Missouri	Nebraska	Nevada	New Hampshire
	Ba5047	Ba5048	Ba5049	Ba5050	Ba5051	Ba5052	Ba5053	Ba5054	Ba5055	Ba5056	Ba5057	Ba5058	Ba5059	Ba5060	Ba5061	Ba5062
Year	Dollars	Dollars	Dollars	Dollars	Dollars	Dollars	Dollars	Dollars	Dollars	Dollars	Dollars	Dollars	Dollars	Dollars	Dollars	Dollars
1810	4.56	7.25	—	—	5.82	2.48	4.67	2.78	4.92	0.84	—	6.60	—	—	—	9.22
1840	2.09	1.88	0.60	—	3.36	0.18	1.60	0.37	0.31	0.54	—	1.82	2.99	—	—	1.89
1850	1.36	1.65	1.15	—	2.50	0.27	0.88	0.19	0.21	0.86	0.00	1.92	2.45	—	—	1.24
1860	0.53	0.73	0.47	0.23	1.81	0.71	0.78	0.10	0.20	0.19	0.05	1.75	1.68	0.55	0.04	0.78

	Per capita value															
	New Jersey	New Mexico	New York	North Carolina	Ohio	Oregon	Pennsylvania	Rhode Island	South Carolina	Tennessee	Texas	Utah	Vermont	Virginia	Washington	Wisconsin
	Ba5063	Ba5064	Ba5065	Ba5066	Ba5067	Ba5068	Ba5069	Ba5070	Ba5071	Ba5072	Ba5073	Ba5074	Ba5075	Ba5076	Ba5077	Ba5078
Year	Dollars	Dollars	Dollars	Dollars	Dollars	Dollars	Dollars	Dollars	Dollars	Dollars	Dollars	Dollars	Dollars	Dollars	Dollars	Dollars
1810	5.27	—	5.24	5.41	6.17	—	5.67	11.70	5.65	6.46	—	—	6.06	5.37	—	—
1840	0.54	—	1.91	1.87	1.22	—	0.75	0.47	1.56	3.48	—	—	2.31	1.97	—	0.41
1850	0.23	0.10	0.41	2.40	0.86	—	0.32	0.18	1.36	3.13	1.25	0.12	0.85	1.52	—	0.14
1860	0.04	0.28	0.18	2.06	0.25	0.88	0.19	0.04	1.16	2.86	0.97	1.66	0.20	0.99	2.89	0.16

Source

Rolla Milton Tryon, *Household Manufactures in the United States, 1640–1860* (Augustus M. Kelley, 1996), Tables XI and XVII, pp. 166 and 308–9.

Documentation

Home manufactures refer to goods produced in a home or plantation household using raw materials produced on the farm on which the manufacturing was done. In the nineteenth-century household economy, home manufactures were thought of as an adjunct to the ordinary work of the farm household. They are distinguished from other forms of manufacturing that were sometimes carried on in households during this era. For example, when a household specialized in the manufacture of a particular good, the system was called "handicrafts," rather than "home manufactures." Where goods were made at home as a stage in a factory operation, the system was called "sweat-shop." Where the raw materials for home-produced goods were supplied from outside the farm, the system was called "outwork." Plantation manufacture, which was carried on primarily for sale, is excluded from home manufactures. The home manufactures valued here are various types of cloth, primarily cotton, flaxen, and woolen goods. Home-manufactured foods – including bread, butter, jellies, and pickles – were excluded.

TABLE Ba5079–5081 Textile output of home manufactures, and the number of textile factories – New York State: 1820–1855

Contributed by Lee A. Craig

	Textile goods produced in home manufactures		
	Yards	Yards per capita	Textile factories
	Ba5079	Ba5080	Ba5081
Year	Yards	Yards	Number
1820 [1]	9,913,374	7.9	—
1825	16,469,422	10.2 [2]	314 [3]
1835	8,773,813	4.0	345
1845	7,089,984	2.7	463
1855	929,241	0.3	889

[1] Data are for the period 1820–1821.

[2] The figure reported in the original source, 8.95 yards per capita, differs from the ratio of total state output to population.

[3] Data on textile factories begins in 1831.

Sources

Rolla Milton Tryon, *Household Manufactures in the United States, 1640–1860* (Augustus M. Kelley, 1996), Table XVI, pp. 289, 304–5, and 307.

Documentation

For a general discussion of the classification of home manufactures, as distinguished from other forms of economic activity in the household, see the text for Table Ba4999–5078.

Tryon's figures for 1820–1821 were taken from data reported by the New York State Assembly. The figures for 1825–1855 are from the New York State censuses. Although Tryon's figures only include textiles, contemporary accounts suggest that, in general, home manufacturing data from the era largely reflected textile production. For a discussion of the *value added* in home manufacturing and its contribution to national output, see the discussion and data in Robert E. Gallman, "Gross National Product in the United States, 1834–1909," in *Output, Employment, and Productivity in the United States after 1800*, National Bureau of Economic Research, Studies in Income and Wealth, volume 30 (Columbia University Press, 1996), Tables A4 and A5; and Thomas Weiss, "Farm Gross Product, Labor Force and Output per Worker in the United States, 1800 to 1900" (unpublished manuscript, University of Kansas, 1990), Table A1.

TABLE Ba5082–5085 Households, by number of boarders and lodgers: 1880–1990

Contributed by Matthew Sobek

		Percentage of households, by number of boarders and lodgers		
	Total households	None	One	Two or more
	Ba5082	Ba5083	Ba5084	Ba5085
Year	Number	Percent	Percent	Percent
1880	10,098,849	92.8	4.7	2.5
1900	16,116,192	89.3	6.8	3.9
1910	20,244,848	89.8	5.9	4.3
1920	24,350,890	91.3	5.2	3.6
1940	34,904,634	93.4	4.5	2.1
1950	43,398,031	95.2	3.2	1.6
1960	52,796,226	97.0	2.3	0.7
1970	63,529,839	97.9	1.6	0.5
1980	80,394,061	98.6	1.1	0.3
1990	93,347,159	98.9	0.8	0.3

Source

Tabulated from the Integrated Public Use Microdata Series (IPUMS). See the Guide to the Millennial Edition for information on the IPUMS.

Documentation

A boarder is a person who pays a fixed stipend for lodging and regular meals in a private home. A lodger is a person who pays for lodging but not for regular meals. These calculations refer to households only and exclude boarders and lodgers in group quarters. The census definition of "group quarters" has changed over time. For 1940–1970, households with more than four unrelated persons (including boarders) were defined as group quarters. In other years, group quarters were defined as dwelling units with more than nine boarders or lodgers.

TABLE Ba5086–5090 Children in primary child care arrangements used by employed mothers, by type of care: 1958–1994

Contributed by Lee A. Craig

		Cared for in			
	Total	Own home	Another home	Organized child care facility	Other facilities
	Ba5086	Ba5087	Ba5088	Ba5089	Ba5090
Year	Thousand	Thousand	Thousand	Thousand	Thousand
1958 [1]	2,039	1,154	553	92	241
1965 [2]	3,794	1,788	1,165	243	599
1977 [3]	4,370	1,481	1,779	568	542
1982	4,826	1,549	2,046	753	463
1984	6,666	1,920	2,533	1,653	553
1985	8,168	2,532	3,022	1,887	727
1986	8,849	2,540	3,602	1,982	726
1987	9,124	2,728	3,248	2,226	931
1988	9,483	2,674	3,490	2,447	948
1990	9,629	2,860	3,380	2,658	732
1991	9,854	3,518	3,055	2,316	966
1993	9,937	3,051	3,190	2,991	706
1994	10,288	3,395	3,220	3,025	658

[1] Includes children less than 6 years of age of mothers employed full-time only.

[2] Includes children less than 6 years of age.

[3] Includes two youngest children less than 5 years of age only.

Sources

U.S. Bureau of the Census, *Primary Child Care Arrangements Used for Preschoolers by Families with Employed Mothers*, selected years, 1977 to 1994. Electronic file. Internet release date: January 14, 1998.

Lynne M. Casper, Mary Hawkins, and Martin O'Connell, *Who's Minding the Kids? Child Care Arrangements: Fall 1991*, U.S. Bureau of the Census, Current Population Reports, series P-70, number 36 (1994).

Marjorie Lueck, Ann C. Orr, and Martin O'Connell, *Trends in Child Care Arrangements of Working Mothers*, U.S. Bureau of the Census, Current Population Reports, series P-23, number 117 (1982).

Who's Minding the Kids? Child Care Arrangements of Working Mothers, Winter 1984–85, The U.S. Bureau of the Census, Current Population Reports, series p-70, number 9 (1987).

Documentation

Except as noted, figures cover children less than age 5 in primary child care arrangements used by employed mothers.

Supplements to the Census Bureau's Current Population Survey have included data on child care arrangements since 1958. Since 1984, these data have been collected by the Census Bureau's Survey of Income and Program Participation. For two-parent households, the information reported in this table was collected from information supplied by the wife and refers to arrangements while *she* was working. For families in which only the mother was present or in which the child was cared for by a legal guardian other than a parent, information was obtained from the mother or the legal guardian. The original documents report subcategories by percentage. For some years, there are minor changes in the organization of certain subcategories. For example, "school-based activities" are sometimes classified with "Organized child care facilities" and sometimes among "Other facilities." As a result, summing across categories does not consistently yield the totals. For a detailed discussion of the survey and its procedures, see Casper, Hawkins, and O'Connell (1994), pp. 1–7 and Appendix C.

More recent data, organized into slightly different categories, are available in *Who's Minding the Kids? Child Care Arrangements: Spring 1999*, Detailed Tables (PPL-168) (n.d.). This is an electronic file available on the Census Bureau's Web site. No author is listed. See, especially, "Historical Table: Primary Child Care Arrangements Used by Employed Mothers of Preschoolers: 1985 to 1999."

Series Ba5090. Includes children who cared for themselves, children cared for by their mother at work (whether work was in or away from the home), children in kindergarten, and other arrangements.

TABLE Ba5091–5095 Year of passage of legislation recognizing married women's property rights and authorizing women's suffrage, by state: 1840–1920[1]

Contributed by Susan B. Carter and Lee A. Craig

	Khan			Geddes and Lueck	Rusk
	Estates	Earnings	Sole trader	Estates and earnings	Female suffrage acts
	Ba5091	Ba5092	Ba5093	Ba5094	Ba5095
State	Year	Year	Year	Year	Year
Alabama	1867	—	—	1887	1912
Arizona	1871	—	1871	1973	—
Arkansas	1873	1873	1868	1873	—
California	1872	1872	1872	1872	1911
Colorado	1874	1874	1874	1868	1893
Connecticut	1856 [2]	1877	1877	1877	—
Delaware	1875	1873	—	1873	—
Florida	—	—	—	1943	—
Georgia	1873	—	—	1873	—
Idaho	1887	—	1887	1915	1896
Illinois	1861	1861	1874	1869	1913 [3]
Indiana	1879	1879	—	1879	1919 [3]
Iowa	1873	1870	1873	1873	1919 [3]
Kansas	1868	1868	1868	1858	1913
Kentucky	—	1873	1873	1873	1920 [3]
Louisiana	—	—	1894	1980	—
Maine	1844	1857	1844	1857	—
Maryland	1860	1860	1860	1860	—
Massachusetts	1845	1874	1860	1846	—
Michigan	1855	—	—	1911	1918
Minnesota	1869	—	1874	1869	1919 [3]
Mississippi	1871	1871	1871	1871	—
Missouri	1879	1879	—	1875	1919 [3]
Montana	1872	1874	1874	1887	1914
Nebraska	1881	1881	1881	1871	1917 [3]
Nevada	1873	1873	1873	1873	1914
New Hampshire	1867	—	1876	1867	—
New Jersey	1852	1874	1874	1874	—
New Mexico	—	—	—	1973	—
New York	1845 [2]	1860	1860	1860	1917
North Carolina	1868	1873	—	1873	—
North Dakota	1877	1877	1877	1877	1920
Ohio	1861	1861	—	1861	1917 [3]
Oklahoma	—	—	—	1910	1918
Oregon	—	1880	1880	1878	1912
Pennsylvania	1848	1872	—	1872	—
Rhode Island	1848	1874	—	1872	1917 [3]
South Carolina	1870	—	—	1887	—
South Dakota	1877	1877	1877	1877	1918
Tennessee	1870	—	—	1919	1919 [3]
Texas	—	—	—	1913	—
Utah	1895	1895	1895	1897	1895
Vermont	1881	—	1881	1888	—
Virginia	1878	—	—	1878	—
Washington	1889	1889	1889	1889	1910
West Virginia	1868 [2]	1893	1893	1893	—
Wisconsin	1850	1872	—	1872	1919 [3]
Wyoming	1876	1876	1876	1869	1889

1 If a year is not shown for series Ba5091–5093, it means that data are not available. However, if a year is not shown for series Ba5095, it means that the state did not ratify a female suffrage act prior to passage of the Nineteenth Amendment to the U.S. Constitution on August 18, 1920.

2 Explicitly accorded a married woman the right to hold a patent for her invention, as if she were unmarried.

3 Presidential race only.

Sources

Series Ba5091–5093. B. Zorina Khan, "Married Women's Property Laws and Female Commercial Activity: Evidence from United States Patent Records, 1790–1895," *Journal of Economic History* 56 (2) (1996): 363–4, Table 1.

TABLE Ba5091–5095 Year of passage of legislation recognizing married women's property rights and authorizing women's suffrage, by state: 1840–1900 *Continued*

Series Ba5094. R. Richard Geddes and Dean Lueck, "The Gains from Self Ownership and the Expansion of Women's Rights," Stanford Law School, John M. Olin Program in Law and Economics, Working Paper number 181 (August 2000), Table 5, p. 58, and R. Richard Geddes and Dean Lueck, "The Gains from Self-Ownership and the Expansion of Women's Rights," *American Economic Review* 92 (September 2002): 1079–92.

Series Ba5095. Jerrold G. Rusk, *A Statistical History of the American Electorate* (CQ Press, 2001), Table 2-20, p. 36.

Documentation

Dates refer to the earliest year of passage of state legislation recognizing the property and voting rights of women. Estate and earnings laws recognized a married women's right to manage and control her estate and her separate earnings, respectively. Sole trader laws recognized a married woman's right to engage in contracts and business without her husband's consent. Female suffrage accorded women the right to vote. It might apply to all political contests or to presidential elections only.

Series Ba5091–5093. Khan's chronology excludes legislation offering married women control only under restricted circumstances, such as her husband's incapacity or abandonment. Khan also excludes laws that allowed the transfer of property control from husband to wife in order to obtain relief from creditors. See notes to her Table 1 for sources and further details.

Series Ba5094. Geddes and Lueck were interested in identifying the timing of wives' control over both their estates and their earnings. To obtain this date for each of the states, they utilized legal treatises published in the late nineteenth century as well as original session laws. To ensure that there were no earlier dates of passage, Geddes and Lueck examined indexes of session laws for all available years prior to the dates obtained in this manner. In some cases, they were able to locate dates of passage earlier than those reported by Khan. Interested readers should consult Geddes and Lueck (2000) for a detailed explanation of differences between their series and that of Khan.

Series Ba5095. Rusk compiled his list of dates at which the various states ratified women's suffrage from state constitutions and relevant state statute volumes. All laws listed were proposed and ratified prior to the Nineteenth Amendment to the U.S. Constitution on August 18, 1920. Rusk defines "ratification" as "the date when a female voting law was ratified by action of a state legislature, a state constitutional convention, a people's vote at a general election, or a governor's proclamation. Such voting provisions went into effect after the ratification date. If the ratification date is the date of a general election (that is, a peoples' vote at a general election), then the female voting law goes into effect after that election and hence has its first effect on suffrage at the next regularly scheduled election in that state."

TABLE Ba5096–5119 Time spent on housework and family care, by sex, employment status, and type of activity: 1965–1985

Contributed by Susan B. Carter

	Women											
	Total				Employed				Nonemployed			
	Total housework	Core housework	Child care	Shopping	Total housework	Core housework	Child care	Shopping	Total housework	Core housework	Child care	Shopping
	Ba5096	Ba5097	Ba5098	Ba5099	Ba5100	Ba5101	Ba5102	Ba5103	Ba5104	Ba5105	Ba5106	Ba5107
Year	Hours per week	Hours per week	Hours per week	Hours per week	Hours per week	Hours per week	Hours per week	Hours per week	Hours per week	Hours per week	Hours per week	Hours per week
1965	40.2	26.9	6.4	7.0	26.1	17.9	2.7	5.7	51.5	34.2	9.3	7.9
1975	32.9	21.3	5.1	6.5	23.7	15.2	3.2	5.3	42.0	27.5	6.8	7.7
1985	30.9	18.7	4.9	7.3	25.6	15.3	3.6	6.7	39.0	23.8	7.0	8.2

Note appears at end of table

(continued)

	Men											
	Total				Employed				Nonemployed			
	Total housework	Core housework	Child care	Shopping	Total housework	Core housework	Child care	Shopping	Total housework	Core housework	Child care	Shopping
	Ba5108	Ba5109	Ba5110	Ba5111	Ba5112	Ba5113	Ba5114	Ba5115	Ba5116	Ba5117	Ba5118	Ba5119
Year	Hours per week	Hours per week	Hours per week	Hours per week	Hours per week	Hours per week	Hours per week	Hours per week	Hours per week	Hours per week	Hours per week	Hours per week
1965	11.5	4.7	1.7	5.1	11.1	4.4	1.8	4.9	15.2	8.3	1.2	5.7
1975	12.2	6.5	1.6	4.2	11.7 [1]	5.8	1.7	4.2	16.1	10.2	1.5	4.4
1985	15.7	9.4	1.4	4.9	14.5	8.4	1.6	4.5	20.3	13.2	1.0	6.1

[1] Includes correction of an arithmetic error in the original.

Source

John P. Robinson and Geoffrey Godbey, *Time for Life: The Surprising Ways Americans Use Their Time* (Pennsylvania State University Press, 1997), Table 3, p. 105.

Documentation

These estimates were derived from time diaries collected from a representative sample of adults ages 18–64. These individuals were asked to focus on a single day and to describe the day's activities in their own words, recording the time the activity was begun and the time it was ended. The time-diary method is widely believed to be the most precise and accurate way of measuring time use. "Core housework" includes cooking, cleaning, laundry, household management, household-related travel, yard work, repair, and pet and plant care. Hours spent in child care were recorded for parents only.

The "employed" are defined as those "working 20 hours or more, the cutoff used in certain government analyses to define the respondent as employed" (Robinson and Godbey 1997, p. 90).

CHAPTER Bb

Slavery

Editors: Stanley L. Engerman, Richard Sutch, and Gavin Wright

SLAVERY

Stanley L. Engerman, Richard Sutch, and Gavin Wright

The "peculiar institution" of slavery cuts a swath through the heart of American history, with effects that lasted long after its abolition by Lincoln's Emancipation Proclamation (1863) and the Thirteenth Amendment to the U.S. Constitution (1865). African slavery on the mainland can be traced back almost to the beginnings of European settlement and was practiced in all parts of British colonial America. But after the Revolution the division of these former colonies into groups of "free" and "slave" states laid the basis for secession and the Civil War (1861–1865), the costliest conflict in American history. The lasting legacies of slavery and the Civil War for the South and for African Americans are still debated in the new millennium, with passions barely diminished by time.

In one sense the statistical record of this history is abundant, though many aspects of slavery's human reality lie beyond the reach of quantitative measurement. The demographic history of African slaves during the colonial period – arrivals and population growth – has been pieced together by scholars from a wide if heterogeneous array of surveys and commercial reports. Beginning with the first federal census of 1790, the slave population may be studied in remarkable geographic detail, by cities and counties as well as states. As the scope of census inquiries expanded in 1840, 1850, and 1860, the surveys of agriculture and manufacturing have formed the primary basis for a flourishing literature on the economics of slavery in the late antebellum period. These sources may be supplemented by others, such as the records of transactions in slaves at leading markets such as New Orleans, probate inventories, and surviving business and plantation accounts. The present chapter presents only a small fraction of the full archival record, focused on basic series that convey a sense of the evolution of the institution and the slave population over time.

Slavery and the Slave Trade in Colonial North America

Its importance in American history notwithstanding, slavery did not originate in the colonies that became the United States, nor did the colonies play a particularly significant role in the transatlantic slave trade. Highly developed systems of slavery existed in ancient Greece and Rome and persisted in medieval Europe, and several different forms of slavery were practiced for centuries in Asia, Africa, and the Americas before the arrival of Columbus.[1] Perhaps a million African slaves were transported to South America on Portuguese and Spanish ships before the first "twenty and odd Negroes" arrived in Virginia in 1619. Over the entire history of the transatlantic slave trade, no more than 8 percent of the coerced African migrants came to mainland North America. The much larger U.S. share in the hemispheric slave population of 1860 (approximately 50 percent) is attributable to the very different demographic experience of slaves in North America than elsewhere in the New World.[2]

By 1619, slavery had been on the decline in England (as elsewhere in western Europe) for centuries. Perhaps for this reason, the legal definition of slavery as perpetual servitude of blacks and their progeny was not fully established in the Chesapeake Bay region until the 1660s. A number of the first generation of African Americans were regarded as "servants" eligible for freedom after a certain term of years, by analogy to the indentured laborers who formed the majority of the workforce in the Upper South during the seventeenth century. In 1664, however, Maryland declared that all blacks held in the colony, and all those imported as slaves in the future, would serve for life, as would their children and later generations; Virginia's policy became equally clear by the end of that decade (Galenson 1996, p. 165). Both the practice and the legal definition of slavery became established in relatively similar form throughout English America.

Slavery was not inflicted exclusively on Africans. During the early settlement of South Carolina, for example, native peoples were frequently captured and sold to planters in the West Indies. With the rise of rice and naval stores as exports after 1700, larger numbers of enslaved Indians were kept in the low country, reaching a peak of roughly 2,000 by 1720 (Menard 1996, p. 287). In this instance, Indian slavery collapsed through the legislative intervention of the Carolina assembly, which was fearful of triggering new outbreaks of war with regional tribes. More broadly, the demographic devastation experienced by the native population made its members unsuitable candidates for enslavement (see the essay on American Indians in Chapter Ag).

Acknowledgments

The authors would like to thank Susan B. Carter for assistance with the tables and for advice on the essay. This work was supported in part by funding from the Center for Social and Economic Policy at the University of California, Riverside, and Stanford University.

[1] A useful historical reference work on global slavery is Drescher and Engerman (1998).

[2] Modern quantitative estimation of the volume of the African slave trade begins with Curtin (1969). Extensive subsequent research has largely confirmed the broad patterns initially proposed by Curtin. For a recent summary, see Eltis (2000), Table 1.1.

Only at the very end of the seventeenth century did the inflow of African slaves become substantial. As of 1690, blacks constituted less than 15 percent of the population in Virginia and Maryland, reflecting the fact that the first two generations of Chesapeake tobacco planters primarily used the labor supplied by white indentured servants (Table Eg1–59). Between 1690 and 1710, the pattern changed radically. Data newly compiled by Lorena Walsh (2001) show that the number of slaves imported into Virginia and Maryland averaged about 750 per year during 1698–1703, then surged to 1,500 per year after 1720 and remained high until the American Revolution (Table Eg214–216). The shift may also be observed in the composition of colonial populations: in Virginia, the proportion of blacks rose from 7 percent in 1680 to 30 percent in 1720 (Table Eg1–59). The reasons for this "transition from servants to slaves" have been intensively studied by economic historians (Gray and Wood 1976; Menard 1977; Galenson 1981). The primary forces may be identified as rising scarcity in the supply of servants; improved life expectancy among African Americans, enhancing their value as slaves for life; and booming demand for Chesapeake tobacco after 1700.

The number of slaves imported into the Lower South colonies of South Carolina and Georgia was not as high, but the slaves' share of the population was much larger. The South Carolina population was more than one third black in 1690, and two thirds black by 1730 (Table Eg1–59). The expansion of Georgia's slave population was delayed by its designation in 1733 as a debtor's colony within which slavery was prohibited. Slaves quickly flowed into Georgia when the restriction was lifted in 1750, pushing the black share in the population above 40 percent by 1770 (Table Eg1–59). During the years 1768–1772, for which detailed figures on the trade are available, more than 40 percent of all imported slaves were sent to Georgia (Table Eg201–213). The contrast in the relative prominence of slavery between the Upper South and the Lower South reflects the adverse health conditions and arduous labor requirements of lowland rice cultivation, whereas tobacco farming continued to be attractive to free family farmers as well as to slave owners.

Although the slave population was highly concentrated in the Southern colonies, it is important to note that slavery existed in all of the colonies, persisting until after the Revolution. The figures show more than 3,000 blacks in Rhode Island in 1748, 9.1 percent of the population; 4,600 blacks in New Jersey in 1745, 7.5 percent of the population; and nearly 20,000 blacks in New York in 1771, 12.2 percent of the population (Tables Eg132–140 and Eg155–168). Most of these blacks are presumed to have been slaves, though the colonial censuses were rarely explicit about status. For an exception, see the 1755 figures for Maryland reported in Table Eg169–181, which indicate that 99 percent of the 42,061 recorded blacks were slaves, though only 60 percent of the 3,608 mulattos were slaves.

Emancipation measures in the Northern states followed in the wake of the Revolution, beginning with Vermont in 1777. But in New York and New Jersey, the struggle to pass an emancipation act was contentious. New York did not do so until 1799, New Jersey not until 1804 (see Table Bb-A). Most of the Northern emancipations were gradual, often applying only to children and only after lengthy periods of "apprenticeship." Thus, one finds enumerations of Negro slaves in Northern states even into the 1840s (Table Bb1–98). The most remarkable case of lingering Northern slavery was in New Jersey, which reported 236 slaves in 1850, and 18 as late as 1860 (series Bb15).[3]

The Demography of Slavery in the Antebellum South

Despite the protracted character of Northern abolition, by the 1790s the country was clearly divided into two sections, one slave and one primarily free, each approximately equal in population and area at the outset. The Northwest Ordinance of 1787 prohibited slavery in the area north of the Ohio River, thus extending the division into the western territories then undergoing rapid settlement. The final step in defining the institutional structure of the era occurred in 1807, when Congress terminated the African slave trade, the constitutional proscription on interference with the trade having expired. After the final influx of Africans between 1793 and 1807, associated with the emergence of cotton as a major export, the Southern states acquiesced in this prohibition. Thus, from this date onward, the growth of the slave population was almost entirely due to natural increase.

Despite this restriction, the slave population grew very rapidly, averaging more than 2 percent per year across the half-century prior to the Civil War (Tables Aa145–184 and Bb1–98). This demographic history was unique among slave systems in the New World (Fogel 1989, pp. 114–53), and was surely not unrelated to the South's willingness to accede to the cessation of the African trade in 1807. Among many implications of the reliance on natural increase, one may note the strikingly equal gender balance of the slave population (Table Aa2093–2140). In 1820, male slaves outnumbered females slightly, at 51.2 percent of the total. By 1840, however, the male and female totals differed by no more than one tenth of 1 percent. This balance is in contrast to slave regimes in which the African trade remained open, in which men typically outnumbered women by large margins. However, the detailed state data found in Table Bb129–166 show somewhat larger numbers of women than men in Eastern states such as Georgia and South Carolina, which some have interpreted as a "division of labor" between slave-exporting and slave-importing states (Sutch 1975).

Many dimensions of American slavery may be illustrated with demographic data. Table Bb1–98 shows the geographic shift of the slave population from the older Eastern states (Virginia, North and South Carolina, and Georgia) to the newer cotton-growing states farther to the west (Alabama, Mississippi, Louisiana, Arkansas, and Texas). Thus Mississippi's slave population increased from 17,088 in 1810 to 436,631 in 1860, while Virginia's grew only from 392,516 to 490,865 over the same period. Nonetheless, one could describe the slave system as "declining" only in Maryland and Delaware during the antebellum era. In Delaware the slave population fell continuously after 1790, so that fewer than 2,000 remained in 1860. In Maryland the decline was more gradual, but by 1860 the number of free blacks nearly equaled the number of slaves.

The demographic data do not tell us what fraction of this forced migration took the form of transactions in slave markets, as opposed to migration of intact plantation groups. Because these magnitudes

[3] The standard account of Northern abolition is Zilversmit (1967). For an account of New Jersey, see Hodges (1997).

TABLE Bb-A Chronology of emancipation: 1761–1888

1761	The Philadelphia Society of Friends votes to exclude slave traders from church membership.
1772	Lord Chief Justice Mansfield rules that slavery is not supported by English law, thus establishing the legal basis for the freeing of England's 15,000 slaves.
1774	The Philadelphia Society of Friends votes to adopt rules forbidding Quakers to buy or sell slaves.
1775	Slavery is abolished in Madeira.
1776	The Society of Friends in England and in Pennsylvania requires members to free their slaves or face expulsion.
1777	The Vermont Constitution prohibits slavery.
1780	The Massachusetts Constitution declares that all men are free and equal by birth; a judicial decision in 1783 interprets this clause as having the force of abolishing slavery.
1780	Pennsylvania adopts a policy of gradual emancipation, freeing the children of all slaves born after November 1, 1780, on their twenty-eighth birthday. The "law of the free womb" is a provision contained in all other cases of gradual emancipation.
1784	Rhode Island and Connecticut pass gradual emancipation laws. Final ending of slavery occurs in 1842 in Rhode Island and 1848 in Connecticut.
1787	The Society for Effecting the Abolition of the Slave Trade is formed in England.
1788	The Société des Amis des Noirs is formed in France. The British Parliament passes legislation regulating the number of slaves per vessel to be carried in the slave trade.
1791	Slaves in St. Domingue (Haiti) rise in insurrection against the French, achieving independence in 1804.
1793	Upper Canada passes a gradual emancipation law. By 1800 there were judicial decisions and legislation effectively limiting slavery elsewhere in Canada. Slavery was ended in 1834 as a result of British legislation.
1794	The French National Convention abolishes slavery in all French territories. This law was repealed by Napoleon in 1802.
1799	New York passes a gradual emancipation law. Legislation for the final ending of slavery was passed in 1817, to take effect in 1827.
1800	U.S. citizens were barred from exporting slaves.
1803	Denmark ends its international slave trade.
1804	Slavery is abolished in independent Haiti. New Jersey adopts a policy of gradual emancipation, but slavery does not finally end until 1864.
1808	England and the United States prohibit engagement in the international slave trade.
1811	Chile enacts a statute for gradual emancipation. Slavery ends in 1823.
1813	Argentina adopts a policy of gradual emancipation. The final ending of slavery occurs in 1853.
1820	England begins using naval power to suppress the international slave trade.
1821	Colombia begins a process of gradual emancipation. Slavery ends in 1852. Gradual emancipation also begins in Ecuador, Peru, and Venezuela, with slavery ending in 1851, 1854, and 1854, respectively.
1824	Slavery is abolished in Central America.
1825	Uruguay begins the process of gradual emancipation. Slavery ends in 1853.
1829	Mexico abolishes slavery.
1831	Bolivia begins the process of gradual emancipation. Slavery ends in 1861.
1834	As the result of legislation passed in 1833, England begins the period of apprenticeship. Slavery is ended in 1838. Compensation is paid to slaveowners.
1841	The Quintuple Treaty is signed by England, France, Russia, Prussia, and Austria, treating the slave trade as piracy and allowing searches of vessels on the high seas in order to suppress the international slave trade.
1842	Paraguay begins the process of gradual emancipation. Slavery does not end until 1869.
1848	Slavery is abolished in all French and Danish colonies.
1851	The slave trade to Brazil is ended.
1862	Slavery is ended in Washington, D.C., with some compensation paid to slaveowners.
1863	Slavery is ended in all Dutch colonies, with a period of apprenticeship. The Emancipation Proclamation (1863) in the United States freed all slaves in the areas of rebellion.
1865	Slavery is abolished in the United States as a result of the passage of the Thirteenth Amendment to the Constitution at the end of the Civil War.
1867	The slave trade to Cuba is ended.
1870	The Moret law starts the process of gradual emancipation in Spanish colonies.
1871	Gradual emancipation is initiated in Brazil.
1873	Slavery is abolished in Puerto Rico.
1886	Slavery is abolished in Cuba.
1888	Slavery is abolished in Brazil.

Sources

Robert William Fogel and Stanley L. Engerman, *Time on the Cross: The Economics of American Negro Slavery* (Little, Brown, 1974), Table 1, pp. 33–34; David Brion Davis, *The Problem of Slavery in the Age of Revolution, 1780–1823* (Cornell University Press, 1975), particularly pp. 23–36; Leslie B. Rout Jr., *The African Experience in Spanish America: 1502 to the Present Day* (Cambridge University Press, 1976), pp. 185–312; Junius P. Rodriguez, *Chronology of World Slavery* (ABC-CLIO, 1999).

must be estimated by indirect means, it is not surprising that quantitative historians have reached widely varying conclusions on this issue (Fogel and Engerman 1974, pp. 44–52; David, Gutman, et al. 1976, pp. 99–133; Tadman 1989, pp. 25–31). The most recent estimates suggest that the relocation was about equally divided between the two modes (Pritchett 2001).

Despite the examples of Delaware and Maryland, we can say with reasonable confidence that the geographic shift in the slave population was not primarily the result of the emancipation of slaves in the Eastern states, a process known as "manumission." The free black population did experience a sharp increase shortly after the Revolution, partly as the result of wartime measures by the British, and partly because the postwar ethos of freedom seemed for a time to be spreading even in the South. In Virginia, the number of free blacks grew from 12,866 in 1790 to 30,570 in 1810, while in Maryland nearly one fourth of the black population was free by the latter year (Table Bb1–98). Thereafter, however, the share of free blacks in the black population failed to increase, drifting downward from 13.2 percent in 1820 to 11.0 percent in 1860 (Table Aa145–184). Within five years of the Nat Turner slave rebellion of 1831, nearly all the Southern states prohibited the freeing of slaves without legislation or court approval, frequently requiring that freed slaves leave the state. By the 1850s, Texas, Mississippi, and Georgia barred manumission altogether. When the census tabulated manumissions in 1860, it counted only 3,018 in a slave population of four million, or fewer than one per thousand (Table Bb219–235). By 1860, fewer than 3 percent of blacks were free in every one of the states of the Lower South (Table Bb1–98).

Another dimension of slave demography is the distribution of slaves among slaveholding units of various sizes. By comparison with slave systems elsewhere in the New World, ownership in the United States was widely dispersed. The 1790 Census figures (not compiled until more than a century later) allow comparisons across seventy years (Table Bb196–208). In the face of historic changes in the geography of slavery (from Southeast to Southwest) and in the primary slave crops (from tobacco to cotton), the size distribution of slaveholdings remained remarkably constant. Only 0.3 percent of the owners held more than 100 slaves in 1790, and by 1860 this proportion had increased merely to 0.6 percent. Although the mean slaveholding varied considerably from state to state – in 1850, for example, from 7.1 in Tennessee to 15 in South Carolina – within each state the average drifted up only slowly over time. The primary split in Southern white society was between slave owners and non–slave owners. As of 1860, in the cotton-growing areas approximately one half of the farms did not own slaves; for the South as a whole, the percentage of slaveowning families declined from 36 in 1830 to 25 in 1860 (Wright 1978, pp. 24–42).

Although slave ownership status was widely dispersed, the matter of scale looked rather different from the perspective of the slaves. Inequality of holdings was such that the "average slave" worked in a relatively large unit. In the cotton-growing areas of 1860, for example, one third of the slaves were part of holdings larger than 50 (Wright 1978, p. 31).

The Economics of Slavery

Rich statistical sources in combination with the enduring and provocative character of the subject have generated a robust and sometimes contentious literature on the economics of American slavery. Beginning with Conrad and Meyer (1958), historical economists have attempted to resolve long-standing debates over the "profitability" of slavery by subjecting the available data to rigorous statistical analysis in light of more precisely defined economic concepts. A core input for most of this research is information on the prices at which slaves were bought and sold in the major markets of the South.

Table Bb209–214 presents four series on the course of slave prices from the early nineteenth century until the Civil War. Series Bb209 is attributable to Ulrich Phillips (1918, 1963), an eminent Southern historian of the early twentieth century and a pioneer in the quantitative study of slavery. The series applies to "prime field hands" and was based on invoices of slave sales, but Phillips never published a precise statement of his sample or selection criteria. Subsequent researchers have concluded that the Phillips price series for New Orleans has an upward bias. Series Bb210, attributable to Stanley L. Engerman, is based on a systematic sample of slave sales in New Orleans from 1804 through 1861, ranging from 2.5 to 5 percent of sales of "males aged 18 to 30, fully guaranteed as without physical or other infirmity." The third series, attributable to Laurence J. Kotlikoff (1979), is from the same underlying source, but pertains to all men 21 to 38 years of age, regardless of their physical condition.

Despite their differences, all three New Orleans series show similar trends and fluctuations across the full period (see Figure Bb-B): an upward surge after 1807, with periods of decline after the peaks of 1819–1820 and 1837–1839; from the trough in the mid-1840s, slave prices surged throughout the 1850s to all-time highs on the eve of secession (approximately $1,500 for a prime field hand). The fluctuations generally follow swings in the business cycle, particularly British demand for American cotton. The overall trend in slave prices is strongly positive.

Following Phillips, some scholars have argued that slavery had become "unprofitable" by the end of the 1850s because slave prices had then reached record high levels. It was pointed out very early by Yasukichi Yasuba (1961) and Richard Sutch (1965), however, that period fluctuations in slave prices had no particular significance for the long-term real returns to investments in slavery. Similar price swings had occurred twice before in the antebellum period.

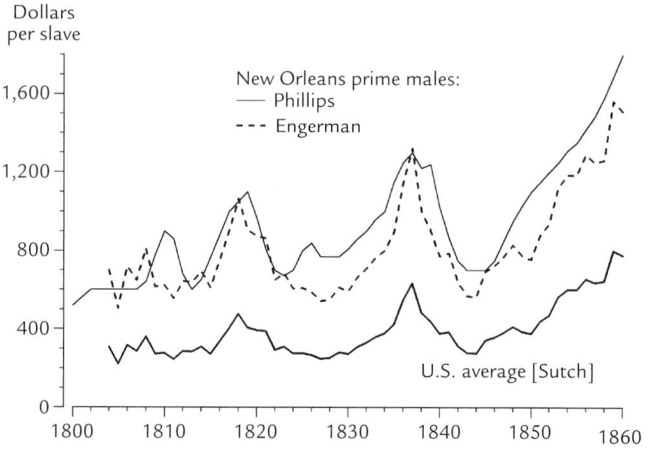

FIGURE Bb-B Slave prices – prime male field hands sold in New Orleans and a U.S. average of all slaves: 1800–1860

Sources

Series Bb209–210 and Bb212.

The deeper significance of this evidence is that slaves were priced, and slave markets were conducted, largely on the basis of expected profitability. Beginning with Conrad and Meyer (1958), virtually all economic studies have confirmed this finding.[4]

Another aspect of the market-oriented nature of American slavery is the structure of slave prices, as opposed to the level and trend in average prices over time. An illustration of price structure is the age–sex price profile presented in Table Bb215–218, developed by Robert W. Fogel and Stanley L. Engerman (1974) from data in probate records. The profiles display a systematic relationship between age and price, with the male profile rising above the female in the late teen years, followed by a peak in both profiles in the late twenties and then a decline. To be sure, these profiles are averages across many hundreds of observations; individual sale prices show considerable dispersion on either side of the line. But detailed statistical analyses show that much of the dispersion can be accounted for by observable traits of the slaves (such as skills or physical defects) or features of the transaction (such as guarantees or credit extension) (Kotlikoff 1979).

Another meaningful approach to measuring the economic returns to slave owners is to focus on the accumulation of wealth in the form of slave value. This is the objective of series Bb212, the "average value of a slave" economywide, which adjusts the prime field hand price for the age, sex, location, and skill of the total slave population each year. In combination with annualized estimates of the slave population (series Bb214), this series allowed Sutch to generate estimates of the overall growth in the stock of slave wealth (series Bb213). Viewed in this way, the enrichment of the slave owners was vast: from $291 million in 1805 to more than $3 billion in 1860, a tenfold increase. Slave capital represented 44 percent of all wealth in the cotton-growing states in 1859, the largest single component (Ransom and Sutch 1988, pp. 138–9).

It hardly needs saying that the high profitability of slavery to the owners did not necessarily enhance the well-being of the other members of the Southern population. This point is clearest in the case of the slaves, who were denied both the immediate fruits of their labor and opportunities for self-advancement through the acquisition of skills and education. But nonslaveholding whites were also affected by the economics of slavery, through competition in land and product markets, and because of slavery's effects on the course of development of the regional economy. Ransom and Sutch (1988) argue that adverse economic effects were the direct consequence of the successful accumulation of wealth in the form of slave value. As in the standard macroeconomic model depicting the burden of public debt, the rise of slave value "crowded out" other forms of wealth in Southern portfolios, reducing other forms of real capital formation. On these grounds, Ransom and Sutch attribute the South's relative lag in transportation, manufacturing, and human capital investment to the effects of capitalization of slave value.

Another developmental issue that has received academic attention is the effect of slavery on urbanization, and vice versa. Table Bb99–128 presents census data on the free and slave populations of ten Southern cities from 1820 to 1860. Although the overall share of the slave population in cities was not large, a port city such as Charleston held a substantial number of slaves (12,652) as of 1820. As Mississippi River commerce grew after 1820, New Orleans became the largest slaveholding city in the country (at 23,448 in 1840). Most notably, however, the table shows that between 1820 and 1860, slaves declined as a share of the population in every one of the ten cities listed, the slave population falling absolutely in six of the ten. Richard Wade (1964) attributes the decline of urban slavery to the growing costs of maintaining the necessary discipline in an urban setting. Escape was much easier than in the countryside, the communities of free blacks often providing refuge and assistance to runaways. Slaves in the cities generally had greater personal freedom, often being hired out rather than employed by their owners, sometimes even being allowed to arrange their own employment. Altogether, according to Wade, the institutional and cultural supports for slavery were being undermined in the cities of the South.

An alternative interpretation, advanced by Claudia Goldin (1976), is that slaves were largely pulled rather than pushed out of the cities because of the strong demand for labor in agriculture, especially during the cotton boom of the 1850s. Because slave prices were rising in both urban and rural markets, the econometric evidence tends to support the Goldin thesis. To be sure, slavery might have required extensive restructuring if the economy of the South had shifted strongly in an urbanized direction. That such a course was feasible is indicated by the exceptional case of Richmond, the slave population of which expanded even in the 1850s because of the growth of its iron and tobacco industries based on slave labor (series Bb117).

The hypothetical course of slavery in the absence of the Civil War cannot be objectively determined on the basis of historical data alone. On the one hand, the extremely limited number of fugitive slaves recorded in 1850 and 1860 (Table Bb236–251) suggests that the institution was not crumbling. Although fears of slave revolts were ubiquitous in the slaveowning South, the compilation of actual cases in Table Bb252–254 does not point toward acceleration of rebellious activity, even as the crisis over slavery came to dominate national politics. Although this sort of evidence is undoubtedly imperfect in many ways, it is sufficient to suggest that the confidence of slave owners in the future of their institution – reflected in the high slave prices of 1860 – had an objective basis.

On the other hand, by 1860 the historical trend had been toward abolition for nearly a century (see Table Bb-A), and there is reason to think that many slaves were aware of this trajectory at some level. Once the war began, plantation discipline proved very insecure whenever fighting drew near, so that slavery did indeed collapse over broad areas of the South as the Union army advanced. Thus the apparent stability of slavery in 1860 may have masked an underlying vulnerability that could not have been suppressed indefinitely, although how long it might have taken in the absence of the Civil War remains uncertain.

[4] On careful reading, this is no more than what Phillips himself argued: "Indeed the peak of this [slave] price movement was evidently cut off by the intervention of war. How great an altitude it might have reached, and what shape its downward slope might have taken had peace continued, it is idle to conjecture. But that a crash must have come is beyond a reasonable doubt" (1918, p. 375).

References

Conrad, Alfred H., and John R. Meyer. 1958. "The Economics of Slavery in the Ante-Bellum South." *Journal of Political Economy* 66 (April): 95–130.

Curtin, Philip D. 1969. *The Atlantic Slave Trade: A Census*. University of Wisconsin Press.

David, Paul A., Herbert G. Gutman, et al. 1976. *Reckoning with Slavery*. Oxford University Press.

Drescher, Seymour, and Stanley L. Engerman. 1998. *A Historical Guide to World Slavery*. Oxford University Press.

Eltis, David. 2000. *The Rise of African Slavery in the Americas*. Cambridge University Press.

Fogel, Robert W. 1989. *Without Consent or Contract: The Rise and Fall of American Slavery*. Norton.

Fogel, Robert W., and Stanley L. Engerman. 1974. *Time on the Cross: The Economics of American Negro Slavery*. Little, Brown.

Galenson, David W. 1981. *White Servitude in Colonial America*. Cambridge University Press.

Galenson, David W. 1996. "The Settlement and Growth of the Colonies." In Stanley L. Engerman and Robert E. Gallman, editors. *The Cambridge Economic History of the United States*. Cambridge University Press.

Goldin, Claudia. 1976. *Urban Slavery in the South, 1820–1860*. University of Chicago Press.

Gray, Ralph, and Betty Wood. 1976. "The Transition from Indentured to Involuntary Labor in Colonial Georgia." *Explorations in Economic History* 13 (October): 353–70.

Hodges, Graham Russell. 1997. *Slavery and Freedom in the Rural North: African Americans in Monmouth County, New Jersey, 1665–1865*. Madison House Publications.

Kotlikoff, Laurence J. 1979. "The Structure of Slave Prices in New Orleans, 1804 to 1862." *Economic Inquiry* 17: 496–517.

Menard, Russell R. 1977. "From Servants to Slaves: The Transformation of the Chesapeake Labor System." *Southern Studies* 16 (Winter): 355–90.

Menard, Russell R. 1996. "Economic and Social Development of the South." In Stanley L. Engerman and Robert E. Gallman, editors. *The Cambridge Economic History of the United States*. Cambridge University Press.

Phillips, Ulrich B. 1918. *American Negro Slavery*. Appleton.

Phillips, Ulrich B. 1963. *Life and Labor in the Old South*. Little, Brown. First published 1929.

Pritchett, Jonathan B. 2001. "Quantitative Estimates of the United States Interregional Slave Trade, 1820–1860." *Journal of Economic History* 61 (June): 467–75.

Ransom, Roger, and Richard Sutch. 1988. "Capitalists without Capital: The Burden of Slavery and the Impact of Emancipation." *Agricultural History* 62 (Summer): 133–60. Reprinted in Morton Rothstein and Daniel Field, editors. 1993. *Quantitative Studies in Agrarian History*. Iowa State University Press.

Sutch, Richard. 1965. "The Profitability of Ante Bellum Slavery – Revisited." *Southern Economic Journal* 31 (April): 365–77.

Sutch, Richard. 1975. "The Breeding of Slaves for Sale and the Westward Expansion of Slavery, 1850–1860." In Stanley L. Engerman and Eugene D. Genovese, editors. *Race and Slavery in the Western Hemisphere: Quantitative Studies*. Princeton University Press.

Tadman, Michael. 1989. *Speculators and Slaves: Masters, Traders and Slaves in the Old South*. University of Wisconsin Press.

Wade, Richard C. 1964. *Slavery in the Cities*. Oxford University Press.

Walsh, Lorena S. 2001. "The Chesapeake Slave Trade: Regional Patterns, African Origins, and Some Implications." *William and Mary Quarterly*, 3rd series, 58 (January): 139–70.

Wright, Gavin. 1978. *The Political Economy of the Cotton South*. Norton.

Yasuba, Yasukichi. 1961. "The Profitability and Viability of Plantation Slavery in the United States." *Economic Studies Quarterly* 12: 60–67. Reprinted in Robert W. Fogel and Stanley L. Engerman, editors. 1972. *The Reinterpretation of American Economic History*. Harper and Row.

Zilversmit, Arthur. 1967. *The First Emancipation: The Abolition of Slavery in the North*. University of Chicago Press.

SLAVE POPULATION

Susan B. Carter

TABLE Bb1–98 Black population, by state and slave/free status: 1790–1860

Contributed by Susan B. Carter

	New England											
	Maine		New Hampshire		Vermont		Massachusetts		Rhode Island		Connecticut	
	Slave	Free	Slave	Free	Slave	Free	Slave	Free	Slave	Free	Slave	Free
	Bb1	Bb2	Bb3	Bb4	Bb5	Bb6	Bb7	Bb8	Bb9	Bb10	Bb11	Bb12
Year	Number	Number	Number	Number	Number	Number	Number	Number	Number	Number	Number	Number
1790	0	536	157	630	0	269	0	5,369	958	3,484	2,648	2,771
1800	0	818	8	852	0	557	0	6,452	380	3,304	951	5,330
1810	0	969	0	970	0	750	0	6,737	108	3,609	310	6,453
1820	0	929	0	786	0	903	0	6,740	48	3,554	97	7,870
1830	2	1,190	3	604	0	881	1	7,048	17	3,561	25	8,047
1840	0	1,355	1	537	0	730	0	8,669	5	3,238	17	8,105
1850	0	1,356	0	520	0	718	0	9,064	0	3,670	0	7,693
1860	0	1,327	0	494	0	709	0	9,602	0	3,952	0	8,627

	Middle Atlantic						East North Central					
	New York		New Jersey		Pennsylvania		Ohio		Indiana		Illinois	
	Slave	Free	Slave	Free	Slave	Free	Slave	Free	Slave	Free	Slave	Free
	Bb13	Bb14	Bb15	Bb16	Bb17	Bb18	Bb19	Bb20	Bb21	Bb22	Bb23	Bb24
Year	Number	Number	Number	Number	Number	Number	Number	Number	Number	Number	Number	Number
1790	21,193	4,682	11,423	2,762	3,707	6,531	0	0	0	0	0	0
1800	20,903	10,417	12,422	4,402	1,706	14,564	0	337	135	163	0	0
1810	15,017	25,333	10,851	7,843	795	22,492	0	1,899	237	393	168	613
1820	10,088	29,279	7,557	12,460	211	30,202	0	4,723	190	1,230	917	457
1830	75	44,870	2,254	18,303	403	37,930	6	9,568	3	3,629	747	1,637
1840	4	50,027	674	21,044	64	47,854	3	17,342	3	7,165	331	3,598
1850	0	49,069	236	23,810	0	53,626	0	25,279	0	11,262	0	5,436
1860	0	49,005	18	25,318	0	56,949	0	36,673	0	11,428	0	7,628

	East North Central		West North Central									
	Michigan		Wisconsin		Minnesota		Iowa		Missouri		North Dakota	
	Slave	Free	Slave	Free	Slave	Free	Slave	Free	Slave	Free	Slave	Free
	Bb25	Bb26	Bb27	Bb28	Bb29	Bb30	Bb31	Bb32	Bb33	Bb34	Bb35	Bb36
Year	Number	Number	Number	Number	Number	Number	Number	Number	Number	Number	Number	Number
1790	0	0	0	0	0	0	0	0	0	0	0	0
1800	0	0	0	0	0	0	0	0	0	0	0	0
1810	24	120	0	0	0	0	0	0	3,011	607	0	0
1820	0	174	0	0	0	0	0	0	10,222	347	0	0
1830	32	261	0	0	0	0	0	0	25,091	569	0	0
1840	0	707	11	185	0	0	16	172	58,240	1,574	0	0
1850	0	2,583	0	635	0	39	0	333	87,422	2,618	0	0
1860	0	6,799	0	1,171	0	259	0	1,069	114,931	3,572	0	0

(continued)

TABLE Bb1–98 Black population, by state and slave/free status: 1790–1860 *Continued*

	West North Central						South Atlantic					
	South Dakota		Nebraska		Kansas		Delaware		Maryland		District of Columbia	
	Slave	Free	Slave	Free	Slave	Free	Slave	Free	Slave	Free	Slave	Free
	Bb37	Bb38	Bb39	Bb40	Bb41	Bb42	Bb43	Bb44	Bb45	Bb46	Bb47	Bb48
Year	Number	Number	Number	Number	Number	Number	Number	Number	Number	Number	Number	Number
1790	0	0	0	0	0	0	8,887	3,899	103,036	8,043	0	0
1800	0	0	0	0	0	0	6,153	8,268	105,635	19,587	3,244	783
1810	0	0	0	0	0	0	4,177	13,136	111,502	33,927	5,395	2,549
1820	0	0	0	0	0	0	4,509	12,958	107,397	39,730	6,377	4,048
1830	0	0	0	0	0	0	3,292	15,855	102,994	52,938	6,119	6,152
1840	0	0	0	0	0	0	2,605	16,919	89,737	62,078	4,694	8,361
1850	0	0	0	0	0	0	2,290	18,073	90,368	74,723	3,687	10,059
1860	0	0	15	67	2	625	1,798	19,829	87,189	83,942	3,185	11,131

	South Atlantic											
	Virginia		West Virginia		North Carolina		South Carolina		Georgia		Florida	
	Slave	Free	Slave	Free	Slave	Free	Slave	Free	Slave	Free	Slave	Free
	Bb49	Bb50	Bb51	Bb52	Bb53	Bb54	Bb55	Bb56	Bb57	Bb58	Bb59	Bb60
Year	Number	Number	Number	Number	Number	Number	Number	Number	Number	Number	Number	Number
1790	292,627	12,866	0	0	100,783	5,041	107,094	1,801	29,264	398	0	0
1800	345,796	20,124	0	0	133,296	7,043	146,151	3,185	59,406	1,019	0	0
1810	392,516	30,570	0	0	168,824	10,266	196,365	4,554	105,218	1,801	0	0
1820	425,148	36,883	0	0	204,917	14,712	258,475	6,826	149,656	1,763	0	0
1830	469,757	47,348	0	0	245,601	19,543	315,401	7,921	217,531	2,486	15,501	844
1840	448,987	49,842	0	0	245,817	22,732	327,038	8,276	280,944	2,753	25,717	817
1850	472,528	54,333	0	0	288,548	27,463	384,984	8,960	381,682	2,931	39,310	932
1860	490,865	58,042	0	0	331,059	30,463	402,406	9,914	462,198	3,500	61,745	932

	East South Central								West South Central			
	Kentucky		Tennessee		Alabama		Mississippi		Arkansas		Louisiana	
	Slave	Free	Slave	Free	Slave	Free	Slave	Free	Slave	Free	Slave	Free
	Bb61	Bb62	Bb63	Bb64	Bb65	Bb66	Bb67	Bb68	Bb69	Bb70	Bb71	Bb72
Year	Number	Number	Number	Number	Number	Number	Number	Number	Number	Number	Number	Number
1790	12,430	114	3,417	361	0	0	0	0	0	0	0	0
1800	40,343	739	13,584	309	0	0	3,489	182	0	0	0	0
1810	80,561	1,713	44,535	1,317	0	0	17,088	240	0	0	34,660	7,585
1820	126,732	2,759	80,107	2,737	41,879	571	32,814	458	1,617	59	69,064	10,476
1830	165,213	4,917	141,603	4,555	117,549	1,572	65,659	519	4,576	141	109,588	16,710
1840	182,258	7,317	183,059	5,524	253,532	2,039	195,211	1,366	19,935	465	168,452	25,502
1850	210,981	10,011	239,459	6,422	342,844	2,265	309,878	930	47,100	608	244,809	17,462
1860	225,483	10,684	275,719	7,300	435,080	2,690	436,631	773	111,115	144	331,726	18,647

	West South Central				Mountain							
	Oklahoma		Texas		Montana		Idaho		Wyoming		Colorado	
	Slave	Free	Slave	Free	Slave	Free	Slave	Free	Slave	Free	Slave	Free
	Bb73	Bb74	Bb75	Bb76	Bb77	Bb78	Bb79	Bb80	Bb81	Bb82	Bb83	Bb84
Year	Number	Number	Number	Number	Number	Number	Number	Number	Number	Number	Number	Number
1790	0	0	0	0	0	0	0	0	0	0	0	0
1800	0	0	0	0	0	0	0	0	0	0	0	0
1810	0	0	0	0	0	0	0	0	0	0	0	0
1820	0	0	0	0	0	0	0	0	0	0	0	0
1830	0	0	0	0	0	0	0	0	0	0	0	0
1840	0	0	0	0	0	0	0	0	0	0	0	0
1850	0	0	58,161	397	0	0	0	0	0	0	0	0
1860	0	0	182,566	355	0	0	0	0	0	0	0	46

TABLE Bb1–98 Black population, by state and slave/free status: 1790–1860 *Continued*

	Mountain								Pacific					
	New Mexico		Arizona		Utah		Nevada		Washington		Oregon		California	
	Slave	Free	Slave	Free	Slave	Free	Slave	Free	Slave	Free	Slave	Free	Slave	Free
	Bb85	Bb86	Bb87	Bb88	Bb89	Bb90	Bb91	Bb92	Bb93	Bb94	Bb95	Bb96	Bb97	Bb98
Year	Number	Number	Number	Number	Number	Number	Number	Number	Number	Number	Number	Number	Number	Number
1790	0	0	0	0	0	0	0	0	0	0	0	0	0	0
1800	0	0	0	0	0	0	0	0	0	0	0	0	0	0
1810	0	0	0	0	0	0	0	0	0	0	0	0	0	0
1820	0	0	0	0	0	0	0	0	0	0	0	0	0	0
1830	0	0	0	0	0	0	0	0	0	0	0	0	0	0
1840	0	0	0	0	0	0	0	0	0	0	0	0	0	0
1850	0	22	0	0	26	24	0	0	0	0	0	207	0	962
1860	0	85	0	0	29	30	0	45	0	30	0	128	0	4,086

Source

U.S. Bureau of the Census, *Negro Population in the United States, 1790–1915* (1918), Table 6, p. 57.

Documentation

The total of the slave and free black populations matches totals given for blacks in Tables Aa2244–6550.

These statistics were compiled by a special U.S. Census Bureau team led by John Cummings. They were published in 1918 in the Census Bureau report cited above and were compiled from Census Bureau publications as well as from unpublished manuscript tables. A considerable amount of scholarship went into the preparation of the special Census Bureau volume that forms the basis for this table. For example, each "state" is defined in the special Census Bureau report according to state boundaries in 1860. Thus, for example, Maine is assigned the appropriate population for counties that would be part of Maine in 1860, even though Maine did not become an independent state until 1820. Likewise, "Virginia" includes counties that would become West Virginia beginning in 1863. This means that zeros in the population columns should be interpreted to mean that no blacks were enumerated in counties that would eventually be included in those 1860 state boundaries. The census did not distinguish between a situation in which no blacks were enumerated because no blacks were found in an enumeration and one in which no blacks were enumerated because no enumeration had taken place.

In 1918, the Census Bureau referred to black persons as "Negroes." The classification of a person as "Negro" reflected common usage at the time rather than an attempt to define biological stock. Persons of mixed parentage, white and another race, were usually classified with the other race. Persons of mixed parentage other than white were usually classified by the race of the father, except that individuals of mixed Negro and Indian origin were classified as Negro unless the Indian stock was clearly predominant or unless the individual was accepted in the community in which he or she resided as an Indian. For further discussion of Census Bureau racial classifications, see Table Aa145–184.

TABLE Bb99–128 Slave and free population of selected Southern cities: 1820–1860

Contributed by Susan B. Carter

	Baltimore			Charleston			Louisville			Mobile			New Orleans		
	Slave	Free black	Free white	Slave	Free black	Free white	Slave	Free black	Free white	Slave	Free black	Free white	Slave	Free black	Free white
	Bb99	Bb100	Bb101	Bb102	Bb103	Bb104	Bb105	Bb106	Bb107	Bb108	Bb109	Bb110	Bb111	Bb112	Bb113
Year	Number	Number	Number	Number	Number	Number	Number	Number	Number	Number	Number	Number	Number	Number	Number
1820	4,357	10,326	48,055	12,652	1,475	10,653	1,031	93	2,886	836 [1]	183 [1]	1,653 [1]	7,355	6,237	13,584
1830	4,120	14,790	61,710	15,354	2,107	12,828	2,406	232	7,703	1,175	372	1,647	9,397	8,041	12,299
1840	3,199	17,967	81,147	14,673	1,558	13,030	3,430	619	17,161	3,869	541	8,262	23,448	19,226	59,519
1850	2,946	25,442	140,666	19,532	3,441	20,012	5,432	1,538	36,224	6,803	715	12,997	17,011	9,905	89,459
1860	2,218	25,680	184,520	13,909	3,237	23,376	4,903	1,917	61,213	7,587	817	20,854	13,385	10,689	144,601

Notes appear at end of table

(continued)

	Norfolk			Richmond			Saint Louis			Savannah			Washington		
	Slave	Free black	Free white	Slave	Free black	Free white	Slave	Free black	Free white	Slave	Free black	Free white	Slave	Free black	Free white
	Bb114	Bb115	Bb116	Bb117	Bb118	Bb119	Bb120	Bb121	Bb122	Bb123	Bb124	Bb125	Bb126	Bb127	Bb128
Year	Number	Number	Number	Number	Number	Number	Number	Number	Number	Number	Number	Number	Number	Number	Number
1820	3,261	599	4,618	4,387	1,235	6,445	1,810 [2]	196 [2]	8,014 [2]	3,075	582	3,866	1,945	1,696	9,606
1830	3,756	928	5,130	6,345	1,960	7,755	2,796 [2]	220 [2]	11,109 [2]	4,000 [3]	452 [3]	4,048 [3]	2,330	3,129	13,367
1840	3,709	1,026	6,185	7,509	1,926	10,718	1,531	531	14,407	4,694	632	5,888	1,713	4,808	16,843
1850	4,295	956	9,075	9,927	2,369	15,274	2,656	1,398	73,806	6,231	686	8,395	2,113	8,158	29,730
1860	3,284	1,046	10,290	11,699	2,576	23,635	1,542	1,755	157,476	7,712	705	13,875	1,774	9,209	50,139

[1] Mobile County.

[2] Saint Louis County.

[3] No census population data were given; figures are approximations based on the manuscript census figures.

Source

Claudia Dale Goldin, *Urban Slavery in the American South, 1820–1860: A Quantitative History* (University of Chicago Press, 1976), Table 13, pp. 52–3.

TABLE Bb129–166 Slave population, by state and sex: 1820–1860

Contributed by Susan B. Carter

	Total		Alabama		Arkansas		District of Columbia		Delaware		Florida	
	Males	Females	Males	Females	Males	Females	Males	Females	Males	Females	Males	Females
	Bb129	Bb130	Bb131	Bb132	Bb133	Bb134	Bb135	Bb136	Bb137	Bb138	Bb139	Bb140
Year	Number	Number	Number	Number	Number	Number	Number	Number	Number	Number	Number	Number
1820	788,025	750,100	21,780	20,099	820	797	3,007	3,370	2,555	1,954	0	0
1830	1,012,823	996,220	59,170	58,379	2,293	2,283	2,852	3,267	1,806	1,486	7,985	7,516
1840	1,246,517	1,240,938	127,360	126,172	10,119	9,816	2,058	2,636	1,371	1,234	13,038	12,679
1850	1,602,535	1,601,778	171,804	171,040	23,658	23,442	1,422	2,265	1,174	1,116	19,804	19,506
1860	1,982,625	1,971,135	217,766	217,314	56,174	54,941	1,212	1,973	860	938	31,348	30,397

Note appears at end of table

(continued)

	Georgia		Kentucky		Louisiana		Maryland		Mississippi		Missouri	
	Males	Females	Males	Females	Males	Females	Males	Females	Males	Females	Males	Females
	Bb141	Bb142	Bb143	Bb144	Bb145	Bb146	Bb147	Bb148	Bb149	Bb150	Bb151	Bb152
Year	Number	Number	Number	Number	Number	Number	Number	Number	Number	Number	Number	Number
1820	75,914	73,740	63,914	62,818	36,566	32,498	56,372	51,025	16,850	15,964	5,341	4,881
1830	108,817	108,714	82,309	82,904	57,911	51,677	53,442	49,552	33,099	32,560	12,439	12,652
1840	139,335	141,609	91,004	91,254	86,529	81,923	46,068	43,669	98,003	97,208	28,742	29,498
1850	188,857	192,825	105,063	105,918	125,874	118,935	45,944	44,424	154,964	154,914	43,484	43,938
1860	229,193	233,005	113,009	112,474	171,977	159,749	44,313	42,876	219,301	217,330	57,360	57,571

Note appears at end of table

(continued)

	New Jersey		North Carolina		South Carolina		Tennessee		Texas		Virginia		Other states	
	Males	Females	Males	Females	Males	Females	Males	Females	Males	Females	Males	Females	Males	Females
	Bb153	Bb154	Bb155	Bb156	Bb157	Bb158	Bb159	Bb160	Bb161	Bb162	Bb163	Bb164	Bb165	Bb166
Year	Number	Number	Number	Number	Number	Number	Number	Number	Number	Number	Number	Number	Number	Number
1820	3,988	3,569	106,551	98,466	130,472	128,003	39,747	40,360	0	0	218,274 [1]	206,879	5,874	5,677
1830	1,059	1,195	124,313	121,288	155,469	159,932	70,216	71,387	0	0	239,077	230,680	566	748
1840	303	371	123,546	122,271	158,678	168,360	91,477	91,582	0	0	228,661	220,426	225	230
1850	96	140	144,581	143,967	187,756	197,228	118,780	120,679	28,700	29,461	240,562	231,966	12	14
1860	6	12	166,469	164,590	196,571	205,835	136,370	139,349	91,189	91,377	249,483	241,382	24	22

[1] Corrects an error in the original.

Sources

U.S. Bureau of the Census, *Statistical View of the United States, Compendium of the Seventh Census* (1854), Table LXXVI, p. 86, and U.S. Bureau of the Census, *Population of the United States in 1860; Compiled from the Original Returns of the Eighth Census* (1864), p. 595.

TABLE Bb167–195 Slaveholding families, by state: 1790–1860

Contributed by Susan B. Carter

		New England						Middle Atlantic		
	United States	Maine	New Hampshire	Vermont	Massachusetts	Rhode Island	Connecticut	New York	New Jersey	Pennsylvania
	Bb167	Bb168	Bb169	Bb170	Bb171	Bb172	Bb173	Bb174	Bb175	Bb176
Year	Number	Number	Number	Number	Number	Number	Number	Number	Number	Number
1790	96,168	0	123	0	0	461	1,563	7,796	4,760 [3]	1,858
1850	347,725	0	0	0	0	0	0	0	200	0
1860	395,216 [2]	0	0	0	0	0	0	0	0	0

	South Atlantic							
	Delaware	Maryland	District of Columbia	Virginia	North Carolina	South Carolina	Georgia	Florida
	Bb177	Bb178	Bb179	Bb180 [1]	Bb181	Bb182	Bb183	Bb184
Year	Number	Number	Number	Number	Number	Number	Number	Number
1790	1,851 [3]	13,777	0	34,026 [3]	16,310	8,859	2,419 [3]	0
1850	809	16,040	1,477	55,063	28,303	25,596	38,456	3,520
1860	587	13,783	1,229	52,128	34,658	26,701	41,084	5,152

	East South Central				West South Central			West North Central			
	Kentucky	Tennessee	Alabama	Mississippi	Arkansas	Louisiana	Texas	Missouri	Kansas	Nebraska	Mountain: Utah
	Bb185	Bb186	Bb187	Bb188	Bb189	Bb190	Bb191	Bb192	Bb193	Bb194	Bb195
Year	Number	Number	Number	Number	Number	Number	Number	Number	Number	Number	Number
1790	1,855 [3]	510 [3]	0	0	0	0	0	0	0	0	0
1850	38,385	33,864	29,295	23,116	5,999	20,670	7,747	19,185	0	0	—
1860	38,645	36,844	33,730	30,943	11,481 [2]	22,033	21,878	24,320	2	6	12

[1] Includes area now in West Virginia.

[2] Includes correction for an error in reporting number of slaveholders in Arkansas in the original publication.

[3] Estimates by the authors of *Negro Population* for areas for which data gathered in 1790 were not available at the time of the preparation of their report.

Sources

1790–1850: U.S. Bureau of the Census, *Negro Population in the United States, 1790–1915* (1918), Table 5, p. 56. 1860: U.S. Bureau of the Census, *Agriculture of the United States in 1860; Compiled from the Original Returns of the Eighth Census* (1864), p. 247.

TABLE Bb196–208 Slaveholders, by size of slaveholdings: 1790–1860

Contributed by Susan B. Carter

	Slaveholders												Average number of slaves per slaveholder
		By number of slaves owned											
	Total	1	2–4	5–9	10–19	20–49	50–99	100–199	200–299	300–499	500–999	1000 or more	
	Bb196	Bb197	Bb198	Bb199	Bb200	Bb201	Bb202	Bb203	Bb204	Bb205	Bb206	Bb207	Bb208
Year	Number	Number	Number	Number	Number	Number	Number	Number	Number	Number	Number	Number	Number
1790	81,885 [2]	20,047	24,912	18,017	11,735	5,274	813	198	38	7 [3]	— [3]	— [3]	6.7
1850	347,525	68,820	105,683	80,765	54,595	29,733	6,196	1,479	187	56	9	2	9.2
1860 [1]	395,216	79,391	113,092	91,809	63,345	36,585	8,636	2,039	230	74	14	1	10.0

[1] Includes correction for an error in reporting number of slaveholders in Arkansas in the original publication.

[2] Includes 844 families for whom the number of slaves owned is unknown.

[3] Slaveholders with 300 or more slaves are included under series Bb205.

Sources

1790: U.S. Bureau of the Census, *A Century of Population Growth: From the First Census of the United States to the Twelfth, 1790–1900* (1909), Table 64, p. 136. 1850: U.S. Bureau of the Census, *Statistical View of the United States, Compendium of the Seventh Census* (1854), Table XC, p. 95. 1860: U.S. Bureau of the Census, *Agriculture of the United States in 1860; Compiled from the Original Returns of the Eighth Census* (1864), p. 247.

Documentation

The 1790 figures were first presented by the Census Bureau in its 1909 publication, *A Century of Population Growth*. They were calculated from census schedules still in existence at that time and therefore do not cover all slaveholders. The estimate for Virginia was based on figures for 1782 and 1783. A Census Bureau comparison of those geographic regions for which schedules were available in both 1790 and 1850 revealed that "in the comparable area practically the same proportion of owners held from 2 to 4 slaves in 1850 as in 1790. There was a considerable decrease, however, in the proportion of families having only 1 slave in 1850 as compared with 1790, and an increase in the proportions in the groups into which those holding between 5 and 300 slaves were divided" (U.S. Bureau of the Census 1909, p. 136).

The 1850 Census notes: "Where the party owns slaves in different counties or in different States, he will be entered more than once. This will disturb the calculation very little, being only the case among the larger properties, and it will account for the fact that a smaller number of such [large] properties are reported in some of the States than are known to exist, particularly in South Carolina, Virginia and Louisiana" (U.S. Bureau of the Census 1854, p. 95).

SLAVE PRICES AND VALUES

Richard Sutch

TABLE Bb209–214 Slave prices, value of the slave stock, and annual estimates of the slave population: 1800–1862

Contributed by Richard Sutch

	Slave prices					
	Prime male field hands, New Orleans					
	Phillips	Engerman	Kotlikoff	Average slave	Value of the slave stock	Slave population
	Bb209	Bb210	Bb211	Bb212	Bb213	Bb214
Year	Dollars	Dollars	Dollars	Dollars	Million dollars	Number
1800	520	—	—	—	—	—
1801	560	—	—	—	—	—
1802	600	—	—	—	—	—
1803	600	—	—	—	—	—
1804	600	700	—	308	—	1,002,545
1805	600	504	—	222	291	1,031,796
1806	600	719	—	317	292	1,061,901
1807	600	647	—	286	351	1,092,883
1808	640	813	—	360	344	1,124,770
1809	780	615	—	272	351	1,157,587
1810	900	624	—	277	316	1,191,362
1811	860	555	—	246	330	1,222,181
1812	680	643	—	286	341	1,253,798
1813	600	638	—	284	377	1,286,232
1814	650	694	—	309	381	1,319,506
1815	765	610	—	272	414	1,353,640
1816	880	753	—	337	468	1,388,657
1817	1,000	900	—	403	578	1,424,580
1818	1,050	1,065	—	477	627	1,461,433
1819	1,100	908	—	407	638	1,499,238
1820	970	875	875	393	610	1,538,022
1821	810	864	762	389	566	1,579,666
1822	700	650	579	294	536	1,622,437
1823	670	683	618	309	488	1,666,367
1824	700	606	498	275	491	1,711,485
1825	800	608	603	277	481	1,757,826
1826	840	588	587	268	477	1,805,421
1827	770	542	568	248	476	1,854,305
1828	770	551	479	253	497	1,904,513
1829	770	611	596	281	526	1,956,080
1830	810	591	579	273	577	2,009,043
1831	860	663	652	308	623	2,052,410
1832	900	707	701	330	697	2,096,713
1833	960	765	797	359	762	2,141,972
1834	1,000	800	714	378	847	2,188,208
1835	1,150	893	881	424	1,005	2,235,442
1836	1,250	1,146	1,069	547	1,222	2,283,696
1837	1,300	1,322	1,263	634	1,295	2,332,992
1838	1,220	1,002	897	484	1,237	2,383,351
1839	1,240	906	823	440	1,056	2,434,798
1840	1,020	773	800	377	997	2,487,355
1841	870	788	746	385	915	2,551,159
1842	750	640	608	314	853	2,616,599
1843	700	569	547	280	778	2,683,718
1844	700	561	547	276	823	2,752,559
1845	700	692	608	342	918	2,823,166
1846	750	723	709	358	1,044	2,895,583
1847	850	771	656	382	1,141	2,969,859
1848	950	830	797	413	1,200	3,046,039
1849	1,030	776	680	387	1,225	3,124,174

(continued)

TABLE Bb209–214 Slave prices, value of the slave stock, and annual estimates of the slave population: 1800–1862 *Continued*

	Slave prices					
	Prime male field hands, New Orleans					
	Phillips	Engerman	Kotlikoff	Average slave	Value of the slave stock	Slave population
	Bb209	Bb210	Bb211	Bb212	Bb213	Bb214
Year	Dollars	Dollars	Dollars	Dollars	Million dollars	Number
1850	1,100	756	697	377	1,286	3,204,313
1851	1,150	878	831	440	1,405	3,272,371
1852	1,200	937	878	471	1,644	3,341,873
1853	1,250	1,122	1,048	565	1,862	3,412,853
1854	1,310	1,189	1,130	601	2,052	3,485,339
1855	1,350	1,185	1,058	600	2,203	3,559,366
1856	1,420	1,291	1,085	656	2,293	3,634,963
1857	1,490	1,249	1,126	636	2,397	3,712,169
1858	1,580	1,262	1,175	645	2,632	3,791,013
1859	1,690	1,564	1,431	801	2,870	3,871,531
1860	1,800	1,513	1,451	778	3,059	3,953,760
1861	—	1,440	1,381	742	—	4,037,735
1862	—	—	1,116	—	—	—

Sources

Richard Sutch, "Appendix: The Value of the Slave Population, 1805–1860," in Roger Ransom and Richard Sutch, "Capitalists without Capital: The Burden of Slavery and the Impact of Emancipation," *Agricultural History* 62 (3) (1988), Tables A.4, pp. 155–6, and A.1, pp. 150–1; Roger Ransom and Richard Sutch, "Who Pays for Slavery?" in Richard F. America, editor, *The Wealth of Races: The Present Value of Benefits from Past Injustices* (Greenwood Press, 1990), Appendix Tables A.1 and A.2, pp. 47–50.

Documentation

Series Bb209. Prices for 1800, 1801, and 1812 were estimated visually by Sutch from Ulrich Bonnell Phillips, *Life and Labor in the Old South* (Little Brown, 1929), p. 177. All other prices are from Alfred H. Conrad and John R. Meyer, "The Economics of Slavery in the Ante-Bellum South," *Journal of Political Economy* 66 (April 1958): 95–130, reprinted in Alfred H. Conrad and John R. Meyer, *The Economics of Slavery and Other Studies in Econometric History* (Aldine, 1964), Table 17, column 6, p. 76.

Series Bb210. Data were supplied to Sutch by Stanley Engerman. They are mean values of the prices included in a sample of invoices of slave sales held in New Orleans. The sample size for each year ranged between 2.5 and 5 percent. The prices averaged refer to "males ages 18 to 30, without skills, fully guaranteed as without physical or other infirmity." Engerman "utilized only those cases in which there was an individual price listed for a separate slave." For most years about fifteen to twenty observations were used in preparing the averages given.

Series Bb211. The data are described in Laurence J. Kotlikoff. "The Structure of Slave Prices in New Orleans, 1804 to 1862," *Economic Inquiry* 17 (October 1979), Chart I, p. 498. The numbers on which the chart was based are taken from Laurence J. Kotlikoff, "Quantitative Description of the New Orleans Slave Market, 1804 to 1862," in Robert W. Fogel and Stanley L. Engerman, editors, *Without Consent or Contract: Technical Papers on Slavery*, Norton, 1992, volume 1, chapter 3. Kotlikoff included all males 21 to 38 years of age, regardless of their physical condition.

Series Bb212. Sutch estimated the average slave value economywide by taking Engerman's estimate of the price of prime field hands in New Orleans, shown in series Bb210, and adjusting it for the age, sex, location, and skill of the total slave population in a given year.

Series Bb213. Sutch estimated the value of the slave stock by multiplying the number of slaves shown in series Bb214 by the three-year moving average of the prices series shown in series Bb212.

Series Bb214. Census year figures are from the decennial censuses, and intercensal figures were estimated by assuming a constant rate of population growth between each pair of census dates.

TABLE Bb215–218 Index of slave values, by age, sex, and region: 1850

Contributed by Richard Sutch

	Old South		New South	
	Males	Females	Males	Females
	Bb215	Bb216	Bb217	Bb218
Age	Index	Index	Index	Index
Under 5	10.19	10.75	15.29	15.54
5–9	31.19	31.11	40.88	40.47
10–13	48.27	45.11	62.71	58.79
14	56.58	51.07	73.84	67.08
15–19	64.43	55.86	85.05	74.37
20–23	72.55	59.56	97.85	81.24
24–25	75.21	59.64	103.17	82.91
26–29	75.47	57.86	105.49	82.18
30–35	71.75	52.00	103.78	77.00
36–39	64.16	43.80	96.41	68.29
40–44	55.10	35.35	85.68	58.42
45–49	43.50	26.00	71.39	46.79
50–54	32.16	17.57	56.31	35.70
55–59	21.87	10.66	42.30	26.16
60 and older	7.29	2.45	24.16	14.46

Source

Richard Sutch, "Appendix: The Value of the Slave Population, 1805–1860," in Roger Ransom and Richard Sutch, "Capitalists without Capital: The Burden of Slavery and the Impact of Emancipation," *Agricultural History* 62 (3) (1988), Tables A.4, pp. 155–6, and A.1, pp. 150–1.

Documentation

The data were provided by Stanley Engerman. For a description of the method used to derive the estimates, see Robert W. Fogel and Stanley L. Engerman, *Time on the Cross* (Little, Brown, 1974), volume 1, Figures 15, 16, and 18, pp. 72 and 76, and volume 2, pp. 79–82. Figures are index numbers in which the price of Louisiana males, age 18 to 30, are set to equal 100, and figures for males of younger and older ages and for females of various ages are expressed in relation to this base. The age breakdown is based on the slave's age in about 1850.

These age-price profiles were developed by Robert Fogel and Stanley Engerman from data in probate records from the "Old South" (defined to include Maryland, Virginia, and North and South Carolina) and the "New South" (defined as Louisiana) for 1846–1855. Probate records show the value of various items in the estate of a recently deceased person. In Louisiana during the period 1846 through 1855, a slave owner's assets would include his or her slaves. The value would be indicated for each, along with descriptive information about the slave, especially the slave's age and sex.

Fogel and Engerman argued that the age-sex and geographical patterns remained stable over the period from 1787 to 1860. See Fogel and Engerman (1974), volume 2, p. 79.

MANUMITTED AND FUGITIVE SLAVES, AND SLAVE REVOLTS

Susan B. Carter

TABLE Bb219–235 Manumitted slaves, by state: 1850–1860

Contributed by Susan B. Carter

	Total	Alabama	Arkansas	Delaware	Florida	Georgia	Kentucky	Louisiana	Maryland
	Bb219	Bb220	Bb221	Bb222	Bb223	Bb224	Bb225	Bb226	Bb227
Year	Number	Number	Number	Number	Number	Number	Number	Number	Number
1850	1,467	16	1	277	22	19	152	159	493
1860	3,018 [1]	101	41	12	17	160	176	517	1,017

Note appears at end of table

(continued)

	Mississippi	Missouri	North Carolina	South Carolina	Tennessee	Texas	Virginia	District of Columbia
	Bb228	Bb229	Bb230	Bb231	Bb232	Bb233	Bb234	Bb235
Year	Number	Number	Number	Number	Number	Number	Number	Number
1850	6	50	2	2	45	5	218	0
1860	182	89	258	12	174	37	277	8

[1] Reflects the correction of an arithmetic error in the original.

Source

U.S. Bureau of the Census, *Statistics of the United States (Including Mortality, Property, Etc.) in 1860* (1866), p. 337.

Documentation

A "manumitted slave" is one who was voluntarily set free by his or her former owner.

TABLE Bb236–251 Fugitive slaves, by state: 1850–1860

Contributed by Susan B. Carter

	Total	Alabama	Arkansas	Delaware	Florida	Georgia	Kentucky	Louisiana
	Bb236	Bb237	Bb238	Bb239	Bb240	Bb241	Bb242	Bb243
Year	Number	Number	Number	Number	Number	Number	Number	Number
1850	1,011	29	21	26	18	89	96	90
1860	803	36	28	12	11	23	119	46

	Maryland	Mississippi	Missouri	North Carolina	South Carolina	Tennessee	Texas	Virginia
	Bb244	Bb245	Bb246	Bb247	Bb248	Bb249	Bb250	Bb251
Year	Number	Number	Number	Number	Number	Number	Number	Number
1850	279	41	60	64	16	70	29	83
1860	115	68	99	61	23	29	16	117

Source

U.S. Bureau of the Census, *Statistics of the United States (Including Mortality, Property, Etc.) in 1860* (1866), p. 338.

Documentation

A "fugitive slave" is one who escaped from his or her owner. The Census Bureau argued for the reliability of these numbers:

> It would scarcely be alleged that these returns are not reliable, being, as they are, made by the persons directly interested, who would be no more likely to err in the number lost than in those retained. Fortunately, however, other means exist of proving the correctness of the results ascertained, by noting the increase of the free colored population, which, with all its artificial accretions, is proven by the census to be less than 13 per cent., in the last ten years, in the free States, whereas the slaves have increased $23^1/_2$ per cent., presenting a natural augmentation altogether conclusive against much loss by escapes; the natural increase being equal to that of the most favored nations, irrespective of immigration, and greater than that of any country in Europe for the same period, and this in spite of the 20,000 manumissions which are believed to have occurred in the past ten years. An additional evidence of the slave population having been attended from year to year, up to the present time, with fewer vicissitudes, is further furnished by the fact that the free colored population, which from 1820 to 1830 increased at the rate of 36 $^1/_5$ per cent., in 1840 exhibited but 20 $^4/_5$ per cent. increase, gradually declining to 1860, when the increase throughout the United States was but one per cent per annum. (U.S. Bureau of the Census 1866, pp. 337–8)

TABLE Bb252–254 Major slave revolts and uprisings, by location and type: 1663–1853

Contributed by Susan B. Carter

	Location	Conspiracy or actual revolt	Type
	Bb252	Bb253	Bb254
Year	State	—	Type
1663	Virginia	Conspiracy	Systematic
1687	Virginia	Conspiracy	Vandalistic
1691	Virginia	Actual	Vandalistic
1708	New York	Actual	Vandalistic
1711	South Carolina	Actual	Vandalistic
1712	New York	Actual	Systematic
1720	South Carolina	Conspiracy	Systematic
1722	Virginia	Conspiracy	Systematic
1730	South Carolina	Conspiracy	Vandalistic
1730	Louisiana	Conspiracy	Vandalistic
1734	Pennsylvania	Conspiracy	Opportunistic
1739	Maryland	Conspiracy	Systematic
1740	South Carolina	Actual	Vandalistic
1774	Georgia	Actual	Vandalistic
1776	North Carolina	Conspiracy	Vandalistic
1792	Virginia	Conspiracy	Systematic
1792	Virginia	Actual	Vandalistic
1793	Virginia	Conspiracy	Systematic
1795	Louisiana	Conspiracy	Vandalistic
1799	Virginia	Actual	Opportunistic
1800	Virginia	Conspiracy	Systematic
1810	Georgia	Conspiracy	Systematic
1811	Louisiana	Actual	Vandalistic
1816	Virginia	Conspiracy	Systematic
1816	South Carolina	Conspiracy	Systematic
1819	Georgia	Conspiracy	Systematic
1822	South Carolina	Conspiracy	Systematic
1826	South Carolina	Actual	Opportunistic
1826	Georgia and Maryland	Actual	Opportunistic
1829	Kentucky	Actual	Opportunistic
1831	Virginia	Actual	Vandalistic
1835	Mississippi	Conspiracy	Vandalistic
1836	Missouri	Conspiracy	Opportunistic
1837	Louisiana	Conspiracy	Systematic
1840	Louisiana	Conspiracy	Systematic
1840	Louisiana	Conspiracy	Opportunistic
1841	Georgia	Conspiracy	Systematic
1845	Maryland	Actual	Opportunistic
1848	Kentucky	Actual	Opportunistic
1849	Georgia	Conspiracy	Opportunistic
1850	Missouri	Actual	Opportunistic
1851	Texas	Actual	Opportunistic
1853	Louisiana	Conspiracy	Systematic

Source

Marion D. De B. Kilson, "Towards Freedom: An Analysis of Slave Revolts in the United States," *Phylon* 24 (1964), Tables 1, 2, and 3, pp. 177, 179, and 180.

Documentation

Kilson's tabulation and classification of major slave revolts and uprisings is based largely on the descriptive account of Herbert Aptheker, *American Negro Slave Revolts*, revised edition (International Publishers, 1963). Kilson supplements Aptheker's enumeration with data from a variety of additional sources with more geographically circumscribed foci.

Kilson defines slave revolts and uprisings as "attempts to achieve freedom by groups of slaves." He distinguishes between those attempts that actually materialized as revolts and those that were quashed while they were still in the conspiracy stage (series Bb253). Kilson also distinguishes among three types of slave revolts. A "systematic" revolt is one "oriented towards overthrowing the slave system itself and establishing a Negro state. It is characterized, therefore, by careful planning and organization which necessitate a considerable period of preparation." As prototypes, he cites the conspiracies of Gabriel Prosser (Virginia, 1800) and Denmark Vesey (South Carolina, 1822). Kilson writes:

> Both Prosser and Vesey planned initially to gain control of a city and thereafter to extend their operations into the surrounding area. Such a plan involves the systematic allocation of tasks to various groups and individuals and the calculation of the numbers of insurgents upon whom reliance could be placed. Further evidence of the rational conception of these uprisings is found in the facts that Gabriel Prosser intended to spare certain sympathetic groups of whites and hoped for aid from poor whites and Indians, and that Vesey hoped to have external aid from the West Indies and Africa to maintain his state after its establishment. (Kilson 1964, pp. 175–6)

Overall, Kilson found seventeen separate incidents that he classified as systematic slave revolts or uprisings.

Kilson classified a second set of slave revolts as "vandalistic." Such a revolt represents a "haphazard expression of opposition to the slave system aimed at the destruction of slave holders and their property. It lacks systematic preparation but may be either of lengthy or of virtually spontaneous conception." He cites Nat Turner's insurrection (Virginia, 1831) as a prototype.

The "opportunistic" revolts are Kilson's third type. Such a revolt is aimed at "escape from servitude." "It is characterized by a group of slaves attempting to escape either to a non-slave area or from removal to areas of more oppressive servitude." Kilson remarks that the only successful slave revolt for which there is evidence was an opportunistic revolt of approximately 1,500 slaves in Colorado County, Texas, who escaped to Mexico in 1851 (see Aptheker 1963, p. 343).

CHAPTER Bc

Education

Editor: Claudia Goldin

EDUCATION

Claudia Goldin

The education and training of a population is a critical input to productivity and thus to economic growth. Education directly increases productivity, and thus the incomes of those who receive schooling, by providing individuals with useful skills and knowledge. Schooling also stimulates invention and innovation and enables the more rapid diffusion of technological advances. The role of education changes with technological progress; some technologies have placed heavy demands on the cognitive skills of workers, whereas others have enabled the substitution of machinery for human skill. Formal education, especially basic literacy, is essential for a well-functioning democracy and enhances responsible citizenship and a sense of community. Religious beliefs have also been important in fostering both public and private education, even in the United States with its long history of separation of church and state. Schooling is also a pure consumption good, enabling people to better understand and enjoy their surroundings. Education can thus play a multitude of roles in the economy, polity, community, and religious and personal lives of a people.

It is perhaps no wonder that educational systems diffused rapidly among the free residents of the world's greatest nineteenth-century democracy. According to some estimates, by the 1840s, primary school enrollment per capita in the United States had exceeded that in Germany, and by this standard Americans had become the best-educated people among those in the world's richer nations (Easterlin 1981). U.S. literacy rates were also extremely high, among, once again, the free population. America borrowed many educational concepts and institutions from Europe but tailored them in particularly American ways. U.S. schools, at almost all levels, were more practical and applied than those in Europe, yet they were not industrial and were rarely vocational.[1] They became, early on, free and publicly funded and were generally permissive in allowing youths to enter each level independent of age, social status (but not race in certain parts of the United States), previous school record, and sex. After the establishment of publicly funded primary schools, girls and boys were educated for about the same number of years, and during the early to mid-twentieth century, a greater proportion of girls than boys attended and graduated from secondary schools (Table Bc258–264).

Although it would be useful to present school enrollment, attendance, and literacy rates for the early to mid-nineteenth century, the data are still fragmentary and subject to many potential biases. They were not included in the previous edition of *Historical Statistics of the United States* (1975), and although there has been considerable research on the subject since then, the data remain imperfect. Part of the problem is that data are incomplete for some geographical areas (for example, see Fishlow 1966) and the amount of detail varies. Massachusetts and New York, for example, have been studied in great depth for 1790 to 1850 (see Kaestle and Vinovskis 1980). But even in those states, enrollment rates that have been estimated for youths 5–19 years old are too high to be consistent with independent evidence on the occupations of youths. Perhaps some youths enrolled in school but did not attend, or perhaps school districts inflated enrollments. Even though precise estimates are beyond the task here, there is general agreement among scholars that by the middle of the nineteenth century U.S. schooling rates were exceptionally high, schooling was widespread among the free population, and literacy was virtually universal, again, among the free population (for illiteracy rates since 1870, see Table Bc793–797).

How the new nation of the United States managed in the short span of a half-century to attain the status of the best-educated country in the world is an involved tale. Until the mid-nineteenth century most education was offered in "common schools" that were publicly operated but often not fully publicly funded. In some districts, parents received a "rate bill" for their children's education. Elsewhere, part of the term was publicly funded and the rate bill supported an extended term. In large cities, such as New York, there were, early on, pauper schools paid for by public funds and private schools for the more fortunate. The details are complicated by the highly local nature of education in the United States. What is perfectly clear, however, is that virtually every state in the nation shifted to publicly funded education at the elementary or common school level in the decades following the American Civil War.

The claim that Americans became the best-educated people in the world by the mid-nineteenth century may, however, be somewhat overstated. Some European countries had, until the beginning

Acknowledgments

Claudia Goldin is grateful to the research assistants who ably helped with this project: Nora Gordon, Marina Jovanovic, Michael Pisetsky, and Alicia Sasser. Caroline Hoxby and Barry Hirsch were consulted on some of the series. Tom Snyder of the U.S. Department of Education, National Center for Education Statistics, gave unstinting help with numerous details, and Shirley Smith of the U.S. Bureau of the Census, Income Division, was generous with her time as well. The data series compilation was funded by a grant from the Spencer Foundation through the National Bureau of Economic Research.

Susan B. Carter thanks Victoria Nayak for her assistance in preparing Tables Bc454–467, Bc480–491, Bc537–567, Bc588–599, Bc621–656, and Bc677–712.

[1] On comparisons among countries, see Ringer (1979).

of the twentieth century, far better institutions of higher education than did the United States. But European educational systems, with few exceptions, were elitist well into the twentieth century. Both secondary and higher education were reserved for those with exceptional abilities, stemming from both family background, with the opportunities it offered, and innate talents. The U.S. system of education, in contrast, was distinctly egalitarian almost from its start. Americans eschewed different systems for different children, and in the early nineteenth century began to embrace the notion that all children should receive a "common," unified, academic education. Despite these claims, however, there were gaping holes in the American educational system. Many, but not all, concern the unequal treatment of African Americans as slaves and then as freed persons.

Slaves received virtually no formal instruction, particularly after Southern states passed laws that prohibited teaching slaves to read (the first was passed in 1830). After emancipation, African-American children attended schools that were both separate from those of whites and unequal in terms of per-student expenditures. But these schools were not nearly as unequal as they were to become, despite the famous dictum of *Plessy v. Ferguson* (1896). The imposition of "Jim Crow" laws and the disenfranchisement of blacks in much of the South in the 1890s led to a decrease in school expenditures per black child relative to that per white child (Margo 1990). Absolute levels also decreased in various states. Southern schools in many states remained de jure segregated throughout the first half of the twentieth century and continued to be segregated even after the famous *Brown v. Board of Education* (1954) case judged such laws to be unconstitutional. Many schools were integrated only after court orders took effect. Even in the North, many blacks attended de jure segregated schools in the early twentieth century. Among the most persistent of the gaping holes in American education has been de facto segregation not just by race, but also by immigrant status and income.[2] Although these deviations from equality of opportunity must not be ignored, they also should not blind us from judging the American experiment with mass education as a grand success story.

The substantial levels of schooling and literacy in the nineteenth-century United States were achieved within a highly decentralized educational system. At present, the federal government still subsidizes only a small fraction (7 percent) of primary and secondary educational expenditures, and even the states do not provide the majority of school revenues (Table Bc902–908). School finance and curriculum decisions are the domain of school districts, and the origin of these districts is yet another detail from the earliest years of the country's educational history.

As the new nation expanded, the township model of school organization, begun in New England, was adopted by many states. But most new states were too rural for township schools, and instead created even smaller jurisdictions. School districts, first counted by the Office of Education in the early 1930s, numbered about 128,000 at that time (series Bc1). Some were not fiscally independent, in the sense of setting their own tax rates, but rather had tax rates set by larger governmental units, such as counties or townships. But many were fiscally independent. Thus, even by the third decade of the twentieth century, the United States had an enormous number of school districts with independent decision-making powers. America's large cities had, by that time, already experienced major school district consolidation, and by the early 1900s schools in virtually all cities with populations exceeding 20,000 had been consolidated into one school district. Consolidation of rural districts occurred slowly until the 1950s. The central point is that most of the decisions regarding elementary and secondary education in America occurred at relatively disaggregated levels – cities, towns, and rural communities.

The large number of school districts across the United States, the vast majority of which were fiscally independent, meant that decisions concerning resources devoted to schools, teachers, education generally, and curriculum were made locally. In many European countries, such decisions were made at a much higher level, often nationally. It is possible that the more disaggregated level of educational decision making fostered education for the masses, particularly during the nineteenth and the early twentieth centuries. Even though some districts were considerably poorer than others, the greater homogeneity within the districts could have greatly enhanced school funding. The reasoning is simple. Education, particularly at the secondary level, was primarily a "private good" that was publicly provided. Families could always opt out of the public system, although they would still pay taxes to support it, and send their children to private school. The greater the homogeneity within the community concerning "tastes" for education, the more citizens will vote to spend on education. If the decision-making unit includes families with widely differing incomes and divergent tastes for education, it is possible that both the bottom and the top segment of the distribution will opt out of the public education system, leaving the middle group with a poorly financed or nonexistent school system. Thus, greater local governance could account for the more rapid and more complete spread of secondary schooling in the United States than in Europe in the early to mid-twentieth century.

The greater level of education in the United States than in Europe until late in the twentieth century is, of course, attributable to a host of factors and not just the decentralization of educational decision making. These other factors include higher levels of wealth, lower relative opportunity cost for youths (that is, a lower wage of youth relative to that of adults), competing religions that valued the ability of the laity to read the Bible, and an ideology of the democratic ideal of universal literacy (Goldin and Katz 1999a, 2003).

Educational Institutions and Education Data

The large number of school districts and the highly localized nature of school finance and administration in the United States complicate the compilation of education data for the United States. Rather than having been collected by one national agency or even many state agencies, most of the series are built up first at the state level from the localities and then at the federal level from surveys of the states. The collection procedure differs from series to series, although most come from the states through the federal government. The federal government began to collect data on education from the states just after the establishment of the Office of Education in 1867.

The Office of Education has had a rather complicated history, but one that is of sufficient importance to the data series to deserve a brief synopsis. The Bureau of Education, the forerunner of today's Department of Education, was established in 1867 and became the Office of Education in 1869, an agency of the Department of the

[2] On early twentieth century ethnic differences, see Perlmann (1988).

Interior, where it stayed for seventy years. It was known as the Bureau of Education for those seventy years, but in 1929 it was renamed the Office of Education. In 1939 it became part of the Federal Security Agency and was, in 1953, included in the new agency of Health, Education, and Welfare (HEW). The Department of Education became a separate cabinet-level agency in 1980. Each of the states also eventually appointed a superintendent or commissioner of education and founded an office, bureau, or board of education. The first state board of education was established in Massachusetts in 1837 and was headed by Horace Mann, an individual best known for his tireless crusade for free common schools.

Most of the data in the series begin with the establishment of the federal Bureau (or Office or Department) of Education. Thus the earliest date for education series is approximately 1870 (Table Bc7–18). As noted previously, this is especially unfortunate with regard to the history of the common and elementary schools. The data for secondary school education suffer less from this omission, as the expansion of high schools began in the late nineteenth century. Private academies, functioning much like secondary schools, proliferated in the mid-nineteenth century, but no reliable data can be found on their numbers and impact. Institutions of higher education in the United States date back to the opening of Harvard University in 1638. But at the aggregate level they, too, can be examined quantitatively only for the years after 1870. As is the case for the secondary schools, there is little lost because only a small fraction of American youth could have been attending colleges and universities before that time.

Despite various problems in assembling the education data series, the relative stability and uniformity of U.S. educational institutions has simplified the task. The levels of education in the United States have not varied much across time and space. "Common school" generally includes youths between ages 6 or 7 and 14 or 15 (or older, if the youth had not attended regularly). That is, common school generally means grades 1–8, even if the schools were "ungraded," occupied a single room, and had but one teacher. Common schools were found mainly in the "open country" or rural areas, and continued to be numerous until the mid-twentieth century (series Bc6). Youths in rural areas often went to common school for longer than 8 years, but the additional time was generally for remedial lessons. Only rarely did it mean they were being taught at the secondary school level (see, for example, Goldin and Katz 1999b). Towns, villages, and cities had graded elementary schools.

Secondary or high school generally means grades 9–12, or ages 14 or 15 to 17 or 18. At the start of the "high school movement" in the early 1900s, however, many high schools in small towns covered only grades 9 to 10 or 11. Several curriculum changes have altered the two levels, elementary and high, across the twentieth century. The "junior high school" was introduced in 1909 (in both Columbus, Ohio, and Berkeley, California) and spread rapidly to other districts. It was adopted to keep pupils, who would otherwise leave at age 14, to grade 9, award them a diploma, and give them practical training, for example, in shop and home economics. Since junior highs included grades 7–9, elementary school was shortened to grades 1–6, and high schools became "senior highs," covering grades from 9 to 12. This system is known as "6–3–3," and the previous one as "8–4." At various points in the past century, some districts returned to the previous model whereas others eliminated the junior high school and introduced the middle school, encompassing grades 5–8. Curriculum changes are far more difficult to track, as will be discussed in the section on secondary schooling.

Most of the education series presented use the school year rather than the calendar year. Those on primary and secondary school enrollment, however, switch in 1965 to "opening fall" enrollment (Table Bc19–37) and those for higher education switch in 1946 (Table Bc523–536). The distinction concerns the period within which enrollments are accumulated. "Opening fall" enrollment is believed to be the more accurate method and counts only those students enrolled at the beginning of the school year, whereas the other method accumulates enrollments from the entire year. The difference is trivial for elementary and secondary school students. For college and university enrollments, however, there could be more substantial differences if students transfer from one institution to another.

Each state, today and in the past, determines what constitutes promotion and graduation. With the establishment of the state universities, graduation from high school often implied automatic college admission (although not automatic graduation). Thus states took great interest in the level of proficiency required to graduate from high school. Similarly, promotion from eighth grade in many states meant admission to public high schools, and many states also took an interest in that transition. In the early twentieth century, particularly after World War I, various states pioneered in the testing of students. A version of the well-known Iowa Test of Educational Development began in the 1920s but was not administered statewide for another decade. The New York and California State Regents also produced their own exams. Only scant evidence exists on time trends regarding elementary and secondary school exam scores (Bishop 1989). One aspect of the history of promotion and graduation is clear. There was considerable age-in-grade retention until the mid-twentieth century, when automatic promotion became a more common phenomenon. Retention rates can be computed using Table Bc19–37 on the fraction of pupils continuing from grade 5. Because these data are for public school students only, the transit of private school students (generally Catholic) to public schools after grade 8 complicates the calculation.

Higher education, at least since the mid-nineteenth century, has been a four-year program, although there are various exceptions and some important changes. One exception is that until the twentieth century, many professional degrees (for example, law, medicine) did not require a baccalaureate degree and thus the first professional degree often included a B.A. Because of this practice, the series on undergraduate enrollment and degrees includes first professional degrees until the mid-twentieth century. Junior (or community) colleges have been two-year institutions ever since the beginning of the twentieth century. Normal (or teacher-training) schools often provided two-year programs, but these grew to four years in some states starting in the 1920s and in most others in the 1940s and 1950s. Teacher-training institutions complicate the higher education data to a considerable degree as the number of women enrolled in them was substantial and program length was not always specified. For that reason, some researchers exclude them in the older data but include them for years after the 1940s (for example, Goldin and Katz 1999b).

Schools at all levels can be under public or private control. At the elementary and secondary levels, the type of control is generally unambiguous in the data series. This is especially true with regard to denominational institutions. The vast majority of private kindergarten to twelfth grade (K–12) schools are denominational. (It is likely that control will be a more ambiguous concept in the future if school vouchers can be used in denominational schools, as they have been in a recent policy experiment involving Catholic schools.) Control of higher education has been a somewhat less transparent concept. In the first place, some institutions of higher education that were under private control received the initial Morrill Land Grant (1862) funds from the state (examples include Cornell University, MIT, Yale, and Rutgers). More important, the federal government supports research at private institutions and allocates student aid on the basis of need, not the control of the institution. All the GI Bills, for example, paid private and public tuitions, and Pell Grants subsidize students at a range of institutions (see Table Bc-A for some details on these programs). Thus, the control of the institution is not necessarily coterminous with the source of

TABLE Bc-A Important state and federal legislation, judicial decisions, and historical events in U.S. education: 1635–1997

1635	Boston Latin School, the first "grammar" or secondary school in the colonies, is opened. Boston Latin was funded, in part, by income from a public land sale, making it the first public school in America.
1638	Harvard University, the first university in America, founded in 1636, is opened to students.
1647	The Old Deluder Satan Act of the General Court of the Colony of Massachusetts Bay is passed. Towns of 50 families or more must establish a public elementary school and towns of 100 families or more must establish a public "grammar" school "with a master capable of preparing young people for university level study."
1785	The first state university is chartered in Georgia.
1785	The Land Ordinance of 1785, "an Ordinance for ascertaining the mode of disposing of Lands in the Western Territory" (north of the Ohio River and east of the Mississippi), passed by the Continental Congress under the Articles of Confederation, reserved section 16 of each congressional township (36-square-mile sections) for the support of public schools within the township.
1787	The Northwest Ordinance, "an Ordinance for the government of the Territory of the United States northwest of the River Ohio," passed by the Continental Congress, noted that because "religion, morality, and knowledge" are essential to good government, "schools and the means of education shall forever be encouraged."
1789	State constitutions provide for the establishment of statewide school systems and, for states entering the union after 1862, contain allotments of federal lands to support state institutions of higher education.
1789	The Tenth Amendment to the U.S. Constitution provides a legal basis for making education a state function. The First Amendment and the Fourteenth Amendment (the latter adopted in 1868) together ensure separation of church and state in the provision of education at the local level.
1819	In *Dartmouth College v. Woodward* the charter of Dartmouth College is determined to be a contract and thus the state legislature of New Hampshire could not abrogate it and set up a state college instead.
1821	The English Classical School, the first high school founded in the United States, is established in Boston, Massachusetts.
1826	Free public schools are required in Massachusetts townships for all children. Although this is mandated in other states later (New York, for example, required the same in 1867), many cities pass their own "free school" legislation ahead of the states.
1827	The Massachusetts Act is passed, requiring towns with 500 families or more to support a public high school (enforcement was incomplete).
1830	The first law prohibiting the teaching of slaves to read is passed in Louisiana; Georgia and Virginia follow in 1831, Alabama in 1832, South Carolina in 1834, and North Carolina in 1835.
1833	Oberlin College (previously Oberlin Collegiate Institute) in Ohio is founded as the first coeducational college in the United States.
1837	Horace Mann is appointed as secretary of the Massachusetts Board of Education to head the first state board of education.
1838	The Central High School in Philadelphia is established.
1850	An amendment to the Land Ordinance of 1785 increased educational allotment to two sections, 16 and 36, for states entering after 1850.
1852	Massachusetts passes the first compulsory school-attendance act in the United States.
1862	Through the Morrill Land Grant Act, Congress grants funds (scrip in federal land) to states to found colleges of mechanical arts (engineering), military science, and agriculture.
1867	The U.S. Bureau of Education is established.
1874	Through the Kalamazoo Decision, the Michigan Supreme Court validates the use of local funds for secondary school education as being similar to their use for elementary (common) school education. The decision influenced later challenges to public high schools in other states.
1887	The Hatch Act provides government support of state agricultural experiment stations, as joint research projects of state agricultural colleges and the U.S. Department of Agriculture.
1890	Through the Second Morrill Land Grant Act, Congress institutes regular appropriations for the land-grant colleges; the "historically black" institutions are set up in response to the demand of this act that nonwhite students be provided facilities.
1896	In *Plessy v. Ferguson* the Supreme Court validates the separation of black and white pupils and establishes the "separate but equal" doctrine.
1909	The first junior high schools are established in Columbus, Ohio, and Berkeley, California.
1914	The Smith-Lever Agriculture Extension Act sets up an agricultural extension.
1917	The Smith-Hughes Vocational Act gave funds to support agriculture, industry, and home economics education and created the Federal Board for Vocational Education.
1918	All states had compulsory school-attendance laws by 1918, although the maximum age of compulsion often exceeded the age at which a work permit could be granted.

TABLE Bc-A Important state and federal legislation, judicial decisions, and historical events in U.S. education: 1635–1997 ***Continued***

1942	The General Educational Development (GED) Program is initiated to provide World War II veterans lacking a high school diploma with an opportunity to earn a secondary school credential; civilians were first able to take the test in 1952.
1943	In *West Virginia Board of Education v. Barnette* the Supreme Court ruled that students who are Jehovah's Witnesses were not obliged to participate in saluting the flag.
1944	Through the GI Bill of Rights the 78th Congress provides subsistence allowances, tuition fees, and supplies for the education and training of veterans of World War II in a wide variety of settings including colleges, high schools, and vocational training institutions.
1950	The National Science Foundation is established to "promote the progress of science; to advance the national health, prosperity, and welfare; to secure the national defense; and for other purposes."
1952	The Korean War GI Bill of Rights extends educational benefits of the 1944 Bill to Korean War veterans and others who served in the armed forces during the war period.
1954	In *Brown v. Board of Education* the Supreme Court holds unconstitutional the deliberate segregation of schools by law on account of race.
1954	The Cooperative Research Program authorizes the U.S. Commissioner of Education to contract with institutions of higher education and state education agencies for educational research.
1958	The National Defense Education Act provides extensive aid to schools and students.
1962	In *Engel v. Vitale* the Supreme Court rules that the state could not enforce prayer in public schools.
1963	The Vocational Education Act further expands agricultural extension.
1964	The Civil Rights Act, Section 1983, outlaws discrimination by sex.
1965	Head Start is established in the Office of Economic Opportunity as a way to serve children of low-income families; it would later be administered by the Administration for Children and Families.
1972	Title IX of the Education Amendments Act protects students from receiving different resources or other disparate treatment on account of sex.
1973	The Federal Pell Grant Program is authorized under the Higher Education Act of 1965, and provides for undergraduate student aid based on need.
1975	The Education for All Handicapped Children Act (EAHCA) requires better access to schools for disabled students.
1975	The Individuals with Disabilities Education Act (IDEA) replaces EAHCA and addresses the failure of many states to comply with EAHCA.
1978	In *University of California Regents v. Bakke* the Supreme Court rules against reverse discrimination; fixed quotas cannot be set.
1980	The Department of Education is established as a separate cabinet-level agency.
1994	The School-to-Work Opportunities Act provides seed money to states and local partnerships of business, labor, government, education, and community organizations to develop school-to-work systems.
1997	The Taxpayer Relief Act sets up Hope Tax Credits, Tax Credits for Lifelong Learning, Education IRAs, and tax deductibility of interest on student loans.

funding. It never was. Harvard University, for example, received funds from the Massachusetts colonial government and afterwards from the state until the early nineteenth century.

This essay ends with a note on the data sources, but there are some details that must be addressed first. As previously mentioned, most of the sources are the administrative records of localities and states. That is why the existence of the U.S. Bureau of Education, which compiled these data, is important to the construction of the series and why the earliest date for the series is about 1870. These administrative sources provide "flow" data rather than "stock" data. That is, they give contemporaneous information on students, teachers, schools, finances, and so on, rather than the number of years of schooling of the population or the number of individuals who ever taught, to provide two examples. They reveal little about student characteristics in terms of age, sex, race, ethnicity, and family background, although some are occasionally indicated. Racial segregation of public schools in the South, for example, allows the calculation of high school graduation by race after 1930 (Table Bc468–479). Some administrative data are given by sex (Table Bc258–264). Because the administrative data are rarely given by age, the contemporaneous "flow" numbers have to be divided by the relevant population group to obtain rates.

Other potential sources of education data are the U.S. decennial population census, the Current Population Survey (CPS), and state censuses. Since 1850 the U.S. census has asked whether an individual had attended (almost any kind of) school (for at least one day) during the preceding year. But not until 1940 did the U.S. population census, and later the CPS, ask about the "stock" of education, that is, school attainment or the "highest grade completed." For the years before 1940, only two states (Iowa and South Dakota) asked questions on educational attainment, and research on the subject has been done using the Iowa State Census of 1915 (Goldin and Katz 1999b).

The relationship between education and income, at the individual level, can be presented for the entire United States beginning only with 1940 (tables Bc814–901). But even the 1940 data are subject to considerable bias. Although the 1940 federal population census was the first to inquire of income and education, both variables contain omissions and biases. Wage and salary income information was requested in 1940, but that from self-employment was first asked for in 1950. The education and income series use comparable income measures for the decennial census years 1940, 1950, and 1960 (wage and salary income) and then switch, by necessity, to a more inclusive measure of income when using the Current Population Survey (Tables Bc814–901). Caution should be exercised in using these data to make inferences about the role of education in enhancing income. One reason is that the aggregate population is used (men 25 years of age or older) and there were large compositional changes between census years. From 1940 to 1950, for example, the fraction of young men with high school diplomas increased substantially. Because these persons had little job market experience, their average earnings were lower than those of older high school graduates and not much higher than those of older individuals without a high school diploma. The compositional change means that, in times of rapid educational advance, the role of more education (here a high school diploma) will not be as apparent than if the series had been divided by age.

"Highest grade completed" was asked in 1940, but many older Americans had not attended graded schools and some went to school for more years than grades. There is considerable evidence that the 1940 Census overstates the high school graduation rate of older Americans to a considerable degree (Goldin 1998). The graduation data are often inconsistent with those from administrative data, although those for lower grades are not. Educational data from the census (and also those from the Current Population Surveys) are also important because they allow tabulation of education by individual and family characteristics (Table Bc38–79).

Even though the U.S. population census asked whether an individual had attended school during the previous year, the answers overstate the number of youths who were actually attending formal day school for at least several months during the year. (They are, however, given for 5- to 19-year-olds in Table Bc438–446 and graphed in Figure Bc-B.) The length of time attended, as previously noted, was "for at least one day" and the type of school was virtually any, including night and commercial schools. Thus, for most of the period under consideration, the administrative data must be relied on for virtually all the series. It should be noted that the terms "enrollment" and "attendance" are used interchangeably in these series. Although the census question concerned attendance of school for at least one day, the convention is to use the term enrollment in this case.

Schools took various forms over the period under discussion. The rural common school of the open country was a simple one-room structure, often situated on someone's quarter section or farm. The town school in almost any era would be recognizable to those reading this essay, although there would be various differences across time. One difference is that elementary and high schools, early on, were often in the same building. Thus, it is impossible to produce separate series on these schools until the 1930s (Table Bc1–6). Some states listed virtually all elementary schools as high schools, whereas others had state laws requiring secondary schools to be separate structures. Similar ambiguities plague issues regarding instructional staff. Each state had regulations concerning who could teach and what the prerequisites were. But these varied enormously across space and time. The series presented here accept the definitions in the administrative records. Someone who taught secondary school students was a secondary school teacher. But there are times when even this distinction is ambiguous.

One last important data issue must be mentioned. Education is "life-long learning." Much of it does not take place in formal settings and is thus difficult to track. The series presented here will, by necessity, omit on-the-job training and also proprietary training institutions. It is possible to study the latter for much of the twentieth century because the Office of Education often collected information on them. Commercial schools proliferated in the 1910s and 1920s, but there is, at present, no readily available, comprehensive, and reliable series on them.

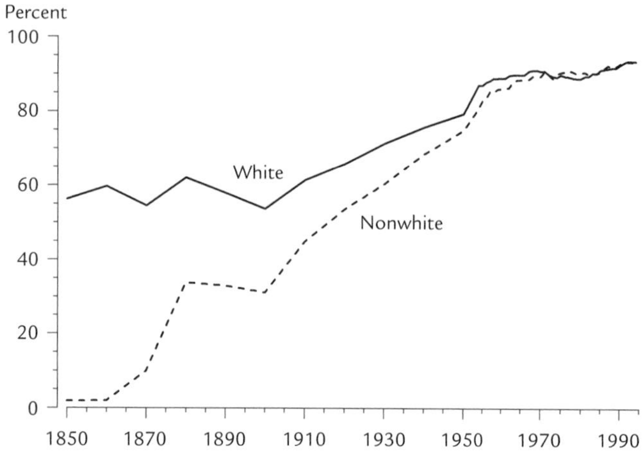

FIGURE Bc-B School enrollment rates, by race: 1850–1994

Sources

Series Bc439–440.

Documentation

Persons ages 5–19.

The Three Transformations of American Education

The United States underwent three transformations of education – primary, secondary, and tertiary. The periodization of the three transformations dates the completion of each schooling level by the majority of youth. The completion of each can be thought of as the moment when an education level was available and taken up by the "masses" or, put another way, when "mass education" reached that level. The first transformation brought most of the youth through common or elementary school (eighth grade) and occurred during the nineteenth century. The second transformation brought the majority of youth through secondary or high school and occurred in the first half of the twentieth century. The third, still ongoing, transformation is bringing the majority of young adults through four-year higher education.

Education is intrinsically a hierarchical process, however. Any state or nation that has elementary schools must also employ teachers with knowledge exceeding that necessary to teach the elementary grades. Thus, although the United States underwent three transformations of education, all three levels had to be in place simultaneously. At times this necessitated borrowing from Europe. In the late nineteenth century, America imported instructional staff for colleges and universities and also exported college students (many of whom returned as trained academics). But the fact that many American institutions of higher learning were founded far in advance of the third transformation is an indication of the importance of the highest levels of education for training at the most elementary levels.

Primary or Common School, and Elementary Education

The first educational transformation occurred over an extended period but moved rapidly during the middle of the nineteenth century when fully free, publicly funded common schools diffused throughout the nation (Kaestle 1983). Although compulsory education laws also began to be passed during the period of the common school transformation, it is believed that they lagged rather than led it. That is, the state laws were passed only after the majority of youths had already gone beyond the compulsory legal age. As noted previously, the most interesting period of common school diffusion predates the era of readily accessible data.

Almost all of the data series concerning K–12 education begin with 1870. The exception is that for school attendance (for 5- to 19-year olds) from the U.S. federal population census (see Table Bc438–446, as well as Figures Bc-B and Bc-C). Beginning with the collection of the administrative information by the Office of Education in 1870, data exist on public and private enrollments by level or grade, where common school students are classified in the K–8 group (Table Bc7–18). More detailed data on students by grade can be computed for the years after 1910 for public school students (Table Bc19–37). But it was not until the late 1910s, with the publication of the *Biennial Survey of Education in the United States*, that data became available to calculate student–teacher ratios (series Bc12). Because the age of students was not collected in most administrative data, rates of attendance have to be computed by assuming an age group (for example, 14–17 for secondary school) and using data on population by age.

According to the data in Tables Bc7–18 and Bc438–446, the transformation to "mass" primary school education (among the free population) was completed by the mid-nineteenth century. The transition, moreover, was similar for boys and girls (Figure Bc-C). Although none of these series reveals the precise fraction of boys and girls at different ages attending school, considerable work by educational historians has shown that, at least in the elementary and secondary grades, girls attended school for more months than did boys for much of the period. Even though a large fraction of youths were enrolled in school, the attendance of those who were enrolled was, on average, between 60 and 70 percent of the school year from the 1850s to the 1910s, or between 80 and 110 days per year (series Bc96). Regrettably, none of the data, as previously reported, says anything about the pre-1850 period.

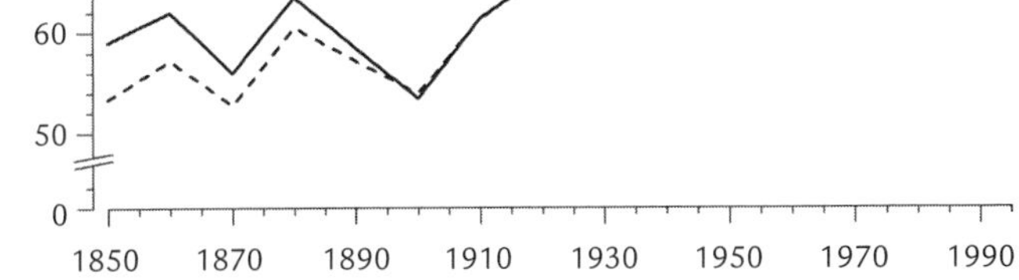

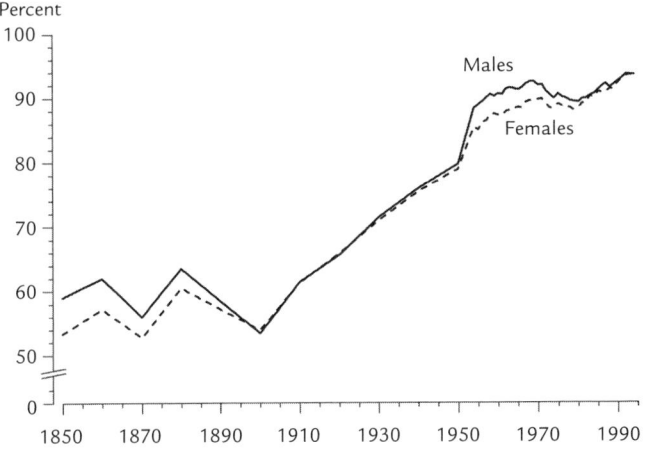

FIGURE Bc-C School enrollment rates for whites, by sex: 1850–1994

Sources

Series Bc442 and Bc445.

Documentation

Persons ages 5–19.

Among the more important changes in elementary public school education since 1970 has been the increase in the fraction of public school youths in "special education programs" (Table Bc80–93), the unionization of teachers (Table Bc447–453), the decrease in classroom size (Table Bc7–18), and the increase in real expenditures per child (Table Bc909–925). The increase in real expenditures per child should not be too surprising because the real cost of teachers (nominal amounts in Table Bc97–106 must be deflated by a price index series) rises with general levels of productivity. But simple decompositions show that the increase in expenditures per pupil cannot be fully explained by the increase in the real wage of teachers, the decrease in classroom size, and the increase in more costly special education students. Administrative costs per pupil, it appears, have greatly increased. Another important recent change is the increase in preschool education (Table Bc429–437).

Most education data measure the quantity of schooling received, in years or grades. The quality of education is an equally important, yet less transparent, aspect. Quality can be proxied by the student–teacher ratio (Table Bc7–18) and the length of the term (series Bc95), to mention two measures that can be used over the long term. Current concern with K–12 educational quality has focused on another measure, that of test scores. Among the most widely used is the National Assessment of Educational Progress (NAEP) (Table Bc273–428). Although the United States has done poorly in international test comparisons, NAEP scores have generally risen since the 1970s. A reconciliation of these two observations is yet to be accomplished.

Secondary or High School

The second transformation of American education was the "high school movement," and it was the most rapid of the three. In 1910, fewer than 10 percent of all U.S. youth graduated high school, but by 1940 the median youth was a high school graduate (Table Bc258–264). In certain parts of the nation (notably, the Pacific, West North Central, and New England states), the "high school movement" was even more rapid (see Table Bc468–479 and Figure Bc-D). In those states, graduation and enrollment rates were as high in the 1930s as they would be until the 1960s (Tables Bc468–479 and Bc492–500). Because the "high school movement" began in the early part of the twentieth century and secondary school attendance was relatively meager before, little is lost from the late starting date for the series.

There was one potentially important predecessor of the public high school in America. "Academies," private institutions that taught material beyond eighth grade and often prepared students for college admission, appeared in the late eighteenth century, particularly in the Northeast, and underwent a growth spurt in the early nineteenth century in both the Northeast and the Midwest. Some of these institutions have survived until today (for example, Andover, Exeter), but most disappeared with the increase in publicly funded secondary schools and a greater demand by parents for a less classically oriented and more practical program of instruction. There are, regrettably, no compilations of their enrollment.[3]

The secondary school graduation rates in Figure Bc-D (and Table Bc468–479) are computed by dividing the administrative data on high school graduates by the number of 17-year-olds in

[3] On the "high school movement" and its origins, see Goldin (1998), Krug (1963), and Reese (1995).

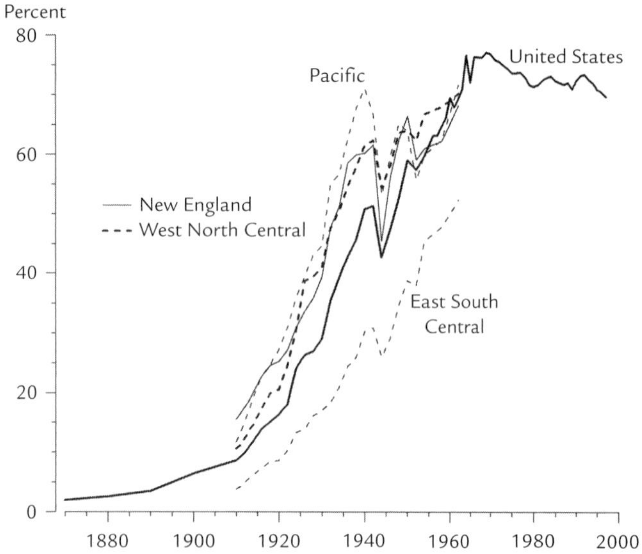

FIGURE Bc-D Public and private secondary school graduation rates – United States and four census divisions: 1870–1997

Sources

Series Bc264, Bc468, Bc472, Bc477, and Bc479.

Documentation

The graduation rate is the number of secondary school graduates in a given year divided by the number of 17-year-olds in that year.

the census division (aggregated up from the states). The secondary school enrollment rates are similarly computed, but the denominator is the number of 14- to 17-year-olds. The fact that some students were older than 17 or younger than 14 may trivially affect the calculation. More important is that the state population data are available only for decennial census years and must be interpolated between them.

It may appear odd that the contemporaneous high school graduation rate in Figure Bc-D is higher in 1970 than it is after. Those data, it will be recalled, were obtained from administrative sources. Data from the major household survey of population – the Current Population Survey – show, to the contrary, that the fraction of 25- to 29-year-olds, for example, claiming to have graduated from high school does not decline from 1975 to 1985 (corresponding to the approximate year of high school graduation of 1966 and 1976). Instead, the fraction graduating high school increases and attains a level that is about 7 percentage points higher than in the administrative records for the same birth cohorts. That is, the contemporaneous public and private high school graduation rate in 1985 is about 73 percent, but it is 86 percent for the same cohorts in the household survey. Most of the difference in the two numbers is accounted for by the General Educational Development (GED) credential (discussed later). The administrative records on high school graduation capture only those who receive diplomas from regular secondary schools, whereas the GED is an examination that can be passed later in life by those who dropped out of high school.

The series in Tables Bc468–479 and Bc492–500 include public and private secondary school students. Also included are college preparatory students in institutions of higher education. Before high schools spread across the nation, many public and private universities and colleges had their own preparatory programs. Youths often entered these programs directly from elementary school or after several years at their local high school. The fraction of secondary school graduates coming from all private programs, including an estimate of those from the preparatory departments of colleges and universities regardless of control, is given in Table Bc501–509.

Secondary schooling spread rapidly in the early twentieth century because schools were built and students in districts already having high schools were enticed to enter and remain. The increased demand for white-collar workers and for trained blue-collar workers spurred an interest in and demand for schooling beyond eighth grade. But in the nineteenth century secondary schools were institutions that generally trained youths to attend university. They often prepped pupils to pass the entrance examination of the local private college or the state university, if it had such an exam. High schools were reinvented beginning in the late nineteenth century to be places of practical and applied learning. They also, of course, retained courses of study to train youth to enter institutions of higher education.

Curriculum is difficult to track because of changes in subject matter, among other details. The Office or Department of Education requested information from secondary schools from 1889–1890 to 1981–1982 on the number of pupils taking various subjects. These data are measured in "pupil courses" and are expressed in Table Bc115–145 as the percentage of pupils taking a course. A course that occupied one hour per week is, by necessity, given equal weight to one that occupied five hours per week. Thus the total can exceed 400 percentage points, even if each student took an average of four full-time courses. The data were systematized in several ways beginning in 1982. Courses were measured in "Carnegie units," in which each Carnegie unit is a one-year course, generally equal to five 45-minute periods per week for the entire year (Table Bc146–257). The course of study for the entire high school program (at graduation) is given in Table Bc146–257, rather than an average for those currently in school (as often the case in Table Bc115–145). Whatever the defects of the historical data, they clearly show that the secondary school curriculum became more practically based and also broader in academic subject matter sometime in the 1920s.

As in the first transformation of American education, one may wonder what the effects of state legislation were in the "high school movement." All states passed compulsory education laws at some point in their history and most were accompanied by related legislation regarding child labor. The laws are complex and, prior to the late 1920s, the maximum compulsory age (often set at age 16) was generally not binding. Rather, youths could be excused if they obtained a work permit and had attained some minimum level of schooling. Although the jury is still out, there is considerable evidence that compulsory education laws did not "cause" much of the high school movement. States did, however, pass other legislation that aided secondary school expansion. One neglected piece of legislation is the "free tuition law." Because school districts were small and numerous in rural areas, not all districts would have had high schools. Families would be responsible to pay tuition to the district with the high school if they lived in a district without one but sent their child to the school. The "free tuition laws" made the sending district responsible for the payment of tuition. Most of these laws were passed in the 1910s and 1920s; Nebraska, for example, passed a "free tuition law" in 1907 and Iowa did in 1913.

A more recent development in secondary schooling is the General Educational Development (GED) credential. The GED was instituted during World War II (in 1942) to give veterans without a high school diploma a chance to earn credit for their informal education outside school. Civilians were allowed to take the examination in 1952. The data on individuals taking (and passing) the exam exist from 1971 and are given in Table Bc265–272.

At the start of this essay, it was noted that, by most accounts, the United States exceeded all other nations in mass elementary school education by the 1840s. It not only retained that lead, but with the "high school movement" it substantially increased it (Goldin and Katz 2003). Although Germany instituted various types of secondary schools in the early twentieth century, neither it nor any other European country was able to put their "masses" through nonvocational full-time secondary school until well after World War II. Thus, when the United States passed the GI Bill of Rights (1944), it could promise to put returning veterans through college because the median 18-year-old was already a high school graduate. No other country could achieve the same objective, nor would any for many years to come.

Tertiary or Higher Education

The third great transformation of American education – that to mass higher education – has been the most prolonged and is still ongoing. Part of the reason for the length of the transition, as noted previously, is that lower levels of education need higher ones to train teachers. All nations require institutions of higher education long before they are to be transformed into nations of highly educated people. Institutions of higher education serve many purposes, of course. Early in American history, for example, these institutions trained ministers, as well as lawyers and military and political leaders.

Institutions of higher education (B.A. granting, four-year) increased steadily in numbers in the United States across the nineteenth century. There was a burst of activity in the 1870s in the public sector and in the 1890s in the private sector.[4] The increase in public universities in the 1870s is attributable to the celebrated Morrill Land Grant Act of 1862, one of many pieces of legislation that had been previously defeated or vetoed but was passed and signed into law during the Civil War's 37th Congress. The Morrill Land Grant Act gave scrip in the form of federal land to each of the states "for the endowment, support and maintenance of at least one college where the leading object shall be – without excluding other scientific and classical studies and including military tactics – to teach branches of learning as are related to agriculture and mechanic arts" (Nevins 1962). The institutions could be publicly controlled, or privately controlled, as they were in states such as New York and New Jersey.

The Morrill Land Grant Act did not, however, set up the first state universities. By 1862 the majority of existing states outside the Northeast (nineteen out of twenty-four) already had a state institution of higher education; some states (for example, Virginia, Ohio) had more than one. States used their Morrill funds in various ways. Some established their first institution of higher education (for example, Nebraska), some gave the money to the existing state institution (for example, Wisconsin), and others established an additional university (for example, Michigan). It should also be noted that the Morrill Land Grant Act of 1862 was but the first of several related acts. An amendment to the original act extended the land grants to states as they entered the union. The second Morrill Act in 1890 set up annual appropriations to the land-grant institutions, and was indirectly responsible for establishing institutions of higher education that are now termed "historically black," by denying funds to states that did not provide facilities to black students (Table Bc719–736).

[4] Goldin and Katz (1999b) analyze institutions surviving to the 1930s.

The series in Table Bc510–522 on the number of institutions of higher education contain several complicated features. One concerns teacher-training institutions, also known as normal schools and teachers' colleges. As mentioned previously, teachers' colleges often began as two-year institutions but later became four-year institutions, able to grant the baccalaureate degree. Many of the state teachers' colleges were later made into the second tier of the state university system (as, for example, in California and Illinois) or the state university system itself (as in New York State). Thus, in the absence of detailed knowledge of the type of degrees awarded in each year, it is impossible to separate the institutions into two-year and four-year schools. Another complication is that state universities often establish separate campuses across the state. Before 1975 these branch campuses were treated as part of the central, or flagship, university, whereas after 1975 they have been treated as separate institutions.

The series on the enrollment of individuals in institutions of higher education (Table Bc523–536) is more complicated than that for elementary and secondary schools. In the first place, until the middle of the twentieth century many students in first-professional-degree programs were simultaneously in an undergraduate program. Undergraduates and first-professional-degree students are, therefore, combined for consistency in the historical series. The computed undergraduate enrollment rates (series Bc524) are therefore more inflated after the 1940s, when almost all professional students had an undergraduate degree, than they are before, when a large fraction of professional students did not have a preprofessional degree. Another difficulty is deciding what age group to use in the denominator. College students more widely disbursed by age than are those in K–12, and the inclusion of the professional and graduate students means that a wider age group is required. The standard is to use 18- to 24-year-olds.

The main gender difference in education in U.S. history has been the greater enrollment of men in colleges and universities, particularly four-year institutions. Ever since the early 1980s, however, women have enrolled in institutions of higher education and received B.A. degrees in greater numbers than have men (see Table Bc568–587 on degrees and Table Bc523–536 on enrollment). As can be seen in Figure Bc-E, the fraction of 20- to 24-year-olds enrolled in school is now greater for women than for men. It should

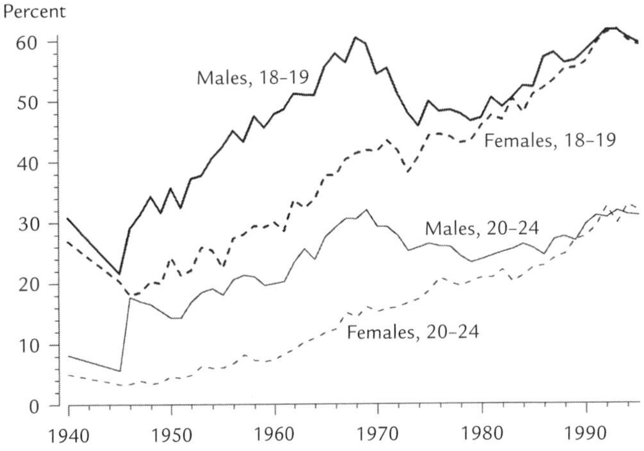

FIGURE Bc-E School enrollment rates, by age and sex: 1940–1995

Sources

Series Bc61, Bc63, Bc75, and Bc77.

also be noted that the fraction of males enrolled in school has only recently exceeded the peak level of the late 1960s. (The same is true for 20- to 24-year-olds.) This anomaly is attributable mainly to the war in Vietnam and draft deferments.

The transition to mass higher education in the United States is the result of several factors. One is the increase in high school graduation early in the twentieth century. Another is the GI Bill for World War II and Korean War veterans. Recent research has estimated the degree to which the GI Bills increased the level of undergraduate education (Stanley 2000). The bills were more than compensatory to returning GIs, as a higher fraction of men in each of the affected cohorts went to college than likely would have occurred had they not served in the wars (for more discussion of the GI Bill, see the essay on veterans in Chapter Ed). The diffusion of the Scholastic Aptitude Test (SAT), particularly in the 1940s, also democratized the admissions procedure for college. Finally, the explosion in the number of public junior colleges (also known as two-year or community colleges) in the 1970s allowed even the financially and scholastically constrained individual to continue in higher education (Table Bc510–522).

Interpretation

This essay has emphasized the leadership of the United States in education – the rapid increase in schooling in the early nineteenth century, the widening lead in the early to mid-twentieth century, and the high levels of tertiary education in the post–World War II period. At the beginning of the twenty-first century, however, many of the world's rich nations, and even some of the "newly industrialized economies," are closing the gap with the United States in educational quantities (for example, years of education, proportion of the population with a bachelor's degree) or, in the case of many European countries, have already closed the gap for young persons. More important, they are rapidly exceeding the United States with respect to educational quality, and even with respect to quantities adjusted by quality, although this concept is difficult to measure.

Many of the virtues of the U.S. educational system, which served Americans so well in the past, are fast becoming disadvantages and drawbacks. The extremely open and permissive system that enabled generations of Americans to continue to secondary school and college now means that there are no rigid standards and no national examinations. In the United States, those who perform in the upper half of the academic standards may be doing well, but those in the bottom half are often left behind. In many European countries, individuals in the bottom half are challenged and sorted by standardized tests or offered technical alternatives to the academic track. In addition, the localized nature of educational finance in the United States is, more and more, coming under attack for its inherent inequities. Affluent districts can afford good schools but poor districts cannot. Attempts at equalization within states, however, often have deleterious and unintended consequences for the school system as a whole, leaving the poor no better off than before and occasionally worse off (Hoxby 2001).

Describing educational change in American history is a much easier task than understanding why change occurred and what its consequences have been. With regard to advances in schooling, it is clear that there is a complicated interrelationship between the demand for educated workers and citizens and the public's response. Compulsory schooling legislation, as pointed out throughout this essay, was *not* the driving force behind "mass education." The public provision and the public funding of education, however, have been strong positive forces in spurring the three great transformations of American education.

But what are the consequences of more education for individuals, the society, and the economy? Many studies demonstrate a positive relationship between education and income and between schooling and productivity (for example, Goldin and Katz 2000). Some critics have claimed that "ability bias" – meaning that the most able continue the longest with their education – imparts an upward bias to these results. But several careful studies using plausibly exogenous variation in years of schooling have found that "ability bias" is a minor factor, and may even have an incorrect sign. Other literature, using cross-country variation in schooling and economic performance, has demonstrated that there are strong correlations between education and income and between schooling and economic growth. But we do not know if the correlations imply causality, for the countries with the highest growth rates could also be ones with institutions and communities that value education and enable human capital formation.

The United States became the richest nation in the world sometime in the late nineteenth century, and it has maintained that position ever since. The extraordinary record of American economic growth would appear to owe something to its achievement of mass education at each of the three levels, but that is a very difficult proposition to prove.

Appendix: A Note on Data Sources

The majority of the series are updated versions of those in *Historical Statistics of the United States* (1975). Many, however, are new to the volume. Most, although not all, of the series are updated annually by the National Center for Education Statistics (NCES) of the U.S. Department of Education and are published in the *Digest of Education Statistics*. Tables from recent editions of the *Digest of Education Statistics* and other NCES publications can be accessed at the NCES Internet site. In the process of updating, the NCES often revises previously published data and thus these series may in the future be altered in small ways by NCES. NCES also published *120 Years of American Education: A Statistical Portrait* (U.S. Department of Education 1993). The series presented here borrow from some of the tables in *120 Years*, which are updated versions of the historical series in the *Digest* and many from *Historical Statistics*.

The primary sources for most of the series begin in 1869–1870 with U.S. Office of Education, *Annual Reports of the Commissioner of Education*. These reports extend to 1916–1917, when they were superseded by the *Biennial Survey of Education in the United States*. The *Biennial*s, published for the even-numbered school years from 1917–1918 to 1957–1958, include general information on the U.S. school systems and reports from the state school systems and those of the cities. The *Biennials* also include a wealth of data on all levels of education and types of school, including private and commercial.

Much of the detailed data in the early *Biennial*s came from surveys of school districts, and complementary data came from surveys of the states. Sometime in the early 1930s, the Office of Education revised some of the earlier data to take account of obvious underreporting from the school districts. The Office never mentioned the procedure that was used nor commented that the revisions were being made. It simply published series with different numbers.[5]

The *Digest of Education Statistics*, published since 1962, picks up where the *Biennials* leave off. Recent tables can be accessed through the NCES Internet site. The sources for the *Digest* are surveys and estimates of the Department of Education and other agencies.

Private school data were often collected by the Office or Department of Education but, beginning in the 1950s, data from the National Catholic Welfare Conference have been relied on for the bulk of private students, those in Catholic schools. The pioneering work of Abbott L. Ferriss in rendering consistent many of the historical education series should also be mentioned (Ferriss 1969).

References

Bishop, John H. 1989. "Is the Test Score Decline Responsible for the Productivity Growth Decline?" *American Economic Review* 79 (March): 178–97.

Easterlin, Richard A. 1981. "Why Isn't the Whole World Developed?" *Journal of Economic History* 41 (March): 1–17.

Ferriss, Abbott L. 1969. *Indicators of Trends in American Education*. Russell Sage Foundation.

Fishlow, Albert. 1966. "The American Common School Revival: Fact or Fancy?" In Henry Rosovsky, editor. *Industrialization in Two Systems: Essays in Honor of Alexander Gerschenkron*. Wiley.

Goldin, Claudia. 1994. "Appendix to How America Graduated from High School: An Exploratory Study, 1910 to 1960." NBER Working Paper number H57 (June).

Goldin, Claudia. 1998. "America's Graduation from High School: The Evolution and Spread of Secondary Schooling in the Twentieth Century." *Journal of Economic History* 58 (June): 345–74.

[5] See Goldin (1994, 1998) for a discussion of the procedure that the Office of Education must have used in the construction of the secondary school data.

Goldin, Claudia, and Lawrence F. Katz. 1999a. "Human Capital and Social Capital: The Rise of Secondary Schooling in America, 1910–1940." *Journal of Interdisciplinary History* 26 (Spring): 683–723.

Goldin, Claudia, and Lawrence F. Katz. 1999b. "The Shaping of Higher Education: The Formative Years in the United States, 1890 to 1940." *Journal of Economic Perspectives* 13 (Winter): 37–62.

Goldin, Claudia, and Lawrence F. Katz. 2000. "Education and Income in the Early Twentieth Century: Evidence from the Prairies." *Journal of Economic History* 60 (September): 782–818.

Goldin, Claudia, and Lawrence F. Katz. 2003. "Why the United States Led in Education: Lessons from Secondary School Expansion, 1910 to 1940." In David Eltis, Frank Lewis, and Kenneth Sokoloff, editors. *Factor Endowments, Labor, and Economic Growth: Essays in Honor of Stanley Engerman*. Cambridge University Press.

Hoxby, Caroline M. 2001. "All School Equalizations Are Not Created Equal." *Quarterly Journal of Economics* 116 (November): 1189–1231.

Kaestle, Carl F. 1983. *Pillars of the Republic: Common Schools and American Society, 1780–1860*. Hill and Wang.

Kaestle, Carl F., and Maris A. Vinovskis. 1980. *Education and Social Change in Nineteenth-Century Massachusetts*. Cambridge University Press.

Krug, Edward A. 1963. *The Shaping of the American High School*. University of Wisconsin Press.

Margo, Robert A. 1990. *Race and Schooling in the South, 1880–1950: An Economic History*. University of Chicago Press.

Nevins, Allan. 1962. *The State Universities and Democracy*. University of Illinois Press.

Perlmann, Joel. 1988. *Ethnic Differences: Schooling and Social Structure among the Irish, Italians, Jews, and Blacks in an American City, 1880–1935*. Cambridge University Press.

Reese, William J. 1995. *The Origins of the American High School*. Yale University Press.

Ringer, Fritz K. 1979. *Education and Society in Modern Europe*. Indiana University Press.

Stanley, Marcus. 2000. "College Education and the Mid-Century G.I. Bills." Ph.D. dissertation, Kennedy School of Government and Public Affairs, Harvard University.

U.S. Bureau of the Census. 1975. *Historical Statistics of the United States: From Colonial Times to the Present*. U.S. Government Printing Office.

U.S. National Center for Education Statistics. 1993. *120 Years of American Education: A Statistical Portrait*. U.S. Government Printing Office.

KINDERGARTEN, ELEMENTARY SCHOOL, AND SECONDARY SCHOOL

Claudia Goldin

TABLE Bc1–6 Public school districts and elementary, secondary, and one-teacher schools, by public–private control: 1916–1996[1]

Contributed by Claudia Goldin

		Schools				
		Elementary		Secondary		
	Public school districts	Total	Public	Total	Public	One-teacher public schools
	Bc1 [2, 3]	Bc2 [4, 5]	Bc3	Bc4 [4, 5]	Bc5	Bc6 [6, 7]
School year ending	Number	Number	Number	Number	Number	Number
1916	—	—	—	—	—	200,100
1918	—	—	—	—	—	196,000
1920	—	—	—	—	—	190,700
1922	—	—	—	—	—	180,800
1924	—	—	—	—	—	169,700
1926	—	—	—	—	—	162,800
1928	—	—	—	—	—	156,100
1930	—	247,581	238,306	27,188	23,930	149,282
1932	127,531	242,484	232,750	29,698	26,409	143,391
1934	—	246,228	236,236	28,041	24,714	139,166
1936	—	242,166	232,174	28,979	25,652	131,101
1938	119,001	231,652	221,660	28,794	25,467	121,178
1940	117,108	—	—	—	—	113,600
1942	115,493	193,397	183,112	28,134	25,123	107,692
1944	111,383	180,190	169,905	31,984	28,973	96,302
1946	101,382	170,090	160,227	27,608	24,314	86,563
1948	94,926	156,831	146,760	28,776	25,484	75,096
1950	83,718	138,600	128,225	27,873	24,542	59,652
1952	71,094	134,429	123,763	27,068	23,746	50,742
1954	63,057	122,614	110,875	29,550	25,637	42,865
1956	54,859	116,799	104,427	29,933	26,046	34,964
1958	47,594	108,511	95,446	29,501	25,507	25,341
1960	40,520	105,427	91,853	29,845	25,784	20,213
1962	35,676	96,672	81,910	29,479	25,350	13,333
1964	31,705	—	77,584	30,882	26,431	9,895
1966	26,983	88,556	73,216	31,203	26,597	6,491
1968	22,010	85,779	70,879	31,311	27,011	4,146
1971	17,995	80,172	65,800	29,122	25,352	1,815
1974	16,730	—	65,070	—	25,906	1,365
1976	16,376	—	63,242	—	25,330	1,166
1977	16,271	79,029	62,644	31,282	25,378	1,111
1979	16,014	78,079	61,982	30,270	24,504	1,056
1981	15,912	77,861	61,069	30,040	24,362	921
1983	15,824	—	59,656	—	23,988	798
1984	15,747	79,954	59,082	31,809	23,947	838
1985	—	—	58,827	—	23,916	825
1987	15,713	—	60,784	—	23,389	763
1988	15,577	82,704	59,754	32,259	23,841	729
1989	15,376	—	60,176	—	23,638	583
1990	15,367	—	60,699	—	23,461	630
1991	15,358	83,563	61,340	32,449	23,460	617
1992	15,173	85,262	61,739	32,530	23,248	569
1993	15,025	—	62,225	—	23,220	430
1994	14,881	86,269	62,726	33,934	23,379	442
1995	14,772	—	63,572	—	23,668	458
1996	14,883	—	63,961	—	23,793	474

[1] Schools with both elementary and secondary programs are included under both elementary and secondary headings.

[2] Includes operating and nonoperating districts.

[3] Because of expanded survey coverage, data after the school year beginning in 1983 are not directly comparable with figures for earlier years.

[4] Data for private schools in most years are partly estimated.

[5] Data for private schools after the school year ending in 1983 are from sample surveys and should not be compared directly to the data for earlier years.

[6] The wording in the reports changes over time from a one-room schoolhouse to a one-teacher schoolhouse, but they appear to be measuring the same construct.

[7] Data prior to 1930 are estimated on the basis of the number of schools that responded to state surveys, whereas subsequent data are the number of schools on file with the state, not all of which responded to the surveys.

Sources

1916–1956, U.S. Bureau of the Census, *Historical Statistics of the United States* (1975), series H412–H417. The original sources are: 1916, U.S. Office of

TABLE Bc1–6 Public school districts and elementary, secondary, and one-teacher schools, by public–private control: 1916–1996 *Continued*

Education, *Annual Report of the United States Commissioner of Education*; 1918–1956, U.S. Office of Education, *Biennial Survey of Education in the United States*, Statistics of State School Systems, various issues; 1958–1996, U.S. Department of Education, *Digest of Education Statistics 1997* (1997), Table 89.

Documentation

A school is defined as a division of the school system consisting of a group of pupils comprising one or more grade levels, organized as one unit with one or more teachers to give instruction of a defined type, and housed in a school plant of one or more buildings. More than one school may be housed in one school plant, as is the case when the elementary and secondary programs are housed in the same school plant. The actual operation of schools is generally the responsibility of local school systems. The local basic administrative unit or school district, series Bc1, is an area organized as a quasi-corporation under the jurisdiction of an elected or appointed board of education responsible for the administration of all public schools in the area. School districts provide the machinery through which local control of schools is exercised, and are largely responsible for the location and size of schools, the types of educational programs and services offered, and the amount of financial support to be provided locally.

A public school is defined as one operated by publicly elected or appointed school officials in which the program and activities are under the control of these officials and that is supported by public funds. School data, prior to 1960, are for public elementary and secondary day schools in the contiguous United States. Excluded are public schools in the outlying areas of the United States, public schools operated directly by the federal government on military reservations or exclusively for Native Americans, public residential schools for special needs children, and subcollegiate departments of institutions of higher education.

Nonpublic schools, although subject to certain regulatory controls of the state, are under the operational control of private individuals or church-affiliated or nonsectarian institutions. Whether operated on a profit or nonprofit basis, nonpublic schools are generally supported by private funds as distinguished from public funds.

Series Bc6. One-teacher public schools are those in which one teacher is employed to teach all grades authorized in the school, regardless of the number of rooms in the building.

TABLE Bc7–18 School enrollment and pupil–teacher ratios, by grades K–8 and 9–12 and by public–private control: 1869–1996[1, 2, 3]

Contributed by Claudia Goldin

	Public and private schools		Public schools					Private schools				
	Enrollment, K–12		Enrollment			Pupils-to-teacher ratio		Enrollment			Pupil–teacher ratio	
	Number	Per 100 persons 5–17 years old	Grades K–12	Grades K–8	Grades 9–12	Grades K–8	Grades 9–12	Grades K–12	Grades K–8	Grades 9–12	Grades K–8	Grades 9–12
	Bc7	Bc8 [4, 5]	Bc9	Bc10	Bc11	Bc12 [6]	Bc13 [6]	Bc14 [7]	Bc15 [7]	Bc16 [7]	Bc17 [6, 7]	Bc18 [6, 7]
School year beginning	Thousand	Per 100	Thousand	Thousand	Thousand	Ratio	Ratio	Thousand	Thousand	Thousand	Ratio	Ratio
1869	—	57.0 [9]	6,872	—	—	—	—	—	—	—	—	—
1870	—	—	7,562	7,481	80	—	—	—	—	—	—	—
1871	—	—	7,815	—	—	—	—	—	—	—	—	—
1872	—	—	8,004	—	—	—	—	—	—	—	—	—
1873	—	—	8,444	—	—	—	—	—	—	—	—	—
1874	—	—	8,786	—	—	—	—	—	—	—	—	—
1875	—	—	8,869	—	—	—	—	—	—	—	—	—
1876	—	—	8,965	—	—	—	—	—	—	—	—	—
1877	—	—	9,439	—	—	—	—	—	—	—	—	—
1878	—	—	9,504	—	—	—	—	—	—	—	—	—
1879	—	65.5 [9]	9,868	9,757	110	—	—	—	—	—	—	—
1880	—	—	10,001	—	—	—	—	—	—	—	—	—
1881	—	—	10,212	—	—	—	—	—	—	—	—	—
1882	—	—	10,652	—	—	—	—	—	—	—	—	—
1883	—	—	10,982	—	—	—	—	—	—	—	—	—
1884	—	—	11,398	—	—	—	—	—	—	—	—	—
1885	—	—	11,664	—	—	—	—	—	—	—	—	—
1886	—	—	11,885	—	—	—	—	—	—	—	—	—
1887	—	—	12,183	—	—	—	—	—	—	—	—	—
1888	13,661	—	12,392	—	—	—	—	1,269	—	—	—	—
1889	14,334	77.3	12,723	12,520 [10]	203	—	—	1,611	1,516 [10]	95	—	13.2
1890	14,541	—	13,050	12,839	212	—	—	1,491	1,392	98	—	—
1891	14,556	—	13,256	13,016	240	—	—	1,300	1,199	101	—	—
1892	14,826	—	13,483	13,229	254	—	—	1,343	1,240	102	—	—
1893	15,314	—	13,995	13,706	289	—	—	1,319	1,200	119	—	—
1894	15,455	—	14,244	13,894	350	—	—	1,211	1,093	118	—	—
1895	15,834	—	14,499	14,118	380	—	—	1,335	1,228	107	—	—
1896	16,140	—	14,823	14,414	409	—	—	1,317	1,209	108	—	—
1897	16,459	—	15,104	14,654	450	—	—	1,355	1,250	105	—	—
1898	16,474	—	15,176	14,700	476	—	—	1,298	1,194	104	—	—
1899	16,855	78.1	15,503	14,984	519	—	—	1,352	1,241	111	—	10.9

Notes appear at end of table

(continued)

TABLE Bc7–18 School enrollment and pupil–teacher ratios, by grades K–8 and 9–12 and by public–private control: 1869–1996 *Continued*

	Public and private schools		Public schools					Private schools				
	Enrollment, K–12		Enrollment			Pupils-to-teacher ratio		Enrollment			Pupil–teacher ratio	
	Number	Per 100 persons 5–17 years old	Grades K–12	Grades K–8	Grades 9–12	Grades K–8	Grades 9–12	Grades K–12	Grades K–8	Grades 9–12	Grades K–8	Grades 9–12
	Bc7	Bc8 [4, 5]	Bc9	Bc10	Bc11	Bc12 [6]	Bc13 [6]	Bc14 [7]	Bc15 [7]	Bc16 [7]	Bc17 [6, 7]	Bc18 [6, 7]
School year beginning	Thousand	Per 100	Thousand	Thousand	Thousand	Ratio	Ratio	Thousand	Thousand	Thousand	Ratio	Ratio
1900	17,072	79.3	15,703	15,161	542	—	—	1,370	1,262	108	—	—
1901	17,126	78.6	15,917	15,367	551	—	—	1,209	1,104	105	—	—
1902	17,205	77.9	16,009	15,417	592	—	—	1,196	1,094	102	—	—
1903	17,560	78.7	16,256	15,620	636	—	—	1,304	1,201	103	—	—
1904	17,806	78.8	16,468	15,789	680	—	—	1,338	1,231	107	—	—
1905	18,056	79.0	16,642	15,919	723	—	—	1,414	1,312	102	—	—
1906	18,292	79.1	16,891	16,140	751	—	—	1,402	1,305	97	—	—
1907	18,537	79.2	17,062	16,292	770	—	—	1,475	1,383	92	—	—
1908	18,917	79.9	17,506	16,665	841	—	—	1,411	1,317	94	—	—
1909	19,372	80.7	17,814	16,899	915	34.4	—	1,558	1,441	117	—	10.5
1910	19,636	80.5	18,035	17,050	985	—	—	1,601	1,471	131	—	—
1911	19,830	80.3	18,183	17,078	1,105	—	—	1,647	1,506	141	—	—
1912	20,348	81.3	18,609	17,474	1,135	—	—	1,739	1,591	148	—	—
1913	20,935	82.1	19,154	17,935	1,219	—	—	1,781	1,626	155	—	—
1914	21,474	82.7	19,704	18,375	1,329	—	—	1,770	1,615	155	—	—
1915	22,172	84.2	20,352	18,896	1,456	—	—	1,820	1,665	157	—	—
1917	22,516	83.1	20,854	18,920	1,934	32.6	23.0	1,662	1,504	159	—	—
1919	23,278	84.4	21,578	19,378	2,200	33.6	21.6	1,699	1,486	214	—	12.3
1921	24,820	87.1	23,239	20,366	2,873	34.3	22.2	1,581	1,355	226	—	—
1923	26,016	86.6	24,289	20,899	3,390	33.9	23.5	1,727	1,473	254	—	—
1925	27,180	90.0	24,741	20,984	3,757	32.6	22.2	2,439	2,143	296	—	—
1927	27,810	89.9	25,180	21,268	3,911	33.1	20.7	2,631	2,289	341	—	—
1929	28,329	90.2	25,678	21,279	4,399	33.2	20.6	2,651	2,310	341	—	14.0
1931	29,061	91.8	26,275	21,135 [10]	5,140	33.0	22.2	2,786	2,383 [10]	403	—	—
1933	29,163	92.4	26,434	20,765 [10]	5,669	33.5	24.9	2,729	2,368 [10]	360	—	—
1935	29,006	92.4	26,367	20,393 [10]	5,975	33.8	22.3	2,639	2,251 [10]	387	34.0	15.3
1937	28,663	92.6	25,975	19,748	6,227	33.2	22.0	2,687	2,241	447	33.4	16.0
1939	28,045	93.0	25,434	18,832	6,601	32.7	22.0	2,611	2,153	458	33.2	15.2
1941	27,179	92.3	24,562	18,175	6,388	32.5	21.3	2,617	2,133	483	32.6	15.3
1943	25,758	89.3	23,267	17,713	5,554	32.9	19.2	2,491	2,070	421	—	—
1945	26,124	91.6	23,300	17,678	5,622	32.6	19.4	2,825	2,259	565	35.0	15.5
1947	26,998	93.2	23,945	18,291	5,653	33.0	18.5	3,054	2,451	602	36.4	14.4
1949	28,492	94.3	25,111	19,387	5,725	32.9	17.7	3,380	2,708	672	35.6	15.9
1951	30,372	97.0	26,563	20,681	5,882	33.4	17.1	3,809	3,154	656	38.3	15.7
1953	33,175	96.7	28,836	22,546	6,290	34.3	16.8	4,339	3,592	747	42.3	15.2
1955	35,872	97.1	31,163	24,290	6,873	30.2	20.9	4,709	3,886	823	40.4	15.7
1956	37,303	97.4	32,334	25,016	7,318	29.6	21.2	4,968	4,092	877	38.8	17.3
1957	38,756	97.7	33,529	25,669	7,860	29.1	21.3	5,227	4,297	931	38.4	17.0
1958	40,290	97.9	34,839	26,581	8,258	28.7	21.7	5,451 [11]	4,459 [11]	993 [11]	38.8 [11]	18.9 [11]
1959	40,857	98.0	35,182	26,911	8,271	28.7	21.5	5,675	4,640	1,035	38.7	18.5
1960	43,070	97.5	37,260	28,439	8,821	28.4	21.7	5,810 [11]	4,752 [11]	1,058 [11]	36.1 [11]	18.6 [11]
1961	44,146	97.5	38,253	28,686	9,566	28.3	21.7	5,893 [11]	4,765 [11]	1,128 [11]	39.0 [11]	19.0 [11]
1962	45,798	98.2	39,746	29,374	10,372	28.5	21.7	6,052 [11]	4,850 [11]	1,202 [11]	36.3 [11]	18.5 [11]
1963	47,199	98.2	41,025	29,915	11,110	28.4	21.5	6,174 [11]	4,910 [11]	1,265 [11]	35.2 [11]	18.6 [11]
1964	47,716	98.1	41,416	30,025	11,391	27.9	21.5	6,300	5,000	1,300	34.2	18.3
1965	48,473	96.9	42,173	30,563	11,610	27.6	20.8	6,300	4,900	1,400	33.3	18.4
1966	49,239	97.2	43,039	31,145	11,894	26.9	20.3	6,200	4,800	1,400	32.7	18.4
1967	49,891	97.1	43,891	31,641	12,250	26.3	20.3	6,000	4,600	1,400	31.1	18.4
1968	50,744	97.6	44,944	32,226	12,718	25.4	20.4	5,800	4,400	1,400	29.9	17.9
1969	51,050	97.5	45,550	32,513	13,037	24.7	20.0	5,500	4,200	1,300	27.8	16.7
1970	51,257	97.5	45,894	32,558	13,336	24.3	19.8	5,363	4,052	1,311	26.5	16.4
1971	51,271	97.5	46,071	32,318	13,753	24.9	19.3	5,200	3,900	1,300	25.7	16.7
1972	50,726	97.0	45,726	31,879	13,848	23.9	19.1	5,000	3,700	1,300	24.0	16.9
1973	50,445	97.2	45,445	31,401	14,044	23.0	19.3	5,000	3,700	1,300	23.6	16.5
1974	50,073	97.2	45,073	30,971	14,103	22.6	18.7	5,000	3,700	1,300	22.6	16.0
1975	49,819	97.6	44,819	30,515	14,304	21.7	18.8	5,000	3,700	1,300	21.5	15.7
1976	49,478	97.7	44,311	29,997	14,314	21.8	18.5	5,167	3,825	1,342	20.9	15.8
1977	48,717	97.6	43,577	29,375	14,203	21.1	18.2	5,140	3,797	1,343	20.0	15.1
1978	47,637	97.1	42,551	28,463	14,088	21.0	17.3	5,086	3,732	1,353	20.2	15.6
1979	46,651	97.1	41,651	28,034	13,616	20.6	17.2	5,000	3,700	1,300	19.7	14.8

Notes appear at end of table

TABLE Bc7–18 School enrollment and pupil–teacher ratios, by grades K–8 and 9–12 and by public–private control: 1869–1996 *Continued*

	Public and private schools		Public schools					Private schools				
	Enrollment, K–12		Enrollment			Pupils-to-teacher ratio		Enrollment			Pupil–teacher ratio	
	Number	Per 100 persons 5–17 years old	Grades K–12	Grades K–8	Grades 9–12	Grades K–8	Grades 9–12	Grades K–12	Grades K–8	Grades 9–12	Grades K–8	Grades 9–12
	Bc7	Bc8 [4, 5]	Bc9	Bc10	Bc11	Bc12 [6]	Bc13 [6]	Bc14 [7]	Bc15 [7]	Bc16 [7]	Bc17 [6, 7]	Bc18 [6, 7]
School year beginning	Thousand	Per 100	Thousand	Thousand	Thousand	Ratio	Ratio	Thousand	Thousand	Thousand	Ratio	Ratio
1980	46,208	97.8	40,877	27,647	13,231	20.4	16.8	5,331	3,992	1,339	18.8	15.0
1981	45,544	98.3	40,044	27,280	12,764	20.3	16.9	5,500	4,100	1,400	18.6	15.2
1982	45,166	98.9	39,566	27,161	12,405	20.2	16.6	5,600	4,200	1,400	18.2	14.9
1983	44,967	99.6	39,252	26,981	12,271	19.9	16.4	5,715	4,315	1,400	18.0	14.4
1984	44,908	99.9	39,208	26,905	12,304	19.7	16.1	5,700	4,300	1,400	17.7	14.4
1985	44,979	100.0	39,422	27,034	12,388	19.5	15.8	5,557	4,195	1,362	17.1	14.0
1986	45,205	100.1	39,753	27,420	12,333	19.3	15.7	5,452	4,116	1,336	16.5	13.6
1987	45,488	100.4	40,008	27,933	12,076	19.3	15.2	5,479	4,232	1,247	16.4	13.1
1988	45,430	100.1	40,189	28,501	11,687	19.0	14.9	5,241	4,036	1,206	16.1	12.8
1989	45,898	101.3	40,543	29,152	11,390	19.0	14.6	5,355	4,162	1,193	15.1	11.7
1990	46,448	102.5	41,217	29,878	11,338	19.0	14.6	5,232	4,095	1,137	16.1	11.3
1991	47,246	102.9	42,047	30,506	11,541	18.9	14.9	5,199	4,074	1,125	16.0	11.1
1992	48,198	103.3	42,823	31,088	11,735	18.9	15.1	5,375	4,212	1,163	16.2	11.3
1993	48,936	103.2	43,465	31,504	11,961	18.8	15.2	5,471	4,280	1,191	16.3	11.5
1994	49,707	102.9	44,111	31,898	12,213	19.0	14.9	5,596	4,360	1,236	16.8	11.2
1995	50,528	102.5	44,840	32,341	12,500	19.1	14.9	5,688	4,427	1,260	16.7	11.3
1996 [8]	—	—	45,229	—	12,874	—	—	—	—	1,293	—	—

[1] In censuses prior to 1965, enrollment data include students who enrolled at any time during the school year. Enrollment ratios based on cumulative enrollment figures tend to be approximately 1 to 2 percentage points higher than counts based on fall enrollment.

[2] In later years, data for grades K–8 include a relatively small number of prekindergarten students. Data for grades 9–12 contain a small number of postgraduate students.

[3] In censuses prior to 1959, data are for the entire school year; thereafter, for fall only.

[4] Population data for 1870 through 1961 include U.S. population overseas; data for later years are for the U.S. resident population only.

[5] Population data for 1870 to 1890 are from the decennial census. Data for later years are based on counts of population for July 1 preceding the school year.

[6] Change in the calculation of the ratio in 1956. See text.

[7] Data for most years are at least partially estimated. Beginning in 1980, data include estimates for an expanded universe of private schools. Therefore, these totals may differ from figures shown in other tables, and direct comparisons with earlier years should not be made.

[8] Public elementary and secondary data are based on "Early Estimates" surveys. The Early Estimates system is designed to allow the National Center for Education Statistics to report data for the school year currently in progress. Other data are projected.

[9] Underlying data are for public elementary and secondary schools only.

[10] Excludes kindergarten.

[11] Estimated by linear interpolation.

Sources

1869–1958, U.S. Department of Education, *120 Years of American Education: A Statistical Portrait* (1993), Table 9. The original sources are: 1869–1915, U.S. Office of Education, *Annual Report of the United States Commissioner of Education*, various issues; 1917–1957, U.S. Office of Education, *Biennial Survey of Education in the United States*, Statistics of State School Systems, various issues; 1959–1996, U.S. Department of Education, *Digest of Education Statistics 1997* (1997), Table 3. When the data in *120 Years* differ from those in *Digest 1997*, the latter is relied on.

Series Bc8, for number of 5- to 17-year-olds, U.S. Bureau of the Census, *Current Population Reports*, series P-25, numbers 519, 917, 1000, 1022, 1045, 1057, and 1092, and *U.S. Population Estimates, by Age, Sex, Race, and Hispanic Origin: 1990–1995*, PPL-41. Series Bc10, 1910–1915, revisions provided by Thomas D. Snyder, of the National Center for Education Statistics. Series Bc12–13 and Bc17–18, for number of teachers, Abbott L. Ferriss, *Indicators of Trends in American Education* (Russell Sage Foundation, 1969), series B-5, B-6, B-9, and B-10.

Documentation

Enrollment and other figures in censuses prior to 1959 for public day schools, grades K–12, include just the contiguous United States. Generally excluded from the entire series are public schools in the outlying areas of the United States, public schools operated directly by the federal government on military bases or exclusively for Native Americans, public residential schools for exceptional children, and subcollegiate departments of institutions of higher education. The excluded category represents a small percentage of all schools. There has been no comprehensive data collection effort for these schools in recent years. Only regular day school pupils are included; pupils enrolled in night schools and summer schools are excluded.

Private school figures are not strictly comparable over time. For example, in some of the earlier years, the figures may include enrollment of secondary pupils in subcollegiate departments of institutions of higher education and normal schools. Enrollment figures in censuses prior to 1976 do not include private schools for exceptional children or private vocational or trade schools. They cover only regular day school pupils. Summer school pupils are excluded in all years.

The enrollment information in the *Biennial Survey of Education* was collected at the state level and represents a cumulative count of the total number of different pupils registered at any time during the school year in each state. Pupils enrolled in two or more states during the school year may be counted more than once. Beginning with 1965, enrollment data come from fall enrollment counts (pupils enrolled in a given school unit on a particular fall date).

Many earlier enrollment series classify enrollments by instructional level (elementary or secondary). The National Center for Education Statistics (NCES) now collects enrollment data by grade, not instructional level. Students enrolled in grades K–8 do not necessarily correspond one-to-one with students enrolled in elementary schools, nor do students enrolled in grades 9–12 correspond one-to-one with students enrolled in secondary schools. Junior high schools with grades 7–9 may be classified as secondary schools, although some of their pupils would be considered as enrolled in elementary grades.

Series Bc8. The figures for total enrollment per 100 persons, 5–17 years old, divide the total enrollment numbers, series Bc7, by the number of persons 5–17 years old as of July 1 of the academic year. For example, for 1992, the ratio is the result of dividing enrollment for the academic year 1992–1993 by the number of persons 5–17 years old on July 1, 1992. This rate has been increasing steadily, and in the 1980s exceeded 100 percent, where it

(continued)

TABLE Bc7–18 School enrollment and pupil–teacher ratios, by grades K–8 and 9–12 and by public–private control: 1869–1996 *Continued*

has remained. This outcome is the result of several factors. The population data come from the census, whereas the enrollment data come from reports from state school systems. Some immigrants are not included in the census but are included in school enrollment data. The school enrollment data can double-count some students; the census should not. Also, some enrolled students are outside of the 5- to 17-year-old age range the July before the school year.

Series Bc12–13 and Bc17–18. The "pupil-teacher ratio" is defined as the number of pupils enrolled divided by the number of classroom teachers. In past series, the methods of counting both pupils and teachers have varied. At times, the pupil counts have been based on average daily attendance or average daily membership, or cumulative enrollment rather than on fall enrollment. Prior to the 1940s, the available figures on "teachers" generally included librarians and guidance and psychological personnel as well as classroom teachers. When considering pupil-teacher ratios by instructional level, there are further complications. Under current NCES data collection practices, teacher data are grouped by instructional level (elementary, secondary), but the enrollment data, as discussed in the preceding, are given by grade level. The mapping from one to the other is not exact in large measure because certain teachers who instruct seventh and eighth grade students often are counted as "secondary school" teachers. After NCES discontinued the collection of teacher and enrollment data by elementary and secondary instructional levels in the mid-1960s, the distribution was estimated based on data collected by the National Education Association (NEA). Proportions of teachers and enrollments by instructional level from the NEA publication "Estimates of School Statistics" were used to distribute counts of teachers and enrollments for the purpose of calculating pupil-teacher ratios by instructional level. The series given here are based on data adjusted for consistency with current definitions, and are not replicable for all years by simply dividing enrollment by teachers. It should also be realized that national averages tend to obscure significant differences in pupil-teacher ratios, such as those between urban and rural areas and between large and small schools.

Series Bc12–13 and Bc17–18. As reported here, the data show a considerable jump between 1954 and 1956. This reflects a change in the calculation of the ratio. Before 1956, some junior high school teachers were classified as secondary school teachers, while their pupils in seventh and eighth grades were classified as elementary school pupils, causing K–8 (or elementary) pupil-teacher ratios to appear higher than they were and 9–12 (or secondary) pupil-teacher ratios to appear lower than they were. The most recent revisions of these data adjust for this bias back to 1956, but not for earlier years.

TABLE Bc19–37 Enrollment in public elementary and secondary schools, by grade: 1910–1995[1]

Contributed by Claudia Goldin

	Total enrollment in public schools	Public schools enrollment, K–8 (elementary)										
		Total	Kindergarten	First grade	Second grade	Third grade	Fourth grade	Fifth grade	Sixth grade	Seventh grade	Eighth grade	Ungraded
	Bc19	Bc20	Bc21 [2]	Bc22	Bc23	Bc24	Bc25	Bc26	Bc27	Bc28	Bc29	Bc30 [3]
School year beginning	Thousand	Thousand	Thousand	Thousand	Thousand	Thousand	Thousand	Thousand	Thousand	Thousand	Thousand	Thousand
1910	18,035	16,878	327	3,890	2,450	2,301	2,201	1,870	1,523	1,258	1,059	—
1911	18,183	16,982	348	3,876	2,445	2,295	2,212	1,880	1,547	1,281	1,098	—
1912	18,609	17,276	370	3,922	2,468	2,316	2,248	1,910	1,589	1,319	1,133	—
1913	19,154	17,722	391	3,986	2,496	2,374	2,288	1,976	1,664	1,369	1,178	—
1914	19,704	18,143	409	4,043	2,536	2,412	2,341	2,022	1,720	1,419	1,241	—
1915	20,352	18,641	434	4,115	2,585	2,476	2,403	2,076	1,784	1,475	1,293	—
1916 [4]	20,603	18,808	434	4,225	2,600	2,504	2,426	2,105	1,814	1,481	1,219	—
1917	20,854	18,920	433	4,323	2,608	2,524	2,441	2,128	1,839	1,483	1,141	—
1918 [4]	21,216	19,149	457	4,322	2,623	2,511	2,499	2,141	1,865	1,537	1,195	—
1919	21,578	19,378	481	4,321	2,638	2,498	2,556	2,153	1,890	1,592	1,248	—
1920 [4]	22,409	19,872	505	4,249	2,743	2,607	2,558	2,221	1,974	1,668	1,346	—
1921	23,239	20,366	529	4,177	2,849	2,716	2,560	2,290	2,058	1,744	1,444	—
1922 [4]	23,764	20,633	569	4,180	2,831	2,756	2,634	2,365	2,089	1,795	1,412	—
1923	24,289	20,899	610	4,184	2,813	2,796	2,708	2,441	2,121	1,846	1,380	—
1924 [4]	24,650	20,999	600	4,049	2,800	2,730	2,696	2,514	2,186	1,931	1,493	—
1925	24,741	20,984	673	3,977	2,820	2,729	2,662	2,473	2,234	1,927	1,488	—
1926 [4]	24,961	21,126	684	4,074	2,818	2,696	2,647	2,454	2,239	1,974	1,539	—
1927	25,180	21,268	695	4,171	2,817	2,662	2,632	2,435	2,243	2,022	1,590	—
1928 [4]	25,429	21,274	709	4,161	2,810	2,697	2,616	2,409	2,250	2,026	1,596	—
1929	25,678	21,279	723	4,151	2,803	2,732	2,599	2,382	2,256	2,030	1,601	—
1930 [4]	25,977	21,207	712	4,041	2,790	2,698	2,594	2,423	2,267	2,041	1,641	—
1931	26,275	21,135	701	3,930	2,776	2,664	2,589	2,463	2,278	2,053	1,682	—
1932 [4]	26,355	20,950	649	3,826	2,704	2,638	2,581	2,448	2,283	2,120	1,701	—
1933	26,434	20,765	602	3,717	2,632	2,612	2,573	2,433	2,288	2,187	1,721	—
1934 [4]	26,401	20,579	604	3,624	2,595	2,568	2,536	2,433	2,304	2,185	1,730	—
1935	26,367	20,393	607	3,530	2,558	2,525	2,499	2,433	2,319	2,182	1,740	—
1936 [4]	26,171	20,070	607	3,424	2,522	2,485	2,451	2,388	2,286	2,178	1,731	—
1937	25,975	19,748	607	3,317	2,487	2,444	2,403	2,342	2,253	2,173	1,722	—
1938 [4]	25,704	19,290	601	3,168	2,410	2,388	2,362	2,295	2,214	2,140	1,712	—
1939	25,434	18,832	595	3,018	2,333	2,332	2,322	2,248	2,176	2,108	1,701	—

Notes appear at end of table

TABLE Bc19–37 Enrollment in public elementary and secondary schools, by grade: 1910–1995 *Continued*

	Total enrollment in public schools	Public schools enrollment, K–8 (elementary)										
		Total	Kindergarten	First grade	Second grade	Third grade	Fourth grade	Fifth grade	Sixth grade	Seventh grade	Eighth grade	Ungraded
	Bc19	Bc20	Bc21 [2]	Bc22	Bc23	Bc24	Bc25	Bc26	Bc27	Bc28	Bc29	Bc30 [3]
School year beginning	Thousand	Thousand	Thousand	Thousand	Thousand	Thousand	Thousand	Thousand	Thousand	Thousand	Thousand	Thousand
1940 [4]	25,296	18,582	613	2,992	2,286	2,263	2,271	2,211	2,156	2,050	1,691	—
1941	24,562	18,175	626	2,931	2,215	2,175	2,197	2,166	2,124	2,061	1,680	—
1942 [4]	24,155	18,033	665	2,919	2,229	2,180	2,149	2,102	2,071	2,023	1,695	—
1943	23,267	17,713	697	2,879	2,221	2,163	2,080	2,017	1,998	1,965	1,694	—
1944 [4]	23,226	17,666	734	2,882	2,266	2,173	2,084	2,008	1,951	1,898	1,671	—
1945	23,300	17,678	773	2,895	2,319	2,191	2,094	2,006	1,910	1,837	1,654	—
1946 [4]	23,659	17,821	873	2,896	2,320	2,205	2,119	2,012	1,907	1,850	1,639	—
1947	23,945	18,291	989	2,951	2,363	2,259	2,183	2,055	1,940	1,898	1,653	—
1948 [4]	24,477	18,818	1,016	3,067	2,503	2,315	2,221	2,089	1,995	1,919	1,694	—
1949	25,111	19,387	1,034	3,170	2,645	2,396	2,254	2,151	2,056	1,947	1,734	—
1950 [4]	25,706	19,900	941	3,053	2,739	2,600	2,358	2,211	2,117	1,995	1,885	—
1951	26,563	20,681	1,272	2,957	2,670	2,718	2,559	2,320	2,166	2,083	1,936	—
1952 [4]	27,507	21,625	1,399	3,358	2,639	2,633	2,684	2,520	2,276	2,143	1,973	—
1953	28,836	22,546	1,474	3,666	2,940	2,569	2,565	2,607	2,449	2,242	2,032	—
1954 [4]	30,045	23,471	1,415	3,518	3,391	2,896	2,535	2,523	2,584	2,432	2,177	—
1955	31,163	24,290	1,564	3,495	3,242	3,291	2,848	2,481	2,470	2,542	2,357	—
1956	32,334	25,016	1,675	3,491	3,241	3,183	3,238	2,808	2,443	2,476	2,460	—
1957	33,529	25,669	1,772	3,587	3,214	3,176	3,128	3,181	2,759	2,458	2,395	—
1958	34,839	26,581	1,834	3,679	3,346	3,179	3,142	3,099	3,136	2,785	2,381	—
1959	36,087	27,602	1,923	3,733	3,436	3,302	3,146	3,118	3,070	3,173	2,701	—
1960 [4]	37,260	28,439	2,000	3,822	3,502	3,405	3,278	3,131	3,095	3,123	3,083	—
1961	38,253	28,686	2,065	3,857	3,568	3,428	3,343	3,218	3,065	3,122	3,021	—
1962 [4]	39,746	29,374	2,162	3,928	3,630	3,518	3,391	3,332	3,190	3,140	3,083	—
1963 [4]	41,025	29,915	2,177	4,023	3,705	3,560	3,467	3,366	3,299	3,241	3,077	—
1964 [4]	42,280	30,652	2,250	4,014	3,800	3,662	3,523	3,465	3,362	3,363	3,212	—
1965	42,068	30,466	2,260	3,915	3,644	3,595	3,476	3,377	3,312	3,297	3,186	404
1966	43,042	31,162	2,370	3,954	3,696	3,615	3,580	3,463	3,369	3,409	3,272	433
1967	43,890	31,643	2,420	3,980	3,723	3,659	3,580	3,562	3,450	3,454	3,357	459
1968	44,903	32,181	2,511	3,926	3,758	3,692	3,629	3,573	3,555	3,552	3,423	561
1969	45,550	32,513	2,545	3,869	3,716	3,720	3,660	3,621	3,568	3,667	3,520	628
1970	45,894	32,558	2,564	3,817	3,654	3,663	3,675	3,635	3,598	3,662	3,601	690
1971	46,071	32,318	2,483	3,570	3,587	3,612	3,623	3,662	3,622	3,710	3,635	814
1972	45,726	31,879	2,503	3,352	3,381	3,533	3,554	3,597	3,639	3,713	3,649	959
1973	45,445	31,401	2,655	3,239	3,192	3,336	3,505	3,538	3,592	3,741	3,676	927
1974	45,073	30,971	2,801	3,198	3,106	3,169	3,345	3,510	3,559	3,712	3,708	863
1975	44,819	30,515	2,972	3,238	3,027	3,038	3,112	3,281	3,476	3,619	3,636	1,116
1976	44,311	29,997	2,918	3,332	3,086	2,986	3,025	3,116	3,298	3,572	3,578	1,084
1977	43,577	29,375	2,742	3,295	3,200	3,059	2,979	3,019	3,111	3,385	3,534	1,051
1978	42,551	28,463	2,652	3,062	3,148	3,158	3,046	2,980	3,036	3,228	3,355	798
1979	41,651	28,034	2,675	2,937	2,909	3,120	3,148	3,055	2,999	3,128	3,171	894
1980	40,877	27,647	2,689	2,894	2,800	2,893	3,107	3,130	3,038	3,085	3,086	924
1981	40,044	27,280	2,688	2,951	2,782	2,806	2,918	3,127	3,180	3,183	3,059	587
1982	39,566	27,161	2,846	2,937	2,790	2,763	2,798	2,912	3,142	3,288	3,123	563
1983	39,252	26,981	2,859	3,080	2,781	2,772	2,758	2,798	2,928	3,247	3,222	535
1984	39,208	26,905	3,009	3,113	2,904	2,765	2,772	2,761	2,831	3,036	3,186	528
1985	39,422	27,034	3,192	3,239	2,941	2,895	2,771	2,776	2,789	2,938	2,982	511
1986	39,753	27,420	3,310	3,358	3,054	2,933	2,896	2,775	2,806	2,899	2,870	520
1987	40,008	27,933	3,389	3,407	3,173	3,046	2,938	2,901	2,811	2,910	2,839	520
1988	40,189	28,501	3,433	3,460	3,223	3,167	3,051	2,945	2,937	2,905	2,853	527
1989	40,543	29,152	3,487	3,485	3,289	3,235	3,182	3,067	2,987	3,027	2,853	540
1990	41,217	29,878	3,609	3,499	3,327	3,297	3,248	3,197	3,110	3,067	2,979	543
1991	42,047	30,506	3,686	3,556	3,360	3,334	3,315	3,268	3,239	3,181	3,020	545
1992	42,823	31,088	3,818	3,542	3,431	3,361	3,342	3,325	3,303	3,299	3,129	539
1993	43,465	31,504	3,922	3,529	3,429	3,437	3,361	3,350	3,356	3,355	3,249	515
1994	44,111	31,898	4,047	3,593	3,440	3,439	3,426	3,372	3,381	3,404	3,302	494
1995	44,840	32,341	4,173	3,671	3,507	3,445	3,431	3,438	3,395	3,422	3,356	502

Notes appear at end of table

(continued)

TABLE Bc19–37 Enrollment in public elementary and secondary schools, by grade: 1910–1995 *Continued*

	Public schools enrollment, secondary						
	Total	Ninth grade	Tenth grade	Eleventh grade	Twelfth grade	Postgraduate	Ungraded
School year beginning	Bc31	Bc32	Bc33	Bc34	Bc35	Bc36	Bc37 [3]
	Thousand	Thousand	Thousand	Thousand	Thousand	Thousand	Thousand
1910	1,157	495	309	208	145	—	—
1911	1,201	501	325	219	156	—	—
1912	1,333	547	359	248	180	—	—
1913	1,432	584	384	266	198	—	—
1914	1,562	639	417	287	219	—	—
1915	1,711	693	460	317	241	—	—
1916 [4]	1,795	743	476	324	251	—	—
1917	1,934	816	507	342	269	—	—
1918 [4]	2,067	867	541	369	290	—	—
1919	2,200	917	576	396	312	—	—
1920 [4]	2,537	1,065	679	456	337	—	—
1921	2,873	1,214	782	516	362	—	—
1922 [4]	3,131	1,271	851	583	426	—	—
1923	3,390	1,328	920	651	490	—	—
1924 [4]	3,651	1,424	970	716	541	—	—
1925	3,757	1,425	1,005	736	592	—	—
1926 [4]	3,834	1,451	1,025	752	607	—	—
1927	3,911	1,476	1,046	768	622	—	—
1928 [4]	4,155	1,551	1,119	824	661	—	—
1929	4,399	1,627	1,192	880	701	—	—
1930 [4]	4,770	1,702	1,290	973	786	18	—
1931	5,140	1,778	1,387	1,067	872	37	—
1932 [4]	5,405	1,816	1,464	1,138	939	48	—
1933	5,669	1,855	1,540	1,209	1,005	59	—
1934 [4]	5,822	1,913	1,580	1,229	1,035	65	—
1935	5,975	1,970	1,620	1,249	1,064	71	—
1936 [4]	6,101	1,975	1,645	1,314	1,107	60	—
1937	6,227	1,979	1,669	1,379	1,151	48	—
1938 [4]	6,414	1,995	1,718	1,433	1,216	52	—
1939	6,601	2,011	1,767	1,486	1,282	55	—
1940 [4]	6,714	2,034	1,793	1,517	1,323	47	—
1941	6,388	1,927	1,706	1,451	1,273	31	—
1942 [4]	6,122	1,898	1,654	1,374	1,170	26	—
1943	5,554	1,775	1,520	1,230	1,010	20	—
1944 [4]	5,560	1,743	1,530	1,237	1,016	35	—
1945	5,622	1,728	1,555	1,256	1,032	50	—
1946 [4]	5,838	1,761	1,583	1,309	1,120	65	—
1947	5,653	1,673	1,503	1,272	1,131	75	—
1948 [4]	5,658	1,709	1,499	1,267	1,126	57	—
1949	5,725	1,761	1,513	1,275	1,134	42	—
1950 [4]	5,806	1,781	1,548	1,313	1,128	37	—
1951	5,882	1,820	1,582	1,338	1,111	31	—
1952 [4]	5,882	1,861	1,579	1,307	1,108	27	—
1953	6,290	1,944	1,717	1,412	1,190	27	—
1954 [4]	6,574	2,028	1,765	1,520	1,246	15	—
1955	6,873	2,143	1,849	1,543	1,326	13	—
1956	7,318	2,368	1,974	1,615	1,349	13	—
1957	7,860	2,480	2,194	1,736	1,431	19	—
1958	8,258	2,412	2,318	1,955	1,538	35	—
1959	8,485	2,412	2,258	2,063	1,747	4	—
1960 [4]	8,821	2,750	2,252	1,997	1,820	2	—
1961	9,566	3,156	2,595	2,018	1,791	7	—
1962 [4]	10,372 [5]	3,172	2,981	2,348	1,866	5	—
1963 [4]	11,110 [5]	3,190	3,006	2,747	2,160	6	—
1964 [4]	11,628 [5]	3,198	3,085	2,778	2,560	7	—
1965	11,602 [5]	3,215	2,993	2,741	2,477	7	169
1966	11,880 [5]	3,318	3,111	2,756	2,508	8	179
1967	12,247	3,395	3,221	2,879	2,525	16	210
1968	12,723	3,508	3,310	2,986	2,650	17	251
1969	13,037	3,568	3,405	3,047	2,732	21	264

Notes appear at end of table

TABLE Bc19–37 Enrollment in public elementary and secondary schools, by grade: 1910–1995 *Continued*

	Public schools enrollment, secondary						
	Total	Ninth grade	Tenth grade	Eleventh grade	Twelfth grade	Postgraduate	Ungraded
	Bc31	Bc32	Bc33	Bc34	Bc35	Bc36	Bc37 [3]
School year beginning	Thousand	Thousand	Thousand	Thousand	Thousand	Thousand	Thousand
1970	13,336	3,654	3,458	3,128	2,775	28	293
1971	13,753	3,781	3,571	3,200	2,864	9	328
1972	13,848	3,779	3,648	3,248	2,873	10	290
1973	14,044	3,801	3,650	3,323	2,918	4	348
1974	14,103	3,832	3,675	3,302	2,955	13	326
1975	14,304	3,879	3,723	3,354	2,986	23	339
1976	14,314	3,825	3,738	3,373	3,015	23	340
1977	14,203	3,779	3,686	3,388	3,026	13	311
1978	14,088	3,726	3,610	3,312	3,023	—	416
1979	13,616	3,526	3,532	3,241	2,969	—	348
1980	13,231	3,377	3,368	3,195	2,925	—	366
1981	12,764	3,286	3,218	3,039	2,907	—	314
1982	12,405	3,248	3,137	2,917	2,787	—	315
1983	12,271	3,330	3,103	2,861	2,678	—	299
1984	12,304	3,440	3,145	2,819	2,599	—	300
1985	12,388	3,439	3,230	2,866	2,550	—	303
1986	12,333	3,256	3,215	2,954	2,601	—	308
1987	12,076	3,143	3,020	2,936	2,681	—	296
1988	11,687	3,106	2,895	2,749	2,650	—	288
1989	11,390	3,141	2,868	2,629	2,473	—	279
1990	11,338	3,169	2,896	2,612	2,381	—	282
1991	11,541	3,313	2,915	2,645	2,392	—	275
1992	11,735	3,352	3,027	2,656	2,431	—	269
1993	11,961	3,487	3,050	2,751	2,424	—	248
1994	12,213	3,604	3,131	2,748	2,488	—	242
1995	12,500	3,704	3,237	2,826	2,487	—	245

[1] Through 1964, includes students who enrolled at any time during the school year. Beginning in 1965, includes only those enrolled at the beginning of the year.

[2] In later years, data contain a relatively small number of prekindergarten students.

[3] Through 1965, enrollment prorated among the regular grades.

[4] Estimated.

[5] Not identical to data in the underlying sources because of the inclusion of seventh and eighth grade enrollments in the secondary school data for several states.

Sources

1910–1980, U.S. Department of Education, *120 Years of American Education: A Statistical Portrait* (1993), Table 10. The underlying sources are U.S. Office of Education, *Annual Report of the Commissioner of Education*, U.S. Office of Education, *Biennial Survey of Education in the United States,* and U.S. Department of Education, *Digest of Education Statistics,* annual issues; 1981–1995, *Digest of Education Statistics 1997*, Table 43.

Documentation

The proportion of eighth graders continuing to ninth grade is often too large, and the proportion of seventh graders continuing to eighth grade is often too small, in these data. For example, the proportion continuing from eighth to ninth grade is above one for most cohorts entering fifth grade since 1925, whereas the proportion continuing from seventh to eighth grade for cohorts entering fifth grade from 1925 to the early 1940s is distinctly too low. On average, however, the proportion continuing from seventh to ninth grade appears reasonable in comparison with the other transition statistics. There are several possible reasons. The number of ninth graders in public schools may be inflated, compared with the number of eighth graders, because many pupils in private schools transfer to public schools for high school. The discrepancies, however, may also be the result of the misclassification of eighth graders as secondary school pupils.

Series Bc30 and Bc37. Ungraded enrollment includes those children enrolled in schools or special programs that do not differentiate by grade level.

Series Bc36. Postgraduate students include those who have finished their requirements for a diploma but are taking classes at a secondary school.

TABLE Bc38–79 School enrollment and school enrollment rates, by age and sex: 1940–1995[1]

Contributed by Claudia Goldin

	Both sexes, by age													
	5–34		5–6		7–13		14–17		18–19		20–24		25–34	
	Enrollment	Rate	Enrollment	Rate	Enrollment	Rate	Enrollment	Rate	Enrollment	Rate	Enrollment	Rate	Enrollment	Rate
	Bc38	Bc39	Bc40	Bc41	Bc42	Bc43	Bc44	Bc45	Bc46	Bc47	Bc48	Bc49	Bc50	Bc51
Year	Thousand	Percent	Thousand	Percent	Thousand	Percent	Thousand	Percent	Thousand	Percent	Thousand	Percent	Thousand	Percent
1940 [2]	26,759 [3]	57.7	1,805	43.0	15,035	95.0	7,709	79.3	1,449	28.9	761	6.6	—	—
1945	25,515 [3]	64.0	2,833	60.4	14,747	98.1	6,956	78.4	668	20.7	311	3.9	—	—
1946	26,924 [3]	61.1	3,030	62.0	14,966	98.3	6,900	79.6	884	22.5	1,144	10.1	—	—
1947	27,746	41.1	3,069	58.0	15,302	98.5	6,737	79.3	1,007	24.3	1,183	10.2	448	2.0
1948	28,390	41.5	3,237	56.0	15,688	98.1	6,824	81.8	1,134	26.9	1,103	9.7	405	1.8
1949	29,283	42.4	3,487	59.3	16,374	98.6	6,778	81.6	1,028	25.3	1,041	9.2	576	2.5
1950	30,073 [4]	51.6	3,304	58.2	17,222	98.7	6,988	83.4	1,199	29.7	1,001	9.2	360 [5]	3.0
1951	30,466 [4]	52.8	3,196	54.5	17,946	99.1	7,216	85.2	974	26.2	846	8.6	288 [5]	2.5
1952	31,980	45.4	3,732	54.7	18,414	98.8	7,440	85.2	1,062	28.8	904	9.7	428	1.8
1953	32,796	46.4	4,038	55.7	18,525	99.4	7,538	85.9	1,180	31.2	981	11.1	534	2.3
1954	36,083	50.0	5,443	77.3	19,952	99.4	7,784	87.1	1,268	32.4	999	11.2	635	2.7
1955	37,426	50.8	5,520	78.1	21,028	99.2	7,970	86.9	1,232	31.5	1,010	11.1	667	2.9
1956	39,353	52.3	5,597	77.6	21,946	99.3	8,413	88.2	1,407	35.4	1,192	12.8	798	3.5
1957	41,166	53.6	5,829	78.6	22,705	99.5	9,067	89.5	1,409	34.9	1,336	14.0	820	3.6
1958	42,900	54.8	6,101	80.4	23,623	99.5	9,446	89.2	1,564	37.6	1,307	13.4	858	3.8
1959	44,370	55.5	6,222	80.0	24,626	99.4	9,839	90.2	1,601	36.8	1,283	12.7	799	3.8
1960	46,259	56.4	6,438	80.7	25,621	99.5	10,240	90.3	1,817	38.4	1,350	13.1	792	3.6
1961	47,708	56.8	6,638	81.7	25,801	99.3	11,163	91.4	1,952	38.0	1,468	13.7	686	3.2
1962	48,704	57.8	6,651	82.2	25,634	99.3	11,740	92.0	2,144	41.8	1,725	15.6	810	3.8
1963	50,356	58.5	6,768	82.7	26,203	99.3	12,517	92.9	2,061	40.9	2,014	17.3	793	3.7
1964	51,660	58.7	6,842	83.3	26,725	99.0	13,014	93.1	2,196	41.6	2,048	16.8	835	3.9
1965	53,769	59.7	6,995	84.4	27,450	99.4	13,033	93.2	2,930	46.3	2,360	19.0	1,001	4.7
1966	55,070	60.0	7,156	85.1	27,895	99.3	13,293	93.7	3,176	47.2	2,547	19.9	1,003	4.6
1967	56,511	60.2	7,352	87.4	28,286	99.3	13,638	93.7	3,026	47.6	3,002	22.0	1,207	5.4
1968	57,564	60.1	7,241	87.6	28,620	99.1	14,118	94.2	3,317	50.4	2,988	21.4	1,280	5.5
1969	58,718	60.1	7,155	88.4	28,844	99.1	14,452	94.0	3,351	50.2	3,380	23.0	1,536	6.4
1970	58,896	59.0	7,000	89.5	28,943	99.2	14,796	94.1	3,322	47.7	3,359	21.5	1,477	6.0
1971	59,630	58.6	6,818	91.6	28,823	99.1	15,144	94.5	3,557	49.2	3,606	21.9	1,682	6.6
1972	58,486	56.9	6,340	91.9	27,907	99.2	15,267	93.3	3,458	46.3	3,692	21.6	1,822	6.8
1973	57,703	55.4	6,228	92.5	27,289	99.2	15,354	92.9	3,284	42.9	3,659	20.8	1,889	6.7
1974	58,252	55.3	6,421	94.2	26,833	99.3	15,529	92.9	3,375	43.1	3,816	21.4	2,278	7.8
1975	58,867	55.1	6,590	94.7	26,104	99.3	15,698	93.6	3,765	46.9	4,121	22.4	2,589	8.5
1976	58,533	54.3	6,701	95.6	25,455	99.2	15,649	93.7	3,768	46.2	4,379	23.3	2,581	8.2
1977	58,078	53.6	6,433	95.8	25,052	99.4	15,529	93.6	3,762	46.2	4,390	22.9	2,912	9.0
1978	56,544	52.2	5,997	95.3	24,597	99.1	15,356	93.7	3,700	45.4	4,245	21.8	2,649	8.0
1979	55,717	51.2	5,846	95.8	24,145	99.2	14,970	93.6	3,693	45.0	4,290	21.7	2,773	8.1
1980	55,068	50.4	5,853	95.7	23,751	99.3	14,411	93.4	3,788	46.4	4,446	22.3	2,819	7.9
1981	56,057	49.7	5,955	94.0	24,025	99.2	14,373	94.1	3,976	49.0	4,700	22.5	3,028	8.0
1982	55,483	49.3	6,070	95.0	23,654	99.0	13,928	94.4	3,837	47.8	4,897	23.5	3,097	8.0
1983	55,120	49.0	6,214	95.5	23,278	99.2	13,791	95.0	3,938	50.4	4,720	22.7	3,179	8.1
1984	54,704	48.6	6,332	94.5	22,854	99.2	13,793	94.7	3,724	50.1	4,886	23.7	3,115	7.7
1985	55,214	48.9	6,697	96.1	22,849	99.2	14,016	94.9	3,716	51.6	4,776	24.0	3,160	7.7
1986	55,340	48.8	6,917	95.3	22,987	99.2	13,868	94.9	3,872	54.6	4,584	23.6	3,112	7.4
1987	55,943	49.3	6,956	95.2	23,521	99.5	13,532	95.0	3,982	55.6	4,792	25.5	3,160	7.5
1988	56,049	49.3	7,044	96.0	24,044	99.7	13,042	95.1	4,059	55.6	4,816	26.1	3,044	7.1
1989	56,338	49.7	6,990	95.2	24,431	99.3	12,747	95.7	4,125	56.0	4,837	27.0	3,208	7.5
1990	57,297	50.6	7,207	96.5	25,016	99.6	12,653	95.8	4,044	57.2	5,083	28.6	3,294	7.7
1991	58,208	51.4	7,178	95.4	25,445	99.6	12,789	96.0	3,969	59.6	5,406	30.2	3,422	8.1
1992	59,021	52.2	7,252	95.5	25,768	99.4	13,133	96.7	4,012	61.4	5,604	31.6	3,251	7.8
1993	59,455	52.6	7,298	95.4	26,110	99.5	13,350	96.5	4,063	61.6	5,389	30.8	3,245	7.9
1994	62,510	53.8	7,752	96.7	26,768	99.3	14,414	96.6	4,180	60.2	5,857	32.0	3,538	8.6
1995	62,897	54.1	7,901	96.0	27,003	98.9	14,648	96.3	4,274	59.4	5,570	31.5	3,500	8.6

Notes appear at end of table

TABLE Bc38–79 School enrollment and school enrollment rates, by age and sex: 1940–1995 *Continued*

	Males, by age													
	5–34		5–6		7–13		14–17		18–19		20–24		25–34	
	Enrollment	Rate	Enrollment	Rate	Enrollment	Rate	Enrollment	Rate	Enrollment	Rate	Enrollment	Rate	Enrollment	Rate
	Bc52	Bc53	Bc54	Bc55	Bc56	Bc57	Bc58	Bc59	Bc60	Bc61	Bc62	Bc63	Bc64	Bc65
Year	Thousand	Percent	Thousand	Percent	Thousand	Percent	Thousand	Percent	Thousand	Percent	Thousand	Percent	Thousand	Percent
1940 [2]	13,615 [3]	58.6	901	42.3	7,607	94.8	3,870	78.9	770	30.8	467	8.2	—	—
1945	12,660 [3]	72.7	1,423	59.6	7,456	97.7	3,475	78.0	192	21.6	114	5.6	—	—
1946	13,941 [3]	64.9	1,514	60.8	7,585	98.0	3,435	79.2	469	29.0	938	17.7	—	—
1947	14,635	44.3	1,549	57.4	7,781	98.6	3,364	78.9	587	31.4	947	17.0	407	3.8
1948	14,991	44.8	1,628	55.1	7,990	98.3	3,436	81.9	682	34.3	898	16.5	358	3.3
1949	15,489	45.8	1,807	60.2	8,330	98.5	3,447	82.5	593	31.6	827	15.4	487	4.5
1950	15,736 [4]	54.8	1,649	56.8	8,773	98.7	3,568	84.4	680	35.7	733	14.3	333 [5]	5.9
1951	15,774 [4]	56.8	1,648	55.1	9,148	99.1	3,614	85.2	534	32.4	602	14.3	228 [5]	4.2
1952	16,644	49.4	1,912	54.8	9,382	98.7	3,758	85.4	612	37.2	630	16.9	350	3.2
1953	16,974	50.2	2,035	55.0	9,405	99.2	3,844	86.8	642	37.7	636	18.5	414	3.7
1954	18,759	54.0	2,746	76.3	10,138	99.2	4,002	88.7	730	40.6	677	19.1	465	4.2
1955	19,573	54.9	2,821	78.1	10,725	99.2	4,096	88.6	752	42.5	686	18.1	494	4.5
1956	20,522	56.3	2,839	77.1	11,179	99.1	4,275	89.1	809	45.1	830	20.6	620	5.7
1957	21,509	57.5	2,963	78.3	11,584	99.5	4,646	91.1	780	43.3	897	21.3	639	5.9
1958	22,497	58.7	3,123	80.6	12,059	99.5	4,854	90.7	898	47.5	915	21.0	648	6.0
1959	23,192	59.1	3,158	79.5	12,556	99.3	5,041	91.4	918	45.6	892	19.6	627	5.9
1960	24,234	60.0	3,292	80.8	13,074	99.5	5,247	91.3	1,063	47.8	936	19.9	621	5.9
1961	24,944	60.4	3,402	82.0	13,167	99.3	5,705	92.2	1,170	48.6	989	20.2	511	4.9
1962	25,452	61.7	3,399	82.6	13,003	99.2	6,032	93.7	1,212	51.2	1,177	23.4	629	6.2
1963	26,243	62.3	3,440	82.7	13,280	99.1	6,402	94.2	1,180	51.0	1,365	25.6	576	5.7
1964	26,851	62.3	3,478	83.4	13,548	98.8	6,658	94.4	1,238	50.9	1,332	23.8	597	5.9
1965	28,059	63.5	3,555	84.4	13,932	99.3	6,613	93.6	1,689	55.6	1,559	27.6	711	7.0
1966	28,733	64.1	3,619	84.5	14,139	99.2	6,770	94.4	1,841	57.8	1,667	29.2	697	6.8
1967	29,368	64.1	3,719	86.6	14,342	99.1	6,975	94.7	1,637	56.3	1,862	30.6	832	7.8
1968	30,051	64.3	3,683	87.3	14,513	98.9	7,199	95.0	1,892	60.4	1,867	30.5	897	8.1
1969	30,583	64.1	3,623	87.7	14,620	98.9	7,374	95.0	1,886	59.4	2,070	32.0	1,011	8.9
1970	30,642	62.6	3,545	88.9	14,688	99.0	7,531	94.8	1,821	54.4	2,062	29.3	996	8.4
1971	31,114	62.1	3,450	90.9	14,633	98.9	7,720	95.3	1,939	55.4	2,217	29.2	1,155	9.4
1972	30,505	60.1	3,220	91.7	14,195	99.1	7,795	94.0	1,857	51.2	2,243	27.8	1,195	9.2
1973	30,012	58.3	3,162	92.2	13,884	99.2	7,845	93.7	1,783	47.9	2,118	25.2	1,220	9.0
1974	30,178	57.9	3,280	94.4	13,650	99.2	7,906	93.3	1,731	45.8	2,202	25.8	1,409	10.0
1975	30,502	57.7	3,346	94.4	13,267	99.0	8,042	94.6	1,940	49.9	2,334	26.4	1,573	10.7
1976	30,209	56.6	3,422	95.6	12,951	99.0	8,014	94.6	1,907	48.2	2,358	26.0	1,557	10.2
1977	29,831	55.6	3,246	94.7	12,751	99.3	7,934	94.3	1,919	48.4	2,401	25.9	1,580	10.0
1978	29,002	54.0	3,054	95.1	12,514	99.0	7,814	93.9	1,902	47.8	2,290	24.3	1,428	8.8
1979	28,459	52.8	3,003	96.3	12,285	99.0	7,680	94.5	1,874	46.6	2,229	23.3	1,388	8.3
1980	27,952	51.6	2,971	95.0	12,110	99.2	7,321	93.7	1,879	47.1	2,299	23.8	1,372	7.9
1981	28,577	51.0	3,051	94.2	12,253	99.1	7,309	94.3	2,018	50.5	2,467	24.4	1,479	8.0
1982	28,255	50.5	3,093	94.7	12,075	99.1	7,108	94.9	1,937	48.9	2,534	25.0	1,508	8.0
1983	28,230	50.4	3,166	95.1	11,887	99.1	7,021	95.1	1,956	50.5	2,582	25.5	1,618	8.4
1984	28,013	50.0	3,220	94.0	11,665	99.1	7,018	94.7	1,924	52.4	2,651	26.3	1,535	7.8
1985	28,087	50.1	3,422	95.3	11,666	99.2	7,186	95.4	1,852	52.2	2,467	25.6	1,494	7.5
1986	28,262	50.0	3,544	96.0	11,768	99.1	7,095	94.9	1,998	57.1	2,305	24.5	1,552	7.5
1987	28,547	50.5	3,580	95.7	12,057	99.7	6,928	95.3	2,047	57.9	2,469	27.2	1,466	7.0
1988	28,483	50.4	3,573	95.9	12,329	99.7	6,679	95.4	2,032	56.2	2,448	27.6	1,422	6.8
1989	28,539	50.4	3,551	95.1	12,509	99.2	6,583	96.1	2,061	56.6	2,339	26.9	1,496	7.1
1990	29,077	51.4	3,705	96.5	12,832	99.6	6,491	95.9	2,038	58.2	2,552	29.6	1,459	6.9
1991	29,612	52.3	3,655	95.0	13,033	99.8	6,584	96.4	1,976	59.8	2,710	31.0	1,653	7.9
1992	29,802	52.7	3,721	95.7	13,197	99.5	6,770	97.3	2,018	61.6	2,666	30.7	1,431	7.0
1993	30,236	53.4	3,750	95.5	13,359	99.6	6,890	97.1	2,049	61.6	2,727	31.8	1,461	7.2
1994	31,586	54.2	3,965	97.0	13,701	99.3	7,358	96.6	2,104	60.4	2,831	31.2	1,628	8.0
1995	31,865	54.6	4,041	95.3	13,800	99.0	7,554	96.7	2,150	59.5	2,711	31.0	1,608	8.0

Notes appear at end of table

(continued)

TABLE Bc38–79 School enrollment and school enrollment rates, by age and sex: 1940–1995 *Continued*

	Females, by age													
	5–34		5–6		7–13		14–17		18–19		20–24		25–34	
	Enrollment	Rate	Enrollment	Rate	Enrollment	Rate	Enrollment	Rate	Enrollment	Rate	Enrollment	Rate	Enrollment	Rate
	Bc66	Bc67	Bc68	Bc69	Bc70	Bc71	Bc72	Bc73	Bc74	Bc75	Bc76	Bc77	Bc78	Bc79
Year	Thousand	Percent	Thousand	Percent	Thousand	Percent	Thousand	Percent	Thousand	Percent	Thousand	Percent	Thousand	Percent
1940 [2]	13,145 [3]	56.9	904	43.7	7,428	95.2	3,840	79.7	680	26.9	294	5.0	—	—
1945	12,855 [3]	57.3	1,410	61.3	7,291	98.4	3,481	78.7	476	20.3	197	3.3	—	—
1946	12,983 [3]	57.5	1,516	63.3	7,381	98.5	3,465	80.1	415	18.0	206	3.4	—	—
1947	13,111	38.0	1,520	58.7	7,521	98.5	3,373	79.8	420	18.5	236	3.9	41	0.3
1948	13,399	38.4	1,608	56.8	7,698	98.0	3,388	81.7	452	20.3	206	3.4	48	0.4
1949	13,794	39.2	1,679	58.4	8,045	98.7	3,331	80.7	435	19.9	215	3.7	89	0.7
1950	14,337 [4]	48.4	1,655	59.5	8,449	98.7	3,420	82.3	519	24.3	268	4.6	27 [5]	0.4
1951	14,692 [4]	49.1	1,548	54.0	8,798	99.1	3,602	85.2	440	21.3	244	4.3	60 [5]	1.0
1952	15,336	41.9	1,820	54.6	9,032	98.9	3,682	85.0	450	22.1	274	4.9	78	0.6
1953	15,822	43.0	2,003	56.6	9,120	99.6	3,695	85.0	538	25.9	346	6.4	120	0.9
1954	17,324	46.3	2,697	78.3	9,813	99.6	3,782	85.4	538	25.4	322	6.0	171	1.4
1955	17,853	47.0	2,700	78.1	10,304	99.1	3,873	85.2	480	22.5	324	6.1	173	1.4
1956	18,801	48.7	2,758	78.2	10,767	99.4	4,138	87.3	598	27.4	362	6.8	178	1.5
1957	19,657	50.0	2,866	79.0	11,121	99.5	4,421	87.8	629	28.1	439	8.2	181	1.5
1958	20,404	51.0	2,978	80.2	11,564	99.4	4,591	87.6	667	29.4	393	7.3	211	1.8
1959	21,178	52.0	3,064	80.5	12,070	99.6	4,798	89.0	683	29.2	391	7.1	172	1.5
1960	22,025	52.8	3,146	80.6	12,547	99.6	4,993	89.2	754	30.0	414	7.4	171	1.7
1961	22,764	53.4	3,236	81.4	12,634	99.3	5,458	90.5	782	28.6	479	8.3	175	1.5
1962	23,252	54.0	3,252	81.7	12,631	99.4	5,708	90.3	932	33.7	548	9.1	181	1.6
1963	24,113	54.9	3,328	82.6	12,923	99.6	6,115	91.6	881	32.3	649	10.3	217	1.9
1964	24,809	55.3	3,364	83.2	13,177	99.2	6,356	91.8	958	33.7	716	10.9	238	2.1
1965	25,710	56.0	3,440	84.4	13,518	99.4	6,420	92.8	1,241	37.7	801	11.8	290	2.6
1966	26,337	56.1	3,537	85.7	13,756	99.5	6,523	92.9	1,335	37.7	880	12.4	306	2.7
1967	27,144	56.5	3,632	88.2	13,944	99.4	6,662	92.6	1,390	40.3	1,139	15.1	375	3.2
1968	27,513	56.1	3,558	88.0	14,106	99.3	6,919	93.4	1,425	41.3	1,121	14.3	383	3.2
1969	28,135	56.3	3,532	89.1	14,223	99.5	7,078	93.1	1,465	41.8	1,310	16.0	526	4.2
1970	28,254	55.5	3,455	90.2	14,255	99.4	7,265	93.4	1,501	41.6	1,297	15.2	480	3.8
1971	28,515	55.2	3,368	92.3	14,190	99.4	7,424	93.7	1,617	43.4	1,389	15.7	527	4.0
1972	27,980	53.8	3,120	92.2	13,712	99.3	7,471	92.6	1,601	41.8	1,449	16.0	627	4.5
1973	27,689	52.6	3,066	92.9	13,405	99.3	7,509	92.1	1,500	38.2	1,540	16.7	669	4.6
1974	28,075	52.7	3,140	93.9	13,183	99.5	7,624	92.5	1,644	40.7	1,615	17.3	869	5.8
1975	28,365	52.6	3,244	95.1	12,837	99.6	7,657	92.6	1,825	44.2	1,786	18.7	1,016	6.5
1976	28,323	52.1	3,279	95.5	12,503	99.3	7,634	92.8	1,861	44.4	2,021	20.8	1,025	6.3
1977	28,246	51.7	3,187	96.9	12,301	99.5	7,594	93.0	1,844	44.0	1,988	20.0	1,332	8.0
1978	27,544	50.4	2,944	95.5	12,083	99.3	7,542	93.5	1,798	43.0	1,955	19.4	1,222	7.1
1979	27,258	49.7	2,843	95.2	11,860	99.4	7,290	92.6	1,819	43.4	2,061	20.2	1,385	7.8
1980	27,115	49.2	2,882	96.4	11,641	99.3	7,089	93.1	1,910	45.8	2,147	20.8	1,446	7.9
1981	27,482	48.4	2,904	93.8	11,771	99.4	7,065	93.9	1,958	47.5	2,234	20.8	1,550	8.0
1982	27,227	48.1	2,977	95.3	11,579	99.3	6,820	94.0	1,899	46.8	2,363	22.1	1,589	8.0
1983	26,891	47.6	3,048	95.8	11,391	99.3	6,770	94.9	1,983	50.3	2,138	20.1	1,561	7.8
1984	26,690	47.3	3,112	95.1	11,190	99.4	6,774	94.7	1,800	47.9	2,235	21.2	1,579	7.7
1985	27,125	47.8	3,274	97.0	11,182	99.3	6,830	94.5	1,864	51.0	2,309	22.5	1,666	8.0
1986	27,079	47.6	3,373	94.6	11,221	99.3 [6]	6,772	94.8 [6]	1,874	52.1 [6]	2,279	22.8 [6]	1,560	7.3 [6]
1987	27,396	48.1	3,376	94.6	11,463	99.4	6,603	94.5	1,936	53.4	2,324	24.0	1,694	7.9
1988	27,565	48.3	3,471	96.0	11,714	99.7	6,363	94.8	2,028	55.2	2,367	24.7	1,622	7.5
1989	27,798	48.9	3,439	95.2	11,922	99.4	6,164	95.3	2,063	55.4	2,498	27.1	1,712	7.9
1990	28,222	49.8	3,502	96.4	12,184	99.7	6,163	95.7	2,006	56.3	2,532	27.7	1,835	8.5
1991	28,596	50.5	3,522	95.8	12,412	99.5	6,205	95.6	1,993	59.4	2,695	29.4	1,769	8.3
1992	29,218	51.7	3,531	95.2	12,571	99.2	6,363	96.0	1,994	61.2	2,938	32.5	1,820	8.6
1993	29,219	51.8	3,547	95.2	12,752	99.4	6,461	95.9	2,014	61.7	2,662	29.8	1,784	8.6
1994	30,924	53.3	3,787	96.4	13,068	99.4	7,056	96.6	2,076	60.0	3,025	32.8	1,911	9.1
1995	31,031	53.5	3,860	96.8	13,203	98.8	7,093	95.7	2,124	59.2	2,859	31.9	1,892	9.2

1 Unless otherwise noted, enrollment data are for October.

2 As of April 1.

3 Ages 5–24.

4 Ages 5–29.

5 Ages 25–29.

6 Value from *120 Years* corrected using U.S. Bureau of the Census, *Current Population Reports*, Population Characteristics, series P-20, "School Enrollment – Social and Economic Characteristics of Students: October 1986" (August 1988).

Sources

1940–1991, U.S. Department of Education, *120 Years of American Education: A Statistical Portrait* (1993), Table 3. The underlying sources are: 1940, U.S. Bureau of the Census, *U.S. Census of Population: 1950*, volume 2, part 1; 1945–1969, *Current Population Reports*, series P-20, numbers 10, 24, 30, 34, 45, 52, 54, 66, 74, 80, 93, 101, 110, 117, 126, 129, 148, 162, 167, 190, 206, and 222; 1970–1991, Current Population Survey, survey data files; 1992–1995, *Current Population Reports*, series P-20, numbers 474, 479, 487, and 495.

TABLE Bc38–79 School enrollment and school enrollment rates, by age and sex: 1940–1995 *Continued*

Documentation

The estimates are based on data obtained in October in the Current Population Survey (CPS) of the Bureau of the Census, except that data shown for 1940 are based on complete enumeration of the population and were published in volume II of the 1950 census reports on population. Except for 1940, data are for the civilian population excluding the relatively small number in institutions. Data shown for 1940 relate to the total population, including those in institutions and all members of the armed forces (about 267,000) enumerated on April 1.

The school enrollment statistics from the CPS are based on replies to the enumerator's inquiry as to whether the person was enrolled in school. In the Census of Population for 1940 and 1950, and in the CPS, 1954–1991, enrollment was defined as enrollment in "regular" schools only - that is, schools where enrollment may lead toward an elementary or high school diploma, or to a college, university, or professional degree. Such schools included public and private nursery schools, kindergartens, elementary and secondary schools, colleges, universities, and professional schools. Enrollment could be either full-time or part-time, day or night.

If a person was receiving regular instruction at home from a tutor and if the instruction was considered comparable to that of a regular school or college, the person was counted as enrolled. Enrollment in a correspondence course was counted only if the person received credit in the regular school system. Enrollments in business and trade schools at the postsecondary level were excluded if the coursework did not lead to a degree.

Children in kindergarten were included in the "regular" school enrollment figures in the CPS beginning in 1950; children enrolled in nursery school were included in 1967. Children enrolled in kindergarten were not included in the "regular" school enrollment figures in the 1950 Census of Population; however, they have been included here to make the data comparable with earlier years and with current practice. In censuses prior to 1950, no attempt was made to exclude children in kindergarten, so the statistics for those years include varying proportions attending kindergarten.

Information on school enrollment is also collected and published by the Department of Education. These data are obtained from reports of school surveys and censuses. They are, however, only roughly comparable with data collected by the Bureau of the Census from households, because of differences in definitions, time references, population coverage, and enumeration methods.

TABLE Bc80–93 Children served in special education programs, by type of disability: 1921–1995[1]

Contributed by Claudia Goldin

School year beginning	Total	As a percentage of total public school enrollment	Learning disabled	Speech impaired	Mentally retarded	Seriously emotionally disturbed	Hard of hearing and deaf	Orthopedically handicapped	Other health-impaired	Visually handicapped	Multi-handicapped	Deaf-blind	Preschool handicapped	Other handicapped
	Bc80	Bc81	Bc82	Bc83	Bc84	Bc85	Bc86	Bc87 [2]	Bc88	Bc89	Bc90	Bc91	Bc92 [3]	Bc93
	Thousand	Percent	Thousand	Thousand	Thousand	Thousand	Thousand	Thousand	Thousand	Thousand	Thousand	Thousand	Thousand	Thousand
1921	—	—	—	—	23	—	4	—	—	—	—	—	—	—
1926	—	—	—	—	52	—	4	—	—	4	—	—	—	—
1929	—	—	—	—	—	10	—	—	—	—	—	—	—	—
1931	161	0.6	—	23	75	14	4	—	—	5	—	—	—	—
1935	294	1.1	—	117	100	13	9	—	—	7	—	—	—	—
1939	310	1.2	—	126	98	10	13	—	—	9	—	—	—	—
1947	356	1.5	—	182	87	15	14	—	—	8	—	—	—	—
1952	475	1.7	—	307	114	—	16	—	—	9	—	—	—	—
1957	838	2.5	—	490	223	29	20	—	—	12	—	—	—	12
1962	1,469	3.7	—	802	432	80	46	—	—	22	—	—	—	22
1965	1,794	4.3	—	990	540	88	51	—	—	23	—	—	—	33
1969	2,677	5.9	—	1,237	830	113	78	—	—	24	—	—	—	126
1976	3,692	8.3	796	1,302	959	283	87	87	141	38	—	—	—	—
1977	3,751	8.6	964	1,223	933	288	85	87	135	35	—	—	—	—
1978	3,889	9.1	1,130	1,214	901	300	85	70	105	32	50	2	—	—
1979	4,005	9.6	1,276	1,186	869	329	80	66	106	31	60	2	—	—
1980	4,142	10.1	1,462	1,168	829	346	79	58	98	31	68	3	—	—
1981	4,198	10.5	1,622	1,135	786	339	75	58	79	29	71	2	—	—
1982	4,255	10.8	1,741	1,131	757	352	73	57	50	28	63	2	—	—
1983	4,298	10.9	1,806	1,128	727	361	72	56	53	29	65	2	—	—
1984	4,315	11.0	1,832	1,126	694	372	69	56	68	28	69	2	—	—
1985	4,317	11.0	1,862	1,125	660	375	66	57	57	27	86	2	—	—
1986	4,374	11.0	1,914	1,136	643	383	65	57	52	26	97	2	—	—
1987	4,447	11.1	1,928	953	582	373	56	47	45	22	77	1	363	—
1988	4,544	11.3	1,987	967	564	376	56	47	43	23	85	2	394	—
1989	4,641	11.4	2,050	973	548	381	57	48	52	22	86	2	422	—
1990	4,762	11.6	2,130	985	534	390	58	49	55	23	96	1	441	—
1991	4,949	11.8	2,234	997	538	399	60	51	58	24	97	1	484	5
1992	5,125	12.0	2,354	996	519	401	60	52	65	23	102	1	531	19
1993	5,309	12.2	2,408	1,014	536	414	64	56	82	24	108	1	578	24
1994	5,378	12.2	2,489	1,015	555	427	64	60	106	24	88	1	519	29
1995	5,573	12.4	2,579	1,022	570	438	67	63	133	25	93	1	544	39

[1] Data for 1976 and later years are for children participating in federal programs.

[2] Includes special health problems.

[3] Prior to 1987, these students were included in the counts by handicapping condition. As of 1987, states are no longer required to report preschool handicapped students (younger than 6 years of age) by handicapping condition.

Sources

U.S. Department of Education, *120 Years of American Education: A Statistical Portrait* (1993), Table 12, updated using U.S. Department of Education, *Digest of Education Statistics 1997* (1997), Table 52.

Documentation

Children served in these programs include "exceptional children" in years prior to 1970. The term applies to pupils who need additional education services, referred to as "special education," because of their physical, intellectual, or personal–social differences from other children. The group includes unusually bright or gifted children, the mentally retarded, the disabled (including the physically handicapped and those with learning disabilities), those with special health problems (such as cardiac involvement and epilepsy), the blind and partially seeing, the deaf and hard of hearing, those with speech impairments, and the emotionally disturbed. Pupils are reported according to the major type of exceptionality for which they were receiving special education.

All data are for children enrolled in special education programs in either public or private schools. The vast majority of the children accounted for are enrolled in public schools.

Data for years after 1970 are based on counts of students participating in PL 94-142, Education of the Handicapped Act, and the successor, Individuals with Disabilities Education Act (IDEA) programs.

Increases since 1987 are in part the result of legislation enacted in the fall of 1986 mandating public school special education services for all handicapped children ages 3–5.

Series Bc81. Equals series Bc80 as a percentage of series Bc9.

TABLE Bc94–96 Average daily attendance, length of school term, and days attended per pupil for public elementary and secondary schools: 1869–1994

Contributed by Claudia Goldin

School year beginning	Average daily student attendance	Average length of school term	Average number of days attended per pupil enrolled
	Bc94	Bc95	Bc96
	Number	Days	Days
1869	4,077,000	132.2	78.4
1870	4,545,000	132.1	79.4
1871	4,659,000	133.4	79.5
1872	4,745,000	129.1	76.5
1873	5,051,000	128.8	77.0
1874	5,248,000	134.4	77.9
1875	5,291,000	133.1	79.4
1876	5,427,000	132.1	80.0
1877	5,783,000	132.0	80.9
1878	5,876,000	130.2	80.5
1879	6,144,000	130.3	81.1
1880	6,146,000	130.0	80.0
1881	6,331,000	131.2	81.3
1882	6,652,000	129.8	81.1
1883	7,056,000	129.1	82.9
1884	7,298,000	130.7	83.6
1885	7,526,000	130.4	84.1
1886	7,682,000	131.3	84.9
1887	7,907,000	132.3	85.9
1888	8,006,000	133.7	86.4
1889	8,154,000	134.7	86.3
1890	8,329,000	135.7	86.6
1891	8,561,000	136.9	88.4
1892	8,856,000	136.3	89.6
1893	9,188,000	139.5	91.6
1894	9,549,000	139.5	93.5
1895	9,781,000	140.5	94.8
1896	10,053,000	142.0	96.3
1897	10,356,000	143.0	98.0
1898	10,389,000	143.0	97.9
1899	10,633,000	144.3	99.0
1900	10,716,000	143.7	98.0
1901	11,064,000	144.7	100.6
1902	11,055,000	147.2	101.7
1903	11,318,000	146.7	102.1
1904	11,482,000	150.9	105.2
1905	11,712,000	150.6	106.0
1906	11,926,000	151.8	107.3
1907	12,154,000	154.1	109.8
1908	12,685,000	155.3	112.6
1909	12,827,000	157.5	113.0
1910	12,872,000	156.8	111.8
1911	13,302,000	158.8	115.6
1912	13,614,000	158.1	115.6
1913	14,216,000	158.7	117.8
1914	14,986,000	159.4	121.2
1915	15,359,000	160.3	120.9
1917	15,549,000	160.7	119.8
1919	16,150,000	161.9	121.2
1921	18,432,000	164.0	130.6
1923	19,132,000	168.3	132.5
1925	19,856,000	169.3	135.9
1927	20,608,000	171.5	140.4
1929	21,265,000	172.7	143.0
1931	22,245,000	171.2	144.9
1933	22,458,000	171.6	145.8
1935	22,299,000	173.0	146.3
1937	22,298,000	173.9	149.3
1939	22,042,000	175.0	151.7
1941	21,031,000	174.7	149.6
1943	19,603,000	175.5	147.9
1945	19,849,000	176.8	150.6
1947	20,910,000	177.6	155.1
1949	22,284,000	177.9	157.9
1951	23,257,000	178.2	156.0
1953	25,643,871	178.6	158.9
1955	27,740,149	178.0	158.5
1957	29,722,275	177.6	157.4
1959	32,477,440	178.0	160.2
1961	34,682,340	179.1	162.3
1963	37,405,058	179.0	163.2
1965	39,154,497	178.9	163.5
1967	40,827,965	178.8	163.2
1969	41,934,376	178.9	161.7
1970	42,428,000	—	—
1971	42,254,272	179.3	161.7
1972	42,179,000	—	—
1973	41,438,054	178.7	159.5
1974	41,524,000	—	—
1975	41,269,720	178.3	161.1
1976	40,832,000	—	—
1977	40,079,590	—	—
1978	39,075,000	—	—
1979	38,288,911	178.5 [1]	160.8 [1]
1980	37,703,744	178.2	160.7
1981	37,094,652	—	—
1982	36,635,868	—	—
1983	36,362,978	—	—
1984	36,404,261	—	—
1985	36,523,103	—	—
1986	36,863,867	—	—
1987	37,050,707	—	—
1988	37,268,072	—	—
1989	37,799,296	—	—
1990	38,426,543	179.8	—
1991	38,960,783	—	—
1992	39,570,462	—	—
1993	40,146,393	—	—
1994	40,720,763	—	—

[1] Estimated by the National Center for Education Statistics.

Sources

1869–1989, U.S. Department of Education, *120 Years of American Education: A Statistical Portrait* (1993), Table 14, although see below for additional source for series Bc94. The underlying sources are: U.S. Office of Education, *Annual Report of the United States Commissioner of Education*, U.S. Office of Education, *Biennial Survey of Education in the United States*, and U.S. Department of Education, *Digest of Education Statistics*, annual issues.

Series Bc94, odd years 1953–1977, and all years 1979–1994, *Digest of Education Statistics 1997*, Table 51. Series Bc95, 1990, *Digest 1997*, Table 39.

Documentation

Figures for average daily attendance in public schools were computed by dividing the total number of days attended by all pupils enrolled by the number of days school was actually in session. Only days when the pupils were under the guidance and direction of teachers are considered as days in session.

TABLE Bc97–106 Public elementary and secondary day school teachers and instructional staff – average annual salary and number, by sex: 1869–1996

Contributed by Claudia Goldin

School year beginning	Instructional staff	Classroom teachers: Elementary and secondary: Total	Classroom teachers: Elementary and secondary: Male	Classroom teachers: Elementary and secondary: Female	Classroom teachers: Elementary	Classroom teachers: Secondary	Average annual salary: Instructional staff	Average annual salary: Classroom teachers: Elementary and secondary	Average annual salary: Classroom teachers: Elementary	Average annual salary: Classroom teachers: Secondary
	Bc97 [1, 2]	Bc98 [3, 4]	Bc99 [3, 4, 5]	Bc100 [3, 4, 5]	Bc101 [4]	Bc102 [4]	Bc103 [6]	Bc104 [7]	Bc105	Bc106
	Thousand	Thousand	Thousand	Thousand	Thousand	Thousand	Dollars	Dollars	Dollars	Dollars
1869	—	201	78	123	—	—	189	—	—	—
1870	—	220	90	130	—	—	—	—	—	—
1871	—	230	95	135	—	—	—	—	—	—
1872	—	238	98	140	—	—	—	—	—	—
1873	—	248	103	145	—	—	—	—	—	—
1874	—	258	109	149	—	—	—	—	—	—
1875	—	260	110	150	—	—	—	—	—	—
1876	—	267	114	153	—	—	—	—	—	—
1877	—	277	119	158	—	—	—	—	—	—
1878	—	280	121	159	—	—	—	—	—	—
1879	—	287	123	164	—	—	195	—	—	—
1880	—	294	123	171	—	—	—	—	—	—
1881	—	299	119	180	—	—	—	—	—	—
1882	—	304	116	188	—	—	—	—	—	—
1883	—	314	119	195	—	—	—	—	—	—
1884	—	326	122	204	—	—	224	—	—	—
1885	—	331	124	208	—	—	—	—	—	—
1886	—	339	127	212	—	—	—	—	—	—
1887	—	347	126	221	—	—	—	—	—	—
1888	—	357	124	232	—	—	—	—	—	—
1889	—	364	126	238	355	9	252	—	—	—
1890	—	368	123	245	—	—	—	—	—	—
1891	—	374	122	253	—	—	—	—	—	—
1892	—	383	122	261	—	—	—	—	—	—
1893	—	389	125	264	—	—	—	—	—	—
1894	—	398	130	268	—	—	286	—	—	—
1895	—	400	130	270	—	—	—	—	—	—
1896	—	405	131	274	—	—	—	—	—	—
1897	—	411	132	279	—	—	—	—	—	—
1898	—	414	131	283	—	—	—	—	—	—
1899	—	423	127	296	403	20	325	—	—	—
1900	—	432	126	306	—	—	—	—	—	—
1901	—	442	121	321	—	—	—	—	—	—
1902	—	449	117	332	—	—	—	—	—	—
1903	—	455	114	341	—	—	—	—	—	—
1904	—	460	111	350	—	—	386	—	—	—
1905	—	466	109	357	—	—	—	—	—	—
1906	—	481	104	377	—	—	—	—	—	—
1907	—	495	104	391	—	—	—	—	—	—
1908	—	506	108	398	—	—	—	—	—	—
1909	—	523	110	413	482	42	485	—	—	—
1910	—	534	110	423	—	—	466	—	—	—
1911	—	547	115	433	—	—	492	—	—	—
1912	—	565	113	452	—	—	512	—	—	—
1913	—	580	115	465	—	—	525	—	—	—
1914	—	604	118	486	—	—	543	—	—	—
1915	—	622	123	499	—	—	563	—	—	—
1917	—	651	105	546	562	84	635	—	—	—
1919	700	680	96	584	576	102	871	—	—	—
1921	756	723	118	605	593	130	1,166	—	—	—
1923	787	761	129	633	617	144	1,227	—	—	—
1925	850	814	139	675	645	170	1,277	—	—	—
1927	868	832	138	694	643	189 [8]	1,364	—	—	—
1929	892	854	142	712	641	213 [8]	1,420	—	—	—
1931	901	872	154	718	640	231	1,417	—	—	—
1933	880	847	162	685	619	228	1,227	—	—	—

Notes appear at end of table

TABLE Bc97–106 Public elementary and secondary day school teachers and instructional staff – average annual salary and number, by sex: 1869–1996 ***Continued***

		Classroom teachers					Average annual salary			
		Elementary and secondary						Classroom teachers		
School year beginning	Instructional staff	Total	Male	Female	Elementary	Secondary	Instructional staff	Elementary and secondary	Elementary	Secondary
	Bc97 [1, 2]	Bc98 [3, 4]	Bc99 [3, 4, 5]	Bc100 [3, 4, 5]	Bc101 [4]	Bc102 [4]	Bc103 [6]	Bc104 [7]	Bc105	Bc106
	Thousand	Thousand	Thousand	Thousand	Thousand	Thousand	Dollars	Dollars	Dollars	Dollars
1935	906	871	179	692	603	268	1,283	—	—	—
1937	919	877	185	692	595	282 [8]	1,374	—	—	—
1939	912	875	195	681	575	300 [8]	1,441	—	—	—
1941	898	859	183	676	559	300 [8]	1,507	—	—	—
1943	865	828	127	701	539	289	1,728	—	—	—
1945	867	831	138	693	542	289	1,995	—	—	—
1947	907	861	162	699	555	306	2,639	—	—	—
1949	962	914	195	719	590	324	3,010	—	—	—
1951	1,012	963	235	728	620	343	3,450	—	—	—
1953	1,098	1,032	254	779	658	375	3,825	—	—	—
1955	1,213	1,141	299	850	733	408	4,156	—	—	—
1957	1,333	1,238	332	906	—	—	4,702	—	—	—
1959	1,464	1,355	393	962	—	—	5,174	4,995	4,815	5,276
1960	—	1,408	—	—	858	550	—	—	—	—
1961	1,588	1,458	451	1,053	—	—	5,700	5,515	5,340	5,775
1963	1,717	1,568	488	1,080	—	—	6,240	5,995	5,805	6,266
1964	—	1,648	—	—	940	708	—	—	—	—
1965	1,885	1,711	544	1,167	965	746	6,935	6,485	6,279	6,761
1966	—	1,789	—	—	1,006	783	—	—	—	—
1967	2,071	1,864	584	1,280	1,040	815	7,630	7,423	7,208	7,692
1968	—	—	—	—	1,076	860	—	—	—	—
1969	2,253	2,023	690	1,333	1,109	908	9,047	8,626	8,412	8,891
1970	—	2,059	676	1,383	1,130	929	9,698	9,268	9,021	9,568
1971	2,322	2,063	688	1,382	1,111	952	10,213	9,705	9,424	10,031
1972	—	2,106	703	1,403	1,142	964	10,634	10,174	9,893	10,507
1973	2,338	2,136	715	1,421	1,151	985	11,254	10,770	10,507	11,077
1974	—	2,165	727	1,438	1,166	998	12,167	11,641	11,334	12,000
1975	2,337	2,198	742	1,456	1,181	1,017	13,124	12,600	12,280	12,937
1976	—	2,189	734	1,455	1,168	1,021	13,840	13,354	12,989	13,776
1977	—	2,209	742	1,467	1,185	1,024	14,698	14,198	13,845	14,602
1978	2,297	2,207	735	1,472	1,191	1,016	15,764	15,032	14,681	15,450
1979	—	2,185	743	1,442	1,191	994	16,715	15,970	15,569	16,459
1980	2,860	2,184	708	1,476	1,189	995	18,404	17,644	17,230	18,142
1981	—	2,127	679	1,439	1,183	945	20,327	19,274	18,853	19,805
1982	—	2,133	679	1,454	1,182	951	21,641	20,695	20,227	21,291
1983	—	2,139	679	1,460	1,186	953	23,005	21,935	21,487	22,554
1984	2,692	2,168	679	1,489	1,208	960	24,666	23,600	23,200	24,187
1985	2,756	2,206	669	1,537	1,237	969	26,362	25,199	24,718	25,846
1986	2,822	2,244	674	1,570	1,271	973	27,706	26,569	26,057	27,244
1987	2,860	2,279	665	1,614	1,307	973	29,219	28,034	27,519	28,798
1988	2,931	2,323	659	1,664	1,353	970	30,850	29,564	29,022	30,218
1989	2,986	2,357	658	1,699	1,387	970	32,638	31,367	30,832	32,049
1990	3,051	2,398	669	1,728	1,426	972	34,401	33,084	32,490	33,896
1991	3,104	2,432	679	1,753	1,459	973	35,556	34,063	33,479	34,827
1992	3,140	2,459	—	—	1,486	972	36,460	35,029	34,350	35,880
1993	3,209	2,504	679	1,825	1,515	989	37,441	35,733	35,233	36,555
1994	3,285	2,552	—	—	1,510	1,041	38,441	36,609	36,084	37,404
1995	—	2,586	—	—	1,529	1,058	39,451	37,560	36,976	38,423
1996	—	2,679	—	—	1,576	1,103	40,580	38,509	37,969	39,310

[1] Full-time equivalent.

[2] Data starting in 1984 not comparable with earlier figures.

[3] For select years prior to 1951, includes a small number of librarians and other non-supervisory instructional staff.

[4] In censuses prior to 1938, number of different persons employed rather than number of positions.

[5] Estimated figures, 1970–1990.

[6] In censuses prior to 1919, computed for teaching positions only; beginning with 1919, also includes supervisors and principals. Data for 1980 and subsequent years are estimates from the National Education Association.

[7] Data for 1970 and subsequent years are estimated by the National Education Association.

[8] Includes teachers in junior high schools.

Sources

Series Bc97. 1919–1969: U.S. Bureau of the Census, *Historical Statistics of the United States* (1975), series H523; 1970–1994: U.S. Department of Education, *Digest of Education Statistics*, annual issues; see, for example, 1996 issue, Table 81, column 8.

(continued)

TABLE Bc97–106 Public elementary and secondary day school teachers and instructional staff – average annual salary and number, by sex: 1869–1996 *Continued*

Series Bc98–100. U.S. Department of Education, *120 Years of American Education: A Statistical Portrait* (1993), Table 14. The series rely on Abbott L. Ferriss, *Indicators of Trends in American Education* (Russell Sage Foundation, 1969), series B-1, B-2, and B-3; U.S. Office of Education, *Biennial Survey of Education in the United States*; and the *Digest of Education Statistics*, which has been used for updates since 1991. See, especially, *Digest of Education Statistics 1996*, Tables 4 and 63. For some years, the Ferriss data have been used in place of those in U.S. Department of Education (1993). The sex breakdown is continued in the *Digest of Education Statistics* sporadically after 1990.

Series Bc101–102. 1870–1954: Ferriss (1969), series B-5 and B-6; subsequent years from *Digest of Education Statistics*, annual issues; see, for example, 1996 issue, Table 63, columns 5, 6, and 7.

Series Bc103. U.S. Department of Education (1993), Table 14, which is from U.S. Bureau of the Census (1975) through 1968, and from the *Digest of Education Statistics* after 1968. Updated data are from *Digest of Education Statistics 1997*, Table 81.

Series Bc104–106. *Digest of Education Statistics 1997*, Table 77.

Documentation

The instructional staff category includes all public elementary and secondary day-school positions that are concerned with teaching or its improvement, including consultants or supervisors of instruction, principals, teachers, guidance personnel, librarians, psychological personnel, and other instructional staff. The category excludes administrative staff, attendance personnel, clerical personnel, and junior college staff.

Classroom teachers are defined as staff members who instruct pupils in self-contained classes or courses, or in classroom situations. The Schools and Staffing Survey (SASS), first conducted in 1987, provides a more precise description of a teacher. For the purposes of SASS, a teacher is any full- or part-time instructor whose primary assignment is to teach in any of the K–12 grades. Beginning in 1993, anyone in a school who taught grades K–12 but whose primary assignment was different work (for example, a principal) was also defined as a teacher. The following individuals were not considered teachers: short-term substitutes, student teachers, nonteaching specialists (such as guidance counselors, librarians, nurses, and psychologists), administrators, teacher aides, or other professional or support staff. SASS classified teachers as elementary or secondary on the basis of the grades they taught rather than the schools in which they taught. An elementary school teacher was one who, when asked for the grades taught, stated below ninth or, if ungraded, identified him- or herself as an elementary school teacher. A secondary school teacher was one who claimed to teach ninth grade or higher, seventh grade and higher with no primary assignments at the elementary level, or if ungraded, identified him- or herself as a secondary school teacher. Previous definitions of elementary and secondary teachers are less precise. In most cases, data have been revised to account for teachers in secondary schools (for example, junior high schools for grades 7–9).

Series Bc98. May not always equal the sum of series Bc101–102, elementary and secondary teachers, or series Bc99–100, male and female teachers.

TABLE Bc107–114 Catholic elementary and secondary school enrollment, staff, and percentage lay staff: 1920–1996[1]

Contributed by Claudia Goldin

	Schools		Enrollment		Instructional staff			
					Elementary		Secondary	
	Elementary	Secondary	Elementary	Secondary	Number	Percentage lay	Number	Percentage lay
School	Bc107	Bc108	Bc109	Bc110	Bc111 [2]	Bc112	Bc113 [2]	Bc114
year	Number	Number	Number	Number	Number	Percent	Number	Percent
1920	6,551	1,552	1,795,673	129,848	41,592	—	7,924	—
1930	7,923	2,123	2,222,598	241,869	58,245	8.6	14,307	—
1936	7,929	1,946	2,103,000	285,000	59,000	5.1	17,000	17.6
1940	7,944	2,105	2,035,182	361,123	60,081	—	20,976	—
1947	—	2,111	—	467,000	—	—	27,000	14.8
1948	8,285	2,150	2,305,000	483,000	62,000	4.8	27,000	14.8
1950	8,589	2,189	2,560,815	505,572	66,525	7.5	27,770	18.0
1952	8,880	2,180	2,842,000	549,000	72,000	8.3	29,000	17.2
1954	9,279	2,296	3,235,000	624,000	77,000	11.7	32,000	18.8
1956	9,615	2,311	3,571,000	705,000	85,000	16.5	35,000	20.0
1960	10,501	2,392	4,373,422	880,369	108,169	26.8	43,733	25.2
1961	10,631	2,376	4,445,000	938,000	111,000	29.7	47,000	29.8
1962	10,676	2,502	4,485,000	1,009,000	112,000	32.1	47,000	27.7
1963	10,775	2,430	4,546,000	1,044,000	115,000	33.0	51,000	31.4
1964	10,832	2,417	4,534,000	1,067,000	118,000	35.6	53,000	34.0
1965	10,879	2,413	4,492,000	1,082,000	120,000	36.7	57,000	33.3
1966	10,769	2,463	4,375,000	1,110,000	120,000	38.3	56,000	35.7
1967	10,350	2,277	4,106,000	1,093,000	124,000	42.7	55,000	38.2
1968	10,113	2,192	3,860,000	1,081,000	126,000	46.0	57,000	40.4
1969	9,695	2,076	3,607,168	1,050,930	133,200 [3]	40.5	62,200 [3]	37.0
1970	9,370	1,980	3,355,478	1,008,088	112,750	53.2	53,458	48.6
1971	8,982	1,859	3,075,785	959,000	106,686	—	52,397	—
1972	8,761	1,743	2,871,000	919,000	105,384	—	50,580	—
1973	8,569	1,728	2,714,000	907,000	102,785	—	51,098	—
1974	8,437	1,690	2,602,000	902,000	100,011	—	50,168	—

Notes appear at end of table

TABLE Bc107–114 Catholic elementary and secondary school enrollment, staff, and percentage lay staff: 1920–1996 *Continued*

	Schools		Enrollment		Instructional staff			
					Elementary		Secondary	
	Elementary	Secondary	Elementary	Secondary	Number	Percentage lay	Number	Percentage lay
	Bc107	Bc108	Bc109	Bc110	Bc111 [2]	Bc112	Bc113 [2]	Bc114
School year	Number	Number	Number	Number	Number	Percent	Number	Percent
1975	8,340	1,653	2,525,000	890,000	99,319	—	49,957	—
1976	8,281	1,623	2,483,000	882,000	100,016	—	50,594	—
1977	8,204	1,593	2,421,000	868,000	99,739	—	50,909	—
1978	8,159	1,564	2,365,000	853,000	98,539	—	49,409	—
1979	8,100	1,540	2,293,000	846,000	97,724	—	49,570	—
1980	8,043	1,516	2,269,000	837,000	96,739	—	49,038	—
1981	7,996	1,498	2,266,000	828,000	96,847	—	49,325	—
1982	7,950	1,482	2,211,412	795,777	97,337	—	49,123	—
1983	7,937	1,464	2,179,000	790,000	98,591	—	48,322	—
1984	7,876	1,449	2,119,000	784,000	99,820	—	50,068	—
1985	7,790	1,430	2,061,000	760,000	96,741	—	49,853	—
1986	7,693	1,409	1,998,000	728,000	93,554	—	48,376	—
1987	7,601	1,391	1,942,000	681,000	93,199	—	46,688	—
1988	7,505	1,362	1,912,000	639,000	93,154	—	44,546	—
1989	7,395	1,324	1,894,000	606,000	94,197	—	42,703	—
1990	7,291	1,296	1,883,906	591,533	91,039	—	40,159	—
1991	7,239	1,269	1,856,302	586,622	109,084	—	44,250	—
1992	7,174	1,249	1,860,937	583,905	109,825	—	44,991	—
1993	7,114	1,231	1,859,947	584,662	112,199	—	45,002	—
1994	7,055	1,238	1,877,782	597,425	117,620 [4]	—	46,599 [4]	—
1995	7,022	1,228	1,884,461	606,650	118,753 [4]	—	48,006 [4]	—
1996	7,005	1,226	1,885,037	612,161	107,548 [4]	—	45,728 [4]	—

[1] Through 1956, data are for school year ending in the year shown; thereafter, for fall (October) of year shown.

[2] Beginning in 1970, includes full-time teaching staff only.

[3] Includes estimates for the nonreporting schools.

[4] Full-time equivalent.

Sources

Series Bc107–111 and Bc113. 1920–1982: U.S. Department of Education, *120 Years of American Education: A Statistical Portrait* (1993), Table 15; 1983–1996: U.S. Department of Education, *Digest of Education Statistics 1997,* Table 62. Data in U.S. Department of Education (1993) are virtually identical to those in the *Digest of Education Statistics,* with the exception of several revised statistics in the 1980s.

Series Bc112. U.S. Bureau of the Census, *Historical Statistics of the United States* (1975), series H539 divided by series Bc111.

Series Bc114. U.S. Bureau of the Census (1975), series H544 divided by series Bc113.

Documentation

These data are reported by the National Catholic Educational Association and are not directly comparable to other series that come from the National Center for Education Statistics because survey procedures and definitions differ. Enrollment excludes prekindergarten. The data for elementary school teachers exclude priests serving as part-time teachers of religion.

The elementary division of the Catholic school system includes five types of schools: (1) parochial schools operated in connection with parishes; (2) interparochial schools under the administrative control of two or more parishes; (3) archdiocesan or diocesan schools under the direct administration of an ordinary and that serve the parishes designated by him; (4) private schools conducted independently of parishes by religious communities; and (5) institutional schools such as industrial schools; those for the blind, deaf, delinquent, or other disadvantaged children; and those conducted in orphanages. In Catholic secondary education there are, broadly, three types of administrative control: (1) central or diocesan, (2) parochial, and (3) private. Many parochial and private schools, however, actually function as diocesan schools.

TABLE Bc115–145 Percentage of public school students enrolled in selected subjects, grades 9–12: 1889–1981[1]

Contributed by Claudia Goldin

	Academic subjects														
	Physical and biological science						Mathematics				Languages and literature				
	Biology	General science	Chemistry	Physiology	Physics	Earth science	Algebra	General mathematics	Geometry	Trigonometry	English	Rhetoric	Spanish	French	German
School year	Bc115	Bc116	Bc117	Bc118	Bc119	Bc120	Bc121	Bc122	Bc123	Bc124	Bc125 [2]	Bc126 [2]	Bc127	Bc128	Bc129
beginning	Percent	Percent	Percent	Percent	Percent	Percent	Percent	Percent	Percent	Percent	Percent	Percent	Percent	Percent	Percent
1889 [5]	—	—	10.10	—	22.21	—	45.39	—	21.33	—	—	—	—	5.84	10.51
1899 [5]	—	—	7.72	27.42	19.04	29.76	56.29	—	27.39	1.91	42.10	38.48	—	7.78	14.33
1909	23.78	—	6.89	15.32	14.61	21.03	56.85	—	30.87	1.87	57.09	57.10	0.67	9.90	23.69
1914	19.25	—	7.38	9.48	14.23	15.34	48.84	—	26.55	1.48	55.82	58.42	2.39	8.80	24.39
1921	14.11	18.27	7.40	5.18	8.93	4.51	40.15	12.38	22.68	1.53	78.60	—	11.30	15.50	0.65
1927	15.94	17.50	7.07	2.68	6.85	2.80	35.22	7.88	19.80	1.27	93.09	—	9.44	14.02	1.84
1933	16.12	17.75	7.56	1.82	6.27	1.75	30.41	7.41	17.06	1.33	90.54	—	6.23	10.87	2.37
1948	18.60	20.80	7.60	1.00	5.40	0.40	26.80	13.05	12.80	2.00	92.90	—	8.20	4.70	0.80
1954 [6]	20.00	—	7.50	—	4.70	—	25.30	12.30	12.50	2.60	—	—	—	—	—
1958 [6]	20.80	19.60	8.10	—	4.70	—	29.90	12.70	13.40	2.70	—	—	—	—	—
1960	21.74	22.22	9.06	0.80	4.89	0.93	28.58	17.37	13.78	3.00	94.64	—	9.82	8.04	1.72
1962 [6]	24.00	17.60	8.30	—	3.80	—	30.40	11.70	14.70	2.00	—	—	—	—	—
1964 [6]	23.20	18.70	9.30	—	4.50	—	28.50	15.40	13.90	2.00	—	—	14.50	12.40	2.70
1972	18.60	11.30	8.70	0.90	2.90	3.80	19.70	13.80	11.60	6.20	89.80	—	12.30	7.60	3.10
1981	24.10	23.00	9.80	1.20	1.00	0.70	29.50	21.70	11.40	3.50	86.50	—	12.30	6.60	2.10

	Academic subjects					Industrial and commercial subjects					Other (generally nonacademic) subjects					
	Languages and literature		History and social sciences													
	Latin	Other foreign language	History	Civics and government	Other social sciences	Typewriting	Industrial subjects	Bookkeeping	Shorthand	Other business subjects	Physical education	Art	Home economics	Music	Agriculture	Miscellaneous
School year	Bc130	Bc131	Bc132	Bc133	Bc134	Bc135	Bc136 [3]	Bc137	Bc138	Bc139 [4]	Bc140	Bc141 [3]	Bc142	Bc143	Bc144	Bc145
beginning	Percent	Percent	Percent	Percent	Percent	Percent	Percent	Percent	Percent	Percent	Percent	Percent	Percent	Percent	Percent	Percent
1889 [5]	34.69	3.05	27.31	—	—	—	—	—	—	—	—	—	—	—	—	—
1899 [5]	50.61	2.85	38.16	21.66	2.38	—	—	—	—	—	—	—	—	—	—	—
1909	49.05	0.75	55.03	15.55	0.96	—	—	—	—	—	—	—	3.78	—	4.66	—
1914	37.32	0.29	50.54	15.72	1.17	—	11.20	3.42	—	—	—	22.90	12.89	31.50	7.17	—
1921	27.50	0.12	50.74	19.30	8.08	13.10	13.70	12.55	8.90	5.36	5.73	14.70	14.27	25.40	5.11	7.03
1927	21.98	0.13	46.51	21.08	8.76	15.17	13.50	10.67	8.69	13.71	15.03	11.70	16.48	26.04	3.66	8.40
1933	16.04	0.23	42.73	19.79	7.71	16.66	21.00	9.85	8.99	16.86	50.66	8.70	16.72	25.54	3.55	9.50
1948	7.80	0.30	42.70	13.24	15.30	22.50	26.60	8.70	7.80	14.50	69.40	9.00	24.20	30.10	6.70	6.46
1954 [6]	—	—	—	—	—	—	—	—	—	—	—	—	—	—	—	—
1958 [6]	—	—	—	—	—	—	—	—	—	—	—	—	—	—	—	—
1960	7.76	0.31	44.35	23.03	16.04	23.15	28.00	7.67	6.70	9.96	73.75	19.33	23.13	28.02	6.18	7.19
1962 [6]	—	—	—	—	—	—	—	—	—	—	—	—	—	—	—	—
1964 [6]	—	—	—	—	—	—	—	—	—	—	—	—	—	—	—	—
1972	1.50	0.30	46.30	15.20	20.00	20.30	3.70	5.80	4.60	9.90	56.90	17.90	20.40	25.10	2.70	30.00
1981	1.10	0.30	44.70	18.70	29.80	21.00	14.80	3.20	3.10	12.30	59.00	24.20	23.90	21.60	3.30	20.10

[1] Subjects in each group are in descending order relative to their enrollments in 1981.

[2] For 1889 to 1914, enrollments in English (termed "English literature") and rhetoric were listed separately. Many students were probably taking the two subjects as part of one course. See text.

[3] Original sources for 1914–1933 give higher numbers for art and lower numbers for industrial subjects than in the revised estimates in *Biennial Survey, 1948–50*. It is likely that the subject of draftsmanship was shifted from art to industrial subjects.

[4] Subject to compositional change. See text.

[5] See text concerning undercounts.

[6] Incomplete listing of subjects in original source.

Sources

1889, *Annual Report of the Commissioner of Education, 1890*, p. 1392; 1899, *Annual Report of the Commissioner of Education, 1900*, Tables 10 and 11, pp. 2138–9; 1909, *Annual Report of the Commissioner of Education, 1910*, Tables 138–140, pp. 1182–4; 1914, *Annual Report of the Commissioner of Education, 1916*, Tables 34, 47–50, pp. 487, 500; 1921, U.S. Office of Education, *Biennial Survey of Education in the United States, 1920–22*, Table 34, p. 599; 1927, U.S. Office of Education, *Biennial Survey of Education in the United States, 1926–28*, Tables 59 and 61, pp. 1057–60; 1933, U.S. Office of Education, *Biennial Survey of Education in the United States, 1936–38*, Table 24, p. 24; 1948, U.S. Office of Education, *Biennial Survey of Education in the United States, 1948–50*, Tables 5 and 7, chapter 5; 1954, 1958, 1962, and 1964, U.S. Department of Education, *120 Years of American Education: A Statistical Portrait* (1993), Table 16; 1960, U.S. Department of Health, Education, and Welfare, Office of Education, *Subject Offerings and Enrollments in Public Secondary Schools, 1965*, Table 7; 1972 and 1981, U.S. National Center for Education Statistics, *A Trend Study of High School Offerings and Enrollments: 1972–73 and 1981–82* (1984), Tables 1 and 2.

Documentation

All series are based on surveys of schools requested by the U.S. Commissioner of Education or the Department (Office) of Education. However, the collection of these data changed over the years. For 1909 to 1933, the percentages are based on the number of pupils enrolled in the last four years of all schools that returned usable questionnaires. For subsequent years, the figures are based on the total number of pupils enrolled in the last four years of all schools. Thus, starting with 1948 schools were sampled and the results were then weighted to approximate the percentages taking specific subjects in all public secondary schools.

The caution noted in the *Biennial Survey, 1948–50*, p. 5, is worth repeating: "Obviously special caution should be used in drawing conclusions. . . . Because subjects are represented . . . only as they have from time to time been judged important in the number of their enrollments, many desirable details are missing. It is possible to do little more than trace the broad outlines of most changes which have occurred. Percentage enrollments in the different investigations reported in the historical table are not precisely comparable. Beginning with 1910 and until the present investigation, the percentage of pupils in each subject is based upon the number of pupils in the schools reporting subject enrollments." By implication, then, the percentages for 1889 and 1899 are based on all students in grades 9–12. Data in these two years may, therefore, seriously understate the percentages taking various courses of study because the denominator may include those in schools responding incompletely or not at all.

In all years, the percentages are intended to give the number of pupils, in grades 9–12, taking specific courses of study during the school year divided by the total number of pupils in those grades. Information was not given concerning whether the subjects listed were semester or full-year courses. Some were clearly full-year courses, others were probably semester courses, and others may have been half-semester in length. If all courses of study were full-year the "all subjects" totals, for 1909–1981 (excluding the four incomplete years), ranging from about 450 and 550, imply that pupils in grades 9–12 were taking about five full-year courses each year.

Prior versions of this table (see, for example, U.S. Department of Education 1993, Table 16) aggregated various subjects and omitted others. The reasons are given in the source for the revised data (*Biennial Survey, 1948–50*): "When necessary, the subjects reported in previous surveys were analyzed, and appropriate components were either recombined, separately listed, or eliminated (with corresponding changes in the number and percentage enrolled) in a manner to yield as close comparability as possible with the data in the current (1948–49) survey." In constructing this table, the original sources were used to obtain greater detail and more accurately reflect changes in curriculum over time. However, there are cases in which the procedure will overstate the number of full-year courses taken. By adding together various other history courses, the percentage taking history may be overstated if students took history courses covering English history and modern history, for example. Previous versions of this table aggregated only U.S. history and English history to form the history group.

Subjects surveyed were intended to include only those for which secondary school credit was given and to exclude extracurricular activities. The large increase in the percentage taking physical education between 1927 and 1933 may represent a change in the category rather than an increase in the activity.

Series Bc115. Includes botany and zoology.

Series Bc120. For 1889–1933, physical geography, astronomy, and geology were reported separately, but subsequently were combined under the heading of earth science. In 1972 and 1981, earth science also includes geology and astronomy.

Series Bc122. Includes arithmetic, business arithmetic, and general mathematics, not all of which are listed in each year.

Series Bc125–126. For 1889–1914, enrollments in English (termed "English literature") and rhetoric were listed separately. In 1909 and 1914, the combined enrollments in these two subjects was 114 percent of the total enrollment and many students were probably taking the two subjects as a part of one course. In 1921, the U.S. Office of Education attempted to collect enrollments in the various English subjects, but it became necessary to combine them all under the heading "English." The Office of Education reported that, in 1921–1922, 78.6 percent of the pupils in schools reporting enrollment by subject (excluding duplicates) were taking one or more English subjects. The implication, therefore, is that about half of the students previously listed as taking both English literature and rhetoric were taking them as part of the same course.

Series Bc131. Includes Greek, Russian, and Italian.

Series Bc132. Includes U.S., English, world, ancient, medieval, and modern history.

Series Bc133. Includes "problems of democracy."

Series Bc134. Includes geography, sociology, economics, consumer education, and psychology.

Series Bc139. Includes business English, business law, commercial geography, commercial history, penmanship, office practice, elementary business training, retailing, cooperative store training, cooperative office training, and salesmanship and advertising. Some of the subjects contained enrollments throughout the years, although some disappeared. The group as a whole, however, appears to reflect an interest in business and commercial subjects that was steady, but subject to compositional change.

Series Bc145. Includes teacher training, journalism, speech and public speaking, hygiene and sanitation, and safety and driver's education.

TABLE Bc146–257 Average number of Carnegie units earned by public high school graduates, by subject field, sex, race, and ethnicity: 1982–1994

Contributed by Claudia Goldin

All persons

Year of graduation	Total	English	History and social studies	Mathematics: Total	Mathematics: Mathematics less than algebra	Mathematics: Mathematics algebra or higher	Science: Total	Science: General science	Science: Biology	Science: Chemistry	Science: Physics	Foreign languages	Arts	Vocational education	Personal use	Computer science
	Bc146	Bc147	Bc148	Bc149	Bc150	Bc151	Bc152	Bc153	Bc154	Bc155	Bc156	Bc157	Bc158	Bc159	Bc160	Bc161 [1]
	Number	Number	Number	Number	Number	Number	Number	Number	Number	Number	Number	Number	Number	Number	Number	Number
1982	21.64	3.90	3.19	2.57	0.92	1.65	2.17	0.74	0.93	0.34	0.17	0.97	1.46	4.68	2.69	0.14
1987	23.06	4.06	3.37	3.05	0.95	2.10	2.53	0.75	1.09	0.48	0.21	1.38	1.43	4.48	2.94	0.49
1990	23.54	4.09	3.50	3.20	0.99	2.21	2.75	0.84	1.14	0.54	0.23	1.59	1.55	4.10	2.95	0.55
1994	24.16	4.20	3.57	3.37	0.85	2.53	3.04	0.87	1.26	0.62	0.28	1.76	1.66	3.87	2.92	0.65

Males

Year of graduation	Total	English	History and social studies	Mathematics: Total	Mathematics: Mathematics less than algebra	Mathematics: Mathematics algebra or higher	Science: Total	Science: General science	Science: Biology	Science: Chemistry	Science: Physics	Foreign languages	Arts	Vocational education	Personal use	Computer science
	Bc162	Bc163	Bc164	Bc165	Bc166	Bc167	Bc168	Bc169	Bc170	Bc171	Bc172	Bc173	Bc174	Bc175	Bc176	Bc177 [1]
	Number	Number	Number	Number	Number	Number	Number	Number	Number	Number	Number	Number	Number	Number	Number	Number
1982	21.44	3.86	3.19	2.65	0.99	1.66	2.24	0.77	0.89	0.35	0.22	0.78	1.29	4.63	2.80	0.16
1987	22.92	4.03	3.35	3.10	1.01	2.09	2.58	0.78	1.05	0.49	0.26	1.18	1.23	4.58	3.13	0.49
1990	23.36	4.04	3.47	3.22	1.06	2.16	2.78	0.87	1.11	0.53	0.28	1.39	1.31	4.23	3.17	0.52
1994	23.98	4.16	3.54	3.36	0.93	2.44	3.02	0.90	1.20	0.60	0.32	1.54	1.43	4.07	3.18	0.65

Females

Year of graduation	Total	English	History and social studies	Mathematics: Total	Mathematics: Mathematics less than algebra	Mathematics: Mathematics algebra or higher	Science: Total	Science: General science	Science: Biology	Science: Chemistry	Science: Physics	Foreign languages	Arts	Vocational education	Personal use	Computer science
	Bc178	Bc179	Bc180	Bc181	Bc182	Bc183	Bc184	Bc185	Bc186	Bc187	Bc188	Bc189	Bc190	Bc191	Bc192	Bc193 [1]
	Number	Number	Number	Number	Number	Number	Number	Number	Number	Number	Number	Number	Number	Number	Number	Number
1982	21.82	3.93	3.20	2.49	0.85	1.64	2.11	0.71	0.97	0.32	0.12	1.14	1.63	4.72	2.60	0.13
1987	23.18	4.09	3.39	3.00	0.89	2.11	2.49	0.73	1.13	0.47	0.16	1.57	1.63	4.38	2.75	0.49
1990	23.70	4.13	3.52	3.18	0.93	2.25	2.72	0.82	1.17	0.54	0.19	1.78	1.77	3.99	2.74	0.57
1994	24.33	4.23	3.61	3.38	0.77	2.62	3.05	0.85	1.31	0.65	0.25	1.97	1.87	3.69	2.68	0.65

Whites

Year of graduation	Total	English	History and social studies	Mathematics: Total	Mathematics: Mathematics less than algebra	Mathematics: Mathematics algebra or higher	Science: Total	Science: General science	Science: Biology	Science: Chemistry	Science: Physics	Foreign languages	Arts	Vocational education	Personal use	Computer science
	Bc194	Bc195	Bc196	Bc197	Bc198	Bc199	Bc200	Bc201	Bc202	Bc203	Bc204	Bc205	Bc206	Bc207	Bc208	Bc209 [1]
	Number	Number	Number	Number	Number	Number	Number	Number	Number	Number	Number	Number	Number	Number	Number	Number
1982	21.75	3.88	3.23	2.61	0.79	1.82	2.25	0.73	0.96	0.37	0.19	1.03	1.52	4.58	2.63	0.15
1987	23.14	4.06	3.33	3.06	0.84	2.22	2.59	0.74	1.12	0.51	0.23	1.38	1.49	4.55	2.86	0.50
1990	23.55	4.08	3.48	3.17	0.89	2.28	2.79	0.83	1.15	0.56	0.25	1.58	1.61	4.13	2.87	0.53
1994	24.31	4.19	3.58	3.39	0.78	2.62	3.12	0.88	1.29	0.66	0.30	1.75	1.74	3.87	2.87	0.64

Blacks

Year of graduation	Total	English	History and social studies	Mathematics: Total	Mathematics: Mathematics less than algebra	Mathematics: Mathematics algebra or higher	Science: Total	Science: General science	Science: Biology	Science: Chemistry	Science: Physics	Foreign languages	Arts	Vocational education	Personal use	Computer science
	Bc210	Bc211	Bc212	Bc213	Bc214	Bc215	Bc216	Bc217	Bc218	Bc219	Bc220	Bc221	Bc222	Bc223	Bc224	Bc225 [1]
	Number	Number	Number	Number	Number	Number	Number	Number	Number	Number	Number	Number	Number	Number	Number	Number
1982	21.25	4.06	3.11	2.55	1.39	1.16	2.04	0.81	0.89	0.25	0.09	0.71	1.25	4.84	2.68	0.16
1987	22.43	4.17	3.37	2.97	1.45	1.52	2.29	0.87	1.02	0.30	0.10	1.07	1.17	4.64	3.08	0.41
1990	23.41	4.25	3.51	3.25	1.33	1.92	2.68	0.97	1.11	0.44	0.16	1.23	1.34	4.39	3.02	0.61
1994	23.60	4.31	3.54	3.26	1.15	2.12	2.80	0.91	1.21	0.50	0.18	1.37	1.36	4.24	3.00	0.65

Hispanics

Year of graduation	Total	English	History and social studies	Mathematics: Total	Mathematics: Mathematics less than algebra	Mathematics: Mathematics algebra or higher	Science: Total	Science: General science	Science: Biology	Science: Chemistry	Science: Physics	Foreign languages	Arts	Vocational education	Personal use	Computer science
	Bc226	Bc227	Bc228	Bc229	Bc230	Bc231	Bc232	Bc233	Bc234	Bc235	Bc236	Bc237	Bc238	Bc239	Bc240	Bc241 [1]
	Number	Number	Number	Number	Number	Number	Number	Number	Number	Number	Number	Number	Number	Number	Number	Number
1982	21.30	3.89	3.03	2.26	1.23	1.03	1.78	0.77	0.79	0.16	0.06	0.76	1.31	5.26	3.02	0.09
1987	23.00	4.03	3.30	2.91	1.40	1.50	2.31	0.82	1.06	0.32	0.11	1.61	1.36	4.20	3.49	0.45
1990	23.85	4.05	3.46	3.22	1.41	1.81	2.49	0.83	1.11	0.42	0.14	1.99	1.48	3.99	3.43	0.59
1994	24.07	4.11	3.49	3.39	1.09	2.30	2.69	0.83	1.19	0.50	0.18	2.10	1.51	3.70	3.36	0.76

Note appears at end of table

(continued)

TABLE Bc146–257 Average number of Carnegie units earned by public high school graduates, by subject field, sex, race, and ethnicity: 1982–1994 *Continued*

	Asians															
				Mathematics			Science									
	Total	English	History and social studies	Total	Mathematics less than algebra	Mathematics algebra or higher	Total	General science	Biology	Chemistry	Physics	Foreign languages	Arts	Vocational education	Personal use	Computer science
Year of graduation	Bc242	Bc243	Bc244	Bc245	Bc246	Bc247	Bc248	Bc249	Bc250	Bc251	Bc252	Bc253	Bc254	Bc255	Bc256	Bc257 [1]
	Number	Number	Number	Number	Number	Number	Number	Number	Number	Number	Number	Number	Number	Number	Number	Number
1982	22.43	3.82	3.18	3.16	0.71	2.44	2.59	0.50	1.09	0.60	0.40	1.96	1.31	3.23	3.17	0.23
1987	24.77	4.01	3.75	3.89	0.64	3.24	3.20	0.59	1.17	0.92	0.53	2.48	1.09	2.95	3.45	0.63
1990	24.08	4.02	3.70	3.64	0.83	2.81	2.97	0.68	1.12	0.74	0.42	2.52	1.30	2.89	3.12	0.55
1994	24.50	4.04	3.68	3.76	0.81	2.95	3.35	0.79	1.22	0.82	0.52	2.62	1.31	2.88	2.92	0.73

[1] Computer courses are included in mathematics and vocational categories.

Sources

U.S. Department of Education, *Digest of Education Statistics 1997* (1997), Table 136. The underlying sources are: U.S. Department of Education, "High School and Beyond," first follow-up survey; "1990 High School Transcript Study," "National Education Longitudinal Study of 1988," second follow-up survey, and "1994 High School Transcript Study."

Documentation

The Carnegie unit is a standard of measurement that represents one credit for the completion of a one-year course.

Vocational education includes nonoccupational vocational education, vocational general introduction, agriculture, business, marketing, health, occupational home economics, trade and industry, and technical courses.

The personal use category includes personal and social courses, religion and theology, and courses not included in other subject fields.

TABLE Bc258–264 Public and private high school graduates, by sex and as a percentage of all 17-year-olds: 1870–1997

Contributed by Claudia Goldin

	High school graduates						
				Type of control			
	Total	Male	Female	Public	Private	Population of 17-year-olds	Graduates as a percentage of all 17-year-olds
School year ending	Bc258 [1]	Bc259 [2, 3]	Bc260 [2, 3]	Bc261	Bc262	Bc263	Bc264 [4]
	Thousand	Thousand	Thousand	Thousand	Thousand	Thousand	Percent
1870	16	7	9	—	—	815	1.96
1871	17	7	9	—	—	—	—
1872	17	8	10	—	—	—	—
1873	18	8	10	—	—	—	—
1874	19	8	11	—	—	—	—
1875	20	9	11	—	—	—	—
1876	20	9	11	—	—	—	—
1877	21	9	11	—	—	—	—
1878	22	10	12	—	—	—	—
1879	23	10	13	—	—	—	—
1880	24	11	13	—	—	946	2.54
1881	25	11	14	—	—	—	—
1882	27	12	15	—	—	—	—
1883	28	13	16	—	—	—	—
1884	31	14	17	—	—	—	—
1885	32	14	18	—	—	—	—
1886	33	15	18	—	—	—	—
1887	32	14	18	—	—	—	—
1888	33	14	19	—	—	—	—
1889	39	16	22	—	—	—	—
1890	44	19	25	—	—	1,259	3.49
1891	48	20	28	—	—	—	—
1892	53	21	32	—	—	—	—
1893	59	24	35	—	—	—	—
1894	65	27	39	—	—	—	—
1895	72	29	43	—	—	—	—
1896	76	31	45	—	—	—	—
1897	80	32	47	—	—	—	—
1898	84	34	50	—	—	—	—
1899	90	36	53	—	—	—	—
1900	95	38	57	—	—	1,489	6.38
1901	97	37	60	—	—	—	—
1902	99	39	61	—	—	—	—
1903	105	41	64	—	—	—	—
1904	112	44	68	—	—	—	—
1905	119	47	72	—	—	—	—
1906	126	50	76	—	—	—	—
1907	127	51	76	—	—	—	—
1908	129	52	77	—	—	—	—
1909	142	57	84	—	—	—	—
1910	156	64	93	123	33	1,814 [5]	8.60
1911	168	69	99	133	35	1,823	9.22
1912	181	74	106	—	—	1,832	9.88
1913	200	82	117	163	37	1,842	10.86
1914	219	90	129	180	39	1,851	11.83
1915	240	99	140	—	—	1,860	12.90
1916	259	108	151	220	39	1,870	13.85
1917	272	110	162	—	—	1,879	14.48
1918	285	112	173	245	40	1,889	15.09
1919	298	118	180	—	—	1,898	15.70
1920	311	124	188	268	43	1,908 [5]	16.30
1921	334	137	198	—	—	1,944	17.18
1922	357	150	207	313	44	1,980	18.03
1923	426	181	244	—	—	2,017	21.12
1924	494	213	281	437	57	2,055	24.04
1925	528	230	298	—	—	2,093	25.23
1926	561	246	315	495	66	2,132	26.31
1927	579	256	323	—	—	2,172	26.66
1928	597	266	330	533	64	2,213	26.98
1929	632	283	349	—	—	2,254	28.04

Notes appear at end of table

(continued)

TABLE Bc258–264 Public and private high school graduates, by sex and as a percentage of all 17-year-olds: 1870–1997 *Continued*

	High school graduates						
				Type of control			
	Total	Male	Female	Public	Private	Population of 17-year-olds	Graduates as a percentage of all 17-year-olds
School year ending	Bc258 [1]	Bc259 [2, 3]	Bc260 [2, 3]	Bc261	Bc262	Bc263	Bc264 [4]
	Thousand	Thousand	Thousand	Thousand	Thousand	Thousand	Percent
1930	667	300	367	599	68	2,296	29.05
1931	747	337	409	—	—	2,327	32.10
1932	827	375	452	747	80	2,330	35.49
1933	871	403	468	—	—	2,335	37.30
1934	915	432	483	843	72	2,334	39.20
1935	965	459	506	—	—	2,348	41.10
1936	1,015	486	530	941	74	2,377	42.70
1937	1,068	505	563	—	—	2,416	44.21
1938	1,120	524	596	1,039	81	2,456	45.60
1940	1,221	579	643	1,136	85	2,403	50.81
1942	1,242	577	666	—	—	2,421	51.30
1944	1,019	424	595	—	—	2,386	42.71
1946	1,080	467	613	—	—	2,278	47.41
1948	1,190	563	627	1,073	117	2,261	52.63
1950	1,200	571	629	1,063	136	2,034	59.00
1952	1,197	569	627	1,056	141	2,086	57.38
1954	1,276	613	664	1,129	147	2,135	59.77
1956	1,415	680	735	1,252	163	2,242	63.11
1957	1,434	690	744	1,270	164	2,272	63.12
1958	1,506	725	781	1,332	174	2,325	64.77
1959	1,627	784	843	1,435	192	2,458	66.19
1960	1,858	895	963	1,627	231	2,672	69.54
1961	1,964	955	1,009	1,725	239	2,892	67.91
1962	1,918	938	980	1,678	240	2,768	69.29
1963	1,943	956	987	1,710	233	2,740	70.91
1964	2,283	1,120	1,163	2,008	275	2,978	76.66
1965	2,658	1,311	1,347	2,360	298	3,684	72.15
1966	2,665	1,323	1,342	2,367	298	3,489	76.38
1967	2,672	1,328	1,344	2,374	298	3,500	76.34
1968	2,695	1,338	1,357	2,395	300	3,532	76.30
1969	2,822	1,399	1,423	2,522	300	3,659	77.12
1970	2,889	1,430	1,459	2,589	300	3,757	76.90
1971	2,937	1,454	1,483	2,638	300	3,872	75.85
1972	3,001	1,487	1,514	2,700	302	3,973	75.53
1973	3,036	1,500	1,536	2,729	306	4,049	74.98
1974	3,073	1,512	1,561	2,763	310	4,132	74.37
1975	3,133	1,542	1,591	2,823	310	4,256	73.61
1976	3,148	1,552	1,596	2,837	311	4,272	73.69
1977	3,152	1,548	1,604	2,837	315	4,272	73.78
1978	3,127	1,531	1,596	2,825	302	4,286	72.96
1979	3,101	1,517	1,584	2,801	300	4,327	71.67
1980	3,043	1,491	1,552	2,748	295	4,262	71.40
1981	3,020	1,483	1,537	2,725	295	4,212	71.70
1982	2,995	1,471	1,524	2,705	290	4,134	72.45
1983	2,888	1,437	1,451	2,598	290	3,962	72.89
1984	2,767	1,313	1,454	2,495	272	3,784	73.12
1985	2,677	1,291	1,386	2,414	263	3,699	72.37
1986	2,643	1,263	1,380	2,383	260	3,670	72.02
1987	2,694	1,301	1,393	2,429	265	3,754	71.76
1988	2,773	1,384	1,389	2,500	273	3,849	72.04
1989	2,727	1,343	1,384	2,459	268	3,842	70.98
1990	2,586	1,285	1,302	2,320	266	3,574	72.36
1991	2,503	1,257	1,254	2,235	268	3,417	73.25
1992	2,482	—	—	2,226	256	3,381	73.41
1993	2,490	—	—	2,233	257	3,433	72.53
1994	2,479	—	—	2,221	258	3,442	72.02
1995	2,531	—	—	2,274	257	3,571	70.88
1996	2,557	—	—	2,293	264	3,629	70.46
1997	2,623	—	—	2,358	265	3,762	69.72

TABLE Bc258–264 Public and private high school graduates, by sex and as a percentage of all 17-year-olds: 1870–1997 *Continued*

[1] Graduates do not include those receiving General Educational Development (GED) credentials.

[2] The sum of males and females may not always equal the total because different sources are used for the series after 1989.

[3] Data for 1984–1991 are estimates based on data published by the Bureau of Labor Statistics.

[4] Graduates not necessarily 17 years old. See text.

[5] Data from U.S. Bureau of the Census, *Historical Statistics of the United States* (1975), not U.S. population census.

Sources

Series Bc258. 1870–1930: U.S. Bureau of the Census, *Historical Statistics of the United States* (1975), series H598, for which the original source is U.S. Office of Education, *Statistical Summary of Education, 1937–38,* Table 15; 1931–1976: U.S. Department of Education, *120 Years of American Education: A Statistical Portrait* (1993), Table 19, the underlying sources of which are: 1931–1938, *Statistical Summary,* Table 15; 1940–1952, U.S. Office of Education, *Biennial Survey of Education in the United States*; 1954–1970, *Projections of Educational Statistics*; and 1971–1976, U.S. Department of Education, *Digest of Education Statistics,* annual issues; 1977–1997: U.S. Department of Education, *Digest of Education Statistics 1997* (1997), Table 99.

Series Bc259–260. 1870–1930: U.S. Bureau of the Census (1975), series H600 and H601, for which the original source is U.S. Office of Education, *Statistical Summary of Education, 1937–38,* Table 15; 1931–1976 and 1984–1991: U.S. Department of Education (1993), Table 19, for which the original sources are the same as for series Bc258 to 1976; 1977–1983: *Digest of Education Statistics 1997,* Table 99.

Series Bc261–262. 1910–1940: for sources see discussion in Claudia Goldin, "America's Graduation from High School: The Evolution and Spread of Secondary Schooling in the Twentieth Century," *Journal of Economic History* 58 (June 1998): 345–74; the public and private breakdown implicit in the Goldin data are applied to the total in series Bc258. Goldin's estimates are derived from the same data as are the official estimates, and differences between the official estimates of all high school graduates and those in Goldin are small (1910, 0.8 percent; 1920, 0.3 percent; 1930, 1.4 percent). Private secondary school data in Goldin include students in the preparatory departments of colleges and universities. 1948–1997: *Digest of Education Statistics 1997,* Table 99.

Series Bc263. 1870–1997: *Digest of Education Statistics 1997,* Table 99, with the exceptions of 1910 and 1920, for which the data implicit in U.S. Bureau of the Census (1975), series H 598 and H 599, are used. Data for the intercensal years from 1911 to 1929 are estimated using an exponential growth rate extrapolation procedure.

Documentation

High school graduates include graduates from public and nonpublic schools and exclude persons granted equivalency certificates, such as the General Educational Development credential. Individuals of any age receiving a high school diploma are included. The official Department (Office) of Education data on the number of graduates differ from those in the contemporaneous publications of the Office of Education particularly prior to the mid-1930s, when the series were substantially revised. There appears to be no extant documentation of the rationale for the revisions, but see Claudia Goldin, "America's Graduation from High School: The Evolution and Spread of Secondary Schooling in the Twentieth Century," *Journal of Economic History* 58 (June 1998): 345–74, for a method that produces estimates close to those of the Department (Office) of Education that are given here. The inference from Goldin's work is that the Department (Office) of Education revisions applied reasonable estimates of undercounts to schools reporting and added to the private school figures students exiting from the preparatory departments of colleges and universities.

Series Bc263. The number of 17-year-olds for 1910 and 1920 given in the U.S. population census is considerably lower than the number of 16- and 18-year-olds. The data implicit in *Historical Statistics* (1975), series H 598 and H 599, appear to have averaged the numbers in the larger group of older teens. Those are the numbers given here.

Series Bc264. Equals the ratio of series Bc258 and series Bc263 multiplied by 100. The division by the number of 17-year-olds is customary and should not be taken to imply that graduates were 17 years old. The estimation of the number of 17-year-olds, and the fact that not all graduates were 17 years old, creates some problems for the year-to-year movement in the overall series. The change in graduation rate from 1963 to 1966 appears to be a function of the number of 17-year-olds rather than the number of graduates. The increase from 1964 to 1965 in the number of 17-year-olds is the largest on record in the United States.

TABLE Bc265–272 General Educational Development (GED) credentials issued, and number and age distribution of test takers: 1971–1995[1]

Contributed by Claudia Goldin

			Test takers					
				By age (as a percentage of total)				
	Credentials issued	Persons completing test battery	Total	19 or younger	20 to 24	25 to 29	30 to 34	35 or older
	Bc265	Bc266	Bc267 [2]	Bc268	Bc269	Bc270	Bc271	Bc272
Year	Thousand	Thousand	Thousand	Percent	Percent	Percent	Percent	Percent
1971	227	—	337	—	—	—	—	—
1972	245	—	419	—	—	—	—	—
1973	249	—	423	—	—	—	—	—
1974	295	412	540	35	27	13	9	17
1975	342	507	652	33	26	14	9	18
1976	337	507	656	31	28	14	10	17
1977	331	488	680	40	24	13	9	14
1978	381	467	641	31	27	13	10	19
1979	435	583	744	35	27	13	8	16
1980	488	708	779	37	27	13	8	15
1981	500	701	770	37	27	13	8	15
1982	494	692	756	37	28	13	8	15
1983	477	678	740	34	29	14	9	15
1984	437	613	676	32	28	15	9	16
1985	427	622	685	33	26	15	10	16
1986	439	648	713	33	26	15	10	16
1987	458	662	729	33	24	15	10	18
1988	421	617	701	36	23	14	10	17
1989	364	554	645	36	24	13	10	16
1990	419	628	727	35	25	14	10	17
1991	471	672	770	33	27	14	10	17
1992	465	653	754	32	28	13	11	16
1993	476	652	757	33	27	14	11	16
1994	499	684	793	34	26	13	10	16
1995	513	698	803	37	25	13	10	15

[1] United States and outlying areas.

[2] Number taking one or more GED subtests. Individuals can take the exam more than one time in a given year.

Source

U.S. Department of Education, *Digest of Education Statistics 1997*, Table 102. The original source is American Council on Education, General Educational Development Testing Service.

Documentation

The General Educational Development (GED) program was initiated in 1942 as a means of providing World War II veterans lacking high school diplomas with an opportunity to earn a secondary school credential. Civilians first took the test in 1952. Currently, all fifty states, the District of Columbia, outlying areas of the United States, ten Canadian provinces and territories, and several foreign countries use and recognize the GED as an alternative high school credential.

The GED credential has become the primary second-chance route to high school certification for high school dropouts in the United States. It is awarded on the basis of a five-test battery covering mathematics, writing, social studies, science, and "interpreting literature and the arts." Individuals with low scores on any of the tests may retake them.

TABLE Bc273–428 Student proficiency in reading, mathematics, and writing, as measured by the National Assessment of Educational Progress (NAEP), by age, sex, race, and ethnicity: 1971–1996[1]

Contributed by Claudia Goldin

	All persons													
	Percentage of 9-year-olds scoring at or above level in							Mean scores in writing among fourth graders	Percentage of 13-year-olds scoring at or above level in					
	Reading			Mathematics					Reading				Mathematics	
	150 level	200 level	250 level	150 level	200 level	250 level	300 level		150 level	200 level	250 level	300 level	200 level	250 level
	Bc273	Bc274	Bc275	Bc276	Bc277	Bc278	Bc279	Bc280	Bc281	Bc282	Bc283	Bc284	Bc285	Bc286
Year	Percent	Percent	Percent	Percent	Percent	Percent	Percent	Number	Percent	Percent	Percent	Percent	Percent	Percent
1971 [2]	90.6	58.7	15.6	—	—	—	—	—	99.8	93.0	57.8	9.8	—	—
1975	93.1	62.1	14.6	—	—	—	—	—	99.7	93.2	58.6	10.2	—	—
1978	—	—	—	96.7	70.4	19.6	0.8	—	—	—	—	—	94.6	64.9
1980	94.6	67.7	17.7	—	—	—	—	—	99.9	94.8	60.7	11.3	—	—
1982	—	—	—	97.1	71.4	18.8	0.6	—	—	—	—	—	97.7	71.4
1984	92.3	61.5	17.2	—	—	—	—	204	99.8	93.9	59.0	11.0	—	—
1986	—	—	—	97.9	74.1	20.7	0.6	—	—	—	—	—	98.6	73.3
1988	92.7	62.6	17.5	—	—	—	—	206	99.9	94.9	58.7	10.9	—	—
1990	90.1	58.9	18.4	99.1	81.5	27.7	1.2	202	99.8	93.8	58.7	11.0	98.5	74.7
1992	92.3	62.0	16.2	99.0	81.4	27.8	1.2	207	99.5	92.7	61.6	15.3	98.7	77.9
1994	92.1	63.3	16.5	99.0	82.0	29.9	1.3	205	99.3	91.7	60.4	14.1	98.5	78.1
1996	92.7	63.7	17.7	99.1	81.5	29.7	1.6	207	99.6	92.8	61.3	13.8	98.8	78.6

	All persons											
	Percentage of 13-year-olds scoring at or above level in		Mean scores in writing among eighth graders	Percentage of 17-year-olds scoring at or above level in								Mean scores in writing among eleventh graders
	Mathematics			Reading				Mathematics				
	300 level	350 level		150 level	200 level	250 level	300 level	200 level	250 level	300 level	350 level	
	Bc287	Bc288	Bc289	Bc290	Bc291	Bc292	Bc293	Bc294	Bc295	Bc296	Bc297	Bc298
Year	Percent	Percent	Number	Percent	Percent	Percent	Percent	Percent	Percent	Percent	Percent	Number
1971 [2]	—	—	—	99.6	96.0	78.6	39.0	—	—	—	—	—
1975	—	—	—	99.7	96.4	80.1	38.7	—	—	—	—	—
1978	18.0	1.0	—	—	—	—	—	99.8	92.0	51.5	7.3	—
1980	—	—	—	99.9	97.2	80.7	37.8	—	—	—	—	—
1982	17.4	0.5	—	—	—	—	—	99.9	93.0	48.5	5.5	—
1984	—	—	267	100.0	98.3	83.1	40.3	—	—	—	—	290
1986	15.8	0.4	—	—	—	—	—	99.9	95.6	51.7	6.5	—
1988	—	—	264	100.0	98.9	85.7	40.9	—	—	—	—	291
1990	17.3	0.4	257	99.9	98.1	84.1	41.4	100.0	96.0	56.1	7.2	287
1992	18.9	0.4	274	99.8	97.1	82.5	43.2	100.0	96.6	59.1	7.2	287
1994	21.3	0.6	265	99.8	96.8	80.8	41.0	100.0	96.5	58.6	7.4	285
1996	20.6	0.6	264	100.0	97.4	81.4	38.6	100.0	96.8	60.1	7.4	283

Notes appear at end of table

(continued)

TABLE Bc273–428 Student proficiency in reading, mathematics, and writing, as measured by the National Assessment of Educational Progress (NAEP), by age, sex, race, and ethnicity: 1971–1996 *Continued*

Males

	Percentage of 9-year-olds scoring at or above level in							Mean scores in writing among fourth graders	Percentage of 13-year-olds scoring at or above level in					
	Reading			Mathematics					Reading				Mathematics	
	150 level	200 level	250 level	150 level	200 level	250 level	300 level		150 level	200 level	250 level	300 level	200 level	250 level
	Bc299	Bc300	Bc301	Bc302	Bc303	Bc304	Bc305	Bc306	Bc307	Bc308	Bc309	Bc310	Bc311	Bc312
Year	Percent	Percent	Percent	Percent	Percent	Percent	Percent	Number	Percent	Percent	Percent	Percent	Percent	Percent
1971 [2]	87.9	52.7	12.0	—	—	—	—	—	99.6	90.7	51.6	7.3	—	—
1975	91.0	56.2	11.5	—	—	—	—	—	99.6	90.9	51.7	7.0	—	—
1978	—	—	—	96.2	68.9	19.2	0.7	—	—	—	—	—	93.9	63.9
1980	92.9	62.7	14.6	—	—	—	—	—	99.8	93.4	55.9	9.1	—	—
1982	—	—	—	96.5	68.8	18.1	0.6	—	—	—	—	—	97.5	71.3
1984	90.4	58.0	15.9	—	—	—	—	201	99.7	92.2	54.0	9.0	—	—
1986	—	—	—	98.0	74.0	20.9	0.7	—	—	—	—	—	98.5	73.8
1988	90.4	58.4	15.8	—	—	—	—	199	99.7	92.8	52.3	8.6	—	—
1990	87.9	53.8	16.1	99.0	80.6	27.5	1.3	195	99.7	91.4	52.4	7.6	98.2	75.1
1992	90.2	56.9	14.2	99.0	81.9	29.4	1.4	198	99.2	90.4	55.5	12.8	98.8	78.1
1994	90.2	59.2	15.2	99.1	82.3	31.5	1.4	196	99.1	88.8	53.3	10.1	98.3	78.9
1996	90.7	57.8	15.0	99.1	82.5	32.7	2.0	200	99.5	90.1	54.8	10.3	98.7	79.8

Males

	Percentage of 13-year-olds scoring at or above level in		Mean scores in writing among eighth graders	Percentage of 17-year-olds scoring at or above level in								Mean scores in writing among eleventh graders
	Mathematics			Reading				Mathematics				
	300 level	350 level		150 level	200 level	250 level	300 level	200 level	250 level	300 level	350 level	
	Bc313	Bc314	Bc315	Bc316	Bc317	Bc318	Bc319	Bc320	Bc321	Bc322	Bc323	Bc324
Year	Percent	Percent	Number	Percent	Percent	Percent	Percent	Percent	Percent	Percent	Percent	Number
1971 [2]	—	—	—	99.4	94.7	74.4	33.9	—	—	—	—	—
1975	—	—	—	99.5	95.3	75.6	33.7	—	—	—	—	—
1978	18.4	1.1	—	—	—	—	—	99.9	93.0	55.1	9.5	—
1980	—	—	—	99.8	96.3	77.9	35.0	—	—	—	—	—
1982	18.9	0.7	—	—	—	—	—	100.0	93.9	51.9	6.9	—
1984	—	—	258	99.9	97.6	79.6	35.4	—	—	—	—	281
1986	17.6	0.5	—	—	—	—	—	99.9	96.1	54.6	8.4	—
1988	—	—	254	100.0	98.5	82.9	37.1	—	—	—	—	282
1990	19.0	0.5	246	99.8	97.0	79.7	36.1	99.9	95.8	57.6	8.8	276
1992	20.7	0.5	264	99.7	96.3	78.4	38.4	100.0	96.9	60.5	9.1	279
1994	23.9	0.8	254	99.7	95.5	76.2	35.6	100.0	97.3	60.2	9.3	276
1996	23.0	0.8	251	99.9	96.3	76.7	32.8	100.0	97.0	62.7	9.5	275

Notes appear at end of table

TABLE Bc273–428 Student proficiency in reading, mathematics, and writing, as measured by the National Assessment of Educational Progress (NAEP), by age, sex, race, and ethnicity: 1971–1996 *Continued*

	Females													
	Percentage of 9-year-olds scoring at or above level in							Mean scores in writing among fourth graders	Percentage of 13-year-olds scoring at or above level in					
	Reading			Mathematics					Reading				Mathematics	
	150 level	200 level	250 level	150 level	200 level	250 level	300 level		150 level	200 level	250 level	300 level	200 level	250 level
	Bc325	Bc326	Bc327	Bc328	Bc329	Bc330	Bc331	Bc332	Bc333	Bc334	Bc335	Bc336	Bc337	Bc338
Year	Percent	Percent	Percent	Percent	Percent	Percent	Percent	Number	Percent	Percent	Percent	Percent	Percent	Percent
1971 [2]	93.2	64.6	19.2	—	—	—	—	—	99.9	95.2	64.0	12.3	—	—
1975	95.3	68.1	17.7	—	—	—	—	—	99.9	95.5	65.5	13.5	—	—
1978	—	—	—	97.2	72.0	19.9	0.8	—	—	—	—	—	95.2	65.9
1980	96.4	72.7	20.7	—	—	—	—	—	99.9	96.1	65.4	13.5	—	—
1982	—	—	—	97.6	74.0	19.6	0.5	—	—	—	—	—	98.0	71.4
1984	94.2	65.2	18.4	—	—	—	—	208	99.9	95.8	64.0	13.2	—	—
1986	—	—	—	97.8	74.3	20.6	0.6	—	—	—	—	—	98.6	72.7
1988	94.9	66.9	19.1	—	—	—	—	213	100.0	96.9	65.0	13.2	—	—
1990	92.4	64.2	20.8	99.1	82.3	27.9	1.0	209	99.9	96.3	65.0	14.5	98.9	74.4
1992	94.4	67.3	18.2	99.0	80.9	26.3	1.0	216	99.8	95.0	67.5	17.7	98.6	77.7
1994	94.0	67.3	17.8	98.9	81.7	28.3	1.1	214	99.6	94.9	67.9	18.4	98.7	77.3
1996	94.6	69.5	20.4	99.1	80.7	26.7	1.2	214	99.8	95.3	67.5	17.1	98.8	77.4

	Females											
	Percentage of 13-year-olds scoring at or above level in		Mean scores in writing among eighth graders	Percentage of 17-year-olds scoring at or above level in								Mean scores in writing among eleventh graders
	Mathematics			Reading				Mathematics				
	300 level	350 level		150 level	200 level	250 level	300 level	200 level	250 level	300 level	350 level	
	Bc339	Bc340	Bc341	Bc342	Bc343	Bc344	Bc345	Bc346	Bc347	Bc348	Bc349	Bc350
Year	Percent	Percent	Number	Percent	Percent	Percent	Percent	Percent	Percent	Percent	Percent	Number
1971 [2]	—	—	—	99.8	97.3	82.6	44.0	—	—	—	—	—
1975	—	—	—	99.8	97.5	84.3	43.6	—	—	—	—	—
1978	17.5	0.9	—	—	—	—	—	99.7	91.0	48.2	5.2	—
1980	—	—	—	99.9	98.1	83.6	40.7	—	—	—	—	—
1982	15.9	0.4	—	—	—	—	—	99.9	92.1	45.3	4.1	—
1984	—	—	276	99.9	99.0	86.8	45.0	—	—	—	—	299
1986	14.1	0.3	—	—	—	—	—	100.0	95.1	48.9	4.7	—
1988	—	—	274	100.0	99.3	88.2	44.4	—	—	—	—	299
1990	15.7	0.2	268	100.0	99.2	88.6	46.8	100.0	96.2	54.7	5.6	298
1992	17.2	0.3	285	99.9	97.9	86.8	48.5	100.0	96.3	57.7	5.2	296
1994	18.7	0.5	278	99.9	98.0	85.6	46.5	100.0	96.0	57.2	5.5	293
1996	18.4	0.5	276	100.0	98.6	86.4	44.7	100.0	96.7	57.6	5.3	292

Notes appear at end of table

(continued)

TABLE Bc273–428 Student proficiency in reading, mathematics, and writing, as measured by the National Assessment of Educational Progress (NAEP), by age, sex, race, and ethnicity: 1971–1996 *Continued*

Non-Hispanic whites

	Percentage of 9-year-olds scoring at or above level in							Mean scores in writing among fourth graders	Percentage of 13-year-olds scoring at or above level in					
	Reading			Mathematics					Reading				Mathematics	
	150 level	200 level	250 level	150 level	200 level	250 level	300 level		150 level	200 level	250 level	300 level	200 level	250 level
	Bc351	Bc352	Bc353	Bc354	Bc355	Bc356	Bc357	Bc358	Bc359	Bc360	Bc361	Bc362	Bc363	Bc364
Year	Percent	Percent	Percent	Percent	Percent	Percent	Percent	Number	Percent	Percent	Percent	Percent	Percent	Percent
1971 [2]	94.0	65.0	18.0	—	—	—	—	—	99.9	96.2	64.2	11.3	—	—
1975	96.0	69.0	17.4	—	—	—	—	—	99.9	96.4	65.5	12.1	—	—
1978	—	—	—	98.3	76.3	22.9	0.9	—	—	—	—	—	97.6	72.9
1980	97.1	74.2	21.0	—	—	—	—	—	100.0	97.1	67.8	13.6	—	—
1982	—	—	—	98.5	76.8	21.8	0.6	—	—	—	—	—	99.1	78.3
1984	95.4	68.6	20.9	—	—	—	—	211	99.9	96.2	65.3	13.1	—	—
1986	—	—	—	98.8	79.6	24.6	0.8	—	—	—	—	—	99.3	78.9
1988	95.1	68.4	20.3	—	—	—	—	215	99.9	96.0	63.7	12.4	—	—
1990	93.5	66.0	22.6	99.6	86.9	32.7	1.5	211	99.9	96.0	64.8	13.3	99.4	82.0
1992	95.8	69.3	19.6	99.6	86.9	32.4	1.4	217	99.8	95.9	68.5	18.1	99.6	84.9
1994	95.7	70.1	19.7	99.6	87.0	35.3	1.5	214	99.6	95.0	68.1	17.2	99.3	85.5
1996	95.9	70.9	21.6	99.6	86.6	35.7	2.0	216	99.8	95.9	70.1	17.2	99.6	86.4

Non-Hispanic whites

	Percentage of 13-year-olds scoring at or above level in		Mean scores in writing among eighth graders	Percentage of 17-year-olds scoring at or above level in								Mean scores in writing among eleventh graders
	Mathematics			Reading				Mathematics				
	300 level	350 level		150 level	200 level	250 level	300 level	200 level	250 level	300 level	350 level	
	Bc365	Bc366	Bc367	Bc368	Bc369	Bc370	Bc371	Bc372	Bc373	Bc374	Bc375	Bc376
Year	Percent	Percent	Number	Percent	Percent	Percent	Percent	Percent	Percent	Percent	Percent	Number
1971 [2]	—	—	—	99.9	97.9	83.7	43.2	—	—	—	—	—
1975	—	—	—	99.9	98.6	86.2	43.9	—	—	—	—	—
1978	21.4	1.2	—	—	—	—	—	100	95.6	57.6	8.5	—
1980	—	—	—	100.0	99.1	86.9	43.3	—	—	—	—	—
1982	20.5	0.6	—	—	—	—	—	100	96.2	54.7	6.4	—
1984	—	—	272	100.0	99.0	88.0	46.3	—	—	—	—	297
1986	18.6	0.4	—	—	—	—	—	100	98.0	59.1	7.9	—
1988	—	—	269	100.0	99.3	88.7	45.4	—	—	—	—	296
1990	21.0	0.4	262	100.0	98.8	88.3	47.5	100	97.6	63.2	8.3	293
1992	22.8	0.4	279	99.9	98.6	88.0	50.1	100	98.3	66.4	8.7	294
1994	25.6	0.7	272	100.0	98.1	86.2	47.7	100	98.4	67.0	9.4	291
1996	25.4	0.8	271	100.0	98.5	86.8	45.1	100	98.7	68.7	9.2	289

Notes appear at end of table

TABLE Bc273–428 Student proficiency in reading, mathematics, and writing, as measured by the National Assessment of Educational Progress (NAEP), by age, sex, race, and ethnicity: 1971–1996 *Continued*

	Blacks													
	Percentage of 9-year-olds scoring at or above level in							Mean scores in writing among fourth graders	Percentage of 13-year-olds scoring at or above level in					
	Reading			Mathematics					Reading				Mathematics	
	150 level	200 level	250 level	150 level	200 level	250 level	300 level		150 level	200 level	250 level	300 level	200 level	250 level
	Bc377	Bc378	Bc379	Bc380	Bc381	Bc382	Bc383	Bc384	Bc385	Bc386	Bc387	Bc388	Bc389	Bc390
Year	Percent	Percent	Percent	Percent	Percent	Percent	Percent	Number	Percent	Percent	Percent	Percent	Percent	Percent
1971 [2]	69.7	22.0	1.6	—	—	—	—	—	98.6	74.2	21.1	0.8	—	—
1975	80.7	31.6	2.0	—	—	—	—	—	98.4	76.9	24.8	1.5	—	—
1978	—	—	—	88.4	42.0	4.1	0.0	—	—	—	—	—	79.7	28.7
1980	84.9	41.3	4.1	—	—	—	—	—	99.3	84.1	30.1	1.8	—	—
1982	—	—	—	90.2	46.1	4.4	0.0	—	—	—	—	—	90.2	37.9
1984	81.3	36.6	4.5	—	—	—	—	182	99.4	85.5	34.6	2.8	—	—
1986	—	—	—	93.9	53.4	5.6	0.1	—	—	—	—	—	95.4	49.0
1988	83.2	39.4	5.6	—	—	—	—	173	99.8	91.3	40.2	4.6	—	—
1990	76.9	33.9	5.2	96.9	60.0	9.4	0.1	171	99.4	87.7	41.7	4.6	95.4	48.7
1992	79.6	36.6	4.6	96.6	59.8	9.6	0.1	175	98.7	82.0	38.4	5.7	95.0	51.0
1994	78.7	38.3	4.4	97.4	65.9	11.1	0.0	173	98.6	80.6	35.6	3.9	95.6	51.0
1996	83.1	41.3	6.6	97.3	65.3	10.0	0.1	182	99.4	82.7	35.1	3.1	96.2	53.7

	Blacks											
	Percentage of 13-year-olds scoring at or above level in		Mean scores in writing among eighth graders	Percentage of 17-year-olds scoring at or above level in								Mean scores in writing among eleventh graders
	Mathematics			Reading				Mathematics				
	300 level	350 level		150 level	200 level	250 level	300 level	200 level	250 level	300 level	350 level	
	Bc391	Bc392	Bc393	Bc394	Bc395	Bc396	Bc397	Bc398	Bc399	Bc400	Bc401	Bc402
Year	Percent	Percent	Number	Percent	Percent	Percent	Percent	Percent	Percent	Percent	Percent	Number
1971 [2]	—	—	—	97.6	81.9	40.1	7.7	—	—	—	—	—
1975	—	—	—	97.7	82.0	43.0	8.1	—	—	—	—	—
1978	2.3	0.0	—	—	—	—	—	98.8	70.7	16.8	0.5	—
1980	—	—	—	99.0	85.6	44.0	7.1	—	—	—	—	—
1982	2.9	0.0	—	—	—	—	—	99.7	76.4	17.1	0.5	—
1984	—	—	247	99.9	95.9	65.7	16.2	—	—	—	—	270
1986	4.0	0.1	—	—	—	—	—	100.0	85.6	20.8	0.2	—
1988	—	—	246	100.0	98.0	75.8	24.9	—	—	—	—	275
1990	3.9	0.1	239	99.6	95.7	69.1	19.7	99.9	92.4	32.8	2.0	268
1992	4.0	0.1	258	99.1	91.6	61.4	16.9	100.0	89.6	29.8	0.9	263
1994	6.4	0.3	245	99.5	93.4	65.7	21.5	100.0	90.6	29.8	0.4	267
1996	4.8	0.1	242	99.8	94.8	67.2	18.0	100.0	90.6	31.2	0.9	267

Notes appear at end of table

(continued)

TABLE Bc273–428 Student proficiency in reading, mathematics, and writing, as measured by the National Assessment of Educational Progress (NAEP), by age, sex, race, and ethnicity: 1971–1996 *Continued*

	Hispanics													
	Percentage of 9-year-olds scoring at or above level in							Mean scores in writing among fourth graders	Percentage of 13-year-olds scoring at or above level in					
	Reading			Mathematics					Reading				Mathematics	
	150 level	200 level	250 level	150 level	200 level	250 level	300 level		150 level	200 level	250 level	300 level	200 level	250 level
	Bc403	Bc404	Bc405	Bc406	Bc407	Bc408	Bc409	Bc410	Bc411	Bc412	Bc413	Bc414	Bc415	Bc416
Year	Percent	Percent	Percent	Percent	Percent	Percent	Percent	Number	Percent	Percent	Percent	Percent	Percent	Percent
1971 [2]	—	—	—	—	—	—	—	—	—	—	—	—	—	—
1975	80.8	34.6	2.6	—	—	—	—	—	99.6	81.3	32.0	2.2	—	—
1978	—	—	—	93.0	54.2	9.2	0.2	—	—	—	—	—	86.4	36.0
1980	84.5	41.6	5.0	—	—	—	—	—	99.7	86.8	35.4	2.3	—	—
1982	—	—	—	94.3	55.7	7.8	0.0	—	—	—	—	—	95.9	52.2
1984	82.0	39.6	4.3	—	—	—	—	189	99.5	86.7	39.0	4.1	—	—
1986	—	—	—	96.4	57.6	7.3	0.1	—	—	—	—	—	96.9	56.0
1988	85.6	45.9	8.6	—	—	—	—	190	99.2	87.4	38.0	4.4	—	—
1990	83.7	40.9	5.8	98.0	68.4	11.3	0.2	184	99.1	85.8	37.2	3.9	96.8	56.7
1992	83.4	43.1	7.2	97.2	65.0	11.7	0.1	189	98.1	83.4	40.9	6.0	98.1	63.3
1994	80.4	37.1	6.4	97.2	63.5	9.7	0.0	189	98.7	82.4	33.9	4.3	97.1	59.2
1996	84.2	47.5	7.5	98.1	67.1	13.8	0.2	191	98.7	86.1	39.8	5.5	96.2	58.3

	Hispanics											
	Percentage of 13-year-olds scoring at or above level in		Mean scores in writing among eighth graders	Percentage of 17-year-olds scoring at or above level in								Mean scores in writing among eleventh graders
	Mathematics			Reading				Mathematics				
	300 level	350 level		150 level	200 level	250 level	300 level	200 level	250 level	300 level	350 level	
	Bc417	Bc418	Bc419	Bc420	Bc421	Bc422	Bc423	Bc424	Bc425	Bc426	Bc427	Bc428
Year	Percent	Percent	Number	Percent	Percent	Percent	Percent	Percent	Percent	Percent	Percent	Number
1971 [2]	—	—	—	—	—	—	—	—	—	—	—	—
1975	—	—	—	99.3	88.7	52.9	12.6	—	—	—	—	—
1978	4.0	0.1	—	—	—	—	—	99.3	78.3	23.4	1.4	—
1980	—	—	—	99.8	93.3	62.2	16.5	—	—	—	—	—
1982	6.3	0.0	—	—	—	—	—	99.8	81.4	21.6	0.7	—
1984	—	—	247	99.8	95.6	68.3	21.2	—	—	—	—	259
1986	5.5	0.2	—	—	—	—	—	99.4	89.3	26.5	1.1	—
1988	—	—	250	99.9	96.3	71.5	23.3	—	—	—	—	274
1990	6.4	0.1	246	99.7	95.9	75.2	27.1	99.6	85.8	30.1	1.9	277
1992	7.0	0.0	265	99.8	93.4	69.2	27.3	100.0	94.1	39.2	1.2	274
1994	6.4	0.0	252	99.0	91.1	63.0	20.1	100.0	91.8	38.3	1.4	271
1996	6.7	0.0	246	99.9	94.0	64.2	20.0	99.9	92.2	40.1	1.8	269

[1] All participants are enrolled in school.

[2] African-American data for reading and mathematics tests include persons of Hispanic origin.

Source

U.S. Department of Education, *Digest of Education Statistics 1997*, Tables 110, 113, and 119. The underlying source is U.S. National Center for Education Statistics, *NAEP 1996 Trends in Academic Progress*, NCES 97-985 (Office of Educational Research and Improvement, 1997).

Documentation

The National Assessment of Educational Progress (NAEP), a series of cross-sectional studies concerning educational achievement nationwide, was designed and initially implemented in 1969. The assessment data were derived from tests written and conducted by the Education Commission of the States (1969–1983) and by the Educational Testing Service (1983 to present). All participants were enrolled in school. Probability samples have been used, stratified by region and, within region, by state, size of community, and socioeconomic level. Sample sizes for the reading proficiency portion of the 1995–1996 NAEP long-term trends study were 5,019 for the 9-year-olds, 5,493 for the 13-year-olds, and 4,669 for the 17-year-olds. Sample sizes in math were 5,414 for 9-year-olds, 5,658 for 13-year-olds, and 3,539 for 17-year-olds.

Tests in reading, writing, and mathematics administered by the Educational Testing Service are graded from 0 to 500. For the reading test, a score of 150 means that the student is able to follow brief written directions and carry out simple, discrete reading tasks. A score of 200 suggests that the student is able to understand, combine ideas, and make inferences based on short uncomplicated passages about specific or sequentially related information. A score of 250 means that the student is able to search for specific information, interrelate ideas, and make generalizations about literature, science, and social studies materials. Students scoring 300 or above are able to find, understand, summarize, and explain relatively complicated literary and informational material.

In mathematics, students scoring 150 or above have knowledge of simple arithmetic facts. A score of 200 suggests beginning skills and understanding of mathematics. At the 250 level, students understand numerical operations and have basic problem-solving skills. At 300, students use moderately complex procedures and reasoning. At 350, students can solve multistep problems and use algebraic methods.

TABLE Bc429–437 Enrollment of 3- to 5-year-olds in preprimary programs, by public–private control and type of program: 1965–1997[1]

Contributed by Claudia Goldin

	Total enrollment	Percentage of children ages 3–5 enrolled	Nursery school			Kindergarten			Enrollment in Head Start
			Total	Public	Private	Total	Public	Private	
	Bc429	Bc430	Bc431	Bc432	Bc433	Bc434	Bc435	Bc436	Bc437
Year	Thousand	Percent	Thousand	Thousand	Thousand	Thousand	Thousand	Thousand	Thousand
1965	3,407	27.1	520	127	393	2,887	2,291	596	561 [2]
1970	4,104	37.5	1,094	332	762	3,009	2,498	511	477
1975	4,955	48.7	1,744	570	1,174	3,210	2,682	528	349
1980	4,878	52.5	1,981	628	1,353	2,897	2,438	459	376
1983	5,384	52.5	2,347	809	1,538	3,039	2,416	623	415
1984	5,480	51.6	2,335	742	1,593	3,144	2,668	476	442
1985	5,865	54.6	2,477	846	1,631	3,388	2,847	541	452
1986	5,971	55.0	2,544	829	1,715	3,426	2,859	567	452
1987	5,931	54.6	2,555	819	1,736	3,376	2,842	534	447
1988	5,978	54.4	2,621	851	1,770	3,356	2,875	481	448
1989	6,026	54.6	2,824	930	1,894	3,201	2,704	497	451
1990	6,659	59.4	3,379	1,199	2,180	3,281	2,772	509	541
1991	6,334	55.7	2,824	996	1,828	3,510	2,967	543	583
1992	6,402	55.5	2,856	1,073	1,783	3,545	2,995	550	621
1993	6,581	55.1	2,984	1,205	1,779	3,597	3,020	577	714
1994	7,514	61.0	4,162	1,848	2,314	3,353	2,819	534	740
1995	7,769	61.8	4,331	1,950	2,381	3,408	2,800	608	751
1996	7,580	61.2	4,147	1,830	2,317	3,433	2,853	580	752
1997	—	—	—	—	—	—	—	—	794

[1] Except for series Bc437, data collected using new procedures starting in 1994. May not be comparable with figures for earlier years.

[2] Summer enrollment only.

Sources

Series Bc429–436, U.S. Department of Education, *Digest of Education Statistics 1997* (1997), Table 46. Series Bc437, Head Start FY:1998 Fact Sheet, Head Start Bureau Internet site.

Documentation

Head Start is a national program that provides developmental services for preschool children ages 3–5 who come from families that meet the federal poverty guidelines. It also provides social services for their families. Head Start began in 1965 in the Office of Economic Opportunity as a way to serve children of low-income families and is now administered by the Administration for Children and Families. As of 1996, Head Start was covered by the 1994 Head Start Reauthorization Act.

TABLE Bc438–446 School enrollment rates, by sex and race: 1850–1994

Contributed by Claudia Goldin

	Both sexes			Males			Females		
	Total	White	Nonwhite	Total	White	Nonwhite	Total	White	Nonwhite
	Bc438	Bc439	Bc440 [1]	Bc441	Bc442	Bc443 [1]	Bc444	Bc445	Bc446 [1]
Year	Percent	Percent	Percent	Percent	Percent	Percent	Percent	Percent	Percent
1850	47.2	56.2	1.8	49.6	59.0	2.0	44.8	53.3	1.8
1860	50.6	59.6	1.9	52.6	62.0	1.9	48.5	57.2	1.8
1870	48.4	54.4	9.9	49.8	56.0	9.6	46.9	52.7	10.0
1880	57.8	62.0	33.8	59.2	63.5	34.1	56.5	60.5	33.5
1890	54.3	57.9	32.9	54.7	58.5	31.8	53.8	57.2	33.9
1900 [2]	50.5	53.6	31.1	50.1	53.4	29.4	50.9	53.9	32.8
1910 [2]	59.2	61.3	44.8	59.1	61.4	43.1	59.4	61.3	46.6
1920 [2]	64.3	65.7	53.5	64.1	65.6	52.5	64.5	65.8	54.5
1930 [2,3]	69.9	71.2	60.3	70.2	71.4	59.7	69.7	70.9	60.8
1940	74.8	75.6	68.4	74.9	75.9	67.5	74.7	75.4	69.2
1950	78.7	79.3	74.8	79.1	79.7	74.7	78.4	78.9	74.9
1954	86.2	87.0	80.8	87.5	88.4	80.9	84.8	85.4	80.7
1955	86.5	87.0	82.9	88.4	88.9	84.6	84.5	85.0	81.2
1956	87.2	87.8	83.6	88.6	89.4	83.6	85.8	86.1	83.5
1957	87.8	88.2	85.3	89.4	90.0	85.6	86.2	86.4	85.0
1958	88.4	88.9	85.1	90.1	90.5	87.2	86.7	87.2	82.9
1959	88.5	88.8	85.9	89.7	90.2	86.8	87.1	87.5	85.0
1960	88.6	89.0	86.1	90.0	90.6	86.6	87.1	87.3	85.7
1961	88.5	88.9	86.3	90.2	90.5	87.7	86.9	87.2	84.9
1962	89.1	89.6	86.3	90.8	91.3	87.6	87.4	87.8	85.0
1963	89.6	89.8	88.0	91.1	91.5	88.7	88.0	88.1	87.3
1964	89.6	89.8	88.4	91.1	91.4	89.2	88.1	88.2	87.6

Notes appear at end of table

(continued)

TABLE Bc438–446 School enrollment rates, by sex and race: 1850–1994 *Continued*

	Both sexes			Males			Females		
	Total	White	Nonwhite	Total	White	Nonwhite	Total	White	Nonwhite
	Bc438	Bc439	Bc440 [1]	Bc441	Bc442	Bc443 [1]	Bc444	Bc445	Bc446 [1]
Year	Percent	Percent	Percent	Percent	Percent	Percent	Percent	Percent	Percent
1965	89.6	89.8	88.5	91.0	91.2	89.8	88.3	88.5	87.2
1966	89.7	89.9	88.5	91.2	91.5	89.9	88.2	88.4	87.2
1967	90.5	90.8	88.6	91.9	92.2	89.8	89.0	89.3	87.4
1968	90.8	91.0	89.4	92.2	92.5	90.5	89.3	89.5	88.4
1969	90.9	91.1	89.5	92.1	92.5	90.0	89.5	89.7	88.9
1970	90.6	90.8	89.4	91.6	91.9	89.6	89.6	89.7	89.1
1971	90.9	90.9	90.8	91.9	92.0	91.3	89.9	89.8	90.3
1972	90.0	90.0	90.1	91.0	91.0	90.9	89.0	89.0	89.3
1973	89.3	89.4	88.9	90.3	90.4	90.1	88.2	88.3	87.7
1974	89.4	89.2	90.1	90.1	89.9	90.9	88.6	88.5	89.3
1975	89.9	89.8	90.4	90.7	90.6	91.1	89.1	89.0	89.6
1976	89.6	89.4	90.8	90.4	90.1	91.9	88.9	88.7	89.6
1977	89.6	89.3	91.1	90.3	89.9	91.9	89.0	88.8	90.2
1978	89.2	89.0	90.6	89.8	89.5	91.6	88.6	88.4	89.7
1979	89.0	88.8	90.2	89.7	89.4	91.5	88.3	88.1	88.8
1980	89.1	88.9	90.4	89.5	89.3	90.4	88.8	88.4	90.4
1981	89.6	89.4	90.5	90.0	89.8	91.4	89.2	89.1	89.7
1982	89.6	89.5	90.0	90.0	89.9	90.6	89.1	89.1	89.4
1983	90.3	90.3	90.3	90.4	90.3	90.8	90.2	90.2	89.8
1984	90.3	90.3	90.2	90.7	90.6	90.9	89.9	90.0	89.5
1985	91.0	91.1	90.7	91.2	91.2	91.4	90.7	90.9	89.9
1986	91.4	91.3	91.6	92.0	91.8	92.6	90.8	90.8	90.7
1987	91.7	91.5	92.3	92.4	92.2	93.2	90.9	90.8	91.4
1988	91.8	91.7	92.2	92.1	91.6	94.5	91.5	91.4	91.9
1989	91.8	91.7	92.1	92.1	92.1	92.2	91.5	91.3	92.0
1990	92.6	92.5	92.8	92.9	92.6	93.8	92.2	92.3	91.8
1991	93.1	93.1	93.2	93.4	93.1	94.2	92.8	93.0	92.2
1992	93.5	93.5	93.4	93.9	93.7	94.8	93.1	93.4	92.0
1993	93.6	93.6	93.3	93.8	93.6	94.5	93.3	93.5	92.4
1994	93.5	93.5	93.6	93.6	93.6	93.6	93.4	93.3	93.5

[1] For 1971–1994, the nonwhite category is calculated by subtracting whites from the total.

[2] Enrollment rates are for 5- to 20-year-olds.

[3] Revised to include Mexicans as white persons.

Sources

1850–1991, U.S. Department of Education, *120 Years of American Education: A Statistical Portrait* (1993), Table 2. The underlying sources are: U.S. Bureau of the Census, *Fifteenth Census (1940) Reports, Population*, volume 2; U.S. Bureau of the Census, *Census of Population: 1950*, volume 2, part 1; U.S. Bureau of the Census, *Census of Population: 1960*, PC(1)-1D; and *Current Population Reports*, series P-20, "School Enrollment: Social and Economic Characteristics of Students," various years, and Current Population Survey, survey data files; 1991–1994, *Current Population Reports*, series P-20, nos. 474, 479, and 487.

Documentation

All figures are expressed as a percentage of 5- to 19-year-olds.

Data for 1850–1950 are based on April 1 counts of population. Data for 1954–1994 are based on October counts.

For decennial census years, the statistics refer to the total population within the specified age group; figures from the Current Population Survey (CPS) refer to the civilian noninstitutional population. Persons not covered in the CPS (armed forces and institutional population) are known to have low enrollment rates.

In the U.S. population census for 1940 and 1950, and in the CPS, 1954–1991, enrollment was defined as enrollment in "regular" schools only – that is, schools in which enrollment may lead toward an elementary or high school diploma, or to a college, university, or professional school degree. Such schools included public and private nursery schools, kindergartens, elementary and secondary schools, colleges, universities, and professional schools. Enrollment could be either full-time or part-time, day or night.

If a person was receiving regular instruction at home from a tutor and if the instruction was considered comparable to that of a regular school or college, the person was counted as enrolled. Enrollment in a correspondence course was counted only if the person received credit in the regular school system. Enrollments in business and trade schools at the postsecondary level were excluded if the coursework did not lead to a degree.

Children enrolled in kindergarten were included in the "regular" school enrollment figures in the CPS beginning in 1950; children enrolled in nursery school were included beginning in 1967. Children enrolled in kindergarten were not included in the "regular" school enrollment figures in the 1950 U.S. population census; however, they have been included here to make the data comparable with earlier years and with current practice. In censuses prior to 1950, no attempt was made to exclude children in kindergarten, so statistics for those years include various proportions attending kindergarten. Also, in censuses prior to 1940, the data were not restricted as to type of school or college the person was attending.

In addition to differences in definition of school enrollment and in population coverage, the enrollment data for different years may differ because of variations in the dates when the questions were asked and the time periods to which enrollment referred. Data from the CPS were obtained in October and refer to enrollment in the current school term. In 1940, 1950, and 1960, the censuses were taken as of April 1, but enrollment related to any time after March 1 in 1940 and any time after February 1 in 1950 and 1960. The corresponding questions in the censuses from 1850 to 1930 applied to a somewhat longer period: in 1850–1900, to the twelve months preceding the census date; and in 1910, 1920, and 1930, to the period between the preceding September 1 and the census date (April 15 in 1910, January 1 in 1920, and April 1 in 1930).

Information on school enrollment is also collected and published by the U.S. Department of Education. These data are obtained from reports of school surveys and censuses. They are, however, only roughly comparable with data collected by the U.S. Bureau of the Census from households, because of differences in definitions, time references, population coverage, and enumeration methods. It is almost always the case that the enrollment percentages in the household survey data exceed those in the school surveys for individuals of roughly comparable ages.

TABLE Bc447–453 Unionization of teachers – NEA and AFT membership, and proportion of teachers unionized or covered by collective bargaining agreements: 1960–1997

Contributed by Claudia Goldin

	Union membership			Union density among school teachers			
	National Educational Association (NEA)			Proportion union members		Proportion covered by collective bargaining agreements	
	Total	K-12 instructional staff	American Federation of Teachers (AFT)	Elementary	Secondary	Elementary	Secondary
	Bc447	Bc448	Bc449	Bc450	Bc451	Bc452	Bc453
Year	Number	Number	Thousand	Proportion	Proportion	Proportion	Proportion
1960	713,994	—	56	—	—	—	—
1961	765,616	—	—	—	—	—	—
1962	812,497	—	58	—	—	—	—
1963	859,505	—	—	—	—	—	—
1964	903,384	—	—	—	—	—	—
1965	943,581	—	—	—	—	—	—
1966	986,113	—	—	—	—	—	—
1967	1,028,456	—	—	—	—	—	—
1968	1,081,660	—	—	—	—	—	—
1969	1,014,275	—	—	—	—	—	—
1970	1,100,155	—	188	—	—	—	—
1971	1,103,485	—	197	—	—	—	—
1972	1,166,203	—	225	—	—	—	—
1973	1,377,998	—	204	—	—	—	—
1974	1,467,186	—	326	0.264	0.286	—	—
1975	1,684,909	—	380	0.288	0.306	—	—
1976	1,886,532	—	323	0.344	0.379	—	—
1977	1,679,689	—	347	0.416	0.455	—	—
1978	1,696,469	—	390	0.505	0.558	—	—
1979	1,709,673	—	452	0.528	0.579	—	—
1980	1,680,566	—	393	0.544	0.599	—	—
1981	1,659,459	—	515	—	—	—	—
1982	1,644,459	—	459	—	—	—	—
1983	1,633,205	1,496,930	457	0.577	0.574	0.691	0.694
1984	1,654,825	1,541,070	—	0.568	0.575	0.672	0.689
1985	1,688,057	1,496,993	470	0.566	0.580	0.667	0.676
1986	1,799,144	—	—	0.546	0.574	0.647	0.684
1987	1,828,649	1,552,236	494	0.578	0.584	0.667	0.675
1988	1,919,773	1,579,689	—	0.564	0.603	0.661	0.693
1989	1,992,917	1,765,862	544	0.554	0.588	0.658	0.673
1990	2,057,286	1,814,669	—	0.560	0.556	0.656	0.666
1991	2,109,866	1,859,480	459	0.558	0.569	0.636	0.661
1992	2,143,170	1,884,001	—	0.540	0.571	0.622	0.667
1993	2,171,682	1,906,694	574	0.582	0.571	0.660	0.659
1994	2,205,661	1,935,642	—	0.570	0.586	0.644	0.665
1995	2,249,703	—	613	0.559	0.584	0.634	0.652
1996	2,279,101	1,998,016	—	0.556	0.578	0.632	0.648
1997	2,323,339	2,034,087	—	0.570	0.561	0.645	0.634

Sources

Series Bc447–448. *NEA Handbook* (National Education Association, annual issues).

Series Bc449. 1960–1983: Leo Troy and Neil Sheflin, *U.S. Union Sourcebook: Membership, Finances, Structure, Directory* (Industrial Relations Data and Information Services, 1985); 1984–1995: U.S. Bureau of the Census, *Statistical Abstract of the United States*, various issues.

Series Bc450–451. 1974–1980: Edward C. Kokkelenberg and Donna R. Sockell, "Union Membership in the United States, 1973–1981," *Industrial and Labor Relations Review* 28 (July 1985): 507.

Series Bc450–453. 1983–1997: Barry T. Hirsch and David A. Macpherson, *Union Membership and Earnings Data Book: Compilations from the Current Population Survey* (Bureau of National Affairs, annual issues). The underlying source is Current Population Survey (CPS) Outgoing Rotation Group (ORG) Earnings Files, 1983–1997.

Documentation

The National Education Association (NEA) has been in existence since 1857, when it was the National Teachers' Association, a professional association of teachers and other instructional staff. As various localities and states granted formal bargaining rights to their public-sector workers in the early 1950s and states passed legislation for school bargaining (beginning with Wisconsin in 1959), local NEA chapters became the bargaining agents for teachers. Although some states still do not allow public-sector employees to bargain collectively, most states passed enabling legislation in the 1960s and 1970s (forty-one states had such legislation in 1975). The American Federation of Teachers (AFT), a union affiliated with the AFL-CIO since its founding in 1916, also has local chapters that are bargaining agents for teachers.

The CPS data include all wage and salary workers who listed their occupation as teacher (elementary or secondary school).

Series Bc447. Includes dues-paying members who are K-12 and higher-education teachers (including substitute teachers), other instructional staff,

(continued)

TABLE Bc447–453 Unionization of teachers – NEA and AFT membership, and proportion of teachers unionized or covered by collective bargaining agreements: 1960–1997 *Continued*

noninstructional staff, NEA staff, and postsecondary school students in training for educational positions. Member status can be active, retired, or lifetime.

Series Bc448. Includes only K–12 teachers and other instructional staff, active and lifetime members. Thus series Bc447 can exceed the total number of public-sector, K–12 active instructional staff. The NEA and AFT data do not, according to Troy and Sheflin (1985), include Canadian members or private school teachers and instructional staff, but there may be a trivial number of private higher education teachers in the NEA membership data.

Series Bc450–453. "Union density" is the proportion of a group (here an occupation) who belong to a union or are represented in a collective bargaining agreement by a union.

TABLE Bc454–467 Characteristics of public school teachers – race, sex, age, teaching experience, annual salary, and terminal degree: 1961–1996

Contributed by Susan B. Carter

	Median age			Sex		Race			Percentage with					
	Both sexes	Male	Female	Male	Female	White	Black	Other	Less than a bachelor's degree	Bachelor's degree	Master's or specialist degree	Ph.D. degree	Median years teaching experience	Average annual salary
	Bc454	Bc455	Bc456	Bc457	Bc458	Bc459	Bc460	Bc461	Bc462	Bc463	Bc464	Bc465	Bc466	Bc467
Year	Years	Years	Years	Percent	Percent	Percent	Percent	Percent	Percent	Percent	Percent	Percent	Years	Dollars
1961	41	34	46	31.3	68.7	—	—	—	14.6	61.9	23.1	0.4	11	5,264
1966	36	33	40	31.1	68.9	—	—	—	7.0	69.6	23.2	0.1	8	6,253
1971	35	33	37	34.3	65.7	88.3	8.1	3.6	2.9	69.6	27.1	0.4	8	9,261
1976	33	33	33	32.9	67.1	90.8	8.0	1.2	0.9	61.6	37.1	0.4	8	12,005
1981	37	38	36	33.1	66.9	91.6	7.8	0.7	0.4	50.1	49.3	0.3	12	17,209
1986	41	42	41	31.2	68.8	89.6	6.9	3.4	0.3	48.3	50.7	0.7	15	24,504
1991	42	43	42	27.9	72.1	86.8	8.0	5.2	0.6	46.3	52.6	0.5	15	31,790
1996	44	46	44	25.6	74.4	90.7	7.3	2.0	0.3	43.6	54.5	1.7	15	35,549

Source

U.S. National Center for Educational Statistics, *Digest of Education Statistics: 1999*, Table 070.

Documentation

All data pertain to spring of the stated year.

Series Bc462–465. Figures for curriculum specialist or professional diploma based on six years of college study are not included.

TABLE Bc468–479 Public and private secondary school graduation rates, by census division and race: 1910–1962[1]

Contributed by Claudia Goldin

	New England	Middle Atlantic	South Atlantic		East South Central		West South Central		East North Central	West North Central	Mountain	Pacific
			All	Whites	All	Whites	All	Whites				
School year ending	Bc468	Bc469	Bc470	Bc471 [2]	Bc472	Bc473 [2]	Bc474	Bc475 [2]	Bc476	Bc477	Bc478	Bc479
	Percent	Percent	Percent	Percent	Percent	Percent	Percent	Percent	Percent	Percent	Percent	Percent
1910	15.5	8.0	4.1	—	3.8	—	4.3	—	12.5	10.6	8.8	11.7
1911	16.5	8.8	4.6	—	4.2	—	5.1	—	13.0	11.1	10.2	13.2
1913	18.7	10.2	5.9	—	5.6	—	6.2	—	15.3	13.6	13.0	17.1
1914	20.1	11.0	6.5	—	6.2	—	6.8	—	16.2	14.6	12.9	19.2
1916	22.8	12.9	7.5	—	7.4	—	7.9	—	18.3	17.4	16.4	22.9
1918	24.6	14.2	8.5	—	8.4	—	11.0	—	21.5	19.9	18.5	24.8
1920	25.3	13.9	8.6	—	8.6	—	12.0	—	20.9	20.5	19.8	27.3
1922	27.2	16.5	10.5	—	10.3	—	13.0	—	25.0	24.6	23.9	30.9
1924	30.9	19.7	13.5	—	13.3	—	16.6	—	29.8	30.4	29.3	35.9
1926	33.7	21.7	15.6	—	13.9	—	18.4	—	31.1	38.7	31.2	39.4
1928	35.9	22.3	17.1	—	16.2	—	19.8	—	33.4	39.4	35.3	43.2
1930	39.4	25.4	19.2	24.2	17.0	21.4	22.5	25.3	36.0	41.0	38.0	44.7
1932	47.8	31.6	22.5	28.8	18.4	23.3	27.6	31.4	43.0	47.6	45.4	55.1
1934	51.2	38.9	25.0	29.7	21.0	24.8	29.5	32.7	49.4	50.4	48.1	56.7
1936	58.6	47.4	30.7	37.8	24.5	29.9	34.3	38.5	53.0	54.5	53.2	62.5
1938	59.9	51.6	35.3	43.2	26.0	31.0	38.1	42.3	54.3	57.8	55.7	67.8
1940	60.2	54.3	37.7	44.4	30.3	35.6	42.7	47.3	57.2	61.5	57.6	71.1
1942 [3]	61.6	57.9	40.9	48.4	30.9	36.4	46.3	51.8	61.8	62.3	58.9	66.6
1944 [3]	45.4	51.4	35.5	41.1	26.0	30.2	37.6	42.0	54.1	54.3	47.6	53.2
1946 [3]	56.3	55.3	31.0	34.9	29.2	33.9	38.3	42.5	57.9	58.2	52.3	59.7
1948 [3]	62.5	62.2	36.9	41.0	34.7	39.7	45.0	50.1	63.7	63.6	58.0	65.3
1950 [3]	66.5	63.1	40.8	44.1	38.8	44.1	45.0	49.6	63.8	64.0	57.3	63.8
1952	59.1	56.7	38.7	42.0	37.9	42.1	44.3	48.1	58.4	62.3	53.9	55.7
1954	61.0	56.1	43.3	46.4	45.5	44.8	51.5	50.1	62.5	66.8	58.8	59.9
1958 [3]	62.2	59.2	47.5	—	47.8	—	53.1	—	62.3	68.0	59.5	62.4
1962	68.2	65.2	54.2	—	52.3	—	57.9	—	65.6	70.2	65.1	71.6

[1] Rates are expressed as a proportion of 17-year-olds; see text.

[2] Derived from the total number of graduates minus those from nonwhite segregated schools.

[3] Extrapolated on the basis of the public secondary school graduate rate because the number of private school graduates cannot be estimated reliably.

Sources

U.S. Office (Department) of Education, *Biennial Surveys of Education of the United States,* various years; U.S. Department of Health, Education, and Welfare, *Statistics of State School Systems* and *Statistics of Non-Public Secondary Schools,* various years; National Catholic Welfare Conference, *Summary of Catholic Education*, various years. See Claudia Goldin, "America's Graduation from High School: The Evolution and Spread of Secondary Schooling in the Twentieth Century," *Journal of Economic History* 58 (June 1998): 345–74, and "Appendix to How America Graduated from High School," National Bureau of Economic Research Historical Working Paper number 57 (June 1994), although some of the numbers have been reestimated.

Documentation

The graduation rate is the number of secondary school graduates in a given year divided by the number of 17-year-olds in that year. Thus, the data represent the contemporaneous graduation rate. The numbers of 17-year-olds (or half the number of 17- and 18-year-olds) by state are from the decennial U.S. population censuses (1910–1970) and are interpolated between census years using a constant growth rate procedure. It does not matter that secondary school graduates can be older (or younger) than 17 years old. The age of 17 is chosen for convenience and because there is generally less understatement for males at that age than after. Graduates can be from public schools (junior highs, senior highs, regular high schools, and so on), private schools (secular and denominational), or the preparatory departments of colleges and universities. The criteria for graduation may depend on state regulations. See Table Bc258–264 for national graduation rates. The data underlying the estimates for the states (aggregated here to the census division level) sum to approximately the aggregate data for the nation by year. See references under sources for details. Because of the lack of private school statistics, these data cannot easily be extended beyond 1962.

See Table Ap-G in Appendix 2 regarding the composition of census regions and divisions.

TABLE Bc480–491 Percentage of 16- to 24-year-olds who did not complete high school, by sex, race, and ethnicity: 1960–1998[1, 2]

Contributed by Susan B. Carter

	Both sexes				Males				Females			
		Non-Hispanic				Non-Hispanic				Non-Hispanic		
	All	White	Black	Hispanic	All	White	Black	Hispanic	All	White	Black	Hispanic
	Bc480	Bc481	Bc482	Bc483	Bc484	Bc485	Bc486	Bc487	Bc488	Bc489	Bc490	Bc491
Year	Percent	Percent	Percent	Percent	Percent	Percent	Percent	Percent	Percent	Percent	Percent	Percent
1960 [3]	27.2	—	—	—	27.8	—	—	—	26.7	—	—	—
1967	17.0	15.4	28.6	—	16.5	14.7	30.6	—	17.3	16.1	26.9	—
1968	16.2	14.7	27.4	—	15.8	14.4	27.1	—	16.5	15.0	27.6	—
1969	15.2	13.6	26.7	—	14.3	12.6	26.9	—	16.0	14.6	26.7	—
1970	15.0	13.2	27.9	—	14.2	12.2	29.4	—	15.7	14.1	26.6	—
1971	14.7	13.4	23.7	—	14.2	12.6	25.5	—	15.2	14.2	22.1	—
1972	14.6	12.3	21.3	34.3	14.1	11.7	22.3	33.7	15.1	12.8	20.5	34.9
1973	14.1	11.6	22.2	33.5	13.7	11.5	21.5	30.4	14.5	11.8	22.8	36.4
1974	14.3	11.9	21.2	33.0	14.2	12.0	20.1	33.8	14.4	11.8	22.1	32.2
1975	13.9	11.4	22.9	29.2	13.3	11.0	23.0	26.7	14.5	11.8	22.9	31.6
1976	14.1	12.0	20.5	31.4	14.1	12.1	21.2	30.3	14.2	11.8	19.9	32.3
1977	14.1	11.9	19.8	33.0	14.5	12.6	19.5	31.6	13.8	11.2	20.0	34.3
1978	14.2	11.9	20.2	33.3	14.6	12.2	22.5	33.6	13.9	11.6	18.3	33.1
1979	14.6	12.0	21.1	33.8	15.0	12.6	22.4	33.0	14.2	11.5	20.0	34.5
1980	14.1	11.4	19.1	35.2	15.1	12.3	20.8	37.2	13.1	10.5	17.7	33.2
1981	13.9	11.4	18.4	33.2	15.1	12.5	19.9	36.0	12.8	10.2	17.1	30.4
1982	13.9	11.4	18.4	31.7	14.5	12.1	21.2	30.5	13.3	10.9	15.9	32.8
1983	13.7	11.2	18.0	31.6	14.9	12.2	19.9	34.3	12.5	10.1	16.2	29.1
1984	13.1	11.0	15.5	29.8	14.0	12.0	16.8	30.6	12.3	10.1	14.3	29.0
1985	12.6	10.4	15.2	27.6	13.4	11.1	16.1	29.9	11.8	9.8	14.3	25.2
1986	12.2	9.7	14.2	30.1	13.1	10.3	15.0	32.8	11.4	9.1	13.5	27.2
1987	12.7	10.4	14.1	28.6	13.2	10.8	15.0	29.1	12.1	10.0	13.3	28.1
1988	12.9	9.6	14.5	35.8	13.5	10.4	15.0	36.0	12.2	8.9	14.1	35.4
1989	12.6	9.4	13.9	33.0	13.6	10.3	14.9	34.4	11.7	8.5	13.0	31.6
1990	12.1	9.0	13.2	32.4	12.3	9.3	11.9	34.3	11.8	8.7	14.4	30.3
1991	12.5	8.9	13.6	35.3	13.0	8.9	13.5	39.2	11.9	8.9	13.7	31.1
1992	11.0	7.7	13.7	29.4	11.3	8.0	12.5	32.1	10.7	7.5	14.8	26.6
1993	11.0	7.9	13.6	27.5	11.2	8.2	12.6	28.1	10.9	7.7	14.4	26.9
1994	11.5	7.7	12.6	30.0	12.3	8.0	14.1	31.6	10.6	7.5	11.3	28.1
1995	12.0	8.6	12.1	30.3	12.2	9.0	11.1	30.0	11.7	8.2	12.9	30.0
1996	11.1	7.3	13.0	29.4	11.4	7.3	13.5	30.3	10.9	7.3	12.5	28.3
1997	11.0	7.6	13.4	25.3	11.9	8.5	13.3	27.0	10.1	6.7	13.5	23.4
1998	11.8	7.7	13.8	29.5	13.3	8.6	15.5	33.5	10.3	6.9	12.2	25.0

[1] Because of changes in collection procedures, data through 1991 may not be comparable with later figures.

[2] Through 1971, persons of Hispanic origin are included under the series for whites and blacks.

[3] Based on the decennial census, taken in April.

Source

U.S. National Center for Education Statistics. *Digest of Education Statistics: 1999*, Table 108.

Documentation

These series refer to "status" dropouts, that is, 16- to 24-year-olds who are not enrolled in school and who have not completed a high school program. People who have received GED credentials are counted as high school completers. Data are based on sample surveys of the civilian noninstitutional population. Except where noted, data were collected in October.

TABLE Bc492–500 Public and private secondary school enrollment rates, by census division: 1910–1962[1]

Contributed by Claudia Goldin

School year ending	New England	Middle Atlantic	South Atlantic	East South Central	West South Central	East North Central	West North Central	Mountain	Pacific
	Bc492	Bc493	Bc494	Bc495	Bc496	Bc497	Bc498	Bc499	Bc500
	Percent	Percent	Percent	Percent	Percent	Percent	Percent	Percent	Percent
1910	28.2	18.5	11.9	10.9	13.7	23.7	23.1	23.0	28.8
1911	29.2	20.1	13.0	11.6	15.8	24.4	23.7	26.0	31.3
1913	32.4	22.1	15.1	13.7	17.7	26.8	27.7	30.8	37.6
1914	35.1	23.7	15.8	14.3	19.0	28.1	29.4	31.9	40.0
1916	39.3	27.7	17.6	16.6	20.5	32.1	33.2	35.6	49.9
1918	40.8	30.0	20.7	17.7	26.6	36.0	37.1	40.2	51.8
1920	43.1	30.5	22.8	19.4	30.9	40.1	43.2	45.2	60.4
1922	46.5	36.9	25.9	21.3	31.6	46.8	47.6	49.7	66.9
1924	48.4	40.0	29.0	25.2	35.5	49.6	51.3	51.7	68.0
1926	51.3	43.8	32.5	26.5	39.1	51.6	55.1	55.5	73.5
1928	54.6	44.9	34.5	29.5	41.6	55.5	58.2	59.4	73.9
1930	59.8	49.8	37.9	31.0	45.5	60.1	60.8	62.8	76.8
1932	71.9	61.0	43.2	34.4	49.5	68.3	66.2	68.1	82.1
1934	75.8	71.5	46.9	37.8	50.6	72.5	69.5	70.6	84.0
1936	79.5	76.4	50.4	39.0	55.9	73.8	71.7	73.1	85.8
1938	79.8	80.3	53.7	41.0	59.9	75.2	74.8	74.5	90.8
1940	78.6	83.6	57.7	44.5	63.6	81.2	77.6	77.0	92.1
1942 [2]	78.5	85.9	60.0	45.7	64.7	78.4	78.7	75.4	89.5
1944 [2]	73.0	79.2	52.3	42.1	57.3	73.4	71.5	66.3	79.1
1946	75.2	83.0	54.9	45.9	56.2	78.0	73.8	69.1	85.2
1948	79.0	85.1	55.7	50.5	58.4	76.4	77.1	72.2	85.4
1950	86.8	86.2	61.9	55.9	61.8	78.9	80.2	75.6	88.0
1952	79.0	77.2	60.0	56.0	62.9	77.7	77.6	73.3	78.6
1954	80.1	79.1	65.2	61.6	68.6	78.4	80.8	79.2	80.5
1956	83.6	80.7	69.1	67.0	73.3	81.7	85.1	82.5	82.3
1958	87.6	76.1	74.9	72.6	77.6	88.0	89.0	86.7	85.6
1962	89.6	89.8	87.6	78.7	83.0	88.8	93.5	92.9	91.1

[1] Rates are expressed as a proportion of 14- to 17-year-olds.

[2] Extrapolated on the basis of the public secondary school enrollment rate, because the number of private secondary school enrollments cannot be estimated reliably

Sources

U.S. Office (Department) of Education, *Biennial Surveys of Education of the United States*, various years; U.S. Department of Health, Education, and Welfare, *Statistics of State School Systems* and *Statistics of Non-Public Secondary Schools*, various years; National Catholic Welfare Conference, *Summary of Catholic Education*, various years. See Claudia Goldin, "America's Graduation from High School: The Evolution and Spread of Secondary Schooling in the Twentieth Century," *Journal of Economic History* 58 (June 1998): 345–74, and "Appendix to How America Graduated from High School," National Bureau of Economic Research Historical Working Paper number 57 (June 1994), although some of the numbers have been reestimated.

Documentation

The enrollment rate is the number of pupils enrolled in ninth, tenth, eleventh, and twelfth grades in a given year divided by the number of 14- to 17-year-olds in that year. Thus, the data represent the contemporaneous enrollment rate. The numbers of 14- to 17-year-olds by state are from the decennial U.S. population censuses (1910–1970) and are interpolated between census years using a constant growth rate procedure. It does not matter that secondary school pupils can be younger than 14 years old or older than 17 years old. The ages are chosen for convenience. Secondary school pupils can be from public schools (junior highs, senior highs, regular high schools, and so on), private schools (secular and denominational), or the preparatory departments of colleges and universities. The data underlying the estimates for the states (aggregated here to the census division level) sum to approximately the aggregate data for the nation by year. See references under sources for details. Because of the lack of private school statistics, these data cannot easily be extended beyond 1962.

See Table Ap-G5 in Appendix 2 regarding the composition of census regions and divisions.

TABLE Bc501–509 Private secondary school graduates as a proportion of all secondary school graduates, by census division: 1910–1962

Contributed by Claudia Goldin

School year ending	New England	Middle Atlantic	South Atlantic	East South Central	West South Central	East North Central	West North Central	Mountain	Pacific
	Bc501	Bc502	Bc503	Bc504	Bc505	Bc506	Bc507	Bc508	Bc509
	Proportion	Proportion	Proportion	Proportion	Proportion	Proportion	Proportion	Proportion	Proportion
1910	0.194	0.216	0.308	0.349	0.189	0.113	0.183	0.196	0.154
1911	0.202	0.217	0.276	0.360	0.182	0.115	0.180	0.201	0.153
1913	0.192	0.205	0.237	0.284	0.168	0.110	0.163	0.145	0.135
1914	0.187	0.194	0.237	0.279	0.145	0.111	0.158	0.161	0.121
1916	0.186	0.177	0.202	0.209	0.114	0.105	0.131	0.136	0.090
1918	0.173	0.176	0.182	0.189	0.095	0.092	0.124	0.148	0.087
1920	0.188	0.168	0.189	0.182	0.077	0.094	0.121	0.124	0.079
1922	0.179	0.154	0.151	0.171	0.075	0.084	0.116	0.108	0.082
1924	0.185	0.144	0.141	0.154	0.064	0.086	0.103	0.081	0.073
1926	0.214	0.139	0.129	0.152	0.077	0.101	0.073	0.087	0.085
1928	0.169	0.143	0.098	0.116	0.059	0.107	0.083	0.049	0.084
1930	0.164	0.138	0.093	0.098	0.049	0.113	0.081	0.050	0.076
1932	0.193	0.129	0.096	0.101	0.047	0.089	0.081	0.044	0.059
1934	0.160	0.110	0.068	0.082	0.040	0.066	0.067	0.039	0.054
1936	0.156	0.095	0.060	0.076	0.041	0.066	0.067	0.032	0.050
1938	0.163	0.098	0.055	0.067	0.038	0.073	0.064	0.034	0.048
1940	0.142	0.101	0.053	0.054	0.034	0.073	0.057	0.035	0.044
1942 [1]	0.149	0.099	0.047	0.057	0.033	0.076	0.061	0.035	0.047
1944 [1]	0.216	0.117	0.052	0.073	0.041	0.097	0.075	0.044	0.059
1946 [1]	0.185	0.113	0.057	0.070	0.042	0.099	0.074	0.041	0.052
1948 [1]	0.177	0.105	0.046	0.063	0.037	0.099	0.072	0.038	0.048
1950 [1]	0.175	0.107	0.040	0.060	0.038	0.107	0.076	0.039	0.049
1952	0.197	0.119	0.042	0.061	0.038	0.117	0.078	0.042	0.056
1954	0.248	0.162	0.049	0.073	0.048	0.149	0.100	0.052	0.074
1956	0.238	0.168	0.050	0.075	0.048	0.149	0.109	0.060	0.070
1958 [1]	0.255	0.222	0.072	0.075	0.067	0.171	0.124	0.070	0.087
1962	0.233	0.202	0.063	0.068	0.062	0.162	0.120	0.064	0.076

[1] The underlying data for the number of private school graduates have been extrapolated on the basis of the public school data, because the number of private secondary school graduates cannot be estimated reliably.

Sources

U.S. Office (Department) of Education, *Biennial Surveys of Education of the United States*, various years; U.S. Department of Health, Education, and Welfare, *Statistics of State School Systems* and *Statistics of Non-Public Secondary Schools*, various years; National Catholic Welfare Conference, *Summary of Catholic Education*, various years. See Claudia Goldin, "America's Graduation from High School: The Evolution and Spread of Secondary Schooling in the Twentieth Century," *Journal of Economic History* 58 (June 1998): 345–74, and "Appendix to How America Graduated from High School," National Bureau of Economic Research Historical Working Paper number 57 (June 1994), although some of the numbers have been reestimated.

Documentation

Graduates can be from public schools (junior highs, senior highs, regular high schools, and so on), private schools (secular and denominational), or the preparatory departments of colleges and universities. The criteria for graduation may depend on state regulations. The data underlying the estimates for the states (aggregated here to the census division level) sum to approximately the aggregate data for the nation by year. See references under sources for details. Because of the lack of private school statistics, these data cannot easily be extended beyond 1962.

See Table Ap-G in Appendix 2 regarding the composition of census regions and divisions.

HIGHER EDUCATION

Susan B. Carter and Claudia Goldin

TABLE Bc510–522 Institutions of higher education – colleges and universities, teacher-training institutions, and medical and dental schools, by public–private control: 1869–1995[1, 2]

Contributed by Claudia Goldin

		Four-year colleges and universities			Teacher-training institutions				Two-year colleges				
	Total institutions	Total	Public	Private	Public teachers colleges	Private teachers colleges	Public normal schools	Private normal schools	Total	Public	Private	Medical schools	Dental schools
School year beginning	Bc510	Bc511	Bc512	Bc513	Bc514 [3]	Bc515 [3]	Bc516	Bc517	Bc518	Bc519	Bc520	Bc521 [4]	Bc522 [4]
	Number	Number	Number	Number	Number	Number	Number	Number	Number	Number	Number	Number	Number
1869	563	—	—	—	—	—	—	—	—	—	—	75	10
1879	811	—	—	—	—	—	—	—	—	—	—	100	14
1889	998	—	—	—	—	—	—	—	—	—	—	133	31
1899	977	—	—	—	—	—	157	148	—	—	—	160	57
1909	951	—	—	—	—	—	191	73	—	—	—	131	54
1915	—	—	—	—	—	—	232	47	—	—	—	95	49
1917	980	—	—	—	—	—	251	57	46	14	32	90	46
1918	1,041	663	—	—	45	—	266	60	52	10	42	85	46
1921	1,162	780	182	598	80	—	239	63	80	17	63	81	45
1923	1,295	869	193	676	88	—	227	67	132	39	93	79	43
1925	1,377	923	208	715	101	—	237	64	153	47	106	79	44
1927	1,415	965	249	716	137	—	143	59	248	114	134	80	40
1929	1,409	941	251	690	134	6	139	52	277	129	148	76	38
1931	1,460	984	279	705	145	10	106	28	342	159	183	76	38
1933	1,418	1,002	282	720	147	11	67	27	322	152	170	77	39
1935	1,628	1,086	292	794	156	12	98	29	415	187	228	77	39
1937	1,690	1,118	298	820	160	14	93	26	453	209	244	77	39
1939	1,707	1,171	305	866	164	40 [5]	80	0 [5]	456	217	239	77	39
1941	1,720	1,259	385	874	238	37	—	—	461	231	230	77	39
1943	1,650	1,237	—	—	—	—	—	—	413	210	203	77	39
1945	1,768	1,304	382	922	217	36	—	—	464	242	222	77	39
1947	1,788	1,316	388	928	229	31	—	—	472	242	230	77	40
1949	1,851	1,327	344	983	183	35	—	—	524	297	227	72	40
1950	1,852	1,312	341	971	—	—	—	—	540	295	245	72	40
1951	1,832	1,326	350	976	—	—	—	—	506	291	215	72	41
1952	1,882	1,355	349	1,006	—	—	—	—	527	290	237	72	41
1953	1,863	1,345	369	976	—	—	—	—	518	293	225	73	42
1954	1,849	1,333	353	980	—	—	—	—	516	295	221	72	42
1955	1,850	1,347	360	987	—	—	—	—	503	290	213	73	42
1956	1,878	1,355	359	996	—	—	—	—	523	297	226	75	43
1957	1,930	1,390	366	1,024	—	—	—	—	540	300	240	75	43
1958	1,947	1,394	366	1,028	—	—	—	—	553	307	246	76	43
1959	2,004	1,422	367	1,055	—	—	—	—	582	328	254	79	45
1960	2,021	1,431	368	1,063	—	—	—	—	590	332	258	79	46
1961	2,033	1,443	374	1,069	—	—	—	—	590	344	246	81	46
1962	2,093	1,468	376	1,092	—	—	—	—	625	364	261	81	46
1963	2,132	1,499	386	1,113	—	—	—	—	633	374	259	82	46
1964	2,175	1,521	393	1,128	—	—	—	—	654	406	248	81	45
1965	2,230	1,551	401	1,150	—	—	—	—	679	420	259	84	47
1966	2,329	1,577	403	1,174	—	—	—	—	752	477	275	83	47
1967	2,374	1,588	414	1,174	—	—	—	—	786	520	266	85	48
1968	2,483	1,619	417	1,202	—	—	—	—	864	594	270	84	48
1969	2,525	1,639	426	1,213	—	—	—	—	886	634	252	86	48
1970	2,556	1,665	435	1,230	—	—	—	—	891	654	237	89	48
1971	2,606	1,675	440	1,235	—	—	—	—	931	697	234	92	48
1972	2,665	1,701	449	1,252	—	—	—	—	964	733	231	97	51
1973	2,720	1,717	440	1,277	—	—	—	—	1,003	760	243	99	52
1974	3,004	1,866	537	1,329	—	—	—	—	1,138	896	242	104	52
1975	3,026	1,898	545	1,353	—	—	—	—	1,128	897	231	107	56
1976	3,046	1,913	550	1,363	—	—	—	—	1,133	905	228	109	57
1977	3,095	1,938	552	1,386	—	—	—	—	1,157	921	236	109	57
1978	3,134	1,941	550	1,391	—	—	—	—	1,193	924	269	109	58
1979	3,152	1,957	549	1,408	—	—	—	—	1,195	926	269	112	58

Notes appear at end of table

(continued)

TABLE Bc510–522 Institutions of higher education – colleges and universities, teacher-training institutions, and medical and dental schools, by public–private control: 1869–1995 *Continued*

		Four-year colleges and universities			Teacher-training institutions				Two-year colleges				
	Total institutions	Total	Public	Private	Public teachers colleges	Private teachers colleges	Public normal schools	Private normal schools	Total	Public	Private	Medical schools	Dental schools
School year beginning	Bc510	Bc511	Bc512	Bc513	Bc514 [3]	Bc515 [3]	Bc516	Bc517	Bc518	Bc519	Bc520	Bc521 [4]	Bc522 [4]
	Number	Number	Number	Number	Number	Number	Number	Number	Number	Number	Number	Number	Number
1980	3,231	1,957	552	1,405	—	—	—	—	1,274	945	329 [6]	116	58
1981	3,253	1,979	558	1,421	—	—	—	—	1,274	940	334 [6]	119	59
1982	3,280	1,984	560	1,424	—	—	—	—	1,296	933	363 [6]	118	59
1983	3,284	2,013	565	1,448	—	—	—	—	1,271	916	355	119	60
1984	3,331	2,025	566	1,459	—	—	—	—	1,306	935	371	120	59
1985	3,340	2,029	566	1,463	—	—	—	—	1,311	932	379	120	59
1986	3,406	2,070	573	1,497	—	—	—	—	1,336	960	376	122	58
1987	3,587	2,135	599	1,536	—	—	—	—	1,452	992	460	122	57
1988	3,565	2,129	598	1,531	—	—	—	—	1,436	984	452	124	58
1989	3,535	2,127	595	1,532	—	—	—	—	1,408	968	440	124	57
1990	3,559	2,141	595	1,546	—	—	—	—	1,418	972	446	—	—
1991	3,601	2,157	599	1,558	—	—	—	—	1,444	999	445	—	—
1992	3,638	2,169	600	1,569	—	—	—	—	1,469	1,024	445	—	—
1993	3,632	2,190	604	1,586	—	—	—	—	1,442	1,021	421	—	—
1994	3,688	2,215	605	1,610	—	—	—	—	1,473	1,036	437	—	—
1995	3,706	2,244	608	1,636	—	—	—	—	1,462	1,047	415	—	—

1 Data for two-year and four-year colleges through 1973 include main campuses only and exclude branch campuses; data for later years include both.

2 Revised survey procedures were used starting in 1986. Data are not entirely comparable with figures for earlier years. The number of branch campuses reporting separately has increased since 1986.

3 Starting in 1941, independent teacher-training institutions are assumed to be in the four-year category.

4 Medical and dental schools are included, as appropriate, in data for two-year and four-year colleges.

5 Private normal schools are assumed to be zero.

6 Large increases are due to the addition of schools accredited by the Accrediting Commission of Career Schools and Colleges of Technology.

Sources

Series Bc510–513 and Bc518–522. 1869 to 1991: unless noted below, U.S. Department of Education, *120 Years of American Education: A Statistical Portrait* (1993), Table 26. The underlying sources are: 1869–1915, U.S. Office of Education, *Annual Report of the United States Commissioner of Education*, various issues; 1917–1957: U.S. Office of Education, *Biennial Survey of Education in the United States*, various issues; and 1958–1991: U.S. Department of Education, *Digest of Education Statistics*, annual issues. 1992–1995, *Digest of Education Statistics 1997*, Table 241.

Series Bc514–517. 1899–1917: U.S. Office of Education, *Annual Report of the United States Commissioner of Education*, various issues; 1919–1949: U.S. Department of Education, *Biennial Survey of Education in the United States*, various issues. Small revisions have been made to series Bc510 from the series in U.S. Department of Education (1993).

Documentation

An institution of higher education is authorized and currently offering either a two-year or four-year degree, or credit transferable to such an institution leading to such a degree. In addition, such an institution must be accredited by an agency recognized as a valid accrediting agency by the Secretary of Education. Institutions reporting include universities, colleges, independent professional schools, junior colleges, and independent teacher-training institutions (including teachers colleges and state, county, city, and private normal schools).

The distinction between public and private is one of control, not funding. Public higher education institutions include those at the federal, state, and municipal levels. Prior to the 1930s many of the publicly controlled historically black institutions in the South were not listed in the *Biennial Surveys of Education in the United States*. The Commissioner of Education, at the time, appears to have categorized most as industrial institutes below the college grade.

The categorization of four- and two-year institutions is based on the highest level of institutional offering, rather than the predominance of the student body. Thus, teachers colleges are included in the four-year group even though, prior to the 1940s, many of their students were in programs of less than four years in length. Normal schools, however, are not included in the four-year group, nor in the two-year group prior to 1941. In the late 1940s and 1950s many of the state teachers colleges were absorbed by state university systems. The increase in four-year institutions from the late 1910s to the early 1920s is largely attributable to the fact that teachers colleges first appeared in *Biennial Survey of Education in the United States, 1918–20* and continued to grow subsequently. (See Claudia Goldin and Lawrence F. Katz, "The Shaping of Higher Education: The Formative Years in the United States, 1890 to 1940," *Journal of Economic Perspectives* 13 (Winter 1999): 37–62.)

The figures for institutions in censuses prior to 1974 represent administrative organizations rather than individual campuses. A university operating one or more branches away from the main campus, for example, is counted as one institution. There is probably some underreporting in some of the earlier years. Since 1946, this underreporting has been corrected by the use of estimated reports prepared from secondary sources for nonrespondent institutions.

Series Bc521. Although the first medical school in the United States was established in 1765, the accuracy of data recorded for years prior to 1900 is questionable. Inspection and classification of medical schools was initiated by the American Medical Association Council on Medical Education in 1904; by 1929 there was only one unapproved school. As far as the data permit, only approved medical and basic science schools are included. Data for 1964 and 1966 show only schools granting M.D. degrees, as reported to the U.S. Office of Education.

Series Bc522. Before the founding of the first dental school in 1840, dental work was done by medical doctors or by persons who were self-taught or apprentice-trained. By 1880, most states required dental practitioners to be dental school graduates. For 1840 and 1926–1930, schools offering courses in dentistry are included; for 1850–1924, schools conferring degrees; for other years through 1962, schools in operation. Data for 1964 and 1966 show only schools granting D.D.S. degrees, as reported to the U.S. Office of Education.

TABLE Bc523–536 Enrollment in institutions of higher education, by sex, enrollment status, and type of institution: 1869–1995[1, 2, 3]

Contributed by Claudia Goldin

School year beginning	Total	Total enrollment as a percentage of population 18 to 24 years old	Males	Females	Full-time enrollment	Part-time enrollment	Four-year institutions	Two-year institutions	Public institutions: Total	Public institutions: Four-year	Public institutions: Two-year	Private institutions: Total	Private institutions: Four-year	Private institutions: Two-year
	Bc523	Bc524 [4]	Bc525	Bc526	Bc527	Bc528	Bc529	Bc530	Bc531	Bc532	Bc533	Bc534	Bc535	Bc536
	Thousand	Percent	Thousand	Thousand	Thousand	Thousand	Thousand	Thousand	Thousand	Thousand	Thousand	Thousand	Thousand	Thousand
1869	63	1.3	49	13	—	—	—	—	—	—	—	—	—	—
1879	116	1.6	78	38	—	—	—	—	—	—	—	—	—	—
1889	157	1.8	100	56	—	—	—	—	—	—	—	—	—	—
1899	238	2.3	152	85	—	—	—	—	—	—	—	—	—	—
1904	264	2.3	—	—	—	—	—	—	—	—	—	—	—	—
1909	355	2.8	215	141	—	—	—	—	—	—	—	—	—	—
1910	354	2.8	—	—	—	—	—	—	—	—	—	—	—	—
1911	356	2.8	—	—	—	—	—	—	—	—	—	—	—	—
1912	361	2.8	—	—	—	—	—	—	—	—	—	—	—	—
1913	379	2.9	—	—	—	—	—	—	—	—	—	—	—	—
1914	404	3.1	—	—	—	—	—	—	—	—	—	—	—	—
1915	441	3.3	—	—	—	—	—	—	—	—	—	—	—	—
1917	441	3.4	—	—	—	—	437	4	—	—	1	—	—	3
1919	598	4.7	315	283	—	—	590	8	—	—	3	—	—	5
1921	681	5.2	—	—	—	—	669	12	—	—	5	—	—	7
1923	823	6.1	—	—	—	—	803	20	—	—	9	—	—	11
1925	941	6.7	—	—	—	—	914	27	—	—	14	—	—	13
1927	1,054	7.2	—	—	—	—	1,010	44	—	—	28	—	—	16
1929	1,101	7.2	620	481	—	—	1,045	56	531	—	37	591	—	19
1931	1,154	7.4	667	487	—	—	1,069	85	582	523	59	572	546	26
1933	1,055	6.7	616	440	—	—	977	78	530	474	56	525	503	23
1935	1,208	7.6	710	499	—	—	1,106	102	614	544	71	594	562	32
1937	1,351	8.4	804	547	—	—	1,229	122	689	607	82	661	622	39
1939	1,494	9.1	893	601	—	—	1,344	150	797	689	108	698	655	42
1941	1,404	8.4	819	585	—	—	1,263	141	732	631	101	672	631	40
1943	1,155	6.8	579	576	—	—	1,066	89	571	511	61	584	556	28
1945	1,677	10.0	928	749	—	—	1,520	156	834	724	110	843	796	47
1946	2,078	12.5	1,418	661	—	—	—	—	—	—	—	—	—	—
1947	2,338	14.2	1,659	679	—	—	2,116	222	1,152	989	163	1,186	1,127	59
1948	2,403	14.7	1,709	694	—	—	2,192	211	1,186	1,032	154	1,218	1,161	57
1949	2,445	15.2	1,722	723	—	—	2,216	229	1,207	1,036	171	1,238	1,179	58
1950	2,281	14.3	1,560	721	—	—	2,064	217	1,140	972	168	1,142	1,092	50
1951	2,102	13.4	1,391	711	—	—	1,902	200	1,038	882	156	1,064	1,020	44
1952	2,134	13.8	1,380	754	—	—	1,896	238	1,101	910	192	1,033	986	47
1953	2,231	14.7	1,423	808	—	—	1,973	258	1,186	976	210	1,045	997	48
1954	2,447	16.2	1,563	883	—	—	2,164	282	1,354	1,112	241	1,093	1,052	41
1955	2,653	17.7	1,733	920	—	—	2,345	308	1,476	1,211	265	1,177	1,134	43
1956	2,918	19.5	1,911	1,007	—	—	2,571	347	1,656	1,359	298	1,262	1,212	50
1957	3,324	22.0	2,171	1,153	—	—	—	—	1,973	—	—	1,351	—	—
1959	3,640	23.8	2,333	1,307	—	—	—	—	2,181	—	—	1,459	—	—
1961	4,145	23.6	2,586	1,559	—	—	—	—	2,561	—	—	1,584	—	—
1963	4,780	27.7	2,962	1,818	3,184	1,596	3,929	850	3,081	2,341	740	1,698	1,588	111
1964	5,280	28.7	3,249	2,031	3,573	1,707	4,291	989	3,468	2,593	875	1,812	1,698	114

Notes appear at end of table

(continued)

TABLE Bc523–536 Enrollment in institutions of higher education, by sex, enrollment status, and type of institution: 1869–1995 *Continued*

School year beginning	Total	Total enrollment as a percentage of population 18 to 24 years old	Males	Females	Full-time enrollment	Part-time enrollment	Four-year institutions	Two-year institutions	Public institutions: Total	Public institutions: Four-year	Public institutions: Two-year	Private institutions: Total	Private institutions: Four-year	Private institutions: Two-year
	Bc523	Bc524 [4]	Bc525	Bc526	Bc527	Bc528	Bc529	Bc530	Bc531	Bc532	Bc533	Bc534	Bc535	Bc536
	Thousand	Percent	Thousand	Thousand	Thousand	Thousand	Thousand	Thousand	Thousand	Thousand	Thousand	Thousand	Thousand	Thousand
1965	5,921	29.8	3,630	2,291	4,096	1,825	4,748	1,173	3,970	2,928	1,041	1,951	1,820	132
1966	6,390	30.7	3,856	2,534	4,439	1,951	5,064	1,326	4,349	3,160	1,189	2,041	1,904	137
1967	6,912	32.2	4,133	2,779	4,793	2,119	5,399	1,513	4,816	3,444	1,372	2,096	1,955	141
1968	7,513	34.1	4,478	3,035	5,210	2,303	5,721	1,792	5,431	3,784	1,646	2,082	1,937	146
1969	8,005	35.0	4,746	3,258	5,499	2,506	5,937	2,068	5,897	3,963	1,934	2,108	1,975	133
1970	8,581	35.8	5,044	3,537	5,816	2,765	6,262	2,319	6,428	4,233	2,195	2,153	2,029	124
1971	8,949	35.3	5,207	3,742	6,077	2,871	6,369	2,579	6,804	4,347	2,457	2,144	2,022	122
1972	9,215	35.8	5,239	3,976	6,072	3,142	6,459	2,756	7,071	4,430	2,641	2,144	2,029	115
1973	9,602	36.5	5,371	4,231	6,189	3,413	6,590	3,012	7,420	4,530	2,890	2,183	2,060	122
1974	10,224	37.9	5,622	4,601	6,370	3,853	6,820	3,404	7,989	4,703	3,285	2,235	2,117	119
1975	11,185	40.3	6,149	5,036	6,841	4,344	7,215	3,970	8,835	4,998	3,836	2,350	2,217	134
1976	11,012	38.8	5,811	5,201	6,717	4,295	7,129	3,883	8,653	4,902	3,752	2,359	2,227	132
1977	11,286	39.0	5,789	5,497	6,793	4,493	7,243	4,043	8,847	4,945	3,902	2,439	2,298	141
1978	11,260	38.3	5,641	5,619	6,668	4,592	7,232	4,028	8,786	4,912	3,874	2,474	2,319	155
1979	11,570	38.8	5,683	5,887	6,794	4,776	7,353	4,217	9,037	4,980	4,057	2,533	2,373	160
1980	12,097	40.2	5,874	6,223	7,098	4,999	7,571	4,526	9,457	5,129	4,329	2,640	2,442	198 [5]
1981	12,372	41.0	5,975	6,397	7,181	5,190	7,655	4,716	9,647	5,166	4,481	2,725	2,489	236 [5]
1982	12,426	41.4	6,031	6,394	7,221	5,205	7,654	4,772	9,696	5,176	4,520	2,730	2,478	252
1983	12,465	42.0	6,024	6,441	7,261	5,204	7,741	4,723	9,683	5,223	4,459	2,782	2,518	264
1984	12,242	42.0	5,864	6,378	7,098	5,144	7,711	4,531	9,477	5,198	4,279	2,765	2,513	252
1985	12,247	43.0	5,818	6,429	7,075	5,172	7,716	4,531	9,479	5,210	4,270	2,768	2,506	261
1986	12,504	45.1	5,885	6,619	7,120	5,384	7,824	4,680	9,714	5,300	4,414	2,790	2,524	266 [6]
1987	12,767	47.1	5,932	6,835	7,231	5,536	7,990	4,776	9,973	5,432	4,541	2,793	2,558	235 [6]
1988	13,055	49.0	6,002	7,053	7,437	5,619	8,180	4,875	10,161	5,546	4,615	2,894	2,634	260
1989	13,539	51.4	6,190	7,349	7,661	5,878	8,388	5,151	10,578	5,694	4,884	2,961	2,693	267
1990	13,819	51.5	6,284	7,535	7,821	5,998	8,579	5,240	10,845	5,848	4,996	2,974	2,730	244
1991	14,359	54.5	6,502	7,857	8,115	6,244	8,707	5,652	11,310	5,905	5,405	3,049	2,802	247
1992	14,487	55.8	6,524	7,963	8,162	6,325	8,765	5,722	11,385	5,900	5,485	3,103	2,865	238
1993	14,305	55.7	6,427	7,877	8,128	6,177	8,739	5,566	11,189	5,852	5,337	3,116	2,887	229
1994	14,279	56.1	6,372	7,907	8,138	6,141	8,749	5,530	11,134	5,825	5,308	3,145	2,924	221
1995	14,262	56.6	6,343	7,919	8,129	6,133	8,769	5,493	11,092	5,815	5,278	3,169	2,955	215

1 Degree-credit enrollment only, 1869–1956; later years include degree-credit and non–degree-credit enrollment.

2 Through 1969, data for two-year branch campuses of four-year institutions are included with the four-year institutions.

3 Cumulative enrollment for the entire academic year, 1869–1945; thereafter, data are for fall only.

4 Measurement of population of 18- to 24-year-olds varies over time. See text.

5 Large increases are attributable to the addition of schools accredited by the National Association of Trade and Technical Schools in 1980 and 1981.

6 Because of imputation techniques, data are not consistent with figures for other years.

Sources

Series Bc523–536, 1869–1988, U.S. Department of Education, *120 Years of Education: A Statistical Portrait* (1993), Table 24. Data for 1923 and previous years based on U.S. Office of Education, *Education for Victory*, volume 3, number 6 (1944). The underlying sources are: U.S. Bureau of the Census, *Historical Statistics of the United States: From Colonial Times to the Present* (1975); U.S. Department of Education, *Digest of Education Statistics*, annual issues. 1989–1995, series Bc523–528, *Digest of Education Statistics 1997*, Tables 6, 172; series Bc529–536, *Digest of Education Statistics 1997*, Table 173. The underlying sources are: U.S. Department of Education, Higher Education General Information Survey (HEGIS), "Fall Enrollment in Colleges and Universities" surveys; and Integrated Postsecondary Education Data System (IPEDS), "Fall Enrollment" surveys.

Documentation

The term "degree-credit enrollment" refers to students whose current program in an institution of higher education consists wholly or principally of work that is creditable toward a bachelor's or higher degree, either in the student's own institution or by transfer to another institution.

Total enrollment includes students in approved four-year, two-year, teacher training, technical, and professional institutions. Professional schools include those giving instruction in law, medicine, dentistry, theology, veterinary medicine, and pharmacology, among other fields. Teacher training

TABLE Bc523–536 Enrollment in institutions of higher education, by sex, enrollment status, and type of institution: 1869–1995 *Continued*

institutions include independent teachers colleges as well as normal schools, particularly in the period before the 1940s. Students in four-year institutions include those attending independent teacher-training institutions even if they attended for fewer than four years. Students can be at the undergraduate, graduate, or professional levels. Until the 1930s and 1940s many students pursuing professional degrees did not yet have a B.A. and earned both simultaneously with the granting of their first professional degree. After the 1940s, the inclusion of students pursuing professional and graduate degrees will overstate those attending school to earn their first postsecondary degree.

Series Bc524. Population ratio data are based on persons 18–24 years old, as of July 1 prior to the opening of school, except for 1899, which is based on July 1 population after the closing of school in June. Population data through 1959 are total population, including armed forces overseas. Data for 1960–1991 are for the resident population. Many students are older than age 24, particularly in the more recent years. In 1995, about 43 percent of college students were older than age 24.

TABLE Bc537–564 Foreign students enrolled in institutions of higher education in the United States and outlying areas, by continent, region, and country of origin: 1980–1997

Contributed by Susan B. Carter

			Europe			Latin America						North America		
	Total	Africa	Total	Eastern	Western	Total	Caribbean	Central America	Mexico	South America	Middle East	Total	Canada	Oceania
	Bc537	Bc538	Bc539	Bc540	Bc541	Bc542	Bc543	Bc544	Bc545	Bc546	Bc547	Bc548	Bc549	Bc550
School year beginning	Number	Number	Number	Number	Number	Number	Number	Number	Number	Number	Number	Number	Number	Number
1980	311,880	38,180	25,330	1,670	23,660	49,810	10,650	12,970	6,730	26,190	84,710	14,790	14,320	4,180
1985	343,780	34,190	34,310	1,770	32,540	45,480	11,100	12,740	5,460	21,640	52,720	16,030	15,410	4,030
1990	407,530	23,800	49,640	4,780	44,860	47,580	12,610	15,950	6,740	19,020	33,420	18,950	18,350	4,230
1991	419,590	21,900	53,710	6,890	46,820	43,200	11,120	12,820	6,650	19,250	31,210	19,780	19,190	3,870
1992	438,620	20,520	58,010	9,800	48,210	43,250	10,270	13,460	7,580	19,530	30,240	21,550	20,970	4,300
1993	449,704	20,569	62,442	12,929	49,496	45,246	10,672	13,886	8,021	20,708	29,509	23,288	22,655	3,857
1994	452,635	20,724	64,811	15,906	48,905	47,239	11,286	14,923	9,003	21,030	30,246	23,394	22,747	4,327
1995	453,787	20,844	67,353	18,032	49,326	47,253	10,737	14,220	8,687	22,296	30,563	23,644	23,005	4,202
1996	457,984	22,078	68,315	19,471	48,844	49,592	11,796	14,524	8,975	23,272	29,841	23,611	22,984	3,690
1997	481,280	23,162	71,616	21,314	50,301	51,368	10,855	15,211	9,559	25,302	30,962	22,613	22,051	3,893

	Asia													
		East Asia						South Central Asia			South East Asia			
	Total	Total	China	Hong Kong	Japan	Republic of Korea	Taiwan	Total	India	Pakistan	Total	Indonesia	Malaysia	Thailand
	Bc551	Bc552	Bc553	Bc554	Bc555	Bc556	Bc557	Bc558	Bc559	Bc560	Bc561	Bc562	Bc563	Bc564
School year beginning	Number	Number	Number	Number	Number	Number	Number	Number	Number	Number	Number	Number	Number	Number
1980	94,640	51,650	2,770	9,660	13,500	6,150	19,460	14,540	9,250	2,990	28,450	3,250	6,010	6,550
1985	156,830	80,720	13,980	10,710	13,360	18,660	23,770	25,800	16,070	5,440	50,310	8,210	23,020	6,940
1990	229,830	146,020	39,600	12,630	36,610	23,360	33,530	42,370	28,860	7,730	41,440	9,520	13,610	7,090
1991	245,810	158,490	42,940	13,190	40,700	25,720	35,550	46,810	32,530	8,120	40,510	10,250	12,650	7,690
1992	260,670	168,410	45,130	14,020	42,840	28,520	37,430	50,430	35,950	8,020	41,830	10,920	12,660	8,630
1993	264,693	171,279	44,381	13,752	43,770	31,076	37,581	48,941	34,796	7,299	44,461	11,744	13,718	9,537
1994	261,789	168,190	39,403	12,935	45,276	33,599	36,407	47,836	33,537	6,989	45,763	11,872	13,617	10,889
1995	259,893	166,717	39,613	12,018	45,531	36,231	32,702	45,401	31,743	6,427	47,774	12,820	14,015	12,165
1996	260,743	167,935	42,503	10,942	46,292	37,130	30,487	44,256	30,641	6,095	48,550	12,461	14,527	13,481
1997	277,508	178,256	46,958	9,665	47,073	42,890	30,855	47,761	33,818	5,821	51,491	13,282	14,597	15,090

Source

U.S. National Center for Education Statistics, *Digest of Education Statistics: 1999*, Table 420.

Documentation

Data refer to students who have not immigrated – that is, those who are not permanent residents or citizens.

Series Bc548. Excludes Mexico and Central America, which are included with Latin America.

TABLE Bc565–567 Percentage of colleges and universities open to men only, women only, and both sexes: 1870–1981[1]

Contributed by Susan B. Carter

School year ending	Men only	Women only	Both women and men
	Bc565	Bc566	Bc567
	Percent	Percent	Percent
1870	59	12	29
1890	37	20	43
1910	27	15	58
1930	15	16	69
1957	13	13	74
1976	4	5	91
1981	3	5	92

[1] Beginning with 1957, data exclude non-degree-granting institutions.

Source

Barbara Miller Solomon, *In the Company of Educated Women: A History of Women and Higher Education in America* (Yale University Press, 1985), Table 1, p. 44.

TABLE Bc568–587 Degrees conferred by institutions of higher education, by degree and sex: 1869–1994[1]

Contributed by Claudia Goldin

School year beginning	Associate degrees: Total	Associate degrees: Males	Associate degrees: Females	Bachelor's degrees: Total	Bachelor's degrees: Males	Bachelor's degrees: Females	Bachelor's degrees: Per 1,000 persons 23 years old	Bachelor's degrees: Per 100 high school graduates four years earlier	Master's degrees: Total	Master's degrees: Males
	Bc568	Bc569	Bc570	Bc571	Bc572	Bc573	Bc574	Bc575	Bc576 [2]	Bc577 [2]
	Number	Number	Number	Number	Number	Number	Per 1000	Per 100	Number	Number
1869	—	—	—	9,371	7,993	1,378	—	—	—	—
1870	—	—	—	12,357	10,484	1,873	—	—	—	—
1871	—	—	—	7,852	6,626	1,226	—	—	794	—
1872	—	—	—	10,807	9,070	1,737	—	—	890	—
1873	—	—	—	11,493	9,593	1,900	—	—	860	—
1874	—	—	—	11,932	9,905	2,027	—	—	661	—
1875	—	—	—	12,005	9,911	2,094	—	—	835	—
1876	—	—	—	10,145	8,329	1,816	—	—	731	—
1877	—	—	—	11,533	9,416	2,117	—	—	816	—
1878	—	—	—	12,081	9,808	2,273	—	—	919	—
1879	—	—	—	12,896	10,411	2,485	—	—	879	868
1880	—	—	—	14,871	12,035	2,836	—	—	922	—
1881	—	—	—	14,998	12,168	2,830	—	—	884	—
1882	—	—	—	15,116	12,294	2,822	—	—	863	—
1883	—	—	—	12,765	10,408	2,357	—	53	901	—
1884	—	—	—	14,734	12,043	2,691	—	59	1,071	—
1885	—	—	—	13,097	10,731	2,366	—	48	859	—
1886	—	—	—	13,402	11,008	2,394	—	48	923	—
1887	—	—	—	15,256	12,562	2,694	—	49	987	—
1888	—	—	—	15,020	12,397	2,623	—	47	1,161	—
1889	—	—	—	15,539	12,857	2,682	—	47	1,015	821
1890	—	—	—	16,840	13,902	2,938	—	53	776	—
1891	—	—	—	16,802	13,840	2,962	—	51	730	—
1892	—	—	—	18,667	15,342	3,325	—	49	1,104	—
1893	—	—	—	21,850	17,917	3,933	—	50	1,223	1,013
1894	—	—	—	24,106	19,723	4,383	—	56	1,334	1,124
1895	—	—	—	24,593	20,076	4,517	—	46	1,478	1,213
1896	—	—	—	25,231	20,550	4,681	—	43	1,413	1,163
1897	—	—	—	25,052	20,358	4,694	—	37	1,440	1,188
1898	—	—	—	25,980	21,064	4,916	—	36	1,542	1,275
1899	—	—	—	27,410	22,173	5,237	19	36	1,583	1,280

Notes appear at end of table

TABLE Bc568–587 Degrees conferred by institutions of higher education, by degree and sex: 1869–1994 *Continued*

	Associate degrees			Bachelor's degrees					Master's degrees	
	Total	Males	Females	Total	Males	Females	Per 1,000 persons 23 years old	Per 100 high school graduates four years earlier	Total	Males
	Bc568	Bc569	Bc570	Bc571	Bc572	Bc573	Bc574	Bc575	Bc576 [2]	Bc577 [2]
School year beginning	Number	Number	Number	Number	Number	Number	Per 1000	Per 100	Number	Number
1900	—	—	—	28,681	23,099	5,582	19	36	1,744	1,405
1901	—	—	—	28,966	23,225	5,741	19	34	1,858	1,464
1902	—	—	—	29,907	23,872	6,035	19	33	1,718	1,385
1903	—	—	—	30,501	24,237	6,264	19	32	1,679	1,340
1904	—	—	—	31,519	24,934	6,585	19	32	1,925	1,538
1905	—	—	—	32,019	25,215	6,804	19	32	1,787	1,366
1906	—	—	—	32,234	25,269	6,965	19	31	1,619	1,215
1907	—	—	—	33,800	26,376	7,424	19	30	1,971	1,511
1908	—	—	—	37,892	29,433	8,459	21	32	2,188	1,713
1909	—	—	—	37,199	28,762	8,437	20	30	2,113	1,555
1910	—	—	—	37,481	28,547	8,934	20	30	2,456	1,821
1911	—	—	—	39,408	29,560	9,848	21	30	3,035	2,215
1912	—	—	—	42,396	31,312	11,084	23	30	3,025	2,021
1913	—	—	—	44,268	32,183	12,085	24	28	3,270	2,256
1914	—	—	—	43,912	31,417	12,495	23	26	3,577	2,638
1915	—	—	—	45,250	31,852	13,398	24	25	3,906	2,934
1917	—	—	—	38,585	26,269	12,316	22	18	2,900	1,806
1919	—	—	—	48,622	31,980	16,642	26	19	4,279	2,985
1921	—	—	—	61,668	41,306	20,362	33	22	5,984	4,304
1923	—	—	—	82,783	54,908	27,875	43	27	8,216	5,515
1925	—	—	—	97,263	62,218	35,045	49	27	9,735	6,202
1927	—	—	—	111,161	67,659	43,502	55	22	12,387	7,727
1929	—	—	—	122,484	73,615	48,869	57	22	14,969	8,925
1931	—	—	—	138,063	83,271	54,792	63	23	19,367	12,210
1933	—	—	—	136,156	82,341	53,815	61	20	18,293	11,516
1935	—	—	—	143,125	86,067	57,058	63	17	18,302	11,503
1937	—	—	—	164,943	97,678	67,265	72	18	21,628	13,400
1939	—	—	—	186,500	109,546	76,954	81	18	26,731	16,508
1941	—	—	—	185,346	103,889	81,457	78	16	24,648	14,179
1943	—	—	—	125,863	55,865	69,998	52	10	13,414	5,711
1945	—	—	—	136,174	58,664	77,510	56	11	19,209	9,484
1947	—	—	—	271,186	175,615	95,571	113	27	42,432	28,931
1948	—	—	—	365,492	263,608	101,884	154	36	50,741	35,212
1949	—	—	—	432,058	328,841	103,217	182	40	58,183	41,220
1950	—	—	—	382,546	278,240	104,306	161	35	65,077	46,196
1951	—	—	—	329,986	225,981	104,005	143	28	63,534	43,557
1952	—	—	—	303,049	199,793	103,256	132	25	60,959	40,946
1953	—	—	—	291,508	186,884	104,624	129	24	56,823	38,147
1954	—	—	—	285,841	182,839	103,002	151	24	58,200	38,739
1955	—	—	—	309,514	198,615	110,899	147	26	59,281	39,393
1956	—	—	—	338,436	221,650	116,786	163	28	61,940	41,329
1957	—	—	—	363,502	241,560	121,942	167	28	65,586	44,229
1958	—	—	—	379,931	252,517	127,414	178	28	72,532	48,360
1959	—	—	—	392,440	254,063	138,377	182	27	74,435	50,898
1960	—	—	—	365,174	224,538	140,636	165	25	84,609	57,830
1961	—	—	—	383,961	230,456	153,505	173	25	91,418	62,603
1962	—	—	—	411,420	241,309	170,111	181	25	98,684	67,302
1963	—	—	—	461,266	265,349	195,917	192	25	109,183	73,850
1964	—	—	—	493,757	282,173	211,584	194	25	121,167	81,319
1965	111,607	63,779	47,828	520,115	299,287	220,828	181	27	140,602	93,081
1966	139,183	78,356	60,827	558,534	322,711	235,823	208	29	157,726	103,109
1967	159,441	90,317	69,124	632,289	357,682	274,607	238	28	176,749	113,552
1968	183,279	105,661	77,618	728,845	410,595	318,250	278	27	193,756	121,531
1969	206,023	117,432	88,591	792,317	451,097	341,220	218	30	208,291	125,624
1970	252,311	144,144	108,167	839,730	475,594	364,136	247	31	230,509	138,146
1971	292,014	166,227	125,787	887,273	500,590	386,683	258	33	251,633	149,550
1972	316,174	175,413	140,761	922,362	518,191	404,171	267	33	263,371	154,468
1973	343,924	188,591	155,333	945,776	527,313	418,463	262	33	277,033	157,842
1974	360,171	191,017	169,154	922,933	504,841	418,092	249	31	292,450	161,570

Notes appear at end of table

(continued)

TABLE Bc568–587 Degrees conferred by institutions of higher education, by degree and sex: 1869–1994 *Continued*

	Associate degrees			Bachelor's degrees					Master's degrees	
	Total	Males	Females	Total	Males	Females	Per 1,000 persons 23 years old	Per 100 high school graduates four years earlier	Total	Males
	Bc568	Bc569	Bc570	Bc571	Bc572	Bc573	Bc574	Bc575	Bc576 [2]	Bc577 [2]
School year beginning	Number	Number	Number	Number	Number	Number	Per 1000	Per 100	Number	Number
1975	391,454	209,996	181,458	925,746	504,925	420,821	242	31	311,771	167,248
1976	406,377	210,842	195,535	919,549	495,545	424,004	234	30	317,164	167,783
1977	412,246	204,718	207,528	921,204	487,347	433,857	229	30	311,620	161,212
1978	402,702	192,091	210,611	921,390	477,344	444,046	225	29	301,079	153,370
1979	400,910	183,737	217,173	929,417	473,611	455,806	218	30	298,081	150,749
1980	416,377	188,638	227,739	935,140	469,883	465,257	218	30	295,739	147,043
1981	434,526	196,944	237,582	952,998	473,364	479,634	222	30	295,546	145,532
1982	449,620	203,991	245,629	969,510	479,140	490,370	227	31	289,921	144,697
1983	452,240	202,704	249,536	974,309	482,319	491,990	225	32	284,263	143,595
1984	454,712	202,932	251,780	979,477	482,528	496,949	230	32	286,251	143,390
1985	446,047	196,166	249,881	987,823	485,923	501,900	236	33	288,567	143,508
1986	436,304	190,839	245,465	991,264	480,782	510,482	241	34	289,349	141,269
1987	435,085	190,047	245,038	994,829	477,203	517,626	252	36	299,317	145,163
1988	436,764	186,316	250,448	1,018,755	483,346	535,409	272	38	310,621	149,354
1989	455,102	191,195	263,907	1,051,344	491,696	559,648	284	40	324,301	153,653
1990	481,720	198,634	283,086	1,094,538	504,045	590,493	301	41	337,168	156,482
1991	504,231	207,481	296,750	1,136,553	520,811	615,742	307	41	352,838	161,842
1992	514,756	211,964	302,792	1,165,178	532,881	632,297	303	43	369,585	169,258
1993	530,632	215,261	315,371	1,169,275	532,422	636,853	302	45	387,070	176,085
1994	539,691	218,352	321,339	1,160,134	526,131	634,003	323	46	397,629	178,598

	Master's degrees		First professional degrees			Doctorate degrees				
	Females	Per 100 bachelor's degrees two years earlier	Total	Males	Females	Total	Males	Females	Average years from receipt of bachelor's to doctorate degree	Per 1,000 bachelor's degrees
	Bc578 [2]	Bc579 [2]	Bc580	Bc581	Bc582	Bc583	Bc584	Bc585	Bc586 [3, 4]	Bc587 [5]
School year beginning	Number	Per 100	Number	Number	Number	Number	Number	Number	Number	Per 1000
1869	—	—	—	—	—	1	1	0	—	—
1870	—	—	—	—	—	13	—	—	—	—
1871	—	8	—	—	—	14	—	—	—	—
1872	—	7	—	—	—	26	—	—	—	—
1873	—	11	—	—	—	13	—	—	—	—
1874	—	6	—	—	—	23	—	—	—	—
1875	—	7	—	—	—	31	—	—	—	—
1876	—	6	—	—	—	39	—	—	—	—
1877	—	7	—	—	—	32	—	—	—	3.4
1878	—	9	—	—	—	36	—	—	—	2.9
1879	11	8	—	—	—	54	51	3	—	5.7
1880	—	8	—	—	—	37	—	—	—	3.7
1881	—	7	—	—	—	46	—	—	—	3.7
1882	—	6	—	—	—	50	—	—	—	4.2
1883	—	6	—	—	—	66	—	—	—	3.8
1884	—	7	—	—	—	77	—	—	—	5.8
1885	—	7	—	—	—	84	—	—	—	2.9
1886	—	6	—	—	—	77	—	—	—	6.4
1887	—	8	—	—	—	140	—	—	—	6.1
1888	—	9	—	—	—	124	—	—	—	8.1
1889	194	7	—	—	—	149	147	2	—	9.0
1890	—	5	—	—	—	187	—	—	—	9.2
1891	—	5	—	—	—	190	—	—	—	13.0
1892	—	7	—	—	—	218	—	—	—	13.2
1893	210	7	—	—	—	279	261	18	—	18.5
1894	210	7	—	—	—	272	247	25	—	18.3

Notes appear at end of table

TABLE Bc568–587 Degrees conferred by institutions of higher education, by degree and sex: 1869–1994 *Continued*

	Master's degrees		First professional degrees			Doctorate degrees				
	Females	Per 100 bachelor's degrees two years earlier	Total	Males	Females	Total	Males	Females	Average years from receipt of bachelor's to doctorate degree	Per 1,000 bachelor's degrees
	Bc578 [2]	Bc579 [2]	Bc580	Bc581	Bc582	Bc583	Bc584	Bc585	Bc586 [3, 4]	Bc587 [5]
School year beginning	Number	Per 100	Number	Number	Number	Number	Number	Number	Number	Per 1000
1895	265	7	—	—	—	271	236	35	—	16.0
1896	250	6	—	—	—	319	299	20	—	19.8
1897	252	6	—	—	—	324	285	39	—	15.2
1898	267	6	—	—	—	345	327	18	—	13.3
1899	303	6	—	—	—	382	359	23	—	14.2
1900	339	7	—	—	—	365	334	31	—	13.7
1901	394	7	—	—	—	293	264	29	—	10.2
1902	333	6	—	—	—	337	302	35	—	11.2
1903	339	6	—	—	—	334	302	32	—	11.8
1904	387	6	—	—	—	369	341	28	—	12.9
1905	421	6	—	—	—	383	358	25	—	13.0
1906	404	5	—	—	—	349	320	29	—	12.6
1907	460	6	—	—	—	391	339	52	—	13.8
1908	475	7	—	—	—	451	397	54	—	13.6
1909	558	6	—	—	—	443	399	44	—	12.5
1910	635	6	—	—	—	497	449	48	—	14.9
1911	820	8	—	—	—	500	436	64	—	15.9
1912	1,004	8	—	—	—	538	481	57	—	14.9
1913	1,014	8	—	—	—	559	486	73	—	15.7
1914	939	8	—	—	—	611	549	62	—	17.2
1915	972	9	—	—	—	667	586	81	—	18.1
1917	1,094	6	—	—	—	556	491	65	—	15.0
1919	1,294	11	—	—	—	615	522	93	7.7	15.6
1921	1,680	12	—	—	—	836	708	128	7.8	18.9
1923	2,701	13	—	—	—	1,098	939	159	8.4	24.3
1925	3,533	12	—	—	—	1,409	1,216	193	8.6	33.6
1927	4,660	13	—	—	—	1,447	1,249	198	8.4	29.8
1929	6,044	13	—	—	—	2,299	1,946	353	8.7	41.7
1931	7,157	16	—	—	—	2,654	2,247	407	9.1	36.7
1933	6,777	13	—	—	—	2,830	2,456	374	8.5	29.1
1935	6,799	13	—	—	—	2,770	2,370	400	9.2	26.6
1937	8,228	15	—	—	—	2,932	2,502	430	9.5	26.4
1939	10,223	16	—	—	—	3,290	2,861	429	9.4	25.3
1941	10,469	13	—	—	—	3,497	3,036	461	8.8	25.5
1943	7,703	7	—	—	—	2,305	1,880	425	9.4	16.5
1945	9,725	15	—	—	—	1,966	1,580	386	11.0	14.1
1947	13,501	31	—	—	—	3,989	3,496	493	10.8	25.9
1948	15,529	25	—	—	—	5,049	4,527	522	10.2	28.7
1949	16,963	21	—	—	—	6,420	5,804	616	10.2	34.4
1950	18,881	18	—	—	—	7,337	6,663	674	9.8	39.5
1951	19,977	15	—	—	—	7,683	6,969	714	9.8	41.5
1952	20,013	16	—	—	—	8,307	7,515	792	9.7	53.4
1953	18,676	17	—	—	—	8,996	8,181	815	9.7	71.5
1954	19,461	19	—	—	—	8,840	8,014	826	9.9	67.5
1955	19,888	20	—	—	—	8,903	8,018	885	10.3	65.4
1956	20,611	22	—	—	—	8,756	7,817	939	10.2	43.0
1957	21,357	21	—	—	—	8,942	7,978	964	10.3	33.0
1958	24,172	21	—	—	—	9,360	8,371	989	10.3	25.6
1959	23,537	20	—	—	—	9,829	8,801	1,028	10.4	22.7
1960	26,779	22	25,253	24,577	676	10,575	9,463	1,112	10.3	27.6
1961	28,815	23	25,607	24,836	771	11,622	10,377	1,245	10.2	35.2
1962	31,382	27	26,590	25,753	837	12,822	11,448	1,374	10.2	42.3
1963	35,333	28	27,209	26,357	852	14,490	12,955	1,535	10.0	49.7
1964	39,848	29	28,290	27,283	1,007	16,467	14,692	1,775	10.0	57.6
1965	47,521	30	30,124	28,982	1,142	18,237	16,121	2,116	10.0	58.9
1966	54,617	32	31,695	30,401	1,294	20,617	18,163	2,454	8.1	54.3
1967	63,197	34	33,939	32,402	1,537	23,089	20,183	2,906	8.1	58.8
1968	72,225	35	35,114	33,595	1,519	26,158	22,722	3,436	8.0	71.6
1969	82,667	33	34,578	32,794	1,784	29,912	25,890	4,022	7.9	77.9

Notes appear at end of table (continued)

TABLE Bc568–587 Degrees conferred by institutions of higher education, by degree and sex: 1869–1994 *Continued*

	Master's degrees		First professional degrees			Doctorate degrees				
	Females	Per 100 bachelor's degrees two years earlier	Total	Males	Females	Total	Males	Females	Average years from receipt of bachelor's to doctorate degree	Per 1,000 bachelor's degrees
	Bc578 [2]	Bc579 [2]	Bc580	Bc581	Bc582	Bc583	Bc584	Bc585	Bc586 [3, 4]	Bc587 [5]
School year beginning	Number	Per 100	Number	Number	Number	Number	Number	Number	Number	Per 1000
1970	92,363	32	37,946	35,544	2,402	32,107	27,530	4,577	7.9	78.0
1971	102,083	32	43,411	40,723	2,688	33,363	28,090	5,273	8.2	72.3
1972	108,903	31	50,018	46,489	3,529	34,777	28,571	6,206	8.4	70.4
1973	119,191	31	53,816	48,530	5,286	33,816	27,365	6,451	8.5	65.0
1974	130,880	32	55,916	48,956	6,960	34,083	26,817	7,266	8.6	65.5
1975	144,523	33	62,649	52,892	9,757	34,064	26,267	7,797	8.6	61.0
1976	149,381	34	64,359	52,374	11,985	33,232	25,142	8,090	8.7	52.6
1977	150,408	34	66,581	52,270	14,311	32,131	23,658	8,473	8.9	44.1
1978	147,709	33	68,848	52,652	16,196	32,730	23,541	9,189	9.0	41.3
1979	147,332	32	70,131	52,716	17,415	32,615	22,943	9,672	9.3	38.8
1980	148,696	32	71,956	52,792	19,164	32,958	22,711	10,247	9.4	37.1
1981	150,014	32	72,032	52,223	19,809	32,707	22,224	10,483	9.6	36.9
1982	145,224	31	73,136	51,310	21,826	32,775	21,902	10,873	9.8	35.5
1983	140,668	30	74,407	51,334	23,073	33,209	22,064	11,145	10.0	35.1
1984	142,861	30	75,063	50,455	24,608	32,943	21,700	11,243	10.2	35.7
1985	145,059	30	73,910	49,261	24,649	33,653	21,819	11,834	10.4	36.4
1986	148,080	30	71,617	46,523	34,041	22,061	22,099	11,980	10.4	37.1
1987	154,154	30	70,735	45,484	22,061	34,870	22,615	12,255	10.5	37.9
1988	161,267	31	70,856	45,046	25,810	35,720	22,648	13,072	10.5	38.8
1989	170,648	33	70,988	43,961	27,027	38,371	24,401	13,970	10.6	41.6
1990	180,686	33	71,948	43,846	28,102	39,294	24,756	14,538	10.4	42.0
1991	190,996	34	74,146	45,071	29,075	40,659	25,557	15,102	10.5	43.5
1992	200,327	34	75,387	45,153	30,234	42,132	26,073	16,059	10.5	44.2
1993	210,985	34	75,418	44,707	30,711	43,185	26,552	16,633	10.8	44.5
1994	219,031	34	75,800	44,853	30,947	44,446	26,916	17,530	10.9	45.6

[1] Through 1959, first professional degrees included with bachelor's degrees.

[2] Through 1959, includes second professional degrees.

[3] Computed from graduation announcements of doctorates (through 1955) and then from personal histories of doctorates collected by the National Research Council of the National Academy of Sciences.

[4] Changes from mean to median beginning in 1966.

[5] Ratio of current doctorate degrees to the number of bachelor's degrees, with appropriate lags. See text.

Sources

Series Bc568–570, U.S. Department of Education, *Digest of Education Statistics 1997* (1997), Table 244. Series Bc571–585, 1869–1988, except where noted below, U.S. Department of Education, *120 Years of American Education: A Statistical Portrait* (1993), Table 28. The underlying sources are: U.S. Bureau of the Census, *Historical Statistics of the United States: From Colonial Times to the Present* (1975); *Current Population Reports*, series P-25, Population Estimates and Projections; U.S. Department of Education, *Digest of Education Statistics*, annual issues. Series Bc586–587, 1877–1994, Abbott L. Ferriss, *Indicators of Trends in American Education* (Russell Sage Foundation, 1969), Appendix D; and National Academy of Sciences, *Doctorate Recipients from United States Universities*, various issues. Series Bc571–573, Bc576–578, and Bc580–585, 1986 to 1994, *Digest of Education Statistics 1997*, Table 244. See also text below for calculated series.

Documentation

The first-level degree (designated as "bachelor's or first professional") is designed as the first degree granted on completion of a course of study in a given field. The degree must be based on at least four years of college work or the equivalent. The same classification (namely, "first level") is given to a degree, for example, LL.B., regardless of whether the degree is based on seven years' preparation, six years' preparation, or less; and regardless of whether the student had previously earned a degree in another field. The first-level degree is ordinarily a bachelor's degree, but important exceptions occur in some professional fields and over time. Before the 1930s and 1940s many students earning their first professional degree did not yet have a bachelor's degree. Thus, part of the series for bachelor's degrees by necessity includes first professional degrees. (See also the text for Table Bc523–536.)

The second-level degree is a degree beyond the first level but below the doctorate and is ordinarily a master's degree. The doctorate (the highest level of earned degrees) includes advanced degrees such as Ph.D., Ed.D., and D.Eng. It includes only earned degrees, not honorary.

Series Bc574, 1989 to 1994. Equals series Bc571 divided by the number of 23-year-olds from *Current Population Reports*, series P-25, numbers 1092 and 1095.

Series Bc575, 1989 to 1994. Equals series Bc571 divided by series Bc258, with appropriate lags.

Series Bc579, 1989 to 1994. Equals series Bc576 divided by series Bc571, with appropriate lags.

Series Bc587, 1877–1988. In making its calculations for the years 1877 through 1916, the U.S. Department of Education assumed that students took eight years to complete their doctorate degrees after receiving their bachelor's degrees. The Department of Education's calculations for 1917 through 1988 use the average years from bachelor's to doctorate degree as reported in series Bc586.

Series Bc587, 1989 to 1994. Equals series Bc583 divided by series Bc571, lagged by the value shown in series Bc586.

TABLE Bc588–599 Medical, dental, and law schools – number of institutions and first professional degrees conferred, by sex: 1950–1997

Contributed by Susan B. Carter

	Dentistry				Medicine				Law			
		First professional degrees conferred				First professional degrees conferred				First professional degrees conferred		
	Institutions	Total	Males	Females	Institutions	Total	Males	Females	Institutions	Total	Males	Females
School year ending	Bc588	Bc589	Bc590	Bc591	Bc592	Bc593	Bc594	Bc595	Bc596	Bc597	Bc598	Bc599
	Number	Number	Number	Number	Number	Number	Number	Number	Number	Number	Number	Number
1950	40	2,579	2,561	18	72	5,612	5,028	584	—	—	—	—
1952	41	2,918	2,895	23	72	6,201	5,871	330	—	—	—	—
1954	42	3,102	3,063	39	73	6,712	6,377	335	—	—	—	—
1956	42	3,009	2,975	34	73	6,810	6,464	346	131	8,262	7,974	288
1958	43	3,065	3,031	34	75	6,816	6,469	347	131	9,394	9,122	272
1960	45	3,247	3,221	26	79	7,032	6,645	387	134	9,240	9,010	230
1962	46	3,183	3,166	17	81	7,138	6,749	389	134	9,364	9,091	273
1964	46	3,180	3,168	12	82	7,303	6,878	425	133	10,679	10,372	307
1966	47	3,178	3,146	32	84	7,673	7,170	503	136	13,246	12,776	470
1968	48	3,422	3,375	47	85	7,944	7,318	626	138	16,454	15,805	649
1970	48	3,718	3,684	34	86	8,314	7,615	699	145	14,916	14,115	801
1971	48	3,745	3,703	42	89	8,919	8,110	809	147	17,421	16,181	1,240
1972	48	3,862	3,819	43	92	9,253	8,423	830	147	21,764	20,266	1,498
1973	51	4,047	3,992	55	97	10,307	9,388	919	152	27,205	25,037	2,168
1974	52	4,440	4,355	85	99	11,356	10,093	1,263	151	29,326	25,986	3,340
1975	52	4,773	4,627	146	104	12,447	10,818	1,629	154	29,296	24,881	4,415
1976	56	5,425	5,187	238	107	13,426	11,252	2,174	166	32,293	26,085	6,208
1977	57	5,138	4,764	374	109	13,461	10,891	2,570	169	34,104	26,447	7,657
1978	57	5,189	4,623	566	109	14,279	11,210	3,069	169	34,402	25,457	8,945
1979	58	5,434	4,794	640	109	14,786	11,381	3,405	175	35,206	25,180	10,026
1980	58	5,258	4,558	700	112	14,902	11,416	3,486	179	35,647	24,893	10,754
1981	58	5,460	4,672	788	116	15,505	11,672	3,833	176	36,331	24,563	11,768
1982	59	5,282	4,467	815	119	15,814	11,867	3,947	180	35,991	23,965	12,026
1983	59	5,585	4,631	954	118	15,484	11,350	4,134	177	36,853	23,550	13,303
1984	60	5,353	4,302	1,051	119	15,813	11,359	4,454	179	37,012	23,382	13,630
1985	59	5,339	4,233	1,106	120	16,041	11,167	4,874	181	37,491	23,070	14,421
1986	59	5,046	3,907	1,139	120	15,938	11,022	4,916	181	35,844	21,874	13,970
1987	58	4,741	3,603	1,138	121	15,428	10,431	4,997	179	36,056	21,561	14,495
1988	57	4,477	3,300	1,177	122	15,358	10,278	5,080	180	35,397	21,067	14,330
1989	58	4,265	3,124	1,141	124	15,460	10,310	5,150	182	35,634	21,069	14,565
1990	57	4,100	2,834	1,266	124	15,075	9,923	5,152	182	36,485	21,079	15,406
1991	55	3,699	2,510	1,189	121	15,043	9,629	5,414	179	37,945	21,643	16,302
1992	52	3,593	2,431	1,162	120	15,243	9,796	5,447	177	38,848	22,260	16,588
1993	55	3,605	2,383	1,222	122	15,531	9,679	5,852	184	40,302	23,182	17,120
1994	53	3,787	2,330	1,457	121	15,368	9,544	5,824	185	40,044	22,826	17,218
1995	53	3,897	2,480	1,417	119	15,537	9,507	6,030	183	39,349	22,592	16,757
1996	53	3,697	2,374	1,323	119	15,341	9,061	6,280	183	39,828	22,508	17,320
1997	52	3,784	2,387	1,397	118	15,571	9,121	6,450	184	40,079	22,548	17,531

Source

U.S. National Center for Education Statistics, *Digest of Education Statistics: 1999*, Table 264.

Documentation

Degrees included: dentistry, D.D.S. or D.M.D; medicine, M.D.; and law, LL.B. or J.D.

Series Bc596–599. Data prior to the 1955–1956 academic year are not shown because they lack comparability with the figures for subsequent years.

TABLE Bc600–620 Doctorate degrees conferred by institutions of higher education, by field of study: 1920–1995[1, 2, 3]

Contributed by Claudia Goldin

	Total	Agriculture and natural resources	Architecture and environmental design	Business and management	Communications	Computer and information sciences	Education	Engineering	Foreign languages	Health sciences	Letters
	Bc600	Bc601	Bc602	Bc603 [4]	Bc604	Bc605	Bc606 [4]	Bc607	Bc608 [4, 5]	Bc609	Bc610 [4, 5]
Year	Number	Number	Number	Number	Number	Number	Number	Number	Number	Number	Number
1920	560	17	—	—	—	—	48	7	42	—	23
1921	661	15	—	—	—	—	33	10	42	—	30
1922	780	27	—	—	—	—	59	15	45	—	34
1923	1,062	45	—	—	—	—	68	14	48	—	44
1924	1,133	32	—	—	—	—	102	14	65	—	57
1925	1,206	36	—	—	—	—	128	16	57	—	55
1926	1,442	29	—	—	—	—	161	27	55	—	71
1927	1,539	42	—	—	—	—	170	33	64	—	63
1928	1,628	56	—	—	—	—	173	51	68	—	70
1929	1,913	60	—	—	—	—	211	41	94	—	69
1930	2,071	61	—	—	—	—	268	64	95	—	96
1931	2,340	62	—	—	—	—	303	67	102	—	108
1932	2,401	83	—	—	—	—	309	68	137	—	129
1933	2,460	75	—	—	—	—	261	92	140	—	114
1934	2,696	91	—	—	—	—	280	119	166	—	137
1935	2,521	80	—	—	—	—	250	111	174	—	136
1936	2,712	60	—	—	—	—	354	70	185	—	144
1937	2,749	59	—	—	—	—	357	98	169	—	161
1938	2,756	68	—	—	—	—	363	75	172	—	159
1939	2,948	69	—	—	—	—	377	69	164	—	173
1940	3,276	94	—	—	—	—	470	107	180	—	174
1941	3,481	93	—	—	—	—	478	122	178	—	189
1942	3,402	101	—	—	—	—	493	98	150	—	177
1943	2,585	75	—	—	—	—	399	53	115	—	124
1944	1,954	46	—	—	—	—	316	64	69	—	74
1945	1,621	54	—	—	—	—	291	68	70	—	72
1946	1,989	44	—	—	—	—	349	102	71	—	114
1947	2,958	81	—	—	—	—	450	119	120	—	165
1948	3,898	101	—	—	—	—	666	257	134	—	166
1949	5,421	182	—	—	—	—	847	450	155	—	179
1950	6,519	252	—	—	—	—	1,032	467	211	—	236
1951	7,331	271	—	—	—	—	1,113	585	201	—	297
1952	7,716	309	—	—	—	—	1,314	570	180	—	263
1953	8,378	332	—	—	—	—	1,425	568	202	—	333
1954	8,706	370	—	—	—	—	1,509	562	216	—	344
1955	8,904	368	—	—	—	—	1,572	651	216	—	327
1956	8,501	352	—	—	—	—	1,636	579	221	—	347
1957	6,187	233	—	—	—	—	834	455	169	—	266
1958	8,773	339	—	—	—	—	1,491	629	189	—	333
1959	9,212	342	—	—	—	—	1,553	699	220	—	340
1960	9,829	440	17	135	0	0	1,591	786	203	107	431
1961	10,575	450	3	172	16	0	1,742	943	232	133	439
1962	11,622	465	1	226	9	0	1,898	1,207	228	148	526
1963	12,822	449	3	250	7	0	2,075	1,378	237	157	565
1964	14,490	555	3	275	12	0	2,348	1,693	326	192	618
1965	16,467	529	10	321	9	6	2,705	2,124	376	173	766
1966	18,237	588	12	387	11	19	3,065	2,304	426	251	801
1967	20,617	637	18	437	5	38	3,529	2,614	478	250	972
1968	23,089	648	15	441	1	36	4,078	2,932	610	243	1,116
1969	26,158	699	32	530	14	64	4,830	3,377	659	283	1,275
1970	29,866	823	35	601	10	107	5,895	3,681	760	357	1,339
1971	32,107	1,086	36	807	145	128	6,403	3,638	781	459	1,857
1972	33,363	971	50	896	111	167	7,044	3,671	841	425	2,023
1973	34,777	1,059	58	923	139	196	7,318	3,492	991	643	2,170
1974	33,816	930	69	981	175	198	7,293	3,312	923	568	2,076
1975	34,083	991	69	1,009	165	213	7,446	3,108	857	609	1,951
1976	34,064	928	82	953	204	244	7,778	2,821	864	577	1,884
1977	33,232	893	73	863	171	216	7,963	2,586	752	538	1,723
1978	32,131	971	73	866	191	196	7,595	2,440	649	638	1,616
1979	32,730	950	96	860	192	236	7,736	2,506	641	705	1,504

Notes appear at end of table

TABLE Bc600–620 Doctorate degrees conferred by institutions of higher education, by field of study: 1920–1995 *Continued*

	Total	Agriculture and natural resources	Architecture and environmental design	Business and management	Communications	Computer and information sciences	Education	Engineering	Foreign languages	Health sciences	Letters
	Bc600	Bc601	Bc602	Bc603 [4]	Bc604	Bc605	Bc606 [4]	Bc607	Bc608 [4, 5]	Bc609	Bc610 [4, 5]
Year	Number	Number	Number	Number	Number	Number	Number	Number	Number	Number	Number
1980	32,615	991	79	792	193	240	7,941	2,507	549	771	1,500
1981	32,958	1,067	93	842	182	252	7,900	2,561	588	827	1,380
1982	32,707	1,079	80	855	200	251	7,680	2,636	536	910	1,313
1983	32,775	1,149	97	809	214	262	7,551	2,831	488	1,155	1,176
1984	33,209	1,172	84	977	219	251	7,473	2,981	462	1,163	1,215
1985	32,943	1,213	89	866	234	248	7,151	3,230	437	1,199	1,239
1986	33,653	1,158	73	969	223	344	7,110	3,410	448	1,241	1,215
1987	34,120	1,049	92	1,098	275	374	6,909	3,820	441	1,213	1,181
1988	34,870	1,142	98	1,109	234	428	6,553	4,191	411	1,261	1,172
1989	35,720	1,183	86	1,100	253	551	6,337	4,523	632	1,437	1,022
1990	38,371	1,295	103	1,093	273	627	6,502	4,981	724	1,536	1,078
1991	39,294	1,185	135	1,185	274	676	6,187	5,272	758	1,613	1,184
1992	40,659	1,214	132	1,242	255	772	6,864	5,499	850	1,661	1,273
1993	42,132	1,173	148	1,346	301	805	7,030	5,843	830	1,767	1,341
1994	43,185	1,278	161	1,364	345	810	6,908	5,979	886	1,902	1,344
1995	44,446	1,264	141	1,394	321	884	6,905	6,128	905	2,069	1,561

	Library sciences	Life sciences	Mathematics	Physical sciences	Psychology	Public affairs	Social sciences and history	Visual and performing arts	Professional fields	Other
	Bc611	Bc612	Bc613	Bc614	Bc615 [4]	Bc616	Bc617	Bc618	Bc619	Bc620
Year	Number	Number	Number	Number	Number	Number	Number	Number	Number	Number
1920	—	104	19	128	35	—	75	—	18	44
1921	—	91	15	174	28	—	120	—	34	69
1922	—	111	17	217	34	—	123	—	32	66
1923	—	169	34	285	65	—	146	—	45	99
1924	—	150	29	330	54	—	166	—	52	82
1925	—	179	28	289	71	—	197	—	56	94
1926	—	198	48	381	74	—	224	—	64	110
1927	—	224	51	342	76	—	270	—	88	116
1928	—	251	42	381	84	—	266	—	77	109
1929	—	271	68	396	122	—	329	—	85	167
1930	—	272	76	474	101	—	339	—	74	151
1931	—	355	82	487	118	—	362	—	107	187
1932	—	334	74	498	105	—	381	—	123	160
1933	—	356	75	589	92	—	403	—	103	160
1934	—	421	91	607	128	—	402	—	103	151
1935	—	359	75	563	112	—	383	—	133	145
1936	—	424	76	653	114	—	359	—	103	170
1937	—	417	74	713	112	—	399	—	80	110
1938	—	478	61	635	116	—	411	—	83	135
1939	—	508	93	689	117	—	438	—	109	142
1940	—	563	103	737	129	—	471	—	94	154
1941	—	517	95	890	113	—	515	—	111	180
1942	—	568	76	812	126	—	466	—	148	187
1943	—	445	44	685	92	—	323	—	105	125
1944	—	301	43	556	68	—	210	—	103	104
1945	—	217	36	354	64	—	194	—	107	94
1946	—	241	54	431	82	—	310	—	80	111
1947	—	406	115	634	122	—	477	—	116	153
1948	—	526	117	898	181	—	496	—	141	215
1949	—	677	147	1,382	276	—	715	—	174	237
1950	—	764	176	1,602	360	—	890	—	219	310
1951	—	840	205	1,682	490	—	1,046	—	250	351
1952	—	935	204	1,731	581	—	983	—	247	399
1953	—	1,148	225	1,697	656	—	1,096	—	241	455
1954	—	1,134	247	1,702	665	—	1,200	—	260	497

Notes appear at end of table

(continued)

TABLE Bc600–620 Doctorate degrees conferred by institutions of higher education, by field of study: 1920–1995 *Continued*

	Library sciences	Life sciences	Mathematics	Physical sciences	Psychology	Public affairs	Social sciences and history	Visual and performing arts	Professional fields	Other
	Bc611	Bc612	Bc613	Bc614	Bc615 [4]	Bc616	Bc617	Bc618	Bc619	Bc620
Year	Number	Number	Number	Number	Number	Number	Number	Number	Number	Number
1955	—	1,113	243	1,703	735	—	1,203	—	269	504
1956	—	973	228	1,621	628	—	1,137	—	275	504
1957	—	819	199	1,302	502	—	797	—	249	362
1958	—	1,140	238	1,652	743	—	1,142	—	344	533
1959	—	1,086	289	1,801	786	—	1,188	—	363	545
1960	19	1,205	303	1,838	641	43	1,211	292	—	567
1961	14	1,193	344	1,991	703	66	1,302	303	—	529
1962	10	1,338	396	2,122	781	67	1,309	311	—	580
1963	17	1,455	490	2,380	844	77	1,461	379	—	598
1964	13	1,625	596	2,455	939	72	1,719	422	—	627
1965	12	1,928	682	2,829	847	87	1,913	428	—	722
1966	19	2,097	782	3,045	1,046	108	2,033	476	—	767
1967	16	2,255	832	3,462	1,231	123	2,388	504	—	828
1968	22	2,784	947	3,593	1,268	129	2,684	528	—	1,014
1969	17	3,051	1,097	3,859	1,551	137	3,016	684	—	983
1970	40	3,289	1,236	4,312	1,668	152	3,638	734	—	1,189
1971	39	3,645	1,199	4,390	1,782	185	3,659	621	—	1,247
1972	64	3,653	1,128	4,103	1,881	219	4,078	572	—	1,466
1973	102	3,636	1,068	4,006	2,089	214	4,230	616	—	1,827
1974	60	3,439	1,031	3,626	2,336	214	4,123	585	—	1,877
1975	56	3,384	975	3,626	2,442	271	4,209	649	—	2,053
1976	71	3,392	856	3,431	2,581	298	4,154	620	—	2,326
1977	75	3,397	823	3,341	2,761	316	3,784	662	—	2,295
1978	67	3,309	805	3,133	2,587	385	3,583	708	—	2,319
1979	70	3,542	730	3,102	2,662	344	3,358	700	—	2,796
1980	73	3,636	724	3,089	2,768	372	3,219	655	—	2,516
1981	71	3,718	728	3,141	2,955	388	3,114	654	—	2,497
1982	84	3,743	681	3,286	2,780	389	3,061	670	—	2,473
1983	52	3,341	698	3,269	3,108	347	2,931	692	—	2,605
1984	74	3,437	695	3,306	2,973	421	2,911	728	—	2,667
1985	87	3,432	699	3,403	2,908	431	2,851	693	—	2,533
1986	62	3,358	742	3,551	3,088	385	2,955	722	—	2,599
1987	57	3,423	725	3,672	3,123	398	2,916	792	—	2,562
1988	46	3,629	750	3,809	2,987	470	2,781	725	—	3,074
1989	61	3,520	915	3,858	3,685	428	2,885	753	—	2,491
1990	42	3,844	966	4,164	3,811	508	3,010	849	—	2,965
1991	56	4,093	1,036	4,290	3,932	430	3,012	838	—	3,138
1992	50	4,243	1,082	4,391	3,373	432	3,218	906	—	3,202
1993	77	4,435	1,189	4,393	3,651	459	3,460	882	—	3,002
1994	45	4,534	1,157	4,650	3,563	519	3,627	1,054	—	3,059
1995	55	4,645	1,226	4,483	3,822	556	3,725	1,080	—	3,282

[1] Doctorates included in professional fields before 1960 are subsequently distributed among those fields listed

[2] Data for censuses prior to 1960 are not directly comparable to those starting in 1960, either because of a change in reporting year or because of changes in field definition.

[3] Through 1956, calendar year basis; thereafter, fiscal year basis. Only the first half of 1957 is shown.

[4] After 1990, series definition changes and figures are not directly comparable to those before.

[5] Subfields included in sources differ. For direct comparability, add series Bc608 and series Bc610, beginning in 1960.

Sources

Series Bc600–601, Bc606–608, Bc610, Bc612–615, Bc617, and Bc619–620, 1920 to 1959, U.S. Bureau of the Census, *Historical Statistics of the United States: From Colonial Times to the Present* (1975). The underlying source for *Historical Statistics* is: National Research Council, Commission on Human Resources, Doctorate Records File. Series Bc600–618 and Bc620, 1960 to 1988, U.S. Department of Education, *120 Years of Education: A Statistical Portrait* (1993), Table 31. The underlying sources for *120 Years* are: U.S. National Center for Education Statistics, "Earned Degrees Conferred" and "Degrees and Other Formal Awards Conferred" surveys; and Integrated Postsecondary Education Data System (IPEDS), "Completions" surveys. Series Bc600–618 and Bc620, 1989 to 1995, U.S. Department of Education, *Digest of Education Statistics 1997*, Table 252.

Documentation

The Doctorate Records File is a virtually complete source of data about persons receiving doctorates since 1920. The doctoral degrees reported are those earned at regionally accredited U.S. universities and include degree titles such as Doctor of Philosophy (Ph.D.), Doctor of Science (Sc.D.), Doctor of Education (Ed.D.), Doctor of Engineering (D.Eng.), and so forth. Professional degrees such as Doctor of Medicine (M.D.), Doctor of Dental Surgery (D.D.S.), and Doctor of Veterinary Medicine (D.V.M.) are excluded.

Information about the doctorate recipients of 1920–1957 was obtained from the graduate schools and is limited to the following: sex; baccalaureate institution and year; master's institution and year; and doctoral institution, year, and field of degree. Since 1957 the information has been obtained from the Survey of Earned Doctorates questionnaire, which is given to the doctoral candidates by the graduate schools at the time all requirements for the degree have been met. The questionnaires are completed by the doctorate recipients, who provide data about their birth date and place, sex, citizenship, marital status, and racial or ethnic group. Information is also provided about their

TABLE Bc600–620 Doctorate degrees conferred by institutions of higher education, by field of study: 1920–1995 *Continued*

educational background from high school to doctorate, sources of financial support in graduate school, and postgraduation employment plans.

Some of the fields included in the groupings are listed below.

Agricultural sciences. Includes agronomy, agricultural economics, agricultural business, soil sciences, conservation and natural resource management, food science and technology, fish and wildlife, animal sciences, forestry, horticulture, and phytopathology.

Communications and communications technologies. Includes communications, advertising, and journalism.

Education. Includes education administration and supervision, special education, and teacher education.

Health sciences. Includes medical laboratory technologies, nursing, pharmacy, and basic medical sciences including biochemistry, biophysics, anatomy, cytology, embryology, immunology, microbiology, bacteriology, animal physiology, and molecular biology.

Letters. Includes English language and literature, comparative literature, composition, and creative writing.

Life sciences. Includes biometrics and biostatistics, botany, ecology, hydrobiology, plant physiology, zoology, genetics, and entomology. Also includes basic medical sciences prior to 1960.

Physical sciences. Includes astronomy, astrophysics, chemistry, geology and related sciences, mineralogy, oceanography, and physics.

Public affairs. Includes public administration, public policy analysis, social work, and public affairs.

Social sciences and history. Includes anthropology, archeology, criminology, demography, economics, geography, history, international relations and affairs, political science and government, sociology, and urban affairs.

Visual and performing arts. Includes dance, film, fine arts and art studies, and music history and theory.

Professional fields. Prior to 1960 includes business administration, journalism, law and jurisprudence, theology, social work, home economics, library and archival science, and speech and hearing sciences.

Other fields. Through 1959, includes other arts and humanities (including applied art, history and criticism of art, music, archaeology, religion, philosophy, linguistics, and speech as a dramatic art), medical sciences, and other unspecified fields. Beginning in 1960, includes area ethnic and cultural studies, home economics and vocational home economics, law, liberal/general studies, military sciences, multidisciplinary and interdisciplinary studies, parks and recreation, philosophy and religion, protective services, theology, and degrees not classified by study.

TABLE Bc621–656 Doctorate degrees conferred by institutions of higher education, by field of study and sex: 1950–1997[1]

Contributed by Susan B. Carter

School year ending	Males: Total	Males: Agriculture and natural resources	Males: Architecture and environmental design	Males: Biological and life sciences	Males: Business and management	Males: Communications	Males: Computer and information sciences	Males: Education	Males: Engineering	Males: English	Males: Modern foreign languages	Males: Health professions and related sciences
	Bc621	Bc622	Bc623	Bc624	Bc625	Bc626	Bc627	Bc628	Bc629	Bc630	Bc631	Bc632
	Number	Number	Number	Number	Number	Number	Number	Number	Number	Number	Number	Number
1950	5,804	—	1	—	—	—	—	797	416	181	135	—
1952	—	—	—	680	—	—	—	—	—	—	—	—
1954	—	—	—	977	—	—	—	—	—	—	—	—
1956	—	—	—	908	127	—	—	—	—	—	—	—
1958	—	—	—	987	105	—	—	—	—	—	—	—
1960	8,801	—	17	1,086	133	—	—	1,279	783	314	100	—
1961	9,463	—	—	—	—	—	—	—	—	—	—	—
1962	10,377	—	—	1,179	221	—	—	—	—	—	—	—
1963	11,448	—	—	—	—	—	—	—	—	—	—	—
1964	12,955	—	—	1,432	268	—	—	—	—	—	—	—
1965	14,692	—	—	—	—	—	—	—	—	—	—	—
1966	16,121	—	—	1,792	370	—	—	—	—	—	—	—
1967	18,163	—	—	—	—	—	—	—	—	—	—	—
1968	20,183	—	15	2,345	427	—	—	3,250	—	717	336	—
1969	22,722	—	—	—	—	—	—	—	—	—	—	—
1970	25,890	—	33	2,820	610	—	—	4,479	3,657	837	369	—
1971	27,530	1,055	33	3,050	736	126	125	4,771	3,615	1,175	425	389
1972	28,090	945	43	3,031	840	96	155	5,104	3,649	1,233	466	362
1973	28,571	1,031	54	2,926	850	114	181	5,191	3,438	1,258	519	485
1974	27,365	897	65	2,740	870	146	189	4,974	3,257	1,208	487	447
1975	26,817	958	58	2,641	897	119	199	4,856	3,042	1,025	442	441
1976	26,267	867	69	2,663	851	154	221	4,826	2,755	967	429	411
1977	25,142	831	62	2,671	775	130	197	4,832	2,513	841	347	366
1978	23,658	909	57	2,511	753	138	181	4,281	2,383	758	282	402
1979	23,541	877	74	2,636	724	138	206	4,174	2,423	708	287	454
1980	22,943	879	66	2,690	642	121	213	4,100	2,412	686	217	435
1981	22,711	940	73	2,666	675	107	227	3,843	2,457	553	259	475
1982	22,224	925	58	2,654	668	136	230	3,612	2,496	511	220	503
1983	21,902	1,004	74	2,266	644	126	228	3,547	2,706	471	183	649
1984	22,064	1,001	62	2,381	730	131	225	3,446	2,816	459	191	574
1985	21,700	1,036	66	2,307	688	143	223	3,172	3,022	470	156	565
1986	21,819	966	56	2,229	729	116	299	3,088	3,181	428	173	604
1987	22,061	871	66	2,225	808	158	322	2,931	3,555	415	162	564
1988	22,615	926	66	2,349	810	134	380	2,739	3,898	428	159	548
1989	22,648	950	63	2,234	800	138	466	2,704	4,123	458	145	609
1990	24,401	1,038	73	2,394	818	145	534	2,776	4,536	480	183	704
1991	24,756	953	101	2,577	876	151	584	2,613	4,787	517	200	694
1992	25,557	963	93	2,620	953	132	669	2,783	4,972	537	222	698
1993	26,073	879	105	2,664	969	146	689	2,867	5,283	550	210	753
1994	26,552	982	111	2,690	980	174	685	2,706	5,315	568	208	789
1995	26,916	962	95	2,771	1,014	162	723	2,621	5,399	665	250	867
1996	26,841	935	96	2,773	974	190	741	2,525	5,580	590	225	919
1997	27,146	884	93	2,738	947	155	721	2,512	5,446	670	247	1,176

Note appears at end of table

TABLE Bc621–656 Doctorate degrees conferred by institutions of higher education, by field of study and sex: 1950–1997 *Continued*

	Males						Females					
	Mathematics	Physical sciences	Psychology	Public affairs	Social sciences	Visual and performing arts	Total	Agriculture and natural resources	Architecture and environmental design	Biological and life sciences	Business and management	Communications
School year ending	Bc633	Bc634	Bc635	Bc636	Bc637	Bc638	Bc639	Bc640	Bc641	Bc642	Bc643	Bc644
	Number	Number	Number	Number	Number	Number	Number	Number	Number	Number	Number	Number
1950	151	—	241	—	—	—	616	—	0	—	—	—
1952	—	—	—	—	—	—	—	—	—	84	—	—
1954	—	—	—	—	—	—	—	—	—	100	—	—
1956	—	—	—	—	—	—	—	—	—	117	2	—
1958	—	—	—	—	—	—	—	—	—	138	5	—
1960	285	1,776	544	—	—	—	1,028	—	0	119	2	—
1961	—	—	—	—	—	—	1,112	—	—	—	—	—
1962	—	—	—	—	—	—	1,245	—	—	159	5	—
1963	—	—	—	—	—	—	1,374	—	—	—	—	—
1964	—	—	—	—	—	—	1,535	—	—	193	7	—
1965	—	—	—	—	—	—	1,775	—	—	—	—	—
1966	—	—	—	—	—	—	2,116	—	—	305	17	—
1967	—	—	—	—	—	—	2,454	—	—	—	—	—
1968	895	3,405	982	—	—	—	2,906	—	0	439	14	—
1969	—	—	—	—	—	—	3,436	—	—	—	—	—
1970	1,140	4,077	1,505	—	—	—	3,976	—	2	469	10	—
1971	1,154	4,144	1,629	132	3,153	483	4,577	31	3	595	21	19
1972	1,075	3,830	1,694	150	3,483	428	5,273	26	7	622	19	15
1973	987	3,738	1,797	160	3,573	449	6,206	28	4	710	52	25
1974	992	3,373	1,987	154	3,383	440	6,451	33	4	699	49	29
1975	936	3,325	1,979	192	3,334	446	7,266	33	11	743	39	46
1976	812	3,132	2,115	192	3,262	447	7,797	61	13	729	49	50
1977	748	3,022	2,127	197	2,957	447	8,090	62	11	726	52	41
1978	722	2,821	1,974	237	2,722	448	8,473	62	16	798	70	53
1979	644	2,752	1,895	215	2,501	454	9,189	73	22	906	97	54
1980	659	2,705	1,921	216	2,357	413	9,672	112	13	946	111	72
1981	656	2,765	2,002	212	2,274	396	10,247	127	20	1,052	120	75
1982	623	2,835	1,856	205	2,237	380	10,483	154	22	1,089	147	64
1983	611	2,811	1,838	184	2,042	404	10,873	145	23	1,075	132	88
1984	614	2,815	1,774	230	2,030	406	11,145	171	22	1,056	199	88
1985	620	2,851	1,739	213	1,933	407	11,243	177	23	1,125	143	91
1986	648	2,963	1,724	171	1,970	396	11,834	192	17	1,129	205	107
1987	628	3,039	1,615	216	2,026	447	11,980	178	26	1,194	254	117
1988	668	3,123	1,573	238	1,849	424	12,255	216	32	1,280	253	100
1989	737	3,088	1,590	210	1,949	446	13,072	233	23	1,286	300	115
1990	794	3,356	1,566	235	2,019	472	13,970	257	30	1,450	275	128
1991	837	3,447	1,520	190	1,956	466	14,538	232	34	1,516	309	123
1992	851	3,429	1,359	204	2,126	504	15,102	251	39	1,623	289	123
1993	906	3,432	1,415	215	2,203	478	16,059	294	43	1,771	377	155
1994	904	3,642	1,346	238	2,317	585	16,633	296	50	1,844	384	171
1995	955	3,428	1,431	274	2,319	545	17,530	302	46	1,874	380	159
1996	962	3,515	1,259	220	2,339	524	17,811	336	45	2,007	394	155
1997	891	3,444	1,350	243	2,479	525	18,730	333	42	2,074	389	145

(continued)

TABLE Bc621–656 Doctorate degrees conferred by institutions of higher education, by field of study and sex: 1950–1997 *Continued*

	Females											
School year ending	Computer and information sciences	Education	Engineering	English	Modern foreign languages	Health professions and related sciences	Mathematics	Physical sciences	Psychology	Public affairs	Social sciences	Visual and performing arts
	Bc645	Bc646	Bc647	Bc648	Bc649	Bc650	Bc651	Bc652	Bc653	Bc654	Bc655	Bc656
	Number	Number	Number	Number	Number	Number	Number	Number	Number	Number	Number	Number
1950	—	156	1	49	33	—	9	—	42	—	—	—
1952	—	—	—	—	—	—	—	—	—	—	—	—
1954	—	—	—	—	—	—	—	—	—	—	—	—
1956	—	—	—	—	—	—	—	—	—	—	—	—
1958	—	—	—	—	—	—	—	—	—	—	—	—
1960	—	312	3	83	50	—	18	62	97	—	—	—
1961	—	—	—	—	—	—	—	—	—	—	—	—
1962	—	—	—	—	—	—	—	—	—	—	—	—
1963	—	—	—	—	—	—	—	—	—	—	—	—
1964	—	—	—	—	—	—	—	—	—	—	—	—
1965	—	—	—	—	—	—	—	—	—	—	—	—
1966	—	—	—	—	—	—	—	—	—	—	—	—
1967	—	—	—	—	—	—	—	—	—	—	—	—
1968	—	828	—	260	155	—	52	188	286	—	—	—
1969	—	—	—	—	—	—	—	—	—	—	—	—
1970	—	1,109	24	376	221	—	96	235	457	—	—	—
1971	3	1,270	23	475	278	77	95	246	515	42	507	138
1972	12	1,544	22	593	287	80	90	273	583	43	598	144
1973	15	1,666	54	677	370	161	102	268	753	38	661	167
1974	9	1,783	55	677	388	131	101	253	885	47	741	145
1975	14	2,119	66	686	387	177	112	301	934	65	878	203
1976	23	2,376	66	705	401	166	97	299	1,042	100	895	173
1977	19	2,506	73	667	381	172	111	319	1,259	95	845	215
1978	15	2,737	57	642	344	252	126	312	1,190	120	872	260
1979	30	2,996	83	606	338	264	125	350	1,333	100	870	246
1980	27	3,214	95	608	305	351	104	384	1,474	126	873	242
1981	25	3,436	104	611	297	367	119	376	1,574	150	848	258
1982	21	3,387	140	590	275	422	98	451	1,605	167	824	290
1983	34	3,510	125	520	268	506	120	458	1,764	163	889	288
1984	26	3,465	165	559	233	590	129	491	1,761	190	881	324
1985	25	3,440	208	571	231	634	114	552	1,708	218	918	289
1986	45	3,517	229	563	253	637	129	588	1,869	211	985	326
1987	52	3,476	263	546	241	649	131	634	1,945	182	890	346
1988	48	3,321	293	553	221	713	128	686	1,907	232	932	303
1989	85	3,633	400	564	244	828	178	770	2,095	218	936	307
1990	93	3,726	445	598	292	832	172	808	2,245	273	991	377
1991	92	3,574	485	667	277	919	199	843	2,412	240	1,056	372
1992	103	4,081	527	736	315	963	231	962	2,014	228	1,092	402
1993	116	4,163	560	791	325	1,014	283	961	2,236	244	1,257	404
1994	125	4,202	664	776	370	1,113	253	1,008	2,217	281	1,310	469
1995	161	4,284	729	896	376	1,202	271	1,055	2,391	282	1,406	535
1996	126	4,151	800	945	354	1,200	247	1,056	2,452	279	1,421	543
1997	136	4,239	764	905	375	1,496	283	1,030	2,703	275	1,510	535

[1] Through 1960, first professional degree recipients included with bachelor's degrees; see Table Bc677–712.

Source

U.S. Department of Education, *Digest of Education Statistics, 1999*, Tables 249, 281, 282, 283, 285, 286, 287, 288, 289, 291, 292, 294, 295, 296, 298, 299, 300, and 302.

Documentation

The subject areas covered in Tables Bc621–656 and Bc677–712 are as follows.

Agriculture and natural resources. Agricultural business and production; agricultural sciences; and conservation and renewable natural resources.

Architecture and environmental design. Prior to 1970: architecture. Beginning in 1970: architecture; city/urban, community, and regional planning; architectural environmental design; interior architecture; landscape architecture; architectural urban design and planning; and architecture and related programs, other.

Biological and life sciences. Biology; biochemistry and biophysics; botany; cell and molecular biology; microbiology/bacteriology; zoology; and other biological sciences.

Business and management. Business management/administrative services; marketing operations/marketing distribution; and consumer and personal services.

Communications. Communications, general; advertising; journalism; broadcast journalism; public relations and organizational communications; radio and television technology; communications, other; and communications technologies.

Computer and information sciences. Computer and information sciences, general; computer programming; data processing technology/technician;

TABLE Bc621–656 Doctorate degrees conferred by institutions of higher education, by field of study and sex: 1950–1997 *Continued*

information science and systems; computer systems analysis; and other information sciences.

Engineering. Engineering; engineering-related technologies; mechanics and repairers; and construction trades beginning 1970.

English. English language and literature, general; comparative literature; English, comparative; English creative writing; literature; creative American literature; English literature; speech and rhetorical studies; English technical and business writing; and English language and literature/letters, other.

Modern foreign languages. Includes degrees conferred in a single language or a combination of modern foreign languages. Excludes degrees in linguistics, Latin, classics, Greek, and other foreign languages.

Health professions and related sciences. Communication disorders sciences; community health liaison; dentistry; dental services; health services administration; health and medical assistants; health and medical diagnostic and treatment services; medical laboratory technologies; predentistry; premedicine; prepharmacy; preveterinary; medicine; medical basic sciences; mental health services; nursing; optometry; pharmacy; epidemiology; rehabilitation and therapeutic services; veterinary medicine; and other health professions.

Mathematics. Mathematics and statistics.

Physical sciences. Physical sciences, general; astronomy; astrophysics; atmospheric science and meteorology; chemistry; geology; miscellaneous physical sciences; physics; science technologies; and other physical sciences.

Public affairs. Public administration; community organization, resources and services; public policy analysis; social work; and other public affairs.

Social sciences. Social sciences, general; anthropology; archeology; criminology; demography and population affairs; economics; geography; history; international relations and affairs; political science and government; sociology; urban/affairs studies; and other social sciences and history.

Visual and performing arts. Prior to 1983: visual and performing arts, general; crafts, folk art, and artisanry; dance; design and applied art; theater arts; film and photographic arts; fine arts; graphic arts technology; music; and precision production. Beginning 1983: visual and performing arts, general; crafts, folk art, and artisanry; dance; design and applied art; theater arts and stagecraft; film/video and photographic arts; fine arts and art studies; music; and visual and performing arts, other.

TABLE Bc657–676 Bachelor's degrees conferred by institutions of higher education, by field of study: 1960–1994

Contributed by Claudia Goldin

School year beginning	Total	Agriculture and natural resources	Architecture and environmental design	Business and management	Communications	Computer and information sciences	Education	Engineering	Foreign languages	Health sciences
	Bc657	Bc658	Bc659	Bc660 [1]	Bc661	Bc662	Bc663 [1]	Bc664	Bc665 [1]	Bc666 [1]
	Number	Number	Number	Number	Number	Number	Number	Number	Number	Number
1960	365,174	5,649	1,674	48,074	1,830	0	91,028	35,698	6,364	11,314
1961	383,961	5,841	1,774	49,017	1,519	0	96,280	34,735	7,906	11,366
1962	411,420	6,013	2,028	50,639	1,687	0	101,338	33,458	9,707	11,854
1963	461,266	6,169	2,059	55,474	2,001	0	111,215	35,226	12,160	11,527
1964	493,757	6,734	2,333	59,288	1,928	87	117,137	36,795	13,859	11,611
1965	520,115	7,178	2,663	62,721	2,357	89	116,448	35,615	15,186	14,965
1966	558,534	7,866	2,937	69,032	2,741	222	118,955	35,954	16,706	15,908
1967	632,289	8,308	3,057	79,074	3,173	459	133,965	37,368	19,128	17,429
1968	728,845	9,965	3,477	93,094	4,269	933	150,985	41,248	21,493	19,825
1969	792,317	11,321	4,105	104,706	5,199	1,544	164,080	44,479	20,895	21,674
1970	839,730	12,672	5,570	114,865	10,802	2,388	176,614	50,046	19,945	25,190
1971	887,273	13,516	6,440	121,360	12,340	3,402	191,220	51,164	18,849	28,570
1972	922,362	14,756	6,962	126,263	14,317	4,304	194,229	51,265	18,964	33,523
1973	945,776	16,253	7,822	131,766	17,096	4,756	185,225	50,286	18,840	41,394
1974	922,933	17,528	8,226	133,010	19,248	5,033	167,015	46,852	17,606	48,858
1975	925,746	19,402	9,146	142,379	21,282	5,652	154,807	46,331	15,471	53,813
1976	919,549	21,467	9,222	150,964	23,214	6,407	143,722	49,283	13,944	57,122
1977	921,204	22,650	9,250	160,187	25,400	7,201	136,141	55,654	12,730	59,168
1978	921,390	23,134	9,273	171,241	26,457	8,719	125,873	62,375	12,821	62,085
1979	929,417	22,802	9,132	184,867	28,616	11,154	118,038	68,893	12,089	63,920
1980	935,140	21,886	9,455	198,983	31,282	15,121	108,074	75,000	11,273	63,649
1981	952,998	21,029	9,728	213,374	34,222	20,267	100,932	80,005	10,756	63,653
1982	969,510	20,909	9,823	226,627	38,567	24,510	97,895	89,018	10,599	64,685
1983	974,309	19,317	9,186	229,478	40,113	32,172	92,299	94,185	10,384	64,288
1984	979,477	18,107	9,325	232,636	42,002	38,878	88,072	95,828	10,827	64,422
1985	987,823	16,823	9,119	237,319	43,076	41,889	87,114	95,660	10,984	64,396
1986	991,264	14,991	8,950	240,546	45,337	39,589	86,936	92,816	11,034	63,103
1987	994,829	14,222	8,603	243,021	46,649	34,523	91,112	88,506	10,926	60,644
1988	1,018,755	13,492	9,150	246,399	48,609	30,454	96,913	85,002	11,693	59,005
1989	1,051,344	12,900	9,364	248,698	51,308	27,257	105,112	81,322	12,386	58,302
1990	1,094,538	13,124	9,781	249,311	52,773	25,083	110,807	78,650	13,133	59,070
1991	1,136,553	15,124	8,453	256,603	54,977	24,557	108,006	77,541	13,903	61,720
1992	1,165,178	16,778	9,167	256,842	54,706	24,200	107,781	78,051	14,387	67,089
1993	1,169,275	18,070	8,975	246,654	51,827	24,200	107,600	78,225	14,378	74,421
1994	1,160,134	19,841	8,756	234,323	48,803	24,404	106,079	78,154	13,775	79,855

Note appears at end of table

(continued)

TABLE Bc657–676 Bachelor's degrees conferred by institutions of higher education, by field of study: 1960–1994 *Continued*

School year beginning	Letters Bc667 [1] Number	Library sciences Bc668 Number	Life sciences Bc669 Number	Mathematics Bc670 [1] Number	Physical sciences Bc671 Number	Psychology Bc672 [1] Number	Public affairs Bc673 [1] Number	Social sciences and history Bc674 [1] Number	Visual and performing arts Bc675 Number	Other Bc676 [1] Number
1960	24,003	439	16,060	13,097	15,452	8,460	1,688	50,221	12,942	21,181
1961	26,609	423	16,915	14,570	15,851	9,578	1,560	55,296	13,609	21,112
1962	30,225	462	19,114	16,078	16,215	10,993	1,957	63,104	14,518	22,030
1963	35,146	510	22,723	18,624	17,456	13,258	2,032	74,729	16,159	24,798
1964	38,836	623	25,166	19,460	17,861	14,626	2,320	81,919	17,391	25,783
1965	42,262	619	26,916	19,977	17,129	16,897	2,960	90,632	18,679	26,822
1966	45,900	701	28,849	21,207	17,739	19,364	3,242	101,550	21,548	28,113
1967	52,467	814	31,826	23,513	19,380	23,819	4,912	117,093	25,521	30,983
1968	59,674	1,000	35,308	27,209	21,480	29,332	5,282	137,517	31,588	35,166
1969	62,583	1,054	37,389	27,442	21,439	33,606	5,762	150,331	35,901	38,807
1970	64,933	1,013	35,743	24,801	21,412	37,880	6,252	155,236	30,394	43,974
1971	64,670	989	37,293	23,713	20,745	43,093	8,221	158,037	33,831	49,820
1972	61,799	1,159	42,233	23,067	20,696	47,695	11,346	155,922	36,017	57,845
1973	55,469	1,164	48,340	21,635	21,178	51,821	12,671	150,298	39,730	70,032
1974	48,534	1,069	51,741	18,181	20,778	50,988	14,730	135,165	40,782	77,589
1975	43,019	843	54,275	15,984	21,465	49,908	16,751	126,287	42,138	86,793
1976	38,849	781	53,605	14,196	22,497	47,373	17,627	116,879	41,793	90,604
1977	36,365	693	51,502	12,569	22,986	44,559	18,078	112,827	40,951	92,293
1978	33,561	558	48,846	12,329	23,207	42,967	17,328	108,059	40,969	91,588
1979	32,541	398	46,370	11,872	23,410	42,093	16,644	103,662	40,892	92,024
1980	32,254	375	43,216	11,433	23,952	41,068	16,707	100,513	40,479	90,420
1981	33,419	307	41,639	12,226	24,052	41,212	16,495	99,705	40,422	89,555
1982	31,829	254	39,982	12,719	23,381	40,460	14,414	95,228	39,794	88,816
1983	32,834	252	38,640	13,764	23,651	39,955	12,570	93,323	40,131	87,767
1984	33,218	197	38,445	15,861	23,704	39,900	11,754	91,570	38,140	86,591
1985	34,552	155	38,524	17,147	21,717	40,628	11,887	93,840	37,241	85,752
1986	36,284	136	38,121	16,999	20,070	42,994	12,328	96,342	36,615	88,073
1987	38,661	119	36,755	16,608	17,806	45,187	12,385	100,460	36,944	91,698
1988	42,470	121	36,059	15,994	17,186	48,910	13,162	108,151	38,227	97,758
1989	47,519	77	37,204	15,176	16,066	53,952	13,908	118,083	39,934	102,776
1990	51,841	90	39,530	15,310	16,344	58,655	14,350	125,107	42,186	119,393
1991	54,951	97	42,941	14,783	16,960	63,513	15,987	133,974	46,522	125,941
1992	56,133	83	47,038	14,812	17,545	66,728	16,775	135,703	47,761	133,599
1993	53,924	62	51,383	14,396	18,400	69,259	17,815	133,680	49,053	136,953
1994	51,901	50	55,984	13,723	19,177	72,083	18,586	128,154	48,690	137,796

[1] Figures prior to 1978 may not be directly comparable to those of later years. See text.

Sources

1960–1977, U.S. Department of Education, *120 Years of Education: A Statistical Portrait* (1993), Table 29; 1978–1994, U.S. Department of Education, *Digest of Education Statistics 1994*, Table 241, and *Digest of Education Statistics 1997*, Table 250. The underlying sources are U.S. Department of Education, "Earned Degrees Conferred" and "Degrees and Other Formal Awards Conferred" surveys; and Integrated Postsecondary Education Data System (IPEDS), "Completions" surveys.

Documentation

In 1991, a new taxonomy for classifying degrees (Classification of Instructional Programs) was introduced. Revised data are available for some years before 1978, and annually thereafter in the *Digest of Education Statistics*. The revised data have been presented for 1978 onward to facilitate annual comparability.

See the text for Table Bc600–620 for field definitions.

TABLE Bc677–712 Bachelor's degrees conferred by institutions of higher education, by field of study and sex: 1950–1997[1]

Contributed by Susan B. Carter

	Males											
	Total	Agriculture and natural resources	Architecture and environmental design	Biological and life sciences	Business and management	Communications	Computer and information sciences	Education	Engineering	English	Modern foreign languages	Health professions and related sciences
School year ending	Bc677	Bc678	Bc679	Bc680	Bc681	Bc682	Bc683	Bc684	Bc685	Bc686	Bc687	Bc688
	Number	Number	Number	Number	Number	Number	Number	Number	Number	Number	Number	Number
1950	328,841	—	2,441	—	—	—	—	31,398	52,071	8,221	1,746	—
1952	—	—	—	8,212	—	—	—	—	—	—	—	—
1954	—	—	—	6,710	—	—	—	—	—	—	—	—
1956	—	—	—	9,515	38,706	—	—	—	—	—	—	—
1958	—	—	—	11,159	48,063	—	—	—	—	—	—	—
1960	254,063	—	1,744	11,654	47,262	—	—	25,556	37,537	7,580	1,548	—
1961	224,538	—	—	—	—	—	—	—	—	—	—	—
1962	230,456	—	—	12,136	45,184	—	—	—	—	—	—	—
1963	241,309	—	—	—	—	—	—	—	—	—	—	—
1964	265,349	—	—	16,321	51,056	—	—	—	—	—	—	—
1965	282,173	—	—	—	—	—	—	—	—	—	—	—
1966	299,287	—	—	19,368	57,516	—	—	—	—	—	—	—
1967	322,711	—	—	—	—	—	—	—	—	—	—	—
1968	357,682	—	2,931	22,986	72,126	—	—	31,926	—	15,700	4,450	—
1969	410,595	—	—	—	—	—	—	—	—	—	—	—
1970	451,097	—	3,888	23,919	96,346	—	—	40,420	44,149	18,650	4,921	—
1971	475,594	12,136	4,906	25,333	104,275	6,989	2,064	44,896	49,646	22,155	4,734	5,788
1972	500,590	12,779	5,667	26,323	109,688	7,964	2,941	49,344	50,638	22,657	4,445	7,005
1973	518,191	13,661	6,042	29,636	112,783	9,074	3,664	51,300	50,652	22,156	4,347	7,754
1974	527,313	14,684	6,665	33,245	114,729	10,536	3,976	48,997	49,490	20,214	4,276	9,388
1975	504,841	15,061	6,791	34,612	111,144	11,455	4,080	44,463	45,838	17,880	3,912	10,930
1976	504,925	15,845	7,396	35,520	113,954	12,458	4,534	42,004	44,871	16,073	3,495	11,456
1977	495,545	16,690	7,249	34,218	115,353	12,932	4,876	39,867	47,065	14,295	3,225	11,947
1978	487,347	17,069	7,054	31,705	116,171	13,480	5,349	37,410	51,945	13,137	2,938	11,593
1979	477,344	16,854	6,876	29,191	118,825	13,266	6,272	33,743	57,201	12,198	2,705	11,205
1980	473,611	16,045	6,596	26,828	122,508	13,656	7,782	30,901	62,488	11,380	2,583	11,391
1981	469,883	15,154	6,800	24,149	125,523	14,179	10,202	27,039	67,301	11,198	2,402	10,519
1982	473,364	14,443	6,825	22,754	129,262	14,917	13,218	24,380	70,899	11,414	2,278	10,105
1983	479,140	14,085	6,403	21,564	131,538	16,161	15,606	23,644	78,096	10,859	2,343	10,218
1984	482,319	13,206	5,895	20,558	129,559	16,604	20,246	22,195	82,092	11,170	2,399	10,040
1985	482,528	12,477	6,019	20,064	127,659	17,175	24,579	21,252	83,232	11,334	2,529	9,741
1986	485,923	11,544	5,824	19,993	128,780	17,639	26,923	20,959	83,117	11,819	2,685	9,630
1987	480,782	10,314	5,617	19,657	128,603	18,110	25,865	20,729	80,104	12,353	2,655	9,134
1988	477,203	9,744	5,271	18,245	129,552	18,527	23,331	20,988	76,372	12,836	2,628	8,929
1989	483,346	9,298	5,545	17,953	131,157	19,215	21,087	21,662	73,436	13,927	2,767	8,872
1990	491,696	8,822	5,703	18,312	132,329	20,218	19,117	23,007	70,071	15,662	2,902	9,118
1991	504,045	8,832	5,788	19,412	131,624	20,645	17,726	23,417	67,738	17,146	3,207	9,596
1992	520,811	9,869	5,805	20,798	135,440	21,497	17,510	22,686	66,716	18,536	3,390	10,189
1993	532,881	11,080	5,940	22,842	135,573	22,028	17,403	23,233	66,836	19,247	3,537	11,347
1994	532,422	11,748	5,764	25,050	129,161	21,359	17,317	24,450	66,597	18,425	3,672	13,062
1995	526,131	12,692	5,741	26,687	121,898	20,404	17,463	25,641	65,933	17,810	3,666	14,443
1996	522,454	13,535	5,340	28,849	116,842	19,760	17,468	26,233	64,956	17,253	3,576	15,432
1997	520,515	13,794	5,090	29,470	116,519	19,688	18,037	26,271	62,648	16,531	3,556	15,877

Note appears at end of table

(continued)

TABLE Bc677–712 Bachelor's degrees conferred by institutions of higher education, by field of study and sex: 1950–1997 *Continued*

	Males						Females					
School year ending	Mathematics	Physical sciences	Psychology	Public affairs	Social sciences	Visual and performing arts	Total	Agriculture and natural resources	Architecture and environmental design	Biological and life sciences	Business and management	Communications
	Bc689	Bc690	Bc691	Bc692	Bc693	Bc694	Bc695	Bc696	Bc697	Bc698	Bc699	Bc700
	Number	Number	Number	Number	Number	Number	Number	Number	Number	Number	Number	Number
1950	4,942	14,013	6,055	—	—	—	103,217	—	122	—	—	—
1952	—	—	—	—	—	—	—	—	—	2,882	—	—
1954	—	—	—	—	—	—	—	—	—	2,569	—	—
1956	—	—	—	—	—	—	—	—	—	2,908	4,107	—
1958	—	—	—	—	—	—	—	—	—	3,149	3,928	—
1960	8,293	—	4,773	—	—	—	138,377	—	57	3,922	3,814	—
1961	—	—	—	—	—	—	140,636	—	—	—	—	—
1962	—	—	—	—	—	—	153,505	—	—	4,779	3,833	—
1963	—	—	—	—	—	—	170,111	—	—	—	—	—
1964	—	—	—	—	—	—	195,917	—	—	6,402	4,418	—
1965	—	—	—	—	—	—	211,584	—	—	—	—	—
1966	—	—	—	—	—	—	220,828	—	—	7,548	5,205	—
1967	—	—	—	—	—	—	235,823	—	—	—	—	—
1968	14,782	16,739	13,792	—	—	—	274,607	—	126	8,840	6,948	—
1969	—	—	—	—	—	—	318,250	—	—	—	—	—
1970	17,177	18,522	19,077	—	—	—	341,219	—	217	10,115	9,234	—
1971	15,498	18,459	21,227	1,726	98,173	12,256	364,136	536	664	10,410	10,454	3,813
1972	14,542	17,663	23,352	2,588	100,895	13,580	386,683	737	773	10,970	11,578	4,376
1973	13,910	17,626	25,117	3,998	99,735	14,267	404,171	1,095	920	12,597	13,361	5,243
1974	12,912	17,674	25,868	4,266	95,650	15,821	418,463	1,569	1,157	15,095	16,911	6,560
1975	10,853	16,992	24,284	4,630	84,826	15,532	418,092	2,467	1,435	17,129	21,587	7,793
1976	9,788	17,353	22,898	5,706	78,691	16,491	420,821	3,557	1,750	18,755	28,080	8,824
1977	8,476	17,996	20,627	5,544	71,128	16,166	424,004	4,777	1,973	19,387	35,412	10,282
1978	7,806	18,090	18,422	5,096	67,217	15,572	433,857	5,581	2,196	19,797	43,520	11,920
1979	7,301	17,985	16,540	4,938	62,852	15,380	444,046	6,280	2,397	19,655	52,416	13,191
1980	6,951	17,864	15,440	4,451	58,511	15,065	455,806	6,757	2,536	19,542	62,359	14,960
1981	6,614	18,064	14,332	4,248	56,131	14,798	465,257	6,732	2,655	19,067	73,460	17,103
1982	6,999	17,866	13,645	4,176	55,196	14,819	479,634	6,586	2,903	18,885	84,112	19,305
1983	7,175	16,993	13,131	3,343	52,771	14,690	490,370	6,824	3,420	18,418	95,089	22,406
1984	7,716	17,116	12,812	2,998	52,154	15,089	491,990	6,111	3,291	18,082	99,919	23,509
1985	8,537	17,069	12,706	2,829	51,226	14,462	496,949	5,630	3,306	18,381	104,977	24,827
1986	9,216	15,755	12,605	2,966	52,724	14,236	501,900	5,279	3,295	18,531	108,539	25,437
1987	9,110	14,372	13,362	2,993	53,949	13,751	510,482	4,677	3,333	18,464	111,943	27,227
1988	8,919	12,389	13,538	2,923	56,377	14,068	517,626	4,478	3,332	18,510	113,469	28,122
1989	8,662	12,077	14,246	3,214	60,121	14,539	535,409	4,194	3,605	18,106	115,242	29,394
1990	8,236	11,031	15,336	3,334	65,887	15,189	559,648	4,078	3,661	18,892	116,369	31,090
1991	8,178	11,176	16,067	3,215	68,701	15,761	590,493	4,292	3,993	20,118	117,687	32,128
1992	7,888	11,431	17,031	3,479	73,001	17,616	615,742	5,255	2,948	22,143	121,163	33,480
1993	7,827	11,825	17,908	3,801	73,589	18,610	632,297	5,698	3,227	24,196	121,269	32,678
1994	7,735	12,223	18,642	3,919	72,006	19,538	636,853	6,322	3,211	26,333	117,493	30,468
1995	7,295	12,497	19,548	3,935	68,139	19,781	634,003	7,149	3,015	29,297	112,425	28,399
1996	7,134	12,578	19,817	4,205	65,872	20,126	642,338	7,896	3,012	32,145	110,260	28,243
1997	6,908	12,228	19,379	4,177	64,115	20,729	652,364	8,808	2,854	34,505	110,114	28,080

TABLE Bc677–712 Bachelor's degrees conferred by institutions of higher education, by field of study and sex: 1950–1997 *Continued*

	Females											
	Computer and information sciences	Education	Engineering	English	Modern foreign languages	Health professions and related sciences	Mathematics	Physical sciences	Psychology	Public affairs	Social sciences	Visual and performing arts
School year	Bc701	Bc702	Bc703	Bc704	Bc705	Bc706	Bc707	Bc708	Bc709	Bc710	Bc711	Bc712
ending	Number	Number	Number	Number	Number	Number	Number	Number	Number	Number	Number	Number
1950	—	30,074	175	9,019	2,731	—	1,440	1,994	3,514	—	—	—
1952	—	—	—	—	—	—	—	—	—	—	—	—
1954	—	—	—	—	—	—	—	—	—	—	—	—
1956	—	—	—	—	—	—	—	—	—	—	—	—
1958	—	—	—	—	—	—	—	—	—	—	—	—
1960	—	63,446	142	12,548	2,979	—	3,106	—	3,288	—	—	—
1961	—	—	—	—	—	—	—	—	—	—	—	—
1962	—	—	—	—	—	—	—	—	—	—	—	—
1963	—	—	—	—	—	—	—	—	—	—	—	—
1964	—	—	—	—	—	—	—	—	—	—	—	—
1965	—	—	—	—	—	—	—	—	—	—	—	—
1966	—	—	—	—	—	—	—	—	—	—	—	—
1967	—	—	—	—	—	—	—	—	—	—	—	—
1968	—	102,039	—	32,277	13,049	—	8,731	2,641	10,027	—	—	—
1969	—	—	—	—	—	—	—	—	—	—	—	—
1970	—	123,544	330	37,760	14,536	—	10,265	2,917	14,602	—	—	—
1971	324	131,411	400	42,187	14,321	19,438	9,439	2,953	16,960	3,740	57,151	18,138
1972	461	141,536	526	41,319	13,692	21,606	9,265	3,082	20,081	4,920	57,165	20,251
1973	640	142,684	613	38,847	13,885	25,810	9,276	3,070	22,823	6,692	56,235	21,750
1974	780	135,910	796	34,376	13,976	32,071	8,849	3,504	26,271	7,700	54,670	23,909
1975	953	122,295	1,014	29,739	13,203	38,160	7,607	3,786	26,961	9,031	50,364	25,250
1976	1,118	112,433	1,460	25,933	11,584	42,502	6,541	4,112	27,380	9,734	47,705	25,647
1977	1,531	103,367	2,218	23,499	10,401	45,381	5,919	4,501	27,234	10,592	45,912	25,627
1978	1,852	98,411	3,709	22,191	9,510	47,841	5,259	4,896	26,457	11,511	45,735	25,379
1979	2,447	92,130	5,174	21,363	8,826	50,880	5,028	5,222	26,157	12,390	45,207	25,589
1980	3,372	87,137	6,405	21,161	8,233	52,529	4,921	5,546	26,653	12,193	45,151	25,827
1981	4,919	81,035	7,699	21,056	7,648	53,130	4,819	5,888	26,736	12,459	44,382	25,681
1982	7,049	76,552	9,106	22,005	7,298	53,548	5,227	6,186	27,567	12,319	44,509	25,603
1983	8,904	74,251	10,922	20,970	6,991	54,467	5,544	6,388	27,329	11,071	42,457	25,104
1984	11,926	70,104	12,093	21,664	6,753	54,248	6,048	6,535	27,143	9,572	41,169	25,042
1985	14,299	66,820	12,596	21,884	7,146	54,681	7,324	6,635	27,194	8,925	40,344	23,678
1986	14,966	66,155	12,543	22,733	7,123	54,766	7,931	5,962	28,023	8,921	41,116	23,005
1987	13,724	66,207	12,712	23,931	7,203	53,969	7,889	5,698	29,632	9,335	42,393	22,864
1988	11,192	70,124	12,134	25,825	7,162	51,715	7,689	5,417	31,649	9,462	44,083	22,876
1989	9,367	75,251	11,566	28,543	7,731	50,133	7,332	5,109	34,664	9,948	48,030	23,688
1990	8,140	82,105	11,251	31,857	8,190	49,184	6,940	5,035	38,616	10,574	52,196	24,745
1991	7,357	87,390	10,912	34,695	8,517	49,474	7,132	5,168	42,588	11,135	56,406	26,425
1992	7,047	85,320	10,825	36,415	8,977	51,531	6,895	5,529	46,482	12,508	60,973	28,906
1993	6,797	84,548	11,215	36,886	9,282	55,742	6,985	5,720	48,820	12,974	62,114	29,151
1994	6,883	83,150	11,628	35,499	9,113	61,359	6,661	6,177	50,617	13,896	61,674	29,515
1995	6,941	80,438	12,221	34,091	8,643	65,412	6,428	6,680	52,535	14,651	60,015	28,909
1996	6,630	79,276	12,481	33,445	8,825	68,604	6,009	7,069	53,474	15,644	60,607	29,170
1997	6,731	78,962	12,509	32,814	8,705	69,754	5,912	7,303	54,812	16,472	60,776	29,354

[1] Through 1960, data include first professional degree recipients.

Source

U.S. Department of Education, *Digest of Education Statistics, 1999*, Tables 249, 281, 282, 283, 285, 286, 287, 288, 289, 291, 292, 294, 295, 296, 298, 299, 300, and 302.

Documentation

See the text for Table Bc621–656.

TABLE Bc713–718 Professional and instructional staff at institutions of higher education, by sex and public–private control: 1869–1993

Contributed by Claudia Goldin

School year beginning	Professional staff: Total	Professional staff: Male	Professional staff: Female	Instructional staff: Total	Instructional staff: Public	Instructional staff: Private
	Bc713	Bc714	Bc715	Bc716	Bc717	Bc718
	Number	Number	Number	Number	Number	Number
1869	5,553	4,887	666	—	—	—
1879	11,522	7,328	4,194	—	—	—
1889	15,809	12,704	3,105	—	—	—
1899	23,868	19,151	4,717	—	—	—
1909	36,480	29,132	7,348	—	—	—
1919	48,615	35,807	12,808	—	—	—
1921	—	—	—	56,486	—	—
1923	—	—	—	63,999	—	—
1925	—	—	—	70,674	—	—
1927	—	—	—	76,080	—	—
1929	—	—	—	82,386	—	—
1931	100,789	71,680	29,109	88,172	—	—
1933	108,873	78,369	30,504	86,914	—	—
1935	121,036	86,567	34,469	92,580	36,697	55,883
1937	135,989	97,362	38,627	102,895	42,156	60,739
1939	146,929	106,328	40,601	110,885	45,718	65,167
1941	151,066	109,309	41,757	114,693	47,988	66,705
1943	150,980	106,254	44,726	105,841	43,707	62,134
1945	165,324	116,134	49,190	125,811	52,335	73,476
1947	223,660	164,616	59,044	174,204	79,062	95,142
1949	246,722	186,189	60,533	190,353	87,707	102,646
1951	244,488	187,136	57,352	183,758	—	—
1953	265,911	204,871	61,040	207,365	100,266	107,099
1955	298,910	230,342	68,568	228,188	113,101	115,087
1957	344,525	267,482	77,043	258,184	131,350	126,834
1959	380,554	296,773	83,781	281,506	144,541	136,965
1961	424,862	332,006	92,856	310,772	162,603	148,169
1963	494,514	385,405	109,109	355,542	196,042	159,500
1966	646,264	—	—	445,484	—	—
1967	709,811	—	—	484,387	—	—
1969	—	—	—	551,000	—	—
1970	—	—	—	574,592	—	—
1972	881,665	639,251	242,414	652,517	—	—
1976	1,073,119	729,169	343,950	793,296	576,658	216,638
1987	1,437,975	850,451	587,524	954,534	689,119	265,415
1989	1,531,071	880,766	650,305	987,518	718,196	269,322
1991	1,595,460	895,591	699,869	1,024,003	754,468	269,535
1993	1,687,287	930,933	756,354	1,118,293	824,112	294,181

Sources

Series Bc713–716, 1869 to 1989, U.S. Department of Education, *120 Years of American Education: A Statistical Portrait* (1993), Table 26. The underlying sources are: 1869–1915, U.S. Office of Education, *Annual Report of the United States Commissioner of Education*, various issues; 1917 to 1957, U.S. Office of Education, *Biennial Survey of Education in the United States*, various issues; and 1958–1989, U.S. Department of Education, *Digest of Education Statistics*, annual issues. Series Bc717–718, 1935–1957, U.S. Department of Education, *Biennial Survey of Education in the United States*, various issues; 1959–1993, and series Bc713–716, 1991 to 1993, *Digest of Education Statistics*, annual issues. For example, the data for 1993 are from *Digest of Education Statistics 1997*, Table 223.

Documentation

See the text for Table Bc510–522 for definitions of institutions of higher education and their control.

Professional staff data include full-time and part-time faculty members. Except in 1932, no attempt has been made to evaluate these services on a full-time equivalent basis. Professional staff figures also include administrative, instructional, research, and other professional personnel. Resident instructional staff, however, exclude administrative and other professional personnel not engaged in instructional activities. Instructional staff include faculty members with titles such as professor, associate professor, assistant professor, instructor, and lecturer, and graduate students who are graduate or teaching fellows.

Series Bc716–718. Instructional staff includes regular faculty, junior faculty, and research assistants.

TABLE Bc719–736 Enrollment in "historically black" colleges and total college enrollment among non-Hispanic blacks, by type of institution: 1976–1995

Contributed by Claudia Goldin

	Enrollment in "historically black" colleges									Total college enrollment among non-Hispanic blacks								
	Public and private institutions			Public institutions			Private institutions			Public and private institutions			Public institutions			Private institutions		
	Total	Four-year	Two-year	Total	Four-year	Two-year	Total	Four-year	Two-year	Total	Four-year	Two-year	Total	Four-year	Two-year	Total	Four-year	Two-year
School year	Bc719	Bc720	Bc721	Bc722	Bc723	Bc724	Bc725	Bc726	Bc727	Bc728	Bc729	Bc730	Bc731	Bc732	Bc733	Bc734	Bc735	Bc736
beginning	Number	Number	Number	Number	Number	Number	Number	Number	Number	Thousand	Thousand	Thousand	Thousand	Thousand	Thousand	Thousand	Thousand	Thousand
1976	222,613	206,676	15,937	156,836	143,528	13,308	65,777	63,148	2,629	1,033.0	603.7	429.3	831.3	421.8	409.5	201.8	182.0	19.8
1977	226,062	209,898	16,164	158,823	145,450	13,373	67,239	64,448	2,791	—	—	—	—	—	—	—	—	—
1978	227,797	211,651	16,146	163,237	150,168	13,069	64,560	61,483	3,077	1,054.4	611.8	442.6	839.5	424.9	414.6	214.9	186.9	28.0
1979	230,124	214,147	15,977	166,315	153,139	13,176	63,809	61,008	2,801	—	—	—	—	—	—	—	—	—
1980	233,557	218,009	15,548	168,217	155,085	13,132	65,340	62,924	2,416	1,106.8	634.3	472.5	876.1	438.2	437.9	230.7	196.1	34.6
1981	232,460	217,152	15,308	166,991	154,269	12,722	65,469	62,883	2,586	—	—	—	—	—	—	—	—	—
1982	228,371	212,017	16,354	165,871	151,472	14,399	62,500	60,545	1,955	1,101.5	612.3	489.2	873.1	420.7	452.4	228.4	191.6	36.8
1983	234,446	217,909	16,537	170,051	155,665	14,386	64,395	62,244	2,151	—	—	—	—	—	—	—	—	—
1984	227,519	212,844	14,675	164,116	151,289	12,827	63,403	61,555	1,848	1,075.8	617.0	458.7	844.0	426.7	417.3	231.8	190.4	41.4
1985	225,801	210,648	15,153	163,677	150,002	13,675	62,124	60,646	1,478	—	—	—	—	—	—	—	—	—
1986	223,275	207,231	16,044	162,048	147,631	14,417	61,227	59,600	1,627	1,082.3	615.1	467.2	853.8	423.7	430.1	228.5	191.4	37.1
1987	227,994	211,654	16,340	165,486	150,560	14,926	62,508	61,094	1,414	—	—	—	—	—	—	—	—	—
1988	239,755	223,250	16,505	173,672	158,606	15,066	66,083	64,644	1,439	1,129.6	656.3	473.3	881.1	448.5	432.6	248.5	207.8	40.7
1989	249,096	232,890	16,206	181,151	166,481	14,670	67,945	66,409	1,536	—	—	—	—	—	—	—	—	—
1990	257,152	240,497	16,655	187,046	171,969	15,077	70,106	68,528	1,578	1,247.0	722.8	524.3	976.5	495.1	481.4	270.6	227.7	42.9
1991	269,335	252,093	17,242	197,847	182,204	15,643	71,488	69,889	1,599	1,335.4	757.8	577.6	1,053.4	516.2	537.2	281.9	241.5	40.4
1992	279,541	261,089	18,452	204,966	188,143	16,823	74,575	72,946	1,629	1,392.9	791.0	601.6	1,100.4	535.4	565.0	292.3	255.7	36.6
1993	282,856	262,430	20,426	208,197	189,032	19,165	74,659	73,398	1,261	1,412.8	813.7	599.0	1,114.3	548.2	566.1	298.5	265.6	32.9
1994	280,071	259,997	20,074	206,520	187,735	18,785	73,551	72,262	1,289	1,448.6	833.6	615.0	1,144.6	561.4	583.2	304.1	272.2	31.9
1995	278,725	259,409	19,316	204,726	186,278	18,448	73,999	73,131	868	1,473.7	852.2	621.5	1,160.7	572.5	588.2	313.0	279.7	33.3

Sources

Series Bc719–727, "historically black" colleges: U.S. Department of Education, *Digest of Education Statistics 1997*, Table 220. Series Bc728–736, non-Hispanic African-American enrollment: *Digest of Education Statistics*, various issues. For example, the most recent data are from *Digest 1997*, Table 206. The underlying sources for all series are U.S. Department of Education, Higher Education General Information Survey (HEGIS), "Fall Enrollment in Colleges and Universities" surveys, and Integrated Postsecondary Education Data System (IPEDS), "Fall Enrollment" surveys.

Documentation

Data are fall enrollments.

"Historically black" colleges and universities are postsecondary academic institutions founded before 1964 whose educational mission has historically been the education of African Americans. Many of the historically black colleges and universities were founded as a result of the second Morrill Act, passed in 1890, which required that states, under penalty of loss of funds, provide facilities to black as well as white students. The first historically black institution in the United States was founded in 1837 just outside of Philadelphia as a secondary school and later became Cheyney University. Among the best known are Wilberforce (1856), Howard University (1866), Tuskegee Institute (1881), and Spelman College (1881), the nation's oldest liberal arts college for black women. There are about 120 historically black colleges and universities, including public and private, four-year and two-year institutions.

EDUCATIONAL ATTAINMENT

Claudia Goldin

TABLE Bc737–792 Years of school completed, by sex, race, and ethnicity: 1940–1997[1, 2, 3]

Contributed by Claudia Goldin

	Percentage of male population completing							Percentage of female population completing						
	Elementary school			High school		College		Elementary school			High school		College	
	0–4 years	5–7 years	8 years	1–3 years	4 years	1–3 years	4 or more years	0–4 years	5–7 years	8 years	1–3 years	4 years	1–3 years	4 or more years
	Bc737	Bc738	Bc739	Bc740	Bc741	Bc742	Bc743	Bc744	Bc745	Bc746	Bc747	Bc748	Bc749	Bc750
Year	Percent	Percent	Percent	Percent	Percent	Percent	Percent	Percent	Percent	Percent	Percent	Percent	Percent	Percent
1940 [4]	15.1	19.0	28.8	14.5	12.2	4.9	5.5	12.4	18.0	27.5	15.9	16.4	6.1	3.8
1950 [4]	12.2	16.9	21.4	16.9	18.2	7.0	7.3	10.0	15.8	20.3	17.9	23.2	7.7	5.2
1960	9.4	14.6	17.8	18.7	21.2	8.6	9.7	7.4	13.1	17.3	19.7	27.8	9.0	5.8
1962	8.7	12.2	16.7	17.4	24.7	8.9	11.4	6.9	11.2	16.5	17.9	31.6	9.3	6.7
1964	8.1	11.4	16.1	17.4	26.3	9.0	11.7	6.3	10.8	15.6	18.5	33.4	8.8	6.8
1965	—	—	—	—	—	—	—	—	—	—	—	—	—	—
1966	7.3	10.7	15.6	17.4	27.7	8.8	12.5	5.7	10.2	14.6	18.8	34.4	9.0	7.4
1967	6.8	10.5	15.1	17.0	28.2	9.6	12.8	5.4	9.8	14.5	18.5	34.8	9.4	7.6
1968	6.5	10.3	14.3	16.9	28.9	9.8	13.3	5.3	9.4	13.9	18.1	35.7	9.5	8.0
1969	6.1	9.9	14.0	16.4	29.7	10.3	13.5	5.1	9.0	13.5	17.9	36.9	9.4	8.2
1970	5.9	9.5	13.6	16.1	30.1	10.8	14.1	4.7	8.7	13.1	17.9	37.5	9.7	8.2
1971	5.6	8.9	13.4	15.8	30.6	11.1	14.6	4.5	8.5	12.7	17.7	37.8	10.3	8.5
1972	5.0	8.6	12.1	16.1	31.4	11.4	15.4	4.2	8.1	11.8	17.8	38.7	10.5	9.0
1973	4.9	8.2	11.5	15.3	32.1	12.0	16.0	4.2	7.7	11.3	17.2	39.2	10.8	9.6
1974	4.9	7.7	11.1	14.7	32.3	12.5	16.9	4.1	7.4	10.7	16.9	39.4	11.4	10.1
1975	4.7	7.5	10.2	14.5	32.3	13.2	17.6	3.8	7.2	10.4	16.6	39.7	11.7	10.6
1976	4.2	7.4	9.5	14.2	32.3	13.8	18.6	3.5	6.8	9.8	16.3	39.9	12.4	11.3
1977	4.0	7.0	9.4	14.0	32.1	14.2	19.2	3.5	6.8	9.2	16.2	39.6	12.7	12.0
1978	3.9	6.9	9.0	13.5	32.1	14.9	19.7	3.4	6.5	9.1	15.9	39.6	13.4	12.2
1979	3.7	6.3	8.6	12.9	32.6	15.4	20.4	3.2	6.1	8.6	15.0	40.2	14.0	12.9
1980	3.6	6.0	8.1	13.1	32.7	15.6	20.9	3.2	6.0	8.2	14.5	40.4	14.2	13.6
1981	3.4	5.8	7.5	12.9	33.6	15.6	21.1	3.1	5.8	7.8	14.1	41.1	14.6	13.4
1982	3.3	5.6	6.9	12.5	34.1	15.7	21.9	2.8	5.5	7.3	14.0	41.4	14.9	14.0
1983	3.2	5.2	6.7	12.1	33.9	15.9	23.0	2.8	5.3	7.0	13.4	41.1	15.4	15.1
1984	2.9	5.1	6.5	11.8	34.6	16.1	22.9	2.6	4.9	6.6	12.9	41.8	15.6	15.7
1985	2.9	5.0	6.3	11.5	34.8	16.5	23.1	2.5	4.5	6.5	12.9	41.3	16.2	16.0
1986	2.8	4.7	6.0	11.3	34.9	17.1	23.2	2.5	4.6	6.0	12.5	41.6	16.7	16.1
1987	2.5	4.6	5.7	11.2	35.4	17.1	23.6	2.4	4.4	5.8	12.1	41.6	17.1	16.5
1988	2.6	4.5	5.0	11.5	35.7	16.8	24.0	2.3	4.2	5.5	12.0	41.8	17.2	17.0
1989	2.7	4.3	4.8	11.0	35.4	17.4	24.5	2.4	4.0	5.2	11.9	41.3	17.2	18.1
1990	2.7	4.2	4.6	10.7	35.5	17.8	24.4	2.2	3.9	4.9	11.5	41.0	18.0	18.4
1991	2.7	3.9	4.5	10.4	36.0	18.2	24.3	2.1	3.7	4.4	11.4	41.0	18.6	18.8
1992	2.3	2.3	5.2	10.6	33.7	21.7	24.3	2.0	2.1	5.3	11.4	38.1	22.4	18.6
1993	2.2	2.2	5.0	10.1	33.2	22.6	24.8	2.0	2.1	5.2	10.9	37.4	23.4	19.2
1995	2.0	2.3	4.2	9.7	31.9	23.8	26.0	1.7	2.0	4.5	10.2	35.7	25.7	20.2
1996	1.9	2.1	4.2	9.9	31.9	24.0	26.0	1.7	2.0	4.3	10.4	35.1	25.1	21.4
1997	1.8	2.2	4.0	10.1	32.1	23.7	26.2	1.6	2.0	4.1	10.1	35.3	25.2	21.7

	Percentage of white male population completing							Percentage of white female population completing						
	Elementary school			High school		College		Elementary school			High school		College	
	0–4 years	5–7 years	8 years	1–3 years	4 years	1–3 years	4 or more years	0–4 years	5–7 years	8 years	1–3 years	4 years	1–3 years	4 or more years
	Bc751	Bc752	Bc753	Bc754	Bc755	Bc756	Bc757	Bc758	Bc759	Bc760	Bc761	Bc762	Bc763	Bc764
Year	Percent	Percent	Percent	Percent	Percent	Percent	Percent	Percent	Percent	Percent	Percent	Percent	Percent	Percent
1940 [4]	12.0	18.1	30.5	15.1	13.0	5.3	5.9	9.8	16.7	29.0	16.5	17.5	6.5	4.0
1950 [4]	9.8	15.9	22.4	17.4	19.3	7.4	7.9	8.1	14.4	21.1	18.2	24.6	8.1	5.4
1960	7.4	13.7	18.4	18.9	22.2	9.1	10.3	6.0	11.9	17.8	19.6	29.2	9.5	6.0
1962	6.9	11.4	17.0	17.3	25.8	9.4	12.2	5.6	10.3	16.8	17.4	33.1	9.9	7.0
1964	6.5	10.5	16.5	17.1	27.6	9.4	12.3	5.2	9.7	15.9	18.1	34.8	9.2	7.1
1965	6.1	10.3	16.4	17.0	28.2	9.3	12.7	4.9	9.3	15.4	18.2	35.6	9.3	7.3
1966	5.7	10.1	15.8	17.1	28.8	9.2	13.3	4.7	9.1	14.9	18.2	35.9	9.4	7.7
1967	5.3	9.7	15.4	16.8	29.1	10.0	13.7	4.4	8.8	14.9	18.0	36.2	9.7	7.9
1968	4.9	9.5	14.7	16.6	29.9	10.3	14.1	4.3	8.5	14.1	17.7	37.2	9.9	8.2
1969	4.8	9.1	14.3	16.1	30.6	10.8	14.3	4.2	8.1	13.7	17.3	38.5	9.8	8.4
1970	4.5	8.8	13.9	15.6	30.9	11.3	15.0	3.9	7.8	13.4	17.3	39.0	10.1	8.6
1971	4.4	8.1	13.7	15.3	31.3	11.6	15.5	3.8	7.5	12.9	17.0	39.2	10.7	8.9
1972	3.9	7.8	12.4	15.6	32.2	12.0	16.2	3.4	7.1	12.0	17.0	40.2	10.9	9.4
1973	3.9	7.5	11.7	14.8	32.8	12.5	16.8	3.4	6.9	11.5	16.5	40.7	11.1	9.9
1974	3.7	7.0	11.3	14.3	33.0	12.9	17.7	3.3	6.6	11.0	16.1	40.8	11.7	10.6
1975	3.6	6.8	10.5	14.0	33.1	13.6	18.4	3.0	6.4	10.6	15.9	41.1	12.1	11.0
1976	3.2	6.6	9.7	13.8	32.9	14.2	19.6	2.9	6.2	9.8	15.6	41.2	12.8	11.6
1977	3.1	6.3	9.6	13.5	32.7	14.6	20.2	2.8	6.1	9.3	15.3	40.9	13.2	12.4
1978	2.9	6.2	9.2	13.0	32.7	15.2	20.7	2.8	5.9	9.2	15.0	40.9	13.7	12.6
1979	2.8	5.7	8.7	12.4	33.1	15.8	21.4	2.6	5.5	8.6	14.1	41.6	14.3	13.3
1980	2.7	5.5	8.3	12.5	33.1	15.8	22.1	2.5	5.3	8.4	13.7	41.6	14.5	14.0
1981	2.7	5.3	7.7	12.3	34.1	15.7	22.2	2.5	5.0	8.1	13.3	42.4	14.9	13.8
1982	2.6	5.1	7.1	11.9	34.5	15.8	23.0	2.3	4.9	7.4	13.1	42.7	15.2	14.4
1983	2.6	4.8	6.8	11.5	34.3	16.1	24.0	2.3	4.8	7.1	12.7	42.2	15.7	15.4
1984	2.3	4.7	6.6	11.1	35.1	16.3	23.9	2.1	4.4	6.6	12.2	42.8	15.8	16.0
1985	2.3	4.6	6.3	10.8	35.3	16.7	24.0	2.1	4.1	6.6	12.1	42.4	16.4	16.3
1986	2.4	4.2	6.1	10.8	35.2	17.3	24.0	2.1	4.2	6.1	11.8	42.5	16.9	16.4
1987	2.1	4.2	5.8	10.6	35.6	17.2	24.5	2.0	4.0	6.0	11.4	42.6	17.3	16.9
1988	2.1	4.1	5.1	10.9	35.9	16.9	25.0	1.9	3.8	5.4	11.2	42.8	17.6	17.3
1989	2.2	3.9	4.8	10.4	35.7	17.6	25.4	1.8	3.5	5.2	11.2	42.3	17.4	18.5
1990	2.2	3.9	4.7	10.1	35.7	18.0	25.3	1.8	3.5	5.0	10.8	41.9	18.1	19.0
1991	2.2	3.6	4.5	9.9	36.1	18.4	25.4	1.8	3.3	4.5	10.5	41.8	18.8	19.3
1992	1.9	2.1	5.2	9.8	33.7	22.2	25.2	1.7	1.9	5.3	10.4	38.8	22.7	19.1
1993	1.8	2.1	4.9	9.3	33.1	23.0	25.7	1.7	1.8	5.2	10.0	38.0	23.6	19.7
1995	1.7	2.1	4.3	9.0	31.7	24.1	27.2	1.5	1.8	4.4	9.3	36.1	25.9	21.0
1996	1.7	2.1	4.3	9.3	31.7	24.1	26.9	1.5	1.9	4.2	9.6	35.9	25.1	21.8
1997	1.6	2.1	4.0	9.4	32.1	23.8	27.0	1.4	1.9	4.1	9.4	35.6	25.2	22.3

Notes appear at end of table

(continued)

TABLE Bc737–792 Years of school completed, by sex, race, and ethnicity: 1940–1997 *Continued*

	Percentage of black male population completing							Percentage of black female population completing						
	Elementary school			High school		College		Elementary school			High school		College	
	0–4 years	5–7 years	8 years	1–3 years	4 years	1–3 years	4 or more years	0–4 years	5–7 years	8 years	1–3 years	4 years	1–3 years	4 or more years
	Bc765	Bc766	Bc767	Bc768	Bc769	Bc770	Bc771	Bc772	Bc773	Bc774	Bc775	Bc776	Bc777	Bc778
Year	Percent	Percent	Percent	Percent	Percent	Percent	Percent	Percent	Percent	Percent	Percent	Percent	Percent	Percent
1940 [4]	46.2	28.1	11.4	7.4	3.8	1.7	1.4	37.5	31.8	12.4	9.9	5.1	2.1	1.2
1950 [4]	36.9	27.1	11.3	12.1	7.5	2.9	2.1	28.6	29.3	12.5	14.8	9.2	3.2	2.4
1960	27.7	23.0	12.3	17.0	12.1	4.4	3.5	19.7	23.7	13.3	20.2	15.2	4.4	3.6
1962	26.1	19.3	13.2	18.2	14.5	4.8	4.0	18.5	19.3	13.9	22.1	18.2	4.0	4.0
1964	22.4	20.5	12.4	21.1	14.6	4.6	4.5	15.7	21.2	12.9	22.7	19.2	4.9	3.4
1965	—	—	—	—	—	—	—	—	—	—	—	—	—	—
1966	23.1	17.2	13.4	20.4	17.2	4.7	3.9	14.0	20.1	11.7	24.7	20.3	5.4	3.7
1967	21.6	19.2	12.7	19.5	18.8	4.8	3.5	13.9	19.4	11.8	23.3	21.3	5.8	4.3
1968	21.0	18.3	10.8	21.0	19.7	5.5	3.7	14.7	18.3	12.8	23.2	21.5	4.7	4.8
1969	18.0	18.3	11.1	20.7	21.4	5.7	4.8	13.4	18.3	11.9	23.9	23.0	5.0	4.5
1970	18.6	16.0	11.1	21.9	22.2	5.7	4.5	12.1	17.4	11.3	24.5	24.4	6.0	4.4
1971	16.7	17.4	10.5	21.5	23.3	5.8	4.7	10.8	17.5	11.1	25.2	24.9	6.2	4.3
1972	15.6	17.4	9.6	21.7	23.8	6.3	5.5	10.6	16.7	9.7	25.8	25.8	6.6	4.8
1973	14.9	15.2	10.8	20.9	25.2	7.1	5.9	10.7	14.5	9.6	25.2	26.3	7.7	6.0
1974	15.9	15.1	9.5	19.7	25.5	8.6	5.7	10.4	14.3	8.5	25.2	28.2	8.0	5.3
1975	15.3	14.7	8.1	20.2	25.2	9.8	6.7	9.8	14.0	8.9	24.0	28.6	8.5	6.2
1976	14.2	15.5	8.7	19.3	26.5	9.5	6.3	9.0	12.6	9.7	23.8	29.5	8.6	6.9
1977	12.0	14.1	8.3	20.1	27.6	11.0	7.0	8.0	13.1	8.8	24.7	29.1	8.9	7.4
1978	11.9	13.4	7.4	19.5	28.0	12.6	7.3	7.9	11.5	8.7	24.5	29.7	10.5	7.1
1979	11.9	12.8	7.5	18.6	29.5	11.3	8.4	7.8	10.7	8.7	23.2	30.4	11.6	7.6
1980	11.4	10.6	7.1	19.8	29.8	13.5	7.7	7.4	11.5	7.3	22.4	31.5	11.7	8.1
1981	9.3	10.2	7.1	20.1	31.1	13.9	8.2	6.8	11.8	6.5	22.4	32.1	12.4	8.2
1982	9.0	10.3	6.5	18.5	32.1	14.5	9.1	6.0	10.9	7.0	21.9	32.8	12.9	8.5
1983	8.8	9.7	6.3	18.7	32.9	13.6	10.0	5.8	9.5	6.9	20.8	34.7	13.3	9.2
1984	8.7	8.9	6.6	18.6	32.9	13.7	10.5	5.7	8.6	6.8	19.3	35.4	13.9	10.4
1985	7.8	9.0	6.0	18.7	31.9	15.3	11.2	4.9	8.3	6.3	19.7	35.5	14.3	11.0
1986	6.7	8.9	5.2	17.7	34.3	15.0	11.2	4.3	7.8	5.9	19.0	36.6	15.6	10.8
1987	5.9	8.6	5.2	17.2	36.5	15.5	11.0	4.3	7.6	5.4	19.0	37.5	15.8	10.4
1988	5.8	8.2	4.6	17.7	37.1	15.5	11.1	4.2	7.1	5.9	19.5	37.5	14.5	11.4
1989	6.1	7.3	5.2	17.2	36.3	16.2	11.7	4.6	7.0	4.7	18.7	36.7	16.5	11.9
1990	6.4	6.6	4.1	17.1	36.8	17.1	11.9	4.2	6.7	4.5	18.2	37.6	18.0	10.8
1991	6.5	6.3	4.3	16.3	38.3	17.0	11.4	3.3	6.6	3.9	19.4	37.2	17.9	11.6
1992	4.7	4.0	5.7	18.5	36.4	18.7	11.9	3.2	3.0	6.1	19.5	35.0	21.2	12.0
1993	4.9	2.7	5.9	17.0	36.9	20.7	11.9	2.7	3.2	5.4	17.6	35.8	23.0	12.4
1995	3.4	3.0	4.7	15.5	37.0	22.8	13.6	1.8	2.2	4.8	17.2	35.6	25.5	12.9
1996	3.0	2.8	4.1	15.9	37.5	24.4	12.4	1.8	2.2	4.8	16.9	33.3	26.4	14.6
1997	3.0	2.7	4.2	16.6	36.5	24.5	12.5	1.5	1.9	4.6	16.0	35.3	26.8	13.9

	Percentage of Hispanic male population completing							Percentage of Hispanic female population completing						
	Elementary school			High school		College		Elementary school			High school		College	
	0–4 years	5–7 years	8 years	1–3 years	4 years	1–3 years	4 or more years	0–4 years	5–7 years	8 years	1–3 years	4 years	1–3 years	4 or more years
	Bc779	Bc780	Bc781	Bc782	Bc783	Bc784	Bc785	Bc786	Bc787	Bc788	Bc789	Bc790	Bc791	Bc792
Year	Percent	Percent	Percent	Percent	Percent	Percent	Percent	Percent	Percent	Percent	Percent	Percent	Percent	Percent
1940 [4]	—	—	—	—	—	—	—	—	—	—	—	—	—	—
1950 [4]	—	—	—	—	—	—	—	—	—	—	—	—	—	—
1960	—	—	—	—	—	—	—	—	—	—	—	—	—	—
1962	—	—	—	—	—	—	—	—	—	—	—	—	—	—
1964	—	—	—	—	—	—	—	—	—	—	—	—	—	—
1965	—	—	—	—	—	—	—	—	—	—	—	—	—	—
1966	—	—	—	—	—	—	—	—	—	—	—	—	—	—
1967	—	—	—	—	—	—	—	—	—	—	—	—	—	—
1968	—	—	—	—	—	—	—	—	—	—	—	—	—	—
1969	—	—	—	—	—	—	—	—	—	—	—	—	—	—
1970	—	—	—	—	—	—	—	—	—	—	—	—	—	—
1971	—	—	—	—	—	—	—	—	—	—	—	—	—	—
1972	—	—	—	—	—	—	—	—	—	—	—	—	—	—
1973	—	—	—	—	—	—	—	—	—	—	—	—	—	—
1974	19.2	17.3	10.0	15.3	21.3	9.7	7.1	19.5	19.2	10.2	16.2	24.2	6.7	4.0
1975	18.2	17.0	10.0	15.3	21.1	10.0	8.3	18.8	18.7	10.6	15.3	24.7	7.5	4.4
1976	17.7	16.9	8.9	15.0	23.7	9.1	8.6	19.6	17.6	10.1	15.4	25.7	7.6	3.9
1977	17.2	15.5	9.0	16.0	23.8	10.4	8.1	18.7	17.6	9.9	16.7	25.0	7.8	4.4
1978	16.4	17.5	8.7	15.2	22.7	11.0	8.6	17.9	18.4	8.8	15.2	26.2	7.6	5.7
1979	17.8	17.0	8.4	14.5	22.9	11.2	8.2	17.5	18.1	8.2	14.5	28.0	8.4	5.3
1980	16.5	15.4	8.5	14.8	24.0	11.7	9.2	15.2	16.6	8.9	15.0	29.2	8.7	6.2
1981	15.2	16.5	9.0	13.8	24.5	11.3	9.7	16.1	16.8	8.7	14.9	27.9	9.8	5.9
1982	14.1	16.3	8.8	12.6	25.9	12.6	9.6	15.3	17.8	8.6	14.3	28.3	9.5	6.2
1983	15.0	15.4	8.0	13.0	27.3	12.0	9.2	14.7	17.8	8.6	14.8	27.4	9.9	6.8
1984	13.6	15.6	8.1	14.1	26.2	12.9	9.5	14.2	16.2	8.9	15.0	28.2	10.5	7.0
1985	13.6	15.8	8.2	13.9	27.2	11.5	9.7	13.4	15.3	9.3	14.7	29.5	10.6	7.3
1986	13.3	15.5	7.3	14.7	27.4	12.3	9.6	12.4	16.2	8.9	14.7	29.4	11.0	7.3
1987	11.9	14.8	7.4	14.2	28.0	14.2	9.7	12.0	15.6	8.8	13.6	30.0	12.5	7.5
1988	11.6	16.1	6.1	14.3	27.1	12.6	12.3	12.7	15.4	7.6	14.4	29.5	12.4	8.1
1989	12.3	15.2	6.8	14.6	26.1	13.9	11.0	12.0	14.9	7.5	14.9	29.6	12.4	8.8
1990	12.9	15.8	7.1	14.0	27.4	13.2	9.8	11.7	15.5	7.3	14.2	30.9	11.7	8.7
1991	12.9	14.8	6.1	14.7	28.5	13.0	10.0	12.1	14.7	6.5	15.5	30.1	11.7	9.4
1992	11.1	12.5	7.2	15.5	27.1	16.4	10.2	12.5	11.7	8.8	15.5	27.5	15.5	8.5
1993	11.4	12.0	8.0	15.6	26.0	17.5	9.5	12.1	11.1	8.3	15.2	27.6	17.1	8.5
1995	10.8	13.6	7.0	15.8	25.6	17.3	10.1	10.4	12.4	8.5	14.9	27.0	18.3	8.4
1996	10.1	12.9	7.1	17.0	26.0	16.8	10.3	10.5	12.2	7.8	16.2	26.0	18.9	8.3
1997	9.2	12.4	7.3	16.3	25.8	18.4	10.6	9.5	12.0	7.8	16.1	26.0	18.5	10.1

[1] In 1992, the U.S. Bureau of the Census changed the categories for educational attainment, the most important relating to transitions that lead to degrees. See text.

[2] As of April for 1946–1960; thereafter, surveys were conducted in March of the year shown.

[3] Through 1962 the census category for blacks included "other races."

[4] Excludes population for whom school years were not reported.

Sources

Series Bc737–764. 1940–1991, U.S. Department of Education, *120 Years of Education: A Statistical Portrait* (1993), Table 4. The underlying sources are: 1940, 1950, U.S. Bureau of the Census, *Census of Population: 1950*, volume 2, *Characteristics of the Population*, part 1, *United States Summary*, Table 115; 1960, U.S. Bureau of the Census, *Census of Population: 1960*, Final Report PC (2)-5B, *Educational Attainment*,

(continued)

TABLE Bc737–792 Years of school completed, by sex, race, and ethnicity: 1940–1997 *Continued*

Table 1; and, for all other years, *Current Population Reports*, series P-20, "Educational Attainment in the United States," various years.

Series Bc765–792. All years, and series Bc737–764, 1992–1997, U.S. Bureau of the Census, *Current Population Reports*, series P-20, "Educational Attainment in the United States," various years. (For example, see *Current Population Reports*, series P-20, "Educational Attainment in the United States," number 505, for the 1997 data.)

Documentation

Data are for persons at least 25 years old. Hispanics can be of any race.

The 1940 U.S. population census was the first to make an inquiry about educational attainment. In 1940, a single question was asked on highest grade of school completed. The 1950 and 1960 Censuses and the various Current Population Surveys (CPS) compute years of school completed from a combination of responses to two questions, one asking for the highest grade of school attended and another whether that grade was finished. Analysis of data from the 1940 Census returns and from surveys conducted by the Bureau of the Census based on the same question wording as in 1940 indicated that respondents frequently reported the year or grade they had last attended, instead of the one completed. There is evidence that, as a result of the change in the questions in 1950, there was less exaggeration in reporting educational attainment than in 1940. A recent study of the 1940 Census has demonstrated that, in comparison with contemporaneous evidence on high school graduation, too large a fraction of Americans claimed to have graduated from high school in the 1940 Census. (See Claudia Goldin, "America's Graduation from High School: The Evolution and Spread of Secondary Schooling in the Twentieth Century," *Journal of Economic History* 58 (June 1998): 345–74.) Thus, there is evidence from a variety of sources that the data on educational attainment from the 1940 Census are upwardly biased.

The 1962 to 1997 CPS data are based on sample surveys and relate to the resident population, including inmates of institutions and members of the armed forces living off post or with their families on post; all other members of the armed forces are excluded.

Beginning in 1992, the CPS changed its educational attainment categories. Rather than reporting years of school completed, it began reporting highest grade, diploma, or degree attained. Further, some categories in the lower grades or years were aggregated. The most important changes occur with transitions that lead to degrees. Thus, the category "four or more years of high school" would now be "high school graduate," if the individual actually graduated. But if the individual did not graduate, the category would be "one to three years of high school." Individuals who received the General Educational Development (GED) degree might previously have been in the "one to three years of high school" group or the "four or more years of high school" group, but would now be included in "high school graduate." "Four or more years of college" would now be "completed bachelor's degree," if the individual received a B.A.

The mappings used here, between the pre-1992 and post-1991 categories, are the following: "zero to four years of elementary school" is a combination of "none" and "first to fourth grade"; "five to seven years elementary" is "fifth and sixth grades"; "eight years elementary" is "seventh and eighth grades"; "one to three years of high school" is the sum of ninth, tenth, and eleventh grades; "four or more years of high school" is "high school graduate"; "one to three years of college" is the sum of "Associate degree, academic," "Associate degree, occupational," and "some college, no degree"; and "four or more years of college" is "completed bachelor's degree," including those who completed higher degrees.

TABLE Bc793–797 Illiteracy rate, by race and nativity: 1870–1979[1]

Contributed by Claudia Goldin

	All persons	White			Black and other races
		All	Native-born	Foreign-born	
	Bc793	Bc794	Bc795	Bc796	Bc797
Year	Percent	Percent	Percent	Percent	Percent
1870	20.0	11.5	—	—	79.9
1880	17.0	9.4	8.7	12.0	70.0
1890	13.3	7.7	6.2	13.1	56.8
1900	10.7	6.2	4.6	12.9	44.5
1910	7.7	5.0	3.0	12.7	30.5
1920	6.0	4.0	2.0	13.1	23.0
1930	4.3	3.0	1.6	10.8	16.4
1940	2.9	2.0	1.1	9.0	11.5
1947	2.7	1.8	—	—	11.0
1950	3.2	—	—	—	—
1952	2.5	1.8	—	—	10.2
1959	2.2	1.6	—	—	7.5
1969	1.0	0.7	—	—	3.6 [2]
1979	0.6	0.4	—	—	1.6 [2]

[1] Data are for persons at least 14 years old.

[2] Based on black population only.

Source

U.S. Department of Education, *120 Years of Education: A Statistical Portrait* (1993), Table 6. The underlying sources are: U.S. Bureau of the Census, *Historical Statistics of the United States: From Colonial Times to the Present* (1975), and U.S. Bureau of the Census, *Current Population Reports*, series P-23, "Ancestry and Language in the United States" (November 1979).

Documentation

Persons were regarded as illiterate if they could not read and write in any language. Information on illiteracy was obtained from direct questions in the U.S. population censuses of 1870–1930. The data for 1947, 1952, 1959, and 1969 were obtained from sample surveys; they exclude the armed forces and inmates of institutions. In 1947, the literacy question was asked only of persons who had completed fewer than five years of school; in 1952, 1959, and 1969, the same general procedure was used but the question was asked of those who had completed less than six years of school.

TABLE Bc793–797 Illiteracy rate, by race and nativity: 1870–1979 *Continued*

The U.S. population censuses and Current Population Surveys examined a very basic level of reading and writing. More recent studies have analyzed functional illiteracy. Functional illiteracy indicates a lack of ability to function effectively in a modern society. These functional illiteracy percentages are substantially higher than earlier studies based on basic illiteracy.

Some variation has existed over the years in the way the question on illiteracy was asked. Since 1930, reference has been made as to whether or not the person was able to read and write. In the U.S. population censuses of 1870 to 1930, two questions were asked, one on whether the person was able to read and another on whether the individual could write. Illiteracy was defined as the inability to write "regardless of ability to read." As the data show that nearly all persons who were able to write could also read, the earlier statistics should be generally comparable with data obtained through the consolidated question used in later years.

Ability to read and write cannot be defined so precisely in a census as to cover all cases. No specific test of the ability to read and write was used, but enumerators were instructed not to classify a person as literate simply because the individual was able to write his or her name.

Data on illiteracy were also collected in the U.S. population censuses of 1840, 1850, and 1860, but are not included here because they are not comparable with statistics for subsequent years, and because of limitations in the quality of data for those early years. In 1840, the head of the family was asked for the total number of illiterates in each family, a method that may have led to some understatement. In 1850, the federal population census became a "nominal census," and questions were asked regarding each member of the household. In 1870, separate questions were asked concerning the ability to read and the ability to write. In addition to changes in the form of the inquiry, the statistics on illiteracy for 1840, 1850, and 1860 related to the population 20 years old and older, whereas in the 1870 and later censuses they referred to the population 10 years old and older.

The percentages of illiterates in the total population 20 years old and older, as recorded in those earlier censuses, were as follows: 1840, 22.0 percent; 1850, 22.6 percent; and 1860, 19.7 percent. The comparable percentages for the white population 20 years old and older in those years were 9.0, 10.7, and 8.9 percent, respectively. The apparent increase in illiteracy of white persons between 1850 and 1870 may be attributable, in part, to the large influx of immigrants, many of whom could not read and write in any language. It is more likely, however, that the apparent increases resulted from improvements in the way the information was obtained at those census dates.

TABLE Bc798–805 College graduation rate, by sex, nativity, and race: 1940–1997[1, 2]

Contributed by Matthew Sobek

	Males				Females			
	Native-born				Native-born			
	White	Black	Other race	Foreign-born	White	Black	Other race	Foreign-born
	Bc798	Bc799	Bc800	Bc801	Bc802	Bc803	Bc804	Bc805
Year	Percent	Percent	Percent	Percent	Percent	Percent	Percent	Percent
1940	6.8	1.5	2.7	4.0	4.9	1.4	0.9	1.7
1950	8.8	1.9	2.7	5.7	6.1	2.6	4.2	3.0
1960	11.7	3.1	9.9	9.7	6.9	3.5	5.0	4.2
1970	16.1	4.6	13.1	16.8	9.5	5.1	9.0	7.8
1980	23.6	9.1	19.3	23.9	15.1	9.1	14.0	14.2
1990	27.1	11.6	22.6	25.9	21.5	12.9	20.0	19.2
1997	30.1	16.3	27.9	27.9	26.6	16.5	25.6	23.9

1 Data pertain to noninstitutionalized persons ages 25–64.

2 Data refer to years of schooling through 1980; attainment of degree thereafter. See text.

Sources

1940–1990, tabulated from the Integrated Public Use Microdata Series (IPUMS). See the Guide to the Millennial Edition for information on IPUMS. 1997, calculated from *Current Population Survey*, 1997 October Supplement.

Documentation

Persons born in U.S. outlying areas are considered foreign-born. Persons who received their schooling outside of the United States were to report the equivalent U.S. grade level in all years. From 1940 to 1980, college graduation is considered equivalent to completion of four years of college. In 1990 and 1997, college graduation means the receipt of a bachelor's degree or higher, rather than a specific number of years of schooling.

TABLE Bc806–813 High school noncompletion rate, by sex, nativity, and race: 1940–1997[1]

Contributed by Matthew Sobek

	Males				Females			
	Native-born				Native-born			
	White	Black	Other race	Foreign-born	White	Black	Other race	Foreign-born
	Bc806	Bc807	Bc808	Bc809	Bc810	Bc811	Bc812	Bc813
Year	Percent	Percent	Percent	Percent	Percent	Percent	Percent	Percent
1940	71.8	93.2	83.6	85.2	67.2	90.9	82.5	86.8
1950	60.9	87.3	67.6	76.5	56.5	84.6	66.7	75.9
1960	52.6	79.9	54.3	67.8	48.7	76.1	56.7	68.4
1970	39.2	66.4	42.6	51.6	37.4	63.7	43.8	53.5
1980	23.5	43.6	27.8	38.7	23.5	41.9	30.9	40.6
1990	12.9	25.0	16.7	31.1	12.2	22.6	17.5	31.2
1997	8.8	16.3	12.4	30.0	8.1	14.5	12.9	28.5

[1] Data pertain to noninstitutionalized persons ages 25–64.

Sources

1940–1990, tabulated from the Integrated Public Use Microdata Series (IPUMS). See the Guide to the Millennial Edition for information on IPUMS. 1997, calculated from *Current Population Survey*, 1997 October Supplement.

Documentation

Persons born in U.S. outlying areas are considered foreign-born. Persons who received their schooling outside of the United States were to report the equivalent U.S. grade level in all years. Graduation from high school equals completion of grade 12 in all years. The 1940–1980 data do not distinguish between the actual receipt of a high school diploma and completion of twelfth grade. In 1980, persons with GEDs were to be reported as having completed twelfth grade. In 1990 and 1997, persons who completed twelfth grade but received no diploma or GED can be identified; these persons are considered graduates for the purposes of this table for the sake of compatibility with other years.

EARNINGS, BY EDUCATION

Claudia Goldin

TABLE Bc814–857 Mean annual income, by years of school completed, sex, and full-time, year-round work status: 1939–1996[1, 2, 3]

Contributed by Claudia Goldin

	Males										
		Elementary school			High school		College				
	All	Less than eight years	Eight years	Eight years or less	One to three years	Four years	One to three years	Some college	Associate degree	Four or more years	Four years only
	Bc814	Bc815	Bc816	Bc817	Bc818	Bc819	Bc820	Bc821	Bc822	Bc823	Bc824
Year	Dollars	Dollars	Dollars	Dollars	Dollars	Dollars	Dollars	Dollars	Dollars	Dollars	Dollars
1939 [4]	—	—	—	—	—	—	—	—	—	—	—
1949 [4]	—	—	—	—	—	—	—	—	—	—	—
1956 [5]	4,423	2,574	3,631	3,041 [4]	4,367	5,183	5,997	—	—	7,877	—
1958 [5]	4,637	2,530	3,677	3,043 [4]	4,452	5,257	6,272	—	—	8,643	7,565
1959 [5]	—	—	—	—	—	—	—	—	—	—	—
1961 [5]	5,472	2,998	4,206	3,544 [4]	5,161	5,946	7,348	—	—	9,817	9,342
1963 [5]	5,837	3,078	4,410	—	5,348	6,557	7,633	—	—	9,811	9,392
1964 [5]	6,106	3,298	4,520	—	5,653	6,738	7,907	—	—	10,284	9,757
1966 [5]	6,908	3,520	4,867	—	6,294	7,494	8,783	—	—	11,739	11,135
1967	7,121	3,606	5,189	4,342	6,335	7,629	8,843	—	—	11,924	11,232
1968	7,705	3,981	5,467	4,679	6,769	8,148	9,397	—	—	12,938	12,418
1969	8,430	4,242	5,809	4,987	7,279	8,827	10,387	—	—	14,079	13,258
1970	8,839	4,434	6,035	5,202	7,629	9,185	10,891	—	—	14,434	13,372
1971	9,292	4,746	6,261	5,463	7,988	9,566	11,045	—	—	15,133	14,158
1972	10,125	5,235	6,756	5,949	8,449	10,433	11,867	—	—	16,201	15,256
1973	10,943	5,525	7,529	6,465	9,125	11,218	12,515	—	—	17,064	15,794
1974 [6]	11,656	5,566	7,499	6,449	9,458	11,884	13,477	—	—	18,265	17,083
1975	12,254	5,845	7,785	6,722	9,534	12,354	13,972	—	—	19,111	17,618
1976	13,163	6,335	8,393	7,284	10,369	13,051	14,600	—	—	20,516	18,796
1977	14,209	6,836	8,772	7,717	10,916	14,017	15,625	—	—	22,125	20,222
1978	15,423	7,149	9,367	8,176	11,784	15,152	16,708	—	—	23,724	22,010
1979 [6]	16,697	7,598	10,168	8,779	12,289	16,288	18,170	—	—	25,544	23,399
1980	17,815	8,201	10,720	9,347	12,968	17,181	19,358	—	—	27,216	25,337
1981	19,190	9,017	11,376	10,058	13,650	18,139	20,767	—	—	29,278	26,694
1982	20,113	8,946	11,663	10,156	13,842	18,598	21,405	—	—	31,055	28,278
1983	20,952	9,261	12,286	10,624	14,295	19,145	22,204	—	—	32,472	29,718
1984	22,373	9,964	12,737	11,204	15,269	20,479	23,185	—	—	34,736	32,056
1985	23,663	10,016	13,217	11,444	15,589	20,916	24,987	—	—	37,570	34,243
1986	24,914	10,414	13,717	11,883	16,136	21,700	26,210	—	—	39,773	36,150
1987 [6]	25,958	—	—	12,615	16,804	22,436	27,562	—	—	40,840	36,907
1988	27,197	—	—	12,712	16,879	23,614	28,306	—	—	42,861	38,397
1989	29,021	—	—	12,852	17,151	24,768	30,034	—	—	46,932	41,911
1990	29,307	—	—	13,008	17,699	24,553	31,032	—	—	46,961	42,281
1991	29,560	—	—	12,944	17,703	24,314	—	29,897	32,084	47,350	41,808
1992 [6]	30,186	—	—	13,208	17,319	24,408	—	29,718	32,046	49,116	42,801
1993	32,496	—	—	13,399	17,651	25,501	—	30,799	32,713	54,682	46,197
1994	34,031	—	—	15,131	17,924	26,634	—	31,339	34,966	56,298	49,094
1995	35,232	—	—	14,748	19,150	27,952	—	33,600	35,812	57,018	48,856
1996	36,830	—	—	15,550	20,464	29,218	—	35,923	37,654	58,527	49,147

Notes appear at end of table

(continued)

TABLE Bc814–857 Mean annual income, by years of school completed, sex, and full-time, year-round work status: 1939–1996 *Continued*

	Females										
		Elementary school			High school		College				
	All	Less than eight years	Eight years	Eight years or less	One to three years	Four years	One to three years	Some college	Associate degree	Four or more years	Four years only
	Bc825	Bc826	Bc827	Bc828	Bc829	Bc830	Bc831	Bc832	Bc833	Bc834	Bc835
Year	Dollars	Dollars	Dollars	Dollars	Dollars	Dollars	Dollars	Dollars	Dollars	Dollars	Dollars
1939 [4]	—	—	—	—	—	—	—	—	—	—	—
1949 [4]	—	—	—	—	—	—	—	—	—	—	—
1956 [5]	—	—	—	—	—	—	—	—	—	—	—
1958 [5]	—	—	—	—	—	—	—	—	—	—	—
1959 [5]	—	—	—	—	—	—	—	—	—	—	—
1961 [5]	—	—	—	—	—	—	—	—	—	—	—
1963 [5]	—	—	—	—	—	—	—	—	—	—	—
1964 [5]	—	—	—	—	—	—	—	—	—	—	—
1966 [5]	—	—	—	—	—	—	—	—	—	—	—
1967	2,868	1,559	1,992	1,766	2,498	3,149	3,713	—	—	5,291	4,759
1968	3,023	1,664	2,153	1,898	2,616	3,321	3,717	—	—	5,349	4,639
1969	3,273	1,745	2,218	1,973	2,819	3,543	4,082	—	—	5,984	5,309
1970	3,493	1,868	2,334	2,092	2,899	3,758	4,367	—	—	6,403	5,701
1971	3,712	1,993	2,455	2,216	3,082	3,952	4,504	—	—	6,734	5,915
1972	3,998	2,154	2,654	2,393	3,284	4,261	4,758	—	—	6,957	6,121
1973	4,258	2,343	2,804	2,560	3,443	4,489	5,216	—	—	7,203	6,383
1974 [6]	4,665	2,592	3,039	2,806	3,741	4,813	5,641	—	—	7,933	7,092
1975	5,051	2,709	3,303	2,992	3,950	5,155	6,060	—	—	8,539	7,537
1976	5,454	2,947	3,550	3,227	4,188	5,603	6,330	—	—	9,048	7,980
1977	5,913	3,130	3,812	3,455	4,473	6,063	7,051	—	—	9,677	8,529
1978	6,170	3,348	3,929	3,627	4,768	6,173	7,123	—	—	9,881	8,595
1979 [6]	6,568	3,603	4,214	3,898	4,892	6,402	7,690	—	—	10,632	9,184
1980	7,381	3,989	4,747	4,349	5,346	7,138	8,814	—	—	11,901	10,614
1981	8,118	4,351	5,291	4,799	5,762	7,817	9,509	—	—	13,033	11,360
1982	8,958	4,659	5,655	5,133	6,119	8,512	10,298	—	—	14,516	12,711
1983	9,624	4,923	5,903	5,394	6,461	8,934	11,030	—	—	15,817	13,793
1984	10,500	5,454	6,500	5,966	7,066	9,610	11,990	—	—	17,254	15,141
1985	11,140	5,582	6,709	6,111	7,306	10,120	12,754	—	—	18,410	16,288
1986	11,719	5,862	6,652	6,237	7,491	10,517	13,255	—	—	19,675	17,603
1987 [6]	12,578	5,970	6,872	6,456	8,057	11,176	14,541	—	—	20,759	18,347
1988	13,400	—	—	6,527	8,073	11,743	15,573	—	—	22,084	19,814
1989	14,372	—	—	7,001	8,743	12,471	16,281	—	—	23,817	21,140
1990	15,124	—	—	7,245	9,124	13,034	16,843	—	—	25,019	22,147
1991	15,636	—	—	7,328	9,022	13,104	—	16,426	19,223	26,224	23,237
1992 [6]	16,209	—	—	7,456	9,235	13,300	—	16,941	19,173	27,371	24,400
1993	17,122	—	—	7,650	9,661	13,844	—	17,173	20,486	28,980	25,579
1994	17,881	—	—	8,288	9,758	14,236	—	17,594	20,496	30,568	26,466
1995	18,819	—	—	8,691	10,263	15,359	—	18,574	22,496	30,269	26,927
1996	20,005	—	—	9,195	10,881	15,848	—	19,828	22,598	32,844	28,926

Notes appear at end of table

TABLE Bc814–857 Mean annual income, by years of school completed, sex, and full-time, year-round work status: 1939–1996 *Continued*

	Male full-time, Year-round workers										
		Elementary school			High school		College				
	All	Less than eight years	Eight years	Eight years or less	One to three years	Four years	One to three years	Some college	Associate degree	Four or more years	Four years only
	Bc836	Bc837	Bc838	Bc839	Bc840	Bc841	Bc842	Bc843	Bc844	Bc845	Bc846
Year	Dollars	Dollars	Dollars	Dollars	Dollars	Dollars	Dollars	Dollars	Dollars	Dollars	Dollars
1939 [4]	1,514	1,070	1,432	1,265	1,522	1,729	1,955	—	—	2,379	2,377
1949 [4]	3,394	2,601	3,104	2,843	3,326	3,607	4,216	—	—	5,009	5,027
1956 [5]	—	—	—	—	—	—	—	—	—	—	—
1958 [5]	—	—	—	—	—	—	—	—	—	—	—
1959 [5]	5,655	4,094	4,971	4,519	5,427	5,909	6,647	—	—	7,802	7,790
1961 [5]	—	—	—	—	—	—	—	—	—	—	—
1963 [5]	—	—	—	—	—	—	—	—	—	—	—
1964 [5]	—	—	—	—	—	—	—	—	—	—	—
1966 [5]	—	—	—	—	—	—	—	—	—	—	—
1967	8,471	5,044	6,555	5,844	7,142	8,316	9,669	—	—	12,954	11,973
1968	9,114	5,557	6,806	6,216	7,640	8,837	10,327	—	—	14,190	13,554
1969	10,087	6,072	7,425	6,797	8,367	9,608	11,515	—	—	15,508	14,670
1970	10,697	6,431	7,947	7,245	8,917	10,080	12,111	—	—	15,946	14,675
1971	11,292	6,806	8,329	7,603	9,437	10,647	12,489	—	—	16,661	15,565
1972	12,349	7,870	9,113	8,508	9,976	11,574	13,678	—	—	17,882	16,972
1973	13,288	8,285	10,144	9,244	10,790	12,546	14,279	—	—	18,738	17,518
1974 [6]	14,440	8,540	10,199	9,412	11,602	13,447	15,403	—	—	20,299	18,925
1975	15,446	9,225	10,853	10,062	11,960	14,251	16,369	—	—	21,301	19,684
1976	16,519	9,686	12,084	10,897	12,936	15,025	17,042	—	—	22,995	20,896
1977	17,820	10,239	12,691	11,447	13,825	16,260	17,998	—	—	24,721	22,585
1978	19,329	11,449	13,784	12,653	15,031	17,580	19,256	—	—	26,449	24,529
1979 [6]	21,079	12,106	15,280	13,767	16,030	19,028	21,027	—	—	28,666	26,241
1980	22,560	13,183	15,709	14,449	16,940	20,222	22,517	—	—	30,476	28,306
1981	24,404	14,500	16,916	15,646	18,015	21,641	24,244	—	—	32,811	29,736
1982	26,056	14,283	17,324	15,740	18,639	22,723	25,421	—	—	34,949	31,822
1983	27,057	15,552	18,220	16,884	19,586	23,161	26,487	—	—	36,529	33,288
1984	28,643	16,482	18,838	17,639	20,376	24,768	27,379	—	—	38,950	35,699
1985	30,267	16,059	19,908	17,896	21,090	25,327	29,305	—	—	42,227	38,191
1986	31,684	16,867	20,545	18,593	22,018	26,211	30,782	—	—	44,274	40,175
1987 [6]	33,056	—	—	19,617	23,138	27,306	32,442	—	—	45,925	41,674
1988	34,226	—	—	19,807	23,201	28,284	33,097	—	—	47,583	42,500
1989	36,466	—	—	20,002	23,259	29,471	34,778	—	—	52,282	46,499
1990	36,755	—	—	20,075	23,493	29,232	35,747	—	—	52,763	47,342
1991	37,688	—	—	20,715	24,709	29,340	—	35,300	37,192	53,854	47,222
1992 [6]	39,047	—	—	20,970	24,238	30,064	—	36,150	36,974	56,062	48,752
1993	41,750	—	—	19,668	24,758	31,447	—	36,614	37,506	62,737	52,606
1994	43,080	—	—	21,462	25,214	32,292	—	37,257	40,402	64,413	56,107
1995	44,337	—	—	21,161	26,000	34,027	—	40,177	40,301	65,409	55,912
1996	46,201	—	—	22,055	27,723	35,413	—	42,637	42,676	67,733	56,161

Notes appear at end of table

(continued)

TABLE Bc814–857 Mean annual income, by years of school completed, sex, and full-time, year-round work status: 1939–1996 *Continued*

	Female full-time, Year-round workers										
		Elementary school			High school		College				
	All	Less than eight years	Eight years	Eight years or less	One to three years	Four years	One to three years	Some college	Associate degree	Four or more years	Four years only
	Bc847	Bc848	Bc849	Bc850	Bc851	Bc852	Bc853	Bc854	Bc855	Bc856	Bc857
Year	Dollars	Dollars	Dollars	Dollars	Dollars	Dollars	Dollars	Dollars	Dollars	Dollars	Dollars
1939 [4]	—	—	—	—	—	—	—	—	—	—	—
1949 [4]	—	—	—	—	—	—	—	—	—	—	—
1956 [5]	—	—	—	—	—	—	—	—	—	—	—
1958 [5]	—	—	—	—	—	—	—	—	—	—	—
1959 [5]	—	—	—	—	—	—	—	—	—	—	—
1961 [5]	—	—	—	—	—	—	—	—	—	—	—
1963 [5]	—	—	—	—	—	—	—	—	—	—	—
1964 [5]	—	—	—	—	—	—	—	—	—	—	—
1966 [5]	—	—	—	—	—	—	—	—	—	—	—
1967	4,670	2,955	3,626	3,333	3,847	4,571	5,502	—	—	7,213	6,678
1968	4,930	3,222	3,744	3,516	4,067	4,904	5,699	—	—	7,416	6,680
1969	5,604	3,645	4,235	3,989	4,560	5,429	6,416	—	—	8,305	7,605
1970	6,046	3,831	4,277	4,084	4,868	5,820	6,950	—	—	8,940	8,439
1971	6,321	4,105	4,480	4,315	5,064	6,016	7,278	—	—	9,471	8,648
1972	6,806	4,408	5,098	4,788	5,428	6,514	7,323	—	—	9,834	8,963
1973	7,236	4,506	5,477	5,024	5,704	6,923	7,932	—	—	10,168	9,429
1974 [6]	8,032	5,081	6,032	5,586	6,329	7,609	8,694	—	—	11,157	10,300
1975	8,633	5,316	6,042	5,718	6,728	8,074	9,344	—	—	11,884	10,728
1976	9,370	5,762	6,682	6,273	7,304	8,784	10,100	—	—	12,815	11,532
1977	9,958	6,216	7,025	6,651	7,578	9,345	10,751	—	—	13,741	12,171
1978	10,874	7,065	7,881	7,484	8,473	10,195	11,385	—	—	14,575	13,018
1979 [6]	11,952	7,579	8,463	8,063	9,274	11,049	12,737	—	—	15,948	14,315
1980	13,369	8,404	9,569	9,017	10,232	12,261	14,245	—	—	17,656	16,294
1981	14,465	9,142	10,573	9,859	10,423	13,257	15,311	—	—	19,124	17,302
1982	15,799	9,226	10,494	9,847	11,184	14,340	16,570	—	—	20,836	18,786
1983	16,722	9,918	11,111	10,516	11,903	14,822	17,391	—	—	22,310	20,136
1984	17,807	10,610	12,111	11,432	13,094	15,595	18,126	—	—	24,126	21,652
1985	18,937	10,227	12,304	11,275	13,378	16,581	19,476	—	—	25,345	23,033
1986	19,735	11,444	11,945	11,690	13,461	16,988	19,979	—	—	27,124	24,926
1987 [6]	20,893	—	—	12,807	14,473	18,001	21,574	—	—	28,300	25,419
1988	21,853	—	—	12,494	14,596	18,444	22,637	—	—	29,799	27,304
1989	23,205	—	—	13,446	15,595	19,427	23,586	—	—	32,059	29,392
1990	24,293	—	—	14,340	16,378	20,199	24,154	—	—	33,756	30,676
1991	25,235	—	—	13,277	16,301	20,450	—	24,174	27,016	35,350	31,907
1992 [6]	26,214	—	—	14,551	16,191	21,047	—	24,868	27,157	36,665	33,378
1993	27,670	—	—	13,914	18,908	22,136	—	25,182	27,918	39,146	34,976
1994	28,809	—	—	14,433	17,120	22,615	—	26,395	28,575	41,630	36,492
1995	29,143	—	—	15,430	18,053	23,326	—	26,647	30,523	40,382	36,546
1996	31,183	—	—	16,510	18,909	23,822	—	29,179	30,857	44,723	39,604

[1] Data are for persons at least 25 years old as of March of the following year.

[2] Year-round, full-time workers are those who worked at least 35 hours per week for at least 50 weeks during the year, except for 1939 (30 weeks) and 1949 and 1959 (40 weeks).

[3] Starting in 1991, modified categories for educational attainment were used. See text.

[4] Based on total money earnings instead of income.

[5] Estimates based on a series of estimated mean values for specific income class intervals. See text.

[6] Data in the original source have been corrected or revised.

Sources

1939, 1949, and 1959, tabulated from the Integrated Public Use Microdata Series (IPUMS) for 1940, 1950, and 1960 (see the Guide to the Millennial Edition for information on IPUMS); 1956–1966, U.S. Bureau of the Census, *Current Population Reports*, series P-60, number 74, Table 1, p. 25; 1967–1996, U.S. Bureau of the Census, *Current Population Reports*, series P-60, "Money Income of Households, Families, and Persons in the United States," various volumes. Most, but not all, relevant series from these publications can be downloaded from the U.S. Bureau of the Census Internet site.

Documentation

Data for revision years (1974, 1979, 1987, and 1992) were obtained directly from the U.S. Bureau of the Census, Income Division, and may not correspond with data in published reports. Portions of several series were also provided by the U.S. Bureau of the Census and may not be available in published reports. These series include: (1) mean total money earnings of male income recipients with less than or equal to eight years of education for the years 1946, 1956, 1958, and 1961 and (2) mean and median income of year-round, full-time men and women with less than or equal to eight years of education for 1967 through 1987.

The data for 1939, 1949, and 1959 were calculated from the Integrated Public Use Microdata Series (IPUMS), 1/100 sample for 1940, 1950, and 1960. The IPUMS is maintained by Steven Ruggles and Matthew Sobek through the Minnesota Historical Census Projects at the University of Minnesota, Minneapolis. Only "sample line" individuals are included in 1950 because only that household member was asked both the wage and education questions.

The sample used for all three years includes all noninstitutionalized men 25 years old and older who were wage and salary workers in either the private

TABLE Bc814–857 Mean annual income, by years of school completed, sex, and full-time, year-round work status: 1939–1996 *Continued*

or government sectors and had nonzero wage and salary earnings. For 1949 and 1959, year-round, full-time is defined as working 35 hours or more per week and 40 weeks or more per year. For 1939, year-round, full-time is defined as working 35 hours or more per week and 30 weeks or more per year because the 1940 Census asked respondents how many full-time equivalent weeks they worked in the previous year.

For those who were top-coded, earnings were imputed at 1.5 times the top-code. (Top-coding is the truncation of earnings at the high end of the distribution.) Weekly wages and earnings were computed by dividing by the reported number of weeks per year. In 1960, weeks are given in intervals and the midpoints of these intervals were used to estimate the number of weeks worked. The top and bottom 1 percent of weekly wage earners were excluded owing to the implausibility of their weekly wages.

The figures for 1939, 1949, and 1959 have not been decomposed by age or potential job-experience groups and may be misleading for periods of substantial education increase such as the decade from 1940 to 1950. In 1939, for example, the overall ratio of weekly earnings among "high school only" graduates to those who left school after eighth grade is 1.21, a number substantially below any of the job-experience group averages. The reason is that high school graduates were much younger than those who left after primary school, and the overall average aggregates across age or job-experience groups. See Claudia Goldin and Robert A. Margo, "The Great Compression: The Wage Structure in the United States at Mid-Century," *Quarterly Journal of Economics* 107 (February 1992): 1–34.

Neither the income concept nor the universe covered is directly comparable for all years shown. Most of the differences, however, are relatively small and are not believed to seriously distort the relationships. The figures for 1939, 1949, and 1959 are based on the 1940, 1950, and 1960 U.S. Census and represent wage and salary earnings only. The 1956, 1958, and 1961 figures for male income recipients with less than or equal to eight years of education represent the total money earnings (not total income) of the civilian noninstitutional male population 25 years old and over. Although the conceptual differences between income and earnings are substantial, the actual differences in the averages are quite small, primarily because the amount of nonearned income is small relative to the total and this type of income tends to be seriously underreported in household surveys of income.

The income concepts for 1956–1996 are comparable because the data are from the Current Population Survey and are total money income of the U.S. civilian noninstitutional population (and members of the U.S. Armed Forces living off post or with their families on post, but excluding all other members of the armed forces). For each person in the sample of working age (14 years and older for 1956–1979 and 15 years and older for 1980–1996) questions were asked on the amount of money income received during the preceding calendar year from each of the following sources: (1) money wages or salary; (2) net income from nonfarm self-employment; (3) net income from farm self-employment; (4) Social Security; (5) dividends, interest (on savings or bonds), and income from estates or trusts or net rental income; (6) public assistance or welfare payments; (7) unemployment compensation, government employee pensions, or veterans' payments; and (8) private pensions, annuities, alimony, regular contributions from persons not living in this household, royalties, and other periodic income. The amounts received represent income before deductions for personal taxes, Social Security, bonds, and so on. The sum of money wages and salaries, net income from self-employment, and income other than earnings represents total money income.

Data since 1990 may not be completely comparable to earlier years owing to changes in the educational attainment categories. For all years, data on years of school completed are derived from the combination of answers to questions concerning the highest grade of school attended by the person and whether or not that grade was finished. Educational attainment applies only to progress in "regular" school. Such schools included graded public, private, and parochial elementary and high schools (both junior and senior high), colleges, universities, and professional schools, whether day schools or night schools. Thus, regular schooling is that which may advance a person toward an elementary school certificate or high school diploma, or a college, university, or professional school degree. Schooling in other than regular schools is counted only if the credits obtained are regarded as transferable to a school in the regular school system.

In 1991, the earlier categories "high school, one to three years" and "high school, four years" were replaced by "ninth through twelfth grade, no degree" and "high school graduate, including equivalency," respectively. Similarly, "college, one to three years" was replaced by "some college, no degree" and "associate degree" (two-year degrees awarded by occupational/vocational programs as well as academic programs). Whereas prior to 1991, "high school, four years" included those with less than one year of college, beginning in 1991, persons with less than one year of college are included in the "some college, no degree" category. Other categories were also replaced in 1991.

Mean income for all years, except those noted below, represents the amount obtained by dividing the total income of a group by the number of income recipients in that group. In the derivation of aggregate amounts based on grouped data for 1956–1966, the number of males in each income interval was multiplied by an estimated mean income. For income intervals below $8,000, the midpoint of each class interval was used; $8,900 was used for the interval $8,000–$9,900; $12,000 for the interval $10,000–$14,999; and $19,000 for the interval $15,000–$24,999. For the $25,000 and over interval, the interpolation was from a Pareto curve fitted to the data for the upper income range.

TABLE Bc858–901 Median annual income, by years of school completed, sex, and full-time, year-round work status: 1939–1996[1, 2, 3]

Contributed by Claudia Goldin

	Males										
		Elementary school			High school		College				
	All	Less than eight years	Eight years	Eight years or less	One to three years	Four years	One to three years	Some college	Associate degree	Four or more years	Four years only
	Bc858	Bc859	Bc860	Bc861	Bc862	Bc863	Bc864	Bc865	Bc866	Bc867	Bc868
Year	Dollars	Dollars	Dollars	Dollars	Dollars	Dollars	Dollars	Dollars	Dollars	Dollars	Dollars
1939 [4]	—	—	—	—	—	—	—	—	—	—	—
1946	2,316	—	—	—	2,345	2,513	—	—	—	—	—
1949 [4]	—	—	—	—	—	—	—	—	—	—	—
1956 [5]	3,608	2,012	3,229	—	3,577	4,413	4,458	—	—	6,038	—
1958 [5]	4,213	2,080	3,508	—	4,367	4,992	5,600	—	—	6,866	6,710
1959 [4]	—	—	—	—	—	—	—	—	—	—	—
1961 [5]	4,795	2,275	3,868	—	4,853	5,552	6,022	—	—	7,697	7,586
1963	5,221	2,397	4,076	3,050	5,153	5,999	6,802	—	—	7,987	7,804
1964	5,410	2,520	3,983	3,131	5,352	6,266	7,032	—	—	8,805	8,430
1965	5,598	2,576	4,210	3,222	5,534	6,458	7,222	—	—	9,048	8,748
1966	6,128	2,784	4,518	3,488	5,982	6,924	7,709	—	—	9,840	9,728
1967	6,466	2,990	4,778	3,717	6,157	7,244	8,155	—	—	10,555	10,090
1968	6,985	3,333	5,096	4,084	6,569	7,731	8,618	—	—	11,257	10,866
1969	7,578	3,429	5,345	4,285	7,079	8,434	9,394	—	—	12,255	11,893
1970	7,891	3,624	5,410	4,420	7,335	8,772	9,879	—	—	12,681	12,144
1971	8,242	3,883	5,469	4,589	7,570	9,088	10,303	—	—	13,126	12,573
1972	8,989	4,150	5,786	4,893	7,976	9,905	10,971	—	—	14,125	13,520
1973	9,800	4,463	6,371	5,258	8,622	10,832	11,670	—	—	14,704	13,939
1974 [6]	10,404	4,509	6,511	5,315	8,919	11,338	12,412	—	—	16,001	14,401
1975	10,878	4,665	6,642	5,473	8,825	11,834	13,060	—	—	16,682	15,659
1976	11,562	4,987	6,959	5,819	9,536	12,393	13,347	—	—	17,323	16,466
1977	12,375	5,402	7,155	6,134	10,023	13,207	14,247	—	—	18,530	17,391
1978	13,377	5,641	7,604	6,520	10,419	14,341	15,459	—	—	20,151	18,774
1979 [6]	14,559	5,881	8,073	6,797	10,947	15,466	16,815	—	—	21,444	20,125
1980	15,579	6,381	8,732	7,444	11,536	16,211	18,010	—	—	23,182	21,838
1981	16,555	7,123	9,270	7,995	11,936	16,989	19,504	—	—	25,486	23,640
1982	16,927	7,218	9,501	8,072	12,079	17,055	19,980	—	—	26,441	24,630
1983	17,577	7,164	10,308	8,400	12,117	17,568	20,327	—	—	28,107	26,152
1984	18,902	7,530	10,325	8,604	12,529	18,825	21,378	—	—	30,298	28,206
1985	19,684	7,857	10,818	8,996	12,870	18,997	22,581	—	—	31,946	29,698
1986	20,538	8,077	11,084	9,240	13,401	19,772	23,738	—	—	33,304	31,602
1987 [6]	21,221	—	—	9,742	14,141	20,262	24,687	—	—	34,148	31,406
1988	22,038	—	—	9,922	14,067	21,186	25,397	—	—	35,697	32,328
1989	22,860	—	—	10,003	14,439	21,650	26,402	—	—	37,553	34,680
1990	23,341	—	—	10,300	15,131	21,713	27,186	—	—	37,860	35,181
1991	23,686	—	—	10,319	14,736	21,546	—	26,591	29,358	39,803	36,067
1992 [6]	23,894	—	—	10,374	14,218	21,645	—	26,318	28,791	40,557	36,745
1993	24,605	—	—	10,895	14,550	21,782	—	26,323	29,736	41,649	37,474
1994	25,465	—	—	11,324	14,584	22,387	—	26,768	30,643	42,027	38,701
1995	26,346	—	—	11,723	15,791	23,365	—	28,004	31,027	43,322	39,040
1996	27,248	—	—	12,174	16,058	24,814	—	29,160	33,065	44,161	39,624

Notes appear at end of table

TABLE Bc858–901 Median annual income, by years of school completed, sex, and full-time, year-round work status: 1939–1996 *Continued*

	Females										
		Elementary school			High school		College				
	All	Less than eight years	Eight years	Eight years or less	One to three years	Four years	One to three years	Some college	Associate degree	Four or more years	Four years only
	Bc869	Bc870	Bc871	Bc872	Bc873	Bc874	Bc875	Bc876	Bc877	Bc878	Bc879
Year	Dollars	Dollars	Dollars	Dollars	Dollars	Dollars	Dollars	Dollars	Dollars	Dollars	Dollars
1939 [4]	—	—	—	—	—	—	—	—	—	—	—
1946	1,130	—	—	—	1,108	1,370	—	—	—	—	—
1949 [4]	—	—	—	—	—	—	—	—	—	—	—
1956 [5]	1,146	724	957	—	941	1,898	1,734	—	—	3,050	—
1958 [5]	1,176	711	909	—	867	2,036	1,865	—	—	3,309	2,903
1959 [4]	—	—	—	—	—	—	—	—	—	—	—
1961 [5]	1,279	791	950	—	994	1,938	1,717	—	—	3,538	3,179
1963	1,611	851	1,186	953	1,582	2,288	2,327	—	—	4,034	3,393
1964	1,726	873	1,297	992	1,636	2,369	2,496	—	—	4,358	3,931
1965	1,828	907	1,388	1,072	1,825	2,544	2,676	—	—	4,664	4,293
1966	1,926	1,009	1,404	1,190	1,913	2,673	2,827	—	—	4,768	4,165
1967	2,106	1,087	1,379	1,218	2,040	2,909	3,083	—	—	5,173	4,426
1968	2,302	1,238	1,590	1,379	2,177	3,073	3,247	—	—	5,305	4,437
1969	2,448	1,277	1,645	1,407	2,338	3,240	3,509	—	—	5,817	5,208
1970	2,595	1,401	1,803	1,565	2,387	3,400	3,722	—	—	6,175	5,362
1971	2,844	1,503	1,883	1,678	2,581	3,594	3,732	—	—	6,620	5,736
1972	3,031	1,664	2,038	1,817	2,692	3,757	4,122	—	—	6,897	6,007
1973	3,268	1,873	2,220	2,017	2,836	3,970	4,564	—	—	7,042	6,214
1974 [6]	3,519	2,132	2,372	2,240	3,129	4,203	4,969	—	—	7,713	6,477
1975	3,913	2,252	2,641	2,396	3,308	4,549	5,403	—	—	8,327	7,459
1976	4,143	2,423	2,854	2,595	3,423	4,925	5,502	—	—	8,540	7,643
1977	4,556	2,524	3,041	2,769	3,679	5,276	6,239	—	—	9,095	8,077
1978	4,636	2,709	3,113	2,882	3,701	5,221	6,204	—	—	9,273	8,090
1979 [6]	4,853	2,884	3,369	3,082	3,938	5,319	6,499	—	—	9,908	8,310
1980	5,492	3,321	3,785	3,527	4,252	5,903	7,529	—	—	11,011	9,607
1981	6,081	3,657	4,225	3,867	4,655	6,495	8,257	—	—	12,085	10,497
1982	6,631	3,868	4,657	4,194	4,930	6,965	8,583	—	—	13,484	11,717
1983	7,139	4,124	4,683	4,380	5,160	7,365	9,524	—	—	14,679	12,492
1984	7,756	4,413	5,167	4,723	5,559	7,839	10,473	—	—	15,871	13,644
1985	8,154	4,615	5,415	4,891	5,689	8,137	11,018	—	—	17,235	15,256
1986	8,582	4,691	5,258	4,886	5,831	8,366	11,574	—	—	18,065	16,126
1987 [6]	9,435	—	—	5,056	6,292	9,143	12,487	—	—	18,872	16,893
1988	10,082	—	—	5,205	6,295	9,748	13,367	—	—	20,465	18,415
1989	10,814	—	—	5,627	6,752	10,439	14,244	—	—	21,659	19,454
1990	11,272	—	—	5,918	7,042	10,653	14,748	—	—	22,509	20,363
1991	11,580	—	—	6,268	7,055	10,818	—	13,963	17,364	23,627	20,967
1992 [6]	11,922	—	—	6,337	7,293	10,901	—	14,401	17,331	25,093	22,383
1993	12,234	—	—	6,480	7,187	11,089	—	14,489	18,346	25,246	22,452
1994	12,766	—	—	6,865	7,618	11,390	—	14,585	17,954	26,237	23,405
1995	13,821	—	—	7,096	8,057	12,046	—	15,552	19,450	26,843	24,065
1996	14,682	—	—	7,276	8,544	12,702	—	16,255	20,460	27,556	25,192

Notes appear at end of table

(continued)

TABLE Bc858–901 Median annual income, by years of school completed, sex, and full-time, year-round work status: 1939–1996 *Continued*

	Male full-time, year-round workers										
		Elementary school			High school		College				
	All	Less than eight years	Eight years	Eight years or less	One to three years	Four years	One to three years	Some college	Associate degree	Four or more years	Four years only
	Bc880	Bc881	Bc882	Bc883	Bc884	Bc885	Bc886	Bc887	Bc888	Bc889	Bc890
Year	Dollars	Dollars	Dollars	Dollars	Dollars	Dollars	Dollars	Dollars	Dollars	Dollars	Dollars
1939 [4]	1,300	1,000	1,300	1,200	1,400	1,500	1,772	—	—	2,080	2,080
1946	—	—	—	—	—	—	—	—	—	—	—
1949 [4]	3,050	2,550	3,050	2,750	3,050	3,250	3,650	—	—	4,250	4,250
1956 [5]	4,462	3,120	4,035	—	4,514	4,887	5,457	—	—	6,980	—
1958 [5]	—	—	—	—	—	—	—	—	—	—	—
1959 [4]	5,250	4,050	4,850	4,450	5,150	5,550	6,050	—	—	7,250	7,150
1961 [5]	—	—	—	—	—	—	—	—	—	—	—
1963	—	—	—	—	—	—	—	—	—	—	—
1964	—	—	—	—	—	—	—	—	—	—	—
1965	—	—	—	—	—	—	—	—	—	—	—
1966	—	—	—	—	—	—	—	—	—	—	—
1967	7,547	4,831	6,133	5,565	6,891	7,732	8,816	—	—	11,571	10,909
1968	8,079	5,307	6,580	5,954	7,324	8,302	9,278	—	—	12,224	11,795
1969	8,978	5,769	7,147	6,498	7,958	9,100	10,311	—	—	13,323	12,960
1970	9,521	6,043	7,535	6,794	8,514	9,567	11,183	—	—	13,871	13,264
1971	10,038	6,310	7,838	7,123	8,945	9,996	11,701	—	—	14,351	13,730
1972	11,148	7,042	8,636	7,863	9,462	11,073	12,428	—	—	15,748	14,879
1973	12,088	7,521	9,406	8,455	10,401	12,017	13,090	—	—	16,576	15,503
1974 [6]	12,704	7,990	9,888	8,888	10,887	12,538	13,703	—	—	17,249	16,413
1975	13,821	8,647	10,600	9,628	11,511	13,542	14,989	—	—	18,450	17,477
1976	14,732	8,991	11,312	10,173	12,301	14,295	15,514	—	—	19,338	18,236
1977	15,726	9,419	12,083	10,509	13,120	15,434	16,235	—	—	20,625	19,603
1978	16,882	10,474	12,965	11,765	14,199	16,396	17,411	—	—	22,095	20,941
1979 [6]	18,691	10,966	14,419	12,337	15,203	18,074	19,337	—	—	23,938	22,322
1980	20,297	11,753	14,674	13,117	16,101	19,469	20,909	—	—	25,849	24,311
1981	21,689	12,866	16,084	14,492	16,938	20,598	22,565	—	—	28,174	26,394
1982	22,857	12,386	16,376	14,220	17,496	21,344	23,633	—	—	30,122	28,030
1983	23,891	14,093	16,438	15,140	17,685	21,823	24,613	—	—	31,800	29,892
1984	25,497	14,624	16,812	15,726	19,120	23,269	25,831	—	—	33,934	31,487
1985	26,365	14,766	18,645	16,607	18,881	23,853	26,960	—	—	35,605	32,822
1986	27,337	14,485	18,541	16,389	20,003	24,701	28,025	—	—	36,665	34,391
1987 [6]	28,232	—	—	16,691	20,863	25,490	29,820	—	—	38,416	35,527
1988	29,331	—	—	17,190	20,777	26,045	30,129	—	—	39,967	36,434
1989	30,380	—	—	17,570	21,062	26,461	31,110	—	—	41,857	38,511
1990	30,650	—	—	17,394	20,905	26,515	31,566	—	—	42,524	39,115
1991	31,613	—	—	17,623	21,402	26,779	—	31,663	33,817	45,138	40,906
1992 [6]	32,157	—	—	17,445	21,411	27,357	—	32,187	33,477	45,890	41,406
1993	32,359	—	—	16,863	21,752	27,370	—	32,077	33,690	47,740	42,757
1994	33,440	—	—	17,532	22,048	28,037	—	32,279	35,794	49,228	43,663
1995	34,551	—	—	18,354	22,185	29,510	—	33,883	35,201	50,481	45,266
1996	35,622	—	—	17,962	22,717	30,709	—	34,845	37,131	51,436	45,846

Notes appear at end of table

TABLE Bc858–901 Median annual income, by years of school completed, sex, and full-time, year-round work status: 1939–1996 *Continued*

	Female full-time, year-round workers										
		Elementary school			High school		College				
	All	Less than eight years	Eight years	Eight years or less	One to three years	Four years	One to three years	Some college	Associate degree	Four or more years	Four years only
	Bc891	Bc892	Bc893	Bc894	Bc895	Bc896	Bc897	Bc898	Bc899	Bc900	Bc901
Year	Dollars	Dollars	Dollars	Dollars	Dollars	Dollars	Dollars	Dollars	Dollars	Dollars	Dollars
1939 [4]	—	—	—	—	—	—	—	—	—	—	—
1946	—	—	—	—	—	—	—	—	—	—	—
1949 [4]	—	—	—	—	—	—	—	—	—	—	—
1956 [5]	2,828	1,811	2,408	—	2,583	3,021	3,440	—	—	3,809	—
1958 [5]	—	—	—	—	—	—	—	—	—	—	—
1959 [4]	—	—	—	—	—	—	—	—	—	—	—
1961 [5]	—	—	—	—	—	—	—	—	—	—	—
1963	—	—	—	—	—	—	—	—	—	—	—
1964	—	—	—	—	—	—	—	—	—	—	—
1965	—	—	—	—	—	—	—	—	—	—	—
1966	—	—	—	—	—	—	—	—	—	—	—
1967	4,372	2,820	3,343	3,139	3,704	4,499	5,253	—	—	6,796	6,372
1968	4,697	3,282	3,601	3,470	3,909	4,835	5,471	—	—	7,220	6,694
1969	5,254	3,603	3,971	3,825	4,427	5,280	6,137	—	—	7,931	7,396
1970	5,616	3,798	4,181	4,005	4,655	5,580	6,604	—	—	8,719	8,156
1971	5,872	3,946	4,400	4,199	4,889	5,808	6,815	—	—	9,162	8,451
1972	6,331	4,221	4,784	4,517	5,253	6,166	7,020	—	—	9,446	8,736
1973	6,791	4,369	5,135	4,756	5,513	6,623	7,593	—	—	9,771	9,057
1974 [6]	7,553	5,091	5,708	5,378	5,933	7,320	8,247	—	—	10,411	9,735
1975	8,117	5,109	5,691	5,460	6,355	7,777	9,126	—	—	11,359	10,349
1976	8,728	5,644	6,433	5,993	6,800	8,377	9,475	—	—	12,109	11,010
1977	9,257	6,074	6,564	6,283	7,387	8,894	10,157	—	—	12,656	11,605
1978	10,121	6,648	7,489	7,079	7,996	9,769	10,634	—	—	13,395	12,347
1979 [6]	11,056	7,373	7,763	7,580	8,507	10,490	11,848	—	—	14,847	13,407
1980	12,156	7,742	8,857	8,216	9,676	11,537	12,954	—	—	16,362	15,143
1981	13,259	8,419	9,723	8,993	10,043	12,332	14,343	—	—	17,795	16,322
1982	14,447	8,424	10,112	9,192	10,661	13,240	15,594	—	—	19,417	17,405
1983	15,292	9,385	10,337	9,849	11,131	13,787	16,536	—	—	20,251	18,452
1984	16,169	9,828	10,848	10,445	11,843	14,569	17,007	—	—	21,889	20,257
1985	17,124	9,736	11,377	10,564	11,836	15,481	17,989	—	—	23,119	21,389
1986	17,675	10,153	11,183	10,688	12,267	15,947	18,516	—	—	24,482	22,412
1987 [6]	18,608	—	—	11,018	12,939	16,549	19,946	—	—	25,735	23,399
1988	19,497	—	—	11,358	13,104	16,810	20,845	—	—	26,804	25,187
1989	20,569	—	—	12,188	13,923	17,524	21,622	—	—	28,815	26,719
1990	21,381	—	—	12,313	14,429	18,323	22,227	—	—	30,392	28,042
1991	22,045	—	—	12,066	14,455	18,837	—	22,144	25,002	31,312	29,087
1992 [6]	23,201	—	—	13,000	14,613	19,462	—	23,223	25,643	32,357	30,394
1993	23,629	—	—	12,415	15,386	19,963	—	23,056	25,883	34,307	31,197
1994	24,399	—	—	12,430	15,133	20,373	—	23,514	25,940	35,378	31,741
1995	24,875	—	—	13,577	15,825	20,463	—	23,997	27,311	35,259	32,051
1996	25,808	—	—	14,414	16,953	21,175	—	25,167	28,083	36,461	33,525

[1] Unless otherwise indicated, data are for persons at least 25 years old as of March of the following year.

[2] Year-round, full-time workers are those who worked at least 35 hours per week for at least 50 weeks during the year, except for 1939 (30 weeks) and 1949 and 1959 (40 weeks).

[3] Starting in 1991, modified categories for educational attainment were used. See text.

[4] Based on total money earnings instead of income.

[5] Persons at least 14 years old (1956). Females at least 14 years old (1958 and 1961).

[6] Data in the original source have been corrected or revised.

Sources

1939 and 1949, Integrated Public Use Microdata Series (IPUMS) for 1940 and 1950 (see the Guide to the Millennial Edition for information on IPUMS); 1956–1996, U.S. Bureau of the Census, *Current Population Reports*, series P-60, "Money Income of Households, Families, and Persons in the United States," various volumes. Most, but not all, relevant series can be downloaded from the U.S. Bureau of the Census Internet site.

Documentation

See the text for Table Bc814–857. Median income for all years is the amount that divides the income distribution into two equal groups, half having income above the median and half having income below the median.

REVENUES AND EXPENDITURES

Claudia Goldin

TABLE Bc902–908 Revenues for public elementary and secondary schools, by level of government: 1889–1995[1]

Contributed by Claudia Goldin

	Revenues				Percentage of total revenues from		
	Total	Federal	State	Local (including intermediate)	Federal	State	Local (including intermediate)
	Bc902	Bc903	Bc904 [2]	Bc905 [2, 3]	Bc906	Bc907	Bc908
School year beginning	Thousand dollars	Thousand dollars	Thousand dollars	Thousand dollars	Percent	Percent	Percent
1889	143,195	—	26,345	97,222	—	21.3	78.7
1890	147,915	—	27,632	100,359	—	21.6	78.4
1891	157,175	—	29,908	105,630	—	22.1	77.9
1892	165,023	—	33,695	108,425	—	23.7	76.3
1893	170,404	—	32,750	112,785	—	22.5	77.5
1894	176,565	—	34,638	118,915	—	22.6	77.4
1895	182,480	—	35,032	124,880	—	21.9	78.1
1896	191,959	—	33,942	130,318	—	20.7	79.3
1897	199,833	—	35,122	135,516	—	20.6	79.4
1898	203,337	—	35,341	144,898	—	19.6	80.4
1899	219,766	—	37,887	149,487	—	20.2	79.8
1900	235,339	—	36,281	163,897	—	18.1	81.9
1901	245,498	—	39,216	173,151	—	18.5	81.5
1902	251,637	—	40,456	173,731	—	18.9	81.1
1903	279,134	—	42,553	193,216	—	18.0	82.0
1904	301,819	—	44,349	210,168	—	17.4	82.6
1905	322,106	—	47,943	223,491	—	17.7	82.3
1906	355,016	—	44,706	231,738	—	16.2	83.8
1907	381,920	—	58,097	259,341	—	18.3	81.7
1908	403,647	—	63,547	288,643	—	18.0	82.0
1909	433,064	—	64,605	312,222	—	17.1	82.9
1910	451,151	—	69,071	333,832	—	17.1	82.9
1911	469,111	—	75,814	346,898	—	17.9	82.1
1912	507,227	—	78,376	375,582	—	17.3	82.7
1913	561,743	—	87,895	425,457	—	17.1	82.9
1914	589,652	—	91,104	456,956	—	16.6	83.4
1915	633,901	—	95,278	488,120	—	16.3	83.7
1917	736,876	1,669	122,256	612,951	0.2	16.6	83.2
1919	970,121	2,475	160,085	807,561	0.3	16.5	83.2
1921	1,444,242	2,891	230,517	1,184,530	0.2	16.3	83.5
1923	1,618,438	3,986	261,997	1,290,239	0.3	16.8	82.9
1925	1,830,017	5,552	284,569	1,539,896	0.3	15.6	84.1
1927	2,025,750	6,174	333,279	1,686,297	0.3	16.5	83.2
1929	2,088,557	7,334	353,670	1,727,553	0.4	16.9	82.7
1931	2,068,029	8,262	410,550	1,649,218	0.4	19.9	79.7
1933	1,810,652	21,548	423,178	1,365,926	1.2	23.4	75.4
1935	1,971,402	9,850 [4]	578,369	1,383,184	0.5	29.3	70.2
1937	2,222,885	26,535	655,996	1,540,353	1.2	29.5	69.3
1939	2,260,527	39,810	684,354	1,536,363	1.8	30.3	68.0
1941	2,416,580	34,305	759,993	1,622,281	1.4	31.4	67.1
1943	2,604,322	35,886	859,183	1,709,253	1.4	33.0	65.6
1945	3,059,845	41,378	1,062,057	1,956,409	1.4	34.7	63.9
1947	4,311,534	120,270	1,676,362	2,514,902	2.8	38.9	58.3
1949	5,437,044	155,848	2,165,689	3,115,507	2.9	39.8	57.3
1951	6,423,816	227,711	2,478,596	3,717,507	3.5	38.6	57.9
1953	7,866,852	355,237	2,944,103	4,567,512	4.5	37.4	58.1
1955	9,686,677	441,442	3,828,886	5,416,350	4.6	39.5	55.9
1957	12,181,513	486,484	4,800,368	6,894,661	4.0	39.4	56.6
1959	14,746,618	651,639	5,768,047	8,326,932	4.4	39.1	56.5
1961	17,527,707	760,975	6,789,190	9,977,542	4.3	38.7	56.9
1963	20,544,182	896,956	8,078,014	11,569,213	4.4	39.3	56.3

Notes appear at end of table

TABLE Bc902–908 Revenues for public elementary and secondary schools, by level of government: 1889–1995 *Continued*

	Revenues				Percentage of total revenues from		
	Total	Federal	State	Local (including intermediate)	Federal	State	Local (including intermediate)
	Bc902	Bc903	Bc904 [2]	Bc905 [2, 3]	Bc906	Bc907	Bc908
School year beginning	Thousand dollars	Thousand dollars	Thousand dollars	Thousand dollars	Percent	Percent	Percent
1965	25,356,858	1,996,954	9,920,219	13,439,686	7.9	39.1	53.0
1967	31,903,064	2,806,469	12,275,536	16,821,063	8.8	38.5	52.7
1969	40,266,923	3,219,557	16,062,776	20,984,589	8.0	39.9	52.1
1970	44,511,292	3,753,461	17,409,086	23,348,745	8.4	39.1	52.5
1971	50,003,645	4,467,969	19,133,256	26,402,420	8.9	38.3	52.8
1972	52,117,930	4,525,000	20,843,520	26,749,412	8.7	40.0	51.3
1973	58,230,892	4,930,351	24,113,409	29,187,132	8.5	41.4	50.1
1974	64,445,239	5,811,595	27,211,116	31,422,528	9.0	42.2	48.8
1975	71,206,073	6,318,345	31,776,101	33,111,627	8.9	44.6	46.5
1976	75,322,532	6,629,498	32,688,903	36,004,134	8.8	43.4	47.8
1977	81,443,160	7,694,194	35,013,266	38,735,700	9.4	43.0	47.6
1978	87,994,143	8,600,116	40,132,136	39,261,891	9.8	45.6	44.6
1979	96,881,165	9,503,537	45,348,814	42,028,813	9.8	46.8	43.4
1980	105,949,087	9,768,262	50,182,659	45,998,166	9.2	47.4	43.4
1981	110,191,257	8,186,466	52,436,435	49,568,356	7.4	47.6	45.0
1982	117,497,502	8,339,990	56,282,157	52,875,354	7.1	47.9	45.0
1983	126,055,419	8,576,547	60,232,981	57,245,892	6.8	47.8	45.4
1984	137,294,678	9,105,569	67,168,684	61,020,425	6.6	48.9	44.4
1985	149,127,779	9,975,622	73,619,575	65,532,582	6.7	49.4	43.9
1986	158,523,693	10,146,013	78,830,437	69,547,243	6.4	49.7	43.9
1987	169,561,974	10,716,687	84,004,415	74,840,873	6.3	49.5	44.1
1988	192,016,374	11,902,001	91,768,911	88,345,462	6.2	47.8	46.0
1989	208,547,573	12,700,784	98,238,633	97,608,157	6.1	47.1	46.8
1990	223,340,537	13,776,066	105,324,533	104,239,939	6.2	47.2	46.7
1991	234,581,384	15,493,330	108,783,449	110,304,605	6.6	46.4	47.0
1992	247,626,168	17,261,252	113,403,436	116,961,481	7.0	45.8	47.2
1994	260,159,468	18,341,483	117,474,209	124,343,776	7.1	45.2	47.8
1995	273,137,899	18,581,511	127,719,673	126,836,715	6.8	46.8	46.4

[1] For 1889–1915 and 1921–1923, totals include receipts not distributed by source. Percentages are based on funds reported by source.

[2] Prior to 1917, includes only taxes and appropriations.

[3] Includes nongovernmental sources (gifts and tuition and transportation fees from patrons), which accounted for 0.4 percent of total revenues in 1967.

[4] Includes only aid for vocational education.

Sources

1889–1988: U.S. Department of Education, *120 Years of American Education: A Statistical Portrait* (1993), Table 21; 1989–1996: U.S. Department of Education, *Digest of Education Statistics 1997*, Table 158. The original sources listed are: U.S. Office of Education, *Annual Report of the United States Commissioner of Education, 1890 to 1917*; U.S. Office of Education, *Biennial Survey of Education in the United States, 1916–18* to *1956–58*; *Statistics of State School Systems, 1959–60* to *1969–70*; *Revenues and Expenditures for Public Elementary and Secondary Education*; and Common Core of Data survey.

Documentation

Revenue receipts are additions to assets (cash) from taxes, appropriations, and other funds that do not incur an obligation that must be met at some future date and do not represent exchanges of property for money. Receipts from county and other intermediate sources are included with local receipts. Other sources of revenue include gifts, tuition, and transportation fees from patrons.

Nonrevenue receipts represent amounts that either incur an obligation that must be met at some future date or change the form of an asset from property to cash and therefore decrease the amount and the value of school property. Money received from loans, sale of bonds, sale of property purchased from capital funds, and proceeds from insurance adjustments constitute most of the nonrevenue receipts. Nonrevenue receipts are not included in the table.

Beginning in 1980, revenues for state education agencies are excluded. Data for 1988 reflect new survey collection procedures and may not be entirely comparable to figures for earlier years.

The source of funds does not adequately capture the fiscal independence of the lower levels of government when there are state laws, such as state equalization laws, that require localities to spend particular amounts. The point is especially true when states set binding maximum amounts that can be raised and spent by local governments.

TABLE Bc909-925 Public elementary and secondary school expenditures – by purpose, per capita, and per pupil: 1869–1996

Contributed by Claudia Goldin

School year beginning	Total expenditures	Current expenditures, day schools: Total	Current expenditures, day schools: Administration	Current expenditures, day schools: Instruction	Current expenditures, day schools: Plant operation and maintenance	Current expenditures, day schools: Other	Capital outlay	Interest on school debt	Other expenditures	Per capita and per pupil expenditures, Current dollars, Total expenditures: Per capita	Current dollars, Total expenditures: Per pupil enrolled	Current dollars, Total expenditures: Per pupil in average daily attendance	Current dollars, Current expenditures: Per pupil in average daily attendance	Constant 1982–1984 dollars, Total expenditures: Per capita	Constant 1982–1984 dollars, Total expenditures: Per pupil enrolled	Constant 1982–1984 dollars, Total expenditures: Per pupil in average daily attendance	Constant 1982–1984 dollars, Current expenditures: Per pupil in average daily attendance
	Bc909	Bc910 [1]	Bc911	Bc912 [2]	Bc913	Bc914 [3]	Bc915 [4,5]	Bc916	Bc917 [6]	Bc918	Bc919	Bc920	Bc921	Bc922	Bc923	Bc924	Bc925
	Million dollars	Million dollars	Million dollars	Million dollars	Million dollars	Million dollars	Million dollars	Million dollars	Million dollars	Dollars	Dollars	Dollars	Dollars	1982–1984 dollars	1982–1984 dollars	1982–1984 dollars	1982–1984 dollars
1869	63	—	—	38	—	—	—	—	—	2	9	16	—	15	69	122	—
1870	69	—	—	43	—	—	—	—	—	—	9	15	—	—	74	123	—
1871	74	—	—	46	—	—	—	—	—	—	9	16	—	—	74	131	—
1872	76	—	—	48	—	—	—	—	—	—	10	16	—	—	83	134	—
1873	80	—	—	51	—	—	—	—	—	—	9	16	—	—	79	140	—
1874	84	—	—	55	—	—	—	—	—	—	10	16	—	—	91	146	—
1875	83	—	—	55	—	—	—	—	—	—	9	16	—	—	84	149	—
1876	79	—	—	55	—	—	—	—	—	—	9	15	—	—	86	143	—
1877	79	—	—	56	—	—	—	—	—	—	8	14	—	—	80	140	—
1878	76	—	—	55	—	—	—	—	—	—	8	13	—	—	80	130	—
1879	78	—	—	56	—	—	—	—	—	2	8	13	—	20	78	127	—
1880	84	—	—	58	—	—	—	—	—	—	8	14	—	—	78	137	—
1881	89	—	—	61	—	—	—	—	—	—	9	14	—	—	88	137	—
1882	97	—	—	65	—	—	—	—	—	—	9	15	—	—	89	149	—
1883	103	—	—	68	—	—	—	—	—	—	9	15	—	—	92	153	—
1884	110	—	—	73	—	—	—	—	—	—	10	15	—	—	104	155	—
1885	113	—	—	76	—	—	—	—	—	—	10	15	—	—	106	160	—
1886	116	—	—	79	—	—	—	—	—	—	10	15	—	—	105	158	—
1887	124	—	—	83	—	—	—	—	—	—	10	16	—	—	105	169	—
1888	133	109	—	88	—	22	23	—	—	—	11	17	14	—	119	184	152
1889	141	114	—	92	—	22	26	—	—	2	11	17	14	22	121	187	154
1890	147	121	—	96	—	25	26	—	—	—	11	18	15	—	121	198	165
1891	156	126	—	100	—	26	29	—	—	—	12	18	15	—	132	198	165
1892	164	134	—	105	—	29	30	—	—	—	12	19	15	—	134	211	167
1893	173	142	—	109	—	33	30	—	—	—	12	19	16	—	140	222	187
1894	176	146	—	114	—	33	29	—	—	—	12	18	15	—	143	214	179
1895	183	151	—	117	—	34	33	—	—	—	13	19	15	—	155	226	179
1896	188	155	—	119	—	36	32	—	—	—	13	19	15	—	156	228	180
1897	194	163	—	124	—	39	31	—	—	—	13	19	16	—	156	228	192
1898	200	169	—	129	—	40	31	—	—	—	13	19	16	—	156	228	192
1899	215	180	—	138	—	42	35	—	—	3	14	20	17	36	167	238	202
1900	228	188	—	143	—	44	40	—	—	3	14	21	18	35	165	247	212
1901	238	198	—	151	—	47	40	—	—	3	15	22	18	35	175	257	210
1902	251	205	—	157	—	48	46	—	—	3	16	—	—	34	181	—	—
1903	273	224	—	168	—	56	49	—	—	3	17	23	19	34	191	258	213
1904	292	235	—	177	—	58	56	—	—	4	18	24	20	45	204	272	227

School year beginning	Total expenditures	Current expenditures, day schools: Total	Current expenditures, day schools: Administration	Current expenditures, day schools: Instruction	Current expenditures, day schools: Plant operation and maintenance	Current expenditures, day schools: Other	Capital outlay	Interest on school debt	Other expenditures	Per capita and per pupil expenditures, Current dollars, Total expenditures: Per capita	Current dollars, Total expenditures: Per pupil enrolled	Current dollars, Total expenditures: Per pupil in average daily attendance	Current dollars, Current expenditures: Per pupil in average daily attendance	Constant 1982–1984 dollars, Total expenditures: Per capita	Constant 1982–1984 dollars, Total expenditures: Per pupil enrolled	Constant 1982–1984 dollars, Total expenditures: Per pupil in average daily attendance	Constant 1982–1984 dollars, Current expenditures: Per pupil in average daily attendance
	Bc909	Bc910 [1]	Bc911	Bc912 [2]	Bc913	Bc914 [3]	Bc915 [4,5]	Bc916	Bc917 [6]	Bc918	Bc919	Bc920	Bc921	Bc922	Bc923	Bc924	Bc925
	Million dollars	Million dollars	Million dollars	Million dollars	Million dollars	Million dollars	Million dollars	Million dollars	Million dollars	Dollars	Dollars	Dollars	Dollars	1982–1984 dollars	1982–1984 dollars	1982–1984 dollars	1982–1984 dollars
1905	308	247	—	186	—	61	61	—	—	4	18	26	21	45	200	289	234
1906	337	272	—	202	—	70	65	—	—	4	20	28	23	43	213	298	245
1907	371	298	—	220	—	78	74	—	—	4	22	31	24	43	238	336	260
1908	401	320	—	237	—	83	82	—	—	5	23	32	25	55	254	353	276
1909	426	356	7	260	—	89	70	—	—	5	24	33	28	53	253	348	295
1910	447	371	6	273	—	91	76	—	—	5	25	35	29	53	264	369	306
1911	483	405	9	295	—	101	78	—	—	5	27	36	30	51	277	370	308
1912	522	438	10	316	—	112	84	—	—	5	28	38	32	51	283	384	323
1913	555	463	12	335	—	116	92	—	—	6	29	39	33	60	290	390	330
1914	605	503	13	358	—	131	103	—	—	6	31	40	34	59	307	396	337
1915	641	537	15	378	—	144	104	—	—	6	31	42	35	55	284	385	321
1917	764	629	25	444	133	27	119	15	—	7	37	49	40	46	245	325	265
1919	1,036	861	37	633	146	46	154	18	3	10	48	64	53	50	240	320	265
1921	1,581	1,235	51	903	203	69	306	36	4	15	68	86	67	89	405	512	399
1923	1,821	1,369	55	1,001	221	92	388	59	5	16	75	95	72	94	439	556	421
1925	2,026	1,538	68	1,127	244	99	411	72	5	17	82	102	77	96	463	576	435
1927	2,184	1,706	77	1,220	278	130	383	92	4	18	87	106	83	105	509	620	485
1929	2,317	1,844	79	1,318	295	152	371	93	10	19	90	108	87	114	539	647	521
1931	2,175	1,810	75	1,333	257	144	211	140	13	18	83	98	81	131	606	715	591
1933	1,720	1,516	64	1,121	203	127	59	137	8	14	65	76	67	104	485	567	500
1935	1,969	1,657	67	1,214	233	142	171	133	8	15	75	88	74	108	540	633	532
1937	2,233	1,870	86	1,360	260	164	239	114	10	17	86	100	84	121	610	709	596
1939	2,344	1,942	92	1,403	268	179	258	131	13	18	92	106	88	129	657	757	629
1941	2,323	2,068	101	1,458	289	220	138	109	9	17	95	110	98	104	583	675	601
1943	2,453	2,293	111	1,591	316	276	54	97	9	18	105	125	117	102	597	710	665
1945	2,907	2,707	133	1,854	372	349	111	77	11	21	125	145	136	108	641	744	697
1947	4,311	3,795	170	2,572	526	527	412	76	28	30	180	203	179	124	747	842	743
1949	5,838	4,687	220	3,112	642	713	1,014	101	36	39	232	259	209	162	963	1,075	867
1951	7,344	5,722	266	3,782	757	917	1,477	114	30	48	276	313	244	181	1,042	1,181	921
1953	9,092	6,791	311	4,552	908	1,020	2,055	154	92	57	315	351	265	212	1,171	1,305	985
1955	10,955	8,251	373	5,502	1,072	1,304	2,387	216	101	66	352	388	294	243	1,294	1,426	1,081
1957	13,569	10,252	443	6,901	1,302	1,605	2,853	342	123	79	405	449	341	273	1,401	1,554	1,180
1959	15,613	12,329	528	8,351	1,508	1,943	2,662	490	133	88	433	472	375	297	1,463	1,595	1,267
1961	18,373	14,729	648	10,016	1,760	2,304	2,862	588	194	100	480	530	419	331	1,589	1,755	1,387
1963	21,325	17,218	745	11,750	1,985	2,738	2,978	701	428	113	519	559	460	365	1,674	1,803	1,484
1965	26,248	21,053	938	14,445	2,386	3,284	3,755	792	648	136	613	654	537	420	1,892	2,019	1,657
1967	32,977	26,877	1,249	18,376	2,864	4,388	4,256	978	866	167	737	786	658	480	2,118	2,259	1,891
1969	40,683	34,218	1,607	23,270	3,512	5,829	4,659	1,171	636	202	877	955	816	521	2,260	2,461	2,103

Notes appear at end of table

(continued)

TABLE Bc909–925 Public elementary and secondary school expenditures – by purpose, per capita, and per pupil: 1869–1996 *Continued*

		Current expenditures, day schools								Per capita and per pupil expenditures							
										Current dollars				Constant 1982–1984 dollars			
										Total expenditures			Current expenditures	Total expenditures			Current expenditures
School year beginning	Total expenditures	Total	Administration	Instruction	Plant operation and maintenance	Other	Capital outlay	Interest on school debt	Other expenditures	Per capita	Per pupil enrolled	Per pupil in average daily attendance	Per pupil in average daily attendance	Per capita	Per pupil enrolled	Per pupil in average daily attendance	Per pupil in average daily attendance
	Bc909	Bc910 [1]	Bc911	Bc912 [2]	Bc913	Bc914 [3]	Bc915 [4,5]	Bc916	Bc917 [6]	Bc918	Bc919	Bc920	Bc921	Bc922	Bc923	Bc924	Bc925
	Million dollars	Million dollars	Million dollars	Million dollars	Million dollars	Million dollars	Million dollars	Million dollars	Million dollars	Dollars	Dollars	Dollars	Dollars	1982–1984 dollars	1982–1984 dollars	1982–1984 dollars	1982–1984 dollars
1970	45,500	38,657	1,789	26,224	3,960	6,684	4,552	1,318	973	223	970	1,049	911	551	2,395	2,590	2,249
1971	48,050	41,818	1,876	28,148	4,325	7,469	4,459	1,378	396	232	1,034	1,128	990	555	2,474	2,699	2,368
1972	51,852	45,423	2,018	30,119	4,677	8,609	4,091	1,547	791	248	1,116	1,211	1,077	559	2,514	2,727	2,426
1973	56,970	50,025	2,276	32,609	5,291	9,849	4,978	1,514	453	270	1,244	1,364	1,207	548	2,523	2,767	2,448
1974	64,846	56,661	2,670	36,482	6,136	11,373	5,746	1,737	702	304	1,424	1,545	1,365	565	2,647	2,872	2,537
1975	70,601	62,054	2,808	39,687	6,675	12,884	6,146	1,846	553	328	1,564	1,697	1,504	576	2,749	2,982	2,643
1976	75,014	66,864	3,273	41,869	7,331	14,391	5,344	1,953	853	341	1,673	1,816	1,638	563	2,761	2,997	2,703
1977	80,844	73,058	3,867	45,024	8,096	16,071	5,245	1,952	589	368	1,842	2,002	1,823	564	2,825	3,071	2,796
1978	86,712	78,951	3,896	48,403	8,565	18,087	5,448	1,955	357	390	2,029	2,210	2,020	537	2,795	3,044	2,782
1979	95,962	86,984	4,264	53,258	9,745	—	6,506	1,874	598	427	2,290	2,491	2,272	518	2,779	3,023	2,757
1980	104,125	94,321	—	—	—	—	—	—	—	458 [7]	2,529 [7]	2,742 [7]	2,502	504 [7]	2,782 [7]	3,017 [7]	2,752
1981	111,186	101,109	—	—	—	—	—	—	—	484 [7]	2,754 [7]	2,973 [7]	2,726	502 [7]	2,854 [7]	3,081 [7]	2,825
1982	118,425	108,268	—	—	—	—	—	—	—	510 [7]	2,966 [7]	3,203 [7]	2,955	512 [7]	2,978 [7]	3,216 [7]	2,967
1983	127,500	115,392	—	—	—	—	—	—	—	544 [7]	3,216 [7]	3,471 [7]	3,173	524 [7]	3,095 [7]	3,341 [7]	3,054
1984	137,000	126,337	—	—	—	—	—	—	—	579 [7]	3,456 [7]	3,722 [7]	3,470	538 [7]	3,212 [7]	3,459 [7]	3,225
1985	148,600	137,165	—	83,463	—	—	—	—	—	622 [7]	3,724 [7]	4,020 [7]	3,756	568 [7]	3,398 [7]	3,668 [7]	3,427
1986	160,900	146,365	—	89,559	—	—	—	—	—	667 [7]	3,995 [7]	4,308 [7]	3,970	587 [7]	3,517 [7]	3,792 [7]	3,495
1987	172,400	157,098	—	96,967	—	—	—	—	—	708 [7]	4,310 [7]	4,654 [7]	4,240	598 [7]	3,643 [7]	3,934 [7]	3,584
1988	192,977	173,099	—	101,016	—	—	14,101	3,213	2,564	785	4,738	5,109	4,645	633	3,821	4,120	3,746
1989	212,770	188,229	—	113,550	—	—	17,781	3,776	2,983	853	5,174	5,550	4,980	653	3,959	4,246	3,810
1990	229,430	202,038	—	122,223	—	—	19,771	4,325	3,296	915	5,486	5,885	5,258	672	4,028	4,321	3,860
1991	241,055	211,210	—	128,476	—	—	20,287	5,164	4,394	951	5,629	6,075	5,421	678	4,012	4,330	3,864
1992	252,935	220,948	—	134,971	—	—	22,172	5,437	4,379	986	5,804	6,281	5,584	682	4,017	4,347	3,864
1993	265,307	231,543	—	141,620	—	—	23,747	5,335	4,682	1,024	5,996	6,492	5,767	691	4,046	4,381	3,891
1994	278,966	243,845	—	150,522	—	—	24,454	5,519	5,149	1,066	6,207 [7]	6,724 [7]	5,988 [7]	699	4,073	4,412	3,929
1995	—	—	—	—	—	—	—	—	—	—	6,484 [7]	7,024 [7]	6,255 [7]	—	4,133	4,477	3,987
1996	—	—	—	—	—	—	—	—	—	—	6,804 [7]	7,371 [7]	6,564 [7]	—	4,239	4,593	4,090

[1] In censuses prior to 1917, includes expenditures for interest.

[2] In censuses prior to 1909, includes only expenditures for salaries of teachers and superintendents.

[3] In censuses prior to 1917, includes plant operation and maintenance; in censuses prior to 1909, includes all current expenditures except salaries of teachers and superintendents.

[4] Beginning in 1965, includes capital outlay by state and local school building authorities.

[5] Included in total, noncurrent. Beginning in 1953, includes expenditures for community services, previously included in "current expenditures, day schools."

[6] Beginning in 1988, includes expenditures for property and for buildings and alterations completed by school district staff or contractors.

[7] Estimated.

Sources

Series Bc909–921, 1869–1989, mainly from U.S. Department of Education, *120 Years of American Education: A Statistical Portrait* (1993), Table 22. Original sources listed in *120 Years* and U.S. Bureau of the Census, *Historical Statistics of the United States* (1975), are as follows. All series, except as noted, 1869–1915, U.S. Office of Education, *Annual Report of the United States Commissioner of Education*, various issues; 1917–1955, U.S. Office of Education, *Biennial Survey of Education in the United States*, various issues; 1957–1989, U.S. Department of Education, *Digest of Education Statistics*, annual issues. Series Bc918 and Bc920, gaps in U.S. Office of Education series computed at U.S. Bureau of the Census on the basis of *Historical Statistics of the United States* (1975), series A29, H492, and H520. Series Bc919, Abbott L. Ferriss, *Indicators of Trends in American Education* (Russell Sage Foundation, 1969), Appendix C.

TABLE Bc909–925 Public elementary and secondary school expenditures – by purpose, per capita, and per pupil: 1869–1996 *Continued*

School years following 1989, series Bc909–910, Bc912, and Bc915–917, U.S. Department of Education, *Digest of Education Statistics 1997*, Table 163. Series Bc919–921, *Digest 1997*, Table 169, columns (6), (2), and (3), respectively.

Documentation

Beginning in 1980 all the components of total current expenditures cannot be subdivided. Thus, total current expenditures, series Bc910, is smaller than the sum of the various components, series Bc911–914. See, for example, *Digest 1997*, Table 163, for other components.

Series Bc911. Expenditures for administration include those for the central office staff for administrative functions and all general control that is systemwide and not confined to one school, subject, or narrow phase of school services.

Series Bc912. Instruction expenditures include salaries of instructional staff and clerical assistants, expenditures for free textbooks, school library books, and supplies, and other expenditures for instruction.

Series Bc913. Plant operation and maintenance expenditures include salaries of custodians, engineers, carpenters, painters, and so on; fuel, light, water, and power; and supplies, expenses, and contractual service.

Series Bc914. Other current expenditures include those for fixed charges and for attendance, health, transportation, food, and miscellaneous services.

Series Bc915. Capital outlay includes expenditures for the acquisition of fixed assets or additions to fixed assets (such as land or existing buildings, improvement of grounds, construction of buildings, additions to buildings, remodeling of buildings, and initial or additional equipment).

Series Bc916. Interest includes interest payments on short-term and current loans from current funds, and on bonds from current and sinking funds.

Series Bc917. Other expenditures include expenditures, when separately reported, for summer schools, community colleges, and adult education.

Series Bc918. Equals series Bc909 divided by population figure in *Digest 1997*, Table 15, averaged over the two years of the school year.

Series Bc922–925. Equal series Bc918–921 deflated by the consumer price index, series Cc1. The deflator year is the end of the school year.

TABLE Bc926–928 Private elementary and secondary school receipts, current expenditures, and capital outlay: 1930–1970

Contributed by Claudia Goldin

School year ending	Receipts	Current expenditures and interest	Capital outlay
	Bc926	Bc927	Bc928
	Million dollars	Million dollars	Million dollars
1930	—	200	37
1940	—	205	25
1948	530	—	—
1950	783	654	136
1952	1,028	—	—
1954	1,354	1,000	400
1956	1,627	1,300	400
1958	2,079	1,500	400
1960	2,412	1,993	419
1962	2,457	1,900	400
1964	3,070	2,500	400
1966	3,600	2,900	500
1968	4,200	3,500	500
1970	4,500	3,900	500

Source

U.S. Bureau of the Census, *Historical Statistics: From Colonial Times to the Present* (1975). The underlying sources are: 1930–1958, Department of Education, *Biennial Survey of Education in the United States*, various issues; 1960 to 1970, U.S. Department of Education, *Digest of Education Statistics*, annual issues; U.S. Department of Education, *Projections of Education Statistics*, annual issues.

Documentation

These series are mainly estimated and do not extend past 1970 because of the infrequency of surveys of private elementary and secondary school institutions. See also the text for Table Bc902–908 and Table 909–925.

Series Bc926. Receipts include revenue and nonrevenue receipts. Revenue receipts represent additions to assets (cash) from taxes, appropriations, and other funds that do not incur an obligation that must be met at some future date and do not represent exchanges of property for money. Nonrevenue receipts represent amounts that either incur an obligation that must be met at some future date or change the form of an asset from property to cash and therefore decrease the amount and the value of school property. Money received from loans, sale of bonds, sale of property purchased from capital funds, and proceeds from insurance adjustments constitutes most of the nonrevenue receipts.

Series Bc927. Current expenditures include expenditures for administration, instruction, plant operation and maintenance, and fixed charges, and for attendance, health, transportation, food, and miscellaneous services.

Series Bc928. Capital outlay includes expenditures for the acquisition of fixed assets or additions to fixed assets (such as land or existing buildings, improvement of grounds, construction of buildings, additions to buildings, remodeling of buildings, and initial or additional equipment).

TABLE Bc929–934 Public school transportation – pupils transported and expenditures per pupil: 1929–1994[1, 2]

Contributed by Claudia Goldin

School year beginning	Pupils transported at public expense: Number	Pupils transported at public expense: As a percentage of pupils in average daily attendance	Expenditures for transportation, Current dollars: Total	Expenditures for transportation, Current dollars: Average per pupil transported	Expenditures for transportation, Constant 1982–1984 dollars: Total	Expenditures for transportation, Constant 1982–1984 dollars: Average per pupil transported
	Bc929	Bc930	Bc931	Bc932	Bc933	Bc934
	Number	Percent	Thousand dollars	Dollars	Thousand dollars	Dollars
1929	1,902,826	8.9	54,823	29	328,281	174
1931	2,419,173	10.9	58,078	24	423,927	175
1933	2,794,724	12.4	53,908	19	402,299	142
1935	3,250,658	14.6	62,653	19	450,741	137
1937	3,769,242	16.9	75,637	20	536,433	142
1939	4,144,161	18.8	83,283	20	594,879	143
1941	4,503,081	21.4	92,922	21	570,074	129
1943	4,512,412	23.0	107,754	24	612,239	136
1945	5,056,966	25.5	129,756	26	665,415	133
1947	5,854,041	28.0	176,265	30	731,390	124
1949	6,947,384	31.2	214,504	31	890,058	129
1951	7,697,130	33.1	268,827	35	1,014,442	132
1953	8,411,719	32.8	307,437	37	1,142,888	138
1955	9,695,819	35.0	353,972	37	1,301,368	136
1957	10,861,689	36.5	416,491	38	1,441,145	131
1959	12,225,142	37.6	486,338	40	1,643,034	135
1961	13,222,667	38.1	576,361	44	1,908,480	146
1963	14,475,778	38.7	673,845	47	2,173,694	152
1965	15,536,567	39.7	787,358	51	2,430,117	157
1967	17,130,873	42.0	981,006	57	2,818,983	164
1969	18,198,577	43.4	1,218,557	67	3,140,611	173
1971	19,474,355	46.1	1,507,830	77	3,607,249	184
1973	21,347,039	51.5	1,858,141	87	3,769,049	176
1975	21,772,483	52.8	2,377,313	109	4,178,054	192
1977	21,800,000	54.4	2,731,041	125	4,188,713	192
1979	21,713,515	56.7	3,833,145	177	4,651,875	215
1980	22,272,000	59.1	4,408,000	198	4,849,285	218
1981	22,246,000	60.0	4,793,000	215	4,966,839	223
1982	22,199,000	60.6	5,000,000	225	5,020,080	226
1983	22,031,000	60.6	5,284,000	240	5,085,659	231
1984	22,320,000	61.3	5,722,000	256	5,317,844	238
1985	22,041,000	60.3	6,123,000	278	5,586,679	254
1986	22,397,000	60.8	6,551,000	292	5,766,725	257
1987	22,158,000	59.8	6,888,000	311	5,822,485	263
1988	22,635,000	60.7	7,550,000	334	6,088,710	269
1989	22,459,000	59.4	8,030,990	358	6,144,598	274
1990	22,000,000	57.3	8,678,954	394	6,372,213	289
1991	23,165,000	59.5	8,769,754	379	6,250,716	270
1992	23,439,000	59.2	9,252,300	395	6,402,976	273
1993	23,857,752	59.4	9,627,155	404	6,496,056	273
1994	23,693,000	58.2	9,889,137	417	6,488,935	274

[1] Expenditures for transportation exclude capital outlay through 1979 and from 1989 to 1994. From 1980 to 1988, total transportation figures include capital outlay.

[2] Number of pupils transported (1977 and 1980–1994) and expenditures for transportation (1980–1988) are estimates based on data appearing in January issues of *School Bus Fleet*.

Source

Series Bc929–932, 1929–1988, U.S. Department of Education, *120 Years of Education: A Statistical Portrait* (1993), Table 13. The underlying sources are: U.S. Department of Education, *Statistics of State School Systems*; U.S. Department of Education, *Revenues and Expenditures for Public Elementary and Secondary Education*; U.S. Department of Education, unpublished data; and Bobbit Publishing, *School Bus Fleet*, January issues. 1989–1994, U.S. Department of Education, *Digest of Education Statistics 1997*, Table 51.

Documentation

More than half of U.S. public school children ride buses to school, often because walking to school would be inconvenient or unsafe. Pupil transportation services are also provided as a result of state or local legislation for reorganization of school systems and consolidation of widely scattered school attendance areas and the objective of school districts to achieve equalization of educational opportunity.

Expenditures of public funds for transportation include salaries, vehicle replacement, supplies and maintenance for vehicles and garages, transportation insurance, contracted services, fares for public transportation, and payments in lieu of transportation.

Data through 1979 are based on reports by state education agencies to the U.S. National Center for Education Statistics. Data for later years are estimates based on data reported by *School Bus Fleet*.

Series Bc930. Equals series Bc929 as a percentage of series Bc94.

Series Bc932. Equals series Bc931 divided by series Bc929.

Series Bc933–934. Equal series Bc931–932 deflated by the consumer price index, series Cc1. The deflator year is the end of the school year.

TABLE Bc935–949 Current-fund revenue of higher education institutions, by source of funds: 1889–1994

Contributed by Claudia Goldin

		Educational and general revenue												Other revenue		
				Government												
School year beginning	Total current-fund revenue	Total	Student tuition and fees	Federal	State	Local	Endowment income	Private gifts and grants	Organized activities related to educational departments	Sales and services of educational activities	Student aid	Other	Hospitals	Independent operations	Auxiliary enterprises
	Bc935	Bc936	Bc937	Bc938 [1]	Bc939	Bc940	Bc941	Bc942	Bc943 [2,3]	Bc944 [3]	Bc945 [4]	Bc946	Bc947 [2,3]	Bc948 [5]	Bc949
	Thousand dollars	Thousand dollars	Thousand dollars	Thousand dollars	Thousand dollars	Thousand dollars	Thousand dollars	Thousand dollars	Thousand dollars	Thousand dollars	Thousand dollars	Thousand dollars	Thousand dollars	Thousand dollars	Thousand dollars
1889	—	21,464	—	—	—	—	—	—	—	—	—	—	—	—	—
1899	—	35,084	—	—	—	—	—	—	—	—	—	—	—	—	—
1909	76,883	67,917	18,463	4,607	20,937	—	12,584	3,551	—	—	—	7,775	—	—	8,966
1919	199,922	172,929	42,254	12,783 [6]	61,690 [6,8]	— [8]	26,482	7,584	—	—	—	22,135	—	—	26,993
1929	554,511	494,092	144,126	20,658	150,847 [8]	— [8]	68,605	26,172	—	—	11,027	72,657	—	—	60,419
1931	566,264	441,987	150,649	— [7]	174,663 [7,8]	— [8]	60,903	29,948	—	—	10,998	14,826	21,008	—	103,269
1933	486,362	380,620	138,257	19,827	117,551 [8]	— [8]	55,534	27,468	—	—	9,653	12,330	17,759	—	87,983
1935	597,585	466,163	158,134	43,234	119,585	21,050	60,090	37,115	—	—	—	26,955	24,943	—	106,479
1937	652,631	494,161	178,996	29,345	140,959	22,091	70,654	36,908	—	—	—	15,208	27,947	—	130,523
1939	715,211	538,511	200,897	38,860	151,222	24,392	71,304	40,453	—	—	—	11,383	32,777	—	143,923
1941	783,720	585,988	201,365	58,232	166,532	27,057	74,075	45,916	—	—	—	12,811	40,308	—	157,424
1943	1,047,298	810,077	154,485	308,162	175,169	26,449	75,196	50,449	—	—	—	20,167	53,577	—	183,644
1945	1,169,394	857,874	214,345	197,250	225,161	31,005	89,763	77,572	—	—	—	22,779	67,084	—	244,436
1947	2,027,051	1,469,172	304,601	526,476	352,281	47,521	86,680	91,468	—	—	23,821	36,324	92,725	—	465,154
1949	2,374,645	1,751,393	394,610	524,319	491,958	61,378	96,341	118,627	—	—	29,535	34,625	111,987	—	511,265
1951	2,562,451	1,916,463	446,591	451,011	611,302	72,013	112,859	149,826	—	—	32,027	40,834	136,442	—	509,546
1953	2,945,550	2,205,901	551,424	417,097	740,043	88,198	127,475	190,899	—	—	32,212	58,553	164,880	—	574,769
1955	3,603,370	2,719,804	722,215	489,800	878,349	106,857	145,000	245,085	—	—	52,364	80,133	191,829	—	691,737
1957	4,641,387	3,650,492	934,203	707,048	1,138,454	129,324	181,585	324,426	46,877	47,302	70,058	71,214	152,078	—	838,817
1959	5,785,537	4,593,485	1,157,481	1,036,988	1,374,476	151,715	206,619	382,570	57,102	45,423	92,902	88,208	187,769	—	1,004,283
1961	7,429,379	5,919,927	1,499,924	1,537,697	1,668,289	191,188	232,289	450,145	65,533	52,252	118,073	104,537	238,567	—	1,270,885
1963	9,543,514	7,642,763	1,892,839	2,160,889	2,110,981	239,851	266,157	550,684	69,443	64,742	148,093	139,082	293,777	—	1,606,974
1965	12,734,225	10,345,108	2,640,641	2,587,893	2,894,893	303,401	288,833	613,718	373,573	34,680	309,855	297,621	250,000 [9]	—	2,139,117
1966	14,561,039	11,111,063	2,972,050	2,200,276	3,371,986	405,561	328,068	765,927	317,627	116,862	394,386	238,320	253,790	951,668	2,244,518
1967	16,825,199	13,288,034	3,380,294	2,695,681	4,181,070	503,661	363,990	848,450	399,821	118,618	497,930	298,519	290,000	765,495	2,481,670
1968	18,874,602	14,901,466	3,814,160	2,924,547	4,812,482	614,462	413,276	915,909	421,301	127,461	571,536	286,332	497,280	708,542	2,767,314
1969	21,515,242	17,144,194	4,419,845	3,146,869	5,787,910	774,803	447,275	1,001,454	484,977	127,800	658,016	295,245	619,578	768,498	2,982,973
1970	23,879,188	19,101,148	5,021,211	3,359,027	6,502,813	907,274	470,655	1,091,654	524,697	137,775	709,101	376,941	821,478	831,324	3,125,238
1971	26,234,258	20,964,859	5,594,095	3,659,506	7,120,982	991,034	480,806	1,208,070	590,448	148,711	764,590	406,616	1,006,865	953,577	3,308,957
1972	28,606,217	22,927,142	6,010,926	3,994,490	7,917,825	1,143,529	515,041	1,300,343	610,342	163,482	800,075	471,090	1,181,390	1,030,751	3,466,934
1973	31,712,452	25,510,428	6,500,101	4,176,226	9,182,189	1,263,145	576,915	1,430,982	611,678	222,382	882,585	664,227	1,436,481	1,031,314	3,734,229
1974	35,686,902	28,373,036	7,232,908	4,990,969	10,857,376	1,424,392	717,915	1,744,967	—	554,882	—	849,625	2,152,079	1,081,585	4,080,202
1975	39,703,166	31,597,873	8,171,942	5,413,847	12,260,885	1,616,975	687,470	1,917,036	—	645,420	—	884,298	2,494,340	1,063,331	4,547,622
1976	43,436,827	34,218,636	9,024,932	5,729,818	13,285,684	1,626,908	764,788	2,105,070	—	779,058	—	902,377	2,859,376	1,439,213	4,919,602
1977	47,034,032	37,581,559	9,855,270	6,112,805	14,746,166	1,744,230	832,286	2,320,368	—	882,715	—	1,087,719	3,268,956	855,696 [10]	5,327,821
1978	51,837,789	41,325,437	10,704,171	6,843,736	16,363,784	1,573,018	985,242	2,489,366	—	1,037,130	—	1,328,991	3,763,453	1,007,590	5,741,309
1979	58,519,982	46,534,023	11,930,340	7,771,726	18,378,299	1,587,552	1,176,627	2,808,075	—	1,239,439	—	1,641,965	4,373,384	1,131,117	6,481,458

Notes appear at end of table

(continued)

TABLE Bc935–949 Current-fund revenue of higher education institutions, by source of funds: 1889–1994 *Continued*

		Educational and general revenue											Other revenue		
	Total current-fund revenue	Total	Student tuition and fees	Government: Federal	Government: State	Government: Local	Endowment income	Private gifts and grants	Organized activities related to educational departments	Sales and services of educational activities	Student aid	Other	Hospitals	Independent operations	Auxiliary enterprises
School	Bc935	Bc936	Bc937	Bc938 [1]	Bc939	Bc940	Bc941	Bc942	Bc943 [2,3]	Bc944 [3]	Bc945 [4]	Bc946	Bc947 [2,3]	Bc948 [5]	Bc949
year beginning	Thousand dollars	Thousand dollars	Thousand dollars	Thousand dollars	Thousand dollars	Thousand dollars	Thousand dollars	Thousand dollars	Thousand dollars	Thousand dollars	Thousand dollars	Thousand dollars	Thousand dollars	Thousand dollars	Thousand dollars
1980	65,584,789	52,048,276	13,773,259	8,478,709	20,106,222	1,790,740	1,364,443	3,176,670	—	1,409,730	—	1,948,503	4,980,346	1,268,877	7,287,290
1981	72,190,856	56,958,692	15,774,038	8,319,817	21,848,791	1,937,669	1,596,813	3,563,558	—	1,582,922	—	2,335,084	5,838,565	1,271,988	8,121,611
1982	77,595,726	60,844,948	17,776,041	8,181,402	23,065,636	2,031,353	1,720,677	4,052,649	—	1,723,484	—	2,293,706	6,531,562	1,449,695	8,769,521
1983	84,417,287	66,296,893	19,714,884	8,782,803	24,706,990	2,192,275	1,873,945	4,415,275	—	1,970,747	—	2,639,973	7,040,662	1,623,363	9,456,369
1984	92,472,694	73,003,805	21,283,329	9,615,221	27,583,011	2,387,212	2,096,298	4,896,325	—	2,126,927	—	3,015,483	7,474,575	1,893,904	10,100,410
1985	100,437,616	79,298,586	23,116,605	10,466,491	29,911,500	2,544,506	2,275,898	5,410,905	—	2,373,494	—	3,199,186	8,226,635	2,238,259	10,674,136
1986	108,809,827	85,488,436	25,705,827	11,224,680	31,309,303	2,799,321	2,377,958	5,952,682	—	2,641,906	—	3,476,760	9,277,834	2,679,369	11,364,188
1987	117,340,109	91,863,743	27,836,781	11,869,932	33,517,166	3,006,263	2,586,441	6,359,282	—	2,918,090	—	3,769,787	10,626,566	2,902,022	11,947,778
1988	128,501,638	100,598,033	30,806,566	12,837,218	36,031,208	3,363,676	2,914,396	7,060,730	—	3,315,620	—	4,268,618	11,991,265	3,056,760	12,855,580
1989	139,635,477	109,241,902	33,926,060	14,016,432	38,349,239	3,639,902	3,143,696	7,781,422	—	3,632,100	—	4,753,051	13,216,664	3,238,442	13,938,469
1990	149,766,051	116,266,700	37,434,462	14,789,530	39,480,874	3,931,239	3,268,629	8,361,265	—	4,054,703	—	4,945,998	15,149,672	3,446,552	14,903,127
1991	161,395,896	124,736,078	41,559,037	16,172,436	40,586,907	4,159,876	3,442,009	8,977,271	—	4,520,890	—	5,317,651	17,240,338	3,660,881	15,758,599
1992	170,880,503	132,454,897	45,346,071	17,375,823	41,247,955	4,444,875	3,627,773	9,659,977	—	5,037,901	—	5,714,523	18,124,015	3,638,741	16,662,850
1993	179,226,601	139,330,947	48,646,538	18,678,021	41,910,288	4,998,306	3,669,536	10,203,062	—	5,294,030	—	5,931,167	18,959,776	3,398,364	17,537,514
1994	189,120,570	148,144,130	51,506,876	19,703,043	44,343,012	5,165,961	3,988,217	10,866,749	—	5,603,251	—	6,967,023	19,100,217	3,540,129	18,336,094

[1] Excludes federally funded research and development centers (FFRDCs) from 1966 to 1989.

[2] In censuses prior to 1957, revenue from hospitals includes organized activities related to educational departments.

[3] After 1973, data are included under sales and services and hospital revenue.

[4] Beginning in 1974, included under the source of student aid money.

[5] Primarily limited to FFRDCs. Where separate data are not shown, included under federal.

[6] Federal includes universities, colleges, and professional schools only; teachers and normal colleges included under state.

[7] Federal included under state.

[8] Local included under state.

[9] Estimated.

[10] Sharp decrease from previous year caused by a change in jurisdiction of one of the FFRDCs.

Source

1889–1989, U.S. Department of Education, *120 Years of American Education: A Statistical Portrait* (1993), Table 33. The underlying sources are: U.S. Office of Education, *Annual Report of the United States Commissioner of Education*; U.S. Office of Education, *Biennial Survey of Education in the United States*; U.S. Department of Education, *Financial Statistics of Institutions of Higher Education*, various issues; U.S. Department of Education, *Digest of Education Statistics*, annual issues; and unpublished data. 1990–1994, *Digest of Education Statistics 1997*, Table 324.

Documentation

Omitted from this table is income that is either so incidental in its nature, so irregular in its frequency, or so minor in its amount as to make its classification difficult or impractical. The most common types of such income are: (1) interest on current funds, (2) rent of institutional property for noninstitutional purposes, (3) transcript fees of students, and (4) library fines.

Series Bc935. Total current-fund revenue represents funds accruing to, or received by, higher education institutions, usable for their recurring day-to-day activities.

Series Bc936. Educational and general revenues are those available to the regular or customary activities of an institution and are part of, contributory to, or necessary to its instructional or research program. Such activities include salaries and travel of faculty and administrative or other employees; purchase of supplies or material for current use in classrooms, libraries, laboratories, or offices; and operation and maintenance of the educational plant.

Series Bc937. Income from students' tuition and fees represents funds (matriculation, tuition, laboratory, library, health, and other fees, but not charges for rooms or meals) regularly paid by students themselves or for them by relatives or philanthropic groups.

Series Bc941. Endowment income is derived from invested funds. Only the income of the endowment funds is to be used for the current purposes of the institution. If funds are temporarily placed in the endowment fund, the right to withdraw them being reserved by the donor or the governing board of the institution concerned, they are known as "funds functioning as endowment" and are not subject to the principle of "once endowment, always endowment."

Series Bc942. Private gifts and grants are voluntary contributions from philanthropically minded individuals and organizations to the various institutions of higher education.

Series Bc943–944. Sales and services of educational activities and of organized activities related to them are frequently referred to as "related activities." The term includes all the incidental earnings of an institution, such as sales of livestock or dairy products of an agricultural school; tuition and other income of a laboratory school, a demonstration school, or a museum; fees for care at a medical or dental clinic; and other income of the nature derived from services directly connected with the instructional program of the institution.

TABLE Bc935–949 Current-fund revenue of higher education institutions, by source of funds: 1889–1994 *Continued*

Series Bc945. Student-aid funds are funds having to do with the provision of scholarships, fellowships, prizes, and student-financed aid of any type not involving employment by or repayment to the institution.

Series Bc946. Other sources of income include annuity and plant funds. Annuity funds are funds acquired subject to the condition that the recipient institution pay a stipulated sum of money annually or at other regular intervals to a designated beneficiary or beneficiaries, not necessarily the same person as the donor. These payments continue until the death of the beneficiary (the last beneficiary, if more than one), at which time the principal of the fund becomes the property of the institution. Plant funds are funds that have been, or are to be, invested in buildings, grounds, furniture, scientific equipment, or other permanent physical property of the institution. Real estate held for direct educational or auxiliary use by the institution is thus part of the plant-fund group.

Series Bc949. Revenue from auxiliary enterprises and activities includes income of dormitories, dining halls, cafeterias, union buildings, college bookstores, university presses, student hospitals, faculty housing, intercollegiate athletic programs, concerts, industrial plants operated on a student self-help basis, and other enterprises conducted primarily for students and staff and intended to be self-supporting.

TABLE Bc950–967 Current-fund expenditures of higher education institutions, by function and per student: 1929–1994

Contributed by Claudia Goldin

		Educational and general expenditures							
	Total current-fund expenditures	Total	Administration and general expense	Instruction and departmental research	Organized research	Libraries	Plant operation and maintenance	Organized activities related to instructional departments	Other sponsored programs
	Bc950	Bc951	Bc952	Bc953	Bc954 [1]	Bc955	Bc956	Bc957 [2]	Bc958
School year beginning	Thousand dollars	Thousand dollars	Thousand dollars	Thousand dollars	Thousand dollars	Thousand dollars	Thousand dollars	Thousand dollars	Thousand dollars
1929	507,142	377,903	42,633	221,598	18,007	9,622	61,061	— [6]	—
1931	536,523	420,633	47,232	232,645	21,978	11,379	56,797	21,297	—
1933	469,329	369,661	43,155	203,332	17,064	13,387	51,046	14,155	—
1935	541,391	419,883	48,069	225,143	22,097	15,531	56,802	20,241	—
1937	614,385	475,191	56,406	253,006	25,213	17,588	62,738	24,031	—
1939	674,688	521,990	62,827	280,248	27,266	19,487	69,612	27,225	—
1941	738,169	572,465	66,968	298,558	34,287	19,763	72,594	37,771	—
1943	974,118	753,846	69,668	334,189	58,456	20,452	81,201	48,415	97,044 [7]
1945	1,088,422	820,326	104,808	375,122	86,812	26,560	110,947	60,604	—
1947	1,883,269	1,391,594	171,829	657,945	159,090	44,208	201,996	85,346	—
1949	2,245,661	1,706,444	213,070	780,994	225,341	56,147	225,110	119,108	—
1951	2,471,008	1,960,481	233,844	823,117	317,928	60,612	240,446	147,854	—
1953	2,882,864	2,345,331	288,147	960,556	372,643	72,944	277,874	186,905	—
1955	3,499,463	2,861,858	355,207	1,140,655	500,793	85,563	324,229	222,007	—
1957	4,509,666	3,734,350	473,945	1,465,603	727,776	109,715	406,226	238,455	—
1959	5,601,376	4,685,258	583,224	1,793,320	1,022,353	135,384	469,943	294,255	—
1961	7,154,526	5,997,007	730,429	2,202,443	1,474,406	177,362	564,225	375,040	—
1963	9,177,677	7,725,433	957,512	2,801,707	1,973,383	236,718	686,054	458,507	—
1965	12,509,489	10,376,630	1,251,107	3,756,175	2,448,300	346,248	844,506	558,170	155,202
1966	14,230,341	10,724,974	1,445,074	4,356,413	1,565,102	415,903	969,275	591,848	350,950
1967	16,480,786	12,847,350	1,738,946	5,139,179	1,933,473	493,266	1,127,290	350,711	514,294
1968	18,481,583	14,718,140	2,277,585	5,941,972	2,034,074	571,572	1,337,903	535,269	668,483
1969	21,043,110	16,845,210	2,627,993	6,883,844	2,144,076	652,596	1,541,698	648,089	769,253
1970	23,375,197	18,714,642	2,983,911	7,804,410	2,209,338	716,212	1,730,664	693,011	890,507
1971	25,559,560	20,441,878	3,344,215	8,443,261	2,265,282	764,481	1,927,553	779,728	1,059,989
1972	27,955,624	22,400,379	3,713,068	9,243,641	2,394,261	840,727	2,141,162	791,290	1,284,085
1973	30,713,581	24,653,849	4,200,955	10,219,118	2,480,450	939,023	2,494,057	838,170	1,355,027
1974	35,057,563	27,547,620	4,495,391	11,797,823	3,132,132	1,001,868	2,786,768	1,253,824	—
1975	38,903,177	30,598,685	5,240,066	13,094,943	3,287,364	1,223,723	3,082,959	1,248,670	—
1976	42,599,816	33,151,681	5,590,669	14,031,145	3,600,067	1,250,314	3,436,705	1,544,646	—
1977	45,970,790	36,256,604	6,177,029	15,336,229	3,919,830	1,348,747	3,795,043	1,781,160	—
1978	50,720,984	39,833,116	6,832,004	16,662,820	4,447,760	1,426,614	4,178,574	2,044,386	—
1979	56,913,588	44,542,843	7,621,143	18,496,717	5,099,151	1,623,811	4,700,070	2,252,577	—
1980	64,052,938	50,073,805	8,681,513	20,733,166	5,657,719	1,759,784	5,350,310	2,513,502	—
1981	70,339,448	54,848,752	9,648,069	22,962,527	5,929,894	1,922,416	5,979,281	2,734,038	—
1982	75,935,749	58,929,218	10,412,233	24,673,293	6,265,280	2,039,671	6,391,596	3,047,220	—
1983	81,993,360	63,741,276	11,561,260	26,436,308	6,723,534	2,231,149	6,729,825	3,300,003	—
1984	89,951,263	70,061,324	12,765,452	28,777,183	7,551,892	2,361,793	7,345,482	3,712,460	—

Notes appear at end of table

(continued)

TABLE Bc950–967 Current-fund expenditures of higher education institutions, by function and per student: 1929–1994 *Continued*

School year beginning	Total current-fund expenditures	Educational and general expenditures: Total	Administration and general expense	Instruction and departmental research	Organized research	Libraries	Plant operation and maintenance	Organized activities related to instructional departments	Other sponsored programs
	Bc950	Bc951	Bc952	Bc953	Bc954 [1]	Bc955	Bc956	Bc957 [2]	Bc958
	Thousand dollars	Thousand dollars	Thousand dollars	Thousand dollars	Thousand dollars	Thousand dollars	Thousand dollars	Thousand dollars	Thousand dollars
1985	97,535,742	76,127,965	13,913,724	31,032,099	8,437,367	2,551,331	7,605,226	4,116,061	—
1986	105,763,557	82,955,555	15,060,576	33,711,146	9,352,309	2,441,184	7,819,032	5,134,267	—
1987	113,786,476	89,157,430	16,171,015	35,833,563	10,350,931	2,836,498	8,230,986	5,305,083	—
1988	123,867,184	96,803,377	17,309,956	38,812,690	11,432,170	3,009,870	8,739,895	5,894,409	—
1989	134,655,571	105,585,076	19,062,179	42,145,987	12,505,961	3,254,239	9,458,262	6,183,405	—
1990	146,087,836	114,139,901	20,751,966	45,496,117	13,444,040	3,343,892	10,062,581	6,706,881	—
1991	156,189,161	121,567,157	21,984,118	47,997,196	14,261,554	3,595,834	10,346,580	6,981,184	—
1992	165,241,040	128,977,968	23,414,977	50,340,914	15,291,309	3,684,852	10,783,727	7,388,118	—
1993	173,350,617	136,024,350	24,489,022	52,775,599	16,117,610	3,908,412	11,368,496	7,769,499	—
1994	182,968,610	144,158,002	25,904,821	55,719,707	17,109,541	4,165,761	11,745,905	8,112,930	—

School year beginning	Educational and general expenditures: Extension and public service	Scholarship and fellowship	Other general expenditures	Auxiliary enterprises	Independent operations	Hospitals	Other current expenditures	Educational and general expenditures per student in fall enrollment: Current dollars	Constant 1982–1984 dollars
	Bc959	Bc960 [3]	Bc961 [4]	Bc962	Bc963 [1]	Bc964 [2]	Bc965 [4]	Bc966 [5]	Bc967 [5]
	Thousand dollars	Thousand dollars	Thousand dollars	Thousand dollars	Thousand dollars	Thousand dollars	Thousand dollars	Dollars	1982–1984 dollars
1929	24,982	—	—	3,127	—	—	126,112 [6]	343	2,054
1931	24,066	—	5,239	90,897	—	—	24,993	364	2,657
1933	20,020	—	7,502	78,730	—	—	20,938	350	2,612
1935	29,426	—	2,580	95,332	—	—	26,176	348	2,504
1937	34,189	—	2,020	115,620	—	—	23,574	352	2,496
1939	35,325	—	—	124,184	—	—	28,514	349	2,493
1941	42,525	—	—	137,328	—	—	28,375	408	2,503
1943	44,421	—	—	199,344	—	—	20,928	653	3,710
1945	55,473	—	—	242,028	—	—	26,068	489	2,508
1947	71,180	—	—	438,988	—	—	52,687	595	2,469
1949	86,674	—	—	476,401	—	—	62,816	698	2,896
1951	97,408	39,272	—	477,672	—	—	32,855	933	3,521
1953	112,227	74,035	—	537,533	—	—	—	1,051	3,907
1955	137,914	95,490	—	637,605	—	—	—	1,079	3,967
1957	175,256	129,935	7,439	775,316	—	—	—	1,124	3,889
1959	205,595	172,050	9,134	916,117	—	—	—	1,287	4,348
1961	244,337	228,765	—	1,157,517	—	—	—	1,447	4,791
1963	297,350	300,370	13,832	1,452,244	—	—	—	1,616	5,213
1965	438,385	425,524	153,013	1,887,744	—	—	245,115	1,753	5,410
1966	226,566	583,390	220,453	2,060,130	951,668	253,790	239,780	1,678	5,024
1967	597,544	712,425	240,222	2,302,419	765,495	290,000	275,523	1,859	5,342
1968	536,527	814,755	—	2,539,183	697,317	526,943	—	1,959	5,338
1969	593,067	984,594	—	2,769,276	757,388	671,236	—	2,104	5,423
1970	588,390	1,098,198	—	2,988,407	829,596	842,552	—	2,181	5,385
1971	615,997	1,241,372	—	3,178,272	940,825	998,585	—	2,284	5,464
1972	669,735	1,322,411	—	3,337,789	1,033,746	1,183,709	—	2,431	5,475
1973	730,560	1,396,488	—	3,613,256	1,014,872	1,431,604	—	2,568	5,209
1974	1,097,788	1,449,542	532,485	4,073,590	1,085,590	2,350,763	—	2,694	5,007
1975	1,238,603	1,635,859	546,498	4,476,841	1,132,016	2,695,635	—	2,736	4,808
1976	1,343,404	1,770,214	584,515	4,858,328	1,434,738	3,155,069	—	3,010	4,967
1977	1,425,294	1,839,298	633,973	5,261,477	855,054	3,597,655	—	3,213	4,928
1978	1,593,097	1,944,599	703,262	5,749,974	1,007,119	4,130,775	—	3,538	4,873
1979	1,816,521	2,200,468	732,385	6,485,608	1,127,728	4,757,409	—	3,850	4,672

Notes appear at end of table

TABLE Bc950–967 Current-fund expenditures of higher education institutions, by function and per student: 1929–1994 *Continued*

	Educational and general expenditures							Educational and general expenditures per student in fall enrollment	
	Extension and public service	Scholarship and fellowship	Other general expenditures	Auxiliary enterprises	Independent operations	Hospitals	Other current expenditures	Current dollars	Constant 1982–1984 dollars
	Bc959	Bc960 [3]	Bc961 [4]	Bc962	Bc963 [1]	Bc964 [2]	Bc965 [4]	Bc966 [5]	Bc967 [5]
School year beginning	Thousand dollars	Thousand dollars	Thousand dollars	Thousand dollars	Thousand dollars	Thousand dollars	Thousand dollars	Dollars	1982–1984 dollars
1980	2,057,770	2,504,525	815,516	7,288,089	1,257,934	5,433,111	—	4,139	4,553
1981	2,203,726	2,684,945	783,854	7,997,632	1,258,777	6,234,287	—	4,433	4,594
1982	2,320,478	2,922,897	856,548	8,614,316	1,406,126	6,986,089	—	4,742	4,761
1983	2,499,203	3,301,673	958,321	9,250,196	1,622,233	7,379,654	—	5,114	4,922
1984	2,861,095	3,670,355	1,015,613	10,012,248	1,867,550	8,010,141	—	5,723	5,319
1985	3,119,533	4,160,174	1,192,449	10,528,303	2,187,361	8,692,113	—	6,216	5,672
1986	3,448,453	4,776,100	1,212,488	11,037,333	2,597,655	9,173,014	—	6,635	5,841
1987	3,786,362	5,325,358	1,317,633	11,399,953	2,822,632	10,406,461	—	6,984	5,904
1988	4,227,323	5,918,666	1,458,397	12,280,063	2,958,962	11,824,782	—	7,415	5,980
1989	4,689,758	6,655,544	1,629,742	13,203,984	3,187,224	12,679,286	—	7,799	5,967
1990	5,076,177	7,551,184	1,707,063	14,272,247	3,349,824	14,325,865	—	8,259	6,064
1991	5,489,298	9,060,000	1,851,393	14,966,100	3,551,592	16,104,313	—	8,466	6,034
1992	5,935,095	10,148,373	1,990,603	15,561,508	3,651,891	17,049,672	—	8,903	6,161
1993	6,242,414	11,238,010	2,115,288	16,429,341	3,387,323	17,509,603	—	9,509	6,416
1994	6,691,485	12,285,328	2,422,524	17,204,917	3,534,332	18,071,359	—	10,108	6,633

[1] Through 1965, expenditures for federally funded research and development centers are included under organized research.

[2] From 1931 through 1965, expenditures for hospitals and independent operations included under organized activities related to instructional departments.

[3] Through 1949, scholarship and fellowship expenditures included under other current expenditures.

[4] Categorization of physical plant assents changes over time. See text.

[5] Data for 1929–1945 are based on school-year enrollment.

[6] Organized activities related to instructional departments included under other current expenditures.

[7] Expenditures for federal contract courses.

Sources

1929–1989, U.S. Department of Education, *120 Years of Education: A Statistical Portrait* (1993), Table 34; 1990–1994, U.S. Department of Education, *Digest of Education Statistics 1997*, Table 334. The underlying sources are: 1929–1958, U.S. Department of Education (Office of Education), *Biennial Survey of Education in the United States*, various issues; 1960 to 1963, U.S. Office of Education, *Higher Education Finances* (1968), and unpublished tabulations; 1965–1994, U.S. Department of Education, *Financial Statistics of Institutions of Higher Education: Current Funds, Revenues and Expenditures*, various issues; and Integrated Postsecondary Education Data System (IPEDS), "Finance" survey.

Documentation

Expenditure data were not tabulated for all institutions of higher education until 1930. Prior to that year, they were collected from land-grant institutions and teacher-education institutions only. Other professional schools and non–land-grant institutions were omitted from the surveys.

The data reflect limitations of survey availability and comparability. Major changes in data collection forms in 1965 and 1974 cause significant comparability problems among the three time periods 1929–1963, 1965–1973, and 1974 to the present. The largest problems affect hospitals, independent operations, organized research, other sponsored programs, extension and public service, and scholarships and fellowships.

Series Bc954. Organized research expenditures cover research programs of sufficient magnitude to warrant carrying them separately in the finance budget.

Series Bc956. Plant operation and maintenance expenditures include wages of janitors and other caretakers; cost of fuel, light, trucking of materials about the campuses and repairs to buildings; and other costs connected with keeping the physical plant in good order.

Series Bc957. Expenditures for conducting laboratory or demonstration schools, medical-school hospitals, dental clinics, home-economics cafeterias, agricultural college creameries, college-operated industries, and other activities closely connected with the instructional program but not actually integral parts of the program are included.

Series Bc958. Includes all separately budgeted programs, other than research, that are supported by sponsors outside the institution. Examples are training programs, workshops, and training and instructional institutes. For years when data are not listed, most expenditures for these programs are included under extension and public service, series Bc959.

Series Bc959. Extension and public service expenditures cover correspondence courses, radio and television courses, adult study courses and other non–degree-credit courses, institutes, public lectures, cooperative extension in land-grant institutions, radio and television stations, and similar media for carrying the work of an institution beyond its traditional and customary campus activities.

Series Bc963. Generally includes only those expenditures associated with federally funded research and development centers (FFRDCs).

Series Bc961 and Bc965. For 1965–1967, series Bc965 includes current expenditures for physical plant assets. Starting in 1968, the educational and general expenditures for physical plant assets are included under series Bc965.

Series Bc967. Equals series Bc966 deflated by the consumer price index, series Cc1. The year of the deflator is that of the end of the school year.

TABLE Bc968–975 Property value, endowments, and liabilities of higher education institutions: 1899–1994[1]

Contributed by Claudia Goldin

School year beginning	Total assets	Physical plant: Total	Physical plant: Land	Physical plant: Buildings	Physical plant: Equipment	Endowment (book value)	Endowment (market value)	Liabilities of plant funds
	Bc968	Bc969	Bc970	Bc971[2]	Bc972	Bc973[3]	Bc974[3]	Bc975
	Thousand dollars	Thousand dollars	Thousand dollars	Thousand dollars	Thousand dollars	Thousand dollars	Thousand dollars	Thousand dollars
1899	448,597	253,599	—	—	—	194,998[4]	—	—
1909	781,255	457,594	92,359	297,153	68,082	323,661[4]	—	—
1919	1,316,404	747,333	128,922	495,920	122,491	569,071[4]	—	—
1929	3,437,117	2,065,049	304,114	1,490,014	270,921	1,372,068[4]	—	—
1935	3,913,028	2,359,418	334,085	1,636,722	388,611	1,553,610[4]	—	—
1937	4,208,695	2,556,075	313,665	1,811,309	431,101	1,652,620	—	—
1939	4,440,063	2,753,780	—	—	—	1,686,283	—	—
1941	4,525,925	2,759,261	—	—	—	1,766,664[4]	—	—
1947	6,076,212	3,691,725	—	—	—	2,384,487	—	—
1949	7,401,187	4,799,964	—	—	—	2,601,223[4]	—	—
1951	9,241,725	6,373,195	—	—	—	2,868,530	—	—
1953	10,717,082	7,523,193	—	—	—	3,193,889	—	—
1955	12,561,046	8,858,907	624,467	6,697,648	1,536,792	3,702,139	—	894,383
1957	15,770,197	11,124,489	733,182	8,540,429	1,850,878	4,645,708	—	1,444,602
1959	18,870,628	13,548,548	842,664	10,472,478	2,233,407	5,322,080	—	1,964,306
1961	22,761,193	16,681,844	1,009,294	12,900,093	2,772,457	6,079,349	—	2,806,868
1963	28,232,362	21,279,346	1,292,691	16,460,867	3,525,788	6,953,016	—	4,190,189
1965	35,274,597	26,851,273	1,758,901	20,653,028	4,439,344	8,423,324	11,126,831	6,071,750
1967	—	34,506,348	2,062,545	26,673,826	5,769,977	—	—	—
1969	52,930,923	42,093,580	3,076,751	31,865,179	7,151,649	10,837,343	11,206,632	9,384,731
1970	57,394,951	46,053,585	3,117,895	35,042,590	7,893,100	11,341,366	13,714,330	9,786,240
1971	62,136,459	50,153,251	3,287,326	38,131,339	8,734,586	11,983,208	15,180,934	10,291,095
1972	66,814,103	53,814,596	3,492,611	40,808,481	9,513,503	12,999,507	15,099,840	10,823,595
1973	71,305,817	58,002,777	3,888,372	43,701,491	10,412,914	13,303,040	13,168,076	11,400,916
1974	75,585,674	62,183,078	4,210,901	46,453,642	11,518,536	13,402,596	14,364,545	12,413,420
1975	80,300,595	66,348,304	4,345,232	49,349,224	12,653,847	13,952,291	15,488,265	12,687,015
1976	85,486,550	70,739,427	4,444,927	52,384,393	13,910,107	14,747,123	16,304,553	13,068,341
1977	90,337,044	74,770,804	4,621,071	55,188,603	14,961,131	15,566,240	16,840,129	13,437,861
1978	95,442,468	78,637,991	4,824,250	57,563,005	16,250,737	16,804,477	18,158,634	13,712,648
1979	102,294,859	83,733,387	5,037,172	60,847,097	17,849,119	18,561,472	20,743,045	14,181,991
1980	109,701,242	88,760,567	5,212,453	64,158,017	19,390,097	20,940,675	23,465,001	14,794,669
1981	117,601,954	94,516,512	5,402,339	67,794,877	21,319,297	23,085,442	24,415,245	15,487,618
1982	127,345,302	100,992,841	5,889,080	71,519,718	23,584,042	26,352,461	32,691,133	16,749,900
1983	137,141,741	107,640,113	6,109,746	75,220,765	26,309,602	29,501,629	32,975,610	18,277,315
1984	148,163,096	114,763,986	6,236,159	79,133,998	29,393,829	33,399,110	39,916,361	22,105,712
1985	160,959,517	122,261,355	6,573,923	82,886,012	32,801,419	38,698,162	50,280,775	25,699,408
1986	—	126,426,171	7,165,445	84,838,657	34,422,069	—	56,585,153	—
1987	—	139,456,342	8,307,789	92,428,615	38,719,937	—	57,391,814	—
1988	—	158,693,085	9,462,095	104,743,145	44,487,845	—	64,155,247	—
1989	—	164,635,000	9,968,000	108,609,000	46,058,000	—	67,978,726	—
1990	—	178,084,000	10,028,000	117,683,000	50,373,000	—	72,048,579	—
1991	—	184,813,238	10,528,395	122,422,566	51,862,277	—	82,534,026	—
1992	—	192,760,817	11,006,451	128,436,599	53,317,767	—	92,239,311	—
1993	—	199,463,715	11,197,662	133,124,680	55,141,373	—	96,012,591	—
1994	—	212,201,113	11,710,436	142,553,837	57,936,840	—	109,706,704	—

[1] All data apply to end of year.

[2] From 1955 through 1967, buildings value includes improvements to land and equipment.

[3] Includes funds functioning as endowment.

[4] Includes annuity funds.

Source

Series Bc968–975, 1899–1985, U.S. Department of Education, *120 Years of Education: A Statistical Portrait* (1993), Table 35. The underlying sources are: 1919–1957, U.S. Office of Education, *Biennial Survey of Education in the United States*; 1959, U.S. Office of Education, *Financial Statistics of Institutions of Higher Education, 1959–60*; 1961–1963, U.S. Office of Education, *Higher Education Finances* (1968); 1965–1985, U.S. Department of Education, Higher Education General Information Survey (HEGIS). 1986–1994, U.S. Department of Education, *Digest of Education Statistics 1997*, Table 351, for which the underlying source is Integrated Postsecondary Education Data System (IPEDS), "Finance" surveys.

Documentation

Data represent moneys received and spent by higher education institutions for expanding their physical holdings (land, buildings, equipment of various sorts) held or utilized primarily for instructional, recreational, or student residence purposes. Real estate held and operated for investment purposes is not included.

Property data represent value of all permanent or quasi-permanent assets, which include land, buildings, and equipment; funds held for investment purposes only (the income from such funds being available for current use); funds subject to annuity or living trust agreements; and funds the principal of which may be lent to students to help defray their living expenses or tuition bills. The term "fund" is used in its accounting sense of cash or other valuable assets (real estate, bonds, stock certificates, and other evidences of ownership or equity).

Series Bc968. Equals series Bc969 plus series Bc973.

TABLE Bc976–1035 Average undergraduate tuition, fees, room, and board in higher education institutions, by type of institution: 1964–1996[1, 2]

Contributed by Claudia Goldin

	Public and private institutions									
	Total tuition, room, and board					Tuition and required fees (in-state)				
	All institutions	Four-year institutions: All	Four-year institutions: Universities	Four-year institutions: Other	Two-year institutions	All institutions	Four-year institutions: All	Four-year institutions: Universities	Four-year institutions: Other	Two-year institutions
	Bc976	Bc977	Bc978	Bc979	Bc980	Bc981	Bc982	Bc983	Bc984	Bc985
School year beginning	Dollars	Dollars	Dollars	Dollars	Dollars	Dollars	Dollars	Dollars	Dollars	Dollars
1964	—	—	—	—	—	—	—	—	—	—
1965	—	—	—	—	—	—	—	—	—	—
1966	—	—	—	—	—	—	—	—	—	—
1967	—	—	—	—	—	—	—	—	—	—
1968	—	—	—	—	—	—	—	—	—	—
1969	—	—	—	—	—	—	—	—	—	—
1970	—	—	—	—	—	—	—	—	—	—
1971	—	—	—	—	—	—	—	—	—	—
1972	—	—	—	—	—	—	—	—	—	—
1973	—	—	—	—	—	—	—	—	—	—
1974	—	—	—	—	—	—	—	—	—	—
1975	—	—	—	—	—	—	—	—	—	—
1976	2,275	2,577	2,647	2,527	1,598	924	1,218	1,210	1,223	346
1977	2,411	2,725	2,777	2,685	1,703	984	1,291	1,269	1,305	378
1978	2,587	2,917	2,967	2,879	1,828	1,073	1,397	1,370	1,413	411
1979	2,809	3,167	3,223	3,124	1,979	1,163	1,513	1,484	1,530	451
1980	3,101	3,499	3,535	3,469	2,230	1,289	1,679	1,634	1,705	526
1981	3,489	3,951	4,005	3,908	2,476	1,457	1,907	1,860	1,935	590
1982	3,877	4,406	4,466	4,356	2,713	1,626	2,139	2,081	2,173	675
1983	4,167	4,747	4,793	4,712	2,854	1,783	2,344	2,300	2,368	730
1984	4,563	5,160	5,236	5,107	3,179	1,985	2,567	2,539	2,583	821
1985 [3]	4,885	5,504	5,597	5,441	3,367	2,181	2,784	2,770	2,793	888
1986	5,206	5,964	6,124	5,857	3,295	2,312	3,042	3,042	3,042	897
1987	5,494	6,272	6,339	6,226	3,263	2,458	3,201	3,168	3,220	809
1988	5,869	6,725	6,801	6,673	3,573	2,658	3,472	3,422	3,499	979
1989	6,207	7,212	7,347	7,120	3,705	2,839	3,800	3,765	3,819	978
1990	6,562	7,602	7,709	7,528	3,930	3,016	4,009	3,958	4,036	1,087
1991	7,074	8,252	8,389	8,164	4,089	3,282	4,399	4,366	4,417	1,186
1992	7,452	8,758	8,934	8,648	4,207	3,517	4,752	4,665	4,795	1,276
1993	7,931	9,296	9,495	9,186	4,449	3,827	5,119	5,104	5,127	1,399
1994	8,306	9,728	9,863	9,646	4,633	4,044	5,391	5,287	5,441	1,488
1995	8,800	10,330	10,560	10,195	4,725	4,338	5,786	5,733	5,812	1,522
1996	9,199	10,825	11,027	10,704	4,896	4,561	6,107	6,050	6,135	1,543

Notes appear at end of table

(continued)

TABLE Bc976–1035 Average undergraduate tuition, fees, room, and board in higher education institutions, by type of institution: 1964–1996 *Continued*

	Public and private institutions									
	Dormitory rooms					Board (seven-day basis)				
	All institutions	Four-year institutions: All	Four-year institutions: Universities	Four-year institutions: Other	Two-year institutions	All institutions	Four-year institutions: All	Four-year institutions: Universities	Four-year institutions: Other	Two-year institutions
	Bc986	Bc987	Bc988	Bc989	Bc990	Bc991	Bc992	Bc993	Bc994	Bc995
School year beginning	Dollars	Dollars	Dollars	Dollars	Dollars	Dollars	Dollars	Dollars	Dollars	Dollars
1964	—	—	—	—	—	—	—	—	—	—
1965	—	—	—	—	—	—	—	—	—	—
1966	—	—	—	—	—	—	—	—	—	—
1967	—	—	—	—	—	—	—	—	—	—
1968	—	—	—	—	—	—	—	—	—	—
1969	—	—	—	—	—	—	—	—	—	—
1970	—	—	—	—	—	—	—	—	—	—
1971	—	—	—	—	—	—	—	—	—	—
1972	—	—	—	—	—	—	—	—	—	—
1973	—	—	—	—	—	—	—	—	—	—
1974	—	—	—	—	—	—	—	—	—	—
1975	—	—	—	—	—	—	—	—	—	—
1976	603	611	649	584	503	748	748	788	719	750
1977	645	654	691	628	525	781	780	818	752	801
1978	688	696	737	667	575	826	825	860	800	842
1979	751	759	803	729	628	895	895	936	865	900
1980	836	846	881	821	705	976	975	1,020	943	1,000
1981	950	961	1,023	919	793	1,083	1,082	1,121	1,055	1,094
1982	1,064	1,078	1,150	1,028	873	1,187	1,189	1,235	1,155	1,165
1983	1,145	1,162	1,211	1,130	916	1,239	1,242	1,282	1,214	1,208
1984	1,267	1,282	1,343	1,242	1,058	1,310	1,311	1,353	1,282	1,301
1985 [3]	1,338	1,355	1,424	1,309	1,107	1,365	1,365	1,403	1,339	1,372
1986	1,405	1,427	1,501	1,376	1,034	1,489	1,495	1,581	1,439	1,364
1987	1,488	1,516	1,576	1,478	1,017	1,549	1,555	1,596	1,529	1,437
1988	1,575	1,609	1,665	1,573	1,085	1,636	1,644	1,715	1,601	1,509
1989	1,638	1,675	1,732	1,638	1,105	1,730	1,737	1,850	1,663	1,622
1990	1,743	1,782	1,848	1,740	1,182	1,802	1,811	1,903	1,751	1,660
1991	1,874	1,921	1,998	1,874	1,210	1,918	1,931	2,026	1,873	1,692
1992	1,939	1,991	2,104	1,926	1,240	1,996	2,015	2,165	1,927	1,692
1993	2,057	2,111	2,190	2,068	1,332	2,047	2,067	2,201	1,992	1,718
1994	2,145	2,200	2,281	2,155	1,396	2,116	2,138	2,295	2,049	1,750
1995	2,264	2,318	2,423	2,260	1,473	2,199	2,226	2,404	2,123	1,730
1996	2,364	2,419	2,518	2,363	1,527	2,275	2,299	2,460	2,206	1,826

Notes appear at end of table

TABLE Bc976–1035 Average undergraduate tuition, fees, room, and board in higher education institutions, by type of institution: 1964–1996 *Continued*

	Public institutions									
	Total tuition, room, and board					Tuition and required fees (in-state)				
	All institutions	Four-year institutions			Two-year institutions	All institutions	Four-year institutions			Two-year institutions
		All	Universities	Other			All	Universities	Other	
	Bc996	Bc997	Bc998	Bc999	Bc1000	Bc1001	Bc1002	Bc1003	Bc1004	Bc1005
School year beginning	Dollars	Dollars	Dollars	Dollars	Dollars	Dollars	Dollars	Dollars	Dollars	Dollars
1964	950	—	1,051	867	638	243	—	298	224	99
1965	983	—	1,105	904	670	257	—	327	241	109
1966	1,026	—	1,171	947	710	275	—	360	259	121
1967	1,064	—	1,199	997	789	283	—	366	268	144
1968	1,117	—	1,245	1,063	883	295	—	377	281	170
1969	1,203	—	1,362	1,135	951	323	—	427	306	178
1970	1,287	—	1,477	1,206	998	351	—	478	332	187
1971	1,357	—	1,579	1,263	1,073	376	—	526	354	192
1972	1,458	—	1,668	1,460	1,197	407	—	566	455	233
1973	1,517	—	1,707	1,506	1,274	438	—	581	463	274
1974	1,563	—	1,760	1,558	1,339	432	—	599	448	277
1975	1,666	—	1,935	1,657	1,386	433	—	642	469	245
1976	1,789	1,935	2,067	1,827	1,491	479	617	689	564	283
1977	1,888	2,038	2,170	1,931	1,590	512	655	736	596	306
1978	1,994	2,145	2,289	2,027	1,691	543	688	777	622	327
1979	2,165	2,327	2,487	2,198	1,822	583	738	840	662	355
1980	2,373	2,550	2,712	2,421	2,027	635	804	915	722	391
1981	2,663	2,871	3,079	2,705	2,224	714	909	1,042	813	434
1982	2,945	3,196	3,403	3,032	2,390	798	1,031	1,164	936	473
1983	3,156	3,433	3,628	3,285	2,534	891	1,148	1,284	1,052	528
1984	3,408	3,682	3,899	3,518	2,807	971	1,228	1,386	1,117	584
1985 [3]	3,571	3,859	4,146	3,637	2,981	1,045	1,318	1,536	1,157	641
1986	3,805	4,138	4,469	3,891	2,989	1,106	1,414	1,651	1,248	660
1987	4,050	4,403	4,619	4,250	3,066	1,218	1,537	1,726	1,407	706
1988	4,274	4,678	4,905	4,526	3,183	1,285	1,646	1,846	1,515	730
1989	4,504	4,975	5,324	4,723	3,299	1,356	1,780	2,035	1,608	756
1990	4,757	5,243	5,585	5,004	3,467	1,454	1,888	2,159	1,707	824
1991	5,135	5,695	6,051	5,459	3,623	1,624	2,119	2,410	1,933	937
1992	5,379	6,020	6,442	5,740	3,799	1,782	2,349	2,604	2,192	1,025
1993	5,694	6,365	6,710	6,146	3,996	1,942	2,537	2,820	2,360	1,125
1994	5,965	6,670	7,077	6,409	4,137	2,057	2,681	2,977	2,499	1,192
1995	6,256	7,014	7,448	6,730	4,217	2,179	2,848	3,151	2,660	1,239
1996	6,534	7,331	7,793	7,028	4,412	2,277	2,986	3,321	2,778	1,283

Notes appear at end of table

(continued)

TABLE Bc976–1035 Average undergraduate tuition, fees, room, and board in higher education institutions, by type of institution: 1964–1996 *Continued*

	Public institutions									
	Dormitory rooms					Board (seven-day basis)				
	All institutions	Four-year institutions: All	Four-year institutions: Universities	Four-year institutions: Other	Two-year institutions	All institutions	Four-year institutions: All	Four-year institutions: Universities	Four-year institutions: Other	Two-year institutions
	Bc1006	Bc1007	Bc1008	Bc1009	Bc1010	Bc1011	Bc1012	Bc1013	Bc1014	Bc1015
School year beginning	Dollars	Dollars	Dollars	Dollars	Dollars	Dollars	Dollars	Dollars	Dollars	Dollars
1964	271	—	291	241	178	436	—	462	402	361
1965	281	—	304	255	194	445	—	474	408	367
1966	294	—	321	271	213	457	—	490	417	376
1967	313	—	337	292	243	468	—	496	437	402
1968	337	—	359	318	278	485	—	509	464	435
1969	369	—	395	346	308	511	—	540	483	465
1970	401	—	431	375	338	535	—	568	499	473
1971	430	—	463	400	366	551	—	590	509	515
1972	476	—	500	455	398	575	—	602	550	566
1973	480	—	505	464	409	599	—	621	579	591
1974	506	—	527	497	424	625	—	634	613	638
1975	544	—	573	533	442	689	—	720	655	699
1976	582	592	614	572	465	728	727	763	692	742
1977	621	631	649	616	486	755	752	785	720	797
1978	655	664	689	641	527	796	793	823	764	837
1979	715	725	750	703	574	867	865	898	833	893
1980	799	811	827	796	642	940	936	969	904	994
1981	909	925	970	885	703	1,039	1,036	1,067	1,006	1,086
1982	1,010	1,030	1,072	993	755	1,136	1,134	1,167	1,103	1,162
1983	1,087	1,110	1,131	1,092	801	1,178	1,175	1,213	1,141	1,205
1984	1,196	1,217	1,237	1,200	921	1,241	1,237	1,276	1,201	1,302
1985 [3]	1,242	1,263	1,290	1,240	960	1,285	1,278	1,320	1,240	1,380
1986	1,301	1,323	1,355	1,295	979	1,398	1,401	1,464	1,348	1,349
1987	1,378	1,410	1,410	1,409	943	1,454	1,456	1,482	1,434	1,417
1988	1,457	1,496	1,483	1,506	965	1,533	1,536	1,576	1,504	1,488
1989	1,513	1,557	1,561	1,554	962	1,635	1,638	1,728	1,561	1,581
1990	1,612	1,657	1,658	1,655	1,050	1,691	1,698	1,767	1,641	1,594
1991	1,731	1,785	1,789	1,782	1,074	1,780	1,792	1,852	1,745	1,612
1992	1,756	1,816	1,856	1,787	1,106	1,841	1,854	1,982	1,761	1,668
1993	1,873	1,934	1,897	1,958	1,190	1,880	1,895	1,993	1,828	1,681
1994	1,959	2,023	1,992	2,044	1,232	1,949	1,967	2,108	1,866	1,712
1995	2,057	2,121	2,104	2,133	1,297	2,020	2,045	2,192	1,937	1,681
1996	2,148	2,212	2,189	2,228	1,346	2,110	2,133	2,283	2,023	1,782

Notes appear at end of table

TABLE Bc976–1035 Average undergraduate tuition, fees, room, and board in higher education institutions, by type of institution: 1964–1996 *Continued*

	Private institutions									
	Total tuition, room, and board					Tuition and required fees (in-state)				
		Four-year institutions					Four-year institutions			
	All institutions	All	Universities	Other	Two-year institutions	All institutions	All	Universities	Other	Two-year institutions
	Bc1016	Bc1017	Bc1018	Bc1019	Bc1020	Bc1021	Bc1022	Bc1023	Bc1024	Bc1025
School year beginning	Dollars	Dollars	Dollars	Dollars	Dollars	Dollars	Dollars	Dollars	Dollars	Dollars
1964	1,907	—	2,202	1,810	1,455	1,088	—	1,297	1,023	702
1965	2,005	—	2,316	1,899	1,557	1,154	—	1,369	1,086	768
1966	2,124	—	2,456	2,007	1,679	1,233	—	1,456	1,162	845
1967	2,205	—	2,545	2,104	1,762	1,297	—	1,534	1,237	892
1968	2,321	—	2,673	2,237	1,876	1,383	—	1,638	1,335	956
1969	2,530	—	2,920	2,420	1,993	1,533	—	1,809	1,468	1,034
1970	2,738	—	3,163	2,599	2,103	1,684	—	1,980	1,603	1,109
1971	2,917	—	3,375	2,748	2,186	1,820	—	2,133	1,721	1,172
1972	3,038	—	3,512	2,934	2,273	1,898	—	2,226	1,846	1,221
1973	3,164	—	3,717	3,040	2,410	1,989	—	2,375	1,925	1,303
1974	3,403	—	4,076	3,156	2,591	2,117	—	2,614	1,954	1,367
1975	3,663	—	4,467	3,385	2,711	2,272	—	2,881	2,084	1,427
1976	3,906	3,977	4,715	3,714	2,971	2,467	2,534	3,051	2,351	1,592
1977	4,158	4,240	5,033	3,967	3,148	2,624	2,700	3,240	2,520	1,706
1978	4,514	4,609	5,403	4,327	3,389	2,867	2,958	3,487	2,771	1,831
1979	4,912	5,013	5,891	4,700	3,751	3,130	3,225	3,811	3,020	2,062
1980	5,470	5,594	6,569	5,249	4,303	3,498	3,617	4,275	3,390	2,413
1981	6,166	6,330	7,443	5,947	4,746	3,953	4,113	4,887	3,853	2,605
1982	6,920	7,126	8,536	6,646	5,364	4,439	4,639	5,583	4,329	3,008
1983	7,508	7,759	9,308	7,244	5,571	4,851	5,093	6,217	4,726	3,099
1984	8,202	8,451	10,243	7,849	6,203	5,315	5,556	6,843	5,135	3,485
1985 [3]	8,885	9,228	11,034	8,551	6,512	5,789	6,121	7,374	5,641	3,672
1986	9,676	10,039	12,278	9,276	6,384	6,316	6,658	8,118	6,171	3,684
1987	10,512	10,659	13,075	9,854	7,078	6,988	7,116	8,771	6,574	4,161
1988	11,189	11,474	14,073	10,620	7,967	7,461	7,722	9,451	7,172	4,817
1989	12,018	12,284	15,098	11,374	8,670	8,147	8,396	10,348	7,778	5,196
1990	12,910	13,237	16,503	12,220	9,302	8,772	9,083	11,379	8,389	5,570
1991	13,907	14,273	17,779	13,189	9,631	9,434	9,775	12,192	9,053	5,752
1992	14,634	15,009	18,898	13,882	9,903	9,942	10,294	13,055	9,533	6,059
1993	15,496	15,904	20,097	14,640	10,406	10,572	10,952	13,874	10,100	6,370
1994	16,207	16,602	21,041	15,363	11,170	11,111	11,481	14,537	10,653	6,914
1995	17,208	17,612	22,502	16,198	11,563	11,864	12,243	15,605	11,297	7,094
1996	18,071	18,476	23,491	17,027	11,889	12,537	12,920	16,531	11,911	7,190

Notes appear at end of table

(continued)

TABLE Bc976–1035 Average undergraduate tuition, fees, room, and board in higher education institutions, by type of institution: 1964–1996 *Continued*

	Private institutions									
	Dormitory rooms					Board (seven-day basis)				
	All institutions	Four-year institutions: All	Four-year institutions: Universities	Four-year institutions: Other	Two-year institutions	All institutions	Four-year institutions: All	Four-year institutions: Universities	Four-year institutions: Other	Two-year institutions
School year beginning	Bc1026	Bc1027	Bc1028	Bc1029	Bc1030	Bc1031	Bc1032	Bc1033	Bc1034	Bc1035
	Dollars	Dollars	Dollars	Dollars	Dollars	Dollars	Dollars	Dollars	Dollars	Dollars
1964	331	—	390	308	289	488	—	515	479	464
1965	356	—	418	330	316	495	—	529	483	473
1966	385	—	452	355	347	506	—	548	490	487
1967	392	—	455	366	366	516	—	556	501	504
1968	404	—	463	382	391	534	—	572	520	529
1969	436	—	503	409	413	561	—	608	543	546
1970	468	—	542	434	434	586	—	641	562	560
1971	494	—	576	454	449	603	—	666	573	565
1972	524	—	622	490	457	616	—	664	598	595
1973	533	—	622	502	483	642	—	720	613	624
1974	586	—	691	536	564	700	—	771	666	660
1975	636	—	753	583	572	755	—	833	718	712
1976	649	651	783	604	607	790	791	882	759	772
1977	698	702	850	648	631	836	838	943	800	811
1978	758	761	916	704	700	889	890	1,000	851	858
1979	827	831	1,001	768	766	955	957	1,078	912	923
1980	918	921	1,086	859	871	1,054	1,056	1,209	1,000	1,019
1981	1,038	1,039	1,229	970	1,022	1,175	1,178	1,327	1,124	1,119
1982	1,181	1,181	1,453	1,083	1,177	1,300	1,306	1,501	1,234	1,179
1983	1,278	1,279	1,531	1,191	1,253	1,380	1,387	1,559	1,327	1,219
1984	1,426	1,426	1,753	1,309	1,424	1,462	1,469	1,647	1,405	1,294
1985 [3]	1,553	1,557	1,940	1,420	1,500	1,542	1,551	1,720	1,490	1,340
1986	1,658	1,673	2,097	1,518	1,266	1,702	1,708	2,063	1,587	1,434
1987	1,748	1,760	2,244	1,593	1,380	1,775	1,783	2,060	1,687	1,537
1988	1,849	1,863	2,353	1,686	1,540	1,880	1,889	2,269	1,762	1,609
1989	1,923	1,935	2,411	1,774	1,663	1,948	1,953	2,339	1,823	1,811
1990	2,063	2,077	2,654	1,889	1,744	2,074	2,077	2,470	1,943	1,989
1991	2,221	2,241	2,860	2,038	1,789	2,252	2,257	2,727	2,098	2,090
1992	2,348	2,362	3,018	2,151	1,970	2,344	2,354	2,825	2,197	1,875
1993	2,490	2,506	3,277	2,261	2,067	2,434	2,445	2,946	2,278	1,970
1994	2,587	2,601	3,469	2,347	2,233	2,509	2,520	3,035	2,362	2,023
1995	2,738	2,751	3,680	2,473	2,371	2,606	2,617	3,218	2,429	2,098
1996	2,873	2,885	3,820	2,597	2,513	2,661	2,670	3,140	2,518	2,186

[1] Because of their low response rate, data for private two-year colleges must be interpreted with caution.

[2] Data collection procedures revised in 1986, affecting board costs. See text.

[3] Room and board data are estimated.

Source

1964–1996, U.S. Department of Education, *Digest of Education Statistics 1997*, Table 312. The underlying sources are: U.S. Department of Education, Higher Education General Information Survey (HEGIS), "Institutional Characteristics of Colleges and Universities" and "Fall Enrollment in Institutions of Higher Education" surveys; Integrated Postsecondary Education Data System (IPEDS), "Fall Enrollment" and "Institutional Characteristics" surveys.

Documentation

Tuition and fee data are for the entire academic year and are similar to "list" tuition and fees rather than average actual charges. Tuition and fees are weighted by the number of full-time-equivalent undergraduates but are not adjusted to reflect student residency. Room and board amounts are based on full-time students.

Because of revisions in data collection procedures, figures for 1986 and later years are not entirely comparable with those for previous years. In particular, data on board rates are somewhat higher than earlier because they reflect a basis of twenty meals per week rather than meals served seven days per week. Because many institutions serve fewer than three meals each day, the 1986 and later data reflect a more accurate accounting of total board costs.

CHAPTER Bd

Health

Editor: Richard H. Steckel

Health, Nutrition, and Physical Well-Being

Richard H. Steckel

Medical scientists have devised numerous measures of the health of individuals. Examples range from those that are easy to observe, such as body temperature, blood pressure, and pulse, to those such as X-rays, ultrasound, and CAT scans that require complex technologies.

In a like manner, social scientists have devised a variety of statistical measures of the health of nations. These can be under three broad headings: health outcomes, the provision of health services, and lifestyle choices that affect health. All are central to any evaluation of a nation's standard of living and quality of life (Engerman 1997).

Long-Term Trends in Summary Measures of Health

At the outset, it should be understood that measuring the health aspects of the quality of life is a complicated endeavor because they include many attributes such as longevity, morbidity (illness or disability), physical vigor, and deaths from various diseases. Health is all the more complicated to measure over long time spans because theories of disease, and therefore the kinds of data collected, have changed over the centuries. Moreover, the data available for study are more limited the farther into the past one searches for them.

Nevertheless, it is possible to provide a brief overview of progress using life expectancy at birth, which is the most widely used measure of health.[1] Over the past 150 years life expectancy has doubled, increasing from 38.3 years in 1850 to 76.7 years in 1998. Childhood mortality greatly affects life expectancy, which was so low in the mid-1800s in large part because mortality rates were very high for this age group. For example, roughly one child in five born alive in 1850 did not survive to age 1, but today the infant mortality rate is under 1 percent. The past century and a half witnessed a significant shift in deaths from early childhood to old age (Cutler and Meara 2001). At the same time, the major causes of death have shifted from infectious diseases caused by germs or microorganisms to degenerative processes that are affected by lifestyle choices, such as diet, smoking, and exercise.

Although the increase in longevity was approximately continuous during the twentieth century, there were substantial fluctuations during the 1800s. Annual data on life expectancy during the nineteenth century are unavailable, however; health fluctuations are considered in the discussion on physical stature later in this section.

The largest gains were concentrated in the first half of the twentieth century, when life expectancy increased from 47.8 years in 1900 to 68.2 years in 1950. Factors behind the growing longevity include the ascent of the germ theory of disease, programs of public health and personal hygiene, better medical technology, higher incomes, better diets, more education, and the emergence of health insurance. Table Bd-A provides a chronology of important medical developments that contributed to improving health. In drawing conclusions, one should keep in mind that the table lists discoveries and first uses of new techniques that often took years or decades to diffuse to large numbers of patients.

The research of Pasteur and Koch was particularly influential in leading to acceptance of the germ theory of disease in the late 1800s.[2] Prior to the work of these scientists, many diseases were thought to have arisen from miasmas or vapors created by rotting vegetation. Thus, swamps were accurately viewed as unhealthy, but not because they were home to mosquitoes and malaria. The germ theory gave public health measures a sound scientific basis, and shortly thereafter cities began cost-effective measures to remove garbage, purify water supplies, and process sewage. The notion that "cleanliness was next to godliness" also emerged in the home, where bathing and the washing of clothes, dishes, and floors became routine.

The discovery of Salvarsan in 1910 led to the first use of an antibiotic (for syphilis), which meant that a drug was effective in altering the course of a disease. This was an important medical event, but broad-spectrum antibiotics were not available until the middle of the century. The most famous of these early drugs was penicillin, which was not manufactured in large quantities until the 1940s. Much of the gain in life expectancy was attained before chemotherapy and a host of other medical technologies became widely available. The cornerstone of improvement in health from the late 1800s to the middle of the twentieth century was, therefore, prevention of disease by reduction in exposure to pathogens and by preparation of the immune system by means of vaccination against diseases such as smallpox and diphtheria.[3]

[1] For more information, see Chapter Ab on vital statistics.

Acknowledgments

Richard H. Steckel is grateful to the Robert Wood Johnson Foundation for financial support. Molly Cooper, Alka Gandhi, and William White provided much valuable research assistance in preparing the tables.

[2] For a discussion of the history of public health, see Smille (1955) and Riley (2001).

[3] For a discussion of medical practices, see Shorter (1996). Weatherall (1996) discusses the evolution of medications.

TABLE Bd-A Chronology of important medical events: 1831–1995

1831	Samuel Guthrie discovers chloroform.
1834	Amalgam used for filling teeth.
1837	Registration Act (birth, deaths, and marriages) passes in England.
1839	Theodor Schwann defines the cell as the basic unit of animal structure.
1841	F. G. J. Henle publishes treatise on microscopic anatomy.
1844	Horace Wells uses nitrous oxide to pull one of his own teeth painlessly.
1846	William Morton uses ether as an anesthetic at the Massachusetts General Hospital.
1847	James Young Simpson uses chloroform to relieve the pain of childbirth.
1848	First Public Health Act sets up General Board of Health in Britain, leading to local medical officers of health; Ignaz Semmelweis introduces antiseptic methods in Vienna.
1849	Elizabeth Blackwell becomes first woman to qualify as a doctor in modern times; Thomas Addison describes anemia.
1853	Smallpox vaccination made compulsory in England.
1858	Medical Reform Act sets up Medical Register and General Medical Council in Britain; first edition of *Gray's Anatomy.*
1861	Louis Pasteur discovers anaerobic bacteria.
1864	International Red Cross founded.
1865	Joseph Lister introduces phenol as a disinfectant in surgery.
1866	Thomas Allbutt develops the clinical thermometer.
1867	First international medical congress in Paris.
1874	Louis Pasteur suggests placing instruments in boiling water to sterilize them.
1876	Robert Koch identifies the anthrax bacillus.
1879	Patrick Manson discovers that mosquitoes transmit filariasis.
1880	Charles Laveran isolates blood parasite that causes malaria.
1881	Louis Pasteur devises a vaccine for anthrax.
1882	Robert Koch isolates the tubercle bacillus.
1883	Robert Koch discovers the cholera vibrio.
1885	Louis Pasteur develops a rabies vaccine.
1889	Johns Hopkins Hospital opens in Baltimore.
1890	Emil von Behring and Shibasabura Kitasato develop vaccines against tetanus and diphtheria; William Halsted introduces surgical gloves.
1893	Johns Hopkins Medical School founded.
1894	First use of diphtheria antitoxin in Britain, by Charles Sherrington.
1895	Wilhelm Röntgen discovers X-rays.
1896	Antoine Becquerel discovers radiation; Scipione Riva-Rocci invents device for measuring blood pressure.
1897	Ronald Ross locates the malaria parasite in the Anopheles mosquito.
1899	London School of Hygiene and Tropical Medicine founded; aspirin introduced.
1900	Karl Landsteiner identifies four major human blood groups (A, O, B, and AB); U.S. Army Yellow Fever Commission founded.
1904	Rockefeller Institute for Medical Research founded in New York.
1905	George Washington Crile performs first direct blood transfusion; J. B. Murphy develops first artificial hip joints.
1906	Frederick Gowland Hopkins starts experiments on "accessory food factors" (vitamins); Charles Sherrington's *The Integrative Action of the Nervous System,* a classic of neurology, is published.
1908	Sulfanilamide first synthesized.
1910	Paul Ehrlich announces his discovery of Salvarsan for syphilis – the beginning of modern chemotherapy.
1913	John Jacob Abel develops first artificial kidney.
1918	Start of influenza pandemic.
1921	F. G. Banting and C. H. Best isolate insulin.
1923	Camille Guérin develops the BCG (bacille Calmette-Guérin) vaccine for tuberculosis.
1926	First enzyme (urease) crystallized by American biochemist James B. Sumner.
1927	Philip Drinker and Louis Shaw develop the "iron lung."
1928	Alexander Fleming discovers penicillin; Albert Szent-Györgyi isolates vitamin C.
1929	Henry Dale and H. W. Dudley demonstrate chemical transmission of nerve impulses.
1932	Armand Quick introduces a test to measure the clotting ability of blood; Gerhard Domagk discovers the first sulfa drug, Prontosil.
1937	Development of vaccine against yellow fever by Max Theiler and of first antihistamine by Daniel Daniel Bovet.
1938	Philip Wiles develops the first total artificial hip replacement, using stainless steel.
1940	Howard Florey and Ernst Chain develop penicillin as an antibiotic.
1941	Normal Gregg links rubella (German measles) in pregnancy with cataracts and other abnormalities in children.
1943	Wilhelm Kolff develops first kidney dialysis machine; Selman Waksman discovers the antibiotic streptomycin.
1945	Fluoridation of water introduced in the United States to prevent tooth decay.

TABLE Bd-A Chronology of important medical events: 1831–1995 *Continued*

1946	Start of first randomized clinical trials of streptomycin for the treatment of tuberculosis.
1948	Philip Hench discovers that cortisone can be used for rheumatoid arthritis.
1952	Open-heart surgery begins with implantation of artificial heart valves.
1953	James Watson and Francis Crick determine the double-helical structure of deoxyribonucleic acid (DNA).
1954	First successful kidney transplant; plastic contact lenses produced.
1957	Albert Sabin develops a live polio vaccine; Clarence Lillehei devises first compact heart pacemaker.
1958	Ian Donald uses ultrasound to diagnosis disorders of the fetus.
1963	Measles vaccine licensed for general use in the United States.
1964	Home kidney dialysis introduced in the United Kingdom and the United States; first Surgeon General's Report on smoking and health.
1967	Christiaan Barnard performs human heart transplant; Rene Favaloro develops coronary bypass operation.
1976	Epidemics of Ebola virus disease in Sudan and Zaire.
1979	World declared free of smallpox.
1980	Experimental vaccine against hepatitis B developed.
1981	AIDS (acquired immune deficiency syndrome) first recognized by U.S. Centers for Disease Control.
1983	First successful human embryo transfers.
1986	Human Genome Project created.
1994	The Americas are declared a polio-free zone.
1995	The World Health Organization (WHO) given license to develop and distribute Manual Patarroyo's malaria vaccine.

Source

Abstracted from Roy Porter, editor, *The Cambridge Illustrated History of Medicine* (Cambridge University Press, 1996), pp. 376–7.

The significant gains in life expectancy do not guarantee that health, broadly defined, increases in proportion. James Riley has argued that as mortality rates fall, morbidity rates (the incidence of illness and disability) rise (Riley 1991). His conclusion is based on the records of friendly societies and other organizations that give information on sick days of adult males; these records show that the number of workdays lost per worker due to illness increased from the eighteenth century to the 1980s. Suchit Arora challenges this analysis, arguing that increased income or more generous sick-leave provisions, rather than objective medical factors, were behind the trend (Arora 2003). His data showed that sickness days in the U.S. military, which give a more objective medical measure of morbidity, declined along with mortality rates during the early twentieth century.

In the past quarter century, historians have increasingly used average heights to assess health aspects of the standard of living (Steckel 1995). Average height is a good proxy for the nutritional status of a population because height at a particular age reflects an individual's history of *net* nutrition, or diet minus claims on the diet made by work (or physical activity) and disease. Growth may cease in poorly nourished children, and repeated bouts of biological stress – whether from food deprivation, hard work, or disease – often lead to stunting or a reduction in adult height. The average heights of children and of adults in countries around the world are highly correlated with their life expectancy at birth and with the logarithm of the per capita GDP in the country where they live (Steckel 2000).

This interpretation of average height has led to its use in studying the health of slaves, health inequality, living standards during industrialization, and trends in mortality. The first important results in the "new anthropometric history" dealt with the nutrition and health of American slaves as determined from stature recorded for identification purposes on slave manifests, which were required in the coastwise slave trade (Steckel 1998). The subject of slave health has been a contentious issue among historians, in part because vital statistics and nutrition information were never systematically collected for slaves (or for the vast majority of the American population in the mid-nineteenth century, for that matter). Yet the height data showed that children were astonishingly small and malnourished, while working slaves were remarkably well fed. Adolescent slaves grew rapidly as teenagers and were reasonably well off in nutritional aspects of health (Steckel 1986).

Figure Bd-B shows the time pattern in height of native-born American men, obtained in historical periods from military muster rolls, and for men and women in recent decades from the National Health and Nutrition Examination Surveys (NHANES series A 52.1).[4] This historical trend is notable for the tall stature during the colonial period, the mid-nineteenth-century decline, and the surge in heights of the past century. Comparisons of average heights from military organizations in Europe show that Americans were taller by two to three inches. Behind this achievement were a relatively good diet, little exposure to epidemic disease, and relative equality in the distribution of wealth. Americans could choose their foods from the best of European and Western Hemisphere plants and animals, and this dietary diversity, combined with favorable weather, meant that Americans never had to contend with harvest failures. Thus, even the poor were reasonably well fed in colonial America.

Loss of stature began in the second quarter of the nineteenth century when the transportation revolution of canals, steamboats,

[4] Average heights increased by more than one inch from 1920 to 1930, when the data source changes from military records to the nationally representative NHANES. This was a period of substantial improvements in public health and personal hygiene, and thus most or all of the increase could have been genuine. But it is also possible that those who served in the military had more net–nutritionally deprived backgrounds on average, which would impart an upward bias to the series in 1930 compared with 1920.

FIGURE Bd-B Height of native-born men and women, by year of birth: 1710–1970

Sources

Series Bd653–654.

and railways brought people into greater contact with diseases.[5] The rise of public schools meant that children were newly exposed to major diseases, such as whooping cough, diphtheria, and scarlet fever. Food prices also rose during the 1830s, and growing inequality in the distribution of income or wealth accompanied industrialization. Business depressions, which were most hazardous for the health of those who were already poor, also emerged with industrialization. The Civil War of the 1860s and its troop movements further spread disease and disrupted food production and distribution. A large volume of immigration also brought new varieties of disease to the United States. Estimates of life expectancy among adults at ages 20, 30, and 50, which were assembled from family histories, also declined in the middle of the nineteenth century (Pope 1992, Table 9.4).

In the twentieth century, heights grew most rapidly for those born between 1910 and 1950, an era when public health and personal hygiene took vigorous hold, incomes rose rapidly, and congestion in housing was reduced. The latter part of the era also witnessed a larger share of income or wealth going to the lower portion of the distribution, implying that the incomes of the less well-off were rising relatively rapidly. Note that most of the rise in heights occurred before modern antibiotics were available, which means that disease prevention – rather than the ability to alter its course after onset – was the most important basis for improvement in health. The growing control that humans have exercised over their environment, particularly increased food supply and reduced exposure to disease, may be leading to biological (but not genetic) evolution of humans with more durable vital organ systems, larger body size, and later onset of chronic diseases (Fogel and Costa 1997).

Between the middle of the twentieth century and the present, however, the average heights of American men have stagnated, increasing by only a small fraction of an inch over the past half-century. Figure Bd-B refers to the native-born, and so recent increases in immigration cannot account for the stagnation. In the absence of other information, one might be tempted to surmise that environmental conditions for growth are so good that most Americans have simply reached their genetic potential for growth. But heights have continued to increase in Europe, which has the same genetic stock from which most Americans descend. By the 1970s, Americans had fallen behind Norway, Sweden, the Netherlands, and Denmark and were on a par with Germany. While heights were essentially flat in America after the 1970s, they continued to increase significantly in Europe (Steckel 2000). Dutch men are now the tallest, averaging six feet, about two inches taller than American men. Lagging heights lead to questions about the adequacy of health care and lifestyle choices in America. As discussed later in this chapter, it is doubtful that lack of resource commitment to health care is the problem, because America invests far more than the Netherlands. Greater inequality and less access to health care could be important factors in the difference. But access to health care alone, whether due to low income or lack of insurance coverage, may not be the only issues – health insurance coverage must be used regularly and wisely. In this regard, Dutch mothers are known for getting regular pre- and postnatal checkups, which are important for early childhood health.

Note that significant differences in health and the quality of life follow from these height patterns. The comparisons are not part of an odd contest that emphasizes height, nor is big per se assumed to be beautiful. Instead, we know that on average, stunted growth has functional implications for longevity, cognitive development, and work capacity. Children who fail to grow adequately are often sick, suffer learning impairments, and have a lower quality of life. Growth failure in childhood has a long reach into adulthood because individuals whose growth has been stunted are at greater risk of death from heart disease, diabetes, and some types of cancer. Therefore, it is important to know why Americans are falling behind.

Other Measures of Health Status

Health also includes the vigor of life while a person is living, which is becoming increasingly relevant as the average lifespan has been extended and as baby boomers in the American population are approaching older ages. This aspect of health can be measured in numerous ways, including the absence (or incidence) of disease, illness, and injury, and by the conditions that limit activity or restrict functions that are normal for someone of a particular age. Compromised or poor health is reflected in days lost from school or work. Biological indicators such as average stature and birth weight also measure important aspects of health.

Some health professionals prefer to measure health by combining length of life and vigor of life in a concept called "quality-adjusted life years." This approach evaluates attributes of health, such as mobility, dexterity, hearing, and so on, as well as the ratings that people give to alternative health states. Overall health at a particular age is gauged on a scale of 0 (most severe state, equivalent to death) to 1 (no disabilities or limitations). Thus, the health quality of life is measured relative to its disability-free level of 1.0. Attractive as this concept may be, it is unavailable for these volumes because data are lacking for historical time series. If sufficient data accumulate using this concept, they may become suitable for future editions.

The example of quality-adjusted life years raises an important issue for this work: the availability of data. These volumes present historical time series, and unlike modern researchers who may

[5] For additional discussion, see Steckel (1995) and Komlos (1998).

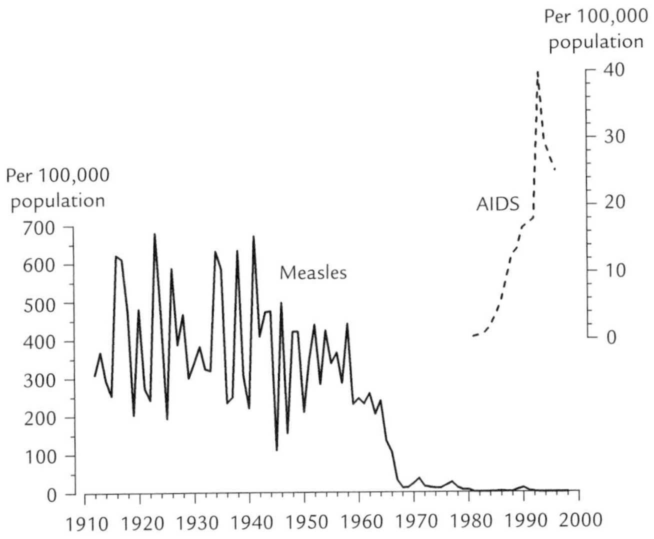

FIGURE Bd-C Incidence of measles and acquired immune deficiency syndrome (AIDS): 1912–1998

Sources

Measles: series Bd458. AIDS: series Aa110 and Bd463.

design surveys or interview people to obtain information, historians are limited to what has already been collected.[6]

Although historians cannot conduct surveys in the past, they have been inventive in using information collected for other purposes. Much of our price history, for example, has been acquired from old newspaper quotes of transaction prices designed to inform contemporary buyers or sellers. Use of average height, which has been discussed, illustrates this point for the history of health.

An important boon to health in the last century was the control or near elimination of numerous severe infectious diseases, such as diphtheria, scarlet fever, whooping cough, and smallpox. Figure Bd-C shows the demise of measles near the middle of the twentieth century. Prior to 1945, this disease fluctuated broadly around 400 cases annually per 100,000 population, but vaccinations nearly eliminated measles by the end of the 1960s. In opposition to this good news has been the rise of AIDS (acquired immune deficiency syndrome) in the 1980s (also in Figure Bd-C). The epidemic peaked in the early to mid-1990s at about 40 cases annually per 100,000 population. Though not nearly as frequent as the major crowd diseases of the early twentieth century, this one is more debilitating and more likely to be fatal.

The National Center for Health Statistics compiles various measures of disability for children, including school-loss days, bed-disability days, and restricted-activity days (series Bd699–701, Bd741–743, and Bd778–780). All climbed approximately 25 percent between the late 1960s and 1980, which is the era when American heights stagnated. In the early 1980s, they abruptly fell to late 1960s levels, but then drifted upward to 1990. Thereafter, two of the measures (bed-disability days and school-loss days) fell to early 1980s levels.

[6] The time series on various diseases are taken from a set of sources that are consistent, but unfortunately, they do not always encompass the time span of most dramatic decline. Although not entirely comparable, the time series presented could be supplemented by evidence on causes of death from insurance records, which are discussed in Dublin and Lotka (1938).

Series Bd920 shows that injury rates have declined over the past several decades. The number rose in the late 1960s and early 1970s, such that annually, more than one third of Americans were injured in some way. These high rates helped spawn a safety movement that has brought injury rates down to about a quarter of the population per year, primarily through lower accident rates at home (series Bd948) and in places outside of work, the home, or automobiles (series Bd957).

Provision of Health Services

Most Americans are accustomed to receiving medical care in doctors' offices or in hospitals, but during the nineteenth century and earlier, most medical care was received in the home. Until the early twentieth century, most babies were born at home under the supervision of midwives (see Banks 1999). Similarly, home health care was commonly provided by relatives or by practical nurses. Various factors led to the rise of hospital-based care near the turn of the twentieth century, including new medical equipment that was expensive and bulky (or nonportable); the growing importance of diagnosis and treatment provided by a team of closely cooperating physicians, nurses, and technicians; the possibility of maintaining a sterile environment for medical procedures; and greater opportunity for monitoring and for rapid response to emergency situations. Nevertheless, much health care is still received at home, particularly by children with minor illnesses, by people who are recovering after treatment in hospitals or clinics, and by older individuals who have lost some capacity for self-care (Kahana, Biegel, and Wykle 1994).

It is doubtful that the practice of medicine a century and a half ago was, on net, beneficial for health. In *Challenges to Contemporary Medicine*, Alan Gregg quotes Lawrence Henderson's statement that "I think it was about the year 1910 or 1912 when it became possible to say of the United States that a random patient with a random disease consulting a doctor chosen at random stood better than a fifty–fifty chance of benefiting from the encounter" (Gregg 1956, p. 13). On the positive side, physicians of the eighteenth century had devised reasonably effective inoculations against smallpox that were replaced in the nineteenth century by the safer technique of vaccination, which created antibodies but did not transmit the disease. Physicians also set broken bones, but many of their actions were misguided because medical scientists lacked the modern germ theory of disease. Thus, most physicians spread infections by washing their hands following, rather than before, surgery. In addition, they also lacked an effective arsenal of medications to alleviate or treat most diseases or disorders. As a result, the demand for doctors remained small and few resources flowed into the medical profession.

Today the public recognizes the contributions of modern medicine to levels of health that are extraordinarily high by standards of the nineteenth century. The transformation began somewhat over a century ago when medical scientists formulated the germ theory of disease, and improved health followed from reduced exposure to pathogens provided by clean water supplies, waste removal, antiseptic practices, and personal hygiene. Table Bd448–462 details the decline of numerous infections diseases, such as typhoid, pertussis (whooping cough), and diphtheria, which eventually followed from the revolution in knowledge.

Bacteriologists of the late nineteenth and early twentieth centuries readily identified numerous infectious agents, leading eventually to several new vaccinations and medications. The most astonishing of these to the general public was the antitoxin against diphtheria, which was developed at Robert Koch's laboratory in 1891. The capability of curing a serious infectious disease significantly upgraded the image of medicine in the public mind. The antibiotic revolution was well underway by the 1940s, when sulfa drugs and penicillin were used to combat a wide array of infections. The obvious success of professional medicine in preventing diseases or finding cures in the first half of the twentieth century led to a substantial increase in the demand for health services.

Society realized very high economic rates of return on its investments in the early years of modern medicine (see Meeker 1980; Preston and Haines 1991). It was relatively cheap to provide clean water and waste removal, and the benefits were enormous. Similarly, the early antibiotics were inexpensive and remarkably effective against many infections.

The average rate of return was far lower per dollar spent on medical care in the second half of the twentieth century. It may seem paradoxical, but the lower return followed partly from the great success of early modern medicine. After the conquest of most infectious diseases, the next challenge for medical science was the treatment and cure of chronic disease. In retrospect, we have learned that these conditions are much more difficult to cure or treat than the infections that caused so many deaths up to the twentieth century. The rise in cancer rates up to the early 1990s is instructive in this regard (series Bd490). While it is evidence of the difficulty of curing cancer, during the previous century infectious diseases would have killed many of these people before their cancers became evident.

Health Insurance

The enormous flow of resources into modern medicine cannot be explained simply by the demise of diseases that were readily prevented by low-cost public health measures or easily treated with chemotherapy. Health insurance, which is now often part of employment benefit packages, emerged to greatly expand the use of medical facilities. The roots of this coverage can be traced to the middle of the nineteenth century, when insurance companies wrote coverage specifically to pay cash benefits following loss of income or inability to work from accidents.[7] In 1875, Americans also borrowed from Europe the concept of mutual aid societies, in which small contributions were collected from groups of workers to pay cash benefits after disability from injury or sickness.

Although single-hospital benefit plans existed as early as 1912 in Rockford, Illinois, the modern approach to health insurance – provision of hospital or medical services to workers – began in 1929 when Justin Ford Kimball established a hospital insurance plan for schoolteachers in Dallas. For a premium of fifty cents a month, the teachers were given up to twenty-one days of hospitalization in a semiprivate room. This approach to coverage became the model for various hospital insurance plans and the Blue Cross plans that spread thereafter.

The success of Blue Cross plans for hospital expenses led physician groups to create a similar model. In 1939, the California Medical Association established the California Physicians Service, which was the first of what were called Blue Shield plans for payments to physicians. Price and wage controls that were imposed

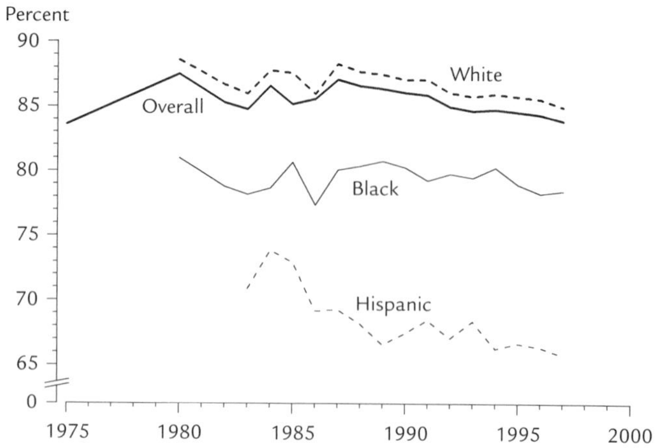

FIGURE Bd-D Percentage of persons covered by health insurance, by race and Hispanic origin: 1975–1997

Sources

Series Bd307, Bd313, Bd315, and Bd317.

during World War II removed the discussion of wages, but working conditions and other forms of compensation were considered. In this environment, unions brought health insurance to the table as an element of collective bargaining. After the war, the Supreme Court affirmed that health insurance and other employee benefits could be negotiated, and thereafter, coverage expanded rapidly. By the 1970s, four systems were providing health care services: commercial insurance companies; nonprofit Blue Cross and Blue Shield groups; managed care plans, which include health maintenance organizations (HMOs); and the government, through plans such as Medicare and Medicaid, which were established in 1965.

But health insurance coverage is not yet universal. Figure Bd-D shows that in the early 1980s, about 85 percent of the American population was covered by some type of health insurance. The coverage rate peaked at 87 percent in 1987, and in the next decade fell to 84 percent. Today somewhat more than 40 million people lack medical insurance in the United States. Figure Bd-D also shows that in the past two decades, coverage rates have remained roughly constant at 86 percent for whites and 79 percent for blacks, but have fallen from 71 percent to 66 percent for Hispanics. Thus, the growing share of Hispanics in the labor force has contributed importantly to the overall decline in coverage within the United States.

While insurance coverage has been enormously beneficial for health, the administration of this coverage has arguably led to abuses. Because the insurance often has low marginal cost (or co-pay amounts), some patients can request tests and procedures of low or questionable value at little cost to themselves. And physicians who may be afraid of malpractice litigation are often happy to oblige, even if the tests being urged by patients have little basis in medical fact. Opposing this view, however, are those who argue that the tests and procedures sponsored by the system are sometimes helpful in making diagnoses. One cannot appraise the "efficiency" of health care administration without some assumptions about the value of health and life and the payoffs from batteries of tests or procedures.

Health care analysts have also suggested that the American health care system has unbalanced priorities, overbuilding acute-care facilities and underbuilding to prevent and manage chronic

[7] For a discussion of the evolution of health insurance, see Raffel and Barsukiewicz (2002), pp. 24–28.

illness and disability. Daniel Fox notes, for example, that about 40 percent of the acute hospital beds in the country have been staffed and empty, at a cost of perhaps $12 billion in 1992 (Fox 1993, p. 127). Whatever the balance (or lack thereof), hospital costs have certainly risen dramatically, increasing 15-fold from 1967 to 1996 (series Bd116) while costs of physicians' services increased 7.5-fold, at a time when the number of hospital beds decreased by more than one third (series Bd119) and the average length of stay declined from about 17 days to 8 days (series Bd174).

Another element in rising health care costs is new technology. Diagnosis and treatment of numerous diseases have gone high tech, and therefore become more expensive. Computerized axial tomography (CAT) scans, magnetic resonance imaging (MRI), and the like were unknown a few decades ago but have become commonplace in the modern medical world. Despite these new machines and techniques, however, modern medicine is largely unsuited to the practice of factory or assembly-line methods that have made manufactured goods so cheap by comparison. Unlike widgets, each individual medical case is potentially different enough to require interviews and medical tests, careful weighing of possible complicating factors, specialized treatment, and individual follow-up. Although some have suggested that computers might eventually help to automate diagnosis and treatment, which would lower costs, medical practice has yet to take significant steps in this direction.

Whatever the explanations for the huge expansion of the medical sector in the American economy, Tables Bd1–447 document this growth in several dimensions: expenditures, prices, facilities and use, personnel, insurance coverage, and administration.

From the perspective of economics, expenditures provide the most comprehensive single measure of resource commitment. Figure Bd-E places American expenditures on medical care as a share of GNP (series Bd34) in comparative international perspective. The figure shows that substantial growth occurred in the past several decades. In 1960, medical expenditures as a share of gross national product were about 5 percent, only slightly above the share in Western European countries with a relatively good health status, such as Denmark, Norway, Sweden, and the Netherlands.[8] Between 1960 and the mid-1970s, the share rose in all these countries to the range of 6–8 percent. But unlike the other countries, the resources devoted to medical care in the United States continued rising and in 1995 absorbed 13.5 percent of GNP, nearly twice that of the other countries shown in figure Bd-E. Thus, it is appropriate to ask whether medical resources in the United States are being efficiently and effectively allocated.

Tables Bd1–103 track this flow of resources in various ways, including type of service, source of funds, type of expenditure, and hospital expenses. Typical of an industry that faces growing demand for its output, Table Bd104–117 shows that medical care prices have also risen dramatically, usually outstripping the gains in prices of other products by a wide margin.

Tables Bd118–293 provide details on resource inputs in the form of facilities and personnel. These include hospitals and beds by type of service and by ownership (Tables Bd118–171), hospital use rates (Table Bd172–189), and numbers of patient contacts (Tables Bd190–211 and Bd285–293). Information on mental health facilities and patients is presented in Tables Bd212–240). Hospital

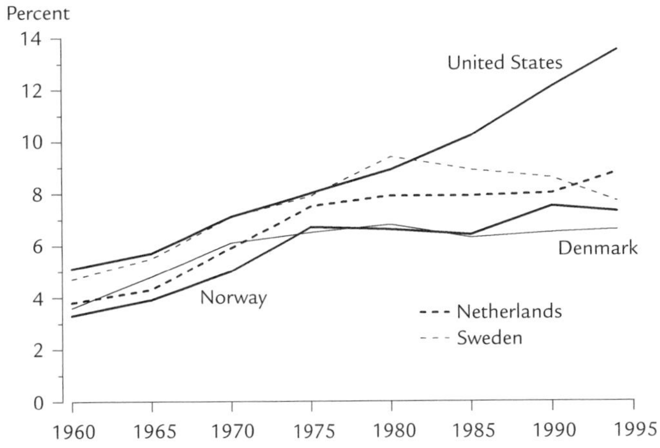

FIGURE Bd-E Health care expenditures as a percentage of gross national product: 1960–1994

Sources

U.S. National Center for Health Statistics, *Health, United States* (1996–1997), Table 117, p. 250.

personnel are documented in Tables Bd257–276. Tables Bd241–256 and Bd277–284 show numbers of physicians, dentists, and nurses, as well as data on facilities for their training. Notably, there has been a dramatic rise between 1967 and the mid-1990s in the number of skilled medical personnel per 100,000 population, with physicians increasing from 162 to nearly 300 and nurses increasing from 322 to approximately 800.

The trends in enrollment of medical students, given in Table Bd241–256, have some connection to the evolution of the American Medication Association (for discussion of the AMA, see Rayack 1967; Berlant 1975). The association was formed in 1846, and in 1904 it established its Council on Medical Education to raise standards for training by advocating a rigorous preparatory curriculum and by urging higher standards for facilities such as libraries and clinics. Between 1904 and 1920, the number of medical schools declined from 160 to 88 and the number of students shrank by approximately 50 percent, as numerous weak institutions closed their doors or merged with stronger schools. In contrast with mildly expansionist policies on enrollment in the 1920s, the AMA strongly advocated limits on enrollment as a way to reverse the declining incomes of physicians in the Depression years of the 1930s. World War II led to a sudden jump in enrollments through accelerated medical programs, which ended following the war. In the face of rising demand for medical education and the strains placed on facilities for training, the AMA favored substantial restrictions in the 1950s. Between 1958 and 1962, this policy was reversed and training capacity was expanded, leading to a doubling of enrollments between the early 1960s and the late 1970s.

Title IX of the Educational Amendments Act of 1972 was a second dynamic factor affecting the pattern of medical education. Prior to the early 1970s, the share of women among degree recipients in medicine and dentistry (and law, too) was relatively low, typically falling well below 10 percent. Within twenty years, however, the share had risen to more than one third and continued to increase in the 1990s.[9]

[8] Life expectancy at birth in each of these countries exceeds that in the United States.

[9] See Chapter Bc on education.

Tables Bd294–447 provide information on the administration of health care delivery. Tables Bd294–317 give data on health insurance coverage, and Table Bd318–326 shows the number of HMOs by plan and type of enrollment. Series Bd318 shows that a dramatic change in health care administration occurred with the rise of HMOs, which grew in number from 176 in 1976 to 651 in 1997. Medicare enrollment, persons served, and utilization are given in Tables Bd327–406, and Tables Bd407–447 depict Medicaid utilization, recipients, and payments.

Lifestyle Choices

Infectious diseases were major causes of death in the first half of the twentieth century. Although personal hygiene was a factor in contagion from some diseases, early in the century several major killers operated though the water supply, the food supply, accumulation of waste, or congestion in housing or place of employment. Thus, many of those who fell ill were victims of events or circumstances outside their control (given their incomes). The eradication of disease could be viewed in large part as the elimination or reduction of forces external to individuals and their lifestyle choices.

Although medical scientists have much to learn about the causes and control of today's major killers, such as heart disease and cancer, it seems clear that individual choices play a more important role in determining longevity and health quality of life than in the early twentieth century. Considerable evidence shows that substances such as tobacco and hard drugs are quite harmful to health. Tables Bd630–652 provide data on drug use and smoking.

Smoking has been on the decline for the past two decades. Series Bd631 on per capita cigarette consumption since 1900 shows that the habit grew significantly after each world war and peaked in the 1960s. Figure Bd-F shows that slightly more than 42 percent of people 18 and older smoked in 1966, but the share declined to about 26 percent in 1990, and has remained roughly constant since that time. The decline in smoking occurred for both men and women and across all education levels, but was substantially more pronounced among the highest education group (Table Bd630–638).

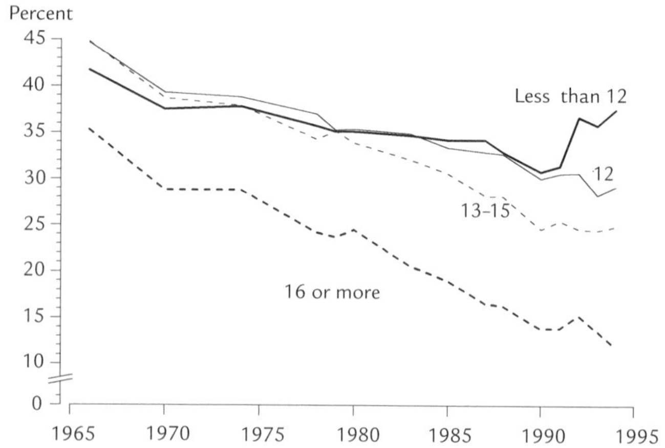

FIGURE Bd-F Percentage of adults who smoke, by years of education: 1966–1994

Sources

Series Bd635–638.

Documentation

Data are for persons age 25 and older.

The National Household Survey on Drug Abuse queries several aspects of drug use, including the number of initiates for various types of drugs. The trends during the 1970s, 1980s, and in the past few years are disturbing. The number of people who first tried cocaine increased from 77,000 in 1968 to 1,389,000 in 1982 (series Bd643). It then fell to 480,000 in 1991 but has once again increased in recent years, reaching 675,000 in 1996. The first use of hallucinogens has also climbed dramatically, from slightly less than 100,000 in 1965 to more than 1,000,000 in 1996 (series Bd645). Most of the gains in this substance occurred in two waves – 1967–1971 and 1992–1996. Initiates to heroin declined from about 100,000 per year in 1970 to 32,000 per year in 1992, but reached 171,000 per year in 1996. Marijuana initiates climbed from 68,000 in 1962 to 3,185,000 in 1975, then fell to 1,376,000 in 1991 and increased to 2,540,000 in 1996 (series Bd639). Overall, drug use grew rapidly in the 1970s and early 1980s, fell off during the middle and late 1980s, but surged again after the early 1990s.

Diet

For many generations, people have known of a connection between health and components of the diet. In the middle of the eighteenth century, for example, experiments established that eating citrus fruits or drinking lime juice could prevent scurvy. The scientific basis of the connection progressed rapidly in the twentieth century, beginning with the discovery of chemical identities for numerous vitamins, which made it readily possible to synthesize additives that fortify many foods. Although it was a significant advance in nutritional science, the success of this effort has not been altogether beneficial, as vitamins acquired a mystique of healing in some circles, leading to excess consumption. Too much vitamin A may cause birth defects, for example, and large intakes of calcium and vitamin D can create kidney stones.

In recent decades, numerous studies have explored the connection between diet and health.[10] A significant portion of the population, particularly well-educated professionals, has absorbed the results of this research and modified lifestyles in accordance with recommendations. It is a demanding process, not only to read the outpouring of research but also to evaluate and act on suggestions. It is challenging for professionals to stay abreast of the field, and even diligent readers in the general public can be confused by highly distilled versions of research that are often presented without perspective by the press.[11] For example, eggs were once portrayed as a villain that raised blood cholesterol, but recent press reports observe that they are high in protein, contain little saturated fat, and pose no significant health risk if consumed in moderation by people without high cholesterol levels.[12] Salt has been linked with hypertension, but it now appears to be harmful only for those at risk for other reasons. No doubt some people concerned about their nutrition have simply thrown up their hands, retreating to dietary habits or to whatever is affordable and tastes good.

The apparent confusion in the field makes it more difficult to assess the responsiveness of the public. Some people may be

---

[10] For additional discussion of nutrition and health, see U.S. Department of Health and Human Services (1988) and Gallagher and Allred (1992).

[11] Adding to the confusion, some recommendations that have been "overturned" were never based on solid evidence, and for various reasons the media has perpetuated some nutritional myths.

[12] See "Health: Eating Smart for Your Heart," *Time,* July 19, 1999, pp. 40–54.

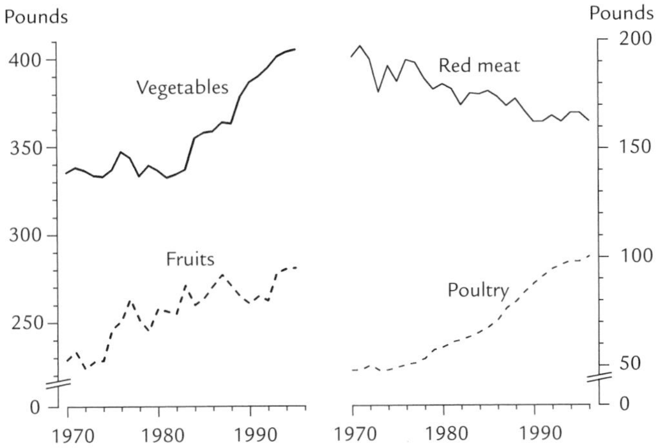

FIGURE Bd-G Per capita food consumption – vegetables, fruits, red meat, and poultry: 1970–1996

Source

Series Bd568–569 and Bd577–580.

Documentation

Figures include both fresh and processed fruits and vegetables.

apathetic, but others trying their best may not change behavior simply because messages have not been consistent and powerful for long periods of time. Yet some recommendations have been consistently proclaimed, among them the benefits of eating fruits and vegetables and the risks of consuming large amounts of saturated fats. The outcomes of dietary choices are presented in Tables Bd559–622. The decline in per capita food consumption after World War II reflects the large increase in the birth rate and the corresponding change in the age distribution of the population. By the time baby boomers reached the teenage years in the 1960s, food consumption per capita had increased.

Evidence discussed in the *Surgeon General's Report on Nutrition and Health* establishes the benefits of consuming fruits and vegetables. Figure Bd-G shows that per capita consumption of fruit (fresh and processed) rose irregularly from about 229 pounds in 1970 to nearly 281 pounds in 1995, a gain of more than 20 percent. The growing year-round availability of fresh fruits and vegetables in grocery stores may have contributed to this trend. Similarly, over the same period, consumption of fresh and processed vegetables also increased by approximately 20 percent, from 335 pounds to 405 pounds. At the same time, per capita consumption of red meat, which tends to be high in saturated fat, declined from 192 pounds to 163 pounds. This decline of 15 percent was replaced in the diet by a gain of more than 50 pounds per person in poultry, which is relatively low in saturated fat. Per capita consumption of total fat fluctuated but remained roughly unchanged at 155 pounds between 1970 and 1994 (series Bd601). Despite a few favorable trends for health in the composition of American diets, there has been an impressive increase in the number of calories consumed per person per day (series Bd598), bolstered by a substantial increase in total caloric sweeteners (series Bd595).

The benefits of moderate physical activity for health are now well established, particularly for reduction of cardiovascular disease, which is the leading cause of death (U.S. Department of Health and Human Services 1996). Unfortunately, it is impossible to obtain a substantial time series of information that consistently measures physical activity or fitness. It is clear, however, that Americans are becoming increasingly obese, and a decline in the physical demands of work combined with a lack of physical recreation are factors contributing to this trend. Activity can be measured in a variety of ways, including self-reports contained in diaries, logs, or recall surveys that tabulate participation in specific types of physical activity. Direct monitoring with mechanical or electronic devices, which detect duration and intensity of activity, is another approach, as is physiological measurement of air intake or carbon dioxide production. All of these approaches, however, are expensive or burdensome for participants, and self-reports may be inaccurate or lack consistency. Physical fitness can be assessed directly though endurance, muscular fitness, or body composition, but these, too, are expensive and burdensome and have not been done over long periods of time for a representative cross section of the population. Given the growing importance of physical fitness to health, however, we can hope that results from a consistent monitoring program will be available in the future.

Conclusions

This chapter documents a revolution in American health over the past century and a half. Important changes have occurred in health status, lifestyle choices, and health care administration. Beginning in the late nineteenth century, cheap and highly effective public health measures led to the eradication or control of several major infectious diseases. By the middle of the twentieth century, chemotherapy had also enabled physicians to reverse numerous diseases after they appeared. These and other progressive steps in health practices led to significant improvements in health, including a gain of twenty-five years in life expectancy and nearly ten centimeters in average height of Americans.

Given the benefits of public health and modern medicine, significant new resources flowed into the industry. Realizing that good health improved productivity, many employers began making health insurance available to workers near the middle of the century. Government-sponsored programs such as Medicare and Medicaid arose in the 1960s and 1970s to expand health care coverage. Recently, employers have increasingly sought HMOs to provide medical services for their employees.

The health achievements of the twentieth century are remarkable in long-term historical perspective, but they should not be a source of complacency. Strains of bacteria resistant to antibiotics are evolving, and new infections such as AIDS and the Ebola virus have appeared in the past quarter century. Americans are falling behind several Western European countries in average height, despite the relatively large share of gross domestic product devoted to health care. Thus, numerous concerns remain for health and for the provision of health care services in America.

References

Arora, Suchit. 2003. "The Relation of Sickness to Deaths: Evidence from the U.S. Army, 1905–39." Unpublished manuscript, April.

Banks, Amanda Carson. 1999. *Birth Chairs, Midwives, and Medicine.* University Press of Mississippi.

Berlant, Jeffrey Lionel. 1975. *Profession and Monopoly: A Study of Medicine in the United States and Great Britain.* University of California Press.

Cutler, David, and Ellen Meara. 2001. "Changes in the Age Distribution of Mortality over the 20th Century." National Bureau of Economic Research Working Paper number W8556, October.

Dublin, Louis I., and Alfred J. Lotka. 1938. *An Era of Health Progress.* Metropolitan Life Insurance Company.

Engerman, Stanley L. 1997. "The Standard of Living Debate in International Perspective: Measures and Indicators." In Richard H. Steckel and Roderick Floud, editors. *Health and Welfare during Industrialization.* University of Chicago Press.

Fogel, Robert W., and Dora L. Costa. 1997. "A Theory of Technophysio Evolution, with Some Implications for Forecasting Population, Health Care Costs, and Pension Costs." *Demography* 34: 49–66.

Fox, Daniel M. 1993. *Power and Illness: The Failure and Future of American Health Policy.* University of California Press.

Gallagher, Charlette R., and John B. Allred. 1992. *Taking the Fear out of Eating: A Nutritionists' Guide to Sensible Food Choices.* Cambridge University Press.

Gregg, Alan. 1956. *Challenges to Contemporary Medicine.* Columbia University Press.

Kahana, Eva, David E. Biegel, and May L. Wykle, editors. 1994. *Family Caregiving across the Lifespan.* Sage Publications.

Komlos, John. 1998. "Shrinking in a Growing Economy? The Mystery of Physical Stature during the Industrial Revolution." *Journal of Economic History* 58: 779–802.

Meeker, Edward. 1980. "Medicine and Public Health." In Glen Porter, editor. *Encyclopedia of American Economic History.* Scribner.

Pope, Clayne L. 1992. "Adult Mortality in America before 1900: A View from Family Histories." In Claudia Goldin and Hugh Rockoff, editors. *Strategic Factors in Nineteenth Century American Economic History: A Volume to Honor Robert W. Fogel.* University of Chicago Press.

Preston, Samuel H., and Michael R. Haines. 1991. *Fatal Years: Child Mortality in Late Nineteenth–Century America.* Princeton University Press.

Raffel, Marshall W., and Camille K. Barsukiewicz. 2002. *The U.S. Health System: Origins and Functions.* Delmar.

Rayack, Elton. 1967. *Professional Power and American Medicine: The Economics of the American Medical Association.* World Publishing.

Riley, James C. 1991. "Working Health Time: A Comparison of Preindustrial, Industrial, and Postindustrial Experience in Life and Health." *Explorations in Economic History* 28: 169–91.

Riley, James C. 2001. *Rising Life Expectancy: A Global History.* Cambridge University Press.

Shorter, Edward. 1996. "Primary Care." In Roy Porter, editor. *The Cambridge Illustrated History of Medicine.* Cambridge University Press.

Smille, Wilson George. 1955. *Public Health: Its Promise for the Future; A Chronicle of the Development of Public Health in the United States, 1607–1914.* Macmillan.

Steckel, Richard H. 1986. "A Peculiar Population: The Health and Nutrition of American Slaves from Childhood to Maturity." *Journal of Economic History* 46: 721–41.

Steckel, Richard H. 1995. "Stature and the Standard of Living." *Journal of Economic Literature* 33: 1903–40.

Steckel, Richard H. 1998. "Strategic Ideas in the Rise of the New Anthropometric History and Their Implications for Interdisciplinary Research." *Journal of Economic History* 58: 803–21.

Steckel, Richard H. 2000. "Alternative Indicators of Health and the Quality of Life." In Jeff Madrick, editor. *Unconventional Wisdom: Alternative Perspectives on the New Economy.* Twentieth Century.

U.S. Department of Health and Human Services. 1988. *The Surgeon General's Report on Nutrition and Health.* Department of Health and Human Services (Public Health Service) Publication number 88-50210. U.S. Government Printing Office.

U.S. Department of Health and Human Services. 1996. *Physical Activity and Health: A Report of the Surgeon General.* Superintendent of Documents.

Weatherall, Miles. 1996. "Drug Treatment and the Rise of Pharmacology." In Roy Porter, editor. *The Cambridge Illustrated History of Medicine.* Cambridge University Press.

EXPENDITURES

Richard H. Steckel

TABLE Bd1–16 Health expenditures, by type: 1929–1995

Contributed by Richard H. Steckel

		Health services and supplies												Research and construction of medical facilities		
	Total	Total	Hospital care	Physicians' services	Dentists' services	Other professional services	Drugs and drug sundries	Eyeglasses and appliances	Nursing home care	Home health care	Expenses for prepayment and administration	Government public health activities	Other health services	Total	Research	Construction
	Bd1	Bd2	Bd3	Bd4	Bd5	Bd6	Bd7	Bd8	Bd9	Bd10 [1]	Bd11	Bd12	Bd13 [1]	Bd14	Bd15	Bd16
Year	Million dollars	Million dollars	Million dollars	Million dollars	Million dollars	Million dollars	Million dollars	Million dollars	Million dollars	Million dollars	Million dollars	Million dollars	Million dollars	Million dollars	Million dollars	Million dollars
1929	3,649	3,436	663	1,004	482	252	606	133	—	—	110	96	91	213	—	213
1935	2,936	2,875	763	773	302	153	475	133	—	—	95	117	64	61	—	61
1940	3,987	3,868	1,011	973	419	174	637	189	33	—	167	153	112	119	3	116
1948	10,612	10,184	3,203	2,611	900	354	1,466	436	150	—	287	306	470	428	89	339
1949	11,576	10,811	3,557	2,633	920	371	1,557	458	168	—	271	338	539	765	105	660
1950	12,662	11,702	3,851	2,747	961	396	1,726	491	187	—	316	361	666	960	117	843
1951	13,992	12,912	4,254	2,868	997	426	1,989	551	207	—	321	416	883	1,080	134	946
1952	14,988	13,949	4,685	3,042	1,098	459	2,071	586	228	—	401	427	952	1,039	150	889
1953	15,745	14,895	5,085	3,278	1,234	499	2,152	612	248	—	498	378	911	850	164	686
1954	16,799	15,946	5,502	3,574	1,406	541	2,181	606	270	—	587	374	904	853	183	670
1955	17,745	16,884	5,900	3,689	1,508	562	2,384	604	312	—	624	377	924	861	210	651
1956	19,246	18,348	6,347	4,067	1,625	610	2,686	668	358	—	620	402	965	898	270	628
1957	21,108	19,885	6,892	4,419	1,737	673	3,010	678	368	—	682	415	1,011	1,223	344	879
1958	22,848	21,442	7,548	4,910	1,850	729	3,242	678	383	—	633	424	1,045	1,406	416	990
1959	24,878	23,354	8,177	5,481	1,894	801	3,525	722	434	—	754	428	1,138	1,524	526	998
1960	26,895	25,185	9,092	5,684	1,977	862	3,657	776	526	—	861	414	1,336	1,710	662	1,048
1961	28,783	26,766	9,921	5,895	2,067	882	3,824	804	606	—	995	452	1,320	2,018	844	1,174
1962	31,295	28,857	10,658	6,498	2,234	902	4,095	908	695	—	1,085	505	1,277	2,438	1,032	1,406
1963	33,530	30,890	11,709	6,891	2,277	921	4,235	952	891	—	1,094	540	1,380	2,640	1,184	1,456
1964	37,461	34,375	12,697	8,065	2,648	940	4,446	1,072	1,214	—	1,172	610	1,511	3,086	1,324	1,762
1965	41,994	38,551	13,885	8,473	2,809	1,033	5,212	1,211	2,072	—	1,736	814	1,306	3,443	1,469	1,912
1966	47,317	43,691	15,640	9,175	2,964	1,159	6,082	2,091	2,457	—	1,762	873	1,486	3,626	1,574	1,960
1967	52,654	48,870	18,259	10,142	3,360	1,258	6,415	1,989	2,889	—	2,020	927	1,612	3,784	1,703	2,006
1968	58,864	54,797	21,016	11,104	3,673	1,424	7,044	2,161	3,383	—	2,156	1,098	1,739	4,068	1,817	2,251
1969	66,155	61,415	24,019	12,648	4,197	1,471	7,674	2,168	3,831	—	2,255	1,272	1,880	4,740	1,823	2,917
1970	74,903	69,583	27,799	14,340	4,750	1,595	8,208	1,926	4,697	—	2,791	1,420	2,058	5,320	1,889	3,431
1971	83,112	77,065	30,769	15,918	5,068	1,628	8,668	1,970	5,635	—	3,321	1,764	2,323	6,047	2,040	4,007
1972	93,501	86,994	34,974	17,162	5,625	1,802	9,344	2,215	6,457	—	4,811	2,006	2,597	6,508	2,267	4,241
1973	103,045	96,291	38,673	19,075	6,531	1,973	10,050	2,480	7,217	—	5,370	2,233	2,690	6,754	2,438	4,316
1974	116,284	108,907	44,769	21,245	7,366	2,230	11,036	2,707	8,567	—	5,169	2,731	3,088	7,377	2,702	4,675
1975	132,120	123,822	52,141	24,932	8,237	2,619	11,813	2,982	10,105	—	4,143	3,157	3,692	8,298	3,239	5,059
1976	148,872	139,823	59,808	27,565	9,448	3,202	12,781	3,219	11,390	—	4,734	3,813	3,863	9,049	3,635	5,414
1977	169,875	160,794	67,721	31,852	10,535	3,566	13,987	3,491	12,810	—	8,511	4,316	4,006	9,081	3,809	5,272
1978	188,643	179,113	75,842	35,802	11,894	4,080	15,374	3,945	15,102	—	7,202	5,284	4,587	9,529	4,323	5,206
1979	212,199	202,318	85,342	40,599	13,607	4,687	16,975	4,353	17,807	—	7,720	6,047	5,180	9,882	4,615	5,267

Note appears at end of table

(continued)

TABLE Bd1–16 Health expenditures, by type: 1929–1995 *Continued*

		Health services and supplies												Research and construction of medical facilities		
	Total	Total	Hospital care	Physicians' services	Dentists' services	Other professional services	Drugs and drug sundries	Eyeglasses and appliances	Nursing home care	Home health care	Expenses for prepayment and administration	Government public health activities	Other health services	Total	Research	Construction
	Bd1	Bd2	Bd3	Bd4	Bd5	Bd6	Bd7	Bd8	Bd9	Bd10 [1]	Bd11	Bd12	Bd13 [1]	Bd14	Bd15	Bd16
Year	Million dollars	Million dollars	Million dollars	Million dollars	Million dollars	Million dollars	Million dollars	Million dollars	Million dollars	Million dollars	Million dollars	Million dollars	Million dollars	Million dollars	Million dollars	Million dollars
1980	247,500	235,600	101,300	46,800	15,400	5,600	18,500	5,100	20,400	—	9,200	7,200	5,900	11,900	5,400	6,500
1981	291,400	278,100	119,900	52,200	15,700	8,200	24,600	4,700	23,500	—	14,200	8,300	6,900	13,200	5,700	7,500
1982	321,200	307,000	134,700	61,800	19,500	7,100	21,800	5,600	26,900	—	12,800	9,300	7,600	14,200	5,900	8,300
1983	355,100	339,800	148,800	68,400	21,800	8,000	23,600	6,500	29,400	—	14,500	10,100	8,600	15,300	6,200	9,100
1984	387,400	371,600	157,900	75,400	25,100	8,800	25,800	7,400	32,000	—	19,100	10,700	9,400	15,800	6,800	9,000
1985	422,600	407,200	168,300	74,000	23,300	16,600	36,200	7,100	34,100	3,800	25,200	12,300	6,400	15,400	7,800	7,600
1986	454,900	438,900	179,800	82,100	24,700	18,600	39,700	8,100	36,700	4,000	24,600	13,500	7,100	16,000	8,500	7,400
1987	494,200	476,900	194,200	93,000	27,100	21,100	43,200	9,100	39,700	4,100	23,000	14,600	7,800	17,300	9,000	8,200
1988	546,100	526,200	212,000	105,100	29,400	23,800	46,300	10,100	42,800	4,500	26,900	16,600	8,700	19,800	10,300	9,500
1989	604,300	583,600	232,400	116,100	31,600	27,100	50,500	10,400	47,500	5,600	33,800	18,900	9,800	20,700	11,000	9,700
1990	697,500	672,900	256,400	146,300	31,600	34,700	59,900	10,500	50,900	13,100	38,600	19,600	11,200	24,500	12,200	12,300
1991	761,700	736,800	282,300	159,200	33,300	38,300	65,600	11,200	57,200	16,100	38,800	21,400	13,600	24,900	12,900	12,000
1992	834,200	806,700	305,400	175,700	37,000	42,100	71,200	11,900	62,300	19,600	42,700	23,400	15,400	27,500	14,200	13,400
1993	892,100	863,100	323,300	182,700	39,200	46,300	75,000	12,500	67,000	23,000	50,900	25,300	17,900	29,000	14,500	14,500
1994	937,100	906,700	335,000	190,600	42,100	49,100	77,700	12,900	72,400	26,300	50,600	28,200	21,700	30,400	15,800	14,600
1995	988,500	957,800	350,100	201,600	45,800	52,600	83,400	13,800	77,900	28,600	47,700	31,400	25,000	30,700	16,600	14,000

[1] Through 1984, home health care included under series Bd13.

Sources

For 1929–1968, U.S. Social Security Administration, *Compendium of National Health Expenditures Data*, Department of Health, Education, and Welfare (DHEW) Publication number (SSA)73-11903 (1973), Table 6.

For 1969–1970, *National Health Expenditures, Calendar Years 1929–71*, Research and Statistics Note, number 3, DHEW Publication number (SSA)73-11701 (1973), Tables 2 and 8.

For 1971–1995, data come from National Center for Health Statistics, *Health, United States* (Public Health Service). Annual issues are published in the year subsequent to the year for which they contain data.

Documentation

This text applies to Table Bd1–16 and Table Bd17–32.

The general method of estimating national health expenditures is to estimate the total outlays for each type of medical service or expenditure and to deduct the amounts paid to public and private hospitals, physicians in private practice, and so on, under each public program. The figures for each public program are allocated by type of expenditure on the basis of published and unpublished reports for each program. Resident population is used to compute per capita expenditures.

Series Bd3 and Bd19. The estimates of expenditures for hospital care are based on the data on hospital finances published by the American Hospital Association and increased slightly to allow for nonreporting and for osteopathic hospitals. Salaries of physicians and dentists on the staffs of hospitals and hospital outpatient facilities are considered a component of hospital care and are, therefore, included. Expenditures for the education and training of physicians and other health personnel are included only where they are not separable from the cost of hospital operations.

Series Bd4–6 and Bd20–22. The estimates of expenditures for the services of physicians, dentists, and other health professions in private practice are based on the gross incomes from self-employment practice reported to the Internal Revenue Service on Schedule C of the income tax return (as shown in U.S. Internal Revenue Service, *Statistics of Income*, an annual bulletin published by the Department of the Treasury). Data are totaled for practitioners in sole proprietorships and partnerships. The total also includes the estimated gross income of offices that are organized as corporations, the gross receipts of medical and dental laboratories estimated to represent patient payments to medical laboratories, and the estimated expenses of group-practice prepayment plans in providing physicians' services (to the extent that these are not included in physicians' income from self-employment). Estimated receipts of physicians for making life insurance examinations are deducted. Salaries of physicians and dentists on the staffs of hospitals and hospital outpatient facilities are considered a component of hospital care, series Bd3. Salaries of visiting nurse associations, estimated from surveys conducted by the National League for Nursing, are added to the private income of other health professionals. Deductions and exclusions are made in the same manner as for expenditures for physicians' and dentists' services.

Series Bd6 and Bd22. Services of registered and practical nurses in private duty, visits of nurses, podiatrists, physical therapists, clinical psychologists, chiropractors, naturopaths, and Christian Science practitioners.

Series Bd7 and Bd23. Include research expenditures of drug companies.

Series Bd7–8 and Bd23–24. The basic source of the estimates for these items is the report of personal consumption expenditures in the U.S. Department of Commerce national income accounts in the monthly *Survey of Current Business*. Total expenditures for drugs and appliances are the sum of the department's estimates and the expenditures under all public programs for these products.

Series Bd8 and Bd24. Include fees of optometrists and expenditures for hearing aids, orthopedic appliances, artificial limbs, crutches, wheelchairs, and so on.

Series Bd9 and Bd25. Expenditures for nursing home care are derived by applying an estimated cost per patient day to the total days of care. Total days of care are estimated by applying an average occupancy rate, as reported by the Federal Housing Administration, to the number of nursing-home beds, as reported by the Division of Hospital and Medical Facilities of the Public Health Service in their annual report, *Hill-Burton State Plan Data*. The cost per patient day was based on unpublished data from a survey of nursing homes financed by the Social Security Administration.

Series Bd11 and Bd27. Include the net cost of insurance and administrative expenses of federally financed health programs. Prepayment expenses represent the difference between the earned premiums or subscription charges of health insurance organizations and their claim or benefit expenditures (expenditures in providing such services in the case of organizations that directly provide services). In other words, it is the amount retained by health insurance organizations for operating expenses, additions to reserves, and profits, and is considered a consumer expenditure. The data on the financial experience of health insurance organizations are reported annually in a *Social Security Bulletin* article on private health insurance. The administration component of this series represents the administrative expenses (where they are reported) of federally financed health programs.

Series Bd12 and Bd28. The federal portion of this series consists of outlays for the organization and delivery of health services and prevention and control of health problems by the Health Services and Mental Health Administration, the National Institutes of Health, and the Environmental Health Service of the Public Health Service. Also included are outlays by other federal agencies for similar health activities. The data for these programs are taken annually from Office of Management and Budget, *Special Analyses, Budget of the United States*. The state and local portion of this series represents expenditures of all state and local health departments and intergovernmental payments to the states and localities for public health activities. It excludes expenditures by other state and local government departments for air-pollution and water-pollution control, sanitation, water supplies, and sewage treatment. The source of these data is *Government Finances,* published annually by the Bureau of the Census.

Series Bd13 and Bd29. Cover expenditures not elsewhere classified. They include, for each public program, the residual amount of expenditures not classified as a specific type of medical service. In addition, they include the following programs: industrial in-plant services and activities of private voluntary health agencies in the private sector, and school health services and nonhospital federal medical activities in the public sector.

Series Bd15 and Bd31. Expenditures for medical research include all such spending by agencies whose primary object is the advancement of human health. Also included are those research expenditures directly related to health that are made by other agencies, such as those of the U.S. Department of Defense or the National Aeronautics and Space Administration. Research expenditures of drug and medical supply companies are excluded because they are included in the cost of the product. The federal amounts represent those reported annually as medical research in the Office of Management and Budget, *Special Analyses, Budget of the United States*. The amounts shown for state and local governments and private expenditures are based on published estimates that have been prepared by the Resources Analysis Branch of the National Institutes of Health, primarily in the periodic publication *Basic Data Relating to the National Institutes of Health*.

Series Bd16 and Bd32. Expenditures for construction represent "value put in place" for hospitals, nursing homes, medical clinics, and medical-research facilities but not for private office buildings providing office space for private practitioners. Excluded are amounts spent for construction of water-treatment or sewage-treatment plants and federal grants for these purposes. The data for value put in place for construction of publicly and privately owned medical facilities in each year are taken from the U.S. Department of Commerce monthly report *Construction Review*.

TABLE Bd17–32 Per capita health expenditures, by type: 1929–1995

Contributed by Richard H. Steckel

		Health services and supplies												Research and construction of medical facilities		
	Total	Total	Hospital care	Physicians' services	Dentists' services	Other professional services	Drugs and drug sundries	Eyeglasses and appliances	Nursing home care	Home health care	Expenses for prepayment and administration	Government public health activities	Other health services	Total	Research	Construction
	Bd17	Bd18	Bd19	Bd20	Bd21	Bd22	Bd23	Bd24	Bd25	Bd26 [1]	Bd27	Bd28	Bd29 [1]	Bd30	Bd31	Bd32
Year	Dollars	Dollars	Dollars	Dollars	Dollars	Dollars	Dollars	Dollars	Dollars	Dollars	Dollars	Dollars	Dollars	Dollars	Dollars	Dollars
1929	29.49	27.77	5.36	8.11	3.90	2.04	4.90	1.07	—	—	0.89	0.78	0.74	1.72	—	1.72
1935	22.65	22.18	5.89	5.96	2.33	1.18	3.67	1.03	—	—	0.73	0.90	0.49	0.47	—	0.47
1940	29.62	28.74	7.51	7.23	3.11	1.29	4.73	1.40	0.25	—	1.24	1.14	0.83	0.88	0.02	0.86
1948	70.97	68.11	21.42	17.46	6.02	2.37	9.80	2.92	1.00	—	1.92	2.05	3.14	2.86	0.60	2.27
1949	76.11	71.08	23.39	17.31	6.05	2.44	10.24	3.01	1.10	—	1.78	2.22	3.54	5.03	0.69	4.34
1950	81.86	75.66	24.90	17.76	6.21	2.56	11.16	3.17	1.21	—	2.04	2.33	4.31	6.21	0.76	5.45
1951	88.95	82.08	27.04	18.23	6.34	2.71	12.64	3.50	1.32	—	2.04	2.64	5.61	6.87	0.85	6.01
1952	93.69	87.19	29.29	19.02	6.86	2.87	12.95	3.66	1.43	—	2.51	2.67	5.95	6.49	0.94	5.56
1953	96.84	91.61	31.27	20.16	7.59	3.07	13.24	3.76	1.53	—	3.06	2.32	5.60	5.23	1.01	4.22
1954	101.54	96.37	33.26	21.60	8.50	3.27	13.18	3.66	1.63	—	3.55	2.26	5.46	5.16	1.11	4.05
1955	105.38	100.27	35.04	21.91	8.96	3.34	14.16	3.59	1.85	—	3.71	2.24	5.49	5.11	1.25	3.87
1956	112.32	107.07	37.04	23.73	9.48	3.56	15.67	3.90	2.09	—	3.62	2.35	5.63	5.24	1.58	3.66
1957	121.00	113.99	39.51	25.33	9.96	3.86	17.25	3.89	2.11	—	3.91	2.38	5.80	7.01	1.97	5.04
1958	128.81	120.88	42.55	27.68	10.43	4.11	18.28	3.82	2.16	—	3.57	2.39	5.89	7.93	2.35	5.58
1959	137.94	129.49	45.34	30.39	10.50	4.44	19.54	4.00	2.41	—	4.18	2.37	6.31	8.45	2.92	5.53

Note appears at end of table

(continued)

TABLE Bd17–32 Per capita health expenditures, by type: 1929–1995 *Continued*

		Health services and supplies												Research and construction of medical facilities		
	Total	Total	Hospital care	Physicians' services	Dentists' services	Other professional services	Drugs and drug sundries	Eyeglasses and appliances	Nursing home care	Home health care	Expenses for prepayment and administration	Government public health activities	Other health services	Total	Research	Construction
	Bd17	Bd18	Bd19	Bd20	Bd21	Bd22	Bd23	Bd24	Bd25	Bd26 [1]	Bd27	Bd28	Bd29 [1]	Bd30	Bd31	Bd32
Year	Dollars	Dollars	Dollars	Dollars	Dollars	Dollars	Dollars	Dollars	Dollars	Dollars	Dollars	Dollars	Dollars	Dollars	Dollars	Dollars
1960	146.30	137.00	49.46	30.92	10.75	4.69	19.89	4.22	2.86	—	4.68	2.25	7.27	9.30	3.60	5.70
1961	154.02	143.23	53.09	31.55	11.06	4.72	20.46	4.30	3.24	—	5.32	2.42	7.06	10.80	4.52	6.28
1962	164.89	152.05	56.16	34.24	11.77	4.75	21.58	4.78	3.66	—	5.72	2.66	6.73	12.85	5.44	7.41
1963	174.15	160.44	60.81	35.79	11.83	4.78	22.00	4.94	4.63	—	5.68	2.80	7.17	13.71	6.15	7.56
1964	191.88	176.07	65.04	41.31	13.56	4.81	22.77	5.49	6.22	—	6.00	3.12	7.74	15.81	6.78	9.03
1965	204.68	187.58	68.81	44.23	14.20	5.25	24.53	6.22	6.72	—	6.54	3.53	7.55	17.10	7.43	9.67
1966	224.89	207.22	77.92	45.78	14.82	5.62	26.55	7.07	7.68	—	8.41	4.43	9.00	17.67	7.87	9.80
1967	250.77	232.42	89.76	50.89	16.62	5.73	27.96	7.96	9.19	—	9.28	4.66	10.38	18.35	8.42	9.92
1968	277.14	257.28	102.49	54.36	17.74	6.22	30.19	8.48	11.17	—	9.83	5.38	11.42	19.86	8.79	11.07
1969	311.06	287.83	116.84	61.37	19.63	6.37	33.04	8.56	12.85	—	10.23	6.38	12.57	23.23	8.81	14.41
1970	343.44	318.45	132.42	68.59	21.20	7.03	35.01	8.95	14.73	—	10.07	7.52	12.91	24.99	8.83	16.15
1971	403.06	373.74	149.22	77.20	24.58	7.90	42.04	9.55	27.33	—	16.11	8.55	11.27	29.33	9.89	19.43
1972	449.09	417.84	167.98	82.43	27.02	8.66	44.88	10.64	31.01	—	23.11	9.63	12.47	31.26	10.89	20.37
1973	490.92	458.75	184.24	90.88	31.11	9.40	47.88	11.82	34.38	—	25.58	10.64	12.82	32.18	11.62	20.56
1974	550.07	515.17	211.77	100.50	34.84	10.55	52.20	12.81	40.53	—	24.45	12.92	14.61	34.90	12.78	22.11
1975	619.99	581.05	244.68	117.00	38.65	12.29	55.43	13.99	47.42	—	19.44	14.81	17.33	38.94	15.20	23.74
1976	693.40	651.25	278.57	128.39	44.01	14.91	59.53	14.99	53.05	—	22.05	17.76	17.99	42.15	16.93	25.22
1977	785.00	743.04	312.94	147.19	48.68	16.48	64.63	16.13	59.20	—	39.33	19.94	18.51	41.96	17.60	24.36
1978	864.94	821.24	347.74	164.15	54.53	18.71	70.49	18.09	69.24	—	33.02	24.23	21.03	43.69	19.82	23.87
1979	964.10	919.21	387.74	184.46	61.82	21.29	77.12	19.78	80.90	—	35.07	27.47	23.53	44.90	20.97	23.93
1980	1,092.49	1,039.97	447.15	206.58	67.98	24.72	81.66	22.51	90.05	—	40.61	31.78	26.04	52.53	23.84	28.69
1981	1,269.90	1,211.94	522.52	227.48	68.42	35.74	107.21	20.48	102.41	—	61.88	36.17	30.07	57.52	24.84	32.68
1982	1,386.49	1,325.20	581.45	266.77	84.17	30.65	94.10	24.17	116.12	—	55.25	40.14	32.81	61.30	25.47	35.83
1983	1,518.87	1,453.43	636.46	292.57	93.25	34.22	100.94	27.80	125.75	—	62.02	43.20	36.78	65.44	26.52	38.92
1984	1,642.74	1,575.74	669.56	319.73	106.43	37.32	109.40	31.38	135.69	—	80.99	45.37	39.86	67.00	28.83	38.16
1985	1,776.20	1,711.47	707.37	311.02	97.93	69.77	152.15	29.84	143.32	15.97	105.92	51.70	26.90	64.73	32.78	31.94
1986	1,894.37	1,827.74	748.75	341.89	102.86	77.46	165.33	33.73	152.83	16.66	102.44	56.22	29.57	66.63	35.40	30.82
1987	2,039.71	1,968.31	801.52	383.84	111.85	87.09	178.30	37.56	163.85	16.92	94.93	60.26	32.19	71.40	37.15	33.84
1988	2,233.55	2,152.16	867.08	429.86	120.25	97.34	189.37	41.31	175.05	18.40	110.02	67.89	35.58	80.98	42.13	38.85
1989	2,448.35	2,364.49	941.58	470.39	128.03	109.80	204.60	42.14	192.45	22.69	136.94	76.57	39.71	83.87	44.57	39.30
1990	2,804.38	2,705.47	1,030.89	588.22	127.05	139.52	240.84	42.22	204.65	52.67	155.20	78.80	45.03	98.51	49.05	49.45
1991	3,021.35	2,922.58	1,119.77	631.48	132.09	151.92	260.21	44.43	226.89	63.86	153.90	84.88	53.95	98.77	51.17	47.60
1992	3,271.23	3,163.39	1,197.60	688.99	145.09	165.09	279.20	46.66	244.30	76.86	167.44	91.76	60.39	107.84	55.68	52.55
1993	3,460.50	3,348.01	1,254.10	708.70	152.06	179.60	290.93	48.49	259.90	89.22	197.44	98.14	69.44	112.49	56.25	56.25
1994	3,599.08	3,482.33	1,286.62	732.03	161.69	188.58	298.42	49.54	278.06	101.01	194.34	108.31	83.34	116.76	60.68	56.07
1995	3,760.13	3,643.35	1,331.74	766.86	174.22	200.08	317.24	52.49	296.32	108.79	181.44	119.44	95.10	116.78	63.14	53.25

[1] Through 1984, home health care included under series Bd29.

Sources

For 1929–1968, U.S. Social Security Administration, *Compendium of National Health Expenditures Data*, Department of Health, Education, and Welfare (DHEW) Publication number (SSA)73-11903 (1973), Table 6.

For 1969–1970, *National Health Expenditures, Calendar Years 1929–71*, Research and Statistics Note, number 3, DHEW Publication number (SSA)73-11701 (1973), Tables 2 and 8.

For 1971–1995, data come from National Center for Health Statistics, *Health, United States* (Public Health Service). Annual issues are published in the year subsequent to the year for which they contain data.

Documentation

See the text for Table Bd1–16.

TABLE Bd33–38 Health expenditures, by source of funds: 1929–1997

Contributed by Richard H. Steckel

	Total		Private			
	Total	As percentage of gross national product	Total	Paid by consumers	Paid by philanthropy and other	Public
	Bd33	Bd34	Bd35	Bd36	Bd37	Bd38
Year	Million dollars	Percent	Million dollars	Million dollars	Million dollars	Million dollars
1929	3,649	3.5	3,154	2,937	217	495
1935	2,936	4.0	2,372	2,288	84	563
1940	3,987	3.9	3,178	3,051	127	811
1948	10,612	3.9	8,208	7,691	517	2,404
1949	11,576	4.3	8,716	8,042	674	2,860
1950	12,662	4.3	9,222	8,425	797	3,440
1951	13,992	4.1	9,846	8,962	884	4,148
1952	14,988	4.2	10,558	9,690	868	4,431
1953	15,745	4.1	11,388	10,629	759	4,357
1954	16,799	4.4	12,421	11,572	849	4,378
1955	17,745	4.2	13,190	12,282	908	4,555
1956	19,246	4.4	14,278	13,374	904	4,968
1957	21,108	4.5	15,648	14,547	1,101	5,461
1958	22,848	4.9	16,932	15,763	1,169	5,918
1959	24,878	4.9	18,596	17,329	267	6,280
1960	26,850	5.1	20,202	18,945	815	6,648
1961	28,768	5.2	21,465	20,015	930	7,302
1962	31,268	5.3	23,290	21,603	1,064	7,977
1963	34,067	5.5	25,343	23,537	1,154	8,724
1964	37,647	5.6	28,290	26,198	1,226	9,356
1965	41,145	5.7	30,867	28,565	1,469	10,278
1966	45,263	5.7	31,600	29,182	1,458	13,663
1967	50,969	6.1	31,964	29,477	1,497	19,005
1968	57,684	6.3	35,879	32,940	1,727	21,804
1969	64,792	6.5	40,247	36,554	1,825	24,545
1970	73,243	7.0	45,537	41,184	2,048	27,706
1971	81,018	7.1	49,829	44,960	2,251	31,189
1972	90,943	7.3	55,808	50,296	2,610	35,135
1973	100,838	7.2	61,550	55,892	2,597	39,288
1974	114,265	7.5	67,667	61,655	2,917	46,597
1975	130,727	7.9	75,695	69,363	3,180	55,032
1976	149,856	8.1	87,434	79,799	4,111	62,422
1977	170,375	8.3	100,158	92,262	4,339	70,217
1978	190,601	8.2	111,048	102,247	5,046	79,553
1979	215,201	8.3	125,054	115,252	5,698	90,147
1980	247,273	8.7	142,493	130,011	7,748	104,780
1981	286,908	9.1	165,715	150,677	9,319	121,193
1982	322,978	9.8	188,397	170,853	10,701	134,581
1983	355,291	9.9	207,746	188,480	11,604	147,545
1984	390,076	9.8	229,938	210,057	12,319	160,139
1985	428,720	10.1	254,518	233,504	14,014	174,202
1986	461,228	10.3	271,397	248,636	15,796	189,831
1987	500,502	10.5	293,291	268,498	16,989	207,210
1988	560,379	10.9	334,251	305,518	19,549	226,127
1989	623,536	11.3	371,413	341,673	20,043	252,123
1990	699,361	12.0	416,187	384,587	20,659	283,174
1991	766,783	12.8	448,859	415,072	22,910	317,923
1992	836,537	13.2	483,553	447,247	24,492	352,984
1993	898,496	13.5	513,172	473,850	26,491	385,323
1994	947,717	13.4	524,908	483,610	28,430	422,810
1995	993,725	13.4	538,507	495,273	30,980	455,218
1996	1,042,522	13.3	561,141	515,233	32,898	481,382
1997	1,092,385	13.1	585,312	535,571	35,032	507,073

Sources

U.S. Social Security Administration. For 1929–1959, *Compendium of National Health Expenditures Data*, Department of Health, Education, and Welfare (DHEW) Publication number (SSA)73-11903 (1973), Tables 3, 4, and 6; *National Health Expenditures, Calendar Years 1929–71*, Research and Statistics Note, number 3, DHEW Publication number (SSA) 73-11701 (1973), Tables 2 and 5. For 1960–1997, data are provided at the Internet site of the Centers for Medicare and Medicaid Services.

(continued)

TABLE Bd33–38 Health expenditures, by source of funds: 1929–1997 *Continued*

Documentation

This text applies to Tables Bd33–44.

See the text for Table Bd1–16 for a discussion of the general method of estimating national health expenditures.

The data for 1960–1970 have been revised and so differ from those in the 1975 edition of *Historical Statistics of the United States*.

Beginning in 1990, published data are revised every year.

Series Bd34. Gross national product from series Ca2.

Series Bd35–37 and Bd40–43. For the most part, private expenditures represent direct payments made by private consumers and insurance benefits paid on their behalf by private insurers. In addition, they include private philanthropy; amounts spent by industry for maintenance of in-plant health services; expenditures made from capital funds for expansion, renovation, or new construction of medical facilities; and outlays for research by private foundations. Series Bd37 includes nonpatient revenues and philanthropy.

Series Bd38 and Bd44. Public funds come from federal, state, and local governments.

Series Bd39–44. Personal health care expenditures include all such expenditures except research, construction, expenses for prepayment and administration, government public health activities, and expenses of private voluntary agencies for fund-raising and general-health activities.

TABLE Bd39–44 Personal health expenditures, by source of funds: 1929–1997

Contributed by Richard H. Steckel

		Private				
	Total	Total	Direct payments	Paid by insurance benefits	Paid by other	Public
	Bd39	Bd40	Bd41	Bd42	Bd43	Bd44
Year	Million dollars	Million dollars	Million dollars	Million dollars	Million dollars	Million dollars
1929	3,202	2,913	28	29	84	289
1935	2,663	2,269	21	95	74	392
1940	3,548	2,980	28	86	94	570
1948	9,473	7,694	6,829	606	259	1,779
1949	10,073	8,078	7,026	767	285	1,995
1950	10,885	8,445	7,133	992	320	2,440
1951	12,031	8,997	7,302	1,353	342	3,035
1952	12,968	9,662	7,697	1,604	361	3,307
1953	13,860	10,525	8,224	1,919	382	3,335
1954	14,818	11,408	8,816	2,179	413	3,410
1955	15,708	12,100	9,132	2,536	432	3,608
1956	17,140	13,221	9,750	3,015	456	3,919
1957	18,591	14,357	10,403	3,474	480	4,235
1958	20,177	15,645	11,266	3,877	502	4,534
1959	21,953	17,141	12,190	4,399	552	4,810
1960	23,618	18,502	18,084	5,016	418	5,117
1961	25,066	19,513	19,059	5,686	454	5,553
1962	26,962	21,047	20,555	6,328	493	5,914
1963	29,467	23,031	22,480	6,942	551	6,436
1964	32,383	25,674	25,059	7,808	614	6,709
1965	35,165	27,910	27,217	8,677	693	7,255
1966	38,839	28,524	27,733	8,895	791	10,315
1967	44,141	28,993	28,062	9,236	931	15,148
1968	49,844	32,405	31,256	10,485	1,149	17,438
1969	56,236	36,508	35,151	12,436	1,357	19,729
1970	63,825	41,313	39,677	14,776	1,636	22,512
1971	70,054	44,681	42,868	16,463	1,813	25,372
1972	78,043	49,313	47,244	18,255	2,069	28,731
1973	87,065	54,744	52,572	20,618	2,173	32,321
1974	99,868	61,434	58,956	24,119	2,478	38,434
1975	114,505	69,211	66,461	28,368	2,750	45,294
1976	130,532	79,284	75,445	33,507	3,839	51,249
1977	147,735	89,669	85,481	39,076	4,188	58,067
1978	164,839	99,333	94,330	44,597	5,002	65,506
1979	187,496	112,798	107,055	52,738	5,743	74,698
1980	217,039	130,053	122,268	62,014	7,785	86,986
1981	252,006	150,737	141,393	72,901	9,344	101,269
1982	283,277	170,088	159,428	83,980	10,660	113,190
1983	311,514	186,564	175,062	92,743	11,502	124,950
1984	341,472	205,208	192,954	102,097	12,254	136,264

TABLE Bd39–44 Personal health expenditures, by source of funds: 1929–1997 *Continued*

		Private				
	Total	Total	Direct payments	Paid by insurance benefits	Paid by other	Public
	Bd39	Bd40	Bd41	Bd42	Bd43	Bd44
Year	Million dollars	Million dollars	Million dollars	Million dollars	Million dollars	Million dollars
1985	376,442	228,754	214,724	114,065	14,031	147,688
1986	410,504	248,746	233,013	124,932	15,733	161,757
1987	449,709	273,234	256,252	140,199	16,982	176,476
1988	499,257	307,813	288,246	160,788	19,567	191,444
1989	550,132	336,612	316,459	183,251	20,154	213,520
1990	614,680	373,536	352,776	207,743	20,761	241,143
1991	679,563	406,200	383,149	229,814	23,050	273,364
1992	740,680	437,115	412,406	250,649	24,709	303,564
1993	790,518	459,128	432,287	265,236	26,841	331,390
1994	833,969	471,969	443,050	274,548	28,920	362,000
1995	879,332	489,191	457,578	286,587	31,613	390,140
1996	923,996	511,405	477,902	299,778	33,503	412,592
1997	969,005	536,651	501,001	313,451	35,650	432,354

Sources

U.S. Social Security Administration. For 1929–1959, *Compendium of National Health Expenditures Data,* Department of Health, Education, and Welfare (DHEW) Publication number (SSA)73-11903 (1973), Tables 3, 4 and 6; *National Health Expenditures, Calendar Years 1929–71,* Research and Statistics Note, number 3, DHEW Publication number (SSA)73-11701 (1973, Tables 2 and 5. 1960–1997, data are provided at the Internet site of the Centers for Medicare and Medicaid Services.

Documentation

See the text for Table Bd33–38.

TABLE Bd45–62 Health expenditures – public and private, by type: 1929–1997

Contributed by Richard H. Steckel

	Total		Private			Public			
						Health and medical services			
	Total	As percentage of gross national product	Health and medical services	Medical research	Medical facilities construction	Veterans' hospital and medical care	General hospital and medical care (Census)	General hospital and medical care (CMS)	Public assistance
	Bd45	Bd46	Bd47	Bd48	Bd49	Bd50	Bd51	Bd52	Bd53
Year	Million dollars	Percent	Million dollars	Million dollars	Million dollars	Million dollars	Million dollars	Million dollars	Million dollars
1929	3,649	3.5	3,049	—	105	49	125	—	—
1935	2,936	4.0	2,362	—	10	50	231	—	—
1940	3,987	3.9	3,145	—	33	63	306	—	—
1948	10,612	3.9	8,068	32	108	554	739	—	—
1949	11,576	4.3	8,456	36	224	579	834	—	26
1950	12,662	4.3	8,885	38	299	582	933	—	76
1951	13,992	4.1	9,449	40	357	613	1,034	—	110
1952	14,988	4.2	10,204	45	309	643	1,137	—	137
1953	15,745	4.1	11,170	51	167	661	1,206	—	165
1954	16,799	4.4	12,152	54	215	701	1,263	—	194
1955	17,745	4.3	12,889	60	241	723	1,384	—	232
1956	19,246	4.4	14,016	70	192	732	1,573	—	270
1957	21,108	4.6	15,224	78	346	769	1,718	—	304
1958	22,848	4.9	16,473	86	373	822	1,803	—	365
1959	24,878	4.9	18,100	106	390	862	1,909	—	451
1960	26,850	5.1	19,598	139	270	922	2,100	108	544
1961	28,768	5.3	20,719	147	344	961	2,179	114	724
1962	31,268	5.3	22,367	153	440	991	2,204	119	957
1963	34,067	5.5	23,908	162	460	1,047	2,360	131	1,106
1964	37,647	5.7	26,837	170	666	1,091	2,481	138	1,355

(continued)

TABLE Bd45–62 Health expenditures – public and private, by type: 1929–1997 *Continued*

	Total		Private			Public			
						Health and medical services			
	Total	As percentage of gross national product	Health and medical services	Medical research	Medical facilities construction	Veterans' hospital and medical care	General hospital and medical care (Census)	General hospital and medical care (CMS)	Public assistance
	Bd45	Bd46	Bd47	Bd48	Bd49	Bd50	Bd51	Bd52	Bd53
Year	Million dollars	Percent	Million dollars	Million dollars	Million dollars	Million dollars	Million dollars	Million dollars	Million dollars
1965	41,145	5.7	29,023	176	622	1,153	2,618	133	1,672
1966	45,263	5.7	30,753	186	734	1,189	2,772	155	2,347
1967	50,969	6.1	31,150	198	744	1,305	2,868	178	3,700
1968	57,684	6.3	33,444	208	947	1,380	2,969	187	4,180
1969	64,792	6.6	37,855	213	1,576	1,521	3,196	229	5,022
1970	73,243	7.0	42,288	215	1,992	1,762	3,560	383	6,310
1971	81,018	7.2	—	233	2,282	2,052	—	552	7,691
1972	90,943	7.3	—	227	2,543	2,380	—	701	8,933
1973	100,838	7.3	—	232	2,674	2,741	—	765	10,154
1974	114,265	7.6	—	252	2,664	3,000	—	897	11,943
1975	130,727	8.0	—	264	2,676	3,496	—	627	14,497
1976	149,856	8.2	—	267	2,982	4,152	—	801	16,379
1977	170,375	8.4	—	220	2,942	4,401	—	807	18,815
1978	190,601	8.3	—	236	3,061	4,989	—	897	20,900
1979	215,201	8.4	—	254	3,322	5,308	—	1,054	23,964
1980	247,273	8.8	—	292	3,863	5,934	—	1,203	28,034
1981	286,908	9.2	—	312	4,744	6,519	—	1,304	32,604
1982	322,978	9.9	—	390	5,765	7,134	—	1,527	34,554
1983	355,291	10.1	—	456	6,473	7,673	—	1,089	37,982
1984	390,076	9.9	—	506	6,248	8,448	—	1,153	41,124
1985	428,720	10.2	—	538	5,574	8,713	—	1,221	44,443
1986	461,228	10.4	—	782	5,398	9,172	—	1,427	48,965
1987	500,502	10.6	—	800	6,090	9,605	—	1,440	53,971
1988	560,379	11.0	—	839	7,316	10,016	—	1,449	58,861
1989	623,536	11.4	—	882	7,645	10,640	—	1,373	66,389
1990	699,361	12.1	—	960	8,692	11,424	—	1,568	80,405
1991	766,783	12.8	—	1,090	8,451	12,367	—	1,721	99,142
1992	836,537	13.2	—	1,183	9,187	13,206	—	1,919	111,906
1993	898,496	13.5	—	1,215	9,991	14,299	—	2,120	126,789
1994	947,717	13.4	—	1,276	9,812	15,291	—	2,331	139,916
1995	993,725	13.4	—	1,325	8,996	15,591	—	2,396	151,615
1996	1,042,522	13.3	—	1,432	9,583	16,471	—	2,664	159,707
1997	1,092,385	13.1	—	1,488	11,103	16,636	—	2,967	165,250

	Public								
	Health and medical services								
	Workers' compensation	Defense Department hospital and medical care	School, maternal, and child health services (Census)	Maternal and child health services (CMS)	School health and state and local hospital funds (CMS)	Other (Census)	Other (CMS)	Medical research	Medical facilities construction
	Bd54 [1]	Bd55	Bd56	Bd57	Bd58	Bd59	Bd60	Bd61 [2]	Bd62
Year	Million dollars	Million dollars	Million dollars	Million dollars	Million dollars	Million dollars	Million dollars	Million dollars	Million dollars
1929	75	29	13	—	—	96	—	—	108
1935	69	29	15	—	—	117	—	—	51
1940	94	75	32	—	—	153	—	3	83
1948	174	280	57	—	—	312	—	57	231
1949	186	325	60	—	—	345	—	69	436
1950	204	584	63	—	—	376	—	79	544
1951	230	976	66	—	—	435	—	94	589
1952	257	1,046	76	—	—	450	—	105	580
1953	282	890	117	—	—	403	—	113	519
1954	305	777	153	—	—	402	—	129	455

Notes appear at end of table

TABLE Bd45–62 Health expenditures – public and private, by type: 1929–1997 *Continued*

	Public								
	Health and medical services								
	Workers' compensation	Defense Department hospital and medical care	School, maternal, and child health services (Census)	Maternal and child health services (CMS)	School health and state and local hospital funds (CMS)	Other (Census)	Other (CMS)	Medical research	Medical facilities construction
	Bd54 [1]	Bd55	Bd56	Bd57	Bd58	Bd59	Bd60	Bd61 [2]	Bd62
Year	Million dollars	Million dollars	Million dollars	Million dollars	Million dollars	Million dollars	Million dollars	Million dollars	Million dollars
1955	325	754	168	—	—	408	—	150	410
1956	345	788	184	—	—	439	—	200	436
1957	362	851	200	—	—	458	—	266	533
1958	380	911	216	—	—	473	—	330	617
1959	405	907	234	—	—	484	—	420	608
1960	564	840	254	152	2,096	474	389	553	439
1961	590	902	284	173	2,203	520	427	736	427
1962	646	942	310	189	2,213	575	476	921	477
1963	681	977	327	208	2,428	618	532	1,054	512
1964	741	921	346	229	2,452	693	601	1,196	584
1965	799	951	377	253	2,589	818	688	1,348	641
1966	911	1,181	451	301	2,735	2,272	869	1,437	640
1967	1,013	1,466	514	337	2,631	5,921	1,046	1,573	764
1968	1,147	1,604	589	391	2,879	7,358	1,199	1,676	868
1969	1,244	1,736	657	452	3,073	8,547	1,423	1,708	990
1970	1,409	1,784	676	425	3,434	9,432	1,665	1,741	1,029
1971	1,437	1,788	—	471	3,557	—	2,031	1,865	1,205
1972	1,568	2,213	—	501	3,895	—	2,185	2,148	1,186
1973	1,877	2,307	—	486	4,330	—	2,388	2,275	1,123
1974	2,177	2,897	—	545	4,888	—	2,802	2,493	1,400
1975	2,431	2,834	—	587	5,171	—	3,170	3,062	1,899
1976	2,740	2,877	—	644	4,939	—	3,574	3,461	2,235
1977	3,190	3,093	—	689	538	—	4,355	3,671	2,026
1978	3,681	3,395	—	727	5,661	—	5,159	4,221	2,014
1979	4,537	3,787	—	805	6,209	—	5,912	4,521	1,885
1980	5,142	4,350	—	892	6,175	—	7,030	5,170	2,015
1981	5,658	5,026	—	908	6,979	—	8,137	5,382	2,428
1982	6,313	5,693	—	959	7,414	—	9,194	5,650	2,481
1983	6,596	6,068	—	1,126	7,594	—	9,841	5,969	2,633
1984	6,856	6,448	—	1,103	7,458	—	10,556	6,632	2,608
1985	7,971	7,498	—	1,262	7,836	—	12,019	7,302	2,569
1986	8,937	8,383	—	1,434	9,986	—	13,132	7,844	2,421
1987	10,606	9,191	—	1,608	11,253	—	14,385	8,329	2,685
1988	12,208	9,761	—	1,695	11,698	—	16,059	9,666	2,890
1989	14,298	10,319	—	1,796	11,624	—	18,582	10,378	2,793
1990	16,067	11,579	—	1,893	11,931	—	20,170	11,254	3,022
1991	17,163	12,849	—	2,014	11,854	—	22,017	11,828	2,982
1992	18,983	12,964	—	2,129	12,029	—	24,051	12,995	3,541
1993	18,549	13,281	—	2,204	13,194	—	25,940	13,272	3,841
1994	18,590	13,221	—	2,294	13,272	—	28,871	14,607	4,100
1995	17,136	13,406	—	2,362	13,141	—	31,136	15,384	4,304
1996	15,215	13,326	—	2,439	13,203	—	34,767	15,718	4,558
1997	14,116	13,432	—	2,523	13,845	—	39,258	16,467	5,060

[1] Beginning 1960, the series includes adjusted data as "workers' compensation" consisting of state, local, and federal funds.

[2] Includes state, local, and federal funds beginning 1960.

Sources

U.S. Social Security Administration. For 1929–1959, *Compendium of National Health Expenditures Data,* Department of Health, Education, and Welfare (DHEW) Publication number (SSA)73-11903 (1973), Tables 6 and 10; *National Health Expenditures, Calendar Years 1929–71,* Research and Statistics Note, number 3, DHEW Publication number (SSA)73-11701 (1973), Tables 2 and 3. For 1960–1997, data are provided at the Internet site of the Centers for Medicare and Medicaid Services (CMS).

Documentation

See the text for Table Bd1–16 for a discussion of the general method of estimating national health expenditures. For additional information, see the Centers for Medicare and Medicaid Services Internet site for information on National Health Accounts.

The data for 1960–1970 have been revised and so differ from the 1975 edition of *Historical Statistics of the United States.*

Series Bd46. Gross national product from series Ca2.

Series Bd50. All veterans with service-connected disabilities are eligible for a wide range of hospital and medical services, as are veterans with non-service-connected disabilities who are unable to pay for care. The medical care program includes inpatient and outpatient hospital and clinic care, nursing bed care (and a community nursing home program where nursing bed facilities are not available), day care centers for psychiatric patients, outpatient dental care, and the provision of prosthetic appliances. All veterans' health and medical benefit data before 1970, together with the administrative costs, are provided by the Veterans Administration.

(continued)

TABLE Bd45–62 Health expenditures – public and private, by type: 1929–1997 *Continued*

Series Bd51

Federal outlays include operation of hospital and medical care units other than military and veterans' facilities and reimbursements to public and private hospitals for the care of federal civilian beneficiaries. Excluded where separately identifiable are training grants and fellowships and expenditures for research and the construction of medical facilities.

Through 1959, the main source of these federal civilian expenditures data was the Office of Management and Budget, *The Budget of the United States Government,* and its *Appendix* and *Special Analyses* published annually. State, local, and county governments also provide hospital and medical care for their residents. Beginning in 1960, data have been published by the Health Care Financing Administration and its successor, the Centers for Medicare and Medicaid Services. State, local, and county governments own and operate long- and short-term general, psychiatric, and tuberculosis hospitals and also pay to or for the support of a few nongovernment facilities.

Through 1959, data represent net expenditures for services. State and local vendor payments for specific programs covered in other series, as well as capital outlays and patient revenues, have been excluded. State and local gross totals, as well as figures on capital outlays and patient revenues, are shown annually in U.S. Bureau of the Census, *Governmental Finances*.

Series Bd52. This series is offered by the Center for Medicare and Medicaid Services to update series Bd51. The difference between these series is that Bd52 includes general hospital and medical expenditures that are not elsewhere categorized (NEC).

Series Bd53

Public assistance programs existed prior to most of the social insurance programs. They comprise old-age assistance, medical assistance for the aged, aid to the blind, aid to families with dependent children, aid to the permanently and totally disabled, medical assistance, and state- and locally financed general assistance programs.

Health expenditures for public assistance include money payments to needy recipients, assistance in kind, and vendor payments on behalf of recipients for medical care and for other goods and services (payments directly to the suppliers of service) made from federal, state, and local funds for categorical assistance programs and from state and local funds for general assistance programs. Administrative expenditures under public assistance programs are included, along with grants for demonstration projects under section 1115 of the Social Security Act.

Beginning in 1966, the Medicaid program, enacted as Title XIX of the Social Security Act in 1965, enabled the states to provide a single health program for the indigent and medically indigent, with federal financial participation. Benefit standards required that a participating state must provide a minimum of five basic services to all Medicaid recipients (inpatient hospital care, outpatient hospital services, other laboratory and X-ray services, skilled nursing home services for individuals age 21 or older, and physicians' services). In addition, states may offer other services – such as drugs and dental care – for which they receive federal matching funds. Wide variation exists among the individual state programs in terms of eligibility and scope and duration of benefits.

Many states, with and without Medicaid programs, contribute additional vendor medical payments out of state and local funds under the category of general assistance.

Vendor payments for medical care under public assistance programs are published annually by the National Center for Social Statistics in *Source of Funds Expended for Public Assistance Payments*.

Series Bd54

Workers' compensation legislation, designed to provide cash benefits and medical care when a worker is injured on the job and an income to survivors if the worker is killed, was the first form of social insurance to develop widely in the United States. "Workmen's Compensation" is now more generally called "Workers' Compensation."

Each of the states operates its own workers' compensation program, independent of any federal legislative or administrative responsibility. As a result, there are wide differences among states in the scope of employment covered, the amount and duration of benefits paid, and the methods used to ensure that compensation will be paid when due.

Workers' compensation expenditures include the following: (1) periodic cash payments to the worker during periods of disability and, in some states, to his or her dependents; (2) death and funeral benefits to the worker's survivors; (3) lump-sum settlements; (4) medical and rehabilitative services; and (5) the administrative costs incurred by government bodies in operating or supervising the programs.

Workers' compensation medical benefits include those for medical and rehabilitative services. Specific medical benefits are included in the law of each state; they are provided without limit as to time and amount in about four fifths of the states.

Medical benefit payments include the estimated amounts paid out by private insurance carriers, by state insurance funds, and by employers as self-insurers. Also included are the amounts paid under the federal workers' compensation programs, such as the Federal Employees' Compensation Act, Longshoremen's and Harbor Workers' Compensation Act, War Hazards Compensation Act, and the Defense Bases Compensation Act. Data for periods prior to 1959 exclude expenditures under the laws in Alaska and Hawai'i.

Workers' compensation medical benefits data are estimated annually by the Social Security Administration, using data primarily compiled by the National Council on Compensation Insurance. The data are published regularly in the *Social Security Bulletin*.

Series Bd55. Active-duty personnel have been provided with complete medical care incident to other necessities of life – food, shelter, and clothing. The armed services provide preventative treatment, curative and rehabilitative services in military hospitals, outpatient clinics, dispensaries, and field and shipboard stations. The series includes the expenses of operating military hospitals, clinics, and other medical facilities; the salaries of military medical personnel; payments for medical care in nonmilitary facilities; and expenditures for the dependents' medical care program.

Series Bd56. School health programs of educational agencies are financed and administered by state and local departments of education. These programs include medical and dental screening, first aid, the salaries of school nurses and/or doctors employed by local school districts, and the expenses of health supplies. Data are from the U.S. Office of Education.

Series Bd56–58. Series Bd57 is an updated version of series Bd56, but it includes maternal and child health services from federal, state, and local funds. Series Bd58 is another updated version of series Bd56, but it includes state and local hospital and school health funds.

Series Bd57

Programs for maternal and child health care at the federal level were established under Title V of the Social Security Act. They were designed to encourage, extend, and improve health services for mothers and children, especially in rural and low-income areas.

Under the maternal and child health program, federal grants are matched and used by state health agencies to provide maternity clinics, well-child and pediatric clinics, inpatient hospital services, health services for schoolchildren, dental care, and immunization.

Under the crippled children's program, federal grants are used by state health and crippled children's agencies to locate crippled children; to provide medical, surgical, corrective, and other services to care for crippled children; and to provide facilities for diagnosis, hospitalization, and aftercare for these children.

Series Bd59

Includes the following: (1) temporary disability insurance, (2) other public health activities, (3) medical vocational rehabilitation, (4) special Office of Economic Opportunity (OEO) programs, and (5) beginning in 1966, health insurance for the aged (Medicare). For a description of other public health activities, see the text for series Bd12. Medical vocational rehabilitation refers to assistance given the physically and mentally handicapped so that they may be prepared for and placed in gainful occupations. Included among vocational rehabilitation basic services are the following: such medical services as study and diagnosis to assess the extent of the disability and the individual's work capacities; medical, surgical and hospital treatment, and related therapy to remove or reduce the disability; and provision of prosthetic

TABLE Bd45–62 Health expenditures – public and private, by type: 1929–1997 *Continued*

devices. Data on federal, state, and local expenditures for this program are provided by the Rehabilitation Services Administration.

The OEO programs are aimed at developing and demonstrating more effective ways of delivering quality health care to poor families. OEO health funds include grants and contracts to aid local health services and resources, and they are reported annually in the *Special Analysis of the Budget* (see the text for series Bd51).

Federal health insurance for the aged (Medicare) became effective July 1, 1966, providing hospital and medical protection to an enrolled population age 65 and older. Benefits under the hospital program (part A) cover specific inpatient hospital services, posthospital services in a "participating" extended-care facility, and home health visits. Under the supplementary medical program (part B), payment is provided for physicians' services (including home and office visits), home health visits, outpatient hospital services, outpatient physical therapy services, diagnostic X-ray and laboratory tests, radiation therapy, prosthetic devices, ambulance services, and certain other medical supplies. Payments for deductibles, coinsurance, and noncovered services are not included here.

Series Bd60. Updates series Bd59 but does not include temporary disability insurance or Medicare. Data concerning Medicare and Medicaid are included in Tables Bd327–447.

HOSPITALS

Richard H. Steckel

TABLE Bd63–72 Hospital assets, by type of control and service: 1947–1977

Contributed by Richard H. Steckel

			Nonfederal hospitals							
							For short-term care			
	Total	Federal hospitals	Total	For psychiatric services	For tuberculosis	For long-term care	Total	Voluntary nonprofit hospitals	For-profit hospitals	State and local government hospitals
	Bd63	Bd64	Bd65	Bd66	Bd67	Bd68	Bd69	Bd70	Bd71	Bd72
Year	Thousand dollars	Thousand dollars	Thousand dollars	Thousand dollars	Thousand dollars	Thousand dollars	Thousand dollars	Thousand dollars	Thousand dollars	Thousand dollars
1947	5,881,000	812,000	5,070,000	966,000	322,000	343,000	3,439,000	2,697,000	129,000	612,000
1948	6,490,000	905,000	5,586,000	1,143,000	395,000	349,000	3,699,000	2,889,000	136,000	675,000
1949	6,946,000	874,000	6,072,000	1,261,000	442,000	435,000	3,934,000	3,101,000	131,000	702,000
1950	7,791,000	1,131,000	6,660,000	1,441,000	421,000	449,000	4,349,000	3,350,000	138,000	861,000
1951	8,206,000	1,439,000	6,766,000	1,476,000	421,000	351,000	4,518,000	3,460,000	141,000	918,000
1952	9,418,000	1,532,000	7,886,000	1,802,000	437,000	509,000	5,138,000	3,901,000	147,000	1,090,000
1953	10,159,000	1,529,000	8,630,000	1,842,000	486,000	562,000	5,739,000	4,348,000	145,000	1,246,000
1954	10,820,000	1,805,000	9,016,000	1,931,000	484,000	422,000	6,177,000	4,709,000	145,000	1,323,000
1955	11,986,000	1,664,000	10,322,000	2,232,000	530,000	575,000	6,985,000	5,223,000	148,000	1,614,000
1956	13,035,000	1,903,000	11,133,000	2,318,000	514,000	766,000	7,535,000	5,741,000	173,000	1,621,000
1957	14,538,000	1,940,000	12,598,000	2,422,000	553,000	818,000	8,805,000	6,505,000	300,000	1,999,000
1958	15,470,000	2,018,000	13,451,000	2,773,000	517,000	742,000	9,419,000	7,221,000	219,000	1,980,000
1959	16,682,000	2,115,000	14,566,000	3,107,000	528,000	777,000	10,154,000	7,807,000	226,000	2,121,000
1960	17,714,000	2,124,000	15,590,000	3,437,000	508,000	787,000	10,858,000	8,422,000	243,000	2,193,000
1961	19,079,000	2,285,000	16,795,000	3,515,000	505,000	992,000	11,783,000	8,949,000	266,000	2,568,000
1962	19,980,000	2,342,000	17,638,000	3,558,000	470,000	1,008,000	12,602,000	9,656,000	288,000	2,658,000
1963	21,309,000	2,450,000	18,859,000	3,716,000	420,000	1,073,000	13,651,000	10,507,000	343,000	2,801,000
1964	23,275,000	2,505,000	20,770,000	4,297,000	442,000	1,143,000	14,888,000	11,423,000	413,000	3,052,000
1965	24,502,000	2,552,000	21,950,000	4,167,000	421,000	998,000	16,364,000	12,476,000	414,000	3,474,000
1966	26,336,000	3,057,000	23,280,000	4,084,000	356,000	1,057,000	17,783,000	13,734,000	412,000	3,637,000
1967	27,922,000	2,817,000	25,105,000	4,189,000	225,000	1,179,000	19,512,000	15,075,000	484,000	3,953,000
1968	31,019,000	3,180,000	27,839,000	4,659,000	317,000	1,085,000	21,778,000	16,954,000	539,000	4,286,000
1969	33,547,000	3,036,000	30,511,000	4,922,000	307,000	1,128,000	24,153,000	18,567,000	647,000	4,938,000
1970	36,159,000	3,183,000	32,976,000	4,816,000	311,000	1,176,000	26,674,000	20,502,000	871,000	5,301,000
1971	38,624,529	3,173,193	35,451,336	4,488,261	317,446	1,036,815	29,608,814	22,637,068	1,030,657	5,941,089
1972	43,157,177	3,255,120	39,902,057	4,926,640	253,298	1,093,248	33,628,871	25,686,359	1,365,064	6,577,448
1973	47,368,625	3,400,844	43,967,781	4,846,193	225,472	1,259,010	37,637,106	28,642,987	1,725,093	7,269,026
1974	51,705,917	3,527,587	48,178,330	4,776,037	166,265	1,396,057	41,839,971	31,481,934	2,287,587	8,070,450
1975	57,302,241	3,707,455	53,594,786	4,804,094	132,403	1,402,761	47,255,528	35,827,499	2,538,099	8,889,930
1976	64,029,012	4,135,145	59,893,867	4,760,951	90,983	1,350,987	53,690,946	40,857,290	3,031,441	9,802,215
1977	72,219,429	4,796,394	67,423,035	4,795,678	87,834	1,406,415	61,133,108	46,686,014	3,493,941	10,953,153

Sources

For 1946–1964, American Hospital Association (AHA), *Hospitals*, Guide Issue, part 2 (August 1, 1965), pp. 448–9; for 1965–1970, *Hospitals*, Guide Issue, part 2 (August 1, 1972), pp. 460–2. For 1971–1977, *AHA Hospital Statistics*. Beginning in 1972, *AHA Hospital Statistics* began to be published separately from *Hospitals*. Each annual issue of *AHA Hospital Statistics* contains data for the previous year. For the years after 1970, data for assets are from Table 3 of these publications.

Documentation

These data are collected through surveys. After 1977, asset data were still collected but no longer published by the AHA. They are maintained as confidential and not released without written permission.

Assets comprise plant assets (land, buildings, equipment, and reserves for construction, improvement, and replacement – less deductions for depreciation), plus all other assets, including endowment fund principal and general and temporary fund balances.

Short-term hospitals are those in which more than 50 percent of all patients admitted have a stay of fewer than thirty days; long-term, those in which 50 percent of all patients admitted have a stay of thirty days or more. General hospitals accept patients for a variety of acute medical and surgical conditions and, for the most part, do not admit cases of contagious disease, tuberculosis, and nervous and mental disease. Special hospitals are those that are devoted to the treatment of some particular disease or group in the population. Among the former are orthopedic, contagious disease, chronic and convalescent, and eye, ear, nose, and throat hospitals; among the latter are maternity, children's, and industrial hospitals. Psychiatric hospitals include those providing temporary or prolonged care for the mentally ill, the mentally retarded, epileptics, and persons with alcoholic or other addictive diseases. Tuberculosis hospitals include sanatoriums or hospitals specifically for the care of tubercular patients.

Government hospitals include those operated by federal, state, and local governments, the latter including county, city, city–county, and hospital district. Nonprofit hospitals are those operated not for profit by churches and by associations of citizens or fraternal organizations. Proprietary hospitals are operated for profit by individuals, partnerships, or corporations.

The data include Alaska beginning in 1958 and Hawai'i the year after.

TABLE Bd73–82 Hospital expenses, by type of control and service: 1946–1996

Contributed by Richard H. Steckel

			Nonfederal hospitals							
							For short-term care			
Year	Total	Federal hospitals	Total	For psychiatric services	For tuberculosis	For long-term care	Total	Voluntary nonprofit hospitals	For-profit hospitals	State and local government hospitals
	Bd73	Bd74	Bd75	Bd76	Bd77	Bd78	Bd79	Bd80	Bd81	Bd82
	Thousand dollars	Thousand dollars	Thousand dollars	Thousand dollars	Thousand dollars	Thousand dollars	Thousand dollars	Thousand dollars	Thousand dollars	Thousand dollars
1946	1,963,000	373,000	1,590,000	262,000	91,000	68,000	1,169,000	848,000	94,000	227,000
1947	2,354,000	405,000	1,949,000	325,000	109,000	81,000	1,434,000	1,048,000	109,000	276,000
1948	2,875,000	480,000	2,396,000	424,000	150,000	98,000	1,724,000	1,264,000	119,000	341,000
1949	3,486,000	764,000	2,722,000	619,000	160,000	101,000	1,842,000	1,333,000	125,000	383,000
1950	3,651,000	712,000	2,938,000	539,000	162,000	117,000	2,120,000	1,523,000	143,000	454,000
1951	3,913,000	743,000	3,169,000	571,000	167,000	117,000	2,314,000	1,688,000	139,000	486,000
1952	4,456,000	925,000	3,531,000	636,000	177,000	141,000	2,577,000	1,879,000	151,000	547,000
1953	4,765,000	853,000	3,912,000	685,000	192,000	167,000	2,868,000	2,080,000	169,000	619,000
1954	5,229,000	927,000	4,303,000	786,000	206,000	190,000	3,121,000	2,276,000	162,000	683,000
1955	5,594,000	837,000	4,757,000	923,000	208,000	192,000	3,434,000	2,508,000	174,000	752,000
1956	6,017,000	968,000	5,049,000	873,000	197,000	236,000	3,743,000	2,739,000	188,000	816,000
1957	6,496,000	1,013,000	5,483,000	870,000	200,000	252,000	4,161,000	3,050,000	200,000	911,000
1958	7,133,000	1,051,000	6,084,000	972,000	195,000	262,000	4,655,000	3,427,000	225,000	1,003,000
1959	7,789,000	1,119,000	6,670,000	1,102,000	208,000	269,000	5,091,000	3,760,000	242,000	1,089,000
1960	8,421,000	1,134,000	7,287,000	1,205,000	192,000	273,000	5,617,000	4,139,000	275,000	1,203,000
1961	9,387,000	1,308,000	8,080,000	1,322,000	192,000	316,000	6,250,000	4,584,000	304,000	1,362,000
1962	10,129,000	1,408,000	8,721,000	1,355,000	182,000	343,000	6,841,000	4,999,000	346,000	1,496,000
1963	10,956,000	1,458,000	9,498,000	1,433,000	158,000	376,000	7,532,000	5,491,000	417,000	1,624,000
1964	12,031,000	1,503,000	10,528,000	1,608,000	163,000	407,000	8,349,000	6,039,000	493,000	1,817,000
1965	12,948,000	1,568,000	11,380,000	1,662,000	165,000	406,000	9,147,000	6,643,000	510,000	1,994,000
1966	14,198,000	1,633,000	12,565,000	1,716,000	147,000	427,000	10,276,000	7,435,000	553,000	2,288,000
1967	16,395,000	1,795,000	14,600,000	1,896,000	94,000	529,000	12,081,000	8,806,000	653,000	2,622,000
1968	19,061,000	2,032,000	17,030,000	2,192,000	133,000	543,000	14,162,000	10,317,000	720,000	3,125,000
1969	22,103,000	2,350,000	19,753,000	2,433,000	143,000	565,000	16,613,000	12,137,000	852,000	3,624,000
1970	25,556,000	2,483,000	23,073,000	2,712,000	152,000	649,000	19,560,000	14,163,000	1,068,000	4,328,000
1971	28,812,353	2,820,618	25,991,735	2,802,989	153,077	636,123	22,399,546	16,343,512	1,213,727	4,842,307
1972	32,667,324	3,147,738	29,519,586	3,133,818	119,056	717,534	25,549,178	18,383,818	1,407,327	5,758,033
1973	36,289,864	3,523,633	32,766,231	3,350,709	114,362	805,464	28,495,696	20,417,540	1,688,833	6,389,323
1974	41,406,109	3,971,156	37,434,953	3,707,934	102,457	873,031	32,751,531	23,494,264	2,046,096	7,211,171
1975	48,706,157	4,539,851	44,166,306	3,997,352	93,015	966,340	39,109,599	27,964,962	2,560,615	8,584,022
1976	55,654,652	5,313,217	50,341,435	4,175,329	63,938	985,911	45,116,257	32,795,957	3,085,305	9,234,995
1977	63,630,098	6,162,623	57,467,475	4,494,319	70,072	1,070,592	51,832,492	37,523,371	3,668,972	10,640,149
1978	70,927,212	6,731,569	64,195,643	4,723,316	68,331	1,056,246	58,347,750	42,261,975	4,179,633	11,906,142
1979	79,796,387	7,265,755	72,530,632	5,136,021	61,969	1,148,249	66,184,393	47,969,105	4,820,242	13,395,046
1980	91,886,325	7,869,259	84,017,066	5,790,705	63,274	1,192,804	76,970,283	55,814,897	5,847,350	15,308,036
1981	107,145,711	8,606,030	98,539,681	6,414,997	67,440	1,318,348	90,738,896	66,288,044	6,856,448	17,594,404
1982	123,218,597	9,506,303	113,712,294	7,047,187	67,665	1,502,958	105,094,485	76,850,296	8,176,943	20,067,246
1983	136,314,556	10,678,554	125,636,002	7,442,268	61,959	1,500,165	116,631,310	85,674,853	9,207,739	21,749,018
1984	144,113,879	11,155,644	132,958,235	7,699,308	58,040	1,651,363	123,549,524	90,883,269	10,251,485	22,414,771
1985	153,326,737	12,335,417	140,991,320	8,344,260	71,600	1,875,679	130,699,781	96,238,548	11,486,229	22,975,004
1986	165,193,654	13,132,702	152,060,953	9,120,351	36,827	1,997,211	140,906,564	103,581,164	12,986,957	24,338,443
1987	178,661,982	13,667,929	164,994,053	9,883,390	42,491	2,159,381	152,908,791	112,396,757	14,067,342	26,444,691
1988	196,704,166	14,601,091	182,103,075	10,854,933	34,934	2,271,301	168,941,906	124,769,726	15,544,743	28,627,437
1989	214,885,884	15,090,523	199,795,362	12,049,267	37,616	2,504,311	185,204,168	136,940,891	17,239,616	31,023,661
1990	234,869,906	15,243,688	219,626,218	12,904,591	50,448	2,743,679	203,927,499	150,692,755	18,821,608	34,413,137
1991	258,507,882	16,798,929	241,708,953	13,484,076	48,816	2,946,164	225,229,897	166,837,334	20,516,299	37,876,264
1992	282,530,997	18,226,802	264,304,195	13,189,454	48,989	2,747,860	248,317,892	183,836,520	22,495,963	41,985,410
1993	301,538,340	19,636,127	281,902,213	12,728,480	53,497	2,737,844	266,382,392	197,242,607	23,076,740	46,063,045
1994	310,833,561	20,005,072	290,828,489	12,280,988	70,114	2,329,643	276,147,743	204,218,746	23,445,407	48,114,617
1995	320,252,158	20,247,675	300,004,483	11,659,471	38,476	2,233,389	286,073,148	209,613,663	26,652,770	49,321,945
1996	330,531,024	22,252,429	308,278,594	11,973,045	35,542	2,349,632	293,920,375	215,950,437	28,384,859	49,419,954

Sources

For 1946–1964, American Hospital Association (AHA), *Hospitals*, Guide Issue, part 2 (August 1, 1965), pp. 448–9; for 1965–1970, *Hospitals*, Guide Issue, part 2 (August 1, 1972), pp. 460–2. For 1971–1996, *AHA Hospital Statistics*, annual issues.

Documentation

Expenses include all expenses covering the twelve-month period, both total and payroll. Payroll expenses include all salaries and wages except those paid to interns, residents, student nurses, and other trainees. All professional fees and those salary expenditures excluded from payroll are defined as nonpayroll expenses and are included in total expenses. The data exclude the cost of new construction.

See the text for Table Bd63–72 for a discussion of hospital types.

The data include Alaska beginning in 1958 and Hawai'i the year after.

TABLE Bd83–94 Hospital expenses per inpatient day, by type of control and service: 1946–1997[1]

Contributed by Richard H. Steckel

	Total						Payroll					
			Nonfederal hospitals						Nonfederal hospitals			
	All hospitals	Federal hospitals	Short-term general and special	Long-term general and special	Psychiatric hospitals	Tuberculosis hospitals	All hospitals	Federal hospitals	Short-term general and special	Long-term general and special	Psychiatric hospitals	Tuberculosis hospitals
	Bd83	Bd84	Bd85	Bd86	Bd87	Bd88	Bd89	Bd90	Bd91	Bd92	Bd93	Bd94
Year	Dollars	Dollars	Dollars	Dollars	Dollars	Dollars	Dollars	Dollars	Dollars	Dollars	Dollars	Dollars
1946	5.21	6.14	9.39	2.97	1.39	4.57	2.93	4.06	4.98	1.64	0.80	2.38
1947	5.42	7.39	11.09	3.03	1.60	5.44	3.07	5.23	5.99	1.64	0.84	2.82
1948	6.35	8.81	13.09	3.81	1.95	6.25	3.60	6.19	7.17	1.99	1.03	3.17
1949	7.70	13.30	14.33	4.07	2.84	6.68	4.53	9.53	7.96	2.35	1.53	3.70
1950	7.98	12.77	15.62	5.39	2.43	7.22	4.79	9.35	8.86	3.32	1.38	4.06
1951	8.26	11.91	16.77	6.30	2.46	7.37	5.01	8.68	9.65	3.89	1.43	4.25
1952	9.14	14.10	18.35	6.63	2.68	7.85	5.63	10.35	10.66	4.05	1.58	4.61
1953	9.73	13.93	19.95	8.26	2.83	8.54	6.10	10.44	11.86	5.28	1.74	5.11
1954	10.67	15.92	21.76	8.53	3.22	9.32	6.83	12.06	13.21	5.63	2.03	5.77
1955	11.24	14.60	23.12	8.06	3.73	10.13	7.20	11.63	14.26	5.36	2.17	6.48
1956	12.16	16.97	24.15	10.20	3.63	10.19	7.98	13.74	14.85	6.84	2.41	6.51
1957	13.48	17.68	26.02	10.33	3.91	11.16	8.76	14.27	15.74	6.79	2.66	7.14
1958	14.74	18.38	28.27	10.32	4.40	12.08	9.63	14.80	17.19	6.91	3.08	7.91
1959	15.65	19.62	30.19	12.50	4.71	12.80	10.37	15.98	18.76	8.39	3.26	8.54
1960	16.46	20.11	32.23	12.82	4.91	13.37	10.92	16.34	20.08	9.01	3.45	8.92
1961	18.46	23.34	34.98	14.49	5.53	14.72	12.25	19.15	21.54	10.12	4.00	9.89
1962	19.73	24.97	36.83	15.10	5.72	15.22	13.12	20.42	22.79	10.62	4.16	10.38
1963	21.00	26.28	38.91	16.57	5.98	15.13	13.93	21.58	24.01	11.61	4.40	10.31
1964	23.20	27.17	41.58	18.91	6.97	15.72	15.38	22.38	25.26	13.21	5.16	10.78
1965	25.29	28.67	44.48	19.79	7.50	17.39	16.70	23.12	27.44	13.96	5.60	12.20
1966	27.94	29.69	48.15	20.59	8.11	19.16	18.27	23.96	29.41	14.39	6.11	13.36
1967	32.54	33.04	54.08	21.45	9.62	21.36	20.76	25.35	32.44	15.10	7.10	14.66
1968	37.78	37.97	61.38	27.00	11.25	25.13	23.78	27.48	36.61	18.58	8.29	17.38
1969	45.01	45.89	70.03	29.77	13.61	29.47	28.11	33.41	41.36	20.60	10.00	20.40
1970	53.95	53.10	81.01	36.17	16.63	34.20	33.16	37.44	47.30	24.00	12.24	23.94
1971	63.82	62.69	92.31	38.44	19.56	38.86	39.07	43.60	53.80	26.46	14.49	26.88
1972	73.89	75.40	105.21	43.91	22.65	41.65	44.17	51.06	59.79	29.69	16.71	28.74
1973	83.67	85.85	114.69	47.40	26.83	48.37	49.18	58.08	63.86	31.52	19.74	33.08
1974	97.23	99.44	128.05	53.44	33.12	54.39	55.93	66.37	69.83	34.98	23.84	36.59
1975	118.69	116.74	151.42	63.01	41.36	75.69	66.12	75.31	80.34	39.85	28.84	47.55
1976	139.64	142.01	172.59	66.59	49.61	84.18	75.71	91.29	88.81	41.40	34.31	54.48
1977	163.60	171.60	198.23	77.08	58.42	95.98	86.75	109.95	99.67	47.68	39.33	59.81
1978	186.58	193.01	222.15	83.13	68.15	112.31	97.85	122.94	110.54	51.78	45.80	69.84
1979	209.67	216.87	248.99	90.59	75.41	128.29	108.95	136.28	123.01	55.37	50.80	79.70
1980	237.09	228.80	281.29	98.27	86.41	168.27	121.19	143.25	136.89	59.50	57.09	98.03
1981	276.78	258.14	325.36	119.01	101.13	179.31	140.83	161.37	158.28	72.17	65.49	106.78
1982	320.84	288.47	377.44	135.99	114.95	229.79	161.48	177.47	182.32	80.31	72.99	128.72
1983	363.54	321.95	426.24	155.93	127.63	254.59	180.66	194.77	203.37	92.88	80.72	137.67
1984	406.13	343.53	480.82	168.26	139.01	268.22	200.11	211.35	226.96	99.35	87.01	139.43
1985	462.17	395.62	551.41	190.39	155.99	360.71	224.22	244.53	255.19	110.48	96.27	188.35
1986	513.00	437.08	612.45	208.88	174.59	373.56	244.05	264.29	277.82	122.49	106.05	186.17
1987	561.17	463.02	671.49	239.27	190.17	300.53	263.15	277.70	300.67	134.56	113.09	149.18
1988	622.93	517.85	742.96	260.40	211.39	303.75	263.15	307.43	331.33	147.10	127.20	159.25
1989	690.78	559.53	819.73	293.02	243.39	308.26	319.07	322.56	363.43	161.29	142.38	161.92
1990	762.88	583.03	900.81	351.68	272.09	442.87	353.13	334.39	401.98	194.75	156.64	228.82
1991	856.73	662.30	1,008.59	381.19	298.30	371.28	394.08	371.86	448.44	203.28	171.19	192.06
1992	957.40	722.43	1,121.26	393.66	319.34	385.11	432.31	394.80	490.10	214.45	182.87	200.81
1993	1,055.65	805.90	1,231.19	429.52	331.38	410.81	469.23	442.43	529.76	229.32	186.04	199.43
1994	1,142.92	872.53	1,329.90	396.17	347.34	458.88	518.27	478.11	586.66	212.75	194.82	221.09
1995	1,235.95	990.72	1,428.41	387.75	357.84	634.99	556.60	529.79	626.99	213.86	201.72	356.05
1996	1,321.10	1,164.68	1,514.28	400.13	385.39	731.44	591.05	597.51	661.21	211.01	220.91	372.32
1997	1,394.64	1,269.72	1,585.03	464.18	378.82	603.89	618.02	657.86	685.84	243.83	212.18	293.51

[1] Wages and salaries of residents, interns, and students excluded beginning in 1952. Full-time equivalent wages and salaries of part-time personnel included from 1954 onward.

Sources

For 1946–1964, American Hospital Association (AHA), *Hospitals,* Guide Issue, part 2 (August 1, 1965), pp. 448–9; for 1965–1970, *Hospitals,* Guide Issue, part 2 (August 1, 1972), pp. 460–2; for 1971–1997, *AHA Hospital Statistics,* annual issues.

Statistical information is also available for purchase on CD-ROM, and custom reports can be requested directly from the AHA.

TABLE Bd83–94 Hospital expenses per inpatient day, by type of control and service: 1946–1997 *Continued*

Documentation

Payroll expenses include all salaries and wages except, beginning in 1952, those paid to interns, residents, and students. From 1954 onward, full-time equivalents of part-time personnel, in addition to full-time personnel, are included. All professional fees and those salary expenditures excluded from payroll are defined as nonpayroll expenses and are included in total expenses. Employee benefits are not included in payroll expenses but are in total expenses.

From 1971 to 1975, payroll and total expenses per inpatient day were reported directly in Table 3 of *AHA Hospital Statistics*. For 1976 and later years, these ratios were calculated from data on expenses and inpatient days, which are reported in another table (5A from 1976 to 1993, 3A in 1994 and 1995, and 2 in 1996 and 1997) of the annual publication.

For information about similar data collected prior to 1946 by the American Medical Association, see the text for Table Bd132–143.

The data include Alaska beginning in 1958 and Hawai'i in 1960.

TABLE Bd95–103 Hospital patient costs, by type of hospital: 1946–1995[1]

Contributed by Richard H. Steckel

	Average cost per day for patients in community hospitals				Average cost per stay for patients in community hospitals				Average daily semiprivate room charge
	Total	Nongovernmental nonprofit	For-profit	State and local government	Total	Nongovernmental nonprofit	For-profit	State and local government	
	Bd95 [2]	Bd96 [3]	Bd97 [3]	Bd98 [3]	Bd99 [2]	Bd100 [3]	Bd101 [3]	Bd102 [3]	Bd103
Year	Dollars	Dollars	Dollars	Dollars	Dollars	Dollars	Dollars	Dollars	Dollars
1946	9	10	10	7	85	88	67	84	—
1950	16	17	15	13	127	130	86	134	—
1955	23	24	21	21	180	181	119	200	—
1960	32	33	31	29	245	246	177	259	—
1961	35	36	33	32	266	270	193	284	—
1962	37	38	35	34	280	283	205	293	—
1963	35	40	38	36	270	303	232	308	—
1964	38	42	43	39	289	327	267	328	—
1965	41	45	44	42	316	350	276	356	—
1966	44	49	47	46	345	387	298	396	—
1967	49	55	52	52	411	451	353	466	—
1968	56	62	56	60	469	516	390	536	—
1969	64	65	60	61	533	537	410	546	—
1970	74	75	71	71	605	615	486	614	—
1971	83	86	81	77	667	693	538	642	—
1972	95	95	92	94	749	763	607	754	—
1973	102	102	103	99	799	811	666	799	—
1974	114	114	113	109	886	896	729	887	—
1975	134	133	133	136	1,030	1,040	876	1,031	—
1976	153	153	156	151	1,176	1,208	1,032	1,133	—
1977	174	175	177	171	1,322	1,363	1,168	1,262	98
1978	194	195	202	189	1,474	1,515	1,317	1,399	105
1979	217	218	226	212	1,642	1,684	1,476	1,561	115
1980	245	246	257	239	1,851	1,902	1,676	1,750	128
1981	284	286	299	274	2,171	2,225	1,953	2,072	144
1982	327	330	340	312	2,501	2,573	2,225	2,364	166
1983	369	374	385	348	2,789	2,869	2,518	2,621	195
1984	411	415	438	385	2,995	3,073	2,749	2,823	203 [4]
1985	460	463	500	433	3,245	3,307	3,033	3,106	213
1986	501	504	552	466	3,533	3,590	3,342	3,405	226
1987	539	544	585	499	3,850	3,914	3,617	3,718	239
1988	586	591	649	539	4,207	4,273	4,023	4,034	255
1989	637	642	708	582	4,588	4,649	4,406	4,430	264
1990	687	692	752	634	4,947	5,001	4,727	4,838	297
1991	752	758	820	696	5,360	5,393	5,134	5,340	—
1992	820	828	889	754	5,794	5,809	5,548	5,871	—
1993	881	898	914	800	6,132	6,178	5,643	6,206	—
1994	931	950	924	859	8,978	8,995	7,724	9,663	—
1995	968	994	947	878	9,229	9,293	7,775	9,942	—

[1] Prior to 1972, hospital units of institutions are included in the data for series Bd95–102.

[2] Beginning in 1963, data are adjusted for outpatient services.

[3] Beginning in 1969, data are adjusted for outpatient services.

[4] Average rate effective July 1.

Sources

American Hospital Association, *Hospital Statistics*, annual issues, except as specified.

Series Bd103. Health Insurance Association of America, *Source Book of Health Insurance Data*, annual issues.

Series Bd99, prior to 1965. Calculated from series Bd95 by multiplying the average cost per day times the average length of stay.

Series Bd100–102, prior to 1969. Computed from series Bd96–98, respectively, by multiplying the average cost per day times the average length of stay.

(continued)

TABLE Bd95–103 Hospital patient costs, by type of hospital: 1946–1995 *Continued*

Documentation

The costs per day and per stay in this table are for community hospitals. Community hospitals are defined as nonfederal short-term general or special hospitals, excluding psychiatric or tuberculosis hospitals, whose facilities and services are available to the public. Examples of special hospitals include obstetrics and gynecology; ear, nose, and throat; and orthopedic. A hospital is considered short-term if the majority of its patients are admitted to units where the average stay is less than thirty days.

Average lengths of stay are reported separately in the original source for total community hospitals, nongovernmental nonprofit community hospitals, for-profit community hospitals, and state and local government community hospitals. These average lengths of stay were used to compute the average cost per stay prior to 1965 for total community hospitals and prior to 1969 for nonprofit, for-profit, and state and local community hospitals. Beginning in the 1982 edition of *Hospital Statistics*, values for average length of stay were printed retroactive to 1965 for total community hospitals and retroactive to 1969 for nonprofit, for-profit, and state and local community hospitals.

Series Bd103. The average daily room charges are the national average cost to a patient for a semiprivate room in a nongovernmental short-term general hospital. Average charges are effective January 1, except for 1984 when the effective date is July 1.

TABLE Bd104–117 Indexes of medical prices: 1935–1996[1]

Contributed by Richard H. Steckel

	All medical care				Professional services								Hospital and other medical services	
			Commodities		Physicians' services									
	Total	Services	Total	Prescriptions	Total	Office visits	House visits	Obstetrical cases	Tonsillectomy and adenoidectomy	Dentists' fees	Optometric examination and eyeglasses	Eye care	Total	Hospital rooms
	Bd104	Bd105	Bd106	Bd107	Bd108	Bd109	Bd110	Bd111	Bd112	Bd113	Bd114	Bd115	Bd116	Bd117 [2]
Year	Index 1967 = 100	Index 1967 = 100	Index 1967 = 100	Index 1967 = 100	Index 1967 = 100	Index 1967 = 100	Index 1967 = 100	Index 1967 = 100	Index 1967 = 100	Index 1967 = 100	Index 1967 = 100	Index 1986 = 100	Index 1967 = 100	Index 1967 = 100
1935	36.1	31.8	70.7	65.4	39.2	38.8	39.1	32.1	41.8	40.8	56.7	—	11.9	14.2
1936	36.3	31.9	70.5	65.4	39.4	38.9	39.6	32.3	41.9	40.9	56.8	—	12.0	14.3
1937	36.6	32.3	70.9	65.7	39.6	39.0	39.7	32.5	42.1	41.8	57.1	—	12.3	14.7
1938	36.7	32.4	71.3	66.2	39.5	38.9	39.6	32.8	42.4	41.9	57.2	—	12.6	15.0
1939	36.7	32.5	71.1	66.2	39.6	39.0	39.6	33.0	42.6	42.0	57.6	—	12.6	15.1
1940	36.8	32.5	70.8	66.2	39.6	39.1	39.6	33.0	41.5	42.0	58.1	—	12.7	15.1
1941	37.0	32.7	71.4	67.0	39.8	39.1	39.6	33.6	41.8	42.0	58.3	—	12.9	15.4
1942	38.0	33.7	73.0	68.8	40.6	39.9	40.4	35.1	43.0	43.1	59.0	—	14.0	16.4
1943	39.9	35.4	73.5	69.4	43.2	42.2	42.5	38.5	45.4	45.1	61.6	—	15.1	17.6
1944	41.1	36.9	74.3	70.6	44.9	44.3	44.0	40.2	47.5	47.6	63.1	—	15.7	18.3
1945	42.1	37.9	74.8	71.5	46.0	45.7	44.7	41.0	48.8	49.6	63.9	—	16.2	18.9
1946	44.4	40.1	76.2	74.0	48.3	48.1	46.6	43.5	51.5	52.5	65.1	—	18.5	21.3
1947	48.1	43.5	81.8	81.3	51.4	51.2	49.5	46.7	55.1	56.9	67.7	—	22.0	24.9
1948	51.1	46.4	86.1	88.1	53.4	53.3	50.8	49.9	58.5	60.0	70.5	—	25.7	28.6
1949	52.7	48.1	87.4	90.2	54.4	54.2	51.9	50.6	60.2	62.4	72.8	—	27.8	30.5
1950	53.7	49.2	88.5	92.6	55.2	54.9	52.9	51.2	60.7	63.9	73.5	—	28.9	31.3
1951	56.3	51.7	91.0	97.1	57.3	56.8	54.6	54.4	62.0	66.4	76.8	—	32.0	34.2
1952	59.3	55.0	91.8	98.3	59.8	59.2	56.3	60.2	64.3	67.8	77.8	—	35.2	37.5
1953	61.4	57.0	92.6	98.3	61.4	61.2	57.6	61.5	66.0	70.0	76.9	—	37.4	39.7
1954	63.4	58.7	93.7	100.2	63.2	63.7	58.8	64.4	67.4	72.3	75.9	—	39.6	42.2
1955	64.8	60.4	94.7	101.6	65.4	65.4	61.2	68.6	69.0	73.0	77.0	—	41.5	44.1
1956	67.2	62.8	96.7	104.7	67.4	67.2	63.5	70.9	69.5	74.4	78.2	—	43.7	46.0
1957	69.9	65.5	99.3	108.2	70.3	69.5	67.5	73.5	71.9	76.2	81.3	—	47.2	48.7
1958	73.2	68.7	102.8	113.1	72.7	72.1	70.1	75.5	74.3	78.6	82.1	—	49.9	51.0
1959	76.4	72.0	104.4	115.7	75.1	74.5	72.8	77.7	77.1	80.5	83.0	—	52.7	53.8
1960	79.1	74.9	104.5	115.3	77.0	75.9	75.0	79.4	80.3	82.1	85.1	—	56.3	57.8
1961	81.4	77.7	103.3	111.5	79.0	77.7	77.2	81.1	81.9	82.5	87.8	—	60.6	62.4
1962	83.5	80.2	101.7	107.1	81.3	80.0	79.7	83.7	83.8	84.7	89.2	—	64.9	66.6
1963	85.6	82.6	100.8	104.5	83.1	82.1	81.6	85.0	85.9	87.1	89.7	—	69.0	70.1
1964	87.3	84.6	100.5	103.1	85.2	84.1	84.1	87.1	88.4	89.4	90.9	—	72.4	73.4
1965	89.5	87.3	100.2	102.0	88.3	87.3	87.6	89.0	91.0	92.2	92.8	—	76.6	77.7
1966	93.4	92.0	100.5	101.8	93.4	92.7	93.5	93.0	94.9	95.2	95.3	—	84.0	84.7
1967	100.0	100.0	100.0	100.0	100.0	100.0	100.0	100.0	100.0	100.0	100.0	—	100.0	100.0
1968	106.1	107.3	100.2	98.3	105.6	105.8	106.5	105.2	104.9	105.5	103.2	—	113.2	112.7
1969	113.4	116.0	101.3	99.6	112.9	113.3	114.5	113.5	110.3	112.9	107.6	—	127.9	126.7
1970	120.6	124.2	103.6	101.2	121.4	122.6	122.4	121.8	117.1	119.4	113.5	—	143.9	141.7
1971	128.6	133.5	105.7	101.2	129.9	131.7	131.4	128.9	124.3	126.4	120.0	—	160.5	157.3
1972	132.4	138.0	105.8	100.9	133.9	135.0	137.0	134.0	130.0	132.4	125.0	—	173.4	173.8
1973	137.0	143.6	105.9	100.4	138.0	139.1	141.4	138.3	133.1	136.1	129.6	—	179.0	181.4
1974	149.4	158.0	108.7	102.0	150.3	154.1	151.2	147.8	142.5	145.7	139.0	—	193.1	198.4

Notes appear at end of table

(continued)

TABLE Bd104–117 Indexes of medical prices: 1935–1996 *Continued*

	All medical care				Professional services								Hospital and other medical services	
			Commodities		Physicians' services									
	Total	Services	Total	Prescriptions	Total	Office visits	House visits	Obstetrical cases	Tonsillectomy and adenoidectomy	Dentists' fees	Optometric examination and eyeglasses	Eye care	Total	Hospital rooms
	Bd104	Bd105	Bd106	Bd107	Bd108	Bd109	Bd110	Bd111	Bd112	Bd113	Bd114	Bd115	Bd116	Bd117 [2]
Year	Index 1967 = 100	Index 1967 = 100	Index 1967 = 100	Index 1967 = 100	Index 1967 = 100	Index 1967 = 100	Index 1967 = 100	Index 1967 = 100	Index 1967 = 100	Index 1967 = 100	Index 1967 = 100	Index 1986 = 100	Index 1967 = 100	Index 1967 = 100
1975	168.1	178.4	118.7	109.0	168.8	173.0	169.4	166.8	164.1	161.8	149.2	—	222.9	232.8
1976	183.7	195.8	126.0	115.2	188.3	193.4	190.0	192.1	179.9	171.6	158.7	—	250.1	265.1
1977	201.8	216.0	134.2	121.9	205.7	211.7	204.9	206.3	201.9	184.1	167.6	—	278.1	298.1
1978	217.9	233.5	143.4	131.3	221.8	—	—	—	—	197.2	—	—	304.8	327.5
1979	237.7	255.9	153.5	141.3	241.8	—	—	—	—	214.3	—	—	337.6	366.0
1980	264.7	285.9	167.9	154.8	269.2	—	—	—	—	240.3	—	—	381.8	412.6
1981	291.5	314.4	186.3	172.3	297.5	—	—	—	—	260.2	—	—	434.6	470.4
1982	326.4	353.0	205.6	191.8	326.4	—	—	—	—	283.9	—	—	498.5	546.8
1983	355.4	384.6	223.2	213.7	351.7	—	—	—	—	301.2	—	—	556.4	609.6
1984	378.0	408.4	239.4	233.5	377.1	—	—	—	—	326.2	—	—	605.5	662.0
1985	401.7	433.0	257.0	256.8	397.8	—	—	—	—	347.3	—	—	647.6	707.4
1986	432.0	466.8	273.3	278.4	426.5	—	—	—	—	367.0	—	—	682.7	745.3
1987	462.1	499.4	290.9	298.7	458.5	—	—	—	—	391.8	—	103.6	736.8	805.8
1988	491.6	530.6	309.8	323.2	491.8	—	—	—	—	418.4	—	108.7	802.5	880.9
1989	528.5	569.1	336.1	353.1	526.0	—	—	—	—	444.6	—	112.2	895.6	964.0
1990	576.2	621.8	363.3	387.3	564.7	—	—	—	—	473.0	—	117.3	991.6	1,070.6
1991	627.3	678.3	392.0	425.2	597.5	—	—	—	—	508.0	—	122.2	1,097.6	1,180.8
1992	674.6	731.0	418.1	457.7	637.3	—	—	—	—	540.9	—	126.8	1,200.9	1,285.0
1993	716.5	781.0	433.0	474.1	674.3	—	—	—	—	573.1	—	129.9	1,305.3	1,398.3
1994	748.9	818.6	446.4	494.0	702.4	—	—	—	—	599.0	—	131.8	1,377.1	1,471.6
1995	782.7	860.2	454.2	500.6	733.8	—	—	—	—	629.2	—	136.5	1,441.6	1,543.1
1996	811.4	892.5	469.6	519.2	759.5	—	—	—	—	657.2	—	139.1	1,514.6	1,604.0

[1] Consumer price index for urban wage earners and clerical workers (CPI-W) used through 1977, consumer price index for all urban consumers (CPI-U) used thereafter. See text for discussion of definitional changes affecting various series.

[2] Private rooms through 1971; semiprivate rooms, 1972–1977; hospital rooms thereafter.

Source

U.S. Bureau of Labor Statistics (BLS), *Consumer Price Index*, July issue of each year. CPI-W used until 1978, at which point the new CPI-U was used. More recent data available in *Consumer Price Index*, issued monthly by the BLS.

Documentation

Although most of the basic data collected for medical care prices have remained unchanged over the past sixty-five years, a number of minor definitional changes have made these series rather complex. Detailed comments are offered below for the categories affected. The CPI index has been reweighted several times over the years, most recently in 1978, 1987, and 1995. Each time, the BLS reindexed each category to 100. For these volumes, the indexes have been recalculated to the 1967 = 100 basis of the 1975 edition of *Historical Statistics*, except in the case of eye care, which is discussed below.

Series Bd106. Until December of 1977, this category was called Drugs and Prescriptions, Total. Since January 1978, essentially the same items have been reported as Medical Care Commodities.

Series Bd108. Until December of 1977, this category was titled Physicians Fees, Total. In January 1978, it was renamed Physicians' Services, and the related subcategories of Office Visits, series Bd109, and Home Visits, series Bd110, were eliminated.

Series Bd114–115. Eye-related professional services were not reported from 1978 to 1986, having been replaced by a series for the cost of eyeglasses. A new series Bd115, capturing eye care costs, was begun with the 1987 revision, using a base of 12/86 = 100. A linkage of the two series is not possible with BLS data.

Series Bd116. Through January of 1972, this category was known as Hospital Services, Daily Service Charges. In February of 1972, it was renamed Hospital Service Charges. From January 1978, essentially the same items have been included in Hospital and Other Medical Services.

Series Bd117. At various times, the CPI has included indexes for private rooms, semiprivate rooms, and hospital rooms, with no series extended continuously. The series presented here represents a compromise between consistency and continuity.

TABLE Bd118–131 Hospitals and beds, by type of hospital: 1946–1997 [American Hospital Association data]

Contributed by Richard H. Steckel

	Total			Nonfederal hospitals									Federal hospitals	
				Short-term general and special			Long-term general and special		Psychiatric		Tuberculosis			
	Hospitals	Beds	Beds per 1,000 population	Hospitals	Beds	Beds per 1,000 population	Hospitals	Beds	Hospitals	Beds	Hospitals	Beds	Hospitals	Beds
	Bd118	Bd119	Bd120	Bd121	Bd122	Bd123	Bd124	Bd125	Bd126	Bd127	Bd128	Bd129	Bd130	Bd131
Year	Number	Number	Per 1,000	Number	Number	Per 1,000	Number	Number	Number	Number	Number	Number	Number	Number
1946	6,125	1,435,778	10.3	4,444	473,059	3.4	389	83,415	476	568,473	412	74,867	404	235,964
1947	6,173	1,400,318	9.8	4,475	465,209	3.2	385	84,758	499	580,273	411	70,307	403	199,771
1948	6,160	1,411,450	9.7	4,499	471,555	3.2	362	77,040	504	601,103	409	75,906	386	185,846
1949	6,277	1,435,288	9.7	4,585	476,584	3.2	395	79,145	507	614,465	414	78,330	376	186,764
1950	6,788	1,455,825	9.6	5,031	504,504	3.3	412	70,136	533	619,530	398	72,178	414	189,477
1951	6,832	1,521,959	9.9	5,066	516,020	3.4	394	62,768	551	655,932	399	72,642	422	214,597
1952	6,903	1,561,809	10.0	5,122	530,669	3.4	405	69,731	546	675,749	391	72,642	439	213,018
1953	6,978	1,580,654	10.0	5,212	545,903	3.4	406	68,039	541	691,855	384	72,253	435	202,604
1954	6,970	1,577,961	9.8	5,212	553,068	3.4	406	70,926	554	691,176	368	73,558	430	189,233
1955	6,956	1,604,408	9.8	5,237	567,612	3.5	402	76,278	542	707,162	347	70,194	428	183,162
1956	6,966	1,607,692	9.6	5,299	586,498	3.5	395	75,646	525	695,331	315	66,096	432	184,121
1957	6,818	1,558,691	9.1	5,309	594,529	3.5	340	77,608	452	641,455	280	62,097	437	183,002
1958	6,786	1,572,036	9.1	5,290	609,732	3.5	321	78,383	475	646,270	261	57,077	439	180,574
1959	6,845	1,612,822	9.1	5,364	619,877	3.5	330	68,323	459	688,410	254	57,392	438	178,820
1960	6,876	1,657,970	9.2	5,407	639,057	3.6	308	67,214	488	722,493	238	52,101	435	177,105
1961	6,923	1,669,789	9.1	5,460	658,521	3.6	321	70,536	483	714,622	222	48,556	437	177,554
1962	7,028	1,689,414	9.1	5,564	676,795	3.6	323	73,474	491	716,781	203	44,687	447	177,677
1963	7,138	1,701,839	9.0	5,684	698,191	3.7	323	73,525	499	714,661	186	39,144	446	176,318
1964	7,127	1,696,039	8.9	5,712	720,810	3.8	300	68,783	487	691,367	187	39,589	441	175,490
1965	7,123	1,703,522	8.8	5,736	741,292	3.8	283	65,897	483	685,175	178	37,196	443	173,962
1966	7,160	1,678,658	8.6	5,812	768,479	3.9	291	67,337	476	639,041	156	30,796	425	173,005
1967	7,172	1,671,125	8.5	5,850	788,446	4.0	331	80,311	470	609,075	105	18,228	416	175,065
1968	7,137	1,663,203	8.3	5,820	805,912	4.0	280	66,517	505	593,916	116	22,213	416	174,645
1969	7,144	1,649,662	8.2	5,853	825,795	4.1	260	63,075	509	570,550	107	20,562	415	169,681
1970	7,123	1,615,771	7.9	5,859	848,232	4.2	236	59,961	519	526,889	101	19,720	408	160,969
1971	7,097	1,555,560	7.5	5,865	866,519	4.2	218	54,364	513	468,745	94	17,773	407	148,159
1972	7,061	1,549,665	7.4	5,843	883,681	4.2	216	53,799	529	456,577	72	12,786	401	142,822
1973	7,123	1,534,726	7.3	5,891	903,324	4.3	229	56,684	543	421,999	63	10,461	397	142,258
1974	7,174	1,512,684	7.2	5,977	931,172	4.4	221	54,236	543	383,480	46	8,162	387	135,634
1975	7,156	1,465,828	6.9	5,979	946,976	4.4	215	51,223	544	329,837	36	5,846	382	131,946
1976	7,082	1,433,515	6.7	5,956	961,175	4.5	197	48,965	528	290,809	21	3,592	380	128,974
1977	7,099	1,407,097	6.5	5,973	973,866	4.5	189	45,119	541	261,207	19	3,315	377	123,590
1978	7,015	1,380,645	6.3	5,935	979,659	4.5	169	41,434	526	234,910	15	2,783	370	121,859
1979	6,988	1,371,849	6.2	5,923	987,687	4.5	165	40,338	527	224,334	12	2,142	361	117,348
1980	6,965	1,364,516	6.0	5,904	992,020	4.4	157	38,602	534	215,032	11	1,534	359	117,328
1981	6,933	1,361,513	5.9	5,879	1,006,774	4.4	146	35,217	549	202,359	11	1,550	348	115,613
1982	6,915	1,359,783	5.9	5,863	1,015,180	4.4	138	34,441	558	195,177	10	1,297	346	113,688
1983	6,888	1,350,361	5.8	5,843	1,021,364	4.4	131	30,486	564	184,582	8	987	342	112,942
1984	6,872	1,338,741	5.7	5,814	1,019,751	4.3	131	30,282	579	175,470	7	930	341	112,308

(continued)

TABLE Bd118–131 Hospitals and beds, by type of hospital: 1946–1997 [American Hospital Association data] *Continued*

	Total			Nonfederal hospitals									Federal hospitals	
				Short-term general and special			Long-term general and special		Psychiatric		Tuberculosis			
	Hospitals	Beds	Beds per 1,000 population	Hospitals	Beds	Beds per 1,000 population	Hospitals	Beds	Hospitals	Beds	Hospitals	Beds	Hospitals	Beds
	Bd118	Bd119	Bd120	Bd121	Bd122	Bd123	Bd124	Bd125	Bd126	Bd127	Bd128	Bd129	Bd130	Bd131
Year	Number	Number	Per 1,000	Number	Number	Per 1,000	Number	Number	Number	Number	Number	Number	Number	Number
1985	6,872	1,317,630	5.5	5,784	1,003,138	4.2	128	30,832	610	170,788	7	849	343	112,023
1986	6,841	1,290,316	5.4	5,728	981,540	4.1	133	29,835	634	167,354	4	458	342	111,129
1987	6,821	1,266,700	5.2	5,659	961,490	4.0	131	28,366	684	166,439	5	614	342	109,791
1988	6,780	1,248,342	5.1	5,579	949,462	3.9	129	27,328	726	165,894	4	462	342	105,196
1989	6,720	1,225,622	5.0	5,497	935,763	3.8	138	27,504	741	161,249	4	475	340	100,631
1990	6,649	1,213,327	4.9	5,420	929,374	3.7	131	24,991	757	160,237	4	470	337	98,255
1991	6,634	1,201,529	4.8	5,370	925,875	3.7	126	24,958	800	153,594	4	470	334	96,632
1992	6,539	1,177,848	4.6	5,321	922,742	3.6	115	22,608	774	141,216	4	420	325	90,862
1993	6,467	1,163,460	4.5	5,289	920,507	3.6	117	20,794	741	133,892	4	420	316	87,847
1994	6,374	1,128,066	4.3	5,256	903,719	3.5	110	19,431	714	120,575	5	518	307	83,823
1995	6,291	1,080,601	4.1	5,220	874,286	3.3	112	18,765	657	110,257	3	214	299	77,079
1996	6,201	1,061,688	4.0	5,160	863,940	3.3	112	18,848	636	105,521	3	208	290	73,171
1997	6,097	1,035,390	—	5,082	855,422	—	125	17,316	601	100,339	4	376	285	61,937

Sources

For 1946–1970, American Hospital Association (AHA), *Hospitals,* Guide Issues, part 2 (1946–1971). For 1971–1997, American Hospital Association, *AHA Hospital Statistics,* annual issues.

More recent data are available from *AHA Hospital Statistics,* published annually. Statistical information is also available for purchase on CD-ROM, and custom reports can be requested directly from the AHA.

Documentation

Statistics of hospitals obtained from the AHA's annual survey of hospitals cover all hospitals accepted for registration by the AHA. To be accepted for registration, a hospital must meet certain requirements, as follows: it must have at least six beds for the care of nonrelated patients for an average stay of more than twenty-four hours per admission; be constructed and equipped to ensure safety of patients and to provide sanitary facilities for their treatment; have an organized medical staff, registered nurse supervision, and nursing care for round-the-clock patient care; maintain clinical records on all patients and submit evidence of patient care by doctors; provide minimal surgical and obstetrical facilities or relatively complete diagnostic and treatment facilities; have diagnostic X-ray and clinical laboratory services readily available; and offer services more intensive than those required merely for room, board, personal services, and general nursing care.

See the text for Table Bd63–72 for a discussion of hospital types.

The number of beds includes beds, cribs, and pediatric bassinets regularly maintained for inpatients during the reporting period. It excludes newborn infant bassinets, but includes isolettes and neonatal intensive care units.

Data from the AHA relate generally to the year ending September 30 or to the fiscal year closest to that date.

The data include Alaska beginning in 1958 and Hawai'i in 1960.

Series Bd120 and Bd123. Total resident population was used in calculating these figures.

TABLE Bd132–143 Hospitals and beds, by type of hospital: 1909–1953 [American Medical Association data]

Contributed by Richard H. Steckel

	Total			General hospitals			Mental hospitals		Tuberculosis hospitals		All other hospitals	
	Hospitals	Beds	Beds per 1,000 population	Hospitals	Beds	Beds per 1,000 population	Hospitals	Beds	Hospitals	Beds	Hospitals	Beds
	Bd132	Bd133	Bd134	Bd135	Bd136	Bd137	Bd138	Bd139	Bd140	Bd141	Bd142	Bd143
Year	Number	Number	Per 1,000	Number	Number	Per 1,000	Number	Number	Number	Number	Number	Number
1909	4,359	421,065	4.7	—	—	—	—	—	—	—	—	—
1914	5,047	532,481	5.4	—	—	—	—	—	—	—	—	—
1918	5,323	612,251	5.9	—	—	—	—	—	—	—	—	—
1920	6,152	817,020	7.7	4,013	311,159	2.9	521	295,382	52	10,150	1,566	200,329
1921	6,236 [1]	—	—	—	—	—	—	—	—	—	—	—
1923	6,830	755,722	6.8	3,793	—	—	593	—	476	—	1,968	—
1924	7,370	813,926	7.1	—	—	—	—	—	—	—	—	—
1925	6,896	802,065	6.9	4,041	293,301	2.5	589	341,480	466	49,131	1,800	118,153
1926	6,946	859,445	7.3	—	—	—	—	—	—	—	—	—
1927	6,807	853,318	7.2	4,322	345,364	2.9	563	373,364	508	63,170	1,414	71,420
1928	6,852	892,934	7.4	4,361	363,337	3.0	553	394,268	508	62,113	1,430	73,216
1929	6,665	907,133	7.4	4,268	357,034	2.9	572	414,386	502	61,310	1,323	74,403
1930	6,719	955,869	7.8	4,302	371,609	3.0	561	437,919	515	65,940	1,341	80,401
1931	6,613	974,115	7.9	4,309	384,333	3.1	587	451,245	509	65,923	1,208	72,614
1932	6,562	1,014,354	8.1	4,305	395,543	3.2	624	479,548	512	69,676	1,121	69,587
1933	6,437	1,027,046	8.2	4,237	386,713	3.1	621	498,955	497	70,682	1,082	70,696
1934	6,334	1,048,101	8.3	4,198	393,425	3.1	614	513,845	495	70,063	1,027	70,768
1935	6,246	1,075,139	8.4	4,257	406,174	3.2	592	529,311	496	70,373	901	69,281
1936	6,189	1,096,721	8.6	4,207	402,605	3.1	584	548,952	506	73,692	892	71,472
1937	6,128	1,124,548	8.7	4,245	412,091	3.2	579	570,616	508	76,751	796	65,090
1938	6,166	1,161,380	8.9	4,286	425,324	3.3	592	591,822	493	76,022	795	68,212
1939	6,226	1,195,026	9.1	4,356	444,947	3.4	600	606,284	480	75,972	790	67,823
1940	6,291	1,226,245	9.3	4,432	462,360	3.5	602	621,284	479	78,246	778	64,355
1941	6,358	1,324,381	9.9	4,518	533,498	4.0	596	638,144	477	82,365	767	70,374
1942	6,345	1,383,827	10.3	4,557	594,260	4.4	586	646,118	468	82,372	734	61,077
1943	6,655	1,649,254	12.3	4,885	850,576	6.3	575	650,993	455	79,860	740	67,825
1944	6,611	1,729,945	13.0	4,833	925,818	7.0	566	648,745	453	79,848	759	75,534
1945	6,511	1,738,944	13.1	4,744	922,549	7.0	563	657,393	449	78,774	755	80,228
1946	6,280	1,468,714	10.5	4,523	641,331	4.6	575	674,930	450	83,187	732	69,266
1947	6,276	1,425,222	9.9	4,539	592,453	4.1	585	680,913	441	81,328	711	70,528
1948	6,335	1,423,520	9.7	4,589	576,459	3.9	586	691,499	438	81,993	722	73,569
1949	6,572	1,439,030	9.7	4,761	574,683	3.9	606	705,423	444	83,470	761	75,454
1950	6,430	1,456,912	9.6	4,713	587,917	3.9	579	711,921	431	85,746	707	71,328
1951	6,637	1,529,988	10.0	4,890	640,207	4.2	596	728,187	430	88,379	721	73,215
1952	6,665	1,541,615	9.9	4,924	640,923	4.1	585	732,929	428	89,571	728	78,192
1953	6,840	1,573,014	9.9	5,087	653,752	4.1	593	749,393	420	88,406	740	81,463

[1] Excludes hospitals with fewer than ten beds.

Sources

1909, 1914, 1918, and 1921: American Medical Association (AMA), *American Medical Directory* (1921 and prior editions).

1920 and 1923–1953: *Journal of the American Medical Association,* Hospital Number issues, for 1920 (April 1921): 1083–1103; for 1923 and 1927–1933 (March 1934): 1008–9; for 1924 (March 1925): 961–70; for 1925 (April 1926): 1009–55; for 1926 (March 1927): 789–839; for 1934–1953 (May 1954): 9–10.

Documentation

Although the AMA's annual census was begun in 1920, complete data on the number of hospital beds classified by type of service are available only from 1925. In addition to information on number of hospitals and beds, the Hospital Number of the AMA journal presented statistics on admissions, average daily census, and births.

Until 1953, when it discontinued registration of hospitals, the AMA collected data annually from all hospitals registered by it, and published them in the Hospital Number of the *Journal of the American Medical Association*. Registration was a basic recognition extended to hospitals and related institutions in accordance with requirements officially adopted by its House of Delegates.

Figures from the AMA presented in Tables Bd132–143, Bd158–171, and Bd202–211 are not entirely comparable with similar data provided by the American Hospital Association (AHA) because the standards required for "listing" or "recognition" of hospitals by the AHA differ from those required by the AMA.

General hospitals accept patients for a variety of acute medical and surgical conditions and, for the most part, do not admit cases of contagious disease, tuberculosis, and nervous and mental disease. The "other" category in the AMA listings includes hospitals devoted to contagious diseases; orthopedics; chronic and convalescent care; diseases of the eye, ear, nose, and throat; and obstetrics and gynecology, as well as children's and industrial hospitals.

Series Bd134 and Bd137. Total resident population was used in calculating these figures.

TABLE Bd144–157 Hospitals and beds, by ownership or control: 1946–1997 [American Hospital Association data]

Contributed by Richard H. Steckel

	Total		Federal government hospitals		State government hospitals		Local government hospitals		Nonprofit church hospitals		Other nonprofit hospitals		Proprietary hospitals	
	Hospitals	Beds	Hospitals	Beds	Hospitals	Beds	Hospitals	Beds	Hospitals	Beds	Hospitals	Beds	Hospitals	Beds
	Bd144	Bd145	Bd146	Bd147	Bd148 [1]	Bd149 [1]	Bd150 [1]	Bd151 [1]	Bd152 [2]	Bd153 [2]	Bd154 [2]	Bd155 [2]	Bd156	Bd157
Year	Number	Number	Number	Number	Number	Number	Number	Number	Number	Number	Number	Number	Number	Number
1946	6,125	1,435,778	404	235,964	—	—	1,504	811,702	—	—	2,921	334,867	1,296	53,245
1947	6,173	1,400,318	403	199,771	—	—	1,490	807,602	—	—	2,981	342,120	1,299	50,825
1948	6,160	1,411,450	386	185,846	—	—	1,474	826,377	—	—	3,022	349,310	1,278	49,917
1949	6,277	1,435,288	376	186,764	—	—	1,511	842,089	—	—	3,044	355,331	1,346	51,104
1950	6,788	1,455,825	414	189,477	—	—	1,654	843,672	—	—	3,250	368,137	1,470	54,539
1951	6,832	1,521,959	422	214,597	—	—	1,701	870,517	—	—	3,297	383,102	1,412	53,743
1952	6,903	1,561,809	439	213,018	—	—	1,747	896,596	—	—	3,348	398,530	1,369	53,665
1953	6,978	1,580,654	435	202,604	556	710,802	1,239	203,836	1,110	157,597	2,259	251,712	1,379	54,103
1954	6,970	1,577,961	430	189,233	552	717,558	1,248	202,312	1,196	169,685	2,225	247,658	1,319	51,515
1955	6,956	1,604,408	428	183,162	552	739,153	1,253	203,179	1,101	162,283	2,339	264,761	1,283	51,870
1956	6,966	1,607,692	432	184,121	553	728,151	1,263	202,368	1,206	176,972	2,304	265,633	1,208	50,447
1957	6,818	1,588,691	437	183,002	543	686,255	1,238	194,740	1,220	180,291	2,291	267,555	1,089	46,848
1958	6,786	1,572,036	439	180,574	548	691,226	1,257	195,778	1,220	183,437	2,288	275,365	1,034	45,656
1959	6,845	1,612,822	438	178,820	555	725,455	1,280	195,328	1,232	186,912	2,328	281,424	1,012	44,883
1960	6,876	1,657,970	435	177,105	556	752,148	1,324	201,322	1,241	192,743	2,338	288,843	982	45,809
1961	6,923	1,669,789	437	177,554	551	745,392	1,374	205,732	1,260	199,284	2,328	294,840	973	46,987
1962	7,028	1,689,414	447	177,677	558	746,490	1,410	208,200	1,259	201,919	2,364	305,189	990	49,939
1963	7,138	1,701,839	446	176,318	561	738,839	1,446	210,527	1,271	205,774	2,392	317,261	1,022	53,120
1964	7,127	1,696,039	441	175,490	555	719,343	1,500	215,891	1,227	210,837	2,424	320,798	980	53,680
1965	7,123	1,703,522	443	173,962	546	707,974	1,495	215,554	1,266	215,723	2,404	336,201	969	54,108
1966	7,160	1,678,658	425	173,005	550	669,118	1,554	218,630	—	—	3,675	563,320	956	54,585
1967	7,172	1,671,125	416	175,065	552	646,929	1,589	216,338	—	—	3,692	578,560	923	54,233
1968	7,137	1,663,203	416	174,645	559	620,455	1,631	218,623	—	—	3,660	594,845	871	54,635
1969	7,144	1,649,662	415	169,681	565	598,064	1,665	220,447	—	—	3,643	606,186	856	55,285
1970	7,123	1,615,771	408	160,969	577	557,571	1,680	219,353	—	—	3,600	618,548	858	59,330
1971	7,097	1,555,560	407	148,159	—	—	2,280	717,816	—	—	3,565	628,537	845	61,048
1972	7,061	1,549,665	401	142,822	—	—	2,300	700,923	—	—	3,515	640,643	845	65,277
1973	7,123	1,534,726	397	142,258	—	—	2,325	667,099	—	—	3,518	652,471	883	72,898
1974	7,174	1,512,684	387	135,634	—	—	2,311	624,131	—	—	3,576	673,395	900	79,524
1975	7,156	1,465,828	382	131,946	—	—	2,306	568,980	—	—	3,562	681,252	906	83,650
1976	7,082	1,433,515	380	128,974	—	—	2,266	525,012	—	—	3,551	692,412	885	87,117
1977	7,099	1,407,097	377	123,590	—	—	2,272	491,138	—	—	3,551	700,904	899	91,465
1978	7,015	1,380,645	370	121,859	—	—	2,232	462,187	—	—	3,532	704,202	881	92,397
1979	6,988	1,371,849	361	117,348	—	—	2,224	447,309	—	—	3,519	711,362	884	95,830
1980	6,965	1,364,516	359	117,328	—	—	2,210	433,380	—	—	3,505	713,685	891	100,123
1981	6,933	1,361,513	348	115,613	—	—	2,157	416,137	—	—	3,525	727,331	903	102,432
1982	6,915	1,359,783	346	113,688	—	—	2,112	405,828	—	—	3,526	733,318	931	106,949
1983	6,888	1,350,361	342	112,942	—	—	2,063	387,877	—	—	3,531	738,301	952	111,241
1984	6,872	1,338,741	341	112,308	—	—	1,990	368,979	—	—	3,539	738,146	1,002	119,308
1985	6,872	1,317,630	343	112,023	—	—	1,933	350,123	—	—	3,544	729,260	1,052	126,224
1986	6,841	1,290,316	342	111,129	—	—	1,870	335,912	—	—	3,517	711,327	1,112	131,948
1987	6,821	1,266,700	342	109,791	—	—	1,860	327,713	—	—	3,466	694,773	1,153	134,423
1988	6,780	1,248,342	342	105,196	—	—	1,849	318,842	—	—	3,440	689,139	1,149	135,165
1989	6,720	1,225,622	340	100,631	—	—	1,811	306,466	—	—	3,424	683,080	1,145	135,445

	Total		Federal government hospitals		State government hospitals		Local government hospitals		Nonprofit church hospitals		Other nonprofit hospitals		Proprietary hospitals	
	Hospitals	Beds	Hospitals	Beds	Hospitals	Beds	Hospitals	Beds	Hospitals	Beds	Hospitals	Beds	Hospitals	Beds
	Bd144	Bd145	Bd146	Bd147	Bd148 [1]	Bd149 [1]	Bd150 [1]	Bd151 [1]	Bd152 [2]	Bd153 [2]	Bd154 [2]	Bd155 [2]	Bd156	Bd157
Year	Number	Number	Number	Number	Number	Number	Number	Number	Number	Number	Number	Number	Number	Number
1990	6,649	1,213,327	337	98,255	—	—	1,785	301,458	—	—	3,388	677,833	1,139	135,781
1991	6,634	1,201,529	334	96,632	—	—	1,768	292,346	—	—	3,368	676,131	1,164	136,420
1992	6,539	1,177,848	325	90,862	—	—	1,717	279,604	—	—	3,363	674,197	1,134	133,185
1993	6,467	1,163,460	316	87,847	—	—	1,708	276,165	—	—	3,338	668,021	1,105	131,427
1994	6,374	1,128,066	307	83,823	—	—	—	—	—	—	—	—	—	—
1995	6,291	1,080,601	299	77,079	—	—	—	—	—	—	—	—	—	—
1996	6,201	1,061,688	290	73,171	—	—	—	—	—	—	—	—	—	—
1997	6,097	1,035,390	285	61,937	—	—	—	—	—	—	—	—	—	—

[1] State hospitals included with local hospitals for 1946–1952 and 1971–1993.

[2] Church-operated and affiliated hospitals included with other nonprofit hospitals for 1946–1952 and 1966–1993.

Sources

For 1946–1970, American Hospital Association (AHA), *Hospitals,* Guide Issues, part 2 (1946–1971). For 1971–1997, American Hospital Association, *AHA Hospital Statistics,* annual issues.

More recent data are available from *AHA Hospital Statistics,* published annually. Statistical information is also available for purchase on CD-ROM, and custom reports can be requested directly from the AHA.

Documentation

See the text for Table Bd118–131.

The data include Alaska beginning in 1958 and Hawai'i in 1960.

Series Bd150–151, Bd154–155, and Bd157. Data were eliminated from the published version. They may still be available directly from the AHA.

TABLE Bd158–171 Hospitals and beds, by ownership or control: 1909–1953 [American Medical Association data]

Contributed by Richard H. Steckel

	Total		Federal government hospitals		State government hospitals		Local government hospitals		Nonprofit church hospitals		Other nonprofit hospitals		Proprietary hospitals	
	Hospitals	Beds	Hospitals	Beds	Hospitals	Beds	Hospitals	Beds	Hospitals	Beds	Hospitals	Beds	Hospitals	Beds
	Bd158	Bd159	Bd160	Bd161	Bd162	Bd163	Bd164	Bd165	Bd166	Bd167	Bd168 [1]	Bd169 [1]	Bd170 [1]	Bd171 [1]
Year	Number	Number	Number	Number	Number	Number	Number	Number	Number	Number	Number	Number	Number	Number
1909	4,359	421,065 [2]	71	8,827	232	189,049	—	—	—	—	—	—	—	—
1914	5,047	532,481	93	12,602	294	232,834	—	—	—	—	—	—	—	—
1918	5,323	612,251	110	18,815	303	262,254	—	—	—	—	—	—	—	—
1923	6,830	755,722	220	53,869	601	302,208	915	115,871	893	77,941	2,439	160,114	1,762	45,719
1924	7,370	813,926	310	62,352	632	321,399	1,050	125,302	1,233	110,760	1,748	131,439	2,397	62,674
1925	6,896	802,065	299	57,091	351	317,264	—	—	—	—	—	—	—	—
1926	6,946	859,445	—	63,553	—	334,984	—	—	—	—	—	—	—	—
1927	6,807	853,318	301	60,444	592	354,786	916	129,939	1,060	108,582	3,938	199,567	—	—
1928	6,852	892,934	294	61,765	595	369,759	924	135,910	1,056	114,613	3,983	210,887	—	—
1929	6,665	907,133	292	59,901	578	385,706	925	136,930	1,024	113,555	3,846	211,041	—	—
1930	6,719	955,869	288	63,581	581	405,309	943	150,836	1,017	116,846	3,890	219,297	—	—
1931	6,613	974,115	291	69,170	576	419,282	949	153,072	1,011	116,935	3,786	215,656	—	—
1932	6,562	1,014,354	301	74,151	568	442,601	935	162,615	1,001	117,555	3,757	217,432	—	—
1933	6,437	1,027,046	295	75,635	557	459,646	924	159,192	984	115,840	3,677	216,733	—	—
1934	6,334	1,048,101	313	77,865	544	473,035	892	166,988	970	113,263	1,676	154,449	1,939	62,501
1935	6,246	1,075,139	316	83,353	526	483,994	882	174,365	970	113,268	1,670	155,300	1,882	64,859
1936	6,189	1,096,721	323	84,234	524	503,306	877	176,300	969	113,288	1,742	162,586	1,754	57,007
1937	6,128	1,124,548	329	97,951	522	508,913	871	181,885	975	115,283	1,718	162,474	1,713	58,042
1938	6,166	1,161,380	330	92,248	523	541,279	875	181,609	981	119,521	1,776	169,980	1,681	56,743
1939	6,226	1,195,026	329	96,338	523	560,575	888	188,233	1,001	120,740	1,839	172,765	1,646	56,375
1940	6,291	1,226,245	336	108,928	521	572,079	910	192,682	998	120,809	1,903	177,681	1,623	54,066
1941	6,358	1,324,381	428	179,202	530	600,320	906	185,989	993	123,331	1,917	182,140	1,584	53,399
1942	6,345	1,383,827	474	220,938	530	606,437	920	188,406	977	126,141	1,949	190,150	1,495	51,755
1943	6,655	1,649,254	827	476,673	531	610,115	926	189,351	1,004	130,488	1,952	192,219	1,415	50,408
1944	6,611	1,729,945	798	551,135	539	609,025	925	192,118	1,020	133,090	1,961	195,624	1,368	48,953
1945	6,511	1,738,944	705	546,384	549	619,642	929	190,692	1,036	135,481	1,954	195,805	1,338	50,940
1946	6,280	1,468,714	464	264,486	557	628,363	941	189,885	1,050	138,096	1,942	198,885	1,326	48,999
1947	6,276	1,425,222	401	213,204	563	626,648	953	190,353	1,051	141,920	1,965	202,661	1,343	50,436
1948	6,335	1,423,520	372	185,098	567	648,386	961	186,283	1,068	144,036	2,016	208,936	1,351	50,781
1949	6,572	1,439,030	361	182,254	573	656,611	1,003	186,290	1,090	146,315	2,067	213,576	1,478	53,984
1950	6,430	1,456,912	355	186,793	552	665,019	1,005	185,229	1,097	150,078	2,072	218,788	1,349	51,005
1951	6,637	1,529,988	388	216,939	554	683,376	1,090	197,405	1,116	154,053	2,121	225,903	1,368	52,312
1952	6,665	1,541,615	386	211,510	549	691,408	1,143	196,705	1,136	158,389	2,146	232,598	1,305	51,005
1953	6,840	1,573,014	392	200,535	550	711,824	1,194	200,645	1,169	164,053	2,206	243,653	1,329	52,304

[1] Proprietary hospitals and beds included with other nonprofit hospitals for 1927–1933.

[2] Agrees with the corresponding entry in Table Bd132–143; U.S. Bureau of the Census, *Historical Statistics of the United States* (1975), had an incorrect figure in this table.

Sources

American Medical Association, *Journal of the American Medical Association,* Hospital Number issues, for 1909, 1914, 1918, and 1934–1953 (May 1954): 4, 7–8; for 1923 and 1927–1933 (March 1934): 1006–7; for 1924 (March 1925): 961–70; for 1925 (April 1926): 1009–55; for 1926 (March 1927): 789–839.

Documentation

See the text for Table Bd132–143.

TABLE Bd172–189 Hospital use rates and average length of stay, by type of hospital: 1946–1996

Contributed by Richard H. Steckel

	All hospitals			Short-term and other general hospitals			Long-term and other general hospitals		
	Per 1,000 resident population			Per 1,000 resident population			Per 1,000 resident population		
	Admissions	Total days	Average length of stay	Admissions	Total days	Average length of stay	Admissions	Total days	Average length of stay
	Bd172	Bd173	Bd174	Bd175	Bd176	Bd177	Bd178	Bd179	Bd180
Year	Per 1,000	Per 1,000	Days	Per 1,000	Per 1,000	Days	Per 1,000	Per 1,000	Days
1946	112	2,688	24.0	97	887	9.1	0.99	165	167
1947	123	—	—	111	—	—	1.04	—	—
1948	115	—	—	103	—	—	0.88	—	—
1949	116	—	—	104	—	—	0.89	—	—
1950	122	3,025	24.7	110	898	8.1	1.08	143	132
1951	123	—	—	109	—	—	1.06	—	—
1952	126	—	—	112	—	—	1.00	—	—
1953	128	—	—	114	—	—	1.01	—	—
1954	126	—	—	114	—	—	0.96	—	—
1955	128	3,028	23.6	116	904	7.8	0.96	145	151
1956	132	—	—	120	—	—	1.05	—	—
1957	135	—	—	123	—	—	1.16	—	—
1958	137	—	—	125	—	—	0.92	—	—
1959	134	—	—	123	—	—	0.84	—	—
1960	139	2,843	20.4	128	968	7.6	0.84	118	141
1961	139	2,777	19.9	128	—	—	0.85	—	—
1962	143	2,763	19.3	131	—	—	0.85	—	—
1963	146	2,769	19.0	134	—	—	0.79	—	—
1964	148	2,713	18.3	136	—	—	0.82	—	—
1965	149	2,646	17.8	137	1,063	7.8	0.86	106	124
1966	149	2,599	17.4	138	1,091	7.9	0.74	106	144
1967	149	2,552	17.2	137	1,131	8.3	0.79	125	159
1968	149	2,530	16.9	137	1,157	8.5	0.75	101	135
1969	153	2,438	16.0	140	1,178	8.4	0.52	94	181
1970	156	2,324	14.9	144	1,185	8.3	0.65	88	136
1971	158	2,189	13.8	146	—	—	0.47	—	—
1972	160	2,124	13.3	148	1,166	7.9	0.51	78	155
1973	164	2,066	12.6	151	1,184	7.8	0.53	81	152
1974	168	2,015	12.0	156	1,210	7.8	0.50	77	153
1975	170	1,926	11.4	157	1,212	7.7	0.48	72	149
1976	171	1,856	10.8	159	1,218	7.7	0.47	69	148
1977	171	1,797	10.5	159	1,208	7.6	0.41	64	155
1978	171	1,743	10.2	159	1,204	7.6	0.36	58	160
1979	172	1,729	10.1	160	1,208	7.6	0.37	58	156
1980	172	1,711	10.0	160	1,208	7.6	0.33	54	160
1981	171	1,687	9.9	159	1,215	7.6	0.34	48	144
1982	169	1,658	9.8	157	1,202	7.6	0.33	48	146
1983	166	1,604	9.6	155	1,170	7.6	0.31	41	133
1984	161	1,505	9.4	149	1,090	7.3	0.33	42	127
1985	153	1,394	9.1	141	996	7.1	0.39	41	108
1986	147	1,341	9.1	135	958	7.1	0.34	40	118
1987	142	1,314	9.2	131	940	7.2	0.33	37	114
1988	139	1,292	9.3	129	930	7.2	0.31	36	117
1989	137	1,260	9.2	126	915	7.3	0.33	35	105
1990	136	1,238	9.1	125	910	7.3	0.36	31	88
1991	133	1,197	9.0	123	886	7.2	0.33	31	93
1992	132	1,157	8.8	122	868	7.1	0.26	27	106
1993	129	1,108	8.6	119	839	7.0	0.23	25	106
1994	127	1,045	8.2	118	797	6.8	0.18	23	124
1995	127	986	7.8	118	762	6.5	0.18	22	120
1996	126	943	7.5	117	732	6.2	0.18	22	120

(continued)

TABLE Bd172–189 Hospital use rates and average length of stay, by type of hospital: 1946–1996 *Continued*

	Psychiatric hospitals			Tuberculosis hospitals			Federal hospitals		
	Per 1,000 resident population			Per 1,000 resident population			Per 1,000 resident population		
	Admissions	Total days	Average length of stay	Admissions	Total days	Average length of stay	Admissions	Total days	Average length of stay
	Bd181	Bd182	Bd183	Bd184	Bd185	Bd186	Bd187	Bd188	Bd189
Year	Per 1,000	Per 1,000	Days	Per 1,000	Per 1,000	Days	Per 1,000	Per 1,000	Days
1946	1.4	1,357	941	0.61	144.0	237	11.4	434	38.2
1947	1.9	—	—	0.66	—	—	8.9	—	—
1948	1.8	—	—	0.77	—	—	8.5	—	—
1949	1.8	—	—	0.86	—	—	8.5	—	—
1950	1.9	1,461	754	0.52	148.2	284	8.5	368	43.3
1951	1.8	—	—	0.54	—	—	10.3	—	—
1952	2.5	—	—	0.49	—	—	10.2	—	—
1953	1.8	—	—	0.49	—	—	9.8	—	—
1954	1.8	—	—	0.55	—	—	8.8	—	—
1955	1.9	1,506	793	0.53	124.9	236	8.6	349	40.5
1956	2.1	—	—	0.45	—	—	8.3	—	—
1957	1.8	—	—	0.42	—	—	8.3	—	—
1958	2.1	—	—	0.40	—	—	8.2	—	—
1959	2.0	—	—	0.45	—	—	8.1	—	—
1960	2.0	1,366	678	0.38	79.7	210	8.2	313	38.2
1961	2.1	1,305	634	0.35	—	—	8.2	306	37.3
1962	2.2	1,275	573	0.33	—	—	8.6	303	35.4
1963	2.3	1,272	551	0.29	—	—	8.5	294	34.7
1964	2.3	1,206	522	0.32	—	—	8.5	289	34.2
1965	2.5	1,145	452	0.27	49.1	183	8.5	283	33.3
1966	2.3	1,080	468	0.23	39.0	170	8.3	281	34.1
1967	2.5	999	401	0.13	22.5	169	8.6	275	32.0
1968	2.7	977	362	0.18	26.5	147	8.9	268	30.3
1969	2.8	888	316	0.18	24.1	135	8.8	254	28.9
1970	2.9	801	273	0.18	21.9	124	8.5	229	26.9
1971	2.9	695	238	0.17	—	—	8.7	218	25.2
1972	2.8	664	237	0.14	13.7	101	8.5	201	23.6
1973	2.8	595	212	0.12	11.3	91	8.9	196	22.0
1974	2.8	530	188	0.10	8.9	89	8.7	189	21.7
1975	2.8	454	160	0.08	5.8	73	9.0	182	20.3
1976	2.8	392	141	0.06	3.5	64	9.3	174	18.7
1977	2.7	355	131	0.06	3.4	59	9.3	166	17.8
1978	2.7	318	119	0.05	2.8	55	9.2	160	17.5
1979	2.6	309	120	0.04	2.2	58	9.0	152	16.9
1980	2.5	296	118	0.03	1.7	48	9.0	152	16.8
1981	2.4	276	114	0.04	1.6	46	8.9	145	16.4
1982	2.5	265	108	0.04	1.3	35	8.7	142	16.4
1983	2.4	249	106	0.03	1.0	33	8.8	142	16.1
1984	2.5	235	96	0.03	0.9	35	8.8	138	15.7
1985	2.5	225	89	0.03	0.8	33	8.8	131	14.8
1986	2.5	218	86	0.02	0.4	27	8.8	125	14.2
1987	2.6	215	81	0.01	0.6	41	8.6	122	14.2
1988	2.8	210	75	0.01	0.5	56	7.6	115	15.1
1989	2.9	201	70	0.01	0.5	57	7.3	109	14.9
1990	2.9	191	66	0.01	0.5	62	7.1	105	14.9
1991	2.9	179	61	0.01	0.5	80	6.6	101	15.3
1992	2.9	162	56	0.01	0.5	83	6.6	99	15.1
1993	2.9	149	52	0.01	0.5	101	6.3	95	15.0
1994	2.9	136	47	0.01	0.6	89	6.1	88	14.4
1995	2.7	124	46	(Z)	0.2	57	5.9	78	13.1
1996	2.7	117	43	(Z)	0.2	75	5.4	72	13.4

(Z) Fewer than .005 admissions.

Sources

Admissions data are from the following American Hospital Association (AHA) sources. For 1946–1953: from *Hospitals,* Guide Issue, volume 28, part 2 (June 1954), p. 16. For 1954, 1956, 1957: from *Hospitals,* Guide Issue, volume 32, part 2 (August 1958), Table 1, p. 364. For 1961–1964: from *Hospitals,* Guide Issue, volume 44, part 2 (August 1970), Table 1, pp. 472–3. For 1955, 1960, 1965–1970: from *Hospitals,* Guide Issue, volume 45, part 2 (August 1971), Table 1, pp. 460–2. For 1971 onward: annual issues of *Hospital Statistics,* Table 3, except 1994 and 1995 in Table 3A, and 1996 and 1997 in Table 2.

Data on inpatient days are from the following sources. For 1946–1953: *Hospitals,* Guide Issue (1954), p. 24. For 1954, 1956, and 1957: *Hospitals,* Guide Issue (1958), Table 1, p. 364. (For 1957, this excludes U.S. Army and "other federal" hospitals, whose data were not included by the AHA. Information from Table 4, pp. 372–3, was used to calculate inpatient days for 1957.) For 1961–1964: *Hospitals,* Guide Issue (1970), Table 1, pp. 472–3. For 1955, 1960, 1965–1970: *Hospitals,* Guide Issue (1971), Table 1, pp. 460–2. For 1971: Information on the smaller classes of hospitals does not appear to be available. For total and federal, inpatient-day calculations used expense data from *Hospital Statistics* (1975), Table 1, pp. 3–5. For 1973–1975: annual editions of *Hospital Statistics,* Table 3. From 1976 onward, inpatient days are

TABLE Bd172–189 Hospital use rates and average length of stay, by type of hospital: 1946–1996 *Continued*

reported directly in the annual editions of *Hospital Statistics*. For 1976–1993, they appear in Table 5A, for 1994 and 1995 in Table 3A, and for 1996 and 1997 in Table 2.

Documentation

See the text for Table Bd63–72 for a description of hospital types, and the text for Table Bd118–131 for additional information on the AHA's data collection practices.

Data on inpatient days were not reported directly by the AHA until 1976. For previous years, these numbers were calculated from reported quantities (for example, total expenses and expenses per patient day, with the quotient representing inpatient days).

Average length of stay is inpatient days divided by admissions.

Series on admissions and inpatient days are expressed as annual rates per 1,000 resident population.

TABLE Bd190–201 Hospital admissions and average daily census, by type of hospital: 1946–1997 [American Hospital Association data]

Contributed by Richard H. Steckel

	All hospitals		Nonfederal hospitals								Federal hospitals	
			Short-term general and special hospitals		Long-term general and special hospitals		Psychiatric hospitals		Tuberculosis hospitals			
	Average daily census	Admissions during year	Average daily census	Admissions during year	Average daily census	Admissions during year	Average daily census	Admissions during year	Average daily census	Admissions during year	Average daily census	Admissions during year
	Bd190	Bd191	Bd192	Bd193	Bd194	Bd195	Bd196	Bd197	Bd198	Bd199	Bd200	Bd201
Year	Thousand	Thousand	Thousand	Thousand	Thousand	Thousand	Thousand	Thousand	Thousand	Thousand	Thousand	Thousand
1946	1,142.0	15,675.0	341.0	13,655.0	63.0	139.0	517.0	202.0	55.0	85.0	166.0	1,593.0
1947	1,190.0	17,689.0	354.0	15,908.0	73.0	149.0	558.0	266.0	55.0	94.0	150.0	1,271.0
1948	1,241.0	16,821.0	361.0	15,072.0	70.0	128.0	595.0	267.0	66.0	112.0	149.0	1,241.0
1949	1,240.0	17,224.0	352.0	15,428.0	68.0	132.0	597.0	269.0	66.0	128.0	157.0	1,268.0
1950	1,253.0	18,483.0	372.0	16,663.0	60.0	164.0	607.0	293.0	62.0	79.0	152.0	1,284.0
1951	1,298.0	18,783.0	378.0	16,677.0	51.0	163.0	636.0	275.0	62.0	83.0	171.0	1,586.0
1952	1,336.0	19,624.0	385.0	17,413.0	58.0	156.0	651.0	392.0	62.0	76.0	180.0	1,586.0
1953	1,342.0	20,184.0	394.0	18,098.0	56.0	160.0	663.0	291.0	62.0	77.0	168.0	1,558.0
1954	1,343.0	20,345.0	393.0	18,392.0	61.0	155.0	668.0	289.0	61.0	89.0	160.0	1,421.0
1955	1,363.0	21,073.0	407.0	19,100.0	65.0	158.0	677.0	312.0	56.0	87.0	157.0	1,415.0
1956	1,356.0	22,090.0	425.0	20,107.0	63.0	175.0	659.0	343.0	53.0	76.0	156.0	1,388.0
1957	1,320.0	22,993.0	438.0	21,002.0	67.0	198.0	609.0	303.0	49.0	71.0	157.0	1,419.0
1958	1,323.0	23,697.0	451.0	21,684.0	67.0	160.0	604.0	359.0	44.0	69.0	157.0	1,425.0
1959	1,363.2	23,605.2	462.0	21,604.6	58.8	148.7	641.5	348.6	44.5	79.4	156.3	1,423.9
1960	1,401.9	25,027.2	477.4	22,970.1	58.4	150.8	672.3	362.5	39.3	68.2	154.5	1,475.5
1961	1,392.9	25,474.4	489.5	23,375.1	59.8	155.4	654.3	376.4	35.8	64.7	153.5	1,502.8
1962	1,406.8	26,531.4	508.8	24,307.3	62.2	158.7	648.6	413.1	32.8	60.5	154.4	1,591.8
1963	1,430.0	27,502.0	530.0	25,267.0	62.0	148.0	657.0	435.0	29.0	55.0	152.0	1,598.0
1964	1,420.9	28,266.2	550.1	25,987.3	59.0	156.8	631.9	441.8	28.4	61.6	151.6	1,618.8
1965	1,402.6	28,811.9	563.4	26,462.9	56.2	166.2	607.1	490.7	26.0	52.1	149.8	1,640.1
1966	1,398.0	29,151.0	588.0	26,897.0	57.0	144.0	582.0	451.0	21.0	45.0	151.0	1,615.0
1967	1,380.4	29,361.4	612.0	26,987.6	67.6	155.3	539.9	492.3	12.1	26.2	148.8	1,699.9
1968	1,378.0	29,766.0	630.0	27,276.0	55.0	149.0	532.0	538.0	14.0	36.0	146.0	1,766.0
1969	1,346.0	30,729.0	651.0	28,254.0	52.0	105.0	490.0	565.0	13.0	36.0	140.0	1,769.0
1970	1,297.7	31,759.1	661.5	29,251.7	49.2	132.0	446.7	598.0	12.2	36.1	128.1	1,741.4
1971	1,236.8	32,663.7	664.8	30,142.4	45.3	97.4	392.6	601.8	10.8	34.1	123.3	1,788.1
1972	1,208.9	33,264.9	664.1	30,776.9	44.7	105.6	378.0	584.7	7.8	28.2	114.3	1,769.5
1973	1,189.0	34,352.1	681.5	31,761.1	46.5	111.6	342.1	588.4	6.5	25.9	112.5	1,865.1
1974	1,167.4	35,506.2	701.3	32,943.2	44.8	106.5	306.8	594.7	5.2	21.2	109.4	1,840.6
1975	1,124.9	36,156.5	708.1	33,519.2	42.1	103.1	264.8	604.1	3.4	16.9	106.5	1,913.2
1976	1,089.7	36,775.8	714.8	34,068.4	40.5	100.3	230.1	597.6	2.1	11.8	102.2	1,997.6
1977	1,065.9	37,059.8	716.7	34,353.2	38.1	89.4	210.8	587.2	2.0	12.5	98.4	2,017.5
1978	1,041.9	37,243.2	719.9	34,575.2	34.8	79.6	189.9	580.2	1.7	11.0	95.6	1,997.2
1979	1,043.5	37,802.1	729.0	35,159.9	34.7	81.3	186.6	567.0	1.3	8.3	91.8	1,985.6
1980	1,059.7	38,892.3	748.4	36,198.3	33.2	75.8	183.2	566.5	1.0	7.8	94.0	2,043.9
1981	1,060.9	39,168.8	764.4	36,493.6	30.4	76.9	173.8	557.6	1.0	8.2	91.3	2,032.5
1982	1,052.7	39,095.0	763.3	36,429.0	30.3	75.7	168.0	568.1	0.8	8.4	90.3	2,013.8
1983	1,027.7	38,886.7	750.1	36,200.6	26.4	72.6	159.7	551.6	0.7	7.3	90.9	2,054.6
1984	9,702.9	37,938.0	702.7	35,202.2	26.9	77.6	151.5	578.2	0.6	6.2	88.7	2,073.9
1985	9,098.1	36,304.1	650.0	33,501.1	27.2	91.6	146.7	602.5	0.5	6.0	85.4	2,102.9
1986	8,826.3	35,219.4	630.6	32,410.2	26.2	81.2	143.2	607.0	0.3	3.6	82.3	2,117.4
1987	8,726.2	34,439.4	624.1	31,632.8	24.7	79.4	142.5	638.5	0.4	3.4	80.9	2,085.3
1988	8,633.8	34,107.0	621.8	31,480.2	23.9	74.8	140.4	687.8	0.3	2.0	77.1	1,862.1
1989	8,526.8	33,742.0	619.2	31,140.9	23.5	81.4	135.7	706.7	0.3	2.1	73.9	1,810.8

(continued)

TABLE Bd190–201 Hospital admissions and average daily census, by type of hospital: 1946–1997 [American Hospital Association data] *Continued*

	All hospitals		Nonfederal hospitals								Federal hospitals	
			Short-term general and special hospitals		Long-term general and special hospitals		Psychiatric hospitals		Tuberculosis hospitals			
	Average daily census	Admissions during year	Average daily census	Admissions during year	Average daily census	Admissions during year	Average daily census	Admissions during year	Average daily census	Admissions during year	Average daily census	Admissions during year
	Bd190	Bd191	Bd192	Bd193	Bd194	Bd195	Bd196	Bd197	Bd198	Bd199	Bd200	Bd201
Year	Thousand	Thousand	Thousand	Thousand	Thousand	Thousand	Thousand	Thousand	Thousand	Thousand	Thousand	Thousand
1990	8,437.2	33,773.6	620.4	31,203.2	21.4	88.3	130.0	721.2	0.3	1.8	71.6	1,759.1
1991	8,270.9	33,566.6	612.2	31,083.8	21.2	83.2	123.9	739.9	0.4	1.6	69.5	1,658.0
1992	8,068.4	33,536.1	605.5	31,052.7	19.1	66.0	112.9	742.1	0.3	1.5	68.9	1,673.7
1993	7,828.4	33,200.5	593.0	30,770.3	17.5	60.0	105.2	743.3	0.4	1.3	66.8	1,625.6
1994	7,450.1	33,125.5	568.8	30,739.3	16.1	47.4	96.9	749.1	0.4	1.7	62.8	1,588.0
1995	7,097.5	33,282.1	549.4	30,966.0	15.8	48.1	88.4	707.9	0.2	1.1	56.0	1,559.1
1996	6,848.8	33,307.2	531.5	31,116.4	16.0	48.9	85.0	719.4	0.1	0.6	52.2	1,421.9
1997	6,727.4	33,624.3	529.2	31,595.2	14.5	55.1	79.8	724.0	0.2	0.7	49.0	1,249.2

Sources

For 1946–1970, American Hospital Association (AHA), *Hospitals,* Guide Issues, part 2 (1946–1971). For 1971–1997, American Hospital Association, *AHA Hospital Statistics,* annual issues.

More recent data are available from *AHA Hospital Statistics,* published annually.

Documentation

See the text for Table Bd118–131.

The data include Alaska beginning in 1958 and Hawai'i in 1960.

TABLE Bd202–211 Hospital admissions and average daily census, by type of hospital: 1923–1953 [American Medical Association data]

Contributed by Richard H. Steckel

	All hospitals		General hospitals		Mental hospitals		Tuberculosis hospitals		Other hospitals	
	Average daily census	Admissions during year	Average daily census	Admissions during year	Average daily census	Admissions during year	Average daily census	Admissions during year	Average daily census	Admissions during year
	Bd202	Bd203	Bd204	Bd205	Bd206	Bd207	Bd208	Bd209	Bd210	Bd211
Year	Thousand	Thousand	Thousand	Thousand	Thousand	Thousand	Thousand	Thousand	Thousand	Thousand
1923	553	—	—	—	—	—	—	—	—	—
1925	629	—	194	—	322	—	40	—	74	—
1927	672	—	228	—	350	—	51	—	43	—
1929	727	—	234	—	395	—	51	—	47	—
1930	763	—	240	—	415	—	56	—	52	—
1931	775	7,156	248	6,322	427	—	56	81	45	—
1932	808	7,228	250	6,304	455	170	60	93	43	662
1933	810	7,038	232	6,072	475	171	60	84	43	711
1934	830	7,147	237	6,292	488	172	60	82	45	601
1935	876	7,717	261	6,875	507	173	61	86	46	583
1936	909	8,647	272	7,756	525	185	63	99	49	607
1937	944	9,222	288	8,350	547	196	65	102	44	574
1938	966	9,421	293	8,546	562	199	66	101	44	576
1939	996	9,879	308	9,018	577	190	65	91	46	580
1940	1,026	10,088	325	9,219	591	190	67	91	43	587
1941	1,087	11,596	364	10,647	603	209	71	101	50	639
1942	1,126	12,546	405	11,634	610	214	70	102	41	596
1943	1,257	15,375	529	14,455	619	209	65	92	43	620
1944	1,299	16,037	570	15,060	619	226	63	88	47	662
1945	1,405	16,257	665	15,228	624	249	60	86	56	694
1946	1,239	15,153	496	14,052	636	271	62	100	45	731
1947	1,217	15,830	457	14,665	652	292	63	99	46	773
1948	1,217	16,423	438	15,160	664	305	66	106	49	852
1949	1,225	16,660	429	15,450	675	308	69	113	51	789
1950	1,243	17,024	433	15,830	688	307	72	113	49	773
1951	1,294	18,237	471	17,066	698	307	74	107	52	757
1952	1,309	18,915	475	17,760	704	312	75	110	55	733
1953	1,333	19,869	477	18,693	719	328	75	108	61	739

TABLE Bd202–211 Hospital admissions and average daily census, by type of hospital: 1923–1953 [American Medical Association data] *Continued*

Sources

American Medical Association, *Journal of the American Medical Association*, Hospital Number issues, for 1925 (April 1926): 1009; for 1923, 1927, and 1929–1933 (March 1934): 1008–9; for 1934–1953 (May 1954): 9–10.

Documentation

See the text for Table Bd132–143.

Average daily census is defined as the average number of inpatients receiving care each day during the twelve-month period, excluding newborns. Admissions refer to the number of patients, excluding newborns, accepted for inpatient service during the twelve-month period.

TABLE Bd212–216 Patients in mental hospitals, by type of hospital: 1904–1970

Contributed by Richard H. Steckel

	All mental hospitals		Federal hospitals	State and county hospitals	Private hospitals
	Total	Per 100,000 population			
	Bd212 [1]	Bd213 [1,2]	Bd214 [3]	Bd215	Bd216
Year	Thousand	Per 100,000	Thousand	Thousand	Thousand
1904	150	183	—	—	—
1910	188	203	—	—	—
1923	268	239	29 [4]	230 [4]	9
1931	353	284	12	332	8
1933	395	315	19	366	10
1934	407	322	21	376	10
1935	422	331	23	389	11
1936	435	340	24	400	11
1937	448	348	27	409	12
1938	462	356	30	421	11
1939	476	364	32	433	11
1940	479	364	34	434	11
1941	496	377	35	450	11
1942	502	383	36	454	12
1943	503	394	38	453	12
1944	510	402	41	456	12
1945	522	409	45	463	13
1946	531	384	49	470	12
1947	544	381	54	477	12
1948	558	384	55	490	13
1949	567	384	54	499	14
1950	580	386	54	513	14
1951	587	389	53	520	14
1952	599	390	53	532	13
1953	612	392	53	545	14
1954	625	393	57	554	14
1955	634	390	60	559	15
1956	628	380	62	551	14
1957	622	369	61	549	14
1958	621	363	62	545	14
1959	618	354	63	542	14
1960	611	343	62	536	14
1961	603	333	63	527	13
1962	591	322	62	516	14
1963	579	311	62	505	13
1964	566	299	62	490	13
1965	550	287	62	475	13
1966	523	270	57	452	14
1967	493	252	53	426	14
1968	457	231	48	399	10
1969	424	212	43	370	11
1970	391	194	43	338	11

[1] Includes patients in state-operated psychopathic hospitals and, through 1950, in city hospitals.

[2] Estimated as of July 1. Total population used prior to 1936; civilian thereafter.

[3] Includes veterans with mental disorders resident in Veterans Administration (VA) hospitals and, through 1965, all patients in public health service hospitals at Fort Worth, Texas, and Lexington, Kentucky.

[4] County hospitals included with federal.

Sources

For 1904, U.S. Census Office, *Insane and Feeble-Minded in Hospitals and Institutions, 1904* (special report). For 1910, U.S. Bureau of the Census, *Insane and Feeble-Minded in Institutions, 1910*. For 1923–1946, *Patients in Mental Institutions*, annual reports, varying titles. For 1947–1966, U.S. National Institute of Mental Health, *Patients in Mental Institutions*, annual issues. For 1967–1970, U.S. National Institute of Mental Health, *Mental Health Statistics*, Series A, Reference Tables, and unpublished data.

Documentation

For 1923–1932, the annual enumerations of patients in mental institutions, conducted by the Bureau of the Census, were confined to state hospitals for mental disease and state institutions for the mentally defective and epileptics. Since 1933, the annual censuses conducted by the Bureau of the Census until 1946 and subsequently by the National Institute of Mental Health (NIMH) have covered all types of hospitals and institutions caring for the mentally ill, the mentally defective, and epileptics. For a discussion of these developments, see the 1947 issue of NIMH, *Patients in Mental Institutions*, pp. 1–4. Additional information on admissions, patients, personnel, and expenditures of institutions for the mentally defective and epileptics, as well as for hospitals for mental diseases, appear in various issues of that report.

The figures represent patients who are resident in hospitals that provide care solely for the mentally ill, as distinguished from the physically ill and from the mentally deficient and epileptic. These hospitals may provide care over an unlimited period of time or temporary care, as in psychopathic hospitals. Hospitals included are those under control of state and local governments, nonprofit and proprietary organizations, the VA, and the federal government in the District of Columbia (included here under state hospitals).

These facilities contain 93 percent of the psychiatric beds. (The other 7 percent are in general hospitals and residential treatment centers for emotionally disturbed children.) The number of resident patients in these hospitals peaked in 1955 (the year during which the use of tranquilizers became widespread in these hospitals) and has decreased since. Coupled with this decrease in residents is an increase in admissions offset by the practice of returning many hospitalized patients to the community for treatment.

There are also programs for preventing hospitalization in the many outpatient psychiatric clinics and community mental health centers. These, along with general hospital psychiatric services, provide about three fourths of the care to the mentally ill in the existing psychiatric facilities.

TABLE Bd217–231 Public institutions for the mentally retarded – facilities, patients, personnel, and maintenance expenditures: 1936–1970

Contributed by Richard H. Steckel

				Admissions, excluding transfers							Full-time personnel		Maintenance expenditures		
														Per average daily resident patient	
	Facilities	Resident patients, beginning of year	Patients per 100,000 population	Number	Per 100,000 population	Patients under treatment	Deaths	Net releases of living persons	Resident patients, end of year	Average daily resident patient population	Total	Per 100 average daily resident patients	Total	Annual	Daily
	Bd217	Bd218	Bd219 [1]	Bd220	Bd221 [2]	Bd222	Bd223	Bd224 [3]	Bd225	Bd226	Bd227 [4]	Bd228 [4]	Bd229 [4, 5]	Bd230 [4, 5]	Bd231 [4, 5]
Year	Number	Number	Per 100,000	Number	Per 100,000	Number	Number	Number	Number	Number	Number	Per 100	Million dollars	Dollars	Dollars
1936	—	92,572	78	10,710	8.4	103,282	2,686	5,792	94,804	—	—	—	—	—	—
1937	—	95,112	79	12,230	9.5	107,342	2,907	5,726	98,709	—	—	—	—	—	—
1938	—	97,516	82	11,226	8.7	108,742	2,555	4,170	102,017	—	—	—	—	—	—
1939	—	96,757	79	10,447	8.0	107,204	2,382	5,241	99,581	—	—	—	—	—	—
1940	—	99,222	80	10,714	8.1	109,936	2,262	6,091	101,533	—	—	—	—	—	—
1941	—	99,720	80	11,980	9.1	111,700	2,310	7,263	102,127	—	—	—	—	—	—
1942	—	109,385	88	11,543	8.8	120,928	2,531	7,831	110,566	—	—	—	—	—	—
1943	—	107,285	89	10,726	8.4	118,011	2,673	7,675	107,663	107,948	—	—	36	333	0.91
1944	—	112,792	94	10,822	8.5	123,614	2,999	7,489	113,126	112,641	15,467	13.7	40	355	0.97
1945	—	112,758	94	11,128	8.7	123,886	2,720	6,967	114,199	113,482	15,926	14.0	43	379	1.04
1946	—	114,199	86	11,216	8.1	125,415	3,063	8,877	113,475	111,648	17,490	15.7	49	439	1.20
1947	—	113,475	88	11,770	8.3	125,245	2,873	3,669	118,703	113,633	18,810	16.6	61	537	1.47
1948	95	119,214	88	12,294	8.5	131,508	2,742	6,315	122,451	119,653	21,554	18.0	75	627	1.72
1949	99	123,557	90	12,384	8.4	135,941	2,833	6,133	126,975	123,717	24,162	19.5	87	703	1.93
1950	96	125,375	90	12,233	6.9	137,608	2,678	5,531	129,399	125,704	25,744	20.1	92	732	2.01
1951	95	130,294	91	11,957	7.9	142,251	2,552	8,216	131,483	127,415	26,902	21.1	103	808	2.21
1952	96	130,743	91	12,262	8.0	143,005	2,721	6,902	133,382	130,076	29,416	22.6	120	923	2.53
1953	98	133,431	91	12,627	8.1	146,058	2,780	6,148	137,130	134,053	31,025	23.1	130	970	2.66
1954	97	136,926	93	13,511	8.5	150,437	2,703	5,517	142,217	138,595	34,336	24.8	141	1,017	2.79
1955	99	141,053	93	13,096	8.1	154,149	2,698	5,581	145,870	142,265	36,333	25.5	153	1,008	2.76
1956	100	145,997	93	12,972	7.8	158,969	2,730	9,998	146,241	145,700	39,470	27.1	169	1,166	3.19
1957	99	147,857	94	13,970	8.3	161,827	2,818	5,616	153,393	149,705	41,235	27.5	190	1,280	3.51
1958	102	152,876	94	13,463	7.9	166,339	3,499	6,050	156,790	153,453	46,218	30.1	215	1,409	3.86
1959	106	156,633	95	13,949	8.0	170,582	3,122	6,262	161,198	158,119	49,892	31.6	235	1,503	4.12
1960	108	158,682	96	14,701	8.3	173,383	3,202	6,451	163,730	163,282	54,277	33.2	266	1,650	4.52
1961	113	163,913	96	14,515	8.0	178,428	3,158	7,979	167,291	166,169	57,666	34.7	288	1,727	4.73
1962	124	170,575	99	14,132	7.7	184,707	3,244	7,764	173,699	175,445	63,810	36.4	326	1,859	5.09
1963	129	174,187	99	15,151	8.1	187,536	3,498	8,156	176,516	179,022	69,494	38.8	354	1,984	5.44
1964	134	177,207	99	15,018	7.9	190,636	3,384	9,292	179,599	181,779	74,128	40.8	397	2,189	6.00
1965	143	181,549	101	17,300	9.1	198,849	3,583	7,993	187,273	189,172	79,056	41.8	442	2,335	6.40
1966	154	189,858	102	14,998	7.8	204,856	3,601	9,268	191,987	192,384	88,974	46.3	505	2,615	7.16
1967	165	192,774	99	15,714	8.1	208,488	3,635	11,665	193,188	194,650	94,900	48.8	577	2,965	8.12
1968	170	193,121	98	14,688	7.4	207,809	3,614	11,675	192,520	193,690	100,804	52.0	673	3,472	9.51
1969	180	192,848	—	14,868	7.4	207,716	3,621	14,701	189,394	191,363	107,737	56.3	765	3,996	10.95
1970	190	189,956	—	14,985	7.5	204,941	3,496	14,702	186,743	187,897	117,327	62.4	871	4,635	12.70

[1] Population estimated as of July 1. Total population used prior to 1936, civilian thereafter.

[2] Based on Bureau of the Census estimated resident population as of July 1.

[3] Excess of patients released alive from the hospital over those returning to the hospital.

[4] Reporting facilities only.

[5] Includes salaries and wages, purchased provisions, fuel, light, water, and so on.

Sources

For 1936–1945, U.S. Bureau of the Census, *Patients in Mental Institutions* (1945), pp. 31, 35–7; for 1946–1970, U.S. Social and Rehabilitation Service, *Residents in Public Institutions for the Mentally Retarded*, annual issues.

TABLE Bd217–231 Public institutions for the mentally retarded – facilities, patients, personnel, and maintenance expenditures: 1936–1970 *Continued*

Documentation

From 1946 to 1968, the National Institute of Mental Health was responsible for collecting and publishing data on the institutionalized mentally retarded in the United States. Since 1969, the annual census of the public institutions of the mentally retarded has been the responsibility of the Social and Rehabilitation Service.

Series Bd220–221. Includes first admissions and readmissions; excludes transfers. First admissions are all patients admitted to a public institution for the mentally retarded without a record of previous care (that is, a record of an admission and a formal discharge), in either a public or private institution anywhere. Thus, a patient coming into a public institution for the mentally retarded from a hospital for mental disease would be considered a first admission. Readmissions are all patients admitted with a record of previous care in a public or private institution. Admissions per 100,000 civilian population, series Bd222, measures the proportion of people coming under care during the year.

Series Bd223. This category includes only deaths occurring among patients resident in the institution and does not include deaths among patients on leave, even though these patients are still on the institution's books.

Series Bd224. Equals series Bd218, plus series Bd221, minus series Bd224, minus series Bd226. This concept takes into account movement of patients into and out of the institution because this quantity is the number of placements in extramural care, plus direct discharge from the institution, less the number of returns from extramural care, all occurring during any one year. National data on placements and returns from extramural care are not available, but net releases may be computed from less detailed movement data. Interpretation of net live releases should be made with caution. This quantity is the net number of live releases from the public institutions in the state system and includes not only direct discharges to the community and placement on leave but also direct discharges to other inpatient facilities outside the state system, such as public mental hospitals, boarding care homes, and public institutions in other states. The number of net releases, rather than the total number of discharges, is used as a measure of movement out of the institution because many discharges occur while patients are already outside the institution on extramural care. The number of net releases may be considered an estimate of the number of effective releases from the institution under the assumption that subtracting returns from leave during the year removes only the short-term visits, leaves, and escapes and retains the effective releases (that is, those from which the patients did not return to the institution within the time period covered).

Series Bd230–231. These are the most commonly used ratios for comparing institution expenditures. Their major limitation is that they do not adequately take into account the number of admissions for which a large share of the expenditure is required. If the patient base were enlarged to include admissions during the year, the resulting sum would be the best available estimate of patients under treatment during the year.

TABLE Bd232–240 Mental health facilities, patients, expenditures, and staff: 1970–1994[1]

Contributed by Richard H. Steckel

					State and county mental hospitals		Expenditures		
	Mental health facilities	Average daily inpatient census	Patients, end of year	Patients per 100,000 civilian population	Patients, end of year	Patients per 100,000 civilians	Total	Per capita	Full-time equivalent staff positions
	Bd232	Bd233	Bd234	Bd235	Bd236	Bd237	Bd238	Bd239	Bd240
Year	Number	Number	Number	Per 100,000	Number	Per 100,000	Thousand 1969 dollars	1969 dollars	Number
1970	3,005	468,831	471,451	236.8	369,969	185.8	3,292,563	16.53	—
1972	3,187	420,930	405,532	198.5	309,000	151.2	3,785,069	18.53	375,984
1974	3,315	346,233	342,597	164.6	215,586	101.9	4,189,067	20.13	403,024
1976	3,480	287,588	284,158	134.4	193,436	90.8	4,414,465	20.88	423,258
1978	3,738	252,304	247,243	115.2	159,500	73.7	4,180,952	19.37	430,051
1980	3,727	233,384	230,216	103.9	140,355	62.6	4,145,598	19.37	—
1982	4,302	211,024	214,065	93.5	125,200	54.6	—	—	—
1984	4,438	224,169	224,347	96.5	117,909	50.0	4,580,116	19.71	440,925
1986	4,747	228,530	237,845	99.6	111,135	46.3	4,828,079	20.15	494,515
1988	4,930	227,836	227,863	93.3	100,615	41.2	5,300,162	21.72	531,072
1990	5,284	224,400	226,953	93.0	90,572	36.4	5,566,274	22.81	563,619
1992	5,498	216,900	214,714	85.2	83,180	33.0	4,995,003	19.83	585,972
1994	5,392	190,500	236,110	91.1	72,096	27.8	5,010,045	19.33	577,669

[1] See the text for discussion of several issues affecting the comparability of the series over time.

Source

Center for Mental Health Statistics, *Mental Health, United States,* annual U.S. Department of Health and Human Services publication. For series Bd233, post-1989 data are published in U.S. Bureau of the Census, *Statistical Abstract of the United States,* cited as "U.S. SAMHSA, Center for Mental Health Services, unpublished data."

Documentation

The data were derived from a series of biennial inventories of specialty mental health organizations and nonfederal general hospitals with mental health services in the United States. The inventories were conducted by the Survey and Analysis Branch, Division of State and Community Systems Development, Center for Mental Health Services, with the cooperation and assistance of the state mental health agencies, the National Association of State Mental Health Program Directors, the American Hospital Association, and the National Association of Psychiatric Healthcare Systems.

These series were originally reported in odd years and then switched to even years in 1986. All the pre-1986 data were originally reported for the odd years prior.

Data for 1979–1980, 1986, 1990, 1992, and 1994 are influenced by factors that affect the comparability of data among these years and earlier years. Since 1979–1980, data are not available for Veterans Administration (VA) medical centers, psychiatric services of nonfederal general hospitals, and

(continued)

TABLE Bd232–240 Mental health facilities, patients, expenditures, and staff: 1970–1994 *Continued*

federally funded community mental health centers (CMHCs); data shown for 1979–1980 are as of 1980–1981 for CMHCs and as of 1977–1978 for VA medical centers and nonfederal general hospitals' psychiatric services. Although the impact of these substitutions on the comparability of the data is unknown, the effect of the change is believed to be small.

A second major revision of the inventory program took place in 1981–1982. As a result of the 1981 shift in the funding of the CMHC program from categorical to block grants, the inventory of the CMHCs was discontinued. Organizations that previously had been classified as CMHCs were reclassified as multiservice mental health organizations, as freestanding psychiatric outpatient clinics, or as separate psychiatric units of nonfederal general hospitals, depending upon the types of services they directly operated and controlled. The biennial Inventory of Mental Health Organizations (IMHO), first used in 1981–1982, was designed to reflect these changes in classification.

A third revision took place in 1983–1984 that changed the definition of multiservice mental health organizations and partial care services. Prior to that time, any organization (1) not classified either as a psychiatric hospital, general hospital with separate psychiatric services, or residential treatment center for emotionally disturbed children, and (2) that offered either inpatient care or residential treatment care and outpatient or partial care was classified as a multiservice mental health organization. In 1983–1984, this definition was broadened to include organizations that offered any two different services and were not classifiable as any of the organizations noted in (1) above. The provision of inpatient or residential treatment care was no longer a prerequisite. As a result, many organizations classified in 1981–1982 and earlier as psychiatric outpatient clinics were classified in 1983–1984 as multiservice mental health organizations.

For partial care services, the definition was broadened in 1983–1984 to include rehabilitation, habitation, and education programs that had previously been excluded. This resulted in a sharp increase in the number and volume of partial care programs.

Another revision occurred in the definition for psychiatric outpatient clinics between 1983–1984 and 1986. In 1983–1984, an organization could be classified as a freestanding psychiatric outpatient clinic if partial care was provided in addition to outpatient services. In 1986, 1990, and 1992, to be so classified an organization had to provide outpatient services only.

The increase in the number of general hospitals with separate psychiatric services also was due to a more concerted effort to identify these organizations in 1980–1981, 1983–1984, and 1986 than previously. In prior years, forms were sent only to those hospitals previously identified as having a separate psychiatric service. In 1980–1981, 1983–1984, 1986, 1990, and 1992, a screener form was sent to general hospitals not previously identified as providing a separate psychiatric service to determine if they had such a service.

Because 1981–1982 data were not available for VA medical centers and nonfederal general hospitals, 1980–1981 data were used where possible. For VA medical centers, 1980–1981 data were available only on bed and patient movement variables for inpatient services. The effect on the comparability of the data resulting from the substitution of data for the previous year is unknown but believed to be small.

Series Bd234–235. The number of residents increased in 1994 because all residential treatment and residential supportive patients were combined with twenty-four-hour care hospital residents; in previous years, residential supportive patients were excluded.

Series Bd238–239. Based on the medical care component of the consumer price index (1969 = 100) (series Cc41).

HEALTH CARE PRACTITIONERS

Richard H. Steckel

TABLE Bd241–256 Physicians, dentists, nurses, and medical, dental, and nursing schools and students: 1810–1995

Contributed by Richard H. Steckel

	Physicians			Medical schools			Dentists		Dental schools			Active professional graduate nurses		Nursing schools		
	Number	Per 100,000 population	Admitted as immigrants	Schools	Medical students	Graduates	Number	Per 100,000 population	Schools	Students	Graduates	Number	Per 100,000 population	Schools	Students	Graduates
	Bd241 [1]	Bd242 [1]	Bd243 [1]	Bd244 [1,2]	Bd245 [1,2]	Bd246 [1,2]	Bd247 [3]	Bd248 [3]	Bd249 [4]	Bd250	Bd251	Bd252	Bd253	Bd254 [5]	Bd255 [5]	Bd256
Year	Number	Per 100,000	Number	Number	Number	Number	Number	Per 100,000	Number	Number	Number	Number	Per 100,000	Number	Number	Number
1810	—	—	—	5	—	—	50	1	—	—	—	—	—	—	—	—
1820	—	—	—	10	—	—	100	1	—	—	—	—	—	—	—	—
1830	—	—	—	20	—	—	300	2	—	—	—	—	—	—	—	—
1840	—	—	—	35	—	—	1,000	6	1	—	—	—	—	—	—	—
1850	40,755 [6]	176 [6]	—	52	—	—	2,923 [6]	13 [6]	2	—	17	—	—	—	—	—
1860	55,055 [6]	175 [6]	—	65	—	—	5,606 [6]	18 [6]	3	—	64	—	—	—	—	—
1870	60,000	150	—	75	—	—	—	—	10	—	147	—	—	—	—	—
1870 [6]	64,414	162	—	—	—	—	7,988	20	—	—	—	—	—	—	—	—
1880	82,000	163	—	100	11,826	3,241	—	—	14	—	315	—	—	15	323	157
1880 [6]	85,671	171	—	—	—	—	12,314	25	—	—	—	—	—	—	—	—
1886	87,521	151	—	—	—	—	—	—	23	—	473	—	—	—	—	—
1890	100,180	159	—	133	15,404	4,454	—	—	31	—	960	—	—	35	1,552	471
1890 [6]	104,805	166	—	—	—	—	17,498	28	—	—	—	—	—	—	—	—
1893	103,090	154	—	—	—	—	—	—	37	—	—	—	—	—	—	—
1896	104,554	147	—	—	—	—	20,063	28	48	—	1,432	—	—	—	—	—
1898	115,524	157	—	—	—	—	23,911	33	54	—	1,894	—	—	—	—	—
1900	119,749	157	160	—	25,171	5,214	25,189	33	57	—	2,091	—	—	432	11,164	3,456
1900 [6]	132,002	173	—	—	—	—	29,665	39	—	—	—	—	—	—	—	—
1901	—	—	100	160	26,417	5,444	—	—	57	—	2,304	—	—	—	—	—
1902	123,196	156	116	160	27,501	5,009	28,109	36	56	—	2,294	—	—	—	—	—
1903	—	—	343	160	27,615	5,698	—	—	55	—	2,198	—	—	—	—	—
1904	128,950	157	907	160	28,142	5,747	—	39	56	—	2,168	—	—	—	—	—
1905	—	—	1,043	158	26,147	5,600	—	—	55	—	2,621	—	—	826	19,824	5,795
1906	134,688	158	725	162	25,204	5,364	35,238	41	55	—	1,519	—	—	—	—	—
1907	—	—	480	159	24,276	4,980	—	—	55	—	1,724	—	—	—	—	—
1908	—	—	504	151	22,602	4,741	36,670	41	55	—	2,005	—	—	—	—	—
1909	134,402	149	332	140	22,145	4,515	—	—	56	—	1,761	—	—	—	—	—
1910	135,000	146	365	131	21,526	4,440	37,684	41	54	—	1,646	50,500 [8]	55	1,129	32,636	8,140
1910 [6]	151,132	164	—	—	—	—	39,997	43	—	—	—	—	—	—	—	—
1911	—	—	429	122	19,786	4,273	—	—	54	—	1,742	—	—	—	—	—
1912	137,199	144	459	118	18,412	4,483	38,866	41	52	—	1,940	—	—	—	—	—
1913	—	—	508	107	17,015	3,981	—	—	51	—	2,022	—	—	—	—	—
1914	142,332	144	504	102	16,502	3,594	42,606	43	48	—	2,254	—	—	—	—	—
1915	—	—	476	96	14,891	3,536	—	—	49	—	2,388	—	—	1,509	46,141	11,118
1916	145,241	142	326	95	14,012	3,518	—	—	49	—	2,835	—	—	—	—	—
1917	—	—	326	96	13,764	3,379	45,988	44	46	—	3,010	—	—	—	—	—
1918	147,812	141	182	90	13,630	2,670	—	—	46	—	3,345	—	—	—	—	—
1919	—	—	236	85	13,052	2,656	—	—	46	—	3,587	—	—	—	—	—

Notes appear at end of table

(continued)

TABLE Bd241–256 Physicians, dentists, nurses, and medical, dental, and nursing schools and students: 1810–1995 *Continued*

	Physicians			Medical schools			Dentists		Dental schools			Active professional graduate nurses		Nursing schools		
	Number	Per 100,000 population	Admitted as immigrants	Schools	Medical students	Graduates	Number	Per 100,000 population	Schools	Students	Graduates	Number	Per 100,000 population	Schools	Students	Graduates
	Bd241 [1]	Bd242 [1]	Bd243 [1]	Bd244 [1, 2]	Bd245 [1, 2]	Bd246 [1, 2]	Bd247 [3]	Bd248 [3]	Bd249 [4]	Bd250	Bd251	Bd252	Bd253	Bd254 [5]	Bd255 [5]	Bd256
Year	Number	Per 100,000	Number	Number	Number	Number	Number	Per 100,000	Number	Number	Number	Number	Per 100,000	Number	Number	Number
1920	—	—	459	85	13,798	3,047	—	—	46	—	906	103,900 [8]	98	1,755	54,953	14,980
1920 [6]	144,977	137	—	—	—	—	56,152	53	—	—	—	—	—	—	—	—
1921	145,404	134	597	83	14,466	3,186	—	—	45	11,745	1,795	—	—	—	—	—
1922	—	—	458	81	15,635	2,520	—	—	45	—	1,765	—	—	—	—	—
1923	145,966	130	704	80	16,960	3,120	—	—	45	13,099	3,271	—	—	—	—	—
1924	—	—	1,391	79	17,728	3,562	—	—	43	—	3,422	—	—	—	—	—
1925	147,010	127	540	80	18,200	3,974	64,481	56	43	11,863	2,590	—	—	—	—	—
1926	—	—	487	79	18,840	3,962	—	—	44	—	2,610	—	—	—	—	—
1927	149,521	126	486	80	19,662	4,035	—	—	40	10,333	2,642	—	—	1,797	77,768	18,623
1928	—	—	454	80	20,545	4,262	67,334	56	40	—	2,563	—	—	—	—	—
1929	152,503	125	398	76	20,878	4,446	—	—	40	8,200	2,442	—	—	1,885	78,771	23,810
1930	—	—	390	76	21,597	4,565	—	—	38	7,813	1,561	214,300 [8]	174	—	—	—
1930 [6]	153,803	125	—	—	—	—	71,055	58	—	—	—	—	—	—	—	—
1931	156,406	126	329	76	21,982	4,735	—	—	38	8,129	1,842	—	—	1,844	100,419	25,971
1932	—	—	259	76	22,135	4,936	—	—	38	8,031	1,840	—	—	1,781	84,290	25,312
1933	—	—	187	77	22,466	4,895	—	—	39	7,508	1,986	—	—	—	—	—
1934	161,359	128	353	77	22,799	5,035	—	—	39	7,160	1,864	—	—	—	—	—
1935	—	—	304	77	22,888	5,101	—	—	39	7,175	1,840	—	—	1,472	67,533	19,600
1936	165,163	129	462	77	22,564	5,183	—	—	39	7,306	1,736	—	—	1,417	69,589	18,600
1937	—	—	533	77	22,095	5,377	—	—	39	7,397	1,739	—	—	1,389	73,286	20,400
1938	169,628	131	738	77	21,587	5,194	—	—	39	7,184	1,704	—	—	1,349	74,305	20,655
1939	—	—	1,384	77	21,302	5,089	—	—	39	7,331	1,794	—	—	1,328	82,095	22,485
1940	175,163	133	1,095	77	21,271	5,097	—	—	39	7,407	1,757	284,200 [8]	216	1,311	85,156	23,600
1940 [6]	165,989	126	—	—	—	—	69,921	53	—	—	—	—	—	—	—	—
1941	—	—	706	77	21,379	5,275	—	—	39	7,720	1,568	—	—	1,303	87,588	24,899
1942	180,496	134	290	77	22,031	5,163	—	—	39	8,355 [7]	1,784	—	—	1,299	91,457	25,613
1943	—	—	218	76	22,631	5,223	—	—	39	8,847 [7]	1,926	—	—	1,297	100,486	26,816
1944	—	—	156	77	48,195 [7]	10,303 [7]	—	—	39	9,014 [7]	2,470	—	—	1,307	112,249	28,276
1945	—	—	202	77	24,028	5,136	—	—	39	8,590 [7]	3,212	—	—	1,295	126,576	31,721
1946	—	—	—	77	23,216	5,826	—	—	39	7,274	2,666	—	—	1,271	126,828	36,195
1947	—	—	—	77	23,900	6,389	72,990	51	40	8,287	2,225	—	—	1,253	106,900	40,744
1948	—	—	—	77	22,739	5,543	—	—	40	8,996	1,755	—	—	1,245	91,643	34,268
1949	201,277	135	1,141	78	23,670	5,094	—	—	41	10,132	1,574	—	—	1,215	88,817	21,379
1950	203,400	134	1,878	79	25,103	5,553	89,441	59	41	11,460	2,565	375,000 [8]	248	1,203	98,712	25,790
1950 [6]	191,947	125	—	—	—	—	74,855	49	—	—	—	—	—	—	—	—
1951	205,500	132	1,388	79	26,186	6,135	—	—	42	11,891	2,830	—	—	1,183	103,433	28,794
1952	207,900	131	1,210	79	27,076	6,080	91,638	58	42	12,169	2,975	—	—	1,167	102,550	29,016 [9]
1953	210,900	131	845	79	27,688	6,668	93,726	58	42	12,370	2,945	—	—	1,148	102,019	29,308
1954	214,200	130	1,040	80	28,227	6,861	95,883	58	43	12,516	3,084	389,600 [8]	237	1,141	103,019	28,539
1955	218,061	130	1,046	81	28,583	6,977	97,529	58	43	12,601	3,081	430,000 [8]	257	1,139	107,572	28,729
1956	—	—	1,388	82	28,639	6,845	99,227	58	43	12,730	3,038	430,000	252	1,125	114,423	30,236
1957	226,625	131	1,990	85	29,130	6,796	100,534	58	45	13,004	3,050	—	—	1,115	114,674	29,933
1958	—	—	1,934	85	29,473	6,861	98,540	56	47	13,279	3,083	460,000	261	1,118	112,989	30,410
1959	236,818	132	1,630	85	29,614	6,860	100,615	56	47	13,509	3,156	—	—	1,126	113,518	30,312

	Physicians			Medical schools			Dentists		Dental schools			Active professional graduate nurses		Nursing schools		
	Number	Per 100,000 population	Admitted as immigrants	Schools	Medical students	Graduates	Number	Per 100,000 population	Schools	Students	Graduates	Number	Per 100,000 population	Schools	Students	Graduates
	Bd241 [1]	Bd242 [1]	Bd243 [1]	Bd244 [1, 2]	Bd245 [1, 2]	Bd246 [1, 2]	Bd247 [3]	Bd248 [3]	Bd249 [4]	Bd250	Bd251	Bd252	Bd253	Bd254 [5]	Bd255 [5]	Bd256
Year	Number	Per 100,000	Number	Number	Number	Number	Number	Per 100,000	Number	Number	Number	Number	Per 100,000	Number	Number	Number
1960	274,833	150	1,574	91	31,999	7,508	101,947	56	47	13,581	3,253	504,000	275	1,119	115,057	30,113
1961	—	—	1,683	92	32,232	7,500	103,596	56	47	13,580	3,290	—	—	1,123	118,849	30,267
1962	270,136	143	1,797	92	32,633	7,530	105,252	56	47	13,513	3,207	550,000	292	1,118	123,012	31,186
1963	289,188	151	2,093	92	33,072	7,631	106,230	56	48	13,576	3,233	—	—	1,128	123,861	32,398
1964	297,089	154	2,249	92	33,595	7,691	107,820	56	48	13,691	3,213	582,000	301	1,142	124,744	35,259
1965	305,115	156	2,012	93	34,089	7,803	109,301	56	49	13,876	3,181	613,188	314	1,153	129,629	34,686
1966	313,559	159	2,552	93	34,516	7,934	111,130	56	49	14,020	3,198	621,000	314	1,191	135,702	35,125
1967	322,045	162	3,326	95	35,212	8,148	112,152	56	49	14,421	3,360	643,000	322	1,219	139,070	38,237
1968	330,732	164	3,128	100	36,368	8,400	113,636	56	50	14,955	3,457	667,000	331	1,262	141,948	41,555
1969	338,942	166	2,756	104	37,712	8,486	115,610	57	52	15,408	3,433	694,000	341	1,287	145,588	42,196
1970	348,328	169	3,158	107	39,666	8,799	116,280	56	53	16,008	3,700	722,000	350	1,328	150,795	43,639
1971	358,523	172	5,800	110	42,638	9,446	117,920	57	53	16,553	3,775	750,000	360	1,343	164,545	47,001
1972	370,534	177	7,100	115	45,954	10,036	119,700	57	52	17,305	3,961	780,000	372	1,350	187,551	51,784
1973	380,679	180	7,100	119	50,125	11,040	121,800	58	56	18,376	4,230	815,000	386	1,363	213,127	59,427
1974	394,448	185	4,500	121	53,666	12,204	103,000	48	58	19,369	4,515	857,000	402	1,359	232,589	67,628
1975	409,042	191	5,400	123	57,213	13,301	127,000	59	59	20,146	4,969	906,000	422	1,359	244,486	74,536
1976	425,016	196	6,200	123	59,649	14,259	110,000	51	59	20,767	5,336	961,000	444	1,360	250,385	77,633
1977	437,800	201	7,100	126	61,900	14,500	113,000	52	59	21,000	5,200	1,011,000	464	1,349	249,541	78,000
1978	454,000	206	4,400	134	64,300	15,400	136,000	62	59	21,500	5,300	1,059,000	481	1,339	245,000	78,000
1979	472,000	208	—	138	68,371	16,172	138,000	61	60	22,200	5,400	—	—	1,374	234,659	77,000
1980	486,500	212	—	140	70,100	16,200	141,000	61	60	22,500	5,300	1,273,000	555	1,385	231,000	76,000
1981	505,000	218	—	142	71,600	16,800	144,000	62	60	22,600	5,600	1,327,000	573	1,401	235,000	74,000
1982	523,000	224	—	142	72,600	17,000	147,000	63	60	22,200	5,400	1,380,000	590	1,432	242,000	74,000
1983	542,000	230	—	142	73,500	17,100	150,000	64	60	21,400	5,800	1,439,000	610	1,466	251,000	77,000
1984	—	—	—	142	73,563	17,792	153,000	64	60	20,588	5,353	1,486,000	625	1,477	237,232	80,000
1985	576,700	240	—	142	73,193	17,677	156,000	65	60	19,563	4,957	1,544,000	643	1,473	217,955	82,075
1986	595,000	246	—	142	72,765	17,417	158,000	65	60	18,673	4,717	1,589,000	656	1,469	193,712	77,027
1987	612,000	250	—	142	72,321	17,491	161,000	66	59	17,885	4,581	1,627,000	665	1,465	182,947	70,561
1988	613,900	249	—	142	71,914	17,239	164,000	66	58	17,094	4,312	1,648,000	668	1,442	184,924	64,839
1989	630,400	253	—	142	71,631	16,927	168,000	68	58	16,412	4,233	1,731,000	696	1,457	201,458	61,660
1990	646,300	256	—	141	71,955	16,961	173,000	69	56	15,951	3,995	1,790,000	710	1,470	221,170	66,088
1991	—	—	—	141	72,614	16,897	179,000	70	55	15,882	3,918	1,853,000	727	1,484	237,598	72,230
1992	686,600	266	—	141	73,517	17,072	183,000	71	55	15,980	3,778	1,907,000	740	1,484	257,983	80,839
1993	703,700	270	—	142	74,451	17,330	187,000	72	54	16,250	3,875	1,976,000	759	1,493	270,228	88,149
1994	719,400	274	—	142	75,218	17,731	190,000	72	54	16,353	3,908	2,044,000	778	1,501	268,350	94,870
1995	756,000	285	—	142	75,445	17,784	—	—	54	16,552	—	2,116,000	798	1,516	261,219	97,052

[1] Beginning 1960, includes osteopaths and their schools.

[2] Beginning 1954, includes Puerto Rico.

[3] Beginning 1958, excludes graduates of year stated.

[4] For 1840 and 1926–1931, schools offering courses in dentistry; for 1850–1925, schools conferring degrees; for other years, schools in operation. Includes Puerto Rico.

[5] Beginning 1950, includes Hawai'i and Puerto Rico.

[6] Census figures.

[7] Reflects enrollment of more than one class in some schools under accelerated programs in operation during World War II.

[8] Census estimate adjusted to exclude student nurses enumerated as graduates.

[9] Includes Hawai'i and Puerto Rico.

Sources

Series Bd241–242. For 1850, Superintendent of the U.S. Census, *Statistical View of the United States. . . a Compendium of the Seventh Census* (1854). For 1860, U.S. Bureau of the Census, *Population of the United States in 1860* (1864). For 1870–1950 (decennial years), U.S. Bureau of the Census, Sixteenth Census Reports, *Comparative Occupation Statistics for the United States, 1870 to 1940*, p. 111; and *U.S. Census of Population, 1950,* volume 2, part 1, pp. 1-266 to 1-269. For 1870–1934, American Medical Association (AMA) and R. G. Leland, *Distribution of Physicians in the United States* (1936), pp. 7, 79. For

(continued)

TABLE Bd241–256 Physicians, dentists, nurses, and medical, dental, and nursing schools and students: 1810–1995 *Continued*

1936–1957, AMA, *American Medical Directory*, volumes 14–20 (periodic editions). The 1958 edition includes a summary for 1906–1957. For 1958–1970, U.S. Public Health Service, *Health Resources Statistics* (1971), p. 147, and unpublished data; compiled from data provided by the AMA and the American Osteopathic Association. For 1970–1977, U.S. National Center for Health Statistics, *Health Resources Statistics,* published annually. For 1978–1995, U.S. Health Resources and Services Administration, unpublished data.

Series Bd243. U.S. Public Health Service, *Foreign Trained Physicians and American Medicine*, Department of Health, Education, and Welfare (DHEW) Publication number (NIH)73-325 (1973), Table A1. Compiled from the U.S. Immigration and Naturalization Service data, *Annual Report*.

Series Bd244–246. For 1810–1840, AMA, *American Medical Directory* (1956). For later years, data are from annual reports of the Council on Medical Education and Hospitals of the AMA as follows. For 1850–1919, *Journal of the American Medical Association* 79 (8) (1922): 629–33. For 1920–1930, *Journal of the American Medical Association* 105 (9) (1935): 686. For 1931–1957, Edward L. Turner, W. S. Wiggins, et al., "Medical Education in the United States and Canada: Fifty-Seventh Annual Report on Medical Education in the United States and Canada by the Council on Medical Education and Hospitals of the American Medical Association," *Journal of the American Medical Association* 165 (11) (1957): 1420. For 1958–1970, U.S. Public Health Service, *Health Resources Statistics* (1971), p. 88, and unpublished data. For 1970–1977, U.S. National Center for Health Statistics, *Health Resources Statistics,* published annually. For 1978–1995, U.S. Health Resources and Services Administration, unpublished data.

Series Bd247–248. For 1810 and 1840, John T. O'Rourke and Leroy M. S. Miner, *Dental Education in the United States* (Saunders, 1941), p. 298. For 1820 and 1830, *Harris' Principles and Practice of Dental Surgery* (Lindsay and Blakiston, 1848), pp. 36–7. For 1850–1950 (decennial years), same sources as for series Bd241–242. For 1896–1928, *Polk's Dental Register and Directory of the United States and Dominion of Canada* (Polk, 1928 and prior editions). For 1947–1957, *Distribution of Dentists in the United States by State, Region, District, and County* (American Dental Association, 1958 and prior editions). For 1958–1970, U.S. Public Health Service, *Health Resources Statistics,* annual issues, and unpublished data; compiled from American Dental Association data. For 1970–1977, U.S. National Center for Health Statistics, *Health Resources Statistics,* published annually. For 1978–1995, U.S. Health Resources and Services Administration, unpublished data.

Series Bd249 and Bd251. For 1840–1945, Harlan Hoyt Horner, *Dental Education Today* (University of Chicago Press, 1947), p. 30. For 1946–1957, American Dental Association Council on Dental Education, *Dental Students' Register,* annual publications. For 1958–1970, U.S. Public Health Service, *Health Resources Statistics* (1971), p. 77, and unpublished data. For 1970–1977, U.S. National Center for Health Statistics, *Health Resources Statistics*, published annually. For post-1977, U.S. Health Resources and Services Administration, unpublished data. Horner's data are compiled from Dorothy Fahs Beck, "The Development of the Dental Profession in the United States" (Ph.D. dissertation, University of Chicago, 1932), and from records of the Council on Dental Education of the American Dental Association. Additional data may be obtained from the following sources cited by Beck: W. J. Gies, *Dental Education in the United States and Canada*, Carnegie Foundation for the Advancement of Teaching, Bulletin number 19 (1926), p. 42; *Polk's Dental Register and Directory of the United States and Canada* (Polk, 1925), p. 35; W. J. Gies, "Additional Remarks on a Reference to the Carnegie Foundation's Study of Dental Education," *Journal of Dental Research* 10 (February 1930): 32; W. J. Greenleaf, *Dentistry,* Career Series, Leaflet number 7 (Office of Education, 1932), pp. 7–10. The Beck tabulation also appears in Frederick B. Noyes, "Dental Education, 1911–36," *Oral Hygiene* 26 (January 1936): 24.

Series Bd250. For 1921–1934, Frederick B. Noyes, "Dental Education, 1911–36," *Oral Hygiene* 26 (January 1936): 28. For 1935–1957, American Dental Association Council on Dental Education, *Dental Students' Register,* annual publications. For 1958–1970, see source for series Bd249. For 1970–1977, U.S. National Center for Health Statistics, *Health Resources Statistics,* published annually. For post-1977, U.S. Health Resources and Services Administration, unpublished data. The sources cited by Noyes are as follows: William J. Gies, "Is the Influx of New Graduates Commensurate with the Demand for Dental Service, or Should the Educational Requirements Be Altered?" *Journal of the American Dental Association* 18 (4) (1931): 593, and Dental Educational Council of America, statistical reports.

Series Bd252–253. For 1910–1950, U.S. Public Health Services, *Health Manpower Source Book 2, Nursing Personnel* (1953), pp. 14–15. For 1954–1955, American Nurses Association, *Facts about Nursing* (1956–1957), p. 8. For 1956–1970, U.S. Public Health Service, *Health Resources Statistics* (1971), p. 177, and unpublished data; compiled from data provided by American Nurses Association. For 1970–1977, U.S. National Center for Health Statistics, *Health Resources Statistics,* published annually. For 1978–1995, U.S. Health Resources and Services Administration, unpublished data.

Series Bd254–256. For 1880–1927 and 1931, U.S. Office of Education, *Biennial Survey of Education in the United States: 1934–36*, volume 2, Chapter 4, p. 294. For 1929 and 1932, Committee on the Grading of Nursing Schools, *The Second Grading of Nursing Schools* (Committee on the Grading of Nursing Schools, 1932), p. 9. For 1935–1939, American Nurses Association, *Facts about Nursing* (1946), pp. 32, 34. For 1940–1955, *Facts about Nursing* (1957), pp. 67, 71. For 1956–1970, U.S. Public Health Service, *Health Resources Statistics* (1971), p. 181; compiled from data provided by the American Nurses Association. For 1978–1995, National League for Nursing, *NLN Data Book,* published annually.

Documentation

Figures for schools and students are for academic session ending in specified year.

See the text for Table Ba470–477 for an explanation of the difference between employed persons and gainful workers.

Series Bd241–242

The census data for 1940 and 1950 are for employed civilian physicians; figures for prior census years are largely for gainful workers and may include physicians not in active medical practice. The 1910 Census figure includes osteopaths; earlier census figures include osteopaths, chiropractors, and healers (not elsewhere classified).

The *American Medical Directory* figures pertain to the total number of physicians, including those retired or not in practice for other reasons and those in the federal service. They exclude graduates of the years concerned. Post-1970, the data represent medical doctors (MDs) and doctors of osteopathy (DOs). The MDs include nonfederal physicians in the fifty states, District of Columbia, Puerto Rico, and other U.S. outlying areas; those with addresses temporarily unknown to the AMA; and federal physicians in the United States and abroad. They exclude physicians with temporary foreign addresses. Data for DOs are estimated.

Series Bd242. Population figures used to compute physician-population rate for census years, 1850–1930, include armed forces overseas; only the civilian population is used for 1940 and 1950. Rates for years prior to 1963, excluding 1960, are based on the Census Bureau's population estimates as of July 1, including armed forces overseas. Rates for years 1960 and 1963–1970 are based on the Census Bureau's estimates of civilian population in the fifty states, District of Columbia, and outlying areas, U.S. citizens in foreign countries, and the armed forces in the United States and abroad as of December 31.

Series Bd244–246. Data on the number of medical schools, students, and graduates prior to 1900 are fragmentary and of dubious accuracy. The first medical school in the United States was founded in 1765. In 1800, three schools graduated students, with the number of schools increasing steadily from 52 in 1850 to a maximum of 162 in 1906. From 1906 to 1929, the number of schools declined sharply, largely because of the inspection and classification system begun in 1904 by the AMA Council on Medical Education. By 1929, only one unapproved school remained. Post-1970, data includes schools of medicine as well as schools of osteopathy.

TABLE Bd241–256 Physicians, dentists, nurses, and medical, dental, and nursing schools and students: 1810–1995 *Continued*

Series Bd244. Covers approved medical and basic science schools.

Series Bd247–248

The census data for 1940 and 1950 are for employed civilian dentists; figures for prior census years are largely for gainful workers and may include dental students and dentists not in active dental practice.

The fourteen editions of *Polk's Dental Register and Directory of the United States and Dominion of Canada* list by state all dentists for 1893–1928. The *American Dental Directory,* first published in 1947, lists by state all dentists, including those retired or not in practice for other reasons and those in the federal dental service. The figures for all dates include graduates of the years concerned.

Series Bd248. Prior to 1963, the population figures used to compute the dentist-population rate are the same as those used for the physician-population rate. See the text for series Bd241–242. Population figures used to compute the dentist-population rate for 1963–1970 include all persons in the United States and in the armed forces overseas as of July 1.

Series Bd249. The first dental school in the United States was organized in 1840. Before that, all physicians practiced some dentistry, a few limiting their practice to this specialty. The dental practitioners who were not physicians learned their trade as apprentices or were self-taught. From 1840 to 1880, apprentice training was the chief source of supply, but by 1880, most states had enacted laws requiring graduation from a dental school.

Series Bd251. Annual figures for graduates for 1841–1924 are also presented in the 1925 *Polk's Dental Register,* p. 34, but the figures for the years far exceed those shown elsewhere in histories of dentistry, as well as those shown here.

Series Bd252–253

The estimates for 1910–1950 were obtained by subtracting student nurses from the number of nurses reported in the decennial censuses. Census data for 1910–1930 are for gainful workers; for 1940 they include employed nurses and those seeking work; and for 1950 they include employed civilian nurses.

The estimates for 1953 and 1955 were prepared jointly by the American Nurses Association, the National League for Nursing, and the Public Health Service. They are based partly on information supplied by hospitals, schools of nursing, public health agencies, boards of education, and nursing homes. Estimates of nurses in private duty, doctors' offices, industry, and other nursing fields were based on the American Nurses Association Inventory of 1951, adjusted according to trends observed in more recent state surveys of nursing needs and resources.

Series Bd253. Population figures used to compute nurse-population rates for 1910–1940 include armed forces overseas. The 1950 rate is based on the civilian population. Rates for 1953–1955 and 1958–1962 are based on the Census Bureau population estimates, including armed forces overseas, as of January 1 of the following year. Rates for 1964–1970 are based on Census Bureau population estimates for civilians and the armed forces in the United States as of December 31.

Series Bd254–256. Nursing education began in this country in 1873 with the opening of three schools. These schools offered students an opportunity to learn by doing, under the tutorship for one year of a superintendent who had been trained in one of the European schools. By 1893, about seventy schools were in operation. As state licensing bodies came into existence, counts of state-approved schools and of their students began to be available. Since only graduates of state-approved schools could stand for licensure examinations, nonapproved schools tended to close as the effect of licensure became felt. Not until 1925 was machinery for approving schools in operation in every state. (U.S. Public Health Service, *Health Manpower Source Book,* volume 2, *Nursing Personnel* (1953), p. 33.) Post-1970, the number of programs and students are as of October 15 of the year shown, and the number of graduates are for the academic year ending in the year shown.

TABLE Bd257–266 Hospital personnel, by type of hospital: 1946–1996[1]

Contributed by Richard H. Steckel

			Nonfederal hospitals							
							Short-term care			
	Total	Federal hospitals	Total	Psychiatric services	Tuberculosis	Long-term care	Total	Voluntary nonprofit hospitals	For-profit hospitals	State and local government hospitals
	Bd257	Bd258	Bd259	Bd260	Bd261	Bd262	Bd263	Bd264	Bd265	Bd266
Year	Number	Number	Number	Number	Number	Number	Number	Number	Number	Number
1946	830,000	162,000	668,000	99,000	36,000	28,000	505,000	362,000	35,000	108,000
1947	883,000	161,000	722,000	117,000	36,000	30,000	539,000	392,000	35,000	111,000
1948	939,000	154,000	785,000	126,000	43,000	30,000	586,000	427,000	34,000	124,000
1949	963,000	161,000	803,000	132,000	45,000	30,000	596,000	435,000	35,000	126,000
1950	1,058,000	169,000	888,000	147,000	45,000	34,000	662,000	473,000	41,000	148,000
1951	1,075,000	197,000	878,000	151,000	47,000	32,000	648,000	464,000	38,000	146,000
1952	1,119,000	206,000	913,000	155,000	47,000	37,000	674,000	486,000	39,000	149,000
1953	1,169,000	198,000	971,000	165,000	47,000	40,000	719,000	520,000	40,000	159,000
1954	1,246,000	195,000	1,051,000	178,000	49,000	46,000	777,000	568,000	40,000	169,000
1955	1,301,000	192,000	1,109,000	188,000	48,000	47,000	826,000	597,000	41,000	188,000
1956	1,375,000	198,000	1,177,000	201,000	45,000	53,000	878,000	639,000	41,000	198,000
1957	1,401,000	186,000	1,215,000	191,000	43,000	55,000	926,000	680,000	43,000	203,000
1958	1,465,000	181,000	1,284,000	203,000	41,000	56,000	984,000	720,000	45,000	219,000
1959	1,520,000	179,000	1,341,000	215,000	41,000	54,000	1,031,000	758,000	46,000	227,000
1960	1,598,000	186,000	1,412,000	238,000	39,000	55,000	1,080,000	792,000	48,000	241,000
1961	1,696,000	202,000	1,494,000	248,000	37,000	60,000	1,149,000	835,000	51,000	263,000
1962	1,763,000	207,000	1,556,000	251,000	34,000	64,000	1,207,000	875,000	57,000	276,000
1963	1,840,000	206,000	1,634,000	261,000	29,000	67,000	1,277,000	921,000	64,000	291,000
1964	1,887,000	193,000	1,693,000	264,000	30,000	67,000	1,333,000	962,000	67,000	304,000

Note appears at end of table

(continued)

TABLE Bd257–266 Hospital personnel, by type of hospital: 1946–1996 *Continued*

			Nonfederal hospitals							
							Short-term care			
	Total	Federal hospitals	Total	Psychiatric services	Tuberculosis	Long-term care	Total	Voluntary nonprofit hospitals	For-profit hospitals	State and local government hospitals
	Bd257	Bd258	Bd259	Bd260	Bd261	Bd262	Bd263	Bd264	Bd265	Bd266
Year	Number	Number	Number	Number	Number	Number	Number	Number	Number	Number
1965	1,952,000	199,000	1,754,000	274,000	29,000	65,000	1,386,000	1,011,000	70,000	306,000
1966	2,106,000	206,000	1,900,000	274,000	24,000	69,000	1,532,000	1,104,000	77,000	352,000
1967	2,203,000	214,000	1,988,000	277,000	15,000	78,000	1,619,000	1,175,000	81,000	363,000
1968	2,309,000	210,000	2,100,000	292,000	19,000	72,000	1,717,000	1,251,000	84,000	382,000
1969	2,426,000	213,000	2,213,000	303,000	18,000	68,000	1,824,000	1,330,000	88,000	407,000
1970	2,537,000	216,000	2,321,000	305,000	18,000	69,000	1,929,000	1,387,000	97,000	444,000
1971	2,588,970	224,980	2,363,990	285,055	16,489	63,227	1,999,219	1,438,276	100,024	460,919
1972	2,670,762	232,132	2,438,630	307,254	12,160	63,306	2,055,910	1,474,434	104,650	476,826
1973	2,768,607	238,473	2,530,134	302,757	10,882	67,330	2,149,165	1,535,447	117,006	496,712
1974	2,918,736	243,694	2,675,042	307,872	9,500	68,949	2,288,721	1,634,296	132,869	521,556
1975	3,022,597	256,146	2,766,451	292,446	7,284	68,035	2,398,686	1,713,682	139,395	545,609
1976	3,107,614	268,858	2,838,756	285,327	4,668	65,979	2,482,782	1,792,665	147,126	542,991
1977	3,212,894	277,526	2,935,368	286,549	4,538	63,399	2,580,882	1,862,708	159,325	558,849
1978	3,280,231	277,393	3,002,838	278,343	4,095	58,436	2,661,964	1,926,510	164,706	570,748
1979	3,381,680	273,243	3,108,437	282,469	3,330	60,578	2,762,060	2,000,005	173,868	588,187
1980	3,491,631	278,746	3,212,885	274,907	2,980	56,271	2,878,727	2,086,789	189,496	602,442
1981	3,661,070	283,423	3,377,647	275,418	2,960	60,624	3,038,645	2,213,417	202,893	622,335
1982	3,958,671	302,183	3,656,488	281,090	2,696	60,685	3,312,017	2,423,690	223,235	665,092
1983	3,707,271	285,510	3,421,761	264,194	2,335	53,192	3,102,040	2,271,594	212,766	617,680
1984	3,629,511	290,444	3,339,067	260,025	2,017	54,423	3,022,602	2,222,954	213,833	585,815
1985	3,625,152	299,471	3,325,681	263,370	2,056	57,552	3,002,703	2,217,131	220,819	564,753
1986	3,647,161	296,348	3,350,813	262,561	985	55,573	3,031,694	2,242,312	228,925	560,457
1987	3,742,196	297,090	3,445,106	269,439	1,191	54,906	3,119,570	2,299,035	242,361	578,174
1988	3,839,880	295,077	3,544,803	280,933	951	53,571	3,209,348	2,373,960	248,726	586,662
1989	3,936,610	288,245	3,648,365	284,176	965	55,779	3,307,445	2,454,848	260,637	591,960
1990	4,063,288	303,471	3,759,817	280,081	1,264	54,983	3,423,489	2,533,805	272,642	617,042
1991	4,164,886	301,344	3,863,542	268,673	997	54,937	3,538,935	2,624,235	281,134	633,566
1992	4,235,573	306,188	3,929,385	255,522	978	48,984	3,623,901	2,692,501	285,446	645,954
1993	4,289,379	319,792	3,969,587	242,071	969	45,368	3,681,179	2,712,534	289,283	679,362
1994	4,270,110	301,404	3,968,706	232,970	1,160	37,581	3,696,995	2,718,785	301,586	671,945
1995	4,272,815	301,454	3,971,361	214,960	677	37,964	3,717,760	2,701,594	342,782	669,511
1996	4,276,109	295,442	3,980,667	211,735	694	39,761	3,728,477	2,711,106	359,418	654,319

[1] Beginning 1951, excludes residents, interns, and students; beginning 1954, includes full-time equivalents of part-time personnel.

Sources

For 1946–1964, American Hospital Association, *Hospitals,* Guide Issue, part 2 (August 1, 1965), pp. 448–9. For 1965–1970, *Hospitals,* Guide Issue, part 2 (August 1, 1972), pp. 460–2. For 1971–1996, *AHA Hospital Statistics,* annual issues.

Documentation

Data on personnel refer to the number of persons on the payroll at the close of the twelve-month reporting period. Except as noted, they include full-time equivalents of part-time personnel but exclude trainees (student nurses, interns, residents, and other trainees), private-duty nurses, and volunteers. Full-time equivalents are calculated on the basis that two part-time persons are equal to one full-time person.

Short-term hospitals are those in which more than 50 percent of all patients admitted have a stay of fewer than thirty days; long-term, those in which 50 percent of all patients admitted have a stay of thirty days or more. General hospitals accept patients for a variety of acute medical and surgical conditions and, for the most part, do not admit cases of contagious disease, tuberculosis, and nervous and mental disease. Special hospitals are those that are devoted to the treatment of some particular disease or group in the population. Among the former are orthopedic, contagious disease, chronic and convalescent, and eye, ear, nose, and throat hospitals; the latter include maternity, children's, and industrial hospitals. Psychiatric hospitals include those providing temporary or prolonged care for the mentally ill, the mentally retarded, epileptics, and persons with alcoholic or other addictive diseases. Tuberculosis hospitals include sanatoriums or hospitals specifically for the care of tubercular patients. Data on long-term and short-term care facilities include both general and special hospitals.

Government hospitals include those operated by federal, state, and local governments, the latter including county, city, city–county, and hospital district. Nonprofit hospitals are those operated not for profit by churches, associations of citizens, or fraternal organizations. Proprietary hospitals are operated for profit by individuals, partnerships, or corporations.

Beginning in 1972, the division of personnel into number of "Registered Nurses" (RNs) and "Licensed Practical Nurses" (LPNs) is available in the original source. Beginning in 1985, the division of personnel into "Physicians and Dentists," "Registered Nurses," "Licensed Practical Nurses," and "Other Salaried Personnel" is available in the original source. Beginning in 1976, RN and LPN personnel per 100 adjusted census figures are also available.

TABLE Bd267–276 Hospital personnel per 100 patients, by type of hospital: 1946–1995[1]

Contributed by Richard H. Steckel

			Nonfederal hospitals							
							Short-term care			
	Total	Federal hospitals	Total	Psychiatric services	Tuberculosis	Long-term care	Total	Voluntary nonprofit hospitals	For-profit hospitals	State and local government hospitals
	Bd267	Bd268	Bd269	Bd270	Bd271	Bd272	Bd273	Bd274	Bd275	Bd276
Year	Per 100	Per 100	Per 100	Per 100	Per 100	Per 100	Per 100	Per 100	Per 100	Per 100
1946	73	97	—	19	66	45	148	156	137	129
1947	79	97	—	21	65	41	151	161	139	126
1948	76	103	—	21	65	43	162	173	145	136
1949	78	102	—	22	68	43	169	180	152	144
1950	84	111	81	24	74	57	178	191	161	149
1951	83	116	—	24	75	63	171	181	155	151
1952	84	115	—	24	76	63	175	184	162	153
1953	87	118	83	25	76	72	183	193	161	161
1954	93	122	89	27	81	76	198	207	178	175
1955	95	122	92	28	85	71	203	210	182	188
1956	101	127	98	31	85	83	207	213	179	195
1957	107	118	104	32	88	82	211	218	185	197
1958	111	116	110	34	93	84	218	224	189	206
1959	112	114	111	34	93	91	223	229	195	210
1960	114	120	113	35	99	95	226	232	196	215
1961	122	132	121	38	103	100	235	240	205	227
1962	125	134	124	39	104	102	237	241	208	232
1963	129	135	128	40	102	108	241	244	214	237
1964	133	128	133	42	105	113	242	247	212	236
1965	139	133	140	45	111	115	246	252	218	234
1966	151	137	152	47	117	120	261	264	234	257
1967	160	144	161	51	122	115	265	268	233	262
1968	168	144	171	55	128	131	272	276	237	270
1969	180	152	183	62	138	131	280	284	244	279
1970	196	169	198	68	146	140	292	292	256	298
1971	209	183	212	73	153	139	301	301	262	308
1972	221	203	223	81	155	142	310	308	267	325
1973	233	212	235	88	168	145	315	314	272	333
1974	250	223	253	100	184	154	326	323	283	351
1975	269	240	272	110	216	162	339	336	288	365
1976	285	263	287	124	225	163	347	346	297	367
1977	301	282	303	136	227	167	360	359	307	382
1978	315	290	317	147	246	168	370	370	319	387
1979	327	298	327	151	252	174	379	379	326	398
1980	329	297	333	150	290	170	385	385	334	402
1981	345	310	348	158	287	200	398	399	348	411
1982	376	335	380	167	334	200	434	438	374	443
1983	361	314	365	165	350	202	414	417	358	422
1984	374	327	379	172	342	203	430	434	375	438
1985	398	351	403	180	378	212	462	466	408	470
1986	413	360	419	183	365	212	481	487	423	483
1987	429	367	435	189	308	222	500	505	448	502
1988	445	383	451	200	303	225	516	521	471	517
1989	462	390	468	209	289	237	534	540	493	530
1990	482	424	487	215	405	257	552	557	510	553
1991	504	434	510	217	277	259	578	582	537	580
1992	525	444	533	226	281	257	598	605	556	593
1993	548	479	554	230	272	259	621	627	572	619
1994	573	480	582	241	278	233	650	659	599	644
1995	602	538	607	243	408	240	677	687	626	669

[1] Beginning in 1951, excludes residents, interns, and students; beginning in 1954, includes full-time equivalents of part-time personnel.

Sources

For 1946–1964, American Hospital Association (AHA), *Hospitals,* Guide Issue, part 2 (August 1, 1965), pp. 448–9. For 1965–1970, *Hospitals,* Guide Issue, part 2 (August 1, 1972), pp. 460–62. For 1971–1995, *AHA Hospital Statistics,* annual issues.

Documentation

See the text for Table Bd257–266.

The data include Alaska beginning in 1958.

TABLE Bd277–284 Physicians, by type of practice: 1950–1997

Contributed by Richard H. Steckel

		Nonfederal			Federal			
	Total	Total	Patient care	Other professional activities	Total	Patient care	Other professional activities	Osteopathy
	Bd277	Bd278	Bd279	Bd280	Bd281	Bd282	Bd283	Bd284
Year	Thousand	Thousand	Thousand	Thousand	Thousand	Thousand	Thousand	Thousand
1950	220.0	—	—	—	—	—	—	10.9
1960	260.5	—	—	—	—	—	—	12.2
1965	292.1	268.1	239.3	15.5	22.8	20.2	2.7	11.1
1970	334.0	281.3	255.0	26.3	—	23.5	6.0	12.3
1971	—	—	—	—	—	—	—	20.8
1972	356.5	325.8 [1]	269.1	24.2	27.6	23.1	4.5	12.8
1973	366.4	334.0	272.9	24.7	26.8	22.4	4.4	13.2
1974	350.6	345.6	278.5	25.1	26.6	22.7	3.9	13.6
1975	366.4	359.7	287.8	24.3	28.2	24.1	4.1	14.1
1976	378.6	373.1	294.7	26.1	27.6	23.7	3.9	14.5
1977	382.0	390.4	315.7	27.9	19.9	16.6	3.3	15.1
1978	401.4	408.0	325.8	29.8	20.2	16.9	3.3	15.7
1979	417.3	427.1	341.5	33.7	18.5	15.3	3.2	16.4
1980	435.5	417.7	361.9	35.2	17.8	14.6	3.2	17.1
1981	444.9	460.1	373.6	37.3	19.8	15.7	4.1	18.0
1982	462.9	479.2	393.3	36.6	19.5	15.4	4.1	18.7
1983	479.4	496.9	408.1	39.3	19.4	15.3	4.0	19.7
1984	—	—	—	—	—	—	—	20.8
1985	511.1	489.5	431.5	44.0	21.6	17.3	4.3	21.9
1986	519.4	544.3	444.7	39.1	21.9	17.4	4.5	23.2
1987	534.7	561.0	461.2	38.4	21.7	17.3	4.5	24.1
1988	521.3	499.6	453.2	46.4	21.7	16.9	4.8	25.3
1989	549.2	528.8	477.2	39.2	20.4	15.9	4.4	26.5
1990	560.0	539.5	487.8	39.0	20.5	16.1	4.4	28.1
1991	—	—	—	—	—	—	—	20.8
1992	594.7	575.5	520.2	38.7	19.2	15.0	4.2	31.1
1993	605.7	584.0	531.7	37.7	21.7	18.8	2.9	32.4
1994	619.8	597.3	543.2	39.9	22.5	19.3	3.2	34.0
1995	646.0	624.9	564.1	40.3	21.1	18.1	3.0	35.7
1996	663.9	643.5	580.7	42.8	20.4	18.2	2.2	37.3
1997	756.7	736.3	603.7	41.5	19.4	16.9	2.4	—

[1] Includes physicians not classified.

Sources

For 1950–1978, *Health Resources Statistics*, annual issues. Beginning in 1979, American Medical Association, *Physician Characteristics and Distribution in the U.S.*, annual issues. U.S. National Center for Health Statistics, *Health, United States*, published annually.

Series Bd284. *Health, United States*, annual. The data prior to 1992 are estimates from the Health Resources and Services Administration, Bureau of Health Professions. Beginning in 1992, lists of active doctors of osteopathy are published annually by the American Osteopathic Association.

More recent data: although *Health Resource Statistics* is no longer in publication, *Physician Characteristics and Distribution in the U.S.* is currently published annually by the American Medical Association.

Documentation

These data refer to active physicians. Active physicians are those currently engaged in patient care or other professional activity for a minimum of twenty hours per week. Federal physicians are those employed full-time by the federal government, including the Army, Navy, Air Force, Veterans Administration, Public Health Service, and other federally funded agencies.

Original data sources provide a further breakdown of "patient care" into "office based" and "hospital based." The latter includes residents, fellows, and hospital staff.

Series Bd280 and Bd283. Other professional activities include medical teaching, administration, research, and "other." Beginning in 1968, they include journalism, law, sales, and so on, as part of other activities in which doctors may be engaged.

TABLE Bd285–293 Physician and dentist contacts with patients: 1958–1995

Contributed by Richard H. Steckel

	Physician contacts						Dentist contacts		
	Both sexes		Men		Women				Percentage of persons with a dental visit
	Total	Per person	Total	Per person	Total	Per person	Total	Per person	
	Bd285	Bd286	Bd287	Bd288	Bd289	Bd290	Bd291	Bd292	Bd293
Year	Million	Number	Million	Number	Million	Number	Million	Number	Percent
1958 [1]	813	4.7	349	4.2	464	5.3	248	1.4	—
1963 [1]	844	4.5	356	4.0	488	5.1	294	1.6	—
1966 [1]	831	4.3	353	3.8	478	4.8	—	—	—
1967	830	4.3	352	3.8	478	4.8	—	—	—
1968	815	4.2	347	3.7	469	4.6	260	1.3	—
1969	840	4.3	355	3.7	485	4.7	293	1.5	—
1970	927	4.5	396	4.1	531	5.1	304	1.5	—
1971	999	4.9	420	4.3	579	5.5	312	1.5	—
1972	1,017	5.0	422	4.3	595	5.6	309	1.5	—
1973	1,031	5.0	430	4.3	601	5.6	333	1.6	—
1974	1,025	4.9	427	4.3	598	5.6	342	1.7	—
1975	1,056	5.0	435	4.3	621	5.7	341	1.6	—
1976	1,041	4.9	435	4.3	606	5.6	336	1.6	—
1977	1,020	4.8	426	4.2	594	5.4	343	1.6	—
1978	1,017	4.8	417	4.0	599	5.4	342	1.6	—
1979	1,022	4.7	422	4.1	600	5.4	366	1.7	—
1980	1,036	4.6	426	4.0	610	5.4	364	1.7	—
1981	1,038	4.6	429	4.0	609	5.2	380	1.7	50.4
1982	1,173	5.2	489	4.5	684	5.8	—	—	—
1983	1,164	5.0	470	4.3	694	5.8	445	1.9	55.3
1984	1,173	5.0	472	4.2	701	5.9	—	—	—
1985	1,231	5.2	498	4.4	733	6.1	—	—	—
1986	1,271	5.3	515	4.5	756	6.2	467	2.0	56.3
1987	1,288	5.3	523	4.5	765	6.2	—	—	—
1988	1,304	5.3	530	4.5	774	6.2	—	—	—
1989	1,323	5.4	552	4.7	771	6.1	492	2.1	57.7
1990	1,364	5.5	558	4.7	806	6.4	—	—	62.3 [2]
1991	1,430	5.8	589	4.9	842	6.6	—	—	58.2 [2]
1992	1,513	6.0	624	5.1	889	6.9	—	—	—
1993	1,551	6.1	634	5.1	917	7.0	—	—	60.8 [2]
1994	1,582	6.1	652	5.2	930	7.0	—	—	—
1995	1,547	5.9	626	4.9	922	6.9	—	—	—

[1] For twelve-month period beginning in July.

[2] Among persons age 25 and older.

Source

U.S. National Center for Health Statistics. Physician visit data come from *Current Estimates from the National Health Interview Survey,* Vital and Health Statistics, series 10, published annually. Dentist visit data come from selected issues of the Vital and Health Statistics, series 10, that were specifically about dental visits. More recent data are available from the National Medical Care Utilization and Expenditure Survey (NMCUES) at a cost.

Documentation

The data come from the National Health Interview Survey (NHIS), which is a nationwide survey by household interview. All information collected in the survey is from reports by responsible family members residing in the household.

In 1982, the NHIS survey and data preparation procedures of the survey were extensively revised. A more complete explanation of these changes is in Appendix IV of series 10, number 150 (1).

A physician contact is defined as a patient consultation with a physician, in person or by telephone, for examination, diagnosis, treatment, or advice. The visit is considered a physician contact if the service is provided by the physician or by another person working under the physician's supervision.

"Contacts per person" is defined as total contacts divided by the relevant population (total, male, or female) of the United States.

Series Bd293. Figures are the percentage of persons with a dental visit within the past year.

HEALTH INSURANCE

Richard H. Steckel

TABLE Bd294–305 Persons with hospital and surgical benefits, by type of private health insurance plan: 1939–1992

Contributed by Richard H. Steckel

	Hospital benefits						Surgical benefits					
	Total						Total					
	Number	Percentage covered	Blue Cross–Blue Shield	Insurance company group policies	Insurance company individual policies	Independent plans	Number	Percentage covered	Blue Cross–Blue Shield	Insurance company group policies	Insurance company individual policies	Independent plans
	Bd294 [1]	Bd295 [1,2]	Bd296	Bd297	Bd298 [3]	Bd299 [4]	Bd300 [1]	Bd301 [1,2]	Bd302	Bd303	Bd304	Bd305
Year	Thousand	Percent	Thousand	Thousand	Thousand	Thousand	Thousand	Percent	Thousand	Thousand	Thousand	Thousand
1939	7,976	6.1	—	—	—	—	3,103	2.4	—	—	—	—
1940	12,312	9.3	6,072	2,500	1,200	2,250	5,350	4.0	260	1,430	850	2,250
1941	16,349	12.4	8,459	3,850	1,500	2,270	6,775	5.1	645	2,300	1,000	2,270
1942	19,695	15.2	10,295	5,080	1,800	2,290	8,140	6.3	815	3,275	1,200	2,290
1943	24,160	18.9	12,696	6,800	2,100	2,319	10,069	7.9	1,065	4,700	1,400	2,323
1944	29,232	22.9	15,828	8,400	2,400	2,495	11,713	9.2	1,583	5,625	1,600	2,375
1945	32,068	24.0	18,961	7,804	2,700	2,670	12,890	9.7	2,335	5,537	1,800	2,420
1946	42,112	29.9	24,342	11,315	3,000	2,820	18,609	13.2	4,236	8,661	2,000	2,460
1947	52,584	36.4	27,646	14,190	7,584	3,040	26,247	18.2	6,187	11,103	4,875	2,550
1948	60,995	41.5	30,619	16,741	11,286	3,280	34,060	23.2	10,516	14,199	6,944	2,670
1949	66,044	44.2	33,576	17,697	14,729	3,623	41,143	27.5	12,842	15,590	9,315	3,026
1950	76,639	50.7	37,645	22,305	17,296	4,445	54,156	35.8	17,253	21,219	13,718	3,760
1951	85,348	55.9	39,412	26,663	20,802	5,290	64,892	42.5	22,052	29,376	15,623	4,510
1952	90,965	58.5	41,353	29,455	21,412	6,120	72,459	46.6	25,775	39,621	18,354	5,258
1953	97,303	61.5	43,684	33,575	21,860	6,973	80,982	51.2	29,527	34,039	17,039	6,007
1954	101,493	62.9	45,355	35,090	22,172	6,680	85,890	53.3	33,081	35,723	16,825	5,970
1955	105,452	64.1	48,924	39,029	24,131	6,545	88,856	54.0	37,396	39,725	18,769	5,930
1956	114,342	68.2	51,455	45,211	25,570	6,430	98,015	58.4	40,542	45,906	18,831	5,899
1957	119,493	69.9	53,282	48,439	26,337	6,411	105,229	61.6	43,305	48,955	20,349	5,990
1958	121,018	69.6	53,623	49,508	26,784	6,389	107,527	61.9	44,331	49,917	20,808	6,080
1959	125,753	71.1	55,054	51,255	28,971	6,380	112,842	63.8	46,386	51,756	22,198	6,188
1960	130,007	72.3	57,464	55,218	30,187	5,994	117,304	65.2	48,266	55,504	23,012	7,336
1961	134,417	73.7	57,960	57,013	30,951	7,102	122,951	67.4	49,374	57,373	24,862	8,494
1962	139,176	75.1	59,618	59,153	32,921	6,937	126,900	68.4	50,876	59,787	25,491	8,287
1963	144,575	76.8	60,698	62,817	34,462	7,165	131,954	70.1	52,371	63,288	26,973	8,608
1964	148,338	77.8	62,429	64,506	35,857	6,840	135,433	71.0	54,473	64,939	27,506	8,297
1965	151,483	78.5	63,662	67,104	37,372	6,984	139,437	72.3	56,330	67,557	29,239	8,684
1966	155,864	80.1	65,638	69,570	38,641	6,633	143,284	73.6	57,916	70,268	29,301	8,325
1967	160,649	81.6	67,513	73,351	37,908	7,050	148,729	75.6	60,433	74,318	28,719	8,580
1968	167,209	84.1	70,510	76,059	39,709	7,277	153,977	77.5	63,279	77,415	28,201	8,752
1969	170,855	85.0	73,211	80,093	41,469	7,702	158,584	78.9	66,595	81,363	29,097	9,950
1970	175,382	86.4	75,464	82,712	43,480	8,131	162,655	80.1	69,110	84,133	30,128	10,532
1971	178,938	87.1	76,349	83,448	46,527	8,545	164,491	80.0	70,395	84,879	30,810	10,860
1972	181,602	87.6	78,605	83,768	49,909	8,990	166,261	80.2	72,433	85,290	32,489	11,490
1973	182,079	87.1	81,541	83,459	50,879	9,169	169,416	81.1	75,136	84,026	35,830	12,132
1974	171,760	81.6	83,845	85,759	28,807	9,484	162,571	77.2	76,873	86,630	18,534	12,539
1975	177,980	83.8	85,762	87,185	30,115	9,092	168,895	79.5	77,803	87,958	18,468	11,395
1976	164,235	76.8	85,528	86,824	26,996	9,227	167,400	77.0	76,952	88,327	16,072	11,462
1977	179,900	83.2	86,000	89,200	28,700	18,100	167,200	76.2	75,400	91,900	14,400	18,900
1978	185,700	85.2	85,800	92,500	36,100	21,500	174,700	78.0	78,000	95,600	16,900	25,000
1979	185,700	84.4	86,100	94,100	34,400	25,500	177,100	78.2	78,200	97,600	17,900	29,100
1980	187,400	82.7	86,700	97,400	33,800	33,200	178,200	77.8	73,600	100,600	17,600	36,900
1981	186,200	81.2	85,800	103,000	25,300	40,300	176,900	76.4	71,800 [5]	105,500	12,400	44,800
1982	188,300	81.3	82,000	103,900	29,400	48,200	180,300	77.1	68,600 [5]	108,000	14,500	52,700
1983	186,600	79.8	79,600	104,600	22,200	53,600	179,100	75.8	66,100 [5]	104,900	13,600	61,800
1984	184,400	78.1	79,400	103,000	20,400	54,400	—	—	—	—	—	—
1985	181,300	75.9	78,700	99,500	21,200	55,100	—	—	—	—	—	—
1986	180,900	75.0	78,000	106,600	12,100	64,900	—	—	—	—	—	—
1987	179,700	73.8	76,900	106,100	10,400	66,900	—	—	—	—	—	—
1988	182,300	74.2	74,000	100,500	10,700	71,300	—	—	—	—	—	—
1989	182,500	73.9	72,500	98,700	10,000	78,600	—	—	—	—	—	—
1990	181,700	73.1	70,900	88,700	10,200	86,200	—	—	—	—	—	—
1991	181,000	71.8	68,100	83,300	9,900	93,500	—	—	—	—	—	—
1992	180,100	70.6	67,500	80,300	8,500	98,600	—	—	—	—	—	—

TABLE Bd294–305 Persons with hospital and surgical benefits, by type of private health insurance plan: 1939–1992 *Continued*

[1] Beginning 1976, net of duplication among persons protected by more than one kind of insuring organization or more than one insurance company policy providing the same type of coverage.

[2] For 1939, based on total population. All other years based on U.S. Bureau of the Census estimates of the civilian population as of end of year.

[3] Beginning in 1977, this category is labeled "individual/family plans" and may not be comparable to earlier years.

[4] Beginning in 1977, this category is labeled "self-insured and HMOs."

[5] Estimated.

Sources

For 1939–1974, U.S. Social Security Administration, *Social Security Bulletin* (February 1976 and earlier issues, June 1977, and September 1978). For 1975–1992, *Statistical Abstract,* various years, and taken from Health Insurance Institute, *Source Book of Health Insurance Data,* published annually.

Documentation

The data for insurance companies are from the Health Insurance Institute, *Source Book of Health Insurance Data,* and were developed from surveys and reports of insurance companies and other health insurance plans, government agencies, and hospital and medical associations. The data for Blue Cross–Blue Shield are from annual reports of the Blue Cross–Blue Shield Associations. The data for independent plans – plans other than Blue Cross–Blue Shield and insurance companies – are from annual surveys of these plans by the Social Security Administration.

In 1970, there were many different health insurance organizations in the United States – 75 Blue Cross plans, 72 Blue Shield plans, about 1,000 commercial insurance companies, and more than 500 independent plans. They insured in varying degree against the costs of hospital and surgical care, other physicians' services, nursing care, dental and vision care, and prescribed drugs.

Health insurance policies, both group and individual, are written by health insurance companies, as well as by life and health, casualty, and multiple-line companies.

Because one plan may provide only one type of benefit and because the benefits may be limited, families frequently carry several forms of health insurance, for example, Blue Cross for hospital insurance, Blue Shield for surgical insurance, in-hospital medical expense insurance, and an insurance policy applicable to all three types of expense. Multiple coverage may also occur when husband and wife are both employed and both cover self, spouse, and dependents under the insurance plan at the workplace.

Hospitalization insurance provides benefits for hospital charges incurred by an insured person because of an illness or injury. Surgical insurance pays benefits toward physicians' surgical fees.

The Social Security Administration publishes its own estimates of the net number (of different persons) and the percentage of the civilian population covered by hospital and surgical insurance. These estimates, which usually run 5–10 percentage points lower than those published by the Health Insurance Institute, are based on household interviews conducted by the National Center for Health Statistics (NCHS) during 1967 and 1968, and on findings of various household surveys by the Health Information Foundation and the Public Health Service in 1953–1963.

Series Bd294–295 and Bd300–301. Net number of different persons covered as estimated by Health Insurance Association of America (HIAA), an association of insurance companies. Estimate of net number enrolled exceeds summary of individual categories for early years because HIAA data include estimated enrollment of college and university health services.

Series Bd299 and Bd305. "Independent plans" include community group and individual practice plans, employer-employee-union group and individual practice plans, private group clinics, and dental service corporations not affiliated with Blue Cross–Blue Shield or insurance companies. In addition, these include self-insured plans, self-administered plans, plans employing third-party administrators, and health maintenance organizations.

TABLE Bd306–317 Persons covered by health insurance, by sex, race, and Hispanic origin: 1975–1997

Contributed by Richard H. Steckel

	All persons		Males		Females		Whites		Blacks		Hispanics	
	Number	Percentage covered	Number	Percentage covered	Number	Percentage covered	Number	Percentage covered	Number	Percentage covered	Number	Percentage covered
	Bd306	Bd307	Bd308	Bd309	Bd310	Bd311	Bd312	Bd313	Bd314	Bd315	Bd316	Bd317
Year	Million	Percent	Million	Percent	Million	Percent	Million	Percent	Million	Percent	Million	Percent
1975	178.2	83.6	—	—	—	—	—	—	—	—	—	—
1980	198.2	87.5	96.1	87.3	102.3	87.8	172.5	88.6	21.6	81.0	—	—
1982	197.6	85.3	96.0	85.2	101.9	85.5	170.5	86.7	21.4	78.8	—	—
1983	196.2	84.8	94.0	83.9	102.2	85.7	169.3	86.0	21.7	78.2	9.9	70.9
1984 [1]	202.1	86.6	—	—	—	—	174.2	87.8	22.1	78.7	10.1	73.9
1985 [1]	234.0	85.2	—	—	—	—	175.2	87.6	23.0	80.7	10.4	73.0
1986 [1]	236.7	85.6	98.8	84.2	105.3	85.1	174.9	86.0	22.4	77.4	13.3	69.2
1987	210.2	87.1	100.7	85.9	109.5	88.3	179.8	88.3	23.6	80.1	13.5	69.3
1988	211.0	86.6	101.0	85.3	110.0	87.8	180.1	87.7	24.0	80.4	13.7	68.2
1989	212.8	86.4	102.1	85.2	110.7	87.6	181.1	87.5	24.6	80.8	13.8	66.6
1990	214.2	86.1	102.5	84.6	111.7	87.5	181.8	87.1	24.8	80.3	14.5	67.5
1991	216.0	85.9	103.1	84.2	112.9	87.6	183.1	87.1	28.9	79.3	15.1	68.5
1992	218.2	85.0	104.3	83.1	113.9	86.7	183.5	86.1	26.0	79.8	17.2	67.1
1993	220.0	84.7	105.3	82.9	114.8	86.4	184.7	85.8	26.3	79.5	18.2	68.4
1994	222.4	84.8	106.8	83.4	115.6	86.3	186.4	86.0	26.9	80.3	18.2	66.3
1995	223.7	84.6	107.5	83.2	116.2	86.0	187.3	85.8	26.8	79.0	19.0	66.7
1996	225.1	84.4	108.3	82.9	116.8	85.8	188.3	85.6	26.8	78.3	19.7	66.4
1997	225.6	83.9	108.6	82.4	117.1	85.2	188.4	85.0	27.2	78.5	20.2	65.8

Note appears on next page

(continued)

TABLE Bd306–317 Persons covered by health insurance, by sex, race, and Hispanic origin: 1975–1997 *Continued*

[1] Data taken from the fourth quarter of the year.

Source

U.S. Bureau of the Census, *Current Population Reports,* "Health Insurance Coverage," P-60 series, annual. More recent data are available at the Census Bureau Internet site, where new annual data are released.

Documentation

These series report persons covered by some type of health insurance. For series involving a percentage of the population, resident population data were used. Beginning in 1992, series involving percentages of the population are based on 1990 census-adjusted population controls.

Series Bd316–317. Given as people of "Spanish origin" for earlier years. People of Hispanic origin may be of any race.

TABLE Bd318–326 Health maintenance organization plans – number and enrollment, by type of plan: 1976–1997

Contributed by Richard H. Steckel

	Plans				Enrollment				
					All plans				
	Total	Individual Practice Association	Group	Mixed	Number	Percentage of population	Individual Practice Association	Group	Mixed
	Bd318	Bd319	Bd320	Bd321	Bd322	Bd323	Bd324	Bd325	Bd326
Year	Number	Number	Number	Number	Million	Percent	Million	Million	Million
1976 [1]	174	41	122	—	6.0	2.8	0.4	5.6	—
1978 [2]	202	70	129	—	7.5	3.4	1.1	6.4	—
1980	235	97	138	—	9.1	4.0	1.7	7.4	—
1982	264	97	167	—	10.8	4.7	1.5	9.3	—
1984	304	125	179	—	15.1	6.4	2.9	12.2	—
1985 [3]	478	244	238	—	21.0	8.9	6.4	14.6	—
1986	623	384	239	—	25.7	10.7	9.9	15.8	—
1987	647	409	238	—	29.2	12.1	12.0	17.2	—
1989	604	385	219	—	31.9	13.0	13.5	18.3	—
1990	572	360	212	—	33.0	13.4	13.7	19.3	—
1991	553	346	168	39	34.0	13.6	13.6	17.1	3.3
1992	555	340	166	49	36.1	14.3	14.7	16.5	4.9
1993	551	332	150	69	38.4	15.1	15.3	15.4	7.7
1994	540	319	117	104	42.2	16.1	16.1	13.6	12.5
1995	550	323	107	120	46.2	17.7	17.4	12.9	15.9
1996	628	366	122	140	52.5	19.9	21.7	13.5	17.2
1997	651	284	98	258	66.8	25.0	26.7	11.0	29.0

[1] Eleven health maintenance organizations (HMOs) with 35,000 enrollment did not report model type.

[2] HMOs with 23,000 enrollment did not report model type.

[3] Increases partly due to changes in reporting methods.

Sources

Office of Health Maintenance Organizations, U.S. Public Health Service, InterStudy; U.S. Bureau of the Census, *Current Population Reports.* Data from all of these sources are published annually by the U.S. National Center for Health Statistics in *Health, United States.*

Documentation

Although health maintenance organizations (HMOs) have technically been in existence since the 1930s, they became popular in the 1970s owing to unexpected increases in health care costs during the 1960s and 1970s. In 1973, legislation was enacted to promote HMOs' growth and to combat these rising medical care costs. The HMO Act required most employers to provide an HMO option to their employees in areas where qualified HMOs were located. Federal funds were allocated to establish and develop HMOs over a five-year period. Owing to their cost-effectiveness, HMOs have attracted Medicare and Medicaid recipients. For these reasons, the growth in HMO plans and enrollment has been very rapid since the 1970s.

Data in this table are for pure HMO enrollment only. This means that the enrollees use only the medical care providers on their HMO's panel.

HMOs in Guam are included starting in 1995.

Series Bd323. Based on the residential population of the United States.

Series Bd319 and Bd324. An individual practice association (IPA) is an HMO that contracts with private-practice physicians to provide medical care.

Series Bd320 and Bd325. Group plans refer to HMOs that provide medical care via a group of physicians directly controlled by the HMO or HMOs, which contract with one or more independent group practices. This category includes staff, group, and network plans – all based on this same idea.

Series Bd321 and Bd326. Mixed plans combine the group and IPA plans. The mixed-plan HMO (also known as a network-based HMO) contracts with two or more multispecialty clinics to treat most of its patients. This type of HMO has quality assurance committees, medical record committees, medical review committees, and other appropriate standards group, all composed of physicians who are members of this network. These did not begin until the mid-1990s. They are constantly changing to adapt to specific needs and, therefore, have become very popular.

TABLE Bd327–332 Medicare – expenditures and enrollees: 1966–1997

Contributed by Richard H. Steckel

	Expenditures			Enrollees		
	Total	Hospital insurance	Supplementary medical insurance	Total	Hospital insurance	Supplementary medical insurance
	Bd327	Bd328	Bd329	Bd330	Bd331	Bd332
Year	Million dollars	Million dollars	Million dollars	Number	Number	Number
1966	1,846	999	203	19,108,822	19,082,454	17,735,966
1967	4,737	3,430	1,307	19,521,000	19,493,895	17,893,012
1968	6,240	4,277	1,702	19,821,000	19,769,701	18,804,815
1969	7,070	4,857	2,061	20,102,741	20,014,235	19,194,708
1970	7,701	5,281	2,212	20,490,908	20,014,235	19,584,387
1971	8,470	5,900	2,377	20,914,896	20,742,250	19,974,692
1972	9,360	6,503	2,614	21,332,120	21,115,261	20,351,273
1973	10,777	7,289	2,844	23,545,363	23,301,082	22,490,534
1974	13,485	9,372	3,728	24,201,042	23,924,145	23,166,570
1975	16,397	11,581	4,735	24,958,552	24,640,497	23,904,551
1976	19,764	13,679	5,622	25,662,921	25,312,575	24,614,402
1977	22,973	16,019	6,505	26,457,899	26,093,919	25,363,468
1978	26,763	18,178	7,755	27,164,222	26,777,263	26,074,085
1979	31,037	21,073	9,265	27,858,742	27,459,157	26,757,329
1980	37,516	25,557	11,245	28,478,245	28,066,894	27,399,658
1981	44,882	30,726	14,028	29,009,934	28,589,504	27,941,227
1982	52,470	36,144	16,227	29,494,219	29,068,966	28,412,282
1983	59,762	39,877	18,984	30,026,082	29,587,295	28,974,535
1984	66,447	43,887	20,552	30,455,368	29,995,971	29,415,397
1985	72,084	48,414	23,880	31,082,801	30,589,468	29,988,763
1986	76,837	50,422	27,299	31,749,708	31,215,529	30,589,728
1987	82,711	50,289	31,740	32,411,204	31,852,860	31,169,960
1988	90,099	53,331	35,230	32,980,033	32,413,038	31,617,082
1989	102,423	60,803	39,783 [1]	33,579,449	33,039,977	32,098,770
1990	111,496	66,997	43,987	34,203,383	33,719,118	32,629,109
1991	121,139	72,570	48,877	34,870,240	34,428,810	33,237,474
1992	136,164	85,015	50,830	35,579,149	35,153,223	33,933,274
1993	148,702	94,391	57,784	36,305,903	35,904,436	34,612,360
1994	166,883	104,545	60,317	36,935,366	36,543,147	35,167,288
1995	185,220	117,604	66,600	37,535,024	37,134,949	35,684,584
1996	200,086	129,929	70,409	38,064,130	37,661,881	36,139,608
1997	214,569	—	—	38,444,739	38,052,242	36,460,143

[1] Includes the impact of the Medicare Catastrophic Coverage Act of 1988.

Source

U.S. Social Security Administration, *Annual Statistical Supplement to the Social Security Bulletin,* published annually.

Documentation

As part of the Social Security Act, Medicare became law on July 30, 1965, and is now one of the major health and medical insurance programs in the United States. This program serves persons 65 years and older and the disabled who are insured under the Social Security program. When Medicare first took effect, it provided only for the aged. Beginning in 1973, Medicare extended insurance to the disabled. In 1983, the program began to include hospice care for terminally ill persons with a life expectancy of six months or less.

The Consolidated Omnibus Budget Reconciliation Act (COBRA), passed in 1985, expanded Medicare protection to almost all state employees hired after March 31, 1986.

Hospital insurance (HI) benefits are premium-free and available to all individuals who are eligible for Social Security. In addition, HI is available for disabled recipients who are entitled to Social Security payments and insured workers with end-stage renal (kidney) disease who require dialysis or a transplant. A 1982 act required that all federal employees be covered for HI protection. Under this protection, the recipients are entitled to (1) inpatient hospital care, (2) inpatient care in a skilled-nursing facility following a hospital stay, (3) home health care, and (4) hospice care.

Supplementary medical insurance (SMI) is offered to all citizens and legal resident aliens of five or more resident years who qualified for HI. This is a voluntary program that requires a monthly premium. Participants can terminate their enrollment at any time. Under this protection, the recipients are entitled to the following services among others: (1) physicians' and surgeons' services that are medically necessary, (2) emergency room services and outpatient surgery, (3) laboratory tests and X-ray films, (4) mental health care, (5) physical and occupational services, (6) radiation therapy, and (7) drugs and biologicals that cannot be self-administered.

Services not covered by HI or SMI include long-term nursing care or custodial care and certain other health care needs, such as eyeglasses, hearing aids, prescription drugs, dentures, and dental care.

See any issue of the *Annual Statistical Supplement to the Social Security Bulletin* for more information regarding the Medicare program.

Series Bd328. Includes administrative expenses and peer-review activity.

Series Bd329. Includes administrative expenses.

TABLE Bd333–359 Medicare – persons served and reimbursements: 1967–1996 [Persons age 65 and older]

Contributed by Richard H. Steckel

	Persons served								
		Hospital insurance				Supplementary medical insurance			
	Total	Total	Inpatient hospital services	Skilled nursing services	Home health services	Total	Physicians' and other medical services	Outpatient services	Home health services
	Bd333	Bd334	Bd335	Bd336	Bd337 [1]	Bd338	Bd339	Bd340	Bd341 [1]
Year	Thousand	Thousand	Thousand	Thousand	Thousand	Thousand	Thousand	Thousand	Thousand
1967	7,154	3,960	3,601	354	126	6,523	6,415	1,511	118
1971	9,425	4,416	4,386	239	167	9,075	8,801	2,171	83
1975	12,032	4,963	4,913	260	329	11,762	11,396	3,768	161
1977	13,584	5,410	5,351	283	481	13,348	12,907	4,911	224
1978	14,464	5,569	5,505	267	540	14,279	13,862	5,432	245
1979	15,221	5,698	5,633	247	601	15,041	14,582	5,928	269
1980	16,271	6,024	5,951	248	675	16,099	15,627	6,629	302
1981	17,036	6,229	6,072	243	881	16,858	16,380	7,096	187
1982	17,023	6,548	6,338	244	1,074	16,807	16,346	7,465	17
1983	17,897	6,691	6,441	257	1,228	17,675	17,209	8,065	20
1984	18,904	6,496	6,195	290	1,398	18,706	18,128	8,743	24
1985	20,347	6,058	5,714	304	1,448	20,186	19,590	9,889	27
1986	21,066	6,018	5,697	294	1,469	20,919	20,316	11,011	30
1987	22,155	6,048	5,752	283	1,447	22,020	21,496	11,939	31
1988	22,942	6,082	5,779	371	1,485	22,808	22,270	12,795	32
1989	23,868	6,155	5,725	613	1,580	23,746	23,283	13,291	36
1990	24,809	6,367	5,906	615	1,818	24,687	24,193	14,055	38
1991	25,190	6,576	6,052	648	2,082	25,053	24,492	14,787	32
1992	25,491	6,746	6,117	759	2,357	25,350	24,745	15,658	35
1993	26,793	6,912	6,109	875	2,669	26,657	26,169	16,496	37
1994	27,223	7,043	6,157	1,026	2,938	27,075	26,476	16,989	37
1995	27,379	7,147	6,148	1,186	3,185	27,234	26,621	17,597	42
1996	27,263	7,139	6,091	1,321	3,290	27,113	26,432	17,875	45

	Persons served, per 1,000 enrollees								
		Hospital insurance				Supplementary medical insurance			
	Total	Total	Hospital insurance for inpatient hospital services	Skilled nursing services	Home health services	Total	Physicians' and other medical services	Outpatient services	Home health services
	Bd342	Bd343	Bd344	Bd345	Bd346 [1]	Bd347	Bd348	Bd349	Bd350 [1,2]
Year	Per 1,000	Per 1,000	Per 1,000	Per 1,000	Per 1,000	Per 1,000	Per 1,000	Per 1,000	Per 1,000
1967	367	203	185	18	7	365	359	77	7
1971	451	213	212	12	8	454	441	109	4
1975	528	221	219	12	15	536	519	172	7
1977	570	231	228	12	21	581	561	214	10
1978	594	232	230	11	23	609	589	231	10
1979	610	232	230	10	25	624	605	246	11
1980	638	240	237	10	27	652	633	269	12
1981	655	243	237	10	34	670	651	282	7
1982	641	251	243	9	41	654	636	290	1
1983	660	251	242	10	46	672	655	307	1
1984	686	240	229	11	52	699	677	327	1
1985	722	219	206	11	52	739	717	362	1
1986	732	213	202	10	52	751	729	395	1
1987	754	210	200	10	50	776	757	421	1
1988	768	208	197	13	51	793	774	445	1
1989	785	206	192	21	53	813	797	455	1

Notes appear at end of table

TABLE Bd333–359 Medicare – persons served and reimbursements: 1967–1996 [Persons age 65 and older] *Continued*

	Persons served, per 1,000 enrollees								
		Hospital insurance				Supplementary medical insurance			
	Total	Total	Hospital insurance for inpatient hospital services	Skilled nursing services	Home health services	Total	Physicians' and other medical services	Outpatient services	Home health services
	Bd342	Bd343	Bd344	Bd345	Bd346 [1]	Bd347	Bd348	Bd349	Bd350 [1, 2]
Year	Per 1,000	Per 1,000	Per 1,000	Per 1,000	Per 1,000	Per 1,000	Per 1,000	Per 1,000	Per 1,000
1990	802	209	194	20	60	832	815	474	1
1991	800	212	195	21	67	830	811	490	1
1992	796	214	194	24	75	825	806	510	1
1993	825	216	191	27	83	856	840	530	1
1994	830	217	190	32	91	861	842	540	1
1995	826	218	188	36	97	858	839	554	1
1996	816	216	185	40	100	848	826	559	1

	Reimbursements to persons served								
		Hospital insurance				Supplementary medical insurance			
	Total	Total	Inpatient hospital services	Skilled nursing services	Home health services	Total	Physicians' and other medical services	Outpatient services	Home health services
	Bd351	Bd352	Bd353	Bd354	Bd355 [1]	Bd356	Bd357	Bd358	Bd359 [1]
Year	Million dollars	Million dollars	Million dollars	Million dollars	Million dollars	Million dollars	Million dollars	Million dollars	Million dollars
1967	4,239	2,967	2,659	274	26	1,272	1,224	38	17
1971	7,349	5,364	5,156	166	42	1,986	1,848	125	13
1975	12,689	9,209	8,840	233	136	3,481	3,050	374	56
1977	18,098	13,179	12,641	293	245	4,919	4,177	649	92
1978	21,063	15,012	14,427	293	293	6,050	5,145	798	107
1979	24,310	17,137	16,477	306	353	7,173	6,045	997	131
1980	29,134	20,353	19,583	331	440	8,781	7,361	1,261	159
1981	34,490	24,153	23,111	361	682	10,336	8,688	1,557	91
1982	41,526	29,214	27,834	388	992	12,311	10,311	1,982	19
1983	46,727	32,141	30,469	413	1,258	14,586	12,105	2,460	22
1984	49,452	33,418	31,428	458	1,532	16,034	13,218	2,790	26
1985	56,199	37,360	35,313	464	1,583	18,839	15,309	3,499	31
1986	60,459	39,285	37,181	474	1,630	21,174	16,887	4,249	38
1987	67,022	41,744	39,578	524	1,643	25,278	16,887	5,097	38
1988	72,900	45,703	43,112	811	1,781	27,196	20,143	5,843	43
1989	82,222	50,448	45,439	2,806	2,202	31,774	25,310	6,407	57
1990	88,778	54,244	48,952	1,886	3,406	34,533	27,379	7,077	78
1991	98,384	61,474	54,366	2,151	4,958	36,910	28,965	7,870	76
1992	107,589	68,598	58,596	3,146	6,856	38,991	29,744	9,145	102
1993	114,247	72,958	59,906	4,136	8,916	41,289	31,258	9,899	131
1994	129,033	83,072	65,722	5,735	11,614	45,961	34,408	11,395	158
1995	138,948	89,631	68,213	7,504	13,914	49,317	37,069	12,045	203
1996	145,322	95,404	71,191	9,157	15,056	499,189	36,865	12,838	215

[1] See the text on elimination of the 100-visit limit on home health services and the three-day prior hospitalization requirement.

[2] Beginning in 1982, a change in legislation resulted in virtually all home health services being paid under hospital insurance.

Source

Social Security Administration, *Annual Statistical Supplement to the Social Security Bulletin,* published annually (Table 8.B1 as of the 2000 issue).

Documentation

See the text for Table Bd327–332.

The Omnibus Reconciliation Act of 1980 eliminated the 100-visit limit on home health services and the three-day prior hospitalization requirement. This made the home health services under hospital insurance the same as under supplementary medical insurance. Because section 1833(D) of the Social Security Act specifies that services that can be paid under hospital insurance cannot be paid under supplementary medical insurance, virtually all home health services are now paid under the hospital insurance program.

Series Bd357. Includes reimbursements for physicians' services, ambulance services, independent laboratory services, durable medical equipment, and prosthetic devices.

TABLE Bd360–386 Medicare – persons served and reimbursements: 1973–1996 [Disabled persons]

Contributed by Richard H. Steckel

	Persons served								
		Hospital insurance				Supplementary medical insurance			
	Total	Total	Inpatient hospital services	Skilled nursing services	Home health services	Total	Physicians' and other medical services	Outpatient services	Home health services
	Bd360	Bd361	Bd362	Bd363	Bd364 [1]	Bd365	Bd366	Bd367	Bd368
Year	Thousand	Thousand	Thousand	Thousand	Thousand	Thousand	Thousand	Thousand	Thousand
1973 [2,3]	—	—	—	—	—	—	—	—	—
1974	792	400	397	8	15	740	691	296	9
1975	975	475	472	8	22	924	865	399	13
1976	1,158	545	541	9	28	1,108	1,036	516	16
1977	1,321	600	595	10	34	1,270	1,189	617	19
1978	1,472	652	647	9	39	1,421	1,320	723	21
1979	1,654	700	694	9	46	1,614	1,523	823	23
1980	1,760	728	721	9	51	1,723	1,631	909	25
1981	1,845	754	739	8	67	1,810	1,717	975	14
1982	1,799	759	739	8	80	1,760	1,671	982	—
1983	1,853	752	729	8	90	1,797	1,714	1,024	—
1984	1,845	700	674	9	100	1,812	1,721	1,029	—
1985	1,944	662	636	10	101	1,916	1,820	1,096	—
1986	2,015	669	645	10	102	1,988	1,888	1,211	—
1987	2,108	665	642	10	97	2,085	1,986	1,288	—
1988	2,182	649	625	13	97	2,156	2,041	1,357	—
1989	2,287	659	627	23	105	2,263	2,159	1,415	—
1990	2,390	680	644	23	122	2,365	2,249	1,496	—
1991	2,466	706	666	23	141	2,439	2,304	1,583	—
1992	2,627	753	703	27	166	2,598	2,453	1,748	—
1993	2,888	812	748	33	199	2,858	2,744	1,936	—
1994	3,126	879	803	42	237	3,094	2,986	2,097	—
1995	3,333	933	844	54	272	3,299	3,184	2,281	—
1996	3,476	964	868	63	293	3,442	3,315	2,407	—

	Persons served, per 1,000 enrollees								
		Hospital insurance				Supplementary medical insurance			
	Total	Total	Inpatient hospital services	Skilled nursing services	Home health services	Total	Physicians' and other medical services	Outpatient services	Home health services
	Bd369	Bd370	Bd371	Bd372	Bd373 [1]	Bd374	Bd375	Bd376	Bd377
Year	Per 1,000	Per 1,000	Per 1,000	Per 1,000	Per 1,000	Per 1,000	Per 1,000	Per 1,000	Per 1,000
1973 [2,3]	—	—	—	—	—	—	—	—	—
1974	411	208	206	4	8	424	396	170	5
1975	450	219	218	4	10	471	442	204	7
1976	484	228	226	4	12	511	478	238	7
1977	520	229	227	4	13	535	501	260	8
1978	527	234	232	3	14	559	519	285	8
1979	568	240	238	3	16	607	573	310	9
1980	594	246	243	3	17	634	600	334	9
1981	615	251	246	3	22	656	622	353	5
1982	609	257	250	3	27	651	618	363	—
1983	629	258	250	3	31	670	639	382	—
1984	640	243	234	3	35	684	649	388	—
1985	669	228	219	4	35	716	680	409	—
1986	681	226	218	4	35	729	692	444	—
1987	696	219	212	3	32	748	712	462	—
1988	704	209	202	4	31	760	720	478	—
1989	721	208	198	7	33	785	749	491	—

Notes appear at end of table

TABLE Bd360–386 Medicare – persons served and reimbursements: 1973–1996 [Disabled persons] *Continued*

	Persons served, per 1,000 enrollees								
		Hospital insurance				Supplementary medical insurance			
	Total	Total	Inpatient hospital services	Skilled nursing services	Home health services	Total	Physicians' and other medical services	Outpatient services	Home health services
	Bd369	Bd370	Bd371	Bd372	Bd373 [1]	Bd374	Bd375	Bd376	Bd377
Year	Per 1,000	Per 1,000	Per 1,000	Per 1,000	Per 1,000	Per 1,000	Per 1,000	Per 1,000	Per 1,000
1990	734	209	198	7	38	804	764	508	—
1991	729	209	197	7	42	799	755	519	—
1992	736	211	197	8	47	807	762	543	—
1993	751	211	195	9	52	825	792	559	—
1994	755	213	194	10	57	831	803	564	—
1995	759	212	192	12	62	837	808	579	—
1996	749	208	187	14	63	828	798	579	—

	Reimbursements to persons served								
		Hospital insurance				Supplementary medical insurance			
	Total	Total	Inpatient hospital services	Skilled nursing services	Home health services	Total	Physicians' and other medical services	Outpatient services	Home health services
	Bd378	Bd379	Bd380	Bd381	Bd382	Bd383	Bd384	Bd385	Bd386
Year	Million dollars	Million dollars	Million dollars	Million dollars	Million dollars	Million dollars	Million dollars	Million dollars	Million dollars
1973	—	173	—	2	1	—	—	—	—
1974	1,049	694	681	7	6	355	206	145	3
1975	1,509	987	968	9	10	522	295	221	5
1976	2,018	1,312	1,286	11	15	705	389	309	7
1977	2,495	1,613	1,582	12	19	882	481	392	9
1978	2,993	1,945	1,909	12	24	1,048	557	480	11
1979	3,747	2,341	2,297	13	31	1,406	810	583	13
1980	4,478	2,765	2,714	13	38	1,713	997	701	16
1981	5,315	3,317	3,243	14	60	1,998	1,199	791	8
1982	6,172	3,878	3,776	14	89	2,294	1,385	909	—
1983	6,711	4,173	4,050	15	108	2,538	1,555	983	—
1984	6,680	4,189	4,048 [4]	15	126	2,490	1,549	941	—
1985	7,495	4,785	4,638	17	130	2,709	1,712	997	—
1986	8,123	5,103	4,949	19	135	3,020	1,871	1,149	—
1987	8,980	5,060	4,908	21	131	3,360	2,099	1,261	—
1988	11,553	5,436	5,264	33	140	3,544	2,162	1,383	—
1989	10,364	6,253	5,936	143	173	4,111	2,623	1,488	—
1990	11,239	6,694	6,345	85	264	4,545	2,831	1,714	—
1991	12,503	7,512	7,045	87	379	4,991	3,054	1,937	—
1992	14,253	8,567	7,876	126	564	5,686	3,285	2,402	—
1993	15,850	9,479	8,566	175	738	6,371	3,693	2,678	—
1994	18,818	11,501	10,230	258	1,013	7,317	4,321	2,996	—
1995	21,024	12,752	11,079	374	1,300	8,272	4,888	3,384	—
1996	22,647	13,790	11,848	464	1,478	8,858	5,125	3,733	—

[1] See the text on elimination of the 100-visit limit on home health services and the three-day prior hospitalization requirement.

[2] For all enrollees younger than age 65, including those with end-stage renal disease.

[3] Disabled enrollees were not covered under Medicare until July 1, 1973. Therefore, figures represent amounts for the last six months of 1973.

[4] Includes estimates of prospective payment system (PPS) pass-through expenditures as reported in the intermediary hospital payment report of the Health Care Financing Administration.

Source

U.S. Social Security Administration, *Annual Statistical Supplement to the Social Security Bulletin,* published annually (Table 8.B2 as of the 2000 issue).

Documentation

See the text for Table Bd327–332.

The Omnibus Reconciliation Act of 1980 eliminated the 100-visit limit on home health services and the three-day prior hospitalization requirement. This made the home health services under hospital insurance the same as under supplementary medical insurance. Because section 1833(D) of the Social Security Act specifies that services that can be paid under hospital insurance cannot be paid under supplementary medical insurance, virtually all home health services are now paid under the hospital insurance program.

Series Bd384. Includes reimbursements for physicians' services, ambulance services, independent laboratory services, durable medical equipment, and prosthetic devices.

TABLE Bd387–396 Medicare – utilization and charges: 1970–1996 [Persons age 65 and older]

Contributed by Richard H. Steckel

	Approved bills for inpatient short-stay hospital care								Supplementary medical insurance	
	Hospital insurance (HI)					Covered charges				
	Number of bills		Covered days of care							
	Total	Per 1,000 HI enrollees	Total	Per 1,000 HI enrollees	Average days of care	Total	Average per day	Percentage of covered charges reimbursed	Allowed charges for physicians' services	Percentage of allowed charges for physicians' services reimbursed
	Bd387	Bd388	Bd389	Bd390	Bd391	Bd392	Bd393	Bd394 [1]	Bd395	Bd396 [2]
Year	Thousand	Per 1,000	Million	Per 1,000	Number	Million dollars	Dollars	Percent	Million dollars	Percent
1970	6,141	307	79	3,947	12.9	5,968	75	78.0	2,310	71.9
1973	6,883	295	78	3,346	11.3	8,198	105	75.6	2,620 [3]	72.9 [3]
1974	7,414	310	81	3,391	10.9	9,643	119	75.6	3,991 [3]	73.5 [3]
1975	7,743	314	82	3,340	10.6	11,845	144	75.3	4,845 [3]	74.4 [3]
1976	8,163	322	86	3,397	10.5	14,542	169	74.7	5,223 [3]	75.0 [3]
1977	8,398	322	87	3,316	10.3	16,918	196	73.4	6,978 [3]	75.7 [3]
1978	8,673	324	88	3,286	10.1	19,621	223	72.2	6,170	76.8
1979	8,955	326	90	3,260	10.0	22,660	253	71.4	9,590 [3]	76.6 [3]
1980	9,621	343	95	3,398	9.9	27,824	292	69.7	9,011	78.0
1981	9,967	349	97	3,390	9.7	33,494	346	68.8	13,225 [3]	77.3 [3]
1982	10,399	358	99	3,407	9.5	40,588	410	67.2	16,468 [3]	76.9 [3]
1983	10,509	355	96	3,247	9.1	45,645	475	64.9	14,574	77.5
1984	9,544	318	80	2,683	8.4	42,699	531	68.8	—	—
1985	9,062	296	80	2,615	8.3	49,236	594	69.4	17,743	78.8
1986	9,337	299	78	2,501	8.4	53,030	679	61.5	—	—
1987	9,279	291	80	2,507	8.6	60,498	757	55.9	—	—
1988	9,384	290	81	2,499	8.5	70,292	864	51.4	23,987	78.4
1989	9,039	274	79	2,391	8.5	78,840	996	50.4	26,274	78.4
1990	9,420	279	82	2,432	8.4	90,846	1,102	47.8	30,447	77.0
1991	9,656	280	83	2,411	8.1	105,596	1,270	45.7	32,138	75.7
1992	10,213	291	84	2,390	7.7	116,977	1,446	47.1	34,083	75.6
1993	9,880	275	81	2,256	7.3	125,444	1,614	46.6	35,255	76.2
1994	10,134	277	79	2,162	7.6	133,591	1,753	46.5	38,151	76.2
1995	10,415	280	76	2,047	7.2	138,489	1,828	47.5	41,409	76.2
1996	10,383	276	72	1,912	6.8	140,606	1,978	48.8	36,212	76.0

[1] Change in reimbursement system in 1980s. See text.

[2] Beginning with calendar year 1973, home health services provided under supplementary medical insurance are reimbursed at 100 percent of the reasonable cost, less any applicable deductions.

[3] Data for this year were not taken from the new source used by the *Social Security Statistical Supplement* beginning in 1990. They are from U.S. Health Care Financing Administration, unpublished data.

Source

U.S. Social Security Administration, *Annual Statistical Supplement to the Social Security Bulletin*, published annually.

Documentation

See the text for Table Bd327–332.

Series Bd394. For most hospitals, the Social Security Amendments of 1983 (P.L. 98-21) replaced the retrospective cost-reimbursement system, the cost-per-case limits, and rate-of-increase ceiling created by the Tax Equity and Fiscal Responsibility Act of 1982. Effective with hospital cost-reporting periods beginning on or after October 1, 1983, Medicare payments for inpatient operating costs are to be based on a fixed amount, determined in advance for each case, according to one of 492 diagnosis-related groups (DRGs) into which a case is classified. The prospective payment is considered payment in full; hospitals are prohibited from charging beneficiaries more than the statutory deductible and coinsurance. Additional payments, determined by diagnostic criteria, are made to hospitals by the program for various "pass-through" costs and additional adjustments. These additional payments are not included in the reimbursed inpatient hospital billing amounts shown in this series.

Series Bd395. Includes physician- or supplier-allowed charges as determined by the carrier and amounts actually billed by the provider's outpatient hospital and home health services.

Series Bd396. Amount reimbursed to or on behalf of the beneficiary – generally 80 percent of the allowed charges, once the beneficiary has satisfied the deductible in the current year. Some radiology and pathology services are reimbursed at a 100 percent rate, regardless of the beneficiary's deductible status.

TABLE Bd397–406 Medicare – utilization and charges: 1973–1996 [Disabled persons]

Contributed by Richard H. Steckel

	Approved bills for inpatient short-stay hospital care								Supplementary medical insurance	
	Hospital insurance (HI)					Covered charges				
	Number of bills		Covered days of care							
	Total	Per 1,000 HI enrollees	Total	Per 1,000 HI enrollees	Average days of care	Total	Average per day	Percentage of covered charges reimbursed	Allowed charges for physicians' services	Percentage of allowed charges for physicians' services reimbursed
	Bd397	Bd398	Bd399	Bd400	Bd401	Bd402	Bd403	Bd404 [1]	Bd405	Bd406
Year	Number	Per 1,000	Number	Per 1,000	Number	Million dollars	Dollars	Percent	Million dollars	Percent
1973	199,645	—	1,970,386	—	9.9	220	112	74.7	—	—
1974	658,768	342	6,808,883	3,532	10.3	881	129	73.7	—	—
1975	799,040	379	7,997,317	4,198	10.0	1,259	157	73.2	367	76.1
1976	921,798	385	9,085,899	3,798	9.9	1,674	184	72.6	414	76.8
1977	1,022,980	391	9,884,543	3,774	9.7	2,097	212	71.7	596	77.4
1978	1,113,252	399	10,587,612	3,791	9.5	2,546	240	70.7	656	77.7
1979	1,218,151	418	11,489,737	3,947	9.4	3,125	272	70.1	925	78.2
1980	1,300,804	429	12,233,699	4,549	9.4	3,824	313	68.6	1,066	78.6
1981	1,343,221	448	12,480,662	4,162	9.3	4,589	368	68.0	1,266	78.8
1982	1,366,404	463	12,551,253	4,249	9.2	5,448	434	66.8	1,541	78.6
1983	1,337,041	458	11,919,411	4,085	8.9	5,955	500	64.9	1,690	78.1
1984	1,162,152	403	9,646,584	3,345	8.3	5,302	550	69.1	1,651	78.2
1985	1,127,463	454	9,159,976	3,739	8.1	5,574	609	69.7	1,823	78.7
1986	1,204,985	407	9,963,430	3,365	8.3	6,908	693	60.5	1,901	78.6
1987	1,141,440	377	9,669,685	3,190	8.5	7,459	771	53.9	—	—
1988	1,139,680	374	9,382,745	3,468	8.2	8,459	902	48.5	2,230	78.1
1989	1,148,650	333	9,443,425	3,526	8.2	9,647	1,022	49.1	2,683	78.4
1990	1,184,500	396	9,788,875	3,464	8.3	11,083	1,132	46.8	2,964	76.0
1991	1,237,630	389	10,042,655	3,545	8.1	13,165	1,311	44.3	3,171	75.6
1992	1,376,235	383	10,780,125	3,082	7.8	16,007	1,485	45.0	3,295	76.2
1993	1,369,080	356	10,481,110	2,871	7.5	17,191	1,640	45.0	3,786	76.2
1994	1,546,225	343	11,010,385	2,660	7.1	19,531	1,774	45.0	4,630	76.2
1995	1,442,000 [2]	328 [2]	10,000,000	2,351	7.2	18,885	1,828	47.5	5,647	76.2
1996	1,572,000 [2]	339 [2]	10,000,000	2,289	6.8	21,011	1,978	48.8	5,411	76.0

[1] Change in reimbursement system in 1980s. See text.

[2] Rounded data.

Source

U.S. Social Security Administration, *Annual Statistical Supplement to the Social Security Bulletin*, published annually.

Documentation

See the text for Table Bd327–332.

Series Bd404. For most hospitals, the Social Security Amendments of 1983 (P.L. 98-21) replaced the retrospective cost-reimbursement system, the cost-per-case limits, and rate-of-increase ceiling created by the Tax Equity and Fiscal Responsibility Act of 1982. Effective with hospital cost-reporting periods beginning on or after October 1, 1983, Medicare payments for inpatient operating costs are to be based on a fixed amount, determined in advance for each case, according to one of 492 diagnosis-related groups (DRGs) into which a case is classified. The prospective payment is considered payment in full; hospitals are prohibited from charging beneficiaries more than the statutory deductible and coinsurance. Additional payments, determined by diagnostic criteria, are made to hospitals by the program for various "pass-through" costs and additional adjustments. These additional payments are not included in the reimbursed inpatient hospital billing amounts shown in this series.

Series Bd405. Includes physician- or supplier-allowed charges as determined by the carrier and amounts actually billed by the provider's outpatient hospital and home health services.

Series Bd406. Amount reimbursed to or on behalf of the beneficiary – generally 80 percent of the allowed charges, once the beneficiary has satisfied the deductible in the current year. Some radiology and pathology services are reimbursed at a 100 percent rate, regardless of the beneficiary's deductible status.

TABLE Bd407–412 Medicaid recipients and days of care, by type of facility: 1975–1996

Contributed by Richard H. Steckel

	General hospitals		Nursing facilities		Intermediate care facilities	
	Recipients discharged	Days of care	Recipients	Days of care	Recipients	Days of care
	Bd407	Bd408	Bd409 [1]	Bd410 [1]	Bd411	Bd412
Year	Thousand	Thousand	Thousand	Thousand	Thousand	Thousand
1975	2,336	22,941	630	78,111	69	9,060
1980	2,255	24,089	606	102,832	121	25,124
1981	2,572	26,468	610	108,066	151	32,640
1982	2,218	21,552	559	92,013	149	35,664
1983	7,410 [2]	23,094	574	100,847	151	39,844
1984	2,263	23,185	559	100,265	141	46,310
1985	2,390	29,562	1,375	277,996	147	47,324
1986	2,564	29,517	1,399	334,016	145	48,418
1987	2,525	23,124	1,371	328,758	140	45,611
1988	2,640	24,022	1,445	344,693	145	46,825
1989	2,701	22,754	1,438	367,228	147	50,276
1990	3,261	27,471	1,461	360,044	146	49,730
1991	3,638	28,998	1,500	387,621	146	50,223
1992	3,866	29,921	1,573	408,191	151	53,538
1993	4,050	31,095	1,610	422,965	149	44,105
1994	3,890	28,941	1,639	400,785	159	54,105
1995	3,743	25,711	1,667	400,123	151	56,878
1996	3,300	23,072	1,594	409,663	140	56,625

[1] Prior to 1985, includes skilled nursing facilities; thereafter, includes skilled nursing facilities and intermediate care facilities for all persons other than the mentally retarded.

[2] Data in the original source appear to be in error but cannot be corrected.

Source

U.S. Health Care Financing Administration, Office of Information Systems, *Statistical Report on Medical Care: Eligibles, Recipients, Payments and Services,* and data published annually from the same source in U.S. Bureau of the Census, *Statistical Abstract of the United States*.

Documentation

Medicaid is one of the major health and medical insurance programs in the United States. The program is funded jointly by the federal government and the states and is state-administered. Medicaid became law in 1965 as part of the Social Security Act. It is a federal- and state-matching entitlement program that provides medical assistance for certain individuals and families with low incomes and resources. Medicaid is the largest program providing medical and health-related services to America's poorest people. It is up to each state to (1) establish eligibility standards; (2) determine the type, amount, duration, and scope of services; (3) set the rate of payment for services; and (4) administer the program. Thus, Medicaid programs vary considerably from state to state, and within each state over time.

Despite broad differences between states, each state is required to provide Medicaid coverage for certain individuals who receive federally assisted income-maintenance payments, as well as for related groups not receiving cash payments. Among others, these mandatory eligible groups include individuals who qualify for Aid to Families with Dependent Children (AFDC) programs in their state; children younger than age 6; pregnant women whose family income is at or below 133 percent of the federal poverty level; and all children born after September 30, 1983, who are younger than age 19, in families with incomes at or below the federal poverty level.

In addition to the mandatory groups to which each state must offer Medicaid, there are mandatory basic services that each state must offer as a part of Medicaid. These services include inpatient hospital services, outpatient hospital services, prenatal care, vaccines for children, physician services, nursing facilities for persons age 21 and older, family planning services and supplies, rural health clinic services, home health care for persons eligible for skilled-nursing services, laboratory and X-ray services, pediatric and family nurse practitioner services, nurse-midwife services, federally qualified health center services and ambulatory services that would be available in other settings, and early and periodic screening, diagnosis, and treatment services for children younger than age 21.

Medicaid acts as a vendor payment program such that states pay recipients directly or through arrangements, for example, with health maintenance organizations (HMOs). Providers that participate in Medicaid must accept the Medicaid reimbursement level as payment in full. With a few exceptions, each state has discretion in determining the reimbursement methodology and resulting payment rate for services. Although states have the option of engaging in cost-sharing aid, certain programs are excluded from this type of payment: emergency services, family planning services and programs that serve pregnant women, children younger than age 18, hospital or nursing home patients (who are expected to contribute most of their income to institutional care), and categorically needy persons enrolled in HMOs.

The federal portion of Medicaid payments is called Federal Medical Assistance Percentage (FMAP). This is determined annually by a formula that compares states' average per capita income level with the national income average. The FMAP cannot be lower than 50 percent nor greater than 83 percent of the total health care costs covered by Medicaid in order to be reimbursed in each state. The wealthier states have a smaller percentage of their costs reimbursed. Most administrative costs are matched at 50 percent for all states. There is no set limit on federal Medicaid payments.

More information is available through a number of sources including the *Annual Statistical Supplement to the Social Security Bulletin,* published annually by the Social Security Administration.

Series Bd411–412. Includes facilities for the mentally retarded only.

TABLE Bd413–430 Medicaid recipients, by program or service: 1972–1997

Contributed by Richard H. Steckel

				Aid to Families with Dependent Children		Inpatient services			
	Total	Age 65 and older	For blindness	Total	Medical assistance only	General hospitals	Mental hospitals	Intermediate care facility services for the mentally retarded	Nursing facility services
	Bd413	Bd414	Bd415	Bd416 [1]	Bd417 [1]	Bd418	Bd419	Bd420	Bd421 [2]
Year	Thousand	Thousand	Thousand	Thousand	Thousand	Thousand	Thousand	Thousand	Thousand
1972	17,600	3,318	108	10,978	—	2,832	40	—	552
1973	19,622	3,496	101	12,725	2,091	3,256	77	29	678
1974	21,117	3,702	129	13,637	2,215	3,241	72	39	646
1975	22,223	3,659	109	14,310	1,816	3,475	64	54	630
1976	22,891	3,644	94	14,749	1,988	3,420	76	77	637
1977	22,920	3,558	93	14,514	1,984	3,662	78	95	641
1978	22,198	3,374	86	14,192	1,878	3,732	70	94	639
1979	21,521	3,768	79	11,807	1,869	3,608	74	114	610
1980	21,605	3,331	92	12,208	2,002	3,680	66	121	606
1981	21,980	3,388	86	12,633	2,135	3,703	90	151	623
1982	21,603	3,759	84	12,557	2,363	3,530	72	149	559
1983	21,554	3,966	77	12,574	2,554	3,696	80	151	574
1984	21,607	3,624	79	12,586	2,697	3,467	35	141	559
1985	21,808	3,523	80	12,484	2,785	3,434	60	147	547
1986	22,500	3,100	82	15,700	—	3,533	45	180	571
1987	23,109	3,224	85	15,767	—	3,767	57	149	572
1988	22,907	3,159	86	15,541	—	3,832	60	145	579
1989	23,511	3,132	95	16,036	—	4,170	90	148	564
1990	25,255	3,202	83	17,230	—	4,593	92	147	601
1991	28,280	3,359	85	20,194	—	5,072	65	146	1,500
1992	30,926	3,742	84	22,058	—	5,768	77	151	1,573
1993	33,432	3,863	84	23,790	—	5,894	75	149	1,610
1994	35,035	4,035	86	24,780	—	5,866	85	159	1,639
1995	36,282	4,119	94	24,767	—	5,561	84	151	1,667
1996	36,118	4,285	95	23,866	—	5,362	93	140	1,594
1997	34,872	3,955	—	6,803	—	4,746	87	136	1,603

	Physicians' services	Dental services	Other practitioners' services	Outpatient hospital services	Clinic services	Laboratory and radiological services	Home health services	Prescribed drugs	Family planning services
	Bd422	Bd423	Bd424	Bd425	Bd426	Bd427	Bd428	Bd429	Bd430
Year	Thousand	Thousand	Thousand	Thousand	Thousand	Thousand	Thousand	Thousand	Thousand
1972	12,282	2,397	1,600	5,215	501	3,523	105	11,139	—
1973	13,278	2,916	1,903	5,295	1,790	3,959	110	12,116	—
1974	14,643	3,434	2,251	5,544	1,854	4,121	135	13,989	—
1975	15,198	3,944	2,673	7,437	1,086	4,738	202	14,155	1,050
1976	15,060	4,174	2,758	6,981	1,922	4,823	227	15,039	1,144
1977	15,636	4,500	2,856	8,333	1,518	5,384	363	15,000	1,335
1978	15,329	4,336	2,974	8,288	1,277	5,574	358	14,736	1,302
1979	15,168	4,401	3,011	7,710	1,497	5,332	359	14,283	1,206
1980	13,765	4,652	3,234	9,705	1,531	3,212	392	13,707	1,129
1981	14,403	5,173	3,582	10,018	1,755	3,822	402	14,256	1,473
1982	13,894	4,868	3,223	9,853	1,702	3,814	377	13,547	1,506
1983	14,056	4,940	3,306	10,069	1,760	4,462	422	13,732	1,538
1984	14,159	4,942	3,353	10,035	2,037	4,822	438	13,935	1,577
1985	14,387	4,672	3,357	10,072	2,121	6,354	535	13,921	1,636
1986	14,895	5,153	3,443	10,688	2,025	7,110	585	14,693	1,733
1987	15,373	5,131	3,542	10,978	2,183	7,596	609	15,083	1,652
1988	15,265	5,072	3,480	10,533	2,256	7,579	569	15,323	1,525
1989	15,686	4,214	3,555	11,344	2,391	7,759	609	15,916	1,564

Notes appear at end of table

(continued)

TABLE Bd413–430 Medicaid recipients, by program or service: 1972–1997 *Continued*

	Physicians' services	Dental services	Other practitioners' services	Outpatient hospital services	Clinic services	Laboratory and radiological services	Home health services	Prescribed drugs	Family planning services
	Bd422	Bd423	Bd424	Bd425	Bd426	Bd427	Bd428	Bd429	Bd430
Year	Thousand	Thousand	Thousand	Thousand	Thousand	Thousand	Thousand	Thousand	Thousand
1990	17,078	4,552	3,873	12,370	2,804	8,959	719	17,294	1,752
1991	19,321	5,209	4,282	14,137	3,511	10,505	813	19,602	2,185
1992	21,627	5,700	4,711	15,120	4,115	11,804	925	22,030	2,550
1993	23,746	6,174	5,229	16,436	4,839	12,970	1,067	23,901	2,538
1994	24,267	6,352	5,409	16,567	5,258	13,412	1,293	24,470	2,566
1995	23,789	6,383	5,528	16,712	5,322	13,064	1,639	23,723	2,501
1996	22,861	6,208	5,342	15,905	5,070	12,607	1,727	22,585	2,366
1997	21,170	5,935	5,142	13,632	4,713	11,074	1,861	20,954	2,091

[1] Beginning 1986, series Bd416 includes Aid to Families with Dependent Children (AFDC) medical assistance.

[2] Category covers "skilled nursing facility services" through 1990; thereafter, it also includes "intermediate care facility services, all other."

Source

U.S. Social Security Administration, *Annual Statistical Supplement to the Social Security Bulletin,* published annually.

Documentation

See the text for Table Bd407–412 for information on the Medicaid program.

Series Bd415. Includes both cash assistance and medical assistance from Supplemental Security Income (SSI).

Series Bd416. Includes adults and children younger than 21 years of age.

TABLE Bd431–447 Medicaid vendor payments, by program or service: 1972–1996

Contributed by Richard H. Steckel

	Total	Persons 65 and older	For blindness	AFDC program recipients	Inpatient services: General hospitals	Inpatient services: Mental hospitals	Intermediate care facility services for the mentally retarded	Nursing facility services	Physicians' services	Dental services	Other practitioners' services	Outpatients hospital services	Clinic services	Laboratory and radiological services	Home health services	Prescribed drugs	Family planning services
	Bd431	Bd432	Bd433	Bd434	Bd435	Bd436	Bd437	Bd438 [1]	Bd439	Bd440	Bd441	Bd442	Bd443	Bd444	Bd445	Bd446	Bd447
Year	Million dollars	Million dollars	Million dollars	Million dollars	Million dollars	Million dollars	Million dollars	Million dollars	Million dollars	Million dollars	Million dollars	Million dollars	Million dollars	Million dollars	Million dollars	Million dollars	Million dollars
1972	6,299	1,925	45	2,101	2,557	113	—	1,472	794	170	59	365	41	81	24	512	—
1973	8,650	3,235	65	2,872	2,660	349	165	1,959	926	206	81	268	237	105	25	609	—
1974	9,983	3,691	80	3,398	2,887	406	203	2,002	1,083	265	101	322	284	96	31	713	—
1975	12,292	4,649	83	4,063	3,411	400	349	2,446	1,248	350	128	377	389	123	70	832	67
1976	14,292	5,192	86	4,598	3,938	527	602	2,488	1,389	382	149	556	341	147	134	957	87
1977	16,277	5,830	99	4,982	4,597	531	975	2,808	1,503	400	148	850	178	156	179	1,018	120
1978	17,966	6,420	102	5,342	4,985	651	1,162	3,094	1,596	395	146	832	196	179	210	1,084	115
1979	20,472	7,046	108	5,905	5,655	778	1,488	3,379	1,625	430	163	847	275	186	263	1,196	109
1980	23,311	8,739	124	6,354	6,412	775	1,989	3,685	1,875	462	198	1,101	320	121	332	1,318	81
1981	27,204	9,926	154	7,271	7,194	877	2,996	4,035	2,101	543	228	1,409	373	147	428	1,535	139
1982	29,399	10,739	172	7,566	7,670	974	3,467	4,427	2,086	492	226	1,438	400	160	496	1,599	133
1983	32,391	11,954	183	8,323	8,813	933	4,079	4,621	2,175	467	226	1,574	479	184	597	1,771	156
1984	33,891	12,815	219	8,373	8,848	1,042	4,256	4,810	2,220	469	232	1,646	594	207	774	1,968	164
1985	37,508	14,096	249	9,160	9,453	1,192	4,731	5,071	2,346	458	251	1,789	714	337	1,120	2,315	195
1986	41,005	15,097	277	10,004	10,373	1,107	5,084	5,660	2,542	533	246	1,968	820	410	1,353	2,706	246
1987	45,050	16,037	309	11,100	11,302	1,409	5,591	5,967	2,776	541	263	2,226	963	475	1,690	2,988	228
1988	48,710	17,135	344	11,731	12,076	1,375	6,022	6,354	2,953	577	284	2,413	1,105	543	2,015	3,294	206
1989	54,500	18,558	409	13,788	13,378	1,470	6,649	6,660	3,408	498	317	2,837	1,249	590	2,572	3,689	227
1990	64,859	21,508	434	17,690	16,674	1,714	7,354	8,026	4,018	593	372	3,324	1,688	721	3,404	4,420	265
1991	77,048	25,453	475	22,129	19,891	2,010	7,680	20,709	4,952	710	437	4,283	2,211	897	4,101	5,424	359
1992	90,814	29,078	530	26,676	23,503	2,196	8,550	23,544	6,102	851	538	5,279	2,818	1,035	4,886	6,765	500
1993	101,709	31,554	589	30,109	25,734	2,161	8,831	25,431	6,952	961	937	6,215	3,457	1,137	5,601	7,970	538
1994	108,270	33,618	644	30,887	26,180	2,057	8,347	27,095	7,189	969	1,040	6,342	3,747	1,176	7,042	8,875	516
1995	120,141	36,527	848	31,487	26,331	2,511	10,383	29,052	7,360	1,019	986	6,627	4,280	1,180	9,406	9,791	514
1996	121,685	36,947	869	29,816	25,176	2,040	9,555	29,630	7,238	1,028	1,094	6,504	4,222	1,208	10,868	10,697	474

[1] Category covers "skilled nursing facility services" through 1990; thereafter, it also includes "intermediate care facility services, all other."

Source

U.S. Social Security Administration, *Annual Statistical Supplement to the Social Security Bulletin,* published annually.

Documentation

See the text for Table Bd407–412 for information on the Medicaid program.

Series Bd434. Aid to Families with Dependent Children (AFDC).

INCIDENCE OF DISEASE

Richard H. Steckel

TABLE Bd448–462 Incidence rates of selected reportable diseases: 1912–1998

Contributed by Richard H. Steckel

	Tuberculosis	Syphilis	Gonorrhea	Malaria	Typhoid and paratyphoid fever	Scarlet fever and streptococcal sore throat	Hepatitis	Brucellosis	Diphtheria	Pertussis (whooping cough)	Measles	Meningococcal infections	Acute poliomyelitis	Smallpox	AIDS
	Bd448 [1, 2, 3]	Bd449	Bd450	Bd451	Bd452 [4]	Bd453 [5]	Bd454 [6]	Bd455	Bd456	Bd457	Bd458	Bd459	Bd460	Bd461	Bd462
Year	Per 100,000	Per 100,000	Per 100,000	Per 100,000	Per 100,000	Per 100,000	Per 100,000	Per 100,000	Per 100,000	Per 100,000	Per 100,000	Per 100,000	Per 100,000	Per 100,000	Per 100,000
1912	—	—	—	—	81.80	138.20	—	—	139.00	—	310.00	—	5.50	30.80	—
1913	—	—	—	—	84.20	143.10	—	—	142.10	—	368.50	3.40	4.00	55.70	—
1914	—	—	—	—	82.40	133.00	—	—	152.50	—	295.80	3.40	2.40	66.40	—
1915	—	—	—	—	74.00	108.60	—	—	132.70	—	254.10	2.90	3.10	50.20	—
1916	—	—	—	—	82.30	114.50	—	—	129.20	—	621.80	2.70	41.10	23.40	—
1917	—	—	—	—	63.00	139.20	—	—	133.00	—	611.60	6.20	4.90	52.70	—
1918	—	—	—	—	50.00	94.50	—	—	101.50	—	474.90	7.20	2.80	83.10	—
1919	—	113.20	147.80	—	42.90	118.30	—	—	144.70	—	203.20	3.10	2.30	63.80	—
1920	—	145.30	175.40	173.00	33.80	151.60	—	—	139.00	—	480.50	2.60	2.20	95.90	—
1921	—	172.30	177.70	174.70	43.50	178.70	—	—	190.70	—	274.50	2.20	5.80	94.70	—
1922	—	157.70	140.40	142.90	33.00	148.10	—	—	156.90	97.70	241.80	1.90	2.00	30.30	—
1923	—	156.20	142.20	124.20	31.00	158.80	—	—	131.40	146.70	680.00	1.90	3.10	27.60	—
1924	—	174.20	144.50	98.40	31.00	164.20	—	—	105.60	145.00	463.70	1.40	4.60	49.60	—
1925	—	181.20	149.30	86.80	40.00	161.90	—	—	82.10	131.20	194.30	1.50	5.30	34.20	—
1926	—	196.10	157.20	98.90	35.50	166.70	—	—	80.70	172.20	587.10	1.80	2.30	28.70	—
1927	—	171.90	140.70	118.20	29.20	179.80	—	—	89.80	152.40	387.60	2.60	8.80	31.60	—
1928	—	174.20	138.30	138.20	22.60	148.90	—	—	75.90	134.30	466.30	4.80	4.30	32.70	—
1929	—	169.20	135.40	134.70	19.10	152.90	—	—	70.10	162.10	300.60	8.70	2.40	34.70	—
1930	101.50	185.40	135.50	80.00	22.10	144.50	—	—	54.10	135.60	340.80	6.80	7.50	39.70	—
1931	100.70	197.40	137.00	56.70	21.40	166.30	—	—	57.10	139.10	382.80	4.40	12.80	24.40	—
1932	97.70	208.20	132.50	55.00	21.40	172.70	—	—	48.00	172.50	323.20	2.50	3.10	9.00	—
1933	91.10	193.40	121.40	100.00	18.60	174.40	—	1.40	40.20	142.60	319.20	2.30	4.00	5.20	—
1934	89.40	186.70	124.10	105.40	17.60	180.00	—	1.60	34.10	209.90	632.60	2.00	5.90	4.30	—
1935	87.90	205.60	130.80	108.10	14.40	211.00	—	1.60	30.80	141.90	584.60	4.60	8.50	6.30	—
1936	83.60	212.60	129.80	104.60	12.40	195.60	—	1.60	23.40	115.00	234.00	5.70	3.50	6.10	—
1937	87.20	264.30	143.40	84.20	12.40	183.50	—	2.10	22.20	166.60	249.60	4.30	7.40	9.10	—
1938	82.40	372.00	153.80	64.90	11.50	152.80	—	3.40	23.50	175.10	633.80	2.20	1.30	11.50	—
1939	79.40	367.10	139.80	63.20	10.00	132.30	—	2.70	18.40	140.00	308.20	1.50	5.60	7.50	—
1940	78.00	359.70	133.80	59.20	7.40	125.90	—	2.50	11.80	139.60	220.70	1.30	7.40	2.10	—
1941	79.30	368.20	146.70	51.10	6.50	104.70	—	2.60	13.50	166.90	671.70	1.50	6.80	1.00	—
1942	87.50	363.40	160.90	44.90	4.60	101.40	—	2.40	12.10	142.90	408.80	2.90	3.10	0.60	—
1943	89.60	447.00	213.60	40.60	4.10	112.00	—	2.80	11.00	142.90	472.00	13.60	9.30	0.60	—
1944	95.00	367.90	236.50	43.40	4.00	150.90	—	3.30	10.60	82.70	474.30	12.30	14.30	0.30	—
1945	86.80	282.30	225.80	47.40	3.70	140.10	—	3.80	14.10	101.00	110.20	6.20	10.30	0.30	—
1946	85.20	271.70	275.00	34.70	2.80	89.60	—	4.20	11.70	78.40	496.80	4.10	18.30	0.20	—
1947	94.10	264.60	284.20	10.50	2.80	65.20	—	4.40	8.50	109.10	155.00	2.40	7.50	0.10	—
1948	93.80	234.70	252.00	6.60	2.50	62.50	—	3.40	6.50	51.10	421.00	2.30	19.00	(Z)	—
1949	90.70	197.30	226.70	2.80	2.70	58.70	—	2.80	5.40	46.70	420.60	2.40	28.30	(Z)	—

Year	Tuberculosis	Syphilis	Gonorrhea	Malaria	Typhoid and paratyphoid fever	Scarlet fever and streptococcal sore throat	Hepatitis	Brucellosis	Diphtheria	Pertussis (whooping cough)	Measles	Meningococcal infections	Acute poliomyelitis	Smallpox	AIDS
	Bd448 [1, 2, 3]	Bd449	Bd450	Bd451	Bd452 [4]	Bd453 [5]	Bd454 [6]	Bd455	Bd456	Bd457	Bd458	Bd459	Bd460	Bd461	Bd462
	Per 100,000	Per 100,000	Per 100,000	Per 100,000	Per 100,000	Per 100,000	Per 100,000	Per 100,000	Per 100,000	Per 100,000	Per 100,000	Per 100,000	Per 100,000	Per 100,000	Per 100,000
1950	80.40	154.20	204.00	1.40	1.60	42.80	2.50	2.30	3.80	80.10	210.10	2.50	22.10	(Z)	—
1951	77.30	131.80	179.50	3.70	1.40	54.90	5.50	2.00	2.60	44.80	345.60	2.70	18.50	(Z)	—
1952	70.50	110.80	161.30	4.50	1.50	73.00	11.80	1.60	1.90	28.90	438.50	3.10	37.20	(Z)	—
1953	53.00	100.80	157.40	0.80	1.40	84.00	21.70	1.30	1.50	23.50	283.70	3.20	22.50	(Z)	—
1954	49.30	87.50	152.00	0.40	1.30	91.70	31.10	1.10	1.30	37.80	423.50	2.80	23.90	(Z)	—
1955	46.90	76.00	149.20	0.30	1.00	89.80	19.50	0.90	1.20	38.20	337.90	2.10	17.60	(Z)	—
1956	41.60	77.10	142.40	0.10	1.00	105.50	11.50	0.80	0.90	19.00	365.90	1.60	9.10	(Z)	—
1957	39.20	78.30	129.80	0.10	0.70	123.30	8.80	0.60	0.70	16.60	285.90	1.60	3.20	(Z)	—
1958	36.50	68.50	129.30	(Z)	0.60	152.40	9.40	0.50	0.50	18.60	440.50	1.50	3.30	(Z)	—
1959	32.50	69.30	137.10	(Z)	0.50	189.60	13.40	0.50	0.50	22.70	230.10	1.20	4.80	(Z)	—
1960	30.80	68.00	139.60	(Z)	0.50	175.80	23.40	0.40	0.50	8.30	245.40	1.30	1.80	(Z)	—
1961	29.40	69.70	147.80	(Z)	0.40	185.00	40.10	0.30	0.30	6.30	231.60	1.20	0.70	(Z)	—
1962	28.70	68.10	142.80	0.10	0.30	170.00	28.90	0.20	0.20	9.60	259.00	1.20	0.50	(Z)	—
1963	28.70	69.30	145.70	0.10	0.30	181.60	23.10	0.20	0.20	9.10	204.20	1.30	0.20	(Z)	—
1964	26.60	62.90	154.50	(Z)	0.30	210.60	20.00	0.20	0.20	6.80	239.40	1.50	0.10	(Z)	—
1965	25.30	59.70	163.80	0.10	0.20	204.30	17.70	0.10	0.10	3.50	135.10	1.60	(Z)	(Z)	—
1966	24.40	57.10	173.60	0.30	0.20	226.80	17.80	0.10	0.10	3.90	104.20	1.70	0.10	(Z)	—
1967	23.10	53.20	193.00	1.00	0.20	238.10	21.20	0.10	0.10	4.90	31.70	1.10	(Z)	(Z)	—
1968	21.30	49.90	219.20	1.20	0.20	226.30	25.70	0.10	0.10	2.40	11.10	1.30	(Z)	(Z)	—
1969	19.40	48.10	245.90	1.50	0.20	238.20	27.30	0.10	0.10	1.60	12.80	1.50	(Z)	(Z)	—
1970	18.30	43.80	285.20	1.50	0.20	239.20	32.00	0.10	0.20	2.10	23.20	1.20	(Z)	(Z)	—
1971	17.07	46.54	324.97	1.15	0.42	—	33.53	0.09	0.10	1.47	36.50	1.10	0.02	(Z)	—
1972	15.79	43.77	368.44	0.36	0.45	—	30.48	0.09	0.07	1.58	15.50	0.64	0.02	(Z)	—
1973	14.77	41.68	401.53	0.11	0.66	—	28.21	0.10	0.11	0.84	12.72	0.66	0.01	(Z)	—
1974	14.25	39.63	428.65	0.14	0.58	—	28.07	0.11	0.13	1.14	10.45	0.64	0.01	(Z)	—
1975	15.95	37.70	469.19	0.18	0.59	—	26.34	0.15	0.14	0.82	11.44	0.69	0.01	(Z)	—
1976	14.96	33.43	466.78	0.22	0.66	—	25.97	0.14	0.06	0.47	19.16	0.75	0.01	(Z)	—
1977	13.93	29.87	463.28	0.25	0.75	—	26.17	0.11	0.04	1.01	26.51	0.84	0.02	(Z)	—
1978	13.08	29.75	464.75	0.34	0.74	—	24.44	0.08	0.03	0.95	12.32	1.15	0.01	(Z)	—
1979	12.57	30.46	456.18	0.41	0.76	—	25.62	0.10	0.03	0.74	6.18	1.24	0.02	(Z)	—
1980	12.25	30.39	443.27	0.91	0.77	—	26.49	0.08	(Z)	0.76	5.96	1.25	(Z)	(Z)	—
1981	11.94	31.75	432.11	0.61	0.80	—	25.26	0.08	(Z)	0.54	1.36	1.54	(Z)	(Z)	—
1982	11.02	32.64	414.90	0.46	0.63	—	24.52	0.07	(Z)	0.82	0.74	1.32	(Z)	(Z)	(Z)
1983	10.19	31.90	384.83	0.35	0.72	—	24.13	0.09	(Z)	1.05	0.64	1.17	0.01	(Z)	(Z)
1984	9.42	29.59	372.02	0.43	0.54	—	24.37	0.06	(Z)	0.96	1.10	1.16	(Z)	(Z)	1.88
1985	9.30	28.30	381.76	0.44	0.48	—	24.92	0.06	(Z)	1.50	1.18	1.04	(Z)	(Z)	3.46
1986	9.44	28.30	373.68	0.47	0.49	—	23.69	0.04	(Z)	1.74	2.61	1.08	(Z)	(Z)	5.36
1987	9.25	35.56	320.83	0.39	0.43	—	23.54	0.05	(Z)	1.16	1.50	1.20	(Z)	(Z)	8.66
1988	9.13	42.08	292.72	0.45	0.45	—	23.10	0.04	(Z)	1.40	1.38	1.21	(Z)	(Z)	12.61
1989	9.46	44.94	297.36	0.51	0.44	—	25.81	0.04	(Z)	1.67	7.33	1.10	(Z)	(Z)	13.58
1990	10.33	53.80	276.60	0.52	0.48	—	22.82	0.03	(Z)	1.84	11.17	0.99	(Z)	(Z)	16.72
1991	10.42	51.69	249.48	0.51	0.45	—	18.73	0.04	(Z)	1.08	3.82	0.84	(Z)	(Z)	17.32
1992	10.46	45.30	201.60	0.43	0.36	—	18.09	0.04	(Z)	1.60	0.88	0.84	(Z)	(Z)	17.83
1993	9.82	39.70	172.40	0.55	0.35	—	16.68	0.05	(Z)	2.55	0.12	1.02	(Z)	(Z)	40.20
1994	9.36	32.00	168.40	0.47	0.35	—	17.05	0.05	(Z)	1.77	0.37	1.11	(Z)	(Z)	30.07
1995	8.70	26.20	149.50	0.55	0.37	—	18.10	0.04	(Z)	1.97	0.12	1.25	(Z)	(Z)	27.20
1996	8.04	19.97	122.80	0.68	0.47	—	17.12	0.05	(Z)	2.94	0.20	1.30	0.01	(Z)	25.21
1997	7.42	17.39	121.40	0.75	0.30	—	16.55	0.04	—	2.46	0.06	1.24	0.01	(Z)	21.85
1998	6.79	14.19	132.88	0.60	0.28	—	13.69	0.03	—	2.74	0.04	1.01	(Z)	(Z)	17.21

Notes appear on next page

(continued)

TABLE Bd448–462 Incidence rates of selected reportable diseases: 1912–1998 *Continued*

(Z) Series Bd451, fewer than 0.05 cases. Series Bd456, fewer than 0.005 cases. Series Bd460, fewer than 0.05 cases through 1970; fewer than 0.005 thereafter. Series Bd462, fewer than 0.005 cases.

[1] Changes in the reporting criteria cause the data after 1974 not to be comparable with those from 1974 and before.

[2] Prior to 1953, active and inactive cases; thereafter, new active cases only.

[3] Includes Alaska and Hawai'i for all years.

[4] Beginning in 1950, excludes paratyphoid fever.

[5] For 1912–1919, excludes streptococcal sore throat.

[6] For 1950–1952, infectious only; thereafter, infectious and serum. Reporting is incomplete.

Sources

For 1912–1919, U.S. Public Health Service, *Public Health Reports,* various issues; for 1920–1950, U.S. National Office of Vital Statistics, *Vital Statistics – Special Reports,* volume 37, number 9 (1953); for 1951–1970, U.S. Centers for Disease Control, *Morbidity and Mortality, Weekly Report,* Annual Supplement, Summary (1960 and 1970); for 1970–1988, U.S. Centers for Disease Control and Prevention, *Morbidity and Mortality, Weekly Report,* volume 37, number 54 (October 1989); for 1989–1998, U.S. Centers for Disease Control and Prevention, *Morbidity and Mortality, Weekly Report,* volume 47, number 53 (December 1999).

Documentation

The rates refer to the number of notifiable diseases occurring within the United States per 100,000 population. For 1920–1970, rates are based on the total resident population. Each state makes its own laws and regulations designating the diseases to be reported, the agencies and persons required to report, and penalties for failure to report. All states have entered voluntarily into a cooperative agreement to report to the federal government.

The notification of disease in the United States began in the colonial period on a local basis, particularly in port cities. It was usually limited to periods when epidemics of pestilential disease threatened or were in progress. Statewide notification was not required until 1883, when Michigan passed a law requiring physicians and householders to report certain diseases to health officers or boards of health. During the next three decades, all states made similar requirements.

In response to the need for nationwide statistical information on epidemic diseases, a law was passed in 1878 providing for the collection of such statistics. By 1912, data were supplied regularly by nineteen states and the District of Columbia on diphtheria, measles, poliomyelitis, scarlet fever, tuberculosis, typhoid fever, and smallpox. State health authorities now report weekly on twenty-five diseases and annually on about forty. Most states require the reporting of additional diseases.

The Public Health Service has changed its form of reporting several times, and some of the rates shown here do not appear in the published reports. Since the data were originally shown only for the individual states, a rate for the country was obtained for each disease by combining the information only for those states reporting it, the denominators being the population of the reporting states.

For trends of sickness and accident among groups of male and female industrial workers (1917–1950, for cases disabling for one day or longer, and 1921–1952, for cases disabling for eight days or longer), see W. M. Gafafer, "Industrial Sickness Absenteeism among Males and Females during 1950," *Public Health Reports* 66 (47) (November 1951): 1550–2. See also "Rates for Specific Causes in 1952 for the Year and Last Two Quarters Industrial Sickness Absenteeism," *Public Health Reports* 68 (11) (November 1953): 1052–5; and S. D. Collins, "Long-Time Trends in Illness and Medical Care," *Public Health Monograph* number 48 (1957), p. 32.

Civilian illness rates for the United States are not available for a long period. However, records of illness (admission to sick report) among the active-duty personnel of the U.S. Army are available back to 1819, and those for the U.S. Navy back to 1865. See U.S. Army, *Annual Reports of the Surgeon General on Medical Statistics,* and U.S. Navy, *Annual Reports of the Surgeon General on Medical Statistics*. For annual days sick per person, computed from army and navy data, see S. D. Collins, "Long-Time Trends in Illness and Medical Care," *Public Health Monograph* number 48 (1957), p. 37.

Series Bd449. Covers syphilis and its sequelae.

Series Bd452. Typhoid and paratyphoid fever include typhus fever borne by fleas (endemic-murine) and by ticks (Rocky Mountain spotted fever).

Series Bd453. Scarlet fever and streptococcal sore throat were not notifiable after 1970.

Series Bd454. After 1980, hepatitis includes infectious (hepatitis A) and serum (hepatitis B), as well as unspecified cases and cases of people who tested positive for antibody to hepatitis C virus but do not have hepatitis.

Series Bd461. The last reported case of smallpox was in 1949.

Series Bd462. Acquired immune deficiency syndrome (AIDS) was not a notifiable disease until 1984. The figures before 1984 represent cases reported to the Centers for Disease Control.

TABLE Bd463–476 AIDS cases reported, by age, sex, and race: 1981–1996[1]

Contributed by Richard H. Steckel

	Age								Sex		Race			
	Total	Under 5	5–12	13–29	30–39	40–49	50–59	60 and over	Male	Female	White non-Hispanic	Black non-Hispanic	Hispanic	Other
	Bd463	Bd464	Bd465	Bd466	Bd467	Bd468	Bd469	Bd470	Bd471	Bd472	Bd473	Bd474	Bd475	Bd476
Year	Number	Number	Number	Number	Number	Number	Number	Number	Number	Number	Number	Number	Number	Number
1981 [2]	858	—	13	202	399	178	61	5	799	59	482	253	119	4
1983	2,073	—	34	460	936	451	161	31	1,916	157	1,181	563	311	18
1984	4,448	—	50	962	2,118	923	313	82	4,155	293	2,696	1,114	605	33
1985	8,232	—	129	1,703	3,868	1,709	627	196	7,646	586	5,012	2,090	1,071	59
1986	13,169	—	186	2,825	6,122	2,689	969	378	12,117	1,052	7,889	3,381	1,780	119
1987	21,478	269	55	4,407	9,773	4,666	1,595	713	19,643	1,835	13,239	5,429	2,601	209
1988	30,657	440	124	6,306	14,105	6,532	2,134	1,016	27,375	3,282	17,029	9,123	4,232	273
1989	33,559	484	101	6,758	15,469	7,327	2,418	1,002	29,921	3,638	18,571	10,254	4,364	370
1990	41,639	583	142	8,160	18,844	9,731	2,929	1,250	36,766	4,873	22,327	13,200	5,669	443
1991	43,653	522	145	7,902	19,875	10,630	3,243	1,336	37,997	5,656	22,125	14,638	6,417	473
1992	45,839	613	137	8,011	20,601	11,599	3,432	1,446	39,507	6,332	22,455	16,053	6,771	560
1993	102,605	674	198	18,801	46,574	26,396	7,385	2,577	86,173	16,432	47,762	38,072	15,529	1,242
1994	77,561	747	220	13,045	34,966	20,617	5,905	2,061	63,684	13,877	32,928	31,103	12,620	910
1995	71,547	554	193	11,612	31,988	19,649	5,604	1,947	58,007	13,540	29,715	29,326	11,577	929
1996	66,886	485	175	10,159	29,990	18,891	5,321	1,865	53,293	13,593	26,324	28,764	10,865	933

[1] Year denotes year in which case was diagnosed. Age denotes age in year in which case was diagnosed.

[2] 1981–1982.

Source

U.S. Centers for Disease Control and Prevention, data published annually in U.S. Bureau of the Census, *Statistical Abstract of the United States.*

TABLE Bd477–484 HIV patients – hospital discharges, days of care, and average length of stay: 1984–1999

Contributed by Richard H. Steckel and Richard Sutch

	Discharges				Days of care		Average length of stay	
			Per 10,000 population					
	HIV patients	All patients	HIV patients	All patients	AIDS patients	All patients	AIDS patients	All patients
	Bd477	Bd478	Bd479	Bd480	Bd481	Bd482	Bd483	Bd484
Year	Thousand	Thousand	Per 10,000	Per 10,000	Thousand days	Thousand days	Days	Days
1984 [1]	10	37,162	0.4	1,585	123	244,652	12.1	6.6
1985 [1]	23	35,056	1.0	1,479	387	226,217	17.1	6.5
1986	44	34,256	1.8	1,437	714	218,496	16.4	6.4
1987	67	33,387	2.8	1,388	936	214,942	14.1	6.4
1988	95	31,146	3.9	1,283	1,277	203,678	13.4	6.5
1989	140	30,947	5.7	1,263	1,731	200,827	12.4	6.5
1990	146	30,788	5.8	1,223	2,188	197,422	14.9	6.4
1991	165	31,098	6.5	1,221	2,108	199,099	12.8	6.4
1992	194	30,951	7.5	1,202	2,136	190,386	11.0	6.2
1993	225	30,825	8.6	1,183	2,561	184,601	11.4	6.0
1994	234	30,843	8.9	1,173	2,317	177,179	9.9	5.7
1995	249	30,722	9.4	1,157	2,326	164,627	9.3	5.4
1996	227	30,545	8.5	1,140	2,123	159,883	9.4	5.2
1997	178	30,914	6.6	1,143	1,448	157,458	8.1	5.1
1998	189	31,827	6.9	1,165	1,503	160,914	8.0	5.1
1999	180	32,132	6.5	1,166	1,310	160,128	7.3	5.0

[1] Listed as data for patients with acquired immune deficiency syndrome (AIDS) as opposed to being HIV (human immunodeficiency virus) positive.

Source

Division of Health Care Statistics, National Center for Health Statistics; *Health, United States, 1993* and *2004* (U.S. Public Health Service).

Documentation

For all series, beginning in 1988, comparisons with data for earlier years should be made with caution as estimates of change may reflect improvements in data collection, rather than true changes in hospital use. These data exclude newborns and are based on civilian population as of July 1 in the respective year.

TABLE Bd485–489 Federal expenditures for HIV research, education, prevention, medical care, and cash assistance: 1982–1997

Contributed by Richard H. Steckel

	Total	Research	Education and prevention	Medical care	Cash assistance
	Bd485	Bd486	Bd487	Bd488	Bd489
Year	Million dollars	Million dollars	Million dollars	Million dollars	Million dollars
1982	8	4	3	1	—
1983	44	24	7	13	—
1984	104	47	15	36	6
1985	205	84	26	81	13
1986	507	193	84	197	33
1987	926	344	197	325	60
1988	1,591	659	367	467	98
1989	2,297	937	396	794	170
1990	3,064	1,142	486	1,187	249
1991	3,806	1,275	528	1,642	360
1992	4,498	1,311	518	2,061	608
1993	5,328	1,361	576	2,523	866
1994	6,329	1,561	619	3,051	1,098
1995	6,821	1,589	658	3,462	1,111
1996	7,522	1,653	635	4,087	1,147
1997 [1]	8,451	1,738	678	4,769	1,266

[1] Preliminary.

Source

Data from U.S. Public Health Service Budget Office, published annually in U.S. National Center for Health Statistics, *Health, United States* (Public Health Service).

Documentation

These data include revisions from earlier data as of the 1998 edition of *Health, United States*. Federal expenditures on human immunodefiency virus-related (HIV-related) activities are estimated at about 35–40 percent of total HIV-related expenditures that include, for example, expenditures covered by private health insurance, out-of-pocket costs to patients, and the states' share of Medicaid, public hospital, and other local expenditures.

TABLE Bd490–512 Cancer incidence rates: 1973–1996[1]

Contributed by Richard H. Steckel

	All cancers	Oral cavity and pharynx	Esophagus	Stomach	Colon/rectum	Liver and intrahepatic bile duct	Pancreas	Larynx	Lung and bronchus	Melanomas of skin	Breast (women)	Cervix uteri (women)
	Bd490	Bd491	Bd492	Bd493	Bd494	Bd495	Bd496	Bd497	Bd498	Bd499	Bd500	Bd501
Year	Per 100,000	Per 100,000	Per 100,000	Per 100,000	Per 100,000	Per 100,000	Per 100,000	Per 100,000	Per 100,000	Per 100,000	Per 100,000	Per 100,000
1973	320.0	11.3	3.4	10.2	46.4	2.3	9.9	4.5	42.5	5.7	82.4	14.2
1974	332.8	11.1	3.6	10.0	47.8	2.2	9.6	4.5	43.9	5.9	94.4	12.7
1975	332.7	11.4	3.5	9.2	47.4	2.2	9.5	4.5	45.3	6.7	88.1	12.4
1976	338.0	11.5	3.7	9.5	49.1	2.2	9.6	4.7	47.8	6.9	85.5	11.9
1977	337.6	11.1	3.5	9.1	49.5	2.2	9.5	4.5	48.9	7.6	84.1	10.9
1978	337.7	11.6	3.6	9.1	49.4	2.3	9.0	4.7	50.2	7.6	84.1	10.5
1979	341.3	12.1	3.7	9.4	49.3	2.2	9.2	4.8	50.9	8.1	85.6	10.6
1980	345.8	11.6	3.7	8.9	50.4	2.2	9.3	4.7	52.3	8.9	85.4	10.2
1981	352.0	11.8	3.5	8.8	50.9	2.4	9.3	4.8	53.9	9.4	88.8	9.0
1982	351.7	11.5	3.7	8.7	49.7	2.4	9.4	4.7	54.9	9.4	89.3	8.9
1983	357.5	11.6	3.7	8.6	50.4	2.4	9.8	4.8	55.0	9.3	93.3	8.8
1984	364.6	11.8	3.6	8.3	51.5	2.4	9.7	4.6	56.8	9.6	97.2	9.2
1985	372.5	11.5	3.8	8.1	52.8	2.6	9.6	4.9	56.1	10.8	104.1	8.5
1986	374.5	11.0	4.0	8.1	51.2	2.7	9.4	4.5	56.9	11.2	106.7	9.0
1987	387.7	11.6	3.9	8.1	49.8	2.8	9.3	4.7	58.5	11.4	113.2	8.3
1988	385.2	10.8	3.8	8.1	48.6	2.8	9.3	4.6	58.7	10.8	110.3	8.8
1989	388.1	10.7	3.7	8.0	48.8	3.0	9.0	4.5	58.0	11.6	106.7	8.9

Note appears at end of table

TABLE Bd490–512 Cancer incidence rates: 1973–1996 *Continued*

	All cancers	Oral cavity and pharynx	Esophagus	Stomach	Colon/rectum	Liver and intrahepatic bile duct	Pancreas	Larynx	Lung and bronchus	Melanomas of skin	Breast (women)	Cervix uteri (women)
	Bd490	Bd491	Bd492	Bd493	Bd494	Bd495	Bd496	Bd497	Bd498	Bd499	Bd500	Bd501
Year	Per 100,000	Per 100,000	Per 100,000	Per 100,000	Per 100,000	Per 100,000	Per 100,000	Per 100,000	Per 100,000	Per 100,000	Per 100,000	Per 100,000
1990	399.7	11.2	4.2	7.4	48.3	3.3	9.0	4.5	58.6	11.6	110.4	8.9
1991	417.3	10.8	3.9	7.7	47.3	3.6	9.0	4.2	59.6	12.3	112.0	8.4
1992	425.6	10.5	3.9	7.4	46.4	3.3	9.3	4.4	59.6	12.5	111.1	8.3
1993	412.1	10.9	4.0	7.2	45.3	3.7	8.7	3.9	57.9	12.4	108.9	8.1
1994	403.8	10.4	3.8	7.2	44.3	3.7	9.0	4.1	57.1	13.0	110.8	7.9
1995	395.2	10.0	3.7	6.6	42.9	3.6	8.7	3.8	56.2	13.5	111.6	7.4
1996	388.6	10.0	4.0	6.6	42.7	4.2	8.6	3.7	54.2	13.8	110.7	7.7

	Ovary (women)	Prostate gland (men)	Testis (men)	Urinary bladder	Kidney and renal pelvis	Brain and nervous system	Thyroid gland	Hodgkin's disease	Non-Hodgkin's lymphoma	All leukemias	All cancers in children 0–14 years old
	Bd502	Bd503	Bd504	Bd505	Bd506	Bd507	Bd508	Bd509	Bd510	Bd511	Bd512
Year	Per 100,000	Per 100,000	Per 100,000	Per 100,000	Per 100,000	Per 100,000	Per 100,000	Per 100,000	Per 100,000	Per 100,000	Per 100,000
1973	14.1	64.1	3.0	14.6	6.7	5.0	3.6	3.3	8.5	10.6	12.7
1974	14.7	65.6	3.3	15.8	6.3	5.1	4.0	3.1	8.9	10.8	13.0
1975	14.1	70.6	3.3	15.5	6.1	5.5	4.1	2.9	9.4	10.6	11.3
1976	13.7	73.5	3.2	15.8	6.9	5.4	4.2	2.6	9.5	11.2	12.9
1977	13.6	76.1	3.8	15.3	6.8	5.8	4.6	2.8	9.3	10.6	12.7
1978	13.2	75.1	3.2	16.1	6.7	5.4	4.3	2.7	10.0	10.6	13.0
1979	13.2	78.0	3.5	16.1	6.5	5.6	3.8	2.8	10.4	10.3	12.9
1980	13.3	79.8	4.0	16.5	6.8	5.8	3.7	2.6	10.5	10.7	12.7
1981	13.2	82.1	3.8	16.7	7.2	5.9	3.8	2.7	11.3	10.4	12.3
1982	13.4	82.2	4.0	16.1	7.1	5.8	4.0	2.8	11.2	10.9	12.8
1983	13.8	84.8	4.2	16.3	7.7	5.7	4.1	2.9	11.6	10.8	12.8
1984	14.1	84.6	4.0	16.9	7.8	5.6	4.2	2.9	12.6	10.9	13.7
1985	14.3	88.3	4.1	16.8	7.7	6.3	4.5	2.8	12.9	11.1	14.3
1986	12.9	91.4	4.3	17.1	8.2	6.2	4.6	2.6	13.1	10.7	14.0
1987	13.9	103.0	4.4	17.5	8.5	6.4	4.3	2.9	13.9	10.9	14.0
1988	14.9	106.2	4.1	16.9	8.5	6.2	4.3	2.9	14.2	10.6	13.2
1989	15.3	113.0	4.9	17.0	8.8	6.2	4.6	2.9	14.3	11.1	14.8
1990	15.2	132.5	4.5	17.1	8.9	6.5	4.7	2.9	15.3	10.5	14.0
1991	15.4	169.2	4.6	16.9	9.1	6.3	4.7	2.8	15.6	10.8	14.9
1992	15.0	190.8	4.6	17.2	9.2	6.3	5.1	2.8	15.3	10.6	13.4
1993	15.0	171.1	4.5	17.3	9.2	6.2	4.8	2.7	15.6	10.4	14.7
1994	14.5	148.4	4.9	16.9	9.7	6.0	5.3	2.7	16.3	10.2	14.0
1995	14.5	139.3	4.2	16.6	9.3	5.9	5.4	2.6	16.2	10.5	13.5
1996	14.1	135.7	4.6	16.2	9.4	5.8	5.5	2.6	15.5	9.7	14.1

[1] The year denotes year of diagnosis. Data is age-adjusted to the 1970 U.S. standard population. See text.

Source

National Cancer Institute, *SEER Cancer Statistics Review, 1973–1996* (1999). Available from the same source at the National Cancer Institute's Internet site.

As of the 1996 *Cancer Statistics Review,* data from 1975 to the present had been revised from early issues.

Documentation

Unless specified, includes males and females. Data collected by the Surveillance, Epidemiology, and End Results (SEER) program.

The cancer incidence rate (this table) is the number of new cases of cancer occurring in a specified population during a year. The cancer mortality rate (Table Bd513–535) is the number of deaths in a specified population during a year with cancer given as the underlying cause of death. Each rate is expressed as the number of cases per 100,000 of the specified population. The age-adjusted rate is a weighted average of the age-specific cancer incidence or mortality rates, where the weights are the proportion of persons in the corresponding age groups of a standard population. This has the effect of eliminating differences in age distributions of two populations as a factor in comparing their rates for all ages combined. For this table, the 1970 U.S. population is used as a standard.

The statistics outlined in the cancer statistics reports must be considered in light of changes in the factors that contribute to cancer incidence (for example, smoking), the manner in which the disease is detected (for example, changes in screening technology or practice), and the introduction of new treatment regimens. All of these changes have the potential to influence the data, which thereby serve as clues to the changes underway in the health care system.

TABLE Bd513–535 Cancer mortality rates: 1973–1996[1]

Contributed by Richard H. Steckel

	Total	Oral cavity and pharynx	Esophagus	Stomach	Colon/rectum	Liver and intrahepatic bile duct	Pancreas	Larynx	Lung and bronchus	Melanomas of skin	Breast (women)	Cervix uteri (women)
	Bd513	Bd514	Bd515	Bd516	Bd517	Bd518	Bd519	Bd520	Bd521	Bd522	Bd523	Bd524
Year	Per 100,000	Per 100,000	Per 100,000	Per 100,000	Per 100,000	Per 100,000	Per 100,000	Per 100,000	Per 100,000	Per 100,000	Per 100,000	Per 100,000
1973	161.5	3.7	3.1	7.5	21.8	2.3	8.9	1.3	34.3	1.5	26.5	4.4
1974	164.4	3.9	3.2	7.3	22.6	2.3	9.2	1.3	34.7	1.6	28.0	4.6
1975	163.4	3.7	3.3	7.5	22.0	2.2	9.4	1.4	35.5	1.6	27.6	3.8
1976	164.5	3.5	3.4	6.6	22.1	2.1	9.0	1.4	37.2	1.7	26.9	4.1
1977	164.0	3.7	3.5	6.5	22.2	2.2	8.9	1.5	37.4	1.7	28.0	3.5
1978	163.3	3.4	3.3	6.6	22.0	2.3	8.6	1.3	38.1	1.8	27.3	3.6
1979	164.4	3.9	3.1	6.6	21.8	2.4	8.7	1.3	39.4	1.8	26.2	3.2
1980	164.4	3.6	3.3	6.1	21.1	2.3	8.4	1.4	40.0	1.9	26.8	2.9
1981	164.2	3.5	3.5	6.2	20.6	2.4	8.5	1.4	40.2	2.0	27.1	3.1
1982	166.2	3.4	3.2	6.1	20.7	2.4	8.8	1.3	41.5	1.9	27.5	2.9
1983	166.3	3.4	3.3	5.7	19.6	2.6	8.7	1.4	42.5	1.9	26.8	2.8
1984	165.3	3.6	3.2	5.8	20.3	2.4	8.9	1.2	42.0	2.1	26.5	2.7
1985	168.0	3.2	3.2	5.6	20.8	2.5	8.6	1.3	43.4	1.9	27.9	2.7
1986	164.6	3.4	3.4	5.4	19.2	2.7	8.6	1.2	42.4	1.9	27.0	2.6
1987	164.3	2.9	3.5	5.1	19.0	2.7	8.3	1.2	43.7	2.1	27.7	2.4
1988	165.4	2.9	3.5	5.1	18.4	2.7	8.4	1.3	44.5	2.1	27.7	2.5
1989	166.9	3.2	3.5	5.0	18.7	2.9	8.4	1.2	44.8	2.0	27.5	2.7
1990	162.2	3.0	3.5	5.0	17.9	3.1	8.0	1.3	44.2	2.0	26.1	2.3
1991	165.9	2.9	3.4	4.9	17.3	3.1	8.4	1.3	45.7	2.2	26.9	2.4
1992	163.2	2.8	3.5	4.7	17.0	3.2	8.3	1.2	44.7	2.0	25.6	2.3
1993	161.5	2.7	3.4	4.6	16.8	3.5	8.3	1.2	44.4	2.1	24.9	2.2
1994	161.1	2.7	3.7	4.5	17.0	3.5	8.2	1.2	44.2	1.9	24.1	2.5
1995	157.5	2.5	3.4	4.2	16.1	3.6	8.1	1.1	43.4	2.0	25.0	2.0
1996	155.6	2.3	3.4	3.9	15.8	3.9	8.1	1.1	42.5	2.1	24.2	2.1

	Ovary (women)	Prostate gland (men)	Testis (men)	Urinary bladder	Kidney and renal pelvis	Brain and nervous system	Thyroid gland	Hodgkin's disease	Non-Hodgkin's lymphoma	All leukemias	All cancers in children 0–14 years old
	Bd525	Bd526	Bd527	Bd528	Bd529	Bd530	Bd531	Bd532	Bd533	Bd534	Bd535
Year	Per 100,000	Per 100,000	Per 100,000	Per 100,000	Per 100,000	Per 100,000	Per 100,000	Per 100,000	Per 100,000	Per 100,000	Per 100,000
1973	8.8	21.7	1.1	4.5	3.1	3.5	0.4	1.3	4.8	6.7	5.8
1974	8.7	21.2	0.7	4.3	3.1	4.1	0.5	1.2	5.0	6.7	5.9
1975	8.7	22.0	0.8	4.3	2.9	3.9	0.4	1.2	4.7	6.7	5.0
1976	9.1	23.4	0.7	4.2	2.9	4.0	0.4	1.0	4.8	6.8	4.7
1977	8.1	22.3	0.6	4.0	3.0	4.1	0.5	0.8	4.9	6.5	4.9
1978	8.2	23.3	0.5	4.0	3.1	3.7	0.4	0.9	5.1	6.5	4.3
1979	8.2	23.1	0.4	3.8	2.8	3.9	0.4	0.8	5.1	6.5	4.6
1980	7.9	23.3	0.5	3.7	2.8	4.0	0.4	0.8	5.3	6.6	4.2
1981	7.7	22.9	0.3	3.6	3.1	4.1	0.4	0.7	5.2	6.2	4.1
1982	7.8	23.4	0.4	3.5	3.0	4.3	0.3	0.7	5.5	6.6	4.3
1983	7.9	23.8	0.3	3.4	3.3	4.0	0.4	0.8	5.5	6.5	4.5
1984	7.2	22.9	0.3	3.6	3.2	3.9	0.4	0.7	5.6	6.4	3.6
1985	7.9	23.6	0.3	3.3	3.0	4.1	0.3	0.7	6.0	6.5	4.0
1986	8.1	24.2	0.2	3.2	3.0	4.1	0.4	0.6	6.3	6.1	4.1
1987	7.7	24.7	0.3	2.9	3.2	4.3	0.3	0.6	5.9	6.4	3.8
1988	8.3	24.3	0.2	3.2	3.2	4.1	0.4	0.5	5.9	6.2	3.6
1989	8.0	25.4	0.2	3.0	3.4	4.1	0.3	0.6	6.2	6.2	2.8
1990	7.6	25.5	0.2	3.2	3.3	4.1	0.3	0.5	6.3	6.1	3.3
1991	7.9	26.4	0.2	3.2	3.2	4.4	0.4	0.5	6.5	6.4	3.4
1992	7.7	26.3	0.2	3.1	3.2	4.0	0.4	0.5	6.6	6.2	2.8
1993	7.7	25.5	0.3	3.2	3.1	4.2	0.4	0.5	6.3	6.3	3.1
1994	8.0	25.5	0.3	3.0	3.3	3.9	0.4	0.5	6.9	6.2	2.6
1995	7.1	23.9	0.2	3.0	3.2	3.8	0.3	0.5	6.6	6.2	2.7
1996	7.1	23.3	0.2	3.0	3.4	4.0	0.3	0.4	6.8	6.1	2.5

[1] The year denotes year of diagnosis. Data is age-adjusted to the 1970 U.S. standard population. See text.

Source

National Cancer Institute, *SEER Cancer Statistics Review, 1973–1996* (1999). Available from the same source at the National Cancer Institute's Internet site.

Documentation

See the text for Table Bd490–512.

TABLE Bd536–558 Cancer survival rates: 1973–1991

Contributed by Richard H. Steckel

Year	All cancers	Oral cavity and pharynx	Esophagus	Stomach	Colon/rectum	Liver	Pancreas	Larynx	Lung and bronchus	Melanomas of skin	Breast (women)	Cervix uteri (women)
	Bd536	Bd537	Bd538	Bd539	Bd540	Bd541	Bd542	Bd543	Bd544	Bd545	Bd546	Bd547
	Percent	Percent	Percent	Percent	Percent	Percent	Percent	Percent	Percent	Percent	Percent	Percent
1973	46.3	50.0	4.2	13.9	46.7	3.6	3.7	61.1	11.0	71.8	72.0	65.0
1974	48.6	53.2	5.0	13.9	48.2	4.3	2.3	68.3	12.0	75.9	73.5	67.4
1975	49.7	52.6	4.0	15.1	49.4	3.3	2.8	63.4	12.1	81.0	75.4	68.8
1976	49.9	53.9	5.0	16.8	51.1	4.0	2.4	64.9	13.0	82.0	74.7	70.0
1977	49.9	51.5	5.8	15.8	51.2	3.5	2.0	70.9	13.1	81.6	75.2	69.8
1978	50.1	54.1	4.6	16.8	51.6	4.0	2.5	67.0	13.7	81.3	74.5	68.3
1979	49.9	52.4	4.7	17.0	52.6	3.5	2.8	63.5	13.5	82.8	74.4	66.9
1980	50.3	54.0	5.8	16.6	52.3	2.9	3.6	67.1	12.9	83.9	75.5	68.5
1981	51.2	53.3	6.9	17.6	55.5	1.9	2.9	69.2	13.3	80.0	76.1	67.4
1982	51.1	50.9	7.7	18.8	55.2	5.4	2.8	67.8	13.9	84.4	77.4	66.0
1983	51.8	52.2	6.4	17.2	55.6	4.8	3.7	69.0	14.1	83.6	76.8	69.7
1984	52.0	52.8	9.4	16.9	55.9	4.5	2.8	63.6	13.2	84.6	78.6	69.1
1985	53.2	54.0	9.1	17.8	58.9	6.9	3.2	68.0	13.7	85.2	78.8	66.6
1986	54.1	53.8	10.8	20.1	60.3	6.3	2.9	65.4	13.2	87.5	80.4	66.3
1987	55.3	54.2	9.0	18.5	59.8	6.8	4.2	67.9	13.3	86.4	83.2	67.3
1988	56.0	50.4	10.0	21.5	60.2	5.1	3.6	66.8	13.3	88.3	84.5	72.7
1989	56.6	51.4	10.1	21.2	60.8	3.4	3.2	63.8	13.9	86.7	84.6	70.9
1990	58.3	54.5	10.6	20.5	61.7	5.6	3.8	64.9	13.7	88.4	84.5	72.2
1991	60.2	51.9	12.3	21.2	62.2	6.2	4.8	67.0	14.0	88.6	84.9	68.3

Year	Ovary (women)	Prostate gland (men)	Testis (men)	Urinary bladder	Kidney and renal pelvis	Brain and nervous system	Thyroid gland	Hodgkin's disease	Non-Hodgkin's lymphoma	All leukemias	All cancers in children 0–14 years old
	Bd548	Bd549	Bd550	Bd551	Bd552	Bd553	Bd554	Bd555	Bd556	Bd557	Bd558
	Percent	Percent	Percent	Percent	Percent	Percent	Percent	Percent	Percent	Percent	Percent
1973	36.1	61.0	73.6	70.4	46.8	17.1	90.9	61.3	42.6	32.4	50.6
1974	38.1	63.7	74.0	71.7	48.9	19.1	88.6	67.7	45.1	35.9	53.1
1975	34.2	67.2	79.8	72.6	52.9	24.2	93.1	71.2	47.5	33.9	55.2
1976	37.8	69.2	81.5	73.2	52.0	23.2	93.9	74.6	48.5	33.4	58.0
1977	38.7	70.0	85.0	73.6	47.2	23.1	92.4	74.1	47.3	38.0	59.4
1978	38.6	70.7	87.3	76.0	54.5	25.2	92.9	74.0	48.8	38.4	63.4
1979	38.0	72.6	89.8	75.2	51.1	25.0	92.1	71.2	48.9	34.8	61.7
1980	39.1	72.4	89.0	75.9	55.5	24.4	93.7	74.8	50.6	38.6	62.4
1981	39.9	74.1	93.9	80.5	48.7	26.2	94.9	76.2	51.6	38.5	64.4
1982	38.0	73.6	92.3	77.3	50.7	25.2	94.0	72.5	51.4	38.6	67.8
1983	42.5	74.1	90.9	77.3	54.3	24.3	94.3	77.9	53.8	39.6	67.3
1984	40.5	74.3	89.9	78.3	56.3	29.4	92.7	78.4	54.2	39.1	66.0
1985	39.7	75.8	92.5	77.1	56.2	25.9	93.0	80.0	53.2	42.0	69.6
1986	38.3	77.7	95.5	78.9	54.6	29.3	94.5	78.6	51.2	41.6	68.2
1987	39.0	81.0	95.3	80.1	58.1	30.5	95.7	79.1	53.0	41.2	69.5
1988	48.1	83.7	94.5	80.1	57.9	31.3	95.2	80.2	52.4	44.2	72.3
1989	47.6	85.5	94.7	80.8	57.2	28.8	94.2	80.6	50.7	43.3	71.3
1990	50.7	89.4	96.1	81.0	60.8	29.7	95.6	81.9	50.7	44.1	73.5
1991	49.6	93.6	95.1	80.4	61.3	33.0	94.6	80.3	51.3	42.5	74.2

Source

National Cancer Institute, *SEER Cancer Statistics Review, 1973–1996* (1999). Available from the same source at the National Cancer Institute's Internet site.

Documentation

Unless specified, series includes males and females. Data collected by the Surveillance, Epidemiology, and End Results (SEER) program.

Figures are five-year relative survival rates. Because a high percentage of cancer occurs in persons 65 years of age or older, many of these individuals die of causes other than their cancer. The relative survival rate corrects for normal mortality by taking the ratio of the observed survival rate for the patient group to the expected survival rate for persons in the general population similar to the patient group with respect to age, sex, race, and calendar year of observation. Thus, because it is obtained by normalizing observed survival for the average life expectancy of the general population of the same age, the relative survival rate is a measure of the influence of cancer on normal life expectancy.

The statistics outlined in the cancer statistics reports must be considered in light of changes in the factors that contribute to cancer incidence (for example, smoking), the manner in which the disease is detected (for example, changes in screening technology or practice), and the introduction of new treatment regimens. All of these changes have the potential to influence the data, which thereby serve as clues to the changes underway in the health care system.

NUTRITION AND HEALTH-RELATED BEHAVIORS

Richard H. Steckel

TABLE Bd559–567 Indexes of per capita consumption of food and selected nutrients: 1909–1970

Contributed by Richard H. Steckel

	Food	Food (use)	Pounds of food	Daily calories	Protein	Fat	Carbohydrates	Iron	Ascorbic acid
	Bd559	Bd560	Bd561	Bd562	Bd563	Bd564	Bd565	Bd566	Bd567
Year	Index 1967 = 100	Index 1967 = 100	Index 1967 = 100	Index 1967 = 100	Index 1967 = 100	Index 1967 = 100	Index 1967 = 100	Index 1967 = 100	Index 1967 = 100
1909	85	—	113	110	106	85	133	90	97
1910	83	—	111	109	104	83	133	89	99
1911	84	—	109	108	103	84	131	88	92
1912	85	—	113	108	104	83	131	88	96
1913	83	—	110	108	102	83	131	86	95
1914	83	—	109	107	100	85	129	84	93
1915	82	—	110	107	99	84	129	85	97
1916	81	—	105	105	98	84	126	83	89
1917	81	—	106	104	98	81	126	85	91
1918	83	—	109	105	99	86	124	89	94
1919	84	—	107	107	99	87	128	88	93
1920	83	—	108	102	95	82	123	85	96
1921	80	—	105	100	93	81	118	82	96
1922	85	—	109	107	96	86	129	84	96
1923	87	—	109	107	98	90	125	86	101
1924	87	92	110	108	98	90	127	85	100
1925	86	91	109	107	97	89	127	83	98
1926	88	92	110	108	96	89	128	84	96
1927	87	90	108	108	97	89	128	84	97
1928	87	89	109	109	96	90	129	84	97
1929	87	90	110	108	96	91	126	83	103
1930	86	89	108	107	95	89	127	83	95
1931	86	89	108	106	94	90	123	82	101
1932	84	87	105	103	93	89	120	80	99
1933	84	88	104	102	92	89	117	79	97
1934	85	89	104	102	93	89	115	81	100
1935	83	85	105	100	90	85	117	78	104
1936	86	88	106	102	93	89	117	81	101
1937	86	89	106	102	92	89	116	79	102
1938	86	88	106	102	92	89	116	80	106
1939	89	91	108	104	94	93	118	81	107
1940	91	93	108	104	95	95	115	83	106
1941	93	95	110	106	96	96	119	84	106
1942	92	94	110	103	99	93	114	90	108
1943	93	97	111	105	102	95	115	94	106
1944	96	100	114	104	101	95	114	102	116
1945	97	101	115	103	104	92	112	104	116
1946	99	103	115	103	104	95	110	106	114
1947	97	100	112	102	99	95	110	100	110
1948	94	96	107	100	96	93	106	95	104
1949	94	95	106	100	96	93	107	95	101
1950	95	96	105	102	96	97	108	96	97
1951	94	95	105	98	95	93	105	94	99
1952	95	96	104	99	96	95	104	94	97
1953	96	97	104	99	97	95	103	95	98
1954	96	97	103	98	96	95	102	93	97
1955	97	99	103	99	97	97	101	94	98
1956	98	100	103	99	98	97	101	95	97
1957	96	98	102	97	97	94	100	94	99
1958	95	96	101	97	96	95	101	94	94
1959	97	98	101	99	97	98	101	94	98
1960	96	96	101	98	97	95	101	95	100
1961	96	97	100	97	97	95	100	95	99
1962	96	96	99	97	96	95	100	95	99
1963	97	98	99	98	98	97	99	96	94
1964	98	98	99	99	99	99	100	97	93

TABLE Bd559–567 Indexes of per capita consumption of food and selected nutrients: 1909–1970 *Continued*

	Food	Food (use)	Pounds of food	Daily calories	Protein	Fat	Carbohydrates	Iron	Ascorbic acid
	Bd559	Bd560	Bd561	Bd562	Bd563	Bd564	Bd565	Bd566	Bd567
Year	Index 1967 = 100	Index 1967 = 100	Index 1967 = 100	Index 1967 = 100	Index 1967 = 100	Index 1967 = 100	Index 1967 = 100	Index 1967 = 100	Index 1967 = 100
1965	97	97	99	98	98	97	99	95	94
1966	98	98	99	99	99	98	99	96	94
1967	100	100	100	100	100	100	100	100	100
1968	101	102	101	102	101	103	101	99	98
1969	102	102	101	102	102	103	102	100	100
1970	103	102	101	103	102	105	102	103	105

Sources

Series Bd559–562, U.S. Department of Agriculture, Economic Research Service, *Food Consumption, Prices, and Expenditures,* Agricultural Economics Report number 135, and its *Supplement* (both 1971), Tables 1, 5, 6, and 35.

Series Bd563–567, U.S. Department of Agriculture, Economic Research Service, *Food Consumption, Prices, and Expenditures,* Agricultural Economics Report number 138, and its *Supplement* (both 1971), Table 38; and National Food Situation, NFS-142 (1972), Table 10.

Documentation

This table was expanded into four separate tables when updated in 1970. The recent information concerning per capita food and nutrient consumption is reported in Tables Bd568–622. These tables have not converted the per capita figures into an index but, rather, have kept the original figures in the units in which the foods and nutrients were consumed (for example, pounds or milligrams).

Three methods are commonly used to measure the total amount of food consumed, or otherwise "disappearing," through the marketing system. Total food consumed is measured in terms of its monetary value, physical weight, or nutritive value.

Civilian disappearance, the residual from all other known uses, normally is the estimate of annual U.S. civilian food consumption. This estimate is usually derived from supply and utilization "balance sheets," which summarize production, imports, and beginning stocks, and then deduct exports, all known nonfood uses, military procurement, and end-of-year inventories of each commodity. The residual, after adjustment for marketing losses up to the retail level, is assumed to have been consumed for food.

The food consumption and food use indexes are based on roughly the same kind of data. But development of the food consumption index at the retail rather than the farm level introduces variations among products in farm-retail marketing margins into its weighting scheme. Consequently, crop products are more heavily weighted in the food consumption index than in the food use index. See Tables 4 and 93 in *Food Consumption, Prices, and Expenditures,* Agricultural Economics Report number 135, and its *Supplement* (both 1971).

Shifts in consumption are reflected in these indexes. A one-pound increase in consumption of a relatively high-priced food (meat, for example) and a simultaneous one-pound decrease in consumption of a relatively low-priced food (potatoes, for example) would result in an increase in both indexes. Major differences in the forms in which food is sold affect the food consumption index. For example, fruits and vegetables sold fresh and those sold in processed form are weighted separately. Accordingly, the index reflects, to a limited extent, the trend toward consumption of more highly processed foods.

The food use index tends to reflect changes in the form of agricultural commodities sold by farmers. Instead of weighting individual food items on the basis of price, as is done in the food consumption index, the food use index weights food groups, such as dairy products, fruits, and vegetables. This difference makes the food consumption index more sensitive to smaller shifts in food consumption patterns than the food use index.

Series Bd559. This index measures per capita consumption (civilian, beginning in 1941) of quantities of individual foods measured in pounds equivalent to the form sold at retail food stores. The quantities used for this series have been combined into indexes on the basis of average 1947–1949 retail prices through 1954 and 1957–1959 prices thereafter; the indexes are linked at 1955. Component indexes for individual groups of animal and crop products are presented in the source (Table 1).

Series Bd560. In concept, this index parallels the food consumption index, except that it combines farm products ultimately used for food (farm weight or an equivalent), weighted by constant prices received by farmers, or an equivalent. It is a component of the system of index numbers that integrates the entire supply and utilization of farm commodities at the farm level (see Tables 91–93 in the source). It is not available in as much detail as the food consumption index but serves as a check on it.

Series Bd561. This index was based on data presented in pounds in the source (Table 6). Pounds of the various foods consumed are totaled on the basis of retail weight, or an equivalent, to achieve consistency in aggregating grossly different foods. Nevertheless, the different forms in which food is marketed and the problems of summing pounds of liquids, solids, and concentrated products make changes in these data difficult to interpret. Quantities of food consumed are roughly equivalent to the weight of food sold (or at least salable) by retail food stores. No aggregation of pounds at the farm level has been made, partly because of the problem of allocating joint raw farm products among various ultimate food and nonfood uses.

Series Bd562. This index was computed from data presented in calories of food energy available for consumption per capita per day in the source (Table 35). These data were in turn based on estimates of per capita food consumption (retail weight), including estimates of the produce of home gardens. No deduction was made for loss or waste of food in the home or use for pet food.

Series Bd563–567. These indexes were computed from data presented in the source in terms of grams and milligrams. The nutritive value of food is measured by the amount of food energy, protein, fat, carbohydrate, and several vitamins and minerals it contains. The data on nutrients are derived by applying composition values to food consumption data reported in terms of retail weight equivalents. Allowances are made for bones, rinds, and peelings, but not for bruises and rot. No deduction is made for nutrient losses that occur in household storage and meal preparation. Quantities of food discarded as plate waste or fed to pets are not deducted. As a result, these data overstate nutrients actually ingested. For additional data on other nutrients, see source. *Food Consumption, Prices, and Expenditures,* Agricultural Economics Report number 135, and its *Supplement* (both 1971).

TABLE Bd568–580 Per capita food consumption – meats, dairy products, fruits, and vegetables: 1970–1996

Contributed by Richard H. Steckel

	Meat and eggs				Dairy products					Fruits and vegetables			
	Red meat	Poultry	Fishery products	Eggs	All	Fluid milk and cream	Butter	Whole- and part-skim-milk cheese	Cottage cheese	Fresh fruits	Processed fruits	Fresh vegetables	Processed vegetables
	Bd568 [1]	Bd569 [1]	Bd570 [1]	Bd571	Bd572 [1]	Bd573	Bd574	Bd575 [1]	Bd576	Bd577	Bd578	Bd579	Bd580
Year	Pounds	Pounds	Pounds	Number	Pounds	Pounds	Pounds	Pounds	Pounds	Pounds	Pounds	Pounds	Pounds
1970	192.4	48.2	11.7	275.9	563.8	275.1	5.4	11.4	5.2	101.2	127.8	152.9	182.5
1971	197.5	48.5	11.5	274.0	557.9	275.6	5.2	12.0	5.3	100.3	133.1	146.7	191.6
1972	191.4	50.5	12.5	267.6	559.6	273.5	5.0	13.0	5.4	94.8	129.2	149.9	186.7
1973	176.2	48.2	12.7	257.0	554.8	268.9	4.8	13.5	5.2	96.4	131.4	146.6	187.1
1974	188.3	48.3	12.1	249.4	535.0	260.3	4.5	14.4	4.6	95.6	132.9	144.5	188.6
1975	181.1	47.1	12.1	245.4	539.1	261.3	4.7	14.3	4.6	101.8	144.5	147.1	189.9
1976	191.0	50.8	12.9	237.3	539.7	260.1	4.3	15.5	4.7	101.5	149.1	146.4	200.9
1977	189.7	51.5	12.6	231.1	540.2	257.5	4.3	16.0	4.7	99.7	163.7	147.0	196.9
1978	182.4	53.5	13.4	237.2	544.3	253.8	4.4	16.8	4.7	103.4	148.0	141.8	191.5
1979	177.5	57.5	13.0	241.1	548.2	250.5	4.5	17.2	4.5	100.1	145.0	146.8	192.6
1980	179.9	58.7	12.4	236.2	543.2	245.5	4.5	17.5	4.5	104.8	153.1	149.3	187.2
1981	177.6	61.0	12.6	232.2	540.6	241.7	4.2	18.2	4.3	103.6	152.6	142.8	189.7
1982	170.1	62.0	12.4	230.2	554.6	235.6	4.3	19.9	4.2	107.4	147.6	148.6	185.7
1983	175.7	63.6	13.3	225.1	572.9	235.9	4.9	20.6	4.1	110.0	161.0	148.5	188.6
1984	175.1	65.5	14.1	222.8	581.9	237.6	4.9	21.5	4.1	112.6	147.4	154.0	200.7
1985	176.7	67.9	15.0	216.5	593.7	240.8	4.9	22.5	4.1	110.6	153.0	156.1	201.9
1986	174.0	71.0	15.4	214.4	591.5	240.3	4.6	23.1	4.1	117.3	153.4	156.2	202.6
1987	169.8	76.7	16.1	210.5	601.2	238.4	4.7	24.1	3.9	121.6	155.4	162.4	201.6
1988	173.1	79.5	15.1	202.4	582.5	234.4	4.5	23.7	3.9	120.6	150.2	167.4	195.8
1989	167.5	84.1	15.6	192.7	563.8	236.2	4.4	23.8	3.6	123.0	141.4	172.3	206.1
1990	162.5	87.9	15.0	186.3	568.5	233.4	4.4	24.6	3.4	116.5	144.1	166.2	220.3
1991	162.4	91.3	14.8	183.0	565.7	233.1	4.4	25.0	3.3	113.2	151.6	163.3	226.6
1992	165.3	94.7	14.7	180.7	565.9	230.5	4.4	26.0	3.1	123.6	138.7	171.3	223.5
1993	162.4	96.6	14.9	179.1	574.0	225.7	4.7	26.2	2.9	124.9	153.4	172.3	228.9
1994	166.6	98.3	15.1	176.9	585.8	226.3	4.8	26.8	2.8	126.5	153.9	175.9	227.7
1995	166.6	98.1	14.9	173.9	584.1	223.2	4.5	27.3	2.7	126.1	154.8	173.5	231.5
1996	162.8	100.3	14.7	174.2 [2]	—	—	—	—	—	—	—	—	—

[1] Computed from unrounded data.

[2] Based on preliminary estimates.

Source

U.S. Department of Agriculture (USDA), *Food Consumption, Prices, and Expenditures, 1970–1995,* Economic Research Service Statistical Bulletin number 939 (1996).

Documentation

The USDA's Economic Research Service annually calculates the amount of food available for human consumption in the United States. This is the only source of time-series data on food and nutrient availability in the country.

The food supply series is based on records of commodity flows from production to end uses. This involves the development of supply and utilization balance sheets for each major commodity from which human foods are produced. Total available supply is the sum of production, beginning inventories, and imports. These three components are either directly measurable or estimated by government agencies using sampling and statistical methods.

The availability of food for human use represents the disappearance of food into the marketing system. Hence, it is often referred to as food disappearance. Per capita food consumption usually is calculated by dividing total food disappearance by the U.S. total population, including the armed forces overseas, on July 1 of each year.

Per capita measures are based on U.S. total population, except series Bd573, which uses U.S. resident population.

Series Bd568. Figures based on carcass weight. Beef-carcass weight is the weight of the chilled hanging carcass, which includes the kidneys and attached internal fat (kidney, pelvic, and heart fat (KPH)), but not the head, feet, and unattached internal organs. Definitions of carcass weight for other red meats differ slightly.

Series Bd569. Ready-to-cook poultry weight is the entire dressed bird, which includes bones, skin, fat, liver, gizzard, and neck.

Series Bd570. The figures are calculated on the basis of raw edible meat, that is, excluding such offal as bones, viscera, and shells.

Series Bd571. Excludes shipments to U.S. territories.

Series Bd572. "USDA donations" and "commercial sales" available separately in the original source.

Series Bd573. Fluid milk figures are aggregates of commercial sales and milk produced and consumed on farms, including whole, lowfat, and skim milk; cream; half-and-half; yogurt; sour cream; and eggnog. Data for these products individually are available in the original source.

Series Bd574. Natural equivalent of cheese and cheese products. Excludes full-skim American and cottage, pot, and baker's cheese. "American" and "other" available separately in original source.

Series Bd577. Includes oranges, tangerines, tangelos, lemons, limes, grapefruits, apples, apricots, avocados, bananas, cantaloupes, cherries, cranberries, grapes, honeydews, kiwifruits, mangoes, nectarines, peaches, pears, pineapples, papayas, plums, strawberries, and watermelons.

Series Bd578. Includes apples, grapes (excluding wine grapes), pineapples, peaches, pears, strawberries, and citrus fruits.

Series Bd579. Includes artichokes, asparagus, snap beans, broccoli, Brussels sprouts, cabbage, carrots, cauliflower, celery, sweet corn, cucumber, eggplant, escarole/endive, garlic, iceberg lettuce, leaf lettuce, lima beans (beginning in 1992), mushrooms, onions, bell peppers, potatoes, radishes, romaine, spinach, sweet potatoes, and tomatoes.

TABLE Bd581–589 Per capita food consumption – beverages: 1970–1995

Contributed by Richard H. Steckel

Year	Milk	Tea	Coffee	Bottled water	Carbonated soft drinks	Selected fruit juices	Beer	Wine	Distilled spirits
	Bd581	Bd582	Bd583	Bd584	Bd585	Bd586	Bd587	Bd588	Bd589
	Gallons	Gallons	Gallons	Gallons	Gallons	Gallons	Gallons	Gallons	Gallons
1970	31.3	6.8	51.0	—	24.3	5.7	28.1	2.0	2.8
1971	31.3	7.2	48.9	—	25.5	5.7	28.6	2.2	2.8
1972	31.0	7.3	50.4	—	26.2	6.2	28.8	2.4	2.8
1973	30.5	7.4	49.4	—	27.6	6.0	29.7	2.4	2.9
1974	29.5	7.5	48.8	—	27.6	6.0	30.7	2.4	2.9
1975	29.5	7.5	45.7	—	28.2	6.6	31.0	2.5	2.9
1976	29.3	7.7	46.8	1.2	30.8	6.9	30.9	2.5	2.8
1977	29.0	7.5	34.9	1.3	33.0	7.0	31.8	2.6	2.8
1978	28.6	7.2	38.7	1.9	34.2	6.5	32.4	2.8	2.8
1979	28.2	6.9	41.1	2.2	34.7	6.8	33.3	2.8	2.8
1980	27.6	7.3	37.2	2.4	35.1	7.2	33.7	2.9	2.7
1981	27.1	7.2	36.0	2.7	35.4	7.4	34.0	3.0	2.7
1982	26.4	6.9	35.7	3.0	35.3	6.8	33.5	3.0	2.6
1983	26.3	7.0	36.0	3.4	35.2	8.4	33.1	3.1	2.5
1984	26.4	7.1	36.5	4.0	35.9	7.3	32.6	3.2	2.5
1985	26.7	7.1	37.3	4.5	35.7	7.7	32.3	3.3	2.4
1986	26.5	7.1	37.3	5.0	35.8	7.8	32.6	3.3	2.2
1987	26.3	6.9	36.2	5.7	41.9	8.3	32.4	3.2	2.2
1988	25.8	7.0	34.6	6.5	44.7	7.9	32.1	3.0	2.1
1989	26.0	6.9	35.4	7.4	45.4	8.2	31.7	2.9	2.0
1990	25.7	6.9	36.2	8.0	46.3	7.3	32.7	2.7	2.0
1991	25.7	7.4	36.2	8.0	47.9	7.8	31.2	2.5	1.9
1992	25.3	8.1	35.1	8.2	48.5	7.3	30.8	2.5	1.9
1993	24.7	8.4	31.7	9.4	50.2	8.5	30.6	2.4	1.8
1994	24.8	8.2	28.6	10.7	51.4	8.7	30.5	2.4	1.7
1995	24.3	8.0	27.8	11.6	51.2	8.7	29.9	2.4	1.7

Source

U.S. Department of Agriculture, *Food Consumption, Prices, and Expenditures, 1970–1995,* Economic Research Service Statistical Bulletin number 939 (1996).

Documentation

See the text for Table Bd568–580.

Soft drinks and alcoholic beverage consumption per capita figures constructed by the Economic Research Service are based on industry data. Milk, soft drink, fruit drink, and alcoholic beverage measures are based on the U.S. resident population as of July 1 of the respective year. Coffee, tea, and fruit juice measures are based on the U.S. total population as of July 1 of the respective year.

Series Bd581. Computed from unrounded data.

Series Bd582. Fluid equivalent conversion factor is 200 six-ounce cups per pound of tea, dry leaf equivalent.

Series Bd583. Includes instant and decaffeinated coffee. Converted to fluid equivalent on the basis of 60 six-ounce cups per pound of regular roasted coffee and 187.5 six-ounce cups per pound of instant coffee. This series includes only people 18 years and older.

Series Bd587. Includes resident population who are 18 years and older.

Series Bd588. Beginning in 1983, includes wine coolers.

TABLE Bd590–597 Per capita food consumption – flour, corn, sugar, sweeteners, and confections: 1970–1995

Contributed by Richard H. Steckel

Year	Wheat flour	Corn products	Flour and cereal	Cane and beet sugar deliveries	Sweeteners: Corn	Sweeteners: Caloric	Sweeteners: Low-calorie	Candy and confectionery products
	Bd590	Bd591	Bd592	Bd593	Bd594	Bd595	Bd596	Bd597
	Pounds	Pounds	Pounds	Pounds	Pounds	Pounds	Pounds	Pounds
1970	110.9	11.1	135.6	101.8	19.1	122.3	5.8	19.9
1971	110.5	10.4	135.1	102.1	19.9	123.4	5.1	19.5
1972	109.8	9.7	133.1	102.3	21.2	125.0	5.1	19.1
1973	112.8	9.8	136.3	100.8	23.4	125.6	5.1	18.6
1974	111.0	10.2	135.5	95.7	25.1	121.9	5.9	17.8
1975	114.5	10.8	139.1	89.2	27.4	118.0	6.1	17.1
1976	119.1	11.0	143.0	93.4	29.2	123.9	6.1	16.9
1977	115.5	12.2	140.9	94.2	31.1	126.6	6.6	16.8
1978	115.2	12.4	138.9	91.4	31.7	124.6	6.9	16.6
1979	116.4	12.8	144.1	89.3	34.9	125.7	7.3	16.4

(continued)

TABLE Bd590–597 Per capita food consumption – flour, corn, sugar, sweeteners, and confections: 1970–1995 *Continued*

	Wheat flour	Corn products	Flour and cereal	Cane and beet sugar deliveries	Sweeteners			Candy and confectionery products
					Corn	Caloric	Low-calorie	
	Bd590	Bd591	Bd592	Bd593	Bd594	Bd595	Bd596	Bd597
Year	Pounds	Pounds	Pounds	Pounds	Pounds	Pounds	Pounds	Pounds
1980	116.9	12.9	144.7	83.6	38.2	123.0	7.7	16.1
1981	115.8	13.3	145.6	79.4	41.6	122.2	8.2	16.3
1982	116.9	13.8	147.9	73.7	45.4	120.4	9.5	16.9
1983	117.7	14.7	147.7	70.3	50.3	121.9	13.0	17.8
1984	119.1	16.0	148.9	66.7	56.6	124.6	15.8	18.5
1985	124.6	17.2	156.4	62.7	64.8	128.8	18.1	18.8
1986	125.6	19.4	162.2	60.0	65.5	127.0	18.5	18.7
1987	129.8	21.7	171.4	62.4	67.7	131.6	19.1	18.8
1988	131.7	21.7	175.5	62.1	69.3	132.7	20.0	19.4
1989	129.6	21.8	174.5	62.8	69.0	133.1	20.3	19.9
1990	136.0	21.9	182.0	64.4	71.1	137.0	22.2	20.3
1991	136.9	22.0	183.6	63.8	72.8	138.0	24.3	20.7
1992	138.8	22.1	186.2	64.6	75.2	141.2	—	21.3
1993	143.3	22.3	191.0	64.3	78.7	144.4	—	21.8
1994	144.5	22.5	194.1	65.0	81.0	147.3	—	22.5
1995	141.7	22.7	192.4	65.5	83.2	150.0	—	23.4

Source

U.S. Department of Agriculture, *Food Consumption, Prices, and Expenditures, 1970–1995,* Economic Research Service Statistical Bulletin number 939 (1996).

Documentation

See the text for Table Bd568–580.

Series Bd591 and Bd594–596. Based on Census of Manufactures data. The original source also offers data on corn sugar and corn syrup.

Series Bd592. Computed from unrounded data.

Series Bd593. Figures based on refined weight. Sugar consumption is total U.S. sugar (cane and beet) deliveries for food and beverages. It does not include sugar imported in blends and mixtures.

Series Bd597. Based on domestic disappearance.

TABLE Bd598–622 Daily per capita food consumption – calories, carbohydrates, protein, fat, cholesterol, and nutrients: 1970–1994

Contributed by Richard H. Steckel

	Food energy	Carbo-hydrates	Protein	Fat				Cholesterol	Micronutrients				
				Total	Saturated	Mono-unsaturated	Poly-unsaturated		Vitamin A	Carotenes	Vitamin E	Vitamin C	Thiamin
	Bd598	Bd599	Bd600	Bd601	Bd602	Bd603	Bd604	Bd605	Bd606	Bd607	Bd608	Bd609	Bd610
Year	Kilocalories	Grams	Grams	Grams	Grams	Grams	Grams	Milligrams	Micrograms	Micrograms	Milligrams	Milligrams	Milligrams
1970	3,300	386	95	154	54	63	26	470	1,500	510	13.7	107	2.0
1971	3,300	387	96	154	55	63	26	470	1,510	520	13.5	108	2.0
1972	3,300	386	95	155	54	63	27	460	1,530	550	13.9	108	2.0
1973	3,200	390	94	150	52	61	27	440	1,520	580	14.4	106	2.0
1974	3,200	383	94	151	52	62	27	440	1,560	600	14.2	108	2.1
1975	3,200	385	93	146	50	59	27	430	1,550	620	14.4	112	2.2
1976	3,300	399	97	152	51	60	29	430	1,580	620	14.7	113	2.3
1977	3,300	398	96	149	51	59	28	430	1,530	580	14.2	112	2.3
1978	3,200	392	95	150	51	59	29	430	1,510	580	14.5	108	2.2
1979	3,300	400	96	151	51	60	30	430	1,530	610	14.6	109	2.3
1980	3,300	406	96	153	52	60	30	430	1,520	600	14.6	112	2.3
1981	3,300	394	96	153	51	61	30	430	1,510	600	14.7	109	2.3
1982	3,300	396	96	152	51	60	30	420	1,510	620	15.0	110	2.3
1983	3,300	400	97	157	53	62	31	430	1,500	600	15.4	115	2.3
1984	3,400	404	98	155	53	62	29	430	1,530	640	14.9	112	2.3
1985	3,500	420	101	163	55	65	32	430	1,520	630	16.2	114	2.4
1986	3,500	425	102	162	54	65	32	420	1,500	610	16.3	118	2.4
1987	3,500	436	103	160	53	64	32	420	1,530	640	16.4	115	2.5
1988	3,600	443	105	161	53	64	33	420	1,470	610	16.9	116	2.5
1989	3,500	445	104	156	51	63	32	410	1,500	640	16.5	115	2.6
1990	3,600	458	105	156	51	63	32	400	1,530	670	16.8	111	2.6
1991	3,600	464	107	155	50	63	32	400	1,500	640	17.0	115	2.6
1992	3,700	473	108	158	52	64	32	410	1,540	670	17.1	117	2.7
1993	3,700	482	108	161	52	66	32	410	1,530	670	17.6	122	2.7
1994	3,800	491	110	159	52	65	31	410	1,520	660	16.9	124	2.7

TABLE Bd598–622 Daily per capita food consumption – calories, carbohydrates, protein, fat, cholesterol, and nutrients: 1970–1994 *Continued*

	Micronutrients											
	Riboflavin	Niacin	Vitamin B6	Folate	Vitamin B12	Calcium	Phosphorus	Magnesium	Iron	Zinc	Copper	Potassium
	Bd611	Bd612	Bd613	Bd614	Bd615	Bd616	Bd617	Bd618	Bd619	Bd620	Bd621	Bd622
Year	Milligrams	Milligrams	Milligrams	Micrograms	Micrograms	Milligrams	Milligrams	Milligrams	Milligrams	Milligrams	Milligrams	Milligrams
1970	2.3	22	2.0	279	9.5	890	1,460	320	15.4	12.2	1.6	3,510
1971	2.3	22	2.0	280	9.5	890	1,470	320	15.6	12.3	1.6	3,500
1972	2.3	22	2.0	279	9.4	890	1,470	330	15.6	12.2	1.6	3,490
1973	2.3	22	1.9	284	8.9	880	1,440	330	15.8	11.8	1.6	3,460
1974	2.3	23	2.0	276	9.2	850	1,430	320	18.1	12.0	1.6	3,410
1975	2.3	24	1.9	298	8.8	840	1,430	320	19.8	11.8	1.7	3,440
1976	2.5	26	2.0	303	9.1	890	1,480	330	23.8	12.3	1.7	3,530
1977	2.4	25	2.0	302	9.0	880	1,470	320	23.3	12.2	1.7	3,460
1978	2.4	25	1.9	291	8.7	880	1,460	320	23.0	12.0	1.6	3,410
1979	2.4	25	2.0	299	8.5	890	1,480	330	16.1	11.9	1.7	3,480
1980	2.4	25	2.0	292	8.4	870	1,460	320	16.0	11.8	1.7	3,440
1981	2.4	26	2.0	292	8.5	860	1,460	320	16.2	11.9	1.7	3,400
1982	2.4	25	2.0	298	8.2	870	1,460	330	16.4	11.9	1.7	3,430
1983	2.4	26	2.0	301	8.4	890	1,490	330	17.4	12.1	1.7	3,490
1984	2.5	26	2.0	295	8.5	900	1,500	330	18.4	12.1	1.7	3,500
1985	2.5	27	2.1	310	8.5	920	1,540	350	19.1	12.5	1.8	3,590
1986	2.5	27	2.1	313	8.4	930	1,570	350	19.2	12.6	1.8	3,650
1987	2.5	27	2.1	304	8.5	930	1,580	350	19.3	12.5	1.8	3,590
1988	2.5	28	2.1	316	8.3	930	1,600	360	19.8	12.7	1.8	3,630
1989	2.5	28	2.2	308	8.2	920	1,600	360	19.8	12.6	1.8	3,630
1990	2.6	28	2.2	311	8.2	940	1,620	370	20.2	12.7	1.8	3,650
1991	2.5	28	2.2	321	8.2	940	1,630	380	20.5	12.8	1.9	3,690
1992	2.6	29	2.3	326	8.3	950	1,660	380	20.8	13.0	1.9	3,750
1993	2.6	29	2.3	329	8.0	950	1,650	380	20.9	13.0	1.9	3,750
1994	2.6	29	2.3	331	8.1	960	1,680	380	21.2	13.2	1.9	3,780

Source

U.S. Department of Agriculture, *Food Consumption, Prices, and Expenditures, 1970–1995,* Economic Research Service Statistical Bulletin number 939 (1996).

Documentation

See the text for Table Bd568–580.

Series Bd606–607. Measured in micrograms, retinol equivalent.

Series Bd608. Measured in milligrams, alpha-TE.

TABLE Bd623–629 Water supply systems with controlled fluoridation – number and population served: 1945–1992[1]

Contributed by Richard H. Steckel

	Operative				Discontinued		
	Number	Communities served	Population served	Percentage of U.S. population served	Number	Communities served	Population served
	Bd623 [2]	Bd624	Bd625	Bd626	Bd627	Bd628	Bd629
Year	Number	Number	Number	Percent	Number	Number	Number
1945	3	6	231,920	0.2	—	—	—
1946	8	12	332,467	0.2	—	—	—
1947	11	16	458,748	0.3	—	—	—
1948	13	26	581,683	0.4	—	—	—
1949	29	49	1,062,779	0.7	—	—	—
1950	62	100	1,578,578	1.0	1	1	16,550
1951	171	368	5,079,321	3.3	2	2	29,450
1952	353	751	13,875,005	8.9	7	7	204,125
1953	482	1,007	17,666,339	11.2	12	12	84,868
1954	572	1,194	22,336,884	13.9	30	32	1,191,370
1955	672	1,347	26,278,820	16.0	47	60	1,604,914
1956	772	1,583	33,905,474	20.3	56	73	1,767,320
1957	879	1,717	36,215,208	21.3	59	84	1,909,455
1958	995	1,890	38,461,589	22.2	65	96	2,001,877
1959	1,081	1,990	39,628,377	22.4	72	103	2,173,363

Notes appear at end of table

(continued)

TABLE Bd623–629 Water supply systems with controlled fluoridation – number and population served: 1945–1992 *Continued*

	Operative				Discontinued		
	Number	Communities served	Population served	Percentage of population served	Number	Communities served	Population served
	Bd623 [2]	Bd624	Bd625	Bd626	Bd627	Bd628	Bd629
Year	Number	Number	Number	Percent	Number	Number	Number
1960	1,172	2,111	41,179,694	22.9	79	110	2,211,230
1961	1,249	2,197	42,201,115	23.1	79	104	2,217,635
1962	1,350	2,321	44,045,392	23.7	83	108	2,243,764
1963	1,482	2,612	46,678,380	24.8	85	111	2,324,486
1964	1,573	2,758	48,363,066	25.3	86	111	2,815,953
1965	1,692	3,030	59,855,024	30.9	89	111	4,018,195
1966	1,785	3,145	62,427,290	31.9	87	112	4,018,710
1967	2,091	3,827	71,916,682	36.4	97	122	3,983,707
1968	2,372	4,229	74,579,666	37.4	98	122	4,628,507
1969	2,653	4,834	80,096,860	39.8	109	146	4,296,868
1970	—	—	83,725,771	41.1	—	—	—
1985	12,358	9,681	130,172,334	54.7	—	—	—
1988	12,263	9,714	132,422,064	53.2	—	—	—
1989	12,874	9,950	135,256,757	54.5	—	—	—
1992	14,351	10,496	144,217,476	55.8	—	—	—

[1] Beginning in 1989, includes water systems that (1) are naturally fluoridated with 0.7 parts per million or more, and (2) have had fluoride added to them, called "adjusted" systems.

[2] Beginning in 1989, "systems" refers to fluoridating systems plus consecutive systems.

Sources

These data continue to be updated, usually quinquennially. A brief list of updated data is also on the Internet site for the Centers for Disease Control.

Series Bd623–625 and Bd627–629. For 1945–1969, U.S. Public Health Service, *Fluoridation Census 1969,* Table 3; for 1970, unpublished data; for post-1970, U.S. Public Health Service, *Fluoridation Census* (1975, 1980, 1985, 1988, 1989, and 1992), Tables 1 and 2.

Series Bd626. For 1945–1970, computed on basis of U.S. resident population in series A7 (in 1975 edition); for post-1970, computed on basis of U.S. population given in respective editions of the *Fluoridation Census.*

Documentation

Controlled fluoridation is defined as the conscious maintenance of the optimal fluoride concentration in the water supply. This may be accomplished by adding fluoride chemicals to fluoride-deficient water; by blending two or more sources of water naturally containing fluoride to the optimal concentration; or by defluoridation (removing fluorides in excess of the recommended level). Water supplies are considered to have natural fluoridation if they contain 0.7 parts per million or more naturally occurring fluoride.

For data through 1970, the current population on controlled fluoridation was estimated by applying the U.S. Bureau of the Census population projection factors to the population on fluoridated water expressed in terms of the 1960 census population. For 1988 and 1989, the Census Bureau's 1988 estimates of population were used. For 1992, the Census Bureau's 1992 population estimates were used.

Through 1970, the data on operative and discontinued systems are based upon the year in which institution, discontinuation, or reinstitution of fluoridation were reported to the U.S. Public Health Service and not necessarily the year in which the event occurred.

Beginning in 1971, data are not reported for discontinued systems. These editions of the *Fluoridation Census* do include the number of naturally fluoridated water systems and number of communities using them, but these data have not been reported here.

TABLE Bd630–638 Cigarette consumption and percentage of persons who smoke, by sex and education: 1900–1994[1]

Contributed by Richard H. Steckel

	Consumption		Percentage who are current cigarette smokers						
			Persons 18 years and older			Persons 25 years and older, by years of education			
	Total	Per capita, persons 18 years and older	All	Males	Females	Less than 12	12	13–15	16 or more
	Bd630	Bd631	Bd632	Bd633	Bd634	Bd635	Bd636	Bd637	Bd638
Year	Billion	Number	Percent	Percent	Percent	Percent	Percent	Percent	Percent
1900	2.5	54	—	—	—	—	—	—	—
1901	2.5	53	—	—	—	—	—	—	—
1902	2.8	60	—	—	—	—	—	—	—
1903	3.1	64	—	—	—	—	—	—	—
1904	3.3	66	—	—	—	—	—	—	—
1905	3.6	70	—	—	—	—	—	—	—
1906	4.5	86	—	—	—	—	—	—	—
1907	5.3	99	—	—	—	—	—	—	—
1908	5.7	105	—	—	—	—	—	—	—
1909	7.0	125	—	—	—	—	—	—	—

Note appears at end of table

TABLE Bd630–638 Cigarette consumption and percentage of persons who smoke, by sex and education: 1900–1994 *Continued*

	Consumption		Percentage who are current cigarette smokers						
			Persons 18 years and older			Persons 25 years and older, by years of education			
	Total	Per capita, persons 18 years and older	All	Males	Females	Less than 12	12	13–15	16 or more
	Bd630	Bd631	Bd632	Bd633	Bd634	Bd635	Bd636	Bd637	Bd638
Year	Billion	Number	Percent	Percent	Percent	Percent	Percent	Percent	Percent
1910	8.6	151	—	—	—	—	—	—	—
1911	10.1	173	—	—	—	—	—	—	—
1912	13.2	223	—	—	—	—	—	—	—
1913	15.8	260	—	—	—	—	—	—	—
1914	16.5	267	—	—	—	—	—	—	—
1915	17.9	285	—	—	—	—	—	—	—
1916	25.2	395	—	—	—	—	—	—	—
1917	35.7	551	—	—	—	—	—	—	—
1918	45.6	697	—	—	—	—	—	—	—
1919	48.0	727	—	—	—	—	—	—	—
1920	44.6	665	—	—	—	—	—	—	—
1921	50.7	742	—	—	—	—	—	—	—
1922	53.4	770	—	—	—	—	—	—	—
1923	64.4	911	—	—	—	—	—	—	—
1924	71.0	982	—	—	—	—	—	—	—
1925	79.8	1,085	—	—	—	—	—	—	—
1926	89.1	1,191	—	—	—	—	—	—	—
1927	97.5	1,279	—	—	—	—	—	—	—
1928	106.0	1,366	—	—	—	—	—	—	—
1929	118.6	1,504	—	—	—	—	—	—	—
1930	119.3	1,485	—	—	—	—	—	—	—
1931	114.0	1,399	—	—	—	—	—	—	—
1932	102.8	1,245	—	—	—	—	—	—	—
1933	111.6	1,334	—	—	—	—	—	—	—
1934	125.7	1,483	—	—	—	—	—	—	—
1935	134.4	1,564	—	—	—	—	—	—	—
1936	152.7	1,754	—	—	—	—	—	—	—
1937	162.8	1,847	—	—	—	—	—	—	—
1938	163.4	1,830	—	—	—	—	—	—	—
1939	172.1	1,900	—	—	—	—	—	—	—
1940	181.9	1,976	—	—	—	—	—	—	—
1941	208.9	2,236	—	—	—	—	—	—	—
1942	245.0	2,585	—	—	—	—	—	—	—
1943	284.3	2,956	—	—	—	—	—	—	—
1944	296.3	3,039	—	—	—	—	—	—	—
1945	340.6	3,449	—	—	—	—	—	—	—
1946	344.3	3,446	—	—	—	—	—	—	—
1947	345.4	3,416	—	—	—	—	—	—	—
1948	358.9	3,505	—	—	—	—	—	—	—
1949	360.9	3,480	—	—	—	—	—	—	—
1950	369.8	3,552	—	—	—	—	—	—	—
1951	397.1	3,744	—	—	—	—	—	—	—
1952	416.0	3,886	—	—	—	—	—	—	—
1953	408.2	3,778	—	—	—	—	—	—	—
1954	387.0	3,546	—	—	—	—	—	—	—
1955	396.4	3,597	—	—	—	—	—	—	—
1956	406.5	3,650	—	—	—	—	—	—	—
1957	422.5	3,755	—	—	—	—	—	—	—
1958	448.9	3,953	—	—	—	—	—	—	—
1959	467.5	4,073	—	—	—	—	—	—	—
1960	484.4	4,171	—	—	—	—	—	—	—
1961	502.5	4,266	—	—	—	—	—	—	—
1962	508.4	4,266	—	—	—	—	—	—	—
1963	523.9	4,345	—	—	—	—	—	—	—
1964	511.3	4,194	—	—	—	—	—	—	—
1965	528.8	4,258	42.4	51.9	33.9	—	—	—	—
1966	541.3	4,287	42.6	52.5	33.9	41.7	44.7	44.8	35.3
1967	549.3	4,280	—	—	—	—	—	—	—
1968	545.6	4,186	—	—	—	—	—	—	—
1969	528.9	3,993	—	—	—	—	—	—	—

(continued)

TABLE Bd630–638 Cigarette consumption and percentage of persons who smoke, by sex and education: 1900–1994 *Continued*

	Consumption		Percentage who are current cigarette smokers						
			Persons 18 years and older			Persons 25 years and older, by years of education			
	Total	Per capita, persons 18 years and older	All	Males	Females	Less than 12	12	13–15	16 or more
	Bd630	Bd631	Bd632	Bd633	Bd634	Bd635	Bd636	Bd637	Bd638
Year	Billion	Number	Percent	Percent	Percent	Percent	Percent	Percent	Percent
1970	536.5	3,985	37.4	44.1	31.5	37.5	39.3	38.7	28.8
1971	555.1	4,037	—	—	—	—	—	—	—
1972	566.8	4,043	—	—	—	—	—	—	—
1973	589.7	4,148	—	—	—	—	—	—	—
1974	599.0	4,141	37.1	43.1	32.1	37.8	38.8	37.9	28.8
1975	607.2	4,122	—	—	—	—	—	—	—
1976	613.5	4,091	—	—	—	—	—	—	—
1977	617.0	4,043	—	—	—	—	—	—	—
1978	616.0	3,970	34.1	38.1	30.7	35.7	37.0	34.3	24.2
1979	621.5	3,861	33.5	37.5	29.9	35.1	35.3	35.2	23.7
1980	631.5	3,849	33.2	37.6	29.3	35.1	35.4	33.9	24.5
1981	640.0	3,836	—	—	—	—	—	—	—
1982	634.0	3,739	—	—	—	—	—	—	—
1983	600.0	3,488	32.1	35.1	29.5	34.7	34.9	32.1	20.6
1984	600.4	3,446	—	—	—	—	—	—	—
1985	594.0	3,370	30.1	32.6	27.9	34.2	33.4	30.6	19.0
1986	583.8	3,274	—	—	—	—	—	—	—
1987	575.0	3,197	28.8	31.2	26.5	34.2	32.9	28.2	16.6
1988	562.5	3,096	28.1	30.8	25.7	32.9	32.7	28.1	16.3
1989	540.0	2,926	—	—	—	—	—	—	—
1990	525.0	2,817	25.5	28.4	22.8	30.8	30.1	24.6	13.9
1991	510.0	2,713	25.7	28.1	23.5	31.4	30.6	25.5	13.9
1992	500.0	2,640	26.5	28.6	24.6	36.7	30.7	24.6	15.3
1993	485.0	2,539	25.0	27.7	22.5	35.8	28.3	24.5	13.6
1994	480.0	2,493	25.5	28.2	23.1	37.5	29.2	24.9	11.9

[1] U.S. military forces overseas are included in the total consumption for 1917–1919 and 1940–1994, and in per capita consumption for 1930–1994.

Sources

Centers for Disease Control and Prevention (CDC) Surveillance Summaries, including "Surveillance for Selected Tobacco-Use Behaviors – United States, 1900–1994" (November 18, 1994), and *Morbidity and Mortality Weekly Report* (MMWR), volume 43, number SS-3 (1994). For 1992 and later, the data were published in *Health, United States, 1996–1997,* but recorded from the National Health Survey conducted by the CDC.

Documentation

Current smokers include those who reported smoking 100 or more cigarettes in a year and currently smoked.

Estimates of cigarette consumption are reported by the U.S. Department of Agriculture (USDA), which uses data from the U.S. Department of the Treasury, the U.S. Department of Commerce, the Tobacco Institute, and other sources. The National Health Interview Survey (NHIS) uses household interviews to provide nationally representative estimates (for the civilian, noninstitutionalized population) of cigarette smoking and other behaviors related to tobacco use. The Behavioral Risk Factor Surveillance System uses telephone surveys of civilian, noninstitutionalized adults, 18 years and older, to provide state-specific estimates of current cigarette smoking and use of smokeless tobacco. The University of Michigan's Institute for Social Research uses school-based, self-administered questionnaires to gather data on cigarette smoking from a representative sample of U.S. high school seniors.

More detailed descriptions of methods used by the USDA, NHIS, Behavioral Risk Factor Surveillance System, and surveys of high school seniors are provided in the MMWR article cited with the sources.

TABLE Bd639–652 First-time drug users – estimated number and mean age, by drug: 1962–1996

Contributed by Richard H. Steckel

	Marijuana		Inhalants		Cocaine		Hallucinogens		Heroin		Alcohol		Cigarettes	
	Users	Mean age	Users	Mean age	Users	Mean age	Users	Mean age	Users	Mean age	Users	Mean age	Users	Mean age
	Bd639	Bd640	Bd641	Bd642	Bd643	Bd644	Bd645	Bd646	Bd647	Bd648	Bd649	Bd650	Bd651	Bd652
Year	Thousand	Number	Thousand	Number	Thousand	Number	Thousand	Number	Thousand	Number	Thousand	Number	Thousand	Number
1962	68	—	—	—	(Z)	—	—	—	—	—	2,199	18.5	2,286	15.6
1963	171	22.4	—	—	—	—	—	—	—	—	2,602	17.1	2,710	15.0
1964	289	18.1	—	—	—	—	—	—	—	—	2,981	18.5	2,950	15.7
1965	617	18.8	119	14.9	—	—	99	19.0	—	—	3,121	17.7	2,974	16.0
1966	900	20.3	93	18.8	—	23.6	154	19.8	—	—	3,663	17.7	2,843	16.2
1967	1,467	19.9	166	15.4	—	—	174	16.5	—	—	3,734	17.5	3,229	15.6
1968	1,590	19.1	160	16.9	77	19.7	428	19.7	—	—	3,768	18.0	3,166	15.4
1969	2,218	19.2	115	15.7	180	18.3	547	17.9	93	17.0	4,231	17.7	3,362	15.5
1970	2,668	19.3	201	18.0	296	19.7	815	18.5	106	19.4	4,022	17.3	3,574	15.7
1971	2,799	18.8	283	15.9	343	19.4	915	18.4	137	18.0	3,638	17.5	3,472	15.2
1972	2,897	18.4	274	19.3	270	19.1	616	18.4	137	17.3	4,488	16.9	3,794	15.3
1973	2,782	18.2	240	16.9	477	20.2	581	18.1	70	18.6	4,420	17.0	3,395	15.5
1974	3,008	18.6	341	19.1	673	21.2	556	18.4	86	22.6	4,425	17.3	3,708	15.0
1975	3,185	18.8	326	17.2	808	21.7	756	19.1	83	19.0	3,988	17.0	3,650	15.2
1976	2,824	18.5	435	18.7	646	21.2	824	17.8	68	18.7	4,060	16.8	3,492	15.5
1977	2,884	19.3	443	18.7	950	21.5	671	19.7	104	21.8	4,575	17.5	3,428	15.7
1978	2,879	17.8	558	18.2	1,041	21.1	715	19.8	54	20.9	4,512	16.9	3,031	15.6
1979	2,585	18.0	436	18.3	999	21.8	710	18.7	66	21.0	4,048	17.3	2,997	15.7
1980	2,492	18.6	485	17.9	1,345	21.1	666	18.9	49	20.6	4,074	17.3	2,753	15.6
1981	2,218	17.8	447	19.1	1,383	21.7	652	19.2	62	20.6	3,627	16.6	2,735	15.6
1982	2,080	18.2	391	17.9	1,389	21.8	665	21.1	50	21.6	3,627	17.1	2,750	15.5
1983	2,044	17.8	439	19.3	1,220	22.0	637	19.1	67	25.1	3,600	16.8	2,739	15.1
1984	1,994	19.6	384	17.9	1,230	21.9	468	18.7	91	27.0	3,509	16.9	2,679	15.5
1985	1,767	17.8	364	16.8	1,174	22.5	508	19.2	39	23.3	3,335	16.6	2,816	15.5
1986	1,871	19.4	365	17.0	1,210	23.1	621	19.1	55	20.1	3,640	17.0	2,782	15.5
1987	1,817	17.9	384	18.1	961	22.6	589	19.5	53	20.5	3,285	17.1	2,566	16.1
1988	1,526	17.3	462	18.8	776	21.4	674	20.4	78	26.2	3,373	17.1	2,484	15.3
1989	1,413	17.8	361	16.9	762	21.9	625	18.6	55	24.3	3,071	16.3	2,503	16.3
1990	1,401	17.3	385	16.5	631	22.7	636	18.5	58	25.9	3,431	16.7	2,645	15.5
1991	1,376	17.5	382	15.4	480	21.4	634	18.5	53	23.5	3,477	16.7	2,567	16.0
1992	1,701	17.7	460	16.7	488	21.0	587	17.9	32	19.6	3,595	16.5	2,707	15.7
1993	1,949	17.0	605	16.4	553	22.4	738	18.2	61	20.2	3,713 [1]	16.4 [1]	2,897 [1]	16.1 [1]
1994	2,393 [1]	16.7 [1]	613 [1]	16.3 [1]	537 [1]	21.7 [1]	876 [1]	18.0 [1]	93 [1]	19.5 [1]	4,150 [2]	17.2 [2]	3,178 [2]	16.0 [2]
1995	2,406 [2]	16.6 [2]	634 [2]	15.8 [2]	653 [2]	19.5 [2]	1,201 [2]	17.3 [2]	117 [2]	19.4 [2]	4,318 [3]	16.2 [3]	3,263 [3]	15.6 [3]
1996	2,540 [3]	16.4 [3]	805 [3]	16.3 [3]	675 [3]	18.7 [3]	1,094 [3]	17.2 [3]	171 [3]	18.1 [3]	—	—	—	—

(Z) Fewer than 500 users.

[1] Estimated using 1995, 1996, and 1997 data only.

[2] Estimated using 1996 and 1997 data only.

[3] Estimated using 1997 data only.

Source

U.S. Substance Abuse and Mental Health Services Administration (SAMHSA), Office of Applied Studies, *Preliminary Results from the 1997 National Household Survey on Drug Abuse* (August 1998). Additionally, this publication may be accessed via the SAMHSA Internet site.

Documentation

This table presents the results from the National Household Survey on Drug Abuse, an annual survey conducted by SAMHSA since 1971. The survey provides estimates of the prevalence of use of alcohol, tobacco, and a variety of illicit drugs, based on a nationally representative sample of the civilian population age 12 and older. Data on mean age pertain to age at the time of first use. The survey covers residents of households, noninstitutional group quarters (shelters, rooming houses, dormitories, etc.), and civilians living on military bases. Persons excluded from the survey include the homeless who never use shelters, active military personnel, and residents of institutional group quarters such as jails and hospitals. Detailed explanations of the survey are available in the source.

In some cases, no value is reported because of low precision.

PHYSICAL WELL-BEING

Richard H. Steckel

TABLE Bd653–687 Selected anthropometric measurements – height, weight, and body mass index: 1710–1989

Contributed by Richard H. Steckel

	Height											
	Native-born American											
			Boys			Girls						
	Men	Women	Age 4	Age 10	Age 16	Age 4	Age 10	Age 16	Men entering Amherst College	Women entering Vassar College	West Point cadets	Citadel cadets
	Bd653	Bd654	Bd655 [1]	Bd656 [1]	Bd657 [1]	Bd658 [1]	Bd659 [1]	Bd660 [1]	Bd661	Bd662	Bd663	Bd664
Birth year	Centimeters	Centimeters	Centimeters	Centimeters	Centimeters	Centimeters	Centimeters	Centimeters	Centimeters	Centimeters	Centimeters	Centimeters
1710	171.5	—	—	—	—	—	—	—	—	—	—	—
1720	171.8	—	—	—	—	—	—	—	—	—	—	—
1730	172.1	—	—	—	—	—	—	—	—	—	—	—
1740	172.1	—	—	—	—	—	—	—	—	—	—	—
1750	172.2	—	—	—	—	—	—	—	—	—	—	—
1760	172.3	—	—	—	—	—	—	—	—	—	—	—
1770	172.8	—	—	—	—	—	—	—	—	—	—	—
1780	173.2	—	—	—	—	—	—	—	—	—	—	—
1790	172.9	—	—	—	—	—	—	—	—	—	—	—
1800	172.9	—	—	—	—	—	—	—	—	—	—	—
1810	173.0	—	—	—	—	—	—	—	—	—	—	—
1820	172.9	—	—	—	—	—	—	—	—	—	172.5	—
1830	173.5	—	—	—	—	—	—	—	—	—	172.0	—
1840	172.2	—	—	—	—	—	—	—	—	—	171.5	—
1850	171.1	—	—	—	—	—	—	—	—	—	170.9	—
1860	170.6	—	—	—	—	—	—	—	171.3 [2]	—	171.1	174.2
1870	171.2	—	—	—	—	—	—	—	169.9	—	172.3	175.0
1880	169.5	—	—	—	—	—	—	—	172.2	160.4 [3]	—	174.8
1890	169.1	—	—	—	—	—	—	—	172.7	161.0	—	173.9
1900	170.0	—	—	—	—	—	—	—	172.7	162.1	—	174.2
1910	172.1	—	—	—	—	—	—	—	173.5	162.1	—	177.4
1920	173.1	—	—	—	—	—	—	—	175.3	164.3	—	179.2
1925	175.7	162.8	—	—	—	—	—	—	175.8	—	—	—
1930	175.8	162.6	—	—	—	—	—	—	177.3	165.4	—	179.6
1935	176.9	163.4	—	—	—	—	—	—	178.1	—	—	—
1940	176.7	163.1	—	—	—	—	—	—	—	166.4	—	—
1945	177.0	163.3	—	—	—	—	—	—	—	—	—	—
1950	177.3	163.1	—	—	—	—	—	—	—	166.1	—	—
1955	177.6	164.1	—	—	—	—	—	—	—	—	—	—
1960	177.9	164.2	—	—	173.3	—	—	163.1	—	—	—	—
1965	177.3	163.3	—	140.7	—	—	141.2	—	—	—	—	—
1970	177.4	163.6	106.0	—	—	103.9	—	—	—	—	—	—
1974	—	—	—	—	176.4	—	—	163.9	—	—	—	—
1977	—	—	—	—	175.3	—	—	162.2	—	—	—	—
1980	—	—	—	141.8	—	—	142.5	—	—	—	—	—
1983	—	—	—	142.2	—	—	143.3	—	—	—	—	—
1986	—	—	105.3	—	—	105.0	—	—	—	—	—	—
1989	—	—	105.2	—	—	105.3	—	—	—	—	—	—

Notes appear at end of table

TABLE Bd653–687 Selected anthropometric measurements – height, weight, and body mass index: 1710–1989 *Continued*

	Height									Weight	
	Adult, free blacks in Maryland		Slaves							Native-born American	
			Age 5		Age 23–49		Adult runaway male				
	Males	Females	Males	Females	Males	Females	African-born	Mainland-born	Unknown birthplace	Men	Women
Birth	Bd665	Bd666	Bd667	Bd668	Bd669	Bd670	Bd671	Bd672	Bd673	Bd674	Bd675
year	Centimeters	Centimeters	Centimeters	Centimeters	Centimeters	Centimeters	Centimeters	Centimeters	Centimeters	Kilograms	Kilograms
1710	—	—	—	—	—	—	—	173.2	172.0	—	—
1720	—	—	—	—	—	—	171.7	173.7	172.2	—	—
1730	—	—	—	—	—	—	173.0	173.0	172.5	—	—
1740	—	—	—	—	—	—	170.4	174.5	171.5	—	—
1750	—	—	—	—	—	—	170.7	173.7	172.2	—	—
1760	169.0	158.4	—	—	—	—	165.1	173.0	172.7	—	—
1770	169.5	159.5	—	—	169.4	159.6	169.9	170.7	172.5	—	—
1780	170.1	158.7	—	—	169.7	159.3	170.7	170.9	172.2	—	—
1790	169.8	159.0	—	—	169.5	159.3	167.6	169.4	172.0	—	—
1800	170.4	158.9	—	—	170.4	159.9	—	—	172.0	—	—
1810	170.3	158.6	100.3	103.3	—	—	—	—	173.0	—	—
1820	170.8	158.1	101.5	100.4	—	—	—	—	—	—	—
1830	170.1	157.6	100.2	98.6	—	—	—	—	—	—	—
1840	169.6	156.6	98.1	98.4	—	—	—	—	—	—	—
1850	—	—	95.5	97.0	—	—	—	—	—	—	—
1860	—	—	—	—	—	—	—	—	—	—	—
1870	—	—	—	—	—	—	—	—	—	—	—
1880	—	—	—	—	—	—	—	—	—	—	—
1890	—	—	—	—	—	—	—	—	—	—	—
1900	—	—	—	—	—	—	—	—	—	—	—
1910	—	—	—	—	—	—	—	—	—	—	—
1920	—	—	—	—	—	—	—	—	—	79.91	68.42
1925	—	—	—	—	—	—	—	—	—	82.32	67.76
1930	—	—	—	—	—	—	—	—	—	81.88	67.11
1935	—	—	—	—	—	—	—	—	—	81.77	65.69
1940	—	—	—	—	—	—	—	—	—	81.36	65.73
1945	—	—	—	—	—	—	—	—	—	80.25	64.60
1950	—	—	—	—	—	—	—	—	—	80.32	65.84
1955	—	—	—	—	—	—	—	—	—	81.97	68.29
1960	—	—	—	—	—	—	—	—	—	81.42	66.69
1965	—	—	—	—	—	—	—	—	—	77.91	65.17
1970	—	—	—	—	—	—	—	—	—	—	—
1974	—	—	—	—	—	—	—	—	—	—	—
1977	—	—	—	—	—	—	—	—	—	—	—
1980	—	—	—	—	—	—	—	—	—	—	—
1983	—	—	—	—	—	—	—	—	—	—	—
1986	—	—	—	—	—	—	—	—	—	—	—
1989	—	—	—	—	—	—	—	—	—	—	—

(continued)

TABLE Bd653–687 Selected anthropometric measurements – height, weight, and body mass index: 1710–1989 *Continued*

	Weight										Body mass index	
	Native-born American						Men					
	Boys			Girls								
	Age 4	Age 10	Age 16	Age 4	Age 10	Age 16	West Point cadets	Citadel cadets	Entering Amherst College	Women entering Vassar College	West Point cadets	Citadel cadets
	Bd676 [1]	Bd677 [1]	Bd678 [1]	Bd679 [1]	Bd680 [1]	Bd681 [1]	Bd682	Bd683	Bd684	Bd685	Bd686	Bd687
Birth year	Kilograms	Kilograms	Kilograms	Kilograms	Kilograms	Kilograms	Kilograms	Kilograms	Kilograms	Kilograms	Number	Number
1710	—	—	—	—	—	—	—	—	—	—	—	—
1720	—	—	—	—	—	—	—	—	—	—	—	—
1730	—	—	—	—	—	—	—	—	—	—	—	—
1740	—	—	—	—	—	—	—	—	—	—	—	—
1750	—	—	—	—	—	—	—	—	—	—	—	—
1760	—	—	—	—	—	—	—	—	—	—	—	—
1770	—	—	—	—	—	—	—	—	—	—	—	—
1780	—	—	—	—	—	—	—	—	—	—	—	—
1790	—	—	—	—	—	—	—	—	—	—	—	—
1800	—	—	—	—	—	—	—	—	—	—	—	—
1810	—	—	—	—	—	—	—	—	—	—	—	—
1820	—	—	—	—	—	—	—	—	—	—	—	—
1830	—	—	—	—	—	—	—	—	—	—	—	—
1840	—	—	—	—	—	—	—	—	—	—	—	—
1850	—	—	—	—	—	—	56.27	—	—	—	19.93	—
1860	—	—	—	—	—	—	58.09	—	60.35 [2]	—	20.32	—
1870	—	—	—	—	—	—	57.45	61.00	59.09	—	20.08	21.35
1880	—	—	—	—	—	—	—	60.68	61.27	53.76 [3]	—	21.33
1890	—	—	—	—	—	—	—	59.00	60.05	53.18	—	21.22
1900	—	—	—	—	—	—	—	61.32	59.73	55.41	—	21.27
1910	—	—	—	—	—	—	—	—	62.23	55.82	—	—
1920	—	—	—	—	—	—	—	69.32	62.82	57.18	—	21.87
1925	—	—	—	—	—	—	—	—	—	—	—	—
1930	—	—	—	—	—	—	—	71.77	63.59	57.05	—	21.92
1935	—	—	—	—	—	—	—	—	—	—	—	—
1940	—	—	—	—	—	—	—	—	67.09	59.05	—	—
1945	—	—	—	—	—	—	—	—	—	—	—	—
1950	—	—	—	—	—	57.84	—	—	71.82	58.50	—	—
1955	—	—	66.17	—	34.56	—	—	—	—	—	—	—
1960	—	35.32	—	—	—	—	—	—	—	—	—	—
1965	17.82	—	—	16.72	—	—	—	—	—	—	—	—
1970	—	—	68.43	—	—	61.67	—	—	—	—	—	—
1974	—	—	72.44	—	—	63.40	—	—	—	—	—	—
1977	—	36.12	—	—	36.80	—	—	—	—	—	—	—
1980	—	38.74	—	—	40.10	—	—	—	—	—	—	—
1983	17.74	—	—	17.34	—	—	—	—	—	—	—	—
1986	17.55	—	—	18.31	—	—	—	—	—	—	—	—
1989	—	—	—	—	—	—	—	—	—	—	—	—

[1] Series uses five-year averages through 1970. See text.

[2] Data for 1860 not available. Value is an average of heights for 1861–1869.

[3] Data for 1880–1883 not available. Value is an average of heights for 1884–1889.

Sources

Series Bd653, 1710–1920. Taken from military records compiled and provided by Richard H. Steckel and Dora L. Costa. See the appendix in Dora L. Costa and Richard H. Steckel's "Long-Term Trends in Health, Welfare and Economic Growth in the United States," in Richard H. Steckel and Roderick Floud, editors, *Health and Welfare during Industrialization* (University of Chicago Press, 1997), pp. 47–90.

Series Bd653, 1925–1970, and series Bd654–660 and Bd674–681. The National Health and Nutrition Examination Survey (NHANES) was conducted by the National Center for Health Statistics (NCHS), part of the Centers for Disease Control and Prevention, U.S. Public Health Service. This survey was conducted in three phases, NHANES I (1971–1975), NHANES II (1976–1980), and NHANES III (1988–1994).

Series Bd661–662 and Bd684–685. Milicent L. Hathaway and Elsie D. Foard, *Heights and Weights of Adults in the United States* (U.S. Department of Agriculture, August 1960).

Series Bd663 and Bd682. From published data in John Komlos, "The Height and Weight of West Point Cadets: Dietary Change in Antebellum America," *Journal of Economic History* 47 (4) (1987): 901, 906.

Series Bd664, Bd683, and Bd687. Peter A. Coclanis and John Komlos, "Nutrition and Economic Development in Post-Reconstruction South Carolina: An Anthropometric Approach," *Social Science History* 19 (1) (1995): 96, 104.

Series Bd665–666. John Komlos, "Towards an Anthropometric History of African-Americans: The Case of the Free Blacks in Antebellum Maryland," in Claudia Goldin and Hugh Rockoff, editors, *Strategic Factors in Nineteenth-Century American Economic History* (University of Chicago Press, 1992), pp. 313, 315.

TABLE Bd653–687 Selected anthropometric measurements – height, weight, and body mass index: 1710–1989 *Continued*

Series Bd667–670. Based on approximately 27,500 manifests that cover the shipping years from 1810 to 1861 analyzed in Richard H. Steckel, "Fluctuations in a Dreadful Childhood: Synthetic Longitudinal Height Data, Relative Prices and Weather in the Short-Term Health of American Slaves," National Bureau of Economic Research Working Paper number WI0993 (December 2004).

Series Bd671–673. John Komlos, "The Height of Runaway Slaves in Colonial America, 1720–1770," in John Komlos, editor, *Stature, Living Standards, and Economic Development: Essays in Anthropometric History* (University of Chicago Press, 1994), p. 108.

Series Bd686. Timothy Cuff, "The Body Mass Index Values of Mid-nineteenth Century West Point Cadets: A Theoretical Application of Waaler's Curves to a Historical Population," *Historical Methods* 26 (4) (1993): 178.

Documentation

Series Bd653, 1925–1970, and series Bd654 and Bd674–675. Calculated as a weighted average of NHANES I (1971–1975), NHANES II (1976–1980), and NHANES III (1988–1994). For NHANES III, the data were not reported by year of birth but, instead, by age. To calculate date of birth for this sample, the midpoint of the NHANES III collection period for phases 1 (1988–1991) and 2 (1991–1994) was used – March 1990 and March 1993 for phase 1 and phase 2, respectively. Then the data were weighted over a five-year period and recorded at the midpoint of that period. For example, 1925 data is an average of heights weighted by number of observations from years 1923 through 1927. The people used for these surveys are the native-born, civilian, noninstitutionalized population of the United States. The heights recorded here are for those men and women, age 20 to 49, who fall into the aforementioned category. The sample sizes for series Bd653 and Bd674 over the years 1925–1970 at five-year intervals are 366, 574, 603, 765, 1,238, 1,519, 1,167, 612, 539, and 421, respectively. The sample sizes for series Bd654 and Bd675 over the years 1925–1970 at five-year intervals are 415, 1,029, 1,119, 1,257, 1,856, 2,295, 1,368, 827, 718, and 568, respectively. Annual data are available in the original survey source.

Series Bd655–660 and Bd676–681. Data pertain to children according to their age at last birthday. The average age of children in series Bd655, Bd658, Bd676, and Bd679 is 4.5 years. The average age of children in series Bd656, Bd659, Bd677, and Bd680 is 10.5 years. The average age of children in series Bd657, Bd660, Bd678, and Bd681 is 16.5 years. For all of these series, the pre-1970 data are five-year averages from NHANES I and II data, which have been calculated in the same way as for series Bd653, 1925–1970, and series Bd654 and Bd674–675. The post-1970 data are from NHANES III and have been recorded by the specific year to which they pertain, rather than the five-year averages used for pre-1970 data, which corrected for the small sample sizes.

Series Bd661–662 and Bd684–685. Annual data are available in the original survey source. The data are for the year given, not birth decade.

Series Bd663–673, Bd682–683, and Bd686–687. The year indicates birth decade.

Series Bd663. The average height of 20-year-old males over all time periods multiplied by the index available in the survey source. From 1843 to 1894, the height data were collected upon admission to the school and recorded in annual reports of medical exams.

Series Bd664. The average height of 19-year-old males over all time periods multiplied by the index available in the survey source.

Series Bd665. Includes men age 21 to 50. See survey source for sample sizes used.

Series Bd666. Includes men age 18 to 50. See survey source for sample sizes used.

Series Bd667–670. Data from ship manifests.

Series Bd671–673. Includes men older than age 22. Rounding up to six feet (or "heaping") was a common practice. These data were taken from advertisements about runaway slaves and thus are subject to rounding concerns. In addition, slaves whose heights were recorded may have been unusually tall.

Series Bd682. Figures are the weights of 18-year-old cadets. For this series, weight data for West Point cadets were recorded only for those cadets who were 170.2 centimeters (67 inches) tall at the time of measurement.

Series Bd686–687. The body mass index (BMI), a measure to assess nutritional status, is a person's weight in kilograms divided by height in meters squared. The optimal value of the BMI lies between 20 and 26. It is considered a good predictor of mortality. The risk of death rises as the BMI diverges in either direction from this optimal range.

Series Bd687. Equals the average BMI of 18-year-olds over the entire time period multiplied by the index available in the survey source.

TABLE Bd688–693 Low-birth-weight infants as a percentage of live births, by race and ethnicity: 1970–1996

Contributed by Richard H. Steckel

	All races	White	Black	Native American or Alaskan Native	Asian or Pacific Islander	Hispanic origin
	Bd688	Bd689	Bd690	Bd691	Bd692	Bd693 [1]
Year	Percent	Percent	Percent	Percent	Percent	Percent
1970	7.93	6.85	13.90	7.97	—	—
1975	7.38	6.27	13.19	6.41	—	—
1980	6.84	5.72	12.69	6.44	6.68	6.12
1981	6.81	5.69	12.72	6.27	6.74	6.12
1982	6.75	5.64	12.61	6.06	6.74	6.23
1983	6.82	5.69	12.82	6.17	6.57	6.29
1984	6.72	5.61	12.58	6.15	6.57	6.15
1985	6.75	5.65	12.65	5.86	6.16	6.16
1986	6.81	5.66	12.77	5.94	6.47	6.13
1987	6.90	5.70	12.98	6.15	6.41	6.24
1988	6.93	5.67	13.26	6.00	6.31	6.17
1989	7.05	5.72	13.51	6.26	6.51	6.18
1990	6.97	5.70	13.25	6.11	6.45	6.06
1991	7.12	5.80	13.55	6.15	6.54	6.15
1992	7.08	5.80	13.31	6.22	6.57	6.10
1993	7.22	5.98	13.34	6.42	6.55	6.24
1994	7.28	6.11	13.24	6.45	6.81	6.25
1995	7.32	6.22	13.13	6.61	6.90	6.29
1996	7.39	6.34	13.01	6.49	7.07	6.28

[1] Changing geographic coverage; see text.

Source

U.S. National Center for Health Statistics: Data computed by the Division of Analysis from data compiled by the Division of Vital Statistics as published annually in *Health, United States* (U.S. Public Health Service).

Documentation

Low-birth-weight infants are born weighing less than 2,500 grams or about 5.5 pounds. Infants of low birth weight are less likely to survive and have a higher risk of disability if they live. Low birth weight may result from premature birth and/or from insufficient growth for the gestational age.

Figures are based on the race or ethnicity of the mother.

Series Bd688–689. Includes persons of both Hispanic and non-Hispanic origin.

Series Bd692. Pacific Islanders include Hawaiians and part-Hawaiians.

Series Bd693. Includes mothers of all races, as persons of Hispanic origin may be of any race. The data are affected by the expansion of the number of states reporting Hispanic origin on birth certificates. That expansion of the reporting area and immigration of Hispanics affect the number of events, composition of the Hispanic population, and maternal and infant health characteristics. The number of states in the reporting area increased from 22 in 1980 to 23 and the District of Columbia (DC) in 1983–1987, 30 and DC in 1988, 47 and DC in 1989, 48 and DC in 1990, 49 and DC in 1991–1992, and 50 and DC in 1993 and later years.

TABLE Bd694–735 Restricted-activity days, by sex, race, age, region, and income: 1967–1995[1]

Contributed by Richard H. Steckel

	Restricted-activity days														
		Sex		Race		Age								Region	
	Total	Males	Females	Whites	Blacks	Under 5	5–17	Under 17	17–24	18–24	25–44	45–64	65 and over	Northeast	Midwest
	Bd694	Bd695	Bd696	Bd697	Bd698	Bd699	Bd700	Bd701	Bd702	Bd703	Bd704	Bd705	Bd706	Bd707	Bd708
Year	Thousand days	Thousand days	Thousand days	Thousand days	Thousand days	Thousand days	Thousand days	Thousand days	Thousand days	Thousand days	Thousand days	Thousand days	Thousand days	Thousand days	Thousand days
1967	2,953,202	1,296,362	1,656,840	—	—	—	—	617,567	231,201	—	627,374	831,531	645,529	—	—
1968	2,996,059	1,347,155	1,648,904	—	—	—	—	668,541	259,169	—	591,838	833,932	642,579	—	—
1969	2,913,817	1,275,536	1,638,281	—	—	—	—	657,652	222,298	—	591,753	816,826	625,228	—	—
1970	2,913,146	1,272,706	1,640,440	—	—	—	—	629,010	250,536	—	627,016	824,152	582,433	—	—
1971	3,175,594	1,390,399	1,785,195	—	—	—	—	723,495	284,622	—	631,851	878,307	657,318	—	—
1972	3,401,746	1,458,277	1,943,469	—	—	—	—	688,109	312,660	—	717,425	956,995	726,557	—	—
1973	3,391,992	1,458,462	1,933,529	—	—	—	—	681,968	339,801	—	731,365	960,693	678,166	—	—
1974	3,565,552	1,564,116	2,001,437	—	—	—	—	673,997	331,249	—	759,573	1,012,728	778,006	—	—
1975	3,733,892	1,574,130	2,159,762	—	—	—	—	681,643	372,909	—	817,581	1,043,594	818,166	—	—
1976	3,840,292	1,666,275	2,174,017	—	—	—	—	668,844	368,461	—	832,780	1,098,752	871,456	—	—
1977	3,772,845	1,618,237	2,154,607	—	—	—	—	671,069	361,069	—	872,257	1,056,391	812,060	—	—
1978	4,011,249	1,678,570	2,332,679	—	—	—	—	665,610	388,993	—	920,781	1,117,812	918,052	—	—
1979	4,105,759	1,755,133	2,350,626	—	—	—	—	639,922	408,235	—	950,349	1,129,547	977,706	—	—
1980	4,165,090	1,802,068	2,363,022	—	—	—	—	670,687	403,167	—	999,217	1,154,825	937,194	—	—
1981	4,295,773	1,880,132	2,415,641	—	—	—	—	620,948	395,648	—	1,073,097	1,214,615	991,465	—	—
1982	3,253,254	1,372,863	1,880,391	2,746,275	438,323	149,193	394,983	—	—	248,122	767,203	891,148	802,606	669,301	754,379
1983	3,318,069	1,364,731	1,953,338	2,813,111	451,903	194,719	406,819	—	—	242,740	789,474	853,667	830,650	715,614	761,601
1984	3,427,193	1,454,136	1,973,057	2,904,705	460,593	183,085	402,211	—	—	268,870	868,087	865,138	839,802	699,696	799,475
1985	3,452,685	1,442,151	2,010,534	2,898,612	489,390	162,841	373,319	—	—	257,766	860,457	902,836	895,466	688,682	743,512
1986	3,596,836	1,497,550	2,099,286	3,047,667	472,812	196,877	425,068	—	—	272,217	899,327	919,475	883,873	699,529	843,761
1987	3,447,742	1,463,593	1,984,149	2,896,268	475,441	185,888	373,037	—	—	251,739	906,920	876,259	853,897	683,563	746,445
1988	3,536,041	1,486,621	2,049,419	2,968,548	487,336	194,020	403,077	—	—	240,383	950,487	867,260	878,813	667,326	761,921
1989	3,693,063	1,558,251	2,134,812	3,086,574	511,335	198,844	452,579	—	—	250,856	1,000,770	871,017	918,996	668,797	812,380
1990	3,669,240	1,558,060	2,111,180	3,056,745	536,079	209,599	383,383	—	—	250,514	970,935	919,089	935,720	656,228	835,979
1991	3,996,402	1,700,766	2,295,636	3,343,859	540,052	211,935	432,499	—	—	252,184	1,088,353	981,232	1,030,200	658,053	906,997
1992	4,096,344	1,739,005	2,357,339	3,384,361	585,873	200,297	398,297	—	—	259,772	1,122,042	1,025,083	1,090,854	683,819	946,331
1993	4,345,986	1,844,009	2,501,977	3,598,321	615,524	214,608	477,248	—	—	242,498	1,224,815	1,129,724	1,057,093	798,154	977,882
1994	4,142,587	1,722,895	2,419,692	3,375,104	607,636	204,255	426,347	—	—	243,520	1,122,933	1,073,017	1,072,514	803,445	879,302
1995	4,097,095	1,747,638	2,349,458	3,391,786	557,998	201,513	424,859	—	—	225,995	1,130,576	1,107,878	1,006,274	754,468	864,689

Note appears at end of table

(continued)

TABLE Bd694–735 Restricted-activity days, by sex, race, age, region, and income: 1967–1995 *Continued*

	Restricted-activity days						Restricted-activity days per person								
	Region		Family income					Sex		Race		Age			
	South	West	Less than $10,000	$10,000–$19,999	$20,000–$34,999	At least $35,000	Total population	Males	Females	Whites	Blacks	Under 5	5–17	Under 17	17–24
	Bd709	Bd710	Bd711	Bd712	Bd713	Bd714	Bd715	Bd716	Bd717	Bd718	Bd719	Bd720	Bd721	Bd722	Bd723
Year	Thousand days	Thousand days	Thousand days	Thousand days	Thousand days	Thousand days	Days	Days	Days	Days	Days	Days	Days	Days	Days
1967	—	—	—	—	—	—	15.3	13.9	16.5	—	—	—	—	9.2	9.9
1968	—	—	—	—	—	—	15.3	14.3	16.3	—	—	—	—	10.0	10.8
1969	—	—	—	—	—	—	14.8	13.4	16.0	—	—	—	—	9.8	9.0
1970	—	—	—	—	—	—	14.6	13.2	15.8	—	—	—	—	9.4	9.7
1971	—	—	—	—	—	—	15.7	14.2	17.0	—	—	—	—	10.9	10.4
1972	—	—	—	—	—	—	16.7	14.8	18.4	—	—	—	—	10.6	11.0
1973	—	—	—	—	—	—	16.5	14.7	18.1	—	—	—	—	10.7	11.7
1974	—	—	—	—	—	—	17.2	15.6	18.7	—	—	—	—	10.7	11.2
1975	—	—	—	—	—	—	17.9	15.6	20.0	—	—	—	—	11.0	12.3
1976	—	—	—	—	—	—	18.2	16.4	19.9	—	—	—	—	11.0	11.9
1977	—	—	—	—	—	—	17.8	15.8	19.6	—	—	—	—	11.2	11.5
1978	—	—	—	—	—	—	18.8	16.3	21.1	—	—	—	—	11.3	12.3
1979	—	—	—	—	—	—	19.0	16.9	21.1	—	—	—	—	11.0	12.8
1980	—	—	—	—	—	—	19.1	17.1	21.0	—	—	—	—	11.6	12.5
1981	—	—	—	—	—	—	19.1	17.3	20.7	—	—	—	—	10.5	12.0
1982	1,145,687	683,888	1,029,928	818,806	700,200	373,226	14.3	12.5	16.0	14.2	16.3	8.6	8.7	—	—
1983	1,184,025	656,828	1,014,836	784,233	689,129	426,963	14.5	12.3	16.5	14.3	16.6	10.9	9.1	—	—
1984	1,231,625	696,397	952,231	801,468	768,733	490,997	14.8	13.0	16.5	14.7	16.6	10.1	9.0	—	—
1985	1,308,277	712,214	893,469	780,839	791,431	568,175	14.8	12.8	16.6	14.5	17.4	9.0	8.3	—	—
1986	1,325,444	728,103	850,604	779,571	829,170	668,969	15.2	13.1	17.2	15.2	16.6	10.8	9.5	—	—
1987	1,220,462	797,272	756,223	750,091	761,358	685,267	14.5	12.7	16.1	14.3	16.4	10.2	8.3	—	—
1988	1,327,989	778,804	754,378	750,829	733,602	725,634	14.7	12.7	16.5	14.6	16.6	10.7	8.9	—	—
1989	1,391,864	820,021	693,856	768,149	751,965	797,505	15.2	13.2	17.0	15.0	17.1	10.6	10.0	—	—
1990	1,404,429	772,605	662,211	758,090	714,685	911,756	14.9	13.1	16.7	14.8	17.7	11.0	8.4	—	—
1991	1,529,302	902,050	711,369	789,232	724,301	983,186	16.1	14.1	17.9	16.1	17.5	10.9	9.4	—	—
1992	1,517,995	948,198	712,350	847,268	750,255	939,639	16.3	14.2	18.2	16.2	18.6	10.2	8.5	—	—
1993	1,563,977	1,005,973	741,457	857,210	848,503	1,085,904	17.1	14.9	19.2	17.0	19.2	10.8	10.0	—	—
1994	1,442,558	1,017,282	680,864	801,490	824,682	1,050,754	16.0	13.6	18.2	15.7	18.4	10.0	8.6	—	—
1995	1,561,006	916,932	649,479	793,876	823,638	1,133,083	15.6	13.7	17.5	15.6	17.0	9.9	8.4	—	—

	Restricted-activity days per person											
	Age				Region				Family income			
	18–24	25–44	45–64	65 and over	Northeast	Midwest	South	West	Less than $10,000	$10,000–$19,999	$20,000–$34,999	At least $35,000
	Bd724	Bd725	Bd726	Bd727	Bd728	Bd729	Bd730	Bd731	Bd732	Bd733	Bd734	Bd735
Year	Days	Days	Days	Days	Days	Days	Days	Days	Days	Days	Days	Days
1967	—	13.8	21.1	35.8	—	—	—	—	—	—	—	—
1968	—	12.9	20.8	35.0	—	—	—	—	—	—	—	—
1969	—	12.8	20.0	33.5	—	—	—	—	—	—	—	—
1970	—	13.4	20.0	30.7	—	—	—	—	—	—	—	—
1971	—	13.3	21.0	34.0	—	—	—	—	—	—	—	—
1972	—	14.7	22.7	36.5	—	—	—	—	—	—	—	—
1973	—	14.6	22.6	33.5	—	—	—	—	—	—	—	—
1974	—	14.8	23.6	38.0	—	—	—	—	—	—	—	—
1975	—	15.6	24.2	38.4	—	—	—	—	—	—	—	—
1976	—	15.5	25.4	40.0	—	—	—	—	—	—	—	—
1977	—	15.8	24.4	36.5	—	—	—	—	—	—	—	—
1978	—	16.2	25.8	40.3	—	—	—	—	—	—	—	—
1979	—	16.2	26.0	41.9	—	—	—	—	—	—	—	—
1980	—	16.5	26.5	39.2	—	—	—	—	—	—	—	—
1981	—	16.7	27.5	39.9	—	—	—	—	—	—	—	—
1982	8.6	11.6	20.2	31.6	13.5	12.8	15.4	15.6	24.6	14.4	10.8	9.3
1983	8.5	11.6	19.3	32.1	14.6	12.9	15.6	14.5	24.1	15.1	10.7	9.9
1984	9.6	12.4	19.5	31.8	13.9	13.4	16.0	15.5	24.3	15.8	12.0	10.2
1985	9.4	11.9	20.3	33.1	13.8	12.7	16.3	15.7	25.8	16.7	12.1	9.9
1986	10.2	12.1	20.6	32.1	13.8	14.6	16.4	15.5	25.4	17.3	13.2	10.5
1987	9.6	11.9	19.5	30.3	13.6	13.0	15.0	16.0	24.2	16.9	12.3	9.9
1988	9.4	12.3	19.0	30.6	13.5	12.8	16.1	15.6	26.6	17.8	12.3	9.7
1989	9.9	12.7	18.9	31.5	13.7	13.6	16.7	15.8	26.5	18.7	13.3	9.9
1990	10.0	12.1	19.7	31.4	13.2	14.0	16.7	14.8	27.3	19.1	13.5	10.3
1991	10.2	13.4	20.8	34.0	13.1	15.2	18.2	16.5	29.8	20.8	13.6	11.0
1992	10.7	13.8	21.1	35.4	13.7	15.4	18.0	17.1	29.0	22.1	14.6	10.3
1993	10.0	15.0	22.7	33.8	15.9	15.8	18.3	17.7	30.2	22.3	15.7	11.2
1994	9.6	13.5	21.3	34.6	15.9	13.9	16.4	17.6	29.1	21.5	15.2	10.5
1995	9.1	13.6	21.4	32.0	14.7	13.9	16.9	16.4	30.0	21.0	15.1	10.6

[1] Beginning in 1982, estimates may not be comparable to earlier estimates because the later data are based on a revised questionnaire and field procedures.

Source

U.S. National Center for Health Statistics, *Vital and Health Statistics,* series 10, published annually.

Documentation

A restricted-activity day is one in which a person cuts down on his or her usual activities because of illness or injury. Restricted-activity days include bed-disability, work-loss, and school-loss days.

The data include estimated totals and rates for the civilian noninstitutionalized population from the National Health Interview Survey.

See Table Ap-G in Appendix 2 regarding the composition of census regions and divisions.

TABLE Bd736–777 Bed-disability days, by sex, race, age, region, and income: 1967–1995[1]

Contributed by Richard H. Steckel

	Bed-disability days														
		Sex		Race		Age								Region	
	Total	Males	Females	Whites	Blacks	Under 5	5–17	Under 17	17–24	18–24	25–44	45–64	65 and over	Northeast	Midwest
	Bd736	Bd737	Bd738	Bd739	Bd740	Bd741	Bd742	Bd743	Bd744	Bd745	Bd746	Bd747	Bd748	Bd749	Bd750
Year	Thousand days	Thousand days	Thousand days	Thousand days	Thousand days	Thousand days	Thousand days	Thousand days	Thousand days	Thousand days	Thousand days	Thousand days	Thousand days	Thousand days	Thousand days
1967	1,109,428	464,461	644,967	—	—	—	—	270,892	100,551	—	232,125	282,447	223,413	—	—
1968	1,233,240	533,071	165,516	—	—	—	—	300,785	114,823	—	245,008	306,694	265,929	—	—
1969	1,197,587	505,768	691,819	—	—	—	—	314,235	98,805	—	235,496	307,880	241,170	—	—
1970	1,222,319	502,566	719,753	—	—	—	—	291,908	115,399	—	242,050	309,858	263,104	—	—
1971	1,238,873	525,750	713,122	—	—	—	—	316,677	124,048	—	231,024	310,753	256,371	—	—
1972	1,319,566	539,167	780,399	—	—	—	—	296,319	136,317	—	273,431	332,397	281,102	—	—
1973	1,310,835	528,282	782,554	—	—	—	—	289,258	151,486	—	275,058	329,668	265,365	—	—
1974	1,391,702	584,282	807,420	—	—	—	—	301,453	135,085	—	296,588	361,499	297,076	—	—
1975	1,371,418	546,363	825,055	—	—	—	—	274,160	154,567	—	305,609	362,902	274,179	—	—
1976	1,500,246	618,512	881,734	—	—	—	—	310,149	159,241	—	316,238	386,485	328,133	—	—
1977	1,458,189	589,209	868,980	—	—	—	—	312,006	141,687	—	326,191	354,574	323,729	—	—
1978	1,524,093	617,418	906,675	—	—	—	—	307,116	174,416	—	330,333	380,759	331,469	—	—
1979	1,455,156	584,715	870,442	—	—	—	—	286,402	159,335	—	331,305	359,365	318,731	—	—
1980	1,520,067	616,258	903,809	—	—	—	—	301,937	152,674	—	368,041	367,351	330,064	—	—
1981	1,553,428	634,377	919,051	—	—	—	—	284,872	162,809	—	361,530	396,808	347,409	—	—
1982	1,444,556	591,850	852,706	1,182,455	226,290	77,642	172,760	—	—	110,669	337,400	372,746	373,338	300,686	311,019
1983	1,529,698	631,915	897,783	1,264,351	235,995	97,542	184,432	—	—	105,438	334,558	374,790	432,538	327,255	333,585
1984	1,508,203	624,172	884,031	1,251,628	221,806	80,666	185,318	—	—	126,539	348,783	368,913	397,984	302,413	345,508
1985	1,435,747	583,310	852,437	1,176,832	225,432	78,871	172,216	—	—	102,674	343,166	367,335	371,485	273,488	326,633
1986	1,547,980	613,113	934,867	1,298,039	220,102	89,762	200,350	—	—	111,208	363,751	371,710	411,199	297,286	368,999
1987	1,474,290	595,016	879,274	1,207,093	234,328	89,956	167,705	—	—	103,048	361,090	358,779	373,713	311,605	309,844
1988	1,519,199	607,386	911,814	1,251,141	233,134	98,274	180,885	—	—	99,546	366,097	362,302	412,094	290,685	314,340
1989	1,579,015	652,452	926,563	1,296,498	239,252	96,358	221,476	—	—	103,686	388,463	353,898	415,134	276,263	324,592
1990	1,521,141	625,349	895,792	1,235,051	248,277	100,817	167,751	—	—	102,200	372,780	371,663	405,930	268,324	330,457
1991	1,612,545	656,879	955,666	1,312,883	245,659	89,829	190,601	—	—	108,503	403,591	373,470	446,552	258,366	329,830
1992	1,585,168	647,620	937,548	1,270,763	259,241	92,247	172,433	—	—	86,060	405,482	374,204	454,741	278,083	330,010
1993	1,707,787	688,269	1,019,518	1,381,081	270,598	94,144	200,310	—	—	101,337	456,712	433,593	421,691	293,553	389,783
1994	1,602,711	623,041	979,670	1,263,995	276,958	91,483	168,898	—	—	97,683	395,735	400,900	448,003	296,801	337,799
1995	1,593,029	677,813	915,217	1,288,777	238,554	99,224	177,537	—	—	92,688	406,470	405,111	411,999	289,925	313,638

	Bed-disability days						Bed-disability days per person								
	Region		Family income					Sex		Race		Age			
	South	West	Less than $10,000	$10,000–$19,999	$20,000–$34,999	At least $35,000	Total population	Males	Females	Whites	Blacks	Under 5	5–17	Under 17	17–24
	Bd751	Bd752	Bd753	Bd754	Bd755	Bd756	Bd757	Bd758	Bd759	Bd760	Bd761	Bd762	Bd763	Bd764	Bd765
Year	Thousand days	Thousand days	Thousand days	Thousand days	Thousand days	Thousand days	Days	Days	Days	Days	Days	Days	Days	Days	Days
1967	—	—	—	—	—	—	5.7	5.0	6.4	—	—	—	—	4.0	3.3
1968	—	—	—	—	—	—	6.3	5.7	6.9	—	—	—	—	4.5	4.8
1969	—	—	—	—	—	—	6.1	5.3	6.8	—	—	—	—	4.7	4.0
1970	—	—	—	—	—	—	6.1	5.2	6.9	—	—	—	—	4.4	4.2
1971	—	—	—	—	—	—	6.1	5.4	6.8	—	—	—	—	4.8	4.5
1972	—	—	—	—	—	—	6.5	5.5	7.4	—	—	—	—	4.6	4.8
1973	—	—	—	—	—	—	6.4	5.3	7.3	—	—	—	—	4.5	5.2
1974	—	—	—	—	—	—	6.7	5.8	7.5	—	—	—	—	4.8	4.6
1975	—	—	—	—	—	—	6.6	5.4	7.6	—	—	—	—	4.4	5.1
1976	—	—	—	—	—	—	7.1	6.1	8.1	—	—	—	—	5.1	5.1
1977	—	—	—	—	—	—	6.9	5.8	7.9	—	—	—	—	5.2	4.5
1978	—	—	—	—	—	—	7.1	6.0	8.2	—	—	—	—	5.2	5.5
1979	—	—	—	—	—	—	6.7	5.6	7.8	—	—	—	—	4.9	5.0
1980	—	—	—	—	—	—	7.0	5.9	8.0	—	—	—	—	5.2	4.7
1981	—	—	—	—	—	—	6.9	5.8	7.9	—	—	—	—	4.8	4.9
1982	549,361	283,490	469,706	359,628	286,026	158,904	6.4	5.4	7.3	6.1	8.4	4.5	3.8	—	—
1983	573,028	295,831	513,842	345,061	293,571	177,435	6.7	5.7	7.6	6.4	8.6	5.5	4.1	—	—
1984	564,126	296,156	454,619	340,075	302,160	210,783	6.5	5.6	7.4	6.3	8.0	4.5	4.2	—	—
1985	552,652	282,975	386,890	329,607	301,667	225,255	6.1	5.2	7.1	5.9	8.0	4.4	3.8	—	—
1986	591,229	290,466	384,962	346,115	326,166	275,957	6.5	5.4	7.7	6.5	7.7	4.9	4.5	—	—
1987	559,230	293,610	355,276	332,454	302,381	270,851	6.2	5.2	7.1	6.0	8.1	4.9	3.7	—	—
1988	589,768	324,407	346,753	333,922	292,823	287,547	6.3	5.2	7.3	6.2	7.9	5.3	4.0	—	—
1989	609,216	368,943	318,556	334,501	296,046	321,029	6.5	5.5	7.4	6.3	8.0	5.1	4.9	—	—
1990	609,175	313,186	296,207	321,300	289,652	339,261	6.2	5.2	7.1	6.0	8.2	5.3	3.7	—	—
1991	675,048	349,301	294,523	323,823	269,109	374,261	6.5	5.4	7.5	6.3	8.0	4.6	4.1	—	—
1992	617,777	359,298	308,268	318,106	289,537	333,909	6.3	5.3	7.3	6.1	8.2	4.7	3.7	—	—
1993	663,033	361,418	312,081	365,581	319,722	396,667	6.7	5.6	7.8	6.5	8.4	4.7	4.2	—	—
1994	599,846	368,263	279,494	311,908	300,618	381,061	6.2	4.9	7.4	5.9	8.4	4.5	3.4	—	—
1995	651,991	337,475	285,679	318,336	330,332	395,698	6.1	5.3	6.8	5.9	7.3	4.9	3.5	—	—

Note appears at end of table

(continued)

TABLE Bd736–777 Bed-disability days, by sex, race, age, region, and income: 1967–1995 *Continued*

	Bed-disability days per person											
	Age				Region				Family income			
	18–24	25–44	45–64	65 and over	Northeast	Midwest	South	West	Less than $10,000	$10,000–$19,999	$20,000–$34,999	At least $35,000
	Bd766	Bd767	Bd768	Bd769	Bd770	Bd771	Bd772	Bd773	Bd774	Bd775	Bd776	Bd777
Year	Days	Days	Days	Days	Days	Days	Days	Days	Days	Days	Days	Days
1967	—	6.1	7.1	12.4	—	—	—	—	—	—	—	—
1968	—	5.3	7.6	14.5	—	—	—	—	—	—	—	—
1969	—	5.1	7.6	12.9	—	—	—	—	—	—	—	—
1970	—	5.1	6.4	6.2	—	—	—	—	—	—	—	—
1971	—	4.9	7.4	13.2	—	—	—	—	—	—	—	—
1972	—	5.6	7.9	14.1	—	—	—	—	—	—	—	—
1973	—	5.5	7.8	13.1	—	—	—	—	—	—	—	—
1974	—	5.8	8.4	14.3	—	—	—	—	—	—	—	—
1975	—	5.8	8.4	12.9	—	—	—	—	—	—	—	—
1976	—	5.9	8.9	15.1	—	—	—	—	—	—	—	—
1977	—	5.9	8.2	14.5	—	—	—	—	—	—	—	—
1978	—	5.8	8.8	14.5	—	—	—	—	—	—	—	—
1979	—	5.6	8.3	13.7	—	—	—	—	—	—	—	—
1980	—	6.1	8.4	13.8	—	—	—	—	—	—	—	—
1981	—	5.6	9.0	14.0	—	—	—	—	—	—	—	—
1982	3.8	5.1	8.4	14.7	6.1	5.3	7.4	6.5	11.2	6.3	4.4	3.9
1983	3.7	4.9	8.5	16.7	6.7	5.7	7.5	6.5	12.2	6.7	4.6	4.1
1984	4.5	5.0	8.3	15.1	6.0	5.8	7.3	6.6	11.6	6.7	4.7	4.4
1985	3.7	4.8	8.3	13.7	5.5	5.6	6.9	6.3	11.2	7.0	4.6	3.9
1986	4.2	4.9	8.3	14.9	5.9	6.4	7.3	6.2	11.5	7.7	5.2	4.3
1987	3.9	4.8	8.0	14.0	6.2	5.4	6.9	5.9	11.4	7.5	4.9	3.9
1988	3.9	4.7	7.9	14.4	5.9	5.3	7.2	6.5	12.2	7.9	4.9	3.8
1989	4.1	4.9	7.9	14.2	5.6	5.5	7.3	7.1	12.2	8.2	5.2	4.0
1990	4.1	4.7	8.0	13.6	5.4	5.5	7.2	6.0	12.2	8.1	5.5	3.8
1991	4.4	5.0	7.9	14.7	5.1	5.5	8.0	6.4	12.3	8.5	5.1	4.2
1992	3.5	5.0	7.7	14.8	5.6	5.4	7.3	6.5	12.6	8.3	5.6	3.7
1993	4.2	5.6	8.7	13.5	5.9	6.3	7.8	6.4	12.7	9.5	5.9	4.1
1994	3.9	4.8	8.0	14.4	5.9	5.3	6.8	6.4	12.0	8.4	5.5	3.8
1995	3.7	4.9	7.8	13.1	5.6	5.0	7.1	6.0	13.2	8.4	6.0	3.7

[1] Beginning in 1982, estimates may not be comparable to earlier estimates because the later data are based on a revised questionnaire and field procedures.

Source

U.S. National Center for Health Statistics, *Vital and Health Statistics,* series 10, published annually.

Documentation

A bed-disability day is one in which a person is kept in bed either all or most of the day because of illness or injury.

The data include estimated totals and rates for the civilian noninstitutionalized population from the National Health Interview Survey.

See Table Ap-G in Appendix 2 regarding the composition of census regions and divisions.

TABLE Bd778–819 Work-loss and school-loss days, by sex, race, age, region, and income: 1967–1995[1]

Contributed by Richard H. Steckel

	School-loss days			Work-loss days											
					Sex		Race		Age					Region	
	Total	Males	Females	Total	Males	Females	Whites	Blacks	17–24	18–24	25–44	45–64	65 and over	Northeast	Midwest
	Bd778 [2]	Bd779 [2]	Bd780 [2]	Bd781	Bd782	Bd783	Bd784	Bd785	Bd786	Bd787	Bd788	Bd789	Bd790	Bd791	Bd792
Year	Thousand days	Thousand days	Thousand days	Thousand days	Thousand days	Thousand days	Thousand days	Thousand days	Thousand days	Thousand days	Thousand days	Thousand days	Thousand days	Thousand days	Thousand days
1967	191,780	96,437	95,343	406,005	251,652	154,353	—	—	59,142	—	154,522	170,043	22,298	—	—
1968	219,229	106,454	112,775	412,639	247,103	165,516	—	—	67,906	—	154,627	171,372	18,720	—	—
1969	242,308	114,258	128,050	397,196	246,531	150,665	—	—	52,506	—	153,884	171,708	19,099	—	—
1970	221,487	107,889	113,598	417,185	242,604	174,581	—	—	61,366	—	161,806	173,369	20,644	—	—
1971	249,583	119,559	130,025	396,210	236,031	160,180	—	—	64,476	—	150,694	163,663	17,377	—	—
1972	235,402	110,532	124,870	428,190	257,863	170,327	—	—	66,533	—	165,609	179,749	16,299	—	—
1973	221,742	103,443	118,299	451,429	263,994	187,435	—	—	85,893	—	184,310	161,997	19,230	—	—
1974	241,844	126,093	115,750	414,302	245,285	169,017	—	—	79,651	—	164,610	156,790	13,243	—	—
1975	217,102	102,500	114,601	433,152	245,786	187,367	—	—	82,413	—	184,187	154,438	12,122	—	—
1976	218,665	104,763	113,901	465,472	269,027	196,444	—	—	84,481	—	203,814	165,524	11,653	—	—
1977	223,450	109,332	114,118	450,289	251,402	198,887	—	—	86,646	—	189,546	160,561	13,536	—	—
1978	220,480	104,450	116,030	486,036	266,154	219,883	—	—	91,734	—	214,643	167,040	12,619	—	—
1979	208,758	101,348	107,409	483,152	261,354	221,797	—	—	105,460	—	208,921	153,964	14,802	—	—
1980	203,984	94,999	108,985	485,324	270,741	214,582	—	—	96,541	—	224,876	150,715	13,191	—	—
1981	191,420	91,884	99,536	491,781	262,062	229,719	—	—	86,071	—	235,077	156,925	13,707	—	—
1982	214,352	102,612	111,740	452,614	225,164	227,451	389,795	53,540	—	72,625	209,116	153,766	17,108	148,592	164,888
1983	224,724	107,126	117,598	419,249	207,088	212,161	362,219	49,996	—	64,980	206,686	131,319	16,264	136,344	171,192
1984	227,130	108,409	118,721	512,498	258,567	253,930	434,884	69,298	—	82,799	262,581	150,131	16,987	162,338	186,440
1985	216,721	99,716	117,005	575,062	287,279	287,784	488,796	76,943	—	81,744	284,780	185,999	22,540	181,992	194,045
1986	226,369	99,472	126,897	607,027	302,032	304,995	522,341	71,679	—	91,140	295,692	191,693	28,501	167,905	218,869
1987	198,330	96,113	102,216	602,625	299,049	303,576	502,336	86,849	—	79,929	309,254	188,867	24,575	168,165	193,971
1988	222,204	106,942	115,262	609,106	306,956	302,151	501,150	89,858	—	83,927	336,853	166,778	21,548	165,675	185,270
1989	259,967	129,345	130,623	658,720	322,121	336,599	542,267	94,693	—	83,430	359,910	187,857	27,523	170,839	214,474
1990	211,787	99,772	112,016	621,471	302,609	318,862	510,840	93,252	—	91,590	321,226	184,072	24,582	166,184	207,581
1991	236,887	113,756	123,161	650,138	312,667	337,471	550,921	82,823	—	74,386	356,682	199,438	19,633	170,312	220,107
1992	214,578	100,939	113,639	597,087	280,440	316,647	480,901	93,932	—	75,945	314,742	183,483	22,917	151,943	199,834
1993	249,928	121,132	128,796	666,067	314,943	351,124	551,643	89,017	—	66,789	368,274	208,371	22,674	178,525	225,570
1994	224,814	104,015	120,799	642,115	310,514	331,601	524,139	91,974	—	68,806	333,629	216,709	22,969	162,866	208,257
1995	228,973	107,455	121,517	656,604	307,403	349,201	535,850	94,870	—	66,412	346,255	216,821	27,115	167,509	206,074

Notes appear at end of table

(continued)

TABLE Bd778–819 Work-loss and school-loss days, by sex, race, age, region, and income: 1967–1995 *Continued*

	Work-loss days						School-loss days			Work-loss days per person				
	Region		Family income								Sex		Race	
	South	West	Less than $10,000	$10,000–$19,999	$20,000–$34,999	At least $35,000	Per child	Per male student	Per female student	Total	Males	Females	Whites	Blacks
	Bd793	Bd794	Bd795	Bd796	Bd797	Bd798	Bd799 [2]	Bd800 [2]	Bd801 [2]	Bd802	Bd803	Bd804	Bd805	Bd806
Year	Thousand days	Thousand days	Thousand days	Thousand days	Thousand days	Thousand days	Days	Days	Days	Days	Days	Days	Days	Days
1967	—	—	—	—	—	—	4.4	4.4	4.4	5.4	5.3	5.6	—	—
1968	—	—	—	—	—	—	4.9	4.7	5.2	5.4	5.2	5.9	—	—
1969	—	—	—	—	—	—	5.4	5.0	5.8	5.2	5.1	5.2	—	—
1970	—	—	—	—	—	—	4.9	4.7	5.1	5.4	5.0	5.9	—	—
1971	—	—	—	—	—	—	5.5	5.2	5.9	5.1	4.9	5.5	—	—
1972	—	—	—	—	—	—	5.3	4.9	5.8	5.3	5.2	5.6	—	—
1973	—	—	—	—	—	—	5.1	4.7	5.5	5.4	5.2	5.8	—	—
1974	—	—	—	—	—	—	5.6	5.7	5.5	4.9	4.8	5.1	—	—
1975	—	—	—	—	—	—	5.1	4.8	5.5	5.2	4.9	5.7	—	—
1976	—	—	—	—	—	—	5.2	4.9	5.5	5.3	4.4	5.3	—	—
1977	—	—	—	—	—	—	5.4	5.2	5.6	5.0	4.7	5.3	—	—
1978	—	—	—	—	—	—	5.4	5.1	5.8	5.2	4.9	5.7	—	—
1979	—	—	—	—	—	—	5.3	5.0	5.5	5.0	4.7	5.4	—	—
1980	—	—	—	—	—	—	5.3	4.8	5.7	5.0	4.9	5.1	—	—
1981	—	—	—	—	—	—	4.9	4.6	5.3	4.9	4.6	5.3	—	—
1982	219,908	133,578	59,954	114,591	147,895	87,403	4.7	4.4	5.0	4.6	4.0	5.3	4.5	5.6
1983	214,117	122,321	55,133	107,199	134,522	84,397	5.0	4.7	5.4	4.2	3.7	4.9	4.1	5.2
1984	237,146	153,704	63,012	125,484	163,187	110,046	5.1	4.8	5.3	4.9	4.4	5.6	4.7	6.8
1985	257,448	158,298	60,085	118,546	192,139	148,188	4.8	4.4	5.3	5.3	4.8	6.0	5.2	7.1
1986	291,785	290,466	55,059	126,060	190,886	164,616	5.0	4.3	5.8	5.5	5.0	6.1	5.4	6.3
1987	268,894	169,924	54,314	108,942	179,215	184,927	4.4	4.2	4.6	5.4	4.8	6.1	5.2	7.6
1988	278,739	201,627	49,422	112,297	175,511	184,873	4.9	4.6	5.2	5.3	4.8	5.8	5.0	7.4
1989	324,145	209,229	47,752	110,749	179,491	213,144	5.7	5.6	5.9	5.6	5.0	6.4	5.4	7.7
1990	271,750	187,744	35,897	104,406	157,302	240,543	4.6	4.3	5.0	5.3	4.7	5.9	5.0	7.5
1991	300,949	195,657	44,819	95,614	168,309	239,787	5.1	4.8	5.5	5.6	4.9	6.3	5.5	6.8
1992	271,934	187,953	34,020	113,773	124,048	230,262	4.6	4.2	5.0	5.1	4.4	5.9	4.8	7.5
1993	317,207	194,693	43,419	105,208	149,292	259,235	5.3	5.0	5.5	5.6	4.8	6.4	5.4	7.1
1994	287,205	208,601	41,608	105,725	155,058	253,890	4.5	4.1	5.0	5.2	4.6	5.9	5.0	6.9
1995	324,920	187,074	36,544	93,962	147,669	298,547	4.5	4.2	4.9	5.3	4.5	6.1	5.1	7.1

	Work-loss days per person												
	Age					Region				Family income			
	17–24	18–24	25–44	45–64	65 and over	Northeast	Midwest	South	West	Less than $10,000	$10,000–$19,999	$20,000–$34,999	At least $35,000
	Bd807	Bd808	Bd809	Bd810	Bd811	Bd812	Bd813	Bd814	Bd815	Bd816	Bd817	Bd818	Bd819
Year	Days	Days	Days	Days	Days	Days	Days	Days	Days	Days	Days	Days	Days
1967	4.2	—	5.0	6.4	6.7	—	—	—	—	—	—	—	—
1968	4.8	—	4.9	6.3	5.8	—	—	—	—	—	—	—	—
1969	3.6	—	4.8	6.3	5.8	—	—	—	—	—	—	—	—
1970	4.1	—	5.1	6.4	6.2	—	—	—	—	—	—	—	—
1971	4.2	—	4.7	6.1	5.5	—	—	—	—	—	—	—	—
1972	3.9	—	5.0	6.6	5.3	—	—	—	—	—	—	—	—
1973	4.7	—	5.3	5.9	6.2	—	—	—	—	—	—	—	—
1974	4.4	—	4.6	5.8	4.4	—	—	—	—	—	—	—	—
1975	4.6	—	5.1	5.8	4.3	—	—	—	—	—	—	—	—
1976	4.4	—	5.3	6.1	4.0	—	—	—	—	—	—	—	—
1977	4.3	—	4.7	5.9	4.2	—	—	—	—	—	—	—	—
1978	4.5	—	5.1	6.1	4.2	—	—	—	—	—	—	—	—
1979	4.9	—	4.7	5.6	4.6	—	—	—	—	—	—	—	—
1980	4.6	—	4.9	5.4	3.9	—	—	—	—	—	—	—	—
1981	4.1	—	4.8	5.7	4.2	—	—	—	—	—	—	—	—
1982	—	3.9	4.3	5.6	5.3	4.7	4.4	4.7	4.8	5.7	4.8	4.6	3.9
1983	—	3.5	4.1	4.8	5.2	4.5	4.6	4.5	4.3	5.3	5.0	4.2	3.5
1984	—	4.4	4.8	5.3	5.2	5.0	4.8	4.8	5.3	6.4	5.0	4.9	2.9
1985	—	4.4	5.0	6.5	7.0	5.7	5.1	5.0	5.3	7.1	6.1	5.8	4.5
1986	—	5.0	5.0	6.5	7.9	5.1	5.7	5.5	4.9	6.3	6.8	5.9	4.4
1987	—	4.5	5.1	6.4	7.1	5.2	5.0	5.0	5.1	7.3	6.0	5.6	4.6
1988	—	4.7	5.3	5.4	5.9	5.1	4.6	5.1	6.0	7.1	6.5	5.7	4.2
1989	—	4.7	5.6	6.0	7.1	5.3	5.3	5.9	6.0	7.7	6.9	6.1	4.5
1990	—	5.4	4.9	5.8	6.1	5.1	5.2	4.9	5.3	6.1	6.8	5.9	4.7
1991	—	4.6	5.5	6.2	5.1	5.2	5.5	5.5	5.5	8.3	6.9	6.3	4.6
1992	—	4.8	4.8	5.5	5.7	4.7	4.8	4.9	5.2	6.0	8.1	4.9	4.3
1993	—	4.2	5.6	6.1	5.6	5.6	5.4	5.7	5.2	7.5	7.5	5.7	4.6
1994	—	4.1	5.0	6.2	5.9	5.0	4.8	4.9	5.5	7.7	7.7	5.8	4.4
1995	—	4.0	5.1	6.0	6.8	5.0	4.8	5.2	5.1	7.3	6.7	5.5	4.8

[1] Beginning in 1982, estimates may not be comparable to earlier estimates because the later data are based on a revised questionnaire and field procedures.

[2] Through 1981, data apply to children ages 6 to 16; thereafter, ages 5 to 17.

Source

U.S. National Center for Health Statistics, *Vital and Health Statistics,* series 10, published annually.

Documentation

A school-loss day is one in which a child loses an entire day of school due to illness or injury. A work-loss day is one in which a person loses an entire workday because of illness or injury.

The data include estimated totals and rates for the civilian noninstitutionalized population from the National Health Interview Survey.

See Table Ap-G in Appendix 2 regarding the composition of census regions and divisions.

TABLE Bd820–879 Persons with activity limitation due to chronic conditions, by sex, race, age, income, and degree of limitation: 1967–1995[1]

Contributed by Richard H. Steckel

	Persons with activity limitation														
		Sex		Race		Age						Family income			
	Total	Males	Females	Whites	Blacks	Under 17	Under 18	17–44	18–44	44–64	65 and over	Less than $10,000	$10,000–$19,999	$20,000–$34,999	At least $35,000
	Bd820	Bd821	Bd822	Bd823	Bd824	Bd825	Bd826	Bd827	Bd828	Bd829	Bd830	Bd831	Bd832	Bd833	Bd834
Year	Thousand	Thousand	Thousand	Thousand	Thousand	Thousand	Thousand	Thousand	Thousand	Thousand	Thousand	Thousand	Thousand	Thousand	Thousand
1967	22,248	11,372	10,876	—	—	1,418	—	4,994	—	7,493	8,343	—	—	—	—
1968	21,329	10,694	10,635	—	—	1,427	—	4,826	—	7,306	7,770	—	—	—	—
1969	22,845	11,578	11,267	—	—	1,760	—	5,362	—	7,810	7,913	—	—	—	—
1970	23,630	11,902	11,728	—	—	1,820	—	5,643	—	8,163	8,003	—	—	—	—
1971	24,817	12,521	12,297	—	—	1,942	—	5,858	—	8,553	8,464	—	—	—	—
1972	25,868	13,006	12,861	—	—	1,921	—	6,407	—	8,926	8,613	—	—	—	—
1973	27,739	13,429	14,310	—	—	2,149	—	6,739	—	9,920	8,932	—	—	—	—
1974	29,292	14,275	15,017	—	—	2,305	—	7,149	—	10,327	9,511	—	—	—	—
1975	29,900	14,379	15,521	—	—	2,283	—	7,454	—	10,222	9,941	—	—	—	—
1976	30,175	14,565	15,611	—	—	2,267	—	7,512	—	10,505	9,891	—	—	—	—
1977	28,577	14,250	14,326	—	—	2,012	—	6,984	—	10,003	9,577	—	—	—	—
1978	30,306	14,748	15,557	—	—	2,309	—	7,501	—	10,244	10,252	—	—	—	—
1979	31,496	15,337	16,159	—	—	2,291	—	8,006	—	10,452	10,747	—	—	—	—
1980	31,410	15,481	15,929	—	—	2,223	—	7,979	—	10,412	10,795	—	—	—	—
1981	32,309	15,806	16,504	—	—	2,216	—	8,151	—	10,574	11,368	—	—	—	—
1983	32,809	15,295	17,514	28,073	4,217	—	3,185	—	8,470	10,751	10,404	10,500	8,326	6,311	3,678
1984	32,085	14,928	17,157	27,535	4,019	—	3,172	—	8,279	10,325	10,309	9,769	7,741	6,575	3,874
1985	32,726	15,312	17,414	28,038	4,091	—	3,221	—	8,391	10,405	10,709	8,899	7,654	7,066	4,674
1986	32,972	15,331	17,641	28,218	4,156	—	3,168	—	8,738	10,369	10,698	8,472	7,785	6,506	5,458
1987	32,204	14,931	17,273	27,488	4,161	—	3,164	—	8,456	10,029	10,555	7,900	7,564	6,577	5,428
1988	33,057	15,450	17,606	28,025	4,311	—	3,394	—	8,835	10,225	10,602	7,389	7,637	6,883	5,893
1989	34,218	16,117	18,101	29,084	4,441	—	3,405	—	9,418	10,215	11,180	7,014	7,972	6,728	6,559
1990	33,753	15,538	18,214	28,713	4,297	—	3,182	—	9,232	10,171	11,167	6,349	7,460	6,417	7,483
1991	35,482	16,734	18,748	30,212	4,451	—	3,796	—	9,746	10,466	11,474	6,363	7,533	6,631	7,798
1992	37,733	17,783	19,950	31,693	5,008	—	4,047	—	10,681	11,063	11,940	6,692	8,084	7,220	8,226
1993	39,331	18,577	20,753	33,028	5,246	—	4,430	—	11,074	11,657	12,170	6,726	8,582	7,898	9,085
1994	39,059	18,206	20,853	32,404	5,396	—	4,711	—	11,094	11,407	11,847	6,544	7,877	8,007	9,488
1995	38,523	18,285	20,238	32,152	5,210	—	4,267	—	10,802	11,734	11,720	6,105	8,377	8,130	9,787

	Percentage of persons with no activity limitation														
		Sex		Race		Age						Family income			
	All persons	Males	Females	Whites	Blacks	Under 17	Under 18	17–44	18–44	45–64	65 and over	Less than $10,000	$10,000–$19,999	$20,000–$34,999	At least $35,000
	Bd835	Bd836	Bd837	Bd838	Bd839	Bd840	Bd841	Bd842	Bd843	Bd844	Bd845	Bd846	Bd847	Bd848	Bd849
Year	Percent	Percent	Percent	Percent	Percent	Percent	Percent	Percent	Percent	Percent	Percent	Percent	Percent	Percent	Percent
1967	88.5	87.8	89.1	—	—	97.9	—	92.7	—	81.1	53.7	—	—	—	—
1968	89.1	88.6	89.5	—	—	97.9	—	93.1	—	81.8	57.6	—	—	—	—
1969	88.4	87.8	89.0	—	—	97.4	—	92.5	—	80.8	57.6	—	—	—	—
1970	88.2	87.6	88.7	—	—	97.3	—	92.3	—	80.2	57.9	—	—	—	—
1971	87.7	87.2	88.3	—	—	97.1	—	92.2	—	79.5	56.3	—	—	—	—
1972	87.3	86.8	87.8	—	—	97.0	—	91.7	—	78.9	56.8	—	—	—	—
1973	86.5	86.5	86.6	—	—	96.6	—	91.5	—	76.7	55.9	—	—	—	—
1974	85.9	85.7	86.0	—	—	96.3	—	91.2	—	75.9	54.1	—	—	—	—
1975	85.7	85.7	85.7	—	—	96.3	—	91.0	—	76.3	53.3	—	—	—	—
1976	85.7	85.7	85.7	—	—	96.3	—	91.1	—	75.7	54.6	—	—	—	—
1977	86.5	86.1	86.9	—	—	96.6	—	91.9	—	76.9	57.0	—	—	—	—
1978	85.8	85.7	85.9	—	—	96.1	—	91.5	—	76.4	55.0	—	—	—	—
1979	85.4	85.3	85.5	—	—	96.1	—	91.2	—	75.9	54.6	—	—	—	—
1980	85.6	85.3	85.9	—	—	96.2	—	91.4	—	76.1	54.8	—	—	—	—
1981	85.6	85.4	85.8	—	—	96.2	—	91.6	—	76.1	54.3	—	—	—	—
1983	85.7	86.2	85.2	85.7	84.5	—	94.9	—	91.2	75.7	59.8	75.1	83.9	90.2	91.5
1984	86.1	86.7	85.7	86.1	85.5	—	94.9	—	91.6	76.7	61.0	75.1	84.7	89.7	92.0
1985	86.0	86.4	85.6	85.9	85.5	—	94.9	—	91.6	76.6	60.4	74.3	83.7	89.2	91.9
1986	86.0	86.6	85.5	85.9	85.4	—	95.0	—	91.3	76.8	61.2	74.7	82.7	89.6	91.4
1987	86.5	87.1	86.0	86.4	85.6	—	95.0	—	91.7	77.7	62.5	74.7	83.0	89.3	92.2
1988	86.3	86.8	85.8	86.2	85.3	—	94.7	—	91.4	77.6	63.0	74.0	81.9	88.5	92.1
1989	85.9	86.3	85.6	85.8	85.1	—	94.7	—	91.0	77.8	61.7	73.2	80.6	88.1	91.8
1990	86.3	87.0	85.6	86.1	85.9	—	95.1	—	91.2	78.2	62.5	73.8	81.2	87.9	91.5
1991	85.7	86.1	85.4	85.5	85.6	—	94.2	—	90.8	77.8	62.1	73.4	80.2	87.5	91.3
1992	85.0	85.4	84.6	84.9	84.1	—	93.9	—	89.9	77.2	61.2	72.7	79.0	85.9	91.0
1993	84.5	85.0	84.1	84.4	83.6	—	93.4	—	89.5	76.6	61.1	72.6	77.6	85.3	90.6
1994	85.0	85.6	84.3	84.9	83.7	—	93.3	—	89.7	77.4	61.8	72.0	78.9	85.2	90.6
1995	85.3	85.7	84.9	85.2	84.1	—	94.0	—	90.0	77.3	62.8	71.8	77.9	85.1	90.8

Note appears at end of table

(continued)

TABLE Bd820–879 Persons with activity limitation due to chronic conditions, by sex, race, age, income, and degree of limitation: 1967–1995 *Continued*

	Percentage of persons with activity limitation														
		Sex		Race		Age						Family income			
	All persons	Males	Females	Whites	Blacks	Under 17	Under 18	17–44	18–44	45–64	65 and over	Less than $10,000	$10,000–$19,999	$20,000–$34,999	At least $35,000
	Bd850	Bd851	Bd852	Bd853	Bd854	Bd855	Bd856	Bd857	Bd858	Bd859	Bd860	Bd861	Bd862	Bd863	Bd864
Year	Percent	Percent	Percent	Percent	Percent	Percent	Percent	Percent	Percent	Percent	Percent	Percent	Percent	Percent	Percent
1967	11.5	12.2	10.9	—	—	2.1	—	7.3	—	18.9	46.3	—	—	—	—
1968	10.9	11.4	10.5	—	—	2.1	—	6.9	—	18.2	42.4	—	—	—	—
1969	11.6	12.2	11.0	—	—	2.6	—	7.5	—	19.2	42.4	—	—	—	—
1970	11.8	12.4	11.3	—	—	2.7	—	7.7	—	19.8	42.1	—	—	—	—
1971	12.3	12.8	11.7	—	—	2.9	—	7.8	—	20.5	43.7	—	—	—	—
1972	12.7	13.2	12.2	—	—	3.0	—	8.3	—	21.1	43.2	—	—	—	—
1973	13.5	13.5	13.4	—	—	3.4	—	8.5	—	23.3	44.1	—	—	—	—
1974	14.1	14.3	14.0	—	—	3.7	—	8.8	—	24.1	45.9	—	—	—	—
1975	14.3	14.3	14.3	—	—	3.7	—	9.0	—	23.7	46.7	—	—	—	—
1976	14.3	14.3	14.3	—	—	3.7	—	8.9	—	24.3	45.4	—	—	—	—
1977	13.5	13.9	13.1	—	—	3.4	—	8.1	—	23.1	43.0	—	—	—	—
1978	14.2	14.3	14.1	—	—	3.9	—	8.5	—	23.6	45.0	—	—	—	—
1979	14.6	14.7	14.5	—	—	3.9	—	8.8	—	24.1	46.0	—	—	—	—
1980	14.4	14.7	14.1	—	—	3.8	—	8.6	—	23.9	45.2	—	—	—	—
1981	14.4	14.6	14.2	—	—	3.8	—	8.4	—	23.9	45.7	—	—	—	—
1983	14.3	13.8	14.8	14.3	15.5	—	5.1	—	8.8	24.3	40.2	24.9	16.1	9.8	8.5
1984	13.9	13.3	14.3	13.9	14.5	—	5.1	—	8.4	23.3	39.0	24.9	15.3	10.3	8.0
1985	14.0	13.6	14.4	14.1	14.5	—	5.1	—	8.4	23.4	39.6	25.7	16.3	10.8	8.1
1986	14.0	13.4	14.5	14.1	14.6	—	5.0	—	8.7	23.2	38.8	25.3	17.3	10.4	8.6
1987	13.5	12.9	14.0	13.6	14.4	—	5.0	—	8.3	22.3	37.5	25.3	17.0	10.7	7.8
1988	13.7	13.2	14.2	13.8	14.7	—	5.3	—	8.6	22.4	37.0	26.0	18.1	11.5	7.9
1989	14.1	13.7	14.4	14.2	14.9	—	5.3	—	9.0	22.2	38.3	26.8	19.4	11.9	8.2
1990	13.7	13.0	14.4	13.9	14.1	—	4.9	—	8.8	21.8	37.5	26.2	18.8	12.1	8.5
1991	14.3	13.9	14.6	14.5	14.4	—	5.8	—	9.2	22.2	37.9	26.6	19.8	12.5	8.7
1992	15.0	14.6	15.4	15.1	15.9	—	6.1	—	10.1	22.8	38.8	27.3	21.0	14.1	9.0
1993	15.5	15.0	15.9	15.6	16.4	—	6.6	—	10.5	23.4	38.9	27.4	22.4	14.7	9.4
1994	15.0	14.4	15.7	15.1	16.3	—	6.7	—	10.3	22.6	38.2	28.0	21.1	14.8	9.4
1995	14.7	14.3	15.1	14.8	15.9	—	6.0	—	10.0	22.7	37.2	28.2	22.1	14.9	9.2

	Percentage of persons with limitation in major activity														
		Sex		Race		Age						Family income			
	All persons	Males	Females	Whites	Blacks	Under 17	Under 18	17–44	18–44	45–64	65 and over	Less than $10,000	$10,000–$19,999	$20,000–$34,999	At least $35,000
	Bd865	Bd866	Bd867	Bd868	Bd869	Bd870	Bd871	Bd872	Bd873	Bd874	Bd875	Bd876	Bd877	Bd878	Bd879
Year	Percent	Percent	Percent	Percent	Percent	Percent	Percent	Percent	Percent	Percent	Percent	Percent	Percent	Percent	Percent
1967	8.7	9.8	7.7	—	—	1.1	—	4.7	—	14.2	40.0	—	—	—	—
1968	9.2	9.7	8.6	—	—	1.2	—	5.3	—	15.5	39.1	—	—	—	—
1969	9.1	9.6	8.7	—	—	1.2	—	5.2	—	15.9	37.5	—	—	—	—
1970	8.9	9.3	8.5	—	—	1.3	—	4.9	—	15.4	36.5	—	—	—	—
1971	9.3	9.7	8.9	—	—	1.5	—	4.9	—	16.0	38.7	—	—	—	—
1972	9.6	10.0	9.2	—	—	1.6	—	5.2	—	16.6	37.9	—	—	—	—
1973	10.2	10.2	10.1	—	—	1.9	—	5.4	—	18.4	37.7	—	—	—	—
1974	10.6	10.7	10.5	—	—	1.9	—	5.6	—	18.9	39.3	—	—	—	—
1975	10.8	10.8	10.8	—	—	1.9	—	5.7	—	18.7	40.5	—	—	—	—
1976	10.8	10.8	10.7	—	—	1.9	—	5.5	—	19.1	39.4	—	—	—	—
1977	10.4	10.9	9.9	—	—	1.8	—	5.2	—	18.6	37.3	—	—	—	—
1978	10.6	10.8	10.3	—	—	2.0	—	5.2	—	18.6	38.3	—	—	—	—
1979	10.9	11.1	10.7	—	—	2.1	—	5.5	—	18.6	39.2	—	—	—	—
1980	10.9	11.2	10.6	—	—	2.0	—	5.5	—	18.8	39.0	—	—	—	—
1981	10.9	11.3	10.6	—	—	2.0	—	5.4	—	19.1	39.2	—	—	—	—
1983	9.9	10.0	9.8	9.7	12.1	—	3.5	—	6.0	18.4	25.4	18.2	11.2	6.5	5.2
1984	9.7	9.7	9.7	9.6	11.1	—	3.6	—	5.8	17.8	24.7	18.0	10.9	7.0	5.1
1985	9.5	9.7	9.4	9.4	11.1	—	3.7	—	5.7	17.5	24.1	18.2	11.3	7.3	5.1
1986	9.4	9.5	9.4	9.3	11.1	—	3.6	—	5.7	17.8	22.7	18.0	12.0	7.0	5.2
1987	9.2	9.0	9.3	9.0	11.2	—	3.5	—	5.6	16.7	22.8	18.8	11.7	7.1	4.7
1988	9.4	9.5	9.4	9.3	11.2	—	3.9	—	5.9	16.9	22.6	18.9	12.7	7.8	5.0
1989	9.6	9.7	9.5	9.5	11.3	—	3.8	—	6.3	16.5	22.8	19.4	13.4	7.9	5.1
1990	9.3	9.1	9.5	9.2	10.7	—	3.6	—	6.2	16.1	22.1	19.2	13.3	8.0	5.2
1991	9.6	9.6	9.6	9.6	11.0	—	4.2	—	6.4	16.3	22.3	19.6	13.7	8.2	5.4
1992	10.3	10.2	10.4	10.2	12.2	—	4.4	—	7.0	17.2	23.2	20.2	14.8	9.4	5.6
1993	10.6	10.5	10.7	10.5	12.6	—	4.6	—	7.3	18.1	22.9	20.9	16.0	9.5	6.0
1994	10.3	10.1	10.5	10.2	12.5	—	4.9	—	7.1	17.1	22.6	21.1	15.0	10.1	5.8
1995	10.1	10.1	10.1	9.9	12.2	—	4.3	—	7.0	17.4	21.5	21.4	15.8	10.0	5.7

[1] Beginning in 1983, estimates may not be comparable to earlier estimates because the later data are based on a revised questionnaire and field procedures.

Source

U.S. National Center for Health Statistics, *Vital and Health Statistics,* series 10, published annually.

Documentation

Persons limited in their major activity are considered either unable to carry on their usual activity or limited in the amount or kind of their usual activity. Examples of major activity include working, keeping house, or engaging in school or preschool activities. Persons limited in other than their major activity include persons restricted in civic, church, recreational, or other activities.

The data include estimated totals and rates for the civilian noninstitutionalized population from the National Health Interview Survey.

TABLE Bd880–959 Persons injured, by sex, age, and place where injury occurred: 1967–1995[1]

Contributed by Richard H. Steckel

	Persons injured															
				Both sexes, by age									Male, by age			
	Total	Male	Female	Under 5	5–17	Under 6	6–16	17–44	18–24	25–44	45–64	65 and over	Under 6	6–16	Under 18	17–44
	Bd880	Bd881	Bd882	Bd883	Bd884	Bd885	Bd886	Bd887	Bd888	Bd889	Bd890	Bd891	Bd892	Bd893	Bd894	Bd895
Year	Thousand	Thousand	Thousand	Thousand	Thousand	Thousand	Thousand	Thousand	Thousand	Thousand	Thousand	Thousand	Thousand	Thousand	Thousand	Thousand
1967	52,967	30,465	22,502	—	—	8,852	12,863	19,832	—	—	8,610	2,810	5,229	8,283	—	11,494
1968	49,011	29,361	19,650	—	—	6,784	13,627	17,707	—	—	7,953	2,941	4,121	8,832	—	11,316
1969	48,712	29,815	18,897	—	—	6,168	13,973	17,239	—	—	8,445	2,888	3,893	8,998	—	11,838
1970	55,964	31,791	24,173	—	—	7,097	15,957	21,024	—	—	7,841	4,045	3,975	9,953	—	12,250
1971	62,539	35,653	26,886	—	—	8,217	17,859	24,052	—	—	8,343	4,067	4,491	10,375	—	15,251
1972	64,259	36,975	27,284	—	—	8,362	17,126	25,250	—	—	9,268	4,253	5,182	10,596	—	15,154
1973	59,973	34,763	25,209	—	—	7,161	16,141	25,470	—	—	7,812	3,390	4,353	9,784	—	15,554
1974	59,139	33,588	25,551	—	—	6,363	15,371	25,739	—	—	8,252	3,414	3,741	9,126	—	15,539
1975	71,903	39,417	32,487	—	—	9,306	17,621	30,434	—	—	10,038	4,505	5,212	11,162	—	17,326
1976	65,428	37,093	28,335	—	—	7,515	14,598	29,166	—	—	10,012	4,137	4,355	9,278	—	17,340
1977	73,927	42,326	31,601	—	—	7,837	17,677	34,069	—	—	9,579	4,765	4,480	11,362	—	20,264
1978	67,159	38,102	29,417	—	—	6,110	15,542	30,861	—	—	10,011	4,996	3,333	9,700	—	18,408
1979	69,127	40,226	28,901	—	—	7,102	13,823	33,807	—	—	10,139	4,256	4,102	8,806	—	20,779
1980	68,089	38,960	29,130	—	—	6,517	15,176	32,732	—	—	9,644	4,020	3,534	10,100	—	19,386
1981	70,252	40,053	30,199	—	—	7,284	14,828	34,364	—	—	9,232	4,544	4,094	8,885	—	20,974
1982	59,968	32,411	27,556	5,009	15,191	—	—	—	10,075	15,571	8,895	5,228	—	—	11,229	—
1983	61,114	32,989	28,124	5,187	15,100	—	—	—	8,692	17,375	8,773	5,988	—	—	12,306	—
1984	61,090	33,714	27,377	5,559	14,019	—	—	—	10,030	18,021	8,605	4,856	—	—	11,919	—
1985	62,565	34,588	27,977	5,478	15,174	—	—	—	9,407	20,283	7,406	4,817	—	—	11,578	—
1986	62,431	34,047	28,383	4,261	15,214	—	—	—	8,422	19,881	8,864	5,788	—	—	11,550	—
1987	62,073	33,646	28,427	4,751	14,392	—	—	—	8,332	20,621	8,043	5,935	—	—	11,079	—
1988	57,703	31,758	25,945	4,934	13,257	—	—	—	8,304	18,646	6,859	5,703	—	—	10,597	—
1989	57,999	31,743	26,256	4,166	12,827	—	—	—	6,929	21,929	7,339	4,809	—	—	10,431	—
1990	58,590	32,855	25,735	5,208	13,280	—	—	—	6,994	19,733	8,828	4,547	—	—	11,344	—
1991	58,263	31,623	26,640	4,490	13,512	—	—	—	7,517	18,806	8,263	5,674	—	—	10,598	—
1992	57,850	31,978	25,872	4,812	13,197	—	—	—	7,298	19,664	6,857	6,021	—	—	10,701	—
1993	58,969	31,671	27,298	4,955	12,212	—	—	—	6,561	20,265	9,110	5,867	—	—	10,048	—
1994	60,452	31,554	28,899	5,218	12,702	—	—	—	7,827	20,322	8,411	5,973	—	—	10,194	—
1995	61,304	33,092	28,212	5,467	14,411	—	—	—	5,793	18,704	11,025	5,904	—	—	12,357	—

	Persons injured														
	Male, by age				Female, by age								At home		
	18–44	45–64	45 and over	65 and over	Under 6	6–16	Under 18	17–44	18–44	45–64	45 and over	65 and over	Total	Male	Female
	Bd896	Bd897	Bd898	Bd899	Bd900	Bd901	Bd902	Bd903	Bd904	Bd905	Bd906	Bd907	Bd908	Bd909	Bd910
Year	Thousand	Thousand	Thousand	Thousand	Thousand	Thousand	Thousand	Thousand	Thousand	Thousand	Thousand	Thousand	Thousand	Thousand	Thousand
1967	—	4,338	—	1,121	3,623	4,580	—	8,339	—	4,272	—	1,689	23,012	10,378	12,633
1968	—	4,050	—	1,043	2,662	4,795	—	6,392	—	3,903	—	1,898	20,475	10,145	10,331
1969	—	4,307	—	780	2,275	4,974	—	5,401	—	4,138	—	2,108	19,681	10,508	9,173
1970	—	4,338	—	1,275	3,122	6,004	—	8,774	—	3,504	—	2,770	21,642	10,078	11,564
1971	—	3,855	—	1,681	3,725	7,485	—	8,801	—	4,488	—	2,386	23,984	11,849	12,134
1972	—	4,188	—	1,855	3,180	6,530	—	10,096	—	5,080	—	2,398	24,040	11,861	12,179
1973	—	3,763	—	1,309	2,807	6,357	—	9,916	—	4,048	—	2,082	22,697	10,754	11,943
1974	—	4,014	—	1,167	2,621	6,245	—	10,199	—	4,238	—	2,247	21,371	9,756	11,615
1975	—	4,412	—	1,305	4,094	6,459	—	13,108	—	5,626	—	3,200	31,197	14,066	17,131
1976	—	4,633	—	1,488	3,160	5,320	—	11,826	—	5,379	—	2,650	25,987	13,526	12,461
1977	—	4,504	—	1,716	3,357	6,315	—	13,805	—	5,075	—	3,049	29,588	14,444	15,145
1978	—	5,145	—	1,515	2,777	5,841	—	12,453	—	4,865	—	3,481	25,413	12,484	12,928
1979	—	5,000	—	1,540	3,000	5,017	—	13,028	—	5,139	—	2,716	24,745	13,021	11,725
1980	—	4,651	—	1,289	2,983	5,076	—	13,346	—	4,994	—	2,731	26,693	13,268	13,425
1981	—	4,380	—	1,719	3,190	5,942	—	13,389	—	4,852	—	2,825	26,909	13,388	13,521
1982	15,400	—	5,782	—	—	—	8,971	—	10,245	—	8,340	—	21,829	10,297	11,533
1983	14,737	—	5,946	—	—	—	7,981	—	11,329	—	8,814	—	22,411	10,658	11,753
1984	16,836	—	4,958	—	—	—	7,659	—	11,215	—	8,503	—	20,401	9,996	10,405
1985	18,148	—	4,863	—	—	—	9,074	—	11,543	—	7,360	—	21,641	9,716	11,926
1986	16,411	—	6,087	—	—	—	7,926	—	11,891	—	8,566	—	22,012	11,012	11,001
1987	16,713	—	5,854	—	—	—	8,063	—	12,240	—	8,124	—	20,968	11,042	9,926
1988	16,024	—	5,136	—	—	—	7,594	—	10,926	—	7,426	—	20,435	9,879	10,556
1989	16,133	—	5,179	—	—	—	6,562	—	12,725	—	6,969	—	17,569	9,220	8,349
1990	15,787	—	5,725	—	—	—	7,144	—	10,940	—	7,651	—	18,577	10,002	8,575
1991	15,084	—	5,941	—	—	—	7,405	—	11,239	—	7,996	—	18,425	7,728	10,697
1992	16,320	—	4,957	—	—	—	7,308	—	10,643	—	7,922	—	18,902	9,420	9,483
1993	15,348	—	6,274	—	—	—	7,118	—	11,478	—	8,702	—	18,869	8,957	9,911
1994	15,853	—	5,506	—	—	—	7,726	—	12,296	—	8,877	—	19,674	9,006	10,667
1995	13,724	—	7,010	—	—	—	7,520	—	10,774	—	9,918	—	17,994	9,614	8,381

Note appears at end of table

(continued)

TABLE Bd880–959 Persons injured, by sex, age, and place where injury occurred: 1967–1995 *Continued*

	Persons injured									Persons injured (per 100)							
	While in a moving motor vehicle			At work			At places other than home, a moving motor vehicle, or work						Both sexes, by age				
	Total	Male	Female	Total	Male	Female	Total	Male	Female	Persons	Male	Female	Under 5	Under 6	5–17	6–16	17–44
	Bd911	Bd912	Bd913	Bd914	Bd915	Bd916	Bd917	Bd918	Bd919	Bd920	Bd921	Bd922	Bd923	Bd924	Bd925	Bd926	Bd927
Year	Thousand	Thousand	Thousand	Thousand	Thousand	Thousand	Thousand	Thousand	Thousand	Per 100	Per 100	Per 100	Per 100	Per 100	Per 100	Per 100	Per 100
1967	3,780	1,578	2,202	9,203	8,032	1,171	18,607	11,772	6,835	27.4	32.7	22.5	—	37.8	—	29.4	28.9
1968	3,414	2,077	1,337	9,287	7,806	1,481	17,382	10,577	6,804	25.1	31.2	19.4	—	29.9	—	30.8	25.3
1969	3,651	1,940	1,711	8,241	6,968	1,273	19,028	11,931	7,097	24.7	31.4	18.5	—	27.9	—	31.2	24.2
1970	3,588	1,821	1,767	7,750	6,602	1,148	24,568	14,547	10,021	28.0	33.0	23.3	—	32.7	—	35.4	28.9
1971	4,741	2,660	2,081	9,631	8,341	1,290	26,068	14,466	11,603	30.9	36.5	25.7	—	38.4	—	39.5	32.2
1972	4,704	2,726	1,978	7,938	6,824	1,114	29,545	16,869	12,677	31.5	37.6	25.8	—	40.3	—	38.8	32.7
1973	3,927	2,265	1,662	9,027	7,493	1,534	26,785	16,113	10,672	29.1	35.0	23.7	—	35.1	—	37.0	32.2
1974	4,311	2,476	1,835	9,254	7,970	1,284	26,356	15,315	11,039	28.5	33.6	23.8	—	32.2	—	35.6	31.9
1975	5,140	2,821	2,319	9,841	7,576	2,264	28,352	16,700	11,652	34.4	39.1	30.0	—	47.7	—	41.5	36.8
1976	4,611	2,151	2,461	9,292	7,496	1,796	27,585	15,435	12,450	31.1	36.5	26.0	—	39.7	—	34.8	34.4
1977	5,033	2,861	2,172	11,414	9,012	2,402	31,435	18,898	12,537	34.8	41.3	28.8	—	42.4	—	42.7	39.3
1978	4,575	2,656	1,919	10,511	8,359	2,152	29,747	16,714	13,033	31.6	36.9	26.6	—	33.2	—	38.3	34.8
1979	5,025	2,834	2,191	12,014	9,316	2,698	30,131	17,209	12,923	32.0	38.6	25.9	—	38.1	—	34.9	37.3
1980	4,392	2,279	2,113	10,826	7,959	2,867	28,211	17,085	11,126	31.2	37.1	25.8	—	34.2	—	39.2	35.3
1981	5,019	2,424	2,595	11,291	9,074	2,216	29,812	17,521	12,291	31.2	36.9	25.9	—	36.2	—	38.2	35.4
1982	3,765	1,964	1,801	9,542	7,504	2,038	16,570	10,084	6,487	26.4	29.6	23.4	28.9	—	33.5	—	—
1983	5,416	2,991	2,425	8,920	7,014	1,905	14,991	9,137	5,854	26.6	29.8	23.7	29.1	—	33.7	—	—
1984	4,473	2,441	2,032	10,634	8,642	1,992	15,138	9,317	5,821	26.4	30.1	22.9	30.8	—	31.5	—	—
1985	5,081	2,584	2,497	11,363	8,008	3,355	17,071	12,042	5,029	26.8	30.6	23.1	30.4	—	33.9	—	—
1986	6,177	2,924	3,253	10,529	6,973	3,556	15,782	10,229	5,554	26.4	29.8	23.3	23.4	—	33.8	—	—
1987	5,808	3,349	2,459	9,131	6,509	2,622	15,801	8,717	7,084	26.0	29.1	23.1	26.1	—	31.9	—	—
1988	4,212	2,038	2,174	10,057	7,536	2,521	15,333	9,692	5,641	24.0	27.2	20.9	26.8	—	29.3	—	—
1989	5,353	2,537	2,816	10,947	7,794	3,154	14,247	8,573	5,674	23.8	26.9	20.9	22.2	—	28.4	—	—
1990	5,469	2,715	2,754	7,277	5,820	1,457	14,215	8,162	6,053	23.8	27.5	20.3	27.3	—	29.1	—	—
1991	4,993	2,963	2,031	8,673	6,363	2,310	15,171	9,941	5,230	23.4	26.2	20.8	23.2	—	29.3	—	—
1992	5,158	3,541	1,617	7,806	5,492	2,314	15,180	8,609	6,571	23.0	26.2	20.0	24.5	—	28.2	—	—
1993	5,594	2,859	2,735	8,752	6,921	1,831	14,224	7,963	6,261	23.2	25.6	20.9	24.9	—	25.7	—	—
1994	3,198	1,782	1,416	8,777	6,540	2,237	15,728	9,686	6,042	23.3	24.9	21.7	25.5	—	25.6	—	—
1995	3,753	1,901	1,852	7,764	4,513	3,251	16,785	9,795	6,990	23.4	25.9	21.0	27.0	—	28.6	—	—

	Persons injured (per 100)															
	Both sexes, by age				Male, by age								Female, by age			
	18–24	25–44	45–64	65 and over	Under 6	6–16	Under 18	17–44	18–44	45–64	45 and over	65 and over	Under 6	6–16	Under 18	17–44
	Bd928	Bd929	Bd930	Bd931	Bd932	Bd933	Bd934	Bd935	Bd936	Bd937	Bd938	Bd939	Bd940	Bd941	Bd942	Bd943
Year	Per 100	Per 100	Per 100	Per 100	Per 100	Per 100	Per 100	Per 100	Per 100	Per 100	Per 100	Per 100	Per 100	Per 100	Per 100	Per 100
1967	—	—	21.8	15.6	43.7	37.4	—	35.5	—	22.9	—	14.4	31.7	21.3	—	22.9
1968	—	—	19.8	16.0	35.6	39.3	—	34.3	—	21.1	—	13.2	24.0	22.0	—	17.3
1969	—	—	20.7	15.5	34.4	39.6	—	35.2	—	22.2	—	9.8	21.1	22.5	—	14.4
1970	—	—	19.0	21.3	35.9	43.5	—	35.4	—	22.1	—	15.8	29.5	27.1	—	22.9
1971	—	—	20.0	21.0	41.1	45.2	—	42.7	—	19.4	—	20.5	35.6	33.7	—	22.6
1972	—	—	21.9	21.3	49.2	47.1	—	40.9	—	20.9	—	22.3	31.2	30.2	—	25.2
1973	—	—	18.4	16.7	41.3	44.4	—	40.8	—	18.7	—	15.6	28.5	29.5	—	24.2
1974	—	—	19.3	16.5	37.0	41.5	—	39.9	—	19.7	—	13.6	27.1	29.5	—	24.4
1975	—	—	23.3	21.2	52.1	51.7	—	43.3	—	21.5	—	14.9	43.0	31.0	—	30.7
1976	—	—	23.1	19.0	45.0	43.4	—	42.3	—	22.5	—	16.6	34.2	25.8	—	27.1
1977	—	—	22.1	21.4	47.5	53.8	—	48.3	—	21.8	—	18.7	37.1	31.1	—	30.9
1978	—	—	23.1	21.9	35.3	47.0	—	42.9	—	24.8	—	16.1	31.0	29.3	—	27.3
1979	—	—	23.3	18.2	42.8	43.7	—	47.2	—	24.1	—	16.0	33.0	25.8	—	27.9
1980	—	—	22.2	16.8	36.3	51.2	—	43.1	—	22.3	—	13.1	32.0	26.7	—	28.0
1981	—	—	20.9	18.3	40.0	44.8	—	44.3	—	20.9	—	16.9	32.3	31.4	—	26.9
1982	35.0	23.6	20.1	20.6	—	—	35.0	—	33.4	—	21.8	—	—	—	29.3	—
1983	30.4	25.5	19.9	23.1	—	—	38.5	—	31.2	—	18.9	—	—	—	26.0	—
1984	35.8	25.7	19.4	18.4	—	—	37.3	—	35.0	—	15.6	—	—	—	25.0	—
1985	34.3	28.2	16.6	17.8	—	—	36.1	—	37.4	—	15.0	—	—	—	29.6	—
1986	31.5	26.8	19.8	21.0	—	—	35.8	—	33.2	—	18.6	—	—	—	25.7	—
1987	31.9	27.1	17.9	21.1	—	—	34.2	—	33.5	—	17.7	—	—	—	26.1	—
1988	32.3	24.1	15.1	19.9	—	—	32.6	—	31.8	—	15.3	—	—	—	24.5	—
1989	27.3	27.8	15.9	16.5	—	—	31.8	—	31.6	—	15.1	—	—	—	21.0	—
1990	28.0	24.6	19.0	15.3	—	—	34.3	—	30.6	—	16.5	—	—	—	22.6	—
1991	30.5	23.2	17.5	18.7	—	—	31.6	—	29.1	—	16.8	—	—	—	23.2	—
1992	30.0	24.2	14.1	19.6	—	—	31.4	—	31.4	—	13.7	—	—	—	22.5	—
1993	27.2	24.8	18.3	18.8	—	—	29.1	—	29.5	—	16.9	—	—	—	21.6	—
1994	31.0	24.5	16.7	19.3	—	—	28.4	—	29.7	—	14.8	—	—	—	22.6	—
1995	23.2	22.5	21.3	18.8	—	—	34.2	—	25.7	—	18.4	—	—	—	21.8	—

(continued)

TABLE Bd880–959 Persons injured, by sex, age, and place where injury occurred: 1967–1995 *Continued*

	Persons injured (per 100)															
	Female, by age				At home			While in a moving motor vehicle			At work (currently employed over 18)			At places other than home, a moving motor vehicle, or work		
	18–44	45–64	45 and over	65 and over	Total	Male	Female	Total	Male	Female	Total	Male	Female	Total	Male	Female
	Bd944	Bd945	Bd946	Bd947	Bd948	Bd949	Bd950	Bd951	Bd952	Bd953	Bd954	Bd955	Bd956	Bd957	Bd958	Bd959
Year	Per 100	Per 100	Per 100	Per 100	Per 100	Per 100	Per 100	Per 100	Per 100	Per 100	Per 100	Per 100	Per 100	Per 100	Per 100	Per 100
1967	—	20.7	—	16.5	11.9	11.1	12.6	2.0	1.7	2.2	4.8	8.6	1.2	9.6	12.6	6.8
1968	—	18.6	—	18.2	10.5	10.8	10.2	1.7	2.2	1.3	4.8	8.3	1.5	8.9	11.2	6.7
1969	—	19.4	—	19.8	10.0	11.1	9.0	1.8	2.0	1.7	4.2	7.3	1.2	9.6	12.6	6.9
1970	—	16.2	—	25.4	10.8	10.5	11.2	1.8	1.9	1.7	3.9	6.9	1.1	12.3	15.1	9.7
1971	—	20.5	—	21.4	11.9	12.1	11.6	2.3	2.7	2.0	4.8	8.5	1.2	12.9	14.8	11.1
1972	—	22.9	—	20.6	11.8	12.0	11.5	2.3	2.8	1.9	3.9	6.9	1.1	14.5	17.1	12.0
1973	—	18.1	—	17.5	11.0	10.8	11.2	1.9	2.3	1.6	4.4	7.6	1.4	13.0	16.2	10.0
1974	—	18.9	—	18.5	10.3	9.8	10.8	2.1	2.5	1.7	4.5	8.0	1.2	12.7	15.3	10.3
1975	—	24.9	—	25.6	14.9	13.9	15.8	2.5	2.8	2.1	4.7	7.5	2.1	13.6	16.6	10.9
1976	—	23.8	—	20.6	12.3	13.3	11.4	2.2	2.1	2.3	4.4	7.4	1.6	13.1	15.2	11.1
1977	—	22.4	—	23.3	13.9	14.1	13.8	2.4	2.8	2.0	5.4	8.8	2.2	14.8	18.5	11.4
1978	—	21.5	—	26.0	11.9	12.1	11.7	2.1	2.6	1.7	4.9	8.1	1.9	13.9	16.2	11.8
1979	—	22.7	—	19.8	11.5	12.5	10.6	2.3	2.7	2.0	5.6	8.9	2.4	14.0	16.5	11.6
1980	—	22.0	—	19.4	12.2	12.6	11.9	2.0	2.2	1.9	5.0	7.6	2.5	12.9	16.2	9.9
1981	—	20.9	—	19.2	12.0	12.3	11.6	2.2	2.2	2.2	5.0	8.4	1.9	13.2	16.1	10.6
1982	21.0	—	21.8	—	9.6	9.4	9.8	1.7	1.8	1.5	5.8	9.7	2.3	7.3	9.2	5.5
1983	22.9	—	22.9	—	9.8	9.6	9.9	2.4	2.7	2.0	5.4	8.9	2.2	6.5	8.3	4.9
1984	22.3	—	21.9	—	8.8	8.9	8.7	1.9	2.2	1.7	6.3	10.8	2.2	6.5	8.3	4.9
1985	22.7	—	18.8	—	9.3	8.6	9.9	2.2	2.3	2.1	6.6	9.9	3.7	7.3	10.7	4.2
1986	23.0	—	21.6	—	9.3	9.6	9.0	2.6	2.6	2.7	6.1	8.5	3.9	6.7	8.9	4.6
1987	23.5	—	20.3	—	8.8	9.6	8.1	2.4	2.9	2.0	5.2	7.8	2.8	6.6	7.6	5.8
1988	20.8	—	18.3	—	8.5	8.5	8.5	1.7	1.7	1.7	5.7	9.0	2.7	6.4	8.3	4.5
1989	23.9	—	16.9	—	7.2	7.8	6.7	2.2	2.1	2.2	6.1	9.1	3.3	5.9	7.3	4.5
1990	20.4	—	18.4	—	7.5	8.4	6.8	2.2	2.3	2.2	4.0	6.7	1.5	5.8	6.8	4.8
1991	20.9	—	19.0	—	7.4	6.4	8.4	2.0	2.5	1.6	4.7	7.3	2.4	6.1	8.2	4.1
1992	19.8	—	18.4	—	7.5	7.7	7.3	2.1	2.9	1.3	4.2	6.2	2.4	6.0	7.0	5.1
1993	21.4	—	19.8	—	7.4	7.2	7.6	2.2	2.3	2.1	4.7	7.8	1.9	5.6	6.4	6.4
1994	22.4	—	20.1	—	7.6	7.1	8.0	1.2	1.4	1.1	4.6	7.2	2.3	6.1	7.7	4.5
1995	19.7	—	22.0	—	6.9	7.5	6.2	1.4	1.5	1.4	4.1	4.9	3.3	6.4	7.7	5.2

[1] Beginning in 1982, estimates may not be comparable to earlier estimates because the later data are based on a revised questionnaire and field procedures.

Source

U.S. National Center for Health Statistics, *Vital and Health Statistics,* series 10, published annually.

Documentation

Data in this table reflect only injuries requiring medical attention or restricted activity.

The data include estimated totals and rates for the civilian noninstitutionalized population from the National Health Interview Survey.

TABLE Bd960–1001 Persons afflicted with acute infective and parasitic conditions, by sex, race, age, region, and income: 1967–1995[1]

Contributed by Richard H. Steckel

	Persons afflicted														
						Age								Region	
	Total	Males	Females	Whites	Blacks	Under 5	Under 6	5–17	6–16	17–44	18–24	25–44	45 and over	Northeast	Midwest
	Bd960	Bd961	Bd962	Bd963	Bd964	Bd965	Bd966	Bd967	Bd968	Bd969	Bd970	Bd971	Bd972	Bd973	Bd974
Year	Thousand	Thousand	Thousand	Thousand	Thousand	Thousand	Thousand	Thousand	Thousand	Thousand	Thousand	Thousand	Thousand	Thousand	Thousand
1967	44,174	21,153	23,020	—	—	—	11,449	—	15,679	12,041	—	—	5,005	—	—
1968	41,592	18,517	23,076	—	—	—	9,935	—	15,944	10,958	—	—	4,755	—	—
1969	49,310	23,191	26,119	—	—	—	13,039	—	17,516	13,934	—	—	4,821	—	—
1970	48,215	22,442	25,773	—	—	—	12,947	—	16,240	13,387	—	—	5,641	—	—
1971	55,099	24,966	30,132	—	—	—	13,284	—	19,690	15,592	—	—	6,533	—	—
1972	46,665	20,355	26,309	—	—	—	11,749	—	13,821	14,179	—	—	6,917	—	—
1973	40,003	18,794	21,209	—	—	—	9,943	—	13,534	12,441	—	—	4,085	—	—
1974	40,465	18,096	22,379	—	—	—	9,371	—	13,062	12,958	—	—	5,074	—	—
1975	47,608	22,083	25,525	—	—	—	10,819	—	14,281	16,649	—	—	5,859	—	—
1976	52,603	24,608	27,995	—	—	—	11,490	—	16,179	17,365	—	—	7,570	—	—
1977	57,694	25,570	32,124	—	—	—	11,391	—	16,835	20,238	—	—	9,231	—	—
1978	52,869	23,558	29,311	—	—	—	11,881	—	14,992	19,794	—	—	6,203	—	—
1979	52,691	23,096	29,594	—	—	—	11,204	—	15,599	18,644	—	—	7,243	—	—
1980	53,580	24,625	28,955	—	—	—	10,728	—	16,442	19,788	—	—	6,621	—	—
1981	53,185	23,287	29,899	—	—	—	12,015	—	14,744	20,957	—	—	5,469	—	—
1982	42,602	17,862	24,740	38,120	3,688	7,661	—	14,766	—	—	4,741	9,628	5,807	11,805	7,616
1983	46,534	19,015	27,519	40,901	5,406	9,172	—	17,249	—	—	5,337	8,696	6,080	11,309	9,662
1984	46,475	21,283	25,191	40,219	5,776	8,235	—	16,013	—	—	5,116	11,996	5,115	13,099	8,240
1985	47,829	20,529	27,301	43,247	4,189	9,087	—	17,462	—	—	4,839	12,369	4,072	12,200	8,418
1986	54,366	23,122	31,244	50,062	3,620	10,093	—	17,920	—	—	5,225	14,476	6,653	12,207	8,504
1987	55,305	23,429	31,876	48,555	5,544	10,361	—	20,211	—	—	5,879	13,830	5,025	11,510	10,696
1988	53,783	23,726	30,057	48,584	4,576	9,405	—	21,082	—	—	4,875	13,204	5,217	9,303	12,288
1989	48,897	21,569	27,329	43,466	4,286	9,987	—	18,691	—	—	3,907	10,608	5,704	9,343	9,339
1990	51,662	22,074	29,588	44,391	6,140	10,454	—	19,737	—	—	5,316	10,195	5,960	10,215	10,277
1991	46,104	21,297	24,807	39,895	5,000	8,895	—	17,736	—	—	3,459	10,112	5,902	10,182	9,120
1992	56,243	23,385	32,858	48,647	6,565	11,590	—	21,155	—	—	5,085	13,156	5,256	12,211	10,946
1993	54,253	23,926	30,327	47,106	5,859	10,842	—	20,042	—	—	4,232	10,992	8,145	11,667	10,735
1994	54,201	23,831	30,370	46,374	6,665	11,210	—	20,778	—	—	4,668	12,066	5,478	12,422	10,477
1995	52,605	23,776	28,830	45,992	5,777	10,545	—	19,942	—	—	4,564	11,199	6,355	12,201	10,289

Note appears at end of table

(continued)

TABLE Bd960–1001 Persons afflicted with acute infective and parasitic conditions, by sex, race, age, region, and income: 1967–1995 *Continued*

	Persons afflicted						Persons afflicted (per 100)								
	Region		Family income									Age			
	South	West	Less than $10,000	$10,000–$19,999	$20,000–$34,999	At least $35,000	Total	Males	Females	Whites	Blacks	Under 5	Under 6	5–17	6–16
	Bd975	Bd976	Bd977	Bd978	Bd979	Bd980	Bd981	Bd982	Bd983	Bd984	Bd985	Bd986	Bd987	Bd988	Bd989
Year	Thousand	Thousand	Thousand	Thousand	Thousand	Thousand	Per 100	Per 100	Per 100	Per 100	Per 100	Per 100	Per 100	Per 100	Per 100
1967	—	—	—	—	—	—	22.8	22.7	23.0	—	—	—	48.9	—	35.9
1968	—	—	—	—	—	—	21.3	19.7	22.8	—	—	—	43.8	—	36.0
1969	—	—	—	—	—	—	25.0	24.4	25.5	—	—	—	59.0	—	39.1
1970	—	—	—	—	—	—	24.1	23.3	24.9	—	—	—	59.7	—	36.1
1971	—	—	—	—	—	—	27.2	25.6	28.8	—	—	—	62.1	—	43.6
1972	—	—	—	—	—	—	22.9	20.7	24.9	—	—	—	56.7	—	31.3
1973	—	—	—	—	—	—	19.4	18.9	19.9	—	—	—	48.8	—	31.0
1974	—	—	—	—	—	—	19.5	18.1	20.9	—	—	—	47.4	—	30.3
1975	—	—	—	—	—	—	22.8	21.9	23.6	—	—	—	55.4	—	33.7
1976	—	—	—	—	—	—	25.0	24.2	25.7	—	—	—	60.7	—	38.5
1977	—	—	—	—	—	—	27.2	25.0	29.3	—	—	—	61.6	—	40.6
1978	—	—	—	—	—	—	24.7	22.8	26.5	—	—	—	64.5	—	36.9
1979	—	—	—	—	—	—	24.4	22.2	20.5	—	—	—	60.0	—	39.4
1980	—	—	—	—	—	—	24.6	23.4	25.7	—	—	—	56.3	—	42.5
1981	—	—	—	—	—	—	23.6	21.4	25.7	—	—	—	59.7	—	38.0
1982	18,454	4,727	8,203	10,363	13,452	7,361	18.8	16.3	21.0	19.6	13.7	44.2	—	32.6	—
1983	19,466	6,097	8,144	9,596	13,646	10,232	20.3	17.2	23.2	20.8	19.8	51.4	—	38.5	—
1984	19,185	5,952	6,768	8,811	14,799	12,587	20.1	19.0	21.0	20.3	20.8	45.6	—	36.0	—
1985	20,843	6,369	4,812	8,502	15,288	14,405	20.5	18.2	22.6	21.7	14.9	50.5	—	39.0	—
1986	24,990	8,666	5,745	9,369	18,543	16,531	23.0	20.2	25.6	25.0	12.7	55.5	—	39.9	—
1987	25,007	8,092	6,807	10,276	15,285	17,578	23.2	20.3	25.9	24.1	19.2	57.0	—	44.8	—
1988	24,660	7,532	5,615	9,227	13,624	19,812	22.3	20.3	24.2	23.9	15.6	51.2	—	46.7	—
1989	21,686	8,530	3,894	7,944	12,678	17,679	20.1	18.3	21.8	21.2	14.3	53.2	—	41.3	—
1990	23,173	7,996	5,585	7,881	10,286	21,021	21.0	18.5	23.3	21.4	20.2	54.8	—	43.3	—
1991	19,659	7,143	4,051	6,505	11,285	19,400	18.5	17.6	19.4	19.2	16.2	45.9	—	38.4	—
1992	25,221	7,865	6,277	6,050	13,296	22,831	22.4	19.1	25.4	23.2	20.9	59.0	—	45.2	—
1993	23,139	8,711	5,712	7,432	11,867	21,689	21.3	19.3	23.2	22.3	18.3	54.4	—	42.2	—
1994	21,466	9,836	3,796	6,863	11,229	24,633	20.9	18.8	22.8	21.6	20.2	54.7	—	41.9	—
1995	23,076	7,040	4,681	8,186	9,945	23,743	20.1	18.6	21.5	21.2	17.6	52.0	—	39.6	—

	Persons afflicted (per 100)											
	Age				Region				Family income			
	17–44	18–24	25–44	45 and over	Northeast	Midwest	South	West	Less than $10,000	$10,000–$19,999	$20,000–$34,999	At least $35,000
	Bd990	Bd991	Bd992	Bd993	Bd994	Bd995	Bd996	Bd997	Bd998	Bd999	Bd1000	Bd1001
Year	Per 100	Per 100	Per 100	Per 100	Per 100	Per 100	Per 100	Per 100	Per 100	Per 100	Per 100	Per 100
1967	17.5	—	—	8.7	—	—	—	—	—	—	—	—
1968	15.7	—	—	8.1	—	—	—	—	—	—	—	—
1969	19.6	—	—	8.1	—	—	—	—	—	—	—	—
1970	18.4	—	—	9.4	—	—	—	—	—	—	—	—
1971	20.9	—	—	10.7	—	—	—	—	—	—	—	—
1972	18.4	—	—	11.1	—	—	—	—	—	—	—	—
1973	15.7	—	—	6.5	—	—	—	—	—	—	—	—
1974	16.0	—	—	8.3	—	—	—	—	—	—	—	—
1975	20.1	—	—	9.1	—	—	—	—	—	—	—	—
1976	20.5	—	—	11.6	—	—	—	—	—	—	—	—
1977	23.4	—	—	14.1	—	—	—	—	—	—	—	—
1978	22.3	—	—	9.4	—	—	—	—	—	—	—	—
1979	20.6	—	—	10.6	—	—	—	—	—	—	—	—
1980	21.3	—	—	9.8	—	—	—	—	—	—	—	—
1981	21.6	—	—	7.9	—	—	—	—	—	—	—	—
1982	—	16.5	14.6	8.3	23.8	12.9	24.7	10.8	19.6	18.2	20.7	18.2
1983	—	18.7	12.8	8.7	23.0	16.4	25.6	13.4	19.3	18.5	21.2	23.7
1984	—	18.2	17.1	7.2	26.1	13.8	24.9	13.3	17.2	17.4	23.1	26.1
1985	—	17.7	17.2	5.7	24.5	14.4	26.0	14.1	13.9	18.2	23.4	25.1
1986	—	19.6	19.5	9.2	24.1	14.7	30.9	18.5	17.2	20.8	29.6	25.9
1987	—	22.5	18.2	6.9	23.0	18.7	30.7	16.3	21.8	23.1	24.8	25.4
1988	—	19.0	17.1	7.0	18.9	20.6	30.0	15.1	19.8	21.9	22.9	26.5
1989	—	15.4	13.5	7.6	19.1	15.7	26.1	16.4	14.9	19.4	22.4	22.0
1990	—	21.2	12.7	7.8	20.5	17.2	27.5	15.3	23.0	19.8	19.4	23.7
1991	—	14.0	12.5	7.6	20.2	15.3	23.4	13.1	17.0	17.1	21.2	21.7
1992	—	20.9	16.2	6.6	24.4	17.8	29.9	14.2	25.6	15.7	25.9	25.0
1993	—	17.5	13.5	10.0	23.3	17.3	27.1	15.3	23.2	19.4	22.0	22.4
1994	—	18.5	14.6	6.7	24.5	16.6	24.4	17.0	16.2	18.4	20.7	24.6
1995	—	18.3	13.5	7.6	23.7	16.5	25.0	12.6	21.6	21.6	18.2	22.2

[1] Beginning in 1982, estimates may not be comparable to earlier estimates because the later data are based on a revised questionnaire and field procedures.

Source

U.S. National Center for Health Statistics, *Vital and Health Statistics,* series 10, published annually.

Documentation

Infective and parasitic conditions include common childhood diseases, intestinal viruses, and viral infections. An acute condition generally lasts less than three months. Only conditions that either caused a person to cut down on his or her daily activities for at least half a day or caused a person to consult a physician were tabulated.

The data include estimated totals and rates for the civilian noninstitutionalized population from the National Health Interview Survey.

See Table Ap-G in Appendix 2 regarding the composition of census regions and divisions.

TABLE Bd1002–1043 Persons afflicted with acute respiratory conditions, by sex, race, age, region, and income: 1967–1995[1]

Contributed by Richard H. Steckel

	Persons afflicted														
						Age								Region	
	Total	Males	Females	Whites	Blacks	Under 5	Under 6	5–17	6–16	17–44	18–24	25–44	45 and over	Northeast	Midwest
	Bd1002	Bd1003	Bd1004	Bd1005	Bd1006	Bd1007	Bd1008	Bd1009	Bd1010	Bd1011	Bd1012	Bd1013	Bd1014	Bd1015	Bd1016
Year	Thousand	Thousand	Thousand	Thousand	Thousand	Thousand	Thousand	Thousand	Thousand	Thousand	Thousand	Thousand	Thousand	Thousand	Thousand
1967	204,581	93,951	110,630	—	—	—	46,546	—	56,314	64,252	—	—	37,469	—	—
1968	238,475	112,972	125,503	—	—	—	44,204	—	65,271	82,943	—	—	46,057	—	—
1969	217,414	98,852	118,563	—	—	—	41,625	—	68,038	69,691	—	—	38,061	—	—
1970	219,764	100,582	119,182	—	—	—	41,422	—	63,698	75,063	—	—	39,581	—	—
1971	235,855	108,481	127,373	—	—	—	45,606	—	73,843	77,462	—	—	38,944	—	—
1972	246,647	110,723	135,924	—	—	—	43,517	—	67,987	90,317	—	—	44,825	—	—
1973	188,817	86,814	102,003	—	—	—	33,222	—	53,128	70,510	—	—	31,957	—	—
1974	195,741	92,228	103,513	—	—	—	34,149	—	56,671	74,696	—	—	30,225	—	—
1975	232,960	107,229	125,732	—	—	—	41,717	—	60,974	90,716	—	—	39,555	—	—
1976	250,704	115,690	135,014	—	—	—	38,588	—	64,798	101,205	—	—	46,113	—	—
1977	232,819	103,716	129,104	—	—	—	37,073	—	61,407	93,703	—	—	40,636	—	—
1978	247,551	113,154	134,398	—	—	—	38,038	—	62,028	103,344	—	—	44,142	—	—
1979	231,431	103,447	127,984	—	—	—	36,650	—	58,616	96,601	—	—	39,563	—	—
1980	253,175	109,170	144,005	—	—	—	38,311	—	61,761	105,086	—	—	48,018	—	—
1981	251,802	115,710	136,092	—	—	—	40,078	—	57,845	108,051	—	—	45,828	—	—
1982	181,087	81,925	99,161	161,506	15,225	27,055	—	51,892	—	—	21,123	49,658	31,359	37,021	49,103
1983	194,841	89,244	105,597	172,606	18,540	29,823	—	56,040	—	—	20,528	54,168	34,283	41,355	55,223
1984	205,387	93,806	111,581	183,095	17,840	31,119	—	60,275	—	—	22,909	57,610	33,474	39,403	56,188
1985	203,491	89,693	113,798	181,924	17,674	27,456	—	53,970	—	—	22,786	60,037	39,241	40,039	52,601
1986	228,842	99,216	129,626	202,523	19,103	32,339	—	62,697	—	—	26,314	64,431	43,060	46,754	62,067
1987	191,049	83,705	107,344	167,148	16,931	29,118	—	50,252	—	—	23,048	56,472	32,160	33,612	47,647
1988	209,342	94,259	115,083	182,920	19,694	30,394	—	59,413	—	—	20,025	61,667	37,844	40,292	52,903
1989	231,854	105,660	126,194	203,414	21,298	32,997	—	62,760	—	—	25,411	70,711	39,974	36,029	59,629
1990	209,825	89,457	120,368	185,081	18,002	32,122	—	55,341	—	—	22,070	59,435	40,857	36,434	58,428
1991	250,214	112,717	137,497	218,178	23,437	35,557	—	69,271	—	—	26,196	71,331	47,859	41,489	69,512
1992	215,358	94,748	120,610	189,682	18,505	31,352	—	55,783	—	—	21,023	65,368	41,832	38,466	58,636
1993	251,551	114,329	137,222	219,654	23,308	36,416	—	65,699	—	—	23,575	77,556	48,305	41,648	67,601
1994	208,930	95,218	113,712	176,767	21,714	31,499	—	51,209	—	—	20,831	63,925	41,467	37,170	55,255
1995	223,037	102,653	120,384	191,845	20,915	32,333	—	61,875	—	—	19,880	66,901	42,048	35,971	64,809

	Persons afflicted						Persons afflicted (per 100)								
	Region		Family income									Age			
	South	West	Less than $10,000	$10,000–$19,999	$20,000–$34,999	At least $35,000	Total	Males	Females	Whites	Blacks	Under 5	Under 6	5–17	6–16
	Bd1017	Bd1018	Bd1019	Bd1020	Bd1021	Bd1022	Bd1023	Bd1024	Bd1025	Bd1026	Bd1027	Bd1028	Bd1029	Bd1030	Bd1031
Year	Thousand	Thousand	Thousand	Thousand	Thousand	Thousand	Per 100	Per 100	Per 100	Per 100	Per 100	Per 100	Per 100	Per 100	Per 100
1967	—	—	—	—	—	—	105.8	100.8	110.4	—	—	—	199.0	—	128.9
1968	—	—	—	—	—	—	122.0	120.1	123.9	—	—	—	194.7	—	147.3
1969	—	—	—	—	—	—	110.1	104.1	115.8	—	—	—	188.5	—	151.9
1970	—	—	—	—	—	—	110.0	104.5	115.1	—	—	—	191.0	—	141.5
1971	—	—	—	—	—	—	116.6	111.1	121.6	—	—	—	213.3	—	163.5
1972	—	—	—	—	—	—	120.8	112.5	128.6	—	—	—	209.9	—	154.1
1973	—	—	—	—	—	—	91.7	87.5	95.7	—	—	—	162.9	—	121.8
1974	—	—	—	—	—	—	94.4	92.2	96.5	—	—	—	172.6	—	131.3
1975	—	—	—	—	—	—	111.4	106.3	116.2	—	—	—	213.8	—	143.7
1976	—	—	—	—	—	—	119.0	113.8	123.8	—	—	—	203.9	—	154.4
1977	—	—	—	—	—	—	109.7	101.3	117.6	—	—	—	200.6	—	148.2
1978	—	—	—	—	—	—	115.8	109.7	121.5	—	—	—	206.6	—	152.8
1979	—	—	—	—	—	—	107.3	99.4	114.7	—	—	—	196.4	—	148.1
1980	—	—	—	—	—	—	116.2	103.8	127.7	—	—	—	201.1	—	159.5
1981	—	—	—	—	—	—	111.9	106.6	116.8	—	—	—	199.3	—	149.2
1982	48,362	46,602	33,872	46,287	54,775	32,517	79.7	74.8	84.3	83.2	56.6	156.2	—	114.5	—
1983	54,582	43,681	40,724	41,274	59,163	35,556	85.0	80.6	89.0	87.9	67.9	167.1	—	125.2	—
1984	54,489	55,307	35,373	46,052	58,153	45,116	88.7	83.9	93.2	92.5	64.3	172.2	—	135.4	—
1985	59,711	51,141	30,404	44,142	54,576	51,257	87.1	79.5	94.2	91.3	62.8	152.5	—	120.6	—
1986	64,746	55,275	32,588	40,305	67,292	64,699	96.8	86.8	106.2	101.1	66.9	177.9	—	139.5	—
1987	55,524	54,266	26,995	35,656	48,968	58,798	80.1	72.5	87.2	82.8	58.5	160.2	—	111.4	—
1988	58,218	57,929	27,310	31,677	52,119	70,256	86.9	80.8	92.6	90.0	67.0	165.3	—	131.5	—
1989	68,811	67,385	28,775	34,277	58,348	78,437	95.2	89.5	100.5	99.1	71.3	175.8	—	138.7	—
1990	57,968	56,994	23,592	34,912	44,880	80,181	85.3	74.9	95.0	89.4	59.3	168.3	—	121.4	—
1991	78,204	61,010	27,449	40,754	55,222	91,235	100.6	93.4	107.4	104.8	75.9	183.5	—	150.1	—
1992	57,668	60,587	24,788	35,708	44,028	78,288	85.6	77.5	93.3	90.6	58.8	159.5	—	119.1	—
1993	71,653	70,650	27,898	38,148	55,270	95,579	98.9	92.4	105.1	103.9	72.8	182.9	—	138.2	—
1994	55,844	60,662	21,517	29,488	46,256	84,246	80.5	75.3	85.4	82.4	65.7	153.8	—	103.4	—
1995	63,372	58,884	22,292	30,819	48,857	93,283	85.2	80.5	89.6	88.3	63.9	159.5	—	122.8	—

Note appears at end of table

(continued)

TABLE Bd1002–1043 Persons afflicted with acute respiratory conditions, by sex, race, age, region, and income: 1967–1995 *Continued*

	Persons afflicted (per 100)											
	Age				Region				Family income			
	17–44	18–24	25–44	45 and over	Northeast	Midwest	South	West	Less than $10,000	$10,000–$19,999	$20,000–$34,999	At least $35,000
	Bd1032	Bd1033	Bd1034	Bd1035	Bd1036	Bd1037	Bd1038	Bd1039	Bd1040	Bd1041	Bd1042	Bd1043
Year	Per 100	Per 100	Per 100	Per 100	Per 100	Per 100	Per 100	Per 100	Per 100	Per 100	Per 100	Per 100
1967	93.5	—	—	65.1	—	—	—	—	—	—	—	—
1968	118.7	—	—	76.7	—	—	—	—	—	—	—	—
1969	97.9	—	—	64.1	—	—	—	—	—	—	—	—
1970	103.1	—	—	65.6	—	—	—	—	—	—	—	—
1971	103.7	—	—	63.7	—	—	—	—	—	—	—	—
1972	117.1	—	—	72.1	—	—	—	—	—	—	—	—
1973	89.2	—	—	50.9	—	—	—	—	—	—	—	—
1974	92.5	—	—	47.5	—	—	—	—	—	—	—	—
1975	109.6	—	—	61.4	—	—	—	—	—	—	—	—
1976	119.5	—	—	70.9	—	—	—	—	—	—	—	—
1977	108.2	—	—	61.9	—	—	—	—	—	—	—	—
1978	116.6	—	—	66.7	—	—	—	—	—	—	—	—
1979	106.5	—	—	59.2	—	—	—	—	—	—	—	—
1980	113.3	—	—	71.2	—	—	—	—	—	—	—	—
1981	111.2	—	—	66.4	—	—	—	—	—	—	—	—
1982	—	73.4	75.1	45.1	74.5	83.1	64.8	106.6	81.0	81.3	84.3	80.6
1983	—	71.9	79.6	48.9	84.1	93.9	71.8	96.3	96.5	79.6	92.1	82.4
1984	—	81.7	82.0	47.3	78.5	94.4	70.8	123.2	90.1	90.7	90.7	93.5
1985	—	83.1	83.4	54.8	80.5	89.8	74.5	113.1	87.8	94.3	83.5	89.2
1986	—	98.5	86.8	59.6	92.4	107.3	79.9	117.8	97.3	89.5	107.5	101.5
1987	—	88.2	74.3	44.0	67.1	83.1	68.2	109.1	86.4	80.1	79.4	85.0
1988	—	77.9	79.7	51.0	81.8	88.8	70.8	116.3	96.2	75.1	87.4	93.8
1989	—	100.0	89.7	53.1	73.6	100.1	82.8	129.8	109.9	83.5	102.9	97.8
1990	—	88.2	74.2	53.5	73.0	97.7	68.8	109.2	97.3	87.9	84.6	90.6
1991	—	106.3	88.0	61.8	82.5	116.4	93.1	111.6	114.9	107.3	103.8	102.3
1992	—	86.4	80.4	52.8	76.9	95.4	68.3	109.1	101.0	92.9	85.9	85.9
1993	—	97.7	95.0	59.6	83.2	109.0	83.9	124.3	113.5	99.4	102.6	98.8
1994	—	82.4	77.1	50.9	73.4	87.4	63.4	105.1	92.1	79.1	85.4	84.0
1995	—	79.7	80.5	50.5	69.9	104.1	68.6	105.5	103.0	81.4	89.4	87.2

[1] Beginning in 1982, estimates may not be comparable to earlier estimates because the later data are based on a revised questionnaire and field procedures.

Source

U.S. National Center for Health Statistics, *Vital and Health Statistics,* series 10, published annually.

Documentation

Respiratory conditions include the common cold, influenza, acute bronchitis, and pneumonia. Only conditions that either caused a person to cut down on his or her daily activities for at least half a day or caused a person to consult a physician were tabulated.

The data include estimated totals and rates for the civilian noninstitutionalized population from the National Health Interview Survey.

See Table Ap-G in Appendix 2 regarding the composition of census regions and divisions.

TABLE Bd1044–1085 Persons afflicted with acute digestive conditions, by sex, race, age, region, and income: 1967–1995[1]

Contributed by Richard H. Steckel

	Persons afflicted														
						Age								Region	
	Total	Males	Females	Whites	Blacks	Under 5	Under 6	5–17	6–16	17–44	18–24	25–44	45 and over	Northeast	Midwest
	Bd1044	Bd1045	Bd1046	Bd1047	Bd1048	Bd1049	Bd1050	Bd1051	Bd1052	Bd1053	Bd1054	Bd1055	Bd1056	Bd1057	Bd1058
Year	Thousand	Thousand	Thousand	Thousand	Thousand	Thousand	Thousand	Thousand	Thousand	Thousand	Thousand	Thousand	Thousand	Thousand	Thousand
1967	16,538	7,836	8,702	—	—	—	3,267	—	3,979	5,573	—	—	3,719	—	—
1968	19,390	9,145	10,246	—	—	—	3,248	—	4,776	7,066	—	—	4,301	—	—
1969	20,141	9,636	10,505	—	—	—	2,726	—	6,767	6,646	—	—	4,002	—	—
1970	23,014	10,024	12,990	—	—	—	2,758	—	7,713	8,782	—	—	3,762	—	—
1971	22,510	9,268	13,242	—	—	—	2,496	—	7,404	8,343	—	—	4,267	—	—
1972	22,965	9,987	12,978	—	—	—	2,679	—	8,016	7,265	—	—	5,005	—	—
1973	17,205	8,927	8,278	—	—	—	2,394	—	4,959	6,849	—	—	3,003	—	—
1974	16,193	6,043	10,150	—	—	—	1,449	—	4,598	7,076	—	—	3,070	—	—
1975	21,618	9,490	12,128	—	—	—	2,858	—	6,059	8,815	—	—	3,886	—	—
1976	21,997	10,314	11,683	—	—	—	2,237	—	6,929	8,629	—	—	4,202	—	—
1977	23,791	10,743	13,049	—	—	—	2,896	—	7,171	8,927	—	—	4,797	—	—
1978	22,878	10,398	12,480	—	—	—	2,580	—	5,417	9,955	—	—	4,926	—	—
1979	24,660	10,660	14,000	—	—	—	2,295	—	6,080	10,900	—	—	5,385	—	—
1980	24,877	11,811	13,066	—	—	—	3,547	—	5,175	12,081	—	—	4,074	—	—
1981	21,771	10,691	11,080	—	—	—	2,039	—	5,945	10,262	—	—	3,526	—	—
1982	14,817	6,784	8,033	12,271	2,122	1,955	—	5,426	—	—	1,930	2,613	2,893	3,351	3,215
1983	17,455	8,468	8,988	14,309	2,704	1,924	—	4,743	—	—	3,637	3,613	3,538	3,618	4,295
1984	17,534	6,327	11,207	15,027	2,179	1,854	—	5,281	—	—	2,889	3,699	3,811	2,651	3,674
1985	16,297	6,904	9,394	13,202	2,741	1,609	—	4,415	—	—	2,725	3,652	3,896	2,951	3,660
1986	14,972	5,860	9,112	12,016	2,130	1,489	—	3,744	—	—	1,919	3,800	4,019	3,420	3,112
1987	15,028	6,959	8,069	11,876	2,655	1,949	—	3,790	—	—	2,067	3,835	3,387	2,774	2,779
1988	15,080	6,877	8,203	11,800	2,745	2,035	—	3,664	—	—	1,675	3,976	3,729	2,624	3,436
1989	14,265	6,798	7,466	11,327	2,324	2,060	—	2,853	—	—	1,639	3,583	4,129	2,024	3,109
1990	13,023	5,432	7,591	10,448	2,057	805	—	3,340	—	—	1,661	3,909	3,307	2,044	3,228
1991	16,452	6,973	9,478	13,746	2,324	1,964	—	4,208	—	—	1,297	4,638	4,345	3,071	4,127
1992	17,594	8,694	8,900	14,225	2,422	2,544	—	4,328	—	—	1,273	4,699	4,750	3,068	3,723
1993	16,085	6,756	9,329	13,062	2,721	1,978	—	3,984	—	—	1,737	4,990	3,397	2,112	3,367
1994	15,863	6,900	8,963	12,149	2,939	2,155	—	4,110	—	—	1,866	3,918	3,813	2,617	3,315
1995	15,828	7,239	8,590	12,275	3,143	2,370	—	3,678	—	—	1,574	4,189	4,017	2,830	3,733

Note appears at end of table

(continued)

TABLE Bd1044–1085 Persons afflicted with acute digestive conditions, by sex, race, age, region, and income: 1967–1995 *Continued*

	Persons afflicted						Persons afflicted (per 100)								
	Region		Family income									Age			
	South	West	Less than $10,000	$10,000–$19,999	$20,000–$34,999	At least $35,000	Total	Males	Females	Whites	Blacks	Under 5	Under 6	5–17	6–16
	Bd1059	Bd1060	Bd1061	Bd1062	Bd1063	Bd1064	Bd1065	Bd1066	Bd1067	Bd1068	Bd1069	Bd1070	Bd1071	Bd1072	Bd1073
Year	Thousand	Thousand	Thousand	Thousand	Thousand	Thousand	Per 100	Per 100	Per 100	Per 100	Per 100	Per 100	Per 100	Per 100	Per 100
1967	—	—	—	—	—	—	8.6	8.4	8.7	—	—	—	14.0	—	9.1
1968	—	—	—	—	—	—	9.9	9.7	10.1	—	—	—	14.3	—	10.8
1969	—	—	—	—	—	—	10.2	10.1	10.3	—	—	—	12.3	—	15.1
1970	—	—	—	—	—	—	11.5	10.4	12.5	—	—	—	12.7	—	17.1
1971	—	—	—	—	—	—	11.1	9.5	12.6	—	—	—	11.7	—	16.4
1972	—	—	—	—	—	—	11.2	10.1	12.3	—	—	—	12.9	—	18.2
1973	—	—	—	—	—	—	8.4	9.0	7.8	—	—	—	11.7	—	11.4
1974	—	—	—	—	—	—	7.8	6.0	9.5	—	—	—	7.3	—	10.6
1975	—	—	—	—	—	—	10.3	9.4	11.2	—	—	—	14.6	—	14.3
1976	—	—	—	—	—	—	10.4	10.1	10.7	—	—	—	11.8	—	16.5
1977	—	—	—	—	—	—	11.2	10.5	11.9	—	—	—	15.7	—	17.3
1978	—	—	—	—	—	—	10.7	10.1	11.3	—	—	—	14.0	—	13.3
1979	—	—	—	—	—	—	11.4	10.2	12.5	—	—	—	12.3	—	15.4
1980	—	—	—	—	—	—	11.4	11.2	11.6	—	—	—	18.6	—	13.4
1981	—	—	—	—	—	—	9.7	9.8	9.5	—	—	—	10.1	—	15.3
1982	4,689	3,561	3,362	4,352	3,617	2,401	6.5	6.2	6.8	6.3	7.9	11.3	—	12.0	—
1983	6,207	3,336	4,154	4,009	4,728	2,509	7.6	7.6	7.6	7.3	9.9	10.8	—	10.6	—
1984	7,074	4,136	3,600	4,866	4,134	3,200	7.6	5.7	9.4	7.6	7.8	10.3	—	11.9	—
1985	6,122	3,563	3,041	2,807	4,886	3,700	7.0	6.1	7.8	6.6	9.7	8.9	—	9.9	—
1986	4,631	3,808	2,488	2,839	5,443	2,330	6.3	5.1	7.5	6.0	7.5	8.2	—	8.3	—
1987	5,814	3,662	2,300	2,925	4,127	3,314	6.3	6.0	6.6	5.9	9.2	10.7	—	8.4	—
1988	5,974	3,047	2,717	3,229	3,305	3,587	6.3	5.9	6.6	5.8	9.3	11.1	—	8.1	—
1989	5,549	3,583	2,334	3,163	2,922	3,916	5.9	5.8	5.9	5.5	7.8	11.0	—	6.3	—
1990	4,678	3,072	1,643	2,016	2,748	4,975	5.3	4.6	6.0	5.0	6.8	4.2	—	7.3	—
1991	5,166	4,088	2,322	2,867	3,445	5,785	6.6	5.8	7.4	6.6	7.5	10.1	—	9.1	—
1992	6,012	4,791	1,867	3,206	3,821	6,016	7.0	7.1	6.9	6.8	7.7	12.9	—	9.2	—
1993	6,050	4,556	2,460	2,733	3,628	4,879	6.3	5.5	7.1	6.2	8.5	9.9	—	8.4	—
1994	5,864	4,067	2,370	2,992	3,073	5,143	6.1	5.5	6.7	5.7	8.9	10.5	—	8.3	—
1995	5,497	3,769	2,433	2,429	2,807	5,794	6.0	5.7	6.4	5.7	9.6	11.7	—	7.3	—

	Persons afflicted (per 100)											
	Age				Region				Family income			
	17–44	18–24	25–44	45 and over	Northeast	Midwest	South	West	Less than $10,000	$10,000–$19,999	$20,000–$34,999	At least $35,000
	Bd1074	Bd1075	Bd1076	Bd1077	Bd1078	Bd1079	Bd1080	Bd1081	Bd1082	Bd1083	Bd1084	Bd1085
Year	Per 100	Per 100	Per 100	Per 100	Per 100	Per 100	Per 100	Per 100	Per 100	Per 100	Per 100	Per 100
1967	8.1	—	—	6.5	—	—	—	—	—	—	—	—
1968	10.1	—	—	7.4	—	—	—	—	—	—	—	—
1969	9.3	—	—	6.7	—	—	—	—	—	—	—	—
1970	12.1	—	—	6.2	—	—	—	—	—	—	—	—
1971	11.2	—	—	7.0	—	—	—	—	—	—	—	—
1972	9.4	—	—	8.1	—	—	—	—	—	—	—	—
1973	8.7	—	—	4.8	—	—	—	—	—	—	—	—
1974	8.8	—	—	4.3	—	—	—	—	—	—	—	—
1975	10.7	—	—	6.0	—	—	—	—	—	—	—	—
1976	10.2	—	—	6.5	—	—	—	—	—	—	—	—
1977	10.3	—	—	7.3	—	—	—	—	—	—	—	—
1978	11.2	—	—	7.4	—	—	—	—	—	—	—	—
1979	12.0	—	—	8.2	—	—	—	—	—	—	—	—
1980	13.0	—	—	6.0	—	—	—	—	—	—	—	—
1981	10.6	—	—	5.1	—	—	—	—	—	—	—	—
1982	—	6.7	4.0	4.2	6.7	5.4	6.3	8.1	8.0	7.6	5.6	6.0
1983	—	12.7	5.3	5.0	7.4	7.3	8.2	7.4	9.8	7.7	7.4	5.8
1984	—	10.3	5.3	5.4	5.3	6.2	9.2	9.2	9.2	9.6	6.4	6.6
1985	—	9.9	5.1	5.4	5.9	6.2	7.6	7.9	8.8	6.0	7.5	6.4
1986	—	7.2	5.1	5.6	6.8	5.4	5.7	8.1	7.4	6.3	8.7	3.7
1987	—	7.9	5.0	4.6	5.5	4.8	7.1	7.4	7.4	6.6	6.7	4.8
1988	—	6.5	5.1	5.0	5.3	5.8	7.3	6.1	9.6	7.7	5.5	4.8
1989	—	6.5	4.5	5.5	4.1	5.2	6.7	6.9	8.9	7.7	5.2	4.9
1990	—	6.6	4.9	4.3	4.1	5.4	5.6	5.9	6.8	5.1	5.2	5.6
1991	—	5.3	5.7	5.6	6.1	6.9	6.1	7.5	9.7	7.5	6.5	6.5
1992	—	5.2	5.8	6.0	6.1	6.1	7.1	8.6	7.6	8.3	7.5	6.6
1993	—	7.2	6.1	4.2	4.2	5.4	7.1	8.0	10.0	7.1	6.7	5.0
1994	—	7.4	4.7	4.7	5.2	5.2	6.7	7.0	10.1	8.0	5.7	5.1
1995	—	6.3	5.0	4.8	5.5	6.0	5.9	6.8	11.2	6.4	5.1	5.4

[1] Beginning in 1982, estimates may not be comparable to earlier estimates because the later data are based on a revised questionnaire and field procedures.

Source

U.S. National Center for Health Statistics, *Vital and Health Statistics*, series 10, published annually.

Documentation

Digestive conditions include dental conditions, indigestion, nausea, and vomiting. Only conditions that either caused a person to cut down on his or her daily activities for at least half a day or caused a person to consult a physician were tabulated.

The data include estimated totals and rates for the civilian noninstitutionalized population from the National Health Interview Survey.

See Table Ap-G in Appendix 2 regarding the composition of census regions and divisions.

TABLE Bd1086–1109 Persons afflicted with chronic circulatory conditions, by age: 1982–1995

Contributed by Richard H. Steckel

	Heart disease						High blood pressure (hypertension)					
		Incidence						Incidence				
			Age						Age			
	Total	Total	Under 18	18–44	45–64	65 and older	Total	Total	Under 18	18–44	45–64	65 and older
	Bd1086	Bd1087	Bd1088	Bd1089	Bd1090	Bd1091	Bd1092	Bd1093	Bd1094	Bd1095	Bd1096	Bd1097
Year	Thousand	Per 1,000	Per 1,000	Per 1,000	Per 1,000	Per 1,000	Thousand	Per 1,000	Per 1,000	Per 1,000	Per 1,000	Per 1,000
1982	16,926	74.5	17.2	34.7	136.8	256.8	26,542	116.9	2.9 [1]	58.9	245.7	390.4
1983	18,978	82.8	19.4	37.1	143.3	303.0	27,813	121.3	1.9 [1]	62.1	263.6	387.9
1984	19,508	84.2	23.4	35.6	137.4	320.0	28,725	124.0	2.7 [1]	59.2	271.0	406.3
1985	19,295	82.6	21.2	40.1	129.0	304.5	29,249	125.1	2.3 [1]	64.1	258.9	414.5
1986	18,458	78.1	21.7	39.3	123.2	276.6	28,969	122.6	1.9 [1]	67.2	250.6	394.4
1987	19,656	82.4	22.2	40.7	126.1	299.2	28,295	118.6	3.2	61.8	252.0	371.1
1988	20,258	84.1	23.3	39.8	135.9	295.8	29,257	121.5	2.3	64.7	257.8	373.0
1989	18,493	75.9	17.1	36.1	118.9	278.9	27,664	113.6	2.2	56.0	229.1	380.6
1990	19,307	78.5	18.9	38.1	118.7	287.3	27,129	110.2	1.8 [1]	55.7	218.3	369.0
1991	20,536	82.6	18.5	38.4	134.1	295.2	27,800	111.8	1.9 [1]	46.3	244.0	372.2
1992	21,584	85.8	19.1	35.7	134.9	324.6	27,816	110.6	1.1 [1]	54.4	226.4	357.6
1993	21,555	83.6	20.3	41.2	119.0	307.3	27,549	108.3	3.1	53.2	217.1	348.5
1994	22,279	85.8	18.1	37.9	135.7	324.9	28,236	108.8	2.7	51.3	222.3	364.0
1995	21,114	80.6	18.6	35.8	120.8	307.7	29,954	114.4	0.6 [1]	52.8	222.7	403.4

	Varicose veins of the lower extremities						Hemorrhoids					
		Incidence						Incidence				
			Age						Age			
	Total	Total	Under 18	18–44	45–64	65 and older	Total	Total	Under 18	18–44	45–64	65 and older
	Bd1098	Bd1099	Bd1100 [1]	Bd1101	Bd1102	Bd1103	Bd1104	Bd1105	Bd1106 [1]	Bd1107	Bd1108	Bd1109
Year	Thousand	Per 1,000	Per 1,000	Per 1,000	Per 1,000	Per 1,000	Thousand	Per 1,000	Per 1,000	Per 1,000	Per 1,000	Per 1,000
1982	6,880	30.3	—	21.9	64.1	77.7	10,449	46.0	0.8	54.0	75.5	76.5
1983	6,838	29.8	0.2	22.1	55.1	87.1	10,924	47.6	1.0	57.5	76.5	74.2
1984	7,188	31.0	0.6	23.3	65.2	74.8	10,119	43.7	0.4	47.9	75.4	77.7
1985	7,141	30.6	0.3	26.4	55.1	75.7	10,359	44.3	1.4	54.7	71.0	61.8
1986	6,856	29.0	—	22.6	56.3	74.6	9,909	41.9	0.9	46.7	73.2	67.8
1987	7,341	30.8	0.7	26.8	54.1	75.7	10,487	44.0	0.6	46.9	79.7	73.7
1988	7,632	31.7	—	26.6	56.8	80.2	11,041	45.8	1.3	53.8	78.2	64.5
1989	7,536	30.9	—	24.8	57.8	78.1	11,489	47.2	0.7	57.2	74.9	69.6
1990	6,976	28.3	0.2	24.6	46.8	74.0	9,446	38.4	1.2	41.0	70.9	58.9
1991	7,938	31.9	0.4	25.9	58.7	79.5	9,298	37.4	0.3	38.0	68.1	67.5
1992	7,281	29.0	0.4	23.8	52.8	70.9	9,562	38.0	0.2	40.2	71.2	60.0
1993	7,641	30.0	0.6	25.1	54.4	71.7	10,111	39.8	0.2	42.1	66.7	74.3
1994	7,260	28.0	—	22.2	50.5	74.7	9,321	35.9	0.4	39.3	62.1	61.7
1995	7,398	28.2	—	22.7	46.2	81.3	9,077	34.7	0.9	36.7	63.6	55.7

[1] Data in original source appear to be in error.

Source

U.S. National Center for Health Statistics, *Vital and Health Statistics,* series 10, published annually.

Documentation

Chronic conditions are defined as conditions that either were first noticed three months or more prior to the reference date of the interview or belong to a group of conditions, such as heart disease or diabetes, that are considered chronic regardless of when they were diagnosed.

The data include estimated totals and rates for the civilian noninstitutionalized population from the National Health Interview Survey.

TABLE Bd1110–1133 Persons afflicted with chronic respiratory conditions, by age: 1982–1995

Contributed by Richard H. Steckel

	Chronic bronchitis						Asthma					
		Incidence						Incidence				
			Age						Age			
	Total	Total	Under 18	18–44	45–64	65 and older	Total	Total	Under 18	18–44	45–64	65 and older
	Bd1110	Bd1111	Bd1112	Bd1113	Bd1114	Bd1115	Bd1116	Bd1117	Bd1118	Bd1119	Bd1120	Bd1121
Year	Thousand	Per 1,000	Per 1,000	Per 1,000	Per 1,000	Per 1,000	Thousand	Per 1,000	Per 1,000	Per 1,000	Per 1,000	Per 1,000
1982	7,709	33.9	33.7	24.5	44.2	52.0	7,899	34.8	40.1	29.0	36.3	40.8
1983	10,864	47.4	59.3	37.9	44.7	58.3	8,787	38.3	45.2	36.1	34.6	36.4
1984	10,925	47.2	49.5	39.5	51.6	63.0	8,388	36.2	42.5	32.1	33.5	41.3
1985	11,618	49.7	55.5	40.5	54.3	62.7	8,612	36.8	47.8	33.4	28.2	38.3
1986	11,379	48.1	63.2	36.5	45.8	60.0	9,690	41.0	51.1	36.4	36.3	42.6
1987	12,749	53.4	62.1	40.4	56.9	75.9	9,565	40.1	52.5	34.5	36.3	38.6
1988	11,894	49.4	54.3	39.0	56.1	64.8	9,934	41.2	49.9	38.7	34.8	41.4
1989	11,974	49.2	50.5	44.5	53.7	55.5	11,621	47.7	61.0	41.3	41.5	51.5
1990	12,584	51.1	53.3	41.5	57.4	70.4	10,311	41.9	57.6	35.2	38.6	36.3
1991	12,549	50.5	53.1	46.7	53.9	52.5	11,735	47.2	62.5	43.4	40.7	37.2
1992	13,494	53.7	53.6	47.0	58.3	69.6	12,375	49.2	63.4	44.9	45.0	39.8
1993	13,820	54.3	59.3	45.8	61.2	61.7	13,074	51.4	71.6	42.5	45.0	48.2
1994	14,021	54.0	55.3	46.7	63.9	60.5	14,562	56.1	69.1	51.7	50.8	50.5
1995	14,533	55.5	53.6	50.2	63.9	64.1	14,787	56.8	74.9	51.6	53.3	39.8

	Chronic sinusitis						Hay fever or allergic rhinitis without asthma					
		Incidence						Incidence				
			Age						Age			
	Total	Total	Under 18	18–44	45–64	65 and older	Total	Total	Under 18	18–44	45–64	65 and older
	Bd1122	Bd1123	Bd1124	Bd1125	Bd1126	Bd1127	Bd1128	Bd1129	Bd1130	Bd1131	Bd1132	Bd1133
Year	Thousand	Per 1,000	Per 1,000	Per 1,000	Per 1,000	Per 1,000	Thousand	Per 1,000	Per 1,000	Per 1,000	Per 1,000	Per 1,000
1982	27,644	121.7	43.0	138.9	179.1	151.7	19,323	85.1	55.1	109.3	87.5	64.6
1983	30,767	134.2	49.5	162.8	182.4	149.6	19,771	86.2	55.4	109.7	91.9	63.1
1984	30,231	130.5	46.6	152.9	176.2	169.4	20,610	89.0	61.4	115.7	84.2	62.9
1985	32,492	139.0	59.6	164.4	184.8	154.5	19,642	84.0	50.3	111.2	90.2	52.4
1986	34,386	145.5	65.8	170.4	187.0	169.4	21,702	91.8	64.3	113.1	95.8	70.4
1987	31,642	132.6	57.6	149.5	192.1	145.3	22,687	95.1	64.0	121.2	93.8	72.5
1988	33,658	139.7	61.4	157.5	188.0	173.0	22,413	93.0	63.4	114.6	99.4	71.4
1989	33,683	138.3	68.9	161.1	173.5	153.4	21,166	86.9	59.7	108.8	87.4	67.9
1990	32,314	131.3	56.7	149.0	181.9	151.7	22,187	90.2	56.5	115.0	95.1	67.7
1991	32,167	129.3	59.6	151.0	171.1	139.5	24,248	97.5	64.6	120.6	107.1	72.9
1992	36,659	145.8	69.3	171.1	187.3	158.7	25,698	102.2	71.4	127.5	101.6	82.8
1993	37,293	146.7	79.6	170.2	185.3	150.0	23,743	93.4	56.7	116.5	106.4	73.3
1994	34,902	134.4	65.1	153.3	179.9	151.1	26,146	100.7	60.5	123.3	120.8	80.0
1995	37,003	141.3	75.6	162.6	179.0	153.4	25,730	98.2	66.2	118.4	115.3	72.9

Source

U.S. National Center for Health Statistics, *Vital and Health Statistics,* series 10, published annually.

Documentation

See the text for Table Bd1086–1109.

TABLE Bd1134–1163 Persons afflicted with chronic skin and musculoskeletal conditions, by age: 1982–1995

Contributed by Richard H. Steckel

	Dermatitis						Arthritis					
		Incidence						Incidence				
			Age						Age			
	Total	Total	Under 18	18–44	45–64	65 and older	Total	Total	Under 18	18–44	45–64	65 and older
	Bd1134	Bd1135	Bd1136	Bd1137	Bd1138	Bd1139	Bd1140	Bd1141	Bd1142	Bd1143	Bd1144	Bd1145
Year	Thousand	Per 1,000	Per 1,000	Per 1,000	Per 1,000	Per 1,000	Thousand	Per 1,000	Per 1,000	Per 1,000	Per 1,000	Per 1,000
1982	8,652	38.1	40.0	40.3	38.2	24.9	30,207	133.0	2.7 [1]	55.3	276.2	495.8
1983	9,108	39.7	37.4	40.8	43.9	34.0	30,115	131.3	2.2	53.6	284.8	471.6
1984	8,719	37.6	38.9	40.3	31.7	35.0	30,784	132.9	2.5 [1]	51.5	285.0	489.7
1985	9,105	39.0	44.5	44.2	28.4	24.4	30,060	128.6	2.2 [1]	52.1	268.5	472.8
1986	9,547	40.4	42.0	44.3	35.4	30.4	30,911	130.8	2.0 [1]	47.9	284.6	480.4
1987	8,698	36.5	32.1	38.3	41.8	31.0	31,438	131.8	2.8	52.8	273.3	482.2
1988	9,025	37.5	34.9	42.5	36.1	27.2	31,292	129.9	2.3	53.3	257.1	485.7
1989	8,420	34.6	35.7	36.0	30.6	33.3	30,999	127.3	1.4 [1]	48.9	253.8	483.0
1990	8,681	35.3	31.0	37.7	37.0	33.1	30,833	125.3	3.0	47.9	249.1	470.1
1991	8,974	36.1	31.5	40.1	36.9	30.8	31,148	125.2	1.6 [1]	47.3	240.8	484.8
1992	10,146	40.4	40.8	40.5	41.4	37.1	33,317	132.5	2.4 [1]	54.1	259.9	481.9
1993	9,896	38.9	35.7	42.0	39.3	34.6	32,642	128.4	2.3	51.4	233.5	493.2
1994	9,192	35.4	37.6	35.7	33.6	32.3	33,446	128.8	2.7	52.3	239.0	501.5
1995	9,333	35.6	35.2	38.0	35.8	28.4	32,663	124.7	2.1 [1]	46.9	232.9	489.5

	Ingrown nails					
		Incidence				
			Age			
	Total	Total	Under 18	18–44	45–64	65 and older
	Bd1146	Bd1147	Bd1148	Bd1149	Bd1150	Bd1151
Year	Thousand	Per 1,000	Per 1,000	Per 1,000	Per 1,000	Per 1,000
1982	4,503	19.8	6.5	18.1	31.8	38.4
1983	4,636	20.2	7.9	18.4	28.6	42.3
1984	5,011	21.6	6.9	22.4	25.6	47.0
1985	5,422	23.2	7.0	22.9	32.5	46.8
1986	5,382	22.8	9.7	20.0	32.9	46.6
1987	5,684	23.8	7.3	25.2	31.6	43.8
1988	6,177	25.6	8.1	28.2	32.1	45.1
1989	5,726	23.5	9.1	23.7	28.1	47.3
1990	6,040	24.5	8.2	23.2	34.0	50.0
1991	5,908	23.8	7.8	24.2	26.6	52.2
1992	6,273	24.9	8.5	26.1	31.2	46.5
1993	6,237	24.5	8.7	23.4	32.7	49.5
1994	5,987	23.1	10.1	20.2	30.9	49.8
1995	5,371	20.5	8.0	20.1	28.9	36.4

TABLE Bd1134–1163 Persons afflicted with chronic skin and musculoskeletal conditions, by age: 1982–1995 *Continued*

	Corns and calluses						Unclassified dry, itching skin					
		Incidence						Incidence				
			Age						Age			
	Total	Total	Under 18	18–44	45–64	65 and older	Total	Total	Under 18	18–44	45–64	65 and older
	Bd1152	Bd1153	Bd1154 [1]	Bd1155	Bd1156	Bd1157	Bd1158	Bd1159	Bd1160	Bd1161	Bd1162	Bd1163
Year	Thousand	Per 1,000	Per 1,000	Per 1,000	Per 1,000	Per 1,000	Thousand	Per 1,000	Per 1,000	Per 1,000	Per 1,000	Per 1,000
1982	4,811	21.2	0.8	16.8	38.9	57.2	3,698	16.3	9.4	14.5	19.6	34.1
1983	4,645	20.3	0.9	16.7	38.2	49.5	4,115	17.9	10.0	18.1	23.1	28.0
1984	4,681	20.2	1.2	16.0	35.6	55.0	3,904	16.9	6.7	17.5	19.2	34.5
1985	5,159	22.1	1.6	20.6	38.0	48.8	4,041	17.3	9.0	16.9	21.5	30.8
1986	4,833	20.4	1.6	19.4	34.0	45.3	4,600	19.5	9.1	21.9	21.0	31.8
1987	4,078	17.1	1.4	14.6	29.3	41.9	4,294	18.0	9.4	19.2	19.1	31.1
1988	4,534	18.8	0.9	16.6	34.0	42.6	4,788	19.9	9.6	20.3	23.3	35.7
1989	4,342	17.8	0.2	14.6	31.5	46.2	4,289	17.6	9.9	17.1	22.9	28.1
1990	4,931	20.0	1.3	18.3	32.7	47.1	5,045	20.5	9.4	21.4	22.6	38.1
1991	4,819	19.4	0.7	16.9	33.2	47.0	4,931	19.8	11.5	18.8	23.2	36.2
1992	4,433	17.6	1.0	13.8	33.2	42.1	5,363	24.9	8.5	26.1	31.2	46.5
1993	5,117	20.1	1.9	17.8	33.9	45.4	5,170	20.3	10.0	19.8	23.9	38.9
1994	4,356	16.8	0.8	15.2	29.0	38.4	6,166	23.7	12.1	23.1	32.9	37.3
1995	4,347	16.6	1.3	12.9	28.7	43.8	6,440	24.6	13.9	22.2	30.2	47.5

[1] Data in original source appear to be in error.

Source

U.S. National Center for Health Statistics, *Vital and Health Statistics,* series 10, published annually.

Documentation

See the text for Table Bd1086–1109.

TABLE Bd1164–1187 Persons afflicted with chronic diabetes, migraine headaches, kidney trouble, and bladder disorders, by age: 1982–1995

Contributed by Richard H. Steckel

	Diabetes						Migraine headaches					
		Incidence						Incidence				
			Age						Age			
	Total	Total	Under 18	18–44	45–64	65 and older	Total	Total	Under 18	18–44	45–64	65 and older
	Bd1164	Bd1165	Bd1166 [1]	Bd1167	Bd1168	Bd1169	Bd1170	Bd1171	Bd1172	Bd1173	Bd1174	Bd1175
Year	Thousand	Per 1,000	Per 1,000	Per 1,000	Per 1,000	Per 1,000	Thousand	Per 1,000	Per 1,000	Per 1,000	Per 1,000	Per 1,000
1982	5,767	25.4	1.4	9.2	57.6	88.9	7,640	33.6	7.8	47.0	49.9	19.2
1983	5,613	24.5	1.8	9.0	58.2	79.5	7,258	31.6	6.4	47.0	42.5	16.9
1984	6,053	26.1	1.4	9.0	53.2	102.9	7,644	33.0	11.0	48.1	40.3	16.7
1985	6,134	26.2	1.9	9.1	51.9	103.8	8,316	35.6	12.7	52.9	41.1	16.0
1986	6,585	27.9	2.4	8.7	63.7	98.3	8,516	36.0	14.6	49.4	45.5	20.8
1987	6,641	27.8	2.0	11.9	56.4	98.2	8,549	35.8	8.4	54.0	45.7	15.6
1988	6,221	25.8	2.2	9.2	54.6	92.4	9,222	38.3	14.2	55.5	45.4	18.4
1989	6,489	26.6	1.8	10.7	58.2	88.2	9,978	41.0	15.5	57.2	51.2	22.8
1990	6,232	25.3	0.6	10.1	50.4	93.4	9,790	39.8	13.7	53.5	56.9	21.0
1991	7,223	29.0	1.1	13.6	57.4	99.3	9,539	38.4	12.6	55.5	47.2	20.6
1992	7,417	29.5	1.3	11.5	56.0	110.4	10,627	42.3	13.3	62.4	50.7	22.5
1993	7,813	30.7	1.5	13.1	61.9	103.5	11,023	43.3	13.2	62.0	59.6	19.3
1994	7,766	29.9	1.4	12.4	63.1	101.2	11,256	43.4	16.1	62.9	52.5	21.8
1995	8,693	33.2	2.6	11.4	63.8	126.4	11,897	45.4	12.7	68.1	58.0	20.2

Notes appear at end of table

(continued)

TABLE Bd1164–1187 Persons afflicted with chronic diabetes, migraine headaches, kidney trouble, and bladder disorders, by age: 1982–1995 *Continued*

	Kidney trouble						Bladder disorders					
		Incidence						Incidence				
			Age						Age			
	Total	Total	Under 18	18–44	45–64	65 and older	Total	Total	Under 18	18–44	45–64	65 and older
	Bd1176	Bd1177	Bd1178	Bd1179	Bd1180	Bd1181	Bd1182	Bd1183	Bd1184	Bd1185	Bd1186	Bd1187
Year	Thousand	Per 1,000	Per 1,000	Per 1,000	Per 1,000	Per 1,000	Thousand	Per 1,000	Per 1,000	Per 1,000	Per 1,000	Per 1,000
1982	3,252	14.3	3.2 [2]	13.2	24.1	28.9	2,665	11.7	3.4 [2]	11.0	15.9	27.6
1983	3,087	13.5	4.3	11.4	20.7	31.1	4,766	17.3	5.1	18.4	22.4	34.2
1984	3,804	16.4	5.0	16.5	25.9	27.1	3,681	15.9	4.3	15.4	21.0	36.9
1985	3,376	14.4	3.0 [2]	14.1	23.8	26.8	3,946	16.9	2.8 [2]	15.9	21.1	46.6
1986	3,966	16.8	4.4	17.3	23.3	32.8	3,770	16.0	2.4 [2]	15.5	22.2	38.5
1987	3,319	13.9	3.2	14.2	20.6	26.2	3,450	14.5	4.2	13.6	19.0	33.5
1988	3,311	13.7	3.1	15.4	17.3	25.6	3,076	12.8	4.1	10.4	17.8	32.4
1989	3,375	13.9	1.8 [2]	15.6	18.2	27.3	3,563	14.6	3.1	14.5	19.9	32.0
1990	3,061	12.4	3.8	11.3	19.6	24.1	3,062	12.4	3.7	10.8	14.5	33.9
1991	3,146	12.6	3.1	12.9	17.3	25.1	3,770	15.2	4.6	14.3	15.6	40.4
1992	3,375	13.4	3.4	14.0	17.1	27.4	3,475	13.8	3.7	13.3	17.8	31.3
1993	3,850	15.1	4.7	15.8	20.5	26.9	4,024	15.8	3.4	13.9	22.3	39.0
1994	3,512	13.5	3.4	15.8	17.2	22.4	3,747	14.4	4.4	12.5	16.9	39.7
1995	3,022	11.5	2.7 [2]	12.7	15.4	21.2	4,135	15.8	2.8 [2]	12.9	19.8	48.3

[1] Data in original source appear to be in error for all years except 1988.

[2] Data in original source appear to be in error.

Source

U.S. National Center for Health Statistics, *Vital and Health Statistics,* series 10, published annually.

Documentation

See the text for Table Bd1086–1109.

TABLE Bd1188–1217 Persons afflicted with chronic visual, hearing, and other impairments, by age: 1982–1995

Contributed by Richard H. Steckel

	Visual impairments						Cataracts					
		Incidence						Incidence				
			Age						Age			
	Total	Total	Under 18	18–44	45–64	65 and older	Total	Total	Under 18	18–44	45–64	65 and older
	Bd1188	Bd1189	Bd1190	Bd1191	Bd1192	Bd1193	Bd1194	Bd1195	Bd1196 [1]	Bd1197	Bd1198	Bd1199
Year	Thousand	Per 1,000	Per 1,000	Per 1,000	Per 1,000	Per 1,000	Thousand	Per 1,000	Per 1,000	Per 1,000	Per 1,000	Per 1,000
1982	8,699	38.3	13.1	31.2	53.4	101.1	5,124	22.6	1.0	2.2 [1]	20.8	154.8
1983	8,081	35.2	10.3	29.5	49.7	92.1	4,766	20.8	0.3	2.7	17.7	143.0
1984	7,941	34.3	9.0	27.2	45.8	100.9	5,064	21.9	0.7	2.4	18.4	150.1
1985	8,496	36.4	10.8	32.8	43.7	96.5	5,832	25.0	2.1	1.8 [1]	24.4	164.0
1986	8,352	35.3	12.2	28.7	46.3	95.0	5,031	21.3	0.6	1.5 [1]	21.1	141.4
1987	7,934	33.3	10.1	29.3	47.3	77.4	5,579	23.4	0.2	1.7	18.6	161.7
1988	8,365	34.7	9.1	29.2	47.7	90.7	6,105	25.3	1.0	2.4	21.6	167.7
1989	7,881	32.4	9.0	27.2	45.1	81.9	5,698	23.4	0.2	3.5	16.1	156.8
1990	7,525	30.6	8.7	28.5	38.5	73.1	5,927	24.1	0.9	2.5	22.1	153.9
1991	7,988	32.1	5.4	28.4	47.5	79.2	6,587	26.5	1.4	2.9	20.2	173.0
1992	8,976	35.7	10.4	30.6	48.9	87.0	6,721	26.7	0.9	2.8	25.8	166.0
1993	9,302	36.6	7.2	31.8	49.4	95.7	6,067	23.9	0.8	2.6	20.0	151.6
1994	8,601	33.1	8.7	29.3	45.1	82.2	6,473	24.9	1.4	3.2	17.3	166.2
1995	8,511	32.5	7.0	28.9	48.3	76.0	6,256	23.9	0.2	2.3	19.3	158.7

Notes appear at end of table

TABLE Bd1188–1217 Persons afflicted with chronic visual, hearing, and other impairments, by age: 1982–1995 *Continued*

	Hearing impairments					
		Incidence				
			Age			
	Total	Total	Under 18	18–44	45–64	65 and older
	Bd1200	Bd1201	Bd1202	Bd1203	Bd1204	Bd1205
Year	Thousand	Per 1,000	Per 1,000	Per 1,000	Per 1,000	Per 1,000
1982	19,776	87.1	19.7	48.8	142.7	299.7
1983	20,698	90.3	18.8	49.8	148.4	314.8
1984	21,190	91.5	24.0	53.6	139.9	311.3
1985	21,198	90.7	19.2	49.8	159.0	294.4
1986	20,732	87.7	20.1	51.8	136.2	295.6
1987	20,994	88.0	16.0	54.1	135.6	296.8
1988	21,864	90.8	17.0	48.7	147.6	315.2
1989	20,246	83.1	15.6	47.8	127.7	286.5
1990	23,296	94.7	21.0	51.1	150.0	321.8
1991	22,680	91.2	16.1	49.7	141.3	320.5
1992	23,777	94.6	15.0	51.4	154.2	320.4
1993	24,160	95.0	17.1	57.1	143.5	314.1
1994	22,400	86.3	17.5	49.4	137.9	286.4
1995	22,465	85.8	14.9	46.2	144.7	283.9

	Tinnitus						Deformity or orthopedic impairment					
		Incidence						Incidence				
			Age						Age			
	Total	Total	Under 18	18–44	45–64	65 and older	Total	Total	Under 18	18–44	45–64	65 and older
	Bd1206	Bd1207	Bd1208 [2]	Bd1209	Bd1210	Bd1211	Bd1212	Bd1213	Bd1214	Bd1215	Bd1216	Bd1217
Year	Thousand	Per 1,000	Per 1,000	Per 1,000	Per 1,000	Per 1,000	Thousand	Per 1,000	Per 1,000	Per 1,000	Per 1,000	Per 1,000
1982	5,130	22.6	1.1	15.6	39.0	73.2	22,522	99.2	31.8	106.5	139.0	168.5
1983	5,380	23.5	1.0	13.6	44.1	79.5	22,152	96.6	27.0	105.9	136.8	161.6
1984	5,673	24.5	1.0	15.5	42.2	83.7	25,277	109.1	34.7	118.5	155.7	172.6
1985	6,228	26.6	0.7	15.0	49.8	91.7	26,314	112.6	33.2	125.3	160.6	170.8
1986	6,315	26.7	3.6	15.3	49.2	85.2	27,381	115.9	32.5	132.2	161.6	172.7
1987	6,235	26.1	1.1	18.4	41.7	85.5	27,725	116.2	35.8	135.4	155.0	165.3
1988	6,361	26.4	1.1	16.0	49.2	83.9	26,878	111.6	28.8	131.4	150.9	161.1
1989	5,867	24.1	1.7	14.4	45.8	73.5	27,998	114.9	29.3	138.3	155.5	155.2
1990	7,149	29.0	2.7	16.5	53.7	92.2	28,899	117.4	28.8	136.3	161.5	174.4
1991	6,490	26.1	1.7	14.3	50.2	82.4	28,725	115.5	25.2	136.4	154.4	177.5
1992	7,779	30.9	1.1	19.5	59.6	89.4	31,605	125.7	32.9	144.3	174.3	185.7
1993	8,845	34.8	2.4	25.0	59.8	97.9	31,182	122.6	29.3	142.2	172.4	178.4
1994	7,033	27.1	2.1	16.2	46.3	90.1	31,068	119.7	28.0	142.4	170.0	165.6
1995	6,805	26.0	1.3	16.1	54.8	67.9	31,784	121.4	29.8	138.8	175.6	178.1

[1] Data in original source appear to be in error.

[2] Data in original source appear to be in error for all years except 1990 and 1993.

Source

U.S. National Center for Health Statistics, *Vital and Health Statistics,* series 10, published annually.

Documentation

See the text for Table Bd1086–1109.

TABLE Bd1218–1235 Persons afflicted with chronic digestive conditions, by age: 1982–1995

Contributed by Richard H. Steckel

	Hernia of the abdominal cavity						Frequent indigestion						Frequent constipation					
		Incidence						Incidence						Incidence				
			Age						Age						Age			
	Total	Total	Under 18	18–44	45–64	65 and older	Total	Total	Under 18	18–44	45–64	65 and older	Total	Total	Under 18	18–44	45–64	65 and older
	Bd1218	Bd1219	Bd1220	Bd1221	Bd1222	Bd1223	Bd1224	Bd1225	Bd1226	Bd1227	Bd1228	Bd1229	Bd1230	Bd1231	Bd1232	Bd1233	Bd1234	Bd1235
Year	Thousand	Per 1,000	Per 1,000	Per 1,000	Per 1,000	Per 1,000	Thousand	Per 1,000	Per 1,000	Per 1,000	Per 1,000	Per 1,000	Thousand	Per 1,000	Per 1,000	Per 1,000	Per 1,000	Per 1,000
1982	4,970	21.9	4.8	10.6	39.5	75.5	5,360	23.6	1.8 [1]	26.1	35.3	47.9	4,431	19.5	6.3	14.8	22.0	65.3
1983	4,698	20.5	4.9	9.0	41.3	65.4	5,493	24.0	2.9 [1]	26.5	35.2	46.2	4,551	19.8	5.9	13.0	24.2	71.7
1984	5,239	22.6	3.0 [1]	9.2	42.0	86.5	5,390	23.3	1.2 [1]	24.8	36.8	47.1	4,707	20.3	6.0	13.3	25.1	72.3
1985	4,802	20.5	4.6	9.6	39.3	66.8	5,697	24.4	1.5 [1]	28.2	35.7	44.9	3,789	16.2	6.2	11.6	15.6	57.5
1986	4,584	19.4	4.7	9.5	36.9	61.2	5,315	22.5	3.9 [1]	25.4	31.3	40.3	4,539	19.2	5.6	14.3	22.1	63.7
1987	4,624	19.4	2.6	9.0	38.7	63.9	6,075	25.5	2.6	28.0	40.5	43.8	4,704	19.7	7.6	14.4	18.2	68.6
1988	4,744	19.7	5.8	9.2	38.9	57.6	5,817	24.1	3.5	27.4	35.2	40.9	4,580	19.0	9.1	12.9	21.9	58.3
1989	4,576	18.8	4.1	9.6	36.9	55.2	5,418	22.2	1.9 [1]	24.5	35.5	38.0	4,529	18.6	8.2	11.9	20.9	61.7
1990	4,179	17.0	1.8 [1]	9.5	29.3	57.1	5,770	23.4	1.7 [1]	27.6	32.7	41.4	3,991	16.2	6.7	12.4	14.3	53.4
1991	4,889	19.7	2.9	9.5	40.6	58.9	5,723	23.0	2.2 [1]	25.3	34.9	41.7	4,609	18.5	6.2	14.1	19.1	59.7
1992	5,228	20.8	5.5	11.2	36.5	62.2	6,374	25.3	3.8	26.9	40.1	43.5	4,296	17.1	6.7	12.8	20.7	48.6
1993	4,900	19.3	2.8	8.0	32.7	71.5	6,253	24.6	2.7	28.0	35.6	42.9	4,460	17.5	5.5	10.3	24.3	57.2
1994	4,778	18.4	1.3 [1]	10.3	31.2	64.4	6,957	26.8	2.0 [1]	31.2	40.9	44.6	4,040	15.6	5.0	12.7	12.3	54.6
1995	4,664	17.8	2.0 [1]	10.4	32.4	54.8	7,198	27.5	3.3	32.2	41.2	43.2	3,644	13.9	4.5	11.3	17.1	38.6

[1] Data in original source appear to be in error.

Source

U.S. National Center for Health Statistics, *Vital and Health Statistics,* series 10, published annually.

Documentation

See the text for Table Bd1086–1109.

CHAPTER Be

Economic Inequality and Poverty

Editors: Peter H. Lindert (Economic Inequality)
Linda Barrington and Gordon M. Fisher (Poverty)

THE DISTRIBUTION OF INCOME AND WEALTH

Peter H. Lindert

Societies are sometimes as concerned about differences as they are about averages. In particular, there has been a long-standing political interest in the issue of how income and wealth are distributed, and how this distribution has changed over time.

Measuring Inequality

The study of income and wealth distribution has been historically motivated by debates over how unequally resources have been distributed and why the distribution is unequal. Estimates of the degree of inequality take the form of size distributions from which summary measures of inequality are derived.

A size distribution of any attribute ranks individuals by how much of that attribute they have, starting with those having it least and proceeding to those having it most. Figure Be-A portrays a conventional summary of a size distribution, in this case a distribution of income. Arranging individuals from the lowest income individual to the highest income individual, and plotting the cumulative share of total income that the lower income group has, traces out a Lorenz curve.

Three summary measures that capture the degree of inequality in this size distribution are (a) top-group income shares, (b) interpercentile income ratios, and (c) the Gini coefficient of inequality. All three kinds of inequality measures are used here to summarize the degree of inequality in the size distributions of income or wealth.[1] Each measure is illustrated in Figure Be-A:

An example of a *top-group income share* is that the top 5 percent of individuals received 32 percent of total income (100 percent minus 68 percent).

An *interpercentile income ratio* is a ratio of a higher percentile income to a lower percentile income. Its usefulness lies in its focus on two known positions on the income spectrum, or Lorenz curve, when the rest of the curve is unknown or less accurately measured. For example, the ratio of the income of an individual at the 95th percentile to the median (50th percentile) income summarizes inequality between these relative ranks. In the figure, this interpercentile income ratio is the ratio of the two slopes shown at the 95th and 50th percentiles of individuals, since each slope shows the relative income of an extra person at that point in the rankings.

The *Gini coefficient* adds up the share of total income that would have to be redistributed to achieve complete equality, assuming that were possible. Because perfect equality is represented by the 45-degree line, the shaded area is a measure of how far the size distribution, the Lorenz curve, departs from complete equality. The Gini coefficient is that shaded area measured as a share of the whole area below and to the right of the 45-degree line. If there were complete equality (so that the Lorenz curve was the 45-degree line itself), the Gini coefficient of inequality would be zero. If one top individual had all the income, the Gini coefficient would be one.

Difficult questions can and should be raised about the concept of a measurable degree of inequality. The first question is: "Inequality over what time span?" Many people probably envision inequalities of income or consumption over entire lifetimes, yet data limitations force the use of incomes within a single year or wealth at a single moment in time. Some of the inequality among individuals in any one year or at any one moment is temporary and only indirectly reflects how unequal they will be over their entire life spans. A second question is: "Inequality of what?" Given that we have only single-year or single-moment measures, should we use income or wealth or consumption, and should the inequalities be measured before or after taxes and transfer payments? None of these economic indicators is a complete measure of individual well-being, which would have to include health and other nonmonetary dimensions. A third difficult question is: "Inequality among whom?" Is the relevant population unit really an individual, of any age? Because people typically share resources within households, a case could be made for measuring income or wealth among households rather than among individuals. If the household unit is chosen, then

Acknowledgments
Linda Barrington and Gordon Fisher thank the following people for research assistance in compiling the tables in this chapter: Mousumi Bhakta, Sumi Gupta, Liam Kavanagh, Bernadette Moton, and Kavita Vashi. Advice and assistance were provided by Caroline Carbaugh and Joe Dalaker, U.S. Census Bureau, in the construction of Table Be371–398. Funding support was provided by the Russell Sage Foundation. The views expressed in this chapter are those of the authors and do not represent the position of the Conference Board or of the U.S. Department of Health and Human Services.

[1] For an advanced treatment of the mathematical properties and problems of alternative inequality measures, see Atkinson and Bourguignon (2000), especially Chapters 1 and 2.

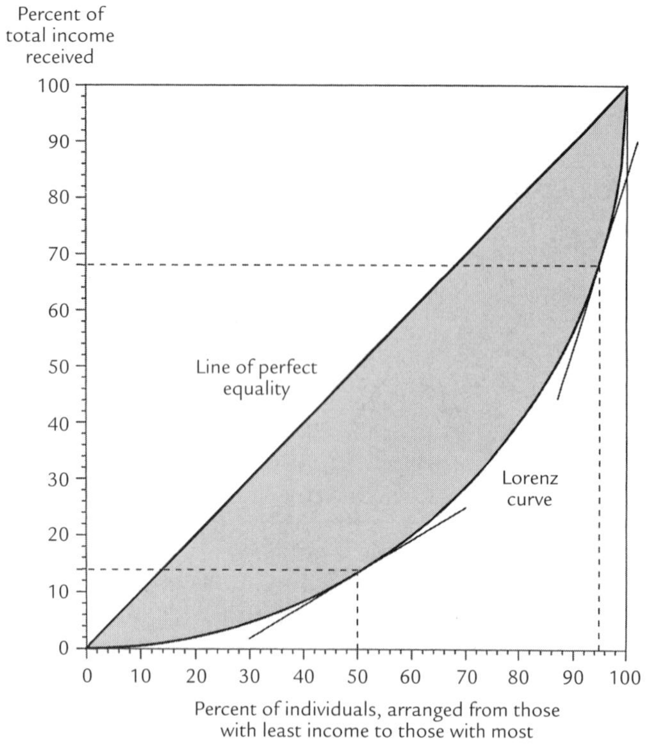

FIGURE Be-A A size distribution of income, portrayed by a Lorenz curve

how should the measure of resources be adjusted for the numbers and ages of the persons sharing those resources? This chapter takes the approach of looking at household (or family) units.

Another major caution about measures of the size distribution of income is that they cannot directly measure the justice or injustice of that distribution. In other words, inequality is not a measure of injustice. Two illustrations of this important distinction relate to the historical series chosen for presentation here.

First, one might wish to know the extent to which income inequality reflects differences in work. Higher incomes can result from longer hours worked per earner or from more earners in the household. Many people would react differently to inequalities based on differences in work than they would to inequalities based on different rewards for the same amount of work. It would be desirable to have historical time series that decompose differences in household income into differences in paid work time versus differences in rates of pay per hour worked. Yet such time series still have too short a time span to be presented here. The exception is Table Be67–84, which shows some ways in which median and mean incomes relate to the number of adults and the number of earners in the family since 1947.

Second, one might wish to know the extent to which each earner's rate of pay, and each household's income, relates to its race, ethnic origin, market work of spouse, or sex of household head. Decades of debate and quantitative studies still have not resolved the controversy over the degree to which such differences have produced income differences through discrimination. Accordingly, this chapter presents differences in median and mean income by race, Hispanic origin, and sex of the householders (Tables Be55–84), with the caution that they cannot directly resolve the issue of how justly income or wealth was distributed in the past.

The History of Measuring Income and Wealth Distributions in America

The development of detailed and informed estimates of the distribution of income and wealth had to wait upon the development of basic income, wealth, and population measures by the Census Bureau, the Internal Revenue Service, other government agencies, and private survey organizations. Only since 1913 has there been the combination of income tax returns, wealth tax returns, nationwide household surveys, and census questions about income.[2] To survey that development, let us begin with the relatively data-rich era since World War II and work back into the relative statistical darkness of the earlier history.

The Current Population Surveys and Related Survey Data since World War II

Since World War II, the measurement of family income has been advanced by a wide array of household surveys. The decennial censuses themselves asked direct income questions, which were preceded by the pioneering attempt of the 1940 census to measure the labor-earnings component of income. Various government agencies continued to survey household income and expenditures in occasional benchmark years. The income tax returns of the Internal Revenue Service took on a new relevance after World War II as the share of households filing income tax returns had shifted from less than 10 percent to more than two thirds. The Social Security Administration also began to develop earnings series for those persons covered under the Old-Age, Survivors, Disability, and Health Insurance (OASDHI) program. The Survey Research Center of the University of Michigan also developed distributions of income for the 1945–1969 period as part of its Survey of Consumer Finances. These different sources could be used to cross check and adjust the weaknesses of each.

The central postwar data set, backed by all these others, is the Census Bureau's Current Population Surveys (CPS), which cover a vast range of demographic, social, and economic characteristics of households and persons. Since 1947, the CPS has included a fairly consistent concept of total money income, measured as all income received in cash, but excluding all income in kind, whether transfer-in-kind from government programs or the household's direct use of goods and services from a business.[3] The CPS yields the conventional estimates of top-group income shares and Gini coefficients, presented in series Be1–15.

Abundant and detailed as these estimates are, the size distributions they yield are subject to all the caveats noted previously, plus one particular caution. This caution relates to the "top-coding" problem with the CPS measurement of money income. The Census Bureau estimates do not record the amounts of income within the top income class. To produce and publish income distribution data, the Census Bureau values all household incomes in the top

[2] Much of the history of early attempts to measure the distribution of income has been detailed in *Historical Statistics of the United States* (1975), Part 1, pp. 284–8.

[3] The types of nongovernment noncash benefits excluded from the "money income" measure include goods produced and consumed on the farm, the family or household use of business transportation and facilities, full or partial payments by business for retirement programs, and medical and educational expenses.

class at the *bottom income* of that top class.[4] For a household member's earnings from longest job, this floor of the top income class was $50,000 for 1967–1976, then $100,000 until it was raised to $300,000 effective in the March 1985 survey, and then to $1 million effective in the March 1994 survey. Clearly, this gives an incomplete view of top incomes.

To gain an impression of the size distribution of income that minimizes the top-coding problem, one can use the fact that the Census Bureau's occasional raising of that top category's floor income has always kept the share of households in that top class below 5 percent of the population. To avoid the effects of top-coding, one can consult series Be16–18, which present interpercentile ratios involving only the 95th, 80th, and 20th percentiles, avoiding the measurement of incomes higher than the 95th percentile.

Income Distributions for 1913–1947

Before the CPS and other systematic annual surveys, government agencies and independent scholars developed credible top-group income shares and even some Gini coefficients from an eclectic data base. A pioneer in these efforts was Simon Kuznets, whose *Shares of Upper Income Groups in Income and Savings* made detailed adjustments to income tax returns to estimate the top-group income shares for 1913–1948 shown in Table Be19–20 (Kuznets 1953). The most widely used estimates spanning the intermediate period from 1929 to 1971 originated in the work of Selma Goldsmith and the Office of Business Economics (OBE) (see Table Be21–26).[5] Neither the Kuznets tax-based estimates nor the eclectic OBE-Goldsmith estimates are known to contain the same top-coding problem found in the later CPS estimates. Similarly, the Piketty-Saez estimates of top income shares among tax units between 1913 and 1998 do not contain this problem (see Table Be27–29).

Before 1913, we lack systematic income distributions because the pre-1913 income tax episodes were very brief and covered only the very highest incomes. For this reason, conjectures about the distribution of economic resources among households before 1913 have to be based on the distribution of wealth, not of income.

Wealth Distributions since 1916, and for Earlier Periods

Since 1916, national taxation on wealth has also yielded top-group shares and Gini coefficients. Systematic estimates by Robert Lampman for the 1922–1956 period have been adjusted and updated by Edward H. Wolff and Marcia Marley.[6] The top-group shares and Gini coefficients are presented in Table Be39–46.

For the long era before World War I, more data survive on national wealth distributions than on national income distributions. A special tax survey of 1798 asked households and other occupants about the value of the real estate they occupied. The Census of 1850 asked people about the total value of the real estate they individually owned, and the Censuses of 1860 and 1870 supplemented these questions with additional queries about the value of their "personal estate" (all assets other than real estate).[7] Aside from these government-generated national returns, the other important estimation of the national distribution of wealth is Alice Hanson Jones's analysis of 919 probate inventories for the thirteen colonies from around the year 1774 (Jones 1977, 1980). Table Be39–46 provides top-group wealth shares and wealth Gini coefficients from these national data sets.

Many other early wealth distributions have been estimated at the state and local levels. The most comprehensive of these is the Steckel-Moehling study of assessed wealth in Massachusetts from 1820 to 1910, summarized in Table Be47–54. Beyond this Massachusetts data set, there are numerous studies of the wealth distributions of regions, cities, and towns extending back to the seventeenth century.[8]

Apparent Long-Run Movements in the Inequality of Income and Wealth

Scholars and news media have long used estimates like those discussed earlier to support conjectures about trends in America's income and wealth gaps. Subject to all the warnings previously noted, one can indeed see some likely trends in the shares of income or wealth received by the top income ranks. To survey these likely trends here, let us start with the earliest, most poorly documented, era and work toward the present.[9]

The Colonial Era

That paucity of data for the thirteen colonies makes it very hazardous to judge movements in the distribution of income and wealth before the 1770s. The only time-series data that even hint at an overall distribution are those local samples of assessed or probated wealth, buttressed by occasional population censuses. The scattered data offer divergent hints about trends in the colonies.

In the South, one particular force must have raised the inequality of wealth across the colonial era. Slavery meant that slaves had essentially zero wealth or disposable income, while the slave owners had extra wealth equal to the market value of the expected profits from slaveowning. Over the colonial period, slaves rose as a share of the Southern colonies' population, from about 7.3 percent in 1680 to 39.3 percent by 1770. Such a great rise in the importance of slavery must have magnified the relative wealth of the richest groups, as well as the share of households having zero wealth. Beyond this observation, however, we lack any time series for the distribution of wealth over the Southern colonies.

In the Middle Atlantic and Northern colonies, the available estimates of the distribution of taxable or probated wealth do not reveal any clear trend in the share held by the richest groups. Wealth inequality seemed to rise in some seaboard regions but not in others, and the westward drift of population was a drift toward areas where land and other wealth were more equally held. On balance, one

[4] A complicating detail is that the dollar brackets refer to CPS questions about kinds of income, not about total household income. The most important kind of income, that from earnings from each household member's longest-held job, is featured here.

[5] For details on the Goldsmith-OBE estimates, again see *Historical Statistics of the United States* (1975), Part 1, pp. 284–8.

[6] Lampman (1962); Wolff and Marley (1989); Wolff (1994); Wolff (1995); and Wolff (in press), cited in the text for series Be39–46.

[7] For extensive analysis of these source materials and the distributions they imply, see Soltow (1989) and (1975).

[8] For a survey and analysis of the local studies of early wealth by Bruce Daniels, Allan Kulikoff, Gloria Main, Jackson Turner Main, Gary Nash, Daniel Scott Smith, and others, see Williamson and Lindert (1980), Chapter 3.

[9] This section draws on the following interpretive surveys of the trends: Williamson and Lindert (1980); Smolensky, Plotnick, et al. (2000); and Lindert (2000). It also uses the studies cited in the earlier footnotes of this chapter, especially when interpreting trends before 1929.

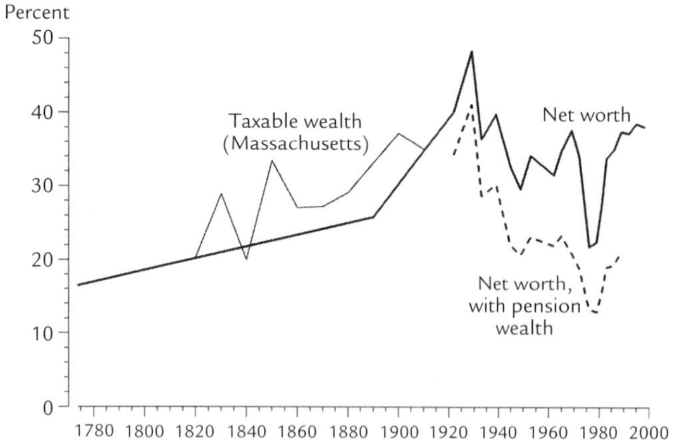

FIGURE Be-B Shares of wealth held by the richest 1 percent of households: 1774–1998

Source

Series Be40, Be43, and Be49.

cannot say whether there was any trend toward, or away from, unequal wealth across the colonial era.

Between 1774 and 1929

Statistical darkness also hangs over the whole century and a half between the end of the colonial era and the eve of the Great Depression.[10] Our best clues are the wealth distribution estimates introduced previously and summarized in Tables Be39–54. Two of these series are shown in Figure Be-B. They suggest that wealth inequality rose over this long period, both in Massachusetts and for the nation as a whole. One cannot yet say how much of this net change occurred before the Civil War, but it is likely that there was some widening of wealth inequality across the whole of the nineteenth century. It is hard to imagine that in the 1770s colonial households were as unequal in their wealth or income as their descendents would become by 1929.

America's long rise of inequality before 1929 seems to testify more to the unusual equality of wealth in the Middle Atlantic and Northern colonies and states in the late eighteenth century than to any unusual degree of inequality, by international standards, in the twentieth century. In particular, Britain, France, and Holland had a less pronounced rise in inequality over the same century and a half, mainly because they started from a position of greater initial inequality not shared by the emerging frontier society of America.[11]

The Leveling Era, 1929–1953

All the available series point to a major narrowing of the gaps in income and wealth over roughly the second quarter of the twentieth century. The change was apparently related to a fundamental shift in earning power in favor of low-paid occupations. This leveling, documented and publicized by Simon Kuznets, became a key exhibit in his suggestion that inequality declines in the later stages of economic development, on the downside of what subsequently became known as the Kuznets curve of rising and falling inequality.[12] It is likely that the equalization was even greater in terms of disposable income, or income after taxes and transfers, than it was in the pretax income distributions featured in this chapter.

A Renewed Rise in Inequality, 1977–1995

After a quarter century without any clear trend in income inequality before or after taxes and transfers, a new widening of income and wealth gaps set in between about 1977 and about 1995. Part of this rise in inequality took the form of another fundamental shift in the earning powers of different occupations, this time an inegalitarian shift. The rest of the rise took the form of shifts in the distributions of income earners and working hours across families. In particular, between 1977 and 1995 there was a shift toward dual-career households, with men and women of high earning power tending more and more to be married to each other, adding to the inequality of total household incomes.

A natural historical question about these trends is whether the inequalities reached by the 1990s were as wide as those back in 1929, another date that might have qualified as a historical peak in inequality. Some of the series in this chapter suggest that the inequality of 1929 was not regained in the 1990s as indicated by the wealth inequality measures that include pension rights in the measure of wealth. Similarly, the America of the 1990s would look less unequal than the America of 1929 if one factored out the effects of the shift toward high-income dual-career couples, which is not a shift in basic rewards for different occupations. On the other hand, other measures suggest that the distribution of income and wealth in the 1990s may have returned to the historic 1929 peak of inequality. Figure Be-C illustrates this possibility by looking at pre-tax income ratios that are free from the top-coding data problem described earlier. It appears that the ratio of a 95th-percentile income or an 80th-percentile income to the median (50th-percentile) income may have been as unequal in 1995 as the corresponding ratio for 1929.

References

Atkinson, A. B., and François Bourguignon, editors. 2000. *Handbook of Income Distribution*, volume 1. Elsevier.

Jones, Alice Hanson. 1977. *American Colonial Wealth: Documents and Methods*, three volumes. Arno Press.

Jones, Alice Hanson. 1980. *Wealth of a Nation to Be.* Columbia University Press.

Kuznets, Simon. 1953. *Shares of Upper Income Groups in Income and Savings.* National Bureau of Economic Research.

Kuznets, Simon. 1955. "Economic Growth and Income Inequality." *American Economic Review* 45 (1): 1–28.

Lampman, Robert J. 1962. *The Share of Top Wealth-Holders in National Wealth, 1922–1956.* Princeton University Press.

Lindert, Peter H. "Three Centuries of Inequality in Britain and America." In A. B. Atkinson and François Bourguignon, editors. *Handbook of Income Distribution*, volume 1. Elsevier.

Morrisson, Christian, and Wayne Snyder. 2000. "The Income Inequality of France in Historical Perspective." *European Review of Economic History* 4 (1): 59–84.

[10] The discussion here focuses on 1929 as a possible all-time peak year for inequality in the distribution of American income and wealth. It may have been the case, however, that inequality was just as high in 1913–1914, on the eve of World War I, as in 1929. The year 1929 is featured here for want of sufficient data on inequality in 1913–1914.

[11] The trends of British income and wealth inequality are summarized in Lindert (2000). On French inequality movements, see Morrisson and Snyder (2000). On inequality in Holland up to 1808, see van Zanden (1995).

[12] Kuznets's classic conjecture of a rise-and-fall pattern for inequality was presented in his presidential address to the American Economic Association (1955).

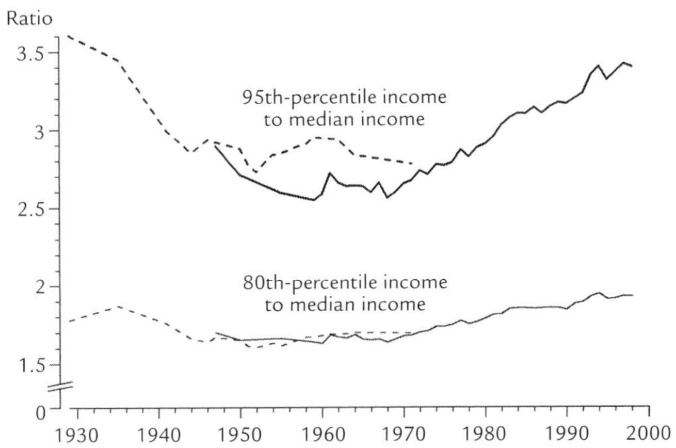

FIGURE Be-C Income inequality – ratios of high-percentile income to the median income: 1929–1998

Source

95th income percentile: series Be16 and Be24. 80th income percentile: series Be17 and Be25.

Documentation

See the text for Tables Be1–18 and Be21–26 for the differences between the series displayed here.

Smolensky, Eugene, Robert Plotnick, et al. 2000. "The Twentieth-Century Record of Inequality and Poverty in the United States." In Stanley L. Engerman and Robert Gallman, editors. *The Cambridge Economic History of the United States*, volume 3. Cambridge University Press.

Soltow, Lee. 1975. *Men and Wealth in the United States, 1850–1870.* Yale University Press.

Soltow, Lee. 1989. *Distribution of Wealth and Income in the United States in 1798.* University of Pittsburgh Press.

Williamson, Jeffrey, and Peter H. Lindert. 1980. *American Inequality: A Macroeconomic History.* Academic Press.

Wolff, Edward N. 1994. "Trends in Household Wealth in the United States, 1962–83 and 1983–89." *Review of Income and Wealth* 40 (2): 143–74.

Wolff, Edward N. 1995. *Top Heavy: A Study of the Increasing Inequality of Wealth in America.* Twentieth Century Fund Press.

Wolff, Edward N. 2001. "Recent Trends in Wealth Ownership, 1983–1998." In Thomas M. Shapiro and Edward N. Wolff, editors. *Assets for the Poor: The Benefits of Spreading Asset Ownership.* Russell Sage Foundation.

Wolff, Edward N., and Marcia Marley. 1989. "Long-Term Trends in U.S. Wealth Inequality: Methodological Issues and Results." In Robert E. Lipsey and Helen Stone Tice, editors. *The Measurement of Saving, Investment, and Wealth*, National Bureau of Economic Research Studies in Income and Wealth, volume 52. University of Chicago Press.

van Zanden, Jan Luiten. 1995. "Tracing the Beginning of the Kuznets Curve: Western Europe during the Early Modern Period." *Economic History Review* 48 (4): 643–64.

POVERTY

Linda Barrington and Gordon M. Fisher

Give me your tired, your poor,
Your huddled masses yearning to breathe free.[1]

American historical myth, especially that of the nineteenth and twentieth centuries, is heavily laden with economic advancement – streets paved with gold and opportunity waiting around every corner. Horatio Alger penned such stories; John D. Rockefeller and Bill Gates embody them. Such anecdotes provide proof for the faithful but hardly a complete chronology of the economic condition of Americans. In reality, how big was the pool of poverty from which the fictional Horatio Alger characters rose? Without a definition of poverty across time, or a count of population therein, the odds of rising above poverty cannot be calculated, and the truth of the myth cannot be tested.

As the United States enters the new millennium, the changing population demographics are dramatic. As of the 2000 U.S. Census of the Population, African Americans are no longer the single largest minority population – the Hispanic population has pulled even. The percentage of the population that is foreign-born again registers in the double digits. One out of ten Americans lives in a state with a "majority minority" population. How pertinent has the American myth been for demographic minorities in the United States? Which Americans face what odds of being poor?

The implicit social contract of capitalism assigns the individual the responsibility of supporting herself in exchange for the ownership of (or property rights to) the additional value that she produces for society. The incidence of poverty is one measure of how well that contract is succeeding.

Although widely accepted time-series estimates exist for gross national product or consumer prices for periods of over a century, an official measurement of America's poor exists only for the last four decades. This is the first volume of *Historical Statistics of the United States* to contain statistics on poverty. At the time of the last edition (1975), the U.S. Census Bureau had been publishing national poverty statistics for less than a decade – not long enough to produce an "historical" series. Now, however, the official series of poverty statistics for the United States covers some four decades. Information on poverty in earlier decades, unfortunately, is still limited. The data series in this chapter compile the official poverty statistics covering the period 1959–1999; some earlier unofficial poverty lines and poverty population estimates are also presented.

The data series on poverty in this chapter are presented in two sections: the first documents the dollar levels that define poverty, and the second, who is poor. The first group of poverty tables answers the question, "What are the income levels below which people are classified as poor in the United States?" (Tables Be85–259). The second group answers the question, "Who and how many are poor?" (Tables Be260–411). These tables present poverty counts, poverty rates, and statistics showing the composition of poverty. The poverty *count* is simply the number of persons or families who are classified as poor. The poverty *rate* is the prevalence of poverty among select demographic groups (for example, what percentage of whites is poor?). The *composition of poverty* tells what share of the poor a certain demographic group comprises (for example, what percentage of the poor is white?).

Note that poverty and inequality, while related, are distinct concepts with separate measures and unique historical trends (see the essay in this chapter on inequality). If the poor are defined as those households with incomes below one half the median household income, it is possible for income to be distributed so equally that no one is poor, as historically has been proven by Sweden. Alternatively, defining poverty independent of contemporary living standards can result in almost universal poverty regardless of the income distribution. Such would be the case, for example, if a modern-day poverty line were simply projected backward to the

[1] "The New Colossus" (1883) by Emma Lazarus, mounted in the base of the Statue of Liberty in 1903.

nineteenth century (with appropriate price adjustments). While measures of both poverty and income distribution are certainly considered important socioeconomic barometers of how broadly the benefits of economic production spread, historical income distribution is not addressed in this essay.

Poverty under Official Measure

Official Poverty Thresholds

Like any definition of poverty, the official U.S. definition of poverty actually has two components – the dollar levels (poverty thresholds) below which people are classified as poor and the definition of income that is compared with those thresholds (Citro and Michael 1995, p. 98). In their present form, the official poverty thresholds for the United States are a matrix of 48 thresholds (dollar figures) that vary by family size, by the number of family members who are children, and (for one- and two-person units only) by the age of the person or family householder.[2] The Census Bureau uses the matrix of 48 thresholds to tabulate poverty population statistics; the thresholds in the matrix may be referred to as the "detailed thresholds." However, the figures commonly cited for general purposes are weighted-average poverty thresholds – one for each family size. For three-person families, for instance, the single weighted-average threshold is generally cited in place of the detailed thresholds for a three-adult family, a two-adult/one-child family, and a one-adult/two-child family. The weighting for the average threshold is based on the total number of families of each subtype according to the Current Population Survey (CPS) for the income year in question. Instead of citing all nine weighted-average thresholds, people often cite a single figure to give a general idea of the poverty thresholds; the figure cited is often the weighted-average threshold for a family of four, although more recently, with average family size having dropped, some people cite the weighted-average three-person threshold. The weighted-average poverty thresholds by family size are presented in Table Be95–112. Tables Be177–259 present the full matrices of official poverty thresholds for the "decennial" income years 1959 through 1999.

History of the Official Poverty Thresholds[3]

The U.S. poverty thresholds were originally developed in 1963–1964 by Mollie Orshansky of the Social Security Administration. She began developing the thresholds as part of a Social Security Administration research project; she was not trying to introduce a new general measure of poverty and, indeed, did not know that the Johnson administration was going to initiate a concerted effort against poverty (called the "War on Poverty") in 1964. In 1965, the Office of Economic Opportunity, the lead agency in the War on Poverty, adopted Orshansky's poverty thresholds as a working or quasi-official definition of poverty. In 1969, the Bureau of the Budget designated the poverty thresholds with some revisions as the federal government's official statistical definition of poverty.

Orshansky based her poverty thresholds on the economy food plan – the cheapest of four food plans developed by the U.S. Department of Agriculture. The Agriculture Department described the economy food plan as being "designed for temporary or emergency use when funds are low."

Orshansky knew from the Department of Agriculture's 1955 Household Food Consumption Survey, the latest available such survey at the time, that families of three or more persons had spent about one third of their after-tax money income on food in 1955; the one-third figure related to families at all income levels, not just those at lower income levels. Orshansky calculated poverty thresholds for families of three or more persons by taking the dollar costs of the economy food plan for families of those sizes and multiplying the costs by a factor of three – the reciprocal of the one-third food-expense-to-income ratio; this factor of three is known as the "multiplier." Although there is no standard term for Orshansky's methodology, it can be characterized as a "component-and-multiplier" methodology. In this methodology, she, in effect, scaled down the food/nonfood consumption pattern of a hypothetical average family to the point where food expenditures equaled the cost of the economy food plan and assumed that the family's nonfood expenditures would then be as adequate as the food plan. The methodology did not assume specific dollar amounts for any budget category other than food. Orshansky derived poverty thresholds for two-person families by multiplying the dollar cost of the food plan for that family size by a somewhat higher multiplier (3.7) also derived from the 1955 survey. She calculated the poverty thresholds for one-person units to be directly proportional (at 80 percent) to the thresholds for two-person units.

The base year for the original poverty thresholds was calendar year 1963. In the absence of valid data usable for that purpose, Orshansky did not adjust her thresholds for geographic variations in living costs. She presented her thresholds as a measure of income inadequacy, not of income adequacy – "if it is not possible to state unequivocally 'how much is enough,' it should be possible to assert with confidence how much, on average, is too little" (Orshansky 1965, p. 3).

Besides the distinctions retained in the official version of the poverty thresholds (family size, number of members who are children, and aged/nonaged status for smaller units), Orshansky also differentiated her original thresholds by the sex of the family head and by farm/nonfarm status. The family size category ranged from one-person units (unrelated individuals, in Census Bureau terminology) to families of seven or more persons. All of these distinctions resulted in a detailed matrix of 124 poverty thresholds (reduced to 48 in a 1981 revision).

Orshansky developed separate poverty thresholds for farm families because the 1955 survey showed that about 40 percent of the food items consumed by all farm families came from their home farm or garden, rather than being purchased for cash. Another reason for having lower thresholds for farm families involved a technical issue about how farm housing expenses were reported for purposes of determining net farm self-employment income in the CPS. The farm thresholds applied specifically to families living on farms, and not to the broader categories of "rural" or nonmetropolitan families. The farm/nonfarm distinction was eliminated in the 1981 revision of the thresholds.

---

[2] There are actually two slightly different versions of the U.S. poverty measure – the poverty thresholds and the poverty guidelines. The poverty thresholds (updated by the Census Bureau) are used to prepare figures on the number of persons and families in poverty. The poverty guidelines (issued by the U.S. Department of Health and Human Services) are a simplification of the thresholds; the guidelines are used to determine financial eligibility for certain federal programs (not including cash public assistance). The guidelines are not discussed further in this chapter.

[3] The material in this section is drawn from Fisher (1992, 1997a). Both the article and the longer manuscript draw on many sources, most notably Orshansky (1965, 1969).

Orshansky developed separate poverty thresholds for aged one- and two-person units because of policy concerns about the economic status of the aged, most of whom lived in such units. The fact that these thresholds for the aged were lower than those for the nonaged was simply a mechanical consequence of the fact that economy food plan costs for aged persons were lower than those for nonaged adults. Orshansky was not claiming that necessary nonfood expenditures for the aged were or should be lower than those for the nonaged. The aged/nonaged distinction for smaller units has been retained in the official thresholds to the present day.

By late 1965, Social Security Administration policymakers and analysts began to express concern about how to adjust the poverty thresholds for increases in the general standard of living (see the following discussion regarding the income elasticity of the poverty line). In 1968, a Social Security Administration plan to raise the thresholds by 8 percent was rejected, but an interagency Poverty Level Review Committee was initiated to reevaluate the poverty thresholds. It decided to adjust the thresholds only for price changes, and not for changes in the general standard of living. In 1969, the Committee decided that the thresholds would be indexed by the Consumer Price Index (CPI) instead of by the per capita cost of the economy food plan, and that farm poverty thresholds would be set at 85 percent rather than 70 percent of corresponding nonfarm thresholds.[4] In August 1969, the Bureau of the Budget designated the poverty thresholds with these revisions as the federal government's official statistical definition of poverty. The series of official poverty thresholds given in this chapter therefore represent the same constant-dollar levels as Orshansky's original nonfarm thresholds for the base year 1963. In 1981, in accordance with recommendations of another interagency committee, several minor changes were made in the poverty thresholds, including the elimination of both the farm/nonfarm differential and the distinction between thresholds for female-headed and male-headed families.

Poverty lines are traditionally dichotomized as "absolute" or "relative." In this context, the phrase "absolute poverty line" is used to denote a poverty definition that is supposedly independent of the living standards, consumption patterns, or development stage of a society.[5] However, the word "absolute" is commonly used rather loosely in this phrase. It is often unclear whether "absolute" refers to (1) the methodology by which a poverty line is developed, (2) the way in which the poverty line is updated, (3) whether the poverty line has been set at a "subsistence" level based on an implicit ranking of "physical" needs as being more important than "social" needs, or (4) some combination of these. Orshansky's poverty thresholds are often called an absolute poverty line. Because the series of official poverty thresholds represent the same constant-dollar levels as Orshansky's original nonfarm thresholds for the base year 1963, the thresholds are "absolute" only in regard to how they are updated. Note that Orshansky herself described the thresholds she constructed as "relatively absolute" because they were developed from calculations that used the consumption patterns at a particular point in time (1955) of the U.S. population as a whole.

Over the years, a number of ad hoc proposals for changes in one aspect or another of the official U.S. poverty measure have been made; often such proposals have focused quite narrowly on one or another particular feature of the poverty thresholds or the income definition used with them.[6] In 1995, however, a report was published proposing a new approach for developing a poverty measure that comprised a set of well-thought-out and mutually consistent changes in all major aspects of the poverty measure (Citro and Michael 1995). The report was produced by the Panel on Poverty and Family Assistance appointed in 1992 by the National Research Council in response to a Congressional committee request for a study of the official U.S. poverty measure to provide a basis for its possible revision. The Panel recommended that a new poverty threshold be developed using actual consumer expenditure data on food, clothing, shelter, and utilities (FCSU), with a small amount added for other necessities. The level of the threshold would be within a range based in part on consideration of various expert family budgets and relative and subjective poverty thresholds. The threshold would be updated annually based on changes in median actual consumption expenditures for FCSU. The threshold would be adjusted for different family sizes and types and to reflect geographic variations in housing costs. The Panel would redefine family resources (income) to be consistent with its threshold concept, including money income and the value of near-money benefits (such as food stamps) that can buy goods and services included in the threshold concept, but excluding expenses that cannot be used to buy these goods and services (for example, income and payroll taxes, child care and other work-related expenses, and out-of-pocket medical care costs, including insurance premiums). Illustrative variations of this Panel's recommendations have been published in several Census Bureau reports on experimental poverty measures since 1999 (for example, Short, Garner, et al. 1999; Short 2001). However, no change has been made in the official poverty measure.

Trends in the Official Poverty Population

Poverty population and poverty rate figures under the Orshansky definition were first published in 1965, but the series was subsequently extended back to 1959, so that there is now some four decades worth of figures (see Figure Be-D). The factor most obviously affecting poverty rates during this period is the business cycle: poverty rates rise during recessions and fall during economic expansions. (During the 1980s and 1990s, poverty rates did not begin to fall until the second or third year of an economic expansion.) Despite the theoretical distinction between poverty and income inequality, the empirical experience with U.S. poverty statistics during the post-1959 period has been that when other factors are held equal, poverty rates increase as income inequality increases (see, for instance, Danziger and Gottschalk 1986).

In 1959, 39.5 million persons – 22.4 percent of all Americans – were in poverty under the official definition in place at that time.[7] These figures remained essentially unchanged during the next two

---

[4] Nonfarm poverty thresholds for the base year 1963 were retained, and the new annual-adjustment and farm/nonfarm provisions were applied to them to yield revised poverty thresholds for both earlier and later years; revised poverty population figures for 1959 and subsequent years were tabulated using the revised thresholds.

[5] For a critique of the notion of an "absolute poverty line," see Townsend (1962). For an alternative classification of methodologies for developing poverty lines, see Callan and Nolan (1991).

[6] As noted by Ruggles (1990, p. 6).

[7] See the documentation for Table Be260–282 for a discussion of the definitional and methodological changes that have taken place in the definition of poverty since the 1960s.

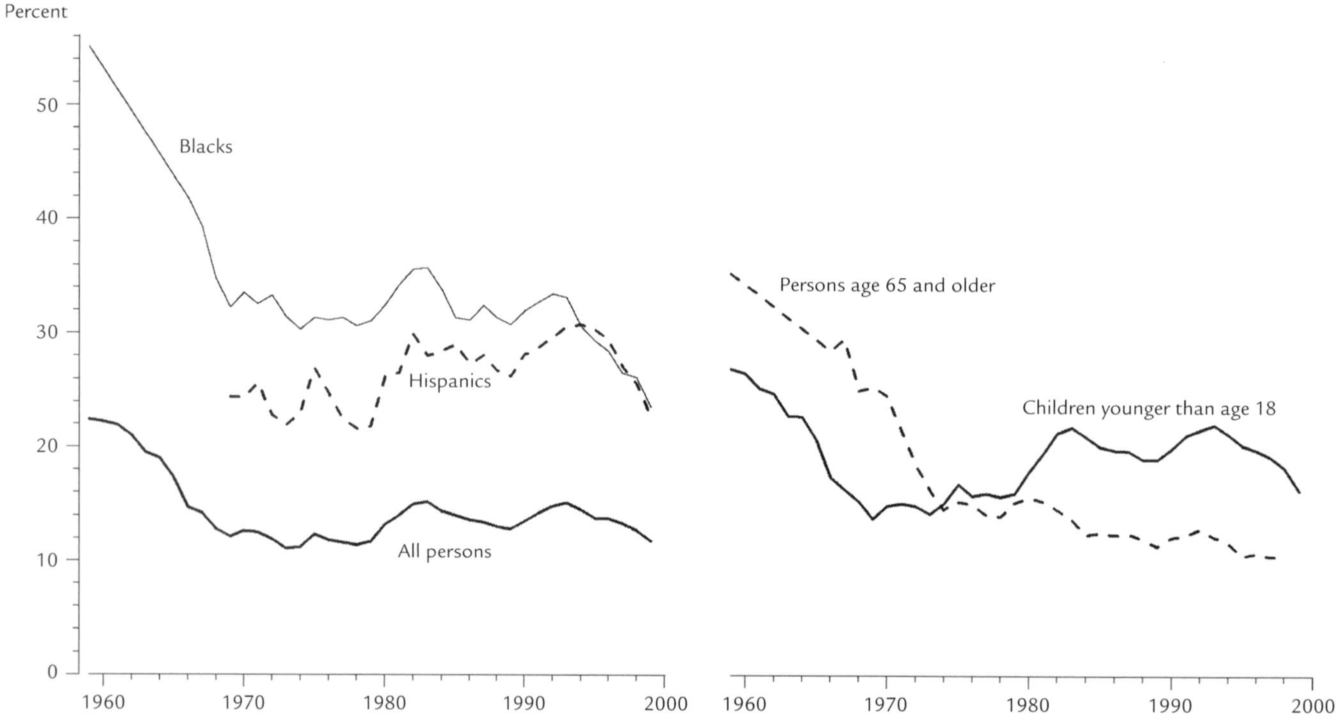

FIGURE Be-D Percentage of persons in poverty, by race, ethnicity, and age: 1959–1999

Source

Series Be272, Be276–277, Be318, and Be335.

years, presumably as a result of the 1960–1961 recession. From 1961 to 1969, during the economic expansion of the 1960s, the poverty rate dropped from 21.9 to 12.1 percent; this was the largest percentage point decrease in the official poverty rate over any eight-year span. During the 1969–1970 recession, the poverty rate rose modestly, to 12.6 percent in 1970. It then fell to its all-time low of 11.1 percent – 23.0 million persons – in 1973. During the 1973–1975 recession, the poverty rate rose to 12.3 percent in 1975. As the economy began to expand again, the rate fell to 11.8 percent in 1976, but then remained statistically unchanged through 1979. As a result of two back-to-back recessions (January–July 1980 and July 1981–November 1982), the poverty rate rose from 11.7 percent in 1979 to 15.0 percent in 1982. The poverty rate remained statistically unchanged in 1983 and dropped to 12.8 percent in 1989. During the 1990–1991 recession, the poverty rate rose to 14.2 percent in 1991. As the economy began to expand again, the rate drifted upward to 15.1 percent in 1993, but fell after that, reaching 12.7 percent in 1998.

For the 1959–1998 period as a whole, the overall poverty rate experienced a net decrease of slightly over two fifths – from 22.4 percent in 1959 to 12.7 percent in 1998. All this net decrease had already occurred by 1973, when the poverty rate fell to 11.1 percent.

Poverty rate trends for large demographic groups of the U.S. population are usually broadly similar to those for all persons, being dominated by ups and downs reflecting the business cycle. The major exception to this generalization is the elderly (persons age 65 or older). The elderly experienced a greater net decrease in poverty from 1959 to 1998 than any other group; their poverty rate dropped from 35.2 percent in 1959 to 10.5 percent in 1998, a reduction of more than two thirds. (The corresponding decrease in the number of elderly persons in poverty was from 5.5 million to 3.4 million, with the growth in the overall elderly population partially offsetting the sharp decrease in the elderly poverty rate.) Much of this decrease was related to the Social Security program. In particular, a decrease in the elderly poverty rate from 29.5 percent in 1967 to 15.7 percent (unrevised, versus 14.6 percent revised) in 1974 was closely correlated with Social Security benefit increases during that period (Fisher 1976). After that, several longish periods of relatively little change in the elderly poverty rate were punctuated by shorter periods of decrease: from 15.3 percent in 1981 to 12.4 percent in 1984, and from 12.9 percent in 1992 to 10.5 percent in 1995. As a result of these decreases in the elderly poverty rate, the proportion of the total poverty population who were elderly persons also decreased – from roughly 19 percent in 1966–1970 to just a little less than 10 percent in 1993–1998. The strong effect of the Social Security program on elderly poverty is, of course, the reason why elderly poverty trends are so different from poverty trends in the general population.

The elderly poverty rate was well above both the overall poverty rate and the poverty rate for children (related children younger than age 18 in families) in 1959 and during the 1960s. The elderly poverty rate first fell below the child poverty rate in 1974 and has remained below the latter since then. The elderly poverty rate first fell below the overall poverty rate in 1982 and has remained below the latter since then.

Children (related children younger than age 18 in families) experienced a more modest net decrease in poverty over this period than did the elderly; their poverty rate was 26.9 percent in 1959 and 18.3 percent in 1998, a reduction of just less than one third. The effects of recessions and economic expansions are clearly visible in changes in the child poverty rate. During the 1960s, the poverty rate for children dropped from 26.9 percent in 1959 to 13.8 percent in 1969 – an all-time low that was essentially equaled in 1973. It continued to rise and fall with the business cycle, varying between 15.7 and 22.0 percent during the 1975–1993 period. From 1993 to 1998, the child poverty rate dropped from 22.0 to 18.3 percent. Because the number of children in the general population grew considerably more slowly than the numbers of working-age adults and elderly persons, the proportion of the total poverty population who were children dropped from 43.6 percent in 1959 to 37.3 percent in 1998.

The black population experienced a considerable net decrease in poverty over the 1959–1998 period; the poverty rate for black persons was 55.1 percent in 1959 and 26.1 percent in 1998, a reduction of slightly more than one half. The largest share of this net reduction had occurred by 1973, when the poverty rate for this group fell to 31.4 percent. Despite the large reduction in the poverty rate among African Americans during the 1960s, the proportion of the total poverty population who were black rose from 25.6 percent in 1959 to 32.2 percent in 1973, and then fell back to 26.4 percent in 1998.

The white population also experienced a noticeable net decrease in poverty over the 1959–1998 period; the poverty rate for white persons was 18.1 percent in 1959 and 10.5 percent in 1998, a reduction of slightly more than two fifths. All this net reduction had already occurred by 1973, when the poverty rate for this group fell to 8.4 percent. The proportion of the total poverty population who were white fell from 72.1 percent in 1959 to 65.9 percent in 1973, and then rose slightly to 68.0 percent in 1998.

Poverty statistics for the Hispanic population are not available for years before 1969. Over the 1969–1998 period as a whole, the poverty rate for Hispanic persons showed relatively little net change; it was 24.4 percent in 1969 and 25.6 percent in 1998. The poverty rate for this group showed considerable variation within this period, falling as low as 22 percent in 1973 and 1977–1979 and rising as high as 30–31 percent in 1982 and 1992–1995. Primarily as a result of the growth in the Hispanic population at all income levels, the proportion of the total poverty population who were Hispanic rose from 8.1 percent in 1969 to 23.4 percent in 1998.

Woman-maintained or female-householder families (families with a female householder, no husband present) experienced a modest net decrease in poverty over the 1959–1998 period; their poverty rate was 42.6 percent in 1959 and 29.9 percent in 1998, a reduction of almost one third. Like that of other demographic groups, the female-householder-family poverty rate is affected by economic conditions, although its decreases during economic expansions are more modest than those for some other groups. During the 1960s, the poverty rate for this group dropped from 42.6 percent in 1959 to 32.3 percent in 1968. It rose to 33.9 percent in 1971 and fell to a new low of 30.4 percent in 1979. It rose to 36.3 percent in 1982, fell to 32.2 percent in 1989, and rose to 35.6 percent in 1993. After 1993, it fell fairly steadily, reaching a new all-time low of 29.9 percent in 1998 (although there was no statistically significant difference between this figure and the 1979 figure).

The proportion of all poor families that are female-householder families rose from 23.0 percent in 1959 to 50.3 percent in 1978 and has fluctuated since then between 45.7 and 54.5 percent (see Figure Be-E). This phenomenon has been termed "the feminization of poverty" (Pearce 1978). It is important to note that the feminization of poverty during the 1960s and 1970s took place while the poverty rate for female-householder families was generally falling; this falling poverty rate was more than offset by the growth in the number of female-householder families at all income levels.[8]

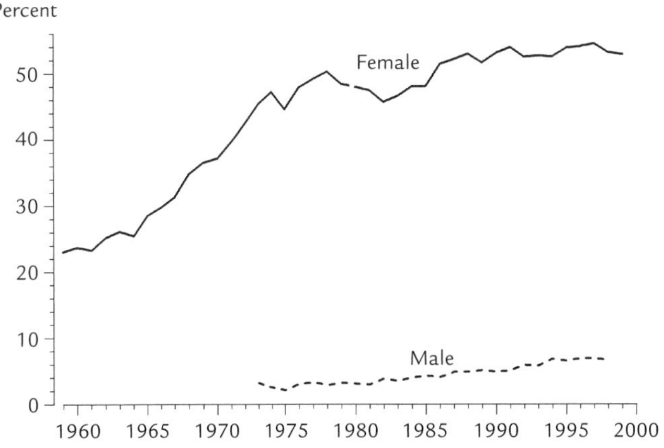

FIGURE Be-E Percentage of families in poverty headed by single householders, by sex: 1959–1999

Source
Series Be305–306.

Poverty statistics for married-couple families are available only for 1973 and subsequent years. Over the 1973–1998 period, the poverty rate for this group showed no net change; it was 5.3 percent in both 1973 and 1998. (The Census Bureau does have poverty statistics for years before 1973 for the slightly larger group comprising married-couple families plus male-householder families, no wife present – a group formerly termed "male-headed" families; for this group, the poverty rate had dropped from 15.8 percent in 1959 to 5.5 percent in 1973, a reduction of two thirds.)

Poverty rates by employment status back to 1966 were estimated by the Census Bureau through a special tabulation (see Figure Be-F) (Barrington 2000). As expected, for all years the poverty rates were lower for employed persons, and lower still for persons employed full-time and year-round. Interestingly, however, the notable downward trend in poverty since the early 1980s that was present for all persons and all employed persons was not present for persons employed full-time and year-round. This implies that increasing work hours for unemployed or underemployed persons has contributed to reducing poverty among them, whereas the wages of the lowest paid full-time, year-round workers have failed to rise in real terms, thus leaving their poverty rate little changed.

Poverty under Unofficial Measures

Minimum Subsistence Budgets and Poverty Lines[9]

In the century before Mollie Orshansky developed her poverty thresholds, numerous unofficial poverty lines and other measures of income inadequacy were developed by American social workers, labor advocates, government employees, researchers, and others, usually because of concerns about inadequate living standards

[8] For an analysis of the feminization of poverty during the 1939–1959 period, see Barrington and Conrad (1994).

[9] Where not otherwise noted, the material in this section is largely drawn from Fisher (1997c). See also Fisher (1998).

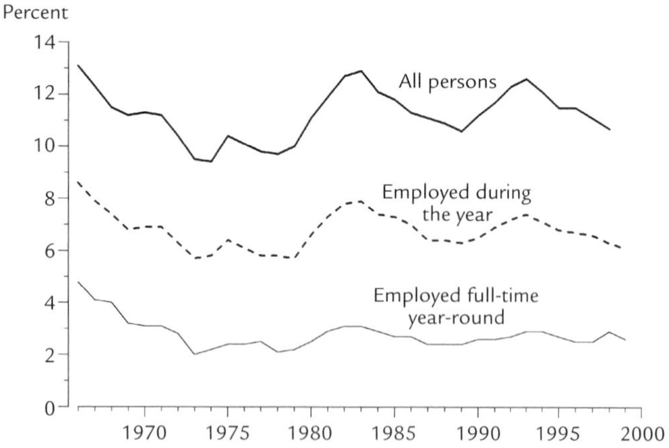

FIGURE Be-F Percentage of persons in poverty, by employment status: 1966–1999

Sources

Series Be389, Be392, and Be395.

Documentation

These series cover persons ages 16 and older.

among working-class and other low-income Americans.[10] Many of these income inadequacy measures were – or were derived from – standard budgets. A standard budget is a list of goods and services that a family of a specified size and composition would need to live at a designated level of well-being, together with the estimated monthly or annual costs of those goods and services.[11]

Standard budgets and other income inadequacy measures can be developed to represent different standards of living – some of them considerably above poverty. It is thus not always immediately clear which of the pre-Orshansky measures correspond to what Orshansky and others during the 1960s called "poverty" – especially because standardized terminology for classifying living standards was slow to develop. Terms applied to different budgets during the 1900–1920 period included "a fair living wage," "a fairly proper standard of living," "a minimum standard," "safe normal living cost," and "lowest 'bare existence.'" To determine which measures corresponded to Orshansky's poverty concept, we employed a widely used classification scheme developed by Dorothy Douglas and an adaptation of that scheme used by Oscar Ornati (Douglas 1923; Ornati 1966). Historical analysis showed that Douglas's "minimum of subsistence level"[12] and Ornati's "minimum subsistence" level corresponded most closely to Orshansky's poverty concept. Accordingly, we excluded from this chapter more generous standard budgets classified at the level of 'minimum health and decency," "minimum adequacy," or "minimum comfort."[13]

There is extensive historical evidence from the United States (including but not limited to the minimum subsistence budgets and poverty lines discussed here) and other countries that successive poverty lines develop as "absolute" poverty lines tend to rise in real terms as the real income of the general population increases; this phenomenon is known as the "income elasticity of the poverty line" (Kilpatrick 1973; Fisher 1995; Fisher 1997b, pp. 171–4; see also Citro and Michael 1995, pp. 32, 33, 98–9, 103, 141, and 319). As one way of illustrating this phenomenon, note that when Orshansky presented her poverty thresholds for 1963, she described families living below these thresholds as "lack[ing] the wherewithal to live at anywhere near a tolerable level" (Orshansky 1965, p. 4). But for 1923, an income level (for a family of five) equal in constant dollars to 102 percent of Orshansky's poverty threshold was described as a "comfort level" income "represent[ing] the attainment of the highest class of wage-earners and the cynosure [center of attention or attraction] of the rest." And for 1907, families with incomes at or above a constant-dollar level equal to 92 percent of Orshansky's five-person threshold were described as "liv[ing] well" and "satisfy[ing] . . . the reasonable ambitions of an American who puts his life into his work."[14] Given the extensive American evidence that poverty lines rise in real terms over time as the real income of the general population rises, we generally included in this chapter only pre-Orshansky poverty lines that were developed and used during a particular time period based on the social standards of that time period. We did not include historical "poverty" lines that represent later standards (for example, the official poverty measure) projected back several decades on the basis of price changes only.[15] In two cases, however, we did include measures developed by late twentieth-century scholars for the late nineteenth century based on standards or relevant data from the late nineteenth century.[16]

Because of the particularized and nonrecurring nature of most pre-Orshansky poverty lines and minimum subsistence budgets, we have presented them in a special table rather than as a formal data series (see Table Be-G).[17] We have included the source and major defining characteristics of each poverty line. For those poverty lines applicable to a particular family size, we also converted the dollar values to constant dollars and expressed them as percentages of the corresponding Orshansky poverty threshold for 1963. For technical reasons, any such efforts to adjust for price changes over long periods of time are at best rough approximations.

---

[10] Because Orshansky seems to have been the first person to use the specific term "poverty threshold," the term "poverty line" is used in this chapter for pre-Orshansky poverty measures.

[11] Innes (1990), p. 138; and Orshansky (1959), p. 10. For reviews of standard budget studies during the early decades of the twentieth century, see National Industrial Conference Board (1921); Douglas (1923); and Bureau of Applied Economics (1932). The standard budget approach fell into disfavor in the United States during the 1960s, 1970s, and 1980s, but enjoyed a resurgence in popularity during the 1990s. For a review of recent American standard budget studies, see Bernstein, Brocht, and Spade-Aguilar (2000).

[12] Concisely defined by a later analyst as follows: "The minimum of subsistence level involves an income adequate to maintain physical existence but makes no allowance for social necessities or for the financing of a major emergency" (Wyand 1937, p. 458).

[13] This is why we excluded the Bureau of Labor Statistics's 1969 lower family budget and the Bureau's 1919 "Tentative Quantity-Cost Budget," both of which have sometimes been incorrectly assumed to be "poverty" or minimum subsistence budgets.

[14] Fisher (1999), pp. 25–6. For a discussion of the case that it is incorrect and anachronistic to apply the U.S. poverty standards of the 1960s to the 1930s, see Barrington (1997).

[15] For analyses that do project the current official poverty measure back over multiple decades on the basis of price changes only, see Ross, Danziger, and Smolensky (1987); and Plotnick, Smolensky, et al. (2000).

[16] Several otherwise similar measures developed by late twentieth-century scholars were not included because they were at levels higher than minimum subsistence.

[17] However, we did include in Table Be85–94 the minimum subsistence budget figures found by Ornati for the 1908–1960 period, and unofficial poverty/low-income lines under the 1940s definition of the Subcommittee on Low-Income Families and the 1950s definition of Robert Lampman.

TABLE Be-G Poverty lines: 1870–1962

Applies to	Study	Poverty line (with family size and the line as a percentage of the Orshansky threshold)	Description	Methodology	Comments
DEFINITIONS BY CONTEMPORARIES					
1870	Henry Oliver and George McNeill, Second Report of the Massachusetts Bureau of Statistics of Labor (1871).	$2 in earnings per workday; $526 annual equivalent allowing for unemployment. Family size: 4 Orshansky: 39 percent	"Poverty or want."	In connection with a table of prices of foods and other necessities, the study noted that "if a man is earning only $2 or less a day, as is the case with thousands of men . . . he must be very near the condition of poverty or want."	First known American use of the word "poverty" together with a specific dollar figure.
1890	James R. Sovereign, Iowa Bureau of Labor Statistics Biennial Report for 1890–91.	$549.84. Family size: 5 Orshansky: 50 percent	"Minimum cost" of "the necessary living expenses of laboring men with families."	Standard budget.	Items excluded from the budget included medical care, street car fares, carpets, and social amusements.
1892	Residents of Hull House (a Chicago settlement house), *Hull House Maps and Papers* (1895).	$10 per week ($520 a year). Family size: 5 Orshansky: 47 percent		None specified.	This poverty line was not stated explicitly. It was inferred by Fisher from a comparison of colors in a Hull House wage map with colors in Charles Booth's London poverty map.
1896	W. E. B. DuBois, *The Philadelphia Negro: A Social Study* (1967 [1899]).	$5 per week ($260 a year). Family size: 5 Orshansky: 26 percent	"Very poor" or "poor."	Essentially Charles Booth's British (London) poverty line converted into dollars.	Probably because it was a "direct translation" of a British poverty line, DuBois's poverty line was markedly lower than other contemporary American poverty lines. DuBois implied he might set a higher poverty line for Philadelphia whites, reflecting a belief at the time that a minimum acceptable standard of living would be different for different occupational or racial/ethnic groups.
1902	New York State Bureau of Labor Statistics, Annual Report for 1902 (1903).	$10 per week ($520 a year). Family size: 4.2 average Orshansky: 59 percent (family of 4)	"About $10 a week . . . is hardly adequate for city dwellers according to American standards."	None specified.	The Bureau noted that its $10 figure was markedly higher than Charles Booth's British (London) poverty line. This investigation also included actual income figures for tenement families.
1903–1905	Louise Bolard More, *Wage-Earners' Budgets: A Study of Standards and Cost of Living in New York City* (1907).	$600. Family size: 4.8 average Orshansky: 56 percent (family of 5)	"Poor."	Expenditure study of 200 families living in the neighborhood of a New York City settlement house where More worked.	Much more prominent in More's book than the poverty figure was her conclusion that a "fair living wage" for a New York City family should be at least $728, but that if one allowed for greater savings to provide for the future, the necessary income would be $800–$900.
1904	Robert Hunter, *Poverty* (1904). Also see Table Be-H for 1900.	$460 for industrial Northern states; $300 for the South. Family size: 5 Orshansky: 43 percent ($460 figure)	The poor were those who "are not able to obtain *those necessaries which will permit them to maintain a state of physical efficiency*" (emphasis in original).	The $460 figure was determined by considering an average actual family expenditure figure from a Massachusetts Bureau of Statistics of Labor survey and three informal estimates of a "necessary income" or "fair wage." These figures ranged from $520 to $754. Hunter chose a lower figure to meet the "physical efficiency" standard.	Hunter derived the "physical efficiency" concept from British poverty researcher Seebohm Rowntree; it was conceptually equivalent to Douglas's later "minimum subsistence" level.

(continued)

TABLE Be-G Poverty lines: 1870–1962 *Continued*

Applies to	Study	Poverty line (with family size and the line as a percentage of the Orshansky threshold)	Description	Methodology	Comments
1905	John Spargo, *The Bitter Cry of the Children* (1906).	$10 per week ($520 a year). Family size: 5 Orshansky: 49 percent	"Primary poverty line."		In one section of his chapter on child labor, Spargo described an investigation of the reasons why children in 213 families were working; he chose this primary poverty line for use in this investigation.
1907–1912	The "Major Report" of the Commission on Industrial Relations, signed by four of the nine commissioners (written by Basil Manly, Director of Research and Investigation). U.S. Commission on Industrial Relations, *Industrial Relations: Final Report . . . to Congress . . .*, volume 1 (1916). Also see Table Be-H for 1908.	$500. Family size: 5 Orshansky: 44 percent	"Abject poverty."	Review of standard budget studies using 1907–1912 prices.	More prominent in the report than the reference to "abject poverty" was the conclusion "that the very least that a family of five persons can live upon in anything approaching decency is $700." The source for the "Major Report" terminology is Allen F. Davis, "The Campaign for the Industrial Relations Commission, 1911–1913," *Mid-America: An Historical Review* 45 (4) (1963): 227 n. 57.
1908	Wood Worcester and Daisy Worthington Worcester, U.S. Bureau of Labor study of cotton mill workers, volume 16 of *Report on Condition of Woman and Child Wage-Earners in the United States* (1911). Also see Table Be-H, Parmelee for 1915.	Fall River, Massachusetts: $484.41 (minimum standard); $731.64 (fair standard). The South: $408.26 (minimum standard); $600.74 (fair standard). Family size: 5 Orshansky: 43 percent (Fall River, minimum); 65 percent (Fall River, fair)	"The minimum standard of living . . . the smallest amount upon which families were . . . apparently maintaining physical efficiency . . . exclud[ing] everything except the bare necessaries of life . . . if the family is not to suffer, the mother must be a woman of rare ability." "The fair standard of living . . . provides not only for physical efficiency but [also] . . . for the development and satisfaction of human attributes."	Standard budget study of cotton mill workers in Fall River, Massachusetts (North), and Atlanta, Georgia, and two North Carolina towns (South).	The minimum standard excluded such items as medical care, schoolbooks, newspapers, and recreation. Ornati classified it as "minimum subsistence" (poverty), and the fair standard as "minimum adequacy," one level above minimum subsistence. However, the Worcesters identified the fair standard as a poverty line, indicating that medical care was also a necessity, and that "[i]nability to buy school books for children, to furnish some simple form of recreation for the family, are unmistakably signs of poverty."
Feb. 1915	Mary Wadley (supervisor) and 5 district workers, Social Service Bureau, Bellevue Hospital (New York City). Included in a 1917 New York City agency report.	$824.356 (third digit due to a precisely calculated food budget). Family size: 5 Orshansky: 68 percent	"Conservative estimates of women who are daily meeting problems arising from poverty, and who have an exact knowledge of the needs of the typical worker's family."	Standard budget.	
1915–1916	Arthur Holder (American Federation of Labor), 1916 Congressional subcommittee hearing on minimum wage for federal workers.	$767.95. Family size: 5 Orshansky: 62 percent	"Estimated Minimum Cost of Bare Existence."	Standard budget for Washington, D.C.	The food portion of the budget was deliberately estimated unrealistically low. The budget excluded such items as a winter overcoat, street car fares, candy, schoolbooks, newspapers, recreation, postage and paper for correspondence, and medical care.
March 1917	Dallas Wage Commission, Report submitted to Dallas, Texas, mayor and Board of Commissioners to guide wage setting for city employees.	$747. Family size: 5 Orshansky: 52 percent	"Lowest 'Bare Existence'" budget allowed for "merely the bare necessities of life . . . nothing for education, recreation or savings."	Standard budget.	The report also included a "safe normal living cost" budget costing $1,081.72, which allowed a family to live in "frugal decency." Ornati classified this budget as "minimum adequacy," one level above minimum subsistence.

Applies to	Study	Poverty line (with family size and the line as a percentage of the Orshansky threshold)	Description	Methodology	Comments
June 1918	William F. Ogburn, Examiner for the National War Labor Board, part 1 of *Memorandum on the Minimum Wage and Increased Cost of Living* (1918).	$1,386. Family size: 5 Orshansky: 78 percent	"Minimum budget . . . American subsistence level."	Standard budget.	The National War Labor Board was established during World War I with the goal of ending labor unrest in war-related industries by arbitrating labor disputes. It requested the *Memorandum* during a 1918 debate on what its living wage principle meant and how (and whether) that principle should be implemented. In his analysis of budgets, Ogburn also included a minimum comfort budget (at $1,760.50), as well as the first known published version of the three-level budget classification scheme that Douglas was to revise into her four-level budget classification scheme. Douglas and Ornati later classified Ogburn's minimum subsistence budget at one level above minimum subsistence.
May 1, 1920	W. Jett Lauck (for United Mine Workers of America), Presentation before U.S. Anthracite Coal Commission (1920).	$1,772. Family size: 5 Orshansky: 71 percent	"Minimum of subsistence . . . subsistence level."	Lauck classified earlier standard budgets, updated them for price changes, and averaged the results.	In the presentation for the United Mine Workers of America, Lauck (a pro-labor economist who had been Secretary of the National War Labor Board) argued for higher wages for miners – "a minimum living wage rate." He also presented an average of "minimum comfort level" budgets at $2,242. Douglas and Ornati later classified some of Lauck's minimum subsistence budgets at one level above minimum subsistence.
1923	Dorothy Douglas, "A Description of Standards of Living," in Paul H. Douglas, Curtice N. Hitchcock, and Willard E. Atkins, editors, *The Worker in Modern Economic Society* (1923).	$1,100–$1,400. Family size: 5 Orshansky: 53–68 percent	"Minimum of subsistence level."	Review of earlier standard budgets.	Douglas's budget classification scheme included four levels: (1) the "comfort level," (2) the "subsistence-plus ('minimum health and decency') level," (3) the "minimum of subsistence level," and (4) the "poverty level," also called the "pauper level" in an earlier article. The poverty/pauper level related to receiving charitable assistance, and so was not analogous to Orshansky's thresholds, but to a 1960s Aid to Families with Dependent Children or General Assistance need standard or payment level.
1928–1929	Louis Reed (Committee on the Costs of Medical Care [a nongovernment group]), *The Ability to Pay for Medical Care*, Committee Publication number 25 (1933). Also see Table Be-H.	$1,200–$1,300. Family size: 5 Orshansky: 58–63 percent	"Minimum subsistence standard of living."	Review of earlier standard budgets.	Reed also estimated that it would take $1,800 to $2,100 to maintain a "minimum comfort" standard of living.
1929	Paul Nystrom, *Economic Principles of Consumption* (1929). Also see Table Be-H.	$1,500. Family size: 4 Orshansky: 86 percent	"Bare subsistence level."	Review of earlier standard budgets.	Nystrom described ten different grades or standards of living ranging from "public and semi-public charges"; "the work-shy, tramps, hobos and incompetents"; "poverty"; and "bare subsistence level" at the bottom to "liberal standards of living" at the top.

(continued)

TABLE Be-G Poverty lines: 1870–1962 *Continued*

Applies to	Study	Poverty line (with family size and the line as a percentage of the Orshansky threshold)	Description	Methodology	Comments
1929	Maurice Leven, Harold Moulton, and Clark Warburton (Brookings Institution), *America's Capacity to Consume* (1934). Also see Table Be-H.	$1,500 (families); $750 (unattached individuals).	"Subsistence and poverty."	The authors divided an estimated income distribution for families and unattached individuals into six economic classes, ranging from "subsistence and poverty" and "minimum comfort" at the bottom to "wealthy" at the top. The authors did not explain how they selected the income ranges associated with each economic class.	The authors' estimated income distribution was based on (nonnational) sample income figures for selected occupational groups, combined with federal income tax return data. One factor that they used as a cross check – the national distribution of residential rents and values of owned homes – was derived from the 1930 Census.
March 1935	Margaret Stecker (U.S. Works Progress Administration), *Intercity Differences in Costs of Living in March 1935, 59 Cities*, Research Monograph 12, Works Progress Administration (1937). Also see Table Be-H, National Resources Planning Board for July 1935–June 1936.	$903.27 (average for 59 cities). Family size: 4 Orshansky: 65 percent	"Emergency budget."	Standard budgets for married, unskilled manual worker's family of four living in 59 cities.	The emergency budget was "a direct concession to conditions produced by the depression, constructed . . . [for] circumstances under which families can and do cut costs temporarily without great physical discomfort" – yet "those forced to exist at the emergency level for an extended period may be subjected to serious health hazards." This budget's food component was an early predecessor of the economy food plan used by Orshansky to develop her poverty thresholds. Stecker also presented a "maintenance" budget with an average cost of $1,260.62.
1935	U.S. Public Health Service, "The National Health Survey: 1935–1936, The Relief and Income Status of the Urban Population of the United States, 1935," preliminary report (1938). Also see Table Be-H.	$1,000 or receiving relief.	"Low income."		"Families" included unrelated individuals.
July 1935–June 1936	President Franklin Delano Roosevelt, Second Inaugural Address (1937), implicitly operationalized in U.S. National Resources Committee, *Consumer Incomes in the United States: Their Distribution in 1935–36* (1938). Also see Table Be-H.	$780 (as implicitly operationalized by the U.S. National Resources Committee).	"One-third of a nation ill-housed, ill-clad, ill-nourished."	Roosevelt's "one-third" was not based on any socioeconomic statistics; it may be conceptualized as an informal estimate by a perceptive nonacademic observer of social conditions. The U.S. National Resources Committee's 1938 report did not refer to Roosevelt's 1937 address, but it did rank "consumer units" (families of all sizes and unrelated individuals) by income and divide the distribution into thirds. The $780 figure was the upper income limit of the lower "third of the Nation."	Roosevelt said, "I see millions of families trying to live on incomes so meager that the pall of family disaster hangs over them day by day . . . . I see one-third of a nation ill-housed, ill-clad, ill-nourished." The $780 figure is unusual as an instance of a poverty line derived from a poverty rate estimate, rather than the reverse. Despite its derivation from an informal estimate, the $780 figure was surprisingly close to the WPA's emergency budget figure of $903.27, especially when one notes that the $780 figure applied to all "consumer units" (average size 3.19 persons), while the $903.27 figure applied specifically to a four-person family.
1950	President Eisenhower's Council of Economic Advisers, *Economic Report of the President* (1954).	$1,500.	"Low incomes . . . poverty."		This may have been an effort to gain public acceptance for a poverty/low-income line lower than the 1949 SLIF's $2,000 family low-income line.

Applies to	Study	Poverty line (with family size and the line as a percentage of the Orshansky threshold)	Description	Methodology	Comments
1951	Walter Reuther (President, Congress of Industrial Organizations [a labor union federation]), *1953 Proceedings of the Fifteenth Constitutional Convention of the Congress of Industrial Organizations, November . . . 1953 . . . .* Also see Table Be-H.	$3,000.	"American families lack[ing] even a bare, decent minimum standard of living . . . low income families."		
1952	President Eisenhower's Council of Economic Advisers. *Economic Report of the President* (1955).	$1,000.	"Low incomes . . . poverty stricken."		This may have been an effort to gain public acceptance for a poverty/low-income line lower than the 1949 SLIF's $2,000 family low-income line.
1955	John Kenneth Galbraith, *The Affluent Society* (1958). Also see Table Be-H.	$1,000.	"The hard core of the very poor."		In setting his unusually low poverty line, Galbraith may have been influenced by the $1,000 figure in the 1955 *Economic Report of the President.*
1957	American Federation of Labor–Congress of Industrial Organizations, Department of Research, *Labor's Economic Review* (February 1959). Also see Table Be-H.	$3,000 (families); $1,500 (unrelated individuals).	"Impoverished Americans . . . not maintaining even a minimum American standard of health and decency."		The $3,000 family poverty line was the same figure that CIO President Walter Reuther had used in his 1953 report, without any adjustment for the inflation that occurred between the reference years 1951 and 1957.
1957	Gabriel Kolko, *Wealth and Power in America: An Analysis of Social Class and Income Distribution* (1962). Also see Table Be-H.	$3,150. Family size: 4 Orshansky: 110 percent	"Emergency standard . . . poverty."	Kolko updated the Works Progress Administration 1930s maintenance and emergency budgets by equating the former with the Bureau of Labor Statistics's (BLS's) postwar City Worker's Family Budget for a family of four, and updating the resulting "maintenance" and "emergency" standards to 1957 roughly in line with price changes. He used a BLS equivalence scale to develop figures for families of other sizes.	Kolko's "maintenance" standard was $4,500 for a family of four. "Between the emergency and maintenance standards, there exists a shadowy area ranging from poverty to hard-pressed insecurity."
1958	Horst Brand, "Poverty in the United States," *Dissent* (Autumn 1960). Also see Table Be-H.	$3,000 (family of 4). The line increased in $500 increments, starting at $1,500 for 1 person and going to $4,500 for a family of 7 or more. Family size: 4 Orshansky: 102 percent	"Poor" – the $3,000 poverty line "covers the subsistence needs of a family of four."	Brand set his four-person poverty line "substantially below" the BLS's City Worker's Family Budget (price-adjusted from the late 1940s), but "well ahead" of public assistance needs standards. He used a BLS equivalence scale to develop poverty lines for other family sizes, rounding the results to the nearest $500.	
1959	Lenore Epstein (employee of the Social Security Administration; later Lenore Bixby), "Some Effects of Low Income on Children and Their Families," *Social Security Bulletin* (February 1961); and "Unmet Need in a Land of Abundance," *Social Security Bulletin* (May 1963). Also see Table Be-H.	$2,675 (married couple with 2 children). Family size: 4 Orshansky: 90 percent	"Low incomes" – a "very conservative definition of low income."	The levels at which families taking only the standard deduction would begin paying taxes – the "taxable limit"	Epstein was assistant director of the Social Security Administration division in which Mollie Orshansky worked. Epstein also presented lines for families of two and six.

(continued)

TABLE Be-G Poverty lines: 1870–1962 *Continued*

Applies to	Study	Poverty line (with family size and the line as a percentage of the Orshansky threshold)	Description	Methodology	Comments
1959	Michael Harrington, *The Other America: Poverty in the United States* (1966 [1962]). Also see Table Be-H.	$3,000–$3,500 (urban family). Family size: 4 Orshansky: 101–118 percent	"Poor . . . existing at levels beneath those necessary for human decency . . . hungry . . . without adequate housing and education and medical care."	After discussing several other poverty lines, Harrington set his poverty line for an urban family of four at roughly half the BLS's recently revised Interim City Worker's Family Budget, recommending (unspecified) adjustments for family size and for farm families.	While the statistical content of Harrington's definitional appendix was modest, few if any statistically detailed analyses of the poverty population have had as great an influence on public policy as his book did.
1959	James Morgan, Martin David, et al., *Income and Welfare in the United States* (1962). Also see Table Be-H.	$3,897. Family size: 4 Orshansky: Not comparable, since this line is applied to money plus nonmoney income, whereas Orshansky's thresholds are applied to money income only.	"Families with small and inadequate incomes . . . poor."	Families were classified as poor if their income (money plus some nonmoney income) was below 90 percent of the Community Council of Greater New York's standard family budget, *and* if they had less than $5,000 in liquid assets. Budget figures were available for all family sizes.	Data were obtained from a survey of 2,800 families conducted by the University of Michigan's Survey Research Center. The four-person family was composed of an employed husband, a wife not working outside the home, and two children aged 8 and 11.
1959	Victor Fuchs, "Toward a Theory of Poverty," in Task Force on Economic Growth and Opportunity, *The Concept of Poverty* (1965). Also see Table Be-H for 1947–1960.	$2,830 (based on family income data from the decennial census); $2,708 (based on family income data from the Current Population Survey).	"Millions of American families who, both in their own eyes and those of others, are poor."	After considering earlier poverty lines, Fuchs concluded that "a meaningful definition of poverty can best be found by setting relative standards." To implement this conclusion, he set a relative poverty line for all families (regardless of family size) at half of median family income.	Fuchs's relative poverty line concept is discussed in the appendix to the current essay; also see series Be110. However, the relative poverty-line figures presented in that series were calculated for a family of four, and thus differ from the figures Fuchs used in his analysis, which were calculated for all families without adjustment for family size. As noted in the essay, Fuchs was the first American to propose a relative (half-of-median-income) definition of poverty.
1960	Selma Goldsmith (employee of the U.S. Department of Commerce), "Low-Income Families and Measures of Income Inequality," *Review of Social Economy* (March 1962). Also see Table Be-H.	$3,000 (families); $2,000 (unrelated individuals).	"Low-income."	"I cannot claim to have made any progress whatsoever [toward defining 'poverty']. . . . These income points [$3,000 and $2,000] were chosen arbitrarily."	The article was originally presented as a paper at the December 1961 meeting of the Catholic Economic Association.
1960	Conference on Economic Progress (a nonprofit research and advocacy group), *Poverty and Deprivation in the United States: The Plight of Two-Fifths of a Nation* (1962). Also see Table Be-H.	$4,000 (families); $2,000 (unrelated individuals).	"Poverty."	The poverty line for families of all sizes was set at roughly two thirds of the average cost of the BLS's Interim City Worker's Family Budget for a family of four. The study argued that overall poverty population figures would be about the same with a single-figure family poverty line as with a poverty line varying by family size. Roughly in line with the BLS equivalence scale for one-person and four-person units, the poverty line for unrelated individuals was set at half the family poverty line.	The study also set lines ($6,000 for families, $3,000 for unrelated individuals) to define "deprivation" – a "condition . . . quite distinguishable from . . . stark poverty, but [which] nonetheless means genuine denial of many of the goods and services which most Americans have come to regard as 'essentials,' and in most cases imposes a continuing sense of insecurity." The study also identified higher income levels ("deprivation-comfort," "comfort-affluence," "affluence or higher") covering the whole income distribution – one of the first studies since the 1930s to do that.

Applies to	Study	Poverty line (with family size and the line as a percentage of the Orshansky threshold)	Description	Methodology	Comments
1962	President Johnson's Council of Economic Advisers, *Economic Report of the President* (January 1964), Chapter 2. Also see Table Be-H.	$3,000 (families); $1,500 (unrelated individuals).	"By the poor we mean those who are not now maintaining a decent standard of living. . . . Poverty is the inability to satisfy minimum needs."	The $3,000 figure was derived from consideration of the minimum wage level, the approximate level at which a family of four started paying federal income taxes, and the highest state Aid to Families with Dependent Children payment level for a family of four. Despite a reference in the CEA chapter to a 1963 Orshansky article, Orshansky's figures were not used in deriving the CEA's $3,000 figure.	The primary author of the chapter was Robert Lampman; see series Be88–94. The $3,000 figure was specified as applying to before-tax annual money income. If the same underlying poverty standard had been applied to money-plus-nonmoney-income data, consistency would have required the use of a dollar figure higher than $3,000.
1962	Walter Heller (Chairman, Council of Economic Advisers), March 1964 Congressional hearing. Also see Table Be-H.	$3,000 (family of 4). The line increased in $500 increments, starting at $1,500 for 1 person and going to $4,000 for a family of 6 or more. Family size: 4 Orshansky: 97 percent	"Poverty."	A refinement of the CEA's $3,000/$1,500 poverty line, varying it by family size.	
1962	Rose Friedman (American Enterprise Institute), *Poverty: Definition and Perspective* (1965). Also see Table Be-H.	$2,195. Family size: household of 4 Orshansky: 71 percent	"Poverty lines . . . the nutritive adequacy definition of poverty."	For each household size from two to seven or more persons, the poverty line was set at the income level at which three fourths of the households of that size met two thirds of the National Research Council's Recommended Daily Allowances. Friedman used data from the 1955 Household Food Consumption Survey, updating the results to 1962 prices.	Friedman criticized the CEA's poverty line and an early version of Orshansky's poverty line as being too high.
ANALYTIC RECONSTRUCTIONS					
1874	Frances Early, "The French-Canadian Family Economy and Standard-of-Living in Lowell, Massachusetts, 1870," in Michael Gordon, editor, *The American Family in Social-Historical Perspective* (3rd edition, 1983).	$585. Family size: 4–6 Orshansky: 42 percent (family of 5)	"Poverty-line annual income."	Early developed poverty lines for several family size ranges using data on 26 French-Canadian families from a family expenditure study in the Sixth Annual Report of the Massachusetts Bureau of Statistics of Labor. Early considered her own summarization of the original interviewers' comments on families' living conditions, as well as whether families' expenditures were more or less than their incomes.	
1880	Michael Haines, "Poverty, Economic Stress, and the Family in a Late Nineteenth-Century American City: Whites in Philadelphia, 1880," in Theodore Hershberg, editor, *Philadelphia: Work, Space, Family, and Group Experience in the Nineteenth Century* (1981).	$464. Family size: 5 Orshansky: 37 percent	"Poverty . . . economic stress . . . estimated 'minimum adequacy' expenditures."	Econometric estimation based on U.S. Commissioner of Labor Carroll Wright's 1889–1890 expenditure survey microdata for families with low income per capita	Haines's "minimum adequacy" is not the same as Ornati's category.

Discussion

Where indicated, poverty rates or counts using the definition given in the study appear in Table Be-H.

The poverty lines represent annual income unless otherwise noted; poverty lines for shorter time periods are also shown in annual terms to facilitate comparisons. Particularly during the earlier part of the period, analysts sometimes did not state the family size to which a measure applied and/or the reference period (for example, "This budget reflects prices as of February 1915," or "This poverty line should be applied to incomes for calendar year 1959.") In such cases, we have presented reasonable assumptions about the values of these variables. Except for poverty lines that were applicable to different family sizes, we converted the dollar values of these poverty lines to 1963 dollars so that they could be expressed as percentages of the corresponding-family-size Orshansky poverty thresholds (for which 1963 was the base year). To make these price adjustments, we used the price index in series Cc1.

Even though our review of pre-Orshansky poverty lines and minimum subsistence budgets was extensive, it was not feasible to include every such poverty line or budget developed during the 1870–1965 period.

Not all of the pre-Orshansky poverty lines and minimum subsistence budgets in Table Be-G were of equal prominence. Even though the four nineteenth-century figures are of great intrinsic historical interest, none of them were cited by later writers.[18] However, Robert Hunter's 1904 book *Poverty* had a significant impact on social reformers and others concerned with the problems of poverty; it was even commented on by Britain's H. G. Wells. Hunter's $460/$300 poverty line was the first known poverty line intended to apply to the nation as a whole rather than to a single city or state, and it was mentioned by a number of contemporary and later writers.

From 1906 into the 1920s, a number of standard budgets and other income inadequacy measures were developed. However, much of the public discussion focused on budgets and other figures that were above the minimum subsistence level. Accordingly, some of the most widely cited budgets and other figures during this period – for instance, those in a 1909 study by Robert Chapin – are not included in Table Be-G (Chapin 1909).

Within the limits of the minimum subsistence level, one of the more widely cited measures during the years before the United States entered World War I was the standard budget for a "minimum standard of living" developed by Wood Worcester and Daisy Worthington Worcester, Special Agents (investigators) working for the U.S. Bureau of Labor (later the Bureau of Labor Statistics). Furthermore, the Worcesters' minimum standard/fair standard distinction was adopted by two reviews of budget studies – one published in 1913 by Scott Nearing and the other in 1916 by Maurice Parmelee (see Table Be-H) (Nearing 1913; Parmelee 1916). Similarly, the U.S. Commission on Industrial Relations's "abject poverty" and "decency" standards were adaptations of the Worcesters' two standards (see Tables Be-G and Be-H).

Several minimum or "bare existence" budgets developed during the 1910s remained in almost total obscurity, but the minimum budget developed by William Ogburn for the National War Labor Board in 1918 was mentioned by several contemporary and later writers; it seems to have been the first budget with which the term "minimum of subsistence level" was used.

Dorothy Douglas's 1923 minimum of subsistence level was by far the most important standard of its type for over a decade. The level and her dollar figures were cited a number of times during the 1920s, while the concept continued to be cited as late as the early 1940s.

Margaret Stecker's emergency budget for the U.S. Works Progress Administration was a minimum subsistence budget cited by various contemporary analysts; in addition, the Textile Workers Union of America issued an upgraded version of this budget in 1944, which they hoped to get accepted as "the lowest conceivable budget . . . for active, patriotic, self-supporting, self-respecting American workers" in connection with the National War Labor Board's directive to eliminate substandard living conditions among American workers during World War II.

Another New Deal–era figure – the National Resources Committee's $780 figure operationalizing President Roosevelt's "one-third of a nation" quotation – was cited by contemporary and later writers as having been an approximate measure of poverty for this period.

The Congressional Subcommittee on Low-Income Families (SLIF) issued a staff report in 1949 that included a low-income line of $2,000 for families of all sizes for 1948 (see Table Be85–94). During the 1950s, there were not large numbers of Americans writing about poverty and poverty lines. However, among those who did so during the 1949–1958 period (and who did not present poverty lines of their own), the large majority cited the SLIF's $2,000 figure.

In 1958, John Kenneth Galbraith published *The Affluent Society*. The book included a chapter on poverty. Galbraith's *conceptual* definition of poverty has often been quoted approvingly by both American and non-American writers.[19] However, his *operational* definition of poverty ($1,000 for families and unrelated individuals) was criticized as being too low, and was not used by other writers.

In 1958 and 1959, a number of people writing about poverty and poverty lines stopped using the SLIF's $2,000 family low-income line and began using higher figures, such as $3,000. The origin of the $3,000 figure used by some of these writers is not immediately clear.

Unofficial poverty lines were developed and published more frequently during the 1958–1963 period than during the 1949–1958 period. Accordingly, no one poverty line dominated the poverty writings of the early 1960s in the same way that the SLIF's $2,000 figure had dominated the writings of the 1949–1958 period. Robert Lampman published low-income lines for 1947 and 1957 ($2,516 for a family of four in 1957) in a 1959 report done for the Congressional Joint Economic Committee (see Table Be85–94). A number of other writers cited Lampman's low-income line, particularly during 1960. Over the next several years, writers either cited other poverty lines or else cited Lampman's low-income line in conjunction with another – generally a higher – poverty line; the higher poverty lines that were cited included the American Federation of Labor–Congress of Industrial Organizations' $3,000/$1,500 poverty line and the Conference on Economic Progress' $4,000/$2,000 poverty line.

In January 1964, when the War on Poverty was announced, President Johnson's Council of Economic Advisers (CEA) set a poverty line of $3,000 for families and $1,500 for unrelated individuals. This became the United States' first quasi-official poverty line and continued to be so for a little over a year.

In January 1965, Mollie Orshansky published a *Social Security Bulletin* article presenting her poverty thresholds. In May 1965, as noted earlier, the Office of Economic Opportunity adopted

---

[18] We did not include in Table Be-G the $600 figure cited by Carroll Wright in the 1875 report of the Massachusetts Bureau of Statistics of Labor. Seeing a reference to families below this level being "in debt and poverty," some twentieth-century analysts have taken the $600 figure to be a poverty line. However, an examination of the broader context of the report shows that the figure is related to the concepts of debt, family deficit (having family expenditure greater than family income), and pauperism, and not to the concept of income inadequacy (poverty).

[19] "In part [poverty] is a physical matter. . . . But . . . it is wrong to rest everything on absolutes. People are poverty-stricken when their income, even if adequate for survival, falls markedly behind that of the community. Then they cannot have what the larger community regards as the minimum necessary for decency; and they cannot wholly escape, therefore, the judgment of the larger community that they are indecent. They are degraded for, in the literal sense, they live outside the grades or categories which the community regards as acceptable" (Galbraith 1964 [1958], Chapter 23, p. 251).

her thresholds as a working definition of poverty; they thus succeeded the CEA's poverty line as the United States' quasi-official poverty line (they were given fully official status as the federal government's statistical definition of poverty in August 1969). The 1965 adoption of Orshansky's thresholds marked the end of the pre-Orshansky period of unofficial poverty lines.

Poverty Population Estimates

Several estimates of the number of Americans in poverty were done by advocates and analysts before Orshansky; these estimates are presented in Table Be-H because they are of interest to historical scholars and social policy historians. These estimates are too scattered – and were done on too many different bases – to be included among the chapter's data series (if one is looking for a single series of pre-1959 poverty estimates, one will be disappointed.) Table Be-H includes estimates of the total number of Americans in poverty, as well as a few estimates of the proportion of major segments of the population (for example, the urban population, or working families) who were in poverty; it does not include poverty rates for small groups of families in a single city.[20] Most of the poverty population estimates in this table were associated with poverty lines or similar measures shown in Table Be-G, although not all of those poverty lines had poverty population estimates associated with them.

As in the case of pre-Orshansky poverty lines, it may be helpful to give a brief assessment of the various pre-Orshansky poverty population estimates and what they can tell us about the incidence of poverty under contemporary definitions.

We found four poverty population estimates for years during the Progressive era and five such estimates for the years 1928–1929. Although each of these two sets of estimates was for years during the same time period, they varied greatly, from about 10 percent to about 50 percent for each set of estimates. The analysts who prepared the individual estimates did the best job that they could to make estimates on the basis of available information, but that information was just too limited. We conclude that their estimates are too weak a basis for us today to make any specific estimate of the poverty rate in the United States (by contemporary standards) during either the Progressive era or the 1928–1929 period. For the period before the mid-1930s, the state of knowledge about the number of Americans in poverty can perhaps best be summed up not in figures but in the words of social insurance theorist and advocate Isaac M. Rubinow:

> How much poverty is there in this, the richest country in the world? . . . Of course, there are no accurate data. We probably know more about the number of poor hogs in this country than the number of poor people. At least, one may have estimates about the hogs. There is a public department to prepare these regularly. There is none to account for the number of poor and dependent. (Rubinow 1929, p. 366)

Only when reasonably good national family income data become available do credible estimates of poverty under contemporary definitions appear. Among the many actions taken by the federal government in response to the Depression were efforts to gather information on the social problems that the New Deal sought to remedy – including low income as well as unemployment. As one government report put it, "Any attempt on the part of Government or business to grapple with basic economic problems must rely heavily on what can be learned of the distribution of income among the various groups of the Nation's consumers" (U.S. National Resources Committee 1938, p. 1). During the mid-1930s, federal agencies conducted two national sample surveys – the Study of Consumer Purchases and the National Health Survey – which collected information on family income as well as other subjects. The addition of limited income questions to the 1940 Decennial Census was presumably motivated by similar concerns. And in March 1940, the U.S. Work Projects Administration (WPA, formerly the Works Progress Administration) initiated the Sample Survey of Unemployment (later the Current Population Survey); when an income supplement was added to this survey in the mid-1940s, it became the principal source of annual national family income data.

One of the earliest survey-based reports with data on the poverty population under a contemporary definition was the preliminary report on the National Health Survey published in 1938 by the U.S. Public Health Service, including data on income in 1935. This report's low-income line was crude, without any adjustment for family size. While it did not aggregate its regional low-income rates into a national rate for all of the 80-plus cities that it covered, it appears that such a national rate would probably have been somewhere in the neighborhood of 45 percent. Including other cities would probably not have changed the national rate greatly, but if the Survey had also included the rural population, the overall national low-income rate for 1935 would probably have been higher – perhaps somewhere between 50 and 60 percent.

A 1942 National Resources Planning Board report included another poverty population estimate based on mid-1930s survey data. The estimate was based on July 1935–June 1936 income data from the Study of Consumer Purchases, combined with some income information from the National Health Survey. This estimate was for urban families only; it thus excluded urban unrelated individuals and rural families and unrelated individuals. It used a poverty line adjusted for family size. It found that 40.0 percent of persons in urban families were either below the WPA emergency budget or in families that had received relief of some kind at some time during 1935–1936. If comparable poverty lines for urban unrelated individuals and the rural population had been available, the overall national poverty rate for 1935–1936 would probably have been higher – perhaps somewhere between 50 and 60 percent.

Intriguingly, we find that extrapolations from these two estimates – using different surveys and different contemporary poverty lines – both suggest that the overall national poverty rate during 1935 or 1935–1936 may perhaps have been in the range of 50 to 60 percent. Even though this estimate is an imprecise range rather than a precise figure, it represents the earliest point at which we can make a statement about the national poverty rate with any confidence.

During the 1990s, Linda Barrington developed an "analytical reconstruction" set of poverty lines for 1939 based on a 1930s Agriculture Department food plan and a multiplier developed from the 1935–1936 Study of Consumer Purchases. She applied these poverty lines to the 1939 earnings (wage and salary) income data collected in the 1940 Decennial Census. As noted in Table Be-H, she came up with an earnings poverty rate of 45.3 percent for

[20] Thus we did not include the estimate of the number of blacks in poverty in Philadelphia found in DuBois (1967 [1899]).

TABLE Be-H Poverty estimates, counts, and rates: 1900–1962

Applies to	Study	Poverty count or rate (with population covered, where necessary)	Measure of poverty and methodology	Comments
COUNTS AND RATES BY CONTEMPORARIES				
1900	Robert Hunter, *Poverty* (1904). Also see Table Be-G for 1904.	Not fewer than 10 million persons (13 percent of the U.S. population); perhaps as many as 15 or 20 million persons (26 percent).	Hunter based this estimate "upon my own observation in various cities . . . , upon the figures of the U.S. Census for 1900 concerning unemployment, upon the reports of the State Boards of Charity, the *Bulletin* of [the] Statistics Department of the city of Boston for 1903[,] the records of the Municipal Court of New York concerning the number of evictions, and the report of the Department of Corrections, concerning the number of pauper burials in New York City." Although Hunter specified poverty lines at $460 for industrial Northern states and $300 for the South, he did not develop his poverty population estimate by applying these lines to estimated national income distribution data.	As indicated in Table Be-G, Hunter's poverty line was assumed to be for 1904. However, in one discussion on estimating the number of persons in poverty, Hunter cited state and national population totals from the 1900 decennial census without attempting to update them to 1904. Accordingly, his poverty population estimate was assumed to be applicable to 1900.
1908	The "Major Report" of the Commission on Industrial Relations, signed by four of the nine commissioners (written by Basil Manly, Director of Research and Investigation). U.S. Commission on Industrial Relations, *Industrial Relations: Final Report . . . to Congress . . .*, volume 1 (1916). Also see Table Be-G for 1907–1912.	"About one-third" of the families of wage earners employed in manufacturing and mining.	"Abject poverty" was defined as having an annual income of $500 or less; the proportion of one third was based on income data on 15,726 immigrant families in a 1909 U.S. Immigration Commission report.	As noted in Table Be-G, the budget studies underlying the Report's "abject poverty" line reflected 1907–1912 prices. However, the income data came from a report published in 1909, so it was assumed to be applicable to 1908.
1910	Newel Howland Comish, *The Standard of Living: Elements of Consumption* (1923).	52 percent of American families were on or below the minimum of subsistence standard or the pauper standard.	On or below pauper the standard (less than $500 a year) or the minimum subsistence standard ($500–799). Comish attributed dollar values to these standards by adapting results from Robert Chapin's study of New York City working-class families in 1907, which did not use the terms "minimum of subsistence" and "pauper." These dollar figures were applied to an estimated family income distribution for 1910, which was not based on a national sample survey or the decennial census.	
1915	Maurice Parmelee, *Poverty and Social Progress* (1916). Also see Table Be-G, Worcester and Worcester for 1908.	Probably higher than 10 percent of the U.S. population (not specified whether persons or families).	$600 a year, presumably for 1915 – an adaptation of the Worcesters' "minimum standard." Parmelee reviewed wages for various occupations and some figures on paupers but did not describe a specific methodology.	
1928–1929	Rexford Tugwell, Thomas Munro, and Roy Stryker, *American Economic Life and the Means of Its Improvement* (3rd edition, 1930).	5 or 6 million families (3 million urban, and 2 or 3 million rural). Population covered: 26 million families.	"Roughly, we shall mean by poverty the whole range below health and decency" (that is, at and below Douglas's minimum of subsistence). They did not give a specific dollar figure for their definition of poverty.	"This . . . is an estimate for normal [non-depression] times . . . . In times of general depression there must be many more." The poverty rate for families would have been between 19 and 23 percent.
1928–1929	Louis Reed (Committee on the Costs of Medical Care [a nongovernment group]), *The Ability to Pay for Medical Care*, Committee Publication number 25 (1933). Also see Table Be-G.	Not less than 10 percent of U.S. families below minimum subsistence.	Reed estimated minimum subsistence for an urban family of five at $1,200 to $1,300 in 1928–1929. He may have applied these figures to an estimated family income distribution for 1928. He did make allowances for an average family size smaller than five and for lower living costs in rural areas.	
1929	Paul Nystrom, *Economic Principles of Consumption* (1929). Also see Table Be-G.	22 million to 23 million persons, comprising 5 million families plus 3 million persons in the lowest two classifications. Population covered: 119 million to 120 million persons.	The estimate given is for persons at or below minimum subsistence – that is, in Nystrom's "public and semi-public charges," "the work-shy, tramps, hoboes and incompetents," "poverty" (pauper level), and "bare subsistence level" groups. Nystrom himself did not total up these four specific groups. Nystrom's "bare subsistence level" dollar figure for a family of four was $1,500. He did not explain how he developed population figures for his various groups.	The poverty/subsistence rate for persons, which Nystrom did not calculate, would have been 18–19 percent.

TABLE Be-H Poverty estimates, counts, and rates: 1900–1962 *Continued*

Applies to	Study	Poverty count or rate (with population covered, where necessary)	Measure of poverty and methodology	Comments
1929	Maurice Leven, Harold Moulton, and Clark Warburton (Brookings Institution), *America's Capacity to Consume* (1934). Also see Table Be-G.	11.7 million families (42 percent of all families) and 2.5 million "unattached" individuals (28 percent of all such individuals) in "subsistence and poverty." Population covered: 27.5 million families and 9 million "unattached" individuals.	The "subsistence and poverty" class comprised families with annual incomes below $1,500 and unattached individuals below $750. The authors presented an estimated income distribution for families and unattached individuals divided into six economic classes, ranging from "subsistence and poverty" at the bottom to "wealthy" at the top. The authors did not explain how they selected the income ranges associated with each economic class.	Their estimated income distribution was based on (nonnational) sample income figures for selected occupational groups, combined with federal income tax return data. One factor that they used as a cross check – the national distribution of residential rents and values of owned homes – was derived from the 1930 Census.
1929 and 1932	Carroll Daugherty, *Labor Problems in American Industry* (4th edition, 1938).	Poverty rate (percent of U.S. families). 1929: 55 percent 1932: 75 percent	Daugherty defined families with "sub-standard incomes" as those living at either the "subsistence plane" or the "poverty [pauper] plane" but did not publish dollar figures defining the subsistence plane. He seems to have applied dollar figures (including unpublished figures for the subsistence plane) to estimated family income distributions for 1929 (Brookings Institution 1934 study – see earlier) and 1932.	Since his dollar figures for 1910 and 1918 were calculated by adjusting 1929 standards for price changes only, they would not have reflected standards contemporary to 1910 and 1918; accordingly, his population estimates for those years are not included here. Because Daugherty only published dollar values for his "poverty [pauper] plane," he was not included in Table Be-G, which was limited to "minimum subsistence" standards.
1935	U.S. Public Health Service, "The National Health Survey: 1935–1936 – The Relief and Income Status of the Urban Population of the United States, 1935," preliminary report (1938). Also see Table Be-G.	Poverty rates (%) — Region: Total / White / "Colored" NE: 37.5 / 35.4 / 73.4 NC: 40.5 / 37.9 / 76.4 S: 52.2 / 36.8 / 90.1 W: 37.5 / 35.7 / 66.7 Regions: Northeast, North Central (Midwest), South, and West. No national totals were shown. Population covered: urban population of persons in families (including unrelated individuals) in more than eighty cities.	Informal "measure of low income," combining families receiving relief with nonrelief families with incomes less than $1,000.	In the terminology of the report, "colored" families included Negro, Mexican, Chinese, and Japanese families. For white families, note that if rural families had been included, the Southern white low-income rate might have diverged more from other regions' white low-income rates.
July 1935–June 1936	President Franklin Delano Roosevelt, Second Inaugural Address (1937), implicitly operationalized in U.S. National Resources Committee, *Consumer Incomes in the United States: Their Distribution in 1935–36* (1938). Also see Table Be-G.	"Millions of families . . . one-third of a nation." 13.2 million consumer units, comprised of 8.5 million families and 4.7 million "single" [unrelated] individuals. Population covered: the "Nation" – 29.4 million families and 10.1 million "single" individuals.	Roosevelt's "one-third" was not based on any socioeconomic statistics; it may be conceptualized as an informal estimate by a perceptive nonacademic observer of social conditions. The Committee operationalized Roosevelt's informal "one-third of a nation" estimate by determining the dollar figure ($780) that was the upper income boundary of the one third of the nation's consumer units with the lowest incomes in the Study of Consumer Purchases.	"I see millions of families trying to live on incomes so meager that the pall of family disaster hangs over them day by day . . . . I see one-third of a nation ill-housed, ill-clad, ill-nourished." If the Committee had made some adjustment for the differing needs of "single" [unrelated] individuals and families of different sizes, its total would presumably have included fewer "single" individuals and more families.
July 1935–June 1936	U.S. National Resources Planning Board (NRPB), *Security, Work, and Relief Policies* (1942). Also see Table Be-G, Margaret Stecker (U.S. Works Progress Administration) for March 1935.	40.0 percent of persons; 51.8 percent of children younger than 16. Population covered: urban families and children in such families.	The NRPB report estimated the number of urban families with incomes below a family-size-adjusted version of the WPA's emergency budget, applying the dollar figures to income data for urban families from the 1935–1936 Study of Consumer Purchases, combined with some income information from the 1935 National Health Survey. Adjusted emergency budget figures were $740 for a family of three, $860 for a family of four, and so on. Note that while these budget figures reflected March 1935 prices, they were applied to income data for July 1935–June 1936.	The Study of Consumer Purchases did not collect income data for consumer units receiving "relief" of some kind (including cash relief, relief vouchers for food and clothing, and work relief) at any time during the twelve-month period. The NRPB report assumed that (urban) families receiving relief generally had incomes below the emergency budget. Families receiving relief accounted for about half its total estimate. These figures were developed to provide one estimate of unmet need for "public aid" (cash transfers – for example, general relief). The NRPB report estimated that 20.8 percent of persons and 25.3 percent of children younger than age 16 in urban families were members of families that had not received some form of relief, yet had incomes below the WPA's emergency budget level. Because the emergency budget was for urban families, the NRPB estimate excluded urban unrelated individuals and rural families and unrelated individuals. If versions of the emergency budget had been available for urban unrelated individuals and rural families and unrelated individuals, presumably even higher proportions of those groups would have been found to have incomes below the budget.

(continued)

TABLE Be-H Poverty estimates, counts, and rates: 1900–1962 *Continued*

<table>
<tr><th>Applies to</th><th>Study</th><th>Poverty count or rate (with population covered, where necessary)</th><th>Measure of poverty and methodology</th><th>Comments</th></tr>
<tr><td>1947, 1957, 1961, and 1963</td><td>Robert Lampman, "The Low Income Population and Economic Growth" (1959 paper for Joint Economic Committee).
See series Be88–94 for accompanying poverty lines.</td><td><table><tr><th>Year</th><th>Count (million)</th><th>Rate (%)</th></tr><tr><td>1947</td><td>36.6</td><td>26.0</td></tr><tr><td>1957</td><td>32.2</td><td>19.1</td></tr><tr><td>1961</td><td>33.0</td><td>18.2</td></tr><tr><td>1963</td><td>31.5</td><td>16.8</td></tr></table>Population covered: U.S. persons.</td><td>For the low-income definition, see the text for series Be88–94. Low-income population figures were calculated from Current Population Survey income data.</td><td>Person counts and rates correcting Lampman's family size assumption and for other years, as calculated by Gordon Fisher (1999):<table><tr><th>Year</th><th>Count (000s)</th><th>Rate (%)</th><th>Year</th><th>Count (000s)</th><th>Rate (%)</th></tr><tr><td>1947</td><td>39,229</td><td>27.3</td><td>1955</td><td>36,078</td><td>22.1</td></tr><tr><td>1948</td><td>41,329</td><td>28.3</td><td>1956</td><td>32,804</td><td>19.7</td></tr><tr><td>1949</td><td>43,643</td><td>29.4</td><td>1957</td><td>33,706</td><td>19.9</td></tr><tr><td>1950</td><td>41,397</td><td>27.6</td><td>1958</td><td>34,773</td><td>20.1</td></tr><tr><td>1951</td><td>39,027</td><td>25.6</td><td>1959</td><td>32,853</td><td>18.6</td></tr><tr><td>1952</td><td>38,395</td><td>24.8</td><td>1960</td><td>33,137</td><td>18.5</td></tr><tr><td>1953</td><td>–</td><td>–</td><td>1961</td><td>32,503</td><td>17.9</td></tr><tr><td>1954</td><td>–</td><td>–</td><td>1962</td><td>31,588</td><td>17.1</td></tr><tr><td></td><td></td><td></td><td>1963</td><td>30,342</td><td>16.2</td></tr></table></td></tr>
<tr><td>1948 and 1954</td><td>SLIF of the U.S. Congress, Joint Committee on the Economic Report, 1949 and 1955 Subcommittee staff reports.
See series Be86–87 for accompanying poverty lines.</td><td><table><tr><th>Year</th><th>Count (million)</th><th>Rate (%)</th></tr><tr><td>1948</td><td>9.6</td><td>25</td></tr><tr><td>1954</td><td>9.4</td><td>22</td></tr></table>Population covered: U.S. families.</td><td>Low-income definition of subcommittee. See series Be86–87 and accompanying text. Low-income population figures calculated from Current Population Survey income data.</td><td>Counts and rates for persons, as calculated by Gordon Fisher (1999):<table><tr><th>Year</th><th>Count (000s)</th><th>Rate (%)</th><th>Year</th><th>Count (000s)</th><th>Rate (%)</th></tr><tr><td>1947</td><td>34,501</td><td>24.0</td><td>1955</td><td>32,538</td><td>19.9</td></tr><tr><td>1948</td><td>36,148</td><td>24.8</td><td>1956</td><td>29,756</td><td>17.9</td></tr><tr><td>1949</td><td>39,141</td><td>26.3</td><td>1957</td><td>30,661</td><td>18.1</td></tr><tr><td>1950</td><td>37,002</td><td>24.6</td><td>1958</td><td>31,650</td><td>18.3</td></tr><tr><td>1951</td><td>34,216</td><td>22.4</td><td>1959</td><td>29,702</td><td>16.8</td></tr><tr><td>1952</td><td>33,340</td><td>21.6</td><td>1960</td><td>29,938</td><td>16.7</td></tr><tr><td>1953</td><td>–</td><td>–</td><td>1961</td><td>29,855</td><td>16.5</td></tr><tr><td>1954</td><td>–</td><td>–</td><td>1962</td><td>28,129</td><td>15.3</td></tr><tr><td></td><td></td><td></td><td>1963</td><td>27,119</td><td>14.5</td></tr></table></td></tr>
<tr><td>1951</td><td>Walter Reuther (President, Congress of Industrial Organizations [a labor union federation]), 1953 Proceedings of the Fifteenth Constitutional Convention of the Congress of Industrial Organizations, November . . . 1953 . . . .
Also see Table Be-G.</td><td>14 million families. Population covered: United States.</td><td>Reuther's low-income line for families was $3,000; he applied it to Current Population Survey income data.</td><td>Based on Current Population Survey income data not rounded to the nearest million, the figure would have been 14.5 million families – 35.9 percent of all families.</td></tr>
<tr><td>1955</td><td>John Kenneth Galbraith, The Affluent Society (1964 [1958]).
Also see Table Be-G.</td><td>7.7 percent of U.S. families.</td><td>Galbraith's poverty line was $1,000; he applied it to Current Population Survey income data.</td><td>Based on Current Population Survey income data, the number of families involved was 3.3 million.</td></tr>
<tr><td>1957</td><td>American Federation of Labor–Congress of Industrial Organizations, Department of Research, Labor's Economic Review (February 1959).
Also see Table Be-G.</td><td>40 million persons. Population covered: United States.</td><td>The poverty line was $3,000 for families and $1,500 for unrelated individuals; they applied it to Current Population Survey income data.</td><td>Based on Current Population Survey data, the corresponding poverty rate would have been 24 percent.</td></tr>
<tr><td>1957</td><td>Gabriel Kolko, Wealth and Power in America: An Analysis of Social Class and Income Distribution (1962).
Also see Table Be-G.</td><td>27.5 percent of all U.S. "spending units" (families and unrelated individuals).</td><td>Kolko's "emergency" standard varied by family size (for example, $3,150 for a family of four); he applied it to Current Population Survey income data.</td><td>An additional 16.5 percent of "spending units" were above Kolko's "emergency" standard but below his "maintenance" standard (e.g., $4,500 for a family of four).</td></tr>
<tr><td>1958</td><td>Horst Brand, "Poverty in the United States," Dissent (Autumn 1960).
Also see Table Be-G.</td><td>42.2 million persons – "close to 25%" of all persons in the United States.</td><td>Brand's poverty line varied by family size (for example, $1,500 for one person; $3,000 for a family of four); he applied it to Current Population Survey income data.</td><td>Based on Current Population Survey data, a more precise poverty rate would have been 24.4 percent.</td></tr>
<tr><td>1959</td><td>Lenore Epstein (employee of the Social Security Administration; later Lenore Bixby), "Some Effects of Low Income on Children and Their Families," Social Security Bulletin (February 1961); and "Unmet Need in a Land of Abundance," Social Security Bulletin (May 1963).
Also see Table Be-G.</td><td>16 million children, nearly one fourth of all American children; almost one fifth of all families; 33 million persons.
Population covered: United States.</td><td>For her low-income lines Epstein used "taxable limits" – the levels at which families taking only the standard deduction would begin paying federal income taxes (for example, $1,325 for a married couple or a mother and child; $2,675 for a married couple with two children). Her figures for families and persons were based on income data for 1959 from the 1960 Decennial Census; the figure for children was based on Current Population Survey data.</td><td></td></tr>
</table>

TABLE Be-H Poverty estimates, counts, and rates: 1900–1962 *Continued*

Applies to	Study	Poverty count or rate (with population covered, where necessary)	Measure of poverty and methodology	Comments
1959	Michael Harrington, *The Other America: Poverty in the United States* (1966 [1962]). Also see Table Be-G.	"Around 50,000,000" persons. Population covered: United States.	Harrington's poverty line was set at $3,000 to $3,500 for an urban family of four. He recommended (unspecified) adjustments for family size and for farm families. One assumes that he applied this poverty line to Current Population Survey income data, but he does not state explicitly what he did.	Based on Current Population Survey data, the corresponding poverty rate would have been about 28 percent.
1959	James Morgan, Martin David, et al., *Income and Welfare in the United States* (1962). Also see Table Be-G.	10.4 million families – "one-fifth of the nation's families." Population covered: United States.	The poverty line varied by family size (for example, $3,897 for a family of four); in addition, the poverty definition included only families with less than $5,000 in liquid assets. This poverty definition was applied to income data from a nationally representative sample survey of 2,800 families by the University of Michigan's Survey Research Center.	This appears to have been the first American study to include an estimate of what was later called the "poverty gap" – the amount that would be required to raise the annual income of every poor individual and family to equal their poverty line (about $10 billion in 1959).
1960	Selma Goldsmith (employee of the U.S. Department of Commerce), "Low-Income Families and Measures of Income Inequality," *Review of Social Economy* (March 1962). Also see Table Be-G.	9.9 million families (21.7 percent) and 5.9 million unrelated individuals (54 percent). Population covered: U.S. families and unrelated individuals.	Goldsmith's low-income line was $3,000 for families and $2,000 for unrelated individuals; she applied it to Current Population Survey income data.	
1960	Conference on Economic Progress (CEP, a nonprofit research and advocacy group), *Poverty and Deprivation in the United States: The Plight of Two-Fifths of a Nation* (1962). Also see Table Be-G.	38.3 million persons – just over one fifth of all persons in the United States.	The poverty line was $4,000 for families and $2,000 for unrelated individuals; it was applied to Office of Business Economics income estimates, which were not based on survey microdata.	An additional 39.1 million persons – just over one fifth of all persons – lived above poverty but in "deprivation." CEP defined deprivation as below $6,000 for families and $3,000 for unrelated individuals.
1962	President Johnson's Council of Economic Advisers, *Economic Report of the President* (January 1964), Chapter 2. Also see Table Be-G.	35 million persons – "nearly a fifth of our fellow citizens." Population covered: U.S. families and persons.	The poverty line was $3,000 for families and $1,500 for unrelated individuals; it was applied to Current Population Survey income data.	An unpublished 1999 recalculation by Gordon Fisher from published Current Population Survey data yielded a figure of 35.1 million persons, or 19.1 percent of all persons, using the CEA definition. The CEA's chapter (like the Morgan, David, et al. 1962 book and Orshansky's January 1965 article) included an estimate of what was later called the "poverty gap." According to the text, this was about $11 billion in 1962 for families only.
1962	Walter Heller (Chairman, Council of Economic Advisers), March 1964 Congressional hearing. Also see Table Be-G.	35.9 million persons (20 percent). Population covered: United States.	Heller refined the CEA's $3,000/$1,500 poverty line, varying it by family size by adding $500 per additional person to the $1,500 one-person figure, up to $6,000 for a family of six or more. He applied this poverty line to Current Population Survey income data.	An unpublished 1999 recalculation by Gordon Fisher from published Current Population Survey data yielded a figure of 36.0 million persons, or 19.5 percent of all persons, using Heller's definition.
1962	Rose Friedman (American Enterprise Institute), *Poverty: Definition and Perspective* (1965). Also see Table Be-G.	4.8 million families – roughly 10 percent of all families in the United States.	Friedman's poverty line varied by family size ($2,195 for four persons); it was set at the income level at which three fourths of the households of that size met two thirds of the National Research Council's Recommended Daily Allowances. Presumably Friedman applied this poverty line to Current Population Survey income data.	Friedman wrote, "further correction for other factors like regional differences, non-money income, and a more realistic estimate of funds available for current consumption would further reduce this estimate" (of 10 percent of all families).
ANALYTIC RECONSTRUCTIONS				
1939	Linda Barrington, "Estimating Earnings Poverty in 1939 . . . ," *Review of Economics and Statistics* (August 1997). Also see Table Be145–176.	45.3 percent of persons in the United States.	Based on wage and salary earnings only (Integrated Public Use Microdata Series, 1940 Census data). "Orshansky-method" poverty line.	Composition of poverty: 14.5 percent of earnings-poor persons lived in female-headed households in 1939. Poverty rates were also presented broken down by age, race, and gender of household head.
1947–1960	Victor Fuchs, "Toward a Theory of Poverty," in Task Force on Economic Growth and Opportunity, *The Concept of Poverty* (1965). Also see Table Be-G for 1959.	Year / Rate (%): 1947 19.0 1948 19.4 1949 20.1 1950 20.0 1951 19.0 1952 19.0 1953 19.9 1954 20.7 1955 19.9 1956 19.5 1957 20.0 1958 19.9 1959 19.9 1960 20.2 Population covered: U.S. families.	Fuchs set his poverty line for families at one half of the median family income without adjusting for family size. Fuchs applied this poverty line to Current Population Survey income data.	Fuchs's poverty rate figures for all years during the 1947–1960 period are included in this table because a relative poverty line by definition reflects contemporary standards for every year for which it is calculated. Fuchs's figures are included here as an "analytical reconstruction" because he calculated them back almost two decades.

(continued)

TABLE Be-H Poverty estimates, counts, and rates: 1900–1962 ***Continued***

Applies to	Study	Poverty count or rate (with population covered, where necessary)	Measure of poverty and methodology	Comments
1929–1960, selected years	Oscar Ornati, *Poverty amid Affluence: A Report on a Research Project Carried Out at the New School for Social Research* (1966).	Year / Persons (million) / Households (%): 1929 31.8 26; 1935–6 33.9 27; 1941 21.6 17; 1944 12.1 10; 1947 21.3 15; 1950 20.1 14; 1951 18.9 12; 1952 17.8 12; 1953 22.7 14; 1954 23.0 14; 1955 19.9 12; 1956 18.1 11; 1957 17.7 10; 1958 22.7 13; 1959 21.3 12; 1960 19.9 11. Ornati did not publish minimum subsistence (poverty) rates for persons, nor did he publish minimum subsistence (poverty) counts for households. Population covered: United States.	From his minimum subsistence figures for a family of four, Ornati calculated needs figures for unrelated individuals. Instead of calculating separate needs figures for families of different sizes, he calculated a single average family needs figure based on the average family size during the year in question. For most years, he applied these needs figures for unrelated individuals and families to income estimates from the U.S. Office of Business Economics.	Ornati's use of a single family poverty line rather than separate lines for different family sizes probably resulted in more poor families but fewer poor persons in families. His use of Office of Business Economics income estimates (which included some private nonmoney income) resulted in lower poverty rates than if he had used Current Population Survey income data (which include money income only) for years for which they were available.

Ornati data:

Year	Persons (million)	Households (%)
1929	31.8	26
1935–6	33.9	27
1941	21.6	17
1944	12.1	10
1947	21.3	15
1950	20.1	14
1951	18.9	12
1952	17.8	12
1953	22.7	14
1954	23.0	14
1955	19.9	12
1956	18.1	11
1957	17.7	10
1958	22.7	13
1959	21.3	12
1960	19.9	11

persons in 1939. Because the 1940 Census did not collect detailed information on nonearnings money income, this poverty rate is biased upward compared with an unobtainable total-money-income poverty rate for 1939. On the other hand, later analysis showed that Barrington's poverty lines were noticeably lower than contemporary (1930s) minimum subsistence level figures;[21] in this respect, her poverty rate is biased downward compared with a poverty estimate based on contemporary minimum subsistence figures. All of this suggests that an unobtainable poverty rate for 1939 calculated from total money income using a contemporary minimum subsistence measure might have been somewhere between 45 and 50 percent. On an a priori basis, it seems reasonable to assume that the "actual" poverty rate for 1939 was probably at least a little lower than that for 1935–1936; however, because of differing income definitions in the Study of Consumer Purchases and the 1940 Decennial Census, as well as other data problems, it will probably never be possible to validate that assumption empirically.

Relatively little public attention was paid to the problem of U.S. poverty during World War II. However, in 1949, the SLIF issued a staff report that included a low-income line of $2,000 for families of all sizes for 1948; this $2,000 figure was cited by the majority of those Americans who wrote about poverty and the poverty line during the 1949–1958 period. The SLIF reported that 25 percent of all families were below this line in 1948 and 22 percent of all families were below it in 1954 (after adjustment for inflation). The corresponding poverty rate for persons for 1948 would also have been 25 percent. If poverty rates for persons under this definition had been calculated for other years during the early postwar period, they would have been between 21.6 and 26.3 percent for the years between 1947 and 1952, and between 17.9 and 19.9 percent for the years between 1955 and 1958.

The near-consensus on the $2,000 figure dissolved beginning in 1958. Some writers in that and immediately following years were using poverty lines of $3,000 or even higher (either for all families or for four-person families). Late in 1959, Robert Lampman published a report using $2,516 for a family of four for 1957. For the years between 1957 and 1961, poverty rates were between 17.9 and 20.1 percent under Lampman's definition (as recalculated by Fisher after correcting for minor errors) and in the 20 to 28 percent range under other definitions (under the no-longer-accepted SLIF definition, the poverty rates for those years would have been between 16.5 and 18.3 percent).

In January 1964, when the War on Poverty was announced, President Johnson's Council of Economic Advisers reported that 35 million persons had been below its $3,000/$1,500 poverty line in 1962. The corresponding poverty rate was 19 percent. Under Lampman's definition as recalculated by Fisher, the poverty rate for that year would have been 17.1 percent. Under the official poverty definition used today, the poverty rate for that year – one year before the base year for Orshansky's thresholds – was 21.0 percent.

Estimates and "guesstimates" of the number of Americans in poverty were done as early as 1904. However, it wasn't until after the mid-1930s, when the Great Depression pushed putting people back to work to the top of the national agenda, that income distribution data from surveys and the decennial census became available, making it possible to prepare reliable estimates of the number of persons or families below a specified poverty line. Furthermore, it was not until the 1960s that, taking thresholds originally developed by Mollie Orshansky for her study of children in poverty, the U.S. government adopted an official poverty definition and began measuring poverty systematically. In 1990, during her tenure as U.S. Commissioner of Labor Statistics, Janet Norwood described the poverty rate estimates for the United States as "a data

[21] Barrington's poverty lines turned out to be quite close to a set of contemporary "poverty" (pauper) level figures published by Carroll Daugherty (1938). However, Daugherty was using Dorothy Douglas's classification of living standards, in which the "poverty" or "pauper" level was one level lower than the minimum of subsistence level – the level that corresponds most closely to Orshansky's poverty concept.

series as sensitive and important as any of the public policy series produced by the federal government" (Norwood 1990, p. 7). Yet, despite this importance, no major overhaul of the poverty measure has been implemented. Embedded still in today's official poverty measurement are American consumption patterns that are almost five decades old. Whether the poverty line in official use today continues in place or is replaced by another poverty line, the way in which poverty is measured will continue both to affect and to be affected by how we view and address the problem of poverty.

Appendix A: Alternative Measures

Minimum Subsistence Budgets

Oscar Ornati found a number of standard budgets from the 1905–1960 period (Ornati 1966). Those budgets that he classified as "minimum subsistence" are included in Table Be85–94. Budgets developed for five-person families were recalculated by Ornati for four-person families. Some of these budgets are also listed in Table Be-G. Ornati's budgets are among the best available evidence for what poverty was by contemporary social standards during different years of the pre-1960 period; however, they should not be viewed as a set of national poverty thresholds for that period. They were not promulgated by a single national authority; many of them were for individual cities, not for the nation as a whole; and the figures were never gathered together and presented in one place until Ornati published his book in 1966.

Lampman Low-Income Lines

The Subcommittee on Low-Income Families (SLIF) – a specially appointed Congressional subcommittee in 1949–1950 and 1955–1956 – published a low-income line for 1948 in a 1949 staff report and used an unpublished low-income line for 1954 in a 1955 staff report (U.S. Congress 1949, 1955). Robert Lampman published low-income lines for 1947 and 1957 in a 1959 report done for the Joint Economic Committee of Congress, and published low-income lines for 1963 in a 1966 book (Lampman 1959, 1966). Because both the SLIF and Lampman used the CPI to adjust their low-income lines over time, Gordon Fisher was able to calculate figures for both low-income lines for other years during the 1947–1963 period using that index; both original and subsequently calculated figures are shown in Table Be-G (Fisher 1999).

The SLIF's low-income line for 1948 and Lampman's low-income lines for 1957 are generally accepted as analogs for the 1940s and 1950s of Orshansky's poverty thresholds. As can be seen in Table Be-G, Ornati's minimum subsistence budget figures for 1948 and 1957 were (respectively) quite close to the SLIF's 1948 figure and Lampman's 1957 figure; this is the major reason for the conclusion that Ornati's "minimum subsistence" level (rather than one of his higher levels) was the conceptual equivalent of Orshansky's poverty concept.

Figure Be-I shows the constant-dollar equivalents of Ornati's minimum subsistence figures, Lampman's low-income lines, the official poverty thresholds, and three alternative poverty lines. Lampman's low-income lines and the official thresholds are adjusted for price changes only, while the budget figures found by Ornati exhibit the income elasticity of the poverty line – the tendency to rise in real terms as the real income of the general population increases. The constant-dollar decrease in the Ornati budget

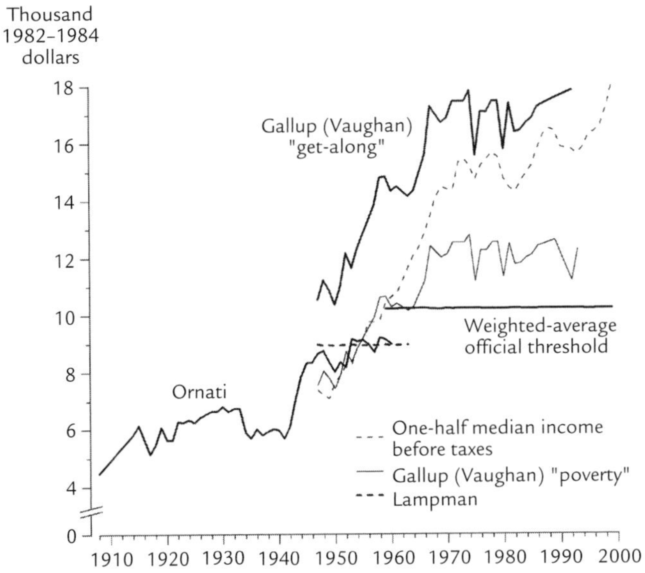

FIGURE Be-I Poverty lines for a family of four: 1908–1999

Sources

Series Be85, Be91, Be102, and Be110–112, converted to constant dollars using the consumer price index in series Cc1.

figures during the 1930s reflects the decrease in the real income of the general population during the Great Depression.

Near-Poverty Lines

One alternative poverty line presented in Table Be95–112 is the near-poverty threshold for a family of four (125 percent of the weighted-average poverty threshold for a family of four). The Census Bureau began publishing statistics on the number of persons below the near-poverty thresholds in 1970, in response to a recommendation of the interagency Poverty Level Review Committee. These near-poverty thresholds were essentially a successor of a higher set of thresholds that Orshansky developed from the Agriculture Department's low-cost food plan (although they were not calculated in the same way). Some analysts concerned about the level of the official thresholds have cited figures on the number of persons below the near-poverty thresholds. Eligibility for a few federal assistance programs has been set at 125 percent of the poverty guidelines.[22]

Another alternative poverty line presented here is the half-of-median-income (relative) poverty line. This definition of poverty was first proposed in the United States by Victor Fuchs.[23] A relative poverty line (unlike a poverty line adjusted only for price changes) changes in real terms as the real standard of living of the society changes, thus reflecting the income elasticity of the poverty line. Although the half-of-the-median income (relative) poverty definition is not used widely in the United States, it has probably been more commonly used than any other non-Orshansky poverty definition.

[22] Eligibility standards for some other federal programs range up to 185 percent of the poverty guidelines.

[23] Fuchs (1965). However, note that Peter Townsend (the dean of post–World War II British poverty studies) had proposed this relative poverty definition in an article published in a British journal three years earlier; see Townsend (1962), pp. 221, 223.

Opinion Polls

In almost every year from 1946 through 1992, the American Institute of Public Opinion's Gallup Poll asked the following question: "What is the smallest amount of money a family of four (husband, wife, and two children) needs each week to get along in this community?" The response to this question is known as the "get-along" amount. This amount is one of the major American sources of evidence for the income elasticity of the poverty line, demonstrating that the general population's assessment of a socially acceptable minimum standard of living depends upon the standard of living of the society as a whole. This evidence from the general population complements the evidence from experts in living standards in the form of the standard budgets found by Ornati (Table Be85–94) and shown in Table Be-G.

In contrast to more than 40 years of the get-along question, the Gallup Poll only asked a "poverty" question in one year (1989) using the following wording: "People who have income below a certain level can be considered poor. That level is called the 'poverty line.' What amount of weekly income would you use as a poverty line for a family of four (husband, wife and two children) in this community?" Vaughan used the get-along amounts for the period 1947–1989 plus the answer to the 1989 Gallup Poll poverty question to construct a social or "subjective" poverty-line series covering that period.[24] That series is presented in Table Be95–112. Vaughan found that his subjective poverty-line series and a relative (half-of-median) poverty-line series were quite close to each other over the whole 1947–1989 period; Vaughan's work and this finding played a significant role in the recommendations for creating a new poverty threshold issued by the National Research Council's Panel on Poverty and Family Assistance (Citro and Michael 1995).

Decennial Measures

For the "decennial" years 1919, 1939, and 1959–1999, detailed matrices of poverty thresholds are provided in Tables Be113–259.[25] The poverty thresholds included in the matrices allow one to determine precisely the official poverty status of an individual or family, given specific family unit characteristics. The matrices for the "decennial" years 1959–1999 present the official poverty thresholds for the United States, adjusted annually for price changes (Tables Be177–259). The matrices for 1919 and 1939 were created by Linda Barrington, duplicating Orshansky's original methodology as closely as possible, but using food plans and multipliers appropriate to the time period of interest (Tables Be113–176) (Barrington 1997, 1999). Because the Orshansky approach underpins these thresholds, they are comparable in *methodology* with the official U.S. poverty thresholds. In other words, the 1919 and 1939 matrices are presumably quite close to poverty thresholds that Orshansky would have developed if she had done for the 1910s and the 1930s what she did in the 1960s. Barrington's poverty thresholds take account of householder gender and the farm status of the family, as Orshansky's did, but not whether the householder was 65 years or older. Note that because of the income elasticity of the poverty line, the 1919 and 1939 poverty thresholds so defined are not comparable in *level* with the official CPI-indexed poverty thresholds of later years.

Regional Variation

Concern over central-city/suburban/nonmetropolitan and regional variation in poverty rates makes the figures in Tables Be343–370 useful time series. It must be remembered, however, that the underlying official definition of poverty does not adjust for geographic variation in the cost of living. The national poverty thresholds are applied uniformly from El Paso, Texas, to New York City.

Working Poor, Severely Poor, and the Aged Poor

The opportunity and the ability of low-income persons to "work their way out of poverty" is an inseparable component of public policy debates over poverty programs and wages. Table Be371–398 provides data on the prevalence of the "working poor" by race. Data are provided for full-time, year-round workers and persons who worked for pay at all during the year. (Note that there is no single official definition of "working poor.") To be classified as a full-time, year-round worker, one had to be employed at least 35 hours per week and at least 50 weeks a year. While some of the data presented in this table can be found in published U.S. Census Bureau documents, the data necessary to calculate the percentage of full-time, year-round workers in poverty back to 1966 were not available. Custom tabulations were produced by the U.S. Census Bureau from the CPS, March 1967 through March 1999 Supplements, to provide these data (see also Barrington 2000).

Table Be399–411 includes figures on persons below the "near-poverty" threshold (125 percent of the poverty threshold) and those who are "severely poor" (below 50 percent of the poverty threshold). These data are presented by race, Hispanic origin, and age. The aged are highlighted in this table, since comparisons between the aged and the general population give somewhat different results depending on whether one uses the poverty threshold or the near-poverty threshold.

Appendix B: Technical Definitions

Units of Analysis – Families and Unrelated Individuals

The "unit of analysis" used by the Census Bureau in the process of determining who is in poverty is actually two "units" – families and unrelated individuals. A *family* is a group of two or more persons related by birth, marriage, or adoption who reside together; all such related persons are considered as members of one family. An *unrelated individual* is a person 15 years old or older (other than an inmate of an institution) who is not living with any relatives. An unrelated individual may be the only person either living in a housing unit or living in a housing unit in which one or more persons who are not related to the individual in question by birth, marriage, or adoption also live. Poverty thresholds for what have been referred to earlier as one-person units are applied to unrelated individuals. Poverty thresholds for two-person units are applied to two-person families, and so on. The Census Bureau has no short term for the concept "families and/or unrelated individuals." However, the term "family unit" has been used unofficially to refer to that concept by

[24] Vaughan (1993). While recognizing that the get-along amount represents a higher living standard than poverty, Vaughan adopted the assumption that the way the get-along amount varies over time in relation to family income would be a good indicator of the way that the public's perception of the poverty line would vary over time in relation to family income (if a poverty question had been asked over an extended period).

[25] The decennial census for a given year (for example, 1990) collects income data for the previous year (in this case 1989). Poverty thresholds for the previous year are applied to those income data to yield poverty population figures.

the poverty guidelines *Federal Register* notice (since 1978) and by some analysts. "Families and/or unrelated individuals" should *not* be referred to as "households" because "household" is a separate and distinct concept; as defined by the Census Bureau, a household consists of all the persons who occupy a housing unit, whether they are related to each other or not. A household may thus contain one or more families and/or one or more unrelated individuals; poverty status for each such family and/or unrelated individual is determined separately.

Persons versus Families

Poverty population figures and poverty rates for persons are presented in most of Tables Be260–411, while poverty population figures and poverty rates for families are limited to Table Be283–309. While correlated, poverty rates for persons and poverty rates for families are distinct statistics and do not always follow the same trend. Trends for the two can vary because of changes in the distribution of families by size, and also because unrelated individuals are included in statistics for all persons but not in statistics for families.

Measuring Poverty

Measuring poverty requires a definition of poverty – a set of poverty thresholds (or lines) and a definition of income that can be compared with those thresholds (see later for the official definition of income). As noted previously, the official poverty thresholds are applied to families and unrelated individuals. The poverty status of a family (or unrelated individual) is determined by comparing the income of the family (or unrelated individual) with the appropriate poverty threshold. If an unrelated individual's income is below the appropriate poverty threshold, he or she is identified as poor. If a family's income (the income of all persons in the family) is below the appropriate poverty threshold, the family and all persons in it are identified as poor. A poverty statistic, such as a poverty count, aggregates the count of poor families or poor persons into a single number. The poverty rate among *persons* is the percentage of all persons (either unrelated individuals or members of families) within a group who are identified as poor. The poverty rate among *families* is the percentage of families within a group who are identified as poor. The Census Bureau also prepares poverty statistics for unrelated individuals, but we have not included such statistics here. It should be noted that the poverty rate is a head-count measure – it is calculated simply by dividing the count of the poor by the size of the relevant total population (for example, the total black population in the case of the black poverty rate). The poverty rate thus reflects the prevalence of poverty – how widespread poverty is – but not the severity of poverty.

The severity of poverty is measured by the poverty gap. For a poor family or unrelated individual, the poverty gap is the difference between their actual income and the applicable poverty threshold. The poverty gap is not defined for individual persons within families, although per capita poverty gaps can be calculated for families. Poverty gaps for individual families and unrelated individuals can be aggregated for the whole poverty population and for segments of the total poverty population. The severity of poverty (measured by the aggregate poverty gap) is not reflected in the poverty rate. The Census Bureau dropped the term "poverty gap" from its poverty reports in 1971 and uses the term "income deficit" instead. However, the term "poverty gap" is still understood and used by other analysts.

Poverty Universe

Poverty statistics for the United States are calculated annually from the CPS. The universe for the CPS includes the civilian noninstitutional population of the United States and members of the armed forces in the United States living off post or with their families on post, but it excludes all other members of the armed forces.[26] The "total CPS population" (or "CPS universe") is derived by subtracting the "civilian institutional population" and "[members of] Armed Forces living without families on post in the United States" from the "total resident (United States) population."

The category "persons for whom poverty status is determined" – sometimes termed the "poverty universe" – is derived by subtracting "unrelated individuals under age 15" (younger than age 14 before income year 1979) from the "total CPS population."[27] In other words, the poverty universe excludes persons in institutional group quarters, persons in military barracks (members of the armed forces living without families on post in the United States), and unrelated individuals age 15/14.

Because of differences in the questionnaires and data collection procedures (including definition of the poverty universe), estimates of the number of persons below the poverty threshold from the decennial censuses will differ slightly from those derived from the CPS. For example, the number of poor persons in 1979 according to the 1980 Decennial Census was 27.4 million, compared with 26.1 million according to the March 1980 CPS. The comparable figures for families in poverty were 5.7 million and 5.5 million, respectively.[28]

Survey Date Inconsistencies

Under the procedure for measuring poverty by the CPS, persons are surveyed in March of a given year – for instance, in March 1999. At that time, they are asked to report their income from various sources during the preceding calendar year – 1998, in this case. The current year and month's population characteristics are recorded, but the previous year's income is used to determine poverty status for that previous year. Assume, for instance, that a surveyed couple had had a child in February 1999. Their family income in 1998 would be compared with the 1998 poverty threshold for a three-person family (specifically, for a two-adult/one-child family) to determine their 1998 poverty status – even though they were only a two-person family in the year in which the income was received. If it were determined that their 1998 income was below the 1998 poverty threshold for a family of three, their child would be included in the count of poor children in 1998, even though she had not been born yet. In other words, poverty in 1998 is determined on the basis of "income-in-1998-of-persons-as-of-March-1999." Accordingly, population counts and demographic characteristics associated with poverty statistics for a given year relate to persons as of March of the following year.

[26] See Current Population Report, series P-60, number 105, Table B, p. 4.

[27] See Current Population Report, series P-60, number 207, pp. v, A-2, and series P-60, number 106, p. 191.

[28] 1980 Census of Population, volume 1, Characteristics of the Population, Chapter C, *General Social and Economic Characteristics*, part 1, United States Summary, PC80-1-C1, December 1983, Table "Thresholds at the Poverty Level in 1979 by Size of Family and Number of Related Children Under 18 Years," p. B-23. For discussion of the differing poverty universe see, for instance, Current Population Report, series P-60, number 95, pp. 2–3.

Poverty Rate versus the Composition of Poverty

The poverty rate indicates what percentage of a demographic group is poor. The composition of poverty indicates what percentage of the poverty population belongs to a certain demographic group. For example, the poverty rate for female-headed families is the percentage of all female-headed families that are poor. The female composition of family poverty is the percentage of all poor families that are female-headed.

The distinction between the poverty rate and the composition of poverty is important. Using a statistical analogy, the poverty rate and the composition of poverty are the opposite conditional probabilities. The impression left by one of these statistics is often quite different from that left by the other. For example, in 1959 the poverty rate among African Americans was 55 percent, but only 25 percent of all poor persons were African Americans. In other words, the majority of African Americans were poor in this year, but the majority of the poor were whites. Time series of both poverty rates and the composition of poverty are included throughout Tables Be260–411.

Income Definition

Definitions of poverty contain two components – the income-based poverty threshold and a definition of income. The definition of income used in the official definition of poverty is before-tax money income. (This definition has been used by the Census Bureau in its annual family income reports since the late 1940s; see the following definition for details.) Accordingly, such statements as "the poverty thresholds do not count noncash benefits" are incorrect; it is the Census Bureau's *income* definition that does not count noncash benefits.

A family's money income is the sum of the incomes received by all family members ages 15 or older.[29] The family's money income is compared with the appropriate poverty threshold to determine the family's poverty status (and thus the poverty status of all persons in the family).

The income definition used to determine poverty status is money income before taxes. In addition to not reflecting personal income taxes that people pay, before-tax money income does not reflect payments for Social Security taxes, union dues, Medicare deductions, and so on, or Earned Income Tax Credit payments that people receive. This income definition also excludes capital gains and noncash benefits from both private and public sources. In other words, money income used to determine poverty status does not reflect the fact that some persons receive such noncash benefits as food stamps, health benefits, rent-free or subsidized housing, goods produced and consumed on the farm, the use of business transportation and facilities, and full or partial payments by business for retirement programs, medical and educational expenses, and so on.

The definition of income that should be used with the poverty thresholds has been a controversial issue for decades. The National Research Council's Panel on Poverty and Family Assistance thoroughly examined this issue in the course of its work. As a result of its examination of the issue, the Panel put great emphasis on the principle that, in poverty measurement, the definition of income used should be consistent with the concept underlying the poverty thresholds. The Panel made a specific recommendation that in developing poverty statistics, any significant change in the definition of income should be accompanied by a consistent adjustment of the poverty thresholds; in particular, the Panel criticized tabulations that add the value of public and private health insurance to families' incomes without adjusting the thresholds to account for medical care needs (Citro and Michael, 1995, pp. 4, 9–10, 37–40, 65–66, 98, 203–206, and 227–231). Because of the Panel's conclusions, we decided not to include figures that made significant changes in the definition of income without making any change in the poverty thresholds.

Revisions in the Poverty Definition and the Underlying Income Series

There have been two revisions in the poverty definition, in 1969 and in 1981. At the time of the 1969 revision, poverty figures for all earlier years back to 1959 were retabulated on the revised basis; accordingly, poverty statistics published since then do not contain any earlier-year figures on the unrevised basis.[30] At the time of the 1981 revision, however, the (by now much longer) series for all earlier years was not retabulated; instead, some figures for income year 1980 were retabulated on the revised basis.

Much more frequent than poverty definition revisions have been revisions in the underlying income data series from the CPS. Every decade the Census Bureau introduces statistical controls from the latest decennial census, thus changing the income series. In addition, about once every decade the Census Bureau implements a new computer processing system for the March supplement to the CPS; this also changes the income series. There have been a few other revisions or corrections in the series for other reasons. Information on all these revisions has been gathered from poverty reports in the Current Population Reports series and summarized in the text for Tables Be260–411.

Each time there is a revision in either the income series or poverty definition, the Census Bureau retabulates some figures for the previous income year on the revised basis, so that people can see how the revision affects the poverty population series. Each revision results in greater or lesser changes in poverty population figures and poverty rate figures. In addition, each revision (except the 1981 poverty redefinition) results in changes in total population figures (the numbers of persons and families at all income levels).

Ideally, a presentation of historical poverty statistics would include both unrevised and revised figures for every year for which they are available. In practice, however, we were only able to include one figure for each year for each statistical series. In general,

[29] For each person 15 years old and older in the March CPS sample, the amount of money income received in the preceding calendar year from each of the following 18 sources is recorded: earnings; unemployment compensation; workers' compensation; Social Security; Supplemental Security Income; public assistance; veterans' payments; survivor benefits; disability benefits; pension or retirement income; interest; dividends; rents, royalties, and estates and trusts; educational assistance; alimony; child support; financial assistance from outside of the household; and other income. The following receipts are not counted as income by the Census Bureau: capital gains people receive (or losses they incur) from the sale of property, including stocks, bonds, a house, or a car (unless the person was engaged in the business of selling such property, in which case the CPS counts the net proceeds as income from self-employment); withdrawals of bank deposits; money borrowed; tax refunds; gifts; and lump-sum inheritances or insurance payments.

[30] Because of the 1969 revision, poverty statistics from documents published before August 1969 should not be used, since they are not comparable with subsequent poverty statistics.

we included the revised figure whenever it was available. In a few cases, however, where both revised and unrevised figures were available for a group but only unrevised figures were available for its components (for example, the child population and its white, black, and Hispanic components), we included the unrevised figure for the whole group as well as for its components.

For any year for which revised figures are available for some statistical series and unrevised figures are available for other statistical series, unrevised figures should not be added to, subtracted from, or divided by revised figures because unrevised figures and revised figures are not strictly comparable with each other.

For some statistical series in these tables, we were able to include poverty figures for 1959 or 1969 from the relevant decennial census when figures were not available for those series for those years from the CPS. For those years, figures from the decennial census should not be added to, subtracted from, or divided by figures from the CPS because the two sets of figures are not strictly comparable with each other.

References

American Federation of Labor–Congress of Industrial Organizations, Department of Research. 1959. "State and Local Tax Burdens Must Be Fairly Shared." *Labor's Economic Review* 4 (2): 1ff.

Barrington, Linda. 1997. "Estimating Earnings Poverty in 1939: A Comparison of Orshansky-Method and Price-Indexed Definitions of Poverty." *Review of Economics and Statistics* 79 (3): 406–14.

Barrington, Linda. 1999. "Absolutely Relative or Relatively Absolute: The Income Elasticity of Orshansky-Method Poverty Lines, 1919–1959." Presented at the Annual Meeting of the Economic History Association, Baltimore, October 10, 1999.

Barrington, Linda. 2000. *Does a Rising Tide Lift All Boats? America's Full-Time Working Poor Reap Limited Gains in the New Economy*, Research Report 1271-00-RR. Conference Board.

Barrington, Linda, and Cecilia A. Conrad. 1994. "At What Cost a Room of Her Own? Factors Contributing to the Feminization of Poverty among Prime-Age Women, 1939–1959." *Journal of Economic History* 54 (2): 342–57.

Bernstein, Jared, Chauna Brocht, and Maggie Spade-Aguilar. 2000. *How Much Is Enough? Basic Family Budgets for Working Families.* Economic Policy Institute.

Brand, Horst. 1960. "Poverty in the United States." *Dissent* 7 (4): 334–54.

Bureau of Applied Economics. 1932. *Standards of Living: A Compilation of Budgetary Studies*, Bulletin number 7, part 2.

Callan, Tim, and Brian Nolan. 1991. "Concepts of Poverty and the Poverty Line." *Journal of Economic Surveys* 5 (3): 243–61.

Chapin, Robert Coit. 1909. *The Standard of Living among Workingmen's Families in New York City.* Charities Publication Committee.

Citro, Constance F., and Robert T. Michael, editors. 1995. *Measuring Poverty: A New Approach.* National Academy Press.

Comish, Newel Howland. 1923. *The Standard of Living: Elements of Consumption.* Macmillan.

Conference on Economic Progress. 1962. *Poverty and Deprivation in the United States: The Plight of Two-Fifths of a Nation.* Conference on Economic Progress.

Council of Economic Advisers. 1954. *Economic Report of the President Transmitted to the Congress January 28, 1954.* U.S. Government Printing Office.

Council of Economic Advisers. 1955. *Economic Report of the President Transmitted to the Congress January 20, 1955.* U.S. Government Printing Office.

Council of Economic Advisers. 1964. *Economic Report of the President Transmitted to the Congress January 1964 Together With the Annual Report of the Council of Economic Advisers.* U.S. Government Printing Office.

Dallas [Texas] Wage Commission, Survey Committee. 1917. *Report of Survey Committee to the Dallas Wage Commission and Submitted by Them to the Honorable Mayor and Board of Commissioners of the City of Dallas . . .*, April 25.

Danziger, Sheldon, and Peter Gottschalk. 1986. "Do Rising Tides Lift All Boats? The Impact of Secular and Cyclical Changes on Poverty." *American Economic Review* 76 (2): 405–10.

Daugherty, Carroll R. 1938. *Labor Problems in American Industry*, fourth edition. Houghton Mifflin.

Davis, Allen F. 1963. "The Campaign for the Industrial Relations Commission, 1911–1913." *Mid-America: An Historical Review* 45 (4): 211–28.

Douglas, Dorothy W. 1923. "A Description of Standards of Living." In Paul H. Douglas, Curtice N. Hitchcock, and Willard E. Atkins, editors. *The Worker in Modern Economic Society.* University of Chicago Press.

Douglas, Paul, and Dorothy Douglas. 1921. "What Can a Man Afford?" *American Economic Review*, 11 (4), supplement number 2: 1ff.

DuBois, W. E. B. 1967 [1899]. *The Philadelphia Negro: A Social Study.* Schocken Books.

Early, Frances H. 1983. "The French-Canadian Family Economy and Standard-of-Living in Lowell, Massachusetts, 1870." In Michael Gordon, editor. *The American Family in Social-Historical Perspective*, third edition. St. Martin's Press.

Epstein, Lenore A. 1961. "Some Effects of Low Income on Children and Their Families." *Social Security Bulletin* 24 (2): 12–17.

Epstein, Lenore A. 1963. "Unmet Need in a Land of Abundance." *Social Security Bulletin* 26 (5): 3–11.

Fisher, Gordon M. 1976. "Poverty among the Aged and Social Security Benefits." In Fred E. Waddell, editor. *The Elderly Consumer.* Human Ecology Center, Antioch College.

Fisher, Gordon M. 1992. "The Development and History of the Poverty Thresholds." *Social Security Bulletin* 55 (4): 3–14.

Fisher, Gordon M. 1995. "Is There Such a Thing as an Absolute Poverty Line over Time? Evidence from the United States, Britain, Canada, and Australia on the Income Elasticity of the Poverty Line." Manuscript, August.

Fisher, Gordon M. 1997a. "The Development of the Orshansky Poverty Thresholds and Their Subsequent History as the Official U.S. Poverty Measure." Manuscript, May 1992, revised September 1997.

Fisher, Gordon M. 1997b. "Disseminating the Administrative Version and Explaining the Administrative and Statistical Versions of the Federal Poverty Measure." *Clinical Sociology Review* 15: 163–82.

Fisher, Gordon M. 1997c. "From Hunter to Orshansky: An Overview of (Unofficial) Poverty Lines in the United States from 1904 to 1965." Manuscript, October 1993, revised August 1997.

Fisher, Gordon M. 1998. "Setting American Standards of Poverty: A Look Back." *Focus* [newsletter of the Institute for Research on Poverty] 19 (2): 47–52.

Fisher, Gordon M. 1999. "How Many Americans Were *Really* in Poverty in 1947? Estimates of the U.S. Poverty Population between 1947 and 1963 under Two Contemporary (1949 and 1959) Definitions of Poverty." Manuscript, October.

Friedman, Rose D. 1965. *Poverty: Definition and Perspective.* American Enterprise Institute for Public Policy Research.

Fuchs, Victor R. 1965. "Toward a Theory of Poverty." In Task Force on Economic Growth and Opportunity, editor. *The Concept of Poverty.* Chamber of Commerce of the United States.

Galbraith, John Kenneth. 1964 [1958]. *The Affluent Society.* New American Library.

Goldsmith, Selma F. 1962. "Low-Income Families and Measures of Income Inequality." *Review of Social Economy* 20 (1): 1–25.

Haines, Michael R. 1981. "Poverty, Economic Stress, and the Family in a Late Nineteenth-Century American City: Whites in Philadelphia, 1880." In Theodore Hershberg, editor. *Philadelphia: Work, Space, Family, and Group Experience in the Nineteenth Century: Essays toward an Interdisciplinary History of the City.* Oxford University Press.

Harrington, Michael. 1966 [1962]. *The Other America: Poverty in the United States.* Penguin Books.

Heller, Walter W. 1964. "Statement . . . " (March 17, 1964), pp. 26 ff. in U.S. House of Representatives, Committee on Education and Labor, *Economic Opportunity Act of 1964: Hearings before the Subcommittee on the War on Poverty Program . . . on H.R. 10440, a Bill to Mobilize the Human and Financial Resources of the Nation to Combat Poverty in the United States – Part 1.*

Hunter, Robert. 1904. *Poverty.* Macmillan.

Hunter, Robert. 1908. "Poverty in the United States." In William D. P. Bliss and Rudolph M. Binder, editors. *The New Encyclopedia of Social Reform....* Funk & Wagnalls.

Innes, Judith Eleanor. 1990. *Knowledge and Public Policy: The Search for Meaningful Indicators.* Transaction Publishers.

Iowa Bureau of Labor Statistics. 1891. *Fourth Biennial Report of the Bureau of Labor Statistics for the State of Iowa, 1890–91.* G. H. Ragsdale.

Kilpatrick, Robert W. 1973. "The Income Elasticity of the Poverty Line." *Review of Economics and Statistics* 55 (3): 327–32.

Kolko, Gabriel. 1962. *Wealth and Power in America: An Analysis of Social Class and Income Distribution.* Frederick A. Praeger.

Lampman, Robert J. 1959. "The Low Income Population and Economic Growth," Study Paper number 12. In U.S. Congress, Joint Economic Committee. *Study Papers Nos. 12 and 13, The Low Income Population and Economic Growth... The Adequacy of Resources for Economic Growth in the United States... Materials Prepared in Connection with the Study of Employment, Growth, and Price Levels...* (December 16, 1959). U.S. Government Printing Office.

Lampman, Robert J. 1966. "Population Change and Poverty Reduction, 1947–75." In Leo Fishman, editor. *Poverty amid Affluence.* Yale University Press.

Lauck, W. Jett. 1920. *Summary, Analysis and Statement.* Presented... on behalf of... the United Mine Workers of America before the United States Anthracite Coal Commission. U.S. Government Printing Office.

Lazarus, Emma. 1989. "The New Colossus." In *The Poems of Emma Lazarus*, volume 1. Houghton Mifflin.

Leven, Maurice, Harold G. Moulton, and Clark Warburton. 1934. *America's Capacity to Consume.* Publication number 56 of the Institute of Economics of the Brookings Institution. Brookings Institution.

[Massachusetts Bureau of Statistics of Labor]. 1871. *[Second] Report of the [Massachusetts] Bureau of Statistics of Labor, Embracing the Account of Its Operations and Inquiries from March 1, 1870, to March 1, 1871.* Wright & Potter.

More, Louise Bolard. 1907. *Wage-Earners' Budgets: A Study of Standards and Cost of Living in New York City.* Greenwich House Series of Social Studies – number 1. Henry Holt.

Morgan, James N., Martin H. David, et al. 1962. *Income and Welfare in the United States* (a study by the Survey Research Center, Institute for Social Research, University of Michigan). McGraw-Hill.

National Industrial Conference Board. 1921. *Family Budgets of American Wage-Earners: A Critical Analysis.* Research Report number 41. Century Company.

Nearing, Scott. 1913. *Financing the Wage-Earner's Family: A Survey of the Facts Bearing on Income and Expenditures in the Families of American Wage-Earners.* B. W. Huebsch.

[New York City] Board of Estimate and Apportionment, Bureau of Personal Service. 1917. *Report on the Increased Cost of Living for an Unskilled Laborer's Family in New York City.* M. B. Brown.

New York State Bureau of Labor Statistics. 1903. *Twentieth Annual Report of the [New York State] Bureau of Labor Statistics for the Year Ended September 30, 1902.* Argus Company.

Norwood, Janet L. 1990. "Distinguished Lecture on Economics in Government: Data Quality and Public Policy." *Journal of Economic Perspectives* 4 (2): 3–12.

Nystrom, Paul H. 1929. *Economic Principles of Consumption.* Ronald Press.

Ogburn, William F. 1918. "Part I. Digest and Critical Analysis." In *Memorandum on the Minimum Wage and Increased Cost of Living* (for members of the National War Labor Board... Submitted by the Secretary [W. Jett Lauck] at the request of the Board at its meeting on July 12, 1918). U.S. Government Printing Office.

Ornati, Oscar, with the editorial assistance of J. Stouder Sweet. 1966. *Poverty amid Affluence: A Report on a Research Project Carried Out at the New School for Social Research.* Twentieth Century Fund.

Orshansky, Mollie. 1959. "Family Budgets and Fee Schedules of Voluntary Agencies," *Social Security Bulletin* 22 (4): 10–17.

Orshansky, Mollie. 1963. "Children of the Poor." *Social Security Bulletin* 26 (7): 3–13.

Orshansky, Mollie. 1965. "Counting the Poor: Another Look at the Poverty Profile." *Social Security Bulletin* 28 (1): 3–29.

Orshansky, Mollie. 1969. "How Poverty Is Measured." *Monthly Labor Review* 92 (2): 37–41.

Parmelee, Maurice. 1916. *Poverty and Social Progress.* Macmillan.

Pearce, Diana. 1978. "The Feminization of Poverty: Women, Work and Welfare." *Urban and Social Change Review* 11 (1 and 2 [combined]) (Special Issue on Women and Work): 28–36.

Plotnick, Robert D., Eugene Smolensky, et al. 2000. "The Twentieth-Century Record of Inequality and Poverty in the United States." In Stanley Engerman and Robert Gallman, editors. *The Cambridge Economic History of the United States,* volume 3, *The Twentieth Century.* Cambridge University Press.

Reed, Louis S. 1933. *The Ability to Pay for Medical Care.* Publications of the Committee on the Costs of Medical Care, number 25. University of Chicago Press.

Residents of Hull-House, A Social Settlement.... 1895. *Hull-House Maps and Papers: A Presentation of Nationalities and Wages in a Congested District of Chicago, Together with Comments and Essays on Problems Growing Out of the Social Conditions.* Thomas Y. Crowell.

Reuther, Walter P. 1953. "Report to the Congress of Industrial Organizations." In *1953 Proceedings of the Fifteenth Constitutional Convention of the Congress of Industrial Organizations, November... 1953....* Congress of Industrial Organizations.

Roosevelt, Franklin D. 1970. "The [Second] Inaugural Address, 1937." In Harold L. Sheppard, editor. *Poverty and Wealth in America.* Quadrangle Books.

Ross, Christine, Sheldon Danziger, and Eugene Smolensky. 1987. "The Level and Trend of Poverty in the United States, 1939–1979." *Demography* 24 (4): 587–600.

Rubinow, Isaac M. 1929. "Can Private Philanthropy Do It?" *Social Service Review* 3 (3): 361–94.

Ruggles, Patricia. 1990. *Drawing the Line: Alternative Poverty Measures and Their Implications for Public Policy.* Urban Institute Press.

Short, Kathleen. 2001. *Experimental Poverty Measures: 1999.* U.S. Census Bureau, Current Population Reports, series P-60, number 216. U.S. Government Printing Office.

Short, Kathleen, Thesia Garner, et al. 1999. *Experimental Poverty Measures: 1990 to 1997.* U.S. Census Bureau, Current Population Reports, series P-60, number 205. U.S. Government Printing Office.

Spargo, John. 1968 [1906]. *The Bitter Cry of the Children.* Quadrangle Books.

Stecker, Margaret Loomis. 1937. *Intercity Differences in Costs of Living in March 1935, 59 Cities.* Research Monograph 12, Works Progress Administration, Division of Social Research. U.S. Government Printing Office.

Townsend, Peter. 1962. "The Meaning of Poverty." *British Journal of Sociology* 13 (3): 210–27.

Tugwell, Rexford Guy, Thomas Munro, and Roy E. Stryker. 1930. *American Economic Life and the Means of Its Improvement*, third edition. Harcourt, Brace.

U.S. Bureau of the Census. 1971. *Current Population Reports*, Series P-23, number 37, *Social and Economic Characteristics of the Population in Metropolitan and Nonmetropolitan Areas: 1970 and 1960.* U.S. Government Printing Office.

U.S. Bureau of the Census. 1973. *Census of Population, 1970*, Subject Reports, Final Report PC(2)-9A, *Low-Income Population.* U.S. Government Printing Office.

U.S. Bureau of the Census. 1974. *Persons of Spanish Origin in the United States: March 1973.* Current Population Reports, series P-20, number 264. U.S. Government Printing Office.

U.S. Bureau of the Census. 1975. *Historical Statistics of the United States, Colonial Times to 1970* (Bicentennial Edition), part 1. U.S. Government Printing Office.

U.S. Bureau of the Census. 1980. *United States Census of the Population: 1980*, volume 1, *Characteristics of the Population,* part 1, Chapter C. U.S. Government Printing Office.

U.S. Bureau of the Census. [1969 through 1999]. Current Population Reports, series P-60 [selected numbers from number 59 through 207], [selected reports on poverty and money income]. U.S. Government Printing Office.

U.S. Bureau of the Census. Unpublished poverty population tabulations for various years.

[U.S. Bureau of Labor]. 1911. *Report on Condition of Woman and Child Wage-Earners in the United States in 19 Volumes*,volume 16, *Family Budgets of Typical Cotton-Mill Workers*, prepared . . . by Wood F. Worcester and Daisy Worthington Worcester. U.S. Government Printing Office.

U.S. Commission on Industrial Relations. 1916. *Industrial Relations: Final Report and Testimony Submitted to Congress . . .* , volume 1. U.S. Government Printing Office.

U.S. Congress, Joint Committee on the Economic Report. 1949. *Low-Income Families and Economic Stability – Materials on the Problem of Low-Income Families Assembled by the Staff of the Subcommittee on Low-Income Families . . . .* U.S. Government Printing Office.

U.S. Congress, Joint Committee on the Economic Report. 1955. *Characteristics of the Low-Income Population and Related Federal Programs – Selected Materials Assembled by the Staff of the Subcommittee on Low-Income Families . . . .* U.S. Government Printing Office.

U.S. Department of Health, Education, and Welfare. 1976. *The Measure of Poverty: A Report to Congress as Mandated by the Education Amendments of 1974.* U.S. Government Printing Office.

U.S. House of Representatives. 1916. *To Fix the Compensation of Certain Employees: Hearings before the Subcommittee of the Committee on Labor . . . on H.R. 11876 . . . March . . . and April . . . 1916.* U.S. Government Printing Office.

U.S. House of Representatives. [1916]. "Minimum Wage Bill . . . Report." [To accompany H.R. 11876] 64th Congress, 1st Session, Report number 742.

U.S. National Resources Committee. 1938. *Consumer Incomes in the United States: Their Distribution in 1935–36.* U.S. Government Printing Office.

U.S. National Resources Planning Board, Committee on Long-Range Work and Relief Policies. 1942. *Security, Work, and Relief Policies.* U.S. Government Printing Office.

U.S. Public Health Service, National Institute of Health, Division of Public Health Methods. 1938. "The National Health Survey: 1935–1936 – The Relief and Income Status of the Urban Population of the United States, 1935." Preliminary Reports, National Health Survey, Population Series, Bulletin C.

Vaughan, Denton R. 1993. "Exploring the Use of the Public's Views to Set Income Poverty Thresholds and Adjust Them over Time." *Social Security Bulletin* 56 (2): 22–46.

Wyand, Charles S. 1937. *The Economics of Consumption.* Macmillan.

DISTRIBUTION OF INCOME

Peter H. Lindert

TABLE Be1–18 Distribution of money income among households: 1947–1998[1]

Contributed by Peter H. Lindert

		Households, share of money income received by the							Household income	
	Number of households	Lowest fifth	Second fifth	Third fifth	Fourth fifth	Top fifth	Top 5 percent	Gini coefficient of income inequality	Mean	Median
	Be1	Be2	Be3	Be4	Be5	Be6	Be7	Be8	Be9	Be10
Year	Thousand	Percent	Percent	Percent	Percent	Percent	Percent	Share	Dollars	Dollars
1947	45,402	3.5	10.6	16.7	23.6	45.6	18.7	0.403	3,215	2,685
1950	49,295	3.1	10.5	17.3	24.1	45.0	18.2	0.404	3,422	2,990
1955	52,778	3.3	10.5	17.4	24.5	44.3	18.8	0.399	4,467	3,909
1959	55,990	3.2	10.6	17.7	24.7	43.9	17.1	0.394	5,306	4,759
1960	56,537	3.2	10.6	17.6	24.7	44.0	17.0	0.394	5,522	4,970
1961	57,504	3.1	10.2	17.2	24.6	44.9	17.7	0.405	5,719	5,009
1962	58,011	3.4	10.4	17.5	24.8	43.9	16.8	0.393	5,921	5,264
1963	58,618	3.4	10.4	17.5	24.8	43.9	16.9	0.393	6,200	5,490
1964	59,892	3.4	10.4	17.3	24.8	44.1	17.2	0.396	6,478	5,696
1965	60,411	3.6	10.6	17.5	24.8	43.6	16.6	0.387	6,795	6,032
1966	61,336	3.8	10.7	17.5	24.7	43.4	16.7	0.384	7,386	6,546
1967	60,446	4.0	10.8	17.3	24.2	43.8	17.5	0.399	8,173	7,143
1968	61,805	4.2	11.1	17.5	24.4	42.8	16.6	0.388	8,749	7,743
1969	62,874	4.1	10.9	17.5	24.5	43.0	16.6	0.391	9,514	8,389
1970	64,374	4.1	10.8	17.4	24.5	43.3	16.6	0.394	10,025	8,734
1971	66,676	4.1	10.6	17.3	24.5	43.5	16.7	0.396	10,370	9,028
1972	68,251	4.1	10.5	17.1	24.5	43.9	17.0	0.401	11,308	9,697
1973	69,859	4.2	10.5	17.1	24.6	43.6	16.6	0.397	12,174	10,512
1974	71,163	4.4	10.6	17.1	24.7	43.1	15.9	0.395	13,103	11,197
1975	72,867	4.4	10.5	17.1	24.8	43.2	15.9	0.397	13,818	11,800
1976	74,142	4.4	10.4	17.1	24.8	43.3	16.0	0.398	14,939	12,686
1977	76,030	4.4	10.3	17.0	24.8	43.6	16.1	0.402	16,084	13,572
1978	77,330	4.3	10.3	16.9	24.8	43.7	16.2	0.402	17,785	15,064
1979	80,776	4.2	10.3	16.9	24.7	44.0	16.4	0.404	19,572	16,461
1980	82,368	4.3	10.3	16.9	24.9	43.7	15.8	0.403	21,081	17,710
1981	83,527	4.2	10.2	16.8	25.0	43.8	15.6	0.406	22,787	19,074
1982	83,918	4.1	10.1	16.6	24.7	44.5	16.2	0.412	24,309	20,171
1983	85,290	4.1	10.0	16.5	24.7	44.7	16.4	0.414	25,609	21,018
1984	86,789	4.1	9.9	16.4	24.7	44.9	16.5	0.415	27,464	22,415
1985	88,458	4.0	9.7	16.3	24.6	45.3	17.0	0.419	29,066	23,618
1986	89,479	3.9	9.7	16.2	24.5	45.7	17.5	0.425	30,759	24,897
1987	91,124	3.8	9.6	16.1	24.3	46.2	18.2	0.426	32,410	26,061
1988	92,830	3.8	9.6	16.0	24.3	46.3	18.3	0.427	34,017	27,225
1989	93,347	3.8	9.5	15.8	24.0	46.8	18.9	0.431	36,520	28,906
1990	94,312	3.9	9.6	15.9	24.0	46.6	18.6	0.428	37,403	29,943
1991	95,669	3.8	9.6	15.9	24.2	46.5	18.1	0.428	37,922	30,126
1992	96,426	3.8	9.4	15.8	24.2	46.9	18.6	0.434	38,840	30,636
1993	97,107	3.6	9.0	15.1	23.5	48.9	21.0	0.454	41,428	31,241
1994	98,990	3.6	8.9	15.0	23.4	49.1	21.2	0.456	43,133	32,264
1995	99,627	3.7	9.1	15.2	23.3	48.7	21.0	0.450	44,938	34,076
1996	101,018	3.7	9.0	15.1	23.3	49.0	21.4	0.455	47,123	35,492
1997	102,528	3.6	8.9	15.0	23.2	49.4	21.7	0.459	49,692	37,005
1998	103,874	3.6	9.0	15.0	23.2	49.2	21.4	0.456	51,855	38,885

Note appears at end of table

TABLE Be1–18 Distribution of money income among households: 1947–1998 *Continued*

	Household income							
	Lower income limit for the					Ratio to the median at the		
	Second fifth	Third fifth	Fourth fifth	Top fifth	Top 5 percent	95th percentile	80th percentile	20th percentile
	Be11	Be12	Be13	Be14	Be15	Be16	Be17	Be18
Year	Dollars	Dollars	Dollars	Dollars	Dollars	Ratio	Ratio	Ratio
1947	1,138	2,211	3,189	4,568	7,775	2.896	1.701	0.424
1950	1,114	2,409	3,460	4,939	8,103	2.710	1.652	0.373
1955	1,475	3,179	4,598	6,498	10,141	2.594	1.662	0.377
1959	1,820	3,800	5,500	7,800	12,130	2.549	1.639	0.382
1960	1,900	3,979	5,750	8,100	12,850	2.586	1.630	0.382
1961	1,900	4,000	5,929	8,437	13,638	2.723	1.684	0.379
1962	2,000	4,160	6,100	8,800	14,000	2.660	1.672	0.380
1963	2,075	4,400	6,487	9,140	14,475	2.637	1.665	0.378
1964	2,200	4,500	6,710	9,609	15,040	2.640	1.687	0.386
1965	2,360	4,850	7,080	10,000	15,910	2.638	1.658	0.391
1966	2,600	5,200	7,640	10,815	17,000	2.597	1.652	0.397
1967	3,000	5,850	8,306	11,841	19,000	2.660	1.658	0.420
1968	3,323	6,300	9,030	12,688	19,850	2.564	1.639	0.429
1969	3,574	6,860	9,920	13,900	21,800	2.599	1.657	0.426
1970	3,687	7,064	10,276	14,661	23,178	2.654	1.679	0.422
1971	3,800	7,244	10,660	15,200	24,138	2.674	1.684	0.421
1972	4,050	7,800	11,530	16,500	26,560	2.739	1.702	0.418
1973	4,418	8,393	12,450	17,985	28,509	2.712	1.711	0.420
1974	4,923	9,094	13,400	19,453	31,085	2.776	1.737	0.440
1975	5,025	9,450	14,246	20,496	32,681	2.770	1.737	0.426
1976	5,479	10,133	15,423	22,192	35,382	2.789	1.749	0.432
1977	5,813	10,900	16,531	24,100	38,961	2.871	1.776	0.428
1978	6,384	12,000	18,146	26,425	42,572	2.826	1.754	0.424
1979	7,009	13,035	20,025	29,097	47,465	2.883	1.768	0.426
1980	7,556	14,100	21,610	31,700	51,500	2.908	1.790	0.427
1981	8,160	15,034	23,396	34,600	56,300	2.952	1.814	0.428
1982	8,520	16,010	24,560	36,670	61,107	3.029	1.818	0.422
1983	9,000	16,773	25,718	38,898	64,600	3.074	1.851	0.428
1984	9,600	17,904	27,506	41,600	69,590	3.105	1.856	0.428
1985	10,000	18,852	29,022	43,809	73,263	3.102	1.855	0.423
1986	10,358	19,783	30,555	46,120	78,226	3.142	1.852	0.416
1987	10,800	20,500	32,000	48,363	80,928	3.105	1.856	0.414
1988	11,382	21,500	33,506	50,593	85,640	3.146	1.858	0.418
1989	12,096	23,000	35,350	53,710	91,750	3.174	1.858	0.418
1990	12,500	23,662	36,200	55,205	94,748	3.164	1.844	0.417
1991	12,588	24,000	37,070	56,760	96,400	3.200	1.884	0.418
1992	12,600	24,140	37,900	58,007	99,020	3.232	1.893	0.411
1993	12,967	24,679	38,793	60,300	104,639	3.349	1.930	0.415
1994	13,426	25,200	40,100	62,841	109,821	3.404	1.948	0.416
1995	14,400	26,914	42,002	65,124	113,000	3.316	1.911	0.423
1996	14,768	27,760	44,006	68,015	119,540	3.368	1.916	0.416
1997	15,400	29,200	46,000	71,500	126,550	3.420	1.932	0.416
1998	16,116	30,408	48,337	75,000	132,199	3.400	1.929	0.414

[1] See text for a discussion of numerous methodological changes.

Source

Census Bureau's Internet site: Current Population Survey (CPS) series P-60, number 184, "Money Income of Households," superseded in 1993 by series P-60, number 189, "Income, Poverty, and Valuation of Noncash Benefits." Tables H-1, H-2, H-4, and H-9, as accessed on June 23, 2000.

Documentation

The Census Bureau's CPS definition of "money income" before taxes includes cash transfers (but not in-kind transfers) from government.

The population unit for the estimates through 1966 consists of families and unrelated individuals living alone; thereafter, the unit is the household.

CPS series P-60, number 184 was superseded in 1993 by CPS series P-60, number 189. The overlapping data for 1993 suggest that the various changes in procedure raised the top 5 percent share by 1 percent of aggregate income, the top 20 percent share by 0.7 percent, and the Gini coefficient by 0.007. The higher new-basis estimates for 1993 are shown here.

Methodological Notes

The following methodological notes apply to the CPS series in Tables Be1–18, Be30–38, and Be55–84.

1947: Based on 1940 Census population controls.

1949: Implementation of expanded income questions to show wage and salary, farm self-employment, nonfarm self-employment, and all other non-earned income separately.

1952: Implementation of 1950 Census population controls.

1961: Implementation of first hot-deck procedure to impute missing income entries (all income data imputed if any missing). Introduction of 1960 Census sample design.

1962: Full implementation of 1960 Census-based sample design and population controls.

1965: Implementation of new procedures to impute missing data only.

1966: Questionnaire expanded to ask eight income questions.

(continued)

TABLE Be1–18 Distribution of money income among households: 1947–1998 *Continued*

1967: Implementation of a new March CPS processing system.

1971: Introduction of 1970 Census sample design and population controls.

1972: Full implementation of 1970 Census-based sample design.

1974: Implementation of a new March CPS processing system. Questionnaire expanded to ask eleven income questions.

1974–75: Estimates were derived using Pareto interpolation and may differ from published data that were derived using linear interpolation.

1976: First-year medians derived using both Pareto and linear interpolation. Prior to this year all medians were derived using linear interpolation.

1979: Implementation of 1980 Census population controls. Questionnaire expanded to show twenty-seven possible values from fifty-one possible sources of income.

1983: Implementation of Hispanic population weighting controls and introduction of 1980 Census sample design.

1985: Recording of amounts for earnings from longest job increased to $299,999. Full implementation of 1980 Census-based sample design.

1987: Implementation of a new March CPS processing system.

1992: Implementation of 1990 Census population controls.

1993: Data collection method changed from paper and pencil to computer-assisted interviewing. In addition, the March 1994 income supplement was revised to allow for the coding of different income amounts on selected questionnaire items. Limits either increased or decreased in the following categories: earnings increased to $999,999; Social Security increased to $49,999; Supplemental Security Income and public assistance increased to $24,999; veterans' benefits increased to $99,999; child support and alimony decreased to $49,999.

1994: Introduction of 1990 Census sample design.

1995: Full implementation of the 1990 Census-based sample design and metropolitan definitions, 7,000 household sample reduction, and revised race edits.

TABLE Be19–20 Distribution of pre-tax money income among individuals covered on tax returns – shares received by the top percentiles: 1913–1948

Contributed by Peter H. Lindert

	Top 1 percent	Top 5 percent
	Be19	Be20
Year	Percent	Percent
1913	14.98	—
1914	13.07	—
1915	14.32	—
1916	15.58	—
1917	14.16	—
1918	12.69	—
1919	12.84	26.10
1920	12.34	25.76
1921	13.50	31.70
1922	13.38	30.39
1923	12.28	28.08
1924	12.91	29.06
1925	13.73	30.24
1926	13.93	30.21
1927	14.39	31.19
1928	14.94	32.06
1929	14.50	31.88
1930	13.82	30.69
1931	13.29	31.96
1932	12.90	32.12
1933	12.14	30.83
1934	12.03	29.13
1935	12.07	28.77
1936	13.37	29.26
1937	13.00	28.51
1938	11.53	27.80
1939	11.80	27.77
1940	11.89	26.83
1941	11.39	25.67
1942	10.06	22.47
1943	9.38	20.86
1944	8.58	18.68
1945	8.81	19.27
1946	8.98	19.96
1947	8.49	—
1948	8.38	—

Source

Simon Kuznets, *Shares of Upper Income Groups in Income and Savings* (Columbia University Press, 1953), pp. 582, 585, 635, 637, 646, 649.

Documentation

All of Kuznets's series refer to income before taxes and to taxpaying units. Unlike the other series in this chapter, the Kuznets series rank recipient units according to money income per person.

Series Be19. Kuznets basic variant.

Series Be20. Kuznets economic variant. This variant is preferred by Kuznets (1953, p. 635) for reasons given in his introduction.

TABLE Be21–26 Distribution of money income among consumer units: 1929–1971

Contributed by Peter H. Lindert

	Consumer units			Household money income – ratio to median at the		
	Share of money income received by					
	Top 20 percent	Top 5 percent	Gini coefficient	95th percentile	80th percentile	20th percentile
	Be21	Be22	Be23	Be24	Be25	Be26
Year	Percent	Percent	Share	Ratio	Ratio	Ratio
1929	30.0	54.4	0.49	3.604	1.780	0.462
1935	26.5	51.7	0.47	3.451	1.871	0.494
1941	24.0	48.8	0.44	2.997	1.759	0.443
1944	20.7	45.8	0.39	2.851	1.661	0.522
1946	21.3	46.1	—	2.935	1.640	0.531
1947	20.9	46.0	0.40	2.919	1.670	0.528
1950	21.4	46.1	0.40	2.878	1.650	0.511
1951	20.7	44.9	—	2.777	1.612	0.522
1952	20.5	44.7	—	2.727	1.606	0.515
1953	19.9	44.7	—	2.788	1.620	0.511
1954	20.3	45.2	0.39	2.837	1.631	0.505
1955	20.3	45.2	—	2.849	1.615	0.521
1956	20.2	45.3	0.39	2.868	1.636	0.522
1957	20.2	45.5	—	2.892	1.650	0.514
1958	20.0	45.5	—	2.905	1.670	0.516
1959	20.0	45.6	—	2.951	1.671	0.504
1960	19.6	45.4	—	2.944	1.680	0.502
1961	19.6	45.5	—	2.941	1.690	0.499
1962	19.6	45.5	0.40	2.935	1.687	0.501
1964	20.0	45.5	—	2.837	1.700	0.472
1970	19.2	44.9	—	2.789	1.696	0.486
1971	19.1	44.6	—	2.781	1.696	0.496

Sources

Selma F. Goldsmith, "Changes in the Size Distribution of Income," in Edwin C. Budd, editor, *Inequality and Poverty* (Harper and Row, 1967), with an update in Budd's introduction and a further extension to 1971 in Daniel B. Radner and John C. Hinrichs, "Size Distribution of Income in 1964, 1970, and 1971," *Survey of Current Business* 54 (10) (1974): 19–31.

Documentation

These estimates mix different sets of primary data. For 1929 they combine tax returns with an independent Brookings Institution estimation of the entire income distribution. For 1935–1936 and 1941, Goldsmith adjusted the results of two household surveys. For later years, the Census Bureau's Current Population Survey series were adjusted to the Office of Business Economics–Goldsmith definitions of income and recipient unit.

TABLE Be27–29 Distribution of income among taxpaying units – shares received by the top percentiles: 1913–1998

Contributed by Peter H. Lindert

	Top 1 percent	Top 5 percent	Top 10 percent
	Be27	Be28	Be29
Year	Percent	Percent	Percent
1913	17.96	—	—
1914	18.16	—	—
1915	17.58	—	—
1916	18.57	—	—
1917	17.60	30.34	40.29
1918	15.88	29.29	39.90
1919	15.87	29.31	39.48
1920	14.46	27.47	38.10
1921	15.47	30.45	42.86
1922	16.29	31.05	42.95
1923	14.99	28.95	40.59
1924	16.32	30.93	43.26
1925	17.60	32.46	44.17
1926	18.01	32.75	44.07
1927	18.68	33.43	44.67
1928	19.60	34.77	46.09
1929	18.42	33.05	43.76
1930	16.42	31.18	43.07
1931	15.27	31.01	44.40
1932	15.48	32.59	46.30
1933	15.77	32.49	45.03
1934	15.87	33.00	45.16
1935	15.63	30.99	43.39
1936	17.64	32.66	44.77
1937	16.45	31.38	43.35
1938	14.73	30.18	43.00
1939	15.39	31.28	44.57
1940	15.73	31.28	44.43
1941	15.01	29.02	41.02
1942	12.91	25.11	35.49
1943	11.48	23.02	32.67
1944	10.54	21.76	31.55
1945	11.07	22.90	32.64
1946	11.76	24.66	34.62
1947	10.95	23.30	33.02
1948	11.27	23.70	33.72
1949	10.95	23.47	33.76
1950	11.36	23.87	33.87
1951	10.52	22.67	32.82
1952	9.76	21.85	32.07
1953	9.08	21.01	31.38
1954	9.39	21.56	32.12
1955	9.18	21.38	31.77
1956	9.09	21.35	31.81
1957	8.98	21.17	31.69
1958	8.83	21.26	32.11
1959	8.75	21.03	32.03
1960	8.36	20.51	31.66
1961	8.34	20.91	31.90
1962	8.27	20.94	32.04
1963	8.16	20.89	32.01
1964	8.02	20.62	31.64
1965	8.07	20.70	31.52
1966	8.37	20.99	31.98
1967	8.43	21.08	32.05
1968	8.35	20.97	31.98
1969	8.02	20.68	31.82
1970	7.80	20.38	31.51
1971	7.79	20.50	31.75
1972	7.75	20.37	31.62
1973	7.74	20.57	31.85
1974	8.12	21.03	32.36
1975	8.01	21.03	32.62
1976	7.89	20.85	32.42
1977	7.90	20.83	32.43
1978	7.95	20.86	32.44
1979	8.03	20.83	32.35
1980	8.18	21.17	32.87
1981	8.03	20.97	32.72
1982	8.39	21.40	33.22
1983	8.59	21.78	33.69
1984	8.89	22.10	33.95
1985	9.09	22.37	34.25
1986	9.13	22.59	34.57
1987	10.75	24.49	36.48
1988	13.17	26.95	38.63
1989	12.61	26.66	38.47
1990	12.98	27.05	38.84
1991	12.17	26.43	38.38
1992	13.48	27.88	39.82
1993	12.82	27.41	39.48
1994	12.85	27.50	39.60
1995	13.33	28.10	40.19
1996	13.85	28.96	40.95
1997	14.32	29.28	41.25
1998	14.58	29.41	41.44

Source

Thomas Piketty and Emmanuel Saez, "Income Inequality in the United States, 1913–1998," National Bureau of Economic Research Working Paper number W8467 (September 2001), Table A1. The main underlying sources were Internal Revenue Service, *Statistics of Income: Individual Income Tax Returns*, and U.S. Bureau of the Census, *Census of Population*.

Documentation

The income measure refers to income after corporate income taxes and employer-paid payroll taxes, but before individual income taxes and individual payments of payroll taxes. It excludes capital gains, though the authors elsewhere consider the effects of including capital gains. Note that the population unit is a tax unit, not a family or household or consumption unit or individual.

TABLE Be30–38 Distribution of household money income after taxes: 1980–1998[1]

Contributed by Peter H. Lindert

	Mean	Median	Share received by							Gini coefficient
			Bottom quintile	Second quintile	Third quintile	Fourth quintile	Top quintile	Top 5 percent		
	Be30	Be31	Be32	Be33	Be34	Be35	Be36	Be37		Be38
Year	Dollars	Dollars	Percent	Percent	Percent	Percent	Percent	Percent		Share
1980	16,272	14,551	4.9	11.6	17.9	25.1	40.6	14.1		0.354
1981	17,495	15,522	4.9	11.5	17.8	25.0	40.9	14.2		0.358
1982	18,926	16,532	4.7	11.3	17.5	24.8	41.8	14.8		0.366
1983	20,147	17,427	4.7	11.1	17.4	24.8	42.1	15.0		0.374
1984	21,564	18,530	4.7	11.0	17.2	24.8	42.3	15.2		0.378
1985	22,646	19,401	4.6	11.0	17.2	24.7	42.6	15.4		0.385
1986	23,683	20,354	4.4	10.9	17.2	24.8	42.6	15.3		0.409
1987	25,110	21,540	4.5	10.9	17.2	24.8	42.5	15.4		0.382
1988	26,371	22,431	4.5	10.9	17.1	24.6	42.9	15.8		0.385
1989	28,156	23,774	4.6	10.8	16.9	24.4	43.3	16.2		0.389
1990	29,188	24,546	4.5	10.8	16.9	24.3	43.5	16.5		0.382
1991	29,640	24,955	4.5	10.8	16.9	24.6	43.2	16.0		0.380
1992	30,425	25,474	4.4	10.6	16.8	24.5	43.6	16.5		0.385
1993	32,092	26,112	4.3	10.4	16.3	24.0	45.0	18.1		0.398
1994	33,315	26,973	4.4	10.4	16.3	23.9	45.1	18.1		0.400
1995	34,592	28,249	4.5	10.5	16.4	23.9	44.6	17.9		0.394
1996	36,008	29,312	4.5	10.5	16.3	24.0	44.7	17.9		0.398
1997	37,656	30,648	4.4	10.5	16.3	24.0	44.8	18.0		0.403
1998	38,963	32,064	4.4	10.6	16.5	24.2	44.3	17.4		0.405

[1] See text for Table Be1–18 for a discussion of numerous methodological changes.

Source

U.S. Census Bureau Internet site, Tables RDI-1, RDI-3, and RDI-5, accessed on June 23, 2000.

Documentation

To estimate after-tax income, the Census Bureau resorts to simulation, rather than actual survey data, to estimate taxes paid.

The Gini coefficient used is described in definition 14 of census experimental Table RDI-5: income after maximum deduction of taxes and maximum addition of transfers in kind.

DISTRIBUTION OF WEALTH

Peter H. Lindert

TABLE Be39–46 Distribution of household wealth: 1774–1998

Contributed by Peter H. Lindert

		Household sector net worth				Household sector total assets		
		Share held by				Share held by		
	Wealth-holder population type	Top 1 percent	Top 10 percent	Gini coefficient	Percentage held by top 1 percent (including pensions and Social Security)	Top 1 percent	Top 10 percent	Gini coefficient
	Be39	Be40	Be41	Be42	Be43	Be44	Be45	Be46
Year	—	Percent	Percent	Share	Percent	Percent	Percent	Share
1774	all households	16.5	59.0	—	—	14.8	55.1	—
1774	free households	14.3	53.2	0.694	—	12.6	49.6	0.642
1774	all adult males	16.5	58.4	—	—	13.2	54.3	—
1774	free adult males	14.2	52.5	0.688	—	12.4	48.7	0.632
1860	all adult males	—	—	—	—	32.7 [1]	76.8 [1]	—
1860	free adult males	—	—	—	—	29.0	73.0	0.832
1870	all adult males	—	—	—	—	27.0	70.0	0.833
1890	families	25.8	72.2	—	—	—	—	—
1922	households	40.1	—	—	34.3	25.5	—	—
1929	households	48.3	—	—	41.1	30.7	—	—
1933	households	36.4	—	—	28.7	—	—	—
1939	households	39.8	—	—	30.2	25.3	—	—
1945	households	32.6	—	—	22.0	20.7	—	—
1949	households	29.6	—	—	20.7	18.8	—	—
1953	households	34.1	—	—	23.1	21.7	—	—
1962	households	31.5	65.9 [1]	0.731	21.9	22.1	—	—
1965	households	34.8	—	—	23.3	23.9	—	—
1969	households	37.6	—	—	20.9	21.6	—	—
1972	households	34.0	—	—	19.0	20.2	—	—
1976	households	21.8	—	—	13.3	12.7	—	—
1979	households	22.4	—	—	12.9	—	—	—
1981	households	27.2	—	—	15.5	—	—	—
1983	households	33.8	69.0 [1]	0.739	19.0	28.6	—	0.703
1986	households	34.9	—	—	19.3	—	—	—
1989	households	37.4	—	—	21.2	—	—	—
1992	households	37.2	—	—	—	—	—	—
1995	households	38.5	—	—	—	—	—	—
1998	households	38.1	—	—	—	—	—	—

[1] Value is mean of range reported in source. See text.

Sources

1774: Alice Hanson Jones, *American Colonial Wealth: Documents and Methods*, volume 3 (Arno Press, 1977), Table 8.1.

1860–1870: Lee Soltow, *Men and Wealth in the United States, 1850–1870* (Yale University Press, 1975), Table 4.2, p. 99.

1890: G. K. Holmes, "The Concentration of Wealth," *Political Science Quarterly* 8 (1893): 589–600.

1922–1989, except for the top 1 percent of net worth: Edward N. Wolff and Marcia Marley, "Long-Term Trends in U.S. Wealth Inequality: Methodological Issues and Results," in Robert E. Lipsey and Helen Stone Tice, editors, *The Measurement of Saving, Investment, and Wealth* (University of Chicago Press, 1989), pp. 765–839; with updating by Wolff, "Trends in Household Wealth in the United States, 1962–83 and 1983–89," *Review of Income and Wealth* 40 (2) (1994): 143–74.

1922–1998, the top 1 percent of net worth: Wolff has offered an updated series rebased to the 1989 Survey of Consumer Finances, a series that also excludes consumer durables. This new series is explained in Edward N. Wolff, "Recent Trends in Wealth Ownership, 1983–1998," in Thomas M. Shapiro and Edward N. Wolff, editors, *Assets and the Disadvantaged: The Benefits of Spreading Asset Ownership* (Russell Sage Foundation, 2001). Wolff has extended this revised top 1 percent series back to 1929 in correspondence with Peter H. Lindert.

Documentation

The varied estimates are discussed and compared in Jeffrey G. Williamson and Peter H. Lindert, *American Inequality: A Macroeconomic History* (Academic Press, 1980), Chapter 3, and also in "Three Centuries of Inequality in Britain and America," in A. B. Atkinson and François Bourguignon, editors, *Handbook of Income Distribution*, volume 1 (Elsevier Science, 2000), pp. 167–216. For an exploration of how sensitive the 1774–1860 comparisons might be with differences in sampling and data definition, see Martin Shanahan and Margaret Corell, "How Much More Unequal? Consistent Estimates of the Distribution of Wealth in the United States between 1774 and 1860," *Journal of Income Distribution* 9 (2000): 27–37.

The 1774 estimates are based on 919 probate inventories. The estimates follow the usual nationality convention (comparable with gross national product, not gross domestic product) of focusing on residents' incomes and wealth, not on income earned or wealth held in this country by residents of other countries. Thus, they are meant to exclude the wealth held in the thirteen Colonies by residents of Britain, the West Indies, Canada, and other places outside these colonies.

TABLE Be39–46 Distribution of household wealth: 1774–1998 *Continued*

For 1860 and 1870, Lee Soltow's spin samples of the census consist of 13,696 men in 1860 and 9,823 men in 1870, where men are defined as males ages 20 and older.

For the top 1 percent of net worth, 1922–1998, Wolff has offered an updated series rebased to the 1989 Survey of Consumer Finances – a series that also excludes consumer durables. This new series is explained in Wolff (2001). Wolff has extended this revised top 1 percent series back to 1922 in correspondence with Peter H. Lindert, and the revisions back to 1922 are shown here.

Means are given in the table for the following ranges reported by the source: series Be41, 58.7–73.0 (1962) and 60.1–77.9 (1983); series Be44, 30.3–35.0 (1860, all adult males); and series Be44, 74.6–79.0 (1860, all adult males).

TABLE Be47–54 Distribution of taxable wealth of male household heads in Massachusetts: 1820–1910

Contributed by Peter H. Lindert

	Share of taxable wealth held by				Standard errors			
					Share of taxable wealth held by			
	Top 20 percent	Top 5 percent	Top 1 percent	Gini coefficient for taxable wealth holding	Top 20 percent	Top 5 percent	Top 1 percent	Gini coefficient for taxable wealth holding
	Be47	Be48	Be49	Be50	Be51	Be52	Be53	Be54
Year	Percent	Percent	Percent	Share	Percent	Percent	Percent	Share
1820	72.0	40.5	20.3	0.720	1.7	2.7	2.8	0.015
1830	77.6	49.2	28.9	0.775	2.2	4.5	5.3	0.020
1840	78.3	45.0	20.0	0.771	1.6	2.8	2.4	0.013
1850	85.8	55.7	33.4	0.836	1.7	4.5	4.6	0.016
1860	88.1	55.7	27.0	0.844	1.4	3.5	3.2	0.012
1870	90.1	56.7	27.2	0.856	1.2	3.3	2.9	0.011
1880	93.7	60.3	29.1	0.877	1.2	4.1	5.0	0.012
1900	97.3	70.5	37.2	0.911	0.9	4.0	5.6	0.011
1910	98.3	68.7	35.0	0.910	0.8	3.8	4.6	0.010

Source

Richard H. Steckel and Carolyn M. Moehling, "Rising Inequality: Trends in the Distribution of Wealth in Industrializing New England," *Journal of Economic History* 61 (1) (2001), Table 3.

Documentation

Steckel and Moehling used tobit regressions to control for the effects of age, occupational group, race, nativity, and illiteracy on men's taxable wealth, in a pooled sample consisting of about a thousand male household heads for each of these ten census years. They then applied the regression patterns to group population weights to estimate the overall distribution of taxable wealth. They estimated the approximate standard errors for each inequality measure by econometric bootstrapping.

MEAN AND MEDIAN INCOME

Peter H. Lindert

TABLE Be55–66 Median and mean money income of households before taxes, and Gini coefficients, by race and ethnicity of householder: 1967–1998[1]

Contributed by Peter H. Lindert

	Households			Household income						Gini coefficient of income inequality		
				Median			Mean					
	White	Black	Hispanic origin	White	Black	Hispanic origin	White	Black	Hispanic origin	White	Black	Hispanic origin
	Be55	Be56	Be57	Be58	Be59	Be60	Be61	Be62	Be63	Be64	Be65	Be66
Year	Thousand	Thousand	Thousand	Dollars	Dollars	Dollars	Dollars	Dollars	Dollars	Share	Share	Share
1967	54,188	5,728	—	7,449	4,325	—	8,281	5,197	—	0.391	0.432	—
1968	55,394	5,870	—	8,062	4,754	—	9,075	5,790	—	0.381	0.412	—
1969	56,248	6,053	—	8,755	5,292	—	9,898	6,300	—	0.383	0.411	—
1970	57,575	6,180	—	9,097	5,537	—	10,351	6,761	—	0.387	0.422	—
1971	59,463	6,578	—	9,443	5,578	—	10,759	6,912	—	0.389	0.419	—
1972	60,618	6,809	2,655	10,173	5,938	7,677	11,725	7,501	8,824	0.393	0.427	0.373
1973	61,965	7,040	2,722	11,017	6,485	8,144	12,627	8,053	9,462	0.389	0.419	0.371
1974	62,984	7,263	2,897	11,710	6,964	8,906	13,579	8,661	10,317	0.387	0.414	0.376
1975	64,392	7,489	2,948	12,340	7,408	8,865	14,288	9,247	10,524	0.390	0.419	0.388
1976	65,353	7,776	3,081	13,289	7,902	9,569	15,496	10,096	11,308	0.391	0.421	0.387
1977	66,934	7,977	3,304	14,272	8,422	10,647	16,729	10,791	12,565	0.394	0.425	0.383
1978	68,028	8,066	3,291	15,660	9,411	11,803	18,387	12,027	13,942	0.394	0.431	0.385
1979	70,766	8,586	3,684	17,259	10,133	13,042	20,325	13,002	15,780	0.396	0.433	0.396
1980	71,872	8,847	3,906	18,684	10,764	13,651	21,913	13,970	16,674	0.394	0.439	0.405
1981	72,845	8,961	3,980	20,153	11,309	15,300	23,742	14,856	18,373	0.397	0.440	0.398
1982	73,182	8,916	4,085	21,117	11,968	15,178	25,311	15,747	18,732	0.403	0.442	0.417
1983	74,376	9,236	4,326	21,902	12,429	15,906	26,455	16,531	19,369	0.404	0.448	0.413
1984	75,328	9,480	4,883	23,647	13,471	16,992	28,597	17,966	21,129	0.405	0.450	0.420
1985	76,576	9,797	5,213	24,908	14,819	17,465	30,259	19,335	21,823	0.411	0.450	0.418
1986	77,284	9,922	5,418	26,175	15,080	18,352	32,040	20,232	23,173	0.415	0.464	0.424
1987	78,519	10,192	5,642	27,458	15,672	19,336	33,795	21,161	24,786	0.415	0.468	0.441
1988	79,734	10,561	5,910	28,781	16,407	20,359	35,468	22,477	25,993	0.416	0.468	0.437
1989	80,163	10,486	5,933	30,406	18,083	21,921	38,041	23,995	27,992	0.422	0.461	0.430
1990	80,968	10,671	6,220	31,231	18,676	22,330	38,912	24,814	27,972	0.419	0.464	0.425
1991	81,675	11,083	6,379	31,569	18,807	22,691	39,523	25,043	28,872	0.418	0.464	0.427
1992	81,795	11,269	7,153	32,209	18,755	22,597	40,594	25,450	28,822	0.423	0.470	0.430
1993	82,387	11,281	7,362	32,960	19,533	22,886	43,285	27,229	30,291	0.444	0.484	0.447
1994	83,737	11,655	7,735	34,028	21,027	23,421	45,034	29,259	31,582	0.448	0.477	0.459
1995	84,511	11,577	7,939	35,766	22,393	22,860	46,729	30,400	31,201	0.442	0.468	0.455
1996	85,059	12,109	8,225	37,161	23,482	24,906	48,994	32,460	34,005	0.446	0.479	0.457
1997	86,106	12,474	8,590	38,972	25,050	26,628	51,902	32,963	35,883	0.453	0.458	0.458
1998	87,212	12,579	9,060	40,912	25,351	28,330	54,207	34,139	38,280	0.450	0.466	0.460

[1] See text for Table Be1–18 for a discussion of numerous methodological changes.

Source

U.S. Census Bureau Internet site, Historical Income Tables H-4 and H-5, accessed June 23, 2000.

Documentation

The source also gives the median and mean incomes for Asia and Pacific Islanders back to 1988, and for non-Hispanic whites back to 1972.

TABLE Be67–84 Median and mean money income of families before taxes, by type of family: 1947–1998[1]

Contributed by Peter H. Lindert

	All families			Married-couple families					
		Family income before taxes		All			Wife in paid labor force		
					Family income before taxes			Family income before taxes	
	Number	Median	Mean	Number	Median	Mean	Number	Median	Mean
	Be67	Be68	Be69	Be70	Be71	Be72	Be73	Be74	Be75
Year	Thousand	Dollars	Dollars	Thousand	Dollars	Dollars	Thousand	Dollars	Dollars
1947	37,237	3,031	—	32,288	3,109	—	—	—	—
1948	38,624	3,187	—	33,538	3,272	—	—	—	—
1949	39,303	3,107	—	34,291	3,195	—	—	3,857	—
1950	39,929	3,319	—	34,556	3,446	—	—	4,003	—
1951	40,578	3,709	—	35,196	3,837	—	8,044	4,631	—
1952	40,832	3,890	—	35,782	4,061	—	9,154	4,900	—
1953	41,202	4,242	—	—	4,371	—	—	5,405	—
1954	41,951	4,167	—	36,395	4,333	—	9,005	5,336	—
1955	42,889	4,418	—	37,200	4,599	—	9,786	5,622	—
1956	43,497	4,780	—	37,849	4,973	—	10,266	5,957	—
1957	43,696	4,966	—	38,112	5,157	—	10,696	6,141	—
1958	44,232	5,087	—	38,585	5,315	—	11,014	6,214	—
1959	45,111	5,417	—	39,335	5,662	—	11,265	6,705	—
1960	45,539	5,620	—	39,624	5,873	—	12,007	6,900	—
1961	46,418	5,735	—	40,405	6,037	—	12,366	7,188	—
1962	47,059	5,956	—	40,923	6,263	—	13,028	7,461	—
1963	47,540	6,249	—	41,311	6,593	—	13,398	7,789	—
1964	47,956	6,569	—	41,647	6,932	—	13,647	8,170	—
1965	48,509	6,957	—	42,108	7,265	—	14,183	8,597	—
1966	49,214	7,532	—	42,553	7,838	—	15,005	9,246	—
1967	50,111	7,933	8,801	43,292	8,441	9,508	15,845	9,956	10,803
1968	50,823	8,632	9,670	43,841	9,144	10,222	16,638	10,686	11,490
1969	51,237	9,433	10,577	44,436	10,001	11,187	17,464	11,629	12,576
1970	51,948	9,867	11,106	44,739	10,516	11,774	17,568	12,276	13,315
1971	53,296	10,285	11,583	45,752	10,990	12,336	18,274	12,853	13,882
1972	54,373	11,116	12,625	46,314	11,903	13,477	18,888	13,897	15,094
1973	55,053	12,051	13,622	46,812	13,028	14,594	19,464	15,237	16,439
1974	55,698	12,902	14,711	47,069	13,923	15,767	20,404	16,221	17,538
1975	56,245	13,719	15,546	47,318	14,867	16,693	20,833	17,237	18,633
1976	56,710	14,958	16,870	47,497	16,203	18,206	21,554	18,731	20,396
1977	57,215	16,009	18,264	47,385	17,616	19,798	21,936	20,268	22,153
1978	57,804	17,640	20,091	47,692	19,340	21,804	23,005	22,109	24,445
1979	59,550	19,587	22,316	49,112	21,429	24,222	24,187	24,861	27,236
1980	60,309	21,023	23,974	49,294	23,141	26,128	24,752	26,879	29,291
1981	61,019	22,388	25,838	49,630	25,065	28,253	25,002	29,247	31,757
1982	61,393	23,433	27,391	49,908	26,019	29,992	25,480	30,342	33,729
1983	61,997	24,580	28,638	50,090	27,286	31,467	26,177	32,107	35,751
1984	62,706	26,433	31,052	50,350	29,612	34,156	26,938	34,668	38,570
1985	63,558	27,735	32,944	50,933	31,100	36,267	27,489	36,431	41,058
1986	64,491	29,458	34,924	51,537	32,805	38,672	28,498	38,346	43,635
1987	65,204	30,970	36,884	51,675	34,879	40,818	29,010	40,751	—
1988	65,837	32,191	38,608	52,100	36,389	42,801	29,713	42,709	—
1989	66,090	34,213	41,506	52,317	38,547	45,995	30,188	45,266	—
1990	66,322	35,353	42,652	52,147	39,895	47,528	30,298	46,777	—
1991	67,173	35,939	43,237	52,457	40,995	48,480	30,923	48,169	—
1992	68,216	36,573	44,221	53,090	41,890	49,755	31,389	49,775	—
1993	68,506	36,959	47,221	53,181	43,005	53,472	32,194	51,204	—
1994	69,313	38,782	49,340	53,865	44,959	55,944	32,902	53,309	—
1995	69,597	40,611	51,353	53,570	47,062	58,377	32,677	55,823	—
1996	70,241	42,300	53,676	53,604	49,707	61,214	33,242	58,381	—
1997	70,884	44,568	56,902	54,321	51,591	64,678	33,535	60,669	—
1998	71,551	46,737	59,589	54,778	54,180	67,875	33,680	63,751	76,431

Note appears at end of table

(continued)

TABLE Be67–84 Median and mean money income of families before taxes, by type of family: 1947–1998 *Continued*

	Married-couple families			Male householder, wife absent			Female householder, husband absent		
	Wife not in paid labor force								
		Family income before taxes			Family income before taxes			Family income before taxes	
	Number	Median	Mean	Number	Median	Mean	Number	Median	Mean
	Be76	Be77	Be78	Be79	Be80	Be81	Be82	Be83	Be84
Year	Thousand	Dollars	Dollars	Thousand	Dollars	Dollars	Thousand	Dollars	Dollars
1947	—	—	—	1,234	2,936	—	3,757	2,172	—
1948	—	—	—	1,287	3,295	—	3,713	2,064	—
1949	—	3,058	—	1,265	2,821	—	3,637	2,103	—
1950	—	3,315	—	1,226	3,115	—	4,040	1,922	—
1951	27,152	3,634	—	1,216	3,452	—	4,030	2,220	—
1952	26,628	3,812	—	1,396	3,615	—	3,842	2,235	—
1953	—	4,117	—	—	4,113	—	—	2,455	—
1954	27,390	4,051	—	1,314	4,014	—	4,225	2,294	—
1955	27,414	4,326	—	1,404	4,190	—	4,239	2,471	—
1956	27,583	4,645	—	1,230	4,167	—	4,366	2,754	—
1957	27,416	4,833	—	1,292	4,581	—	4,310	2,763	—
1958	27,571	4,983	—	1,285	4,260	—	4,332	2,741	—
1959	28,070	5,317	—	1,233	4,613	—	4,494	2,764	—
1960	27,617	5,520	—	1,202	4,860	—	4,609	2,968	—
1961	28,039	5,592	—	1,293	5,069	—	4,643	2,993	—
1962	27,895	5,764	—	1,334	5,711	—	4,741	3,131	—
1963	27,913	6,039	—	1,243	5,710	—	4,882	3,211	—
1964	28,000	6,338	—	1,182	5,792	—	5,006	3,458	—
1965	27,925	6,592	—	1,179	6,148	—	4,992	3,532	—
1966	27,548	7,128	—	1,197	6,432	—	5,172	4,010	—
1967	27,447	7,611	8,760	1,210	6,814	7,899	5,333	4,294	5,305
1968	27,203	8,215	9,447	1,229	7,321	8,185	5,439	4,477	5,549
1969	26,972	8,879	10,288	1,221	8,340	9,662	5,580	4,822	5,915
1970	27,172	9,304	10,778	1,258	9,012	10,476	5,950	5,093	6,213
1971	27,478	9,744	11,307	1,353	8,722	9,911	6,191	5,114	6,388
1972	27,426	10,556	12,363	1,453	10,305	11,657	6,607	5,342	6,862
1973	27,348	11,418	13,281	1,438	10,742	12,219	6,804	5,797	7,228
1974	26,665	12,231	14,411	1,399	11,658	13,343	7,230	6,488	8,106
1975	26,486	12,752	15,166	1,444	12,995	14,686	7,482	6,844	8,463
1976	25,944	13,931	16,386	1,500	12,860	14,733	7,713	7,211	9,058
1977	25,449	15,063	17,768	1,594	14,518	16,355	8,236	7,765	9,811
1978	24,686	16,156	19,343	1,655	15,966	18,784	8,458	8,537	10,689
1979	24,925	17,706	21,297	1,733	16,808	20,047	8,705	9,880	12,014
1980	24,542	18,972	22,938	1,933	17,519	20,820	9,082	10,408	12,953
1981	24,628	20,325	24,696	1,986	19,889	22,607	9,403	10,960	13,773
1982	24,428	21,299	26,094	2,016	20,140	22,907	9,469	11,484	14,635
1983	23,913	21,890	26,777	2,030	21,845	24,949	9,878	11,789	15,052
1984	23,412	23,582	29,078	2,228	23,325	27,037	10,129	12,803	16,501
1985	23,445	24,556	30,650	2,414	22,622	27,525	10,211	13,660	17,647
1986	23,038	25,803	32,533	2,510	24,962	29,472	10,445	13,647	17,743
1987	22,664	26,640	—	2,834	25,208	30,786	10,696	14,683	19,489
1988	22,387	27,220	—	2,847	26,827	32,501	10,890	15,346	20,144
1989	22,129	28,747	—	2,884	27,847	34,756	10,890	16,442	21,730
1990	21,849	30,265	—	2,907	29,046	34,685	11,268	16,932	22,140
1991	21,534	30,075	—	3,025	28,351	34,611	11,692	16,692	21,946
1992	21,701	30,174	—	3,065	27,576	34,070	12,061	17,025	22,441
1993	20,988	30,218	—	2,914	26,467	33,585	12,411	17,443	23,635
1994	20,962	31,176	—	3,228	27,751	34,663	12,220	18,236	24,105
1995	20,893	32,375	—	3,513	30,358	37,238	12,514	19,691	25,249
1996	20,362	33,748	—	3,847	31,600	40,013	12,790	19,911	26,196
1997	20,786	36,027	—	3,911	32,960	42,546	12,652	21,023	27,954
1998	21,098	37,161	54,217	3,977	35,681	43,913	12,796	22,163	28,990

[1] See text for Table Be1–18 for a discussion of numerous methodological changes.

Source

U.S. Census Bureau Internet site, Table F-7, accessed on June 28, 2000.

Documentation

The source also gives data by households as opposed to families. The household data extend back only to 1980, however, and the categories of household types differ from those of family types.

POVERTY LINES

Linda Barrington and Gordon M. Fisher

TABLE Be85–94 Minimum subsistence budgets and poverty lines, by family size: 1908–1963

Contributed by Gordon M. Fisher

		Poverty lines								
		Subcommittee on Low-Income Families		Lampman						
					Families					
	Minimum subsistence budget (Ornati)	Families	Unrelated individual	1 person (unrelated individual)	2 persons	3 persons	4 persons	5 persons	6 persons	7 or more persons
	Be85	Be86	Be87	Be88	Be89	Be90	Be91	Be92	Be93	Be94
Year	Dollars	Dollars	Dollars	Dollars	Dollars	Dollars	Dollars	Dollars	Dollars	Dollars
1908	413	—	—	—	—	—	—	—	—	—
1914	582	—	—	—	—	—	—	—	—	—
1915	620	—	—	—	—	—	—	—	—	—
1917	657	—	—	—	—	—	—	—	—	—
1918	829	—	—	—	—	—	—	—	—	—
1919	1,051	—	—	—	—	—	—	—	—	—
1920	1,128	—	—	—	—	—	—	—	—	—
1921	1,007	—	—	—	—	—	—	—	—	—
1922	1,054	—	—	—	—	—	—	—	—	—
1923	1,068	—	—	—	—	—	—	—	—	—
1924	1,083	—	—	—	—	—	—	—	—	—
1925	1,093	—	—	—	—	—	—	—	—	—
1926	1,136	—	—	—	—	—	—	—	—	—
1927	1,136	—	—	—	—	—	—	—	—	—
1928	1,136	—	—	—	—	—	—	—	—	—
1929	1,137	—	—	—	—	—	—	—	—	—
1930	1,137	—	—	—	—	—	—	—	—	—
1931	1,008	—	—	—	—	—	—	—	—	—
1932	923	—	—	—	—	—	—	—	—	—
1933	876	—	—	—	—	—	—	—	—	—
1934	791	—	—	—	—	—	—	—	—	—
1935	780	—	—	—	—	—	—	—	—	—
1936	836	—	—	—	—	—	—	—	—	—
1937	836	—	—	—	—	—	—	—	—	—
1938	836	—	—	—	—	—	—	—	—	—
1939	836	—	—	—	—	—	—	—	—	—
1940	836	—	—	—	—	—	—	—	—	—
1941	836	—	—	—	—	—	—	—	—	—
1942	993	—	—	—	—	—	—	—	—	—
1943	1,215	—	—	—	—	—	—	—	—	—
1944	1,379	—	—	—	—	—	—	—	—	—
1945	1,498	—	—	—	—	—	—	—	—	—
1946	1,627	—	—	—	—	—	—	—	—	—
1947	1,929	1,858	929	920	1,302	1,674	2,000	2,296	2,572	2,981
1948	2,107	2,000	1,000	990	1,401	1,801	2,152	2,470	2,767	3,208
1949	1,990	1,980	990	980	1,387	1,783	2,130	2,445	2,739	3,175
1950	1,932	2,000	1,000	990	1,401	1,801	2,152	2,470	2,767	3,208
1951	2,171	2,160	1,080	1,069	1,513	1,945	2,324	2,668	2,989	3,464
1952	2,171	2,208	1,104	1,093	1,547	1,989	2,376	2,728	3,056	3,541
1953	2,444	2,226	1,113	1,101	1,558	2,004	2,394	2,748	3,079	3,568
1954	2,444	2,234	1,117	1,106	1,565	2,012	2,404	2,760	3,092	3,583
1955	2,444	2,228	1,114	1,102	1,560	2,005	2,396	2,751	3,081	3,571
1956	2,444	2,260	1,130	1,119	1,583	2,036	2,432	2,792	3,128	3,625
1957	2,444	2,338	1,169	1,157	1,638	2,106	2,516	2,888	3,236	3,750
1958	2,662	2,402	1,201	1,188	1,682	2,163	2,584	2,966	3,323	3,851
1959	2,662	2,424	1,212	1,200	1,699	2,184	2,609	2,995	3,356	3,889
1960	2,662	2,462	1,231	1,217	1,723	2,216	2,647	3,038	3,404	3,945
1961	—	2,486	1,243	1,230	1,741	2,239	2,675	3,070	3,440	3,986
1962	—	2,516	1,258	1,245	1,762	2,266	2,707	3,107	3,482	4,035
1963	—	2,548	1,274	1,261	1,785	2,296	2,742	3,148	3,527	4,088

(continued)

TABLE Be85–94 Minimum subsistence budgets and poverty lines, by family size: 1908–1963 *Continued*

Sources

Series Be85. Oscar Ornati, *Poverty amid Affluence: A Report on a Research Project Carried Out at the New School for Social Research* (Twentieth Century Fund, 1966).

Series Be86–87. Gordon Fisher, "How Many Americans Were *Really* in Poverty in 1947? Estimates of the U.S. Poverty Population between 1947 and 1963 under Two Contemporary (1949 and 1959) Definitions of Poverty," presented to the Annual Meeting of the Economic History Association, October 10, 1999, Baltimore, Maryland, Appendix A. The 1948 figures are from U.S. Congress, Joint Committee on the Economy Report, *Low-Income Families and Economic Stability – Materials on the Problem of Low-Income Families Assembled by the Staff of the Subcommittee on Low-Income Families* (1949).

Series Be88 and Be94. Gordon Fisher (1999), Appendix B, except as noted for specific dates and series.

Series Be88–93, 1947, and series Be88–94, 1957. Robert J. Lampman, "The Low Income Population and Economic Growth," Study Paper number 12, pp. 1–36, in U.S. Congress, Joint Economic Committee, *Study Papers Nos. 12 and 13, The Low Income Population and Economic Growth . . . The Adequacy of Resources for Economic Growth in the United States . . . Materials Prepared in Connection with the Study of Employment, Growth, and Price Levels . . .* December 16, 1959.

Series Be88–94, 1963. Robert J. Lampman, "Population Change and Poverty Reduction, 1947–1975," in Leo Fishman, editor, *Poverty amid Affluence* (Yale University Press, 1966), p. 23.

Documentation

Refer to the appendixes to the essay on poverty in this chapter for additional discussion of the tables, as well as for various technical definitions and descriptions.

Series Be85. Ornati analyzed the costs of about sixty standard budgets prepared during the 1905–1960 period. (A standard budget is a list of goods and services that a family of a specified size and composition – and sometimes of a specified social class or occupational group – would need to live at a designated level of well-being, together with the estimated monthly or annual costs of those goods and services.) Ornati classified the standard budgets into three categories – minimum subsistence, minimum adequacy, and minimum comfort. Only the values he provided for minimum subsistence budgets are included here. Of Ornati's three categories, "minimum subsistence" best corresponds to the standard represented by Mollie Orshansky's original 1963 poverty thresholds – later to be adopted as the first official poverty line of the United States. Ornati's minimum subsistence levels are also very close to the Sub-committee on Low-Income Family (SLIF) family poverty line and Lampman's four-person poverty line. Ornati provided dollar figures for each budget that he analyzed. He standardized the budgets to that of a four-person family; when the original budget was for a five-person family, he recalculated the budget for a four-person family. For those years during the 1905–1960 period for which he did not have a budget in a given category, he provided dollar figures by interpolation. The figures in series Be85 are for only those years for which Ornati had actual "minimum subsistence" budgets – his interpolated figures are not included because they do not represent actual budgets. From a review of his descriptive and tabular material, it appears that Ornati did not have actual "minimum subsistence" budgets for 1905–1907, 1909–1913, and 1916.

Series Be86–87. Data represent poverty lines under SLIF definitions, calculated by Fisher.

Series Be88–94. Data represent poverty lines under Lampman definitions, calculated by Fisher.

TABLE Be95–112 Weighted-average official poverty thresholds and selected alternative poverty lines, by family size: 1947–1999[1]

Contributed by Linda Barrington and Gordon M. Fisher

	Weighted-average official poverty threshold – nonfarm								
	1 person (unrelated individual)			Families					
				2 persons					
	All	Younger than 65	65 and older	All	Householder younger than 65	Householder 65 and older	3 persons	4 persons	5 persons
	Be95	Be96	Be97	Be98	Be99	Be100	Be101	Be102	Be103
Year	Dollars	Dollars	Dollars	Dollars	Dollars	Dollars	Dollars	Dollars	Dollars
1947	—	—	—	—	—	—	—	—	—
1948	—	—	—	—	—	—	—	—	—
1949	—	—	—	—	—	—	—	—	—
1950	—	—	—	—	—	—	—	—	—
1951	—	—	—	—	—	—	—	—	—
1952	—	—	—	—	—	—	—	—	—
1953	—	—	—	—	—	—	—	—	—
1954	—	—	—	—	—	—	—	—	—
1955	—	—	—	—	—	—	—	—	—
1956	—	—	—	—	—	—	—	—	—
1957	—	—	—	—	—	—	—	—	—
1958	—	—	—	—	—	—	—	—	—
1959	1,467	1,503	1,397	1,894	1,952	1,761	2,324	2,973	3,506
1960	1,490	1,526	1,418	1,924	1,982	1,788	2,359	3,022	3,560
1961	1,506	1,545	1,433	1,942	2,005	1,808	2,383	3,054	3,597
1962	1,519	1,562	1,451	1,962	2,027	1,828	2,412	3,089	3,639
1963	1,539	1,581	1,470	1,988	2,052	1,850	2,442	3,128	3,685
1964	1,558	1,601	1,488	2,015	2,079	1,875	2,473	3,169	3,732

Note appears at end of table

TABLE Be95–112 Weighted-average official poverty thresholds and selected alternative poverty lines, by family size: 1947–1999 *Continued*

	Weighted-average official poverty threshold – nonfarm								
	1 person (unrelated individual)			Families					
				2 persons					
	All	Younger than 65	65 and older	All	Householder younger than 65	Householder 65 and older	3 persons	4 persons	5 persons
	Be95	Be96	Be97	Be98	Be99	Be100	Be101	Be102	Be103
Year	Dollars	Dollars	Dollars	Dollars	Dollars	Dollars	Dollars	Dollars	Dollars
1965	1,582	1,626	1,512	2,048	2,114	1,906	2,514	3,223	3,797
1966	1,628	1,674	1,556	2,107	2,175	1,961	2,588	3,317	3,908
1967	1,675	1,722	1,600	2,168	2,238	2,017	2,661	3,410	4,019
1968	1,748	1,797	1,667	2,262	2,333	2,102	2,774	3,553	4,188
1969	1,840	1,893	1,757	2,383	2,458	2,215	2,924	3,743	4,415
1970	1,954	2,010	1,861	2,525	2,604	2,348	3,099	3,968	4,680
1971	2,040	2,098	1,940	2,633	2,716	2,448	3,229	4,137	4,880
1972	2,109	2,168	2,005	2,724	2,808	2,530	3,339	4,275	5,044
1973	2,247	2,307	2,130	2,895	2,984	2,688	3,548	4,540	5,358
1974	2,495	2,562	2,364	3,211	3,312	2,982	3,936	5,038	5,950
1975	2,724	2,797	2,581	3,506	3,617	3,257	4,293	5,500	6,499
1976	2,884	2,959	2,730	3,711	3,826	3,445	4,540	5,815	6,876
1977	3,075	3,152	2,906	3,951	4,072	3,666	4,833	6,191	7,320
1978	3,311	3,392	3,127	4,249	4,383	3,944	5,201	6,662	7,880
1979	3,689	3,778	3,479	4,725	4,878	4,390	5,784	7,412	8,775
1980	4,190	4,290	3,949	5,363	5,537	4,983	6,565	8,414	9,966
1981	4,620	4,729	4,359	5,917	6,111	5,498	7,250	9,287	11,007
1982	4,901	5,019	4,626	6,281	6,487	5,836	7,693	9,862	11,684
1983	5,061	5,180	4,775	6,483	6,697	6,023	7,938	10,178	12,049
1984	5,278	5,400	4,979	6,762	6,983	6,282	8,277	10,609	12,566
1985	5,469	5,593	5,156	6,998	7,231	6,503	8,573	10,989	13,007
1986	5,572	5,701	5,255	7,138	7,372	6,630	8,737	11,203	13,259
1987	5,778	5,909	5,447	7,397	7,641	6,872	9,056	11,611	13,737
1988	6,022	6,155	5,674	7,704	7,958	7,157	9,435	12,092	14,304
1989	6,310	6,451	5,947	8,076	8,343	7,501	9,885	12,674	14,990
1990	6,652	6,800	6,268	8,509	8,794	7,905	10,419	13,359	15,792
1991	6,932	7,086	6,532	8,865	9,165	8,241	10,860	13,924	16,456
1992	7,143	7,299	6,729	9,137	9,443	8,487	11,186	14,335	16,952
1993	7,363	7,518	6,930	9,414	9,728	8,740	11,522	14,763	17,449
1994	7,547	7,710	7,108	9,661	9,976	8,967	11,821	15,141	17,900
1995	7,763	7,929	7,309	9,933	10,259	9,219	12,158	15,569	18,408
1996	7,995	8,163	7,525	10,233	10,564	9,491	12,516	16,036	18,952
1997	8,183	8,350	7,698	10,473	10,805	9,712	12,802	16,400	19,380
1998	8,316	8,480	7,818	10,634	10,972	9,862	13,003	16,660	19,680
1999	8,501	8,667	7,990	10,869	11,214	10,075	13,290	17,029	20,127

	Weighted-average official poverty threshold – nonfarm					Alternative poverty thresholds for 4-person families			
	Families							Gallup Poll Standard	
	6 persons	7 persons or more	7 persons	8 persons	9 persons or more	Near poverty	One-half median income before taxes	"Get-along"	"Poverty"
	Be104	Be105	Be106	Be107	Be108	Be109	Be110	Be111	Be112
Year	Dollars	Dollars	Dollars	Dollars	Dollars	Dollars	Dollars	Dollars	Dollars
1947	—	—	—	—	—	—	1,646	2,350	1,688
1948	—	—	—	—	—	—	1,734	2,700	1,939
1949	—	—	—	—	—	—	1,689	2,586	1,857
1950	—	—	—	—	—	—	1,838	2,495	1,792
1951	—	—	—	—	—	—	2,061	2,860	2,054
1952	—	—	—	—	—	—	2,187	3,224	2,315
1953	—	—	—	—	—	—	2,214	3,110	2,233
1954	—	—	—	—	—	—	2,384	3,320	2,384

(continued)

TABLE Be95–112 Weighted-average official poverty thresholds and selected alternative poverty lines, by family size: 1947–1999 *Continued*

	Weighted-average official poverty threshold – nonfarm					Alternative poverty thresholds for 4-person families			
	Families							Gallup Poll Standard	
	6 persons	7 persons or more	7 persons	8 persons	9 persons or more	Near poverty	One-half median income before taxes	"Get-along"	"Poverty"
	Be104	Be105	Be106	Be107	Be108	Be109	Be110	Be111	Be112
Year	Dollars	Dollars	Dollars	Dollars	Dollars	Dollars	Dollars	Dollars	Dollars
1955	—	—	—	—	—	—	2,460	—	—
1956	—	—	—	—	—	—	2,660	—	—
1957	—	—	—	—	—	—	2,744	3,888	2,792
1958	—	—	—	—	—	—	2,843	4,273	3,068
1959	3,944	4,849	—	—	—	3,716	3,035	4,316	3,099
1960	4,002	4,921	—	—	—	3,778	3,148	4,240	3,045
1961	4,041	4,967	—	—	—	3,818	3,219	4,328	3,108
1962	4,088	5,032	—	—	—	3,861	3,378	4,323	3,104
1963	4,135	5,092	—	—	—	3,910	3,569	4,328	3,108
1964	4,193	5,156	—	—	—	3,961	3,744	4,438	3,187
1965	4,264	5,248	—	—	—	4,029	3,900	—	—
1966	4,388	5,395	—	—	—	4,146	4,171	5,044	3,622
1967	4,516	5,550	—	—	—	4,263	4,497	5,772	4,145
1968	4,706	5,789	—	—	—	4,441	4,917	—	—
1969	4,958	6,101	—	—	—	4,679	5,312	6,136	4,406
1970	5,260	6,468	—	—	—	4,960	5,584	6,552	4,705
1971	5,489	6,751	—	—	—	5,171	5,813	7,072	5,078
1972	5,673	6,983	—	—	—	5,344	6,404	—	—
1973	6,028	7,435	—	—	—	5,675	6,855	7,748	5,564
1974	6,699	8,253	—	—	—	6,298	7,485	8,788	6,311
1975	7,316	9,022	—	—	—	6,875	7,924	8,372	6,012
1976	7,760	9,588	—	—	—	7,269	8,658	9,724	6,983
1977	8,261	10,216	—	—	—	7,739	9,362	10,348	7,431
1978	8,891	11,002	—	—	—	8,328	10,214	11,388	8,178
1979	9,914	12,280	—	—	—	9,265	11,256	12,688	9,111
1980	11,269	13,955	12,761	14,199	16,896	10,518	12,166	13,000	9,335
1981	12,449	—	14,110	15,655	18,572	11,609	13,137	15,808	11,352
1982	13,207	—	15,036	16,719	19,698	12,328	13,810	15,808	11,352
1983	13,630	—	15,500	17,170	20,310	12,723	14,592	16,380	11,763
1984	14,207	—	16,096	17,961	21,247	13,261	15,549	17,368	12,472
1985	14,696	—	16,656	18,512	22,083	13,736	16,389	18,148	13,032
1986	14,986	—	17,049	18,791	22,497	14,004	17,358	18,928	13,592
1987	15,509	—	17,649	19,515	23,105	14,514	18,543	—	—
1988	16,146	—	18,232	20,253	24,129	15,115	19,526	—	—
1989	16,921	—	19,162	21,328	25,480	15,843	20,382	21,788	15,646
1990	17,839	—	20,241	22,582	26,848	16,699	20,726	—	—
1991	18,587	—	21,058	23,605	27,942	17,405	21,528	—	—
1992	19,137	—	21,594	24,053	28,745	17,919	22,126	25,028	15,714
1993	19,718	—	22,383	24,838	29,529	18,454	22,581	—	17,744
1994	20,235	—	22,923	25,427	30,300	18,926	23,506	—	—
1995	20,804	—	23,552	26,237	31,280	19,461	24,844	—	—
1996	21,389	—	24,268	27,091	31,971	20,045	25,759	—	—
1997	21,886	—	24,802	27,593	32,566	20,500	26,675	—	—
1998	22,228	—	25,257	28,166	33,339	20,825	28,031	—	—
1999	22,727	—	25,912	28,967	34,417	21,286	29,991	—	—

[1] Beginning with income year 1980, separate official poverty thresholds for farm families were abolished, as were distinctions by sex of householder. See text.

Sources

Series Be95–108. U.S. Census Bureau Internet site, Historical Poverty Tables, Table 1, "Weighted Average Poverty Thresholds for Families of Specified Size: 1959 to 1999." For series Be107, the 1991 value is from *Current Population Reports*, series P-60, number 181, Table A-3, p. A-8.

Series Be110. Computed by dividing by 2 the median four-person pre-tax income found in the following sources. For all years except those noted: "Size of Family–Families (All Races) by Median and Mean Income 1947 to 1998," Table F-8, U.S. Bureau of the Census, Internet site, Historical Income Tables. For 1953 and 1954: Denton R. Vaughan, "Exploring the Use of the Public's Views to Set Income Poverty Thresholds and Adjust Them over Time," *Social Security Bulletin* 56 (2) (1993), Table 1, p. 30. For 1999: *Current Population Reports*, Consumer Income, "Money Income in the United States, 1999," series P-60, number 209, September 2000, Table 4 "Median Income of Families by Selected Characteristics, Race and Hispanic Origin of Householder: 1999, 1998, and 1997."

Series Be111–112. Vaughan (1993), Table 1, pp. 30–1. Exceptions for specific dates are as noted. For series Be111–112, the values for 1992 were obtained from Constance F. Citro and Robert T. Michael, editors, *Measuring Poverty: A New Approach* (National Research Council, 1995), Table 2-4, pp. 138–9. For series Be112, the value for 1993 was obtained by adjusting the 1992 constant-dollar figure found in Citro and Michael (1995), Table 2-4, pp. 138–9, into current dollars using the consumer price index for all urban consumers.

TABLE Be95–112 Weighted-average official poverty thresholds and selected alternative poverty lines, by family size: 1947–1999 *Continued*

Documentation

Refer to the appendixes to the essay on poverty in this chapter for additional discussion of the tables, as well as for various technical definitions and descriptions.

Series Be95–108

The Census Bureau uses a detailed threshold matrix to tabulate poverty population statistics (for example, Table Be251–259), which distinguishes by the number of adults and children in the family. However, for general purposes, the single weighted-average line for each sized family is commonly used. See the essay on poverty in this chapter for further discussion.

For income years 1959–1979, there were separate official poverty thresholds for farm and nonfarm families (and unrelated individuals). For these years, the weighted average is computed only from the nonfarm poverty lines. The separate farm thresholds, which had been lower in value than the nonfarm poverty thresholds, were eliminated for income year 1980 and subsequent years. Thus, for 1980 and subsequent years, the poverty status of a family living on a farm was determined using the same poverty line that had previously been reserved for nonfarm families. "Farm" referred only to family units actually living on farms, and not to all family units living in nonmetropolitan or "rural" areas. Correspondingly, "nonfarm" family units were a broader category than family units living in metropolitan areas, or "urban" family units. Also beginning in income year 1980, the separate thresholds for families with female householder and male householder were eliminated. For 1980 and subsequent years, the weighted average of the poverty thresholds for these two types of families were applied to all types of families, regardless of the sex of householder. Finally, beginning in 1980, the thresholds by size of family were extended from seven or more persons to nine or more persons. For a complete discussion of the threshold modifications, see Current Population Reports, series P-60, number 133.

Series Be109. The "Near Poverty Threshold" is 125 percent of the weighted-average nonfarm poverty threshold for a four-person family. The series was constructed by multiplying series Be102 by 1.25.

Series Be111. Through 1992, the American Institute of Public Opinion's Gallup Poll asked the following question: "What is the smallest amount of money a family of four (husband, wife, and two children) needs each week to get along in this community?" The response to this question is known as the "get-along" amount. See the essay on poverty in this chapter for further discussion.

Series Be112. In 1989, the Gallup Poll asked the following "poverty" question: "People who have income below a certain level can be considered poor. That level is called the 'poverty line.' What amount of weekly income would you use as a poverty line for a family of four (husband, wife, and two children) in this community?" Denton R. Vaughan used this 1989 data in conjunction with the get-along amounts to estimate the series provided here.

TABLE Be113–144 Poverty lines, by family size, sex of head, farm–nonfarm residence, and number of related children younger than age 18: 1919

Contributed by Linda Barrington

Nonfarm

Size of family	0 children		1 child		2 children		3 children		4 children		5 children		6 children		7 or more children	
	Male head	Female head	Male head	Female head	Male head	Female head	Male head	Female head	Male head	Female head	Male head	Female head	Male head	Female head	Male head	Female head
	Be113	Be114	Be115	Be116	Be117	Be118	Be119	Be120	Be121	Be122	Be123	Be124	Be125	Be126	Be127	Be128
	Dollars	Dollars	Dollars	Dollars	Dollars	Dollars	Dollars	Dollars	Dollars	Dollars	Dollars	Dollars	Dollars	Dollars	Dollars	Dollars
1	690	690	—	—	—	—	—	—	—	—	—	—	—	—	—	—
2	784	784	668	664	—	—	—	—	—	—	—	—	—	—	—	—
3	1,155	1,047	938	1,043	830	914	—	—	—	—	—	—	—	—	—	—
4	1,425	1,425	1,320	1,316	1,110	1,297	1,028	1,094	—	—	—	—	—	—	—	—
5	1,779	1,779	1,575	1,673	1,473	1,654	1,292	1,458	1,163	1,352	—	—	—	—	—	—
6	2,108	2,009	1,911	2,003	1,713	1,889	1,636	1,698	1,413	1,694	1,380	1,303	—	—	—	—
7	2,439	2,439	2,246	2,242	2,053	2,225	1,977	2,038	1,759	1,938	1,630	1,651	1,619	1,544	—	—
8	2,846	2,748	2,651	2,549	2,455	2,531	2,281	2,343	2,158	2,339	2,028	1,952	1,919	—	1,669	1,720
9 or more	3,226	3,129	3,031	2,832	2,835	2,814	2,662	2,723	2,440	2,621	2,408	2,332	—	—	1,952	—

Farm

Size of family	0 children		1 child		2 children		3 children		4 children		5 children		6 children		7 or more children	
	Male head	Female head	Male head	Female head	Male head	Female head	Male head	Female head	Male head	Female head	Male head	Female head	Male head	Female head	Male head	Female head
	Be129	Be130	Be131	Be132	Be133	Be134	Be135	Be136	Be137	Be138	Be139	Be140	Be141	Be142	Be143	Be144
	Dollars	Dollars	Dollars	Dollars	Dollars	Dollars	Dollars	Dollars	Dollars	Dollars	Dollars	Dollars	Dollars	Dollars	Dollars	Dollars
1	212	212	—	—	—	—	—	—	—	—	—	—	—	—	—	—
2	241	241	205	204	—	—	—	—	—	—	—	—	—	—	—	—
3	355	321	288	320	255	281	—	—	—	—	—	—	—	—	—	—
4	437	437	405	404	341	398	316	336	—	—	—	—	—	—	—	—
5	546	546	484	514	452	508	370	448	357	415	—	—	—	—	—	—
6	647	617	587	615	526	580	503	521	434	520	424	400	—	—	—	—
7	749	749	690	688	630	683	607	626	540	550	500	507	497	474	—	—
8	874	844	814	783	754	777	700	719	662	718	622	599	589	—	512	528
9 or more	990	960	930	869	—	864	817	836	479	805	739	716	—	—	599	—

Source

Linda Barrington, "Absolutely Relative or Relatively Absolute: The Income Elasticity of Orshansky-Method Poverty Lines, 1919–1959," presented to the Annual Meeting of the Economic History Association, October 10, 1999, Baltimore, Maryland.

Documentation

Refer to the appendixes to the essay on poverty in this chapter for additional discussion of the tables, as well as for various technical definitions and descriptions.

In general, lower poverty lines were established for families with a female householder because of the lower caloric needs of women, and thus lower minimum food costs underpinning the poverty line. The typical age distribution of children and gender distribution of adults other than the household head also differed by sex of householder, affecting the underlying food costs and poverty line. Lower farm poverty lines resulted from the lower proportion of food value purchased (the higher proportion of food grown at home).

TABLE Be145–176 Poverty lines, by family size, sex of head, farm–nonfarm residence, and number of related children younger than age 18: 1939 [Barrington]

Contributed by Linda Barrington

Nonfarm

Size of family	0 children		1 child		2 children		3 children		4 children		5 children		6 children		7 or more children	
	Male head	Female head	Male head	Female head	Male head	Female head	Male head	Female head	Male head	Female head	Male head	Female head	Male head	Female head	Male head	Female head
	Be145	Be146	Be147	Be148	Be149	Be150	Be151	Be152	Be153	Be154	Be155	Be156	Be157	Be158	Be159	Be160
	Dollars	Dollars	Dollars	Dollars	Dollars	Dollars	Dollars	Dollars	Dollars	Dollars	Dollars	Dollars	Dollars	Dollars	Dollars	Dollars
1	439	439	—	—	—	—	—	—	—	—	—	—	—	—	—	—
2	500	500	466	469	—	—	—	—	—	—	—	—	—	—	—	—
3	586	563	536	563	499	506	—	—	—	—	—	—	—	—	—	—
4	743	743	718	720	658	688	626	623	—	—	—	—	—	—	—	—
5	912	912	865	890	830	838	775	795	735	750	—	—	—	—	—	—
6	1,069	1,047	1,025	1,027	967	997	937	935	878	912	853	833	—	—	—	—
7	1,204	1,204	1,182	1,184	1,129	1,134	1,077	1,097	1,040	1,052	995	995	922	935	—	—
8	1,401	1,401	1,356	1,379	1,321	1,329	1,271	1,289	1,209	1,244	1,187	1,167	1,094	1,129	1,037	1,015
9 or more	1,563	1,563	1,541	1,563	1,483	1,511	1,453	1,451	1,394	1,428	1,349	1,349	1,276	1,289	1,217	1,197

Farm

Size of family	0 children		1 child		2 children		3 children		4 children		5 children		6 children		7 or more children	
	Male head	Female head	Male head	Female head	Male head	Female head	Male head	Female head	Male head	Female head	Male head	Female head	Male head	Female head	Male head	Female head
	Be161	Be162	Be163	Be164	Be165	Be166	Be167	Be168	Be169	Be170	Be171	Be172	Be173	Be174	Be175	Be176
	Dollars	Dollars	Dollars	Dollars	Dollars	Dollars	Dollars	Dollars	Dollars	Dollars	Dollars	Dollars	Dollars	Dollars	Dollars	Dollars
1	277	277	—	—	—	—	—	—	—	—	—	—	—	—	—	—
2	316	316	297	297	—	—	—	—	—	—	—	—	—	—	—	—
3	370	355	340	355	312	316	—	—	—	—	—	—	—	—	—	—
4	471	471	451	455	417	436	394	394	—	—	—	—	—	—	—	—
5	575	575	548	563	525	529	490	502	463	471	—	—	—	—	—	—
6	675	660	644	648	610	629	590	590	556	575	536	525	—	—	—	—
7	760	760	745	748	714	718	683	691	656	664	629	629	583	590	—	—
8	887	887	856	872	837	841	802	814	764	787	748	741	691	714	652	640
9 or more	988	988	972	988	937	953	918	918	880	903	853	853	806	814	768	756

Source

Linda Barrington, "Estimating Poverty in 1939: A Comparison of Orshansky Method and Price Indexed Definitions of Poverty," *Review of Economics and Statistics* 79 (3) (August 1997): 406–14.

Documentation

See the text for Table Be113–144.

TABLE Be177–204 Official poverty thresholds, by family size, sex of head, farm–nonfarm residence, and number of related children younger than age 18: 1959

Contributed by Linda Barrington and Gordon M. Fisher

Nonfarm

Size of family (age of the head)	0 children		1 child		2 children		3 children		4 children		5 children		6 or more children	
	Male head	Female head	Male head	Female head	Male head	Female head	Male head	Female head	Male head	Female head	Male head	Female head	Male head	Female head
	Be177	Be178	Be179	Be180	Be181	Be182	Be183	Be184	Be185	Be186	Be187	Be188	Be189	Be190
	Dollars	Dollars	Dollars	Dollars	Dollars	Dollars	Dollars	Dollars	Dollars	Dollars	Dollars	Dollars	Dollars	Dollars
1 (under 65)	1,572	1,454	—	—	—	—	—	—	—	—	—	—	—	—
1 (65 and over)	1,412	1,394	—	—	—	—	—	—	—	—	—	—	—	—
2 (under age 65)	1,965	1,815	2,201	1,982	—	—	—	—	—	—	—	—	—	—
2 (65 and over)	1,764	1,742	2,201	1,982	—	—	—	—	—	—	—	—	—	—
3	2,288	2,213	2,362	2,109	2,496	2,332	—	—	—	—	—	—	—	—
4	3,016	2,836	3,061	3,000	2,955	2,986	3,105	2,955	—	—	—	—	—	—
5	3,640	3,476	3,683	3,581	3,565	3,565	3,476	3,536	3,550	3,417	—	—	—	—
6	4,175	4,056	4,189	4,130	4,100	4,100	4,011	4,070	3,892	3,937	3,952	3,817	—	—
7 or more	5,258	5,094	5,303	5,169	5,199	5,154	5,109	5,109	4,991	4,976	4,812	4,872	4,769	4,634

Farm

Size of family (age of the head)	0 children		1 child		2 children		3 children		4 children		5 children		6 or more children	
	Male head	Female head	Male head	Female head	Male head	Female head	Male head	Female head	Male head	Female head	Male head	Female head	Male head	Female head
	Be191	Be192	Be193	Be194	Be195	Be196	Be197	Be198	Be199	Be200	Be201	Be202	Be203	Be204
	Dollars	Dollars	Dollars	Dollars	Dollars	Dollars	Dollars	Dollars	Dollars	Dollars	Dollars	Dollars	Dollars	Dollars
1 (under 65)	1,336	1,236	—	—	—	—	—	—	—	—	—	—	—	—
1 (65 and over)	1,200	1,185	—	—	—	—	—	—	—	—	—	—	—	—
2 (under age 65)	1,670	1,543	1,871	1,685	—	—	—	—	—	—	—	—	—	—
2 (65 and over)	1,499	1,481	1,871	1,685	—	—	—	—	—	—	—	—	—	—
3	1,945	1,881	2,008	1,793	2,122	1,982	—	—	—	—	—	—	—	—
4	2,564	2,462	2,602	2,550	2,512	2,538	2,639	2,512	—	—	—	—	—	—
5	3,094	2,955	3,131	3,044	3,030	3,030	2,955	3,006	3,018	2,904	—	—	—	—
6	3,549	3,448	3,561	3,511	3,485	3,485	3,409	3,460	3,308	3,346	3,359	3,244	—	—
7 or more	4,469	4,330	4,508	4,394	4,419	4,381	4,343	4,343	4,242	4,230	4,090	4,141	4,054	3,939

Source

Mollie Orshansky, 1965, "Counting the Poor: Another Look at the Poverty Profile," *Social Security Bulletin* 28 (1): 3–29, and unpublished data from the U.S. Social Security Administration.

Documentation

Refer to the appendixes to the essay on poverty in this chapter for additional discussion of the tables, as well as for various technical definitions and descriptions.

Since its construction, the official poverty threshold has distinguished between families of heads younger than age 65 and those with heads age 65 and older. The poverty threshold is set lower for those age 65 and older. This level was established because of the lower caloric needs of the elderly, and thus lower minimum food costs underpinning the poverty threshold. Similarly, lower poverty thresholds were generally set for families with a female head because of the lower caloric needs of women, and thus lower minimum food costs underpinning the poverty threshold. The typical age distribution of children and gender distribution of adults other than the household head also differed by sex of head, affecting the underlying food costs and poverty line. Lower farm thresholds resulted from the lower proportion of food value purchased (the higher proportion of food grown at home).

TABLE Be205–232 Official poverty thresholds, by family size, sex of head, farm–nonfarm residence, and number of related children younger than age 18: 1969

Contributed by Gordon M. Fisher

	Nonfarm													
	0 children		1 child		2 children		3 children		4 children		5 children		6 or more children	
	Male head	Female head	Male head	Female head	Male head	Female head	Male head	Female head	Male head	Female head	Male head	Female head	Male head	Female head
Size of family	Be205	Be206	Be207	Be208	Be209	Be210	Be211	Be212	Be213	Be214	Be215	Be216	Be217	Be218
(age of head)	Dollars	Dollars	Dollars	Dollars	Dollars	Dollars	Dollars	Dollars	Dollars	Dollars	Dollars	Dollars	Dollars	Dollars
1 (younger than 65)	1,980	1,830	—	—	—	—	—	—	—	—	—	—	—	—
1 (65 and older)	1,770	1,750	—	—	—	—	—	—	—	—	—	—	—	—
2 (younger than 65)	2,470	2,280	2,770	2,490	—	—	—	—	—	—	—	—	—	—
2 (65 and older)	2,220	2,190	2,770	2,490	—	—	—	—	—	—	—	—	—	—
3	2,880	2,780	2,970	2,650	3,140	2,930	—	—	—	—	—	—	—	—
4	3,790	3,640	3,850	3,770	3,720	3,750	3,900	3,720	—	—	—	—	—	—
5	4,570	4,370	4,630	4,500	4,480	4,480	4,370	4,440	4,460	4,290	—	—	—	—
6	5,250	5,100	5,270	5,190	5,150	5,150	5,040	5,120	4,890	4,950	4,970	4,800	—	—
7 or more	6,610	6,400	6,670	6,500	6,540	6,480	6,420	6,420	6,270	6,260	6,050	6,120	5,990	5,830

	Farm													
	0 children		1 child		2 children		3 children		4 children		5 children		6 or more children	
	Male head	Female head	Male head	Female head	Male head	Female head	Male head	Female head	Male head	Female head	Male head	Female head	Male head	Female head
Size of family	Be219	Be220	Be221	Be222	Be223	Be224	Be225	Be226	Be227	Be228	Be229	Be230	Be231	Be232
(age of head)	Dollars	Dollars	Dollars	Dollars	Dollars	Dollars	Dollars	Dollars	Dollars	Dollars	Dollars	Dollars	Dollars	Dollars
1 (younger than 65)	1,680	1,550	—	—	—	—	—	—	—	—	—	—	—	—
1 (65 and older)	1,510	1,490	—	—	—	—	—	—	—	—	—	—	—	—
2 (younger than 65)	2,100	1,940	2,350	2,120	—	—	—	—	—	—	—	—	—	—
2 (65 and older)	1,880	1,860	2,350	2,120	—	—	—	—	—	—	—	—	—	—
3	2,440	2,360	2,520	2,250	2,670	2,490	—	—	—	—	—	—	—	—
4	3,220	3,100	3,270	3,210	3,160	3,190	3,320	3,160	—	—	—	—	—	—
5	3,890	3,710	3,940	3,830	3,810	3,810	3,710	3,780	3,790	3,650	—	—	—	—
6	4,460	4,330	4,480	4,410	4,380	4,380	4,290	4,350	4,160	4,210	4,220	4,080	—	—
7 or more	5,620	5,440	5,670	5,520	5,560	5,510	5,460	5,460	5,330	5,320	5,140	5,210	5,100	4,950

Source

U.S. Census Bureau, *Census of the Population: 1970*, Subject Reports, Final Report PC (2)-9A, "Low Income Population," Table A-1, "Poverty Cutoffs and Weighted Average Thresholds at the Poverty Level in 1969 by Size of Family and Presence of Related Children under 18 Years Old, and Sex of Head: 1970," p. 457.

Documentation

See the text for Table Be177–204.

TABLE Be233–241 Official poverty thresholds, by family size and number of related children younger than age 18: 1979

Contributed by Gordon M. Fisher

Size of family (age of the head)	0 children	1 child	2 children	3 children	4 children	5 children	6 children	7 children	8 or more children
	Be233	Be234	Be235	Be236	Be237	Be238	Be239	Be240	Be241
	Dollars	Dollars	Dollars	Dollars	Dollars	Dollars	Dollars	Dollars	Dollars
1 (younger than 65)	3,774	—	—	—	—	—	—	—	—
1 (65 and older)	3,479	—	—	—	—	—	—	—	—
2 (younger than 65)	4,858	5,000	—	—	—	—	—	—	—
2 (65 and older)	4,385	4,981	—	—	—	—	—	—	—
3	5,674	5,839	5,844	—	—	—	—	—	—
4	7,482	7,605	7,356	7,382	—	—	—	—	—
5	9,023	9,154	8,874	8,657	8,525	—	—	—	—
6	10,378	10,419	10,205	9,999	9,693	9,512	—	—	—
7	11,941	12,016	11,759	11,580	11,246	10,857	10,429	—	—
8	13,356	13,473	13,231	13,018	12,717	12,334	11,936	11,835	—
9 or more	16,066	16,144	15,929	15,749	15,453	15,046	14,667	14,586	14,024

Source

U.S. Bureau of the Census, *1980 Census of Population*, volume 1, *Characteristics of the Population*, Chapter C, "General Social and Economic Characteristics," part 1, United States Summary, PC80-1-C1, December 1983, Table "Thresholds at the Poverty Level in 1979 by Size of Family and Number of Related Children under 18 Years," p. B-23.

Documentation

Refer to the appendixes to the essay on poverty in this chapter for additional discussion of the tables, as well as for various technical definitions and descriptions.

This table gives the poverty thresholds applied to the 1980 Decennial Census (1979 income). They are not those applied to the 1980 Current Population Survey (CPS) (1979 income). The thresholds for income year 1979 used in the 1980 Decennial Census were the revised and less detailed "48-cell matrix" of poverty thresholds. In contrast, the thresholds for income year 1979 used in the March 1980 Current Population Survey were the "124-cell matrix," which distinguished between farm and nonfarm families and the sex of the householder. For the 1980 Census "48-cell matrix," the separate thresholds for families with female householder and male householder were eliminated. The weighted average of the poverty thresholds for these two types of families were applied to all types of families, regardless of the sex of householder. The distinction between farm and nonfarm families was also abolished in the 1980 Census. Farm families and farm unrelated individuals no longer had a lower set of poverty thresholds than nonfarm families and individuals. Instead, nonfarm poverty thresholds were applied to all families and unrelated individuals regardless of residence. Also beginning with the 1980 Census, the thresholds by size of family were extended from seven or more persons to nine or more persons (U.S. Bureau of the Census 1980). The poverty rates appearing in Tables Be260–411 for the income year 1979 are from the CPS and therefore based upon the extended 124-cell matrix thresholds (not presented here). The thresholds presented here are appropriate for interpretation of, or for use with, 1980 Census data, but not for 1980 (income year 1979) CPS poverty statistics. For a complete discussion of the threshold modifications, see Current Population Reports, series P-60, number 133.

See also the text for Table Be177–204.

TABLE Be242–250 Official poverty thresholds, by family size and number of related children younger than age 18: 1989

Contributed by Linda Barrington and Gordon M. Fisher

Size of family (age of householder)	0 children	1 child	2 children	3 children	4 children	5 children	6 children	7 children	8 or more children
	Be242	Be243	Be244	Be245	Be246	Be247	Be248	Be249	Be250
	Dollars	Dollars	Dollars	Dollars	Dollars	Dollars	Dollars	Dollars	Dollars
1 (younger than 65)	6,451	—	—	—	—	—	—	—	—
1 (65 and older)	5,947	—	—	—	—	—	—	—	—
2 (younger than 65)	8,303	8,547	—	—	—	—	—	—	—
2 (65 and older)	7,495	8,515	—	—	—	—	—	—	—
3	9,699	9,981	9,990	—	—	—	—	—	—
4	12,790	12,999	12,575	12,619	—	—	—	—	—
5	15,424	15,648	15,169	14,798	14,572	—	—	—	—
6	17,740	17,811	17,444	17,092	16,569	16,259	—	—	—
7	20,412	20,540	20,101	19,794	19,224	18,558	17,828	—	—
8	22,830	23,031	22,617	22,253	21,738	21,084	20,403	20,230	—
9 or more	27,463	27,596	27,229	26,921	26,415	25,719	25,089	24,933	23,973

Source

U.S. Census Bureau Internet site, "Poverty Thresholds: 1989," as of April 13, 2000.

Documentation

Refer to the appendixes to the essay on poverty in this chapter for additional discussion of the tables, as well as for various technical definitions and descriptions.

Since its construction, the official poverty threshold has distinguished between families of householders younger than age 65 and those with householders age 65 and older. The poverty threshold is set lower for those who are age 65 and older because of the lower caloric needs of the elderly, and thus lower minimum food costs underpinning the poverty threshold. The official poverty threshold no longer distinguishes between male and female householders or between farm and nonfarm families. See the text for Table Be233–241.

TABLE Be251–259 Official poverty thresholds, by family size and number of related children younger than age 18: 1999

Contributed by Linda Barrington and Gordon M. Fisher

Size of family (age of householder)	0 children	1 child	2 children	3 children	4 children	5 children	6 children	7 children	8 or more children
	Be251	Be252	Be253	Be254	Be255	Be256	Be257	Be258	Be259
	Dollars	Dollars	Dollars	Dollars	Dollars	Dollars	Dollars	Dollars	Dollars
1 (younger than 65)	8,667	—	—	—	—	—	—	—	—
1 (65 and older)	7,990	—	—	—	—	—	—	—	—
2 (younger than 65)	11,156	11,483	—	—	—	—	—	—	—
2 (65 and older)	10,070	11,440	—	—	—	—	—	—	—
3	13,032	13,410	13,423	—	—	—	—	—	—
4	17,184	17,465	16,895	16,954	—	—	—	—	—
5	20,723	21,024	20,380	19,882	19,578	—	—	—	—
6	23,835	23,930	23,436	22,964	22,261	21,845	—	—	—
7	27,425	27,596	27,006	26,595	25,828	24,934	23,953	—	—
8	30,673	30,944	30,387	29,899	29,206	28,327	27,412	27,180	—
9 or more	36,897	37,076	36,583	36,169	35,489	34,554	33,708	33,499	32,208

Source

U.S. Census Bureau Internet site, "Poverty Thresholds: 1999," as of April 13, 2000.

Documentation

See the text for Table Be242–250.

CHARACTERISTICS OF THE POVERTY POPULATION

Linda Barrington and Gordon M. Fisher

TABLE Be260–282 Persons below poverty threshold, by sex, race, and Hispanic origin: 1959–1999[1]

Contributed by Linda Barrington and Gordon M. Fisher

	Persons for whom poverty status is determined						Persons in poverty					
	Total	Male	Female	White	Black	Hispanic	Total	Male	Female	White	Black	Hispanic
	Be260 [2]	Be261 [3]	Be262 [3]	Be263	Be264	Be265 [4]	Be266 [2]	Be267 [3]	Be268 [3]	Be269	Be270	Be271 [4]
Year	Thousand	Thousand	Thousand	Thousand	Thousand	Thousand	Thousand	Thousand	Thousand	Thousand	Thousand	Thousand
1959	176,557	—	—	156,956	18,013 [7]	—	39,490	—	—	28,484	9,927 [7]	—
1960	179,503	—	—	158,863	—	—	39,851	—	—	28,309	—	—
1961	181,277	—	—	160,306	—	—	39,628	—	—	27,890	—	—
1962	184,276	—	—	162,842	—	—	38,625	—	—	26,672	—	—
1963	187,258	—	—	165,309	—	—	36,436	—	—	25,238	—	—
1964	189,710	—	—	167,313	—	—	36,055	—	—	24,957	—	—
1965	191,413	—	—	168,732	—	—	33,185	—	—	22,496	—	—
1966	193,388	93,718	99,637	170,247	21,206	—	28,510	12,225	16,265	19,290	8,867	—
1967 [5]	195,672	94,796	100,861	172,038	21,590	—	27,769	11,813	15,951	18,983	8,486	—
1968	197,628	95,681	101,919	173,732	21,944	—	25,389	10,793	14,578	17,395	7,616	—
1969	199,517	96,802 [6]	103,037 [6]	175,349	22,011	8,935 [8]	24,147	10,292 [6]	13,978 [6]	16,659	7,095	2,178 [8]
1970	202,183	98,228 [6]	104,248 [6]	177,376	22,515	8,957 [6]	25,420	10,879 [6]	14,632 [6]	17,484	7,548	2,177 [6]
1971	204,554	99,232	105,298	179,398	22,784	9,178	25,559	10,708	14,841	17,780	7,396	2,350
1972	206,004	99,804	106,168	180,125	23,144	10,577	24,460	10,190	14,258	16,203	7,710	2,414
1973	207,621	100,694	106,898	181,185	23,512	10,795	22,973	9,642	13,316	15,142	7,388	2,366
1974	209,362	101,523 [6]	107,743 [6]	182,376	23,699	—	23,370	10,313 [6]	13,881 [6]	15,736	7,182	2,575
1975	210,864	102,211	108,652	183,164	24,089	11,117	25,877	10,908	14,970	17,770	7,545	2,991
1976	212,303	102,955	109,348	184,165	24,399	11,269	24,975	10,373	14,603	16,713	7,595	2,783
1977	213,867	103,629	110,238	185,254	24,710	12,046	24,720	10,340	14,381	16,416	7,726	2,700
1978	215,656	104,480	111,175	186,450	24,956	12,079	24,497	10,017	14,480	16,259	7,625	2,607
1979	222,903	105,542 [6]	112,306 [6]	191,742	25,944	13,371	26,072	10,535 [6]	14,810 [6]	17,214	8,050	2,921
1980	225,027	108,990	116,037	192,912	26,408	13,600	29,640	12,207 [6]	17,065 [6]	20,049	8,555	3,566
1981	227,157	110,010	117,147	194,504	26,834	14,021	31,822	13,360	18,462	21,553	9,173	3,713
1982	229,412	111,175	118,237	195,919	27,216	14,385	34,398	14,842	19,556	23,517	9,697	4,301
1983	231,700	112,280 [6]	119,332 [6]	197,496	27,678	16,544	35,303	15,182 [6]	20,084 [6]	23,984	9,882	4,633
1984	233,816	113,391	120,425	198,941	28,087	16,916	33,700	14,537	19,163	22,955	9,490	4,806
1985	236,594	114,970	121,624	200,918	28,485	18,075	33,064	14,140	18,923	22,860	8,926	5,236
1986	238,554	115,915	122,640	202,282	28,871	18,758	32,370	13,721	18,649	22,183	8,983	5,117
1987	240,982	117,123 [6]	123,767 [6]	203,605	29,362	19,395	32,221	14,029 [6]	18,518 [6]	21,195	9,520	5,422
1988	243,530	118,399	125,131	205,235	29,849	20,064	31,745	13,599	18,146	20,715	9,356	5,357
1989	245,992	119,704	126,288	206,853	30,332	20,746	31,528	13,366	18,162	20,785	9,302	5,430
1990	248,644	121,073	127,571	208,611	30,806	21,405	33,585	14,211	19,373	22,326	9,837	6,006
1991	251,192	122,418	128,774	210,133	31,313	22,070	35,708	15,082	20,626	23,747	10,242	6,339
1992	256,549	125,288	131,261	213,060	32,411	25,646	38,014	16,222	21,792	25,259	10,827	7,592
1993	259,278	126,668	132,610	214,899	32,910	26,559	39,265	16,900	22,365	26,226	10,877	8,126
1994	261,616	127,838	133,778	216,460	33,353	27,442	38,059	16,316	21,744	25,379	10,196	8,416
1995	263,733	128,852	134,880	218,028	33,740	28,344	36,425	15,683	20,742	24,423	9,872	8,574
1996	266,218	130,353	135,865	219,656	34,110	29,614	36,529	15,611	20,918	24,650	9,694	8,697
1997	268,480	131,376	137,105	221,200	34,458	30,637	35,574	15,187	20,387	24,396	9,116	8,308
1998	271,059	132,408	138,652	222,837	34,877	31,515	34,476	14,712	19,764	23,454	9,091	8,070
1999	—	—	—	—	—	—	32,258	—	—	21,922	8,360	7,439

Notes appear at end of table

TABLE Be260–282 Persons below poverty threshold, by sex, race, and Hispanic origin: 1959–1999 *Continued*

	Percentage in poverty						Percentage of persons in poverty who are				
	All persons	Males	Females	Whites	Blacks	Hispanics	Male	Female	White	Black	Hispanic
	Be272 [2]	Be273 [3]	Be274 [3]	Be275	Be276	Be277 [4]	Be278 [3]	Be279 [3]	Be280	Be281	Be282 [4]
Year	Percent	Percent	Percent	Percent	Percent	Percent	Percent	Percent	Percent	Percent	Percent
1959	22.4	—	—	18.1	55.1 [7]	—	—	—	72.1	25.6 [7]	—
1960	22.2	—	—	17.8	—	—	—	—	71.0	—	—
1961	21.9	—	—	17.4	—	—	—	—	70.4	—	—
1962	21.0	—	—	16.4	—	—	—	—	69.1	—	—
1963	19.5	—	—	15.3	—	—	—	—	69.3	—	—
1964	19.0	—	—	14.9	—	—	—	—	69.2	—	—
1965	17.3	—	—	13.3	—	—	—	—	67.8	—	—
1966	14.7	13.0	16.3	11.3	41.8	—	42.9	57.1	67.7	31.1	—
1967 [5]	14.2	12.5	15.8	11.0	39.3	—	42.5	57.4	68.4	30.6	—
1968	12.8	11.3	14.3	10.0	34.7	—	42.5	57.4	68.5	30.0	—
1969	12.1	10.6 [6]	13.6 [6]	9.5	32.2	24.4 [8]	42.4 [6]	57.6 [6]	69.0	29.4	8.1 [8]
1970	12.6	11.1 [6]	14.0 [6]	9.9	33.5	24.3 [6]	42.6 [6]	57.3 [6]	68.8	29.7	8.5 [6]
1971	12.5	10.8	14.1	9.9	32.5	25.6	41.9	58.1	69.6	28.9	9.2
1972	11.9	10.2	13.4	9.0	33.3	22.8	41.7	58.3	66.2	31.5	9.9
1973	11.1	9.6	12.5	8.4	31.4	21.9	42.0	58.0	65.9	32.2	10.3
1974	11.2	10.2 [6]	12.9 [6]	8.6	30.3	23.0	42.5 [6]	57.2 [6]	67.3	30.7	11.0
1975	12.3	10.7	13.8	9.7	31.3	26.9	42.2	57.9	68.7	29.2	11.6
1976	11.8	10.1	13.4	9.1	31.1	24.7	41.5	58.5	66.9	30.4	11.1
1977	11.6	10.0	13.0	8.9	31.3	22.4	41.8	58.2	66.4	31.3	10.9
1978	11.4	9.6	13.0	8.7	30.6	21.6	40.9	59.1	66.4	31.1	10.6
1979	11.7	10.0 [6]	13.2 [6]	9.0	31.0	21.8	41.6 [6]	58.4 [6]	66.0	30.9	11.2
1980	13.2	11.2 [6]	14.7 [6]	10.4	32.4	26.2	41.7 [6]	58.3 [6]	67.6	28.9	12.0
1981	14.0	12.1	15.8	11.1	34.2	26.5	42.0	58.0	67.7	28.8	11.7
1982	15.0	13.4	16.5	12.0	35.6	29.9	43.1	56.9	68.4	28.2	12.5
1983	15.2	13.5 [6]	16.8 [6]	12.1	35.7	28.0	43.0 [6]	57.0 [6]	67.9	28.0	13.1
1984	14.4	12.8	15.9	11.5	33.8	28.4	43.1	56.9	68.1	28.2	14.3
1985	14.0	12.3	15.6	11.4	31.3	29.0	42.8	57.2	69.1	27.0	15.8
1986	13.6	11.8	15.2	11.0	31.1	27.3	42.4	57.6	68.5	27.8	15.8
1987	13.4	12.0 [6]	15.0 [6]	10.4	32.4	28.0	43.1 [6]	56.9 [6]	65.8	29.5	16.8
1988	13.0	11.5	14.5	10.1	31.3	26.7	42.8	57.2	65.3	29.5	16.9
1989	12.8	11.2	14.4	10.0	30.7	26.2	42.4	57.6	65.9	29.5	17.2
1990	13.5	11.7	15.2	10.7	31.9	28.1	42.3	57.7	66.5	29.3	17.9
1991	14.2	12.3	16.0	11.3	32.7	28.7	42.2	57.8	66.5	28.7	17.8
1992	14.8	12.9	16.6	11.9	33.4	29.6	42.7	57.3	66.4	28.5	20.0
1993	15.1	13.3	16.9	12.2	33.1	30.6	43.0	57.0	66.8	27.7	20.7
1994	14.5	12.8	16.3	11.7	30.6	30.7	42.9	57.1	66.7	26.8	22.1
1995	13.8	12.2	15.4	11.2	29.3	30.3	43.1	56.9	67.1	27.1	23.5
1996	13.7	12.0	15.4	11.2	28.4	29.4	42.7	57.3	67.5	26.5	23.8
1997	13.3	11.6	14.9	11.0	26.5	27.1	42.7	57.3	68.6	25.6	23.4
1998	12.7	11.1	14.3	10.5	26.1	25.6	42.7	57.3	68.0	26.4	23.4
1999	11.8	—	—	9.8	23.6	22.8	—	—	68.0	25.9	23.1

[1] Tabulation procedures changed numerous times, affecting the comparability of the series over time. See the essay on poverty in this chapter for additional information on methodology changes.

[2] Includes other races not shown separately.

[3] For income years 1966–1974, figures exclude family heads and spouses ages 14 and 15.

[4] Hispanics can be of any race. Tabulation procedures changed in 1972, affecting Hispanic counts. See documentation.

[5] Overestimate of poverty population. See documentation.

[6] Not revised. See documentation.

[7] Derived from 1-in-1,000 sample. See documentation.

[8] Derived from 5-percent sample. See documentation.

Sources

U.S. Bureau of the Census, March *Current Population Survey* (CPS). Data were obtained from the Internet site of the U.S. Census Bureau, Poverty and Health Statistics Branch/HHES Division. Series Be260, Be263–266, Be269–272, and Be275–277, from Historical Poverty Tables, Table 2; series Be261–262, Be267–268, and Be273–274, from *Historical Poverty Tables*, Table 7; series Be278–282, based on series Be266–271. Exceptions are noted.

For all series, the figures for 1999 were found in *Current Population Reports* (CPR) series P-60, number 210, Table A, p. vi.

Series Be260. 1991: CPR series P-60, number 207, Table B-1, p. B-2.

Series Be263–264. 1995–1998: CPR series P-60, numbers 194, 198, 201, and 207, respectively, from Table 2, pp. 3–4.

Series Be265. 1995, 1996, and 1998: CPR series P-60, numbers 194, 198, 207, respectively, from Table 2, p. 5.

Series Be265, Be271, and Be277. 1969: U.S. Bureau of the Census, *1970 Census of Population*, Report PC(2)-9A, Table 1, pp. 7–8; 1970: CPR series P-60, number 81, Table 7, p. 50; 1971: CPR series P-60, number 86, Table 11, p. 70; 1972: CPR series P-60, number 99, Table 16, p. 19.

Series Be266. 1997–1998: CPR series P-60, numbers 201 and 207, respectively, Table 2, p. 2.

Series Be266, Be269–272, and Be275–277. 1980: CPR series P-60, number 134, from Table 14, pp. 20, 21; 1997: CPR series P-60, number 201, Table 2, pp. 2, 3, 5.

Series Be267. 1998: CPR series P-60, number 207, Table 2, p. 2.

Series Be269, Be271–272, and Be275. 1997 CPR series P-60, number 201, Table 2, pp. 2, 3, 5.

Series Be270. 1998: CPR series P-60, number 207, from Table 2, p. 4.

Series Be276. 1966: CPR series P-60, number 68, Table A-1, p. 107.

(continued)

TABLE Be260–282 Persons below poverty threshold, by sex, race, and Hispanic origin: 1959–1999 *Continued*

Series Be276–277. 1996: CPR series P-60, number 198, Table 2, pp. 4 and 5, respectively.

Series Be277. 1991: CPR series P-60, number 207, Table B-1, p. B-5.

Documentation

Refer to the appendixes to the essay on poverty in this chapter for additional discussion of the tables, as well as for various technical definitions and descriptions.

According to the Census Bureau, the racial or ethnic categorization of persons is that of the individual, regardless of the racial or ethnic categorization of the family householder. Although this has been the case for some years, it was not always so. A supplementary P-60 poverty report issued in 1974 indicates (CPR series P-60, number 95, p. 3) that in the main P-60 poverty reports for income years 1971 and 1972, persons were classified by the race of the family head (and not by their own race). The contributors of this table have not been able to determine when that situation changed to what it is today.

Series Be278–282. Calculated by dividing series Be267–271, respectively, by series Be266. Exceptions for specific dates are as noted.

Series Be278–279. Figures for 1969, 1970, 1974, 1979, 1980, 1983, and 1987 were constructed by dividing the numerator series by the unrevised total persons in poverty for that year because the numerator is an unrevised figure. The unrevised figures for the total persons in poverty used in the denominator to calculate the value in these series are as follows (in thousands) – 1969: 24,289 (CPR series P-60, number 86, Table 1, p. 29); 1970: 25,522 (CPR series P-60, number 81, Table A, p. 2); 1974: 24,260 (CPR series P-60, number 106, Table E, p. 10); 1979: 25,345 (CPR series P-60, number 133, Table E, p. 8); 1980: 29,272 (CPR series P-60, number 133, Table D, p. 6); 1983: 35,266 (CPR series P-60, number 152, Table B, p. 3); and 1987: 32,546 (CPR series P-60, number 166, Table E, p. 15).

Series Be281. The 1959 figure was constructed by dividing the numerator value by the 1959 total persons in poverty from the 1-in-1,000 sample of the 1960 Decennial Census, because the numerator is from this source. The decennial census figure for the total persons in poverty used in the denominator to calculate this value is 38,766 thousand (CPR series P-60, number 91, Table L, p. 13).

Series Be282. The 1969 figure was constructed by dividing the numerator value by the 1969 total persons in poverty from the 5-percent sample of the 1970 Decennial Census because the numerator is from this source. The decennial census figure for the total persons in poverty used in the denominator to calculate this value is 26,931 thousand (1970 Census of Population, Report PC(2)-9A, Table 1, p. 1). The 1970 figure is constructed by dividing the numerator value by the unrevised total persons in poverty for that year because the numerator is an unrevised figure. The unrevised figure for the total persons in poverty used in the denominator to calculate this value is 25,522 thousand (CPR series P-60, number 81, Table A, p. 2).

Methodology Changes

Changes in methodology affecting the comparability of data in Tables Be260–411 are described here.

Tables Be260–411 contain both unrevised and revised (or revised-and-corrected) figures, which are not strictly comparable. In the case of percentages, unrevised figures were constructed by dividing an unrevised numerator by the corresponding unrevised poverty count figure. The unrevised denominator may not appear in the source series used in the computation of other figures for the series.

The Census Bureau classifies persons separately by race (black/white/other) and ethnicity (Hispanic/not Hispanic). Accordingly, persons of Hispanic origin may be of any race. Poverty data for Hispanics are available for income year 1969 from the 1970 Decennial Census, and for 1970 and subsequent years from the CPS. Beginning with data for income year 1972, the Census Bureau revised procedures for producing figures on Hispanics; it changed the CPS sample design, question wording, and allocation procedures affecting persons younger than age 14. Figures for 1972 and 1973 were tabulated under both unrevised and revised procedures. Accordingly, data for 1972 (revised) and subsequent years are not strictly comparable with data for earlier years. See CPR series P-60, number 98, p. 163, and series P-20, number 264, pp. 7–9.

Some figures for income year 1959, where noted, were derived from the 1-in-1,000 sample of the 1960 Decennial Census. See CPR series P-60, number 76, p. 24, and series P-23, number 37, pp. 6–9, 12–13. Such figures are not comparable with figures derived from the CPS for that year.

Beginning with data for income year 1967, the Census Bureau implemented a new March CPS processing system. Figures for 1966 were retabulated on the revised basis. See CPR series P-60, number 68, pp. 15–17.

Coding errors and computer income editing procedures resulted in partially offsetting misestimates of the 1967 poverty population. The net impact of these errors was to overestimate the poverty population by about 0.12 million families. Accordingly, 1967 poverty data are not strictly comparable with 1966 (revised) and 1968 data. See CPR series P-60, number 68, pp. 15–16, and number 81, p. 24.

Some figures derived for income year 1969 were derived from the 5-percent sample of the 1970 Decennial Census. See 1970 Census of the Population, Report PC(2)-9A, pp. vi, 1 (Table 1 headnote). Such figures are not comparable with figures derived from the CPS for that year.

Beginning with CPS data for income year 1971, the Census Bureau implemented 1970 Decennial Census population controls. Some figures for 1969 and 1970 were retabulated on the revised basis. See CPR series P-60, number 86, p. 22.

Beginning with data for income year 1975, the Census Bureau implemented a new March CPS processing system. In addition, the Bureau expanded the March 1975 CPS questionnaire to ask eleven rather than nine income questions. Some figures for 1974 were retabulated on the revised basis. See CPR series P-60, number 106, pp. 6–12.

Beginning with data for income year 1979, the Census Bureau made several modifications to the March CPS, including a more detailed income questionnaire (expanded to show twenty-seven possible values from fifty-one possible sources of income), implementation of the "householder" concept in place of the earlier "head" concept, and exclusion of unrelated subfamilies from the count of all families. See CPR series P-60, number 130, pp. 6, 8–10.

Beginning with CPS data for income year 1980, the Census Bureau implemented 1980 Decennial Census population controls. Some figures for 1979 were retabulated on the revised basis. See CPR series P-60, number 133, pp. 7–8.

Beginning with data for income year 1981, the Census Bureau implemented a slightly modified definition of poverty. A limited number of figures for 1980 were retabulated on the revised basis. See CPR series P-60, number 133, pp. 2–6, 9, and number 138, pp. 2–4, 7 (footnote 2).

Beginning with data for income year 1984, the Census Bureau implemented population weighting controls for Hispanics. Data based on these new population controls for Hispanics are not directly comparable with data for prior years. Some figures for 1983 were retabulated on the revised basis. In addition, a correction was made to the revised 1983 figures to implement a revised method of imputing interest income. See CPR series P-60, number 152, pp. 2–3.

Beginning with data for income year 1988, the Census Bureau implemented a new March CPS processing system. Some figures for 1987 were retabulated on the revised basis. In addition, a correction was made to the revised 1987 figures because of several minor errors in the CPS computer file. See CPR series P-60, number 166, pp. 14–17, and number 171, pp. 2 (including footnote 2), 12 (footnote r).

Data for income year 1991 were corrected after the release of the 1991 Income and Poverty reports. Weights for nine-person records had been omitted in the original file. The errors, which were quite small, involved figures for the total population but not figures for the poverty population. See CPR series P-60, number 184, p. ix, and series P-60, number 207, p. B-17 (footnote r).

Beginning with CPS data for income year 1993, the Census Bureau implemented 1990 Decennial Census population controls. Some figures for 1992 were retabulated on the revised basis. See CPR series P-60, number 188, Appendix B.

Beginning with data for income year 1993, the Census Bureau changed the CPS data collection method from paper-and-pencil interviewing to computer-assisted interviewing. The Bureau also made several other changes in data collection and processing procedures. See CPR series P-60, number 188, Appendix C.

TABLE Be283–309 Families below poverty threshold, by family type and the sex, race, and Hispanic origin of the household head: 1959–1999[1]

Contributed by Linda Barrington and Gordon M. Fisher

	Families for whom poverty status is determined							Number of families in poverty						
			Single householder							Single householder				
	Total	Married couple	Male	Female	White	Black	Hispanic	Total	Married couple	Male	Female	White	Black	Hispanic
	Be283 [2]	Be284	Be285	Be286	Be287	Be288	Be289 [3]	Be290 [2]	Be291	Be292	Be293	Be294	Be295	Be296 [3]
Year	Thousand	Thousand	Thousand	Thousand	Thousand	Thousand	Thousand	Thousand	Thousand	Thousand	Thousand	Thousand	Thousand	Thousand
1959	45,054	39,335	1,226	4,493	40,820	3,863 [5]	—	8,320	—	—	1,916	6,185	1,860 [5]	—
1960	45,435	39,624	1,202	4,609	41,104	—	—	8,243	—	—	1,955	6,115	—	—
1961	46,341	40,405	1,293	4,643	41,888	—	—	8,391	—	—	1,954	6,205	—	—
1962	46,998	40,923	1,334	4,741	42,437	—	—	8,077	—	—	2,034	5,887	—	—
1963	47,436	41,311	1,243	4,882	42,663	—	—	7,554	—	—	1,972	5,466	—	—
1964	47,836	41,648	1,182	5,006	43,081	—	—	7,160	—	—	1,822	5,258	—	—
1965	48,278	42,107	1,179	4,992	43,496	—	—	6,721	—	—	1,916	4,824	—	—
1966	49,065	42,723	1,141	5,202	44,110	4,558	—	5,784	—	—	1,721	4,106	1,620	—
1967 [4]	49,835	43,292	1,210	5,333	44,813	4,589	—	5,667	—	—	1,774	4,056	1,555	—
1968	50,511	43,842	1,228	5,441	45,437	4,646	—	5,047	—	—	1,755	3,616	1,366	—
1969	51,586	44,436	1,559	5,591	46,261	4,887	2,004 [6]	5,008	—	—	1,827	3,574	1,365	424 [6]
1970	52,227	44,739	1,487	6,001	46,601	5,027	—	5,260	—	—	1,952	3,708	1,481	—
1971	53,296	45,752	1,353	6,191	47,641	5,157	—	5,303	—	—	2,100	3,751	1,484	—
1972	54,373	46,314	1,452	6,607	48,477	5,265	2,312	5,075	—	—	2,158	3,441	1,529	477
1973	55,053	46,812	1,438	6,804	48,919	5,440	2,365	4,828	2,482	154	2,193	3,219	1,527	468
1974	55,698	47,069	1,399	7,230	49,440	5,491	2,475	4,922	2,474	125	2,324	3,352	1,479	526
1975	56,245	47,318	1,445	7,482	49,873	5,586	2,499	5,450	2,904	116	2,430	3,838	1,513	627
1976	56,710	47,497	1,500	7,713	50,083	5,804	2,583	5,311	2,606	162	2,543	3,560	1,617	598
1977	57,215	47,385	1,594	8,236	50,530	5,806	2,764	5,311	2,524	177	2,610	3,540	1,637	591
1978	57,804	47,692	1,654	8,458	50,910	5,906	2,741	5,280	2,474	152	2,654	3,523	1,622	559
1979	59,550	49,112	1,733	8,705	52,243	6,184	3,029	5,461	2,640	176	2,645	3,581	1,722	614
1980	60,309	49,294	1,933	9,082	52,710	6,317	3,235	6,301	3,085	196	3,021	4,275	1,825	759
1981	61,019	49,630	1,986	9,403	53,269	6,413	3,305	6,851	3,394	205	3,252	4,670	1,972	792
1982	61,393	49,908	2,016	9,469	53,407	6,530	3,369	7,512	3,789	290	3,434	5,118	2,158	916
1983	62,015	50,081	2,038	9,896	53,890	6,681	3,788	7,647	3,815	268	3,564	5,220	2,161	981
1984	62,706	50,350	2,228	10,129	54,400	6,778	3,939	7,277	3,488	292	3,498	4,925	2,094	991
1985	63,558	50,933	2,414	10,211	54,991	6,921	4,206	7,223	3,438	311	3,474	4,983	1,983	1,074
1986	64,491	51,537	2,510	10,445	55,676	7,096	4,403	7,023	3,123	287	3,613	4,811	1,987	1,085
1987	65,204	51,675	2,833	10,696	56,086	7,202	4,576	7,005	3,011	340	3,654	4,567	2,117	1,168
1988	65,837	52,100	2,847	10,890	56,492	7,409	4,823	6,874	2,897	336	3,642	4,471	2,089	1,141
1989	66,090	52,317	2,884	10,890	56,590	7,470	4,840	6,784	2,931	348	3,504	4,409	2,077	1,133
1990	66,322	52,147	2,907	11,268	56,803	7,471	4,981	7,098	2,981	349	3,768	4,622	2,193	1,244
1991	67,175	52,457	3,025	11,693	57,225	7,716	5,177	7,712	3,158	392	4,161	5,022	2,343	1,372
1992	68,216	53,090	3,065	12,061	57,669	7,982	5,733	8,144	3,385	484	4,275	5,255	2,484	1,529
1993	68,506	53,181	2,914	12,411	57,881	7,993	5,946	8,393	3,481	488	4,424	5,452	2,499	1,625
1994	69,313	53,865	3,228	12,220	58,444	8,093	6,202	8,053	3,272	549	4,232	5,312	2,212	1,724
1995	69,597	53,570	3,513	12,514	58,872	8,055	6,287	7,532	2,982	493	4,057	4,994	2,127	1,695
1996	70,241	53,604	3,847	12,790	58,934	8,455	6,631	7,708	3,010	531	4,167	5,059	2,206	1,748
1997	70,884	54,321	3,911	12,652	59,515	8,408	6,961	7,324	2,821	508	3,995	4,990	1,985	1,721
1998	71,551	54,778	3,977	12,796	60,077	8,452	7,273	7,186	2,879	476	3,831	4,829	1,981	1,648
1999	—	—	—	—	—	—	—	6,676	2,673	—	3,531	4,377	1,898	1,525

Notes appear at end of table

(continued)

TABLE Be283–309 Families below poverty threshold, by family type and the sex, race, and Hispanic origin of the household head: 1959–1999 *Continued*

	Percentage of families in poverty							Percentage of families in poverty headed by					
			Single householder						Single householder				
	All families	Married couple	Male	Female	White	Black	Hispanic	Married couple	Male	Female	White	Black	Hispanic
	Be297 [2]	Be298	Be299	Be300	Be301	Be302	Be303 [3]	Be304	Be305	Be306	Be307	Be308	Be309 [3]
Year	Percent	Percent	Percent	Percent	Percent	Percent	Percent	Percent	Percent	Percent	Percent	Percent	Percent
1959	18.5	—	—	42.6	15.2	48.1 [5]	—	—	—	23.0	74.3	23.3 [5]	—
1960	18.1	—	—	42.4	14.9	—	—	—	—	23.7	74.2	—	—
1961	18.1	—	—	42.1	14.8	—	—	—	—	23.3	73.9	—	—
1962	17.2	—	—	42.9	13.9	—	—	—	—	25.2	72.9	—	—
1963	15.9	—	—	40.4	12.8	—	—	—	—	26.1	72.4	—	—
1964	15.0	—	—	36.4	12.2	—	—	—	—	25.4	73.4	—	—
1965	13.9	—	—	38.4	11.1	—	—	—	—	28.5	71.8	—	—
1966	11.8	—	—	33.1	9.3	35.5	—	—	—	29.8	71.0	28.0	—
1967 [4]	11.4	—	—	33.3	9.1	33.9	—	—	—	31.3	71.6	27.4	—
1968	10.0	—	—	32.3	8.0	29.4	—	—	—	34.8	71.6	27.1	—
1969	9.7	—	—	32.7	7.7	27.9	21.2 [6]	—	—	36.5	71.4	27.3	7.8 [6]
1970	10.1	—	—	32.5	8.0	29.5	—	—	—	37.1	70.5	28.2	—
1971	10.0	—	—	33.9	7.9	28.8	—	—	—	39.6	70.7	28.0	—
1972	9.3	—	—	32.7	7.1	29.0	20.6	—	—	42.5	67.8	30.1	9.4
1973	8.8	5.3	10.7	32.2	6.6	28.1	19.8	51.4	3.2	45.4	66.7	31.6	9.7
1974	8.8	5.3	8.9	32.1	6.8	26.9	21.2	50.3	2.5	47.2	68.1	30.0	10.7
1975	9.7	6.1	8.0	32.5	7.7	27.1	25.1	53.3	2.1	44.6	70.4	27.8	11.5
1976	9.4	5.5	10.8	33.0	7.1	27.9	23.1	49.1	3.1	47.9	67.0	30.4	11.3
1977	9.3	5.3	11.1	31.7	7.0	28.2	21.4	47.5	3.3	49.1	66.7	30.8	11.1
1978	9.1	5.2	9.2	31.4	6.9	27.5	20.4	46.9	2.9	50.3	66.7	30.7	10.6
1979	9.2	5.4	10.2	30.4	6.9	27.8	20.3	48.3	3.2	48.4	65.6	31.5	11.2
1980	10.4	6.3	10.1	33.3	8.1	28.9	23.5	49.0	3.1	47.9	67.8	29.0	12.0
1981	11.2	6.8	10.3	34.6	8.8	30.8	24.0	49.5	3.0	47.5	68.2	28.8	11.6
1982	12.2	7.6	14.4	36.3	9.6	33.0	27.2	50.4	3.9	45.7	68.1	28.7	12.2
1983	12.3	7.6	13.2	36.0	9.7	32.3	25.9	49.9	3.5	46.6	68.3	28.3	12.8
1984	11.6	6.9	13.1	34.5	9.1	30.9	25.2	47.9	4.0	48.1	67.7	28.8	13.6
1985	11.4	6.7	12.9	34.0	9.1	28.7	25.5	47.6	4.3	48.1	69.0	27.5	14.9
1986	10.9	6.1	11.4	34.6	8.6	28.0	24.7	44.5	4.1	51.4	68.5	28.3	15.4
1987	10.7	5.8	12.0	34.2	8.1	29.4	25.5	43.0	4.9	52.2	65.2	30.2	16.7
1988	10.4	5.6	11.8	33.4	7.9	28.2	23.7	42.1	4.9	53.0	65.0	30.4	16.6
1989	10.3	5.6	12.1	32.2	7.8	27.8	23.4	43.2	5.1	51.7	65.0	30.6	16.7
1990	10.7	5.7	12.0	33.4	8.1	29.3	25.0	42.0	4.9	53.1	65.1	30.9	17.5
1991	11.5	6.0	13.0	35.6	8.8	30.4	26.5	40.9	5.1	54.0	65.1	30.4	17.8
1992	11.9	6.4	15.8	35.4	9.1	31.1	26.7	41.6	5.9	52.5	64.5	30.5	18.8
1993	12.3	6.5	16.8	35.6	9.4	31.3	27.3	41.5	5.8	52.7	65.0	29.8	19.4
1994	11.6	6.1	17.0	34.6	9.1	27.3	27.8	40.6	6.8	52.6	66.0	27.5	21.4
1995	10.8	5.6	14.0	32.4	8.5	26.4	27.0	39.6	6.5	53.9	66.3	28.2	22.5
1996	11.0	5.6	13.8	32.6	8.6	26.1	26.4	39.1	6.9	54.1	65.6	28.6	22.7
1997	10.3	5.2	13.0	31.6	8.4	23.6	24.7	38.5	6.9	54.5	68.1	27.1	23.5
1998	10.0	5.3	12.0	29.9	8.0	23.4	22.7	40.1	6.6	53.2	67.2	27.6	22.9
1999	9.3	4.8	—	27.8	7.3	21.9	20.2	40.0	—	52.9	65.6	28.4	22.8

[1] Tabulation procedures changed numerous times, affecting the comparability of the poverty series over time. See documentation for Table Be260–282.

[2] Includes other races not shown separately.

[3] Hispanics can be of any race. Tabulation procedures changed in 1972, affecting Hispanic counts. See documentation for Table Be260–282.

[4] Overestimate of poverty population. See documentation for Table Be260–282.

[5] Derived from 1-in-1,000 sample.

[6] Derived from 5-percent sample.

Sources

U.S. Bureau of the Census, March *Current Population Survey* (CPS). Data for the following series were obtained from the Internet site of the U.S. Census Bureau, Poverty and Health Statistics Branch/HHES Division. Series Be283–303, from *Historical Poverty Tables*, Table 4; series Be304–309, based on series Be290–296. Exceptions for specific dates are as noted.

In all series, the figures for 1999 were found in *Current Population Reports* (CPR) series P-60, number 210, Table A, p. vi.

Series Be283 and Be287. 1966: CPR series P-60, number 68, Table K, p. 16.

Series Be284. 1966: CPR series P-60, number 59, Table H, p. 18.

Series Be285–286. 1966: U.S. Bureau of the Census, *Historical Statistics of the United States* (1975), part 1, p. 296, series G184 and G185, respectively.

Series Be286 and Be300. 1992 and 1993: CPR series P-60, number 188, Table D-6, p. D-21; 1994: CPR series P-60, number 189, Table 9, p. 26.

Series Be288. 1966: unpublished tabulation prepared for the Office of Economic Opportunity by the U.S. Census Bureau.

Series Be288, Be295, and Be302. 1959: CPR series P-60, number 91, Table K, p. 12.

Series Be289. 1972: CPR series P-60, number 94, Table 11, p. 12.

Series Be289 and Be303. 1969: 1970 Census of Population, *Report* PC(2)-9A, Table 1, p. 7–8; 1972: CPR series P-60, number 94, Table 11, p. 12.

Series Be290–303. 1980: CPR series P-60, number 134, Table 14, pp. 20–1.

Series Be292. 1991: CPR series P-60, number 207, Table B-3, p. B-10.

Series Be293. 1992–1993: CPR series P-60, number 188, Table D-6, p. D-21.

Series Be295. 1966: CPR series P-60, number 68, Table A-2, p. 108.

Series Be296. 1969: 1970 Census of Population, *Report* PC(2)-9A, Table 1, p. 7; 1972: CPR series P-60, number 94, Table 11, p. 12.

Series Be300. 1994: CPR series P-60, number 189, Table 9, p. 26.

Series Be302. 1966: CPR series P-60, number 68, Table A-2, p. 108.

Series Be303. 1972: CPR series P-60, number 94, Table 11, p. 12.

Documentation

Refer to the appendixes to the essay on poverty in this chapter for additional discussion of the tables, as well as for various technical definitions and descriptions.

A family is a group of two people or more (one of whom is the householder) related by birth, marriage, or adoption and residing together; all such people (including related subfamily members) are considered as members of one family. Beginning with the March 1980 CPS (data for income year 1979), unrelated subfamilies (referred to in the past as secondary families) are no longer included in the count of families, nor are the members of unrelated subfamilies included in the count of family members. The number of families is equal to the number of family households; however, the count of family members differs from the count of family household members because family household members include any nonrelatives living in the household.

The marital status classification "married" excludes those who are never married, widowed, and divorced. These terms refer to the marital status at the time of the enumeration. A married couple, as defined for census purposes, is a husband and wife enumerated as members of the same household. The married couple may or may not have children living with them. The expression "husband-wife" or "married-couple" before the term "household," "family," or "subfamily" indicates that the household, family, or subfamily is maintained by a husband and wife. The number of married couples equals the count of married-couple families plus the count of related and unrelated married-couple subfamilies. "Single," when used as a marital status category, is the sum of never-married, widowed, and divorced people. "Single," when used in the context of "single-parent family/household," means only one parent is present in the home. The parent may be never-married, widowed, divorced, or married, spouse absent.

The racial or ethnic categorization of the family is based on the racial or ethnic categorization of the family householder. The householder refers to the person (or one of the people) in whose name the housing unit is owned or rented (maintained) or, if there is no such person, any adult member, excluding roomers, boarders, or paid employees. Beginning with the March 1980 CPS, if the house is owned or rented jointly by a married couple, the householder may be either the husband or the wife. The person designated as the householder is the "reference person" to whom the relationship of all other household members, if any, is recorded.

The number of householders is equal to the number of households. Also, the number of family householders is equal to the number of families.

Beginning with the 1980 CPS, the U.S. Census Bureau replaced the terms "head of household" and "head of family" with "householder" and "family householder," respectively, in response to greater sharing of household responsibilities among the adult members of the household and family. Specifically, beginning in 1980, the Census Bureau discontinued its longtime practice of always classifying the husband as the reference person (head) when he and his wife are living together.

Series Be304–309. Calculated by dividing series Be291–296, respectively, by series Be290. Exceptions for specific dates are as noted.

Series Be308. The figure for 1959 was constructed by dividing the numerator value from series Be295 by the 1959 total persons in poverty from the 1-in-1,000 sample of the 1960 Decennial Census because the numerator is from this source. The decennial census figure for the total persons in poverty in 1959 used in the denominator to calculate this value is 7,974 thousand, as reported in CPR series P-23, number 37, Table 19, p. 72. The figure for 1969 was constructed by dividing the numerator value from series Be296 by the 1969 total persons in poverty from the 5-percent sample of the 1970 Decennial Census because the numerator is from this source. The decennial census figure for the total persons in poverty in 1969 used in the denominator to calculate the 1969 value is 5,461 thousand, as reported in 1970 Census of the Population, *Report* PC(2)-9A, Table 1, pp. 1, 7.

TABLE Be310–322 Persons age 65 and older below poverty threshold, by the race and Hispanic origin: 1959–1999[1]

Contributed by Linda Barrington and Gordon M. Fisher

	Persons 65 and older													Percentage of persons in poverty who are 65 and older
	For whom poverty status is determined				Number in poverty				Percentage in poverty				
	Total	White	Black	Hispanic	Total	White	Black	Hispanic	Total	White	Black	Hispanic	
	Be310 [2]	Be311 [3]	Be312 [3]	Be313 [3]	Be314 [2]	Be315	Be316	Be317 [3]	Be318 [2]	Be319	Be320	Be321 [3]	Be322 [2]
Year	Thousand	Thousand	Thousand	Thousand	Thousand	Thousand	Thousand	Thousand	Percent	Percent	Percent	Percent	Percent
1959 [4]	15,557	14,344	1,138	—	5,481	4,744	711	—	35.2	33.1	62.5	—	14.1
1966	17,929	16,514	1,311	—	5,114	4,357	722	—	28.5	26.4	55.1	—	17.9
1967 [5]	18,240	16,791	1,341	—	5,388	4,646	715	—	29.5	27.7	53.3	—	19.4
1968	18,559	17,062	1,374	—	4,632	3,939	655	—	25.0	23.1	47.7	—	18.2
1969	18,899 [6]	17,370 [6]	1,373 [6]	398 [7]	4,787 [6]	4,052 [6]	689 [6]	134 [7]	25.3 [6]	23.3 [6]	50.2 [6]	33.6 [7]	19.7 [6]
1970	19,470	17,767	1,540	—	4,793	4,011	735	—	24.6	22.6	47.7	—	18.9
1971	19,827	18,087	1,584	—	4,273	3,605	623	—	21.6	19.9	39.3	—	16.7
1972	20,117	18,340	1,603	—	3,738	3,072	640	—	18.6	16.8	39.9	—	15.3
1973	20,602	18,754	1,672	381	3,354	2,698	620	95	16.3	14.4	37.1	24.9	14.6
1974	—	—	—	—	3,085	2,460	591	117	14.6	12.8	34.3	28.9	13.2
1975	21,662	19,654	1,795	420	3,317	2,634	652	137	15.3	13.4	36.3	32.6	12.8
1976	22,100	20,020	1,852	464	3,313	2,633	644	128	15.0	13.2	34.8	27.7	13.3
1977	22,468	20,316	1,930	518	3,177	2,426	701	113	14.1	11.9	36.3	21.9	12.9
1978	23,175	20,950	1,954	539	3,233	2,530	662	125	14.0	12.1	33.9	23.2	13.2
1979	24,194	21,898	2,040	574	3,682	2,911	740	154	15.2	13.3	36.2	26.8	14.1
1980	24,686	22,325	2,054	582	3,871 [8]	3,042 [8]	783 [8]	179 [8]	15.7 [8]	13.6 [8]	38.1 [8]	30.8 [8]	13.2 [6]
1981	25,231	22,791	2,102	568	3,853	2,978	820	146	15.3	13.1	39.0	25.7	12.1
1982	25,738	23,234	2,124	596	3,751	2,870	811	159	14.6	12.4	38.2	26.6	10.9
1983	26,313	23,754	2,197	782	3,625	2,776	791	173	13.8	11.7	36.0	22.1	10.3
1984	26,818	24,206	2,238	819	3,330	2,579	710	176	12.4	10.7	31.7	21.5	9.9
1985	27,322	24,629	2,273	915	3,456	2,698	717	219	12.6	11.0	31.5	23.9	10.5
1986	27,975	25,173	2,331	906	3,477	2,689	722	204	12.4	10.7	31.0	22.5	10.7
1987	28,487	25,602	2,387	885	3,563	2,704	774	243	12.5	10.6	32.4	27.5	11.1
1988	29,022	26,001	2,436	1,005	3,481	2,593	785	225	12.0	10.0	32.2	22.4	11.0
1989	29,566	26,479	2,487	1,024	3,363	2,539	763	211	11.4	9.6	30.7	20.6	10.7
1990	30,093	26,898	2,547	1,091	3,658	2,707	860	245	12.2	10.1	33.8	22.5	10.9
1991	30,590	27,297	2,606	1,143	3,781	2,802	880	237	12.4	10.3	33.8	20.8	10.6
1992	30,430	27,256	2,504	1,298	3,928	2,989	838	287	12.9	11.0	33.5	22.1	10.3
1993	30,799	27,580	2,510	1,390	3,755	2,939	702	297	12.2	10.7	28.0	21.4	9.6
1994	31,267	27,985	2,557	1,428	3,663	2,846	700	323	11.7	10.2	27.4	22.6	9.6
1995	31,658	28,436	2,478	1,458	3,318	2,572	629	342	10.5	9.0	25.4	23.5	9.1
1996	31,877	28,464	2,616	1,516	3,428	2,667	661	370	10.8	9.4	25.3	24.4	9.4
1997	32,082	28,553	2,691	1,617	3,376	2,569	700	384	10.5	9.0	26.0	23.8	9.5
1998	32,394	28,759	2,723	1,696	3,386	2,555	718	356	10.5	8.9	26.4	21.0	9.8
1999	—	—	—	—	3,167	—	—	—	—	—	—	—	9.8

[1] Tabulation procedures changed numerous times, affecting the comparability of the poverty series over time. See documentation for Table Be260–282.

[2] Includes other races not shown separately.

[3] Hispanics can be of any race. Tabulation procedures changed in 1972, affecting Hispanic counts. See documentation for Table Be260–282.

[4] Derived from 1-in-1,000 sample.

[5] Overestimate of poverty population. See documentation for Table Be260–282.

[6] Not revised.

[7] Derived from 5-percent sample.

[8] Not revised. However, the figure is consistent with any 1980 "total persons" or "total families" figures because slight modifications in the poverty definition did not affect such totals for this year.

Sources

U.S. Bureau of the Census, March Current Population Survey (CPS). Data were obtained from the Internet site of the U.S. Census Bureau, Poverty and Health Statistics Branch/HHES Division. Series Be310–321, from *Historical Poverty Tables*, Table 3; series Be322, based on series Be266 and Be314. Exceptions for specific dates are noted.

In all series, the figures for 1999 were found in *Current Population Reports* (CPR) series P-60, number 210, Table A, p. vi.

Series Be311. Figures for the following years were obtained from CPR series P-60: 1959, number 91, Table L, p. 13; 1969, number 76, Table 4, p. 40; 1970, number 91, Table L, p. 13; 1971, number 86, Table 9, p. 64; 1972, number 91, Table 9, p. 50; 1973, number 98, Table 6, p. 35.

Series Be312. Figures for the following years were obtained from CPR series P-60: 1959, number 91, Table L, p. 13; 1970, number 91, Table L, p. 13.

Series Be313. 1969: 1970 Census of Population, *Report* PC (2)-9A, Table 1, p. 7; 1973 and 1975: CPR series P-60, number 98, Table 46, p. 139, and number 106, Table 42, p. 177, respectively.

Series Be314. 1992: CPR series P-60, number 188, Table D-5, p. D-17.

Series Be316 and Be320. 1970: CPR series P-60, number 91, Table L, p. 13.

Series Be317 and Be321. 1969: 1970 Census of Population, *Report* PC (2)-9A, Table 1, pp. 7–8.

Documentation

Refer to the appendixes to the essay on poverty in this chapter for additional discussion of the tables, as well as for various technical definitions and descriptions.

Series Be322. Calculated by dividing series Be314 by series Be266. Exceptions for specific dates are as noted. 1959: calculated by dividing series Be314 by 1959 total persons in poverty from the 1-in-1,000 sample of the 1960 Decennial Census (38,766 thousand) as found in CPR series P-60, number 91, Table L, p. 13; 1969: calculated by dividing series Be314 by *unrevised* 1969 total persons in poverty (24,289 thousand) as found in CPR series P-60,

TABLE Be310–322 Persons age 65 and older below poverty threshold, by the race and Hispanic origin: 1959–1999 *Continued*

number 86, Table 1, p. 29; 1980: calculated by dividing series Be314 by *unrevised* 1980 total persons in poverty (29,272 thousand) as found in CPR series P-60, number 133, Table D, p. 6.

According to the Census Bureau, the racial or ethnic categorization of persons is that of the individual, regardless of the racial or ethnic categorization of the family householder. Although this has been the case for some years, it was not always so. A supplementary P-60 poverty report issued in 1974 indicates (CPR series P-60, number 95, p. 3) that, in the main P-60 poverty reports for income years 1971 and 1972, persons were classified by the race of the family head (and not by their own race). The contributors of this table have not been able to determine when that situation changed to what it is today.

TABLE Be323–342 Related children in families below poverty threshold, by the sex, race, and Hispanic origin of the household head: 1959–1999[1]

Contributed by Linda Barrington and Gordon M. Fisher

	Related children younger than 18 in families for whom poverty status is determined					Related children in families					
						Number in poverty					
							Younger than 18				
	Total	In white families	In black families	In Hispanic families	In female-headed households	Younger than 6	Total	In white families	In black families	In Hispanic families	In female-headed households
	Be323[2]	Be324	Be325	Be326[3]	Be327	Be328	Be329[2]	Be330	Be331	Be332[3]	Be333
Year	Thousand	Thousand	Thousand	Thousand	Thousand	Thousand	Thousand	Thousand	Thousand	Thousand	Thousand
1959	63,995	—	7,664[5]	—	5,741	6,268[5]	17,208	11,386	5,022[5]	—	4,145
1960	65,275	—	—	—	5,987	—	17,288	11,229	—	—	4,095
1961	65,792	—	—	—	6,212	—	16,577	10,614	—	—	4,044
1962	67,385	—	—	—	6,419	—	16,630	10,382	—	—	4,506
1963	68,837	—	—	—	6,838	—	15,691	9,749	—	—	4,554
1964	69,364	—	—	—	7,098	—	15,736	9,573	—	—	4,422
1965	69,638	—	—	—	7,106	—	14,388	8,595	—	—	4,562
1966	69,869	59,579	9,470[6]	—	7,323	4,261	12,146	7,204	4,774	—	4,262
1967[4]	70,058	59,583	9,631[6]	—	7,820	3,996	11,427	6,729	4,558	—	4,246
1968	70,035	59,416	9,741[6]	—	7,987	3,559	10,739	6,373	4,188	—	4,409
1969	68,746	58,578	9,290	3,939[7]	—	3,079	9,501	5,667	3,677	1,156[7]	4,247
1970	68,815	58,472	9,448	—	—	3,561[8]	10,235	6,138	3,922	—	4,689
1971	68,474	58,119	9,414	—	9,127	3,499	10,344	6,341	3,836	—	4,850
1972	67,592	57,181	9,426	—	9,600	3,276	10,082	5,784	4,025	—	5,094
1973	66,626	56,211	9,405	4,910	9,929	3,097	9,453	5,462	3,822	1,364	5,171
1974	—	55,320	9,384	4,939	—	3,294[8]	9,967	6,079	3,713	1,414	5,361
1975	64,750	54,126	9,374	4,896	10,622	3,460	10,882	6,748	3,884	1,619	5,597
1976	63,729	53,167	9,291	4,736	10,739	3,270	10,081	6,034	3,758	1,424	5,583
1977	62,823	52,299	9,253	5,000	11,238	3,326	10,028	5,943	3,850	1,402	5,658
1978	61,987	51,409	9,168	4,972	11,232	3,184	9,722	5,674	3,781	1,354	5,687
1979	62,646	51,687	9,172	5,426	11,595	3,415	9,993	5,909	3,745	1,505	5,635
1980	62,168	51,002	9,287	5,211	11,539	3,986[8]	11,114[8]	6,817[8]	3,906[8]	1,718[8]	5,866[8]
1981	61,756	50,553	9,291	5,291	12,059	4,422	12,068	7,429	4,170	1,874	6,305
1982	61,565	50,305	9,269	5,436	11,946	4,821	13,139	8,282	4,388	2,117	6,696
1983	61,578	50,183	9,245	5,977	12,172	5,118	13,427	8,534	4,273	2,251	6,747
1984	61,681	50,192	9,356	5,982	12,536	4,938	12,929	8,086	4,320	2,317	6,772
1985	62,019	50,358	9,405	6,346	12,531	4,832	12,483	7,838	4,057	2,512	6,712
1986	62,009	50,356	9,467	6,511	12,763	4,619	12,257	7,714	4,037	2,413	6,943
1987	62,423	50,360	9,546	6,692	13,066	4,792	12,275	7,398	4,234	2,606	7,019
1988	62,906	50,590	9,681	6,908	13,146	4,800	11,935	7,095	4,148	2,576	6,955
1989	63,225	50,704	9,847	7,040	13,316	4,868	12,001	7,164	4,257	2,496	6,808
1990	63,908	51,028	9,980	7,300	13,793	5,198	12,715	7,696	4,412	2,750	7,363
1991	64,800	51,627	10,178	7,473	14,545	5,483	13,658	8,316	4,637	2,977	8,065
1992	67,256	53,110	10,823	8,829	15,319	6,082	14,521	8,752	5,015	3,440	8,368
1993	68,040	53,614	10,969	9,188	15,844	6,097	14,961	9,123	5,030	3,666	8,503
1994	68,819	54,221	11,044	9,621	15,924	5,878	14,610	8,826	4,787	3,956	8,427
1995	69,425	54,532	11,198	10,011	16,637	5,670	13,999	8,474	4,644	3,938	8,364
1996	69,411	54,599	11,155	10,255	16,213	5,333	13,764	8,488	4,411	4,090	7,990
1997	69,844	54,870	11,193	10,625	16,175	5,049	13,422	8,441	4,116	3,865	7,928
1998	70,253	55,126	11,176	10,921	16,550	4,775	12,845	7,935	4,073	3,670	7,627
1999	—	—	—	—	—	4,170	11,510	—	—	—	—

Notes appear at end of table

(continued)

TABLE Be323–342 Related children in families below poverty threshold, by the sex, race, and Hispanic origin of the household head: 1959–1999 *Continued*

	Related children in families						Percentage of persons in poverty who are		
	Percentage in poverty								
		Younger than 18							
	Younger than 6	In all families	In white families	In black families	In Hispanic families	In female-headed households	Younger than 18	Younger than 6	Related children younger than 18 in female-headed households (no spouse present)
	Be334	Be335 [2]	Be336	Be337	Be338 [3]	Be339	Be340	Be341	Be342
Year	Percent	Percent	Percent	Percent	Percent	Percent	Percent	Percent	Percent
1959	26.0 [5]	26.9	20.6	65.5 [5]	—	72.2	43.6	16.2 [5]	10.5
1960	—	26.5	20.0	—	—	68.4	43.4	—	10.3
1961	—	25.2	18.7	—	—	65.1	41.8	—	10.2
1962	—	24.7	17.9	—	—	70.2	43.1	—	11.7
1963	—	22.8	16.5	—	—	66.6	43.1	—	12.5
1964	—	22.7	16.1	—	—	62.3	43.6	—	12.3
1965	—	20.7	14.4	—	—	64.2	43.4	—	13.7
1966	18.1	17.4	12.1	50.6	—	58.2	42.6	14.9	14.9
1967 [4]	17.5	16.3	11.3	47.4	—	54.3	41.2	14.4	15.3
1968	16.1	15.3	10.7	43.1	—	55.2	42.3	14.0	17.4
1969	14.8	13.8	9.7	39.6	29.3 [7]	54.4	39.3	12.8	17.6
1970	16.6 [8]	14.9	10.5	41.5	—	53.0	40.3	14.0 [8]	18.4
1971	16.9	15.1	10.9	40.4	—	53.1	40.5	13.7	19.0
1972	16.1	14.9	10.1	42.7	—	53.1	41.2	13.4	20.8
1973	15.7	14.2	9.7	40.6	27.8	52.1	41.1	13.5	22.5
1974	16.9 [8]	15.1	11.0	39.6	28.6	51.5	42.6	13.6 [8]	22.9
1975	18.2	16.8	12.5	41.4	33.1	52.7	42.1	13.4	21.6
1976	17.7	15.8	11.3	40.4	30.1	52.0	40.4	13.1	22.4
1977	18.1	16.0	11.4	41.6	28.0	50.3	40.6	13.5	22.9
1978	17.2	15.7	11.0	41.2	27.2	50.6	39.7	13.0	23.2
1979	17.8	16.0	11.4	40.8	27.7	48.6	38.3	13.1	21.6
1980	20.3 [8]	17.9 [8]	13.4 [8]	42.1 [8]	33.0 [8]	50.8 [8]	38.0 [8]	13.6 [8]	20.0 [8]
1981	22.0	19.5	14.7	44.9	35.4	52.3	37.9	13.9	19.8
1982	23.3	21.3	16.5	47.3	38.9	56.1	38.2	14.0	19.5
1983	24.6	21.8	17.0	46.2	37.7	55.4	38.0	14.5	19.1
1984	23.4	21.0	16.1	46.2	38.7	54.0	38.4	14.7	20.1
1985	22.6	20.1	15.6	43.1	39.6	53.6	37.8	14.6	20.3
1986	21.6	19.8	15.3	42.7	37.1	54.4	37.9	14.3	21.4
1987	22.1	19.7	14.7	44.4	38.9	53.7	38.1	14.9	21.8
1988	21.8	19.0	14.0	42.8	37.3	52.9	37.6	15.1	21.9
1989	21.9	19.0	14.1	43.2	35.5	51.1	38.1	15.4	21.6
1990	23.0	19.9	15.1	44.2	37.7	53.4	37.9	15.5	21.9
1991	24.0	21.1	16.1	45.6	39.8	55.4	38.2	15.4	22.6
1992	25.7	21.6	16.5	46.3	39.0	54.6	38.2	16.0	22.0
1993	25.6	22.0	17.0	45.9	39.9	53.7	38.1	15.5	21.7
1994	24.5	21.2	16.3	43.3	41.1	52.9	38.4	15.4	22.1
1995	23.7	20.2	15.5	41.5	39.3	50.3	38.4	15.6	23.0
1996	22.7	19.8	15.5	39.5	39.9	49.3	37.7	14.6	21.9
1997	21.6	19.2	15.4	36.8	36.4	49.0	37.7	14.2	22.3
1998	20.6	18.3	14.4	36.4	33.6	46.1	37.3	13.9	22.1
1999	18.0	16.3	—	—	—	—	35.7	12.9	—

[1] Tabulation procedures changed numerous times, affecting the comparability of the poverty series over time. See documentation for Table Be260–282.

[2] Includes other races not shown separately.

[3] Hispanics can be of any race. Tabulation procedures changed in 1972, affecting Hispanic counts. See documentation for Table Be260–282.

[4] Overestimate of poverty population. See documentation for Table Be260–282.

[5] Derived from 1-in-1,000 sample.

[6] Figure (from an unpublished tabulation for the Office of Economic Opportunity) differs slightly from the corresponding figure tabulated for – but not published in – the standard 1968 poverty report, even though there is no difference in the underlying data source or population coverage. Compare, for instance, the 1968 poverty population figures from *Current Population Reports* (CPR) series C-60, number 68, Table 1, p. 21 (25,389 thousand) and CPR series P-60, number 95, Table 1, p. 4 (25,377 thousand). Accordingly, dividing the figure in series Be331 by this figure may produce a result that differs by one or two tenths of a percentage point from the corresponding figure appearing in series Be337.

[7] Derived from 5-percent sample.

[8] Not revised.

Sources

U.S. Bureau of the Census, March *Current Population Survey* (CPS). Data were obtained from the Internet site of the U.S. Census Bureau, Poverty and Health Statistics Branch/HHES Division. Series Be323–326, Be329–332, and Be335–338, from *Historical Poverty Tables*, Table 3; series Be328 and Be334, from *Historical Poverty Tables*, Table 20; series Be327 and Be333, from *Historical Poverty Tables*, Table 10; series Be339, constructed by dividing series Be333 by series Be327; series Be340–342, calculated by dividing series Be328–329 and Be333, respectively, by series Be266. Exceptions for specific dates are noted.

TABLE Be323–342 Related children in families below poverty threshold, by the sex, race, and Hispanic origin of the household head: 1959–1999 *Continued*

In all series, the figures for 1999 were found in CPR series P-60, number 210, Table A, p. vi.

Series Be324–325. 1966–1968: from unpublished tabulation prepared for the Office of Economic Opportunity by the U.S. Census Bureau.

Series Be325. 1959: CPR series P-23, number 37, Table 3, p. 24.

Series Be326 and Be338. 1969: 1970 Census of the Population, *Report* PC(2)-9A, Table 1, pp. 7 and 8, respectively.

Series Be327. 1963–1974: CPR series P-60, number 68, Table 1, p. 24, and unpublished tabulations prepared for the Office of Economic Opportunity by the U.S. Census Bureau. As of August 9, 2000, *Historical Poverty Tables*, Table 10, contained data errors throughout these years.

Series Be328 and Be334. 1959: CPR series P-23, number 37, Table 19, pp. 72 and 76, respectively; 1969: CPR series P-60, number 124, Table A, p. 2; 1979: CPR series P-60, number 127, Table 16, pp. 26 and 27, respectively. Figures for 1966–1968 were obtained from unpublished tabulations prepared for the Office of Economic Opportunity by the U.S. Census Bureau; figures for 1983–1987 were obtained from other unpublished Census Bureau tabulations.

Series Be328. 1992: CPR series P-60, number 188, Table B-2, p. B-4.

Series Be330. 1961–1964: CPR series P-60, number 68, Table 1, p. 21; 1992: CPR series P-60, number 188, Table D-5, p. D-18.

Series Be331. 1959: CPR series P-23, number 37, Table 19, p. 75; 1992: CPR series P-60, number 188, Table D-5, p. D-19.

Series Be332. 1969: 1970 Census of the Population, *Report* PC(2)-9A, Table 1, p. 7; 1992: CPR series P-60, number 188, Table D-5, p. D-20.

Series Be333. 1974: CPR series P-60, number 106, Table 1, p. 15.

Series Be336. 1961–1964: CPR series P-60, number 68, Table 1, p. 24; 1969: 1970 Census of the Population, *Report* PC(2)-9A, Table 1, p. 8.

Series Be337. 1959: CPR series P-23, number 37, Table 19, p. 79.

Series Be339. 1963–1968: CPR series P-60, number 68, Table 1, p. 24; and figures for 1969 and 1970 were obtained from CPR series P-60, number 86, Table 1, p. 31.

Series Be340. 1980: calculated by dividing the 1980 figure from series Be329 by *unrevised* 1980 total persons in poverty (29,272 thousand), from CPR series P-60, number 133, Table D, p. 6.

Series Be341. 1959: calculated by dividing the 1959 figure from series Be328 by the 1959 total persons in poverty from the 1-in-1,000 sample of the 1960 Decennial Census (38,766 thousand), from CPR series P-60, number 91, Table L, p. 13. Figures for 1970, 1974, and 1980 were calculated by dividing the 1970, 1974, and 1980 figures from series Be328 by the *unrevised* total persons in poverty, respectively, 1970: 25,522 thousand (CPR series P-60, number 81, Table A, p. 2); 1974: 24,260 thousand (CPR series P-60, number 106, Table E, p. 10); and 1980: 29,272 thousand (CPR series P-60, number 133, Table D, p. 6).

Series Be342. 1980: calculated by dividing the 1980 figure from series Be333 by the *unrevised* 1980 total persons in poverty, 29,272 thousand (CPR series P-60, number 133, Table D, p. 6).

Documentation

Refer to the appendixes in the essay on poverty in this chapter for additional discussion of the tables, as well as various technical definitions and descriptions.

For this table, 1980 figures were available on both the unrevised and revised basis for related children younger than age 18 in poverty, but only on the *unrevised* basis for the white, black, and Hispanic components of that group. To have consistent figures within the table, the *unrevised* figures are presented for the former group as well as for its components.

The term "children," as used in tables on living arrangements of children younger than age 18, are all persons younger than age 18, excluding people who maintain households, families, or subfamilies as a reference person or spouse. Related children in a family include own children and all other children younger than age 18 in the household who are related to the householder by birth, marriage, or adoption. The count of related children in families was formerly restricted to never-married children. However, beginning with data for 1968 the U.S. Census Bureau included ever-married children under the category of related children. This change added approximately 20,000 children to the total number of related children in March 1968. Note, however, that the term "children" is sometimes used differently in the text of recent CPS reports. Beginning with the report for income year 1987, the term "children" is sometimes used to refer to all persons younger than age 18 without exclusion.

A family is a group of two people or more (one of whom is the householder) related by birth, marriage, or adoption and residing together; all such people (including related subfamily members) are considered to be members of one family. Beginning with the March 1980 CPS (data for income year 1979), unrelated subfamilies (referred to in the past as secondary families) are no longer included in the count of families, nor are the members of unrelated subfamilies included in the count of family members. The number of families is equal to the number of family households; however, the count of family members differs from the count of family household members because family household members include any nonrelatives living in the household.

The racial or ethnic categorization of the family is based on the racial or ethnic categorization of the family householder. The householder refers to the person (or one of the people) in whose name the housing unit is owned or rented (maintained) or, if there is no such person, any adult member, excluding roomers, boarders, or paid employees. Beginning with the March 1980 CPS, if the house is owned or rented jointly by a married couple, the householder may be either the husband or the wife. The person designated as the householder is the "reference person" to whom the relationship of all other household members, if any, is recorded.

The number of householders is equal to the number of households. Also, the number of family householders is equal to the number of families.

Specifically, beginning with the March 1980 CPS, the U.S. Census Bureau replaced the terms "head of household" and "head of family" with "householder" and "family householder," respectively, in response to greater sharing of household responsibilities among the adult members of the household and family. Specifically, beginning in 1980, the Census Bureau discontinued its longtime practice of always classifying the husband as the reference person (head) when he and his wife are living together.

TABLE Be343–354 Persons below poverty threshold, by metropolitan residence: 1959–1999[1]

Contributed by Linda Barrington and Gordon M. Fisher

	Number of poor persons				Percentage of residents who are poor				Percentage of poor living in			
	Metropolitan areas				Metropolitan areas				Metropolitan areas			
	Total	Central cities	Noncentral cities	Nonmetropolitan areas	Total	Central cities	Noncentral cities	Nonmetropolitan areas	Total	Central cities	Noncentral cities	Nonmetropolitan areas
	Be343	Be344	Be345	Be346	Be347	Be348	Be349	Be350	Be351	Be352	Be353	Be354
Year	Thousand	Thousand	Thousand	Thousand	Percent	Percent	Percent	Percent	Percent	Percent	Percent	Percent
1959 [2]	17,019	10,437	6,582	21,747	15.3	18.3	12.2	33.2	43.9	26.9	17.0	56.1
1967 [3]	13,832	8,649	5,183	13,936	10.9	15.0	7.5	20.2	49.8	31.1	18.7	50.2
1968	12,871	7,754	5,117	12,518	10.0	13.4	7.3	18.0	50.7	30.5	20.2	49.3
1969	13,084	7,993	5,091	11,063	9.5	12.7	6.8	17.9	54.2	33.1	21.1	45.8
1970	13,317	8,118	5,199	12,103	10.2	14.2	7.1	16.9	52.4	31.9	20.5	47.6
1971	14,561	8,912	5,649	10,999	10.4	14.2	7.2	17.2	57.0	34.9	22.1	43.0
1972	14,508	9,179	5,329	9,952	10.3	14.7	6.8	15.3	59.3	37.5	21.8	40.7
1973	13,759	8,594	5,165	9,214	9.7	14.0	6.4	14.0	59.9	37.4	22.5	40.1
1974	13,851	8,373	5,477	9,519	9.7	13.7	6.7	14.2	59.3	35.8	23.4	40.7
1975	15,348	9,090	6,259	10,529	10.8	15.0	7.6	15.4	59.3	35.1	24.2	40.7
1976	15,229	9,482	5,747	9,746	10.7	15.8	6.9	14.0	61.0	38.0	23.0	39.0
1977	14,859	9,203	5,657	9,861	10.4	15.4	6.8	13.9	60.1	37.2	22.9	39.9
1978	15,090	9,285	5,805	9,407	10.4	15.4	6.8	13.5	61.6	37.9	23.7	38.4
1979	16,135	9,720	6,415	9,937	10.7	15.7	7.2	13.8	61.9	37.3	24.6	38.1
1980	18,157	10,674	7,483	11,483	11.9	17.2	8.3	15.7	61.3	36.0	25.2	38.7
1981	19,347	11,231	8,116	12,475	12.6	18.0	8.9	17.0	60.8	35.3	25.5	39.2
1982	21,247	12,696	8,551	13,152	13.7	19.9	9.3	17.8	61.8	36.9	24.9	38.2
1983 [4]	21,750	12,872	8,878	13,516	13.8	19.8	9.6	18.3	61.7	36.5	25.2	38.3
1985	23,275	14,177	9,097	9,789	12.7	19.0	8.4	18.3	70.4	42.9	27.5	29.6
1986	22,657	13,295	9,362	9,712	12.3	18.0	8.4	18.1	70.0	41.1	28.9	30.0
1987	23,054	13,697	9,357	9,167	12.3	18.3	8.3	17.0	71.5	42.5	29.0	28.5
1988	23,059	13,615	9,444	8,686	12.2	18.1	8.3	16.0	72.6	42.9	29.7	27.4
1989	22,917	13,592	9,326	8,611	12.0	18.1	8.0	15.7	72.7	43.1	29.6	27.3
1990	24,510	14,254	10,255	9,075	12.7	19.0	8.7	16.3	73.0	42.4	30.5	27.0
1991	26,827	15,314	11,513	8,881	13.7	20.2	9.6	16.1	75.1	42.9	32.2	24.9
1992	28,380	16,346	12,034	9,634	14.2	20.9	9.9	16.9	74.7	43.0	31.7	25.3
1993	29,615	16,805	12,810	9,650	14.6	21.5	10.3	17.2	75.4	42.8	32.6	24.6
1994	29,610	16,098	13,511	8,449	14.2	20.9	10.3	16.0	77.8	42.3	35.5	22.2
1995	28,342	16,269	12,072	8,083	13.4	20.6	9.1	15.6	77.8	44.7	33.1	22.2
1996	28,211	15,645	12,566	8,318	13.2	19.6	9.4	15.9	77.2	42.8	34.4	22.8
1997	27,273	15,018	12,255	8,301	12.6	18.8	9.0	15.9	76.7	42.2	34.4	23.3
1998	26,997	14,921	12,076	7,479	12.3	18.5	8.7	14.4	78.3	43.3	35.0	21.7
1999	24,816	13,123	11,693	7,442	11.2	16.4	8.3	14.3	76.9	40.7	36.2	23.1

[1] Tabulation procedures changed numerous times, affecting the comparability of the poverty series over time. See documentation for Table Be260–282.

[2] Derived from 1-in-1,000 sample.

[3] Overestimate of poverty population. See documentation for Table Be260–282.

[4] Not revised.

Sources

U.S. Bureau of the Census, March *Current Population Survey* (CPS). Data were obtained from the Internet site of the U.S. Census Bureau, Poverty and Health Statistics Branch/HHES Division. Series Be343–350, from *Historical Poverty Tables*, Table 8. Exceptions for specific dates are as noted.

In all series, the figures for 1999 were found in Current Population Report (CPR) series P-60, number 210, Table A, p. vi.

Series Be343–350. The figures for 1959 were derived from the 1-in-1,000 sample of the 1960 Decennial Census. See CPR series P-60, number 76, p. 24, and series P-23, number 37, pp. 6–9, 12–13. The figures for 1980 were obtained from the CPR series P-60, number 134, Table 14, p. 21.

Series Be351–354. Based on series Be343–346.

Documentation

Refer to the appendixes to the essay on poverty in this chapter for additional discussion of the tables, as well as for various technical definitions and descriptions.

The definition of metropolitan area (Standard Metropolitan Statistical Area, SMSA) is not constant over time. Data for income years 1959 through 1968 use metropolitan area (SMSA) definitions based on the 1960 Decennial Census. (See CPR series P-23, number 37, pp. 1, 9, and series P-60, number 86, pp. 13–14, 22.) Data for income years 1969 (revised), 1970 (revised), and 1971 through 1983 use metropolitan area (SMSA) definitions based on the 1970 Decennial Census. (See CPR series P-60, number 86, pp. 13–14, 22, number 147, pp. 175, 183, and number 158, p. 167.) Data for income years 1985 through 1993 use metropolitan area (Metropolitan Statistical Area) definitions announced in 1984 and based on the 1980 Decennial Census. (See CPR series P-60, number 158, pp. 159, 167, and series P-60, number 194, Appendix E.) And data for income years 1994 and subsequent years use metropolitan area definitions based on the 1990 Decennial Census. (See CPR series P-60, number 194, Appendix E.)

It is important to emphasize that "metropolitan" and "nonmetropolitan" areas should not be referred to as "urban" and "rural." The Census Bureau's urban/rural distinction is quite different from its metropolitan/nonmetropolitan distinction. Although the Census Bureau's definition of "urban" has several elements, it has always included incorporated places of 2,500 or more persons. (See "Urban and Rural Definitions" on the Census Bureau's Internet site.) This definition is entirely appropriate in its historical context. However, it is questionable whether most people would consider an incorporated place of just 2,500 persons as "urban." Because of the confusion over differing popular and technical uses of these words, it is probably better to avoid the words "urban" and "rural" entirely.

TABLE Be343–354 Persons below poverty threshold, by metropolitan residence: 1959–1999 *Continued*

Metropolitan-nonmetropolitan residence is defined by the U.S. Census Bureau as follows. The general concept of a metropolitan area is one of a large population nucleus, together with adjacent communities that have a high degree of economic and social integration with that nucleus. Some metropolitan areas are defined around two or more nuclei. The metropolitan area classification is a statistical standard, developed for use by federal agencies in the production, analysis, and publication of data on metropolitan areas. The metropolitan areas are designated and defined by the Federal Office of Management and Budget, following a set of official published standards. These standards were developed by the interagency Federal Executive Committee on Metropolitan Areas, with the aim of producing definitions that are as consistent as possible for all metropolitan areas nationwide. Each metropolitan area must contain either a place with a minimum population of 50,000 or a Census Bureau–defined urbanized area and a total metropolitan area population of at least 100,000 (75,000 in New England). A metropolitan area comprises one or more central counties, and a metropolitan area may also include one or more outlying counties that have closed economic and social relationships with the central county. An outlying county must have a specified level of commuting to the central counties and also must meet certain standards regarding metropolitan character, such as population density, urban population, and population growth. In New England, metropolitan areas are composed of cities and towns rather than whole counties. The territory, population, and housing units in metropolitan areas are referred to as "metropolitan." The territory, population, and housing units located outside the metropolitan area are referred to as "nonmetropolitan."

Central city residence is defined by the U.S. Census Bureau as follows. The metropolitan category is subdivided into "inside central city" and "outside central city." The largest central city and, in some cases, up to two additional central cities are included in the title of the metropolitan area; there are also central cities that are not included in any metropolitan area title. A metropolitan central city does not include any part of that city that extends outside the metropolitan area boundary.

Series Be351–354. Constructed by dividing series Be343–346, respectively, by series Be266. Exceptions for the denominator are as noted. 1959: the 1959 total persons in poverty from the 1-in-1,000 sample of the 1960 Decennial Census (38,766 thousand), as found in CPR series P-60, number 91, Table L, p. 13. 1980: the revised 1980 total persons in poverty (29,640 thousand), as found in CPR series P-60, number 133, Table D, p. 6. 1983: the unrevised 1983 total persons in poverty (35,266 thousand), as found in CPR series P-60, number 152, Table B, p. 3.

TABLE Be355–370 Persons below poverty threshold, by region: 1959–1999[1]

Contributed by Linda Barrington and Gordon M. Fisher

	Persons for whom poverty status is determined				Number of persons in poverty				Percentage in poverty				Percentage of poor population residing in			
	Northeast	South	Midwest	West	Northeast	South	Midwest	West	Northeast	South	Midwest	West	Northeast	South	Midwest	West
	Be355	Be356	Be357	Be358	Be359	Be360	Be361	Be362	Be363	Be364	Be365	Be366	Be367	Be368	Be369	Be370
Year	Thousand	Thousand	Thousand	Thousand	Thousand	Thousand	Thousand	Thousand	Percent	Percent	Percent	Percent	Percent	Percent	Percent	Percent
1959 [2]	—	53,941	—	—	—	19,116	—	—	—	35.4	—	—	—	49.3	—	—
1967 [3]	—	—	—	—	—	12,976	—	—	—	22.1	—	—	—	46.7	—	—
1969	—	58,834	—	—	4,108	11,090	5,424	3,525	8.6	17.9	9.6	10.4	17.0	45.9	22.5	14.6
1970	47,597	61,825	56,286	33,809	4,204	11,462	5,842	3,947	8.7	18.6	10.3	11.3	16.5	45.1	23.0	15.5
1971	—	—	—	—	4,512	11,182	5,764	4,101	9.3	17.5	10.3	11.4	17.7	43.7	22.6	16.0
1972	48,584	63,746	56,107	36,116	4,266	10,928	5,258	4,008	8.7	16.9	9.3	11.1	17.4	44.7	21.5	16.4
1973	48,853	64,579	56,502	36,070	4,207	10,061	4,864	3,841	8.6	15.3	8.6	10.5	18.3	43.8	21.2	16.7
1974	48,829	65,613	56,437	36,742	4,247	10,319	4,994	3,811	8.8	15.4	8.8	10.1	18.2	44.2	21.4	16.3
1975	—	66,986	—	—	4,904	11,059	5,459	4,454	10.2	16.2	9.7	11.7	19.0	42.7	21.1	17.2
1976	48,154	68,095	56,397	38,218	4,949	10,354	5,657	4,015	10.2	15.2	9.9	10.5	19.8	41.5	22.7	16.1
1977	48,508	68,236	57,157	38,402	4,956	10,249	5,589	3,927	10.2	14.8	9.8	10.1	20.0	41.5	22.6	15.9
1978	48,823	69,148	56,969	38,927	5,050	10,255	5,192	4,000	10.4	14.7	9.1	10.0	20.6	41.9	21.2	16.3
1979	48,576	69,910	57,313	39,858	5,058	11,098	5,639	4,276	10.4	15.0	9.7	10.1	19.4	42.6	21.6	16.4
1980	—	—	—	—	5,402	12,504	6,729	5,005	11.1	16.7	11.6	11.5	18.2	42.2	22.7	16.9
1981	48,533	75,001	58,054	43,439	5,815	13,256	7,142	5,609	11.9	17.4	12.3	12.7	18.3	41.7	22.4	17.6
1982	48,944	76,034	58,183	43,997	6,364	13,967	7,772	6,296	13.0	18.1	13.3	14.1	18.5	40.6	22.6	18.3
1983	49,054	77,375	58,228	44,754	6,605	13,504	8,511	6,682	13.4	17.2	14.6	14.6	18.7	38.3	24.1	18.9
1984	—	—	—	—	6,531	12,792	8,303	6,074	13.2	16.2	14.1	13.1	19.4	38.0	24.6	18.0
1985	49,374	79,195	58,749	46,498	5,751	12,921	8,191	6,201	11.6	16.0	13.9	13.0	17.4	39.1	24.8	18.8
1986	49,413	80,604	58,745	47,832	5,211	13,106	7,641	6,412	10.5	16.1	13.0	13.2	16.1	40.5	23.6	19.8
1987	49,572	81,646	58,702	48,634	5,378	13,297	7,370	6,176	10.9	16.1	12.5	12.4	16.7	41.3	22.9	19.2
1988	—	—	—	—	5,089	13,530	6,804	6,322	10.1	16.1	11.4	12.7	16.0	42.6	21.4	19.9
1989	50,272	83,817	59,493	49,948	5,061	12,943	7,043	6,481	10.0	15.4	11.9	12.5	16.1	41.1	22.3	20.6
1990	50,520	84,044	59,428	52,000	5,794	13,456	7,458	6,877	11.4	15.8	12.4	13.0	17.3	40.1	22.2	20.5
1991	50,799	85,097	59,914	52,835	6,177	13,783	7,989	7,759	12.2	16.0	13.2	14.3	17.3	38.6	22.4	21.7
1992	50,789	85,895	60,371	54,136	6,414	15,198	8,060	8,343	12.6	17.1	13.3	14.8	16.9	40.0	21.2	21.9
1993	50,808	88,763	60,793	56,186	6,839	15,375	8,172	8,879	13.3	17.1	13.4	15.6	17.4	39.2	20.8	22.6
1994	51,474	89,654	61,158	56,992	6,597	14,729	7,965	8,768	12.9	16.1	13.0	15.3	17.3	38.7	20.9	23.0
1995	51,185	91,717	61,379	57,335	6,445	14,458	6,785	8,736	12.5	15.7	11.0	14.9	17.7	39.7	18.6	24.0
1996	51,429	92,027	61,773	58,503	6,558	14,098	6,654	9,219	12.7	15.1	10.7	15.4	18.0	38.6	18.2	25.2
1997	51,455	93,123	61,940	59,700	6,474	13,748	6,493	8,858	12.6	14.6	10.4	14.6	18.2	38.6	18.3	24.9
1998	51,202	94,235	62,498	60,545	6,357	12,992	6,501	8,625	12.3	13.7	10.3	14.0	18.4	37.7	18.9	25.0
1999	51,742	94,640	63,155	61,522	5,678	12,538	6,210	7,833	10.9	13.1	9.8	12.6	17.6	38.9	19.3	24.3

[1] Tabulation procedures changed numerous times, affecting the comparability of the poverty series over time. See documentation for Table Be260–282.

[2] Derived from 1-in-1,000 sample.

[3] Overestimate of poverty population. See documentation for Table Be260–282.

Sources

U.S. Bureau of the Census, March *Current Population Survey* (CPS). Data for the following series were obtained from the Internet site of the U.S. Census Bureau, Poverty and Health Statistics Branch/HHES Division. Series Be355–366, from *Historical Poverty Tables*, Table 9; series Be367–370, based on series Be266 and Be359–362. Exceptions for specific dates are noted.

In all series, the figures for 1999 were found in *Current Population Reports* (CPR) series P-60, number 210, Table A, p. vi.

Series Be356. Figures for the following years were obtained from the CPR series P-60: 1967, number 86, Table 3, p. 35; 1974, number 103, Table 20, p. 43.

Series Be359. Figures are from the CPR series P-60 as follows: 1970 from number 133, Table 4, p. 19; 1974 from number 124, Table 4, p. 24; 1979 from number 133, Table E, p. 8; 1980 from number 138, Table B, p. 4; 1983 from number 152, Table A, p. 2; 1987 from unpublished Census Bureau tabulation; 1997 from number 201, Table A, p. vii.

Series Be360. Figures are from the CPR series P-60 as follows: 1967 from number 86, Table 3, p. 35; 1970 from number 133, Table 4, p. 19; 1974 from number 124, Table 4, p. 24; 1979 from number 133, Table E, p. 8; 1980 from number 138, Table B, p. 4; 1983 from number 152, Table A, p. 2; 1987 from unpublished Census Bureau tabulation.

Series Be361. Figures are from the CPR series P-60 as follows: 1970 from number 133, Table 4, p. 19; 1974 from number 124, Table 4, p. 24; 1978 from number 124, Table 8, p. 40; 1979 from number 133, Table E, p. 8; 1980 from number 138, Table B, p. 4; 1983 from number 152, Table A, p. 2; 1987 from unpublished Census Bureau tabulation.

Series Be362–363 and Be365–366. Figures are from the CPR series P-60 as follows: 1970 from number 133, Table 4, p. 19; 1974 from number 124, Table 4, p. 24; 1979 from number 133, Table E, p. 8; 1980 from number 138, Table B, p. 4; 1983 from number 152, Table A, p. 2; 1987 from unpublished Census Bureau tabulation.

Series Be364. Figures are from the CPR series P-60 as follows: 1967 calculated from numbers in number 86, Table 3, p. 35; 1970 from number 133, Table 4, p. 19; 1974 from number 124, Table 4, p. 24; 1979 from number 133, Table E, p. 8; 1980 from number 138, Table B, p. 4; 1983 from number 152, Table A, p. 2; 1987 from unpublished Census Bureau tabulation.

Documentation

Refer to the appendixes to the essay on poverty in this chapter for additional discussion of the tables, as well as for various technical definitions and descriptions.

Revised figures were used wherever possible. If revised figures were unavailable, unrevised figures were used if consistency across series for a particular year could be maintained. For example, if an unrevised figure for the total population and an unrevised figure for the poverty count both existed, these would be divided to obtain an unrevised poverty rate. However, available figures were never used to "back out" a missing figure for a larger population group. For example, suppose total persons was unavailable on a revised basis, but both a revised poverty rate and a revised count of persons in poverty were available. The latter two statistics would not have been used to back out the total persons on a revised basis. Rather, the total persons cell would be left empty and noted as "not available."

See Appendix 2 regarding the composition of census regions and divisions.

Series Be367–370. Calculated by dividing series Be359–362, respectively, by series Be266. Exceptions are as noted.

Series Be367. 1980: calculated by dividing series Be363 by the *revised* 1980 total persons in poverty (29,640 thousand), from CPR series P-60, number 33, Table D, p. 6.

Series Be368. 1959 and 1980: calculated by dividing series Be364 by the following: for 1959, total persons in poverty from the 1-in-1,000 sample of the 1960 Decennial Census (38,766 thousand), from CPR series P-60, number 91, Table L, p. 13; for 1980, the 1980 *revised* total persons in poverty (29,640 thousand), from CPR series P-60, number 91, Table L, p. 13.

Series Be370. 1980: calculated by dividing series Be366 by the *revised* 1980 total persons in poverty (29,640 thousand), from CPR series P-60, younger than number 91, Table L, p. 13.

TABLE Be371–398 Persons ages 16 and older below poverty threshold, by employment status and race: 1966–1999

Contributed by Linda Barrington

	Persons for whom poverty is determined			Number of persons in poverty			Persons employed during the year						Persons employed full-time year-round		
										In poverty					
	Total	White	Nonwhite	Total	White	Nonwhite	Total	White	Nonwhite	Total	White	Nonwhite	Total	White	Nonwhite
	Be371	Be372	Be373	Be374	Be375	Be376	Be377	Be378	Be379	Be380	Be381	Be382	Be383	Be384	Be385
Year	Thousand	Thousand	Thousand	Thousand	Thousand	Thousand	Thousand	Thousand	Thousand	Thousand	Thousand	Thousand	Thousand	Thousand	Thousand
1966	130,183	116,424	13,759	16,990	12,366	4,624	86,910	77,256	9,654	7,510	4,839	2,671	50,098	45,378	4,720
1967	132,503	118,412	14,092	16,254	11,986	4,268	89,020	79,025	9,995	7,048	4,668	2,380	51,770	46,662	5,108
1968	134,698	120,325	14,372	15,488	11,527	3,961	90,964	80,824	10,140	6,745	4,565	2,180	52,361	47,148	5,213
1969	138,110	123,068	15,042	15,424	11,428	3,996	92,890	82,491	10,399	6,281	4,286	1,995	52,844	47,583	5,261
1970	140,165	124,863	15,302	15,863	11,743	4,120	93,657	83,398	10,259	6,458	4,561	1,897	51,976	46,752	5,225
1971	143,772	127,838	15,934	16,088	11,916	4,172	94,935	84,614	10,321	6,583	4,728	1,854	53,187	47,922	5,265
1972	146,154	129,513	16,641	15,252	10,887	4,365	96,795	86,184	10,611	6,127	4,348	1,779	55,180	49,383	5,797
1973	148,638	131,470	17,168	14,123	10,050	4,072	100,175	89,016	11,159	5,692	4,014	1,677	56,864	50,938	5,926
1974	151,528	133,837	17,691	14,287	10,144	4,142	101,472	90,166	11,305	5,868	4,231	1,637	55,207	49,595	5,612
1975	154,094	135,791	18,303	16,012	11,579	4,433	101,240	89,944	11,296	6,472	4,838	1,634	55,032	49,345	5,687
1976	156,600	137,774	18,826	15,769	11,144	4,625	104,219	92,578	11,641	6,346	4,644	1,703	56,578	50,598	5,981
1977	159,062	139,718	19,343	15,654	11,011	4,642	107,096	94,991	12,104	6,222	4,610	1,611	58,847	52,476	6,371
1978	161,580	141,704	19,877	15,683	11,069	4,613	110,290	97,603	12,687	6,390	4,667	1,723	62,187	55,410	6,777
1979	167,842	146,415	21,428	16,832	11,628	5,204	114,993	101,407	13,586	6,601	4,763	1,838	64,706	57,481	7,224
1980	170,269	148,048	22,221	18,960	13,268	5,693	115,752	101,904	13,848	7,674	5,635	2,038	64,936	57,547	7,389
1981	172,537	149,862	22,675	20,600	14,543	6,057	116,794	102,825	13,969	8,524	6,454	2,070	65,292	57,689	7,603
1982	174,537	151,164	23,373	22,122	15,678	6,444	116,277	102,192	14,085	9,013	6,866	2,147	63,973	56,523	7,450
1983	176,758	152,790	23,969	22,773	15,955	6,818	117,575	103,243	14,332	9,329	7,079	2,250	66,744	58,683	8,061
1984	178,587	154,025	24,562	21,567	15,320	6,248	121,148	105,818	15,330	8,999	6,783	2,216	70,419	61,679	8,739

(continued)

TABLE Be371–398 Persons ages 16 and older below poverty threshold, by employment status and race: 1966–1999 *Continued*

	Persons for whom poverty is determined			Number of persons in poverty			Persons employed during the year						Persons employed full-time year-round		
										In poverty					
	Total	White	Nonwhite	Total	White	Nonwhite	Total	White	Nonwhite	Total	White	Nonwhite	Total	White	Nonwhite
	Be371	Be372	Be373	Be374	Be375	Be376	Be377	Be378	Be379	Be380	Be381	Be382	Be383	Be384	Be385
Year	Thousand	Thousand	Thousand	Thousand	Thousand	Thousand	Thousand	Thousand	Thousand	Thousand	Thousand	Thousand	Thousand	Thousand	Thousand
1985	181,034	155,856	25,178	21,302	15,387	5,915	123,466	107,434	16,032	9,008	6,821	2,187	72,422	63,202	9,220
1986	183,093	157,312	25,781	20,719	14,747	5,973	125,763	109,194	16,569	8,743	6,609	2,134	74,427	64,850	9,577
1987	185,096	158,580	26,516	20,546	14,083	6,463	128,316	111,250	17,066	8,258	6,063	2,195	77,015	67,142	9,873
1988	186,802	159,643	27,159	20,323	13,832	6,491	130,450	112,728	17,722	8,363	6,027	2,336	79,627	69,012	10,614
1989	188,479	160,770	27,709	19,952	13,772	6,180	132,817	114,458	18,359	8,376	6,179	2,197	81,117	70,050	11,067
1990	190,216	161,931	28,285	21,242	14,720	6,522	133,534	115,012	18,523	8,716	6,422	2,294	80,932	69,799	11,133
1991	191,875	162,873	29,002	22,530	15,613	6,918	133,423	114,576	18,848	9,208	6,755	2,453	80,396	69,398	10,998
1992	195,065	164,479	30,587	23,951	16,630	7,321	135,064	115,197	19,866	9,739	7,167	2,572	81,828	70,102	11,726
1993	197,166	165,932	31,234	24,833	17,234	7,598	136,354	116,191	20,163	10,144	7,437	2,707	83,386	71,136	12,249
1994	198,954	167,074	31,879	24,108	16,824	7,284	138,469	117,528	20,941	9,829	7,193	2,636	85,764	72,825	12,939
1995	200,722	168,522	32,200	23,078	16,236	6,841	139,723	118,723	21,000	9,484	7,016	2,468	88,173	74,796	13,377
1996	203,381	170,254	33,126	23,471	16,480	6,991	142,200	120,241	21,959	9,586	7,095	2,490	90,252	76,269	13,983
1997	205,348	171,599	33,749	22,753	16,259	6,494	143,967	121,083	22,884	9,444	6,945	2,499	92,631	77,831	14,799
1998	207,777	173,141	34,635	22,256	15,817	6,439	145,566	122,220	23,346	9,133	6,727	2,407	95,772	80,418	15,353
1999	—	—	—	—	—	—	148,295	124,041	—	9,113	6,614	—	97,941	81,713	—

	Persons employed full-time year-round			Percentage in poverty									Percentage of poor persons employed during the year
	In poverty						Employed during the year			Employed full-time year-round			
	Total	White	Nonwhite	Total	White	Nonwhite	Total	White	Nonwhite	Total	White	Nonwhite	
	Be386	Be387	Be388	Be389	Be390	Be391	Be392	Be393	Be394	Be395	Be396	Be397	Be398
Year	Thousand	Thousand	Thousand	Percent	Percent	Percent	Percent	Percent	Percent	Percent	Percent	Percent	Percent
1966	2,385	1,554	831	13.1	10.6	33.6	8.6	6.3	27.7	4.8	3.4	17.6	44.2
1967	2,141	1,476	665	12.3	10.1	30.3	7.9	5.9	23.8	4.1	3.2	13.0	43.4
1968	2,110	1,474	635	11.5	9.6	27.6	7.4	5.6	21.5	4.0	3.1	12.2	43.5
1969	1,677	1,212	464	11.2	9.3	26.6	6.8	5.2	19.2	3.2	2.5	8.8	40.7
1970	1,629	1,218	412	11.3	9.4	26.9	6.9	5.5	18.5	3.1	2.6	7.9	40.7
1971	1,673	1,252	422	11.2	9.3	26.2	6.9	5.6	18.0	3.1	2.6	8.0	40.9
1972	1,526	1,112	414	10.4	8.4	26.2	6.3	5.0	16.8	2.8	2.3	7.1	40.2
1973	1,140	816	324	9.5	7.6	23.7	5.7	4.5	15.0	2.0	1.6	5.5	40.3
1974	1,223	984	239	9.4	7.6	23.4	5.8	4.7	14.5	2.2	2.0	4.3	41.1
1975	1,310	1,058	252	10.4	8.5	24.2	6.4	5.4	14.5	2.4	2.1	4.4	40.4
1976	1,355	1,035	320	10.1	8.1	24.6	6.1	5.0	14.6	2.4	2.0	5.3	40.2
1977	1,446	1,140	305	9.8	7.9	24.0	5.8	4.9	13.3	2.5	2.2	4.8	39.7
1978	1,306	1,043	262	9.7	7.8	23.2	5.8	4.8	13.6	2.1	1.9	3.9	40.7
1979	1,394	1,068	327	10.0	7.9	24.3	5.7	4.7	13.5	2.2	1.9	4.5	39.2

	Persons employed full-time year-round			Percentage in poverty									Percentage of poor persons employed during the year
	In poverty						Employed during the year			Employed full-time year-round			
	Total	White	Nonwhite	Total	White	Nonwhite	Total	White	Nonwhite	Total	White	Nonwhite	
	Be386	Be387	Be388	Be389	Be390	Be391	Be392	Be393	Be394	Be395	Be396	Be397	Be398
Year	Thousand	Thousand	Thousand	Percent	Percent	Percent	Percent	Percent	Percent	Percent	Percent	Percent	Percent
1980	1,644	1,271	373	11.1	9.0	25.6	6.6	5.5	14.7	2.5	2.2	5.0	40.5
1981	1,881	1,506	375	11.9	9.7	26.7	7.3	6.3	14.8	2.9	2.6	4.9	41.4
1982	1,999	1,619	380	12.7	10.4	27.6	7.8	6.7	15.2	3.1	2.9	5.1	40.7
1983	2,064	1,659	405	12.9	10.4	28.4	7.9	6.9	15.7	3.1	2.8	5.0	41.0
1984	2,076	1,654	422	12.1	9.9	25.4	7.4	6.4	14.5	2.9	2.7	4.8	41.7
1985	1,972	1,575	397	11.8	9.9	23.5	7.3	6.3	13.6	2.7	2.5	4.3	42.3
1986	2,007	1,577	430	11.3	9.4	23.2	7.0	6.1	12.9	2.7	2.4	4.5	42.2
1987	1,821	1,435	386	11.1	8.9	24.4	6.4	5.4	12.9	2.4	2.1	3.9	40.2
1988	1,929	1,455	474	10.9	8.7	23.9	6.4	5.3	13.2	2.4	2.1	4.5	41.2
1989	1,908	1,453	455	10.6	8.6	22.3	6.3	5.4	12.0	2.4	2.1	4.1	42.0
1990	2,076	1,538	538	11.2	9.1	23.1	6.5	5.6	12.4	2.6	2.2	4.8	41.0
1991	2,103	1,639	463	11.7	9.6	23.9	6.9	5.9	13.0	2.6	2.4	4.2	40.9
1992	2,211	1,670	541	12.3	10.1	23.9	7.2	6.2	12.9	2.7	2.4	4.6	40.7
1993	2,408	1,853	554	12.6	10.4	24.3	7.4	6.4	13.4	2.9	2.6	4.5	40.9
1994	2,520	1,853	667	12.1	10.1	22.8	7.1	6.1	12.6	2.9	2.5	5.2	40.8
1995	2,418	1,827	591	11.5	9.6	21.2	6.8	5.9	11.8	2.7	2.4	4.4	41.1
1996	2,263	1,720	543	11.5	9.7	21.1	6.7	5.9	11.3	2.5	2.3	3.9	40.8
1997	2,345	1,751	595	11.1	9.5	19.2	6.6	5.7	10.9	2.5	2.2	4.0	41.5
1998	2,804	2,126	678	10.7	9.1	18.6	6.3	5.5	10.3	2.9	2.6	4.4	41.0
1999	2,499	1,863	—	—	—	—	6.1	5.3	—	2.6	2.3	—	—

Source

Series Be371–397 were obtained from custom tabulations produced by the U.S. Census Bureau from the *Current Population Survey* (CPS), March 1967 through 1999 Supplements. Series Be398 was computed by dividing series Be380 by series Be374. For all series, figures for 1999 were found in *Current Population Reports* (CPR) series P-60, number 210, Table 3, p. 18.

Documentation

Refer to the appendixes in the essay on poverty in this chapter for additional discussion of the tables, as well as for various technical definitions and descriptions.

Employed persons are those who have any work experience during the preceding calendar year. A person with work experience is one who, during the preceding calendar year, did any work for pay or profit or worked without pay on a family-operated farm or business at any time during the year, on a part-time or full-time basis. Full-time year-round employees worked full-time (thirty-five or more hours per week) and fifty or more weeks during the previous calendar year.

In this custom tabulation produced from the CPS, the racial or ethnic categorization of persons is that of the individual, regardless of the racial or ethnic categorization of the family householder.

Due to changes in methodology, data are not strictly comparable over time.

1967: Implementation of a new March CPS processing system.

1971: Implementation of 1970 Census population controls.

1974: Implementation of a new March CPS processing system. Questionnaire expanded to ask eleven income questions.

1979: Implementation of 1980 Census population controls. Questionnaire expanded to show twenty-seven possible values from fifty-one possible sources of income.

1987: Implementation of a new March CPS processing system.

1992: Implementation of 1990 Census population controls.

1993: Data collection method changed from paper-and-pencil to computer-assisted interviewing. In addition, the March 1994 income supplement was revised to allow for the coding of different income amounts on selected questionnaire items. Limits either increased or decreased in the following categories: earnings increased to $999,999; Social Security increased to $49,999; Supplemental Security Income and public assistance increased to $24,999; veterans' benefits increased to $99,999; child support and alimony decreased to $49,999.

TABLE Be399–411 Persons below 50 and 125 percent of poverty threshold, by age, race, and Hispanic origin: 1959–1998[1]

Contributed by Linda Barrington and Gordon M. Fisher

	Number of persons						Percentage of persons						Percentage of persons below 125 percent of poverty threshold who are age 65 and older
		Below 125 percent of poverty threshold						Below 125 percent of poverty threshold					
			Age 65 and older						Age 65 and older				
	Below 50 percent of poverty threshold	Total	All races	White	Black	Hispanic	Below 50 percent of poverty threshold	All races	All races	White	Black	Hispanic	
	Be399	Be400	Be401 [2]	Be402	Be403	Be404 [3]	Be405	Be406	Be407 [2]	Be408	Be409	Be410 [3]	Be411
Year	Thousand	Thousand	Thousand	Thousand	Thousand	Thousand	Percent	Percent	Percent	Percent	Percent	Percent	Percent
1959	—	54,942	—	—	—	—	—	31.1	—	—	—	—	—
1960	—	54,560	—	—	—	—	—	30.4	—	—	—	—	—
1961	—	54,280	—	—	—	—	—	30.0	—	—	—	—	—
1962	—	53,119	—	—	—	—	—	28.8	—	—	—	—	—
1963	—	50,778	—	—	—	—	—	27.1	—	—	—	—	—
1964	—	49,819	—	—	—	—	—	26.3	—	—	—	—	—
1965	—	46,163	—	—	—	—	—	24.1	—	—	—	—	—
1966	—	41,267	—	—	—	—	—	21.3	—	—	—	—	—
1967 [4]	—	39,206	—	—	—	—	—	20.0	—	—	—	—	—
1968	—	35,905	—	—	—	—	—	18.2	—	—	—	—	—
1969	—	34,875 [6]	6,647 [6]	5,739 [6]	843 [6]	—	—	17.5 [6]	35.2 [6]	33.0 [6]	61.4 [6]	—	19.1 [6]
1970	—	35,752 [6]	6,529 [6]	5,626 [6]	854 [6]	—	—	17.7 [6]	33.9 [6]	31.8 [6]	60.1 [6]	—	18.3 [6]
1971	—	36,501	6,274	5,350	875	—	—	17.8	31.6	29.6	55.2	—	17.2
1972	—	34,653	5,730	4,838	841	—	—	16.8	28.5	26.4	52.5	—	16.5
1973	—	32,828	5,522	4,563	899	—	—	15.8	26.8	24.3	53.8	—	16.8
1974	—	33,666	5,228	4,283	880	167	—	16.1	24.7	22.3	51.2	41.2	15.5
1975	7,733	37,182	5,495	4,516	925	181	3.7	17.6	25.4	23.0	51.5	43.1	14.8
1976	7,016	35,509	5,521	4,559	907	177	3.3	16.7	25.0	22.8	49.0	38.2	15.5
1977	7,474	35,659	5,502	4,451	976	173	3.5	16.7	24.5	21.9	50.6	33.5	15.4
1978	7,708	34,155	5,421	4,380	972	201	3.6	15.8	23.4	20.9	49.7	37.3	15.9
1979	8,553	36,616	5,986	4,905	1,019	226	3.8	16.4	24.7	22.4	49.9	39.3	16.3
1980	9,804 [5]	40,658 [5]	6,346 [5]	5,151 [5]	1,093 [5]	245 [5]	4.4 [5]	18.1 [5]	25.7 [5]	23.1 [5]	53.2 [5]	42.1 [5]	15.6 [5]
1981	11,189	43,748	6,354	5,142	1,126	232	4.9	19.3	25.2	22.6	53.6	40.9	14.5
1982	12,806	46,520	6,106	4,889	1,095	244	5.6	20.3	23.7	21.0	51.6	40.9	13.1
1983	13,590	47,150	5,784	4,618	1,063	288	5.9	20.3	22.0	19.4	48.4	36.8	12.3
1984	12,770	45,288	5,684	4,590	1,022	284	5.5	19.4	21.2	19.0	45.7	34.7	12.6
1985	12,380	44,166	5,706	4,621	1,021	319	5.2	18.7	20.9	18.8	44.9	34.8	12.9
1986	12,677	43,486	5,743	4,602	1,043	298	5.3	18.2	20.5	18.3	44.7	32.9	13.2
1987	12,469	43,032	5,765	4,588	1,053	356	5.2	17.9	20.2	17.9	44.1	40.2	13.4
1988	12,676	42,551	5,812	4,544	1,141	334	5.2	17.5	20.0	17.5	46.8	33.2	13.7
1989	11,983	42,653	5,643	4,444	1,095	334	4.9	17.3	19.1	16.8	44.0	32.6	13.2
1990	12,914	44,837	5,712	4,423	1,150	365	5.2	18.0	19.0	16.4	45.1	33.5	12.7
1991	14,059	47,527	6,038	4,697	1,208	398	5.6	18.9	19.7	17.2	46.3	34.8	12.7
1992	15,547	50,592	6,224	4,928	1,143	448	6.1	19.7	20.5	18.1	45.7	34.5	12.3
1993	15,971	51,801	6,077	4,892	1,010	493	6.2	20.0	19.7	17.7	40.2	35.5	11.7
1994	15,404	50,401	5,841	4,721	951	513	5.9	19.3	18.7	16.9	37.2	35.9	11.6
1995	13,892	48,761	5,591	4,488	941	505	5.3	18.5	17.7	15.8	38.0	34.7	11.5
1996	14,412	49,310	5,862	4,757	958	551	5.4	18.5	18.4	16.7	36.6	36.3	11.9
1997	14,594	47,853	5,440	4,287	989	572	5.4	17.8	17.0	15.0	36.8	35.3	11.4
1998	13,914	46,036	5,447	4,231	1,057	550	5.1	17.0	16.8	14.7	38.8	32.4	11.8

[1] Tabulation procedures changed numerous times, affecting the comparability of the poverty series over time. See methodology changes text for Table Be260–282.

[2] Includes other races not shown separately.

[3] Hispanics can be of any race. Tabulation procedures changed in 1972, affecting Hispanic counts. See methodology changes text for Table Be260–282.

[4] Overestimate of poverty population. See methodology changes text for Table Be260–282.

[5] Not revised. See methodology changes text for Table Be260–282. However, the figure is consistent with any 1980 "total persons" or "total families" figures because slight modifications in the poverty definition did not affect such totals for this year.

[6] Not revised. See methodology changes text for Table Be260–282.

Sources

U.S. Bureau of the Census, March Current Population Survey. Data were obtained from the Internet site of the Bureau of the Census, Poverty and Health Statistics Branch/HHES Division. Series Be399 and Be405, from *Historical Poverty Tables*, Table 22; series Be400 and Be406, from *Historical Poverty Tables*, Table 6; series Be401–404 and Be407–410, from *Historical Poverty Tables*, Table 12; series Be411, calculated by dividing series Be401 by series Be400. Exceptions for specific dates are as noted.

Series Be400. Figures are from the *Current Population Reports* (CPR) series P-60 as follows: 1969 from number 81, Table 2, p. 31; 1970 from number 81, Table 2, p. 31.

Series Be401. Figures are from the CPR series P-60 as follows: 1969 through 1972 from number 95, Table 9, p. 29; 1973 from number 98, Table 49, p. 144; 1974 from number 103, Table 18, p. 36.

Series Be402. Figures are from the CPR series P-60 as follows: 1969 through 1972 from number 95, Table 9, p. 29; 1973 from number 98, Table 49, p. 144; 1974 from number 103, Table 18, p. 36; 1977 from number 116, Table 18, p. 24.

TABLE Be399–411 Persons below 50 and 125 percent of poverty threshold, by age, race, and Hispanic origin: 1959–1998 *Continued*

Series Be403. Figures are from the CPR series P-60 as follows: 1969 through 1972 from number 95, Table 9, p. 29; 1973 from number 98, Table 49, p. 144; 1974 from number 103, Table 18, p. 36.

Series Be404. Figures are from the CPR series P-60 as follows: 1974, 1975, and 1978 from number 124, Table 2, p. 19; 1976 from number 107, Table 18, p. 24; 1977 from number 116, Table 18, p. 24; 1979 and 1980 from number 133, Table 2, p. 14; 1981 from number 138, Table 2, p. 10; 1982 from number 144, Table 2, p. 10; 1983 and 1984 from number 152, Table 2, p. 8; 1985 from number 154, Table 16, p. 24; 1986 from number 157, Table 17, p. 28.

Series Be406. 1969–1970: CPR series P-60, number 81, Table 2, p. 32.

Series Be407. 1969–1970: calculated by dividing series Be401 by that year's *unrevised* total aged persons. These figures were 18,899 thousand and 19,254 thousand for 1969 and 1970, respectively, as found in CPR series P-60, number 95, Table 9, p. 29; 1971–1972: calculated by dividing series Be401 by that year's total aged persons as found in CPR series P-60, number 95, Table 9, p. 29; 1973: calculated by dividing series Be401 by the population age 65 and older for whom poverty status was determined (from Census Bureau's Internet site, Historical Poverty Tables, Table 3); 1974: CPR series P-60, number 103, Table 18, p. 36.

Series Be408. 1969–1970: calculated by dividing series Be402 by that year's *unrevised* total white aged persons as found in CPR series P-60, number 95, Table 9, p. 29; 1971–1972: calculated by dividing series Be402 by that year's total white aged persons from CPR series P-60, number 95, Table 9, p. 29; 1974: CPR series P-60, number 103, Table 18, p. 36; 1977: CPR series P-60, number 116, Table 18, p. 24. Figures for 1973 were calculated by dividing series Be402 by the population of whites age 65 and older for whom poverty status was determined (Census Bureau's Internet site, *Historical Poverty Tables*, Table 3). Additional figures for the denominator were obtained from CPR series P-60 as follows: 1959 from number 91, Table L, p. 13; 1969 from number 76, Table 4, p. 40; 1970 from number 91, Table L, p. 13; 1971 from number 86, Table 9, p. 64; 1972 from number 91, Table 9, p. 50; 1973 from number 98, Table 6, p. 35.

Series Be409. 1969–1970: calculated by dividing series Be403 by that year's *unrevised* total black aged persons as found in CPR series P-60, number 95, Table 9, p. 29; 1971–1972 were obtained by dividing series Be403 by that year's total black aged persons from CPR series P-60, number 95, Table 9, p. 29; 1974: CPR series P-60, number 103, Table 18, p. 36; 1979: CPR series P-60, number 133, Table 2, p. 14. Figures for 1973 were calculated by dividing series Be403 by the population of blacks age 65 and older for whom poverty status was determined (Census Bureau's Internet site, *Historical Poverty Tables*, Table 3). Additional figures for the denominator were obtained from CPR series P-60 as follows: 1959 from number 91, Table L, p. 13; 1970 from number 91, Table L, p. 13.

Series Be410. Figures are from the CPR series P-60 as follows: 1974, 1975, and 1978 from number 124, Table 2, p. 19; 1976 from number 107, Table 18, p. 24; 1977 from number 116, Table 18, p. 24; 1979 and 1980 from number 133, Table 2, p. 14; 1981 from number 138, Table 2, p. 10; 1982 from number 144, Table 2, p. 10; 1983 and 1984 from number 152, Table 2, p. 8; 1985 from number 154, Table 16, p. 24; 1986 from number 157, Table 17, p. 28; 1998 from number 207, Table 2, p. 5.

Documentation

Refer to the appendixes in the essay on poverty in this chapter for additional discussion of the tables, as well as for various technical definitions and descriptions.

Beginning with the poverty report for income year 1997, the Census Bureau refers to people below 50 percent of the poverty threshold as "severely poor." (See CPR series P-60, number 201, p. xii). Beginning with the poverty report for income year 1970, the Census Bureau refers to people between 100 percent and 125 percent of the poverty threshold as "the near poor." (See CPR series P-60, number 81, p. 14.)

According to the Census Bureau, the racial or ethnic categorization of persons is that of the individual, regardless of the racial or ethnic categorization of the family householder. Although this has been the case for some years, it was not always so. A supplementary P-60 poverty report issued in 1974 indicates (CPR, series P-60, number 95, p. 3) that in the main P-60 poverty reports for income years 1971 and 1972, persons were classified by the race of the family head (and not by their own race). The contributors of this table have not been able to determine when that situation changed to what it is today.

CHAPTER Bf

Social Insurance and Public Assistance

Editor: Price V. Fishback

Associate Editors: Joan Underhill Hannon, Melissa A. Thomasson, and Stephen T. Ziliak

INTRODUCTION

Price V. Fishback

Social welfare spending is a broad category that includes provisions for maintaining health, income, and welfare in good times and bad. The category covers a wide range of types of spending: assistance to the poor; social insurance expenditures in programs such as Social Security, unemployment insurance, and workers' compensation; private purchases of health and life insurance; and direct expenditures on health care and education. Decisions on social welfare spending are made both by governments through public programs and by individuals in their private decisions about how much to spend on charity, insurance, education, and their own health. Prior to the twentieth century, social welfare spending was largely the responsibility of individuals, extended families, and cities and towns. In consequence, we have only limited and scattered quantitative evidence on the extent of public assistance programs, and we know relatively little about the share of private spending devoted to the general category. Our sense is that social welfare spending was a smaller proportion of overall spending in the eighteenth and nineteenth centuries than in the twentieth century. Certainly, the extent of public programs was much smaller. Much more research needs to be done before we can develop a comprehensive picture of the nature of social welfare spending prior to the 1920s.

As the American economy developed, more centralized layers of government began to accept responsibility for public programs for social welfare spending. For example, during the nineteenth century towns and later states began to develop educational programs for children, while in the Progressive era in the late nineteenth and early twentieth centuries, state governments began establishing workers' compensation and mothers' pensions programs. The federal government became more heavily involved with social welfare spending during the Great Depression, and the levels of social welfare spending both public and private have expanded rapidly since. The rise in federal activity has also led to expanded efforts to collect data on social welfare activities. Most of the evidence on social welfare spending at the national level has been collected and developed by the Social Security Administration, which was formed in the 1930s. Thus, we have a relatively comprehensive picture of social welfare spending from approximately 1929 to the present. We have several goals in this chapter: first, to provide in one place a consistent set of time series over a long period that show the extent and nature of public assistance available in various cities and states in the nineteenth century; second, to give a sense of the nature of both public programs and private spending described by the social welfare statistics of the twentieth century; third, to examine long-term trends in social welfare spending in the context of changes in the economy; and finally, to warn users about features that may cause peculiarities in the data.

PUBLIC ASSISTANCE: COLONIAL TIMES TO THE 1920S

Stephen T. Ziliak with Joan Underhill Hannon

The category of social welfare expenditure called public assistance includes all types of noncontributory, tax-financed payments of relief to the poor. Payments of public assistance are made sometimes in cash and sometimes in kind, both to the poor who reside in households and to the poor who reside in institutions. For example, the present-day "food stamp," had it been in circulation from colonial times to the 1920s, would be counted here as public assistance in kind. Until the 1920s, all payments in cash and in kind were called

Acknowledgments

For helpful comments, Joan Hannon and Steve Ziliak thank Susan Carter, Price Fishback, Brian Gratton, Monty Hindman, Peter Lindert, Robert Margo, John Schwarz, Matthew Sobek, and Richard Sutch. For research assistance, the work of Erin Mooney (Government Publications, Emory University), Susan Pozzanghera (Bowling Green State University), and the staff of the University of Iowa Government Publications Division is gratefully acknowledged. This work was made possible in part by grants from the Faculty Development Fund (Saint Mary's College of California) and the Office of Sponsored Programs (Bowling Green State University).

Price Fishback and Melissa Thomasson thank the Economics Department and the College of Business and Public Administration at the University of Arizona for financial support. Kari Beardsley, Amanda Ebel, Emie Portwood, and Kwok-Chung Wong provided help in collecting and computerizing the information. We received invaluable help from representatives at various government agencies: Ann Bixby at the Social Security Administration, Mike Finucan at the Office of Personnel Management, Marla Huddleston at the Railroad Retirement Board, Dan Peed at the Department of Labor, and Dora Teimouri at the U.S. Rehabilitation Service. A number of colleagues, including Susan Carter, Lee A. Craig, Brian Gratton, Joan Underhill Hannon, Monty Hindman, Shawn Kantor, Carolyn Moehling, John Schwartz, Matt Sobek, Richard Sutch, John Wallis, and Stephen Thomas Ziliak provided valuable help and advice on our essay and the organization and choice of tables.

public outdoor relief, or just outrelief.[1] By contrast with outdoor relief, the "poorhouse" is counted by the Census Bureau and here as an institution of indoor relief, an almshouse where the poor reside at public expense.

Public Assistance Began in Colonial Times

A common misconception concerning the origin of taxation for public assistance is that it was born of the deep and persistent unemployment of the Great Depression, and that its first cry was President Roosevelt's signing of the Social Security Act in 1935. In fact, public assistance for the poor, a compulsory tax for both indoor and outdoor relief, can be traced without interruption to colonial times.

The first schemes of public assistance in the New World were influenced by British examples, the financial and legal responsibility for the destitute being assumed by the town, the parish, or the county. Indeed, the colonies stayed close to the spirit of Britain's "43rd of Elizabeth," the so-called Elizabethan Poor Law of 1601.[2] The Elizabethan Poor Law laid the basis in England for the English poor law system. It also laid the basis for poor laws in the British colonies of America. The colony of Rhode Island, for instance, would adopt the Elizabethan Poor Law with hardly a revision. The Act made it compulsory for each "parish" (or town) to provide for the poor by levying a rate on property held within the jurisdiction. The Act set in motion the idea that public responsibility for the poor should be guaranteed through a program of compulsory taxation. It enabled various means of providing tax-financed relief, including but not limited to outdoor relief for the aged and infirm poor, apprenticing of pauper children to farmers, and construction of poorhouses for the able-bodied. Administration was to be the responsibility of an unpaid "overseer of the poor." There were exceptions to the British pattern. In the colony of New Netherland (1609–1664), the ecclesiastical practice of the Dutch Reformed Church put a profound stamp upon colonial poor laws, and the Dutch system was only gradually replaced by an English system in developing New York (Schneider 1938, Chapter 1).

More so than would Britain, the American colonies, and then later the states, would adjust the poor laws to facilitate differences in local or regional economic conditions and culture. Thus, for example, the little-known municipal practice of "auctioning" the poor had faded from much of New England by the late 1820s, and yet auctioning did not leave a less settled Indiana until the 1840s (Shaffer, Keefer, and Breckinridge 1941, pp. 12–41; Ziliak 2003). Indeed, ridding a burdened house of its children at auction to the lowest bidder (lowest, because the tax would subsidize the taker) was a legal form of assistance in Arkansas as late as 1903 (U. S. Department of Commerce and Labor 1906, p. 41). And while poorhouses could be found in New England in the late seventeenth century, the Old Northwest Territories would not see the poorhouse as common until the 1830s.

Quantitative research on public assistance in colonial America is relatively scant. But clearly, as one can see in the work of Professor Gary Nash on Boston, Philadelphia, and New York City, American struggles with poverty, and collective strategies to deal with it, came early (see Tables Bf1–16). While the Continental Congress "was debating independence in the handsome brick statehouse at Fifth and Chestnut streets, the managers of the Philadelphia almshouse, eight blocks away, were penning a doleful report on the care of the poor. In it they admitted their doubt that they could any longer cope with the spiraling problem of poverty and disclosed that 'of the 147 Men, 178 women, and 85 Children [admitted to the almshouse during the previous year] most of them [are] naked, helpless and emaciated with Poverty and Disease to such a Degree, that some have died in a few Days after their Admission.'"[3] The almshouse in colonial Philadelphia, like most almshouses throughout the entire antebellum period, was a miscellaneous receptacle for human distress. One almshouse could serve as a hostel, a hospice, and a home for the disabled. The immigrant widow and the common laborer could share quarters with the insane, the helpless, and the emaciated, as they did in colonial Philadelphia.

From colonial times to the present, the history of public assistance is in part a history of increasingly specialized "goods" and "services" being redistributed to increasingly diverse populations. Taking the long view, it is a history of an increasingly centralized system of administration and finance, evolving from the township trustee to the federal government, from local property taxes to the federal income tax. But in closer range, the history of public assistance is in many regards what historians call a "nonlinear" history, a story filled with surprising switchbacks and sometimes radical reversals. The tables published here give but a small sense of the uneven appearance of quantitative data across time and space, an indication of the sometimes vast difference in the practices of local and regional care for the poor.

County Asylums Dominated the Discourse of Poverty in the Nineteenth Century, Although Outdoor Relief Was More Often Provided

The volume of quantitative evidence increases as one proceeds to the 1820s and beyond. The work of Joan Underhill Hannon, although limited to the state of New York, provides evidence on local and regional difference in care for the poor since the 1820s (Tables Bf156–187). A large and economically diverse state, the New York of the nineteenth century is fertile ground for studying the influence of industrialization, urbanization, commercialization, and immigration on both dependency rates and local relief policy. The state as a whole is clearly not representative of the nation with respect to any of these factors. But the urban–rural variation *within* New York State is suggestive both of the variation one might expect to find across states and of the ways in which one might expect New York's history to be unique.

Throughout the nineteenth century, dependency rates – or what officials called the "pauperism rates"[4] – and relief expenditures per capita were higher in New York City than in the rest of the state. But over the course of the century, pauperism grew more rapidly outside of the city. In 1823, New York City's pauperism

[1] "Relief" replaced the older terms for a short time in the 1930s before "welfare" gained currency for the rest of the century.

[2] Trattner (1974), Chapters 1–3; Webb and Webb (1927); Rose (1971). Also see Table Bf-A.

[3] Nash (1976a), p. 4; *Philadelphia Gazette*, May 29, 1776. While this chapter was in the final stages of preparation, some quantitative evidence on pauper apprenticeship began to emerge. See, in particular, Murray and Herndon (2001).

[4] The pauperism rate is defined as the ratio of public relief recipients to the size of the state population.

TABLE Bf-A Important legislation and events affecting social welfare policy: 1601–1997

1601	Elizabethan Poor Law: The "43rd of Elizabeth" laid the basis for the Poor Laws in England and in the British colonies of America. The Act set in motion the idea that public responsibility for the poor should be guaranteed through a program of compulsory taxation.
1610–1660	"Sieckentroosters" and Dutch Poor Relief in New Netherland: The Dutch colony of New Netherland (New York) established public responsibility for the poor, financed by donations to the Dutch Reformed Church. As early as 1626, two "sieckentroosters" were employed by the Church to visit and comfort the sick of present-day Manhattan, perhaps as America's first social workers.
1662	Act of Settlement: Applicants for public assistance had to prove residence in the parish or town to which they applied. The Act connected the idea of entitlement to relief to the prerequisite of local residence. Settlement laws were passed and enforced in the United States throughout the nineteenth and twentieth centuries.
1775	First military pension program established by the Continental Congress. Set the precedent for military pensions for future wars.
1787	Free African Society organized by Richard Allen and Absalom Jones, in Philadelphia. The Society was a self-help and charitable organization for blacks. It was probably the first success among what would become a long line of independent black social organizations.
1824	New York's Act to Provide for the Establishment of County Poorhouses established that New York counties were to build poorhouses to provide shelter to applicants for public assistance. A number of states in New England, the Middle Atlantic, and the Middle West passed similar legislation during the antebellum period.
1862	Federal Civil War Disability Pensions were established for regular recruits and volunteers in the Union Army. Initially, the criteria for the eligibility and size of pensions were strictly tied to service-related injuries. The Arrears Act of 1879 loosened that tie, and the 1890 Dependent Pension Act ended it. By 1910, 28 percent of all men aged 65 and over and some 300,000 widows, orphans, and other dependents received benefits from veterans' pension programs.
1863	Massachusetts established the first Board of State Charities. Between 1863 and the 1900s, individual states established a central authority over the state's institutions of public assistance. In many states, the central authority administered corrections, health, and lunacy, in addition to public assistance.
1865	New York State legislature authorized the establishment of the Willard Asylum, the first state hospital for the chronically mentally ill, preparing the state for the removal of mentally ill paupers from poorhouses to state hospitals.
1874	The first annual National Conference on Charities and Corrections (NCCC) brought together leaders of the nation's public relief and private charitable organizations to discuss the similarity of their problems. The Charity Organization Society (COS), a quasi-private organization, dominated the agenda of the NCCC until 1905 when Jane Addams, a Progressive and a leader of the settlement house movement, was elected as its president.
1874	First private pension program established by railroads.
1875	The New York Children's Act ordered the removal of all children between the ages of 2 and 16 from poorhouses to orphanages and other facilities. Other states passed similar acts over the last quarter of the nineteenth century. Reaction to the resulting family breakup and overcrowding of orphans' homes provided a basis for the Progressive-era movement toward Mothers' Pensions.
1877	The first COS was established in Buffalo, New York. During the last quarter of the nineteenth century, the COS led the movement that would abolish public outdoor relief in ten of the largest cities and bring sharp reductions to many other cities. The COS sought to replace public assistance with a voluntaristic and "scientific charity" based on distinctions between the "worthy" and the "unworthy" poor. By 1893, there was a COS in 100 cities across the nation.
1880	New York State Care Act: The Act required that all of the mentally ill in county institutions be moved to state hospitals and that the state assume complete responsibility for care of the insane poor. Other states created similar legislation during the late nineteenth century.
1893–1894	An early experiment with public works: With the initiative of their COSs, the municipalities of Indianapolis and New York City used tax dollars to put to work many thousands of adults who had been thrown out of work during the depression.
1899	Charity Organization Society and the State of Indiana. The Indiana Legislature directed the Indiana Board of State Charities to implement the principles of the COS.
1908	Federal Employers Liability Act declared unconstitutional. The Act increased the range of accidents for which railroad employers were required to make payments to injured workers by limiting their legal defenses in lawsuits.
1908	Provision of workers' compensation to federal employees involved in workplace accidents.
1911	First permanent workers' compensation acts passed by California, Illinois, Kansas, Massachusetts, New Hampshire, New Jersey, Ohio, Washington, and Wisconsin. Most other states and territories established the program over the next nine years. Mississippi was the last to establish a program in 1948. Workers' compensation provided payments to the families of workplace accident victims and took the place of the earlier common law rules based on employer liability.
1911	First state Mothers' Pension law passed in Illinois. By 1920, forty states had established mothers' pensions to provide regular payments to impoverished mothers of dependent children. These programs served as a model for the Aid to Dependent Children program established by the Social Security Act of 1935.
1915	First state Old-Age Pension law passed by Alaskan territory. Provided pensions for elderly with low incomes to allow them to live outside the almshouse. By 1934, thirty states and territories had passed legislation.

(continued)

TABLE Bf-A Important legislation and events affecting social welfare policy: 1601–1997 *Continued*

1917	First state department of public welfare established in Illinois to increase state financing and control of public assistance. Other states developed public welfare departments in the 1920s.
1920	Civil Service Retirement Act. Established a regular system of pensions for all federal government employees.
1920	State–federal rehabilitation programs first enacted under the Smith–Fess Act.
1921	Shephard–Towner Act passed to provide federal grants to states to improve public health programs. Program ended by 1930.
1932	Reconstruction Finance Corporation established. Among its many tasks, the RFC made loans to local governments to help finance public assistance and work relief.
1932	First state unemployment insurance law passed by Wisconsin, but no benefits were paid before the Social Security Act established the state–federal program in 1935.
1933	New Deal programs began providing emergency funding for work relief and direct relief of the unemployed.
1934	Federal Railroad Retirement pension program enacted. Declared unconstitutional and replaced by new law in 1935.
1935	First federal public housing project begins construction under the Public Works Administration's Public Housing program.
1935	Social Security Act passed. The Act established the Old-Age, Survivors Insurance pension program and set up state–federal programs for unemployment insurance, old-age assistance, aid to the blind, and aid to dependent children.
1936	Veterans' bonus of up to $2 billion paid to World War I veterans.
1937	U.S. Housing Authority established to aid in the building of public housing.
1938	Federal Railroad Unemployment Insurance program enacted.
1939	Social Security Act amended to make the Old-Age, Survivors Insurance program a pay-as-you-go system in which current tax revenues fund payments to Social Security pension recipients.
1940	First Social Security Old-Age Insurance pension checks issued.
1946	Federal Railroad Disability Insurance program enacted.
1950	Farm and domestic employees and nonfarm self-employed persons are covered for first time under Social Security Old-Age Insurance pension program.
1950	Federal government establishes program to fund payments to medical vendors for care of low-income persons.
1950	Social Security Act amended to provide aid to the totally and permanently disabled.
1954	Self-employed farmers covered under Social Security pension program.
1959	First payments made under Social Security Disability Insurance program.
1960	Federal government initiated a program for medical assistance to the elderly.
1962	Aid to Families with Dependent Children (AFDC) superseded the aid to dependent children program as coverage expands to include adults caring for dependent children.
1962	First year that Food Stamps are provided for low-income persons under pilot program. First Food Stamp Act was passed in 1964.
1962	Manpower Development and Training Act along with the Equal Opportunity Act of 1964 established work-experience training programs.
1965	Legislation established the U.S. Department of Housing and Urban Administration.
1965	Medicaid program established to build upon and take over earlier programs for paying vendors for the provision of medical care to persons with low incomes.
1965	Medicare established to offer federal health insurance for the elderly.
1965	Omnibus Budget and Reconciliation Act (OBRA) homogenized resource limits across states and increased the AFDC benefit reduction rate to 100 percent.
1969	Black Lung Benefits program established by the federal government to provide disability payments to miners with black lung disease.
1969	Federal government established an emergency assistance program.
1972	Supplemental Security Income program superseded the old-age assistance, aid to the blind, and disability programs.
1972	The Women, Infants and Children program for nutritional supplementation was started as a pilot program and became permanent in 1974.
1973	Congress passed the Comprehensive Education and Training Act to replace earlier job training programs and to provide block grants for decentralized training.
1981	Low-Income Home Energy Assistance Program established to provide block grants to help low-income households meet their energy expenses.
1983	Job Training Partnership Act replaced Comprehensive Education and Training Act. Private industry councils work with county welfare agents to connect welfare-to-work with wage subsidies.
1987	Federal Employees Retirement System (FERS) established. The FERS offered a broader range of retirement benefits than the original Civil Service Retirement System.
1988	Family Support Act. Attempted to change welfare programs from eligibility and monitoring programs to explicit programs for moving households into self-sufficiency. Child support laws were strengthened, and work was required from most of the able-bodied.
1996	Personal Responsibility and Work Opportunity Reconciliation Act. The Act removed the federal control of public assistance that had been enabled by the Social Security Act of 1935 and strengthened by amendments in 1962. In particular, the individual states were no longer required to provide a poor person with a cash welfare benefit.
1997	Temporary Assistance for Needy Families program (TANF) replaced the AFDC program. TANF was by 1998 operating in about forty states. Each state is enforcing a four- or five-year lifetime limit on the receipt of cash benefits and requiring (however differently) some amount of waged employment from drug-free participants.

rate was almost twelve times that in the rest of the state; by the end of the century, that difference would shrink to a factor of less than three (though many would still regard the difference economically and morally significant). Since New York City spent fewer dollars per recipient, the city-to-state differential in per capita expenditures (which narrowed across the antebellum period before widening again in the late nineteenth century) can probably be attributed entirely to the city's higher pauperism rate (Hannon 1997b, Tables 1 and 4).

Outside New York City, pauperism rates and expenditures per capita were positively correlated with urbanization, though urbanization and population density are found to have had little or no independent effect after controlling for other variables (Hannon 1997a, Tables 2, A1, A2, A3, and A4).

Given the relationships between urbanization, dependency, and expenditures within the state, it should not be surprising to find in the nationwide data a relatively high level of dependency in New York State. The work of Stephen Ziliak on the number of paupers in the nation's almshouses shows that the New York figures are not out of line with the averages for the New England and Middle Atlantic states (Tables Bf34–155) (Ziliak 2002a). Yet as one might expect, the almshouse rate in New York greatly exceeded the national average in 1880 and 1890. Still, the almshouse rates should not be used synonymously with pauperism rates. Pauperism rates include *all* recipients of public assistance, indoor and outdoor. Moreover, each state and each county used indoor relief and outdoor relief with different criteria for eligibility and in the context of local economic conditions.

The history of public assistance, when viewed from a long-run perspective, is also a history of withdrawal – though never complete – from the explicitly punitive, correctional, and mental health institutions. Most Americans now would not consider the auctioning system of the 1800s or the whippings of the 1700s a "good" or "service"; the practices hardly deserve the word "assistance." Likewise, most Americans in the Victorian period would have shuddered at the very idea of the 1970s "welfare right" (Gordon 1990; Ziliak 1996b).

The separation of spheres, and its division of labor, would come slowly, unevenly, and with sudden reversals. In his study of relief in New York in 1823, John Yates, the Secretary of the State of New York, could still include pauper auctions as part of New York's public assistance programs (Hannon 1984). State Departments of Public Welfare, formed as recently as the 1920s, were preceded for sixty years by "State Boards of Charities and Corrections" and by "State Boards of Charities, Corrections, and Lunacy" (National Conference of Charities and Corrections 1893, pp. 33–51). To take one more example, at the end of the nineteenth century the very idea of a poor person would be transformed and expanded by caseworkers who were studying the nascent field of psychology – this shift occurred at the same time that public assistance was being abolished in the largest cities and as the notion of "structural unemployment" was coming into vogue.

The Evolution of Relief in New York Was Probably Typical

The evolution of public assistance in nineteenth-century New York can probably be regarded as fairly typical of Northern states, although sometimes ahead of its time. New York State was a leading participant in each major reform movement of the nineteenth century, and the state's poor law often served as a model for other states (Schneider 1938; Trattner 1974; Leiby 1978; Katz 1983). Prior to 1824, public relief in New York State was the responsibility of town governments, and the forms of relief varied from town to town. Under its 1824 poor law, as revised in 1827, New York State transferred primary responsibility to county governments (though towns in many counties continued to assume responsibility for temporary outdoor relief). The 1824 law required that each county establish a poorhouse; and although many counties were exempted from this provision, by 1840 almost every county operated a poorhouse. By mandate of state law, all public relief recipients, except those deemed to be in need of only temporary assistance not to exceed $10 during the year, were to be supported in a county poorhouse. Public assistance evolved with a similar pattern of development in the states of the Old Northwest Territory, which looked to Pennsylvania for their first model (Kennedy 1934, Chapter 1).

The 1827 revision of New York's poor law required county superintendents of the poor to submit annual reports to the Secretary of State, who in turn was directed to present a report to the state legislature. Annual reporting began in most states forty to seventy years later with the establishment of a Board of State Charities. In New York, the first *Annual Report* appeared in 1830. Most counties reported only on poorhouse relief until 1839, when they were directed to include temporary outdoor relief in their reports. The data in Tables Bf156–187 are constructed from the county-level data contained in these reports. When compared with the almost negligible use of the poorhouse found by Secretary Yates in 1823, the data from the period from the 1820s through the 1840s document a dramatic rise of the poorhouse as a share of both total expenditures on public relief (Tables Bf156–187). Likewise, the dramatic rise of the poorhouse can be seen in the series constructed by Priscilla Clement for the city of Philadelphia, 1800–1854 (Tables Bf17–27).

Though much of the historical literature locates the impetus of enthusiasm in America's *cities*, in antebellum New York State both the support for and the usage of the poorhouse was, if anything, more prevalent in rural–agricultural areas (Hannon 1985, pp. 243–7, 1996; Cray 1988, pp. 100–135). In 1840, for example, New York City sent 29 percent of its paupers to the poorhouse, whereas 44 percent of paupers in the rest of the state were supported in poorhouses (calculated from Table Bf176–187). Quantitative evidence from other states is required to determine the representativeness of New York City's policy. To take what must be an extreme illustration, in 1840 about 93 percent of Philadelphia's paupers were supported in the almshouse (Table Bf23–27).

The work of Stephen Ziliak on paupers in almshouses during the period 1850–1923 shows vast differences in almshouse usage by state, by census region, and over time (Tables Bf34–155) (Ziliak 2002a). For example, the length of time a pauper stayed in an almshouse varied immensely. In 1880, the average length of stay in a Delaware almshouse was eight years and in a Texas almshouse, one year. Length of stay was no doubt related to age (among other factors), and the age structure of the population in the East was much older than that of the West. But poorhouse usage varied over time and space in nearly every social and economic variable. Nationwide the able-bodied paupers were never more than one third the total almshouse population. In the nineteenth century, the able-bodied share of the almshouse population fell at each census enumeration and hit a low of about 7 percent in the 1920s. To take one more example of difference, in 1923 the ratio of men to women in the population of the United States was near unity. In the almshouses of the Deep South, the ratio of men to women was also near unity. But in the almshouses of the Middle West and especially of the Pacific and Mountain regions the ratio of men to women was as high as 5:1 (Ziliak 2002a, Figures 3 and 8 and Table 1).

Oliver Twist Was Not the Typical Pauper of an Almshouse

The almshouses erected during the antebellum period remained central to the administrative structure of relief systems, and in New York they absorbed well over half of the funds of local public relief for the remainder of the century (Table Bf156–175). Across the Northern states, the almshouse bulked large in administrative and financial budgets. Yet nationwide, the percentage of the population living in almshouses was not particularly large (Tables Bf34–155). This was especially true in the second half of the nineteenth century and in the early twentieth century. Between 1850 and the 1920s, the fraction of the population living in almshouses peaked at 2.7 persons per 1,000. From its peak (in 1860), the fraction of the population living in almshouses fell at each census enumeration to a low of 0.08 percent in 1923 (Ziliak 2002a, Figures 5 and 6). During the same period, local officials provided outdoor relief to an increasing share of all public relief recipients (Table Bf176–187). This trend was caused by the relatively high cost of almshouse relief (calculated from Tables Bf156–187) and by a dawning recognition of the many environmental, as opposed to personal, causes of poverty (Hannon 1985). But this was also a trend toward the provision of increasingly specialized services to increasingly diverse populations. The miscellaneous poorhouse of colonial America was seen to be inhumane by the standards of the late nineteenth century. From New York to California, the almshouse evolved into an "old folks home," a home for aged, unskilled, "feeble-minded," and physically disabled men and women; there were more natives than immigrants and more whites than blacks, and most almshouse dwellers had never been married and had no children alive or able and willing to care for them. Oliver Twist, the waif of Dickens' fiction commonly associated with the bowels of the poorhouse and the even darker workhouse, was in fact hardly seen in such places. By 1915, just 0.1 percent of all paupers in almshouses were, like Oliver, children with neither parent living. A better literary characterization of a pauper in an almshouse is Mrs. Thomson of Edward Eggleston's *The Hoosier School-Master* (1871) or Grampa Joad of John Steinbeck's *The Grapes of Wrath* (1939). Outdoor relief, though expanding at a tremendous rate, was going instead into the homes of able-bodied adults who experienced short spells of illness or industrial unemployment (Ziliak 1997). Yet total *institutional* usage was all the while expanding. This was as true of public institutions as it was of private institutions. As almshouse usage fell with each census enumeration, the usage of insane asylums, orphans' homes, homes for the "friendless," homes for "fallen women," homes for the "blind, deaf, and dumb," and homes for the feeble-minded increased more than proportionately (Ziliak 2002a, Table 2). An array of charities, many of them hybrids of public and private schemes, emerged to meet the special needs of new immigrant and urban poverty. Between 1880 and 1895, Indianapolis gave birth to more than thirty new charities. Among them one finds the Alpha Home for Aged Colored Women, the German Lutheran Orphan's Home, the Ladies' Hebrew Benevolent Society, and the Socialistic Sick Benefit Society (Ziliak 1996a). Indianapolis was not unique.

"Welfare" Was Widely Abolished in the Late Nineteenth Century

The midcentury expansion of outdoor relief was rather abruptly halted when the downturns of the 1870s and the 1880s swelled pauper applications (Table Bf176–187). In response to crippled municipal budgets and a rising fear of pauperism and other vice, the Charity Organization Societies (COSs) launched a crusade against public outdoor relief (Ziliak 1996a, 1997; Hannon 1997b; Kauffman and Kiesling 1997).

Ten of the nation's largest cities abolished public outdoor relief, and many others sharply reduced it. The numbers affected were not small. In Brooklyn more than 46,000 people were directly affected by the abolition of 1879. Leaders of the COS orchestrated the abolition.[5] The COS did not object to the provision of material relief. Rather, they were advocates of a voluntaristic and "scientific charity." Although their practices and achievements varied, the COSs sharpened the old distinction between "worthy" and "unworthy" poor; they revived a notion of friendship and morality in the delivery of public assistance; they brought "scientific method" to the study of poverty; they centralized service delivery and data exchange; they established state boards and national conferences of charity; they started industrial schools and commercial clubs; and they gave birth to modern social and case work. According to Stephen Ziliak, the abolition of public outdoor relief had at least two large effects: It induced a large increase in private charitable donations as well as in expenditures on workhouses and other correctional facilities. And yet instead of helping the poor to achieve self-reliance, abolition seems to have merely shifted the dependence from public to private rolls, and from benevolent societies to departments of corrections. For example, the length of time that a family stayed on relief rolls did not change with the abolition of welfare. In fact, the length of time a family stays on relief has not changed much at all since the 1820s, hovering in most decades between eight and thirteen months (Ziliak 1996a, 2002b, Table 3). The percentage of families leaving relief rolls for higher earnings is also relatively stable: between 33 and 40 percent. Similarly, the research of Stephen Ziliak and of Stanley Lebergott lends some support to the idea that middle-class charity – in spite of occasional and localized spasms – is rather constant: The ratio of the nation's expenditures on indoor and outdoor relief to the average earnings of common labor has remained relatively steady over a long sweep of nineteenth- and twentieth-century history, between 25 and 30 percent nationwide (Table Bf28–33) (Lebergott 1976, pp. 61–65; Ziliak 2002b). As yet there is little evidence suggesting that the abolition of welfare was productive of increases in the self-reliance of the poor. To take just one more example, not a single laborer advanced to a higher occupational category while under the care of the Indianapolis Charity Organization Society.

Despite the crusades against public outdoor relief – or perhaps because of it – total institutional usage was rising and diversifying in the latter part of the nineteenth century. This rise correlated

[5] The COS was imported from London to Buffalo, New York, in 1877. By 1893, there was a COS in 100 cities of the United States.

with increasing degrees of administrative control at the state level. Pauper children were removed from county almshouses and placed in private households or in state institutions that would try to address specific physical or mental disadvantages. Yet estimates of the numbers involved suggest that the local systems continued to support almost three quarters of the relief population in New York and Indiana at the end of the century, and so far there is little reason for thinking that other states deviated markedly from this pattern (Butler 1916; Hannon 1997a, Figure 2; Ziliak 2002a). Under stress from the depression of 1893–1894, public outdoor relief returned. But the more dramatic appearance of the welfare state, of course, waited for the twentieth century.

Alternatives to local relief in the late nineteenth and early twentieth centuries included federal pensions for veterans of the Civil War and, in many states, mothers' pensions (on which Aid to Dependent Children [ADC] was later modeled). By 1910, according to Theda Skocpol, 28 percent of all American men aged 65 and over, and some 300,000 widows, orphans, and other dependents were receiving benefits under the veterans' benefits programs. That is, the number of widows and dependents receiving veterans' pensions was more than four times the total number of paupers living in almshouses. By 1920, forty states had enacted mothers' pensions, under which local governments provided regular payments to impoverished mothers of dependent children (Skocpol 1992, pp. 160–204, 424–79). Still, the enumeration of paupers in almshouses in each decennial census from 1850 to 1880 and the special censuses of paupers in almshouses conducted by the Bureau of the Census in 1904, 1910, and 1923 attest to the continuing symbolic importance of the county poorhouse in the twentieth century (Tables Bf34–155) (Ziliak 2002a).

Public Assistance Has Been Entwined with Health and Corrections

The historical process of separating matters of public assistance from matters of crime and mental illness is a process that parallels the great twentieth-century expansions of criteria for eligibility for relief and of the sovereignty of the poor as consumer. Throughout the nineteenth century, there were moments when especially those who worked most closely with the poor acknowledged economic and social causes of poverty, but the belief that the roots of poverty lie in the character of the poor themselves and the idea that the provision of public relief itself creates dependency were dominant forces shaping public relief policy (Katz 1983; Hannon 1997a; Ziliak 1997). The twentieth century certainly did not eliminate these ideas from popular opinion, academic scholarship, or public policy debate. They continue to provide ideological support for reversals of a long-run evolution of programs for public assistance that, at least for native whites, lay less and less blame for poverty on the character of the poor person. The separation of public assistance from crime and "lunacy" has been a slow process of conceding ground to causes of poverty that lay outside the domain of personal responsibility. Perhaps most important, these causes have included recognition of the uncertain and sometimes volatile breakdown of markets and of marriage, as well as recognition of the facts of institutional racism, patriarchy, and mental and physical difference.

At the same time that public assistance was being divorced from corrections and mental healthcare, and as the power of local self-government and local control were being diminished, the sovereignty of the poor was expanding: The movements were from auctions to workhouses to free government cheese; from the spectacle of bread lines to cashable checks in the mail, confidential and unrestricted, like cash. The Personal Responsibility and Work Opportunity Reconciliation Act of 1996 made way for a substantial reversal of these developments.

The history of public assistance can, of course, be seen as a history of race, of class, and of gender struggles to define work, home, and the American Dream. From early nineteenth-century lists of the "causes of pauperism," on which immigration occupied the number one spot, through the Americanization efforts of early social workers to restrictions on the eligibility of immigrants under the 1996 Personal Responsibility and Work Opportunity Reconciliation Act, the immigrant poor are often subjected to a nineteenth-century distinction between "worthy" and "unworthy." Similarly, from gender and racial segregation of nineteenth-century poorhouse residents through the fight for mothers' pensions and ADC, to provisions of the Personal Responsibility and Work Opportunity Reconciliation Act that allow states to deny benefits to unmarried teen mothers and to impose family caps, the historical evolution of welfare policy is integrally linked with the politics of race, gender, and the American family (Skocpol 1992; Gordon 1994; Mink 1995; Quadagno 1996; Green 1999). To take just one example, in the first half of the nineteenth century, a free "Negro or mulatto" could enter the state of Ohio only "by giving to the clerk of the common pleas court a freehold security to the amount of five hundred dollars, which was later used for his support in case he became a pauper" (Kennedy 1934, pp. 23–36).

Previous editions of the *Historical Statistics of the United States* have published statistics on public assistance. Most of the previously published data series begin their run in 1936. A few of the previously published data series were traced back to 1890.[6] Statistical data for the centuries before the 1930s were omitted from the previous editions of *Historical Statistics of the United States*. The omission was not caused by an absence of publicly financed relief programs in earlier times nor by a dearth of primary source data: they are plentiful. At the time of the publication of the previous editions, there was simply a lack of historical research into the identification, collection, and analysis of such data.

A statistical portrait of public assistance in the United States from colonial times to the 1920s is beginning to emerge. The tables published here are but a small sample of the data on public assistance that historians now know exist. There is a long way to go before we have a quantitative account of public assistance whose completeness is akin to that of our national income statistics. For example, while historians are aware that public assistance is entwined financially and administratively with the history of private charities, historians are just beginning to uncover the economic significance of the relation between the two sectors (Ziliak 1996a, 1997; Hannon 1997b; Kauffman and Kiesling 1997; Kiesling and Margo 1997). Thus the data assembled here are more voluminous for particular geographic regions, periods of time, and kinds of relief, reflecting both the varied development of public and private schemes over time and place and the relative infancy of quantitative historical scholarship on public assistance in the United States.

[6] For example, in *Historical Statistics of the United States* (1975), series H 346–367 traces public assistance at the local, state, and federal levels to 1936; and series H1–31 ("Social Welfare Expenditures under Public Programs") extend back to 1890.

References

Butler, Amos. 1916. "A Century of Progress: A Study of Public Charities and Correction, 1790–1915." Holliday Collection, Indiana Room, Indiana State Library.

Cray, Robert E., Jr. 1988. *Paupers and Poor Relief in New York City and Its Rural Environs, 1700–1830.* Temple University Press.

Gordon, Linda, editor. 1990. *Women, the State, and Welfare.* University of Wisconsin Press.

Gordon, Linda. 1994. *Pitied but Not Entitled: Single Mothers and the History of Welfare.* Harvard University Press.

Green, Elna C., editor. 1999. *Before the New Deal: Social Welfare in the South, 1830–1930.* University of Georgia Press.

Hannon, Joan Underhill. 1984. "Poverty and the Antebellum Northeast: The View from New York State's Poor Relief Rolls." *Journal of Economic History* 44 (4): 1007–32.

Hannon, Joan Underhill. 1985. "Poor Relief Policy in Antebellum New York State: The Rise and Decline of the Poorhouse." *Explorations in Economic History* 22 (January): 233–56.

Hannon, Joan Underhill. 1996. "Why Poorhouses? Determinants of Local Relief Policy in Nineteenth-Century New York State." Paper presented to the Social Science History Association, New Orleans.

Hannon, Joan Underhill. 1997a. "Public Relief Dependency before the Welfare State: The Interplay of Life Cycles, Labor Markets, and Policy in Nineteenth-Century New York State." Paper presented to the Allied Social Science Association (January).

Hannon, Joan Underhill. 1997b. "Shutting Down Welfare: Two Cases from America's Past." *Quarterly Review of Economics and Finance* 37 (2): 419–38.

Herndon, Ruth Wallis. 2001. *Unwelcome Americans: Living on the Margin in Early New England.* University of Pennsylvania Press.

Katz, Michael B. 1983. *Poverty and Policy in American History.* Academic Press.

Kauffman, Kyle D., and L. Lynne Kiesling. 1997. "Was There a Nineteenth-Century Welfare Magnet in the United States? Preliminary Results from New York City and Brooklyn." *Quarterly Review of Economics and Finance* 37 (2): 439–48.

Kennedy, Aileen E. 1934. *The Ohio Poor Law and Its Administration.* University of Chicago Press.

Kiesling, L. Lynne, and Robert A. Margo. 1997. "Explaining the Rise in Antebellum Pauperism, 1850–1860: New Evidence." *Quarterly Review of Economics and Finance* 37 (2): 405–18.

Lebergott, Stanley. 1976. *The American Economy: Income, Wealth, and Want.* Princeton University Press.

Leiby, James. 1978. *A History of Social Welfare and Social Work in the United States.* Columbia University Press.

Mink, Gwendolyn. 1995. *The Wages of Motherhood: Inequality in the Welfare State, 1917–1942.* Cornell University Press.

Nash, Gary B. 1976a. "Poverty and Poor Relief in Pre-Revolutionary Philadelphia." *William and Mary Quarterly* 33: 3–30.

National Conference of Charities and Corrections. 1893. Committee Report, "History of State Boards." *Proceedings of the National Conference of Charities and Corrections.* Geo. H. Ellis.

Quadagno, Jill. 1996. *The Color of Welfare: How Racism Undermined the War on Poverty.* Oxford University Press.

Rose, Michael E. 1971. *The English Poor Law.* Barnes & Noble.

Schneider, David M. 1938. *The History of Public Welfare in New York State, 1609–1866.* University of Chicago Press.

Shaffer, Alice, Mary Wysor Keefer, and Sophonisba P. Breckinridge. 1941. *The Indiana Poor Law.* University of Chicago Press.

Skocpol, Theda. 1992. *Protecting Soldiers and Mothers: The Political Origins of Social Policy in the United States.* Harvard University Press.

Trattner, Walter. 1974. *From Poor Law to Welfare State.* Free Press.

U.S. Bureau of the Census. 1906. *Paupers in Almshouses.* U.S. Government Printing Office.

Webb, Sidney, and Beatrice Webb. 1927. *English Local Government: English Poor Law History: Part I, The Old Poor Law.* Longmans, Green.

Ziliak, Stephen. 1996a. "The End of Welfare and the Contradiction of Compassion." *Independent Review* 1 (1): 55–73.

Ziliak, Stephen T. 1996b. "Essays on Self-Reliance: The United States in the Era of 'Scientific Charity.'" Ph.D. dissertation, University of Iowa.

Ziliak, Stephen T. 1997. "Kicking the Malthusian Vice: Lessons from the Abolition of 'Welfare' in the Late Nineteenth Century." *Quarterly Review of Economics and Finance* 37 (2): 449–68.

Ziliak, Stephen T. 2002a. "Pauper Fiction in Economic Science: 'Paupers in Almshouses' and the Odd Fit of *Oliver Twist*." *Review of Social Economy* 60 (2): 159–81.

Ziliak, Stephen T. 2002b. "Some Tendencies of Social Welfare and the Problem of Interpretation." *Cato Journal* 21 (Winter): 499–513.

SOCIAL WELFARE: 1929 TO THE PRESENT

Price V. Fishback and Melissa A. Thomasson

Probably the most dramatic change in the American economy over the course of the twentieth century has been the growth of social welfare spending by both public and private entities. A key component of that growth has been an expansion in *public* social welfare programs. These programs aid individuals and families in obtaining education and in obtaining insurance against financial hardship in old age and against the risks of workplace disability and unemployment. They also provide financial and other resources for low-income households. The programs sometimes supplement and sometimes replace the provisions of such services by private enterprise or by households. In fact, private spending on these social welfare issues may have been greater than public spending at the turn of the century and is roughly two thirds of the level of public social welfare spending today.

The Social Security Administration (SSA) is the primary source for public social welfare statistics. The SSA defines social welfare spending to include "expenditures on social insurance, income maintenance, health and medical care, education, housing, veterans' benefits, and other welfare services directed specifically toward promoting the economic and social welfare of individuals and families." There is certainly the potential for endless debate over the adequacy of this definition. The SSA chose the definition in part to be compatible with international definitions of social welfare spending used by the Organization for Economic Co-operation and Development (OECD) and the International Labour Office (ILO). Awareness of the potential limitations of the definition and its implied categories has led the SSA to provide the statistics at a low enough level of disaggregation that those with alternative definitions can regroup the data appropriately.

Prior to the 1930s, social welfare spending was primarily the responsibility of state and local governments. As seen in this chapter's essay on public assistance from colonial times to the 1920s and tables contributed by Joan Hannon and Stephen Ziliak on public assistance in the nineteenth century, some local governments provided relief to the poor, but the amounts varied substantially from place to place. Public schools were supported by local taxes, and beginning in the mid-nineteenth century they were maintained by a combination of state and local taxes. In the mid-1850s, states began to establish institutions for the mentally ill and other dependent groups, and state boards of health were in operation in many states by the early 1900s. The federal government largely confined its social welfare responsibilities to aiding veterans of military service, although the pensions for Civil War veterans and their widows and children benefited a substantial segment of society (see Skocpol 1992; Orloff 1993). During the Progressive era in the early 1900s, reformers pressed state governments for an extensive series of social welfare programs, including workers' compensation laws, unemployment insurance, state-provided health insurance, old-age pensions, and mothers' aid pensions for widowed mothers. Of all these programs, only workers' compensation and the mothers' aid pensions were adopted in a large number of states by 1929. By the mid-1930s a number of states had adopted old-age relief plans, while only Wisconsin had enacted unemployment insurance, and they had not yet started paying benefits by the time the Social Security Act established unemployment insurance as a joint federal–state program.

Prior to the Great Depression, social insurance and many social welfare activities were not considered to be under the purview of the federal government. When the Great Depression led to an unemployment rate of nearly 25 percent in 1933, Franklin Roosevelt and the New Dealers made the argument that the Depression was a national emergency that must be dealt with using federal programs. The New Deal provided emergency assistance to large numbers of unemployed workers and then in 1935 established several long-term social insurance programs with the Social Security Act. Federal actions during the 1930s set precedents for the expansion of the federal government into additional programs that were introduced in later years. After the federal government became involved in the social welfare business, the collection of statistics aggregated to a national level expanded rapidly. Consequently, most of the statistics presented in this chapter are from 1929 to the present. Few national statistics are available for the earlier periods. There was enormous variation across cities, counties, and states in the provision of such services, and we have only shreds of evidence available.

It is important to offer a caveat about use of the statistics on social welfare expenditures. The vast majority of the statistics available on social welfare spending are reported by the SSA in the *Social Security Bulletin* and the *Social Security Bulletin Annual Supplement*. The first lesson to be learned in examining the long time series is that the series are often revised in response to new data, methods, and conceptual definitions. The SSA often publishes the revised versions of the recent data, but in many cases it offers revised information for only those earlier years ending in 0 and 5. In most cases, we try to present the revisions that were available through 1997. Discussions with the people at the SSA who compile the statistics suggest that a search for "the" number in any single year would be futile. The numbers are estimates from surveys, reports of other agencies, and other sources. In a number of settings, the fundamental information is collected only every second, third, fifth, or tenth year, and the observations for the intervening years are interpolations. Thus, the reported observations for each year should be treated as rough approximations of the "true" level. The people at the SSA are careful to try to maintain consistency in the definitions of the series. However, even the revisions are subject to measurement error, and year-to-year fluctuations between a revised statistic for a year ending in 0 or 5 with neighboring years are likely to be subject to measurement error. There is some comfort in our finding that many of the revisions are within 3 percent of the prior reported estimates. This caveat suggests that the data are useful for showing long-term trends over decades but are more sensitive to measurement error in examining year-to-year changes.

A preliminary word on the organization of tables is also in order. Tables Bf188–270 report annual information on social welfare spending under public programs based on the OECD definitions for the period 1929 to the mid-1990s. The tables offer a breakdown of social welfare spending for programs under each of the broad categories of social insurance, public aid, health and medical programs, veterans' programs, education, public housing, and other programs. Many of the programs are funded by several layers of government; therefore, Table Bf196–211 shows the extent to which federal and state or local governments provide the funding for each of the broad categories. Governments are not the only source of social welfare spending. Tables Bf773–892 offer information on social welfare spending by private entities, which account for as much as 13 percent of gross domestic product (GDP) in today's economy. Tables Bf271–772 offer information about specific public programs: the numbers of people affected, the monies spent, and the sources of funding. There are a large number of tables in this area because the development of social welfare programs over the course of the twentieth century has been complicated. The federal, state, and local governments have developed an array of programs to meet different aspects of social welfare. Views have changed about the optimal way to meet these goals. As a result, long-term programs have been redesigned, and even if they have kept the same name, the nature of data collection for the new goals changes the series collected. In other cases, new agencies are developed to take over the duties of the original program. Finally, new programs are added to the list. This has led us in some cases to report multiple overlapping series on the same issues.

Aggregate Trends

The dramatic increase in public social welfare spending in the United States has been one of the major economic trends in the twentieth century. The broadest conceptual measure of public social welfare spending is in series Bf188, which is the series collected by the SSA to be compatible with the OECD/ILO definitions of public social welfare spending. Between 1929 and 1993, social welfare spending in public programs in 1992 dollars (adjusted for inflation by the GDP deflator) has grown at an average annual rate of 6.1 percent per year, nearly double the annual average growth rate of 3.3 percent for real GDP.[1] To give a sense of the size of public social welfare spending, it is useful to compare it to the overall size of the economy by describing the spending as a comparative percentage to GDP. There is one important caveat about this comparison. When social welfare expenditures are compared to GDP in percentage terms, it should not be presumed that this is the contribution of social welfare expenditures to GDP. The GDP is defined as the market value of the output of final goods and services in the economy, while a significant percentage of the social welfare expenditures are transfer payments that would not be considered as additions to the final goods and services measured by the GDP.

[1] The annual average growth rate for social welfare spending between 1929 and 1993 is calculated as $[(S_{1993}/S_{1929})^{(1/(1993-1929))} - 1]*100$, where S_{year} refers to the value for the variable in that year. All other average annual growth rates in the chapter are calculated in the same way using the endpoints of the period examined. The information on nominal GDP, GDP in 1992 dollars, and the GDP deflator used to convert nominal dollars to 1992 dollars is derived from the nominal and real GDP series rounded to billions of dollars that formed the basis for the tables in the Council of Economic Advisors, Economic Report of the President Transmitted to Congress February 1998, pp. 280–2. In Chapter Ca, there is an updated set of GDP numbers.

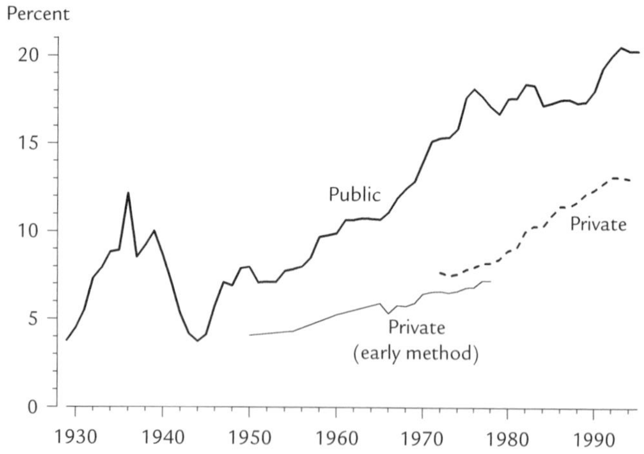

FIGURE Bf-B Public and private social welfare expenditures as a percentage of gross domestic product: 1929–1995

Sources

Series Bf188, Bf773, and Bf781 expressed as a percentage of series Ca1.

Figure Bf-B shows that social welfare spending from public sources rose from roughly 3.8 percent as large as GDP in 1929 to 20.6 percent by 1993. The estimate for 1929 should be considered a very rough estimate because of our lack of accumulated statistics for state and local governments. However, it is likely that the true value is close to this figure. Estimates for 1890 and 1913 prepared for *Historical Statistics of the United States* (1975) suggest that public social welfare spending was approximately 2.4 percent as large as GDP in 1890 and 2.5 percent as large as GDP in 1913.[2] Impressionistic comparisons seem consistent with these estimates. As seen in Chapter Bc, children have spent increasingly longer periods of time in school over their lifetimes. Spending on veterans' programs peaked between 1890 and 1913, as the number of Civil War veterans began to dwindle. Old-age pension programs were typically provided for federal workers in 1920 before they were available to most state and local governments. Finally, public assistance spending by state and local governments was clearly meager relative to the levels we see during and after the 1930s. Social welfare spending spiked above 10 percent as large as GDP during the mid-1930s owing to a combination of low output during the heart of the Great Depression and the large-scale public assistance spending by the Works Progress Administration (WPA) and other New Deal agencies. By the end of World War II, social welfare spending had returned to pre-Depression percentages relative to GDP. We then see its substantial rise over the course of the next fifty years.

The rise in public social welfare spending during the twentieth century was accompanied by a substantial increase in the share of social welfare spending from federal funds (calculated from Table Bf196–211). It is not always obvious how to determine precisely whether the federal government or the state and local governments are the source of the funds. Many programs involved combined activity by the state and local governments and the federal government, and, in a number of cases, the federal government provides grants of funds to be administered by state and local governments in ways that might vary from state to state. The text for Table Bf196–211 describes several situations where the SSA statistics and the national income product accounts (NIPA) have treated the source of the same grants differently. The description that follows is based on the decisions made by the SSA.

Estimates from *Historical Statistics of the United States* (1975) place the federal government's share of social welfare spending in 1890 at 36 percent, primarily as a result of the Civil War Pension program. As the number of Civil War veterans declined, the federal share fell to 20 percent by 1913 (see pp. 332, 341). In 1929, the first year of the SSA's long-term time series, the federal government continued to fund about 20 percent of public social welfare expenditures. The federal share spiked above 60 percent during the New Deal and was at 56 percent during the military mobilization and demobilization of World War II. A long-term secular rise followed through the end of the Carter administration. Since the early 1980s, the share has fallen slowly to below 60 percent, as the federal government has sought to shift more of the responsibility to state and local governments.

The data in Table Bf196–211 show that the federal share of social welfare spending varies greatly across categories. The federal government has always provided nearly all of the funding for veterans' programs and the lion's share of funding for public housing projects and subsidies. In contrast, the federal share of public educational spending has traditionally been below 10 percent because the focus of public educational spending is on elementary and secondary schools, which are primarily the responsibility of state and local governments. After the New Deal fueled a dramatic increase in federal activity, public aid has become largely a shared responsibility between the federal government and the state and local governments. Since 1929, the federal share of public social insurance expenditures has risen markedly from 20 percent in 1929 to over 80 percent in the early 1990s. The rise is largely the result of the rapid expansions in the federal old-age and Medicare programs, which account for roughly 47 and 22 percent of social insurance expenditures, respectively (see series Bf189 and Bf214–215). State and local governments still provide workers' compensation for nonfederal government workers, administer roughly 80 percent of the funds for unemployment insurance, and operate public employee retirement systems that account for 40 percent of the total of federal, state, and local systems.

Social Insurance Programs

The leading contributor to the long-term rise in public social welfare expenditures has been social insurance programs (see series Bf189 and table Bf212–224). As seen in Figure Bf-C, social insurance expenditures have risen from less than 1 percent as large as GDP in 1929 to 10 percent as large as GDP by 1993. The social insurance programs, as defined by the SSA, include the federal Social Security programs for Old-Age, Survivors Insurance (OASI) and Disability Insurance (DI); the Medicare programs for Hospital Insurance (HI) and Supplementary Medical Insurance (SMI); the state programs for workers' compensation insurance; the federal Black Lung Benefits program; temporary disability programs in a handful of states; the federal–state programs for Unemployment Insurance (UI); and retirement and disability programs for federal employees (including the military), state and local employees, and railroad workers. All these programs operate at least to some extent

[2] The estimates are based on Musgrave and Culbertson (1953) and J. Frederic Dewhurst and Associates (1955) and reports of official agencies. See U.S. Bureau of the Census (1975), pp. 330, 340–1.

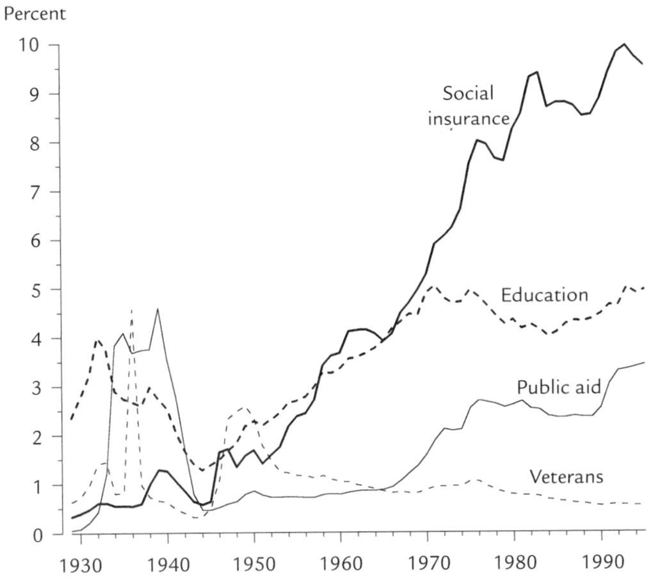

FIGURE Bf-C Public social welfare expenditures as a percentage of gross domestic product, by type of program: 1929–1995

Sources

Series Bf189–190 and Bf192–193 expressed as a percentage of series Ca1.

Documentation

Not shown from Table Bf188–195 are the following lesser categories: health and medical programs (series Bf191), housing (series Bf194), and other social welfare programs (series Bf195). Together they accounted for 0.4 percent of gross domestic product in 1929 and 1.9 percent in 1995.

like insurance. Individuals and/or their employers pay premiums or taxes into a fund. In turn, when the individual reaches old age, is disabled, is unemployed, or is injured on the job, depending on the program, the individual receives payments. In actual operation, it is not always easy to draw the line between the programs defined as social insurance in the SSA statistics and those defined as public assistance. For example, the aged persons receiving Social Security OASI payments in the early 1940s had contributed little, if anything, into the program before they began receiving benefits. Further, many of the early cohorts receiving Social Security received more in benefits than they would have received if they had contributed the amounts to an actuarially sound private pension fund.

Among the industrial nations, the United States was a latecomer in the widespread public provision of social insurance. Germany under Bismarck led the way in the 1880s with sickness, accident, old-age, and disability insurance programs. A number of European countries followed suit. Except for federal provisions for the military, government provision of widespread social insurance did not begin until the majority of states adopted workers' compensation laws in the 1910s and the federal government established unemployment insurance and old-age insurance under the Social Security Act of 1935. Only a handful of states have established temporary disability insurance programs.[3]

[3] The states establishing temporary disability programs are California, Hawai'i, New Jersey, New York, and Rhode Island, as well as the territory of Puerto Rico. There are also government-run railroad temporary disability programs. See Social Security Administration, *SSBASS* (1997), Table 9.C.1.

Old-Age and Disability Insurance

The earliest forms of social insurance by the federal government were limited to disability pension programs for the military (Clark, Craig, and Wilson, 1999, 2003). Before 1855, the military pension systems were primarily disability plans, with the notable exception of officer's pensions from the Revolutionary War. The Continental Congress created the first military pension plan for naval personnel in November 1775 and an army plan a year later. Subsequent revisions to the army plan offered life annuities to officers who remained in the line for the duration of the war. In addition, several colonies offered plans for their militia and naval personnel. All these plans were compromised by the woeful financial state of Revolutionary public finance. Eventually, the Revolutionary pensions were reorganized and ultimately assumed by the federal government after ratification of the Constitution. At that time, the army plan was placed on a "pay-as-you-go" basis, but until its bankruptcy in 1842, the navy plan was funded with monies from the liquidation of prizes. Veterans of subsequent military conflicts, most conspicuously the War of 1812 and the Mexican War, were offered similar plans. Although confusion surrounding antebellum pension records makes an exact accounting problematic, by 1861 roughly 10,500 veterans, widows, or dependents were receiving $1,036,064 in pensions benefits, most of which was for disabilities. In 1855, Congress created the first systematic retirement plan for naval officers. In 1861, that plan was revised, and army officers were included. The Act of 1861, and its subsequent amendments, allowed officers to retire at 75 percent of their active-duty pay after forty years of service. The Civil War, which began in the same year, added substantially to the pension rolls and the pressure on the Treasury to finance those liabilities (Clark, Craig, and Wilson, 1999, 2003). The benefits expanded more widely after the Civil War because of the substantial percentage of the Northern population that participated in the Civil War and later became eligible for Civil War veterans' disability pensions. Definitions of eligibility were broadened enough over time that the Civil War disability program has been considered a precursor of old-age programs for the general public.[4]

Prior to 1920, nonmilitary civil servants received pensions on a case-by-case basis at the discretion of the Congress. The federal government established retirement programs for all federal employees under the 1920 Civil Service Retirement Act (Graebner 1980; Johnson and Libecap 1994; Craig 1995). Since 1987, the

[4] See Skocpol (1992) and Orloff (1993), pp. 134–7. The original law for Civil War pensions in 1862 extended only to soldiers actually injured in combat or to dependents of those killed or disabled. As a result, expenditures on Civil War pensions began declining in the 1870s. The 1879 Arrears Act allowed soldiers who "discovered" Civil War–related disabilities to sign up and receive in one lump sum all the payments they would have been eligible for since the 1860s. In 1890, the Dependent Pension Act severed the tie to combat-related injuries; any veteran serving ninety days in the military was eligible if at some point he became disabled for manual labor. In practice, old age alone became a sufficient disability. A 1906 law declared that the age of 62 and over was a permanent specific disability within the meaning of the pension laws. At the turn of the century, about 15 percent of the elderly in America were receiving Civil War pensions because veterans accounted for about 30 percent of American men over age 65. In the North and Midwest, the proportion receiving pensions was about 40 to 48 percent. Confederate veterans were left out of the system, although some states provided pensions. Georgia was the most generous, with a pension that was less than one seventh as generous as the Northern pension of $360 per year.

federal employee retirement programs have been in transition. Almost all new federal employees hired after 1983 are now under the Federal Employees Retirement System (FERS), which combines Social Security benefits, a basic benefit plan, and opportunities for employees to save in tax-deferred annuities similar to 401(k) plans. Employees hired prior to 1983 are still under the Civil Service Retirement System but have the option to transfer to the FERS.[5]

As of 1929, retirement programs for public employees, including the military (series Bf217), accounted for roughly one third of social insurance expenditures, while state workers' compensation programs (series Bf223) accounted for roughly two thirds. Expenditures for public employee retirement programs have continued to expand at an average annual rate nearly 2.4 times as fast as real GDP, as public employment has expanded and benefit levels have increased (see Tables Bf290–348 and Bf735–745). Even so, the expansion of other social insurance programs has been even more rapid, such that the public employees' share of public social insurance expenditures has declined to 22 percent in the 1990s.

Prior to the 1930s, there were virtually no old-age insurance programs for the general public that resemble the current Social Security old-age pension plan. Between 1915 and 1935, twenty-eight states and two territories passed "old-age pension" plans. These programs appear to be largely relief programs for the aged with low incomes that would allow them to live outside institutions (Stevens 1970, pp. 20–4; Quadagno 1988, pp. 51–75; Costa 1998 pp. 166–7). In compliance with the SSA's categories, we discuss them in more detail in the section on public assistance programs. As the Depression deepened, the federal government became involved in providing public assistance, and there was substantial grassroots public pressure for some type of federal old-age pension plan.[6] The Social Security Act of 1935 established the OASI (the bulk of series Bf214) and UI (the bulk of series Bf218) programs. In 1957 the program was expanded to include DI, and in 1966 the Medicare HI and SMI programs were established for the elderly (series Bf215).

The railroads led the way in establishing private retirement pension programs beginning in 1874. In the 1930s, the federal government established railroad social insurance systems that were separate from the Social Security systems. The railroad system for retirement was established in 1934, 1935, and 1937 (series Bf216 and Table Bf746–761); for unemployment in 1938 (series Bf219 and Table Bf497–510); and for temporary disability benefits in 1946 (series Bf220).[7] Because railroad employment has declined over the past thirty years, expenditures on temporary disability and unemployment insurance in the railroad systems peaked in the early 1960s, while expenditures in the railroad retirement system peaked in the early 1980s.

Even though the first old-age pension checks were not issued until 1940, the Social Security and Railroad Retirement Acts immediately gave retirement coverage to a large segment of the population. Employees with wages and salaries equivalent to roughly 85 percent of total wages and salaries were covered by OASI retirement programs by 1937 (see series Bf272 and Bf274). After dropping during World War II to a low of 72 percent, the figure rose to its long-run level of over 95 percent in the mid-1950s. The self-employed were not covered by the Old-Age, Survivors, Disability, and Health Insurance (OASDHI) system until the 1950 amendments to the Social Security Act. The earnings of the self-employed covered by the OASDHI system (series Bf279) expanded very rapidly during the 1950s, as additional amendments to the Social Security Act expanded the types of self-employment covered under the Act.

Since the introduction of Social Security, there has been a significant rise in life expectancy, a significant population growth during the baby boom, and an increase in labor force participation by women. All these factors have contributed to a substantial increase in the number of workers with earnings that are taxable for contributions to the OASDHI trust funds (series Bf381). Although the number of workers with taxable earnings has increased rapidly over the past six decades, the benefits paid out to Social Security recipients have risen at an even faster pace. After the Social Security Act was amended in 1939 to allow the OASI to become a pay-as-you-go system funded by contributions of taxes by current workers, the size of the tax burden on current workers has risen dramatically over time. Average earnings per worker in covered employment have risen at an average annual rate of roughly 1.6 percent per year from $9,382 in 1937 to $22,618 in 1997 (1992 dollars in both cases). Yet, the rise in benefits paid has been even faster. OASI benefits in 1992 dollars per worker with taxable earnings started at a low of around $10 when the old-age benefits were first paid out in 1940 and have risen to just under $2,000 per worker with taxable earnings in the 1990s.

The rise in the tax burden has been driven by expansions in coverage, increases in average benefits, a rise in the percentage of the population reaching retirement age, and an increase in the longevity of the retirees. Since 1940, the number of families receiving old-age benefits per wage earner reporting taxable incomes in Table Bf-D has increased from below 1 per 100 to nearly 19 per 100 in the early 1990s. The OASI program provides benefits not only to the retired and their dependents but also to the survivors of deceased workers. Following World War II, generally 70 to 80 percent of the benefits in the OASI program have been paid to the retired workers and their dependents with the remainder going to the survivors of deceased workers (see series Bf396–397 and Bf401). As a result, the number of families receiving survivor benefits has risen to about 4 families per 100 wage earners reporting taxable income.

The SSA began paying benefits to disabled workers in 1959 under the DI program, and the number of beneficiary families of disabled workers has risen to a similar level of about 4 families for every 100 wage earners (series Bf416–421).[8] It is anticipated that as the baby boom generation reaches retirement age, the number of families receiving OASI and DI benefits will continue to rise relative to the number of wage earners, putting increasing pressure on the Social Security system.

[5] See the text for Table Bf735–745 for more specific details on the operation of the Civil Service Retirement System and the FERS.

[6] For discussions and other sources on the introduction of Social Security and later amendments to the law, see Graebner (1980), chapter 7; Weaver (1982); Ball (1988); Berkowitz and McQuaid (1992); Costa (1998), Chapter 8; and Schieber and Shoven (1999).

[7] See also Tables Bf290–348 for information on beneficiaries and payments under the railroad systems. The 1934 version of the Railroad Retirement law was declared unconstitutional and replaced by a new act in 1935. For a description of the introduction of the Railroad Retirement law, see Graebner (1980), pp. 153–80.

[8] For a discussion of the introduction of DI, see Berkowitz and McQuaid (1992), pp. 136–41, 186–8; and Weaver (1982), pp. 137–40.

TABLE Bf-D Long-term changes in key indicators for the Old-Age, Survivors Insurance program under Social Security: 1940–1996

	Ratios to the number of workers with taxable earnings					Ratio of benefits to average monthly earnings of workers in covered employment				
						Retired-worker family				
	Workers fully insured	Retired-worker families receiving old-age benefits	Survivor families receiving benefits	OASI benefits paid per worker with taxable earnings	Average earnings of workers in covered employment	Male worker only	Female worker only	Survivor family: widowed mother or father and one child	Disabled-worker family: worker, spouse, and one child	Maximum benefit payable to men at retirement
Year	Ratio	Ratio	Ratio	1992 dollars	1992 dollars	Ratio	Ratio	Ratio	Ratio	Ratio
1940	0.68	0.003	0.001	9	9,382	0.27	0.22	0.40	—	0.49
1950	1.24	0.036	0.010	109	12,439	0.24	0.18	0.41	—	0.24
1960	1.16	0.108	0.027	633	15,712	0.26	0.20	0.43	0.61	0.39
1970	1.16	0.140	0.039	1,015	18,735	0.27	0.21	0.45	0.55	0.40
1980	1.24	0.169	0.041	1,541	19,492	0.38	0.30	0.63	0.74	0.58
1990	1.23	0.183	0.038	1,783	21,621	0.40	0.31	0.60	0.63	0.58
1996	1.22	0.184	0.035	1,913	22,618	0.40	0.31	0.59	0.60	0.60

	Percentage of recipients age 80 and older		Percentage of recipients accepting reduced benefits		Tax rates for employer and employee each			Maximum taxable earnings	OASI trust fund assets
	Male	Female	Male	Female	OASI	DI	HI		
Year	Percent	Percent	Percent	Percent	Percent	Percent	Percent	Million 1992 dollars	dollars
1940	1.8	0.6	—	—	1.00	—	—	27,901	18,889
1950	7.1	3.7	—	—	1.50	—	—	16,408	75,046
1960	12.1	7.2	—	33.4	2.75	0.25	—	20,627	87,336
1970	15.9	14.4	35.9	58.5	3.65	0.55	0.60	25,590	106,475
1980	15.6	18.3	54.8	69.1	4.52	0.56	1.05	42,931	37,831
1990	16.6	22.7	64.6	72.6	5.60	0.60	1.45	54,806	228,834
1996	18.5	25.9	68.0	74.4	5.26	0.94	1.45	56,890	453,165

Sources

GDP deflator used to convert nominal dollars to 1992 dollars: the deflator derived from the nominal and real GDP series rounded to billions of dollars that formed the basis for tables in the Council of Economic Advisors, Economic Report of the President Transmitted to Congress February 1998 (U.S. Government Printing Office, 1998), pp. 280–2.

Workers with taxable earnings: series Bf381.

Workers fully insured for retirement or survivor benefits: series Bf377.

Retired-worker families receiving old-age benefits: sum of series Bf408 and Bf411.

Survivor families receiving benefits: sum of series Bf412–415.

Benefits paid: series Bf395.

Average annual earnings of workers in covered employment: series Bf384 divided by series Bf381. Average monthly earnings of workers in covered employment: average annual earnings divided by 12.

Ratio of benefits to average earnings of workers in covered employment: series Bf462, Bf463, Bf466, Bf472, and Bf474, each expressed as a ratio to the average monthly earnings of workers in covered employment.

Percentage of beneficiaries age 80 and over: series Bf431 and Bf441.

Percentage of beneficiaries accepting reduced benefits: for men, series Bf425 and Bf435.

Tax rates for employer and employee each: series Bf389–391.

Maximum taxable earnings: series Bf386.

OASI trust fund assets: series Bf451.

The increase in the number of families receiving benefits has been driven partly by increases in the life span of the retirees as well as increasing numbers of people accepting reduced benefits for early retirement. The average age of retired-workers beneficiaries has risen by 5 years for males and 6.4 years for females between 1940 and 1996 (series Bf426 and Bf436). Meanwhile the percentage of beneficiaries aged 80 and over in Table Bf-D has risen from below 2 percent in 1940 to over 18.5 percent for males and 25.9 percent for females in 1996. These averages and percentages understate the true rise in life expectancy because women and men became eligible to draw reduced benefits at age 62 in 1956 and 1961, respectively.[9] The monthly benefits are reduced to allow for the increased length of time that the retired worker accepts the benefits.[10] Despite these administrative reductions in benefits, the percentage of male beneficiaries accepting reduced benefits listed

[9] As of 1997, the reduction in OASI benefits for a person who accepted benefits between age 62 and the retirement age of 65 (rising to 67 next decade) was five ninths of 1 percent for each month of entitlement prior to age 65 up to a maximum of 20 percent.

[10] The SSA reports average monthly benefits for those with full benefits and those with reductions for early acceptance. The ratio of average monthly benefits paid to beneficiaries with reduced benefits to average monthly benefits for those with full benefits has remained stable at around 75 percent for both men and women since 1985 (see Table Bf476–483). The ratio gives the impression that people lose more from early retirement than they actually do. Through 1979, the SSA came up with a calculation of what workers who had reductions for early retirement would have received without the reduction (see Table Bf476–483). The ratios of the average reduced benefits to the average benefits they would have received without reduction were roughly 90 percent over the period. Thus, the differences between average benefits for early retirees and regular retirees is caused by differences in the lifetime labor force participation, age at retirement, and possible income differences at the time of retirement of the two groups.

in Table Bf-D has risen from less than 5 percent to 68 percent in 1996, while the percentage for women has risen from 7.5 percent in 1956 to 74.4 percent in 1996.

Another contributor to the rise in spending on Old-Age, Survivors, and Disability Insurance pensions has been a long-term rise in average monthly benefits. Over the past fifty-five years, the average monthly benefits reported in Table Bf461–475 have risen faster than the average monthly earnings for wage and salary earners covered by Social Security (series Bf381 and Bf384). Figure Bf-E shows the ratio of average monthly family benefits to the monthly earnings of wage earners for several different retirement categories. During the 1940s, benefits rose very slowly in nominal terms, and beneficiaries lost ground relative to inflation and average monthly earnings. In the 1950 Social Security Amendments, Congress adjusted benefits upward to accommodate for much of the lost ground during the 1940s. Through periodic adjustments, Congress kept the ratio of benefits to earnings roughly stable through the 1960s. In 1972, Congress established cost of living adjustment (COLA) clauses that allowed benefits to rise with the rate of inflation. During the 1970s, the ratio of benefit levels to monthly earnings rose sharply by roughly 40 to 60 percent. The rapid growth in the 1970s caused Congress to establish new benefit computation rules in 1977 for workers who became newly eligible or died

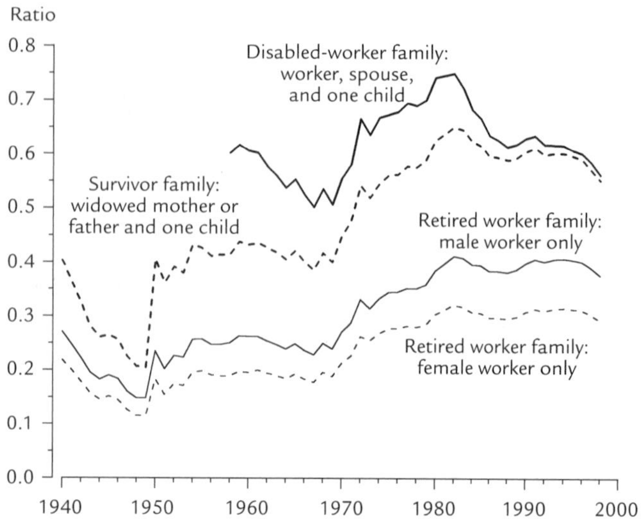

FIGURE Bf-E Old-Age, Survivors, and Disability Insurance – ratio of the family benefit to average earnings of workers in covered employment, by family type: 1940–1998

Sources

Calculated from series Bf381, Bf384, Bf462–463, Bf466, and Bf472.

Documentation

This figure is based on average monthly benefits received by various types of families under the Old-Age, Survivors, and Disability Insurance (OASDI) program. Four family types are displayed: disabled-worker family (worker, spouse, and one child), series Bf472; survivor family (widowed mother or father and one child), series Bf466; retired-worker family (male worker only), series Bf462; and retired-worker family (female worker only), series Bf463. These monthly benefits are displayed here as a ratio of the average monthly earnings for wage and salary earners covered by OASDI, which is computed from series Bf381 and Bf384.

after 1978.[11] Since 1980 male retired workers have received average monthly benefits that are about 40 percent of the average monthly earnings in covered employment (series Bf462). Disabled-worker families have not fared as well (series Bf469–474). In figure Bf-E, the monthly benefits for a disabled worker with a wife and one child started at 60 percent of the average workers' monthly earning when the program was introduced in 1958. They then dropped to around 50 percent by 1969 and then started a sharp climb to 74 percent in the early 1980s. However, by the 1990s disabled-worker benefits had fallen back to around 60 percent. For comparisons of monthly benefits paid to different genders, see Tables Bf-D and Bf476–483.

Medicare

Studies in the early 1960s showed that the majority of elderly who had applied for means-tested public assistance to the elderly had been seeking help to pay their medical bills.[12] Congress responded by amending Title II of the Social Security Act in 1965 to establish Medicare, a health insurance program for the aged. The Medicare program consists of two separate but coordinated programs: Part A, Hospital Insurance; and Part B, Supplementary Medical Insurance. Expenditures on the Medicare program since 1966 account for a substantial part of the increase in social insurance expenditures. Starting at zero in 1965, Medicare expenditures accounted for 22.5 percent of all social insurance expenditures in 1993 and were 2.25 percent as large as GDP (see series Bf215).

The HI program is funded by the HI taxes collected from wage and salary earnings (see series Bf391 and Bf394) and therefore is available to all Social Security recipients without payment of any monthly insurance premiums. The HI program tries to use basic insurance methods to limit overuse of hospital services by requiring that the insured pay deductibles and copayments, which are described in Table Bf535–544. Persons who do not qualify for Social Security benefits but who obtain SMI may purchase HI for a monthly premium, which rose from $33 in 1973 to $311 in 1997 (series Bf539).

The Medicare program also offers voluntary SMI coverage for physicians' visits and other medical services (see the text for Table Bf545–557). After individuals reach the proper age or disability status, they can purchase insurance for a monthly premium, which is deducted from the individual's Social Security check (see series Bf542). The government supplements this premium from

[11] Generally, all the retirement and survivor series follow a similar path relative to monthly earnings (series Bf461–468 compared with average monthly earnings for wage and salary earners covered by Social Security, which is calculated as series Bf384 divided by series Bf381 and then divided by 12). The average monthly benefits are influenced by demographic factors and variations in the lifetime labor force activities of the retirees and the survivors. For detailed descriptions about the formulas used to calculate benefits, see Social Security Administration, *SSBASS* (1997), pp. 39–75. The maximum benefits for men in the year they retire give an indication of the potential earnings. The maximum started at about 50 percent of average monthly earnings, dropped during the 1940s, steadied at about 40 percent in the 1950s and 1960s, jumped above 60 percent in the early 1980s, dipped in the late 1980s, and has stayed around 60 percent in the 1990s (see series Bf475 compared with average monthly earnings for wage and salary workers covered by Social Security).

[12] For more discussion of the introduction of Medicare, see Weaver (1982), pp. 151–8.

general revenues (series Bf543–544). The insured pays a deductible of the first $100 for medical care during the year and then a copayment of 20 percent of the cost of treatment (series Bf540–541). The SMI program aspect of Medicare is partially funded by premiums from purchasers of the insurance, with the remainder largely based on general tax revenues because there is no specific tax designated for this program. The premiums paid by participants (series Bf559) covered over 50 percent of the expenditures on medical coverage under the SMI plan (series Bf564) in the early 1970s. Since 1979, premiums have covered less than 30 percent of the costs of the medical coverage provided.

Because health care costs have risen sharply since 1966 – the consumer price index (CPI) for medical care has risen by an average annual rate of 7.3 percent per year – the Medicare program has raised premiums and deductibles at an even faster average annual rate of 10 percent per year for the HI inpatient hospital deductible (series Bf535) and 13 percent per year for the SMI monthly premium (series Bf542). The Medicare program has tried to control costs further by limiting the amounts that hospitals and physicians can receive in payment for treatments.

Funding the Old-Age, Survivors, Disability, and Hospital Insurance Programs

When the OASI system was originally established in 1935, the original intent of the Roosevelt administration appears to have been to establish a pension fund with accumulated reserves, although the initial tax rate established was below the levels needed to make the fund actuarially sound. Congress and the administration abandoned this goal with the Social Security Amendment of 1939 (Meriam 1946, p. 87; Weaver 1982, pp. 111–24; McSteen 1985, p. 39; Quadagno 1988, pp. 119–21; Berkowitz and McQuaid 1992, pp. 123–5, 130–6; Schieber and Shoven 1999, pp. 49–76). Since 1940, the OASDHI program has been a pay-as-you-go system funded by taxes on earnings for wage and salary workers and the self-employed. Workers and employers each pay a separate and matching tax (the self-employed pay the combined rate for workers and employers) to the federal government to fund the system. The rapid long-term rise in beneficiaries relative to the working population and the increase in average benefits relative to average workers' earnings has led to increases in the tax rates to fund the various programs. As seen in Table Bf-D, with only the OASI program to fund, the OASI tax rate was 1 percent for employers and 1 percent for workers on incomes up to $3,000 in the late 1930s and 1940s. The OASI tax rate has risen to 5.35 percent each in 1999 on incomes up to $72,600. The introduction of DI in 1957 tacked on an additional tax of 0.25 percent, which rose to 0.85 percent in 1997. Finally, the introduction of Medicare led to an additional tax of 0.35 percent, which since quadrupled to 1.45 percent in 1997. As of 1999, the total OASDHI tax rate paid by the worker was 7.65 percent, which was matched by the same 7.65 percent rate paid by the employer (see Table Bf377–394).

Not only has the tax rate risen, but the annual earnings subject to the tax rate have risen faster than the average workers' average annual earnings. Total earnings subject to tax have risen close to 90 percent of the earnings of covered workers (series Bf385 divided by series Bf384), while the percentage of workers reaching the maximum has fallen from 36 percent in 1965 to less than 6 percent in the early 1990s. The rise in earnings subject to Medicare taxes followed the same path until the 1990s and then the Omnibus Budget Reconciliation Act of 1993 repealed the maximum. The OASDHI taxes are in many ways more regressive than the income tax. While the income tax does not apply to the lowest income earners, the OASDHI taxes are drawn on the first dollar of earnings. Further, the maximum limits on earnings subject to tax mean that the earners in the top 5 percent of the income distribution do not pay taxes on income beyond the limits. However, it should be noted that the working poor receive some relief from the OASDHI payroll taxes through the earned income tax credit.

The monies from the OASDHI taxes go into trust funds and are to be paid out of these trust funds. The information on assets, receipts, and expenditures for the OASI trust fund appears in Table Bf442–460. The government still maintains a trust fund. Certainly, discussions of the trust fund have dominated the discussions of Social Security in the political arena of the 1990s. It is a pay-as-you-go system with taxpayers paying the OASDHI taxes into the trust fund each year and benefits being paid out each year without a tight actuarial relationship between the two. In fact, the initial recipients of the Social Security benefits received a relatively large subsidy compared to the amounts that they paid into the system. Each succeeding generation that reached retirement has paid in taxes an increasing share of the pension benefits they received. The programs are sound in the sense that should the benefit claims exceed the monies allocated for benefits in the trust fund, the government is able to redirect resources away from other government expenditures to pay the benefits.

Assets in the OASI trust fund slowly built up from 1937 through 1956 in both real and nominal terms because it took time for the benefits paid each year to rise slowly toward 100 percent of receipts collected. The trust fund stayed relatively stable until the early 1980s when increases in tax rates and the arrival of the baby boom bulge in their prime working years caused assets in the fund in 1992 dollars to rise twelve-fold between 1984 and 1996. The process for funding the Medicare HI program is similar (see Table Bf558–567 for details), although assets in the fund declined drastically in 1982 when Congress allowed the OASI trust fund to borrow nearly half the fund to meet a substantial gap between receipts and expenditures. When the loan was repaid in 1985 and 1986, the assets rose sharply and continued to rise through 1992 as a result of an increase in the HI tax (series Bf391). During the 1990s there has been extensive discussion of possible problems with the Medicare trust fund because benefit expenditures have exceeded payroll tax collections. The shortfall in tax collections has the potential to increase in the future because the ratio of taxpayers to those eligible for Medicare is expected to fall, while the elderly population is living longer and health care costs per person are expected to increase.

The assets of the trust fund are largely "invested" in government securities (see series Bf451–452). The government securities are promises by the federal government to repay the principal of the securities plus the stated interest back into the fund sometime in the future. In essence, the federal government has been borrowing money from the trust fund assets each year to fund current government spending on programs other than Social Security. People have begun to worry because the baby boom generation is expected to begin reaching retirement age during the period 2010 to 2030, and the number of recipients per worker is expected to rise sharply. Given a continuation of the status quo, we can anticipate that the assets in the trust fund eventually will be depleted, as expenditures on benefits exceed OASI tax receipts. Thus, the payment of Social Security benefits will begin to be covered by other tax receipts, leaving less room for funding of other government programs unless there are cuts in OASI benefits or increases in the OASI taxes.[13]

Workers' Compensation

At the turn of the twentieth century, prior to the introduction of state workers' compensation laws, workers could obtain compensation for workplace accidents under the common law if they could show that the employer was negligent. However, such a worker might still be denied compensation if the employer could invoke any of three defenses: The worker had known about and assumed the risk (assumption of risk); the worker's own negligence had contributed to the accident (contributory negligence); or a fellow worker had caused the accident (fellow-servant). A study analyzing several state surveys of families of workers who died in workplace accidents found that between 1900 and 1910 about half of such families received some compensation from the worker's employer, primarily in out-of-court settlements. The average compensation for those families who received a positive amount was about a year's income. When workers' compensation was introduced in the various states in the 1910s, all workers who experienced accidents arising out of or in the course of employment were to receive compensation. The present value of the streams of payments for fatal accidents ranged from roughly two to four times annual income across the states. The average amount of accident compensation received by injured workers and the families of fatalities probably went up between 70 to 200 percent with the introduction of workers' compensation (Fishback and Kantor 2000, Chapters 2 and 3).

During the late 1890s and early 1900s a number of states passed employer liability laws to limit some of the employers' defenses.[14] In the railroad industry, the Federal Employer Liability Act (FELA) of 1908 retained negligence liability but eliminated the fellow-servant defense and weakened the contributory negligence defenses. The assumption-of-risk defense was later eliminated in 1939. Common law rules of negligence without the three defenses continue to govern workplace accident compensation for railroad workers today.[15]

Dissatisfaction with the existing common law system and the results of employer liability laws led employers, workers, and insurance companies to press for the enactment of workers' compensation, which would eliminate the fault basis for compensation. The federal government led the way by establishing a workers' compensation law for federal employees in 1908. As shown in Table Bf-F, between 1911 and 1920 forty-three states enacted workers' compensation laws to require employers to provide compensation for all accidents arising out of and in the course of employment that caused a worker to lose more than a few days of working time. The laws established basic parameters for compensation of injuries. After a waiting period of a few days, workers would receive up to two thirds of their wages during the period of their disability, although the payments were typically capped by a weekly maximum. In turn, employers were required either to purchase insurance from a private or state fund, depending on the state, or to show that they had adequate resources to cover payments to injured workers. Workers' compensation rules vary across states along several dimensions. More detail on the variations in rules through 1929 can be found in Fishback and Kantor (2000), and information for the modern era is available in annual volumes titled *Analysis of Workers' Compensation Laws*, published by the U.S. Chamber of Commerce.

The number of workers covered by workers' compensation rose quickly when the states began adopting a permanent law during that period. When workers' compensation was first introduced, a number of types of employment were exempted, including agricultural workers, domestic servants, many railroad workers in interstate commerce, and, in some states, workers in nonhazardous employments. Further, workers hired by employers with fewer than three to five workers (varying by state) are exempted from the law. By 1940 employees earning wages and salaries accounting for 75 percent of wage and salary disbursements were covered by workers' compensation laws (series Bf283 divided by series Bf273). At the time that Mississippi, the last state to adopt workers' compensation, adopted in 1948, the percentage rose to about 78.1 percent. Since that time, a decline in domestic servitude, railroading, and agricultural employment, as well as expansions of workers' compensation coverage, has led to payroll coverage of about 92 percent.

Since 1929, real expenditures on workers' compensation programs, which continue to be administered by the states, have grown at an average annual rate of 5 percent per year (series Bf223, adjusted for inflation by the GDP deflator). The growth has been caused by expansions in the coverage of injuries and occupational diseases, as well as increases in benefits, even though workplace accident rates have declined since the beginning of the century.[16] Workers' compensation costs as a percentage of covered payroll generally stayed around 1 percent until the late 1960s and early 1970; since then, costs have risen along a strong upward trend to nearly 2.5 percent in 1990 (series Bf520). The rise was driven in part by increased payments for benefits and medical coverage (series Bf521), as well as the introduction of the Black Lung Benefits program for coal miners in 1969.[17] The rise in benefits can

[13] For additional discussions of earlier crises and the potential crisis in financing Social Security and Medicare, see Weaver (1982); Berkowitz and McQuaid (1992); Wolfe (1993); Murphy and Welch (1998); and Schieber and Shoven (1999).

[14] For descriptions of these laws, see Fishback and Kantor (2000), Appendix G.

[15] For a description of the Railroad Compensation system, see Transportation Research Board (1994) and Kim and Fishback (1993).

[16] Although workers' compensation was originally established to insure workers again workplace accidents, the programs in most states were expanded to cover occupation-related diseases. Starting with California in 1915, states began expanding the coverage of workers' compensation laws to include payments to workers' disabled by occupational diseases. By 1939, twenty-three states covered at least some occupational diseases. The states include California (1915), North Dakota (1925), Minnesota (1927), Connecticut (1930), Kentucky (1930), New York (1930), Illinois (1931), Missouri (1931), New Jersey (1931), Ohio (1931), Massachussetts (1932), Nebraska (1935), North Carolina (1935), Wisconsin (1935), West Virginia (1935), Rhode Island (1936), Delaware (1937), Indiana (1937), Michigan (1937), Pennsylvania (1937), Washington (1937), Idaho (1939), and Maryland (1939) (Balkan 1998, p. 64). As of July 1953, every state but Mississippi and Wyoming had at least some coverage for occupation diseases (U.S. Bureau of Labor Statistics 1953, p. 21). By the 1980s, all states had some form of coverage.

[17] The workers' compensation series on costs as a percentage of the covered payroll contains some employer contributions to the Black Lung Benefits program, while the benefits series does not include benefits associated with the Black Lung Benefits program.

TABLE Bf-F The presence of state social welfare programs in the early 1900s

State	Workers' Compensation: year permanently enacted	Mothers' Pensions: year enacted (through 1935)	Old-Age Pensions: year enacted (through 1935)	Aid to the Blind: making cash payments as of August 1, 1935
Alabama	1919	1931	—	No
Alaska	1915	1917	1915	No
Arizona	1913	1917	1933	No
Arkansas	1939	1917	—	Yes
California	1911	1913	1929	Yes
Colorado	1915	1912	1927	Yes
Connecticut	1913	1919	—	Yes
Delaware	1917	1917	1931	No
Florida	1935	1919	—	No
Georgia	1920	—	—	No
Hawai'i	1915	1919	1933	No
Idaho	1917	1913	1931	Yes
Illinois	1911	1911	—	Yes
Indiana	1915	1919	1933	Yes
Iowa	1913	1913	1934	Yes
Kansas	1911	1915	—	Yes
Kentucky	1916	1928	1926	Yes
Louisiana	1914	1920	—	Yes
Maine	1915	1917	1933	Yes
Maryland	1912	1916	1927	Yes
Massachusetts	1911	1913	1930	No
Michigan	1912	1913	1933	No
Minnesota	1913	1913	1929	Yes
Mississippi	1948	1928	—	No
Missouri	1926	1917	—	Yes
Montana	1915	1915	1923	No
Nebraska	1913	1913	1933	Yes
Nevada	1913	1913	1925	Yes
New Hampshire	1911	1913	1931	Yes
New Jersey	1911	1913	1931	Yes
New Mexico	1917	1931	—	No
New York	1913	1915	1930	Yes
North Carolina	1929	1923	—	No
North Dakota	1919	1915	1933	No
Ohio	1911	1913	1933	Yes
Oklahoma	1915	1915	—	Yes
Oregon	1913	1913	1933	Yes
Pennsylvania	1915	1913	1934	Yes
Rhode Island	1912	1923	—	No
South Carolina	1935	—	—	No
South Dakota	1917	1913	—	No
Tennessee	1919	1915	—	No
Texas	1913	1917	—	No
Utah	1917	1913	1929	Yes
Vermont	1915	1917	—	No
Virginia	1918	1918	—	No
Washington	1911	1913	1933	Yes
West Virginia	1913	1915	1931	No
Wisconsin	1911	1913	1925	Yes
Wyoming	1915	1915	1929	Yes

Sources

Workers' compensation laws: Fishback and Kantor (2000), pp. 103–4.

Mothers' Pension laws: for laws enacted prior to 1920, see Thompson (1919), pp. 7–11; and for laws enacted after 1920, see Skocpol (1992), p. 457. See also Moehling (2002).

Old-Age Pensions: Stevens (1970), pp. 20–4; and U.S. Committee on Economic Security (1937), pp. 160–71.

Aid to the Blind: "Public Provision for Pensions for the Blind in 1934," *Monthly Labor Review* 41 (3) (September 1935): 584–601; reprinted in Stevens (1970), pp. 29–31.

Documentation

Workers' compensation laws. The year listed is the date at which a permanent law was enacted. New York passed a compulsory law in 1910 and an elective law in 1910, but the compulsory law was declared unconstitutional, and the elective law saw little use. New York passed a compulsory law in 1913 after passing a constitutional amendment. Kentucky originally enacted a law in 1914, but that law was declared unconstitutional. The permanent law for Kentucky was enacted in 1916. The Missouri General Assembly passed a workers' compensation law in 1919, but it failed to receive enough votes in a referendum in 1920. Another law passed in 1921 was defeated in a referendum in 1922 and an initiative on the ballot was again defeated in 1924. Missouri voters finally approved a workers' compensation law in a 1926 referendum on a 1925 legislative act (see Kantor and Fishback 1994). Maryland (1902) and Montana (1909) passed earlier laws specific to miners that were declared unconstitutional.

Mothers' Pension laws. State provisions in Missouri (1911), California (pre-1913), Wisconsin (1912), Michigan (1911), and Oklahoma (1908) endowed funds similar to Mothers' Pensions in indirect ways. Some of the provisions were limited to specific cities, and others were indirect means of providing funds to dependent children. Arizona in a 1914 referendum passed a Mothers' Pension and Old-Age Pension system that hinged on the abolishment of the almshouses in the state, but it was found unconstitutional

(continued)

TABLE Bf-F The presence of state social welfare programs in the early 1900s *Continued*

(Thompson 1919, pp. 7–9). The 1917 Arizona law was also considered "unworkable," and a new law was enacted in 1921 (Lundberg 1921). More detail on the specifics of Mothers' Pension laws as of 1934 are available in Stevens (1970), pp. 28–9, and U.S. Committee on Economic Security (1937), pp. 233–49. There is some disagreement about whether Alabama had adopted a Mothers' Pension law in 1931; members of the Children's Bureau and later the U.S. Social Security Administration considered the law to be more in the nature of a poor-relief statute than the provision of long-term care for children (Abbott 1934; Bucklin 1939).

Old-Age Pensions. Arizona set up an Old-Age Pension subject to the elimination of almshouses in a referendum in 1915, but the pension was declared unconstitutional. Pennsylvania passed an Old-Age Pension law in 1923, but it was declared unconstitutional in 1924. Nevada also passed an act in 1923 that was replaced by the 1925 act listed in this table.

be explained in part by a series of amendments to state laws in the 1970s that sharply increased the weekly maximums that could be paid for benefits.

During the 1980s and early 1990s, rising medical expenditures have been a prime contributor to rising costs. Expenditures on medical and hospital benefits have risen to 40 percent of workers' compensation expenditures since 1980 after accounting for less than one third of worker's compensation expenditures for the rest of the century (see series Bf224 as a percentage of series Bf223; see also series Bf513 as a percentage of series Bf512). In the early 1990s, employers and insurers have begun managing their health care costs more closely and have limited the growth of medical costs. Similarly, disability benefits as a percentage of covered payroll have risen over time as reforms of workers' compensation expanded the range of workplace injuries and diseases covered (series Bf515 as a percentage of series Bf283). In contrast, the percentage of the payrolls spent on paying the survivors of fatal accidents has stayed relatively constant at below 0.1 percent from the 1940s through 1970 and again from the 1980s to the present. There is one blip in the survivors of fatally injured series that needs some explanation (series Bf516). The percentage of covered payroll paid out to survivors of the fatally injured rose sharply between 1970 and 1973 because the federal Black Lung Benefits program was put into effect. The impact of the Black Lung Benefits program was so dramatic because of the accumulation of a number of years of survivors all being added to the system in the span of three years. As soon as the Black Lung Benefits program stabilized, the survivors' benefits reached a steady state of about 0.1 percent of the payroll and have declined in the 1990s.

The general rise in workers' compensation benefits as a share of the payroll should not necessarily be considered a sign that workplaces have become more dangerous. Workers' compensation has increasingly provided benefits for a wide range of injuries and diseases for which compensation would not have been awarded earlier in the century. The series on the occupational injury and illness rate for all occupations shows that the number of cases of injury and illness per 100 workers in the private sectors has fallen by 32 percent since 1972, while the number of lost workday cases has stayed roughly constant (series Ba4750–4751).

Although the states establish the basic rules for compensation, employers can obtain insurance to cover their compensation responsibilities from private insurance carriers in the majority of states and from government-sponsored insurance funds in roughly half of the states, or employers can self-insure as long as they demonstrate sufficient resources to handle their benefit obligations. Between the end of World War II and 1970, the distribution of benefits paid by these various insurers stayed relatively constant. The percentage of benefits paid by private insurers was roughly 62 percent, by state and federal funds roughly 25 percent, and by self-insurers about 12 to 15 percent (series Bf517–519, each as a percentage of series Bf512). The introduction of the Black Lung Benefits program in 1970 led to a sharp rise in the state and federal insurance funds, as a large number of workers not previously covered received federal coverage for black lung disease. Since 1973, the trend has been to return more of the insurance activity to private insurers, and many employers have increasingly self-insured.

Black lung (pneumoconiosis), which struck large numbers of long-time coal miners, is one of the most notorious occupational diseases. The Federal Coal Mine Health and Safety Act of 1969 established a Black Lung Benefits program to provide monthly benefit payments to coal miners who are totally disabled and to the widows and dependents of coal miners who died as a result of pneumoconiosis. Table Bf525–534 shows the number of persons receiving black-lung benefits under the two administrative systems.[18] The SSA is responsible for the payment and administration of benefits with respect to claims filed through June 30, 1973 (and for certain survivor cases before December 31, 1973). The Black Lung Benefits Act of 1972 transferred to the Department of Labor jurisdiction over all claims after July 1, 1973. The number of recipients of black-lung benefits peaked around 1980 at over 500,000 people. The annual number of beneficiaries has halved since, in part as a result of declines in the number of underground coal miners. Another contributor to the decline has been the deadliness of the disease, which has caused the number of miners and their dependents who receive benefits to fall sharply; meanwhile, the number of widows receiving benefits has fallen at a much slower pace.

Unemployment Insurance

Although a few firms had experimented with unemployment insurance between 1894 and the 1930s, public provision of modern unemployment insurance was not established at any level of government prior to the 1930s (Lescohier 1966, pp. 259–69). A number of state legislatures considered the adoption of unemployment insurance during the late 1910s and 1920s, but only Wisconsin adopted a law in 1932 and began to administer it (Brandeis 1966, pp. 616–24; Berkowitz and McQuaid 1992, pp. 109–15). The Wisconsin system had not yet begun paying benefits when the Social Security Act of 1935 established UI as a federally mandated program run by the states. The states collect payroll taxes from employers to fund the system. Wisconsin,

[18] The miners receive benefits that are 37.5 percent of the monthly pay rate for federal employees in the first step of grade GS-2, adjusted for the number of dependents. If a miner or surviving spouse is receiving workers' compensation, unemployment compensation, or disability insurance payments under state law, the black-lung benefit is offset by the amount being paid under these other programs. The program is funded by a tax paid by employers per ton of coal mined.

based on its early start, was ready to pay benefits as early as 1936, while the remaining states first had to pass enabling legislation and then accumulate reserves for two years before the programs could begin paying out funds to unemployed workers. By 1938, roughly 75 percent of payrolls were covered by unemployment insurance (series Bf280 divided by series Bf273). The percentage rose to a peak of 98 percent in 1979 and fell back to about 92.4 percent in 1994. Covered employment includes employment in industrial and commercial establishments of eight or more for the period 1941–1955 and four or more for 1956–1970.[19]

To fund the system, employers pay taxes on employee earnings up to a specific maximum per employee in each state. Part of the taxes (0.4 percent of taxable wages in 1970) is remitted to the federal government, which in turn provides grants to the states for the cost of administering unemployment insurance and employment services. The payroll contribution rates for individual employers vary to some extent in response to the unemployment experience of workers in the employer's operation.

Unemployed workers begin receiving benefits in most states after a waiting period of one week is served. In the late 1930s the benefits typically replaced 50 percent of weekly earnings up to a weekly maximum benefit level. The weekly maximum has often served to reduce the percentage of average weekly wages paid to roughly 33 to 41 percent between 1940 and 1970, with a rate in 1995 around 35.5 percent (series Bf489). Since 1940, average weekly benefits in 1992 dollars have risen at a relatively slow average annual rate of less than 1 percent per year from $103.3 in 1940 to $173.9 in 1996 (series Bf488 deflated by GDP deflator). The states establish a maximum number of weeks that unemployed workers can receive payments. These durations ranged from 12 to 22.6 weeks in the late 1930s, depending on the state. The maximums have risen such that by 1970 workers could receive benefits for up to 20 to 36 weeks depending on the state. The average actual duration varies with the business cycle from as low as 7.7 weeks during the extraordinarily tight labor markets during World War II to over 14 weeks in 1958 and 1961, and again in 1995 (series Bf490).

As the labor force has expanded, average weekly benefits have risen, as has the maximum duration of benefits. Total benefits paid in 1992 dollars rose from $2 billion in 1941 to more than $20 billion in the 1990s (series Bf493 deflated by the GDP deflator). As a result, expenditures on unemployment insurance and employment service programs rose along a trend to where they comprised 6.2 percent of social insurance expenditures in 1993 (series Bf218). Of course, unemployment claims are cyclical, with total benefits paid peaking during recessions and declining during economic booms. The unemployed receiving insurance as a percentage of the covered employment payroll was as low as 2.0 percent in 1969 and as high as 6 percent in 1975 and 6.6 percent in 1958 (series Bf485 as a percentage of series Bf484).

Public Assistance Programs

The second leading contributor to the rise in public social welfare spending is public assistance programs. As of 1996, the governments of the United States provided benefits to low-income households through a large number of programs: Aid to Families with Dependent Children (AFDC, which has since been replaced by Temporary Assistance to Needy Families), Medicaid, the Women, Infants and Children (WIC) programs, Food Stamps, General Assistance, work relief programs, Old-Age Assistance, Aid to the Blind, and Aid to the Permanently and Totally Disabled. In most cases, these programs are means-tested or provide funds to those with disability. Again, it should be noted that the division of social welfare programs into the specific categories of social insurance and public assistance is somewhat arbitrary and based on the statutory programs and the administrative structure of the programs. Users of the statistics might want to regroup programs into alternative categories.

Over the past seventy years, public aid expenditures, as defined by the SSA, rose from 0.1 percent as large as GDP in 1929 to more than 3 percent as large as GDP in the early 1990s (series Bf190). Prior to the 1930s, public assistance was exclusively the responsibility of state and local governments. There was enormous variation across counties and states in the provision of such services.

In the first few decades of the twentieth century, a number of state governments began to legislate forms of public aid that foreshadowed the aid programs for dependent children, the blind, and the elderly established by the Social Security Act of 1935. During the 1910s, a large number of states enacted mothers' pension laws, which provided for public assistance for dependent children in their own homes. The eligibility for such aid varied from state to state, but aid was most often provided for women with preteen children where the support of the husband was absent.[20] Table Bf-F gives an indication of the timing of the enactment of the mothers' pension laws. The U.S. Department of Labor reported that in forty states with mothers' aid laws about 121,000 children were receiving aid at any given time in 1921 and 1922 (U.S. Department of Labor 1932, p. 99). By June 1931, approximately 250,000 children were receiving $35 million in aid in forty-four states and the District of Columbia. Still, the total public assistance expenditures were relatively small, as the SSA estimates that public aid expenditures were roughly 0.1 percent as large as GDP in 1929.[21]

The states were slower to introduce old-age pensions, which provided public funds to low-income elderly living outside of public almshouses and charity institutions. The dates of enactment of the various laws appear in Table Bf-F. The Alaskan territory led the way in 1915. Arizona citizens passed a referendum to establish old-age pensions, but the program was declared unconstitutional in 1916. At the end of 1928, Alaska, Colorado, Kentucky, Maryland, Montana, Nevada, and Wisconsin had laws that gave each county in the state the option to provide pensions. Yet only Montana and Wisconsin appeared to have established operative systems that were paying pensions totaling $222,599 to 1,221 persons. From 1929 forward, the trend in legislation was to make the old-age assistance systems mandatory for counties. By 1932, eighteen

[19] In some of the states, the covered employment also represents employment in smaller establishments and for additional groups of workers, such as state and local employees or seamen. Although the federal law requires only employers to pay taxes, some states require some workers to contribute as well.

[20] Details on the various eligibility rules as of 1919 can be found in Thompson (1919, pp. 11–19). For a snapshot as of 1934, see Stevens (1970), pp. 28–9.

[21] For descriptions of the mothers' pensions laws as of 1934, see Stevens (1970), pp. 28–9, reprinting materials from pp. 301–10 of U.S. Committee on Economic Security, 1937. For a general discussion of the development of mothers' pensions and their impact, see the work of Theda Skocpol (1992) and Carolyn Moehling (2002).

states were paying out pensions totaling $22.5 million to 102,537 persons.[22]

The final group that received cash assistance payments through state programs was the blind. Many states were generally involved in providing some form of educational and vocational training for blind children, workshops for the adult blind, and field work in providing medical assistance and aid in procuring employment. By August 1935, twenty-seven states were providing cash payments to the blind. Estimates by the U.S. Department of Labor showed that in 1934 approximately two thirds of the blind population was receiving some form of cash grants. The average value of monthly grants across the twenty-seven states was nearly $20, but the averages ranged from a low of $0.83 in Arkansas to a high of $33.12 in California.[23]

During the Great Depression, state and local governments increased their expenditures fivefold between 1929 and 1932 in response to the dramatic rise in unemployment. When the unemployment rate reached nearly 25 percent of the labor force in 1933, state and local governments and private charitable organizations claimed to be overwhelmed. During the first hundred days of the Roosevelt administration, a series of New Deal Emergency Assistance programs were established (see Table Bf663–678).[24] The initial program was the Federal Emergency Relief Administration (FERA) which spent nearly $200 million between 1933 and 1935 for direct relief to families and work relief for able-bodied workers (about $2 billion in 1992 dollars). In an attempt to increase federal employment through work relief in the short run, the Civil Works Administration (CWA) spent more than $700 million between November 1933 and March 1934. Meanwhile, the Civilian Conservation Corps spent more than $230 million per year for the rest of the decade as they worked to conserve forests, farmland, and other natural sites while providing work and educational opportunities for young men. Possibly the most famous of the New Deal programs was the Works Progress Administration (WPA), later renamed the Works Projects Administration, which provided work relief for unemployed "employables." The WPA spent between $1 billion and $2 billion per year from 1936 through 1940 building schools, roads, post offices, sidewalks, and a host of other projects. The National Youth Administration and the Farm Security Administration were smaller programs that, respectively, employed students and provided aid to farmers in obtaining their own farms. In sum, well over thirty New Deal programs provided aid of some sort during the 1930s. The sudden influx of federal monies caused public aid expenditures to rise as high as 4.6 percent as large as GDP between 1934 through 1940, a percentage that has not been reached again during the long-term rise in public aid expenditures over the past 60 years (series Bf190).

Activities at the state and local level did not cease in 1933 when the federal government began providing relief through New Deal programs. As can be seen in Table Bf621–633, public assistance provided by state and local governments to the aged, dependent children, and the blind and general assistance rose from $837 million in 1933 to $1,665 million in 1935 (more than 85 percent of the expenditures were for general assistance). The number of cases receiving general assistance was 3.2 million in 1933, 5.4 million in 1934, and 2.9 million in 1935. When the WPA replaced the FERA, the federal government disclaimed responsibility for what it defined as unemployables, low-income people who were not considered capable of working. State and local expenditures on direct relief to the unemployables are included under the heading "general assistance" in the public assistance tables (series Bf625 and Bf638). To help fill the void for some groups and building on the precedents established by earlier state legislation, the Social Security Act of 1935 established three joint state and federal programs for Old-Age Assistance, Aid to the Blind, and Aid to Dependent Children (ADC). In October 1950, Congress amended the Social Security Act to provide aid to the totally and permanently disabled. The Old-Age Assistance, Aid to the Blind, ADC, and Aid to the Disabled programs under the Social Security Act are designed to be joint programs with the federal government providing grants to the states and the states providing additional funds and administering the programs.

A number of the programs have gone through administrative changes. Through legislation enacted in 1972 and effective in 1974, the Supplemental Security Income (SSI) program superseded the Aid to the Blind, Old-Age Assistance, and Aid to the Disabled programs, except in the U.S. territories of Guam, Puerto Rico, and the Virgin Islands.[25] The program for ADC began paying benefits to support payments for a mother or other relative caring for the child in 1950. Under the Public Welfare Amendments of 1962, the program was renamed Aid to Families with Dependent Children to reflect expanded coverage of the adults caring for the dependent children. The AFDC and the Emergency Assistance (EA) programs (series Bf637 and Bf639) have been replaced by the Temporary Assistance for Needy Families (TANF) program under the Personal Responsibility and Work Opportunity Reconciliation Act of 1996. The act was designed to limit the length of time that families could receive assistance and to promote a return to the workforce by those who are able.

The two public aid programs with the fastest growth have been the programs aiding children and the disabled. The number of recipients in the ADC program grew at an average annual rate of 7 percent per year between the end of World War II and the change to AFDC in 1962. The number of recipients then exploded at an average annual rate of 12 percent per year from 1962 through 1971 to reach nearly 10 million. The average monthly number of recipients leveled off at around 11 million before jumping sharply again from 1989 through 1994 to more than 14 million (series Bf630 and Bf644).[26] Annual payments show a generally similar

---

[22] See Brandeis (1966), pp. 613–6; Stevens (1970), pp. 20–24, based on U.S. Committee on Economic Security (1937), pp. 156–70; Quadagno (1988), pp. 51–75; and Costa (1998), pp. 166–7.

[23] U.S. Department of Labor (1935), pp. 584–601. See also Stevens (1970), pp. 29–31.

[24] The Hoover administration in 1932 established the Reconstruction Finance Corporation, which made some loans to state and local governments to help finance relief expenditures in addition to its loans to banks and industries. The loans do not appear in the tables on emergency relief spending because they were expected to be repaid and, thus, were not considered a net cost to the federal government. The impact of the loans will appear in the estimates of assistance provided by state and local governments.

[25] For more information on the extent of state supplementation under SSI, see Table Bf591–598.

[26] To develop a long-term time series for average monthly benefits, number of recipients, and total spending over the period 1936 to 1973 for AFDC (formerly ADC), General Assistance, Old-Age Assistance, Aid to the Blind, and Aid to the Permanently and Totally Disabled, users will be forced to splice together two sets of series reported by the SSA in Tables Bf621–662 The U.S. Social

pattern, although it is somewhat amplified by changes in monthly benefits per recipient, which were around $83 (1992 dollars) in the late 1930s (series Bf624 and Bf637). The average benefits rose above $150 (1992 dollars) through the transition to AFDC and into the 1970s. They stayed in the same range during the 1980s but fell off to around $124 prior to the transition to TANF. This decline in the average benefits per recipient may reflect a decline in the average number of children in the families receiving benefits. Just as the average number of children in families in the overall population has fallen, so it appears has the average number of children in families receiving AFDC. The share of the recipients who are children rose slowly from around 73 percent in 1936 to a peak of around 77 percent circa 1960, just before the transition to AFDC. Since then, the share experienced a secular decline to around 65 to 66 percent in the 1990s (series Bf645 as a share of series Bf644 and series Bf631 as a share of series Bf630).

The SSA began offering federal aid to the permanently and totally disabled in October 1950. The program grew from aiding 69,000 recipients in its first year to 1.2 million recipients in 1973 (series Bf628 and Bf642). Since the SSI program was established in 1974, the number of recipients has more than tripled from 1.6 million in 1974 to more than 5 million in 1995, as the coverage of disabilities has expanded (series Bf614 and Bf642). In contrast, the number of recipients of Aid to the Blind rose from 45,000 in 1936 to a peak more than 100,000 in the early 1960s, fell to 78,000 in 1973, and then rose again to an average annual number of about 84,000 in the 1990s (series Bf613, Bf627, and Bf641). The development of the Social Security old-age pensions and Medicare for retired workers and survivors has reduced the number of Old-Age Assistance recipients since 1950 and kept benefits low (series Bf609, Bf626, and Bf640). The number of Old-Age Assistance recipients rose from 1.1 million in 1936 to 2.7 million in 1950, but it fell back to 1.5 million in 1995.[27] Meanwhile, average monthly benefits in 1992 dollars rose to about $250 in the late 1950s and have generally fallen below that level since 1970.[28]

Average monthly benefits in the Aid to the Blind program (series Bf619, Bf650, and Bf657) and permanently disabled programs (series Bf620, Bf651, and Bf658) have risen somewhat faster than inflation since their beginnings. Average monthly benefits in 1992 dollars in the Aid to the Blind program rose from $250 per month per recipient in 1936 to more than $350 under the SSI program in 1995. Meanwhile, Aid to the Permanently Disabled rose from less than $250 in 1950 to more than $350 in the 1990s (in 1992 dollars). Recipients in both programs experienced spikes in 1974 with the transition to SSI and again in 1978. It should be noted that the average benefits in all three programs are well under the statutory maximums. The difference is determined by the extent of disability and the resources available to the person and his or her family.[29]

The General Assistance programs are state-run programs. The expansion of the federal programs for increasing numbers of categories has appeared to reduce the pressure on the states for general assistance. After the huge numbers receiving relief during the 1930s, the number of recipients of general assistance has generally never been higher than 1.4 million in any year (series Bf632 and Bf646). However, the General Assistance program experienced a rapid growth rate of 6.3 percent per year during the initial stages of the War on Poverty in 1964 to 1970. Average monthly benefits per recipient of General Assistance in 1992 dollars have generally been lower than those of Aid to the Blind and Aid to the Disabled, peaking around $250 in 1977 and falling back to $210 in 1982 (series Bf654 or series Bf661 deflated by GDP deflator). Since that time, information on spending in monthly benefits has not been available.

When the federal government established Medicare in 1965 to provide medical insurance for retired workers, it also developed Medicaid to build on and then take over earlier programs for paying vendors for the provision of medical care to persons with low incomes. Medicaid established a federal–state matching entitlement program that provides medical assistance for certain individuals and families with low incomes and resources. The program is a jointly funded, cooperative venture between the federal and state governments. Each state establishes its own eligibility standards, range of services, rates of payment, and administration.

The federal government first became involved in helping to fund payments to vendors of medical care in October 1950 through a Title I amendment to the Social Security Act. The expenditures were made under the programs for assistance to the elderly, blind, disabled, and families with dependent children, which typically involved federal, state, and local activities. The federal government

---

and Rehabilitation Service reported information on AFDC to the SSA through 1975. However, beginning in the *Social Security Bulletin, Annual Statistical Supplement, 1976* (p. 200), data on the public assistance programs were reported from a different source, and the new series reported were considered not comparable. In later years, the SSA has reported a consistent series for 1960 to the present and for the years 1960, 1955, 1950, 1945, 1940, and 1936. Both sources are reported here to allow users to develop their own means of interpolating the annual information for the years prior to 1960. Correlations of the monthly benefit figures between the two sets of series are very high. In Table Bf649–662, the correlations between the two versions of the series for the overlapping years of 1936, 1940, 1945, 1950, 1955, and 1960–1973 are 0.998 for average monthly benefits for Old-Age Assistance, 0.999 for Aid to the Blind, 0.998 for Aid to the Permanently and Totally Disabled, 0.977 for AFDC per family, 0.998 for AFDC per recipient, and 0.999 for General Assistance.

[27] Annual information on the number of recipients, amount of payments, and monthly benefits for Old-Age Assistance, Aid to the Blind, and Aid to the Disabled is provided in Tables Bf599–662. In addition to the problems described in the text, a consistent series for the entire period 1936 to 1996 requires that information on the SSI versions of the programs in Table Bf599–620 for the years after 1974 be combined with the information for the territories of Guam, the Virgin Islands, and Puerto Rico, which have remained under the old programs in Table Bf634–648. This fact helps to explain the precipitous drops in each of these series in Tables Bf634–662.

[28] The monthly benefits comparisons for Old-Age Assistance, Aid to the Blind, and Aid to the Permanently and Totally Disabled splice together three series. The three programs were superseded by SSI in 1974 in all states and the District of Columbia, so the series shows the average benefits paid under SSI to this group (the benefits are artificially high in comparison with the earlier years because the low benefits for recipients in Guam, Puerto Rico, and the Virgin Islands are not included). So for the Old-Age Assistance program, we have used series Bf618 from 1974 to 1996, series Bf649 for the period 1936–1959, and series Bf656 for the period 1960–1973.

[29] The average monthly benefits listed in series Bf603 are lower than the maximum benefits available because the benefits are adjusted downward as households have access to increasing resources. The monthly SSI benefit rate for persons who are eligible for the maximum rose from $140 for an individual ($195 for a couple) in 1974 to $484 for an individual ($726 for a couple) in 1997. The SSI also provides an additional increment for an "essential person" in the household rising from $70 in 1974 to $242 in 1997. See Social Security Administration, *SSBASS* (1997), p. 92, for listing of legislative history of maximum benefits.

was not involved in medical assistance under the General Assistance programs, which were financed entirely from state and local funds. Medical assistance for the aged under Title I of the Social Security Act was initiated in October 1960 under the 1960 Social Security amendments (series Bf585). The earlier programs for medical care vendor payments (except for General Assistance) were rolled into the Medicare program in 1970.

From the time the federal government became involved in helping to fund payments to medical vendors in 1951 until Medicaid was legislated in 1965, the medical vendor payments skyrocketed at an average annual growth rate of 18.9 percent per year from $527 million in 1951 to $7.8 billion in 1966 (series Bf582 adjusted by the GDP deflator to express the amounts in 1992 dollars). State and local governments were likely to have already been providing some payments to medical care vendors prior to 1951 because the $47 million dollars in General Assistance spending in 1951 was not financed by any federal spending (series Bf590).

Since 1972, the number of Medicaid recipients has grown at roughly 3 percent per year, while vendor payments in 1992 dollars have risen by 7.6 percent per year. Average payments per recipient in 1992 dollars have risen 4.6 percent per year from $1,070 in 1972 to $3,057 in 1996 (series Bf568 and Bf575, with adjustments by the GDP deflator).

In the late 1960s, Congress established a series of additional programs for persons with low incomes. In 1969, Congress established an Emergency Assistance program, which has been rolled into the TANF program and has been aiding more than 50,000 families per month. The Food Stamp program, which began in the early 1960s, was designed to provide low-income households with a means for obtaining an adequate diet by providing them with coupons redeemable for food and for garden seeds and plants. The percentage of the population participating in the Food Stamp program rose sharply in the 1970s to more than 9 percent, dipped during the late 1980s, and was above 10 percent in the mid-1990s (series Aa110 and Bf689). Meanwhile the average monthly value of bonus coupons in 1992 dollars fell sharply during the 1960s to a trough of less than $23 and rose to nearly $70 in the mid-1990s (series Bf691 deflated by GDP deflator).

Another form of public aid, included in series Bf231, has been the development of work-experience training programs. The Manpower Development and Training Act of 1962 and the Equal Opportunity Act of 1964 "spawned a myriad of categorical programs in almost frantic succession" (Franklin and Ripley 1984, p. 6). In 1973, Congress passed the Comprehensive Employment and Training Act (CETA) in a political compromise that replaced the profusion of earlier programs. Whereas the earlier programs tended to be federally run, CETA provided block grants for more decentralized programs. CETA was replaced in 1983 by the Job Training Partnership Act, which furthered the process of decentralization.

Legislation in 1981 established the Low-Income Home Energy Assistance (LIHEAP) program. Block grants administered by Health and Human Services (HHS) are provided to the states to assist low-income households in meeting home energy expenses (Table Bf708–716). Since 1982, between 5 and 9 percent of American households annually receive such assistance. Average LIHEAP assistance expenditures per household in most programs have been in the $60 to $300 range (1992 dollars). The largest annual average expenditures are in the weatherization program, which typically involves capital expenditures, starting at around $400 in 1982 and rising to more than $1,600 in the mid-1990s (1992 dollars).

Health and Medical Programs

The most controversial area of social welfare spending over the past two decades has been public programs for health and medical care. The SSA offers two sets of series on public expenditures on health and medical programs. The first set includes direct spending on public hospitals, military health care, public medical research, school health programs, and medical facilities (series Bf191 and Bf232–240). Expenditures on medical care through veterans' programs, social insurance programs such as Medicare, and public assistance programs such as Medicaid are not included in these series but are listed under the series on public expenditures on health and medical care under other programs (series Bf241). The reason for the exclusion is that these types of expenditures are already included under other parts of the public social welfare expenditures tables.

Those users who seek to combine all health and medical expenditures into one category, no matter how the funds were administered, will find the series on all public expenditures on health and medical care programs useful. Series Bf242 combines expenditures for health and medical care programs with all of the other spending on health and medicine for workers' compensation, public aid, veterans' programs, and Medicare. These totals for all public expenditures are then separated into the categories of health and medical services, research, and facilities construction.

Direct public expenditures on health and medical care programs outside of expenditures under Medicare, Medicaid, and veterans' programs have grown from about 0.3 percent as large as GDP in 1929 to about 1 percent as large as GDP since the 1970s (series Bf191). In general, the federal share of these direct health and medical expenditures has risen from roughly 12 percent in the 1930s to more than 40 percent in the 1990s (see series Bf199 and Bf207). The federal share sharply spiked to 77 percent when federal spending on military health care caused public health care expenditures to exceed 1 percent of GDP in 1943 to 1945.

Although the data in the tables begin in 1929, there was a history of public spending on health and medical care in earlier years. As just one example of a combined federal and state program, consider the spending by the U.S. Children's Bureau authorized by the Shephard–Towner Maternity and Infancy Act of 1921. The Act appropriated about $7 million in federal money for grants in aid to states for the promotion of maternal and infant health and welfare and was distributed between 1922 and 1929. According to the Children's Bureau, this legislation led to expansion of the Birth Registration and Death Registration Areas, establishment of state child-hygiene bureaus and divisions, establishment of permanent state health centers for mothers and children, and, perhaps most important, an accompanying increase in state appropriations for infant and maternal health (U.S. Children's Bureau 1930, pp. 1–3; see also Berkowitz and McQuaid 1992, pp. 73–7). In the SSA listings, the Shephard–Towner spending would appear under series Bf236. The lack of values in the early 1930s in this SSA series may reflect an inability to effectively determine state and local spending on this issue.

Expenditures on health and medical care under other administrative structures include medical expenditures under workers' compensation, under Medicare, and under Medicaid and other public assistance payments to vendors (series Bf241). The expenditures fluctuated between $1 billion and $2 billion (1992 dollars) until the introduction of Medicare in 1966. Rising health care costs have contributed to an explosion in these expenditures since that time, as they grew to more than $10 billion by 1979 and doubled to more than $20 billion by 1989 (1992 dollars).

During the post–World War II era, the United States has probably been the world leader in medical research, partially as a result of public financing. Public expenditures on medical research were under $30 million until 1947 when in one year they jumped to 149.7 million (series Bf237, converted to 1992 dollars). They first reached $1 billion in 1957 and then experienced another rapid rise to more than $5 billion by 1966. They held steady between $5.5 billion and $6 billion into the mid-1970s and have risen steadily since to more than $13 billion today. On the other hand, public spending on medical facilities construction peaked between $3 billion and $4 billion in the late 1970s and has tailed off since (series Bf240, converted to 1992 dollars).

Education Programs

Public expenditures on education have also outstripped GDP since 1929, growing in real terms at an average annual rate of about 4.5 percent per year. As Claudia Goldin notes in the essay on education in Chapter Bc, one of the keys to growth in the American standard of living has been our educational system. Since World War II, educational expenditures have risen from 1.7 percent as large as GDP in 1947 to roughly 5 percent as large as GDP in 1993. The fastest growth in educational expenditures, as defined by the OECD, occurred in the 1960s and 1970s, when average annual rates of growth in real expenditures neared 8 percent per year. Over the course of the twentieth century, the mix of spending has gone through several changes. As a larger share of the population in each new generation has extended their schooling beyond high school, the shares of public spending on higher education have increased from less than 10 percent to just over 20 percent of public educational spending (series Bf258). Following a sharp rise immediately after World War II, the higher education share peaked in 1984 at around 24 percent and has since declined to just above 20 percent as renewed emphasis was placed on elementary and secondary education. Public spending on vocational and adult education received a boost during the New Deal and then expanded rapidly to a peak of 7 percent of educational spending during World War II (series Bf260). Interest in vocational and adult education was renewed in the 1960s, but spending was virtually eliminated in the mid-1980s. One caveat about the vocational and adult education series: they do not include job training programs such as CETA.

Veterans' Programs

The U.S. government has always provided social insurance, hospitals, and medical care for its veterans (see Clark, Craig, and Wilson 2000). As discussed earlier, pensions for Civil War veterans set precedents for establishing old-age pensions for the general public. Public spending for veterans since 1929 typically has been less than 1 percent of GDP except during periods immediately following major wars (series Bf192). The most unusual increase in the series came when Congress voted to pay a "veterans' bonus" of $2 billion dollars ($20 billion 1992 dollars) in 1936 over Franklin Roosevelt's veto. The bonus provided for the immediate payment to veterans of World War I of their adjusted compensation certificates, which were supposed to come due in 1945. The bonus caused a one-time jump in the veterans' "welfare and other" series and caused the overall veterans' series to rise to 4.6 percent as large as GDP in 1936 (series Bf192 and Bf254).

Between 1929 and the end of World War II, except for 1936, two thirds of the veterans' spending was for pensions (series Bf247). The disability pension program, which is described in more detail in Table Bf762–772, accounts for roughly 50 to 60 percent of veterans' spending, except for the immediate aftermath of World War II.[30] Immediately following World War II, the GI bill, designed to provide educational opportunities for returning veterans, caused veterans' educational spending to rise to around 40 percent of veterans' spending for 1947–1950 (series Bf252). The educational spending tailed off to less than 10 percent by 1960 and remained below 10 percent until the early 1970s, when the aftermath of the Vietnam War led to more educational programs for returning veterans. As in other areas, health and medical spending for veterans has become increasingly important. Health and medical spending accounted for less than 10 percent of veterans' spending prior to World War II. Since World War II, health and medical spending has consistently outpaced all other forms of spending, rising to 42 percent of veterans' spending by 1993.[31]

Public Housing Programs

Public expenditures on housing consist of payments for public housing and housing subsidies for low- and moderate-income families. Federal public housing expenditures got their start under the Housing Division of the Public Works Administration (PWA) during the New Deal with a strong burst of building activity in late 1935 and 1936. The PWA projects were then taken over by the U.S. Housing Authority in 1937, which began a new public housing building program, spending about $40 million per year during the late 1930s (1992 dollars). The spending jumped to close to $100 million per year during World War II and then jumped more than $1 billion in 1946 and 1947 (1992 dollars). Spending fell back to $43 million in 1949 and then rose continuously to about $1.8 billion in 1969 (1992 dollars). Since legislation in 1965, the U.S. Department of Housing and Urban Development (HUD) has overseen the housing programs.[32] After the Housing and Urban

---

[30] Included among the array of veterans' benefits are two major cash programs: the Service-Connected Disability Compensation program and the Nonservice-Connected Disability and Pension program. The service-connected program pays monthly benefits to honorably discharged veterans who are disabled as a result of injury or disease incurred while in or aggravated by active military duty. In addition, the surviving spouse, dependent children, and certain parents of veterans who die as the result of an injury or disease incurred while in or aggravated by active military duty are also eligible for compensation under the Dependency and Indemnity Compensation (DIC) program. Both disability compensation and DIC benefits are not means-tested. The second cash program provides for means-tested monthly benefits for honorably discharged wartime veterans with limited income and resources who are permanently and totally disabled as a result of a condition not related to their military service. The amount of benefit varies with the number of the veteran's dependents and the severity of the veteran's condition. Pensions for nonservice-connected death are based on need and are paid to surviving spouses and dependent children of deceased wartime veterans.

[31] Additional discussion of the veterans' programs can be found in Chapter Ed.

[32] HUD oversees a wide variety of programs not included in these expenditures, including the Federal Housing Administration (FHA), which insures loans for mortgages and home rehabilitation, and the General National Mortgage Association (Ginnie Mae).

Development Act of 1970 established a national growth policy, public housing expenditures skyrocketed in the 1970s, rising more than 18 percent per year to a level of $11.4 billion in 1980 (1992 dollars). The growth rate slowed to 7 percent per year in the 1980s. Since 1989, the annual expenditures have been around $20 billion (1992 dollars). Government expenditures on housing were focused on public housing provision until the beginning of the 1950s, when state governments began providing subsidies for housing for low- and moderate-income families that accounted for 39 percent of the public housing expenditures. The focus of spending soon returned to public housing through the rest of the 1950s, and then shifted back toward subsidies at the federal, state, and local levels through the mid-1970s, when resources devoted to public housing began increasing again (see series Bf194, Bf202, Bf210, and Bf262).

Other Public Social Welfare Programs

The catchall category in Table Bf263–270 includes spending on vocational rehabilitation, child nutrition, child welfare spending, ACTION, and Office of Economic Opportunity (OEO) programs. Expenditures in these areas have risen about 5 percent per year in real terms since 1929, with the most rapid growth occurring during the 1960s during the War on Poverty. Most of the increase in this miscellaneous category is on programs for child nutrition, including surplus foods under the National School Lunch and Child Nutrition Act. The special OEO and ACTION programs got their start in the mid-1960s. In 1971–1972 the VISTA, foster grandparents, and other volunteer programs were consolidated under the ACTION rubric. Expenditures rose through 1973 and had a significant one-year increase to $3.8 billion at the end of the Carter administration; successive administrations have reduced the spending well below $1 billion per year (1992 dollars).

Private Social Welfare

The impressive growth of public social welfare expenditures and programs sometimes causes us to forget that private entities play an important role in providing assistance to low-income households, insurance, health care spending, and education. Consequently, the growth in public spending has been complemented by similarly rapid growth in private spending on social welfare services. The SSA has developed two sets of estimates of private social welfare expenditures for the periods 1950–1978 and 1972 to the present. Neither of the series is a precise private counterpart of the SSA's public social welfare expenditure series. As seen in Figure Bf-B, private social welfare expenditures have risen from less than 5 percent as large as GDP in 1950 to 13 percent as large as GDP in the 1990s. We do not have good aggregate estimates for private social welfare spending for earlier periods.

Prior to the introduction of the public social welfare programs of the twentieth century, households followed a number of strategies for protecting themselves against misfortune. In the early 1900s, compared with today, households faced greater risk of workplace injury, similar risk of unemployment, and greater risk of disability and illness. With only limited access to public social insurance and relief at the local level, individuals and families developed a number of strategies for dealing with these problems. Many of these methods cannot be easily measured and turned into aggregate national statistics. To deal with the problems of old age, the elderly often lived with their children and their families or in close proximity to relatives. To deal with unemployment, illness, injury, or death, a number of families sent wives and children into the work force.[33] To varying degrees, employers and unions also provided some aid for families of workers injured on the job or fallen ill (Berkowitz and McQuaid 1992, pp. 11–34, 50–67; Jacoby 1997, pp. 10–34).

Both in past and present labor markets, varying combinations of competition for labor among employers and collective bargaining have forced employers to pay higher wages for jobs with greater risks of injury or unemployment. Estimates of the implicit value of life implied by the higher wages have risen over time to a range of approximately $1 million to $10 million in modern labor markets (Moore and Viscusi 1990; Fishback 1998). The higher wages probably did not fully compensate workers for their expected losses, but households used the higher wages to purchase limited amounts of life and accident insurance and to obtain some protection against accidents and sickness by joining mutual societies through employers or fraternal organizations. A number of households accumulated precautionary savings, but these were often not large enough to protect against the loss of the household head's income for more than a few months. Others used pawn shops and other informal sources of credit to tide them over (Haines 1985; Rotella and Alter 1993). People with low incomes without these resources sometimes obtained limited support from local governments, charities, or community groups.

The introduction of public social welfare programs may have partially replaced many of these private mechanisms for dealing with the risks and vicissitudes of life. Social Security pensions appear to have freed the elderly to maintain separate households. Increases in benefits for workers' compensation and unemployment insurance have been shown in a number of studies to be associated with reductions in the wages paid by employers (Moore and Viscusi 1990; Fishback 1998). A number of economists have found evidence that Social Security and other social insurance programs reduce precautionary savings and insurance purchases by households (Feldstein 1974, 1982; Leimer and Lesnoy 1982; Fishback and Kantor 2000). Even charitable donations and organizational activities have been found to be crowded out by public programs in some studies (Abrams and Schmitz 1984; Ziliak 1996, 1997). On the other hand, many of these changes have been marginal responses that apparently have been swamped by other factors because private social welfare spending over the past fifty years has followed an upward trend similar to the one displayed by public social welfare spending (see Figure Bf-B).

The most rapid growth in private social welfare spending since 1972 has come in expansions in the category for income maintenance spending, which is essentially expenditures for employee benefit plans for retirement pensions, life and disability insurance, and supplemental unemployment insurance (series Bf790–795). Since 1972, expenditures on these plans have risen at an average annual rate of 6.3 percent per year after adjusting for inflation. The largest expansion within employee benefit plans has been in private pension plans, which have risen more than

[33] For descriptions of various family strategies, see Modell (1979); Graebner (1980); Goldin (1981); Haines (1985); Keyssar (1986); Rotella and Alter (1993), Haber and Gratton (1994), and Costa (1998).

fivefold in real terms between 1972 and 1994, in part as a result of the expansion of pension options available to employers (Kerns 1995). This rise in private pensions continues a longer trend from the beginning of the twentieth century. The railroad industry was the leader in providing pension plans in the late nineteenth century, and a few other large firms followed suit (Latimer 1932). In 1920, approximately 3 million workers were covered by pension plans (Craig 1995, p. 309; see also Ransom, Sutch, and Williamson 1993). By 1950 approximately 10 million private employees were covered by employer pension plans, and the number had tripled by 1970 (see Table Bf836–853). Similar stories can be told for life insurance, disability insurance, and health insurance benefits, although the growth rates in disability insurance and life insurance expenditures over the past twenty years have not matched the growth in pension spending (Tables Bf786–835 and Bf854–874).

Expenditures of private funds on welfare services by private social service agencies, such as family service agencies, adoption services, group foster homes, the YMCA, the Boy Scouts, and a wide range of other programs, have risen nearly as fast as spending on income maintenance – 6 percent per year in real terms since 1972 (series Bf777).[34]

Even the slowest-growing category of private social welfare spending – education – has grown at an average annual rate of 3.6 percent per year in real terms between 1972 and 1994. This growth is slightly faster than the growth in public spending on education. About 50 percent of the private spending throughout the period has been on current operations in higher education, while about 13 to 15 percent is devoted to current operations in vocational education (see Kerns 1995, p. 69).

An important component of private social welfare spending is expenditures on health care. The U.S. health care system contrasts with the public health care systems of many other countries in that our system is financed by a mixture of direct private spending, spending under health insurance (often provided as benefits by employers), and public programs. Private health expenditures in 1992 dollars have grown at a pace of approximately 5 percent per year since 1960 (series Bf876 deflated by the GDP deflator).[35] Despite this rapid growth, the expansion of Medicare and Medicaid has caused the privately financed share of health care expenditures to fall from 75 percent in 1960 to 54 percent in the 1990s (series Bf876 as a percentage of series Bf875).

One of the major changes in the financing of health care expenditures has been the rise in the role of private health insurance. While payments from health insurers financed only 29 percent of private health expenditures in 1960, by the 1990s health insurance paid for roughly 60 percent of all private health expenditures (series Bf879 as a percentage of series Bf876). This figure might understate the involvement of insurers in medical transactions because the leading alternative category – series Bf878, out-of-pocket medical expenditures by consumers – includes the consumer payments of copayments and deductibles required by health insurers. The rise in the extent of private health insurance coverage of the population has been even more dramatic. Since 1940, the number of people with private health insurance has risen sharply from 12 million to more than 180 million in the 1990s (series Bf887). The rise has been dramatic, but the absence of universal coverage of the population has been a leading public policy issue during the 1990s and early twenty-first century.

The current system of health insurance coverage evolved from "sickness" insurance, which was the primary form of health insurance sold in the early part of the twentieth century through the 1930s. Sickness insurance was designed to replace lost income from illness rather than to pay medical bills. Sickness insurance is still sold today, but the majority of the private protections against lost income from sickness are found in employer programs (Tables Bf854–874).

As medical care became more effective and expensive, Blue Cross (and later Blue Shield) was an early leader in developing health insurance that paid for the direct costs of obtaining medical care. The "Blues" provided coverage to roughly half of the people with insurance in 1940 (series Bf891 as a percentage of series Bf887). A substantial part of the rise in health insurance coverage of medical costs has come from group insurance plans through the person's employer. Tables Bf802–835 show the dramatic rise in health insurance coverage for employees between 1950 and 1976, the point at which these series were no longer collected. The rise was driven in part by federal tax policies during World War II, which were later clarified and encoded by the Internal Revenue Code of 1954, which freed employers from paying taxes on the value of health insurance provided to their workers (Thomasson 1998). The most recent trend in the health insurance industry has been the rise in the number of people covered by health maintenance organizations (HMOs) and other managed care plans. Over the past twenty years the percentage of persons insured by HMOs, managed care plans, and miscellaneous insurance has risen from 10 percent to nearly two thirds (series Bf892 as a percentage of series Bf887).

Summary

"Expansion" is the single best word to use in describing social welfare expenditures during the twentieth century in America. Expenditures have risen at a much faster rate than GDP as the coverage of programs has expanded and the average payments to beneficiaries have increased. Public programs have proliferated, and private social welfare spending has also risen at a rapid pace. Social welfare spending from both public and private sources has grown from less than 10 percent as large as GDP to more than 30 percent as large as GDP over the past ninety years. The result has been a dramatic change in the institutional landscape with regard to social insurance and public assistance. Responsibility for many forms of social welfare activity has shifted from the individual and private organizations to state and local governments to the federal government, although the federal programs are often administered and funded in conjunction with state and local governments. Some public programs, such as Social Security, have expanded in ways that have led to significant public discussion of the possibility of future breakdowns in the government's ability to maintain the promises made to the workers who are currently funding them. Similar problems have arisen in our complex public–private system of health care. The discussions have led to new proposals of innovative ways of dealing with these issues, which in turn may well lead to more complex arrangements in the future.

---

[34] More extensive information on private philanthropy is available in Chapter Bg.

[35] The SSA obtained its estimates for private spending on health care (series Bf774) from the Health Care Financing Administration, which has reported a longer time series for 1960–1997 in series Bf876.

References

Abbott, Grace. 1934. "Recent Trends in Mothers' Aid." *Social Service Review* 8: 191–210.

Abrams, Burton A., and Mark D. Schmitz. 1984. "The Crowding-Out Effect of Governmental Transfers on Private Charitable Contributions: Cross-Section Evidence." *National Tax Journal* 37 (4): 563–8.

Balkan, Sule. 1998. "Social Insurance Programs and Compensating Wage Differentials in the United States." Ph.D. dissertation, University of Arizona.

Ball, Robert M. 1988. "The Original Understanding on Social Security: Implications for Later Developments." In Theodore R. Marmor and Jerry L. Mashaw, editors. *Social Security: Beyond the Rhetoric of Crisis*. Princeton University Press.

Berkowitz, Edward, and Kim McQuaid. 1992. *Creating the Welfare State: The Political Economy of Twentieth-Century Reform*, revised edition. University of Kansas Press.

Brandeis, Elizabeth. 1966. "Labor Legislation." In John R. Commons and Associates, editors. *History of Labor in the United States,* volume 3. Augustus M. Kelley, reprint of 1935 edition.

Bucklin, Dorothy R. 1939. "Public Aid for the Care of Dependent Children in Their Own Homes, 1932–38." *Social Security Bulletin* 2 (April): 25.

Clark, Robert L., Lee A. Craig, and Jack W. Wilson. 1999. "Privatization of Public-Sector Pensions: The U.S. Navy Pension Fund, 1800–1842." *Independent Review* 3 (4): 549–64.

Clark, Robert L., Lee A. Craig, and Jack W. Wilson. 2000. "The Life and Times of a Public-Sector Pension Plan before Social Security: The U.S. Navy Pension Plan in the Nineteenth Century." In Olivia Mitchell and Edwin Hustead, editors. *Pensions in the Public Sector*. University of Pennsylvania Press.

Clark, Robert L., Lee A. Craig, and Jack W. Wilson. 2003. *A History of Public-Sector Pensions in the United States*. University of Pennsylvania Press.

Costa, Dora. 1998. *The Evolution of Retirement: An American Economic History, 1880–1990.* University of Chicago Press.

Craig, Lee A. 1995. "The Political Economy of Public–Private Compensation Differentials: The Case of Federal Pensions." *Journal of Economic History* 55 (2): 304–20.

Feldstein, Martin. 1974. "Social Security, Induced Retirement, and Aggregate Capital Accumulation." *Journal of Political Economy* 82 (September/October): 905–26.

Feldstein, Martin. 1982. "Social Security and Private Saving: Reply." *Journal of Political Economy* 90 (June): 630–42.

Fishback, Price. 1998. "Operations of 'Unfettered' Labor Markets: Exit and Voice in American Labor Markets at the Turn of the Century." *Journal of Economic Literature* 36 (June): 722–65.

Fishback, Price, and Shawn Everett Kantor. 2000. *Prelude to the Welfare State: The Origins of Workers' Compensation*. University of Chicago Press.

Franklin, Grace, and Randall Ripley. 1984. *CETA: Politics and Policy, 1973–1982*. University of Tennessee Press.

Goldin, Claudia. 1981. "Family Strategies and the Family Economy in the Late Nineteenth Century: The Role of Secondary Workers." In Theodore Hershberg, editor. *Philadelphia: Work, Space, and Group Experience in the Nineteenth Century*. Oxford University Press.

Graebner, William. 1980. *A History of Retirement: The Meaning and Function of an American Institution, 1885–1978*. Yale University Press.

Haber, Carole, and Brian Gratton. 1994. *Old Age and the Search for Security: An American Social History*. Indiana University Press.

Haines, Michael R. 1985. "The Life Cycle, Savings, and Demographic Adaptation: Some Historical Evidence for the United States and Europe." In Alice S. Rossi, editor. *Gender and the Life Course*. Aldine.

J. Frederic Dewhurst and Associates. 1955. *America's Needs and Resources*. Twentieth Century Fund.

Jacoby, Sanford M. 1997. *Modern Manors: Welfare Capitalism since the New Deal*. Princeton University Press.

Johnson, Ronald N., and Gary D. Libecap. 1994. *The Federal Civil Service System and the Problem of Bureaucracy: The Economics and Politics of Institutional Change*. University of Chicago Press.

Kantor, Shawn E., and Price V. Fishback. 1994. "Coalition Formation and the Adoption of Workers' Compensation: The Case of Missouri, 1911 to 1926." In Claudia D. Goldin and Gary D. Libecap, editors. *The Regulated Economy: A Historical Approach to Political Economy*. University of Chicago Press.

Kerns, Wilmer. 1995. "Private Social Welfare Expenditures, 1995." *Social Security Bulletin* 58 (1): 66–73.

Keyssar, Alexander. 1986. *Out of Work: The First Century of Unemployment in Massachusetts*. Cambridge University Press.

Kim, Seung-Wook, and Price V. Fishback. 1993. "Institutional Change, Compensating Differentials, and Accident Risk in Railroading, 1892–1945." *Journal of Economic History* 53 (December): 796–823.

Latimer, Murray Webb. 1932. *Industrial Pension Systems in the United States and Canada.* Industrial Relations Counselors.

Leimer, Dean R., and Selig Lesnoy. 1982. "Social Security and Private Saving: New Time-Series Evidence." *Journal of Political Economy* 90 (June): 606–29.

Lescohier, Don D. 1966 (1935). "Working Conditions." In John R. Commons and Associates, editors. *History of Labor in the United States,* volume 3. Augustus M. Kelley, reprint of 1935 edition.

Lundberg, Emma O. 1921. "Aid to Mothers with Dependent Children." *Annals of the American Academy of Political and Social Science* 98 (November): 97–105.

McSteen, Martha. 1985. "Fifty Years of Social Security." *Social Security Bulletin* 48 (8): 36–44.

Meriam, Lewis. 1946. *Relief and Social Security*. Brookings Institution Press.

Modell, John. 1979. "Changing Risks, Changing Adaptations: American Families in the Nineteenth and Twentieth Centuries." In Allan J. Lichtman and Joan R. Challinor, editors. *Kin and Communities: Families in America.* Smithsonian Institution Press.

Moehling, Carolyn. 2002. "Mothers' Pensions and Female Headship." Working paper, Yale University Economics Department.

Moore, Michael J., and W. Kip Viscusi. 1990. *Compensation Mechanisms for Job Risks: Wages, Workers' Compensation, and Product Liability*. Princeton University Press.

Murphy, Kevin, and Finis Welch. 1998. "Perspectives on the Social Security Crisis and Proposed Solutions." *American Economic Review* 88 (2): 142–50.

Musgrave, R. A., and J. J. Culbertson. 1953. "The Growth of Public Expenditures in the U.S., 1890–1948." *National Tax Journal* 6 (2): 97–115.

Orloff, Ann Shola. 1993. *The Politics of Pensions: A Comparative Analysis of Britain, Canada, and the United States*. University of Wisconsin Press.

Quadagno, Jill. 1988. *The Transformation of Old Age Security: Class and Politics in the American Welfare State*. University of Chicago Press.

Ransom, Roger, Richard Sutch, and Samuel H. Williamson. 1993. "Inventing Pensions: The Origins of the Company-Provided Pensions in the United States, 1900–1940." In K. W. Schaie and W. A. Achenbaum, editors. *Societal Impact on Aging: Historical Perspectives.* Springer.

Rotella, Elyce, and George Alter. 1993. "Working-Class Debt in the Late Nineteenth-Century United States." *Journal of Family History* 18 (Spring): 111–34.

Schieber, Sylvester J., and John B. Shoven. 1999. *The Real Deal: The History and Future of Social Security*. Yale University Press.

Skocpol, Theda. 1992. *Protecting Soldiers and Mothers: The Political Origins of Social Policy in the United States*. Belknap Press of Harvard University Press.

Social Security Administration. Various years. *Social Security Bulletin: Annual Statistical Supplement (SSBASS).*

Stevens, Robert B., editor. 1970. *Statutory History of the United States: Income Security*. Chelsea House.

Thomasson, Melissa. 1998. "From Sickness to Health: The Twentieth-Century Development of the Demand for Health Insurance." Ph.D. dissertation, University of Arizona.

Thompson, Laura. 1919. "Laws Relating to 'Mothers' Pensions' in the United States, Canada, Denmark, and New Zealand." *U.S. Department of Labor, Children's Bureau Publication number 63, Legal Series number 4.* U.S. Government Printing Office.

Transportation Research Board. 1994. *Compensating Injured Railroad Workers under the Federal Employers' Liability Act, Special Report 241*. National Academy Press.

U.S. Bureau of Labor Statistics. 1953. "Workmen's Compensation in the United States." *Bulletin number 1149*.

U.S. Bureau of the Census. 1975. *Historical Statistics of the United States: Colonial Times to 1970*.

U.S. Children's Bureau. 1930. *Eighteenth Annual Report of the Children's Bureau*.

U.S. Committee on Economic Security. 1937. *Social Security in America: The Factual Background of the Social Security Act as Summarized from Staff Reports to the Committee on Economic Security*.

U.S. Department of Labor. 1932. *Annual Report, 1932*.

U.S. Department of Labor. 1935. "Public Provision for Pensions for the Blind in 1934." *Monthly Labor Review* 41 (3): 584–601.

Weaver, Carolyn L. 1982. *The Crisis in Social Security: Economic and Political Origins*. Duke University Press.

Wolfe, John. 1993. *The Coming Health Crisis: Who Will Pay for Care for the Aged in the Twenty-First Century*? University of Chicago Press.

Ziliak, Stephen. 1996. "The End of Welfare and the Contradiction of Compassion." *Independent Review* 1 (1): 55–73.

Ziliak, Stephen. 1997. "Kicking the Malthusian Vice: Lessons from the Abolition of 'Welfare' in the Late Nineteenth Century." *Quarterly Review of Economics and Finance* 37 (2): 449–68.

POOR RELIEF

Joan Underhill Hannon and Stephen T. Ziliak

TABLE Bf1–7 Poor relief in Philadelphia – recipients, expenditures, and tax levied: 1709–1775

Contributed by Stephen T. Ziliak

			Poor relief				
	Population	Poor tax levied per annum	Expenditures	Expenditures per 1,000 population	Recipients	Recipients per 1,000 population	Expenditures per recipient
	Bf1	Bf2	Bf3	Bf4	Bf5	Bf6	Bf7
Period	Number	Pence	Pounds	Pounds per 1,000	Number	Per 1,000	Pounds
1709	2,500	1.5	158	59	13	4.8	12.00
1739	9,100	3.0	800	83	80 [1]	8.3 [1]	10.00 [1]
1756–1758	15,600	3.0	1,175	72	110 [1]	6.7 [1]	10.90 [1]
1765	18,100	5.0	2,385	123	310	16.0	7.14
1768–1771	19,700	6.0	3,681	175	590	28.1	6.50
1772–1775	22,300	6.0	3,868	163	720	30.3	5.70

[1] Estimate based on the known number of outreliefers plus an estimated 40 to 50 inmates in the small almshouse.

Source

Gary B. Nash, "Poverty and Poor Relief in Pre-Revolutionary Philadelphia," *William and Mary Quarterly* 33 (1976): 3–30. Table 1, p. 9.

Documentation

All values are in Philadelphia currency. The data are derived from numerous archival sources. For example, the figures for 1768 to 1775 are derived from the annual reports of the Records of the Contributors of Relief to the Poor, Treasurer's Accounts, City Archives, Philadelphia. The figures for 1739, on the other hand, are found in the Philadelphia Poor Day Book, 1739. "Although food prices rose steeply in the 1770s, there was general stability in prices and sterling exchange rates in Philadelphia during the colonial period, so money values have not been converted to English sterling" (Nash 1976, p. 9).

Series Bf2. The source suggests that the tax was a flat tax on any assessable property.

TABLE Bf8–16 Poor relief expenditures in Boston, Philadelphia, and New York: 1700–1775

Contributed by Stephen T. Ziliak

	Boston			Philadelphia			New York		
		Poor relief			Poor relief			Poor relief	
	Population	Average annual expenditure	Expenditure per 1,000 population	Population	Average annual expenditure	Expenditure per 1,000 population	Population	Average annual expenditure	Expenditure per 1,000 population
	Bf8	Bf9	Bf10	Bf11	Bf12	Bf13	Bf14	Bf15	Bf16
Period	Number	Pounds sterling	Pounds sterling per 1,000	Number	Pounds sterling	Pounds sterling per 1,000	Number	Pounds sterling	Pounds sterling per 1,000
1700–1710	7,500	173	23	2,450	119	48	4,500	—	—
1711–1720	9,830	181	18	3,800	—	—	5,900	249	32
1721–1730	11,840	273	23	6,600	—	—	7,600	276	25
1731–1740	15,850	498	31	8,800	471	49	10,100	351	21
1741–1750	16,240	806	50	12,000	—	—	12,900	389	21
1751–1760	15,660	1,204	77	15,700	1,083	67	13,200	667	39
1761–1770	15,520	1,909	123	22,100	2,842	129	18,100	1,667	92
1771–1775	15,500	2,478	158	27,900	3,785	136	22,600	2,778	123

Source

Gary B. Nash, "Urban Wealth and Poverty in Pre-Revolutionary America," *Journal of Interdisciplinary History* 6 (4) (1976): 545–84. Table 4, p. 557.

Documentation

See the text for Table Bf1–7 for a description of the data source for Philadelphia.

Between 1754 and 1775, the town records of Boston provide, with few interruptions, an annual report of the treasurer on disbursements to the Overseers of the Poor. These reports provide direct counts. For the period 1700–1720, Nash "estimated poor relief costs at one-third the town expenses (given yearly in Boston Town Records), the ratio that prevailed in the five years between 1727 and 1737 when poor relief expense figures are given" (Nash 1976, p. 556 n. 24).

The figures for New York have been reconstructed from the Minutes and Accounts of the Church Warden and Vestrymen of the City of New York, 1696–1715, New York Historical Society; and Minutes of the Meetings of the Justices, Church Wardens, and Vestrymen of the City of New York, 1694–1747, New York Public Library. The salary of the clergymen for the Society for the Propagation of the Gospel, which was included in these expenditures, has been subtracted from the yearly totals. Nash reports that "the New York

TABLE Bf8–16 Poor relief expenditures in Boston, Philadelphia, and New York: 1700–1775 *Continued*

records after 1747 have apparently not survived, but the level of expenditures on the eve of the Revolution was reported by the vestrymen and churchwardens in a petition to the Continental Congress in May 1776" (1976, p. 556 n. 25).

All values, which in the inventories are given in Massachusetts and Pennsylvania currency, have been converted to sterling. Nash used the conversion figures given in U.S. Bureau of the Census, *Historical Statistics of the United States, Colonial Times to 1957* (1960), p. 773, and filled in the missing years from the price per ounce of silver cited in the inventories for these years. For Philadelphia, the yearly sterling equivalents for Pennsylvania currency are taken from Anne Bezanson, Robert D. Gray, and Marian Hussey, *Prices in Colonial Pennsylvania* (University of Pennsylvania Press, 1935), p. 431.

TABLE Bf17–22 Tax assessments and expenditures for the poor in Philadelphia: 1800–1854[1]

Contributed by Stephen T. Ziliak

			Almshouse expenditures		Outdoor expenditures	
	Poor-tax assessment	Total expenditures for the poor	Total	Percentage of total expenditures	Total	Percentage of total expenditures
	Bf17	Bf18	Bf19 [2]	Bf20	Bf21	Bf22
Fiscal year beginning	Dollars	Dollars	Dollars	Percent	Dollars	Percent
1800	50,000	47,212	25,330 [4]	54	21,882	46
1801	75,000	59,830	37,568 [4]	63	22,262	37
1802	60,000	73,507	38,004 [4]	52	35,503	48
1803	75,000	79,684	50,192	63	29,492	37
1804	70,000	91,702	55,202	60	36,500	40
1805	90,000	96,025	62,309	65	33,716	35
1806	90,000	89,795	57,942	65	31,854	35
1807	91,160	103,856	67,537	65	36,318	35
1808	90,000	113,952	79,414	70	34,537	30
1809	83,000	113,049	76,704	68	36,345	32
1810	88,000	92,203	58,154	63	34,049	37
1811	102,954	88,040	49,023	56	39,067	44
1812	102,595	—	—	—	—	—
1813	90,000	103,981	45,409	44	58,572	56
1814	100,000	120,488	64,424	53	56,064	47
1815	110,000	124,660	70,788	57	53,872	43
1816	110,000	117,892	63,222	54	54,670	46
1817	150,000	107,598	52,031	48	55,567	52
1818	135,000	116,408	48,811	42	67,596	58
1819	135,000	98,014	51,393	52	46,621	48
1820	140,000	95,010	51,501	54	43,509	46
1821	130,000	97,847	50,511	52	47,337	48
1822	105,940	111,120	59,506	54	51,530	46
1823	114,468	129,125	57,227	44	71,898	56
1824	132,317	110,020	52,423	49	55,597	51
1825	129,383	100,170	52,842	52	47,329	48
1826	89,961	119,798	70,789	59	49,009	41
1827	80,000	83,088	52,419	63	30,669	37
1828	90,000	82,154	55,190	67	26,964	33
1829	90,000	83,508	53,877	65	29,631	35
1830	80,564	86,614	54,494	63	32,120	37
1831	91,828	106,139	69,513	66	36,626	34
1832	139,891	106,252	64,814	61	41,438	39
1833	—	101,597	68,308	67	33,289	33
1835	168,942	114,092	97,720	86	16,372	14
1836	—	112,107	100,297	89	11,810	11
1837	—	130,360	114,933	88	15,427	12
1838	—	122,612	105,921	86	16,691	14
1839	169,043	111,292	84,902	76	26,390	24
1840	—	98,763	70,621	72	28,142	28
1841	—	120,035	88,910	74	31,125	26
1842	181,094	115,511	80,755	70	34,756	30
1843	178,003	113,034	79,489	70	33,546	30
1844	194,825	—	—	—	—	—

Notes appear at end of table

(continued)

TABLE Bf17–22 Tax assessments and expenditures for the poor in Philadelphia: 1800–1854 *Continued*

			Almshouse expenditures		Outdoor expenditures	
	Poor-tax assessment	Total expenditures for the poor	Total	Percentage of total expenditures	Total	Percentage of total expenditures
Fiscal year beginning	Bf17	Bf18	Bf19 [2]	Bf20	Bf21	Bf22
	Dollars	Dollars	Dollars	Percent	Dollars	Percent
1845	161,025	144,074	105,245	73	38,829	27
1846	197,265	129,345	91,463	71	37,882	29
1847	191,013	144,598	106,207	73	38,391	27
1848	189,425	148,297	100,683	68	47,613	32
1849	191,037	166,346	117,759	70	48,587	30
1850	208,018	167,204	121,485	73	45,719	27
1852	259,583	176,434	120,878	69	55,557	31
1853	—	193,277	127,558	66	65,719	34
1854 [3]	—	143,771	115,665	80	28,107	20

[1] Through 1802, the fiscal year began in March; thereafter in May.

[2] Beginning in 1821, expenditures of the children's asylum and board of youngsters in the Shelter for Colored Orphans and of the sick in the city hospital are included with the almshouse expenditures. In the annual accounts, they are included with outdoor expenditures.

[3] May to December.

[4] Almshouse figures include the amount paid the Pennsylvania Hospital for boarding some insane patients.

Source

Priscilla Clement, *Welfare and the Poor in the Nineteenth-Century City: Philadelphia, 1800–1854* (Fairleigh Dickinson University Press, 1985), Appendix 1, pp. 174–7.

Documentation

The underlying sources for the data are many and are documented in detail in Clement (1985), Appendix 1. There are some discrepancies (though apparently small in magnitude) in the year-to-year comparability of figures.

Series Bf17. The tax assessment was usually levied in January for the fiscal year that began in March or May.

Series Bf19. Expenditures are direct costs of caring for the poor in the almshouse. The figures include salaries paid to almshouse employees and the cost of materials used in the [almshouse] factory.

Series Bf21. Expenditures include sums spent for outdoor cash aid, medical attendance, and wood as well as for the amount paid in salaries to employees of the guardians of the poor.

TABLE Bf23–27 Public relief recipients in Philadelphia, by type of relief: 1800–1854[1]

Contributed by Stephen T. Ziliak

	Public relief				
	Total	Almshouses and children's asylum	Outdoor pensioners	Medical aid	Fuel aid
Fiscal year beginning	Bf23	Bf24	Bf25	Bf26	Bf27
	Number	Number	Number	Number	Number
1800	1,390	788	602	—	—
1801	—	948	—	—	—
1802	—	804	—	—	—
1803	—	1,101	—	—	—
1804	—	1,196	—	—	—
1805	1,180 [2]	1,270	590	—	—
1806	2,000	1,455	545	—	—
1807	—	1,406	—	—	—
1808	—	1,581	—	—	—
1809	—	1,611	—	—	—
1810	2,500	1,755	745	—	—
1811	2,106	1,796	310	—	—
1812	—	1,830	—	—	—
1813	—	1,820	—	—	—
1814	3,145	1,891	1,254	—	—
1815	3,462	2,254	1,208	—	—
1816	3,852	2,653	1,199	—	—
1817	4,082	2,843	1,239	—	—
1818	—	—	1,249	—	—
1819	5,530	4,049	1,481	—	—

Notes appear at end of table

TABLE Bf23–27 Public relief recipients in Philadelphia, by type of relief: 1800–1854 *Continued*

	Public relief				
	Total	Almshouses and children's asylum	Outdoor pensioners	Medical aid	Fuel aid
	Bf23	Bf24	Bf25	Bf26	Bf27
Fiscal year beginning	Number	Number	Number	Number	Number
1820	5,237	3,907	1,330	—	—
1821	4,834	3,566	1,268	—	—
1822	5,119	3,897	1,222	—	—
1823	5,387	4,378	1,009	—	—
1824	4,508	3,666	842	—	—
1825	4,591	3,578	1,013	—	—
1826	5,059	4,025	1,034	—	—
1827	4,110	3,411	699	—	—
1828	4,276	4,024	252	—	—
1829	4,360	3,651	709	2,875	2,128
1830	3,450	2,730	720	—	—
1831	4,171	3,501	670	—	3,197
1832	—	—	760	2,285	3,175
1833	4,198	3,400	798	—	—
1834	—	—	916	—	—
1835	2,512	2,512	0	—	—
1836	2,692	2,692	0	—	—
1837	2,896	2,896	0	—	3,685
1838	2,420	2,420	0	—	2,742
1839	3,131	3,008	123	—	—
1840	2,891	2,696	195	—	2,889
1841	3,161	2,985	176	2,437	4,498
1842	3,060	2,869	191	3,164	7,575
1843	3,187	2,958	229	2,808	6,650
1845	3,475	3,223	252	3,077	7,040
1846	4,810	4,503	307	3,190	7,720
1847	4,520	4,303	217	2,864	6,903
1848	4,775	4,504	271	2,882	8,868
1849	5,146	4,885	261	3,491	8,821
1850	5,041	4,854	187	—	—
1851	—	6,719	—	—	—
1852	—	5,017	—	—	—
1853	—	5,407	—	—	—
1854	—	3,244	—	—	—

[1] Through 1802, the fiscal year began in March; thereafter in May.

[2] Total is given as reported in the source, but it does not equal the sum of series Bf24–25.

Source

Priscilla Clement, *Welfare and the Poor in the Nineteenth-Century City: Philadelphia, 1800–1854* (Fairleigh Dickinson University Press, 1985), Appendix 2, pp. 178–80.

Documentation

The underlying sources for the data are many and are documented in detail in Clement (1985), Appendix 2. There are some discrepancies (though apparently small in magnitude) in the year-to-year comparability of figures. See Clement (1985), Appendix 2, "Sources."

Series Bf24. Almshouse and asylum figures represent total admissions; they may be somewhat inflated, then, because some people were admitted more than once in a year.

Series Bf25. Single people and heads of families. The number of children in these families is not included in these figures but may have amounted to 40 percent of those on pensions in some years.

Series Bf26–27. Numbers of medical and fuel aid recipients were given annually in most years after 1800. Many outdoor pensioners received both fuel and medical aid so there may be a great deal of overlap, which is impossible to measure because there are no extant lists of aid recipients.

TABLE Bf 28–33 Pauper support, by state: 1850–1870

Contributed by Stephen T. Ziliak

	Average pauper support			Pauper support as a ratio to income of common laborer		
	1850	1860	1870	1850	1860	1870
	Bf28	Bf29	Bf30	Bf31	Bf32	Bf33
State	Dollars	Dollars	Dollars	Percent	Percent	Percent
United States	59	87	119	21.6	26.4	24.0
Alabama	56	87	119	25.7	29.1	31.6
Arkansas	103	94	139	44.2	29.1	32.2
California	—	388	276	—	41.3	38.4
Colorado	—	—	601	—	—	77.2
Connecticut	55	56	111	23.3	17.1	22.0
Delaware	65	51	91	26.7	18.8	18.8
District of Columbia	—	89	94	—	28.6	—
Florida	15	43	67	4.7	11.9	18.0
Georgia	33	38	88	14.7	13.7	26.0
Illinois	104	106	235	53.9	32.4	47.2
Indiana	99	96	110	57.9	31.5	22.7
Iowa	122	123	205	47.3	39.9	39.0
Kansas	—	20	138	—	5.3	23.7
Kentucky	74	80	90	34.4	26.5	20.8
Louisiana	— [1]	70	105	— [1]	16.2	19.8
Maine	43	49	101	18.2	15.0	21.1
Maryland	36	104	101	16.7	39.8	21.1
Massachusetts	71	89	194	27.2	28.1	39.0
Michigan	66	80	132	32.2	24.8	27.0
Minnesota	—	—	69	—	46.1	12.7
Mississippi	71	89	120	24.1	22.7	26.6
Missouri	105	90	103	45.1	29.5	22.4
Montana	—	—	742	—	—	39.8
Nebraska	—	— [2]	121	—	— [2]	18.3
Nevada	—	—	439	—	—	47.1
New Hampshire	72	67	110	36.7	22.9	27.2
New Jersey	59	71	119	29.2	21.3	23.3
New York	64	75	189	30.8	23.7	40.5
North Carolina	38	58	83	22.6	24.3	32.5
Ohio	57	— [3]	154	32.8	— [3]	30.9
Oregon	—	526	306	—	—	46.4
Pennsylvania	61	86	143	38.4	24.9	27.9
Rhode Island	66	70	154	29.5	21.4	33.0
South Carolina	40	45	109	19.5	17.6	34.7
Tennessee	53	69	75	29.4	26.4	20.9
Texas	— [2]	105	105	— [2]	27.0	26.6
Utah	—	344	122	—	57.0	—
Vermont	64	65	100	28.6	20.1	22.3
Virginia	34	46	92	16.8	18.3	29.3
Washington	—	935	264	—	103.0	33.9
West Virginia	—	—	81	—	—	20.5
Wisconsin	62	64	134	28.1	19.6	28.0

[1] Aggregate expenditures greater than in 1860.

[2] Fewer than 10 persons enumerated.

[3] June 1 count above yearly total.

Source

Stanley Lebergott, *The American Economy: Income, Wealth, and Want* (Princeton University Press, 1976), pp. 64–5. Notes on pp. 61–4. Data for daily wages of common labor are taken from Lebergott, *Manpower in Economic Growth* (McGraw-Hill, 1964), p. 541, and multiplied by 311 to give an annual rate (Lebergott 1976, p. 63).

Documentation

The estimates for relief payments were computed from data in *A Compendium of the Ninth Census* (U.S. Census Office, 1872, pp. 533–4). According to Lebergott, "the estimates . . . were computed . . . by dividing the count of paupers as of June 1 into the 'annual cost of support' for an entire year. The June 1 count is probably below a yearly average so far as seasonality is concerned. But the peak of immigrant flows in the spring would tend to bring it above average. Because 40 percent of the June 1 count was in New York, Pennsylvania, and Massachusetts – centers for immigrant arrival – the importance of this latter factor is probably substantial. We therefore accept the June 1 count as a fair annual average" (Lebergott 1976, p. 61).

Lebergott's data for New York State cannot be replicated with Hannon's county-level data from New York State. The reason for the discrepancy is unresolved. L. Lynne Kiesling and Robert Margo have examined the census manuscripts for the antebellum period, 1850 and 1860. They have found that some of Lebergott's other state totals cannot be replicated by aggregating the county-level data (L. Lynne Kiesling and Robert A. Margo, "Explaining the Rise in Antebellum Pauperism, 1850–1860: New Evidence," *Quarterly Review of Economics and Finance* 37 (2) (1997): 405–17). Margo points out (in correspondence to Ziliak) that the numerator (the pauper expenditures) and the denominator (the average wage) of Lebergott's "generosity" figure are unweighted, even in cases where census agents performed the arithmetic correctly. Margo suggests that it would be better to produce a generosity figure built up from the county-level data, and then weighted by, for example, the number of paupers in each county.

TABLE Bf34–149 Paupers enumerated in almshouses, by region and state: 1880–1923[1]

Contributed by Stephen T. Ziliak

	Paupers enumerated											
	Total, United States	New England							Middle Atlantic			
		Total	Maine	New Hampshire	Vermont	Massachusetts	Rhode Island	Connecticut	Total	New York	New Jersey	Pennsylvania
	Bf34	Bf35	Bf36	Bf37	Bf38	Bf39	Bf40	Bf41	Bf42	Bf43	Bf44	Bf45
Year	Number	Number	Number	Number	Number	Number	Number	Number	Number	Number	Number	Number
1880	66,203	9,835	1,505	1,198	655	4,533	526	1,418	24,098	12,452	2,462	9,184
1890	73,044	9,500	1,161	1,143	543	4,725	490	1,438	21,643	10,272	2,718	8,653
1904	81,764	11,495	1,152	1,140	414	5,934	788	2,067	21,783	10,793	1,936	9,054
1910	84,198	11,886	945	991	383	6,555	768	2,244	23,772	12,031	2,135	9,606
1923	78,090	9,529	745	870	234	5,629	889	1,162	18,564	8,740	1,764	8,060

	Paupers enumerated											
	East North Central						West North Central					
	Total	Ohio	Indiana	Illinois	Michigan	Wisconsin	Total	Minnesota	Iowa	Missouri	North Dakota	South Dakota
	Bf46	Bf47	Bf48	Bf49	Bf50	Bf51	Bf52	Bf53	Bf54	Bf55	Bf56	Bf57
Year	Number	Number	Number	Number	Number	Number	Number	Number	Number	Number	Number	Number
1880	16,474	6,974	3,052	3,684	1,746	1,018	3,337	227	1,165	1,477	—	—
1890	20,279	7,400	2,927	5,395	1,916	2,641	5,336	365	1,621	2,378	35	53
1904	21,127	8,172	3,120	5,635	2,594	1,606	6,618	547	2,019	2,465	184	159
1910	21,358	8,078	3,114	5,421	2,970	1,775	6,366	687	1,779	2,388	81	145
1923	21,405	6,872	3,128	6,415	3,262	1,728	7,298	1,032	1,711	2,712	120	171

	Paupers enumerated											
	West North Central		South Atlantic									
	Nebraska	Kansas	Total	Delaware	Maryland	District of Columbia	Virginia	West Virginia	North Carolina	South Carolina	Georgia	Florida
	Bf58	Bf59	Bf60	Bf61	Bf62	Bf63	Bf64	Bf65	Bf66	Bf67	Bf68	Bf69
Year	Number	Number	Number	Number	Number	Number	Number	Number	Number	Number	Number	Number
1880	113	355	6,975	387	1,187	184	2,117	711	1,275	519	550	45
1890	291	593	8,100	299	1,599	221	2,193	792	1,483	578	901	24
1904	464	780	8,298	278	1,633	230	1,915	881	1,519	686	1,032	124
1910	551	735	7,706	366	1,681	276	1,688	808	1,389	478	813	207
1923	573	979	6,875	277	1,368	313	1,211	702	1,474	451	872	207

	Paupers enumerated											
	East South Central					West South Central					Mountain	
	Total	Kentucky	Tennessee	Alabama	Mississippi	Total	Arkansas	Louisiana	Oklahoma	Texas	Total	Montana
	Bf70	Bf71	Bf72	Bf73	Bf74	Bf75	Bf76	Bf77	Bf78	Bf79	Bf80	Bf81
Year	Number	Number	Number	Number	Number	Number	Number	Number	Number	Number	Number	Number
1880	3,361	1,366	1,136	514	345	315	105	—	—	210	152	—
1890	4,240	1,578	1,545	623	494	809	223	122	—	464	367	132
1904	4,768	1,678	1,812	761	517	1,689	575	149	52	913	1,283	314
1910	4,266	1,522	1,569	739	436	1,630	534	187	48	861	1,652	415
1923	4,097	1,457	1,477	768	395	2,075	578	174	250	1,073	1,778	324

Note appears at end of table

(continued)

TABLE Bf34–149 Paupers enumerated in almshouses, by region and state: 1880–1923 *Continued*

	Paupers enumerated									
	Mountain						Pacific			
	Idaho	Wyoming	Colorado	Arizona	Utah	Nevada	Total	Washington	Oregon	California
	Bf82	Bf83	Bf84	Bf85	Bf86	Bf87	Bf88	Bf89	Bf90	Bf91
Year	Number	Number	Number	Number	Number	Number	Number	Number	Number	Number
1880	7	—	46	4	—	95	1,656	11	51	1,594
1890	20	—	87	23	62	43	2,770	71	99	2,600
1904	70	—	398	146	184	171	4,703	306	257	4,140
1910	97	19	510	271	181	159	5,562	564	352	4,646
1923	193	62	667	206	188	138	6,469	769	580	5,120

	Paupers enumerated per 100,000 population											
		New England							Middle Atlantic			
	Total, United States	Total	Maine	New Hampshire	Vermont	Massachusetts	Rhode Island	Connecticut	Total	New York	New Jersey	Pennsylvania
	Bf92	Bf93	Bf94	Bf95	Bf96	Bf97	Bf98	Bf99	Bf100	Bf101	Bf102	Bf103
Year	Per 100,000	Per 100,000	Per 100,000	Per 100,000	Per 100,000	Per 100,000	Per 100,000	Per 100,000	Per 100,000	Per 100,000	Per 100,000	Per 100,000
1880	132.0	245.2	231.9	345.3	197.1	254.2	190.2	227.7	229.6	245.0	217.7	214.4
1890	116.5	202.1	175.6	303.6	163.3	211.0	141.8	192.7	170.4	171.3	188.1	164.6
1904	100.0	193.5	161.8	272.4	118.9	197.2	167.7	210.2	129.2	136.0	91.3	133.2
1910	91.5	181.4	127.3	230.2	107.6	194.7	141.5	201.3	123.1	132.0	84.1	125.3
1923	71.5	125.1	96.2	194.9	66.4	141.5	143.3	80.2	80.6	81.6	53.2	89.6

	Paupers enumerated per 100,000 population											
	East North Central						West North Central					
	Total	Ohio	Indiana	Illinois	Michigan	Wisconsin	Total	Minnesota	Iowa	Missouri	North Dakota	South Dakota
	Bf104	Bf105	Bf106	Bf107	Bf108	Bf109	Bf110	Bf111	Bf112	Bf113	Bf114	Bf115
Year	Per 100,000	Per 100,000	Per 100,000	Per 100,000	Per 100,000	Per 100,000	Per 100,000	Per 100,000	Per 100,000	Per 100,000	Per 100,000	Per 100,000
1880	147.0	218.1	154.3	119.7	106.7	77.4	54.2	29.1	71.7	68.1	—	—
1890	150.5	201.5	133.5	141.0	91.5	156.6	60.0	28.0	84.8	88.8	19.2	16.1
1904	125.7	186.6	120.8	110.1	101.2	74.2	61.2	29.3	90.6	77.7	44.6	34.0
1910	117.0	169.5	115.3	96.1	105.7	76.1	54.7	33.1	80.0	72.5	14.0	24.8
1923	96.0	114.2	104.6	95.7	83.9	63.8	57.1	41.8	69.8	79.0	18.0	26.3

	Paupers enumerated per 100,000 population											
	West North Central		South Atlantic									
	Nebraska	Kansas	Total	Delaware	Maryland	District of Columbia	Virginia	West Virginia	North Carolina	South Carolina	Georgia	Florida
	Bf116	Bf117	Bf118	Bf119	Bf120	Bf121	Bf122	Bf123	Bf124	Bf125	Bf126	Bf127
Year	Per 100,000	Per 100,000	Per 100,000	Per 100,000	Per 100,000	Per 100,000	Per 100,000	Per 100,000	Per 100,000	Per 100,000	Per 100,000	Per 100,000
1880	25.0	35.6	91.8	264.0	127.0	103.6	140.0	115.0	91.1	52.1	35.7	16.7
1890	27.5	41.6	91.4	177.5	153.4	95.9	132.4	103.8	92.3	50.2	49.0	6.1
1904	41.7	50.3	74.9	145.5	138.1	77.3	99.3	83.6	75.7	48.9	43.7	20.3
1910	46.2	43.5	63.2	180.9	129.8	83.4	81.9	66.2	63.0	31.5	31.2	27.5
1923	43.3	54.7	47.6	121.3	91.8	71.5	51.0	46.0	55.6	26.1	29.4	20.2

TABLE Bf34–149 Paupers enumerated in almshouses, by region and state: 1880–1923 *Continued*

	Paupers enumerated per 100,000 population									
	East South Central					West South Central				
	Total	Kentucky	Tennessee	Alabama	Mississippi	Total	Arkansas	Louisiana	Oklahoma	Texas
	Bf128	Bf129	Bf130	Bf131	Bf132	Bf133	Bf134	Bf135	Bf136	Bf137
Year	Per 100,000	Per 100,000	Per 100,000	Per 100,000	Per 100,000	Per 100,000	Per 100,000	Per 100,000	Per 100,000	Per 100,000
1880	60.2	82.9	73.7	40.7	30.5	9.4	13.1	—	—	13.2
1890	66.0	84.9	87.4	41.2	88.3	17.8	19.8	10.9	—	20.8
1904	60.7	76.3	87.1	39.2	31.5	23.0	40.9	10.0	4.7	27.2
1910	50.7	66.5	71.8	34.6	24.3	18.6	33.9	11.3	2.9	22.1
1923	45.4	59.5	62.1	32.0	22.1	19.5	32.1	9.5	11.8	22.1

	Paupers enumerated per 100,000 population											
	Mountain								Pacific			
	Total	Montana	Idaho	Wyoming	Colorado	Arizona	Utah	Nevada	Total	Washington	Oregon	California
	Bf138	Bf139	Bf140	Bf141	Bf142	Bf143	Bf144	Bf145	Bf146	Bf147	Bf148	Bf149
Year	Per 100,000	Per 100,000	Per 100,000	Per 100,000	Per 100,000	Per 100,000	Per 100,000	Per 100,000	Per 100,000	Per 100,000	Per 100,000	Per 100,000
1880	23.3	—	21.5	—	23.7	9.9	—	152.6	148.6	14.6	29.2	184.3
1890	31.7	99.9	23.7	—	21.1	38.6	29.8	94.0	148.0	20.3	31.6	215.2
1904	63.4	107.7	31.6	—	62.8	95.8	59.0	301.7	153.6	41.1	50.6	228.9
1910	62.7	110.4	29.8	13	63.8	132.6	48.5	194.2	132.7	49.4	52.3	195.4
1923	50.6	54.6	42.0	30	68.4	56.0	40.1	178.3	109.3	54.5	71.4	138.5

[1] Enumeration date June 1 through 1890; January 1 thereafter.

Source

Paupers in Almshouses: 1923 (U.S. Government Printing Office, 1926), Table 4, p. 7. Notes for Table 4 appear in the report on pp. 1–5, 7.

Documentation

The data report the number of paupers in public almshouses only. The data do not report the number of paupers receiving relief in their own homes–those receiving "outdoor relief" – and they do not include the number of paupers residing in privately financed almshouses or asylums. Therefore, the data cannot be used as the only indicator of the extent of pauperism.

A great store of statistical data on indoor institutions – almshouses, poorhouses, workhouses, insane asylums, and houses of refuge – can be found in the annual reports of the (variously named) State Boards of Charities and Corrections, and in the county-level reports that comprise them. One may also find state and national information on the laws and practices of public assistance in the annual *Proceedings of the National Conference of Charities and Corrections*.

Although the word "pauper" slid away from American vocabularies for most of the twentieth century, the Bureau of the Census used the term during the first quarter of the twentieth century to categorize anyone who received public assistance. Prior to 1923, the Bureau of the Census took seven different censuses relating to paupers. A census of paupers was taken as a part of each decennial census from 1850 to 1880, while for 1904, 1910, and again for 1923, a special census of paupers in public almshouses was taken. The Bureau defined a public almshouse as an institution supported or controlled by town, municipal, county, or state authorities and used for the shelter of persons who are without means of self-support and who have no relatives able and willing or legally bound to aid them. The censuses of 1904, 1910, and 1923 included all public almshouses in the United States. The enumerations were made chiefly by officials of the institutions and covered not only the paupers who were inmates of almshouses on a given date but also those admitted in the course of one year and those who were discharged or transferred, or who died during one year.

No almshouse was maintained in New Mexico in the years covered by this table.

For a quantitative analysis of these pauper census data, see Stephen T. Ziliak, "Pauper Fiction in Economic Science: 'Paupers in Almshouses' and the Odd Fit of *Olive Twist*," *Review of Social Economy* 60 (2)(2002): 159–81. A quantitative analysis of poorhouses in New York State may be found in Joan Underhill Hannon, "Shutting Down Welfare: Two Cases from America's Past," *Quarterly Review of Economics and Finance* 37 (2) (1997): 419–38; Joan Underhill Hannon, "Poor Relief Policy in Antebellum New York State: The Rise and Decline of the Poorhouse," *Explorations in Economic History* 22 (1985): 233–56; and Joan Underhill Hannon, "Poverty and the Antebellum Northeast: The View from New York State's Poor Relief Rolls," *Journal of Economic History* 44 (4) (1984): 1007–32. For a general introduction to the history of the almshouse, see David J. Rothman, *The Discovery of the Asylum* (Little, Brown, 1971), and Michael B. Katz, *In the Shadow of the Poorhouse* (Basic Books, 1986).

TABLE Bf150–155 Paupers admitted to almshouses, by region and state: 1904–1922

Contributed by Stephen T. Ziliak

	Paupers admitted			Paupers per 100,000 population		
	1904	1910	1922	1904	1910	1922
	Bf150	Bf151	Bf152	Bf153	Bf154	Bf155
Region and state	Number	Number	Number	Per 100,000	Per 100,000	Per 100,000
United States	81,412	88,313	63,807	99.5	96.0	58.4
New England	12,990	14,716	10,036	218.7	224.6	131.7
Maine	828	860	839	116.3	115.8	108.3
New Hampshire	646	812	830	154.4	188.6	186.0
Vermont	231	269	215	66.4	75.6	61.0
Massachusetts	8,398	9,520	6,481	279.1	282.8	162.9
Rhode Island	551	526	419	117.2	96.9	67.5
Connecticut	2,336	2,729	1,252	237.6	244.8	86.4
Middle Atlantic	23,400	23,927	14,250	138.8	123.9	61.9
New York	12,073	12,724	6,043	152.1	139.6	56.4
New Jersey	1,589	1,736	1,116	74.9	68.4	33.7
Pennsylvania	9,738	9,467	7,093	143.3	123.5	78.9
East North Central	16,901	17,116	15,604	100.6	93.8	70.0
Ohio	7,091	5,825	4,150	161.9	122.2	69.0
Indiana	1,800	1,741	1,739	69.7	64.5	58.2
Illinois	4,446	5,590	5,949	86.9	99.1	88.7
Michigan	2,476	2,783	2,944	96.5	99.0	75.7
Wisconsin	1,092	1,177	822	50.4	50.4	30.3
West North Central	3,578	4,585	4,137	33.1	39.4	32.4
Minnesota	517	815	563	27.7	39.3	22.8
Iowa	896	823	766	40.2	37.0	31.3
Missouri	1,123	1,151	1,124	35.4	34.9	32.7
North Dakota	163	114	86	39.5	19.8	12.9
South Dakota	150	160	138	32.1	27.4	21.2
Nebraska	174	1,101	1,009	15.6	92.3	76.3
Kansas	555	421	451	35.8	24.9	25.2
South Atlantic	7,227	7,945	6,396	65.2	65.2	44.3
Delaware	183	430	283	95.8	212.5	123.9
Maryland	1,617	1,949	1,845	131.8	150.5	123.9
District of Columbia	148	171	155	49.7	51.7	35.4
Virginia	2,159	2,404	1,211	111.9	116.6	51.0
West Virginia	719	531	495	68.2	43.5	32.4
North Carolina	863	728	801	43.0	33.0	30.2
South Carolina	432	285	254	30.8	18.8	14.7
Georgia	726	514	511	30.8	19.7	17.2
Florida	380	933	841	62.3	124.0	82.1
East South Central	3,448	3,086	2,128	43.9	36.7	23.6
Kentucky	1,013	1,133	666	46.1	49.5	27.2
Tennessee	1,460	1,227	785	70.2	56.2	33.0
Alabama	748	481	520	38.5	22.5	21.6
Mississippi	227	245	157	13.8	13.6	8.8
West South Central	2,045	2,068	1,723	27.8	23.5	16.2
Arkansas	982	849	728	69.8	53.9	40.5
Louisiana	75	112	50	5.1	6.8	2.7
Oklahoma	87	61	229	7.9	3.7	10.8
Texas	901	1,046	716	26.8	26.8	14.7
Mountain	2,528	3,505	2,375	125.0	133.1	67.5
Montana	759	926	473	260.4	246.2	79.9
Idaho	168	177	148	75.9	54.4	32.2
Wyoming	—	53	44	—	36.3	21.3
Colorado	694	697	905	109.5	87.2	92.7
Arizona	436	1,015	527	285.9	496.7	143.4
Utah	124	181	111	39.8	48.5	23.7
Nevada	347	456	167	612.2	556.9	215.7
Pacific	9,295	11,365	7,158	303.7	271.1	120.9
Washington	420	1,247	566	56.4	109.2	40.1
Oregon	545	504	465	107.4	74.9	57.3
California	8,330	9,614	6,127	460.5	404.4	165.7

Source

Paupers in Almshouses: 1923 (U.S. Government Printing Office, 1926), Table 5, p. 8. Notes: pp. 1–5, 8.

Documentation

See the text for Table Bf34–149.

No almshouse was maintained in New Mexico in the years covered by this table, nor in Wyoming in 1904.

TABLE Bf156–175 Local public poor relief expenditures and the value of pauper labor in New York State and New York City, by type of relief: 1840–1895

Contributed by Joan Underhill Hannon

	New York State						New York City					
	Local public expenditures						Local public expenditures					
	Public relief – including or excluding poorhouse repairs and improvements			Connected with county and city poorhouses – including or excluding poorhouse repairs and improvements		Value of pauper labor in city and county poorhouses	Public relief – including or excluding poorhouse repairs and improvements			Connected with city poorhouse – including or excluding poorhouse repairs and improvements		Value of pauper labor in city poorhouse
	Including	Excluding	Temporary outdoor relief	Including	Excluding		Including	Excluding	Temporary outdoor relief	Including	Excluding	
	Bf156	Bf157	Bf158	Bf159	Bf160	Bf161	Bf162	Bf163	Bf164	Bf165	Bf166	Bf167
Year	Dollars	Dollars	Dollars	Dollars	Dollars	Dollars	Dollars	Dollars	Dollars	Dollars	Dollars	Dollars
1840	—	493,596	146,315	—	347,281	—	—	188,683	28,019	—	160,664	—
1841	—	508,214	150,205	—	358,009	55,211	—	195,997	24,060	—	171,937	27,551
1842	—	485,793	163,128	—	322,665	32,611	—	170,188	26,894	—	143,294	2,979
1843	—	558,741	240,205	—	318,536	58,895	—	192,908	55,748	—	137,160	26,983
1844	—	537,932	214,268	—	323,664	37,754	—	205,143	50,859	—	154,284	6,000
1846	—	538,133	225,131	—	313,002	—	—	205,604	65,134	—	140,470	—
1847	—	674,843	257,662	—	417,181	—	—	312,113	96,019	—	216,094	—
1848	—	—	—	—	—	—	—	—	—	—	—	—
1849	—	797,985	331,328	—	466,657	—	—	308,508	91,074	—	217,434	—
1850	—	691,064	295,730	—	395,334	—	—	231,986	76,255	—	155,731	—
1851	—	786,755	340,358	—	446,397	—	—	264,329	71,904	—	192,425	—
1852	—	939,731	409,814	—	529,917	—	—	304,465	91,189	—	213,276	—
1853	—	930,974	345,765	—	585,209	—	—	296,286	82,136	—	214,150	—
1854	—	1,057,923	380,100	—	677,823	—	—	346,828	83,705	—	263,123	—
1855	—	1,316,048	504,484	—	811,564	—	—	444,925	121,861	—	323,064	—
1856	—	1,315,805	455,812	—	859,993	—	—	442,509	95,522	—	346,987	—
1857	—	1,218,034	443,383	—	774,651	—	—	428,457	108,756	—	319,701	—
1858	—	1,425,269	625,002	—	800,267	—	—	490,883	139,731	—	351,152	—
1859	—	1,297,699	586,511	—	711,188	—	—	436,434	111,702	—	324,732	—
1860	—	1,286,701	524,551	—	762,150	—	—	474,529	88,833	—	385,696	—
1861	—	1,284,032	485,189	—	798,843	—	—	463,930	69,162	—	394,768	—
1862	—	1,187,152	475,687	—	711,465	—	—	404,431	94,718	—	309,713	—
1863	—	1,382,044	551,711	—	830,333	—	—	439,056	83,751	—	355,305	—
1864	—	1,803,757	682,086	—	1,121,671	—	—	497,556	99,630	—	397,926	—
1865	—	2,252,606	761,087	—	1,491,519	—	—	741,568	104,803	—	636,765	—
1866	—	2,205,268	740,727	—	1,464,541	—	—	701,279	90,529	—	610,750	—
1867	—	2,306,709	759,840	—	1,546,869	—	—	669,555	70,441	—	599,114	—
1868	—	2,472,286	888,874	—	1,583,412	—	—	777,479	135,858	—	641,621	—
1869	—	2,326,951	866,583	—	1,460,368	—	—	717,219	128,385	—	588,834	—
1870	2,625,349	2,415,785	916,809	1,708,540	1,498,976	—	814,463	740,551	126,360	688,103	614,191	—
1871	2,337,853	2,180,068	716,487	1,621,366	1,463,581	—	814,719	752,104	123,732	690,987	628,372	—
1872	2,266,649	2,163,015	747,159	1,519,490	1,415,856	—	823,021	772,735	104,051	718,970	668,684	—
1873	2,580,806	2,503,373	841,958	1,738,848	1,661,415	—	877,649	828,689	104,165	773,484	724,524	—
1874	2,648,146	2,525,039	1,021,946	1,626,200	1,503,093	—	790,103	777,283	102,102	688,001	675,181	—
1875	2,643,908	2,502,904	944,671	1,699,237	1,558,233	—	833,363	756,396	95,521	737,842	660,875	—
1876	2,563,607	2,499,267	931,877	1,631,730	1,567,390	—	786,877	759,253	74,395	712,482	684,858	—
1877	2,737,795	2,643,362	1,095,231	1,642,564	1,548,131	—	799,425	771,545	83,248	716,177	688,297	—
1878	2,519,429	2,414,610	938,450	1,580,979	1,476,160	—	755,705	732,515	59,430	696,275	673,085	—
1879	2,403,342	2,312,033	788,766	1,614,576	1,523,267	—	827,537	801,775	59,909	767,628	741,866	—
1880	2,301,816	1,958,742	743,258	1,558,558	1,215,484	—	854,305	841,993	58,701	795,604	783,292	—
1881	—	—	—	—	—	—	—	—	—	—	—	—
1882	—	—	—	—	—	—	—	—	—	—	—	—
1883	2,659,290	2,538,165	636,917	2,022,373	1,901,248	—	1,070,320	1,010,270	57,488	1,012,832	952,782	—
1884	2,568,653	2,460,920	651,305	1,917,348	1,809,615	—	949,304	910,364	38,995	910,309	871,369	—
1885	2,644,120	2,543,007	732,514	1,911,606	1,810,493	—	930,833	894,038	63,100	867,733	830,938	—
1886	2,946,429	2,832,239	811,687	2,134,742	2,020,552	—	1,175,382	1,118,882	74,699	1,100,683	1,044,183	—
1887	2,909,244	2,849,956	734,071	2,175,173	2,115,885	—	1,164,713	1,164,713	69,365	1,095,348	1,095,348	—
1888	3,797,968	3,731,889	756,010	3,041,958	2,975,879	—	1,898,611	1,898,611	62,030	1,836,581	1,836,581	—
1889	3,801,615	3,432,340	742,389	3,059,226	2,689,951	—	1,802,663	1,502,432	61,975	1,740,688	1,440,457	—
1890	3,036,717	2,898,174	710,886	2,325,831	2,187,288	—	1,635,127	1,537,027	40,000	1,595,127	1,497,027	—
1891	3,627,996	3,368,216	710,476	2,917,520	2,657,740	—	1,571,390	1,396,663	39,940	1,531,450	1,356,723	—
1892	3,147,063	3,045,502	663,369	2,483,694	2,382,133	—	1,121,724	1,094,474	40,000	1,081,724	1,054,474	—
1893	3,857,476	3,657,874	671,698	3,185,778	2,986,176	—	1,790,188	1,760,488	40,000	1,750,188	1,720,488	—
1894	3,939,240	3,784,940	758,488	3,180,752	3,026,452	—	1,828,102	1,805,957	82,500	1,745,602	1,723,457	—
1895	3,839,829	3,739,783	743,654	3,096,175	2,996,129	—	1,814,875	1,794,675	60,000	1,754,875	1,734,675	—

(continued)

TABLE Bf156–175 Local public poor relief expenditures and the value of pauper labor in New York State and New York City, by type of relief: 1840–1895 *Continued*

	New York State, excluding New York City						Population of counties covered by public poor relief data	
	Local public expenditures							
	Public relief – including or excluding poorhouse repairs and improvements			Connected with county and city poorhouses – including or excluding poorhouse repairs and improvements				
	Including	Excluding	Temporary outdoor relief	Including	Excluding	Value of pauper labor in city and county poorhouses	New York State	New York State, excluding New York City
	Bf168	Bf169	Bf170	Bf171	Bf172	Bf173	Bf174	Bf175
Year	Dollars	Dollars	Dollars	Dollars	Dollars	Dollars	Number	Number
1840	—	304,913	118,296	—	186,617	28,500	2,210,040	1,897,330
1841	—	312,217	126,145	—	186,072	27,660	2,264,902	1,941,278
1842	—	315,605	136,234	—	179,371	29,632	2,284,270	1,949,352
1843	—	365,833	184,457	—	181,376	31,912	2,375,145	2,028,538
1844	—	332,789	163,409	—	169,380	31,754	2,256,578	1,897,874
1846	—	332,529	159,997	—	172,532	35,075	2,552,473	2,156,048
1847	—	362,730	161,643	—	201,087	25,951	2,672,359	2,249,020
1848	—	360,124	177,103	—	183,021	32,046	—	2,027,248
1849	—	489,477	240,254	—	249,223	31,155	2,837,114	2,354,345
1850	—	459,078	219,475	—	239,603	36,277	2,764,045	2,248,498
1851	—	522,426	268,454	—	253,972	32,590	2,777,283	2,240,660
1852	—	635,266	318,625	—	316,641	39,272	2,900,492	2,341,931
1853	—	634,688	263,629	—	371,059	30,115	2,781,408	2,200,012
1854	—	711,095	296,395	—	414,700	26,647	2,920,427	2,315,263
1855	—	871,123	382,623	—	488,500	24,382	3,056,005	2,426,101
1856	—	873,296	360,290	—	513,006	27,305	3,142,345	2,479,352
1857	—	789,577	334,627	—	454,950	22,920	2,966,809	2,268,988
1858	—	934,386	485,271	—	449,115	24,953	3,283,127	2,548,650
1859	—	861,265	474,809	—	386,456	28,223	3,418,462	2,645,402
1860	—	812,172	435,718	—	376,454	38,448	3,313,667	2,499,998
1861	—	820,102	416,027	—	404,075	23,766	3,283,893	2,488,482
1862	—	782,721	380,969	—	401,752	26,667	3,175,676	2,398,113
1863	—	942,988	467,960	—	475,028	40,264	3,323,461	2,563,346
1864	—	1,306,201	582,456	—	723,745	33,170	3,469,725	2,726,666
1865	—	1,511,038	656,284	—	854,754	27,495	3,424,714	2,698,328
1866	—	1,503,989	650,198	—	853,791	29,105	3,358,869	2,593,676
1867	—	1,637,154	689,399	—	947,755	31,555	3,698,820	2,892,746
1868	—	1,694,807	753,016	—	941,791	36,041	3,578,741	2,729,603
1869	—	1,609,732	738,198	—	871,534	25,849	3,666,146	2,771,643
1870	1,810,886	1,675,235	790,449	1,020,437	884,786	32,537	3,978,362	3,036,070
1871	1,523,134	1,427,963	592,755	930,379	835,208	27,526	3,841,832	2,880,414
1872	1,443,628	1,390,280	643,108	800,520	747,172	30,247	3,861,122	2,880,189
1873	1,703,157	1,674,684	737,793	965,364	936,891	33,255	4,216,052	3,215,209
1874	1,858,043	1,747,757	919,844	938,199	827,913	37,345	4,086,236	3,065,077
1875	1,810,545	1,746,508	849,150	961,395	897,358	32,537	4,336,503	3,294,617
1876	1,776,730	1,740,014	857,482	919,248	882,532	27,526	4,525,032	3,452,162
1877	1,938,370	1,871,817	1,011,983	926,387	859,834	30,247	4,479,337	3,374,601
1878	1,763,724	1,682,095	879,020	884,704	803,075	33,255	4,584,337	3,446,707
1879	1,575,805	1,510,257	728,857	846,948	781,400	37,345	4,617,888	3,446,427
1880	1,447,511	1,116,749	684,557	762,954	432,192	73,622	4,413,530	3,207,231
1881	1,208,520	1,088,071	669,639	538,881	418,432	42,410	2,634,505	2,634,505
1882	1,259,676	1,214,267	609,479	650,197	604,788	34,507	2,951,550	2,951,550
1883	1,588,970	1,527,895	579,429	1,009,541	948,466	63,106	6,495,255	5,203,536
1884	1,619,349	1,550,556	612,310	1,007,039	938,246	73,934	4,888,560	3,567,044
1885	1,713,287	1,648,970	669,414	1,043,873	979,556	85,462	4,992,472	3,640,471
1886	1,771,047	1,713,357	736,988	1,034,059	976,369	86,460	5,049,364	3,666,176
1887	1,744,531	1,685,243	664,706	1,079,825	1,020,537	101,928	5,273,216	3,858,121
1888	1,899,357	1,833,278	693,980	1,205,377	1,139,298	97,557	5,477,201	4,029,463
1889	1,998,952	1,929,908	680,414	1,318,538	1,249,494	98,822	5,526,731	4,045,596
1890	1,401,590	1,361,147	670,886	730,704	690,261	66,987	4,799,547	3,284,246
1891	2,056,606	1,971,553	670,536	1,386,070	1,301,017	93,603	5,515,215	3,953,373
1892	2,025,339	1,951,028	623,369	1,401,970	1,327,659	124,636	5,674,781	4,064,968
1893	2,067,288	1,897,386	631,698	1,435,590	1,265,688	80,255	5,791,579	4,132,323
1894	2,111,138	1,978,983	675,988	1,435,150	1,302,995	104,187	5,951,105	4,240,886
1895	2,024,954	1,945,108	683,654	1,341,300	1,261,454	97,535	5,883,048	4,120,301

TABLE Bf156–175 Local public poor relief expenditures and the value of pauper labor in New York State and New York City, by type of relief: 1840–1895 *Continued*

Sources

Previously unpublished data compiled from the following sources: New York Secretary of State, *Annual Reports of the Secretary of State in Relation to the Statistics of the Poor, 1831–1896,* in New York State Legislature, Assembly, *Assembly Documents 1831*, volume 1, number 66; *1832*, volume 1, number 33; *1833*, volume 2, number 38; *1834*, volume 3, number 173; *1835*, volume 3, number 185; *1836*, volume 2, number 72; *1837*, volume 3, number 270; *1838*, volume 6, number 311; *1839*, volume 3, number 146; *1840*, volume 8, number 332; *1841*, volume 7, number 227; *1842*, volume 5, number 121; *1843*, volume 2, number 38; *1845*, volume 5, number 197; *1850*, volume 6, number 169; *1851*, volume 5, number 147; *1853*, volume 6, number 120; *1854*, volume 4, number 144; *1856*, volume 5, number 214; *1858*, volume 1, number 10; *1859*, volume 3, number 101; *1860*, volume 2, number 71; *1861*, volume 2, number 60; *1863*, volume 8, number 230; *1864*, volume 8, number 198; *1865*, volume 7, number 147; *1866*, volume 7, number 165; *1867*, volume 7, number 145; *1868*, volume 9, number 88; *1869*, volume 6, number 79; *1870*, volume 6, number 124; *1871*, volume 3, number 46; *1872*, volume 3, number 48; *1873*, volume 3, number 32; *1877*, volume 9, number 142; *1880*, volume 3, number 62; *1881*, volume 4, number 64; *1882*, volume 2, number 34; *1884*, volume 5, number 59; *1885*, volume 5, number 45; *1886*, volume 3, number 45; *1887*, volume 7, number 46; *1890*, volume 10, number 58; *1891*, volume 12, number 60; *1892*, volume 6, number 43; *1893*, volume 10, number 58; *1894*, volume 10, number 72; *1895*, volume 13, number 74; *1896*, volume 18, number 84; and New York State Legislature, Senate, *Senate Documents, 1844*, volume 2, number 73; *1847*, volume 3, number 100; *1848*, volume 3, number 79; *1849*, volume 3, number 83; *1855*, volume 3, number 72; *1857*, volume 4, number 131; *1862*, volume 4, number 65; *1874*, volume 4, number 62; *1875*, volume 4, number 52; *1876*, volume 3, number 46; *1878*, volume 2, number 28; *1879*, volume 2, number 34; *1883*, volume 2, number 25; *1888*, volume 5, number 44; and *1889*, volume 6, number 40.

Documentation

See the essay in this chapter on public assistance, colonial times to the 1920s, for additional information on public relief in New York.

Five-year averages of real public relief expenditures per recipient and per capita appear in Joan Underhill Hannon, "Shutting Down Welfare: Two Cases from America's Past," *Quarterly Review of Economics and Finance* 37 (2) (1997): 419–38. Data reported here reflect minor revisions and corrections to the real relief expenditures per capita and per recipient and the poorhouse expenditures as a share of total reported as five-year averages by region for the period 1835–1859 in Joan Underhill Hannon, "Poor Relief Policy in Antebellum New York State: The Rise and Decline of the Poorhouse," *Explorations in Economic History* 22 (Academic Press, 1985), pp. 233–56, and in Joan Underhill Hannon, "The Generosity of Antebellum Poor Relief," *Journal of Economic History* 44 (3) (1984): 810–21.

Over the second half of the nineteenth century, state law gradually transferred some categories of relief recipients out of the system covered by the series on local relief expenditures. Most significantly, an 1865 act required the removal of insane paupers from poorhouses to state asylums, and an 1875 act mandated the removal of children from poorhouses to orphanages or other charitable institutions. Though local governments paid for the support of the insane and children in these institutions, these expenditures are not included in the data on local public relief expenditures, series Bf156–173. Some evidence on their magnitude is reported in Hannon (1997).

Tables B and C in each *Annual Report* from 1840 to 1895 provide the data on expenses connected with county poorhouses and expenses of administering temporary relief in total and for various subcomponents by county and for the whole state. The reported state totals are not used here for several reasons. First, each year some counties failed to report on some or all expenditure categories; the published state totals simply treat such missing data as zeros. Second, to have series on expenditures that cover the same counties each year as the data on recipients, series Bf176–187, counties that failed to report or reported internally inconsistent data on recipients were eliminated. The public relief expenditure data, series Bf156–173, and the public relief recipient data, series Bf176–187, cover the same set of counties for which consistent and complete data were available in any given year, but the included counties vary slightly from year to year. In no year do the covered counties represent less than 80 percent of the state's non–New York City population; but year-to-year fluctuations in the level of expenditures may reflect changes in county coverage, and per capita figures should not be calculated using total state population in the denominator. For this purpose, series Bf174–175 provide the population of counties covered by public poor relief data for New York State and for the state excluding New York City, assuming constant exponential population growth in each county between census years.

Prior to 1870, the reported subcomponents of poorhouse expenditures are payments to superintendents of the poor, payments to keepers and poorhouse officers, payments to constables and other officers, payments for supplies for the county poorhouse, payments for transportation of paupers, payments to physicians for attendance and medicine, and miscellaneous expenses connected with the poorhouse. The total of these components is included in the series on poorhouse expenditures excluding repairs and improvements of buildings and grounds, series Bf160, Bf166, and Bf172. In 1870, an additional category, expenditures for repairs and improvements of buildings and grounds, appears, providing the basis for the series on poorhouse expenditures including repairs and improvements of buildings and grounds, series Bf159, Bf165, and Bf171.

Series including or excluding poorhouse repairs and improvements refer to expenditures for both poorhouse buildings and grounds.

Series Bf156–157, Bf162–163, and Bf168–169. The series on total expenditures including and excluding repairs and improvements are the sum of the poorhouse and temporary outdoor relief columns. The data on expenditure subcomponents are used to divide both poorhouse and outdoor relief expenditures between administrative and direct relief costs in Hannon (1997).

Series Bf158 and Bf164–165. The subcomponents included in the series on expenditures for temporary outdoor relief are payments to overseers of the poor for their services, payments to justices of the peace for their services, and payments for relieving indigent persons temporarily not included in the two foregoing.

Series Bf161, Bf167, and Bf173. Many county poorhouses maintained farms on which residents worked. Pauper labor was also used in the daily operations of the poorhouse; and picking oakum, breaking stones, or chopping wood were common winter tasks. The series on the value of pauper labor in the poorhouse are from Table D of each year's *Annual Report on Statistics of the Poor.*

TABLE Bf176–187 Local public relief recipients in New York State and New York City, by type of relief: 1840–1895

Contributed by Joan Underhill Hannon

	New York State			New York City				New York State, excluding New York City			Population of counties covered by public poor relief data	
	Persons relieved or supported	Persons receiving temporary outdoor relief	Persons supported in county and city poorhouses	Persons relieved or supported	Persons receiving temporary outdoor relief	Families receiving temporary outdoor relief	Persons supported in city poorhouse	Persons relieved or supported	Persons receiving temporary outdoor relief	Persons supported in county and city poorhouses	New York State	New York State, excluding New York City
	Bf176	Bf177	Bf178	Bf179	Bf180	Bf181	Bf182	Bf183	Bf184	Bf185	Bf186	Bf187
Year	Number	Number	Number	Number	Number	Number	Number	Number	Number	Number	Number	Number
1840	57,935	36,843	21,092	27,553	19,690	—	7,863	30,382	17,153	13,229	2,210,040	1,897,330
1841	62,230	41,679	20,551	28,221	20,461	—	7,760	34,009	21,218	12,791	2,264,902	1,941,278
1842	60,314	39,745	20,569	29,951	21,960	—	7,991	30,363	17,785	12,578	2,284,270	1,949,352
1843	84,667	62,512	22,155	40,765	32,777	—	7,988	43,902	29,735	14,167	2,375,145	2,028,538
1844	99,582	78,546	21,036	61,163	52,920	—	8,243	38,419	25,626	12,793	2,256,578	1,897,874
1846	99,432	73,047	26,385	58,049	45,272	—	12,777	41,383	27,775	13,608	2,552,473	2,156,048
1847	105,525	74,486	31,039	54,647	40,000	—	14,647	50,878	34,486	16,392	2,672,359	2,249,020
1848	—	—	—	—	—	—	—	54,291	39,179	15,112	—	2,027,248
1849	101,201	66,408	34,793	31,770	18,066	—	13,704	69,431	48,342	21,089	2,837,114	2,354,345
1850	114,840	84,089	30,751	50,251	38,054	—	12,197	64,589	46,035	18,554	2,764,045	2,248,498
1851	122,505	87,855	34,650	56,526	41,140	—	15,386	65,979	46,715	19,264	2,777,283	2,240,660
1852	153,466	113,265	40,201	61,416	46,634	—	14,782	92,050	66,631	25,419	2,900,492	2,341,931
1853	128,831	94,798	34,033	55,823	41,622	—	14,201	73,008	53,176	19,832	2,781,408	2,200,012
1854	135,979	97,613	38,366	58,183	42,136	—	16,047	77,796	55,477	22,319	2,920,427	2,315,263
1855	198,600	160,571	38,029	101,166	85,136	—	16,030	97,434	75,435	21,999	3,056,005	2,426,101
1856	177,766	142,177	35,589	91,225	75,861	—	15,364	86,541	66,316	20,225	3,142,345	2,479,352
1857	171,794	136,035	35,759	91,660	73,811	—	17,849	80,134	62,224	17,910	2,966,809	2,268,988
1858	258,263	214,633	43,630	130,213	110,822	—	19,391	128,050	103,811	24,239	3,283,127	2,548,650
1859	228,456	184,874	43,582	107,872	87,850	—	20,022	120,584	97,024	23,560	3,418,462	2,645,402
1860	218,459	175,587	42,872	112,625	91,543	—	21,082	105,834	84,044	21,790	3,313,667	2,499,998
1861	308,912	267,389	41,523	208,050	189,433	—	18,617	100,862	77,956	22,906	3,283,893	2,488,482
1862	251,129	218,340	32,789	152,703	138,270	—	14,433	98,426	80,070	18,356	3,175,676	2,398,113
1863	259,079	221,186	37,893	159,453	143,618	—	15,835	99,626	77,568	22,058	3,323,461	2,563,346
1864	267,296	227,500	39,796	161,224	143,938	—	17,286	106,072	83,562	22,510	3,469,725	2,726,666
1865	277,749	228,269	49,480	169,963	143,758	—	26,205	107,786	84,511	23,275	3,424,714	2,698,328
1866	267,938	219,581	48,357	161,220	135,629	—	25,591	106,655	83,889	22,766	3,358,869	2,593,676
1867	261,982	212,440	49,542	156,924	133,660	—	23,264	105,058	78,780	26,278	3,698,820	2,892,746
1868	360,524	310,521	50,003	247,996	222,764	—	25,232	112,528	87,757	24,771	3,578,741	2,729,603
1869	—	—	49,543	—	—	19,616	26,552	147,727	124,736	22,991	3,666,146	2,771,643
1870	—	—	56,671	—	—	5,834	29,761	124,366	97,456	26,910	3,978,362	3,036,070
1871	—	—	56,462	—	—	4,970	30,288	80,929	54,755	26,174	3,841,832	2,880,414
1872	—	—	55,554	—	—	8,429	31,805	95,219	71,470	23,749	3,861,122	2,880,189
1873	—	—	58,893	—	—	9,263	31,880	98,307	71,294	27,013	4,216,052	3,215,209
1874	—	—	66,753	—	—	11,511	33,326	146,410	112,983	33,427	4,086,236	3,065,077
1875	—	—	63,346	—	—	27,153	27,846	175,856	140,356	35,500	4,336,503	3,294,617
1876	—	—	60,679	—	—	6,431	27,094	182,019	148,434	33,585	4,525,032	3,452,162
1877	—	—	62,259	—	—	15,391	28,802	207,568	174,111	33,457	4,479,337	3,374,601
1878	—	—	61,370	—	—	13,519	30,365	185,736	154,731	31,005	4,584,337	3,446,707
1879	—	—	57,897	—	—	15,101	31,102	107,867	81,072	26,795	4,617,888	3,446,427
1880	—	—	54,881	—	—	13,749	30,947	92,347	68,813	23,534	4,413,530	3,207,231
1881	—	—	14,122	—	—	—	—	71,917	57,795	14,122	2,634,505	2,634,505
1882	—	—	13,789	—	—	—	—	64,866	51,077	13,789	2,951,550	2,951,550
1883	—	—	63,531	—	—	9,215	38,771	80,744	55,984	24,760	6,495,255	5,203,536
1884	—	—	65,706	—	—	7,851	40,744	73,885	48,923	24,962	4,888,560	3,567,044
1885	—	—	67,606	—	—	8,890	39,928	81,626	53,948	27,678	4,992,472	3,640,471
1886	—	—	65,577	—	—	8,093	38,972	73,897	47,292	26,605	5,049,364	3,666,176
1887	—	—	67,639	—	—	5,172	40,938	71,716	45,015	26,701	5,273,216	3,858,121
1888	—	—	70,260	—	—	7,607	42,664	77,100	49,504	27,596	5,477,201	4,029,463
1889	—	—	75,800	—	—	7,687	48,921	80,272	53,393	26,879	5,526,731	4,045,596
1890	169,011	103,283	65,728	98,102	49,195	6,597	48,907	70,909	54,088	16,821	4,799,547	3,284,246
1891	208,018	131,768	76,250	124,393	74,458	8,471	49,935	83,625	57,310	26,315	5,515,215	3,953,373
1892	213,359	134,493	78,866	132,832	79,099	8,746	53,733	80,527	55,394	25,133	5,674,781	4,064,968
1893	206,452	121,148	85,304	126,252	67,806	7,138	58,446	80,200	53,342	26,858	5,791,579	4,132,323
1894	191,253	102,615	88,638	76,683	21,153	—	55,530	114,570	81,462	33,108	5,951,105	4,240,886
1895	206,324	135,966	70,358	95,237	56,302	—	38,935	111,087	79,664	31,423	5,883,048	4,120,301

TABLE Bf176–187 Local public relief recipients in New York State and New York City, by type of relief: 1840–1895 *Continued*

Source

Previously unpublished data compiled from the following sources: New York Secretary of State *Annual Reports of the Secretary of State In Relation to the Statistics of the Poor, 1831–1896,* in New York State Legislature, Assembly, *Assembly Documents 1831*, volume 1, number 66; *1832*, volume 1, number 33; *1833*, volume 2, number 38; *1834,* volume 3, number 173; *1835*, volume 3, number 185; *1836*, volume 2, number 72; *1837*, volume 3, number 270; *1838,* volume 6, number 311; *1839,* volume 3, number 146; *1840,* volume 8, number 332; *1841,* volume 7, number 227; *1842*, volume 5, number 121; *1843*, volume 2, number 38; *1845,* volume 5, number 197; *1850*, volume 6, number 169; *1851*, volume 5, number 147; *1853,* volume 6, number 120; *1854*, volume 4, number 144; *1856,* volume 5, number 214; *1858,* volume 1, number 10; *1859,* volume 3, number 101; *1860,* volume 2, number 71; *1861*, volume 2, number 60; *1863*, volume 8, number 230; *1864,* volume 8, number 198; *1865*, volume 7, number 147; *1866,* volume 7, number 165; *1867,* volume 7, number 145; *1868*, volume 9, number 88; *1869*, volume 6, number 79; *1870*, volume 6, number 124; *1871*, volume 3, number 46; *1872*, volume 3, number 48; *1873*, volume 3, number 32; *1877,* volume 9, number 142; *1880,* volume 3, number 62; *1881,* volume 4, number 64; *1882,* volume 2, number 34; *1884*, volume 5, number 59; *1885,* volume 5, number 45; *1886,* volume 3, number 45; *1887*, volume 7, number 46; *1890*, volume 10, number 58; *1891,* volume 12, number 60; *1892,* volume 6, number 43; *1893,* volume 10, number 58; *1894,* volume 10, number 72; *1895,* volume 13, number 74; *1896*, volume 18, number 84; and New York State Legislature, Senate, *Senate Documents, 1844,* volume 2, number 73; *1847*, volume 3, number 100; *1848*, volume 3, number 79; *1849,* volume 3, number 83; *1855,* volume 3, number 72; *1857,* volume 4, number 131; *1862,* volume 4, number 65; *1874,* volume 4, number 62; *1875,* volume 4, number 52; *1876,* volume 3, number 46; *1878,* volume 2, number 28; *1879,* volume 2, number 34; *1883,* volume 2, number 25; *1888*, volume 5, number 44; and *1889,* volume 6, number 40, and from New York State Board of Charities, *Annual Reports, 1875–1897*.

Documentation

See the essay in this chapter on public assistance, colonial times to the 1920s, for additional information on public relief in New York.

Five-year averages of relief recipients as a percentage of the population and of the fraction of all recipients supported in the poorhouse appear in Joan Underhill Hannon, "Shutting Down Welfare: Two Cases from America's Past," *Quarterly Review of Economics and Finance* 37 (2) (1997): 419–38. Relief recipient data reported here reflect minor corrections and revisions to that reported for 1835–1860 in Joan Underhill Hannon, "Poverty in the Antebellum Northeast: The View from New York State's Poor Relief Rolls," *Journal of Economic History* 44 (4) (1984): 1007–32, and Joan Underhill Hannon, "Poor Relief Policy in Antebellum New York State: The Rise and Decline of the Poorhouse," *Explorations in Economic History* (Academic Press, 1984), Tables 1 and 5.

Over the second half of the nineteenth century, state law gradually transferred some categories of relief recipients out of the system of local outdoor and poorhouse relief. Most significantly, an 1865 act required the removal of insane paupers from poorhouses to state asylums, and an 1875 act mandated the removal of children from poorhouses to orphanages or other charitable institutions. Though local governments paid for the support of the insane and children in these institutions, the recipients are not included in the data on local public relief recipients, series Bf176–185. Estimates of the number of recipients involved are reported in Joan Underhill Hannon, "Public Relief Dependency before the Welfare State: The Interplay of Life Cycles, Labor Markets, and Policy in Nineteenth Century New York State" (unpublished manuscript presented to the American Economic Association, January 1997), Figure 2.

The relief recipient data are constructed from two tables in the New York Secretary of State's *Annual Reports on Statistics of the Poor.* Table A reports by county the whole number of paupers relieved or supported and the number of persons temporarily relieved during the year ended December 1 of each year. Table E reports by county the number of persons received into and born in the poorhouse and the number who left the poorhouse (died, bound out, discharged, or absconded) during the year, along with the number remaining in the poorhouse on December 1. Unfortunately, some counties failed to provide information in some categories; and in deriving state totals, the published reports did not distinguish between zeros and missing data. Moreover, individual county reports on the number of recipients are often internally inconsistent.

The reports offer three logical ways to calculate the number supported in the poorhouse during the year. First, one can subtract the number temporarily relieved outdoors from the total relieved and supported. Second, one can add the number in the poorhouse at the end of the previous year to the number received and born in the poorhouse during the year. Third, one can take the sum of those reported leaving the poorhouse during the year and those remaining in the poorhouse at year-end. The three methods often yielded different results. Sometimes the reason for the discrepancy was readily apparent. Quite often, for example, it was clear that a county had included those already in the poorhouse at the end of the previous year in the number for those received during the year, producing by method 2 a figure that was too high by exactly the number in the house at the end of the previous year. If the source of the discrepancy could not be identified and corrected, the figures reported for number of persons supported in county and city poorhouses during the year (series Bf178, Bf182, and Bf185) for the period from 1840 to 1875 are based on the following procedure: If the differences between the three estimates were small (on the order of less than 5 percentage points), the middle figure was used. If the unexplained discrepancy was large, the data for that county were not used for that year.

Beginning in 1875, all issues of *Annual Reports of the New York State Board of Charities* include data on local public relief. Though the State Board of Charities worked with the same county superintendents' annual reports to the Secretary of State, the Board of Charities did not simply replicate the tables from the Secretary of State's *Annual Reports*. Instead, the Board of Charities calculated the number of poorhouse recipients according to the second procedure described earlier (the sum of the number in the poorhouse at the end of the previous years, and those received and those born in the poorhouse during the year). They added the resulting figure to the number temporarily relieved outdoors to get the total number relieved and supported. The figures reported by the State Board of Charities are always internally consistent but do not always match those reported by the Secretary of State. Often, notes to the tables indicate that the Board of Charities returned a report to the county superintendent for correction or clarification. For the period 1875–1895, the three methods outlined here were used to derive estimates of the number supported in the poorhouse from the *Annual Reports of the Secretary of State* and those were compared with the figure reported by the State Board of Charities. If one of the estimates matched that of the Board of Charities or if the differences between them were small, the figure from the Board of Charities was used. If there were large inexplicable discrepancies, the data for that county were not used for that year.

Series Bf176, Bf179, and Bf183. Calculated as the sum of the series on persons receiving temporary outdoor relief and those supported in the poorhouse. The series include only those counties for which both poorhouse and temporary outdoor recipient data are available. Though the counties included in the data set are the same for all series in a given year, included counties vary from year to year. As a result, the raw data may not accurately reflect year-to-year fluctuations in the total number of recipients; and per capita figures should not be calculated using total state population in the denominator. For this purpose, series Bf186–187 provide the population of counties covered by public poor relief data for New York State and for the state excluding New York City, assuming constant exponential population growth in each county between Census years.

Series Bf180–181. For 1840–1868, the data come directly from the *Annual Reports of the Secretary of State.* From 1869 through 1893, all issues of the *Annual Reports of the Secretary of State* report the number of families receiving temporary outdoor relief in New York City, series Bf181, rather than the number of individuals. For four of those years, 1890–1893, the number of persons receiving temporary outdoor relief in New York City is reported in the *Annual Report of the State Board of Charities,* and those figures are included in series Bf180.

Series Bf184. Derived from the *Annual Reports of the Secretary of State*, but includes only those counties for which data on the number supported in the poorhouse are also available.

SOCIAL WELFARE EXPENDITURES

Price V. Fishback and Melissa A. Thomasson

TABLE Bf188–195 Public expenditures on social welfare: 1890–1995[1]

Contributed by Price V. Fishback and Melissa A. Thomasson

	Total	Social insurance	Public aid	Health and medical programs	Veterans' programs	Education	Housing	Other social welfare programs
	Bf188	Bf189	Bf190	Bf191	Bf192	Bf193	Bf194	Bf195
Fiscal year	Million dollars	Million dollars	Million dollars	Million dollars	Million dollars	Million dollars	Million dollars	Million dollars
1890	318.0	—	— [4]	18.0	113.0	146.0	—	41.0 [4]
1913	1,000.0	15.0	— [4]	150.0	196.0	525.0	—	114.0 [4]
1929	3,921.2	342.4	60.0	351.1	657.9	2,433.7	—	76.2
1930	4,084.9	360.9	77.8	378.1	667.8	2,522.8	—	77.5
1931	4,200.8	368.3	164.0	405.8	744.3	2,439.6	—	78.8
1932	4,303.4	355.3	255.9	434.5	825.0	2,351.8	—	80.9
1933	4,462.2	343.9	689.1	417.6	818.8	2,104.0	—	88.8
1934	5,832.0	361.8	2,530.5	400.3	529.5	1,913.8	0.4	95.8
1935	6,548.3	406.3	2,997.6	427.2	597.5	2,007.5	13.2	99.0
1936	10,184.2	455.6	3,079.4	453.9	3,825.5	2,227.6	41.7	100.5
1937	7,858.2	545.2	3,436.0	500.1	892.7	2,375.7	3.1	105.4
1938	7,923.5	848.6	3,232.9	539.5	627.3	2,563.0	3.9	108.2
1939	9,212.9	1,181.2	4,229.6	575.2	606.1	2,503.7	3.4	113.8
1940	8,795.1	1,271.8	3,597.0	615.5	629.0	2,561.2	4.2	116.4
1941	8,953.4	1,330.0	3,523.7	724.4	612.9	2,617.2	8.9	136.4
1942	8,609.2	1,375.6	2,777.1	948.7	645.4	2,694.2	14.3	153.9
1943	8,283.1	1,258.7	1,549.7	1,885.8	623.3	2,793.3	13.6	158.6
1944	8,227.6	1,255.7	1,031.5	2,225.1	720.0	2,800.4	13.3	181.6
1945	9,205.3	1,409.4	1,030.6	2,354.2	1,125.8	3,076.3	11.1	197.9
1946	12,797.9	3,652.1	1,150.6	1,904.1	2,402.9	3,296.8	158.7	232.7
1947	17,337.0	4,160.0	1,441.8	1,367.0	5,682.5	4,089.0	280.9	315.6
1948	18,652.3	3,602.8	1,702.0	1,416.0	6,638.2	4,897.3	27.3	368.8
1949	21,164.9	4,185.8	2,089.1	1,753.1	6,926.7	5,806.6	7.7	395.9
1950	23,508.4	4,946.6	2,496.2	2,063.5	6,865.7	6,674.1	14.6	447.7
1951	24,054.7	4,772.2	2,591.7	2,782.8	5,996.0	7,415.1	35.0	461.9
1952	25,576.4	5,671.0	2,584.7	3,331.3	5,255.6	8,245.7	37.1	451.0
1953	27,044.9	6,607.3	2,727.9	3,190.4	4,734.7	9,230.9	50.6	503.0
1954	29,546.8	8,264.7	2,788.2	3,099.1	4,630.9	10,084.4	67.4	612.1
1955	32,639.9	9,834.9	3,003.0	3,103.1	4,833.5	11,157.2	89.3	619.0
1956	35,130.6	10,646.1	3,114.7	3,307.1	5,061.2	12,154.4	111.7	735.4
1957	39,350.4	12,471.8	3,308.5	3,775.8	5,118.8	13,732.3	120.2	823.0
1958	45,456.9	15,956.7	3,615.4	4,090.9	5,426.7	15,312.6	134.2	920.4
1959	49,821.4	18,286.5	3,997.9	4,400.6	5,472.3	16,498.3	156.2	1,009.6
1960	52,293.3 [2]	19,306.7	4,101.1	4,463.8 [2]	5,479.2	17,626.2	176.8	1,139.4
1961	58,236.0	22,364.9	4,444.3	4,927.0	5,623.7	19,337.2	196.1	1,342.8
1962	62,658.8	24,193.8	4,945.3	5,229.8	5,654.1	21,004.6	216.6	1,414.5
1963	66,766.2	25,613.5	5,295.9	5,593.5	5,751.2	22,670.7	248.1	1,593.4
1964	71,491.1	26,971.3	5,642.1	6,003.5	5,861.5	24,989.0	277.7	1,746.0
1965	77,083.8	28,122.8	6,283.4	6,155.0	6,031.1	28,107.8	318.1	2,065.6
1966	87,802.8 [3]	31,934.6	7,301.1	6,740.0	6,358.3	32,825.1	334.9	2,308.8
1967	99,465.1	37,338.7	8,811.0	7,383.0	6,898.3	35,807.8	377.8	2,848.5
1968	113,553.4	42,740.4	11,091.6	8,172.0	7,246.7	40,589.7	427.6	3,285.4
1969	126,970.7	48,772.1	13,439.1	8,828.0	7,933.6	43,673.1	532.3	3,792.5
1970	145,555.1 [2]	54,691.2	16,487.8	9,606.0 [2]	9,078.1	50,845.5	701.2	4,145.3
1971	171,256.7 [3]	66,368.8	21,262.0	10,437.0	10,455.0 [3]	56,704.7	1,046.2 [3]	4,983.0
1972	190,315.2	74,809.4	26,078.2	11,824.0	11,522.3	59,385.1	1,332.4	5,363.8
1973	213,293.9 [3]	86,165.6	28,691.4	12,799.0	13,026.4	64,733.7	2,179.6	5,698.2 [3]
1974	238,641.6 [3]	99,001.4	31,520.4	14,198.0	14,112.4	70,533.9	2,554.0	6,721.5 [3]
1975	289,173.0	123,013.1	41,446.6	16,742.0	17,018.9	80,834.1	3,171.7	6,946.6
1976	331,613.8 [3]	145,703.4	49,023.4 [3]	18,356.0	18,958.0	87,729.7	3,370.8	8,472.5
1977	360,458.8 [3]	160,881.3	53,812.4 [3]	19,441.0	19,014.3	93,878.3	4,358.1	9,071.4
1978	394,265.6 [3]	175,089.6	59,925.8 [3]	22,201.0	19,744.0 [3]	101,517.8	5,224.7	10,562.7
1979	430,066.9 [3]	194,287.5	65,307.0 [3]	24,040.0	20,601.6	109,261.5	5,493.1	11,076.2

Notes appear at end of table

TABLE Bf188–195 Public expenditures on social welfare: 1890–1995 *Continued*

	Total	Social insurance	Public aid	Health and medical programs	Veterans' programs	Education	Housing	Other social welfare programs
	Bf188	Bf189	Bf190	Bf191	Bf192	Bf193	Bf194	Bf195
Fiscal year	Million dollars	Million dollars	Million dollars	Million dollars	Million dollars	Million dollars	Million dollars	Million dollars
1980	492,713.7 [2]	229,754.4	72,703.1	27,263.0 [2]	21,465.5	121,049.6	6,879.0	13,599.1
1981	552,882.8 [3]	267,394.8	83,634.0	29,588.0	23,440.9 [3]	130,108.5	6,733.5 [3]	11,983.1
1982	601,344.9 [3]	302,614.8	82,206.2 [3]	32,870.0	24,708.1	138,089.3	9,202.1	11,654.4
1983	649,229.1	331,161.2	88,330.7	34,090.0	25,801.9	146,415.4	10,963.5	12,466.4
1984	678,112.1	341,120.2	92,979.4	35,722.0	26,274.9	157,188.9	11,531.8	13,294.9
1985	732,249.5 [3,2]	369,595.2	98,361.8	39,053.0 [2]	27,041.7 [3]	172,047.5	12,598.5	13,551.8
1986	781,725.2	390,770.1	104,200.2	43,953.0	27,444.9	189,234.6	11,961.8 [3]	14,160.6
1987	834,121.9	412,873.9	112,115.1	48,067.0	28,050.8	204,563.7	13,173.5	15,277.9
1988	887,951.2 [3]	434,051.3	119,723.4	53,096.0	29,663.4 [3]	219,382.2	16,555.9	15,479.0
1989	957,394.6 [3]	468,051.7 [3]	128,609.8	57,123.0	30,103.7 [3]	238,771.0	18,126.7	16,608.7
1990	1,048,950.8	513,821.8	146,811.1	61,684.0	30,916.2	258,331.6	19,468.5	17,917.6
1991	1,159,626.4	561,175.2	181,334.4	65,810.0	32,857.3	277,147.1	21,522.6	19,779.8
1992	1,266,867.1	618,938.8	207,953.0	70,114.0	35,642.0	292,070.6	20,617.2	21,531.5
1993	1,366,754.1 [3]	659,209.9	220,999.8	74,717.0 [3]	36,378.3	331,996.8	20,782.3	22,670.0
1994	1,435,819.3 [3]	683,778.7	238,025.3	80,235.0 [3]	37,894.8	344,091.0	27,032.0	24,762.5
1995	1,505,136.4	705,483.3	253,530.0	85,507.0	39,072.0	365,625.3	29,361.1	26,557.7

1 See text on inclusion of Alaska, Hawai'i, and outlying areas.

2 The data reported in the 1997 and 1999 source articles do not precisely match the data in the July 1995 source, owing to revisions in the procedures for estimating health expenditures. The differences for them are typically less than $500 million.

3 Revised figure. See text.

4 Public aid included with other social welfare services.

Sources

Estimates presented for 1890 and 1913 were based primarily on the following: R. A. Musgrave and J. J. Culbertson, "The Growth of Public Expenditures in the U.S., 1890–1948," *National Tax Journal* (June 1953): 97–115; J. Frederic Dewhurst and Associates, *America's Needs and Resources* (Twentieth Century Fund, 1955); and reports of official agencies. Data for 1929–1989, U.S. Social Security Administration, *Social Welfare Expenditures under Public Programs in the United States, 1929–90* (July 1995); Ann Kallman Bixby, "Public Social Welfare Expenditures, Fiscal Year 1992," *Social Security Bulletin* 58 (2) (1995): 65–73. Data for 1990–1995 are from Ann Kallman Bixby, "Public Social Welfare Expenditures, Fiscal Year 1994," *Social Security Bulletin* 60 (3) (1997): 42; and Ann Kallman Bixby, "Public Social Welfare Expenditures, Fiscal Year 1995," *Social Security Bulletin* 62 (2) (1999): 88.

The information is updated annually in the *Social Security Bulletin* and the *Social Security Bulletin: Annual Statistical Supplement*, Table 3.A3.

Documentation

The material for the period 1929–1964 was first reported in Ida C. Merriam and Alfred M. Skolnik, *Social Welfare Expenditures under Public Programs in the United States, 1929–1966,* Research Report number 25 (U.S. Social Security Administration, 1968). This report included a compendium of detailed data covering each year from 1929 to 1966, and a complete description of the methodology used in formulating the series. In situations where the published information for a year differs in the sources, the number published later was used with one exception: there was a misprint for the 1991 data in the 1996 *Annual Statistical Supplement*, and so the data for 1991 are from Summer 1995 *Social Security Bulletin*.

Information on the state and local breakdown for all of the programs in Tables Bf212–270 from 1929 through 1989 is available in U.S. Social Security Administration (July 1995); Merriam and Skolnik (1968); and the annual articles in the *Social Security Bulletin*. For example, see Ann Kallman Bixby, "Public Social Welfare Expenditures, Fiscal Year 1994," *Social Security Bulletin* 60 (3) (1997): 43–4; and Ann Kallman Bixby, "Public Social Welfare Expenditures, Fiscal Year 1995," *Social Security Bulletin* 62 (2) (1999): 89, 90.

Scattered data relating to social welfare programs in particular localities or states may be found in other sources. The definitions used in these sources, however, are highly variable and the original source of the data is frequently not indicated. No data comparable to those shown for 1929–1993 are readily available.

Social welfare expenditures include the areas of income maintenance, health, education, housing, veterans' benefits, and other welfare services directed specifically toward promoting the economic and social welfare of individuals and families. The social welfare expenditures data collected by the U.S. Social Security Administration fit the definitions of social welfare spending used by the Organization for Economic Co-operation and Development and the International Labour Office. Expenditures are grouped on the basis of statutory programs and administrative structure rather than strictly by function. Finally, the economic status of the individual or family receiving benefits is not a criterion for inclusion in the series. Rather, the requirement is that the funds be expended through the government apparatus in compliance with or as a result of public law. For further information about the components of these series, see the text for Tables Bf212–270.

Social welfare expenditures under public programs represent payments from federal, state, and local revenues (general and special) and trust funds. They include capital outlays as well as administrative expenses unless otherwise noted. Some payments abroad are included. Programs or services financed by loans are excluded. The expenditures are reported on a fiscal year basis. Through 1976, the fiscal year ended June 30 for the federal government, most states, and some localities. Beginning in 1977, federal fiscal years end on September 30.

Data on federal programs include expenditures in Alaska and Hawai'i for all years; state and local data include expenditures in Alaska and Hawai'i from the year of their admission to the Union. Data include federal expenditures (and matching local expenditures under grant programs) in Puerto Rico, the Virgin Islands, Guam, Trust Territory of the Pacific, American Samoa, and the Panama Canal Zone, as well as expenditures to beneficiaries of some of the income-maintenance programs residing in foreign countries, and that part of Defense Department education and health expenses incurred abroad.

Wherever possible, data for federal, federal-state, and federal-local programs were drawn from published and unpublished materials of the appropriate federal agencies and from the annual *Budget of the United States Government*. The principal source for state, state-local, and local program statistics has been the census of governments. To bridge gaps, especially for early years of the series, and to augment fragmentary data, the U.S. Social Security Administration has estimated expenditures for certain years for some programs (e.g., state and local public employee retirement benefits and administration). The series are often revised in response to new data, new benchmarks, and changes in reporting from other sources. The U.S. Social Security Administration often publishes the revised versions of the recent data but in many cases offers revised information for earlier years for years ending in 0 and 5. Discussions with the people at the U.S. Social Security Administration who compile the statistics suggest that a search for "the" number in any single year would be futile. The numbers are basically estimates from surveys, reports of other agencies, and other sources, and they

(continued)

TABLE Bf188–195 Public expenditures on social welfare: 1890–1995 *Continued*

should be treated as rough approximations of the "true" level. The people at the U.S. Social Security Administration are very careful to try to maintain consistency in the definitions of the series. However, even the revisions are subject to measurement error, and year-to-year fluctuations between a revised statistic for a year ending in 0 or 5 with neighboring years are likely to be subject to measurement error. The majority of revisions are within 1 or 2 percent of the prior reported estimates.

The footnoted revisions to the table are based on corrections to the information reported in the sources that arise from cross checking the sums of series that should add up to totals in that category. In all cases, the corrections are based on new sums using the most disaggregated data reported in the source and then recalculating the sums. For example, if there was a discrepancy between the all government spending in a category and the sum of state and local plus federal spending in the category, we used the sum of state and local plus federal spending unless there was an obvious error. For the data presented here, efforts were made to account for all differences from 1965 to the present. Differences between the total series and the sums of the subcategories of $0.1 million in years prior to 1965 were left unaltered because they might be the result of rounding error.

TABLE Bf196–211 Public expenditures on social welfare, by federal or state–local source of funds: 1890–1995

Contributed by Price V. Fishback and Melissa A. Thomasson

	Federal funds								State and local funds							
	Total	Social insurance	Public aid	Health and medical programs	Veterans' programs	Education	Housing	Other social welfare programs	Total	Social insurance	Public aid	Health and medical programs	Veterans' programs	Education	Housing	Other social welfare programs
	Bf196	Bf197	Bf198	Bf199	Bf200	Bf201	Bf202	Bf203	Bf204	Bf205	Bf206	Bf207	Bf208	Bf209	Bf210	Bf211
Year	Million dollars	Million dollars	Million dollars	Million dollars	Million dollars	Million dollars	Million dollars	Million dollars	Million dollars	Million dollars	Million dollars	Million dollars	Million dollars	Million dollars	Million dollars	Million dollars
1890	115.0	—	—	—	—	—	—	—	203.0	—	—	—	—	—	—	—
1913	196.0	—	—	—	—	—	—	—	804.0	—	—	—	—	—	—	—
1929	798.4	55.9	—	46.7	657.9	36.5	—	1.4	3,122.8	286.5	60.0	304.4	—	2,397.2	—	74.8
1930	817.1	60.3	—	47.4	667.8	40.1	—	1.5	3,267.8	300.6	77.8	330.7	—	2,482.7	—	76.0
1931	911.0	68.9	—	50.8	744.3	45.3	—	1.7	3,289.8	299.4	164.0	355.0	—	2,394.3	—	77.1
1932	1,002.3	74.6	—	55.1	825.0	45.9	—	1.7	3,301.1	280.8	255.9	379.4	—	2,305.9	—	79.2
1933	1,338.8	81.2	344.8	51.8	818.8	40.7	—	1.7	3,123.4	262.8	344.4	365.8	—	2,063.3	—	87.2
1934	2,771.0	94.6	2,003.8	48.0	529.5	93.0	0.4	1.6	3,061.1	267.2	526.7	352.3	—	1,820.7	—	94.2
1935	3,207.2	118.9	2,373.7	49.5	597.5	52.7	13.2	1.7	3,341.1	287.4	623.9	377.7	—	1,954.8	—	97.2
1936	6,505.9	132.9	2,309.6	54.5	3,825.5	138.6	41.7	3.2	3,678.3	322.7	769.8	399.3	—	2,089.1	—	97.4
1937	3,788.1	193.3	2,494.1	69.7	880.4	143.4	3.1	4.1	4,070.1	351.8	942.0	430.3	12.4	2,232.3	—	101.3
1938	3,254.6	295.2	2,075.3	72.6	615.1	187.5	3.9	5.0	4,669.0	553.4	1,157.6	466.9	12.3	2,375.5	—	103.3
1939	3,986.8	357.8	2,870.7	79.0	596.3	72.7	3.4	6.9	5,226.2	823.3	1,358.9	496.2	9.8	2,431.0	—	107.0
1940	3,443.1	393.8	2,243.1	96.6	619.8	74.7	4.2	10.9	5,351.0	878.0	1,352.8	518.9	9.2	2,486.6	—	105.5
1941	3,660.3	470.0	2,187.6	231.5	604.5	135.8	8.9	22.0	5,293.1	860.0	1,336.1	492.9	8.3	2,481.5	—	114.4
1942	3,605.3	531.7	1,698.0	470.7	636.9	217.9	14.3	35.8	5,003.9	843.9	1,079.1	478.0	8.5	2,476.3	—	118.1
1943	3,684.2	565.1	818.3	1,382.7	616.9	251.3	13.6	36.2	4,598.9	693.6	731.3	503.1	6.5	2,542.0	—	122.5
1944	3,758.7	630.8	427.5	1,725.4	713.4	192.7	13.3	55.6	4,468.9	624.8	604.0	499.7	6.6	2,607.7	—	126.0
1945	4,339.4	734.9	420.1	1,801.4	1,118.5	187.3	11.1	66.1	4,865.9	674.5	610.4	552.8	7.4	2,889.0	—	131.8
1946	6,343.3	1,912.6	449.2	1,273.3	2,348.5	126.5	158.7	74.5	6,454.6	1,739.5	701.5	630.7	54.4	3,170.4	—	158.1
1947	9,794.1	2,605.0	617.2	554.7	5,504.4	129.4	280.9	102.5	7,542.9	1,555.0	824.7	812.4	178.1	3,959.6	—	213.1
1948	9,481.7	2,039.8	724.0	421.2	6,001.1	140.7	27.3	127.6	9,170.6	1,563.1	977.9	994.7	637.1	4,756.6	—	241.2
1949	10,252.4	2,103.1	941.5	522.0	6,399.8	138.5	7.7	139.8	10,912.5	2,082.7	1,147.6	1,231.1	526.9	5,668.1	—	256.0
1950	10,541.1	2,103.0	1,103.2	603.5	6,386.2	156.7	14.6	174.0	12,967.3	2,843.6	1,393.0	1,460.0	479.5	6,517.5	—	273.7
1951	11,125.6	2,723.5	1,196.4	1,169.8	5,661.3	180.3	21.6	172.7	12,929.1	2,048.8	1,395.3	1,613.0	334.7	7,234.8	13.4	289.1
1952	11,729.9	3,342.1	1,211.3	1,585.7	5,112.9	307.9	25.1	144.9	13,846.5	2,328.9	1,373.4	1,745.5	142.8	7,937.8	12.0	306.1
1953	12,244.2	4,224.0	1,360.8	1,380.3	4,620.6	429.3	37.9	191.3	14,800.6	2,383.3	1,367.1	1,810.1	114.1	8,801.6	12.7	311.7
1954	12,990.3	5,093.6	1,419.5	1,209.6	4,528.1	418.8	53.8	267.0	16,556.5	3,171.1	1,368.7	1,889.6	102.8	9,665.6	13.7	345.1
1955	14,622.9	6,385.0	1,504.2	1,150.3	4,771.9	485.1	74.7	251.7	18,017.1	3,449.9	1,498.8	1,952.8	61.6	10,672.1	14.6	367.3
1956	16,211.7	7,534.1	1,555.4	1,256.0	4,972.0	475.7	92.0	326.6	18,918.8	3,112.0	1,559.3	2,051.0	89.2	11,678.7	19.7	408.8
1957	18,129.5	8,926.4	1,690.0	1,410.4	5,079.6	540.5	101.2	381.3	21,220.9	3,545.3	1,618.5	2,365.4	39.3	13,191.8	19.0	441.6
1958	20,631.2	10,856.5	1,834.9	1,567.1	5,305.3	607.8	110.6	349.0	24,825.8	5,100.2	1,780.5	2,523.8	121.4	14,704.8	23.7	571.4
1959	23,550.3	13,054.0	2,082.1	1,716.5	5,411.2	766.7	127.8	392.0	26,271.1	5,232.6	1,915.8	2,684.1	61.1	15,731.5	28.4	617.6
1960	24,956.7	14,307.2	2,116.9	1,737.1	5,367.4	867.9	143.5	416.7	27,336.6	4,999.4	1,984.2	2,726.8	111.9	16,758.3	33.2	722.8
1961	27,402.6	15,965.7	2,337.3	1,949.4	5,539.4	1,000.5	159.2	451.1	30,833.4	6,399.2	2,107.1	2,977.6	84.3	18,336.7	36.9	891.7
1962	30,624.4	18,289.5	2,741.3	2,241.9	5,558.9	1,089.6	173.4	529.9	32,034.3	5,904.3	2,204.1	2,987.9	95.2	19,915.0	43.2	884.6
1963	32,674.9	19,417.1	2,999.3	2,441.0	5,731.2	1,322.6	192.6	571.1	34,091.3	6,196.3	2,296.6	3,152.5	20.0	21,348.1	55.5	1,022.3
1964	34,928.0	20,646.1	3,208.2	2,749.1	5,842.6	1,619.5	212.1	650.4	36,563.1	6,325.3	2,433.9	3,254.3	18.9	23,369.5	65.6	1,095.6

(continued)

TABLE Bf196–211 Public expenditures on social welfare, by federal or state–local source of funds: 1890–1995 *Continued*

	Federal funds								State and local funds							
	Total	Social insurance	Public aid	Health and medical programs	Veterans' programs	Education	Housing	Other social welfare programs	Total	Social insurance	Public aid	Health and medical programs	Veterans' programs	Education	Housing	Other social welfare programs
	Bf196	Bf197	Bf198	Bf199	Bf200	Bf201	Bf202	Bf203	Bf204	Bf205	Bf206	Bf207	Bf208	Bf209	Bf210	Bf211
Year	Million dollars	Million dollars	Million dollars	Million dollars	Million dollars	Million dollars	Million dollars	Million dollars	Million dollars	Million dollars	Million dollars	Million dollars	Million dollars	Million dollars	Million dollars	Million dollars
1965	37,591.2	21,806.7	3,593.9	2,660.0	6,010.7	2,469.8	238.1	812.0	39,492.6	6,316.1	2,689.5	3,495.0	20.4	25,638.0	80.0	1,253.6
1966	45,242.7 [1]	25,663.6	4,366.0	3,010.0	6,337.0 [1]	4,580.5	250.8	1,034.8	42,560.1	6,271.0	2,935.1	3,730.0	21.3	28,244.6	84.1	1,274.0
1967	53,173.9	30,544.8	5,244.4	3,588.0	6,875.2	5,278.8	283.0	1,359.7	46,291.2	6,793.9	3,566.6	3,795.0	23.1	30,529.0	94.8	1,488.8
1968	60,168.3	35,390.0	6,455.1	4,087.0	7,214.2	5,000.3	325.1	1,696.6	53,385.1	7,350.4	4,636.5	4,085.0	32.5	35,589.4	102.5	1,588.8
1969	68,146.3	40,847.4	7,829.0	4,334.0	7,883.0	4,922.9	425.5	1,904.5	58,824.4	7,924.7	5,610.1	4,494.0	50.6	38,750.2	106.8	1,888.0
1970	77,130.1	45,245.6	9,648.6	4,568.0	8,951.6	5,875.8	581.6	2,258.9	68,425.0	9,445.6	6,839.2	5,038.0	126.5	44,969.7	119.6	1,886.4
1971	92,346.8 [1]	53,902.6	12,990.3	4,909.0	10,330.1 [1]	6,597.4	871.1 [1]	2,746.3	78,909.9	12,466.2	8,271.7	5,528.0	124.9	50,107.3	175.1	2,236.7
1972	105,869.6	61,248.5	16,291.3	5,865.0	11,405.2	6,721.3	1,183.2	3,155.1	84,445.6	13,560.9	9,786.9	5,959.0	117.1	52,663.8	149.2	2,208.7
1973	122,154.3	72,248.8	18,061.0	6,286.0	12,903.3	7,359.6	1,749.7	3,545.9	91,139.6 [1]	13,916.8	10,630.4	6,513.0	123.1	57,374.1	429.9	2,152.3 [1]
1974	136,723.5	82,832.3	20,387.7	6,677.0	13,873.8	7,041.5	2,009.1	3,902.1	101,918.1 [1]	16,169.1	11,132.7	7,521.0	238.6	63,492.4	544.9	2,819.4 [1]
1975	166,884.2	99,715.0	27,275.8	7,890.0	16,569.8	8,629.3	2,540.7	4,263.6	122,288.8	23,298.1	14,170.8	8,852.0	449.1	72,204.8	631.0	2,683.0
1976	196,672.6 [1]	119,600.2	32,670.1 [1]	9,079.0	18,796.1	9,023.2	2,906.0	4,598.0	134,941.2 [1]	26,103.2	16,353.3 [1]	9,277.0	161.9	78,706.5	464.8	3,874.5
1977	217,895.5	134,744.7	35,655.2	9,419.0	18,860.6	9,741.0	4,005.5	5,469.5	142,563.3 [1]	26,138.6	18,157.2 [1]	10,022.0	153.7	84,137.3	352.6	3,601.9
1978	239,788.7 [1]	147,364.7	40,392.5	10,724.0	19,570.3 [1]	10,900.8	4,887.3	5,949.1	154,476.9 [1]	27,724.9	19,533.3 [1]	11,477.0	173.7	90,617.0	337.4	4,613.6
1979	263,446.2	163,879.3	44,247.2	11,282.0	20,411.9	12,108.0	5,069.2	6,448.6	166,620.7 [1]	30,408.2	21,059.8 [1]	12,758.0	189.7	97,153.5	423.9	4,627.6
1980	303,165.5	191,162.0	49,394.2	12,840.0	21,253.6	13,452.2	6,277.6	8,785.9	189,548.2	38,592.4	23,308.9	14,423.0	211.9	107,597.4	601.4	4,813.2
1981	345,179.5 [1]	224,573.5	56,818.1	13,837.0	23,228.8 [1]	13,372.4	6,045.2 [1]	7,304.5	207,703.3	42,821.3	26,815.9	15,751.0	212.1	116,736.1	688.3	4,678.6
1982	370,172.2	250,551.4	53,434.1	14,883.0	24,462.8	11,916.9	8,423.8	6,500.2	231,172.7 [1]	52,063.4	28,772.1 [1]	17,987.0	245.3	126,172.4	778.3	5,154.2
1983	402,252.0	274,315.4	57,834.8	15,153.0	25,561.0	12,399.3	9,960.5	7,028.0	246,977.1	56,845.8	30,495.9	18,937.0	240.9	134,016.1	1,003.0	5,438.4
1984	421,194.1	288,742.6	59,868.1	16,029.0	25,969.8	13,009.5	10,225.9	7,349.2	256,918.0	52,377.6	33,111.3	19,693.0	305.1	144,179.4	1,305.9	5,945.7
1985	450,790.6 [1]	310,174.7	63,479.9	18,029.0	26,703.8 [1]	13,796.2	11,058.8	7,548.2	281,458.9	59,420.5	34,881.9	21,024.0	337.9	158,251.3	1,539.7	6,003.6
1986	472,761.8 [1]	326,016.3	67,299.1	19,440.0	27,072.1	15,022.4	10,089.6 [1]	7,822.3	308,963.4	64,753.8	36,901.1	24,513.0	372.8	174,212.2	1,872.2	6,338.3
1987	497,932.1	342,932.7	70,934.9	20,813.0	27,640.8	16,062.0	11,044.2	8,504.5	336,189.8	69,941.2	41,180.2	27,254.0	410.0	188,501.7	2,129.3	6,773.4
1988	527,470.8 [1]	360,268.1	75,989.6	22,875.0	29,254.4	16,966.4	14,005.9	8,111.4	360,480.4	73,783.2	43,733.8	30,221.0	409.0	202,415.8	2,550.0	7,367.6
1989	565,107.9 [1]	387,286.5 [1]	81,730.7 [1]	24,117.0	29,638.2 [1]	18,659.9	15,183.9	8,491.7	392,286.7	80,765.2	46,879.1	33,006.0	465.5	220,111.1	2,942.8	8,117.0
1990	616,640.6	422,256.6	92,858.5	27,206.0	30,427.7	18,374.0	16,612.4	8,905.4	432,310.2	91,565.2	53,952.6	34,478.0	488.5	239,957.6	2,856.1	9,012.2
1991	676,384.2	453,534.4	113,234.9	29,672.0	32,331.2	19,084.5	18,696.1	9,831.1	483,242.2	107,640.8	68,099.5	36,138.0	526.1	258,062.6	2,826.5	9,948.7
1992	750,237.3	496,075.6	138,703.7	31,685.0	35,087.2	20,059.6	17,949.6	10,676.6	516,629.8	122,863.2	69,249.3	38,429.0	554.8	272,011.0	2,667.6	10,854.9
1993	805,335.7	534,211.9	151,850.5	33,189.0	35,806.3	20,454.9	18,984.8	10,838.3	561,418.4	124,998.0	69,149.3	41,528.0	572.0	311,541.9	1,797.5	11,831.7
1994	852,875.7	557,320.7	162,674.7	34,770.0	37,261.6	24,084.2	24,987.2	11,777.3	582,943.6	126,458.0	75,350.6	45,465.0	633.2	320,006.8	2,044.8	12,985.2
1995	888,357.3	579,803.7	170,260.0	36,767.0	38,384.9	23,472.0	27,276.0	12,393.7	616,779.1	125,679.6	83,270.0	48,740.0	687.1	342,153.3	2,085.1	14,164.0

[1] Revised figure. See text for Table Bf188–195.

Sources

Estimates presented for 1890 and 1913 were primarily based on the following: R. A. Musgrave and J. J. Culbertson, "The Growth of Public Expenditures in the U.S., 1890–1948," *National Tax Journal* (June 1953): 97–115; J. Frederic Dewhurst and Associates, *America's Needs and Resources* (Twentieth Century Fund, 1955); and reports of official agencies. Data for 1929–1989, U.S. Social Security Administration, *Social Welfare Expenditures under Public Programs in the United States, 1929–90* (July 1995); Ann Kallman Bixby, "Public Social Welfare Expenditures, Fiscal Year 1992," *Social Security Bulletin* 58 (2) (1995): 65–73. Data for 1990–1995 come from Ann Kallman Bixby, "Public Social Welfare Expenditures, Fiscal Year 1994," *Social Security Bulletin* 60 (3) (1997): 43–4; and Ann Kallman Bixby, "Public Social Welfare Expenditures, Fiscal Year 1995," *Social Security Bulletin* 62 (2) (1999): 89, 90. More detailed breakdowns for all of the programs in Tables Bf212–270 from 1929 through 1989 are available in these sources, as well. See the text for Table Bf188–195 for further discussion of the sources.

Documentation

Federal grants-in-aid are classified as expenditures from federal funds (contrary to the practice in the national income accounts, which include them as expenditures from state and local funds). Benefit payments under the state unemployment insurance programs are classified as expenditures from state funds (in the national income accounts, they are classified as federal expenditures, based on the fact that the state unemployment insurance trust funds are held and invested by the Secretary of the Treasury). Federal grants to the states for the administration of unemployment insurance and the employment service are classified as expenditures from federal funds, as are the benefits paid under the temporary extended unemployment insurance acts of 1958 and 1961.

The expenditures for state and federal funds for each category should sum to the expenditures reported for each category in Table Bf188–195. In some cases during the period 1990 through 1995, there are disparities. The differences arise because revisions for Table Bf188–195 have been reported later than revisions for Table Bf196–211.

TABLE Bf212–224 Public expenditures on social welfare – social insurance: 1929–1995

Contributed by Price V. Fishback and Melissa A. Thomasson

		Old-Age, Survivors, Disability, and Health Insurance (OASDHI)								State temporary disability insurance		Workers' compensation	
	Total	Total	Old-Age, Survivors, and Disability Insurance	Health Insurance (Medicare)	Railroad Retirement	Public employee retirement	Unemployment insurance and employment services	Railroad unemployment insurance	Railroad temporary disability insurance	Total	On hospital and medical benefits	Total	On hospital and medical benefits
	Bf212	Bf213	Bf214	Bf215	Bf216	Bf217	Bf218	Bf219	Bf220	Bf221	Bf222	Bf223	Bf224
Year	Million dollars	Million dollars	Million dollars	Million dollars	Million dollars	Million dollars	Million dollars	Million dollars	Million dollars	Million dollars	Million dollars	Million dollars	Million dollars
1929	342.4	—	—	—	—	113.1	—	—	—	—	—	229.3	75.0
1930	360.9	—	—	—	—	122.1	—	—	—	—	—	238.8	75.0
1931	368.3	—	—	—	—	135.6	—	—	—	—	—	232.7	75.0
1932	355.3	—	—	—	—	146.4	—	—	—	—	—	209.0	68.0
1933	343.9	—	—	—	—	163.6	—	—	—	—	—	180.3	58.0
1934	361.8	—	—	—	—	186.2	—	—	—	—	—	172.7	55.0
1935	406.3	—	—	—	—	208.8	—	—	—	—	—	188.4	65.0
1936	455.6	0.5	0.5	—	0.6	233.0	17.6	—	—	—	—	204.0	73.0
1937	545.2	19.5	19.5	—	5.8	244.2	45.1	—	—	—	—	230.6	75.0
1938	848.6	26.1	26.1	—	85.5	256.8	236.2	—	—	—	—	244.0	80.0
1939	1,181.2	36.5	36.5	—	110.0	269.5	516.7	1.7	—	—	—	246.7	80.0
1940	1,271.8	40.4	40.4	—	116.8	283.4	553.0	18.9	—	—	—	259.2	90.0
1941	1,330.0	91.2	91.2	—	124.7	297.9	507.0	21.1	—	—	—	288.1	98.0
1942	1,375.6	137.0	137.0	—	129.5	322.0	451.8	11.4	—	—	—	323.8	104.0
1943	1,258.7	176.8	176.8	—	133.7	305.4	281.2	3.9	—	0.8	—	356.8	110.0
1944	1,255.7	217.2	217.2	—	137.6	331.7	173.5	3.7	—	4.6	—	387.3	116.0
1945	1,409.4	266.8	266.8	—	145.0	355.0	216.7	4.3	—	5.1	—	416.6	122.0
1946	3,652.1	357.9	357.9	—	156.5	412.6	2,255.9	24.2	—	4.8	—	440.0	132.0
1947	4,160.0	466.4	466.4	—	177.8	510.1	2,453.7	51.2	—	15.6	—	485.2	150.0
1948	3,602.8	559.1	559.1	—	229.8	579.5	1,600.8	35.9	28.6	33.3	—	535.7	168.0
1949	4,185.8	660.5	660.5	—	287.9	649.1	1,876.2	50.5	32.0	50.0	—	579.6	180.0
1950	4,946.6	784.1	784.1	—	306.4	817.9	2,190.1	119.6	31.1	72.1	2.2	625.1	193.0
1951	4,772.2	1,568.5	1,568.5	—	321.8	920.0	1,062.8	28.3	28.9	142.7	9.8	699.2	216.0
1952	5,671.0	2,067.0	2,067.0	—	400.4	998.7	1,189.4	26.3	27.7	174.7	12.2	786.8	245.0
1953	6,607.3	2,716.9	2,716.9	—	466.5	1,123.5	1,143.2	57.8	45.4	198.0	14.9	856.1	270.0
1954	8,264.7	3,364.2	3,364.2	—	518.0	1,250.6	1,871.8	100.4	46.6	210.5	17.6	902.5	295.0
1955	9,834.9	4,436.3	4,436.3	—	556.0	1,388.5	2,080.6	158.7	54.2	217.5	20.0	943.0	315.0
1956	10,646.1	5,485.2	5,485.2	—	607.5	1,577.3	1,623.5	59.7	52.3	232.7	22.4	1,007.9	335.0
1957	12,471.8	6,665.9	6,665.9	—	685.5	1,785.3	1,841.6	88.1	52.0	269.8	26.3	1,083.6	355.0
1958	15,956.7	8,221.1	8,221.1	—	729.9	2,026.3	3,302.5	176.0	54.7	304.1	31.9	1,142.2	370.0
1959	18,286.5	9,615.9	9,615.9	—	790.2	2,342.5	3,731.1	200.2	57.0	327.0	38.4	1,222.7	390.0
1960	19,306.7	11,032.3	11,032.3	—	934.7	2,569.9	2,829.6	215.2	68.5	347.9	40.2	1,308.5	420.0
1961	22,364.9	12,160.8	12,160.8	—	996.1	2,870.2	4,280.0	213.4	58.0	385.2	43.8	1,401.4	450.0
1962	24,193.8	13,984.8	13,984.8	—	1,036.9	3,189.7	3,853.8	163.2	56.8	407.1	45.5	1,501.4	475.0
1963	25,613.5	15,344.6	15,344.6	—	1,077.3	3,569.3	3,390.6	122.8	52.8	444.2	48.4	1,611.8	510.0
1964	26,971.3	16,201.1	16,201.1	—	1,107.3	4,056.7	3,273.8	92.6	50.1	467.7	50.4	1,722.0	545.0
1965	28,122.8	16,997.5	16,997.5	—	1,128.1	4,528.5	3,002.6	76.7	46.5	483.5	50.9	1,859.4	580.0
1966	31,934.6	20,295.2	20,231.6	63.6	1,211.6	5,145.4	2,662.4	52.4	42.6	507.5	54.3	2,017.5	640.0
1967	37,338.7	24,580.7	21,186.1	3,394.6	1,278.4	5,903.6	2,752.2	38.5	38.4	529.6	53.7	2,217.3	715.0
1968	42,740.4	28,748.4	23,401.2	5,347.2	1,416.6	6,581.9	2,928.6	46.2	36.1	574.3	54.6	2,408.3	790.0
1969	48,772.1	33,388.7	26,791.0	6,597.7	1,550.7	7,493.8	2,947.1	44.3	58.5	648.1	57.7	2,640.9	875.0

(continued)

TABLE Bf212–224 Public expenditures on social welfare – social insurance: 1929–1995 *Continued*

		Old-Age, Survivors, Disability, and Health Insurance (OASDHI)								State temporary disability insurance		Workers' compensation	
	Total	Total	Old-Age, Survivors, and Disability Insurance	Health Insurance (Medicare)	Railroad Retirement	Public employee retirement	Unemployment insurance and employment services	Railroad unemployment insurance	Railroad temporary disability insurance	Total	On hospital and medical benefits	Total	On hospital and medical benefits
	Bf212	Bf213	Bf214	Bf215	Bf216	Bf217	Bf218	Bf219	Bf220	Bf221	Bf222	Bf223	Bf224
Year	Million dollars	Million dollars	Million dollars	Million dollars	Million dollars	Million dollars	Million dollars	Million dollars	Million dollars	Million dollars	Million dollars	Million dollars	Million dollars
1970	54,691.2	36,835.4	29,686.2	7,149.2	1,609.9	8,658.7	3,819.5	38.5	61.1	717.7	62.6	2,950.4	985.0
1971	66,368.8	43,122.8	35,247.8	7,875.0	1,928.9	10,226.1	6,665.3	49.6	53.0	773.1	68.4	3,550.0	1,090.0
1972	74,809.4	48,229.1	39,409.9	8,819.2	2,141.2	11,920.4	7,651.0	86.0	42.1	783.7	68.3	3,955.9	1,185.0
1973	86,165.6	57,766.6	48,287.8	9,478.8	2,477.5	14,010.8	6,065.9	45.2	34.9	848.2	69.8	4,916.5	1,355.0
1974	99,001.4	66,286.6	54,939.1	11,347.5	2,692.6	16,677.5	6,661.5	25.6	31.5	915.4	70.7	5,710.7	1,610.0
1975	123,013.1	78,429.9	63,648.5	14,781.4	3,085.1	20,118.6	13,835.9	41.6	32.9	990.0	72.9	6,479.1	2,470.0
1976	145,703.4	90,440.7	72,663.3	17,777.4	3,499.6	23,441.4	19,585.2	148.2	78.6	1,022.4	75.5	7,487.3	2,205.0
1977	160,883.3 [1]	105,410.1	83,861.3	21,548.8	3,818.6	26,495.9	15,448.8	107.3	81.8	1,042.2	75.7	8,478.6 [1]	2,530.0
1978	175,089.6	117,431.9	92,242.7	25,189.2	4,019.8	29,935.8	12,598.4	134.0	73.4	1,124.6	77.7	9,771.7	2,830.5
1979	194,287.5	131,719.4	102,595.8	29,123.6	4,310.6	33,929.8	11,313.1	86.9	65.6	1,232.2	75.9	11,629.9	3,250.0
1980	229,754.4	152,110.4	117,118.9	34,991.5	4,768.7	39,490.2	18,326.4	155.4	68.7	1,377.4	49.6	13,457.2	3,725.0
1981	267,394.8	180,425.0	137,970.2	42,454.8	5,323.4	45,743.7	19,022.3	208.1	60.9	1,596.9	50.3	15,014.5	4,165.0
1982	302,614.8 [1]	204,567.8	154,144.3	50,423.5	5,766.4	50,464.2	23,256.5	298.8	62.2	1,695.7	52.5	16,503.2	4,640.0
1983	331,161.2	224,709.2	167,778.9	56,930.3	6,081.5	54,937.5	25,349.7	386.6	61.3	1,766.9	55.7	17,868.5	5,082.0
1984	341,120.2	238,254.0	175,773.2	62,480.8	6,143.8	58,887.8	16,103.5	183.3	46.7	1,817.7	56.0	19,683.4	6,010.0
1985	369,595.2	257,535.1	186,150.8	71,384.3	6,275.6	63,044.0	18,343.8	138.4	50.6	1,944.1	55.3	22,263.6	7,080.0
1986	390,770.1	271,980.0	196,077.4	75,902.6	6,354.5	66,910.8	18,549.6	140.2	57.8	2,067.3	54.7	24,709.9	8,365.9
1987	412,873.9	286,339.7	204,708.4	81,631.3	6,549.1	72,151.7	18,045.7	124.1	64.9	2,545.4	56.4	27,053.3	9,618.3
1988	434,051.3	300,048.2	216,438.7	83,609.5	6,675.9	78,051.3	16,117.8	82.1	18.3	2,753.6	62.4	30,303.8	11,110.3
1989	468,051.7	324,109.5	229,557.5	94,552.0	6,971.2	83,799.9	16,381.3	64.4	35.0	2,886.3	67.3	33,804.1	12,825.0
1990	513,821.8 [1]	355,264.5	245,555.5	109,709.0	7,229.9	90,391.2	19,973.7	64.6	40.3	3,224.2	62.5	37,633.4	14,305.5
1991	561,175.2	382,289.8	265,638.8	116,651.0	7,531.8	97,271.3	28,405.3	71.0	23.4	3,879.2	65.8	41,703.4	16,009.5
1992	618,938.8	416,564.0	284,317.7	132,246.3	7,737.1	103,699.4	41,166.0	67.4	27.5	4,009.4	69.7	45,668.0	17,914.2
1993	659,209.9	449,276.8	301,183.3	148,093.5	7,920.6	112,559.5	40,720.8	60.3	25.9	3,316.0	53.7	45,330.0	17,712.3
1994	683,778.7	477,339.7	315,947.0	161,392.7	8,025.2	119,253.1	31,251.1	53.5	29.3	3,200.8	52.1	44,626.0	16,200.0
1995	705,483.3	495,355.8	331,642.3	164,713.2	8,106.2	128,001.8	26,302.0	48.4	30.0	3,189.1	43.2	43,450.0	16,700.0

[1] Revised figure. See text for Table Bf188–195.

Sources

Data for 1929–1989, U.S. Social Security Administration, *Social Welfare Expenditures under Public Programs in the United States, 1929–90* (July 1995); Ann Kallman Bixby, "Public Social Welfare Expenditures, Fiscal Year 1992," *Social Security Bulletin* 58 (2) (1995): 65–73. Data for 1990–1995 are from Ann Kallman Bixby, "Public Social Welfare Expenditures, Fiscal Year 1994," *Social Security Bulletin* 60 (3) (1997): 42; and Ann Kallman Bixby, "Public Social Welfare Expenditures, Fiscal Year 1995," *Social Security Bulletin* 62 (2) (1999): 88, 94. Most of the series in this table are annually updated in the *Social Security Bulletin: Annual Statistical Supplement*, Table 3.A3. See the text for Table Bf188–195 for further discussion of the sources.

Documentation

More information on social insurance programs is available in Tables Bf271–348, Bf377–496, Bf511–567, and Bf735–761.

Social insurance programs involve situations where workers and/or employers pay taxes or premiums into funds and are then insured against the specific risk covered by that program. For example, in the Social Security program, workers and employers pay taxes and then are covered so that they receive benefits when they reach retirement age or become disabled. Other programs insure workers against the risk of unemployment, temporary disability, workplace accidents or diseases, and requirements for medical care in old age.

Series Bf213. The sum of series Bf214–215.

Series Bf215, Health Insurance (Medicare). Includes Hospital Insurance and Supplementary Medical Insurance.

Series Bf216, Railroad Retirement. Excludes the financial interchange between Old-Age, Survivors, and Disability Insurance and the Railroad Retirement system.

Series Bf217, Public Employee Retirement. Includes the military retirement system. Excludes refunds of employee contributions, while administrative expenses are not available for some programs.

TABLE Bf212–224 Public expenditures on social welfare – social insurance: 1929–1995 *Continued*

Series Bf218, unemployment insurance and employment services. Includes unemployment compensation under state programs, programs for federal employees, trade adjustment and training allowances, and payments under the extended, emergency, disaster, and special unemployment insurance programs.

Series Bf221. State temporary disability insurance programs are found in California, New Jersey, New York, Puerto Rico, and Rhode Island. The programs provide cash and medical benefits for temporary disability. They include private plans where applicable and state administrative costs. Hawai'i also offers temporary disability insurance, but data on the Hawaiian program are not available.

Series Bf223–224. Workers' compensation expenditures include cash and medical benefits paid under public law by private insurance carriers, state funds, and self-insurers. Administrative costs of private carriers and self-insurers are not available. Beginning in 1969–1970, the series include the federal Black Lung Benefits program.

TABLE Bf225–231 Public expenditures on social welfare – public aid: 1929–1995

Contributed by Price V. Fishback and Melissa A. Thomasson

		Public assistance					
	Total	Total	Medical payments	Social services	Supplemental Security Income	Food Stamps	Other public aid
	Bf225	Bf226	Bf227	Bf228	Bf229	Bf230	Bf231
Year	Million dollars	Million dollars	Million dollars	Million dollars	Million dollars	Million dollars	Million dollars
1929	60.0	59.9	—	—	—	—	0.1
1930	77.8	77.5	—	—	—	—	0.3
1931	164.0	145.0	—	—	—	—	19.0
1932	255.9	189.9	—	—	—	—	66.0
1933	689.1	344.4	—	—	—	—	344.8
1934	2,530.5	435.9	—	—	—	—	2,094.6
1935	2,997.6	623.9	—	—	—	—	2,373.7
1936	3,079.4	655.8	—	—	—	—	2,423.6
1937	3,436.0	779.5	—	—	—	—	2,656.6
1938	3,232.9	990.9	—	—	—	—	2,242.0
1939	4,229.6	1,102.2	—	—	—	—	3,127.4
1940	3,597.0	1,124.3	—	—	—	—	2,472.7
1941	3,523.7	1,108.2	—	—	—	—	2,415.5
1942	2,777.1	1,061.5	—	—	—	—	1,715.6
1943	1,549.7	1,011.5	—	—	—	—	538.2
1944	1,031.5	1,014.5	—	—	—	—	17.0
1945	1,030.6	1,028.8	—	—	—	—	1.7
1946	1,150.6	1,148.4	—	—	—	—	2.2
1947	1,441.8	1,441.7	—	—	—	—	0.2
1948	1,702.0	1,701.6	—	—	—	—	0.3
1949	2,089.1	2,088.5	—	—	—	—	0.6
1950	2,496.2	2,490.2	51.3	—	—	—	6.0
1951	2,591.7	2,584.9	100.7	—	—	—	6.8
1952	2,584.7	2,584.1	119.1	—	—	—	0.5
1953	2,727.9	2,727.5	154.4	—	—	—	0.4
1954	2,788.2	2,776.3	175.5	—	—	—	11.9
1955	3,003.0	2,941.1	211.9	—	—	—	61.9
1956	3,114.7	3,023.7	252.7	—	—	—	91.0
1957	3,308.5	3,230.6	287.6	—	—	—	77.9
1958	3,615.4	3,539.5	320.2	—	—	—	75.9
1959	3,997.9	3,890.9	410.0	—	—	—	107.0
1960	4,101.1	4,041.7	492.7	—	—	—	59.4
1961	4,444.3	4,301.0	588.9	—	—	—	143.4
1962	4,945.3	4,675.0	812.4	—	—	—	270.3
1963	5,295.9	5,029.0	1,000.8	—	—	—	267.0
1964	5,642.1	5,381.1	1,147.6	—	—	—	261.0
1965	6,283.5	5,874.9	1,367.1	—	—	—	408.5
1966	7,301.1	6,497.0	1,724.9	—	—	—	804.1
1967	8,811.0	7,832.4	2,475.1	—	—	—	978.6
1968	11,091.6	9,886.5	3,723.2	547.3	—	—	1,205.1
1969	13,439.1	11,925.9	4,595.6	554.5	—	—	1,513.2

(continued)

TABLE Bf225–231 Public expenditures on social welfare – public aid: 1929–1995

Contributed by Price V. Fishback and Melissa A. Thomasson

		Public assistance					
	Total	Total	Medical payments	Social services	Supplemental Security Income	Food Stamps	Other public aid
	Bf225	Bf226	Bf227	Bf228	Bf229	Bf230	Bf231
Year	Million dollars	Million dollars	Million dollars	Million dollars	Million dollars	Million dollars	Million dollars
1970	16,487.8	14,433.5	5,212.7	712.6	—	577.0	1,477.3
1971	21,262.0	18,075.0	6,277.5	950.4	—	1,576.3	1,610.7
1972	26,078.2	21,895.0	7,751.6	2,160.5	—	1,866.8	2,316.4
1973	28,691.4	24,002.6	9,208.7	2,306.3	45.7	2,212.9	2,430.2
1974	31,520.4	23,827.4	10,371.9	2,155.1	2,831.5	2,838.9	2,022.6
1975	41,446.6	27,409.4	13,550.6	2,622.4	6,091.6	4,693.9	3,251.7
1976	49,023.4 [1]	31,384.5	15,708.8	2,799.4	6,540.3 [1]	5,699.7	5,398.9
1977	53,812.4	35,376.0	18,351.7	3,216.8	6,818.9	5,472.0	6,145.5
1978	59,925.8	37,360.3	20,471.9	2,840.1	7,193.7	5,139.5	10,232.3
1979	65,307.0	40,497.1	23,491.0	2,725.8	7,532.3	6,816.1	10,461.5
1980	72,703.1	45,064.3	27,570.1	2,342.8	8,226.5	9,083.3	10,329.0
1981	83,634.0	51,744.7	32,492.3	2,489.9	9,288.0	11,136.4	11,464.9
1982	82,206.2	53,860.0	34,804.6	2,567.5	9,753.0	10,761.0	7,832.2
1983	88,330.7	57,181.6	37,180.6	2,507.9	10,793.8	12,540.7	7,814.6
1984	92,979.4	61,906.0	40,194.8	2,788.9	11,136.7	12,375.2	7,561.5
1985	98,361.8	66,170.2	43,859.6 [2]	2,742.8	11,840.0	12,512.7	7,838.9
1986	104,200.2	70,839.6	47,242.9	2,670.7	12,887.4	12,397.0	8,076.2
1987	112,115.1 [1]	78,249.2	53,121.4	2,696.8 [1]	13,638.0 [1]	12,362.1	7,865.8
1988	119,723.4	84,152.2	58,039.4	2,700.0	14,687.1	13,071.1	7,813.0
1989	128,609.8	91,290.6	64,548.3	2,670.5	15,823.3	13,589.3	7,906.6
1990	146,811.1	105,093.8	76,175.1	2,753.2	17,230.4	16,254.5	8,232.4
1991	181,334.4	133,664.2	101,909.0	2,822.5	19,646.2	19,471.3	8,552.7
1992	207,953.0	152,018.2	117,622.1	2,707.6	23,423.2	23,232.9	9,278.7
1993	220,999.8	160,625.0	125,138.0	3,712.9	26,506.2	24,496.7	9,371.9
1994	238,025.3	171,755.1	134,204.5	3,645.2	30,085.5	25,273.6	10,911.1
1995	253,530.0	187,219.0	150,869.0	3,729.0	30,138.0	25,319.0	10,854.0

[1] Revised figure. See text for Table Bf188–195.

[2] The data reported in the 1997 and 1999 source articles for the year 1980 is 44,182.7, which does not precisely match the data in the July 1995 source owing to revisions in the procedures for estimating health expenditures.

Sources

Estimates presented for 1890 and 1913 were based primarily on the following: R. A. Musgrave and J. J. Culbertson, "The Growth of Public Expenditures in the U.S., 1890–1948," *National Tax Journal* (June 1953): 97–115; J. Frederic Dewhurst and Associates, *America's Needs and Resources* (Twentieth Century Fund, 1955); and reports of official agencies. Data for 1929–1989, U.S. Social Security Administration, *Social Welfare Expenditures under Public Programs in the United States, 1929–90* (July 1995); Ann Kallman Bixby, "Public Social Welfare Expenditures, Fiscal Year 1992," *Social Security Bulletin* 58 (2) (1995): 65–73. Data for 1990–1995 are from Ann Kallman Bixby, "Public Social Welfare Expenditures, Fiscal Year 1994," *Social Security Bulletin* 60 (3) (1997): 42; and Ann Kallman Bixby, "Public Social Welfare Expenditures, Fiscal Year 1995," *Social Security Bulletin* 62 (2) (1999): 88, 94. Most of the series in this table are annually updated in the *Social Security Bulletin: Annual Statistical Supplement*, Table 3.A3. See the text for Table Bf188–195 for further discussion of the sources.

Documentation

More information on the public aid programs is available in Tables Bf568–678 and Bf689–716.

Series Bf225. Includes cash payments and medical assistance under Aid to Families with Dependent Children (AFDC), Medicaid, emergency assistance, WIC (Women, Infants and Children), General Assistance programs, public assistance, work relief, other emergency aid, surplus food for the needy, food stamps, repatriate and refugee assistance, social services and work incentive activities, and the Job Corps, Neighborhood Youth Corps, and work-experience training programs under the Economic Opportunity Act and related laws. It is the sum of series Bf226 and Bf229–231. Certain other economic opportunity programs are included in series Bf195 as anti-poverty programs.

Series Bf226. The figures on public assistance include cash payments and medical assistance under the following programs: AFDC, Medicaid, emergency assistance, WIC, and general assistance from state and local funds. It also includes social services. Beginning in 1969, work incentive program expenditures are included.

Series Bf229. Supplemental Security Insurance (SSI) was established by Congress in 1972, with payments beginning in January 1974. SSI replaced the former federal–state programs of Old-Age Assistance, Aid to the Blind, and Aid to the Permanently and Totally Disabled.

Series Bf231. Includes work relief, other emergency aid, surplus food for the needy, repatriate and refugee assistance, work-experience training programs, the WIC program beginning in 1974, and Low-Income Home Energy Assistance beginning in 1981.

TABLE Bf232–245 Public expenditures on social welfare – health and medical programs: 1929–1995

Contributed by Price V. Fishback and Melissa A. Thomasson

	Expenditures, by program										Expenditures, by function			
	Under health and medical programs													
		Hospital and medical care												
	Total	Total	Civilian programs	Under Defense Department	Maternal and child health programs	Medical research	School health (education agencies)	Other public health activities	Medical facility construction	Under other programs	Total	Health and medical services	Medical research	Medical facilities construction
	Bf232	Bf233	Bf234	Bf235	Bf236	Bf237	Bf238	Bf239	Bf240	Bf241	Bf242	Bf243	Bf244	Bf245
Year	Million dollars	Million dollars	Million dollars	Million dollars	Million dollars	Million dollars	Million dollars	Million dollars	Million dollars	Million dollars	Million dollars	Million dollars	Million dollars	Million dollars
1929	351.1	146.3	117.1	29.2	6.2	—	9.4	88.8	100.4	126.0	477.1	372.5	0.0	104.6
1930	378.1	162.7	133.7	29.0	—	—	9.7	102.3	103.4	134.4	512.5	400.5	0.0	112.0
1931	405.8	179.1	150.2	29.0	—	0.3	10.1	108.6	107.7	143.4	549.3	431.8	0.3	117.2
1932	434.5	218.2	187.9	30.3	—	1.6	10.5	115.0	89.2	146.1	580.6	476.2	1.6	102.8
1933	417.6	232.4	204.5	28.0	—	0.9	10.0	114.6	59.8	128.1	545.9	471.1	0.9	73.9
1934	400.3	226.3	199.4	26.9	—	0.3	9.3	114.9	49.6	97.4	497.8	444.6	0.3	52.9
1935	427.2	253.1	225.3	27.7	6.9	0.3	10.0	112.2	44.8	116.0	543.2	495.1	0.3	47.8
1936	453.9	267.1	237.5	29.7	2.5	0.5	10.6	121.0	52.1	128.4	582.3	526.7	0.5	55.1
1937	500.1	277.6	245.9	31.7	9.9	1.4	12.1	132.1	66.8	137.7	637.6	560.0	1.4	76.2
1938	539.5	289.5	255.9	33.6	11.6	1.7	13.5	147.7	75.5	144.9	684.4	597.5	1.7	85.2
1939	575.2	290.2	255.3	34.9	13.0	2.0	15.0	153.3	101.7	149.0	724.2	609.0	2.0	113.2
1940	615.5	343.0	297.6	45.4	13.8	2.6	16.4	154.5	85.2	166.1	781.6	679.5	2.6	99.5
1941	724.4	472.9	315.1	157.8	16.0	2.5	17.8	152.4	62.7	168.1	892.4	822.5	2.5	67.4
1942	948.7	661.3	311.7	349.6	17.3	2.4	19.2	154.6	93.8	176.8	1,125.4	1,025.0	2.4	98.0
1943	1,885.8	1,456.3	325.4	1,130.9	17.7	2.6	20.6	177.4	211.2	185.7	2,071.5	1,854.9	2.6	214.0
1944	2,225.1	1,866.8	335.0	1,531.8	46.7	2.6	21.9	163.4	123.7	203.9	2,429.0	2,297.6	2.6	128.8
1945	2,354.2	1,995.9	364.8	1,631.1	62.1	2.5	23.3	178.0	92.4	225.2	2,579.4	2,468.2	2.5	108.7
1946	1,904.1	1,528.6	400.6	1,128.0	53.3	3.5	24.6	230.3	63.8	378.0	2,282.1	2,178.9	3.5	99.7
1947	1,367.0	963.9	567.6	396.2	35.2	25.6	24.7	260.0	57.7	731.6	2,098.6	1,848.3	27.0	223.3
1948	1,416.0	941.4	696.3	245.1	30.6	47.0	24.7	287.5	84.6	736.7	2,152.5	1,989.2	49.6	113.7
1949	1,753.1	1,096.5	782.4	314.1	31.4	60.8	27.7	325.1	211.5	904.4	2,657.4	2,242.4	65.1	349.9
1950	2,063.5	1,222.3	886.1	336.2	29.8	69.2	30.6	350.8	360.8	1,001.9	3,065.4	2,470.2	72.9	522.3
1951	2,782.8	1,812.1	980.0	832.0	33.4	79.6	31.2	370.7	455.8	1,030.1	3,812.8	3,162.6	84.6	565.6
1952	3,331.3	2,207.5	1,087.7	1,119.8	36.5	99.4	31.8	462.1	494.0	1,151.8	4,483.1	3,767.1	103.3	612.7
1953	3,190.4	2,157.9	1,185.5	972.4	39.9	102.1	45.1	391.6	453.8	1,187.4	4,377.8	3,724.2	107.2	546.4
1954	3,099.1	2,035.7	1,227.4	808.3	90.1	113.5	58.3	363.9	437.5	1,236.7	4,335.7	3,725.6	118.8	491.3
1955	3,103.1	2,042.4	1,297.6	744.8	92.9	132.8	65.9	383.7	385.4	1,317.5	4,420.6	3,862.4	138.7	419.5
1956	3,307.1	2,233.7	1,471.2	762.5	104.2	154.0	73.4	369.6	372.2	1,382.2	4,689.3	4,127.2	161.7	400.4
1957	3,775.8	2,489.2	1,675.5	813.6	113.3	226.0	79.5	435.0	432.7	1,470.6	5,246.2	4,536.9	238.5	470.8
1958	4,090.9	2,649.4	1,760.7	888.7	122.1	278.0	85.6	394.5	561.2	1,584.6	5,675.4	4,788.0	291.7	595.7
1959	4,400.6	2,778.1	1,844.6	933.6	133.4	350.1	93.3	454.1	591.5	1,764.3	6,164.9	5,158.5	367.6	638.8
1960 [1]	4,463.8	2,853.3	1,973.2	880.1	141.3	448.9	101.0	401.2	518.1	1,931.3	6,395.1	5,346.8	470.6	577.7
1961	4,927.0	3,150.7	2,226.0	924.7	152.4	576.1	115.0	426.6	506.2	2,131.6	7,058.6	5,895.2	603.2	560.2
1962	5,229.8	3,138.9	2,132.8	1,006.1	174.1	780.5	129.0	478.1	529.2	2,407.7	7,637.5	6,237.5	818.3	581.7
1963	5,593.5	3,270.5	2,274.6	995.8	190.3	920.3	128.4	531.5	552.6	2,710.7	8,304.2	6,718.8	963.0	622.4
1964	6,003.5	3,536.0	2,446.3	1,089.7	211.7	1,042.5	127.7	548.7	536.9	2,967.4	8,970.9	7,261.3	1,096.0	613.6

Note appears at end of table

(continued)

TABLE Bf232–245 Public expenditures on social welfare – health and medical programs: 1929–1995 *Continued*

	Expenditures, by program										Expenditures, by function			
	Under health and medical programs													
		Hospital and medical care												
	Total	Total	Civilian programs	Under Defense Department	Maternal and child health programs	Medical research	School health (education agencies)	Other public health activities	Medical facility construction	Under other programs	Total	Health and medical services	Medical research	Medical facilities construction
	Bf232	Bf233	Bf234	Bf235	Bf236	Bf237	Bf238	Bf239	Bf240	Bf241	Bf242	Bf243	Bf244	Bf245
Year	Million dollars	Million dollars	Million dollars	Million dollars	Million dollars	Million dollars	Million dollars	Million dollars	Million dollars	Million dollars	Million dollars	Million dollars	Million dollars	Million dollars
1965	6,155.0	3,391.0	2,510.0	881.0	239.0	1,227.0	140.0	614.0	544.0	3,283.3	9,438.3	7,531.0	1,286.3	621.0
1966	6,740.0	3,720.0	2,682.0	1,038.0	274.0	1,374.0	157.0	663.0	552.0	3,843.7	10,583.7	8,505.6	1,442.6	635.5
1967	7,383.0	3,982.0	2,630.0	1,352.0	326.0	1,425.0	178.0	832.0	640.0	8,091.7	15,474.7	13,275.6	1,499.1	700.0
1968	8,172.0	4,300.0	2,759.0	1,541.0	352.0	1,617.0	205.0	927.0	771.0	11,477.3	19,649.3	17,143.5	1,684.9	820.9
1969	8,828.0	4,564.0	2,933.0	1,631.0	430.0	1,620.0	225.0	1,103.0	886.0	13,804.3	22,632.3	19,997.2	1,701.2	933.9
1970 [1]	9,606.0	4,983.0	3,301.0	1,682.0	450.0	1,684.0	247.0	1,312.0	930.0	15,357.0	24,963.0	22,186.7	1,775.4	1,000.9
1971	10,437.0	5,527.0	3,702.0	1,825.0	420.0	1,694.0	272.0	1,492.0	1,032.0	17,499.7	27,936.7	25,057.7	1,761.9	1,117.1
1972	11,824.0	6,114.0	4,051.0	2,063.0	516.0	1,938.0	281.0	1,870.0	1,105.0	20,451.7	32,275.7	29,039.9	2,021.0	1,214.8
1973	12,799.0	6,910.0	4,591.0	2,319.0	474.0	2,173.0	300.0	1,925.0	1,017.0	23,068.4	35,867.4	32,483.6	2,262.0	1,121.8
1974	14,198.0	7,565.0	4,981.0	2,584.0	516.0	2,242.0	325.0	2,454.0	1,096.0	26,568.8	40,766.8	37,231.9	2,320.0	1,214.9
1975	16,742.0	8,836.0	6,019.0	2,817.0	567.0	2,648.0	352.0	2,815.0	1,524.0	34,609.4	51,351.4	46,949.7	2,741.0	1,660.7
1976	18,356.0	8,993.0	6,136.0	2,857.0	614.0	3,307.0	369.0	3,272.0	1,801.0	40,043.6	58,399.6	52,985.4	3,401.0	2,013.2
1977	19,441.0	9,336.0	6,313.0	3,023.0	680.0	3,392.0	435.0	3,981.0	1,617.0	47,433.2	66,874.2	61,502.0	3,509.8	1,862.4
1978	22,201.0	10,247.0	6,933.0	3,314.0	718.0	4,029.0	496.0	5,061.0	1,650.0	54,084.9	76,285.9	70,202.5	4,163.5	1,919.9
1979	24,040.0	11,363.0	7,681.0	3,682.0	779.0	4,271.0	519.0	5,640.0	1,468.0	61,930.9	85,970.9	79,825.8	4,401.1	1,744.0
1980 [1]	27,263.0	12,303.0	8,105.0	4,198.0	870.0	4,924.0	575.0	6,931.0	1,660.0	72,833.0	100,096.0	93,044.5	5,068.5	1,983.0
1981	29,588.0	13,376.0	8,536.0	4,840.0	921.0	5,193.0	612.0	8,062.0	1,424.0	86,452.0	116,040.0	108,852.7	5,328.3	1,859.0
1982	32,870.0	15,195.0	9,614.0	5,581.0	912.0	5,454.0	649.0	9,024.0	1,636.0	98,056.5	130,926.5	123,220.9	5,589.3	2,116.3
1983	34,090.0	15,156.0	9,098.0	6,058.0	1,114.0	5,693.0	685.0	9,603.0	1,839.0	108,005.3	142,095.3	133,938.2	5,844.6	2,312.5
1984	35,722.0	15,608.0	9,260.0	6,348.0	1,093.0	6,273.0	726.0	10,460.0	1,562.0	118,019.1	153,741.1	145,150.1	6,463.3	2,127.7
1985 [1]	39,053.0	16,565.0 [2]	9,143.0	7,422.0 [2]	1,222.0	6,891.0	788.0 [2]	11,912.0	1,675.0	132,231.8	171,284.8	162,034.2	7,117.6	2,133.0
1986	43,953.0	19,474.0	11,275.0	8,199.0	1,376.0	7,561.0	842.0	13,245.0	1,455.0	141,866.0	185,819.0	175,999.7	7,747.2	2,072.1
1987	48,067.0	21,986.0	12,856.0	9,130.0	1,584.0	7,847.0	888.0	14,271.0	1,491.0	155,342.8	203,409.8	193,090.5	8,056.5	2,262.8
1988	53,096.0	23,927.0	14,257.0	9,670.0	1,666.0	9,132.0	944.0	15,983.0	1,444.0	164,596.5	217,692.5	205,937.1	9,347.3	2,408.1
1989	57,123.0	24,584.0	14,426.0	10,158.0	1,775.0	9,800.0	1,028.0 [2]	18,261.0	1,675.0	184,155.3	241,278.3	228,922.8	10,034.7	2,320.8
1990	61,684.0	25,971.0	14,809.0	11,162.0	1,865.0	10,848.0	1,113.0	19,354.0	2,533.0	212,788.0	274,472.0	260,408.0	11,086.0	2,978.0
1991	65,810.0	28,251.0	15,511.0	12,740.0	1,981.0	11,312.0	1,194.0	20,881.0	2,191.0	248,417.0	314,227.0	299,692.0	11,568.0	2,967.0
1992	70,114.0	28,664.0	15,895.0	12,769.0	2,106.0	12,599.0	1,230.0	22,980.0	2,535.0	283,060.0	353,174.0	336,925.0	12,869.0	3,380.0
1993	74,717.0 [2]	30,617.0	17,208.0	13,409.0	2,185.0	12,779.0	1,320.0 [2]	24,772.0	3,044.0	306,993.0	381,710.0	364,858.0	13,058.0	3,794.0
1994	80,235.0 [2]	31,562.0	18,428.0	13,134.0	2,272.0	13,988.0	1,489.0 [2]	27,685.0	3,239.0	328,545.0	408,780.0	390,482.0	14,280.0	4,018.0
1995	85,507.0	31,904.0	18,482.0	13,422.0	2,348.0	14,982.0	1,667.0	30,808.0	3,798.0	349,568.0	435,075.0	415,424.0	15,271.0	4,380.0

[1] The data reported in the 1997 and 1999 source articles do not precisely match the data in the July 1995 source, due to revisions in the procedures for estimating health expenditures. The differences are typically less than $500 million.

[2] Revised figure. See text for Table Bf188–195.

Sources

Data for 1929–1989, U.S. Social Security Administration, *Social Welfare Expenditures under Public Programs in the United States, 1929–90* (July 1995); Ann Kallman Bixby, "Public Social Welfare Expenditures, Fiscal Year 1992," *Social Security Bulletin* 58 (2) (1995): 65–73. Data for 1990–1995 are from Ann Kallman Bixby, "Public Social Welfare Expenditures, Fiscal Year 1994," *Social Security Bulletin* 60 (3) (1997): 42; and Ann Kallman Bixby, "Public Social Welfare Expenditures, Fiscal Year 1995," *Social Security Bulletin* 62 (2) (1999): 88, 94. Most of the series in this table are annually updated in the *Social Security Bulletin: Annual Statistical Supplement*, Table 3.A3. See the text for Table Bf188–195 for further discussion of the sources.

Documentation

The U.S. Social Security Administration reports information on health and medical care on the basis of statutory programs and administrative structure, rather than strictly by function; therefore, all health and medical expenditures are not reported under the category health and medical programs in the reporting of the Social Welfare Expenditures.

TABLE Bf232–245 Public expenditures on social welfare – health and medical programs: 1929–1995 *Continued*

Series Bf232. The sum of series Bf233 and Bf236–240. The estimates for health and medical programs are derived from the Census of Governments and the U.S. Budget. They include net public expenditures for hospital and medical care (after deduction of fee payments), hospital construction, school health, community and related public health services, and maternal and child health services. They exclude state and local expenditures for domiciliary care in institutions other than mental and tuberculosis. They also exclude expenditures for health and medical services provided in connection with Old-Age, Survivors, Disability, and Health Insurance, state temporary disability insurance, workers' compensation, public assistance, vocational rehabilitation, and veterans' and antipoverty programs; these are included in the total expenditures shown for those programs. Also excluded are international health activities. Omitted from the health category, but included under education in Table Bf255–262, are expenditures for medical schools and other health training institutions.

Series Bf233. The sum of series Bf234–235.

Series Bf235. Includes medical care for military dependents.

Series Bf236. Includes services for disabled children.

Series Bf241. Sums the expenditures listed under other administrative structures, including expenditures on Medicare, series Bf215; health and medical benefits under state temporary disability insurance, series Bf222; workers' compensation health and medical benefits, series Bf224; public assistance medical payments, series Bf227; veterans' hospital and medical care, series Bf249; veterans' hospital construction, series Bf250; veterans' medical and prosthetic research, series Bf251; and vocational rehabilitation spending on medical services and medical research, series Bf265–266.

Series Bf242. Includes health and medical expenditures under all public programs. This series is the sum of series Bf232 and Bf241. It is also the sum of series Bf243–245 (see Bixby 1995, p. 73). When comparing the two sets of sums, there are some rounding errors in some years. In 1992 through 1994, there are some discrepancies between the two sums greater than $0.2 million but smaller than 0.02 percent of the value of the series.

Series Bf243, expenditures on health and medical services. The series is the sum of expenditures under the following: medicare, series Bf215; state temporary disability insurance spending on health and medical benefits, series Bf222; workers' compensation spending on health and medical care, series Bf224; public assistance medical payments, series Bf227; hospital and medical care for civilians, series Bf234; hospital and medical care under the Defense Department, series Bf235; maternal and child health programs, series Bf236; other public health activities, series Bf239; veterans' hospital and medical care, series Bf249; medical vocational rehabilitation, series Bf265; and school health expenditures by education agencies (series not listed in education tables).

Series Bf244, medical research expenditures. The series is the sum of expenditures under the following: health and medical programs, series Bf237; veterans' programs, series Bf251; and vocational rehabilitation, series Bf266.

Series Bf245, medical facilities construction. The series is the sum of spending under both health and medical programs and veterans' programs, series Bf240 and Bf250.

TABLE Bf246–254 Public expenditures on social welfare – veterans' programs: 1929–1995

Contributed by Price V. Fishback and Melissa A. Thomasson

			Health and medical programs						
	Total	Pensions and compensation	Total	Hospital and medical care	Hospital construction	Medical and prosthetic research	Education	Life insurance	Welfare and other
	Bf246	Bf247	Bf248	Bf249	Bf250	Bf251	Bf252	Bf253	Bf254
Year	Million dollars	Million dollars	Million dollars	Million dollars	Million dollars	Million dollars	Million dollars	Million dollars	Million dollars
1929	657.9	434.7	50.9	46.7	4.2	—	—	136.4	35.8
1930	667.8	433.4	59.4	50.7	8.6	—	—	140.0	35.0
1931	744.3	504.4	68.3	58.7	9.5	—	—	137.7	34.0
1932	825.0	562.2	77.8	64.3	13.6	—	—	146.0	39.0
1933	818.8	565.0	69.9	55.8	14.1	—	—	145.3	38.6
1934	529.5	333.0	42.2	38.9	3.3	—	—	124.6	29.8
1935	597.5	386.5	50.8	47.8	3.0	—	—	122.8	37.5
1936	3,825.5	411.3	55.1	52.1	3.0	—	—	117.7	3,241.4
1937	892.7 [1]	409.0	62.1	52.8	9.4	—	—	113.1	308.4
1938	627.3	415.2	64.6	54.8	9.7	—	—	107.8	39.8
1939	606.1	429.7	68.6	57.2	11.5	—	—	76.3	31.3
1940	629.0	443.3	75.8	61.5	14.3	—	—	77.0	32.9
1941	612.9	448.4	69.9	65.1	4.7	—	—	68.7	25.8
1942	645.4	445.7	72.4	68.2	4.2	—	—	60.4	67.0
1943	623.3	457.8	75.1	72.3	2.8	—	—	67.0	23.3
1944	720.0	513.1	87.0	82.0	5.1	—	—	93.7	26.2
1945	1,125.8	766.6	101.8	85.5	16.3	—	9.8	201.2	46.4
1946	2,402.9	1,279.5	243.8	207.9	35.9	—	368.9	376.0	134.7
1947	5,682.5	1,834.4	578.0	411.1	165.6	1.4	2,273.3	440.9	556.0
1948	6,638.2	1,910.6	563.5	531.8	29.1	2.6	2,630.2	433.1	1,100.8
1949	6,926.7	1,980.1	718.2	575.5	138.4	4.3	2,817.9	452.3	958.2
1950	6,865.7	2,092.1	748.0	582.8	161.5	3.7	2,691.6	475.7	858.3
1951	5,996.0	2,113.8	695.8	581.0	109.8	5.0	2,019.3	515.0	652.1
1952	5,255.6	2,183.7	766.7	644.2	118.7	3.9	1,380.7	554.9	369.6
1953	4,734.7	2,448.6	739.2	641.5	92.6	5.1	706.8	538.8	301.4
1954	4,630.9	2,507.1	739.9	680.8	53.8	5.3	596.4	538.1	249.4

Note appears at end of table

(continued)

TABLE Bf246–254 Public expenditures on social welfare – veterans' programs: 1929–1995 *Continued*

			Health and medical programs						
	Total	Pensions and compensation	Total	Hospital and medical care	Hospital construction	Medical and prosthetic research	Education	Life insurance	Welfare and other
	Bf246	Bf247	Bf248	Bf249	Bf250	Bf251	Bf252	Bf253	Bf254
Year	Million dollars	Million dollars	Million dollars	Million dollars	Million dollars	Million dollars	Million dollars	Million dollars	Million dollars
1955	4,833.5	2,689.7	761.1	721.5	34.1	5.6	706.1	490.2	186.5
1956	5,061.2	2,805.4	759.9	725.2	28.2	6.5	809.5	476.2	210.2
1957	5,118.8	2,886.4	786.9	738.4	38.1	10.4	816.2	476.9	152.5
1958	5,426.7	3,126.7	843.8	799.3	34.5	10.0	736.9	490.0	229.3
1959	5,472.3	3,303.9	904.5	844.4	47.3	12.8	608.7	485.6	169.6
1960	5,479.2	3,402.7	954.0	879.4	59.6	15.1	409.6	494.1	218.8
1961	5,623.7	3,664.8	1,019.9	947.4	54.0	18.4	257.6	492.7	188.9
1962	5,654.1	3,749.1	1,041.3	962.0	52.5	26.8	157.2	499.5	207.1
1963	5,751.2	3,912.6	1,112.7	1,013.0	69.8	29.9	100.8	489.4	135.7
1964	5,861.5	4,001.7	1,172.8	1,063.0	76.7	33.2	69.6	471.6	145.7
1965	6,031.1	4,141.4	1,228.7	1,114.8	77.0	36.9 [1]	40.9	434.3	185.8
1966	6,358.3	4,409.3	1,285.1	1,160.9	83.5	40.7	34.4	442.1	187.4
1967	6,898.3	4,499.4	1,358.8	1,251.7	60.0	47.1	296.9	548.4	194.8
1968	7,246.7	4,644.1	1,438.7	1,342.5	49.9	46.3	465.7	503.8	194.4
1969	7,933.6	4,987.0	1,530.9	1,430.8	47.9	52.2	679.4	492.9	243.4
1970	9,078.1	5,393.8	1,784.1	1,651.4	70.9	61.8	1,018.5	502.3	379.4
1971	10,455.0 [1]	5,877.5	2,026.0 [1]	1,873.0	85.1	67.9	1,622.4	526.6	402.5
1972	11,522.3	6,209.3	2,431.4	2,255.6	109.8	66.0	1,924.6	523.7	433.3
1973	13,026.4	6,605.8	2,766.1	2,587.3	104.8	74.0	2,647.9	532.2	474.4
1974	14,112.4	6,777.4	2,983.5	2,786.6	118.9	78.0	3,206.9	538.5	606.2
1975	17,018.9	7,578.5	3,516.8	3,287.1	136.7	93.0	4,433.8	556.1	933.7
1976	18,958.0	8,279.7	4,060.9	3,754.7	212.2	94.0	5,350.6	564.3	702.5
1977	19,014.3	9,081.9	4,670.6	4,321.2	245.4	104.0	3,925.5	607.2	729.1
1978	19,744.0	9,676.5	5,237.5	4,855.6	269.9	112.0	3,405.6	614.3	810.1
1979	20,601.6	10,578.2	5,700.9	5,307.9	276.0	117.0	2,794.1	638.2	890.2
1980	21,465.5	11,306.0	6,203.9	5,749.9	323.0	131.0	2,400.7	664.5	890.4
1981	23,440.9	12,453.6	6,999.6	6,429.3	435.0	135.3	2,335.6	709.0	943.1
1982	24,708.1	13,301.6	7,825.8	7,210.2	480.3	135.3	1,816.3	747.0	1,017.4
1983	25,801.9	13,894.9	8,387.7	7,762.6	473.5	151.6	1,707.5	744.0	1,067.8
1984	26,274.9	14,050.5	8,935.9	8,179.9	565.7	190.3	1,402.0	719.0	1,167.5
1985	27,041.7 [1]	14,333.0	9,492.6 [1]	8,808.0	458.0	226.6	1,170.8	795.5	1,249.8
1986	27,444.9	14,493.2	9,923.1	9,119.8	617.1	186.2	866.8	893.0	1,268.8
1987	28,050.8	14,522.1	10,503.0	9,521.7	771.8	209.5	742.2	937.9	1,345.6
1988	29,663.4	14,913.9	11,331.0	10,151.5	964.1	215.3	653.0	963.1	1,802.4
1989	30,103.7	15,279.2	11,662.9	10,782.3	645.8	234.7	647.3	1,002.2	1,512.1
1990	30,916.2	15,792.6	12,004.1	11,321.4	445.0	237.7	522.8	1,037.8	1,558.9
1991	32,857.3	16,284.3	13,221.5	12,189.6	776.4	255.5	569.5	1,039.3	1,742.7
1992	35,642.0	16,539.3	15,442.0	13,451.8	844.9	270.4	772.0	1,113.7	1,775.0
1993	36,378.3	17,205.2	15,410.5	14,382.5	749.6	278.6	937.7	904.7	1,920.2
1994	37,984.8	17,481.0	16,231.4	15,089.5	778.8	292.3	1,098.3	971.5	2,112.6
1995	39,072.0	18,070.4	16,654.4	15,714.0	581.9	289.1	1,118.2	946.3	2,282.7

[1] Revised figure. See text for Table Bf188–195.

Sources

Data for 1929–1989, U.S. Social Security Administration, *Social Welfare Expenditures under Public Programs in the United States, 1929–90* (July 1995); Ann Kallman Bixby, "Public Social Welfare Expenditures, Fiscal Year 1992," *Social Security Bulletin* 58 (2) (1995): 65–73. Data for 1990–1995 are from Ann Kallman Bixby, "Public Social Welfare Expenditures, Fiscal Year 1994," *Social Security Bulletin* 60 (3) (1997): 42; and Ann Kallman Bixby, "Public Social Welfare Expenditures, Fiscal Year 1995," *Social Security Bulletin* 62 (2) (1999): 88. Most of the series in this table are annually updated in the *Social Security Bulletin: Annual Statistical Supplement*, Table 3.A3. See the text for Table Bf188–195 for further discussion of the sources.

Documentation

The estimates for veterans programs were obtained from the *Annual Report of Veterans Administration*, supplemented by unpublished data.

Series Bf246. The sum of series Bf247–248 and Bf252–254.

Series Bf247 and Bf252. Series Bf247 includes burial awards and, beginning in 1965, subsistence payments to disabled veterans undergoing training and special allowances for survivors of veterans who did not qualify under Old-Age, Survivors, Disability, and Health Insurance. Beginning in 1973–1974, subsistence payments to disabled veterans undergoing training shifted from the pensions and compensation to the education series.

Series Bf248. The sum of series Bf249–251.

Series Bf253. Excludes the service persons' group life insurance program.

Series Bf254. The most unusual increase in the series came when Congress voted to pay a "veterans' bonus" in 1936 over Franklin Roosevelt's veto. The bonus provided for the immediate payment to veterans of World War I of their adjusted compensation certificates, which were supposed to come due in 1945.

TABLE Bf255–262 Public expenditures on social welfare – education and housing: 1929–1995

Contributed by Price V. Fishback and Melissa A. Thomasson

	Education						Housing	
		Elementary and secondary education		Higher education		Vocational and adult education		
	Total	Total	Construction	Total	Construction		Total	Public housing
	Bf255	Bf256	Bf257	Bf258	Bf259	Bf260	Bf261	Bf262
Year	Million dollars	Million dollars	Million dollars	Million dollars	Million dollars	Million dollars	Million dollars	Million dollars
1929	2,433.7	2,216.2	377.0	182.1	0.2	34.9	—	—
1930	2,522.8	2,288.2	370.9	196.1	30.9	37.9	—	—
1931	2,439.6	2,217.5	290.9	180.4	—	41.1	—	—
1932	2,351.8	2,144.4	202.0	164.3	0.9	42.4	—	—
1933	2,104.0	1,911.1	135.1	153.1	—	39.2	—	—
1934	1,913.8	1,732.8	112.5	143.2	14.4	37.3	0.4	0.4
1935	2,007.5	1,820.1	123.3	147.9	—	39.1	13.2	13.2
1936	2,227.6	2,012.5	255.0	154.8	—	50.8	41.7	41.7
1937	2,375.7	2,143.8	288.8	177.5	—	53.9	3.1	3.1
1938	2,563.0	2,296.6	355.9	199.3	19.4	66.6	3.9	3.9
1939	2,503.7	2,221.4	248.4	208.6	20.0	73.0	3.4	3.4
1940	2,561.2	2,267.4	258.0	217.6	20.6	75.4	4.2	4.2
1941	2,617.2	2,255.2	197.8	225.9	17.1	135.2	8.9	8.9
1942	2,694.2	2,262.8	138.2	251.0	13.6	178.7	14.3	14.3
1943	2,793.3	2,324.4	95.8	269.3	12.4	197.8	13.6	13.6
1944	2,800.4	2,392.2	53.9	261.5	11.3	144.4	13.3	13.3
1945	3,076.3	2,620.6	82.5	314.4	42.3	139.2	11.1	11.1
1946	3,296.8	2,834.0	111.1	363.5	73.5	97.9	158.7	158.7
1947	4,089.0	3,479.1	263.2	497.2	130.5	111.3	280.9	280.9
1948	4,897.3	4,130.1	413.7	633.6	191.0	131.7	27.3	27.3
1949	5,806.6	4,889.5	719.8	769.1	245.8	145.6	7.7	7.7
1950	6,674.1	5,596.2	1,019.4	914.7	310.3	160.8	14.6	14.5
1951	7,415.1	6,329.9	1,251.5	912.4	234.3	169.9	35.0	21.4
1952	8,245.7	7,115.0	1,483.6	947.9	161.7	179.0	37.1	25.0
1953	9,230.9	8,034.4	1,774.2	1,012.9	155.1	178.5	50.6	37.9
1954	10,084.4	8,815.5	2,066.4	1,081.5	146.9	183.9	67.4	53.8
1955	11,157.2	9,734.3	2,231.9	1,214.4	198.6	204.9	89.3	74.7
1956	12,154.4	10,578.8	2,395.5	1,349.9	244.4	221.9	111.7	92.0
1957	13,732.3	11,856.5	2,629.6	1,628.8	333.0	241.2	120.2	101.2
1958	15,312.6	13,150.8	2,868.1	1,893.0	423.9	261.1	134.2	110.6
1959	16,498.3	14,139.1	2,757.3	2,062.5	389.7	283.2	156.2	127.8
1960	17,626.2	15,109.0	2,661.8	2,190.7	357.9	298.0	176.8	143.5
1961	19,337.2	16,448.4	2,762.0	2,546.0	458.8	316.5	196.1	159.2
1962	21,004.6	17,743.6	2,862.2	2,877.7	554.8	353.7	216.6	173.3
1963	22,670.7	18,915.5	2,920.1	3,299.6	653.8	420.6	248.1	191.4
1964	24,989.0	20,688.1	2,978.0	3,740.0	703.0	512.9	277.7	206.5
1965	28,107.8	22,357.7	3,267.0	4,826.4	1,081.4	853.9	318.1	234.5
1966	32,825.1	25,566.0	3,754.9	6,023.7	1,482.3	1,108.1	334.9	249.2
1967	35,807.8	27,741.5	3,970.4	6,628.9	1,439.2	1,296.1	377.8	275.8
1968	40,589.7	31,675.4	4,255.8	7,327.7	1,323.1	1,435.3	427.6	293.7
1969	43,673.1	33,705.3	4,654.1	8,173.9	1,447.0	1,648.3	532.3	360.1
1970	50,845.5	38,632.3	4,659.1	9,907.0	1,566.9	2,144.4	701.2	459.9
1971	56,704.7	42,910.8	4,551.9	10,834.9	1,565.5	2,718.1	1,046.2	608.2
1972	59,385.1	44,524.1	4,458.9	11,582.6	1,481.9	3,021.0	1,332.4	731.1
1973	64,733.7	48,076.9	5,008.4	12,940.0	1,483.2	3,453.9	2,179.6	1,101.9
1974	70,533.9	52,459.2	4,978.9	13,955.8	1,386.3	3,880.4	2,554.0	1,233.1
1975	80,834.1	59,745.6	5,746.0	16,384.1	1,512.7	4,441.3	3,171.7	1,456.4
1976	87,729.7	63,234.9	5,920.1	18,741.9	1,557.7	5,504.9	3,370.8	1,716.0
1977	93,878.3	68,218.5	6,235.1	20,034.4	1,505.7	5,312.0	4,358.1	2,763.5
1978	101,517.8	73,133.1	5,245.2	21,893.3	1,458.5	6,133.3	5,224.7	3,626.0
1979	109,261.5	77,714.6	5,449.3	24,129.8	1,417.4	7,029.4	5,493.1	3,775.8
1980	121,049.6	87,149.9	6,524.0	26,175.9	1,528.1	7,375.2	6,879.0	4,680.6
1981	130,108.5	92,327.7	6,756.9	29,615.2	1,751.6	7,854.9	6,733.5	4,587.3
1982	138,089.3	97,419.5	6,772.2	32,369.1	1,991.7	7,997.2	9,202.1	6,643.5
1983	146,415.4	102,651.7	7,199.5	35,067.7	2,058.6	8,386.4	10,963.5	7,594.3
1984	157,188.9	110,066.7	7,258.0	37,796.8	1,962.4	9,069.4	11,531.8	8,408.2

(continued)

TABLE Bf255–262 Public expenditures on social welfare – education and housing: 1929–1995 *Continued*

	Education						Housing	
		Elementary and secondary education		Higher education				
	Total	Total	Construction	Total	Construction	Vocational and adult education	Total	Public housing
	Bf255	Bf256	Bf257	Bf258	Bf259	Bf260	Bf261	Bf262
Year	Million dollars	Million dollars	Million dollars	Million dollars	Million dollars	Million dollars	Million dollars	Million dollars
1985	172,047.5	120,696.6	8,358.0	41,130.4	2,346.6	9,891.2	12,598.5	9,340.3
1986	189,234.6	142,721.9	10,009.0	45,033.1	2,638.0	1,207.6	11,961.8	8,350.0
1987	204,563.7	154,917.5	11,325.0	48,022.1	3,086.9	1,247.4	13,173.5	9,230.7
1988	219,382.2	167,834.9	11,789.0	49,898.3	3,199.3	1,288.0	16,555.9	12,176.5
1989	238,771.0	183,170.7	14,584.0	54,028.5	3,313.0	1,209.2	18,126.7	13,210.9
1990	258,331.6	199,224.3	10,636.0	57,424.3	3,953.0	1,293.3	19,468.5	14,521.8
1991	277,147.1	215,798.8	12,363.0	59,582.6	3,981.1	1,314.3	21,522.6	16,177.4
1992	292,070.6	226,905.4	14,681.0	63,259.9	4,869.5	1,451.8	20,617.2	15,302.0
1993	331,996.8	252,506.5	22,288.0	77,558.1	8,990.3	1,494.9	20,782.3	15,302.0
1994	344,091.0	261,006.2	19,692.8	81,091.2	9,891.8	1,503.8	27,032.0	24,724.4
1995	365,625.3	277,874.5	24,809.9	85,743.8	10,490.3	1,508.0	29,361.1	24,724.4

Sources

Data for 1929–1989, U.S. Social Security Administration, *Social Welfare Expenditures under Public Programs in the United States, 1929–90* (July 1995); Ann Kallman Bixby, "Public Social Welfare Expenditures, Fiscal Year 1992," *Social Security Bulletin* 58 (2) (1995): 65–73. Data for 1990–1995 come from Ann Kallman Bixby, "Public Social Welfare Expenditures, Fiscal Year 1994," *Social Security Bulletin* 60 (3) (1997): 42; and Ann Kallman Bixby, "Public Social Welfare Expenditures, Fiscal Year 1995," *Social Security Bulletin* 62 (2) (1999): 88. Most of the series in this table are annually updated in the *Social Security Bulletin: Annual Statistical Supplement*, Table 3.A3. See the text for Table Bf188–195 for further discussion of the sources.

Documentation

The primary basis for the education estimates are the various federal and state expenditures series compiled by the U.S. Office of Education and appearing in the annual editions of the *Digest of Educational Statistics*. Data from these sources, however, are adjusted to fit the conceptual framework for these social welfare expenditures series. For example, the latter omit the various student and school construction loan programs and certain research and development expenditures that have subordinate educational objectives. Also excluded are in-house training programs conducted outside of educational institutions and expenditures for international education (except for U.S.-operated schools abroad).

In addition, certain programs included in the U.S. Office of Education series, such as veterans' benefits, manpower and training programs, school meals, and health-related research facilities, are included elsewhere in the social welfare expenditures series and are therefore not included as education expenditures.

Series Bf255–260. The education data include public expenditures for support, maintenance, and operation of local, state, and federal elementary–secondary, vocational, adult, and higher education institutions.

Series Bf255, public expenditures on education. The sum of series Bf256, Bf258, and Bf260. Includes expenditures for the support of students, the construction of educational facilities, and the administrative operations of state and local departments of education and the U.S. Office of Education. Federal administrative expenditures (U.S. Department of Education) and research costs are included only in total spending, series Bf255. State and local expenditures for vocational and adult education are not available after 1985.

Series Bf261. The data on housing expenditures are supplied principally by the U.S. Department of Housing and Urban Development and confined to outlays for housing owned or operated by a public body ("public housing") and to programs designed to provide subsidized housing for low- and moderate-income families (for example, rent supplements, homeownership and rental housing assistance, and rehabilitation grants). Excluded from the series are urban renewal and city demonstration programs, as well as mortgage and loan insurance programs and programs providing credit facilities for home-financing institutions.

TABLE Bf263–270 Public expenditures on social welfare – other programs: 1929–1995

Contributed by Price V. Fishback and Melissa A. Thomasson

		Vocational rehabilitation						
	Total	Total	Medical care	Medical research	Child nutrition	Child welfare	Special OEO and ACTION programs	Social welfare, not elsewhere classified
	Bf263	Bf264	Bf265	Bf266	Bf267	Bf268	Bf269	Bf270
Year	Million dollars	Million dollars	Million dollars	Million dollars	Million dollars	Million dollars	Million dollars	Million dollars
1929	76.2	1.6	0.1	—	—	—	—	74.7
1930	77.5	1.8	0.1	—	—	—	—	75.7
1931	78.8	2.1	0.2	—	—	—	—	76.7
1932	80.9	2.3	0.2	—	—	—	—	78.7
1933	88.8	2.2	0.2	—	—	—	—	86.6
1934	95.8	2.1	0.2	—	—	—	—	93.7
1935	99.0	2.3	0.2	—	—	26.0	—	70.7
1936	100.5	2.7	0.3	—	0.2	26.1	—	71.5
1937	105.4	3.4	0.5	—	0.2	35.4	—	66.4
1938	108.2	4.0	0.4	—	0.6	47.6	—	56.1
1939	113.8	4.1	0.3	—	1.3	46.4	—	62.0
1940	116.4	4.2	0.3	—	4.0	45.0	—	63.3
1941	136.4	4.8	0.3	—	13.7	43.6	—	74.3
1942	153.9	5.3	0.4	—	23.3	42.1	—	83.1
1943	158.6	5.7	0.6	—	23.4	46.2	—	83.4
1944	181.6	6.6	0.8	—	34.4	50.2	—	90.5
1945	197.9	10.2	1.4	—	47.4	55.5	—	84.9
1946	232.7	14.2	2.2	—	57.1	60.7	—	100.7
1947	315.6	20.0	3.5	—	100.3	79.3	—	116.0
1948	368.8	25.1	5.2	—	117.1	98.5	—	128.1
1949	395.9	26.5	6.2	—	131.8	101.9	—	135.7
1950	447.7	30.0	7.4	—	160.2	104.9	—	152.6
1951	461.9	31.0	7.8	—	166.0	108.4	—	156.4
1952	451.0	33.4	8.7	—	154.2	113.4	—	149.9
1953	503.0	35.2	8.9	—	191.9	120.5	—	155.3
1954	612.1	36.7	8.7	—	240.3	126.2	—	208.9
1955	619.0	42.4	9.1	0.3	239.6	135.1	—	201.8
1956	735.4	56.3	11.0	1.2	294.4	145.6	—	239.1
1957	823.0	66.5	12.7	2.1	364.0	159.7	—	232.8
1958	920.4	77.8	15.0	3.7	325.4	176.4	—	340.8
1959	1,009.6	86.9	16.7	4.7	368.4	184.8	—	369.4
1960	1,139.4	96.3	17.7	6.6	398.7	211.5	—	432.9
1961	1,342.8	109.0	20.4	8.7	405.5	224.5	—	603.7
1962	1,414.5	128.6	22.5	11.0	463.7	246.6	—	575.5
1963	1,593.4	148.5	26.0	12.8	479.8	268.8	—	696.3
1964	1,746.0	182.4	31.2	20.3	521.6	314.6	—	727.4
1965	2,065.6	210.4	34.2	22.4	617.4	354.3	51.7	831.8
1966	2,308.8	298.6	47.9	27.9	537.4	400.5	287.3	785.0
1967	2,848.5	410.2	67.5	27.0	588.5	453.3	451.7	944.8
1968	3,285.4	466.0	102.0	21.6	705.9	505.6	608.1	999.8
1969	3,792.5	583.1	118.4	29.0	743.1	566.6	663.3	1,236.4
1970	4,145.3	703.7	133.8	29.6	896.0	585.4	752.8	1,207.4
1971	4,983.0	800.8	162.8	—	1,204.5	596.8	784.9	1,596.0
1972	5,363.8	875.4	179.2	17.0	1,502.4	532.0	782.7	1,671.3
1973	5,698.2	911.7	175.0	15.0	1,707.0	526.0	894.9	1,658.6
1974	6,721.5	967.5	185.2	—	2,025.8	510.0	766.7	2,451.5
1975	6,946.6	1,036.4	217.7	—	2,517.6	597.0	638.3	2,157.3
1976	8,472.5	1,189.7	216.0	—	2,806.3	752.6	572.1	3,151.8
1977	9,071.4	1,251.9	242.6	13.8	3,268.3	810.0	748.7	2,992.5
1978	10,562.7	1,297.6	255.6	22.5	3,584.9	800.0	881.4	3,998.8
1979	11,076.2	1,309.2	276.4	13.1	4,374.6	800.0	896.9	3,695.5
1980	13,599.1	1,251.1	279.4	13.5	4,852.3	800.0	2,302.7	4,393.0
1981	11,983.1	1,195.1	290.0	—	4,870.7	172.7	814.5	4,930.1
1982	11,654.4	1,233.7	310.1	—	4,490.6	160.2	521.5	5,248.4
1983	12,466.4	1,333.2	369.0	—	4,981.4	160.1	457.4	5,534.3
1984	13,294.9	1,447.7	341.6	—	5,198.9	165.0	479.1	6,004.2

(continued)

TABLE Bf263–270 Public expenditures on social welfare – other programs: 1929–1995 *Continued*

		Vocational rehabilitation						
	Total	Total	Medical care	Medical research	Child nutrition	Child welfare	Special OEO and ACTION programs	Social welfare, not elsewhere classified
	Bf263	Bf264	Bf265	Bf266	Bf267	Bf268	Bf269	Bf270
Year	Million dollars	Million dollars	Million dollars	Million dollars	Million dollars	Million dollars	Million dollars	Million dollars
1985	13,551.8	1,536.7	360.0	—	5,308.5	200.0	503.8	6,002.8
1986	14,160.6	1,615.9	376.8	—	5,676.7	197.9	504.5	6,165.6
1987	15,277.9	1,773.4	412.4	—	6,230.6	222.5	519.6	6,531.8
1988	15,479.0	1,905.5	444.0	—	6,250.0	239.4	153.3	6,930.8
1989	16,608.7	1,999.0	499.9	—	6,644.9	246.7	162.9	7,555.2
1990	17,917.6	2,126.6	531.6	—	7,165.4	252.6	169.4	8,203.6
1991	19,779.8 [1]	2,235.8	559.0	—	7,966.9	273.9	191.9	9,111.3
1992	21,531.5	2,446.8	611.7	—	8,775.8	273.9	193.8	9,841.2
1993	22,670.0	2,379.1	594.8	—	9,392.4	294.6	208.3	10,395.6
1994	24,762.5	2,560.1	640.0	—	10,099.1	294.6	204.4	11,604.3
1995	26,557.7	2,630.3	658.0	—	10,653.4	292.0	222.0	12,760.0

[1] Revised figure. See text for Table Bf188–195.

Sources

Data for 1929–1989, U.S. Social Security Administration, *Social Welfare Expenditures under Public Programs in the United States, 1929–90* (July 1995); Ann Kallman Bixby, "Public Social Welfare Expenditures, Fiscal Year 1992," *Social Security Bulletin* 58 (2) (1995): 65–73. Data for 1990–1993, *Social Security Bulletin: Annual Statistical Supplement* (1996), Table 3.A3, p. 141; for 1994–1995, *Social Security Bulletin: Annual Statistical Supplement* (1999), Table 3.A3, p. 139. Information for the 1990s on series Bf265 is from Ann Kallman Bixby, "Public Social Welfare Expenditures, Fiscal Year 1994," *Social Security Bulletin* 60 (3) (1997): 42; and Ann Kallman Bixby, "Public Social Welfare Expenditures, Fiscal Year 1995," *Social Security Bulletin* 62 (2) (1999): 88. The series in this table are annually updated in the *Social Security Bulletin: Annual Statistical Supplement*, Table 3.A3. See the text for Table Bf188–195 for further discussion of the sources.

Documentation

Series Bf263. The sum of series Bf264 and Bf267–270.

Series Bf264, vocational rehabilitation. Includes vocational rehabilitation spending on medical services and research, series Bf265–266. Vocational rehabilitation spending on medical research is no longer available separately after 1980.

Series Bf267, child nutrition. Includes surplus food for schools and programs under the National School Lunch and Child Nutrition Acts.

Series Bf268, child welfare. Represents primarily child welfare services under the Social Security Act. State and local data on child welfare spending are not available after 1980. Beginning in 1968–1969, administrative expenditures are excluded.

Series Bf269, U.S. Office of Economic Opportunity (OEO) and ACTION programs. Includes domestic programs consolidated in 1972 under ACTION (VISTA, foster grandparents, and other domestic volunteer programs) and special OEO programs. After 1987, represents ACTION funds only.

Series Bf270, social welfare spending, not elsewhere classified. Federal expenditures include spending on the following: institutional care primarily in the form of surplus food for institutions; the administrative and related expenses of the Secretary of Health and Human Services; Indian welfare and guidance; aging and juvenile delinquency; and certain manpower and human development programs. State and local expenditures include amounts for institutional care, anti-poverty and manpower programs, day care, child placement and adoption services, foster care, legal assistance, care of transients, and other unspecified welfare services. In the original source, spending on institutional care is reported separately from social welfare spending, not elsewhere classified. However, there was a definitional change such that the information on state and local spending on anti-poverty programs, foster care, legal assistance to the needy, and care of transients that was listed under spending on institutional care prior to 1970 was moved to the category social welfare spending not elsewhere classified after 1969. To ensure consistency, the data are presented as a combined series here.

SOCIAL WELFARE PROGRAMS

Price V. Fishback and Melissa A. Thomasson

TABLE Bf271–283 Employment covered under selected government social insurance programs – estimated payrolls: 1937–1996

Contributed by Price V. Fishback and Melissa A. Thomasson

Year	Total earnings in employment, including self-employment	Wage and salary disbursements: Total	Wage and salary disbursements: Civilian	Wages and salaries in employment covered by retirement programs: Total	Wages and salaries in employment covered by retirement programs: OASDHI	Wages and salaries in employment covered by retirement programs: Railroad	Wages and salaries in employment covered by retirement programs: Federal civil service	Wages and salaries in employment covered by retirement programs: State and local government	Net earnings of self-employed covered by OASDHI	Wages and salaries in civilian employment covered by other programs: Unemployment insurance: Total	Unemployment insurance: State programs	Unemployment insurance: Railroad	Workers' compensation
	Bf271	Bf272	Bf273	Bf274 [1, 2]	Bf275 [3]	Bf276 [3]	Bf277	Bf278	Bf279	Bf280	Bf281	Bf282 [3]	Bf283
	Million dollars	Million dollars	Million dollars	Million dollars	Million dollars	Million dollars	Million dollars	Million dollars	Million dollars	Million dollars	Million dollars	Million dollars	Million dollars
1937	57,624	44,421	44,067	37,943	32,770	2,265	1,050	1,858	—	—	—	2,265	—
1938	52,157	40,860	40,495	33,755	28,635	2,010	1,139	1,971	—	28,210	26,200	2,010	—
1939	55,901	44,056	43,668	36,892	31,488	2,149	1,221	2,034	—	31,218	29,069	2,149	—
1940	81,272	48,227	47,664	41,660	35,600	2,280	1,430	2,350	—	34,632	32,352	2,280	35,500
1941	78,369	60,862	58,996	52,499	45,300	2,697	1,912	2,590	—	44,682	41,985	2,697	—
1942	105,347	81,516	75,348	67,714	58,000	3,394	3,600	2,720	—	57,942	54,548	3,394	—
1943	134,159	105,527	91,394	81,640	69,400	4,100	5,100	3,040	—	69,971	65,871	4,100	—
1944	146,763	116,942	96,909	86,443	73,100	4,523	5,600	3,220	—	73,409	68,886	4,523	—
1945	148,901	117,479	95,660	85,438	71,300	4,530	5,840	3,768	—	70,941	66,411	4,530	74,000
1946	148,700	112,000	104,200	93,618 [4]	79,000	4,883 [4]	5,195 [4]	5,500	—	78,300	73,400	4,883 [4]	80,000
1947	159,000	123,100	118,900	107,462 [4]	92,100	5,113 [4]	4,809 [4]	5,440 [4]	—	91,700	86,600	5,113 [4]	91,500
1948	176,400	135,500	131,400	118,458 [4]	101,900	5,539 [4]	4,469 [4]	6,550 [4]	—	101,600	96,100	5,539 [4]	105,000
1949	171,100	134,800	130,300	117,780 [4]	99,600	5,133 [4]	5,707 [4]	7,340 [4]	—	99,000	93,900	5,133 [4]	103,000
1950	185,700	147,000	141,700	128,900	109,400	5,327 [4]	6,068 [4]	8,000	—	108,400	103,100	5,327 [4]	113,500
1951	214,500	171,300	162,300	152,576 [4]	131,200	6,101 [4]	6,395 [4]	8,900	16,300	123,800	118,700	6,101 [4]	131,500
1952	228,700	185,400	174,600	164,734 [4]	135,200	6,185 [4]	6,929 [4]	9,820 [4]	16,300	134,700	127,800	6,900	141,500
1953	240,400	198,600	188,000	177,447 [4]	154,000	6,147 [4]	6,950 [4]	10,670 [4]	16,900	145,300	139,200	6,147 [4]	153,500
1954	238,000	196,800	186,500	176,660 [4]	153,200	5,630 [4]	6,980 [4]	11,650 [4]	16,700	142,700	137,100	5,630 [4]	153,000
1955	254,500	211,700	201,500	193,291 [4]	169,400	5,801 [4]	8,290 [4]	12,400	24,400	154,400	148,600	5,801 [4]	168,000
1956	272,300	228,200	218,300	210,700	186,200	6,206 [4]	9,560 [4]	13,700	28,100	170,700	164,500	6,206 [4]	181,500
1957	284,500	239,300	229,100	227,893 [4]	203,100	6,177 [4]	10,116 [4]	15,500	28,200	179,800	173,600	6,177 [4]	190,000
1958	288,200	240,500	230,200	229,624 [4]	205,600	5,722 [4]	11,102 [4]	17,000	28,300	177,100	171,400	5,722 [4]	192,000
1959	306,600	258,900	247,000	246,957 [4]	222,500	5,751 [4]	11,406 [4]	18,600	29,700	192,700	186,900	5,751 [4]	209,000
1960	319,100	271,900	261,500	260,600	234,300	5,648 [4]	11,952 [4]	20,300	29,100	200,600	195,000	5,648 [4]	220,000
1961	328,000	279,500	268,900	266,872 [4]	238,800	5,345 [4]	13,227 [4]	22,200	29,900	204,300	199,000	5,345 [4]	226,500
1962	357,900	298,000	286,800	284,838 [4]	255,700	5,381 [4]	13,557 [4]	24,100	31,300	218,000	212,600	5,381 [4]	241,000
1963	363,900	313,400	301,900	298,770 [4]	268,200	5,350 [4]	14,620 [4]	26,100	31,600	228,400	223,000	5,350 [4]	254,000
1964	388,600	336,100	323,700	321,135 [4]	288,400	5,446 [4]	15,789 [4]	28,500	33,500	244,600	239,200	5,446 [4]	272,000
1965	418,900	362,000	349,100	342,944 [4]	308,600	5,590 [4]	16,254 [4]	31,300	40,200	263,500	257,900	5,590 [4]	292,000
1966	458,900	398,400	382,300	382,200	344,200	5,676 [4]	17,640 [4]	34,700	43,900	289,600	283,900	5,676 [4]	321,000
1967	488,200	427,000	409,900	411,300	374,700	5,734 [4]	19,105 [4]	39,200	44,700	307,700	302,000	5,734 [4]	342,000
1968	533,600	470,000	450,700	451,800	410,500	5,878 [4]	21,537 [4]	42,700	46,300	337,200	331,300	5,878 [4]	376,000
1969	582,700	515,700	496,000	495,900	452,500	6,092 [4]	23,127 [4]	47,000	46,900	371,800	365,700	6,092 [4]	414,000
1970	614,900	548,700	528,000	528,300	480,000	6,281 [4]	26,335 [4]	53,100	47,900	389,000	382,700	6,281 [4]	441,000
1971	650,300	580,900	560,200	555,300	505,200	6,600	27,800	57,400	50,600	417,800	411,200	6,600	469,000
1972	712,000	635,200	613,500	615,600	559,100	7,200	29,800	66,100	54,500	499,500	492,300	7,200	512,000
1973	796,500	702,700	680,500	682,200	619,800	7,900	31,700	74,000	62,800	558,800	550,900	7,900	578,000
1974	854,500	765,700	742,900	744,900	678,100	8,400	34,300	81,000	65,600	621,500	613,100	8,400	637,000
1975	896,400	806,400	783,300	783,200	717,200	8,300	36,800	86,800	70,400	693,800	685,500	8,300	678,000
1976	984,000	889,900	866,400	869,000	797,900	9,300	38,600	98,900	76,800	768,400	759,100	9,300	750,000
1977	1,087,300	983,800	959,500	966,700	887,500	10,000	41,600	105,500	80,600	853,500	843,500	10,000	827,000
1978	1,222,300	1,105,100	1,078,400	1,079,900	999,800	10,900	44,700	112,200	88,100	1,055,400	1,044,500	10,900	922,000
1979	1,369,700	1,237,600	1,210,600	1,207,100	1,117,900	12,500	48,300	118,500	99,800	1,187,800	1,175,300	12,500	1,041,000
1980	1,552,700	1,372,000	1,342,300	1,318,100	1,229,200	13,100	52,300	122,900	97,700	1,308,800	1,290,000	13,100	1,136,000
1981	1,697,200	1,510,400	1,475,300	1,444,700	1,347,600	13,400	56,300	135,200	98,900	1,432,600	1,419,500	13,400	1,247,000
1982	1,716,600	1,586,100	1,546,300	1,529,300	1,423,300	12,700	59,100	142,600	98,600	1,500,100	1,487,400	12,700	1,301,000
1983	1,867,100	1,676,200	1,633,900	1,613,600	1,502,100	12,500	62,200	153,500	109,300	1,583,200	1,570,700	12,500	1,382,000
1984	2,073,300	1,838,800	1,793,800	1,774,800	1,665,000	13,200	64,800	162,300	117,200	1,739,200	1,726,000	13,200	1,516,000

Notes appear at end of table

(continued)

TABLE Bf271–283 Employment covered under selected government social insurance programs – estimated payrolls: 1937–1996 *Continued*

	Total earnings in employment, including self-employment	Wage and salary disbursements		Wages and salaries in employment covered by retirement programs					Net earnings of self-employed covered by OASDHI	Wages and salaries in civilian employment covered by other programs			
										Unemployment insurance			
		Total	Civilian	Total	OASDHI	Railroad	Federal civil service	State and local government		Total	State programs	Railroad	Workers' compensation
	Bf271	Bf272	Bf273	Bf274 [1, 2]	Bf275 [3]	Bf276 [3]	Bf277	Bf278	Bf279	Bf280	Bf281	Bf282 [3]	Bf283
Year	Million dollars	Million dollars	Million dollars	Million dollars	Million dollars	Million dollars	Million dollars	Million dollars	Million dollars	Million dollars	Million dollars	Million dollars	Million dollars
1985	2,231,300	1,975,400	1,927,500	1,896,100	1,782,300	12,800	70,100	175,300	130,000	1,870,000	1,857,200	12,800	1,618,000
1986	2,376,800	2,094,800	2,044,800	2,011,200	1,896,200	12,200	72,400	189,900	139,000	1,982,900	1,970,700	12,200	1,725,000
1987	2,573,100	2,249,700	2,197,500	2,157,500	2,042,000	11,900	74,200	203,000	155,800	2,045,500	2,033,600	11,900	1,845,000
1988	2,767,300	2,443,000	2,389,800	2,342,600	2,224,700	12,000	79,600	218,800	208,100	2,205,100	2,193,100	12,000	1,997,400
1989	2,933,700	2,586,400	2,531,400	2,492,700	2,367,800	12,100	83,400	235,000	210,000	2,336,200	2,324,100	12,100	2,115,000
1990	3,109,700	2,742,800	2,685,300	2,636,400	2,510,000	11,800	87,600	238,800	193,800	2,491,600	2,479,800	11,800	2,442,000
1991	3,190,500	2,827,600	2,765,900	2,694,700	2,565,000	12,000	92,300	271,400	195,500	2,548,900	2,536,900	12,000	2,552,900
1992	3,410,200	2,986,400	2,925,400	2,850,700	2,711,000	12,700	98,000	296,300	205,800	2,697,300	2,684,600	12,700	2,699,600
1993	3,540,400	3,089,600	3,031,400	2,964,600	2,821,000	12,400	100,800	307,000	212,000	2,797,900	2,785,500	12,400	2,802,100
1994	3,712,300	3,240,700	3,185,800	3,102,100	2,954,000	12,500	102,900	320,300	221,500	2,946,200	2,933,700	12,500	2,948,700
1995	3,918,500	3,429,500	3,373,300	3,294,000	3,140,000	12,600	104,300	341,400	234,900	3,129,200	3,116,600	12,600	3,122,600
1996	4,152,800	3,632,500	3,576,000	3,489,400	3,328,000	12,800	107,200	364,500	254,200	3,327,400	3,314,600	12,800	—

[1] Beginning in 1953, data are adjusted for duplication of payrolls covered by both Old-Age, Survivors, Disability, and Health Insurance (OASDHI) and state and local government retirement systems. Beginning in 1984, data are adjusted for duplication of payrolls covered by both OASDHI and the federal civil service retirement system.

[2] Beginning in 1975, OASDHI estimates include a small amount of taxable wages in American business in U.S. territories and possessions.

[3] Beginning in 1957, includes military wages. Beginning in 1975, includes a small amount of taxable wages on American business in U.S. territories and possessions.

[4] Revised from original source.

Sources

1937–1939, unpublished data from U.S. Social Security Administration; 1940–1945, *U.S. Social Security Bulletin, Annual Statistical Supplement, 1971*, Table 6; 1946 to present, *U.S. Social Security Bulletin, Annual Statistical Supplement, 1999*, Table 3.B2, p. 141.

Documentation

This table reports data for total earnings and total wages and salaries in employment covered by various government social insurance programs. Total earnings include the earnings of people who are self-employed. For state unemployment insurance, OASDHI, railroad retirement, and railroad unemployment insurance, data include taxable plus nontaxable wages and salaries in employment covered by the programs.

The U.S. Bureau of Economic Analysis (formerly Office of Business Economics) is the original source for total earnings and wage and salary disbursements, series Bf271–273. The U.S. Social Security Administration is the original source for payrolls covered by state and local government retirement systems and by workers' compensation, series Bf278 and Bf283. Data for series Bf274–277 and Bf279–282 are based on reports of the agencies administering the programs specified.

Series Bf283. Data for payrolls in employment covered by workers' compensation programs exclude railroad employees because accident compensation for railroad employees is based on negligence liability rules under the federal Employers' Liability Act of 1908 and amendments.

TABLE Bf284–289 Employment covered under government social insurance programs – number of workers: 1934–1989

Contributed by Price V. Fishback and Melissa A. Thomasson

	Civilian population covered by public retirement programs			Civilian population covered by other social insurance programs		
	OASDHI	Railroad Retirement System	Public employee retirement systems	Workers' compensation	Unemployment insurance	Temporary disability insurance
	Bf284	Bf285	Bf286	Bf287	Bf288	Bf289
Year	Million	Million	Million	Million	Million	Million
1934	—	1.4	17.0	—	—	—
1939	24.0	1.2	2.0	22.0	22.6	—
1944	30.8	1.7	4.7	33.0	31.6	0.2
1949	34.3	1.4	4.4	35.3	33.1	5.3
1954	45.3	1.2	4.6	40.4	37.2	10.7
1955	51.8	1.3	4.7	42.9	41.7	11.2
1956	53.2	1.2	4.5	44.1	43.8	11.5
1957	53.7	1.1	3.9	43.1	43.2	11.2
1958	53.4	1.0	3.9	42.7	42.6	11.0
1959	55.4	0.9	3.8	45.1	44.1	11.4
1960	55.7	0.9	3.9	44.6	43.7	11.3
1961	56.1	0.8	4.0	46.0	44.6	11.8
1962	57.3	0.8	4.0	46.8	45.4	12.3
1963	58.5	0.8	3.7	48.2	46.3	12.5
1964	60.1	0.8	3.9	50.0	47.9	12.7
1965	62.8	0.8	4.1	52.5	50.3	13.3
1966	64.9	0.7	4.6	55.1	52.8	13.7
1967	65.7	0.7	4.6	56.3	53.8	14.0
1968	67.1	0.7	4.6	58.3	55.5	14.2
1969	68.6	0.7	3.9	60.1	57.0	14.8
1970	69.1	0.6	5.5	59.0	55.8	14.6
1971	69.8	0.6	5.2	60.5	57.1	14.8
1972	72.6	0.6	5.2	63.7	66.0	16.0
1973	75.6	0.6	5.3	68.0	69.0	16.0
1974	75.2	0.6	5.3	67.8	69.5	15.7
1975	75.7	0.5	6.0	68.6	69.7	15.7
1976	80.3	0.5	6.1	70.4	72.1	16.2
1977	82.1	0.5	6.2	74.2	75.8	16.7
1978	83.2	0.5	6.4	74.5	85.8	18.0
1979	87.6	0.5	6.4	77.4	87.9	18.1
1980	89.3	0.5	6.6	79.1	90.4	18.4
1981	89.5	0.5	6.4	79.8	89.9	18.4
1982	88.9	0.4	6.4	77.8	87.9	18.1
1983	92.7	0.4	6.4	80.9	91.3	18.7
1984	98.0	0.4	6.0	83.4	95.8	18.9
1985	100.3	0.3	6.0	85.1	98.2	19.8
1986	102.9	0.3	5.9	87.2	100.2	20.3
1987	106.0	0.3	5.9	90.0	103.7	21.6
1988	108.4	0.3	5.8	92.8	106.9	21.8
1989	110.3	0.3	5.8	95.3	109.1	—

Sources

U.S. Social Security Administration, 1934, unpublished data; 1939–1989, *Social Security Bulletin, Annual Statistical Supplement*. 1985–1989 from 1990 volume, 1984 from 1989 volume, 1983 from 1986 volume, 1979–1982 from 1984–1985 volume, 1977–1978 from 1983 volume, 1970, 1975–1976 from 1982 volume, 1971–1974 from 1974 volume, 1968–1969 from 1972 volume, 1967, 1965, 1964 from 1971 volume. Earlier figures were collected from earlier volumes for the 1975 edition of *Historical Statistics of the United States*.

Documentation

For further information, see also the text for Tables Bf212–224, Bf271–283, and Bf377–394. More details on these programs can be found in Tables Bf326–348, Bf377–496, Bf511–567, and Bf735–761. The U.S. Social Security Administration stopped reporting this table in the *Annual Statistical Supplement* after the 1990 issue.

All series are as of December for the period 1954 to 1989. Monthly averages are reported prior to 1954. Monthly averages for 1954 are 45.3 for Old-Age, Survivors, Disability, and Health Insurance (OASDHI), 1.2 for railroad, 4.5 for public employees retirement, 39.7 for workers' compensation, 36.6 for unemployment insurance, and 10.6 for temporary disability.

Series Bf284. Beginning in 1955, includes persons covered under both a government retirement system and OASDHI (about 5.3 million in December 1970). Excludes members of the armed forces and persons whose coverage was authorized on an elective or optional basis but not in effect (about 3.5 million in December 1970). Also excludes railroad employees jointly covered by OASDHI and their own retirement program.

Series Bf286, public employee retirement. Excludes persons covered under both a government retirement system and OASDHI.

Series Bf288, unemployment insurance. Includes state, railroad, and federal employee programs.

Series Bf289, temporary disability insurance. Includes state and railroad programs, but excludes government employees covered by sick-leave provisions.

TABLE Bf290–325 Social insurance and veterans' programs – cash benefits: 1940–1988

Contributed by Price V. Fishback and Melissa A. Thomasson

		Retirement programs						Disability programs				
					Public employees							
	Total	Total	OASDHI	Railroad	Federal	State and local	Veterans	Total	OASDHI	Workers' compensation	Veterans	Railroad
	Bf290	Bf291	Bf292	Bf293	Bf294	Bf295	Bf296	Bf297	Bf298	Bf299	Bf300	Bf301
Year	Million dollars	Million dollars	Million dollars	Million dollars	Million dollars	Million dollars	Million dollars	Million dollars	Million dollars	Million dollars	Million dollars	Million dollars
1940	1,540.3	330.8	17.2	83.3	103.2	103.0	24.1	476.5	0.0	129.0	293.7	30.8
1941	1,418.2	325.7	55.1	88.4	50.9	106.8	24.4	501.1	0.0	149.0	296.1	31.5
1942	1,499.8	369.4	80.3	91.6	53.2	115.4	29.0	523.8	0.0	170.0	296.3	31.2
1943	1,370.6	459.1	97.3	94.6	109.7	124.9	32.6	543.2	0.0	182.0	298.7	31.2
1944	1,629.9	523.1	119.0	98.7	121.7	134.5	49.3	700.9	0.0	227.0	407.0	31.0
1945	2,604.1	591.7	148.1	106.2	141.0	143.0	53.4	954.4	0.0	241.0	644.5	30.9
1946	5,768.9	748.7	230.3	117.8	112.8	158.0	57.4	1,536.8	0.0	251.0	1,211.6	31.4
1947	5,409.3	899.6	299.8	138.5	231.9	175.0	54.2	2,021.5	0.0	281.0	1,621.7	38.5
1948	5,298.7	1,048.9	366.9	150.1	277.7	190.0	64.2	2,135.3	0.0	312.0	1,647.0	58.5
1949	6,578.5	1,242.9	454.5	168.9	354.8	203.0	61.7	2,181.9	0.0	333.0	1,630.5	72.0
1950	6,321.5	1,423.5	651.4	176.9	286.9	250.0	58.2	2,441.9	0.0	360.0	1,674.0	77.3
1951	6,834.4	2,189.3	1,321.1	187.1	345.9	273.0	62.4	2,487.3	0.0	416.0	1,585.6	81.6
1952	7,734.3	2,574.0	1,539.3	267.3	370.2	310.0	87.2	2,632.1	0.0	460.0	1,635.0	93.9
1953	8,937.6	3,300.2	2,175.3	267.3	413.9	343.0	86.3	2,850.8	0.0	491.0	1,754.2	92.5
1954	11,136.1	3,953.8	2,698.0	324.9	466.9	385.0	79.1	2,975.6	0.0	498.0	1,842.3	104.0
1955	12,166.8	5,157.4	3,747.7	335.9	538.0	460.0	75.8	3,185.2	0.0	521.0	1,981.8	103.1
1956	13,294.6	5,964.9	4,361.2	379.8	628.0	525.0	71.1	3,344.2	0.0	578.0	2,030.7	110.7
1957	15,848.9	7,503.1	5,687.8	420.2	725.1	606.0	64.1	3,590.9	56.7	617.0	2,116.4	118.3
1958	19,946.6	8,516.5	6,476.7	449.4	848.9	685.0	56.5	4,083.4	246.2	647.0	2,325.7	121.3
1959	20,862.8	9,910.5	7,607.0	523.1	965.7	765.0	49.7	4,527.9	456.7	700.0	2,424.7	66.2
1960	22,610.1	10,754.6	8,196.1	594.4	1,076.4	845.0	42.7	4,859.6	568.2	755.0	2,529.7	146.7
1961	26,101.4	11,868.2	9,031.9	617.5	1,241.4	940.0	37.4	5,402.2	887.1	791.0	2,646.8	150.5
1962	27,050.8	13,138.8	10,161.9	638.4	1,295.8	1,011.1	31.7	5,851.3	1,105.1	879.0	2,724.3	156.1
1963	28,723.4	14,238.0	10,794.6	653.7	1,627.8	1,135.0	26.9	6,187.3	1,210.2	932.0	2,819.1	159.0
1964	29,973.3	15,122.2	11,281.5	667.5	1,891.0	1,260.0	22.3	6,466.1	1,308.8	1,001.0	2,846.0	161.7
1965	32,571.5	16,786.8	12,541.5	705.3	2,130.0	1,390.0	19.9	7,041.0	1,573.2	1,074.0	3,026.4	149.4
1966	34,984.9	18,276.9	13,417.1	739.1	2,549.5	1,555.0	16.3	7,600.5	1,781.4	1,143.0	3,173.2	164.5
1967	37,727.6	19,823.2	14,361.5	817.3	2,896.2	1,735.0	13.3	8,041.9	1,938.9	1,284.0	3,197.9	171.6
1968	42,483.3	22,726.1	16,533.5	936.5	3,285.1	1,960.0	11.0	8,725.0	2,294.3	1,374.0	3,264.7	187.5
1969	46,227.6	24,709.6	1,769.1	965.5	3,787.3	2,250.0	8.8	9,775.6	2,542.2	1,519.0	3,706.2	193.0
1970	55,609.4	29,401.5	21,075.2	1,112.9	4,549.5	2,660.0	4.0	11,000.8	3,067.0	1,674.0	3,930.9	219.3
1971	65,679.2	34,338.7	24,540.2	1,272.7	5,377.7	3,145.0	3.1	12,557.5	3,758.2	1,846.0	4,252.6	253.0
1972	72,781.4	38,797.2	27,383.8	1,372.2	6,268.8	3,770.0	2.3	14,029.1	4,473.2	2,009.0	4,497.6	288.5
1973	84,670.2	46,472.4	33,084.6	1,539.3	7,426.8	4,415.0	1.7	16,371.4	5,718.0	2,312.0	4,618.3	368.1
1974	98,646.7 [1]	53,593.5	37,451.9	1,679.9	9,265.5	5,195.0	1.2	18,849.5 [1]	6,902.9	2,701.0	5,133.4	403.9
1975	123,235.2	61,543.3	42,432.0	1,965.7	11,299.7	5,845.0	0.8	21,883.5	8,413.9	3,248.0	5,583.2	403.0
1976	135,288.6	69,662.4	48,069.0	2,147.1	12,760.8	6,685.0	0.6	25,037.8	9,965.7	3,809.0	6,147.4	420.8
1977	145,450.6 [1]	77,683.9 [1]	53,591.0	2,297.5	14,145.1	7,650.0	0.3	28,208.4 [1]	11,462.6	4,495.0	6,708.9	455.2
1978	155,286.3	86,755.7	59,818.3	2,417.1	15,884.3	8,636.0	—	30,808.2	12,518.9	5,217.0	7,009.5	471.9
1979	174,214.7 [1]	97,465.5	66,947.0	2,627.6	18,124.9	9,766.0	—	34,858.9	13,708.0	6,199.0	7,905.3	510.8
1980	207,796.8	113,252.0	77,905.0	2,930.6	21,624.1	10,792.3	—	39,659.4	15,437.0	7,245.0	8,602.2	564.4
1981	231,599.4	132,518.1	92,478.0	3,234.2	24,677.3	12,128.6	—	44,332.0	17,199.0	8,166.0	9,524.4	610.1
1982	261,158.7	149,074.7	104,885.0	3,530.6	27,157.3	13,501.8	—	46,610.7	17,338.0	8,909.0	10,203.2	668.3
1983	275,108.1	161,326.8	114,048.0	3,698.1	28,856.7	14,724.0	—	48,063.0	17,530.0	9,519.0	10,488.6	673.8
1984	282,978.9	173,419.4	123,804.2	3,761.6	29,716.6	16,137.0	—	50,133.3	17,897.1	10,852.0	10,577.7	681.1
1985	301,528.6	187,531.6	132,298.0	3,862.1	32,188.5	19,183.0	—	52,129.1	18,645.7	12,646.4	10,748.0	696.3
1986	316,272.1 [1]	198,226.7	140,418.2	3,942.8	32,258.7	21,607.0	—	55,155.6	19,524.5	13,333.0	10,886.1	705.8
1987	328,642.0	209,074.6	146,836.1	4,060.5	33,640.0	24,538.0	—	57,770.6	20,413.6	14,179.3	11,209.8	738.4
1988	345,022.7	223,530.0	156,695.7	4,192.8	36,020.4	26,621.1	—	60,309.2	21,386.1	15,737.8	11,346.9	776.5

Notes appear at end of table

TABLE Bf290–325 Social insurance and veterans' programs – cash benefits: 1940–1988 *Continued*

	Disability programs				
	Public employees		State temporary disability insurance	Railroad temporary disability	Black lung
	Federal	State and local			
	Bf302	Bf303	Bf304	Bf305	Bf306
Year	Million dollars	Million dollars	Million dollars	Million dollars	Million dollars
1940	13.0	10.0	0.0	0.0	—
1941	14.0	10.5	0.0	0.0	—
1942	14.9	11.4	0.0	0.0	—
1943	16.2	12.2	2.9	0.0	—
1944	17.3	13.5	5.0	0.0	—
1945	18.9	14.5	4.7	0.0	—
1946	22.0	16.0	4.8	0.0	—
1947	24.8	18.0	26.0	11.4	—
1948	31.4	20.0	35.6	30.8	—
1949	35.3	22.0	59.1	30.1	—
1950	189.3	24.0	89.3	28.1	—
1951	201.9	28.0	147.8	26.3	—
1952	211.0	30.0	167.7	34.7	—
1953	248.0	35.0	185.0	45.2	—
1954	256.0	45.0	186.0	49.2	—
1955	279.7	55.0	192.7	52.0	—
1956	297.8	62.0	215.5	49.5	—
1957	309.2	68.0	254.0	51.3	—
1958	343.1	75.0	273.1	51.9	—
1959	374.1	85.0	287.1	66.2	—
1960	396.9	95.0	311.3	56.9	—
1961	425.2	105.0	341.6	55.0	—
1962	456.6	114.0	364.9	51.4	—
1963	499.9	125.0	392.8	49.5	—
1964	552.8	140.0	409.9	46.0	—
1965	596.3	155.0	426.0	40.8	—
1966	681.7	175.0	442.8	38.8	—
1967	747.5	195.0	472.5	34.6	—
1968	812.5	220.0	530.9	41.0	—
1969	904.9	255.0	598.0	57.4	—
1970	1,056.8	255.0	664.6	56.2	77.0
1971	1,210.7	280.0	680.0	44.7	232.0
1972	1,372.4	315.0	707.8	35.7	330.0
1973	1,536.7	365.0	775.3	27.9	650.0
1974	1,810.8	425.0	842.3	30.2	600.0
1975	2,212.3	490.0	890.4	47.6	595.0
1976	2,535.9	565.0	916.7	84.4	593.0
1977	2,869.6	630.0	939.9	74.2	573.0
1978	3,192.5	712.0	1,027.5	66.9	591.0
1979	3,571.9	804.0	1,161.0	60.9	1,033.0
1980	4,160.1	1,210.7	1,299.8	63.2	1,077.0
1981	4,728.8	1,490.2	1,525.1	58.4	1,030.0
1982	5,141.8	1,811.0	1,567.9	55.6	916.0
1983	5,364.4	1,987.0	1,580.2	50.1	870.0
1984	5,498.0	2,178.0	1,584.1	42.0	823.0
1985	4,862.5	1,848.0	1,843.5	42.6	796.0
1986	5,913.1	1,833.0	2,067.3	57.8	838.0
1987	5,995.9	1,807.0	2,545.4	72.4	808.8
1988	5,494.9	1,960.9	2,753.6	63.7	788.8

	Survivor programs (paid monthly)							
				Public employees				
	Total	OASDHI	Railroad	Federal	State and local	Veterans	Workers' compensation	Black lung
	Bf307	Bf308	Bf309	Bf310	Bf311	Bf312	Bf313	Bf314
Year	Million dollars	Million dollars	Million dollars	Million dollars	Million dollars	Million dollars	Million dollars	Million dollars
1940	161.5	6.4	1.4	—	16.0	105.7	32.0	—
1941	192.3	25.5	1.6	(Z)	16.5	111.8	37.0	—
1942	214.2	41.7	1.6	(Z)	17.7	111.2	42.0	—
1943	239.0	57.8	1.7	(Z)	18.4	116.1	45.0	—
1944	282.1	76.9	1.8	(Z)	19.0	144.3	40.0	—
1945	417.8	99.7	2.0	0.1	20.0	254.2	42.0	—
1946	530.8	130.1	1.8	0.2	21.0	333.6	44.0	—
1947	623.1	153.1	19.3	0.2	22.0	382.5	46.0	—
1948	700.6	176.7	36.0	0.9	23.0	413.9	50.0	—
1949	799.3	201.4	39.3	4.3	25.0	477.4	52.0	—
1950	901.8	276.9	43.9	8.4	26.0	491.6	55.0	—
1951	1,178.7	506.8	49.5	14.0	29.0	519.4	60.0	—
1952	1,353.6	591.5	74.1	20.0	30.0	573.0	65.0	—
1953	1,569.7	743.5	83.3	27.3	32.0	613.5	70.0	—
1954	1,740.8	880.0	93.2	33.9	35.0	628.8	70.0	—
1955	2,068.4	1,107.5	121.8	40.6	40.0	688.4	70.0	—
1956	2,247.8	1,244.1	133.2	51.3	45.0	699.2	75.0	—
1957	2,604.8	1,520.7	143.8	60.6	51.0	748.7	80.0	—
1958	2,891.1	1,720.1	153.9	75.7	57.0	794.3	90.0	—
1959	3,322.3	2,063.3	180.9	97.1	62.0	819.1	100.0	—
1960	3,671.6	2,316.2	201.3	109.6	75.0	864.6	105.0	—
1961	4,150.5	2,658.6	217.1	123.3	85.0	956.5	110.0	—
1962	4,565.3	3,011.1	233.9	136.8	91.8	976.7	115.0	—
1963	4,869.1	3,216.0	244.2	160.6	105.0	1,018.3	125.0	—
1964	5,176.5	3,416.4	255.0	180.8	115.0	1,074.2	135.0	—
1965	5,871.5	3,979.0	278.4	199.4	125.0	1,149.7	140.0	—
1966	6,620.4	4,612.8	291.4	242.3	140.0	1,184.0	150.0	—
1967	7,014.8	4,854.0	307.6	288.0	165.0	1,245.2	155.0	—
1968	8,192.3	5,839.5	350.6	321.8	175.0	1,340.3	165.0	—
1969	8,774.1	6,219.3	367.0	368.6	195.0	1,439.2	185.0	—
1970	10,271.5	7,427.6	424.0	444.7	200.0	1,545.2	197.0	33.0
1971	11,815.9	8,566.7	476.8	513.9	220.0	1,678.8	213.0	146.7
1972	13,069.8	9,418.2	514.3	587.1	250.0	1,840.2	235.0	225.0
1973	16,429.2	12,327.8	657.7	675.1	290.0	1,818.5	265.0	395.0
1974	18,349.0	13,839.3	723.9	841.1	340.0	1,934.7	315.0	355.0
1975	20,716.1	15,544.0	914.0	1,058.9	390.0	2,084.1	365.0	360.0
1976	23,052.7	17,297.5	1,002.5	1,226.4	450.0	2,261.3	430.0	385.0
1977	25,367.0 [1]	19,210.3	1,071.1	1,392.1	450.0	2,368.5	482.0	393.0
1978	26,878.3	20,193.5	1,132.3	1,602.7	508.0	2,481.7	531.0	429.0
1979	30,722.0 [1]	23,140.0	1,223.7	1,858.8	575.0	2,649.5	610.0	665.0
1980	34,986.0	26,654.0	1,371.6	2,231.6	663.9	2,754.9	675.0	635.0
1981	40,136.7	30,875.0	1,527.1	2,615.0	767.3	2,952.3	730.0	670.0
1982	43,631.6	33,612.0	1,644.1	2,905.4	857.0	3,113.1	795.0	705.0
1983	45,615.1	35,164.0	1,671.3	3,174.9	903.0	3,191.9	810.0	700.0
1984	44,971.1	33,916.6	1,678.6	3,565.8	990.0	3,230.1	880.0	710.0
1985	46,289.2	34,806.9	1,702.3	3,792.5	968.0	3,309.5	980.0	730.0
1986	45,667.8	33,785.4	1,722.0	3,983.6	1,002.0	3,374.8	1,032.0	768.0
1987	47,068.2	35,028.7	1,736.9	4,324.7	1,041.0	3,123.0	1,067.3	746.6
1988	48,601.9	35,663.8	1,762.5	4,634.6	1,129.0	3,499.3	1,184.6	728.1

Notes appear at end of table

(continued)

TABLE Bf290–325 Social insurance and veterans' programs – cash benefits: 1940–1988 *Continued*

	Lump-sum payments						Unemployment programs				
				Public employee retirement							
	Total	OASDHI	Railroad retirement	Federal	State and Local	Veterans' programs	Total	State unemployment insurance	Railroad unemployment insurance	Veterans' unemployment allowances	Training and related allowances
	Bf315	Bf316	Bf317	Bf318	Bf319	Bf320	Bf321	Bf322	Bf323	Bf324	Bf325
Year	Million dollars	Million dollars	Million dollars	Million dollars	Million dollars	Million dollars	Million dollars	Million dollars	Million dollars	Million dollars	Million dollars
1940	36.8	11.8	2.5	6.0	12.5	4.0	534.7	518.7	16.0	—	—
1941	40.3	13.3	3.4	6.2	13.0	4.4	358.9	344.3	14.5	—	—
1942	42.0	15.0	4.1	6.3	12.6	4.1	350.4	344.1	6.3	—	—
1943	48.7	17.8	5.6	7.6	13.4	4.4	80.6	79.6	0.9	—	—
1944	56.7	22.1	6.6	8.2	15.0	4.8	67.1	62.4	0.6	4.1	—
1945	65.3	26.1	8.1	10.5	15.5	5.0	574.9	445.9	2.4	126.6	—
1946	74.2	27.3	9.1	14.3	16.0	7.5	2,626.1	1,094.9	40.0	1,491.3	—
1947	79.0	29.5	6.1	14.1	16.0	13.3	1,587.9	776.2	39.4	772.4	—
1948	81.8	32.3	8.9	11.2	17.0	12.4	1,248.4	793.3	28.6	426.6	—
1949	83.3	33.2	11.5	8.2	18.0	12.4	2,227.5	1,737.3	103.6	386.6	—
1950	86.7	32.7	12.7	8.5	20.0	12.7	1,467.6	1,373.1	59.8	34.7	—
1951	116.1	57.3	12.7	8.2	25.0	12.9	862.8	840.4	20.2	2.1	—
1952	131.0	63.3	13.7	8.8	30.0	15.1	1,043.6	988.2	41.8	3.5	—
1953	166.3	87.5	18.4	9.4	35.0	16.1	1,050.6	962.2	46.7	41.7	—
1954	174.3	92.2	16.3	10.0	40.0	16.2	2,291.6	2,026.9	157.1	107.7	—
1955	195.6	112.9	16.1	9.8	40.0	16.8	1,560.2	1,379.2	93.3	87.7	—
1956	197.1	109.3	14.5	10.7	45.0	17.5	1,540.7	1,409.3	70.4	60.9	—
1957	237.0	138.8	16.4	11.5	50.0	20.2	1,913.1	1,766.4	93.5	53.1	—
1958	245.5	132.9	19.9	13.0	55.0	24.7	4,210.1	3,899.2	228.8	82.0	—
1959	297.0	171.3	17.8	12.2	58.0	37.7	2,805.0	2,563.1	224.5	17.4	—
1960	299.5 [1]	164.3	20.0	12.7	63.0	39.5	3,024.7	2,866.7	157.7	0.4	—
1961	322.4	171.1	20.6	14.9	73.0	42.8	4,358.2	4,156.3	201.9	—	20.0
1962	346.5	183.4	22.0	16.9	80.0	44.1	3,149.0	3,012.6	132.7	—	3.7
1963	381.3	205.9	24.1	15.7	85.0	50.7	3,047.6	2,926.5	99.4	—	21.6
1964	407.5	216.4	24.4	18.1	95.0	53.6	2,801.0	2,670.8	78.4	—	51.8
1965	420.5	216.9	22.2	19.6	105.0	56.8	2,451.6	2,283.4	60.5	—	107.6
1966	456.6	237.1	25.2	20.3	115.0	59.0	2,030.6	1,852.2	39.3	—	139.1
1967	483.9	252.2	24.3	20.1	125.0	62.4	2,363.9	2,183.4	40.6	—	139.8
1968	512.3	269.2	23.6	22.0	130.0	67.5	2,327.7	2,151.3	40.4	—	136.0
1969	545.2	291.2	26.2	23.9	135.0	68.9	2,423.0	2,261.6	37.0	—	124.4
1970	582.2	293.6	26.4	24.2	165.0	73.0	4,353.3	4,183.7	38.7	—	130.9
1971	604.2	305.6	26.5	24.5	175.0	72.5	6,362.9	6,130.8	75.7	—	156.4
1972	645.7	319.8	30.5	20.0	200.0	75.4	6,239.6	6,043.2	51.5	—	144.9
1973	700.7	328.8	27.5	21.1	240.0	83.3	4,696.5	4,542.7	30.6	—	123.1
1974	779.0	327.3	28.2	23.4	275.0	125.2	7,075.7	6,943.7	22.2	—	109.8
1975	807.8	337.0	25.0	21.4	300.0	124.4	18,284.6	18,188.1	89.5	—	7.0
1976	863.7	332.5	23.6	22.5	350.0	135.2	16,672.0	16,537.2	134.7	—	—
1977	753.6	312.0	18.6	22.0	270.0	131.0	13,437.6	13,337.8	99.8	—	—
1978	828.8	344.5	16.3	29.4	304.0	134.6	10,015.3	9,890.8	124.5	—	—
1979	873.8	340.0	15.4	22.5	345.0	150.8	10,294.5	10,212.0	82.5	—	—
1980	963.6	395.0	13.6	25.7	351.6	177.7	18,935.9	18,756.5	179.4	—	—
1981	862.0	332.0	13.0	44.8	368.9	103.3	13,750.6	13,542.8	207.8	—	—
1982	770.0	203.0	11.0	40.2	397.7	118.2	21,071.7	20,733.0	338.7	—	—
1983	822.5	205.0	10.7	39.2	452.0	115.6	19,280.7 [1]	18,992.1	288.6	—	—
1984	811.6	140.0	10.5	43.2	495.0	122.9	13,643.5	13,495.5	148.0	—	—
1985	817.8	142.9	9.3	39.5	502.0	124.1	14,760.9	14,629.2	131.7	—	—
1986	1,105.7	136.2	9.6	62.2	778.0	119.7	16,116.3 [1]	15,988.0	128.3	—	—
1987	337.8 [2]	138.0	9.3	56.2	—	134.3	14,390.8	14,276.2	114.6	—	—
1988	352.1	142.1	7.7	68.7	—	133.6	12,229.5	12,158.7	70.8	—	—

(Z) Less than $50,000.

[1] Revised from the original source.

[2] The sharp drop relative to previous years is the result of the unavailability of series Bf319.

Sources

U.S. Social Security Administration, *Social Security Bulletin, Annual Statistical Supplement*, For the years 1985–1988: 1990, pp. 106–7; for 1970, 1980, 1983–1985: 1987, pp. 256–7; for 1982: 1986, pp. 252–3; for 1981: 1984–1985, pp. 223–4; for 1975, 1978, 1979: 1982, pp. 220–1; for 1977: 1981, pp. 66–7; for 1976: 1980, pp. 67–8; for 1973–1974: 1975, p. 50; for 1972: 1974, p. 47; for 1971: 1973, pp. 43–4; for 1940, 1950, 1955, 1960, 1965, 1970–1972: 1973, p. 43; for 1969: 1970, p. 29; for 1966, 1967: 1968, p. 28; for 1962–1964: 1965, p. 6; for 1961: 1964, p. 6; for 1958–1959: 1962, p. 6; for 1956–1957: 1960, p. 6; for 1951–1954: 1957, p. 14; for 1944–1949: 1952, p. 27; for 1943: 1946, p. 3; for 1942: 1945, p. 18; for 1941: 1944, p. 23.

TABLE Bf290–325 Social insurance and veterans' programs – cash benefits: 1940–1988 *Continued*

The U.S. Social Security Administration stopped publishing the data for Tables Bf290–348 in the *Annual Statistical Supplement* after the 1990 issue. More recent data at higher levels of aggregation are published in the quarterly *Social Security Bulletin*, Tables 4.A1 and 4.A2. The data are reported through 1997 at a more aggregate level in Tables Bf349–376. Most of the data are derived from operating statistics of the administering agencies.

Documentation

Tables Bf290–348 are usually published in combination. The following discussion pertains to both tables where appropriate.

Revisions of the series that are sums of several series were made when there were significant discrepancies with the published numbers for those aggregates and after double-checking the original source and earlier published versions of the series involved.

Beneficiary data for workmen's compensation are not available.

Series Bf290. The sum of series Bf291, Bf297, Bf307, Bf315, and Bf321. Differs from the total listed in series H125 of *Historical Statistics of the United States* (1975) because lump-sum payments have been included. The majority of social insurance programs make a stream of payments to recipients over time, which are reported as monthly cash payments. In some cases, the programs pay lump sums to beneficiaries, which are listed in series Bf315–320.

Series Bf291. The sum of series Bf292–296.

Series Bf291–306. Retirement and disability benefits series include benefits to spouses and children where applicable.

Series Bf294–295, Bf302–303, Bf310–311, and Bf318–319. The public employee benefits series include refunds of contributions to employees who leave service.

Series Bf294, Bf302, Bf310, Bf318, Bf328, Bf334, and Bf341. Series for the federal government systems include federal civil service and other contributory systems and federal noncontributory systems. Prior to 1954, retirement data, series Bf294 and Bf328, include unknown amounts and numbers of disability and survivor payments. Beneficiaries of the military retirement programs under the Uniformed Services Contingency Option Act of 1953 included under the federal government survivorship retirement program, in series Bf341, represent the number of families.

Series Bf296, Bf300, Bf312, Bf320, Bf330, Bf333, and Bf344. The veterans' retirement series cover veterans of the Civil War, the Indian Wars, the Spanish-American War, the Boxer Rebellion, and the Philippine Insurrection. Beginning October 1951, they include all service pensions.

Series Bf296 and Bf330. Beginning in 1978, the retirement data for veterans are no longer available separately.

Series Bf297. The sum of series Bf298–306.

Series Bf299 and Bf313. For the basis of estimates of workers' compensation payments, see the text for Table Bf511–524. Series Bf313 includes a small but unknown amount of lump-sum death payments.

Series Bf300 and Bf332, veterans' disability payments and beneficiaries. Covers pensions and compensation, clothing allowance (beginning 1973), and subsistence payments to disabled veterans undergoing training (1944–1973).

Series Bf303 and Bf329. Estimates of the operations of the state and local government retirement programs prior to 1950 are based primarily on the Bureau of the Census, *Annual Compendium of State Government Finances* and *Compendium of City Government Finances*. These present fiscal year data (which were averaged to secure calendar year figures) for state-administered and city-administered systems. Data on county-administered systems (not reported, and not many in that period) were estimated by the U.S. Social Security Administration. After 1950 extensive use was made of the 1957, 1962, and 1967 Census of Governments Reports, *Employee-Retirement Systems of State and Local Governments* for benchmark purposes. Beginning 1959, data from the Census Bureau's annual *Finances of Employee-Retirement Systems of State and Local Governments* were used, with certain adjustments through the year 1966 (no adjustments between 1967 and 1970). Two fiscal years are averaged to approximate calendar year data.

Series Bf304 and Bf336, state temporary disability insurance. Covers cash benefits payable in California, New Jersey, New York, Rhode Island, and Puerto Rico under public and private plans. The beneficiary data exclude private-plan beneficiaries in New Jersey. Beginning in 1980, includes data for Hawai'i.

Series Bf307. The sum of series Bf308–314.

Series Bf312 and Bf343, veterans' survivor payments and beneficiaries. Covers special allowances for survivors of veterans who did not qualify under Old-Age, Survivors, Disability, and Health Insurance (OASDHI; Servicemen's and Veterans' Survivor Benefit Act of 1956).

Series Bf315. The sum of series Bf316–320.

Series Bf320. The lump-sum veterans' payments are for burial of deceased veterans.

Series Bf321. The sum of series Bf322–325.

Series Bf322 and Bf345, state unemployment insurance. Covers payments made by the states as agents of the federal government under the federal employees' unemployment compensation program and under the Ex-Servicemen's Compensation Act of 1958 until 1981. Also covers payments under extended unemployment insurance programs. Beginning in 1961, covers program in Puerto Rico. Covers payments under the Automotive Products Trade Act of 1965 and the Trade Expansion Act of 1962, beginning in January 1970.

Series Bf324 and Bf348. Veterans' allowances are paid under the Servicemen's Readjustment Assistance Act of 1944 (terminated July 1949) and the Veterans' Readjustment Assistance Act of 1952 (terminated January 1960). Series Bf324 includes allowances for self-employed, but series Bf348 does not. For example, veterans' allowances to the self-employed were as follows: in 1945, $11.67 million paid to 12,100 veterans (average monthly number); in 1950, $1.666 million paid to 1,500 veterans; and a negligible amount thereafter.

Series Bf325 and Bf348, training and related allowances. Fall under the Area Redevelopment Act of 1961 (November 1961–June 1966) and the Manpower Development and Training Act of 1962. The training allowances are based on unemployment insurance in the state of training, and allowances for transportation and maintenance when training is away from home.

Series Bf326, Bf331, and Bf339. The information on beneficiaries for OASDHI is the average monthly number. The source for the 1985–1988 figures claim it is the number on rolls June 30, but this appears to be a misprint.

Series Bf327–330, Bf332, Bf334–335, and Bf340–343. Number on rolls as of June 30.

Series Bf336, Bf345, and Bf347. Average weekly number.

Series Bf337 and Bf346. Average number during the fourteen-day registration period.

Series Bf342. Number of families.

TABLE Bf326–348 Social insurance and veterans' programs – beneficiaries: 1940–1988

Contributed by Price V. Fishback and Melissa A. Thomasson

	Retirement programs					Disability programs					
			Public employees						Public employees		
Year	OASDHI	Railroad	Federal	State and local	Veterans	OASDHI	Veterans	Railroad	Federal	State and local	State temporary disability insurance
	Bf326	Bf327	Bf328	Bf329	Bf330	Bf331	Bf332	Bf333	Bf334	Bf335	Bf336
	Thousand	Thousand	Thousand	Thousand	Thousand	Thousand	Thousand	Thousand	Thousand	Thousand	Thousand
1940	77.2	102.0	80.8	113.0	33.8	—	576.3	39.3	15.5	14.3	—
1941	271.5	112.6	51.0	117.2	39.1	0.0	583.6	40.3	17.6	15.0	—
1942	351.8	115.2	53.6	126.7	44.5	0.0	579.6	39.7	19.1	16.3	0.0
1943	406.3	119.4	56.2	136.0	49.5	0.0	599.1	39.6	20.5	17.6	4.1
1944	463.4	121.5	90.1	146.0	52.4	0.0	763.6	39.1	21.2	19.5	5.9
1945	591.8	129.1	101.1	155.0	60.4	0.0	1,083.7	39.0	23.7	21.0	5.4
1946	842.7	139.7	122.9	167.0	62.5	0.0	2,010.1	39.3	27.3	23.0	5.6
1947	1,068.1	147.1	147.1	180.0	61.6	0.0	2,283.7	51.2	31.6	25.0	23.0
1948	1,294.9	156.0	166.8	190.0	59.8	0.0	2,252.0	63.0	35.8	27.0	24.2
1949	1,574.6	164.3	206.9	200.0	57.4	0.0	2,260.0	70.0	39.7	29.0	28.0
1950	1,918.1	174.8	184.3	222.0	54.1	0.0	2,314.1	76.0	99.0	32.0	55.2
1951	2,756.8	182.0	122.4	230.0	57.3	0.0	2,319.1	79.1	106.9	35.0	71.3
1952	3,187.3	268.6	218.2	250.0	78.4	0.0	2,343.9	80.3	116.5	38.0	75.0
1953	3,888.7	288.5	231.6	270.0	71.8	0.0	2,437.0	81.9	130.2	42.0	83.4
1954	4,589.6	307.7	153.7	292.0	65.7	0.0	2,527.7	84.9	139.2	45.0	81.7
1955	5,443.2	329.2	271.1	335.0	59.8	0.0	2,609.0	87.1	146.8	42.0	96.3
1956	6,190.9	347.3	296.5	375.0	56.0	0.0	2,682.5	89.8	153.6	43.0	102.3
1957	7,623.3	363.6	332.2	424.0	50.4	123.7	2,746.1	91.2	156.8	44.0	114.4
1958	8,738.1	383.3	369.8	465.0	44.3	205.1	2,806.2	92.6	170.2	46.0	115.7
1959	9,631.0	405.4	401.6	500.0	38.8	377.9	2,895.4	95.6	180.5	50.0	118.7
1960	10,309.7	440.0	442.2	535.0	33.2	542.6	2,976.0	96.6	192.2	55.0	121.1
1961	11,127.5	463.7	497.3	575.0	28.8	891.7	3,078.2	99.2	204.9	58.0	128.5
1962	12,248.2	474.1	549.4	600.0	24.3	1,161.0	3,125.9	99.6	218.9	61.0	135.7
1963	13,038.1	489.2	618.3	650.0	20.5	1,380.0	3,160.2	100.9	230.7	65.0	144.6
1964	13,588.8	495.0	687.4	690.0	16.9	1,518.5	3,180.2	102.2	244.2	70.0	146.5
1965	13,918.2	498.4	747.3	725.0	14.0	1,653.9	3,202.9	102.5	257.1	69.0	148.9
1966	14,670.3	525.1	832.2	775.0	11.3	1,883.3	3,173.0	100.3	274.1	72.0	152.1
1967	15,665.4	530.9	899.5	832.0	9.1	2,057.4	3,173.0	100.3	287.4	75.0	157.0
1968	16,062.4	541.9	974.8	903.0	7.1	2,257.3	3,156.9	99.1	298.1	80.0	164.4
1969	16,430.4	550.3	1,044.0	978.0	5.5	2,416.2	3,154.6	96.5	315.2	87.0	172.3
1970	16,869.6	552.5	1,119.4	1,085.0	3.1	2,572.7	3,178.0	95.1	332.8	86.0	180.9
1971	17,402.5	557.9	1,210.1	1,165.0	2.4	2,806.6	3,220.0	95.6	349.6	89.0	178.0
1972	17,953.3	560.1	1,301.7	1,241.0	1.8	3,097.3	3,267.1	97.3	364.2	92.0	171.9
1973	18,685.7	558.8	1,424.9	1,320.0	1.3	3,408.8	3,255.5	99.6	381.7	95.0	177.2
1974	19,408.9	554.0	1,556.3	1,395.0	1.0	3,712.3	3,240.3	101.7	401.7	104.0	181.7
1975	20,014.5	579.4	1,644.1	1,480.0	0.6	4,142.1	3,226.1	101.7	421.2	105.0	175.7
1976	20,624.3	587.2	1,755.6	1,580.0	0.4	4,523.6	3,235.4	100.8	437.8	110.0	176.7
1977	21,239.0	591.6	1,822.6	1,837.0	0.2	4,750.4	3,262.8	99.8	459.4	152.0	171.5
1978	21,832.4	594.2	1,903.8	1,959.0	—	4,865.7	3,273.0	15.7	480.6	169.0	175.4
1979	22,421.1	591.7	2,051.0	2,097.0	—	4,822.7	3,241.6	14.4	486.9	181.0	189.3
1980	22,267.3	589.4	2,062.0	2,146.0	—	4,728.7	3,193.9	95.2	511.5	208.0	199.2
1981	23,612.3	576.7	2,136.9	2,275.0	—	4,599.2	3,145.0	93.6	521.5	229.0	224.2
1982	24,148.2	584.4	2,190.7	2,404.0	—	4,173.8	3,008.0	91.6	528.5	250.0	216.4
1983	24,749.3	580.4	2,254.2	2,403.0	—	3,874.9	3,030.0	89.2	540.0	246.0	223.7
1984	25,237.0	592.0	2,318.4	2,809.1	—	3,808.0	2,985.0	87.3	507.0	222.6	191.4
1985	25,739.0	566.3	2,405.7	2,912.0	—	3,808.0	2,933.2	85.3	476.1	223.0	169.4
1986	26,156.6	575.4	2,464.5	3,089.0	—	3,715.2	2,893.7	83.7	469.7	212.0	147.5
1987	26,755.0	567.6	2,498.9	3,269.0	—	4,034.0	2,850.0	82.7	461.7	196.0	151.6
1988	27,168.0	561.7	2,573.8	3,302.0	—	4,047.0	2,811.0	81.7	453.9	198.0	156.7

TABLE Bf326–348 Social insurance and veterans' programs – beneficiaries: 1940–1988 *Continued*

	Disability programs		Survivor programs						Unemployment programs			
	Railroad temporary disability	Black lung	OASDHI	Railroad	Public employees: Federal	Public employees: State and local	Veterans	Black lung	State unemployment insurance	Railroad unemployment insurance	Veterans' unemployment allowances	Training and related allowances
	Bf337	Bf338	Bf339	Bf340	Bf341	Bf342	Bf343	Bf344	Bf345	Bf346	Bf347	Bf348
Year	Thousand	Thousand	Thousand	Thousand	Thousand	Thousand	Thousand	Thousand	Thousand	Thousand	Thousand	Thousand
1940	—	—	35.7	3.0	(Z)	25.0	323.2	—	982.4	41.5	—	—
1941	—	—	168.5	3.6	(Z)	26.0	318.5	—	523.0	22.4	—	—
1942	—	—	255.1	3.8	(Z)	28.0	315.9	—	192.6	3.3	—	—
1943	—	—	341.5	4.1	(Z)	29.0	322.7	—	64.4	0.7	—	—
1944	—	—	402.8	4.2	0.2	30.0	342.0	—	79.3	0.8	10.1	—
1945	—	—	533.5	4.4	0.3	32.0	537.3	—	465.0	3.3	88.9	—
1946	—	—	661.0	4.5	0.4	34.0	790.5	—	1,152.2	52.7	1,359.3	—
1947	23.6	—	767.4	40.5	0.4	35.0	901.5	—	852.4	52.6	760.6	—
1948	33.2	—	872.4	101.6	2.0	36.0	950.0	—	821.1	38.2	434.9	—
1949	33.6	—	983.9	121.8	9.4	38.0	971.2	—	1,666.1	120.4	387.5	—
1950	31.2	—	1,093.9	136.3	18.3	40.0	991.2	—	1,305.0	76.4	32.1	—
1951	28.9	—	1,286.8	146.8	30.2	42.0	1,011.2	—	796.9	29.0	2.8	—
1952	31.5	—	1,484.6	149.9	40.0	44.0	1,044.2	—	873.6	42.6	15.1	—
1953	33.2	—	1,687.5	157.7	50.4	46.0	1,086.0	—	812.1	40.2	33.5	—
1954	31.5	—	1,891.9	167.2	61.5	48.0	1,122.2	—	1,614.9	110.4	89.3	—
1955	31.9	—	2,096.6	196.5	71.9	50.0	1,154.2	—	1,099.5	63.2	72.4	—
1956	30.3	—	2,282.3	210.6	82.9	53.0	1,173.9	—	1,037.0	47.6	50.7	—
1957	30.7	—	2,633.0	220.7	65.4	55.0	1,176.9	—	1,250.2	59.6	44.6	—
1958	30.5	—	2,912.2	231.3	109.2	57.0	1,187.9	—	2,771.9	129.8	67.2	—
1959	29.1	—	3,189.3	242.3	140.1	58.0	1,210.4	—	1,762.6	79.1	14.4	—
1960	28.0	—	3,446.0	251.3	153.4	70.0	1,262.0	—	1,723.0	74.0	1.6	—
1961	29.7	—	3,770.7	259.3	167.1	76.0	1,492.7	—	2,581.5	96.1	—	0.2
1962	28.2	—	3,965.7	265.2	180.8	78.0	1,595.5	—	1,729.0	66.0	—	2.9
1963	27.4	—	4,226.8	275.0	195.6	85.0	1,706.7	—	1,622.9	49.6	—	21.2
1964	25.8	—	4,458.7	282.5	212.0	90.0	1,814.5	—	1,439.7	39.4	—	50.7
1965	23.5	—	4,680.8	288.4	226.8	92.0	1,899.7	—	1,188.5	31.1	—	74.8
1966	21.5	—	5,227.9	294.6	241.9	98.0	1,970.0	—	960.7	22.6	—	65.0
1967	19.6	—	5,511.4	305.9	258.3	108.0	2,041.2	—	1,059.6	25.9	—	67.4
1968	19.7	—	5,823.7	314.6	275.7	110.0	2,253.1	—	986.7	21.0	—	61.4
1969	24.6	—	6,115.0	318.9	290.7	115.0	2,175.6	—	976.0	16.7	—	52.1
1970	24.9	25.1	6,369.3	324.3	306.9	120.0	2,284.1	1.5	1,620.3	17.7	—	60.0
1971	20.5	132.1	6,587.8	326.3	326.2	125.0	2,332.5	64.9	1,959.9	43.3	—	70.0
1972	17.9	165.0	6,826.5	332.3	345.6	130.0	2,390.5	84.5	1,698.1	21.6	—	48.4
1973	14.9	274.4	7,023.3	334.4	364.6	135.0	2,367.7	126.5	1,465.5	14.1	—	45.8
1974	14.4	336.4	7,197.2	335.5	392.1	146.0	2,294.6	146.5	1,984.2	9.7	—	18.7
1975	14.0	333.2	7,301.8	337.6	414.5	145.0	2,257.5	151.6	3,514.7	25.9	—	—
1976	17.9	321.1	7,416.1	337.0	436.0	150.0	2,220.7	156.0	2,595.0	28.2	—	—
1977	17.0	298.4	7,516.7	337.0	452.9	282.0	2,191.3	159.0	2,298.1	21.6	—	—
1978	15.7	281.0	7,560.7	335.1	472.8	290.0	2,137.8	159.0	2,028.5	25.2	—	—
1979	14.4	268.6	7,591.0	332.8	510.8	311.0	1,982.9	161.2	2,112.0	18.0	—	—
1980	14.5	252.2	8,259.7	330.1	509.9	253.0	1,464.9	157.8	2,830.0	38.0	—	—
1981	13.7	162.7	7,635.2	326.1	541.4	248.0	1,374.0	213.8	3,191.0	52.0	—	—
1982	13.5	146.7	7,434.5	324.1	567.6	243.0	1,300.0	207.8	3,897.0	77.0	—	—
1983	12.9	133.8	7,310.3	310.2	596.3	246.0	1,227.0	199.5	2,337.0	43.0	—	—
1984	11.3	172.0	7,196.0	321.7	593.9	242.3	1,157.0	151.1	2,167.0	29.2	—	—
1985	11.4	155.8	7,162.0	310.8	615.4	243.0	1,081.8	147.8	2,409.0	26.5	—	—
1986	12.0	140.5	7,126.8	289.1	644.3	237.0	1,035.3	144.0	2,391.0	24.0	—	—
1987	11.0	126.9	7,184.0	285.0	664.0	233.0	979.0	139.9	2,032.0	17.0	—	—
1988	10.3	114.1	7,222.0	279.1	688.0	235.0	932.0	135.4	1,833.0	13.3	—	—

(Z) Fewer than fifty beneficiaries.

Sources

U.S. Social Security Administration, *Social Security Bulletin, Annual Statistical Supplement*, For the years 1985–1988: 1990, pp. 106–7; for 1970, 1980, 1983–1985: 1987, pp. 256–7; for 1982: 1986, pp. 252–3; for 1981: 1984–1985, pp. 223–4; for 1975, 1978, 1979: 1982, pp. 220–1; for 1977: 1981, pp. 66–7; for 1976: 1980, pp. 67–8; for 1973–1974: 1975, p. 50; for 1972: 1974, p. 47; for 1971: 1973, pp. 43–4; for 1940, 1950, 1955, 1960, 1965, 1970–1972: 1973, p. 43; for 1969: 1970, p. 29; for 1966, 1967: 1968, p. 28; for 1962–1964: 1965, p. 6; for 1961: 1964, p. 6; for 1958–1959: 1962, p. 6; for 1956–1957: 1960, p. 6; for 1951–1954: 1957, p. 14; for 1944–1949: 1952, p. 27; for 1943: 1946, p. 3; for 1942: 1945, p. 18; for 1941: 1944, p. 23. The U.S. Social Security Administration stopped publishing this table in the *Annual Statistical Supplement* after the 1990 issue.

The U.S. Social Security Administration stopped publishing the data for Tables Bf290–348 in the *Annual Statistical Supplement* after the 1990 issue. More recent data at higher levels of aggregation are available in Table Bf364–376 and are published in the quarterly *Social Security Bulletin*, Table 4.A2. Most of the data are derived from operating statistics of the administering agencies.

Documentation

See the text for Table Bf290–325.

TABLE Bf349–363 Social insurance and veterans' programs – cash benefits: 1940–1997

Contributed by Price V. Fishback and Melissa A. Thomasson

		Retirement, disability, and survivor benefits							Unemployment benefits		Temporary disability benefits				
		Paid on monthly basis					Lump-sum payments								
				Public employee retirement											
Year	Total	OASDI	Railroad retirement	Federal civil service	Other	Veterans' pensions and compensation	OASDI	Other	Under state laws	Railroad	Under state laws	Railroad	Workers' compensation benefits	Public assistance payments	Supplemental Security Income payments
	Bf349	Bf350	Bf351	Bf352	Bf353	Bf354	Bf355	Bf356	Bf357	Bf358	Bf359	Bf360	Bf361	Bf362	Bf363
	Million dollars	Million dollars	Million dollars	Million dollars	Million dollars	Million dollars	Million dollars	Million dollars	Million dollars	Million dollars	Million dollars	Million dollars	Million dollars	Million dollars	Million dollars
1940	2,171	24	116	62	183	424	12	25	519	16	—	—	161	631	—
1950	8,395	928	298	184	600	2,224	33	54	1,408	60	89	28	415	2,074	—
1960	25,564	11,081	942	805	1,793	3,437	164	135	2,867	158	311	57	860	2,954	—
1970	59,323	31,570	1,756	2,797	6,369	5,480	294	289	4,184	39	645	56	1,981	4,864	—
1980	227,884	120,272	4,867	15,043	25,559	11,358	250	606	18,757	176	1,300	63	9,632	12,144	7,858
1985	328,304	186,083	6,265	22,841	40,028	14,084	143	680	14,639	134	1,808	47	15,170	15,276	11,107
1990	434,753	244,757	7,259	29,396	58,349	15,717	131	212	18,059	61	3,099	58	23,029	19,272	15,175
1991	478,224	264,216	7,571	31,777	63,317	16,246	132	284	25,450	67	3,731	56	25,694	21,227	18,503
1992	507,013	281,393	7,748	30,691	69,209	16,316	88	188	24,967	60	3,858	52	27,754	22,329	22,324
1993	—	296,156	7,904	32,948	76,096	16,865	81	110	21,547	51	3,101	49	27,618	21,038	24,730
1994	—	311,496	8,002	35,715	81,447	18,747	94	113	21,646	45	3,201	56	27,426	23,270	26,078
1995	—	326,671	8,085	37,689	88,015	17,975	119	116	22,010	40	3,189	55	26,750	22,712	27,871
1996	—	341,011	8,129	39,170	—	—	127	123	21,751	42	—	51	—	—	29,388
1997	—	355,550	8,224	41,223	—	—	128	108	19,771	43	—	61	—	—	31,427

Source

U.S. Social Security Administration, *Social Security Bulletin* 62 (4) (1999), Table 4.A1, p. 81. The Social Security Administration bases the information on reports of administrative agencies on a checks-issued basis (including retroactive payments) where available.

Documentation

This table and Table Bf364–376 provide overviews of various public income-maintenance programs. They are companions to Tables Bf290–348. The U.S. Social Security Administration stopped publishing the more disaggregated data for Tables Bf290–348 in the *Annual Statistical Supplement* after the 1990 issue. This table provides a more aggregated and updated version of the same data. These are the series that, as of 1999, are being updated in the quarterly *Social Security Bulletin*. In published sources, the U.S. Social Security Administration does not report revisions for years prior to 1990 except for years divisible by 5 and 10. The public income-maintenance payments include payments outside the United States and benefits to spouses and children where applicable.

Series Bf349. Emergency relief funds of $1630.3 million are included in the 1940 total and not included elsewhere. Includes training allowances to unemployed workers under Area Redevelopment Act and manpower Development and Training Act for 1961–1975, not shown separately. Beginning December 1980, the series also includes public assistance revisions for 1940–1979.

Series Bf350. Retirement and survivor benefits beginning in 1940; disability benefits beginning in 1957. Beginning October 1966, includes special benefits authorized by 1966 legislation for persons aged 72 or older not insured under the regular or transitional provisions of the Social Security Act.

Series Bf351. Includes annuities to widows under joint-and-survivor elections before 1947. Beginning February 1967, includes supplemental annuities for career railroad employees.

Series Bf352–353. Excludes refunds of contributions to employees who leave service.

Series Bf352. Beginning January 1988, includes both Civil Service Retirement System and Federal Employee Retirement System benefits. Beginning 1994, includes annual data only.

Series Bf353. Represents federal contributory systems other than civil service, federal noncontributory systems for civilian employees and career military personnel, and systems for state and local employees.

Series Bf354. Payments to veterans and survivors of deceased veterans, including special allowances for survivors of veterans who did not qualify under Old-Age, Survivors, Disability, and Health Insurance (OASDHI; Servicemen's and Veteran's Survivor Benefit Act of 1956) and through June 1973, subsistence payments to disabled veterans undergoing training.

Series Bf355–356. The lump-sum payments are death payments.

Series Bf356. Includes annual and monthly payments for Railroad Retirement, veteran's programs, and federal civil service retirement. For "other" public employee systems, includes annual data only. Lump-sum data are not available for state and local retirement systems after 1986. Beginning 1993, annual data include civil service and Railroad Retirement only.

TABLE Bf349–363 Social insurance and veterans' programs – cash benefits: 1940–1997 *Continued*

Series Bf357. Annual and monthly totals include regular state Unemployment Insurance program and payments made by states as agents of the federal government under the Federal Employees' Unemployment Compensation program and under the Ex-Servicemen's Compensation Act of 1958. Annual data are only for payments under Servicemen's Readjustment Act of 1944, Veterans' Readjustment Act of 1962, Trade Expansion Act of 1962, Disaster Relief Act of 1970, and the Temporary and Permanent Extended Unemployment Insurance programs. Beginning in 1961, includes program in Puerto Rico. Beginning in 1981, state Unemployment Insurance and Ex-Servicemen's Compensation Act only. Beginning July 1987, state programs only.

Series Bf358–359. Benefits in Rhode Island (from 1943), in California (from 1947), in New Jersey (from 1949), in New York (from 1950), in Puerto Rico (from 1970), in Hawai'i (from 1972), including payments under private plans where applicable.

Series Bf360. Benefits began in 1947.

Series Bf361. Workers' compensation benefits include those under federal workers' compensation laws and under state laws paid by private insurance carriers, state funds, and self-insurers. Beginning in 1959, includes data for Alaska and Hawai'i. Monthly data refer only to federal Black Lung Benefits administered by the Social Security Administration (starting in 1970).

Series Bf362. Includes Aid to Families with Dependent Children and General Assistance. Through 1973, includes Old-Age Assistance, Aid to the Blind, and Aid to the Permanently and Totally Disabled (see text for series Bf363). Includes payments to intermediate-care facilities (July 1968–December 1971) and payments for emergency assistance, beginning July 1969. Includes money payments under medical assistance for the aged (1960–1969). Excludes medical vendor payments. Starting in 1974, includes money payments to the aged, blind, and disabled in Guam, Puerto Rico, and the Virgin Islands under federally aided public assistance programs.

Series Bf363. The Supplemental Security Income program supersedes the public assistance programs of Old-Age Assistance. Aid to the Blind, and Aid to the Permanently and Totally Disabled in the fifty states and the District of Columbia, beginning in 1974 – beginning in 1978, in the Northern Mariana Islands. Annual totals include payments under state-administered supplementation programs.

TABLE Bf364–376 Public income-maintenance programs – beneficiaries of cash payments: 1940–1997

Contributed by Price V. Fishback and Melissa A. Thomasson

	Retirement and disability programs					Survivor programs					Unemployment programs		
	OASDI									Railroad temporary disability			
	Retirement	Disability	Railroad	Federal civil service	Veterans'	OASDI	Railroad	Federal civil service	Veterans'		Under state laws	Railroad	Black lung
	Bf364	Bf365	Bf366	Bf367	Bf368	Bf369	Bf370	Bf371	Bf372	Bf373	Bf374	Bf375	Bf376
Year	Thousand	Thousand	Thousand	Thousand	Thousand	Thousand	Thousand	Thousand	Thousand	Thousand	Thousand	Thousand	Thousand
1940	148	—	146	65	610	74	3	—	323	—	667	74	—
1950	2,326	—	256	161	2,366	1,152	142	25	1,010	32	838	35	—
1960	10,599	687	553	379	3,064	3,558	256	154	1,393	34	2,165	102	—
1970	17,096	2,665	653	697	3,210	6,468	326	308	2,301	22	2,045	21	—
1980	23,336	4,685	685	1,296	3,189	7,601	330	450	1,748	16	2,830	38	400
1985	25,991	3,907	652	1,454	2,924	7,160	311	501	1,067	12	2,409	29	295
1986	26,551	3,993	641	1,489	2,876	7,164	306	516	1,006	12	2,391	24	276
1987	26,995	4,945	633	1,518	2,836	7,150	302	532	955	1	2,032	17	259
1988	27,384	4,074	627	1,543	2,797	7,169	296	548	911	9	1,736	8	242
1989	27,853	4,129	622	1,585	2,771	7,169	290	561	868	7	1,716	8	226
1990	38,368	4,266	613	1,590	2,741	7,198	284	562	831	7	2,596	9	211
1991	28,819	4,513	602	1,616	2,700	7,260	278	573	790	8	2,849	9	196
1992	29,302	4,890	590	1,647	2,673	7,315	270	589	775	7	2,620	6	182
1993	29,634	5,254	576	1,681	2,658	7,358	264	607	706	7	2,349	6	168
1994	29,914	5,584	560	1,666	2,660	7,385	257	597	678	6	2,088	4	155
1995	30,141	5,858	542	1,704	2,668	7,388	250	607	656	6	2,099	5	144
1996	30,311	6,072	528	1,716	—	7,354	241	618	—	6	2,197	3	131
1997	30,638	6,153	512	1,731	—	7,180	233	621	—	6	2,076	3	119

Source

U.S. Social Security Administration, *Social Security Bulletin* 62 (4) (1999), Table 4.A2, p. 82. The U.S. Social Security Administration bases the information on reports of administrative agencies.

Documentation

This is a companion table to Tables Bf290–363. See the text for Table Bf349–363 for further details on programs.

Series Bf364–366. Beneficiaries include auxiliaries or dependents.

Series Bf364. Beginning October 1966, Old-Age, Survivors, and Disability Insurance (OASDI) retirement benefits include special benefits authorized by 1966 legislation for persons aged 72 or older and not insured under the regular or transitional provisions of the Social Security Act.

Series Bf367. Beginning January 1988, includes both Civil Service Retirement System and Federal Employee Retirement System beneficiaries.

Series Bf372. Monthly number at end of quarter.

Series Bf373 and Bf375. Average number during fourteen-day registration period.

Series Bf374. Average weekly number in December. Includes regular state Unemployment Insurance, the Federal Employees' Unemployment Compensation program, and the Ex-Servicemen's Compensation program through 1981. Excludes federal employees' program thereafter. Beginning July 1987, includes state programs only.

Series Bf376. Includes dependents and survivors. Data refer only to programs administered by the U.S. Social Security Administration.

TABLE Bf377–394 Old-Age, Survivors, Disability, and Health Insurance – covered workers, earnings, employers, and tax rates: 1937–1999

Contributed by Price V. Fishback and Melissa A. Thomasson

	Workers fully insured for retirement and/or survivor benefits				Workers reported with taxable earnings			Earnings	
	Total	Permanently insured	Workers insured in event of disability	Living workers (estimated)	Total	With maximum taxable earnings	New entrants into covered employment	Total in covered employment	Reported taxable earnings
	Bf377	Bf378	Bf379	Bf380	Bf381	Bf382	Bf383	Bf384	Bf385
Year	Thousand	Thousand	Thousand	Thousand	Thousand	Thousand	Thousand	Million dollars	Million dollars
1937	—	—	—	—	32,904	1,031	32,904	32,200	29,620
1938	—	—	—	—	31,822	—	3,930	28,497 [2]	26,502
1939	—	—	—	—	33,751	—	4,450	32,226 [2]	29,745
1940	24,200	1,100	—	40,700	35,390	1,196	4,430	35,700	32,970
1941	25,800	1,400	—	44,800	40,980	—	6,440	45,489 [2]	41,850
1942	28,100	1,800	—	50,900	46,360	—	7,960	58,176 [2]	52,940
1943	29,900	2,300	—	58,500	47,660	—	7,340	69,665 [2]	62,420
1944	31,900	2,800	—	65,400	46,300	—	4,690	73,299 [2]	64,430
1945	33,400	3,400	—	69,600	46,390	6,361	3,480	71,600	62,950
1946	35,400	8,600	—	72,400	48,840	6,477	3,080	79,300	69,090
1947	37,300	11,600	—	75,200	48,910	9,620	2,680	92,400	78,370
1948	38,900	13,200	—	77,400	49,020	12,061	2,640	102,300	84,120
1949	40,100	14,900	—	79,400	46,800	11,740	1,960	100,000	81,810
1950	59,800	21,000	—	80,800	48,280	13,936	2,520	109,800	87,500
1951	62,800	22,900	—	82,700	58,120	14,270	6,000	148,900	120,770
1952	68,200	25,600	—	88,000	59,580	16,606	3,500	159,900	128,640
1953	71,000	27,700	—	90,800	60,840	19,013	3,090	173,000	135,870
1954	70,200	29,900	31,900	93,100	59,610	18,866	2,360	171,900	133,520
1955	70,500	32,500	35,400	94,700	65,200	16,704	4,760	196,100	157,540
1956	74,000	36,100	37,200	98,600	67,610	19,236	3,660	216,800	170,720
1957	76,100	38,300	38,400	101,400	70,590	21,095	3,380	233,900	181,380
1958	76,500	40,300	43,400	103,800	69,770	21,328	2,450	236,500	180,720
1959	76,700	42,200	46,400	105,300	71,700	19,112	3,180	255,000	202,310
1960	84,400	47,600	48,500	107,400	72,530	20,310	3,130	265,200	207,000
1961	88,500	53,300	50,500	109,400	72,820	21,265	2,990	270,700	209,640
1962	89,800	54,900	51,500	111,200	74,820	23,154	3,360	289,000	219,050
1963	91,300	56,600	52,300	113,300	75,540	24,570	3,520	302,300	225,550
1964	92,800	58,300	53,300	115,600	77,430	26,717	3,890	324,500	236,390
1965	94,800	60,200	55,000	118,100	80,680	29,136	4,620	351,700	250,730
1966	97,200	61,900	55,700	121,300	84,600	20,498	5,080	390,700	312,540
1967	99,900	63,300	56,900	125,000	87,040	22,948	4,530	422,300	329,960
1968	102,600	64,500	70,100	127,900	89,380	19,120	4,830	460,000	375,840
1969	105,000	65,700	72,400	130,800	92,060	22,577	5,160	502,800	402,550
1970	108,300	67,300	74,500	133,500	93,090	24,224	4,440	531,600	415,600
1971	110,800	68,500	76,100	135,900	93,340	26,404	4,470	559,700	426,960
1972	113,500	69,800	77,800	138,200	96,240	24,074	5,150	617,900	484,110
1973	116,800	71,300	80,400	140,600	99,830	20,250	5,670	686,700	561,850
1974	120,200	72,700	83,300	142,900	101,330	15,310	4,940	746,700	636,760
1975	123,100	74,300	85,300	145,200	100,200	15,070	4,120	787,600	664,660
1976	126,000	76,100	87,000	148,300	102,600	15,330	4,700	874,700	737,700
1977	129,000	78,100	89,300	151,000	105,800	15,700	5,070	960,100	816,550
1978	133,300	80,300	93,700	153,700	110,600	17,050	5,460	1,092,600	915,600
1979	137,300	83,000	98,000	156,400	112,700	11,236	4,883	1,222,200	1,067,000
1980	140,400	85,300	100,300	159,000	113,000	9,903	4,243	1,328,800	1,180,700
1981	142,900	88,000	102,600	161,500	113,000	8,594	4,090	1,450,900	1,294,100
1982	144,700	90,700	104,500	164,000	111,800	7,929	3,408	1,516,600	1,365,300
1983	146,500	94,000	105,400	—	112,100	7,044	3,914	1,615,200	1,454,100
1984	148,300	96,900	107,100	—	116,300	7,421	4,743	1,800,800	1,608,800
1985	150,900	100,000	109,600	—	119,800	7,766	4,756	1,936,800	1,722,600
1986	153,200	103,300	111,600	—	122,900	7,624	4,641	2,081,800	1,844,400
1987	155,700	107,400	113,500	—	125,600	7,735	4,956	2,237,000	1,960,000
1988	158,300	110,600	115,700	—	129,600	8,483	5,489	2,432,800	2,088,400
1989	161,300	113,600	118,100	—	131,700	8,110	4,856	2,578,700	2,239,500

Notes appear at end of table

TABLE Bf377–394 Old-Age, Survivors, Disability, and Health Insurance – covered workers, earnings, employers, and tax rates: 1937–1999 ***Continued***

	Workers fully insured for retirement and/or survivor benefits				Workers reported with taxable earnings			Earnings	
	Total	Permanently insured	Workers insured in event of disability	Living workers (estimated)	Total	With maximum taxable earnings	New entrants into covered employment	Total in covered employment	Reported taxable earnings
	Bf377	Bf378	Bf379	Bf380	Bf381	Bf382	Bf383	Bf384	Bf385
Year	Thousand	Thousand	Thousand	Thousand	Thousand	Thousand	Thousand	Million dollars	Million dollars
1990	164,000	116,400	120,100	—	133,600	7,575	4,012	2,703,800	2,358,000
1991	165,900	118,800	121,500	—	133,000	7,483	3,541	2,760,500	2,422,500
1992	167,500	121,100	122,900	—	134,000	7,667	3,918	2,917,800	2,532,900
1993	169,100	123,600	124,400	—	136,100	7,617	4,204	3,022,900	2,636,100
1994	170,800	125,900	126,200	—	138,200	7,517	4,570	3,169,100	2,785,200
1995	173,000	128,300	128,100	—	141,000	8,192	4,612	3,359,100	2,919,900
1996	175,200	130,800	129,900	—	143,500	8,654	4,611	3,568,200	3,075,600
1997	177,500	133,400	132,000	—	146,700	—	—	3,852,600	3,291,000
1998	179,500	135,700	133,800	—	148,500	—	—	4,120,500	3,512,100
1999	181,800	137,900	136,000	—	—	—	—	—	—

	Annual maximum taxable earnings per worker			Contribution rate					
				For employer and employee each			For self-employed persons		
	Under OASDI	Under HI (Medicare)	Employers reporting taxable wages	Old-Age, Survivors Insurance (OASI)	Disability Insurance (DI)	Health Insurance (HI)	Old-Age, Survivors Insurance (OASI)	Disability Insurance (DI)	Health Insurance (HI)
	Bf386 [1]	Bf387 [1]	Bf388	Bf389	Bf390	Bf391	Bf392	Bf393	Bf394
Year	Dollars	Dollars	Thousand	Percent	Percent	Percent	Percent	Percent	Percent
1937	3,000	—	2,420	1.000	—	—	—	—	—
1938	3,000	—	2,240	1.000	—	—	—	—	—
1939	3,000	—	2,370	1.000	—	—	—	—	—
1940	3,000	—	2,500	1.000	—	—	—	—	—
1941	3,000	—	2,650	1.000	—	—	—	—	—
1942	3,000	—	2,660	1.000	—	—	—	—	—
1943	3,000	—	2,390	1.000	—	—	—	—	—
1944	3,000	—	2,470	1.000	—	—	—	—	—
1945	3,000	—	2,610	1.000	—	—	—	—	—
1946	3,000	—	3,020	1.000	—	—	—	—	—
1947	3,000	—	3,250	1.000	—	—	—	—	—
1948	3,000	—	3,300	1.000	—	—	—	—	—
1949	3,000	—	3,320	1.000	—	—	—	—	—
1950	3,000	—	3,350	1.500	—	—	—	—	—
1951	3,600	—	4,700	1.500	—	—	2.2500	—	—
1952	3,600	—	4,740	1.500	—	—	2.2500	—	—
1953	3,600	—	4,700	1.500	—	—	2.2500	—	—
1954	3,600	—	4,720	2.000	—	—	3.0000	—	—
1955	4,200	—	4,910	2.000	—	—	3.0000	—	—
1956	4,200	—	5,240	2.000	—	—	3.0000	—	—
1957	4,200	—	5,190	2.000	0.250	—	3.0000	0.3750	—
1958	4,200	—	5,270	2.000	0.250	—	3.0000	0.3750	—
1959	4,800	—	5,520	2.250	0.250	—	3.3750	0.3750	—
1960	4,800	—	5,670	2.750	0.250	—	4.1250	0.3750	—
1961	4,800	—	5,860	2.750	0.250	—	4.1250	0.3750	—
1962	4,800	—	5,910	2.875	0.250	—	4.3250	0.3750	—
1963	4,800	—	6,000	3.375	0.250	—	5.0250	0.3750	—
1964	4,800	—	6,090	3.375	0.250	—	5.0250	0.3750	—
1965	4,800	—	6,090	3.375	0.250	—	5.0250	0.3750	—
1966	6,600	6,600	5,990	3.500	0.350	0.35	5.2750	0.5250	0.35
1967	6,600	6,600	5,920	3.550	0.350	0.50	5.3750	0.5250	0.50
1968	7,800	7,800	5,820	3.325	0.475	0.60	5.0875	0.7125	0.60
1969	7,800	7,800	5,790	3.725	0.475	0.60	5.5875	0.7125	0.60

Notes appear at end of table

(continued)

TABLE Bf377–394 Old-Age, Survivors, Disability, and Health Insurance – covered workers, earnings, employers, and tax rates: 1937–1999

Contributed by Price V. Fishback and Melissa A. Thomasson

	Annual maximum taxable earnings per worker			Contribution rate					
				For employer and employee each			For self-employed persons		
	Under OASDI	Under HI (Medicare)	Employers reporting taxable wages	Old-Age, Survivors Insurance (OASI)	Disability Insurance (DI)	Health Insurance (HI)	Old-Age, Survivors Insurance (OASI)	Disability Insurance (DI)	Health Insurance (HI)
	Bf386 [1]	Bf387 [1]	Bf388	Bf389	Bf390	Bf391	Bf392	Bf393	Bf394
Year	Dollars	Dollars	Thousand	Percent	Percent	Percent	Percent	Percent	Percent
1970	7,800	7,800	5,690	3.650	0.550	0.60	5.4750	0.8250	0.60
1971	7,800	7,800	5,760	4.050	0.550	0.60	6.0750	0.8250	0.60
1972	9,000	9,000	5,710	4.050	0.550	0.60	6.0750	0.8250	0.60
1973	10,800	10,800	5,760	4.300	0.550	1.00	6.2050	0.7950	1.00
1974	13,200	13,200	5,750	4.375	0.575	0.90	6.1850	0.8150	0.90
1975	14,100	14,100	5,720	4.375	0.575	0.90	6.1850	0.8150	0.90
1976	15,300	15,300	5,840	4.375	0.575	0.90	6.1850	0.8150	0.90
1977	16,500	16,500	5,920	4.375	0.575	0.90	6.1850	0.8150	0.90
1978	17,700	17,700	—	4.275	0.775	1.00	6.0100	1.0900	1.00
1979	22,900	22,900	—	4.330	0.750	1.05	6.0100	1.0400	1.05
1980	25,900	25,900	—	4.520	0.560	1.05	6.2725	0.7775	1.05
1981	29,700	29,700	—	4.700	0.650	1.30	7.0250	0.9750	1.30
1982	32,400	32,400	—	4.575	0.825	1.30	6.8125	1.2375	1.30
1983	35,700	35,700	—	4.775	0.625	1.30	7.1125	0.9375	1.30
1984	37,800	37,800	—	5.200	0.500	1.30	10.4000	1.0000	2.60
1985	39,600	39,600	—	5.200	0.500	1.35	10.4000	1.0000	2.70
1986	42,000	42,000	—	5.200	0.500	1.45	10.4000	1.0000	2.90
1987	43,800	43,800	—	5.200	0.500	1.45	10.4000	1.0000	2.90
1988	45,000	45,000	—	5.530	0.530	1.45	11.0600	1.0600	2.90
1989	48,000	48,000	—	5.530	0.530	1.45	11.0600	1.0600	2.90
1990	51,300	51,300	—	5.600	0.600	1.45	11.2000	1.2000	2.90
1991	53,400	125,000	—	5.600	0.600	1.45	11.2000	1.2000	2.90
1992	55,500	130,200	—	5.600	0.600	1.45	11.2000	1.2000	2.90
1993	57,600	135,000	—	5.600	0.600	1.45	11.2000	1.2000	2.90
1994	60,600	—	—	5.260	0.940	1.45	10.5200	1.8800	2.90
1995	61,200	—	—	5.260	0.940	1.45	10.5200	1.8800	2.90
1996	62,700	—	—	5.260	0.940	1.45	10.5200	1.8800	2.90
1997	65,400	—	—	5.350	0.850	1.45	10.7000	1.7000	2.90
1998	68,400	—	—	5.350	0.850	1.45	10.7000	1.7000	2.90
1999	72,600	—	—	5.350	0.850	1.45	10.7000	1.7000	2.90

[1] Data in some years based on automatic adjustment. See text.

[2] Data error in original source, which cannot be corrected.

Sources

U.S. Social Security Administration, *Social Security Bulletin: Annual Statistical Supplement* (1997), Table 4.B1, p. 167, Table 4.C1, p. 178; (1999), Table 4.B1, p. 165, Table 4.C1, p. 176, Table 2.A3, p. 36. Series Bf380 and Bf388 are reported in the *Social Security Bulletin: Annual Statistical Supplement* (1981), pp. 84, 96 and (1987), p. 104.

Documentation

The Old-Age, Survivors, and Disability Insurance (OASDI) program provides monthly benefits to retired and disabled workers and their dependents and to survivors of insured workers. Benefits are paid as a matter of earned right to workers who gain insured status and to their eligible spouses, children, and survivors. A person builds protection under the OASDI program through taxes on earnings from employment covered under Social Security. In 1965, a comprehensive health insurance program (Medicare) for persons 65 years old and older was established. The program consists of a compulsory hospital insurance plan covering hospital and related services and a voluntary supplementary medical insurance plan covering physicians' and related medical services. The hospital insurance plan is financed through contributions made while the individual is working (except that federal general revenues are used to finance the benefits for certain elderly persons who reach retirement age without becoming insured under the Social Security Act). The supplementary medical insurance plan is financed through voluntary contributions by the elderly matched by the federal government general revenues.

The national system of Old Age, Survivors, Disability, and Health Insurance (OASDHI) originally covered employees in industry and commerce. Beginning in 1951, coverage was extended to regularly employed agricultural and domestic workers, to most urban self-employed persons, and, on a voluntary group basis, to employees of nonprofit organizations and to employees of state and local governments not covered by separate retirement programs. During the 1950s, coverage was further extended to self-employed farmers and additional farmworkers, to most professional self-employed persons and, on a voluntary basis, to most state and local government employees covered by their own retirement system. As of January 1957, military personnel were covered on a compulsory basis. Free wage credits for military service from September 1940 through December 1956 are reflected in benefits paid during the years covered by the series (primarily in benefits to young survivors) but do not enter into the count of covered workers or taxable earnings. The additional cost of benefits paid as a result of these credits is met by transfers to the trust funds from general revenues. In 1965, self-employed doctors of

TABLE Bf377–394 Old-Age, Survivors, Disability, and Health Insurance – covered workers, earnings, employers, and tax rates: 1937–1999 *Continued*

medicine were covered, and in 1967 the previous elective coverage of ministers became compulsory unless exemption was claimed on grounds of conscience or religious principle.

When the OASDHI program began in 1937, fewer than 60 percent of all persons who worked in paid employment during an average week were covered. Following the 1950 amendments, the proportion rose to 75 percent and by 1970 was more than 90 percent. In the mid-1990s about 96 percent of all jobs in the United States were covered. Workers excluded from coverage fall into five major categories: (1) federal civilian employees hired before January 1, 1984, (2) railroad workers, (3) certain employees of state and local governments who are covered under a retirement system, (4) household workers and farm workers whose earnings do not meet certain minimum requirements, and (5) persons with very low net earnings from self-employment (generally less than $400 annually). Federal civil servants hired prior to 1984 and railroad employees are covered, separately, by compulsory, contributory retirement systems of their own. The railroad system is closely coordinated with OASDHI.

To qualify for cash benefits, a worker must have worked a sufficient time in covered employment to have acquired an insured status (see series Bf377–379). Workers are considered "fully insured" when they meet the minimum requirements for insurance; they become "permanently insured" when they become eligible for a required-worker benefit. Workers are insured in the event of disability if they are considered fully insured and have contributed a sufficient amount to receive disability insurance. Under the 1939 amendments, workers were generally "fully insured" for benefits if they had worked in covered employment half the time after 1936 and before age 65 and had a minimum of six calendar quarters of coverage. Subsequent liberalizations permitted a person to become fully insured if he had been in covered work roughly equal to one fourth of the time between 1950 (or age 21, if later) and retirement age or death. Based on the rules in 1970, if a worker died before acquiring a fully insured status but was "currently insured" 1.5 years of employment out of the 3 preceding years, death-survivor benefits may be paid to his young widow with children. To be insured for disability benefits, circa 1970, a worker must generally have worked for at least five out of the ten years before onset of disability. The 1965 amendments eased the eligibility requirements for persons 72 years old and older who were not eligible for cash benefits by introducing a transitional insured status under which a special flat monthly benefit may be paid to persons with three to five quarters of coverage. A 1966 amendment extended these special monthly benefits to certain persons 72 years old and older who could not meet even these minimal requirements. Lump-sum payments became payable in 1937; monthly benefits, in 1940. The original Social Security Act provided for monthly old-age benefits only. Amendments adopted in 1939 added benefits for dependents and survivors of the insured worker. Benefits for disabled persons were added in 1956, and benefits for the dependents of disabled persons, in 1958. Beginning in 1966, the cost of rehabilitation services furnished to disability beneficiaries was also paid by the program. A complete discussion of insured status can be found in the *Social Security Bulletin: Annual Statistical Supplement*, 1997, p. 372.

Since 1940, the OASDHI program has been a pay-as-you-go system funded by taxes on earnings for wage and salary workers and the self-employed. An employer deducts Social Security contributions from a worker's pay and adds an equal amount for his tax as employer. The money is forwarded to the Internal Revenue Service and deposited into federal trust funds from which the benefits and administrative expenses are paid. Self-employed persons pay their Social Security contributions with their federal income tax. For example, the information in series Bf386–394 shows that in 1990 a typical worker would pay a tax on earnings up to a maximum of $51,300 of 5.6 percent for Old-Age, Survivors Insurance (OASI), start 0.6 percent for Disability Insurance (DI), and 1.4 percent for Medicare. The employer would pay the matching amount. The self-employed would pay both the worker and employer share, or 11.2 percent for OASI, 1.2 percent for DI, and 2.8 percent for Medicare. The Omnibus Budget Reconciliation Act of 1993 repealed the Medicare maximum so that now all earnings are subject to the Medicare tax. In 1984 the total contribution rate for OASDHI for employers and employees each (the sum of series Bf389–391) includes an automatic tax credit of 0.3 percent for remuneration paid in the calendar year 1984 under the Federal Insurance Contributions Act. During the period 1984 to 1989, the total contribution rate for OASDHI for self-employed (the sum of series Bf392–394) includes an automatic tax credit of 2.7 percent of earnings for self-employed income for taxable years beginning in 1984, 2.3 percent for taxable years beginning in 1985, and 2.0 percent for taxable years beginning in 1986, 1987, 1988, and 1989. During this period, scheduled taxes were credited to the Social Security Trust funds, monies for tax credits were paid from the Treasury, and the reduced tax rates were paid by employees and the self-employed. For more information, see *Social Security Bulletin, Annual Statistical Supplement, 1997*, Table 2.A4, p. 35. Unlike the income tax, the OASDHI taxes are drawn on the first dollar of earnings; however, the working poor receive some relief from the OASDHI payroll taxes through the earned income tax credit.

Series Bf380. The estimated total number of living workers is the estimated number of persons who had covered employment any time during the period from 1937 to the year shown. It is not adjusted to reflect the effect of provisions that coordinate the OASDHI and Railroad Retirement programs and wage credits for military service. It is only partially adjusted to eliminate duplicate counts of persons with taxable earnings reported on more than one Social Security number.

Series Bf381–385. Relate only to wage and salary workers for the period 1937–1950. Beginning in 1951, the data include self-employed workers and earnings.

Series Bf383. New entrants into covered employment are workers reported with first taxable earnings under the program in a specified year. During the period 1937–1994, 276.2 million different persons were reported with taxable earnings.

Series Bf382–383 and Bf385. Preliminary estimates are based on data from the Bureau of Labor Statistics and the National Income and Product Accounts.

Series Bf381–383, Bf385, and Bf387. Data for 1996 are preliminary estimates based on data from the Bureau of Labor Statistics and the National Income and Product Accounts.

Series Bf386–387. Data for 1975–1978, 1982–1989, and 1993–1996 are based on automatic adjustment under 1972a Act (as modified by 1973a and 1973b Acts), in proportion to increases in the average wage level. The maximum earnings taxable for HI in 1991 is based on 1990 legislation.

Series Bf388. No longer reported in statistical supplement after 1977.

TABLE Bf395–407 Old-Age and Survivors Insurance – benefits, by type of beneficiary: 1937–1998

Contributed by Price V. Fishback and Melissa A. Thomasson

		Annual benefits paid to											
			Retired workers and dependents				Survivors						
	Total	Total	Total	Retired workers	Spouses	Children	Total	Surviving children	Widowed mothers and fathers	Widows and widowers	Parents	Special age-72 beneficiaries	Lump-sum death payments
	Bf395	Bf396	Bf397	Bf398	Bf399	Bf400	Bf401	Bf402	Bf403	Bf404	Bf405	Bf406	Bf407
Year	Million dollars	Million dollars	Million dollars	Million dollars	Million dollars	Million dollars	Million dollars	Million dollars	Million dollars	Million dollars	Million dollars	Million dollars	Million dollars
1937	1	—	—	—	—	—	—	—	—	—	—	—	1
1938	10	—	—	—	—	—	—	—	—	—	—	—	10
1939	14	—	—	—	—	—	—	—	—	—	—	—	14
1940	35	24	17	15	2	(Z)	6	3	2	(Z)	(Z)	—	9
1941	88	75	51	44	7	1	24	13	8	2	(Z)	—	13
1942	131	116	76	65	10	1	40	21	13	5	(Z)	—	15
1943	166	148	93	79	13	1	55	29	16	9	1	—	18
1944	209	187	113	97	16	1	73	39	20	14	1	—	22
1945	274	248	148	126	21	2	100	52	27	20	1	—	26
1946	378	350	222	189	31	2	128	66	32	28	1	—	28
1947	466	437	288	245	40	3	149	77	34	37	2	—	29
1948	556	524	352	300	49	4	172	86	36	48	2	—	32
1949	667	634	437	373	60	5	197	95	39	60	2	—	33
1950	961	928	651	557	88	6	277	135	49	89	3	—	33
1951	1,885	1,828	1,321	1,135	175	11	507	260	82	156	9	—	57
1952	2,194	2,131	1,539	1,328	200	12	592	298	92	191	10	—	63
1953	3,006	2,919	2,175	1,884	275	16	744	369	114	248	12	—	87
1954	3,670	3,578	2,698	2,340	338	21	880	430	133	304	13	—	92
1955	4,968	4,855	3,748	3,253	466	29	1,108	532	163	396	16	—	113
1956	5,715	5,605	4,361	3,793	536	33	1,244	581	177	469	17	—	109
1957	7,347	7,209	5,688	4,888	756	43	1,521	651	198	653	19	—	139
1958	8,327	8,194	6,474	5,567	851	56	1,720	720	223	757	20	—	133
1959	9,842	9,670	7,607	6,548	982	77	2,063	855	263	921	25	—	171
1960	10,677	10,512	8,196	7,053	1,051	92	2,316	945	286	1,057	28	—	164
1961	11,862	11,690	9,032	7,802	1,124	106	2,659	1,080	316	1,232	31	—	171
1962	13,356	13,173	10,162	8,813	1,216	134	3,011	1,171	336	1,470	34	—	183
1963	14,217	14,011	10,795	9,391	1,258	146	3,216	1,222	348	1,612	34	—	206
1964	14,914	14,698	11,281	9,854	1,277	150	3,416	1,275	354	1,754	33	—	216
1965	16,737	16,521	12,542	10,984	1,383	175	3,979	1,515	388	2,041	35	—	217
1966	18,267	18,030	13,373	11,727	1,429	216	4,613	1,812	415	2,351	35	44	237
1967	19,468	19,215	14,049	12,372	1,456	221	4,854	1,855	420	2,545	34	313	252
1968	22,642	22,373	16,204	14,278	1,673	253	5,839	2,207	478	3,117	37	330	269
1969	24,209	23,917	17,395	15,385	1,750	260	6,219	2,322	490	3,371	36	303	291
1970	28,796	28,503	20,770	18,438	2,029	303	7,428	2,760	574	4,055	39	305	294
1971	33,413	33,107	24,219	21,544	2,323	352	8,602	3,168	630	4,763	41	285	306
1972	37,122	36,802	27,057	24,143	2,532	382	9,428	3,433	679	5,326	43	263	320
1973	45,741	45,412	32,793	29,336	3,000	457	12,356	4,002	801	7,505	48	264	329
1974	51,618	51,291	37,211	33,369	3,309	533	13,843	4,399	898	8,497	49	237	327
1975	58,509	58,172	42,432	38,079	3,719	634	15,544	4,888	1,009	9,597	50	196	337
1976	65,699	65,366	47,936	43,083	4,117	736	17,257	5,336	1,113	10,757	51	174	332
1977	73,113	72,801	53,575	48,186	4,559	830	19,070	5,759	1,191	12,068	52	157	312
1978	80,352	80,008	59,159	53,255	4,983	921	20,707	6,093	1,284	13,278	51	142	344
1979	90,556	90,216	66,947	60,379	5,554	1,014	23,140	6,608	1,409	15,071	52	128	340
1980	105,074	104,678	77,905	70,358	6,405	1,142	26,654	7,389	1,572	17,638	55	119	394
1981	123,795	123,463	92,478	83,614	7,543	1,321	30,875	8,307	1,760	20,749	58	110	332
1982	138,800	138,596	104,885	95,123	8,539	1,223	33,612	8,204	1,861	23,488	59	100	203
1983	149,502	149,297	114,048	103,578	9,328	1,143	35,164	7,911	1,771	25,425	56	85	205
1984	157,862	157,651	120,952	109,957	9,860	1,135	36,628	7,775	1,474	27,325	53	71	212
1985	167,360	167,152	128,479	116,823	10,517	1,140	38,616	7,762	1,474	29,330	51	57	207
1986	176,845	176,642	135,902	123,584	11,152	1,166	40,693	7,843	1,457	31,345	48	47	203
1987	183,644	183,441	141,293	128,513	11,598	1,183	42,112	7,846	1,388	32,833	44	36	203
1988	195,522	195,314	150,498	136,987	12,292	1,219	44,787	8,120	1,392	35,233	43	29	208
1989	207,997	207,770	160,331	146,027	13,054	1,249	47,418	8,254	1,401	37,723	41	21	206

Note appears at end of table

TABLE Bf395–407 Old-Age and Survivors Insurance – benefits, by type of beneficiary: 1937–1998 *Continued*

	Annual benefits paid to												
		Retired workers and dependents				Survivors							
	Total	Total	Total	Retired workers	Spouses	Children	Total	Surviving children	Widowed mothers and fathers	Widows and widowers	Parents	Special age-72 beneficiaries	Lump-sum death payments
	Bf395	Bf396	Bf397	Bf398	Bf399	Bf400	Bf401	Bf402	Bf403	Bf404	Bf405	Bf406	Bf407
Year	Million dollars	Million dollars	Million dollars	Million dollars	Million dollars	Million dollars	Million dollars	Million dollars	Million dollars	Million dollars	Million dollars	Million dollars	Million dollars
1990	222,993	222,787	172,025	156,756	13,953	1,316	50,746	8,564	1,437	40,705	39	16	206
1991	240,436	240,234	185,533	169,142	14,986	1,405	54,689	9,022	1,490	44,139	38	12	202
1992	254,939	254,734	196,676	179,372	15,810	1,494	58,049	9,431	1,521	47,060	37	9	206
1993	267,804	267,590	206,359	188,440	16,356	1,563	61,225	9,897	1,547	49,746	36	6	214
1994	279,118	278,898	214,891	196,400	16,854	1,637	64,003	10,293	1,551	52,124	34	4	220
1995	291,682	291,464	224,378	205,315	17,348	1,715	67,083	10,717	1,573	54,761	32	3	218
1996	302,914	302,697	232,937	213,423	17,715	1,799	69,759	11,217	1,486	57,025	31	1	218
1997	316,311	316,095	243,590	223,554	18,154	1,882	72,505	11,660	1,466	59,349	30	1	216
1998	326,817	326,599	252,659	232,324	18,395	1,940	73,940	11,936	1,435	60,540	29	(Z)	218

(Z) Less than $500,000.

Source

U.S. Social Security Administration, *Social Security Bulletin: Annual Statistical Supplement* (1999), Table 4.A5, p. 163.

Documentation

For additional information about the Old-Age, Survivors, and Disability Insurance program, see the text for Table Bf377–394.

Amounts are benefits paid from the Old-Age, Survivors Insurance Trust Fund.

TABLE Bf408–421 Old-Age, Survivors, Disability, and Health Insurance – families receiving current-pay benefits, by selected family groups: 1940–1998

Contributed by Price V. Fishback and Melissa A. Thomasson

	Retired-worker families receiving benefits for				Survivor families receiving benefits for				Disabled-worker families receiving benefits for					
	Worker only					Widowed mother or father and			Worker only					
	Total	Male	Female	Both worker and wife	Nondisabled widow only	One child	Two children	Three or more children	Total	Male	Female	Worker, wife, and one child	Worker, wife, and two or more children	Worker and spouse
	Bf408	Bf409	Bf410	Bf411	Bf412	Bf413	Bf414	Bf415	Bf416	Bf417	Bf418	Bf419	Bf420	Bf421
Year	Thousand	Thousand	Thousand	Thousand	Thousand	Thousand	Thousand	Thousand	Thousand	Thousand	Thousand	Thousand	Thousand	Thousand
1940	78	65	12	30	4	10	6	3	—	—	—	—	—	—
1941	136	114	22	57	15	20	13	4	—	—	—	—	—	—
1942	176	146	30	77	29	29	17	7	—	—	—	—	—	—
1943	206	161	45	92	46	34	20	11	—	—	—	—	—	—
1944	315	253	62	135	69	67	36	20	—	—	—	—	—	—
1945	416	338	78	181	95	86	48	24	—	—	—	—	—	—
1946	473	381	92	216	127	66	37	22	—	—	—	—	—	—
1947	590	471	119	269	164	69	39	23	—	—	—	—	—	—
1948	708	560	148	321	210	73	41	24	—	—	—	—	—	—
1949	872	687	186	390	261	78	44	26	—	—	—	—	—	—
1950	1,240	939	301	498	314	82	53	33	—	—	—	—	—	—
1951	1,618	1,162	456	614	384	92	61	49	—	—	—	—	—	—
1952	1,894	1,306	588	699	454	103	68	56	—	—	—	—	—	—
1953	2,321	1,543	778	839	540	113	74	64	—	—	—	—	—	—
1954	2,744	1,780	964	958	637	116	82	72	—	—	—	—	—	—
1955	3,266	2,054	1,212	1,124	700	126	86	80	—	—	—	—	—	—
1956	3,662	2,133	1,528	1,359	912	128	88	83	—	—	—	—	—	—
1957	4,344	2,361	1,983	1,726	1,089	142	97	92	—	—	—	—	—	—
1958	4,872	2,587	2,285	1,902	1,224	156	105	99	223	176	48	—	—	—
1959	5,321	2,755	2,565	2,029	1,380	160	106	108	275	206	69	15	15	18
1960	5,742	2,922	2,820	2,122	1,527	172	113	114	357	261	96	22	32	22
1961	6,470	3,336	3,134	2,214	1,677	185	120	121	459	332	127	34	59	25
1962	7,134	3,666	3,468	2,324	1,835	191	128	131	542	384	158	43	78	26
1963	7,606	3,867	3,739	2,368	1,984	191	131	137	599	416	183	48	93	27
1964	7,982	3,998	3,984	2,392	2,129	191	134	142	650	446	203	50	99	30
1965	8,386	4,137	4,249	2,400	2,332	182	135	153	714	481	232	54	109	30
1966	8,897	4,301	4,596	2,418	2,541	180	140	164	780	518	262	58	128	33
1967	9,247	4,416	4,831	2,429	2,696	181	140	172	847	556	290	59	138	37
1968	9,641	4,558	5,082	2,430	2,836	181	144	177	914	596	318	64	149	39
1969	10,039	4,707	5,332	2,440	2,984	180	148	178	987	640	347	69	154	41
1970	10,533	4,904	5,629	2,457	3,080	183	155	182	1,054	680	374	77	164	43
1971	11,128	5,149	5,979	2,481	3,258	190	159	185	1,165	749	416	86	178	47
1972	11,653	5,364	6,288	2,507	3,325	188	166	184	1,287	821	467	98	198	52
1973	12,379	5,663	6,716	2,565	3,444	209	174	195	1,425	902	523	113	208	57
1974	12,948	5,862	7,086	2,583	3,536	218	176	178	1,586	989	598	123	224	62
1975	13,520	6,134	7,385	2,618	3,606	221	182	176	1,750	1,080	671	137	250	66
1976	14,056	6,351	7,705	2,647	3,706	219	186	171	1,883	1,152	730	144	257	72
1977	14,597	6,564	8,033	2,681	3,805	221	190	167	2,000	1,222	782	152	263	80
1978	15,148	6,791	8,357	2,697	3,894	228	186	158	2,043	1,245	798	155	256	81
1979	15,748	7,044	8,704	2,710	3,964	234	187	147	2,050	1,248	802	154	242	80

	Retired-worker families receiving benefits for				Survivor families receiving benefits for				Disabled-worker families receiving benefits for					
	Worker only					Widowed mother or father and			Worker only					
	Total	Male	Female	Both worker and wife	Nondisabled widow only	One child	Two children	Three or more children	Total	Male	Female	Worker, wife, and one child	Worker, wife, and two or more children	Worker and spouse
	Bf408	Bf409	Bf410	Bf411	Bf412	Bf413	Bf414	Bf415	Bf416	Bf417	Bf418	Bf419	Bf420	Bf421
Year	Thousand	Thousand	Thousand	Thousand	Thousand	Thousand	Thousand	Thousand	Thousand	Thousand	Thousand	Thousand	Thousand	Thousand
1980	16,314	7,286	9,028	2,736	4,033	239	184	134	2,061	1,257	804	154	228	80
1982	17,519	7,852	9,667	2,784	4,191	236	165	106	1,969	1,208	760	124	163	78
1983	18,162	8,166	9,996	2,830	4,271	161	141	92	1,961	1,215	746	85	143	80
1984	18,613	8,362	10,251	2,839	4,520	159	135	79	1,993	1,241	752	83	140	76
1985	19,132	8,601	10,531	2,861	4,606	158	131	74	2,039	1,267	772	84	140	76
1986	19,664	8,849	10,816	2,883	4,666	151	123	68	2,096	1,301	795	82	136	74
1987	20,137	9,064	11,074	2,893	4,709	141	115	62	2,154	1,338	816	79	132	74
1988	20,567	9,264	11,302	2,896	4,749	137	112	61	2,194	1,353	841	77	125	71
1989	21,036	9,495	11,541	2,903	4,788	137	109	58	2,262	1,390	872	75	120	67
1990	21,537	9,752	11,786	2,914	4,825	133	106	57	2,370	1,448	922	75	118	63
1991	21,978	9,985	11,992	2,918	4,850	130	106	55	2,523	1,529	994	76	119	61
1992	22,434	10,218	12,216	2,928	4,871	129	103	54	2,738	1,643	1,094	78	125	61
1993	22,796	10,404	12,392	2,912	4,870	126	103	53	2,935	1,743	1,192	78	127	59
1994	23,124	10,573	12,552	2,885	4,862	123	100	51	3,121	1,830	1,292	76	128	57
1995	23,433	10,732	12,701	2,845	4,841	120	97	49	3,305	1,909	1,396	75	124	55
1996	23,705	10,874	12,831	2,799	4,815	117	78	41	3,473	1,973	1,500	61	104	53
1997	24,124	11,027	13,097	2,759	4,657	113	74	37	3,593	2,006	1,588	57	91	53
1998	24,409	11,163	13,246	2,703	4,589	111	69	34	3,769	2,074	1,695	52	80	53

Sources

U.S. Social Security Administration, *Social Security Bulletin: Annual Statistical Supplement* (1973), Table 29, p. 59; (1983), Table 98, p. 172; (1988), Table 5.H1, p. 218; (1999), Table 5.H1, p. 233.

Documentation

For additional information about the Old-Age, Survivors, and Disability Insurance (OASDI) program, see the text for Table Bf377–394.

This table reports the number of families receiving current-pay benefits under OASDI. Beneficiary families are decomposed into retired-worker families, survivors of insured persons, and disabled-worker families. Data for 1981 are not available.

Series Bf411 and Bf419–420. A wife's entitlement is based on her age for series Bf411. In the disabled-worker categories, a wife's entitlement is based on care of children.

TABLE Bf422–431 Old-Age, Survivors, and Disability Insurance – benefits in current-payment status for male retired-worker beneficiaries, by age: 1940–1998[1]

Contributed by Price V. Fishback and Melissa A. Thomasson

	Beneficiaries					Retired worker current-pay beneficiaries – distribution by age				
			With reduction in benefits for early retirement							
	Total	With full benefits	Number	Percent	Average age of beneficiaries	62–64	65–69	70–74	75–79	80 and older
	Bf422	Bf423	Bf424	Bf425	Bf426	Bf427	Bf428	Bf429	Bf430	Bf431
Year	Number	Number	Number	Percent	Years	Percent	Percent	Percent	Percent	Percent
1940	99,000	99,000	—	—	68.8	—	74.4	17.4	6.4	1.8
1941	175,000	175,000	—	—	69.8	—	65.6	23.0	8.9	2.6
1942	224,000	224,000	—	—	70.5	—	57.3	28.6	10.9	3.3
1943	261,000	261,000	—	—	71.1	—	49.2	34.1	12.7	4.0
1944	323,000	323,000	—	—	71.5	—	42.7	38.6	14.2	4.6
1945	447,000	447,000	—	—	71.7	—	39.9	40.2	15.1	4.7
1946	610,000	610,000	—	—	71.9	—	38.0	41.1	15.7	5.2
1947	756,000	756,000	—	—	72.1	—	36.5	40.4	17.4	5.8
1948	900,000	900,000	—	—	72.3	—	35.6	39.1	18.9	6.4
1949	1,100,000	1,100,000	—	—	72.3	—	36.3	37.0	19.8	6.8
1950	1,469,000	1,469,000	—	—	72.2	—	39.1	33.7	20.2	7.1
1951	1,819,000	1,819,000	—	—	72.3	—	38.8	32.4	21.2	7.6
1952	2,052,000	2,052,000	—	—	72.6	—	36.9	32.9	21.7	8.5
1953	2,438,000	2,438,000	—	—	72.6	—	37.3	32.5	21.3	8.9
1954	2,803,000	2,803,000	—	—	72.6	—	37.2	32.8	20.6	9.4
1955	3,252,000	3,252,000	—	—	72.7	—	35.7	34.8	20.0	9.5
1956	3,572,271	3,572,271	—	—	72.9	—	34.2	35.2	20.3	10.3
1957	4,198,000	4,198,000	—	—	72.9	—	34.9	34.2	20.4	10.5
1958	4,617,000	4,617,000	—	—	73.0	—	33.9	34.3	20.6	11.2
1959	4,937,000	4,937,000	—	—	73.1	—	34.0	33.7	20.9	11.5
1960	5,216,668	5,216,668	—	—	73.2	—	33.8	33.1	21.1	12.1
1961	5,764,685	5,491,000	273,000	4.7	72.8	4.1	32.7	31.0	20.2	11.9
1962	6,244,000	5,587,000	657,000	10.5	72.7	6.5	31.4	30.4	19.4	12.3
1963	6,497,000	5,552,000	945,000	14.5	72.7	7.0	30.9	29.8	19.7	12.6
1964	6,657,000	5,460,000	1,197,000	18.0	72.8	7.2	30.0	29.7	19.8	13.3
1965	6,825,078	5,389,166	1,435,912	21.0	72.9	6.9	29.7	29.5	19.9	14.0
1966	7,034,000	5,345,000	1,689,000	24.0	73.1	6.9	29.5	29.2	19.8	14.5
1967	7,160,000	5,215,000	1,946,000	27.2	73.1	6.8	29.5	28.5	20.2	14.9
1968	7,309,000	5,108,000	2,202,000	30.1	73.1	7.0	29.5	28.0	20.0	15.5
1969	7,459,000	5,002,000	2,457,000	32.9	73.2	7.1	29.9	27.3	20.0	15.8
1970	7,688,460	4,930,400	2,758,060	35.9	72.6	7.5	30.1	26.9	19.6	15.9
1971	7,951,809	4,878,482	3,073,327	38.6	72.5	8.0	30.7	26.1	19.3	15.9
1972	8,230,847	4,833,280	3,397,567	41.3	72.4	8.4	31.2	26.0	18.5	15.9
1973	8,610,361	4,817,041	3,793,320	44.0	72.3	8.7	31.9	25.7	17.9	15.8
1974	8,832,270	4,737,114	4,095,156	46.4	72.3	8.9	32.2	25.9	17.3	15.7
1975	9,163,776	4,711,571	4,452,077	48.6	72.3	9.3	32.2	25.6	17.1	15.8
1976	9,420,659	4,633,096	4,787,563	50.8	72.3	9.4	32.3	25.8	16.7	15.8
1977	9,723,815	4,591,745	5,132,070	52.8	72.2	9.6	32.4	25.7	16.7	15.6
1978	9,928,463	4,535,918	5,392,545	54.3	72.2	9.2	32.4	25.9	16.8	15.6
1979	10,192,475	4,606,965	5,585,510	54.8	72.2	9.2	32.3	25.9	16.9	15.7
1980	10,460,735	4,586,539	5,874,196	54.8	72.2	9.5	32.1	25.8	16.9	15.6
1981	10,767,000	4,586,149	6,180,832	57.4	72.2	9.9	31.8	25.7	17.1	15.5
1982	11,030,000	4,647,057	6,382,785	57.9	72.2	10.3	31.3	25.6	17.1	15.6
1983	11,358,000	4,751,287	6,607,070	58.2	72.2	10.6	31.0	25.8	17.0	15.5
1984	11,573,000	4,702,805	6,870,106	59.4	72.2	10.8	30.3	25.9	17.3	15.7
1985	11,816,956	4,655,477	7,161,479	60.6	72.3	10.9	30.2	25.9	17.3	15.7
1986	12,080,376	4,621,111	7,459,265	61.7	72.4	10.9	30.3	25.7	17.3	15.8
1987	12,295,034	4,587,974	7,707,060	62.7	72.4	10.9	30.2	25.5	17.4	16.0
1988	12,486,962	4,563,777	7,923,185	63.5	72.4	10.7	30.0	25.5	17.6	16.2
1989	12,718,425	4,566,059	8,152,366	64.1	72.5	10.5	30.1	25.1	17.8	16.4
1990	12,853,832	4,592,911	8,390,921	64.6	72.5	10.3	30.0	25.3	17.8	16.6
1991	13,222,776	4,621,584	8,601,192	65.0	72.6	10.2	29.5	25.7	17.9	16.7
1992	13,470,502	4,649,446	8,821,056	65.5	72.7	10.0	29.2	25.8	17.8	17.1
1993	13,645,386	4,645,649	8,999,737	66.0	72.8	9.9	28.9	25.9	17.9	17.5
1994	13,790,997	4,639,089	9,151,908	66.4	72.8	9.8	28.3	26.2	17.9	17.8

Note appears at end of table

TABLE Bf422–431 Old-Age, Survivors, and Disability Insurance – benefits in current-payment status for male retired-worker beneficiaries, by age: 1940–1998 *Continued*

	Beneficiaries					Retired worker current-pay beneficiaries – distribution by age				
			With reduction in benefits for early retirement							
	Total	With full benefits	Number	Percent	Average age of beneficiaries	62–64	65–69	70–74	75–79	80 and older
	Bf422	Bf423	Bf424	Bf425	Bf426	Bf427	Bf428	Bf429	Bf430	Bf431
Year	Number	Number	Number	Percent	Years	Percent	Percent	Percent	Percent	Percent
1995	13,913,531	4,559,535	9,353,996	67.2	72.9	9.5	28.0	26.1	18.3	18.1
1996	14,010,875	4,478,565	9,532,310	68.0	73.1	9.2	27.6	25.8	18.9	18.5
1997	14,116,818	4,371,503	9,745,315	69.0	73.2	9.0	27.2	25.8	19.2	18.8
1998	14,200,826	4,371,895	9,828,931	69.2	73.3	9.0	26.6	25.6	19.5	19.2

[1] Data reported in 1988 and 1990–1996 for series Bf426–431 are based on a 10 percent sample.

Sources

U.S. Social Security Administration, *Social Security Bulletin, Annual Statistical Supplement* (1981), Table 81, p. 149; (1988), Table 5.B5, p. 184, Table 5.B8, p. 184; (1997), Table 5.B5, p. 211, Table 5.B8, p. 211; (1999), Table 5.B5, p. 206, Table 5B.8, p. 209.

Documentation

For additional information about the Old-Age, Survivors, and Disability Insurance (OASDI) program, see the text for Table Bf377–394.

This table provides information on the number of male retired workers who receive benefits under the OASDI program. Men became eligible to draw reduced OASDI benefits at age 62 in 1961. The OASDI tables do not include a number of persons receiving Railroad Retirement benefits who would be eligible for Social Security benefits had they applied.

TABLE Bf432–441 Old-Age, Survivors, and Disability Insurance – benefits in current-payment status for female retired-worker beneficiaries, by age: 1940–1998[1]

Contributed by Price V. Fishback and Melissa A. Thomasson

	Beneficiaries					Retired worker current-pay beneficiaries – distribution by age				
			With reduction in benefits for early retirement							
	Total	With full benefits	Number	Percent	Average age of beneficiaries	62–64	65–69	70–74	75–79	80 and older
	Bf432	Bf433	Bf434	Bf435	Bf436	Bf437	Bf438	Bf439	Bf440	Bf441
Year	Number	Number	Number	Percent	Years	Percent	Percent	Percent	Percent	Percent
1940	13,000	13,000	—	—	68.1	—	82.6	12.8	3.9	0.6
1941	25,000	25,000	—	—	68.9	—	75.2	18.2	5.4	1.2
1942	36,000	36,000	—	—	69.5	—	68.4	23.5	6.5	1.6
1943	45,000	45,000	—	—	70.0	—	60.4	29.8	7.8	1.9
1944	55,000	55,000	—	—	70.5	—	52.6	36.1	9.1	2.3
1945	71,000	71,000	—	—	70.8	—	47.1	40.0	10.2	2.6
1946	92,000	92,000	—	—	71.1	—	43.3	42.5	11.2	3.0
1947	119,000	119,000	—	—	71.4	—	41.2	42.6	13.0	3.3
1948	148,000	148,000	—	—	71.6	—	39.9	41.3	15.0	3.7
1949	186,000	186,000	—	—	71.7	—	39.8	39.0	17.0	4.2
1950	302,000	302,000	—	—	71.1	—	48.4	32.9	15.0	3.7
1951	459,000	459,000	—	—	70.8	—	51.5	30.6	14.2	3.7
1952	592,000	592,000	—	—	71.0	—	50.2	30.9	14.7	4.1
1953	784,000	784,000	—	—	71.1	—	49.8	30.9	14.8	4.6
1954	972,000	972,000	—	—	71.2	—	49.0	31.2	14.8	5.0
1955	1,222,000	1,222,000	—	—	71.3	—	47.8	32.3	14.6	5.2
1956	1,540,159	1,425,130	115,029	7.5	70.9	7.3	42.5	30.7	14.0	5.5
1957	1,999,000	1,613,000	386,000	19.3	70.5	13.3	39.7	28.2	13.4	5.5
1958	2,303,000	1,735,000	569,000	24.7	70.7	13.0	38.3	28.7	13.9	6.1
1959	2,589,000	1,825,000	764,000	29.5	70.8	12.9	37.5	28.8	14.4	6.6
1960	2,844,801	1,895,597	949,204	33.4	71.0	12.6	36.3	29.0	15.0	7.2
1961	3,160,000	1,977,000	1,183,000	37.4	71.1	13.0	35.4	28.5	15.4	7.6
1962	3,494,000	2,060,000	1,434,000	41.0	71.2	13.3	34.3	28.5	15.7	8.2
1963	3,766,000	2,111,000	1,655,000	44.0	71.4	13.0	33.5	28.3	16.4	8.8
1964	4,011,000	2,138,000	1,873,000	46.7	71.6	12.9	32.3	28.1	17.1	9.5

Note appears at end of table

(continued)

TABLE Bf432–441 Old-Age, Survivors, and Disability Insurance – benefits in current-payment status for female retired-worker beneficiaries, by age: 1940–1998 *Continued*

	Beneficiaries					Retired worker current-pay beneficiaries – distribution by age				
			With reduction in benefits for early retirement		Average age of beneficiaries					
	Total	With full benefits	Number	Percent		62–64	65–69	70–74	75–79	80 and older
	Bf432	Bf433	Bf434	Bf435	Bf436	Bf437	Bf438	Bf439	Bf440	Bf441
Year	Number	Number	Number	Percent	Years	Percent	Percent	Percent	Percent	Percent
1965	4,275,506	2,192,220	2,083,286	48.7	71.8	12.2	31.6	28.1	17.6	10.5
1966	4,624,000	2,307,000	2,317,000	50.1	72.1	11.8	31.0	27.7	18.1	11.4
1967	4,859,000	2,338,000	2,521,000	51.9	72.2	11.4	30.7	27.1	18.7	12.1
1968	5,111,000	2,345,000	2,766,000	54.1	72.3	11.3	30.4	26.5	18.8	13.1
1969	5,363,000	2,321,000	3,042,000	56.7	72.4	11.4	30.3	25.8	18.8	13.8
1970	5,660,715	2,351,895	3,308,820	58.5	72.0	11.5	30.1	25.4	18.7	14.4
1971	5,975,130	2,371,290	3,603,840	60.3	72.1	11.7	30.2	24.7	18.4	15.1
1972	6,324,628	2,402,222	3,922,406	62.0	72.0	11.9	30.3	24.5	17.9	15.5
1973	6,754,201	2,526,938	4,227,263	62.6	72.0	11.9	30.7	24.2	17.3	15.8
1974	7,126,251	2,525,675	4,600,576	64.6	72.1	11.8	30.6	24.2	17.0	16.4
1975	7,424,353	2,527,259	4,897,094	66.0	72.2	11.8	30.4	24.2	16.9	16.7
1976	7,744,756	2,670,201	5,074,555	65.5	72.3	11.6	30.2	24.4	16.7	17.1
1977	8,108,669	2,672,843	5,435,826	67.0	72.3	11.7	30.0	24.3	16.7	17.3
1978	8,429,522	2,684,147	5,745,375	68.2	72.5	11.3	29.7	24.4	16.8	17.8
1979	8,777,697	2,772,090	6,005,607	68.4	72.5	11.2	29.5	24.3	17.0	17.9
1980	9,101,350	2,810,659	6,290,691	69.1	72.6	11.2	29.2	24.2	17.1	18.3
1981	9,428,000	2,838,899	6,589,482	69.9	72.7	11.1	28.9	24.0	17.4	18.6
1982	9,733,000	2,899,564	6,833,824	70.2	72.8	11.2	28.3	24.0	17.5	19.0
1983	10,060,000	2,989,500	7,070,890	70.3	72.9	11.1	28.0	23.9	17.6	19.4
1984	10,334,000	3,034,277	7,299,273	70.6	73.1	11.1	27.2	24.0	17.8	19.9
1985	10,614,974	3,065,482	7,549,492	71.1	73.3	11.0	26.9	23.9	17.9	20.2
1986	10,900,572	3,089,833	7,811,739	71.7	73.3	10.8	26.7	23.8	18.0	20.7
1987	11,144,650	3,102,818	8,041,832	72.2	73.4	10.7	26.4	23.6	18.1	21.2
1988	11,371,264	3,136,139	8,235,125	72.4	73.5	10.5	26.0	23.6	18.2	21.7
1989	11,608,179	3,185,150	8,423,029	72.6	73.6	10.2	26.1	23.1	18.4	22.2
1990	11,854,268	3,247,328	8,606,940	72.6	73.7	9.9	25.9	23.0	18.5	22.7
1991	12,065,943	3,306,543	8,759,400	72.6	73.9	9.5	25.4	23.2	18.6	23.2
1992	12,287,225	3,370,997	8,916,228	72.6	74.0	9.3	25.2	23.1	18.5	23.8
1993	12,458,919	3,423,336	9,035,583	72.5	74.1	9.0	24.9	23.0	18.6	24.4
1994	12,616,759	3,470,886	9,145,873	72.5	74.2	9.0	24.3	23.2	18.4	25.0
1995	12,759,275	3,381,828	9,377,447	73.5	74.3	8.8	24.0	23.2	18.5	25.4
1996	12,887,197	3,305,513	9,581,684	74.4	74.4	8.7	23.6	22.9	18.8	25.9
1997	13,157,754	3,301,783	9,855,971	74.9	74.5	8.6	23.2	23.0	19.0	26.3
1998	13,309,709	3,327,769	9,981,940	75.0	74.6	8.7	22.8	22.8	19.0	26.7

[1] Data in 1988, 1990–1996 for series Bf436–441 are based on a 10 percent sample.

Sources

Social Security Bulletin, Annual Statistical Supplement (1981), Table 81, p. 149; (1988), Table 5.B5, p. 184, Table 5B.8, p. 184; (1999) Table 5.B5, p. 206, Table 5B.8, p. 209.

Documentation

For additional information about the Old-Age, Survivors, and Disability Insurance (OASDI) program, see the text for Table Bf377–394.

The OASDI tables do not include a number of persons receiving Railroad Retirement benefits who would be eligible for Social Security benefits had they applied.

This table provides information on the number of female retired workers who receive benefits under the OASDI program. Women became eligible to receive reduced benefits from the OASI program at age 62 in 1956.

TABLE Bf442–460 Old-Age, Survivors Insurance trust fund – receipts, expenditures, and assets: 1937–1998

Contributed by Price V. Fishback and Melissa A. Thomasson

	Old-Age and Survivors Insurance Trust Fund								
	Receipts					Expenditures			
	Total	Net contributions	Taxation of benefits	Payments from the general fund of the Treasury	Net interest	Total	Benefit payments	Administrative expenses	Transfers to Railroad Retirement program
	Bf442	Bf443	Bf444	Bf445	Bf446	Bf447	Bf448	Bf449	Bf450
Year	Million dollars	Million dollars	Million dollars	Million dollars	Million dollars	Million dollars	Million dollars	Million dollars	Million dollars
1937	767	765	—	—	2	1	1	—	—
1938	375	360	—	—	15	10	10	—	—
1939	607	580	—	—	27	14	14	—	—
1940	368	325	—	—	43	61	35	26	—
1941	845	789	—	—	56	114	88	26	—
1942	1,085	1,012	—	—	72	159	131	28	—
1943	1,328	1,239	—	—	88	195	166	29	—
1944	1,422	1,316	—	—	107	238	209	29	—
1945	1,420	1,285	—	—	134	304	274	30	—
1946	1,447	1,295	—	—	152	418	378	40	—
1947	1,722	1,557	—	1	164	512	466	46	—
1948	1,969	1,685	—	3	281	607	556	51	—
1949	1,816	1,666	—	4	146	721	667	54	—
1950	2,928	2,667	—	4	257	1,022	961	61	—
1951	3,784	3,363	—	4	417	1,966	1,885	81	—
1952	4,184	3,819	—	—	365	2,282	2,194	88	—
1953	4,359	3,945	—	—	414	3,094	3,006	88	—
1954	5,610	5,163	—	—	447	3,741	3,670	92	−21
1955	6,167	5,713	—	—	454	5,079	4,968	119	−7
1956	6,697	6,172	—	—	526	5,841	5,715	132	−5
1957	7,381	6,825	—	—	556	7,507	7,347	162	−2
1958	8,117	7,566	—	—	552	8,646	8,327	194	124
1959	8,584	8,052	—	—	532	10,308	9,842	184	282
1960	11,382	10,866	—	—	516	11,198	10,677	203	318
1961	11,833	11,285	—	—	548	12,432	11,862	239	332
1962	12,585	12,059	—	—	526	13,973	13,356	256	361
1963	15,063	14,541	—	—	521	14,920	14,217	281	423
1964	16,258	15,689	—	—	569	15,613	14,914	296	403
1965	16,610	16,017	—	—	593	17,501	16,737	328	436
1966	21,302	20,580	—	78	644	18,967	18,267	256	444
1967	24,034	23,138	—	78	818	20,382	19,468	406	508
1968	25,040	23,719	—	382	939	23,557	22,643	476	438
1969	29,554	27,947	—	442	1,165	25,176	24,210	474	491
1970	32,220	30,256	—	449	1,515	29,848	28,798	471	579
1971	35,877	33,723	—	488	1,667	34,542	33,414	514	613
1972	40,050	37,781	—	475	1,794	38,522	37,124	674	724
1973	48,344	45,975	—	442	1,928	47,175	45,745	647	783
1974	54,688	52,081	—	447	2,159	53,397	51,623	865	909
1975	59,605	56,816	—	425	2,364	60,395	58,517	896	982
1976	66,276	63,362	—	614	2,301	67,876	65,705	959	1,212
1977	72,412	69,572	—	613	2,227	75,309	73,121	981	1,208
1978	78,094	75,471	—	615	2,008	83,064	80,361	1,115	1,589
1979	90,274	87,919	—	557	1,797	93,133	90,573	1,113	1,448
1980	105,841	103,456	—	540	1,845	107,678	105,083	1,154	1,442
1981	125,362	122,627	—	675	2,060	126,695	123,803	1,307	1,585
1982	125,198	123,673	—	680	845	142,119	138,806	1,519	1,793
1983	150,584	138,337	—	5,541	6,706	153,999	149,221	1,528	2,251
1984	169,328	164,122	2,835	105	2,266	161,883	157,841	1,638	2,404

(continued)

TABLE Bf442–460 Old-Age, Survivors Insurance trust fund – receipts, expenditures, and assets: 1937–1998 *Continued*

	Old-Age and Survivors Insurance Trust Fund								
	Receipts					Expenditures			
	Total	Net contributions	Taxation of benefits	Payments from the general fund of the Treasury	Net interest	Total	Benefit payments	Administrative expenses	Transfers to Railroad Retirement program
	Bf442	Bf443	Bf444	Bf445	Bf446	Bf447	Bf448	Bf449	Bf450
Year	Million dollars	Million dollars	Million dollars	Million dollars	Million dollars	Million dollars	Million dollars	Million dollars	Million dollars
1985	184,239	176,958	3,208	2,203	1,871	171,150	167,248	1,592	2,310
1986	197,394	190,741	3,424	160	3,069	181,000	176,813	1,601	2,585
1987	210,737	202,735	3,257	55	4,690	187,668	183,587	1,524	2,557
1988	240,770	229,775	3,384	43	7,568	200,020	195,454	1,776	2,790
1989	264,653	250,195	2,439	34	11,985	212,489	207,971	1,673	2,845
1990	286,652	267,530	4,848	−2,089	16,363	227,519	222,987	1,563	2,969
1991	299,286	272,574	5,864	19	20,829	245,634	240,467	1,792	3,375
1992	311,161	280,992	5,852	14	24,303	259,861	254,883	1,830	3,148
1993	323,277	290,905	5,335	10	27,027	273,104	267,755	1,996	3,353
1994	328,271	293,323	4,995	7	29,946	284,133	279,068	1,645	3,420
1995	342,801	304,620	5,490	−129	32,820	297,760	291,630	2,077	4,052
1996	363,741	321,557	6,471	7	35,706	308,217	302,861	1,802	3,554
1997	397,169	349,946	7,426	2	39,795	322,073	316,257	2,128	3,688
1998	424,848	371,207	9,149	1	44,491	332,324	326,762	1,899	3,662

	Old-Age and Survivors Insurance Trust Fund			Disability Insurance trust fund						
				Receipts			Expenditures			
	Total assets (year end)	Assets invested in U.S. government securities	Cash balances	Total	Net contributions	Other sources	Total	Benefit payments	Other expenditures	Assets (year end)
	Bf451	Bf452	Bf453	Bf454	Bf455	Bf456	Bf457	Bf458	Bf459	Bf460
Year	Million dollars	Million dollars	Million dollars	Million dollars	Million dollars	Million dollars	Million dollars	Million dollars	Million dollars	Million dollars
1937	766	513	253	—	—	—	—	—	—	—
1938	1,132	862	269	—	—	—	—	—	—	—
1939	1,724	1,435	289	—	—	—	—	—	—	—
1940	2,031	2,017	14	—	—	—	—	—	—	—
1941	2,762	2,736	26	—	—	—	—	—	—	—
1942	3,688	3,655	33	—	—	—	—	—	—	—
1943	4,820	4,779	42	—	—	—	—	—	—	—
1944	6,005	5,967	38	—	—	—	—	—	—	—
1945	7,121	7,054	66	—	—	—	—	—	—	—
1946	8,150	8,079	71	—	—	—	—	—	—	—
1947	9,360	9,268	92	—	—	—	—	—	—	—
1948	10,722	10,556	166	—	—	—	—	—	—	—
1949	11,816	11,728	88	—	—	—	—	—	—	—
1950	13,721	13,331	391	—	—	—	—	—	—	—
1951	15,540	15,017	522	—	—	—	—	—	—	—
1952	17,442	16,960	481	—	—	—	—	—	—	—
1953	18,707	18,291	416	—	—	—	—	—	—	—
1954	20,576	19,863	713	—	—	—	—	—	—	—
1955	21,663	21,102	561	—	—	—	—	—	—	—
1956	22,519	21,831	689	—	—	—	—	—	—	—
1957	22,393	21,566	827	709	702	7	59	57	2	649
1958	21,864	20,953	911	991	966	25	261	249	12	1,379
1959	20,141	19,151	990	931	891	40	485	457	28	1,825
1960	20,324	19,128	1,196	1,063	1,010	53	600	568	32	2,289
1961	19,725	18,404	1,321	1,104	1,038	66	956	887	69	2,437
1962	18,337	17,060	1,277	1,114	1,046	68	1,183	1,105	78	2,368
1963	18,480	17,154	1,327	1,165	1,099	66	1,297	1,210	87	2,235
1964	19,125	17,758	1,367	1,218	1,154	64	1,407	1,309	98	2,047

TABLE Bf442–460 Old-Age, Survivors Insurance trust fund – receipts, expenditures, and assets: 1937–1998 *Continued*

	Old-Age and Survivors Insurance Trust Fund			Disability Insurance trust fund						
				Receipts			Expenditures			
	Total assets (year end)	Assets invested in U.S. government securities	Cash balances	Total	Net contributions	Other sources	Total	Benefit payments	Other expenditures	Assets (year end)
	Bf451	Bf452	Bf453	Bf454	Bf455	Bf456	Bf457	Bf458	Bf459	Bf460
Year	Million dollars	Million dollars	Million dollars	Million dollars	Million dollars	Million dollars	Million dollars	Million dollars	Million dollars	Million dollars
1965	18,235	16,643	1,592	1,247	1,188	59	1,687	1,573	114	1,606
1966	20,570	18,789	1,781	2,079	2,006	73	1,947	1,784	163	1,739
1967	24,222	22,513	1,708	2,379	2,286	93	2,089	1,950	139	2,029
1968	25,704	23,258	2,446	3,454	3,316	138	2,458	2,311	147	3,025
1969	30,082	27,886	2,197	3,792	3,599	193	2,716	2,557	159	4,100
1970	32,454	29,935	2,519	4,774	4,481	293	3,259	3,085	174	5,614
1971	33,789	—	—	5,031	4,620	411	4,000	3,783	217	6,645
1972	35,318	—	—	5,572	5,107	465	4,759	4,502	257	7,457
1973	36,487	—	—	6,443	5,932	511	5,973	5,764	209	7,927
1974	37,777	—	—	7,378	6,826	552	7,196	6,957	239	8,109
1975	36,987	—	—	8,035	7,444	591	8,790	8,505	285	7,354
1976	35,388	—	—	8,757	8,233	524	10,366	10,055	311	5,745
1977	32,491	—	—	9,570	9,138	432	11,945	11,547	398	3,370
1978	27,520	—	—	13,810	13,413	397	12,954	12,599	355	4,226
1979	24,660	—	—	15,590	15,114	476	14,186	13,786	400	5,630
1980	22,823	—	—	13,871	13,255	616	15,872	15,515	357	3,629
1981	21,490	—	—	17,078	16,738	340	17,658	17,192	466	3,049
1982	22,088	—	—	22,715	21,995	720	17,992	17,376	616	2,691
1983	19,672	—	—	20,682	17,991	2,691	18,177	17,524	653	5,195
1984	27,117	—	—	17,309	15,945	1,364	18,546	17,898	648	3,959
1985	35,842	—	—	19,301	17,191	2,110	19,478	18,827	651	6,321
1986	39,081	—	—	19,439	18,399	1,040	20,522	19,853	669	7,780
1987	62,149	—	—	20,303	19,691	612	21,425	20,519	906	6,658
1988	102,899	—	—	22,699	22,039	660	22,494	21,695	799	6,864
1989	155,063	—	—	24,795	23,993	802	23,753	22,911	842	7,905
1990	214,197	—	—	28,791	28,539	252	25,616	24,829	787	11,079
1991	267,849	—	—	30,390	29,137	1,253	28,571	27,695	876	12,898
1992	319,150	—	—	31,430	30,136	1,294	32,004	31,112	892	12,324
1993	369,322	—	—	32,301	31,185	1,116	35,662	34,613	1,049	8,963
1994	413,460	—	—	52,841	51,373	1,468	38,879	37,744	1,135	22,925
1995	458,502	—	—	56,696	54,401	2,295	42,055	40,923	1,132	37,566
1996	514,028	—	—	60,710	57,325	3,385	45,351	44,189	1,162	52,924
1997	589,121	—	—	60,499	56,037	4,462	47,034	45,695	1,339	66,389
1998	681,645	—	—	64,357	58,966	5,390	49,931	48,207	1,724	80,815

Source

U.S. Social Security Administration, *Social Security Bulletin: Annual Statistical Supplement* (1999), Tables 4.A1 and 4.A2, pp. 159–160. For series Bf452–453, April issues of the *Social Security Bulletin*.

Documentation

See also the text for Table Bf377–394.

The Old-Age, Survivors, and Disability Insurance (OASDI) taxes collected from employees, employers, and the self-employed are credited to the Old-Age, Survivors Insurance (OASI) and Disability Insurance (DI) trust funds. Benefits are financed principally through these contributions on a pay-as-you-go basis. In addition, the trust funds receive income from the following: interest on investments of trust fund assets in securities issued or guaranteed by the U.S. government; federal general revenues to finance the cost of benefits attributable to military and other gratuitous wage credits; revenues resulting from the inclusion of Social Security benefits in adjusted gross income for federal income tax purposes; and special age-72 benefits (covered by transfers from the general fund of payments for costs of benefits to certain uninsured persons who attained age 72 before 1972). The OASI program is currently administered by the Social Security Administration (SSA). Prior to 1995, SSA was a component of the Department of Health and Human Services.

Series Bf442. The sum of series Bf443–446.

Series Bf447. The sum of series Bf448–450.

Series Bf443 and Bf455. Beginning in 1983, the net contributions to the OASI and DI trust funds include transfers from the general fund of the Treasury representing contributions that would have been paid on deemed wage credits for military service in 1957 and later if such credits were considered to be covered wages.

Series Bf445 and Bf456. Includes payments for the following: in 1947–1951 (OASI) and in 1966 and later (both funds), costs of noncontributory wage credits for military service performed before 1957; in 1971–1982, costs of deemed wage credits for military service performed after 1956; and starting in 1968 (OASI only), costs of benefits to certain uninsured persons who attained age 72 before 1968.

Series Bf446 and Bf456. Includes net profits or losses on marketable investments. Beginning in 1967, administrative expenses are charged currently to the trust fund on an estimated basis with a final adjustment, including interest, made in the following fiscal year. Beginning in October 1973 for the OASI fund and in July 1974 for the DI fund, the figures shown in series Bf446 and Bf456 include relatively small amounts of gifts to the fund. Figures for the period 1983–1986 reflect payments from a borrowing trust fund to

(continued)

TABLE Bf442–460 Old-Age, Survivors Insurance trust fund – receipts, expenditures, and assets: 1937–1998 *Continued*

a lending trust fund for interest on amounts owed under the interfund borrowing provisions. During 1983–1990 the series reflect interest paid from the trust fund to the general fund on advance tax transfers. Finally, the amount shown for the OASI fund in series Bf446 for 1985 includes an interest adjustment of $88 million on unnegotiated checks issued prior to April 1985. For the DI fund in series Bf456, the amount shown for 1985 includes an interest adjustment of $14.8 million on unnegotiated checks issued before April 1985. In 1987, other receipts from the DI trust fund, series Bf456, include $195 million in transfers from the DI trust fund to the general fund of the Treasury to correct estimated amounts transferred for calendar years 1984 and 1985.

Series Bf452–453. Unavailable after 1970.

Series Bf454. The sum of series Bf455–456.

Series Bf456. Other receipts in the DI trust fund include income from taxation of benefits, payments from the general fund of the Treasury, and net interest.

Series Bf457. The sum of series Bf458–459.

Series Bf458. Benefit payments from the DI trust fund include payments for vocational rehabilitation services furnished to disabled persons receiving benefits because of their disabilities. Beginning in 1983, amounts are reduced by amount of reimbursement for unnegotiated benefit checks.

Series Bf459. Other expenditures of the DI trust fund include administrative expenses and transfers to the Railroad Retirement program.

TABLE Bf461–475 Old-Age, Survivors and Disability Insurance – average monthly family benefit, by selected family groups: 1940–1999

Contributed by Price V. Fishback and Melissa A. Thomasson

	OASDI average monthly family benefit														OASDI maximum benefits payable to men at time of retirement
	Retired-worker families, receiving benefits for				Survivors' families, receiving benefits for				Disabled-worker families, receiving benefits for						
		Worker only				Widowed mother or father and				Worker only		Worker and			
Year	Total	Male worker only	Female worker only	Worker and wife	Nondisabled widow only	One child	Two children	Three or more children	Total	Male worker	Female worker	Spouse and one child	Spouse and two or more children	Spouse	
	Bf461	Bf462	Bf463	Bf464	Bf465	Bf466	Bf467	Bf468	Bf469	Bf470	Bf471	Bf472	Bf473	Bf474	Bf475
	Dollars	Dollars	Dollars	Dollars	Dollars	Dollars	Dollars	Dollars	Dollars	Dollars	Dollars	Dollars	Dollars	Dollars	Dollars
1940	22.1	22.8	18.4	36.4	20.3	33.9	47.1	51.3	—	—	—	—	—	—	41.2
1941	22.2	22.9	18.5	36.3	20.2	33.7	46.6	51.0	—	—	—	—	—	—	41.6
1942	22.5	23.3	18.7	36.8	20.2	33.9	46.5	50.7	—	—	—	—	—	—	42.0
1943	22.9	23.8	19.1	37.5	20.2	34.2	46.9	50.4	—	—	—	—	—	—	42.4
1944	23.0	24.1	19.3	37.9	20.2	34.4	47.3	50.1	—	—	—	—	—	—	42.8
1945	23.5	24.5	19.5	38.5	20.2	34.1	47.7	50.4	—	—	—	—	—	—	43.2
1946	23.9	24.9	19.6	39.0	20.2	34.6	48.2	51.4	—	—	—	—	—	—	43.6
1947	24.2	25.3	19.9	39.6	20.4	35.4	48.8	52.2	—	—	—	—	—	—	44.0
1948	24.6	25.8	20.1	40.4	20.6	36.0	49.8	53.0	—	—	—	—	—	—	44.4
1949	25.3	26.5	20.6	41.4	20.8	36.5	50.4	54.0	—	—	—	—	—	—	44.8
1950	42.2	44.6	34.8	71.7	36.5	76.9	93.9	92.4	—	—	—	—	—	—	45.2
1951	40.3	43.2	33.0	70.2	36.0	77.3	93.8	92.0	—	—	—	—	—	—	68.5
1952	47.1	50.7	39.1	81.6	40.7	87.5	106.0	101.3	—	—	—	—	—	—	68.5
1953	48.8	52.9	40.6	85.0	40.9	90.1	111.9	109.0	—	—	—	—	—	—	85.0
1954	56.5	61.6	47.0	99.1	46.3	103.9	130.5	126.8	—	—	—	—	—	—	85.0
1955	59.1	64.6	49.8	103.5	48.7	106.8	135.4	133.2	—	—	—	—	—	—	98.5
1956	59.9	66.1	51.1	105.9	50.1	109.9	141.0	138.7	—	—	—	—	—	—	103.5
1957	60.9	68.3	52.2	108.4	51.1	114.3	146.3	144.8	72.8	73.5	69.8	—	—	—	108.5
1958	62.6	70.7	53.5	111.2	51.9	117.0	151.7	150.7	81.7	84.7	70.6	170.1	165.5	—	108.5
1959	68.7	78.0	58.7	121.6	56.7	129.7	170.7	178.6	87.9	91.9	76.1	182.8	188.3	135.6	116.0
1960	69.9	79.9	59.6	123.9	57.7	131.7	188.0	181.7	87.9	91.9	76.9	184.7	192.2	135.5	119.0
1961	71.9	81.2	62.0	126.6	64.9	135.0	189.3	182.8	87.7	91.5	77.7	186.5	193.8	136.3	120.0
1962	72.5	81.8	62.6	127.9	65.9	137.3	190.7	186.8	88.0	92.1	78.1	185.8	194.7	136.9	121.0
1963	73.2	82.6	63.4	129.4	66.9	139.4	192.5	190.4	88.6	92.9	78.8	186.7	196.1	137.9	122.0
1964	73.9	83.6	64.3	130.7	67.9	141.6	193.4	192.1	89.2	93.8	79.3	187.7	197.1	138.1	123.0
1965	80.1	90.5	70.0	141.5	73.9	153.0	219.8	218.1	95.4	100.7	85.0	201.0	216.3	145.9	131.7
1966	80.6	91.2	70.7	142.5	74.3	154.3	221.9	218.8	95.8	101.2	85.2	202.0	217.8	146.0	132.7
1967	81.7	92.5	71.9	144.2	75.2	155.9	224.4	221.7	96.2	101.8	85.5	202.9	217.3	146.0	135.9
1968	95.0	107.1	84.2	166.3	86.8	179.0	257.1	253.4	109.2	115.6	97.2	229.7	242.0	167.4	156.0
1969	96.6	109.0	85.7	168.9	87.8	182.2	255.8	253.6	109.9	116.6	97.6	230.7	241.3	169.7	160.5
1970	114.2	128.7	101.6	198.9	102.4	213.0	291.1	289.9	128.1	136.3	113.1	264.1	273.2	199.2	189.8
1971	127.4	143.7	113.3	222.3	114.4	238.3	320.0	315.6	142.7	152.6	124.9	290.2	296.7	221.6	213.1
1972	157.1	177.0	140.2	272.5	138.3	290.0	383.1	376.1	175.0	188.2	151.8	356.3	362.8	274.2	216.1
1973	161.6	180.1	146.0	276.7	158.4	297.8	391.0	377.9	178.2	192.8	153.2	364.8	367.2	278.6	266.1
1974	183.1	204.2	164.6	312.3	178.8	335.0	438.4	421.9	200.0	217.8	170.6	409.9	411.3	314.0	274.6

(continued)

TABLE Bf461–475 Old-Age, Survivors and Disability Insurance – average monthly family benefit, by selected family groups: 1940–1999 *Continued*

	OASDI average monthly family benefit														
	Retired-worker families, receiving benefits for				Survivors' families, receiving benefits for				Disabled-worker families, receiving benefits for						OASDI maximum benefits payable to men at time of retirement
		Worker only				Widowed mother or father and				Worker only		Worker and			
Year	Total	Male worker only	Female worker only	Worker and wife	Nondisabled widow only	One child	Two children	Three or more children	Total	Male worker	Female worker	Spouse and one child	Spouse and two or more children	Spouse	
	Bf461	Bf462	Bf463	Bf464	Bf465	Bf466	Bf467	Bf468	Bf469	Bf470	Bf471	Bf472	Bf473	Bf474	Bf475
	Dollars	Dollars	Dollars	Dollars	Dollars	Dollars	Dollars	Dollars	Dollars	Dollars	Dollars	Dollars	Dollars	Dollars	Dollars
1975	201.6	225.5	181.8	343.9	195.9	367.2	468.6	461.8	218.9	240.0	185.0	441.0	454.0	344.0	316.3
1976	218.8	245.1	197.1	373.1	211.0	399.8	503.4	499.7	237.4	261.4	199.4	482.2	495.7	377.0	364.0
1977	236.8	265.9	213.1	404.4	226.5	436.8	546.6	538.6	265.5	283.8	213.8	525.8	538.1	407.5	412.7
1978	256.6	288.9	230.3	437.5	243.6	474.0	591.9	582.8	277.9	308.5	230.2	568.0	585.9	443.0	459.8
1979	287.0	324.0	257.1	488.6	270.3	532.9	655.0	646.7	308.9	343.6	254.8	632.7	655.7	497.1	503.4
1980	333.0	377.1	297.4	566.6	311.6	612.8	759.2	740.5	355.4	396.2	291.7	727.0	746.1	573.0	572.0
1981	—	—	—	—	—	—	—	—	—	—	—	—	—	—	677.0
1982	408.9	465.5	362.9	702.5	379.0	735.6	885.5	867.9	424.2	474.2	344.7	847.4	858.2	690.7	679.3
1983	429.7	490.0	380.4	742.9	400.6	774.8	923.0	884.5	439.4	490.9	355.4	867.9	881.8	716.2	709.5
1984	448.2	511.6	396.4	781.2	416.3	805.3	948.3	906.6	454.0	507.6	365.7	881.5	885.5	740.4	703.6
1985	465.8	531.8	412.0	813.9	434.3	829.6	981.5	924.9	466.9	523.1	374.6	898.1	895.2	765.0	717.2
1986	475.2	542.6	420.1	831.3	444.9	841.7	994.0	939.8	470.7	527.8	377.4	896.9	888.3	773.3	760.1
1987	499.2	570.4	440.8	873.3	468.7	882.1	1,032.3	968.9	491.6	552.0	392.6	929.4	918.3	815.5	789.2
1988	522.7	597.2	461.7	914.1	493.6	921.8	1,070.4	1,012.9	512.2	576.1	409.5	960.2	938.4	855.4	838.6
1989	552.1	630.7	487.4	965.6	522.8	967.8	1,120.0	1,064.6	539.3	607.1	431.2	1,009.4	971.9	903.7	899.6
1990	588.3	671.9	519.1	1,026.6	557.9	1,020.2	1,177.7	1,124.6	570.4	642.8	456.8	1,062.1	1,016.0	960.8	975.0
1991	614.7	702.0	542.1	1,071.7	584.9	1,059.8	1,216.8	1,160.6	592.3	668.4	475.5	1,098.0	1,043.3	1,004.7	1,022.9
1992	637.8	728.1	562.3	1,110.5	609.0	1,086.9	1,252.4	1,190.8	609.5	688.7	490.7	1,122.1	1,057.4	1,045.0	1,088.7
1993	659.1	751.9	581.2	1,145.4	632.2	1,114.2	1,282.6	1,229.4	625.5	707.2	506.0	1,143.0	1,074.2	1,078.2	1,128.8
1994	682.3	777.8	601.8	1,183.7	657.1	1,150.1	1,328.4	1,271.0	646.2	731.8	525.0	1,177.6	1,100.0	1,118.6	1,147.5
1995	704.8	803.0	621.8	1,220.6	681.6	1,184.5	1,365.5	1,299.8	667.6	757.4	544.8	1,205.5	1,130.9	1,159.9	1,199.1
1996	730.0	831.1	644.2	1,262.1	708.7	1,222.5	1,450.6	1,347.2	690.6	785.3	566.0	1,245.9	1,148.5	1,200.6	1,248.9
1997	750.2	853.7	663.1	1,294.6	733.2	1,250.3	1,502.6	1,358.0	708.0	806.6	583.6	1,280.2	1,165.9	1,238.5	1,326.6
1998	765.1	870.5	676.4	1,317.7	750.9	1,277.0	1,537.7	1,393.2	720.0	820.2	597.4	1,300.4	1,189.4	1,261.9	1,342.8
1999	—	—	—	—	—	—	—	—	—	—	—	—	—	—	1,373.1

Sources

Social Security Bulletin: Annual Statistical Supplement (1973), Table 29, p. 59; *Social Security Bulletin: Annual Statistical Supplement* (1983), Table 98, pp. 172–3; *Social Security Bulletin: Annual Statistical Supplement* (1988), Table 5.H1, p. 218; *Social Security Bulletin: Annual Statistical Supplement* (1999), Table 5.H1, p. 233, Table 2.A28, p. 73.

Documentation

This table reports the average monthly benefit paid to families receiving current-pay benefits under Old-Age, Survivors, and Disability Insurance (OASDI). Beneficiary families are decomposed into retired-worker families, survivors of insured persons, and disabled-worker families. For more information on OASDI, see the text for Table Bf377–394.

The OASDI tables do not include a number of persons receiving Railroad Retirement benefits who would be eligible for Social Security benefits had they applied. Data for 1981 are not available, except for series Bf475.

For fully insured workers who retire at the normal retirement age (currently age 65), benefits payable are equal to 100 percent of the primary insurance amount (PIA). The normal retirement age is scheduled to rise from age 65 to 67, with the first increase affecting workers who reach age 62 in the year 2000.

Workers who retire before the normal retirement age can receive benefits at a permanently reduced rate beginning at age 62. The amount of the reduction depends upon the number of benefit payments received before the normal retirement age. The annual rate of reduction is $6\frac{2}{3}$ percent for each of the first three years and, eventually, 5 percent for each of the next two years the worker receives benefits before the normal retirement age. Disabled workers may receive reduced benefits if they previously received a reduced retirement benefit. Workers who postpone their retirements beyond the normal retirement age have their benefits increased through the delayed retirement credit for each month benefits are foregone as a result of earnings above the exempt amount.

TABLE Bf461–475 Old-Age, Survivors and Disability Insurance – average monthly family benefit, by selected family groups: 1940–1999 *Continued*

Spouses of retired or disabled workers are eligible for monthly benefits at age 62. Their benefits are equal to 50 percent of the worker's PIA for the first entitlement at the normal retirement age but are permanently reduced if payments begin earlier. The annual rate of reduction is 8 $^1/_3$ percent for the first three years and, eventually, 5 percent for the next two years. Children of retired or disabled workers are also eligible to receive monthly benefits equal to 50 percent of the worker's PIA, as are spouses younger than age 65 who are caring for at least one child younger than age 16 or disabled child age 18 or older of the worker.

Widows and widowers of fully insured workers are first eligible for monthly benefits at age 60, or at age 50 if they are disabled. The benefit amount payable to widows and widowers first entitled to benefits at age 60 or before is equal to 71.5 percent of the worker's PIA, plus any delayed retirement credit the deceased worker would be receiving. For those widows and widowers first entitled to benefits at age 62 or later, the benefit is limited (if the worker had received benefits before normal retirement age) to the greater of the amount the worker would be receiving if still living, or 82.5 percent of the PIA.

Children of deceased workers are eligible to receive monthly benefits equal to 75 percent of the worker's PIA, as are mothers and fathers younger than age 65 who are caring for at least one child younger than age 16 or a disabled child. A dependent parent age 62 or older is eligible for monthly benefits equal to 82.5 percent, and each of two dependent parents, for benefits equal to 75 percent of the deceased worker's PIA. For detailed information, consult the *Social Security Bulletin, Annual Statistical Supplement* (1997), p. 59.

Series Bf464 and Bf472–473. For series Bf464, a wife's entitlement is based on her age. In the disabled-worker categories, a wife's entitlement is based on care of children.

Series Bf475. Assumes the workers began to work at age 22, retired at the beginning of the year, and had no prior period of disability. The observation in 1968 is effective in February of that year. In 1982, the figure was derived from the transitional guarantee computation based on the 1978 PIA table. The benefit for women was identical except for the period 1962 to 1977, when the male maximum was approximately 97 percent of the female maximum.

TABLE Bf476–483 Old-Age, Survivors, Disability, and Health Insurance – average monthly benefit received by retired workers, by sex: 1940–1998

Contributed by Price V. Fishback and Melissa A. Thomasson

	Men				Women			
			With reduction for early retirement				With reduction for early retirement	
	All benefits	Without reduction for early retirement	Before reduction	After reduction	All benefits	Without reduction for early retirement	Before reduction	After reduction
	Bf476	Bf477	Bf478	Bf479	Bf480	Bf481	Bf482	Bf483
Year	Dollars	Dollars	Dollars	Dollars	Dollars	Dollars	Dollars	Dollars
1940	23.17	23.17	—	—	18.37	18.37	—	—
1941	23.32	23.32	—	—	18.48	18.48	—	—
1942	23.71	23.71	—	—	18.73	18.73	—	—
1943	24.17	24.17	—	—	19.06	19.06	—	—
1944	24.48	24.48	—	—	19.35	19.35	—	—
1945	24.94	24.94	—	—	19.51	19.51	—	—
1946	25.30	25.30	—	—	19.64	19.64	—	—
1947	25.68	25.68	—	—	19.91	19.91	—	—
1948	26.21	26.21	—	—	20.11	20.11	—	—
1949	26.92	26.92	—	—	20.58	20.58	—	—
1950	45.67	45.67	—	—	35.05	35.05	—	—
1951	44.44	44.44	—	—	33.03	33.03	—	—
1952	52.16	52.16	—	—	39.17	39.17	—	—
1953	54.46	54.46	—	—	40.66	40.66	—	—
1954	63.34	63.34	—	—	47.05	47.05	—	—
1955	66.40	66.40	—	—	49.93	49.93	—	—
1956	68.23	68.23	—	—	51.16	51.16	53.64	48.20
1957	70.47	70.47	—	—	52.23	52.98	55.33	49.08
1958	72.74	72.74	—	—	53.55	54.62	57.06	50.27
1959	80.11	80.11	—	—	58.81	60.34	63.18	55.16
1960	81.90	81.90	—	—	59.70	61.60	64.19	55.80
1961	83.13	83.84	76.94	69.01	62.00	64.87	65.84	57.20
1962	33.79	85.26	80.03	71.24	62.61	66.10	66.41	57.59
1963	84.69	36.81	81.63	72.21	63.42	67.48	67.11	58.23
1964	85.58	88.37	82.72	72.85	64.28	69.01	67.88	58.87
1965	92.60	96.10	90.14	79.40	70.10	75.40	73.82	64.50
1966	93.26	97.37	90.98	80.26	70.79	76.40	75.47	65.21
1967	94.49	99.33	92.53	81.53	71.92	78.28	76.46	66.01
1968	109.08	115.02	106.95	95.29	84.24	91.89	88.90	77.75
1969	110.96	117.78	109.16	97.06	85.71	94.51	90.13	78.99

(continued)

TABLE Bf476–483 Old-Age, Survivors, Disability, and Health Insurance – average monthly benefit received by retired workers, by sex: 1940–1998 *Continued*

	Men				Women			
			With reduction for early retirement				With reduction for early retirement	
	All benefits	Without reduction for early retirement	Before reduction	After reduction	All benefits	Without reduction for early retirement	Before reduction	After reduction
	Bf476	Bf477	Bf478	Bf479	Bf480	Bf481	Bf482	Bf483
Year	Dollars	Dollars	Dollars	Dollars	Dollars	Dollars	Dollars	Dollars
1970	130.53	139.10	128.89	115.30	101.20	111.70	105.60	93.77
1971	146.13	156.39	144.06	129.84	113.60	126.24	118.05	105.29
1972	179.44	192.37	176.93	161.04	140.11	156.20	144.53	130.26
1973	182.60	197.00	181.00	164.20	145.80	164.00	148.84	135.00
1974	206.56	223.55	205.80	186.91	165.47	186.21	171.40	154.09
1975	227.80	247.20	228.20	207.20	181.80	205.90	190.57	169.38
1976	247.70	269.81	249.60	226.30	197.08	223.51	200.14	183.17
1977	268.40	293.20	271.90	246.24	212.60	242.50	222.10	197.83
1978	291.60	319.90	296.60	267.85	229.70	263.80	240.50	213.81
1979	326.80	359.30	332.60	299.95	256.50	296.70	262.90	237.99
1980	380.20	419.60	—	349.50	296.80	346.50	—	274.60
1981 [1]	431.10	479.50	—	395.10	334.50	394.00	—	308.80
1982	469.60	528.20	—	426.90	362.20	432.60	—	332.40
1983	495.00	565.50	—	444.30	379.60	460.50	—	345.40
1984	517.80	598.30	—	462.70	396.50	487.00	—	358.90
1985	538.40	627.50	—	480.50	412.10	511.00	—	372.00
1986	549.80	644.60	—	491.00	420.50	525.10	—	379.10
1987 [1]	577.50	679.20	—	516.90	441.20	553.70	—	397.70
1988	604.90	713.40	—	542.40	462.00	582.60	—	416.20
1989	638.90	755.20	—	573.80	487.90	617.10	—	439.10
1990	679.30	803.60	—	611.20	518.60	656.80	—	466.40
1991	709.30	840.50	—	638.90	541.60	687.00	—	486.80
1992	735.50	872.50	—	663.30	561.80	712.90	—	504.70
1993	759.30	901.70	—	685.80	580.70	736.90	—	521.50
1994	785.20	932.80	—	710.50	601.30	762.10	—	540.20
1995	810.20	963.70	—	735.40	621.20	780.40	—	563.80
1996	838.10	997.80	—	763.10	643.70	788.00	—	593.90
1997	860.50	1,025.10	—	786.60	662.50	771.30	—	626.10
1998	876.90	1,044.50	—	802.40	675.90	785.40	—	639.50

[1] Data based on unedited monthly estimates.

Sources

Social Security Bulletin, Annual Statistical Supplement (1971), Table 76, p. 95; (1981), Table 91, pp. 160–1; (1988), Table 5.B8, p. 189; (1999), Table 5.B8, p. 209.

Documentation

This table provides information on the average monthly benefit received by retired workers under the Old-Age, Survivors Insurance program. Benefits payable to workers who retire at the normal retirement age, currently age 65, are equal to 100 percent of the primary insurance amount (PIA). The normal retirement age is scheduled to rise gradually from 65 to 67, with the first increase affecting workers who reach age 62 in the year 2000. Retired workers are eligible to receive benefits at a permanently reduced rate beginning at age 62. The extent of reduction depends on the number of benefit payments received for months before the normal retirement age. The annual rate of reduction amounts to $6\frac{2}{3}$ percent for each of the first three years, and eventually (after the age for full benefits is established at age 67) 5 percent for each of the next two years the worker receives benefits before the normal retirement age. Workers receiving benefits at age 62 are eligible to receive benefits equal to 80 percent of the PIA ($6\frac{2}{3}$ multiplied by 3). This rate will decline to 75 and 70 percent, respectively, as the normal retirement age increases.

Workers who postpone their retirement beyond the normal retirement age have their benefits increased through the delayed retirement credit for each month benefits are foregone owing to earnings above the exempt amount. Spouses of retired workers are eligible for monthly benefits at age 62. Their benefits are equal to 50 percent of the worker's PIA for the first entitlement at the normal age but are permanently reduced if payments to the retired worker begin earlier. The annual rate of reduction is $8\frac{2}{3}$ percent for the first three years, and eventually 5 percent for the next two years the spouse receives benefits before reaching the normal retirement age. Children of retired workers are also eligible to receive monthly benefits equal to 50 percent of the worker's PIA, as are spouses younger than age 65 who are caring for at least one child younger than age 16 or disabled child age 18 or older of the worker. For more information, see the summary of Old-Age, Survivors, and Disability Insurance benefit types and levels (*Social Security Bulletin, Annual Statistical Supplement,* 1997, p. 59).

The OASI tables do not include a number of persons receiving Railroad Retirement benefits who would be eligible for Social Security benefits had they applied.

Series Bf478 and Bf482. These series are believed to show what the worker would have earned upon retirement at age 65 if they had not retired early. The series were no longer reported in the annual statistical supplements after 1979.

TABLE Bf484–496 Unemployment Insurance – coverage, benefits, and financing: 1938–1997

Contributed by Price V. Fishback and Melissa A. Thomasson

Year	Average monthly covered employment	Average weekly insured unemployment	First payments	Average weekly initial claims	Average weekly benefit amount	Average weekly benefit as percentage of average weekly wage	Average actual duration of benefit payments	Claimants exhausting benefits	Average actual duration of benefits for exhaustees	Total benefits paid	Total contributions collected	Taxable wages paid in covered employment during year	Net reserves, balance as of end of year
	Bf484	Bf485	Bf486	Bf487	Bf488	Bf489	Bf490	Bf491	Bf492	Bf493	Bf494	Bf495	Bf496
	Number	Number	Number	Number	Dollars	Percent	Weeks	Number	Weeks	Thousand dollars	Thousand dollars	Thousand dollars	Thousand dollars
1938	19,969,577	—	—	—	10.94	43.1	0.0	—	0.0	393,783	818,501	25,775,045	1,110,625
1939	21,418,945	—	448,336	—	10.66	40.8	0.0	3,056,446	0.0	429,298	824,876	28,463,115	1,537,797
1940	23,092,402	—	5,220,073	—	10.56	39.1	9.8	2,590,183	0.0	518,700	853,750	30,110,665	1,817,110
1941	26,804,701	—	3,439,323	164,000	11.06	36.6	9.4	1,543,533	12.1	344,324	1,006,328	38,676,791	2,524,463
1942	29,347,087	—	2,815,127	122,000	12.66	35.3	10.0	1,077,753	12.6	344,083	1,139,333	49,720,608	3,387,888
1943	30,825,503	—	664,015	36,000	13.84	33.6	9.0	193,891	14.3	79,644	1,325,423	59,048,952	4,715,510
1944	30,043,750	—	533,406	29,000	15.90	35.9	7.7	101,745	13.8	62,384	1,317,049	60,637,087	6,071,925
1945	28,405,595	—	2,822,922	116,000	18.77	41.6	8.5	250,440	14.5	445,867	1,161,883	58,544,835	6,914,010
1946	30,229,654	—	4,479,029	189,000	18.50	39.6	13.4	1,985,928	18.5	1,094,845	911,836	63,690,396	6,860,044
1947	32,272,248	1,008,737	3,983,603	187,000	17.83	34.6	11.1	1,271,821	17.8	775,142	1,095,522	72,981,066	7,303,287
1948	33,084,302	1,001,517	4,008,393	210,000	19.03	34.1	10.7	1,027,530	18.0	789,931	999,635	78,536,164	7,602,964
1949	31,695,005	1,975,629	7,363,767	340,000	20.48	36.0	11.8	1,934,709	18.7	1,735,991	986,906	76,267,263	7,009,585
1950	32,886,694	1,503,050	5,211,889	252,000	20.76	34.4	13.0	1,853,336	19.3	1,373,113	1,191,435	81,545,274	6,972,181
1951	34,857,403	969,105	4,127,134	218,000	21.09	32.2	10.1	810,580	17.9	840,411	1,492,506	90,242,251	7,781,930
1952	35,576,997	1,024,294	4,384,030	222,000	22.79	33.0	10.4	931,362	19.3	998,238	1,367,676	94,669,424	8,327,427
1953	36,667,115	994,865	4,227,616	225,000	23.58	32.3	10.1	764,420	19.2	962,219	1,347,632	99,629,885	8,912,680
1954	35,371,999	1,865,202	6,590,464	315,000	24.93	33.5	12.8	1,768,927	20.0	2,026,868	1,136,151	96,539,455	8,218,954
1955	36,590,254	1,254,508	4,508,404	235,000	25.04	32.1	12.4	1,272,231	20.3	1,350,264	1,208,788	101,574,717	8,260,724
1956	38,983,356	1,212,182	4,665,218	235,000	27.02	33.3	11.4	980,790	20.0	1,380,728	1,463,261	109,817,323	8,573,431
1957	39,670,705	1,447,468	5,574,620	278,000	28.17	33.5	11.5	1,139,246	20.5	1,733,876	1,544,233	112,829,744	8,659,312
1958	38,110,003	2,513,000	7,833,252	369,000	30.54	35.3	14.8	2,506,896	21.7	3,512,732	1,470,841	109,154,231	6,831,292
1959	39,544,909	1,665,071	5,816,912	277,000	30.40	33.4	13.1	1,675,963	21.7	2,279,018	1,955,664	115,302,625	6,674,297
1960	40,198,155	1,902,610	6,753,531	331,000	32.87	35.2	12.7	1,603,518	21.4	2,726,849	2,288,440	119,181,579	6,418,822
1961	40,059,163	2,286,604	7,067,370	350,000	33.80	35.4	14.7	2,366,012	21.8	3,422,558	2,449,942	119,344,649	5,567,780
1962	41,286,214	1,780,248	6,073,470	302,000	34.56	34.9	13.1	1,638,466	21.6	2,675,565	2,951,841	125,537,437	6,038,626
1963	42,013,516	1,789,424	6,040,577	298,000	35.28	34.6	13.3	1,572,071	21.6	2,775,222	3,018,817	129,569,191	6,421,119
1964	43,200,252	1,602,940	5,497,903	268,000	35.96	33.8	13.0	1,370,982	21.9	2,521,575	3,047,288	136,337,595	7,090,270
1965	45,098,297	1,325,720	4,813,229	232,000	37.19	33.8	12.2	1,087,384	21.3	2,166,011	3,053,646	143,988,969	8,172,316
1966	47,684,227	1,059,551	4,139,041	203,000	39.76	34.7	11.2	780,749	21.1	1,771,292	3,030,126	156,958,490	9,664,712
1967	48,792,640	1,203,072	4,619,249	225,635	41.25	34.7	11.4	867,446	20.9	2,092,364	2,678,119	161,096,708	10,702,198
1968	50,354,124	1,109,204	4,196,559	198,135	43.43	34.3	11.6	848,037	21.2	2,029,957	2,551,573	171,389,505	11,715,954
1969	52,362,457	1,100,269	4,212,022	196,904	46.17	34.4	11.4	810,718	21.4	2,125,809	2,545,161	181,762,193	12,636,017
1970	52,168,445	1,805,002	6,397,173	292,346	50.31	35.7	12.3	1,302,628	22.1	3,847,312	2,505,814	182,707,427	11,902,575
1971	52,079,721	2,165,758	6,627,071	293,942	54.35	36.5	14.4	2,057,217	22.7	4,951,507	2,636,599	182,755,684	9,725,314
1972	56,618,236	1,849,442	5,713,209	262,755	56.68	36.7	14.2	1,811,376	22.7	4,481,854	3,896,620	236,355,573	9,402,983
1973	59,911,079	1,629,342	5,328,998	244,692	59.00	36.1	13.4	1,495,092	22.5	4,005,191	4,995,166	254,896,173	10,882,144
1974	61,254,089	2,258,700	7,729,590	355,788	64.34	36.6	12.6	1,926,133	22.4	5,977,411	5,218,967	265,375,024	10,520,181
1975	59,143,407	3,973,770	11,160,948	473,846	70.23	37.1	15.7	4,195,023	22.4	11,753,643	5,210,885	261,521,631	3,070,231
1976	61,208,766	2,990,703	8,560,107	381,269	75.16	37.1	14.9	3,262,282	22.6	8,972,637	7,532,078	301,106,223	871,380
1977	63,602,710	2,647,475	7,985,105	375,962	78.79	36.4	14.2	2,776,387	22.1	8,345,948	9,170,529	324,182,674	950,381
1978	68,565,923	2,354,216	7,568,310	342,827	83.67	36.4	13.3	2,030,423	22.5	7,722,347	11,193,446	411,988,796	4,554,185
1979	71,631,725	2,424,513	8,075,003	384,115	89.68	36.0	13.1	2,037,095	22.4	8,556,908	12,095,041	444,278,867	8,582,608

(continued)

TABLE Bf484–496 Unemployment Insurance – coverage, benefits, and financing: 1938–1997 *Continued*

Year	Average monthly covered employment	Average weekly insured unemployment	First payments	Average weekly initial claims	Average weekly benefit amount	Average weekly benefit as percentage of average weekly wage	Average actual duration of benefit payments	Claimants exhausting benefits	Average actual duration of benefits for exhaustees	Total benefits paid	Total contributions collected	Taxable wages paid in covered employment during year	Net reserves, balance as of end of year
	Bf484	Bf485	Bf486	Bf487	Bf488	Bf489	Bf490	Bf491	Bf492	Bf493	Bf494	Bf495	Bf496
	Number	Number	Number	Number	Dollars	Percent	Weeks	Number	Weeks	Thousand dollars	Thousand dollars	Thousand dollars	Thousand dollars
1980	71,258,455	3,355,747	9,992,123	479,769	99.66	36.6	14.9	3,071,943	22.7	13,768,135	11,414,649	458,643,511	6,591,827
1981	71,965,970	3,044,857	9,407,372	450,846	106.61	35.9	14.4	2,989,177	23.0	13,221,592	11,624,545	478,414,824	5,745,115
1982	70,331,861	4,058,646	11,648,448	579,252	119.34	37.7	15.9	4,174,709	23.2	20,649,840	12,206,070	477,471,932	2,644,584
1983	70,817,863	3,394,666	8,907,190	441,653	123.59	37.2	17.5	4,179,622	23.4	17,755,392	14,548,669	532,288,687	5,803,331
1984	75,204,621	2,474,809	7,742,547	371,773	123.47	35.5	14.4	2,606,145	22.8	12,598,229	18,757,690	586,020,262	2,204,797
1985	77,467,012	2,616,958	8,372,070	390,294	128.14	35.3	14.2	2,572,059	22.7	14,124,342	19,296,983	611,969,897	10,069,416
1986	79,093,152	2,642,644	8,360,752	376,227	135.65	35.8	14.5	2,687,723	22.9	15,402,735	18,111,266	638,038,517	15,402,260
1987	81,352,396	2,300,399	7,203,357	326,153	140.55	35.5	14.6	2,408,471	22.7	13,617,007	17,576,976	667,498,815	23,174,690
1988	83,984,776	2,080,582	6,860,662	312,882	144.97	34.9	13.7	1,979,285	22.7	12,579,703	17,720,628	705,002,395	31,103,671
1989	86,164,595	2,157,666	7,368,766	328,819	151.73	35.4	13.2	1,940,390	22.9	13,641,569	16,451,876	738,265,107	36,870,882
1990	87,008,189	2,521,564	8,628,557	387,001	161.56	36.0	13.4	2,323,255	23.1	17,320,777	15,221,274	759,670,530	37,937,017
1991	84,905,782	3,341,935	10,074,550	447,593	169.88	36.4	15.4	3,472,019	23.2	24,582,501	14,510,670	751,666,268	30,488,785
1992	85,098,137	3,245,191	9,243,338	407,344	173.64	35.4	16.2	3,838,011	23.3	23,956,510	16,972,655	776,502,595	25,846,579
1993	86,850,536	2,751,441	7,884,326	342,309	179.62	36.0	15.9	3,203,897	23.4	20,687,678	19,831,045	807,165,885	28,001,956
1994	89,690,770	2,669,872	7,959,281	342,730	182.16	35.7	15.5	2,977,468	23.2	20,433,832	21,802,069	856,255,509	31,343,551
1995	92,328,088	2,571,951	8,035,229	357,041	187.29	35.5	14.7	2,661,773	23.1	20,122,189	21,970,828	889,901,028	35,403,296
1996	94,685,734	2,595,585	7,989,615	351,361	189.45	34.5	14.9	2,738,963	23.2	20,634,904	21,577,968	923,895,199	38,631,922
1997	97,837,884	2,322,573	7,325,279	321,511	192.76	33.5	14.6	2,484,911	23.0	18,605,353	21,247,040	970,110,253	43,833,157

Sources

All series except series Bf487. *Unemployment Insurance Financial Data Handbook number 394* from the Information Technology Support Center (ITSC) in Maryland.

Series Bf487. Through 1966, data were collected by the Bureau of the Census from monthly issues of the U.S. Manpower Administration's *Unemployment Statistics*. Beginning in 1967, data are from evidence posted February 24, 2000, on the U.S. Department of Labor, Employment Training Administration Internet site.

Documentation

ITSC is a collaboration of state employment security agencies, the Department of Labor (DOL), and private sector partners. Most of these data were compiled from monthly and quarterly statistical and accounting reports submitted by the State Employment Security agencies to the U.S. Employment and Training Administration of the U.S. Department of Labor. Revised data and corrections have been incorporated into this edition to the extent possible. Data contained in this handbook may not be identical with state records.

The Social Security Act of 1935 established Unemployment Insurance (UI) as a federally mandated program run by the states. The states collect payroll taxes from employers to fund the system. After the Social Security Act passed, the states had to pass enabling legislation and then wait two years to accumulate enough reserves to begin paying benefits. Because Wisconsin had passed an unemployment insurance act prior to 1935, it was the first state to pay benefits. By 1938, roughly 75 percent of payrolls were covered by unemployment insurance. The percentage rose to a peak of 98 percent in 1979 and fell back to about 92.4 percent in 1994.

To fund the system, employers pay taxes on employee earnings up to a specific maximum per employee in each state. Part of the taxes (0.4 percent of taxable wages in 1970) is remitted to the federal government, which in turn provides grants to the states for the cost of administering unemployment insurance and employment services. The payroll contribution rates for individual employers vary to some extent in response to the unemployment experience of workers in the employer's operation.

Reimbursable coverage has been excluded from series Bf484 and Bf493–495. However, the claims resulting from reimbursable coverage have not been excluded from series Bf485–486 and Bf488–492.

In June 1962, employees engaged in the agricultural aspects of the sugar cane industry who were previously covered under a special unemployment insurance law were brought under the Puerto Rico Employment Security Act of 1957.

Series Bf484. Average monthly covered employment represents the twelve-month average of the covered employees reported to states by each employer for 1938–1944 for the last payroll period in the month. For 1945–1962, data represent the twelve-month average for the payroll period ending nearest the fifteenth day of the month. After 1963, data represent the twelve-month average for the payroll period including the twelfth day of the month. Covered employment represents employment in industrial and commercial establishments of eight or more for the period 1941–1955 and four or more for 1956 to 1970. In some states, the covered employment also represents employment in smaller establishments and for additional groups of workers, such as state and local employees or seamen. Although the federal law requires only employers to pay taxes, some states require some workers to contribute as well.

Series Bf484–485. Beginning in 1964, the series on the average number of weekly insured employment, series Bf485, includes workers in the sugar cane industry, while series Bf484 excludes them.

Series Bf487. Calculated as an average for the year of the number of initial claims for unemployment insurance filed each week. An initial claim is "any notice of unemployment filed (1) to request a determination of entitlement to and eligibility for compensation or (2) to begin a second or subsequent period of eligibility within a benefit year or period of eligibility."

Series Bf489. Unemployed workers begin receiving benefits in most states after a waiting period of one week is served. In the late 1930s, the benefits typically replaced 50 percent of weekly earnings up to a weekly maximum benefit level. The weekly maximum has often served to reduce benefits as a percent of average weekly wages to roughly 33 to 41 percent. From 1938 through 1970, the percentage of the weekly wage has reimbursable coverage in the numerator but not in the denominator.

Series Bf490. The states establish maximum durations for payments that ranged from 12 to 22.6 weeks in the late 1930s. The maximums rose such that by 1970 workers could receive benefits for up to 20 to 36 weeks, depending on the state. The average actual duration of benefit payments is calculated as the number of weeks compensated during the year divided by the number of first payments.

Series Bf492. The number of weeks compensated for all individuals exhausting benefits divided by the total number of people who receive benefits for the maximum number of weeks during the year.

Series Bf493. Excludes reconversion unemployment benefits for seamen of $1,018,777 in 1947, $3,330,528 in 1948, $1,286,940 in 1949, $311,739 in 1950, and $1,941 in 1951.

Series Bf494. Includes state unemployment taxes paid by employers and the contributions from employees in states that tax workers. Also includes penalties and interest for those states in which the law requires that these items be used to pay benefits. The data in this series have been adjusted for refunds of contributions. Contributions collected are the cash payments received during the calendar year and are not equal to total collections due for that year. In 1938 and 1939, the series includes receipts from railroads and related employers subject to the Railroad Unemployment Insurance Act after 1939.

Series Bf495. Wages paid to covered employees who are subject to state unemployment insurance taxes during the calendar year.

Series Bf496. Total reserves minus the balance of federal loans to state reserve funds.

TABLE Bf497–510 Railroad unemployment insurance and sickness benefits – applications, claims, beneficiaries, and payments: 1940–1998

Contributed by Price V. Fishback and Melissa A. Thomasson

	Unemployment benefits							Sickness benefits						
					Payments							Payments		
	Applications received	Claims received	Beneficiaries	Accounts exhausted	Number	Total amount	Average amount	Applications received	Claims received	Beneficiaries	Accounts exhausted	Number	Total amount	Average amount
	Bf497	Bf498	Bf499	Bf500	Bf501	Bf502	Bf503	Bf504	Bf505	Bf506	Bf507	Bf508	Bf509	Bf510
Year	Number	Number	Number	Number	Number	Thousand dollars	Dollars	Number	Number	Number	Number	Number	Thousand dollars	Dollars
1940	211,000	1,258,000	161,000	29,000	1,001,000	14,810	—	—	—	—	—	—	—	—
1941	181,000	517,000	164,000	27,000	999,000	17,699	—	—	—	—	—	—	—	—
1942	90,000	101,000	80,000	11,000	448,000	8,890	—	—	—	—	—	—	—	—
1943	22,000	27,000	18,000	3,000	79,000	1,753	—	—	—	—	—	—	—	—
1944	7,000	35,000	5,000	(Z)	21,000	547	—	—	—	—	—	—	—	—
1945	9,000	847,000	6,000	1,000	27,000	728	26.47	—	—	—	—	—	—	—
1946	201,000	1,763,000	157,000	15,000	731,000	20,517	28.01	—	—	—	—	—	—	—
1947	257,000	1,347,000	225,000	48,000	1,583,000	46,617	29.41	—	—	—	—	—	—	—
1948	267,000	1,706,000	210,000	22,000	1,146,000	32,426	28.57	235,000	800,000	150,000	16,000	734,000	26,604	39.66
1949	347,000	3,731,000	286,000	20,000	1,531,000	46,745	30.70	214,000	922,000	179,000	21,000	873,000	29,823	40.29
1950	562,000	1,028,000	506,000	83,000	3,475,000	113,769	32.72	197,000	896,000	160,000	22,000	852,000	29,487	41.16
1951	233,000	905,000	181,000	17,000	912,000	24,780	27.53	186,000	826,000	143,000	22,000	783,000	27,003	40.96
1952	220,000	1,305,000	162,000	11,000	823,000	22,741	28.06	192,000	801,000	143,000	20,000	758,000	25,898	41.35
1953	264,000	2,118,000	224,000	15,000	1,202,000	53,849	45.26	207,000	918,000	158,000	24,000	878,000	43,526	58.87
1954	316,000	2,785,000	265,000	34,000	1,981,000	95,541	48.68	203,000	942,000	154,000	26,000	902,000	44,904	60.47
1955	371,000	1,123,000	320,000	77,000	2,594,000	152,668	59.06	205,000	961,000	151,000	27,000	912,000	52,388	68.63
1956	177,000	1,553,000	149,000	22,000	1,022,000	55,456	54.98	200,000	930,000	150,000	26,000	889,000	50,040	69.40
1957	279,000	2,746,000	221,000	28,000	1,434,000	83,154	58.23	194,000	915,000	145,000	25,000	875,000	50,028	71.29
1958	391,000	2,765,000	312,000	67,000	2,595,000	169,214	65.42	204,000	942,000	153,000	25,000	896,000	52,544	73.05
1959	265,000	2,026,000	300,000	90,000	2,636,000	193,118	67.09	171,000	876,000	139,000	26,000	842,000	54,757	76.28
1960	254,000	2,663,000	221,000	51,000	—	208,554	79.49	190,000	880,000	142,000	26,000	847,000	66,080	90.42
1961	359,000	2,048,000	319,000	68,000	2,546,000	206,651	80.40	169,000	828,000	128,000	24,000	788,000	54,974	91.44
1962	231,000	1,572,000	215,000	50,000	1,995,000	156,788	78.79	168,000	798,000	125,000	22,000	764,000	54,120	91.75
1963	213,000	1,188,000	191,000	34,000	1,506,000	116,789	78.38	156,000	751,000	121,000	21,000	718,000	50,035	91.55
1964	172,000	979,000	152,000	24,000	1,137,000	86,563	77.42	150,000	727,000	114,000	20,000	693,000	47,349	91.30

Notes appear at end of table

(continued)

TABLE Bf497–510 Railroad unemployment insurance and sickness benefits – applications, claims, beneficiaries, and payments: 1940–1998 *Continued*

	Unemployment benefits							Sickness benefits						
					Payments							Payments		
	Applications received	Claims received	Beneficiaries	Accounts exhausted	Number	Total amount	Average amount	Applications received	Claims received	Beneficiaries	Accounts exhausted	Number	Total amount	Average amount
	Bf497	Bf498	Bf499	Bf500	Bf501	Bf502	Bf503	Bf504	Bf505	Bf506	Bf507	Bf508	Bf509	Bf510
Year	Number	Number	Number	Number	Number	Thousand dollars	Dollars	Number	Number	Number	Number	Number	Thousand dollars	Dollars
1965	153,000	727,000	127,000	19,000	926,900	71,260	78.97	142,000	688,000	106,000	20,000	647,800	43,984	91.37
1966	175,000	525,000	153,000	10,000	696,000	47,673	71.26	134,000	631,000	101,000	18,000	594,700	40,447	91.15
1967	98,000	751,000	81,000	8,000	496,300	34,413	74.44	127,000	591,000	92,000	16,000	552,900	36,477	91.00
1968	275,000	516,000	233,000	9,000	710,900	41,698	61.45	121,000	560,000	88,000	14,000	522,600	34,052	90.80
1969	112,000	438,000	96,000	8,000	485,000	40,840	88.85	128,000	684,000	93,000	16,000	646,300	55,747	110.63
1970	98,000	438	79,000	6,000	407,400	35,028	91.84	121,000	707,000	91,000	17,000	674,000	57,927	112.87
1971	330,600	748,700	249,000	8,300	682,200	44,957	68.34	113,800	671,500	86,000	15,200	632,800	50,140	113.26
1972	392,100	1,095,300	317,000	14,100	1,015,800	80,684	82.28	108,700	612,000	82,000	12,600	571,200	39,407	112.48
1973	128,000	505,800	105,000	7,800	476,100	41,193	91.46	97,800	527,300	74,000	9,800	491,800	31,634	112.09
1974	60,600	274,000	48,000	4,000	254,500	22,417	95.19	94,800	487,300	71,000	8,500	450,000	28,053	111.45
1975	108,600	443,400	77,900	4,800	411,600	37,549	94.28	89,600	453,300	67,400	7,900	417,900	29,564	111.26
1976	133,000	875,100	105,300	20,500	826,500	142,983	175.87	103,000	511,800	76,900	11,200	473,000	74,930	204.92
1977	102,500	640,800	84,600	13,400	604,500	111,239	190.75	107,600	549,900	82,200	12,400	514,200	77,973	230.63
1978	112,200	652,700	94,900	10,500	614,900	112,393	195.05	107,800	511,300	81,800	11,100	482,200	71,197	232.06
1979	124,800	580,600	97,200	7,100	531,900	100,795	198.69	103,500	485,800	78,300	10,100	454,700	64,235	231.73
1980	136,900	650,200	101,600	11,200	596,500	112,706	198.79	102,800	468,300	76,800	9,500	428,500	60,043	231.04
1981	156,200	1,116,700	121,900	27,900	1,070,600	216,028	208.84	99,700	458,600	75,200	9,400	422,300	60,613	231.88
1982	210,000	1,322,900	152,400	36,000	1,247,400	247,674	208.27	94,100	444,300	71,800	9,300	409,800	54,716	232.15
1983	236,700	2,023,500	182,900	67,600	1,894,500	394,364 [1]	212.95	82,300	423,300	62,900	10,000	388,200	56,721	234.65
1984	132,700	1,123,400	115,600	34,400	1,065,800	216,348 [1]	207.94	72,100	370,600	57,200	8,800	345,600	45,434	234.10
1985	105,300	695,200	81,700	16,100	648,500	126,426 [1]	201.03	67,000	342,100	51,600	8,000	316,900	43,783	234.16
1986	112,300	754,500	87,600	17,400	706,800	140,452 [1]	205.56	63,500	356,400	49,500	8,800	329,400	47,397	233.87
1987	90,400	680,000	75,200	17,000	630,200	118,573	206.88	58,200	346,800	45,200	9,100	319,100	55,735	232.82
1988	68,500	456,100	54,400	10,600	417,800	85,774	209.76	54,500	323,600	41,700	8,400	295,200	24,834	232.85
1989	49,200	306,000	35,200	6,600	258,200	60,798	247.44	47,700	286,300	33,700	7,600	245,000	32,136	271.35
1990	39,600	298,900	29,900	5,600	230,900	57,215	249.72	41,900	270,400	28,200	6,100	208,700	32,566	285.74
1991	46,100	309,500	30,500	5,900	245,400	60,102	264.45	37,800	257,100	25,600	5,300	192,000	32,567	289.93
1992	32,900	280,700	26,400	5,900	236,600	55,104	269.48	34,200	233,000	23,600	5,300	184,900	12,037	290.93
1993	27,200	215,300	20,700	4,300	182,500	49,188	289.30	31,700	205,000	21,800	4,600	167,600	21,546	307.33
1994	22,600	187,700	18,600	4,000	158,700	40,441	293.38	30,900	205,100	21,600	4,700	170,000	25,437	312.94
1995	23,700	158,000	18,700	2,900	129,900	37,357	312.84	29,100	196,200	21,000	4,300	163,000	24,198	336.36
1996	22,400	162,400	16,800	3,400	134,800	40,678	314.31	28,000	194,100	20,400	4,400	162,900	25,759	337.84
1997	19,500	130,200	15,300	2,700	105,500	38,249	357.69	27,400	184,300	20,500	4,300	154,600	32,475	372.03
1998	13,700	86,800	11,300	2,100	71,500	27,034	375.04	26,600	171,100	20,500	4,300	147,500	33,058	385.40

(Z) Fewer than 500 accounts.

[1] Includes supplemental extended unemployment benefits paid to certain workers. See text.

Source

U.S. Railroad Retirement Board, *Statistical Tables: Data through Fiscal Year 1998*, Tables C1 and C2.

Documentation

The Railroad Unemployment Insurance Act of 1938 was established to provide unemployment benefits for railroad workers who were often denied coverage under state programs because of the interstate nature of their employment. The Act established a system of benefits for unemployed railroad workers that was financed entirely by railroad employers and administered by the Railroad Retirement Board. The Railroad system covers the entire United States and is similar to the Unemployment Insurance (UI) system described in the text for Table Bf484–496.

In 1940 a uniform benefit year was established, and sickness benefits were added in 1946. As of 1997, contribution rates for employers ranged from 0.65 to 12 percent, and benefits were paid for compensable days of unemployment and sickness at a daily rate of 60 percent of the employee's wage subject to a $42.00 maximum and a $12.70 minimum.

Between 1946 and 1997, several amendments have changed benefit levels and employer contribution requirements. For a full, detailed history of the Railroad Unemployment Insurance System, see the *1997 Railroad Retirement and Unemployment Insurance Systems Handbook*.

All data are reported in a June–July benefit year, rather than a fiscal year.

Series Bf501. From 1983 to 1985, includes beneficiaries who received supplemental extended unemployment benefits.

Series Bf501–503 and Bf508–510. Not adjusted for recoveries or settlements of underpayments.

Series Bf502. For 1983–1986, includes supplemental extended unemployment benefits paid to certain workers with less than ten years of service. These benefits totaled $37,731,000 in 1982–1983, $13,395,000 in 1983–1984, $654,000 in 1984–1985, and $22,400 in 1985–1986 and were financed from general revenues.

Series Bf503 and Bf510. Represents the average amount per two-week claim period. Over the period 1940–1965, beneficiaries are based on a 10 percent sample for unemployment and sickness payments and a 20 percent sample for maternity. From 1966 to 1975, the number of beneficiaries is based on a 20 percent sample, while universal data are used after 1975.

Series Bf504–510. Includes maternity benefits.

TABLE Bf511–524 Workers' compensation – workers covered, benefit payments, and costs: 1939–1998

Contributed by Price V. Fishback and Melissa A. Thomasson

		Benefits paid											NASI estimates		
				Disability and survivor benefits			Source of payments			Per $100 of covered payroll			Per $100 of covered payroll	
	Workers covered	Total	Medical and hospitalization benefits	Total	Disability	Survivor	Private insurance carriers	Disbursements from state and federal funds	Employers' self-insurance	Cost of programs	Benefits paid	Workers covered	Cost of programs	Benefits paid
	Bf511	Bf512	Bf513	Bf514	Bf515	Bf516 [1]	Bf517	Bf518	Bf519	Bf520	Bf521	Bf522	Bf523	Bf524
Year	Million	Million dollars	Million dollars	Million dollars	Million dollars	Million dollars	Million dollars	Million dollars	Million dollars	Dollars	Dollars	Million	Dollars	Dollars
1939	—	235	85	150	120	30	122	68	44	—	—	—	—	—
1940	24.6	256	95	161	129	32	135	73	48	1.19	0.72	—	—	—
1941	—	291	100	191	157	34	160	77	54	—	—	—	—	—
1942	—	329	108	221	185	36	190	81	57	—	—	—	—	—
1943	—	353	112	241	203	38	213	81	59	—	—	—	—	—
1944	—	385	120	265	225	40	237	86	63	—	—	—	—	—
1945	—	408	125	283	241	42	253	91	65	—	—	—	—	—
1946	32.7	434	140	294	250	44	270	96	68	0.91	0.54	—	—	—
1947	—	486	160	326	280	46	302	110	74	—	—	—	—	—
1948	36.0	534	175	359	309	50	335	121	78	0.96	0.51	—	—	—
1949	35.3	566	185	381	329	52	353	132	81	0.98	0.55	—	—	—
1950	36.9	615	200	415	360	55	381	149	85	0.89	0.54	—	—	—
1951	38.7	709	233	476	416	60	444	170	94	0.90	0.54	—	—	—
1952	39.4	785	260	525	460	65	491	193	101	0.94	0.55	—	—	—
1953	40.7	841	280	561	491	70	524	210	107	0.97	0.55	—	—	—
1954	39.8	876	308	568	498	70	540	225	110	0.98	0.57	—	—	—
1955	41.4	916	325	591	521	70	563	238	115	0.91	0.55	—	—	—
1956	43.0	1,002	350	652	577	75	618	259	125	0.92	0.55	—	—	—
1957	43.3	1,062	360	702	617	85	661	271	130	0.91	0.56	—	—	—
1958	42.5	1,112	375	737	647	90	694	285	132	0.91	0.58	—	—	—
1959	44.0	1,210	410	800	700	100	753	316	141	0.89	0.58	—	—	—

Note appears at end of table

(continued)

TABLE Bf511–524 Workers' compensation – workers covered, benefit payments, and costs: 1939–1998 *Continued*

		Benefits paid											NASI estimates		
				Disability and survivor benefits			Source of payments			Per $100 of covered payroll				Per $100 of covered payroll	
	Workers covered	Total	Medical and hospitalization benefits	Total	Disability	Survivor	Private insurance carriers	Disbursements from state and federal funds	Employers' self-insurance	Cost of programs	Benefits paid	Workers covered	Cost of programs	Benefits paid
	Bf511	Bf512	Bf513	Bf514	Bf515	Bf516 [1]	Bf517	Bf518	Bf519	Bf520	Bf521	Bf522	Bf523	Bf524
Year	Million	Million dollars	Million dollars	Million dollars	Million dollars	Million dollars	Million dollars	Million dollars	Million dollars	Dollars	Dollars	Million	Dollars	Dollars
1960	44.9	1,295	435	860	755	105	810	325	160	0.93	0.59	—	—	—
1961	45.0	1,374	460	914	804	110	851	347	176	0.95	0.61	—	—	—
1962	46.2	1,489	495	994	879	115	924	371	194	0.96	0.62	—	—	—
1963	47.3	1,582	525	1,057	932	125	988	388	207	0.99	0.62	—	—	—
1964	48.8	1,707	565	1,142	1,007	135	1,070	412	226	1.00	0.63	—	—	—
1965	50.8	1,814	600	1,214	1,074	140	1,124	445	244	1.00	0.61	—	—	—
1966	53.7	2,000	680	1,320	1,170	150	1,239	486	275	1.02	0.61	—	—	—
1967	55.0	2,189	750	1,439	1,284	155	1,363	524	303	1.07	0.63	—	—	—
1968	56.8	2,376	830	1,546	1,381	165	1,482	556	338	1.07	0.62	—	—	—
1969	59.0	2,634	920	1,714	1,529	185	1,641	607	386	1.08	0.62	—	—	—
1970	59.2	3,031	1,050	1,981	1,751	230	1,843	755	432	1.11	0.66	—	—	—
1971	59.4	3,563	1,130	2,433	2,068	365	2,005	1,098	460	1.11	0.67	—	—	—
1972	62.3	4,061	1,250	2,811	2,351	460	2,179	1,379	504	1.14	0.68	—	—	—
1973	66.3	5,103	1,480	3,623	2,953	670	2,514	1,998	592	1.17	0.70	—	—	—
1974	68.0	5,781	1,760	4,021	3,351	670	2,971	2,086	724	1.24	0.75	—	—	—
1975	67.2	6,598	2,030	4,568	3,843	725	3,422	2,324	852	1.32	0.83	—	—	—
1976	69.6	7,584	2,380	5,204	4,394	810	3,976	2,570	1,039	1.49	0.87	—	—	—
1977	72.1	8,630	2,680	5,950	5,075	875	4,629	2,750	1,250	1.71	0.92	—	—	—
1978	75.6	9,796	2,980	6,816	5,851	965	5,256	3,043	1,497	1.86	0.94	—	—	—
1979	78.6	12,027	3,520	8,507	7,232	1,275	6,157	4,022	1,848	1.95	1.01	—	—	—
1980	78.8	13,618	3,947	9,671	8,359	1,312	7,029	4,330	2,259	1.96	1.07	—	—	—
1981	78.3	15,054	4,431	10,623	9,224	1,399	7,876	4,595	2,583	1.85	1.08	—	—	—
1982	77.0	16,407	5,058	11,349	9,862	1,488	8,647	4,768	2,993	1.75	1.16	—	—	—
1983	78.0	17,575	5,681	11,894	10,385	1,509	9,265	5,061	3,249	1.67	1.17	—	—	—
1984	81.9	19,685	6,424	13,261	11,666	1,595	10,610	5,405	3,671	1.66	1.21	—	—	—
1985	84.3	22,217	7,498	14,719	13,060	1,659	12,341	5,744	4,132	1.82	1.30	—	—	—
1986	86.0	24,613	8,642	15,971	14,328	1,643	13,827	6,248	4,538	1.99	1.37	—	—	—
1987	88.4	27,317	9,912	17,406	15,775	1,631	15,453	6,782	5,082	2.07	1.43	—	—	—
1988	91.3	30,703	11,518	19,215	17,613	1,602	17,512	7,447	5,744	2.16	1.49	—	—	—
1989	93.7	34,316	13,424	20,892	19,171	1,721	19,918	7,965	6,433	2.27	1.58	103.9	2.04	1.43
1990	95.1	38,237	15,187	23,051	21,212	1,839	22,222	8,766	7,249	2.36	1.66	105.5	2.13	1.49
1991	93.6	42,170	16,832	25,337	23,373	1,964	24,515	9,711	7,944	2.40	1.79	103.7	2.16	1.64
1992	94.6	45,668	18,252	26,408	24,410	1,998	25,280	10,664	9,724	2.39	1.86	104.3	2.13	1.66
1993	96.1	45,330	17,521	25,403	23,450	1,952	24,129	10,578	10,623	2.44	1.78	106.2	2.17	1.58
1994	99.0	44,586	17,194	27,503	25,458	2,045	22,306	10,753	11,527	2.30	1.70	109.4	2.05	1.52
1995	102.1	43,373	16,733	26,779	24,800	1,979	21,145	10,996	11,232	2.05	1.56	112.8	1.83	1.39
1996	—	42,065	16,609	25,456	—	—	20,510	10,700	10,855	—	—	114.6	1.67	1.28
1997	—	40,586	15,447	25,139	—	—	20,617	10,097	9,872	—	—	117.7	1.46	1.14
1998	—	41,693	16,427	25,266	—	—	22,215	10,352	9,126	—	—	120.9	1.35	1.08

[1] Sharp jump between 1970 and 1973 is in large part the result of the introduction of the federal Black Lung Benefits program.

Sources

For series Bf511–521, 1939–1967, Alfred M. Skolnik and Daniel N. Price, "Another Look at Workmen's Compensation," *Social Security Bulletin* 33 (October 1970): 3–25; 1968–1991, U.S. Social Security Administration, *Social Security Bulletin, Annual Statistical Supplement* (1994), Table 9.B1, p. 333; 1992–1993, Jack Schmulowitz, "Workers' Compensation: Coverage, Benefits, and Costs, 1992–93," *Social Security Bulletin* 58 (Summer 1995): 51–7. The Social Security Administration stopped collecting and publishing these data in 1995. The National Academy of Social Insurance (NASI) with the help of Jack Schmulowitz published updated information for 1994 and 1995 in National Academy of Social Insurance, "Workers' Compensation: Benefits, Coverage and Costs, 1994–1995 New Estimates." For series Bf512 and Bf517–519 for years 1987 through 1998 and for series Bf522–524, National Academy of Social Insurance, "Workers' Compensation: Benefits, Coverage and Costs, 1997–1998 New Estimates." The publication is available at the NASI Internet site. The NASI continues to publish annual updates.

Documentation

Workers' compensation programs provide medical and hospital care and income-maintenance protection to workers whose disabilities are the result of work-related injuries or illnesses. The programs also provide survivor benefits to the dependents of deceased workers whose deaths result from job-related accidents and/or occupational diseases. The first permanent workers' compensation law was established by the Federal Employer Liability Act in 1908, which provided limited benefits for certain federal employees engaged in hazardous work. Nine states had enacted their own workers' compensation laws by 1911, forty-one states by 1920, forty-four by 1930, forty-six prior to 1939, and all forty-eight by 1948. Alaska and Hawai'i each adopted workers' compensation in 1915 as territories, long before becoming states in 1959.

The figures include estimated payments under state worker's compensation laws (forty-six states in 1939; forty-eight states, 1948–1957; fifty states after Alaska and Hawai'i are included from 1959 to the present) and under federal workers' compensation laws covering employees of the federal government, private employees in the District of Columbia, and longshoremen and harbor workers. Beginning in 1970, the data include the federal Black Lung Benefits program for disabled coal miners and their dependents.

Most of the state workers' compensation laws exempt employment in agriculture, domestic service, and casual labor; about half exempt employers who have fewer than a specified number of employees. In the original laws, occupational diseases were not covered. The number of laws covering occupational diseases expanded. For the past fifty years nearly all states have made occupational diseases, or at least specified diseases, compensable.

To make certain that benefit payments will be made when due, the covered employer is required by law to obtain insurance from a private insurance carrier or from a state insurance fund or to give proof of his qualifications to carry his own risk, which is known as self-insurance.

There is substantial variation in the benefit payments across states. Detailed descriptions of the benefit rules are published annually by the U.S. Chamber of Commerce in *Analysis of Workers' Compensation Laws* and the U. S. Bureau of Labor Statistics in *Workers' Compensation Laws*.

Estimates of workers' compensation payments depend on a variety of sources of published information, supplemented by correspondence with state agencies. Data on payments by private insurance companies and some of the competitive state funds are obtained from annual issues of *Spectator: Insurance by States of Fire, Marine, Casualty, Surety and Miscellaneous Lines* and from the A. M. Best Company. Data on payments made by the remaining state funds are obtained from annual or biennial reports issued by state workmen's compensation bureaus or divisions, or state insurance departments, and from the annual publication of the Bureau of the Census, *State Government Finances*. Data on payments by self-insurers in some states are obtained directly from state reports. For most states, however, estimates are calculated using one of several ratios (for example, reported accidents, claims filed, taxes paid) that exist between firms that are insured with private carriers or state funds and firms that self-insure. For more details on estimation procedures in the 1990s, see the publications by the NASI in the source listings.

Series Bf511. Estimates are monthly averages.

Series Bf512. The sum of series Bf513–514, although the sums during the 1990s may not match series Bf512 because published sources provide more recent updates for series Bf512 than for the subcategories. It is also the sum of series Bf517–519.

Series Bf512–519. After 1992, includes estimated benefits paid under deductible provisions. Provisions for payments of deductibles are a relatively new development of the 1990s, and data were not previously available.

Series Bf514. The sum of series Bf515–516.

Series Bf517. Net cash and medical benefits paid by private insurance companies under standard workers' compensation policies.

Series Bf518. Includes net cash and medical benefits paid by competitive and exclusive state funds and federal workers' compensation programs, and, starting in 1970, cash benefits paid by the federal Black Lung Benefits program. Data for fiscal years for some funds.

Series Bf519. Cash and medical benefits paid by self-insurers plus the value of medical benefits paid by employers carrying workers' compensation policies that exclude standard medical coverage. Estimated from available state data.

Series Bf520. Includes benefits paid by self-insurers with an additional 5–10 percent added to allow for administrative costs plus the premiums written by private carriers and state funds. Also includes benefits paid and administrative costs of federal system for government employees. According to Schmulowitz (1992, notes to Tables 5 and 6, p. 57), this includes the portion of the federal Black Lung Benefits program financed from employer contributions. This series equals the sum of benefits divided by the size of the covered payroll.

Series Bf521. Excludes programs financed from general revenue – most federal Black Lung Benefits programs and supplemental pensions in a few states. Through 1991, the sources give this figure directly. In updates for 1992–1995, this figure was calculated as benefits per $1 of cost multiplied by cost per $100 of payroll.

Series Bf522–524. These are estimates for coverage of workers and, consequently, employers' costs and benefits per $100 of payroll based on the methods for estimating coverage used in the publications from the NASI. These are the estimates that will be updated in future years. For descriptions of the difference in the procedures for estimating these series, see the NASI publication for 1994–1995 in the source notes (pp. 9–13).

TABLE Bf525–534 Black Lung Benefits – recipients and payments: 1970–1998

Contributed by Price V. Fishback and Melissa A. Thomasson

	Persons receiving benefits								Benefits paid by Social Security Administration	
	Claim filed prior to July 1, 1973				Claim filed after July 1, 1973					
	Total	Miners	Widows	Dependents	Total	Miners	Widows	Dependents	Monthly amount	Annual amount
	Bf525	Bf526	Bf527	Bf528	Bf529	Bf530	Bf531	Bf532	Bf533	Bf534
Year	Number	Number	Number	Number	Number	Number	Number	Number	Thousand dollars	Thousand dollars
1970	111,976	43,921	24,889	43,166	—	—	—	—	12,500	111,000
1971	231,729	77,213	67,358	87,158	—	—	—	—	27,200	378,900
1972	298,963	101,802	88,067	109,094	—	—	—	—	37,800	554,400
1973	461,491	159,837	124,154	177,500	—	—	—	—	63,700	1,045,200
1974	487,216	169,097	134,700	183,419	—	—	—	—	71,500	951,300
1975	482,311	165,405	139,407	177,499	—	—	—	—	75,500	947,700
1976	469,655	158,087	142,495	169,073	—	—	—	—	77,400	963,300
1977	457,399	148,720	144,543	164,136	—	—	—	—	80,500	942,200
1978	439,970	138,648	145,829	155,493	—	—	—	—	82,300	965,100
1979	418,948	129,558	146,527	142,863	83,887	30,739	19,366	33,177	86,500	983,100
1980	399,477	120,235	146,603	132,639	139,073	52,922	26,739	58,223	91,400	1,032,000
1981	376,505	111,249	146,173	119,083	163,401	62,787	30,517	68,266	91,700	1,081,300
1982	354,569	102,234	144,863	107,472	173,972	61,727	32,689	78,738	90,800	1,076,000
1983	333,358	93,694	142,967	96,697	166,043	64,181	35,178	65,871	86,300	1,055,800
1984	313,822	85,658	140,995	87,169	163,166	62,785	36,495	62,982	85,300	1,038,000
1985	294,846	77,836	138,328	78,682	160,437	60,906	37,827	60,817	83,700	1,025,000
1986	275,783	70,253	135,003	70,497	156,892	59,014	38,895	58,058	78,900	971,000
1987	258,988	63,573	131,561	63,854	153,769	57,095	40,346	55,345	76,800	940,000
1988	241,626	56,977	127,322	57,327	150,123	54,920	41,607	52,553	73,500	904,000
1989	225,764	51,048	123,220	51,496	145,289	52,258	42,691	49,245	72,000	882,000
1990	210,678	45,643	118,705	46,330	139,854	49,306	43,404	45,996	70,000	863,400
1991	196,419	40,703	114,046	41,670	134,205	46,450	43,831	42,745	68,400	844,400
1992	182,396	35,971	109,091	37,334	128,761	43,723	43,967	39,846	66,500	822,500
1993	168,365	31,664	103,334	33,367	123,213	40,866	44,103	36,964	64,100	794,300
1994	155,172	27,828	97,414	29,930	117,569	37,970	44,073	34,194	60,600	751,900
1995	143,011	24,573	91,517	26,921	111,769	35,220	43,688	31,499	56,100	696,700
1996	131,143	21,477	85,559	24,107	105,923	32,452	43,155	28,923	52,600	654,600
1997	119,233	18,488	79,238	21,507	100,352	29,839	42,468	26,601	49,255	614,888
1998	109,271	15,964	73,420	19,887	—	—	—	—	46,204	576,389

Sources

Series Bf525–528 and Bf533–534, *Social Security Bulletin: Annual Statistical Supplement* (1999), Table 9.D1, p. 338. Series Bf529–532, U.S. Department of Labor, *Office of Workers' Compensation Programs Annual Report to Congress, FY 1996*.

Documentation

Established by the federal Coal Mine Health and Safety Act of 1969, the Black Lung Benefits program provides monthly benefit payments to coal miners who are totally disabled as a result of pneumoconiosis, to the widows of coal miners who died as a result of pneumoconiosis, and to their dependents. Until October 1, 1997, the Social Security Administration has been responsible for the payment and administration of benefits with respect to Part B claims filed through June 30, 1973 (and for certain survivor cases before December 31, 1973). As a result, series Bf525–528 and Bf533–534 reflect payments made to beneficiaries resulting from Part B claims made prior to July 1, 1973. These payments are financed from the general funds of the Treasury.

Under the Black Lung Benefits Act of 1972, the U.S. Department of Labor (DOL) has jurisdiction over Part C claims (generally claims arising July 1, 1973, and later). Different financing provisions are applicable to these claims. Data on claims filed with the DOL are included in series Bf529–532.

Under the law, the basic Black Lung Benefits rate is 37.5 percent of the monthly pay rate for federal employees in the first step of grade GS-2. The basic rate to a miner or widow may be increased according to the number of qualified dependents: 50 percent of the basic benefit rate if one dependent qualifies, 75 percent for two dependents, and 100 percent for three or more dependents. Because Black Lung payments are tied directly to federal employee salary scales, increases are automatically payable when federal salaries are increased. If a miner or surviving spouse is receiving workers' compensation, unemployment compensation, or Disability Insurance payment under state law, the Black Lung Benefit is offset by the amount being paid under these other programs.

All coal mine operators are required to pay an excise tax, based on their tonnage and price of coal sold, to support payment of benefits to miners under the Act and to pay for the cost of administering the Act. In addition, coal mine operators are required, either directly or through insurance, to provide for the payment of benefits to miners when they are the responsible employer of the miners. Benefits for recipients who worked in mines before 1970, for whom an employer cannot be designated responsible, or for whom the employer defaults on payments are paid from a trust fund funded by taxes on coal production.

TABLE Bf535–544 Medicare cost sharing and premium amounts: 1966–1999[1]

Contributed by Price V. Fishback and Melissa A. Thomasson

	Hospital Insurance					Supplementary Medical Insurance				
	Deductible and copayment							Monthly premium		
		Inpatient hospital daily copayment							Government contribution for	
	Inpatient hospital deductible (IHD) first 60 days	Days 61–90	Lifetime reserve days after 90 days	Skilled-nursing facility daily copayment after 20 days	Monthly premium for voluntary purchase by persons not covered by the HI program	Annual deductible	Coinsurance rate	Individual contributions for all enrollees	Aged enrollees	Disabled enrollees
	Bf535	Bf536	Bf537	Bf538	Bf539	Bf540	Bf541	Bf542	Bf543	Bf544
Year	Dollars	Dollars	Dollars	Dollars	Dollars	Dollars	Percent	Dollars	Dollars	Dollars
1966	40	10	—	—	—	50	20	3.00	3.00	—
1967	40	10	—	5.00	—	50	20	3.00	3.00	—
1968	40	10	20	5.00	—	50	20	4.00	4.00	—
1969	44	11	22	5.50	—	50	20	4.00	4.00	—
1970	52	13	26	6.50	—	50	20	5.30	5.30	—
1971	60	15	30	7.50	—	50	20	5.60	5.60	—
1972	68	17	34	8.50	—	50	20	5.80	5.80	—
1973	72	18	36	9.00	33	60	20	6.30	6.30	22.70
1974	84	21	42	10.50	36	60	20	6.70	6.70	29.30
1975	92	23	46	11.50	40	60	20	6.70	8.30	30.30
1976	104	26	52	13.00	45	60	20	7.20	14.20	30.80
1977	124	31	62	15.50	54	60	20	7.70	16.90	42.30
1978	144	36	72	18.00	63	60	20	8.20	18.60	41.80
1979	160	40	80	20.00	69	60	20	8.70	18.10	41.30
1980	180	45	90	22.50	78	60	20	9.60	23.00	41.40
1981	204	51	102	25.50	89	60	20	11.00	34.20	62.20
1982	260	65	130	32.50	113	75	20	12.20	37.00	72.00
1983	304	76	152	38.00	113	75	20	12.20	41.80	80.00
1984	356	89	178	44.50	155	75	20	14.60	43.80	94.00
1985	400	100	200	50.00	174	75	20	15.50	46.50	89.90
1986	492	123	246	61.50	214	75	20	15.50	46.50	66.10
1987	520	130	260	65.00	226	75	20	17.90	53.70	88.10
1988	540	135	270	67.50	234	75	20	24.80	74.40	72.40
1989 [2]	560	—	—	25.25	156	75	20	31.90	83.70	40.70
1990	592	148	296	74.00	175	75	20	28.60	85.40	59.20
1991	628	157	314	78.50	177	100	20	29.90	95.30	82.10
1992	652	163	326	81.50	192	100	20	31.80	89.80	129.80
1993	676	169	338	84.50	221	100	20	36.60	104.40	129.20
1994	696	174	348	87.00	245	100	20	41.10	82.50	111.10
1995	716	179	358	89.50	261	100	20	46.10	100.10	165.50
1996	736	184	368	92.00	289	100	20	42.50	127.30	167.70
1997	760	190	380	95.00	311	100	20	43.80	131.40	177.00
1998	764	191	382	95.50	309	100	20	43.80	132.00	150.40
1999	768	192	384	96.00	309	100	20	45.50	139.10	160.50

[1] Information in the table based on rules beginning in July, through 1983, and in January thereafter.

[2] Program changes in this year produce irregularities in some series. See text.

Source

Social Security Bulletin: Annual Statistical Supplement (1999), Table 2.C.1, p. 106.

Documentation

Medicare was established as part of the Social Security Amendments of 1965 as a health insurance program for the aged that complemented retirement, survivors, and disability benefits under Title II of the Social Security Act. It consists of two separate but coordinated programs: Part A (Hospital Insurance, or HI) and Part B (Supplementary Medical Insurance, or SMI).

For a full, detailed summary of Medicare and a history of its provisions, consult the *Social Security Bulletin: Annual Statistical Supplement*, 1997.

These series do not reflect Medicare changes in the Balanced Budget Act of 1997, enacted August 5 (Public Law 105-33).

HI provides beneficiaries with four kinds of care: (1) inpatient hospital care, (2) inpatient care in a skilled-nursing facility, (3) home health care, and (4) hospice care. As of January 1, 1996, once a Medicare beneficiary has paid the inpatient hospital deductible (IHD), series Bf535, all remaining hospital costs for the first sixty days in a benefit period are paid by Medicare. From the sixty-first day through the ninetieth day in a benefit period, the patient pays a daily coinsurance amount, series Bf536, equal to one fourth the amount of the inpatient hospital deductible. Further, since 1968, each HI beneficiary has a "lifetime reserve" of sixty days that may be used when the covered days within a benefit period have been exhausted. Lifetime reserve days may be used only once, and the patient must pay one half the inpatient hospital deductible as the daily coinsurance amount, series Bf537. Since 1967, the HI program has provided the opportunity for care in a skilled-nursing facility. After twenty days, the patient pays a coinsurance payment per day of one eighth of the IHD, series Bf538.

Some special changes in 1989 led to certain odd figures in that year. After the IHD for the first sixty days, series Bf535, had been paid by the beneficiary, Medicare paid the balance of expenses for covered hospital services, regardless of the number of days of hospitalization; hence, no values are included in series Bf536–537. Also, the beneficiary paid a coinsurance rate equal to 20 percent of the estimated average daily cost of covered skilled-nursing facility care for the first eight days of care.

(continued)

TABLE Bf535–544 Medicare cost sharing and premium amounts: 1966–1999 *Continued*

Individuals who are eligible for Social Security or Railroad Retirement benefits are eligible for premium-free HI when they reach age 65. Workers and their spouses with a sufficient period of Medicare-only coverage in federal, state, or local government employment are also eligible at age 65. HI is also provided to disabled beneficiaries who have been entitled to Social Security or Railroad Retirement disability benefits for at least twenty-four months, and government employees with Medicare-only coverage who have been disabled for more than twenty-nine months. Insured workers and their spouses and children who have end-stage renal disease and who require kidney dialysis or a kidney transplant are eligible regardless of age.

Since July 1973, most persons age 65 or older and otherwise ineligible for HI have been permitted to enroll voluntarily and pay the monthly premium for HI if they also enroll in SMI. Beginning in 1993, Omnibus Budget Reconciliation legislation stipulated that individuals and their spouses with at least thirty quarters of Social Security coverage were eligible for a reduced premium over the period 1994–1997. The reduced premiums for each year in this period were $184, $183, $188, and $187, respectively.

Financing for the HI program is provided through a tax on earnings that is separate from the tax used to finance Old-Age, Survivors, and Disability Insurance (OASDI) benefits. Prior to January 1991, the OASDI and HI taxes were applied to the same maximum earnings base. Since that time, the earnings base for HI has increased; the Omnibus Budget Reconciliation Act of 1993 repealed the dollar limit and wages and self-employment income subject to HI taxes. The HI contribution rate of 1.45 percent applies equally to employers and employees, and the rate for the self-employed equals the combined rate of 2.9 percent. Income from contributions is channeled into the federal HI trust fund, from which HI benefits and administrative costs are paid. After 1977, the Health Care Financing Administration (HCFA) assumed responsibility for administering the program from the Social Security Administration.

The SMI program covers medically necessary services and supplies such as the following: (1) physician's, surgeon's, and some Medicare-approved practitioners' services; (2) services in an emergency room or outpatient clinic; (3) laboratory tests, X-rays, and other radiology services; (4) mental health care in a partial hospitalization psychiatric program; (5) ambulatory surgical center services; (6) physical and occupational therapy, and speech pathology services; (7) comprehensive outpatient rehabilitation facility services, and certain treatments of a mental illness; (8) radiation therapy, renal (kidney) dialysis and transplants, and heart and liver transplant under certain limited conditions; (9) approved durable medical equipment for home use; and (10) certain drugs and biologicals.

Cost-sharing contributions are required for participants in SMI. Beneficiaries must pay the following: an annual deductible, series Bf540; coinsurance payments as a percentage of the bill, series Bf541; charges above the Medicare allowed charge; and charges for services that are not covered by Medicare. Noncovered services include routine physical examinations, long-term nursing care, and certain other health care needs such as eyeglasses. In addition, the insured pays a monthly premium, series Bf542. The government then pays a supplemental premium for the aged and, since July 1973, for the disabled, series Bf543–544.

Except for aliens, all persons age 65 and older and all disabled persons entitled to coverage under HI are eligible to enroll in the SMI program on a voluntary basis by paying a monthly premium. Premiums are channeled into the federal SMI trust fund, and the program is administered by HCFA.

Series Bf540–541. Beginning in April 1968, professional inpatient services of pathologists and radiologists were not subject to either a deductible or coinsurance for SMI. However, after 1980, the pathologists' and radiologists' services were not subject to a deductible or coinsurance only as long as the physician accepted assignment (agreed to accept Medicare's determination of "reasonable charges" as the full fee for the service). Effective in October 1982, these services once again became subject to coinsurance. In 1973 only, home health services were not subject to coinsurance under SMI. In 1981 only, home health services were not subject to a deductible.

Series Bf542. In 1973, the monthly premium for SMI for the enrollee was reduced temporarily to $5.80 in July and $6.10 in August by the Cost of Living Council. For 1989, the monthly premium reported in the table includes the standard monthly SMI premium and a supplemental monthly flat premium under the Medicare Catastrophic Coverage Act of 1988. The amount shown is for most Part B enrollees. Residents of Puerto Rico and other territories and commonwealths, as well as other persons enrolled in Part B only, paid different supplemental flat premiums, so that the amount shown in the table is larger than the amount paid by these individuals. The Omnibus Budget Reconciliation Act of 1989 revised the methodology for determining the 1990 SMI premium for enrollees. Before the revision, the rate would have been $29.

Series Bf542–543. The monthly premium for SMI for both the enrollee and the government did not change to $4 until April 1968.

TABLE Bf545–557 Medicare trust fund for hospital insurance – receipts, expenditures, and assets: 1966–1998

Contributed by Price V. Fishback and Melissa A. Thomasson

	Receipts								Expenditures				
					Reimbursements from general revenues						Administrative expenses		
Year	Total	Payroll taxes	Income from taxation of benefits	Railroad retirement account transfers	Uninsured persons	Military wage credits	Premium receipts from voluntary enrollees	Interest on investments and other income	Total	Benefit payment	Total	As a percentage of benefit payments	Trust fund assets at year-end
	Bf545	Bf546	Bf547	Bf548	Bf549	Bf550	Bf551	Bf552	Bf553	Bf554	Bf555	Bf556	Bf557
	Million dollars	Million dollars	Million dollars	Million dollars	Million dollars	Million dollars	Million dollars	Million dollars	Million dollars	Million dollars	Million dollars	Percent	Million dollars
1966	1,943	1,858	—	16	26	11	—	32	999	891	108	12.1	944
1967	3,559	3,152	—	44	301	11	—	51	3,430	3,353	77	2.3	1,073
1968	5,287	4,116	—	54	1,022	22	—	74	4,277	4,179	99	2.4	2,083
1969	5,279	4,473	—	64	617	11	—	113	4,857	4,739	118	2.5	2,505
1970	5,979	4,881	—	66	863	11	—	158	5,281	5,124	157	3.1	3,202
1971	5,732	4,921	—	66	503	48	—	193	5,900	5,751	150	2.6	3,034
1972	6,403	5,731	—	63	381	48	—	180	6,503	6,318	185	2.9	2,935
1973	10,821	9,944	—	99	451	48	2	278	7,289	7,057	232	3.3	6,467
1974	12,024	10,844	—	132	471	48	5	523	9,372	9,099	272	3.0	9,119
1975	12,980	11,502	—	138	621	48	7	664	11,581	11,315	266	2.4	10,517
1976	13,766	12,727	—	143	—	141	9	746	13,679	13,340	339	2.5	10,605
1977	15,856	14,114	—	—	803	143	12	784	16,019	15,737	283	1.8	10,442
1978	19,213	17,324	—	214	688	141	13	834	18,178	17,682	496	2.8	11,477
1979	22,825	20,768	—	191	734	141	16	975	21,073	20,623	450	2.2	13,228
1980	26,097	23,848	—	244	697	141	18	1,149	25,577	25,064	512	2.0	13,749
1981	35,725	32,959	—	276	659	207	22	1,603	30,726	30,342	384	1.3	18,748
1982	37,998	34,586	—	351	808	207	24	2,022	36,144	35,631	513	1.4	8,164
1983	44,570	37,259	—	358	878	3,456	27	2,593	39,877	39,337	540	1.4	12,858
1984	46,720	42,288	—	351	752	250	33	3,046	43,887	43,257	629	1.5	15,691
1985	51,397	47,576	—	371	766	−719	41	3,362	48,414	47,580	834	1.8	20,499
1986	59,267	54,583	—	364	566	91	43	3,619	50,422	49,758	664	1.3	39,957
1987	64,064	58,648	—	368	447	94	38	4,469	50,289	49,496	793	1.6	53,732
1988	69,239	62,449	—	364	475	80	41	5,830	53,331	52,517	815	1.6	69,640
1989	76,721	68,369	—	379	515	86	55	7,317	60,803	60,011	792	1.3	85,558
1990	80,372	72,013	—	367	413	−993	122	8,451	66,997	66,239	758	1.1	98,933
1991	88,839	77,851	—	352	605	89	432	9,510	72,570	71,549	1,021	1.4	115,202
1992	93,836	81,745	—	374	621	86	522	10,487	85,015	83,895	1,121	1.3	124,022
1993	98,187	84,133	—	400	367	81	675	12,531	94,391	93,487	904	1.0	127,818
1994	109,570	95,280	1,639	413	506	80	907	10,745	104,545	103,282	1,263	1.2	132,844
1995	115,027	98,421	3,913	396	462	61	954	10,820	117,604	116,368	1,236	1.1	130,267
1996	124,603	110,585	4,069	401	419	−2,293	1,199	10,222	129,929	128,632	1,297	1.0	124,942
1997	130,154	114,670	3,558	419	481	70	1,319	9,637	139,452	137,762	1,690	1.2	115,643
1998	140,547	124,317	5,067	419	34	67	1,316	9,327	135,771	133,990	1,782	1.3	120,419

Source

Social Security Bulletin, Annual Statistical Supplement (1999), Table 8.A.1, p. 311. The original source of the series is the 1996 Annual Report of the Board of Trustees of the federal Hospital Insurance (HI) trust fund, Table II.D2.

Documentation

This table provides information on the Medicare trust fund for HI. The trust fund reports data on receipts from payroll taxes, premiums of voluntary enrollees, transfers from Railroad Retirement accounts, and reimbursements from general revenues for uninsured persons and military wage credits. The table also provides information on expenditures for benefit payments and administrative expenses. For more detailed information on the Medicare program itself, see the text for Table Bf535–544.

Series Bf548–549. For series Bf548, no transfer occurred in 1977 because of the change in transfer dates from August to June. The 1978 transfer reflects benefits and administrative costs from July 1977 to September 1978. Similarly, for series Bf549, no transfer occurred in 1976 because of the change in transfer dates from December to March. The 1977 transfer reflects benefits and administrative expenses from July 1976 to September 1977.

Series Bf550. In 1977, includes $2 million in reimbursements from general revenues for costs arising from the granting of deemed wage credits to persons of Japanese ancestry who were interned during World War II. The data reported for 1938 reflect the lump-sum general revenue transfer, as provided for in section 151 of Public Law 98-21. Amounts in 1985, 1990, and 1996 include a lump-sum general revenue transfer as provided for in section 151 of Public Law 98-21. The amounts transferred were −$805 million, −$1,100 million, and −$2,366 million, respectively.

Series Bf552. Includes recoveries of amounts reimbursed from the trust fund that are not obligations of the trust fund, as well as a small amount of miscellaneous income. In 1993, includes $1,805 million transferred from Supplementary Medical Insurance (SMI) Catastrophic Coverage Reserve Fund as provided for by Public Law 102-394.

Series Bf554. Amounts reported as benefit payments include the costs of Peer Review Organizations, beginning with the implementation of the Prospective Payment System on October 1, 1983. In 1998, includes monies transferred from the SMI trust fund for home health agency costs, as provided for by Public Law 105-33.

Series Bf555. Data on administrative expenses include the costs of experimental and demonstration projects.

Series Bf557. In 1982, total assets reported exclude $12,437 million loaned to the Old-Age, Survivors Insurance trust fund. Repayments of $1,824 million and $10,613 million occurred in 1985 and 1986, respectively. Amounts reported in those years reflect the repayments.

TABLE Bf558–567 Medicare trust fund for Supplementary Medical Insurance – receipts, expenditures, and assets: 1966–1998

Contributed by Price V. Fishback and Melissa A. Thomasson

	Receipts						Expenditures			
		Premiums from participants								
	Total	Total	Aged premiums	Disabled premiums	Government contributions	Interest and other income	Total	Benefit payments	Administrative expenses	Trust fund assets at year-end
	Bf558	Bf559	Bf560	Bf561	Bf562	Bf563	Bf564	Bf565	Bf566	Bf567
Year	Million dollars	Million dollars	Million dollars	Million dollars	Million dollars	Million dollars	Million dollars	Million dollars	Million dollars	Million dollars
1966	324	322	322	—	0	2	203	128	75	122
1967	1,597	640	640	—	933	24	1,307	1,197	110	412
1968	1,711	832	832	—	858	21	1,702	1,518	184	421
1969	1,839	914	914	—	907	18	2,061	1,865	196	199
1970	2,201	1,096	1,096	—	1,093	12	2,212	1,975	237	188
1971	2,639	1,302	1,302	—	1,313	24	2,377	2,117	260	450
1972	2,808	1,382	1,382	—	1,389	37	2,614	2,325	289	643
1973	3,312	1,550	1,491	59	1,705	57	2,844	2,526	318	1,111
1974	4,124	1,804	1,664	140	2,225	95	3,728	3,318	410	1,506
1975	4,673	1,918	1,759	158	2,648	107	4,735	4,273	462	1,444
1976	5,977	2,060	1,878	183	3,810	107	5,622	5,080	542	1,799
1977	7,805	2,247	2,030	217	5,386	172	6,505	6,038	467	3,099
1978	9,056	2,470	2,221	248	6,287	299	7,755	7,252	503	4,400
1979	9,768	2,719	2,451	267	6,645	404	9,265	8,708	557	4,902
1980	10,874	3,011	2,707	304	7,455	408	11,245	10,635	610	4,530
1981	15,374	3,722	3,356	366	11,291	361	14,028	13,113	915	5,877
1982	16,580	3,697	3,341	356	12,284	599	16,227	15,455	772	6,230
1983	19,824	4,236	3,845	391	14,861	727	18,984	18,106	878	7,070
1984	23,180	5,167	4,721	445	17,054	959	20,552	19,661	891	9,698
1985	25,106	5,613	5,105	508	18,250	1,243	23,880	22,947	933	10,924
1986	24,665	5,722	5,218	504	17,802	1,141	27,299	26,239	1,060	8,291
1987	31,844	7,409	6,747	661	23,560	875	31,740	30,820	920	8,394
1988	35,825	8,761	7,983	778	26,203	861	35,230	33,970	1,260	8,990
1989	44,349	12,263	9,793	993	30,852	1,234	39,783	38,294	1,489	13,556
1990	45,913	11,320	10,311	1,008	33,035	1,558	43,987	42,468	1,519	15,482
1991	51,224	11,934	10,846	1,088	37,602	1,688	48,877	47,336	1,541	17,828
1992	57,237	14,077	12,814	1,263	41,359	1,801	50,830	49,260	1,570	24,235
1993	57,679	14,193	12,731	1,462	41,465	2,021	57,784	55,784	2,000	24,131
1994	55,607	17,386	15,569	1,817	36,203	2,018	60,317	58,618	1,699	19,422
1995	60,306	19,717	17,651	2,066	39,007	1,582	66,599	64,972	1,627	13,130
1996	85,609	18,763	16,654	2,109	65,035	1,811	70,408	68,598	1,810	28,332
1997	81,924	19,289	17,079	2,210	60,171	2,464	74,124	72,757	1,368	36,131
1998	87,711	20,933	18,594	2,338	64,068	2,711	77,630	76,125	1,505	46,212

Source

Social Security Bulletin: Annual Statistical Supplement (1999), Table 8.A2, p. 312. The original source for the series is the *1999 Annual Report of the Board of Trustees of the Federal Supplementary Insurance Trust Fund*, Table II.D2, and unpublished Treasury reports.

Documentation

For more detailed information on Medicare, consult the text for Table Bf535–544.

This table provides information on the Medicare trust fund for Supplementary Medical Insurance (SMI). The trust fund reports data on receipts from participant premiums, government contributions, and interest and other income. The table also provides information on expenditures for benefit payments and administrative expenses.

Series Bf558, Bf563–564, and Bf566–567. Data for 1989 include the impact of the Medicare Catastrophic Coverage Act of 1988.

Series Bf559. The receipts from premiums from participants in 1989 include catastrophic coverage premiums of $1.5 billion that were not distributed between aged and disabled enrollees.

Series Bf559–562. Section 708 of Title VII of the Social Security Act modified the provisions for the delivery of Social Security benefit checks when the regularly designated delivery day falls on a Saturday, Sunday, or legal public holiday. Delivery of benefit checks normally due in January 1982 occurred on December 31, 1981. The SMI premiums withheld from the checks ($264 million) and the general revenue matching contributions ($883 million) are thus included in 1981 premium income and general revenue income and are not included in the 1982 data. Similarly, delivery of benefit checks normally due in January 1988 occurred on December 31, 1987. The SMI premiums withheld from the checks ($692 million) and the general revenue matching contributions ($2,178 million) are thus included in 1987 premium income and general revenue income and are not included in the 1988 data. Delivery of benefit checks normally due in January 1993 occurred on December 31, 1992. The SMI premiums withheld from the checks ($1,089 million) and the general revenue matching contributions ($3,175 million) are thus included in 1992 premium income and general revenue income and are not included in the 1993 data. Delivery of benefit checks normally due in January 1999 occurred on December 31, 1998. The SMI premiums withheld from the checks ($1,512 million) and the general revenue matching contributions ($4,711 million) are thus added to the SMI trust fund on December 31, 1998. These amounts are excluded from the premium income and general revenue income for 1999.

Series Bf562. Government contributions include certain interest-adjustment items.

TABLE Bf558–567 Medicare trust fund for Supplementary Medical Insurance – receipts, expenditures, and assets: 1966–1998 *Continued*

Series Bf563. Interest and other income includes recoveries of amounts reimbursed from the trust fund that are not obligations of the trust fund, and other miscellaneous income. The data reported under trust fund year-end assets depends on the total net assets as well as the liabilities of the program. In 1989, the total premiums received include $1.5 billion as catastrophic coverage premiums that are not distributed between aged and disabled enrollees.

Series Bf565. Includes the impact of the transfer to the Hospital Insurance (HI) trust fund of the SMI reserve fund on March 31, 1993, as specified in Public Law 102-394. Actual benefit payments for fiscal year 1993 are $53,979 million; the amount transferred was $1,805 million. In 1998, the benefit payments are less monies transferred from the HI trust fund for home health agency costs, as provided by the Balanced Budget Act of 1997.

TABLE Bf568–581 Medicaid recipients and vendor payments, by eligibility category: 1972–1997

Contributed by Price V. Fishback and Melissa A. Thomasson

	Recipients							Vendor payments						
	Total	Age 65 or older	Blind	Permanently and totally disabled	Dependent children younger than 21	Adults in families with dependent children	Other Medicaid recipients	Total	Age 65 or older	Blind	Permanently and totally disabled	Dependent children younger than 21	Adults in families with dependent children	Other recipients
	Bf568	Bf569	Bf570	Bf571	Bf572	Bf573	Bf574	Bf575	Bf576	Bf577	Bf578	Bf579	Bf580	Bf581
Fiscal year	Thousand	Thousand	Thousand	Thousand	Thousand	Thousand	Thousand	Million dollars	Million dollars	Million dollars	Million dollars	Million dollars	Million dollars	Million dollars
1972	17,606	3,318	108	1,625	7,841	3,137	1,576	6,300	1,925	45	1,354	1,139	962	875
1973	19,622	3,496	101	1,804	8,659	4,066	1,495	8,639	3,235	65	2,015	1,426	1,446	452
1974	21,462	3,732	135	2,222	9,478	4,392	1,502	9,983	3,691	80	2,388	1,694	1,704	425
1975	22,007	3,615	109	2,355	9,598	4,529	1,800	12,242	4,358	93	3,052	2,186	2,062	492
1976	22,815	3,612	97	2,572	9,924	4,774	1,836	14,091	4,910	96	3,824	2,431	2,288	542
1977	22,831	3,636	92	2,710	9,651	4,785	1,959	16,239	5,499	116	4,767	2,610	2,606	641
1978	21,965	3,376	82	2,636	9,376	4,643	1,852	17,992	6,308	116	5,505	2,748	2,673	643
1979	21,520	3,364	79	2,674	9,106	4,570	1,727	20,472	7,046	108	6,774	2,884	3,021	638
1980	21,605	3,440	92	2,819	9,333	4,877	1,499	23,311	8,739	124	7,497	3,123	3,231	596
1981	21,890	3,367	86	2,993	9,581	5,187	1,364	27,204	9,926	154	9,301	3,508	3,763	552
1982	21,603	3,240	84	2,806	9,563	5,356	1,434	29,399	10,739	172	10,233	3,473	4,093	689
1983	21,554	3,371	77	2,844	9,535	5,592	1,129	32,391	11,954	183	11,184	3,836	4,487	747
1984	21,607	3,238	79	2,834	9,634	5,600	1,187	33,891	12,815	219	11,758	3,979	4,420	700
1985	21,814	3,061	80	2,937	9,757	5,518	1,214	37,508	14,096	249	13,203	4,414	4,746	798
1986	22,515	3,140	82	3,100	10,029	5,647	1,362	41,005	15,097	277	14,635	5,135	4,880	980
1987	23,109	3,224	85	3,296	10,168	5,599	1,418	45,050	16,037	309	16,507	5,508	5,592	1,078
1988	22,907	3,159	86	3,401	10,037	5,503	1,343	48,710	17,135	344	18,250	5,848	5,883	1,198
1989	23,511	3,132	95	3,496	10,318	5,717	1,175	54,500	18,558	409	20,476	6,892	6,897	1,268
1990	25,255	3,202	83	3,635	11,220	6,010	1,105	64,859	21,508	434	23,969	9,100	8,590	1,257
1991	28,280	3,359	85	3,983	13,415	6,778	658	77,048	25,453	475	27,798	11,690	10,439	1,193
1992	30,926	3,742	84	4,378	15,104	6,954	664	90,814	29,078	530	33,326	14,491	12,185	1,204
1993	33,432	3,863	84	4,932	16,285	7,505	763	101,709	31,554	589	38,065	16,504	13,605	1,391
1994	35,053	4,035	87	5,372	17,194	7,586	779	108,270	33,618	644	41,654	17,302	13,585	1,467
1995	36,282	4,119	92	5,767	17,164	7,604	1,537	120,141	36,527	848	48,570	17,976	13,511	2,708
1996	36,118	4,285	95	6,126	16,739	7,127	1,746	121,685	36,947	869	51,196	17,544	12,275	2,746
1997	34,872	3,955	—	6,129	15,266	6,803	2,719	124,430	37,721	—	54,130	15,658	12,307	4,612

Sources

For 1972, 1975, 1980, 1985–1996, *Social Security Bulletin, Annual Statistical Supplement* (1999), Table 8.E2, p. 329. For 1973–1974, 1976–1979, *Social Security Bulletin, Annual Statistical Supplement* (1988), Tables 7.E2 and 7.F2, pp. 300–2.

Documentation

Medicaid was established under Title XIX of the Social Security Act in 1965. It established a federal–state matching entitlement program that provides medical assistance for certain individuals and families with low incomes and resources. The program is a jointly funded, cooperative venture between the federal and state governments. Each state establishes its own eligibility standards, range of services, rates of payment, and administration. Consequently, the Medicaid programs vary considerably across states and within states over time. The preceding categories give a general indication of the types of people eligible for Medicare – individuals who qualify for Supplemental Security Income, Aid to Families with Dependent Children (now Temporary Assistance for Needy Families), children younger than 6 and pregnant women whose family incomes are near the poverty line, some Medicare participants, and a series of other needy individuals.

More detail on the program can be found in *Social Security Bulletin, Annual Statistical Supplement* (1997), pp. 108–13, or at the Internet site for the Health-Care Financing Administration.

Figures are the unduplicated number of recipients and total vendor payments. Beginning in fiscal year 1980, recipients' categories do not add to an unduplicated total because of the small number of recipients that are in more than one category during the year.

TABLE Bf582–590 Public assistance – vendor payments for medical care, by program: 1951–1975

Contributed by Price V. Fishback and Melissa A. Thomasson

	Total								
	Amount	As percentage of total public assistance payments	Title XIX (Medicaid)	For the aged under Title I	Old-Age Assistance	Aid to the Blind	Aid to the Permanently and Totally Disabled	Aid to Families with Dependent Children	General assistance
	Bf582	Bf583	Bf584	Bf585	Bf586	Bf587	Bf588	Bf589	Bf590
Year	Thousand dollars	Percent	Thousand dollars	Thousand dollars	Thousand dollars	Thousand dollars	Thousand dollars	Thousand dollars	Thousand dollars
1951	103,179	4.3	—	—	41,728	1,196	3,445	10,413	46,397
1952	139,539	5.7	—	—	64,520	1,888	9,187	12,839	51,105
1953	165,721	6.5	—	—	83,395	2,351	13,591	15,069	51,315
1954	190,851	7.2	—	—	92,676	2,545	17,124	16,772	61,733
1955	231,544	8.4	—	—	117,748	3,170	21,302	21,197	68,127
1956	268,866	9.4	—	—	141,918	3,892	26,062	24,833	72,161
1957	302,143	9.8	—	—	158,799	4,642	27,722	33,332	77,648
1958	357,758	10.4	—	—	176,827	5,688	31,342	51,114	92,786
1959	456,944	12.5	—	—	254,389	6,846	41,268	58,143	96,298
1960	522,228	13.8	—	5,348	295,743	7,950	50,110	61,093	101,983
1961	688,320	16.8	—	113,387	316,479	8,513	60,294	79,384	110,262
1962	924,978	20.8	—	250,830	388,434	9,854	77,409	96,336	102,115
1963	1,064,664	22.6	—	329,391	412,906	10,895	97,698	110,569	103,206
1964	1,255,131	24.7	—	444,970	432,237	11,577	117,692	137,832	110,823
1965	1,480,119	27.0	—	585,501	452,289	12,255	144,165	164,845	121,063
1966	2,007,626	31.8	1,193,768	293,442	277,766	5,623	78,485	74,059	84,484
1967	2,872,696	36.8	2,510,531	63,916	160,627	2,996	38,309	30,210	66,106
1968	4,096,133	41.9	3,783,095	65,267	105,294	2,698	36,598	27,193	75,989
1969	4,681,110	40.5	4,360,445	58,873	103,566	2,702	40,311	31,317	83,311
1970	5,605,610	38.7	5,506,940	—	—	—	—	—	98,670
1971	6,953,129	39.0	6,842,098	—	—	—	—	—	111,031
1972	8,804,716	44.0	8,707,524	—	—	—	—	—	97,192
1973	9,919,266	46.4	9,806,853	—	—	—	—	—	112,413
1974	11,782,345	57.0	11,476,418	—	—	—	—	—	305,927
1975	14,555,229	57.9	14,177,418	—	—	—	—	—	377,811

Source

Social Security Administration, *Social Security Bulletin: Annual Statistical Supplement* (1975), p. 187.

Documentation

The series here show the precursors of Medicaid in federal government provision of medical assistance. Beginning October 1, 1950, under the 1950 amendments, federal participation in vendor payments for medical care became possible in the assistance to old-age, blind, disabled, and families with dependent children programs. The federal government was not involved in medical assistance under the General Assistance programs, which were financed entirely from state and local funds. Medical assistance for the aged under Title I of the Social Security Act, series Bf585, was initiated in October 1960 under the 1960 amendments. Medicaid medical assistance under Title XIX of the Social Security Act, series Bf584, was initiated January 1966 under the 1965 amendments. Beginning in January 1970, medical assistance replaced the original medical assistance for the aged program under Title I and the medical vendor payments under Old-Age Assistance, Aid to the Blind, Aid to the Permanently and Totally Disabled, and Aid to Families with Dependent Children.

Series Bf584. Beginning in 1972, Medicaid spending under Title XIX includes payments for institutional services in intermediate care facilities.

Series Bf590. Complete data are not available.

TABLE Bf591–598 Supplemental Security Income program – persons receiving payments from federal or state governments: 1974–1998

Contributed by Price V. Fishback and Melissa A. Thomasson

				State supplementation				
					Federally administered		State-administered	
	Total	Federal and/or federally administered state supplementation	Federal with or without state supplementation	Total	Total	State supplement only	Total	State supplement only
	Bf591	Bf592	Bf593	Bf594	Bf595	Bf596	Bf597	Bf598
Year	Number	Number	Number	Number	Number	Number	Number	Number
1974	4,027,572	3,996,064	—	—	—	—	300,724	31,508
1975	4,359,625	4,314,275	3,893,419	1,987,409	1,684,018	420,856	303,391	45,350
1976	4,285,785	4,235,939	3,799,069	1,912,550	1,638,173	436,870	274,377	49,846
1977	4,287,299	4,237,692	3,777,856	1,927,340	1,657,645	459,836	269,695	49,607
1978	4,265,473	4,216,925	3,754,663	1,946,921	1,681,403	462,262	265,518	48,548
1979	4,202,727	4,149,575	3,687,119	1,941,572	1,684,283	462,456	257,289	53,152
1980	4,194,100	4,142,017	3,682,411	1,934,239	1,684,765	459,606	249,474	52,083
1981	4,067,421	4,018,875	3,590,103	1,874,844	1,625,279	428,772	249,565	48,546
1982	3,908,466	3,857,590	3,473,301	1,798,400	1,550,405	384,289	247,995	50,876
1983	3,955,767	3,901,497	3,589,521	1,811,614	1,557,714	311,976	253,900	54,270
1984	4,093,956	4,029,333	3,698,758	1,875,187	1,607,234	330,575	267,953	64,623
1985	4,200,177	4,138,021	3,799,092	1,915,503	1,660,847	338,929	254,656	62,156
1986	4,346,652	4,269,184	3,921,661	2,002,746	1,723,401	347,523	279,345	77,468
1987	4,457,847	4,384,999	4,019,297	2,078,503	1,806,847	365,702	271,656	72,848
1988	4,541,441	4,463,869	4,088,988	2,154,759	1,884,675	374,881	270,084	77,572
1989	4,672,577	4,593,059	4,206,390	2,224,122	1,949,585	386,669	274,537	79,518
1990	4,888,180	4,817,127	4,412,131	2,343,803	2,058,273	404,996	285,530	71,053
1991	5,199,539	5,118,470	4,729,639	2,512,220	2,204,329	388,831	307,891	81,069
1992	5,646,877	5,566,189	5,202,249	2,684,371	2,371,564	363,940	312,807	80,688
1993	6,064,502	5,984,330	5,635,995	2,849,887	2,536,349	348,335	313,538	80,172
1994	6,377,111	6,295,786	5,965,130	2,950,470	2,628,431	330,658	322,039	81,325
1995	6,515,753	6,514,134	6,194,493	2,817,408	2,517,805	319,641	299,603	61,619
1996	6,676,729	6,613,718	6,325,531	2,731,681	2,421,470	288,187	310,211	63,011
1997	6,564,613	6,494,985	6,211,867	3,029,449	2,372,479	283,118	656,970	69,628
1998	6,649,465	6,566,069	6,289,070	3,072,392	2,411,707	276,999	660,685	83,396

Sources

U.S. Social Security Administration, *Social Security Bulletin: Annual Statistical Supplement* (1999), Table 7.A3, p. 287. Annual data from earlier years are from *Social Security Bulletin: Annual Statistical Supplement* (1983) and *Social Security Bulletin: Annual Statistical Supplement* (1988).

Documentation

The Supplemental Security Income (SSI) program was implemented in 1974 and superseded the former programs of Old-Age Assistance, Aid to the Blind, and Aid to the Permanently and Totally Disabled, except in the U.S. territories of Puerto Rico, Guam, and the Virgin Islands. SSI provides income support to persons age 65 and older, and blind or disabled adults and children. The federal payment is based on the individual's countable income, although not all income is counted against the federal SSI benefit level. States have the option to supplement the SSI floor and are required to supplement the federal benefit rate under certain circumstances.

A detailed legislative history and program summary is available in the *Social Security Bulletin: Annual Statistical Supplement* (1997).

Data are reported in December of every year. In 1974, data were unavailable for some series in December, but were reported in January. These series are listed in the *Social Security Bulletin Annual Statistical Supplement* (1997), pp. 287–90.

Administration of SSI Payments

The administration of SSI payments is complex. Some persons receive only federal payments, others receive both federal payments and a state supplementation, and some receive federally administered state supplements. Details are described next.

Series Bf591. Sum of series Bf592 and Bf598.

Series Bf592. Includes persons receiving a federal payment, as well as those receiving a state supplement administered by the federal government. Equals series Bf593 plus series Bf596.

Series Bf593. Includes persons receiving a federal payment of some form, either a federal payment alone or a federal payment with a state supplement. The state supplementations are administered sometimes by the federal government and sometimes by the state government.

Series Bf594. Sum of series Bf595 and Bf597.

Series Bf595. Includes persons receiving either federally administered state supplements only, or both a federal payment and a federally administered state supplement.

Series Bf596. Includes persons receiving only federally administered state supplementation.

Series Bf597. Includes persons receiving either federally administered state supplementation only or both a federal payment and state-administered state supplementation.

Series Bf598. Includes persons receiving only state-administered state supplementation.

TABLE Bf599–620 Supplemental Security Income program – beneficiaries, payments, and monthly benefits, by source of funds and disability status: 1974–1999

Contributed by Price V. Fishback and Melissa A. Thomasson

	Total SSI payments				SSI average monthly benefit					
								State supplementation		
	Total	Federal	Federally administered state supplementation	State administered state supplementation	Total	Federally administered	Federal	Total	Federally administered	State administered
	Bf599	Bf600	Bf601	Bf602	Bf603	Bf604	Bf605	Bf606	Bf607	Bf608
Year	Thousand dollars	Thousand dollars	Thousand dollars	Thousand dollars	Dollars	Dollars	Dollars	Dollars	Dollars	Dollars
1974	5,245,719	3,833,161	1,263,652	148,906	114.76	112.83	—	—	—	37.75
1975	5,878,224	4,313,538	1,402,534	162,152	116.36	114.39	96.17	66.86	70.71	45.59
1976	6,065,842	4,512,061	1,388,154	165,627	121.53	119.70	101.72	70.24	73.63	50.00
1977	6,306,041	4,703,292	1,430,794	171,955	126.39	124.52	106.61	72.39	75.36	53.68
1978	6,552,068	4,880,691	1,490,947	180,430	131.79	129.61	111.98	73.02	75.00	58.91
1979	7,075,394	5,279,181	1,589,544	206,669	157.87	155.65	123.89	106.45	112.26	71.23
1980	7,940,734	5,866,354	1,848,286	226,094	170.42	167.77	143.35	96.93	99.15	79.85
1981	8,593,414	6,517,727	1,838,969	236,718	185.49	182.73	160.29	95.46	97.78	80.31
1982	8,981,328	6,907,043	1,798,453	275,832	198.87	195.83	174.72	94.75	95.81	88.08
1983	9,404,227	7,422,524	1,711,319	270,384	214.69	211.68	188.94	94.42	94.81	92.01
1984	10,371,790	8,281,017	1,792,089	298,684	221.87	219.01	196.16	97.46	97.61	96.60
1985	11,060,476	8,777,341	1,972,597	310,538	228.66	226.06	200.84	103.06	103.82	98.05
1986	12,081,025	9,498,047	2,243,332	339,646	246.93	244.48	215.40	114.14	115.47	105.93
1987	12,951,091	10,029,197	2,562,700	359,194	254.23	251.58	218.39	122.95	124.76	110.85
1988	13,786,207	10,734,202	2,670,561	381,444	263.09	260.18	227.49	122.80	122.68	123.60
1989	14,979,898	11,606,066	2,954,668	419,164	277.65	274.63	238.83	131.61	131.70	130.90
1990	16,598,680	12,893,805	3,239,154	465,721	303.19	299.22	261.47	140.11	139.79	141.01
1991	18,524,229	14,764,795	3,230,844	528,590	324.44	320.53	286.03	132.99	130.55	150.46
1992	22,232,503	18,246,934	3,435,476	550,093	361.63	358.49	329.74	121.70	118.08	149.14
1993	24,556,867	20,721,613	3,269,540	565,714	348.18	344.92	317.41	113.22	108.50	151.00
1994	25,876,570	22,175,233	3,115,854	585,483	353.86	350.54	325.26	107.22	101.46	154.15
1995	27,627,658	23,919,430	3,117,850	590,378	361.58	358.40	334.12	109.31	105.24	143.91
1996	28,791,924	25,264,878	2,987,596	539,450	366.40	362.75	339.24	110.00	104.58	152.31
1997	29,052,089	25,457,387	2,913,181	681,521	—	—	—	—	—	—
1998	30,216,345	26,404,793	3,003,415	608,137	—	—	—	—	—	—
1999	—	—	—	—	—	—	—	—	—	—

	Total SSI payments for assistance to			Persons receiving payments under program for			Federal monthly benefit rates			SSI average monthly benefits for		
	Aged	Blind	Disabled	Aged	Blind	Disabled	Individual in own household	Couple in own household	Increment for "essential person" in household	Aged	Blind	Disabled
	Bf609	Bf610	Bf611	Bf612	Bf613	Bf614	Bf615	Bf616	Bf617	Bf618	Bf619	Bf620
Year	Thousand dollars	Thousand dollars	Thousand dollars	Number	Number	Number	Dollars	Dollars	Dollars	Dollars	Dollars	Dollars
1974	2,503,407	130,195	2,601,936	2,307,722	75,528	1,644,322	146	219	73	93.15	143.30	143.78
1975	2,604,792	130,936	3,142,476	2,333,685	75,315	1,950,625	158	237	79	92.99	148.96	143.07
1976	2,508,483	137,793	3,419,543	2,175,442	77,223	2,032,675	168	252	84	96.33	155.32	147.21
1977	2,448,724	146,070	3,710,788	2,077,945	78,363	2,130,991	178	267	89	98.75	161.39	152.05
1978	2,432,738	152,210	3,965,611	1,995,982	78,028	2,191,145	189	284	94	102.96	167.19	156.78
1979	2,525,374	166,835	4,380,932	1,903,369	78,108	2,220,827	208	312	104	125.66	214.56	183.80
1980	2,734,270	190,075	5,013,948	1,838,381	79,139	2,276,130	238	357	119	131.75	215.70	200.06
1981	2,818,143	206,263	5,566,157	1,707,166	79,198	2,280,525	265	397	133	141.56	230.33	216.81
1982	2,824,003	216,936	5,908,841	1,578,968	77,929	2,251,013	284	426	143	150.06	244.79	231.48
1983	2,813,897	229,374	6,356,975	1,545,999	79,446	2,329,596	304	437	153	162.30	259.74	247.87
1984	2,974,122	248,762	7,143,212	1,562,064	80,948	2,449,947	314	472	157	162.55	268.30	258.08
1985	3,034,596	264,162	7,754,588	1,529,674	82,622	2,586,741	325	488	163	168.30	277.32	262.71
1986	3,096,142	277,102	8,699,773	1,506,496	83,557	2,755,401	336	504	168	178.20	290.23	283.08
1987	3,194,145	291,174	9,457,787	1,483,353	83,876	2,888,852	340	510	170	187.24	299.74	288.29
1988	3,298,922	302,135	10,176,906	1,464,459	83,316	2,992,606	354	532	177	193.32	309.47	295.86
1989	3,476,324	315,692	11,180,155	1,471,216	83,267	3,117,095	368	553	184	203.83	322.97	311.20

(continued)

TABLE Bf599–620 Supplemental Security Income program – beneficiaries, payments, and monthly benefits, by source of funds and disability status: 1974–1999 *Continued*

	Total SSI payments for assistance to			Persons receiving payments under program for			Federal monthly benefit rates			SSI average monthly benefits for		
	Aged	Blind	Disabled	Aged	Blind	Disabled	Individual in own household	Couple in own household	Increment for "essential person" in household	Aged	Blind	Disabled
	Bf609	Bf610	Bf611	Bf612	Bf613	Bf614	Bf615	Bf616	Bf617	Bf618	Bf619	Bf620
Year	Thousand dollars	Thousand dollars	Thousand dollars	Number	Number	Number	Dollars	Dollars	Dollars	Dollars	Dollars	Dollars
1990	3,736,104	334,120	12,520,568	1,484,160	84,109	3,319,911	386	579	193	218.81	345.17	339.43
1991	3,890,412	346,828	14,268,192	1,497,817	85,227	3,615,438	407	610	204	228.15	355.33	363.54
1992	4,139,612	370,769	17,710,514	1,504,586	86,070	4,055,105	422	633	211	234.35	366.06	408.72
1993	4,250,092	374,998	19,925,929	1,507,463	86,169	4,469,711	434	652	217	243.62	363.94	383.11
1994	4,366,528	372,461	21,131,001	1,499,367	85,609	4,790,658	446	669	223	250.13	369.30	386.04
1995	4,467,146	375,512	22,778,547	1,479,415	84,273	5,010,326	458	687	229	256.92	374.76	392.27
1996	4,507,202	371,869	23,905,578	1,446,321	82,815	5,145,850	470	705	235	268.04	382.97	393.78
1997	4,531,973	374,857	24,006,254	1,395,845	81,449	5,078,995	484	726	242	—	—	—
1998	4,424,877	366,452	25,304,721	1,369,206	81,029	5,190,815	494	741	—	—	—	—
1999	—	—	—	—	—	—	500	751	—	—	—	—

Sources

Most recent data for series Bf599–602 and Bf609–616, U.S. Social Security Administration, *Social Security Bulletin: Annual Statistical Supplement* (1999), Tables 7.A3 and 7.A4, pp. 287–8 and Table 2.B1, p. 90; (1997), Tables 7.A3 and 7.A4, pp. 288–9; and Table 2.B.1, p. 90. Most recent data for series Bf603–608 and Bf616–620, U.S. Social Security Administration, *Social Security Bulletin: Annual Statistical Supplement*, 1997, Tables 7.A3, and 7.A5, pp. 288–9 and Table 2.B.1, p. 92. Annual data from earlier years is from *Social Security Bulletin: Annual Statistical Supplement* (1981, 1983, and 1988).

Documentation

See Table Bf591–598 for a discussion of the Supplemental Security Income program.

Series Bf603–608 and Bf618–620. The series for average monthly payments reported here include retroactive payments. The *Annual Statistical Supplements* for 1998 and 1999 report the series excluding retroactive payments, which can be as much as 7 percent of average payments.

Series Bf612–614 and Bf618–620. As of December.

Series Bf615–617. The rates effective July 1 (1974–1983) and January 1 thereafter. Information for series Bf617 is no longer reported for years after 1996.

TABLE Bf621–633 Public assistance – recipients and annual payments, by program: 1933–1975 [Earlier estimates]

Contributed by Price V. Fishback and Melissa A. Thomasson

	Annual payments					Recipients							
									Aid to Families with Dependent Children				
	Old-Age Assistance	Aid to the Blind	Aid to the Permanently and Totally Disabled	Aid to Families with Dependent Children	General assistance	Old-Age Assistance	Aid to the Blind	Aid to the Permanently and Totally Disabled	Families	All persons	Children	General assistance	Institutional services in intermediate-care facilities
	Bf621 [1]	Bf622 [1]	Bf623 [1]	Bf624	Bf625	Bf626 [1]	Bf627 [1]	Bf628 [1]	Bf629	Bf630	Bf631	Bf632	Bf633
Year	Thousand dollars	Thousand dollars	Thousand dollars	Thousand dollars	Thousand dollars	Thousand	Thousand	Thousand	Thousand	Thousand	Thousand	Thousand	Thousand
1933	26,071	5,839	—	40,504	758,752	107	25	—	112	—	285	—	—
1934	32,244	7,073	—	40,636	1,200,615	206	33	—	113	—	280	—	—
1935	64,966	7,970	—	41,727	1,433,182	378	35	—	117	—	286	—	—
1936	155,500	12,800	—	49,700	437,100	1,106	45	—	162	546	404	4,545	—
1937	309,600	16,200	—	70,500	406,700	1,579	56	—	229	769	568	4,840	—
1938	394,900	19,000	—	97,600	475,600	1,779	67	—	281	935	688	5,177	—
1939	433,500	20,400	—	114,800	482,100	1,912	70	—	316	1,042	764	4,675	—
1940	472,800	21,700	—	133,400	392,200	2,070	73	—	372	1,222	895	3,618	—
1941	540,100	22,900	—	153,300	273,200	2,238	77	—	391	1,288	944	2,068	—
1942	593,400	24,600	—	158,400	180,400	2,230	79	—	349	1,158	851	1,000	—
1943	650,000	25,000	—	140,400	110,900	2,149	76	—	272	916	676	558	—
1944	690,700	25,300	—	135,100	89,300	2,066	72	—	254	862	639	477	—
1945	725,700	26,500	—	149,500	86,300	2,056	71	—	274	943	701	507	—
1946	819,800	30,700	—	208,400	120,400	2,196	77	—	346	1,190	885	673	—
1947	986,400	36,200	—	294,000	164,200	2,332	81	—	416	1,426	1,060	739	—
1948	1,128,200	41,300	—	362,800	198,500	2,498	86	—	475	1,632	1,214	842	—
1949	1,372,900	48,400	—	472,400	281,300	2,736	93	—	599	2,048	1,521	1,337	—

Notes appear at end of table

TABLE Bf621–633 Public assistance – recipients and annual payments, by program: 1933–1975 [Earlier estimates] *Continued*

	Annual payments					Recipients							
	Old-Age Assistance	Aid to the Blind	Aid to the Permanently and Totally Disabled	Aid to Families with Dependent Children	General assistance	Old-Age Assistance	Aid to the Blind	Aid to the Permanently and Totally Disabled	Aid to Families with Dependent Children: Families	Aid to Families with Dependent Children: All persons	Aid to Families with Dependent Children: Children	General assistance	Institutional services in intermediate-care facilities
	Bf621 [1]	Bf622 [1]	Bf623 [1]	Bf624	Bf625	Bf626 [1]	Bf627 [1]	Bf628 [1]	Bf629	Bf630	Bf631	Bf632	Bf633
Year	Thousand dollars	Thousand dollars	Thousand dollars	Thousand dollars	Thousand dollars	Thousand	Thousand	Thousand	Thousand	Thousand	Thousand	Thousand	Thousand
1950	1,453,900	52,600	8,000	547,200	292,800	2,786	97	69	651	2,233	1,661	866	—
1951	1,427,600	54,500	54,300	548,800	194,500	2,701	97	124	592	2,041	1,523	664	—
1952	1,462,900	59,600	81,500	538,000	169,500	2,635	98	161	596	1,991	1,495	587	—
1953	1,513,300	63,600	102,000	544,000	151,300	2,582	100	192	547	1,941	1,464	618	—
1954	1,497,600	65,200	119,800	573,100	196,000	2,553	102	222	604	2,173	1,639	880	—
1955	1,488,000	67,800	134,600	612,200	214,000	2,538	104	241	602	2,192	1,661	743	—
1956	1,529,000	72,900	150,100	634,900	197,200	2,499	107	266	615	2,270	1,731	731	—
1957	1,609,400	78,700	172,200	716,800	211,100	2,480	108	290	667	2,497	1,912	907	—
1958	1,647,400	81,500	196,600	839,900	303,300	2,438	110	325	755	2,486	2,181	1,246	—
1959	1,620,700	83,600	217,300	937,200	342,000	2,370	108	346	776	2,946	2,265	1,107	—
1960	1,626,000	86,100	236,400	994,400	319,500	2,305	107	369	803	3,073	2,370	1,244	—
1961	1,569,000	84,500	255,600	1,148,800	351,400	2,229	103	389	916	3,566	2,753	1,069	—
1962	1,566,100	83,900	281,100	1,289,800	289,500	2,183	99	428	932	3,789	2,844	900	—
1963	1,610,300	85,100	317,700	1,355,500	277,400	2,152	97	464	954	3,930	2,951	872	—
1964	1,606,600	86,200	355,600	1,496,500	270,300	2,120	95	509	1,012	4,219	3,170	779	—
1965	1,594,200	77,300	416,800	1,644,100	260,600	2,087	85	557	1,054	4,396	3,316	677	—
1966	1,630,100	84,700	487,200	1,849,900	251,900	2,073	84	588	1,127	4,666	3,526	663	—
1967	1,698,100	87,000	573,600	2,249,700	323,100	2,073	83	646	1,297	5,309	3,986	782	—
1968	1,673,200	87,800	655,800	2,823,800	419,500	2,027	81	702	1,522	6,086	4,555	826	14
1969	1,746,700	91,400	786,800	3,533,300	474,500	2,074	81	803	1,875	7,313	5,413	860	92
1970	1,866,100	97,500	975,500	4,857,200	632,400	2,082	81	935	2,552	9,659	7,033	1,056	163
1971	1,919,700	100,700	1,185,300	6,230,400	760,600	2,024	80	1,068	2,918	10,653	7,707	982	196
1972	1,894,000	104,700	1,392,900	7,019,600	741,000	1,933	80	1,169	3,123	11,069	7,986	865	—
1973	1,749,300	103,000	1,566,100	7,291,900	688,100	1,820	78	1,275	3,156	10,815	7,813	700	—
1974	4,800	100	3,000	7,990,800	825,400	19	(Z)	17	3,312	11,006	7,885	851	—
1975	4,600	100	2,900	9,348,900	1,138,000	19	(Z)	17	3,555	11,389	8,090	977	—

(Z) Fewer than 500 recipients.

[1] Beginning in 1974, includes only Puerto Rico, Guam, and the Virgin Islands. See text.

Sources

U.S. Social Security Administration, *Social Security Bulletin, Annual Statistical Supplement* (1975), Table 175, and *Social Security Bulletin, Annual Statistical Supplement* (1966), Table 113. For years 1933–1935: *Social Security Bulletin* 14 (9) (1951): 43.

Documentation

Prior to 1935 public assistance was a state and local responsibility. After the Social Security Administration Act of 1935, assistance programs financed in part by federal grants-in-aid were in effect on a statewide basis in 1936 in forty-two states for Old-Age Assistance, twenty-seven states for Aid to Dependent Children, and twenty-five states for Aid to the Blind. Programs have been in effect in the forty-eight contiguous states and the District of Columbia beginning 1938 for Old-Age Assistance, 1955 for Aid to Dependent Children, and 1953 for Aid to the Blind. Approval of the first plans for Aid to the Permanently and Totally Disabled was effective October 1950 and, in 1957, forty-four states and the District of Columbia were participating. Assistance payments for all the previously mentioned programs were still financed in part from federal funds and, with the exception of Nevada (Aid to the Permanently and Totally Disabled), these programs were in effect in all fifty states, the District of Columbia, Guam, Puerto Rico, and the Virgin Islands until 1974. General assistance, provided from state or local funds or both, is available to certain other categories of needy persons in all fifty-four jurisdictions.

Beginning in the *Social Security Bulletin, Annual Statistical Supplement* (1976), p. 200, data on the Public Assistance programs were reported from a different source, and the new series reported were considered not comparable with the previously listed series. See Table Bf634–648 for modern information on these programs back to 1960 and for 1955, 1950, 1945, 1940, and 1936.

Series Bf621–623 and Bf626–628. Beginning in 1974, includes only Puerto Rico, Guam, and the Virgin Islands, because the Old-Age Assistance, Aid to the Blind, and Totally Disabled programs for the United States were superceded by Supplementary Security Income, except in those territories.

Series Bf626–633. In December.

Series Bf630. Aid to Families with Dependent Children (AFDC) recipients include children and one or both parents, or one caretaker relative other than a parent, in families in which the requirements of such adults were considered in determining the amount of assistance. The figure is partially estimated before 1950. The program for Aid to Dependent Children began paying benefits to support payments for a mother or other relative caring for the child in 1950. Under the Public Welfare Amendments of 1962, the program was renamed Aid to Families with Dependent Children to reflect expanded coverage of the adults caring for the dependent children. The AFDC and the Emergency Assistance programs have been replaced by the Temporary Assistance for Needy Families program under the Personal Responsibility and Work Opportunity Reconciliation Act of 1996. The Act was designed to limit the length of time that families could receive assistance and promote a return to the workforce by those who are able. The original source may contain a typographical error for 1958 because the percentage of recipients who are children – series Bf631 divided by series Bf630 – is unusually high. The value reported here is believed to be true.

Series Bf632. Partly estimated. For certain periods, the series excludes data for Florida, Idaho, Indiana, Kentucky, Nebraska, Nevada, New Mexico, Tennessee, Texas, and Vermont. The number of recipients in 1933–1935 was not reported, but the number of cases was 3.246 million in 1933, 5.368 million in 1934, 2.89 million in 1935, and 1.51 million in 1936.

TABLE Bf634–648 Public assistance – recipients and annual payments, by program: 1936–1997 [Later estimates]

Contributed by Price V. Fishback and Melissa A. Thomasson

	Annual payments						Average monthly number of recipients								
										TANF/AFDC					
											Recipients				
	Old-Age Assistance	Aid to the Blind	Aid to the Permanently and Totally Disabled	TANF/AFDC	General assistance	Emergency assistance	Old-Age Assistance	Aid to the Blind	Aid to the Permanently and Totally Disabled	Families	Total	Children	General assistance	Emergency assistance	States with emergency assistance programs
	Bf634 [1]	Bf635 [1]	Bf636 [1]	Bf637	Bf638	Bf639	Bf640 [1]	Bf641 [1]	Bf642 [1]	Bf643	Bf644	Bf645	Bf646 [2]	Bf647	Bf648
Year	Thousand dollars	Thousand dollars	Thousand dollars	Thousand dollars	Thousand dollars	Thousand dollars	Thousand	Thousand	Thousand	Thousand	Thousand	Thousand	Thousand	Thousand	Number
1936	155,484	12,811	—	49,678	437,134	—	738	42.7	—	147	534	361	4,545	—	—
1940	475,704	21,838	—	133,770	404,963	—	1,986	71.6	—	349	1,182	840	3,618	—	—
1945	726,550	26,557	—	149,667	87,930	—	2,044	71.2	—	259	907	656	507	—	—
1950	1,461,624	52,698	7,967	551,653	298,262	—	2,783	95.5	63	644	2,205	1,637	866	—	—
1955	1,490,352	67,958	135,168	617,841	214,266	—	2,539	103.5	234	612	2,214	1,673	785	—	—
1960	1,629,541	86,231	237,366	1,000,784	322,465	—	2,330	107.4	359	787	3,005	2,314	1,071	—	—
1961	1,571,309	84,739	256,910	1,156,769	355,991	—	2,261	104.6	379	869	3,354	2,587	1,182	—	—
1962	1,571,162	84,039	282,711	1,298,774	292,709	—	2,196	99.9	409	931	3,676	2,818	902	—	—
1963	1,615,023	85,335	318,948	1,365,851	279,623	—	2,159	97.4	448	947	3,876	2,909	861	—	—
1964	1,612,983	86,558	357,856	1,510,352	272,737	—	2,131	96.2	488	992	4,118	3,091	782	—	—
1965	1,600,708	85,121	417,720	1,660,186	259,225	—	2,105	91.5	536	1,039	4,329	3,256	703	—	—
1966	1,633,675	85,615	487,301	1,863,925	263,866	—	2,077	84.4	572	1,088	4,513	3,411	636	—	—
1967	1,702,091	87,711	574,574	2,266,400	325,847	—	2,067	83.0	617	1,217	5,014	3,771	713	—	—
1968	1,676,632	88,885	658,589	2,849,298	421,211	—	2,032	81.3	674	1,410	5,705	4,275	789	—	—
1969	1,752,730	92,204	788,079	3,563,427	472,360	6,699	2,043	80.3	758	1,698	6,706	4,985	817	7.5	23
1970	1,862,412	98,292	999,861	4,852,964	618,319	11,396	2,061	80.4	877	2,208	8,466	6,214	957	7.5	23
1971	1,888,878	100,840	1,189,636	6,203,528	760,559	19,843	2,055	80.5	1,004	2,762	10,241	7,434	1,009	11.1	24
1972	1,876,755	105,515	1,390,509	6,909,260	740,499	44,180	2,003	80.6	1,133	3,049	10,947	7,905	889	19.9	27
1973	1,743,465	104,373	1,609,572	7,212,035	688,502	39,265	1,852	78.2	1,217	3,148	10,949	7,902	746	18.8	29
1974	4,725	88	2,947	7,916,563	825,408	64,031	19	0.5	17	3,230	10,864	7,822	758	31.3	29
1975	4,599	79	2,953	9,210,995	1,138,211	77,516	18	0.4	17	3,498	11,346	8,095	964	38.3	29
1976	4,783	75	3,066	10,140,543	1,227,865	55,673	19	0.4	17	3,579	11,304	8,001	934	27.5	26
1977	7,938	76	3,426	10,603,820	1,237,609	66,132	19	0.4	18	3,588	11,050	7,773	861	32.8	26
1978	5,076	82	3,754	10,730,415	1,205,381	80,919	19	0.4	19	3,522	10,570	7,402	793	34.5	26
1979	9,448	170	9,064	11,068,864	1,230,744	84,043	19	0.4	20	3,509	10,312	7,179	796	35.7	24
1980	8,873	135	8,702	12,475,245	1,442,278	113,238	19	0.3	21	3,712	10,774	7,419	945	48.6	27
1981	9,400	159	10,364	12,981,115	—	123,467	19	0.3	22	3,835	11,079	7,527	1,006	49.1	27
1982	8,039	139	9,869	12,877,906	—	102,344	19	0.3	22	3,542	10,258	6,903	1,141	27.5	27
1983	7,889	136	9,846	13,837,228	—	125,246	18	0.3	22	3,686	10,761	7,098	1,299	30.0	27
1984	7,839	129	10,057	14,503,710	—	141,137	18	0.3	22	3,714	10,831	7,144	1,364	32.1	27
1985	7,620	134	10,412	15,195,835	—	157,304	18	0.3	23	3,701	10,855	7,198	1,326	32.6	28
1986	7,532	135	10,976	16,033,074	—	178,284	17	0.3	24	3,763	11,038	7,334	1,303	34.8	28
1987	7,434	137	10,825	16,372,535	—	213,903	17	0.3	24	3,776	11,027	7,366	1,168	42.4	29
1988	7,354	131	11,012	16,826,794	—	278,906	17	0.3	24	3,749	10,915	7,329	1,106	48.8	30
1989	7,273	139	11,559	17,465,943	—	296,841	17	0.3	25	3,799	10,993	7,420	1,105	48.7	31

	Annual payments						Average monthly number of recipients								
										TANF/AFDC					
											Recipients				
	Old-Age Assistance	Aid to the Blind	Aid to the Permanently and Totally Disabled	TANF/AFDC	General assistance	Emergency assistance	Old-Age Assistance	Aid to the Blind	Aid to the Permanently and Totally Disabled	Families	Total	Children	General assistance	Emergency assistance	States with emergency assistance programs
	Bf634 [1]	Bf635 [1]	Bf636 [1]	Bf637	Bf638	Bf639	Bf640 [1]	Bf641 [1]	Bf642 [1]	Bf643	Bf644	Bf645	Bf646 [2]	Bf647	Bf648
Year	Thousand dollars	Thousand dollars	Thousand dollars	Thousand dollars	Thousand dollars	Thousand dollars	Thousand	Thousand	Thousand	Thousand	Thousand	Thousand	Thousand	Thousand	Number
1990	8,530	157	12,352	19,066,541	—	348,986	17	0.3	26	4,057	11,695	7,917	1,220	56.0	33
1991	11,088	218	19,006	20,930,600	—	302,894	17	0.3	27	4,467	12,930	8,715	1,332	59.7	34
1992	7,504	139	13,189	21,655,881	—	272,853	17	0.3	28	4,829	13,773	9,303	1,184	52.7	34
1993	8,791	131	14,044	22,688,016	—	387,113	16	0.3	28	5,012	14,205	9,574	1,161	56.8	35
1994	9,398	119	13,267	22,827,399	—	802,258	16	0.3	27	5,035	14,164	9,570	1,105	60.5	49
1995	8,124	106	12,636	21,608,686	—	3,447,361	16	0.2	26	4,798	13,417	9,134	922	84.1	50
1996	8,076	99	12,163	20,583,810	—	2,716,705	15	0.2	25	4,443	12,320	8,458	744	69.8	51
1997	—	—	—	22,031,399	—	403,138	—	—	—	3,747	10,375	7,277	645	81.8	34

[1] Beginning in 1974, includes only Puerto Rico, Guam, and the Virgin Islands. The Supplemental Security Income (SSI) program superseded these programs elsewhere.

[2] For the period 1936–1950, reports data collected as of December of each year.

Source

U.S. Social Security Administration, *Social Security Bulletin, Annual Statistical Supplement* (1999), Table 9.G1, p. 342, Table 9.K1, p. 351, and Table 9.L1, p. 352.

Documentation

See the text for Table Bf621–633 for more information.

Series Bf637 and Bf643–645. Thirty-four states had converted to Temporary Assistance to Needy Families from Aid to Families with Dependent Children as of January 1, 1997; eight phased in over the next five months; the remaining twelve waited until July 1, 1997.

Series Bf639 and Bf647. Reporting on emergency assistance was initiated in July 1969. These data represent the latest revisions provided by the Social Security Administration. The revised annual data for the period 1936–1959 are not available except in years ending in 0 and 5. Table Bf621–633 presents earlier estimates for these programs reported in a different way for the period 1936–1975.

Series Bf638. After 1980 information was not available.

TABLE Bf649–662 Public assistance – average monthly payment, by program: 1936–1997

Contributed by Price V. Fishback and Melissa A. Thomasson

	Earlier estimates							Later estimates						
	Old-Age Assistance	Aid to the Blind	Aid to the Permanently and Totally Disabled	Aid to Families with Dependent Children		General assistance	Institutional services, intermediate-care facilities	Old-Age Assistance	Aid to the Blind	Aid to the Permanently and Totally Disabled	Temporary Assistance to Needy Families/Aid to Families with Dependent Children		General assistance	Emergency assistance per family
				Per family	Per person						Per family	Per person		
	Bf649 [1]	Bf650 [1]	Bf651 [1]	Bf652	Bf653	Bf654 [2]	Bf655	Bf656 [1]	Bf657 [1]	Bf658 [1]	Bf659	Bf660	Bf661	Bf662 [3]
Year	Dollars	Dollars	Dollars	Dollars	Dollars	Dollars	Dollars	Dollars	Dollars	Dollars	Dollars	Dollars	Dollars	Dollars
1936	18.80	26.10	—	29.85	8.80	8.00	—	17.55	25.00	—	28.15	7.75	8.00	—
1937	19.45	27.20	—	31.50	9.35	8.50	—	—	—	—	—	—	—	—
1938	19.55	25.20	—	31.95	9.60	7.90	—	—	—	—	—	—	—	—
1939	19.30	25.45	—	31.75	9.65	8.30	—	—	—	—	—	—	—	—
1940	20.25	25.35	—	32.40	9.85	8.30	—	19.96	24.43	—	31.98	9.43	8.30	—
1941	21.25	25.80	—	33.65	10.20	9.40	—	—	—	—	—	—	—	—
1942	23.35	26.55	—	36.25	10.95	11.65	—	—	—	—	—	—	—	—
1943	26.65	27.95	—	41.55	12.35	14.55	—	—	—	—	—	—	—	—
1944	28.45	29.30	—	45.60	13.40	15.60	—	—	—	—	—	—	—	—
1945	30.90	33.50	—	52.05	15.15	16.55	—	29.62	31.07	—	48.18	13.75	16.55	—
1946	35.30	36.65	—	62.25	18.10	18.45	—	—	—	—	—	—	—	—
1947	37.40	39.60	—	63.00	18.40	20.60	—	—	—	—	—	—	—	—
1948	42.00	43.55	—	71.90	20.90	22.40	—	—	—	—	—	—	—	—
1949	44.75	46.10	—	74.20	21.70	21.25	—	—	—	—	—	—	—	—
1950	43.05	46.00	44.10	71.45	20.85	22.25	—	43.76	45.96	42.35	71.33	17.64	22.25	—
1951	44.55	48.05	46.45	75.80	22.00	22.90	—	—	—	—	—	—	—	—
1952	48.80	53.50	48.40	82.10	23.45	23.30	—	—	—	—	—	—	—	—
1953	48.90	54.05	47.90	82.30	23.20	22.05	—	—	—	—	—	—	—	—
1954	48.70	54.35	48.35	83.70	23.25	22.85	—	—	—	—	—	—	—	—
1955	50.05	55.55	48.75	85.50	23.50	23.30	—	48.92	54.72	48.24	84.17	23.26	22.74	—
1956	53.25	60.00	50.70	91.50	24.80	23.45	—	—	—	—	—	—	—	—
1957	55.50	62.20	52.35	95.15	25.40	22.70	—	—	—	—	—	—	—	—
1958	56.95	63.55	53.80	100.40	26.65	24.05	—	—	—	—	—	—	—	—
1959	56.70	65.60	54.15	103.70	27.30	25.05	—	—	—	—	—	—	—	—
1960	58.90	67.45	56.15	108.35	28.35	24.85	—	58.27	66.92	55.18	105.75	27.75	25.10	—
1961	57.60	68.05	57.05	114.65	29.45	26.15	—	57.91	67.50	56.50	110.97	28.74	25.11	—
1962	61.55	71.95	58.50	119.10	29.30	26.30	—	59.61	70.12	57.63	116.30	29.44	27.03	—
1963	62.80	73.95	59.85	122.40	29.70	27.45	—	62.34	72.98	59.30	120.19	29.36	27.07	—
1964	63.65	76.15	62.25	131.30	31.50	30.50	—	63.07	74.97	61.12	126.88	30.57	29.07	—
1965	63.10	81.35	66.50	136.95	32.85	31.65	—	63.37	77.54	64.95	133.20	31.96	30.72	—
1966	68.05	86.85	74.75	150.10	36.25	36.20	—	65.54	84.56	70.94	142.83	34.42	34.60	—
1967	70.15	90.45	80.60	161.70	39.50	39.40	—	68.61	88.08	77.64	155.19	37.67	38.07	—
1968	69.55	92.15	82.65	168.15	42.05	44.70	—	68.76	91.06	81.47	168.41	41.62	44.51	—
1969	73.90	98.75	90.15	176.05	45.15	50.25	153.05	71.51	95.72	86.68	174.89	44.28	48.15	117.23
1970	77.65	104.35	97.65	187.90	49.65	57.85	246.80	75.32	101.93	95.06	183.13	47.77	53.82	126.14
1971	77.50	106.50	102.25	190.90	52.30	64.80	265.70	76.60	104.39	98.78	187.16	50.48	62.82	148.54
1972	79.95	112.85	106.15	191.75	54.10	72.10	284.00	78.07	109.03	102.29	188.87	52.60	69.44	184.91
1973	76.15	112.00	109.75	195.20	56.95	82.00	—	78.44	111.29	110.25	190.91	54.89	76.87	174.05
1974	—	—	—	217.75	65.50	96.35	—	20.48	14.97	14.39	204.27	60.72	90.70	170.38

	Earlier estimates							Later estimates						
	Old-Age Assistance	Aid to the Blind	Aid to the Permanently and Totally Disabled	Aid to Families with Dependent Children		General assistance	Institutional services, intermediate-care facilities	Old-Age Assistance	Aid to the Blind	Aid to the Permanently and Totally Disabled	Temporary Assistance to Needy Families/Aid to Families with Dependent Children		General assistance	Emergency assistance per family
				Per family	Per person						Per family	Per person		
	Bf649 [1]	Bf650 [1]	Bf651 [1]	Bf652	Bf653	Bf654 [2]	Bf655	Bf656 [1]	Bf657 [1]	Bf658 [1]	Bf659	Bf660	Bf661	Bf662 [3]
Year	Dollars	Dollars	Dollars	Dollars	Dollars	Dollars	Dollars	Dollars	Dollars	Dollars	Dollars	Dollars	Dollars	Dollars
1975	—	—	—	—	—	—	—	20.74	15.22	14.67	219.44	67.65	98.40	168.85
1976	—	—	—	—	—	—	—	21.01	15.78	14.98	236.10	74.75	109.56	168.43
1977	—	—	—	—	—	—	—	21.75	16.91	15.94	246.27	79.97	119.74	168.05
1978	—	—	—	—	—	—	—	22.31	18.59	16.72	253.89	84.60	126.62	195.24
1979	—	—	—	—	—	—	—	41.52	39.35	38.02	262.86	89.45	128.84	195.92
1980	—	—	—	—	—	—	—	39.18	35.85	34.61	280.03	96.49	127.18	194.29
1981	—	—	—	—	—	—	—	41.18	42.97	39.57	282.04	97.64	—	209.51
1982	—	—	—	—	—	—	—	35.53	36.94	36.57	303.02	103.60	—	278.54
1983	—	—	—	—	—	—	—	35.99	36.45	36.85	312.82	107.16	—	283.15
1984	—	—	—	—	—	—	—	36.18	37.28	37.41	325.44	111.60	—	276.97
1985	—	—	—	—	—	—	—	35.97	38.91	37.61	342.15	116.65	—	312.98
1986	—	—	—	—	—	—	—	36.02	38.65	37.78	355.04	121.05	—	362.45
1987	—	—	—	—	—	—	—	36.07	39.78	37.71	361.37	123.73	—	358.29
1988	—	—	—	—	—	—	—	35.90	38.86	37.99	374.07	128.47	—	420.89
1989	—	—	—	—	—	—	—	35.59	41.80	38.71	383.14	132.40	—	461.45
1990	—	—	—	—	—	—	—	42.18	41.32	39.92	391.67	135.86	—	476.50
1991	—	—	—	—	—	—	—	55.19	55.97	57.98	390.44	134.89	—	422.07
1992	—	—	—	—	—	—	—	37.66	38.45	39.05	373.71	131.03	—	431.41
1993	—	—	—	—	—	—	—	44.88	39.63	41.43	377.24	133.10	—	568.17
1994	—	—	—	—	—	—	—	48.76	39.22	40.50	377.78	134.30	—	1,105.95
1995	—	—	—	—	—	—	—	43.13	37.58	41.15	375.31	134.21	—	3,415.93
1996	—	—	—	—	—	—	—	43.58	37.57	40.36	386.10	139.23	—	3,033.42
1997	—	—	—	—	—	—	—	—	—	—	490.01	176.95	—	410.74

[1] Beginning in 1974, includes only Puerto Rico, Guam, and the Virgin Islands. The Supplemental Security Income (SSI) program superseded these programs elsewhere.

[2] For 1936–1950, as of December of each year.

[3] For 1983–1997, excludes family count and expenditures for states providing only partial data.

Sources

Series Bf649–654, 1950–1975: U.S. Social Security Administration, *Social Security Bulletin, Annual Statistical Supplement* (1974), Table 155; 1936–1949: *Social Security Bulletin, Annual Statistical Supplement* (1966), Table 113, p. 115. Series Bf655–661, U.S. Social Security Administration, *Social Security Bulletin, Annual Statistical Supplement* (1999), Table 9.G1, p. 342, Table 9.K1, p. 351, and Table 9.L1, p. 352.

Documentation

See the text for Tables Bf621–648 for more information about the public assistance programs.

This table reports two sets of alternative series. In 1976, the Social Security Administration stated that the data in series Bf656–661 are not comparable with series Bf649–654 because of a change in source (p. 200). Although not identical, the series are very closely related. The correlations between the two versions of the series for the overlapping years of 1936, 1940, 1945, 1950, 1955, and 1960–1973 are 0.998 for Old-Age Assistance, 0.999 for Aid to the Blind, and 0.998 for Aid to the Permanently and Totally Disabled. The correlations for overlapping years of 1936, 1940, 1945, 1950, 1955, and 1960–1974 are 0.977 for Aid to Families with Dependent Children (AFDC) per family, 0.998 for AFDC per recipient, and 0.999 for general assistance.

All series include nonmedical vendor payments.

TABLE Bf663–678 Public assistance and federal work programs – recipients, assistance, persons employed, and earnings: 1933–1943

Contributed by Price V. Fishback and Melissa A. Thomasson

	Number of cases		Persons employed					
				National Youth Administration				
	Federal Emergency Relief Administration	Farm Security Administration	Civilian Conservation Corps	Student work program	Out-of-school work program	Works Projects Administration	Civil Works Administration	Other federal emergency projects
	Bf663	Bf664	Bf665	Bf666	Bf667	Bf668	Bf669	Bf670
Year	Thousand	Thousand	Thousand	Thousand	Thousand	Thousand	Thousand	Thousand
1933	101	—	290	—	—	—	3,597	264
1934	459	—	330	—	—	—	—	331
1935	96	130	459	283	—	2,667	—	408
1936	11	135	328	411	178	2,243	—	506
1937	—	109	284	304	136	1,594	—	235
1938	—	115	275	372	240	3,156	—	167
1939	—	96	266	434	296	2,109	—	141
1940	—	45	246	449	326	1,826	—	22
1941	—	26	126	333	283	1,023	—	2
1942	—	—	—	86	—	300	—	—
1943	—	—	—	—	—	—	—	—

	Payments for assistance or earnings							
			Earnings					
				National Youth Administration				
	Federal Emergency Relief Administration	Farm Security Administration subsistence program	Civilian Conservation Corps	Student work program	Out-of-school work program	Works Projects Administration	Civil Works Administration	Other federal emergency projects
	Bf671	Bf672	Bf673	Bf674	Bf675	Bf676	Bf677	Bf678
Year	Thousand dollars	Thousand dollars	Thousand dollars	Thousand dollars	Thousand dollars	Thousand dollars	Thousand dollars	Thousand dollars
1933	5,753	—	140,736	—	—	—	214,956	30,718
1934	61,069	—	260,957	—	—	—	503,060	275,161
1935	114,996	2,541	332,851	6,364	—	238,018	—	289,897
1936	3,873	20,365	292,397	26,329	28,883	1,592,039	—	498,415
1937	467	35,894	245,756	24,287	32,664	1,186,266	—	324,639
1938	—	22,579	230,318	19,598	41,560	1,751,053	—	186,505
1939	—	19,055	230,513	22,707	51,538	1,565,515	—	247,285
1940	—	18,282	215,846	26,864	65,211	1,269,617	—	92,604
1941	—	12,281	155,604	25,118	94,032	937,366	—	12,904
1942	—	6,271	34,030	11,328	32,009	503,055	—	730
1943	—	—	—	3,794	—	46,737	—	—

Sources

U.S. Social Security Administration, *Social Security Bulletin* 14 (9) (1951): 43 and *Social Security Bulletin: Yearbook* (1945), p. 21.

Documentation

The estimates shown here for 1933–1939 are very similar to those in the National Resources Planning Board report on *Security, Work, and Relief Policies* (1942), Appendixes 9 and 10.

The National Youth Administration (NYA) and Works Projects Administration programs were discontinued before the end of 1943.

Each of the individual programs provided the data about their operations to the Social Security Administration, except in the following cases. The data for the Federal Emergency Relief Administration (FERA), series Bf663 and Bf671, and for the NYA through June 1939, series Bf666–667 and Bf674–675, were provided by the Works Projects Administration.

Deeming that the depressed economy was a national emergency, the Roosevelt administration established a series of New Deal programs to aid the needy and the unemployed. The initial program was the FERA, which provided direct relief to families and work relief for able-bodied workers, series Bf671. The Civil Works Administration (CWA) provided work relief between November 1933 and March 1934. Meanwhile, the Civilian Conservation Corps (CCC) provided work and educational opportunities for young men, as they worked to conserve forests, farmland, and other natural sites. The Works Progress Administration (WPA), later renamed the Works Projects Administration, provided work relief for unemployed "employables" while building schools, roads, post offices, sidewalks, and a host of other projects. The NYA and the Farm Security Administration (FSA) were smaller programs that, respectively, employed students and provided aid to farmers in obtaining their own farms.

Series Bf663 and Bf671. FERA programs provided direct relief, work relief, emergency education, student aid, rural rehabilitation, and transient programs.

TABLE Bf663–678 Public assistance and federal work programs – recipients, assistance, persons employed, and earnings: 1933–1943 *Continued*

Series Bf664 and Bf672. FSA programs included emergency grant vouchers and cases receiving only FSA commodities and the value of such commodities. These were dropped from the series in June 1942 because the appropriation was drastically reduced and payments were limited to need occasioned by natural disasters.

Series Bf665–670 and Bf672–678. Information on the CCC, NYA, WPA, and the other federal agencies excludes administrative employees and their earnings and cost of materials, equipment, and other items incidental to operation of work programs.

Series Bf665 and Bf673, CCC figures. Average number of enrolled persons. Earnings were estimated by multiplying average monthly number of persons enrolled by average expenditures per enrollee for cash allowances, clothing, shelter, subsistence and medical care, and certain other items. Beginning July 1941, average expenditures per enrolled were estimated at $67.20 for enrollees other than Indians, $60.50 for Indians.

Series Bf666–667 and Bf674–675, NYA. Persons employed during month, except for the out-of-school program after June 1941, in which case the data represent the average of weekly employment counts. Information on the out-of-school program of the NYA is no longer included as public assistance after June 1942 because the purpose of the program changed from employment based on need to training for war industry.

Series Bf668 and Bf676, WPA. Average weekly number employed on projects financed from WPA funds. Beginning July 1942, earnings represent expenditures (approved vouchers) for labor during month.

Series Bf670 and Bf678, other federal projects. Average number of weekly employed persons during the monthly period ending on the fifteenth, on projects financed in whole or in part from emergency federal funds other than CCC, NYA, WPA, and CWA. Beginning with October 1941, the data include only employment and earnings on projects financed from Public Works Administration funds. Data are from the Bureau of Labor Statistics.

TABLE Bf679–688 Public child health and welfare service programs – children and mothers served: 1937–1970

Contributed by Price V. Fishback and Melissa A. Thomasson

	Children served in Crippled Children's Program		Mothers served in maternity medical clinics		Children served in child health clinics				Children served by child welfare programs	
					Infants		Other children			
	Number	Rate per 10,000 children	Number	Rate per 1,000 live births	Number	Rate per 1,000 infants	Number	Rate per 1,000 children (1 to 4 years old)	Number	Rate per 10,000 under 21
	Bf679	Bf680	Bf681 [1]	Bf682	Bf683	Bf684	Bf685	Bf686	Bf687	Bf688
Year	Thousand	Per 10,000	Number	Per 1,000	Number	Per 1,000	Number	Per 1,000	Number	Per 10,000
1937	110	24	75,193	31	127,365	66	200,022	25	—	—
1938	114	24	119,623	48	156,749	80	266,466	32	—	—
1939	127	26	125,667	51	138,280	69	277,703	33	—	—
1940	127	26	146,440	55	175,357	84	299,174	34	—	—
1941	147	30	167,002	61	185,139	85	314,238	36	—	—
1942	133	27	161,367	52	185,562	78	307,344	33	—	—
1943	115	24	147,599	46	185,729	67	264,817	28	—	—
1944	125	27	129,596	43	169,799	66	266,774	26	—	—
1945	130	27	116,961	31	169,965	67	256,815	24	241,000	51
1946	155	32	130,909	37	187,045	75	275,969	25	250,000	51
1947	175	34	151,117	38	245,514	69	320,263	28	255,000	50
1948	195	37	152,691	41	263,819	81	379,472	31	260,000	50
1949	207	39	168,234	45	294,998	91	398,582	31	265,000	50
1950	214	39	175,270	47	302,892	94	420,334	31	270,000	49
1951	229	41	188,541	48	402,279	120	580,344	41	277,000	50
1952	238	42	180,265	45	433,911	126	576,260	41	279,000	49
1953	252	43	177,580	44	411,907	117	591,959	41	282,000	48
1954	271	45	190,667	47	446,772	123	576,966	39	289,000	48
1955	278	45	188,988	46	448,058	121	576,896	39	289,400	46
1956	296	46	225,624	—	517,243	139	769,102	—	297,500	46
1957	313	47	240,630	—	557,801	144	768,476	—	318,000	48
1958	325	47	250,630	58	607,291	140	812,371	—	328,300	48
1959	339	49	235,638	54	629,258	145	854,210	—	344,500	49
1960	355	49	253,638	59	614,883	142	865,494	—	382,500	54
1961	372	50	276,771	64	598,736	138	898,919	—	403,900	56
1962	385	50	267,741	63	606,015	143	893,745	—	422,800	56
1963	396	51	271,084	65	593,362	142	915,868	—	457,300	60
1964	423	54	276,187	70	605,480	147	902,013	—	487,500	62
1965	—	—	—	—	—	—	—	—	531,600	67
1966	437	54	282,432	77	679,688	184	1,084,318	—	573,800	71
1967	476	60	366,373	98	603,661	161	1,028,225	—	607,000	74
1968	475	59	292,000	83	591,000	169	1,019,000	—	656,000	80
1969	483	59	346,000	97	515,000	144	871,000	—	694,000	85
1970	492	61	331,499	89	622,708	167	851,081	—	652,000	80

Note appears on next page

(continued)

TABLE Bf679–688 Public child health and welfare service programs – children and mothers served: 1937–1970 *Continued*

[1] Prior to 1956, includes antepartum service only.

Sources

Series Bf679–686, 1937–1969, U.S. Children's Bureau, *Statistical Series*, and U.S. Social Security Administration, unpublished data; 1970, U.S. Health Services Administration, unpublished data. Series Bf687–688, U.S. Social and Rehabilitation Service, *Child Welfare Statistics* (1969), and *Children Served by Public Welfare Agencies and Voluntary Child Welfare Agencies and Institutions*, Reports CW-1 and E-9.

Documentation

Series Bf679–680. Data represent general coverage of state reports: 1937–1947, for services administered or financed in whole or in part by official state agencies under the Social Security Act; 1948–1949, for services provided or purchased by official state agencies exclusive of prediagnostic services; 1950–1956, for "physician's services" consisting of clinic service, hospital care, convalescent home care, and other services by physicians. Data for 1937 are for forty-five states, the District of Columbia, Alaska, Hawai'i (Georgia, Louisiana, and Oregon not participating). For 1938, Georgia and Oregon are also included and, for 1939, Louisiana is included (except for first quarter). Puerto Rico was excluded beginning with the last half of 1940, and the Virgin Islands were excluded beginning the last half of 1947; prior to these dates, they were included. Arizona, which did not participate from 1950 through 1956, is excluded for those years. Rates for each year are based on the population of states participating in those years.

Series Bf679–685. Calendar year basis through 1964; fiscal year thereafter.

Series Bf681–686. Maternal and child health programs include services administered or supervised by official state health agencies. Reports were received each year except 1941 from forty-eight states, the District of Columbia, Alaska, and Hawai'i. Missouri was not participating in 1941. Puerto Rico is included beginning with 1940, and the Virgin Islands are included beginning with the last half of 1947.

Series Bf686. Not computed after 1956 because older children were included in the program.

TABLE Bf689–707 Food programs – participation, benefits, payments, and costs: 1962–1999

Contributed by Price V. Fishback and Melissa A. Thomasson

	Food Stamps			Women, Infants, and Children program			Federal cost of school food programs		
	Average number of persons participating	Annual benefit	Annual average monthly benefit per person	Total participation	Program costs	Average monthly benefit per person	Cash payments	Commodity costs	Total costs
	Bf689	Bf690	Bf691	Bf692	Bf693	Bf694	Bf695	Bf696	Bf697
Year	Thousand	Thousand dollars	Dollars	Thousand	Million dollars	Dollars	Million dollars	Million dollars	Million dollars
1962	143	13,153	7.66	—	—	—	—	—	—
1963	226	18,639	6.87	—	—	—	—	—	—
1964	367	28,643	6.50	—	—	—	—	—	—
1965	424	32,494	6.39	—	—	—	—	—	—
1966	864	64,781	6.25	—	—	—	—	—	—
1967	1,447	105,455	6.07	—	—	—	—	—	—
1968	2,211	172,982	6.52	—	—	—	—	—	—
1969	2,878	228,587	6.62	—	—	—	310.5	272.0	582.5
1970	4,340	550,806	10.58	—	—	—	412.2	265.2	677.4 [1]
1971	9,368	1,522,904	13.55	—	—	—	642.8	277.3	920.1
1972	11,103	1,794,875	13.47	—	—	—	853.9	312.1	1,166.0
1973	12,190	2,102,133	14.37	—	—	—	1,007.5	331.0	1,338.5
1974	12,896	2,725,988	17.62	88	10.4	15.68	1,193.7	316.1	1,509.8
1975	17,063	4,386,144	21.42	344	89.3	18.58	1,498.0	423.5	1,921.5
1976	18,557	5,310,133	23.85	520	142.6	19.60	1,743.7	418.6	2,162.3
1977	17,058	5,057,700	24.71	848	255.9	20.80	1,868.9	540.8	2,409.7
1978	16,044	5,165,209	26.83	1,181	379.6	21.99	2,124.8	542.9	2,667.7
1979	17,710	6,484,538	30.51	1,483	525.4	24.09	2,348.3	744.9	3,093.2
1980	21,077	8,685,521	34.34	1,914	727.7	25.43	2,712.4	904.5	3,616.9
1981	22,430	10,615,964	39.44	2,119	871.6	27.84	2,813.1	895.2	3,708.3
1982	21,716	10,205,799	39.18	2,189	948.8	28.83	2,521.0	757.0	3,278.0
1983	21,630	11,153,867	42.98	2,537	1,126.0	29.62	2,763.0	800.9	3,563.9
1984	20,858	10,696,100	42.74	3,045	1,388.1	30.58	2,887.7	827.4	3,715.1
1985	19,910	10,744,200	44.99	3,138	1,489.3	31.69	2,973.5	801.3	3,774.8
1986	19,428	10,604,950	45.49	3,312	1,582.9	31.82	3,136.4	821.9	3,958.3
1987	19,113	10,500,344	45.78	3,429	1,679.6	32.68	3,259.4	888.2	4,147.6
1988	18,644	11,149,051	50.00	3,593	1,797.5	33.28	3,417.2	813.7	4,230.9
1989	18,766	11,676,436	51.85	4,118	1,910.9	30.14	3,537.2	763.9	4,301.1
1990	20,038	14,184,028	59.01	4,517	2,122.2	30.20	3,829.4	619.7	4,449.1
1991	22,629	17,307,235	63.89	4,893	2,301.1	29.84	4,229.5	699.3	4,928.8
1992	25,403	20,899,531	68.57	5,403	2,596.7	30.21	4,662.7	707.2	5,369.9
1993	26,982	22,005,194	67.96	5,921	2,825.5	29.76	4,968.8	668.4	5,637.2
1994	27,476	23,749,813	69.01	6,477	3,169.5	29.91	5,267.6	725.3	5,992.9
1995	26,619	22,765,849	71.27	6,894	3,441.4	30.41	5,531.8	693.6	6,225.4
1996	25,533	22,440,298	73.23	7,188	3,695.3	31.19	5,796.9	693.0	6,489.9
1997	22,851	19,555,263	71.31	7,407	3,844.1	31.67	6,165.7	619.7	6,785.4
1998	19,787	16,879,929	71.09	7,367	3,889.9	31.75	6,390.7	728.2	7,118.9
1999	—	—	—	7,311	3,945.7	32.53	6,675.6	704.9	7,380.5

Note appears at end of table

TABLE Bf689–707 Food programs – participation, benefits, payments, and costs: 1962–1999 *Continued*

	National School Lunch program			School Breakfast program					Child and Adult Care Food program	
	Average monthly participation	Meals served	Percentage of free and reduced-price meals served	Total monthly participation	Meals served	Percentage of free and reduced-price meals served	Special Milk program: half-pints served	Summer Food Service program: meals served	Meals served	Percentage of free and reduced-price meals
	Bf698	Bf699	Bf700	Bf701	Bf702	Bf703	Bf704	Bf705	Bf706	Bf707
Year	Million	Million	Percent	Million	Million	Percent	Million	Million	Million	Percent
1962	—	—	—	—	—	—	—	—	—	—
1963	—	—	—	—	—	—	—	—	—	—
1964	—	—	—	—	—	—	—	—	—	—
1965	—	—	—	—	—	—	—	—	—	—
1966	—	—	—	—	—	—	—	—	—	—
1967	—	—	—	—	—	—	—	—	—	—
1968	—	—	—	—	—	—	—	—	—	—
1969	19.4	3,368.2	15.1	0.22	39.7	71.0	2,944.4	2.2	8	78.2
1970	22.4	3,565.1	20.7	0.45	71.8	71.5	2,901.9	8.2	42	80.3
1971	24.1	3,848.3	26.1	0.80	125.5	76.3	2,570.0	29.0	81	83.5
1972	24.4	3,972.1	32.4	1.04	169.3	78.5	2,498.2	73.5	103	85.4
1973	24.7	4,008.8	35.0	1.19	194.1	83.4	2,560.7	65.4	118	87.1
1974	24.6	3,981.6	37.1	1.37	226.7	82.8	1,425.9	63.6	163	88.6
1975	24.9	4,063.0	40.3	1.82	294.7	82.1	2,139.0	84.3	224	87.6
1976	25.6	4,147.9	43.1	2.20	353.6	84.2	2,206.8	104.8	254	80.6
1977	26.2	4,250.0	44.8	2.49	434.3	85.7	2,204.4	170.4	311	82.6
1978	26.7	4,294.1	44.4	2.80	478.8	85.3	1,990.8	120.3	339	81.8
1979	27.0	4,357.4	43.6	3.32	565.6	84.1	1,821.1	121.8	382	79.8
1980	26.6	4,387.0	45.1	3.60	619.9	85.2	1,794.8	108.2	431	82.6
1981	25.8	4,210.6	48.6	3.81	644.2	86.9	1,533.1	90.3	547	91.0
1982	22.9	3,755.0	50.2	3.32	567.4	89.3	201.9	68.2	493	85.5
1983	23.0	3,803.3	51.7	3.36	580.7	90.3	189.0	71.3	536	84.4
1984	23.4	3,826.2	51.0	3.43	589.2	89.7	174.4	73.8	591	84.0
1985	23.6	3,890.1	49.1	3.44	594.9	88.6	166.9	77.2	640	83.7
1986	23.7	3,942.5	49.1	3.50	610.6	88.7	161.8	77.1	678	83.6
1987	23.9	3,939.9	48.6	3.61	621.5	88.4	162.3	79.9	725	83.2
1988	24.2	4,032.9	47.4	3.68	642.5	87.5	193.6	80.3	792	83.2
1989	24.3	4,004.9	47.2	3.81	658.4	86.8	188.7	86.0	866	83.5
1990	24.1	4,009.1	48.3	4.07	707.5	86.7	181.2	91.2	966	83.9
1991	24.2	4,050.9	50.4	4.44	772.1	87.3	177.0	96.2	1,063	84.5
1992	24.6	4,101.9	53.0	4.92	852.6	88.0	174.4	107.4	1,182	85.4
1993	24.9	4,137.7	54.8	5.36	923.6	87.9	167.3	113.4	1,298	85.4
1994	25.3	4,201.8	55.9	5.83	1,001.6	87.4	158.8	116.9	1,414	85.3
1995	25.7	4,253.4	56.4	6.32	1,078.9	86.8	151.4	120.3	1,508	85.2
1996	25.9	4,313.2	56.9	6.58	1,125.7	86.5	144.3	125.4	1,546	85.2
1997	26.3	4,409.0	57.6	6.92	1,191.2	86.5	140.6	128.5	1,572	85.3
1998	26.6	4,424.9	57.8	7.14	1,221.0	86.1	133.6	134.8	1,602	84.7
1999	26.9	4,513.2	57.6	7.37	1,267.6	85.4	126.9	134.6	1,637	84.2

[1] Corrected from original source using sum of series Bf695–696.

Sources

Series Bf689–691. U.S. Social Security Administration, *Social Security Bulletin: Annual Statistical Supplement* (1999), Table 9.H.1, p. 344. The original source for the series is the U.S. Department of Agriculture (USDA), Food and Consumer Service.

Series Bf692–707. Internet site for the USDA, Food and Nutrition Service.

More detail on these programs and others and recent updates have been posted at the U.S. Food and Nutrition Service Internet site. See also U.S. Food and Nutrition Service, "Annual Historical Review of FNS Programs."

Documentation

The U.S. Food and Nutrition Service administers a series of programs designed to provide food to low-income persons. These include food stamp, school meals, and summer feeding programs, and programs to feed women, infants, and children and the elderly.

Food Stamp Program

The Food Stamp program was designed to provide low-income persons with a means for obtaining an adequate diet. Under this program, single persons and individuals living in households meeting nationwide standards for income and assets may receive coupons redeemable for food and for garden seeds and plants. To qualify for the program, as of 1996, a household must have (1) less than $2,000 in disposable assets ($3,000 if one member is aged 60 or older), (2) gross income below 130 percent of the poverty guidelines for the household size, and (3) net income, after subtracting the deductions, of less than 100 percent of the poverty guidelines. Households with a person aged 60 or older, or a disabled person receiving Supplemental Security Income (SSI), Social Security (Old-Age, Survivors, and Disability Insurance, or OASDI), state general assistance or veterans' disability benefits (or interim disability assistance pending approval of any of the previously mentioned programs) may have gross income exceeding 130 percent of the poverty guidelines if the income is lower than 100 percent of the poverty guidelines after subtracting the preceding deductions. One- and two-person households in which all members receive Temporary Assistance to Needy Families (TANF) or SSI are categorically eligible for food stamps without meeting these income criteria.

Initiated on a pilot basis in 1961, the Food Stamp Act of 1964 formally established the program, with twenty-two states participating. Currently,

(continued)

TABLE Bf689–707 Food programs – participation, benefits, payments, and costs: 1962–1999 *Continued*

the Food Stamp program is in effect in the fifty states, the District of Columbia, Guam, and the Virgin Islands. Since July 1982, Puerto Rico has been receiving a block grant for nutrition assistance instead of participating in the Food Stamp program. Authorization for this program extended through September 30, 2002.

The Food Stamp program is administered nationally by the U.S. Food and Consumer Service and operates through local welfare offices and the nation's food marketing and banking systems. Since August 1, 1980, persons receiving or applying for SSI payments have been permitted to apply for food stamps through local Social Security district offices. The federal government, through general revenues, pays the entire cost of the food stamp benefits, but federal and state agencies share administrative costs.

Originally, food stamp coupons were purchased by participants. The difference between the face value of the coupons and the amount paid by the participant was known as the bonus value. Effective January 1, 1979, the purchase requirement was eliminated, and participants could directly receive the bonus.

Between 1974 and 1979, SSI recipients were made ineligible for food stamps in Massachusetts, Wisconsin, California, and selected counties in New York and Virginia because those areas supplemented SSI payments in amounts that included the value of food stamps. As of 1983 and 1992, SSI recipients were returned to the Food Stamp program in Massachusetts and Wisconsin, respectively, when these states chose to stop including a value for food stamps in the SSI supplement.

The U.S. Food and Nutrition Service has several additional programs to strengthen the nutritional safety net beyond those included here. These include an emergency food assistance program to provide commodity foods to states for distribution to supplement food stocks of households, soup kitchens, and food banks; and food distribution programs for women, infants, children, the elderly, Puerto Ricans, and Native Americans. More information can be found at the Internet sites listed in the sources.

After July 1, 1982, residents of Puerto Rico are not included in the data.

Other Food Programs

Series Bf692–694. The Special Supplemental Nutrition Program for Women, Infants, and Children (WIC) is designed to improve the health of low-income pregnant women, breastfeeding and nonbreastfeeding new mothers, and infants and children up to 5 years old. WIC provides supplemental foods, nutrition education, and access to health services. Participants redeem vouchers for specific foods that contain nutrients frequently lacking in the diet of low-income mothers and children.

Series Bf695–705. The School Food programs include the National School Lunch program, School Breakfast program, and Special Milk program. The National School Lunch program and the School Breakfast program provide funding and commodity foods to nonprofit food services in elementary and secondary schools, and in residential child care facilities. Depending on income, students qualify for free or reduced-price meals, which must meet federal nutritional guidelines. The Special Milk program as of 1999 furnishes milk to all children in approved schools, camps, and child care institutions that have no federally supported meal program. The federal cost of the school food programs does not include payments for the federal share of state administrative expenses. The commodity food costs represent the value of food distributed.

Series Bf698–700. The average monthly participation in the National School Lunch program is a nine-month average covering October through May plus September. Total lunches served includes free and reduced-price lunches, which are determined by the income of the household of the recipient, and full-price lunches for students from higher income households.

Series Bf701–703. The total monthly participation in the School Breakfast program is a nine-month average covering October through May plus September.

Series Bf704. The Omnibus Budget Reconciliation Act of 1981 limited School Milk program participation to schools and institutions that do not participate in other child nutrition programs. The Act became effective in fiscal year 1982. Public Law 99-500 in 1987 (effective October 1988) permitted the National School Lunch program or the School Breakfast program to offer milk to pre-kindergarten and kindergarten children attending half-day sessions who have no access to meal service programs.

Series Bf705. For 1969–1975, data are for the summer component of the Special Food Service program. There was a transitional quarter between 1976 and 1977, which was the interim between the old definition of the fiscal year (July through June) and the current one (October through September). During that period 198 million meals were served.

Series Bf706–707. The Child and Adult Care Food program supplies commodity foods and reimburses for meals in child and adult day care centers, and family and group day care homes for children. The 1969–1975 data are for the year-round component of the Special Food Service program.

TABLE Bf708–716 Low-Income Home Energy Assistance program – obligations and households receiving assistance: 1982–1996

Contributed by Price V. Fishback and Melissa A. Thomasson

	Estimated home energy assistance obligations for				Households receiving assistance for				
							Energy crisis intervention		
	Heating	Cooling	Energy crisis intervention	Weatherization and energy-related home repair	Heating	Cooling	Winter	Summer	Weatherization and energy-related home repair
	Bf708	Bf709	Bf710	Bf711	Bf712	Bf713	Bf714	Bf715	Bf716
Year	Dollars	Dollars	Dollars	Dollars	Number	Number	Number	Number	Number
1982	1,124,476,630	51,498,572	138,941,133	136,195,046	5,990,176	1,075,061	707,123	—	430,830
1983	1,343,267,155	33,020,830	191,771,756	195,463,612	6,414,448	529,036	972,894	25,342	482,620
1984	1,372,772,591	32,374,067	225,795,893	186,662,906	6,443,637	537,598	963,743	28,841	180,748
1985	1,466,721,924	29,135,118	191,407,205	227,096,051	6,545,616	511,333	857,809	27,196	217,864
1986	1,351,903,078	35,620,945	199,178,003	193,420,839	6,359,924	535,553	951,945	114,194	191,316
1987	1,280,302,113	29,581,262	197,719,071	220,419,633	6,495,409	366,721	1,060,425	60,797	172,372
1988	1,145,560,993	21,151,405	190,046,023	170,292,505	5,827,481	309,044	981,775	57,750	156,770
1989	1,017,024,757	12,341,113	187,442,779	147,952,928	5,595,268	126,977	890,616	20,384	142,584
1990	1,030,150,903	25,007,676	188,844,316	133,479,484	5,459,631	358,823	1,058,067	37,340	148,104
1991	1,098,583,280	27,416,776	220,795,517	129,279,737	5,769,346	374,483	1,004,634	39,399	127,587
1992	990,903,081	22,645,002	197,218,623	134,816,010	5,906,292	384,468	950,275	25,570	106,066
1993	948,596,196	22,274,975	183,189,522	146,444,590	5,282,993	143,279	956,435	47,169	111,295
1994	1,062,552,111	24,862,636	225,583,805	214,342,289	5,663,040	145,684	1,127,832	24,532	126,086
1995	884,846,144	43,883,481	212,713,182	159,076,150	5,147,619	341,041	932,263	77,915	102,817
1996	696,801,144	17,597,204	167,622,219	135,835,358	3,974,152	128,538	804,560	59,992	91,503

Source

U.S. Social Security Administration, *Social Security Bulletin: Annual Statistical Supplement* (1999), Tables 9.J1 and 9.J3, pp. 346, 350; a legislative history of the Low-Income Home Energy Assistance program (LIHEAP) is on pp. 128–9.

Documentation

Under LIHEAP, block grants administered by Health and Human Services (HHS) are provided to the states to assist eligible households to meet home energy expenses. In addition to the fifty states, grants were provided in fiscal year 1995 to the District of Columbia, the Commonwealth of Puerto Rico, five insular areas, and 123 Indian tribes or tribal organizations.

The unit of eligibility for energy assistance is the household, defined as any individual or group of individuals who are living together as one economic unit for which residential energy is customarily purchased in common, either directly or through rent. Under the Act, households can be eligible for assistance on the basis of income, or are categorically eligible if they already receive Aid to Families with Dependent Children (replaced by the Temporary Assistance for Needy Families program), Supplemental Security Income, food stamps, or need-tested veterans' benefits. To be eligible on the basis of income, households must have incomes less than either 150 percent of the income guidelines or 60 percent of the state's median income, whichever is greater. As of 1995, no household may be excluded from eligibility on the basis of income alone if household income is less than 110 percent of the poverty guidelines.

States make payments directly to eligible households or to home energy suppliers on behalf of eligible households. Payments can be provided in cash, fuel, or prepaid utility bills or as vouchers, stamps, or coupons that can be used in exchange for energy supplies. Payments are to vary in such a way that the highest level of assistance is furnished to households with the lowest income and the highest energy costs in relation to income, taking into account family size.

With respect to the series that are reported for the number of households receiving assistance, note that an unduplicated total of households assisted cannot be derived from the data because the same household may be included under more than one type of assistance. In addition, the data for the number of households that received heating and cooling assistance include households that received combined heating and cooling assistance in Arizona, California, and Florida, and households in Hawai'i that received assistance without differentiation between heating and cooling assistance. Further, the total number of households receiving energy crisis intervention in winter includes households that received expedited heating assistance in Maryland, Massachusetts, and New Hampshire.

TABLE Bf717–721 Vocational rehabilitation caseload and expenditures: 1921–1999

Contributed by Price V. Fishback and Melissa A. Thomasson

	Persons		Expenditures		
	Served	Rehabilitated	Total	Federal	State
	Bf717	Bf718	Bf719	Bf720	Bf721
Year	Number	Number	Thousand dollars	Thousand dollars	Thousand dollars
1921	—	523	285	93	191
1922	—	1,898	736	312	424
1923	—	4,530	1,188	525	663
1924	—	5,664	1,243	551	691
1925	—	5,825	1,187	520	668
1926	—	5,604	1,274	579	695
1927	—	5,092	1,407	631	775
1928	—	5,012	1,541	654	887
1929	—	4,645	1,490	665	825
1930	—	4,605	1,700	739	960
1931	—	5,184	2,043	933	1,110
1932	—	5,592	2,186	998	1,187
1933	—	5,613	2,176	999	1,177
1934	—	8,062	2,080	916	1,164
1935	—	9,422	2,248	1,032	1,216
1936	—	10,338	2,603	1,230	1,373
1937	—	11,091	3,319	1,513	1,806
1938	63,666	9,844	3,862	1,791	2,071
1939	63,575	10,747	3,992	1,833	2,159
1940	65,624	11,890	4,108	1,972	2,136
1941	78,320	14,576	4,711	2,282	2,429
1942	91,572	21,757	5,205	2,557	2,648
1943	129,207	42,618	5,630	2,762	2,868
1944	145,059	43,997	6,372	4,052	2,320
1945	161,050	41,925	9,856	7,135	2,720
1946	169,796	36,106	13,749	10,002	3,747
1947	170,143	43,880	19,313	14,189	5,124
1948	191,063	53,131	24,589	17,707	6,862
1949	216,997	58,020	25,819	18,216	7,603
1950	255,724	59,597	29,347	20,340	9,007
1951	231,544	66,193	30,273	21,001	9,271
1952	228,490	63,632	32,689	22,122	10,567
1953	221,849	61,308	34,583	22,948	11,636
1954	211,219	55,825	35,366	22,965	12,403
1955	209,039	57,981	38,629	23,812	14,818
1956	221,128	65,640	46,221	28,830	17,391
1957	238,582	70,940	54,282	33,648	20,634
1958	258,444	74,317	63,727	39,365	24,362
1959	280,384	80,739	71,206	43,932	27,274
1960	297,950	88,275	78,711	48,144	30,567
1961	320,963	92,501	88,150	53,898	34,252
1962	345,635	102,377	101,390	61,956	39,404
1963	368,696	110,136	113,111	69,325	43,785
1964	399,852	119,708	133,259	82,195	51,065
1965	441,332	134,859	154,140	94,713	59,427
1966	499,464	154,279	213,639	144,629	69,009
1967	569,907	173,594	303,846	225,268	78,578
1968	680,415	207,918	377,646	282,337	95,309
1969	781,614	241,390	455,865	340,858	115,007
1970	875,911	266,975	557,707	431,764	125,943
1971	1,001,660	291,272	631,000	489,000	142,000
1972	1,111,045	326,138	697,000	548,000	149,000
1973	1,176,445	360,726	730,000	572,000	158,000
1974	1,201,661	361,138	810,000	636,000	174,000
1975	1,244,338	324,039	867,000	673,000	194,000
1976	1,238,446	303,328	898,000	700,000	198,000
1977	1,204,487	291,202	956,000	733,000	223,000
1978	1,167,991	294,396	986,000	755,000	231,000
1979	1,127,551	298,325	1,063,000	813,000	250,000

TABLE Bf717–721 Vocational rehabilitation caseload and expenditures: 1921–1999 *Continued*

	Persons		Expenditures		
	Served	Rehabilitated	Total	Federal	State
	Bf717	Bf718	Bf719	Bf720	Bf721
Year	Number	Number	Thousand dollars	Thousand dollars	Thousand dollars
1980	1,095,139	277,136	1,076,000	817,000	259,000
1981	1,038,232	255,881	1,118,000	850,000	268,000
1982	958,537	226,924	1,167,000	858,000	309,000
1983	938,923	216,231	1,254,000	937,000	317,000
1984	936,180	225,772	1,366,000	1,038,000	328,000
1985	931,779	227,652	1,452,000	1,100,000	352,000
1986	923,774	223,354	1,506,000	1,144,000	362,000
1987	917,482	219,616	1,649,000	1,275,000	374,000
1988	918,942	218,241	1,776,000	1,373,000	403,000
1989	928,998	220,408	1,867,000	1,446,000	421,000
1990	937,971	216,112	1,910,000	1,525,000	385,000
1991	941,771	202,831	2,092,000	1,622,000	470,000
1992	949,053	191,890	2,240,000	1,731,000	509,000
1993	1,048,527	193,994	2,241,000	1,691,000	550,000
1994	1,193,661	203,035	2,517,000	1,891,000	626,000
1995	1,250,314	209,509	2,714,000	2,054,000	660,000
1996	1,225,156	213,520	2,844,000	2,104,000	740,000
1997	1,198,231	211,502	3,046,000	2,164,000	882,000
1998	1,210,604	223,668	—	—	—
1999	1,202,286	229,829	—	—	—

Sources

Series Bf717–718. Through 1989, from U.S. Department of Education, Rehabilitation Services Administration, *Annual Report to the President and to the Congress on Federal Activities Related to the Rehabilitation Act of 1973, as amended, Fiscal Year 1990,* p. 136; 1990–1993, from the *Annual Report for the Fiscal Year 1993*, p. 262; 1994 and thereafter, from unpublished information provided by the administration.

Series Bf719–721. U.S. Bureau of the Census, *Statistical Abstract of the United States*, which reports the information from annual issues of U.S. Social and Rehabilitation Service, *Caseload Statistics of State Vocational Rehabilitation Agencies in Fiscal Years and State Vocational Rehabilitation Agency Program Data in Fiscal Years*. Annual updates are often reported in the *Statistical Abstract* before the annual reports of the administration are issued.

Documentation

The state-federal program of vocational rehabilitation assists persons with disabilities, and especially persons with severe disabilities, to reach successful employment outcomes. Persons with severe disabilities are persons whose physical or mental impairment seriously limits one or more functional capacities in terms of an employment outcome, and whose vocational rehabilitation can be expected to require multiple vocational rehabilitation services over an extended period of time. The percentage of persons served with severe disabilities has risen from 58 percent in 1980 to 79 percent in 1997.

Series Bf717. Includes active cases accepted for rehabilitation services during the year plus active cases on hand at beginning of the year.

Series Bf718. Persons rehabilitated refers to persons who are successfully placed into gainful employment.

Series Bf719–721. These series present data on expenditures only under the basic support provisions of the Vocational Rehabilitation Act. As of 1970, federal funds were allotted to fifty-four states and territories in support of basic programs for providing vocational rehabilitation services. The federal allotment was based on population and per capita income. In 1970, expenditures were at the matching rates of 80 percent for the federal government and 20 percent for the state; in 1995, the matching rates were 78.7 and 21.3 percent, respectively.

TABLE Bf722–734 Federal employee and civil service retirement systems – annuitants: 1925–1997

Contributed by Price V. Fishback and Melissa A. Thomasson

	Total	Mandatory retirement	Optional with 30 years service	Optional with less than 30 years service	Normal	Disabled	Deferred	Involuntary	Hazardous duty	Air traffic controllers	Members of Congress	Transferred from other systems	Voluntary early
	Bf722	Bf723	Bf724	Bf725	Bf726	Bf727	Bf728	Bf729	Bf730	Bf731	Bf732	Bf733	Bf734
Year	Number	Number	Number	Number	Number	Number	Number	Number	Number	Number	Number	Number	Number
1925	11,689	9,741	—	—	—	1,948	—	—	—	—	—	—	—
1930	17,768	12,504	—	—	—	3,994	—	1,270	—	—	—	—	—
1935	48,655	23,853	4,310	—	—	9,886	—	10,606	—	—	—	—	—
1940	62,027	30,216	6,318	—	—	15,294	—	10,199	—	—	—	—	—
1945	85,011	28,904	16,388	5,766	—	23,389	2,104	8,460	—	—	—	—	—
1950	155,135	27,503	32,827	14,711	—	42,869	27,446	8,177	219	—	52	1,331	—
1955	226,180	27,718	57,716	26,081	—	61,043	43,339	7,715	1,435	—	107	1,026	—
1956	246,362	27,835	64,776	30,316	—	66,093	47,069	7,484	1,714	—	103	972	—
1957	276,408	28,766	77,354	35,546	—	73,074	51,420	7,299	1,922	—	122	905	—
1958	311,992	30,476	87,057	42,051	—	84,493	57,164	7,707	2,087	—	114	843	—
1959	338,898	32,486	92,888	47,957	—	92,723	61,538	8,095	2,263	—	161	787	—
1960	365,391	33,977	97,518	89,318	—	101,940	30,848	8,500	2,405	—	143	742	—
1961	396,523	35,608	104,160	97,854	—	112,060	33,960	9,345	2,657	—	163	716	—
1962	426,031	37,122	109,543	106,787	—	121,859	36,823	10,132	2,939	—	158	668	—
1963	453,099	38,587	114,575	115,615	—	129,834	39,517	10,877	3,287	—	187	620	—
1964	482,131	39,944	119,603	124,551	—	139,378	42,055	12,211	3,613	—	184	592	—
1965	508,731	41,134	123,840	131,831	—	149,174	44,408	13,669	3,910	—	223	542	—
1966	560,992	41,570	140,386	148,288	—	160,904	46,899	17,646	4,570	—	221	508	—
1967	580,771	41,046	143,896	155,078	—	166,928	48,912	19,319	4,869	—	235	488	—
1968	604,873	41,151	148,834	163,539	—	172,768	51,116	21,542	5,241	—	225	457	—
1969	628,572	40,819	154,042	172,915	—	178,334	53,034	23,219	5,549	—	249	411	—
1970	662,223	40,197	162,890	184,506	—	185,081	55,107	27,922	5,922	—	232	366	—
1971	711,323	39,425	172,776	197,638	—	195,732	57,716	41,147	6,302	—	254	333	—
1972	758,469	38,508	187,159	208,624	—	205,413	60,045	51,361	6,807	—	246	306	—
1973	843,520	37,230	214,097	223,861	—	219,786	62,342	78,042	7,602	28	265	267	—
1974	938,654	35,762	249,204	240,234	—	238,543	65,268	100,046	9,017	133	251	196	—
1975	989,786	34,179	262,289	242,221	—	257,774	68,784	113,813	10,071	189	287	179	—
1976	1,038,337	33,241	278,043	247,901	—	279,326	70,791	116,749	11,603	245	281	157	—
1977	1,096,561	32,194	297,838	253,510	—	306,380	72,678	120,278	12,899	322	317	145	—
1978	1,148,142	31,512	319,172	260,301	—	323,446	75,035	122,712	15,117	421	303	123	—
1979	1,189,942	29,611	342,157	266,875	—	333,230	76,460	124,543	16,074	545	341	106	—
1980	1,247,886	—	—	—	681,537	343,251	76,753	128,259	16,937	703	347	99	—
1981	1,320,439 [1]	—	—	—	738,356	347,500	78,542	97,199	17,827	987	391	4,658	34,979
1982	1,357,687	—	—	—	769,916	348,068	79,885	99,052	18,488	1,259	373	4,915	35,731
1983	1,388,616	—	—	—	804,236	343,457	80,753	99,819	19,081	1,478	378	3,821	35,593
1984	1,420,194	—	—	—	837,368	337,871	80,974	101,622	19,506	1,773	373	5,218	35,489
1985	1,454,206	—	—	—	876,692	331,675	80,849	101,887	19,915	2,123	377	5,503	35,185
1986	1,491,571	—	—	—	916,313	325,978	81,114	102,850	20,477	2,483	362	5,724	36,270
1987	1,504,140	—	—	—	934,269	318,436	80,172	103,638	20,917	2,850	369	5,762	37,727
1988	1,548,363	—	—	—	973,533	311,263	79,830	105,467	21,553	3,354	351	6,139	46,873
1989	1,571,418	—	—	—	1,000,986	304,571	78,761	105,929	22,105	3,760	352	6,426	48,528
1990	1,584,785	—	—	—	1,021,950	297,257	77,429	105,982	22,830	4,113	342	6,868	48,014
1991	1,614,306	—	—	—	1,054,589	289,723	76,437	106,732	23,478	4,505	346	7,398	51,098
1992	1,604,444	—	—	—	1,040,441	281,690	75,088	119,822	23,652	4,639	336	7,396	51,380
1993	1,652,667	—	—	—	1,059,486	274,401	73,297	123,056	24,042	4,828	391	7,742	85,424
1994	1,666,226	—	—	—	1,063,518	268,375	71,652	125,102	25,147	5,177	381	7,844	99,030
1995	1,703,467	—	—	—	1,077,004	263,377	70,428	128,641	26,690	5,379	404	8,320	123,224
1996	1,718,898	—	—	—	1,078,296	259,885	69,000	127,582	28,022	5,596	401	8,631	141,485
1997	1,730,952	—	—	—	1,079,935	256,595	67,319	126,619	29,196	5,753	423	8,784	156,328

[1] Data revised from original source.

Source

Civil Service Retirement and Disability Fund Annual reports, unpublished data.

Documentation

The Office of Personnel Management is no longer required to prepare annual reports. Historical data (before 1989) are unaudited. For further information, contact the Office of Personnel Management. See also the text for Table Bf735–745.

These series combine annuitants covered under the Civil Service Retirement System (CSRS) and the Federal Employees Retirement System (FERS). Systematic provision for the retirement of federal civil service employees started with the original retirement act (Public Law 66-215), which was signed May 22, 1920, and initially covered about 330,000 employees in the classified civil service. The Act provided only for mandatory and disability retirement after fifteen years of service with annual annuities ranging from $180 to $720 based on length of service and the average salary for the ten years preceding retirement. Benefits have continued to evolve to the present time. They are now financed by both employee and government contributions to the retirement fund, and they provide benefits based on length of service and the average salary over the highest three years of pay. Additional information on the CSRS from 1921 through 1970 can be found in the text for Table Bf735–745. As of September 30, 1978, the former mandatory

TABLE Bf722–734 Federal employee and civil service retirement systems – annuitants: 1925–1997 *Continued*

separation requirement for federal employees who attain age 70 was removed. In 1979, the Office of Personnel Management began to administer the program, which was replaced by a new FERS in 1987.

As of 1999, almost all federal employees hired after 1983 are automatically included in the FERS program. The FERS provides three types of benefits: the basic Social Security benefits, a basic annuity component based on contributions by the employer and the government, and the opportunity to participate in a Thrift Savings Plan, which is essentially a tax-deferred savings and investment plan similar to the 401(k) for corporations. Generally, the basic annuity component of FERS is 1 percent of the employee's "high-3" year's average pay, multiplied by years of service. If the employee retires at age 62, or later, with at least twenty years of service, a factor of 1.1 percent is used rather than 1 percent. The tax-deferred savings plan allows employees to contribute up to 10 percent of their income. The government automatically contributes to the employee's account an amount equal to 1 percent of basic pay, and, if the employee contributes, the government matches the contribution up to a maximum of 4 percent of the employee's salary to the plan. A special retirement supplement designed to approximate the retiree's eventual Social Security benefits may be provided to compensate the retiree for any lack of Social Security benefits for those retiring prior to reaching the age of 62. Retirees may be eligible for the supplement if they retired after the minimum retirement age with thirty years of service, at age 60 with twenty years of service, or upon involuntary retirement. Law enforcement officers and firefighters who retire at age 50 with twenty years of service or at any age with twenty-five years of service are also eligible for the supplement. This supplement is also payable, after attainment of the minimum retirement age, to discontinued service and involuntary retirees as well as to members of the Senior Executive Service (SES) who are removed from SES status and who retire at the age of 50 with twenty years of service or at any age with twenty-five years of service.

Employees hired prior to 1984 are typically included under the CSRS, although they have the option to transfer to the FERS. Many of the features of the CSRS plans are the same as in 1973, although as of September 30, 1978, mandatory retirement was eliminated for federal employees. CSRS-covered employees may also participate in the Thrift Savings Plan, but their participation is limited to 5 percent of salary and no government contribution is made.

As of 1997, there are two requirements that all retiring employees must meet for the CSRS. First, the employee must have at least five years of civilian service with the federal government. Second, unless retiring because of total disability, the employee must have been employed under the CSRS for at least one year of the last two preceding final separation. There is no "1-out-of-2" requirement under FERS as there is under CSRS. Employees are eligible for immediate retirement if they meet these general requirements and any combination of the following age/service requirements. (1) Employees may elect optional voluntary early retirement, series Bf734, at a minimum age of 62 with at least five years of service; at age 60 with at least twenty years of service; or at age 55 with thirty years of service. (2) Law enforcement officers may retire at age 50 with twenty years of service. (3) Employees at any age with at least twenty-five years of service may retire when the agency is undergoing a major reduction in force. In the latter category, benefits may be reduced.

Series Bf722. For 1920–1979, equals the sum of series Bf723–725 and Bf727–733. For 1980–1997, equals the sum of series Bf726–734.

Series Bf723–726. The employees who retired under the "normal" rules are reported from 1920 to 1979 in three categories: mandatory retirement, optional retirement with thirty or more years of service, and optional retirement with less than thirty years of service. Starting with 1980, these three series were replaced by a single series for normal retirement (series Bf726). In 1979, when both sets of series were reported, series Bf723–725 summed to series Bf726. Series Bf723 ends in 1979 because the mandatory retirement age requirement was abolished.

Series Bf727. Employees of any age with at least five years of service may qualify for disability retirement if they become disabled for useful and efficient service.

Series Bf728. An employee who meets the five-year service requirement for retirement and who is separated from the federal service for any reason before meeting the age requirement for a general annuity may receive a deferred annuity that is payable upon attaining age 62. For 1945–1955, the information for the series was listed in the original source under the title "optional retirement with 5 years service at age 62."

Series Bf729. Employees age 50 or older with at least twenty years of service, or at any age with at least twenty-five years of service, may qualify for discontinued service retirement with a reduced annuity in cases of involuntary separation from the federal service. Involuntary separations include any separation against the will and without the consent of the employee, other than "for cause" for misconduct or delinquency. The most common cause of an involuntary separation was a reduction in force. Employees who decline "reasonable offers" of other positions are not eligible for discontinued service annuities. A reasonable offer is defined as the offer of another position in your agency and commuting area for which you are qualified and that is no more than two grades or pay levels below your current grade or pay level.

Series Bf730–733. There are several categories of federal employees who operate under special retirement rules, including those under hazardous duty, air traffic controllers, members of Congress, and annuitants who were transferred from other systems. The hazardous duty series is referred to as "law enforcement and firefighters" after 1980, but the data are comparable over time.

Series Bf734. Refers to annuitants who chose voluntary early retirement. Annuitants fall under this category when they volunteer to retire when an agency undergoes a major reorganization, reduction in force, or transfer of function, and a significant percentage of the employees will be separated or reduced in pay. At that point, the head of the agency can ask the Office of Personnel Management (OPM) to permit early optional retirement for eligible employees to lessen the impact of involuntary separations and demotions. After the agency head obtains approval, workers with at least twenty-five years of service, or workers at least age 50 with twenty or more years, may retire voluntarily on an immediate annuity. The annuity is reduced by 2 percent for each year younger than age 55.

TABLE Bf735–745 Civil service retirement annuities and payments: 1921–1970[1]

Contributed by Price V. Fishback and Melissa A. Thomasson

	Annuities					Lump-sum payments to					
			In force			Separated employees		Deceased employees		Deceased annuitants	
	Certified	Terminated	Total	Disability	Annual value	Payments	Amount paid	Payments	Amount paid	Payments	Amount paid
	Bf735	Bf736	Bf737	Bf738	Bf739	Bf740 [2]	Bf741 [2]	Bf742 [2]	Bf743 [2]	Bf744 [2]	Bf745 [2]
Year	Thousand	Thousand	Thousand	Thousand	Million dollars	Thousand	Million dollars	Thousand	Million dollars	Thousand	Million dollars
1921	7	1	6	1	4	26	0.3	—	—	—	—
1922	2	—	8	1	4	71	2.2	—	—	—	—
1923	3	2	9	1	5	58	2.8	—	—	—	—
1924	2	(Z)	11	2	6	45	2.9	—	—	—	—
1925	2	1	12	2	6	37	2.7	—	—	—	—
1926	2	1	13	2	7	34	3.4	—	—	—	—
1927	3	2	14	3	10	32	3.9	—	—	—	—
1928	3	2	15	3	11	28	3.8	—	—	—	—
1929	3	1	17	4	12	26	4.1	—	—	—	—
1930	3	2	18	4	13	28	5.0	—	—	—	—
1931	7	2	23	5	22	24	4.2	—	—	—	—
1932	5	2	26	6	24	21	3.9	—	—	—	—
1933	9	2	33	7	32	17	4.8	—	—	—	—
1934	14	2	45	9	44	22	8.0	—	—	—	—
1935	7	3	49	10	48	16	5.8	—	—	—	—
1936	6	4	51	11	50	12	2.6	3	2.7	2	1.2
1937	5	3	53	12	52	14	3.1	3	2.9	2	1.3
1938	6	3	56	13	55	18	3.8	3	3.1	2	1.4
1939	6	4	58	14	57	15	2.7	3	3.2	2	1.4
1940	7	3	62	15	60	15	2.9	3	3.7	2	1.5
1941	8	4	66	17	63	21	3.6	4	4.3	3	1.7
1942	8	5	69	18	66	46	5.6	4	3.9	3	1.7
1943	10	5	74	20	71	111	7.2	6	5.0	3	2.0
1944	10	6	78	21	76	390	21.5	9	5.2	3	2.3
1945	12	5	85	23	82	901	62.4	16	7.4	3	2.5
1946	16	5	96	27	93	—	179.8 [3]	—	— [3]	—	2.6
1947	22	7	111	32	103	943	178.9	17	10.4	4	3.7
1948	22	7	126	35	134	432	112.8	11	9.4	4	3.5
1949	31	9	148	39	154	229	61.4	6	3.9	5	4.7
1950	33	9	172	43	182	239	88.2	5	3.7	7	4.2
1951	36	11	197	46	206	167	64.9	4	4.0	8	3.9
1952	31	12	216	48	227	147	71.0	4	4.3	8	3.6
1953	38	13	241	52	289	136	81.4	4	5.2	8	3.8
1954	41	13	269	56	324	123	89.0	4	5.4	8	3.4
1955	42	14	297	61	358	101	73.3	4	5.7	8	3.6
1956	47	17	327	66	441	164	84.2	4	6.0	8	3.6
1957	61	19	369	73	516	184	99.3	4	6.7	8	3.7
1958	70	21	418	84	635	199	114.7	4	7.4	9	3.9
1959	81	23	476	93	723	144	95.4	4	7.3	9	3.7
1960	65	26	515	102	792	153	114.2	4	7.8	9	3.6
1961	72	28	559	112	883	131	103.7	4	8.7	9	3.6
1962	73	30	602	122	975	137	108.6	4	8.7	11	6.2
1963	73	32	643	130	1,127	131	105.8	4	9.0	13	6.1
1964	79	34	688	139	1,240	128	108.2	4	9.7	16	6.0
1965	78	37	729	149	1,354	121	112.5	5	10.2	15	7.3
1966	105	38	796	161	1,688	129	139.2	5	11.2	15	7.5
1967	77	42	831	167	1,881	164	157.1	5	10.5	16	7.6
1968	83	42	872	173	2,089	190	160.1	5	12.0	18	8.5
1969	86	48	910	178	2,315	207	198.8	5	12.3	15	8.2
1970	99	50	959	185	2,660	215	197.5	5	12.8	19	10.0

(Z) Fewer than 500 annuities.

[1] Years ending June 30.

[2] Deceased employees and deceased annuitants included with separated employees through 1935.

[3] Amount paid to beneficiaries of deceased employees included with amount paid to separated employees.

Source

U.S. Civil Service Commission, *Civil Service Retirement, Federal Employees Group Life Insurance, Federal Employees Health Benefits, retired Federal Employees Health Benefits*, various annual issues.

Documentation

The original retirement act (Public Law 66-215) was signed May 22, 1920, and initially covered about 330,000 employees in the classified civil service. The Act provided only for mandatory and disability retirement after fifteen years of service with annual annuities ranging from $180 to $720 based on length of service and the average salary for the ten years preceding retirement. The average annuity in the year following enactment was $568.

At the time these data were collected in the early 1970s, the retirement law in effect (passed in 1973) provided optional retirement on full annuity at age 55 with thirty years of service, age 60 with twenty years of service, or age 62

TABLE Bf735–745 Civil service retirement annuities and payments: 1921–1970 *Continued*

with five years of service; disability retirement was permitted at any age with five years of service; involuntary retirement at any age after twenty-five years of service, or at age 50 with twenty years of service. Deferred annuities were payable at age 62 with five years of service. Mandatory retirement was age 70 with fifteen years of service, and the average salary was the highest three years of salary. Employees contributed 7 percent of their pay to the retirement system. The annuity formula provided 1.5 percent of average salary for the first five years service, 1.75 percent for the next five years, and 2 percent for any remaining service, up to a maximum of 80 percent of average salary. Disability annuitants received the greater of the preceding computation or a guaranteed minimum of 40 percent of average salary or regular formula using service projected to age 60, whichever was less. The law also contained special hazardous duty positions for legislative branch employees. About 2.7 million employees were covered by the system, and the average annual annuity in 1970 was $4,920. For a more detailed depiction of timing of the major changes in the provisions of the Civil Service Retirement System between 1920 and 1970, see *Historical Statistics of the United States* (1975), pp. 336–7.

Lump-sum payments or refunds are paid to persons leaving the federal service and withdrawing contributions and to survivors of deceased employees and of deceased annuitants. In the case of deceased employees with no survivor annuity payable, accumulated deductions (contributions) are paid. In the case of deceased annuitants whose annuity paid has not equaled contributions, the unexpended balance is paid.

These series from the previous edition of *Historical Statistics of the United States* could not be updated owing to changes in the retirement systems for federal employees that creates problems with data comparability. See Table Bf722–734 for data on the number of annuitants since 1925, as well as descriptions of the modern retirement system. As of 1999, almost all federal employees hired after 1983 are automatically included in the Federal Employee Retirement System (FERS) program.

Series Bf735, annuities certified. Represents the number of employee and survivor annuitants added to the roll during the year.

Series Bf736, annuities terminated. Represents the employee and survivor annuitants dropped from the roll during the year; it is derived by adding the prior year's number in force to the current number certified and subtracting the current number in force.

Series Bf737, annuities in force. Represents total employee and survivor annuitants in active annuity status as of June 30. The annual value is the average monthly annuity as of June 30 projected to an annual basis.

TABLE Bf746–761 Railroad retirement benefits – number and amount, by type of beneficiary: 1937–1997

Contributed by Price V. Fishback, Richard Sutch, and Melissa A. Thomasson

			Favorable actions on applications for retirement and survivor monthly benefits				Recipients of monthly benefits actually paid by current payment status					Benefit payments				
	Railroad employees	Recipients	Total	Retirees	Spouse	Survivors	Total	Retirees	Spouse	Survivors	Lump-sum death benefits awarded	Total	Retirement annuities and pensions	Spouse annuities	Total survivor annuities	Total lump-sum survivor payments
	Bf746	Bf747	Bf748	Bf749	Bf750	Bf751	Bf752	Bf753	Bf754	Bf755	Bf756	Bf757	Bf758	Bf759	Bf760	Bf761
Fiscal year	Thousand	Thousand	Number	Number	Number	Number	Number	Number	Number	Number	Number	Million dollars	Million dollars	Million dollars	Million dollars	Million dollars
1937	1,279	7	8,000	7,000	—	(Z)	7,000	7,000	—	(Z)	—	5.0	4.0	—	(Z)	—
1938	1,093	117	110,000	107,000	—	2,000	108,000	107,000	—	1,000	1,000	83.0	82.0	—	1.0	—
1939	1,151	163	38,000	35,000	—	3,000	132,000	130,000	—	3,000	15,000	107.0	104.0	—	1.0	(Z)
1940	1,195	173	25,000	23,000	—	2,000	144,000	141,000	—	3,000	13,000	114.0	111.0	—	1.0	1.0
1941	1,322	182	22,000	21,000	—	2,000	153,000	150,000	—	3,000	13,000	122.0	117.0	—	2.0	2.0
1942	1,470	186	18,000	16,000	—	1,000	157,000	153,000	—	4,000	13,000	127.0	122.0	—	2.0	3.0
1943	1,591	191	17,000	16,000	—	1,000	160,000	156,000	—	4,000	15,000	131.0	124.0	—	2.0	4.0
1944	1,670	197	19,000	18,000	—	1,000	164,000	160,000	—	4,000	15,000	135.0	128.0	—	2.0	5.0
1945	1,680	210	22,000	21,000	—	1,000	171,000	167,000	—	4,000	20,000	143.0	133.0	—	2.0	6.0
1946	1,622	224	28,000	27,000	—	1,000	185,000	181,000	—	4,000	20,000	154.0	143.0	—	2.0	8.0
1947	1,598	265	63,000	29,000	—	34,000	231,000	194,000	—	37,000	15,000	173.0	159.0	—	7.0	9.0
1948	1,558	376	121,000	43,000	—	78,000	320,000	218,000	—	102,000	21,000	225.0	188.0	—	31.0	7.0
1949	1,403	427	67,000	36,000	—	31,000	356,000	234,000	—	122,000	34,000	283.0	234.0	—	38.0	7.0
1950	1,421	461	65,000	38,000	—	27,000	387,000	251,000	—	137,000	33,000	302.0	248.0	—	42.0	12.0
1951	1,476	484	57,000	32,000	—	24,000	408,000	261,000	—	147,000	31,000	317.0	259.0	—	45.0	12.0
1952	1,429	568	137,000	30,000	85,000	21,000	503,000	268,000	81,000	154,000	26,000	394.0	296.0	23.0	62.0	13.0
1953	1,405	609	77,000	33,000	23,000	20,000	531,000	279,000	91,000	161,000	27,000	460.0	324.0	41.0	79.0	13.0
1954	1,250	638	77,000	36,000	19,000	22,000	562,000	294,000	99,000	169,000	29,000	512.0	362.0	46.0	85.0	16.0
1955	1,239	696	106,000	38,000	21,000	47,000	616,000	310,000	107,000	200,000	24,000	550.0	376.0	49.0	110.0	19.0
1956	1,220	730	89,000	38,000	20,000	31,000	651,000	323,000	114,000	214,000	23,000	601.0	396.0	62.0	127.0	16.0
1957	1,150	757	83,000	37,000	20,000	26,000	679,000	336,000	119,000	224,000	21,000	678.0	455.0	69.0	139.0	15.0
1958	984	798	92,000	42,000	21,000	29,000	710,000	350,000	126,000	234,000	24,000	721.0	482.0	73.0	149.0	15.0
1959	949	824	94,000	44,000	21,000	28,000	746,000	369,000	132,000	245,000	22,000	781.0	519.0	81.0	164.0	18.0
1960	909	873	115,000	45,000	42,000	28,000	794,000	384,000	157,000	254,000	22,000	926.0	602.0	110.0	195.0	18.0
1961	836	906	98,000	43,000	26,000	29,000	821,000	397,000	166,000	259,000	23,000	987.0	641.0	118.0	207.0	20.0
1962	815	932	93,000	41,000	23,000	29,000	838,000	405,000	168,000	265,000	22,000	1,027.0	661.0	118.0	227.0	21.0
1963	790	951	94,000	42,000	22,000	30,000	861,000	416,000	173,000	272,000	23,000	1,068.0	686.0	119.0	240.0	21.0
1964	775	970	91,000	40,000	21,000	30,000	879,000	423,000	174,000	282,000	23,000	1,096.0	704.0	119.0	250.0	23.0
1965	753	980	85,000	36,000	19,000	29,000	889,000	426,000	174,000	288,000	23,000	1,118.0	716.0	118.0	259.0	24.0
1966	741	1,002	104,000	35,000	41,000	28,000	921,000	429,000	197,000	294,000	20,000	1,200.0	737.0	148.0	293.0	24.0
1967	713	1,022	103,000	50,000	24,000	29,000	950,000	445,000	200,000	306,000	20,000	1,266.0	780.0	162.0	299.0	23.0
1968	683	1,040	115,000	60,000	25,000	29,000	989,000	470,000	204,000	314,000	20,000	1,403.0	869.0	183.0	327.0	24.0
1969	659	1,050	114,000	55,000	26,000	33,000	1,016,000	489,000	208,000	319,000	21,000	1,536.0	941.0	208.0	362.0	24.0
1970	640	1,051	99,000	48,000	24,000	27,000	1,036,000	501,000	210,000	324,000	19,000	1,594.0	963.0	214.0	391.0	25.0
1971	611	—	113,832	60,067	24,823	28,951	1,067,121	525,712	212,075	329,334	—	1,909.7	1,178.5	256.4	448.7	26.0
1972	589	—	106,362	54,260	22,831	29,271	1,084,241	540,509	211,449	332,283	—	2,121.9	1,320.9	282.5	486.3	26.1
1973	584	—	99,088	51,601	21,976	25,511	1,098,454	553,256	210,793	334,405	—	2,456.8	1,511.9	319.4	598.7	32.2
1974	592	—	94,745	46,358	21,020	27,367	1,106,832	561,864	209,518	335,450	—	2,670.5	1,621.2	340.1	681.4	26.8
1975	548	—	137,034	79,526	32,101	25,407	1,160,312	603,028	219,644	337,640	—	3,060.4	1,838.2	384.2	811.4	27.9
1976	540	—	106,729	57,301	26,326	23,102	1,182,028	620,974	223,838	337,216	—	3,469.5	2,040.6	440.7	964.0	26.6
(TQ)	—	—	27,902	14,417	7,204	6,281	1,186,012	623,820	225,220	336,972	—	916.9	534.2	118.7	257.3	23.7
1977	546	—	95,992	45,775	26,292	23,925	1,201,055	633,331	230,758	336,966	—	3,786.9	2,212.8	499.1	1,054.6	6.7
1978	542	—	87,104	41,261	23,642	22,201	1,203,895	636,284	232,472	335,139	—	3,988.1	2,323.8	529.3	1,118.3	20.3
1979	554	—	83,538	40,177	22,323	21,038	1,204,719	638,183	233,611	332,925	—	4,274.9	2,492.4	572.1	1,194.8	16.7

			Favorable actions on applications for retirement and survivor monthly benefits				Recipients of monthly benefits actually paid by current payment status					Benefit payments				
	Railroad employees	Recipients	Total	Retirees	Spouse	Survivors	Total	Retirees	Spouse	Survivors	Lump-sum death benefits awarded	Total	Retirement annuities and pensions	Spouse annuities	Total survivor annuities	Total lump-sum survivor payments
	Bf746	Bf747	Bf748	Bf749	Bf750	Bf751	Bf752	Bf753	Bf754	Bf755	Bf756	Bf757	Bf758	Bf759	Bf760	Bf761
Fiscal year	Thousand	Thousand	Number	Number	Number	Number	Number	Number	Number	Number	Number	Million dollars	Million dollars	Million dollars	Million dollars	Million dollars
1980	532	—	83,476	40,511	22,268	20,697	1,203,006	639,314	233,916	329,776	—	4,730.6	2,754.9	634.9	1,327.2	15.6
1981	503	—	82,854	41,176	21,346	20,321	1,202,364	641,787	233,977	326,427	—	5,286.6	3,070.7	709.1	1,492.8	13.6
1982	440	—	84,395	39,985	21,613	22,787	1,200,427	642,640	234,009	323,621	—	5,725.6	3,342.1	755.9	1,617.0	13.8
1983	395	—	81,260	38,687	20,231	22,323	1,193,226	640,985	232,367	319,730	—	6,041.1	3,548.7	805.5	1,676.1	10.6
1984	395	—	72,237	33,176	18,587	20,461	1,182,606	635,821	230,433	316,218	—	6,099.9	3,602.6	815.2	1,670.8	10.8
1985	372	—	68,334	31,316	18,286	18,720	1,165,202	626,521	227,284	311,274	—	6,251.0	3,699.8	839.6	1,702.4	11.3
1986	342	—	69,330	31,875	17,850	19,590	1,151,861	619,548	224,642	307,551	—	6,329.5	3,760.6	847.4	1,711.9	9.3
1987	320	—	68,224	32,903	18,040	17,271	1,139,782	614,024	222,303	303,342	—	6,520.3	3,897.4	876.2	1,737.0	9.5
1988	312	—	67,057	32,297	17,776	16,973	1,124,645	607,088	220,093	297,264	—	6,675.9	4,017.6	897.4	1,752.9	9.7
1989	308	—	66,572	30,403	19,583	16,577	1,111,630	600,065	220,483	290,977	—	6,938.6	4,198.0	942.9	1,789.5	7.9
1990	296	—	60,743	27,689	17,036	16,006	1,094,112	590,660	218,475	284,878	—	7,194.6	4,376.5	980.4	1,829.6	8.1
1991	285	—	55,181	24,434	15,641	15,096	1,074,199	579,377	215,733	278,993	—	7,490.8	4,573.5	1,019.7	1,890.9	8.0
1992	276	—	52,298	23,277	14,442	14,566	1,050,546	566,804	212,036	271,619	—	7,693.9	4,705.1	1,048.8	1,933.1	6.7
1993	271	—	49,014	20,691	12,719	15,597	1,024,439	552,339	206,967	265,050	—	7,872.3	4,825.7	1,070.4	1,969.1	6.8
1994	266	—	44,378	19,205	11,847	13,315	998,280	536,856	201,327	258,014	—	7,978.9	4,890.7	1,088.3	1,993.6	7.2
1995	265	—	42,072	17,771	10,407	13,886	967,175	521,400	195,082	250,611	—	8,059.2	4,963.1	1,079.7	2,009.5	6.3
1996	257	—	38,635	16,707	9,576	12,343	936,428	505,483	188,281	242,581	—	8,113.6	5,013.3	1,075.9	2,018.5	6.8
1997	253	—	38,293	16,788	9,175	12,323	906,741	490,448	181,399	234,816	—	8,205.7	5,091.0	1,075.3	2,033.8	5.9

(Z) Series Bf751 and Bf755, fewer than 500 benefits. Series Bf760–761, less than $500,000.

Sources

U.S. Bureau of the Census, *Historical Statistics of the United States* (1975), series H271–286; *The Railroad Retirement Board Statistical Supplement to 1980 Annual Report*, Tables B-1, B-2, B-3; *The Railroad Retirement Board: Statistical Tables through FY 1990*, Tables B-1, B-2, B-3; *The Railroad Retirement Board: Statistical Tables through FY 1998*, Tables B-1, B-2, B-3, D-1. Updates are available from the Internet site of the Railroad Retirement Board.

Documentation

The Railroad Retirement and Carriers' Taxing Act of 1937 established the railroad retirement system for railroad employees as a program separate from the Social Security system. The 1937 Act provided annuities to retired employees based on their earnings and service. The system was to be administered by the U.S. Railroad Retirement Board. Annuities were paid at age 65 or later regardless of length of service, although persons between the ages of 60 and 64 could receive benefits (at reduced levels) after thirty years of service. Disabled workers could receive a full annuity for disability only if they were totally and permanently disabled and had thirty years of service. Persons between the ages of 60 and 64 could receive a reduced annuity after less than thirty years of service. Under the 1937 Act, survivor benefits were limited to a lump sum of 4 percent of the employee's creditable earnings, less any previously made annuity payments. The system was financed by taxes on employers and employees. Initially, employers and employees each contributed 2.75 percent of an employee's earnings up to $300 monthly.

Amendments in 1946 lessened the restrictions on disability payments and divided jurisdiction for survivor's benefits between the Railroad Retirement Board and the Social Security Administration. In 1951, further amendments added annuities for the spouses of retired railroad employees and made provisions for Social Security to assume the jurisdiction of benefits for employees with less than ten years of railroad service. The intention of the latter amendments was to ensure that Railroad Retirement benefits would be no less than the benefits that would be given under Social Security for similar service. In 1965, the Railroad Retirement tax base was coordinated with that of Social Security, and Medicare benefits were extended to railroad retirees and their families.

The Railroad Retirement Act of 1974 restructured the original act into a two-tier system of benefits in order to eliminate duplications in Railroad Retirement and Social Security benefits. The first tier takes into account both Railroad Retirement and nonrailroad Social Security credits and provides benefits equal to Social Security benefits. The second tier focuses on railroad service exclusively and provides benefits comparable to those in other industries with pension systems that provide benefits over and above Social Security. Subsequent amendments in the 1980s and 1990s changed some eligibility requirements as well as employer and employee tax contributions.

For a complete, detailed history of the Railroad Retirement System, see the U.S. Railroad Retirement Board's *Railroad Retirement Handbook*, available at its Internet site.

Series Bf746. Represents the mid-monthly calendar year average of the number of railroad employees.

Series Bf747 and Bf756. As reported in *Historical Statistics of the United States* (1975), series H272 and H281. Derived, in part, from otherwise unpublished data.

Series Bf748. Includes annuities to parents from 1981 forward.

Series Bf757. Includes a small amount of payments for Hospital Insurance benefits for services in Canada.

Series Bf755. Includes annuities temporarily being paid at spouse annuity rates, pending final adjudication of survivor annuities.

Series Bf759. Beginning in 1982, includes divorced spouse annuities. Further disaggregated information is available from the Railroad Retirement Board.

Series Bf760. Includes survivor (option) and parents' annuities.

TABLE Bf762–772 Veterans' benefits – number of payments, by eligibility category: 1940–1998

Contributed by Price V. Fishback and Melissa A. Thomasson

		Disability compensation or pension									
		Service-connected							Non-service-connected		
			Under age 65			Age 65 or older					
				With disability rating			With disability rating				
	Total	All ages	Total	Less than 70 percent	70–100 percent	Total	Less than 70 percent	70–100 percent	All ages	Under age 65	Age 65 or older
	Bf762	Bf763	Bf764	Bf765	Bf766	Bf767	Bf768	Bf769	Bf770	Bf771	Bf772
Year	Thousand	Thousand	Thousand	Thousand	Thousand	Thousand	Thousand	Thousand	Thousand	Thousand	Thousand
1940	610	385	—	—	—	—	—	—	189	—	—
1945	1,144	912	—	—	—	—	—	—	159	—	—
1950	2,368	1,990	—	—	—	—	—	—	290	—	—
1955	2,699	2,076	—	—	—	—	—	—	531	—	—
1956	2,739	2,083	2,026	1,841	185	57	43	14	597	319	278
1957	2,797	2,074	2,004	1,825	179	70	53	17	670	304	366
1958	2,850	2,064	1,980	1,807	173	84	65	19	741	279	462
1959	2,934	2,053	1,952	1,781	171	101	78	23	841	257	584
1960	3,009	2,027	1,908	1,746	162	119	93	26	947	219	728
1961	3,107	2,000	1,868	1,711	158	131	104	27	1,077	182	895
1962	3,150	1,987	1,849	1,693	156	138	109	29	1,138	166	972
1963	3,181	1,989	1,844	1,686	158	145	115	30	1,170	165	1,005
1964	3,197	1,993	1,846	1,684	162	147	117	30	1,186	176	1,010
1965	3,217	1,992	1,846	1,679	167	146	117	29	1,210	197	1,013
1966	3,201	1,993	1,850	1,677	173	143	115	28	1,196	221	975
1967	3,182	1,999	1,858	1,683	175	141	114	27	1,173	243	930
1968	3,164	2,011	1,873	1,696	177	138	112	26	1,145	265	880
1969	3,160	2,039	1,904	1,712	192	135	110	25	1,114	286	828
1970	3,181	2,091	1,950	1,754	196	141	116	25	1,086	310	776
1971	3,222	2,146	1,995	1,780	215	151	128	23	1,073	335	738
1972	3,269	2,183	2,022	1,804	218	161	135	26	1,086	381	705
1973	3,257	2,204	2,028	1,806	222	176	150	26	1,053	402	651
1974	3,241	2,211	2,018	1,796	222	193	165	28	1,030	410	620
1975	3,227	2,220	2,006	1,784	222	214	185	29	1,006	430	576
1976	3,236	2,232	1,996	1,767	229	236	209	27	1,003	456	547
1977	3,280	2,248	1,989	1,759	230	258	226	32	1,032	505	527
1978	3,284	2,259	1,971	1,741	230	288	254	34	1,025	516	509
1979	3,241	2,267	1,944	1,717	227	323	285	38	974	500	474
1980	3,196	2,274	1,912	1,689	223	362	320	42	922	467	455
1981	3,154	2,279	1,873	1,656	217	406	359	47	875	438	437
1982	3,096	2,274	1,818	1,606	210	456	404	52	824	406	418
1983	3,044	2,263	1,744	1,544	200	519	461	58	781	373	408
1984	2,980	2,251	1,666	1,476	190	585	520	65	729	339	390
1985	2,931	2,240	1,589	1,408	181	651	579	72	690	306	384
1986	2,883	2,225	1,505	1,335	169	720	641	79	658	274	384
1987	2,844	2,212	1,428	1,268	160	784	698	86	631	244	387
1988	2,804	2,199	1,361	1,209	153	838	746	92	606	219	387
1989	2,776	2,192	1,302	1,156	146	890	792	98	584	196	388
1990	2,746	2,184	1,253	1,113	140	931	828	102	562	175	387
1991	2,709	2,179	1,238	1,098	140	941	838	103	530	156	375
1992	2,674	2,181	1,245	1,104	141	936	833	103	493	138	354
1993	2,660	2,198	1,265	1,122	143	932	828	104	462	128	335
1994	2,659	2,218	1,290	1,144	146	928	824	104	441	122	319
1995	2,669	2,236	1,310	1,158	152	926	819	107	433	120	313
1996	2,671	2,253	1,330	1,171	158	923	814	109	418	116	302
1997	2,667	2,263	1,346	1,178	168	917	805	112	404	112	292
1998	2,668	2,277	1,372	1,191	180	905	790	115	391	110	281

Source

U.S. Social Security Administration, *Social Security Bulletin: Annual Statistical Supplement* (1999), Table 9.F1, p. 341. The original source of the series is published and unpublished data from the U.S. Department of Veteran's Affairs.

Documentation

Two major cash programs are available to veterans. The Disability Compensation program pays monthly benefits to honorably discharged veterans who are disabled as a result of injury or disease incurred while in or aggravated by active military duty. The amount of payment depends on the degree of disability, rated as the percentage impairment of earning capacity, graduated in intervals from 10 to 100 percent. Veterans with a 30 percent service-connected disability are also entitled to an additional allowance for dependents.

The surviving spouse, dependent children, and certain parents of veterans who die as the result of an injury or disease incurred while in or aggravated

TABLE Bf762–772 Veterans' benefits – number of payments, by eligibility category: 1940–1998 *Continued*

by active military duty are also eligible for compensation under the Dependency and Indemnity Compensation (DIC) program. The amount paid is based on the number of dependents and the degree of disability. DIC benefits may also be paid if the veteran was receiving or was entitled to receive compensation for a service-connected disability at the time of his or her death. Both Disability Compensation and DIC benefits are not means-tested.

Means-tested monthly benefits are provided to honorably discharged wartime veterans with limited income and resources who are permanently and totally disabled as a result of a condition not related to their military service. The amount of benefit varies with the number of the veteran's dependents and the severity of the veteran's condition. Pensions for non-service-connected death are based on need and are paid to surviving spouses and dependent children of deceased wartime veterans. For a pension to be payable, the veteran generally must have met the same service requirements established for the non-service-connected disability pension program.

Data reported are as of June 30 (1940–1956), June 20 (1957–1976), and September 30 thereafter.

Series Bf762. Does not always equal the sum of series Bf763 and Bf770 because there are persons receiving payments under special acts and as retired emergency and reserve offices included in the total but excluded from distribution.

Series Bf763. The sum of series Bf764 and Bf767.

Series Bf764. The sum of series Bf765–766.

Series Bf767. The sum of series Bf768–769.

Series Bf770. The sum of series Bf771–772.

PRIVATE WELFARE

Price V. Fishback and Melissa A. Thomasson

TABLE Bf773–785 Private social welfare expenditures: 1950–1994

Contributed by Price V. Fishback and Melissa A. Thomasson

	Private social welfare expenditures					Social welfare expenditures as a percentage of GDP			Private social welfare expenditures, earlier method				
	Total	Health and medical care	Income maintenance	Education	Welfare services	Public and private	Public	Private	Total	Health and medical care	Income maintenance	Education	Welfare services
	Bf773	Bf774	Bf775	Bf776	Bf777	Bf778	Bf779	Bf780	Bf781	Bf782	Bf783	Bf784	Bf785
Year	Million dollars	Million dollars	Million dollars	Million dollars	Million dollars	Percent	Percent	Percent	Million dollars	Million dollars	Million dollars	Million dollars	Million dollars
1950	—	—	—	—	—	—	—	—	12,027	965	8,962	1,615	685
1955	—	—	—	—	—	—	—	—	17,997	1,895	12,909	2,343	850
1960	—	—	—	—	—	—	—	—	27,829	3,535	19,461	3,745	1,088
1965	—	—	—	—	—	—	—	—	42,687	5,975	29,357	5,980	1,375
1966	—	—	—	—	—	—	—	—	42,245	—	31,464	6,648	—
1967	—	—	—	—	—	—	—	—	48,531	—	32,315	7,456	—
1968	—	—	—	—	—	—	—	—	52,679	8,840	33,523	8,566	1,750
1969	—	—	—	—	—	—	—	—	58,611	10,170	37,041	9,500	1,900
1970	—	—	—	—	—	—	—	—	67,353	11,660	43,810	9,883	2,000
1971	—	—	—	—	—	—	—	—	74,380	13,100	48,387	10,793	2,100
1972	95,362	55,800	17,123	14,894	7,545	23.5	16.6	7.7	82,127	14,835	53,214	11,778	2,300
1973	104,083	61,500	18,063	16,223	8,297	23.4	16.7	7.5	90,610	16,640	58,715	12,655	2,600
1974	114,084	67,700	19,660	17,754	8,970	23.8	17.0	7.6	99,592	18,725	64,535	13,432	2,900
1975	128,556	75,700	23,336	19,453	10,067	25.2	18.2	7.9	111,658	21,630	72,333	14,695	3,000
1976	145,570	87,400	25,004	21,418	11,748	26.8	19.7	8.0	125,187	24,605	80,777	16,405	3,400
1977	167,276	100,200	30,662	22,879	13,535	26.6	19.3	8.3	146,769	27,800	97,243	17,876	3,850
1978	189,590	111,000	36,743	25,257	16,590	25.6	18.2	8.3	165,978	31,400	110,778	19,500	4,300
1979	217,279	125,100	44,703	27,936	19,540	25.3	17.7	8.3	—	—	—	—	—
1980	250,534	142,500	53,564	31,694	22,776	26.1	18.1	9.0	—	—	—	—	—
1981	285,585	165,700	58,741	35,416	25,728	26.9	18.7	9.2	—	—	—	—	—
1982	328,111	188,400	72,445	39,199	28,067	28.2	19.2	10.1	—	—	—	—	—
1983	366,635	207,700	84,652	42,891	31,392	28.9	19.6	10.4	—	—	—	—	—
1984	406,535	229,600	95,759	46,427	34,749	27.6	18.3	10.4	—	—	—	—	—
1985	462,283	253,900	118,871	50,513	38,999	27.6	17.8	11.1	—	—	—	—	—
1986	512,287	271,000	143,670	54,406	43,211	28.0	17.7	11.6	—	—	—	—	—
1987	544,584	293,000	143,589	60,394	47,601	28.8	18.5	11.6	—	—	—	—	—
1988	600,132	333,100	148,858	65,595	52,579	29.3	18.7	11.9	—	—	—	—	—
1989	668,806	369,800	167,260	72,434	59,312	29.4	18.5	12.3	—	—	—	—	—
1990	720,718	413,100	164,772	78,263	64,583	29.7	18.5	12.5	—	—	—	—	—
1991	764,439	441,000	170,754	83,687	68,998	31.3	19.8	12.9	—	—	—	—	—
1992	830,628	477,000	187,461	90,145	76,022	32.4	20.6	13.3	—	—	—	—	—
1993	873,871	505,100	192,340	95,532	80,899	33.0	21.1	13.3	—	—	—	—	—
1994	921,465	528,600	204,736	101,832	86,297	—	—	13.3	—	—	—	—	—

Sources

Series Bf773–780. Wilmer Kerns, "Private Social Welfare Expenditures, 1972–94," *Social Security Bulletin* 60 (1) (1997): 54–5. Series Bf781–785: for the years 1950, 1955, 1960, 1965, 1970, and 1974–1978, Alma W. McMillan and Ann Kallman Bixby, "Social Welfare Expenditures, Fiscal Year 1978," *Social Security Bulletin* 43 (5) (1980): 16; for the years 1971–1973, Alfred M. Skolnik and Sophie R. Dales, "Social Welfare Expenditures, Fiscal Year, 1976," *Social Security Bulletin* 40 (1) (1977): 17; for the year 1969, Alfred M. Skolnik and Sophie R. Dales, "Social Welfare Expenditures, 1972–73," *Social Security Bulletin* 37 (1) (1974): 17; for the year 1968, Alfred M. Skolnik and Sophie R. Dales, "Social Welfare Expenditures, 1971–72," *Social Security Bulletin* 35 (12) (1972): 16; and for the years 1966 and 1967, Alfred M. Skolnik and Sophie R. Dales, "Social Welfare Expenditures, 1968–69," *Social Security Bulletin* 32 (12) (1969): 17.

Documentation

The Social Security Administration (SSA) has estimated private social welfare expenditures for 1972 to the present for calendar years – see series Bf773–777 and Bf779 – using methodologies described first in Milton P. Glanz, Wilmer L. Kerns, and Jack Schmulowitz, "Private Social Welfare Expenditures," 1972–84," *Social Security Bulletin* 50 (5) (1987): 59–67. Through the late 1970s, the SSA used an alternative methodology to develop earlier estimates for fiscal years during the period 1950–1978 but ended the series because of data-source and methodology limitations.

Series Bf773–777. All estimates are on a calendar-year basis in current-year dollars. The private social welfare expenditures series are estimates of private-sector financing of social welfare programs in the United States. They complement the parallel public social welfare expenditures series but do not have a one-to-one relationship with them. Conceptually, private expenditures can be grouped into four major categories: health and medical care, income maintenance, education, and welfare services.

Series Bf774. The health and medical care expenditures data are from the Health Care Financing Administration. They include spending on health services and supplies (rising from 94.2 percent in 1972 to 97.6 percent in 1994), noncommercial medical research (0.2 to 0.4 percent), and medical facilities construction (5.2 percent in 1972, declining to 2.2 percent in 1974).

Series Bf775. Income maintenance expenditures represent outlay for employee benefit plans in the private sector, including group life insurance,

TABLE Bf773–785 Private social welfare expenditures: 1950–1994 *Continued*

sickness and disability insurance, long-term disability insurance, and private pension plans.

Series Bf776. The SSA developed a methodology for estimating private expenditures for education that has produced estimates similar to those by the Bureau of Economic Analysis, using an alternative methodology. Both agencies have modified their procedures over the past ten to fifteen years, and the series are approaching convergence. For discussion of the procedures for the period 1972–1994, see Wilmer Kerns, "Private Social Welfare Expenditures, 1972–90," *Social Security Bulletin* 55 (3) (1992): 62–63.

Series Bf777. The welfare services estimates are based on an indicator series developed by the U.S. Bureau of Economic Analysis for the national income and product accounts on personal consumption expenditures. The data are collected by the Census Bureau from its Census of Service Industries. Public funds are excluded from the estimates for private social services. The services include individual and family services (19.6 percent in 1992), residential care (18.2 percent), civic and social/fraternal organizations (18.1), child day care (10.9), job training and vocational rehabilitation services (9.4), and social services not elsewhere classified (23.9).

Series Bf778. Fiscal year basis.

Series Bf780. Adjusts for overlap that occurs when payments received under public or private income-maintenance programs are used to purchase medical care, educational services, or residential care.

TABLE Bf786–801 Private social welfare expenditures – disaggregations of major categories: 1960–1997

Contributed by Price V. Fishback and Melissa A. Thomasson

	Private health expenditures				Private social welfare expenditures on income maintenance						Private social welfare expenditures on education					
	Total	Health services and supplies	Medical research	Construction of medical facilities	Total	Group life insurance for all wage and salary workers	Private pension plan	Sickness and disability insurance	Long-term disability	Supplemental unemployment benefits	Total	Elementary, secondary, and nursery schools	Higher education	Commercial and vocational schools	Private construction of schools	Sickness and disability insurance payments
	Bf786	Bf787	Bf788	Bf789	Bf790	Bf791	Bf792	Bf793	Bf794	Bf795	Bf796	Bf797	Bf798	Bf799	Bf800	Bf801
Year	Million dollars	Million dollars	Million dollars	Million dollars	Million dollars	Million dollars	Million dollars	Million dollars	Million dollars	Million dollars	Million dollars	Million dollars	Million dollars	Million dollars	Million dollars	Million dollars
1960	20,203	19,496	139	568	—	—	—	—	—	—	—	—	—	—	—	—
1961	21,466	20,606	147	713	—	—	—	—	—	—	—	—	—	—	—	—
1962	23,291	22,232	153	905	—	—	—	—	—	—	—	—	—	—	—	—
1963	25,343	24,237	162	945	—	—	—	—	—	—	—	—	—	—	—	—
1964	28,290	26,944	170	1,176	—	—	—	—	—	—	—	—	—	—	—	—
1965	30,867	29,417	176	1,273	—	—	—	—	—	—	—	—	—	—	—	—
1966	31,600	30,120	186	1,294	—	—	—	—	—	—	—	—	—	—	—	—
1967	31,964	30,561	198	1,205	—	—	—	—	—	—	—	—	—	—	—	—
1968	35,879	34,262	208	1,410	—	—	—	—	—	—	—	—	—	—	—	—
1969	40,247	38,047	213	1,987	—	—	—	—	—	—	—	—	—	—	—	—
1970	45,537	42,957	215	2,364	—	—	—	—	—	—	—	—	—	—	—	—
1971	49,829	46,915	233	2,682	—	—	—	—	—	—	—	—	—	—	—	—
1972	55,808	52,522	227	3,060	17,123	3,180	9,710	3,999	—	234	14,894	3,941	8,224	1,761	968	2,649
1973	61,550	58,211	232	3,107	18,063	—	—	—	—	—	16,223	4,461	8,940	1,985	837	—
1974	67,667	64,288	252	3,128	19,660	3,195	12,638	—	—	400	17,754	5,218	9,810	2,071	655	3,277
1975	75,695	72,274	264	3,158	23,336	3,380	14,398	5,058	—	500	19,453	5,911	10,293	2,682	567	3,396
1976	87,434	83,807	267	3,360	25,004	3,523	17,091	—	—	200	21,418	6,302	11,153	3,303	660	3,906
1977	100,158	96,621	220	3,317	30,662	3,832	22,064	—	—	190	22,879	6,481	12,120	3,618	660	4,277
1978	111,048	107,432	236	3,380	36,743	4,193	27,316	—	—	248	25,257	7,323	13,136	4,069	729	4,692
1979	125,054	121,193	254	3,607	44,703	4,564	31,602	—	—	400	27,936	8,130	14,656	4,344	806	5,772
1980	142,493	138,041	292	4,161	53,564	5,075	37,605	8,630	1,282	972	31,694	9,338	16,520	4,661	1,175	6,280
1981	165,715	160,297	312	5,107	58,741	5,746	44,569	—	—	491	35,416	10,251	19,000	4,994	1,171	6,437
1982	188,397	181,844	390	6,163	72,445	6,269	54,380	9,178	1,688	930	39,199	10,727	21,993	5,123	1,356	6,884
1983	207,746	200,372	456	6,919	84,652	6,510	66,743	9,171	1,817	411	42,891	11,569	24,249	5,661	1,412	6,993
1984	229,938	222,755	506	6,677	95,759	6,899	76,683	—	1,874	282	46,427	12,362	26,490	6,175	1,400	7,498
1985	254,518	248,018	538	5,962	118,871	7,489	98,570	10,570	1,937	305	50,513	13,121	28,758	6,934	1,700	8,026
1986	271,398	264,844	782	5,771	143,670	7,797	122,384	10,748	2,253	488	54,406	13,550	31,243	7,513	2,100	8,046
1987	293,291	285,982	800	6,509	143,589	8,166	120,672	11,822	2,293	636	60,394	14,496	33,788	8,410	3,700	8,896
1988	334,251	325,592	839	7,820	148,858	8,418	124,871	12,789	2,295	485	65,595	15,435	36,608	10,652	2,900	9,636
1989	371,413	362,361	882	8,170	167,260	9,063	141,286	13,616	2,892	403	72,434	16,861	40,288	11,985	3,300	9,869
1990	416,187	405,939	960	9,288	164,772	9,278	138,114	13,680	2,926	774	78,263	17,546	43,952	12,665	4,100	10,362
1991	448,859	438,737	1,090	9,033	170,754	9,472	143,314	13,844	3,172	952	83,687	17,960	47,978	12,849	4,900	10,615
1992	483,553	472,546	1,183	9,824	187,461	10,184	158,857	14,684	3,143	593	90,145	19,312	52,024	13,709	5,100	—
1993	513,172	501,275	1,215	10,682	192,340	10,693	163,158	15,132	2,900	457	95,532	20,201	55,908	14,523	4,900	—
1994	524,908	513,136	1,276	10,496	204,736	11,229	174,452	15,901	2,895	259	101,832	21,222	59,675	15,535	5,400	—
1995	538,507	527,555	1,325	9,628	—	—	—	—	—	—	—	—	—	—	—	—
1996	561,141	549,454	1,432	10,254	—	—	—	—	—	—	—	—	—	—	—	—
1997	585,312	571,946	1,488	11,877	—	—	—	—	—	—	—	—	—	—	—	—

TABLE Bf786–801 Private social welfare expenditures – disaggregations of major categories: 1960–1997 *Continued*

Sources

For series Bf786–789, see the Health Care Financing Administration Internet site, National Health Care Expenditures. See also *Health Care Financing Review, Statistical Supplement, 1998*. For series Bf790–800, Wilmer Kerns, "Private Social Welfare Expenditures, 1972–94," *Social Security Bulletin* 60 (1) (1997): 54–9 and "Role of the Private Sector in Financing Social Welfare Programs, 1972–92," *Social Security Bulletin* 58 (1) (1995): 66–73. There are some exceptions for the income-maintenance expenditures: the figures for 1974 and 1976–1978 are from Wilmer Kerns and Milton P. Glanz, "Private Social Welfare Expenditures, 1972–95," *Social Security Bulletin* 51 (8) (1988): 8; and the figures for 1979 and 1984 are from Wilmer Kerns, "Private Social Welfare Expenditures, 1972–92," *Social Security Bulletin* 57 (3) (1992): 63. For series Bf801, see Wilmer Kerns, "Social Welfare Expenditure, 1972–1991," *Social Security Bulletin* 57 (1) (1994): 92, and Kerns and Glanz (1988).

Documentation

For more detail on health care expenditures and the source, see the text for Table Bf875–886.

Series Bf786. Identical to series Bf876, and the sum of series Bf787–789.

Series Bf787. Health services and supplies include "personal health care," comprising therapeutic goods or services rendered to treat or prevent a specific disease or condition in a specific person, and services, including hospital services, physician services, dental service, durable and nondurable medical devices, nursing home care, program administration, and net costs of health insurance. The series represents spending for care rendered during the year. It is the sum of personal health care expenditures, government public health activity, and program administration. It is distinguished from research and construction expenditures, which represent an investment in the future health care system.

Series Bf788–789. Includes noncommercial biomedical research and the construction of health care facilities.

Series Bf790. Identical to series Bf775.

Series Bf790–795. In the years 1980 through 1994, the subcategories should sum to series Bf790. Prior to that time, series Bf790 includes information on accidental death and dismemberment. Missing information on sickness and disability in some years (see discussion that follows) also prevent the subcategories from summing to the total. See the text for Table Bf773–785 for more detail.

Series Bf791. Includes programs for government civilian employees in order to maintain consistency with data reported for years prior to 1988. The estimates are further adjusted to exclude group policies not based directly on employer–employee relationships, such as insurance for credit card holders, mortgage insurance, fraternal societies, savings or investment groups, professional societies and employee associations; the excluded categories account for about 8 percent of total life insurance benefits. The totals also include accidental death and dismemberment benefits for the 1972–1979 period. After 1979, the Health Insurance Association of America eliminated this item from their questionnaire.

Series Bf792. Based on mandatory form 5500 reports filed with the Internal Revenue Service and forwarded to the Department of Labor. Defined-contribution benefit plans included 401(k)-type plans, into which employees can contribute a portion of their salaries with or without employer contributions on a tax-deferred basis. Another form of pension coverage is the employee stock ownership plan. Benefits paid include benefits from all employment-related pension plans to which employees contribute (such as thrift plans). However, withdrawals from individual savings plans, individual retirement accounts, and Keogh plans are not included. More detail on specific types of pension plan expenditures is available in the source.

Series Bf793. Sickness and disability benefits are sick leave and payments for short-term sickness and disability from private and self-insurance. After 1980 long-term and short-term disability benefits are estimated separately. This series does not correspond exactly to the series on short-term sickness benefits in Tables Bf854–874. For the years 1972–1986, Kerns and Glanz (1988, p. 8) report figures on sickness and disability benefits, but the estimates for the overlapping years do not match up with the data on sickness and disability reported in this table.

Series Bf793 and Bf801. In the 1995 Kerns article, there was a change in the method of calculating sickness and disability insurance payments that led to substantial changes in the numbers reported. Series Bf801 was included for persons who were interested in having a consistent series for changes during the 1970s and early 1980s. Kerns seems to consider series Bf793 to be the superior estimate.

Series Bf794. Long-term disability benefits, as a rule, commence on the first day of the seventh month of disability. The figures are estimated from data supplied by the Health Insurance Association of America. Long-term disability benefits paid under the provisions of employment-related pension plans are included in the private pension category.

Series Bf795. Data on supplemental unemployment benefits are taken from the national income and product accounts (NIPA) series on other labor income by industry and by type. Most of these benefits are paid to automobile workers under management-union contractual agreements.

Series Bf796. Identical to series Bf776, and the sum of series Bf797–800.

Series Bf796–800. The education spending figures are derived from methods developed by both the Social Security Administration (SSA) and the U.S. Bureau of Economic Analysis (BEA). For consistency, the SSA is now using the BEA's NIPA estimates with two minor adjustments. The SSA estimates include school construction costs funded by private sources, which the BEA reports elsewhere. The BEA estimate for education includes contributions from foundations and from nonprofit research funds, which are excluded by the SSA.

Series Bf801. Covers private industry wage and salary workers.

TABLE Bf802–813 Employee-benefit plans – estimated number of workers covered, by type of benefit: 1950–1975

Contributed by Price V. Fishback and Melissa A. Thomasson

	All wage and salary workers							Wage and salary workers in private industry				
			With hospitalization coverage					With coverage for temporary disability including formal sick leave				
	With life insurance and death benefits	With accidental death and dismemberment coverage	Total	Written in compliance with California temporary disability law	With surgical coverage	With regular medical coverage	With major medical expenses coverage	Total	In compliance with state temporary disability laws	With coverage for long-term disability	With supplemental unemployment coverage	With retirement coverage
	Bf802	Bf803	Bf804	Bf805	Bf806	Bf807	Bf808	Bf809	Bf810	Bf811	Bf812	Bf813
Year	Million	Million	Million	Million	Million	Million	Million	Million	Million	Million	Million	Million
1950	19.4	8.1	24.3	1.2	17.7	8.2	—	20.1	6.6	—	—	9.8
1951	20.8	9.5	27.1	1.4	21.7	10.7	—	21.7	6.8	—	—	10.8
1952	22.3	10.7	28.8	1.5	24.2	12.7	0.2	22.4	7.0	—	—	11.3
1953	24.2	11.8	31.0	1.5	26.9	15.8	0.5	23.4	7.0	—	—	12.6
1954	25.7	14.0	31.1	1.4	27.8	17.5	0.8	22.9	6.7	—	—	13.4
1955	28.1	15.6	32.8	1.4	30.2	20.2	2.2	23.5	6.8	—	1.0	14.2
1956	29.8	17.3	35.1	1.5	32.4	22.0	3.5	24.7	7.1	—	2.0	15.5
1957	31.2	18.4	36.4	1.6	34.2	23.9	4.9	24.9	7.2	—	1.9	16.7
1958	31.7	18.7	36.2	1.4	34.1	24.5	5.9	23.8	6.8	—	1.7	17.2
1959	33.5	19.7	37.2	1.5	35.4	26.1	7.2	24.4	6.9	—	1.9	18.2
1960	34.2	20.9	39.3	1.2	37.4	28.2	8.8	24.5	6.8	—	1.7	18.7
1961	35.5	21.3	39.9	1.1	38.0	29.8	10.3	24.6	6.8	—	1.9	19.2
1962	36.4	22.6	41.0	0.9	39.0	31.3	11.7	25.3	6.8	—	1.8	19.7
1963	37.8	24.7	42.6	0.3	40.8	33.3	13.2	23.6	6.2	0.7	1.8	20.3
1964	40.1	26.5	43.9	0.3	41.8	35.4	14.7	23.9	6.2	1.2	2.0	20.9
1965	41.9	28.4	45.7	0.3	43.4	38.2	16.6	24.5	6.4	1.9	2.1	21.8
1966	43.5	28.5	47.2	0.4	45.2	40.2	18.3	25.5	6.6	2.3	2.2	22.7
1967	45.7	30.4	48.7	0.4	47.0	42.5	20.2	26.0	6.7	3.7	2.2	24.3
1968	48.2	33.7	50.1	0.4	48.3	43.6	21.7	27.9	6.7	4.6	2.2	24.8
1969	49.0	36.5	52.1	0.4	50.6	46.1	23.4	29.4	6.9	5.5	2.2	26.0
1970	52.0	38.7	53.1	0.4	51.5	48.0	24.6	29.7	7.1	7.0	2.2	26.1
1971	53.5	39.2	53.2	0.4	51.7	48.3	25.7	30.1	6.9	7.9	2.2	26.4
1972	55.6	40.7	54.2	0.4	52.9	49.4	26.4	31.3	7.1	9.5	2.0	27.5
1973	57.8	42.7	56.8	0.4	55.4	53.7	27.6	32.0	7.2	10.6	2.1	29.2
1974	60.6	44.3	57.6	0.4	56.1	54.9	28.2	31.7	7.0	11.1	2.0	29.8
1975	62.4	46.5	58.2	0.4	56.6	56.1	29.6	31.1	7.0	11.5	1.9	30.3

Sources

Martha Remy Yohalem, "Employee-Benefit Plans, 1975," *Social Security Bulletin* 38 (11) (1977): 20, and Alfred M. Skolnik, "Twenty-five Years of Employee-Benefit Plans," *Social Security Bulletin* 39 (9) (1976): 5.

Documentation

An "employee-benefit plan," as defined here, is any type of plan sponsored or initiated unilaterally or jointly by employers or employees and providing benefits that stem from the employment relationship and are not underwritten or paid directly by government (federal, state, or local). In general, the intent is to include plans that provide in an orderly predetermined fashion (1) income maintenance when regular earnings are cut off because of death, accident, sickness, retirement, or unemployment, and (2) benefits to meet medical expenses associated with illness or injury. The plans exclude workers' compensation required by statute and employer's liability.

Government employees who are covered by plans underwritten by nongovernmental organizations are included in the series, whether or not the government unit contributes (as an employer) to the financing of the program. Specifically included here are plans providing government employees with group life insurance, accidental death and dismemberment insurance, and hospital, surgical, regular medical, and major-medical expense insurance. Retirement and sick-leave plans for government employees, which are financed and administered directly by government, are excluded from the series.

Coverage data are generally based on the number of active participants (those currently employed) and may include persons who have been temporarily laid off or retired. The practice of continuing coverage for a retired worker is particularly prevalent in group life insurance. Many group life and health plans permit a person on layoff to continue coverage in the group for three to six months, and, in some cases, even longer. In addition, workers who have terminated employment may carry vested pension rights; these persons are often included in the total coverage group. No attempt has been made to correct the coverage data for such limitations; therefore, the proportion that covered employees represent of all employed workers and the proportion that contributions represent of aggregate payrolls are somewhat overstated. Nevertheless, long-run growth patterns for the various types of plans remain valid.

Series Bf802. Group and wholesale life insurance coverage is based on data from the Institute of Life Insurance, *Group Life Insurance and Group Annuity Coverage in the United States*, annual issues, modified to exclude group plans not related to employment. It also excludes coverage under servicemen's group life insurance plans. Self-insured death-benefit plan coverage is based on data for various trade-union, mutual benefits association, and company-administered plans.

Series Bf803. Accidental death and dismemberment coverage is from Health Insurance Association of America, *Group Health Insurance Coverage in the United States*, annual issues.

Series Bf804 and Bf806–807. Data on hospitalization, surgical, and regular medical coverage are from Marjorie Smith Mueller and Paula A. Piro, "Private Health Insurance in 1974: A Review of Coverage, Enrollment, and Financial Experience," *Social Security Bulletin* 39 (3) (1976): 3–20; Health Insurance Association of America, *Group Health Insurance Coverage in the United States*,

TABLE Bf802–813 Employee-benefit plans – estimated number of workers covered, by type of benefit: 1950–1975 *Continued*

annual issues; and Health Insurance Institute, *Source Book of Health Insurance Data* (1975–1976). Data are modified to exclude participants not actively employed and to allow for duplication resulting from participation in more than one plan, using benchmark data from a special household survey of employed workers conducted in conjunction with the April 1972 Current Population Survey. The data are adjusted to include employees covered by group comprehensive major-medical expenses insurance.

Series Bf804–805. Hospitalization coverage includes private hospital plans written in compliance with state temporary disability insurance law in California, shown separately in series Bf805.

Series Bf808. Major medical expenses coverage represents coverage under group supplementary and comprehensive major-medical insurance underwritten by commercial insurance carriers.

Series Bf809–810. Temporary disability and formal sick leave programs include private plans written in compliance with state temporary disability insurance laws in California, Hawai'i, New Jersey, and New York, shown separately in series Bf810. The data are from *A Survey of Accident and Health Coverage in the United States* (Health Insurance Council, 1950) and the Health Insurance Association of America and Health Insurance Institute and are adjusted to exclude credit, accident, and health insurance. Data for 1950 are modified slightly to adjust for the effect of state temporary disability insurance laws on formal paid sick leave and self-insured plan coverage. Before 1963, this series includes group long-term disability, which was minimal before that time.

Series Bf811. The long-term disability coverage series reported separately in 1963 comes from Health Insurance Institute, *Source Book of Health Insurance Data* (1975–1976).

Series Bf812. Information on supplemental unemployment insurance is based on trade-union and industry reports and "Financing Supplemental Unemployment Benefit Plans," *Monthly Labor Review*, November 1969, and a 1976 survey of reports filed with the U.S. Department of Labor under the Welfare and Pension Plans Disclosure Act. The data exclude dismissal wage and separation allowances, except when financed from supplemental unemployment benefit funds covering temporary and permanent layoffs.

Series Bf813. Retirement coverage is estimated by the Social Security Administration from data furnished primarily by the Institute of Life Insurance and the Securities and Exchange Commission. The data are adjusted for duplication resulting from participation in more than one plan and the vesting of benefits, using benchmark data from a special household survey of employed workers conducted in conjunction with the April 1972 Current Population Survey. The series includes pay-as-you-go and deferred profit-sharing plans, plans of nonprofit organizations, union pension plans, and railroad plans supplementing the federal Railroad Retirement program. It excludes beneficiaries as well as pension plans for federal, state, and local government employees, tax-sheltered annuity plans, and plans for the self-employed.

TABLE Bf814–824 Employee-benefit plans – estimated employer and employee contributions, by type of benefit: 1950–1975

Contributed by Price V. Fishback and Melissa A. Thomasson

	All wage and salary workers							Wage and salary workers in private industry			
				Health benefits				Temporary and long-term disability			
	Total	Life insurance and death benefits	Accidental death and dismemberment benefits	Total	Hospitalization benefits	Surgical and regular medical benefits	Major medical benefits	Total	In compliance with state temporary disability laws	Supplemental unemployment benefits	Retirement benefits
	Bf814	Bf815	Bf816	Bf817	Bf818	Bf819	Bf820	Bf821	Bf822	Bf823	Bf824
Year	Million dollars	Million dollars	Million dollars	Million dollars	Million dollars	Million dollars	Million dollars	Million dollars	Million dollars	Million dollars	Million dollars
1950	3,940	480	18	856	562	294	—	505	76	—	2,080
1951	4,986	524	23	1,139	727	412	—	640	144	—	2,660
1952	5,677	620	27	1,373	881	493	—	687	156	—	2,970
1953	6,630	694	31	1,664	1,071	593	—	766	187	—	3,475
1954	6,989	732	34	1,924	1,221	684	18	785	178	—	3,515
1955	7,857	881	43	2,194	1,385	770	39	859	179	40	3,840
1956	8,911	1,002	50	2,595	1,603	898	94	914	177	125	4,225
1957	10,042	1,077	57	2,996	1,806	1,021	169	1,023	217	170	4,720
1958	10,521	1,179	61	3,286	1,945	1,076	266	1,049	232	125	4,820
1959	11,715	1,292	66	3,774	2,230	1,187	357	1,098	233	125	5,360
1960	12,530	1,416	70	4,257	2,505	1,282	470	1,179	239	118	5,490
1961	13,482	1,557	75	4,924	2,834	1,440	651	1,215	255	102	5,610
1962	14,758	1,677	80	5,508	3,159	1,596	753	1,311	255	152	6,030
1963	15,881	1,867	92	5,993	3,472	1,684	837	1,360	244	148	6,420
1964	17,657	2,044	99	6,726	3,885	1,876	965	1,397	238	112	7,280
1965	19,919	2,233	116	7,520	4,333	2,109	1,078	1,574	258	116	8,360
1966	21,683	2,376	131	8,042	4,547	2,300	1,195	1,754	280	130	9,250
1967	23,419	2,538	142	8,549	4,703	2,552	1,294	1,897	311	113	10,180
1968	26,889	2,937	169	10,076	5,539	2,915	1,621	2,333	342	125	11,250
1969	30,569	3,222	190	11,595	6,341	3,363	1,890	2,702	399	110	12,750
1970	39,861	3,577	224	13,878	7,569	3,998	2,310	3,075	417	109	14,000
1971	39,861	3,869	229	15,703	8,578	4,489	2,635	3,227	443	194	16,640
1972	45,429	4,343	284	18,248	9,528	5,152	3,568	3,750	499	264	18,540
1973	50,460	4,394	303	20,500	10,512	5,938	4,050	3,939	522	224	21,100
1974	57,741	4,711	329	23,068	11,437	7,022	4,609	4,383	517	230	25,020
1975	67,302	5,089	331	27,087	13,273	8,162	5,652	4,704	580	240	29,850

Source

Martha Remy Yohalem, "Employee-Benefit Plans, 1975," *Social Security Bulletin* 38 (11) (1977): 23, and Alfred M. Skolnik, "Twenty-five Years of Employee-Benefit Plans," *Social Security Bulletin* 39 (9) (1976): 8.

Documentation

See the text for Table Bf802–813 for more information. See the parallel table Bf825–835 for data on benefits paid.

Employee-benefit plans have become the predominant way through which most workers and their families obtain basic medical care protection, and they provide many services and protections not originally included. The increasing dollar amounts of benefits paid under employee-benefit plans, however, do not necessarily represent real gains – in terms of increased quality of care and adequacy of protection provided – for individual employees. Some of the rise in aggregate expenditures is the result of growth in the number of employees and dependents covered, increased per unit cost of providing specific services and benefits, and increased utilization of services.

Measuring the magnitude of real gain in health care benefits is particularly difficult. See Herbert E. Klarman, Dorothy P. Rice, Barbara S. Cooper, and H. Louis Stettler III, *Sources of Increase in Selected Medical Care Expenditures, 1929–1969*, Staff Paper number 4 (Social Security Administration, Office of Research and Statistics, 1970). The utilization of medical and hospital services is influenced by a number of factors such as the age distribution of the workforce, variations in incidence of sickness, shifts in types of services used, and the tendency for private plans to provide supplemental rather than basic protection to the elderly, as the result of Medicare.

Series Bf815 and Bf826. Group and wholesale life insurance contributions and benefits are based, respectively, on data from Institute of Life Insurance, *Group Life Insurance and Group Annuity Coverage in the United States* (annual issues) and Institute of Life Insurance, *Life Insurance Fact Book 1976*. The data have been modified to exclude group and service plans not related to employment. Also excludes premiums for, and benefits paid under, servicemen's group life insurance. Self-insured and unfunded death benefits are based on 1976 survey of various trade-union, mutual benefit association, and company-administered and jointly administered plans filed with the U.S. Department of Labor under the Welfare and Pension Plan Disclosures Act.

Series Bf816 and Bf827. Accidental death and dismemberment contributions and benefits are from Health Insurance Association of America, *Group Health Insurance Coverages in the United States* (annual issues) and unpublished data from the Institute of Life Insurance.

Series Bf818 and Bf829. Hospitalization contributions and benefits include private hospital plans written in compliance with state temporary disability insurance law in California.

Series Bf818–819 and Bf829–830. Information on the hospitalization and surgical and regular medical contributions and benefits are from Marjorie Smith Mueller, "Private Health Insurance in 1975: Coverage, Enrollment, and Financial Experience," *Social Security Bulletin* 40 (6) (1977): 3–21; Health Insurance Association of America, *Group Health Insurance Coverages in the United States* (annual issues); and Marjorie Smith Mueller and Paula A. Piro, "Private Health Insurance in 1974," *Social Security Bulletin* 39 (3) (1976): 3–20. In estimating contributions for, and benefits paid to, employees under plans other than group insurance and union and company plans, it was assumed that the proportion of subscription income, and benefits attributable to, employed groups increased gradually from 75 percent in 1950–60 to 85 percent in 1974.

TABLE Bf814–824 Employee-benefit plans – estimated employer and employee contributions, by type of benefit: 1950–1975 *Continued*

Series Bf820 and Bf831. Major medical contributions and benefits represent either premiums or benefits for group supplementary and comprehensive major-medical insurance underwritten by commercial insurance carriers. Data are from Health Insurance Association of America *Group Health Insurance Coverages in the United States* (annual issues).

Series Bf821–822 and Bf832–833. Temporary disability contributions and benefits are from Daniel N. Price, "Cash Benefits for Short-Term Sickness," *Social Security Bulletin* 39 (7) (1976): 22–34 and from unpublished Social Security Administration information. The data include private plans written in compliance with state temporary disability insurance laws in California, New Jersey, and New York (Hawai'i information not available), shown separately in series Bf822 and Bf833. This information includes contributions under long-term disability plans, not available separately.

Series Bf823 and Bf834. Supplemental unemployment contributions and benefits are based on trade union and industry reports, Emerson H. Beier, "Financing Supplemental Unemployment Benefit Plans," *Monthly Labor Review* 92 (11) (1969): 31–35, and a 1976 survey of reports filed with the Department of Labor under the Welfare and Pension Plans Disclosure Act. The data exclude dismissal wage and separation allowances, except when financed from supplemental unemployment benefit funds covering temporary and permanent layoffs.

Series Bf824 and Bf835. Retirement data are estimated by the Social Security Administration from the data compiled in the American Council of Life Insurance, *Pension Facts 1976* and the Securities and Exchange Commission, *1975 Survey of Private Noninsured Pension Funds*. The data include benefits and contributions paid under pay-as-you-go and deferred profit-sharing plans, plans of nonprofit organizations, union pension plans, and railroad plans supplementing the federal Railroad Retirement program. Excluded are benefits and contributions paid under plans for federal, state, and local employees, under tax-sheltered annuity plans, and under plans for the self-employed.

TABLE Bf825–835 Employee-benefit plans – estimated benefits paid, by type of benefit: 1950–1975

Contributed by Price V. Fishback and Melissa A. Thomasson

	All wage and salary workers							Wage and salary workers in private industry			
				Health benefits				Temporary disability benefits paid, including formal sick leave			
	Total	Life insurance and death benefits	Accidental death and dismemberment benefits	Total	Hospitalization benefits	Surgical and regular medical benefits	Major medical benefits	Total	In compliance with state temporary disability laws	Supplemental unemployment benefits	Retirement benefits
	Bf825	Bf826	Bf827	Bf828	Bf829	Bf830	Bf831	Bf832	Bf833	Bf834	Bf835
Year	Million dollars	Million dollars	Million dollars	Million dollars	Million dollars	Million dollars	Million dollars	Million dollars	Million dollars	Million dollars	Million dollars
1950	1,816	310	16	709	478	231	—	411	54	—	370
1951	2,385	363	17	1,012	660	352	—	545	113	—	450
1952	2,747	405	20	1,202	791	411	—	600	128	—	520
1953	3,183	463	22	1,446	954	492	—	632	140	—	620
1954	3,531	509	25	1,643	1,080	553	10	644	132	—	710
1955	4,076	582	26	1,903	1,242	637	24	715	135	—	850
1956	4,829	650	31	2,320	1,495	758	67	824	151	5	1,000
1957	5,595	779	37	2,722	1,714	877	131	897	178	20	1,140
1958	6,275	851	42	3,055	1,893	929	233	902	184	135	1,290
1959	7,000	919	43	3,464	2,108	1,024	332	960	190	75	1,540
1960	7,813	1,018	47	3,898	2,355	1,116	427	1,038	196	91	1,720
1961	8,808	1,122	58	4,482	2,676	1,244	562	1,046	201	130	1,970
1962	9,963	1,237	69	5,083	3,005	1,411	667	1,143	204	102	2,330
1963	10,849	1,342	83	5,536	3,312	1,472	752	1,201	198	97	2,590
1964	12,032	1,430	88	6,242	3,731	1,642	869	1,221	191	62	2,990
1965	13,567	1,550	90	7,012	4,161	1,848	1,004	1,333	198	62	3,520
1966	14,966	1,707	97	7,428	4,312	1,980	1,136	1,462	208	82	4,190
1967	16,295	1,899	101	7,837	4,389	2,142	1,306	1,549	222	119	4,790
1968	19,234	2,137	121	9,415	5,289	2,468	1,658	1,927	252	105	5,530
1969	22,224	2,385	129	10,984	6,128	2,934	1,922	2,177	281	100	6,450
1970	26,115	2,493	151	13,323	7,344	3,564	2,415	2,542	307	246	7,360
1971	29,341	2,704	171	14,962	8,253	3,960	2,749	2,619	310	296	8,590
1972	32,872	2,939	182	16,539	8,872	4,480	3,187	2,978	329	234	10,000
1973	36,210	3,197	212	18,267	9,646	5,185	3,435	3,205	354	110	11,220
1974	42,012	3,385	256	21,381	11,059	6,293	4,029	3,660	382	400	12,930
1975	47,887	3,563	286	24,929	13,064	7,404	4,461	3,799	401	500	14,810

Sources

Martha Remy Yohalem, "Employee-Benefit Plans, 1975," *Social Security Bulletin* 38 (11) (1977): 24, and Alfred M. Skolnik, "Twenty-five Years of Employee-Benefit Plans," *Social Security Bulletin* 39 (9) (1976): 10.

Documentation

See the text for Table Bf814–824 for a discussion of these series and the text for Table Bf802–813 for additional information.

TABLE Bf836–853 Private pension and deferred profit-sharing plans – estimated coverage, contributions, reserves, beneficiaries, and payments: 1930–1970

Contributed by Price V. Fishback and Melissa A. Thomasson

	Coverage			Employer contributions			Employee contributions		
	Total	Insured plans	Noninsured plans	Total	Insured plans	Noninsured plans	Total	Insured plans	Noninsured plans
	Bf836	Bf837	Bf838	Bf839	Bf840	Bf841	Bf842	Bf843	Bf844
Year	Thousand	Thousand	Thousand	Million dollars	Million dollars	Million dollars	Million dollars	Million dollars	Million dollars
1930	2,700	—	—	130	—	—	70	—	—
1935	2,700	—	—	140	—	—	90	—	—
1940	4,100	—	—	180	—	—	130	—	—
1945	6,400	—	—	830	—	—	160	—	—
1950	9,800	2,600	7,200	1,750	720	1,030	330	200	130
1951	11,000	2,900	8,100	2,280	820	1,460	380	210	170
1952	11,700	3,200	8,500	2,540	910	1,630	430	240	190
1953	13,200	3,400	9,800	2,990	1,010	1,980	485	260	225
1954	14,200	3,600	10,600	3,000	1,030	1,970	515	270	245
1955	15,400	3,800	11,600	3,280	1,100	2,180	560	280	280
1956	16,900	4,100	12,800	3,600	1,110	2,490	625	290	335
1957	18,100	4,400	13,700	4,030	1,220	2,810	690	300	390
1958	18,800	4,500	14,300	4,100	1,250	2,850	720	310	410
1959	19,900	4,800	15,100	4,590	1,330	3,260	770	330	440
1960	21,200	4,900	16,300	4,710	1,190	3,520	780	300	480
1961	22,200	5,100	17,100	4,830	1,180	3,650	780	290	490
1962	23,100	5,200	17,900	5,200	1,240	3,960	830	310	520
1963	23,800	5,400	18,400	5,560	1,390	4,170	860	300	560
1964	24,600	6,000	18,600	6,370	1,520	4,850	910	310	600
1965	25,300	6,200	19,100	7,370	1,770	5,600	990	320	670
1966	26,300	6,900	19,400	8,210	1,850	6,360	1,040	330	710
1967	27,500	7,700	19,800	9,050	2,010	7,040	1,130	340	790
1968	28,000	7,900	20,100	9,940	2,240	7,700	1,230	340	890
1969	29,000	8,700	20,300	11,520	3,030	8,490	1,360	350	1,010
1970	29,700	9,300	20,400	12,580	2,860	9,720	1,420	350	1,070

	Reserves			Monthly beneficiaries			Benefit payments		
	Total	Insured plans	Noninsured plans	Total	Insured plans	Noninsured plans	Total	Insured plans	Noninsured plans
	Bf845	Bf846	Bf847	Bf848	Bf849	Bf850	Bf851	Bf852	Bf853
Year	Billion dollars	Billion dollars	Billion dollars	Thousand	Thousand	Thousand	Million dollars	Million dollars	Million dollars
1930	0.8	—	—	100	—	—	90	—	—
1935	1.3	—	—	110	—	—	100	—	—
1940	2.4	—	—	160	—	—	140	—	—
1945	5.4	—	—	310	—	—	220	—	—
1950	12.1	5.6	6.5	450	150	300	370	80	290
1951	14.5	6.6	8.0	540	170	370	450	100	350
1952	17.3	7.7	9.7	650	200	450	520	120	400
1953	20.5	8.8	11.7	750	230	520	620	140	480
1954	23.8	10.0	13.8	880	270	610	710	160	550
1955	27.5	11.3	16.1	980	290	690	850	180	670
1956	31.4	12.5	18.9	1,090	320	770	1,000	210	790
1957	36.1	14.1	22.1	1,240	370	870	1,140	240	900
1958	40.9	15.6	25.2	1,400	430	970	1,290	290	1,000
1959	46.6	17.6	29.1	1,590	500	1,090	1,540	340	1,200
1960	52.0	18.8	33.1	1,780	540	1,240	1,720	390	1,330
1961	57.8	20.2	37.5	1,910	570	1,340	1,970	450	1,520
1962	63.5	21.6	41.9	2,100	630	1,470	2,330	510	1,820
1963	69.9	23.3	46.6	2,280	690	1,590	2,590	570	2,020
1964	77.7	25.2	52.4	2,490	740	1,750	2,990	640	2,350
1965	86.5	27.3	59.2	2,750	790	1,960	3,520	720	2,800
1966	95.5	29.3	66.2	3,110	870	2,240	4,190	810	3,380
1967	106.2	31.9	74.2	3,410	930	2,480	4,790	910	3,880
1968	117.8	34.8	83.1	3,770	1,010	2,760	5,530	1,030	4,500
1969	127.8	37.2	90.6	4,180	1,070	3,110	6,450	1,160	5,290
1970	137.1	40.1	97.0	4,720	1,220	3,500	7,360	1,330	6,030

TABLE Bf836–853 Private pension and deferred profit-sharing plans – estimated coverage, contributions, reserves, beneficiaries, and payments: 1930–1970 *Continued*

Sources

U.S. Social Security Administration, *Social Security Bulletin* 22 (4) (1959): 12; 29 (4) (1966): 11; and 35 (4) (1972): 20. These series were compiled by the U.S. Social Security Administration from releases of the Institute of Life Insurance, U.S. Securities and Exchange Commission (SEC), U.S. Department of Labor, Internal Revenue Service, and various other reports, such as those of nonprofit organizations and the annual statements of the leading life insurance companies writing group annuities. Information was also received from various industrial concerns. In addition, for the earlier years, M. W. Latimer's studies were utilized; see M. W. Latimer, *Industrial Pension Systems in the United States and Canada* (Industrial Relations Counselors, 1932).

Documentation

These series present estimates with respect to formal private pension and deferred profit-sharing plans. Included are plans covering employees of industrial and nonprofit organizations. Most of them are funded, although some of the noninsured plans are on a pay-as-you-go basis. The majority are single-employer plans with an increasing number of industry-wide or area-wide multiemployer plans.

Under insured plans, insurance carriers are the medium through which benefits are provided; sponsors of the plans pay premiums to these carriers. Under noninsured plans, the sponsors themselves perform the functions of insurance carriers.

Series Bf836–838. Excludes annuitants and potential members who have not yet met the entrance requirements (age and/or service). Employees under both insured and noninsured plans are included only once – under the insured plans. The larger groups under insured plans are covered by group annuity contracts, whereas individual-policy pension trusts cover smaller groups.

Series Bf839–844. Contributions to insured plans are on a net basis, with dividends and refunds deducted. Contributions to noninsured plans are, for the most part, on a gross basis, refunds appearing as benefit payments. For pay-as you-go plans, contributions have been assumed to equal benefit payments.

Series Bf846. Reserves for insured plans were furnished to the Social Security Administration by the Institute of Life Insurance.

Series Bf847. Reserves for noninsured plans include those of corporate pension plans, obtained from releases of the SEC. To these were added estimated reserves of noninsured nonprofit organization and multiemployer plans.

Series Bf848–850. Covers those in receipt of periodic payments at the end of the year, thus excluding those receiving lump sums during the year.

Series Bf852. Net amounts.

Series Bf853. Payments for the noninsured plans were obtained by adding to the SEC data the estimated payments under formal pay-as-you-go plans and under noninsured multiemployer and nonprofit organization plans. The data from the SEC include lump sums and refunds from corporate pension funds (types not segregated). Therefore, dividing the payments for the year by the mean number of beneficiaries results in an overstatement of the average annual periodic payment.

TABLE Bf854–863 Short-term disability programs – benefits provided for income loss from sickness, by type of insurance: 1948–1983

Contributed by Price V. Fishback and Melissa A. Thomasson

		Benefits provided as protection against income loss from short-term sickness								
				Group benefits						
					Workers in private industry					
Year	Estimated income loss from nonoccupational short-term sickness	Total	Through individual insurance	Total	Total	Private cash-sickness insurance and self-insurance	Publicly operated cash-sickness funds	Sick leave	Sick leave for government employees	Old-Age, Survivors, and Disability Insurance program (sixth month of disability)
	Bf854	Bf855	Bf856	Bf857	Bf858	Bf859	Bf860	Bf861	Bf862	Bf863
	Million dollars	Million dollars	Million dollars	Million dollars	Million dollars	Million dollars	Million dollars	Million dollars	Million dollars	Million dollars
1948	4,582	761	141	620	361	146	57	158	259	—
1949	4,445	848	150	698	398	172	62	164	300	—
1950	4,816	942	153	789	474	231	63	180	315	—
1951	5,494	1,153	157	996	606	344	61	201	390	—
1952	5,834	1,304	177	1,127	674	382	75	218	453	—
1953	6,163	1,413	209	1,204	722	397	91	235	481	—
1954	6,114	1,478	230	1,248	747	399	103	245	500	—
1955	6,565	1,620	250	1,370	825	442	109	273	545	—
1956	7,052	1,806	278	1,528	937	525	114	299	591	—
1957	7,386	1,958	307	1,651	1,024	567	127	330	626	—
1958	7,477	2,093	353	1,740	1,044	556	141	346	696	—
1959	7,749	2,236	390	1,847	1,123	601	164	359	724	—
1960	8,591	2,430	393	2,037	1,211	638	172	400	826	—
1961	8,664	2,561	426	2,135	1,241	626	195	420	894	—
1962	9,653	2,776	419	2,358	1,355	671	212	472	1,003	—
1963	10,213	2,997	447	2,550	1,445	675	244	526	1,105	—
1964	10,296	3,101	484	2,617	1,485	716	264	505	1,133	—
1965	11,333	3,349	483	2,866	1,602	767	269	566	1,264	—
1966	12,268	3,637	513	3,124	1,735	843	273	619	1,389	—
1967	12,844	3,898	527	3,371	1,834	869	285	680	1,537	—
1968	14,585	4,622 [1]	609	4,013	2,247	1,124	320	803	1,766	—
1969	15,307	5,104	635	4,469	2,551	1,247	374	930	1,918	—
1970	16,757	5,888	694	5,194	2,953	1,476	411	1,066	2,242	—
1971	17,146	6,137	731	5,406	3,030	1,489	411	1,130	2,376	—
1972	19,507	6,874	772	6,102	3,390	1,614	412	1,364	2,712	—
1973	21,059	7,461	795	6,666	3,650	1,736	446	1,469	2,906	110
1974	21,804	8,232	851	7,381	4,144	2,024	485	1,634	3,107	130
1975	23,595	9,003	973	8,030	4,328	2,011	538	1,779	3,542	160
1976	26,447	9,819	881	8,938	4,900	2,267	581	2,052	3,868	170
1977	28,225	10,559	940	9,619	5,285	2,344	582	2,359	4,145	190
1978	32,811	11,751	1,210	10,541	5,782	2,403	609	2,770	4,579	180
1979	36,072	13,371	1,322	12,049	6,987	3,216	699	3,072	4,892	170
1980	38,529	14,426	1,280	13,146	7,633	3,271	770	3,593	5,337	175
1981	41,278	15,113	1,291	13,822	8,011	2,959	953	4,099	5,640	170
1982	42,558	16,269	1,595	14,674	8,498	2,931	987	4,581	6,026	150
1983	45,615	16,411	1,152	15,259	8,615	2,708	1,007	4,899	6,490	157

[1] Data in the original source have been corrected or revised.

Sources

Daniel N. Price, "Cash Benefits for Short-Term Sickness: Thirty Five Years of Data, 1948–83," *Social Security Bulletin* 45 (5) (1986): 5–19. A new series using different methodologies was developed in the 1990s; see Table Bf864–874.

Documentation

Protection against loss of earnings in periods of nonoccupational disability is provided in a number of ways. For wage and salary workers in private industry, the most common method is through group or individual insurance policies sold by commercial insurance companies that pay cash amounts during specified periods of disability. Employers may also self-insure, providing either cash benefits or paid sick leave. Some unions, union management trust funds, fraternal societies, and mutual benefit associations also pay cash disability benefits. In addition, employers often use a paid-sick leave plan to supplement benefits under insurance plans, and workers may, as individuals, purchase insurance to supplement the protection provided through their jobs. Private insured protection may be obtained through voluntary action by the employer or the employee, or it may come about as the result of compulsory programs. For further discussion and more detailed information see the original source.

Nonoccupational short-term sickness is defined as short-term or temporary non-work-connected disability (lasting not more than six months) and the first six months of long-term disability.

Beginning in 1959, the data are adjusted to reflect changes in sickness experience (average number of days of disability), as reported in the Health Interview Survey of the Public Health Service. Income loss was estimated by multiplying the annual payroll by estimated average number of days lost as a result of sickness and dividing by the average number of workdays in the year. The average days lost assumed for wage and salary workers was 7; for federal government employees was 8; and for state and local government employees was 7.5 for 1948–1966, 7.35 for 1967, 7.2 for 1968, and 7 for 1969–1983; and for self-employed was 7. Estimated workdays were 255, 260, 255, and 300, respectively. Payroll information for groups came from the U.S. Department of Commerce estimates of payrolls and for self-employed of annual farm and nonfarm proprietors' income. See source for more detail.

Series Bf855. The sum of series Bf856–857 and Bf863.

Series Bf857. The sum of series Bf858 and Bf862.

Series Bf858. The sum of series Bf859–861.

Series Bf859. Private cash sickness insurance and self-insurance includes a small but undetermined amount of group disability insurance benefits paid to government workers and to self-employed persons through farm, trade, or professional associations.

Bf863. Calculated by subtracting series Bf858 and Bf862 from series Bf857.

TABLE Bf864–874 Short-term disability programs – cash benefits provided for income loss, by type of insurance: 1970–1994

Contributed by Price V. Fishback and Melissa A. Thomasson

		Benefits provided as protection against short-term income loss									
					Employment-related benefits						
						For workers in private sector					
	Estimated total income loss due to injury or illness for wage and salary workers	Total	Old-Age, Survivors, and Disability Insurance program (sixth month of disability)	Obtained through individual insurance	Total	Total	Private cash-sickness insurance and self-insurance	Publicly operated cash-sickness funds	Employment-related sick leave	Workers' compensation	Sick leave for government employees
	Bf864	Bf865	Bf866	Bf867	Bf868	Bf869	Bf870	Bf871	Bf872	Bf873	Bf874
Year	Million dollars	Million dollars	Million dollars	Million dollars	Million dollars	Million dollars	Million dollars	Million dollars	Million dollars	Million dollars	Million dollars
1970	13,635	8,556	—	772	7,784	4,196	1,476	411	2,309	928	2,660
1975	20,439	13,164	160	973	12,031	5,997	2,011	538	3,448	2,037	3,998
1980	33,746	21,910	175	1,280	20,455	9,984	3,271	770	5,943	4,430	6,041
1985	48,484	29,840	195	1,796	27,849	12,440	2,601	1,179	8,660	6,922	8,487
1986	—	31,256	194	1,774	29,288	12,713	2,275	1,255	9,183	7,594	8,982
1987	—	34,509	220	2,062	32,227	14,275	2,692	1,696	9,887	8,361	9,591
1988	60,185	37,255	207	2,057	34,992	15,391	2,903	1,779	10,710	9,335	10,266
1989	63,862	40,167	224	2,451	37,492	16,364	2,732	1,907	11,725	10,161	10,967
1990	68,296	42,925	274	2,701	39,950	16,834	2,711	2,269	11,855	11,242	11,873
1991	69,542	45,378	311	2,588	42,480	17,555	2,605	2,817	12,133	12,388	12,537
1992	73,783	48,402	396	3,497	44,509	18,456	2,703	2,975	12,778	12,937	13,115
1993	76,816	48,317	403	3,560	44,355	18,310	2,608	2,349	13,353	12,429	13,616
1994	81,101	49,374	412	3,263	45,699	19,039	2,558	2,370	14,111	12,500	14,160

Sources

Wilmer Kerns, "Cash Benefits for Short-Term Sickness, 1970–1994," *Social Security Bulletin* 60 (1) (1997): 49–53. The Social Security Disability Insurance benefits, series Bf865, are from the *Annual Statistical Supplement of the Social Security Bulletin*, Table 6.C1.

Documentation

These series are estimated using methods different from those in Table Bf854–863. Short-term disability programs are designed to provide income, continuing up to six months, for workers who are unable to perform their jobs because of temporary illness or injury. If the injury or illness requires a prolonged absence from work, this short-term income serves as a bridge between employment and long-term disability benefits. Income replacement for short-term disability is available through a variety of private employment plans and in several states through mandatory public programs (see the text for Table Bf290–325). The Social Security Disability Insurance program now provides monthly benefits to severely disabled insured workers and their dependents after a waiting period of five calendar months. Sickness or injury that occurs outside of the workplace, and is non-job-related, is classified as nonoccupational illness. Three programs protect workers from this kind of illness: temporary disability insurance in certain states, paid sick leave, and employment-related group insurance. Some individuals also purchase individual insurance policies. Another class of income protection is provided by workers' compensation programs, which cover job-related illnesses or occupational illnesses. For further discussion of methods of estimation, see the original source.

Series Bf864. Assumes the following days of work loss per employee and work days per year: 5.3 days in a 255-day work year for persons employed in the private sector; 8 days in a 260-day work year for federal public employees; 7 days in a 255-day work year for state and local public employees; and 7 days in a 300-day work year for the self-employed.

Series Bf865. The sum of series Bf866–868.

Series Bf868. The sum of series Bf869 and Bf873–874.

Series Bf869. The sum of series Bf870–872.

TABLE Bf875–886 Health care expenditures, by source of funds: 1960–1997

Contributed by Price V. Fishback and Melissa A. Thomasson

		From private funds					From public funds					
			Consumer payments					By type of government		By program		
Year	Total	Total	Total	Out of pocket	From private health insurance	Other	Total	Federal	State and local	Medicaid	Medicare	From public funds besides Medicare and Medicaid
	Bf875	Bf876	Bf877	Bf878	Bf879	Bf880	Bf881	Bf882	Bf883	Bf884	Bf885	Bf886
	Million dollars	Million dollars	Million dollars	Million dollars	Million dollars	Million dollars	Million dollars	Million dollars	Million dollars	Million dollars	Million dollars	Million dollars
1960	26,850	20,203	18,945	13,067	5,878	1,258	6,648	2,914	3,734	0	0	6,648
1961	28,768	21,466	20,015	13,373	6,642	1,450	7,302	3,327	3,976	0	0	7,302
1962	31,268	23,291	21,603	14,227	7,376	1,688	7,977	3,787	4,190	0	0	7,977
1963	34,067	25,343	23,537	15,537	7,999	1,807	8,724	4,231	4,493	0	0	8,724
1964	37,647	28,290	26,198	17,252	8,946	2,093	9,356	4,460	4,896	0	0	9,356
1965	41,145	30,867	28,565	18,540	10,026	2,302	10,278	4,820	5,458	0	0	10,278
1966	45,263	31,600	29,182	18,839	10,344	2,418	13,663	7,614	6,049	1,311	1,846	10,506
1967	50,969	31,964	29,477	18,826	10,651	2,487	19,005	12,106	6,899	3,157	4,939	10,909
1968	57,684	35,879	32,940	20,771	12,169	2,940	21,804	14,190	7,615	3,558	6,240	12,006
1969	64,792	40,247	36,554	22,715	13,839	3,693	24,545	16,049	8,496	4,194	7,070	13,281
1970	73,243	45,537	41,184	24,901	16,283	4,353	27,706	17,816	9,890	5,316	7,700	14,690
1971	81,018	49,829	44,960	26,405	18,555	4,869	31,189	20,403	10,786	6,728	8,470	15,991
1972	90,943	55,808	50,296	28,989	21,307	5,512	35,135	22,974	12,161	8,350	9,360	17,425
1973	100,838	61,550	55,892	31,954	23,938	5,658	39,288	25,199	14,089	9,463	10,778	19,047
1974	114,265	67,667	61,656	34,837	26,818	6,012	46,597	30,575	16,022	11,116	13,485	21,996
1975	130,727	75,695	69,363	38,094	31,269	6,332	55,032	36,407	18,625	13,497	16,396	25,139
1976	149,856	87,434	79,799	41,938	37,861	7,634	62,422	42,952	19,470	15,248	19,764	27,410
1977	170,375	100,158	92,262	46,405	45,858	7,896	70,217	47,693	22,524	17,534	22,973	29,710
1978	190,601	111,048	102,247	49,733	52,513	8,802	79,553	54,325	25,228	19,542	26,763	33,248
1979	215,201	125,054	115,252	54,317	60,936	9,802	90,147	61,384	28,763	22,416	31,037	36,694
1980	247,273	142,493	130,011	60,254	69,758	12,482	104,780	71,958	32,823	26,135	37,516	41,129
1981	286,908	165,715	150,677	68,492	82,185	15,039	121,193	83,711	37,482	30,378	44,883	45,932
1982	322,978	188,397	170,852	75,448	95,404	17,545	134,581	93,038	41,543	32,117	52,470	49,994
1983	355,291	207,746	188,480	82,319	106,162	19,266	147,545	103,126	44,419	35,333	59,761	52,451
1984	390,077	229,938	210,057	90,857	119,200	19,880	160,139	113,207	46,932	38,249	66,446	55,444
1985	428,721	254,518	233,504	100,659	132,846	21,014	174,202	123,171	51,032	41,253	72,084	60,865
1986	461,229	271,398	248,636	108,081	140,555	22,762	189,831	132,634	57,197	45,542	76,838	67,451
1987	500,502	293,291	268,498	116,053	152,446	24,793	207,211	143,096	64,115	50,419	82,711	74,081
1988	560,379	334,251	305,518	127,458	178,060	28,733	226,127	156,359	69,769	55,118	90,100	80,909
1989	623,536	371,413	341,673	133,208	208,466	29,740	252,123	174,766	77,357	62,250	102,423	87,450
1990	699,361	416,187	384,587	145,032	239,554	31,601	283,174	195,181	87,993	75,373	111,496	96,305
1991	766,783	448,859	415,072	153,335	261,737	33,787	317,923	222,550	95,374	93,942	121,138	102,843
1992	836,537	483,553	447,247	161,758	285,490	36,306	352,984	251,759	101,225	106,370	136,164	110,450
1993	898,496	513,172	473,850	167,051	306,800	39,322	385,323	275,353	109,970	121,748	148,702	114,873
1994	947,717	524,908	483,610	168,502	315,109	41,298	422,810	301,171	121,638	134,592	166,883	121,335
1995	993,725	538,507	495,273	170,991	324,282	43,235	455,218	325,989	129,229	146,105	185,220	123,893
1996	1,042,522	561,141	515,233	178,124	337,108	45,908	481,382	348,009	133,373	154,106	200,086	127,190
1997	1,092,385	585,312	535,571	187,551	348,020	49,741	507,073	367,050	140,023	159,890	214,569	132,614

Source

Internet site of the Health Care Financing Administration, National Health Care Expenditures. See also U.S. Department of Health and Human Services, Health Care Financing Administration, Office of Research and Demonstrations, *Health Care Financing Review, Statistical Supplement* (1998).

Documentation

Substantially more detail on health care expenditures is available from the source. For earlier sources using a different methodology and some differing categories for the period 1929, 1935, 1940, 1945, 1950, 1955, 1960–1975, see Ida C. Merriam, "Social Welfare Expenditures, 1964–5," *Social Security Bulletin* 28 (10) (1965): 10, and Alfred M. Skolnik and Sophie R. Dales, "Social Welfare Expenditures, Fiscal Year, 1974," *Social Security Bulletin* 38 (1) (1935): 15.

Since 1964, the U.S. Department of Health and Human Services has published an annual series of statistics presenting total national health expenditures during each year. The basic aim of these statistics, termed national health accounts (NHA), is to "identify all goods and services that can be characterized as relating to health care in the nation, and determine the amount of money used for the purchase of these goods and services" (D. Rice, B. Cooper, and R. Gibson, "U.S. National Health Accounts: Historical Perspectives, Current Issues, and Future Projections," in Emile Levy, editor, *La Santé Fait ses Comptes (Accounting for Health)* (Economica, 1982)). The essential framework for the accounts consists of a matrix of operational categories classifying and defining the sources of health care dollars and services purchased with these funds. The NHA are compatible with the national income and product accounts generally, but bring together in one place a picture of the nation's health economy.

Out-of-pocket expenditure includes direct spending by consumers for all health care goods and services. Included in this estimate is the amount paid out of pocket for services not covered by insurance, the amount of coinsurance and deductibles required by private health insurance and by public programs such as Medicare and Medicaid (and not paid by some other third party), and the payment to providers for services and goods that exceed the usual, customary, or reasonable charges reimbursed by third parties. Enrollee premiums for private health insurance and Medicare Supplementary Medical Insurance (SMI) are not included with under out-of-pocket expenditures.

(continued)

TABLE Bf875–886 Health care expenditures, by source of funds: 1960–1997 *Continued*

Counting the cost of the premiums and the benefits that are paid by the insurer would overstate the funding received by the provider of care. Similarly, coinsurance and deductible amounts paid by supplementary medigap policies are excluded. For most services, out-of-pocket spending estimates for 1980 through 1989 are based on information from the consumer expenditure (CE) survey conducted by the Department of Labor. Sources other than the CE are used for other categories.

Surveys of the non-institutional population's health care use and financing patterns have been conducted periodically over the past three decades. For 1963 and 1970, the Center for Health Administration Studies and the National Opinion Research Center, both at the University of Chicago, surveyed individuals for the purpose of providing "reliable and valid statistics of medical care use and expenditures for . . . public policy and research activities" (Research Triangle Institute, *Benchmark Studies of the National Health Accounts*, HCFA contract number 500-86-0042, prepared for the Health Care Financing Administration, March 1987). These studies were followed in 1977 by the National Medical Care Expenditure Survey (National Center for Health Services Research, *Department of Health and Human Services: Data from the National Medical Care and Utilization Survey* (1977)) and in 1980 by the National Medical Care and Utilization Survey (National Center for Health Statistics, *Department of Health and Human Services: Data from the National Medical Care Utilization and Expenditure Survey* (1980)). (Expenditure information from the national medical expenditure survey covering 1987 recently became available. Data from this source will be integrated into the NHA during the next benchmark revision.) These surveys have provided information used to determine the amount of out-of-pocket spending in historical periods.

At the NHE level, private health insurance expenditures equal the premiums earned by private health insurers. This figure is decomposed to benefits incurred (personal health care expenditures) and net cost, the difference between premiums and benefits. In addition to the traditional insurers such as commercial carriers and Blue Cross and Blue Shield, the NHA category for private health insurance includes a number of other plans. Health maintenance organizations are included here, as are self-insured plans. Estimates of private health insurance benefits by type of service were developed in conjunction with out-of-pocket spending. Both relied on periodic historical surveys to determine the relative share of private health insurance and out-of-pocket spending. Surveys by medical trade associations, the Visiting Nurse Association, and the federal government augmented the person survey data. Estimates of total premiums earned by private health insurers are derived from the data series on the financial experience of private health insurance organizations compiled and analyzed by the Health Care Financing Administration (HCFA) (R. H. Arnett and G. Trapnell, "Private Health Insurance: New Measures of a Complex and Changing Industry. *Health Care Financing Review* 6 (2) (1984)). Data for these estimates are furnished by the Health Insurance Association of America, the National Underwriter Company, Blue Cross and Blue Shield Association, Group Health Association of America, and a survey of self-insured and prepaid health plans conducted by HCFA. These estimates are verified using the Bureau of Labor Statistics (1980–1990) employment cost index and CE survey.

Estimates of Medicare spending for health services and supplies are based on information received from Medicare actuaries, reports submitted by Medicare contractors, and administrative and statistical records. Medicaid estimates are based primarily on financial information reports filed by the state Medicaid agencies on Form HCFA-64. These reports provide total program expenditures and service distributions. Prior to the availability of the Form HCFA-64 in 1979, state statistical reports (Form HCFA-2082) were used to develop service distributions. The federal share of Medicaid spending was taken from federal budget outlay data (Executive Office of the President, 1960–1991; Bureau of Government Financial Operations, 1960–1991) For further information, see the Center for Medicare and Medicaid Services Web site. Several adjustments to reported program data are necessary to fit the estimates into the framework of the NHA. An estimate of Medicaid buy-ins to Medicare is deducted to avoid double counting when the programs are presented together. An estimate of hospital-based home health care spending is added to hospital care expenditures and subtracted from home health care expenditures. That portion of reported program expenditures for intermediate care facilities for the mentally retarded estimated to cover services in hospital-based facilities (40 percent of the total) is counted as hospital care rather than nursing home care.

All health care expenditures that are channeled through any program established by public law are treated as a public expenditure in the NHA. For example, expenditures under workers' compensation programs are included with government expenditures, even though they involve benefits paid by insurers from premiums that have been collected from private sources. Similarly, premiums paid by enrollees for Medicare SMI are treated as public, rather than private, expenditure because payment of benefits is made by a public program. However, Medicare coinsurance and deductibles are included under out-of-pocket payments because they are paid directly by the beneficiary to the provider of service.

To be included in the NHA, a program must have provision of care or treatment of disease as its primary focus. For this reason, nutrition, sanitation, and antipollution programs are excluded. Another example of this is "Meals on Wheels," which is excluded from the NHA because it is viewed as a nutrition program rather than a health service program. Statistics on federal program expenditures are based, in part, on data reported by the budget offices of federal agencies. Several differences exist from spending reported in the federal budget because of the conceptual framework on which the NHA are based.

Series Bf875. The sum of series Bf876 and Bf881.

Series Bf876. The sum of series Bf878–880.

Series Bf881. The sum of series Bf882–883. It is also the sum of series Bf884–886.

TABLE Bf887–892 Private health insurance – persons insured, by type of insurer: 1940–1995

Contributed by Price V. Fishback and Melissa A. Thomasson

		By insurance companies				
	Total	Total	Group policies	Individual/family policies	Blue Cross and Blue Shield plans	Other plans
	Bf887	Bf888	Bf889	Bf890	Bf891	Bf892
Year	Million	Million	Million	Million	Million	Million
1940	12.0	3.7	2.5	1.2	6.0	2.3
1945	32.0	10.5	7.8	2.7	18.9	2.7
1950	76.6	37.0	22.3	17.3	38.8	4.4
1955	101.4	53.5	38.6	19.9	50.7	6.5
1960	122.5	69.2	54.4	22.2	58.1	6.0
1961	125.8	70.4	56.1	22.4	58.7	7.1
1962	129.4	72.2	58.1	23.1	60.1	6.9
1963	133.5	74.5	61.5	23.5	61.0	7.2
1964	136.3	75.8	63.1	34.0	62.1	6.8
1965	138.7	77.6	65.4	24.4	63.3	7.0
1966	142.4	80.4	67.8	24.9	54.3	6.6
1967	146.4	82.6	71.5	24.6	67.2	7.1
1968	151.9	85.7	74.1	25.3	70.1	7.3
1969	155.0	88.8	77.9	25.9	82.7	7.7
1970	158.8	89.7	80.5	26.7	85.1	8.1
1971	161.8	91.5	80.6	27.8	76.5	8.5
1972	164.1	93.7	81.5	29.1	78.2	8.1
1973	168.5	94.5	83.6	27.5	81.3	9.6
1974	173.1	97.0	85.4	28.8	83.8	11.1
1975	178.2	99.5	87.2	30.1	86.4	13.1
1976	176.9	97.0	86.8	27.0	86.6	14.9
1977	179.9	100.4	89.2	28.7	86.0	18.1
1978	185.7	106.0	92.5	36.1	85.8	21.5
1979	185.7	104.1	94.1	34.4	86.1	25.5
1980	187.4	105.5	97.4	33.8	86.7	33.2
1981	186.2	105.9	103.0	25.3	85.8	40.3
1982	188.3	109.6	103.9	29.4	82.0	48.2
1983	186.6	105.9	104.6	22.2	79.6	53.6
1984	184.4	103.1	103.0	20.4	79.4	54.4
1985	181.3	100.4	99.5	21.2	78.7	55.1
1986	180.9	98.2	106.6	12.1	78.0	64.9
1987 [1]	179.7	96.7	106.1	10.4	76.9	66.9
1988 [1]	182.3	92.6	100.5	10.7	74.0	71.3
1989 [2]	182.5	88.9	98.7	10.0	72.5	78.6
1990 [2]	181.7	83.1	88.7	10.2	70.9	86.2
1991	181.0	78.0	83.3	9.9	68.1	93.5
1992	180.7	76.6	82.1	8.5	67.5	97.9
1993	180.9	74.7	80.9	7.4	65.9	105.7
1994	182.2	75.8	82.4	7.0	65.2	112.9
1995	185.3	76.6	83.3	7.0	65.6	120.1

[1] Revised Health Insurance Association of America survey form.

[2] Change in methodology.

Source

Source Book of Health Insurance Data (1998), Table 2.10, p. 39.

Documentation

This table reports information collected by the Health Insurance Association of American on the number of privately insured Americans covered through commercial insurance companies, through Blue Cross and Blue Shield plans, and under other types of policies such as health maintenance organizations and other managed care plans.

Series Bf887–888. Refers to the net total of persons protected so that duplication among persons protected by more than one insuring organization or more than one policy providing the same type of coverage has been eliminated.

Series Bf887. Excludes hospital indemnity coverage that may have been included in prior editions. For 1975 and later, data include the number of persons covered in Puerto Rico and other U.S. territories and possessions.

CHAPTER Bg

Nonprofit, Voluntary, and Religious Entities

Editor: Peter Dobkin Hall

Nonprofit, Voluntary, and Religious Entities

Peter Dobkin Hall with Colin B. Burke

The purpose of this essay is to review and rationalize the assumptions governing the definition of the entities and activities covered by this chapter, to touch on some of the difficulties inherent in certain kinds of historical data, and to suggest guidelines for the future collection of data on the domain of voluntary, nonprofit, and religious enterprises.

In undertaking the unprecedented effort to conceptualize and assemble data for this chapter, the editors in chief of the Millennial Edition were well aware of the often contested and always ambiguous nature of most of the fundamental issues and institutions to be covered, as well as the fragmentary and discontinuous quality of many of the data sets. We warned them that, under these circumstances, we would not be able to produce a definitive set of historical statistics. The best we could expect to achieve would be to gather and evaluate existing statistics and to convene the major scholarly and institutional stakeholders in these data in order to identify gaps and strive for consensus about definitions, with the hope that these efforts would lead in coming years to more adequate data collection efforts.

The data in the chapter document several major types of nonproprietary entities and activities, including the following.

"Traditional" voluntary associations: incorporated or unincorporated membership organizations supported by dues, sales of goods and services, donations, or bequests. These include both charitable/public benefit entities (for example, the scouts) and noncharitable/mutual benefit entities (for example, trade associations, cooperatives, and fraternal orders).

Charitable trusts: funds placed in trust for charitable, educational, and religious purposes. They may be freestanding unincorporated entities, embedded in charitable corporations, or administered by commercial enterprises, such as banks and financial services companies.

Charitable tax-exempt nonprofit entities: incorporated or unincorporated entities and charitable trusts registered under section 501(c)(3) of the Internal Revenue Code and chartered as nonstock corporations under state law. These include most charitable and educational organizations, such as nonprofit hospitals, organized charities, and educational institutions.

Noncharitable nonprofit entities: incorporated or unincorporated nonprofit entities described in sections 501(c)(1)–(2) and (4)–(27) of the Internal Revenue Code. These include such mutual benefit organizations as social clubs, veterans' organizations, labor unions, burial societies, trade associations, cooperatives, political parties, and "other associations that may roughly be described as carrying forward the private interests of the members, but subject to the nondistribution constraint" (Simon 1987, p. 69).

Congregations, churches, religious orders, denominations, and other religious bodies. Religious bodies are not required to incorporate, register with the Internal Revenue Service (IRS), or file reports with tax authorities, although increasing numbers of these entities are doing so as they become involved with the provision of social welfare and other services funded by government. Since 1970, many religious bodies have incorporated and received exempt status.

Faith-based, "religiously tied," or denominational service providers. These may or may not be separately incorporated as secular entities, and they may or may not be registered with the IRS as charitable tax-exempts. Not all "faith-based" organizations are religious bodies, and many religious bodies provide services through secular corporations.[1]

These types should not be regarded as categorical: entities that counted as "traditional" voluntary associations or charities in censuses of early-nineteenth-century organizations (see Tables Bg1–27) might be classified as charitable tax-exempt or noncharitable exempt entities in statistical series based on IRS data. Religiously tied service providers appear in different guises – as religious bodies, as 501(c)(3) charitable tax-exempts, as "benevolent institutions," or as traditional voluntary associations, depending on when they were enumerated, by whom, and for what purpose.

Compilers of education statistics have the advantage of relatively fixed definitions for major institutional types and roles, which enable them to know, when they present long statistical series, that "school" and "education" mean more or less the same thing in 1800 as in 1990. Thus, as in Table Bg166–175, we are able to present data on schools from the beginning of the nineteenth century to the present. Nonprofits statisticians, in contrast,

Acknowledgments

The research on which this chapter is based has been generously supported by the AAFRC Trust for Philanthropy; the Aspen Institute's Nonprofit Sector Research Fund; the Ford Foundation; the Lilly Endowment, Inc.; the Institution for Social and Policy Studies, Yale University; and the Hauser Center for Nonprofit Organizations, Harvard University.

[1] On this, see Jeavons (1998), Chaves (2001), and Hall (2002).

labor under the task of trying to account, in a reasonably coherent way, for an organizational population and sets of activities whose meanings are fungible and contested: terms such as "charitable," "church," and "religious" have very different meanings today than they had a century ago. In consequence, users of this chapter will have to accept an inevitable degree of fragmentation and discontinuity in the data we offer. It would be nice to be able to assemble statistical series presenting the growth of the nonprofit sector from de Tocqueville's time to our own. We *can* offer data on various kinds of traditional voluntary associations. We *do* have numbers on organizations classified as nonprofit by the IRS. But the extent to which the former can be counted as part of the latter is a hotly contested question.

The data sets in this chapter include information on each of the major organizational types, as well as information on growth and change within these organizational populations, their revenues and sources of revenue, expenditures, assets, location, membership, clientage, and goods and services produced or provided. By using data from other chapters in these volumes (on education, health care, the labor force), readers should be able to track the changing significance of nonprofit ownership within particular industries.

Although *Historical Statistics of the United States* generally favors national aggregations of data, we have tried, wherever possible, to include data on regional and state trends and patterns (such as Tables Bg620–675 on charitable giving, Table Bg41–54 on the location of foundations, and Tables Bg349–449 on religion). Because of interest in the geographical distribution, density, and patterns of diffusion of nonproprietary entities of various types (Hall 1982; Bowen, Nygren, et al. 1994; Schneider 1996; Gamm and Putnam 1999); variations in regional generosity (Wolpert 1989, 1993); and regional and local variations and changes in the allocation of tasks among nonprofit, for-profit, and government service providers within particular industries or activity areas (Hansmann 1997; Hall 1999b), we urge that data stakeholders give greater attention to collecting statistics about these issues in the future.

In this essay, we review the problems connected with compiling statistics on nonprofit and related entities, shifting definitions and concepts about them, and the forces driving those shifts.

Defining and Differentiating Voluntary, Nonprofit, and Faith-Based Entities

Earlier editions of *Historical Statistics of the United States* gave scant attention to the universe of voluntary, nonprofit, and religious entities. Envisioned as a reference work for public planners and produced by the Census Bureau (see Appendix 3), the volumes focused primarily on the activities of interest to governmental and other public institutions – particularly economic and defense planners and policymakers (Anderson 1988).

But it was not only the statist bias of census bureaucrats that buttressed indifference to nongovernmental institutions. The domain itself, as represented in numbers and significance before the 1970s, hardly seemed to warrant attention. As late as 1953, when congressional committees, responding with alarm to reports of the growing number of foundations and other tax-exempt entities, requested information about them from the IRS, they were assured by the Commissioner of Internal Revenue that a mere 32,000 registered organizations did not justify the agency's gathering or publishing statistics about them (U.S. House of Representatives 1953, p. 64). Systematic data gathering on these "foundations and other tax-exempt entities" began only in the mid-1960s, when the population of registered tax-exempts passed the 200,000 mark and when their assets, their influence, and the privileges accorded their financial supporters sparked another bout of regulatory enthusiasm in an increasingly tax-sensitive public (on the swelling population of nonprofits, see Table Bg55–64; on their growing assets, expenditures, and revenues, see Table Bg65–74).

Regulatory activism and increasing public concern led in 1969 to the passage of tax reforms that greatly increased government oversight of tax-exempt entities. Provisions of the act requiring the filing of detailed annual reports to federal tax authorities greatly enhanced both the quantity and the quality of information on the numbers, activities, and revenues of nonprofits. These data provided scholars and policymakers with the information needed for the systematic analysis of statistics of income and wealth to assess the impact of tax policy on philanthropic giving, as well as the revenues, expenditures, and activities of philanthropic institutions. By the mid-1970s, there was sufficient information about tax-exempts – and sufficient interest in their role and significance – to justify the inclusion of modest sections titled "Philanthropy" and "Religion" in the Bicentennial Edition of *Historical Statistics*, as well as some attention to nonpublic, voluntary, and private service provision in chapters focusing on education and health care.

Governmental attention stimulated efforts by tax-exempt organizations and the trade associations and lobbying groups representing them to gather and disseminate information in the hope of influencing legislation and public opinion. In the late 1940s, the Russell Sage Foundation began publishing studies of foundations (Harrison and Andrews 1946), philanthropic giving (Andrews 1950), corporation giving (Andrews 1952), attitudes toward giving (Andrews 1953), and – beginning in 1960 – an annual directory of foundations, and it established the Foundation Library Center, which compiled and disseminated reference materials on grantmakers and grantmaking (Andrews 1973). (On the proliferation of independent, community, and corporate foundations, especially in the decades following World War II, see Tables Bg28–54.) In 1955, the American Association of Fund-Raising Counsel – a trade association of fund-raising firms and consultants – began publishing *Giving USA*, which presented trend data on philanthropic revenues and expenditures. In 1956, a consortium of foundations convened a meeting of scholars and philanthropic executives to set forth a research agenda on philanthropy – the first of what would become a long line of enterprises in subsidized academic scholarship (*Report* 1956).

Efforts to gather information and frame concepts about private nonprofit entities and activities intensified after the passage of the 1969 Tax Reform Act. By the early 1970s, the first scholarly society, the Association of Voluntary Action Scholars (AVAS), began convening annual research conferences and publishing a journal (the *Journal of Voluntary Action Research*). By the mid-1970s, the U.S. Department of the Treasury cosponsored a privately funded body, the Commission of Philanthropy and Public Needs (better known as the Filer Commission, after its chair, corporate executive John Filer), to study and report on the scope, scale, role, and function of philanthropic and other tax-exempt organizations.

In addition to six volumes of research papers covering every aspect of voluntary and philanthropic activity (Commission 1977), the commission offered a uniquely encompassing view of "diverse domain charitable tax-exempt enterprise" as a distinct and coherent institutional "sector." It also sought to identify and highlight the significant commonalities of these enterprises – the most important of which were their treatment under the federal tax code and the fact that they were legally constrained from distributing their financial surpluses in the form of dividends ("the nondistribution constraint"). Although couched in a language and set of concepts drawn from economics and public policy that justified inclusion of all exempt activity in this newly defined "nonprofit," "independent," or "third" sector, this new characterization also drew on the more traditional rhetorics and rationales for private charity. The most important came from de Tocqueville, whose *Democracy in America* had not only stressed the importance of voluntary associations in public life but also asserted – without evidence – that their development was inextricably interwoven with the growth of other democratic institutions (de Tocqueville 1835). This linkage posited a sectoral concept that was extraordinarily inclusive – not only encompassing all presently existing tax-exempt entities but also treating them as continuous with all earlier voluntary associations.

Shortcomings of the Nonprofit Sector Concept

The new conception of an all-encompassing nonprofit sector that was independent of government and business was not without its critics. Historian Barry Karl argued that the "sanitary language designating a third or independent sector" conflated the rhetoric of scholarly research with the advocacy agenda of the tax-exempt industries. Substitution of the term "nonprofit" for "philanthropy" or "charity," he wrote, suggested an organizational conception that was "presumably efficient, subject to cost-accounting standards of performance and principles of effective management," in order to highlight its public-serving aspects and to obscure its ties to private interests (Karl 1987, pp. 984–5). Others, such as the lawyer-economist Henry Hansmann, criticized the concept's imprecision, particularly its conflation of organizations that, despite their common status as tax-exempt entities, differed in important ways. He argued that nonprofits supported by private donations (such as the United Way) were significantly different from commercial nonprofits whose revenues derived from the sale of goods and services (such as the National Geographic Society) and from mutual benefit organizations in which members pooled resources in order to receive benefits (such as the Knights of Columbus and other fraternal orders) (Hansmann 1987). Policy scientist Lester Salamon offered a detailed critique of the failure of the sector concept to engage the important relationships between nonprofits and government, arguing that the modern American state was increasingly dependent on nonprofits to carry out its responsibilities (Salamon 1987).

The shortcomings of the nonprofit sector concept became clearer with the passage of time. The election of Ronald Reagan, who promised massive federal spending reductions in order to free traditional voluntary organizations from the heavy hand of Big Government, called attention to the extent of the supposedly "independent" sector's reliance on direct and indirect government subsidy. Urban Institute researchers, studying the projected impact of proposed cuts, found that the contribution of federal funds to nonprofit revenues ranged from 12 percent to 90 percent, depending on the industry (Salamon and Abramson 1982); cuts of this magnitude would devastate this sector. (On the growing significance of government as a source of revenue for nonprofits, see Tables Bg65–74, Bg176–187, Bg220–233, and Bg251–264.)

With the 1989 publication of Burton Weisbrod's *Nonprofit Economy*, the IRS's statistics on exempt organization registrations became easily accessible, offering a view of the sector's historical development that was strikingly at odds with the conventional notion that the growth of government diminished the significance of private initiative. Instead, these data portrayed an explosive proliferation of tax-exempt entities after 1950, growth that paralleled the growth of Big Government.

Perhaps the greatest shortcoming of the nonprofit sector concept as originally formulated was its failure to include religious entities and activities – which comprised 40 percent of the organizations in the tax-exempt universe and accounted for as much as two thirds of its donated revenues and volunteer labor force. This omission was problematic both quantitatively, because of the sheer numerical significance of religion in American institutional life, and qualitatively, because of the important and well-documented ties between religious bodies and secular agencies. Studies such as Lloyd Warner and Paul Lunt's Yankee City project had found religious organizations to be the single most important factor shaping associational life in modern American communities, with a single congregation serving as anchor for nearly half of Yankee City's secular associations (Warner and Lunt 1941).

In the 1990s, three additional factors called further attention to the limitations of conceptualizing nonprofits as an organizational sector clearly distinct from business and government. First, efforts to establish market economies and democratic polities in formerly authoritarian states directed the attention of scholars and policymakers to the interdependence of economies, polities, and the civic values and organizations that appeared to be a necessary condition for their success. The entities comprising "civil society" appeared to include two very different kinds of entities: grassroots voluntary associations and quasi-governmental "nonprofit organizations," each of which appeared to have very different implications for the vitality and viability of economic, political, and governmental institutions (Putnam 1993; J. Hall 1995). The application of these critical perspectives to American organizational life not only produced an intense – and still unresolved – scholarly debate about the origins and characteristics of civil society and its impact on democratic institutions (Skocpol 1996; Gamm and Putnam 1999; Skocpol and Fiorina 1999; D. Smith 2000), but also gave rise to historical studies that underscored the important differences between traditional grassroots voluntary associations and the charitable tax-exempt nonprofit organizations of the post–World War II decades.

Second, the enactment of public policies favoring devolution (the shifting of tasks from the federal to state and local governments) and privatization (the shifting of these tasks from government to secular and religious actors in the private sectors) focused attention on the allocation of tasks among government, for-profit, and nonprofit service providers. These issues had initially emerged in the 1980s, in response to charges that nonprofits were competing unfairly with for-profit enterprises (U.S. Small Business Administration 1984) and, more compellingly, in connection with the growing number of conversions of nonprofit health care providers to for-profit ownership (Gray 1991; Schlesinger 1994). Both of these debates served to undermine the arguments advanced by some nonprofit sector theorists that certain kinds of goods and services possessed qualities that favored their provision by nonprofits and government rather than by for-profit providers (Olson 1971) – since these hypotheses could explain neither the enormous growth of commercial activity by supposedly donative and voluntary nonprofit entities nor the impressive success of for-profit service providers in industries assumed to be peculiarly suitable for nonproprietary firms.

Historical studies undertaken in connection with these debates demonstrated conclusively that the role of voluntary and nonprofit firms had varied significantly over time in many of the industries. Health care, which had been dominated by proprietary and government providers, became largely nonprofit by the 1960s – and then, with shifts in government policy, began converting to for-profit ownership in the 1980s (Starr 1982; Fox 1986; Stevens 1989). Before the end of the nineteenth century, a lively rivalry had flourished between for-profit and nonprofit arts organizations; by the 1960s, almost all performing arts organizations had become nonprofit (DiMaggio 1986a, 1986b). Before the 1960s, most independent day schools were proprietary; today, virtually all are nonprofits (Hall 1999a). Even when entities were organized as nonprofits, most functioned as commercial enterprises, providing goods and services for fees. Even for Harvard University, the nation's oldest nonprofit, income earned from tuition, fees, and government grants and contracts has been more important as a source of revenue than donative income from gifts, bequests, and endowments (Harris 1970, p. 210).

Devolution and privatization also directed attention to the fact that studies of the nonprofit sector had largely ignored the role of state-level activity, particularly the important differences in chronologies of organizational development, organizational density (Bowen, Nygren, et al. 1994; Schneider 1996), and philanthropic capacity (Wolpert 1989, 1993). While nationally aggregated data might serve the needs of those arguing for the ubiquity (and, hence, the legitimacy) of nonprofits, they served as a poor predictor of organizational and community capacity to provide essential services to needy populations who once benefited from federal programs (Smith and Lipsky 1993; Gronbjerg 1994; Salamon 1996).

The Elusive Public/Private Distinction

We so take for granted the notion of a clear distinction between public and private domains that we frequently overlook the extent to which this seemingly immutable boundary has developed and changed over time. Only in the 1980s, with the public debate over devolution and privatization, did we begin to appreciate this complex process.

The Supreme Court's decision in the 1819 Dartmouth College case had long been regarded as a landmark in the evolution of American corporations. Under English law, corporations had been treated as contingent delegations of government power and, as such, entirely subject to government authority. Thus, when the state of New Hampshire took control of Dartmouth College from its trustees, it believed that it was acting within the law. Although its actions were upheld in its own courts, New Hampshire lost in the U.S. Supreme Court, which, in a remarkable instance of judicial activism, ruled that Dartmouth College was a constitutionally protected contract between private citizens. In doing so, it extended civil rights from individuals to corporations and, in doing so, created a private domain of associational activity.

Before the 1980s, it was generally assumed that the Court had acted merely to protect a private college from unwarranted government interference. We now understand that the contest between Dartmouth's trustees and the state of New Hampshire was only one episode in a protracted struggle that played out in courts and legislatures throughout the new nation in the fifty years following the Revolution over whether corporations should be permitted to exist and, if so, whether they should be treated as public or private institutions (Davis 1918; Zollmann 1924; Miller 1961; Whitehead 1976; Hall 1982, 1987, 1992). As a result, few charitable corporations or voluntary associations were formed before 1820 (Wright 1992).

Because of the nature of the federal system, the Supreme Court's decision in the Dartmouth case did not entirely settle the issue. Because neither the Bill of Rights nor decisions by the U.S. Supreme Court were binding on the states until after the ratification of the Fourteenth Amendment, state legislatures and courts – many of them outspokenly hostile to private corporations and private charities – continued to shape policies and practices within their own jurisdictions, where the vast majority of incorporations took place. Most corporations chartered before the Dartmouth case remained unaffected by it and only slowly changed their bylaws to take advantage of their privatized status. Harvard College, perhaps the oldest American eleemosynary corporation (chartered in 1636), continued to be what must be considered a public corporation – with the entire state senate sitting ex officio as its Board of Overseers – until 1865, when the alumni began electing representatives to fill these positions. Yale (established in 1701) had a similarly public character between 1792 – when governor, lieutenant governor, and eight senior members of the upper house of the legislature joined the corporation – until 1870, when these were replaced by alumni representatives. Following New England practice, the governing boards of western colleges – including institutions established under denominational sponsorship – were frequently appointed by the governor and included elected officials sitting ex officio as members (Hall 1987). The combination of full or partial government presence on boards and significant, if often erratic, levels of state support makes it difficult to define these institutions as clearly public or private before the charities law reforms of the late nineteenth century brought about a greater degree of uniformity, at least in major industrial states such as Massachusetts, New York, Ohio, and Illinois.

Debate on these questions continues, fueled by contemporary privatization of education, social services, health care, and other services that, for most of the twentieth century, have been considered to be public responsibilities. (In contrast, during the nineteenth century, these services were commonly provided by private contractors.) Beginning in the 1950s, governments broadened their use of nonprofit entities, using them as vehicles for economic development, urban renewal, and related purposes. Although these entities were technically private corporations, the fact that they were completely controlled and funded by government and engaged in governmental tasks has raised interesting legal questions about how community development corporations and entities such as port, housing, water, and redevelopment authorities should be treated under freedom-of-information, sovereign immunity, and other statutes governing the activities of public agencies. In the 1970s and 1980s, the court-ordered movement of the mentally disabled from state institutions into a largely nonprofit system of group homes – entities entirely funded by government and often accorded special statutory status as facilities operating on behalf of the state – has further blurred distinctions between public and private domains.

The complexity of government support for nonprofits poses particular dilemmas for those who have and will be compiling statistics on nonprofit social service providers in the future. Government revenues for service providers often take a number of forms, including contracts, vouchers, and bonded funding for capital expenditures. Contractual arrangements usually involve multiple government agencies at federal, state, and local levels. The huge sums of money involved and the welfare of clients render accurate and comprehensive statistics on revenues and services a public policy issue of the first importance. But its complexity may mean that for historical statisticians of the future, as for those concerned about cost and quality of care today, the system is unmonitorable.

Charitables and Noncharitables

Among the greatest difficulties in compiling historical statistics on nonprofit organizations are, first, changes in the way government agencies have classified charitable and noncharitable nonprofits and, second, the ways in which such changes in tax and regulatory policy have served as incentives for firms to alter their ownership status and their classification under the tax code.

Tax regimes are dynamic, not static. They change with the nature of the state and its priorities. In the late nineteenth and early twentieth centuries, governments generally saw themselves as following and fostering market activity, rather than regulating or directing it. Accordingly, tax burdens at all levels were relatively light and regulatory mechanisms minimal. With the evident failure of market self-regulation in the 1930s and the rise of the welfare/warfare state in the 1940s, national stability was seen to depend on economic management by the federal government. To engage in this task, the federal government embraced a variety of management tools, chief of which was the use of tax policy to selectively encourage private sector activity.

To encourage transfers of revenue from wealthy individuals and corporations, the federal government imposed high tax rates on incomes and estates – but permitted these taxpayers to reduce their obligations through gifts to organizations designated as exempt by the IRS. Prior to 1950, all exempt organizations had been tossed into a catchall part of the code, section 101. In the massive revision of the IRS Code completed in 1954, exempt organizations were carefully classified, with varying amounts of benefit to donors and the organizations themselves, according to policymakers' calculus of public benefit. Initially, the basic rationale behind the 501(c) taxonomy was to differentiate public from private and mutual benefit entities. Over the years, lawmakers drew increasingly fine distinctions between types of organizations whose activities they shaped with regulations and tax incentives. This use of tax policy to engineer organizational activity was not only applied to nonprofits. It was also used to shape economic policy, as in the case of benefits enjoyed by the oil and gas industries.

Ironically, as Tables Bg590–619 suggest, the attempt to substitute tax savings for more traditional benevolent and expressive motives seems to have been less than successful (Burke 2001). While tax savings undoubtedly affected high-income earners who itemized their deductions and, in their estate plans, were highly attentive to the tax code, they did not significantly affect Americans of the lower and middle classes who, as nonitemizers, received no tax benefit for giving. With high tax rates and generous tax benefits for charitable giving, the wealthy and corporations established foundations at a record rate, while the proportion of their annual incomes given for charity increased very little. But the nonitemizers, to whom no benefits accrued for giving, continued to give – usually to religious bodies – at rates often exceeding those of the wealthy (Schervish and Havens 1995). Overall, charitable giving per capita rose, but at a slower pace than real income; see Figure Bg-A.

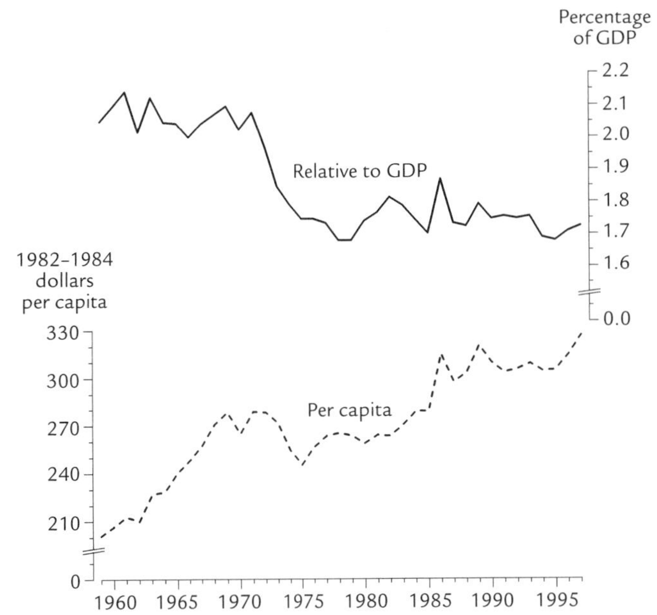

FIGURE Bg-A Estimated philanthropic and charitable giving – per capita and relative to gross domestic product: 1959–1997

Sources

Estimated giving: series Bg590. Population: series Aa7. Gross domestic product (GDP): series Ca1. Consumer price index used to convert per capita giving to real (1982–1984) dollars: series Cc1.

The federal government used other tools of economic management to influence institutional life. In areas such as health care, government grants were made available to nonprofit and public hospitals to fund research and construction of facilities. Higher education benefited both from grant and contract revenues and from indirect funding, the most notable example of which is the GI Bill of Rights, a voucher program that underwrote the tuitions of veterans. Subsidized loan programs underwrote graduate education in a variety of disciplines and professions. In the 1960s, when federal funding of higher education hit its peak, more than one third of the annual revenues of private universities such as Harvard and Yale came from government (see Tables Bg207–233).

From the standpoint of donors and nonprofit organizations and their managers, government tax, regulatory, and spending policies became the incentive structures that largely determined whether an activity would be organized as a business or a nonprofit and, if the latter, what type of nonprofit. As these policies changed after 1954, the allocation of tasks shifted among nonprofits, for-profits, and government, along with the location of firms within the IRS's classificatory scheme.

Since 1954, entities designated as charitable under the IRS Code have had to be considered as parts of a larger universe of firms that have no owners (nonstock corporations) and are prohibited from distributing their surpluses in the form of dividends. Put in quantitative terms, the 554,614 501(c)(3) charitables registered with the IRS in 1992 were a component of a population of 1,085,206 entities that included 396,000 religious congregations (most of which were not registered with the IRS) and 530,592 noncharitable nonprofits – including such entities as corporations organized under act of Congress [501(c)(1)], title-holding corporations for exempt organizations [501(c)(2)], teachers' retirement fund associations [501(c)(11)], benevolent life insurance and other mutual benefit or cooperative companies [501(c)(12)], cemetery companies [501(c)(13)], state-chartered credit unions and mutual reserve banks [501(c)(14)], agricultural cooperatives [501(c)(16)], employee-funded pension trusts [501(c)(18)], black lung benefit trusts [501(c)(21)], withdrawal liability payment funds [501(c)(22)], title-holding corporations or trusts with multiple parents [501(c)(25)], state-sponsored high-risk health coverage organizations [501(c)(26)], state-sponsored workers' compensation reinsurance organizations [501(c)(27)], religious and apostalic organizations [501(d)], cooperative hospital service organizations [501(e)], cooperative service organizations of operating educational organizations [501(f)], child care organizations [501(k)], and farmers' cooperative associations [512(a)]. Included within these categories of noncharitable nonprofits are social welfare and civic organizations, labor unions, trade associations, fraternal and sororal organizations, social clubs, veterans' organizations, and political parties. (On the changing population of various types of nonprofit organizations since the 1960s, see Tables Bg75–101 and Bg600–605.)

While the 501(c)(3) "charitables" enjoy a wide range of privileges under federal and state tax regimes, including exemption from taxes on corporate income, sales, and real estate and, for their supporters, deductibility of donations, the noncharitables enjoy these benefits selectively. Some, such as churches and apostolic organizations, not only have the same tax privileges as secular charitables but also operate under vastly lighter regulatory burdens. Others, such as many mutual benefit entities, enjoy only exemption from federal corporate taxation. Restrictions on advocacy and lobbying also vary, with most charitables suffering significant limitations on political activity, while trade associations and trade unions are generally unrestricted.

Perhaps the most important factor shaping the organizational demography of nonprofits in the postwar decades has been legislators' and policymakers' increasingly expansive definition of charity. Originally freighted with the notion, inherited from English law, that it involved relief of the needy – dependent, disabled, ignorant, or distressed people – through religious, educational, or charitable interventions, charity is defined by modern tax writers far more broadly, in terms of nondistribution of surpluses and absence of private benefit. As the definition of charity has broadened, the range of entities that could qualify for the coveted 501(c)(3) charitable tax-exempt status expanded to include publishers of books and periodicals (such as *The Nation*, *Ms.*, and *National Geographic*), radio and television broadcasters, and, if appropriate educational programs were initiated, trade associations. The impact of this policy shift was dramatic: in 1967, there were twice as many noncharitables as charitables among the exempt organizations registered

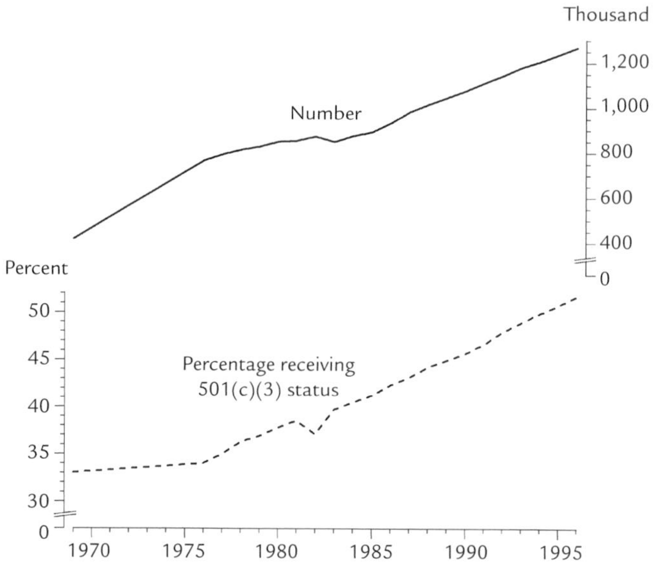

FIGURE Bg-B Active tax-exempt organizations, farmers' cooperatives, and nonexempt charitable trusts – total number and the percentage receiving 501(c)(3) status: 1969–1996

Sources

Total: the sum of series Bg75–101. Percentage receiving 501(c)(3) status: series Bg77 expressed as a percentage of the total.

with the IRS; by 1995, the number of charitables had surpassed noncharitables (see Figure Bg-B). Many of the new charitables were noncharitables that had taken advantage of the IRS's increasingly permissive definition of charity and the tax benefits associated with charitable tax-exempt status.

The growing gap between the technical definition of charity embraced by policymakers, the tax-exempt bar, and nonprofit managers and the notions of charity held by average Americans became dramatically evident after 9/11, when public outrage greeted the Red Cross's handling of donations for Twin Towers victims. Under the law, diverting donations for institutional purposes was perfectly legal. But donors, who wanted their money to relieve the suffering, felt cheated and expressed their dismay forcefully.

A labile policy environment, combined with increasingly sophisticated organizational leadership, does not produce neat or easily understood statistical series. In light of this, data on organizational populations, their activities, and their sources of support cannot be taken as self-explanatory. They must be viewed critically and contextually in terms of the changing nature of government and its policies.

Religious Organizations

The final factor standing in the way of gathering representative statistics on nonprofits involves religious organizations and their activities. While religious bodies in many ways resemble their secular nonprofit counterparts, they have always been accorded special treatment by tax and regulatory authorities because of protections for religious expression embodied in the federal Constitution. Under the Constitution there is no guaranteed right to form voluntary associations; in contrast, government is prohibited from restricting (or supporting) religious expression. The consequence is special treatment accorded religion under federal and state tax and regulatory regimes: religious bodies are not required to incorporate or file tax returns; they and their supporters enjoy tax exemption and deductibility of donations without having to bear the burden of proof imposed on secular organizations and their donors. As a result, the quality and quantity of statistical information available on religious bodies is fragmentary and often of problematic quality.

A further obstacle is the immense – and increasing – variety of religious organizations, making difficult any clear definition of what constitutes a church, a religion, or a devotional activity. Religious bodies vary enormously in their organizational characteristics, ranging from freestanding congregations through federated organizations, some tightly coupled (such as the Roman Catholic Church) and others loosely coupled (such as the Southern Baptist Convention). With this variety, it is difficult to make meaningful statistical comparisons between religious groups. Variable criteria of what constitutes church membership complicate any effort to construct a coherent statistical portrait of American religion. Until the 1990s, the IRS thought it knew the answer to the question "What is a church?" But after a three-decade battle with the Church of Scientology, which concluded in 1993 with the IRS's granting it 501(c)(3) status, the agency conceded its inability to set forth authoritative definitions in this area (see Frantz 1997).

The definitional murkiness is further compounded in efforts to deal with service provision by religious or faith-based entities. In fact, there have never been universally accepted definitions of what constituted a religious, sectarian, or faith-based service provider. The sporadic and selective attention of federal agencies to these entities, however defined, and the virtual exclusion of religious bodies and activities from the research agendas of nonprofits and organizational scholars have long posed formidable obstacles to the gathering and analysis of credible statistics on these organizations. The fact that religious entities provide services directly through congregations and other bodies exempt from federal and state registration and reporting requirements, as well as through affiliated secular corporations – community development corporations, hospitals, schools, and social welfare agencies – further complicates matters.[2] While there may be substantial data on the latter entities compiled by government, trade associations, and industry accrediting agencies, the lack of information on the former stands in the way of any attempt to compile fully integrated measures of their role and significance in private service provision.

Finally, the entire topic of religion and faith-based activity and its place in the nonprofit domain has been obscured by pervasive ignorance and confusion about the nature of religious and religiously tied organizations in the American polity. Although contemporary debate over faith-based social service provision revolves around the "strict separation" of church and state originating in the federal courts, beginning in the 1940s the import of those decisions has been widely misunderstood. They focus almost exclusively on school funding; long-standing government subsidies of church-controlled organizations, such as Catholic Charities USA, the Salvation Army, and Lutheran Social Services, remain unaffected. In fact, government is the largest single source of revenue for these agencies.

The controversy over charitable choice and related proposals to increase the role of religious bodies in social welfare provision appears to be grounded more in politics than in principle. Before the 1990s, few objections were raised either to the massive government subsidies received by large Protestant, Catholic, and Jewish social service agencies or to the funds granted to inner-city congregations for running job-training, neighborhood revitalization, and other antipoverty programs during the 1960s. The present debate seems to center on policies that would reallocate funds from the large sectarian agencies that had traditionally benefited from government largesse to evangelical congregations that have not historically provided social services and to small religiously tied service providers (Cnaan and Milofsky 1997; Cnaan 1999; Wineburg 2001; Walsh 2002). The lack of knowledge about these entities makes it difficult to assess or project their capacity to manage and sustain the social services that charitable-choice initiatives propose to entrust to them – and underscores the need for more complete and reliable statistics on religious bodies of every kind.

Organizational Complexity

Historical statistics generally do not do justice to the complexity of organizations. Most of the extant historical statistics on charitable, religious, and other nonprofit organizations concern freestanding entities, giving either aggregate data on national entities without providing information about state and local subunits or data on local subunits without providing information about the larger organizational matrixes of which they were part. Contemporary hybrids, changelings, and organizational complexes operating simultaneously in several sectors present challenges to future statistical scholarship that urgently need to be met.

Since the nineteenth century, much of the scholarship, legislation, and jurisprudence on nonprofits has been based on an ideal typology of freestanding, donatively supported membership organizations, religious and secular, that hardly did justice to the complexity of the organizational universe as it actually existed. Although little attention was devoted to them until very recently, federated or franchiseform organizations – national organizations with state and local chapters – were among the most important types of nonprofit organizations (Young 1989; Oster 1992; Hunter 1993; Skocpol and Ganz 1997). By the time of the Civil War, the major religious denominations and fraternal and sororal organizations, whose members numbered in the hundreds of thousands, belonged to these kinds of entities. Franchiseform organizations – or "national associations," as Theda Skocpol calls them – varied in structure: some were tightly coupled, with authority wielded from the top; others were loosely coupled, with state and local chapters exercising power over national headquarters. This organizational form became more common in the twentieth century, as trade and professional associations, as well as entities such as the Red Cross and the Community Chest, organized as franchiseforms.

In recent years, changes in tax, regulatory, and funding environments have driven nonprofits to become organizationally more complex, heterogeneous, and less clearly bounded from government and business. IRS restrictions on commercial and advocacy activities by charities have encouraged nonprofits to create wholly owned for-profit subsidiaries to carry out otherwise impermissible activities, while increasing numbers of business corporations have

[2] On this variety, see Jeavons (1994, 1998); Chaves (2001), and Hall (2002).

found nonprofit instrumentalities to be useful for a variety of purposes. Changes in government and other third-party reimbursement policies have driven nonprofits in health and certain social service industries to join national and regional franchise systems or to affiliate with holding companies in order to reduce costs and create efficiencies of scale in purchasing and allocating clients. Other policy changes not only have produced the conversion of many nonprofit hospitals and health insurance plans to for-profit ownership but have also created complex nestings of nonprofit and for-profit corporations which are, in turn, often embedded in national franchiseform organizations. In many states, for example, providers of services to the disabled – most of them parts of national chains – became members of nonprofit umbrella agencies that, through a combination of nonprofit and for-profit subsidiaries, purchased supplies, acquired and developed real estate, and conducted lobbying, advocacy, and litigation on behalf of the disabled (Hall 1999b). In health care, many hospitals, while retaining their nonprofit form, have come under the control of for-profit hospital chains either by means of contracts to manage their operations or by allocating to the chain a controlling number of seats on governing boards. These arrangements have produced constellations of interlocked for-profit, nonprofit, and sometimes governmental agencies. These organizational hybrids are difficult to classify, as growing bodies of literature and litigation about them suggest.

Additional ambiguities in organizational characteristics and activities, which have yet to be adequately measured, involve complex federated or franchiseform organizational structures, hybrid agencies that have developed under contemporary contracting regimes, and the social investment and contributions mechanisms and activities of business corporations. Of these, the franchiseform organizations are the ones most overlooked and most demanding of our attention. They are among the oldest and most common types of nonproprietary entities – embracing not only such venerable organizations as the Freemasons and denominationally structured religious bodies but also contemporary health, advocacy, emergency relief, community service, and other agencies. Despite their obvious prominence, these larger structures have been almost entirely ignored in favor of studies of particular chapters, lodges, or units (Young 1989; Oster 1992; Hunter 1993; Skocpol and Ganz 1997). This bias toward the analysis of firms, rather than the formal larger systems in which they are embedded, requires rethinking and, from the standpoint of historical statisticians, recalculating.

Besides public "authorities" and corporations that administer the utilities and transportation infrastructures of many states, devolution and privatization have given rise to a host of entities that are difficult to locate in standard sectoral or activity taxonomies. The most important of these entities are the group homes that are now the major locus for service provision to the disabled. While most are incorporated as charitable tax-exempt nonprofits, they are treated under the law as hybrid entities – both as households and as licensed service providers (Hall 1996, 1999b). This taxonomic ambiguity has had significant legal consequences because of the courts' willingness to exempt these facilities from the zoning protections that normally constrain the nonresidential uses of property ("City of Edmonds" 1995). To complicate matters, group homes, though operating on the community level, are increasingly likely to be units of national or regional franchiseform entities.

The Charity of Business and the Business of Charity

While trade and industry groups, such as the National Bureau of Economic Research (Williams and Croxton 1930), the American Association of Fund-Raising Counsel, the Foundation Center, and the Council for Aid to Education (H. Smith 1983, 1984), have been gathering and analyzing statistics on corporate contributions since the 1920s, the full scale of business social investment activities remains unclear (on corporate philanthropic activities, see Tables Bg28–54). This is due, in part, to the fact that substantial portions of such funds are disbursed as direct expenses – for community affairs, public relations, and the like – for which no charitable deductions are claimed. The question remains as to whether political contributions, corporate sponsorships, and the costs of "cause-related marketing" – all major growth areas in recent decades – should be included in enumerations of corporate social expenditure. Because business firms are not generally required to disclose the organizations and causes to which they contribute funds, the full range and impact of corporate civic participation remains far from clear (H. Smith 1998). Finally, because corporations were limited by law in types and amounts of giving before 1954, a significant proportion of contributions took the form of individual donations by corporate officers. A study of giving to Harvard by firms and their officers in the mid-1920s showed that while only 10 percent of the university's annual gift income came from corporations, the amount given by these firms and their top officers totaled nearly 30 percent of annual gifts received (Hall 1989).

Despite their professed high purposes, nonprofit enterprises have had to be as concerned about their finances as businesses; or, as contemporary nonprofit managers put it, "no margin, no mission." Like businesses, nonprofits gather and analyze financial information to inform management decisions, to convince donors and funders of their probity and efficacy, and to satisfy the demands of regulators and tax authorities. Aggregate statistics sectorwide on nonprofit revenues, expenditures, and assets date back only to the 1970s (see Tables Bg28–54, Bg65–74, and Bg130–165). However, particular industries have been assembling such statistics since the 1920s. (See Table Bg28–40 for foundations, Tables Bg234–250 for hospitals and health care, and Table Bg251–264 for arts and culture.) Because financial records tend to be preserved, they constitute an extraordinary – and largely unused – statistical resource. When they have been used, as in Seymour Harris's *The Economics of Harvard* or George Pierson's *Yale Book of Numbers*, they provide extraordinarily deep and detailed data about the scale, scope, and priorities of institutions (Harris 1970; Pierson 1983). (For examples of these data, see Table Bg220–233.)

Since the 1960s, as nonprofits have had to negotiate increasingly complex funding environments – staying in the black by seeking revenues from mixes of donations, grants, and contracts from public and private sources and from earned income – their management has become increasingly sophisticated and entrepreneurial. This has produced cries of alarm about "commerciality" – the displacement of traditional charitable goals in the pursuit of healthy bottom lines (Weisbrod 1998). Here, representative statistics can serve as a healthy corrective by showing that most nonprofit organizations except the truly charitable ones have historically depended more on earned income than on donations. The nation's oldest nonprofits, Harvard and Yale, have always drawn the greater part of their annual revenues from tuitions, fees, grants, contracts, and the sale of goods and services than from gifts, bequests, and endowment income (see Table Bg220–233). A similar distribution of sources of income is found in health care: of the private hospitals, most were for-profit enterprises until after World War II; even after most of the "proprietaries" converted to nonprofit ownership, earned income remained their major source of revenue (see Tables Bg234–250). While human services providers would seem, by the nature of their activities, to be protected from the necessity to be entrepreneurial, they have shown themselves to be remarkably adept at locating opportunities for earning revenues. Kirsten Gronbjerg's 1994 study of nonprofit funding, which broke down the income sources of a representative midsize human services provider, showed it drawing revenue from multiple federal, state, and local agencies (including voucher income), from foundations, corporations, and federated funders, and from rents and sales of goods and services.

Recent changes in public policy should greatly improve the quality of financial statistics on nonprofits. In 1998, the IRS began requiring all nonprofits to make their annual tax returns (Form 990s) available to the public. Most of these are now available at the Internet site of GuideStar, a national database of nonprofit organizations. In contrast to the situation before 1998, when tax data were available on a very limited basis only to accredited researchers who could go to Washington and work with IRS tapes and files, we can expect that with the passage of time, large aggregations of sector-wide financial data will be available to the general public and to scholars.

Conceptualization, Quantification, and the Dilemmas of "Legibility"

Had editors of earlier editions of *Historical Statistics of the United States* commissioned chapters on nonprofits, they would have proceeded from very different sets of assumptions about their scope, scale, role, and public significance than the editors of the current edition. Although the population of nonprofits grew dramatically and the range of activities in which they engage broadened impressively in the decades after 1949, there was a notable and perhaps inevitable lag between rapidly changing institutional realities and the perceptions of scholars and policymakers. In 1949, when the first edition appeared, the vast majority of nonprofits were religious bodies and voluntary membership associations. By the 1960 and 1975 editions, most of the voluntary associations had disappeared and been replaced by section 501(c) entities, increasing numbers of which – though not engaged in the kinds of charitable, educational, or religious activities to which charities had traditionally devoted themselves – sought classification as 501(c)(3) or 501(c)(4) exempt entities. Small wonder that the editors of the 1975 edition confined their efforts on nonprofits to small chapters on religious affiliation and philanthropy, rather than trying to capture the larger domain of rapidly changing nonprofits. And they can hardly be faulted for the modesty of their achievement, since the concept of nonprofits as a coherent and clearly defined institutional sector was invented only in the late 1970s.

Only now, after nearly three decades of intensive study, has it become possible to take the first steps toward a comprehensive view of nonprofit activity. But doing so runs the risk of imposing on extraordinarily complex, diverse, and locally variable institutions and practices standardized definitions and measures necessary for a synoptic view (Scott 1998). The problem with such quantified simplifications, which stem from the needs of states to centrally record and monitor the activities, is that – embedded in statutory, tax, and regulatory regimes – they take on the power to shape organizational activity and individual behavior. Rather than serving merely as a scheme of classification intended to set forth the variety of tax and regulatory treatments meted out to various kinds of organizations and activities according to the extent to which they serve public rather than private interests, the tax code becomes an incentive structure for tax and estate planners, entrepreneurs, and managers. The distorting effect of the tax code is abundantly evident in statistics of individual giving, which show declines in the proportion of annual household income given for charity, despite increases in potential tax benefits to donors (see Tables Bg606–675; see also Burke 2001, pp. 186–7). This suggests that moral and religious commitments may be more powerful motives for giving than economic calculation.

Because the universe of nonproprietary entities and activities had its greatest period of growth concomitant with the rise of the welfare state, the evolution and crystallization of concepts defining it display the power of "legibility" with particular force. The irrational, complex, diverse, and manifestly unstandardized domain of voluntary associations "of a thousand kinds" that so astonished de Tocqueville in the 1820s – even when it was still embryonic – grew through the course of the nineteenth and the first half of the twentieth centuries to fill a public space that had, for the most part, been defined in terms of individual and collective rights that government was forbidden to impair.

Efforts to create governmental capacities for social engineering can be dated to the Progressive era, with the adoption of comprehensive federal budgeting and, during the 1920s, with the systematic gathering of statistics on virtually every aspect of American life by the U.S. Department of Commerce (Hawley 1974, 1977; Webber and Wildavsky 1986). These initiatives depended to a large extent on voluntary efforts of trade associations, industry groups, and state and municipal agencies. Under such auspices, these statistics inevitably contained built-in biases and elements of advocacy and self-promotion.

The universalization of the personal income tax during World War II and the implementation of economic and national defense planning in the late 1940s definitively transformed this unregulated domain of entities that mediated between citizens and the formal agencies of government into a target for what James Scott would call "state initiated social engineering" (Scott 1998, p. 4). Constrained by deeply rooted traditions of hostility to strong central government, the policymakers of the postwar era devised a unique alternative to the European-style bureaucratic welfare state. The American welfare state, as it emerged after the war, combined elements of centralization (particularly the federalization of revenue gathering and policy planning) and decentralization (under which the actual implementation of national policy was allocated to states and localities and to private sector actors).

Tax policy and the targeted use of federal spending played key roles in this process, influencing patterns of investment and employment, the formation of human capital (particularly through grants and contracts to universities), health and human services provision (through incentives for charitable giving), and forms of ownership (through funding favoring "voluntary" over proprietary entities). The Hill–Burton Program (the Hospital Survey and Construction Act of 1946), for example, in making massive federal aid available to "voluntary" and public hospitals, fueled a tidal wave of

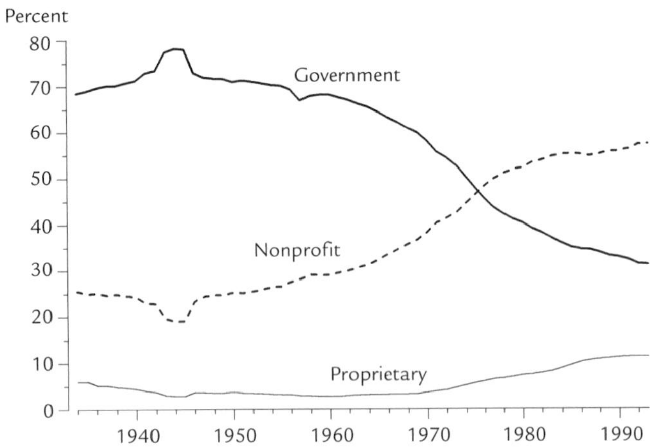

FIGURE Bg-C Hospital beds, by ownership or control: 1934–1993

Sources
Through 1945, Table Bd158–171; thereafter, Table Bd144–157.

conversions of ownership in the health care industry. To this were added generous federal research grants through the federal medical and science institutes. Between 1934 and 1990, hospital beds controlled by nonprofit hospitals increased from under 30 percent to nearly 60 percent, while the government's share fell from over 70 percent to slightly more than 30 percent (see Figure Bg-C). During this period, percentage of proprietary hospitals dropped from over 30 percent to about 17 percent (see Tables Bd144–171). Federal investment in such programs as the GI Bill of Rights, combined with grants and contracts, fueled a similarly explosive growth of higher education. While public institutions benefited from these programs, they also provided powerful incentives for the establishment and expansion of new private institutions.

Although there is little evidence to suggest that anyone in the 1940s anticipated the explosive growth of the charitable tax-exempt domain, there can be no disputing the impact of new tax policies on decision making by the wealthy (who began creating foundations at a record rate), corporations (which began aggressively seeking legal and regulatory sanction for contributing to nonprofits), and fund-raisers and charitable advocacy groups (which began intensive efforts to sell wealthy individuals and foundations on the value of charitable giving) (Andrews 1952; Ruml 1952; Cutlip 1965; Curti and Nash 1965). Indeed, it was the very success of these efforts and some of the surprising loopholes taken advantage of by tax lawyers and estate planners that first attracted unfavorable congressional attention to the rapidly growing tax-exempt universe. Among the more notorious schemes was the New York University (NYU) Law School's acquisition of the Mueller Macaroni Company, then the world's largest pasta manufacturer. Because all of its profits went to support the school, NYU sought tax-exempt status for the enterprise ("Macaroni Monopoly" 1968; Sharpe 1996). The scheme that enabled the Ford Motor Company to pass from its founder to his heirs without paying a penny in taxes – while at the same time creating the world's largest foundation – helped to focus Congress's attention on "foundations and other tax-exempt entities" in overhauling the Internal Revenue Code (MacDonald 1955).

The revised IRS Code, enacted in 1954, was as much a mechanism for gathering revenue as it was a device for steering the surplus wealth of individuals and corporations to activities and institutions favored by the government. Although Congress strove conscientiously to grasp the changing nature of the growing tax-exempt universe, it is clear from statements made at congressional hearings that legislators and tax officials had a very imperfect understanding of these entities, and they also failed to anticipate how powerfully new tax policies would stimulate their proliferation. While the new code increased government's capacity to oversee nonprofits, it remained a largely underregulated domain, encouraging a variety of abuses that would make them objects of particular scrutiny when Congress again revised the tax code in 1969.

By the 1970s, increasing regulatory scrutiny and demands for demonstrable efficiency and effectiveness by government agencies that funded nonprofits helped to stimulate the final stage of the so-called legibility process: the reform and standardization of nonprofit incorporation statutes and the professionalization of nonprofit management. Both had the effect of shifting nonprofits from a charitable paradigm based on voluntary labor and donative support to a corporate paradigm based on trained employees, government subsidy, and earned revenues.

The needs of the modern state were not the only forces impacting the conceptualization of nonprofits and their activities. As the state sought to make voluntary and nonprofit activity legible, affected industries sought to influence the policy process with their own sets of concepts, definitions, and measures. Congressional investigations of foundations in the 1950s and 1960s and the foundations' inability to block the passage of the Tax Reform Act of 1969 led philanthropic leaders to reconsider their relationship to the rest of the tax-exempt universe. Confronted by a hostile Congress, philanthropy's leaders had defended themselves by using the language of political philosophy derived from de Tocqueville and the Founding Fathers. When they discovered that the lingua franca of public policy had become the language of law and economics, they strategically embraced it – little knowing that doing so would powerfully transform the institutions they sought to defend.

"Has philanthropy become all *law*?" wrote an outraged executive of the Council on Foundations in the midst of the congressional hearings on the 1969 Tax Reform Act. "Is it irrecoverably committed to lawyers instead of its traditional practitioners?" (Goheen 1974). Philanthropy had indeed become very nearly "all law" – and the law itself had increasingly become all economics. Out of this came the effort to conceptually capture the domain of de Tocqueville's thousand kinds of voluntary associations and the growing population of tax-exempt organizations of the post–World War II decades as part of a third, independent, or nonprofit sector.

Religion Statistics

"To represent the religious history of America statistically and geographically is to generalize dangerously and to court disaster openly." (Gaustad 1962)

Religious bodies have been gathering data about themselves since the eighteenth century, and government agencies have done so periodically since the mid-nineteenth century (notably, information on religious bodies collected as part of the population censuses of 1850–1880 and the censuses of religious bodies for 1890, 1906, 1916, 1926, and 1936). Nevertheless, the intrinsic complexity and diversity of religious organizations – whose variations in polity lead to differences in such fundamentals as the interrelationships and relative significance of operating units, lines of authority and accountability, methods of financial accounting, and definitions of membership – pose formidable obstacles to compiling and presenting historical statistics that are either continuous or comparable.

As Roger Finke and Rodney Stark note in their important but controversial 1992 study *The Churching of America, 1776–1990*, the quality of religion statistics is variable and their meaning contestable. The federal census takers, for example, collected masses of information about

> the history, doctrine, organizational features of every religious body in the nation, along with detailed statistics on such things as total membership (also separated by age and sex), Sunday School enrollment, number of congregations, value of church property, amount of debt, total expenditures, ministers'salaries, contributions to foreign missions, and so on – presented separately for every state . . . [as well as] membership data by counties and for all cities having more than 25,000 inhabitants. (Finke and Stark 1992, pp. 9–10)

But despite this wealth of valuable data, our statistical understanding of American religion is deeply flawed. Because religious groups define membership and affiliation differently, statistical series on membership in one group are not strictly comparable with data from others. Since much of the data were collected by religious groups themselves, they are of questionable reliability because congregations had incentives to make themselves appear popular and prosperous to denominational executives and because denominations often wanted to appear wealthier and larger than they actually were (Fry 1933; Webber 1933). Moreover, even if we had reliable and representative data on membership, it would tell us little about the relative influence and public presence of groups regionally and locally (see Figure Bg-D, for example).

Scholars have only recently turned their attention to these questions, investigating such things as the relative generosity and stinginess of religious groups in giving and volunteering (Ronsvalle and Ronsvalle 1997; Iannacone 1998), their effectiveness in promoting civic engagement (Verba, Schlozman and Brady 1995), and their role in providing social services (Wuthnow 1991; Cnaan 1999; Wineburg 2001; Walsh 2002). Ambitious efforts have also been made to define the place of religion in the nonprofit sector (Wuthnow 1986; Hodgkinson, Weitzman, and Kirsch 1988a, 1988b, 1993; Wuthnow, Hodgkinson, et al. 1990; Hall 1990; Hodgkinson, Weitzman, Toppe, and Noga 1992; Cherry and Sherrill 1992; Demerath, Hall, et al. 1998). These questions are of interest not only to scholars of religious demography (including such issues as the vitality of "mainline" denominations and the implications of increasing religious pluralism), but also – in the wake of welfare reform and its charitable-choice provisions – to policymakers concerned about the capacity of religious groups to provide the "safety net" needed for the dependent and disabled. While valuable data have been collected to illuminate these questions, none were of sufficient temporal depth to include in this chapter.

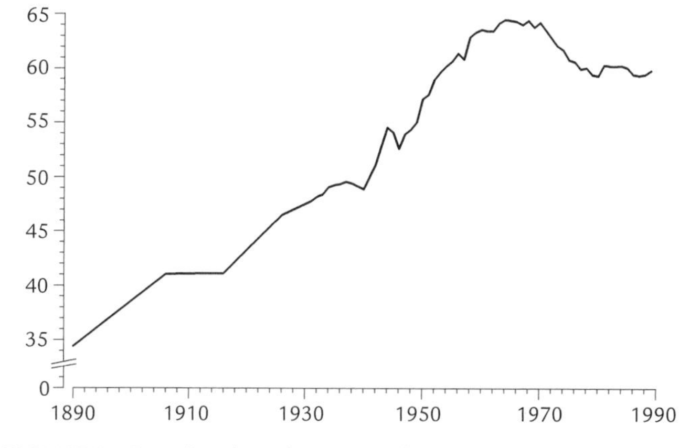

FIGURE Bg-D Church and congregation membership as a percentage of the population: 1890–1989

Sources

Series Aa7 and Bg320.

Even if *Historical Statistics* had presented the full range of information on religious bodies collected by the Census Bureau and denominational enumerators, it would have provided scant insight into the place of religious entities and activities in the larger domain of nonproprietary entities, because the definition of faith-based service provision and faith-based or religiously tied associations and organizations is as fraught with variability and ambiguity as the far simpler question of membership. Because theological orientations, established practices, and other factors – such as state statutes and regulatory norms – introduce variations in not only *what services* religious groups are likely to provide but also *how they are provided* (directly by congregations' religious orders or denomination bodies, through affiliated secular entities, or through ecumenical/interchurch bodies), it is extraordinarily difficult to locate and present reliable comparable data on these entities and activities. Where possible, we have attempted to present both data on the role of faith-based service provision within particular industries (such as education and health care) and data on service provision within and among religious or faith-based bodies.

Although groups such as Independent Sector have conducted quantitative studies of faith-based service provision (Hodgkinson, Weitzman, and Kirsch 1988a, 1993) – and have gathered a great deal of valuable information in the course of doing so – these bold and costly initiatives have, in using congregations as their basic unit of analysis, ignored the complexity and variability of faith-based service provision. Although congregations have historically been the primary locus of devotional activity for most religious groups, their significance as platforms for service provision varies over time and among traditions.

The Roman Catholic Church presents an excellent example of the problematic nature of the congregation as the primary or sole unit of analysis. The Catholic Church is, of all American religious groups, probably the most active provider of the widest range of educational, health, and human services. But few of these are supplied under congregational auspices. Most are delivered by a complex of secular corporations (most Catholic hospitals and social service agencies, as well as increasing numbers of schools, are separately incorporated and governed by lay boards), religious orders (whose members often administer or work in secular corporations), or diocesan bodies. Catholic Charities USA, perhaps the largest faith-based charity, is a secular corporation that is substantially supported by government subsidies. The Knights of Columbus, one of the largest faith-based financial service enterprises, is a secular corporation whose charter ties it closely to the church. Covenant House, the scandal-plagued human services empire founded by Father Bruce Ritter, is a secular corporation with a lay board (composed of prominent Catholics) but headed by a member of a religious order. All of these are Catholic service providers – but any analysis that depended solely on either congregational data or even revenues derived from Catholic donors would offer a very partial glimpse into the full dimensions of the service activities connected with the church.

The limited and fragmentary quality of available data precludes this discussion from offering much more than a hint of these kinds of activities. At this point, the best we can offer are figures on faith-based service provision in certain industries.

A final caveat on religion statistics involves the ongoing transformation of American religious life and demography. Over the long term, the major organizational trend in religious life since the beginning of the nineteenth century has been the emergence of large denominational and interdenominational bodies. More recently, however, new countertrends have become evident, particularly the establishment of impressive numbers of freestanding congregations. Although many of these are transient "storefront" enterprises, increasing numbers of these entities ("superchurches") command memberships that can be counted in the thousands and sometimes tens of thousands (Trueheart 1996). Even if superchurches were not an issue, the proliferation of smaller freestanding congregations over the past two decades amounts, in some communities, to as many as half of the active congregations (Hall 1999a). As the population of these entities increases, the dependability of data collected by denominational and ecumenical bodies is likely to become increasingly questionable.

A related trend involves the rise of alternative forms of worship (for example, the Church of Scientology) and para-church organizations (for example, Habitat for Humanity and Alcoholics Anonymous), for whom ministry and devotional activity are not exercised in congregations nor do they follow familiar forms of worship (Wuthnow 1994). Some of these involve impressive numbers of participants in their activities and, if their significance continues to increase, will demand greater and more scrupulous attention.

Shifts in religious demography, particularly increasing populations of people affiliated with faiths outside the Judeo–Christian traditions, though obviously important features of a changing and more diverse human population, have been largely ignored by collectors of religion statistics. The 1975 edition of *Historical Statistics* confines itself solely to "mainline" Christian bodies, omitting accounts of such important African American groups as the African Methodist Episcopal Church and black Baptist sects, as well as Jewish denominations. Little of the recent scholarship on religious membership and financial trends has given attention to the activities of Islamic or Asian groups, whose membership is now believed to number in the millions.

What Counts and Why?

In the course of the protracted debate over the nature of the nonprofit sector, the fact that categorical and classificatory schemes are merely representations, created for the convenience of individuals or agencies, has often been overlooked. The usefulness of such representations varies according to the needs of researchers and policymakers. Representing nonprofits as a "sector" may be very useful if we are concerned with tax and regulatory issues as they affected exempt organizations after 1954 (when the current IRS taxonomy of exempt organizations was promulgated). This category would not be particularly useful if we wish to understand the allocation of tasks among public agencies, business firms, and nonprofits with industries or to examine interorganizational relationships that cross sectoral boundaries. Put another way, road maps are useful if we are traveling by car; they are useless if we are navigating waterways.

Over time, reasons for compiling historical statistics have changed, as has an understanding of what kinds of historical statistics we needed to compile. When the first edition of *Historical Statistics* appeared, hard on the heels of the passage of the Employment Act of 1946 and the creation of the Council of Economic Advisors – which signaled the federal government's determination to manage the nation's economy – the intention was to "bring together within a single cover the most important of the comprehensive statistical series measuring the economic development of the United States over the past century or more" for the use of the "larger policy making community" (U.S. Bureau of the Census 1949, p. vi; Anderson 1988, p. 192; and the essay on the origins of *Historical Statistics* in Appendix 3). The purpose of *Historical Statistics*, as originally formulated, was to create a resource for government planners concerned with managing the economy, maintaining domestic and international political stability, and mobilizing the nation in the event of war (U.S. Department of Commerce 1954). For these purposes, the range of institutions and activities considered pertinent to the effort were more or less restricted to wealth and income, population characteristics, natural and human resources, public and private finance, and physical infrastructure – domains affected by or otherwise relevant to then-current public policies. Philanthropy, nonprofit organizations, religion, and related institutions and activities were not considered germane to these concerns.

At the beginning of the twenty-first century, the needs of researchers and policymakers and the nature of government itself have changed, and with them our understanding of the kinds of information needed for informed public and private planning. Half a century of devolution and privatization has diffused the tasks of policy planning and implementation to state and municipal governments and to nonprofit agencies created or subsidized by public funds, including religious bodies and universities, which, before World War II, were supported entirely by revenues from private sources. Moreover, since the collapse of authoritarian regimes in the 1990s and the effort to put in their place market democracies, we have discovered that economic and political systems depend on "civil society," formal and informal associations and organizations that produce the norms of trust and reciprocity essential to orderly exchange and governance (Putnam 1993, 2000; Fukuyama 1995). All of this has made the acquisition of usable knowledge about nonprofits and related entities compellingly important.

References

Anderson, Margo J. 1988. *The American Census: A Social History*. Yale University Press.

Andrews, F. Emerson. 1950. *Philanthropic Giving*. Russell Sage Foundation.

Andrews, F. Emerson. 1952. *Corporation Giving*. Russell Sage Foundation.

Andrews, F. Emerson. 1953. *Attitudes toward Giving*. Russell Sage Foundation.

Andrews, F. Emerson. 1973. *The Foundation Watcher*. Franklin and Marshall College.

Bowen, William G., Thomas I. Nygren, et al. 1994. *The Charitable Nonprofits: An Analysis of Institutional Dynamics and Characteristics*. Jossey-Bass.

Burke, Colin B. 2001. "Nonprofit History's New Numbers (and the Need for More)." *Nonprofit and Voluntary Sector Quarterly* 30 (2) (June): 174–203.

Chaves, Mark. 2001. "Religious Congregations and Welfare Reform: Assessing the Potential." In Andrew Walsh, editor. *Can Charitable Choice Work? Covering Religion's Impact on Urban Affairs and Social Services*. Leonard E. Greenberg Center for the Study of Religion in Public Life, Trinity College.

Cherry, Conrad, and Rowland A. Sherrill. 1992. *Religion, the Independent Sector, and American Culture*. Scholars Press.

"City of Edmonds, Petitioner v. Oxford House, Inc., et al." 1995. Number 94-23 Supreme Court of the United States. 115 S. Ct. 1776; 131 L. Ed. 2d 801.

Cnaan, Ram. 1999. *The Newer Deal: Social Work and Religion in Partnership*. Columbia University Press.

Cnaan, Ram, and Carl Milofsky, editors. 1997. *Small Religious Nonprofits. Nonprofit and Voluntary Sector Quarterly* 26 (Supplemental Issue).

Commission on Philanthropy and Public Needs. 1977. *Research Papers*. 6 volumes. U.S. Department of the Treasury.

Curti, Merle, and Roderick Nash. 1965. *Philanthropy and the Shaping of American Higher Education*. Rutgers University Press.

Cutlip, Scott M. 1965. *Fund Raising in the United States*. Rutgers University Press.

Davis, Joseph S. 1918. *Essays in the Earlier History of American Corporations*. 2 volumes. Harvard University Press.

Demerath, N. J., III, Peter Dobkin Hall, et al., editors. 1998. *Sacred Companies: Organizational Aspects of Religion and Religious Aspects of Organizations*. Oxford University Press.

de Tocqueville, Alexis. 1835. *Democracy in America*. Translated by Henry Reeve. Vintage Books, 1945.

DiMaggio, Paul J. 1986a. "Cultural Entrepreneurship in Nineteenth Century Boston." In Paul J. DiMaggio, editor. *Nonprofit Enterprise in the Arts: Studies in Mission and Constraint*. Oxford University Press.

DiMaggio, Paul J. 1986b. "Can Culture Survive the Marketplace?" In Paul J. DiMaggio, editor. *Nonprofit Enterprise in the Arts: Studies in Mission and Constraint*. Oxford University Press.

Finke, Roger, and Rodney Stark. 1992. *The Churching of America, 1776–1990: Winners and Losers in Our Religious Economy*. Rutgers University Press.

Fox, Daniel M. 1986. *Health Policies, Health Politics: The British and American Experience, 1911–1965*. Princeton University Press.

Frantz, Douglas. 1997. "The Shadowy Story behind Scientology's Tax-Exempt Status." *New York Times* (March 9).

Fry, C. Luther. 1933. "Changes in Religious Organizations." In *Recent Social Trends in the United States: Report of the President's Research Committee on Social Trends*, volume 2. McGraw-Hill.

Fukuyama, Francis. 1995. *Trust: The Social Virtues and the Creation of Prosperity.* Free Press.

Gamm, Gerald, and Robert Putnam. 1999. "Association Building in America, 1840–1950." *Journal of Interdisciplinary History* 29 (4) (March): 511–58.

Gaustad, Edwin. 1962. *Historical Atlas of Religion in America*. Harper & Row.

Goheen, Robert. 1974. Memorandum to Eugene Struckhoff. Council on Foundations files, Agency File 8/73-4/74, Rockefeller Archives Center.

Gray, Bradford H. 1991. *The For-Profit Motive and Patient Care: The Changing Accountability of Doctors and Hospitals*. Twentieth Century Fund.

Gronbjerg, Kirsten. 1994. *Understanding Nonprofit Funding*. Jossey-Bass.

Hall, John A., editor. 1995. *Civil Society: Theory, History, Comparison.* Polity Press.

Hall, Peter Dobkin. 1982. *The Organization of American Culture, 1700–1900: Institutions, Elites, and the Origins of American Nationality.* New York University Press.

Hall, Peter Dobkin. 1987. "The Spirit of the Ordinance of 1787: Organizational Values, Voluntary Associations, and Higher Education in Ohio, 1803–1830." In Paul H. Mattingly and Edward W. Stevens Jr., editors. *"... Schools and the Means of Education Shall Forever Be Encouraged": A History of Education in the Old Northwest.* Ohio University Libraries.

Hall, Peter Dobkin. 1989. "Business Giving and Social Investment in the United States." In Richard Magat, editor. *Philanthropic Giving: Studies in Varieties and Goals.* Oxford University Press.

Hall, Peter Dobkin. 1990. "The History of Religious Philanthropy in the United States." In Robert Wuthnow, Virginia A. Hodgkinson, et al., editors. *Faith and Philanthropy in America*. Jossey-Bass.

Hall, Peter Dobkin. 1992. *Inventing the Nonprofit Sector and Other Essays on Philanthropy, Voluntarism, and Nonprofit Organizations*. Johns Hopkins University Press.

Hall, Peter Dobkin. 1996. "There's No Place Like Home: Contracting Human Services in Connecticut, 1970–1995." PONPO Working Paper number 235. Program on Non-Profit Organizations, Yale University.

Hall, Peter Dobkin. 1999a. "Vital Signs: Associational Populations and Ecologies in New Haven, Connecticut, 1850–1990." In Morris Fiorina and Theda Skocpol, editors. *Civic Engagement in American Democracy*. Brookings Institution Press.

Hall, Peter Dobkin. 1999b. "Blurred Boundaries, Hybrids, and Changelings: The Fortunes of Nonprofit Organizations in the Late Twentieth Century." In George E. Marcus, editor. *Critical Anthropology Now: Unexpected Contexts, New Constituencies, Changing Genres.* American College of Research.

Hall, Peter Dobkin. 2002. "Historical Perspectives on Religion, Government, and Social Welfare in America." In Andrew Walsh, editor. *Can Charitable Choice Work? Covering Religion's Impact on Urban Affairs and Social Services*. Leonard E. Greenberg Center for the Study of Religion and Public Life, Trinity College.

Hansmann, Henry. 1987. "Economic Theories of the Nonprofit Sector." In W. W. Powell, editor. *The Nonprofit Sector: A Research Handbook*. Yale University Press.

Hansmann, Henry. 1997. *Ownership of Enterprise*. Harvard University Press.

Harris, Seymour. 1970. *The Economics of Harvard*. McGraw-Hill.

Harrison, Shelby M., and F. Emerson Andrews. 1946. *American Foundations for Social Welfare.* Russell Sage Foundation.

Hawley, Ellis W., editor. 1974. *Herbert Hoover as Secretary of Commerce: Studies in New Era Thought and Practice*. University of Iowa Press.

Hawley, Ellis W. 1977. "Herbert Hoover, the Commerce Secretariat, and the Vision of an 'Associative State.'" In E. J. Perkins, editor. *Men and Organizations: The American Economy in the Twentieth Century*. Putnam's.

Hodgkinson, Virginia A., Murray S. Weitzman, and Arthur D. Kirsch. 1988a. *From Belief to Commitment: The Activities and Finances of Religious Congregations in the United States, 1992.* Independent Sector.

Hodgkinson, Virginia A., Murray S. Weitzman, and Arthur D. Kirsch. 1988b. "Demographic Trends in Religious Insitutions: Preliminary Findings from a National Survey of the Activities and Finances of Religious Institutions in the United States." In *Looking Forward to the Year 2000: Public Policy and Philanthropy.* Spring Research Forum Working Papers, Independent Sector.

Hodgkinson, Virginia A., Murray S. Weitzman, and Arthur D. Kirsch. 1993. *From Belief to Commitment: The Activities and Finances of Religious Congregations in the United States, 1992.* Independent Sector.

Hodgkinson, Virginia A., Murray S. Weitzman, Christopher M. Toppe, and Stephen M. Noga. 1992. *Nonprofit Almanac, 1992–1993*. Jossey-Bass.

Hunter, Albert. 1993. "National Federations: The Role of Voluntary Organizations in Linking Macro and Micro Orders in Society." *Nonprofit and Voluntary Sector Quarterly* 22 (3) (Summer): 121–36.

Iannacone, Laurence R. 1998. "Why Strict Churches Are Strong." In N. J. Demerath III, Peter Dobkin Hall, et al. *Sacred Companies: Organizational Aspects of Religion and Religious Aspects of Organizations*. Oxford University Press.

Jeavons, Thomas. 1994. *When the Bottom Line Is Faithfulness: Management of Christian Service Organizations.* Indiana University Press.

Jeavons, Thomas. 1998. "Identifying Characteristics of 'Religious' Organizations." In N. J. Demerath III, Peter Dobkin Hall, et al. *Sacred Companies: Organizational Aspects of Religion and Religious Aspects of Organizations*. Oxford University Press.

Karl, Barry. 1987. "Nonprofit Institutions." *Science* 236 (May 22): 984–5.

"The Macaroni Monopoly: The Developing Concept of Unrelated Business Income of Exempt Organizations." 1968. *Harvard Law Review* 81: 1280–94.

MacDonald, Dwight. 1955. *The Ford Foundation: The Men and the Millions*. Reynal.

Miller, Howard S. 1961. *The Legal Foundations of American Philanthropy*. State Historical Society of Wisconsin.

Olson, Mancur. 1971. *The Logic of Collective Action: Public Goods and the Theory of Groups*. Harvard University Press.

Oster, Sharon. 1992. "Nonprofit Organizations as Franchise Operations." *Nonprofit Management and Leadership* 2 (Spring): 223–38.

Pierson, George W. 1983. *The Yale Book of Numbers: Historical Statistics of the College and University, 1701–1976*. Yale University Press.

Putnam, Robert D. 1993. *Making Democracy Work: Civic Traditions in Modern Italy*. Princeton University Press.

Putnam, Robert D. 2000. *Bowling Alone: The Collapse and Revival of American Community*. Simon & Schuster.

Report of the Princeton Conference on the History of Philanthropy. 1956. Russell Sage Foundation.

Ronsvalle, John, and Sylvia Ronsvalle. 1997. *The State of Church Giving through 1995*. Empty Tomb.

Ruml, Beardsley. 1952. *Manual of Corporate Giving*. National Planning Association.

Salamon, Lester M. 1987. "Of Market Failure, Voluntary Failure, and Third-Party Government: Toward a Theory of Government – Nonprofit Relations in the Modern Welfare State." In Susan Ostrander, Stuart Langton, and Jon Van Til, editors. *Shifting the Debate: Public/Private Sector Relations in the Modern Welfare State*. Transaction Press.

Salamon, Lester M. 1996. *Partners in Public Service: Government–Nonprofit Relations in the Modern Welfare State*. Johns Hopkins University Press.

Salamon, Lester, and Alan Abramson. 1982. *The Federal Budget and the Nonprofit Sector*. Urban Institute Press.

Schervish. Paul G., and John J. Havens. 1995. "Do the Poor Pay More: Is the U-Shaped Curve Correct?" *Nonprofit and Voluntary Sector Quarterly* 24 (1) (Spring): 79–90.

Schlesinger, Mark. 1994. "Mismeasuring the Consequences of Ownership: External Influences and the Comparative Performance of Public, For-Profit, and Private Nonprofit Organizations." PONPO Working Paper number 205. Program on Non-Profit Organizations, Yale University.

Schneider, J. C. 1996. "Philanthropic Styles in the United States: Toward a Theory of Regional Differences." *Nonprofit and Voluntary Sector Quarterly* 25 (2): 190–210.

Scott, James C. 1998. *Seeing Like a State: How Certain Schemes to Improve the Human Condition Have Failed*. Yale University Press.

Sharpe, Donald L. 1996. "Unfair Business Competition and the Tax on Income Destined for Charity: Forty-Six Years Later." *Florida Tax Review* 3: 367–470.

Simon, John G. 1987. "The Tax Treatment of Nonprofit Organizations: A Review of Federal and State Policies." In W. W. Powell, editor. *The Nonprofit Sector: A Research Handbook*. Yale University Press.

Skocpol, Theda. 1996. "The Tocqueville Problem: Civic Engagement in American Democracy." *Social Science History* 21 (4) (Winter): 106–9.

Skocpol, Theda, and Morris Fiorina. 1999. *Civic Engagement in American Democracy*. Brookings Institution Press.

Skocpol, Theda, and Marshall Ganz. 1997. "Casting Wider Nets." Paper presented to the Conference on Civic Engagement in American Democracy, Portland, Maine, September 26–28.

Smith, David H. 2000. *Grassroots Associations*. Sage Publications.

Smith, Hayden W. 1983. *A Profile of Corporate Contributions*. Council for Aid to Education.

Smith, Hayden W. 1984. *Corporate Contributions Research since the Filer Commission*. Council for Aid to Education.

Smith, Hayden W. 1998. "Mandating the Disclosure of Corporate Charitable Contributions." PONPO Working Paper number 254. Program on Non-Profit Organizations, Yale University.

Smith, Steven R., and Michael Lipsky. 1993. *Nonprofits for Hire: The Welfare State in the Age of Contracting*. Harvard University Press.

Starr, Paul. 1982. *The Social Transformation of American Medicine*. Basic Books.

Stevens, Rosemary. 1989. *In Sickness and in Wealth: American Hospitals in the Twentieth Century*. Basic Books.

Trueheart, Charles. 1996. "Welcome to the Next Church." *Atlantic Monthly* 278 (2): 37–58.

U.S. Bureau of the Census, 1949. *Historical Statistics of the United States, 1789–1945*. U.S. Government Printing Office.

U.S. Department of Commerce. 1954. *A Supplement to the Survey of Current Business: National Income 1954 Edition*. U.S. Government Printing Office.

U.S. House of Representatives, 82nd Congress, 2nd Session. 1953. *Hearings before the Select Committee to Investigate Foundations and Comparable Organizations*. U.S. Government Printing Office.

U.S. Small Business Administration. 1984. *Unfair Competition by Nonprofit Organizations with Small Business: An Issue for the 1980s*. Small Business Administration.

Verba, Sidney, Kay Lehman Schlozman, and Henry E. Brady. 1995. *Voice and Equality: Civic Voluntarism in American Politics*. Harvard University Press.

Walsh, Andrew, editor. 2002. *Can Charitable Choice Work? Covering Religion's Impact on Urban Affairs and Social Services*. Leonard E. Greenberg Center for the Study of Religion and Public Life, Trinity College.

Warner, W. Lloyd, and Paul S. Lunt. 1941. *The Social Life of a Modern Community*. Yale University Press.

Webber, Carolyn, and Aaron Wildavsky. 1986. *A History of Taxation and Expenditure in the Western World*. Simon & Schuster.

Webber, Herman C., editor. 1933. *Yearbook of American Churches: A Record of Religious Activities in the United States for the Year 1932*. Round Table Press.

Weisbrod, Burton. 1989. *The Nonprofit Economy*. Harvard University Press.

Weisbrod, Burton. 1998. *To Profit or Not to Profit: The Commercial Transformation of the Nonprofit Sector*. Cambridge University Press.

Whitehead, John S. 1976. *The Separation of College and State: Columbia, Dartmouth, Harvard, and Yale, 1776–1876*. Yale University Press.

Williams, Pierce, and Frederick E. Croxton. 1930. *Corporate Contributions to Organized Community Welfare Services*. National Bureau of Economic Research.

Wineburg, Robert J. 2001. *A Limited Partnership: The Politics of Religion, Welfare, and Social Service*. Columbia University Press.

Wolpert, Julian. 1989. "Prudence and Parsimony: A Regional Perspective." *Nonprofit and Voluntary Sector Quarterly* 18 (3): 223–36.

Wolpert, Julian. 1993. *Patterns of Generosity in America: Who's Holding the Safety Net?* Twentieth Century Fund.

Wright, Conrad Edick. 1992. *The Transformation of Charity in Post-Revolutionary Massachusetts*. Northeastern University Press.

Wuthnow, Robert. 1986. *The Restructuring of American Religion*. Princeton University Press.

Wuthnow, Robert. 1991. *Acts of Compassion: Caring for Others and Helping Ourselves*. Princeton University Press.

Wuthnow, Robert, editor. 1994. *"I Come Away Stronger": How Small Groups Are Shaping American Religion*. William B. Eerdmans.

Wuthnow, Robert, Virginia A. Hodgkinson, et al. 1990. *Faith and Philanthropy in America*. Jossey-Bass.

Young, D. M. 1989. "Local Autonomy in a Franchise Age: Structural Change in National Voluntary Organizations." *Nonprofit and Voluntary Sector Quarterly* 18: 101–17.

Zollmann, Carl. 1924. *American Law of Charities*. Bruce Publishing Company.

NONPROFIT INSTITUTIONS

Colin B. Burke

TABLE Bg1–14 Voluntary and nonprofit associations per capita, by region and type of association, and in selected cities: 1840–1990

Contributed by Colin B. Burke

	21 cities							All types, by region				New Haven, Connecticut		
													Secular	
	All types	Benevolent	Religious, nonchurch	Business	Women's	Youth	Secular	Eastern	Southern	Midwestern	Western	All types	Locally based	Nationally based
	Bg1	Bg2	Bg3	Bg4	Bg5	Bg6	Bg7	Bg8	Bg9	Bg10	Bg11	Bg12	Bg13	Bg14
Date	Per 1,000	Per 1,000	Per 1,000	Per 1,000	Per 1,000	Per 1,000	Per 1,000	Per 1,000	Per 1,000	Per 1,000	Per 1,000	Per 1,000	Per 1,000	Per 1,000
1840	2.0	0.05	0.20	—	0.05	0.05	0.20	—	—	—	—	—	—	—
1850	1.5	0.15	0.25	0.01	0.15	0.10	0.30	—	—	—	—	2.1	1.9	0.2
1860	2.5	0.20	0.80	0.05	0.10	0.10	0.40	—	2.0	2.5	—	2.3	0.7	0.5
1870	2.5	0.10	0.65	0.02	0.10	0.10	0.30	2.0	2.0	3.0	3.5	2.6	—	—
1880	3.0	0.20	1.00	0.05	0.15	0.10	0.60	2.5	4.0	3.5	3.0	4.0	—	—
1890	4.0	0.20	1.20	0.05	0.30	0.20	0.65	3.5	4.0	5.0	4.0	3.8	—	—
1900	5.0	0.20	1.20	0.08	0.50	0.15	0.70	3.5	6.0	5.0	5.0	4.2	2.1	2.2
1910	5.0	0.20	1.00	0.10	0.50	0.10	0.70	3.5	5.5	5.5	5.0	4.5	—	—
1920	4.5	0.15	0.85	0.13	0.55	0.15	0.50	3.0	4.5	4.5	6.0	3.7	—	—
1930	—	—	—	—	—	—	—	—	—	—	—	4.2	2.7	1.4
1940	—	—	—	—	—	—	—	—	—	—	—	3.8	—	—
1950	—	—	—	—	—	—	—	—	—	—	—	4.0	—	—
1960	—	—	—	—	—	—	—	—	—	—	—	3.9	—	—
1970	—	—	—	—	—	—	—	—	—	—	—	4.5	—	—
1980	—	—	—	—	—	—	—	—	—	—	—	4.7	—	—
1990	—	—	—	—	—	—	—	—	—	—	—	4.8	4.3	0.5

Sources

Series Bg1–11: unpublished data developed by Gerald Gamm and Robert D. Putnam. Series Bg12–14: unpublished data developed by Peter Dobkin Hall.

Documentation

Figures are expressed per 1,000 persons in local population.

Series Bg1–11. Estimated from graphs in the unpublished papers provided by Gamm and Putnam. These scholars surveyed city directories and other relevant lists for the following cities: St. Louis; Boston; San Francisco; Milwaukee; Denver; Lowell, Massachusetts; Charleston; Des Moines; Portland, Oregon; Peoria, Illinois; Galveston; Little Rock; Burlington, Vermont; Brookline, Massachusetts; Leadville, Colorado; Adrian, Michigan; Bath, Maine; Bowling Green, Kentucky; Perkin, Illinois; Junction City, Kansas; and Boise, Idaho.

TABLE Bg15–27 Charitable and voluntary organizations founded in New England and Massachusetts, by type: 1600–1829[1]

Contributed by Colin B. Burke

	New England						Massachusetts						
	All types	Mutual benefit	Humanitarian	Religious missionary	Secular reform	All types, charitable	All types, nonprofit institutions and organizations	Charitable	Worship/ ritual	Mutual aid	Humanitarian charitable	Religious missionary	Secular reform
	Bg15	Bg16	Bg17	Bg18	Bg19	Bg20	Bg21	Bg22	Bg23	Bg24	Bg25	Bg26	Bg27
Period	Number	Number	Number	Number	Number	Number	Number	Number	Number	Number	Number	Number	Number
1600–1769	42	37	4	0	1	24	330	4	290	19	4	0	1
1770–1779	—	—	—	—	—	—	61	0	39	—	—	—	—
1780–1789	36	32	3	1	0	18	109	4	67	14	3	1	0
1790–1799	112	103	6	1	2	39	312	9	162	33	5	1	0
1800–1809	158	107	9	42	0	59	329	17	171	41	3	15	0
1810–1819	1,001	85	39	890	87	474	502	150	150	18	23	395	38
1820–1829	—	—	—	—	—	—	634	148	299	—	—	—	—

[1] For series Bg15–20 and Bg24–27, data pertain to the following actual dates: 1600s–1769, 1770–1789, 1790–1797, 1798–1807, 1808–1817.

Sources

Series Bg15–20 and Bg24–27. Conrad Edick Wright, *The Transformation of Charity in Post-Revolutionary New England* (Northeastern University Press, 1992).

Series Bg21–23. Richard D. Brown, "The Emergence of Voluntary Associations in Massachusetts, 1760–1830," *Journal of Voluntary Action Research* 2 (2) (1973): 71.

Documentation

Series Bg21. Brown had a broader approach to voluntary organizations than did other researchers dealing with the nonprofit sector. His count of all voluntary institutions included businesses (profit-seeking), civic organizations, occupational institutions and organizations, and educational institutions and organizations. This series includes all these voluntary organizations and institutions except the profit-seeking ones.

TABLE Bg28–40 Foundations, community trusts, and nonprofit organizations – number, endowment income, and grant expenditures, by sector: 1921–1997

Contributed by Colin B. Burke

	Grant expenditures of 100 large foundations and community trusts						Income from endowments		Foundations				
	Total	For education	For health	For religion	Independent foundations	Private foundations	Foundations	Nonprofit organizations (not foundations)	Active	Independent	Company-sponsored	Community	Operating
	Bg28	Bg29	Bg30	Bg31	Bg32	Bg33	Bg34	Bg35	Bg36	Bg37	Bg38	Bg39	Bg40
Year	Dollars	Dollars	Dollars	Dollars	Number	Number	Million dollars	Million dollars	Number	Number	Number	Number	Number
1921	36,344,509	15,071,660	11,489,743	751,980	—	—	—	—	—	—	—	—	—
1922	42,546,462	15,199,995	20,274,609	564,141	—	—	—	—	—	—	—	—	—
1923	38,792,664	14,965,386	14,132,775	237,546	—	—	—	—	—	—	—	—	—
1924	45,796,876	25,161,574	11,375,477	216,849	—	—	—	—	—	—	—	—	—
1925	40,152,292	14,712,889	14,719,113	261,801	—	—	—	—	—	—	—	—	—
1926	46,788,000	17,807,472	17,779,147	353,180	—	—	—	—	—	—	—	—	—
1927	56,737,014	28,409,699	17,158,882	391,168	—	—	—	—	—	—	—	—	—
1928	83,743,490	27,905,812	30,221,779	2,539,906	—	—	—	—	—	—	—	—	—
1929	65,813,941	31,104,881	19,833,440	1,543,603	—	—	82	435	—	—	—	—	—
1930	61,704,783	32,661,152	15,156,159	714,799	—	—	94	414	122	—	—	—	—
1931	54,605,000	13,579,000	17,144,000	370,000	—	—	89	393	—	—	—	—	—
1932	—	—	—	—	—	—	70	372	—	—	—	—	—
1933	—	—	—	—	—	—	63	352	—	—	—	—	—
1934	34,211,000	9,220,000	9,167,000	40,000	—	—	66	376	—	—	—	—	—
1935	—	—	—	—	—	—	68	400	—	—	—	—	—
1936	—	—	—	—	—	—	80	424	—	—	—	—	—
1937	38,478,000	9,170,000	13,496,000	275,000	—	—	105	449	—	—	—	—	—
1938	—	—	—	—	—	—	87	450	—	—	—	—	—
1939	—	—	—	—	—	—	86	452	—	—	—	—	—
1940	40,390,000	11,697,000	12,274,000	1,224,000	—	—	96	461	—	—	—	—	—
1941	—	—	—	—	—	—	103	470	—	—	—	—	—
1942	—	—	—	—	—	—	109	473	—	—	—	—	—
1943	—	—	—	—	—	—	108	477	—	—	—	—	—
1944	—	—	—	—	—	—	142	524	505	—	—	—	—
1945	—	—	—	—	—	—	148	570	—	—	—	—	—
1946	—	—	—	—	—	—	155	560	—	—	—	—	—
1947	—	—	—	—	—	—	199	550	—	—	—	—	—
1948	—	—	—	—	—	—	225	580	—	—	—	—	—
1949	—	—	—	—	—	—	242	611	—	—	—	—	—
1950	—	—	—	—	—	—	277	663	—	—	—	—	—
1951	—	—	—	—	—	—	315	716	—	—	—	—	—
1952	—	—	—	—	—	—	323	794	—	—	—	—	—
1953	—	—	—	—	—	—	333	872	—	—	—	—	—
1954	—	—	—	—	—	—	341	950	4,164	—	—	—	—
1955	—	—	—	—	—	—	386	1,080	3,795	—	—	—	—
1956	—	—	—	—	—	—	407	1,100	—	—	—	—	—
1957	247,894,000	116,175,000	35,214,000	8,520,000	—	—	449	1,200	—	—	—	—	—
1958	—	—	—	—	—	—	450	1,200	—	—	—	—	—
1959	—	—	—	—	—	—	475	1,200	5,202	—	—	—	—
1960	—	—	—	—	—	—	—	—	5,143	—	—	—	—
1962	—	—	—	—	—	—	—	—	6,007	—	—	—	—
1965	—	—	—	—	—	—	—	—	6,803	—	—	—	—
1968	—	—	—	—	—	—	—	—	5,454	—	—	—	—
1972	—	—	—	—	—	—	—	—	2,533	—	—	—	—
1974	—	—	—	—	—	26,889	—	—	—	—	—	—	—

(continued)

TABLE Bg28–40 Foundations, community trusts, and nonprofit organizations – number, endowment income, and grant expenditures, by sector: 1921–1997
Continued

	Grant expenditures of 100 large foundations and community trusts						Income from endowments		Foundations				
	Total	For education	For health	For religion	Independent foundations	Private foundations	Foundations	Nonprofit organizations (not foundations)	Active	Independent	Company-sponsored	Community	Operating
	Bg28	Bg29	Bg30	Bg31	Bg32	Bg33	Bg34	Bg35	Bg36	Bg37	Bg38	Bg39	Bg40
Year	Dollars	Dollars	Dollars	Dollars	Number	Number	Million dollars	Million dollars	Number	Number	Number	Number	Number
1975	—	—	—	—	21,877	—	—	—	2,823	—	—	—	—
1976	—	—	—	—	21,447	—	—	—	2,818	—	—	—	—
1977	—	—	—	—	22,152	27,691	—	—	—	—	—	—	—
1978	—	—	—	—	22,484	29,659	—	—	3,138	—	—	—	—
1979	—	—	—	—	22,535	27,980	—	—	3,178	2,470	545	81	42
1980	—	—	—	—	22,088	—	—	—	3,363	—	—	—	—
1981	—	—	—	—	21,967	—	—	—	—	2,618	602	95	48
1982	—	—	—	—	23,770	28,468	—	—	4,063	—	—	—	—
1983	—	—	—	—	24,261	29,863	—	—	—	—	—	—	—
1984	—	—	—	—	24,859	—	—	—	—	—	—	—	—
1985	—	—	—	—	25,639	31,221	—	—	4,402	3,466	723	134	79
1986	—	—	—	—	—	35,172	—	—	—	—	—	—	—
1987	—	—	—	—	27,661	35,907	—	—	5,148	4,100	781	160	107
1988	—	—	—	—	30,338	37,141	—	—	—	—	—	—	—
1989	—	—	—	—	31,990	38,773	—	—	6,615	5,383	904	175	153
1990	—	—	—	—	32,401	40,166	—	—	—	—	—	—	—
1991	—	—	—	—	33,356	41,348	—	—	—	—	—	—	—
1992	—	—	—	—	35,765	42,426	—	—	8,729	7,277	1,010	233	209
1993	—	—	—	—	37,571	44,004	—	—	6,334	5,146	813	218	157
1994	—	—	—	—	—	—	—	—	6,785	5,547	839	230	169
1995	—	—	—	—	40,140	—	—	—	7,292	6,018	841	248	185
1997	—	—	—	—	—	—	—	—	7,960	6,601	869	286	204

Sources

Series Bg28–31. Raymond Rich Associates, *American Foundations and Their Fields* (Twentieth Century Fund, 1939), various issues, and, Edward C. Lindeman, *Wealth and Culture: A Study of One Hundred Foundations and Community Trusts and Their Operations during the Decade 1921–1930* (Transaction Books, 1988).

Series Bg32. Virginia Ann Hodgkinson, Murray S. Weitzman, et al., *Nonprofit Almanac 1996–1997: Dimensions of the Independent Sector* (Jossey-Bass, 1996), Table 2.20, and Foundation Center, *Guide to United States Foundations: Their Trustees, Officers, and Donors* (Foundation Center, 1996).

Series Bg33. U.S. Internal Revenue Service, *Statistics of Income Bulletin* (various years, especially spring issues).

Series Bg34–35. Frank G. Dickinson, "The Changing Position of Philanthropy in the American Economy," Occasional Paper number 110, National Bureau of Economic Research (Columbia University Press, 1970), Table 2.5.

Series Bg36–40. Foundation Center, *The Foundation Directory* (Foundation Center, various years), and Raymond Rich Associates, *American Foundations and Their Fields*.

Documentation

Estimates of the number and finances of foundations, especially those for the years before the 1960s, have focused on the larger "charitable" foundations, those which have underwritten so many other nonprofit organizations. In contrast, reports based on federal tax records include organizations that may never have been active. That is one of the reasons for the great differences in the estimates of numbers, assets, and expenditures of foundations in Tables Bg28–54.

Series Bg32. Based on tax records and includes all foundations, not just those with significant assets. Note the difference between these estimates and those in series Bg33, which are based on Internal Revenue Service files.

Series Bg34–35. See the text in David C. Hammack, editor, *Making the Nonprofit Sector in the United States – A Reader* (Indiana University Press, 1998), and D. M. Young, "Local Autonomy in a Franchise Age: Structural Change in National Voluntary Organizations," *Nonprofit and Voluntary Sector Quarterly* 18 (1989): 101–17. See Young for an explanation of their methods of estimating income before the mid-1950s.

Series Bg36. Covers foundations listed in *Foundation Directory*. This series gives higher estimates than others in the table perhaps because of its more inclusive definition of a foundation.

Series Bg36–40. Includes only larger or more active and prominent foundations. The *Foundation Directory*'s compilers altered its criteria of "large" and "prominent" several times. In 1962, 1965, 1968–1969, and 1972, they raised the amount of assets and total amount of grants issued by a foundation to qualify it for inclusion. By 1972 a foundation had to have at least $1,000,000 in assets to qualify.

TABLE Bg41–54 Foundations and endowments – number, assets, revenues, disbursements, and foundings, by type and in selected states: 1921–1997

Contributed by Colin B. Burke

	Foundations		Private 501(c)(3) foundations					Foundations in Massachusetts, Connecticut, New York, and California			Foundations founded			
	Assets	Gifts and contributions received	Assets	Revenue	Grants made	Foundations with assets of at least $10 million	Disbursements of community trusts	Number	Assets	Foundation expenditures on research	All types	Independent	Corporate	Community
	Bg41	Bg42	Bg43	Bg44	Bg45	Bg46	Bg47	Bg48	Bg49	Bg50	Bg51	Bg52	Bg53	Bg54
Year	Thousand dollars	Million dollars	Thousand dollars	Thousand dollars	Thousand dollars	Number	Thousand dollars	Number	Million dollars	Thousand dollars	Number	Number	Number	Number
1921	—	—	—	—	—	—	375	—	—	—	—	—	—	—
1922	—	—	—	—	—	—	350	—	—	—	—	—	—	—
1923	—	—	—	—	—	—	350	—	—	—	—	—	—	—
1924	—	—	—	—	—	—	400	—	—	—	—	—	—	—
1925	—	—	—	—	—	—	500	—	—	—	159	125	5	20
1926	—	—	—	—	—	—	550	—	—	—	—	—	—	—
1927	—	—	—	—	—	—	600	—	—	—	—	—	—	—
1928	—	—	—	—	—	—	700	—	—	—	—	—	—	—
1929	—	—	—	—	—	—	852	—	—	—	—	—	—	—
1930	853,000	—	—	—	—	—	941	72	707	—	—	—	—	—
1931	—	—	—	—	—	—	1,002	—	—	—	—	—	—	—
1932	—	—	—	—	—	—	1,107	—	—	—	—	—	—	—
1933	—	—	—	—	—	—	1,026	—	—	—	—	—	—	—
1934	—	—	—	—	—	—	1,060	—	—	—	—	—	—	—
1935	—	—	—	—	—	—	1,129	—	—	—	198	179	7	5
1936	—	—	—	—	—	—	1,109	—	—	10,022	—	—	—	—
1937	—	—	—	—	—	—	1,150	142	—	—	—	—	—	—
1938	—	—	—	—	—	—	1,757	—	—	—	—	—	—	—
1939	—	—	—	—	—	—	1,278	—	—	—	—	—	—	—
1940	—	—	—	—	—	—	2,225	183	—	—	—	—	—	—
1941	—	—	—	—	—	—	1,606	—	—	—	—	—	—	—
1942	—	—	—	—	—	—	1,725	—	—	—	—	—	—	—
1943	—	—	—	—	—	—	1,740	—	—	—	—	—	—	—
1944	1,402,000	—	—	—	—	—	1,918	272	789	—	—	—	—	—
1945	—	—	—	—	—	—	2,022	—	—	—	778	681	63	20
1946	—	—	—	—	—	—	2,205	—	—	44,454	—	—	—	—
1947	—	—	—	—	—	—	2,250	—	—	—	—	—	—	—
1948	—	—	—	—	—	—	3,362	—	—	—	—	—	—	—
1949	—	—	—	—	—	—	3,855	—	—	—	—	—	—	—
1953	—	252	—	—	—	—	—	—	—	23,225	—	—	—	—
1954	4,524,000	291	—	—	—	—	—	1,698	2,826	—	—	—	—	—
1955	—	330	—	—	—	—	—	1,551	—	—	1,858	1,488	318	30
1956	—	369	—	—	—	—	—	—	—	—	—	—	—	—
1957	—	408	—	—	—	—	—	—	—	—	—	—	—	—
1958	—	447	—	—	—	—	—	—	—	—	—	—	—	—
1959	11,518,000	486	—	—	—	—	—	2,034	7,836	—	—	—	—	—

(continued)

TABLE Bg41–54 Foundations and endowments – number, assets, revenues, disbursements, and foundings, by type and in selected states: 1921–1997 *Continued*

	Foundations		Private 501(c)(3) foundations					Foundations in Massachusetts, Connecticut, New York, and California			Foundations founded			
	Assets	Gifts and contributions received	Assets	Revenue	Grants made	Foundations with assets of at least $10 million	Disbursements of community trusts	Number	Assets	Foundation expenditures on research	All types	Independent	Corporate	Community
	Bg41	Bg42	Bg43	Bg44	Bg45	Bg46	Bg47	Bg48	Bg49	Bg50	Bg51	Bg52	Bg53	Bg54
Year	Thousand dollars	Million dollars	Thousand dollars	Thousand dollars	Thousand dollars	Number	Thousand dollars	Number	Million dollars	Thousand dollars	Number	Number	Number	Number
1960	—	525	—	—	—	—	—	2,019	—	—	—	—	—	—
1961	—	567	—	—	—	—	—	—	—	—	—	—	—	—
1962	14,511,000	729	—	—	—	—	—	2,391	9,004	—	—	—	—	—
1963	—	793	—	—	—	—	—	2,391	8,937	—	—	—	—	—
1964	—	952	—	—	—	—	—	2,721	10,608	—	—	—	—	—
1965	19,927,000	1,043	—	—	—	—	—	2,711	10,481	—	1,670	1,420	174	36
1966	—	1,135	—	—	—	—	—	—	—	—	—	—	—	—
1967	—	1,215	—	—	—	—	—	—	—	—	—	—	—	—
1968	25,180,700	1,300	—	—	—	—	—	2,157	11,457	—	—	—	—	—
1972	31,510,000	—	—	—	—	—	—	941	14,198	—	—	—	—	—
1973	27,306,000	—	—	—	—	—	—	—	11,427	—	—	—	—	—
1974	—	—	25,514,367	3,263,351	1,953,060	—	—	—	—	—	—	—	—	—
1975	29,649,000	—	—	—	—	—	—	1,018	12,903	—	983	811	100	54
1976	28,635,000	—	—	—	—	—	—	1,022	12,368	—	—	—	—	—
1977	—	—	—	—	—	471	—	1,191	—	—	—	—	—	—
1978	32,359,000	—	—	—	—	—	—	1,124	13,723	—	—	—	—	—
1979	38,522,000	—	44,600,000	6,013,129	2,801,000	—	—	—	15,984	—	—	—	—	—
1980	41,594,000	—	—	—	—	626	—	—	17,054	—	—	—	—	—
1981	—	—	—	—	—	—	—	—	18,989	—	—	—	—	—
1982	—	—	62,886,606	9,126,529	4,429,979	—	—	—	24,644	—	—	—	—	—
1983	—	—	71,934,891	12,131,748	4,363,354	—	—	—	—	—	—	—	—	—
1984	—	—	—	—	—	—	—	—	1,180	—	—	—	—	—
1985	63,075,000	—	97,089,280	16,412,533	5,244,114	—	—	1,532	43,442	—	3,082	2,618	303	71
1986	—	—	113,175,809	20,031,228	6,205,413	—	—	—	—	—	—	—	—	—
1987	89,916,000	—	114,301,195	17,116,794	6,770,100	1,272	—	1,790	37,296	—	—	—	—	—
1988	—	—	128,889,124	16,280,190	7,379,690	1,343	—	—	—	—	—	—	—	—
1989	106,940,000	—	151,694,261	19,916,920	8,801,108	1,477	—	2,264	42,560	—	—	—	—	—
1990	—	—	164,828,987	19,521,182	8,880,590	1,593	—	—	52,730	—	—	—	—	—
1991	—	—	189,571,401	24,610,028	10,146,287	1,741	—	—	—	—	—	—	—	—
1992	134,191,000	—	192,207,531	23,566,388	10,910,350	1,928	—	3,060	50,932	—	—	—	—	—
1993	151,182,000	—	207,536,468	25,415,288	11,652,564	2,066	—	2,216	57,033	—	—	—	—	—
1994	162,145,000	—	222,542,546	29,859,556	12,308,958	—	—	2,331	62,164	—	—	—	—	—
1995	173,513,000	—	263,386,454	32,289,714	12,858,843	2,347	—	2,513	66,733	—	687	594	58	13
1997	207,373,860	—	—	—	—	—	—	2,696	77,086	—	—	—	—	—

Sources

Series Bg41 and Bg48–49. Compiled using data in *The Foundation Directory* (Foundation Center, various editions), and Raymond Rich Associates, *American Foundations and Their Fields* (Twentieth Century Fund, 1939 and other editions).

Series Bg42. Ralph L. Nelson, "Private Philanthropy – Estimated Fund Flows, by Donors and Recipients, 1929–1970," in *Historical Statistics of the United States* (1975), pp. 339, 359.

Series Bg43–45. Alicia Meckstroth and Paul Arnsberger, *A 20-Year Review of the Nonprofit Sector, 1975–1995* (U.S. Internal Revenue Service Special Projects Section, 1999).

TABLE Bg41–54 Foundations and endowments – number, assets, revenues, disbursements, and foundings, by type and in selected states: 1921–1997 *Continued*

Series Bg46 and Bg51–54. Virginia Ann Hodgkinson, Murray S. Weitzman, et al., *Nonprofit Almanac 1996–1997: Dimensions of the Independent Sector* (Jossey-Bass, 1996), Table 2.23.

Series Bg47. Shelby M. Harrison and F. Emerson Andrews, *American Foundations for Social Welfare* (Russell Sage Foundation, 1946).

Series Bg50. National Science Foundation, *Patterns of Research and Development Resources* (1999).

Documentation

Note that the estimates for foundations that are based on tax files, such as those published by the Statistics of Income Division and Special Studies Special Projects Section of the IRS, are different from those found in publications by such institutions as the Foundation Center. This is owing to the greater inclusiveness of the tax files, which contain the names of several thousand more foundations than do the files of the foundation-watch centers, and to the use of different accounting procedures and definitions.

Series Bg41 and Bg48–49. Covers foundations listed in *The Foundation Directory*. The year is approximate as a result of data reporting practices.

Series Bg43–45. Covers private 501(c)(3) foundations reporting their finances to the IRS. Assets reported in terms of fair-market values.

Series Bg44. Revenue is defined as income minus the cost of doing business. The IRS changed its definition of revenue after the issuance of its 1970s special reports on the nonprofit sector.

Series Bg50. Covers thirty-seven foundations.

Series Bg51–54. The source defined a "large" foundation as one with at least $1 million in assets or one making at least $100,000 in grants during the previous year.

These series cover large foundations active in 1994. The data represent the middle year of the decade in which the foundation was born, except for 1995, which covers only 1900–1994.

TABLE Bg55–64 Nonprofit and tax-exempt institutions – number, employment, employee compensation, and applications for tax-exempt status: 1929–1997

Contributed by Colin B. Burke

		Tax-exempt organizations		IRS 501(c)(3) and (c)(4) organizations				Applications for tax-exempt nonprofit status		
					Independent sector					
	Nonprofit institutions, gross domestic product	Number	Tax returns filed	Charitable nonprofit organizations	Wages and salaries	Full- and part-time employees	Volunteers	Approved	Declined	Returned without approval, or withdrawn
	Bg55	Bg56	Bg57	Bg58	Bg59	Bg60	Bg61	Bg62	Bg63	Bg64
Year	Billion dollars	Number	Number	Number	Billion dollars	Thousand	Thousand	Number	Number	Number
1929	1.1	—	—	—	—	—	—	—	—	—
1930	1.2	—	—	—	—	—	—	—	—	—
1931	1.1	—	—	—	—	—	—	—	—	—
1932	1.0	—	—	—	—	—	—	—	—	—
1933	0.9	—	—	—	—	—	—	—	—	—
1934	1.0	—	—	—	—	—	—	—	—	—
1935	1.0	—	—	—	—	—	—	—	—	—
1936	1.0	—	—	—	—	—	—	—	—	—
1937	1.1	—	—	—	—	—	—	—	—	—
1938	1.1	—	—	—	—	—	—	—	—	—
1939	1.1	—	—	—	—	—	—	—	—	—
1940	1.2	—	—	—	—	—	—	—	—	—
1941	1.3	—	—	—	—	—	—	—	—	—
1942	1.4	—	—	—	—	—	—	—	—	—
1943	1.6	80,250	—	17,450	—	—	—	—	—	—
1944	1.8	—	—	—	—	—	—	—	—	—
1945	2.0	—	—	—	—	—	—	—	—	—
1946	2.4	93,458	—	24,766	—	—	—	—	—	—
1947	2.8	—	—	—	—	—	—	—	—	—
1948	3.2	—	—	—	—	—	—	—	—	—
1949	3.6	—	—	—	—	—	—	—	—	—
1950	3.9	—	—	—	—	—	—	—	—	—
1951	4.3	—	—	—	—	—	—	—	—	—
1952	4.6	—	—	—	—	—	—	—	—	—
1953	5.1	—	—	—	—	—	—	—	—	—
1954	5.5	—	—	—	—	—	—	—	—	—
1955	6.1	—	—	—	—	—	—	—	—	—
1956	6.6	—	—	—	—	—	—	5,373	342	1,482
1957	7.3	—	—	—	—	—	—	5,015	371	1,723
1958	8.0	—	—	—	—	—	—	4,865	311	1,855
1959	8.9	—	—	—	—	—	—	4,920	317	1,557

(continued)

TABLE Bg55–64 Nonprofit and tax-exempt institutions – number, employment, employee compensation, and applications for tax-exempt status: 1929–1997 *Continued*

		Tax-exempt organizations		IRS 501(c)(3) and (c)(4) organizations				Applications for tax-exempt nonprofit status		
					Independent sector					
	Nonprofit institutions, gross domestic product	Number	Tax returns filed	Charitable nonprofit organizations	Wages and salaries	Full- and part-time employees	Volunteers	Approved	Declined	Returned without approval, or withdrawn
	Bg55	Bg56	Bg57	Bg58	Bg59	Bg60	Bg61	Bg62	Bg63	Bg64
Year	Billion dollars	Number	Number	Number	Billion dollars	Thousand	Thousand	Number	Number	Number
1960	10.1	—	—	—	—	—	—	4,907	330	1,433
1961	10.7	—	—	—	—	—	—	4,780	362	1,439
1962	11.8	—	—	—	—	—	—	4,554	416	1,359
1963	12.8	—	—	—	—	—	—	4,871	328	1,102
1964	14.0	—	—	—	—	—	—	6,936	463	1,436
1965	15.3	—	—	—	—	—	—	11,929	717	1,668
1966	17.2	—	—	—	—	—	—	13,445	885	1,972
1967	19.2	309,000	—	—	—	—	—	13,672	814	2,136
1968	21.7	358,000	—	—	—	—	—	14,640	935	2,429
1969	25.0	416,000	—	—	—	—	—	—	—	—
1970	27.9	—	—	—	—	—	—	—	—	—
1971	31.1	—	—	—	—	—	—	—	—	—
1972	34.3	535,000	—	—	—	—	—	—	—	—
1973	38.2	630,000	—	—	—	—	—	—	—	—
1974	42.6	673,000	—	—	31.2	4,849	3,500	—	—	—
1975	47.4	692,000	—	—	—	—	—	—	—	—
1976	51.7	762,689	—	—	—	—	—	—	—	—
1977	56.5	789,666	—	406,000	46.7	5,471	3,271	36,017	2,389	8,661
1978	63.2	810,048	—	—	—	—	—	35,214	2,192	10,354
1979	71.0	824,536	—	—	—	—	—	35,342	2,536	10,637
1980	81.0	846,433	443,674	449,000	63.5	6,162	4,060	36,980	1,914	10,640
1981	91.5	851,012	408,750	—	—	—	—	36,854	1,639	13,853
1982	102.0	838,650	443,705	454,000	80.7	6,543	4,481	38,434	1,510	12,160
1983	112.9	842,751	437,026	—	—	—	—	38,604	1,180	14,163
1984	123.9	838,319	393,244	483,000	91.6	6,677	4,694	44,173	1,389	19,006
1985	133.6	858,745	431,156	—	—	—	—	44,205	1,076	14,216
1986	145.9	897,424	487,183	—	—	—	—	43,007	987	16,347
1987	165.6	939,105	522,751	560,588	116.0	7,390	5,059	43,964	1,012	17,542
1988	186.8	969,177	489,952	585,955	130.4	7,907	5,375	41,335	632	16,334
1989	205.7	992,561	490,129	605,376	143.9	8,319	5,691	—	—	—
1990	228.5	1,024,766	484,000	632,355	156.2	8,652	5,784	41,569	781	15,407
1991	248.3	1,055,545	512,551	—	—	—	—	38,801	705	11,158
1992	269.0	1,085,206	530,592	688,773	184.2	9,128	5,500	—	—	—
1993	285.8	1,118,131	542,969	718,015	—	—	—	43,975	545	14,199
1994	301.7	1,138,598	522,000	730,888	204.6	9,656	5,462	—	—	—
1995	319.5	1,164,789	560,057	—	—	—	—	50,613	619	16,062
1996	333.1	1,188,510	573,265	—	—	—	—	48,635	577	18,800
1997	349.4	—	—	—	—	—	—	—	—	—

Sources

Series Bg55. U.S. Bureau of Economic Analysis, *National Income and Product Accounts of the United States* (1998) and *Survey of Current Business* (published annually).

Series Bg56–58 and Bg62–64. U.S. Internal Revenue Service, *Annual Report of the Commissioner* (U.S. Government Printing Office, published annually), and *Databook* (published annually); and Burton A. Weisbrod, *The Nonprofit Economy* (Harvard University Press, 1988), Tables A.2, A.9.

Series Bg59–61. Virginia Ann Hodgkinson, Murray S. Weitzman, et al., *Nonprofit Almanac 1996–1997: Dimensions of the Independent Sector* (Jossey-Bass, 1996), pp. 44–5.

Documentation

See also the text for Table Bg65–74.

The Internal Revenue Service (IRS) files on nonprofit organizations have remained central to estimates of the number and types of voluntary and charitable organizations. However, the files have limited value for those wishing to describe or evaluate the nonprofit world in the United States. They do not contain a list of all formal or informal voluntary groups in the country, the number of which may exceed nine million. The files do not even include all formal organizations. For example, religious organizations are not required to file with the service, and organizations that had less than a certain amount of yearly income (recently, $25,000) are not required to file a return. In addition, many voluntary organizations do not opt for the tax advantages provided by recognition by the government. The Business Master File contains an unknown number of inactive organizations, and the segment of the file originating before the 1960s has special weaknesses. A rewarding discussion of the potentials and limits of the IRS's data appears in William G. Bowen, Thomas I. Nygren, et al., *The Charitable Nonprofits* (Jossey-Bass, 1994).

One of the more influential nonprofit professional organizations has preferred to combine many of the 501(c)(3) and (c)(4) organizations and call them "the independent sector" (IS). The figures for this sector are different from those provided by the IRS for several reasons. The IS series have been based on somewhat different data sources, somewhat different accounting methods, and a much less inclusive definition of relevant organizations.

Series Bg55. A very inclusive definition of nonprofit institutions is used for this series. According to the documents provided by the U.S. Bureau of Economic Analysis, nonprofit institutions include "religious organizations,

TABLE Bg55–64 Nonprofit and tax-exempt institutions – number, employment, employee compensation, and applications for tax-exempt status: 1929–1997 *Continued*

social and athletic clubs, labor organizations, nonprofit schools and hospitals, charitable and welfare organizations and other nonprofit organizations providing services to individuals." Wages and salaries and imputed values of food and housing provided free to clergy and employees of nonprofit institutions are core values for the series. The broad definition of nonprofit organizations and the inclusion of imputed compensation help account for the difference between this series and other estimates of wages and salaries in the sector. Note, however, that the nonprofit gross domestic product as a percentage of total gross national product yields a smaller figure than when wages and salaries, alone, are compared. This is due to the composition of the gross domestic product. Also note that this series does not include wages and salaries within private households.

Series Bg56. Excludes taxable farmers' organizations and taxable foundations. For a list of the rather wide range of organizations that can receive tax-exempt status (some twenty-nine types), see Internal Revenue Service, *Annual Report* or *Databook*.

Series Bg58. The organizations in this series most fit the common image of voluntary and charitable institutions. IRS 501(c)(3) organizations are "Religious, educational, charitable, scientific, etc." IRS 501(c)(4) entities are civic leagues or social welfare organizations. Note that donations to IRS 501(c)(3) organizations have been tax deductible, a special inducement for funding and supporting them, and that in recent years, IRS 501(c)(4) organizations have not been regarded by many as "charitable." For a more precise description of the IRS categories, see Internal Revenue Service, *Annual Report* or *Databook*.

Series Bg59. Does not include the estimated dollar value of volunteers' time.

TABLE Bg65–74 Charitable nonprofit and independent sector organizations – assets, expenditures, and revenues, by source: 1943–1995[1]

Contributed by Colin B. Burke

	501(c)(3) charitable nonprofit organizations			501(c)(3) and (c)(4) independent sector organizations						
				Sources of support						
	Total revenue	Fair market value of assets	Contributions received	Total funds received	Private contributions	Private payments for services and goods	Government payments	Other income	Government payments to all but health and education nonprofits	Operating expenditures
	Bg65	Bg66	Bg67	Bg68	Bg69	Bg70	Bg71	Bg72	Bg73	Bg74
Year	Thousand dollars	Thousand dollars	Thousand dollars	Thousand dollars	Thousand dollars	Billion dollars	Billion dollars	Billion dollars	Billion dollars	Billion dollars
1943	—	—	—	1,018,300	367,866	—	—	—	—	—
1946	—	—	—	1,621,163	486,216	—	—	—	—	—
1960	—	—	—	—	—	—	—	—	—	18.4
1961	—	—	—	—	—	—	—	—	—	19.4
1962	—	—	—	—	—	—	—	—	—	21.4
1963	—	—	—	—	—	—	—	—	—	23.4
1964	—	—	—	—	—	—	—	—	—	25.4
1965	—	—	—	—	—	—	—	—	—	27.8
1966	—	—	—	—	—	—	—	—	—	31.3
1967	—	—	—	—	—	—	—	—	—	34.9
1968	—	—	—	—	—	—	—	—	—	39.4
1969	—	—	—	—	—	—	—	—	—	45.4
1970	—	—	—	—	—	—	—	—	—	50.7
1971	—	—	—	—	—	—	—	—	—	56.5
1972	—	—	—	—	—	—	—	—	—	62.4
1973	—	—	—	—	—	—	—	—	—	69.4
1974	—	—	—	76,300,000	—	29.2	29.2	—	—	77.4
1975	54,148,000	108,508,657	17,109,471	—	—	—	—	—	—	86.2
1976	—	—	—	—	—	—	—	—	—	94.0
1977	95,400,000	139,000,000	—	111,100,000	29,200,000	41.7	29.5	10.7	12.9	102.7
1978	127,000,000	174,100,000	—	—	—	—	—	—	—	116.4
1979	—	—	—	—	—	—	—	—	—	131.3
1980	—	—	—	159,900,000	—	61.7	—	—	—	150.4
1981	—	—	—	—	—	—	—	—	—	170.7
1982	196,303,700	279,638,066	41,272,737	211,900,000	46,200,000	82.1	59.5	24.1	23.0	191.1
1983	224,047,813	331,226,616	46,382,698	—	—	—	—	—	—	208.5
1984	—	—	—	—	—	—	—	—	—	225.1
1985	268,389,632	423,544,289	55,770,719	—	—	—	—	—	—	242.4
1986	292,483,178	489,180,002	60,115,290	—	—	—	—	—	—	292.7
1987	310,765,938	529,514,045	61,686,060	316,700,000	72,600,000	129.2	88.5	26.4	33.7	292.2
1988	354,646,576	583,573,213	69,061,529	—	—	—	—	—	—	326.0
1989	398,628,410	655,425,991	76,973,160	—	—	154.8	105.3	37.0	—	358.5

Note appears at end of table

(continued)

TABLE Bg65–74 Charitable nonprofit and independent sector organizations – assets, expenditures, and revenues, by source: 1943–1995 *Continued*

	501(c)(3) charitable nonprofit organizations			501(c)(3) and (c)(4) independent sector organizations						
				Sources of support						
	Total revenue	Fair market value of assets	Contributions received	Total funds received	Private contributions	Private payments for services and goods	Government payments	Other income	Government payments to all but health and education nonprofits	Operating expenditures
	Bg65	Bg66	Bg67	Bg68	Bg69	Bg70	Bg71	Bg72	Bg73	Bg74
Year	Thousand dollars	Thousand dollars	Thousand dollars	Thousand dollars	Thousand dollars	Billion dollars	Billion dollars	Billion dollars	Billion dollars	Billion dollars
1990	435,566,954	697,315,389	85,332,140	—	—	—	—	—	—	396.4
1991	491,105,661	777,471,601	87,461,613	—	—	—	—	—	—	431.8
1992	523,729,927	849,324,435	94,992,327	508,500,000	93,700,000	198.7	159.4	56.7	53.0	469.8
1993	566,067,394	926,847,263	103,052,916	—	—	—	—	—	—	499.1
1994	589,101,858	993,381,198	110,723,736	—	—	—	—	—	—	—
1995	663,370,551	1,143,078,681	127,742,791	—	—	—	—	—	—	—

[1] Data for the 1940s not strictly comparable with later data. See text.

Sources

Series Bg65–67. Alicia Meckstroth and Paul Arnsberger, *20-Year Review of the Nonprofit Sector, 1975–1995* (U.S. Internal Revenue Service Special Projects Section, 1999).

Series Bg68–74. Virginia Ann Hodgkinson, Murray S. Weitzman, et al., *Nonprofit Almanac 1996–1997: Dimensions of the Independent Sector* (Jossey-Bass, 1997), Tables 4.2 and 1.8, and data from earlier Independent Sector (IS) publications, all of which relied heavily on data from the *Census of Service Industries* and the *Survey of Current Business*; Internal Revenue Service, *Statistics of Income Bulletin* (1945 and 1946), Supplements.

Documentation

See also the text for Table Bg55–64.

The organizations included in these series – especially those in series Bg65–67 – are the ones that best fit the common view of the charitable role of nonprofit institutions. However, the common and formal categorizations of "charitable" and nonprofit organizations have changed over time, and even in the 1990s the boundaries of subsectors are variously defined. The Internal Revenue Service (IRS) has more than two dozen categories for tax-exempt organizations and restricts the term "charitable" to those granted the 501(c)(3) status. The IRS has complex rules for granting (c)(3) charity status and has two major subcategories for (c)(3) organizations: public charities and private foundations. The 501(c)(4) category is reserved for what the IRS terms "social welfare" organizations, and the IRS now reports on (c)(3) and (c)(4) organizations separately. Also, the IRS frequently reports on the "public charity" (c)(3) organizations without including statistics on (c)(3) private foundations. For IRS data on (c)(3) private foundations, see series Bg43–45.

One of the more influential nonprofit professional organizations has preferred to combine many of the (c)(3) and (c)(4) organizations together and call them the "independent sector" (IS). The figures for this sector are different from those provided by the IRS for several reasons. The IS series have been based on somewhat different data sources, somewhat different accounting methods, and a much less inclusive definition of relevant organizations. The subsectors included in the combined (c)(3)–(c)(4) IS series are: Health, Education/Research, Religious, Social-Legal Service, Civic-Social-Fraternal, Arts-Culture, and Foundations. Note that some very important organizations within those subsectors are not included in the IS series.

IRS 501(c)(3) and (c)(4) organizations are granted federal tax exemptions and are expected to provide service to the community. The (c)(3) public charity organizations are presently called the "charitable nonprofits" by the IRS, and they and the (c)(3) private foundations receive the special advantage of offering their donors tax deductibility for their contributions. Although not granted all the exemption benefits of the (c)(3)s, the types of organizations presently granted (c)(4) status were once perceived as being part of a general nonprofit universe. Thus, the IRS statistics for the 1940s were included in the combined (c)(3)–(c)(4) IS series.

It should be recognized that the IRS requirements concerning the amount of charitable activity and spending needed to gain and maintain (c)(3) or even (c)(4) status have changed over time. Some observers have expressed concern that in the last two or three decades regulatory policy changes have allowed a significant increase in the number of nonprofit organizations and their financial powers, while there has been a decline in the amount of charitable activity and popular participation. For an example of such observations, see Gilbert M. Gaul and Neill A. Borowski, *Free Ride: The Tax-Exempt Economy* (Andrews and McMeel, 1993).

Note that the data for the 1940s is not strictly comparable to that of the later period because different definitions and methods were employed. Caution should also be exercised when using these series to make inferences about the charitable role of religious organizations. Not all religious charitable activity is reflected by the series.

There are many other limits to the usefulness of the IRS data, and readers are cautioned not to interpret the IRS or IS series as capturing all nonprofit activity. For a useful exploration of the limitations, see David R. Stevenson, Thomas H. Pollack, et al., *State Nonprofit Almanac, 1997: Profiles of Charitable Organizations* (Urban Institute Press, 1997), Appendix A.

Series Bg65. Revenue is defined as receipts minus cost of goods sold, sales and rental expenses, and so on.

Series Bg65–67. Does not include private foundations.

Series Bg74. This series was based on a different table (1.8) in Hodgkinson, Weitzman, et al. (1997) than the one used to anchor the other IS series, and it covers a somewhat broader range of organizations.

TABLE Bg75–101 Active tax-exempt organizations, farmer's cooperatives, and nonexempt charitable trusts, by type: 1969–1996

Contributed by Colin B. Burke

	Active 501													
	(c)(1) corporations organized under Act of Congress	(c)(2) titleholding corporations	(c)(3) religious, charitable, etc. organizations	(c)(4) social welfare organizations	(c)(5) labor, agricultural organizations	(c)(6) business leagues	(c)(7) social and recreation clubs	(c)(8) fraternal benevolent societies	(c)(9) voluntary employees' beneficiary societies	(c)(10) domestic fraternal beneficiary societies	(c)(11) teachers' retirement funds	(c)(12) benevolent life insurance associations	(c)(13) cemetery companies	(c)(14) credit unions
	Bg75	Bg76	Bg77 [1]	Bg78	Bg79	Bg80	Bg81	Bg82	Bg83	Bg84	Bg85	Bg86	Bg87	Bg88
Year	Number	Number	Number	Number	Number	Number	Number	Number	Number	Number	Number	Number	Number	Number
1969	961	3,992	137,487	104,546	77,737	27,594	36,189	989	4,330	467	14	4,211	3,809	5,022
1970	—	0	—	—	—	—	—	—	—	—	—	—	—	—
1971	—	0	—	—	—	—	—	—	—	—	—	—	—	—
1972	—	0	—	—	—	—	—	—	—	—	—	—	—	—
1973	—	0	—	—	—	—	—	—	—	—	—	—	—	—
1974	—	0	—	—	—	—	—	—	—	—	—	—	—	—
1975	—	0	—	—	—	—	—	—	—	—	—	—	—	—
1976	1,067	5,114	259,523	125,415	87,412	42,120	47,820	141,725	6,271	11,612	14	4,685	4,959	4,686
1977	1,072	5,223	276,455	129,496	87,656	44,100	50,031	141,438	6,486	12,410	13	4,801	5,264	5,074
1978	25	5,272	293,947	125,317	87,531	45,325	49,964	140,963	6,827	12,199	11	4,863	5,529	5,118
1979	110	5,324	304,315	127,254	85,479	46,940	50,577	137,417	7,122	16,525	10	4,891	5,752	5,149
1980	42	5,358	319,842	129,553	85,774	48,717	51,922	137,449	7,738	16,178	12	4,945	5,947	5,639
1981	45	5,355	327,758	129,101	84,489	48,908	51,958	135,798	7,995	15,995	11	4,973	6,025	5,665
1982	24	5,522	322,826	131,578	86,322	51,056	54,036	116,549	8,703	18,570	13	5,071	6,290	6,074
1983	24	5,567	335,767	129,209	79,775	51,714	53,467	88,272	9,303	16,871	12	5,125	6,412	5,754
1984	24	5,679	352,884	130,344	76,763	53,303	56,060	92,431	10,145	16,116	11	5,200	6,845	6,053
1985	21	5,758	366,071	131,250	76,632	54,217	57,343	94,435	10,668	15,924	11	6,244	7,239	6,032
1986	24	5,859	393,051	133,490	76,236	57,064	58,625	95,623	10,776	17,931	11	5,392	7,600	6,068
1987	24	5,977	422,103	138,485	75,238	59,981	60,145	98,979	10,927	17,813	11	5,572	7,942	6,652
1988	24	6,026	447,525	138,430	73,200	61,257	60,877	99,568	12,360	18,574	11	5,682	8,148	6,786
1989	—	—	—	—	—	—	—	—	—	16,178	—	4,973	—	—
1990	9	6,278	489,891	142,473	71,653	65,896	62,723	100,321	14,210	18,350	10	5,873	8,565	6,352
1991	9	6,408	516,554	142,811	72,009	68,442	63,922	98,840	14,706	18,360	10	5,984	8,781	6,219
1992	9	6,529	546,100	142,673	71,012	70,871	64,681	93,544	14,986	21,415	10	6,103	9,025	5,559
1993	9	6,739	575,690	142,325	70,416	72,901	64,924	93,728	15,048	20,827	11	6,177	9,184	5,637
1994	9	6,967	599,745	140,143	68,144	74,273	65,273	92,284	14,835	21,215	11	6,221	9,294	5,391
1995	10	7,025	626,226	139,451	66,662	75,695	65,501	92,115	14,081	21,046	11	6,291	9,433	5,225
1996	20	7,100	654,186	139,512	64,955	77,274	60,845	91,972	14,486	20,925	13	6,343	9,562	5,157

Note appears at end of table

(continued)

TABLE Bg75–101 Active tax-exempt organizations, farmer's cooperatives, and nonexempt charitable trusts, by type: 1969–1996 *Continued*

	Active 501										Active farmers' cooperatives		
	(c)(15) mutual insurance companies	(c)(16) corporations to finance crop operation	(c)(17) supplemental unemployment benefit trusts	(c)(18) employee-funded pension trusts	(c)(19) war veterans' organizations	(c)(20) legal service organizations	(c)(21) black lung trusts	(d) religious/apostolic organizations	(e) cooperative hospitals	(f) cooperative service organizations of educational organizations	521	Taxable	Active nonexempt charitable trusts
	Bg89	Bg90	Bg91	Bg92	Bg93	Bg94	Bg95	Bg96	Bg97	Bg98	Bg99	Bg100	Bg101
Year	Number	Number	Number	Number	Number	Number	Number	Number	Number	Number	Number	Number	Number
1969	1,728	39	674	—	—	—	—	40	—	—	6,462	—	—
1970	—	—	—	—	—	—	—	—	—	—	—	—	—
1971	—	—	—	—	—	—	—	—	—	—	—	—	—
1972	—	—	—	—	—	—	—	—	—	—	—	—	—
1973	—	—	—	—	—	—	—	—	—	—	—	—	—
1974	—	—	—	—	—	—	—	—	—	—	—	—	—
1975	—	—	—	—	—	—	—	—	—	—	—	—	—
1976	1,454	30	790	4	13,960	—	—	59	—	—	3,969	—	—
1977	1,450	31	800	4	14,305	—	—	63	—	—	3,794	—	—
1978	1,408	28	807	4	21,233	4	—	67	—	—	3,606	—	—
1979	1,312	26	794	3	22,210	11	—	67	—	—	3,312	—	—
1980	1,140	22	806	4	22,247	46	—	67	—	—	2,965	—	—
1981	1,009	22	798	4	21,858	61	—	58	112	—	2,960	—	—
1982	1,073	22	784	3	23,851	90	9	68	107	—	2,791	—	28,297
1983	1,017	22	771	3	22,130	116	12	72	98	—	2,713	—	31,248
1984	938	19	747	3	22,100	140	14	81	90	—	2,973	—	32,908
1985	967	18	726	3	23,062	167	15	82	82	—	2,542	1,233	27,973
1986	949	18	712	3	24,716	191	19	82	81	0	2,453	2,133	29,858
1987	950	18	728	5	24,749	210	21	88	80	1	2,405	3,150	36,421
1988	1,079	17	704	9	26,122	207	22	93	79	1	2,347	3,300	39,888
1989	—	—	—	—	—	—	—	—	—	—	—	—	—
1990	1,137	19	667	8	27,460	197	22	94	76	1	2,129	3,276	45,401
1991	1,147	20	644	8	27,962	206	23	93	72	1	2,372	3,219	48,900
1992	1,157	23	625	8	28,096	217	23	92	68	1	2,086	3,161	52,021
1993	1,165	22	611	4	29,974	213	22	96	69	1	1,950	3,123	56,518
1994	1,161	23	601	4	30,282	181	25	99	68	1	1,866	2,537	62,103
1995	1,185	23	583	3	30,828	141	25	107	61	1	1,810	2,982	68,134
1996	1,212	23	565	2	31,464	131	25	113	54	1	1,773	2,930	75,362

[1] Counts may be incomplete. See text.

Sources

U.S. Internal Revenue Service, *Annual Report* (various years), *Databook* (various years), and *Statistics of Income Bulletin* (1945 and 1946), Supplements; and Burton A. Weisbrod, *The Nonprofit Economy* (Harvard University Press, 1988), p. 176.

Documentation

The organizations in these series are those on the Internal Revenue Service (IRS) Exempt Organization Master File. The organizations granted some type of federal tax exemption under section 501(c) of the IRS Code cover a wide range of activities. Those organizations formally termed "charitable" by IRS analysts and accorded a 501(c)(3) status include universities, schools, United Way campaigns, hospitals, social service organizations, private foundations, and other organizations that operate programs, provide services, or make grants to support charitable activities. The (c)(3) organizations must serve the public good, not private interests, and they are restricted from influencing legislation and politics. In return, (c)(3) organizations are not only exempt from most federal taxation but may also receive tax-deductible contributions, a privilege not granted to the other 501 tax-exempt organizations. That encourages individuals to contribute to the (c)(3) organizations due to tax savings. Most organizations that fit the traditional definition of charitable institutions are granted a (c)(3) status, although some experts in the field accord those with a (c)(4) status membership in the "independent" or charitable sector. It should be recognized that the IRS requirements concerning the amount of charitable activity and spending needed to gain and maintain (c)(3) or (c)(4) status have changed over time. Some observers have expressed concern that in the last two or three decades, IRS policy changes have allowed a significant increase in the number of nonprofit organizations and their financial powers, while there has been a decline of the importance of charitable activity and popular participation in

TABLE Bg75–101 Active tax-exempt organizations, farmer's cooperatives, and nonexempt charitable trusts, by type: 1969–1996 *Continued*

their operations. For an example of such observations, see Gilbert M. Gaul and Neill A. Borowski, *Free Ride: The Tax-Exempt Economy* (Andrews and McMeel, 1993).

Series Bg77. The IRS used a different set of categories during the 1940s. If organizations with codes that appeared to fit the post-1960 definition of (c)(3) organizations are tallied, these values are obtained for the series in 1943 and 1946: 8,901 and 14,424, respectively. Also, the IRS cautions that their (c)(3) files remain an incomplete count of charitable and religious organizations: "Certain organizations, such as churches, their integrated auxiliaries and conventions and associations of churches, need not apply for recognition of exemption unless they desire to receive a ruling. When issued the ruling letter goes to the central organization on the Master File where it is counted as one entity in the figure as stated above. However, this one ruling may represent a large number of subordinate units, as in the case of larger religious sects. An exception are subordinate units considered nonintegrated auxiliaries, which are included in the above figures since they may be required to file information returns as prescribed under IRC sec. 6033" (IRS, *Annual Report* (1981), Table 20).

TABLE Bg102–113 Tax-exempt organizations – receipts and IRS 990 returns filed, by state and type of organization: 1946

Contributed by Colin B. Burke

	All types			Type 6			Type 7			Type 8		
	IRS 990 returns filed	Total receipts	Business receipts	IRS 990 returns filed	Total receipts	Business receipts	IRS 990 returns filed	Total receipts	Business receipts	IRS 990 returns filed	Total receipts	Business receipts
	Bg102	Bg103	Bg104	Bg105	Bg106	Bg107	Bg108	Bg109	Bg110	Bg111	Bg112	Bg113
State	Number	Thousand dollars	Thousand dollars	Number	Thousand dollars	Thousand dollars	Number	Thousand dollars	Thousand dollars	Number	Thousand dollars	Thousand dollars
Alabama	744	28,001	21,105	106	5,743	2,707	45	697	61	55	2,120	1,695
Alaska	9	1,795	1,790	1	60	59	0	0	0	4	479	475
Arizona	351	16,152	13,129	47	2,811	2,275	29	536	128	17	424	146
Arkansas	591	25,061	22,923	40	710	190	29	501	114	51	718	372
California	7,565	1,280,474	1,163,655	1,616	92,747	51,442	622	19,010	2,985	1,033	20,730	12,893
Colorado	284	62,468	51,046	205	9,464	4,183	118	1,670	218	118	4,383	3,424
Connecticut	2,016	69,907	49,338	435	20,125	7,318	115	1,687	243	280	7,673	6,558
Delaware	207	52,998	49,203	64	3,541	483	8	97	3	17	1,588	1,534
District of Columbia	426	128,367	80,733	87	29,355	17,551	117	21,414	6,718	44	18,053	15,165
Florida	745	138,902	133,008	102	3,217	1,116	51	870	58	46	1,986	1,387
Georgia	738	65,707	58,194	149	6,762	3,118	45	1,051	118	30	2,535	2,020
Hawai'i	201	14,538	7,535	48	5,859	3,406	14	690	164	6	237	12
Idaho	654	62,993	61,054	41	746	261	33	392	32	74	898	524
Illinois	8,692	584,102	419,693	1,101	95,686	47,426	768	54,273	12,402	921	21,291	8,118
Indiana	2,137	296,657	248,595	170	13,276	4,692	107	2,992	1,059	214	11,516	8,211
Iowa	2,401	147,691	133,287	178	6,195	2,861	117	1,257	215	331	3,377	2,367
Kansas	2,709	89,026	77,871	507	7,148	4,409	173	1,368	239	402	4,244	1,976
Kentucky	796	75,255	69,489	111	3,770	2,085	72	1,411	223	31	1,655	1,542
Louisiana	880	38,064	27,203	97	4,533	954	70	2,672	560	38	1,551	338
Maine	397	30,662	28,316	93	3,384	1,848	12	70	0	40	174	108
Maryland	1,913	168,464	99,829	374	33,031	12,730	203	15,554	600	186	7,261	1,691
Massachusetts	4,046	515,370	451,022	1,123	82,639	40,489	204	7,923	3,141	254	19,387	14,543
Michigan	6,170	299,373	225,704	830	67,519	39,298	441	8,812	2,088	1,107	29,972	26,989
Minnesota	4,059	754,456	724,652	336	28,017	12,961	199	3,646	528	583	9,244	6,954
Mississippi	559	70,855	69,055	70	3,116	2,521	41	502	23	19	381	252
Missouri	2,314	332,375	299,006	288	22,946	9,904	159	5,270	1,560	158	5,748	1,719
Montana	815	41,996	39,613	23	1,254	1,006	44	409	57	53	696	465
Nebraska	1,041	111,125	100,944	84	10,648	4,126	57	913	171	228	5,980	4,917
Nevada	70	555	234	4	8	0	6	36	9	15	75	50
New Hampshire	428	23,603	21,652	119	3,156	2,123	20	369	21	32	1,876	1,822
New Jersey	2,819	128,518	98,141	368	26,450	16,273	146	2,833	412	304	9,672	8,176
New Mexico	153	8,677	8,415	5	188	180	4	28	0	43	300	223
New York	8,449	1,582,506	1,045,068	2,126	431,821	123,507	1,013	87,083	12,314	707	67,737	43,464
North Carolina	1,148	72,362	59,408	240	18,147	8,448	71	812	103	35	4,117	3,599
North Dakota	629	109,811	108,629	35	1,616	1,244	17	202	23	17	544	522
Ohio	5,245	550,579	473,857	516	50,501	35,678	337	13,814	3,081	301	25,540	19,909
Oklahoma	1,190	108,584	100,850	125	5,305	2,513	120	3,294	742	77	1,402	1,010
Oregon	1,691	139,655	125,311	157	10,072	6,949	123	2,199	192	158	1,645	903
Pennsylvania	6,456	400,068	296,868	708	60,114	33,079	346	10,802	1,762	743	46,230	28,727
Rhode Island	422	28,471	23,891	98	5,919	3,297	27	354	81	46	3,403	3,285

(continued)

TABLE Bg102–113 Tax-exempt organizations – receipts and IRS 990 returns filed, by state and type of organization: 1946 *Continued*

	All types			Type 6			Type 7			Type 8		
	IRS 990 returns filed	Total receipts	Business receipts	IRS 990 returns filed	Total receipts	Business receipts	IRS 990 returns filed	Total receipts	Business receipts	IRS 990 returns filed	Total receipts	Business receipts
	Bg102	Bg103	Bg104	Bg105	Bg106	Bg107	Bg108	Bg109	Bg110	Bg111	Bg112	Bg113
State	Number	Thousand dollars	Thousand dollars	Number	Thousand dollars	Thousand dollars	Number	Thousand dollars	Thousand dollars	Number	Thousand dollars	Thousand dollars
South Carolina	455	19,867	16,998	74	3,197	1,434	24	274	39	35	707	389
South Dakota	463	54,028	53,126	30	1,182	958	31	310	38	6	60	56
Tennessee	850	51,987	41,676	82	2,604	1,416	55	2,234	79	129	1,308	594
Texas	3,522	218,338	187,936	427	19,725	8,926	305	5,895	1,047	182	4,796	1,536
Utah	528	86,968	84,644	26	415	233	30	631	55	38	342	259
Vermont	219	32,457	31,609	50	1,840	1,454	7	189	2	18	52	2
Virginia	1,277	91,982	81,623	191	10,418	6,595	100	1,495	309	74	3,645	1,593
Washington	3,539	310,466	286,903	362	16,183	12,562	282	5,558	1,690	520	9,017	7,040
West Virginia	651	11,170	5,498	53	2,195	1,197	37	1,180	7	49	801	541
Wisconsin	4,192	311,216	289,511	263	13,759	7,638	203	4,215	1,571	444	3,863	2,728
Wyoming	308	8,063	7,049	21	197	42	9	37	5	29	379	261

Source

U.S. Internal Revenue Service, *Supplement to the Statistics of Income for 1946* (October 1949), Part 2.

Documentation

These series are based on financial reports filed with the Internal Revenue Service. Like the early censuses of charitable and nonprofit organizations, the series are not complete lists of organizations in the sectors. The Revenue Act of 1943 required tax-exempt organizations to submit annual financial reports, but many types of "nonprofit," "tax-exempt," and "voluntary" organizations were not required to file reports. In addition, the IRS knew that many organizations falling under the rule for mandatory filing did not do so, especially during the first few years of the new requirements. (See *Supplement to the Statistics of Income for 1943*, Part 2, p. 2).

Organizations not required to file reports included the following: (1) religious organizations exempt under section 101(6); (2) educational organizations exempt under section 101(6) that maintained a regular faculty, curriculum, student body, and place of instruction; (3) charitable organizations or institutions devoted to preventing cruelty to animals or children and that received support from government sources or contributions from the general population; (4) organizations controlled by exempt religious organizations; (5) fraternal organizations, beneficiary societies, orders, or associations solely exempt under section 101(6); and (6) corporations wholly owned by the U.S. government or a wholly owned subsidiary of such an organization.

Series Bg102–104. These series are for nineteen categories of section 101 tax-exempt organizations: labor organizations; agricultural and horticultural organizations; mutual savings banks; building and loan or savings and loan associations (not federal), cooperative banks, and credit unions (not federal); cemetery companies; literary, library, scientific, research, educational, or charitable organizations and hospitals and foundations; business and trade associations; civic organizations and local associations of employees devoted to charitable, educational, or recreational purposes; clubs organized for pleasure or recreation; local benevolent life insurance associations; mutual ditch, irrigation, telephone, and rural electrification organizations; mutual insurance companies other than life or marine, farmers' mutual hail, cyclone, fire, or casualty insurance companies; farmers' cooperative associations; financing associations organized by farmers' cooperatives; financing and holding companies of tax-exempt organizations; federal credit unions, federal savings and loan associations, intermediate credit banks, national farm loan associations, production credit associations, and so on; employees' beneficiary associations; teachers' retirement funds (local); and U.S. employees' beneficiary associations.

Series Bg105–107. Covers organizations that most fit the common definition of charitable organizations: literary, library, scientific, research, educational, or charitable organizations and hospitals and foundations.

Series Bg108–110. Covers organizations that encompass business and trade associations.

Series Bg111–113. Covers civic organizations and local associations of employees devoted to charitable, educational, or recreational purposes.

TABLE Bg114–129 Benevolent institutions, by state, type of institutional control, and recipient of care: 1910

Contributed by Colin B. Burke

	Benevolent institutions, by type of institutional control, for the care of							
	Children				Adults, or adults and children			
	Government agency	Religious denomination	Other agencies or groups	Nongovernmental groups receiving government appropriations	Government agency	Religious denomination	Other agencies or groups	Nongovernmental groups receiving government appropriations
	Bg114	Bg115	Bg116	Bg117	Bg118	Bg119	Bg120	Bg121
State	Number	Number	Number	Number	Number	Number	Number	Number
Alabama	0	8	0	1	5	4	2	2
Arizona	0	2	0	0	0	2	0	0
Arkansas	0	5	4	1	1	4	3	1
California	2	29	25	63	2	22	25	11
Colorado	2	5	7	2	1	3	0	1
Connecticut	7	5	11	2	0	15	20	2
Delaware	0	3	2	0	0	6	0	0
District of Columbia	2	7	5	3	3	9	14	5
Florida	0	3	4	2	1	4	1	2
Georgia	0	11	11	5	1	13	12	6
Idaho	0	0	2	2	1	0	0	0
Illinois	2	36	26	20	4	39	45	10
Indiana	18	12	17	9	3	21	16	12
Iowa	2	10	6	5	1	13	13	3
Kansas	1	7	8	12	3	9	3	8
Kentucky	0	19	6	7	1	16	4	4
Louisiana	0	19	5	16	2	9	8	11
Maine	1	4	7	6	1	13	5	4
Maryland	0	25	11	20	2	12	17	18
Massachusetts	0	27	22	1	4	83	43	6
Michigan	1	9	14	6	1	15	15	2
Minnesota	2	12	2	3	1	10	18	2
Mississippi	0	6	1	—	1	1	0	2
Missouri	1	24	7	0	2	15	20	4
Montana	1	1	1	1	1	2	1	1
Nebraska	2	5	2	0	3	3	8	1
Nevada	0	1	0	0	0	0	0	1
New Hampshire	0	11	6	7	1	11	4	1
New Jersey	1	19	30	8	4	29	26	0
New Mexico	0	2	0	0	0	1	0	0
New York	3	82	69	102	5	97	119	42
North Carolina	1	11	5	2	1	6	3	2
North Dakota	0	1	1	0	1	1	0	1
Ohio	51	31	24	8	3	32	48	2
Oklahoma	0	2	3	0	0	3	1	1
Oregon	0	3	3	3	1	5	5	3
Pennsylvania	5	54	46	33	2	78	85	49
Rhode Island	1	7	5	2	1	12	6	2
South Carolina	1	4	5	1	2	3	9	2
South Dakota	0	1	1	0	2	0	0	0
Tennessee	1	9	5	4	2	9	6	4
Texas	2	10	8	3	2	11	11	1
Utah	0	2	1	1	0	1	2	1
Vermont	0	0	4	0	1	5	3	0
Virginia	0	14	18	3	2	15	10	4
Washington	1	4	9	4	1	8	10	6
West Virginia	0	4	5	2	0	3	2	0
Wisconsin	3	13	3	3	1	10	13	3
Wyoming	0	1	0	0	1	0	0	0

(continued)

TABLE Bg114–129 Benevolent institutions, by state, type of institutional control, and recipient of care: 1910 *Continued*

	Benevolent institutions, by type of institutional control, for the care of				Benevolent hospitals and sanatoriums, by type of institutional control			
	The blind and deaf							
	Government agency	Religious denomination	Other agencies or groups	Nongovernmental groups receiving government appropriations	Government agency	Religious denomination	Other agencies or groups	Nongovernmental groups receiving government appropriations
	Bg122	Bg123	Bg124	Bg125	Bg126	Bg127	Bg128	Bg129
State	Number	Number	Number	Number	Number	Number	Number	Number
Alabama	3	0	0	0	4	3	4	2
Arizona	0	0	0	0	3	5	4	0
Arkansas	2	0	0	0	5	6	4	2
California	2	1	0	0	23	16	27	5
Colorado	1	0	0	0	6	20	19	0
Connecticut	0	0	3	2	4	5	19	20
Delaware	0	0	0	—	1	1	3	4
District of Columbia	0	0	2	2	5	4	7	9
Florida	1	0	0	0	8	1	8	2
Georgia	2	0	0	0	9	4	14	5
Idaho	1	0	0	0	1	4	1	1
Illinois	3	1	2	0	9	63	60	31
Indiana	2	0	0	0	9	21	21	15
Iowa	2	0	0	0	9	27	16	9
Kansas	2	0	0	0	4	18	13	18
Kentucky	2	0	0	0	6	12	7	8
Louisiana	1	1	0	0	4	6	2	2
Maine	1	0	0	0	2	3	16	14
Maryland	3	1	1	2	8	11	24	25
Massachusetts	1	0	7	4	37	14	78	22
Michigan	3	1	0	0	13	12	41	15
Minnesota	2	0	0	—	12	30	27	9
Mississippi	2	0	0	0	2	4	4	4
Missouri	2	1	1	0	7	27	23	3
Montana	1	0	0	0	3	10	3	1
Nebraska	2	0	0	0	5	14	4	2
Nevada	0	0	0	0	0	0	0	—
New Hampshire	0	0	0	—	5	5	16	12
New Jersey	1	1	1	0	15	15	33	43
New Mexico	1	0	0	0	3	6	10	6
New York	3	6	9	11	50	59	144	138
North Carolina	1	0	0	0	4	7	20	8
North Dakota	2	0	0	0	1	8	2	1
Ohio	2	0	3	1	13	31	37	27
Oklahoma	2	0	0	0	1	2	3	0
Oregon	1	0	0	0	2	7	3	3
Pennsylvania	2	0	9	4	15	25	144	137
Rhode Island	1	0	0	0	6	2	9	5
South Carolina	1	0	0	0	3	1	5	3
South Dakota	2	0	0	0	2	6	1	1
Tennessee	2	1	0	1	7	2	7	1
Texas	3	0	0	0	11	12	14	4
Utah	1	0	0	0	2	3	2	2
Vermont	0	0	0	—	1	2	8	2
Virginia	1	0	0	0	6	22	1	15
Washington	0	0	0	—	13	15	8	5
West Virginia	1	0	0	0	4	5	7	0
Wisconsin	4	1	0	0	8	26	16	6
Wyoming	0	0	0	—	4	0	2	0

Source

U.S.Bureau of the Census, *Benevolent Institutions 1910* (1914).

Documentation

This census was the most comprehensive and precise and, for the purposes of the study of the nonprofit and voluntary sectors, the most useful of a series of Census Bureau attempts to define and survey the charitable and benevolent sector. Unfortunately, its predecessors, including the special censuses of 1896 and 1904, were not compatible with this census, and after this 1910 effort there was no directly comparable census report.

Although this 1910 Census is the best available survey, it has its own weaknesses, as admitted by its editors in their introduction to the volume. They were not satisfied with the classifications of institutions, had to rely upon questionnaires sent to known institutions, and had to use a loose definition of benevolence.

TABLE Bg114–129 Benevolent institutions, by state, type of institutional control, and recipient of care: 1910 *Continued*

Benevolent institutions were defined as "those for the benefit of the sick, the needy, and the dependent, exclusive of those covered by the special reports on paupers, the insane and the feeble-minded. The great majority are conducted by private persons or corporations both with and without financial assistance, whether from public authorities or private benefaction. Some are charitable in the sense that inmates are cared for free of all charge; others are benevolent rather than charitable, in that they provide succor and relief for persons who are not destitute, but whose means or circumstances are inadequate for the full provision of their need. In most cases the income, from whatever source received, is applied to the purposes of the institution." For the quotation and further details, see the source, pp. 12–14.

Series Bg114–117. Covers institutions especially designed for children: orphanages, children's homes and asylums, receiving homes for societies for the protection and care of children, detention homes connected with juvenile courts, and similar institutions that received children as resident inmates, sometimes for a short period. The series do not include day nurseries or homes open for only a part of the year.

Series Bg117, Bg121, Bg125, and Bg129. Includes denominational or other agencies or groups reporting the receipt of government appropriations. The census reported its figures using three subcategories of religious denominations: Protestant, Roman Catholic, and Jewish. These categories have been summed to arrive at the figures in the denominational category. When used to indicate the type of organization that controlled an institution, the category "other" included the following: church-related but nondenominational organizations, secular benevolent institutions, fraternal organizations, and for-profit institutions that also served benevolent functions.

Series Bg118–121. Focuses on those institutions primarily for the care of adults and includes "homes for the permanent care of the aged, infirm, or destitute; for the temporary shelter of the homeless, the unemployed, or wayfarers; for the protection and relief of the unfortunate, wayward or fallen; and for special classes, as convalescents, incurable, epileptics, and others. Children are received when they accompany their parents or when, for any reason, they can not appropriately be received into the institutions specially for the care of children, particularly in the case of self-supporting, delinquent, or wayward minors." See the source, pp. 12–14.

Series Bg122–125. Covers institutions that made special provision for the care and training of the blind and deaf and received persons unable to meet the cost of their care and education. Institutions run on a distinctively business basis were excluded.

Series Bg126–129. Covers institutions "which may be regarded as benevolent institutions in distinction from those which are conducted on a distinctively business basis," including private corporate hospitals that received patients for free or part-pay treatment at their own expense or on contract with public or private benevolent organizations. Dispensaries were not included, nor were those county institutions that had hospitals connected with pauper asylums. See the source, pp. 12–14.

TABLE Bg130–165 Tax-exempt service organizations – payroll and number, by state and type of organization: 1977–1992

Contributed by Colin B. Burke

	Annual payroll											
	Selected health services			Nursing and personal care facilities			Legal aid societies and similar legal services			Social services		
	1977	1987	1992	1977	1987	1992	1977	1987	1992	1977	1987	1992
	Bg130	Bg131	Bg132	Bg133	Bg134	Bg135	Bg136	Bg137	Bg138	Bg139	Bg140	Bg141
State	Thousand dollars	Thousand dollars	Thousand dollars	Thousand dollars	Thousand dollars	Thousand dollars	Thousand dollars	Thousand dollars	Thousand dollars	Thousand dollars	Thousand dollars	Thousand dollars
Alabama	180,667	1,120,353	1,866,302	6,166	14,419	25,943	755	—	—	42,684	71,003	117,973
Alaska	78,443	216,836	317,428	—	11,959	6,425	—	2,383	2,389	16,430	54,486	79,296
Arizona	420,198	1,063,197	1,647,970	8,288	19,832	73,498	1,955	4,542	5,840	37,625	130,203	232,100
Arkansas	220,462	609,300	988,138	—	9,696	19,682	—	—	2,929	37,570	88,724	141,319
California	3,896,083	9,510,524	14,244,050	50,956	204,353	272,343	17,707	44,363	87,850	393,025	1,290,177	2,078,582
Colorado	273,448	1,123,650	1,797,176	13,046	—	54,181	1,807	5,083	7,227	42,441	129,334	221,375
Connecticut	484,721	1,586,778	2,546,943	20,855	80,607	190,102	3,856	4,363	9,203	65,326	276,665	417,586
Delaware	79,043	265,954	465,120	—	—	25,836	—	—	—	13,548	36,918	56,888
District of Columbia	219,748	243,537	1,432,622	—	17,178	25,378	4,125	—	13,494	77,934	780,455	374,798
Florida	581,852	3,290,004	5,696,470	24,734	114,815	279,117	3,211	10,285	17,673	122,438	435,982	735,414
Georgia	148,577	1,957,676	3,095,973	12,467	64,221	61,462	2,684	6,552	12,013	56,651	142,146	228,220
Hawai'i	72,795	394,417	701,520	3,325	14,169	14,029	—	—	—	19,278	44,800	92,937
Idaho	41,799	194,258	331,010	—	7,887	16,485	—	—	—	10,017	21,997	39,311
Illinois	1,685,425	4,759,541	6,900,360	55,425	216,073	389,309	5,724	11,091	20,395	223,393	1,470,095	954,943
Indiana	4,788,791	1,891,336	2,983,728	18,063	62,691	140,565	2,024	3,088	5,989	83,005	323,305	348,004
Iowa	273,488	1,049,112	1,626,502	38,335	101,418	189,775	859	2,170	2,881	57,545	133,854	284,285
Kansas	238,201	609,300	1,304,719	17,600	9,696	105,288	600	—	—	32,537	88,724	161,471
Kentucky	254,093	987,835	1,607,201	15,650	47,838	85,490	808	3,635	5,405	57,743	107,048	158,042
Louisiana	204,564	1,273,072	2,037,997	7,538	30,338	66,348	1,546	4,255	5,952	46,776	11,174	165,545
Maine	144,984	458,814	737,397	7,390	26,380	46,355	—	1,473	2,384	27,956	73,972	132,361
Maryland	454,478	1,761,896	2,835,486	24,027	91,846	183,009	—	—	10,180	63,980	227,400	451,068
Massachusetts	1,081,622	3,585,945	5,580,542	34,183	139,989	277,697	3,862	9,467	16,785	156,569	608,215	929,556
Michigan	1,226,942	4,018,992	5,927,125	32,180	126,182	253,567	5,393	10,253	24,215	145,716	459,000	706,441
Minnesota	582,691	2,184,727	3,532,701	78,341	232,740	383,608	2,422	4,816	10,350	100,622	282,579	452,997
Mississippi	78,936	708,576	1,078,094	—	7,142	17,529	1,446	3,022	3,521	41,553	66,066	75,086

(continued)

TABLE Bg130–165 Tax-exempt service organizations – payroll and number, by state and type of organization: 1977–1992 ***Continued***

	Annual payroll											
	Selected health services			Nursing and personal care facilities			Legal aid societies and similar legal services			Social services		
	1977	1987	1992	1977	1987	1992	1977	1987	1992	1977	1987	1992
	Bg130	Bg131	Bg132	Bg133	Bg134	Bg135	Bg136	Bg137	Bg138	Bg139	Bg140	Bg141
State	Thousand dollars	Thousand dollars	Thousand dollars	Thousand dollars	Thousand dollars	Thousand dollars	Thousand dollars	Thousand dollars	Thousand dollars	Thousand dollars	Thousand dollars	Thousand dollars
Missouri	573,891	2,849,459	3,273,357	31,960	101,567	142,401	2,044	4,295	6,813	87,102	281,283	374,771
Montana	72,381	265,728	418,339	3,302	12,369	21,994	—	—	—	21,251	42,129	66,290
Nebraska	144,853	557,351	905,250	23,390	60,644	79,117	583	1,143	—	32,102	82,764	120,831
Nevada	13,949	189,015	300,203	—	—	—	444	—	—	10,512	23,106	43,370
New Hampshire	88,937	336,004	589,445	3,282	8,439	—	0	—	—	16,833	63,754	113,503
New Jersey	867,004	2,938,949	5,151,633	29,723	128,306	240,111	4,060	9,057	14,959	127,525	328,272	594,203
New Mexico	71,743	392,314	660,211	3,945	18,895	36,023	862	2,235	3,288	19,566	48,014	91,240
New York	2,958,794	10,515,113	17,424,557	237,423	842,278	1,438,261	37,199	93,457	156,062	619,104	1,682,575	2,805,800
North Carolina	298,505	1,805,993	3,338,138	13,297	60,673	115,514	1,062	5,789	8,499	69,916	202,236	357,338
North Dakota	95,694	310,855	484,408	14,824	51,642	90,893	—	—	817	9,816	35,331	56,344
Ohio	1,466,585	4,864,092	6,881,584	65,094	246,972	421,255	3,288	13,207	22,268	189,225	487,340	770,748
Oklahoma	193,599	941,818	1,318,555	6,187	20,602	28,676	—	—	2,940	40,708	73,896	154,114
Oregon	222,800	854,742	1,403,258	12,936	35,989	64,752	1,721	6,251	10,410	47,378	133,346	235,588
Pennsylvania	1,744,455	5,888,587	9,304,398	111,175	358,747	688,647	14,518	20,256	33,905	276,646	759,568	1,181,798
Rhode Island	162,877	531,109	808,924	7,156	—	60,205	—	—	—	20,480	68,551	116,971
South Carolina	121,382	842,335	1,441,624	—	14,503	32,520	1,043	3,084	5,075	29,184	76,159	131,750
South Dakota	71,556	295,410	454,658	12,397	34,070	55,342	—	640	986	11,514	33,123	59,782
Tennessee	346,236	1,584,123	2,543,390	11,173	41,198	67,240	591	2,962	5,196	48,464	126,573	217,688
Texas	746,997	4,145,181	6,810,214	34,567	118,863	166,910	4,020	14,805	21,711	179,960	454,998	749,054
Utah	78,633	389,911	592,165	1,555	5,724	17,006	—	2,351	3,467	8,155	30,711	73,370
Vermont	64,885	203,026	336,323	2,759	8,628	16,802	794	—	—	17,774	32,890	58,090
Virginia	356,554	1,680,263	2,821,609	15,188	47,801	113,218	1,158	6,507	9,060	68,714	231,810	379,166
Washington	334,152	1,574,980	2,947,861	18,062	66,031	122,390	1,429	10,830	20,377	82,742	221,877	427,139
West Virginia	166,842	675,799	967,923	4,628	16,143	30,219	755	1,702	3,541	16,542	53,773	106,313
Wisconsin	558,867	1,743,732	2,843,895	46,323	184,956	284,024	1,509	3,137	5,501	95,806	228,287	398,109
Wyoming	13,038	—	185,835	1,430	—	11,156	228	—	—	5,135	23,837	42,376

	Annual payroll											
	Child day care services			Membership organizations, except religious			Business associations			Civic, social, and fraternal associations		
	1977	1987	1992	1977	1987	1992	1977	1987	1992	1977	1987	1992
	Bg142	Bg143	Bg144	Bg145	Bg146	Bg147	Bg148	Bg149	Bg150	Bg151	Bg152	Bg153
State	Thousand dollars	Thousand dollars	Thousand dollars	Thousand dollars	Thousand dollars	Thousand dollars	Thousand dollars	Thousand dollars	Thousand dollars	Thousand dollars	Thousand dollars	Thousand dollars
Alabama	7,652	11,174	18,624	33,119	54,993	79,481	6,436	13,898	22,643	10,313	24,900	33,178
Alaska	—	6,984	7,594	22,175	24,390	34,339	1,682	5,122	8,714	7,991	15,766	19,746
Arizona	2,765	8,993	8,057	35,568	63,177	89,583	4,639	11,085	17,938	16,933	33,579	39,454
Arkansas	3,848	9,632	9,042	16,652	29,907	42,209	3,002	5,881	8,772	6,905	13,041	18,772
California	44,508	168,648	217,069	491,344	808,828	1,096,218	77,384	179,294	252,823	133,733	310,689	398,636
Colorado	4,524	9,760	22,071	55,498	123,436	192,953	9,624	33,796	54,747	14,488	35,182	53,629
Connecticut	5,799	19,270	38,831	62,822	125,591	149,994	13,139	28,689	37,068	27,036	60,418	67,516
Delaware	2,165	5,257	7,477	10,147	4,327	27,704	976	845	5,819	4,564	10,284	15,697
District of Columbia	6,272	22,040	22,390	388,022	624,107	978,939	128,148	352,694	579,979	44,716	83,633	114,758
Florida	15,349	53,374	82,917	101,328	276,622	430,939	18,185	63,119	92,707	41,146	122,317	175,993
Georgia	11,439	26,689	33,685	57,345	112,481	185,328	16,228	38,938	56,786	17,380	40,055	63,488
Hawai'i	3,723	15,748	14,983	19,612	101,963	49,053	3,424	23,418	11,651	7,234	21,089	27,422
Idaho	1,247	1,870	3,717	10,812	16,160	23,027	1,523	45,660	6,407	4,724	7,750	10,518
Illinois	30,163	98,118	89,477	356,832	592,626	823,707	79,688	179,950	334,054	90,712	163,663	191,877
Indiana	7,569	18,991	29,942	86,440	126,088	182,273	10,260	22,120	31,531	37,990	72,435	108,443
Iowa	4,700	10,558	19,695	54,156	69,929	107,110	19,091	23,953	34,060	15,549	26,215	35,334
Kansas	4,592	9,632	14,429	39,791	66,540	89,538	5,837	14,874	22,671	19,391	27,733	33,063
Kentucky	4,860	11,562	18,559	30,063	57,034	83,996	5,319	11,653	22,490	8,999	29,918	38,111
Louisiana	4,722	13,093	15,208	38,736	55,259	75,981	11,535	19,217	25,807	9,508	21,783	33,187
Maine	1,616	7,449	9,691	11,173	26,265	37,527	1,747	5,903	11,639	4,738	14,453	18,125

TABLE Bg130–165 Tax-exempt service organizations – payroll and number, by state and type of organization: 1977–1992 *Continued*

	Annual payroll											
	Child day care services			Membership organizations, except religious			Business associations			Civic, social, and fraternal associations		
	1977	1987	1992	1977	1987	1992	1977	1987	1992	1977	1987	1992
	Bg142	Bg143	Bg144	Bg145	Bg146	Bg147	Bg148	Bg149	Bg150	Bg151	Bg152	Bg153
State	Thousand dollars	Thousand dollars	Thousand dollars	Thousand dollars	Thousand dollars	Thousand dollars	Thousand dollars	Thousand dollars	Thousand dollars	Thousand dollars	Thousand dollars	Thousand dollars
Maryland	9,126	21,785	34,958	76,888	145,596	219,037	14,076	34,687	48,647	20,639	53,890	69,546
Massachusetts	16,625	68,877	115,886	107,786	217,341	246,320	11,554	53,135	61,118	42,346	95,395	102,559
Michigan	9,796	23,991	42,490	175,694	171,136	238,813	23,787	46,936	69,836	46,556	81,429	109,581
Minnesota	8,929	19,270	29,783	84,241	140,444	194,056	13,137	29,970	43,390	32,161	75,192	101,722
Mississippi	21,826	19,984	20,644	16,284	25,675	35,518	3,654	7,184	9,906	6,349	10,234	14,012
Missouri	7,954	21,892	35,127	103,980	150,678	195,580	15,743	36,696	50,226	31,106	60,106	75,368
Montana	1,224	2,245	3,461	14,798	17,460	21,961	2,404	3,723	5,099	6,664	10,148	9,879
Nebraska	2,783	5,054	7,931	27,005	39,542	53,932	4,876	7,941	12,449	13,319	22,966	28,853
Nevada	990	2,321	6,103	14,113	19,588	29,777	2,263	4,453	7,269	3,820	8,488	12,429
New Hampshire	2,746	7,599	11,210	11,689	26,572	34,693	1,646	6,091	7,488	5,200	13,704	17,199
New Jersey	25,469	49,427	85,882	104,328	159,581	229,074	13,625	40,421	77,156	42,156	68,654	81,687
New Mexico	2,968	5,864	11,808	17,135	27,172	39,997	2,287	6,838	9,881	9,086	13,056	18,386
New York	77,174	198,513	322,457	555,449	694,204	923,695	98,139	180,189	274,052	158,280	307,118	366,689
North Carolina	12,708	28,094	46,483	51,961	104,933	183,403	13,418	29,085	43,032	22,508	48,566	75,127
North Dakota	603	1,841	2,901	13,112	24,310	30,940	1,799	4,385	6,996	7,459	15,174	17,744
Ohio	16,566	35,397	56,006	214,804	247,723	343,783	23,989	53,416	79,411	62,433	112,268	155,151
Oklahoma	5,521	10,853	16,256	35,293	58,042	86,011	7,445	14,717	22,586	13,190	21,871	35,385
Oregon	6,886	11,693	16,953	47,722	69,125	107,736	9,575	19,930	30,810	15,485	30,887	48,415
Pennsylvania	26,875	59,997	89,243	261,622	312,891	443,076	21,495	49,198	72,982	87,827	157,031	198,643
Rhode Island	1,812	4,622	8,664	18,200	30,151	46,787	2,665	6,296	6,973	7,686	13,641	21,005
South Carolina	3,043	7,433	14,723	19,110	45,650	74,906	4,136	11,151	18,286	8,175	22,437	36,044
South Dakota	565	1,763	5,446	9,062	16,752	25,334	1,535	3,209	6,313	4,650	10,220	12,111
Tennessee	6,263	16,437	26,557	47,163	83,231	151,029	8,034	23,224	67,276	16,316	35,930	51,525
Texas	29,329	70,459	104,637	155,521	333,082	478,048	36,099	89,212	146,490	56,004	143,939	207,483
Utah	331	3,872	8,945	14,175	21,227	33,556	2,352	4,878	8,643	5,982	10,214	13,207
Vermont	2,090	3,479	6,439	5,503	13,659	22,485	1,254	3,375	7,478	2,476	7,486	10,441
Virginia	7,629	19,242	35,197	89,724	301,574	478,749	32,628	133,497	226,827	21,044	56,849	78,811
Washington	6,883	23,735	38,257	83,583	131,882	212,416	11,243	24,505	37,144	31,280	61,556	94,137
West Virginia	1,858	5,017	9,867	23,358	27,083	36,712	2,727	4,570	6,297	8,318	14,254	18,933
Wisconsin	7,922	22,603	40,560	78,318	125,971	176,840	14,137	30,983	49,805	25,739	54,237	71,352
Wyoming	—	4,690	5,559	7,383	—	14,166	2,137	—	4,959	3,301	5,879	7,071

	Annual payroll									Number of organizations		
	Noncommercial educational, scientific, and research organizations			Producers, orchestras, and entertainers			Museums, art galleries, and botanical and zoological gardens			Educational services		
	1977	1987	1992	1977	1987	1992	1977	1987	1992	1977	1987	1992
	Bg154	Bg155	Bg156	Bg157	Bg158	Bg159	Bg160	Bg161	Bg162	Bg163	Bg164	Bg165
State	Thousand dollars	Thousand dollars	Thousand dollars	Thousand dollars	Thousand dollars	Thousand dollars	Thousand dollars	Thousand dollars	Thousand dollars	Number	Number	Number
Alabama	675	—	—	753	4,695	6,649	986	1,704	2,772	31	41	60
Alaska	206	943	1,121	—	949	2,431	258	818	1,312	15	28	30
Arizona	6,829	2,911	—	2,203	10,162	14,041	3,028	9,825	14,792	43	52	68
Arkansas	813	—	7,868	318	—	1,996	319 [1]	—	904	23	29	48
California	46,532	244,899	643,064	33,326	99,892	158,078	12,607 [1]	92,373	124,466	385	424	690
Colorado	6,702	—	—	2,786	—	18,416	1,422 [1]	—	8,901	67	81	106
Connecticut	3,536	6,873	10,734	4,217	10,408	13,372	5,684	13,203	23,975	150	136	169
Delaware	890	—	3,568	—	—	—	3,348 [1]	—	13,864	17	17	18
District of Columbia	60,362	148,077	192,203	5,481	14,554	15,446	2,848 [1]	13,011	22,058	64	73	115
Florida	7,855	14,932	26,491	3,705	20,018	38,976	3,454	16,074	28,845	99	117	174
Georgia	3,832	—	—	2,898	12,890	21,979	1,297	8,171	17,055	58	68	103
Hawai'i	—	18,169	25,006	—	—	17,337	3,007	7,927	14,379	41	43	51
Idaho	503	—	—	—	—	1,336	—	386	—	11	12	12
Illinois	16,656	—	—	8,080	27,532	49,697	20,810 [1]	66,555	103,429	169	169	217
Indiana	1,667	4,568	6,319	3,051	9,978	15,764	3,619	10,457	19,577	42	58	82

Note appears at end of table

(continued)

TABLE Bg130–165 Tax-exempt service organizations – payroll and number, by state and type of organization: 1977–1992 *Continued*

	Annual payroll									Number of organizations		
	Noncommercial educational, scientific, and research organizations			Producers, orchestras, and entertainers			Museums, art galleries, and botanical and zoological gardens			Educational services		
	1977	1987	1992	1977	1987	1992	1977	1987	1992	1977	1987	1992
	Bg154	Bg155	Bg156	Bg157	Bg158	Bg159	Bg160	Bg161	Bg162	Bg163	Bg164	Bg165
State	Thousand dollars	Thousand dollars	Thousand dollars	Thousand dollars	Thousand dollars	Thousand dollars	Thousand dollars	Thousand dollars	Thousand dollars	Number	Number	Number
Iowa	281	—	—	434	2,638	4,311	1,067	2,746	4,615	20	21	35
Kansas	556	—	—	179	—	1,160	548	—	4,140	29	29	54
Kentucky	869	1,615	1,843	1,807	6,979	10,697	1,520	—	7,534	41	38	75
Louisiana	1,685	4,206	—	2,041	2,116	3,880	1,350	4,998	7,503	42	39	60
Maine	—	13,350	—	493	1,725	2,487	475	2,373	4,173	76	69	101
Maryland	5,278	14,993	39,480	3,480	10,574	16,587	2,690	9,981	19,530	70	85	106
Massachusetts	86,423	100,457	—	9,168	24,925	41,097	17,091	37,797	51,468	207	244	333
Michigan	12,595	54,628	60,630	4,887	18,607	22,712	9,551	18,704	23,827	78	109	125
Minnesota	5,873	6,277	—	6,629	22,957	31,880	5,601	22,741	31,985	47	66	113
Mississippi	—	349	1,749	126	—	1,243	268	1,094	1,523	9	19	25
Missouri	11,838	—	65,446	6,539	17,289	25,756	3,670	10,495	18,369	65	86	109
Montana	1,662	2,770	4,020	—	—	1,182	198	848	1,455	13	14	22
Nebraska	1,305	446	689	650	2,067	—	1,118	3,656	6,705	24	25	39
Nevada	—	—	—	—	424	1,790	52	529	1,211	12	18	22
New Hampshire	408	—	507	512	1,171	2,004	944	1,996	3,734	32	32	42
New Jersey	5,232	11,603	19,653	3,326	11,836	16,527	2,700 [1]	—	—	135	153	175
New Mexico	5,418	916	16,282	1,296	4,793	7,262	510	1,112	2,353	30	32	44
New York	193,663	271,233	451,830	75,717	173,432	247,110	17,110	178,111	253,687	747	802	871
North Carolina	2,603	21,833	—	2,177	8,506	13,314	2,553	6,612	12,702	53	54	88
North Dakota	—	—	—	—	—	1,079	193	200	792	8	5	14
Ohio	6,915	14,655	21,023	11,099	38,147	56,784	17,256	42,382	62,832	163	165	184
Oklahoma	5,147	—	—	768	—	6,246	1,890	3,813	5,742	22	37	46
Oregon	8,449	11,822	26,881	2,075	9,865	16,096	3,644	7,966	14,805	57	70	81
Pennsylvania	23,923	54,176	88,708	9,766	33,518	49,979	13,538	32,095	57,836	359	434	546
Rhode Island	927	3,604	—	843	2,523	—	1,060	2,408	3,465	37	37	48
South Carolina	145	—	—	348	1,892	4,041	1,049	2,930	4,214	20	21	29
South Dakota	—	163	—	31	—	—	277	1,100	1,607	8	11	14
Tennessee	3,728	7,974	—	2,090	10,480	15,413	2,221	6,181	15,591	62	50	90
Texas	18,307	—	—	13,019	33,469	58,749	8,366	32,206	50,912	150	207	284
Utah	3,052	3,567	4,138	2,361	5,705	7,592	713	—	—	20	18	25
Vermont	736	—	1,281	230	753	1,271	915	2,554	4,176	52	62	84
Virginia	8,378	—	61,022	1,882	9,353	15,347	8,209	42,697	51,887	64	93	150
Washington	8,348	36,039	65,674	4,583	16,094	25,576	2,075	7,197	14,296	59	96	152
West Virginia	—	—	—	478	784	2,305	254	703	1,329	37	26	40
Wisconsin	1,854	4,651	4,427	3,261	10,595	19,515	1,938	8,704	15,563	48	81	93
Wyoming	103	—	—	—	—	—	—	—	2,726	7	14	21

[1] Noncommercial only.

Source

U.S.Bureau of the Census, *Census of Service Industries* (1977, 1987, and 1992).

Documentation

Only institutions that had a paid workforce were included in these censuses.

The series correspond to the following Standard Industrial Classification (SIC) codes. See the Introduction to Part D for a discussion of SIC codes. Series Bg130: SIC 80. Series Bg131–132: SIC 8011 (part), 8021 (part), 805, 806, 808, 809. Series Bg133–135: SIC 805. Series Bg136–137: SIC 81. Series Bg138: SIC 8111 (part). Series Bg139 and Bg141: SIC 83. Series Bg142–144: SIC 835. Series Bg145: SIC 86, except 866. Series Bg146–147: SIC 861, 862, 864, 869. Series Bg148–150: SIC 861. Series Bg151–153: SIC 864. Series Bg154: SIC 892. Series Bg155–156: SIC 8733. Series Bg157–159: SIC 792. Series Bg160: SIC 84, 7999 (part). Series Bg161–162: SIC 84. Series Bg163–165: SIC 823, 824, and 829.

TABLE Bg166–175 Private and nonprofit elementary, secondary, and higher education – schools, enrollment, and personal consumption expenditures: 1800–1999

Contributed by Colin B. Burke

	Enrollment				Private schools			Private two-year and four-year colleges		
	Private schools									
	Elementary	Secondary	Higher education	Liberal arts colleges	Elementary	Secondary	Private liberal arts/general purpose colleges and universities	Excluding branch campuses	Including branch campuses	Personal consumption expenditures on private education and research
	Bg166 [1]	Bg167 [2]	Bg168 [3]	Bg169	Bg170 [4]	Bg171 [4]	Bg172 [5]	Bg173	Bg174 [6]	Bg175
Year	Thousand	Thousand	Thousand	Number	Number	Number	Number	Number	Number	Million dollars
1800	—	—	—	1,156	—	—	30	—	—	—
1810	—	—	—	1,939	—	—	34	—	—	—
1820	—	—	—	2,566	—	—	51	—	—	—
1830	—	—	—	4,947	—	—	99	—	—	—
1840	—	—	—	8,328	—	—	132	—	—	—
1850	—	—	—	9,931	—	—	204	—	—	—
1860	—	—	—	16,600	—	—	—	—	—	—
1870	—	—	—	23,000	—	—	327	—	—	—
1880	—	—	—	33,000	—	—	377	—	—	—
1889	1,516	95 [12]	—	44,000	—	—	—	—	—	—
1890	—	—	—	—	—	—	430	—	—	—
1899	1,241	111 [13]	—	—	—	—	—	—	—	—
1900	—	—	—	82,000	—	—	422	—	—	—
1909	1,441 [7]	117 [14]	—	—	—	—	—	—	—	—
1919	1,486 [8]	214	—	—	—	—	—	—	—	—
1929	2,310	341 [15]	—	—	—	—	—	—	—	800
1930	—	—	—	—	9,275	3,258	—	—	—	800
1931	—	—	—	—	—	—	—	—	—	800
1932	—	—	—	—	9,734	3,289	—	—	—	700
1933	—	—	—	—	—	—	—	—	—	500
1934	—	—	—	—	9,992	3,327	—	—	—	600
1935	—	—	—	—	—	—	—	—	—	600
1936	—	—	—	—	9,992	3,327	—	—	—	600
1937	—	—	—	—	—	—	—	—	—	700
1938	—	—	—	—	9,992	3,327	—	—	—	700
1939	2,153	458	698 [16]	—	—	—	—	—	—	700
1940	—	—	—	—	—	—	—	1,105	—	700
1941	—	—	—	—	—	—	—	—	—	800
1942	—	—	—	—	10,285	3,011	—	—	—	900
1943	—	—	—	—	—	—	—	—	—	1,100
1944	—	—	—	—	10,285	3,011	—	—	—	1,100
1945	—	—	—	—	—	—	—	—	—	1,100
1946	—	—	—	—	9,863	3,294	—	—	—	1,200
1947	—	—	—	—	—	—	—	—	—	1,500
1948	—	—	—	—	10,071	3,292	—	—	—	1,700
1949	2,708 [9]	672 [9]	1,304 [9]	—	—	—	—	—	—	1,800
1950	—	—	—	—	10,375	3,331	—	1,210	—	1,900
1951	—	—	—	—	—	—	—	1,216	—	2,100
1952	—	—	—	—	10,666	3,322	—	1,191	—	2,200
1953	—	—	—	—	—	—	—	1,243	—	2,400
1954	—	—	—	—	11,739	3,913	—	1,201	—	2,500
1955	—	—	—	—	—	—	—	1,201	—	2,800
1956	—	—	—	—	12,372	3,887	—	1,200	—	3,100
1957	—	—	—	—	—	—	—	1,222	—	3,400
1958	—	—	—	—	13,065	3,994	—	1,264	—	3,700
1959	4,640 [10]	1,035	1,459 [10]	—	—	—	—	1,274	—	4,000
1960	—	—	—	—	13,574	4,061	—	1,309	—	4,300
1961	—	—	—	—	—	—	—	1,321	—	4,700
1962	—	—	—	—	14,762	4,129	—	1,315	—	5,100
1963	—	—	—	—	—	—	—	1,353	—	5,500
1964	5,000 [11]	1,300 [10]	1,812 [10]	—	—	4,451	—	1,372	—	6,100
1965	4,900	1,400	1,951	—	—	—	—	1,376	—	6,900
1966	4,800	1,400	2,041	—	15,340	4,606	—	1,409	—	7,800
1967	4,600	1,400	2,096	—	—	—	—	1,449	—	8,700
1968	4,400	1,400	2,082	—	14,900	4,300	—	1,440	—	9,900
1969	4,200	1,300	2,108	—	—	—	—	1,472	—	11,100

Notes appear at end of table

(continued)

TABLE Bg166–175 Private and nonprofit elementary, secondary, and higher education – schools, enrollment, and personal consumption expenditures: 1800–1999 *Continued*

	Enrollment				Private schools			Private two-year and four-year colleges		
	Private schools									
	Elementary	Secondary	Higher education	Liberal arts colleges	Elementary	Secondary	Private liberal arts/general purpose colleges and universities	Excluding branch campuses	Including branch campuses	Personal consumption expenditures on private education and research
	Bg166 [1]	Bg167 [2]	Bg168 [3]	Bg169	Bg170 [4]	Bg171 [4]	Bg172 [5]	Bg173	Bg174 [6]	Bg175
Year	Thousand	Thousand	Thousand	Number	Number	Number	Number	Number	Number	Million dollars
1970	4,025	1,311	2,153	—	14,372 [17]	3,770 [17]	—	1,465	—	12,500
1971	3,900	1,300	2,144	—	—	—	—	1,467	—	13,700
1972	3,700	1,300	2,144	—	—	—	—	1,469	—	15,100
1973	3,700	1,300	2,183	—	—	—	—	1,483	—	16,600
1974	3,700	1,300	2,235	—	—	—	—	1,520	—	18,300
1975	3,700	1,300	2,350	—	—	—	—	1,533	1,571	20,500
1976	3,825	1,342	2,359	—	—	—	—	1,546	1,584	22,400
1977	3,797	1,343	2,439	—	—	—	—	1,554	1,591	24,000
1978	3,732	1,353	2,474	—	16,400	5,900	—	1,585	1,622	26,600
1979	3,700	1,300	2,533	—	16,100	5,800	—	1,646	1,660	29,600
1980	3,992	1,339	2,640	—	—	—	—	1,665	1,677	33,300
1981	4,100	1,400	2,725	—	16,792	5,678	—	1,722 [18]	1,734 [18]	37,500
1982	4,200	1,400	2,730	—	—	—	—	1,743 [18]	1,755 [18]	41,200
1983	4,315	1,400	2,782	—	—	7,862	—	1,775 [18]	1,787 [18]	45,000
1984	4,300	1,400	2,765	—	20,872	—	—	1,792	1,803	48,700
1985	4,195	1,362	2,768	—	—	7,387	—	1,817	1,830	52,900
1986	4,116	1,336	2,790	—	20,252	—	—	1,829	1,842	56,900
1987	4,232	1,247	2,793	—	—	8,418	—	—	1,873	61,400
1988	4,036	1,206	2,894	—	22,959	—	—	—	1,996	68,200
1989	4,162	1,193	2,961	—	—	—	—	—	1,963	75,400
1990	4,095	1,137	2,974	—	—	8,989	—	—	1,972	80,700
1991	4,074	1,125	3,049	—	22,223	9,282	—	—	1,992	86,100
1992	4,212	1,163	3,102	—	23,523	—	—	—	2,003	93,100
1993	4,280	1,191	3,117	—	23,543	10,555	—	—	2,014	98,500
1994	4,360	1,236	3,097	—	—	—	—	—	2,007	104,700
1995	4,431	1,269	3,128	—	—	—	—	—	2,047	—
1996	4,493	1,304	3,151	—	—	—	—	—	2,051	—
1997	4,547	1,329	3,240	—	—	—	—	—	—	—
1998	4,587	1,346	3,261	—	—	—	—	—	—	—
1999	4,610	1,367	3,297	—	—	—	—	—	—	—

1 For 1994, preliminary; for 1995, estimated; for 1996–1999, projected.

2 For 1959–1973, estimated; for 1994–1999, projected.

3 For 1994, preliminary; for 1995–1999, projected.

4 Partly estimated.

5 For 1800–1860, the figures are for colleges active in the decade. For 1870–1900, the figures are for the year reported.

6 Because of revised survey procedures, data beginning in 1987 are not entirely comparable with figures for earlier years. The number of branch campuses reporting separately has increased since 1986–1987.

7 1900–1910.

8 1919–1920.

9 1949–1950.

10 Fall.

11 Fall, estimated.

12 1889–1890.

13 1899–1900.

14 1909–1910.

15 1929–1930.

16 1939–1940.

17 1970–1971.

18 Large increases are due to the addition of schools accredited by the Accrediting Commission of Career Schools and Colleges of Technology.

Sources

Series Bg166–168, Bg170–171, and Bg173–174. U.S. National Center for Educational Statistics, *Digest of Education Statistics* (especially the 1997 edition).

Series Bg169. Colin B. Burke, *American Collegiate Populations: A Test of the Traditional View* (New York University Press, 1982), p. 216.

Series Bg172. Burke (1982), p. 17; *Report of the United States Commissioner of Education* (various years) for lists of male or coeducational colleges and universities.

Series Bg175. U.S. Bureau of Economic Analysis, *National Income and Product Accounts of the United States* (1998), Tables 2.4.

Documentation

Nationwide statistics on education have been collected and published primarily by the U.S. Office of Education and the U.S. Bureau of the Census. Coverage before the Civil War was weak, especially for secondary and higher education. The later nineteenth century also suffered from relative inattention. Only in the last generation have scholars turned to the construction of series for the nineteenth century.

Data on education have also been collected and published by other federal, state, and local governmental agencies, and by independent research organizations. The Office of Education generally obtained data from reports of state and local school systems and institutions of higher learning. These data relate to school enrollment and attendance, graduates, instructional staff, curricula, school district organization, receipts, and expenditures for elementary and secondary schools, and enrollment, faculty, degrees conferred, income, expenditures, property, and plant-fund operations for institutions of higher education.

The Office of Education issued statistical reports on elementary and secondary education in the *Biennial Survey of Education in the United States*. Chapter 1, "Statistical Summary of Education," and Chapter 2, "Statistics of

TABLE Bg166–175 Private and nonprofit elementary, secondary, and higher education – schools, enrollment, and personal consumption expenditures: 1800–1999 *Continued*

State School Systems," are primary sources for some series since 1870. For 1870–1917, statistics were included as part of the *Annual Report of the United States Commissioner of Education*. For 1918–1958, a report had been issued for each even-numbered school year under the title "derived measures relating to education." Beginning with 1941 and ending with 1951, Chapter 2 was supplemented by an abridged report issued as a circular for each odd-numbered school year. Data from the odd-year biennial circulars have not been included in the present compilation. Biennial survey data are based on report forms completed by state departments of education (a copy of the report form appears in the *Biennial Survey* of 1952–1954). Beginning with the *Biennial Survey* of 1952–1954, these forms have been completed by education officials in accordance with detailed instructions contained in the Office of Education's "Handbook I, the Common Core of State Educational Information." Prior to that date, the forms were completed in accordance with various circulars of information distributed by the Office of Education.

Since 1962, the annual publication *Digest of Education Statistics* has provided an abstract of statistical information covering the broad field of American education from kindergarten through graduate school. The *Digest* utilizes materials from numerous sources, including the statistical surveys and estimates of the Office of Education and other appropriate agencies, both governmental and nongovernmental. It is divided into five chapters: (1) all levels of education, (2) elementary and secondary education, (3) higher education, (4) federal programs of education, and (5) selected statistics related to education in the United States. One of the major factors in presenting accurate statistical data on a national basis is the uniformity with which all recording units use standard terms, definitions, and procedures. Prior to 1909, this was controlled only by definitions on the questionnaires requesting information. Since 1909, the Office of Education, in cooperation with other national and state organizations, has improved uniform recording and reporting by means of national committees, publications, and national and regional conferences.

A major problem in the collection and processing of comprehensive nationwide school statistics is that of getting all schools to respond within reasonable time limits. The school authorities are not compelled to report to the Office of Education. There is some evidence that the proportion of schools reporting has increased over the years. This increase is most evident in the data for secondary schools. Prior to 1930, a complete list of public secondary day schools had not been compiled, and consequently there is no way to measure the degree of response in the earlier years. In 1930, there were 23,930 public secondary day schools on file, and reports were received from 22,237. In 1938, the number of schools on file increased to 25,308, and the number reporting was 25,091. In 1952, there were 23,757 schools, and replies were received from all but 12 schools. The data for the missing schools were estimated, and the published totals for 1952 cover all public secondary day schools.

Since 1870, there have been both major and minor changes in the collection patterns and in the administration of the program. Some patterns lasted for many years. With voluntary response and no field service (until 1924), response rates varied in their completeness for both reporting in general and for specific items. The completeness of the coverage is not always made evident in the publication. Field service supplemented returns by mail for the 1923–1924 biennial chapters. Visits were made to state departments of education and to colleges and universities in order to complete the coverage from basic or secondary records that were available in the state departments of education or at individual schools and institutions. The introduction of sampling in recent years has also ensured adequate coverage. The data in these historical tables will not always agree with similar data in the publications cited as sources for a specific year because tabulations were "kept open" for many years, and as data came in, they were added and reflected in future historical tables.

Series Bg168. See the text for series Bg173–174 for the definition of higher education.

Series Bg169. For 1800–1860, "college" was defined as an institution with a college charter that operated a college-level program. For 1870–1900, colleges were chartered male or coeducational institutions that had a liberal or general curriculum. For the post-Civil War era, see the lists in the reports of the Commissioner of Education. Caution should be exercised when using those reports. Preliminary analysis suggests that the commissioner's staff was unable to keep the files up to date.

Series Bg172. Excludes women's colleges. The number of government-controlled colleges (state colleges and universities) in operation at any time during a decade was as follows: 1800–1810, 2; 1810–1820, 4; 1820–1830, 8; 1830–1840, 6; 1840–1850, 10; 1850–1860, 14; 1870, 23; 1880, 33; 1890, 48; 1900, 48. Also see the text for series Bg169.

Series Bg173–174. The *Digest of Education Statistics* defined institutions of higher education as "including those colleges designated as institutions of higher education by the Higher Education General Information Survey system, even if they have a less than 2-year program, and includes branch campuses. Beginning in 1980, total includes some schools accredited by the Accrediting Commission of Career Schools and Colleges of Technology" (1995, p. 14). Series Bg174 uses a different definition of higher educational institutions than does series Bg173, and it includes branch campuses.

Series Bg175. "For private institutions, equals current expenditures (including consumption of fixed capital) less receipts – such as those from meals, rooms, and entertainments – accounted for separately in consumer expenditures, and less expenditures for research and development funded under contracts and grants. For government institutions, equals student payment of tuition" (*National Income and Product Accounts*, 1998, p. 108). Although the institutions involved are a mixture of public and private entities, the series seems to reflect private investments in education and thus serves as an indicator for nongovernmental spending on education. Detailed estimates by the U.S. Department of Commerce of consumer expenditures for commodities and services since 1929 were first published in the *Survey of Current Business* (June 1944). The figures on personal consumption expenditures for commodities were first calculated by the "commodity flow methods" developed by Simon Kuznets, "Commodity Flow and Capital Formation," National Bureau of Economic Research (1938). Estimates of personal consumption expenditures for services are based on a variety of source materials that cannot be summarized briefly. For further detail, see *National Income and Product Accounts*, 1954 and 1992 editions. As defined by the Department of Commerce, personal consumption expenditures represent the market value of purchases of goods and services by individuals and nonprofit institutions and the value of food, clothing, housing, and financial services received by them as income in kind. Rental value of owner-occupied houses is included; purchases of dwellings, which are classified as capital goods, are excluded.

TABLE Bg176–187 Private and nonprofit elementary, secondary, and higher education – expenditures, employment, and receipts, by source and type of institution: 1948–1995

Contributed by Colin B. Burke

	Private elementary and secondary schools		Nonprofit education and research							Nonprofit employment		
			Receipts					Expenditures				
	Receipts	Expenditures	Total	Private contributions	Charges, fees, dues, etc.	Other nongovernment	Government	Operating expenditures	Construction and capital improvements	Colleges and universities	Select educational services	Elementary and secondary schools
	Bg176	Bg177 [1]	Bg178	Bg179	Bg180	Bg181	Bg182	Bg183	Bg184	Bg185	Bg186	Bg187
Year	Million dollars	Million dollars	Billion dollars	Billion dollars	Billion dollars	Billion dollars	Billion dollars	Billion dollars	Billion dollars	Thousand	Thousand	Thousand
1948	530	—	—	—	—	—	—	—	—	—	—	—
1949	—	411	—	—	—	—	—	—	—	—	—	—
1950	783	—	—	—	—	—	—	—	—	—	—	—
1951	—	517	—	—	—	—	—	—	—	—	—	—
1952	1,028	—	—	—	—	—	—	—	—	—	—	—
1953	—	641	—	—	—	—	—	—	—	—	—	—
1954	1,354	—	—	—	—	—	—	—	—	—	—	—
1955	—	772	—	—	—	—	—	—	—	—	—	—
1956	1,627	—	—	—	—	—	—	—	—	—	—	—
1957	—	956	—	—	—	—	—	—	—	—	—	—
1958	2,079	—	—	—	—	—	—	—	—	—	—	—
1959	—	1,100	—	—	—	—	—	—	—	—	—	—
1960	2,412	—	—	—	—	—	—	—	—	—	—	—
1961	—	1,300	—	—	—	—	—	—	—	—	—	—
1962	2,457	—	—	—	—	—	—	—	—	—	—	—
1963	—	1,500	—	—	—	—	—	—	—	—	—	—
1964	3,070	—	—	—	—	—	—	—	—	—	—	—
1965	—	1,800	—	—	—	—	—	—	—	—	—	—
1966	3,600	—	—	—	—	—	—	—	—	—	—	—
1967	—	2,100	—	—	—	—	—	—	—	—	—	—
1968	4,200	—	—	—	—	—	—	—	—	—	—	—
1969	—	2,500	—	—	—	—	—	—	—	—	—	—
1970	4,500	2,700	—	—	—	—	—	—	—	—	—	—
1971	—	2,900	—	—	—	—	—	—	—	—	—	—
1972	—	3,100	—	—	—	—	—	—	—	637.0	47.0	435.0
1973	—	3,400	—	—	—	—	—	—	—	—	—	—
1974	—	4,000	20.9	—	14.6	—	2.6 [3]	18.0	—	653.0	49.0	443.0
1975	—	4,500	—	—	—	—	—	—	—	—	—	—
1976	—	5,000	—	—	—	—	—	—	—	—	—	—
1977	—	5,700	27.4	2.4	14.5	5.5	4.4	23.7	2.1	702.6	49.4	427.7
1978	—	6,300	—	—	—	—	—	—	—	—	—	—
1979	—	7,200	—	—	—	—	—	—	—	—	—	—
1980	—	8,200	37.6	—	19.5	—	6.0	31.0	3.0	727.0	52.0	495.0
1981	—	9,300	—	—	—	—	—	—	—	749.0	52.0	506.0
1982	—	10,300	47.7	4.0	25.3	10.3	8.1	40.5	3.8	753.2	53.5	527.9
1983	—	11,500	52.1	—	27.8	—	—	44.7	3.9	767.6	53.2	537.7
1984	—	12,400	57.1	—	30.5	—	—	48.7	4.2	770.2	54.7	547.7
1985	—	13,200	—	—	—	—	—	—	—	—	—	—
1986	—	14,300	—	—	—	—	—	—	—	—	—	—
1987	—	15,300	70.0	9.1	38.7	9.1	12.8	62.3	4.9	907.8	68.2	565.5
1988	—	16,400	—	—	—	—	—	—	—	974.3	68.2	608.1
1989	—	18,200	85.4	—	46.4	—	14.7	76.9	4.9	1,003.9	68.2	648.3
1990	—	19,500	—	—	—	—	—	—	—	988.1	68.2	657.0
1991	—	20,200	—	—	—	—	—	—	—	—	—	—
1992	—	21,500	94.5	12.0	53.8	9.8	18.9	84.5	6.4	1,000.3	63.0	674.0
1993	—	22,200	—	—	—	—	—	—	—	—	—	—
1994	—	23,500	—	—	—	—	—	—	—	1,064.5	64.9	744.0
1995	—	24,800 [2]	—	—	—	—	—	—	—	—	—	—

[1] For "term" years, for example, 1949–1950.

[2] Estimated.

[3] Data in original source are in error and cannot be corrected.

Sources

Series Bg176. Based on data from the U.S. Office of Education: for 1930–1958, *Biennial Survey of Education in the United States* (various years), and for 1960–1970, *Digest of Education Statistics* and *Projections of Educational Statistics* (annual issues, 1962–1974). Included as series H509 in *Historical Statistics of the United States* (1975).

Series Bg177. U.S. National Center for Educational Statistics, *Digest of Education Statistics* (1995 and annual editions), Table 31.

TABLE Bg176–187 Private and nonprofit elementary, secondary, and higher education – expenditures, employment, and receipts, by source and type of institution: 1948–1995 *Continued*

Series Bg178–187. Virginia Ann Hodgkinson, Murray S. Weitzman, et al., *The Nonprofit Almanac, 1996–1997: Dimensions of the Independent Sector* (Jossey-Bass, 1997), Tables 4.2 and 5.6, and subsequent editions titled *The New Nonprofit Almanac*.

Documentation

For a description of the data underlying the estimates provided in the publications of the Independent Sector and for the limitations of the Internal Revenue Services data on nonprofit educational institutions, see Hodgkinson, Weitzman, et al. (1996), pp. xxv–xxvii and 216–17.

Note that most of the series included in this table use the Standard Industrial Classification (SIC) codes, rather than the newer concepts and classifications of the National Taxonomy of Exempt Entities (NTEE), which seem better suited to the study of the nonprofit world. The NTEE classifications could not be employed because the SIC categories were the ones used to generate the original series. See the introduction to Part D for a discussion of SIC codes. On NTEE, see Hodgkinson, Weitzman, et al. (1996), pp. 271–309. The SIC codes relevant to specific series are as follows: series Bg178–183: SIC 82,873, 892e; series Bg184: SIC 873, 892e; series Bg185–186: SIC 822; series Bg187: SIC 821.

Series Bg177. Estimated by the *Digest of Education Statistics* staff.

Series Bg179 and Bg181. Data incompatible with series in earlier editions of *Historical Statistics*.

TABLE Bg188–193 College foundings and failures in the United States, and active and failed nonproprietary entities in New Haven: 1800–1991

Contributed by Colin B. Burke

	Liberal arts colleges		Failures of two- and four-year colleges		Nonproprietary entities in New Haven, Connecticut	
	Founded	Failed	Private	Public	Active	"Died" during previous 20 years
	Bg188	Bg189	Bg190	Bg191	Bg192	Bg193
Period	Number	Number	Number	Number	Number	Number
1800–1809	12	1	—	—	—	—
1810–1819	8	1	—	—	—	—
1820–1829	23	4	—	—	—	—
1830–1839	56	6	—	—	—	—
1840–1849	42	13	—	—	—	—
1850–1859	88	15	—	—	—	—
1870	—	—	—	—	130	—
1899	—	—	—	—	—	85
1900	—	—	—	—	460	—
1929	—	—	—	—	—	256
1930	—	—	—	—	676	—
1959	—	—	—	—	—	427
1960	—	—	7	1 [2]	427	—
1961	—	—	2	0	—	—
1962	—	—	0	0	—	—
1963	—	—	6	1	—	—
1964	—	—	4	4	—	—
1965	—	—	4	4	—	—
1966	—	—	6	3	—	—
1967	—	—	14	0	—	—
1968	—	—	20	1	—	—
1969	—	—	15	3	—	—
1970	—	—	23	9	—	—
1971	—	—	9	3	—	—
1972	—	—	17	2	—	—
1973	—	—	18	0	—	—
1974	—	—	14	3	—	—
1975	—	—	6	2	—	—
1976	—	—	8	0	—	—
1977	—	—	12	0	—	—
1978	—	—	9	0	—	—
1979	—	—	6	0	—	—
1980	—	—	4	0	—	—
1981	—	—	7	0	—	—
1982	—	—	7	0	—	—
1983	—	—	4	0	—	—
1984	—	—	4	0	—	—
1985	—	—	9	1	—	—
1986	—	—	24 [1]	1	—	—
1988	—	—	14	8	—	—
1989	—	—	12	6	630	310
1990	—	—	10	6	—	—
1991	—	—	10	3	—	—

[1] For 1986–1987 and 1987–1988.

[2] For 1960–1961.

Sources

Series Bg188–189, Colin B. Burke, *American Collegiate Populations: A Test of the Traditional View* (New York University Press, 1982), pp. 17–18; series Bg190–191, U.S. National Center for Educational Statistics, *Digest of Education Statistics* (U.S. Government Printing Office, 1996), Table 238; series Bg192–193, unpublished data supplied by Peter Dobkin Hall.

Documentation

The original sources used different terms for what were, essentially, college failures. Except where noted, the data are for the year in which the institution failed.

Series Bg188–189. For the comparative base of all colleges operating in the era, see Table Bg166–175.

Series Bg190–191. Excludes branch campuses.

Series Bg192–193. Nonproprietary entities are defined as all organizations and associations not established for the personal benefit of their principals, a definition which allows the inclusion of all the institutions typically referred to by terms such as voluntary, membership, and nonprofit organizations.

TABLE Bg194–206 Liberal arts college enrollment rates and private liberal arts colleges, by state and region: 1800–1860

Contributed by Colin B. Burke

	Private liberal arts colleges in operation						Liberal arts college enrollment as a percentage of white male population, ages 15–20						
	1800–1809	1810–1819	1820–1829	1830–1839	1840–1849	1850–1859	1800	1810	1820	1830	1840	1850	1860
	Bg194	Bg195	Bg196	Bg197	Bg198	Bg199	Bg200	Bg201	Bg202	Bg203	Bg204	Bg205	Bg206
State/region	Number	Number	Number	Number	Number	Number	Percent	Percent	Percent	Percent	Percent	Percent	Percent
Maine	1	1	2	2	2	2	0.00	0.20	0.10	0.20	0.40	0.30	0.40
New Hampshire	1	1	1	1	1	1	1.20	2.80	1.30	0.90	1.80	1.10	1.80
Vermont	2	2	2	3	3	3	1.10	1.60	1.70	0.80	1.70	1.20	1.50
Massachusetts	2	2	3	3	4	5	1.40	1.70	1.40	1.60	1.50	1.40	1.80
Rhode Island	1	1	1	1	1	1	1.00	3.30	3.80	2.00	3.20	2.10	2.30
Connecticut	1	1	2	3	3	3	1.70	2.00	2.70	2.80	3.70	3.10	3.30
New York	2	3	4	6	9	13	—	—	—	—	—	—	0.82
New Jersey	2	2	2	2	3	3	—	—	—	—	—	—	1.67
Pennsylvania	4	5	7	13	13	16	—	—	—	—	—	—	0.90
Ohio	—	1	5	10	16	24	—	—	—	—	—	—	1.12
Indiana	—	1	1	4	6	9	—	—	—	—	—	—	0.75
Illinois	—	—	—	4	6	13	—	—	—	—	—	—	0.54
Michigan	—	—	—	1	3	3	—	—	—	—	—	—	0.87
Wisconsin	—	—	—	—	1	4	—	—	—	—	—	—	0.81
Minnesota	—	—	—	—	—	1	—	—	—	—	—	—	0.56
Iowa	—	—	—	—	1	9	—	—	—	—	—	—	0.69
Missouri	—	—	—	6	8	10	—	—	—	—	—	—	1.09
Kansas	—	—	—	—	—	0	—	—	—	—	—	—	—
Delaware	0	0	0	1	1	1	—	—	—	—	—	—	1.44
Maryland	2	2	2	4	5	8	—	—	—	—	—	—	0.79
District of Columbia	1	1	2	2	2	3	—	—	—	—	—	—	5.86
Virginia	3	3	3	6	8	10	—	—	—	—	—	—	2.03
North Carolina	0	0	0	2	2	3	—	—	—	—	—	—	2.02
South Carolina	2	2	2	2	2	4	—	—	—	—	—	—	3.11
Georgia	0	0	0	3	4	3	—	—	—	—	—	—	1.53
Florida	—	—	—	—	0	0	—	—	—	—	—	—	0.00
Kentucky	3	3	5	8	9	8	—	—	—	—	—	—	1.15
Tennessee	1	1	3	5	9	15	—	—	—	—	—	—	1.98
Alabama	—	—	—	1	3	5	—	—	—	—	—	—	1.38
Mississippi	—	1	1	4	4	6	—	—	—	—	—	—	1.80
Arkansas	—	—	0	0	0	0	—	—	—	—	—	—	0.00
Louisiana	1	0	1	2	4	8	—	—	—	—	—	—	0.80
Texas	—	—	—	—	1	5	—	—	—	—	—	—	0.27
Oregon	—	—	—	—	—	2	—	—	—	—	—	—	—
California	—	—	—	—	—	3	—	—	—	—	—	—	—
New England	—	—	—	—	—	—	1.22	1.79	1.51	1.29	1.68	1.28	1.67
Mid-Atlantic	—	—	—	—	—	—	0.72	0.64	0.59	0.58	0.79	0.78	0.93
South Atlantic	—	—	—	—	—	—	0.38	0.71	0.64	0.63	1.11	1.28	1.90
Southwest	—	—	—	—	—	—	—	—	—	0.91	1.52	1.20	1.21
Midwest	—	—	—	—	—	—	—	—	—	0.38	0.60	0.59	0.94

Source

Colin B. Burke, *American Collegiate Populations: A Test of the Traditional View* (New York University Press, 1982), Table 1.2, Tables 2.1–2.25, Appendix A, and passim.

Documentation

Series Bg194–199. Includes nonstate colleges and universities that had charters and operated a college-level program. The numbers of state liberal arts/general purpose universities in operation during the period were as follows: Alabama, 1830–1860, 1; Delaware, 1850, 1; Georgia, 1810–1860, 1; Indiana, 1820, 2, 1830–1860, 1; Louisiana, 1820–1830, 1, 1850–1860, 1; Maryland, 1850–1860, 1; Michigan, 1850–1860, 1; Mississippi, 1840–1860, 1; Missouri, 1840–1860, 1; North Carolina, 1800–1860, 1; Ohio, 1820–1860, 1; South Carolina, 1800–1860, 1; Virginia, 1820–1860, 1; Wisconsin, 1850–1860, 1.

Series Bg200–206. Includes students enrolled in private and public (state) liberal arts/general purpose colleges and universities. The enrollments include students whose homes were not in the state in which their college was located. The figures in the series are the result of dividing the number of students enrolled in college in a state by the number of white males, ages 15–20, resident in the college's state. The percentage of students enrolled in public (state) colleges and universities nationwide was as follows: 1800s, 1 percent; 1810s, 11 percent; 1820s, 8 percent; 1830s, 7 percent; 1840s, 7 percent; 1850s, 13 percent.

States and regions not listed in the table had no data.

TABLE Bg207–219 Higher education expenditures, endowment income, receipts, and voluntary support, by source: 1919–1995[1]

Contributed by Colin B. Burke

	Private higher education			All higher education									
	Receipts			Voluntary support									
	Total	Nongovernment sources	Expenditures	Total	Private gifts and grants	Alumni	Nonalumni	Foundations	Corporations	Religious organizations	Other sources	Endowment income	Earnings from endowments
	Bg207 [2]	Bg208 [2]	Bg209	Bg210	Bg211	Bg212	Bg213	Bg214	Bg215	Bg216	Bg217	Bg218 [3]	Bg219
Year	Million dollars	Million dollars	Million dollars	Million dollars	Thousand dollars	Million dollars	Million dollars	Million dollars	Million dollars	Million dollars	Million dollars	Million dollars	Thousand dollars
1919	—	—	—	—	7,584	—	—	—	—	—	—	—	26,482
1929	—	—	341	—	26,172	—	—	—	—	—	—	87	68,605
1930	—	—	—	—	—	—	—	—	—	—	—	83	—
1931	—	—	—	—	—	—	—	—	—	—	—	79	—
1932	—	—	—	—	—	—	—	—	—	—	—	70	—
1933	—	—	—	—	—	—	—	—	—	—	—	70	—
1934	—	—	—	—	—	—	—	—	—	—	—	75	—
1935	—	—	—	—	—	—	—	—	—	—	—	80	—
1936	—	—	—	—	—	—	—	—	—	—	—	85	—
1937	—	—	—	—	—	—	—	—	—	—	—	90	—
1938	—	—	—	—	—	—	—	—	—	—	—	90	—
1939	—	—	367	—	40,453	—	—	—	—	—	—	90	71,304
1940	—	—	—	—	—	—	—	—	—	—	—	92	—
1941	—	—	—	—	—	—	—	—	—	—	—	94	—
1942	—	—	—	—	—	—	—	—	—	—	—	95	—
1943	—	—	—	—	—	—	—	—	—	—	—	95	—
1944	—	—	—	—	—	—	—	—	—	—	—	105	—
1945	—	—	—	—	—	—	—	—	—	—	—	114	—
1946	—	—	—	—	—	—	—	—	—	—	—	112	—
1947	—	—	—	—	—	—	—	—	—	—	—	110	—
1948	727	434	—	—	—	—	—	—	—	—	—	116	—
1949	—	—	1,233	240	118,627	60	60	60	28	19	16	122	96,341
1950	854	547	—	—	—	—	—	—	—	—	—	113	—
1951	—	—	1,309	—	—	—	—	—	—	—	—	117	—
1952	1,372	1,098	—	—	—	—	—	—	—	—	—	138	—
1953	—	—	1,502	—	—	—	—	—	—	—	—	146	—
1954	1,512	1,282	—	—	—	—	—	—	—	—	—	157	—
1955	—	—	1,832	—	—	—	—	—	—	—	—	172	—
1956	2,127	1,861	—	—	—	—	—	—	—	—	—	189	—
1957	—	—	2,293	—	—	—	—	—	—	—	—	218	—
1958	2,551	2,189	—	—	—	—	—	—	—	—	—	231	—
1959	—	—	3,244	815	382,569	—	194	163	130	80	57	257	206,619
1960	3,295	2,731	—	—	—	191	—	—	—	—	—	303	—
1961	—	—	3,911	—	—	—	—	—	—	—	—	321	—
1962	4,201	3,335	—	—	—	—	—	—	—	—	—	345	—
1963	—	—	5,057	—	—	—	—	—	—	—	—	374	—
1964	5,398	4,039	—	—	—	—	—	—	—	—	—	408	—

Notes appear at end of table

(continued)

TABLE Bg207–219 Higher education expenditures, endowment income, receipts, and voluntary support, by source: 1919–1995 *Continued*

	Private higher education			All higher education									
	Receipts			Voluntary support									
	Total	Nongovernment sources	Expenditures	Total	Private gifts and grants	Alumni	Nonalumni	Foundations	Corporations	Religious organizations	Other sources	Endowment income	Earnings from endowments
	Bg207 [2]	Bg208 [2]	Bg209	Bg210	Bg211	Bg212	Bg213	Bg214	Bg215	Bg216	Bg217	Bg218 [3]	Bg219
Year	Million dollars	Million dollars	Million dollars	Million dollars	Thousand dollars	Million dollars	Million dollars	Million dollars	Million dollars	Million dollars	Million dollars	Million dollars	Thousand dollars
1965	—	—	6,588	1,440	—	310	350	357	230	105	85	445	—
1966	6,944	5,022	—	—	—	—	—	—	—	—	—	485	—
1967	—	—	7,824	—	—	—	—	—	—	—	—	527	—
1968	8,335	6,364	—	—	—	—	—	—	—	—	—	580	—
1969	—	—	9,041	—	1,129,438	—	—	—	—	—	—	633	516,038
1970	9,498	7,443	9,513	1,860	—	458	495	418	259	104	126	668	—
1971	—	—	10,184	—	—	—	—	—	—	—	—	—	—
1972	—	—	10,779	—	—	—	—	—	—	—	—	—	—
1973	—	—	11,484	—	—	—	—	—	—	—	—	—	—
1974	—	—	12,852	—	—	—	—	—	—	—	—	—	—
1975	—	—	13,869	2,410	1,917,036	588	569	549	379	130	195	—	687,470
1976	—	—	15,226	—	2,105,070	—	—	—	—	—	—	—	764,788
1977	—	—	16,467	—	2,320,368	—	—	—	—	—	—	—	832,286
1978	—	—	18,187	—	2,489,366	—	—	—	—	—	—	—	985,242
1979	—	—	21,031	—	2,828,075	—	—	—	—	—	—	—	1,176,627
1980	—	—	23,965	4,230	3,176,670	1,049	1,007	922	778	140	334	—	1,364,443
1981	—	—	26,502	—	3,563,558	—	—	—	—	—	—	—	1,596,813
1982	—	—	29,018	—	4,052,649	—	—	—	—	—	—	—	1,720,677
1983	—	—	31,473	—	4,415,275	—	—	—	—	—	—	—	1,873,945
1984	—	—	34,553	—	4,896,325	—	—	—	—	—	—	—	2,096,298
1985	—	—	37,616	7,400	5,410,905	1,825	1,781	—	1,702	211	518	—	2,275,898
1986	—	—	42,222	—	5,952,682	—	—	—	—	—	—	—	2,377,958
1987	—	—	45,516	—	6,359,282	—	—	—	—	—	—	—	2,586,441
1988	—	—	50,398	—	7,060,730	—	—	—	—	—	—	—	2,914,396
1989	—	—	54,169	9,800	7,781,422	2,540	2,230	1,920	2,170	240	700	—	3,143,696
1990	—	—	59,288	10,200	8,361,265	2,680	2,310	2,030	2,230	240	710	—	3,268,629
1991	—	—	63,814	10,700	8,977,271	2,870	2,500	2,090	2,260	240	770	—	3,442,009
1992	—	—	67,220	11,200	9,659,977	2,980	2,530	2,200	2,400	250	840	—	3,627,773
1993	—	—	70,884	12,350	10,203,062	3,410	2,800	2,540	2,510	240	850	—	3,669,536
1994	—	—	74,900 [4]	—	—	—	—	—	—	—	—	—	—
1995	—	—	78,400 [4]	—	—	—	—	—	—	—	—	—	—

[1] Data apply to the academic year except as indicated.

[2] Year ending.

[3] Calendar year.

[4] Estimated.

Sources

Series Bg207–208. Series H510 and H512, *Historical Statistics of the United States* (1975), which used data from the U.S. National Center for Educational Statistics, *Digest of Education Statistics* (various years) and *Biennial Survey of Education*.

Series Bg209. *Digest of Education Statistics* (1995 and 1996), Table 31.

Series Bg210–217 and Bg219. *Digest of Education Statistics* (1995 and 1996), Tables 332, 333, and 334, which were based on data provided by the Council for Aid to Education.

Series Bg218. Series H403, *Historical Statistics* (1975). The underlying sources are Ralph L. Nelson, "Estimates of Balance Sheets and Income Statements of Foundations and Colleges and Universities," supplementary volume 1 of *Institutional Investor Study Report of the Securities and Exchange Commission* (1965), Appendix A-III; Nelson, *The Investment Policies of Foundations* (Russell Sage Foundation, 1967), Chapter 2; and Nelson, *Private Giving in the American Economy, 1960–1972* (Commission on Private Philanthropy and Public Needs, 1973).

Documentation

Most of the series in the table (those not titled as private) include earnings of and contributions to all colleges and universities. Because the income was from voluntary, nongovernmental sources, such giving and income, despite their recipients, are indicators of the role of "giving" in education.

Series Bg211–217 and Bg219. Voluntary support excludes income from endowment and other invested funds, as well as all support received from federal, state, and local governments and their agencies and contract research.

Series Bg211. Beginning in the 1969–1970 academic year, private grants represent nongovernmental revenue for sponsored research, student aid, and other sponsored programs.

Series Bg218. Constructed by Ralph Nelson in the 1970s. Although more recent estimates have yielded different levels of giving and income, Nelson's series was included to provide continuity and because it is based upon a somewhat more traditional and limited definition of higher education and its constituent institutions. See the associated notes in *Historical Statistics* (1975) for an insight into his methods.

TABLE Bg220–233 Income of Yale and Harvard Universities, by source: 1636–1975

Contributed by Colin B. Burke

	Harvard income								Yale income					
	Total	Endowment funds	Gifts for current use	Individual donations	Colony grants to the college	Government grants and contracts	Student charges	Other sources	Government programs, grants, and contracts	Individual donations	Student charges	Endowment funds	Gifts and grants	Colony grants
	Bg220	Bg221	Bg222	Bg223	Bg224	Bg225	Bg226	Bg227	Bg228	Bg229 [1]	Bg230	Bg231	Bg232	Bg233
Period	Dollars	Dollars	Dollars	Dollars	Dollars	Dollars	Dollars	Dollars	Dollars	Dollars	Dollars	Dollars	Dollars	Dollars
1636–1640	—	—	—	1,936 [2]	2,002 [2]	—	—	—	—	—	—	—	—	—
1641–1645	—	—	—	4,826	—	—	—	—	—	—	—	—	—	—
1646–1650	—	—	—	333	445	—	—	—	—	—	—	—	—	—
1651–1655	—	—	—	1,475	666	—	—	—	—	—	—	—	—	—
1656–1660	—	—	—	6,785	1,665	—	—	—	—	—	—	—	—	—
1661–1665	—	—	—	266	—	—	—	—	—	—	—	—	—	—
1666–1670	—	—	—	4,754	66	—	—	—	—	—	—	—	—	—
1671–1675	—	—	—	7,745	1,831	—	—	—	—	—	—	—	—	—
1676–1680	—	—	—	900	1,665	—	—	—	—	—	—	—	—	—
1681–1685	—	—	—	7,041	1,998	—	—	—	—	—	—	—	—	—
1686–1690	—	—	—	2,558	1,665	—	—	—	—	—	—	—	—	—
1691–1695	—	—	—	462	1,332	—	—	—	—	—	—	—	—	—
1696–1700	—	—	—	3,724	1,831	—	—	—	—	—	—	—	—	—
1701–1705	—	—	—	1,498	—	—	—	—	—	134	—	—	—	1,335
1706–1710	—	—	—	1,232	2,337	—	—	—	—	—	—	—	—	1,335
1711–1715	—	—	—	2,970	2,758	—	—	—	—	1,424	—	—	—	3,627
1716–1720	—	—	—	9,171	11,107	—	—	—	—	5,416	—	—	—	1,758
1721–1725	—	—	—	8,259	907	—	—	—	—	828	—	—	—	4,005
1726–1730	—	—	—	5,153	4,485	—	—	—	—	1,941	—	—	—	2,203
1731–1735	—	—	—	2,496	2,345	—	—	—	—	12,608	—	—	—	2,448
1736–1740	—	—	—	2,643	654	—	—	—	—	67	—	—	—	2,997
1741–1745	—	—	—	2,973	378	—	—	—	—	352	—	—	—	2,679
1746–1750	—	—	—	1,277	942	—	—	—	—	53	—	—	—	5,233
1751–1755	—	—	—	1,112	9,459	—	—	—	—	159	—	—	—	4,520
1756–1760	—	—	—	2,584	2,946	—	—	—	—	968	—	—	—	—

Notes appear at end of table

(continued)

TABLE Bg220–233 Income of Yale and Harvard Universities, by source: 1636–1975 *Continued*

	Harvard income								Yale income					
	Total	Endowment funds	Gifts for current use	Individual donations	Colony grants to the college	Government grants and contracts	Student charges	Other sources	Government programs, grants, and contracts	Individual donations	Student charges	Endowment funds	Gifts and grants	Colony grants
	Bg220	Bg221	Bg222	Bg223	Bg224	Bg225	Bg226	Bg227	Bg228	Bg229 [1]	Bg230	Bg231	Bg232	Bg233
Period	Dollars	Dollars	Dollars	Dollars	Dollars	Dollars	Dollars	Dollars	Dollars	Dollars	Dollars	Dollars	Dollars	Dollars
1761–1765	—	—	—	17,397	33,507	—	—	—	—	1,041	—	—	—	—
1766–1770	—	—	—	6,336	14,142	—	—	—	—	109	—	—	—	3,595
1771–1775	—	—	—	12,989	6,594	—	—	—	—	62	—	—	—	1,282
1776–1780	—	—	—	1,814	3,203	—	—	—	—	1,290	—	—	—	—
1781–1785	—	—	—	1,800	4,878	—	—	—	—	3,233	—	—	—	—
1786–1790	—	—	—	7,905	3,220	—	—	—	—	1,458	—	—	—	—
1791–1795	—	—	—	9,163	—	—	—	—	—	1,122	—	—	—	—
1796–1800	—	—	—	4,000	—	—	—	—	—	—	—	—	—	40,629 [3]
1801–1805	—	—	—	33,333	—	—	—	—	—	—	—	—	—	—
1809–1810	35,592	16,515	—	—	—	—	16,977	2,100	—	2,000	—	—	—	—
1819–1820	83,805	17,431	5,866	—	—	—	64,387	15,923	—	6,000	—	—	—	8,785 [4]
1829–1830	51,605	22,293	—	—	—	—	25,699	3,612	—	93,512	—	—	—	7,000 [5]
1839–1840	90,609	31,079	1,087	—	—	—	52,825	5,618	—	138,130	—	—	—	—
1849–1850	92,214	40,113	1,474	—	—	—	47,767	2,859	—	53,950	—	—	—	—
1859–1860	156,171	73,088	7,965	—	—	—	73,244	1,874	—	406,990	—	—	—	—
1869–1870	305,079	185,488	3,661	—	—	—	114,405	1,220	—	1,178,129	—	—	—	—
1879–1880	574,401	252,736	68,503	—	—	—	242,397	9,765	—	1,552,007	—	—	—	—
1889–1890	1,005,144	414,119	161,828	—	—	—	380,950	48,247	—	3,972,671	—	—	—	—
1899–1900	1,487,636	534,061	60,933	—	—	—	754,231	138,350	—	3,282,476	487,022	255,697	20,000	—
1909–1910	2,035,108	803,868	166,879	—	—	—	775,376	288,985	—	—	—	—	—	—
1919–1920	4,183,492	1,895,122	422,533	—	—	—	1,468,406	397,432	—	—	894,498	1,388,206	—	—
1929–1930	13,911,721	5,342,101	2,100,670	—	—	—	5,022,131	1,446,819	—	—	—	—	587,661	—
1939–1940	14,115,498	5,123,926	1,679,744	—	—	—	3,514,759	3,797,069	21,211	—	2,562,127	—	1,104,555	—
1949–1950	30,311,683	7,547,609	4,880,181	—	—	—	12,306,543	5,577,350	—	—	—	—	—	—
1959–1960	74,552,070	16,774,216	12,599,300	—	—	18,116,153	22,141,965	4,920,437	6,880,457	—	13,489,842	12,173,584	6,807,943	—
1962–1963	102,896,078	21,813,969	15,022,827	—	—	31,177,512	27,061,669	7,820,102	—	—	—	—	—	—
1974–1975	—	—	—	—	—	—	—	—	51,000,000	—	40,406,063	34,059,866	19,133,964	—

[1] Starting with 1795, value is for the decade ending at the last year indicated.

[2] Precise starting date not specified by source.

[3] For the period 1791–1800.

[4] For the period 1811–1815.

[5] For the period 1826–1830.

Sources

Series Bg220–222 and Bg225–227. Seymour E. Harris, *Economics of Harvard* (McGraw-Hill, 1970), Table 24.5, p. 210.

Series Bg223–224, Bg229, and Bg233. Jesse Brundage Sears, *Philanthropy in the History of American Higher Education: With a New Introduction by Roger L. Geiger* (Transaction Publishers, 1990), Table 3, p. 23.

Series Bg228 and Bg230–232. George Wilson Pierson, *The Yale Book of Numbers: Historical Statistics of the College and University, 1701–1976* (Yale University Press, 1983).

Documentation

Series Bg232. Combines several series in the source that listed income from various types of gifts and private grants.

TABLE Bg234–247 Health care expenditures, philanthropic revenue of health care institutions, nonprofit nursing homes, and hospital assets, employment, and expenses, by type and nonprofit status: 1923–1996

Contributed by Colin B. Burke

	Philanthropic giving to the health sector	Philanthropic revenues of hospitals and health care institutions	Expenditures on health care, philanthropic and other	Hospitals					Nonprofit nursing homes	Nonprofit hospitals				
				Church-sponsored	Church-controlled	Other nonprofit (AMA)	Other nonprofit (AHA)	Nonprofit		Assets	Personnel	Employment	Expenses (AMA)	Expenses (AHA)
	Bg234	Bg235	Bg236	Bg237	Bg238	Bg239	Bg240	Bg241	Bg242	Bg243	Bg244 [1]	Bg245	Bg246	Bg247
Year	Billion dollars	Million dollars	Million dollars	Number	Number	Number	Number	Number	Number	Million dollars	Thousand	Thousand	Million dollars	Billion dollars
1923	—	—	—	893	—	2,439	—	—	—	—	—	—	—	—
1924	—	—	—	1,233	—	1,748	—	—	—	—	—	—	—	—
1927	—	—	—	1,060	—	3,938	—	—	—	—	—	—	—	—
1928	—	—	—	1,056	—	3,983	—	—	—	—	—	—	—	—
1929	—	—	217	1,024	—	3,846	—	—	—	—	—	—	—	—
1930	—	97	—	1,017	—	3,890	—	—	—	—	—	—	—	—
1931	—	—	—	1,011	—	3,786	—	—	—	—	—	—	—	—
1932	—	—	—	1,001	—	3,757	—	—	—	—	—	—	—	—
1933	—	—	—	984	—	3,677	—	—	—	—	—	—	—	—
1934	—	—	—	970	—	1,676	—	—	—	—	—	—	—	—
1935	—	36	84	970	—	1,670	—	—	—	—	—	—	—	—
1936	—	—	—	969	—	1,742	—	—	—	—	—	—	—	—
1937	—	—	—	975	—	1,718	—	—	—	—	—	—	—	—
1938	—	—	—	981	—	1,776	—	—	—	—	—	—	—	—
1939	—	—	—	1,001	—	1,839	—	—	—	—	—	—	—	—
1940	—	56	127	998	—	1,903	—	—	—	—	—	—	—	—
1941	—	—	—	993	—	1,917	—	—	—	—	—	—	—	—
1942	—	—	—	977	—	1,949	—	—	—	—	—	—	—	—
1943	—	—	—	1,004	—	1,952	—	—	—	—	—	—	—	—
1944	—	—	—	1,020	—	1,961	—	—	—	—	—	—	—	—
1945	—	330	—	1,036	—	1,954	—	—	—	—	—	—	—	—
1946	—	—	—	1,050	—	1,942	2,921 [2]	—	—	—	505	—	848	—
1947	—	—	—	1,051	—	1,965	2,981 [2]	—	—	2,697	539	—	1,048	—
1948	—	—	517	1,068	—	2,016	3,022 [2]	—	—	2,889	586	—	1,264	—
1949	—	—	674	1,090	—	2,067	3,044 [2]	—	—	3,101	596	—	1,333	—
1950	—	515	797	1,097	—	2,072	3,250 [2]	—	—	3,350	662	—	1,523	—
1951	—	—	884	1,116	—	2,121	3,297 [2]	—	—	3,460	648	—	1,688	—
1952	—	—	868	1,136	—	2,146	3,348 [2]	—	—	3,901	674	—	1,879	—
1953	—	—	759	1,169	1,110	2,206	2,259	—	—	4,348	719	—	2,080	—
1954	—	—	849	—	1,196	—	2,225	—	—	4,709	777	—	2,276	—
1955	—	632	908	—	1,101	—	2,339	—	—	5,223	826	—	2,508	—
1956	—	900	904	—	1,206	—	2,304	—	—	5,741	878	—	2,739	—
1957	—	—	1,101	—	1,220	—	2,291	—	—	6,505	926	—	3,050	—
1958	—	750	1,169	—	1,220	—	2,288	—	—	7,221	984	—	3,427	—
1959	1.11	—	1,267	—	1,232	—	2,328	—	—	7,807	1,031	—	3,760	—

Notes appear at end of table

(continued)

TABLE Bg234–247 Health care expenditures, philanthropic revenue of health care institutions, nonprofit nursing homes, and hospital assets, employment, and expenses, by type and nonprofit status: 1923–1996 *Continued*

	Philanthropic giving to the health sector	Philanthropic revenues of hospitals and health care institutions	Expenditures on health care, philanthropic and other	Hospitals: Church-sponsored	Hospitals: Church-controlled	Hospitals: Other nonprofit (AMA)	Hospitals: Other nonprofit (AHA)	Hospitals: Nonprofit	Nonprofit nursing homes	Nonprofit hospitals: Assets	Nonprofit hospitals: Personnel	Nonprofit hospitals: Employment	Nonprofit hospitals: Expenses (AMA)	Nonprofit hospitals: Expenses (AHA)
	Bg234	Bg235	Bg236	Bg237	Bg238	Bg239	Bg240	Bg241	Bg242	Bg243	Bg244 [1]	Bg245	Bg246	Bg247
Year	Billion dollars	Million dollars	Million dollars	Number	Number	Number	Number	Number	Number	Million dollars	Thousand	Thousand	Million dollars	Billion dollars
1960	0.95	947	1,428	—	1,241	—	2,338	—	—	8,422	1,080	—	4,139	—
1961	1.09	1,087	1,602	—	1,260	—	2,328	—	—	8,949	1,149	—	4,584	—
1962	1.25	1,246	1,858	—	1,259	—	2,364	—	—	9,656	1,207	—	4,999	—
1963	1.35	1,349	1,969	—	1,271	—	2,392	—	—	10,507	1,277	—	5,491	—
1964	1.55	1,546	2,295	—	1,227	—	2,424	—	—	11,423	1,333	—	6,039	—
1965	1.60	1,602	2,348	—	1,266	—	2,404	—	—	12,476	1,386	—	6,643	—
1966	1.69	1,685	2,422	—	—	—	3,675 [2]	—	—	13,734	1,532	—	7,435	—
1967	1.91	1,907	2,485	—	—	—	3,692 [2]	—	—	15,075	1,619	—	8,806	—
1968	2.08	2,080	2,717	—	—	—	3,660 [2]	—	—	16,954	1,717	—	10,317	—
1969	2.31	2,305	3,432	—	—	—	3,643 [2]	—	—	18,567	1,824	—	12,137	—
1970	2.40	2,400	3,742	—	—	—	3,600 [2]	—	—	20,502	1,929	—	14,163	—
1971	2.61	—	—	—	—	—	—	3,826	3,587	—	—	—	—	—
1972	2.80	—	—	—	—	—	—	—	—	—	—	1,704.0	—	—
1973	3.10	—	—	—	—	—	—	—	—	—	—	—	—	—
1974	3.37	—	—	—	—	—	—	—	—	—	—	1,859.0	—	—
1975	3.61	—	—	—	—	—	—	—	—	—	—	—	—	—
1976	3.92	—	—	—	—	—	—	—	—	—	—	—	—	—
1977	4.09	—	—	—	—	—	—	—	—	—	—	2,121.1	—	—
1978	4.52	—	—	—	—	—	—	—	—	—	—	—	—	—
1979	4.94	—	—	—	—	—	—	—	—	—	—	—	—	—
1980	5.34	—	—	—	—	—	—	3,547	3,460	—	—	2,366.0	—	55.8
1981	5.79	—	—	—	—	—	—	—	—	—	—	2,496.0	—	—
1982	6.15	—	—	—	—	—	—	—	—	—	—	2,593.7	—	—
1983	6.68	—	—	—	—	—	—	—	—	—	—	2,612.8	—	—
1984	6.84	—	—	—	—	—	—	—	—	—	—	2,575.6	—	—
1985	7.72	—	—	—	—	—	—	—	—	—	—	—	—	96.1
1986	8.44	—	—	—	—	—	—	3,548	4,378	—	—	—	—	—
1987	9.22	—	—	—	—	—	—	3,504	—	—	—	2,664.8	—	—
1988	9.58	—	—	—	—	—	—	3,489	—	—	—	2,784.8	—	—
1989	9.93	—	—	—	—	—	—	3,463	—	—	—	2,903.7	—	139.9
1990	9.90	—	—	—	—	—	—	3,431	—	—	—	2,993.8	—	150.7
1991	9.68	—	—	—	—	—	—	3,398	7,180	—	—	—	—	166.8
1992	10.24	—	—	—	—	—	—	3,390	—	—	—	3,252.0	—	183.8
1993	10.83	—	—	—	—	—	—	3,367 [3]	—	—	—	—	—	197.2
1994	11.53	—	—	—	—	—	—	—	—	—	—	3,252.0	—	204.2
1995	12.59	—	—	—	—	—	—	—	—	—	—	—	—	209.6
1996	13.98	—	—	—	—	—	—	—	—	—	—	—	—	—

[1] Beginning 1951, excludes residents, interns, and students; 1954, includes full equivalents of part-time personnel.

[2] Includes church-affiliated and operated institutions.

[3] For 1993–1995, the American Hospital Association's "*Hospital Statistics*" lists 3,154, 3,139, and 3,092 nonprofit hospitals, respectively.

Sources

Series Bg234. Ann E. Kaplan, editor, *Giving USA, 1996* (AAFRC Trust for Philanthropy, 1996), and unpublished data provided by the American Association of Fund-Raising Counsel (AAFRC) from 1997–1998 studies.

Series Bg235. Series H409 in *Historical Statistics of the United States* (1975), which was based on data compiled by Ralph L. Nelson, City University of New York, Queens College, in 1973.

Series Bg236. Series B240 in *Historical Statistics of the United States* (1975). The underlying sources are, for 1929–1968, *Compendium of National Health Expenditures Data*, U.S. Department of Health, Education, and Welfare (DHEW) Publication number (SSA) 73-11903, Table 6; and for 1969–1970, *National Health Expenditures, Calendar Years 1929–71*, Research and Statistics Note number 3, 1973, DHEW Publication number (SSA) 73-11701, Tables 2 and 8.

Series Bg237. Series B353 in *Historical Statistics* (1975), which was based on data in American Medical Association (AMA), *Journal of the American Medical Association*, "Hospitals" issues: for 1909, 1914, 1918, and 1934–1953, (May 1954): 4, 7–8; for 1923 and 1927–1933, (March 1934): 1006–7; for 1924, (March 1925): 961–70; for 1925, (April 1926): 1009–55; for 1926, (March 1927): 789–839.

Series Bg238 and Bg240. Series B339 and B341 in *Historical Statistics* (1975), which were based upon data in American Hospital Association (AHA), *Hospitals*, Guide Issue, part 2 (published annually).

Series Bg239. Series B355 in *Historical Statistics* (1975), which was based on data in *Journal of the American Medical Association*, "Hospitals" issues: for 1909, 1914, 1918, and 1934–1953, (May 1954): 4, 7–8; for 1923 and 1927–1933, (March 1934): 1006–7; for 1924, (March 1925): 961–70; for 1925, (April 1926): 1009–55; for 1926, (March 1927): 789–839.

Series Bg241–242. National Center for Health Statistics, unpublished data.

Series Bg243–244 and Bg246. Series B420 in *Historical Statistics* (1975), which was based on data in *Journal of the American Medical Association,* "Hospitals" issues: for 1946–1964, (August 1, 1965): 448–9; and for 1965–1970, (August 1, 1972): 460–2.

Series Bg245. Virginia Ann Hodgkinson, Murray S. Weitzman, et al., *The Nonprofit Almanac, 1996–1997: Dimensions of the Independent Sector* (Jossey-Bass, 1996), and allied Independent Sector publications.

Series Bg247. AHA, *Hospital Statistics* (published annually).

Documentation

As with statistical series about other segments of the nonprofit sector, the statistics on health care are marked by periods of inattention and by ongoing struggles over the definition of terms and categories. There are no reliable series for the nineteenth century. In the twentieth century, the statistics for hospitals, for example, have been the product of different organizations: the AMA, the AHA, the National Center for Health Statistics, and the Census Bureau. Each has had a different approach.

Series Bg234. Estimates differ from those presented by the Internal Revenue Service in issues of its *Statistics of Income Bulletin,* especially those for 1958.

Series Bg235. Based on estimates made by the Research and Statistics staff of the U.S. Social Security Administration as published in *Social Security Bulletin* and on estimates made by the AAFRC as published in *Giving USA*. These estimates were verified for general trends from a variety of data sources (federated campaign allocations, national health agencies, church benevolences distributions, and so forth).

Series Bg236. For the general method of estimating national health expenditures, see the text for series B221–235 in *Historical Statistics* (1975).

Series Bg243 and Bg246. Assets comprise plant assets (land, buildings, equipment, and reserves for construction, improvement, and replacement, less deductions for depreciation) plus all other assets, including endowment fund principal and general and temporary fund balances. Expenses include all expenses covering the twelve-month period, both total and payroll. Payroll expenses include all salaries and wages except those paid to interns, residents, student nurses, and other trainees. All professional fees and those salary expenditures excluded from payroll are defined as nonpayroll expenses and are included in the total.

Series Bg244. Data on personnel refer to the number of persons on the payroll at the close of the twelve-month reporting period. Except as noted, they include full-time equivalents of part-time personnel but exclude trainees (student nurses, interns, residents, and other trainees), private duty nurses, and volunteers. Full-time equivalents are calculated on the basis that two part-time persons are equal to one full-time person. See also the general note for series B305–400 and B413–422 in *Historical Statistics* (1975).

Series Bg245. Standard Industrial Classification (SIC) code 806. See the introduction to Part D for a discussion of SIC codes.

TABLE Bg248–250 Blue Cross subscribers, subscription income, and benefit expenditures: 1940–1970

Contributed by Colin B. Burke

Year	Subscription income	Benefit expenditures	Subscribers
	Bg248	Bg249	Bg250
	Million dollars	Million dollars	Thousand
1940	—	—	6,072
1941	—	—	8,469
1942	—	—	10,295
1943	—	—	12,696
1944	—	—	15,828
1945	—	—	18,961
1946	—	—	24,342
1947	—	—	27,646
1948	365	308	30,619
1949	455	383	33,576
1950	574	491	37,645
1951	685	605	39,412
1952	881	736	41,353
1953	989	851	43,684
1954	1,133	985	45,355
1955	1,292	1,147	48,924
1956	1,493	1,353	51,455
1957	1,668	1,543	53,282
1958	1,867	1,768	53,623
1959	2,157	1,995	55,054
1960	2,482	2,287	57,464
1961	2,805	2,585	57,960
1962	3,119	2,894	59,618
1963	3,399	3,180	60,698
1964	3,785	3,574	62,429
1965	4,169	3,913	63,662
1966	4,328	3,975	65,638
1967	4,555	4,083	67,513
1968	5,187	4,840	70,510
1969	6,156	5,903	73,211
1970	7,371	7,060	75,464

Sources

Series Bg248. Series B403 in *Historical Statistics of the United States* (1975), based on data supplied by the Blue Cross–Blue Shield Association.

Series Bg249–250. Series X957 and X958 in *Historical Statistics* (1975), based on data supplied by the Blue Cross–Blue Shield Association and its annual reports.

VOLUNTARY ASSOCIATIONS

Colin B. Burke

TABLE Bg251–264 Arts, humanities, and public broadcasting organizations – income, expenditures, giving, employment, and buildings: 1814–1997

Contributed by Colin B. Burke

			Nonprofit arts and cultural organizations							Income of public broadcasting				
			Income											
	Giving to arts, humanities, and cultural organizations	Philanthropic giving to museums and orchestras	Private payments	Other income	Government payments	Current operating expenditures	Personal consumption expenditures on theater entertainment of nonprofit institutions	Number of museum buildings	Employment in nonprofit arts and cultural institutions	Total	Subscribers, auctions/marathons	Business and industry	Foundations	Federal government
	Bg251 [1]	Bg252	Bg253	Bg254	Bg255	Bg256	Bg257	Bg258	Bg259	Bg260	Bg261	Bg262	Bg263	Bg264
Year	Million dollars	Million dollars	Million dollars	Million dollars	Million dollars	Million dollars	Million dollars	Number	Number	Million dollars	Million dollars	Million dollars	Million dollars	Million dollars
1814	—	—	—	—	—	—	—	1	—	—	—	—	—	—
1824	—	—	—	—	—	—	—	2	—	—	—	—	—	—
1844	—	—	—	—	—	—	—	3	—	—	—	—	—	—
1855	—	—	—	—	—	—	—	4	—	—	—	—	—	—
1860	—	—	—	—	—	—	—	5	—	—	—	—	—	—
1870	—	—	—	—	—	—	—	8	—	—	—	—	—	—
1880	—	—	—	—	—	—	—	20	—	—	—	—	—	—
1890	—	—	—	—	—	—	—	33	—	—	—	—	—	—
1900	—	—	—	—	—	—	—	68	—	—	—	—	—	—
1910	—	—	—	—	—	—	—	108	—	—	—	—	—	—
1920	—	—	—	—	—	—	—	157	—	—	—	—	—	—
1924	—	4	—	—	—	—	—	—	—	—	—	—	—	—
1925	—	4	—	—	—	—	81	—	—	—	—	—	—	—
1926	—	4	—	—	—	—	146	—	—	—	—	—	—	—
1927	—	4	—	—	—	—	174	—	—	—	—	—	—	—
1928	—	5	—	—	—	—	195	—	—	—	—	—	—	—
1929	—	5	—	—	—	—	100	—	—	—	—	—	—	—
1930	—	5	—	—	—	—	100	255	—	—	—	—	—	—
1931	—	5	—	—	—	—	100	—	—	—	—	—	—	—
1932	—	6	—	—	—	—	100	—	—	—	—	—	—	—
1933	—	5	—	—	—	—	—	—	—	—	—	—	—	—
1934	—	4	—	—	—	—	—	—	—	—	—	—	—	—
1935	—	4	—	—	—	—	—	—	—	—	—	—	—	—
1936	—	4	—	—	—	—	100	—	—	—	—	—	—	—
1937	—	4	—	—	—	—	100	—	—	—	—	—	—	—
1938	—	4	—	—	—	—	100	380	—	—	—	—	—	—
1939	—	4	—	—	—	—	100	—	—	—	—	—	—	—
1940	—	4	—	—	—	—	100	—	—	—	—	—	—	—
1941	—	4	—	—	—	—	100	—	—	—	—	—	—	—
1942	—	5	—	—	—	—	100	—	—	—	—	—	—	—
1943	—	6	—	—	—	—	100	—	—	—	—	—	—	—
1944	—	6	—	—	—	—	100	—	—	—	—	—	—	—

Note appears at end of table

(continued)

TABLE Bg251–264 Arts, humanities, and public broadcasting organizations – income, expenditures, giving, employment, and buildings: 1814–1997 *Continued*

			Nonprofit arts and cultural organizations							Income of public broadcasting				
			Income											
	Giving to arts, humanities, and cultural organizations	Philanthropic giving to museums and orchestras	Private payments	Other income	Government payments	Current operating expenditures	Personal consumption expenditures on theater entertainment of nonprofit institutions	Number of museum buildings	Employment in nonprofit arts and cultural institutions	Total	Subscribers, auctions/marathons	Business and industry	Foundations	Federal government
	Bg251 [1]	Bg252	Bg253	Bg254	Bg255	Bg256	Bg257	Bg258	Bg259	Bg260	Bg261	Bg262	Bg263	Bg264
Year	Million dollars	Million dollars	Million dollars	Million dollars	Million dollars	Million dollars	Million dollars	Number	Number	Million dollars	Million dollars	Million dollars	Million dollars	Million dollars
1945	—	7	—	—	—	—	100	—	—	—	—	—	—	—
1946	—	6	—	—	—	—	200	—	—	—	—	—	—	—
1947	—	8	—	—	—	—	200	—	—	—	—	—	—	—
1948	—	8	—	—	—	—	200	—	—	—	—	—	—	—
1949	—	—	—	—	—	—	200	—	—	—	—	—	—	—
1950	—	—	—	—	—	—	200	—	—	—	—	—	—	—
1951	—	—	—	—	—	—	200	—	—	—	—	—	—	—
1952	—	—	—	—	—	—	200	—	—	—	—	—	—	—
1953	—	—	—	—	—	—	200	—	—	—	—	—	—	—
1954	—	—	—	—	—	—	200	—	—	—	—	—	—	—
1955	—	—	—	—	—	—	200	—	—	—	—	—	—	—
1956	—	—	—	—	—	—	300	—	—	—	—	—	—	—
1957	—	—	—	—	—	—	300	—	—	—	—	—	—	—
1958	—	—	—	—	—	—	300	—	—	—	—	—	—	—
1959	397	—	—	—	—	—	300	—	—	—	—	—	—	—
1960	408	—	—	—	—	—	300	—	—	—	—	—	—	—
1961	415	—	—	—	—	—	300	—	—	—	—	—	—	—
1962	410	—	—	—	—	—	400	—	—	—	—	—	—	—
1963	485	—	—	—	—	—	400	—	—	—	—	—	—	—
1964	435	—	—	—	—	—	400	—	—	—	—	—	—	—
1965	436	—	—	—	—	—	400	—	—	—	—	—	—	—
1966	536	—	—	—	—	—	400	—	—	—	—	—	—	—
1967	559	—	—	—	—	—	500	—	—	—	—	—	—	—
1968	604	—	—	—	—	—	500	—	—	—	—	—	—	—
1969	718	—	—	—	—	—	500	—	—	—	—	—	—	—
1970	663	—	—	—	—	—	500	—	—	—	—	—	—	—
1971	1,010	—	—	—	—	—	500	—	—	—	—	—	—	—
1972	1,100	—	—	—	—	—	600	—	52,000	—	—	—	—	—
1973	1,260	—	—	—	—	—	600	—	—	—	—	—	—	—
1974	1,150	—	—	—	—	1,200	700	—	56,000	—	—	—	—	—
1975	1,240	—	—	—	—	1,300	800	—	—	—	—	—	—	—
1976	1,380	—	—	—	—	—	900	—	—	—	—	—	—	—
1977	2,320	—	500	300	200	1,500	1,100	—	65,700	—	—	—	—	—
1978	2,400	—	—	—	—	—	1,300	—	—	—	—	—	—	—
1979	2,730	—	—	—	—	—	1,500	—	—	—	—	—	—	—
1980	3,150	—	—	—	—	2,500	1,800	—	78,000	705	102	72	24	193
1981	3,660	—	—	—	—	—	2,100	—	80,000	—	—	—	—	—
1982	4,690	—	1,400	700	800	3,300	2,200	—	89,100	—	—	—	—	—
1983	4,210	—	—	—	—	—	2,500	—	93,400	899	196	120	25	164
1984	4,500	—	—	—	—	—	2,800	—	98,200	974	215	145	28	167

			Nonprofit arts and cultural organizations								Income of public broadcasting				
	Giving to arts, humanities, and cultural organizations	Philanthropic giving to museums and orchestras	Income: Private payments	Income: Other income	Income: Government payments	Current operating expenditures	Personal consumption expenditures on theater entertainment of nonprofit institutions	Number of museum buildings	Employment in nonprofit arts and cultural institutions	Total	Subscribers, auctions/marathons	Business and industry	Foundations	Federal government
	Bg251 [1]	Bg252	Bg253	Bg254	Bg255	Bg256	Bg257	Bg258	Bg259	Bg260	Bg261	Bg262	Bg263	Bg264
Year	Million dollars	Million dollars	Million dollars	Million dollars	Million dollars	Million dollars	Million dollars	Number	Number	Million dollars	Million dollars	Million dollars	Million dollars	Million dollars
1985	5,080	—	—	—	—	—	3,200	—	—	1,096	240	171	43	179
1986	5,830	—	—	—	—	—	3,900	—	—	1,134	269	171	38	186
1987	6,310	—	1,800	900	900	5,200	4,100	—	121,700	1,293	298	196	48	243
1988	6,790	—	—	—	—	—	4,500	—	137,000	1,348	321	213	51	248
1989	7,500	—	—	—	—	—	4,700	—	146,700	1,549	347	242	69	264
1990	7,890	—	—	—	—	—	5,800	—	157,800	1,581	364	262	71	267
1991	8,810	—	—	—	—	—	6,000	—	—	1,721	384	290	70	333
1992	9,320	—	2,000	1,700	1,200	7,700	6,800	—	165,400	1,790	404	300	80	374
1993	9,570	—	—	—	—	—	7,800	—	—	1,790	412	301	100	370
1994	9,680	—	—	—	—	—	8,200	—	177,900	1,795	420	301	97	330
1995	9,960	—	—	—	—	—	9,000	—	—	1,917	447	294	109	338
1996	10,920	—	—	—	—	—	—	—	—	—	—	—	—	—
1997	10,620	—	—	—	—	—	—	—	—	—	—	—	—	—

[1] For 1959–1966, the data in original source are in error and cannot be corrected.

Sources

Series Bg251. Ann E. Kaplan, editor, *Giving USA: Annual Report on Philanthropy* (AAFRC Trust for Philanthropy, published annually), and unpublished data provided by the American Association of Fund-Raiding Counsel from 1997–1998 studies.

Series Bg252. Edward C. Jenkins, *Philanthropy in America: An Introduction to the Practices and Prospects of Organizations Supported by Gifts and Endowments* (Association Press, 1950).

Series Bg253–256 and Bg259. Virginia Ann Hodgkinson, Murray S. Weitzman, et al., *Nonprofit Almanac, 1996–1997: Dimensions of the Independent Sector* (Jossey-Bass, 1996).

Series Bg257. U.S. Bureau of Economic Analysis, *National Income and Product Accounts of the United States* (1998), and *Survey of Current Business* (various years).

Series Bg258. Lawrence Vail Coleman, *The Museum in America: A Critical Study*, 3 volumes (American Association of Museums, 1939).

Series Bg260–264. Corporation for Public Broadcasting (CPB), *Public Broadcasting Income* (various years), and unpublished data.

Documentation

For a discussion of deficiencies of the data on the arts, see Deborah A. Kaple et al., "Data on Arts Organizations: A Review and Needs Assessment, with Design Implications," Working Paper number 2, Center for Arts and Cultural Policy Studies, Princeton University, Department of Sociology, November 1996.

Series Bg251. Includes gifts and contributions to nonprofit organizations by individuals, foundations, businesses, and corporations. National Taxonomy of Exempt Entities Category A institutions are the recipients.

Series Bg253. The source reports payments for goods and services, not contributions.

Series Bg253–256 and Bg259. Includes Standard Industrial Classification (SIC) industries 483, 792, and 84. See the introduction to Part D for a discussion of SIC codes.

Series Bg254. Includes endowment income; excludes private and government contributions.

Series Bg257. Includes plays, operas, and the like; excludes athletics. Note that the title for this series changed after the publication of *Historical Statistics of the United States* (1975), although the series reflects continuity in definition. In the 1990s, the *Survey of Current Business* titled the series as "Legitimate Theater and Opera and Entertainments of Nonprofit Institutions."

Series Bg260–264. Data are for operating year of the corporation.

TABLE Bg265–279 Membership and income of fraternal and service organizations, by organization: 1847–1999

Contributed by Colin B. Burke

	Membership								National Red Cross						
												Income			
												National organization		Including local chapters	
	Masonic orders	Benevolent and Protective Order of Elks	Modern Woodmen of America	Kiwanis	Improved Order of Redmen	Rotary, worldwide	Lions International	National Parent Teacher Association	Membership	Adult volunteers	Junior membership	Total	From contributions	Total	From contributions
	Bg265	Bg266	Bg267	Bg268	Bg269	Bg270	Bg271	Bg272	Bg273	Bg274	Bg275	Bg276	Bg277	Bg278	Bg279
Year	Number	Number	Number	Number	Number	Number	Number	Number	Number	Number	Number	Million dollars	Million dollars	Million dollars	Million dollars
1847	—	—	—	—	491	—	—	—	—	—	—	—	—	—	—
1850	—	—	—	—	3,175	—	—	—	—	—	—	—	—	—	—
1851	—	—	—	—	4,709	—	—	—	—	—	—	—	—	—	—
1852	—	—	—	—	4,276	—	—	—	—	—	—	—	—	—	—
1853	—	—	—	—	5,242	—	—	—	—	—	—	—	—	—	—
1854	—	—	—	—	6,251	—	—	—	—	—	—	—	—	—	—
1855	—	—	—	—	7,220	—	—	—	—	—	—	—	—	—	—
1856	—	—	—	—	7,953	—	—	—	—	—	—	—	—	—	—
1857	—	—	—	—	7,042	—	—	—	—	—	—	—	—	—	—
1858	—	—	—	—	7,742	—	—	—	—	—	—	—	—	—	—
1859	—	—	—	—	9,266	—	—	—	—	—	—	—	—	—	—
1860	—	—	—	—	9,096	—	—	—	—	—	—	—	—	—	—
1863	—	—	—	—	7,018	—	—	—	—	—	—	—	—	—	—
1864	—	—	—	—	7,835	—	—	—	—	—	—	—	—	—	—
1865	—	—	—	—	7,835	—	—	—	—	—	—	—	—	—	—
1866	—	—	—	—	10,238	—	—	—	—	—	—	—	—	—	—
1867	—	—	—	—	12,160	—	—	—	—	—	—	—	—	—	—
1868	—	—	—	—	19,491	—	—	—	—	—	—	—	—	—	—
1869	—	—	—	—	19,571	—	—	—	—	—	—	—	—	—	—
1870	—	—	—	—	22,784	—	—	—	—	—	—	—	—	—	—
1871	—	243	—	—	26,954	—	—	—	—	—	—	—	—	—	—
1872	—	271	—	—	31,540	—	—	—	—	—	—	—	—	—	—
1873	—	268	—	—	36,248	—	—	—	—	—	—	—	—	—	—
1874	—	385	—	—	39,953	—	—	—	—	—	—	—	—	—	—
1875	—	376	—	—	40,504	—	—	—	—	—	—	—	—	—	—
1876	—	418	—	—	39,516	—	—	—	—	—	—	—	—	—	—
1877	—	—	—	—	36,422	—	—	—	—	—	—	—	—	—	—
1878	—	820 [1]	—	—	31,057	—	—	—	—	—	—	—	—	—	—
1879	—	929	—	—	28,075	—	—	—	—	—	—	—	—	—	—
1880	—	1,060	—	—	27,214	—	—	—	—	—	—	—	—	—	—
1881	—	1,339	—	—	28,366	—	—	—	—	—	—	—	—	—	—
1882	—	1,806	—	—	29,965	—	—	—	—	—	—	—	—	—	—
1883	—	2,400	—	—	35,119	—	—	—	—	—	—	—	—	—	—
1884	—	3,051	—	—	41,497	—	—	—	—	—	—	—	—	—	—
1885	—	3,949	—	—	43,619	—	—	—	—	—	—	—	—	—	—
1886	—	5,511	—	—	50,263	—	—	—	—	—	—	—	—	—	—
1887	—	7,334	—	—	63,200	—	—	—	—	—	—	—	—	—	—
1888	—	8,952 [2]	—	—	78,781	—	—	—	—	—	—	—	—	—	—
1889	—	10,549	—	—	88,070	—	—	—	—	—	—	—	—	—	—

	Membership								National Red Cross						
												Income			
												National organization		Including local chapters	
Year	Masonic orders	Benevolent and Protective Order of Elks	Modern Woodmen of America	Kiwanis	Improved Order of Redmen	Rotary, worldwide	Lions International	National Parent Teacher Association	Membership	Adult volunteers	Junior membership	Total	From contributions	Total	From contributions
	Bg265	Bg266	Bg267	Bg268	Bg269	Bg270	Bg271	Bg272	Bg273	Bg274	Bg275	Bg276	Bg277	Bg278	Bg279
	Number	Number	Number	Number	Number	Number	Number	Number	Number	Number	Number	Million dollars	Million dollars	Million dollars	Million dollars
1890	—	13,067	—	—	96,626	—	—	—	—	—	—	—	—	—	—
1891	—	15,742	5,499	—	97,518	—	—	—	—	—	—	—	—	—	—
1892	—	18,424	10,229	—	139,127	—	—	—	—	—	—	—	—	—	—
1893	—	21,844	14,057	—	122,314	—	—	—	—	—	—	—	—	—	—
1894	—	22,068	20,272	—	133,785	—	—	—	—	—	—	—	—	—	—
1895	—	27,610	33,027	—	133,485	—	—	—	—	—	—	—	—	—	—
1896	750,000	32,025	50,110	—	149,245	—	—	—	—	—	—	—	—	—	—
1898	—	44,252 [3]	88,481	—	162,422	—	—	—	—	—	—	—	—	—	—
1899	—	60,129	113,473	—	178,664	—	—	—	—	—	—	—	—	—	—
1900	—	77,351	129,837	—	194,785	—	—	—	—	—	—	—	—	—	—
1901	—	99,827	153,017	—	212,549	—	—	—	—	—	—	—	—	—	—
1902	—	128,679	176,028	—	237,361	—	—	—	—	—	—	—	—	—	—
1903	—	155,434	207,176	—	290,373	—	—	—	—	—	—	—	—	—	—
1904	—	177,527	237,252	—	311,984	12	—	—	—	—	—	—	—	—	—
1905	989,176	199,370	274,592	—	329,371	—	—	—	—	—	—	—	—	—	—
1906	—	225,016	330,720	—	354,582	—	—	—	—	—	—	—	—	—	—
1907	1,229,001	254,532	389,169	—	385,332	200	—	—	—	—	—	—	—	—	—
1908	—	284,321	439,285	—	388,644	510	—	—	—	—	—	—	—	—	—
1909	—	304,899	500,369	—	391,924	1,500	—	—	—	—	—	—	—	—	—
1910	1,309,697	331,228	563,466	—	403,723	2,500	—	20,103	—	—	—	—	—	—	—
1911	—	359,677	606,466	—	411,395	5,000	—	—	—	—	—	—	—	—	—
1912	—	384,026	642,300	—	405,115	10,000	—	31,672	—	—	—	—	—	—	—
1913	—	408,281	692,447	—	402,125	15,000	—	23,367	—	—	—	—	—	—	—
1914	—	428,658	722,637	—	388,017	20,700	—	69,441	—	—	—	—	—	—	—
1915	1,671,427	453,516	751,058	—	377,955	27,000	—	59,852	—	—	—	—	—	—	—
1916	—	474,690	804,291	650	372,614	32,000	800	85,452	—	—	—	—	—	—	—
1917	—	493,733	842,546	3,700	362,617	38,800	1,526	122,250	—	—	—	—	—	—	—
1918	—	527,522	893,615	7,900	344,834	45,000	2,364	98,843	—	—	—	—	—	—	—
1919	—	645,678 [4]	962,109	13,000	372,465	56,800 [4]	6,451	119,500	—	—	—	—	—	—	—
1920	2,056,596	767,661	646,719	20,000	400,522	70,000	13,739	189,282	—	—	—	—	—	—	—
1921	—	812,657	542,510	36,047	386,053	81,000	25,429	278,727	—	—	—	—	—	—	—
1922	—	826,825	506,882	57,797	364,844	88,700	32,477	401,308	—	—	—	—	—	—	—
1923	—	839,429	495,274	74,875	347,028	101,700	36,943	530,546	—	—	—	—	—	—	—
1924	3,077,161	832,083	490,751	86,066	323,480	108,000	43,647	651,133	—	—	—	—	—	—	—
1925	3,157,566	825,960	508,444	92,125	305,555	120,000	49,230	875,240	—	—	—	6.9	4.6	—	—
1926	3,218,375	816,000	497,019	96,326	289,273	129,000	52,965	967,766	3,012,055	—	4,947,715	3.2	2.2	—	—
1927	3,267,241	808,658	491,280	99,796	264,535	137,000	60,859	1,134,714	3,087,789	—	5,357,109	23.7 [8]	22.1	—	—
1928	3,295,872	779,973	480,691	100,371	252,711	144,000	70,479	1,275,401	4,058,949	—	5,838,628	6.9	4.6	—	—
1929	3,295,125	761,461	457,643	101,465	240,523	153,000	79,414	1,392,741	4,127,946	—	5,832,986	10.7	7.1	—	—

Notes appear at end of table

(continued)

TABLE Bg265–279 Membership and income of fraternal and service organizations, by organization: 1847–1999 *Continued*

	Membership								National Red Cross						
												Income			
												National organization		Including local chapters	
	Masonic orders	Benevolent and Protective Order of Elks	Modern Woodmen of America	Kiwanis	Improved Order of Redmen	Rotary, worldwide	Lions International	National Parent Teacher Association	Membership	Adult volunteers	Junior membership	Total	From contributions	Total	From contributions
	Bg265	Bg266	Bg267	Bg268	Bg269	Bg270	Bg271	Bg272	Bg273	Bg274	Bg275	Bg276	Bg277	Bg278	Bg279
Year	Number	Number	Number	Number	Number	Number	Number	Number	Number	Number	Number	Million dollars	Million dollars	Million dollars	Million dollars
1930	3,279,778	707,887	456,277	102,750	217,306	157,000	80,456	1,481,105	4,130,066	—	7,106,288	4.1	2.1	—	—
1931	3,216,307	640,591	388,770	98,442	193,318	155,000	79,203	1,511,203	4,075,649	—	—	14.3	12.9	—	—
1932	3,069,645	556,764	351,818	91,248	158,701	146,300	75,022	1,393,454	4,004,459	—	—	3.7	2.5	—	—
1933	2,901,758	500,171	343,516	75,493	142,534	150,000	77,218	1,243,715	3,701,866	—	6,629,866	3.6	2.6	—	—
1934	2,760,451	465,043	355,838	74,577	130,251	162,400	78,871	1,465,910	3,802,384	—	6,968,405	3.6	2.5	—	—
1935	2,659,218	466,520	362,596	79,772	123,233	170,000	85,539	1,727,603	3,837,941	—	7,752,243	3.3	2.3	—	—
1936	2,591,309	472,153	371,298	85,404	114,784	183,000	91,948	1,877,171	4,137,636	—	8,351,298	11.6	10.5	—	—
1937	2,549,772	479,494	369,507	90,107	107,563	200,998	104,774	2,056,777	4,904,316	—	8,577,198	29.2	25.7	—	—
1938	2,514,595	473,927	361,316	95,026	98,536	209,887	120,251	2,222,218	5,523,585	—	9,070,958	5.1	4.2	—	—
1939	2,482,291	475,599	355,522	99,725	91,744	213,791	137,727	2,291,479	5,668,680	—	7,556,306	5.2	4.3	—	—
1940	2,457,263	490,417	346,827	104,489	87,228	211,415	147,407	2,379,599	7,139,263	—	8,588,398	15.4	14.6	—	—
1941	2,451,301	506,887	338,738	108,900	85,468	208,363	147,311	2,480,188	9,190,474	—	9,749,053	15.6	14.7	—	—
1942	2,478,892	547,718	336,272	111,609	82,337	209,689	150,024	2,685,041	15,129,833	—	14,887,792	68.0	64.6	—	—
1943	2,561,844	627,513	339,868	111,618	81,726	227,913	177,579	2,612,346	28,962,883 [6]	—	17,281,502	90.7	89.7	—	—
1944	2,719,607	705,570	348,507	123,792	85,366	247,212	218,184	3,054,950	36,544,151	—	18,466,340	154.3	149.5	—	—
1945	2,896,343	792,339	363,459	139,149	87,506	279,881	279,116	3,487,198	36,645,333	—	19,905,400	165.3	163.5	—	—
1946	3,097,713	877,271	386,179	152,110	92,539	300,529	326,448	3,910,106	21,986,171	—	19,326,847	71.0	68.2	—	—
1947	3,281,371	925,679	405,212	168,633	94,923	318,259	358,144	4,486,855	18,110,170	—	19,270,811	64.7	57.5	—	—
1948	3,426,155	965,387	421,948	180,032	92,693	329,342	—	5,127,896	18,098,250	—	19,414,788	43.3	39.6	—	—
1949	3,545,757	1,004,985	426,700	186,902	88,461	341,716	—	5,774,358	18,138,767	—	19,314,427	40.1	37.8	—	—
1950	3,644,634	1,041,264	429,490	194,128	81,346	349,867	—	6,167,079	18,090,000	—	19,283,438	31.3	29.0	—	—
1951	3,726,744	1,069,868	426,162	198,544	78,824	361,641	—	6,589,516	18,635,000	—	19,334,800	32.8	30.5	—	—
1952	3,808,364	1,097,003	431,763	203,801	75,809	374,855	—	7,219,165	20,829,000	—	19,076,000	43.0	41.7	—	—
1953	3,893,530	1,122,803	438,591	211,106	71,195	392,628	—	7,953,806	20,894,000	—	—	42.1	40.6	—	—
1954	3,964,118	1,149,613	437,333	219,242	66,465	418,933	—	8,822,694	23,196,000	—	21,256,000	47.6	44.9	—	—
1955	4,009,925	1,173,494	437,554	228,905	67,872	433,798	—	9,409,282	23,000,000	—	—	40.5	38.8	88.7	81.3
1956	4,053,323	1,195,509	430,731	238,595	64,716	449,758	—	10,130,352	23,000,000	—	21,819,300	54.2	52.2	104.2	79.9
1957	4,085,676	1,214,163	423,817	243,574	57,732	464,245	—	10,694,474	25,000,000	—	20,400,000	48.2	45.7	99.9	86.6
1958	4,099,928	1,232,007	421,791	246,523	53,835	480,469	—	11,018,156	—	—	—	46.7	44.5	99.0	86.1
1959	4,103,161	1,260,007	412,993	249,936	52,280	498,616	—	11,926,552 [5]	24,200,000	—	20,500,000	43.0	40.8	94.1	85.9
1960	4,099,219	1,280,524	410,009	253,293	50,301	513,059	—	12,074,289	23,900,000	—	20,300,000	43.3	40.0	96.0	84.5
1961	4,086,499	1,294,604	411,278	255,221	—	528,297	—	12,074,507	24,885,700	—	19,816,300	45.3	41.9	98.4	86.9
1962	4,063,563	1,315,319	412,308	255,876	46,288	542,432	—	12,131,318	26,400,000	—	—	—	—	100.1	86.3
1963	4,034,020	1,333,482	414,696	257,968	—	558,638	—	11,992,726	28,600,000	—	17,800,000 [7]	43.8	40.1	102.3	87.8
1964	4,005,605	1,361,455	430,801	258,963	42,516	581,436	—	11,791,431	25,700,000	—	—	45.3	41.1	101.9	88.3
1965	3,987,690	1,388,561	560,210	262,431	—	599,945	—	11,710,117	28,222,000	—	—	46.8	42.1	105.0	91.7
1966	3,948,193	1,417,435	564,924	266,555	38,778	620,827	—	11,029,396	—	—	—	47.6	43.3	106.8	94.0
1967	3,910,509	1,452,187	570,546	266,303	—	639,112	—	10,738,541	30,464,000	—	—	54.6	49.7	119.2	103.7
1968	3,868,854	1,480,412	582,577	267,262	35,794	660,259	—	10,249,740	31,617,200	—	—	54.1	49.7	124.5	106.7
1969	3,817,846	1,508,050	589,993	268,460	—	682,183	—	9,681,209	33,396,000	—	—	50.3	44.5	122.9	103.8

	Membership								National Red Cross						
												Income			
												National organization		Including local chapters	
	Masonic orders	Benevolent and Protective Order of Elks	Modern Woodmen of America	Kiwanis	Improved Order of Redmen	Rotary, worldwide	Lions International	National Parent Teacher Association	Membership	Adult volunteers	Junior membership	Total	From contributions	Total	From contributions
	Bg265	Bg266	Bg267	Bg268	Bg269	Bg270	Bg271	Bg272	Bg273	Bg274	Bg275	Bg276	Bg277	Bg278	Bg279
Year	Number	Number	Number	Number	Number	Number	Number	Number	Number	Number	Number	Million dollars	Million dollars	Million dollars	Million dollars
1970	3,763,213	1,520,731	597,654	269,754	34,423	706,372	522,525	9,210,911	33,587,000	—	—	70.2	63.8	147.1	125.5
1971	3,718,718	1,531,912	608,860	269,340	—	725,271	528,448	8,590,622	35,833,166	—	—	64.0	56.8	175.1	119.0
1972	3,991,507	1,541,784	623,774	271,188	32,051	742,493	539,273	8,236,649	36,424,000	—	—	—	—	177.4	113.0
1973	3,611,448	1,558,772	639,986	276,189	—	761,074	548,149	7,658,014	36,465,000	—	—	—	—	211.0	146.6
1974	3,561,767	1,582,735	658,398	278,966	31,136	779,373	556,315	7,057,030	30,868,000	1,475,907	—	75.9	64.6	219.6	128.0
1975	3,512,628	1,611,139	685,632	281,768	—	796,806	564,413	6,620,764	30,945,000	—	—	71.7	57.8	248.7	125.6
1976	3,470,980	1,624,702	717,463	286,402	29,907	813,704	658,391	6,403,854	—	1,387,415	—	76.0	61.0	285.1	129.3
1977	3,418,844	1,634,488	748,030	290,062	—	845,092	570,727	6,329,348	—	1,441,364	—	98.9	59.0	347.3	135.4
1978	3,360,409	1,644,496	781,190	297,682	29,807	851,547	569,478	6,170,141	—	1,382,749	—	103.0	60.0	377.8	141.8
1979	3,304,334	1,649,267	835,000	302,046	—	895,740	569,022	6,069,438	—	—	—	—	—	426.9	152.1
1980	3,251,528	1,640,247	875,000	302,453	23,932	907,943	564,158	5,893,047	—	—	—	—	—	484.3	204.4
1981	3,188,175	1,631,508	908,000	—	—	925,571	565,297	5,288,135	—	1,405,743	—	—	—	561.9	203.9
1982	3,121,746	1,621,378	930,000	—	22,294	961,256	566,565	5,341,984	—	1,374,579	—	—	—	637.1	205.3
1983	3,060,242	1,613,647	967,500	—	—	991,047	565,736	5,413,162	—	1,457,658	—	—	—	722.2	238.4
1984	2,992,289	1,594,954	958,800	—	21,120	1,013,033	557,139	5,604,821	—	1,443,108	—	—	—	786.6	262.2
1985	2,914,421	1,560,825	933,973	—	—	1,038,747	549,656	5,842,974	—	1,734,604	—	—	—	850.7	283.4
1986	2,839,962	1,529,871	925,466	—	19,496	1,056,888	542,566	6,168,429	—	1,415,249	—	—	—	972.7	341.0
1987	2,763,828	1,500,665	928,747	—	—	1,091,056	537,368	6,466,350	—	—	—	—	—	—	—
1988	2,862,537	1,475,028	934,716	—	18,754	1,121,230	528,768	6,642,956	—	1,137,876	—	—	—	1,000.4	315.4
1989	2,608,935	1,448,043	947,328	—	—	1,143,296	521,230	6,858,550	—	—	—	—	—	1,140.2	333.4
1990	2,531,643	1,421,864	955,363	—	—	1,155,810	514,960	7,029,248	—	—	—	—	—	1,465.6	520.0
1991	2,452,676	1,387,273	—	—	—	1,171,348	510,939	6,825,100	—	—	—	—	—	1,410.0	386.1
1992	2,371,863	1,353,376	—	—	—	1,190,102	502,679	6,820,514	—	—	—	—	—	—	—
1993	2,293,949	1,317,825	—	—	—	—	490,946	6,748,735	—	—	—	—	—	1,567.0	394.7
1994	2,225,611	1,282,017	—	—	—	1,206,112	483,831	6,785,639	—	—	—	—	—	—	—
1995	2,153,316	1,244,898	—	—	—	1,213,748	478,452	6,487,791	—	—	—	—	—	—	—
1996	—	—	—	—	—	—	—	6,515,030	—	—	—	—	—	1,813.9	573.0
1997	—	—	—	—	—	—	—	—	—	—	—	—	—	1,939.6	573.0
1998	—	—	—	—	—	—	—	—	—	—	—	—	—	2,080.4	655.0
1999	—	—	—	—	—	—	—	—	—	—	—	—	—	2,421.5	817.3

[1] For 1877–1878.

[2] For 1888–1889.

[3] For 1898–1899.

[4] For 1919–1920.

[5] For 1959–1960.

[6] Membership criteria were liberalized in this year.

[7] Junior membership was not reported after this year.

[8] Figure includes $20 million for Mississippi flood relief.

Sources

Series Bg265. Unpublished data supplied by the Masonic Service Association of the United States.

Series Bg266. *Grandlodge Proceedings, Benevolent and Protective Order of Elks* (Office of the Grand Secretary, 1996), and James R. Nicholson, Lee A. Donaldson, et al., *History of the Order of Elks, 1868–1998*, revised edition (Benevolent and Protective Order of Elks, 1992).

Series Bg267. Leland A. Larson and James R. Cook, *The Woodmen Story: Our First 100 Years* (Woodmen of the World Life Insurance Society, 1992).

Series Bg268. L. A. "Larry" Hapgood, *The Men Who Wear the K: The Story of Kiwanis* (Kiwanis International, 1981).

Series Bg269. Robert E. Davis, *The Improved Order of Redmen and Degree of Pochahontas, 1765–1988* (Robert E. Davis, ca. 1990).

Series Bg270. *Historical Review of Rotary* (Rotary International, ca. 1995), and unpublished data supplied by Rotary International.

(continued)

TABLE Bg265–279 Membership and income of fraternal and service organizations, by organization: 1847–1999 *Continued*

Series Bg271. Data provided by Lions Clubs International.

Series Bg272. Unpublished data provided by Annie Wang, Librarian, National Parent Teacher Association.

Series Bg273–279. Red Cross, annual reports.

Documentation

The reporting years varied from organization to organization and within organizations over time.

Series Bg270. Rotary membership figures are for the worldwide membership of Rotary International. Rotary was unable to provide membership statistics for just the United States.

Series Bg271. Lions International was unable to provide membership totals for just the United States, but it did report approximate U.S. membership totals for 1916–1947 and 1970–1995. For the early period, the figures represent membership in the United States and a few Central and South American countries. In the later period, the numbers include "USA Affiliates, Bermudas, and Bahamas."

Series Bg276 and Bg278. Includes all revenues of the organization.

Series Bg277 and Bg279. Includes all income defined by the organizations as contributions.

TABLE Bg280–291 Membership in the Boy Scouts and Girl Scouts, and survey respondent membership in selected voluntary associations: 1911–1997

Contributed by Colin B. Burke

	Boy Scout members		Girl Scout members		National sample surveys							
					Number of voluntary organization memberships	Percent reporting membership in						
	Boys	Men and boys	Girls	Adults		Fraternal organization	Nationality organization	Professional group	Service club	Veterans' organization	Youth group	Sample size
	Bg280	Bg281	Bg282	Bg283	Bg284	Bg285	Bg286	Bg287	Bg288	Bg289	Bg290	Bg291
Year	Number	Number	Number	Number	Number	Percent	Percent	Percent	Percent	Percent	Percent	Number
1911	—	61,495	—	—	—	—	—	—	—	—	—	—
1912	—	97,495	8,000 [1]	—	—	—	—	—	—	—	—	—
1913	—	115,634	—	—	—	—	—	—	—	—	—	—
1914	—	127,685	—	—	—	—	—	—	—	—	—	—
1915	143,782	182,303	—	—	—	—	—	—	—	—	—	—
1916	—	245,183	—	—	—	—	—	—	—	—	—	—
1917	—	783,574	—	—	—	—	—	—	—	—	—	—
1918	—	418,984	32,000	2,100	—	—	—	—	—	—	—	—
1919	—	462,060	39,000	3,300	—	—	—	—	—	—	—	—
1920	376,537	478,528	47,000	5,000	—	—	—	—	—	—	—	—
1921	—	513,015	63,500	7,000	—	—	—	—	—	—	—	—
1922	—	534,415	65,000	8,000	—	—	—	—	—	—	—	—
1923	—	587,578	69,453	11,777	—	—	—	—	—	—	—	—
1924	—	696,620	77,647	12,068	—	—	—	—	—	—	—	—
1925	—	756,857	97,335	14,696	—	—	—	—	—	—	—	—
1926	—	783,574	114,817	17,496	—	—	—	—	—	—	—	—
1927	—	785,633	139,760	21,653	—	—	—	—	—	—	—	—
1928	—	819,791	162,575	24,059	—	—	—	—	—	—	—	—
1929	—	833,897	174,452	26,913	—	—	—	—	—	—	—	—
1930	623,382	847,051	203,523	33,725	—	—	—	—	—	—	—	—
1931	—	878,358	227,230	40,187	—	—	—	—	—	—	—	—
1932	—	878,461	245,216	45,626	—	—	—	—	—	—	—	—
1933	—	904,240	259,829	50,184	—	—	—	—	—	—	—	—
1934	—	973,589	297,732	58,020	—	—	—	—	—	—	—	—
1935	—	1,027,833	312,672	66,961	—	—	—	—	—	—	—	—
1936	—	1,069,837	322,225	72,348	—	—	—	—	—	—	—	—
1937	—	—	354,419	80,723	—	—	—	—	—	—	—	—
1938	—	1,242,009	415,701	96,051	—	—	—	—	—	—	—	—
1939	—	1,357,993	452,239	107,151	—	—	—	—	—	—	—	—
1940	1,106,000	1,449,412	508,893	123,030	—	—	—	—	—	—	—	—
1941	—	1,522,302	541,550	134,067	—	—	—	—	—	—	—	—
1942	—	1,553,080	579,563	142,037	—	—	—	—	—	—	—	—
1943	—	1,613,783	663,302	154,003	—	—	—	—	—	—	—	—
1944	—	1,866,356	818,003	194,462	—	—	—	—	—	—	—	—
1945	1,534,000	1,977,463	936,595	236,912	—	—	—	—	—	—	—	—
1946	—	2,063,397	957,599	256,314	—	—	—	—	—	—	—	—
1947	—	2,141,984	1,030,095	293,867	—	—	—	—	—	—	—	—
1948	—	2,210,766	1,072,495	312,369	—	—	—	—	—	—	—	—
1949	—	2,579,515	1,136,179	332,117	—	—	—	—	—	—	—	—

Notes appear at end of table

TABLE Bg280–291 Membership in the Boy Scouts and Girl Scouts, and survey respondent membership in selected voluntary associations: 1911–1997 *Continued*

	Boy Scout members		Girl Scout members		National sample surveys							
						Percent reporting membership in						
	Boys	Men and boys	Girls	Adults	Number of voluntary organization memberships	Fraternal organization	Nationality organization	Professional group	Service club	Veterans' organization	Youth group	Sample size
	Bg280	Bg281	Bg282	Bg283	Bg284	Bg285	Bg286	Bg287	Bg288	Bg289	Bg290	Bg291
Year	Number	Number	Number	Number	Number	Percent	Percent	Percent	Percent	Percent	Percent	Number
1950	2,072,000	2,795,222	1,267,742	378,367	—	—	—	—	—	—	—	—
1951	—	2,942,779	1,372,412	412,285	—	—	—	—	—	—	—	—
1952	—	3,183,266	1,490,257	447,660	—	—	—	—	—	—	—	—
1953	—	3,395,884	1,607,279	486,829	—	—	—	—	—	—	—	—
1954	—	3,774,015	1,753,870	542,915	—	—	—	—	—	—	—	—
1955	3,056,000	4,175,134	2,025,067	617,549	—	—	—	—	—	—	—	—
1956	—	4,526,302	2,387,727	669,821	—	—	—	—	—	—	—	—
1957	—	4,751,495	2,387,727 [2]	726,688	—	—	—	—	—	—	—	—
1958	—	4,950,885	2,529,554	764,850	—	—	—	—	—	—	—	—
1959	—	5,043,195	2,622,480	779,198	—	—	—	—	—	—	—	—
1960	3,783,000	5,160,958	2,645,730	773,408	—	—	—	—	—	—	—	—
1961	—	5,210,294	2,984,565	769,331	—	—	—	—	—	—	—	—
1962	3,909,000	5,322,167	2,687,717	747,386	—	—	—	—	—	—	—	—
1963	4,016,000	5,446,910	2,835,633	693,360	—	—	—	—	—	—	—	—
1964	—	5,583,700	3,035,117	625,697	—	—	—	—	—	—	—	—
1965	4,231,000	5,732,708	3,030,009	616,841	—	—	—	—	—	—	—	—
1966	4,289,000	5,831,521	2,968,239	625,574	—	—	—	—	—	—	—	—
1967	4,461,000	6,058,508	3,022,375	629,148	—	—	—	—	—	—	—	—
1968	4,608,000	6,247,160	3,154,619	602,405	—	—	—	—	—	—	—	—
1969	4,592,000	6,183,086	3,249,644	671,759	—	—	—	—	—	—	—	—
1970	4,683,000	6,287,284	3,247,737	658,651	—	—	—	—	—	—	—	—
1971	4,806,000	6,427,026	3,235,248	667,586	—	—	—	—	—	—	—	—
1972	—	6,524,640	3,109,826	616,494	—	—	—	—	—	—	—	—
1973	—	6,405,225	2,952,516	585,311	—	—	—	—	—	—	—	—
1974	—	5,803,885	2,754,730	536,061	—	13.68	3.50	13.01	8.89	8.89	10.31	1,484
1975	3,933,000	5,318,070	2,723,000	494,966	1.77	10.74	2.48	11.68	8.32	6.98	9.66	1,490
1976	3,600,000	4,884,082	2,623,225	536,991	—	—	—	—	—	—	—	—
1977	3,466,000	4,718,138	2,582,522	557,448	1.84	10.20	3.40	12.94	10.65	8.24	10.26	1,530
1978	3,303,000	4,493,491	2,510,983	572,369	1.73	10.18	2.55	13.19	8.36	6.46	8.94	1,532
1979	3,176,000	4,284,469	2,338,914	572,362	—	—	—	—	—	—	—	—
1980	3,207,000	4,326,082	2,250,026	534,322	1.58	10.42	2.52	12.81	8.92	7.36	7.97	1,468
1981	3,244,000	4,355,723	2,275,958	553,500	—	—	—	—	—	—	—	—
1982	3,425,000	4,542,449	2,247,141	572,061	—	—	—	—	—	—	—	—
1983	3,567,214	4,688,953	2,280,977	607,150	1.75	9.44	3.56	15.76	10.32	6.63	10.51	1,599
1984	3,657,000	4,748,511	2,247,256	623,828	—	9.10	3.33	15.34	10.39	6.86	9.37	1,473
1985	3,755,000	4,845,040	2,172,353	629,582	—	—	—	—	—	—	—	—
1986	4,037,000	5,170,979	2,248,398	669,223	1.87	8.98	4.63	15.37	11.29	5.85	10.54	1,470
1987	4,180,000	5,347,098	2,274,055	672,814	1.64	8.85	2.47	13.47	8.96	5.77	8.36	1,819
1988	4,228,000	5,377,493	2,345,234	706,722	1.75	8.43	2.21	13.54	11.03	8.43	10.73	997
1989	4,247,000	5,363,593	2,415,099	759,703	1.55	9.08	3.38	17.68	9.66	7.54	9.28	1,035
1990	4,293,000	5,445,899	2,480,270	788,360	1.53	9.68	4.56	15.57	9.68	7.12	10.46	899
1991	4,150,000	5,319,226	2,560,718	821,988	1.45	9.05	4.52	16.32	8.95	6.98	8.55	1,017
1992	4,146,000	5,339,660	2,647,336	862,977	—	—	—	—	—	—	—	—
1993	4,165,000	5,355,401	2,613,036	826,692	1.60	7.95	4.73	18.07	12.39	6.72	9.93	1,057
1994	4,188,000	5,377,920	2,561,378	801,830	1.61	9.98	3.52	18.59	9.98	7.83	10.37	511
1995	4,256,000	5,456,617	—	783,860	—	—	—	—	—	—	—	—
1996	4,398,677	5,628,806	—	806,630	—	—	—	—	—	—	—	—
1997	—	—	2,670,672	854,733	—	—	—	—	—	—	—	—

[1] Estimated.

[2] Original data appear to be in error and cannot be corrected.

Sources

Series Bg280–283. Unpublished data provided by the Boy Scouts and Girl Scouts of America.

Series Bg284. National Organization for Research at the University of Chicago data cited in Everett G. Ladd, "The Data Just Don't Show an Erosion of Social Capital," *Public Perspective* 7 (4) (1996): 9.

Series Bg285–291. Compiled and computed from the National Opinion Research Center's General Social Survey data.

Documentation

Series Bg284. Mean number reported in national surveys.

Series Bg285–291. The sample size for the General Social Survey data was the same for each question during a year. Those interested in the statistical power of the estimates may use series Bg291 to return the other series to the original absolute numbers.

TABLE Bg292–293 Organized bowling teams and membership: 1896–1996

Contributed by Colin B. Burke

	WIBC membership	Bowling teams
	Bg292	Bg293
Year	Number	Number
1896	—	60
1897	—	75
1898	—	100
1899	—	120
1900	—	150
1901	—	200
1902	—	220
1903	—	400
1904	—	470
1905	—	630
1906	—	970
1907	—	1,266
1908	—	1,320
1909	—	1,300
1910	—	1,400
1911	—	1,200
1912	—	1,700
1913	—	1,700
1914	—	1,500
1915	—	2,100
1916	40	3,200
1917	412	3,300
1918	641	3,100
1919	1,005	2,700
1920	1,220	5,100
1921	1,920	4,800
1922	2,219	7,500
1923	2,885	11,000
1924	3,769	10,000
1925	4,576	12,000
1926	5,357	15,000
1927	6,095	18,000
1928	7,757	22,000
1929	8,985	27,000
1930	9,400	43,000
1931	9,746	44,000
1932	8,386	39,000
1933	10,483	29,000
1934	13,409	32,000
1935	15,886	41,000
1936	22,308	52,000
1937	36,160	64,000
1938	51,913	93,000
1939	81,776	103,000
1940	127,705	132,000
1941	183,737	163,000
1942	200,610	190,000
1943	212,581	150,000
1944	252,540	151,000
1945	250,478	172,000
1946	301,064	184,000
1947	362,779	250,117
1948	432,926	284,777
1949	495,880	310,299
1950	542,723	320,878
1951	582,703	322,277
1952	630,421	333,300
1953	665,427	351,506
1954	706,193	368,231
1955	764,456	386,912
1956	865,603	425,089
1957	1,005,157	492,249
1958	1,231,529	571,457
1959	1,543,362	714,395
1960	1,906,098	858,869
1961	2,212,339	—
1962	2,453,783	—
1963	2,607,370	—
1964	2,736,393	—
1965	2,821,747	—
1966	2,896,693	1,248,427
1967	2,941,739	—
1968	2,968,268	—
1969	2,988,077	—
1970	3,058,977	—
1971	3,184,711	—
1972	3,343,965	—
1973	3,531,061	—
1974	3,692,694	—
1975	3,870,947	—
1976	4,043,631	1,454,727
1977	4,209,220	—
1978	4,232,143	—
1979	4,187,053	—
1980	4,112,012	—
1981	4,064,861	—
1982	3,947,229	—
1983	3,886,718	—
1984	3,713,751	—
1985	3,555,679	—
1986	3,351,411	1,466,743
1987	3,184,196	—
1988	3,026,468	—
1989	2,859,570	—
1990	2,711,909	—
1991	2,523,000	1,283,075
1992	2,403,000	1,199,017
1993	2,191,000	1,136,370
1994	2,036,000	1,115,185
1995	1,916,761	1,078,553
1996	—	1,023,785

Sources

Series Bg292. A. W. Karcher and Karen Sytsma, editors, *WIBC: The First 75 Years 1916–1991, A History of the Women's International Bowling Congress* (WIBC, n.d.), and unpublished data supplied by the Women's International Bowling Congress.

Series Bg293. American Bowling Congress, *Annual Report*; *Historical Statistics of the United States* (1975), Series H863; and unpublished data provided by the staff of the American Bowling Congress's *Bowling Magazine*.

Documentation

Although there has been much interest among scholars in participation in group recreational activities, statistics on recreation have not been widely and rigorously compiled nor published in a systematic way. One major difficulty is that recreation, as a field of human activity and of social science research, has not been clearly defined in a manner accepted by all students. This general problem, and some of the consequent statistical problems, were explored in the study by Marion Clawson, "Statistical Data Available for Economic Research on Certain Types of Recreation," *Journal of the American Statistical Association* (March 1959): 281–305. In general, many more data are available in the files of public agencies or private groups than have been published, and much of the publication is in forms not physically permanent or likely to be preserved in libraries and other reference sources. For years prior to 1958, particularly for individual states and other geographic areas, some data may be found in a report by Clawson, *Statistics on Outdoor Recreation* (Resources for the Future, 1958).

Series Bg292. Memberships were assigned to years on the basis of the data provided by the WIBC. Note that *Statistical Abstract of the United States* assigned data one year earlier than the years in this series.

Series Bg293. The data cover organized tenpin bowling leagues of the American Bowling Congress, the WIBC, and the American Junior Bowling Congress.

TABLE Bg294–307 Voluntary organizations and employees, by state and type of organization: 1935

Contributed by Colin B. Burke

	Organizations							Employees						
	Trade and professional associations	Chambers of Commerce and boards of trade	Civic organizations	War veterans' organizations	Fraternal organizations	Youth organizations	Welfare and relief organizations	Trade and professional associations	Chambers of Commerce and boards of trade	Civic organizations	War veterans' organizations	Fraternal organizations	Youth organizations	Welfare and relief organizations
	Bg294	Bg295	Bg296	Bg297	Bg298	Bg299	Bg300	Bg301	Bg302	Bg303	Bg304	Bg305	Bg306	Bg307
State	Number	Number	Number	Number	Number	Number	Number	Number	Number	Number	Number	Number	Number	Number
Alabama	31	13	3	2	34	18	9	128	49	6	—	153	159	—
Arizona	9	14	3	1	18	8	3	37	30	10	—	61	54	15
Arkansas	21	26	3	6	45	12	11	110	52	4	12	158	58	32
California	418	136	39	—	483	121	114	2,057	592	132	—	1,496	1,270	1,402
Colorado	7	18	3	2	98	23	17	115	60	14	—	304	237	97
Connecticut	38	14	6	10	92	65	51	177	49	18	22	269	732	394
Delaware	0	0	0	2	7	3	2	0	0	0	—	32	161	—
District of Columbia	90	4	1	6	12	5	15	682	—	—	101	106	293	133
Florida	32	40	8	2	36	13	9	214	132	16	—	114	87	17
Georgia	63	22	9	6	70	37	28	768	56	14	8	261	222	153
Idaho	7	9	0	2	41	8	3	31	16	0	—	127	55	4
Illinois	319	56	12	14	237	105	93	3,325	488	228	64	907	2,248	863
Indiana	68	33	12	28	264	62	45	400	183	38	144	1,014	664	378
Iowa	39	28	4	28	164	50	22	178	97	8	61	561	374	102
Kansas	21	21	2	3	54	24	13	76	76	—	—	186	141	70
Kentucky	25	15	1	8	99	23	25	227	50	—	17	266	290	491
Louisiana	35	15	3	3	40	15	12	260	70	5	10	145	115	64
Maine	5	14	2	2	51	17	8	29	15	—	—	190	104	26
Maryland	25	4	5	1	27	16	13	70	—	12	—	142	484	229
Massachusetts	75	32	17	31	178	133	117	306	161	68	56	538	1,577	776
Michigan	83	36	9	15	160	57	42	405	139	51	60	761	763	381
Minnesota	149	25	11	13	155	46	60	344	279	33	57	453	591	994
Mississippi	3	17	2	3	19	14	2	109	35	—	—	52	69	—
Missouri	128	31	14	8	84	46	54	727	156	61	85	319	632	890
Montana	14	17	2	4	54	9	6	36	31	—	5	202	61	13
Nebraska	33	20	1	4	91	19	14	130	90	—	27	487	204	137
Nevada	2	1	0	1	11	1	0	—	—	0	—	26	—	0
New Hampshire	4	8	1	4	23	18	7	93	14	—	7	60	109	37
New Jersey	39	12	5	12	139	90	56	301	59	18	22	570	1,251	374
New Mexico	4	7	2	—	7	3	1	—	13	—	—	16	21	—
New York	579	80	41	30	368	223	327	6,566	420	208	68	1,362	5,097	4,821
North Carolina	46	26	4	2	36	36	14	124	157	7	—	106	296	45
North Dakota	5	8	3	1	21	9	6	17	21	6	—	93	64	—
Ohio	186	48	22	35	438	143	139	1,172	234	112	97	1,847	2,351	1,792
Oklahoma	36	44	3	4	35	18	10	217	119	8	11	111	139	46

(continued)

TABLE Bg294–307 Voluntary organizations and employees, by state and type of organization: 1935 *Continued*

	Organizations							Employees						
	Trade and professional associations	Chambers of Commerce and boards of trade	Civic organizations	War veterans' organizations	Fraternal organizations	Youth organizations	Welfare and relief organizations	Trade and professional associations	Chambers of Commerce and boards of trade	Civic organizations	War veterans' organizations	Fraternal organizations	Youth organizations	Welfare and relief organizations
	Bg294	Bg295	Bg296	Bg297	Bg298	Bg299	Bg300	Bg301	Bg302	Bg303	Bg304	Bg305	Bg306	Bg307
State	Number	Number	Number	Number	Number	Number	Number	Number	Number	Number	Number	Number	Number	Number
Oregon	51	27	3	—	51	13	18	318	94	8	—	189	142	231
Pennsylvania	143	38	18	92	430	167	147	1,089	203	68	249	1,712	2,144	2,210
Rhode Island	12	5	3	3	20	12	15	58	55	7	6	83	213	60
South Carolina	9	12	1	0	16	18	7	33	33	—	—	45	96	—
South Dakota	5	6	1	1	25	6	1	20	18	—	—	93	49	—
Tennessee	63	13	9	7	66	30	38	237	78	26	18	272	294	196
Texas	67	118	9	12	99	45	18	321	278	30	39	366	463	132
Utah	16	5	1	—	20	2	5	76	43	—	—	75	—	29
Vermont	5	4	1	1	21	9	5	77	7	—	—	49	33	13
Virginia	44	19	10	0	68	40	36	197	75	22	5	207	379	230
Washington	115	23	15	—	202	47	52	652	119	22	—	637	313	363
West Virginia	20	10	2	0	54	28	13	66	25	—	0	186	225	50
Wisconsin	72	24	6	12	99	33	31	243	116	28	70	585	536	270
Wyoming	4	5	3	—	50	6	2	12	—	3	—	91	12	—

Source

U.S. Bureau of the Census, *Census of Business, 1935: Non-profit Organizations, Office Buildings, and Miscellaneous* (May 1937).

Documentation

The Census Bureau advised that this census was incomplete and provided some details of its failings (p. 2 of the source). Despite these faults, the census seems informative. These series should be compared to those of the Internal Revenue Service for the 1940s (Table Bg41–54).

TABLE Bg308–319 Voluntary membership organizations – number, indicators of economic significance, employment, employee compensation, expenditures, and income, by source: 1909–2000

Contributed by Colin B. Burke and Susan B. Carter

	National income originating in nonprofit membership organizations	Personal consumption expenditures for recreation, clubs, and fraternal organizations	Nonprofit membership organizations			Nonprofit civic, social, and fraternal organizations						Fraternal, ethnic, foreign interest, and nationality organizations
						Expenditures		Income				
			Total compensation of employees	Wage and salary accruals per FTE employee	FTE employees	Annual wages and salaries	Operating expenditures	Private contributions	Private payments	Government payments	Other receipts	
	Bg308	Bg309	Bg310	Bg311	Bg312	Bg313	Bg314	Bg315	Bg316	Bg317	Bg318	Bg319
Year	Million dollars	Million dollars	Million dollars	Million dollars	Thousand	Billion dollars	Billion dollars	Billion dollars	Billion dollars	Billion dollars	Billion dollars	Number
1909	—	121	—	—	—	—	—	—	—	—	—	—
1914	—	140	—	—	—	—	—	—	—	—	—	—
1919	—	242	—	—	—	—	—	—	—	—	—	—
1921	—	242	—	—	—	—	—	—	—	—	—	—
1923	—	242	—	—	—	—	—	—	—	—	—	—
1925	—	275	—	—	—	—	—	—	—	—	—	—
1927	—	283	—	—	—	—	—	—	—	—	—	—
1929	640	302	605	1712	351	—	—	—	—	—	—	—
1930	649	294	612	1698	358	—	—	—	—	—	—	—
1931	626	277	589	1653	354	—	—	—	—	—	—	—
1932	569	242	531	1545	341	—	—	—	—	—	—	—
1933	527	208	487	1442	335	—	—	—	—	—	—	—
1934	532	199	492	1440	339	—	—	—	—	—	—	—
1935	528	197	489	1435	338	—	—	—	—	—	—	—
1936	546	198	507	1465	342	—	—	—	—	—	—	—
1937	547	203	509	1497	332	—	—	—	—	—	—	—
1938	556	200	519	1529	331	—	—	—	—	—	—	—
1939	556	199	521	1546	328	—	—	—	—	—	—	—
1940	599	203	565	1408	390	—	—	—	—	—	—	—
1941	640	203	606	1379	427	—	—	—	—	—	—	—
1942	716	205	682	1482	448	—	—	—	—	—	—	—
1943	819	217	785	1679	455	—	—	—	—	—	—	—
1944	916	236	883	1795	479	—	—	—	—	—	—	—
1945	983	281	952	1876	493	—	—	—	—	—	—	—
1946	1,193	359	1166	1984	572	—	—	—	—	—	—	—
1947	1,308	397	1280	2077	599	—	—	—	—	—	—	—
1948	1,492	435	1464	2090	647	—	—	—	—	—	—	—
1949	1,686	454	—	—	—	—	—	—	—	—	—	—
1950	1,803	462	—	—	—	—	—	—	—	—	—	—
1951	1,971	477	—	—	—	—	—	—	—	—	—	—
1952	2,096	498	—	—	—	—	—	—	—	—	—	—
1953	2,310	517	—	—	—	—	—	—	—	—	—	—
1954	2,486	539	—	—	—	—	—	—	—	—	—	—
1955	2,675	569	—	—	—	—	—	—	—	—	—	—
1956	2,873	611	—	—	—	—	—	—	—	—	—	—
1957	3,120	653	—	—	—	—	—	—	—	—	—	—
1958	3,378	692	—	—	—	—	—	—	—	—	—	—
1959	3,620	721	—	—	—	—	—	—	—	—	—	—

(continued)

TABLE Bg308–319 Voluntary membership organizations – number, indicators of economic significance, employment, employee compensation, expenditures, and income, by source: 1909–2000 *Continued*

	National income originating in nonprofit membership organizations	Personal consumption expenditures for recreation, clubs, and fraternal organizations	Nonprofit membership organizations			Nonprofit civic, social, and fraternal organizations						Fraternal, ethnic, foreign interest, and nationality organizations
						Expenditures		Income				
			Total compensation of employees	Wage and salary accruals per FTE employee	FTE employees	Annual wages and salaries	Operating expenditures	Private contributions	Private payments	Government payments	Other receipts	
	Bg308	Bg309	Bg310	Bg311	Bg312	Bg313	Bg314	Bg315	Bg316	Bg317	Bg318	Bg319
Year	Million dollars	Million dollars	Million dollars	Million dollars	Thousand	Billion dollars	Billion dollars	Billion dollars	Billion dollars	Billion dollars	Billion dollars	Number
1960	3,870	733	—	—	—	—	—	—	—	—	—	—
1961	4,041	763	—	—	—	—	—	—	—	—	—	—
1962	4,298	773	—	—	—	—	—	—	—	—	—	—
1963	4,562	808	—	—	—	—	—	—	—	—	—	—
1964	4,907	854	—	—	—	—	—	—	—	—	—	—
1965	5,306	879	—	—	—	—	—	—	—	—	—	—
1966	5,785	934	—	—	—	—	—	—	—	—	—	—
1967	6,346	988	—	—	—	—	—	—	—	—	—	—
1968	6,955	1,047	—	—	—	—	—	—	—	—	—	—
1969	7,762	1,112	—	—	—	—	—	—	—	—	—	—
1970	8411	1,158	—	—	—	—	—	—	—	—	—	—
1971	—	1,500	—	—	—	—	—	—	—	—	—	—
1972	—	1,500	—	—	—	—	—	—	—	—	—	—
1973	—	1,600	—	—	—	—	—	—	—	—	—	—
1974	—	1,800	—	—	—	1.2	3.2	0.8	—	—	—	—
1975	—	2,000	10879	7616	1335	—	—	—	—	—	—	—
1976	—	2,100	11317	7936	1327	—	—	—	—	—	—	—
1977	—	2,200	12400	8751	1316	1.5	4.0	1.3	0.5	2.1	0.4	—
1978	—	2,100	13708	9591	1324	—	—	—	—	—	—	—
1979	—	2,500	14718	10373	1312	—	—	—	—	—	—	—
1980	—	2,900	16153	11420	1304	1.9	5.1	1.4	0.7	2.7	0.4	435
1981	—	3,400	17198	12248	1291	—	—	—	—	—	—	—
1982	—	4,100	18349	13005	1311	2.1	5.6	1.7	0.8	2.9	0.4	—
1983	—	4,400	19696	13885	1297	2.3	6.1	1.9	0.8	3.2	0.5	—
1984	—	4,700	21235	14814	1296	2.5	6.7	2.1	0.9	3.5	0.5	—
1985	—	5,500	21920	15100	1296	—	—	—	—	—	—	492
1986	—	6,100	23796	16210	1310	—	—	—	—	—	—	—
1987	—	6,700	25477	16553	1377	3.2	8.6	3.1	1.2	4.5	0.6	—
1988	—	7,100	28220	17546	1482	3.5	—	—	—	—	—	544
1989	—	8,000	30640	17898	1571	3.8	10.6	3.4	2.0	4.5	1.1	570
1990	—	8,700	32900	18327	1641	4.1	—	—	—	—	—	573
1991	—	9,500	35070	17466	1827	—	—	—	—	—	—	565
1992	—	10,200	36298	20066	1636	4.2	13.6	4.6	3.0	4.9	1.7	561
1993	—	11,100	39412	20990	1688	—	—	—	—	—	—	567
1994	—	11,800	41874	22016	1710	4.4	—	—	—	—	—	548
1995	—	12,700	44427	22733	1767	—	—	—	—	—	—	552
1996	—	14,000	46584	23479	1805	—	—	—	—	—	—	—
1997	—	14600	49511	24348	1863	—	—	—	—	—	—	541
1998	—	15000	54147	25306	1948	—	—	—	—	—	—	—
1999	—	15800	58431	26538	2002	—	—	—	—	—	—	—
2000	—	—	62661	27722	2052	—	—	—	—	—	—	—

TABLE Bg308–319 Voluntary membership organizations – number, indicators of economic significance, employment, employee compensation, expenditures, and income, by source: 1909–2000 *Continued*

Sources

Series Bg308. *Historical Statistics* (1975), Series T14.

Series Bg309. 1909–1970. *Historical Statistics* (1975), Series H887. 1971–1997: U.S. Bureau of Economic Analysis, *National Income and Product Accounts,* various years.

Series Bg310–312. U.S. Bureau of Economic Analysis, *National Income and Product Accounts,* various years.

Series Bg313–318. Virginia Ann Hodgkinson, Murray S. Weitzman, et al., *Nonprofit Almanac 1996–1997: Dimensions of the Independent Sector* (Jossey-Bass, 1996), Table 4.2, and earlier editions.

Series Bg319. Gale Research, *Encyclopedia of Associations* (published annually).

Documentation

The National Income and Product Accounts (NIPA) are the underlying source for most of the estimates of the income of nonprofit membership and fraternal organizations. The terms used by NIPA to categorize the nonprofit data have varied over time. There have also been variations in the types of institutions included. In the 1970s, NIPA ceased to categorize service industries according to nonprofit status.

Series Bg308. Data represent value added at factor cost. For a detailed discussion of terms, see the U.S. Bureau of Economic Analysis publications defining the NIPA series.

Series Bg309. Consists of dues and fees excluding insurance premiums. For consumer expenditures on other items, see Table Cd153–263.

Series Bg310. Measures wage and salary income per person-year of full-time work. Wages and salaries comprise all payments accruing to persons in an employee status as compensation for their work. Included are commissions, tips, and bonuses, as well as cash payments commonly referred to as wages and salaries, together with the value of those payments in kind that clearly represent an addition to the recipient's income. Income in kind is valued, so far as possible, at its cost to the employer. Service industries in which such income is a perceptible portion of wages and salaries include hotels and other lodging places and educational services. The series does not include dismissal pay, directors' fees, employer contributions to social insurance funds and private pension plans, nor accident compensation payments.

Series Bg312. These figures are in terms of full-time equivalent employment, which measures person-years of full-time employment and its equivalent work performed by part-time workers. Full-time employment is defined simply in terms of the number of hours that are customary at a particular time and place. For a full explanation of the concept, see *Survey of Current Business* (available online at the Internet site of the U.S. Bureau of Economic Analysis). Unpaid family workers are excluded due to unresolved difficulties in their definition and measurement.

Series Bg313–318. Data apply to Standard Industrial Classification (SIC) industry 864. See the introduction to Part D for a discussion of SIC codes.

Series Bg318. Includes endowment income.

Series Bg319. Assembled from the various editions of *Encyclopedia of Associations,* which list the larger or more prominent active associations.

RELIGION

Colin B. Burke

TABLE Bg320–333 Religious organizations – membership, churches and synagogues, clergy, and attendance, by denomination and region: 1776–1998

Contributed by Colin B. Burke

				Clergy		Percentage of population sample reporting church or synagogue								
							Attendance in last seven days							
								By denomination			By region			
	Church membership	Churches and church edifices	Churches	Total	Female	Membership	All denominations	Protestants	Catholics	Jews	East	Midwest	South	West
	Bg320	Bg321	Bg322	Bg323	Bg324	Bg325 [1]	Bg326	Bg327	Bg328	Bg329	Bg330	Bg331	Bg332	Bg333
Year	Number	Number	Thousand	Number	Number	Percent	Percent	Percent	Percent	Percent	Percent	Percent	Percent	Percent
1776	—	3,228 [2]	—	—	—	—	—	—	—	—	—	—	—	—
1850	—	38,061	—	26,842	—	—	—	—	—	—	—	—	—	—
1860	—	54,000	—	37,529	—	—	—	—	—	—	—	—	—	—
1870	—	63,082	—	43,874	67	—	—	—	—	—	—	—	—	—
1880	—	—	—	88,203	165	—	—	—	—	—	—	—	—	—
1890	21,699,000	142,487	—	111,942	1,143	—	—	—	—	—	—	—	—	—
1900	—	—	—	108,728	3,405	—	—	—	—	—	—	—	—	—
1906	35,068,058	192,795	—	—	—	—	—	—	—	—	—	—	—	—
1910	—	—	—	118,018	685	—	—	—	—	—	—	—	—	—
1916	41,927,000	203,432	—	—	—	—	—	—	—	—	—	—	—	—
1920	—	—	—	127,270	1,787	—	—	—	—	—	—	—	—	—
1926	54,576,346	210,924	—	—	—	—	—	—	—	—	—	—	—	—
1930	—	—	—	148,848	3,276	—	—	—	—	—	—	—	—	—
1931	59,268,764	—	—	—	—	—	—	—	—	—	—	—	—	—
1932	60,157,392	—	—	—	—	—	—	—	—	—	—	—	—	—
1933	60,812,624	—	—	—	—	—	—	—	—	—	—	—	—	—
1934	62,007,376	—	—	—	—	—	—	—	—	—	—	—	—	—
1935	62,678,177	—	—	—	—	—	—	—	—	—	—	—	—	—
1936	63,221,996	179,742	—	—	—	73	—	—	—	—	—	—	—	—
1937	63,848,094	—	—	—	—	73	—	—	—	—	—	—	—	—
1938	64,156,895	—	—	—	—	—	—	—	—	—	—	—	—	—
1939	—	—	—	—	—	72	41	—	—	—	—	—	—	—
1940	64,501,594	—	—	140,077	3,308	72	37	—	—	—	—	—	—	—
1942	68,501,186	—	—	—	—	74	36	—	—	—	—	—	—	—
1944	72,492,699	—	—	—	—	75	58	—	—	—	—	—	—	—
1945	71,700,142	—	—	—	—	75	—	—	—	—	—	—	—	—
1946	73,673,182	—	—	—	—	76	—	—	—	—	—	—	—	—
1947	77,386,188	—	—	—	—	76	45	—	—	—	—	—	—	—
1948	79,435,605	—	—	—	—	75	—	—	—	—	—	—	—	—
1949	81,862,328	—	—	—	—	—	—	—	—	—	—	—	—	—
1950	86,830,490	—	—	168,419	6,847	—	39	—	—	—	—	—	—	—
1951	88,673,006	—	—	—	—	—	—	—	—	—	—	—	—	—
1952	92,277,129	—	—	—	—	73	—	—	—	—	—	—	—	—
1953	94,842,845	—	—	—	—	—	—	—	—	—	—	—	—	—
1954	97,482,611	—	—	—	—	—	46	40	60	—	52	45	48	37
1955	100,162,529	—	—	—	—	—	49	—	—	—	53	—	50	35
1956	103,224,954	—	—	—	—	—	46	44	76	—	52	50	53	42
1957	104,189,678	—	—	—	—	—	47	40	74	18	—	—	—	—
1958	109,557,741	—	—	—	—	—	49	44	74	—	52	54	51	35
1959	112,226,905	—	—	—	—	—	47	—	—	—	—	—	—	—
1960	114,449,217	—	—	202,000	4,700	—	47	—	—	—	—	—	—	—
1961	116,109,929	—	—	—	—	—	47	41	71	21	49	49	47	36
1962	117,946,002	—	—	—	—	—	46	—	—	—	—	—	—	—
1963	120,965,238	—	—	—	—	—	46	38	71	17	59	—	48	35
1964	123,307,449	—	—	—	—	—	45	38	67	15	49	44	44	34
1965	124,682,422	—	—	—	—	73	44	—	67	—	—	—	—	—
1966	125,778,656	—	—	—	—	—	44	38	68	22	47	48	45	33
1967	126,445,110	—	—	—	—	—	43	39	66	—	46	48	47	34
1968	128,469,636	—	—	—	—	—	43	38	65	—	46	45	44	32
1969	128,505,084	—	—	—	—	—	42	37	63	22	45	46	40	35

Notes appear at end of table

TABLE Bg320–333 Religious organizations – membership, churches and synagogues, clergy, and attendance, by denomination and region: 1776–1998 *Continued*

				Clergy		Percentage of population sample reporting church or synagogue								
							Attendance in last seven days							
								By denomination			By region			
	Church membership	Churches and church edifices	Churches	Total	Female	Membership	All denominations	Protestants	Catholics	Jews	East	Midwest	South	West
	Bg320	Bg321	Bg322	Bg323	Bg324	Bg325 [1]	Bg326	Bg327	Bg328	Bg329	Bg330	Bg331	Bg332	Bg333
Year	Number	Number	Thousand	Number	Number	Percent	Percent	Percent	Percent	Percent	Percent	Percent	Percent	Percent
1970	131,045,053	—	—	219,000	—	—	42	38	60	19	43	47	44	33
1971	131,389,642	—	—	—	—	—	40	37	57	19	39	40	45	33
1972	131,424,564	—	—	—	—	—	40	—	—	19	—	—	—	—
1973	131,245,139	—	—	—	—	—	40	37	55	—	38	43	44	29
1974	131,671,743	—	332	—	—	—	40	—	—	—	—	—	—	—
1975	131,012,953	—	—	—	—	71	40	38	54	—	—	—	—	—
1976	131,897,539	—	—	—	—	71	42	40	55	—	—	—	—	—
1977	131,812,470	—	333	—	—	70	41	39	55	—	—	—	—	—
1978	133,388,776	—	—	—	—	68	41	40	52	—	—	—	—	—
1979	133,469,690	—	—	—	—	68	40	40	52	—	38	46	41	33
1980	134,816,943	—	336	—	—	69	41	39	53	—	—	—	—	—
1981	138,452,614	—	—	—	—	68	41	—	—	—	40	45	42	29
1982	139,603,059	—	339	—	—	67	41	—	—	—	—	—	—	—
1983	140,816,385	—	—	293,000	16,408	69	40	—	—	—	—	—	—	—
1984	142,172,138	—	338	—	—	68	40	—	—	—	38	42	44	33
1985	142,926,363	—	—	—	—	71	42	—	—	—	41	44	46	34
1986	142,799,662	—	—	—	—	69	40	—	—	—	—	—	—	—
1987	143,830,806	—	346	—	—	69	40	—	—	—	—	—	—	—
1988	145,383,739	—	349	—	—	65	42	—	—	—	37	48	45	36
1989	147,607,394	—	351	—	—	67	43	—	—	—	—	—	—	—
1990	—	—	351	—	—	69	40	—	—	—	—	—	—	—
1991	—	—	—	—	—	66 [3]	41	—	—	—	—	—	—	—
1992	—	—	396	—	—	71	40	—	—	—	—	—	—	—
1993	—	—	—	—	—	71	38	—	—	—	—	—	—	—
1994	—	—	—	—	—	70	40	—	—	—	—	—	—	—
1995	—	—	—	—	—	67	43	—	—	—	—	—	—	—
1996	—	—	—	354,000	43,542	66	38	45	47	—	—	—	—	—
1997	—	—	—	—	—	65	40	45	45	25	—	—	—	—
1998	—	—	—	—	—	67	—	—	—	—	—	—	—	—

[1] Prior to 1995, the estimate was based on one sample per year; thereafter, several samples per year were averaged.

[2] Estimate from Charles Paullin, which was checked against Edwin Scott Gaustad's graphs.

[3] Percentages varied among the samples by some 2 points in either direction over a year.

Sources

Series Bg320. U.S. Bureau of the Census, Censuses of 1850–1890, *Religious Bodies* (1906–1936), and National Council of Churches *Yearbook of American and Canadian Churches* (title and editors vary), annual issues.

Series Bg321. U.S. Bureau of the Census, Censuses of 1850–1890, *Religious Bodies* (1906–1936); Edwin Scott Gaustad, *Historical Atlas of Religion in America*, revised edition (Harper and Row, 1976); and Charles O. Paullin, *Atlas of the Historical Geography of the United States* (Carnegie Institution, 1932).

Series Bg322. *Yearbook of American and Canadian Churches* (various years).

Series Bg323–324. U.S. Bureau of the Census, Censuses 1850–1990, *Current Population Survey*.

Series Bg325–333. *The Gallup Poll, 1935–1971* (Random House, 1972); *The Gallup Poll, 1972–1978* (Scholarly Resources, 1978); *The Gallup Poll* (Scholarly Resources, published annually); and *Religion in America, Gallup Survey* (Princeton Research Center, 1989).

Documentation

National statistics for all religious bodies on an interdenominational basis were compiled at intervals from 1850 to 1936 by the U.S. Bureau of the Census. The compilations were of varying scope and quality. Weaknesses in the 1936 census, primarily due to lack of cooperation by several denominations and related political issues concerning government involvement in religion, led the Census Bureau to end its religious series. Since the 1930s, those interested in national religious statistics have had to rely upon estimates generated and published by several nongovernmental organizations. None of those sources has had the capability of matching the comprehensiveness of the better U.S. Census surveys. The effort of *The Christian Herald*, an early religious periodical, was superseded by that of the National Council of the Churches of Christ in the United States of America in the *Yearbook of American and Canadian Churches* (title varies), and then by the more recent and more detailed *Churches and Church Membership in the United States* (available at the Internet site of the Evangelical Lutheran Church of America), which has appeared approximately once a decade since the mid-1950s. These publications presented statistical data furnished by the major denominations but have found it difficult to identify churches and congregations not formally affiliated with a denomination.

Despite recent efforts to standardize reporting and to gather uniform statistics for special studies (see *Churches and Church Membership*), estimates concerning the denominations continue to be based upon denominational data collection and definitions. The problematic nature of the postcensus data on denominations was evident to the experts who constructed the series for the earlier editions of *Historical Statistics of the United States*:

> Practically all national religious bodies compile reports or estimates from time to time based on records kept by local churches (congregations or parishes), or from estimates furnished by the local churches. Probably about half the national bodies receive reports from their local churches annually and then issue the figures to their constituencies or to the public. The bodies which report annually the figures systematically received from their local churches are mainly the larger denominations. The other national bodies report their statistics at irregular intervals. For those

(continued)

TABLE Bg320–333 Religious organizations – membership, churches and synagogues, clergy, and attendance, by denomination and region: 1776–1998 *Continued*

denominations which have standard forms, the records are kept locally as determined by the national body. For other denominations, the records are kept in accordance with the wishes of the local churches. The statistics are gathered by the denominations for their own, often different, purposes, thus leading to variety in the forms used and in the nature of the information gathered. In addition, local church records are usually kept by persons untrained in the keeping of statistical records, or persons with only the most elementary instruction or experience. (p. 389)

In addition to the many practicalities that limited the accuracy of the statistics on religious organizations, there were and there continue to be problems of definition and, thus, specification. The Census Bureau employed a variety of names and definitions for such mundane but important indicators as church accommodations and even church buildings. For example, sittings, seats, and accommodations were used at different times to indicate the seating capacity of churches. In some censuses, churches were equated with congregations, while in others, clear distinctions were made between organizations and edifices.

Of perhaps greater importance to the task of estimating the U.S. population's commitment to religion are the varying definitions of membership used by the denominations, the changes of membership criteria within the denominations over time, and the absence of any census estimates of total national membership before the Census of 1890. As described in some detail below, denominations make their own definitions of membership, adherence, or affiliation. Some include all those baptized or living within an area. Other denominations, in contrast, restrict "membership" to those adults who have fulfilled rigorous theological and participatory requirements and categorize others who are associated with the denomination as adherents or affiliates. In the eighteenth and early nineteenth centuries, a few denominations seem to have counted as members only the full communicants who headed families. In recent years, some denominations have counted and reported both full members (communicants) and adherents. Other denominations continue to report only one type of member.

Those weaknesses have led to the employment of rather complex estimating procedures in order to create series for "inclusive" membership for each denomination which, it is hoped for at least a portion of the post–World War II era, provide a basis for denominational comparison and for judging levels of religious adherence over time and space. For example, see *Churches and Church Membership in the United States* (1980), p. xiii, as well as Table Bg450–549.

The difficulties caused by the varying definitions of membership (over denominations and time), combined with the absence of direct counts of any type of membership for all denominations until the census of 1890, have led other students of American religion to apply a range of advanced statistical methods and strong assumptions in order to create comparable membership series for the eighteenth and early nineteenth centuries. For an example of such estimates, see Roger Finke and Rodney Stark, *The Churching of America, 1776–1990: Winners and Losers in Our Religious Economy* (Rutgers University Press, 1992).

Denominational Membership Criteria and the Census Data

Many denominations altered their criteria for membership status in the nineteenth and early twentieth centuries. The trend was toward liberalization and inclusion. However, some degree of stability was achieved by the 1920s. The 1975 edition of *Historical Statistics* stated that the bodies reporting made no major changes in their definitions between the Census of Religious Bodies (1926) and the late 1970s. Although similar analyses of membership criteria have not been presented since 1975, the running comments in such publications as the *Yearbook of American and Canadian Churches* indicate continued stability.

The definitions used since 1926 for the larger bodies are as follows. The Eastern churches report estimates of the total number of persons within the cultural or nationality group served. The Jewish congregations report on the number of Jews in communities having congregations. The Roman Catholic Church, the Lutheran bodies, and the Protestant Episcopal Church report as members the total number of baptized persons, including infants. Most Protestant bodies report as members those persons who have attained full membership, usually at about age 13. One relatively large body, the Church of Christ, Scientist, forbade the enumeration of its members and the publication of statistics of affiliation. The local churches of this body reported a total membership of 268,915 in the Census of Religious Bodies for 1936. A few relatively small bodies also did not report membership figures to compilers of national data. However, it is believed that the figures presented here cover all but a fraction of total religious affiliation.

See also the text for Table Bg334–348.

Details of the Censuses

Special note must be taken in the case of the data for 1936 in relation to other years. The compilation for that year was less complete than those of other years for reasons noted here.

Limited information on religious bodies (number of congregations and buildings, and value of edifices) was first published in the census report for 1850, and similar information was included in the reports for 1860 and 1870. In 1880, the figures gathered by the Census Office were not published. In 1890, the Census Office collected figures from religious organizations concerning membership, number and value of edifices, number of ministers, and so on. The 1906 Census of Religious Bodies (two parts) was the first to be compiled by means of a questionnaire mailed to the pastors or clerks of the local churches. The Jewish congregations reported heads of families only (101,457, principally male, persons). It is indicated that in most denominations, 99 percent of the local churches to which forms were mailed made returns. The 1916 Census reported 41,926,854 members, a figure adjusted in the 1926 report to read 43,311,648 persons, for reasons given there. The Jewish congregations reported only heads of families (357,135 persons). The methods used in the 1916 and 1926 Censuses were essentially the same as those used in the 1936 Census.

Students of church statistics regard the compilation of 1926 as probably the most adequate one ever made. In this census, every local organization was classed as a church whether it was commonly known as a church, a congregation, a meeting, a society, a mission, a station, a chapel, or by some other term: "A local church may have had officers and an enrolled membership, or it may have been little more than an association or fellowship, but to be included in this enumeration it must have had a religious purpose and a distinctive membership" (1926 Census). For all denominations except the Jewish congregations, the 1926 Census reported 50,495,104 members, compared with a corrected total figure, partly estimated, of 42,954,512 persons in 1916. The Jewish congregations reported "all Jews in communities where there is a congregation," whereas in 1916 they reported only "heads of families, seat holders, and other contributors." The figures for Jews were admittedly incomplete. With this census also, the Lutheran bodies, the Protestant Episcopal Church, and the Christian Reformed Church began to report on a more inclusive basis than in previous censuses.

The data for the 1936 Census were obtained by means of a schedule for local church organizations mailed to the clergyman or the lay clerk of the local parish or congregation. The data collected were for the year 1936, or refer "to the church record year most nearly conforming to the end of that year." The Census Bureau established contact with persons in authority in the various religious bodies in order to secure lists of pastors or clerks of the local religious organizations. Special agents were employed for the purpose of securing data from "some loosely organized denominations, or those averse to publishing the statistics of their organizations." The census received only halfhearted support from a few denominations, and the total membership figures would undoubtedly have been much larger if all churches had furnished statistics. The incompleteness of returns is also reflected by the fact that the total value of church edifices – series H792 in *Historical Statistics* (1975) – is lower in 1936 than in 1926. A private compilation for 1936, published in the *Christian Herald* (July 1937) and based on official reports of the religious bodies, listed 244,147 local churches. It seems probable that about 20 percent of the officers of active local churches in 1936 did not report to the Census Bureau. The *Christian Herald* stated, for example, that the *Southern Baptist Handbook* for 1937 reported 4,482,315 members for 1936, while the Census Bureau reported only 2,700,155 members. Differences among the

TABLE Bg320–333 Religious organizations – membership, churches and synagogues, clergy, and attendance, by denomination and region: 1776–1998 *Continued*

religious bodies in defining the term "member" were noted. The Jewish congregations, continuing on a basis begun in 1926, reported "all persons of the Jewish faith living in communities in which local congregations are situated. Among the Roman Catholic and Eastern churches, all persons, even infants, are considered members, provided they have been baptized according to the rites of the church. The Protestant Episcopal Church, and the Lutheran bodies, because they also count as members all baptized persons in the congregation, tend toward the more inclusive definition of the term" (1936 Census). In the large majority of Protestant bodies, the term "member" was applied only to "communicants," or to persons who attained full membership, usually at age 13.

The Census Bureau usually secured information for the year indicated, but it also accepted a figure for the church year nearest to that for which data were sought. In the compilations of private agencies, the "latest information" is published for each denomination; in a number of instances, the actual figures of a denomination are for a previous period. The lag is usually only of several years' duration, but in a few instances (for small bodies), the actual figures are from much earlier compilations.

Series Bg320. Inclusive membership used when available. Data presented are not directly comparable from census period to census period, and caution must be exercised when using the post-1936 estimates of total membership, which were based on the annual surveys reported in the *Yearbook of American and Canadian Churches* (various years). Its editor realized that it did not cover all denominations and churches, although it probably received information for well over 90 percent of organizations. The *Yearbook*'s experts had to estimate its "inclusive" membership figures for the many denominations that reported the number of full members only. After the 1989 edition, the *Yearbook* refrained from making estimates of total U.S. membership and confined its estimates to the membership for the larger denominations. For other estimates of total "inclusive" or "adherent" membership, see Table Bg450–549. Special note must be taken in the case of the data for 1936 in relation to other census-based estimates. The compilation for that year was less complete than that of other years for reasons noted above.

Series Bg321–322. In cases when the census presented figures for organizations or congregations as well as churches, the data in the church or edifice category was selected.

Series Bg323. The census volumes indicate that the definition of clergy was changed several times, even in the late twentieth century. Detailed explanations were not provided, however.

Series Bg324. Note the erratic figures for some periods. These suggest changes in definition, ones that were not explained in the census tables.

Series Bg330–333. The regional categories were usually given as follows: East: Maine, New Hampshire, Rhode Island, New York, Connecticut, Vermont, Massachusetts, New Jersey, Pennsylvania, West Virginia, Delaware, District of Columbia, Maryland; Midwest: Ohio, Indiana, Illinois, Missouri, Minnesota, Wisconsin, Iowa, North Dakota, South Dakota, Kansas, Nebraska, Montana; South: Kentucky, Tennessee, Virginia, North Carolina, South Carolina, Georgia, Florida, Alabama, Mississippi, Texas, Arkansas, Oklahoma, Louisiana; and West: Arizona, New Mexico, Colorado, Nevada, Montana, Idaho, Wyoming, Utah, California, Washington, Oregon, Alaska, Hawai'i.

TABLE Bg334–348 Church and congregation membership, by denomination: 1790–1995

Contributed by Colin B. Burke

Year	Catholic Church	Catholic Church	Presbyterian Church	Presbyterian Church USA	Protestant Episcopal Church	Protestant Episcopal Church	Methodist Church	Methodist Church	Seventh-Day Adventist Churches	Southern Baptist Church	Salvation Army	Buddhist churches (temple or religion)	Old Catholic and Polish churches	Eastern churches	Jewish congregations
	Bg334	Bg335	Bg336	Bg337	Bg338	Bg339	Bg340	Bg341	Bg342	Bg343	Bg344	Bg345	Bg346	Bg347	Bg348
	Thousand	Number	Thousand	Number	Thousand	Number	Thousand	Number	Number	Number	Number	Thousand	Thousand	Thousand	Thousand
1790	—	—	—	—	—	—	58	—	—	—	—	—	—	—	—
1791	—	—	—	—	—	—	76	—	—	—	—	—	—	—	—
1792	—	—	—	—	—	—	66	—	—	—	—	—	—	—	—
1793	—	—	—	—	—	—	68	—	—	—	—	—	—	—	—
1794	—	—	—	—	—	—	67	—	—	—	—	—	—	—	—
1795	—	—	—	—	—	—	61	—	—	—	—	—	—	—	—
1796	—	—	—	—	—	—	57	—	—	—	—	—	—	—	—
1797	—	—	—	—	—	—	59	—	—	—	—	—	—	—	—
1798	—	—	—	—	—	—	60	—	—	—	—	—	—	—	—
1799	—	—	—	—	—	—	62	—	—	—	—	—	—	—	—
1800	—	—	—	—	—	—	65	—	—	—	—	—	—	—	—
1801	—	—	—	—	—	—	73	—	—	—	—	—	—	—	—
1802	—	—	—	—	—	—	87	—	—	—	—	—	—	—	—
1803	—	—	—	—	—	—	104	—	—	—	—	—	—	—	—
1804	—	—	—	—	—	—	114	—	—	—	—	—	—	—	—
1805	—	—	—	—	—	—	120	—	—	—	—	—	—	—	—
1806	—	—	—	—	—	—	131	—	—	—	—	—	—	—	—
1807	—	—	—	—	—	—	145	—	—	—	—	—	—	—	—
1808	—	—	—	—	—	—	153	—	—	—	—	—	—	—	—
1809	—	—	—	—	—	—	164	—	—	—	—	—	—	—	—
1810	—	—	—	—	—	—	175	—	—	—	—	—	—	—	—
1811	—	—	—	—	—	—	185	—	—	—	—	—	—	—	—
1812	—	—	—	—	—	—	196	—	—	—	—	—	—	—	—
1813	—	—	—	—	—	—	215	—	—	—	—	—	—	—	—
1814	—	—	—	—	—	—	212	—	—	—	—	—	—	—	—
1815	—	—	—	—	—	—	212	—	—	—	—	—	—	—	—
1816	—	—	—	—	—	—	215	—	—	—	—	—	—	—	—
1817	—	—	—	—	—	—	226	—	—	—	—	—	—	—	—
1818	—	—	—	—	—	—	230	—	—	—	—	—	—	—	—
1819	—	—	—	—	—	—	242	—	—	—	—	—	—	—	—
1820	—	—	—	—	—	—	258	—	—	—	—	—	—	—	—
1821	—	—	—	—	—	—	282	—	—	—	—	—	—	—	—
1822	—	—	—	—	—	—	299	—	—	—	—	—	—	—	—
1823	—	—	—	—	—	—	314	—	—	—	—	—	—	—	—
1824	—	—	—	—	—	—	330	—	—	—	—	—	—	—	—
1825	—	—	—	—	—	—	342	—	—	—	—	—	—	—	—
1826	—	—	127	—	—	—	362	—	—	—	—	—	—	—	—
1827	—	—	135	—	—	—	384	—	—	—	—	—	—	—	—
1828	—	—	146	—	—	—	423	—	—	—	—	—	—	—	—
1829	—	—	163	—	—	—	450	—	—	—	—	—	—	—	—
1830	—	—	173	—	—	—	478	—	—	—	—	—	—	—	—
1831	—	—	182	—	—	—	515	—	—	—	—	—	—	—	—
1832	—	—	217	—	—	—	551	—	—	—	—	—	—	—	—
1833	—	—	234	—	—	—	602	—	—	—	—	—	—	—	—
1834	—	—	248	—	—	—	641	—	—	—	—	—	—	—	—

Year	Catholic Church	Catholic Church	Presbyterian Church	Presbyterian Church USA	Protestant Episcopal Church	Protestant Episcopal Church	Methodist Church	Methodist Church	Seventh-Day Adventist Churches	Southern Baptist Church	Salvation Army	Buddhist churches (temple or religion)	Old Catholic and Polish churches	Eastern churches	Jewish congregations
	Bg334	Bg335	Bg336	Bg337	Bg338	Bg339	Bg340	Bg341	Bg342	Bg343	Bg344	Bg345	Bg346	Bg347	Bg348
	Thousand	Number	Thousand	Number	Thousand	Number	Thousand	Number	Number	Number	Number	Thousand	Thousand	Thousand	Thousand
1835	—	—	—	—	—	—	655	—	—	—	—	—	—	—	—
1836	—	—	219	—	—	—	651	—	—	—	—	—	—	—	—
1837	—	—	221	—	—	—	700	—	—	—	—	—	—	—	—
1838	—	—	178	—	—	—	744	—	—	—	—	—	—	—	—
1839	—	—	128	—	—	—	798	—	—	—	—	—	—	—	—
1840	—	—	127	—	—	—	856	—	—	—	—	—	—	—	—
1841	—	—	134	—	—	—	917	—	—	—	—	—	—	—	—
1842	—	—	140	—	—	—	1,072	—	—	—	—	—	—	—	—
1843	—	—	159	—	—	—	1,175	—	—	—	—	—	—	—	—
1844	—	—	166	—	—	—	1,143	—	—	—	—	—	—	—	—
1845	—	—	172	—	—	—	995	—	—	352,000	—	—	—	—	—
1846	—	—	175	—	—	—	1,168	—	—	367,000	—	—	—	—	—
1847	—	—	179	—	—	—	1,102	—	—	377,000	—	—	—	—	—
1848	—	—	192	—	—	—	1,196	—	—	386,000	—	—	—	—	—
1849	—	—	201	—	—	—	1,158	—	—	405,000	—	—	—	—	—
1850	—	—	207	—	—	—	1,186	—	—	—	—	—	—	—	—
1851	—	—	210	—	—	—	1,223	—	—	424,000	—	—	—	—	—
1852	—	—	210	—	—	—	1,254	—	—	467,000	—	—	—	—	—
1853	—	—	219	—	—	—	1,121	—	—	496,000	—	—	—	—	—
1854	—	—	225	—	—	—	1,187	—	—	519,000	—	—	—	—	—
1855	—	—	231	—	—	—	1,326	—	—	542,000	—	—	—	—	—
1856	—	—	233	—	—	—	1,348	—	—	569,000	—	—	—	—	—
1857	—	—	244	—	—	—	1,372	—	—	580,000	—	—	—	—	—
1858	—	—	259	—	—	—	1,510	—	—	618,000	—	—	—	—	—
1859	—	—	279	—	—	—	1,561	—	—	639,000	—	—	—	—	—
1860	—	—	292	—	—	—	1,661	—	—	650,000	—	—	—	—	—
1861	—	—	300	—	—	—	1,617	—	—	—	—	—	—	—	—
1862	—	—	303	—	—	—	1,549	—	—	—	—	—	—	—	—
1863	—	—	227	—	—	—	1,581	—	—	—	—	—	—	—	—
1864	—	—	231	—	—	—	1,438	—	—	—	—	—	—	—	—
1865	—	—	232	—	—	—	1,381	—	—	—	—	—	—	—	—
1866	—	—	238	—	—	—	1,428	—	—	—	—	—	—	—	—
1867	—	—	245	—	—	—	1,565	—	—	—	—	—	—	—	—
1868	—	—	251	—	—	—	1,667	—	—	—	—	—	—	—	—
1869	—	—	258	—	—	—	1,748	—	—	—	—	—	—	—	—
1870	—	—	445	—	—	—	1,822	—	—	—	—	—	—	—	—
1871	—	—	454	—	—	—	1,915	—	—	—	—	—	—	—	—
1872	—	—	466	—	—	—	1,987	—	—	—	—	—	—	—	—
1873	—	—	470	—	—	—	2,026	—	—	1,099,000	—	—	—	—	—
1874	—	—	493	—	—	—	2,118	—	—	1,200,000	—	—	—	—	—
1875	—	—	503	—	—	—	2,185	—	—	1,249,000	—	—	—	—	—
1876	—	—	531	—	—	—	2,224	—	—	1,342,000	—	—	—	—	—
1877	—	—	553	—	—	—	2,346	—	—	1,418,000	—	—	—	—	—
1878	—	—	563	—	—	—	2,412	—	—	1,484,000	—	—	—	—	—
1879	—	—	568	—	—	—	2,633	—	—	1,516,000	—	—	—	—	—

(continued)

TABLE Bg334–348 Church and congregation membership, by denomination: 1790–1995 *Continued*

Year	Catholic Church	Catholic Church	Presbyterian Church	Presbyterian Church USA	Protestant Episcopal Church	Protestant Episcopal Church	Methodist Church	Methodist Church	Seventh-Day Adventist Churches	Southern Baptist Church	Salvation Army	Buddhist churches (temple or religion)	Old Catholic and Polish churches	Eastern churches	Jewish congregations
	Bg334	Bg335	Bg336	Bg337	Bg338	Bg339	Bg340	Bg341	Bg342	Bg343	Bg344	Bg345	Bg346	Bg347	Bg348
	Thousand	Number	Thousand	Number	Thousand	Number	Thousand	Number	Number	Number	Number	Thousand	Thousand	Thousand	Thousand
1880	—	—	573	—	—	—	2,694	—	—	1,673,000	—	—	—	—	—
1881	—	—	575	—	—	—	2,665	—	—	961,000	—	—	—	—	—
1882	—	—	585	—	—	—	2,727	—	—	915,000	—	—	—	—	—
1883	—	—	593	—	—	—	2,794	—	—	935,000	—	—	—	—	—
1884	—	—	607	—	—	—	2,907	—	—	975,000	—	—	—	—	—
1885	—	—	627	—	—	—	2,974	—	—	1,013,000	—	—	—	—	—
1886	—	—	648	—	—	—	3,059	—	—	1,072,000	—	—	—	—	—
1887	—	—	681	—	—	—	3,104	—	—	1,126,000	—	—	—	—	—
1888	—	—	706	—	—	—	3,168	—	—	1,166,000	—	—	—	—	—
1889	—	—	739	—	—	—	3,290	—	—	1,195,000	—	—	—	—	—
1890	—	—	761	—	—	—	3,442	—	—	1,236,000	—	—	—	—	—
1891	8,277	—	790	—	—	—	3,511	—	—	1,282,000	—	—	—	—	—
1892	8,618	—	812	—	—	—	3,619	—	—	1,322,000	—	—	—	—	—
1893	8,806	—	837	—	—	—	3,705	—	—	1,363,000	—	—	—	—	—
1894	8,902	—	877	—	—	—	3,841	—	—	1,431,000	—	—	—	—	—
1895	9,078	—	903	—	—	—	3,990	—	—	1,469,000	—	—	—	—	—
1896	9,411	—	924	—	—	—	4,086	—	—	1,529,000	—	—	—	—	—
1897	9,596	—	939	—	—	—	4,134	—	—	1,569,000	—	—	—	—	—
1898	9,857	—	955	—	—	—	4,230	—	—	1,587,000	—	—	—	—	—
1899	9,907	—	961	—	—	—	4,186	—	—	1,608,000	—	—	—	—	—
1900	10,130	—	983	—	—	—	4,226	—	—	1,658,000	—	—	—	—	—
1901	10,775	—	1,000	—	—	—	4,302	—	—	1,683,000	—	—	—	—	—
1902	10,977	—	1,024	—	—	—	4,354	—	—	1,737,000	—	—	—	—	—
1903	11,290	—	1,044	—	—	—	4,389	—	—	1,806,000	—	—	—	—	—
1904	11,887	—	1,068	—	—	—	4,477	—	—	1,833,000	—	—	—	—	—
1905	12,463	—	1,090	—	—	—	4,518	—	—	1,899,000	—	—	—	—	—
1906	12,652	—	1,127	—	—	—	4,612	—	—	1,947,000	—	—	—	—	—
1907	13,089	—	1,305	—	—	—	4,735	—	65,000	2,015,000	—	—	—	—	—
1908	13,877	—	1,276	—	—	—	4,851	—	65,000	2,139,000	—	—	—	—	—
1909	14,235	—	1,299	—	—	—	4,977	—	65,000	2,219,000	—	—	—	—	—
1910	14,347	—	1,315	—	—	—	5,073	—	64,000	2,332,000	—	—	—	—	—
1911	14,619	—	1,331	—	—	—	5,168	—	65,000	2,421,000	—	—	—	—	—
1912	15,016	—	1,353	—	—	—	5,261	—	66,000	2,446,000	—	—	—	—	—
1913	15,154	—	1,388	—	—	—	5,402	—	69,000	2,523,000	—	—	—	—	—
1914	16,068	—	1,428	—	—	—	5,394	—	69,000	2,589,000	—	—	—	—	—
1915	16,309	—	1,493	—	—	—	5,698	—	74,000	2,686,000	—	—	—	—	—
1916	16,584	—	1,541	—	—	—	5,829	—	76,000	2,744,000	35,954	—	—	—	—
1917	17,023	—	1,579	—	—	—	5,970	—	83,000	2,844,000	—	—	—	—	—
1918	17,416	—	1,604	—	—	—	6,006	—	88,000	2,887,000	—	—	—	—	—
1919	17,549	—	1,571	—	—	—	5,937	—	91,000	2,961,000	—	—	—	—	—
1920	17,736	—	1,603	—	—	—	6,140	—	91,000	3,149,000	—	—	—	—	—
1921	17,886	—	1,686	—	—	—	6,289	—	94,000	3,220,000	—	—	—	—	—
1922	18,105	—	1,718	—	—	—	6,444	—	96,000	3,366,000	—	—	—	—	—
1923	18,261	—	1,760	—	—	—	6,522	—	98,000	3,494,000	—	—	—	—	—
1924	18,560	—	1,787	—	—	—	6,604	—	102,000	3,575,000	—	—	—	—	—

Year	Catholic Church	Catholic Church	Presbyterian Church	Presbyterian Church USA	Protestant Episcopal Church	Protestant Episcopal Church	Methodist Church	Methodist Church	Seventh-Day Adventist Churches	Southern Baptist Church	Salvation Army	Buddhist churches (temple or religion)	Old Catholic and Polish churches	Eastern churches	Jewish congregations
	Bg334	Bg335	Bg336	Bg337	Bg338	Bg339	Bg340	Bg341	Bg342	Bg343	Bg344	Bg345	Bg346	Bg347	Bg348
	Thousand	Number	Thousand	Number	Thousand	Number	Thousand	Number	Number	Number	Number	Thousand	Thousand	Thousand	Thousand
1925	18,654	—	1,829	—	—	—	7,066	—	103,000	3,649,000	—	—	—	—	—
1926	18,879	—	1,868	—	—	—	6,830	—	105,000	3,617,000	74,408	—	—	—	—
1927	19,483	—	1,886	—	1,789	—	7,171	—	107,000	3,674,000	—	—	—	—	—
1928	19,689	—	1,919	—	1,878	—	7,248	—	108,000	3,706,000	—	—	—	—	—
1929	20,113	—	1,959	—	1,876	—	7,245	—	112,000	3,771,000	—	—	—	—	—
1930	20,204	—	1,937	—	1,939	—	7,319	—	114,000	3,850,000	—	—	—	—	—
1931	20,215	—	1,950	—	1,957	—	7,247	—	121,000	3,945,000	—	—	—	—	—
1932	20,236	—	1,958	—	1,986	—	7,301	—	128,000	4,066,000	—	—	—	—	—
1933	20,268	—	1,917	—	2,015	—	7,153	—	136,000	4,174,000	—	—	—	—	—
1934	20,323	—	1,934	—	2,040	—	7,254	—	143,000	4,277,000	—	—	—	—	—
1935	20,523	—	1,921	—	2,038	—	7,320	—	149,000	4,389,000	—	—	—	—	—
1936	20,735	—	1,915	—	2,068	—	7,346	—	152,000	4,482,000	103,038	—	—	—	—
1937	20,959	—	1,928	—	2,095	—	7,387	—	155,000	4,596,000	—	—	—	—	—
1938	21,167	—	1,906	—	2,110	—	7,507	—	162,000	4,770,000	—	—	—	—	—
1939	21,407	21,284,455	1,930	—	2,157	—	7,590	—	167,000	4,949,000	—	—	—	—	—
1940	21,403	—	1,971	2,690,969	2,172	1,996,434	7,360	—	175,000	5,104,000	238,357	—	—	—	—
1941	22,293	—	1,961	—	2,162	—	7,683	—	181,000	5,238,000	—	—	—	—	—
1942	22,556	—	1,986	—	2,168	—	7,838	—	186,000	5,367,000	—	—	—	—	—
1943	22,945	—	1,996	—	2,189	—	7,979	—	190,000	5,493,000	—	—	—	—	—
1944	23,420	—	2,040	—	2,228	—	8,046	—	196,000	5,668,000	—	—	—	—	—
1945	23,964	—	2,104	—	2,270	—	8,084	—	201,000	5,866,000	—	—	—	—	—
1946	24,402	—	2,115	—	2,301	—	8,430	—	208,000	6,079,000	—	—	—	—	—
1947	25,268	24,402,124	2,203	2,969,382	2,350	2,155,514	8,568	—	216,000	6,271,000	205,881	—	—	—	—
1948	26,076	—	2,266	—	2,437	—	8,651	—	223,000	6,489,000	—	—	—	—	—
1949	26,718	—	2,319	—	2,512	—	8,793	—	230,000	6,761,000	—	—	—	—	—
1950	27,766	28,634,878	2,364	—	2,541	2,417,464	8,936	—	237,000	7,080,000	209,341	—	—	—	—
1951	28,635	—	2,360	3,210,635	2,643	—	9,066	—	246,000	7,373,000	—	73	337	1,859	5,000
1952	29,408	—	2,438	—	2,716	—	9,180	—	254,000	7,634,000	—	73	367	2,354	5,000
1953	30,425	—	2,492	—	2,791	—	9,152	—	261,000	7,886,000	—	63	366	2,100	5,000
1954	31,648	—	2,567	—	2,907	—	9,223	—	270,000	8,169,000	—	63	368	2,024	5,500
1955	32,576	33,396,647	2,645	3,701,635	3,014	2,852,965	9,313	—	277,000	8,475,000	249,641	63	368	2,387	5,500
1956	33,574	—	2,743	—	3,111	—	9,445	—	283,000	8,709,000	—	63	351	2,598	5,500
1957	34,564	—	2,775	—	3,163	—	9,567	—	292,000	8,966,000	—	10	469	2,540	5,500
1958	36,024	—	3,160	—	3,275	—	9,692	—	305,000	9,207,000	—	10	488	2,545	5,500
1959	39,505	—	3,210	—	3,359	—	9,815	—	312,000	9,485,000	—	20	484	2,808	5,500
1960	40,871	42,104,900	3,259	4,161,860	3,444	3,269,325	9,884	—	318,000	9,731,000	254,141	20	590	2,699	5,367
1961	42,105	—	3,249	—	3,520	—	10,046	—	329,000	9,978,000	—	60	573	2,800	5,365
1962	42,882	—	3,278	—	3,565	—	10,153	—	336,000	10,193,000	—	60	597	3,002	5,509
1963	43,847	—	3,292	—	3,587	—	10,235	—	346,000	10,395,000	—	60	498	3,094	5,585
1964	44,874	—	3,303	—	3,591	—	10,304	—	355,000	10,601,000	—	110	491	3,167	5,600
1965	45,640	46,246,175	3,309	3,984,460	3,616	3,429,153	10,332	—	365,000	10,772,000	287,991	92	484	3,172	5,600
1966	46,246	—	3,298	—	3,647	—	10,311	—	374,000	10,949,000	—	—	—	—	5,725
1967	46,864	—	3,269	—	3,585	—	10,289	—	385,000	11,142,000	—	—	580	2,651	5,725
1968	47,468	—	3,230	—	3,588	—	10,991	—	396,000	11,332,000	—	100	599	2,660	5,725
1969	47,873	—	3,173	—	3,536	—	10,790	—	408,000	11,489,000	—	100	818	3,745	5,780

(continued)

TABLE Bg334–348 Church and congregation membership, by denomination: 1790–1995 *Continued*

	Catholic Church	Catholic Church	Presbyterian Church	Presbyterian Church USA	Protestant Episcopal Church	Protestant Episcopal Church	Methodist Church	Methodist Church	Seventh-Day Adventist Churches	Southern Baptist Church	Salvation Army	Buddhist churches (temple or religion)	Old Catholic and Polish churches	Eastern churches	Jewish congregations
	Bg334	Bg335	Bg336	Bg337	Bg338	Bg339	Bg340	Bg341	Bg342	Bg343	Bg344	Bg345	Bg346	Bg347	Bg348
Year	Thousand	Number	Thousand	Number	Thousand	Number	Thousand	Number	Number	Number	Number	Thousand	Thousand	Thousand	Thousand
1970	47,872	48,214,729	3,096	4,045,408	3,475	3,285,826	10,672	—	420,000	11,629,000	326,934	100	848	3,850	5,870
1971	—	43,390,990	—	—	—	3,217,365	—	10,509,198	433,906	11,824,676	335,684	100	867	3,848	5,870
1972	—	48,460,427	—	—	—	3,062,734	—	10,334,521	449,188	12,065,333	358,626	100	913	3,740	6,115
1973	—	48,465,438	—	—	—	2,917,165	—	10,192,265	464,276	12,295,400	361,571	60	848	3,706	6,115
1974	—	48,701,835	—	—	—	2,907,293	—	10,063,046	479,799	12,513,378	366,471	60	849	3,696	6,115
1975	—	48,881,872	—	3,535,825	—	2,857,513	—	9,861,028	495,699	12,733,124	384,817	60	846	3,696	6,115
1976	—	49,325,752	—	—	—	2,882,064	—	9,861,028	509,792	12,917,992	380,618	60	846	3,755	6,115
1977	—	49,836,176	—	—	—	2,818,830	—	9,785,534	522,317	13,078,239	396,238	60	801	3,753	5,775
1978	—	49,602,035	—	—	—	2,815,359	—	9,731,779	535,705	13,191,394	414,035	60	809	3,633	5,781
1979	—	49,812,178	—	—	—	2,841,350	—	9,653,711	553,089	13,372,757	414,659	60	937	3,822	5,861
1980	—	50,449,842	—	3,362,086	—	2,786,004	—	9,519,407	571,141	13,600,126	417,359	60	924	3,853	5,920
1981	—	51,207,579	—	—	—	2,767,440	—	9,457,012	588,536	13,782,644	414,999	60	921	3,823	5,921
1982	—	52,088,774	—	3,157,372	—	2,794,139	—	9,504,164	606,310	13,991,709	419,475	100	925	3,860	5,725
1983	—	52,392,934	—	3,122,213	—	2,794,680	—	—	623,563	14,170,051	428,046	70	1,150	4,034	5,728
1984	—	52,286,043	—	3,092,151	—	2,775,424	—	—	638,929	14,341,822	420,971	100	1,025	4,053	5,817
1985	—	52,654,904	—	3,048,235	—	2,739,422	—	9,192,172	651,954	14,477,364	427,825	100	1,024	4,026	5,834
1986	—	52,893,217	—	2,896,138	—	2,504,507	—	—	666,199	14,613,618	432,893	100	829	3,980	5,814
1987	—	53,496,862	—	2,967,781	—	2,462,300	—	9,124,575	675,200	14,722,617	434,002	100	826	3,973	5,943
1988	—	54,918,949	—	2,929,608	—	2,455,422	—	9,055,145	687,200	14,812,844	433,448	—	—	—	—
1989	—	57,019,948	—	2,886,482	—	2,433,413	—	8,904,824	701,781	14,907,826	445,566	—	—	—	—
1990	—	58,568,015	—	3,788,009	—	2,446,050	—	—	717,446	15,038,409	445,991	—	—	—	—
1991	—	58,267,424	—	3,778,358	—	2,471,880	—	8,789,101	733,026	15,232,347	446,407	—	—	—	—
1992	—	59,220,723	—	3,748,085	—	—	—	—	748,687	15,358,866	—	—	—	—	—
1993	—	59,858,042	—	3,796,766	—	2,504,682	—	8,646,595	761,703	15,398,642	—	—	—	—	—
1994	—	60,190,605	—	3,698,136	—	—	—	8,584,125	775,349	15,614,060	443,246	—	—	—	—
1995	—	60,280,000	—	3,669,000	—	2,537,000	—	8,539,000	791,000	15,663,000	453,000	—	—	—	—

Sources

Series Bg334. *The Official Catholic Directory* (P. J. Kenedy, published annually), and unpublished data.

Series Bg335, Bg337, Bg339, Bg341, and Bg344. National Council of Churches, *Yearbook of American and Canadian Churches* (editors and title vary), annual issues.

Series Bg336. For 1826–1926: *Presbyterian Statistics through One Hundred Years to 1926* (General Council, Presbyterian Church, 1927). For 1927–1957: Presbyterian Church (unpublished data). For 1958–1970: *The United Presbyterian Church in the United States of America* (published annually); *Minutes of the General Assembly*.

Series Bg338. *The Episcopal Church Annual* (Morehouse-Gorham; previously Morehouse Barlow).

Series Bg340. For 1790–1948: Statistical Office of the Methodist Church, "Methodist History as Revealed in Statistical Form," loose insert in *The Methodist Fact Book* (Division of National Missions of the Board of Missions of the Methodist Church, 1949). For 1949–1955: *The Methodist Fact Book* (1957).

Series Bg342. For 1907–1970: Statistical Secretary of the Seventh-Day Adventist Church, unpublished data. For 1971–1995: *Yearbook of American and Canadian Churches*.

Series Bg343. For 1845–1970: Southern Baptist Convention, *Southern Baptist Handbook* (Convention Press, 1970). For 1971–1995: *Yearbook of American and Canadian Churches*.

Series Bg345–348. For 1890–1926 and 1936: U.S. Bureau of the Census, *Religious Bodies* (various years). For 1931–1935, 1937, and 1945–1949: *The Christian Herald*, various issues. For 1938–1944 and 1950–1970: *Yearbook of American Churches* (National Council of the Churches of Christ, various years). For 1970–1987: *Yearbook of American and Canadian Churches*.

Documentation

The U.S. Bureau of the Census usually secured information for the year indicated, but it also accepted a figure for the church year nearest to that for which data were sought. In the compilations of private agencies, the "latest information" was published for each denomination; in a number of instances, the actual figures of a denomination were for a previous period. The lag is usually only of several years' duration. Data for certain years, which do not appear in these series, appeared in the *Christian Herald*.

These data are not fully comparable, as some series or portions of them include only the "communicant" or adult membership. For definition of membership used by the larger groups (Eastern churches, Jewish congregations, Roman Catholic Church, and Protestant bodies), see below and the text for Table Bg320–333.

Series Bg334. The continuous history of the Roman Catholic Church in this country began in Maryland in 1634. Certain of the typographical errors appearing in the annual published reports issued by the source have been corrected in this series. Figures are compiled from reports by dioceses and parishes.

Series Bg336. Figures include persons who attained full membership, usually at age 13. Foreign members were excluded. In 1958, the United Presbyterian Church of North America merged with the Presbyterian Church in the United States of America to form the United Presbyterian Church in the United States of America. This was the largest of eight Presbyterian churches in the United States. The other large Presbyterian church, located primarily in the South, was the Presbyterian Church in the United States.

Series Bg337. On mergers, see the text for series Bg336.

Series Bg338. This body entered the colonies with the earliest settlers (1607) as the Church of England. It became autonomous as the Protestant Episcopal Church in the U.S.A. and adopted its present name in 1789. In 1967, the General Convention adopted "The Episcopal Church" as an alternative name. Data include "communicants" residing abroad, numbering less than one half of 1 percent of the total communicants during the period covered by the figures.

Series Bg340. The Methodist Church was formed in 1939 by a merger of the Methodist Episcopal Church; the Methodist Episcopal Church, South; and the Methodist Protestant Church. Figures include all three bodies prior to 1939. Members are persons who attained full membership, usually at age 13. The Evangelical United Brethren Church was formed in 1946 with the merger of the Evangelical Church and the Church of the United Brethren in Christ. The United Methodist Church was formed in 1968 by a merger of the Methodist Church and the Evangelical United Brethren Church. The United Methodist Church was the largest of nearly twenty separate Methodist denominations. Three large black Methodist denominations, for which there were no annual statistical reports, were the African Methodist Episcopal Church, the African Methodist Episcopal Zion Church, and the Christian Methodist Episcopal Church.

Series Bg342. This Protestant body developed out of an interdenominational movement in the early decades of the nineteenth century but was not formally organized until 1863. The members of this body were mainly 13 years of age and over. The latest year for which age grouping was reported was 1936, when the local churches of the body reported that only about 3 percent of their members were younger than 13 years of age.

Series Bg343. In 1845, Southern Baptists withdrew from the General Missionary Convention over the question of slavery and other matters and formed the Southern Baptist Convention. Membership in the Southern Baptist Convention consists only of individuals who present themselves to the church, request membership, and are baptized. Infant baptism was and is not practiced.

TABLE Bg349–399 Churches, by state: 1850–1990

Contributed by Colin B. Burke

	Alabama	Alaska	Arizona	Arkansas	California	Colorado	Connecticut	Delaware	District of Columbia	Florida	Georgia	Hawai'i	Idaho	Illinois	Indiana	Iowa	Kansas
	Bg349	Bg350	Bg351	Bg352	Bg353	Bg354	Bg355	Bg356	Bg357	Bg358	Bg359	Bg360	Bg361	Bg362	Bg363	Bg364	Bg365
Year	Number	Number	Number	Number	Number	Number	Number	Number	Number	Number	Number	Number	Number	Number	Number	Number	Number
1850	1,373	—	—	362	28	—	734	180	46	177	1,862	—	—	1,223	2,032	193	—
1860	1,875	—	—	1,008	293	—	802	220	68	319	2,393	—	—	2,424	2,933	949	97
1870 [1]	1,958	—	4	1,141	532	47	902	252	112	390	2,698	—	12	3,459	3,106	1,446	301
1890 [1]	6,013	34	70	3,791	1,505	463	1,175	401	205	1,793	7,008	—	143	7,352	5,944	4,539	2,854
1906 [2]	8,845	—	235	6,133	2,816	1,248	1,345	465	285	3,341	10,013	—	673	9,252	6,800	6,247	4,970
1916 [2]	9,381	—	443	6,961	3,721	1,448	1,400	484	338	4,384	10,697	—	1,045	9,207	6,767	5,714	4,689
1926	9,896	—	587	6,807	4,659	1,688	1,541	508	399	4,640	10,898	—	1,002	9,556	6,781	5,175	4,530
1936	7,981	—	650	5,063	4,904	1,585	1,570	436	460	4,002	9,754	—	921	8,498	5,944	4,567	3,686
1952	5,620	—	767	3,715	6,794	1,578	1,363	490	389	3,528	5,749	—	658	8,265	6,164	4,593	3,727
1971	6,078	326	1,176	3,568	7,552	1,683	1,422	413	292	4,948	6,255	353	629	8,468	6,092	4,074	3,382
1980	8,054	579	2,096	5,493	11,421	2,373	1,725	463	376	6,818	7,485	558	1,393	9,358	6,590	4,534	3,869
1990	8,447	—	2,766	5,029	14,427	2,813	1,944	523	343	8,577	8,300	758	1,600	9,799	7,134	4,560	3,958

Notes appear at end of table

(continued)

TABLE Bg349-399 Churches, by state: 1850-1990 *Continued*

	Kentucky	Louisiana	Maine	Maryland	Massachusetts	Michigan	Minnesota	Mississippi	Missouri	Montana	Nebraska	Nevada	New Hampshire	New Jersey	New Mexico	New York	North Carolina
	Bg366	Bg367	Bg368	Bg369	Bg370	Bg371	Bg372	Bg373	Bg374	Bg375	Bg376	Bg377	Bg378	Bg379	Bg380	Bg381	Bg382
Year	Number	Number	Number	Number	Number	Number	Number	Number	Number	Number	Number	Number	Number	Number	Number	Number	Number
1850	1,845	306	945	909	1,475	399	3	1,016	880	—	—	—	626	813	73	4,134	1,795
1860	2,179	572	1,167	1,016	1,636	807	260	1,441	1,577	—	63	—	681	1,123	100	5,287	2,270
1870 [1]	2,696	599	1,104	1,389	1,764	1,415	582	1,800	2,082	11	108	19	624	1,384	152	5,474	2,497
1890 [1]	4,768	2,520	1,342	2,369	2,458	3,761	2,619	5,001	6,121	164	1,822	41	774	2,204	381	7,942	6,512
1906 [2]	6,502	3,793	1,528	2,725	2,963	5,584	4,699	7,344	9,154	539	3,292	86	830	2,694	621	8,840	8,545
1916 [2]	7,312	4,005	1,601	2,907	3,058	5,501	5,007	7,873	8,457	1,325	3,279	129	884	3,118	1,075	9,031	9,705
1926	7,192	4,215	1,447	2,959	3,359	5,709	5,132	7,863	7,951	1,297	3,007	158	821	3,670	1,095	10,638	10,297
1936	5,286	3,751	1,289	2,442	3,227	5,367	4,794	6,354	6,016	1,138	2,710	153	737	3,716	1,030	10,543	8,029
1952	5,733	3,004	1,295	2,466	2,848	5,573	4,399	4,136	6,421	946	2,494	171	705	3,106	831	8,141	8,029
1971	6,101	3,125	1,228	2,725	2,584	6,257	4,038	4,382	6,627	995	2,242	231	650	3,093	1,142	7,880	8,985
1980	6,704	3,960	1,298	3,107	2,945	6,595	4,818	5,395	7,571	1,273	2,684	475	774	3,708	1,594	8,989	10,281
1990	7,255	4,025	1,336	3,519	3,382	7,229	4,961	5,433	7,666	1,415	2,629	664	896	4,183	1,824	10,878	11,331

	North Dakota	Ohio	Oklahoma	Oregon	Pennsylvania	Rhode Island	South Carolina	South Dakota	Tennessee	Texas	Utah	Vermont	Virginia	Washington	West Virginia	Wisconsin	Wyoming
	Bg383	Bg384	Bg385	Bg386	Bg387	Bg388	Bg389	Bg390	Bg391	Bg392	Bg393	Bg394	Bg395	Bg396	Bg397	Bg398	Bg399
Year	Number	Number	Number	Number	Number	Number	Number	Number	Number	Number	Number	Number	Number	Number	Number	Number	Number
1850	—	3,936	—	9	3,566	228	1,182	—	2,014	341	9	599	2,383	—	—	365	—
1860	—	5,210	—	75	5,337	310	1,267	—	2,311	1,034 [3]	21	697	3,105	12	—	1,070	—
1870 [1]	10	6,284	—	135	5,668	283	1,308	—	2,842	164	164	744	2,405	36	1,018	1,466	12
1890 [1]	335	8,857	41	592	9,624	386	3,967	774	5,792	5,638	280	802	4,894	532	2,160	3,286	43
1906 [2]	1,960	9,754	4,464	1,286	12,628	493	5,366	1,798	7,951	12,260	534	899	6,587	1,753	4,018	4,854	226
1916 [2]	2,518	9,497	5,372	1,602	13,211	503	5,663	2,177	8,514	14,566	611	853	7,120	2,364	4,630	4,898	354
1926	2,435	9,809	5,281	1,500	13,843	551	5,752	2,217	8,556	15,062	714	758	7,566	2,280	4,968	4,883	438
1936	2,147	8,864	4,045	1,453	13,461	529	4,263	1,924	6,243	11,190	730	670	6,078	2,145	3,922	4,636	399
1952	1,899	8,654	4,052	1,703	11,976	480	3,853	1,677	6,425	10,563	759	746	5,667	2,273	4,189	4,365	381
1971	1,562	8,932	4,085	1,721	10,927	455	4,331	1,479	6,608	11,223	223	638	5,952	2,372	3,821	4,179	361
1980	1,695	10,060	5,329	2,628	12,386	498	4,994	1,718	8,529	16,111	2,422	716	6,496	3,381	4,159	4,698	628
1990	1,622	11,086	5,707	2,908	13,264	554	5,509	1,781	9,246	16,961	3,319	764	7,490	4,092	4,443	5,023	766

[1] Edifices.

[2] Excludes Jewish congregations.

[3] Data in the original source appear to be in error but cannot be corrected.

Sources

For 1850-1890: U.S. Bureau of the Census, Censuses of 1850-1890. For 1906-1936: U.S. Bureau of the Census, *Religious Bodies* (1906-1936). For 1952-1990: Glenmary Research Center, *Churches and Church Membership in the United States* (title and editors vary), 1955-1990.

Documentation

See the text for Table Bg320-333.

For 1952-1990, the date shown is approximate. In 1952, 112 denominations reported. For the years 1971, 1980, and 1990, the following numbers of major religious groups reported: 53, 111, and 133, respectively.

TABLE Bg400–449 Estimates of church accommodations, by state: 1850–1890[1]

Contributed by Colin B. Burke

	Alabama	Alaska	Arizona	Arkansas	California	Colorado	Connecticut	Delaware	District of Columbia	Florida	Georgia	Idaho	Illinois	Indiana	Iowa	Kansas	Kentucky
	Bg400	Bg401	Bg402	Bg403	Bg404	Bg405	Bg406	Bg407	Bg408	Bg409	Bg410	Bg411	Bg412	Bg413	Bg414	Bg415	Bg416
Year	Number	Number	Number	Number	Number	Number	Number	Number	Number	Number	Number	Number	Number	Number	Number	Number	Number
1850	440,155	—	—	60,226	10,200	—	307,299	55,741	34,120	44,960	627,617	—	486,576	709,655	43,529	—	671,053
1860	550,494	—	—	216,183	97,721	—	374,686	68,560	50,040	68,990	763,812	—	798,346	1,047,211	256,891	32,650	778,025
1870	510,810	—	2,400	264,225	165,558	17,495	338,735	87,899	63,655	78,920	801,148	2,150	1,201,403	1,008,380	431,709	102,085	876,439
1890	1,702,527	4,800	19,230	1,041,040	422,609	120,862	443,979	111,172	114,420	391,132	2,108,566	29,527	2,260,619	1,890,300	1,203,185	706,334	1,504,736

	Louisiana	Maine	Maryland	Massachusetts	Michigan	Minnesota	Mississippi	Missouri	Montana	Nebraska	Nevada	New Hampshire	New Jersey	New Mexico	New York	North Carolina	North Dakota
	Bg417	Bg418	Bg419	Bg420	Bg421	Bg422	Bg423	Bg424	Bg425	Bg426	Bg427	Bg428	Bg429	Bg430	Bg431	Bg432	Bg433
Year	Number	Number	Number	Number	Number	Number	Number	Number	Number	Number	Number	Number	Number	Number	Number	Number	Number
1850	109,615	321,167	379,465	693,133	120,117	100	294,104	251,068	—	—	—	237,417	346,133	28,650	1,914,154	572,924	—
1860	206,196	370,814	377,022	757,995	250,794	60,960	445,963	500,616	—	7,010	—	231,363	461,796	79,400	2,155,828	611,423	—
1870	213,955	376,038	499,770	882,317	456,226	158,266	485,398	691,520	3,850	32,210	8,000	210,090	573,303	81,500	2,280,876	718,310	2,800 [2]
1890	617,245	408,452	718,459	1,102,772	1,097,060	691,631	1,330,542	1,859,589	33,942	409,462	9,890	250,035	803,017	107,925	2,868,490	2,192,835	69,590

	Ohio	Oklahoma	Oregon	Pennsylvania	Rhode Island	South Carolina	South Dakota	Tennessee	Texas	Utah	Vermont	Virginia	Washington	West Virginia	Wisconsin	Wyoming
	Bg434	Bg435	Bg436	Bg437	Bg438	Bg439	Bg440	Bg441	Bg442	Bg443	Bg444	Bg445	Bg446	Bg447	Bg448	Bg449
Year	Number	Number	Number	Number	Number	Number	Number	Number	Number	Number	Number	Number	Number	Number	Number	Number
1850	1,457,769	—	—	1,576,245	102,040	460,530	—	625,695	64,815	4,200	234,534	858,086	—	—	97,773	—
1860	1,966,648	—	19,230	2,112,920	147,520	451,256	—	728,661	271,148	12,950	213,235	1,067,840	4,775	—	293,699	—
1870	2,084,386	—	38,425	2,332,288	125,183	491,425	—	878,199	199,100	86,110	270,614	765,127	6,000	297,315	423,015	3,500
1890	2,815,712	8,605	142,843	3,592,019	166,384	1,199,908	149,728	1,811,942	1,567,745	89,695	237,000	1,490,675	126,109	587,338	845,208	8,385

[1] The census used varying names for seating capacity because of the varied practices of the denominations: for 1850–1860, accommodations; for 1870, sittings; and for 1890, approximate seating capacity.

[2] Dakota Territory.

Source

U.S. Bureau of the Census, Censuses of 1850–1890, *Religious Bodies* (1906).

Documentation

See the text for Table Bg320–333.

TABLE Bg450–549 Estimates of church membership, by state and sex: 1890–1990[1]

Contributed by Colin B. Burke

	Both sexes															
	Alabama	Alaska	Arizona	Arkansas	California	Colorado	Connecticut	Delaware	District of Columbia	Florida	Georgia	Hawai'i	Idaho	Illinois	Indiana	Iowa
	Bg450	Bg451	Bg452	Bg453	Bg454	Bg455	Bg456	Bg457	Bg458	Bg459	Bg460	Bg461	Bg462	Bg463	Bg464	Bg465
Year	Number	Number	Number	Number	Number	Number	Number	Number	Number	Number	Number	Number	Number	Number	Number	Number
1890	559,171	14,852	29,972	296,208	280,619	86,837	309,341	48,679	94,203	141,734	679,051	—	24,036	1,202,588	693,860	556,817
1906	824,209	—	45,057	778,901	611,464	205,666	502,560	71,251	136,759	221,318	1,029,037	—	74,578	2,077,197	938,405	788,667
1916	1,010,544	—	118,042	584,166	903,767	262,855	740,585	88,534	167,245	328,632	1,236,475	—	137,447	2,592,020	1,199,564	988,036
1926	1,217,179	—	153,086	621,107	1,522,211	352,863	956,728	110,142	238,871	528,380	1,350,184	—	162,679	3,363,385	1,382,818	1,080,158
1936	1,138,472	—	165,020	570,219	1,928,439	355,272	1,050,927	112,785	271,724	555,317	1,264,287	—	178,316	3,556,852	1,350,288	1,080,989
1952	1,046,460	—	336,938	598,593	4,306,690	550,993	1,215,346	140,847	374,215	1,007,983	1,337,252	—	259,547	4,670,691	1,715,289	1,404,005
1971	1,645,794	111,252	839,667	880,433	6,692,785	916,743	1,797,210	236,868	240,279 [2]	2,799,114 [2]	2,118,091	291,471	381,760	6,136,362	1,211,591	1,762,704
1980	2,235,178	123,434	1,073,012	1,284,100	8,157,986	1,057,709	1,913,148	239,532	312,444	3,753,873	2,570,084	328,288	472,497	6,297,355	2,458,653	1,783,704
1990	2,867,460	—	1,577,427	1,425,192	12,585,339	1,294,376	2,047,646	306,364	374,160	5,672,756	3,730,757	390,827	507,426	6,848,422	2,634,841	1,681,062

	Both sexes															
	Kansas	Kentucky	Louisiana	Maine	Maryland	Massachusetts	Michigan	Minnesota	Mississippi	Missouri	Montana	Nebraska	Nevada	New Hampshire	New Jersey	New Mexico
	Bg466	Bg467	Bg468	Bg469	Bg470	Bg471	Bg472	Bg473	Bg474	Bg475	Bg476	Bg477	Bg478	Bg479	Bg480	Bg481
Year	Number	Number	Number	Number	Number	Number	Number	Number	Number	Number	Number	Number	Number	Number	Number	Number
1890	336,575	606,397	399,991	159,846	379,418	942,751	569,504	532,590	430,557	735,839	32,478	194,466	5,877	102,941	508,351	105,749
1906	458,190	858,324	426,179	212,988	473,257	1,562,621	982,479	834,442	657,381	1,199,239	98,984	345,803	14,944	190,298	857,548	137,009
1916	626,996	968,308	866,184	256,914	621,838	1,972,766	1,250,375	1,058,308	762,846	1,388,194	145,663	473,730	16,976	212,894	1,366,245	210,629
1926	747,078	1,051,504	1,037,008	294,092	758,366	2,500,204	1,786,831	1,282,188	800,509	1,581,278	152,387	561,553	19,769	223,674	1,983,781	215,563
1936	691,438	913,482	1,136,123	313,353	751,600	2,609,101	1,786,839	1,352,662	778,864	1,392,860	160,138	566,806	27,881	237,736	2,357,432	243,936
1952	887,643	1,320,412	1,440,910	376,705	1,118,039	3,145,023	2,693,781	1,836,015	738,028	1,932,329	276,229	707,954	60,165	282,727	2,786,070	441,774
1971	1,184,802	1,764,374	2,178,589	444,794	1,677,329	3,593,205	4,070,237	2,522,913	1,132,375	2,391,454	323,738	896,127	184,561	370,751	3,655,814	643,408
1980	1,263,168	2,413,059	2,413,059	461,335 [3]	1,695,948	3,709,251	3,952,916	2,653,161	1,387,371	2,634,435	348,301	992,303	233,781	407,939	3,988,369	767,737
1990	1,354,657	2,227,747	2,975,409	447,053	2,311,814	3,942,101	4,686,550	2,837,418	1,806,049	2,944,890	341,247	1,006,572	386,312	438,374	4,734,822	889,298

	Both sexes																
	New York	North Carolina	North Dakota	Ohio	Oklahoma	Oregon	Pennsylvania	Rhode Island	South Carolina	South Dakota	Tennessee	Texas	Utah	Vermont	Virginia	Washington	West Virginia
	Bg482	Bg483	Bg484	Bg485	Bg486	Bg487	Bg488	Bg489	Bg490	Bg491	Bg492	Bg493	Bg494	Bg495	Bg496	Bg497	Bg498
Year	Number	Number	Number	Number	Number	Number	Number	Number	Number	Number	Number	Number	Number	Number	Number	Number	Number
1890	2,171,822	685,194	59,496	1,215,409	4,901	70,524	1,726,640	148,008	508,485	85,490	551,673	677,151	128,115	106,315	569,235	58,798	189,917
1906	3,591,974	824,385	159,053	1,742,872	257,100	120,229	2,977,022	264,712	665,933	161,053	697,570	1,226,906	172,814	147,223	793,546	191,976	301,565
1916	4,340,423	1,096,642	263,829	2,347,173	426,687	183,137	4,267,980	351,360	801,990	229,260	841,704	1,800,478	281,128	146,968	961,767	292,736	432,358
1926	6,799,146	1,407,005	304,936	2,866,386	581,083	232,731	5,213,023	452,044	873,528	294,622	1,018,033	2,280,366	369,591	161,123	1,172,447	384,182	531,983
1936	7,150,501	1,274,722	315,659	2,934,248	587,425	249,275	5,412,246	473,361	710,163	278,567	918,809	2,298,966	372,699	169,792	1,017,531	367,261	491,607
1952	8,919,263	1,620,339	390,081	3,685,458	947,654	421,859	6,178,459	599,682	847,446	381,358	1,323,396	4,132,478	505,196	199,167	1,278,816	726,089	658,326
1971	8,567,413	2,578,641	473,332	5,043,970	1,410,323	961,085	6,981,986	712,787	1,356,819	460,456	1,965,320	6,294,555	885,332	231,449	2,011,887	1,108,916	706,179
1980	8,721,288	3,173,793	482,574	5,346,227	1,754,071	949,471	7,231,834	715,569	1,605,231	462,277	2,492,387	7,781,967	898,578	244,730	2,232,913	1,280,918	744,864
1990	11,813,403	3,977,923	484,628	5,437,630	2,102,290	915,285	7,290,699	769,964	2,157,820	474,010	2,984,916	10,896,401	1,374,097	236,757	2,966,083	1,612,516	741,998

	Both sexes		Female														
	Wisconsin	Wyoming	Alabama	Arizona	Arkansas	California	Colorado	Connecticut	Delaware	District of Columbia	Florida	Georgia	Idaho	Illinois	Indiana	Iowa	Kansas
	Bg499	Bg500	Bg501	Bg502	Bg503	Bg504	Bg505	Bg506	Bg507	Bg508	Bg509	Bg510	Bg511	Bg512	Bg513	Bg514	Bg515
Year	Number	Number	Number	Number	Number	Number	Number	Number	Number	Number	Number	Number	Number	Number	Number	Number	Number
1890	556,355	11,705	—	—	—	—	—	—	—	—	—	—	—	—	—	—	—
1906	1,000,903	23,945	455,838	18,802	419,082	322,981	105,861	264,356	38,151	72,723	125,215	583,173	36,827	842,686	514,938	428,603	253,826
1916	1,288,427	41,687	—	—	—	—	—	—	—	—	—	—	—	—	—	—	—
1926	1,472,890	62,975	608,969	79,643	348,083	738,468	179,623	454,806	54,542	126,317	286,403	601,788	82,531	1,547,348	729,950	576,348	410,616
1936	1,605,820	67,770	648,094	75,104	325,712	909,171	172,777	459,395	56,313	135,394	307,051	680,267	91,777	1,368,867	689,856	558,784	370,682
1952	2,129,928	126,606	—	—	—	—	—	—	—	—	—	—	—	—	—	—	—
1971	2,972,647	158,198	—	—	—	—	—	—	—	—	—	—	—	—	—	—	—
1980	3,038,209	287,484	—	—	—	—	—	—	—	—	—	—	—	—	—	—	—
1990	3,160,201	216,375	—	—	—	—	—	—	—	—	—	—	—	—	—	—	—

	Female																
	Kentucky	Louisiana	Maine	Maryland	Massachusetts	Michigan	Minnesota	Mississippi	Missouri	Montana	Nebraska	Nevada	New Hampshire	New Jersey	New Mexico	New York	North Carolina
	Bg516	Bg517	Bg518	Bg519	Bg520	Bg521	Bg522	Bg523	Bg524	Bg525	Bg526	Bg527	Bg528	Bg529	Bg530	Bg531	Bg532
Year	Number	Number	Number	Number	Number	Number	Number	Number	Number	Number	Number	Number	Number	Number	Number	Number	Number
1890	—	—	—	—	—	—	—	—	—	—	—	—	—	—	—	—	—
1906	432,232	239,099	119,971	229,087	813,961	387,461	414,771	370,870	636,001	49,285	184,718	6,474	100,340	408,929	59,746	1,794,081	463,395
1916	—	—	—	—	—	—	—	—	—	—	—	—	—	—	—	—	—
1926	535,541	534,650	160,243	361,992	1,205,820	572,646	632,789	438,690	805,776	77,845	291,260	10,229	112,913	945,609	109,609	2,590,271	757,355
1936	464,920	525,865	164,660	361,039	1,088,101	828,089	655,822	427,030	687,125	82,506	289,266	14,755	125,627	758,441	121,007	2,583,233	702,532
1952	—	—	—	—	—	—	—	—	—	—	—	—	—	—	—	—	—
1971	—	—	—	—	—	—	—	—	—	—	—	—	—	—	—	—	—
1980	—	—	—	—	—	—	—	—	—	—	—	—	—	—	—	—	—
1990	—	—	—	—	—	—	—	—	—	—	—	—	—	—	—	—	—

	Female																
	North Dakota	Ohio	Oklahoma	Oregon	Pennsylvania	Rhode Island	South Carolina	South Dakota	Tennessee	Texas	Utah	Vermont	Virginia	Washington	West Virginia	Wisconsin	Wyoming
	Bg533	Bg534	Bg535	Bg536	Bg537	Bg538	Bg539	Bg540	Bg541	Bg542	Bg543	Bg544	Bg545	Bg546	Bg547	Bg548	Bg549
Year	Number	Number	Number	Number	Number	Number	Number	Number	Number	Number	Number	Number	Number	Number	Number	Number	Number
1890	—	—	—	—	—	—	—	—	—	—	—	—	—	—	—	—	—
1906	76,480	875,713	139,515	66,459	1,505,424	131,202	375,754	78,242	373,888	654,454	86,664	82,472	436,929	99,422	159,538	503,178	10,598
1916	—	—	—	—	—	—	—	—	—	—	—	—	—	—	—	—	—
1926	152,886	1,418,011	324,157	122,807	2,465,139	228,132	477,470	150,618	552,718	1,186,325	168,816	86,933	621,310	201,688	277,879	720,871	32,818
1936	152,825	1,388,464	323,876	131,254	2,412,708	230,876	395,692	132,664	501,632	1,173,171	184,981	88,106	544,120	183,951	258,731	778,497	35,506
1952	—	—	—	—	—	—	—	—	—	—	—	—	—	—	—	—	—
1971	—	—	—	—	—	—	—	—	—	—	—	—	—	—	—	—	—
1980	—	—	—	—	—	—	—	—	—	—	—	—	—	—	—	—	—
1990	—	—	—	—	—	—	—	—	—	—	—	—	—	—	—	—	—

Notes appear on next page

(continued)

TABLE Bg450–549 Estimates of church membership, by state and sex: 1890–1990 *Continued*

[1] Coverage and membership definition vary over time; see text. For 1952–1990, the year shown is approximate.

[2] Estimated.

[3] Data in the original source appear to be in error but cannot be corrected.

Sources

For 1890: U.S. Bureau of the Census, Census of 1890. For 1906–1936: U.S. Bureau of the Census, *Religious Bodies* (1906–1936). For 1952–1990: Glenmary Research Center, *Churches and Church Membership in the United States* (title and editors vary), 1955–1990.

Documentation

See the text for Table Bg320–333. As discussed there, the census used differing definitions and names for membership in the churches because of the varied practices of the denominations. "Communicants" was a somewhat more restrictive definition than "membership" or "adherents." Additional information for each year as follows:

1890. Communicants.

1906. Inclusive membership.

1916. Inclusive membership, partly estimated by census experts. Jewish congregations excluded.

1926. Inclusive membership. 7,576,913 persons did not have their gender reported.

1936. Membership. Includes Jewish congregations. The addition of Jewish congregations added some 4,600,000 persons to total membership. 10,029,328 persons did not have gender reported.

1952. Inclusive, "adherent" membership.

1971. Inclusive, "adherent" membership. Adherents were partly estimated because several denominations reported full members only. It was found that reported adherents were 2.4 times the number of reported full members. Note that the multiplier reached as high as 7 in some states and as low as 1.2 in others.

1980. Inclusive, "adherent" membership. 111 major religious bodies were surveyed. The estimation procedures for adherents was explained on p. xiii of Glenmary Research Center, *Churches and Church Membership in the United States* (title and editors vary), 1956–1990. The source claimed that its survey matched 91 percent of the number of full members reported by the *Yearbook of American and Canadian Churches.*

1990. 133 major religious bodies were surveyed.

TABLE Bg550–556 Personal expenditures on religious activities, and charitable and philanthropic giving to religion, by denomination: 1900–1996

Contributed by Colin B. Burke

	Personal consumption expenditures on			Philanthropic giving to			
	Religious and welfare activities	Religion	Religious giving	Protestant churches	Roman Catholic Church	Jewish religious organizations	Other denominations
	Bg550	Bg551	Bg552	Bg553	Bg554	Bg555	Bg556
Year	Billion dollars	Million dollars	Million dollars	Million dollars	Million dollars	Million dollars	Million dollars
1900	—	226	—	—	—	—	—
1901	—	225	—	—	—	—	—
1902	—	227	—	—	—	—	—
1903	—	237	—	—	—	—	—
1904	—	237	—	—	—	—	—
1905	—	238	—	—	—	—	—
1906	—	245	—	—	—	—	—
1907	—	262	—	—	—	—	—
1908	—	266	—	—	—	—	—
1909	—	265	—	—	—	—	—
1910	—	257	—	—	—	—	—
1911	—	277	—	—	—	—	—
1912	—	287	—	—	—	—	—
1913	—	297	—	—	—	—	—
1914	—	314	—	—	—	—	—
1915	—	332	—	—	—	—	—
1916	—	346	—	—	—	—	—
1917	—	366	—	—	—	—	—
1918	—	411	—	—	—	—	—
1919	—	442	—	—	—	—	—
1920	—	523	—	—	—	—	—
1921	—	574	—	—	—	—	—
1922	—	618	—	—	—	—	—
1923	—	664	—	—	—	—	—
1924	—	729	—	—	—	—	—
1925	—	790	—	—	—	—	—
1926	—	832	—	—	—	—	—
1927	—	867	—	—	—	—	—
1928	—	905	—	—	—	—	—
1929	1.2	949	838	596	201	37	4

TABLE Bg550–556 Personal expenditures on religious activities, and charitable and philanthropic giving to religion, by denomination: 1900–1996 *Continued*

	Personal consumption expenditures on			Philanthropic giving to			
	Religious and welfare activities	Religion	Religious giving	Protestant churches	Roman Catholic Church	Jewish religious organizations	Other denominations
	Bg550	Bg551	Bg552	Bg553	Bg554	Bg555	Bg556
Year	Billion dollars	Million dollars	Million dollars	Million dollars	Million dollars	Million dollars	Million dollars
1930	1.3	—	787	554	195	34	4
1931	1.2	—	696	490	175	29	3
1932	1.0	—	579	400	151	24	3
1933	0.9	—	505	348	134	20	3
1934	0.9	—	516	358	134	20	3
1935	0.9	—	534	374	136	21	3
1936	0.9	—	569	398	141	25	4
1937	0.9	—	593	415	149	26	3
1938	1.0	—	605	423	152	26	4
1939	1.0	—	598	417	152	26	3
1940	1.1	—	612	428	155	26	2
1941	1.1	—	680	481	166	29	4
1942	1.3	—	736	529	172	31	5
1943	1.5	—	809	596	175	33	4
1944	1.7	—	889	665	183	38	3
1945	1.8	—	1,009	765	194	45	5
1946	2.1	—	1,186	911	218	51	6
1947	2.1	—	1,335	1,017	255	54	9
1948	2.3	—	1,589	1,211	305	62	11
1949	2.3	—	1,811	1,390	335	75	12
1950	2.4	—	1,962	1,503	360	78	20
1951	2.6	—	2,175	1,973	396	85	22
1952	3.0	—	2,391	1,870	401	91	29
1953	3.2	—	2,650	2,090	433	99	28
1954	3.4	—	2,905	2,296	474	106	29
1955	3.5	—	3,166	2,507	514	113	33
1956	4.0	—	3,497	2,785	538	133	41
1957	4.2	—	3,778	3,011	582	141	44
1958	4.5	—	4,036	3,236	607	147	46
1959	5.0	—	4,271	3,398	670	151	51
1960	5.3	—	—	—	—	—	—
1961	5.6	—	—	—	—	—	—
1962	5.8	—	—	—	—	—	—
1963	6.2	—	—	—	—	—	—
1964	7.1	—	—	—	—	—	—
1965	7.7	—	—	—	—	—	—
1966	8.5	—	—	—	—	—	—
1967	9.4	—	—	—	—	—	—
1968	10.3	—	—	—	—	—	—
1969	11.0	—	—	—	—	—	—
1970	12.1	—	—	—	—	—	—
1971	13.5	—	—	—	—	—	—
1972	15.2	—	—	—	—	—	—
1973	16.3	—	—	—	—	—	—
1974	18.0	—	—	—	—	—	—
1975	19.7	—	—	—	—	—	—
1976	22.3	—	—	—	—	—	—
1977	24.8	—	—	—	—	—	—
1978	29.4	—	—	—	—	—	—
1979	33.4	—	—	—	—	—	—
1980	38.3	—	—	—	—	—	—
1981	43.2	—	—	—	—	—	—
1982	47.4	—	—	—	—	—	—
1983	51.8	—	—	—	—	—	—
1984	58.8	—	—	—	—	—	—
1985	62.6	—	—	—	—	—	—
1986	69.7	—	—	—	—	—	—
1987	74.4	—	—	—	—	—	—
1988	83.3	—	—	—	—	—	—
1989	90.4	—	—	—	—	—	—

(continued)

TABLE Bg550–556 Personal expenditures on religious activities, and charitable and philanthropic giving to religion, by denomination: 1900–1996 *Continued*

	Personal consumption expenditures on			Philanthropic giving to			
	Religious and welfare activities	Religion	Religious giving	Protestant churches	Roman Catholic Church	Jewish religious organizations	Other denominations
	Bg550	Bg551	Bg552	Bg553	Bg554	Bg555	Bg556
Year	Billion dollars	Million dollars	Million dollars	Million dollars	Million dollars	Million dollars	Million dollars
1990	100.4	—	—	—	—	—	—
1991	104.1	—	—	—	—	—	—
1992	115.6	—	—	—	—	—	—
1993	121.3	—	—	—	—	—	—
1994	131.2	—	—	—	—	—	—
1995	139.8	—	—	—	—	—	—
1996	150.5	—	—	—	—	—	—

Sources

Series Bg550. U.S. Bureau of Economic Analysis, *National Income and Product Accounts of the United States (NIPA)*, 1998, Table 2.4; *Survey of Current Business* (published annually).

Series Bg551. Stanley Lebergott, *Consumer Expenditures: New Measures and Old Motives* (Princeton University Press, 1996), Table A1.

Series Bg552–556. Frank Greene Dickinson, *The Changing Position of Philanthropy in the American Economy* (National Bureau of Economic Research, 1970), Table 3.1.

Documentation

Series Bg550. Previously, this series was presented as two incompatible series divided at 1970. The 1998 *NIPA* revisions led to this unified series: "For nonprofit institutions, equals current expenditures (including consumption of fixed capital) of religious, social welfare, foreign relief, and political organizations, museums, libraries and foundations. The expenditures are net of receipts – such as those from meals, rooms and entertainments – accounted for separately in consumer expenditures and excludes relief payments within the United States and expenditures by foundations for education and research" (*NIPA,* 1998, volume 1, p. 108).

Series Bg551. Religious consumption only; welfare spending not included.

TABLE Bg557–570 Charitable and philanthropic giving – religious and secular – by purpose and denomination: 1910–1992

Contributed by Colin B. Burke

		Expenditures from philanthropic funds									Private organization expenditures for social work, New York City			
	Total giving by religious organizations	All expenditures by churches	All welfare expenditures	Church-related welfare	All secular welfare	All health and welfare expenditures	Church expenditures for health and welfare	Church-related expenditures for health	Secular health care and services	Religious giving abroad	Total	Catholic	Jewish	Protestant and nonsectarian
	Bg557	Bg558	Bg559	Bg560	Bg561	Bg562	Bg563	Bg564	Bg565	Bg566	Bg567	Bg568	Bg569	Bg570
Year	Billion dollars	Million dollars	Million dollars	Million dollars	Million dollars	Million dollars	Million dollars	Million dollars	Million dollars	Million dollars	Thousand dollars	Thousand dollars	Thousand dollars	Thousand dollars
1910	—	—	—	—	—	—	—	—	—	—	14,796	3,708	1,795	9,293
1911	—	—	—	—	—	—	—	—	—	—	15,269	3,709	1,895	9,664
1912	—	—	—	—	—	—	—	—	—	—	16,276	3,914	2,067	10,295
1913	—	—	—	—	—	—	—	—	—	—	16,911	3,998	2,177	10,736
1914	—	—	—	—	—	—	—	—	—	—	17,892	4,179	2,449	11,264
1915	—	—	—	—	—	—	—	—	—	—	19,514	4,695	2,619	12,200
1916	—	—	—	—	—	—	—	—	—	—	20,514	4,548	2,878	13,050
1917	—	—	—	—	—	—	—	—	—	—	23,387	4,903	3,367	15,117
1918	—	—	—	—	—	—	—	—	—	—	30,533	5,097	3,867	21,570
1919	—	—	—	—	—	—	—	—	—	—	34,793	5,721	4,766	24,306
1920	—	—	—	—	—	—	—	—	—	—	37,315	6,425	5,615	25,275
1921	—	—	—	—	—	—	—	—	—	—	37,744	6,978	6,137	24,630
1922	—	—	—	—	—	—	—	—	—	—	37,946	7,064	6,207	24,674
1923	—	—	—	—	—	—	—	—	—	—	39,468	7,277	6,659	25,532
1924	—	—	—	—	—	—	—	—	—	—	41,529	7,541	7,081	26,907
1925	—	—	—	—	—	—	—	—	—	—	43,720	7,827	7,633	28,260
1926	—	—	—	—	—	—	—	—	—	—	46,189	8,243	8,081	29,864
1927	—	—	—	—	—	—	—	—	—	—	48,245	8,209	8,473	31,564
1928	—	—	—	—	—	—	—	—	—	—	50,890	8,719	8,956	33,225
1929	—	—	—	—	—	—	—	—	—	42	53,648	9,196	9,458	34,994
1930	—	875	247	89	167	369	105	25	26	40	—	—	—	—
1931	—	—	—	—	—	—	—	—	—	36	—	—	—	—
1932	—	—	—	—	—	—	—	—	—	27	—	—	—	—
1933	—	—	—	—	—	—	—	—	—	21	—	—	—	—
1934	—	—	—	—	—	—	—	—	—	22	—	—	—	—
1935	—	574	165	45	120	216	60	15	26	20	—	—	—	—
1936	—	—	—	—	—	—	—	—	—	22	—	—	—	—
1937	—	—	—	—	—	—	—	—	—	24	—	—	—	—
1938	—	—	—	—	—	—	—	—	—	26	—	—	—	—
1939	—	—	—	—	—	—	—	—	—	32	—	—	—	—
1940	—	627	200	50	150	271	65	15	38	30	—	—	—	—
1941	—	—	—	—	—	—	—	—	—	33	—	—	—	—
1942	—	—	—	—	—	—	—	—	—	30	—	—	—	—
1943	—	—	—	—	—	—	—	—	—	38	—	—	—	—
1944	—	—	—	—	—	—	—	—	—	58	—	—	—	—
1945	—	1,158	790	115	625	1,155	150	35	280	77	—	—	—	—
1946	—	—	—	—	—	—	—	—	—	150	—	—	—	—
1947	—	—	—	—	—	—	—	—	—	211	—	—	—	—
1948	—	—	—	—	—	—	—	—	—	248	—	—	—	—
1949	—	—	—	—	—	—	—	—	—	180	—	—	—	—

(continued)

TABLE Bg557–570 Charitable and philanthropic giving – religious and secular – by purpose and denomination: 1910–1992 *Continued*

		Expenditures from philanthropic funds									Private organization expenditures for social work, New York City			
	Total giving by religious organizations	All expenditures by churches	All welfare expenditures	Church-related welfare	All secular welfare	All health and welfare expenditures	Church expenditures for health and welfare	Church-related expenditures for health	Secular health care and services	Religious giving abroad	Total	Catholic	Jewish	Protestant and nonsectarian
	Bg557	Bg558	Bg559	Bg560	Bg561	Bg562	Bg563	Bg564	Bg565	Bg566	Bg567	Bg568	Bg569	Bg570
Year	Billion dollars	Million dollars	Million dollars	Million dollars	Million dollars	Million dollars	Million dollars	Million dollars	Million dollars	Million dollars	Thousand dollars	Thousand dollars	Thousand dollars	Thousand dollars
1950	—	1,963	850	200	600	1,440	260	60	335	163	—	—	—	—
1951	—	—	—	—	—	—	—	—	—	132	—	—	—	—
1952	—	—	—	—	—	—	—	—	—	144	—	—	—	—
1953	—	—	—	—	—	—	—	—	—	175	—	—	—	—
1954	—	—	—	—	—	—	—	—	—	206	—	—	—	—
1955	—	3,100	1,150	290	780	1,925	380	90	465	163	—	—	—	—
1956	—	—	—	—	—	—	—	—	—	218	—	—	—	—
1957	—	—	—	—	—	—	—	—	—	199	—	—	—	—
1958	—	—	—	—	—	—	—	—	—	207	—	—	—	—
1959	—	3,900	—	468	—	—	—	118	—	219	—	—	—	—
1960	—	4,092	—	480	—	—	—	122	—	—	—	—	—	—
1977	3.4	—	—	—	—	—	—	—	—	—	—	—	—	—
1980	4.4	—	—	—	—	—	—	—	—	—	—	—	—	—
1982	5.7	—	—	—	—	—	—	—	—	—	—	—	—	—
1983	6.3	—	—	—	—	—	—	—	—	—	—	—	—	—
1984	6.8	—	—	—	—	—	—	—	—	—	—	—	—	—
1987	8.3	—	—	—	—	—	—	—	—	—	—	—	—	—
1989	6.1	—	—	—	—	—	—	—	—	—	—	—	—	—
1992	7.0	—	—	—	—	—	—	—	—	—	—	—	—	—

Sources

Series Bg557. Virginia Ann Hodgkinson, Murray S. Weitzman, et al., *The Nonprofit Almanac, 1996–1997: Dimensions of the Independent Sector* (Jossey-Bass, 1996), Table 4.2, and other Independent Sector publications.

Series Bg558–565. *Social Security Bulletin* (various years), especially Thomas Karter, "Voluntary Agency Expenditures, 1930–1955," *Social Security Bulletin* (February 1958).

Series Bg566. Frank Greene Dickinson, *The Changing Position of Philanthropy in the American Economy* (National Bureau of Economic Research, 1970).

Series Bg567–570. New York Research Bureau of the Welfare Council, *Financial Trends in Organized Social Work in New York City* (Welfare Council, ca. 1931), p. 39.

Documentation

Series Bg557. Covers Standard Industrial Classification (SIC) industry 866, religious organizations. See the introduction to Part D for a discussion of SIC codes. This series estimates the amount churches spend on nonsacerdotal activities.

TABLE Bg571–577 Charitable and philanthropic giving to religion, other sources of religious income, and average contributions to churches by members: 1921–1999

Contributed by Colin B. Burke

		Average contributions to churches			Contributions and payments to religious organizations		
	Giving to religion	By full members (50 denominations)	For congregational purposes and benevolence (29 denominations)	By church members (11 denominations)	Private contributions	Private sector payments and purchases	Philanthropic revenues of religious organizations
	Bg571	Bg572	Bg573	Bg574	Bg575	Bg576	Bg577
Year	Billion dollars	Dollars	Dollars	Dollars	Billion dollars	Billion dollars	Million dollars
1921	—	—	—	16.10	—	—	—
1922	—	—	—	18.95	—	—	—
1923	—	—	—	22.03	—	—	—
1924	—	—	—	23.03	—	—	—
1925	—	—	—	21.19	—	—	—
1926	—	—	—	21.61	—	—	—
1927	—	—	—	22.67	—	—	—
1928	—	—	—	20.56	—	—	—
1929	—	—	—	21.60	—	—	—
1930	—	—	—	20.18	—	—	787
1931	—	—	—	17.07	—	—	—
1932	—	—	—	14.22	—	—	—
1933	—	—	—	11.95	—	—	—
1934	—	—	—	11.79	—	—	—
1935	—	—	—	12.05	—	—	534
1936	—	—	—	12.87	—	—	—
1937	—	—	—	13.56	—	—	—
1938	—	—	—	13.76	—	—	—
1939	—	—	—	13.10	—	—	—
1940	—	—	—	13.15	—	—	612
1941	—	—	—	14.56	—	—	—
1942	—	—	—	15.22	—	—	—
1943	—	—	—	16.24	—	—	—
1944	—	—	—	18.30	—	—	—
1945	—	—	—	21.29	—	—	1,009
1946	—	—	—	23.25	—	—	—
1947	—	—	—	25.27	—	—	—
1948	—	—	—	28.68	—	—	—
1949	—	—	—	31.69	—	—	—
1950	—	—	—	33.17	—	—	1,962
1951	—	—	—	35.67	—	—	—
1952	—	—	—	38.28	—	—	—
1955	—	—	—	—	—	—	3,166
1956	—	—	—	—	—	—	3,497
1958	—	—	—	—	—	—	4,036
1959	4.76	—	—	—	—	—	—
1960	5.01	—	—	—	—	—	4,550
1961	5.23	69.00	—	—	—	—	4,764
1962	5.45	68.76	—	—	—	—	4,835
1963	5.84	69.87	—	—	—	—	5,029
1964	6.14	72.04	—	—	—	—	5,273
1965	6.72	77.75	—	—	—	—	5,866
1966	7.22	—	—	—	—	—	5,937
1967	7.58	—	—	—	—	—	6,390
1968	8.42	95.31	96.58	—	—	—	6,283
1969	9.02	99.68	100.63	—	—	—	6,464
1970	9.34	96.84	103.82	—	—	—	6,854
1971	10.07	103.94	109.43	—	—	—	—
1972	10.10	110.29	116.91	—	—	—	—
1973	10.53	118.16	127.23	—	—	—	—
1974	11.84	127.16	138.74	—	—	—	—
1975	12.81	138.54	149.93	—	—	—	—
1976	14.18	149.07	162.63	—	—	—	—
1977	16.98	159.33	175.40	—	17.0	—	—
1978	18.35	176.37	192.57	—	—	—	—
1979	20.17	197.44	211.15	—	—	—	—

(continued)

TABLE Bg571–577 Charitable and philanthropic giving to religion, other sources of religious income, and average contributions to churches by members: 1921–1999 *Continued*

		Average contributions to churches			Contributions and payments to religious organizations		
	Giving to religion	By full members (50 denominations)	For congregational purposes and benevolence (29 denominations)	By church members (11 denominations)	Private contributions	Private sector payments and purchases	Philanthropic revenues of religious organizations
	Bg571	Bg572	Bg573	Bg574	Bg575	Bg576	Bg577
Year	Billion dollars	Dollars	Dollars	Dollars	Billion dollars	Billion dollars	Million dollars
1980	22.23	213.41	231.90	—	22.3	—	—
1981	25.05	239.71	255.08	—	—	—	—
1982	28.06	261.95	275.73	—	28.1	—	—
1983	31.84	278.67	292.62	—	31.9	—	—
1984	35.55	300.40	315.34	—	35.6	—	—
1985	38.21	321.77	335.63	—	—	—	—
1986	41.68	344.42	352.84	—	—	—	—
1987	43.51	356.67	367.23	—	43.6	3.1	—
1988	45.15	376.04	381.92	—	—	—	—
1989	47.77	399.63	403.02	—	48.5	3.4	—
1990	49.79	—	419.52	—	—	—	—
1991	50.00	—	433.69	—	—	—	—
1992	54.91	410.59	445.16	—	55.1	3.9	—
1993	55.29	425.78	457.76	—	—	—	—
1994	60.21	421.23	477.21	—	—	—	—
1995	66.26	469.18	498.20	—	—	—	—
1996	70.66	373.41	—	—	—	—	—
1997	74.97	497.24	—	—	—	—	—
1998	—	557.93	—	—	—	—	—
1999	—	557.05	—	—	—	—	—

Sources

Series Bg571. Ann E. Kaplan, editor, *Giving USA, 1996* (AAFRC Trust for Philanthropy, 1996), and unpublished data provided by the American Association of Fund-Raising Counsel (AAFRC) from 1997–1998 studies.

Series Bg572. National Council of Churches, *Yearbook of American and Canadian Churches* (title and editors vary) annual issues.

Series Bg573–574. John L. Ronsvalle and Sylvia Ronsvalle, *The State of Church Giving through 1995* (Empty Tomb, 1997), pp. 9 and 115.

Series Bg575–576. Virginia Ann Hodgkinson, Murray S. Weitzman, et al., *The Nonprofit Almanac, 1996–1997: Dimensions of the Independent Sector* (Jossey-Bass, 1996), Table 4.3.

Series Bg577. Data compiled by Ralph L. Nelson, City University of New York, Queens College, reported in *Historical Statistics of the United States* (1975), series H406.

Documentation

Series Bg575–576. Covers Standard Industrial Classification (SIC) industry 866, religious organizations. See the Introduction to Part D for a discussion of SIC codes.

Series Bg577. The estimates shown here differ from those presented in the 1970s editions of *Statistical Abstract of the United States*. Reasons for the differences include differences in estimating procedures, definition and scope of particular categories, and the need to make projections. The source of the *Statistical Abstract* estimates was the original estimates in *Giving USA* (AAFRC Trust for Philanthropy, annual issues). In the annual *Giving USA*, the objective was to present contemporary estimates, which required projection of historical data. According to Ralph L. Nelson, his estimates reflected a greater opportunity to use historical benchmarks and the availability of the time and research resources required to handle more thoroughly the problems of data refinement and estimation. For a description of data sources for this series and the estimation procedures, see Frank Greene Dickinson, *The Changing Position of Philanthropy in the American Economy* (National Bureau of Economic Research, 1970), Chapter 3, and the documentation prepared by Nelson for the Carnegie Corporation and for the Commission on Private Philanthropy and Public Needs.

TABLE Bg578–589 Catholic personnel and education – priests, nuns, schools, pupils, teachers, and philanthropic school revenue: 1890–1998

Contributed by Colin B. Burke

		Catholic sisters (nuns)		Philanthropic revenue of parochial schools	Catholic elementary schools				Catholic secondary schools			
	Catholic priests	Total	Teaching in Catholic schools		Number	Pupils enrolled	Religious teachers	Lay teachers	Number	Pupils enrolled	Religious teachers	Lay teachers
	Bg578 [1]	Bg579 [1]	Bg580	Bg581	Bg582	Bg583	Bg584	Bg585	Bg586	Bg587	Bg588	Bg589
Year	Number	Number	Number	Million dollars	Number	Thousand	Thousand	Thousand	Number	Thousand	Thousand	Thousand
1890	8,463	—	—	—	—	—	—	—	—	—	—	—
1902	12,429	—	—	—	—	—	—	—	—	—	—	—
1911	17,084	—	—	—	—	—	—	—	—	—	—	—
1920	21,124	—	—	—	6,551	1,796	—	—	1,552	130	—	—
1930	27,043	—	—	153	7,923	2,223	53	5	—	—	—	—
1935	—	—	—	75	—	—	—	—	—	—	—	—
1936	—	—	—	—	7,929	2,103	50	—	1,946	285	14	3
1940	34,048	—	—	115	7,944	2,035	—	—	2,105	361	—	—
1945	—	—	—	146	—	—	—	—	—	—	—	—
1947	—	—	—	—	—	—	—	—	2,111	467	23	4
1948	—	—	—	—	8,285	2,305	59	3	2,150	483	23	4
1950	50,347	147,370	82,048	428	8,589	2,561	62	—	2,189	506	23	5
1952	—	—	—	—	8,880	2,842	66	6	2,180	549	24	5
1954	—	—	—	—	9,279	3,235	67	9	2,296	624	26	6
1955	—	—	—	697	—	—	—	—	—	—	—	—
1956	—	—	—	801	9,615	3,571	71	14	2,311	705	28	7
1958	—	—	—	896	—	—	—	—	—	—	—	—
1960	64,269	168,527	98,471	993	10,501	4,373	79	29	2,392	880	33	11
1961	—	—	—	1,058	10,631	4,445	78	33	2,376	938	34	14
1962	—	—	—	1,120	10,676	4,485	77	36	2,502	1,009	34	13
1963	—	—	—	1,180	10,775	4,546	77	38	2,430	1,044	35	16
1964	—	—	—	1,203	10,832	4,534	76	42	2,417	1,067	36	18
1965	—	—	—	1,154	10,879	4,492	76	44	2,413	1,082	38	19
1966	—	—	—	1,239	10,769	4,375	74	46	2,463	1,110	36	20
1967	—	—	—	1,235	10,350	4,106	70	53	2,277	1,093	34	21
1968	—	—	—	1,293	10,113	3,860	68	58	2,192	1,081	33	23
1969	—	—	—	1,391	9,695	3,607	56	54	2,076	1,051	29	23
1970	70,815	160,931	85,616	1,422	9,362	3,359	52	60	1,981	1,008	27	26
1975	—	—	—	—	8,340	2,525	35	64	1,653	898	20	30
1980	66,562	126,517	41,135	—	8,043	2,269	25	72	1,516	837	14	35
1981	—	—	—	—	7,996	2,266	24	73	1,490	828	14	35
1982	—	—	—	—	7,950	2,225	22	75	1,482	801	13	36
1983	—	120,699	—	—	7,937	2,180	21	78	1,464	788	12	36
1984	—	—	—	—	7,891	2,120	20	80	1,449	782	12	38
1985	64,861	—	—	—	7,806	2,057	18	79	1,430	762	11	39
1986	—	—	—	—	7,693	1,998	17	77	1,409	728	10	38
1987	—	—	—	—	7,601	1,942	15	78	1,391	681	10	37
1988	—	—	—	—	7,501	1,912	14	80	1,362	639	8	36
1989	—	—	—	—	7,395	1,893	12	82	1,324	606	8	35
1990	60,693	103,329	19,012	—	7,291	1,884	11	80	1,296	592	6	34
1991	—	—	—	—	7,239	1,964	12	96	1,269	587	6	37
1992	59,401	99,327	17,453	—	7,174	1,984	11	98	1,249	584	6	38
1993	—	—	—	—	7,114	1,992	12	100	1,231	585	7	38
1994	—	—	—	—	7,056	2,004	11	107	1,238	615	6	40
1995	—	—	—	—	7,022	2,011	10	109	1,228	624	6	42
1996	—	—	11,217	—	—	—	—	—	—	—	—	—
1998	53,793	85,412	—	—	—	—	—	—	—	—	—	—

[1] Years are approximate due to nature of reporting in source.

Sources

Series Bg578–580. *The Official Catholic Directory* (P. J. Kenedy, published annually).

Series Bg581. For 1929–1959 estimates, Frank Greene Dickinson, *The Changing Position of Philanthropy in the American Economy* (National Bureau of Economic Research, 1970), Chapter 3. 1960–1970 estimates (and also 1929–1959) prepared by Ralph L. Nelson for the Carnegie Corporation and for the Commission on Private Philanthropy and Public Needs.

Series Bg582–589. U.S. Office of Education, *Biennial Survey of Education in the United States* (1930–1932, 1934–1936, and 1946–1948), and *Digest of Education Statistics* (1972–1999). For 1947 and 1952–1963, National Catholic Welfare Conference, *Summary of Catholic Education* (published biennially). For 1950 and 1964–1970, *Statistical Report on Catholic Elementary and Secondary Schools for the Years 1967–68 to 1969–70* (National Catholic Educational Association, 1970), and *A Report on U.S. Catholic Schools, 1970–71* (National Catholic Educational Association, 1971); *Official Catholic Directory* (P. J. Kenedy, various years); and U.S. National Center for Educational Statistics, *Digest of Education Statistics* (various years).

(continued)

TABLE Bg578–589 Catholic personnel and education – priests, nuns, schools, pupils, teachers, and philanthropic school revenue: 1890–1998 *Continued*

Documentation

The Catholic school system includes five types of schools: (1) Parochial schools are operated in connection with parishes. (2) Interparochial schools are under the administrative control of two or more parishes. (3) Archdiocesan or diocesan schools are under the direct administration of an ordinary and serve the parishes designated by him. (4) Private schools are conducted independently of parishes by religious communities. (5) Institutional schools include industrial schools; schools for blind, deaf, delinquent, or subnormal children; and schools conducted in orphanages. In Catholic secondary education there are, broadly, three types of administrative control, defined generally along the lines described above: (1) central or diocesan, (2) parochial, and (3) private. However, many parochial and private schools really function as diocesan schools. The data for elementary school teachers exclude priests serving as part-time teachers of religion.

Series Bg578. Includes all types of male Catholic clergy.

Series Bg584 and Bg588. Includes priests, brothers, and sisters.

PHILANTHROPY

Colin B. Burke

TABLE Bg590–599 Philanthropic and charitable giving, and philanthropic revenue of nonprofit organizations: 1900–1997

Contributed by Colin B. Burke

	Philanthropic and charitable giving									
			By individuals					Giving to Community Chest and United Way Fund campaigns		
	Estimated total giving	Charitable contributions	By individuals	Gifts of living donors	Consumer expenditures on welfare	Charitable bequests	Charitable bequests	United States and Canada	United States	Philanthropic revenue of nonprofit organizations
	Bg590	Bg591	Bg592	Bg593	Bg594	Bg595	Bg596	Bg597	Bg598	Bg599
Year	Million dollars	Thousand dollars	Million dollars	Million dollars	Million dollars	Million dollars	Million dollars	Dollars	Dollars	Million dollars
1900	—	—	—	—	100	—	—	—	—	—
1901	—	—	—	—	100	—	—	—	—	—
1902	—	—	—	—	100	—	—	—	—	—
1903	—	—	—	—	100	—	—	—	—	—
1904	—	—	—	—	100	—	—	—	—	—
1905	—	—	—	—	100	—	—	—	—	—
1906	—	—	—	—	100	—	—	—	—	—
1907	—	—	—	—	100	—	—	—	—	—
1908	—	—	—	—	100	—	—	—	—	—
1909	—	—	—	—	100	—	—	—	—	—
1910	—	—	—	—	100	—	—	—	—	—
1911	—	—	—	—	100	—	—	—	—	—
1912	—	—	—	—	100	—	—	—	—	—
1913	—	—	—	—	100	—	—	—	—	—
1914	—	—	—	—	108	—	—	—	—	—
1915	—	—	—	—	114	—	—	—	—	—
1916	—	—	—	—	115	—	—	—	—	—
1917	—	—	—	—	317	—	—	—	—	—
1918	—	—	—	—	456	—	—	—	—	—
1919	—	—	—	—	205	—	—	19,651,334	—	—
1920	—	—	—	—	312	—	—	22,781,834	—	—
1921	—	—	—	—	266	—	—	28,568,453	—	—
1922	—	467,760	—	—	266	—	—	40,280,649	—	—
1923	—	649,141	—	—	265	—	—	50,351,190	—	—
1924	—	644,906	—	—	285	—	—	58,003,965	—	—
1925	—	596,099	—	—	248	—	—	63,677,235	—	—
1926	—	755,767	—	—	256	—	—	66,432,072	—	—
1927	—	695,409	—	—	280	—	—	68,664,042	—	—
1928	—	832,735	—	—	275	—	—	73,276,688	—	—
1929	—	803,555	—	1,084	298	154	—	75,972,555	—	—
1930	—	768,525	—	969	—	223	—	84,796,505	—	1,474
1931	—	640,235	—	805	—	220	—	101,377,537	—	—
1932	—	609,464	—	751	—	191	—	77,752,954	—	—
1933	—	479,502	—	700	—	96	—	70,609,078	—	—
1934	—	559,732	—	790	—	146	—	69,781,478	—	—
1935	—	591,991	—	828	—	106	—	77,367,634	—	969
1936	—	660,247	—	985	—	128	—	81,707,787	—	—
1937	—	747,741	—	1,057	—	127	—	83,898,234	—	—
1938	—	733,546	—	1,001	—	200	—	86,561,920	—	—
1939	—	814,088	—	1,177	—	179	—	89,751,702	—	—
1940	—	1,052,352	—	1,254	—	143	—	94,161,098	—	1,212
1941	—	1,551,332	—	1,520	—	175	—	108,812,899	—	—
1942	—	2,132,374	—	1,944	—	155	—	166,538,363	—	—
1943	—	2,653,761	—	2,449	—	186	—	214,757,782	—	—
1944	—	2,905,331	—	2,567	—	202	—	225,934,893	—	—
1945	—	3,173,073	—	2,762	—	192	—	201,859,357	—	2,611
1946	—	3,391,808	—	3,088	—	186	—	173,512,638	—	—
1947	—	3,918,277	—	3,559	—	223	—	181,716,355	—	—
1948	—	4,098,753	—	3,898	—	296	—	193,307,693	—	—
1949	—	4,218,868	—	3,966	—	206	—	198,120,167	—	—

(continued)

TABLE Bg590–599 Philanthropic and charitable giving, and philanthropic revenue of nonprofit organizations: 1900–1997 *Continued*

	Philanthropic and charitable giving									
			By individuals					Giving to Community Chest and United Way Fund campaigns		
	Estimated total giving	Charitable contributions	By individuals	Gifts of living donors	Consumer expenditures on welfare	Charitable bequests	Charitable bequests	United States and Canada	United States	Philanthropic revenue of nonprofit organizations
	Bg590	Bg591	Bg592	Bg593	Bg594	Bg595	Bg596	Bg597	Bg598	Bg599
Year	Million dollars	Thousand dollars	Million dollars	Million dollars	Million dollars	Million dollars	Million dollars	Dollars	Dollars	Million dollars
1950	—	4,663,714	—	4,359	—	274	—	218,421,521	—	4,429
1951	—	—	—	5,051	—	301	—	246,813,142	—	—
1952	—	—	—	5,521	—	328	—	272,257,433	—	—
1953	—	—	—	6,036	—	355	—	293,898,475	—	—
1954	—	—	—	6,216	—	398	—	308,303,285	—	—
1955	—	—	—	6,735	—	466	—	—	329,990,528	6,751
1956	—	—	—	7,317	—	534	—	—	367,720,884	7,537
1957	—	—	—	7,735	—	602	—	—	398,967,291	—
1958	—	—	—	8,078	—	669	—	—	409,446,729	8,613
1959	10,400	—	8,680	8,545	—	810	510	—	438,675,048	—
1960	11,050	—	9,160	—	—	951	670	—	456,983,942	9,996
1961	11,690	—	9,500	—	—	913	950	—	479,086,478	10,663
1962	11,830	—	9,890	—	—	876	700	—	501,437,619	11,295
1963	13,140	—	10,860	—	—	1,020	880	—	520,325,952	12,008
1964	13,600	—	11,190	—	—	1,164	950	—	558,559,954	12,552
1965	14,710	—	11,820	—	—	1,309	1,020	—	597,738,826	13,468
1966	15,790	—	12,440	—	—	1,515	1,310	—	639,085,139	14,011
1967	17,030	—	13,410	—	—	1,721	1,400	—	676,729,723	15,254
1968	18,850	—	14,750	—	—	1,927	1,600	—	716,422,803	15,985
1969	20,660	—	15,930	—	—	2,132	2,000	—	764,327,412	16,947
1970	21,040	—	16,190	—	—	2,087	2,130	—	786,985,155	18,052
1971	23,440	—	17,640	—	—	—	3,000	—	812,924,645	—
1972	24,440	—	19,370	—	—	—	2,100	—	858,812,200	—
1973	25,590	—	20,530	—	—	—	2,000	—	916,400,000	—
1974	26,880	—	21,600	—	—	—	2,070	—	978,764,132	—
1975	28,560	—	23,530	—	—	—	2,230	—	1,022,906,395	—
1976	31,850	—	26,320	—	—	—	2,300	—	1,104,329,744	—
1977	35,210	—	29,550	—	—	—	2,120	—	1,204,825,000	—
1978	38,570	—	32,100	—	—	—	2,600	—	1,317,745,690	—
1979	43,110	—	36,590	—	—	—	2,230	—	1,423,461,336	—
1980	48,630	—	40,710	—	—	—	2,860	—	1,526,000,000	—
1981	55,280	—	45,990	—	—	—	3,580	—	1,680,000,000	—
1982	59,110	—	47,630	—	—	—	5,210	—	1,780,000,000	—
1983	63,210	—	52,060	—	—	—	3,880	—	1,950,000,000	—
1984	68,580	—	56,460	—	—	—	4,040	—	2,145,000,000	—
1985	71,690	—	57,390	—	—	—	4,770	—	2,330,000,000	—
1986	83,250	—	67,090	—	—	—	5,700	—	2,440,000,000	—
1987	82,210	—	64,530	—	—	—	6,580	—	2,600,000,000	—
1988	88,044	—	69,980	—	—	—	6,570	—	2,780,000,000	—
1989	98,430	—	79,450	—	—	—	6,970	—	2,980,000,000	—
1990	101,370	—	81,040	—	—	—	7,640	—	3,110,000,000	—
1991	105,010	—	84,270	—	—	—	7,780	—	3,170,000,000	—
1992	110,410	—	87,700	—	—	—	8,150	—	3,404,000,000	—
1993	116,540	—	92,000	—	—	—	8,540	—	3,047,000,000	—
1994	119,170	—	92,520	—	—	—	10,010	—	3,078,000,000	—
1995	124,310	—	95,690	—	—	—	10,730	—	3,148,000,000	—
1996	133,460	—	102,350	—	—	—	11,480	—	3,248,000,000	—
1997	143,460	—	109,260	—	—	—	12,630	—	—	—

Sources

Series Bg590, Bg592, and Bg596. Ann E. Kaplan, editor, *Giving USA, 1996* (AAFRC Trust for Philanthropy, 1996), and unpublished data provided by the American Association of Fund-Raising Counsel (AAFRC) from 1997–1998 studies.

Series Bg591. John Price Jones, *The American Giver: A Review of American Generosity* (Inter-River Press, 1956), Table 1.

Series Bg593. Frank Greene Dickinson, *The Changing Position of Philanthropy in the American Economy* (National Bureau of Economic Research 1970), Table 2.5.

Series Bg594. Stanley Lebergott, *Consumer Expenditures: New Measures and Old Motives* (Princeton University Press, 1996), Table A1.

Series Bg595 and Bg599. Data compiled by Ralph L. Nelson, City University of New York, Queens College, reported in *Historical Statistics of the United States* (1975).

TABLE Bg590–599 Philanthropic and charitable giving, and philanthropic revenue of nonprofit organizations: 1900–1997 *Continued*

Series Bg597–598. Eleanor L. Brilliant, *The United Way: Dilemmas of Organized Charity* (Columbia University Press, 1993), p. 271, and unpublished data provided by United Way Research Services, 1997.

Documentation

Series Bg590. This series includes charitable and philanthropic contributions by individuals, corporations, and foundations, as well as bequests by individuals. Like other estimates of total giving, it rests upon federal income, corporate, and estate/gift tax information, as well as surveys by organizations such as the Foundation Center and the Council for Aid to Education. The estimating procedures originally developed by Ralph L. Nelson in the 1970s were and are central to the most widely accepted "giving" series. His procedures are used to estimate missing information, such as contributions by those who did not seek tax deductions, and to interpolate and extrapolate series and their components. Nelson's estimates appeared in *Historical Statistics* (1975) and were used by the major investigations of the nonprofit sector during the 1970s. However, his estimating procedures have recently been refined with the help of the staff of the AAFRC Trust for Philanthropy and have been used on more precise data to create this new estimate of total giving and, as indicated below, many of its components. The new methods and data are described in *Giving USA, 1996,* p. 201.

Series Bg591. These estimates were created by the first national organization to monitor the charitable and philanthropic sectors. It includes John Price Jones's estimates of contributions by those filing income taxes, contributions by those who did not, gifts of property by individuals, charitable bequests, foundation grants, and corporate gifts. Note that not all of these components were included before 1936.

Series Bg592. This series includes only giving by individuals and families. Based on U.S. Internal Revenue Service (IRS), *Statistics of Income: Individual Income Tax Returns* (published annually), and on the estimating procedures originated by Nelson, the series includes estimates of contributions by those who did not file for deductions for charitable contributions and includes estimates for years with missing data. This series replaces previous estimates of contributions by living donors for the period and, while not fully compatible, it parallels series Bg593 for 1929–1959. See *Giving USA, 1996,* p. 195, for technical details. Note that debates continue over the methods and assumptions used to estimate individual giving. See Hayden W. Smith, "Some Thoughts on the Validity of Estimates of Charitable Giving," *Voluntas* 7 (2) (1993): 251–2, and Virginia Ann Hodgkinson, Murray S. Weitzman, et al., *The Nonprofit Almanac, 1996–1997: Dimensions of the Independent Sector* (Jossey-Bass, 1996), pp. 311–14.

Series Bg593. Applying improved estimating procedures to the data provided in *Statistics of Income: Individual Income Tax Returns*, and building on the work of Harry Kahn, this series replaces earlier estimates, such as series H399 in *Historical Statistics* (1975). Like the earlier series, this one compensates for "overreporting" of contributions and contains estimates of contributions by those not reporting them to the IRS. See C. Harry Kahn, *Personal Deductions in the Federal Income Tax* (Princeton University Press, 1960).

Series Bg594. These data are based upon estimated income of personnel in sectors related to welfare, such as social workers, rather than on tax data. This series may be estimating government as well as private "expenditures," but it remains the only series for the early years of the century. See Lebergott's description on p. 89 of *Consumer Expenditures*.

Series Bg595. This was series H400 in *Historical Statistics of the United States* (1975). It is based on charitable bequests reported on estate tax returns as tabulated in U.S. Internal Revenue Service, *Statistics of Income: Estate and Gift Tax Returns* (various years). For years in which no tabulations were made, estimates were based on linear interpolation between years for which tabulations were available.

Series Bg596. Based upon data in *Statistics of Income: Estate and Gift Tax Returns* and various sources, this series includes estimates of bequest amounts not reported to the IRS and employs estimating procedures initiated by Nelson. See *Giving USA, 1996,* p. 198.

Series Bg597–598. Based on the official records of the organizations.

Series Bg599. Created by Nelson and published as series H405 in *Historical Statistics* (1975), this series gauges the amount of giving through estimates of the charitable income received by nonprofit institutions. For insights into the techniques and sources used, refer to the text and sources for series H398–411 in *Historical Statistics of the United States* (1975).

TABLE Bg600–605 Philanthropic and charitable giving and philanthropic revenue, by cause: 1930–1997

Contributed by Colin B. Burke

	Philanthropic and charitable giving to				Philanthropic revenues	
	Human services	Public and society benefit organizations	Environmental causes	Unclassified causes	Youth service, race relations, and welfare organizations	Other major nonprofit service organizations
	Bg600	Bg601	Bg602	Bg603	Bg604	Bg605
Year	Million dollars	Million dollars	Million dollars	Million dollars	Million dollars	Million dollars
1930	—	—	—	—	167	60
1935	—	—	—	—	120	63
1940	—	—	—	—	150	100
1945	—	—	—	—	675	205
1950	—	—	—	—	685	392
1955	—	—	—	—	850	611
1956	—	—	—	—	900	503
1958	—	—	—	—	1,116	758
1959	1,630	290	—	1,050	—	—
1960	1,630	314	—	1,480	1,108	1,166
1961	1,690	318	—	1,570	1,163	1,248
1962	1,770	312	—	1,120	1,218	1,400
1963	1,970	374	—	1,440	1,256	1,562
1964	1,920	387	—	1,320	1,296	1,448

(continued)

TABLE Bg600–605 Philanthropic and charitable giving and philanthropic revenue, by cause: 1930–1997 *Continued*

	Philanthropic and charitable giving to				Philanthropic revenues	
	Human services	Public and society benefit organizations	Environmental causes	Unclassified causes	Youth service, race relations, and welfare organizations	Other major nonprofit service organizations
	Bg600	Bg601	Bg602	Bg603	Bg604	Bg605
Year	Million dollars	Million dollars	Million dollars	Million dollars	Million dollars	Million dollars
1965	2,070	380	—	1,490	1,335	1,573
1966	2,010	390	—	1,880	1,484	1,684
1967	2,070	411	—	2,370	1,621	2,064
1968	2,310	428	—	2,630	1,825	2,239
1969	2,710	561	—	2,800	1,950	2,414
1970	2,920	455	—	2,660	2,050	2,839
1971	3,010	684	—	3,310	—	—
1972	3,160	820	—	3,480	—	—
1973	3,070	620	—	3,910	—	—
1974	3,020	670	—	3,780	—	—
1975	2,940	790	—	4,340	—	—
1976	3,020	1,030	—	5,040	—	—
1977	3,570	1,220	—	3,410	—	—
1978	3,870	1,080	—	2,630	—	—
1979	4,480	1,230	—	2,810	—	—
1980	4,910	1,460	—	4,600	—	—
1981	5,620	1,790	—	5,210	—	—
1982	6,330	1,680	—	1,930	—	—
1983	7,160	1,890	—	2,070	—	—
1984	7,880	1,940	—	1,220	—	—
1985	8,500	2,220	—	−2,940	—	—
1986	9,130	2,450	—	1,370	—	—
1987	9,840	2,870	1,990	−7,310	—	—
1988	10,490	3,210	2,220	−4,420	—	—
1989	11,390	3,840	1,910	−270	—	—
1990	11,820	4,920	2,490	−2,990	—	—
1991	11,110	4,930	2,760	−1,700	—	—
1992	11,570	5,050	2,940	−4,410	—	—
1993	12,470	5,440	3,000	−4,400	—	—
1994	11,710	6,050	3,330	−8,200	—	—
1995	11,700	7,100	3,750	−13,940	—	—
1996	12,160	7,570	3,810	−1,568	—	—
1997	12,660	8,380	4,090	−15,960	—	—

Sources

Series Bg600–603. Ann E. Kaplan, editor, *Giving USA, 1996* (AAFRC Trust for Philanthropy, 1996), and unpublished data provided by the American Association of Fund-Raising Counsel (AAFRC) from 1997–1998 studies.

Series Bg604–605. Data compiled by Ralph L. Nelson, City University of New York, Queens College, reported in *Historical Statistics of the United States* (1975).

Documentation

Series Bg600–602. Based on a survey of relevant organizations. These series include charitable/philanthropic giving, not other types of income received or generated by nonprofit organizations. See *Giving USA, 1996,* pp. 200, 201, and 206, for a description of the series, the estimation procedures, and the organizations that provided the underlying data.

Series Bg603. *Giving USA, 1996* describes this series as a residual one that includes funds not specifically identified in its surveys of organizations; funds reported as personal tax deductions but not included in organizations' income; and funds handled by intermediary organizations (p. 201). The 1997–1998 revision of this series highlights the importance of transfers of funds between nonprofit organizations. Such transfers account for the negative values. For insight into the interplay of funds reported by donors and by recipients in the estimating procedures, see p. 201 in *Giving USA, 1996* and the 1998 edition.

Series Bg604. Constructed by Ralph L. Nelson, this was series H410 in *Historical Statistics* (1975). It was annotated with the following (p. 339): "This has been the most profoundly changing category over this 4-decade period, reflecting changing social needs, government programs, and support patterns. Many sources of information were used, the most comprehensive being 'Expenditures from public and private funds for organized income maintenance and welfare service programs' presented in the *Social Security Bulletin*."

Series Bg605. Constructed by Nelson, this was series H411 in *Historical Statistics* (1975). It was annotated as follows (p. 339): "It is a comprehensive series covering a large number of important nonprofit/voluntary sectors. It includes philanthropic receipts of (1) independent nonsectarian primary and secondary schools, (2) church foreign missions and private foreign relief, (3) foundations' net endowment increase, project and administrative expense, (4) civic and cultural support, and (5) charity raffles."

TABLE Bg606–619 Charitable giving and average charitable contributions as reported by individuals on income tax returns and in surveys, by income level: 1918–1995

Contributed by Colin B. Burke

	Income and charitable contributions reported on income tax returns												Average charitable contribution, reported on surveys, for those with income	
		Charitable contributions claimed as deductions				Average charitable contribution for those with income								
	Total	Total	Average, by those who itemized deductions	Gross income	Total charitable contributions	Under $5,000	Under $5,000	$10,000 to $25,000	$5,000 or greater	Greater than $49,999	$5,000 to $10,000	$50,000 to $100,000	Less than $10,000	$49,999 to $60,000
	Bg606	Bg607	Bg608	Bg609	Bg610	Bg611	Bg612	Bg613	Bg614	Bg615	Bg616	Bg617	Bg618	Bg619
Year	Million dollars	Thousand dollars	Dollars	Thousand dollars	Thousand dollars	Dollars	Dollars	Dollars	Dollars	Dollars	Dollars	Dollars	Dollars	Dollars
1918	234	—	—	—	—	—	—	—	—	—	—	—	—	—
1919	291	—	—	—	—	—	—	—	—	—	—	—	—	—
1920	349	—	—	—	—	—	—	—	—	—	—	—	—	—
1921	319	—	—	—	—	—	—	—	—	—	—	—	—	—
1922	343	—	—	25,871,903	425,214	34	—	340	—	2,079	—	—	—	—
1923	422	—	—	29,318,922	536,757	49	—	363	—	2,378	—	—	—	—
1924	441	—	—	29,778,990	533,181	42	—	326	—	2,151	—	—	—	—
1925	371	—	—	25,272,020	439,587	46	—	369	—	1,787	—	—	—	—
1926	395	—	—	25,417,432	482,199	49	—	320	—	1,905	—	—	—	—
1927	423	—	—	26,226,546	507,697	48	—	319	—	1,895	—	—	—	—
1928	459	—	—	28,987,630	532,893	46	—	303	—	1,652	—	—	—	—
1929	441	—	—	29,946,948	528,877	48	—	298	—	1,724	—	—	—	—
1930	357	—	—	22,414,440	424,035	48	—	339	—	2,258	—	—	—	—
1931	242	—	—	17,268,445	328,296	48	—	395	—	2,497	—	—	—	—
1932	231	—	—	14,392,074	303,728	47	—	429	—	2,819	—	—	—	—
1933	185	—	—	13,393,826	252,250	41	—	362	—	2,044	—	—	—	—
1934	200	—	—	15,092,461	272,822	39	—	336	—	2,216	—	—	—	—
1935	227	—	—	17,006,476	305,277	40	—	307	—	2,032	—	—	—	—
1936	312	—	—	21,888,371	381,172	39	—	269	—	1,832	—	—	—	—
1937	352	—	—	24,454,099	440,010	39	—	295	—	2,127	—	—	—	—
1938	310	—	—	21,311,467	407,419	42	—	343	—	2,357	—	—	—	—
1939	387	—	—	—	494,790	—	—	—	—	—	—	—	—	—
1940	570	—	—	—	734,643	—	36	—	313	—	—	—	—	—
1941	876	1,002,187	—	—	1,186,163	—	36	—	300	—	—	—	—	—
1942	1,320	1,445,060	—	—	1,796,280	—	41	—	287	—	—	—	—	—
1943	1,813	1,836,000	—	—	2,197,000	—	45	—	279	—	—	—	—	—
1944	1,235	—	—	—	2,337,208	—	41	—	288	—	—	—	—	—
1945	1,424	1,423,586	182	—	2,554,455	—	37	—	329	—	—	—	—	—
1946	1,559	1,638,982	187	—	2,666,645	—	37	—	318	—	—	—	—	—
1947	1,875	1,969,641	189	—	3,143,673	—	42	—	318	—	—	—	—	—
1948	1,756	1,878,080	212	—	3,217,231	—	42	—	265	—	—	—	—	—
1949	1,897	2,029,550	209	—	3,311,670	—	42	—	327	—	—	—	—	—
1950	2,129	2,258,009	219	—	3,714,115	—	45	—	259	—	—	—	—	—
1952	2,968	3,114,739	—	—	—	—	—	—	—	—	253	2,531	—	—
1953	3,383	3,552,448	265	—	—	—	—	—	—	—	—	—	—	—
1954	3,671	3,891,173	277	—	—	—	—	—	—	—	252	2,649	—	—

(continued)

TABLE Bg606–619 Charitable giving and average charitable contributions as reported by individuals on income tax returns and in surveys, by income level: 1918–1995 *Continued*

	Income and charitable contributions reported on income tax returns												Average charitable contribution, reported on surveys, for those with income	
	Charitable contributions claimed as deductions					Average charitable contribution for those with income								
	Total	Total	Average, by those who itemized deductions	Gross income	Total charitable contributions	Under $5,000	Under $5,000	$10,000 to $25,000	$5,000 or greater	Greater than $49,999	$5,000 to $10,000	$50,000 to $100,000	Less than $10,000	$49,999 to $60,000
	Bg606	Bg607	Bg608	Bg609	Bg610	Bg611	Bg612	Bg613	Bg614	Bg615	Bg616	Bg617	Bg618	Bg619
Year	Million dollars	Thousand dollars	Dollars	Thousand dollars	Thousand dollars	Dollars	Dollars	Dollars	Dollars	Dollars	Dollars	Dollars	Dollars	Dollars
1955	—	4,650,171	—	—	—	—	—	—	—	—	—	—	—	—
1956	4,650	4,877,793	284	—	—	—	—	—	—	—	242	2,742	—	—
1958	—	5,693,836	285	—	—	—	—	—	—	—	244	2,947	—	—
1959	—	—	—	—	—	—	—	—	—	—	234	—	—	—
1960	—	6,758,928	280	—	—	—	—	—	—	—	240	2,822	—	—
1962	—	7,519,578	284	—	—	—	—	—	—	—	227	2,809	—	—
1964	—	8,326,986	309	—	—	—	—	—	—	—	229	—	—	—
1966	—	9,119,990	319	—	—	—	—	—	—	—	223	—	—	—
1968	—	11,138,925	370	—	—	—	—	—	—	—	221	—	—	—
1970	—	12,892,734	364	—	—	—	—	—	—	—	247	—	—	—
1972	—	13,213,956	513	—	—	—	—	—	—	—	284	—	—	—
1973	—	13,895,720	495	—	—	—	—	—	—	—	—	—	—	—
1974	—	14,960,838	538	—	—	—	—	—	—	—	—	—	—	—
1975	—	15,393,331	624	—	—	—	—	—	—	—	—	—	—	—
1976	—	16,710,718	643	—	—	—	—	—	—	—	423	2,013	—	—
1977	—	17,266,462	754	—	—	—	—	—	—	—	583	1,965	—	—
1978	—	19,691,249	764	—	—	—	—	—	—	—	518	1,825	—	—
1979	—	22,210,838	838	—	—	—	—	—	—	—	519	1,784	—	—
1980	—	25,809,608	970	—	—	—	—	—	—	—	—	—	—	—
1981	—	30,800,722	1,062	—	—	—	—	—	—	—	623	1,754	—	—
1982	—	33,471,694	1,097	—	—	—	—	—	—	—	639	1,709	—	—
1983	—	37,677,955	1,176	—	—	—	—	—	—	—	641	1,777	—	—
1984	—	42,209,811	1,223	—	—	—	—	—	—	—	672	1,708	170	—
1985	—	47,962,848	1,326	—	—	—	—	—	—	—	617	1,757	—	—
1986	—	54,454,471	1,477	—	—	—	—	—	—	—	—	—	—	—
1987	—	49,623,907	1,539	—	—	—	—	—	—	—	869	1,609	172	1,015
1988	—	50,949,273	1,750	—	—	—	—	—	—	—	869	1,660	—	—
1989	—	55,459,205	1,903	—	—	—	—	—	—	—	812	1,792	379	1,096
1990	—	57,242,757	1,779	—	—	—	—	—	—	—	989 [1]	1,794	—	—
1991	—	60,575,565	2,050	—	—	—	—	—	—	—	961	1,836	239	1,230
1992	—	63,843,281	1,962	—	—	—	—	—	—	—	984	1,927	—	—
1993	—	68,354,293	2,042	—	—	—	—	—	—	—	997	1,930	207	1,042
1994	—	70,544,542	2,364	—	—	—	—	—	—	—	1,065	1,901	—	—
1995	—	74,824,415	2,169	—	—	—	—	—	—	—	—	—	295	1,001

TABLE Bg606–619 Charitable giving and average charitable contributions as reported by individuals on income tax returns and in surveys, by income level: 1918–1995 *Continued*

[1] Estimated.

Sources

Series Bg606. C. Harry Kahn, *Personal Deductions in the Federal Income Tax* (Princeton University Press, 1960), Table D.1, p. 209.

Series Bg607–608. U.S. Internal Revenue Service, *Statistics of Income Bulletin* (published annually), and *Annual Report* (various years).

Series Bg609, Bg611, Bg613, and Bg615. John Price Jones, editor, *The Yearbook of Philanthropy, 1940* (Inter-River Press, 1940).

Series Bg610, Bg612, and Bg614. John Price Jones, editor, *The American Giver: A Review of American Generosity* (Inter-River Press, 1954).

Series Bg616–617. U.S. Internal Revenue Service, *Statistics of Income Bulletin* (published annually), *Annual Report* (various years), and *Databook* (various years).

Series Bg618–619. The Gallup Organization, *Giving and Volunteering in the United States* (Independent Sector, various years), and Virginia Ann Hodgkinson, Murray S. Weitzman, et al., *The Nonprofit Almanac, 1996–1997: Dimensions of the Independent Sector* (Jossey-Bass, 1996).

Documentation

Charitable deductions itemized on individual federal income tax returns have been the foundation for most of the estimates of individual giving and remain central despite the introduction of population surveys of charitable behavior. The use of tax data brings many inferential problems, however. For example, since the introduction of the income tax in the early twentieth century, there have been significant changes in the percentage of the population required to file a return and changes in the nature and levels of allowable deductions. The tax laws encourage those with large incomes to itemize deductions and also encourage those with exceptionally high levels of contributions during a particular year to itemize. The returns thus provide a partial and skewed picture of the amount of giving and of charitable behavior. Many efforts have been made to compensate for the shortcomings of the tax data. For example, various assumptions have been made to estimate the giving of "nonfilers" in different income levels in order to arrive at national totals. For an insight into the history of the use of the income tax returns, see Kahn (1960).

Series Bg607. Compiled by the table contributors from issues of the IRS *Annual Report* and *Statistics of Income Bulletin,* and from IRS data published in *Giving USA* (various years).

Series Bg611–619. Income levels based upon adjusted gross income.

Series Bg618–619. Extensive population surveys have been conducted to make estimates free of the influence of tax laws. The estimates in these series are based on sample surveys conducted by the Gallup Organization for Independent Sector. Income and contribution levels were self-reported.

TABLE Bg620–624 Average charitable contributions in selected states, as reported on federal income tax returns: 1922–1937

Contributed by Colin B. Burke

	Alabama	California	Massachusetts	New York	Ohio
	Bg620	Bg621	Bg622	Bg623	Bg624
Year	Dollars	Dollars	Dollars	Dollars	Dollars
1922	64.71	37.18	58.54	91.21	68.40
1923	74.24	72.37	65.06	87.54	74.31
1924	80.31	42.12	67.14	96.36	82.27
1925	126.38	63.20	96.13	140.27	124.20
1926	132.34	69.55	104.99	153.76	129.20
1927	131.57	71.32	113.58	168.32	139.07
1928	126.44	72.56	126.08	184.56	149.47
1929	122.70	72.16	124.44	187.97	141.34
1930	110.68	60.61	101.76	153.35	124.28
1931	99.88	53.30	86.95	126.27	117.00
1932	74.13	45.78	68.26	101.52	87.12
1933	67.68	38.95	64.40	87.58	41.26
1934	63.02	38.89	64.24	87.66	66.39
1935	67.33	39.35	66.67	87.48	62.99
1936	68.71	41.41	73.78	94.53	71.69
1937	65.52	40.86	72.90	96.56	63.85

Source

John Price Jones, editor, *The Yearbook of Philanthropy, 1940* (Inter-River Press, 1940).

Documentation

These series report claimed deductions for cash and value of goods. The series were based upon data provided by the Internal Revenue Service to the *Yearbook of Philanthropy*.

See the text for Table Bg606-619 for a discussion of the use of tax data to measure charitable contributions.

TABLE Bg625–675 Average charitable deductions reported on federal income tax returns, by state: 1960–1995

Contributed by Colin B. Burke

	Alabama	Alaska	Arizona	Arkansas	California	Colorado	Connecticut	Delaware	District of Columbia	Florida	Georgia	Hawai'i	Idaho	Illinois	Indiana	Iowa	Kansas
	Bg625	Bg626	Bg627	Bg628	Bg629	Bg630	Bg631	Bg632	Bg633	Bg634	Bg635	Bg636	Bg637	Bg638	Bg639	Bg640	Bg641
Year	Dollars	Dollars	Dollars	Dollars	Dollars	Dollars	Dollars	Dollars	Dollars	Dollars	Dollars	Dollars	Dollars	Dollars	Dollars	Dollars	Dollars
1960	305	367	260	320	240	234	365	609	343	255	300	193	268	309	297	218	260
1966	352	248	297	392	292	232	386	609	476	318	348	223	310	366	340	277	283
1970	421	369	320	406	362	300	405	506	505	391	433	260	361	398	597	460	355
1975	812	556	607	941	546	550	604	648	813	710	694	397	792	628	682	534	706
1978	1,000	939	766	764	764	660	820	915	976	999	966	571	1,214	808	880	964	851
1981	1,234	1,321	1,005	1,184	848	813	922	1,038	1,152	1,141	1,114	678	1,281	909	960	870	1,094
1993	2,966	2,411	1,962	3,000	2,168	1,903	2,031	2,097	3,369	2,608	2,627	1,795	2,554	2,300	2,325	2,010	2,264
1995	3,266	2,530	2,124	3,249	2,323	2,105	2,156	2,243	3,605	2,812	2,789	1,778	2,874	2,446	2,499	2,156	2,665

	Kentucky	Louisiana	Maine	Maryland	Massachusetts	Michigan	Minnesota	Mississippi	Missouri	Montana	Nebraska	Nevada	New Hampshire	New Jersey	New Mexico	New York	North Carolina
	Bg642	Bg643	Bg644	Bg645	Bg646	Bg647	Bg648	Bg649	Bg650	Bg651	Bg652	Bg653	Bg654	Bg655	Bg656	Bg657	Bg658
Year	Dollars	Dollars	Dollars	Dollars	Dollars	Dollars	Dollars	Dollars	Dollars	Dollars	Dollars	Dollars	Dollars	Dollars	Dollars	Dollars	Dollars
1960	302	306	188	274	272	259	272	302	296	220	268	227	212	314	280	353	312
1966	329	365	258	345	317	315	318	378	330	259	332	328	252	364	285	372	373
1970	355	447	270	348	368	364	341	447	360	288	369	337	280	426	340	406	416
1975	592	654	471	568	502	569	548	723	665	500	719	590	457	587	606	583	735
1978	758	986	571	736	623	703	644	1,007	909	627	880	789	531	740	904	738	844
1981	1,003	1,272	761	853	696	798	884	1,308	1,167	767	861	925	733	888	1,043	923	1,026
1993	2,264	2,798	1,556	2,138	1,766	2,023	1,940	3,042	2,497	1,800	2,294	2,049	1,461	2,044	2,093	2,395	2,526
1995	2,327	3,008	1,638	2,271	1,920	2,287	2,099	3,431	2,505	2,505	2,380	2,330	1,639	2,038	2,303	2,503	2,755

	North Dakota	Ohio	Oklahoma	Oregon	Pennsylvania	Rhode Island	South Carolina	South Dakota	Tennessee	Texas	Utah	Vermont	Virginia	Washington	West Virginia	Wisconsin	Wyoming
	Bg659	Bg660	Bg661	Bg662	Bg663	Bg664	Bg665	Bg666	Bg667	Bg668	Bg669	Bg670	Bg671	Bg672	Bg673	Bg674	Bg675
Year	Dollars	Dollars	Dollars	Dollars	Dollars	Dollars	Dollars	Dollars	Dollars	Dollars	Dollars	Dollars	Dollars	Dollars	Dollars	Dollars	Dollars
1960	220	277	293	212	315	247	317	264	310	351	256	213	314	219	305	240	222
1966	270	336	346	245	360	274	387	306	392	418	460	257	368	253	350	274	229
1970	346	356	416	316	406	289	405	345	456	488	513	261	391	327	422	285	249
1975	673	641	819	567	651	475	789	634	911	905	1,066	426	577	582	747	477	613
1978	923	803	1,155	703	865	611	1,081	878	1,059	1,230	1,519	611	803	777	1,072	594	1,029
1981	945	897	1,404	896	964	657	1,110	1,022	1,483	1,441	1,776	881	1,009	1,004	1,011	666	1,020
1993	2,209	1,987	2,698	1,953	2,101	1,463	2,580	2,641	3,435	3,111	4,137	1,477	2,138	2,174	2,407	1,718	3,290
1995	2,634	2,101	2,890	2,153	2,231	1,543	2,859	2,872	3,810	3,408	4,588	1,727	2,332	2,333	2,573	1,910	3,966

Sources

U.S. Internal Revenue Service, *Statistics of Income Bulletin* (various years), and *Annual Report* (various years).

Documentation

Total contributions (cash and value of donated goods) and the number of returns with charitable deductions were used to compile these series. Unfortunately, the Internal Revenue Service did not publish statistics by state for all years.

See the text for Table Bg606–619 for a discussion of the use of tax data to measure charitable contributions.

TABLE Bg676–690 Corporate charitable and philanthropic giving, by sector, and large corporate foundation assets: 1929–1997

Contributed by Colin B. Burke

		Corporate contributions		Corporate donations						Corporate philanthropic donations					
	Corporate philanthropy	Total	Adjusted total	Total	Health sector	Education sector	Cultural sector	Civic and community betterment	Religious sector	Total	Health and human services	Education	Culture and arts	Civic and community betterment	Larger corporate foundations' assets
	Bg676	Bg677	Bg678	Bg679	Bg680	Bg681	Bg682	Bg683	Bg684	Bg685	Bg686	Bg687	Bg688	Bg689	Bg690
Year	Million dollars	Million dollars	Million dollars	Thousand dollars	Thousand dollars	Thousand dollars	Thousand dollars	Thousand dollars	Thousand dollars	Million dollars	Thousand dollars	Thousand dollars	Thousand dollars	Thousand dollars	Million dollars
1929	32	—	—	—	—	—	—	—	—	—	—	—	—	—	—
1930	35	—	—	—	—	—	—	—	—	—	—	—	—	—	—
1931	40	—	—	—	—	—	—	—	—	—	—	—	—	—	—
1932	31	—	—	—	—	—	—	—	—	—	—	—	—	—	—
1933	27	—	—	—	—	—	—	—	—	—	—	—	—	—	—
1934	27	—	—	—	—	—	—	—	—	—	—	—	—	—	—
1935	28	—	—	—	—	—	—	—	—	—	—	—	—	—	—
1936	30	—	26.7	—	—	—	—	—	—	—	—	—	—	—	—
1937	33	—	29.6	—	—	—	—	—	—	—	—	—	—	—	—
1938	27	—	25.2	—	—	—	—	—	—	—	—	—	—	—	—
1939	31	—	29.2	—	—	—	—	—	—	—	—	—	—	—	—
1940	38	—	35.0	—	—	—	—	—	—	—	—	—	—	—	—
1941	58	—	51.2	—	—	—	—	—	—	—	—	—	—	—	—
1942	98	—	82.9	—	—	—	—	—	—	—	—	—	—	—	—
1943	159	—	132.1	—	—	—	—	—	—	—	—	—	—	—	—
1944	234	—	196.1	—	—	—	—	—	—	—	—	—	—	—	—
1945	266	—	225.5	—	—	—	—	—	—	—	—	—	—	—	—
1946	214	—	186.2	—	—	—	—	—	—	—	—	—	—	—	—
1947	241	—	210.2	16,100	10,626	2,254	—	—	—	—	—	—	—	—	—
1948	239	—	211.5	—	—	—	—	—	—	—	—	—	—	—	—
1949	223	—	201.0	—	—	—	—	—	—	—	—	—	—	—	—
1950	252	—	224.9	—	—	—	—	—	—	—	—	—	—	—	—
1951	343	—	309.2	—	—	—	—	—	—	—	—	—	—	—	—
1952	399	—	375.6	—	—	—	—	—	—	—	—	—	—	—	—
1953	495	—	473.9	—	—	—	—	—	—	—	—	—	—	—	—
1954	314	—	340.1	—	—	—	—	—	—	—	—	—	—	—	—
1955	415	—	427.6	38,360	19,397	11,975	1,224	—	191	—	—	—	—	—	—
1956	418	—	435.4	—	—	—	—	—	—	—	—	—	—	—	—
1957	419	—	441.8	—	—	—	—	—	—	—	—	—	—	—	—
1958	395	—	423.4	—	—	—	—	—	—	—	—	—	—	—	—
1959	482	510	506.9	101,400	45,700	39,590	—	2,940	400	—	—	—	—	—	—
1960	482	510	511.8	—	—	—	—	—	—	—	—	—	—	—	—
1961	512	540	540.2	—	—	—	—	—	—	—	—	—	—	—	—
1962	595	540	611.1	154,142	63,104	64,531	—	8,239	589	—	—	—	—	—	—
1963	657	580	664.5	—	—	—	—	—	—	—	—	—	—	—	—
1964	729	630	727.0	—	—	—	—	—	—	—	—	—	—	—	—
1965	785	740	775.5	209,296	89,921	80,344	5,833	12,099	1,053	—	—	—	—	—	—
1966	805	790	797.8	—	—	—	—	—	—	—	—	—	—	—	—
1967	830	820	824.1	—	—	—	—	—	—	—	—	—	—	—	—
1968	1,005	900	967.3	—	—	—	—	—	—	—	—	—	—	—	—
1969	1,055	930	1,012.0	—	—	—	—	—	—	—	—	—	—	—	—

(continued)

TABLE Bg676–690 Corporate charitable and philanthropic giving, by sector, and large corporate foundation assets: 1929–1997 *Continued*

		Corporate contributions		Corporate donations						Corporate philanthropic donations					
	Corporate philanthropy	Total	Adjusted total	Total	Health sector	Education sector	Cultural sector	Civic and community betterment	Religious sector	Total	Health and human services	Education	Culture and arts	Civic and community betterment	Larger corporate foundations' assets
	Bg676	Bg677	Bg678	Bg679	Bg680	Bg681	Bg682	Bg683	Bg684	Bg685	Bg686	Bg687	Bg688	Bg689	Bg690
Year	Million dollars	Million dollars	Million dollars	Thousand dollars	Thousand dollars	Thousand dollars	Thousand dollars	Thousand dollars	Thousand dollars	Million dollars	Thousand dollars	Thousand dollars	Thousand dollars	Thousand dollars	Million dollars
1970	797	820	811.2	—	—	—	—	—	—	—	—	—	—	—	—
1971	1,100	850	865.6	—	—	—	—	—	—	—	—	—	—	—	—
1972	—	970	980.8	—	—	—	—	—	—	—	—	—	—	—	—
1973	—	1,060	1,113.0	—	—	—	—	—	—	—	—	—	—	—	—
1974	—	1,100	1,163.6	—	—	—	—	—	—	—	—	—	—	—	—
1975	1,100	1,150	1,226.8	—	—	—	—	—	—	436.8	180,000	158,400	33,000	45,200	1,211
1976	—	1,330	1,422.5	—	—	—	—	—	—	—	—	—	—	—	—
1977	1,791	1,540	1,676.1	—	—	—	—	—	—	593.9	227,500	219,700	73,200	68,300	1,626
1978	1,600	1,700	1,806.5	—	—	—	—	—	—	—	—	—	—	—	—
1979	1,900	2,050	2,191.7	—	—	—	—	—	—	—	—	—	—	—	2,008
1980	2,200	2,250	2,330.7	—	—	—	—	—	—	994.6	337,900	375,800	108,700	116,800	—
1981	2,700	2,640	2,614.8	—	—	—	—	—	—	1,170.0	393,300	429,800	139,600	136,600	2,491
1982	3,200	3,110	3,026.8	—	—	—	—	—	—	1,281.6	397,300	522,200	145,800	149,300	—
1983	3,700	3,670	3,669.9	—	—	—	—	—	—	1,278.4	367,600	498,800	145,200	188,800	2,996
1984	4,300	4,130	3,932.2	—	—	—	—	—	—	1,444.3	399,900	561,700	154,700	271,600	—
1985	4,800	4,630	4,430.9	—	—	—	—	—	—	1,694.7	494,100	650,000	187,500	279,500	3,938
1986	5,100	—	4,932.3	—	—	—	—	—	—	1,673.7	468,600	718,000	198,700	220,500	—
1987	5,500	—	4,936.1	—	—	—	—	—	—	1,658.4	450,500	610,000	178,600	236,100	4,966
1988	5,600	—	5,052.0	—	—	—	—	—	—	1,645.7	480,200	614,100	183,600	212,100	—
1989	5,800	—	5,345.2	—	—	—	—	—	—	1,820.1	481,000	699,800	201,200	253,500	5,517
1990	5,900	—	5,500.0	—	—	—	—	—	—	2,051.5	580,200	789,200	243,600	254,500	5,740
1991	6,000	—	5,250.0	—	—	—	—	—	—	2,245.5	608,900	783,600	265,400	253,500	5,948
1992	5,920	—	5,910.0	—	—	—	—	—	—	2,061.4	570,800	764,700	243,600	214,300	6,340
1993	6,050	—	6,470.0	—	—	—	—	—	—	1,976.4	535,600	746,600	214,267	211,383	6,423
1994	6,110	—	6,980.0	—	—	—	—	—	—	1,193.2	493,824	653,435	189,313	227,257	—
1995	7,400	—	7,320.0	—	—	—	—	—	—	—	—	—	—	—	—
1996	—	—	7,630.0	—	—	—	—	—	—	—	—	—	—	—	—
1997	—	—	8,200.0	—	—	—	—	—	—	—	—	—	—	—	—

Sources

Series Bg676. Through 1970 compiled by Ralph L. Nelson, City University of New York, Queens College, reported in *Historical Statistics of the United States* (1975); thereafter, unpublished data provided by the American Association of Fund-Raising Counsel (AAFRC).

Series Bg677. Ann E. Kaplan, editor, *Giving USA, 1996* (AAFRC Trust for Philanthropy, 1996), and unpublished data provided by the AAFRC from 1997–1998 studies.

Series Bg678. Hayden W. Smith, "Improved Measures of Corporate Contributions: Adjustments to the IRS Tax File on Corporate Giving to Include Corporate Foundations, and Other Matters," PONPO Working Paper number 169 and ISPS Working Paper number 1269, Program on Non-Profit Organizations and Institution for Social and Policy Studies (Yale University, October 1991), p. 29, and unpublished data provided by Smith.

Series Bg679–684. Ralph L. Nelson, *Economic Factors in the Growth of Corporation Giving* (National Bureau of Economic Research, 1970), Appendix, Table XVI.

Series Bg685–689. U.S. Bureau of the Census, *Statistical Abstract of the United States* (various years), and Conference Board, *Annual Survey of Corporate Contributions* (National Bureau of Economic Research, various years).

Series Bg690. Virginia Ann Hodgkinson, Murray S. Weitzman, et al., *Nonprofit Almanac, 1996–1997: Dimensions of the Independent Sector* (Jossey-Bass, 1997), and Foundation Center, *Foundation Giving: Yearbook of Facts and Figures* (Foundation Center, various years).

Documentation

The corporate tax files of the Internal Revenue Service (IRS) have been used as the basis of many estimates of charitable and philanthropic giving. But the compilers have employed varying interpretations of the domain of corporations and have used differing accounting definitions and procedures. In addition, some of the important groups that have compiled the statistics of corporate giving have focused on the activities of the larger corporations and corporate donors. The criteria for inclusion in such series have varied over time and institution. The work of the Conference Board and the Foundation Center

TABLE Bg676–690 Corporate charitable and philanthropic giving, by sector, and large corporate foundation assets: 1929–1997 *Continued*

has been the basis for most of these estimates, but series vary because of estimation procedures and criteria for inclusion. The publications of Nelson and Smith provide insights into criteria, methods, and sources of primary data.

Series Bg676. Through 1970, this is series H401 in *Historical Statistics* (1975). It was based on the larger "tracked" corporations. It was incorporated and updated in *Giving USA,* until the AAFRC implemented a new estimation model that led to the much higher estimates in series Bg677. See *Giving USA, 1996,* pp. 88 and 199.

Series Bg677. This series is a newer estimate by the staff of AAFRC. It includes the contributions to in-house corporate foundations, as well as donations to noncorporate recipients in its concept of "giving." See *Giving USA, 1996,* pp. 88 and 199, and unpublished reports and data from 1997–1998 AAFRC studies. This series, which originally ran through 1997, was replaced by series Bg678 starting with the year 1986.

Series Bg678. Smith began, like many others, with the data provided by the IRS. However, recognizing the analytical importance of corporations' contributions to their in-house foundations and the contributions of those foundations to other than corporate recipients, he used new techniques and measures to construct a series that seems to better reflect the amount of realized corporate giving per year. Smith's publications also provide insight into defects in the IRS corporate tax files. See Smith (1991), Appendix C.

Series Bg680–684. These series also reflect the activities of the larger corporations and corporate donors and are from Nelson's National Bureau of Economic Research/Russell Sage Foundation work.

Series Bg685–689. Based on the Conference Board series. They cover larger corporations and corporate donors. See *Nonprofit Almanac, 1996–1997,* p. 123, for a description.

Series Bg690. Corporate foundations in this series are ones that are controlled, to a significant degree, by the donor corporation and that focus their work on corporate-related projects and recipients. The series includes corporate foundations with assets of at least $1 million or those making grants in the year reported. As of 1993, larger foundations held nearly 96 percent of assets and awarded 98 percent of grants of corporate foundations.

TABLE Bg691–697 International charitable and philanthropic giving by U.S. charitable organizations, by religious affiliation: 1919–1996

Contributed by Colin B. Burke

		Private institutional remittances				Registered voluntary organizations	
	Total private foreign philanthropy	Nonsectarian	Protestant	Catholic	Religious giving abroad	Revenue and receipts	Payment received from U.S. government
	Bg691	Bg692	Bg693	Bg694	Bg695	Bg696	Bg697
Year	Million dollars	Million dollars	Million dollars	Million dollars	Million dollars	Dollars	Dollars
1919	—	82.0	37.0	6.0	—	—	—
1920	—	60.0	37.0	6.0	—	—	—
1921	—	48.0	37.0	6.0	—	—	—
1922	—	35.0	37.0	6.0	—	—	—
1923	—	31.0	36.7	6.0	—	—	—
1924	—	20.0	38.1	6.0	—	—	—
1925	—	15.0	39.4	6.1	—	—	—
1926	—	14.0	33.3	7.2	—	—	—
1927	—	13.3	33.6	6.5	—	—	—
1928	—	12.6	34.0	6.0	—	—	—
1929	343	12.7	33.3	5.3	42	—	—
1930	306	9.6	32.6	4.6	40	—	—
1931	279	6.2	30.4	2.9	36	—	—
1932	217	8.0	23.7	2.1	27	—	—
1933	191	8.5	17.7	1.8	21	—	—
1934	162	8.3	16.7	1.6	22	—	—
1935	162	6.6	16.2	1.5	20	—	—
1936	176	6.1	16.6	1.8	22	—	—
1937	175	9.1	17.0	1.7	24	—	—
1938	153	11.7	16.5	2.1	26	—	—
1939	151	10.7	16.0	2.4	32	—	—
1940	178	19.2	16.5	3.0	30	—	—
1941	179	49.4	17.8	3.3	33	—	—
1942	123	35.0	15.9	2.3	30	—	—
1943	249	76.8	19.6	3.5	38	—	—
1944	357	123.5	23.2	7.1	58	—	—
1945	473	156.4	32.3	7.9	77	—	—
1946	650	150.0	54.0	23.0	150	—	—
1947	669	79.0	73.0	25.0	211	—	—
1948	683	61.0	78.0	23.0	248	—	—
1949	521	41.0	78.0	20.0	180	—	—

(continued)

TABLE Bg691–697 International charitable and philanthropic giving by U.S. charitable organizations, by religious affiliation: 1919–1996 *Continued*

		Private institutional remittances				Registered voluntary organizations	
	Total private foreign philanthropy	Nonsectarian	Protestant	Catholic	Religious giving abroad	Revenue and receipts	Payment received from U.S. government
	Bg691	Bg692	Bg693	Bg694	Bg695	Bg696	Bg697
Year	Million dollars	Million dollars	Million dollars	Million dollars	Million dollars	Dollars	Dollars
1950	444	33.0	65.0	23.0	163	—	—
1951	386	25.0	58.0	21.0	132	—	—
1952	417	31.0	63.0	21.0	144	—	—
1953	476	40.0	72.0	30.0	175	—	—
1954	486	36.0	84.0	19.0	206	—	—
1955	444	24.0	84.0	26.0	163	—	—
1956	503	32.0	87.0	34.0	218	—	—
1957	535	39.0	99.0	40.0	199	312,188,540	—
1958	525	45.0	106.0	31.0	207	341,329,850	—
1959	563	46.0	111.0	31.0	219	—	—
1960	—	53.0	126.0	37.0	—	—	—
1965	—	—	—	—	—	433,974,467	215,279,000
1967	—	—	—	—	—	671,699,266	240,185,000
1968	—	—	—	—	—	556,886,558	224,314,000
1969	—	—	—	—	—	557,052,871	193,293,871
1970	—	—	—	—	—	614,970,331	205,579,000
1971	—	—	—	—	—	652,126,685	221,322,685
1972	—	—	—	—	—	680,878,213	207,812,213
1973	—	—	—	—	—	949,174,717	260,857,717
1974	—	—	—	—	—	950,774,176	353,588,176
1975	—	—	—	—	—	868,000,000	320,000,000
1978	—	—	—	—	—	1,156,000,000	448,000,000
1979	—	—	—	—	—	1,500,000,000	618,000,000
1980	—	—	—	—	—	1,800,000,000	742,000,000
1981	—	—	—	—	—	1,876,503,040	731,000,000
1982	—	—	—	—	—	2,072,659,000	831,659,000
1983	—	—	—	—	—	2,467,529,000	1,001,000,000
1988	—	—	—	—	—	3,380,897,115	1,010,172,000
1989	—	—	—	—	—	4,744,053,696	1,097,035,599
1990	—	—	—	—	—	4,229,477,037	1,067,292,000
1991	—	—	—	—	—	4,564,133,000	1,097,035,000
1992	—	—	—	—	—	6,184,776,040	1,811,720,040
1993	—	—	—	—	—	7,110,463,000	2,069,115,000
1994	—	—	—	—	—	7,321,890,560	2,429,938,000
1995	—	—	—	—	—	7,222,472,117	2,380,259,000
1996	—	—	—	—	—	8,725,158,000	2,410,582,000

Sources

Series Bg691. Frank Greene Dickinson, *The Changing Position of Philanthropy in the American Economy* (National Bureau of Economic Research, 1970), Table 4.1.

Series Bg692–694. *U.S. Balance of Payments: Statistical Supplement,* revised edition (1962), and Merle Curti, *American Philanthropy Abroad* (Rutgers University Press, 1963).

Series Bg695. Dickinson (1970), Table 4–7.

Series Bg696–697. U.S. Agency for International Development, *Voluntary Foreign Aid Programs: Report of American Voluntary Agencies Engaged in Overseas Relief and Development Registered with the U.S. Agency for International Development* (1950s–1997; published annually, but title varies).

Documentation

There have been varied definitions of "private" international charity and aid. Some scholars have included individual giving. Some have included government goods and funds processed by voluntary organizations. But most have included in their series only the funds and value of goods generated within and delivered by formal voluntary organizations.

Series Bg691. Dickinson used a very inclusive definition of private philanthropy, which led to the higher estimates than those found in other series.

Series Bg692–695. Institutional remittances only.

Series Bg696–697. Includes data on organizations that registered with the U.S. Agency for International Development (USAID) and its predecessors. That registration qualified an organization to receive government aid and grants. Organizations are not required to register, and not all do. However, it is believed that most organizations register and that their revenues constitute the bulk of foreign private institutional aid. Unfortunately, USAID's and its predecessors' reports used different formats over the decades, and some early issues of the reports did not find their way to major depositories. Series Bg696 includes private and government funds and the value of goods. By the 1960s, the series included the value of shipping provided by the government.

INDEX

Note: The number before the colon is the volume; the number after the colon is the page. A number range indicates inclusive pages in the same volume. Numbers in italics refer to pages in essays; numbers not in italics refer to pages in statistical tables.

Abolition of slavery, *1:694–5. See also* Emancipation
Abortions, induced, 1:418–19
Accidental death and dismemberment coverage, employee benefits, 2:824–7
Accidents and fatalities, 1:463–6, 1:483–5, 1:745 *See also* Injuries and fatalities
  air transportation, 4:970–2
  motor vehicle, *4:765,* 4:840–2
Acquired immune deficiency syndrome (AIDS)
  cases reported, 2:567
  incidence, *2:503,* 2:564–6
Acreage. *See* Cropland; Farms; Land; *specific crops*
Administration Party, 5:200–3
Advertising
  expenditures, 4:1030–4
  magazine, 4:752–6, 4:759
  newspaper, 4:752–8
  outdoor, 4:752–6
  radio, 4:1030–3
  television, 4:1033–4
Afghanistan, U.S. population born in, 1:610
Africa
  bilateral exchange rates, 5:575–8
  crude oil reserves, 4:344–5
  emigration to, 1:551
  exports to, 5:534–9
  immigration from, 1:550, 1:555–8, 1:583–5
  imports from, 5:540–5
  refugees and asylees from, 1:635
  slave trade, *2:369–70*
  U.S. direct investment in, by industry, 5:473–8
  U.S. government foreign grants and credits, 5:483–97
  U.S. population born in, 1:605, 1:608–11
Agricultural land. *See* Land: farm
Agriculture. *See also* Agriculture, U.S. Department of; Crops; Farmers and farm managers; Farms; *specific products*
  balance sheets, 4:234–5
  colonial, 5:700–3
  commodities, price indexes, 3:192–5
  corporations, 3:499–502, 3:521, 3:539–47, 3:563–5
  crops, 4:89–192
  earnings, annual, 2:272–3
  employment, 2:117–19, *4:10, 4:12*
  exports, *4:31, 4:36*
  fertilizer, 4:83–5
  finance, *4:28–31,* 4:226–42
  government outlays for, 4:252
  imports, *4:31*
  income, *4:28–31,* 4:226–42
  injury and illness rates, 2:332–3
  inputs, *4:19–22,* 4:215–18
  labor force, 2:110–11
Agriculture (*continued*)
  labor force participants engaged in, 2:101
    by nativity, 2:108–9
    by race, 2:104–7
    by sex, 2:102–7
  livestock, 4:89–192
  national income originating in, 3:32–5
  outputs, *4:19–22,* 4:193–6, 4:215–18
  partnerships, 3:499–502, 3:521
  patents granted, 3:430–44
  prices received by farmers, *4:29*
  productivity, *4:19–27,* 4:193–225
    labor hours, by commodity, 4:209–10
    multifactor indexes of, 4:218–19
    total factor productivity (TFP), 4:215–18
  programs and policy, *4:32–4*
  proprietorships, 3:499–502
  regulation laws, 4:273
  research and development, 3:453–5, *4:22–3, 4:25–6*
    federal and state, 4:220–2
    private-sector spending, 4:223
  union membership, 2:347
  value added, *4:29–30*
  wages and salaries, 2:254–5, 2:282–3, 2:292
Agriculture, U.S. Department of
  budget authority, 4:256–7
  employees, 4:259–60
  outlays, 4:257–8
AIDS. *See* Acquired immune deficiency syndrome
Air Force. *See* Armed forces
Air quality, *3:338–9. See also* Emissions; Environment; Pollution
  pollutants, *3:339,* 3:368, 3:370
Air transportation, *4:771–4,* 4:954–72
  accidents and fatalities, 4:970–2
  aircraft, 4:954–6, 4:959–62
    operational, *4:774*
    production and exports, 4:963–4
  airports, 4:959–62
  cargo, 4:954–62
  departures, 4:962
  employees, 4:793
  expenses, 4:965–6, 4:968
  fares, 4:795
  fuel consumption, 4:959–62
  international, 4:957–8
    aircraft, 4:957–8
    airline revenues and expenses, 4:966–7, 4:969
    arrivals and departures, 4:962
    cargo, 4:957–8
    mileage flown, 4:957–8
    passengers, 4:957–8
  mileage flown, 4:954–62
  passengers, 4:954–8, 4:962
  pilots, 4:959–62
  revenues, 4:788–9, 4:965–6, 4:968
Alabama. *See* State data
Alaska. *See also* State data
  government revenues and expenditures, 5:621–3
  imports and exports, 5:610–14
  infant mortality, 5:597–8
  population, 1:39, 5:594–6
Albania, U.S. population born in, 1:602, 1:607, 1:609
Albany, 3:407, 3:414. *See also* Metropolitan areas
Alcohol
  abuse, 5:297–307
  consumer expenditures on, *3:227,* 3:230–42, 3:273–5, 3:278–86
  first-time use, 2:581
    high school seniors reporting use, 5:306–7
  persons using, 5:297–9
  price indexes, 3:161–2, 3:180–6, 3:192–5
Aleut population. *See* American Indian, Aleut, or Eskimo population
Algeria, U.S. population born in, 1:610
Aliens. *See* Immigration
Alliance Party, 5:172–9
Almonds, acreage, price, and production, 4:140–2
Almshouses, *2:698,* 2:721–3, 2:725–8
Aluminum production, 4:315–18
America First party, 5:172–9
American Independent Party, 5:172–9, 5:184–92
American Indian, Aleut, or Eskimo population, 1:48–51, *1:715–24,* 1:726–77
  by age, 1:735–6
  arrests, 5:226–32
  births and birth rates, 1:392–6, 1:399–417, 1:435–8
    low-birth-weight infants, 2:586
  Bureau of Indian Affairs, 1:753
  communities, *1:722–4*
  deaths and death rates, 1:392–6, 1:458–73, 1:487
    casualties during hostile engagements, 5:381–403
    cause of death, 1:745
  definition, *1:715*
  divorce rates, 1:392–6
  education, *1:14,* 1:773–7
  emigrants, 4:783–4
  employment, 1:767–72
  epidemics, 1:742–3
  federal expenditures, 1:757–66
  fertility rates, 1:399–408
  health and medical care, *1:720–1,* 1:742–6, 1:763
  homeownership rates, 4:510–12
  homicides, 4:783–4, 5:242–7
  hostile engagements with, 5:381–403
  infant mortality rates, 1:392–6, 1:744
  labor force, *1:721*
  land, *1:722–4,* 1:747–56
    claims, 1:748
    natural resources, *1:721–4,* 1:747–56
    by state, 1:749–52
    U.S. purchase, 1:747

American Indian (*continued*)
- life expectancy, 1:746
- marital status, 1:392–6
- marriage rates, 1:392–6
- occupations, 1:767–72
- by region, 1:726–34, 1:737–41
- reservations, 1:757–66
- by sex, 1:735–6
- by state, 1:727–34, 1:737–9
- suicides, 5:242–7
- tribes, *1:719,* 1:726–41, 1:765–6
- urban–rural residence, 1:740–1
- veterans, 1:777, 5:412
- vital statistics, 1:742–6

American Party, 5:172–9
American Samoa. *See also* Outlying areas
- education, 5:599–603
- employment, 5:605–7
- government revenues and expenditures, 5:621–3
- imports and exports, 5:610–12
- infant mortality, 5:597–8
- population, 1:39, 5:594–5
- price indexes, consumer, 5:619–20
- telephones in, 5:617–18
- unemployment, 5:607
- visitor arrivals, 5:615–16

Amtrak, 4:953
Amusements
- national income originating in, 4:1080–1
- spectator, consumer expenditures on, 3:243–66

Angola, U.S. population born in, 1:610
Antebellum South
- banking, *3:589–90, 3:617–18*
- slavery, *2:370–2*

Anthracite. *See* Coal
Anthropometric measurements, 2:614
Anti-Federalist Party, 5:172–9
Antigua and Barbuda, U.S. population born in, 1:611
Anti-Jackson Party, 5:172–9
Antilles, U.S. population born in, 1:611
Anti-Masonic Party, 5:172–9, 5:200–3
Apparel and textile products, 4:583–617
- consumer expenditures on, 3:230–66, 3:273–5, 3:278–86
- cotton sheeting, prices, 3:71, 3:207–11
- manufacturing, 4:583–617
- for men and boys, 3:163–4
- output, 4:627–46
- patents granted, 3:430–44
- price indexes, 3:160, 3:163–4, 3:167, 3:171–2, 3:175–7, 3:180–6, 3:199–201
- for women and girls, 3:163–4

Apples, price and production, 4:124–7
Appliances
- electrical, patents granted, 3:430–44
- household
  - consumer expenditures on, 3:267–72
  - state government expenditures on, 5:58–64
- value of, as commodities produced, 3:267–70

Apportionment, of the House of Representatives, *5:147–8,* 5:161–4
Aquaculture production, 4:372
Aqueducts, *4:1070*
Arab states, immigration from, 1:566–70
Argentina
- immigration from, 1:577–80
- U.S. population born in, 1:612

Arizona. *See* State data
Arkansas. *See* State data
Armed forces, *5:333–9,* 5:350–439. *See also* Wars and battles
- and arms control, *5:339*
- branches of, *5:321–2, 5:338–9*
- characteristics, by war, 5:363–4
- draftees, 5:363–5

Armed forces (*continued*)
- military pay, 5:363–4
- mission, *5:334*
- personnel, *5:334,* 5:363–4
- population, 1:28–30
- research and development in, 3:453–5
- reserve components of, *5:339*
- Selective Service registrants, 5:363–5
- weaponry, *5:339*

Armenia, U.S. population born in, 1:603
Arms control, *5:339,* 5:404–5
Army. *See* Armed forces
Arrests, 5:223–36
- by age, 5:226–32
- by offense, 5:228–32
- by race and ethnicity, 5:226–32
- by sex, 5:226–7

Arthritis, 2:616–17
Artificial limbs, 3:267–72
Artisans, wages of, 2:262–3
Arts, 4:1120–3. *See also* National Endowment for the Arts
- attendance, 4:1120
- revenues and expenses, 4:1121

Aruba, U.S. population born in, 1:611
Asia and Pacific Islands. *See also* Asian and Pacific Islander population
- aliens naturalized from, 1:644–7
- bilateral exchange rates, 5:575–8
- crude oil reserves, 4:344–5
- emigration to, 1:551
- exports to, 5:534–9
- immigration from, 1:550, 1:555–8, 1:566–70
- imports from, 5:540–5
- Pacific Islands, U.S. population born in, 1:608, 1:611
- refugees and asylees from, 1:635
- U.S. direct investment in, 5:473–8
- U.S. government foreign grants and credits, 5:483–97
- U.S. population born in, 1:603–4, 1:607–8, 1:610–11

Asian and Pacific Islander population, 1:48–51
- arrests, 5:226–32
- births and birth rates, 1:392–6, 1:399–417, 1:435–6, 1:438
- deaths and death rates, 1:392–6, 1:458–73, 1:487
- divorce rates, 1:392–6
- fertility rates, 1:399–408
- homeownership rates, 4:510–12
- homicides, 5:242–7
- immigration to Hawai'i, 1:554
- infant mortality rates, 1:392–6
- low-birth-weight infants, 2:586
- marriage rates, 1:392–6
- suicides, 5:242–7
- veterans, 5:412

Asparagus, acreage, price, and production, 4:146–9
Assaults, aggravated, 5:225
Assets. *See* Net worth
Asthma, 2:615
Asylees, 1:632–5
Asylums. *See* Children's asylums; Hospitals
Atlantic Islands, U.S. population born in, 1:605, 1:608
Atomic Energy Commission, 3:453–5
Australia
- bilateral exchange rates, 5:575–8
- emigration to, 1:551
- exports to, 5:534–9
- immigration from, 1:555–8, 1:583–5
- imports from, 5:540–5
- refugees and asylees from, 1:635
- U.S. population born in, 1:605, 1:608, 1:611

Austria, U.S. population born in, 1:602, 1:606, 1:609
Automobiles. *See also* Motor vehicles
- auto repair, services, and parking
  - consumer expenditures on, 3:230–66
  - full-time employment, 2:117–19
  - national income originating in, 3:32–5, 4:1080–1
  - persons engaged in, 4:1079–80
  - price indexes, 3:165–6
  - production employees, 2:130–2
  - wages and salaries, 2:282–3
- consumer expenditures on, 3:230–66, 3:270–5
- exports, 4:832
- financing, 4:829
- imports, 4:832
- insurance, 4:834
- interest rates, consumer installment credit and finance company, 4:833
- ownership, 4:829
- parts, consumer expenditures on, 3:270–2
- price indexes, 3:165–6, 3:170, 3:173–4
- production, 3:116–20
- sales, domestic, 4:832
- value of, as commodities produced, 3:267–70

Avocados, price and production, 4:124–7
Azores. *See* Portugal

Baby boom, *1:385, 1:695–6*
Bahamas, U.S. population born in, 1:611
Balance of payments, 5:452–97
Baltimore, *1:387,* 3:407, 3:414. *See also* Metropolitan areas
Bandwidth, *4:980*
Bangladesh, U.S. population born in, 1:610
Bankers' acceptances, 3:810–11
Banking, *3:589–91, 3:617–21. See also* Banks
- automated teller machines, 3:670
- consumer expenditures on, 3:230–42
- National Banking Era, *3:586–8, 3:602–3*
- point-of-sale terminals, 3:670
- reforms, *3:591–2, 3:621–2*

Bankruptcies, 3:531–52
Banks, 3:632–70. *See also* Banking; Federal Deposit Insurance Corporation; Federal Home Loan Banks; Federal Reserve System; Mutual savings banks; Savings Association Insurance Fund; Savings institutions
- assets
  - of commercial banks, 3:650–2, 3:660–2, 3:707–8
  - by deposit insurance status, 3:715–17
  - by type of bank, 3:715–17
- branch banking, 3:665–8, 3:718–19
- closed, 3:136–40, 3:697–706
- commercial
  - assets, 3:650–2, 3:660–2, 3:707–8
  - branches, 3:718–19
  - expenses, 3:713–14
  - by Federal Reserve membership, 3:660–2
  - income, 3:711–2
  - insured, 3:707–8, 3:711–14, 3:718–19
  - liabilities, 3:653–5, 3:709–10
  - number, 3:650–2, 3:660–2, 3:711–12, 3:718–19
  - offices, 3:718–19
  - reserves, 3:629–30
  - by type, 3:660–2
- debits, 3:662–4
- deposit turnover, 3:662–4
- loans
  - business, short-term, 3:816–19
  - during the Great Depression, 3:130–5

Banks (*continued*)
interest rates, 3:816–19
number, 3:715–17
state, 3:632–8
Bar iron, 5:740–4
Barbados, U.S. population born in, 1:611
Barley, acreage, price, and production, 4:97–101
Battle campaigns, 5:372–403. *See also* Wars and battles
Bauxite production, 4:315–18
Beef. *See* Cattle
Belgium, U.S. population born in, 1:602, 1:606, 1:609
Belize, U.S. population born in, 1:611
Bell companies, 4:1017–19
Benefits. *See* Employee benefits
Benevolent and Protective Order of Elks, 2:888–92
Benevolent institutions, 2:865–7. *See also* Nonprofit institutions
Bermuda, U.S. population born in, 1:612
Birth registration areas, 1:397–8
Births and birth rates, *1:13,* 1:391–6, 1:399–439. *See also* Birth registration areas; Fertility
Black lung, 2:761, 2:788. *See also* Coal; Mining
Black population, 1:36, 1:48–51, 1:61–5, 1:105–6
age, 1:71
births and birth rates, 1:391–6, 1:399–417, 1:428–30, 1:433–8, 1:615
fertility rates, 1:391, 1:399–408, 1:426–7
low-birth-weight infants, 2:586
colonial, 5:651–5
consumer expenditures by, 3:280, 3:282–4
crime
arrests, 5:226–32
delinquency, 5:281–6
high school seniors involved in, 5:286–96
homicides, 5:242–7
lynching victims, 5:251–5
victimization, 5:270–5
deaths and death rates, 1:392–6, 1:458–73, 1:487
divorce rates, 1:392–6
drug abuse, 5:298–9, 5:303–5
earnings, *2:45,* 2:294
education, *1:15,* 2:418–20, 2:425–30, 2:436
college graduation rates, 2:469
high school noncompletion rates, 2:470
illiteracy rates, 2:468–9
school enrollment rates, 2:431–2
years of school completed, 2:464–8
fertility rates, 1:391, 1:399–408, 1:426–7
firearm possession, 5:310
health and illness
activity limitation, 2:596–9
AIDS, 2:567
digestive conditions, 2:611–13
infective and parasitic conditions, 2:605–7
respiratory conditions, acute, 2:608–10
restricted-activity days, 2:587–9
health insurance coverage, *2:504,* 2:551–2
height, 2:582–5
householders, 1:660–2, 1:679–84
housing
homeownership rates, 4:509, 4:510–12
housing units, occupied by, 4:506–8
illegitimate births to, 1:420–4
illiteracy, 2:468–9
immigration, 1:544
income, 1:618, 2:660
in institutions, 1:669–70
Black population (*continued*)
labor force, 2:91–2
participation, 1:616
life expectancy, 1:391, 1:440–2, 1:447
marital status
divorce rates, 1:392–6
marriage rates, 1:392–6, 1:685–7
of mothers, 1:673–5
migration, 1:495–7, 1:505–18, 1:523
mortality, 1:458–61, 1:485–7
infant mortality rates, 1:391–6
in poverty, *2:628,* 2:674–83, 2:690–1
prisoners, *5:213,* 5:258–9, 5:262–3
by state, 1:180–379, 2:375–7
substance use and abuse
drug abuse, 5:298–9, 5:303–5
high school seniors reporting, 5:306–7
suicides, 5:242–7
unemployment rate, 1:617
union membership, 2:350
urban area, population residing in, 1:107–8
veterans, 5:412
victimization of, 5:270–5
wages
ratios, black to white, 2:286
union and nonunion, 2:351
Bladder disorders, 2:617–18
Blind population. *See also* Visual impairments
aid to, 2:795, 2:798–803
benevolent institutions for, 2:865–7
Blue-collar workers, *2:38.* *See also* Employment; Labor; Labor force; Labor unions; Laborers; Occupations
Blue Cross insurance policies, 2:550–51, 2:835, 2:884
Blue Shield insurance policies, 2:550–51, 2:835
Boating, 4:1115–17
Body mass index, 2:582–5
Bolivia, U.S. population born in, 1:612
Bombing incidents, 5:255
Bonds. *See also* Equity and bond markets; Securities and bond markets
Confederate States of America, *5:776–8,* 5:802
sales, 3:770
yields, 3:812–6, 3:826–7
Books, *4:984–5,* 4:1050–9. *See also* Books and maps; Printing and publishing, books; Reading
Books and maps, consumer expenditures on, 3:230–66, 3:270–2. *See also* Books; Reading
Border control, 1:648–52
Border patrol, 1:650–1
Boston. *See also* Metropolitan areas
colonial commerce, 5:718–20
colonial population, 5:655
poor relief, 2:720–1
travel times, 4:779
Bowling
participation, 4:1115–17
teams and membership, 2:894
Boy Scout membership, 2:892–3
Brain cancer, 2:568–71
Brazil
immigration from, 1:579–80
U.S. population born in, 1:612
Breast cancer, 2:568–71
Bricks, prices, 3:217–24
British Isles, U.S. population born in, 1:601. *See also specific countries*
British North America, imports and exports, 5:732–34, 5:737–44
Broccoli, acreage, price, and production, 4:146–9
Brokerage services, consumer expenditures on, 3:230–42
Brokers' loans, 3:773
Bronchitis, 2:615
Bronchus cancer, 2:568–71
Brucellosis, 2:564–6
Buckwheat, 4:106–9
Buddhist temples, membership, 2:904–9
Buffalo (American bison) population, 1:754
Buildings
nonresidential, 4:470–3
public, 4:470–1, 4:476–7, 4:479–80
residential, 4:470–3
value of new construction, 4:468–80
Bulgaria, U.S. population born in, 1:602, 1:607, 1:609
Bureau of Indian Affairs
employees, 1:764
land under jurisdiction, 1:753
Burglaries, 5:225
Burma, U.S. population born in, 1:610
Business, 3:554–5. *See also* Corporations; Mergers, business; Partnerships, business
acquisitions, 3:553–60
assets, 3:561–79
bankruptcies, 3:531–52
big business, rise of, *3:486–9*
divestitures, number and value, 3:556
enterprises, 3:557–60
establishments, 3:557–60
colonial, 5:706
failures (*see* Business: bankruptcies)
firms, 3:529–30
income tax, 3:561–79
incorporations (*see* Corporations)
joint ventures, 3:554–5
labor force participants engaged in, 2:101
by nativity, 2:108–9
by race, 2:104–7
by sex, 2:102–7
by legal status, 3:495–530
leveraged buyouts, 3:556
liabilities, 3:550–1, 3:561–79
loans, interest rates of, 3:816–19
organizations, *3:477–93,* 3:495–582
events, legislation, and judicial decisions relating to, *3:492*
partnerships, *3:480–2, 3:491*
active, 3:495–520
persons engaged in, 4:1079–80
proprietorships, *3:480–2*
active, 3:495–520
receipts, 3:561–79
services, 1:621–2, 1:772
national income originating in, 4:1080–1
Business cycles, *3:71–7,* 3:78–207
chronology, 3:78–9
construction, *4:397–8*
gross domestic product trends, *3:73*
indicators, *3:75–6*
nomenclature, *3:72*
seasonal adjustments, *3:76*
trend-cycle decomposition, *3:72–5*
turning dates and duration, 3:78–9
Business fluctuations. *See* Business cycles

Cabbage, acreage, price, and production, 4:150–5
California. *See also* State data
foundations in, 2:855–7
migration to, overland, 4:783–4
Calluses and corns, 2:616–17
Calorie consumption, 2:576–7
Cambodia, U.S. population born in, 1:610

Cameroon, U.S. population born in, 1:610
Canada
aliens naturalized from, 1:644–7
crude oil reserves, 4:344–5
emigration to, 1:551, 1:553
immigration from, 1:571–6
investment in United States, by industry, 5:479–82
labor union membership, 2:336–9
U.S. direct investment in, by industry, 5:473–8
U.S. population born in, 1:604, 1:608, 1:612
Canal Zone. *See also* Outlying areas
education, 5:599–603
employment, 5:605–7
population, 1:39, 5:594–5
telephones in, 5:617–18
Canals. *See also* Panama Canal
cargo moved on, 4:885, 4:888
construction, land grants aiding, 3:355,
federal aid for, 4:780
freight rates, 4:881, 4:888
investment, 4:882
Cancer, 2:568–71
Candy and confections, consumption, 2:575–6
Canola oil, price and production, 4:138–9
Cantaloupe, acreage, price, and production, 4:131–4
Cape Verde, U.S. population born in, 1:611
Capital (financial), *3:287–95,* 3:298–332
colonial, *5:638–9*
definition, *3:287–90*
manufacturing, capital (physical) formation of, 4:676–98
equipment and structures, 4:680–3
by industry division, 4:689–92
residential capital formation, 4:520–2
Carbohydrates, consumption, 2:576–7
Carbon dioxide, emissions, 3:368, 3:370
Carbon monoxide, emissions, 4:851
Caribbean
immigration from, 1:571–4, 1:576
refugees and asylees from, 1:635
U.S. direct investment in, by industry, 5:473–8
U.S. population born in, 1:604, 1:611
Carnegie units, earned by public high school graduates, 2:418–20
Carrots, acreage, price, and production, 4:150–55
Cast iron ware, 5:744–6
Casualties, military, *5:335,* 5:350–66
active duty military deaths, 5:350–52
definition, *5:338*
in hostile engagements with American Indians, 5:381–403
Cataracts, 2:618–19
Catholic Church. *See also* Catholic schools; Churches and congregations; Religious institutions
charitable and philanthropic giving to, 2:914–16
education, 2:921–2
membership, 2:904–9
personnel, 2:921–2
Catholic schools, 2:414–5, 2:921–2. *See also* Education; Educational services
Cattle
beef slaughtering, 4:172–8
number, 4:165–9, 4:171
price, production, 4:165–9
value per head, 4:165–9
Cauliflower, acreage, price, and production, 4:150–5
Celery, acreage, price, and production, 4:155–60
Cellular telephone industry, 4:1025
Cement, 4:323–8
Census regions and divisions, *5:815, 5:817*
map, *5:816*
Central America
immigration from, 1:571–6
U.S. population born in, 1:604, 1:608, 1:611–12
Cereal and bakery products, consumer price indexes, 3:161–2
Cervix and uterus cancer, 2:568–71
Chain stores, 4:728
Chambers of Commerce, 2:895–6
Charitable giving, *2:841, 2:844–5,* 2:923–34
corporate, 2:931–3
by income level, 2:927–9
international, by U.S. organizations, 2:933–4
philanthropic revenue, 2:925–6
religious and secular, 2:914–16, 2:917–20
by state, 2:929–30
Charitable trusts, *2:842*
by type, 2:861–3
Charleston. *See also* Metropolitan areas
colonial
commerce, 5:726–9
pitch, tar, and turpentine exported from, 5:768–9
population, 5:655
price of rice in, 5:688–90
price indexes, wholesale, 3:187–91
rice exported from, 5:767
timber and timber products exported from, 5:770–2
travel times, 4:779
Chemicals and allied products
farm, *4:13–14*
manufacturing, 4:583–617
output, 4:627–46
patents granted, 3:430–44
price indexes, 3:171–2, 3:175–7, 3:180–6, 3:199–201
Chickens, 4:187–92
Child and Adult Care Food Program, 2:806–8
Children
under age 5, per 1,000 women, 1:426
benevolent institutions for, 2:865–7
born, 1:412–24
cancer in, 2:568–71
child care arrangements, 2:366
deaf-blind, 2:410
dependent, aid to families of
medical care, vendor payments for, 2:795
payments, 2:798–9, 2:802–3
recipients, 2:798–9
disabled, 2:410
emotionally disturbed, 2:410
enrolled in school (*see* Education)
health and medical care
clinics, 2:805–6
nutrition, expenditures on, 2:749–50
public, 2:805–6
living arrangements of, 1:670–2
orphans, immigrant, 1:631
in poverty, 2:668–73, 2:681–3 (*see also* Poverty: families in)
special education programs for, 2:410
Children's asylums, 2:722–3
Chile
immigration from, 1:579–80
U.S. population born in, 1:612
China
immigration from, 1:566–70
space launches, commercial, 3:458
U.S. population born in, 1:603, 1:607, 1:610
China and household utensils
consumer expenditures on, 3:270–2
value of, as commodities produced, 3:267–70
Cholesterol consumption, 2:576–7
Chrome, 4:318–20
Churches and congregations, 2:900–3, 2:911, 2:921–2. *See also* Religious institutions; *specific religions*
charitable and philanthropic giving to, 2:914–16
clergy, 2:900–3
membership
by sex, 2:912–14
by state, 2:912–14
number
by denomination, 2:904–9
by state, 2:909–11
Cigarettes, cigars, and tobacco. *See also* Smoking; Tobacco
cigarettes
consumption, 2:578–80
first-time use, 2:581
high school seniors reporting use of, 5:306–7
consumer expenditures on, *3:227,* 3:230–66, 3:273–5, 3:278–86
production, 3:116–20
value of, as commodities produced, 3:267–70
Cigars. *See* Cigarettes, cigars, and tobacco
Cincinnati. *See also* Metropolitan areas
price indexes, 3:195–6
Circulatory conditions, 2:614
Cities. *See* Metropolitan areas; *specific cities*
Citizens Party, 5:172–9
Citizenship status, 1:597–601, 1:614, 1:635. *See also* Immigration
Civic organizations, 2:895–6
Civil War
banking after, *3:590–1, 3:619–21*
casualties, 5:350–51
cost, 5:370
draftees, 5:363–4
military pay, 5:363–4
personnel, 5:350–1
veterans, *5:341–5*
Clay, 4:326–8
Clergy, 2:900–3. *See also* Religious institutions
Clerical, sales, and kindred occupations, 2:145–6
American Indians in, 1:768–70
earnings in, 2:280
females in, 2:165–6, 2:195–6, 2:205–6
immigrants, arriving, with prior occupation in, 1:590–6, 1:618–20
males in, 2:155–6, 2:175–6, 2:185–6
wages, 2:262–3
workers
economically active, 2:236, 2:238
by nativity, 2:215–16, 2:225–6
by race, 2:175–6, 2:185–6, 2:195–6, 2:205–6
Clothing and personal furnishings. *See* Apparel and textile products
Coal. *See also* Black lung; Mining
anthracite, 4:308–11
prices, 3:212–17
bituminous, 4:300–3
injuries and fatalities in mining of, 2:335
consumption, 4:337–9, 4:693
energy production, 4:335–9
fuel mineral production, 4:288–94
imports and exports, 4:341–44, 5:734–6
mining, employees, 3:467–9, 4:286–7
Coalition Party, 5:200–3
Coast Guard. *See* Armed forces
Cocaine
first-time use, 2:581
persons using, 5:297–9
Coffee, 4:694–5, 5:553–60
Cohorts, *1:691–6,* 1:697–714
baby boom, *1:695–6*
definition, *1:691*
Colleges and universities, *2:395–6,* 2:439–63. *See also* Harvard University; Yale University

Colleges and universities (*continued*)
colleges
failures, 2:875
foundings, 2:875
liberal arts, 2:876
consumer expenditures on, 3:230–42
degrees conferred, 2:444–8
by field of study, 2:450–61
by sex, 2:454–7, 2:459–61
dental schools, 2:449, 2:541–5
endowments, 2:492, 2:877–9
enrollments, 2:441–3
expenditures by
by function, 2:489–91
nonprofit, 2:874–5
per student, 2:489–91
foreign students enrolled in, 2:443
graduation rates, 1:712–14, 2:469
"historically black," 2:463
law schools, 2:449
liabilities, 2:492
medical schools, 2:449, 2:541–5
nonprofits, 2:871–5
nursing schools, 2:541–5
private, 2:871–5
professors and instructors, 2:142
female, 2:162, 2:192, 2:202
male, 2:152, 2:172, 2:182
by nativity, 2:212, 2:222
by race, 2:172, 2:182, 2:192, 2:202
property values, 2:492
public–private control, 2:462
receipts, 2:877–9
revenues, 2:487–9
single-sex institutions, 2:444
staff, 2:462
undergraduate fees, 2:493–8
veterans enrolled in, under GI Bills, *5:347*
voluntary support, 2:877–9
Colombia
immigration from, 1:577–80
U.S. population born in, 1:612
Colon cancer, 2:568–71
Colorado. *See* State data
Commerce. *See* Foreign trade
Commerce, U.S. Department of, 5:106–8
Commercial banks. *See* Banks
Commodities. *See specific commodities*
Commodity Credit Corporation, 4:253–5, 4:270–71
Commonwealth Land Party, 5:172–9
Communications, *4:977–98,* 4:999–1059. *See also specific media*
bandwidth, *4:980*
business incorporations, 3:539–47
corporations, 3:510–11, 3:525, 3:572–3
definition, *4:977*
delivery services, 4:1038–49
employees, 1:621–2, 1:772, 4:999–1000
Internet, *4:996–7,* 4:1026
limited liability companies, 3:525
national income originating in, 3:32–5
newspapers and books, *4:984–5,* 4:1050–9
partnerships, 3:510–11, 3:525
patents granted, 3:436–44
periodicals, 4:1050–9
postal service, *4:981–4,* 4:1038–49
proprietorships, 3:510–11
radio, *4:993–6,* 4:1027–37
telegraph, *4:985–8,* 4:1001–26
telephone, *4:988–93,* 4:1001–26
television, *4:993–6,* 4:1027–37
United Parcel Service, 4:1049
U.S. direct investment in, in foreign countries, 5:473–8
U.S. Postal Service, 4:1038–49
Communist Party, 5:172–9
Community and regional development, government expenditures on, 5:106–8
Community trusts, 2:853–4
Computers, 3:459–62
consumer expenditures on, 3:243–66
patents granted, 3:430–44
performance indicators, 3:461–2
price indexes, 3:460–1
purchase, by type, 3:459–60
technology, *3:417*
Confederate States of America, *5:773–81,* 5:783–805
blockades, *5:779–80,* 5:788
bonds, *5:776–8,* 5:802
chronology, *5:774–5*
cotton, *5:778–80,* 5:789, 5:802
government finance, *5:778–9,* 5:800–5
map, *5:775*
money, *5:776–8,* 5:791–9
population, 5:783–90
prices and price indexes, *5:776–8, 5:780,* 5:791–9, 5:804–5
taxable property, 5:787
wage indexes, 5:793–4
war cost, *5:778–9*
Congress
bills and resolutions, *5:149,* 5:195–9
vetoed, 5:197
elections and voter turnout, 5:169–94
political party affiliations, 5:200–3
Connecticut. *See also* State data
colonial population, 5:660
Conservation and development
government expenditures on, 3:365
new construction for, 4:468–75, 4:477–8
Constipation, 2:620
Constitution Party, 5:172–9
Constitutional Union Party, 5:172–9
Construction, 1:621–2, 1:772, *4:395–403,* 4:406–572. *See also* Construction materials
business incorporations, 3:539–47
canal, 3:355
contracts awarded, 4:433–6
corporations, 3:505–7, 3:568–9
cost indexes, 4:406–49
definition, *4:395*
earnings, 2:272–3, 2:277–9
employees, 2:110–14, 2:117–19, 4:448–9
female, 2:114–16, 2:129–32
expenditures, gross and net, 4:419–24
firms, 3:529–30, 3:558, 4:448–9
heavy, 4:448–9
highway, 4:812
housing units, 4:490–1
indexes and measures of activity, *4:397,* 4:425–32
injury and illness rates, occupational, 2:332–3
labor force participants engaged in, 2:101
by nativity, 2:108–9
by race, 2:104–7
by sex, 2:102–7
national income originating in, 3:32–5
new, 4:419–24
output, 4:406–49
partnerships, 3:505–7, 3:523
private, 4:406–8, 4:419–24
proprietorships, 3:505–7
public, 4:406–8, 4:419–24, 4:465–75, 4:477–8
by sector, 4:450–80
union membership, 2:347
value, 4:406–13, 4:433–4, 4:450–80
value-in-place series, *4:401–3*
wages and salaries, 2:292
work stoppages, 2:359–61
Construction materials, 4:437–41, 4:647–52
Consumer credit, interest rates, 3:828–30
Consumer expenditures. *See* Consumption
Consumer goods. *See* Consumption
Consumer Party, 5:172–9
Consumption
beverages, 2:575
communications, 4:1059
consumer units
by income class, 3:285–6
income distribution, 2:655
by type of expenditure, 3:273–5
electric utility, 4:347–8
energy, *4:278,* 4:337–40
expenditures, *3:225–8,* 3:270–2, 3:276–86
on consumer durables, 3:270–2
data sources, *3:226*
definition, *3:225*
for domestic service, *2:60*
by families, 3:276, 3:286
by family characteristics, 3:276
for food, *2:59*
by government, 3:40–2, 3:48–50, 3:53–6
personal, 3:40–4, 3:53–6, 4:1107–8
for religious activities, 2:914–16
for school, 2:871–3
for transportation, 4:801
trends, *3:283–4*
by type, 3:230–75
fishery products, 4:370–71
food, *2:507,* 2:572–7
fuel
airplane, 4:959–62
motor vehicle, 4:837–40
goods production, 3:116–20, 4:647–52
domestic, 3:267–70
manufacturing, 4:693–5
lumber, *4:282*
petroleum, 4:797
power, 4:676–98
price indexes, 3:141–5, *3:149,* 3:158–70
alcohol, 3:161–2
apparel, 3:160, 3:163–4, 3:167
automobile, 3:165–6
electric, gas, and sanitary services, 3:163–4, 3:167
energy, 3:165–6
entertainment and recreation services, 3:165–6
food and beverages, 3:160–2, 3:167
fuel and other utilities, 3:163–4
health and medical care, 3:165–6
housing, 3:160, 3:163–4, 3:167
in outlying areas, 5:619–20
personal care, 3:165–6
telephone services, 3:163–4
transportation, 3:165–6
urban areas, 3:161–6
recreation, *4:1067,* 4:1107–8
services, *4:1067,* 4:1107–8
value, 3:267–70
Contract labor, *2:9–10,* 2:110–11
Copper
imports and exports, 4:329–33
prices, 3:217–24, *4:277*
production, 4:308–11, 4:321–3
Copyrights, 3:422–45
Corn
acreage and production, 4:97–101
colonial prices, 5:685–6
and Commodity Credit Corporation, 4:253–5
commodity program provisions, 4:245–8
consumption, 2:575–6
inventory, 4:97–100
price, *4:35,* 4:97–101

Numbers in italics refer to pages in essays; numbers not in italics refer to pages in statistical tables.

Corn (*continued*)
price support, *4:35*
sweet, acreage, price, and production, 4:155–60
Corn oil, 4:138–9
Corporate income tax, 3:561–9
Corporations, *3:482–6*. *See also* S-corporations
in agriculture, forestry, and fishing industries, 3:499–502, 3:563–5
assets, 3:561–79, 3:581–2
balance sheets, 3:561–82
capital, 3:581–2
charitable giving, 2:931–3
in construction industries, 3:505–7, 3:568–9
in distribution industries, 3:574–5
dividends, 3:561–79, 3:581–2
in finance, insurance, and real estate industries, 3:514–15, 3:576–7
during the Great Depression, 3:129
income, 3:581–2
income tax, corporate, 3:561–79
incorporations, 3:531–52
in New England, *3:483*, 3:548
in New Jersey, *3:483*
number and liabilities, 3:550–1
by type of incorporation law, *3:483*, 3:531–6, 3:548
liabilities, 3:561–79, 3:581–2
in manufacturing industries, 3:508–9, 3:570–1, 4:702–4
in mining industries, 3:503–5, 3:566–7
profits, national income originating in, 3:29–30
receipts of, 3:561–79
saving of, 3:298–9
securities of, 3:764–6
in service industries, 3:578–9
in trade, wholesale, and retail industries, 3:512–13
in transportation, communications, and utilities industries, 3:572–3
Correctional institutions, *5:222*, *5:820–1* *See also* Prisoners
population, *1:13*, 1:669–70
state and federal, 5:256–61
Corruption, public, federal prosecution of, 5:331
Costa Rica, U.S. population born in, 1:611
Cotton and cottonseed
acreage, 4:110–15
Commodity Credit Corporation, owned by, 4:253–5
Confederate States of America, *5:778*
cotton, 5:778–9, 5:802
consumption, 4:694–5
cottonseed oil, price and production, 4:138–9
exports, 5:546–53
freight rates, 4:884
inventory, 4:110–14
prices, 3:71, 3:207–11, 4:110–14, *5:778*
production, 4:110–15
Courier services, 4:857
Courts, *5:220–2*, 5:311–31
juvenile courts, 5:326–9
state courts, 5:326
U.S. District Courts, 5:321–5
U.S. Supreme Court, 5:315–20
Crab. *See* Shellfish
Craftsmen, foremen, and kindred workers, 2:146–8
American Indian, 1:768–70
economically active, 2:238–41
immigrants, prior occupation of, 1:590–6, 1:618–20
by nativity, 2:216–18, 2:226–8
by race, 2:176–8, 2:186–8, 2:196–8, 2:206–8
by sex, 1:618–20, 1:768–70, 2:156–8, 2:166–8, 2:176–8, 2:186–8, 2:196–8, 2:206–8
Credit cards, 3:669
Credit market debt, 3:789–90
outstanding, 3:777, 3:784–8
by sector, 3:784–8
Credit unions, 3:687–8. *See also* National Credit Union Administration
Crime, *5:209–22*, 5:223–36
criminal behavior, definition, *5:210–11*
estimated, 5:236
justice, criminal, *5:211*
known to police, by type of offense, 5:223–4
measurement, *5:209–10*
property
high school seniors involved in, 5:278–9, 5:286–91
known to police, *5:215*, 5:223–5
by race and sex, 5:286–91
victimization, 5:234–5, 5:274–5
public corruption, 5:331
rates, by type of offense, 5:224–5
recorded, 5:236
statistics, reliability of, *5:211–17*
urban, by type of offense, 5:225
victims, *5:209–19*, 5:236
high school seniors as, 5:267–96
of personal crimes, 5:232–3
of property crimes, 5:232–5, 5:269, 5:274–5
by type of offense, 5:232–5
of violent crimes, 5:234–5, 5:267–8, 5:270–3
Crippled Children's Program, 2:805–6
Cropland, 3:360–1. *See also* Crops; *specific crops*
acreage harvested, 4:89–91
acreage reduction programs, *4:35*, 4:267–8
harvested, *4:11*, *4:15*
use, *4:15*, 4:89–91
utilization, *4:15–17*
yield, per acre, 4:89–91
Crops, *4:15–18*, 4:89–192. *See also* Cropland
acreage, *4:16* (*see also specific crops*)
greenhouse, 4:143
insurance programs for, 4:268–9
inventory, 4:101–4
nursery, 4:143
in outlying areas, 5:608–9
output, 4:193–6, 5:785
yields, *4:21*, 4:199–201
Crude oil reserves, 4:344–5
Cuba
aliens naturalized from, 1:644–7
immigration from, 1:571–4, 1:576
U.S. population born in, 1:604, 1:608, 1:611
Cucumbers, acreage, price, and production, 4:155–60
Currency
in circulation, 3:588–92, 3:608–16
coin, 3:588, 3:608–13
paper notes, 3:588, 3:592–3, 3:608–13, 3:623
stock of, 3:589–92, 3:614–16
U.S. Treasury, 3:589–92, 3:614–16
value of, 3:592–3, 3:623
Cyprus, U.S. population born in, 1:610
Czechoslovakia, U.S. population born in, 1:602, 1:606, 1:609

Dairy products
consumption, 2:574
livestock kept for milk, 4:178–86
prices and price indexes, 3:161–2, 4:178–86
production, 4:178–86
Dams, *4:1070*
federal government owned, 4:1101–2
Deaf and hard-of-hearing population
benevolent institutions for, 2:865–7
special education programs for, 2:410
Deaf-blind children, special education programs for, 2:410
Death registration areas, 1:397–8
Deaths and death rates, 1:391–6, 1:458–85, 1:487, 1:745. *See also* Accidents and fatalities; Casualties; Death registration areas; Mortality rates
causes of, *1:387*, 1:463–6, 1:483–5, 1:745
motor vehicle, *4:765*, 4:840–6
trends in, *1:387*
Debt, *3:593–4*, *3:624–5*, 3:774–811
credit market, 3:784–8
outstanding, 3:778–90
government, *5:6*
federal, 5:80–1, 5:96–9, 5:100–2
by level, 5:25–6
mortgage, 3:777
private, 3:774–6
public, 3:774–6
Defense. *See also* Armed forces
government expenditures for, 5:19–25
federal, 5:32–7, 5:91–4, 5:105–8, 5:369
national, *5:333–9*, 5:350–439
veterans' benefits, 5:367–8
research and development, 3:453–5
Deformities, 2:618–19
Degrees conferred, 2:444–9
bachelor's, 2:457–61
doctorate, 2:450–7
by field of study, 2:450–61
by sex, 2:454–7, 2:459–61
Delaware. *See* State data
Delinquency
by high school seniors, 5:267–96
violent crimes, by race and sex, 5:281–6
Democratic Party
congressional affiliations with, 5:200–3
House candidates, votes cast, 5:193
party identification, 5:204
presidential affiliations with, 5:200–3
presidential candidates, 5:172–9
presidential elections
electoral votes, 5:180–3
popular votes, 5:184–92
Senate candidates, votes cast, 5:194
Democratic-Republican Party, 5:172–9, 5:200–3
Denmark, U.S. population born in, 1:601, 1:606, 1:609. *See also* Scandinavia
Dental care. *See also* Dentists
consumer expenditures on, 3:230–66
price indexes, 3:165–6
Dentists, 2:541–5, 2:549
Department stores, sales and inventories, 4:737
Deportation, 1:648–9
Deposit insurance, 3:693–730. *See also* Federal Deposit Insurance Corporation
Savings Association Insurance Fund, 3:730
Depository institution reserve funds
requirements, 3:627–8
sources, uses, and reserves, 3:594–5, 3:625–7
Depressions, *3:71–7*. *See also* Business cycles; Great Depression
definition, *3:71*, *3:207–11*
Dermatitis, 2:616–17
Diabetes, 2:617–18
Diet, *2:506–7*. *See also* Nutrition
Digestive conditions, 2:611–13, 2:620
Diphtheria, 2:564–6

Numbers in italics refer to pages in essays; numbers not in italics refer to pages in statistical tables.

Disability programs. *See also* Old-Age, Survivors, and Disability Insurance Programs
long-term, 2:824–7
payments, 2:798–801
recipients, 2:798–801
short-term, benefits, 2:830–2
Supplemental Security Income Program, 2:797–8
temporary, 2:824–7
vendor payments for medical care, 2:795
veterans, 2:754–9
Disabled persons
activity limitation, degree of, 2:596–9
children, 2:410
education, 2:410
Medicare, 2:558–9
Disease. *See also specific diseases*
in American Indian population, 1:742–3, 1:745
deaths caused by, 1:745
incidence, 2:564–71
Distribution industries, 1:621–2, 1:768–9. *See also* Retail trade; Wholesale trade
business incorporations, 3:539–47
dividends, 3:574–5
earnings, 2:273, 2:277–9
employees, 2:111–14, 4:713–14, 4:716–17
economically active, 2:235
female, 2:114
full-time, 2:117–19
production, 2:115–16, 2:129–32
firms, 3:512–13, 3:526, 3:529–30, 3:559–60, 3:574–5, 4:716–17
hours of work, 2:305–7
injury and illness rates, 2:332–3
inventory, 4:717–19
labor force, 2:110–11
labor force participants engaged in, 2:101
by nativity, 2:108–9
by race, 2:104–7
by sex, 2:102–7
national income originating in, 3:32–5, 4:713
union membership, 2:347
wages and salaries, 2:282–3, 2:292–3, 4:715
work stoppages, 2:359–61
workplace size, *2:53,* 2:324
District courts
civil and criminal cases, by disposition, 5:321–2
civil and criminal trials, 5:323
offenders convicted and sentenced, 5:324–5
District of Columbia. *See* State data
Dividends
agriculture, forestry, and fishing, 3:563–5
construction, 3:568–9
corporate, 3:561–79, 3:581–2
distribution industries, 3:574–5
finance, 3:576–7
insurance, 3:576–7
manufacturing, 3:570–1
mining, 3:566–7
in personal income, 3:36–7
real estate, 3:576–7
S-corporations, 3:580
service industries, 3:578–9
transportation, communication, and utilities, 3:572–3
Divorce, 1:72–101, 1:392–6, 1:688–9, 1:705–6
Dollar. *See* Currency
Domestic workers. *See also* Service industries
consumer expenditures on, *2:60*
immigrants, prior occupation as, 1:593–6, 1:618–20
by sex, 1:618–20, *2:39*
Dominica, U.S. population born in, 1:611
Dominican Republic
immigration from, 1:571–4, 1:576
U.S. population born in, 1:611
Draft. *See* Selective Service
Drugs. *See also* Drugs, illicit; Drugs and toilet and household preparations; Prescription drugs
patents granted, 3:430–44
price indexes, 3:183–6, 3:199–201
Drugs, illicit, 5:297–307
first-time users, 2:581
high school seniors reporting use of, 5:300–5
persons using, 5:297–9
by age, race, ethnicity, and sex, 5:298–9
by drug, 5:297–9
rates of use, *5:216*
Drugs and toilet and household preparations, commodity value, 3:267–70
Dry goods and notions, 3:267–70
Ducks, wild, 3:376
Durable goods
consumer expenditures on, 3:270–2
manufacturing, 4:671–2
personal consumer expenditures on, 3:42–4
value, 3:267–70
Duties. *See* Tariffs

Earnings. *See also* Income; Wages and salaries
annual and daily, 2:265
by industry, 2:271–5
by occupation, 2:271–2
by education, 2:471–9
by industry, 2:270, 2:277–9
labor
skilled, 2:270
unskilled, 2:280
manufacturing, 2:279, 2:281
hourly and weekly, 2:275–6
by industry, 2:287–90
by region and urban–rural location, 2:261
median, by race and sex, *2:45*
by race, *2:45,* 2:294
by region, 2:260–1
by sex, *2:45,* 2:259, 2:294
Eastern Church, 2:904–9. *See also* Churches and congregations; Religious institutions
Economic fluctuations. *See* Business cycles
Economic growth, 3:4
Economic Recovery Party, 5:172–9
Economic sectors, 4:1, 4:1123
agriculture, *4:7–37,* 4:39–273
coverage, *4:5*
Ecuador
immigration from, 1:577–80
U.S. population born in, 1:612
Education, *2:387–97,* 2:398–498. *See also* Colleges and universities; Educational services
American Indian, 1:773–7
attainment, 2:464–70
Carnegie units earned, 2:418–20
Catholic schools, 2:414–15, 2:921–2
by cohort, 1:709–14
common school, *2:392–3*
consumer expenditures on, *3:227,* 3:230–66, 3:273–5, 3:278–86
degrees conferred, 2:444–8
elementary school, *2:392–3,* 2:402–9
enrollment, 2:399–402
by age, *2:395–6,* 2:406–9
Catholic school, 2:414–15
high school, 2:437
public school, 2:402–5
by race, *2:392,* 2:431–2
Education (*continued*)
rates, *2:393,* 2:406–9
by sex, *2:395–6,* 2:406–9, 2:431–2
by subject, 2:416–17
expenditures, 2:480–98
government, 5:19–25, 5:45–51, 5:58–64, 5:73–9, 5:106–8
per capita, 2:482–5
per pupil, 2:482–5
of private schools, 2:485
of public schools, 2:480–5
by purpose, 2:482–5
General Educational Development credentials issued, 2:424
graduation rates, 2:421–3
secondary school, *2:394,* 2:435
by sex, 2:421–3
high school, *2:393,* 2:402–9
completion, 2:436
enrollment rates, 2:437
graduation rates, *2:394,* 2:435
noncompletion rate, 2:470
illiteracy rate, 2:468–9
kindergarten, 2:406–9, 2:431
labor force participation rates, 2:88
legislation and historical events, *2:390–1*
nonprofit schools
consumer expenditures on, 2:871–3
employment, 2:874–5
enrollment, 2:871–3
receipts and expenditures, 2:874–5
nursery school, 2:431
patents granted, 3:436–44
preprimary programs, 2:431
private schools, 2:398–402
consumer expenditures on, 2:871–3
employment, 2:874–5
enrollment, 2:871–3
expenditures, 2:485, 2:874–5
graduates, 2:421–3, 2:438
receipts, 2:874–5
public schools, 2:398–402, 2:416–17
enrollment, 2:402–5
expenditures, 2:480–6
graduates, 2:421–3
transportation, 2:486
pupil–teacher ratios, 2:399–402
research and development, 3:453–5
revenues, 2:480–98
by level of government, 2:480–1
school attendance, 2:411
secondary school (*see* Education: high school)
smokers, 2:578–80
special education programs, 2:410
student proficiency tests, 2:425–30
and work absence, 2:317
years of school completed, 2:464–8
Educational services, 1:621–2, 2:142, 2:152. *See also* Education
females in, 2:162, 2:192, 2:202
labor force, 2:110–11, 4:1079–80
labor force participants engaged in, 2:101
by nativity, 2:108–9
by race, 2:104–7
by sex, 2:102–7
males in, 2:172, 2:182
national income originating in, 4:1080–1
by nativity, 2:212, 2:222
persons engaged in, 4:1079–80
by race, 2:172, 2:182, 2:192, 2:202
teachers and instructional staff, 2:462
by age, 2:434
Catholic school, 2:414–15
number, 2:412–14
by race, 2:434
salary, 2:412–14, 2:434

Educational services (*continued*)
by sex, 2:434
union membership, 2:433–4
wages and salaries, 2:282–3, 2:293
Eggplant, acreage, price, and production, 4:155–60
Eggs, number, price, production, and sales, 4:187–91
Egypt, U.S. population born in, 1:610
Eire. *See* Ireland
El Salvador
immigration from, 1:571–6
U.S. population born in, 1:611
Elderly
homes for dependent, 1:669–70
Medicare utilization and charges, 2:558
poor, *2:646*
Elections, *5:141–58,* 5:161–207. *See also* Electoral votes; Popular votes
chronology, *5:153–8*
Congress, 5:169–94
House of Representatives, 5:193
Senate, 5:194
presidential, 5:171–94
state methods for selecting electors, 5:171
voter turnout, 5:165–70
survey data, *5:151–2*
voter turnout, 5:165–70,
Electoral votes, *5:147–8*
by candidate, 5:172–9
by party and state, 5:180–3
Electric, gas, and sanitary services
consumer expenditures on, 3:230–66
full-time employment, 2:117–19
national income originating in, 3:32–5
price indexes, 3:163–4, 3:167
union membership, 2:347
wages and salaries, 2:282–3, 2:292
Electrical equipment
manufacturing, 4:583–617
output, physical, 4:627–46
patents granted, 3:430–44
Electricity
prices and price indexes, 3:163–4, 3:167, 3:180–6, 3:199–201, *4:280*
Elementary school, *2:392–3,* 2:402–9. *See also* Education
Elks, Benevolent and Protective Order of, 2:888–92
Emancipation, *2:371. See also* Slavery
Emigrant and nonemigrant, *1:524–5,* 1:541–54
Emigration. *See* Immigration; Migration, internal
Emissions
carbon dioxide, 3:368–70
carbon monoxide, 4:851
lead, 4:854
motor vehicle, 4:851–4
nitrogen oxide, 4:852
organic compounds, volatile, 4:853
pollutants, 3:368, 3:370
Emotionally disturbed children, special education programs for, 2:410
Employee benefits, *2:52*
accidental death and dismemberment coverage, 2:824–7
benefits paid, 2:827
compensation, 2:283–4, 2:291, 2:322–3, *2:708–10*
coverage, 2:325
disability coverage, 2:824–7
employee contributions for, 2:826–7
employer contributions for, 2:826–7
health benefits, 2:824–7
insurance, 2:291
paid days off, 2:325
plans, workers covered, 2:824–5
Employee benefits (*continued*)
social insurance, 2:751–3
supplements, 2:283–4, 2:291
unemployment insurance, 2:824–7
Employee compensation. *See also* Employee benefits; Wages and salaries
government, 5:132–7
national income originating in, 3:29–30
railroads, 4:940
Employees. *See also* Labor; Labor force; *specific industries*
full-time workers, *2:51*
Pullman Company, 4:952
Employer compensation, 2:322–3
Employment, 2:77–100. *See also specific industries*
by age, 2:314–5
American Indian, 1:767–72
benefits, *2:52*
cost indexes, 2:295–300
definition, *2:13*
earnings, 2:265
full-time, 2:117–19, 2:312–15
Great Depression, 3:121–5
and housework and family care, 2:368
by industry, 1:621–2, 1:772, 2:101–29
injuries, work-related, *2:52,* 2:330–1, 2:600–4
job duration, *2:50–2,* 2:318–19
layoffs, *2:51*
on merchant vessels, U.S. flag, 4:900
of mothers, 2:366
by nativity, 1:616, 1:621–2
in outlying areas, 5:605–7
in poverty, *2:630,* 2:687–9
production, 2:115–16, 2:129–32
by race, 2:314–15
rates, 2:85–6
by sex, 2:77, 2:87–8, 2:312–15
by state, 2:67–74
time spent at paid work, 2:316
turnover, *2:50–2*
unfair practice complaints, 2:353
union membership, 2:350
wages, by sector, union and nonunion, 2:351
by weeks worked, 2:312–13
work absence, by cause, 2:317
work stoppages, 2:354–6
by industry, 2:359–61
by issue, 2:357–8
work-loss days, 2:593–5
Energy, 4:335–57
consumption
per capita, *4:278*
renewable, 4:340
by source, 4:337–9
efficiency, *4:279–80*
federal government expenditures on, 5:106–8
imports and exports, by type of fuel, 4:341
price indexes, consumer, 3:165–6
production
renewable, 4:340
by source, 4:335–7
products, consumption, 4:693
renewable, 4:340
research and development, 3:453–5
by source, 4:335–40
Engineers
civil, annual earnings, 2:261
technical, economically active, 2:232–3
England. *See also* Great Britain
colonial foreign commerce, 5:710–13, 5:737–44, 5:746, 5:748, 5:751–4, 5:756–8, 5:761–3
U.S. population born in, 1:601, 1:606, 1:609
Entertainment and recreation services, 1:621–2, 1:772
consumer expenditures on, 3:273–5, 3:285–6
labor force participants engaged in, 2:101
by nativity, 2:108–9
by race, 2:104–7
by sex, 2:102–7
price indexes, 3:165–6
Environment, *3:333, 3:343,* 3:345, 3:414
air quality, *3:338–9*
ducks, wild, 3:376
environmental indicators, *3:338*
expenditures on, by government, 3:365–6, 4:252, 5:19–25, 5-32–9, 5:45–51, 5:58–68, 5:73–9, 5:106–8
expenditures on, private, 3:365–6
forestland damaged by insects, 3:377
geese and swans, wild, 3:375
herring gull egg contaminants, 3:373–4
municipal solid waste disposal, *3:339–40*
oil spills, 3:373
water quality, *3:338–9*
wildlife preservation, *3:340–1*
Equity and bond markets, 3:756–73. *See also* Stock market
brokers' loans, 3:773
mutual funds, 3:771
Eskimo population. *See* American Indian, Aleut, or Eskimo population
Esophagus cancer, 2:568–71
Establishments. *See* Firms
Estonia, U.S. population born in, 1:602, 1:607, 1:609
Ethiopia, U.S. population born in, 1:610. *See also* Africa
Ethnicity, *1:4–16. See also specific ethnicities*
Europe
aliens naturalized from, 1:644–7
bilateral exchange rates, 5:567–72
Confederate cotton exported to, 5:790
exports to, 5:534–9
immigration from, 1:549–50, 1:555–8, 1:560–5
imports from, 5:540–5
investment in United States, by industry, 5:479–82
refugees and asylees from, 1:635
space launches, commercial, 3:458
U.S. direct investment in, by industry, 5:473–8
U.S. government foreign grants and credits, 5:483–97
U.S. population born in, 1:601–3, 1:606–7, 1:609
Western, crude oil reserves, 4:344–5
Exchange rates, *5:441–51,* 5:452–585
bilateral, *5:450–1,* 5:578–83
Africa, 5:575–8
Americas, 5:572–5
Asia, 5:575–8
Australia, 5:575–8
Europe, 5:567–72
definition, *5:448*
dollar-sterling, *5:449–50,* 5:561–6
multilateral, *5:451,* 5:584–5
parity, *5:449,* 5:561–3
Execution, 5:256–66
Expenditures. *See specific institution or specific function*
Exports, 5:498–560. *See also* Foreign trade; *specific commodity or specific service*
colonial, *5:636,* 5:669–70, 5:703, 5:710–16, 5-734–5, 5:739–40, 5:743–7, 5:758–67, 5:770–2
commodities, selected, 5:546–53
Confederate cotton, 5:789
cotton freight rates, 4:884

Numbers in italics refer to pages in essays; numbers not in italics refer to pages in statistical tables.

Exports (*continued*)
by country of destination, 5:534–9
crude and manufactured goods, 5:520–2
indexes of quantity and unit value of, 5:523–8
gold and silver, 5:498–503
goods, 5:506, 5:508
merchandise
outlying areas, 5:610–12
price indexes and terms of trade, 5:515–19
price indexes, 3:187–91
by broad end-use class, 5:533
programs, federal expenditures on, 4:262
services, 5:507
waterborne, *4:768–9,* 4:869–71, 4:896–7

Faculty. *See* Education; Educational services
Families. *See also* Households
composition, *1:653–5, 1:658, 1:660–89*
consumer expenditures by, 3:276–84
by income class, 3:276–84
by occupation, 3:280, 3:282–6
by race, 3:280–4
female householder, husband absent
income, 2:661–2
in poverty, 2:677–9
homeownership rates, 4:510–12
income, by type of family, 2:661–2
living arrangements, *1:655–7*
male householder, wife absent
income, 2:661–2
in poverty, 2:677–9
married couple
income, 2:661–2
in poverty, 2:677–9
minimum subsistence budgets, 2:663–4
multigenerational, *1:655–6*
patriarchal, *1:657–8*
in poverty, *2:629, 2:645,* 2:677–9
poverty measurement
minimum subsistence budgets, 2:663–4
poverty lines, 2:663–9
poverty thresholds, 2:664–7, 2:670–3
single parents, *1:656–7,* 1:670–2
in poverty, *2:629*
subfamilies, by race and sex, 1:664–5
urban, consumer expenditures by, 3:278–84
Far East, U.S. government foreign grants and credits, 5:483–97
Farm Credit System, 4:270–2
Farm laborers, 2:151, 2:161
earnings, 2:260
economically active, 2:249
female, 2:171, 2:201, 2:211
male, 2:181, 2:191
by nativity, 2:221, 2:231
by race, 2:181, 2:191, 2:201, 2:211
wages, 2:255–6
Farm policy, *4:31–7,* 4:243–73
commodity program provisions, selected, 4:245–51
direct commodity program, 4:243–5
New Deal, *4:34–5*
post–World War II, *4:35–7*
Farm population, *1:492,* 1:519, 4:39–44. *See also* Farmers and farm managers
by region, 4:44–50
by state, 4:44–50
Farm products, 4:228. *See also* Food and beverages; *specific commodities*
demand, *4:18*
exports and imports, 4:236–7
prices and price indexes, 3:171–2, 3:175–7, 3:180–6, 3:192–5, 3:199–201, *4:18*
value of, 4:64–6
Farm Service Agency, 4:270–1
Farm value, food
consumer expenditures on, 4:241–2
as portion of retail cost of food, 4:240
Farmer–Labor Party, 5:172–9
Farmers and farm managers, 2:144
by age, 4:68–9
American Indian, 1:768–70
characteristics, *4:12–13*
economically active, 2:234
immigrants, prior occupation, 1:590–6, 1:618–20
by nativity, 2:214, 2:221, 2:224, 2:231
by number of days worked off farm, 4:70
prices received and paid by, 4:238–9
by race, 2:174, 2:181, 2:184, 2:191, 2:194, 2:201, 2:204, 2:211, 4:66–7, 4:71–3
by region, 4:66–7
by residence on or off farm, 4:68
by sex, 1:618–20, 1:768–70, 2:154, 2:164, 2:171, 2:174, 2:181, 2:184, 2:191, 2:194, 2:201, 2:204, 2:211, 4:66–7
by tenure, 4:71–4
trips to market, 4:779
wealth, *4:29–30*
by years on present farm, 4:69
Farmers' cooperatives, *2:842,* 2:861–3, 4:86–8
Farmers Home Administration, 4:271–2
Farming, forestry, and fishing. *See also* Fishing; Forestry
American Indian population in, 1:771
employees, 2:115–16, 2:129–32
by sex, 1:771
Farms, *4:10–14,* 4:39–88. *See also* Agriculture; Farm laborers; Farmers and farm managers
acreage, *4:21,* 4:54–7
balance sheets, 4:234–5
buildings, 4:57–64, 4:73–4
cash receipts, *4:12*
chemicals, *4:13–14*
cropland harvested, *4:11*
by use, *4:15*
crops, *4:15–18* (*see also specific crops*)
acreage of major crops, *4:16*
yield per acre, average, *4:21*
deaths, by type of injury, 4:79
employment, *4:10, 4:12,* 4:77–8
expenses, 4:229–30
federal government outlays for, 4:258
fertilizer, 4:84–5
food retail cost, farm-value component of, 4:240
gross domestic product originating in, 3:50–2
housing units, 4:506–8
income, 3:29–30, *4:28,* 4:229–30
input
costs, *4:28–9*
expenditures, 4:197–9
indexes, 4:204–6
output per unit of, 4:207–8
labor force, 2:110–11 (*see also* Farmers and farm managers)
land, 3:360–3, *4:11,* 4:39–44, 4:76 (*see also* Agricultural land)
by operator tenure, 4:73–4
by region, 4:50–3, 4:57–64
by size of farm, 4:76
by state, 4:50–3, 4:57–64
utilization, *4:15–17*
value, 4:57–64, 4:73–4
livestock, *4:15–18*
loans, non–real estate, 4:271–2
machinery and equipment, *4:13–14,* 4:80–2
marketing, 4:231–3, 4:241–2
mortgages, 4:74
national income originating in, 4:226–7
net income, *4:12*
Farms (*continued*)
number, *4:10–11,* 4:39–44
output, 4:226–7
gross, 4:228
indexes, 4:204–8
by region, 4:207–8
productivity, 4:204–6
property value, 4:39–44
real estate debt, 4:270–1
revenues, *4:28–9*
size, *4:12,* 4:75–6
structures, *4:10–14,* 4:39–88
Fat, consumption, 2:576–7
FDIC. *See* Federal Deposit Insurance Corporation
Federal Deposit Insurance Corporation (FDIC)
assessment rate, 3:695–6
assets, 3:693–4
banks closed, 3:697–706
deposit insurance coverage, 3:697–8
income and expenses, 3:695–6
insured deposits, 3:693–4
savings institutions insured by, 3:720–2
Federal Home Loan Banks, 3:681, 3:689–91, 4:516–18
Federal Housing Administration, mortgage insurance, 4:553–5
Federal income tax
rates, 5:110–18
by income group, 5:114–18
returns, 5:110–18
corporate, 5:110–11
individual, 5:112–13
Federal Reserve Act, *3:591–2, 3:621–2*
Federal Reserve System
Banks, 3:656–9
commercial bank membership, 3:660–2
currency held in, 3:589–92, 3:614–16
interest rates, 3:593–4, 3:624–5
margin requirements, 3:772
monetary policy, 3:593–4, 3:624–5
Federal Savings and Loan Insurance Corporation, 3:726–8
Federal work programs, 2:804–5
Federalist Party, 5:172–9, 5:200–3
Federated States of Micronesia. *See also* Outlying areas
education, 5:599–603
employment, 5:605–7
exports, 5:610–12
government revenues and expenditures, 5:624–5
gross domestic product, 5:604–5
imports, 5:612–14
infant mortality, 5:597–8
population, 1:39, 5:594–5
telephones in, 5:617–18
visitor arrivals, 5:615–16
Feeds, price indexes, 3:171–2, 3:175–7, 3:180–6, 3:199–201
Fertility, 1:391, 1:399–439. *See also* Birth registration areas; Births and birth rates
decline, *1:382–5*
rates, *1:382*
ratios, 1:426–7
Fertilizer
consumption, 4:84–5
farmers' expenditures on, 4:84–5
liming materials, 4:84–5
quantity used, 4:83
Fetal deaths, 1:419, 1:458–61
Finance, 1:621–22, 1:772, 3:692, 3:810–11
colonial, 5:692–9
government, *5:3–9,* 5:10–140
Confederate States of America, 5:800–5
federal, *5:6–8,* 5:10–109
local, *5:6,* 5:10–79

Finance (*continued*)
state, *5:5–6,* 5:10–79
terms and concepts, *5:4–5*
war, *5:5*
U.S. direct investment in foreign countries, 5:473–8
Finance companies, 3:692, 3:810–11
employees, 3:683–4
Financial industries
agricultural, *4:28–31,* 4:226–42
business incorporations, 3:539–47
debt, *3:593–4, 3:624–5*
earnings, 2:277–9
employees, 2:111–14
female, 2:114
production, 2:115–16, 2:129–32
employment, full-time, 2:117–19
flow of funds, *3:593–4, 3:624–5*
hours of work, 2:305–7
injury and illness rates, 2:332–3
labor force participants engaged in, 2:101
by nativity, 2:108–9
by race, 2:104–7
by sex, 2:102–7
national income originating in, *4:1065,* 4:1073–5
patents granted, 3:436–44
persons engaged in, 4:1076–7
self-employed in, *4:1066*
wages and salaries, 2:282–3
Financial institutions, *3:583–95,* 3:596–831. *See also* Banks; Savings institutions
credit unions, 3:687–8
depository, reserve funds, 3:594–5, 3:625–8
regulation, *3:589–92, 3:614–16*
Financial markets, *3:583–95,* 3:596–831
Finland, U.S. population born in, 1:601, 1:607, 1:609
Firearms, possession of, 5:308–10
Firms
business, 3:557–60
colonial, 5:706
construction, 3:558
distribution industry, 3:559–60, 4:716–17
employees, 3:557–60
by industry, 3:557–60
manufacturing, 3:559, 4:579–620
colonial, 5:706
corporate, 4:618–20
definition, *4:577–8*
noncorporate, 4:618–20
mineral industry, 4:285
mining, 3:558
number, 3:557–60
payroll, 3:557–60
retail trade
service, 4:738–41
by type of business, 4:720–2
service industry, 3:560, 4:1082–92
wholesale trade
employment, 4:742–9
operating expenses, 4:742–8
sales, 4:742–8
by type of business, 4:742–8
First Bank of the United States, 3:638
Fish. *See also* Fisheries; Meat, poultry, fish, seafood, and eggs; Shellfish
aquaculture production, 4:372
canned, 4:365
colonial prices, 5:675–6
crab, 4:368–9
cured, 4:365
domestic production, 4:366–7
dried fish meal scrap, 4:366–7
Fish (*continued*)
fish oils and other marine oils, 4:366–7
fresh and frozen, 4:365
groundfish fillets and steaks, 4:366–7
imports and exports, 4:358–9
industrial, 4:365
landed catches, 4:360–2
disposition, 4:365
shellfish, 4:363–4
lobster, 4:368–9
processed, 4:366–7
supply, 4:368–9
yield, 4:358–9
Fish oils and other marine oils, 4:366–7
Fisheries, *4:275–84,* 4:358–75
landed catches, 4:360–5
production
canned, 4:366–9
consumption, 4:370–1
sealskin harvesting, 4:375
whale processing, 4:375
whaling products, output, 4:373–4
Fishing. *See also* Farming, forestry, and fishing; Forestry and fishing
colonial, 5:700–3
recreational
catch, 4:369
harvest, 4:369
participants, 4:369
trips, 4:369
Flaxseed, 4:97–101
Floor coverings, 3:267–70
Florida. *See* State data
Flour, consumption, 2:575–6
Flow of funds, 3:310–12, *3:593–4, 3:624–5,* 3:774–811
balance sheets
households, 3:799–804
national, 3:791–5
nonfarm, 3:805–9
nonfinancial corporate businesses, 3:805–9
nonprofit organizations, 3:799–804
personal sector, 3:796–8
Flowers and plants, consumer expenditures on, 3:230–42
Food and beverages
candy and confections, 2:575–6
Child and Adult Care Food Program, 2:806–8
consumed away from home, price indexes, 3:161–2
consumer expenditures on, *2:59, 3:227,* 3:230–66, 3:273–5, 3:278–86
beverages, 2:575
by farm value and marketing bill components, 4:241–2
food, 2:575–7
by location, 4:241–2
consumption of, *2:507,* 2:572–7
corn, 2:575–6
dairy products, 2:574
federal government outlays for, 4:258
flour, 2:575–6
fruit and vegetables, 2:574
industries, 3:470
manufacturing, 4:583–617
meat, 2:574
output, 4:627–46
patents granted, 3:430–44
per capita, 2:572–4
by families, 3:278–86
price indexes, 3:160–2, 3:167
retail cost, farm-value component of, 4:240
sugar, 2:575–6
sweeteners, 2:575–6
value of, as commodities produced, 3:267–70
Food programs, 2:806–8
Food stamps, 2:741–2, 2:806–8
Foreign countries, U.S. direct investment in, 5:473–8
Foreign trade. *See also* Exports; Imports
coal
anthracite, 4:304–7
bituminous, 4:300–3
petroleum, 4:298–9
uranium, 4:354
Foreign-born population, 1:31–4, 1:36, 1:166–7, 1:170–71, *1:524. See also* Immigration; *specific countries or regions of origin*
age, 1:71, 1:172–4
birth rate, 1:439
characteristics, *1:537–8,* 1:597–626
citizenship status, 1:597–601
by country of birth, 1:601–9
education
college graduation rate, 2:469
enrolled in U.S. institutions of higher education, 2:443
high school noncompletion rate, 2:470
illiteracy rate, 2:468–9
English speaking, 1:614
geographic concentration of, 1:613
income, 1:618
labor force, 1:616, 1:699–700, *2:23,* 2:109
migration, intercensal, 1:509–18
occupations, 2:141, 2:222–31, 2:253
race, 1:166–7
sex, 1:166–7, 1:172–4, 1:597–601
Forestland, *4:280–1*
acreage, 4:376
growing stock, 4:376
insect-damaged, 3:377
sawtimber, 4:376
Forestry, *4:280–1,* 4:376–94. *See also* Farming, forestry, and fishing; Forestland; Forestry and fishing; National Forest System
forest fires, 4:382–3
forest products industries, *4:275–84*
stumpage prices, *4:282,* 4:393–4
Forestry and fishing, 1:621–2, 1:772
business incorporations, 3:539–47
corporations, 3:499–502, 3:563–5
employment, full-time, 2:117–19
injury and illness rates, 2:332–3
labor force, 2:110–11
labor force participants engaged in, 2:101
by nativity, 2:108–9
by race, 2:104–7
by sex, 2:102–7
limited liability companies, 3:521
national income originating in, 3:32–5
partnerships, 3:499–502, 3:521
patents granted, 3:430–44
proprietorships, 3:499–502
union membership, 2:347
wages and salaries, 2:282–3
Fossil fuels
consumption, 4:347–8
energy consumption, 4:337–9
energy production, 4:335–7
fuel mineral production, value, 4:292–4
Foundations, nonprofit, 2:853–7
France
U.S. government foreign grants and credits to, 5:483–97
U.S. population born in, 1:602, 1:606, 1:609
Fraternal organizations
employees, 2:895–6
income, 2:888–92
membership, 2:888–92
by state, 2:895–6
Free Soil Party, 5:172–9

Freight
  colonial foreign commerce, tobacco, 5:731
  domestic interstate, haul length, 4:798
  inland, 4:781
  railroad
    speed, 4:929–31, 4:947
    traffic and revenue, 4:932–4, 4:948
    traffic volume, 4:929–31, 4:947
  rates
    canal, 4:881
    cotton, 4:884
    keelboat, 4:879
    railroad, 4:879
    steamboat, 4:879
  revenue, 4:794, 4:921
  traffic
    Great Lakes, 4:891–2
    railroad, 4:919
    Sault Ste. Marie canals, 4:888
  transportation bills, 4:796
  trucking services, expenses and operating revenue, 4:857
  water transportation, 4:782
Fruit. *See also specific fruits*
  bearing acreage, 4:122–4
  consumption, 2:574
  price indexes, 3:161–2
Fuel. *See also* Fossil fuels; Gasoline; Motor fuel; *specific fuels*
  aid, 2:722–3
  airplane, 4:959–62
  efficiency, 4:346
  lighting products and, value of, as commodities produced, 3:267–70
  mineral
    imports and exports, 4:342–4
    production, 4:288–94
  motor vehicle, 4:837–40, 4:847–9
  nuclear, inventories, 3:370–1
  price indexes, 3:163–4, 3:171–2, 3:175–7, 3:180–86, 3:199–201
  railroad, 4:944–5
  wood, 4:337–9
Funeral and burial expenses, expenditures on, 3:230–66
Furniture and fixtures, manufacturing, 4:583–617
Furniture and household durables
  consumer expenditures on, 3:230–42, 3:270–5, 3:278–86
  price indexes, 3:173–7, 3:180–6
  value of, as commodities produced, 3:267–70
Furs
  imported into England, 5:748
  price indexes, 3:192–5

Garlic, acreage, price, and production, 4:155–60
Gas. *See also* Electric, gas, and sanitary services; Gasoline; Natural gas
  consumer expenditures on, 3:230–66, 3:273–5
  pipelines, mileage, 4:975
  price indexes, consumer, 3:163–4
  utilities
    customers, 4:356–7
    gross domestic product, 4:1094
    output indexes, 4:1093
    productivity, 4:1093
    sales and revenues, by type of service, 4:356–7
Gasoline
  fuel mineral production, value, 4:292–4
  tax rates, 4:850
General Educational Development (GED) credentials issued, 2:424
Geography, *3:333, 3:343,* 3:345, 3:414. *See also* Land
Georgia. *See* State data
Geothermal energy, 4:335–40
Germany
  immigration from, *1:534,* 1:560–5
  investment in United States, by industry, 5:479–82
  U.S. population born in, 1:602, 1:606, 1:609
Ghana, U.S. population born in, 1:611
GI Bills, veterans enrolled in training programs and higher education institutions under, *5:347,* 5:438–9
Gifts and contributions, by consumers, 3:278–84, 3:286
Girl Scouts, membership, 2:892–3
Gold
  Confederacy, prices of, 5:804–5
  exports and imports, 5:498–503
  production, 4:315–18, 4:321–3
  stock, U.S. monetary, 3:584, 3:596–7
Golfing, participation, 4:1115–17
Gonorrhea, 2:564–6
Geese, wild, 3:375
Government. *See also* Government, federal; Government, local; Government, state; Government, state and local
  American Indian relations, *1:724*
  assets and liabilities, 3:322–4
  bond yields, 3:827
  colonial, 5:707–9
  Confederate States of America, 5:800–5
  debt, *5:6,* 5:25–6
  employees, 1:621–2, 2:111–14, *5:3–9,* 5:10–140
    compensation, 5:132–7
    earnings, 2:273
    economically active, 2:234
    female, 2:114
    full-time employment, 2:117–19
    by level, branch, and major function of government, 5-138–40
    production, 2:129
    terms and concepts, *5:4–5*
    union membership, 2:347
    wages and salaries, 2:282–3, 2:293
  expenditures, consumer, 3:40–2, 3:48–50, 3:53–6
  farm policy, *4:32–4*
  finance, *5:3–9,* 5:10–140
    Confederate States of America, *5:778–9,* 5:800–5
    federal, *5:6–8*
    history, *5:3–4*
    local, *5:6*
    state, *5:5–6*
    terms and concepts, *5:4–5*
    war, *5:5*
  gross domestic product, contribution to, 3:50–2
  hospitals, 2:523–4, 2:530–2
  industries, national income originating in, 3:32–5
  investment, gross, 3:48–50, 3:53–6
  labor force participants engaged in, 2:101
    by nativity, 2:108–9
    by race, 2:104–7
    by sex, 2:102–7
  by level and type, 5:10
  national income originating in, 3:31–2
  outlying areas, 5:621–5
  patents granted, 3:436–44
  payroll, by level and type of government, 5:125–7
  revenue, *5:6–7,* 5:10–17, 5:621–5
  saving, 3:298–9
  structures, net stock, *4:396,* 4:414–19
Government, federal. *See also* Government
  assets and liabilities, 3:322–4
  buildings, value of new construction, 4:476–7, 4:479–80
  construction, public, value of new, 4:470–80
  consumer expenditures by, 3:48–50, 3:53–6
  dams owned by, 4:1101–2
  debt, 5:80–81, 5:102
    by type, 5:96–9, 5:100–1
    where held, 5:109
  employees
    by government branch and location relative to capital, 5-127–9
    pay, 5:130–1
  finances, 5:10–109
  gross domestic product, contribution to, 3:50–2
  highways, 4:811, 4:813–16
  hydroelectric power plants owned by, 4:1101–2
  income tax, federal, returns and rates, 5:110–18
  investments by, 3:48–50, 3:53–6
  Office of Management and Budget, 5:102–9
  research and development, by agency, 3:453–5
  revenue, 5:80–1, 5:102
    by source, 5:27–30, 5:82–4, 5:103–4
  tax revenue, internal, by source, 5:85–90
Government, local. *See also* Government; Government, state and local
  expenditures, 5:72–9
  revenue, by source, 5:69–72
Government, state. *See also* Government; Government, state and local
  expenditures, 5:56–68
  revenues, by source, 5:52–5
Government, state and local, 2:739–41. *See also* Government, local; Government, state
  assets and liabilities, 3:322–4
  buildings, value of new construction, 4:476–7, 4:479–80
  construction, public, value of new, 4:470–80
  expenditures, 5:56–68
    by character and object, 5:43–4
    consumer, 3:48–50, 3:53–6
    criminal justice, 5:311–14
    environment, 3:365–6
    by function, 5:45–51
    natural resources, 3:365
    social welfare, 2:737–8
  finance, 5:10–79
  gross domestic product, contribution to, 3:50–2
  highway debt, 4:826–9
  highway finance, 4:817–21
  hospitals, 2:520–4, 2:527–8, 2:530–7, 2:539–40, 2:545–6
  investments by, 3:48–50, 3:53–6
Graduates, high school
  Carnegie units earned by, 2:418–20
  private school, 2:421–3
  public school, 2:421–3
Grapefruit, acreage, price, and production, 4:128–30
Grapes, price and production, 4:124–7
Grazing, 3:358–9, 4:265–6
Great Britain. *See also* England; Ireland; Scotland; Wales
  colonial foreign commerce, 5:754–6
  immigration from, *1:534,* 1:560–4
  U.S. population born in, 1:606
Great Depression, *3:76–7,* 3:116–45
  banking, 3:136–40
  corporations with profits, 3:29
  interest rates, 3:130–5
  loans, 3:130–5
  manufacturing, employment and hours, 3:121–5
  money, 3:136–40

Great Depression (*continued*)
prices, 3:141–5
production, goods, 3:116–20
stock market indicators, 3:126–8
wages and salaries, 3:141–5
Great Lakes, freight traffic, 4:891–2
Greece
immigration from, 1:560–5
U.S. population born in, 1:603, 1:607, 1:609
Green Party, 5:172–9
Greenback–Labor Party, 5:172–9
Grenada, U.S. population born in, 1:611
Gross domestic product (GDP), 3:23–8. *See also* Gross national product
colonial, 5:671–3
growth rates, *3:5*
by major components, 3:40–2
Okun-Phillips decomposition, 3:84–8
outlying areas, 5:604–5
potential, 3:84–9
price deflators, implicit, 3:53–4
quantity indexes, 3:55–6
real, chain-weighted, *3:11*
rebasing estimates of, *3:12*
by sector of origin, 3:50–2
slave economy, *3:16*
trends and fluctuations, 3:80–8
Gross national product (GNP). *See also* Gross domestic product
Balke-Gordon series, *3:15,* 3:65–6
Gallman series, *3:14,* 3:67–8
Kuznets-Kendrick series, *3:13–14*
slave economy, 3:69
Standard series, *3:14,* 3:63–4
Group insurance policies, 2:835
Group quarters, residents of, *1:654,* 1:669–70. *See also* Households
Guam. *See also* Outlying areas
consumer price indexes, 5:619–20
education, 5:599–603
employment, 5:605–7
exports, 5:610–12
government revenues and expenditures, 5:621–3
gross domestic product, 5:604–5
imports, 5:612–14
infant mortality, 5:597–8
population, 1:39, 5:594–5
telephones in, 5:617–18
unemployment, 5:607
visitor arrivals, 5:615–16
Guatemala
immigration from, 1:574–6
U.S. population born in, 1:611
Guyana
immigration from, 1:579–80
U.S. population born in, 1:612
Gypsum, production, 4:323–5

Haiti
immigration from, 1:571–4, 1:576
U.S. population born in, 1:611
Hallucinogens
first-time use, 2:581
persons using, 5:297–8
Harbors, 4:780, 4:883
Harvard University, income, 2:879–80
Hawai'i. *See also* Outlying areas; State data
consumer price indexes, 5:619–20
crop production, 5:608–9
education, 5:599–601
employment, 5:605–7
exports, 5:610–12
government revenues and expenditures, 5:621–3
gross domestic product, 5:604–5
immigration to, 1:554
Hawai'i (*continued*)
imports, 5:612–14
infant mortality, 5:597–8
population, 1:39, 5:594–5
by sex and ethnic group, 5:596
telephones in, 5:617–18
unemployment, 5:607
visitor arrivals, 5:615–16
Hay, acreage, price, and production, *4:16,* 4:106–9
Hay fever, 2:615
Hazelnuts, acreage, price, and production, 4:140–2
Headaches, migraine, 2:617–18
Health and medical care, 1:466, *2:499–507,* 2:509–620. *See also* Disease; Hospitals; Nutrition
American Indian, *1:720–1,* 1:742–6, 1:763
consumer expenditures for, *3:227,* 3:230–66, 3:273–5, 3:278–86
disease incidence, 2:564–71
expenditures, 2:509–19, 2:743–5, 2:881–3
federal government, 5:106–8
per capita, 2:511–12
personal, 2:514–15
programs, 2:734–6, 2:743–5
public and private, 2:515–19
by source of funds, 2:513–15, 2:833–4
by type, 2:509–12, 2:515–19
facility construction expenditures, public, 2:743–5
height, *2:502*
institutions, philanthropic revenue of, 2:881–3
insurance, *2:504–6,* 2:550–63
maternal and child, 2:743–5
measures, *2:499–502, 2:502–3*
medical aid, 2:722–3
medical research expenditures, public, 2:743–5
patents granted, 3:436–44
practitioners, 2:541–9
price indexes, 2:525–6, 3:165–6
programs, *2:714–15,* 2:734–6, 2:743–5
research and development, 3:453–5
U.S. Department of Veterans Affairs, 5:429–33
Health insurance, *2:504–6,* 2:550–63. *See also* Health maintenance organizations; *specific plans*
expenditures on
consumer, 3:243–66
public, 2:739–41
hospital and surgical benefits, by plan, 2:550–1
Medicaid, 2:560
Medicare, 2:553–9
persons covered
by race, *2:504,* 2:551–2
by sex, 2:551–2
plans, 2:550–1
private, persons injured, 2:835
Health maintenance organizations (HMOs)
group plans, 2:552
individual practice associations, 2:552
number and enrollment, by type of plan, 2:552
Health professions, education, 2:449, 2:541–5
Health services
expenditures on, 2:509–11, 2:515–19
national income originating in, 4:1080–1
persons engaged in, 4:1079–80
practitioners, 2:541–9
price index, 2:525–6
professional, 2:525–6
Health-related behaviors, 2:572–81
Hearing impairments, 2:618–19. *See also* Deaf and hard-of-hearing population
Heart disease, 2:614
Heating and cooking apparatus, value of, as commodities produced, 3:267–70. *See also* Appliances
Height, 2:582–5
Hemorrhoids, 2:614
Hepatitis, 2:564–6
Hernia, 2:620
Heroin
first-time use, 2:581
persons using, 5:297–8
Herring gull eggs, 3:373–4
Hides, skins, leather, and related products, price indexes, 3:171–2, 3:175–7, 3:180–6, 3:192–5. *See also* Leather and leather products
High blood pressure, 2:614
High school, *2:393. See also* Education; Graduates, high school
Highways, *4:762–6*
construction, 4:812
contracts awarded, 4:812
value of new, 4:468–75, 4:477–8
debt, state and local government, 4:826–9
fatalities and injuries, 4:842–3
federal aid, 4:811
finance
county and township, 4:822–3
federal government, 4:813–16
local government, 4:820–1
municipal, 4:824–5
state government, 4:817–19
motor vehicle distance traveled, 4:835–6
motor vehicle speed, 4:855
public, 4:470–5, 4:477–8
railroads, grade crossings, 4:943
value of new construction, 4:468–9
by financing, 4:470–1
by ownership, 4:470–5, 4:477–8
Hispanic population, *1:24,* 1:177–9
AIDS cases reported, 2:567
births and birth rates, 1:429–30, 1:433
low-birth-weight infants, 2:586
Central and South American, 1:429–30
Cuban, 1:177–8, 1:429–33
drug abuse, 5:298–9, 5:303–5
earnings, 2:294
education, *1:15,* 2:418–20, 2:425–30, 2:436, 2:464–8
health insurance coverage, *2:504,* 2:551–2
homeownership rates, 4:510–12
homicides, 5:242–7
housing units occupied, 4:506–8
income, 2:660
juvenile delinquents, 5:264–6
labor force, 2:91–2
marriage rates, 1:687
Mexican, 1:429–33, 1:177–8
mortality, 1:485–7
nativity, 1:177–8
in poverty, *2:628,* 2:674–83, 2:690–1
Puerto Rican, 1:429–33, 1:177–8
race, 1:177–8
residence, 1:177–8
sex, 1:177–9
Spanish, 1:177–8
substance use and abuse
drug abuse, 5:298–9, 5:303–5
by high school seniors, 5:306–7
suicides, 5:242–7
unemployment rate, 2:95
union membership, 2:350
veterans, 5:412
Historical Statistics of the United States
guide to, 1:xxv–xxviii, 2:xi–xiv, 3:xi–xiv, 4:xi–xiv, 5:xi–xiv
origin and evolution, *5:334, 5:821–4*
HIV. *See* Human immunodeficiency virus
HMOs. *See* Health maintenance organizations
Hodgkin's disease, 2:568–71
Hogs, 3:116–20, 4:165–9, 4:171

Homeownership, 1:615
owner-occupied units, *4:399*
rates, 4:509–12
vacancy rates, 4:513–14
Homicides, 1:745, 5:237–55. *See also* Crime
criminal, 5:225
negligent, 5:225
New York City, number, indictments, and rates, 5:248–9
Philadelphia, number, indictments, and rates, 5:248–9
police officers killed, 5:250
by race and ethnicity, 5:242–7
rates, *5:214,* 5:239–41
reported, 5:239–41
Honduras
immigration from, 1:574–6
U.S. population born in, 1:612
Honey, commodity program provisions, 4:249–51
Honeydew melons, acreage, price, and production, 4:161–4
Hong Kong
immigration from, 1:566–70
U.S. population born in, 1:610
Horse-drawn passenger vehicles and accessories, *4:762–6*
consumer expenditures on, 3:270–2
value of, as commodities produced, 3:267–70
Horses and mules, 4:170–1
Hospitals, 2:520–40
admissions, 2:535–7
assets, 2:520
average daily census, 2:535–7
beds, 2:527–32, *2:846*
consumer expenditures on, 3:230–66
expenses, 2:521–3
per inpatient day, 2:522–3
by type of control and service, 2:521–3
for-profit, 2:523–4
general and special care, 2:522–3, 2:527–9, 2:533, 2:535–7
government, federal, 2:520–3, 2:534
admissions and average daily census, 2:535–7
assets, 2:520
average length of stay, 2:534
expenses, 2:521–3
mental, 2:537
number of beds, 2:527–8
physicians, 2:548
government, state and local, 2:523–4
insurance, 2:791
length of stay, 2:533–5
long-term care, 2:520–3, 2:533, 2:535–7
mental and psychiatric
admissions and average daily census, 2:535–7
assets, 2:520
average length of stay, 2:534
children's, 2:722–3
county, *2:694–7*
expenditures, 2:539–40
expenses, 2:521–3
facilities, 2:539–40
federal, 2:537
number of beds, 2:527–9
patients, 2:537, 2:539–40
personnel, 2:545–7
population in, 1:669–70
private, 2:537
staff, 2:539–40
state and county, 2:537
for mentally retarded, 2:538–9
nonfederal, 2:520–3, 2:527–8 2:535–7
Hospitals (*continued*)
nonprofit, 2:523–4
assets, employment, and expenditures, 2:881–3
number of beds, 2:530–2
number of beds, 2:527–8
patient care, 2:548
patient costs, 2:523–4
payroll, 2:522–3
personnel, 2:545–7
per 100 patients, 2:547
physicians, 2:548
price indexes, 2:525–6, 3:165–6
private, 2:537
proprietary, 2:530–2
short-term care, 2:520–3, 2:527–8, 2:533, 2:535–7, 2:545–7
tuberculosis, 2:520–3, 2:527–9, 2:534–7
use rates, 2:533–5
Hotel and lodging service industries
national income originating in, 4:1080–1
persons engaged in, 4:1079–80
House of Representatives
apportionment, 5:161–3
political party affiliations, 5:200–3
votes cast, by party, 5:193
Household operation, consumer expenditures on, 3:230–66, 3:273–5, 3:278–86
Household production, *2:59–62, 2:60–2,* 2:363–8
gross domestic product originating in, 3:50–2
production, *2:59–62,* 2:363–8
textile output, 2:365
value, by state, 2:363–4
Households. *See also* Families
asset holdings, *3:295*
boarders and lodgers, 2:365
composition, *1:653–5, 1:658*
definition, *1:654–5,* 1:660–2
farm and nonfarm, 1:666–7
firearm possession, 5:309
flow of funds balance sheets, 3:799–804
head of, 1:679–84
by race, 1:660–2
by sex, 1:660–3
income, by type of family, 2:661–2
individual, *1:655*
married couples, *1:655*
money income, distribution, 2:652–4, 2:657
national income originating in, 3:31–2
net worth, *3:295,* 3:314–16
number, *1:654*
population, 1:668, 1:679–84
in poverty, 2:677–9
size, 1:668
types, 1:660–3
unmarried mothers with children, 1:673–4
wealth, distribution, 2:658–9
Housework and family care, time spent, 2:368
Housing, *4:395–403,* 4:406–572. *See also* Mortgages
characteristics, *4:398*
consumer expenditures on, 3:230–66, 3:273–5, 3:278–86
expenditures
government, 5:19–25
government, federal, 5:32–7, 5:106–8
government, local, 5:73–9
government, state and local, 5:45–51
intergovernmental, federal, 5:37–9
intergovernmental, state, 5:65–8
public, 2:734–6, 2:747–8
houses for sale, 4:492–4, 4:495–7
insurance, mortgage, 4:550–5
manufactured homes, 4:498–9
nonfarm, 4:562–4
Housing (*continued*)
prices and price indexes
consumer, 3:163–4
median asking price, 4:515
by region, 4:519–20
repeat sales, 4:519–20
single-family, 4:515–19
public housing programs, *2:715–16*
social welfare, 2:747–8
stock, 4:523–5
units, 4:500–2, 4:506–8
units started, 4:481–91
Human immunodeficiency virus (HIV), 2:567–8
Human resources, government expenditures, 5:106–8
Humanities, 4:1120–3. *See also* National Endowment for the Humanities
Hungary, U.S. population born in, 1:602, 1:606, 1:609
Hydroelectric power
consumption, 4:337–40
plants, 4:1101–2
production, 4:335–7, 4:340
Hypertension, 2:614

Iceland, U.S. population born in, 1:601, 1:606, 1:609
Idaho. *See* State data
Illegitimate births. *See* Births and birth rates
Illinois. *See* State data
Illiteracy rate, 2:468–9
Immigrants. *See under* Immigration
Immigration, 1:157–65, *1:539,* 1:541–652, *1:694*
admissions, 1:627–40, 1:652
by birthplace and residence, 1:555–85
border control, 1:648–52
citizenship status, 1:597–601, 1:614
definition, 1:523
deportation, 1:648–9
immigrants, *1:524–5,* 1:541–54
by age, 1:588–9
characteristics, *1:535–6,* 1:586–96
by country of origin, *1:532–5,* 1:555–85, 1:601–9
by occupation, *1:536,* 1:590–6, 1:618–20
by race, 1:544
by sex, *1:535,* 1:586–7
legislation and regulation, *1:525–31,* 1:630
native population, by nativity of parents, 1:598–9, 1:600–1, 1:614
naturalization, *1:531,* 1:641–7
net, 1:547–8
nonimmigrants, *1:536–7,* 1:636–40
numbers, *1:536–7,* 1:547–8, 1:551–2, 1:630, 1:636–40
persons entering by ship, 4:901
Immigration and Naturalization Service, 1:650–1
Imports, 3:40–2, 3:46–7, 3:53–6, 5:498–560. *See also* Tariffs
agricultural, *4:31*
Charleston, 3:187–91
colonial, 5:710–16, 5:737–8, 5:740–2, 5:744–8, 5:752–62
by country of origin, 5:540–5
energy, by type of fuel, 4:341
farm products, 4:236–7
fishery products, 4:358–9
gold and silver, 5:498–503
goods, 5:506, 5:508, 5:520–8
lumber, 4:387–9
merchandise
duties, 5:510–14
outlying areas, 5:612–14
price indexes and terms of trade, 5:515–19

Numbers in italics refer to pages in essays; numbers not in italics refer to pages in statistical tables.

Imports (*continued*)
metals, 4:329–33
mineral fuels, 4:342–4
nonfuel nonmetals, 4:333–4
passenger cars and trucks, 4:832
price indexes, 5:515–19, 5:533
wholesale, 3:187–95, 3:197–8
pulpwood, woodpulp, paper and board, and newsprint, 4:391–3
of select commodities, 5:553–60
services, 5:507
timber products, 4:384–6
waterborne
percentage carried by U.S. vessels, *4:768–9*
tonnage, 4:896–7
value, by flag of carrier, 4:869–71
Improved Order of Redmen, 2:888–92
Incarceration, 5:256–66. *See also* Correctional institutions; Prisoners
Income, 1:618. *See also* Earnings; National income; Wages and salaries
agricultural, *4:28–31,* 4:226–42
colonial, *5:632–4*
corporations, net, 3:581–2
definition, *2:648*
disposable, personal, 3:16
distribution of, *2:621–4,* 2:652–7
Lorenz curve, *2:622*
dividend, as component of personal income, 3:36–7
family
measuring, *2:622–3*
by type of family, 2:661–2
farm, *4:12, 4:28,* 4:229–30
national income originating in, 3:29–30
interest, as component of personal income, 3:36–7
mean, 2:660–2
by education, 2:471–5
by race and ethnicity, 2:660
median, 1:618, *2:625,* 2:660–2
by education, 2:476–9
by race and ethnicity, 2:660
nonfarm, 3:29–30
personal, 3:38–9
disposition of, 3:38–9
by source, 3:36–7
pre-tax, distribution, 2:654
proprietors' income, as component of personal income, 3:36–7
rental income, as component of personal income, 3:36–7
Income maintenance programs, 2:761
Income tax. *See also* Federal income tax
agriculture, forestry, and fishing, 3:563–5
assessments, 2:721–2
construction, 3:568–9
corporate, 3:561–79
distribution industries, 3:574–5
finance, insurance, and real estate, 3:576–7
manufacturing, 3:570–1
mining, 3:566–7
service industries, 3:578–9
taxpayers, income distribution, 2:656
transportation, communication, and utilities, 3:572–3
Incorporation law, *3:483,* 3:531–6, 3:548
manufacturing companies chartered in New York, 3:549
Incorporations, business, 3:531–52
capital stock, authorized, 3:537–8
by industry, 3:539–48
in New England, *3:483,* 3:548
in New Jersey, *3:483*
Incorporations (*continued*)
number and liabilities, 3:550–1
by type of incorporation law, *3:483,* 3:531–6, 3:548
Indentured servitude, *2:9–10*
Independent Federalist Party, 5:172–9
Independent Party
party identification, 5:204
presidential candidates, 5:172–9
presidential elections, popular votes, 5:184–92
India
immigration from, 1:566–70
U.S. population born in, 1:603, 1:607, 1:610
Indian Health Services, 1:763
Indiana. *See* State data
Indians. *See* American Indian, Aleut, or Eskimo population
Indigestion, 2:620
Indigo, 5:749–50
Indonesia, U.S. population born in, 1:610
Industrial classification systems, *4:3–5. See also* North American Industry Classification System; Standard Industrial Classification system
Industrial production indexes, 3:97–110
by industry group, 4:663–9
by market group, 4:654–62
Industries, *1:693–4, 2:35–6. See also specific industries*
Inequality, economic, *2:621–49,* 2:652–91
measuring, *2:621–2*
Infant mortality, 1:391–6, 1:458–62, 1:744, 5:597–8
Infectious disease epidemics, 1:742
Infective and parasitic conditions, 2:605–7
Inflation, *3:149*
rates, gross domestic product, 3:84–8
Information technology, *3:417. See also* Computers
Ingrown nails, 2:616–17
Inhalants, first-time drug use, 2:581
Injuries and fatalities. *See also* Accidents and fatalities
bituminous coal industry, 2:335
bombing incidents, 5:255
farm, 4:79
motor vehicle, 2:600–4
place where injury occurred, 2:600–4
railroad industry, 2:333–5
work related, *2:52,* 2:330–1, 2:600–4
by industry, 2:332–3
mining, 2:326–9
Institutions of higher education. *See* Colleges and universities
Instruments and related products, manufacturing, 4:583–617
Insurance. *See also* Deposit insurance; Federal Deposit Insurance Corporation; Social insurance
automobile, premiums written and losses paid, 4:834
business incorporations, 3:539–47
companies, 3:514–15, 3:527, 3:576–7
company policies, group and individual, 2:550–1
consumer expenditures on, 3:230–66, 3:273–5, 3:278–84, 3:286
crop, 4:268–9
deposit, 3:693–730 (*see also* Deposit insurance)
disability, *2:703–6,* 2:739–41, 2:761, 2:824–7
earnings, 2:277–9
employee benefits, 2:291
employees, 2:111–14, 3:683–4
female, 2:114
production, 2:115–16, 2:129–32
employment, 2:117–19
Insurance (*continued*)
group health, 2:291
health, *2:504–6,* 2:550–63, 2:739–41 (*see also* Health insurance)
home mortgage, 4:550–5
hospital, Medicare trust fund for, 2:791
hours of work, 2:305–7
industry, 1:621–2, 1:772
injury and illness rates, 2:332–3
labor force participants engaged in, 2:101
by nativity, 2:108–9
by race, 2:104–7
by sex, 2:102–7
life, 3:230–42, 3:731–55 (*see also* Life insurance)
Medicare trust fund for, 2:792–3
old-age, *2:703–6*
personal, 3:278–84
policies, group, 2:835
private, 2:835
property, 3:731–55
railroad, 2:739–41
social, 2:291, *2:693–717*
disability, *2:703–6*
expenditures, public, 2:734–6
programs, *2:702–11*
supplementary medical, 2:792–3
unemployment, *2:710–11,* 2:781–3
expenditures, public, 2:739–41
wages and salaries, 2:282–3, 2:293
Insurance trust, government expenditures, 5:19–25
federal, 5:32–7
local, 5:45–51, 5:73–9
state, 5:45–51, 5:58–64
Intellectual property, *3:415–6*
Intercensal migration, 1:505–18
Intercity motor carriers, 4:856
Interest
expenditures, federal government, 5:52–5, 5:95
income, as component of personal income, 3:36–7
paid, by consumers, 3:16
on public debt, federal government, 5:105–6
rates, *3:594–5, 3:625–7,* 3:812–31
consumer credit, 3:828–30
Federal Reserve, 3:593–4, 3:624–5
during the Great Depression, 3:130–5
household savings, 3:828–30
money market, 3:820–5
mortgage, 3:831
short-term business loans, bank rates, 3:816–19
yields, *3:594–5, 3:625–7,* 3:812–31
corporate bonds, 3:826
government bonds, 3:827
long-term bond, 3:812–16
International affairs and finance, federal government expenditures on, 5:95, 5:106–8
International investment, 5:466–9
in United States, by country and industry, 5:479–82
U.S. direct investment in foreign countries, 5:473–8
International relations, 5:1–805
government expenditures for, 5:19–25
federal, 5:32–7
International trade, *5:441–51,* 5:452–585
balance of payments, 5:452–97
exports and imports, 5:498–560
goods and services, *5:444–8*
data collection, *5:445–7*
terminology, *5:447–8*
U.S. direct investment in foreign countries, 5:473–8

International transactions, *5:441–4*
  annual averages, by decade, *5:441–4*
  colonial, *5:441,* 5:710–12
Internet, *4:996–7,* 4:1026
Investments
  construction as, *4:395–7*
  definition, *3:289–90*
  farm, 4:193–225
  gross
    federal government, 3:40–2
    government, 3:48–50
    private domestic, 3:40–2, 3:44–5, 3:53–6
    by sector and type, 3:306–9
  manufacturing, 4:684–8
Iowa. *See* State data
Iran
  immigration from, 1:566–9, 1:569–70
  U.S. population born in, 1:610
Iraq, U.S. population born in, 1:610
Ireland (Eire). *See also* Northern Ireland
  immigration from, *1:534,* 1:560–5
  U.S. population born in, 1:601, 1:606, 1:609
Iron. *See* Bar iron; Cast iron ware; Iron ore; Pig iron; Wrought iron
Iron ore
  imports and exports, 4:329–33
  production, 4:308–11, 4:321–3
Irrigation, 3:364
Israel
  immigration from, 1:566–70
  U.S. population born in, 1:610
Italy
  immigration from, 1:560–5
  U.S. population born in, 1:603, 1:607, 1:609

Jacksonian Party, 5:200–3
Jamaica
  immigration from, 1:571–4, 1:576
  U.S. population born in, 1:611
Japan
  immigration from, 1:566–70
  investment in United States, by industry, 5:479–82
  U.S. population born in, 1:603, 1:607, 1:610
Jewelry, silverware, clocks, and watches
  consumer expenditures on, 3:270–2
  value of, as commodities produced, 3:267–70
Jewish congregations. *See also* Religious institutions; Synagogues
  charitable and philanthropic giving to, 2:914–16
  membership, 2:904–9
Jobless Party, 5:172–9
Joint ventures, business, 3:554–5
Jordan, U.S. population born in, 1:610
Justice, *5:209–22,* 5:223–31
  administration of, federal government expenditures on, 5-106–8
  criminal, 5:311–31
    administration of, *5:211*
    expenditures on, by level of government, 5:311–14
  system, *5:220–2*
Juvenile delinquents, 5:264–6. *See also* Delinquency

Kansas. *See* State data
Keelboats, 4:879–80
Kentucky. *See* State data
Kenya, U.S. population born in, 1:610
Kidney cancer, 2:568–71
Kidney disorders, 2:617–18
Kindergarten, 2:406–9, 2:431
Kiwanis, 2:888–92
Korea
  immigration from, 1:566–70
  U.S. population born in, 1:603, 1:607, 1:610
Korean Conflict
  characteristics, 5:363–4
  draftees, 5:363–4
  estimated cost, 5:370
  medical care, 5:363–4
  military pay, 5:363–4
  military personnel and casualties, 5:350–1
Kuwait, U.S. population born in, 1:610

Labor, *1:777,* 2:63–368. *See also* Labor force; Labor unions; Laborers
  agricultural productivity indexes, *4:21*
  colonial, 5:665–70
  contract, *2:9–10*
  division of, *2:4–5*
  earnings, 2:270, 2:280
  farm, wages, 2:255–6
  human, capital, *2:7–8*
  laws, *2:9–12*
  nonfarm, productivity, *3:419*
  skilled, earnings, by industry, 2:270
  slave, *2:10*
  technology, *2:8*
  unskilled, 2:280
  wages, *2:40–6*
    common, 2:262–4
    farm, 2:255–6
Labor force, 1:616, *2:13–33,* 2:63–76. *See also* Employment; Labor; Laborers; Unemployment
  by age, 2:63–4, 2:89
  American Indian, *1:721,* 1:767–72
  characteristics, *2:17–23*
  civilian, 2:82–4
  cohorts, 1:697–702
  definition, *2:13*
  female, *1:692,* 1:700–2, *2:15, 2:26–9, 2:39,* 2:90 (*see also* Women in labor force)
    marital status, 1:616, 1:701–2, *2:11,* 2:93
    by race, *2:39,* 2:92
  by industry, 2:110–11
  male, 2:63–4, 2:89, 2:91
  occupations, 1:618–20, *2:38*
  participation, *2:23–9, 2:35–6*
    by age, 1:697–702, *2:16–17, 2:25,* 2:64–6, 2:78–9, 2:94
    American Indian, 1:767–8
    by education, 2:88
    foreign-born, *2:23*
    immigrant, 1:616, 1:699, 1:700
    by marital status, 1:701–2, 2:80–2, 2:94
    by race, 1:698–702, *2:24,* 2:64–6, 2:80–2
    by sex, 1:697–702, 1:767–8, *2:24–6,* 2:64–6, 2:77–82, 2:94
  by race, 2:63–6, 2:91
  union membership, *2:55–7,* 2:336–45, 2:347–50
  wages, hourly, 2:351
Labor Party, 5:172–9
Labor unions, *2:54–9,* 2:234
  affiliations, *2:56–7,* 2:340–1
  contracts, workers covered by, 2:350
  density, *2:56*
  elections and results, 2:352
  membership, *2:55–6,* 2:336–9
    by affiliation, 2:340–2
    by age, 2:350
    characteristics, *2:57*
    full-time status, 2:350
    by industry, 2:343–5, 2:347–9
    manufacturing, 2:346, 2:348–9
    by race, 2:350
    by sex, 2:349–50
  organizing, *2:8, 2:54–5*
  public opinion concerning, 2:362
  strikes, *2:58–9*
Labor unions (*continued*)
  unfair practice complaints, 2:353
  wages, 2:351
  wages affected by, *2:57–8*
  work stoppages, 2:354–61
Laborers, 2:151. *See also* Labor; Labor force
  American Indian, 1:768–70
  economically active, 2:249–52
  farm, 2:151
    earnings, 2:260
    economically active, 2:249
    female, 2:171, 2:201, 2:211
    male, 2:161, 2:181, 2:191
    by nativity, 2:221, 2:231
    by race, 2:181, 2:191, 2:201, 2:211
  immigrants, 1:593–6, 1:618–20
  by nativity, 2:221, 2:231
  by race, 2:181, 2:191, 2:201, 2:211
  by sex, 1:618–20, 1:768–70, 2:161, 2:171, 2:181, 2:191, 2:201, 2:211
  unskilled
    earnings, 2:280
    wages, *2:44,* 2:256–7
Lamb, slaughtering, prices, and production, 4:172–8
Land, 3:345, 3:364. *See also* Cropland; Forestland
  agricultural, 4:211
    drainage and irrigation, 3:362–3
  American Indian, *1:722–4,* 1:747–56
    claims, 1:748
    by state, 1:749–52
    U.S. purchase, 1:747
  area of United States 1:12, 1:108–39, 1:157–65, *3:333* (*see also* Outlying areas)
    conterminous United States, 1:26–39
    by state, 3:346, 3:349
    by territory, 3:346, 3:349
    by use, 3:360–1
  colonial, 5:700
  expenditures, for government management of, 3:365
  farm, 3:360–1, *4:11,* 4:39–44
    by operator tenure, 4:73–4
    by region, 4:50–3, 4:57–64
    by size of farm, 4:76
    by state, 4:50–3, 4:57–64
    utilization, *4:15–17*
    value, 4:73–4
  forest, 3:360–1
    insect-damaged, 3:377
  grants
    public, 3:355
    railroad use of federal, 4:919
  grazing, 3:358–9, 4:265–6
  nonfarm, 3:360–1
  private, by use, 3:362,
  productivity indexes, *4:21*
  revenue from, 3:356, 3:358
  territorial expansion of United States, *3:333–6,* 3:345
  utilization, *3:337–8,* 3:362, *4:15–17*
  vacant, 3:350, 3:354
Laos, U.S. population born in, 1:610
Larcenies and thefts, 5:225. *See also* Crime
Lard, price and production, 4:138–9
Latin America. *See also* Central America; South America; *specific countries*
  crude oil reserves, 4:344–5
  U.S. direct investment in, by industry, 5:473–8
Latvia, U.S. population born in, 1:602, 1:607, 1:609
Law enforcement, *5:209–22,* 5:223–31
  officers, 5:330
Lawyers. *See under* Legal services
Layoffs, *2:51.* *See also* Unemployment

Lead
emissions, motor vehicle, 4:854
exports, 4:329–33
imports, 4:329–33
production, 4:311–14, 4:321–3
Learning disabilities, special education programs for individuals with, 2:410
Leather and leather products. *See also* Hides, skins, leather, and related products
manufacturing, 4:583–617
output, physical, 4:627–46
Lebanon, U.S. population born in, 1:610
Legal services
consumer expenditures for, 3:230–66
lawyers, by sex and employment setting, 5:329–30
national income originating in, 4:1080–1
persons engaged in, 4:1079–80
Legitimate births. *See* Births and birth rates
Lemons, acreage, price, and production, 4:128–30
Lettuce, acreage, price, and production, 4:161–4
Leukemia, 2:568–71
Leveraged buyouts, number and value, 3:556
Liabilities. *See specific institutions*
Liberia, U.S. population born in, 1:611
Libertarian Party, 5:172–9
Liberty Party, 5:172–9
Libya, U.S. population born in, 1:610
Life expectancy, 1:391, 1:440–2, 1:447, 1:746
Life insurance, 3:731–55
benefit payments, 3:741–3
companies, 3:731–5, 3:738–40, 3:744–8
finances, 3:751–4
operating results, 3:754–5
resources, 3:754–5
consumption expenditures for, 3:230–66, 3:273–5
employee benefits, 2:824–7
finances, 3:751–4
in force, by type, 3:731–5
policy reserves, 3:747–8
sales, by type of insurance, 3:736–7
surplus, 3:747–8
veteran, 5:428
Lighting
electrical patents granted, 3:430–44
price of, 3:169
Lignite, fuel mineral production value, 4:292–4
LIHEAP. *See* Low-Income Home Energy Assistance Program
Lime, 4:323–8
Limes, acreage, price, and production, 4:128–30
Linseed oil, price and production, 4:138–9
Lions International, 2:888–92
Liquor stores, government owned
government expenditures on, 5:19–25
local government expenditures on, 5:73–9
state and local government expenditures on, 5:45–51
state government expenditures on, 5:58–64
Lithuania, U.S. population born in, 1:602, 1:607, 1:609
Liver cancer, 2:568–71
Livestock, *4:15–18,* 4:89–192. *See also specific animals*
agricultural output values, 4:193–6
colonial, 5:700
farm, *4:15–18*
industry changes, *4:17–18*
farm marketings, cash receipts, 4:231–3
products, productivity indicators, 4:202–3
in slave states, 5:784
Loans
brokers', 3:773
Confederate, bond yields on domestic, 5:802
credit unions, 3:687–8
Loans (*continued*)
farm, non–real estate, 4:271–2
during the Great Depression, 3:130–5
interest rates, business, 3:816–19
veterans, 5:436–7
Lobster, 4:368–9
Long-term disability coverage, 2:824–7
Lorenz curve, *2:622*
Los Angeles, water supply and consumption, 4:1098
Louisiana. *See also* State data
price indexes, 3:197–8
Louisville, steamboat trade, 4:878
Low-birth-weight infants, 2:586
Low-Income Home Energy Assistance Program (LIHEAP), 2:809
Lumber
consumption, *4:282*
exports, 4:387–9
forest products industries, *4:281–2*
hardwood, 4:387–91
imports, 4:387–9
manufacturing, 4:583–617
price indexes, 3:173–7, 3:180–6, 3:192–5, 3:199–201
production, 4:387–91
softwood, 4:387–91
stumpage, prices, *4:282*
Lung cancer, 2:568–71
Luxembourg, U.S. population born in, 1:602, 1:606, 1:609
Lymphoma, 2:568–71
Lynching victims, *5:219,* 5:252–5
by race, 5:251–5

Macadamia nuts, acreage, price, and production, 4:140–2
Macau, U.S. population born in, 1:610
Machinery and equipment
manufacturing, 4:583–617
output, 4:627–46
price indexes, 3:173–4
Magazines and newspapers. *See also* Newspapers; Periodicals
advertising distribution, 4:752–6
consumption expenditures on, 3:230–66
Magnesium production, 4:315–18
Maine. *See also* State data
colonial agriculture, 5:700
colonial population, 5:657
Malaria, 2:564–6
Malaysia, U.S. population born in, 1:610
Malta, U.S. population born in, 1:609
Managers, officials, and proprietors, 2:144–5
American Indian, 1:768–70
economically active, 2:234–6
immigrants, 1:590–6, 1:618–20
by nativity, 2:214–15, 2:224–5
by race, 2:174–5, 2:184–5, 2:194–5, 2:204–5
by sex, 1:618–20, 1:768–70, 2:154–5, 2:164–5, 2:174–5, 2:184–5, 2:194–5, 2:204–5
specialty occupations, 1:771
Manganese production, 4:318–20
Manufactured homes, 4:498–9
Manufacturing, 1:621–2, 1:772, *4:573–8,* 4:579–704
assets, fixed, 4:684–8
business incorporations, 3:539–47
capital, 4:676–98
depreciation, 4:680–3
expenditures, 4:579–620
by industry division, 4:689–92
purchases, 4:680–3
value of equipment and structures, 4:680–3
Manufacturing (*continued*)
colonial, 5:704–6
business establishments, 5:706
vessel, 5:704–5
companies and corporations, 3:508–9, 3:524, 3:529–30, 3:559, 4:579–620
assets, 3:570–1
cash dividends, 1:579–80
chartered in New York, 3:549
control, 4:702
dividends, 3:570–1
income tax, 3:570–1
liabilities, 3:570–1
profits, 4:703–4
receipts, 3:570–1
retained earnings, 4:703–4
sales, 4:703–4
stockholder equity, 4:703–4
definition, *4:573, 4:577–8*
durable goods, 4:671–2
employees, 2:111–14, 4:676–98
earnings, 2:275–6, 2:279, 2:287–90, 3:141–5
economically active, 2:239, 2:243–6, 2:249–52
female, 2:114
during the Great Depression, 3:121–5
production workers, 2:309
employment, *4:574,* 4:579–617, 4:673–5
equipment, power, 4:583–617, 4:696
expenditures, capital, 4:579–620
foreign direct investment in United States by country, 5:479–82
full-time employment, 2:117–19
during the Great Depression, 3:121–5, 3:141–5
hours of work
daily, 2:301–3
during the Great Depression, 3:121–5
by industry, 2:302–3
overtime, 2:315
by sex, 2:309
by skill, 2:309
weekly, *2:47,* 2:303–8
household (*see* Household production)
indexes
industrial production, 4:663–9
by industry group, 4:670
industrial concentration, legal form, and economic performance, 4:699–704
by industry, 4:583–617
injuries, 2:330–3
inputs, 4:676–98
inventories, 4:579–82
investment, 4:684–8
labor force, 2:110–11
labor force participants engaged in, 2:101
by nativity, 2:108–9
by race, 2:104–7
by sex, 2:102–7
by legal form of organization, 4:618–20
mergers, *3:487,* 3:553–6
national income originating in, 3:32–5
nondurable goods, 4:671–2
output, 4:621–75
consumption of, 4:693–5
by type of commodity, 4:621–6
patents granted, 3:430–44
payroll, 4:579–620
power
consumption of, 4:697–8
equipment horsepower, 4:696
price indexes, 4:621–6
production
capacity, 4:673–5

Numbers in italics refer to pages in essays; numbers not in italics refer to pages in statistical tables.

Manufacturing (*continued*)
indexes, 4:652–3, 4:670
products, 4:627–46
consumption of, 4:676–98
in slave states, 5:786
turnover rates, *2:51,* 2:320–2
union membership, 2:346–9
U.S. direct investment in foreign countries, 5:473–8
value added, 4:579–620
wages and salaries, 2:266–9, 2:282–3, 2:292
work stoppages, 2:359–61
workplace size, *2:53,* 2:323–4
Marijuana
first-time use, 2:581
persons using, 5:297–9
Marine Corps. *See* Armed forces
Marital status. *See also* Marriage; Married couples; Married women
by age, 1:703–4
births and birth rates, 1:433–6, 1:439
cohorts, 1:703–8
homeownership rates by, 4:510–12
hours of work by, 2:311–12
labor force participation rates by, 2:80–2, 2:94
of mothers with children, 1:674–5, *1:656*
population by, 1:40–101, 1:703–4
colonial, 5:658, 5:660
of women in labor force, 1:616, 2:80–2, 2:93
Marriage, 1:392–6. *See also* Marital status; Married couples; Married women
age at first, *1:13,* 1:685–7
rates, 1:688–9
singulate mean age, *1:383*
Married couples, *1:655. See also* Marital status; Marriage; Married women
income of, 2:661–2
in poverty, 2:677–9
Married women. *See also* Marital status; Marriage; Married couples
labor force participation rate, 2:94
labor rights, *2:11*
property rights legislation, 2:367–8
Marshall Islands. *See also* Outlying areas
consumer price indexes, 5:619–20
crop production, 5:608–9
education, 5:599–603
employment, 5:605–7
exports, 5:610–12
government revenues and expenditures, 5:624–5
gross domestic product, 5:604–5
imports, 5:612–14
infant mortality, 5:597–8
population, 1:39, 5:594–5
telephones in, 5:617–18
unemployment, 5:607
visitor arrivals, 5:615–16
Maryland. *See also* State data
business incorporations, 3:539–47
colonial population, 5:663
colonial prices
corn, 5:685–6
tobacco, 5:681–5
wheat, 5:687–8
slaves imported into, 5:670
turnpikes, 4:783
wages, farm labor, 2:255–6
Masonic orders, 2:888–92
Massachusetts. *See also* State data
charitable and voluntary organizations, 2:852
charitable giving, 2:929
colonial
agriculture, acreage and livestock, 5:700
cod fishery, 5:701
Massachusetts (*continued*)
government taxes, annual, 5:709
population, 5:659
death rates, 1:483–5
foundations, 2:855–7
infant mortality, 1:462
wage indexes, agriculture, 2:254–5
wealth, 2:659
Maternal and child health programs, 2:743–5
Maternity medical clinics, 2:805–6
Mathematics, student proficiency, 2:425–30
Measles, *2:503,* 2:564–6
Meat, poultry, fish, seafood, and eggs. *See also* Cattle; Chickens; Fish; Lamb; Pork; Turkeys
consumption, 2:574
eggs, 4:187–91
poultry, 4:187–91
price indexes, 3:161–2, 3:192–5
slaughtering, 3:116–20, 4:172–8
Medicaid
recipients, 2:560
days of care, 2:560
by eligibility, 2:794
by program or service, 2:561–2
vendor payments
by eligibility, 2:794
by program or service, 2:563
Medical facilities, construction expenditures, 2:509–11, 2:515–19
Medicare, *2:706–7*
charges, 2:558–9
cost sharing, 2:789–90
disabled persons, 2:558
enrollees, 2:553
expenditures, 2:553
federal government, 5:106–8
public, 2:739–41
persons served, 2:554–7
premium amounts, 2:789–90
reimbursements, 2:554–7
trust fund
hospital insurance, 2:791
insurance, supplementary medical, 2:792–3
utilization, 2:558–9
Melanoma, 2:568–71
Meningococcal infection, 2:564–6
Mental health facilities, 2:539–40. *See also under* Hospitals
Mentally retarded population
hospitals, 2:538–9
public institutions, 2:538–9
admissions, 2:538–9
deaths, 2:538–9
facilities, 2:538–9
maintenance expenditures, 2:538–9
patients, 2:538–9
personnel, 2:538–9
releases, 2:538–9
special education programs, 2:410
Merchant vessels
built, *4:769,* 4:871–2, 4:881, 4:886–7, 4:893–4
documented, 4:871–2, 4:881, 4:886–7
gross tonnage, by region, 4:874–6
number and tonnage, 4:858–63
launched, number and tonnage, 4:889–90
owned, number and tonnage, 4:889–90
tonnage, gross
by region, 4:881, 4:886–7
by type of service, 4:910
trade, 4:858–63
types, 4:858–63
under U.S. flag
Merchant vessels (*continued*)
employment, 4:900
number and tonnage, 4:902–9
wage rates, 4:900
Mergers, business, 3:553–6
manufacturing and mining, *3:487,* 3:553–6
number, capitalization, and type, 3:553–6
number and assets, 3:554–5
number and value, 3:556
Metals and metal products, 4:583–617
exports, 4:329–33
fabricated, 4:583–617
imports, 4:329–33
mining, employees, 4:286–7
output, 4:627–46
patents granted, 3:430–44
price indexes, 3:173–7, 3:180–6, 3:199–201
production, by type, 4:308–20
Methodist Church, membership, 2:904–9. *See also* Churches and congregations; Religious institutions
Metropolitan areas, 1:108–39, 1:157–65. *See also specific cities*
firearm possession, 5:310
homeownership rates, 4:510–12
houses, multifamily, 4:495–7
housing units started, 4:481–90
persons in poverty, 2:684–5
Mexican War
casualties, 5:350–1
estimated cost, 5:370
military personnel, 5:350–1
Mexico
agricultural worker immigrants from, 1:638
aliens naturalized from, 1:644–7
immigration from, 1:571–6
U.S. population born in, 1:604, 1:608
Michigan. *See* State data
Mid-Atlantic States. *See* Regional data
Middle East
crude oil reserves, 4:344–5
U.S. direct investment in, by industry, 5:473–8
Migraine headaches, 2:617–18
Migration, colonial, 5:665–70
Migration, internal, *1:489–93,* 1:495–521
by birthplace and residence, *1:491,* 1:495–8
definition, *1:489*
intercensal, 1:505–18
mobility status, 1:520–1
by nativity, 1:492, 1:509–18
by race, 1:495–8, 1:505–18, 1:523
trends, *1:491–3*
Migration, international. *See* Immigration
Military. *See also* Armed forces; Military personnel
battle campaigns, 5:372–403, 5:372–80
expenditures, 5:367–71
facilities, value of new construction, 4:468–9
service, *1:695*
Military personnel, *5:336–7,* 5:350–66
active duty, *5:334*
by branch of service, 5:353–9
by sex, 5:353–9
by branch of service, 5:350–1
deaths, 5:352
female, *5:337*
reserve, *5:339,* 5:360–3
by branch of service and reserve status, 5:360–3
by war, 5:350–1
Milk. *See also* Dairy products
commodity program provisions, 4:249–51
livestock kept for, 4:178–86
marketing, 4:264–5
Mineral fuels. *See also specific fuels*
imports and exports, 4:342–4
production, 4:288–94

Numbers in italics refer to pages in essays; numbers not in italics refer to pages in statistical tables.

Mineral industries, 1:621–2, 1:772, *4:275–84*. *See also* Mining
earnings, 2:272–3, 2:277–9
employees, 2:111–14, 4:285
female, 2:114
full-time, 2:117–19
by industry division, 4:286–7
output, 3:467–9
production, 2:115–16, 2:129–32
establishments, 4:285
expenses, 4:285
fuel mineral production, 4:288–94
hours of work, 2:305–8
injuries and fatalities, 2:326–33, 2:335
labor force, 2:110–11
labor force participants engaged in, 2:101
by nativity, 2:108–9
by race, 2:104–7
by sex, 2:102–7
national income originating in, 3:32–5
operations, 4:285
patents granted, 3:430–44
receipts of, 4:285
union membership in, 2:347
value added in, 4:285
wages and salaries, 2:282–3, 2:292
work stoppages, 2:359–61
Mineral production
metal, 4:308–23
nonmetal, 4:323–5
cement, 4:323–8
lime, 4:326–8
pyrites, 4:323–5
stone, 4:323–8
Mineral products
patents granted, 3:430–44
price indexes, producer and wholesale, 3:173–4
Minerals
American Indian land, 1:755–6
operations, 4:285
Minimum wage, 2:284–5
Mining, 4:285–334. *See also* Mineral industries
accidents, bituminous coal mining, 2:335
business incorporations, 3:539–47
clay, 4:326–8
companies and corporations, 3:503–5, 3:522, 3:558, 3:566–7
employees, 4:286–7
coal mining, 4:286–7
gypsum, crude, 4:323–5
industrial production indexes, 4:663–9
injuries and fatalities, 2:326–9
lime, 4:323–5
limited liability companies, 3:522
mergers, *3:487*, 3:553–6
output, 3:467–9
phosphate rock, 4:323–8
potash, 4:323–5
salt, 4:323–8
sand and gravel, 4:323–8
stone, 4:326–8
sulfur, 4:323–8
U.S. direct investment in foreign countries, 5:473–8
Minnesota. *See* State data
Mississippi. *See* State data
Missouri. *See* State data
Modern Woodmen of America, 2:888–92
Molybdenum
imports and exports, 4:329–33
production, 4:318–23
Monetary aggregates, *3:583–5*, 3:596–622
definition, *3:585*, *3:601*
Divisia, 3:591–2, 3:621–2
Monetary aggregates (*continued*)
Federal Reserve Board, 3:590–1, 3:619–21
U.S. monetary gold stock, 3:584, 3:596–7
Monetary policy, *3:588–9*, *3:592*, *3:604–7*, 3:623–31
definition, *3:588*, *3:608–13*
Monetary values, 3:592–3, 3:623, *5:809–12*
Money. *See also* Currency; Monetary policy
colonial, *5:643–4*
Confederate States of America, *5:776–8*, 5:791–9
money stock, 5:791–2
during the Great Depression, 3:136–40
high-powered, 3:631
market rates, 3:820–5
monetary aggregates, *3:583–5*, 3:596–622
monetary standards, 3:592–3, 3:623
stock, and components, 3:585–9, 3:598–607
value of the dollar, 3:592–3, 3:623
Montana. *See* State data
Montserrat, U.S. population born in, 1:611
Monuments and tombstones, 3:267–70
Morocco, U.S. population born in, 1:610
Mortality rates, 1:467, 1:458–73, 1:487, *1:695*. *See also* Deaths and death rates
decline, *1:385–7*
infant, *1:388*
maternal, 1:458–61
neonatal, 1:458–61
Mortgages, *4:395–403*, 4:406–572
conventional single-family
delinquencies and foreclosures, 4:571–2
terms, 4:565–8
debt, 3:777
by financing, 4:532–5
by holder, 4:526–39
by property type, 4:526–39
by type, 4:526–31
delinquencies, 4:569–72
farm
owner-operated, 4:74
foreclosures, 4:569–72
insurance, 4:550–5
interest rates, 3:831
multifamily residential property, 4:547–9
nonfarm residential, 4:526–39, 4:541, 4:562–4
nonfarm structure, 4:526–35
one- to four-family homes, 4:540, 4:542–6
by property, 3:777, 4:526–39, 4:545–6, 4:549
residential, *4:399–401*, 4:526–72
nonfarm, 4:526–39
secondary, 4:470–1, 4:556–9
secondary residential, 4:470–1, 4:556–9
securities related to, 4:560–2
terms, 4:562–8
by type of holder, 3:777
Motion picture attendance, 4:1123
Motor fuel. *See also* Gasoline
consumption, 4:847–9
fuel efficiency, vehicles, 4:346
price indexes, consumer, 3:165–7
Motor vehicles, *4:762–6*, 4:806–57. *See also* Automobiles
accidents, 4:843–4
alternative-fuel, 4:346
deaths and death rates, *4:765*, 4:843–6
distance traveled, 4:835–40
emissions
carbon monoxide, 4:851
lead, 4:854
nitrogen oxide, 4:852
organic compounds, volatile, 4:853
Motor vehicles (*continued*)
factory sales, 4:831
fatalities and injuries, 2:600–4, 4:840–2
motor vehicle accidents, 4:843
fuel consumption, 4:847–9
by motor vehicle type, 4:837–40
fuel efficiency, 4:346
registrations, 4:830, 4:837–40
speed, highway, 4:855
thefts, 5:225
Motorcycles and bicycles, 3:267–70
Mountain States. *See* Regional data
Multifamily residential property. *See also* Housing
houses for sale, 4:495–7
mortgages, 4:547–9
Municipal solid waste disposal, *3:339–40*
Murder, prisoners executed for, 5:262–3. *See also* Homicides
Musculoskeletal conditions, 2:616–17
Museums, 2:885–7
Music, radio, and television consumption expenditures, 3:230–42
Musical instruments, commodity value, 3:267–70. *See also* Radios and musical instruments
Mutual funds, 3:771
Mutual savings banks, 3:671–82. *See also* Banks
insured, 3:724–5

NAICS. *See* North American Industry Classification System
Nails, prices, 3:212–17
NAIRU. *See* Nonaccelerating inflation rate of unemployment
NASA. *See* National Aeronautics and Space Administration
National Aeronautics and Space Administration (NASA), 3:453–5
National Assessment of Educational Progress, 2:425–30
National Banks, 3:641–9
National Collegiate Athletic Association, attendance, 4:1118–19
National Credit Union Administration, 3:691–2
National defense, 3:53–6
National Economic Recovery Party, 5:172–9
National Endowment for the Arts, 4:1122
National Endowment for the Humanities, 4:1122
National Forest System, 4:377–81
National income, *3:3–19*, 3:21–69
definition, *3:3*
National income and product accounts (NIPA), *3:6–10*
National Labor Relations Board
elections and results, 2:352
unfair practice complaints, 2:353
National Party, 5:172–9
National product, *3:3–19*, 3:21–69
National saving, *3:290*
net, personal, corporate, and government, 3:298–9
rates, *3:290*, 3:312–13
National Science Foundation, 3:453–5
National security, federal government expenditures for, 5:95
National States Rights Party, 5:172–9
National wealth, 3:325–32
estimating, *3:294–5*
by type of asset, 3:325–9
Nativity. *See* Immigration; Population; *specific countries of origin*
NATO. *See* North Atlantic Treaty Organization
Natural gas, 4:335–9, 4:341–4
fuel production, 4:288–91
Natural Law Party, 5:172–9

Numbers in italics refer to pages in essays; numbers not in italics refer to pages in statistical tables.

Natural resources, *3:333, 3:341*
belonging to American Indians, *1:721–4,* 1:747–56
definition, *3:333*
government expenditures for, 3:365
federal, 4:252, 5:106–8
industries, *4:275–84,* 4:285–394
energy, 4:335–57
fisheries, 4:358–75
forestry, 4:376–94
mining, 4:285–334
Naturalization, *1:531,* 1:641–7. *See also* Citizenship status; Immigration
alien, 1:641–7
Naval vessels, 4:912–13
Navy, 3:453–5. *See also* Armed forces
NCAA. *See* National Collegiate Athletic Association
Near East, U.S. government foreign grants and credits, 5:483–97
Nebraska. *See* State data
Nectarines, acreage, price, and production, 4:131–4
Nepal, U.S. population born in, 1:610
Net worth, *3:295,* 3:314–16
Netherlands
investment in United States, by industry, 5:479–82
U.S. population born in, 1:602, 1:606, 1:609
Nevada. *See* State data
New Alliance Party, 5:172–9
New Deal
banking reforms, *3:591–2, 3:621–2*
farm policies, *4:34–5*
New England. *See also* Regional data
charitable and voluntary organizations, 2:852
codfish prices, 5:675–6
incorporations, business, *3:483,* 3:548
towns settled and incorporated, 5:665–8
turnpike mileage and cost, 4:783
New Hampshire, 5:658. *See also* State data
New Haven. *See also* Metropolitan areas
college foundings and failures, 2:875
nonprofit and voluntary institutions per capita, 2:851
New Jersey. *See also* State data
business incorporations, *3:483,* 3:539–47
colonial agriculture, 5:700
colonial population, 5:662
New Mexico. *See* State data
New Orleans. *See also* Metropolitan areas
cotton freight rates, 4:884
price indexes, 3:197–8
steamboat trade, 4:878
travel times to, 4:779
New York. *See also* State data
business incorporations, 3:539–47
canals, 4:881, 4:885
charitable giving, 2:929
colonial population, 5:660–1
cotton freight rates, 4:884
foundations, 2:855–7
household manufacturing, 2:365
manufacturing companies chartered in, 3:549
poor relief expenditures, 2:729–31
public relief, *2:697–8,* 2:732–3
New York City. *See also* Metropolitan areas
colonial population, 5:655
homicides, number, indictments, and rates, 5:248–9
poor relief, 2:720–1, 2:729–31
public relief recipients, 2:732–3
rental housing, price indexes, 3:168
travel times, 4:779
vessels clearing, in colonial foreign commerce, 5:720–2
New York Stock Exchange sales, 3:770. *See also* Stock market
New Zealand
immigration from, 1:583–5
U.S. population born in, 1:611
Newport, Rhode Island, colonial population, 5:655. *See also* Metropolitan areas
Newspapers, *4:984–5,* 4:1050–9. *See also* Magazines and newspapers
advertising, 4:752–8
circulation, 4:915–53, 4:1055
daily, number and circulation, *4:984*
newsprint consumption, 4:1059
number, 4:1055–8
pages per issue, 4:1059
Newsprint, 4:391–3, 4:1059
Nicaragua
immigration from, 1:574–6
U.S. population born in, 1:612
Nickel, 4:318–20
Nigeria, U.S. population born in, 1:611
NIPA. *See* National income and product accounts
Nitrogen oxide emissions, 4:852
Nobel prizes
American recipients, by field and country of birth, 1:623–6
by category, 3:457
by recipient's country of residence, 3:457
Nonaccelerating inflation rate of unemployment (NAIRU), 3:84–8
Non-Hodgkin's lymphoma, 2:568–71
Nonmetals, nonfuel imports and exports, 4:333–4
Nonprofit arts, humanities, and cultural institutions, 2:885–7. *See also* Nonprofit institutions
Nonprofit institutions, *2:837–48,* 2:851–84
assets, *3:295*
benevolent, 2:851, 2:865–7
business, 2:851
charitable, *2:841–2,* 2:859–60
definition, *2:837, 2:838–9*
employee compensation, 2:857–9
employment, 2:857–9
endowment income, 2:853–4
farmers' cooperatives, 2:861–3
flow of funds balance sheets, 3:799–804
grant expenditures, 2:853–4
gross domestic product, as component of, 3:50–2
net worth, *3:295,* 3:314–6
noncharitable, *2:841–2*
nonexempt charitable trusts, 2:861–3
number, 2:853–4, 2:857–9
per capita, 2:851
personal saving, 3:304–6
public/private, *2:840–1*
religious, 2:851 (*see also* Religious institutions; *specific religions*)
revenue, philanthropic, 2:923–5
secular, 2:851
schools, 2:871–5
tax-exempt organizations, 2:861–4, 2:867–70
women's, 2:851
youth, 2:851
Nonresidential structures
net stock, 4:414–19
composition, *4:396*
value of new construction, by type, 4:455–60
North America
emigration from, 1:555–8, 1:571–6
immigration to, 1:551
map of, *5:629*
refugees and asylees from, 1:635
U.S. population born in, 1:604, 1:612
North American Industry Classification System (NAICS), 4:5
North Atlantic Treaty Organization (NATO), 5:371
North Carolina, 5:751. *See also* State data
North Central States. *See* Regional data
North Dakota. *See* State data
Northern Ireland. *See also* Ireland
immigration from, *1:534*
U.S. population born in, 1:601, 1:606, 1:609
Northern Mariana Islands. *See also* Outlying areas
consumer price indexes, 5:619–20
education, 5:599–603
employment, 5:605–7
exports, 5:610–12
government revenues and expenditures, 5:624–5
gross domestic product, 5:604–5
imports, 5:612–14
infant mortality, 5:597–8
population, 1:39, 5:594–5
telephones in, 5:617–18
unemployment, 5:607
visitor arrivals, 5:615–16
Norway, U.S. population born in, 1:601, 1:606, 1:609. *See also* Scandinavia
Nuclear fuel and waste inventory, 3:370–1
Nuclear power
energy consumption, 4:337–9
energy production, 4:335–7
plants, 4:353
Nuclear weapons, 5:404–5, *5:335–6*
U.S. strategic, 5:404
Nullifiers Party, 5:172–9
Nursery school, 2:431
Nurses, 2:541–5
Nursing facilities
Medicaid recipients and days of care, 2:560
nonprofit, 2:881–3
Nursing homes
consumer expenditures, 3:243–66
U.S. Department of Veterans Affairs, 5:435
Nutrient consumption. *See also* Food and beverages; Nutrition
daily, 2:576–7
per capita, 2:572–3
Nutrition, *2:499–507,* 2:572–81. *See also* Food and beverages; Nutrient consumption
calorie consumption, 2:576–7
carbohydrate consumption, 2:576–7
child, public expenditures for, 2:749–50
cholesterol consumption, 2:576–7
diet, *2:506–7*
fat consumption, 2:576–7
lifestyle choices, *2:506*
nutrient consumption, 2:572–3, 2:576–7
protein consumption, 2:576–7
Nuts, tree, 4:122–4. *See also specific nuts*

OASDHI. *See* Old-Age, Survivors, Disability, and Health Insurance
Oats, acreage, price, and production, *4:16,* 4:92–6
Occupations, *1:693–4, 2:35–40,* 2:133–253. *See also* Employment; *specific occupations*
of American Indians, 1:767–72
blue collar, *2:38*
consumer expenditures by occupation class, 3:286
distribution, *2:38*
earnings, 2:271–2
of economically active population, 2:232–53
employment, cost indexes, 2:295–300
groups, major, 2:133
immigrants by, *1:536,* 1:590–6, 1:618–20
by nativity, 2:212–131, 2:253
by race, 2:136–9, 2:172–211, 2:253
by sex, 1:618–20, 1:770, 2:134–9, 2:152–211, 2:253
skill differential, *2:42*

Numbers in italics refer to pages in essays; numbers not in italics refer to pages in statistical tables.

Occupations (*continued*)
wages, 2:266
white collar, *2:38–9*
Ocean shipping, 4:877
Oceania
bilateral exchange rates, 5:575–8
emigration to, 1:551
exports to, 5:534–9
immigration from, 1:555–8, 1:583–5
imports from, 5:540–5
refugees and asylees from, 1:635
U.S. population born in, 1:605, 1:608, 1:611
Ohio. *See also* State data
business incorporations, 3:539–47
canals, 4:881
charitable giving, 2:929
Ohio River Valley, wholesale price indexes, 3:195–6
Oil. *See also specific oils*
crude
imports and exports, 4:342–4
reserves, by country, 4:344–5
employees, 4:286–7
pipelines, 4:973–5
spills, U.S. water, 3:373
Oklahoma. *See* State data
Old-age assistance
payments, 2:798–803
recipients, 2:798–801
Old-Age, Survivors, and Disability Insurance Programs
benefits, 2:766–7, 2:777–9
disability, 2:761
retired-worker beneficiaries, 2:770–2
retirement, 2:761
trust fund, receipts, expenditures, and assets, 2:773–6
Old-Age, Survivors, Disability, and Health Insurance (OASDHI)
benefits
families receiving current-pay, 2:768–9
retired worker, by sex, 2:779–80
covered workers, 2:762–5
earnings, 2:762–5
employers, 2:762–5
expenditures for, public, 2:739–41
funding, *2:707–8*
self-employment net earnings and coverage, 2:751–2
tax rates, 2:762–5
Onions, acreage, price, and production, 4:161–4
Operatives and kindred workers, 2:148–9
American Indian, 1:770
economically active, 2:242–6
immigrants, 1:590–6, 1:618–20
by nativity, 2:218–19, 2:228–9
by race, 2:178–9, 2:188–9, 2:198–9, 2:208–9
by sex, 1:618–20, 1:770, 2:158–9, 2:168–9, 2:178–9, 2:188–9, 2:198–9, 2:208–9
Ophthalmic products and artificial limbs, 3:267–72
Opposition Party, 5:200–3
Oranges, acreage, price, and production, 4:128–30
Orchestras, 2:885–7
Oregon, 4:783–4. *See also* State data
Organizations. *See specific organizations*
Orphans, immigrant, 1:631
Orthopedic impairment, 2:410, 2:618–19
Outdoor pensioners, public relief, 2:722–3
Outlying areas, *5:587–92,* 5:594–625. *See also specific outlying areas*
acquisition and political status, *5:590–1*
consumer price indexes, 5:619–20
crop production, 5:608–9
definition, *5:587*
economic statistics, 5:604–20
education, 5:599–603
Outlying areas (*continued*)
employment, 5:605–7
exports, 5:610–12
government, 5:621–5
gross domestic product, 5:604–5
imports, 5:612–14
infant mortality, 5:597–8
population, 1:39, 5:594–603
revenues, 5:621–3
social statistics, 5:594–603
telephones in, 5:617–18
territorial expansion of the United States, *3:335–6*
unemployment, 5:607
visitor arrivals, 5:615–16
vital facts, *5:589*
Ovarian cancer, 2:568–71

Pacific Islands. *See* Asia and Pacific Islands
Pacific States. *See* Regional data
Pakistan, U.S. population born in, 1:610
Palau. *See also* Outlying areas
education, 5:599–603
employment, 5:605–7
exports, 5:610–12
government revenues and expenditures, 5:624–5
gross domestic product, 5:604–5
imports, 5:612–14
infant mortality, 5:597–8
population, 1:39, 5:594–5
telephones in, 5:617–18
unemployment, 5:607
visitor arrivals, 5:615–16
Palestine, U.S. population born in, 1:604, 1:607, 1:610
Panama
immigration from, 1:574–6
U.S. population born in, 1:612
Panama Canal, 4:895
Pancreas cancer, 2:568–71
Paper. *See also* Pulp, paper, and allied products; Stationery and supplies
and board, 4:391–3
commercial, 3:810–11
manufacturing, paper and allied products, 4:583–617
patents granted, 3:430–44
Paraguay, U.S. population born in, 1:611
Parent Teacher Association, 2:888–92
Parks and recreation, government expenditures on, 3:365
Partnerships, business, *3:480–2*
active, 3:512–13
agriculture, forestry, and fishing, 3:499–502
construction, 3:505–7
finance, insurance, and real estate, 3:514–15
manufacturing, 3:508–9
mining, 3:503–5
number, 3:495–520
profit, 3:495–520
receipts, 3:495–520
services, 3:516–17
transportation, communications, and utilities, 3:510–11
agriculture, forestry, and fishing, 3:499–502
construction, 3:505–7, 3:523
distribution of firms and firm receipts, *3:480*
finance, insurance, and real estate, 3:514–15, 3:527
general, *3:491,* 3:520–8
construction, 3:523
distribution industries, 3:526
finance, insurance, and real estate, 3:527
manufacturing, 3:524
mining, 3:522
number, partners, and profit, 3:520–8
Partnerships (*continued*)
services, 3:528
transportation, communications, and utilities, 3:525
limited, *3:491*
construction, 3:523
distribution industries, 3:526
finance, insurance, and real estate, 3:527
manufacturing, 3:524
mining, 3:522
number, partners, and profit, 3:520–8
services, 3:528
transportation, communications, and utilities, 3:525
manufacturing, 3:508–9, 3:524
mining, 3:503–5, 3:522
trade, wholesale and retail, 3:512–13
transportation, communications, and utilities, 3:510–11, 3:525
Patents, 3:422–45
applications filed, 3:425–9
granted, 3:430–44
issued, 3:425–9
Paupers
almshouse admittance of, 2:728
enumerated in almshouses, 2:725–7
support, 2:724
Peace and Freedom Party, 5:172–9
Peaches, price and production, 4:124–7
Peanuts
acreage, price, and production, 4:119–21
commodity program provisions, 4:249–51
Pears, production and price, 4:135–7
Pecans, acreage, price, and production, 4:140–2
Pennsylvania, 3:539–47. *See also* State data
Pension, private
beneficiaries, 2:828–9
consumer expenditures, 3:273–5
contributions, 2:828–9
coverage, estimated, 2:828–9
payments, 2:828–9
profit sharing, 2:291
reserves, 2:828–9
People's Party
presidential candidates, 5:172–9
presidential elections, popular votes, 5:184–92
Peppers, acreage, price, and production, 4:161–4
Periodicals, 4:1050–9. *See also* Magazines and newspapers
circulation, 4:1055
number, 4:1055, 4:1057–8
Perishable commodities, 3:267–70
Persian Gulf War, 5:350–1
Personal care
consumer expenditures on, 3:230–66, 3:273–5, 3:278–86
price indexes, 3:165–6
Personal income, 1:618
Personal saving, 3:298–9
by assets and liabilities, 3:300–6
derivation, 3:310–12
nonagricultural individuals, 3:304–6
nonprofit institutions, 3:304–6
rates, *3:291,* 3:312–13
Personal service industries
national income originating in, 4:1080–1
persons engaged in, 4:1079–80
Pertussis (whooping cough), 2:564–6
Peru
immigration from, 1:579–80
U.S. population born in, 1:612
Petroleum, *4:279*
coal products and, 4:583–617
consumption, 4:693
energy, 4:337–9
transportation, 4:797

Petroleum (*continued*)
crude, 4:298–9
energy production, 4:335–7
foreign countries' direct investment in the United States, 5:479–82
fuel mineral production, 4:288–91
imports and exports, 4:341
patents granted, 3:430–44
product, physical, 4:627–46
products, imports and exports, 4:342–4
refineries, input and output, 4:295
U.S. direct investment in foreign countries, 5:473–8
Philadelphia. *See also* Metropolitan areas
colonial population, 5:655
colonial prices
select commodities, 5:677–80
ships, 5:680–1
homicides, number, indictments, and rates, 5:248–9
poor relief, 2:720–2
price indexes, 3:192–5
public relief recipients, 2:722–3
vessels clearing, in colonial foreign commerce, 5:722–4
wages, 2:258
Philanthropic giving, *2:841,* 2:923–34
Catholic school, 2:921–2
corporate, 2:931–3
international, by the United States, 2:933–4
religious and secular, 2:914–20
revenue, 2:923–6
Philippines. *See also* Outlying areas
consumer price indexes, 5:619–20
crop production, 5:608–9
education, 5:599–603
emigration from, 1:566–70
exports, 5:610–12
government revenues and expenditures, 5:621–3
imports, 5:612–14
population, 1:39, 5:594–5
U.S. population born in, 1:604, 1:607, 1:610
Phosphate rock
imports and exports, 4:333–4
production, 4:323–5
value, 4:326–8
Physicians, 2:541–5
expenditures for, 3:230–66
patient care, 2:548
patient contacts, 2:549
price indexes, consumer, 3:165–6
by type of practice, 2:548
Pig iron
imports and exports, 4:329–33, 5:737–40
production, 3:116–20, 4:308–11
Pipelines, *4:774,* 4:973–5
gas, 4:975
oil, 4:973–5
operating revenues, 4:788–9
Plastic. *See* Rubber and plastic products
Plate glass, 3:116–20
Pleasure craft, commodity value, 3:267–70. *See also* Vessels
Plums, production and price, 4:135–7
Point-of-sale terminals, 3:670
Poland
immigration from, 1:560–5
U.S. population born in, 1:602, 1:606, 1:609
Poliomyelitis, 2:564–6
Political party affiliations, 5:200–7
administrations, 5:200–3
Congress, 5:200–3
president, 5:200–3
Politics, *5:141–58,* 5:161–207
chronology, *5:153–8*
party affiliation, 5:200–7
Politics (*continued*)
party identification, *5:150–1*
policy mood, *5:151,* 5:205
public opinion on, *5:150–2,* 5:200–7
survey data, *5:151–2*
Pollution. *See also* Emissions; Environment
air pollutants, *3:339*
concentration, 3:368
emissions, 3:368, 3:370
motor vehicle, 4:851–4
control and abatement, government expenditures for, 3:365
Poor relief, 2:720–33
almshouses, *2:698*
expenditures, 2:721–2
paupers admitted to, 2:728
paupers enumerated in, 2:725–7
public relief, 2:722–3
expenditures, 2:720–2, 2:729–31
pauper support, 2:724–8
recipients, 2:720
tax levied, 2:720
Poorhouses, 2:732–3
Popular votes, *5:147–8*
by candidate, 5:172–9
by party and state, 5:184–92
Population, *1:1–24. See also* Foreign-born population; Poverty population; Slave population; *specific races*
age, 1:36, 1:40–101
American Indian, *1:715–24,* 1:726–77 (*see also* American Indian, Aleut, or Eskimo population)
reservations, 1:757–62
black, 1:36, 1:48–51, 1:61–5, 1:105–6 (*see also* Black population)
change, *1:3–4*
demographic components of, 1:31–4
net increase, *1:4,* 1:157–65
characteristics, *1:4, 1:17–24,* 1:24–379, 2:674–91
citizenship, 1:597–601, 1:614
civilian, 1:28–30
colonial, 5:651–64
city, 5:655
by race, colony, or locality, 5:651–5
by select characteristics, 5:657–64
Confederate States of America, 5:783–90
definition, *1:3*
density, 1:26–7
economically active, 2:232–53
farm, *1:492,* 1:519, *4:10–11,* 4:39–44
regional, 4:44–50
state, 4:44–50
foreign-born, 1:31–4, 1:36, 1:166–7, 1:170–1, *1:523–4,* 1:597–626, (*see also* Foreign-born population)
gender, *1:5–7*
geographic distribution, *1:11*
growth, 1:35–6
Hispanic, 1:177–9 (*see also* Hispanic population)
in households (*see also* Families; Households)
immigration, 1:157–65, *1:539,* 1:541–652 (*see also* Immigration)
in institutions, *1:13,* 1:669–70
marital status, 1:40–101, 1:72–101, 1:703–8 (*see also* Marital status)
migration, *1:489–93,* 1:495–521
nativity, 1:166–74, 1:180–379, 1:613, 1:615–22
foreign-born, 1:166–7, 1:170–1, 1:597–601, 1:613
Hispanic population, 1:177–8
labor force participants, 2:108–9
native-born, 1:169, 1:174, 1:615
Population (*continued*)
prisoner, *5:213* (*see also* Prisoners)
by race (*see specific races*)
residence
conterminous United States, 1:26–39, 1:157–65
farm, *1:492,* 1:519
metropolitan areas, 1:108–39
outlying areas, 1:39, 5:594–603
regions, 1:37–8
rural, 1:37–38, 1:102–49, 1:613, 1:740–1
urban, 1:36–8, 1:102–49, 1:613, 1:740–1
sex, 1:40–101, 1:36, 1:40–43, 1:48–56
American Indian, 1:735–6
in households, 1:679–84
institutional, 1:669–70
slave, 1:48–51, 1:175–6, 2:375–80 (*see also* Slave population)
total, 1:28–30
vital statistics (*see* Vital statistics)
white, 1:36, 1:48–51, 1:57–60, 1:105–6
Populist Party, 5:172–9
Pork
hogs, 3:116–20
prices, and production, 4:172–8
Portugal
immigration from, 1:560–4, 1:564–5
U.S. population born in, 1:603, 1:607, 1:609
Postal Savings System, 3:685–6
Postal service, *4:981–4. See also* Postal Service, U.S.
post offices and pieces handled, *4:982*
Postal Service, U.S., 4:1038–49
employees, 4:1042–6
finances, 4:1038–42
by class of mail, 4:1042–6
items issued, 4:1038–42
pieces handled, 4:1038–42
by class of mail, 4:1042–6
post offices, 4:1038–42
rates
single letter, by distance, 4:1046
by zone and type of mail, 4:1047–8
Potash, 4:329–34
Potatoes, 4:116–19
Poultry. *See* Meat, poultry, fish, seafood, and eggs; *specific types of poultry*
Poverty, *2:621–49,* 2:652–91. *See also* Poverty lines; Poverty population
aged poor, *2:646*
children in, 2:668–73, 2:681–3
counts and rates, *2:640–4*
definitions, *2:625–49*
families in, *2:629, 2:645,* 2:663–73, 2:680–1
opinion polls, *2:646*
regional variation, *2:646*
thresholds, official, *2:626*
by age, 2:680–1, 2:687–9
families below, 2:677–9
by family size, 2:664–7, 2:670–3
history, *2:626–7*
by number of children younger than age 18, 2:670–3
persons below, 2:674–6
by residence, 2:670–3, 2:684–7
by sex of head of household, 2:670–3
Poverty lines, *2:629–39, 2:645,* 2:663–73. *See also* Poverty; Poverty population
Poverty population
by age, *2:628*
characteristics of, 2:674–91
definition, *2:647*
by employment status, *2:630*
persons below poverty threshold, 2:674–6, 2:690–1

Numbers in italics refer to pages in essays; numbers not in italics refer to pages in statistical tables.

Poverty population (*continued*)
by sex, 2:674–6
by race and ethnicity, *2:628,* 2:674–6
rates, *2:640–4*
severely poor, *2:646*
working poor, *2:646*
Power
consumption, 4:347–8, 4:676–98
manufacturing, 4:697–8
equipment, 4:583–617, 4:696
Precipitation
annual, at climatological stations, 3:395, 3:406
chemistry, by region, 3:367
normal, averages, 3:381–2
total, at long-record city stations, 3:407, 3:414
Precision production, craft, and repair, 1:771
Preference system, alien admissions, 1:628–9. *See also* Immigration
Pregnancy rates, 1:417–19
Presbyterian Church membership, 2:904–9
Prescription drugs. *See also* Drugs
consumption expenditures for, 3:230–66
price indexes, 3:165–6, 3:180–3
Presidents, political party affiliations of, 5:200–3
Presidential approval rating, *5:151–2,* 5:206–7
Presidential vetoes, *5:149*
Prices and price indexes, *3:147–56, 3:158–224*
aggregate, *3:151–3*
agricultural commodities, 3:192–5
apparel and textile products
consumer, 3:160, 3:163–4, 3:167
producer, 3:171–2
wholesale, 3:171–2, 3:175–7, 3:180–6, 3:199–201
automobile, 3:170, 3:173–4
colonial, 5:674–91, 5:822–4
Confederate States of America, *5:776–8, 5:780,* 5:791–9
monthly commodity, 5:797–9
wholesale commodity prices, 5:794–5
consumer, 3:141–5, *3:149, 3:154–6,* 3:158–70
outlying areas, 5:619–20 (*see also specific commodities*)
urban area, 3:161–6
during the Great Depression, 3:141–5
inflation, *3:149*
price index construction/use, *3:147–51*
price level, changes in, *3:148–50*
producer, 3:141–5, *3:149,* 3:153–4, 3:171–201
rent, residential, 3:160, 3:163–4, 3:167–9
wholesale, *3:149,* 3:153–4, 3:171–201
by city, 3:187–201
by commodity, 3:171–7, 3:180–6, 3:192–5, 3:199–201, 3:202–24
exports and imports, 3:187–91
by stage of processing, 3:179
Printing and publishing, books. *See also* Books
manufacturing summary, 4:583–617
value of, as commodities, 3:267–70
Prisoners, *5:222, 5:820–1. See also* Correctional institutions
executed, by race and offense, 5:262–3
population, by race, *5:213*
released, by type of release, 5:260–1
sentenced
by race, 5:258–9
by sex, 5:256–7
in state and federal institutions, 5:256–9
Prisons. *See* Correctional institutions
Private business enterprises, national income originating in, 3:31–2
Private household workers, 2:150
American Indian, 1:768–70
economically active, 2:246
immigrants, 1:593–6, 1:618–20
by industry, 2:121–2
by nativity, 2:220, 2:230
by race, 2:180, 2:190, 2:200, 2:210
by sex, 1:618–20, 1:768–70, 2:160, 2:170, 2:180, 2:190, 2:200, 2:210
wages and salaries, 2:282–3, 2:293
Production workers, by industry, 2:115–16, 2:129–31. *See also specific industries*
Productivity, *3:415–21,* 3:422–75
agricultural, *4:19–27* (*see also* Agriculture: productivity)
definition, *3:418–19*
employee output
food and beverage industry, 3:470–1
manufacturing industry, 3:472–3
mining and mineral industry, 3:467–9
per hour, 3:469, 3:471, 3:473, 3:475
service industry, 3:474–5
utilities, 3:474–5
fluctuations, *3:420–1*
indexes
by sector, 3:463–7
by type of good, 3:466–7
by type of input, 3:463–5
labor, nonfarm, *3:419*
national, 3:463–7
total factor productivity (TFP), *3:419–20,* 4:215–18
trends, *3:420–1*
Professional, technical, and kindred workers, 1:772, 2:142–4
American Indian, 1:770
economically active, 2:232–4
immigrant, 1:590–6, 1:618–20
by nativity, 2:212–14, 2:222–4
by race, 2:172–4, 2:182–4, 2:192–4, 2:202–4
by sex, 1:618–20, 1:770, 2:152–4, 2:162–4, 2:172–4, 2:182–4, 2:192–4, 2:202–4
Profit-sharing plans, 2:828–9
Progressive Party
presidential candidates, 5:172–9
presidential elections, popular votes received, 5:184–92
Prohibition Party, 5:172–9
Property
damage, bombing incidents, 5:255
insurance, 3:731–55
taxable, Confederacy, 5:787
Property liability insurance
business assets, 3:749–50
policyholders' surplus, 3:749–50
premiums written, 3:749–50
Proprietors' income
national income originating in, 3:29–30
personal, 3:36–7
Proprietorships, *3:480–2,* 3:512–13
active, 3:512–13
agriculture, forestry, and fishing, 3:499–502
construction, 3:505–7
finance, insurance, and real estate, 3:514–15
manufacturing, 3:508–9
mining, 3:503–5
number, 3:495–520
profit, 3:495–520
receipts, 3:495–520
services, 3:516–17
transportation, communications, and utilities, 3:510–11
by firm size, *3:480*
by sector, 3:495–520
trade, wholesale and retail, 3:512–13
Prostate cancer, 2:568–71
Protein consumption, 2:576–7
Protestant Episcopal Church
charitable and philanthropic giving to, 2:914–16
membership, 2:904–9
Prunes, production and price, 4:135–7
Public assistance, *2:693–717,* 2:720–835
almshouses, *2:698,* 2:722–3
children's asylums, 2:722–3
emergency, 2:800–3
expenditures, public, 2:734–6
fuel aid, 2:722–3
medical aid, 2:722–3, 2:795
old-age, 2:795
outdoor pensioners, 2:722–3
payments, 2:798–803
recipients, 2:798–801, 2:804–5
relief, *2:697–8*
recipients, by type of relief, 2:732–3
recipients, in Philadelphia, 2:722–3
Public broadcasting, 2:885–7
employment, 2:885–7
expenditures, 2:885–7
giving, 2:885–7
income, 2:885–7, 4:1037
stations, 4:1037
Public domain, *3:333, 3:336–7,* 3:349–50
acquisition, 3:349
cost, 3:349
disposal of, 3:350, 3:354
grazing on, 3:358–9
revenue, 3:356, 3:358
sales, 3:354–5
by use, 3:362
Public safety, government expenditures on, 5:19–25
federal, 5:32–7
intergovernmental, 5:65–8
local, 5:45–51, 5:73–9
state, 5:45–51, 5:58–64
Public transit. *See also under* Transportation
employees, 4:802–4
equipment, 4:802–4
fares, 4:795
mileage, 4:802–4
passengers, 4:802–4
revenue, 4:802–4
trips, 4:802–4
vehicle miles operated, 4:804–5
Puerto Rico. *See also* Outlying areas
consumer price indexes, 5:619–20
crop production, 5:608–9
education, 5:599–603
employment, 5:605–7
exports, 5:610–12
government revenues and expenditures, 5:621–3
gross domestic product, 5:604–5
imports, 5:612–14
infant mortality, 5:597–8
population, 1:39, 5:594–5
telephones in, 5:617–18
unemployment, 5:607
visitor arrivals, 5:615–16
Pullman Company, 4:952
Pulp, paper, and allied products
exports and imports, 4:391–3
price indexes, 3:173–4
production, 4:391–3
Pulpwood, 4:391–3
Pyrites
imports and exports, 4:333–4
production, 4:323–5

Quits, *2:51*
Quota system, alien admissions, 1:627–8

Numbers in italics refer to pages in essays; numbers not in italics refer to pages in statistical tables.

Race. *See specific races*
Radio, *4:993–6,* 4:1027–37. *See also* Public broadcasting
advertising
distribution, 4:752–6
expenditures, 4:1030–3
broadcast systems, *4:994*
employment, 4:1030–3
finances, 4:1030–3
households with, 4:1027–30
patents granted, 3:430–44
sets, *4:994,* 4:1027–30
stations, 4:1027–30
special and safety stations, 4:1035–6
Radios and musical instruments, consumption expenditures for, 3:270–2
Radiotelegraph rates, 4:1005–7
Railroads, *4:770–1,* 4:915–53. *See also* Amtrak; Pullman Company
capital expenditures, 4:920, 4:922, 4:935–7, 4:949
construction, public land grants aiding, 3:355
disability insurance, 2:739–41, 2:761
dividends, 4:937–9, 4:950
electric, 4:941
employees, 4:792
compensation, 4:940
equipment, 4:916–17, 4:923–8, 4:945–6
expenses, 4:937–9, 4:950
federal aid for internal improvements, 4:780
federal land grants, 4:919
freight services
operations, 4:947–8
rates, 4:879
revenue, 4:921, 4:932–4
speed, 4:929–31
traffic, 4:919, 4:929–34
volume, 4:921, 4:929–31
fuel received, 4:944–5
highway grade crossings, 4:943
income, 4:937–9, 4:950
indexes, 4:922
injuries and fatalities, 2:330–1, 2:333–5
inputs, 4:922
insurance, unemployment, 2:783–5
interest, 4:937–9, 4:950
investment, by region, 4:915
map, *4:772*
mileage, *4:771,* 4:916–18, 4:923–8, 4:931, 4:945–6
operating revenues, 4:788–9
outputs, 4:922
passenger fares, 4:795, 4:880
passenger services
revenue, 4:921, 4:923–8, 4:945–6
speed, 4:929–31
traffic, 4:923–31, 4:945–6
volume, 4:921, 4:929–31
productivity, 4:922
property investment, capital, and capital expenditures, 4:920, 4:922, 4:935–7, 4:949
purchases, 4:944–5, 4:951
receipts, 4:919
retirement, 2:739–41, 2:761, 2:816–17
revenues, 4:921–8, 4:932–4, 4:945–6, 4:948
road mileage operated, 4:919
sickness benefits, 2:783–5
speeds and travel time, 4:880
tax accruals, 4:942
ties and rails laid, 4:944–5, 4:951
transportation firms, employees, 4:792
work hours, 2:308
Railways, electric, 4:941
Rape
prisoners executed for, 5:262–3
rates, *5:218*
Rape (*continued*)
urban, 5:225
Reading. *See also specific media*
consumer expenditures on, 3:273–5, 3:278–86
student proficiency, 2:425–30
Real estate, 1:621–2, 1:772
business incorporations, 3:539–47
companies and corporations, 3:514–15, 3:576–7
earnings, 2:277–9
employees, 2:111–14, 3:683–4
female, 2:114
production, 2:115–16, 2:129–32
employment
full-time, 2:117–19
hours of work, 2:305–7
injury and illness rates, 2:332–3
farm, debt, 4:270–1
labor force participants engaged in, 2:101
by nativity, 2:108–9
by race, 2:104–7
by sex, 2:102–7
wages and salaries, 2:282–3, 2:293
Receipts. *See specific industries*
Recessions, *3:71–7. See also* Depressions
definition, *3:71, 3:207–11*
Recreation, 4:1107–19. *See also* Entertainment and recreation services
activities, participation, 4:1115–17
consumption expenditures for, 3:230–66, 3:278–86
goods, personal, 4:1107–8
services, personal, 4:1108–9
government expenditures for, 3:365
national income originating in, 4:1080–1
Red Cross, National, 2:888–92
Reform Party, 5:172–9
Refugees and asylees, 1:632–5
Regional data. *See also* Census regions and divisions
agricultural productivity, 4:212–14
multifactor, 4:218–19
American Indian population, 1:726–34, 1:737–41
Antebellum South
banking, *3:589–90, 3:617–18*
slave values, 2:383
slavery, *2:370–2*
canal investment, state and private, 4:882
charitable and voluntary organizations, 2:852
colonial
business establishments, 5:706
wealth, private, per free person, 5:672–3
earnings
farm laborers, 2:260
monthly, 2:261
education
liberal arts colleges, 2:876
school attendance, 1:773
farms
acreage, 4:54–7
buildings, 4:57–64
laborers, earnings, 2:260
land, 4:50–3, 4:57–64
operators, 4:66–7, 4:72–3
output, 4:207–8
population, 4:44–50
products, value of sold, 4:64–6
fertility ratios, 1:426–7
firearm possession, 5:310
homeownership rates, 4:509–12
homes, manufactured, 4:498–9
houses, for sale
multifamily, 4:495–7
price indexes, repeat sales, 4:519–20
single-family, 4:492–4
housing units
Regional data (*continued*)
occupied, 4:506–8
started, 4:489–90
started and authorized by permit, 4:481–8
illness
acute infective and parasitic conditions, 2:605–7
bed-disability days, 2:590–2
digestive conditions, acute, 2:611–13
respiratory conditions, acute, 2:608–10
restricted-activity days, 2:587–9
work-loss and school-loss days, 2:593–5
land, agricultural, 4:212–14
lynching victims, 5:252–5
merchant vessels, gross tonnage, 4:874–6, 4:881, 4:886–7
migration
internal, *1:493,* 1:498
international, 1:544
nonprofit and voluntary institutions, 2:851
paupers
admitted to almshouses, 2:728
enumerated in almshouses, 2:725–7
poverty, *2:646*
persons below thresholds, 2:686–7
precipitation
chemistry, 3:367
climatological stations, 3:381–2, 3:395, 3:406
railroad investment, 4:915
religious institutions, attendance, 2:900–3
shellfish bed closures, 3:372
slavery, *2:370–2*
slave values, 2:383
temperatures
at climatological stations, 3:378, 3:380, 3:383–4
vacancy rates, 4:513–14
wages of common labor, 2:264
work-loss and school-loss days, 2:593–5
bed-disability days, 2:590–2
restricted-activity days, 2:587–9
Regional economic development. *See* Community and regional development
Religious institutions, *2:837–48,* 2:900–22. *See also specific religions*
attendance, 2:900–3
charitable and philanthropic giving to, 2:919–20
by denomination, 2:914–16
churches and congregations, *2:847,* 2:900–3
accommodations, 2:911
membership, 2:904–9, 2:912–14
by state, 2:909–10
clergy, 2:900–3
consumption expenditures on, 3:230–42
definition, *2:837–9*
expenditures for and contributions to, personal, 2:914–16
income, sources, 2:919–20
membership, 2:900–3
per capita, 2:851
synagogues, 2:900–3
Renewable energy, 4:340
Rent, residential
multifamily houses, 4:495–7
price indexes, 3:160, 3:163–4, 3:167, 3:169
New York City, 3:168
Rental income
national income originating in, 3:29–30
personal, 3:36–7
Repair services, 1:621–2, 1:772
Republican Party, 5:172–9, 5:200–3
congressional affiliations with, 5:200–3
House candidates, votes cast, 5:193
party identification, 5:204
presidential affiliations with, 5:200–3
presidential candidates, 5:172–9

Republican party (*continued*)
presidential elections
electoral votes, 5:180–3
popular votes, 5:184–92
Senate candidates, votes cast, 5:194
Research and development, 3:446–58
agricultural
federal and state, 4:220–2
private-sector spending, 4:223
expenditures for, 3:446–52
industrial, 3:455–6
federal obligations, by agency, 3:453–5
industrial, expenditures, 3:455–6
Reservoirs, *4:1070*
Residential structures, private
stock, *4:396,* 4:414–19
value of new construction, by type, 4:450–4
Respiratory conditions, 2:608–10, 2:615
Retail trade, 4:720–41
chain stores, 4:728
department store sales and stocks, 4:737
establishments, by type of business, 4:720–2
margins, by type of business, 4:732
multiunit firms, sales, 4:729–31
persons engaged in, by type of business, 4:724–6
sales, by type of business, 4:722–4, 4:733–7
service establishments, 4:738–41
by type of business, 4:726–8
Retirement. *See also* Old-Age, Surviors, and Disability Insurance Programs; Old-Age, Survivors, Disability, and Health Insurance
beneficiaries, 2:779–80
female, 2:771–2
male, 2:770–1
civil service, 2:812–15
employee benefits, 2:824–7
federal employees, 2:812–13
medical care, vendor payments for, 2:795
public employees, 2:739–41
railroad, 2:761
benefits, 2:816–17
expenditures, public, 2:739–41
veterans programs, 2:754–9
Revolutionary War
casualties, 5:350–1
estimated cost, 5:370
military personnel, 5:350–1
Rhinitis, 2:615
Rhode Island, 5:659. *See also* State data
Rice
acreage, price, and production, 4:92–6
colonial prices, wholesale, 5:688–90
commodity program provisions, 4:245–8
exports, colonial
from Charleston, 5:767
from South Carolina and Georgia, 5:763–6
Right to Life Party, 5:172–9
Rivers and streams
federal aid for internal improvements, 4:780
federal expenditures and appropriations, 4:883
improvements, land grants aiding, 3:355
water quality, 3:371–2
Roads and streets, 4:806–57
federal aid for internal improvements, 4:780
mileage
by jurisdiction, 4:807–9
municipal streets, 4:806–8
public, 4:808–10
rural, 4:806–8
state highway, 4:810
by surface type, 4:809–10
by urban-rural location, 4:809–10
municipal streets
mileage, 4:807–8
surfaced mileage, 4:806
Roads and streets (*continued*)
public, mileage, 4:808–10
rural
mileage, 4:807–8
surfaced mileage, 4:806
Robberies, 5:225. *See also* Crime
Romania, U.S. population born in, 1:603, 1:607, 1:609
Rotary, 2:888–92
Rubber and plastic products
imports, 5:553–60
manufacturing, 4:583–617
patents granted, 3:430–44
price indexes, 3:171–2
Rural areas, 1:102–4
American Indian population, 1:740–1
births and birth rates, 1:439
earnings, 2:261
fertility ratios, 1:426–7
population, 1:37–8, 1:102–49, 1:613
by state, 1:180–379
Rural Electrification Administration, 4:1103–4
Rural Utilities Service, 4:1103–4
Russia. *See also* Soviet Union and Baltic states; Union of Soviet Socialist Republics
space launches, commercial, 3:458
U.S. population born in, 1:603, 1:606
Rye, acreage, price, and production, 4:106–9

Salaried employees, consumer expenditures on, 3:280, 3:282–6
Salt
production, 4:323–5
value, 4:326–8
Salvation Army, 2:904–9
San Francisco. *See also* Metropolitan areas
gold-dollar exchange rates, 3:199–201
price indexes, 3:199–201
travel times, 4:779
Sand and gravel, 4:323–8
Sanitation. *See also* Electric, gas, and sanitary services
city, operating and capital costs for, 4:1105
government expenditures on, *4:1070*
gross domestic product, as component of, 4:1094
Saudi Arabia, U.S. population born in, 1:610
Savings, *3:287–95,* 3:298–332
corporate, 3:298–9
definitions, *3:287–90*
government, 3:298–9
gross, by sector and type, 3:306–9
household, interest rates, 3:828–30
national, *3:290,* 3:298–9
net, 3:298–9
rates, *3:290,* 3:312–13
personal, *3:291,* 3:298–9
by assets and liabilities, 3:300–6
derivation, 3:310–12
rates, 3:312–13
private, *3:290, 3:292–4*
Savings and loan associations
assets, 3:676–80
expenses, 3:682
Federal Home Loan Bank, 3:681
income, 3:682
insured
assets, 3:680
expenses, 3:682
income, 3:682
liabilities, 3:680
number, 3:680
liabilities, 3:678–80
number, 3:674–5, 3:678–80
Savings Association Insurance Fund, 3:729–30
Savings institutions, 3:671–82. *See also* Federal Savings and Loan Insurance Corporation; Mutual savings banks; Savings Association Insurance Fund
failed, 3:723
insured, 3:723
FDIC-insured, 3:720–2
Scandinavia. *See also specific countries*
immigration from, *1:534,* 1:560–5
U.S. population born in, 1:601
Scarlet fever, 2:564–6
School Lunch Program, 2:806–8
Schools. *See* Education
Science, *3:415–21,* 3:422–75. *See also* Science, space, and technology
definition, *3:415*
Science, space, and technology, federal government expenditures on, 5:106–8
Scientists
natural, 2:143
by nativity, 2:213, 2:223
by race, 2:173, 2:183, 2:193, 2:203
by sex, 2:153, 2:163, 2:173, 2:183, 2:193, 2:203
social, 2:144
by nativity, 2:214, 2:224
by race, 2:174, 2:184, 2:194, 2:204
by sex, 2:154, 2:164, 2:174, 2:184, 2:194, 2:204
S-corporations
assets, 3:580
dividends, 3:580
liabilities, 3:580
limited liability, *3:491*
receipts, 3:580
Scotland
colonial foreign commerce, 5:714–16
U.S. population born in, 1:601, 1:606, 1:609
Seafood. *See* Meat, poultry, fish, seafood, and eggs; Shellfish; *specific types of seafood*
Sealskin harvesting, 4:375
Second Bank of the United States
assets, 3:639
dividend rates, 3:640
liabilities, 3:639
profits, 3:640
Secondary school enrollment, outlying areas, 5:602–3. *See also* Education
Securities and bond markets, *3:592–3, 3:623,* 3:756–73. *See also* Equity and bond markets; Stock market
equity securities, 3:789–90
mortgage related, 4:560–2
state and local government, 3:767
stock and bond sales, 3:768–9
yields, during the Great Depression, 3:130–5
Selective Service
defendants charged with violation of Act, 5:366
draftees, 5:363–4
registrants, by classification, 5:365
Self-employment, 1:617
by industry, 2:120–7, *4:1066*
rate, 2:126–7
by sex, 2:126–7
Semidurable commodities value, 3:267–70
Senate
political party affiliations, 5:200–3
votes cast, by party, 5:194
Senegal, U.S. population born in, 1:611
Separations, marital, *2:51.* *See also* Divorce; Marital status
Service industries, 1:621–2, 1:772, 2:150–1. *See also specific service industries*
administrative organizations, central, 3:560
business incorporations, 3:539–47
consumer behavior, *4:1067*

Numbers in italics refer to pages in essays; numbers not in italics refer to pages in statistical tables.

Service industries (*continued*)
consumption, 3:230–42, *4:1067*
earnings, 2:273, 2:277–9
employees, 2:111–14, 4:1073–92
economically active, 2:246–7
full-time, 2:117–19
hours of work, 2:305–7
output per employee, 3:474–5
production, 2:115–16, 2:129–32
by sex, 2:114, 2:160, 2:170
establishments, 3:560, 4:1082–92
firms, 3:529–30, 3:560, 3:578–9
gross product and national income originating in, 3:32–5, *4:1062, 4:1065,* 4:1074–5, 4:1077–8, 4:1080–1
injury and illness rates, occupational, 2:332–3
labor force, 2:110–11, *4:1062,* 4:1076–7, 4:1079–80
labor force participants engaged in, 2:101
by nativity, 2:108–9
by race, 2:104–7
by sex, 2:102–7
limited liability companies, 3:528
output, 4:1073–81
payroll, 4:1087–8
proprietorships, partnerships, and corporations, 3:516–7, 3:528
receipts, 4:1082–92
revenue, 4:1087
sector definition, *4:1062–3*
self-employed in, *4:1066*
by sex, 2:180, 2:190, 2:200, 2:210
union membership, 2:347
value added, 4:1073–4
wages and salaries, 2:282–3, 2:293
workplace size, *2:53,* 2:324
Service occupations, 2:888–92
Seventh-Day Adventist Church membership, 2:904–9
Sewers, *4:1070*
government expenditures for, 3:365
value of new construction, 4:468–9
by financing, 4:470–1
by ownership, 4:470–5, 4:477–8
Sheep
number, 4:165–9, 4:171
price, production, and value per head, 4:165–9
Shellfish
aquaculture production, 4:372
bed closures, by region, 3:372
fishery products, 4:368–9
landed catches, 4:363–5
Shipbuilding, private shipyard, 4:912–13
Shoes, 3:163–4
value of, as commodities produced, 3:267–70
women's, production, 3:116–20
SIC. *See* Standard Industrial Classification system
Sierra Leone, U.S. population born in, 1:611
Silk
consumption, 4:694–5
exported from South Carolina and Georgia, 5:749–50
imported, raw, 5:553–60
trade between England and Carolinas, 5:751
Silver
bonds, Confederate States of America, 5:802
exports, 5:498–503
imports, 5:498–503
production, 4:315–18, 4:321–3
Singapore, U.S. population born in, 1:610
Single parents, *1:656–7,* 1:670–2, 1:674–5. *See also* Marital status
Single Party, 5:172–9
Single persons. *See* Marital status
Sinusitis, 2:615
Skin conditions, 2:616–17
Slave labor, *2:10,* 2:110–11
prices, *2:372,* 2:381–3
by state
female, 2:76
male, 2:75
Slave owners. *See* Slaveholders
Slave population, 1:48–51, 1:175–6, 2:375–80
by city (Southern), 2:377
colonial, 5:658, 5:663
estimates, annual, 2:381–2
fugitive, 2:384–5
height, 2:582–5
manumitted, 2:384–5
by race, 5:783
by sex, 2:378
by state, 2:375–8, 5:658, 5:663, 5:783
Slave revolts, 2:384–5
Slave states, 5:784–6
Slave trade, *2:369–70*
by colony, 5:669–70
by origin or destination, 5:669–70
prices, *2:372,* 2:381–3
colonial, 5:690–1
Slaveholders
families, by state, 2:379
by size of slaveholdings, 2:380
Slavery, *2:369–73*
abolition, *1:694–5*
in Antebellum South, *2:370–2*
in colonial North America, *2:369–70*
definition, *2:369*
economics, *2:372–3*
gross domestic product and gross national product, *3:16,* 3:23–8, 3:69
emancipation, *2:371*
Smallpox
in American Indians, 1:743
incidence, 2:564–6
Smoking, cigarette, by education and sex, *2:506,* 2:578–80. *See also* Cigarettes, cigars, and tobacco; Tobacco
Snap beans, acreage, price, and production, 4:146–9
Social insurance, 2:291, *2:693–717,* 2:720–835. *See also* Social Security
disability, *2:703–6*
expenditures, public, 2:734–8
old-age, *2:703–6*
personal contributions for, 3:16
programs, *2:702–11*
employment covered under, 2:751–3
government, 2:751–2
veterans, 2:754–61
Social Security
consumer expenditures, 3:273–5
government expenditures, 5:105–8
income, supplemental, 2:741–2
Old-Age, Survivors Insurance Programs under, *2:705*
Social services and income maintenance, government expenditures for, 5:19–25
federal, 5:32–9
local, 5:45–51, 5:73–9
state, 5:45–51, 5:58–68
Social services and membership organizations
national income originating in, 4:1080–1
persons engaged in, 4:1079–80
Social welfare
definition, *2:693*
expenditures, 2:734–50
federal government, 2:737–8
funding source, 2:737–8
private, 2:820–3
on programs, 2:743–6
public, 2:734–6, 2:739–50
state and local government, 2:737–8
Social welfare (*continued*)
housing, 2:747–8
policies, legislation and event affecting, *2:695–6*
private, *2:716–17,* 2:820–3
programs, *2:716,* 2:743–6, 2:751–819
public assistance, *2:693–9, 2:711–14*
Socialist Labor Party, 5:172–9
Socialist Party, 5:172–9
Socialist Workers Party, 5:172–9
Solar collectors, 4:355
Solar energy, 4:340
Solid waste, *4:1071*
disposal, *4:1071,* 4:1106
generation, *4:1071,* 4:1106
management
government expenditures for, 3:365
municipal, 3:370
Somalia, U.S. population born in, 1:610
Sorghum, price, 4:92–6
South Africa, U.S. population born in, 1:611
South America
immigration from, 1:555–8, 1:577–80
immigration to, 1:551
refugees and asylees from, 1:635
U.S. population born in, 1:604, 1:608, 1:612
South Atlantic States. *See* Regional data
South Carolina. *See also* State data
colonial
finances, 5:708
indigo and silk exported from, 5:749–50
price indexes, 3:187–91
silk trade between England and, 5:751
South Central States. *See* Regional data
South Dakota. *See* State data
Southern Baptist Church membership, 2:904–9
Soviet Union, U.S. population born in, 1:603, 1:606, 1:609. *See also* Russia; Soviet Union and Baltic states
Soviet Union and Baltic states, immigration from, 1:560–5
Soybeans
acreage, price, production, and stocks, *4:16,* 4:92–6, 4:138–9
commodity program provisions, 4:249–51
oil, 4:138–9
Space launches, commercial, 3:458
Spain
immigration from, 1:560–5
U.S. population born in, 1:603, 1:607, 1:609
Spanish–American War
casualties, 5:350–1
characteristics, 5:363–4
draftees, 5:363–4
estimated cost, 5:370
medical care, 5:363–4
military pay, 5:363–4
military personnel, 5:350–1, 5:363–4
Speech impairment, special education programs for individuals with, 2:410
Sports, 4:1107–19
professional, attendance at selected, 4:1113–14
Sri Lanka, U.S. population born in, 1:610
St. Kitts-Nevis, U.S. population born in, 1:611
St. Lucia, U.S. population born in, 1:611
St. Vincent and the Grenadines, U.S. population born in, 1:611
Standard Industrial Classification (SIC) system, *4:5*
State data. *See also* Confederate States of America; *specific states*
American Indians
lands, 1:749–52
population, 1:727–34, 1:737–9
benevolent institutions, 2:865–7

State data (*continued*)
charitable contributions, 2:929–30
churches and congregations, 2:909–14
congressional representation
apportionment population, 5:164
number of Representatives, 5:164
education, 1:773
elections, presidential
electoral votes, 5:180–3
methods, 5:171
popular votes, 5:184–92
farms, 4:44–66
household manufacturing, 2:363–4
incorporations, business, 3:531–6
land area, 3:346, 3:349
liberal arts colleges, 2:876
migration, interstate, *1:489–93,* 1:495–7, 1:505–18, 1:523
paupers, 2:724–8
population, 1:39, 1:180–379
black, 2:375–7
slave, 2:378, 2:384–5
white, colonial, 5:656
precipitation, at climatological stations, 3:381–2, 3:395, 3:406
railroads, federal land grants used by, 4:919
slavery
fugitive slaves, 2:384–5
manumitted slaves, 2:384–5
slave labor, 2:75–6
slave population, 2:378
slave revolts, 2:384–5
slave states, 5:783–4
slave/free status of black population, 2:375–7
slaveholding families, 2:379
social welfare programs, *2:709–10*
tax-exempt organizations, 2:863–4, 2:867–70
temperatures, at climatological stations, 3:378, 3:380, 3:383, 3:394
voluntary institutions, 2:895–6
voting rights, constitutional extensions of, *5:142*
women's suffrage, authorization, 2:367–8
workers, 2:67–74
Statehood, *5:815*
territorial legislation dates and admission to United States, *5:816*
States and census regions map, *5:814–17*
States' Rights Party
presidential candidates, 5:172–9
presidential elections, popular votes, 5:184–92
Stationery and supplies, commodity value, 3:267–70
Steamboats, 4:878–80
Steel rails, prices, wholesale, 3:212–17
Stock market
common stock prices, 3:756–60
indicators, during the Great Depression, 3:126–8
sales, New York Stock Exchange, 3:770
stock dividend yields, 3:760–3
Stomach cancer, 2:568–71
Stone, clay, and glass products, 4:583–617
Stone mining value, 4:326–8
Straight Democratic Party, 5:172–9
Strawberries, acreage, price, and production, 4:131–4
Streets. *See also* Highways; Roads and streets
public, value of new construction, 4:470–8
value of new construction, 4:468–9
by financing, 4:470–1
by ownership, 4:470–5, 4:477–8
Streptococcal sore throat, 2:564–6
Strikes, labor, *2:58–9*
Stumpage prices, *4:282,* 4:393–4
Sudan, U.S. population born in, 1:610
Sugar
consumption, 2:575–6
imports, 5:553–60
prices, 3:202, 3:78–207, 4:261
Sugar beets
acreage, price, and production, 4:119–21
commodity program provisions, 4:249–51
Sugarcane
acreage, price, and production, 4:119–22
commodity program provisions, 4:249–51
Suicide, 1:745, 5:237–55
by race and ethnicity, 5:242–7
rates, 5:237–9
Sulfur
exports, 4:333–4
imports, 4:333–4
production and value, 4:323–8
Sunflower seeds and oil, 4:138–9
Supplemental Security Income Program, 2:796
beneficiaries, 2:797–8
benefits, 2:797–8
payments, 2:797–8
Supplementary medical insurance, Medicare trust fund for, 2:792–3
Supreme Court cases, number and disposition, 5:315–20
Suriname, U.S. population born in, 1:612
Survivor programs, veterans, 2:754–9. *See also* Old-Age, Survivors, and Disability Insurance Programs
Swans, wild population, 3:375
Sweden, U.S. population born in, 1:601, 1:606, 1:609. *See also* Scandinavia
Sweeteners, consumption of, 2:575–6
Switzerland
investment in United States, by industry, 5:479–82
U.S. population born in, 1:602, 1:606, 1:609
Synagogues, 2:900–3. *See also* Churches and congregations; Religious institutions
charitable and philanthropic giving to, 2:914–16
membership in, 2:904–9
Syphilis, 2:564–6
Syria, U.S. population born in, 1:604, 1:607, 1:610

Taiwan, U.S. population born in, 1:610
Tanzania, U.S. population born in, 1:610
Tariffs, 5:510–14
Taxes. *See also* Federal income tax; Income tax
colonial, 5:663, 5:707–9
Confederate States of America, property, 5:787
gasoline, 4:850
Old-Age, Survivors, Disability, and Health Insurance, 2:762–5
poor relief, levied, 2:720
railroad, accruals, 4:942
Tax-exempt organizations, *2:842*
employee compensation, 2:857–9
employment, 2:857–9
IRS returns, 2:863–4
number, 2:857–9, 2:867–70
payroll, 2:867–70
receipts, 2:863–4
by state, 2:863–4, 2:867–70
by type, 2:861–4, 2:867–70
Taxpayers, income distribution, 2:656
Taxpayers Party, 5:172–9
Tea imports, 5:553–60
from England, by colony, 5:762–3
Teachers. *See* Educational services
Technical, sales, and administrative support, 1:771
Technology, *3:415–21,* 3:422–75
computer, *3:417*
definition, *3:415*
improvements, *2:8*
Technology (*continued*)
information, *3:417*
technological progress, *3:415–16*
Telegraph, *4:985–8,* 4:1001–26. *See also* Telephone and telegraph cable
domestic, 4:1001–5
employees, 4:1001–5, 4:1022–4
finances, 4:1001–5, 4:1022–4
international, 4:1022–4
messages, 4:1001–5, 4:1022–4
ocean cable, 4:1022–4
rates, 4:1005–7
wire, domestic, 4:1001–5
Telephone, 4:1001–26. *See also* Telephone and telegraph cable
access lines, wire, and plant, 4:1008–12
cellular, 4:1025
conversations, average daily, 4:1013–15
employees, 4:1008–12, 4:1022–5
finances, 4:1017–24
international, 4:1022–4
in outlying areas, 5:617–18
rates, 4:1015–16
services, *4:988–93*
consumption expenditures, 3:230–42
price indexes, 3:163–4
Telephone and telegraph cable, international rates, 4:1005–7
Teletypewriter exchange (TWX) rates, 4:1005–7
Television, *4:993–6,* 4:1027–37. *See also* Public broadcasting
advertising
distribution, 4:752–6
expenditures, 4:1033–4
broadcast systems, *4:994*
employment, 4:1033–4
finances, 4:1033–34
households with sets, 4:1027–30
patents granted, 3:430–44
sets, production, 4:1027–30
stations, 4:1027–30
Temperatures
mean annual
at climatological stations, 3:383, 3:394
at long-record city stations, 3:407, 3:414
normal averages, at climatological stations, 3:378, 3:380
Tennessee. *See* State data
Tennessee Valley Authority, 4:1101–2
Territorial expansion, *5:334–5*
outlying areas, *3:335–6*
of United States, *3:333–5*
Territories, land area, 3:346, 3:349. *See also* Outlying areas; Territorial expansion
Terrorism, *5:336*
Testis cancer, 2:568–71
Texas. *See* State data
Thailand, U.S. population born in, 1:610
Thefts, 5:225. *See also* Crime
Thrift institutions, monetary aggregates, 3:589–90, 3:617–18
Thyroid gland cancer, 2:568–71
Timber and timber products
American Indian land, 1:754–5
exports, from Charleston and Savannah, 5:770–2
products, 4:384–6
Tinnitus, 2:618–19
Tires and tubes, 3:267–70
Tobacco. *See also* Cigarettes, cigars, and tobacco; Smoking
acreage, 4:110–14
colonial foreign trade, 5:752–62
colonial freight rates, 5:731

Numbers in italics refer to pages in essays; numbers not in italics refer to pages in statistical tables.

Tobacco (*continued*)
commodity program provisions, 4:249–51
consumption expenditures for, *3:227,* 3:230–66, 3:273–5, 3:278–86
leaf, exports, 5:546–53
manufacturing summary, 4:583–617
patents granted, 3:430–44
prices, 4:110–14
colonial, 5:681–5
production, 4:110–14
Tomatoes, acreage, price, and production, 4:161–4
Toys
consumption expenditures for, 3:230–42
durable, 3:230–42
nondurable, 3:230–42
toys, games, and sporting goods, commodity value, 3:267–70
Trade. *See specific trades*
Trade and professional organizations, 2:895–6
Trade industries. *See* Distribution industries
Trade patents granted, 3:436–44
Trademarks, 3:422–45
Transistors, performance indicators, 3:461–2
Transportation, *4:761–77,* 4:779–975. *See also* Transportation, communications, and other public utilities; *specific transportation modes*
bills, freight and passenger, 4:796
business incorporations, 3:539–47
consumption expenditures for, *3:227,* 3:230–66, 3:273–5
family, 3:278–86
personal, 4:801
data sources, *4:774–7*
definition, *4:761*
employees, 4:793, 4:1092
equipment
manufacturing summary, 4:583–617
output, physical, 4:627–46
expenditures, government, 4:799, 5:19–25
federal, 5:32–9, 5:106–8
local, 5:45–51, 5:73–9
state, 5:45–51, 5:58–68
fares, 4:795, 4:800
farmers' trips to market, length and hauling costs, 4:779
federal aid for internal improvements, 4:780
firms, 3:510–11, 3:525, 3:572–3
air, 4:793
land, 4:791–2
railroad, 4:792
water, 4:793
freight, inland rates, 4:781
horse-drawn passenger vehicles and accessories, 3:267–72, 4:762–6
intercity motor carriers, 4:856
modes, 4:779–805
national income originating in, 3:32–5
operating revenues, 4:788–9
partnerships, general and limited, 3:510–11, 3:525
patents granted, 3:436–44
petroleum consumption, 4:797
pipeline, *4:774,* 4:973–5
price indexes, 3:173–4
private
consumer expenditures for, 3:243–66, 3:273–5, 3:285–6
price indexes, 3:165–6
proprietorships, 3:510–11
public
consumption expenditures for, 3:243–66, 3:273–5, 3:285–6
price indexes, 3:165–6
research and development, 3:453–5
Transportation (*continued*)
roads, 4:806–57
school, public, 2:486
travel times between selected cities, 4:779
U.S. direct investment in foreign countries, 5:473–8
vehicles, 4:806–57
wagons, 3:355, *4:762–6*
water, *4:766–70,* 4:858–914
freight shipments, 4:782
Transportation, communications, and other public utilities
earnings, annual, 2:272–3
employees, 2:111–14
female, 2:114
production, 2:115–16, 2:130–2
employment, 1:621–2, 1:772
full-time, 2:117–19
hours, weekly, 2:305–7
injury and illness rates, occupational, 2:332–3
labor force, 2:110–11
labor force participants engaged in, 2:101
by nativity, 2:108–9
by race, 2:104–7
by sex, 2:102–7
union membership, 2:347
wages and salaries, 2:282–3, 2:292
work stoppages, 2:359–61
Travel, 4:1107–19
foreign
consumption expenditures for, 3:230–66
to United States, 4:1109–12
Trespassing, 5:279–80, 5:292–6
Trinidad and Tobago
immigration from, 1:576
U.S. population born in, 1:611
Trucking services, expenses and operating revenue, 4:857
Trust companies, insured, 3:707–8
assets, 3:707–8
expenses, 3:713–14
income, 3:711–12
liabilities, 3:709–10
number, 3:707–8, 3:711–12
Trust Territory of the Pacific, 5:624–5. *See also* Outlying areas
Tuberculosis
hospitals, 2:520–3
admissions, 2:535–7
average daily census, 2:535–7
average length of stay, 2:534
number of beds, 2:527–9
personnel, 2:545–7
incidence, 2:564–6
Tungsten, 4:318–20
Tunisia, U.S. population born in, 1:611
Turkey
in Asia
immigration from, 1:566–70
U.S. population born in, 1:604, 1:607, 1:610
in Europe, U.S. population born in, 1:603, 1:607
Turkeys
number, price, production, and sales, 4:187–91
value per head, 4:187–92
Turnover rates, *2:50–2*
Turnpike mileage and cost, 4:783. *See also* Highways; Roads and streets
Turpentine prices, 3:217–24
Typhoid, and paratyphoid fever, 2:564–6

Uganda, U.S. population born in, 1:610
Unemployment, *2:29–33,* 2:77–100, 3:89–96
by age, 2:95
definition, *2:13–14, 2:29–30*
duration, 2:96–8
Unemployment (*continued*)
employee benefits, supplemental, 2:824–7
insurance, *2:710–11,* 2:781–3
expenditures, public, 2:739–41
railroad, 2:783–5
by nativity, 1:617
outlying areas, 5:607
by race, 1:617, *2:32,* 2:95–100
rates, 1:617, *2:31–2,* 2:95, 3:76, 3:84–96
by reason, 2:99–100
by sex, 1:617, *2:32,* 2:77, 2:87–8, 2:95–100
veterans, programs for, 2:754–9
Unfair practice complaints, 2:353
Union of Soviet Socialist Republics (USSR), U.S. population born in, 1:603, 1:606, 1:609. *See also* Russia; Soviet Union and Baltic states
Union Party, 5:172–9
Unionist Party, 5:200–3
United Arab Emirates, U.S. population born in, 1:610
United Kingdom. *See also* England; Ireland; Scotland; Wales
Confederate cotton imported into, 5:789
immigration from, 1:564–5
investment in United States, by industry, 5:479–82
United Parcel Service, 4:1049
Universities. *See* Colleges and universities
Unmarried mothers with children, living arrangements, 1:673–4
Unpaid family workers
by industry, 2:120–3
by sex, 2:128
Uranium
discharged commercial reactor fuel, 4:354
foreign trade, 4:354
fuel mineral production, 4:288–91
value, 4:292–4
production, 4:288–91, 4:354
Urban areas. *See also* Metropolitan areas; *specific cities*
American Indian population, 1:740–1
births and birth rates, of married women, 1:439
earnings in, 2:261
fertility ratios in, 1:426–7
housing units, occupied, 4:506–8
metropolitan, 1:108–39, 1:157–65
population, 1:36–8, 1:102–49, 1:613
by state, 1:180–379
price indexes, 3:161–6
by size, 1:102–4
by type, 1:107–8
Urinary and bladder cancer, 2:568–71
Uruguay, U.S. population born in, 1:612
U.S. agencies. *See specific agencies*
U.S. map, current census regions and divisions, *5:816*
USSR. *See* Union of Soviet Socialist Republics
Utah, 4:783–4. *See also* State data
Uterus cancer, 2:568–71
Utilities, *4:1061–71,* 4:1073–1123. *See also* Rural Electrification Administration; Rural Utilities Service; *specific utilities*
business incorporations, 3:539–47
consumption expenditures for, 3:243–66, 3:273–5, 3:278–86
dams, reservoirs, and aqueducts, *4:1070*
definition, *4:1061*
electricity
consumption, 4:347–8
gross domestic product, 4:1094
output indexes, 4:1093
productivity, 4:1093
employees, 4:1082–92, 4:1096
employment, 4:1073–81

Numbers in italics refer to pages in essays; numbers not in italics refer to pages in statistical tables.

Utilities (*continued*)
establishments, 4:1082–92, 4:1096
expenditures, government, 5:19–25
local, 5:45–51, 5:73–9
state, 5:45–51, 5:58–64
gas, 4:356–7
industrial production, indexes, 4:663–9, 4:1095
by legal status, 3:510–11, 3:525, 3:572–3
output, 4:1073–81
price indexes, 3:163–4
privately owned, value of new construction, 4:460–4
public
employment, 1:621–2, 1:772
receipts, 4:1082–92
sewers, *4:1070*
solid waste, *4:1071*
U.S. direct investment in foreign countries, 5:473–8
waterworks, *4:1069*

Vacancy rates, 4:513–14
Vanadium, 4:318–20
Vandalism, 5:279–80, 5:292–6
Varicose veins, 2:614
Veal slaughtering, 4:172–8
Vegetables. *See also specific vegetables*
acreage and production, for fresh market and processing, 4:144–5
commercial acreage and production, 4:144–5
consumption, 2:574
processed, consumer price indexes, 3:161–2
Venezuela
immigration from, 1:579–80
U.S. population born in, 1:612
Vermont, 5:658. *See also* State data
Vessels. *See also* Merchant vessels
colonial foreign commerce, 5:718–30
colonial manufacturing, 5:704–5
colonial prices, Philadelphia, 5:680–1
commercial, shipbuilding in private shipyard, 4:912–13
foreign, entered and cleared, 4:864–8
tonnage, 4:873
U.S., entered and cleared, 4:864–8
water transport, number and tonnage, 4:914
Veterans, *5:333–49,* 5:350–439. *See also* Veterans Affairs, U.S. Department of
by age, 5:406–7, 5:412
American Indian, 1:777
benefits, *5:343,* 5:367–8
number of payments, 2:818–19
number receiving, 5:421–7
chronology, *5:341*
in civil life, by period of service, 5:408–11
Civil War, *5:341–5*
colonial, *5:341–2*
compensation
expenditures for, 5:421–6
by period of service, 5:424–7
definition, *5:340*
education, higher, *5:347*
expenditures, public, 2:734–6, 2:745–6
female, 5:411
GI Bills, 5:438–9
life insurance for, 5:428
loans, guaranteed or insured
defaults on, 5:437
number and amount, by purpose of loan, 5:436–7
lump-sum payments to, 2:754–9
organizations, 2:895–6
pensions
expenditures, 5:421–6
by period of service, 5:424–7
Veterans (*continued*)
population, *5:343*
postwar era, *5:347–8*
programs, *2:715,* 2:761
beneficiaries, 2:758–9
cash benefits, 2:754–7, 2:760–1
expenditures, public, 2:734–6, 2:745–6
by race and Hispanic origin, 5:412
research and development for, 3:453–5
by sex, 5:412
World War I, *5:342–5*
World War II, *5:345–7*
Veterans Affairs, U.S. Department of
expenditures
by function, 5:413–17
by period of service, 5:418–20
hospital and domiciliary care authorized by, 5:429–30
medical centers, 5:433–4
nursing home care authorized by, 5:435
outpatient medical care authorized by, 5:432–3
patients treated, 5:431
Veterans Loan Program, 5:437
Veterans service and benefits, government expenditures, 5:95, 5:105–8
Victimization. *See* Crime
Video and audio goods, musical instruments, and computer goods, consumption expenditures for, 3:243–66
Video cassette recorders, *4:994*
Vietnam, U.S. population born in, 1:610
Vietnam Conflict
casualties, 5:350–1
characteristics, 5:363–4
draftees, 5:363–4
estimated cost, 5:370
medical care, 5:363–4
military pay, 5:363–4
personnel, 5:350–1, 5:363–4
Virgin Islands. *See also* Outlying areas
crop production, 5:608–9
education, 5:599–601
employment, 5:605–7
exports, 5:610–12
government revenues and expenditures, 5:624–5
gross domestic product, 5:604–5
imports, 5:612–14
infant mortality, 5:597–8
population, 1:39, 5:594–5
telephones in, 5:617–18
unemployment, 5:607
visitor arrivals, 5:615–16
Virginia. *See also* State data
colonial
population, by age, sex, race, and free/slave status, 5:664
prices, 5:681–8
taxes, government, 5:709
slaves imported into, 5:670
tobacco exported from, 5:760–1
Visual impairments, 2:618–19. *See also* Blind population
Vital statistics, *1:381–9,* 1:391–487
of American Indian population, 1:742–6
births and birth rates, 1:391–6, 1:399–439
child/woman ratio, 1:429–30
deaths and death rates, *1:387,* 1:458–73, 1:487
definition, *1:381*
divorce rates, 1:392–6
fertility rates, *1:382–5,* 1:391, 1:399–439
illegitimate births, 1:420–4
infant mortality, 1:391–6, 1:458–62
life expectancy, 1:391, 1:440
marriage rates, *1:383,* 1:392–6, 1:433–6, 1:439
Vital statistics (*continued*)
mortality rates, *1:385–9,* 1:458–73, 1:487
registration areas, birth and death, 1:397–8
reproduction rate, 1:424–5
Vocational rehabilitation
caseloads, 2:810–11
expenditures, 2:749–50, 2:810–11
Voluntary institutions, *2:837–48,* 2:885–99
arts, 2:885–7
bowling teams, 2:894
definition, *2:837–9*
economic significance indicators, 2:897–9
employees, 2:895–9
compensation, 2:897–9
expenditures, 2:897–9
fraternal organizations, 2:888–92
humanities, 2:885–7
income, 2:897–9
membership, 2:892–4
number, 2:897–9
per capita, 2:851
public broadcasting, 2:885–7
public/private, *2:840–41*
service organizations, 2:888–92
by type of organization, 2:895–6
Voter participation and turnout, *5:143–7,* 5:165–70
congressional election, 5:169–70
estimates, *5:145–6*
historical variations, *5:146–7*
presidential elections, *5:146,* 5:165–70
Voting rights, *5:141–3. See also* Women's suffrage
constitutional extensions of, by state, *5:142*

Wages and salaries, *2:40–6,* 2:254–300. *See also* Earnings
accruals, by industry, 2:282–3, 2:292–3
Confederacy, 5:793–4
disbursements, 2:751–2
distribution industry, 4:715
farm labor, 2:255–6
federal government employees, 5:130–1
during the Great Depression, 3:141–5
income, personal, 3:36–7
indexes, 2:254–5
inequality, *2:40–6,* 2:285–6
labor union impact on, *2:57–8*
manufacturing
by industry, 2:267–9
by occupation, 2:266
merchant vessels, U.S. flag, 4:900
minimum, 2:284–5
Old-Age, Survivors, Disability, and Health Insurance Program coverage, 2:762–5
ratios, black/white, 2:286
regional data, common labor, 2:264
retirement program coverage, 2:751–2
skill differential, *2:42*
trends, *2:44–6*
unskilled labor, *2:44,* 2:256–7
Wagons, *4:762–6*
road construction, public land grants aiding, 3:355
Wales, U.S. population born in, 1:601, 1:606, 1:609
Walnuts, acreage, price, and production, 4:140–2
War of 1812
casualties, 5:350–1
estimated cost, 5:370
military personnel, 5:350–1
Wars and battles, *5:333–9,* 5:350–439. *See also specific wars and conflicts*
battle campaigns, 5:372–403
casualties, *5:335*
cost, by war, 5:370
definition, *5:334, 5:821–2*

Wars and battles (*continued*)
  major, *5:335*
  minor, *5:336*
Washington. *See* State data
Water, 3:345, 3:364
  area of U.S., 1:12
  consumption expenditures for, 3:230–66
  fluoridation, 2:577–8
  irrigation, 3:364
  Los Angeles, supply and consumption, 4:1098
  power, 4:1099–1100
  public domain, acquisition and cost, 3:349
  public utility, 3:364
  quality, *3:338–9,* 3:371–2
  resources, government expenditures on, 3:365
  self-supplied, 3:364
  supply systems, number and population served, 2:577–8
  use, 3:364
Water facilities
  public, value of new construction, 4:470–5, 4:477–8
  value of new construction, 4:468–9
    by financing, 4:470–1
    by ownership, 4:470–5, 4:477–8
  waterworks, *4:1069*
    city, by type of ownership, 4:1097
    government expenditures, *4:1070*
    public ownership change, year of, 4:1097
    year built, 4:1097
Water transportation, *4:766–70,* 4:858–914
  canal and steamboat routes map, *4:768–9*
  cargo tonnage, 4:898–9
  exports, 4:869–71, 4:896–7
  firms, employees, 4:793
  freight shipments, 4:782
  imports, 4:869–71, 4:896–7
  ocean shipping, 4:877
  operating revenues, 4:788–9
  persons entering the United States by ship, 4:901
  steamboat trade, 4:878
  vessels
    number and tonnage, 4:914
    repairs and conversions, private shipyard, 4:911
Watermelon, acreage, price, and production, 4:131–4
Wealth, *3:287–95,* 3:298–332
  colonial, 5:671–3
  definition, *3:287–90*
  distribution, *2:621–4,* 2:658–9
    colonial, *5:632–4*
    measuring, *2:622–3*
    shares, *2:624*
  farmers, *4:29–30*
  fixed reproducible tangible, by type of asset, 3:330–2
  national, *3:294–5,* 3:325–32
  private physical, in British North America, 3:167, *5:632*
  residential formation of, 4:520–2
  taxable, 2:659
Weaponry, armed forces, *5:339*
Weapons treaties and agreements, 5:405
Weather, *3:341–3,* 3:378, 3:414
  precipitation at climatological stations, 3:381–2, 3:395, 3:406
  research, *3:341–2*
  temperatures
    mean annual, 3:383, 3:394, 3:407, 3:414
    normal averages, at climatological stations, 3:378, 3:380
Web sites, 4:1026. *See also* Internet
Weight, 2:582–5
Weights and measures, *5:809*
  crop-to-pound conversion, *5:812–13*
  International System (SI), *5:809, 5:811*
  metric system, *5:809, 5:811*
  monetary values and, *5:807–12*
  U.S. Customary System, *5:810*
  U.S.–metric unit conversion, *5:811*
Welfare, *2:1–368. See also* Social welfare
  child, 2:805–6
    expenditures, public, 2:749–50
  children and mothers served, 2:805–6
  private, 2:820–35
  research and development, 3:453–5
  social, *2:700–17*
Welfare and relief organizations, 2:895–6
West Indies, U.S. population born in, 1:608
West Virginia, 2:255–6. *See also* State data
Western States. *See* Regional data
Whaling
  colonial fishing, 5:702
  products
    output, 4:373–4
    whale processing, 4:375
Wheat. *See also* Wheat flour
  acreage, 4:102–5
  commodity program provisions, 4:245–8
  exports, 5:546–53
  prices, 3:78–207, 4:102–4
    colonial, 5:687–8
  production, 4:102–4
  stocks, 4:102–4
Wheat flour, prices, 3:202, 3:78–207
Whig Party
  congressional affiliations with, 5:200–3
  presidential affiliations with, 5:200–3
  presidential candidates, 5:172–9
  presidential elections, popular votes, 5:184–92
White-collar workers
  occupational distribution, *2:38*
  women, *2:39*
White population, 1:36, 1:40–1, 1:48–51, 1:57–60, 1:105–6
  age, median, 1:71
  births and birth rates, 1:391–6, 1:399–417, 1:428–30, 1:432–8, 1:615
    fertility rates, 1:391, 1:399–408, 1:426–7
    illegitimate births, 1:420–4
    low-birth-weight infants, 2:586
  colonial, 5:651–6
  crime
    arrests, 5:226–32
    delinquency, 5:264–6, 5:281–96
    homicides, 5:242–7
    lynching victims, 5:251–5
  deaths and death rates, 1:392–6, 1:458–73, 1:487
  drug abuse, 5:298–9, 5:303–5
  education, 2:418–20, 2:425–30, 2:435–6
    college graduation rate, 2:469
    high school noncompletion rate, 2:470
    illiteracy rate, 2:468–9
    school enrollment rates, *2:392–3,* 2:431–2
    years of school completed, 2:464–8
  employment and earnings
    earnings, *2:45,* 2:294
    employment, 2:314–15
    hours of work, 2:310–11
    occupations, 2:136, 2:138, 2:172–81, 2:192–201, 2:253
    wages, union and nonunion, 2:351
  farm operators, 4:66–7, 4:71–3
  firearm possession, 5:310
  foreign-born, 1:170–71
  health and illness, 2:587–613
  health insurance coverage, *2:504,* 2:551–2
  householder, 1:660–2, 1:679–84
White population (*continued*)
  housing
    homeownership rates, 4:509–12
    housing units, occupied, 4:506–8
  immigration, 1:544–6
  income
    individual, 1:618
    mean, 2:660
    median, 2:660
  in institutions, 1:669–70
  labor force, 2:63–4, 2:91–2
    participation, *2:24,* 2:64, 2:80
  life expectancy, 1:391, 1:440–2, 1:447
  marital status, 1:72–101
    divorce rates, 1:392–6
    marriage rates, 1:392–6, 1:685–7
    of mothers, 1:673–5
  migration, 1:505–18, 1:523
    internal, 1:495–501
    international, 1:544–6
  mortality, 1:458–61, 1:485–7
    infant mortality rates, 1:391–6
  native-born, 1:169
  in poverty
    adults, 2:687–9
    children, 2:681–3
    families, 2:677–9, 2:681–3
    persons, 2:674–6, 2:680–1, 2:690–1
  prisoners, *5:213*
    executed, by offense, 5:262–3
    sentenced, 5:258–9
  by state, 1:180–379
  substance use and abuse
    drug abuse, 5:298–9, 5:303–5
    high school seniors reporting, 5:306–7
  suicides, 5:242–7
  unemployment, 1:617, *2:32,* 2:95–100
  union membership, 2:350
  in urban areas, 1:107–8
  veterans, 5:412
Wholesale trade, 4:742–51
  employment, 4:742–9
  operating expenses, 4:742–8
  sales, 4:742–8
    ratios, 4:750–1
  stocks, 4:750–1
  by type of business, 4:742–8
  wholesalers, 4:750–1
Whooping cough. *See* Pertussis
Widowed population, 1:72–101, 1:707–8
  current-pay benefits received by, 2:768–9
Wildlife preservation, *3:340–1*
Wind energy, 4:340
Winter wheat. *See* Wheat
Wisconsin. *See* State data
Women in labor force, *1:692,* 1:700–2, *2:15, 2:26–9, 2:39,* 2:66
  by age, 2:65–6, 2:90, 2:94
  marital status, 1:616, 1:701–2, *2:11,* 2:80–2, 2:93–4
  occupations, 2:162–71
  participation, 2:65–6, 2:80–2
  by presence of children, 2:80–2, 2:94
  by race, *2:39,* 2:65–6, 2:80–2, 2:92
  servants, *2:39*
  slave labor, 2:76
  by state, 2:69–70, 2:73–4
  white-collar workers, *2:39*
Women's suffrage, authorization by state, 2:367–8
Wood and waste energy, 4:340
Woodland, 3:360–1
Woodpulp, 4:391–3
Wool
  commodity program provisions, 4:249–51
  consumption, 4:694–5
  prices, wholesale, 3:71, 3:207–11
  shorn, price and production, 4:110–14

Numbers in italics refer to pages in essays; numbers not in italics refer to pages in statistical tables.

Work, *2:1–62,* 2:63–368. *See also* Employment
Work, hours of, *2:46–54,* 2:301–35
  by age, 2:310–11
  full-time status, 2:312–13
  hours paid, 2:316–17
  by industry, 2:302–4
  manufacturing, 2:301
    overtime hours, 2:315
    weekly, 2:303–4, 2:308
  by marital status, 2:311–12
  nonagricultural employment, 2:310–12
    by industry, 2:304–7
  overtime, 2:315
  by race, 2:310–11
  by sex, 2:309–12
  trends and cycles, *2:48–9*
  variation, *2:50*
  weekly, *2:47–8*
    by industry, 2:303–4
    manufacturing, 2:303–8
    nonagricultural employment, 2:304–7
Work force. *See* Labor force
Work stoppages, 2:354–6
  by industry, 2:359–61
  by issue, 2:357–8
Worker's compensation, 2:291, *2:708–10*
  benefit payments, 2:785–7
  costs, 2:785–7
  expenditures, public, 2:739–41
  by industry, 2:283–4
  workers covered, 2:785–7
Worker's League Party, 5:172–9
Worker's World Party, 5:172–9
Working conditions, *2:46–54,* 2:301–35
  employee benefits, *2:52*
  illness rates, by industry, 2:332–3
  injuries, work-related, *2:52,* 2:326–33
  job duration, *2:50–2,* 2:320–2
  turnover, *2:50–2,* 2:318–19
  workplace size, *2:52–4,* 2:323–4
Working poor, *2:646*
Work-loss days, 2:593–5
Workplace size, *2:52–4,* 2:323–4
Work-related injuries, *2:52. See also* Injuries and fatalities
World War I
  casualties, 5:350–1
  draftees, 5:363–4
  estimated cost, 5:370
  medical care, 5:363–4
  military pay, 5:363–4
World War I (*continued*)
  personnel, 5:350–1, 5:363–4
  veterans, *5:342–7*
World War II
  casualties, 5:350–1
  draftees, 5:363–4
  estimated cost, 5:370
  medical care, 5:363–4
  military pay, 5:363–4
  personnel, 5:350–1, 5:363–4
  veterans, *5:345–7*
Writing, student proficiency, 2:425–30
Wrought iron, exported from England, 5:746
Wyoming. *See* State data

Yale University, income, by source, 2:879–80
Yemen, U.S. population born in, 1:610
Youth organizations, 2:895–6
Yugoslavia, U.S. population born in, 1:603, 1:606, 1:609

Zaire, U.S. population born in, 1:610
Zambia, U.S. population born in, 1:610
Zimbabwe, U.S. population born in, 1:610
Zinc
  imports and exports, 4:329–33
  production, 4:311–14, 4:321–3